# THE POLITICAL HISTORY

OF THE

# UNITED STATES OF AMERICA

DURING THE

# PERIOD OF RECONSTRUCTION,

(FROM APRIL 15, 1865, TO JULY 15, 1870,)

INCLUDING A

CLASSIFIED SUMMARY OF THE LEGISLATION OF THE THIRTY-NINTH, FORTIETH, AND FORTY-FIRST CONGRESSES.
WITH THE VOTES THEREON;

TOGETHER WITH THE

ACTION, CONGRESSIONAL AND STATE, ON THE FOURTEENTH AND FIF-TEENTH AMENDMENTS TO THE CONSTITUTION OF THE UNITED STATES,

AND THE OTHER

IMPORTANT EXECUTIVE, LEGISLATIVE, POLITICO-MILITARY, AND JUDICIAL FACTS OF THAT PERIOD.

SECOND EDITION.

---

By Hon. EDWARD McPHERSON, LL.D.,
CLERK OF THE HOUSE OF REPRESENTATIVES OF THE UNITED STATES.

---

NEGRO UNIVERSITIES PRESS
NEW YORK

50389

Originally published in 1875
by Solomons & Chapman

Reprinted 1969 by
Negro Universities Press
A DIVISION OF GREENWOOD PUBLISHING CORP.
NEW YORK

SBN 8371-1946-4

# PREFACE.

———•———

This volume is a reprint of my Political Manuals, issued in 1866, 1867, 1868, 1869, and 1870, with revision and corrections to date and with some additions, and includes the political facts of the most momentous legislative period in the history of our country—that between April 15, 1865, and July 15, 1870. During it occurred the great controversy between President JOHNSON and the Thirty-ninth and Fortieth Congresses, which resulted, among many minor features of significance and importance, in the enactment of the Civil Rights act and the Tenure-of-Office act; the overthrow of the Presidential plan of Reconstruction; the remission to military rule of the lately insurrectionary States, except Tennessee; the prescription by Congress of the terms of their restoration; and the adoption, by Congress and the requisite number of State Legislatures, of the Fourteenth Amendment to the Constitution of the United States, which distinctly defines citizenship and places it under constitutional protection, and of the Fifteenth Amendment, which settles upon a new basis the question of suffrage in the United States, and modifies the relations of the States to it—all which measures indicate the era referred to as unquestionably the most remarkable in our legislative history.

It has been my effort to preserve in these pages the record of the various steps by which these ends have been reached, so that it may be entirely practicable for the student of them to trace their development from the first suggestion to the final shape.

A glance at the Table of Contents and the Index will indicate the scope of the work, and the thoroughness and detail which characterize it; and a close examination of its pages will, I trust, leave no room to doubt that it has been prepared in a spirit of fairness and impartiality, and that it may be accepted as an actual contribution to the political history of our times.

The general plan of the work is the same as that of the Political History of the United States during the Rebellion, but differs from it chiefly in its having been arranged in annual parts. The advantage in this is, that it exhibits more · clearly the growth of legislation and of public sentiment on each question, year by year. The disadvantage is, a small increase in the labor of investigation.

iii

It is hoped, however, that the completeness of the Index, both as to subjects, persons, and parties, will enable all, without difficulty, to command ready access to the multitude of facts which will be found in these pages.

Part I contains a full statement of the Orders and Proclamations and the general action of President JOHNSON, in the development of his policy of restoring the insurrectionary States to their places in the Union, by calling constitutional conventions in each, on an indicated basis, and by suggesting certain action therein as preliminary to restoration. It also contains the legislation of those organizations respecting the colored population recently freed, and the various Messages, Speeches, Letters, and Proclamations of the PRESIDENT in vindication of his policy and in resistance to that of Congress. This part will also be found to contain the full text of the majority and minority reports of the Joint Congressional Committee on Reconstruction, with the text of the Fourteenth Amendment, as finally adopted by Congress and submitted to the Legislatures for their action. This amendment having been rejected by the Legislatures in the insurrectionary States, chosen under the action of President JOHNSON, Congress subsequently adopted the decisive measure of dividing those States into five Military Districts, providing for their re-organization on the basis of, substantially, Universal Manhood Suffrage, and prescribing the conditions on which they would be entitled to representation in Congress.

Part II contains the texts of these various measures, the Veto Messages of the PRESIDENT in disapproval of them, and the various Votes by which they were passed over the veto by two-thirds of each House.

Part III contains all the proceedings connected with the proposed impeachment of President JOHNSON by the Fortieth Congress, with the Articles of Impeachment in full, the answer of President JOHNSON, the Replication of the House, and the Judgment of the Senate thereon. It also contains a digest of the Orders of the Military Commanders and their general action under the various Reconstruction acts, with an abstract of the Constitutions prepared by the Conventions called under them.

Parts IV and V contain the remaining record of Reconstruction, the final votes in Congress upon the adoption of the Fifteenth Constitutional Amendment, President GRANT'S action thereon, the votes of the various State Legislatures, and the final certificate of the Secretary of State announcing its ratification as an amendment to the Constitution. Besides these great measures, the interest in which will scarcely abate as long as our present system of government remains, in this volume will be found all the Decisions of the Supreme Court of the United States during this period, on the more important public questions which came before it, such as the *Habeas Corpus*, the Legal-Tender, and the Test-Oath cases; the right of States to tax National Banks; the right of the United

States to tax State Banks; the right of a State to tax persons passing through it; the validity of contracts in confederate money, and the effect of express contracts to pay coined dollars; and sundry opinions in United States Circuit and State courts. Besides, in it will be found all the votes in Congress upon general questions, such as the Public Credit act, Banking and Currency legislation, the Tenure-of-Office act, the Civil Rights act, Internal Revenue, Tariff, and Land-grant legislation; the various Messages, Proclamations, and Orders of Presidents JOHNSON and GRANT; the votes of Congress on political declaratory resolutions; the platforms of parties, both State and National, from 1866 to 1870; the returns of State and Presidential elections; Tables of Population, Public Debt, Land-grants, Taxation, Registration, Disfranchisement, Expenditures and Appropriations, Revenue receipts and reductions, Lists of the Cabinets of Presidents JOHNSON and GRANT, and of the Members of the Thirty-ninth, Fortieth, and Forty-first Congresses; and an extended political and military miscellany, which will be found to include almost every thing of permanent interest connected with national politics during the period referred to.

This volume takes up the thread where it was dropped by that on the Rebellion, and it is naturally a companion to it. That gives the record of the steps by which Secession was accomplished and Disunion attempted, as well as of those by which Secession was resisted and Disunion defeated. This gives the equally portentous record of the means by which, the War over, the Government and people of the United States reaped its fruits, and especially the memorable steps by which four millions of slaves, formerly knows as chattels, became incorporated, first into the civil, and next into the political, body.

In the various votes given, the names of Republicans are printed in Roman, of Democrats, and of those who generally co-operated with them, in *italic*.

EDWARD McPHERSON.

WASHINGTON, D. C., *April* 20, 1871.

# TABLE OF CONTENTS.

## PART I--1866.

# PART II--1867.

# PART III--1868.

## PART IV--1869.

## PART V--1870.

# POLITICAL MANUAL FOR 1866.

## I.

## CONSTITUTION OF THE UNITED STATES.

WE the People of the United States, in order to form a more perfect Union, establish Justice, insure domestic Tranquillity, provide for the common defence, promote the general Welfare, and secure the Blessings of Liberty to ourselves and our Posterity, do ordain and establish this CONSTITUTION for the United States of America.

### ARTICLE I.

SECTION 1. All legislative Powers herein granted shall be vested in a Congress of the United States, which shall consist of a Senate and House of Representatives.

SEC. 2. The House of Representatives shall be composed of Members chosen every second Year by the People of the several States, and the Electors in each State shall have the Qualifications requisite for Electors of the most numerous Branch of the State Legislature.

No Person shall be a Representative who shall not have attained to the Age of twenty-five Years, and been seven Years a Citizen of the United States, and who shall not, when elected, be an Inhabitant of that State in which he shall be chosen.

Representatives and direct Taxes shall be apportioned among the several States which may be included within this Union, according to their respective Numbers, which shall be determined by adding to the whole Number of free Persons, including those bound to Service for a Term of Years, and excluding Indians not taxed, three fifths of all other Persons. The actual Enumeration shall be made within three Years after the first Meeting of the Congress of the United States, and within every subsequent Term of ten Years, in such Manner as they shall by Law direct. The Number of Representatives shall not exceed one for every thirty Thousand, but each State shall have at Least one Representative; and until such enumeration shall be made, the State of New Hampshire shall be entitled to chuse three, Massachusetts eight, Rhode Island and Providence Plantations one, Connecticut five, New York six, New Jersey four, Pennsylvania eight, Delaware one, Maryland six, Virginia ten, North Carolina five, South Carolina five, and Georgia three.

When vacancies happen in the Representation from any State, the Executive Authority thereof shall issue Writs of Election to fill such Vacancies.

The House of Representatives shall chuse their Speaker and other Officers; and shall have the sole Power of Impeachment.

SEC. 3. The Senate of the United States shall be composed of two Senators from each State, chosen by the Legislature thereof, for six Years; and each Senator shall have one Vote.

Immediately after they shall be assembled in Consequence of the first Election, they shall be divided as equally as may be into three Classes. The Seats of the Senators of the first Class shall be vacated at the Expiration of the second Year, of the second Class at the Expiration of the fourth Year, and of the third Class at the Expiration of the sixth Year, so that one-third may be chosen every second Year; and if Vacancies happen by Resignation, or otherwise, during the Recess of the Legislature of any State, the Executive thereof may make temporary Appointments until the next Meeting of the Legislature, which shall then fill such Vacancies.

No Person shall be a Senator who shall not have attained to the Age of thirty Years, and been nine Years a Citizen of the United States, and who shall not, when elected, be an Inhabitant of that State for which he shall be chosen.

The Vice President of the United States shall be President of the Senate, but shall have no Vote, unless they be equally divided.

The Senate shall chuse their other Officers, and also a President pro tempore, in the Absence of the Vice President, or when he shall exercise the Office of President of the United States.

The Senate shall have the sole Power to try all Impeachments. When sitting for that Purpose, they shall be on Oath or Affirmation. When the President of the United States is tried, the Chief Justice shall preside: And no Person shall be convicted without the Concurrence of two thirds of the Members present.

Judgment in Cases of Impeachment shall not extend further than to removal from Office, and Disqualification to hold and enjoy any Office of honour, Trust or Profit under the United States: but the Party convicted shall nevertheless be liable and subject to Indictment, Trial, Judgment and Punishment, according to Law.

SEC. 4. The Times, Places and Manner of holding Elections for Senators and Representatives, shall be prescribed in each State by the Legislature thereof; but the Congress may at any time by Law make or alter such Regulations, except as to the place of chusing Senators.

The Congress shall assemble at least once in every Year, and such Meeting shall be on the first Monday in December, unless they shall by Law appoint a different Day.

Sec. 5. Each House shall be the Judge of the Elections, Returns and Qualifications of its own Members, and a Majority of each shall constitute a Quorum to do Business; but a smaller Number may adjourn from day to day, and may be authorized to compel the Attendance of absent Members, in such Manner, and under such Penalties as each House may provide.

Each House may determine the Rules of its Proceedings, punish its Members for disorderly Behaviour, and, with the Concurrence of two thirds, expel a Member.

Each House shall keep a Journal of its Proceedings, and from time to time publish the same, excepting such Parts as may in their Judgment require Secrecy; and the Yeas and Nays of the Members of either House on any question shall, at the Desire of one fifth of those Present, be entered on the Journal.

Neither House, during the Session of Congress, shall, without the Consent of the other, adjourn for more than three days, nor to any other Place than that in which the two Houses shall be sitting.

Sec. 6. The Senators and Representatives shall receive a Compensation for their Services, to be ascertained by Law, and paid out of the Treasury of the United States. They shall in all Cases, except Treason, Felony and Breach of the Peace, be privileged from Arrest during their Attendance at the Session of their respective Houses, and in going to and returning from the same; and for any Speech or Debate in either House, they shall not be questioned in any other Place.

No Senator or Representative shall, during the Time for which he was elected, be appointed to any civil Office under the Authority of the United States, which shall have been created, or the Emoluments whereof shall have been encreased during such time; and no Person holding any Office under the United States, shall be a Member of either House during his Continuance in Office.

Sec. 7. All Bills for raising Revenue shall originate in the House of Representatives; but the Senate may propose or concur with Amendments as on other Bills.

Every Bill which shall have passed the House of Representatives and the Senate, shall, before it becomes a Law, be presented to the President of the United States; If he approve he shall sign it, but if not he shall return it, with his Objections to that House in which it shall have originated, who shall enter the Objections at large on their Journal, and proceed to reconsider it. If after such Reconsideration two thirds of that House shall agree to pass the Bill, it shall be sent, together with the Objections, to the other House, by which it shall likewise be reconsidered, and if approved by two thirds of that House, it shall become a Law. But in all such Cases the Votes of both Houses shall be determined by yeas and Nays, and the Names of the Persons voting for and against the Bill shall be entered on the Journal of each House respectively. If any Bill shall not be returned by the President within ten Days (Sundays excepted) after it shall have been presented to him, the Same shall be a law, in like Manner as if he had signed it, unless the Congress by their Adjournment prevent its return, in which Case it shall not be a Law.

Every Order, Resolution, or Vote to which the Concurrence of the Senate and House of Representatives may be necessary (except on a question of Adjournment) shall be presented to the President of the United States; and before the Same shall take Effect, shall be approved by him, or being disapproved by him, shall be repassed by two-thirds of the Senate and House of Representatives, according to the Rules and Limitations prescribed in the Case of a Bill.

Sec. 8. The Congress shall have Power

To lay and collect Taxes, Duties, Imposts and Excises, to pay the Debts and provide for the common Defence and general Welfare of the United States; but all Duties, Imposts and Excises shall be uniform throughout the United States;

To borrow Money on the credit of the United States;

To regulate Commerce with foreign Nations, and among the several States, and with the Indian Tribes;

To establish an uniform Rule of Naturalization, and uniform Laws on the subject of Bankruptcies throughout the United States;

To coin Money, regulate the Value thereof, and of foreign Coin, and fix the Standard of Weights and Measures;

To provide for the Punishment of counterfeiting the Securities and current Coin of the United States;

To establish Post Offices and post Roads;

To promote the progress of Science and useful Arts, by securing for limited Times to Authors and Inventors the exclusive Right to their respective Writings and Discoveries;

To constitute Tribunals inferior to the supreme Court;

To define and punish Piracies and Felonies committed on the high Seas, and Offences against the Law of Nations;

To declare War, grant Letters of Marque and Reprisal, and make Rules concerning Captures on Land and Water;

To raise and support Armies, but no Appropriation of Money to that Use shall be for a longer Term than two years;

To provide and maintain a Navy;

To make Rules for the Government and Regulation of the land and naval Forces;

To provide for calling forth the Militia to execute the Laws of the Union, suppress Insurrections and repel Invasions;

To provide for organizing, arming, and disciplining, the Militia, and for governing such Part of them as may be employed in the Service of the United States, reserving to the States respectively, the Appointment of the Officers, and the Authority of training the Militia according to the Discipline prescribed by Congress;

To exercise exclusive Legislation in all Cases whatsoever, over such District (not exceeding ten Miles square) as may, by Cession of particular States, and the Acceptance of Congress, become the Seat of the Government of the United States, and to exercise like Authority over all Places purchased by the Consent of the Legislature of the State in which the Same shall be, for the Erection of Forts, Magazines, Arsenals, Dock-Yards, and other needful Buildings;—And

To make all Laws which shall be necessary and proper for carrying into Execution the foregoing Powers, and all other Powers vested by this Constitution in the Government of the United States, or in any Department or Officer thereof.

SEC. 9. The Migration or Importation of such Persons as any of the States now existing shall think proper to admit, shall not be prohibited by the Congress prior to the Year one thousand eight hundred and eight, but a Tax or Duty may be imposed on such Importation, not exceeding ten dollars for each Person.

The Privilege of the Writ of Habeas Corpus shall not be suspended, unless when in Cases of Rebellion or Invasion the public Safety may require it.

No Bill of Attainder or ex post facto Law shall be passed.

No Capitation, or other direct, Tax shall be laid, unless in Proportion to the Census or Enumeration herein before directed to be taken.

No Tax or Duty shall be laid on Articles exported from any State.

No Preference shall be given by any Regulation of Commerce or Revenue to the Ports of one State over those of another; nor shall Vessels bound to, or from, one State, be obliged to enter, clear, or pay Duties in another.

No Money shall be drawn from the Treasury, but in Consequence of Appropriations made by Law; and a regular Statement and Account of the Receipts and Expenditures of all public Money shall be published from time to time.

No Title of Nobility shall be granted by the United States: and no Person holding any Office of Profit or Trust under them, shall, without the Consent of the Congress, accept of any present, Emolument, Office, or Title, of any kind whatever, from any King, Prince, or foreign State.

SEC. 10. No State shall enter into any Treaty, Alliance, or Confederation; grant Letters of Marque and Reprisal; coin Money; emit Bills of Credit; make any Thing but gold and silver Coin a Tender in Payment of Debts; pass any Bill of Attainder, ex post facto Law, or Law impairing the Obligation of Contracts, or grant any Title of Nobility.

No State shall, without the consent of the Congress, lay any Imposts or Duties on Imports or Exports, except what may be absolutely necessary for executing it's inspection Laws: and the net Produce of all Duties and Imposts, laid by any State on Imports or Exports, shall be for the Use of the Treasury of the United States; and all such Laws shall be subject to the Revision and Controul of the Congress.

No State shall, without the Consent of Congress, lay any Duty of Tonnage, keep Troops, or Ships of War in time of Peace, enter into any Agreement or Compact with another State, or with a foreign Power, or engage in War, unless actually invaded, or in such imminent Danger as will not admit of Delay.

## ARTICLE II.

SEC. 1. The executive Power shall be vested in a President of the United States of America. He shall hold his Office during the Term of four Years, and, together with the Vice President, chosen for the same term, be elected as follows

Each State shall appoint, in such Manner as the Legislature thereof may direct, a Number of Electors, equal to the whole Number of Senators and Representatives to which the State may be entitled in the Congress: but no Senator or Representative, or person holding an Office of Trust or Profit under the United States, shall be appointed an Elector.

[The Electors shall meet in their respective States, and vote by Ballot for two Persons, of whom one at least shall not be an Inhabitant of the same State with themselves. And they shall make a list of all the Persons voted for, and of the Number of Votes for each; which List they shall sign and certify, and transmit sealed to the Seat of the Government of the United States, directed to the President of the Senate. The President of the Senate shall, in the Presence of the Senate and House of Representatives, open all the Certificates, and the Votes shall then be counted. The Person having the greatest Number of Votes shall be the President, if such Number be a Majority of the whole Number of Electors appointed; and if there be more than one who have such Majority, and have an equal Number of Votes, then the House of Representatives shall immediately chuse by Ballot one of them for President; and if no Person have a Majority, then from the five highest on the List the said House shall in like Manner chuse the President. But in chusing the President, the Votes shall be taken by States, the Representation from each State having one Vote; A Quorum for this Purpose shall consist of a Member or Members from two-thirds of the States, and a Majority of all the States shall be necessary to a Choice. In every Case, after the Choice of the President, the Person having the greatest Number of Votes of the Electors shall be the Vice President. But if there should remain two or more who have equal Votes, the Senate shall chuse from them by Ballot the Vice President.*]

The Congress may determine the Time of chusing the Electors, and the Day on which they shall give their Votes; which Day shall be the same throughout the United States.

No Person except a natural born Citizen, or a Citizen of the United States, at the time of the Adoption of this Constitution, shall be eligible to the Office of President; neither shall any Person be eligible to that Office who shall not have attained to the Age of thirty-five Years, and been fourteen Years a Resident within the United States.

In Case of the Removal of the President from Office, or of his Death, Resignation, or Inability

---

* This clause of the Constitution has been annulled. See twelfth article of the Amendments.

to discharge the Powers and Duties of the said Office, the same shall devolve on the Vice President, and the Congress may by Law provide for the Case of Removal, Death, Resignation, or Inability, both of the President and Vice President, declaring what Officer shall then act as President, and such Officer shall act accordingly, until the Disability be removed, or a President shall be elected.

The President shall, at stated Times, receive for his Services, a Compensation, which shall neither be encreased nor diminished during the Period for which he shall have been elected, and he shall not receive within that Period any other Emolument from the United States, or any of them.

Before he enter on the Execution of his Office, he shall take the following Oath or Affirmation:—

"I do solemnly swear (or affirm) that I will faithfully execute the Office of President of the United States, and will to the best of my Ability, preserve, protect and defend the Constitution of the United States."

SEC. 2. The President shall be Commander in Chief of the Army and Navy of the United States, and of the Militia of the several States, when called into the actual Service of the United States; he may require the Opinion, in writing, of the principal Officer in each of the executive Departments, upon any Subject relating to the Duties of their respective Offices, and he shall have Power to grant Reprieves and Pardons for Offences against the United States, except in Cases of Impeachment.

He shall have Power, by and with the Advice and Consent of the Senate, to make Treaties, provided two thirds of the Senators present concur; and he shall nominate, and by and with the Advice and Consent of the Senate, shall appoint Ambassadors, other public Ministers and Consuls, Judges of the supreme Court, and all other Officers of the United States, whose Appointments are not herein otherwise provided for, and which shall be established by Law: but the Congress may by Law vest the Appointment of such inferior Officers, as they think proper, in the President alone, in the Courts of Law, or in the Heads of Departments.

The President shall have Power to fill up all Vacancies that may happen during the Recess of the Senate, by granting Commissions which shall expire at the End of their next Session.

SEC. 3. He shall from time to time give to the Congress Information of the State of the Union, and recommend to their Consideration such Measures as he shall judge necessary and expedient; he may, on extraordinary Occasions, convene both Houses, or either of them, and in Case of Disagreement between them, with Respect to the Time of Adjournment, he may adjourn them to such Time as he shall think proper; he shall receive Ambassadors and other public Ministers; and he shall take Care that the Laws be faithfully executed, and he shall Commission all the officers of the United States.

SEC. 4. The President, Vice President and all civil Officers of the United States, shall be removed from Office on Impeachment for, and Conviction of, Treason, Bribery, or other high Crimes and Misdemeanors.

## ARTICLE III.

SEC. 1. The judicial Power of the United States, shall be vested in one supreme Court, and in such inferior Courts as the Congress may from time to time ordain and establish. The Judges, both of the supreme and inferior Courts, shall hold their Offices during good Behavior, and shall, at stated Times, receive for their Services, a Compensation, which shall not be diminished during their Continuance in Office.

SEC. 2. The judicial Power shall extend to all cases, in Law and Equity, arising under this Constitution, the Laws of the United States, and Treaties made, or which shall be made, under their Authority;—to all Cases affecting Ambassadors, other public Ministers, and Consuls;—to all Cases of admiralty and maritime Jurisdiction;—to Controversies to which the United States shall be a Party;—to Controversies between two or more States;—between a State and Citizens of another State;—between Citizens of different States,—between Citizens of the same State claiming Lands under Grants of different States, and between a State or the Citizens thereof, and foreign States, Citizens or Subjects.

In all Cases affecting Ambassadors, other public Ministers and Consuls, and those in which a State shall be Party, the supreme Court shall have original Jurisdiction. In all the other Cases before mentioned, the supreme Court shall have appellate Jurisdiction, both as to Law and Fact, with such Exceptions, and under such Regulations as the Congress shall make.

The Trial of all Crimes, except in Cases of Impeachment, shall be by Jury; and such Trial shall be held in the State where the said Crimes shall have been committed; but when not committed within any State, the Trial shall be at such Place or Places as the Congress may by Law have directed.

SEC. 3. Treason against the United States, shall consist only in levying War against them, or in adhering to their Enemies, giving them Aid and Comfort. No Person shall be convicted of Treason unless on the Testimony of two Witnesses to the same overt Act, or on Confession in open Court.

The Congress shall have Power to declare the Punishment of Treason, but no Attainder of Treason shall work Corruption of Blood, or Forfeiture except during the Life of the Person attainted.

## ARTICLE IV.

SEC. 1. Full Faith and Credit shall by given in each State to the public Acts, Records, and judicial Proceedings of every other State. And the Congress may by general Laws prescribe the Manner in which such Acts, Records and Proceedings shall be proved, and the Effect thereof.

SEC. 2. The Citizens of each State shall be entitled to all Privileges and Immunities of Citizens in the several States.

A Person charged in any State with Treason, Felony, or other Crime, who shall flee from Justice, and be found in another State, shall on Demand of the executive Authority of the State from which he fled, be delivered up, to be removed to the State having Jurisdiction of the Crime.

No Person held to Service or Labour in one

State, under the Laws thereof, escaping into another, shall, in Consequence of any Law or Regulation therein, be discharged from such Service or Labour, but shall be delivered up on Claim of the Party to whom such Service or Labour may be due.

SEC. 3. New States may be admitted by the Congress into this Union; but no new State shall be formed or erected within the Jurisdiction of any other State; nor any State formed by the Junction of two or more States, or Parts of States, without the Consent of the Legislatures of the States concerned as well as of the Congress.

The Congress shall have Power to dispose of and make all needful Rules and Regulations respecting the Territory or other Property belonging to the United States; and nothing in this Constitution shall be so construed as to Prejudice any Claims of the United States, or of any particular State.

SEC. 4. The United States shall guarantee to every State in this Union a Republican Form of Government, and shall protect each of them against Invasion; and on Application of the Legislature, or of the Executive (when the Legislature cannot be convened) against domestic Violence.

## ARTICLE V.

The Congress, whenever two thirds of both Houses shall deem it necessary, shall propose Amendments to this Constitution, or, on the Application of the Legislatures of two thirds of the several States, shall call a Convention for proposing Amendments, which, in either Case, shall be valid to all Intents and Purposes, as Part of this Constitution, when ratified by the Legislatures of three fourths of the several States, or by Conventions in three fourths thereof, as the one or the other Mode of Ratification may be proposed by the Congress; Provided that no Amendment which may be made prior to the Year one thousand eight hundred and eight shall in any Manner affect the first and fourth Clauses in the Ninth Section of the first Article; and that no State, without its Consent, shall be deprived of its equal Suffrage in the Senate.

## ARTICLE VI.

All Debts contracted and Engagements entered into, before the Adoption of this Constitution, shall be as valid against the United States under this Constitution, as under the Confederation.

This Constitution, and the Laws of the United States which shall be made in Pursuance thereof; and all Treaties made, or which shall be made, under the authority of the United States, shall be the supreme Law of the Land; and the Judges in every State shall be bound thereby, any Thing in the Constitution or Laws of any State to the Contrary notwithstanding.

The Senators and Representatives before mentioned, and the Members of the several State Legislatures, and all executive and judicial Officers, both of the United States and of the several States, shall be bound by Oath or Affirmation, to support this Constitution; but no religious Test shall ever be required as a Qualification to any Office or public Trust under the United States.

## ARTICLE VII.

The Ratification of the Conventions of nine States, shall be sufficient for the Establishment of this Constitution between the States so ratifying the Same.

### Amendments.

ART. 1. Congress shall make no law respecting an establishment of religion, or prohibiting the free exercise thereof; or abridging the freedom of speech, or of the press; or the right of the people peaceably to assemble, and to petition the Government for a redress of grievances.

ART. 2. A well regulated Militia, being necessary to the security of a free State, the right of the people to keep and bear Arms, shall not be infringed.

ART. 3. No Soldier shall, in time of peace be quartered in any house, without the consent of the Owner, nor in time of war, but in a manner to be prescribed by law.

ART. 4. The right of the people to be secure in their persons, houses, papers, and effects, against unreasonable searches and seizures, shall not be violated, and no Warrants shall issue, but upon probable cause, supported by Oath or affirmation, and particularly describing the place to be searched, and the persons or things to be seized.

ART. 5. No person shall be held to answer for a capital, or otherwise infamous crime, unless on a presentment or indictment of a Grand Jury, except in cases arising in the land or naval forces, or in the Militia, when in actual service in time of War or public danger; nor shall any person be subject for the same offence to be twice put in jeopardy of life or limb; nor shall be compelled in any Criminal Case to be a witness against himself, nor be deprived of life, liberty, or property, without due process of law; nor shall private property be taken for public use, without just compensation.

ART. 6. In all criminal prosecutions, the accused shall enjoy the right to a speedy and public trial, by an impartial jury of the State and district wherein the crime shall have been committed, which district shall have been previously ascertained by law, and to be informed of the nature and cause of the accusation; to be confronted with the witnesses against him; to have Compulsory process for obtaining Witnesses in his favour, and to have the Assistance of Counsel for his defence.

ART. 7. In Suits at common law, where the value in controversy shall exceed twenty dollars, the right of trial by jury shall be preserved, and no fact tried by a jury shall be otherwise re-examined in any Court of the United States, than according to the rules of the common law.

ART. 8. Excessive bail shall not be required, nor excessive fines be imposed, nor cruel and unusual punishments inflicted.

ART. 9. The enumeration in the Constitution, of certain rights, shall not be construed to deny or disparage others retained by the people.

ART. 10. The powers not delegated to the United States by the Constitution, nor prohibited by it to the States, are reserved to the States respectively, or to the people.

ART. 11. The Judicial power of the United

States shall not be construed to extend to any suit in law or equity, commenced or prosecuted against one of the United States by Citizens of another State, or by Citizens or Subjects of any Foreign State.

ART. 12. The Electors shall meet in their respective states, and vote by ballot for President and Vice-President, one of whom, at least, shall not be an inhabitant of the same state with themselves; they shall name in their ballots the person voted for as President, and in distinct ballots the person voted for as Vice-President, and they shall make distinct lists of all persons voted for as President, and of all persons voted for as Vice-President, and of the number of votes for each, which lists they shall sign and certify, and transmit sealed to the seat of the government of the United States, directed to the President of the Senate;—The President of the Senate shall, in presence of the Senate and House of Representatives, open all the certificates and the votes shall then be counted;—The person having the greatest number of votes for President, shall be the President, if such number be a majority of the whole number of Electors appointed; and if no person have such majority, then from the persons having the highest numbers not exceeding three on the list of those voted for as President, the House of Representatives shall choose immediately, by ballot, the President. But in choosing the President, the votes shall be taken by states, the representation from each state having one vote; a quorum for this purpose shall consist of a member or members from two thirds of the states, and a majority of all the states shall be necessary to a choice. And if the House of Representatives shall not choose a President whenever the right of choice shall devolve upon them, before the fourth day of March next following, then the Vice-President shall act as President, as in the case of the death or other constitutional disability of the President. The person having the greatest number of votes as Vice-President, shall be the Vice-President, if such number be a majority of the whole number of Electors appointed, and if no person have a majority, then from the two highest numbers on the list, the Senate shall choose the Vice-President; a quorum for the purpose shall consist of two thirds of the whole number of Senators, and a majority of the whole number shall be necessary to a choice. But no person constitutionally ineligible to the office of President shall be eligible to that of Vice-President of the United States.

---

### Mr. Seward's Certificate of the Anti-Slavery Amendment, known as the 13th Amendment.

WILLIAM H. SEWARD, SECRETARY OF STATE OF THE UNITED STATES,

*To all to whom these presents may come, greeting:*
Know ye, that whereas the Congress of the United States on the 1st of February last passed a resolution which is in the words following, namely:

"A resolution submitting to the Legislatures of the several States a proposition to amend the Constitution of the United States.

"*Resolved by the Senate and House of Representatives of the United States of America in Congress assembled, (two-thirds of both Houses concurring,)* That the following article be proposed to the Legislatures of the several States as an amendment to the Constitution of the United States, which, when ratified by three fourths of said Legislatures, shall be valid, to all intents and purposes, as a part of the said Constitution, namely:

### ARTICLE XIII.

"SEC. 1. Neither slavery nor involuntary servitude, except as a punishment for crime, whereof the party shall have been duly convicted, shall exist within the United States, or any place subject to their jurisdiction.

"SEC. 2. Congress shall have power to enforce this article by appropriate legislation."

And whereas it appears from official documents on file in this Department that the amendment to the Constitution of the United States, proposed as aforesaid, has been ratified by the Legislatures of the States of Illinois, Rhode Island, Michigan, Maryland, New York, West Virginia, Maine, Kansas, Massachusetts, Pennsylvania, Virginia, Ohio, Missouri, Nevada, Indiana, Louisiana, Minnesota, Wisconsin, Vermont, Tennessee, Arkansas, Connecticut, New Hampshire, South Carolina, Alabama, North Carolina, and Georgia—in all, twenty-seven States;

And whereas the whole number of States in the United States is thirty-six, and whereas the before specially-named States, whose Legislatures have ratified the said proposed amendment, constitute three-fourths of the whole number of States in the United States:

Now, therefore, be it known that I, William H. Seward, Secretary of State of the United States, by virtue and in pursuance of the second section of the act of Congress approved the twentieth of April, eighteen hundred and eighteen, entitled "An act to provide for the publication of the laws of the United States and for other purposes," do hereby certify that the amendment aforesaid has become valid, to all intents and purposes, as a part of the Constitution of the United States.

In testimony whereof I have hereunto set my hand and caused the seal of the Department of State to be affixed.

Done at the city of Washington this eighteenth day of December, in the year of our Lord [SEAL] one thousand eight hundred and sixty-five, and of the Independence of the United States of America the ninetieth.

WILLIAM H. SEWARD,
*Secretary of State.*

[New Jersey, Oregon, California and Iowa ratified subsequently to the date of this certificate, as did Florida in the same form as South Carolina and Alabama.]

# II.

# PRESIDENT JOHNSON'S ORDERS AND PROCLAMATIONS.

## Respecting Commercial Intercourse with Insurrectionary States, April 29, 1865.

EXECUTIVE CHAMBER,
WASHINGTON, *April 29*, 1865.

Being desirous to relieve all loyal citizens and well-disposed persons, residing in insurrectionary States, from unnecessary commercial restrictions, and to encourage them to return to peaceful pursuits, *It is hereby ordered:*

I. That all restrictions upon internal, domestic, and coastwise commercial intercourse be discontinued in such parts of the States of Tennessee, Virginia, North Carolina, South Carolina, Georgia, Florida, Alabama, Mississippi, and so much of Louisiana as lies east of the Mississippi river, as shall be embraced within the lines of national military occupation, excepting only such restrictions as are imposed by acts of Congress and regulations in pursuance thereof, prescribed by the Secretary of the Treasury, and approved by the President; and excepting also from the effect of this order the following articles contraband of war, to wit: arms, ammunition, all articles from which ammunition is manufactured, gray uniforms and cloth, locomotives, cars, railroad iron, and machinery for operating railroads, telegraph wires, insulators, and instruments for operating telegraphic lines.

II. All existing military and naval orders in any manner restricting internal, domestic, and coastwise commercial intercourse and trade with or in the localities above named be, and the same are hereby revoked; and that no military or naval officer, in any manner, interrupt or interfere with the same, or with any boats or other vessels engaged therein, under proper authority, pursuant to the regulations of the Secretary of the Treasury.

ANDREW JOHNSON.

## Executive Order for the Trial of the Alleged Assassins of President Lincoln, May 1, 1865.

EXECUTIVE CHAMBER,
WASHINGTON CITY, *May 1*, 1865.

Whereas, the Attorney General of the United States hath given his opinion:

That the persons implicated in the murder of the late President, Abraham Lincoln, and the attempted assassination of the Honorable William H. Seward, Secretary of State, and in an alleged conspiracy to assassinate other officers of the Federal Government at Washington city, and their aiders and abettors, are subject to the jurisdiction of, and lawfully triable before, a military commission:

It is *Ordered:* 1st, That the Assistant Adjutant General detail nine competent military officers to serve as a commission for the trial of said parties, and that the Judge Advocate General proceed to prefer charges against said parties for their alleged offences, and bring them to trial before said military commission; that said trial or trials be conducted by the said Judge Advocate General, and as recorder thereof, in person, aided by such assistant and special judge advocates as he may designate; and that said trials be conducted with all diligence consistent with the ends of justice: the said commission to sit without regard to hours.

2d. That Brevet Major General Hartranft be assigned to duty as special provost marshal general, for the purpose of said trial, and attendance upon said commission, and the execution of its mandates.

3d. That the said commission establish such order or rules of proceedings as may avoid unnecessary delay, and conduce to the ends of public justice.

ANDREW JOHNSON.

---

ORDER FOR THE EXECUTION OF THE SENTENCE OF THE COMMISSION.

EXECUTIVE MANSION, *July 5*, 1865.

The foregoing sentences in the cases of David E. Herold, G. A. Atzerodt, Lewis Payne, Michael O'Laughlin, Edward Spangler, Samuel Arnold, Mary E. Surratt and Samuel A. Mudd, are hereby approved, and it is ordered that the sentences of said David E. Herold, G. A. Atzerodt, Lewis Payne, and Mary E. Surratt, be carried into execution by the proper military authority, under the direction of the Secretary of War, on the 7th day of July, 1865, between the hours of 10 o'clock, a. m., and 2 o'clock, p. m., of that day. It is further ordered, that the prisoners, Samuel Arnold, Samuel A. Mudd, Edward Spangler, and Michael O'Laughlin, be confined at hard labor in the penitentiary at Albany, New York, during the period designated in their respective sentences.

ANDREW JOHNSON,
*President.*

[By an order dated July 15, the place of confinement, as to the four last mentioned, was changed to the "military prison at Dry Tortugas, Florida."]

---

## For the Arrest of Jefferson Davis, Clement C. Clay, and others, May 2, 1865.

Whereas it appears from evidence in the Bureau of Military Justice that the atrocious murder of the late President, Abraham Lincoln, and the attempted assassination of the Honorable William H. Steward, Secretary of State, were incited, concerted, and procured by and between Jefferson Davis, late of Richmond, Virginia, and Jacob Thompson, Clement C. Clay, Beverly Tucker, George N. Sanders, William C. Cleary, and other rebels and traitors against the Government of the United States, harbored in Canada:

Now, therefore, to the end that justice may be done, I, Andrew Johnson, President of the United States, do offer and promise for the arrest of said persons, or either of them, within the limits of the United States, so that they can be brought to trial, the following rewards:

One hundred thousand dollars for the arrest of Jefferson Davis.

Twenty-five thousand dollars for the arrest of Clement C. Clay.*

Twenty-five thousand dollars for the arrest of Jacob Thompson, late of Mississippi.

Twenty-five thousand dollars for the arrest of George N. Sanders.

Twenty-five thousand dollars for the arrest of Beverly Tucker.

Ten thousand dollars for the arrest of William C. Cleary, late clerk of Clement C. Clay.

The Provost Marshal General of the United States is directed to cause a description of said persons, with notice of the above rewards, to be published.

In testimony whereof, I have hereunto set my hand and caused the seal of the United States to be affixed.

Done at the city of Washington this second day of May, in the year of our Lord one thousand eight hundred and sixty-five, [L. S.] and of the Independence of the United States of America the eighty-ninth.

ANDREW JOHNSON.

By the President:
W. HUNTER, Acting Secretary of State.

### Executive Order to Re-establish the Authority of the United States, and Execute the Laws within the Geographical Limits known as the State of Virginia.

EXECUTIVE CHAMBER,
WASHINGTON CITY, *May 9*, 1865.

ORDERED—*First.* That all acts and proceedings of the political, military, and civil organizations which have been in a state of insurrection and rebellion, within the State of Virginia, against the authority and laws of the United States, and of which Jefferson Davis, John Letcher, and William Smith were late the respective chiefs, are declared null and void. All persons who shall exercise, claim, pretend, or attempt to exercise any political, military, or civil power, authority, jurisdiction, or right, by, through, or under Jefferson Davis, late of the

city of Richmond, and his confederates, or under John Letcher or William Smith and their confederates, or under any pretended political, military, or civil commission or authority issued by them, or either of them, since the 17th day of April, 1861, shall be deemed and taken as in rebellion against the United States, and shall be dealt with accordingly.

*Second.* That the Secretary of State proceed to put in force all laws of the United States, the administration whereof belongs to the Department of State, applicable to the geographical limits aforesaid.

*Third.* That the Secretary of the Treasury proceed, without delay, to nominate for appointment, assessors of taxes and collectors of customs and internal revenue, and such other officers of the Treasury Department as are authorized by law, and shall put into execution the revenue laws of the United States within the geographical limits aforesaid. In making appointments, the preference shall be given to qualified loyal persons residing within the districts where their respective duties are to be performed. But if suitable persons shall not be found residents of the districts, then persons residing in other States or districts shall be appointed.

*Fourth.* That the Postmaster General shall proceed to establish post offices and post routes, and put into execution the postal laws of the United States within the said States, giving to loyal residents the preference of appointment; but if suitable persons are not found, then to appoint agents, &c., from other States.

*Fifth.* That the district judge of said district proceed to hold courts within said State, in accordance with the provisions of the acts of Congress. The Attorney General will instruct the proper officers to libel and bring to judgment, confiscation, and sale, property subject to confiscation, and enforce the administration of justice within said State, in all matters civil and criminal within the cognizance and jurisdiction of the Federal courts.

*Sixth.* That the Secretary of War assign such assistant provost marshal general, and such provost marshals in each district of said State as he may deem necessary.

*Seventh.* The Secretary of the Navy will take possession of all public property belonging to the Navy Department within said geographical limits, and put in operation all acts of Congress in relation to naval affairs having application to the said State.

*Eighth.* The Secretary of the Interior will also put in force the laws relating to the Department of the Interior.

*Ninth.* That to carry into effect the guarantee of the Federal Constitution of a republican form of State government, and afford the advantage and security of domestic laws, as well as to complete the re-establishment of the authority of the laws of the United States, and the full and complete restoration of peace within the limits aforesaid, Francis H. Pierpoint, Governor of the State of Virginia, will be aided by the Federal Government, so far as may be necessary, in the lawful measures which he may take for the extension and administration of the State Government throughout the geographical limits of said State.

---

* Mr. CLAY was released under this order:

WAR DEPARTMENT, ADJUTANT GENERAL'S OFFICE,
WASHINGTON, *April* 17, 1866.

Maj. Gen. N. A. MILES, *Commanding, &c., Fortress Monroe, Virginia:*

*Ordered,* That Clement C. Clay, Jr., is hereby released from confinement, and permitted to return to and remain in the State of Alabama, and to visit such other places in the United States as his personal business may render absolutely necessary, upon the following conditions, viz: that he takes the oath of allegiance to the United States, and gives his parole of honor to conduct himself as a loyal citizen of the same, and to report himself in person at any time and place to answer any charges that may hereafter be prepared against him by the United States.

Please report receipt and execution of this order.

By order of the President of the United States:
E. D. TOWNSEND,
*Assistant Adjutant General.*

In testimony whereof, I have hereunto set my [SEAL.] hand and caused the seal of the United States to be affixed.

ANDREW JOHNSON.

By the President:
W. HUNTER, *Acting Secretary of State.*

## Equality of Rights with all Maritime Nations, May 10, 1865.

Whereas the President of the United States, by his proclamation of the nineteenth day of April, one thousand eight hundred and sixty-one, did declare certain States therein mentioned in insurrection against the Government of the United States;

And whereas armed resistance to the authority of this Government in the said insurrectionary States may be regarded as virtually at an end, and the persons by whom that resistance, as well as the operations of insurgent cruisers, were directed, are fugitives or captives;

And whereas it is understood that some of those cruisers are still infesting the high seas, and others are preparing to capture, burn, and destroy vessels of the United States:

Now, therefore, be it known, that I, Andrew Johnson, President of the United States, hereby enjoin all naval, military, and civil officers of the United States, diligently to endeavor, by all lawful means, to arrest the said cruisers, and to bring them into a port of the United States, in order that they may be prevented from committing further depredations on commerce, and that the persons on board of them may no longer enjoy impunity for their crimes.

And I further proclaim and declare, that if, after a reasonable time shall have elapsed for this proclamation to become known in the ports of nations claiming to have been neutrals, the said insurgent cruisers and the persons on board of them shall continue to receive hospitality in the said ports, this Government will deem itself justified in refusing hospitality to the public vessels of such nations in ports of the United States, and in adopting such other measures as may be deemed advisable towards vindicating the national sovereignty.

In witness whereof, I have hereunto set my hand and caused the seal of the United States to be affixed.

Done at the city of Washington, this tenth day of May, in the year of our Lord one [L. S.] thousand eight hundred and sixty-five, and of the independence of the United States of America the eighty-ninth.

ANDREW JOHNSON.

By the President:
W. HUNTER, *Acting Secretary of State.*

## Commercial Intercourse and the Blockade, May 22, 1865.

Whereas, by the proclamation of the President of the eleventh day of April last, certain ports of the United States therein specified, which had previously been subject to blockade, were, for objects of public safety, declared, in conformity with previous special legislation of Congress, to be closed against foreign commerce during the national will, to be thereafter expressed and made known by the President; and whereas events and circumstances have since occurred which, in my judgment, render it expedient to remove that restriction, except as to the ports of Galveston, La Salle, Brazos de Santiago (Point Isabel,) and Brownsville, in the State of Texas:

Now, therefore, be it known that I, Andrew Johnson, President of the United States, do hereby declare that the ports aforesaid, not excepted as above, shall be open to foreign commerce from and after the first day of July, next; that commercial intercourse with the said ports may, from that time, be carried on, subject to the laws of the United States, and in pursuance of such regulations as may be prescribed by the Secretary of the Treasury. If, however, any vessel from a foreign port shall enter any of the before-named excepted ports in the State of Texas, she will continue to be held liable to the penalties prescribed by the act of Congress approved on the thirteenth day of July, eighteen hundred and sixty-one, and the persons on board of her to such penalties as may be incurred, pursuant to the laws of war, for trading, or attempting to trade, with an enemy.

And I, Andrew Johnson, President of the United States, do hereby declare and make known that the United States of America do, henceforth, disallow to all persons trading, or attempting to trade, in any ports of the United States in violation of the laws thereof, all pretence of belligerent rights and privileges, and I give notice that, from the date of this proclamation, all such offenders will be held and dealt with as pirates.

It is also ordered that all restrictions upon trade heretofore imposed in the territory of the United States east of the Mississippi river, save those relating to contraband of war, to the reservation of the rights of the United States to property purchased in the territory of an enemy, and to the twenty-five per cent. upon purchases of cotton, are removed. All provisions of the internal revenue law will be carried into effect under the proper officers.

In witness whereof I have hereunto set my hand and caused the seal of the United States to be affixed.

Done at the city of Washington, this twenty-second day of May, in the year of our Lord one thousand eight hundred and [SEAL.] sixty-five, and of the Independence of the United States of America the eighty-ninth.

ANDREW JOHNSON.

By the President:
W. HUNTER, *Acting Secretary of State.*

## Of Amnesty, May 29, 1865.

WHEREAS the President of the United States, on the 8th day of December, A. D. eighteen hundred and sixty-three, and on the 26th day of March, A. D. eighteen hundred and sixty-four, did, with the object to suppress the existing rebellion, to induce all persons to return to their loyalty, and to restore the authority of the United States, issue proclamations offering amnesty and pardon to certain persons who had directly, or by implication, participated in the said rebellion; and whereas many persons who had so engaged in said rebellion, have, since the issuance of said proclamations, failed or neglected to take the benefits offered thereby; and whereas many persons who have been justly deprived of all claim to amnesty and pardon thereunder by reason of their participation, directly or by implication, in said rebellion, and continued hostility to the Government of the United States since the date of said proclamations, now desire to apply for and obtain amnesty and pardon:

To the end, therefore, that the authority of the Government of the United States may be restored, and that peace, order, and freedom may be established, I, Andrew Johnson, President of the United States, do proclaim and declare that I hereby grant to all persons who have, directly or indirectly, participated in the existing rebellion, except as hereinafter excepted, amnesty and pardon, with restoration of all rights of property, except as to slaves, and except in cases where legal proceedings, under the laws of the United States providing for the confiscation of property of persons engaged in rebellion, have been instituted; but upon the condition, nevertheless, that every such person shall take and subscribe the following oath (or affirmation), and thenceforward keep and maintain said oath inviolate; and which oath shall be registered for permanent preservation, and shall be of the tenor and effect following, to wit:

" I, —— ——, do solemnly swear (or affirm), in presence of Almighty God, that I will henceforth faithfully support, protect, and defend the Constitution of the United States, and the union of the States thereunder; and that I will, in like manner, abide by and faithfully support all laws and proclamations which have been made during the existing rebellion, with reference to the emancipation of slaves: So help me God."

The following classes of persons are excepted from the benefits of this proclamation :

1st. All who are or shall have been pretended civil or diplomatic officers or otherwise domestic or foreign agents of the pretended government.

2d. All who left judicial stations under the United States to aid the rebellion.

3d. All who shall have been military or naval officers of said pretended confederate government above the rank of colonel in the army, or lieutenant in the navy.

4th. All who left seats in the Congress of the United States to aid the rebellion.

5th. All who resigned or tendered resignations of their commissions in the army or navy of the United States, to evade duty in resisting the rebellion.

6th. All who have engaged in any way in treating otherwise than lawfully as prisoners of war, persons found in the United States service as officers, soldiers, seamen, or in other capacities.

7th. All persons who have been or are absentees from the United States for the purpose of aiding the rebellion.

8th. All military and naval officers, in the rebel service, who were educated by the Government in the Military Academy at West Point or the United States Naval Academy.

9th. All persons who held the pretended offices of governors of States in insurrection against the United States.

10th. All persons who left their homes within the jurisdiction and protection of the United States, and passed beyond the Federal military lines into the pretended confederate States for the purpose of aiding the rebellion.

11th. All persons who have been engaged in the destruction of the commerce of the United States upon the high seas, and all persons who have made raids into the United States from Canada, or been engaged in destroying the commerce of the United States upon the lakes and rivers that separate the British Provinces from the United States.

12th. All persons who, at the time when they seek to obtain the benefits hereof by taking the oath herein prescribed, are in military, naval, or civil confinement, or custody, or under bonds of the civil, military, or naval authorities, or agents of the United States, as prisoners of war, or persons detained for offences of any kind, either before or after conviction.

13th. All persons who have voluntarily participated in said rebellion, and the estimated value of whose taxable property is over twenty thousand dollars.

14th. All persons who have taken the oath of amnesty as prescribed in the President's proclamation of December 8, A. D. 1863, or an oath of allegiance to the Government of the United States since the date of said proclamation, and who thenceforward kept and maintained the same inviolate.

*Provided*, That special application may be made to the President for pardon by any person belonging to the excepted classes; and such clemency will be liberally extended as may be consistent with the facts of the case and the peace and dignity of the United States.

The Secretary of State will establish rules and regulations for administering and recording said amnesty oath, so as to insure its benefit to the people, and guard the Government against fraud.

In testimony whereof, I have hereunto set my hand, and caused the seal of the United States to be affixed.

Done at the City of Washington, the twenty-ninth day of May, in the year of our Lord one thousand eight hundred and sixty-five, and of the Independence of the United States the eighty-ninth.

[SEAL.]

ANDREW JOHNSON.

By the President:
WILLIAM H. SEWARD, *Secretary of State.*

—

### CIRCULAR.

DEPARTMENT OF STATE,
WASHINGTON, *May* 29, 1865.

SIR: A copy of the President's amnesty proclamation of this date is herewith appended. By a clause in the instrument, the Secretary of State is directed to establish rules and regulations for administering and recording the amnesty oath, so as to insure its benefit to the people and guard the Government against fraud. Pursuant to this injunction,. you are informed that the oath prescribed in the proclamation may be taken and subscribed before any commissioned officer, civil, military, or naval, in the service of the United States, or any civil or military officer of a loyal State or Territory, who, by the laws thereof, may be qualified for administering oaths. All officers who receive such oaths are hereby authorized to give certified copies thereof to the persons respectively by whom they were made. And such officers are hereby required to transmit the originals of such oaths, at as early a day as may be convenient, to this Department, where they will be deposited, and remain in the archives of the Government. A register thereof will be kept in the Department, and on application, in proper cases, certificates will be issued of such records in the customary form of official certificates.

I am, sir, your obedient servant,
WILLIAM H. SEWARD.

### Appointing William W. Holden Provisional Governor of North Carolina, May 29, 1865.

Whereas the fourth section of the fourth article of the Constitution of the United States declares that the United States shall guarantee to every State in the Union a republican form of government, and shall protect each of them against invasion and domestic violence; and whereas the President of the United States is, by the Constitution, made commander-in-chief of the army and navy, as well as chief civil executive officer of the United States, and is bound by solemn oath faithfully to execute the office of President of the United States, and to take care that the laws be faithfully executed; and whereas the rebellion, which has been waged by a portion of the people of the United States against the properly constituted authorities of the Government thereof, in the most violent and revolting form, but whose organized and armed forces have now been almost entirely overcome, has, in its revolutionary progress, deprived the people of the State of North Carolina of all civil government; and whereas it becomes necessary and proper to carry out and enforce the obligations of the United States to the people of North Carolina, in securing them in the enjoyment of a republican form of government:

Now, therefore, in obedience to the high and solemn duties imposed upon me by the Constitution of the United States, and for the purpose of enabling the loyal people of said State to organize a State government, whereby justice may be established, domestic tranquillity insured, and loyal citizens protected in all their rights of life, liberty, and property, I, Andrew Johnson, President of the United States, and Commander-in-Chief of the army and navy of the United States, do hereby appoint William W. Holden Provisional Governor of the State of North Carolina, whose duty it shall be, at the earliest practicable period, to prescribe such rules and regulations as may be necessary and proper for convening a convention, composed of delegates to be chosen by that portion of the people of said State who are loyal to the United States, and no others, for the purpose of altering or amending the constitution thereof; and with authority to exercise, within the limits of said State, all the powers necessary and proper to enable such loyal people of the State of North Carolina to restore said State to its constitutional relations to the Federal Government, and to present such a republican form of State government as will entitle the State to the guarantee of the United States therefor, and its people to protection by the United States against invasion, insurrection, and domestic violence; *Provided*, that in any election that may be hereafter held for choosing delegates to any State convention, as aforesaid, no person shall be qualified as an elector, or shall be eligible as a member of such convention, unless he shall have previously taken the oath of amnesty, as set forth in the President's proclamation of May 29, A. D. 1865, and is a voter qualified as prescribed by the Constitution and laws of the State of North Carolina, in force immediately before the 20th day of May, 1861, the date of the so-called ordinance of secession; and the said convention when convened, or the Legislature that may be thereafter assembled, will prescribe the qualification of electors, and the eligibility of persons to hold office under the Constitution and laws of the State, a power the people of the several States composing the Federal Union have rightfully exercised from the origin of the Government to the present time.

And I do hereby direct:

*First.* That the military commander of the Department, and all officers and persons in the military and naval service aid and assist the said Provisional Governor in carrying into effect this proclamation, and they are enjoined to abstain from, in any way, hindering, impeding, or discouraging the loyal people from the organization of a State Government, as herein authorized.

*Second.* That the Secretary of State proceed to put in force all laws of the United States, the administration whereof belongs to the State Department, applicable to the geographical limits aforesaid.

*Third.* That the Secretary of the Treasury proceed to nominate for appointment assessors of taxes and collectors of customs and internal revenue, and such other officers of the Treasury Department as are authorized by law, and put in execution the revenue laws of the United States within the geographical limits aforesaid. In making appointments, the preference shall be given to qualified loyal persons residing within the districts where their respective duties are to be performed. But, if suitable residents of the districts shall not be found, then persons residing in other States or districts shall be appointed.

*Fourth.* That the Postmaster General proceed to establish post offices and post routes, and put into execution the postal laws of the United States within the said State, giving to loyal residents the preference of appointment; but if suitable residents are not found, then to appoint agents, &c., from other States.

*Fifth.* That the district judge for the judicial district in which North Carolina is included proceed to hold courts within said State, in accordance with the provisions of the act of Congress. The Attorney General will instruct the proper officers to libel, and bring to judgment, confiscation and sale, property subject to confiscation, and enforce the administration of justice within said State in all matters within the cognizance and jurisdiction of the Federal courts.

*Sixth.* That the Secretary of the Navy take possession of all public property belonging to the Navy Department, within said geographical limits, and put in operation all acts of Congress in relation to naval affairs having application to the said State.

*Seventh.* That the Secretary of the Interior put in force the laws relating to the Interior Department, applicable to the geographical limits aforesaid.

In testimony whereof, I have hereunto set my hand and caused the great seal of the United States to be affixed.

Done at the city of Washington, this twenty-ninth day of May, in the year of our Lord one thousand eight hundred and [L. S.] sixty-five, and of the Independence of the United States the eighty-ninth.

ANDREW JOHNSON.

By the President:

WILLIAM H. SEWARD, *Secretary of State.*

1865, June 13—A like proclamation was issued, appointing WILLIAM L. SHARKEY, Provisional Governor of Mississippi.

1865, June 17—JAMES JOHNSON appointed Provisional Governor of Georgia.

1865, June 17—ANDREW J. HAMILTON appointed Provisional Governor of Texas.

1865, June 21—LEWIS E. PARSONS appointed Provisional Governor of Alabama.

1865, June 30—BENJAMIN F. PERRY appointed Provisional Governor of South Carolina.

1865, July 13—WILLIAM MARVIN appointed Provisional Governor of Florida.

### Orders Respecting Freedmen.

EXECUTIVE MANSION,
WASHINGTON, D. C., *June* 2, 1865.

Whereas, By an act of Congress, approved March 3, 1865, there was established in the War Department a Bureau of Refugees, Freedmen, and Abandoned Lands, and to which, in accordance with the said act of Congress, is committed the supervision and management of all abandoned lands, and the control of all subjects relating to refugees and freedmen from rebel States, or from any district of country within the territory embraced in the operations of the army, under such rules and regulations as may be prescribed by the head of the bureau, and approved by the President; and whereas, it appears that the management of abandoned lands, and subjects relating to refugees and freedmen, as aforesaid, have been, and still are, by orders based on military exigencies, or legislation based on previous statutes, partly in the hands of military officers disconnected with said bureau, and partly in charge of officers of the Treasury Department; it is therefore *Ordered,* That all officers of the Treasury Department, all military officers and others in the service of the United States, turn over to the authorized officers of said bureau all abandoned lands and property contemplated in said act of Congress, approved March third, eighteen hundred and sixty-five, establishing the Bureau of Refugees, Freedmen, and Abandoned Lands, that may now be under or within their control. They will also turn over to such officers all funds collected by tax or otherwise for the benefit of refugees or freedmen, or accruing from abandoned lands or property set apart for their use, and will transfer to them all official records connected with the administration of affairs which pertain to said Bureau.

ANDREW JOHNSON.

By order of the Secretary of War:

E. D. TOWNSEND, *Ass't Adj't General.*

---

### CIRCULAR No. 15.

WAR DEPARTMENT,
BUREAU REFUGEES, FREEDMEN,
AND ABANDONED LANDS,
WASHINGTON, D. C., *September* 12, 1865.

I. Circular No. 13, of July 28, 1865, from this bureau, and all portions of circulars from this bureau conflicting with the provisions of this circular, are hereby rescinded.

II. This bureau has charge of such "tracts of land within the insurrectionary States as shall have been abandoned, or to which the United States shall have acquired title by confiscation or sale, or otherwise," and no such lands now in its possession shall be surrendered to any claimant except as hereinafter provided.

III. Abandoned lands are defined in section 2 of the act of Congress approved July 2, 1864, as lands, "the lawful owner whereof shall be voluntarily absent therefrom, and engaged either in arms or otherwise in aiding or encouraging the rebellion."

IV. Land will not be regarded as confiscated until it has been condemned and sold by decree of the United States court for the district in which the property may be found, and the title thereto thus vested in the United States.

V. Upon its appearing satisfactorily to any assistant commissioner that any property under his control is not abandoned as above defined, and that the United States has acquired no title to it by confiscation, sale or otherwise, he will formally surrender it to the authorized claimant or claimants, promptly reporting his action to the Commissioner.

VI. Assistant commissioners will prepare accurate descriptions of all confiscated and abandoned lands under their control, keeping a record thereof themselves, and forwarding monthly to the Commissioner copies of these descriptions in the manner prescribed in circular No. 10, of July 11, 1865, from this bureau.

They will set apart so much of said lands as is necessary for the immediate use of loyal refugees and freedmen, being careful to select for this purpose those lands which most clearly fall under the control of this bureau, which selection must be submitted to the Commissioner for his approval.

The specific division of lands so set apart into lots, and the rental or sale thereof, according to section 4 of the law establishing the bureau, will be completed as soon as practicable, and reported to the Commissioner.

VII. Abandoned lands held by this bureau may be restored to owners pardoned by the President, by the assistant commissioners, to whom applications for such restoration should be forwarded, so far as practicable, through the superintendents of the districts in which the lands are situated.

Each application must be accompanied by—

1st. Evidence of special pardon by the President, or a copy of the oath of amnesty prescribed in the President's proclamation of May 29, 1865, when the applicant is not included in any of the classes therein excepted from the benefits of said oath.

2d. Proof of title.

Officers of the bureau through whom the application passes will indorse thereon such facts as may assist the assistant commissioner in his decision, stating especially the use made by the bureau of the land.

VIII. No land under cultivation by loyal refugees or freedmen will be restored under this circular, until the crops now growing shall be secured for the benefit of the cultivators, unless full and just compensation be made for their labor and its products, and for their expenditures.   O. O. HOWARD,
*Major General, Commissioner.*

Approved:   ANDREW JOHNSON,
*President of the United States.*

## For the Return to Persons Pardoned, of their Property.

EXECUTIVE OFFICE, *August* 16, 1865.

Respectfully returned to the Commissioner of Bureau Refugees, Freedmen, &c. The records of this office show that B. B. Leake was specially pardoned by the President on the 27th ultimo, and was thereby restored to all his rights of property, except as to slaves. Notwithstanding this, it is understood that the possession of his property is withheld from him. I have, therefore, to direct that General Fisk, assistant commissioner at Nashville, Tennessee, be instructed by the Chief Commissioner of Bureau of Freedmen, &c., to relinquish possession of the property of Mr. Leake, held by him as assistant commissioner, &c., and that the same be immediately restored to the said Leake. The same action will be had in all similar cases.*

ANDREW JOHNSON,
*President United States.*

To O. O. HOWARD,
*Maj. General, Com'r Freedmen's Affairs.*

## Respecting Commercial Intercourse, and the Suppression of the Rebellion in the State of Tennessee, June 13, 1865.

Whereas by my proclamation of the twenty-ninth of April, one thousand eight hundred and sixty-five, all restrictions upon internal,

*Extract from letter of General Howard, April 23, 1866, in reply to resolution of the House of Representatives of March 5, 1866:

"In complying with these definite instructions, the bureau has been compelled to part with the greater portion of the property once under its control. Except in the very few cases where property has been actually sold under the act of July 17, 1862, and in that portion of South Carolina and Georgia embraced in the provisions of General Sherman's Field Order No. 15, its tenure of property has been too uncertain to justify allotments to freedmen.

| | Acres. |
|---|---|
| Property seized under act of July, 1862, and restored by this bureau | 15,452 |
| Abandoned property allotted to freedmen and restored by this bureau | 14,652 |
| Abandoned property not allotted to freedmen restored by this bureau | 400,000 |
| Total | 430,104" |

domestic, and commercial intercourse, with certain exceptions therein specified and set forth, were removed "in such parts of the States of Tennessee, Virginia, North Carolina, South Carolina, Georgia, Florida, Alabama, Mississippi, and so much of Louisiana as lies east of the Mississippi river, as shall be embraced within the lines of national military occupation; * *"

And whereas by my proclamation of the twenty-second of May, one thousand eight hundred and sixty-five, for reasons therein given, it was declared that certain ports of the United States which had been previously closed against foreign commerce, should, with certain specified exceptions be reopened to such commerce, on and after the first day of July next, subject to the laws of the United States, and in pursuance of such regulations as might be prescribed by the Secretary of the Treasury;

And whereas I am satisfactorily informed, that dangerous combinations against the laws of the United States no longer exist within the State of Tennessee; that the insurrection heretofore existing within said State has been suppressed; that within the boundaries thereof the authority of the United States is undisputed; and that such officers of the United States as have been duly commissioned are in the undisturbed exercise of their official functions:

Now, therefore, be it known that I, Andrew Johnson, President of the United States, do hereby declare that all restrictions upon internal, domestic, and coastwise intercourse and trade, and upon the removal of products of States heretofore declared in insurrection, reserving and excepting only those relating to contraband of war, as hereinafter recited, and also those which relate to the reservation of the rights of the United States to property purchased in the territory of an enemy, heretofore imposed in the territory of the United States east of the Mississippi river, are annulled, and I do hereby direct that they be forthwith removed; and that on and after the first day of July next all restriction upon foreign commerce with said ports, with the exception and reservation aforesaid, be likewise removed; and that the commerce of such States shall be conducted under the supervision of the regularly appointed officers of the customs provided by law; and such officers of the customs shall receive any captured and abandoned property that may be turned over to them, under the law, by the military or naval forces of the United States, and dispose of such property as shall be directed by the Secretary of the Treasury.

The following articles contraband of war are excepted from the effect of this proclamation: arms, ammunition, all articles from which ammunition is made, and gray uniforms and cloth.

And I hereby also proclaim and declare that the insurrection, so far as it relates to, and within the State of Tennessee, and the inhabitants of the said State of Tennessee as re-organized and constituted under their recently adopted constitution and re-organization, and accepted by them, is suppressed, and therefore, also, that all the disabilities and disqualifications attaching to said State and the inhabitants thereof consequent upon any proclamations, issued by virtue of the fifth section of the act entitled "An act further to provide for the collection of duties on imports and for other purposes," approved the thirteenth day of July, one thousand eight hundred and sixty-one, are removed.

But nothing herein contained shall be considered or construed as in any wise changing or impairing any of the penalties and forfeitures for treason heretofore incurred under the laws of the United States, or any of the provisions, restrictions, or disabilities set forth in my proclamation, bearing date the twenty-ninth day of May, one thousand eight hundred and sixty-five, or as impairing existing regulations for the suspension of the habeas corpus, and the exercise of military law in cases where it shall be necessary for the general public safety and welfare during the existing insurrection; nor shall this proclamation affect, or in any way impair, any laws heretofore passed by Congress, and duly approved by the President, or any proclamations or orders, issued by him, during the aforesaid insurrection, abolishing slavery, or in any way affecting the relations of slavery, whether of persons or of property; but on the contrary, all such laws and proclamations heretofore made or issued are expressly saved, and declared to be in full force and virtue.

In testimony whereof, I have hereunto set my hand, and caused the seal of the United States to be affixed.

Done at the city of Washington, this thirteenth day of June, in the year of our Lord one thousand eight hundred and [SEAL.] sixty-five, and of the independence of the United States of America the eighty-ninth.    ANDREW JOHNSON.

By the President:
WILLIAM H. SEWARD, *Secretary of State.*

---

### Blockade Rescinded, June 23, 1865.

Whereas by the proclamation of the President of the fifteenth and twenty-seventh of April, eighteen hundred and sixty-one, a blockade of certain ports of the United States was set on foot; but whereas the reasons for that measure have ceased to exist:

Now, therefore, be it known that I, Andrew Johnson, President of the United States, do hereby declare and proclaim the blockade aforesaid to be rescinded as to all the ports aforesaid, including that of Galveston and other ports west of the Mississippi river, which ports will be open to foreign commerce on the first of July next, on the terms and conditions set forth in my proclamation of the twenty-second of May last.

It is to be understood, however, that the blockade thus rescinded was an international measure for the purpose of protecting the sovereign rights of the United States. The greater or less subversion of civil authority in the region to which it applied, and the impracticability of at once restoring that in due efficiency, may, for a season, make it advisable to employ the army and navy of the United States towards carrying the laws into effect, wherever such employment may be necessary.

In testimony whereof, I have hereunto set my hand and caused the seal of the United States to be affixed.

Done at the city of Washington this twenty-third day of June, in the year of our Lord one thousand eight hundred and [L. S.] sixty-five, and of the Independence of the United States the eighty-ninth.
ANDREW JOHNSON.

By the President:
W. HUNTER, *Acting Secretary of State.*

---

### Further Removal of Restrictions, August 29, 1865.

Whereas by my proclamations of the thirteenth and twenty-fourth of June, one thousand eight hundred and sixty-five, removing restrictions, in part, upon internal, domestic, and coastwise intercourse and trade with those States recently declared in insurrection, certain articles were excepted from the effect of said proclamations as contraband of war; and whereas the necessity for restricting trade in said articles has now, in a great measure, ceased: It is hereby ordered, that on and after the 1st day of September, 1865, all restrictions aforesaid be removed, so that the articles declared by the said proclamations to be contraband of war may be imported into and sold in said States, subject only to such regulations as the Secretary of the Treasury may prescribe.

In testimony whereof, I have hereunto set my hand and caused the seal of the United States to be affixed.

Done at the city of Washington this twenty-ninth day of August, in the year of our Lord one thousand eight hundred and [L. S.] sixty-five, and of the Independence of the United States of America the ninetieth.
ANDREW JOHNSON.

By the President:
WILLIAM H. SEWARD, *Secretary of State.*

---

### Passports for Paroled Prisoners.

DEPARTMENT OF STATE,
WASHINGTON, *August* 25, 1865.

Paroled prisoners asking passports as citizens of the United States, and against whom no special charges may be pending, will be furnished with passports upon application therefor to the Department of State in the usual form. Such passports will, however, be issued upon the condition that the applicants do not return to the United States without leave of the President. Other persons implicated in the rebellion, who may wish to go abroad, will apply to the Department of State for passports, and the applications will be disposed of according to the merits of the several cases.

By the President of the United States.
WILLIAM H. SEWARD.

---

### Paroling certain State Prisoners.

EXECUTIVE OFFICE,
WASHINGTON, *October* 11, 1865.

Whereas the following named persons, to wit: John A. Campbell, of Alabama; John H. Reagan, of Texas; Alexander H. Stephens, of Georgia; George A. Trenholm, of South Carolina; and Charles Clark, of Mississippi, lately engaged in rebellion against the United States Government, who are now in close custody, have made their submission to the authority of the United States and applied to the President for pardon under his proclamation; and whereas, the authority of the Federal Government is sufficiently restored in the aforesaid States to admit of the enlargement of said persons from close custody, it is ordered that they be released on giving their respective paroles to appear at such time and place as the President may designate, to answer any charge that he may direct to be preferred against them; and also that they will respectively abide until further orders in the places herein designated, and not depart therefrom: John A. Campbell, in the State of Alabama; John H. Reagan, in the State of Texas; Alexander H. Stephens, in the State of Georgia; George A. Trenholm, in the State of South Carolina; and Charles Clark, in the State of Mississippi. And if the President should grant his pardon to any of said persons, such person's parole will be thereby discharged.

ANDREW JOHNSON,
President.

## Martial Law Withdrawn from Kentucky, October 12, 1865.

Whereas by a proclamation of the fifth day of July, one thousand eight hundred and sixty-four, the President of the United States, when the civil war was flagrant, and when combinations were in progress in Kentucky for the purpose of inciting insurgent raids into that State, directed that the proclamation suspending the writ of *habeas corpus* should be made effectual in Kentucky, and that martial law should be established there and continue until said proclamation should be revoked or modified;

And whereas since then the danger of insurgent raids into Kentucky has substantially passed away:

Now, therefore, be it known that I, Andrew Johnson, President of the United States, by virtue of the authority vested in me by the Constitution, do hereby declare that the said proclamation of the fifth day of July, one thousand eight hundred and sixty-four, shall be, and is hereby, modified in so far that martial law shall be no longer in force in Kentucky from and after the date hereof.

In testimony whereof, I have hereunto set my hand and caused the seal of the United States to be affixed.

Done at the city of Washington this twelfth day of October, in the year of our Lord one thousand eight hundred and sixty-five, and of the Independence of the United States of America the ninetieth.

[L. S.]

ANDREW JOHNSON.

By the President:
W. HUNTER, *Acting Secretary of State.*

## Annulling the Suspension of the Habeas Corpus, December 1, 1865

Whereas by the proclamation of the President of the United States of the fifteenth day of September, one thousand eight hundred and sixty-three, the privilege of the writ of *habeas corpus* was, in certain cases therein set forth, suspended throughout the United States;

And whereas the reasons for that suspension may be regarded as having ceased in some of the States and Territories:

Now, therefore, be it known that I, Andrew Johnson, President of the United States, do hereby proclaim and declare that the suspension aforesaid, and all other proclamations and orders suspending the privilege of the writ of *habeas corpus* in the States and Territories of the United States, are revoked and annulled excepting as to the States of Virginia, Kentucky, Tennessee, North Carolina, South Carolina, Georgia, Florida, Alabama, Mississippi, Louisiana, Arkansas, and Texas, the District of Columbia, and the Territories of New Mexico and Arizona.

In witness whereof, I have hereunto set my hand and caused the seal of the United States to be affixed.

Done at the city of Washington this first day of December, in the year of our Lord one thousand eight hundred and sixty-five, and of the Independence of the United States of America the ninetieth.

[L. S.]

ANDREW JOHNSON.

By the President:
WILLIAM H. SEWARD, *Secretary of State.*

## Announcing that the Rebellion has ended, April 2, 1866.

Whereas, by proclamations of the fifteenth and nineteenth of April, one thousand eight hundred and sixty-one, the President of the United States, in virtue of the power vested in him by the Constitution and the laws, declared that the laws of the United States were opposed, and the execution thereof obstructed in the States of South Carolina, Georgia, Alabama, Florida, Mississippi, Louisiana, and Texas, by combinations too powerful to be suppressed by the ordinary course of judicial proceedings, or by the powers vested in the marshals by law;

And whereas, by another proclamation made on the sixteenth day of August, in the same year, in pursuance of an act of Congress approved July thirteenth, one thousand eight hundred and sixty-one, the inhabitants of the States of Georgia, South Carolina, Virginia, North Carolina, Tennessee, Alabama, Louisiana, Texas, Arkansas, Mississippi, and Florida (except the inhabitants of that part of the State of Virginia lying west of the Alleghany mountains, and to such other parts of that State and the other States before named, as might maintain a loyal adhesion to the Union and the Constitution, or might be from time to time occupied and controlled by forces of the United States engaged in the dispersion of insurgents) were declared to be in a state of insurrection against the United States;

And whereas, by another proclamation of the first day of July, one thousand eight hundred and sixty-two, issued in pursuance of an act of Congress approved June 7, in the same year, the insurrection was declared to be still existing in the States aforesaid, with the exception of certain specified counties in the State of Virginia;

And whereas, by another proclamation made on the second day of April, one thousand eight hundred and sixty-three, in pursuance of the act of Congress of July 13, one thousand eight hundred and sixty-one, the exceptions named in the proclamation of August 16, one thousand eight hundred and sixty-one were revoked, and the inhabitants of the States of Georgia, South Carolina, North Carolina, Tennessee, Alabama, Louisiana, Texas, Arkansas, Mississippi, Florida, and Virginia, (except the forty-eight counties of Virginia designated as West Virginia, and the ports of New Orleans, Key West, Port Royal, and Beaufort, in South Carolina,) were declared to be still in a state of insurrection against the United States.

And whereas the House of Representatives, on the 22d day of July, one thousand eight hundred and sixty-one, adopted a resolution in the words following, namely:

"*Resolved by the House of Representatives of the Congress of the United States,* That the present deplorable civil war has been forced upon the country by the disunionists of the southern States, now in revolt against the constitutional Government, and in arms around the capital; that in this national emergency Congress, banishing all feelings of mere passion or resentment, will recollect only its duty to the whole country; that this war is not waged on our part in any spirit of oppression, nor for any purpose of conquest or subjugation, nor purpose of overthrowing or interfering with the rights or established institutions of those States; but to defend and maintain the supremacy of the Constitution and to preserve the Union with all the dignity, equality, and rights of the several States unimpaired; that as soon as these objects are accomplished, the war ought to cease."

And whereas the Senate of the United States, on the 25th day of July, one thousand eight hundred and sixty-one, adopted a resolution in the words following, to wit:

"*Resolved,* That the present deplorable civil war has been forced upon the country by the disunionists of the southern States, now in revolt against the constitutional Government, and in arms around the capital; that in this national emergency Congress, banishing all feeling of mere passion or resentment, will recollect only its duty to the whole country; that this war is not prosecuted on our part in any spirit of oppression nor for any purpose of conquest or subjugation, nor purpose of overthrowing or interfering with the rights or established institutions of those States, but to defend and maintain the supremacy of the Constitution and all laws made in pursuance thereof, and to preserve the Union with all the dignity, equality, and rights of the several States unimpaired; that as soon as these objects are accomplished, the war ought to cease."

And whereas these resolutions, though not joint or concurrent in form, are substantially identical, and as such may be regarded as having expressed the sense of Congress upon the subject to which they relate;

And whereas, by my proclamation of the thirteenth day of June last, the insurrection in the State of Tennessee was declared to have been suppressed, the authority of the United States therein to be undisputed, and such United States officers as had been duly commissioned to be in the undisputed exercise of their official functions;

And whereas there now exists no organized armed resistance of misguided citizens or others to the authority of the United States in the States of Georgia, South Carolina, Virginia, North Carolina, Tennessee, Alabama, Louisiana, Arkansas, Mississippi, and Florida, and the laws can be sustained and enforced therein by the proper civil authority, State or Federal, and the people of the said States are well and loyally disposed, and have conformed or will conform in their legislation to the condition of affairs growing out of the amendment to the Constitution of the United States, prohibiting slavery within the limits and jurisdiction of the United States:

And whereas, in view of the before recited premises, it is the manifest determination of the American people that no State, of its own will, has the right or the power to go out of, or separate itself from, or be separated from the American Union, and that therefore each State ought to remain and constitute an integral part of the United States;

And whereas the people of the several beforementioned States have, in the manner aforesaid, given satisfactory evidence that they acquiesce in this sovereign and important resolution of national unity;

And whereas it is believed to be a fundamental principle of government that people who have revolted, and who have been overcome and subdued, must either be dealt with so as to induce them voluntarily to become friends, or else they must be held by absolute military power, or devastated, so as to prevent them from ever again doing harm as enemies, which last-named policy is abhorrent to humanity and freedom;

And whereas the Constitution of the United States provides for constituent communities only as States and not as Territories, dependencies, provinces, or protectorates;

And whereas such constituent States must necessarily be and by the Constitution and laws of the United States are made equals and placed upon a like footing as to political rights, immunities, dignity, and power, with the several States with which they are united;

And whereas the observance of political equality as a principle of right and justice is well calculated to encourage the people of the aforesaid States to be and become more and more constant and persevering in their renewed allegiance;

And whereas standing armies, military occupation, martial law, military tribunals, and the suspension of the privilege of the writ of *habeas corpus* are, in time of peace, dangerous to public liberty, incompatible with the individual rights of the citizen, contrary to the genius and spirit of our free institutions, and exhaustive of the national resources, and ought not, therefore, to be sanctioned or allowed, except in cases of actual necessity, for repelling invasion or suppressing insurrection or rebellion;

And whereas the policy of the Government of the United States, from the beginning of the insurrection to its overthrow and final suppression, has been in conformity with the principles herein set forth and enumerated:

Now, therefore, I, Andrew Johnson, President of the United States, do hereby proclaim and declare that the insurrection which heretofore existed in the States of Georgia, South Carolina, Virginia, North Carolina, Tennessee,

Alabama, Louisiana, Arkansas, Mississippi and Florida is at an end, and is henceforth to be so regarded.*

In testimony whereof, I have hereunto set my hand, and caused the seal of the United States to be affixed.

[SEAL.] Done at the city of Washington, the second day of April, in the year of our Lord one thousand eight hundred and sixty-six, and of the Independence of the United States of America the ninetieth.

ANDREW JOHNSON.

By the President:

WM. H. SEWARD, *Secretary of State.*

---

### Order in Relation to Appointments to Office.

EXECUTIVE MANSION, *April* 7, 1866.

It is eminently right and proper that the Government of the United States should give earnest and substantial evidence of its just appreciation of the services of the patriotic men who, when the life of the nation was imperiled, entered the army and navy to preserve the integrity of the Union, defend the Government, and maintain and perpetuate unimpaired its free institutions. It is therefore directed:

*First.* That in appointments to office in the several executive departments of the General Government and the various branches of the public service connected with said departments, preference shall be given to such meritorious and honorably discharged soldiers and sailors, particularly those who have been disabled by wounds received or diseases contracted in the line of duty, as may possess the proper qualifications.

*Second.* That in all promotions in said departments and the several branches of the public service connected therewith, such persons shall have preference, when equally eligible and

---

* The following official telegraphic correspondence shows the scope of the proclamation, in the opinion of the President:

AUGUSTA, GA., *April* 7, 1866.

Maj. Gen. O. O. HOWARD:

Does the President's recent proclamation remove martial law in this State? If so, Gen. Brannan does not feel authorized to arrest parties who have committed outrages on freed people or Union refugees. Please answer by telegraph.

DAVIS TILLSON,
*Brig. Gen. of Vols.*

[Answer.]

ADJUTANT GENERAL'S OFFICE, WAR DEPARTMENT,
WASHINGTON, *April* 17, 1866.

The President's proclamation does not remove martial law, or operate in any way upon the Freedmen's Bureau in the exercise of its *legitimate* jurisdiction. It is not expedient, however, to resort to military tribunal in any case where justice can be attained through the medium of civil authority. E. D. TOWNSEND, A. A. G.

---

TO GOVERNOR WORTH, OF NORTH CAROLINA.

WASHINGTON, D. C., *April* 27, 1866.

To Gov. WORTH: I am directed by the President to inform you that by his proclamation of April 2, 1866, it was not intended to interfere with military commissions at that time or previously organized, or trials then pending before such commissions, unless by special instructions the accused were to be turned over the civil authorities. General Ruger has been instructed to proceed with the trial to which you refer; but before the execution of any sentence rendered by said commission, to report all the proceedings to the War Department for examination and revision. There has been an order this day prepared, and which will soon be issued, which will relieve and settle all embarrassment growing out of a misconstruction of the proclamation, of which I will send you a copy. Edmund COOPER, *Acting Private Secretary to the President.*

---

qualified, over those who have not faithfully and honorably served in the land and naval forces of the United States.

ANDREW JOHNSON.

---

### Order in Relation to Trials by Military Courts and Commissions.

WAR DEPARTMENT,
ADJUTANT GENERAL'S OFFICE,
WASHINGTON, *May* 1, 1866.

*General Orders No.* 26:

Whereas some military commanders are embarrassed by doubts as to the operation of the proclamation of the President, dated the 2d day of April, 1866, upon trials by military courts-martial and military offenses, to remove such doubts, it is ordered by the President that—

Hereafter, whenever offenses committed by civilians are to be tried where civil tribunals are in existence which can try them, their cases are not authorized to be, and will not be, brought before military courts-martial or commissions, but will be committed to the proper civil authorities. This order is not applicable to camp followers, as provided for under the 60th Article of War, or to contractors and others specified in section 16, act of July 17, 1862, and sections 1 and 2, act of March 2, 1863. Persons and offenses cognizable by the Rules and Articles of War, and by the acts of Congress above cited, will continue to be tried and punished by military tribunals as prescribed by the Rules and Articles of War and acts of Congress, hereinafter cited, to wit:

*Sixtieth of the Rules and Articles of War.* All sutlers and retainers to the camp, and all persons whatsoever serving with the armies of the United States in the field, though not enlisted soldiers, are to be subject to orders according to the rules and discipline of war.    *    *    *

By order of the Secretary of War:

E. D. TOWNSEND,
*Assistant Adjutant General.*

---

### Against the Fenian Invasion of Canada, June 6, 1866.

Whereas it has become known to me that certain evil-disposed persons have, within the territory and jurisdiction of the United States, begun and set on foot, and have provided and prepared, and are still engaged in providing and preparing, means for a military expedition and enterprise, which expedition and enterprise is to be carried on from the territory and jurisdiction of the United States against colonies, districts, and people of British North America, within the dominions of the United Kingdom of Great Britain and Ireland, with which said colonies, districts, and people, and kingdom the United States are at peace;

And whereas the proceedings aforesaid constitute a high misdemeanor, forbidden by the law of the United States, as well as by the law of nations:

Now, therefore, for the purpose of preventing the carrying on of the unlawful expedition and enterprise aforesaid, from the territory and jurisdiction of the United States, and to maintain the public peace, as well as the national honor, and enforce obedience and respect to the laws of the United States, I, Andrew Johnson, President of the United States, do admonish and warn all good citizens of the United States against taking part in or in any wise aiding, countenancing, or abetting said unlawful proceedings, and I do exhort all judges, magistrates, marshals, and officers in the service of the United States, to employ all their awful authority and power to prevent and defeat the aforesaid unlawful proceedings, and to arrest and bring to justice all persons who may be engaged therein.*

And, pursuant to the act of Congress in such case made and provided, I do furthermore authorize and empower Major General George G. Meade, commander of the Military Division of the Atlantic, to employ the land and naval forces of the United States and the militia thereof, to arrest and prevent the setting on foot and carrying on the expedition and enterprise aforesaid.

In testimony whereof, I have hereunto set my hand, and caused the seal of the United States to be affixed.

Done at the city of Washington the sixth day of June, in the year of our Lord one [SEAL.] thousand eight hundred and sixty-six, and of the Independence of the United States the ninetieth.

ANDREW JOHNSON.

By the President:
WILLIAM H. SEWARD, *Secretary of State.*

---

* *Circular to the District Attorneys and Marshals of the United States.*

ATTORNEY GENERAL'S OFFICE, WASHINGTON, D. C., June 5, 1866.—By direction of the President you are hereby instructed to cause the arrest of all prominent, leading, or conspicuous persons called Fenians, whom you may have probable cause to believe have been or may be guilty of violations of the neutrality laws of the United States.

JAMES SPEED,
*Attorney General.*

---

# III.

# ACTION OF THE CONVENTIONS AND LEGISLATURES OF THE LATELY INSURRECTIONARY STATES.

## NORTH CAROLINA.

1865, April 27—Gen. Schofield announced the cessation of hostilities within that State.

April 28—Gen. Schofield issued an order that, under the emancipation proclamation, all persons heretofore held as slaves are now free, and that it is the duty of the army to maintain their freedom.

May 29—William W. Holden appointed Provisional Governor.

June 12—Provisional Governor Holden issued his proclamation announcing his purpose to order an election for a convention, and to appoint justices of the peace to administer the oath of allegiance and conduct the election, &c.

July —President Johnson ordered the cotton of the State to be restored to her, and the proceeds of all that had been sold to be paid to her agents.

August 8—Provisional Governor Holden fixed Thursday, September 21, for the election of a convention.

Voters' qualifications are thus prescribed:

"No person will be allowed to vote who is not a voter qualified as prescribed by the constitution and laws of the State in force immediately before the 20th day of May, 1861, except that the payment of poll tax shall not be required.

"All paroled soldiers of the army and navy of the pretended Confederate States, or of this State, and all paroled officers of the army and navy of the pretended Confederate States, or of this State, under and including the rank of colonel, if of the army, and under and including the rank of lieutenant, if of the navy, will be allowed to vote, pro-

vided they are not included in any of the fourteen excluded classes of the President's amnesty proclamation; and, provided further, that they are citizens of the State in accordance with the terms prescribed in the preceding paragraph.

"No person will be allowed to vote who does not exhibit to the inspectors a copy of the amnesty oath, as contained in the President's proclamation of May 29, 1865, signed by himself and certified by at least two justices of the peace.'

The convention to meet October 2.

September 29—The colored people of the State met in convention in Raleigh, and petitioned for legislation to secure compensation for labor, and enable them to educate their children, and asking protection for the family relation, and for the repeal of oppressive laws making unjust discriminations on account of race or color.

October 2—Convention met.

October 7—The secession ordinance declared "null and void."

October 9—An ordinance passed, declaring slavery forever prohibited within the State.

October 10—Ordinance passed, providing for an election for Governor, members of the Legislature, and seven members of Congress November 9, the Provisional Governor to give the certificates. Each member of the Legislature, and each voter to be qualified "according to the now existing constitution of the State": *Provided,* That no one shall be eligible to a seat, or be capable of voting, who, being free in all respects, shall not, before May 29, 1865, have taken President Lincoln's amnesty oath, or have taken President Johnson's oath, and who shall not in either case be of the excepted classes. All persons who have preferred petitions for pardon shall be deemed to have been pardoned if the fact of being pardoned shall be announced by the Governor, although the pardon may not have been received. The payment of a public tax shall not be required as a qualification of the voter in the elections in November next.

October 12—Convention tabled a proposition to prohibit the payment of the war debt created by the State in aid of the rebellion.

October 16—Ordinance passed, dividing the State into seven congressional districts.

October 17—Resolution adopted, requesting Congress to repeal the "test-oath."

October 18—President Johnson sent this telegram:

EXECUTIVE OFFICE,
WASHINGTON, D. C., *October* 18, 1865.

W. W. HOLDEN, *Provisional Governor:*

Every dollar of the debt created to aid the rebellion against the United States should be repudiated finally and forever. The great mass of the people should not be taxed to pay a debt to aid in carrying on a rebellion which they in fact, if left to themselves, were opposed to. Let those who have given their means for the obligations of the State look to that power they tried to establish in violation of law, constitution, and will of the people. They must meet their fate. It is their misfortune, and cannot be recognized by the people of any State professing themselves loyal to the government of the United States and in the Union. I repeat that the loyal people of North Carolina should be exonerated from the payment of every dollar of indebtedness created to aid in carrying on the rebellion. I trust and hope that the people of North Carolina will wash their hands of everything that partakes in the slightest degree of the rebellion, which has been so recently crushed by the strong arm of the Government in carrying out the obligations imposed by the Constitution of the Union. ANDREW JOHNSON,
*President of the United States.*

October 19—Ordinance passed, that no officer of this State who may have taken an oath of office to support the constitution of the Confederate States, shall be capable of holding under the State any office of trust or profit which he held when he took such oath, until he may be appointed or re-elected to the same; and all the offices lately held by such persons are hereby declared vacant.

October 19—Convention—yeas 84, nays 12—passed an ordinance prohibiting the assumption of the State debt created in aid of the rebellion. An amendment to refer this question to a vote of the people, lost.

November 9—Election of State officers and Representatives in Congress. Same day, ordinances repealing secession ordinance and anti-slavery ordinance, submitted to popular vote, and approved.

November 13—Legislature met.

December 1—The Legislature ratified, with six dissenting voices, the anti-slavery amendment.

December 9—Jonathan Worth declared elected Governor, by a vote of 32,529 to 25,809 for Prov. Gov. Holden.

December 15—Governor Worth qualified.

1866, May 24—The Convention re-assembled. A motion to adjourn *sine die* was tabled, 61 to 30.

---

## MISSISSIPPI.

1865, May 10—Governor Clark called an extra session of the Legislature for the 18th, to order a State Convention.

May 21—Major General Canby telegraphed as follows to Major General Warren, commanding the department: "By direction of the President, you will not recognize any officer of the Confederate or State government, within the limits of your command, as authorized to exercise in any manner whatever the functions of their late offices. You will prevent, by force if necessary, any attempt of any of the legislatures of the States in insurrection to assemble for legislative purposes, and will imprison any members or other persons who may attempt to exercise these functions in opposition to your orders."

June 13—William L. Sharkey appointed Provisional Governor.

July 1—Prov. Gov. Sharkey issued a proclamation appointing local officers, and fixing an election for a Convention—August 7th—voters to have these qualifications:

"Voters for delegates to this convention must possess the qualifications required by the constitution and laws as they existed prior to the 9th day of January, 1861, and must also produce a certificate that they have taken, before a competent officer, the amnesty oath prescribed by the proclamation of the 29th of May, 1865, which certificate shall be attached to or accompanied by a copy of the oath, and no one will be eligible as a member of this convention who has not also taken this oath."

August 14—Convention met.

August 15—President Johnson sent this telegram:

EXECUTIVE OFFICE,
WASHINGTON, D. C., *August* 15, 1865.

Governor W. L. SHARKEY, *Jackson, Miss.:*

I am gratified to see that you have organized your Convention without difficulty. I hope that without delay your Convention will amend your State constitution, abolishing slavery and denying to all future legislatures the power to legislate that there is property in man; also that they will adopt the amendment to the Constitution of the United States abolishing slavery. If you could extend the elective franchise to all persons of color who can read the Constitution of the United States in English and write their names, and to all persons of color who own real estate valued at not less than two hundred and fifty dollars, and pay taxes thereon, you would completely disarm the adversary and set an example the other States will follow. This you can do with perfect safety, and you thus place the southern States, in reference to free persons of color, upon the same basis with the free States. I hope and trust your convention will do this, and, as a consequence, the radicals, who are wild upon negro franchise, will be completely foiled in their attempt to keep the southern States from renewing their relations to the Union by not accepting their senators and representatives.*

ANDREW JOHNSON, *President of the U. S.*

**August 21**—Ordinance passed that " the institution of slavery having been destroyed in the State of Mississippi," neither slavery nor involuntary servitude, &c., shall hereafter exist in the State.

**August 21**—An election ordered for first Monday in October for State and county officers, and Representatives in Congress in the several congressional districts as they were fixed by the legislature in 1857.

**August 22**—Secession ordinance declared null and void.

**October 7**—The colored citizens of Mississippi met in convention, and protested against the reactionary policy prevailing, and expressing the fear that the Legislature will pass such proscriptive laws as will drive the freedmen from the State, or practically re-enslave them.

**October 16**—Legislature met.

**October 17**—Benjamin G. Humphreys inaugurated Governor.

**November 20**—Governor Humphreys sent a message recommending that negroes be permitted to sue and be sued, and give testimony, and that the freedmen be encouraged to engage in pursuits of industry, and that a militia bill be passed, " to protect our people against insurrection, or any possible combination of vicious white men and negroes."

**November 24**—Bill passed " reserving twenty per cent. of the revenue of the State as a fund for the relief of destitute disabled Confederate and State soldiers, and their widows, and for the support and education of indigent children of deceased or disabled Confederate or State soldiers, to be distributed annually," &c.

**November 27**—The joint committee reported against ratifying the anti-slavery amendment, for reasons given ; and the Legislature adopted it.

**November 29**—The Legislature adopted a memorial to the Congress of the United States, asking for the repeal of the " test oath." November 22, one for the pardon of Jacob Thompson. November 8, one for the pardon of Jefferson Davis.

**December 1**—The name of Jones county changed to Davis.

**December 5**—Bill passed, taxing each male inhabitant of the State, between 21 and 60, $1, and authorizing any person having in his or her employ any one subject to the tax, to pay it and charge it to the person for whom paid. All officers and enlisted men who have herefore received

*As bearing upon this point, this letter from the late President Lincoln, on a similar occasion, has value:

EXECUTIVE MANSION,
WASHINGTON, *March* 13, 1864.

Hon MICHAEL HAHN:

MY DEAR SIR: I congratulate you on having fixed your name in history as the first free State Governor of Louisiana. Now you are about to have a convention, which, among other things, will probably define the elective franchise. I barely suggest, for your private consideration, whether some of the colored people may not be let in, as, for instance, the very intelligent, and especially those who have fought gallantly in our ranks. They would probably help, in some trying time to come, to keep the jewel of liberty in the family of freedom. But this is only a suggestion, not to the public, but to you alone.

Truly yours,     A. LINCOLN.

pensions, and have forfeited the same by taking a part in the late war against the United States, shall be exempt from poll tax.

## GEORGIA.

**1865, May 3**—Gov. Joseph E. Brown issued a proclamation calling an extra meeting of the Legislature for 22d.

**May 14**—Maj. Gen. Gillmore issued an order annulling this proclamation, and directing the persons interested not to heed it.

**June 17**—James Johnson appointed Provisional Governor.

**July 13**—Prov. Gov. Johnson issued a proclamation fixing the first Wednesday in October for an election for delegates to a Convention—these to be the qualifications of voters :

"That no person at such election shall be qualified as an elector, or shall be eligible as a member of such convention, unless he shall have previously thereto taken and subscribed to the oath of amnesty, as set forth in the President's proclamation of May 29, A. D. 1865, and is a voter qualified as prescribed by the constitution and laws of the State of Georgia, in force immediately before the 19th of January, A. D. 1861, the date of the so-called ordinance of secession."

**October 7**—Names of members elect requiring pardons sent to the President, and pardons returned, as in each of the other States.

**October 25**—Convention met.

**October 30**—Secession ordinance repealed ; ordinance passed dividing the State into seven congressional districts.

**November 4**—Slavery declared abolished, "the Government of the United States having, as a war measure, proclaimed all slaves held or owned in this State emancipated from slavery, and having carried that proclamation into full practical effect." "*Provided*, That acquiescence in the action of the Government of the United States is not intended to operate as a relinquishment, or waiver, or estoppel, of such claim for compensation of loss sustained by reason of the emancipation of his slaves, as any citizen of Georgia may hereafter make upon the justice and magnanimity of that Government."

**November 8**—The State debt of Georgia, incurred in aid of the rebellion, declared null and void—yeas 133, nays 117. Pending this proposition these telegrams were sent :

MILLEDGEVILLE, GA., *October* 27, 1865.

His Excellency ANDREW JOHNSON,
*President of the United States :*

We need some aid to repeal the war debt. Send me word on the subject. What should the Convention do ?     J. JOHNSON,
*Provisional Governor of Georgia.*

EXECUTIVE OFFICE,
WASHINGTON, D. C., *October* 28, 1865.

JAMES JOHNSON, *Provisional Governor :*

Your despatch has been received. The people of Georgia should not hesitate one single moment in repudiating every single dollar of debt created for the purpose of aiding the rebellion against the Government of the United States. It will not do to levy and collect taxes from a State and people that are loyal and in the Union, to pay a debt that was created to aid in an effort to take them out, and thereby subvert the Constitution of the United States. I do not believe the great mass of the people of the State of Georgia, when left uninfluenced, will ever submit to the payment of a debt which was the main cause of bringing on their past and present suffering, the result of the rebellion. Those who vested their capital in the creation of this debt must meet their fate, and take it as one of the inevitable results of the rebellion, though it may seem hard to them. It should at once be made known at home and abroad, that no debt contracted for the purpose of dissolving the Union of the States can or ever will be paid by taxes levied on the people for such purpose.

ANDREW JOHNSON,
*President of the United States.*

Hon. W. H. SEWARD:

We are pressed on the war debt. What should the Convention do?  J. JOHNSON,
*Provisional Governor of Georgia.*
MILLEDGEVILLE, *October 27, 1865.*

His Excellency JAMES JOHNSON,
*Provisional Governor of Georgia:*

Your several telegrams have been received. The President of the United States cannot recognize the people of any State as having resumed the relations of loyalty to the Union that admits as legal, obligations contracted or debts created in their name, to promote the war of the rebellion.  WILLIAM H. SEWARD.
WASHINGTON, *October 28, 1865.*

November 8—Convention adjourned.

November 15—Election held for State officers and Representatives in Congress.

December 4—Legislature met.

December 5—Legislature ratified the anti-slavery amendment.

1866, January—A convention of colored persons at Augusta advocated a proposition to give those who could write and read well, and possessed a certain property qualification, the right of suffrage.

March 10—Bill passed legislature, authorizing an extra tax, the amount to be fixed by the grand juries, but not to exceed two per cent. upon the State tax, for the benefit of indigent soldiers, and the indigent families of deceased soldiers of the Confederate and State troops. Artificial arms and legs to be furnished disabled soldiers.

## ALABAMA.

1865, June 21—Lewis E. Parsons appointed Provisional Governor.

July 20—Provisional Governor Parsons issued a proclamation, fixing August 31 for an election for a Convention, under these restrictions: "But no person can vote in said election, or be a candidate for election, who is not a legal voter as the law was on that day; and if he is excepted from the benefit of amnesty, under the President's proclamation of the 29th May, 1865, he must have obtained a pardon.

"Every person must vote in the county of his residence, and, before he is allowed to do so, must take and subscribe the oath of amnesty prescribed in the President's proclamation of the 29th of May, 1865, before some one of the offi-

cers hereinafter appointed for that purpose in the county where he offers to vote; and any person offering to vote in violation of these rules or the laws of Alabama on the 11th of January, 1861, will be punished.

September 12—Convention met.

September 18—Election for State officers fixed for first Monday in November—the Provisional Governor authorized to order an election for Representatives in Congress.

September 20—Slavery abolished, "as the institution of slavery has been destroyed in the State of Alabama." Secession ordinance declared "null and void." Rebel State debt repudiated, 60 to 19.

September 30—Convention adjourned.

November 20—Legislature met.

December 2—Anti-slavery amendment ratified in this form:

1st. That the foregoing amendment to the Constitution of the United States be, and the same is hereby, ratified, to all intents and purposes, as part of the Constitution of the United States.

2d. That this amendment to the Constitution of the United States is adopted by the Legislature of Alabama with the understanding that it does not confer upon Congress the power to legislate upon the political status of freedmen in this State.

3d. That the governor of the State be, and he is hereby, requested to forward to the President of the United States an authenticated copy of the foregoing preamble and resolutions.

December 5—The President sent this response

His Excellency L. E. PARSONS.
*Provisional Governor:*

The President congratulates you and the country upon the acceptance of the congressional amendment of the Constitution of the United States by the State of Alabama, which vote, being the twenty-seventh, fills up the complement of two-thirds, and gives the amendment finishing effect as a part of the organic law of the land.  WILLIAM H. SEWARD.
WASHINGTON, *December 5, 1865.*

1866, January 8—The Legislature re-assembled.

Gov. R. M. Patton vetoed three bills. He vetoed the bill to regulate contracts with freedmen, because no special law is necessary. He adds:

"Information from various parts of the State shows that negroes are everywhere making contracts for the present year upon terms that are entirely satisfactory to the employers. They are also entering faithfully upon the discharge of the obligations contracted. There is every prospect that the engagement formed will be observed with perfect good faith. I therefore think that special laws for regulating contracts between whites and freedmen would accomplish no good, and might result in much harm."

Governor Patton has also vetoed the bill "to extend the criminal laws of the State, applicable to free persons of color, to freedmen, free negroes and mulattoes." He says ·

"The bill proposes to apply to the freedmen a system of laws enacted for the government of free negroes residing in a community where slavery existed. I have carefully examined the laws which, under this bill, would be applied to the freedmen; and I think that a mere recital of some of their provisions will show the impolicy and injustice of enforcing them upon the negroes in their new condition."

Governor Patton has also vetoed " a bill entitled an act to regulate the relations of master and apprentice, as relate to freedmen, free negroes and mulattoes," because he deems the present laws amply sufficient for all purposes of apprenticeship, without operating upon a particular class of persons.

The Legislature passed a tax bill, of which these are two sections:

"12. To sell, or expose for sale, for one year, at any one place, any pictorial or illustrated weekly, or any monthly paper, periodical or magazine, *published outside the limits of this State, and not in a foreign country*, and to vend the same on the streets, or on boats or railroad cars, *fifty* dollars."

"13. To keep a news depot for one year, in any city, town or village, for the sale of any newspaper, periodical or magazine, not including pictorials provided for in the preceding paragraph, ten dollars."

The Legislature passed some joint resolutions on the state of the Union, of which this, the fourth, is the most important:

" That Alabama will not voluntarily consent to change the adjustment of political power as fixed by the Constitution of the United States, and to constrain her to do so, in her present prostrate and helpless condition, with no voice in the councils of the nation, would be an unjustifiable breach of faith; and that her earnest thanks are due to the President for the firm stand he has taken against amendments to the Constitution forced through in the present condition of affairs."

The code became operative June 1st, under a proclamation of Governor Patton.

## SOUTH CAROLINA.

1865, May 2—Gov. Magrath issued a proclamation that the confederate stores within the State should be turned over to State officers, to be distributed among the people.

May 8—Gov. Magrath summoned the State officers to Columbia to resume their duties.

May 14—Maj. Gen. Gillmore issued an order annulling the Governor's acts, and notifying the persons interested not to heed his proclamations.

June 30—Benjamin F. Perry was appointed Provisional Governor.

July 20—Prov. Gov. Perry issued a proclamation fixing the first Monday of September for an election for a State Convention—the qualifications of voters being thus prescribed:

Every loyal citizen who had taken the amnesty oath, and not within the excepted classes in the President's proclamation, will be entitled to vote, provided he was a legal voter under the constitution as it stood prior to the secession of South Carolina. And all who are within the excepted classes must take the oath and apply for a pardon, in order to entitle them to vote or become members of the convention.

September 13—Convention met.

September 15—Secession ordinance repealed, 107 to 3.

September 19—Slavery declared abolished "the slaves in South Carolina having been emancipated by the action of the United States authorities."

September 27—Election ordered for third Wednesday in October, for State officers. Ordinance passed, creating four congressional districts.

September 29—Convention adjourned.

October 18—James L. Orr elected Governor

October    —Legislature met.

This telegraphic correspondence occurred:

EXECUTIVE OFFICE,
WASHINGTON, D. C., *October 28*, 1865.
B. F. PERRY, *Provisional Governor:*

Your last two despatches have been received and the pardons suggested have been ordered. I hope that your Legislature will have no hesitancy in adopting the amendment to the Constitution of the United States abolishing slavery. It will set an example which will no doubt be followed by the other States, and place South Carolina in a most favorable attitude before the nation. I trust in God that it will be done. The nation and State will then be left free and untrammeled to take that course which sound policy, wisdom, and humanity may suggest.

ANDREW JOHNSON, *President.*

———

EXECUTIVE OFFICE,
WASHINGTON, D. C., *October 31*, 1865.
B. F. PERRY, *Provisional Governor:*

There is a deep interest felt as to what course the Legislature will take in regard to the adoption of the amendment to the Constitution of the United States abolishing slavery, and the assumption of the debt created to aid in the rebellion against the government of the United States. If the action of the convention was in good faith, why hesitate in making it a part of the Constitution of the United States?

I trust in God that restoration of the Union will not now be defeated, and all that has so far been well done thrown away. I still have faith that all will come out right yet.

This opportunity ought to be understood and appreciated by the people of the southern States.

If I know my own heart and every passion which enters it, my earnest desire is to restore the blessings of the Union, and tie up and heal every bleeding wound which has been caused by this fratricidal war. Let us be guided by love and wisdom from on high, and Union and peace will once more reign throughout the land.

ANDREW JOHNSON.

———

COLUMBIA, S. C., *November 1*, 1865.
His Excellency ANDREW JOHNSON,
*President United States:*

I will send you to-day the whole proceedings of the State Convention, properly certified, as you request.

The debt contracted by South Carolina during the rebellion is very inconsiderable. Her expenditures for war purposes were paid by the confederate government. She has assumed no debt, or any part of any debt, of that government. Her whole State debt at this time is only about six millions, and that is mostly for railroads and building new State-house prior to the war. The members of the Legislature say they have received no official information of the amendment of the Federal Constitution abolishing slavery. They have no objection to adopting the first section of the amendment proposed; but they fear that the second section may be construed to give Congress power of local legislation over the negroes, and white men, too, after the abolishment of slavery. In good faith South Carolina has abolished slavery, and never will wish to restore it again.

The Legislature is passing a code of laws providing ample and complete protection for the negro. There is a sincere desire to do everything necessary to a restoration of the Union, and tie up and heal every bleeding wound which has been caused by this fratricidal war. I was elected United States Senator by a very flattering vote. The other Senator will be elected to-day. B. F. PERRY,
*Provisional Governor.*

---

WASHINGTON, *November 6*, 1865.
His Excellency B. F. PERRY, *Prov. Gov.:*
Your despatch to the President of November 4 has been received. He is not entirely satisfied with the explanations it contains. He deems necessary the passage of adequate ordinances declaring that all insurrectionary proceedings in the State were unlawful and void *ab initio.* Neither the Constitution nor laws direct official information to the State of amendments to the Constitution submitted by Congress. Notices of the amendment by Congress abolishing slavery were nevertheless given by the Secretary of State at the time to the States which were then in communication with this Government. Formal notice will immediately be given to those States which were then in insurrection.

The objection you mention to the last clause of the constitutional amendment is regarded as querulous and unreasonable, because that clause is really restraining in its effect, instead of enlarging the powers of Congress. The President considers the acceptance of the amendment by South Carolina as indispensable to a restoration of her relations with the other States of the Union. WILLIAM H. SEWARD.

November 7—Provisional Governor Perry sent a message communicating these telegrams, and recommending the ratification, and that they "place on record the construction which had been given to the amendment by the executive department of the Federal Government."

November 13—The Legislature ratified the anti-slavery amendment, in this form:

1. *Resolved, &c.,* That the aforesaid proposed amendment of the Constitution of the United States be, and the same is hereby, accepted, and adopted and ratified by this State.

2. That a certified copy of the foregoing preamble and resolution be forwarded by his excellency the Provisional Governor to the President of the United States, and also to the Secretary of State of the United States.

3. That any attempt by Congress towards legislating upon the political status of former slaves, or their civil relations, would be contrary to the Constitution of the United States as it now is, or as it would be altered by the proposed

amendment, in conflict with the policy of the President, declared in his amnesty proclamation, and with the restoration of that harmony upon which depend the vital interests of the American Union.

Respecting the repudiation of the rebel State debt, this telegraphic correspondence took place:

DEPARTMENT OF STATE,
WASHINGTON, *Nov.* 20, 1865.
His Excellency B. F. PERRY,
*Provisional Governor:*
Your despatch of this date was received at half-past 10 o'clock this morning. This freedom of loyal intercourse between South Carolina and her sister States is manifestly much better and wiser than separation. The President and the whole country are gratified that South Carolina has accepted the congressional amendment to the Constitution abolishing slavery. Upon reflection South Carolina herself would not care to come again into the councils of the Union incumbered and clogged with debts and obligations which had been assumed in her name in a vain attempt to subvert it. The President trusts that she will lose no time in making an effective organic declaration, disavowing all debts and obligations created or assumed in her name or behalf in aid of the rebellion. The President waits further events in South Carolina with deep interest.

You will remain in the exercise of your functions of provisional governor until relieved by his express directions. WM. H. SEWARD.

---

COLUMBIA, *November* 27, 1865.
Hon. W. H. SEWARD: Your telegram of the 20th instant was not received in due time, owing to my absence from Columbia. The Convention having been dissolved, it is impracticable to enact any organic law in regard to the war debt. That debt is very small, as the expenditures of South Carolina were reimbursed by the confederate government. The debt is so mixed up with the ordinary expenses of the State that it cannot be separated. In South Carolina all were guilty of aiding the rebellion, and no one can complain of being taxed to pay the trifling debt incurred by his own assent in perfect good faith. The Convention did all that the President advised to be done, and I thought it wrong to keep a revolutionary body in existence and advised their immediate dissolution, which was done. There is now no power in the Legislature to repudiate the debt if it were possible to separate it from the other debts of the State. Even then it would fall on widows and orphans whose estates were invested in it for safety. B. F. PERRY,
*Provisional Governor.*

---

DEPARTMENT OF STATE,
WASHINGTON, *November* 30, 1865
SIR: I have the honor to acknowledge the receipt of your telegram of the 27th instant, informing me, that as the Convention had been dissolved, it was impossible to adopt the President's suggesstion to repudiate the insurgent debt, and to inform you that while the objections which you urge to the adoption of that proceeding are of a serious nature, the Presi-

dent cannot refrain from awaiting with interest an official expression upon that subject from the Legislature.*

I have the honor to be, sir, your obedient servant, WILLIAM H. SEWARD.

His Excellency B. F. PERRY.

November—The colored State Convention addressed a memorial to Congress, asking that equal suffrage be conferred upon them in common with the white men of the State.

November 22—Election held for Representatives in Congress.

Respecting their admission there was this telegraphic correspondence:

COLUMBIA, S. C., *November* 27, 1865.

President JOHNSON:

Will you please inform me whether the South Carolina members of Congress should be in Washington at the organization of the House. Will the Clerk of the House call their names if their credentials are presented to him? Will the test oath be required, or will it be refused by Congress? If the members are not allowed to take their seats they do not wish to incur the trouble and expense of going on, and the mortification of being rejected. Do give your views and wishes.

B. F. PERRY,
*Provisional Governor.*

---

EXECUTIVE OFFICE,
*Washington, D. C., November* 27, 1865.

B. F. PERRY, *Provisional Governor:*

I do not think it necessary for the members elect from South Carolina to be present at the organization of Congress. On the contrary, it will be better policy to present their certificates of election after the two Houses are organized, and then it will be a simple question under the Constitution of the members taking their seats. Each House must judge for itself the election, returns, and qualifications of its own members. As to what the two Houses will do in reference to the oath now required to be taken before the members can take their seats is unknown to me, and I do not like to predict; but, upon the whole, I am of opinion that it would be better for the question to come up and be disposed of after the two Houses have been organized.

I hope that your Legislature will adopt a code in reference to free persons of color that will be acceptable to the country, at the same time doing justice to the white and colored population.

ANDREW JOHNSON,
*President of the United States.*

---

## FLORIDA.

1865, April 8—Abraham K. Allison, President of the rebel Senate, of Florida, announced the death of John Milton, rebel Governor, and appointed June 7 for election of a successor.

May 14—Major General Gillmore issued an order annulling this proclamation, and com-

---

* December 21—Before adjourning, the subject of the repudiation of the war debt was referred to the Committee on Federal Relations, who recommended the appointment of a special joint committee of both Houses to inquire into the amount of such debt due by the State, and to whom due: and to report at the next regular session of the Legislature, which will be in November, 1866.

---

manding the people to give it no heed whatever.

July 13—William Marvin appointed Provisional Governor.

August 3—Provisional Governor Marvin called an election for delegates to a convention for October 10th—these provisions governing the election:

"Every free white male person of the age of twenty-one years and upwards, and who shall be at the time of offering to vote a citizen of the United States, and who shall have resided and had his home in this State for one year next preceding the election, and for six months in the county in which he may offer to vote, and who shall have taken and subscribed the oath of amnesty, as set forth in the President's proclamation of amnesty of the 29th day of May, 1865, and if he comes within the exceptions contained in said proclamation, shall have taken said oath, and have been specially pardoned by the President, shall be entitled to vote in the county where he resides, and shall be eligible as a member of said convention, and none others. Where the person offering to vote comes within the exceptions contained in the amnesty proclamation, and shall have taken the amnesty oath, and shall have made application to the President for a special pardon through the Provisional Governor, and shall have been recommended by him for such pardon, the inspectors or judges of the election may, in most instances, properly presume that such pardon has been granted though, owing to the want of mail facilities, it may not have been received by the party at the time of the election.

"Free white soldiers, seamen, and marines in the army or navy of the United States, who were qualified by their residence to vote in said State at the time of their respective enlistments, and who shall have taken and subscribed the amnesty oath, shall be entitled to vote in the county where they respectively reside. But no soldier, seaman, or marine not a resident in the State at the time of his enlistment shall be allowed to vote."

October 25—Convention met.

October 28.—Secession ordinance annulled.

November 6—Slavery abolished—"slavery having been destroyed in the State by the Government of the United States." Same ordinance gives colored people the right to testify in all cases where the person or property of such person is involved, but denies them the right to testify where the interest of the white class are involved.

Same day—Rebel State debt repudiated. A bill was first passed submitting this question to a vote of the people: but this was reconsidered, on finding this was a condition of recognition by the executive branch of the government, and the direct repudiation adopted.

November 29—Election held under an ordinance of the Convention for State officers and Representative in Congress.

December 18—Legislature met.

December 28—Anti-slavery amendment ratified, with this declaratory resolution a part of the ratifying instrument:

"*Resolved,* That this amendment to the Constitution of the United States is adopted by the Legislature of the State of Florida, with the understanding that it does not confer upon the Congress the power to legislate upon the political status of the freedmen in this State."

Pending this action, this telegraphic correspondence took place:

DEPARTMENT OF STATE,
WASHINGTON, *September* 12, 1865.

SIR: Your excellency's letter of the 29th ultimo, with the accompanying proclamation, has been received and submitted to the President. The steps to which it refers, towards reorganizing the government of Florida, seem to be in the main judicious, and good results from them may be hoped for. The presumption to which the proclamation refers, however, in favor of insurgents who may wish to vote, and who may have applied for, but not received, their pardons, is not entirely approved. All applications for pardons will be duly considered, and will be disposed of as soon as may be practicable. It must, however, be distinctly understood that the restoration to which your proclamation refers will be subject to the decision of Congress.

I have the honor to be, your excellency's obedient servant, WILLIAM H. SEWARD.

His Excellency WILLIAM MARVIN.

—

OFFICE OF THE PROVISIONAL GOVERNOR,
TALLAHASSEE, FLA., *October* 7, 1865.

* * * I have said that the Convention will, in good faith, abolish slavery; but I think it probable that the Legislature, which will be elected and convened at an early period, will feel some reluctance against ratifying the proposed amendment to the Constitution of the United States. The principal argument urged against the ratification is, that the Legislature will thereby assist to impose abolition on Kentucky and Delaware, which have not yet abolished slavery. If the President should think it desirable that the Legislature should ratify the proposed amendment, either with a view to promote a more complete reconciliation between the North and the South, or for any other reason, he possibly may not deem it amiss to communicate to me his wishes on the subject. His wishes on the subject would be very potent in the State.

The military authorities in the State, under the command of Major General Foster, are rendering me every possible assistance in sending out notices and proclamations of the election, in the absence of mail facilities, and no disagreements exist between us.

I have the honor to be, very respectfully, your obedient servant,

WM. MARVIN, *Provisional Governor.*
Hon. W. H. SEWARD, *Secretary of State.*

—

DEPARTMENT OF STATE,
WASHINGTON, *November* 1, 1865.

His Excellency WILLIAM MARVIN,
*Provisional Governor:*

Your letter of October 7 was received and submitted to the President. He is gratified with the favorable progress towards reorganization in Florida, and directs me to say that he regards the ratification by the Legislature of the congressional amendment of the Constitution of the United States as indispensable to a successful restoration of the true legal relations between Florida and the other States, and equally indispensable to the return of peace and harmony throughout the Republic.

WILLIAM H. SEWARD.

—

## VIRGINIA.

1865, April 4—President Lincoln visited Richmond.

April 7—An informal meeting of private individuals, among whom were five or six members of the rebel legislature in Richmond, was had to consider a suggestion that the Legislature reassemble to call a Convention to restore Virginia to the Union, said to be with the concurrence of President Lincoln.

April 12—This address was published in the Richmond *Whig:*

ADDRESS TO THE PEOPLE OF VIRGINIA.

The undersigned, members of the Legislature of the State of Virginia, in connection with a number of the citizens of the State, whose names are attached to this paper, in view of the evacuation of the city of Richmond by the Confederate government and its occupation by the military authorities of the United States, the surrender of the army of northern Virginia, and the suspension of the jurisdiction of the civil power of the State, are of the opinion that an immediate meeting of the General Assembly of the State is called for by the exigencies of the situation. The consent of the military authorities of the United States to a session of the Legislature in Richmond, in connection with the Governor and Lieutenant Governor, to their free deliberation upon public affairs, and to the ingress and departure of all its members under safe conduct, has been obtained.

The United States authorities will afford transportation from any point under their control to any of the persons before mentioned.

The matters to be submitted to the Legislature are the restoration of peace to the State of Virginia, and the adjustment of the questions, involving life, liberty and property, that have arisen in the State as a consequence of war.

We, therefore, earnestly request the Governor, Lieutenant Governor, and members of the Legislature, to repair to this city by the 25th of April, instant.

We understand that full protection to persons and property will be afforded in the State, and we recommend to peaceful citizens to remain at their homes and pursue their usual avocations with confidence that they will not be interrupted.

We earnestly solicit the attendance in Richmond, on or before the 25th of April, instant, of the following persons, citizens of Virginia, to confer with us as to the best means of restoring peace to the State of Virginia. We have secured safe conduct from the military authorities of the United States for them to enter the city and depart without molestation:

Hons. R. M. T. Hunter, A. T. Caperton, Wm. C. Rives, John Letcher, A. H. H. Stuart, R. L. Montague, Fayette McMullen, J. P. Holcombe, Alex. Rives, B. Johnson Barbour, Jas. Barbour, Wm. L. Goggin. J. B. Baldwin, Thos. S. Gholson, Waller Staples, S. D. Miller, Thos. J. Randolph, Wm. T. Early, R. A. Claybrook, John Critcher Williams, T. H. Eppes, and those other persons for whom passports have been procured, and especially others whom we consider it unnecessary to mention.          Signed—

A. J. Marshall, Senator from Fauquier.

John Wesson, Senator from Marion.

James Venable, Senator elect from Petersburg.

David J. Burr, of the House of Delegates, from Richmond.

David J. Saunders, of the House of Delegates, Richmond city.

L. S. Hall, of the House of Delegates, Wetzel county.

J. J. English, of the House of Delegates, Henrico county.

Wm. Ambers, of the House of Delegates, Chesterfield county.

A. M. Keetz, House Delegates, Petersburg.

H. W. Thomas, Second Auditor, Richmond.

Lieutenant L. L. Moncure, Chief Clerk, Second Auditor's office.

Joseph Mayo, Mayor, city of Richmond.

Robert S. Howard, Clerk Hustings Court, Richmond city.

Thomas W. Dudley, Sergeant, Richmond city.

Littleton Tazewell, Commonwealth's Attorney, Richmond city.

Wm. T. Joynes, Judge of the Circuit Court, Petersburg.

John A. Meredith, Judge of the Circuit Court, Richmond.

Wm. H. Lyons, Judge of the Hustings Court, Richmond.

Wm. C. Wickham, Member of Congress, Richmond.

Benjamin S. Ewell, President of William and Mary College.

Nat. Tyler, editor Richmond *Enquirer.*

R. F. Walker, publisher, *Examiner.*

J. R. Anderson, Richmond.

R. R. Howison, Richmond.

W. Goddin, Richmond.

P. G. Bagley, Richmond.

F. J. Smith, Richmond.

Franklin Sterns, Henrico.

John Lyon, Petersburg.

Thomas B. Fisher, Fauquier.

Wm. M. Harrison, Charles City.

Cyrus Hall, Ritchie.

Thos. W. Garnett, King and Queen.

James A. Scott, Richmond.

I concur in the preceding recommendation.
                              J. A. CAMPBELL.

Approved for publication in the *Whig* and in handbill form.          G. WEITZEL,
                    *Major General Commanding.*
RICHMOND, VA., *April 11*, 1865.

April 12—Said authority revoked in this telegram from President Lincoln to Major General Weitzel, being the last telegram ever transmitted by the former:

OFFICE U. S. MILITARY TELEGRAPH,
              WAR DEPARTMENT,
        WASHINGTON, D. C., *April 12*, 1865.
Major General WEITZEL, *Richmond, Va.:*

I have just seen Judge Campbell's letter to you of the 7th. He assumes, as appears to me, that I have called the insurgent Legislature of Virginia together, as the rightful Legislature of the State, to settle all differences with the United States. I have done no such thing. I spoke of them not as a legislature, but as "the gentlemen who have *acted* as the Legislature of Virginia in support of the rebellion." I did this on purpose to exclude the assumption that I was recognizing them as a *rightful* body. I dealt with them as men having power *de facto* to do a specific thing, to wit, "to withdraw the Virginia troops and other support from resistance to the General Government," for which, in the paper handed to Judge Campbell, I promised a specific equivalent, to wit, a remission to the people of the State, except in certain cases, the confiscation of their property. I meant this and no more. Inasmuch, however, as Judge Campbell misconstrues this, and is still pressing for an armistice, contrary to the explicit statement of the paper I gave him; and particularly as Gen. Grant has since captured the Virginia troops, so that giving a consideration for their withdrawal is no longer applicable, let my letter to you and the paper to Judge Campbell both be withdrawn or countermanded, and he be notified of it. Do not now allow them to assemble; but if any have come, allow them safe return to their homes.
                              A. LINCOLN.

May 9—President Johnson issued an executive order recognizing the Pierpoint Administration as that of. Virginia. (See President Johnson's Orders, p. 8.)

June 19—Legislature met.

June 20—Bill passed prescribing means by which persons who have been disfranchised by the third article of the constitution may be restored to the rights of voters. [It provides, substantially, that persons, otherwise qualified as voters, who take the amnesty oath and an oath to uphold the executive government of Virginia, shall be qualified as voters.]

June 21—Bill passed submitting to a vote of the people whether the legislature to be chosen at the next election should have power to alter or amend the third article of the constitution, which is in these words:

"No person shall vote or hold office under this constitution who has held office under the so-called Confederate government, or under any rebellious State government, or who has been a member of the so-called Confederate Congress, or a member of any State Legislature in rebellion against the authority of the United States, excepting therefrom the county officers."

June 23—Legislature adjourned.

October 12—Election held for Representatives in Congress. The vote on empowering the Legislature to alter the third article almost unanimously affirmative.

December 4—Legislature assembled. A bill passed, providing that all qualified voters heretofore identified with "the rebellion," and not excluded from the amnesty proclamation by President Johnson (with the exception of those embraced in the "$20,000 clause,") can appear before a notary public, or other persons authorized to administer oaths, under the restored Government, and recover the right of suffrage, by taking the amnesty oath of the 29th of May, 1865, an oath to support the restored Government of Virginia, and to protect and defend the Constitution of the United States. He also becomes eligible to office, unless he has "held office under the so-called Confederate government, or under any rebellious State government, or has been a member of the so-called Confederate Congress, or a member of any State Legislature in rebellion against the authority of the United States," excepting therefrom county officers.

---

## TENNESSEE.

1865, March 4—William G. Brownlow elected Governor, under the organization effected by Andrew Johnson, Military Governor. Brownlow received 23,352 votes, scattering 37.

June 5—Franchise act passed, with these provisions:

SEC. 1. *Be it enacted, &c.*, That the following persons, to wit:

1. Every white man twenty-one years of age, a citizen of the United States and a citizen of the county wherein he may offer his vote six months next preceding the day of election, and publicly known to have entertained unconditional Union sentiments from the outbreak of the rebellion until the present time; and

2. Every white man, a citizen of the United States and a citizen of the county wherein he may offer his vote six months next preceding the day of election, having arrived at the age of twenty-one years since March 4, 1865: *Provided,* That he has not been engaged in armed rebellion against the authority of the United States voluntarily; and

3. Every white man of lawful age coming from another State, and being a citizen of the United States, on proof of loyalty to the United States, and being a citizen of the county wherein he may offer his vote six months next preceding the day of election; and

4. Every white man, a citizen of the United States and a citizen of this State, who has served as a soldier in the army of the United States, and has been or may be hereafter honorably discharged therefrom; and

5. Every white man of lawful age, a citizen of the United States and a citizen of the county wherein he may offer his vote six months next preceding the day of election, who was conscripted by force into the so-called confederate army, and was known to be a Union man, on proof of loyalty to the United States, established by the testimony of two voters under the previous clauses of this section; and

6. Every white man who voted in this State at the presidential election in November, 1864, or voted on the 22d of February, 1865, or voted on the 4th of March, 1865, in this State, and all others who had taken the "oath of allegiance" to the United States, and may be known by the judges of election to have been true friends to the Government of the United States, and would have voted in said previously mentioned elections if the same had been holden within their reach. shall be entitled to the privileges of the elective franchise.

SEC. 2. That all persons who are or shall have been civil or diplomatic officers or agents of the so-called Confederate States of America, or who have left judicial stations under the United States or the State of Tennessee to aid, in any way, the existing or recent rebellion against the authority of the United States, or who are or shall have been military or naval officers of the so-called Confederate States, above the rank of captain in the army or lieutenant in the navy; or who have left seats in the United States Congress or seats in the Legislature of the State of Tennessee, to aid in said rebellion, or have resigned commissions in the army or navy of the United States, and afterward have voluntarily given aid to said rebellion; or persons who have been engaged in treating otherwise than lawfully, as prisoners of war, persons found in the United States service as officers, soldiers, seamen, or in any other capacities; or persons who have been or are absentees from the United States for the purpose of aiding the rebellion; or persons who held pretended offices under the government of States in insurrection against the United States; or persons who left their homes within the jurisdiction and protection of the United States, or fled before the approach of the national forces and passed beyond the Federal military lines into the so-called Confederate States, for the purpose of aiding the rebellion, shall be denied and refused the privilege of the elective franchise in this State for the term of fifteen years from and after the passage of this act.

SEC. 3. That all other persons, except those mentioned in section one of this act, are hereby and henceforth excluded and denied the exercise of the privilege of the elective franchise in this State for the term of five years from and after the passage of this act.

SEC. 4. That all persons embraced in section three of this act, after the expiration of said five years, may be readmitted to the privilege of the elective franchise by petition to the circuit or chancery court, on proof of loyalty to the United States, in open court, upon the testimony of two or more loyal citizens of the United States.

July 15—President Johnson sent this telegram:

WASHINGTON, D. C.—3.50 P. M.,
*July 16, 1865.*

*To Governor W. G. Brownlow :*

I hope, as I have no doubt you will see, that the laws passed by the last Legislature are faithfully executed, and that all illegal voters in the approaching election be kept from the polls, and that the election of members of Congress be conducted fairly. Whenever it becomes necessary for the execution of the law and the protection of the ballot-box, you will call upon General Thomas for sufficient military force to sustain the civil authority of the State. I have just read your address, which I most heartily endorse. ANDREW JOHNSON,
*President U. S. A.*

1866, April 12—An amendment to the franchise act passed the House, 41 to 15.

May 3—The Senate passed it, 13 to 6. Its principal provisions are:

SEC. 1. That every white male inhabitant of this State of the age of twenty-one years, a citizen of the United States and a resident of the county wherein he may offer his vote six months next preceding the day of election, shall be entitled to the privilege of the elective franchise, subject to the following exceptions and disqualifications, to wit:

First. Said voter shall have never borne arms against the Government of the United States for the purpose of aiding the late rebellion, nor have voluntarily given aid, comfort, countenance, counsel, or encouragement to any rebellion against the authority of the United States Government, nor aided, countenanced, or encouraged acts of hostility thereto.

Second. That said voter shall have never sought, or voluntarily accepted, any office, civil or military, or attempted to exercise the functions of any office, civil or military, under the authority or pretended authority of the so-called Confederate States of America, or of any insurrectionary State whatever, hostile or opposed to the authority of the United States Government, with the intent and desire to aid said rebellion or insurrectionary authority.

Third. That said voter shall have never voluntarily supported any pretended government, power, or authority hostile or inimical to the authority of the United States, by contributions in money or property, by persuasion or influence, or in any other way whatever: *Provided,* That the foregoing restrictions and disqualifications shall not apply to any white citizen who may have served in and been honorably discharged from the army or navy of the United States since the 1st day of January, 1862, nor to those who voted in the Presidential election in November, 1864, or voted in the election for " ratification or rejection " in February, 1865, or voted in the election held on the 4th day of March of the same year for Governor and members of the Legislature, nor to those who have been appointed to any civil or military office by Andrew Johnson, Military Governor, or William G. Brownlow, Governor of Tennessee, all of whom are hereby declared to be qualified voters upon their complying with the requirements of this act: *Provided,* That this latter clause shall not apply to any commission issued upon any election which may have been held.

SEC. 2. That the Governor of the State shall, within sixty days after the passage of this act, appoint a commissioner of registration for each and every county in the State, who shall, without delay, enter upon the discharge of his duties, and who shall have full power to administer the necessary oaths provided by this act.

May 19—A bill was passed to disqualify certain persons from holding office, civil or military. It excludes those persons who held civil or diplomatic offices, or were agents of the so-called Confederate States, or who left judicial stations under the United States, or the State of Tennessee, to aid the rebellion, or who were military or naval officers of the so-called Confederate States, above the rank of captain in the army, or lieutenant in the navy, or who left seats in the United States Congress, or seats in the Legislature of the State of Tennessee, to aid the rebellion, or who resigned commissions in the army or navy of the United States and afterward gave voluntary aid to the rebellion, or who absented themselves from the State of Tennessee to give such aid, or who held offices under the States in insurrection against the United States with intent to aid the rebellion, or who ever held office in the State of Tennessee of legislative, judicial, or executive character, under an oath to support the constitution of the State of Tennessee, and who violated said oath, and gave voluntary aid or countenance to the rebellion, that each and all be excluded from all offices, State, county, or municipal.

It also provides that any qualified voter shall not be excluded from office by the provisions of this bill, as amended.

May  —The Senate rejected a suffrage bill, 16 to 5, which proposed to allow all blacks and whites of legal age to vote, and exclude all, after 1875, who cannot read.

May 28—The Legislature adjourned until November 28.

## TEXAS.

1865, June 17—Andrew J. Hamilton appointed Provisional Governor.

1866, March  —Convention met.

April 2—Convention adjourned. The Constitution to be voted on, June 5. It abolishes slavery, and annuls the Secession Ordinance. The war debt has been repudiated. Five years residence required for eligibility to the Legislature. White population is the basis of representation for State purposes. An ordinance passed exempting all persons who, under authority of civil or military power, had inflicted injury upon persons during the war, from accountability therefor.

## ARKANSAS.

1865, October 30—President Johnson sent this telegram to Governor Isaac Murphy, elected Governor under the free State organization formerly made.

EXECUTIVE OFFICE, WASHINGTON, D. C.,
October 30, 1865.

To Gov. MURPHY, Little Rock, Arkansas:

There will be no interference with your present organization of State government. I have learned from E. W. Gantt, Esq., and other sources, that all is working well, and you will proceed and resume the former relations with the Federal Government, and all the aid in the power of the Government will be given in restoring the State to its former relations.

ANDREW JOHNSON, *Pres't of the U. S.*

## LOUISIANA.

There was no interference with the State organization formerly made.

1865, November  —J. M. Wells was elected Governor, and Albert Voorhis, Lieut. Governor

November 23—Legislature met in extra session again, under proclamation of the Governor.

December 22—Legislature adjourned.

1866, March  —J. T. Monroe elected mayor of New Orleans, and James O. Nixon an alderman.

March 19—General Canby issued an order suspending them from the exercise of any of the functions of these offices until the pleasure of the President be made known—as they come within the excepted class of the President's proclamation. They were subsequently pardoned, on application, and took the offices.

# IV.

# LEGISLATION RESPECTING FREEDMEN.

## NORTH CAROLINA.

1866, March 10—The act "concerning negroes, and persons of color, or of mixed blood," passed by the Legislature, declares that "negroes and their issue, even where one ancestor in each succeeding generation to the fourth inclusive, is white, shall be deemed persons of color." It gives them all the privileges of white persons before the courts in the mode of prosecuting, defending, continuing, removing, and transferring their suits at law and in equity, and makes them eligible as witnesses, when not otherwise incompetent, in " all controversies at law and in equity where the rights of persons or property of persons of color shall be put in issue, and would be concluded by the judgment or decree of court; and also in pleas of the State, where the violence, fraud, or injury alleged shall be charged to have been done by or to persons of color. In all other civil and criminal cases such evidence shall be deemed inadmissible, unless by consent of the parties of record : *Provided,* That this section shall not go into effect until jurisdiction in matters relating to freedmen shall be fully committed to the courts of this State : *Provided further,* That no person shall be deemed incompetent to bear testimony in such cases, because of being a party to the record or in interest."

The criminal laws of the State are extended in their operation to embrace persons of color, and the same punishment is inflicted on them as on the whites, except for rape, which, if a white female is the victim, is a capital crime for a black. The law regarding apprentices is so amended as to make its provisions applicable to blacks, but it gives the former masters the preference, and declares that they should be regarded as the most suitable persons. Provision is also made for legalizing the marriages of the blacks contracted during slavery, and for punishment of illicit cohabitation. All which is modified by a proviso that the act shall not take effect until after the Freedmen's Bureau is removed. Where men and women, lately slaves, now cohabit together in the relation of husband and wife, they shall be deemed to have been lawfully married at the time of the commencement of such cohabitation ; and they are required to go before the clerk of the county court, acknowledge the cohabitation, of which record shall be made, and shall be *prima facie* evidence of the statements made.

All contracts between any persons whatever, whereof one or more of them shall be a person of color, for the sale or purchase of any horse, mule, ass, jennet, neat cattle, hog, sheep, or goat, whatever may be the value of such articles, and all contracts between such persons for any other article or articles of property whatever of the value of ten dollars or more, and all contracts executed or executory between such persons for the payment of money of the value of ten dollars or more, shall be void as to all persons whatever, unless the same be put in writing and signed by the vendors or debtors, and witnessed by a white person who can read and write.

Marriage between white persons and persons of color shall be void ; and every person authorized to solemnize the rites of matrimony, who shall knowingly solemnize the same between such persons, and every clerk of a court who shall knowingly issue license for their marriage, shall be deemed guilty of a misdemeanor, and, moreover, shall pay a penalty of five hundred dollars to any person suing for the same.

---

## MISSISSIPPI.
### An Act to regulate the Relation of Master and Apprentice relative to Freedmen, Free Negroes, and Mulattoes, November 22, 1865.

Sec. 1 provides that it shall be the duty of all sheriffs, justices of the peace, and other civil officers of the several counties in this State to report to the probate courts of their respective counties semi-annually, at the January and July terms of said courts, all freedmen, free negroes, and mulattoes, under the age of eighteen, within their respective counties, beats, or districts, who are orphans, or whose parent or parents have not the means, or who refuse to provide for and support said minors, and thereupon it shall be the duty of said probate court to order the clerk of said court to apprentice said minors to some competent and suitable person, on such terms as the court may direct, having a particular care to the interest of said minors: *Provided,* That the former owner of said minors shall have the preference when, in the opinion of the court, he or she shall be a suitable person for that purpose.

Sec. 2 provides that the said court shall be fully satisfied that the person or persons to whom said minor shall be apprenticed shall be a suitable person to have the charge and care of said minor, and fully to protect the interest of said minor: *Provided,* That said apprentice shall be bound by indenture, in case of males until they are twenty-one years old, and in case of females until they are eighteen years old.

Sec. 3 provides that in the management and control of said apprentices said master or mistress shall have power to inflict such moderate corporeal chastisement as a father or guardian is allowed to inflict on his or her child or ward at common law: *Provided,* That in no case shall cruel or inhuman punishment be inflicted.

Sec. 4 provides that if any apprentice shall leave the employment of his or her master or

29

mistress, without his or her consent, said master or mistress may pursue and recapture said apprentice, and bring him or her before any justice of the peace of the county, whose duty it shall be to remand said apprentice to the service of his or her master or mistress; and in the event of a refusal on the part of said apprentice so to return, then said justice shall commit said apprentice to the jail of said county, on failure to give bond, until the next term of the county court; and it shall be the duty of said court, at the first term thereafter, to investigate said case, and if the court shall be of opinion that said apprentice left the employment of his or her master or mistress without good cause, to order him or her to be punished, as provided for the punishment of hired freedmen, as may be from time to time provided for by law for desertion, until he or she shall agree to return to his or her master or mistress: *Provided*, That the court may grant continuances, as in other cases: *And provided further*, That if the court shall believe that said apprentice had good cause to quit his said master or mistress, the court shall discharge said apprentice from said indenture, and also enter a judgment against the master or mistress, for not more than one hundred dollars, for the use and benefit of said apprentice, to be collected on execution, as in other cases.

Sec. 5 provides that if any person entice away any apprentice from his or her master or mistress, or shall knowingly employ an apprentice, or furnish him or her food or clothing, without the written consent of his or her master or mistress, or shall sell or give said apprentice ardent spirits without such consent, said person so offending shall be deemed guilty of a high misdemeanor, and shall on conviction thereof before the county court, be punished as provided for the punishment of persons enticing from their employer hired freedmen, free negroes, or mulattoes.

Sec. 6 makes it the duty of all civil officers to report any minors within their respective counties to said probate court for apprenticeship.

Sec. 9 provides that it shall be lawful for any freedman, free negro, or mulatto, having a minor child or children, to apprentice the said minor child or children as provided for by this act.

Sec. 10 provides that in all cases where the age of the freedman, free negro, or mulatto cannot be ascertained by record testimony, the judge of the county court shall fix the age.

### The Vagrant Act, November 24, 1865.

Sec. 1 defines who are vagrants.

Sec. 2 provides that all freedmen, free negroes, and mulattoes in this State, over the age of eighteen years, found on the second Monday in January, 1866, or thereafter, with no lawful employment or business, or found unlawfully assembling themselves together, either in the day or night time, and all white persons so assembling with freedmen, free negroes, or mulattoes, or usually associating with freedmen, free negroes, or mulattoes on terms of equality, or living in adultery or fornication with a freedwoman, free negro, or mulatto, shall be deemed vagrants, and on conviction thereof shall be fined in the sum of not exceeding, in the case of a freedman, free negro or mulatto, fifty dollars, and a white man two hundred dollars and im-

prisoned, at the discretion of the court, the free negro not exceeding ten days, and the white man not exceeding six months.

Sec. 3 gives all justices of the peace, mayors, and aldermen jurisdiction to try all questions of vagrancy, and it is made their duty to arrest parties violating any provisions of this act, investigate the charges, and, on conviction, punish as provided. It is made the duty of all sheriffs, constables, town constables, city marshals, and all like officers, to report to some officer having jurisdiction all violations of any of the provisions of this act, and it is made the duty of the county courts to inquire if any officer has neglected any of these duties, and if guilty to fine him not exceeding $100, to be paid into the county treasury.

Sec. 5 provides that all fines and forfeitures collected under the provisions of this act shall be paid into the county treasury for general county purposes, and in case any freedman, free negro or mulatto, shall fail for five days after the imposition of any fine or forfeiture upon him or her, for violation of any of the provisions of this act to pay the same, that it shall be, and is hereby made, the duty of the sheriff of the proper county to hire out said freedman, free negro or mulatto, to any person who will, for the shortest period of service, pay said fine or forfeiture and all costs: *Provided*, A preference shall be given to the employer, if there be one, in which case the employer shall be entitled to deduct and retain the amount so paid from the wages of such freedman, free negro or mulatto, then due or to become due; and in case such freedman, free negro or mulatto cannot be hired out, he or she may be dealt with as a pauper.

Sec. 6 provides that the same duties and liabilities existing among white persons of this State shall attach to freedmen, free negroes and mulattoes, to support their indigent families and all colored paupers; and that in order to secure a support for such indigent freedmen, free negroes and mulattoes, it shall be lawful, and it is hereby made the duty of the boards of county police of each county in this State, to levy a poll or capitation tax on each and every freedman, free negro or mulatto, between the ages of eighteen and sixty years, not to exceed the sum of one dollar annually to each person so taxed, which tax when collected shall be paid into the county treasurer's hands, and constitute a fund to be called the freedmen's pauper fund, which shall be applied by the commissioners of the poor for the maintenance of the poor of the freedmen, free negroes and mulattoes, of this State, under such regulations as may be established by the boards of the county police in the respective counties of this State.

Sec. 7 provides that if any freedman, free negro or mulatto shall fail or refuse to pay any tax levied according to the provisions of the sixth section of this act, it shall be *prima facie* evidence of vagrancy, and it shall be the duty of the sheriff to arrest such freedman, free negro or mulatto, or such persons refusing or neglecting to pay such tax, and proceed at once to hire, for the shortest time, such delinquent tax-payer to any one who will pay the said tax, with the accruing costs, giving preference to the employer, if there be one.

**An Act to confer Civil Rights on Freedmen, and for other Purposes, November 25, 1865.**

SECTION 1 provides that all freedmen, free negroes and mulattoes may sue and be sued, implead and be impleaded in all the courts of law and equity of this State, and may acquire personal property and choses in action by descent or purchase, and may dispose of the same in the same manner and to the same extent that white persons may: *Provided*, That the provisions of this section shall not be so construed as to allow any freedman, free negro or mulatto to rent or lease any lands or tenements, except in incorporated towns or cities, in which places the corporate authorities shall control the same.

SEC. 2 provides that all freedmen, free negroes and mulattoes may intermarry with each other in the same manner and under the same regulations that are provided by law for white persons: *Provided*, That the clerk of probate shall keep separate records of the same.

SEC. 3 further provides that all freedmen, free negroes and mulattoes, who do now and have heretofore lived and cohabited together as husband and wife shall be taken and held in law as legally married, and the issue shall be taken and held as legitimate for all purposes. That it shall not be lawful for any freedman, free negro or mulatto to intermarry with any white person; nor for any white person to intermarry with any freedman, free negro or mulatto; and any person who shall so intermarry shall be deemed guilty of felony, and on conviction thereof, shall be confined in the State penitentiary for life; and those shall be deemed freedmen, free negroes and mulattoes who are of pure negro blood, and those descended from a negro to the third generation, inclusive, though one ancestor of each generation may have been a white person.

SEC. 4 provides that in addition to cases in which freedmen, free negroes and mulattoes are now by law competent witnesses, freedmen, free negroes and mulattoes shall be competent in civil cases, when a party or parties to the suit, either plaintiff or plaintiffs, defendant or defendants; also in cases where freedmen, free negroes and mulattoes are either plaintiff or plaintiffs, defendant or defendants, and a white person or white persons is or are the opposing party or parties, plaintiff or plaintiffs, defendant or defendants. They shall also be competent witnesses in all criminal prosecutions where the crime charged is alleged to have been committed by a white person upon or against the person or property of a freedman, free negro or mulatto: *Provided*, That in all cases said witnesses shall be examined in open court on the stand, except, however, they may be examined before the grand jury, and shall in all cases be subject to the rules and tests of the common law as to competency and credibility.

SEC. 5 provides that every freedman, free negro, and mulatto shall on the second Monday of January, one thousand eight hundred and sixty-six, and annually thereafter, have a lawful home or employment, and shall have written evidence thereof, as follows, to wit: If living in any incorporated city, town, or village, a license from the mayor thereof, and if living outside of any incorporated city, town, or village, from the member of the board of police of his beat, authorizing him or her to do irregular and job work, or a written contract, as provided in section six of this act; which licenses may be revoked for cause at any time by the authority granting the same.

SEC. 6 provides that all contracts for labor made with freedmen, free negroes, and mulattoes, for a longer period than one month, shall be in writing and in duplicate, attested and read to said freedman, free negro, or mulatto by a beat, city, or county officer or two disinterested white persons of the county in which the labor is to be performed, of which each party shall have one; and said contracts shall be taken and held as entire contracts, and if the laborer shall quit the service of the employer before the expiration of his term of service without good cause, he shall forfeit his wages for that year up to the time of quitting.

SEC. 7. provides that every civil officer shall, and every person may arrest and carry back to his or her legal employer any freedman, free negro, or mulatto who shall have quit the service of his or her employer before the expiration of his or her term of service without good cause; and said officer and person shall be entitled to receive for arresting and carrying back every deserting employé aforesaid the sum of five dollars, and ten cents per mile from the place of arrest to the place of delivery, and the same shall be paid by the employer and held as a set-off for so much against the wages of said deserting employé: *Provided*, That said arrested party after being so returned may appeal to a justice of the peace or member of the board of the police of the county, who, on notice to the alleged employer, shall try, summarily, whether said appellant is legally employed by the alleged employer and has good cause to quit said employer; either party shall have the right of appeal to the county court, pending which the alleged deserter shall be remanded to the alleged employer, or otherwise disposed of as shall be right and just; and the decision of the county court shall be final.

SEC. 8 provides that upon affidavit made by the employer of any freedman, free negro, or mulatto, or other credible person, before any justice of the peace or member of the board of police, that any freedman, free negro, or mulatto, legally employed by said employer, has illegally deserted said employment, such justice of the peace or member of the board of police shall issue his warrant or warrants, returnable before himself or other such officer, directed to any sheriff, constable, or special deputy, commanding him to arrest said deserter and return him or her to said employer, and the like proceedings shall be had as provided in the preceding section; and it shall be lawful for any officer to whom such warrant shall be directed to execute said warrant in any county of this State, and that said warrant may be transmitted without indorsement to any like officer of another county to be executed and returned as aforesaid, and the said employer shall pay the cost of said warrants and arrest and return, which shall be set off for so much against the wages of said deserter.

SEC. 9 provides that if any person shall persuade, or attempt to persuade, entice, or cause any freedman, free negro, or mulatto to desert from the legal employment of any person before the expiration of his or her term of service, or shall knowingly employ any such deserting freedman, free negro, or mulatto, or shall knowingly give or sell to any such deserting freedman, free negro, or mulatto any food, raiment, or other thing, he or she shall be guilty of a misdemeanor, and upon conviction shall be fined not less than twenty-five dollars and not more than two hundred dollars and the costs; and if said fine and costs shall not be immediately paid, the court shall sentence said convict to not exceeding two months' imprisonment in the county jail, and he or she shall, moreover, be liable to the party injured in damages: *Provided,* If any person shall, or shall attempt to, persuade, entice, or cause any freedman, free negro, or mulatto to desert from any legal employment of any person with the view to employ said freedman, free negro, or mulatto without the limits of this State, such person, on conviction, shall be fined not less than fifty dollars and not more than five hundred dollars and costs; and if said fine and costs shall not be immediately paid the court shall sentence said convict to not exceeding six months' imprisonment in the county jail.

SEC. 10 provides that it shall be lawful for any freedman, free negro, or mulatto to charge any white person, freedman, free negro, or mulatto, by affidavit, with any criminal offence against his or her person or property, and upon such affidavit the proper process shall be issued and executed as if said affidavit was made by a white person, and it shall be lawful for any freedman, free negro, or mulatto, in any action, suit, or controversy pending or about to be instituted in any court of law or equity in this State, to make all needful and lawful affidavits as shall be necessary for the institution, prosecution, or defence of such suit or controversy.

SEC. 11 provides that the penal laws of this State, in all cases not otherwise specially provided for, shall apply and extend to all freedmen, free negroes, and mulattoes.

### An Act Supplementary to "An Act to confer Civil Rights upon Freedmen," and for other purposes, December 2, 1865.

SEC. 1 provides that in every case where any white person has been arrested and brought to trial, by virtue of the provisions of the tenth section of the above recited act, in any court in this State, upon sufficient proof being made to the court or jury, upon the trial before said court, that any freedman, free negro or mulatto has falsely and maliciously caused the arrest and trial of said white person or persons, the court shall render up a judgment against said freedman, free negro or mulatto for all costs of the case, and impose a fine not to exceed fifty dollars, and imprisonment in the county jail not to exceed twenty days; and for a failure of said freedmen, free negro or mulatto to pay, or cause to be paid, all costs, fines and jail fees, the sheriff of the county is hereby authorized and required, after giving ten days' public notice, to proceed to hire out at public outcry, at the court-house of the county, said freedman,

free negro or mulatto, for the shortest time to raise the amount necessary to discharge said freedman, free negro or mulatto from all costs, fines, and jail fees aforesaid.

### An Act to punish certain Offences therein named, and for other purposes, November 29, 1865.

SEC. 1. *Be it enacted, &c.,* That no freedman, free negro, or mulatto, not in the military service of the United States Government, and not licensed to do so by the board of police of his or her county, shall keep or carry fire-arms of any kind, or any ammunition, dirk, or bowie-knife; and on conviction thereof, in the county court, shall be punished by fine, not exceeding ten dollars, and pay the costs of such proceedings, and all such arms or ammunition shall be forfeited to the informer; and it shall be the duty of every civil and military officer to arrest any freedman, free negro, or mulatto found with any such arms or ammunition, and cause him to be committed for trial in default of bail.

SEC. 2. That any freedman, free negro, or mulatto, committing riots, routes, affrays, trespasses, malicious mischief and cruel treatment to animals, seditious speeches, insulting gestures, language, or acts, or assaults on any person, disturbance of the peace, exercising the functions of a minister of the gospel without a license from some regularly organized church, vending spirituous or intoxicating liquors, or committing any other misdemeanor, the punishment of which is not specifically provided for by law, shall, upon conviction thereof, in the county court, be fined not less than ten dollars, and not more than one hundred dollars, and may be imprisoned, at the discretion of the court, not exceeding thirty days.

SEC. 3. That if any white person shall sell, lend, or give to any freedman, free negro, or mulatto, any fire-arms, dirk, or bowie-knife, or ammunition, or any spirituous or intoxicating liquors, such person or persons so offending, upon conviction thereof, in the county court of his or her county, shall be fined not exceeding fifty dollars, and may be imprisoned, at the discretion of the court, not exceeding thirty days.

SEC. 4. That all the penal and criminal laws now in force in this State, defining offences, and prescribing the mode of punishment for crimes and misdemeanors committed by slaves, free negroes or mulattoes, be and the same are hereby re-enacted, and declared to be in full force and effect, against freedmen, free negroes, and mulattoes, except so far as the mode and manner of trial and punishment have been changed or altered by law.

SEC. 5. That if any freedman, free negro or mulatto, convicted of any of the misdemeanors provided against in this act, shall fail or refuse, for the space of five days after conviction, to pay the fine and costs imposed, such person shall be hired out by the sheriff or other officer, at public outcry, to any white person who will pay said fine and all costs, and take such convict for the shortest time.

### GEORGIA.

1865, December 15—Free persons of color are made competent witnesses in all courts in cases where a free person of color is a party, or the offence charged is against the person or property of a free person of color. Persons of color now living as husband and wife are declared to be so, except a man has two or more reputed wives, or a wife two or more reputed husbands; in such event, they shall select one and the marriage ceremony be performed. .

1866, Feb. 23—All male inhabitants, white and black, between sixteen and fifty, subject to work on the public roads, except such as are specially exempted.

March 7—Any officer knowingly issuing any marriage license to parties, either of whom is of African descent and the other a white person, shall be guilty of a misdemeanor, and on conviction be fined from two hundred to five hundred dollars, or imprisoned for three months, or both. Any officer or minister marrying such persons shall be fined from five hundred to one thousand dollars, and imprisoned six months, or both.

March 9—That among persons of color the parent shall be required to maintain his or her children, whether legitimate or illegitimate. That children shall be subjected to the same obligations, in relation to their parents, as those which existing relation to white persons. That every colored child hereafter born, is declared to be the legitimate child of his mother, and also of his colored father, if acknowledged by such father.

### To Amend the Penal Code.

March 12—The 4,435th section of the Penal Code shall read as follows:

All persons wandering or strolling about in idleness, who are able to work, and who have no property to support them; all persons leading an idle, immoral, or profligate life, who have no property to support them, and are able to work and do not work; all persons able to work having no visible and known means of a fair, honest, and reputable livelihood; all persons having a fixed abode, who have no visible property to support them, and who live by stealing or by trading in, bartering for, or buying stolen property; and all professional gamblers living in idleness, shall be deemed and considered vagrants, and shall be indicted as such, and it shall be lawful for any person to arrest said vagrants and have them bound over for trial to the next term of the county court, and upon conviction, they shall be fined and imprisoned or sentenced to work on the public works, for not longer than a year, or shall, in the discretion of the court, be bound out to some person for a time not longer than one year, upon such valuable consideration as the court may prescribe; the person giving bond in a sum not exceeding $300, payable to said court and conditioned to clothe and feed, and provide said convict with medical attendance for and during said time: *Provided*, That the defendant may, at any time, before conviction, be discharged, upon paying costs and giving bond and security in a sum not exceeding $200, payable to said court, and condition for the good behavior and industry of defendant for one year.

March 8—The wilful and malicious burning of an occupied dwelling-house of another on a farm, or plantation, or elsewhere, shall be punished with death; also burglary in the night; also stealing a horse or mule, unless recommended by the jury to the mercy of the court.

March 17—County courts organized, as in other States, for hearing of "cases arising out of the relation of master and servant," &c. Where such cases shall go against the servant, the judgment for costs upon written notice to the master shall operate as a garnishment against him, and he shall retain a sufficient amount for the payment thereof, out of any wages due to said servant, or to become due during the period of service, and may be cited at any time by the collecting officer to make answer thereto.

March 17—SEC. 1. That all negroes, mulattoes, mestizoes, and their descendants having one eighth negro or African blood in their veins, shall be known in this State as "persons of color."

2. That persons of color shall have the right to make and enforce contracts, to sue, be sued, to be parties and give evidence, to inherit, to purchase, lease, sell, hold, and convey real and personal property, and to have full and equal benefit of all laws and proceedings for the security of person and estate, and shall not be subjected to any other or different punishment, pain or penalty, for the commission of any act or offense, than such as are prescribed for white persons committing like acts or offenses.

March 20—Crimes defined in certain sections named, as felonies are reduced below felonies, and all other crimes, punishable by fine or imprisonment or either, shall be likewise punishable by a fine not exceeding $1,000, imprisonment not exceeding six months, whipping not exceeding thirty-nine lashes, to work in a chain-gang on the public works not to exceed twelve months, and any one or more of these punishments may be ordered in the discretion of the judge.

### ALABAMA.

December  —Bill passed, " making it unlawful for any freedmen, mulatto, or free person of color in this State to own fire-arms, or carry about his person a pistol or other deadly weapon," under a penalty of a fine of $100 or imprisonment three months. Also, making it unlawful for any person to sell, give, or lend fire-arms or ammunition of any description whatever to any freedman, free negro, or mulatto, under a penalty of not less than $50 not more than $100 at the discretion of the jury.

December 9—This bill passed: That all freedmen, free negroes, and mulattoes, shall have the right to sue and be sued, plead and be impleaded in all the different and various courts of this State, to the same extent that white persons now have by law. And they shall be competent to testify only in open court, and only in cases in which freedmen, free negroes, and mulattoes are parties, either plaintiff or defendant, and in civil or criminal cases, for injuries in the persons and property of freedmen, free negroes, and mulattoes, and in all cases, civil or criminal, in which a freedman, free negro, or mulatto, is a witness against a white person, or a white person against a freedman, free negro, or mulatto, the parties shall be competent witnesses, and neither interest in the question or suit, nor marriage, shall disqualify any witness from testifying in open court.

1866, Febuary 16.—A law was enacted, of

which section 1 provides that it shall not be lawful for any person to interfere with, hire, employ, or entice away, or induce to leave the service of another, any laborer or servant who shall have stipulated or contracted, in writing, to serve for any given number of days, weeks, or months, or for one year, so long as the said contract shall be and remain in force and binding upon the parties thereto, without the consent of the party employing or to whom said service is due and owing in writing, or in the presence of some veritable white person; and any person who shall knowingly interfere with, hire, employ, or entice away, or induce to leave the service aforesaid, without justifiable excuse therefor, before the expiration of said term of service so contracted and stipulated as aforesaid, shall be guilty of a misdemeanor, and on conviction thereof, must be fined in such sum, not less than fifty nor more than five hundred dollars, as the jury trying the same may assess, and in no case less than double the amount of the injury sustained by the party from whom such laborer or servant was induced to leave, one-half to go to the party injured and the other to the county as fines and forfeitures.

Sec. 2 provides that the party injured shall be a competent witness in all prosecutions under this act, notwithstanding his interest in the fine to be assessed.

Sec. 3 provides that when any laborer or servant, having contracted as provided in the first section of this act, shall afterward be found, before the termination of said contract, in the service or employment of another, that fact shall be *prima facie* evidence that such person is guilty of violation of this act, if he fail and refuse to forthwith discharge the said laborer or servant, after being notified and informed of such former contract and employment.

A new penal code was adopted.

The material changes introduced by the new penal code are briefly these:

*First.* Whipping and branding are abolished, as legal punishments, and a new punishment is introduced, entitled "hard labor for the county." This "hard labor for the county" is put under the control of the court of county commissioners, who are authorized to employ a superintendent of the convicts, to make regulations for their government and labor, to put them to work on the public roads, bridges, &c., or to hire them out to railroad companies or private individuals.

*Second.* For all offences which were heretofore punishable by fine, or by fine and imprisonment, either in the county jail or in the penitentiary, the jury may still impose a fine; to which the court, in its discretion, may superadd imprisonment or hard labor, within specified limits in each case.

*Third.* The dividing line between grand and petit larceny, is raised from twenty to one hundred dollars; grand larceny being made a felony, that is, it may be punished by imprisonment in the penitentiary; while petit larceny is only a misdemeanor, punishable by fine, or by fine and imprisonment in the county jail.

*Fourth.* A county court is established for the trial of misdemeanors.

*Fifth.* Justices of the peace have jurisdiction of a few minor offences, such as vagrancy, larceny of less than ten dollars, and assaults, affrays, &c., in which no weapon is used. The proceedings before them conform substantially to proceedings before the county court.

The new code makes no distinction on account of color, only marriages between white persons and negroes are prohibited. It went into effect June 1, 1866.

The Governor vetoed three bills referring to persons of color. See page 21.

## SOUTH CAROLINA.

### An Act Preliminary to the Legislation induced by the Emancipation of Slaves, October 19, 1865.

Section 3 provides that all free negroes, mulattoes, and mestizoes, all freedwomen, and all descendants through either sex of any of these persons, shall be known as *persons of color*, except that every such descendant who may have of Caucasian blood seven eighths, or more, shall be deemed a white person.

Sec. 4 provides that the statutes and regulations concerning slaves are now inapplicable to persons of color; and although such persons are not entitled to social or political equality with white persons, they shall have the right to acquire, own, and dispose of property, to make contracts, to enjoy the fruits of their labor, to sue and be sued, and to receive protection under the law in their persons and property.

Sec. 5 provides that all rights and remedies respecting persons or property, and all duties and liabilities under laws, civil and criminal, which apply to white persons, are extended to persons of color, subject to the modifications made by this act and the other acts hereinbefore mentioned.

### An Act to Amend the Criminal Law, December 19, 1865.

Section 1 provides that either of the crimes specified in this first section shall be felony, without benefit of clergy, to wit: For a person of color to commit any wilful homicide, unless in self-defence; for a person of color to commit an assault upon a white woman, with manifest intent to ravish her; for a person of color to have sexual intercourse with a white woman by personating her husband; for any person to raise an insurrection or rebellion in this State; for any person to furnish arms or ammunition to other persons who are in a state of actual insurrection or rebellion, or permit them to resort to his house for advancement of their evil purpose; for any person to administer, or cause to be take by any other person, any poison, chloroform, soporific, or other destructive thing, or to shoot at, stab, cut, or wound any other person, or by any means whatsoever to cause bodily injury to any other person, whereby, in any of these cases, a bodily injury dangerous to the life of any other person is caused, with intent, in any of these cases, to commit the crime of murder, or the crime of rape, or the crime of robbery, burglary, or larceny; for any person who had been transported under sentence to return to this State within the period of prohibition contained in the sentence; or for a person to steal a horse or mule, or cotton packed in a bale ready for market.

Sec. 10 provides that a person of color who is in the employment of a master engaged in husbandry shall not have the right to sell any corn, rice, peas, wheat, or other grain, any flour, cotton, fodder, hay, bacon, fresh meat of any kind, poultry of any kind, animal of any kind, or any other product of a farm, without having written evidence from such master, or some person authorized by him, or from the district judge or a magistrate, that he has the right to sell such product; and if any person 'shall, directly or indirectly, purchase any such product from such person of color without such written evidence, the purchaser and seller shall each be guilty of a misdemeanor.

Sec. 11 provides that it shall be a misdemeanor for any person not authorized to write or give to a person of color a writing which professes to show evidence of the right of that person of color to sell any product of a farm which, by the section last preceding, he is forbidden to sell without written evidence; and any person convicted of this misdemeanor shall be liable to the same extent as the purchaser in the section last preceding is made liable; and it shall be a misdemeanor for a person of color to exhibit as evidence of his right to sell any product a writing which he knows to be false or counterfeited, or to have been written or given by any person not authorized.

Sec. 13 states that persons of color constitute no part of the militia of the State, and no one of them shall, without permission in writing from the district judge or magistrate, be allowed to keep a fire-arm, sword, or other military weapon, except that one of them, who is the owner of a farm, may keep a shot-gun or rifle, such as is ordinarily used in hunting, but not a pistol, musket, or other fire-arm or weapon appropriate for purposes of war. The district judge or a magistrate may give an order, under which any weapon unlawfully kept may be seized and sold, the proceeds of sale to go into the district court fund. The possession of a weapon in violation of this act shall be a misdemeanor which shall be tried before a district court or a magistrate, and in case of conviction, shall be punished by a fine equal to twice the value of the weapon so unlawfully kept, and if that be not immediately paid, by corporeal punishment.

Sec. 14 provides that it shall not be lawful for a person of color to be the owner, in whole or in part, of any distillery where spirituous liquors of any kind are made, or of any establishment where spirituous liquors of any kind are sold by retail; nor for a person of color to be engaged in distilling any spirituous liquors, or in retailing the same in a shop or elsewhere. A person of color who shall do anything contrary to the prohibitions herein contained shall be guilty of a misdemeanor, and, upon conviction, may be punished by fine or corporeal punishment and hard labor, as to the district judge or magistrate before whom he may be tried shall seem meet.

Sec. 22 provides that no person of color shall migrate into and reside in this State, unless, within twenty days after his arrival within the same, he shall enter into a bond, with two freeholders as sureties, to be approved by the judge of the district court or a magistrate, in a penalty of one thousand dollars, conditioned for his good behavior, and for his support, if he should become unable to support himself.

Sec. 24 provides that when several persons of color are convicted of one capital offence, the jury which tries them may recommend one or more to mercy, for reasons which, in their opinion, mitigate the guilt; the district judge shall report the case, with his opinion, and the Governor shall do in the matter as seems to him meet. The same may be done when one only is convicted of capital offence. Before sentence of death shall be executed in any case, time for application to the Governor shall be allowed.

Sec. 27 provides that whenever, under any law, sentence imposing a fine is passed, if the fine and costs be not immediately paid, there shall be detention of the convict, and substitution of other punishment. If the offence should not involve the *crimen falsi*, and be infamous, the substitution shall be, in the case of a white person, imprisonment for a time proportioned to the fine, at the rate of one day for each dollar; and in the case of a person of color, enforced labor, without unnecessary pain or restraint, for a time proportioned to the fine, at the rate of one day for each dollar. But if the offence should be infamous, there shall be substituted for a fine, for imprisonment, or for both, hard labor, corporeal punishment, solitary confinement, and confinement in tread-mill or stocks, one or more, at the discretion of the judge of the superior court, the district judge, or the magistrate, who pronounces the sentence. In this act, and in respect to all crimes and misdemeanors, the term servants shall be understood to embrace an apprentice as well as a servant under contract.

Sec. 29 provides that, upon view of a misdemeanor committed by a person of color, or by a white person toward a person of color, a magistrate may arrest the offender, and, according to the nature of the case, punish the offender summarily, or bind him in recognizance with sufficient sureties to appear at the next monthly sitting of the district court, or commit him for trial before the district court.

Sec. 30 provides that, upon view of a misdemeanor committed by a person of color, any person present may arrest the offender and take him before a magistrate, to be dealt with as the case may require. In case of a misdemeanor committed by a white person toward a person of color, any person may complain to a magistrate, who shall cause the offender to be arrested, and, according to the nature of the case, to be brought before himself, or be taken for trial in the district court.

## An Act to establish District Courts, December 19, 1865.

Courts are established to have "exclusive jurisdiction, subject to appeal, of all civil causes where one or both the parties are persons of color, and of all criminal cases wherein the accused is a person of color, and also of all cases of misdemeanors affecting the person or property of a person of color, and of all cases of bastardy, and of all cases of vagrancy, not tried before a magistrate."

An indictment against a white person for the homicide of a person of color shall be tried in the superior court of law, and so shall other indictments in which a white person is accused of a capital felony affecting the person or property of a person of color.

In every case, civil and criminal, in which a person of color is a party, or which affects the person or property of a person of color, persons of color shall be competent witnesses. The accused, in such a criminal case, and the parties in every such civil case, may be witnesses, and so may every other person who is a competent witness; and in every such case, either party may offer testimony as to his own character, or that of his adversary or of the prosecutor, or of the third person mentioned in an indictment.

December 21—"*An act to establish and regulate the domestic relations of persons of color, and to amend the law in relation to paupers and vagrancy,*" establishes the relation of husband and wife, declares those now living as such to be husband and wife, and provides that persons of color desirous hereafter to marry shall have the contract duly solemnized. A parent may bind his child over two years of age as an apprentice to serve till 21 if a male, 18 if a female. All persons of color who make contracts for service or labor shall be known as servants, and those with whom they contract as masters.

"Colored children between 18 and 21, who have neither father nor mother *living in the district in which they are found*, or whose parents are paupers, or unable to afford them a comfortable maintenance, *or whose parents are not teaching them habits of industry and honesty*, or are persons of notoriously bad character, or are vagrants, or have been convicted of infamous offences, and colored children, *in all cases where they are in danger of moral contamination*, may be bound as apprentices by the district judge or one of the magistrates for the aforesaid term."

It "provides that no person of color shall pursue or practice the art, trade, or business of an artisan, mechanic, or shopkeeper, or any other trade, employment, or business, (besides that of husbandry, or that of a servant under a contract for service or labor,) on his own account and for his own benefit, or in partnership with a white person, or as agent or servant of any person, until he shall have obtained a license therefor from the judge of the district court, which license shall be good for one year only. This license the judge may grant upon petition of the applicant, and upon being satisfied of his skill and fitness, and of his good moral character, and upon payment by the applicant to the clerk of the district court of one hundred dollars if a shopkeeper or pedlar, to be paid annually, and ten dollars if a mechanic, artisan, or to engage in any other trade, also to be paid annually: *Provided, however*, That upon complaint being made and proved to the district judge of an abuse of such license, he shall revoke the same: *And provided, also*, That no person of color shall practice any mechanical

art or trade unless he shows that he has served an apprenticeship in such trade or art, or is now practicing such trade or art."

Former slaves, now helpless, who were on a farm Nov. 10, 1865 and six months previous shall not be evicted by the owner from the house occupied by them before January 1, 1867.

It "provides that if the district court fund, after payment of the sums with which it is charged, on account of the salary of the judge of the district court, superintendent of convicts, jurors, and other expenses of the court and of convicts, shall be insufficient to support indigent persons of color, who may be proper charges on the public, the board aforesaid shall have power to impose for that purpose, whenever it may be required, a tax of one dollar on each male person of color between the ages of eighteen and fifty years, and fifty cents on each unmarried female person of color between the ages of eighteen and forty-five, to be collected in each precinct by a magistrate thereof: *Provided*, That the said imposition of a tax shall be approved in writing by the judge of the district court, and that his approval shall appear in the journals of that court."

### Order of General Sickles, disregarding the Code, January 17, 1866.

1866, January 17—Major General Sickles issued this order:

HEADQ'RS DEP'T OF SOUTH CAROLINA, *January* 17, 1866.

[G. O., No. 1.]—I. To the end that civil rights and immunities may be enjoyed; that kindly relations among the inhabitants of the State may be established; that the rights and duties of the employer and the free laborer respectively may be defined; that the soil may be cultivated and the system of free labor undertaken; that the owners of estates may be secure in the possession of their lands and tenements; that persons able and willing to work may have employment; that idleness and vagrancy may be discountenanced, and encouragement given to industry and thrift; and that humane provision may be made for the aged, infirm and destitute, the following regulations are established for the government of all concerned in this department.

II. All laws shall be applicable alike to all the inhabitants. No person shall be held incompetent to sue, make complaint, or to testify, because of color or caste.

III. All the employments of husbandry or the useful arts, and all lawful trades or callings, may be followed by all persons, irrespective of color or caste; nor shall any freedman be obliged to pay any tax or any fee for a license, nor be amenable to any municipal or parish ordinance, not imposed upon all other persons.

IV. The lawful industry of all persons who live under the protection of the United States, and owe obedience to its laws, being useful to the individual, and essential to the welfare of society, no person will be restrained from seeking employment when not bound by voluntary agreement, nor hindered from traveling from place to place, on lawful business. All combinations or agreements which are intended to hinder, or may so operate as to hinder, in any way, the employment of labor—or to limit compensation for labor—or to compel labor to be involuntarily performed in certain places or for certain persons; as well as all combinations or agreements to prevent the sale or hire of lands or tenements, are declared to be misdemeanors; and any person or persons convicted thereof shall be punished by fine not exceeding $500, or by imprisonment, not to exceed six months, or by both such fine and imprisonment.

V. Agreements for labor or personal service of any kind, or for the use and occupation of lands and tenements, or for any other lawful purpose, between freedmen and other persons, when fairly made, will be immediately enforced against either party violating the same.

VI. Freed persons, unable to labor, by reason of age or infirmity, and orphan children of tender years, shall have allotted to them by owners suitable quarters on the premises where they have been heretofore domiciled as slaves, until adequate provision, approved by the general commanding, be made for them by the State or local authorities, or otherwise; and they shall not be removed from the premises, unless for disorderly behavior, misdemeanor, or other offence committed by the head of a family or a member thereof.

VII. Able-bodied freedmen, when they leave the premises in which they may be domiciled, shall take with them and provide for such of their relatives as by the laws of South Carolina all citizens are obliged to maintain.

VIII. When a freed person, domiciled on a plantation, refuses to work there, after having been offered employment by the owner or lessee, on fair terms, approved by the agent of the Freedmen's Bureau, such freedman or woman shall remove from the premises within ten days after such offer and due notice to remove by the owner or occupant.

IX. When able-bodied freed persons are domiciled on premises where they have been heretofore held as slaves, and are not employed thereon or elsewhere, they shall be permitted to remain, on showing to the satisfaction of the commanding officer of the post that they have made diligent and proper efforts to obtain employment.

X. Freed persons occupying premises without the authority of the United States, or the permission of the owner, and who have not been heretofore held there as slaves, may be removed by the commanding officer of the post, on the complaint of the owner, and proof of the refusal of said freed persons to remove after ten days' notice.

XI. Any person employed or domiciled on a plantation or elsewhere, who may be rightfully dismissed by the terms of agreement, or expelled for misbehavior, shall leave the premises, and shall not return without the consent of the owner or tenant thereof.

XII. Commanding officers of districts will establish within their commands respectively suitable regulations for hiring out to labor, for a period not to exceed one year, all vagrants who cannot be advantageously employed on roads, fortifications and other public works. The proceeds of such labor shall be paid over to the assistant commissioner of the Freedmen's Bureau, to provide for aged and infirm refugees, indigent freed people and orphan children.

XIII. The vagrant laws of the State of South Carolina, applicable to free white persons, will be recognized as the only vagrant laws applicable to the freedmen; nevertheless, such laws shall not be considered applicable to persons who are without employment, if they shall prove that they have been unable to obtain employment, after diligent efforts to do so.

XIV. It shall be the duty of officers commanding posts to see that issues of rations to freedmen are confined to destitute persons who are unable to work because of infirmities arising from old age or chronic diseases, orphan children too young to work, and refugee freedmen returning to their homes with the sanction of the proper authorities; and in ordering their issues, commanding officers will be careful not to encourage idleness or vagrancy. District commanders will make consolidated reports of these issues tri-monthly.

XV. The proper authorities of the State in the several municipalities and districts shall proceed to make suitable provision for their poor, without distinction of color; in default of which the general commanding will levy an equitable tax on persons and property sufficient for the support of the poor.

XVI. The constitutional rights of all loyal and well-disposed inhabitants to bear arms will not be infringed; nevertheless this shall not be construed to sanction the unlawful practice of carrying concealed weapons, nor to authorize any person to enter with arms on the premises of another against his consent. No one shall bear arms who has borne arms against the United States, unless he shall have taken the amnesty oath prescribed in the proclamation of the President of the United States, dated May 20, 1865, or the oath of allegiance, prescribed in the proclamation of the President, dated December 8, 1863, within the time prescribed therein. And no disorderly person, vagrant, or disturber of the peace, shall be allowed to bear arms.

XVII. To secure the same equal justice and personal liberty to the freedmen as to other inhabitants, no penalties or punishments different from those to which all persons are amenable shall be imposed on freed people; and all crimes and offences which are prohibited under existing laws shall be understood as prohibited in the case of freedmen; and if committed by a freedman, shall, upon conviction, be punished in the same manner as if committed by a white man.

XVII. Corporeal punishment shall not be inflicted upon any person other than a minor, and then only by the parent, guardian, teacher, or one to whom said minor is lawfully bound by indenture of apprenticeship.

XIX. Persons whose conduct tends to a breach of the peace may be required to give security for their good behavior, and in default thereof shall be held in custody.

XX. All injuries to the person or property committed by or upon freed persons shall be punished in the manner provided by the laws of South Carolina for like injuries to the persons or property of citizens thereof. If no provision be made by the laws of the State, then the punishment for such offences shall be according to the course of common law; and in the case of any injury to the person or property, not prohibited by the common law, or for which the punishment shall not be appropriate, such sentence shall be imposed as, in the discretion of the court before which the trial is had, shall be deemed proper, subject to the approval of the general commanding.

XXI. All arrests for whatever cause will be reported tri-monthly, with the proceedings thereupon, through the prescribed channel, to the general commanding.

XXII. Commanding officers of districts, subdistricts, and posts, within their commands respectively, in the absence of the duly-appointed agent, will perform any duty appertaining to the ordinary agents of the Bureau of Refugees, Freedmen, and Abandoned Lands, carefully observing for their guidance all orders published by the commissioner or assistant commissioner, or other competent authority.

XXIII. District commanders will enforce these regulations by suitable instructions to sub-district and post commanders, taking care that justice be done, that fair dealing between man and man be observed, and that no unnecessary hardship, and no cruel or unusual punishments be imposed upon any one.

By command of D. E. SICKLES, Major General.

Official:                W. L. M. BURGER,
                    *Assistant Adjutant General.*

---

### FLORIDA.

### An Act to Establish and Organize a County Criminal Court, January 11, 1866.

SEC. 1 gives the court jurisdiction in cases of assault, assault and battery, assault with intent to kill, riot, affray, larceny, robbery, arson, burglary, malicious mischief, vagrancy, and all misdemeanors, and all offences against religion, chastity, morality, and decency: *Provided*, That the punishment of the same does not affect the life of the offender. The Governor to appoint the judge. In the proceedings, "no presentment, indictment, or written pleadings, shall be required." Where a fine is imposed, and not paid, the party may be put to such labor as the county commissioner may direct, the compensation for which to go in payment of the fine and cost of prosecution; "or the said county commissioner may hire out, at public outcry, the said party to any person who will take him or her for the shortest time, and pay the fine, forfeiture, and penalty imposed, and cost of prosecution."

### An Act to Extend to all the Inhabitants of the State the Benefit of Courts of Justice, and the Processes thereof, January 11, 1866.

SEC. 1 provides that the judicial tribunals of this State, with the processes thereof, shall be accessible to all the inhabitants of the State, without distinction of color, for the prosecution and defence of all the rights of person and property, subject only to the restrictions contained in the constitution of the State.

SEC. 2 provides that all laws heretofore passed, with reference to slaves, free negroes, and mulattoes, except the act to prevent their migration into the State, and the act prohibiting the sale of fire-arms and ammunition to them, be, and the same are hereby, repealed; and all the criminal laws of this State applicable to white persons now in force, and not in conflict with, or modified by, the legislation of the present session of the General Assembly, shall be deemed and held to apply equally to all the inhabitants of the same without distinction of color.

### An act to Establish and Enforce the Marriage Relation between Persons of Color. January 11, 1866.

SEC. 1 requires all the colored inhabitants, claiming to be living together in the relation of husband and wife, and who have not been joined as such agreeably to the laws, and who shall mutually desire to continue in that relation, within nine months from the passage of this act, to appear before some person legally authorized to perform the marriage ceremony, and be regularly joined in the holy bonds of matrimony.

SEC. 2 provides that the issue of such prior cohabitation shall be legitimated by the act of marriage so regularly contracted as aforesaid, and be thenceforth entitled to all the rights and privileges of a legitimate offspring.

SEC. 5 provides that after the expiration of the time limited in the first section, all laws applicable to or regulating the marriage relation between white persons shall deemed to apply to the same relation between the colored population of the State.

### An Act in Addition to An Act concerning Marriage Licenses. January 12, 1866.

SEC. 1 provides that if any white female resident shall hereafter attempt to intermarry, or shall live in a state of adultery or fornication, with any negro, mulatto, or other person of color, she shall be deemed to be guilty of a misdemeanor, and upon conviction shall be fined in a sum not exceeding one thousand dollars, or be confined in the public jail not exceeding three months, or both, at the discretion of the jury; and shall, moreover, be disqualified to testify as a witness against any white person.

SEC. 2 provides that if any negro, mulatto, or other person of color, shall hereafter live in a state of adultery or fornication with any white female resident within the limits of this State, he shall be deemed to be guilty of a misdemeanor, and upon conviction shall be fined in a sum not exceeding one thousand dollars, or be made to stand in the pillory for one hour and be whipped not exceeding thirty-nine stripes, or both, at the discretion of the jury.

SEC. 3 provides that every person who shall have one eighth or more of negro blood shall be deemed and held to be a person of color.

SEC. 4 provides that in existing cases, upon petition to the circuit judge, parties coming within the provisions of this act and liable to be punished under the same, may by order and judgment of said judge be relieved from the penalties thereof, when in his opinion justice and equity shall so require.

SEC. 5 provides that in all cases where marriages have heretofore been contracted and solemnized between white persons and persons of color, and where the parties have continued to live as man and wife, the said marriages are hereby legalized, and neither of the parties shall be subject to the provisions of this or of any other act.

## An Act to Require the Children of Destitute Persons to Provide for the Support of said Persons, January 11, 1866.

SEC. 1 requires the children of natural parents who are unable to support themselves to make provision for their support. In case of neglect, and proof before a justice of the peace or judge, that officer shall make an order of assessment on the children for the necessary amount, which order shall carry with it the right of enforcement by execution, and shall have the force of a writ of garnishment on the wages of such children.

## An Act to Punish Vagrants and Vagabonds, January 12, 1866.

SEC. 1. Defines as a vagrant "every ablebodied person why has no visible means of living and shall not be employed at some labor to support himself or herself, or shall be leading an idle, immoral, or profligate course of life;" and may be arrested by any justice of the peace or judge of the county criminal court and be bound "in sufficient surety" for good behavior and future industry for one year. Upon refusing or failing to give such security, he or she may be committed for trial, and if convicted sentenced to labor or imprisonment not exceeding twelve months, by whipping not exceeding thirty-nine stripes, or being put in the pillory. If sentenced to labor, the "sheriff or other officer of said court shall hire out such person for the term to which he or she shall be sentenced, not exceeding twelve months aforesaid, and the proceeds of such hiring shall be paid into the county treasury." All vagrants going armed may be disarmed by the sheriff, constable, or police officer.

## An Act in Relation to Contracts of Persons of Color, January 12, 1866.

SEC. 1 Provides that all contracts with persons of color shall be made in writing and fully explained to them before two credible witnesses, which contract shall be in duplicate, one copy to be retained by the employer and the other filed with some judicial officer of the State and county in which the parties may be residing at the date of the contract, with the affidavit of one or both witnesses, setting forth that the terms and effect of such contract were fully explained to the colored person, and that he, she, or they had voluntarily entered into and signed the contract and no contract shall be of any validity against any person of color unless so executed and filed: *Provided*, That contracts for service or labor may be made for less time than thirty days by parol.

SEC. 2 Provides, that whereas is is essential to the welfare and prosperity of the entire population of the State that the agricultural interest be sustained and placed upon a permanent basis, it is provided that when any person of color shall enter into a contract as aforesaid, to serve as a laborer for a year, or any other specified term, on any farm or plantation in this State, if he shall refuse or neglect to perform the stipulations of his contract by wilful disobedience of orders, wanton impudence or disrespect to his employer, or his authorized agent, failure or refusal to perform the work assigned to him, idleness, or abandonment of the premises or the employment of the party with whom the contract was made, he or she shall be liable, upon the complaint of his employer or his agent, made under oath before any justice of the peace of the county, to be arrested and tried before the criminal court of the county, and upon conviction shall be subject to all the pains and penalties prescribed for the punishment of vagrancy: *Provided*, That it shall be optional with the employer to require that such laborer be remanded to his service, instead of being subjected to the punishment aforesaid: *Provided, further*, That if it shall on such trial appear that the complaint made is not well founded, the court shall dismiss such complaint, and give judgment in favor of such laborer against the employer, for such sum as may appear to be due under the contract, and for such damages as may be assessed by the jury.

SEC. 3 provides that when any employé as aforesaid shall be in the occupancy of any house or room on the premises of the employer by virtue of his contract to labor, and he shall be adjudged to have violated his contract; or when any employé as aforesaid shall attempt to hold possession of such house or room beyond the term of his contract, against the consent of the employer, it shall be the duty of the judge of the criminal court, upon the application of the employer, and due proof made before him, to issue his writ to the sheriff of the court, commanding him forthwith to eject the said employé and to put the employer into full possession the premises: *Provided*, Three days' previous notice shall be given to the employé of the day of trial.

SEC. 4 provides that if any person employing the services or labor of another, under contract entered into as aforesaid, shall violate his contract by refusing or neglecting to pay the stipulated wages or compensation agreed upon, or any part thereof, or by turning off the employé before the expiration of the term, unless for sufficient cause, or unless such right is reserved by the contract, the party so employed may make complaint thereof before the judge of the criminal court, who shall at an early day, on reasonable notice to the other party, cause the same to be tried by a jury summoned for the purpose, who, in addition to the amount that may be proved to be due under the contract, may give such damages as they in their discretion may deem to be right and proper, and the judgment thereon shall be a first lien on the crops of all kinds in the cultivation of which such labor may have been employed: *Provided*, That either party shall be entitled to an appeal to the circuit court, as in case of appeal from justices of the peace.

SEC. 5 provides that if any person shall entice, induce, or otherwise persuade any laborer or employé to quit the service of another to which he was bound by contract, before the expiration of the term of service stipulated in said contract, he shall be guilty of a misdemeanor, and upon conviction shall be fined in a sum not exceeding one thousand dollars, or shall stand in the pillory not more than three hours, or be whipped not more than thirty-nine stripes on the bare back, at the discretion of the jury.

SEC. 6 applies the provisions of this act to all contracts between employers and employés relating to the lumber, rafting, or milling business, and to all other contracts with persons of color to do labor and to perform service.

## An Act prescribing additional Penalties for the Commission of Offences against the State, and for other purposes, January 15, 1866.

SEC. 1 provides that whenever in the criminal laws of this State, heretofore enacted, the punishment of the offence is limited to fine and imprisonment, or to fine or imprisonment, there shall be superadded, as an alternative, the punishment of standing in the pillory for an hour, or whipping not exceeding thirty-nine stripes on the bare back, or both, at the discretion of the jury.

SEC. 3 makes a felony, punishable with death, the exciting, or attempting to excite, by writing, speaking, or by other means, an insurrection or sedition amongst any portion or class of the population.

SEC. 12 makes it unlawful for any negro, mulatto, or person of color to own, use, or keep in possession or under control any bowie-knife, dirk, sword, fire-arms, or ammunition of any kind, unless by license of the county judge of probate, under a penalty of forfeiting them to the informer, and of standing in the pillory one hour, or be whipped not exceeding thirty-nine stripes, or both, at the discretion of the jury.

SEC. 14 forbids colored and white persons respectively from intruding upon each other's public assemblies, religious or other, or public vehicle set apart for their exclusive use, under punishment of pillory or stripes, or both.

SEC. 15 provides that persons forming a military organization not authorized by law, or aiding or abetting it, shall be fined not exceeding $1,000 and imprisonment not exceeding six months, or be pilloried for one hour, and be whipped not exceeding thirty-nine stripes, at the discretion of the jury—the penalties to be three-fold upon persons who accepted offices in such organizations.

SEC. 19 prohibits any person from hunting within the enclosure of another without his consent, under penalty of a fine of $1,000, or imprisonment not exceeding six months, or the pillory for one hour, and being whipped not exceeding thirty-nine stripes. So, if a person takes, rides, or uses any horse, mule, ass, or ox, without the consent of the owner, whether the person so using is in the employ of the owner or not: so, by SEC. 17, if a person shall move into any tenant house or other building without leave of the person in charge, or illegally take possession of any church or school-house, educational or charitable building, or cut down trees exceeding $1 in value, with a view to convert the same to his own use. Burglary is punishable with death, or fine of $1,000 and imprisonment not exceeding six months, or standing in the pillory one hour, and being whipped not

exceeding thirty-nine stripes. An assault upon a white female, with intent to commit a rape, or being accessory thereto, is punishable with death.

## An Act Prescribing additional Penalties for the Commission of Offenses against the State, January 15, 1866.

SEC. 12 provides that it shall not be lawful for any negro, mulatto, or other person of color, to own, use, or keep in his possession or under his control any bowie-knife, dirk, sword, fire-arms, or ammunition of any kind, unless he first obtain a license to do so from the judge of probate of the county in which he may be a resident for the time being; and the said judge of probate is hereby authorized to issue license, upon the recommendation of two respectable citizens of the county, certifying to the peaceful and orderly character of the applicant; and any negro, mulatto, or other person of color, so offending, shall be deemed to be guilty of a misdemeanor, and upon conviction shall forfeit to the use of the informer all such fire-arms and ammunition, and in addition thereto, shall be sentenced to stand in the pillory for one hour, or be whipped, not exceeding thirty-nine stripes, or both, at the discretion of the jury.

SEC. 14 provides that if any negro, mulatto, or other person of color, shall intrude himself into any religious or other public assembly of white persons, or into any railroad car or other public vehicle set apart for the exclusive accommodation of white people, he shall be deemed to be guilty of a misdemeanor, and upon conviction shall be sentenced to stand in the pillory for one hour, or be whipped, not exceeding thirty-nine stripes, or both, at the discretion of the jury; nor shall it be lawful for any white person to intrude himself into any religious or other public assembly of colored persons, or into any railroad car or other public vehicle, set apart for the exclusive accommodation of persons of color, under the same penalties.

## An Act to Raise a Revenue for the State of Florida, January 16, 1866.

SECTION 1 imposes a yearly capitation tax of three dollars upon every male inhabitant between twenty-one and fifty-five, except paupers and insane or idiotic persons. In default of payment the tax collector is hereby authorized and required to seize the body of the said delinquent and hire him out, after five days' public notice, before the door of the public court-house, to any person who will pay the said tax and the costs incident to the proceedings growing out of said arrest, and take him into his service for the shortest period of time: *Provided*, That if said delinquent be in the employment of another the said employer may pay the tax and costs, and the said payment shall be good as a credit against the amount that may be due by the employer as wages to the said delinquent.

## An Act Concerning Schools for Freedmen, January 16, 1866.

Provision is made for schools for freedmen—supported by a tax of one dollar upon all male persons of color between twenty-one and fifty-five, and a tuition fee to be collected from each pupil—the schools to be in charge of a superintendent and assistants; no person to teach without a certificate; and the fee, five dollars, to go to the school fund for freedmen, and the certificate good for one year, subject to be cancelled by the superintendent for incompetency, immorality or other sufficient cause. The superintendent "to establish schools for freedmen when the number of children of persons of color in any county or counties will warrant the same: *Provided*, The funds provided for shall be sufficient to meet the expenses thereof."

By another act, the interest from the school fund of the State is applied to the education of indigent white children.

### An Act concerning Testimony, January 16, 1866.

SECTION 3 provides that this act shall not be construed to authorize the testimony of colored persons to be taken by depositions in writing or upon written interrogatories, otherwise than in such manner as will enable the court or jury to judge of the credibility of the witness.

### VIRGINIA.

These are some of the provisions in the recently-enacted laws of Virginia respecting colored persons:

That no contract between a white person and a colored person, for the labor or service of the latter for a longer period than two months, shall be binding on such colored person, unless the contract be in writing, signed by such white person or his agent and by such colored person, and duly acknowledged before a justice or notary public, or clerk of the county or corporation court, or overseer of the poor, or two or more credible witnesses, in the county or corporation court in which the white person may reside, or in which the labor or service it to be performed. And it shall be the duty of the justice, notary, clerk or overseer of the poor, or the witnesses, to read and explain the contract to the colored person, before taking his acknowledgment thereof, and to state that this has been done in the certificate of acknowledgment of the contract.

"§ 5. The writing by which any minor is bound an apprentice, shall specify his age, and what art, trade, or business he is to be taught. The master, whether it is expressly provided therein or not, shall be bound to teach him the same, and shall also be bound to teach him reading, writing, and common arithmetic, including the rule of three."

The marital relation between colored persons is regulated by law. The colored person must procure a license the same as the whites, and persons celebrating a marriage are obliged to report it to the county clerks, and whether white or colored.

Where colored persons, before the passage of this act, shall have undertaken and agreed to occupy the relation to each other of husband and wife, and shall be cohabiting together as such at the time of its passage, whether the rites of marriage shall have been celebrated between them or not, they shall be deemed husband and wife, and be entitled to the rights and privileges, and subject to the duties and obligations, of that relation in like manner as if they had been duly married, and all their children shall be deemed legitimate, whether born before or after the pass-age of this act. And when the parties have ceased to cohabit before the passage of this act, in consequence of the death of the woman, or from any other cause, all the children of the woman, recognized by the man to be his, shall be deemed legitimate.

Bigamy, too, is punished in the case of the negro as of the white person, and also intermarriage within the prohibited degrees. And all persons officiating in the rites of marriage without due authority of law are punished by fine and imprisonment.

Under the old code these provisions applied only to white persons.

*Be it enacted*, That every person having one fourth or more of negro blood shall be deemed a colored person, and every person not a colored person having one fourth or more of Indian blood shall be deemed an Indian.

2. All laws in respect to crimes and punishments, and in respect to criminal proceedings, applicable to white persons, shall apply in like manner to colored persons and to Indians, unless when it is otherwise specially provided.

3. The following acts and parts of acts are hereby repealed, namely: All acts and parts of acts relating to slaves and slavery; chapter one hundred and seven of the code of eighteen hundred and sixty, relating to free negroes; chapter two hundred of said code relating to offences by negroes; chapter two hundred and twelve of said code, relating to proceedings against negroes; chapter ninety-eight of said code, relating to patrols; sections twenty-five to forty-seven, both inclusive, of chapter one hundred ninety-two of said code; sections twenty-six to thirty, both inclusive, and sections thirty-three to thirty-seven, both inclusive, of chapter one hundred and ninety-eight of said code; the fifth paragraph, as enumerated in section two of chapter two hundred and three, of said code; all acts and parts of acts imposing on negroes the penalty of stripes, where the same penalty is not imposed on white persons; and all other acts and parts of acts inconsistent with this act are hereby repealed.—General Terry issued this order:

### The Virginia Vagrant Act—General Terry orders its Non-Enforcement.

#### GENERAL ORDERS—NO 4.

HEADQUARTERS, DEPARTMENT OF VA.,
RICHMOND, *January* 24, 1866.

By a statute passed at the present session of the Legislature of Virginia, entitled "A bill providing for the punishment of vagrants," it is enacted, among other things, that any justice of the peace, upon the complaint of any one of certain officers therein named, may issue his warrant for the apprehension of any person alleged to be a vagrant and cause such person to be apprehended and brought before him; and that if upon due examination said justice of the peace shall find that such person is a vagrant within the definition of vagrancy contained in said statute, he shall issue his warrant, directing such person to be employed for a term not exceeding three months, and by any constable of the county wherein the proceedings are had be hired out for the best wages which can be procured, his wages to be applied to the support of himself and his family. The said statute further provides, that in case any vagrant so hired shall, during his term of service, run away from his employer without sufficient cause, he shall be apprehended on the warrant of a justice of the peace and returned to the custody of his employer, who shall then have, free from any other hire, the services of such vagrant for one month in addition to the original terms of hiring, and that the employer shall then have power, if authorized by a justice of the peace, to work such vagrant with ball and chain. The said statute specifies the persons who shall be considered vagrants and liable to the penalties imposed by it. Among those declared to be vagrants are all persons who, not having the wherewith to support their families, live idly and without employment, and refuse to work for the usual and common wages given to other laborers in the like work in the place where they are.

In many counties of this State meetings of employers have been held, and unjust and wrongful combinations have been entered into for the purpose of depressing the wages of the freedmen below the real value of their labor, far below the prices formerly paid to masters for labor performed by their slaves. By reason of these combinations wages utterly inadequate to the support of themselves and families have, in many places, become the usual and common wages of the freedmen. The effect of the statute in question will be, therefore, to compel the freedmen, under penalty of punishment as criminals, to accept and labor for the wages established by these combinations of employers. It places them wholly in the power of their employers, and it is easy to foresee that, even where no such combination now exists, the temptation to form them offered by the statute will be too strong to be resisted, and that such inadequate wages will become the common and usual wages throughout the State. The ultimate effect of the statute will be to reduce the freedmen to a condition of servitude worse than that from which they have been emancipated—a condition which will be slavery in all but its name.

It is therefore ordered that no magistrate, civil officer or other person shall in any way or manner apply or attempt to apply the provisions of said statute to any colored person in this department.

By command of Major General A. H. TERRY,
ED. W. SMITH, *Assistant Adjutant General.*

January 26—President Johnson refused to interfere with this order. The Legislature took no further action on the question.

February 28—This bill passed in relation to the testimony of colored persons:

*Be it enacted,* That colored persons and Indians shall, if otherwise competent, and subject to the rules applicable to other persons, be admitted as witnesses in the following cases:

1. In all civil cases and proceedings at law or in equity, in which a colored person or an Indian is a party, or may be directly benefited or injured by the result.

2. In all criminal proceedings in which a

colored person or an Indian is a party, or which arise out of an injury done, attempted, or threatened to the person, property, or rights of a colored person or Indian, or in which it is alleged in the presentment, information, or indictments, or in which the court is of opinion from the other evidence that there is probable cause to believe that the offence was committed by a white person in conjunction or co-operation with a colored person or Indian.

3. The testimony of colored persons shall, in all cases and proceedings, both at law and in equity, be given *ore tenus,* and not by deposition, and in suits in equity, and in all other cases in which the deposition of the witness would regularly be part of the record, the court shall, if desired by any party, or if deemed proper by itself, certify the facts proved by such witnesses, or the evidence given by him as far as credited by the court, as the one or the other may be proper under the rules of law applicable to the case, and such certificate shall be made part of the record.

March 4—The Legislature adjourned.

### TENNESSEE.

1866, January 25—This bill became a law:

That persons of African and Indian descent are hereby declared to be competent witnesses in all the courts of this State, in as full a manner as such persons are by an act of Congress competent witnesses in all the courts of the United States, and all laws and parts of laws of the State excluding such persons from competency are hereby repealed: *Provided, however,* That this act shall not be so construed as to give colored persons the right to vote, hold office, or sit on juries in this State; and that this provision is inserted by virtue of the provision of the 9th section of the amended constitution, ratified February 22, 1865.

May 26—This bill became a law:

An act to define the term "persons of color," and to declare the rights of such persons.

SEC. 1. That all negroes, mulattoes, mestizoes, and their descendants, having any African blood in their veins, shall be known in this State as "persons of color."

SEC. 2. That persons of color shall have the right to make and enforce contracts, to sue and be sued, to be parties and give evidence, to inherit, and to have full and equal benefits of all laws and proceedings for the security of person and estate, and shall not be subject to any other or different punishment, pains, or penalty, for the commission of any act or offence than such as are prescribed for white persons committing like acts or offences.

SEC. 3. That all persons of color, being blind, deaf and dumb, lunatics, paupers, or apprentices, shall have the full and perfect benefit and application of all laws regulating and providing for white persons, being blind, or deaf and dumb, or lunatics or paupers, or either (in asylums for their benefit) and apprentices.

SEC. 4. That all acts or parts of acts or laws, inconsistent herewith, are hereby repealed: *Provided,* That nothing in this act shall be so construed as to admit persons of color to serve on a jury: *And provided further,* That the provisions of this act shall not be so construed as to require the education of colored and white children in the same school.

SEC. 5. That all free persons of color who were living together as husband and wife in this State while in a state of slavery are hereby declared to be man and wife, and their children legitimately entitled to an inheritance in any property heretofore acquired, or that may hereafter be acquired, by said parents, to as full an extent as the children of white citizens are now entitled by the existing laws of this State.

May 26—All the freedmen's courts in Tennessee were abolished by the assistant commander, the law of the State making colored persons competent witnesses in all civil courts.

## TEXAS.

A colored man is permitted by the new constitution to testify orally where any one of his race is a party, allows him to hold property, and to sue and be sued.

## LOUISIANA.

1865, December .—"An act to provide for and regulate labor contracts for agricultural pursuits" requires all such laborers to make labor contracts for the next year within the first ten days of January—the contracts to be in writing, to be with heads of families, to embrace the labor of all the members, and be binding on all minors thereof. Each laborer, after choosing his employer, "shall not be allowed to leave his place of employment until the fulfillment of his contract, unless by consent of his employer, or on account of harsh treatment, or breach of contract on the part of employer; and if they do so leave, without cause or permission, they shall forfeit all wages earned to the time of abandonment." Wages due shall be a lien upon the crops; and one half shall be paid at periods agreed by the parties, "but it shall be lawful for the employer to retain the other moiety until the completion of the contract." Employers failing to comply, are to be fined double the amount due to laborer. These are the eighth and ninth sections in full:

SEC. 8. That in case of sickness of the laborer, wages for the time lost shall be deducted, and where the sickness is feigned for purposes of idleness, and also on refusal to work according to contract, double the amount of wages shall be deducted for the time lost, and also where rations have been furnished; and should the refusal to work be continued beyond three days, the offender shalll be reported to a justice of the peace, and shall be forced to labor on roads, levees, and other public works, without pay, until the offender consents to return to his labor.

SEC. 9. That, when in health, the laborer shall work ten hours during the day in summer, and nine hours during the day in winter, unless otherwise stipulated in the labor contract; he shall obey all proper orders of his employer or his agent; take proper care of his work mules, horses, oxen, stock; also of all agricultural implements; and employers shall have the right to make a reasonable deduction from the laborer's wages for injuries done to animals or agricultural implements committed to his care, or for bad or negligent work. Bad work shall not be allowed. Failing to obey reasonable orders, neglect of duty, and leaving home without permission, will be deemed disobedience; impudence, swearing, or indecent language to or in the presence of the employer, his family or agent, or quarrelling and fighting with one another, shall be deemed disobedience. For any disobedience a fine of one dollar shall be imposed on the offender. For all lost time from work hours, unless in case of sickness, the laborer shall be fined twenty-five cents per hour. For all absence from home without leave the laborer will be fined at the rate of two dollars per day. Laborers will not be required to labor on the Sabbath except to take the necessary care of stock and other property on plantations and do the necessary cooking and household duties, unless by special contract. For all thefts of the laborer from the employer of agricultural products, hogs, sheep, poultry or any other property of the employer, or wilful destruction of property or injury, the laborer shall pay the employer double the amount of the value of the property stolen, destroyed or injured, one half to be paid to the employer and the other half to be placed in the general fund provided for in this section. No live stock shall be allowed to laborers without the permission of the employer. Laborers shall not receive visitors during work hours. All difficulties arising between the employers and laborers, under this section, shall be settled, and all fines be imposed, by the former; if not satisfactory to the laborers, an appeal may be had to the nearest justice of the peace and two freeholders, citizens, one of said citizens to be selected by the employer and the other by the laborer; and all fines imposed and collected under this section shall be deducted from the wages due, and shall be placed in a common fund, to be divided among the other laborers employed on the plantation at the time when their full wages fall due, except as provided for above.

December 21—This bill became a law:

SEC. 1. That any one who shall persuade or entice away, feed, harbor, or secrete any person who leaves his or her employer, with whom she or he has contracted, or is assigned to live, or any apprentice who is bound as an apprentice, without the permission of his or her employer, said person or persons so offending shall be liable for damages to the employer, and also, upon conviction thereof, shall be subject to pay a fine of not more than five hundred dollars, nor less than ten dollars, or imprisonment in the parish jail for not more than twelve months nor less than ten days, or both, at the discretion of the court.

SEC. 2. That it shall be duty of the judges of this State to give this act especially in charge of the grand juries at each jury term of their respective courts.

A new vagrant act is thus condensed in the New Orleans *Picayune:*

It adopts the same definition of vagrancy as in the act of 1855, and provides that any person charged with vagrancy shall be arrested on the warrant of any judge or justice of the peace; and if said judge or justice of the peace shall be satisfied by the confession of the offender, or by competent testimony, that he is a vagrant within this said description, he shall make a certificate of the same, which shall be filed with the clerk of the court of the parish and in the city of New Orleans. The certificate shall be filed in the offices of the recorders, and the said justice or other officer shall require the party accused to enter into bond, payable to the Governor of Louisiana, or his successors in office, in such sums as said justice of the peace or other officer shall prescribe, with security, to be approved by said officer, for his good behavior and future industry for the period of one year; and upon his failing or refusing to give such bond and security, the justice or other officer shall issue his warrant to the sheriff or other officer, directing him to detain and to hire out such vagrant for a period not exceeding twelve months, or to cause him to labor on the public works, roads and levees, under such regulations as shall be made by the municipal authorities: *Provided,* That if the accused be a person who has abandoned his employer before his contract expired, the preference shall be given to such employer of hiring the accused: *And provided further,* That in the city of New Orleans the accused may be committed to the work-house for a time not exceeding six months, there to be kept at hard labor on the public works, roads, or levees. The proceeds of hire in the cases herein provided for to be paid into the parish treasury for the benefit of paupers: *And provided further,* That the persons hiring such vagrant shall be compelled to furnish such clothing, food, and medical attention as they may furnish their other laborers.

---

# V.

# PRESIDENT JOHNSON'S INTERVIEWS AND SPEECHES.

1865, April 15—Andrew Johnson qualified as President, Chief Justice Chase administering the oath of office.

### Remarks at an Interview with Citizens of Indiana.

1865, April 21—A delegation was introduced by Governor O. P. Morton, to whose address President Johnson responded, stating that he did not desire to make any expression of his future policy more than he had already made, and adding:

But in entering upon the discharge of the duties devolving upon me by the sad occurrence of the assassination of the Chief Magistrate of the nation, and as you are aware, in surrounding circumstances which are peculiarly embarrassing and responsible, I doubt whether you are aware how much I appreciate encouragement and countenance from my fellow-citizens of Indiana. The most courageous individual, the most determined will, might justly shrink from entering upon the discharge of that which lies before me; but were I a coward, or timid, to receive the countenance and encouragement I have from you, and from various other parts of the country, would make me a courageous and determined man. I mean in the proper sense of the term, for there is as much in moral courage and the firm, calm discharge of duty, as in physical courage. But, in entering upon the duties imposed upon me by this calamity, I require not only courage, but determined will, and I assure you that on this occasion your encouragement is peculiarly acceptable to me. In reference to what my administration will be, while I occupy my present position, I must refer you to the past. You may look back to it as evidence of what my course will be; and, in reference to this diabolical and fiendish rebellion sprung upon the country, all I have to do is to ask you to also go back and take my course in the past, and from that determine what my future will be. Mine has been but one straightforward and unswerving course, and I see no reason now why I should depart from it.

As to making a declaration, or manifesto, or message, or what you may please to call it, my past is a better foreshadowing of my future course than any statement on paper that might be made. Who, four years ago, looking down the stream of time, could have delineated that which has transpired since then? Had any one done so, and presented it, he would have been looked upon as insane, or it would have been thought a fable—fabulous as the stories of the Arabian Nights, as the wonders of the lamp of Aladdin, and would have been about as readily believed.

If we knew so little four years ago of what has passed since then, we know as little what events will arise in the next four years; but as these events arise I shall be controlled in the disposition of them by those rules and principles by which I have been guided heretofore. Had it not been for extraordinary efforts, in part owing to the machinery of the State, you would have had rebellion as rampant in Indiana as we had it in Tennessee. Treason is none the less treason whether it be in a free State or in a slave State; but if there could be any difference in such a crime, he who commits treason in a free State is a greater traitor than he who commits it in a slave State. There might be some little excuse in a man based on his possession of the peculiar property, but the traitor in a free State has no excuse, but simply to be a traitor.

Do not, however, understand me to mean by

this that any man should be exonerated from the penalties and punishments of the crime of treason. The time has arrived when the American people should understand what crime is, and that it should punished, and its penalties enforced and inflicted. We say in our statutes and courts that burglary is a crime, that murder is a crime, that arson is a crime, *and that treason is a crime;* and the Constitution of United States, and the laws of the United States, say that treason shall consist in levying war against them, and giving their enemies aid and comfort. I have just remarked that burglary is a crime and has its penalties, that murder is a crime and has its penalties, and so on through the long catalogue of crime.

To illustrate by a sad event, which is before the minds of all, and which has draped this land in mourning. Who is there here who would say if the assassin who has stricken from our midst one beloved and revered by all, and passed him from time to eternity, to that bourne whence no traveler returns, who, I repeat, who, here would say that the assassin, if taken, should not suffer the penalties of his crime? Then, if you take the life of one individual for the murder of another, and believe that his property should be confiscated, what should be done with one who is trying to assassinate this nation? What should be done with him or them who have attempted the life of a nation composed of thirty millions of people?

We were living at a time when the public mind had almost become oblivious of what treason is. The time has arrived, my countrymen, when the American people should be educated and taught what is crime, and that treason is a crime, and the highest crime known to the law and the Constitution. Yes, treason against a State, treason against all the States, treason against the Government of the United States, *is* the highest crime that can be committed, and those engaged in it should suffer all its penalties.

I know it is very easy to get up sympathy and sentiment where human blood is about to be shed, easy to acquire a reputation for leniency and kindness, but sometimes its effects and practical operations produce misery and woe to the mass of mankind. Sometimes an individual whom the law has overtaken, and on whom its penalties are about to be imposed, will appeal and plead with the Executive for the exercise of clemency. But before its exercise he ought to ascertain what is mercy and what is not mercy. It is a very important question, and one which deserves the consideration of those who moralize upon crime and the morals of a nation, whether in some cases action should not be suspended here and transferred to Him who controls all. There, if innocence has been invaded, if wrong has been done, the Controller and Giver of all good, one of whose attributes is mercy, will set it right.

It is not promulging anything that I have not heretofore said to say that traitors must be made odious, that treason must be made odious, that traitors must be punished and impoverished.

They must not only be punished, but their social power must be destroyed. If not, they will still maintain an ascendency, and may again become numerous and powerful; for, in the words of a former Senator of the United States, "When traitors become numerous enough, treason becomes respectable." And I say that, after making treason odious, every Union man and the Government should be remunerated out of the pockets of those who have inflicted this great suffering upon the country. But do not understand me as saying this in a spirit of anger, for, if I understand my own heart, the reverse is the case; and, while I say that the penalties of the law, in a stern and inflexible manner, should be executed upon conscious, intelligent, and influential traitors—the leaders, who have deceived thousands upon thousands of laboring men who have been drawn into this rebellion—and while I say, as to the leaders, *punishment*, I also say leniency, conciliation, and amnesty to the thousands whom they have misled and deceived; and in reference to this, as I remarked, I might have adopted your speech as my own.

As my honorable friend knows, I long since took the ground that this Government was sent upon a great mission among the nations of the earth; that it had a great work to perform, nd that in starting it was started in perpetuity. Look back for one single moment to the Articles of Confederation, and then come down to 1787, when the Constitution was formed—what do you find? That we, "the people of the United States, in order to form a more perfect government," &c. Provision is made for the admission of new States, to be added to old ones embraced within the Union. Now, turn to the Constitution: we find that amendments may be made, by a recommendation of two thirds of the members of Congress, if ratified by three fourths of the States. Provision is made for the admission of new States; no provision is made for the secession of old ones.

The instrument was made to be good in perpetuity, and you can take hold of it, not to break up the Government, but to go on perfecting it more and more as it runs down the stream of time.

We find the Government composed of integral parts. An individual is an integer, and a number of individuals form a State; and a State itself is an integer, and the various States form the Union, which is itself an integer—they all making up the Government of the United States. Now we come to the point of my argument, so far as concerns the perpetuity of the Government. We have seen that the Government is composed of parts, each essential to the whole, and the whole essential to each part. Now, if an individual (part of a State) declare war against the whole, in violation of the Constitution, he, as a citizen, has violated the law, and is responsible for the act as an individual. There may be more than one individual, it may go on till they become parts of States. Sometime the rebellion may go on increasing in numbers till the State machinery is overturned, and the country becomes like a man that is paralyzed on one side. But we find in the Constitution a great panacea provided. It provides that the United States (that is, the great integer) shall guarantee to each State (the integers composing the whole) in this Union a republican form of government. Yes, if rebellion had been rampant, and set aside the machinery of a State for a time, there stands the great law to remove the paralysis and revitalize it, and put it on its feet again. When we come to understand our system of government, though it be complex, we see how beautifully one part moves in harmony with another; then we see our Government is to be a perpetuity, there being no provision for pulling it down, the Union being its vitalizing power, imparting life to the whole of the States that move around it like planets round the sun, receiving thence light and heat and motion.

Upon this idea of destroying States, my position has been heretofore well known, and I see no cause to change it now, and I am glad to hear its reiteration on the present occasion. Some are satisfied with the idea that States are to be lost in territorial and other divisions; are to lose their character as States. But their life breath has been only suspended, and it is a high constitutional obligation we have to secure each of these States in the possession and enjoyment of a republican form of government. A State may be in the Government with a peculiar institution, and by the operation of rebellion lose that feature; but it was a State when it went into rebellion, and when it comes out without the institution it is still a state.

I hold it as a solemn obligation in any one of these States where the rebel armies have been beaten back or expelled—I care not how small the number of Union men, if enough to man the ship of State, I hold it, I say, a high duty to protect and secure to them a republican form of government. This is no new opinion. It is expressed in conformity with my understanding of the genius and theory of our Government. Then in adjusting and putting the Government upon its legs again, I think the progress of this work must pass into the hands of its friends. If a State is to be nursed until it again gets strength, it must be nursed by its friends, not smothered by its enemies.[*]

---

[*] On this and other points, President Johnson declared himself in his Nashville speech of June 9, 1864, from which these extracts are taken:

The question is, whether man is capable of self-government? I hold with Jefferson that government was made for the convenience of man, and not man for government. The laws and constitutions were designed as instruments to promote his welfare. And hence, from this principle, I conclude that governments can and ought to be changed and amended to conform to the wants, to the requirements and progress of the people, and the enlightened spirit of the age. Now, if any of your secessionists have lost faith in men's capability for self-government, and feel unfit for the exercise of this great right, go straight to rebeldom, take Jeff. Davis, Beauregard, and Bragg for your masters, and put their collars on your necks.

And let me say that now is the time to secure these fundamental principles, while the land is rent with anarchy and upheaves with the throes of a mighty revolution. While society is in this disordered state, and we are seeking security, let us fix the foundation of the Government on principles of eternal justice which will endure

Now, permit me to remark, that while I have opposed dissolution and disintegration on the one

---

for all time. There is an element in our midst who are for perpetuating the institution of slavery. Let me say to you, Tennesseeans and men from the Northern States, that slavery is dead. It was not murdered by me. I told you long ago what the result would be if you endeavored to go out of the Union to save slavery; and that the result would be bloodshed, rapine, devastated fields, plundered villages and cities and, therefore, I urged you to remain in the Union. In trying to save slavery, you killed it and lost your own freedom. Your slavery is dead, but I did not murder it. As Macbeth said to Banquo's bloody ghost:

> "'Never shake thy gory locks at me;
> Thou canst not say I did it.'"

Slavery is dead, and you must pardon me if I do not mourn over its dead body; you can bury it out of sight. In restoring the State leave out that disturbing and dangerous element and use only those parts of the machinery which will move in harmony.

But in calling a convention to restore the State, who shall restore and re-establish it? Shall the man who gave his influence and his means to destroy the Government? Is he to participate in the great work of reorganization? Shall he who brought this misery upon the State be permitted to control its destinies? If this be so, then all this precious blood of our brave soldiers and officers so freely poured out will have been wantonly spilled. All the glorious victories won by our noble armies will go for nought, and all the battle-fields which have been sown with dead heroes during the rebellion will have been made memorable in vain.

Why all this carnage and devastation? It was that treason might be put down and traitors punished. Therefore I say that traitors should take a back seat in the work of restoration. If there be but five thousand men in Tennessee loyal to the Constitution, loyal to freedom, loyal to justice, these true and faithful men should control the work of reorganization and reformation absolutely. I say that the traitor has ceased to be a citizen, and in joining the rebellion has become a public enemy. He forfeited his right to vote with loyal men when he renounced his citizenship and sought to destroy our Government. We say to the most honest and industrious foreigner who comes from England or Germany to dwell among us, and to add to the wealth of the country, "Before you can be a citizen you must stay here for five years." If we are so cautious about foreigners, who voluntarily renounce their homes to live with us, what should we say to the traitor, who, although born and reared among us, has raised a parricidal hand against the Government which always protected him? My judgment is that he should be subjected to a severe ordeal before he is restored to citizenship. A fellow who takes the oath merely to save his property, and denies the validity of the oath, is a perjured man, and not to be trusted. Before these repenting rebels can be trusted, let them bring forth the fruits of repentance. He who helped to make all these

hand, on the other I am equally opposed to consolidation, or the centralization of power in the hands of a few. Sir, all this has been extorted from me by the remarks you have offered, and as I have already remarked, I might have adopted your speech as my own. I have detained you longer than I expected, but Governor Morton is responsible for that.

I scarcely know how to express my feeling in view of the kindness you have manifested on this occasion. Perhaps I ought not to add what I am about to say, but human nature is human nature. Indiana first named me for the Vice Presidency, though it was unsolicited by me. Indeed, there is not a man can say that I ever approached him on the subject. My eyes were turned to my own State. If I could restore her, the measure of my ambition was complete. I thank the State of Indiana for the confidence and regard she manifested toward me, which has resulted in what is now before me, placing me in the position I now occupy.

In conclusion, I will repeat that the vigor of my youth has been spent in advocating those great principles at the foundation of our Government, and, therefore, I have been by many denounced as a demagogue, I striving to please the

widows and orphans, who draped the streets of Nashville in mourning, should suffer for his great crime. The work is in our own hands. We can destroy this rebellion. With Grant thundering on the Potomac before Richmond, and Sherman and Thomas on their march toward Atlanta, the day will ere long be ours. Will any madly persist in rebellion? Suppose that an equal number be slain in every battle, it is plain that the result must be the utter extermination of the rebels. Ah! these rebel leaders have a strong personal reason for holding out to save their necks from the halter; and these leaders must feel the power of the Government! Treason must be made odious, and traitors must be punished and impoverished. Their great plantations must be seized, and divided into small farms, and sold to honest, industrious men. The day for protecting the lands and negroes of these authors of the rebellion is past. It is high time it was. I have been most deeply pained at some things which have come under my observation. We get men in command who, under the influence of flattery, fawning, and caressing, grant protection to the rich traitor, while the poor Union man stands out in the cold, often unable to get a receipt or a voucher for his losses. [Cries of "That's so!" from all parts of the crowd.] The traitor can get lucrative contracts, while the loyal man is pushed aside, unable to obtain a recognition of his just stripes and shoulder-straps. I want them all to hear what I say. I have been on a gridiron for two years at the sight of these abuses. I blame not the Government for these things, which are the work of weak or faithless subordinates. Wrongs will be committed under every form of government and every administration. For myself, I mean to stand by the Government till the flag of the Union shall wave over every city, town, hilltop, and cross-roads, in its full power and majesty.

people. I am free to say to you that my highest ambition was to please the people, for I believe that when I pleased them, I was pretty nearly right, and being in the right, I didn't care who assailed me. But I was going to say I have always advocated the principle, that government was made for man—not man for goverment; even as the good Book says that the Sabbath was made for man—not man for the Sabbath.

So far as in me lies, those principles shall be carried out; and, in conclusion, I tender you my profound and sincere thanks for your respect and support in the performance of the arduous duties now devolving upon me.

### To Virginia Refugees.

April 24, 1865—A large number of Southern refugees had an interview, Hon. John C. Underwood making an address; to which the President replied:

It is hardly necessary for me on this occasion to say that my sympathies and impulses in connection with this nefarious rebellion beat in unison with yours. Those who have passed through this bitter ordeal, and who participated in it to a great extent, are more competent, as I think, to judge and determine the true policy which should be pursued. [Applause.]

I have but little to say on this question in response to what has been said. It enunciates and expresses my own feelings to the fullest extent, and in much better language than I can at the present moment summon to my aid.

The most that I can say is, that entering upon the duties that have devolved upon me under circumstances that are perilous and responsible, and being thrown into the position I now occupy unexpectedly, in consequence of the sad event—the heinous assassination which has taken place—in view of all that is before me, and the circumstances that surround me, I cannot but feel that your encouragement and kindness are peculiarly acceptable and appropriate.

I do not think you have been familiar with my course, if you who are from the South deem it necessary for me to make any professions as to the future on this occasion, or to express what my course will be upon questions that may arise. If my past life is no indication of what my future will be, my professions were both worthless and empty; and in returning you my sincere thanks for this encouragement and sympathy, I can only reiterate what I have said before, and, in part, what has just been read.

As far as clemency and mercy are concerned, and the proper exercise of the pardoning power, I think I understand the nature and character of the latter. In the exercise of clemency and mercy, that pardoning power should be exercised with caution. I do not give utterance to my opinions on this point in any spirit of revenge or unkind feelings. Mercy and clemency have been pretty large ingredients in my compound. Having been the executive of a State, and thereby placed in a position in which it was necessary to exercise clemency and mercy, I have been charged with going too far, being too lenient; and I have become satisfied that mercy without justice is a crime, and that when mercy and clemency are exercised by the executive it should always be done in view of justice, and in that manner alone is properly exercised that great prerogative.

The time has come, as you who have had to drink this bitter cup are fully aware, when the American people should be made to understand the true nature of crime. Of crime, generally, our people have a high understanding, as well as of the necessity for its punishment; but in the catalogue of crimes there is one—and that the highest known to the law and the Constitution—of which, since the days of Jefferson and Aaron Burr, they have become oblivious; that is TREA-SON. Indeed, one who has become distinguished in treason and in this rebellion said, that "when traitors become numerous enough, treason becomes respectable," and to become a traitor was to constitute a portion of the aristocracy of the country.

God protect the people against such an aristocracy.

Yes, the time has come when the people should be taught to understand the length and breath, the depth and height of treason. An individual occupying the highest position among us was lifted to that position by the free offering of the American people—the highest position on the habitable globe. This man we have seen, revered, and loved; one who, if he erred at all, erred ever on the side of clemency and mercy; that man we have seen treason strike through a fitting instrument; and we have beheld him fall like a bright star falling from its sphere.

Now, there is none but would say, if the question came up, what should be done with the individual who assassinated the chief magistrate of a nation—he is but a man, one man after all; but if asked what should be done with the assassin, what should be the penalty, the forfeit exacted, I know what response dwells in every bosom. It is, that he should pay the forfeit with his life. And hence we see that these are times when mercy and clemency without justice become a crime. The one should temper the other and bring about the proper mean. And if we would say this when the case was the simple murder of one man by his fellow man, what should we say when asked what shall be done with him, or them, or those who have raised impious hands to take away the life of a nation composed of thirty millions of people? What would be the reply to that question? But while in mercy we remember justice, in the language that has been uttered, I say justice toward the leaders, the conscious leaders; but I also say amnesty, conciliation, clemency, and mercy to the thousands of our countrymen who you and I know have been deceived or driven into this infernal rebellion.

And so I return to where I started from, and again repeat, that it is time our people were taught to know that treason is a crime—not a mere political difference, not a mere contest between two parties, in which one succeeded, and the other has simply failed. They must know it is treason, for if they had succeeded, the life of the nation would have been reft from it, the Union would have been destroyed.

Surely the Constitution sufficiently defines treason. It consists in levying war against the United States, and in giving their enemies aid

and comfort. With this definition it requires the exercise of no great acumen to ascertain who are traitors. It requires no great perception to tell us who have levied war against the United States, nor does it require any great stretch of reasoning to ascertain who has given aid to the enemies of the United States. And when the Government of the United States does ascertain who are the conscious and intelligent traitors, the penalty and the forfeit should be paid.

I know how to appreciate the condition of being driven from one's home. I can sympathize with him whose all has been taken from him; with him who has been denied the place that gave his children birth; but let us, withal, in the restoration of true government, proceed temperately and dispassionately, and hope and pray that the time will come, as I believe, when we all can return and remain at our homes, and treason and traitors be driven from our land; [applause;] when again law and order shall reign, and the banner of our country be unfurled over every inch of territory within the area of the United States.

In conclusion, let me thank you most profoundly for this encouragement and manifestation of your regard and respect, and assure you that I can give no greater assurance regarding the settlement of this question than that I intend to discharge my duty, and in that way which shall in the earliest possible hour bring back peace to our distracted country, and hope the time is not far distant when our people can all return to their homes and firesides, and resume their various avocations.

### Interview with George L. Stearns.

WASHINGTON, D. C., *Oct.* 3, 1865, 11½, A. M.

I have just returned from an interview with President Johnson, in which he talked for an hour on the process of reconstruction of rebel States. His manner was as cordial, and his conversation as free as in 1863, when I met him daily in Nashville.

His countenance is healthier, even more so than when I first knew him.

I remarked that the people of the North were anxious that the process of reconstruction should be thorough, and they wished to support him in the arduous work, but their ideas were confused by the conflicting reports constantly circulated, and especially by the present position of the Democratic party. It is industriously circulated in the Democratic clubs that he was going over to them. He laughingly replied, " Major, have you never known a man who for many years had differed from your views because you were in advance of him, claim them as his own when he came up to your standpoint?"

I replied, " I have, often." He said, " So have I," and went on : " The Democratic party finds its old position untenable, and is coming to ours; if it has come up to our position, I am glad of it. You and I need no preparation for this conversation; we can talk freely on this subject, for the thoughts are familiar to us; we can be perfectly frank with each other." He then commenced with saying that the States are in the Union, which is whole and indivisible.

Individuals tried to carry them out, but did not succeed, as a man may try to cut his throat and be prevented by the bystanders; and you cannot say he cut his throat because he tried to do it.

Individuals may commit treason and be punished, and a large number of individuals may constitute a rebellion, and be punished as traitors. Some States tried to get out of the Union, and we opposed it honestly, because we believed it to be wrong; and we have succeeded in putting down the rebellion. The power of those persons who made the attempt has been crushed, and now we want to reconstruct the State governments, and have the power to do it. The State institutions are prostrated, laid out on the ground, and they must be taken up and adapted to the progress of events; this cannot be done in a moment. We are making very rapid progress—so rapid I sometimes cannot realize it. It appears like a dream.

We must not be in too much of a hurry; it is better to let them reconstruct themselves than to force them to it; for if they go wrong the power is in our hands, and we can check them in any stage, to the end, and oblige them to correct their errors; we must be patient with them. I did not expect to keep out all who were excluded from the amnesty, or even a large number of them; but I intended they should sue for pardon, and so realize the enormity of the crime they had committed.

You could not have broached the subject of equal suffrage at the North seven years ago, and we must remember that the changes of the South have been more rapid, and they have been obliged to accept more unpalatable truth than the North has; we must give them time to digest a part, for we cannot expect such large affairs will be comprehended and digested at once. We must give them time to understand their new position.

I have nothing to conceal in these matters, and have no desire or willingness to take indirect courses to obtain what we want.

Our Government is a grand and lofty structure; in searching for its foundation we find it rests on the broad basis of popular rights. The elective franchise is not a natural right, but a political right. I am opposed to giving the States too much power, and also to a great consolidation of power in the central government.

If I interfered with the vote in the rebel States, to dictate that no negro shall vote, I might do the same for my own purposes in Pennsylvania. Our only safety lies in allowing each State to control the right of voting by its own laws, and we have the power to control the rebel States if they go wrong. If they rebel we have the army, and can control them by it, and, if necessary, by legislation also. If the General Government controls the right to vote in the States, it may establish such rules as will restrict the vote to a small number of persons, and thus create a central despotism.

My position here is different from what it would be if I was in Tennessee.

There I should try to introduce negro suffrage gradually; first those who had served in the army; those who could read and write; and perhaps a property qualification for others, say $200 or $250.

It would not do to let the negro have aniversal suffrage now; it would breed a war of races.

There was a time in the Southern States when the slaves of large owners looked down upon non-slaveowners because they did not own slaves; the larger the number of slaves the masters owned the prouder they were, and this has produced hostility between the mass of the whites and the negroes. The outrages are mostly from non-slaveholding whites against the negro, and from the negro upon the non-slaveholding whites.

The negro will vote with the late master, whom he does not hate, rather than with the non-slaveholding white, whom he does hate. Universal suffrage would create another war, not against us, but a war of races.

Another thing: This Government is the freest and best on earth, and I feel sure is destined to last; but to secure this we must elevate and purify the ballot. I for many years contended at the South that slavery was a political weakness; but others said it was political strength; they thought we gained three-fifths representation by it; I contended that we lost two-fifths.

If we had no slaves we should have had twelve Representatives more, according to the then ratio of representation. Congress apportions representation by States, not districts, and the State apportions by districts.

Many years ago I moved in the Legislature that the apportionment of Representatives to Congress in Tennessee should be by qualified voters.

The apportionment is now fixed until 1872; before that time we might change the basis of representation from population to qualified voters, North as well as South, and, in due course of time, the States, *without regard* to color, might extend the elective franchise to all who possessed certain mental, moral, or such other qualifications as might be determined by an enlightened public judgment.

BOSTON, *October* 18, 1865.

The above report was returned to me by President Johnson with the following endorsement. GEORGE L. STEARNS.

I have read the within communication and find it substantially correct.

I have made some verbal alterations.

—— A. J.

## Address to the Colored Soldiers.

October 10, 1865—The first colored regiment of District of Columbia troops, recently returned from the South, marched to the Executive Mansion, and were addressed by the President, as follows:

MY FRIENDS: My object in presenting myself before you on this occasion is simply to thank you, members of one of the colored regiments which have been in the service of the country to sustain and carry its banner and its laws triumphantly in every part of this broad land. I appear before you on the present occasion merely to tender you my thanks for the compliment you have paid me on your return home, to again be associated with your friends and your relations, and those you hold most sacred and dear. I have but little to say. It being unusual in this Government and in most of the other governments to have colored troops engaged in their cause, you have gone forth as events have shown, and served with patience and endurance in the cause of your country. This is your country as well as anybody else's country. This is the country in which you expect to live, and in which you should expect to do something by your example in civil life, as you have done in the field. This country is founded upon the principle of equality; and at the same time the standard by which persons are to be estimated is according to their merit and their worth. And you observe, no doubt, that for him who does his duty faithfully and honestly, there is always a just public judgment that will appreciate and measure out to him his proper reward.

I know that there is much well calculated in this Government, and since the late rebellion commenced, to excite the white against the black, and the black against the white man. These are things that you should all understand, and at the same time prepare yourselves for what is before you. Upon the return of peace and the surrender of the enemies of the country, it should be the duty of every patriot and every one who calls himself a Christian to remember that with a termination of the war his resentments should cease—that angry feelings should subside, and that every man should become calm and tranquil, and be prepared for what is before him.

This is another part of your mission. You have been engaged in the effort to sustain your country in the past, but the future is more important to you than the period in which you have just been engaged. One great question has been settled in this Government, and that is the question of slavery. The institution of slavery made war upon the United States, and the United States has lifted its strong arms in vindication of the Government and of free government, and in lifting the arm and appealing to the God of battles, it was decided that the institution of slavery must go down. This has been done, and the Goddess of Liberty, in bearing witness over many of our battle-fields since the struggle commenced, has made her loftiest flight and proclaimed that true liberty has been established upon a more permanent and enduring basis than heretofore. But this is not all; and as you have paid me the compliment to call upon me, I shall take the privilege of saying one or two words as I am before you.

Now, when the sword is returned to its scabbard, when your arms are reversed, and when the olive-branch of peace is extended, resentment and revenge should subside. Then what is to follow? You do understand, no doubt—and if you do not you cannot understand too soon—that simple liberty does not mean the privilege of going into the battle-field, or into the service of the country as a soldier. It means other things as well; and now when you have laid down your arms there are other objects of equal importance before you—now that the Government has triumphantly passed through this mighty rebellion, after the most gigantic battles the world ever saw.

The problem is before you, and it is best that you should understand it, and I therefore speak simply and plainly. Will you now, when you have retired from the army of the United States and taken the position of the citizen—when you have returned to the avocations of peace—will you give evidence to the world that you are capable and competent to govern yourselves? This is what you will have to do.

Liberty is not a mere idea, a mere vagary; when you come to examine this question of liberty you should not be mistaken in a mere idea for the reality. It does not consist in idleness. Liberty does not consist in being worthless. Liberty does not consist in doing in all things as we please; and there can be no liberty without law. In a government of freedom and liberty there must be law, and there must be obedience and submission to the law, without regard to color. Liberty—and may I not call you my countrymen?—liberty consists in the glorious privileges of freedom—consists in the glorious privileges of worth—of pursuing the ordinary avocations of peace with energy, with industry, and with economy; and that being done, all those who have been industrious and economical are permitted to appropriate and enjoy the products of their own labor. This is one of the great blessings of freedom; and hence we might ask the question and answer it by stating that liberty means freedom to work and enjoy the products of your own labor.

You will soon be mustered out of the ranks. It is for you to establish the great fact that you are fit and qualified to be free. Hence, freedom is not a mere idea, but it is something that exists in fact. Freedom is not simply the principle to live in idleness. Liberty does not mean simply to resort to the low saloons and other places of disreputable character. Freedom and liberty do not mean that the people ought to live in licentiousness, but liberty means simply to be industrious and to be virtuous, to be upright in all our dealings and relations with men; and to those now before me, members of the last regiment of colored volunteers from the District of Columbia, and the capital of the United States, I have to say, that a great deal depends upon yourselves; you must give evidence that you are competent for the rights that the government has guaranteed to you.

Hence, each and all of you must be measured according to his merit. If one man is more meritorious than the other, they cannot be equals, and he is the most exalted that is the most meritorious, without regard to color; and the idea of having a law passed in the morning that will make a white man black before night and a black man a white man before day is absurd. That is not the standard; it is your own conduct; it is your own merit; it is the development of your own talents and of your intellectual and moral qualities.

Let this, then, be your course; adopt systems of morality; abstain from all licentiousness; and let me say one thing here, for I am going to talk plainly. I have lived in a Southern State all my life, and know what has too often been the case. There is one thing you should esteem higher and more supreme than almost all others, and that is the solemn contract with all the penalties in the association of married life. Men and women should abstain from those qualities and habits that too frequently follow a war. Inculcate among your children and among your associates, notwithstanding you are just back from the army of the United States, that virtue, that merit, that intelligence are the standards to be observed, and those which you are determined to maintain during your future lives. He that is meritorious and virtuous, intellectual and well informed, must stand highest, without regard to color. It is the very basis upon which heaven itself rests—each individual takes his degree in the sublimer and more exalted regions in proportion to his merits and his virtue.

Then I shall say to you on this occasion, in returning to your homes and firesides, after feeling conscious and proud of having faithfully done your duty, return with the determination that you will perform your duty in the future as you have performed it in the past. Abstain from all those bickerings and jealousies and revengeful feelings which too often spring up between different races.

There is a great problem before us, and I may as well allude to it here in this connection, and that is, whether this race can be incorporated and mixed with the people of the United States --to be made a harmonious and permanent ingredient in the population. This is a problem not yet settled, but we are in the right line to do so. Slavery raised its head against the Government, and the Government raised its strong arm and struck it to the ground; hence, that part of the problem is settled. The institution of slavery is overthrown. But another part remains to be solved, and that is, can four millions of people, reared as they have been, with all their prejudices of the whites—can they take their places in the community, and be made to work harmoniously and congruously in our system? This is a problem to be considered. Are the digestive powers of the American Government sufficient to receive this element in a new shape, and digest it and make it work healthfully upon the system that has incorporated it?

This is the question to be determined. Let us make the experiment, and make it in good faith. If that cannot be done, there is another problem that is before us. If we have to become a separate and distinct people (although I trust that the system can be made to work harmoniously, and that the great problem will be settled without going any further)—if it should be so that the two races cannot agree and live in peace and prosperity, and the laws of Providence require that they should be separated—in that event, looking to the far distant future, and trusting in God that it may never come—if it should come, Providence, that works mysteriously, but unerringly and certainly, will point out the way, and the mode, and the manner by which these people are to be separated, and they are to be taken to their land of inheritance and promise, for such a one is before them. Hence we are making the experiment.

Hence, let me again impress upon you the importance of controlling your passions, developing your intellect, and of applying your physical powers to the industrial interests of the country; and that is the true process by which this question can be settled. Be patient, persevering, and forbearing, and you will help to solve this problem. Make for yourselves a reputation in this cause, as you have won for yourselves a reputation in the cause in which you have been engaged. In speaking to the members of this regiment, I want them to understand that, so far as I am concerned, I do not assume or pretend that I am stronger than the laws or course of nature, or that I am wiser than Providence itself. It is our duty to try and discover what these great laws are which are the foundation of all things, and, having discovered what they are, conform our action and conduct to them and to the will of God, who ruleth all things. He holds the destinies of nations in the palm of his hand, and He will solve the questions and rescue these people from the difficulties that have so long surrounded them. Then let us be patient, industrious, and persevering. Let us develop our intellectual and moral worth.

I trust what I have said may be understood and appreciated. Go to your homes and lead peaceful, prosperous, and happy lives, in peace with all men. Give utterance to no word that would cause dissensions, but do that which will be creditable to yourselves and to your country. To the officers who have led and so nobly commanded you in the field I also return my thanks, for the compliment you and they have conferred upon me.

## Interview with Senator Dixon, of Connecticut.

January 28, 1866—The following is the substance of the conversation, as telegraphed that night over the country:

The President said he doubted the propriety at this time of making further amendments to the Constitution. One great amendment had already been made, by which slavery had forever been abolished within the limits of the United States, and a national guarantee thus given that the institution should never exist in the land. Propositions to amend the Constitution were becoming as numerous as preambles and resolutions called to consider the most ordinary questions connected with the administration of local affairs. All this, in his opinion, had a tendency to diminish the dignity and prestige attached to the Constitution of the country, and to lessen the respect and confidence of the people in their great charter of freedom. If, however, amendments are to be made to the Constitution, changing the basis of representation and taxation, (and he did not deem them at all necessary at the present time,) he knew of none better than a simple proposition, embraced in a few lines, making in each State the number of qualified voters the basis of representation, and the value of property the basis of direct taxation. Such a proposition could be embraced in the following terms:

"Representatives shall be apportioned among the several States which may be included within this Union according to the number of qualified voters in each State.

"Direct taxes shall be apportioned among the several States which may be included within this Union according to the value of all taxable property in each State."

An amendment of this kind would, in his opinion, place the basis of representation and direct taxation upon correct principles. The qualified voters were, for the most part, men who were subject to draft and enlistment when it was necessary to repel invasion, suppress rebellion, and quell domestic violence and insurrection. They risk their lives, shed their blood and peril their all to uphold the Government, and give protection, security, and value to property. It seemed but just that property should compensate for the benefits thus conferred, by defraying the expenses incident to its protection and enjoyment.

Such an amendment, the President also suggested, would remove from Congress all issues in reference to the political equality of the races. It would leave the States to determine absolutely the qualifications of their own voters with regard to color; and thus the number of Representatives to which they would be entitled in Congress would depend upon the number upon whom they conferred the right of suffrage.

The President, in this connection, expressed the opinion that the agitation of the negro franchise question in the District of Columbia at this time was the mere entering-wedge to the agitation of the question throughout the States, and was ill-timed, uncalled-for, and calculated to do great harm. He believed that it would engender enmity, contention, and strife between the two races, and lead to a war between them, which would result in great injury to both, and the certain extermination of the negro population. Precedence, he thought, should be given to more important and urgent matters, legislation upon which was essential to the restoration of the Union, the peace of the country, and the prosperity of the people.

### Interview with a Colored Delegation respecting Suffrage.

February 7, 1866—The delegation of colored representatives from different States of the country, now in Washington, to urge the interests of the colored people before the Government, had an interview with the President.

The President shook hands kindly with each member of the delegation.

#### ADDRESS OF GEORGE T. DOWNING.

Mr. GEORGE T. DOWNING then addressed the President as follows:

We present ourselves to your Excellency, to make known with pleasure the respect which we are glad to cherish for you—a respect which is your due, as our Chief Magistrate. It is our desire for you to know that we come feeling that we are friends meeting a friend. We should, however, have manifested our friendship by not coming to further tax your already much burdened and valuable time; but we have another object in calling. We are in a passage to equality before the law. God hath made it by opening a Red Sea. We would have your assistance through the same. We come to you in the name of the colored people of the United States. We are delegated to come by some who have unjustly worn iron manacles on their bodies—by some whose minds have been manacled by class legislation in States called free. The colored people of the States of Illinois, Wisconsin, Alabama, Mississippi, Florida, South Carolina, North Carolina, Virginia, Maryland, Pennsylvania, New York, New England States, and District of Columbia have specially delegated us to come.

Our coming is a marked circumstance, noting determined hope that we are not satisfied with an amendment prohibiting slavery, but that we wish it enforced with appropriate legislation. This is our desire. We ask for it intelligently, with the knowledge and conviction that the fathers of the Revolution intended freedom for every American; that they should be protected in their rights as citizens, and be equal before the law. We are Americans, native born Americans. We are citizens; we are glad to have it known to the world that you bear no doubtful record on this point. On this fact, and with confidence in the triumph of justice, we base our hope. We see no recognition of color or race in the organic law of the land. It knows no privileged class, and therefore we cherish the hope that we may be fully enfranchised, not only here in this District, but throughout the land. We respectfully submit that rendering anything less than this will be rendering to us less than our just due; that granting anything less than our full rights will be a disregard of our just rights and of due respect for our feelings. If the powers that be do so it will be used as a license, as it were, or an apology, for any community, or for individuals thus disposed, to outrage our rights and feelings. It has been shown in the present war that the Government may justly reach its strong arm into States, and demand from them, from those who owe it allegiance, their assistance and support. May it not reach out a like arm to secure and protect its subjects upon who it has a claim?

#### ADDRESS OF FRED. DOUGLASS.

Following upon Mr. Downing, Mr. Fred. Douglass advanced and addressed the President, saying:

Mr. President, we are not here to enlighten you, sir, as to your duties as the Chief Magistrate of this Republic, but to show our respect, and to present in brief the claims of our race to your favorable consideration. In the order of Divine Providence you are placed in a position where you have the power to save or destroy us, to bless or blast us—I mean our whole race. Your noble and humane predecessor placed in our hands the sword to assist in saving the nation, and we do hope that you, his able successor, will favorably regard the placing in our hands the ballot with which to save ourselves.

We shall submit no argument on that point. The fact that we are the subjects of Government, and subject to taxation, subject to volunteer in the service of the country, subject to being drafted, subject to bear the burdens of the State, makes it not improper that we should ask to share in the privileges of this condition.

I have no speech to make on this occasion. I simply submit these observations as a limited expression of the views and feelings of the delegation with which I have come.

### RESPONSE OF THE PRESIDENT.

In reply to some of your inquiries, not to make a speech about this thing, for it is always best to talk plainly and distinctly about such matters, I will say that if I have not given evidence in my course that I am a friend of humanity, and to that portion of it which constitutes the colored population, I can give no evidence here. Everything that I have had, both as regards life and property, has been perilled in that cause, and I feel and think that I understand—not to be egotistic—what should be the true direction of this question, and what course of policy would result in the melioration and ultimate elevation, not only of the colored, but of the great mass of the people of the United States. I say that if I have not given evidence that I am a friend of humanity, and especially the friend of the colored man, in my past conduct, there is nothing that I can now do that would. I repeat, all that I possessed, life, liberty, and property, have been put up in connection with that question, when I had every inducement held out to take the other course, by adopting which I would have accomplished perhaps all that the most ambitious might have desired. If I know myself, and the feelings of my own heart, they have been for the colored man. I have owned slaves and bought slaves, but I never sold one. I might say, however, that practically, so far as my connection with slaves has gone, I have been their slave instead of their being mine. Some have even followed me here, while others are occupying and enjoying my property with my consent. For the colored race my means, my time, my all has been perilled; and now at this late day, after giving evidence that is tangible, that is practical, I am free to say to you that I do not like to be arraigned by some who can get up handsomely-rounded periods and deal in rhetoric, and talk about abstract ideas of liberty, who never perilled life, liberty, or property. This kind of theoretical, hollow, unpractical friendship amounts to but very little. While I say that I am a friend of the colored man, I do not want to adopt a policy that I believe will end in a contest between the races, which if persisted in will result in the extermination of one or the other. God forbid that I should be engaged in such a work!

Now, it is always best to talk about things practically and in a common sense way. Yes, I have said, and I repeat here, that if the colored man in the United States could find no other Moses, or any Moses that would be more able and efficient than myself, I would be his Moses to lead him from bondage to freedom; that I would pass him from a land where he had lived in slavery to a land (if it were in our reach) of freedom. Yes, I would be willing to pass with him through the Red sea to the Land of Promise, to the land of liberty; but I am not willing, under either circumstance, to adopt a policy which I believe will only result in the sacrifice of his life and the shedding of his blood. I think I know what I say. I feel what I say; and I feel well assured that if the policy urged by some be persisted in, it will result in great injury to the white as well as to the colored man. There is a great deal of talk about the sword in one hand accomplishing an end, and the ballot accomplishing another at the ballot-box.

These things all do very well, and sometimes have forcible application. We talk about justice; we talk about right; we say that the white man has been in the wrong in keeping the black man in slavery as long as he has. That is all true. Again, we talk about the Declaration of Independence and equality before the law. You understand all that, and know how to appreciate it. But, now, let us look each other in the face; let us go to the great mass of colored men throughout the slave States; let us take the condition in which they are at the present time—and it is bad enough, we all know—and suppose, by some magic touch you could say to every one, "you shall vote to-morrow;" how much would that ameliorate their condition at this time?

Now, let us get closer up to this subject, and talk about it. [The President here approached very near to Mr. Douglass.] What relation has the colored man and the white man heretofore occupied in the South? I opposed slavery upon two grounds. First, it was a great monopoly, enabling those who controlled and owned it to constitute an aristocracy, enabling the few to derive great profits and rule the many with an iron rod, as it were. And this is one great objection to it in a government, it being a monopoly. I was opposed to it secondly upon the abstract principle of slavery. Hence, in getting clear of a monopoly, we are getting clear of slavery at the same time. So you see there were two right ends accomplished in the accomplishment of the one.

Mr. DOUGLASS. Mr. President, do you wish—

The PRESIDENT. I am not quite through yet. Slavery has been abolished. A great national guarantee has been given, one that cannot be revoked. I was getting at the relation that subsisted between the white man and the colored men. A very small proportion of white persons compared with the whole number of such owned the colored people of the South. I might instance the State of Tennessee in illustration. There were there twenty-seven non-slaveholders to one slaveholder, and yet the slave power controlled the State. Let us talk about this matter as it is. Although the colored man was in slavery there, and owned as property in the sense and in the language of that locality and of that community, yet, in comparing his condition and his position there with the non-slaveholder, he usually estimated his importance just in proportion to the number of slaves that his master owned with the non-slaveholder.

Have you ever lived upon a plantation?

Mr. DOUGLASS. I have, your excellency.

The PRESIDENT. When you would look over and see a man who had a large family, struggling hard upon a poor piece of land, you thought a great deal less of him than you did of your own master's negro, didn't you?

Mr. DOUGLASS. Not I!

The PRESIDENT. Well, I know such was the case with a large number of you in those sections. Where such is the case we know there is an enmity, we know there is a hate. The poor white man, on the other hand, was opposed to the slave and his master; for the colored man and his master combined kept him in slavery, by depriving him of a fair participation in the labor and productions of the rich land of the country.

Don't you know that a colored man, in going to hunt a master (as they call it) for the next year, preferred hiring to a man who owned slaves rather than to a man who did not? I know the fact, at all events. They did not consider it quite as respectable to hire to a man who did not own negroes as to one who did.

Mr. DOUGLASS. Because he wouldn't be treated as well.

The PRESIDENT. Then that is another argument in favor of what I am going to say. It shows that the colored man appreciated the slave owner more highly than he did the man who didn't own slaves. Hence the enmity between the colored man and the non-slaveholders. The white man was permitted to vote before—government was derived from him. He is a part and parcel of the political machinery.

Now, by the rebellion or revolution—and when you come back to the objects of this war, you find that the abolition of slavery was not one of the objects; Congress and the President himself declared that it was waged on our part in order to suppress the rebellion—the abolition of slavery has come as an incident to the suppression of a great rebellion—as an incident, and as an incident we should give it the proper direction.

The colored man went into this rebellion a slave; by the operation of the rebellion he came out a freedman—equal to a freeman in any other portion of the country. Then there is a great deal done for him on this point. The non-slaveholder who was forced into the rebellion, who was as loyal as those that lived beyond the limits of the State, but was carried into it, lost his property, and in a number of instances the lives of such were sacrificed, and he who has survived has come out of it with nothing gained, but a great deal lost.

Now, upon the principle of justice, should they be placed in a condition different from what they were before? On the one hand, one has gained a great deal; on the other hand, one has lost a great deal, and, in a political point of view, scarcely stands where he did before.

Now, we are talking about where we are going to begin. We have got at the hate that existed between the two races. The query comes up, whether these two races, situated as they were before, without preparation, without time for passion and excitement to be appeased, and without time for the slightest improvement, whether the one should be turned loose upon the other, and be thrown together at the ballot-box with this enmity and hate existing between them. The query comes up right there, whether we don't commence a war of races. I think I understand this thing, and especially is this the case when you force it upon a people without their consent.

You have spoken about government. Where is power derived from? We say it is derived from the people. Let us take it so, and refer to the District of Columbia by way of illustration. Suppose, for instance, here, in this political community, which, to a certain extent, must have government, must have laws, and putting it now upon the broadest basis you can put it—take into consideration the relation which the white has heretofore borne to the colored race—is it proper to force upon this community, without their consent, the elective franchise, without regard to color, making it universal?

Now, where do you begin? Government must have a controlling power—must have a lodgment. For instance, suppose Congress should pass a law authorizing an election to be held at which all over twenty-one years of age, without regard to color, should be allowed to vote, and a majority should decide at such election that the elective franchise should not be universal; what would you do about it? Who would settle it? Do you deny that first great principle of the right of the people to govern themselves? Will you resort to an arbitrary power, and say a majority of the people shall receive a state of things they are opposed to?

Mr. DOUGLASS. That was said before the war.

The PRESIDENT. I am now talking about a principle; not what somebody else said.

Mr. DOWNING. Apply what you have said, Mr. President, to South Carolina, for instance, where a majority of the inhabitants are colored.

The PRESIDENT. Suppose you go to South Carolina; suppose you go to Ohio. That doesn't change the principle at all. The query to which I have referred still comes up when government is undergoing a fundamental change. Government commenced upon this principle; it has existed upon it; and you propose now to incorporate into it an element that didn't exist before. I say the query comes up in undertaking this thing whether we have a right to make a change in regard to the elective franchise in Ohio, for instance: whether we shall not let the people in that State decide the matter for themselves.

Each community is better prepared to determine the depositary of its political power than anybody else, and it is for the Legislature, for the people of Ohio to say who shall vote, and not for the Congress of the United States. I might go down here to the ballot-box to-morrow and vote directly for universal suffrage; but if a great majority of the people said no, I should consider it would be tyrannical in me to attempt to force such upon them without their will. It is a fundamental tenet in my creed that the will of the people must be obeyed. Is there anything wrong or unfair in that?

Mr. DOUGLASS (smiling.) A great deal that is wrong, Mr. President, with all respect.

The PRESIDENT. It is the people of the States that must for themselves determine this thing. I do not want to be engaged in a work that will commence a war of races. I want to begin the work of preparation, and the States, or the people in each community, if a man demeans himself well, and shows evidence that this new state of affairs will operate, will protect him in all his rights, and give him every possible advantage when they become reconciled socially and politically to this state of things. Then will this new order of things work harmoniously; but forced upon the people before they are prepared for it, it will be resisted, and work inharmoniously. I feel a conviction that driving this matter upon the people, upon the community, will result in the injury of both races, and the ruin of one or the other. God knows I have no desire but the good of the whole human race. I would it were so that all you advocate could be done in the twinkling of an eye; but it is not in the nature of things, and I do not assume or pretend to be wiser than Providence, or stronger than the laws of nature.

Let us now seek to discover the laws governing this thing. There is a great law controlling it; let us endeavor to find out what that law is, and conform our actions to it. All the details will then properly adjust themselves and work out well in the end,

God knows that anything I can do I will do. In the mighty process by which the great end is to be reached, anything I can do to elevate the races, to soften and ameliorate their condition I will do, and to be able to do so is the sincere desire of my heart.

I am glad to have met you, and thank you for the compliment you have paid me.

Mr. Douglass. I have to return to you our thanks, Mr. President, for so kindly granting us this interview. We did not come here expecting to argue this question with your excellency, but simply to state what were our views and wishes in the premises. If we were disposed to argue the question, and you would grant us permission, of course we would endeavor to controvert some of the positions you have assumed.

Mr. Downing. Mr. Douglass, I take it that the President, by his kind expressions and his very full treatment of the subject, must have contemplated some reply to the views which he has advanced, and in which we certainly do not concur, and I say this with due respect.

The President. I thought you expected me to indicate to some extent what my views are on the subjects touched upon in your statement.

Mr. Downing. We are very happy, indeed, to have heard them.

Mr. Douglass. If the President will allow me, I would like to say one or two words in reply. You enfranchise your enemies and disfranchise your friends.

The President. All I have done is simply to indicate what my views are, as I supposed you expected me to, from your address.

Mr. Douglass. My own impression is that the very thing that your excellency would avoid in the southern States can only be avoided by the very measure that we propose, and I would state to my brother delegates that because I perceive the President has taken strong grounds in favor of a given policy, and distrusting my own ability to remove any of those impressions which he has expressed, I thought we had better end the interview with the expression of thanks. (Addressing the President.) But if your excellency will be pleased to hear, I would like to say a word or two in regard to that one matter of the enfranchisement of the blacks as

a means of preventing the very thing which your excellency seems to apprehend—that is a conflict of races.

The President. I repeat, I merely wanted to indicate my views in reply to your address, and not to enter into any general controversy, as I could not well do so under the circumstances.

Your statement was a very frank one, and I thought it was due to you to meet it in the same spirit.

Mr. Douglass. Thank you, sir.

The President. I think you will find, so far as the South is concerned, that if you will all inculcate there the idea in connection with the one you urge, that the colored people can live and advance in civilization to better advantage elsewhere than crowded right down there in the South, it would be better for them.

Mr. Douglass. But the masters have the making of the laws, and we cannot get away from the plantation.

The President. What prevents you?

Mr. Douglass. We have not the single right of locomotion through the Southern States now.

The President. Why not; the government furnishes you with every facility.

Mr. Douglass. There are six days in the year that the negro is free in the South now, and his master then decides for him where he shall go, where he shall work, how much he shall work—in fact, he is divested of all political power. He is absolutely in the hands of those men.

The President. If the master now controls him or his action, would he not control him in his vote?

Mr. Douglass. Let the negro once understand that he has an organic right to vote, and he will raise up a party in the Southern States among the poor, who will rally with him. There is this conflict that you speak of between the wealthy slaveholder and the poor man.

The President. You touch right upon the point there. There is this conflict, and hence I suggest emigration. If he cannot get employment in the South, he has it in his power to go where he can get it.

In parting, the President said that they were both desirous of accomplishing the same ends, but proposed to do so by following different roads.

Mr. Douglass, on turning to leave, remarked to his fellow delegates: "The President sends us to the people, and we go to the people."

The President. Yes, sir; I have great faith in the people. I believe they will do what is right. ──

## Reply of the Colored Delegation to the President.

*To the Editor of the Chronicle:*

Will you do us the favor to insert in your columns the following reply of the colored delegation to the President of the United States?

Geo. T. Downing,
*In behalf of the Delegation.*

Mr. President: In consideration of a delicate sense of propriety, as well as your own repeated intimations of indisposition to discuss or to listen to a reply to the views and opinions you were pleased to express to ns in your elaborate speech to-day, the undersigned would respectfully take this method of replying thereto. Believing as we do that the views and opinions you expressed in that address are entirely unsound and prejudicial to the highest interests of our race as well as our country at large, we cannot do other than expose the same, and, as far as may be in our power, arrest their dangerous influence. It is not necessary at this time to call attention to more than two or three features of your remarkable address:

1. The first point to which we feel especially bound to take exception is your attempt to found a policy opposed to our enfranchisement, upon the alleged ground of an existing hostility on the part of the form er slaves toward the poor white people of the South. We admit the existence of this hostility, and hold that it is entirely reciprocal. But you obviously commit an error by drawing an argument from an incident of a state of slavery, and making it a basis for a policy adapted to a state of freedom. The hostility between the whites and blacks of the South is easily explained. It has its root and sap in the relation of slavery, and was incited on both sides by the cunning of the slave masters. Those masters secured their ascendency over both the poor whites and the blacks by putting enmity between them.

They divided both to conquer each. There was no earthly reason why the blacks should not hate and dread the poor whites when in a state of slavery, for it was from this class that their masters received their slave-catchers, slave-drivers, and overseers. They were the men called in upon all occasions by the masters when any fiendish outrage was to be committed upon the slave. Now, sir, you cannot but perceive that, the cause of this hatred removed, the effect must be removed also. Slavery is abolished. The cause of antagonism is removed, and you must see that it is altogether illogical (and "putting new wine into old bottles," "mending new garments with old cloth") to legislate from slave-holding and slave-driving premises for a people whom you have repeatedly declared your purpose to maintain in freedom.

2. Besides, even if it were true, as you allege, that the hostility of the blacks toward the poor whites must necessarily project itself into a state of freedom, and that this enmity between the two races is even more intense in a state of freedom than in a state of slavery, in the name of Heaven, we reverently ask, how can you, in view of your professed desire to promote the welfare of the black man, deprive him of all means of defence, and clothe him whom you regard as his enemy in the panoply of political power? Can it be that you would recommend a policy which would arm the strong and cast down the defenceless? Can you, by any possibility of reasoning, regard this as just, fair, or wise? Experience proves that those are oftenest abused who can be abused with the greatest impunity. Men are whipped oftenest who are whipped easiest. Peace betwen races is not to be secured by degrading one race and exalting another, by giving power to one race and withholding it from another; but by maintaining a state of equal justice between all classes. First pure, then peaceable.

3. On the colonization theory you were pleased to broach, very much could be said. It is impossible to suppose, in view of the usefulness of the black man in time of peace as a laborer in the South, and in time of war as a soldier at the North, and the growing respect for his rights among the people, and his increasing adaptation to a high state of civilization in this his native land, there can ever come a time when he can be removed from this country without a terrible shock to its prosperity and peace. Besides, the worst enemy of the nation could not cast upon its fair name a greater infamy than to suppose that negroes could be tolerated among them in a state of the most degrading slavery and oppression, and must be cast away, driven into exile, for no other cause than having been freed from their chains.

GEORGE T. DOWNING,<br>JOHN JONES,<br>WILLIAM WHIPPER,<br>FREDERICK DOUGLASS,<br>LEWIS H. DOUGLASS,<br>and others.

WASHINGTON, *February* 7, 1866.

### Remarks at an Interview with the Committee of the Legislature of Virginia.

February 10, 1866—A committee of the Senate and House of Delegates of Virginia called upon the President, for the purpose of presenting him with resolutions adopted by the General Assembly of Virginia. After some remarks by Mr. John B. Baldwin, chairman of the delegation, the President responded:

In reply, gentlemen, to the resolutions you have just presented, to me, and the clear and forcible and concise remarks which you have made in explanation of the position of Virginia, I shall not attempt to make a formal speech, but simply to enter into a plain conversation in regard to the condition of things in which we stand.

As a premise to what I may say, permit me first to tender you my thanks for this visit, and next to express the gratification I feel in meeting so many intelligent, responsible, and respectable men of Virginia, bearing to me the sentiments which have been expressed in the resolutions of your Legislature and the remarks accompanying them.

They are, so far as they refer to the Constitution of the country, the sentiments and the principles embraced in the charter of the Government. The preservation of the Union has been, from my entrance into public life, one of my cardinal tenets. At the very incipiency of this rebellion I set my face against the dissolution of the Union of the States. I do not make this allusion for the purpose of bringing up anything which has transpired which may be regarded as of an unkind or unpleasant character, but I believed then, as I believe now, and as you have most unmistakably indicated, that the security and the protection of the rights of all the people were to be found in the Union; that we were certainly safer in the Union than we were out of it.

Upon this conviction I based my opposition to the efforts which were made to destroy the Union. I have continued those efforts, notwithstanding the perils through which I have passed, and you are not unaware that the trial has been a severe one. When opposition to the Government came from one section of the country, and that the section in which my life had been passed, and with which my interests were identified, I stood, as I stand now, contending for the Union, and asseverating that the best and surest way to obtain our rights and to protect our interests was to remain in the Union, under the protection of the Constitution.

The ordeal through which we have passed during the last four or five years demonstrates most conclusively that that opposition was right; and to-day, after the experiment has been made and has failed; after the demonstration has been most conclusively afforded that this Union cannot be dissolved, that it was not designed to be dissolved, it is extremely gratifying to me to meet gentlemen as intelligent and as responsible as yourselves, who are willing and anxious to accept and do accept the terms laid down in the Constitution and in obedience to the laws made in pursuance thereof.

We were at one period separated; the separation was to me painful in the extreme; but now, after having gone through a struggle in which the powers of the Government have been tried, when we have swung around to a point at which we meet to agree and are willing to unite our efforts for the preservation of the Government, which I believe is the best in the world, it is exceedingly gratifying to me to meet you to-day, standing upon common ground, rallying around the Constitution and the Union of these States, the preservation of which, as I conscientiously and honestly believe, will result in the promotion and the advancement of this people.

I repeat, I am gratified to meet you to-day, expressing the principles and announcing the sentiments to which you have given utterance, and I trust that the occasion will long be remembered. I have no doubt that your intention is to carry out and comply with every single principle laid down in the resolutions you have submitted. I know that some are distrustful; but I am of those who have confidence in the judgment, in the integrity, in the intelligence, in the virtue of the great mass of the American people; and having such confidence, I am willing to trust them, and I thank God that we have not yet reached that point where we have lost all confidence in each other.

The spirit of the Government can only be preserved, we can only become prosperous and great as a people, by mutual forbearance and confidence. Upon that faith and confidence alone can the Government be successfully carried on.

On the cardinal principle of representation to which you refer I will make a single remark. That principle is inherent; it constitutes one of the fundamental elements of this Government. The representatives of the States and of the people should have the qualifications prescribed by the Constitution of the United States, and *those qualifications most unquestionably imply*

*loyalty.* He who comes as a representative, having the qualifications prescribed by the Constitution to fit him to take a seat in either of the deliberative bodies which constitute the national legislature, must necessarily, according to the intendment of the Constitution, *be a loyal man,* willing to abide by and devoted to the Union and the Constitution of the States. He cannot be for the Constitution, he cannot be for the Union, he cannot acknowledge obedience to all the laws, unless he is loyal. When the people send such men in good faith, they are entitled to representation through them.

In going into the recent rebellion or insurrection against the Government of the United States we erred; and in returning and resuming our relations with the Federal Government, I am free to say that all the responsible positions and places ought to be confined distinctly and clearly to men who are loyal. If there were only five thousand loyal men in a State, or a less number, but sufficient to take charge of the political machinery of the State, those five thousand men, or the lesser number, are entitled to it, if all the rest should be otherwise inclined. I look upon it as being fundamental that the exercise of political power should be confined to loyal men; and I regard that as implied in the doctrines laid down in these resolutions and in the eloquent address by which they have been accompanied. I may say, furthermore, that after having passed through the great struggle in which we have been engaged, we should be placed upon much more acceptable ground in resuming all our relations to the General Government if we presented men unmistakably and unquestionably loyal to fill the places of power. This being done, I feel that the day is not far distant—I speak confidingly in reference to the great mass of the American people—when they will determine that this Union shall be made whole, and the great right of representation in the councils of the nation be acknowledged.

Gentlemen, that is a fundamental principle. "No taxation without representation" was one of the principles which carried us through the Revolution. This great principle will hold good yet; and if we but perform our duty, if we but comply with the spirit of the resolutions presented to me to-day, the American people will maintain and sustain the great doctrines upon which the Government was inaugurated. It can be done, and it will be done; and I think that if the effort be fairly and fully made, with forbearance and with prudence, and with discretion and wisdom, the end is not very far distant.

It seems to me apparent that from every consideration the best policy which could be adopted at present would be a restoration of these States and of the Government upon correct principles. We have some foreign difficulties, but the moment it can be announced that the Union of the States is again complete, that we have resumed our career of prosperity and greatness, at that very instant, almost, all our foreign difficulties will be settled; for there is no power upon the earth which will care to have a controversy or a rupture with the Government of the United States under such circumstances.

If these States be fully restored, the area for

the circulation of the national currency, which is thought by some to be inflated to a very great extent, will be enlarged, the number of persons through whose hands it is to pass will be increased, the quantity of commerce in which it is to be employed as a medium of exchange will be enlarged; and then it will begin to approximate what we all desire, a specie standard. If all the States were restored—if peace and order reigned throughout the land, and all the industrial pursuits—all the avocations of peace—were again resumed, the day would not be very far distant when we could put into the commerce of the world $250,000,000 or $300,000,000 worth of cotton and tobacco, and the various products of the Southern States, which would constitute, in part, a basis of this currency.

Then, instead of the cone being inverted, we should reverse the position, and put the base at the bottom, as it ought to be; and the currency of the country will rest on a sound and enduring basis; and surely that is a result which is calculated to promote the interests not only of one section, but of the whole country, from one extremity to the other. Indeed, I look upon the restoration of these States as being indispensable to all our greatness.

Gentlemen, I know nothing further that I could say in the expression of my feelings on this occasion—and they are not affected—more than to add, that I shall continue in the same line of policy which I have pursued from the commencement of the rebellion to the present period. My efforts have been to preserve the Union of the States. I never, for a single moment, entertained the opinion that a State could withdraw from the Union of its own will. That attempt was made. It has failed. I continue to pursue the same line of policy which has been my constant guide. I was against dissolution. Dissolution was attempted; it has failed; and now I cannot take the position that a State which attempted to secede is out of the Union, when I contended all the time that it could not go out, and that it never has been out. I cannot be forced into that position. Hence, when the States and their people shall have complied with the requirements of the Government, I shall be in favor of their resuming their former relations to this Government in all respects.

I do not intend to say anything personal, but you know as well as I do that at the beginning, and indeed before the beginning, of the recent gigantic struggle between the different sections of the country, there were extreme men South and there were extreme men North. I might make use of a homely figure—which is sometimes as good as any other, even in the illustrations of great and important questions—and say that it has been hammer at one end of the line and anvil at the other; and this great Government, the best the world ever saw, was kept upon the anvil and hammered before the rebellion, and it has been hammered since the rebellion; and there seems to be a disposition to continue the hammering until the Government shall be destroyed. I have opposed that system always, and I oppose it now.

The Government, in the assertion of its powers and in the maintenance of the principles of the constitution, has taken hold of one extreme, and with the strong arm of physical power has put down the rebellion. Now, as we swing around the circle of the Union, with a fixed and unalterable determination to stand by it, if we find the counterpart or the duplicate of the same spirit that played to this feeling and these persons in the South, this other extreme, which stands in the way must get out of it, and the Government must stand unshaken and unmoved on its basis. The Government must be preserved.

I will only say, in conclusion, that I hope all the people of this country, in good faith and in the fullness of their hearts, will, upon the principles which you have enunciated here to-day, of the maintenance of the Constitution and the preservation of the Union, lay aside every other feeling for the good of our common country, and with uplifted faces to heaven swear that our gods and our altars and all shall sink in the dust together rather than that this glorious Union shall not be preserved.

I am gratified to find the loyal sentiment of the country developing and manifesting itself in these expressions; and now that the attempt to destroy the government has failed at one end of the line, I trust we shall go on determined to preserve the Union in its original purity against all opposers.

I thank you, gentlemen, for the compliment you have paid me, and I respond most cordially to what has been said in your resolutions and address, and I trust in God that the time will soon come when we can meet under more favorable auspices than we do now.

----

### Speech of the 22d February, 1866.

*[Report of National Intelligencer.]*

After returning his thanks to the committee which had waited upon him and presented him with the resolutions which had been adopted, the President said: The resolutions, as I understand them, are complimentary of the policy which has been adopted and pursued by the Administration since it came into power. I am free to say to you on this occasion that it is extremely gratifying to me to know that so large a portion of our fellow-citizens indorse the policy which has been adopted and which is intended to be carried out.

This policy has been one which was intended to restore the glorious Union—to bring those great States, now the subject of controversy, to their original relations to the Government of the United States. And this seems to be a day peculiarly appropriate for such a manifestation as this—the day that gave birth to him who founded the Government—that gave birth to the Father of our Country—that gave birth to him who stood at the portal when all these States entered into this glorious Confederacy. I say that the day is peculiarly appropriate to the indorsement of measures for the restoration of the Union that was founded by the Father of his Country. Washington, whose name this city bears, is embalmed in the hearts of all who love their Government. [A voice, "So is Andy Johnson."] Washington, in the language of his eulogists, was first in peace, first in war, and first in the hearts of his countrymen. No people can claim him—no nation can appropriate him. His eminence is acknowledged throughout the civilized world by all those who love free government. I have had the pleasure of a visit from the association which has been directing its efforts towards the completion of a monument erected to his name. I was prepared to meet them and give them my humble influence and countenance in aid of the work. Let the monument be erected to him who founded the Government, and that almost within the throw of a stone from the spot from which I now address you. Let it be completed. Let the pledges which all these States and corporations and associations have put in that monument be preserved as an earnest of our faith in and love of this Union, and let the monument be completed. And in connection with Washington, in speaking of the pledges that have been placed in that monument, let me refer to one from my own State—God bless her!—which has struggled for the preservation of this Union in the field and in the councils of the nation. Let me repeat, that she is now struggling in consequence of an innovation that has taken place in regard to her relation with the Federal Government growing out of the rebellion—she is now struggling to renew her relations with this Government and take the stand which she has occupied since 1796. Let me repeat the sentiment which that State inscribed upon her stone that is deposited within the monument of freedom and in commemoration of Washington; she is struggling to stand by the sentiment inscribed on that stone, and she is now willing to maintain that sentiment. And what is the sentiment? It is the sentiment which was enunciated by the immortal and the illustrious Jackson—"The Federal Union, it must be preserved."

Were it possible for that old man, who in statue is before me and in portrait behind me, to be called forth—were it possible to communicate with the illustrious dead, and he could be informed of the progress in the work of faction, and rebellion, and treason—that old man would turn over in his coffin, he would rise, shake off the habiliments of the tomb, and again extend that long arm and finger and reiterate the sentiment before enunciated, "the Federal Union, it must be preserved." But we witness what has transpired since his day. We remember what he said in 1833. When treason and treachery and infidelity to the Government and the Constitution of the United States stalked forth, it was his power and influence that went forth and crushed it in its incipiency. It was then stopped. But it was only stopped for a time, and the spirit continued. There were men disaffected towards the Government in both the North and South. There were peculiar institutions in the country to which some were adverse and others attached. We find that one portion of our countrymen advocated an institution in the South which others opposed in the North. This resulted in two extremes. That in the South reached a point at which the people there were disposed to dissolve the Government of the United States, and they sought to preserve their peculiar institutions. (What I say on this oc-

casion I want to be understood.) There was a portion of our countrymen opposed to this, and they went to that extreme that they were willing to break up the Government to destroy this peculiar institution of the South.

I assume nothing here to-day but the citizen—one of you—who has been pleading for his country and the preservation of the Constitution. These two parties have been arrayed against each other, and I stand before you as I did in the Senate of the United States in 1860. I denounced there those who wanted to disrupt the Government, and I portrayed their true character. I told them that those who were engaged in the effort to break up the Government were traitors. I have not ceased to repeat that, and, as far as endeavor could accomplish it, to carry out the sentiment. I remarked, though, that there were two parties. One would destroy the Government to preserve slavery; the other would break up the Government to destroy slavery. The objects to be accomplished were different, it is true, so far as slavery was concerned; but they agreed in one thing—the destruction of the Government, precisely what I was always opposed to; and whether the disunionists came from the South or from the North, I stand now where I did then, vindicating the Union of these States and the Constitution of our country. The rebellion manifested itself in the South. I stood by the Government. I said I was for the Union with slavery. I said I was for the Union without slavery. In either alternative I was for the Government and the Constitution. The Government has stretched forth its strong arm, and with its physical power it has put down treason in the field. That is, the section of country that arrayed itself against the Government has been conquered by the force of the Government itself. Now, what had we said to those people? We said: "No compromise; we can settle this question with the South in eight and forty hours."

I have said it again and again, and I repeat it now, "disband your armies, acknowledge the supremacy of the Constitution of the United States, give obedience to the law, and the whole question is settled."

What has been done since? Their armies have been disbanded. They come now to meet us in a spirit of magnanimity and say, "We were mistaken; we made the effort to carry out the doctrine of secession and dissolve this Union, and having traced this thing to its logical and physical results, we now acknowledge the flag of our country, and promise obedience to the Constitution and the supremacy of the law."

I say, then, when you comply with the Constitution, when you yield to the law, when you acknowledge allegiance to the Government—I say let the door of the Union be opened, and the relation be restored to those that had erred and had strayed from the fold of our fathers.

Who has suffered more than I have? I ask the question. I shall not recount the wrongs and the sufferings inflicted upon me. It is not the course to deal with a whole people in a spirit of revenge. I know there has been a great deal said about the exercise of the pardon power, as regards the Executive; and there is no one who has labored harder than I to have the principals, the intelligent and conscious offenders, brought to justice and have the principle vindicated that "treason is a crime."

But, while conscious and intelligent traitors are to be punished, should whole communities and States be made to submit to the penalty of death ? I have quite as much asperity, and perhaps as much resentment, as a man ought to have; but we must reason regarding man as he is, and must conform our action and our conduct to the example of Him who founded our holy religion.

I came into power under the Constitution of the country, and with the approbation of the people, and what did I find ? I found eight millions of people who were convicted, condemned under the law, and the penalty was death ; and, through revenge and resentment, were they all to be annihilated? Oh! may I not exclaim, how different would this be from the example set by the Founder of our holy religion, whose divine arch rests its extremities on the horizon while its span embraces the universe ! Yes, He that founded this great scheme came into the world and saw men condemned under the law, and the sentence was death. What was his example? Instead of putting the world or a nation to death, He went forth on the cross and testified with His wounds that He would die and let the world live. Let them repent; let them acknowledge their rashness ; let them become loyal, and let them be supporters of our glorious stripes and stars, and the Constitution of our country. I say let the leaders, the conscious, intelligent traitors, meet the penalties of the law. But as for the great mass, who have been forced into the rebellion—misled in other instances—let there be clemency and kindness, and a trust and a confidence in them. But, my countrymen, after having passed through this rebellion, and having given as much evidence of enmity to it as some who croak a great deal about the matter— when I look back over the battle-field and see many of those brave men in whose company I was, in localities where the contest was most difficult and doubtful, and who yet were patient; when I look back over these fields, and where the smoke has scarcely passed away ; where the blood that has been shed has scarcely been absorbed—before their bodies have passed through the stages of decomposition—what do I find? The rebellion is put down by the strong arm of the Government in the field. But is this the only way in which we can have rebellions? This was a struggle against a change and a revolution of the Government, and before we fully get from the battle-fields— when our brave men have scarcely returned to their homes and renewed the ties of affection and love to their wives and their children—we are now almost inaugurated into another rebellion.

One rebellion was the effort of States to secede, and the war on the part of the Government was to prevent them from accomplishing that, and thereby changing the character of our Government and weakening its power. When the Government has succeeded, there is an attempt now to concentrate all power in the hands of a few at the federal head, and thereby bring about a consolidation of the Republic, which is equally objectionable with its dissolution. We find a power assumed and attempted to be exercised of a most extraordinary character. We see now that governments can be revolutionized without going into the battle-field; and sometimes the revolutions most distressing to a people are effected without the shedding of blood. That is, the substance of your Government may be taken away, while there is held out to you the form and the shadow. And now, what are the attempts, and what is being proposed ? We find that by an irresponsible central directory nearly all the powers of Congress are assumed, without even consulting the legislative and executive departments of the Government. By a resolution reported by a committee, upon whom and in whom the legislative power of the Government has been lodged, that great principle in the Constitution which authorizes and empowers the legislative department, the Senate and House of Representatives, to be the judges of elections, returns, and qualifications of its own members, has been virtually taken away from the two respective branches of the national legislature, and conferred upon a committee, who must report before the body can act on the question of the admission of members to their seats. By this rule they assume a State is out of the Union, and to have its practical relations restored by that rule, before the House can judge of the qualifications of its own members. What position is that? You have been struggling for four years to put down a rebellion. You contended at the beginning of that struggle that a State had not a right to go out. You said it had neither the right nor the power, and it has been settled that the States had neither the right nor the power to go out of the Union. And when you determine by the executive, by the military, and by the public judgment, that these States cannot have any right to go out, this committee turns around and assumes that they are out, and that they shall not come in

I am free to say to you, as your Executive, that I am not prepared to take any such position. I said in the Senate, in the very inception of this rebellion, that the States had no right to secede. That question has been settled. Thus determined, I cannot turn round and give the lie direct to all that I profess to have done during the last four years. I say that when the States that attempted to secede comply with the Constitution, and give sufficient evidence of loyalty, I shall extend to them the right hand of fellowship, and let peace and union be restored. I am opposed to the Davises, the Toombses, the Slidells, and the long list of such. But when I perceive, on the other hand, men—[A voice, "Call them off"]—I care not by what name you call them— still opposed to the Union, I am free to say to you that I am still with the people. I am still for the preservation of these States, for the preservation of this Union, and in favor of this great Government accomplishing its destiny.

[Here the President was called upon to give the names of three of the members of Congress to whom he had alluded as being opposed to the Union.]

The gentleman calls for three names. I am talking to my friends and fellow-citizens here. Suppose I should name to you those whom I look upon as being opposed to the fundamental principles of this Government, and as now laboring to destroy them. I say Thaddeus Stevens, of Pennsylvania; I say Charles Sumner, of Massachusetts; I say Wendell Phillips, of Massachusetts. [A voice, "Forney!"]

I do not waste my fire on dead ducks. I stand for the country, and though my enemies may traduce, slander, and vituperate, I may say, that has no force.

In addition to this, I do not intend to be governed by real or pretended friends, nor do I intend to be bullied by my enemies. An honest conviction is my sustenance, the Constitution my guide. I know, my countrymen, that it has been insinuated—nay, said directly, in high places—that if such a usurpation of power had been exercised two hundred years ago, in particular reigns, it would have cost an individual his head. What usurpation has Andrew Johnson been guilty of? [Cries of "None."] My only usurpation has been committed by standing between the people and the encroachments of power. And because I dared say in a conversation with a fellow-citizen and a Senator too, that I thought amendments to the constitution ought not to be so frequent, lest the instrument lose all its sanctity and dignity, and be wholly lost sight of in a short time, and because I happened to say in conversation that I thought that such and such an amendment was all that ought to be adopted, it was said that I had suggested such a usurpation of power as would have cost a king his head in a certain period! In connection with this subject, one has exclaimed that we are in the "midst of an earthquake and he trembled." Yes, there is an earthquake approaching, there is a groundswell coming, of popular judgment and indignation. The American people will speak, and by their instinct, if in no other way, know who are their friends, when and where and in whatever position I stand—and I have occupied many positions in the government, going through both branches of the legislature. Some gentleman here behind me says, "And was a tailor." Now, that don't affect me in the least. When I was a tailor I always made a close fit, and was always punctual to my customers, and did good work.

[A voice. No patchwork.]

The PRESIDENT. No, I did not want any patchwork. But we pass by this digression. Intimations have been thrown out—and when principles are involved and the existence of my country imperiled, I will, as on former occasions, speak what I think. Yes! Cost him his head! Usurpation! When and where have I been guilty of this? Where is the man in all the positions I have occupied, from that of alderman to the Vice Presidency, who can say that Andrew Johnson ever made a pledge that he did not redeem, or ever made a promise that he violated, or that he acted with falsity to the people! They may talk about beheading; but when I am beheaded I want the American people to be the witness. I do not want by inuendoes of an indirect character in high places to have one say to a man who has assassination broiling in his heart, "there is a fit subject," and also exclaim that the "presidential obstacle" must be got out of the way, when possibly the intention was to institute assassination. Are those who want to destroy our institutions and change the character of the Government not satisfied with the blood that has been shed? Are they not satisfied with one martyr? Does not the blood of Lincoln appease the vengeance and wrath of the opponents of this Government? Is their thirst still unslaked? Do they want more blood? Have they not honor and courage enough to effect the removal of the presidential obstacle otherwise than through the hands of the assassin? I am not afraid of assassins; but if it must be, I would wish to be encountered where one brave man can oppose another. I hold him in dread only who strikes cowardly. But if they have courage enough to strike like men, (I know they are willing to wound, but they are afraid to strike;) if my blood is to be shed because I vindicate the Union and the preservation of this Government in its original purity and character, let it be so; but when it is done, let an altar of the Union be erected, and then, if necessary, lay me upon it, and the blood that now warms and animates my frame shall be poured out in a last libation as a tribute to the Union; and let the opponents of this Government remember that when it is poured out the blood of the martyr will be the seed of the church. The Union will grow. It will continue to increase in strength and power, though it may be cemented and cleansed with blood.

I have talked longer, my countrymen, than I intended. With many acknowledgments for the honor you have done me, I will say one word in reference to the amendments to the Constitution of the United States. Shortly after I reached Washington, for the purpose of being inaugurated Vice President, I had a conversation with Mr. Lincoln. We were talking about the condition of affairs, in reference to matters in my own State. I said we had called a convention and demanded a constitution abolishing slavery in the State, which provision was not contained in the President's proclamation. This met with his approbation, and he gave me encouragement. In talking upon the subject of amendments to the Constitution, he said, "when the amendment to the Constitution now proposed is adopted by three-fourths of the States, I shall be pretty nearly or quite done as regards forming amendments to the Constitution if there should be one other adopted." I asked what that other amendment suggested was, and he replied, "I have labored to preserve this Union. I have toiled four years. I have been subjected to calumny and misrepresentation, and my great and sole desire has been to preserve these States intact under the Constitution, as they were before; and there should be an amendment to the Constitution which would *compel* the States to send their Senators and Representatives to the Congress of the United States." He saw, as part of the doctrine of secession, that the States could, if they were prepared, withdraw their Senators and Representatives; and he wished to remedy this evil by the adoption of the amendment suggested. Even that portion of the Constitutio which differs from other organic law says that no State shall be deprived of its representation. We now find the position taken that States shall not be recognized; that we will impose taxation; and where taxes are to be imposed the Representatives elect from thence are met at the door, and told: "No; you must pay taxes, but you cannot participate in a Government which is to affect you for all time." Is this just? [Voices—"No! No!"] We see, then, where we are going. I repeat, that I am for the Union. I am for preserving all the States. They may have erred, but let us admit those into the counsels of the nation who are unmistakably loyal. Let the man who acknowledges allegiance to the Government, and swears to support the Constitution, (he cannot do this in good faith unless he is loyal; no amplification of the oath can make any difference; it is mere detail, which I care nothing about;) let him be unquestionably loyal to the Constitution of the United States and its Government, and willing to support it in its peril, and I am willing to trust him. I know that some do not attach so much importance to the principle as I do. One principle that carried us through the revolution was, that there should be no taxation without representation. I hold that that principle, which was laid down by our fathers for the country's good then, is important to its good now. If it was worth battling for then, it is worth battling for now. It is fundamental, and should be preserved so long as our Government lasts. I know it was said by some during the rebellion that the Constitution had been rolled up as a piece of parchment, and should be put away, and that in time of rebellion there was no constitution. But it is now unfolding; it must now be read and adjusted and understood by the American people.

I come here to-day to vindicate, in so far as I can in these remarks, the Constitution; to save it, as I believe; for it does seem that encroachment after encroachment is to be pressed; and as I resist encroachments on the Government, I stand to-day prepared to resist encroachments on the Constitution, and thereby preserve the Government. It is now peace, and let us have peace. Let us enforce the Constitution. Let us live under and by its provisions. Let it be published in blazoned characters, as though it were in the heavens, so that all may read and all may understand it. Let us consult that instrument, and, understanding its principles, let us apply them. I tell the opponents of this Government, and I care not from what quarter they come—East or West, North or South—"you that are engaged in the work of breaking up this Government are mistaken. The Constitution and the principles of free government are deeply rooted in the American heart." All the powers combined, I care not of what character they are, cannot destroy the image of freedom. They may succeed for a time, but their attempts will be futile. They may as well attempt to lock up the winds or chain the waves. Yes, they may as well attempt to repeal it, (as it would seem the Constitution can be,) by a con-

current resolution; but when it is submitted to the popular judgment, they will find it just as well to introduce a resolution repealing the law of gravitation; and the idea of preventing the restoration of the Union is as about as feasible as resistance to the great law of gravity which binds all to a common centre. This great law of gravitation will bring back those States to harmony and their relations to the Federal Government, and all machinations North and South cannot prevent it. All that is wanting is time, until the American people can understand what is going on, and be ready to accept the view just as it appears to me. I would to God that the whole American people could be assembled here to-day as you are. I could wish to have an amphitheatre large enough to contain the whole thirty millions, that they could be here and witness the great struggle to preserve the Constitution of our fathers. They could at once see what it is, and how it is, and what kind of spirit is manifested in the attempt to destroy the great principles of free government; and they could understand who is for them and who is against them, and who was for ameliorating their condition. Their opposers could be placed before them, and there might be a regular contest, and in the first tilt the enemies of the country would be crushed. I have detained you longer than I intended; but in this struggle I am your instrument. Where is the man or woman, in private or public life, that has not always received my attention and my time? Sometimes it is said, "that man Johnson is a lucky man." I will tell you what constitutes good fortune. Doing right and being for the people. The people in some particular or other, notwithstanding their sagacity and judgment, are frequently underrated or underestimated; but somehow or other the great mass of the people will find out who is for them and who is against them. You must indulge me in this allusion, when I say I can lay my hand on my bosom and say that in all the positions in which I have been placed—many of them as trying as any in which mortal man could be put —so far, thank God, I have not deserted the people, nor do I believe they will desert me. What sentiment have I swerved from? Can my calumniators put their finger on it? Can they dare indicate a discrepancy or a deviation from principle?

Have you heard them at any time quote my predecessor, who fell a martyr to his course, as coming in controversy with anything I advocated? An inscrutable Providence saw proper to remove him to, I trust, a better world than this, and I came into power. Where is there one principle in reference to this restoration that I have departed from? Then the war is not simply upon me, but it is upon my predecessor. I have tried to do my duty. I know some are jealous in view of the White House, and I say all that flummery has as little influence on me as it had heretofore. The conscious satisfaction of having performed my duty to my country, my children, and my God, is all the reward which I shall ask.

In conclusion of what I have to say, let me ask this vast concourse, this sea of upturned faces, to go with me—or I will go with you— and stand around the Constitution of our country; it is again unfolded, and the people are invited to read and understand it, and to maintain its provisions. Let us stand by the principles of our fathers, though the heavens fall; and then, though factions array their transient forces to give vituperation after vituperation in the most virulent manner, I intend to stand by the Constitution as the chief ark of our safety, as the palladium of our civil and religious liberty. Yes, let us cling to it as the mariner clings to the last plank when the night and the tempest close around him.

Accept my thanks, gentlemen, for the indulgence you have given me in my extemporaneous remarks. Let us go on, forgetting the past and looking only upon the future, and trusting in Him that can control all that is on high and here below, and hoping that hereafter our Union will be restored, and that we will have peace on earth and good will towards man.

## Speech to the Colored People of the District of Columbia, Celebrating the Third Anniversary of their Emancipation.

April 19, 1866—I have nothing more to say to you on this occasion than to thank you for this compliment you have paid me in presenting yourselves before me on this your day of celebration. I come forward for the purpose of indicating my approbation and manifesting my appreciation of the respect thus offered or conferred.

I thank you for the compliment, and I mean what I say. And I will remark in this connection to this vast concourse that the time will come, and that, too, before a great while, when the colored population of the United States will find out who have selected them as a hobby and a pretence by which they can be successful in obtaining and maintaining power, and who have been their true friends, and wanted them to participate in and enjoy the blessings of freedom.

The time will come when it will be made known who contributed as much as any other man, and who, without being considered egotistic, I may say contributed more, in procuring the great national guarantee of the abolition of slavery in all the States, by the ratification of the amendment to the Constitution of the United States—giving a national guarantee that slavery shall no longer be permitted to exist or be re-established in any State or jurisdiction of the United States.

I know how easy it is to cater to prejudices, and how easy it is to excite feelings of prejudice and unkindness. I care not for that. I have been engaged in this work in which my all has been periled. I was not engaged in it as a

hobby, nor did I ride the colored man for the sake of gaining power. What I did was for the purpose of establishing the great principles of freedom. And, thank God, I feel and know it to be so, that my efforts have contributed as much, if not more, in accomplishing this great national guarantee, than those of any other living man in the United States.

It is very easy for colored men to have pretended friends, ensconced in high places, and far removed from danger, whose eyes have only abstractly gazed on freedom; who have never exposed their limbs or property, and who never contributed a sixpence in furtherance of the great cause, while another periled his all, and put up everything sacred and dear to man, and those whom he raised and who lived with him now enjoy his property with his consent, and receive his aid and assistance; yet some who assume, and others who have done nothing, are considered the great defenders and protectors of the colored man.

I repeat, my colored friends, here to-day, the time will come, and that not far distant, when it will be proved who is practically your best friend.

My friendship, so far as it has gone, has not been for place or power, for I had these already. It has been a principle with me, and I thank God the great principle has been established, that wherever any individual, in the language of a distinguished orator and statesman, treads American soil, his soul swells within him beyond the power of chains to bind him, in appreciation of the great truth that he stands forth redeemed, regenerated, and disenthralled by the genius of universal emancipation!

Then let me mingle with you in celebration of the day which commenced your freedom. I do it in sincerity and truth, and trust in God the blessings which have been conferred may be enjoyed and appreciated by you, and that you may give them a proper direction.

There is something for all to do. You have high and solemn duties to perform, and you ought to remember that freedom is not a mere idea. It must be reduced to practical reality. Men in being free have to deny themselves many things which seem to be embraced in the idea of universal freedom.

It is with you to give evidence to the world and the people of the United States, whether you are going to appreciate this great boon as it should be, and that you are worthy of being freemen. Then let me thank you with sincerity for the compliment you have paid me by passing through here to-day and paying your respects to me. I repeat again, the time will come when you will know who has been your best friend, and who has not been your friend from mercenary considerations. Accept my thanks.

# VI.

# SPECIAL AND VETO MESSAGES OF PRESIDENT JOHNSON,

## WITH THE

## VOTES IN CONGRESS ON THE PASSAGE OF THE VETOED BILLS.

**The Annual Message, December 4, 1865.**

The following extracts relate to reconstruction:

I found the States suffering from the effects of a civil war. Resistance to the General Government appeared to have exhausted itself. The United States had recovered possession of their forts and arsenals, and their armies were in the occupation of every State which had attempted to secede. Whether the territory within the limits of those States should be held as conquered territory, under military authority emanating from the President as the head of the army, was the first question that presented itself for decision.

Now, military governments, established for an indefinite period, would have offered no security for the early suppression of discontent; would have divided the people into the vanquishers and the vanquished; and would have envenomed hatred, rather than have restored affection. Once established, no precise limit to their continuance was conceivable. They would have occasioned an incalculable and exhausting expense. Peaceful emigration to and from that portion of the country is one of the best means that can be thought of for the restoration of harmony, and that emigration would have been prevented; for what emigrant from abroad, what industrious citizen at home, would place himself willingly under military rule? The chief persons who have followed in the train of the army would have been dependents on the General Government, or men who expected profit from the miseries of their erring fellow-citizens. The powers of patronage and rule which would have been exercised, under the President, over a vast and populous and naturally wealthy region, are greater than, unless under extreme necessity, I should be willing to intrust to any one man; they are such as, for myself, I could never, unless on occasions of great emergency, consent to exercise. The wilful use of such powers, if continued through a period of years, would have endangered the purity of the general administration and the liberties of the States which remained loyal.

Besides, the policy of military rule over a conquered territory would have implied that the States whose inhabitants may have taken part in the rebellion had, by the act of those inhabitants, ceased to exist. But the true theory is, that all pretended acts of secession were, from the beginning, null and void. The States cannot commit treason, nor screen the individual citizens who may have committed treason, any more than they could make valid treaties or engage in lawful commerce with any foreign power. The States attempting to secede placed themselves in a condition where their vitality was impaired, but not extinguished—their functions suspended, but not destroyed.

But if any State neglects or refuses to perform its offices, there is the more need that the General Government should maintain all its authority, and, as soon as practicable, resume the exercise of all its functions. On this principle I have acted, and have gradually and quietly, and by almost imperceptible steps, sought to restore the rightful energy of the General Government and of the States. To that end, provisional governors have been appointed for the States, conventions called, governors elected, legislatures assembled, and Senators and Representatives chosen to the Congress of the United States. At the same time, the Courts of the United States, as far as could be done, have been reopened, so that the laws of the United States may be enforced through their agency. The blockade has been removed and the custom-houses re-established in ports of entry, so that the revenue of the United States may be collected. The Post Office Department renews its ceaseless activity, and the General Government is thereby enabled to communicate promptly with its officers and agents. The courts bring security to persons and property; the opening of the ports invites the restoration of industry and commerce; the post office renews the facilities of social intercourse and of business. And is it not happy for us all, that the restoration of each one of these functions of the General Government brings with it a blessing to the States over which they are extended? Is it not a sure promise of harmony and renewed attachment to the Union that, after all that has happened, the return of the General Government is known only as a beneficence?

I know very well that this policy is attended with some risk; that for its success it requires at least the acquiescence of the States which it concerns; that it implies an invitation to those States, by renewing their allegiance to the United States, to resume their functions as States of the Union. But it is a risk that must be taken; in the choice of difficulties, it is the smallest risk; and to diminish, and, if possible, to remove all danger, I have felt it incumbent on me to assert one other power of the General Government—the power of pardon. As no State can throw a defence over the crime of treason, the power of pardon is exclusively vested in the executive government of the United States. In exercising that power, I have taken every precaution to connect it with the clearest recognition of the binding force of the laws of the United States, and an unqualified acknowledgment of the great social change of condition in regard to slavery which has grown out of the war.

The next step which I have taken to restore the constitutional relations of the States, has been an invitation to them to participate in the high office of amending the Constitution. Every patriot must wish for a general amnesty at the earliest epoch consistent with public safety. For this great end there is a need of a concurrence of all opinions, and the spirit of mutual conciliation. All parties in the late terrible conflict must work together in harmony. It is not too much to ask, in the name of the whole people, that, on the one side, the plan of restoration shall proceed in conformity with a willingness to cast the disorders of the past into oblivion; and that, on the other, the evidence of sincerity in the future maintenance of the Union shall be put beyond any doubt by the ratification of the proposed amendment to the Constitution, which provides for the abolition of slavery forever within the limits of our country. So long as the adoption of this amendment is delayed, so long will doubt and jealousy and uncertainty prevail. This is the measure which will efface the sad memory of the past; this is the measure which will most certainly call population and capital and security to those parts of the Union that need them most. Indeed, it is not too much to ask of the States which are now resuming their places in the family of the Union to give this pledge of perpetual loyalty and peace. Until it is done, the past, however much we may desire it, will not be forgotten. The adoption of the amendment reunites us beyond all power of disruption. It heals the wound that is imperfectly closed; it removes slavery, the element which has so long perplexed and divided the country; it makes of us once more a united people, renewed and strengthened, bound more than ever to mutual affection and support.

The amendment to the Constitution being adopted, it would remain for the States, whose powers have been so long in abeyance, to resume their places in the two branches of the national legislature, and thereby complete the work of restoration. Here it is for you, fellow-citizens of the Senate, and for you, fellow-citizens of the House of Representatives, to judge, each of you for yourselves, of the elections, returns, and qualifications of your own members.

The full assertion of the powers of the General Government requires the holding of circuit courts of the United States within the districts where their authority has been interrupted. In the present posture of our public affairs, strong objections have been urged to holding those courts in any of the States where the rebellion has existed; and it was ascertained, by inquiry, that the circuit court of the United States would not be held within the district of Virginia during the autumn or early winter, nor until Congress should have "an opportunity to consider and act on the whole subject." To your deliberations the restoration of this branch of the civil authority of the United States is therefore necessarily referred, with the hope that early provision will be made for the resumption of all its functions. It is manifest that treason, most flagrant in character, has been committed. Persons who are charged with its commission should have fair and impartial trials in the highest civil tribunals of the country, in order that the Constitution and the laws may be fully vindicated; the truth clearly established and affirmed that treason is a crime, that traitors should be punished and the offence made infamous; and, at the same time, that the question be judicially settled, finally and forever, that no State of its own will has the right to renounce its place in the Union.

The relations of the General Government towards the four millions of inhabitants whom the war has called into freedom have engaged my most serious consideration. On the propriety of attempting to make the freedmen electors by the proclamation of the Executive, I took for my counsel the Constitution itself, the interpretations of that instrument by its authors and their contemporaries, and recent legislation by Congress. When, at the first movement towards independence, the Congress of the United States instructed the several States to institute governments of their own, they left each State to decide for itself the conditions for the enjoyment of the elective franchise. During the period of the confederacy, there continued to exist a very great diversity in the qualifications of electors in the several States; and even within a State a distinction of qualification prevailed with regard to the officers who were to be chosen. The Constitution of the United States recognises the diversities when it enjoins that, in the choice of members of the House of Representatives of the United States, "the electors in each State shall have the qualifications requisite for electors of the most numerous branch of the State legislature." After the formation of the Constitution, it remained, as before, the uniform usage for each State to enlarge the body of its electors, according to its own judgment; and, under this system, one State after another has proceeded to increase the number of its electors, until now universal suffrage, or something very near it, is the general rule. So fixed was this reservation of power in the habits of the people, and so unquestioned has been the interpretation of the Constitution, that during the civil war the late President never harbored the purpose—certainly never avowed the purpose—of disregarding it; and in the acts of Congress, during that period, nothing can be found which during the continuance of hostilities, much less after their close, would have sanctioned any departure by the Executive from a policy which has so uniformly obtained. Moreover, a concession of the elective franchise to the freedmen, by act of the President of the United States, must have been extended to all colored men, wherever found, and so must have established a change of suffrage in the Northern, Middle, and Western States, not less than in the

Southern and Southwestern. Such an act would have created a new class of voters, and would have been an assumption of power by the President which nothing in the Constitution or laws of the United States would have warranted.

On the other hand, every danger of conflict is avoided when the settlement of the question is referred to the several States. They can, each for itself, decide on the measure, and whether it is to be adopted at once and absolutely, or introduced gradually and with conditions. In my judgment, the freedmen, if they show patience and manly virtues, will sooner obtain a participation in the elective franchise through the States than through the General Government, even if it had power to intervene. When the tumult of emotions that have been raised by the suddenness of the social change shall have subsided, it may prove that they will receive the kindliest usage from some of those on whom they have heretofore most closely depended.

But while I have no doubt that now, after the close of the war, it is not competent for the General Government to extend the elective franchise in the several States, it is equally clear that good faith requires the security of the freedmen in their liberty and in their property, their right to labor, and their right to claim the just return of their labor. I cannot too strongly urge a dispassionate treatment of this subject, which should be carefully kept aloof from all party strife. We must equally avoid hasty assumptions of any natural impossibility for the two races to live side by side, in a state of mutual benefit and good will. The experiment involves us in no inconsistency; let us, then, go on and make that experiment in good faith, and not be too easily disheartened. The country is in need of labor, and the freedmen are in need of employment, culture, and protection. While their right of voluntary migration and expatriation is not to be questioned, I would not advise their forced removal and colonization. Let us rather encourage them to honorable and useful industry, where it may be beneficial to themselves and to the country; and, instead of hasty anticipations of the certainty of failure, let there be nothing wanting to the fair trial of the experiment. The change in their condition is the substitution of labor by contract for the status of slavery. The freedman cannot fairly be accused of unwillingness to work, so long as a doubt remains about his freedom of choice in his pursuits, and the certainty of his recovering his stipulated wages. In this the interests of the employer and the employed coincide. The employer desires in his workmen spirit and alacrity, and these can be permanently secured in no other way. And if the one ought to be able to enforce the contract, so ought the other. The public interest will be best promoted if the several States will provide adequate protection and remedies for the freedmen. Until this is in some way accomplished, there is no chance for the advantageous use of their labor; and the blame of ill success will not rest on them.

I know that sincere philanthropy is earnest for the immediate realization of its remotest aims; but time is always an element in reform. It is one of the greatest acts on record to have brought four millions of people into freedom.

The career of free industry must be fairly opened to them: and then their future prosperity and condition must, after all, rest mainly on themselves. If they fail, and so perish away, let us be careful that the failure shall not be attributable to any denial of justice. In all that relates to the destiny of the freedmen, we need not be too anxious to read the future; many incidents which, from a speculative point of view, might raise alarm, will quietly settle themselves.

Now that slavery is at an end or near its end, the greatness of its evil, in the point of view of public economy, becomes more and more apparent. Slavery was essentially a monopoly of labor, and as such locked the States where it prevailed against the incoming of free industry. Where labor was the property of the capitalist, the white man was excluded from employment, or had but the second best chance of finding it; and the foreign emigrant turned away from the region where his condition would be so precarious. With the destruction of the monopoly, free labor will hasten from all parts of the civilized world to assist in developing various and immeasurable resources which have hitherto lain dormant. The eight or nine States nearest the Gulf of Mexico have a soil of exuberant fertility, a climate friendly to long life, and can sustain a denser population than is found as yet in any part of our country. And the future influx of population to them will be mainly from the North, or from the most cultivated nations in Europe. From the sufferings that have attended them during our late struggle, let us look away to the future, which is sure to be laden for them with greater prosperity than has ever before been known. The removal of the monopoly of slave labor is a pledge that those regions will be peopled by a numerous and enterprising population, which will vie with any in the Union in compactness, inventive genius, wealth, and industry.

### Message on the late Insurrectionary States.

*To the Senate of the United States:*

In reply to the resolution adopted by the Senate on the 12th instant, I have the honor to state that the rebellion waged by a portion of the people against the properly-constituted authorities of the Government of the United States has been suppressed; that the United States are in possession of every State in which the insurrection existed; and that, as far as could be done, the courts of the United States have been restored, post offices re-established, and steps taken to put into effective operation the revenue laws of the country.

As the result of the measures instituted by the Executive, with the view of inducing a resumption of the functions of the States comprehended in the inquiry of the Senate, the people in North Carolina, South Carolina, Georgia, Alabama, Mississippi, Louisiana, Arkansas, and Tennessee, have reorganized their respective State governments, and "are yielding obedience to the laws and Government of the United States" with more willingness and greater promptitude than under the circumstances could reasonably have been anticipated. The proposed amendment to the Constitution, providing for the abolition of slavery forever within the limits of the country, has been ratified by each one of those States, with the exception of Mississippi, from which no official information has yet been received; and in nearly all of them measures have been adopted or are now pending, to confer upon freedmen rights and privileges which are essential to their comfort, protection, and security. In Florida and Texas the people are making commendable progress in restoring their State governments, and no doubt is entertained that they will at an early period be in a condition to resume all of their practical relations to the Federal Government.

In "that portion of the Union lately in rebellion" the aspect of affairs is more promising than, in view of all the circumstances, could well have been expected. The people throughout the entire South evince a laudable desire to renew their allegiance to the Government, and to repair the devastations of war by a prompt and cheerful return to peaceful pursuits. An abiding faith is entertained that their actions will conform to their professions, and that, in acknowledging the supremacy of the Constitution and the laws of the United States, their loyalty will be unreservedly given to the Government, whose leniency they cannot fail to appreciate, and whose fostering care will soon restore them to a condition of prosperity.

It is true that in some of the States the demoralizing effects of the war are to be seen in occasional disorders; but these are local in character, not frequent in occurrence, and are rapidly disappearing as the authority of civil law is extended and sustained. Perplexing questions were naturally to be expected from the great and sudden change in the relations between the two races; but systems are gradually devoloping themselves under which the freedman will receive the protection to which he is justly entitled, and by means of his labor make himself a useful and independent member of the community in which he has his home. From all the information in my possession, and from that which I have recently derived from the most reliable authority, I am induced to cherish the belief that sectional animosity is surely and rapidly merging itself into a spirit of nationality, and that representation, connected with a properly-adjusted system of taxation, will result in a harmonious restoration of the relations of the States to the national Union.

The report of Carl Schurz is herewith transmitted, as requested by the Senate. No reports from Hon. John Covode have been received by the President. The attention of the Senate is invited to the accompanying report of Lieutenant General Grant, who recently made a tour of inspection through several of the States whose inhabitants participated in the rebellion.

ANDREW JOHNSON.

WASHINGTON, D. C., *December* 18, 1865.

---

### Accompanying Report of General Grant.

HEADQUARTERS ARMIES OF THE U. S.,
WASHINGTON, D. C., *December* 18, 1865.

SIR: In reply to your note of the 16th inst., requesting a report from me giving such information as I may be possessed of, coming within the scope of the inquiries made by the Senate of the United States in their resolution of the 12th instant, I have the honor to submit the following:

With your approval, and also that of the honorable Secretary of War, I left Washington city on the 27th of last month for the purpose of making a tour of inspection through some of the Southern States, or States lately in rebellion, and to see what changes were necessary to be made in the disposition of the military forces of the country; how these forces could be reduced and expenses curtailed, &c.; and to learn, as far as possible, the feelings and intentions of the citizens of those States toward the General Government.

The State of Virginia being so accessible to Washington city, and information from this quarter therefore being readily obtained, I hastened through the State without conversing or meeting with any of its citizens. In Raleigh, North Carolina, I spent one day; in Charleston, South Carolina, two days; Savannah and Augusta, Georgia, each one day. Both in traveling and while stopping, I saw much and conversed freely with the citizens of those States, as well as with officers of the army who have been stationed among them. The following are the conclusions come to by me:

I am satisfied that the mass of thinking men of the South accept the present situation of affairs in good faith. The questions which have heretofore divided the sentiments of the people of the two sections—slavery and States rights, or the right of a State to secede from the Union —they regard as having been settled forever by the highest tribunal—arms—that man can resort to. I was pleased to learn from the leading men whom I met, that they not only accepted the decision arrived at as final, but, now that the smoke of battle has cleared away and time has been given for reflection, that this decision has been a fortunate one for the whole country, they receiving like benefits from it with those who opposed them in the field and in council.

Four years of war, during which law was executed only at the point of the bayonet throughout the States in rebellion, have left the people possibly in a condition not to yield that ready obedience to civil authority the American people have generally been in the habit of yielding. This would render the presence of small garrisons throughout those States necessary until such time as labor returns to its proper channels, and civil authority is fully established. I did not meet any one, either those holding places under the Government or citizens of the Southern States, who think it practicable to withdraw the military from the South at present. The white and the black mutually require the protection of the General Government.

There is such universal acquiescence in the authority of the General Government throughout the portions of the country visited by me, that the mere presence of a military force, without regard to numbers, is sufficient to maintain order. The good of the country and economy require that the force kept in the interior, where there are many freedmen, (elsewhere in the Southern States than at forts upon the sea-coast no force is necessary,) should all be white troops. The reasons for this are obvious without mentioning many of them. The presence of black troops, lately slaves, demoralizes labor both by their advice and by furnishing in their camps a resort for the freedmen for long distances around. White troops generally excite no opposition, and therefore a small number of them can maintain order in a given district. Colored troops must be kept in bodies sufficient to defend themselves. It is not the thinking men who would use violence toward any class of troops sent among them by the General Government, but the ignorant in some cases might, and the late slave seems to be imbued with the idea that the property of his late master should by right belong to him, or at least should have no protection from the colored soldier. There is danger of collisions being brought on by such causes.

My observations lead me to the conclusion that the citizens of the Southern States are anxious to return to self-government within the Union as soon as possible; that while reconstructing, they want and require protection from the Government; that they are in earnest in wishing to do what they think is required by the Government, not humiliating to them as citizens, and that if such a course was pointed out they would pursue it in good faith. It is to be regretted that there cannot be a greater commingling at this time between the citizens of the two sections, and particularly of those intrusted with the law-making power.

I did not give the operations of the Freedmen's Bureau that attention I would have done if more time had been at my disposal. Conversations on the subject, however, with officers connected with the bureau lead me to think that in some of the States its affairs have not been conducted with good judgment or economy, and that the belief, widely spread among the freedmen of the Southern States, that the lands of their former owners will, at least in part, be divided among them, has come from the agents of this bureau. This belief is seriously interfering with the willingness of the freedmen to make contracts for the coming year. In some form the Freedmen's Bureau is an absolute necessity until civil law is established and enforced, securing to the freedmen their rights and full protection. At present, however, it is independent of the military establishment of the country, and seems to be operated by the different agents of the bureau according to their individual notions. Everywhere General Howard, the able head of the bureau, made friends by the just and fair instructions and advice he gave; but the complaint in South Carolina was, that when he left things went on as before. Many, perhaps the majority, of the agents of the Freedmen's Bureau advise the freedmen that by their own industry they must expect to live. To this end they endeavor to secure employment for them, and to see that both contracting parties comply with their engagements. In some instances, I am sorry to say, the freedman's mind does not seem to be disabused of the idea that a freedman has the right to live without care or provision for the future. The effect of the belief in division of lands is idleness and accumulation in camps,

towns, and cities. In such cases I think it will be found that vice and disease will tend to the extermination, or great reduction of the colored race. It cannot be expected that the opinions held by men at the South for years can be changed in a day; and therefore the freedmen require for a few years not only laws to protect them, but the fostering care of those who will give them good counsel, and in whom they can rely.

The Freedmen's Bureau, being separated from the military establishment of the country, requires all the expense of a separate organization. One does not necessarily know what the other is doing, or what orders they are acting under. It seems to me this could be corrected by regarding every officer on duty with troops in the Southern States as agents of the Freedmen's Bureau, and then have all orders from the head of the bureau sent through department commanders. This would create a responsibility that would secure uniformity of action throughout all the South; would insure the orders and instructions from the head of the bureau being carried out; and would relieve from duty and pay a large number of employés of the Government.

I have the honor to be, very respectfully, your obedient servant, U. S. GRANT,
Lieutenant General.

His Excellency A. JOHNSON,
· President of the United States.

### Veto of the Freedmen's Bureau Bill, February 19, 1866.

*To the Senate of the United States:*

I have examined with care the bill which originated in the Senate, and has been passed by the two Houses of Congress, to amend an act entitled "An act to establish a Bureau for the relief of Freedmen and Refugees," and for other purposes. Having, with much regret, come to the conclusion that it would not be consistent with the public welfare to give my approval to the measure, I return the bill to the Senate with my objections to its becoming a law.

I might call to mind, in advance of these objections, that there is no immediate necessity for the proposed measure. The act to establish a bureau for the relief of freedmen and refugees, which was approved in the month of March last, has not yet expired. It was thought stringent and extensive enough for the purpose in view in time of war. Before it ceases to have effect, further experience may assist to guide us to a wise conclusion as to the policy to be adopted in time of peace.

I share with Congress the strongest desire to secure to the freedmen the full enjoyment of their freedom and property, and their entire independence and equality in making contracts for their labor; but the bill before me contains provisions which, in my opinion, are not warranted by the Constitution, and are not well suited to accomplish the end in view.

The bill proposes to establish, by authority of Congress, military jurisdiction over all parts of the United States containing refugees and freedmen. It would, by its very nature, apply with most force to those parts of the United States in which the freedmen most abound; and it expressly extends the existing temporary jurisdiction of the freedmen's bureau, with greatly enlarged powers, over those States "in which the ordinary course of judicial proceedings has been interrupted by the rebellion." The source from which this military jurisdiction is to emanate is none other than the President of the United States, acting through the War Department and the Commissioner of the Freedmen's Bureau. The agents to carry out this military jurisdiction are to be selected either from the army or from civil life; the country is to be divided into districts and sub-districts, and the number of salaried agents to be employed may be equal to the number of counties or parishes in all the United States where freedmen and refugees are to be found.

The subjects over which this military jurisdiction is to extend in every part of the United States include protection to "all employés, agents, and officers of this bureau in the exercise of the duties imposed" upon them by the bill. In eleven States it is further to extend over all cases affecting freedmen and refugees discriminated against "by local law, custom, or prejudice." In those eleven States, the bill subjects any white person who may be charged with depriving a freedman of "any civil rights or immunities belonging to white persons" to imprisonment or fine, or both, without, however, defining the "civil rights and immunities" which are thus to be secured to the freedmen by military law. This military jurisdiction also extends to all questions that may arise respecting contracts. The agent who is thus to exercise the office of a military judge may be a stranger, entirely ignorant of the laws of the place, and exposed to the errors of judgment to which all men are liable. The exercise of power, over which there is no legal supervision, by so vast a number of agents as is contemplated by the bill, must, by the very nature of man, be attended by acts of caprice, injustice, and passion.

The trials, having their origin under this bill, are to take place without the intervention of a jury, and without any fixed rules of law or evidence. The rules on which offences are to be "heard and determined" by the numerous agents are such rules and regulations as the President, through the War Department, shall prescribe. No previous presentment is required, nor any indictment charging the commission of a crime against the laws; but the trial must proceed on charges and specifications. The punishment will be—not what the law declares, but such as a court-martial may think proper; and from these arbitrary tribunals there lies no appeal, no writ of error to any of the courts in which the Constitution of the United States vests exclusively the judicial power of the country.

While the territory and the classes of actions and offences that are made subject to the measure are so extensive, the bill itself, should it become a law, will have no limitation in point of time, but will form a part of the permanent legislation of the country. I cannot reconcile a system of military jurisdiction of this kind with the words of the Constitution, which declare that "no person shall be held to answer for a capital or otherwise infamous crime unless upon a presentment or indictment of a grand jury, except in cases arising in the land and naval forces, or in the militia when in actual service in time of war or public danger;" and that "in all criminal prosecutions the accused shall enjoy the right to a speedy and public trial, by an impartial jury of the State or district wherein the crime shall have been committed." The safeguards which the experience and wisdom of ages taught our fathers to establish as securities for the protection of the innocent, the punishment of the guilty, and the equal administration of justice, are to be set aside, and, for the sake of a more vigorous interposition in behalf of justice, we are to take the risks of the many acts of injustice that would necessarily follow from an almost countless number of agents, established in every parish or county, in nearly a third of the States of the Union, over whose decisions there is to be no supervision or control by the federal courts. The power that would be thus placed in the hands of the President is such as in time of peace certainly ought never to be intrusted to any one man.

If it be asked whether the creation of such a tribunal within a State is warranted as a measure of war, the question immediately presents itself whether we are still engaged in war. Let us not unnecessarily disturb the commerce, and credit, and industry of the country, by declaring to the American people and to the world that the United States are still in a condition of civil war. At present there is no part of our country in which the authority of the United States is disputed. Offences that may be committed by individuals should not work a forfeiture of the rights of whole communities. The country has returned or is returning to a state of peace and industry, and the rebellion is, in fact, at an end. The measure, therefore, seems to be as inconsistent with the actual condition of the country as it is at variance with the Constitution of the United States.

If, passing from general considerations, we examine the bill in detail, it is open to weighty objections.

In time of war it was eminently proper that we should provide for those who were passing suddenly from a condition of bondage to a state of freedom.* But this bill proposes to make the

---

*I have obtained from an official source the following statement, not of the number of persons relieved, but of the number of rations issued by the Freedmen's Bureau, in each State, from June 1, 1865, to April 1, 1866—ten months:

| | Refugees. | Freedmen. | Total. |
|---|---|---|---|
| Virginia | 4,635 | 1,676,127 | 1,680,762 |
| North Carolina | 4,474 | 902,776 | 907,450 |
| South Carolina and Georgia | 24,974 | 861,653 | 886,627 |
| Alabama | 879,353 | 364,215 | 1,243,568 |
| Louisiana | 4,330 | 296,431 | 300,761 |
| Texas | 166 | 3,521 | 3,687 |
| Mississippi | 33,489 | 308,391 | 341,880 |
| Arkansas | 1,004,862 | 715,572 | 1,720,434 |
| Kentucky and Tennessee | 87,180 | 306,960 | 394,140 |
| District of Columbia | 3,834 | 440,626 | 444,460 |
| | 2,047,297 | 5,876,272 | 7,923,569 |

Total number of rations issued to freedmen for ten months............................................. 5,876,272
Total number of rations issued to refugees......... 2,047,297

Total number of rations issued to whites and blacks *for ten months*, from June 1, 1865, to April 1, 1866............ ................................. 7,923,569

Freedmen's Bureau, established by the act of 1865, as one of many great and extraordinary military measures to suppress a formidable rebellion, a permanent branch of the public administration, with its powers greatly enlarged. I have no reason to suppose, and I do not understand it to be alleged, that the act of March, 1865, has proved deficient for the purpose for which it was passed, although at that time, and for a considerable period thereafter, the Government of the United States remained unacknowledged in most of the States whose inhabitants had been involved in the rebellion. The institution of slavery, for the military destruction of which the Freedmen's Bureau was called into existence as an auxiliary, has been already effectually and finally abrogated throughout the whole country by an amendment of the Constitution of the United States, and practically its eradication has received the assent and concurrence of most of those States in which it at any time had an existence. I am not, therefore, able to discern in the condition of the country anything to justify an apprehension that the powers and agencies of the Freedmen's Bureau, which were effective for the protection of freedmen and refugees during the actual continuance of hostilities and of African servitude, will now, in a time of peace, and after the abolition of slavery, prove inadequate to the same proper ends. If I am correct in these views there can be no necessity for the enlargement of the powers of the bureau for which provision is made in the bill.

The third section of the bill authorizes a general and unlimited grant of support to the destitute and suffering refugees and freedmen, their wives and children. Succeeding sections make provision for the rent or purchase of landed estates for freedmen, and for the erection for their benefit of suitable buildings for asylums and schools—the expenses to be defrayed from the treasury of the whole people. The Congress of the United States has never heretofore thought itself empowered to establish asylums beyond the limits of the District of Columbia, except for the benefit of our disabled soldiers and sailors. It has never founded schools for any class of our own people; not even for the orphans of those who have fallen in the defence of the Union, but has left the care of education to the much more competent and efficient control of the States, of communities, of private associations, and of individuals. It has never deemed itself authorized to expend the public money for the rent or purchase of homes for the thousands, not to say millions, of the white race who are honestly toiling from day to day for their subsistence. A system for the support of indigent persons in the United States was never contemplated by the authors of the Constitution; nor can any good reason be advanced why, as a permanent establishment, it should be founded for one class or color of our people more than another. Pending the war many refugees and freedmen received support from the Government, but it was never intended that they should thenceforth be fed, clothed, educated, and sheltered by the United States. The idea on which the slaves were assisted to freedom was, that on becoming free they would be a self-sustaining population. Any legislation that shall imply that they are not expected to attain a self-sustaining condition must have a tendency injurious alike to their character and their prospects.

The appointment of an agent for every county and parish will create an immense patronage; and the expense of the numerous officers and their clerks, to be appointed by the President, will be great in the beginning, with a tendency steadily to increase. The appropriations asked by the Freedmen's Bureau, as now established for the year 1866, amount to $11,745,000 It may be safely estimated that the cost to be incurred under the pending bill will require double that amount—more than the entire sum expended in any one year under the administration of the second Adams. If the presence of agents in every parish and county is to be considered as a war measure, opposition, or even resistance, might be provoked; so that, to give effect to their jurisdiction, troops would have to be stationed within reach of every one of them, and thus a large standing force be rendered necessary. Large appropriations would, therefore, be required to sustain and enforce military jurisdiction in every county or parish from the Potomac to the Rio Grande. The condition of our fiscal affairs is encouraging; but, in order to sustain the present measure of public confidence, it is necessary that we practice, not merely customary economy, but, as far as possible, severe retrenchment.

In addition to the objections already stated, the fifth section of the bill proposes to take away land from its former owners without any legal proceedings being first had, contrary to that provision of the Constitution which declares that no person shall "be deprived of life, liberty, or property without due process of law." It does not appear that a part of the lands to which this section refers may not be owned by minors, or persons of unsound mind, or by those who have been faithful to all their obligations as citizens of the United States. If any portion of the land is held by such persons, it is not competent for any authority to deprive them of it. If, on the other hand, it be found that the property is liable to confiscation, even then it cannot be appropriated to public purposes until, by due process of law, it shall have been declared forfeited to the Government.

There is still further objection to the bill on grounds seriously affecting the class of persons to whom it is designed to bring relief. It will tend to keep the mind of the freedman in a state of uncertain expectation and restlessness, while to those among whom he lives it will be a source of constant and vague apprehension.

Undoubtedly the freedman should be protected, but he should be protected by the civil authorities, especially by the exercise of all the constitutional powers of the courts of the United States and of the States. His condition is not so exposed as may at first be imagined. He is in a portion of the country where his labor cannot well be spared. Competition for his services from planters, from those who are constructing or repairing railroads, and from capitalists in his vicinage, or from other States, will enable him to command almost his own terms. He also possesses a perfect right to change his place of abode; and if, therefore, he does not find in one community or State a mode of life suited to his desires, or proper remuneration for his labor, he can move to another, where that labor is more esteemed and better rewarded. In truth, however, each State, induced by its own wants and interests, will do what is necessary and proper to retain within its borders all the labor that is needed for the development of its resources. The laws that regulate supply and demand will maintain their force, and the wages of the laborer will be regulated thereby. There is no danger that the exceedingly great demand for labor will not operate in favor of the laborer.

Neither is sufficient consideration given to the ability of the freedmen to protect and take care of themselves. It is no more than justice to them to believe that as they have received their freedom with moderation and forbearance, so they will distinguish themselves by their industry and thrift, and soon show the world that in a condition of freedom they are self-sustaining, capable of selecting their own employment and their own places of abode, of insisting for themselves on a proper remuneration, and of establishing and maintaining their own asylums and schools. It is earnestly hoped that, instead of wasting away, they will, by their own efforts, establish for themselves a condition of respectability and prosperity. It is certain that they can attain to that condition only through their own merits and exertions.

In this connexion the query presents itself whether the system proposed by the bill will not, when put into complete operation, practically transfer the entire care, support, and control of four millions of emancipated slaves to agents, overseers, or task-masters, who, appointed at Washington, are to be located in every county and parish throughout the United States containing freedmen and refugees? Such a system would inevitably tend to a concentration of power in the Executive, which would enable him, if so disposed, to control the action of this numerous class, and use them for the attainment of his own political ends.

I cannot but add another very grave objection to this bill. The Constitution imperatively declares, in connection with taxation, that each State SHALL have at least one Representative, and fixes the rule for the number to which, in future times, each State shall be entitled. It also provides that the Senate of the United States SHALL be composed of two Senators from each State; and adds, with peculiar force, "that no State, without its consent, shall be deprived of its equal suffrage in the Senate." The original act was necessarily passed in the absence of the States chiefly to be affected, because their people were then contumaciously engaged in the rebellion. Now the case is changed, and some, at least, of those States are attending Congress by loyal representatives, soliciting the allowance of the constitutional right of representation. At the time, however, of the consideration and the passage of this bill, there was no Senator or Representative in Congress from the eleven States which are to be mainly affected by its provisions. The very fact that reports were and are made against the good disposition

of the people of that portion of the country is an additional reason why they need, and should have, Representatives of their own in Congress, to explain their condition, reply to accusations, and assist, by their local knowledge, in the perfecting of measures immediately affecting themselves. While the liberty of deliberation would then be free, and Congress would have full power to decide according to its judgment, there could be no objection urged that the States most interested had not been permitted to be heard. The principle is firmly fixed in the minds of the American people, that there should be no taxation without representation. Great burdens have now to be borne by all the country, and we may best demand that they shall be borne without murmur when they are voted by a majority of the representatives of all the people. I would not interfere with the unquestionable right of Congress to judge, each house for itself, "of the elections, returns, and qualifications of its own members." But that authority cannot be construed as including the right to shut out, in time of peace, any State from the representation to which it is entitled by the Constitution. At present all the people of eleven States are excluded—those who were most faithful during the war not less than others. The State of Tennessee, for instance, whose authorities engaged in rebellion, was restored to all her constitutional relations to the Union by the patriotism and energy of her injured and betrayed people. Before the war was brought to a termination they had placed themselves in relations with the General Government, had established a State government of their own, and, as they were not included in the emancipation proclamation, they, by their own act, had amended their constitution so as to abolish slavery within the limits of their State. I know no reason why the State of Tennessee, for example, should not fully enjoy "all her constitutional relations to the United States."

The President of the United States stands towards the country in a somewhat different attitude from that of any member of Congress. Each member of Congress is chosen from a single district or State; the President is chosen by the people of all the States. As eleven States are not at this time represented in either branch of Congress, it would seem to be his duty, on all proper occasions, to present their just claims to Congress. There always will be differences of opinion in the community, and individuals may be guilty of transgressions of the law, but these do not constitute valid objections against the right of a State to representation. I would in nowise interfere with the discretion of Congress with regard to the qualifications of members; but I hold it my duty to recommend to you, in the interests of peace and in the interests of Union, the admission of every State to its share in public legislation, when, however insubordinate, insurgent, or rebellious its people may have been, it presents itself not only in an attitude of loyalty and harmony, but in the persons of representatives whose loyalty cannot be questioned under any existing constitutional or legal test. It is plain that an indefinite or permanent exclusion of any part of the country from representation must be attended by a spirit of disquiet and complaint. It is unwise and dangerous to pursue a course of measures which will unite a very large section of the country against another section of the country, however much the latter may preponderate. The course of emigration, the development of industry and business, and natural causes, will raise up at the South men as devoted to the Union as those of any other part of the land. But if they are all excluded from Congress; if, in a permanent statute, they are declared not to be in full constitutional relations to the country, they may think they have cause to become a unit in feeling and sentiment against the Government. Under the political education of the American people, the idea is inherent and and ineradicable, that the consent of the majority of the whole people is necessary to secure a willing acquiescence in legislation.

The bill under consideration refers to certain of the States as though they had not "been fully restored in all their constitutional relations to the United States." If they have not, let us at once act together to secure that desirable end at the earliest possible moment. It is hardly necessary for me to inform Congress that, in my own judgment, most of those States, so far, at least, as depends upon their own action, have already been fully restored, and are to be deemed as entitled to enjoy their constitutional rights as members of the Union.* Reasoning from the

*In response to this suggestion, this action took place in Congress:

## When Representatives shall be Admitted from States declared in Insurrection.

### IN HOUSE.

February 20, 1866—Mr. Stevens, from the Committee on Reconstruction, reported this concurrent resolution:

*Resolved by the House of Representatives,* (the Senate concurring,) That, in order to close agitation upon a question which seems likely to disturb the action of the Government, as well as to quiet the uncertainty which is agitating the minds of the people of the eleven States which have been declared to be in insurrection, no Senator or Representative shall be admitted into either branch of Congress from any of said States until Congress shall have declared such State entitled to such representation.

Which was agreed to—yeas 109, nays 40, as follow:

YEAS—Messrs. Allison, Anderson, James M. Ashley, Baker, Baldwin, Banks, Baxter, Beaman, Benjamin, Bidwell, Bingham, Blaine, Boutwell, Brandegee, Bromwell, Broomall, Buckland, Sidney Clarke, Cobb, Conkling, Cook, Cullom, Dawes, Defrees, Deming, Donnelly, Driggs, Eckley, Eggleston, Eliot, Farnsworth, Farquhar, Ferry, Garfield, Grinnell, Griswold, Abner C. Harding, Hart, Hayes, Henderson, Higby, Holmes, Hooper, Hotchkiss, Asahel W. Hubbard, Chester D. Hubbard, Demas Hubbard, jr., John H. Hubbard, James R. Hubbell, Hulburd, Ingersoll, Jenckes, Julian, Kelley, Kelso, Ketcham, Laflin, George V. Lawrence, William Lawrence, Loan, Longyear, Lynch, Marston, McClurg, McIndoe, McKee, McRuer, Mercur, Moorhead, Morrill, Morris, Moulton, Myers, O'Neill, Orth, Paine, Patterson, Perham, Pike, Plants, Pomeroy, Price, William H. Randall, John H. Rice, Sawyer, Schenck, Scofield, Shellabarger, Sloan, Spalding, Starr, Stevens, Thayer, John L. Thomas, jr., Trowbridge, Upson, Van Aernam, Burt Van Horn, Ward, Warner, Ellihu B. Washburne, William B. Washburn, Welker, Wentworth, Williams, James F. Wilson, Stephen F. Wilson, Windom, Woodbridge—109.

Constitution itself, and from the actual situation of the country, I feel not only entitled, but bound to assume that, with the federal courts restored, and those of the several States in the full exercise of their functions, the rights and interests of all classes of the people will, with the aid of the military in cases of resistance to the laws, be essentially protected against unconstitutional infringement or violation. Should this expectation unhappily fail, which I do not anticipate, then the Executive is already fully armed with the powers conferred by the act of March, 1865, establishing the Freedmen's Bureau, and hereafter, as heretofore, he can employ the land and naval forces of the country to suppress insurrection or to overcome obstructions to the laws.

In accordance with the Constitution I return the bill to the Senate, in the earnest hope that a measure involving questions and interests so important to the country will not become a law, unless, upon deliberate consideration by the people, it shall receive the sanction of an enlightened public judgment.                   ANDREW JOHNSON.

WASHINGTON, *February* 19, 1866.

### Copy of the Bill Vetoed.

AN ACT to amend an act entitled "An act to establish a Bureau for the relief of Freedmen and Refugees," and for other purposes.

*Be it enacted, &c.,* That the act to establish a

NAYS—Messrs. *Bergen, Boyer, Brooks, Chanler, Coffroth, Dawson, Eldridge, Finck, Glossbrenner, Goodyear, Grider,* Hale, *Aaron Harding, Hogan, Humphrey, Kerr,* Latham, *Marshall, McCullough,* Newell, *Niblack, Nicholson,* Phelps, *Radford, Samuel J. Randall,* Raymond, *Ritter, Rogers, Ross,* Rousseau, *Shanklin, Sitgreaves,* Smith, *Taber, Taylor, Thornton, Trimble, Voorhees,* Whaley, *Wright*—40.

February 21—A motion to reconsider the above vote having been entered, Mr. Stevens moved to lay it on the table; which was agreed to—yeas 108, nays 38, as follow:

YEAS—Messrs. Allison, Anderson, Delos R. Ashley, James M. Ashley, Baker, Baldwin, Banks, Barker, Baxter, Beaman, Benjamin, Bidwell, Bingham, Blaine, Boutwell, Brandegee, Bromwell, Broomall, Buckland, Reader W. Clarke, Cobb, Conkling, Cook, Cullom, Dawes, Defrees, Deming, Donnelly, Driggs, Dumont, Eckley, Eggleston, Eliot, Farquhar, Ferry, Garfield, Grinnell, Griswold, Abner C. Harding, Hart, Hayes, Henderson, Higby, Holmes, Hooper, Asahel W. Hubbard, Demas Hubbard, jr., John H. Hubbard, James R. Hubbell, Hulburd, Ingersoll, Jenckes, Julian, Kelley, Ketcham, Laflin, George V. Lawrence, William Lawrence, Loan, Longyear, Lynch, Marston, Marvin, McClurg, McIndoe, McRuer, Mercur, Moorhead, Morrill, Morris, Moulton, O'Neill, Orth, Paine, Perham, Pike, Plants, Pomeroy, Price, William H. Randall, Alexander H. Rice, John H. Rice, Rollins, Sawyer, Schenck, Scofield, Shellabarger, Sloan, Spalding, Starr, Stevens, Thayer, Francis Thomas, John L. Thomas, jr., Trowbridge, Upson, Van Aernam, Burt Van Horn, Ward, Warner, Ellihu B. Washburne, William B. Washburn, Welker, Wentworth, Williams, James F. Wilson, Stephen F. Wilson, Windom—108.

NAYS—Messrs. *Ancona,* Bergen, *Boyer, Brooks, Coffroth, Dawson,* Delano, *Denison, Eldridge, Finck, Glossbrenner, Goodyear, Grider,* Robert S. Hale, *Hogan, Edwin N. Hubbell, James M. Humphrey, Kerr,* Latham, *Marshall, McCullough,* Newell, *Niblack, Nicholson, Noell,* Phelps, *Radford, Ritter, Rogers, Ross,* Rousseau, *Shanklin, Sitgreaves, Strouse, Taber, Taylor, Trimble,* Whaley—38.

March 2—The SENATE passed the resolution—yeas 29, nays 18, as follow:

YEAS—Messrs. Anthony, Brown, Chandler, Clark, Conness, Cragin, Creswell, Fessenden, Foster, Grimes, Harris, Henderson, Howe, Kirkwood, Lane of Indiana, Morrill, Nye, Poland, Pomeroy, Ramsey, Sherman, Sprague, Sumner, Trumbull, Wade, Willey, Williams, Wilson, Yates—29.

NAYS—Messrs. *Buckalew, Cowan, Davis,* Dixon, Doolittle, *Guthrie, Hendricks, Johnson,* Lane of Kansas, *McDougall,* Morgan, *Nesmith,* Norton, *Riddle, Saulsbury,* Stewart, *Stockton,* Van Winkle—18.

bureau for the relief of freedmen and refugees, approved March three, eighteen hundred and sixty-five, shall continue in force until otherwise provided by law, and shall extend to refugees and freedmen in all parts of the United States; and the President may divide the section of country containing such refugees and freedmen into districts, each containing one or more States, not to exceed twelve in number, and, by and with the advice and consent of the Senate, appoint an assistant commissioner for each of said districts, who shall give like bond, receive the compensation, and perform the duties prescribed by this and the act to which this is an amendment; or said bureau may, in the discretion of the President, be placed under a commissioner and assistant commissioners, to be detailed from the army; in which event each officer so assigned to duty shall serve without increase of pay or allowances.

SEC. 2. That the commissioner, with the approval of the President, and when the same shall be necessary for the operations of the bureau, may divide each district into a number of sub-districts, not to exceed the number of counties or parishes in such district, and shall assign to each sub-district at least one agent, either a citizen, officer of the army, or enlisted man, who, if an officer, shall serve without additional compensation or allowance, and if a citizen or enlisted man, shall receive a salary of not less than five hundred dollars nor more than twelve hundred dollars annually, according to the services rendered, in full compensation for such services; and such agent shall, before entering on the duties of his office, take the oath prescribed in the first section of the act to which this is an amendment. And the commissioner may, when the same shall be necessary, assign to each assistant commissioner not exceeding three clerks, and to each of said agents one clerk, at an annual salary not exceeding one thousand dollars each, provided suitable clerks cannot be detailed from the army. And the President of the United States, through the War Department and the commissioner, shall extend military jurisdiction and protection over all employés, agents, and officers of this bureau in the exercise of the duties imposed or authorized by this act or the act to which this is additional.

SEC. 3. That the Secretary of War may direct such issues of provisions, clothing, fuel, and other supplies, including medical stores and transportation, and afford such aid, medical or otherwise, as he may deem needful for the immediate and temporary shelter and supply of destitute and suffering refugees and freedmen, their wives and children, under such rules and regulations as he may direct: *Provided*, That no person shall be deemed "destitute," "suffering," or "dependent upon the Government for support," within the meaning of this act, who, being able to find employment, could by proper industry and exertion avoid such destitution, suffering, or dependence.

SEC. 4. That the President is hereby authorized to reserve from sale, or from settlement, under the homestead or pre-emption laws, and to set apart for the use of freedmen and loyal refugees, male or female, unoccupied public lands in Florida, Mississippi, Alabama, Louisiana, and Arkansas, not exceeding in all three millions of acres of good land; and the commissioner, under the direction of the President, shall cause the same from time to time to be allotted and assigned, in parcels not exceeding forty acres each, to the loyal refugees and freedmen, who shall be protected in the use and enjoyment thereof for such term of time and at such annual rent as may be agreed on between the commissioner and such refugees or freedmen. The rental shall be based upon a valuation of the land, to be ascertained in such manner as the commissioner may, under the direction of the President, by regulation prescribe. At the end of such term, or sooner, if the commissioner shall assent thereto, the occupants of any parcels so assigned, their heirs and assigns, may purchase the land and receive a title thereto from the United States in fee, upon paying therefor the value of the land ascertained as aforesaid.

SEC. 5. That the occupants of land under Major General Sherman's special field order, dated at Savannah, January sixteen, eighteen hundred and sixty-five, are hereby confirmed in their possession for the period of three years from the date of said order, and no person shall be disturbed in or ousted from said possession during said three years, unless a settlement shall be made with said occupant, by the former owner, his heirs or assigns, satisfactory to the commissioner of the Freedmen's Bureau: *Provided*, That whenever the former owners of lands occupied under General Sherman's field order shall make application for restoration of said lands, the commissioner is hereby authorized, upon the agreement and with the written consent of said occupants, to procure other lands for them by rent or purchase, not exceeding forty acres for each occupant, upon the terms and conditions named in section four of this act, or to set apart for them, out of the public lands assigned for that purpose in section four of this act, forty acres each, upon the same terms and conditions.

SEC. 6. That the commissioner shall, under the direction of the President, procure in the name of the United States, by grant or purchase, such lands within the districts aforesaid as may be required for refugees and freedmen dependent on the Government for support; and he shall provide or cause to be erected suitable buildings for asylums and schools. But no such purchase shall be made, nor contract for the same entered into, nor other expense incurred, until after appropriations shall have been provided by Congress for such purposes. And no payment shall be made for lands purchased under this section, except for asylums and schools, from any moneys not specifically appropriated therefor. And the commissioner shall cause such lands from time to time to be valued, allotted, assigned, and sold in manner and form provided in the fourth section of this act, at a price not less than the cost thereof to the United States.

SEC. 7. That whenever in any State or district in which the ordinary course of judicial proceedings has been interrupted by the rebellion, and wherein, in consequence of any State or local law, ordinance, police or other regulation, custom, or prejudice, any of the civil rights or immunities belonging to white persons, including the right to make and enforce contracts, to sue, be parties, and give evidence, to inherit, purchase, lease, sell, hold and convey real and personal property, and to have full and equal benefit of all laws and proceedings for the security of person and estate, including the constitutional right of bearing arms, are refused or denied to negroes, mulattoes, freedmen, refugees, or any other persons, on account of race, color, or any previous condition of slavery or involuntary servitude, or wherein they or any of them are subjected to any other or different punishment, pains, or penalties, for the commission of any act or offence than are prescribed for white persons committing like acts or offences, it shall be the duty of the President of the United States, through the commissioner, to extend military protection and jurisdiction over all cases affecting such persons so discriminated against.

SEC. 8. That any person who, under color of any State or local law, ordinance, police, or other regulation or custom, shall, in any State or district in which the ordinary course of judicial proceedings has been interrupted by the rebellion, subject, or cause to be subjected, any negro, mulatto, freedman, refugee, or other person, on account of race or color, or any previous condition of slavery or involuntary servitude, or for any other cause, to the deprivation of any civil right secured to white persons, or to any other or different punishment than white persons are subject to for the commission of like acts or offences, shall be deemed guilty of a misdemeanor, and be punished by fine not exceeding one thousand dollars, or imprisonment not exceeding one year, or both; and it shall be the duty of the officers and agents of this bureau to take jurisdiction of, and hear and determine all offences committed against the provisions of this section, and also of all cases affecting negroes, mulattoes, freedmen, refugees, or other persons who are discriminated against in any of the particulars mentioned in the preceding section of this act, under such rules and regulations as the President of the United States, through the War Department, shall prescribe. The jurisdiction conferred by this and the preceding section on the officers and agents of this bureau shall cease and determine whenever the discrimination on account of which it is conferred ceases, and in no event to be exercised in any State in which the ordinary course of judicial proceedings has not been interrupted by the rebellion, nor in any such State after said State shall have been fully restored in all its constitutional relations to the United States, and the courts of the State and of the United States within the same are not disturbed or stopped in the peaceable course of justice.

SEC. 9. That all acts, or parts of acts, inconsistent with the provisions of this act, are hereby repealed.

The votes on passing this bill were:

IN SENATE.

1866, January 25—The bill passed—yeas 37, nays 10, as follow:

YEAS—Messrs. Anthony, Brown, Chandler, Clark, Conness, Cragin, Creswell, Dixon, Doolittle, Fessenden, Foot,

Foster, Grimes, Harris, Henderson, Howard, Howe, Kirkwood, Lane of Indiana, Lane of Kansas, Morgan, Morrill, Norton, Nye, Poland. Pomeroy, Ramsey, Sherman, Sprague, Stewart, Sumner, Trumbull, Van Winkle, Wade, Williams, Wilson, Yates—37.

NAYS—Messrs. *Buckalew, Davis, Guthrie, Hendricks, Johnson, McDougall, Riddle, Saulsbury, Stockton, Wright*—10.

IN HOUSE.

February 6—The bill passed—yeas 137, nays 33, as follow:

YEAS—Messrs. Alley, Allison, Ames, Anderson, Delos R. Ashley, James M. Ashley, Baker, Baldwin, Banks, Barker, Baxter, Beaman, Benjamin, Bidwell, Bingham, Blaine, Blow, Boutwell, Brandegee, Bromwell, Broomall, Bundy, Reader W. Clarke, Sidney Clarke, Cobb, Conkling, Cook, Cullom, Darling, Davis, Dawes, Defrees, Delano, Deming, Dixon, Donnelly, Driggs, Dumont, Eckley, Eggleston, Eliot, Farnsworth, Farquhar, Ferry, Garfield, Grinnell, Griswold, Hale, Abner C. Harding, Hart, Hayes, Henderson, Higby, Hill, Holmes, Hooper, Hotchkiss, Asahel W. Hubbard, Chester D. Hubbard, Demas Hubbard, John H. Hubbard, James R. Hubbell, James Humphrey, Ingersoll, Jenckes, Julian, Kasson, Kelley, Kelso, Ketcham, Kuykendall, Laflin, Latham, George V. Lawrence, William Lawrence, Loan, Longyear, Lynch, Marston, Marvin, McClurg, McIndoe, McKee, McRuer, Mercur, Miller, Moorhead, Morrill, Morris, Moulton, Myers, Newell, O'Neill, Orth, Paine, Patterson, Perham, Phelps, Pike, Plants, Pomeroy, Price, William H. Randall, Raymond, Alexander H. Rice, John H. Rice, Rollins, Sawyer, Schenck, Scofield, Shellabarger, Sloan, Smith, Spalding, Starr, Stevens, Stilwell, Thayer, Francis Thomas, John L. Thomas, Trowbridge, Upson, Van Aernam, Burt Van Horn, Robert T. Van Horn, Ward, Warner, Ellihu B. Washburne, William B. Washburn, Welker, Wentworth, Whaley, Williams, James F. Wilson, Stephen F. Wilson, Windom, Woodbridge—137.

NAYS—Messrs. *Boyer, Brooks, Chanler, Dawson, Eldridge, Finck, Glossbrenner, Grider, Aaron Harding, Harris, Hogan, Edwin N. Hubbell, James M. Humphrey, Kerr, Le Blond Marshall, McCullough, Niblack, Nicholson, Noell, Samuel J. Randall, Ritter, Rogers, Ross,* Rousseau, *Shanklin, Sitgreaves, Strouse, Taber, Taylor, Thornton, Trimble, Wright*—33.

February 21—In Senate, the vote on passing the bill, notwithstanding the objections of the President, was—yeas 30, nays 18, as follow:

YEAS—Messrs. Anthony, Brown, Chandler, Clark, Conness, Cragin, Creswell, Fessenden, Foster, Grimes, Harris, Henderson, Howard, Howe, Kirkwood, Lane of Indiana, Lane of Kansas, Morrill, Nye, Poland, Pomeroy, Ramsey, Sherman, Sprague, Sumner, Trumbull, Wade, Williams, Wilson, Yates—30.

NAYS—Messrs. *Buckalew,* Cowan, *Davis,* Dixon, Doolittle, *Guthrie, Hendricks, Johnson, McDougall,* Morgan, *Nesmith,* Norton, *Riddle, Saulsbury,* Stewart, *Stockton,* Van Winkle, Willey—18.

Two-thirds not having voted therefor, the bill failed.

**Veto of the Civil Rights Bill, March 27, 1866.**

*To the Senate of the United States:*

I regret that the bill which has passed both Houses of Congress, entitled "An act to protect all persons in the United States in their civil rights, and furnish the means of their vindication," contains provisions which I cannot approve, consistently with my sense of duty to the whole people, and my obligations to the Constitution of the United States. I am therefore constrained to return it to the Senate, the house in which it originated, with my objections to its becoming a law.

By the first section of the bill all persons born in the United States, and not subject to any foreign power, excluding Indians not taxed, are declared to be citizens of the United States. This provision comprehends the Chinese of the Pacific States, Indians subject to taxation, the people called Gipsies, as well as the entire race designated as blacks, people of color, negroes, mulattoes, and persons of African blood. Every individual of these races, born in the United

States, is by the bill made a citizen of the United States. It does not purport to declare or confer any other right of citizenship than federal citizenship. It does not purport to give these classes of persons any *status* as citizens of States, except that which may result from their *status* as citizens of the United States. The power to confer the right of State citizenship is just as exclusively with the several States as the power to confer the right of federal citizenship is with Congress.

The right of federal citizenship thus to be conferred on the several excepted races before mentioned, is now, for the first time, proposed to be given by law. If, as is claimed by many, all persons who are native-born already are, by virtue of the Constitution, citizens of the United States, the passage of the pending bill cannot be necessary to make them such. If, on the other hand, such persons are not citizens, as may be assumed from the proposed legislation to make them such, the grave question presents itself, whether, when eleven of the thirty-six States are unrepresented in Congress at the present time, it is sound policy to make our entire colored population and all other excepted classes citizens of the United States? Four millions of them have just emerged from slavery into freedom. Can it be reasonably supposed that they possess the requisite qualifications to entitle them to all the privileges and immunities of citizens of the United States? Have the people of the several States expressed such a conviction? It may also be asked whether it is necessary that they should be declared citizens, in order that they may be secured in the enjoyment of the civil rights proposed to be conferred by the bill? Those rights are, by federal as well as State laws, secured to all domiciled aliens and foreigners, even before the completion of the process of naturalization; and it may safely be assumed that the same enactments are sufficient to give them protection and benefits to those for whom this bill provides special legislation. Besides, the policy of the Government, from its origin to the present time, seems to have been that persons who are strangers to and unfamiliar with our institutions and our laws should pass through a certain probation, at the end of which, before attaining the coveted prize, they must give evidence of their fitness to receive and to exercise the rights of citizens, as contemplated by the Constitution of the United States. The bill, in effect, proposes a discrimination against large numbers of intelligent, worthy, and patriotic foreigners, and in favor of the negro, to whom, after long years of bondage, the avenues to freedom and intelligence have just now been suddenly opened. He must, of necessity, from his previous unfortunate condition of servitude, be less informed as to the nature and character of our institutions than he who, coming from abroad, has to some extent, at least, familiarized himself with the principles of a government to which he voluntarily intrusts "life, liberty, and the pursuit of happiness." Yet it is now proposed, by a single legislative enactment, to confer the rights of citizens upon all persons of African descent born within the extended limits of the United States, while persons of foreign birth, who make our

land their home, must undergo a probation of five years, and can only then become citizens upon proof that they are "of good moral character, attached to the principles of the Constitution of the United States, and well disposed to the good order and happiness of the same."

The first section of the bill also contains an enumeration of the rights to be enjoyed by these classes, so made citizens, "in every State and Territory in the United States." These rights are, "to make and enforce contracts, to sue, be parties, and give evidence; to inherit, purchase, lease, sell, hold, and convey real and personal property;" and to have "full and equal benefit of all laws and proceedings for the security of person and property as is enjoyed by white citizens." So, too, they are made subject to the same punishments, pains, and penalties in common with white citizens, and to none other. Thus a perfect equality of the white and colored races is attempted to be fixed by federal law in every State of the Union, over the vast field of State jurisdiction covered by these enumerated rights. In no one of these can any State ever exercise any power of discrimination between the different races. In the exercise of State policy over matters exclusively affecting the people of each State, it has frequently been thought expedient to discriminate between the two races. By the statutes of some of the States, northern well as southren, it is enacted, for instance, that no white person shall intermarry with a negro or mulatto. Chancellor Kent says, speaking of the blacks, that "marriages between them and the whites are forbidden in some of the States where slavery does not exist, and they are prohibited in all the slaveholding States; and when not absolutely contrary to law, they are revolting, and regarded as an offence against public decorum."

I do not say that this bill repeals State laws on the subject of marriage between the two races; for, as the whites are forbidden to intermarry with the blacks, the blacks can only make such contracts as the whites themselves are allowed to make, and therefore connot, under this bill, enter into the marriage contract with the whites. I cite this discrimination, however, as an instance of the State policy as to discrimination, and to inquire whether, if Congress can abrogate all State laws of discrimination between the two races in the matter of real estate, of suits, and of contracts generally, Congress may not also repeal the State laws as to the contract of marriage between the two races? Hitherto every subject embraced in the enumeration of rights contained in this bill has been considered as exclusively belonging to the States. They all relate to the internal police and economy of the respective States. They are matters which in each State concern the domestic condition of its people, varying in each according to its own peculiar circumstances and the safety and well-being of its own citizens. I do not mean to say that upon all these subjects there are not federal restraints—as, for instance, in the State power of legislation over contracts, there is a federal limitation that no State shall pass a law impairing the obligations of contracts; and, as to crimes, that no State shall pass an *ex post facto* law; and, as to money, that no State shall make anything but gold and silver a legal tender. But where can we find a federal prohibition against the power of any State to discriminate, as do most of them, between aliens and citizens, between artificial persons called corporations and natural persons, in the right to hold real estate? If it be granted that Congress can repeal all State laws discriminating between whites and blacks in the subjects covered by this bill, why, it may be asked, may not Congress repeal, in the same way, all State laws discriminating between the two races on the subjects of suffrage and office? If Congress can declare by law who shall hold lands, who shall testify, who shall have capacity to make a contract in a State, then Congress can by law also declare who, without regard to color or race, shall have the right to sit as a juror or as a judge, to hold any office, and, finally, to vote, "in every State and Territory of the United States." As respects the Territories, they come within the power of Congress, for as to them the law-making power is the federal power; but as to the States no similar provision exists vesting in Congress the power "to make rules and regulations" for them.

The object of the second section of the bill is to afford discriminating protection to colored persons in the full enjoyment of all the rights secured to them by the preceding section. It declares "that any person who, under color of any law, statute, ordinance, regulation, or custom, shall subject, or cause to be subjected, any inhabitant of any State or Territory to the deprivation of any right secured or protected by this act, or to different punishment, pains, or penalties, on account of such person having at any time been held in a condition of slavery or involuntary servitude, except as a punishment for crime, whereof the party shall have been duly convicted, or by reason of his color or race, than is prescribed for the punishment of white persons, shall be deemed guilty of a misdemeanor, and, on conviction, shall be punished by a fine not exceeding one thousand dollars, or imprisonment not exceeding one year, or both, in the discretion of the court." This section seems to be designed to apply to some existing or future law of a State or Territory which may conflict with the provisions of the bill now under consideration. It provides for counteracting such forbidden legislation by imposing fine and imprisonment upon the legislators who may pass such conflicting laws, or upon the officers or agents who shall put or attempt to put them into execution. It means an official offence—not a common crime committed against law upon the persons or property of the black race. Such an act may deprive the black man of his property, but not of the right to hold property. It means a deprivation of the right itself, either by the State judiciary or the State legislature. It is therefore assumed that under this section members of State legislatures who should vote for laws conflicting with the provisions of the bill, that judges of the State courts who should render judgments in antagonism with its terms, and that marshals and sheriffs who should, as ministerial officers, execute processes sanctioned by State laws and issued by State judges in execution of their judgments, could be brought before other tribunals, and there subjected to fine and imprisonment for the performance of the duties which such State laws might impose. The legislation thus proposed invades the judicial power of the State. It says to every State court or judge, if you decide that this act is unconstitutional; if you refuse, under the prohibition of a State law, to allow a negro to testify; if you hold that over such a subject-matter the State law is paramount, and "under color" of a State law refuse the exercise of the right to the negro, your error of judgment, however conscientious, shall subject you to fine and imprisonment! I do not apprehend that the conflicting legislation which the bill seems to contemplate is so likely to occur as to render it necessary at this time to adopt a measure of such doubtful constitutionality.

In the next place, this provision of the bill seems to be unnecessary, as adequate judicial remedies could be adopted to secure the desired end, without invading the immunities of legislators, always important to be preserved in the interest of public liberty; without assailing the independence of the judiciary, always essential to the preservation of individual rights; and without impairing the efficiency of ministerial officers, always necessary for the maintenance of public peace and order. The remedy proposed by this section seems to be, in this respect, not only anomalous, but unconstitutional; for the Constitution guarantees nothing with certainty if it does not insure to the several States the right of making and executing laws in regard to all matters arising within their jurisdiction, subject only to the restriction that, in cases of conflict with the Constitution and constitutional laws of the United States, the latter should be held to be the supreme law of the land.

The third section gives the district courts of the United States exclusive "cognizance of all crimes and offences committed against the provisions of this act," and concurrent jurisdiction with the circuit courts of the United States of all civil and criminal cases "affecting persons who are denied, or cannot enforce in the courts or judicial tribunals of the State or locality where they may be, any of the rights secured to them by the first section." The construction which I have given to the second section is strengthened by this third section, for it makes clear what kind of denial or deprivation of the rights secured by the first section was in contemplation. It is a denial or deprivation of such rights "in the courts or judicial tribunals of the State." It stands, therefore, clear of doubt that the offence and the penalties provided in the second section are intended for the State judge, who, in the clear exercise of his functions as a judge, not acting ministerially but judicially, shall decide contrary to this federal law. In other words, when a State judge, acting upon a question involving a conflict between a State law and a federal law, and bound, according to his own judgment and responsibility, to give an impartial decision between the two, comes to the conclusion that the State law is valid and the federal law is invalid, he must not follow the dictates of his own judgment, at the peril of fine and imprisonment. The legislative department of the Government of the United States thus takes from the judicial department of the States the sacred and exclusive duty of judicial decision, and converts the State judge into a mere ministerial officer, bound to decide according to the will of Congress.

It is clear that, in States which deny to persons whose rights are secured by the first section of the bill any one of those rights, all criminal and civil cases affecting them will, by the provisions of the third section, come under the exclusive cognizance of the federal tribunals. It follows that if, in any State which denies to a colored person any one of all those rights, that person should commit a crime against the laws of a State—murder, arson, rape, or any other crime—all protection and punishment through the courts of the State are taken away, and he can only be tried and punished in the federal courts. How is the criminal to be tried? If the offence is provided for and punished by federal law, that law, and not the State law, is to govern. It is only when the offence does not happen to be within the purview of federal law that the federal courts are to try and punish him under any other law. Then resort is to be had to the "common law, as modified and changed" by State legislation, "so far as the same is not inconsistent with the Constitution and laws of the United States." So that over this vast domain of criminal jurisprudence provided by each State for the protection of its own citizens, and for the punishment of all persons who violate its criminal laws, federal law, whenever it can be made to apply, displaces State law. The question here naturally arises, from what source Congress derives the power to transfer to federal tribunals certain classes of cases embraced in this section? The Constitution expressly declares that the judicial power of the United States "shall extend to all cases in law and equity arising under this Constitution, the laws of the United States, and treaties made, or which shall be made under their authority; to all cases affecting ambassadors, other public ministers and consuls; to all cases of admiralty and maritime jurisdiction; to controversies to which the United States shall be a party; to controversies between two or more States, between a State and citizens of another State, between citizens of different States, between citizens of the same State claiming land under grants of different States, and between a State, or the citizens thereof, and foreign States, citizens, or subjects," Here the judicial power of the United States is expressly set forth and defined; and the act of September 24, 1789, establishing the judicial courts of the United States, in conferring upon the federal courts jurisdiction over cases originating in State tribunals, is careful to confine them to the classes enumerated in the above-recited clause of the Constitution. This section of the bill undoubtedly comprehends cases and authorizes the exercise of powers that are not, by the Constitution, within the jurisdiction of the courts of the United States. To transfer them to those courts would be an exercise of authority well calculated to excite distrust and alarm on the part of all the States; for the bill applies alike to all of them—as well to those that have as to those that have not been engaged in rebellion.

It may be assumed that this authority is incident to the power granted to Congress by the Constitution, as recently amended, to enforce, by appropriate legislation, the article declaring that "neither slavery nor involuntary servitude, except as a punishment for crime whereof the party shall have been duly convicted, shall exist within the United States, or any place subject to their jurisdiction." It cannot, however, be justly claimed that, with a view to the enforcement of this article of the Constitution, there is at present any necessity for the exercise of all the powers which this bill confers. Slavery has been abolished, and at present nowhere exists within the jurisdiction of the United States; nor has there been, nor is it likely there will be, any attempt to revive it by the people or the States. If, however, any such attempt shall be made, it will then become the duty of the General Government to exercise any and all incidental powers necessary and proper to maintain inviolate this great constitutional law of freedom.

The fourth section of the bill provides that officers and agents of the Freedmen's Bureau shall be empowered to make arrests, and also that other officers may be specially commissioned for that purpose by the President of the United States. It also authorizes circuit courts of the United States and the superior courts of the Territories to appoint, without limitation, commissioners, who are to be charged with the performance of *quasi* judicial duties. The fifth section empowers the commissioners so to be selected by the courts to appoint in writing, under their hands, one or more suitable persons from time to time to execute warrants and other processes described by the bill. These numerous official agents are made to constitute a sort of police, in addition to the military, and are authorized to summon a *posse comitatus*, and even to call to their aid such portion of the land and naval forces of the United States, or of the militia, "as may be necessary to the performance of the duty with which they are charged." This extraordinary power is to be conferred upon agents irresponsible to the Government and to the people, to whose number the discretion of the commissioners is the only limit, and in whose hands such authority might be made a terrible engine of wrong, oppression, and fraud. The general statutes regulating the land and naval forces of the United States, the militia, and the execution of the laws, are believed to be adequate for every emergency which can occur in time of peace. If it should prove otherwise Congress can at any time amend those laws in such a manner as, while subserving the public welfare, not to jeopard the rights, interests, and liberties of the people.

The seventh section provides that a fee of ten dollars shall be paid to each commissioner in every case brought before him, and a fee of five dollars to his deputy, or deputies, "for each person he or they may arrest and take before any such commissioner," "with such other fees as may be deemed reasonable by such commission," "in general for performing such other duties as may be required in the premises." All these fees are to be "paid out of the Treasury of the United States," whether there is a conviction or not; but in case of conviction they are to be recoverable from the defendant. It seems to me that under the influence of such temptations bad men might convert any law, however beneficent, into an instrument of persecution and fraud.

By the eighth section of the bill the United States courts, which sit only in one place for white citizens, must migrate, with the marshal and district attorney, (and necessarily with the clerk, although he is not mentioned,) to any part of the district upon the order of the President, and there hold a court "for the purpose of the more speedy arrest and trial of persons charged with a violation of this act;" and there the judge and officers of the court must remain, upon the order of the President, "for the time therein designated."

The ninth section authorizes the President, or such person as he may empower for that purpose, "to employ such part of the land or naval forces of the United States or of the militia as shall be necessary to prevent the violation and enforce to due execution of this act." This language seems to imply a permanent military force, that is to be always at hand, and whose only business is to be the enforcement of this measure over the vast region where it is intended to operate.

I do not propose to consider the policy of this bill. To me the details of the bill seem fraught with evil. The white race and the black race of the South have hitherto lived together under the relation of master and slave—capital owning labor. Now, suddenly, that relation is changed, and, as to ownership, capital and labor are divorced. They stand now each master of itself. In this new relation, one being necessary to the other, there will be a new adjustment, which both are deeply interested in making harmonious. Each has equal power in settling the terms, and, if left to the laws that regulate capital and labor, it is confidently believed that they will satisfactorily work out the problem. Capital, it is true, has more intelligence, but labor is never so ignorant as not to understand its own interests, not to know its own value, and not to see that capital must pay that value.

This bill frustrates this adjustment. It intervenes between capital and labor, and attempts to settle questions of political economy through the agency of numerous officials, whose interest it will be to foment discord between the two races; for as the breach widens their employment will continue, and when it is closed their occupation will terminate.

In all our history, in all our experience as a people, living under federal and State law, no such system as that contemplated by the details of this bill has ever before been proposed or adopted. They establish for the security of the colored race safeguards which go infinitely beyond any that the General Government has ever provided for the white race. In fact, the distinction of race and color is, by the bill, made to operate in favor of the colored and against the white race. They interfere with the municipal legislation of the States, with the relations existing exclusively between a State and its citizens, or between inhabitants of the same

State—an absorption and assumption of power by the General Government which, if acquiesced in, must sap and destroy our federative system of limited powers, and break down the barriers which preserve the rights of the States. It is another step, or rather stride, towards centralization, and the concentration of all legislative powers in the national Government. The tendency of the bill must be to resuscitate the spirit of rebellion, and to arrest the progress of those influences which are more closely drawing around the States the bonds of union and peace.

My lamented predecessor, in his proclamation of the 1st of January, 1863, ordered and declared that all persons held as slaves within certain States and parts of States therein designated were, and thenceforward should be free, and, further, that the executive government of the United States, including the military and naval authorities thereof, would recognize and maintain the freedom of such persons. This guarantee has been rendered especially obligatory and sacred by the amendment of the Constitution abolishing slavery throughout the United States. I, therefore, fully recognize the obligation to protect and defend that class of our people, whenever and wherever it shall become necessary, and to the full extent compatible with the Constitution of the United States.

Entertaining these sentiments, it only remains for me to say, that I will cheerfully co-operate with Congress in any measure that may be necessary for the protection of the civil rights of the freedmen, as well as those of all other classes of persons throughout the United States, by judicial process, under equal and impartial laws, in conformity with the provisions of the Federal Constitution.

I now return the bill to the Senate, and regret that, in considering the bills and joint resolutions—forty-two in number—which have been thus far submitted for my approval, I am compelled to withhold my assent from a second measure that has received the sanction of both Houses of Congress.

ANDREW JOHNSON.
WASHINGTON, D. C., *March* 27, 1866.

#### Copy of the Bill Vetoed.

AN ACT to protect all persons in the United States in their civil rights, and furnish the means of their vindication.

*Be it enacted, &c.,* That all persons born in the United States and not subject to any foreign power, excluding Indians, not taxed, are hereby declared to be citizens of the United States; and such citizens of every race and color, without regard to any previous condition of slavery or involuntary servitude, except as a punishment for crime whereof the party shall have been duly convicted, shall have the same right in every State and Territory in the United States to make and enforce contracts; to sue, be parties, and give evidence; to inherit, purchase, lease, sell, hold, and convey real and personal property; and to full and equal benefit of all laws and proceedings for the security of person and property as is enjoyed by white citizens, and shall be subject to like punishment, pains, and penalties, and to none other, any law, statute ordinance, regulation, or custom, to the contrary notwithstanding.

Sec. 2. That any person who, under color of any law, statute, ordinance, regulation, or custom, shall subject, or cause to be subjected, any inhabitant of any State or Territory to the deprivation of any right secured or protected by this act, or to different punishment, pains, or penalties on account of such person having at any time been held in a condition of slavery or involuntary servitude, except as a punishment for crime whereof the party shall have been duly convicted, or by reason of his color or race, than is prescribed for the punishment of white persons, shall be deemed guilty of a misdemeanor, and, on conviction, shall be punished by fine not exceeding one thousand dollars, or imprisonment not exceeding one year, or both, in the discretion of the court.

Sec. 3. That the district courts of the United States, within their respective districts, shall have, exclusively of the courts of the several States, cognizance of all crimes and offences committed against the provisions of this act, and also, concurrently with the circuit courts of the United States, of all causes, civil and criminal, affecting persons who are denied or cannot enforce in the courts or judicial tribunals of the State or locality where they may be any of the rights secured to them by the first section of this act; and if any suit or prosecution, civil or criminal, has been or shall be commenced in any State court against any such person, for any cause whatsoever, or against any officer, civil or military, or other person, for any arrest or imprisonment, trespasses, or wrongs done or committed by virtue or under color of authority derived from this act or the act establishing a bureau for the relief of freedmen and refugees, and all acts amendatory thereof, or for refusing to do any act upon the ground that it would be inconsistent with this act, such defendant shall have the right to remove such cause for trial to the proper district or circuit court in the manner prescribed by the "Act relating to *habeas corpus* and regulating judicial proceedings in certain cases," approved March three, eighteen hundred and sixty-three, and all acts amendatory thereof. The jurisdiction in civil and criminal matters hereby conferred on the district and circuit courts of the United States shall be exercised and enforced in conformity with the laws of the United States, so far as such laws are suitable to carry the same into effect; but in all cases where such laws are not adapted to the object, or are deficient in the provisions necessary to furnish suitable remedies and punish offences against law, the common law, as modified and changed by the constitution and statutes of the State wherein the court having jurisdiction of the cause, civil or criminal, is held, so far as the same is not inconsistent with the Constitution and laws of United States, shall be extended to and govern said courts in the trial and disposition of such cause, and, if of a criminal nature, in the infliction of punishment on the party found guilty.

Sec. 4. That the district attorneys, marshals, and deputy marshals of the United States, the commissioners appointed by the circuit court and territorial courts of the United States, with powers of arresting, imprisoning, or bailing offenders against the laws of the United States, the officers and agents of the Freedmen's Bureau, and every other officer who may be specially empowered by the President of the United States, shall be, and they are hereby, specially authorized and required, at the expense of the United States, to institute proceedings against all and every person who shall violate the provisions of this act, and cause him or them to be arrested and imprisoned, or bailed, as the case may be, for trial before such court of the United States or territorial court as by this act has cognizance of the offence. And with a view to affording reasonable protection to all persons in their constitutional rights of equality before the law, without distinction of race or color, or previous condition of slavery or involuntary servitude, except as a punishment for crime, whereof the party shall have been duly convicted, and to the prompt discharge of the duties of this act, it shall be the duty of the circuit courts of the United States and the superior courts of the Territories of the United States, from time to time, to increase the number of commissioners, so as to afford a speedy and convenient means for the arrest and examination of persons charged with a violation of this act. And such commissioners are hereby authorized and required to exercise and discharge all the powers and duties conferred on them by this act, and the same duties with regard to offences created by this act, as they are authorized by law to exercise with regard to other offences against the laws of the United States.

Sec. 5. That it shall be the duty of all marshals and deputy marshals to obey and execute all warrants and precepts issued under the provisions of this act, when to them directed; and should any marshal or deputy marshal refuse to receive such warrant or other process when tendered, or to use all proper means diligently to execute the same, he shall, on conviction thereof, be fined in the sum of one thousand dollars, to the use of the person upon whom the accused is alleged to have committed the offence. And the better to enable the said commissioners to execute their duties faithfully and efficiently, in conformity with the Constitution of the United States and the requirements of this act, they are hereby authorized and empowered, within their counties respectively, to appoint, in writing, under their hands, any one or more suitable persons, from time to time, to execute all such warrants and other process that may be issued by them in the lawful performance of their respective duties; and the persons so appointed to execute any warrant or process as aforesaid shall have authority to summon and call to their aid the bystanders or the *posse comitatus* of the proper county, or such portion of the land and naval forces of the United States, or of the militia, as may be necessary to the performance of the duty with which they are charged, and to insure a faithful observance of the clause of the Constitution which prohibits slavery, in conformity with the provisions of this act; and said warrants shall run and be executed by said officers anywhere in the State or Territory within which they are issued.

Sec. 6. That any person who shall knowingly

and wilfully obstruct, hinder or prevent any officer, or other person charged with the execution of any warrant or process issued under the provisions of this act, or any person or persons lawfully assisting him or them, from arresting any person for whose apprehension such warrant or process may have been issued, or shall rescue or attempt to rescue such person from the custody of the officer, other person or persons, or those lawfully assisting as aforesaid, when so arrested pursuant to the authority herein given and declared, or shall aid, abet, or assist any person so arrested as aforesaid, directly or indirectly, to escape from the custody of the officer or other person legally authorized as aforesaid, or shall harbor or conceal any person for whose arrest a warrant or process shall have been issued as aforesaid, so as to prevent his discovery and arrest after notice or knowledge of the fact that a, warrant has been issued for the apprehension of such person, shall, for either of said offences, be subject to a fine not exceeding one thousand dollars, and imprisonment not exceeding six months, by indictment and conviction before the district court of the United States for the district in which said offence may have been committed, or before the proper court of criminal jurisdiction, if committed within any one of the organized Territories of the United States.

SEC. 7. That the district attorneys. the marshals, their deputies, and the clerks of the said district and territorial courts shall be paid for their services the like fees as may be allowed to them for similar services in other cases; and in all cases where the proceedings are before a commissioner, he shall be entitled to a fee of ten dollars in full for his services in each case, inclusive of all services incident to such arrest and examination. The person or persons authorized to execute the process to be issued by such commissioners for the arrest of offenders against the provisions of this act shall be entitled to a fee of five dollars for each person he or they may arrest and take before any such commissioner as aforesaid, with such other fees as may be deemed reasonable by such commissioner for such other additional services as may be necessarily performed by him or them, such as attending at the examination, keeping the prisoner in custody, and providing him with food and lodging during his detention, and until the final determination of such commissioner, and in general for performing such other duties as may be required in the premises; such fees to be made up in conformity with the fees usually charged by the officers of the courts of justice within the proper district or county, as near as may be practicable and paid out of the treasury of the United States on the certificate of the judge of the district within which the arrest is made, and to be recoverable from the defendant as part of the judgment in case of conviction.

SEC. 8. That whenever the President of the United States shall have reason to believe that offences have been, or are likely to be committed against the provisions of this act within any judicial district, it shall be lawful for him, in his discretion, to direct the judge, marshal, and district attorney of such district to attend at such place within the district, and for such time as he may designate, for the purpose of the more speedy arrest and trial of persons charged with a violation of this act; and it shall be the duty of every judge or other officer, when any such requisition shall be received by him, to attend at the place and for the time therein designated.

SEC. 9. That it shall be lawful for the President of the United States, or such person as he may empower for that purpose, to employ such part of the land or naval forces of the United States, or of the militia, as shall be necessary to prevent the violation and enforce the due execution of this act.

SEC. 10. That upon all questions of law arising in any cause under the provisions of this act, a final appeal may be taken to the Supreme Court of the United States.

The votes on this bill were:

1866, February 2—The SENATE passed the bill —yeas 33, nays 12, as follow:

YEAS—Messrs. Anthony, Brown, Chandler, Clark, Conness, Cragin, Dixon, Fessenden, Foster, Foster, Harris, Henderson, Howard, Howe, Kirkwood, Lane of Indiana, Lane of Kansas, Morgan, Morrill, Nye, Poland, Pomeroy, Ramsey. Sherman, Sprague, Stewart, Sumner, Trumbull, Wade, Willey, Williams, Wilson, Yates—33.

NAYS—Messrs. *Buckalew*, Cowan, *Davis, Guthrie, Hendricks, McDougall, Nesmith*, Norton, *Riddle, Saulsbury, Stockton*, Van Winkle—12.

**March 9**—The bill being before the HOUSE,

Mr. ELDRIDGE moved that it lie on the table; which was disagreed to—yeas 32, nays 118, as follow:

YEAS—Messrs. *Ancona, Boyer, Brooks, Chanler, Coffroth, Dawson, Denison, Eldridge, Glossbrenner, Goodyear, Grider, Aaron Harding, Harris, Hogan, Edwin N. Hubbell, Kerr, Le Blond, Marshall, Niblack, Nicholson, Radford, Ritter, Rogers, Ross, Rousseau, Shanklin, Sitgreaves, Taber, Taylor, Thornton, Trimble, Winfield*.—32.

NAYS—Messrs. Alley, Allison, Ames, Anderson, D. R. Ashley, James M. Ashley, Baker, Baldwin, Banks, Baxter, Beaman, Bidwell, Bingham, Blaine, Blow, Boutwell, Bromwell, Broomall, Buckland, Bundy, Sidney Clarke, Cobb, Conkling, Cook, Cullom, Darling, Davis, Defrees, Delano, Deming, Dixon, Donnelly, Driggs, Dumont, Eliot, Farnsworth, Farquhar, Ferry, Grinnell, Abner C. Harding, Hart, Hayes, Henderson, Higby, Hill, Holmes, Hooper, Asahel W. Hubbard, Chester D. Hubbard, Demas Hubbard, jr., John H. Hubbard, Hulburd, James Humphrey, Ingersoll, Jenckes, Julian, Kelley, Kelso, Ketcham, Kuykendall, Latham, George V. Lawrence, William Lawrence, Loan, Longyear, Lynch, Marston. Marvin, McClurg, McKee, McRuer, Mercur, Miller, Moorhead, Morrill, Morris, Moulton, Myers, O'Neill, Orth, Paine, Perham, Phelps, Pike, Plants, Price, Raymond, Alexander H. Rice, John H. Rice, Sawyer, Schenck, Scofield, Shellabarger, Sloan, Spalding, Starr, Stevens, Thayer, Francis Thomas, John L. Thomas, jr., Trowbridge, Upson, Van Aernam, Burt Van Horn, Robert T. Van Horn, Ward, Warner, Ellihu B. Washburne, Henry D. Washburn, William B. Washburn, Welker, Wentworth, Whaley, Williams, James F. Wilson, Stephen F. Wilson, Windom, Woodbridge.—118.

**March 13**—The bill passed—yeas 111, nays 38, as follow:

YEAS—Messrs. Alley, Allison, Ames, Anderson, James M. Ashley, Baker, Baldwin, Banks, Baxter, Beaman, Bidwell, Blaine, Blow, Boutwell, Bromwell, Broomall, Buckland, Bundy, Sidney Clarke, Cobb, Conkling, Cook, Cullom, Darling. Davis, Dawes, Delano, Deming, Dixon, Donnelly, Driggs, Dumont, Eliot, Farnsworth, Farquhar, Ferry, Garfield, Grinnell, Abner C. Harding, Hart, Hayes, Higby, Hill, Holmes, Hooper, Asahel W. Hubbard, Chester D. Hubbard, Demas Hubbard, John H. Hubbard, Hulburd, James Humphrey, Ingersoll, Jenckes, Julian, Kelley, Kelso, Ketcham, Kuykendall, Laflin, George V. Lawrence, William Lawrence, Loan, Longyear, Lynch, Marston, Marvin, McClurg, McRuer, Mercur, Miller, Moorhead, Morrill, Morris, Moulton, Myers, Newell, O'Neill, Orth, Paine. Perham, Pike, Plants, Price, Alexander H. Rice, Sawyer, Schenck, Scofield, Shellabarger, Sloan, Spalding, Starr, Stevens, Thayer, Francis Thomas, John L. Thomas, Trowbridge, Upson, Van Aernam, Burt Van Horn, Ward, Warner, Ellihu B. Washburne, William B. Washburn, Welker, Wentworth, Whaley, Williams, James F. Wilson, Stephen F. Wilson, Windom, Woodbridge—111.

NAYS—Messrs. *Ancona, Bergen*, Bingham, *Boyer, Brooks*,

*Coffroth, Dawson, Denison, Glossbrenner, Goodyear, Grider, Aaron Harding, Harris, Hogan, Edwin N. Hubbell, Jones, Kerr,* Latham, *Le Blond, Marshall, McCullough, Nicholson,* Phelps, *Radford, Samuel J. Randall,* William H. Randall, *Ritter, Rogers, Ross,* Rousseau, *Shanklin, Sitgreaves,* Smith, *Taber, Taylor, Thornton, Trimble, Winfield—38.*

March 15—The Senate concurred in the House amendments.

March 27—The bill was vetoed.

April 6—The SENATE passed the bill, notwithstanding the objections of the President, by a vote of 33 yeas to 15 nays, as follow:

YEAS—Messrs. Anthony, Brown, Chandler, Clark, Conness, Cragin, Creswell, Edmunds, Fessenden, Foster, Grimes, Harris, Henderson, Howard, Howe, Kirkwood, Lane of Indiana, Morgan, Morrill, Nye, Poland, Pomeroy, Ramsey, Sherman, Sprague, Stewart, Sumner, Trumbull, Wade, Willey, Williams, Wilson, Yates—33.

NAYS—Messrs. *Buckalew,* Cowan, *Davis,* Doolittle, *Guthrie, Hendricks, Johnson,* Lane of Kansas, *McDougall, Nesmith,* Norton, *Riddle, Saulsbury,* Van Winkle, *Wright—15.*

April 9—The HOUSE OF REPRESENTATIVES again passed it—yeas 122, nays 41, as follow:

YEAS—Messrs. Alley, Allison, Delos R. Ashley, James M. Ashley, Baker, Baldwin, Banks, Barker, Baxter, Beaman, Benjamin, Bidwell, Boutwell, Brandegee, Bromwell, Broomall, Buckland, Bundy, Reader W. Clarke, Sidney Clarke, Cobb, Colfax, Conkling, Cook, Cullom, Darling, Davis, Dawes, Defrees, Delano, Deming, Dixon, Dodge, Donnelly, Eckley, Eggleston, Eliot, Farnsworth, Farquhar, Ferry, Garfield, Grinnell, Griswold, Hale, Abner C. Harding, Hart, Hayes, Henderson, Higby, Hill, Holmes, Hooper, Hotchkiss. Asahel W. Hubbard, Chester D. Hubbard, John H. Hubbard, James R. Hubbell, Hulburd, James Humphrey, Ingersoll, Jenckes, Kasson, Kelley, Kelso, Ketcham, Laflin, George V. Lawrence, William Lawrence, Loan, Longyear, Lynch, Marston, Marvin, McClurg, McIndoe, McKee, McRuer, Mercur, Miller, Moorhead, Morrill, Morris, Moulton, Myers, Newell, O'Neill, Orth, Paine, Patterson, Perham, Pike, Plants, Pomeroy, Price, Alexander H. Rice, John H. Rice, Rollins, Sawyer, Schenck, Scofield, Shellabarger, Spalding, Starr, Stevens, Thayer, Francis Thomas, John L. Thomas, jr., Trowbridge, Upson, Van Aernam, Burt Van Horn, Robert T. Van Horn, Ward, Ellihu B. Washburne, Henry D. Washburn, William B. Washburn, Welker, Wentworth, James F. Wilson, Stephen F. Wilson, Windom, Woodbridge.—122.

NAYS—Messrs. *Ancona, Bergen, Boyer, Coffroth, Dawson, Denison, Eldridge, Finck, Glossbrenner, Aaron Harding, Harris, Hogan, Edwin N. Hubbell, James M. Humphrey,* Latham, *Le Blond, Marshall, McCullough, Niblack, Nicholson, Noell,* Phelps, *Radford, Samuel J. Randall,* William H. Randall, *Raymond, Ritter, Rogers, Ross,* Rousseau, *Shanklin, Sitgreaves,* Smith, *Strouse, Taber, Taylor, Thornton, Trimble,* Whaley, *Winfield, Wright.—41.*

Whereupon the Speaker of the House declared the bill a law.

---

### Veto of the Colorado Bill, May 15, 1866

*To the Senate of the United States:*

I return to the Senate, in which house it originated, the bill which has passed both Houses of Congress, entitled "An act for the admission of the State of Colorado into the Union," with my objections to its becoming a law at this time.

*First.* From the best information which I have been able to obtain, I do not consider the establishment of a State government at present necessary for the welfare of the people of Colorado. Under the existing Territorial government all the rights, privileges, and interests of the citizens are protected and secured. The qualified voters choose their own legislators and their own local officers, and are represented in Congress by a delegate of their own selection. They make and execute their own municipal laws, subject only to revision by Congress—an authority not likely to be exercised, unless in extreme or extraordinary cases. The population is small, some estimating it so low as twenty-five thousand, while advocates of the bill reckon

the number at from thirty-five thousand to forty thousand souls. The people are principally recent settlers, many of whom are understood to be ready for removal to other mining districts beyond the limits of the Territory, if circumstances shall render them more inviting. Such a population cannot but find relief from excessive taxation if the territorial system, which devolves the expenses of the executive, legislative, and judicial departments upon the United States, is for the present continued. They cannot but find the security of person and property increased by their reliance upon the national executive power for the maintenance of law and order against the disturbances necessarily incident to all newly organized communities.

*Second.* It is not satisfactorily established that a majority of the citizens of Colorado desire, or are prepared for an exchange of a territorial for a State government. In September, 1864, under the authority of Congress, an election was lawfully appointed and held, for the purpose of ascertaining the views of the people upon this particular question. 6,192 votes were cast, and of this number a majority of 3,152 was given against the proposed change. In September, 1865, without any legal authority, the question was again presented to the people of the Territory, with a view of obtaining a reconsideration of the result of the election held in compliance with the act of Congress approved March 21, 1864. At this second election 5,905 votes were polled, and a majority of 155 was given in favor of a State organization. It does not seem to me entirely safe to receive this, the last mentioned result, so irregularly obtained, as sufficient to outweigh the one which had been legally obtained in the first election. Regularity and conformity to law are essential to the preservation of order and stable government, and should, as far as practicable, always be observed in the formation of new States.

*Third.* The admission of Colorado, at this time, as a State into the federal Union, appears to me to be incompatible with the public interests of the country. While it is desirable that territories, when sufficiently matured, should be organized as States, yet the spirit of the Constitution seems to require that there should be an approximation towards equality among the several States comprising the Union. No State can have less or more than two Senators in Congress. The largest State has a population of four millions; several of the States have a population exceeding two millions; and many others have a population exceeding one million. A population of 127,000 is the ratio of apportionment of representatives among the several States.

If this bill should become a law, the people of Colorado, thirty thousand in number, would have in the House of Representatives one member, while New York, with a population of four millions, has but thirty-one; Colorado would have in the electoral college three votes, while New York has only thirty-three; Colorado would have in the Senate two votes, while New York has no more.

Inequalities of this character have already occurred, but it is believed that none have happened where the inequality was so great. When such inequality has been allowed, Congress is supposed to have permitted it on the ground of some high public necessity, and under circumstances which promised that it would rapidly disappear through the growth and development of the newly admitted State. Thus, in regard to the several States in what was formerly called the "northwest territory," lying east of the Mississippi, their rapid advancement in population rendered it certain that States admitted with only one or two representatives in Congress, would, in a very short period, be entitled to a great increase of representation. So, when California was admitted on the ground of commercial and political exigencies, it was well foreseen that that State was destined rapidly to become a great, prosperous, and important mining and commercial community. In the case of Colorado, I am not aware that any national exigency, either of a political or commercial nature, requires a departure from the law of equality, which has been so generally adhered to in our history.

If information submitted in connection with this bill is reliable, Colorado, instead of increasing, has declined in population. At an election for members of a territorial legislature held in 1861, 10,530 votes were cast. At the election before mentioned, in 1864, the number of votes cast was 6,192; while at the irregular election held in 1865, which is assumed as a basis for legislative action at this time, the aggregate of votes was 5,905. Sincerely anxious for the welfare and prosperity of every Territory and State, as well as for the prosperity and welfare of the whole Union, I regret this apparent decline of population in Colorado; but it is manifest that it is due to emigration which is going on from that Territory into other regions within the United States, which either are in fact, or are believed by the inhabitants of Colorado to be, richer in mineral wealth and agricultural resources. If, however, Colorado has not really declined in population, another census, or another election under the authority of Congress, would place the question beyond doubt, and cause but little delay in the ultimate admission of the Territory as a State, if desired by the people.

The tenor of these objections furnishes the reply which may be expected to an argument in favor of the measure derived from the enabling act which was passed by Congress on the 21st day of March, 1864. Although Congress then supposed that the condition of the Territory was such as to warrant its admission as a State, the result of two years' experience shows that every reason which existed for the institution of a territorial instead of a State government in Colorado, at its first organization, still continues in force.

The condition of the Union at the present moment is calculated to inspire caution in regard to the admission of new States. Eleven of the old States have been for some time, and still remain, unrepresented in Congress. It is a common interest of all the States, as well those represented as those unrepresented, that the integrity and harmony of the Union should be restored as completely as possible, so that all those who are expected to bear the burdens of the Federal Government shall be consulted concerning the admission of new States; and that in the mean time no new State shall be prematurely and unnecessarily admitted to a participation in the political power which the Federal Government wields, not for the benefit of any individual State or section, but for the common safety, welfare, and happiness of the whole country.

ANDREW JOHNSON.

WASHINGTON, D. C., *May* 15, 1866.

### Copy of the Bill.

AN ACT for the admission of the State of Colorado into the Union.

Whereas, on the twenty-first day of March, anno Domini eighteen hundred and sixty-four, Congress passed an act to enable the people of Colorado to form a constitution and State government, and offered to admit said State, when so formed, into the Union upon compliance with certain conditions therein specified; and whereas it appears by a message of the President of the United States, dated January twelve, eighteen hundred and sixty-six, that the said people have adopted a constitution, which upon due examination is found to conform to the provisions and comply with the conditions of said act, and to be republican in its form of government, and that they now ask for admission into the Union:

*Be it enacted, &c.*, That the constitution and State government which the people of Colorado have formed for themselves be, and the same is hereby, ratified, accepted, and confirmed, and that the said State of Colorado shall be, and is hereby, declared to be one of the United States of America, and is hereby admitted into the Union upon an equal footing with the original States, in all respects whatsoever.

SEC. 2. *And be it further enacted*, That the said State of Colorado shall be, and is hereby, declared to be entitled to all the rights, privileges, grants, and immunities, and to be subject to all the conditions and restrictions, of an act entitled "An act to enable the people of Colorado to form a constitution and a State government, and for the admission of such State into the Union on an equal footing with the original States," approved March twenty-first, eighteen hundred and sixty-four.

The votes on this bill were:

IN SENATE.

March 13—The bill was rejected—yeas 14, nays 21, as follow:

YEAS—Messrs. Chandler, Cragin, Kirkwood, Lane of Indiana, Lane of Kansas, *McDougall*, Nesmith, Norton, Pomeroy, Ramsey, Sherman, Stewart, Trumbull, Williams—14.

NAYS—Messrs. *Buckalew*, Conness, Creswell, *Davis*, Doolittle, Fessenden, Foster, Grimes, *Guthrie*, Harris, *Hendricks*, Morgan, Morrill, Poland, *Riddle*, Sprague, *Stockton*, Sumner, Van Winkle, Wade, Wilson—21.

Mr. Wilson entered a motion to reconsider the vote.

April 25—The Senate voted to reconsider; yeas 19, nays 13. (Same as below.)

The bill was then passed—yeas 19, nays 13, as follow:

YEAS—Messrs. Chandler, Clark, Conness, Cragin, Creswell, Howard, Howe, Kirkwood, Lane of Indiana, Nye, Pomeroy, Ramsey, Sherman, Sprague, Stewart, Trumbull, Van Winkle, Willey, Wilson—19.

NAYS—Messrs. *Buckalew*, *Davis*, Doolittle, Edmunds, Foster, Grimes, *Guthrie*, *Hendricks*, *McDougall*, Morgan, Poland, *Riddle*, Sumner—13.

### In House.

May 3—The bill was passed—yeas 81, nays 57, as follow:

YEAS—Messrs. Ames, Anderson, Delos R. Ashley, James M. Ashley, Baker, Banks, Barker, Beaman, Benjamin, Bidwell, Bingham, Blow, Brandegee, Bromwell, Buckland, Bundy, Reader W. Clarke, Sidney Clarke, Cobb, Conkling Cullom, Defrees, Deming, Dixon, Dodge, Donnelly, Driggs, Dumont, Eckley, Farquhar, Ferry, Garfield, Grinnell, Abner C. Harding, Hart, Henderson, Holmes, Hotchkiss, Asahel W. Hubbard, Chester D. Hubbard, James R. Hubbell, Ingersoll, Jenckes, Kasson, Kelso, Ketcham, Laflin, Latham, George V. Lawrence, William Lawrence, Loan, Longyear, Marston, McClurg, McKee, Mercur, Miller, Moorhead, Moulton, Myers, O'Neill, Orth, Patterson, Plants, Alexander H Rice, Rollins, Sawyer, Schenck, Shellabarger, Smith, Spalding, Francis Thomas, Trowbridge, Upson, Van Aernam, Burt Van Horn, Robert T. Van Horn, Warner, Welker, Whaley, Williams—81.

NAYS—Messrs. Allison, Alley, *Ancona*, Baxter, *Bergen*, Blaine, Boutwell, *Boyer*, Broomall, *Chanler*, *Coffroth*, Darling, *Dawson*, *Denison*, *Eldridge*, Eliot, *Finck*, *Glossbrenner*, Grider, Griswold, *Aaron Harding*, *Harris*, Higby, James Humphrey, Julian, Kelley, Kuykendall, *Le Blond*, Lynch, *Marshall*, *McCullough*, McRuer, Morrill, Morris, Newell, *Niblack*, Paine, Perham, Pike, Raymond, John H. Rice, *Ritter*, *Ross*, Rousseau, *Shanklin*, Stevens, Stilwell, *Strouse*, Taylor, Thornton, Ellihu B. Washburne, Henry D. Washburn, James F. Wilson, Windom, *Winfield*, Woodbridge, *Wright*—57.

Up to the time this page is put to press, no vote has been taken on the re-passage of the vetoed bill. When taken, it will be inserted in a subsequent page.

___

### Message Respecting the Proposed Constitutional Amendment on Representation, &c., June 22, 1866.

*To the Senate and House of Representatives:*

I submit to Congress a report of the Secretary of State, to whom was referred the concurrent resolution of the 18th instant,* respecting a submission to the legislatures of the States of an additional article to the Constitution of the United States.

It will be seen from this report that the Secretary of State had, on the 16th instant, transmitted to the Governors of the several States certified copies of the joint resolution passed on the 13th instant, proposing an amendment to the Constitution.

Even in ordinary times any question of amending the Constitution must be justly regarded as of paramount importance. This importance is at the present time enhanced by the fact that the joint resolution was not submitted by the two Houses for the approval of the President, and that of the thirty-six States which constitute the Union eleven are excluded from representation in either House of Congress, although, with the single exception of Texas, they have been entirely restored to all their functions as States, in conformity with the organic law of the land, and have appeared at the national capital by Senators and Representatives, who have applied for and have been refused admission to the vacant seats.

___

* This resolution passed the House under a suspension of the rules, which was agreed to, yeas 92, nays 25, (the latter all Democrats,) by a vote of yeas 87, nays 20, on a count by tellers. It passed the Senate same day without a division; and is a copy of a concurrent resolution passed in 1864, requesting President Lincoln to submit the anti-slavery amendment, changed only as to the phraseology descriptive of the amendment.

Nor have the sovereign people of the nation been afforded an opportunity of expressing their views upon the important questions which the amendment involves. Grave doubts therefore may naturally and justly arise as to whether the action of Congress is in harmony with the sentiments of the people, and whether State legislatures, elected without reference to such an issue, should be called upon by Congress to decide respecting the ratification of the proposed amendment.

Waiving the question as to the constitutional validity of the proceedings of Congress upon the joint resolution proposing the amendment, or as to the merits of the article which it submits through the executive department to the legislatures of the States, I deem it proper to observe that the steps taken by the Secretary of State, as detailed in the accompanying report, are to be considered as purely ministerial, and in no sense whatever committing the Executive to an approval or a recommendation of the amendment to the State legislatures or to the people. On the contrary, a proper appreciation of the letter and spirit of the Constitution, as well as of the interests of national order, harmony, and union, and a due deference for an enlightened public judgment, may at this time well suggest a doubt whether any amendment to the Constitution ought to be proposed by Congress and pressed upon the legislatures of the several States for final decision until after the admission of such loyal Senators and Representatives of the now unrepresented States as have been, or may hereafter be, chosen in conformity with the Constitution and laws of the United States.

ANDREW JOHNSON.

WASHINGTON, D. C., *June 22, 1866.*

___

*To the President.*

The Secretary of State, to whom was referred the concurrent resolution of the two Houses of Congress of the 18th instant, in the following words: "That the President of the United States be requested to transmit forthwith to the executives of the several States of the United States copies of the article of amendment proposed by Congress to the State legislatures to amend the Constitution of the United States, passed June 13, 1866, respecting citizenship, the basis of representation, disqualification for office, and validity of the public debt of the United States, &c., to the end that the said States may proceed to act upon the said article of amendment, and that he request the executive of each State that may ratify said amendment to transmit to the Secretary of State a certified copy of such ratification," has the honor to submit the following report, namely: That on the 16th instant the Hon. Amasa Cobb, of the Committee of the House of Representatives on Enrolled Bills, brought to this Department and deposited therein an enrolled resolution of the two Houses of Congress, which was thereupon received by the Secretary of State and deposited among the rolls of the Department, a copy of which is hereunto annexed. Thereupon the Secretary of State, upon the 16th instant, in conformity with the proceeding which was adopted by him in 1865, in regard to the then proposed and afterwards adopted congressional amendment of the Constitution of the United States concerning the prohibition of slavery, transmitted certified copies of the annexed resolution to the Governors of the several States, together with a certificate and circular letter. A copy of both of these communications are hereunto annexed.

Respectfully submitted,
WILLIAM H. SEWARD.
DEPARTMENT OF STATE, *June* 20, 1866.

[*Circular.*]
DEPARTMENT OF STATE, *June* 16, 1866.
*To his Excellency*
*Governor of the State of*
SIR: I have the honor to transmit an attested copy of a resolution of Congress, proposing to the legislatures of the several States a fourteenth article to the Constitution of the United States. The decisions of the several legislatures upon the subject are required by law to be communicated to this Department. An acknowledgment of the receipt of this communication is requested by Your excellency's most obedient servant,
WILLIAM H. SEWARD.

# VII.

# MAJORITY AND MINORITY REPORTS

## OF THE

## JOINT COMMITTEE ON RECONSTRUCTION.

### The Majority Report.

June 18, 1866—Mr. FESSENDEN in the Senate, and Mr. STEVENS in the House, submitted this

REPORT:

*The Joint Committee of the two Houses of Congress, appointed under the concurrent resolution of December* 13, 1865, *with direction to " inquire into the condition of the States which formed the so-called Confederate States of America, and report whether they or any of them are entitled to be represented in either House of Congress, with leave to report by bill or otherwise," ask leave to report:*

That they have attended to the duty assigned them as assiduously as other duties would permit, and now submit to Congress, as the result of their deliberations, a resolution proposing amendments to the Constitution, and two bills, of which they recommend the adoption.

Before proceeding to set forth in detail their reasons for the conclusion to which, after great deliberation, your committee have arrived, they beg leave to advert, briefly, to the course of proceedings they found it necessary to adopt, and to explain the reasons therefor.

The resolution under which your committee was appointed directed them to inquire into the condition of the Confederate States, and report whether they were entitled to representation in Congress. It is obvious that such an investigation, covering so large an extent of territory and involving so many important considerations, must necessarily require no trifling labor, and consume a very considerable amount of time. It must embrace the condition in which those

States were left at the close of the war; the measures which have been taken towards the reorganization of civil government, and the disposition of the people towards the United States; in a word, their fitness to take an active part in the administration of national affairs.

As to their condition at the close of the rebellion, the evidence is open to all, and admits of no dispute. They were in a state of utter exhaustion. Having protracted their struggle against federal authority until all hope of successful resistance had ceased, and laid down their arms only because there was no longer any power to use them, the people of those States were left bankrupt in their public finances, and shorn of the private wealth which had before given them power and influence. They were also necessarily in a state of complete anarchy, without governments and without the power to frame governments except by the permission of those who had been successful in the war. The President of the United States, in the proclamations under which he appointed provisional governors, and in his various communications to them, has, in exact terms, recognized the fact that the people of those States were, when the rebellion was crushed, "deprived of all civil government," and must proceed to organize anew. In his conversation with Mr. Stearns, of Massachusetts, certified by himself, President Johnson said "the State institutions are prostrated, laid out on the ground, and they must be taken up and adapted to the progress of events." Finding the Southern States in this condition, and Congress having failed to provide for the contingency, his duty was obvious. As President of the United States he had no power, except to execute the laws of the land as Chief Magistrate. These laws gave him no authority over the subject of reorganization; but by the Constitution he was commander-in-chief of the army and navy of the United States. These Confederate States embraced a portion of the people of the Union who had been in a state of revolt, but had been reduced to obedience by force of arms. They were in an abnormal condition, without civil government, without commercial connections, without national or international relations, and subject only to martial law. By withdrawing their representatives in Congress, by renouncing the privilege of representation, by organizing a separate government, and by levying war against the United States, they destroyed their State constitutions in respect to the vital principle which connected their respective States with the Union and secured their federal relations; and nothing of those constitutions was left of which the United States were bound to take notice. For four years they had a *de facto* government, but it was usurped and illegal. They chose the tribunal of arms wherein to decide whether or not it should be legalized, and they were defeated. At the close of the rebellion, therefore, the people of the rebellious States were found, as the President expresses it, "deprived of all civil government."

Under this state of affairs it was plainly the duty of the President to enforce existing national laws, and to establish, as far as he could, such a system of government as might be provided for by existing national statutes. As commander-in-chief of a victorious army, it was his duty, under the law of nations and the army regulations, to restore order, to preserve property, and to protect the people against violence from any quarter until provision should be made by law for their government. He might, as President, assemble Congress and submit the whole matter to the law-making power; or he might continue military supervision and control until Congress should assemble on its regular appointed day. Selecting the latter alternative, he proceeded, by virtue of his power as commander-in-chief, to appoint provisional governors over the revolted States. These were regularly commissioned, and their compensation was paid, as the Secretary of War states, "from the appropriation for army contingencies, because the duties performed by the parties were regarded as of a temporary character; ancillary to the withdrawal of military force, the disbandment of armies, and the reduction of military expenditure; by provisional organizations for the protection of civil rights, the preservation of peace, and to take the place of armed force in the respective States." It cannot, we think, be contended that these governors possessed, or could exercise, any but military authority. They had no power to organize civil governments, nor to exercise any authority except that which inhered in their own persons under their commissions. Neither had the President, as commander-in-chief, any other than military power. But he was in exclusive possession of the military authority. It was for him to decide how far he would exercise it, how far he would relax it, when and on what terms he would withdraw it. He might prop-

erly permit the people to assemble, and to initiate local governments, and to execute such local laws as they might choose to frame not inconsistent with, nor in opposition to, the laws of the United States. And, if satisfied that they might safely be left to themselves, he might withdraw the military forces altogether, and leave the people of any or all of these States to govern themselves without his interference. In the language of the Secretary of State, in his telegram to the provisional governor of Georgia, dated October 28, 1865, he might "recognize the people of any State as having resumed the relations of loyalty to the Union," and act in his military capacity on this hypothesis. All this was within his own discretion, as military commander. But it was not for him to decide upon the nature or effect of any system of government which the people of these States might see fit to adopt. This power is lodged by the Constitution in the Congress of the United States, that branch of the government in which is vested the authority to fix the political relations of the States to the Union, whose duty is to guarantee to each State a republican form of government, and to protect each and all of them against foreign or domestic violence, and against each other. We cannot, therefore, regard the various acts of the President in relation to the formation of local governments in the insurrectionary States, and the conditions imposed by him upon their action, in any other light than as intimations to the people that, as commander-in-chief of the army, he would consent to withdraw military rule just in proportion as they should, by their acts, manifest a disposition to preserve order among themselves, establish governments denoting loyalty to the Union, and exhibit a settled determination to return to their allegiance, leaving with the law-making power to fix the terms of their final restoration to all their rights and privileges as States of the Union. That this was the view of his power taken by the President is evident from expressions to that effect in the communications of the Secretary of State to the various provisional governors, and the repeated declarations of the President himself. Any other supposition inconsistent with this would impute to the President designs of encroachment upon a co-ordinate branch of the government, which should not be lightly attributed to the Chief Magistrate of the nation.

When Congress assembled in December last the people of most of the States lately in rebellion had, under the advice of the President, organized local governments, and some of them had acceded to the terms proposed by him. In his annual message he stated, in general terms, what had been done, but he did not see fit to communicate the details for the information of Congress. While in this and in a subsequent message the President urged the speedy restoration of these States, and expressed the opinion that their condition was such as to justify their restoration, yet it is quite obvious that Congress must either have acted blindly on that opinion of the President, or proceeded to obtain the information requisite for intelligent action on the subject. The impropriety of proceeding wholly on the judgment of any one man, however exalted his station, in a matter involving the welfare of the republic in all future time, or of adopting any plan, coming from any source, without fully understanding all its bearings and comprehending its full effect, was apparent. The first step, therefore, was to obtain the required information. A call was accordingly made on the President for the information in his possession as to what had been done, in order that Congress might judge for itself as to the grounds of the belief expressed by him in the fitness of States recently in rebellion to participate fully in the conduct of national affairs. This information was not immediately communicated. When the response was finally made, some six weeks after your committee had been in actual session, it was found that the evidence upon which the President seemed to have based his suggestions was incomplete and unsatisfactory. Authenticated copies of the new constitutions and ordinances adopted by the conventions in three of the States had been submitted, extracts from newspapers furnished scanty information as to the action of one other State, and nothing appears to have been communicated as to the remainder. There was no evidence of the loyalty of those who had participated in these conventions, and in one State alone was any proposition made to submit the action of the conventions to the final judgment of the people.

Failing to obtain the desired information, and left to grope for light wherever it might be found, your committee did not deem it either advisable or safe to adopt, without further examination, the suggestions of the President, more especially as he had not deemed it expedient to remove the military force, to suspend martial law, or to restore the writ of *habeas corpus*, but still thought it necessary to exercise over the people of the rebellious States his military power and jurisdiction. This conclusion derived still greater force from the fact, undisputed, that in all these States, except Tennessee and perhaps Arkansas, the elections which were held for State officers and members of Congress had resulted, almost universally, in the defeat of candidates who had been true to the Union, and in the election of notorious and unpardoned rebels, men who could not take the prescribed oath of office, and who made no secret of their hostility to the Government and the people of the United States. Under these circumstances, anything like hasty action would have been as dangerous as it was obviously unwise. It appeared to your committee that but one course remained, viz: to investigate carefully and thoroughly the state of feeling and opinion existing among the people of these States; to ascertain how far their pretended loyalty could be relied upon, and thence to infer whether it would be safe to admit them at once to a full participation in the Government they had fought for four years to destroy. It was an equally important inquiry whether their restoration to their former relations with the United States should only be granted upon certain conditions and guarantees which would effectually secure the nation against a recurrence of evils so disastrous as those from which it had escaped at so enormous a sacrifice.

To obtain the necessary information recourse could only be had to the examination of witnesses whose position had given them the best means of forming an accurate judgment, who could state facts from their own observation, and whose character and standing afforded the best evidence of their truthfulness and impartiality. A work like this, covering so large an extent of territory, and embracing such complicated and extensive inquiries, necessarily required much time and labor. To shorten the time as much as possible, the work was divided and placed in the hands of four sub-committees, who have been diligently employed in its accomplishment. The results of their labors have been heretofore submitted, and the country will judge how far they sustain the President's views, and how far they justify the conclusions to which your committee have finally arrived.

A claim for the immediate admission of Senators and Representatives from the so-called Confederate States has been urged, which seems to your committee not to be founded either in reason or in law, and which cannot be passed without comment. Stated in a few words, it amounts to this: That inasmuch as the lately insurgent States had no legal right to separate themselves from the Union, they still retain their positions as States, and consequently the people thereof have a right to immediate representation in Congress without the imposition of any conditions whatever; and further, that until such admission Congress has no right to tax them for the support of the Government. It has even been contended that until such admission all legislation affecting their interests is, if not unconstitutional, at least unjustifiable and oppressive.

It is believed by your committee that all these propositions are not only wholly untenable, but, if admitted, would tend to the destruction of the Government.

It must not be forgotten that the people of these States, without justification or excuse, rose in insurrection against the United States. They deliberately abolished their State goverernments so far as the same connected them politically with the Union as members thereof under the Constitution. They deliberately renounced their allegiance to the Federal Government, and proceeded to establish an independent government for themselves. In the prosecution of this enterprise they seized the national forts, arsenals, dock-yards, and other public property within their borders, drove out from among them those who remained true to the Union, and heaped every imaginable insult and injury upon the United States and its citizens. Finally they opened hostilities, and levied war against the Government.

They continued this war for four years with the most determined and malignant spirit, killing in battle and otherwise large numbers of loyal people, destroying the property of loyal citizens on the sea and on the land, and entailing on the Government an enormous debt, incurred to sustain its rightful authority. Whether legally and constitutionally or not, they did, in fact, withdraw from the Union and made themselves subjects of another government of their own creation. And they only yielded when, after a long, bloody, and wasting war, they were compelled by utter exhaustion to lay down their arms; and this they did not willingly, but declaring that they yielded because they could no longer resist, affording no evidence whatever of repentance for their crime, and expressing no regret, except that they had no longer the power to continue the desperate struggle.

It cannot, we think, be denied by any one, having a tolerable acquaintance with public law, that the war thus waged was a civil war of the greatest magnitude. The people waging it were necessarily subject to all the rules which, by the law of nations, control a contest of that character, and to all the legitimate consequences following it. One of those consequences was that, within the limits prescribed by humanity, the conquered rebels were at the mercy of the conquerors. That a government thus outraged had a most perfect right to exact indemnity for the injuries done and security against the recurrence of such outrages in the future would seem too clear for dispute. What the nature of that security should be, what proof should be required of a return to allegiance, what time should elapse before a people thus demoralized should be restored in full to the enjoyment of political rights and privileges, are questions for the law-making power to decide, and that decision must depend on grave considerations of the public safety and the general welfare.

It is moreover contended, and with apparent gravity, that, from the peculiar nature and character of our Government, no such right on the part of the conqueror can exist; that from the moment when rebellion lays down its arms and actual hostilities cease, all political rights of rebellious communities are at once restored; that, because the people of a State of the Union were once an organized community within the Union, they necessarily so remain, and their right to be represented in Congress at any and all times, and to participate in the government of the country under all circumstances, admits of neither question nor dispute. If this is indeed true, then is the Government of the United States powerless for its own protection, and flagrant rebellion, carried to the extreme of civil war, is a pastime which any State may play at, not only certain that it can lose nothing in any event, but may even be the gainer by defeat. If rebellion succeeds, it accomplishes its purpose and destroys the Government. If it fails, the war has been barren of results, and the battle may be still fought out in the legislative halls of the country. Treason, defeated in the field, has only to take possession of Congress and the cabinet.

Your committee does not deem it either necessary or proper to discuss the question whether the late Confederate States are still States of this Union, or can even be otherwise. Granting this profitless abstraction, about which so many words have been wasted, it by no means follows that the people of those States may not place themselves in a condition to abrogate the powers and privileges incident to a State of the Union, and deprive themselves of all pretence of right to exercise those powers and enjoy those privileges. A State within the Union has obligations to discharge as a member of the Union. It must submit to federal laws and uphold federal authority. It must have a government republican in form, under and by which it is connected with the General Government, and through which it can discharge its obligations. It is more than idle, it is a mockery, to contend that a people who have thrown off their allegiance, destroyed the local government which bound their States to the Union as members thereof, defied its authority, refused to execute its laws, and abrogated every provision which gave them political rights within the Union, still retain, through all, the perfect and entire right to resume, at their own will and pleasure, all their privileges within the Union, and especially to participate in its government, and to control the conduct of its affairs. To admit such a principle for one moment would be to declare that treason is always master and loyalty a blunder. Such a principle is void by its very nature and essence, because inconsistent with the theory of government, and fatal to its very existence.

On the contrary, we assert that no portion of the people of this country, whether in State or Territory, have the right, while remaining on its soil, to withdraw from or reject the authority of the United States. They must obey its laws as paramount, and acknowledge its jurisdiction. They have no right to secede; and while they can destroy their State governments, and place themselves beyond the pale of the Union, so far as the exercise of State privileges is concerned, they cannot escape the obligations imposed upon them by the Constitution and the laws, nor impair the exercise of national authority. The Constitution, it will be observed, does not act upon States, as such, but upon the people; while, therefore, the people cannot escape its authority, the States may, through the act of their people, cease to exist in an organized form, and thus dissolve their political relations with the United States.

That taxation should be only with the consent of the taxed, through their own representatives, is a cardinal principle of all free governments; but it is not true that taxation and representation must go together under all circumstances, and at every moment of time. The people of the District of Columbia and of the Territories are taxed, although not represented in Congress. If it is true that the people of the so-called Confederate States had no right to throw off the authority of the United States, it is equally true that they are bound at all times to share the burdens of government. They cannot, either legally or equitably, refuse to bear their just proportion of these burdens by voluntarily abdicating their rights and privileges as States of the Union, and refusing to be represented in the councils of the nation, much less by rebellion against national authority and levying war. To hold that by so doing they could escape taxation would be to offer a premium for insurrection, to reward instead of punishing for treason. To hold that as soon as government is restored to its full authority it can be allowed no time to secure itself against similar wrongs in the future, or else omit the ordinary exercise of its constitutional power to compel equal contribution from all towards the expenses of government, would be unreasonable in itself and unjust to the nation. It is sufficient to reply that the loss of representation by the people of the insurrectionary States was their own voluntary choice. They might abandon their privileges, but they could not escape their obligations; and surely they have no right to complain if, before resuming those privileges, and while the people of the United States are devising measures for the public safety, rendered necessary by the act of those who thus disfranchised themselves, they are compelled to contribute their just proportion of the general burden of taxation incurred by their wickedness and folly.

Equally absurd is the pretense that the legislative authority of the nation must be inoperative so far as they are concerned, while they, by their own act, have lost the right to take part in it. Such a proposition carries its own refutation on its face.

While thus exposing fallacies which, as your committee believe, are resorted to for the purpose of misleading the people and distracting their attention from the questions at issue, we freely admit that such a condition of things should be brought, if possible, to a speedy termination. It is most desirable that the Union of all the States should become perfect at the earliest moment consistent with the peace and welfare of the nation ; that all these States should become fully represented in the national councils, and take their share in the legislation of the country. The possession and exercise of more than its just share of power by any section is injurious, as well to that section as to all others. Its tendency is distracting and demoralizing, and such a state of affairs is only to be tolerated on the ground of a necessary regard to the public safety. As soon as that safety is secured it should terminate.

Your committee came to the consideration of the subject referred to them with the most anxious desire to ascertain what was the condition of the people of the States recently in insurrection, and what, if anything, was necessary to be done before restoring them to the full enjoyment of all their original privileges. It was undeniable that the war into which they had plunged the country had materially changed their relations to the people of the loyal States. Slavery had been abolished by constitutional amendment. A large proportion of the population had become, instead of mere chattels, free men and citizens. Through all the past struggle these had remained true and loyal, and had, in large numbers, fought on the side of the Union. It was impossible to abandon them without securing them their rights as free men and citizens. The whole civilized world would have cried out against such base ingratitude, and the bare idea is offensive to all right-thinking men. Hence it became important to inquire what could be done to secure their rights, civil and political. It was evident to your committee that adequate security could only be found in appropriate constitutional provisions. By an original provision of the Constitution, representation is based on the whole number of free persons in each State, and three-fifths of all other persons. When all become free, represen-

tation for all necessarily follows. As a consequence the inevitable effect of the rebellion would be to increase the political power of the insurrectionary States, whenever they should be allowed to resume their positions as States of the Union. As representation is by the Constitution based upon population, your committee did not think it advisable to recommend a change of that basis. The increase of representation necessarily resulting from the abolition of slavery was considered the most important element in the questions arising out of the changed condition of affairs, and the necessity for some fundamental action in this regard seemed imperative. It appeared to your committee that the rights of these persons by whom the basis of representation had been thus increased should be recognized by the General Government. While slaves, they were not considered as having any rights, civil or political. It did not seem just or proper that all the political advantages derived from their becoming free should be confined to their former masters, who had fought against the Union, and withheld from themselves, who had always been loyal. Slavery, by building up a ruling and dominant class, had produced a spirit of oligarchy adverse to republican institutions, which finally inaugurated civil war. The tendency of continuing the domination of such a class, by leaving it in the exclusive possession of political power, would be to encourage the same spirit, and lead to a similar result. Doubts were entertained whether Congress had power, even under the amended Constitution, to prescribe the qualifications of voters in a State, or could act directly on the subject. It was doubtful, in the opinion of your committee, whether the States would consent to surrender a power they had always exercised, and to which they were attached. As the best, if not the only, method of surmounting the difficulty, and as eminently just and proper in itself, your committee came to the conclusion that political power should be possessed in all the States exactly in proportion as the right of suffrage should be granted, without distinction of color or race. This it was thought would leave the whole question with the people of each State, holding out to all the advantage of increased political power as an inducement to allow all to participate in its exercise. Such a provision would be in its nature gentle and persuasive, and would lead, it was hoped, at no distant day, to an equal participation of all, without distinction, in all the rights and privileges of citizenship, thus affording a full and adequate protection to all classes of citizens, since all would have, through the ballot-box, the power of self-protection.

Holding these views, your committee prepared an amendment to the Constitution to carry out this idea, and submitted the same to Congress. Unfortunately, as we think, it did not receive the necessary constitutional support in the Senate, and therefore could not be proposed for adoption by the States. The principle involved in that amendment is, however, believed to be sound, and your committee have again proposed it in another form, hoping that it may receive the approbation of Congress.

Your committee have been unable to find, in the evidence submitted to Congress by the President, under date of March 6, 1866, in compliance with the resolutions of January 5 and February 27, 1866, any satisfactory proof that either of the insurrectionary States, except, perhaps, the State of Tennessee, has placed itself in a condition to resume its political relations to the Union. The first step towards that end would necessarily be the establishment of a republican form of government by the people. It has been before remarked that the provisional governors, appointed by the President in the exercise of his military authority, could do nothing by virtue of the power thus conferred towards the establishment of a State government. They were acting under the War Department and paid out of its funds. They were simply bridging over the chasm between rebellion and restoration. And yet we find them calling conventions and convening legislatures. Not only this, but we find the conventions and legislatures thus convened acting under executive direction as to the provisions required to be adopted in their constitutions and ordinances as conditions precedent to their recognition by the President. The inducement held out by the President for compliance with the conditions imposed was, directly in one instance, and presumably, therefore, in others, the immediate admission of Senators and Representatives to Congress. The character of the conventions and legislatures thus assembled was not such as to inspire confidence in the good faith of their members. Governor Perry, of South Carolina, dissolved the convention assembled in that State before the suggestion had reached Columbia from Washington that the rebel war debt should be repudiated, and gave as his reason that it was a "revolutionary body." There is no evidence of the loyalty or disloyalty of the members of those conventions and legislatures except the fact of pardons being asked for on their account. Some of these States now claiming representation refused to adopt the conditions imposed. No reliable information is found in these papers as to the constitutional provisions of several of these States, while in not one of them is there the slightest evidence to show that these "amended constitutions," as they are called, have ever been submitted to the people for their adoption. In North Carolina alone an ordinance was passed to that effect, but it does not appear to have been acted on. Not one of them, therefore, has been ratified. Whether, with President Johnson, we adopt the theory that the old constitutions were abrogated and destroyed, and the people "deprived of all civil government," or whether we adopt the alternative doctrine that they were only suspended and were revived by the suppression of the rebellion, the new provisions must be considered as equally destitute of validity before adoption by the people. If the conventions were called for the sole purpose of putting the State government into operation, they had no power either to adopt a new constitution or to amend an old one without the consent of the people. Nor could either a convention or a legislature change the fundamental law without power previously conferred. In the view of your committee, it follows, there-fore, that the people of a State where the constitution has been thus amended might feel themselves justified in repudiating altogether all such unauthorized assumptions of power, and might be expected to do so at pleasure.

So far as the disposition of the people of the insurrectionary States, and the probability of their adopting measures conforming to the changed condition of affairs, can be inferred from the papers submitted by the President as the basis of his action, the prospects are far from encouraging. It appears quite clear that the anti-slavery amendments, both to the State and Federal Constitutions, were adopted with reluctance by the bodies which did adopt them, while in some States they have been either passed by in silence or rejected. The language of all the provisions and ordinances of these States on the subject amounts to nothing more than an unwilling admission of an unwelcome truth. As to the ordinance of secession, it is, in some cases, declared "null and void," and in others simply "repealed;" and in no instance is a refutation of this deadly heresy considered worthy of a place in the new constitution.

If, as the President assumes, these insurrectionary States were, at the close of the war, wholly without State governments, it would seem that, before being admitted to participation in the direction of public affairs, such governments should be regularly organized. Long usage has established, and numerous statutes have pointed out, the mode in which this should be done. A convention to frame a form of government should be assembled under competent authority. Ordinarily, this authority emanates from Congress; but, under the peculiar circumstances, your committee is not disposed to criticise the President's action in assuming the power exercised by him in this regard. The convention, when assembled, should frame a constitution of government, which should be submitted to the people for adoption. If adopted, a legislature should be convened to pass the laws necessary to carry it into effect. When a State thus organized claims representation in Congress, the election of representatives should be provided for by law, in accordance with the laws of Congress regulating representation, and the proof that the action taken has been in conformity to law should be submitted to Congress.

In no case have these essential preliminary steps been taken. The conventions assembled seem to have assumed that the constitutions which had been repudiated and overthrown were still in existence, and operative to constitute the States members of the Union, and to have contented themselves with such amendments as they were informed were requisite in order to insure their return to an immediate participation in the Government of the United States. Not waiting to ascertain whether the people they represented would adopt even the proposed amendments, they at once ordered elections of representatives to Congress, in nearly all instances before an executive had been chosen to issue writs of election under the State laws, and such elections as were held were ordered by the conventions. In one instance, at least, the writs of election were signed by the provisional governor. Glaring irregularities and unwarranted assumptions of power are manifest in several cases, particularly in South Carolina, where the convention, although disbanded by the provisional governor on the ground that it was a revolutionary body, assumed to redistrict the State.

It is quite evident from all these facts, and indeed from the whole mass of testimony submitted by the President to the Senate, that in no instance was regard paid to any other consideration than obtaining immediate admission to Congress, under the barren form of an election in which no precautions were taken to secure regularity of proceedings or the assent of the people. No constitution has been legally adopted except, perhaps, in the State of Tennessee, and such elections as have been held were without authority of law. Your committee are accordingly forced to the conclusion that the States referred to have not placed themselves in a condition to claim representation in Congress, unless all the rules which have, since the foundation of the Government, been deemed essential in such cases should be disregarded.

It would undoubtedly be competent for Congress to waive all formalities and to admit these Confederate States to representation at once, trusting that time and experience would set all things right. Whether it would be advisable to do so, however, must depend upon other considerations of which it remains to treat. But it may well be observed, that the inducements to such a step should be of the very highest character. It seems to your committee not unreasonable to require satisfactory evidence that the ordinances and constitutional provisions which the President deemed essential in the first instance will be permanently adhered to by the people of the States seeking restoration, after being admitted to full participation in the government, and will not be repudiated when that object shall have been accomplished. And here the burden of proof rests upon the late insurgents who are seeking restoration to the rights and privileges which they willingly abandoned, and not upon the people of the United States who have never undertaken, directly or indirectly, to deprive them thereof. It should appear affirmatively that they are prepared and disposed in good faith to accept the results of the war, to abandon their hostility to the Government, and to live in peace and amity with the people of the loyal States, extending to all classes of citizens equal rights and privileges, and conforming to the republican idea of liberty and equality. They should exhibit in their acts something more than an unwilling submission to an unavoidable necessity—a feeling, if not cheerful, certainly not offensive and defiant. And they should evince an entire repudiation of all hostility to the General Government, by an acceptance of such just and reasonable conditions as that Government should think the public safety demands. Has this been done? Let us look at the facts shown by the evidence taken by the committee.

Hardly is the war closed before the people of these insurrectionary States come forward and haughtily claim, as a right, the privilege of par-

ticipating at once in that Government which they had for four years been fighting to overthrow. Allowed and encouraged by the Executive to organize State governments, they at once placed in power leading rebels, unrepentant and unpardoned, excluding with contempt those who had manifested an attachment to the Union, and preferring, in many instances, those who had rendered themselves the most obnoxious. In the face of the law requiring an oath which would necessarily exclude all such men from federal offices, they elect, with very few exceptions, as Senators and Representatives in Congress men who had actively participated in the rebellion, insultingly denouncing the law as unconstitutional. It is only necessary to instance the election to the Senate of the late vice president of the Confederacy, a man who, against his own declared convictions, had lent all the weight of his acknowledged ability and of his influence as a most prominent public man to the cause of the rebellion and who, unpardoned rebel as he is, with that oath staring him in the face, had the assurance to lay his credentials on the table of the Senate. Other rebels of scarcely less note or notoriety were selected from other quarters. Professing no repentance, glorying apparently in the crime they had committed, avowing still, as the uncontradicted testimony of Mr. Stephens and many others proves, an adherence to the pernicious doctrine of secession, and declaring that they yielded only to necessity, they insist, with unanimous voice, upon their rights as States, and proclaim that they will submit to no conditions whatever as preliminary to their resumption of power under that Constitution which they still claim the right to repudiate.

Examining the evidence taken by your committee still further, in connection with facts too notorious to be disputed, it appears that the southern press, with few exceptions, and those mostly of newspapers recently established by northern men, abound with weekly and daily abuse of the institutions and people of the loyal States; defends the men who led, and the principles which incited, the rebellion; denounces and reviles southern men who adhered to the Union; and strives, constantly and unscrupulously, by every means in its power, to keep alive the fire of hate and discord between the sections; calling upon the President to violate his oath of office, overturn the Government by force of arms, and drive the representatives of the people from their seats in Congress. The national banner is openly insulted, and the national airs scoffed at, not only by an ignorant populace, but at public meetings, and once, among other notable instances, at a dinner given in honor of a notorious rebel who had violated his oath and abandoned his flag. The same individual is elected to an important office in the leading city of his State, although an unpardoned rebel, and so offensive that the President refuses to allow him to enter upon his official duties. In another State the leading general of the rebel armies is openly nominated for governor by the speaker of the house of delegates, and the nomination is hailed by the people with shouts of satisfaction, and openly indorsed by the press.

Looking still further at the evidence taken

by your committee, it is found to be clearly shown, by witnesses of the highest character, and having the best means of observation, that the Freedmen's Bureau, instituted for the relief and protection of freedmen and refugees, is almost universally opposed by the mass of the population, and exists in an efficient condition only under military protection, while the Union men of the South are earnest in its defence, declaring with one voice that without its protection the colored people would not be permitted to labor at fair prices, and could hardly live in safety. They also testify that without the protection of United States troops Union men, whether of northern or southern origin, would be obliged to abandon their homes. The feeling in many portions of the country towards the emancipated slaves, especially among the uneducated and ignorant, is one of vindictive and malicious hatred. This deep-seated prejudice against color is assiduously cultivated by the public journals, and leads to acts of cruelty, oppression, and murder, which the local authorities are at no pains to prevent or punish. There is no general disposition to place the colored race, constituting at least two fifths of the population, upon terms even of civil equality. While many instances may be found where large planters and men of the better class accept the situation, and honestly strive to bring about a better order of things, by employing the freedmen at fair wages and treating them kindly, the general feeling and disposition among all classes are yet totally averse to the toleration of any class of people friendly to the Union, be they white or black; and this aversion is not unfrequently manifested in an insulting and offensive manner.

The witnesses examined as to the willingness of the people of the South to contribute, under existing laws, to the payment of the national debt, prove that the taxes levied by the United States will be paid only on compulsion and with great reluctance, while there prevails, to a considerable extent, an expectation that compensation will be made for slaves emancipated and property destroyed during the war. The testimony on this point comes from officers of the Union army, officers of the late rebel army, Union men of the Southern States, and avowed secessionists, almost all of whom state that, in their opinion, the people of the rebellious States would, if they should see a prospect of success, repudiate the national debt.

While there is scarcely any hope or desire among leading men to renew the attempt at secession at any future time, there is still, according to a large number of witnesses, including A. H. Stephens, who may be regarded as good authority on that point, a generally prevailing opinion which defends the legal right of secession, and upholds the doctrine that the first allegiance of the people is due to the States, and not to the United States. This belief evidently prevails among leading and prominent men as well as among the masses everywhere, except in some of the northern counties of Alabama and the eastern counties of Tennessee.

The evidence of an intense hostility to the Federal Union, and an equally intense love of the late Confederacy, nurtured by the war, is decisive. While it appears that nearly all are willing to submit, at least for the time being, to the federal authority, it is equally clear that the ruling motive is a desire to obtain the advantages which will be derived from a representation in Congress. Officers of the Union army on duty, and northern men who go South to engage in business, are generally detested and proscribed. Southern men who adhered to the Union are bitterly hated and relentlessly persecuted. In some localities prosecutions have been instituted in State courts against Union officers for acts done in the line of official duty, and similar prosecutions are threatened elsewhere as soon as the United States troops are removed. All such demonstrations show a state of feeling against which it is unmistakably necessary to guard.

The testimony is conclusive that after the collapse of the Confederacy the feeling of the people of the rebellious States was that of abject submission. Having appealed to the tribunal of arms, they had no hope except that by the magnanimity of their conquerors their lives, and possibly their property, might be preserved. Unfortunately, the general issue of pardons to persons who had been prominent in the rebellion, and the feeling of kindness and conciliation manifested by the Executive, and very generally indicated through the northern press, had the effect to render whole communities forgetful of the crime they had committed, defiant towards the Federal Government, and regardless of their duties as citizens. The conciliatory measures of the Government do not seem to have been met even half way. The bitterness and defiance exhibited toward the United States under such circumstances is without a parallel in the history of the world. In return for our leniency we receive only an insulting denial of our authority. In return for our kind desire for the resumption of fraternal relations we receive only an insolent assumption of rights and privileges long since forfeited. The crime we have punished is paraded as a virtue, and the principles of republican government which we have vindicated at so terrible cost are denounced as unjust and oppressive.

If we add to this evidence the fact that, although peace has been declared by the President, he has not, to this day, deemed it safe to restore the writ of *habeas corpus*, to relieve the insurrectionary States of martial law, nor to withdraw the troops from many localities, and that the commanding general deems an increase of the army indispensable to the preservation of order and the protection of loyal and well-disposed people in the South, the proof of a condition of feeling hostile to the Union and dangerous to the Government throughout the insurrectionary States would seem to be overwhelming.

With such evidence before them, it is the opinion of your committee—

I. That the States lately in rebellion were, at the close of the war, disorganized communities, without civil government, and without constitutions or other forms, by virtue of which political relations could legally exist between them and the Federal Government.

II. That Congress cannot be expected to recognize as valid the election of representatives from disorganized communities, which, from the very nature of the case, were unable to present their claim to representation under those established and recognized rules, the observance of which has been hitherto required.

III. That Congress would not be justified in admitting such communities to a participation in the government of the country without first providing such constitutional or other guarantees as will tend to secure the civil rights of all citizens of the Republic; a just equality of representation; protection against claims founded in rebellion and crime; a temporary restoration of the right of suffrage to those who have not actively participated in the efforts to destroy the Union and overthrow the Government; and the exclusion from positions of public trust of at least a portion of those whose crimes have proved them to be enemies to the Union, and unworthy of public confidence.

Your committee will, perhaps, hardly be deemed excusable for extending this report further; but inasmuch as immediate and unconditional representation of the States lately in rebellion is demanded as a matter of right, and delay, and even hesitation, is denounced as grossly oppressive and unjust, as well as unwise and impolitic, it may not be amiss again to call attention to a few undisputed and notorious facts, and the principles of public law applicable thereto, in order that the propriety of that claim may be fully considered and well understood.

The State of Tennessee occupies a position distinct from all the other insurrectionary States, and has been the subject of a separate report, which your committee have not thought it expedient to disturb. Whether Congress shall see fit to make that State the subject of separate action, or to include it in the same category with all others, so far as concerns the imposition of preliminary conditions, it is not within the province of this committee either to determine or advise.

To ascertain whether any of the so-called Confederate States "are entitled to be represented in either House of Congress," the essential inquiry is, whether there is, in any one of them, a constituency qualified to be represented in Congress. The question how far persons claiming seats in either House possess the credentials necessary to enable them to represent a duly qualified constituency is one for the consideration of each House separately, after the preliminary question shall have been finally determined.

We now propose to re-state, as briefly as possible, the general facts and principles applicable to all the States recently in rebellion.

First. The seats of the senators and representatives from the so-called Confederate States became vacant in the year 1861, during the second session of the Thirty-sixth Congress, by the voluntary withdrawal of their incumbents, with the sanction and by direction of the legislatures or conventions of their respective States. This was done as a hostile act against the Constitution and Government of the United States, with a declared intent to overthrow the same by forming a southern confederation. This act of declared hostility was speedily followed by an organiza-

tion of the same States into a confederacy, which levied and waged war, by sea and land, against the United States. This war continued more than four years, within which period the rebel armies besieged the national capital, invaded the loyal States, burned their towns and cities, robbed their citizens, destroyed more than 250,000 loyal soldiers, and imposed an increased national burden of not less than $3,500,000,000, of which seven or eight hundred millions have already been met and paid. From the time these confederated States thus withdrew their representation in Congress and levied war against the United States, the great mass of their people became and were insurgents, rebels, traitors, and all of them assumed and occupied the political, legal, and practical relation of enemies of the United States. This position is established by acts of Congress and judicial decisions, and is recognized repeatedly by the President in public proclamations, documents, and speeches.

Second. The States thus confederated prosecuted their war against the United States to final arbitrament, and did not cease until all their armies were captured, their military power destroyed, their civil officers, State and confederate, taken prisoners or put to flight, every vestige of State and confederate government obliterated, their territory overrun and occupied by the federal armies, and their people reduced to the condition of enemies conquered in war, entitled only by public law to such rights, privileges, and conditions as might be vouchsafed by the conqueror. This position is also established by judicial decisions, and is recognized by the President in public proclamations, documents, and speeches.

Third. Having voluntarily deprived themselves of representation in Congress, for the criminal purpose of destroying the Federal Union, and having reduced themselves, by the act of levying war, to the condition of public enemies, they have no right to complain of temporary exclusion from Congress; but on the contrary, having voluntarily renounced the right to representation, and disqualified themselves by crime from participating in the Government, the burden now rests upon them, before claiming to be reinstated in their former condition, to show that they are qualified to resume federal relations. In order to do this, they must prove that they have established, with the consent of the people, republican forms of government in harmony with the Constitution and laws of the United States, that all hostile purposes have ceased, and should give adequate guarantees against future treason and rebellion—guarantees which shall prove satisfactory to the Government against which they rebelled, and by whose arms they were subdued.

Fourth. Having, by this treasonable withdrawal from Congress, and by flagrant rebellion and war, forfeited all civil and political rights and privileges under the Constitution, they can only be restored thereto by the permission and authority of that constitutional power against which they rebelled and by which they were subdued.

Fifth. These rebellious enemies were conquered by the people of the United States, acting through all the co-ordinate branches of the Government, and not by the executive department alone. The powers of conqueror are not so vested in the President that he can fix and regulate the terms of settlement and confer congressional representation on conquered rebels and traitors. Nor can he, in any way, qualify enemies of the Government to exercise its law-making power. The authority to restore rebels to political power in the Federal Government can be exercised only with the concurrence of all the departments in which political power is vested; and hence the several proclamations of the President to the people of the Confederate States cannot be considered as extending beyond the purposes declared, and can only be regarded as provisional permission by the commander-in-chief of the army to do certain acts, the effect and validity whereof is to be determined by the constitutional government, and not solely by the executive power.

Sixth. The question before Congress is, then, whether conquered enemies have the right, and shall be permitted at their own pleasure and on their own terms, to participate in making laws for their conquerors; whether conquered rebels may change their theatre of operations from the battle-field, where they were defeated and overthrown, to the halls of Congress, and, through their representatives, seize upon the Government which they fought to destroy; whether the national treasury, the army of the nation, its navy, its forts and arsenals, its whole civil administration, its credit, its pensioners, the widows an orphans of those who perished in the war, the public honor, peace and safety, shall all be turned over to the keeping of its recent enemies without delay, and without imposing such conditions as, in the opinion of Congress, the security of the country and its institutions may demand.

Seventh. The history of mankind exhibits no example of such madness and folly. The instinct of self-preservation protests against it. The surrender by Grant to Lee, and by Sherman to Johnston, would have been disasters of less magnitude, for new armies could have been raised, new battles fought, and the Government saved. The anti-coercive policy, which, under pretext of avoiding bloodshed, allowed the rebellion to take form and gather force, would be surpassed in infamy by the matchless wickedness that would now surrender the halls of Congress to those so recently in rebellion, until proper precautions shall have been taken to secure the national faith and the national safety.

Eighth. As has been shown in this report, and in the evidence submitted, no proof has been afforded by Congress of a constituency in any one of the so-called Confederate States, unless we except the State of Tennessee, qualified to elect Senators and Representatives in Congress. No State constitution, or amendment to a State constitution, has had the sanction of the people. All the so-called legislation of State conventions and legislatures has been had under military dictation. If the President may, at his will, and under his own authority, whether as military commander or chief executive, qualify persons to appoint Senators and elect Representatives, and empower others to appoint and elect them, he thereby practically controls the organization of the legislative department. The con-

stitutional form of government is thereby practically destroyed, and its powers absorbed in the Executive. And while your committee do not for a moment impute to the President any such design, but cheerfully concede to him the most patriotic motives, they cannot but look with alarm upon a precedent so fraught with danger to the Republic.

Ninth. The necessity of providing adequate safeguards for the future, before restoring the insurrectionary States to a participation in the direction of public affairs, is apparent from the bitter hostility to the Government and people of the United States yet existing throughout the conquered territory, as proved incontestably by the testimony of many witnesses and by undisputed facts.

Tenth. The conclusion of your committee therefore is, that the so-called Confederate States are not at present entitled to representation in the Congress of the United States; that, before allowing such representation, adequate security for future peace and safety should be required; that this can only be found in such changes of the organic law as shall determine the civil rights and privileges of all citizens in all parts of the Republic, shall place representation on an equitable basis, shall fix a stigma upon treason, and protect the loyal people against future claims for the expenses incurred in support of rebellion and for manumitted slaves, together with an express grant of power in Congress to enforce those provisions. To this end they offer a joint resolution for amending the Constitution of the United States, and the two several bills designed to carry the same into effect, before referred to.

Before closing this report, your committee beg leave to state that the specific recommendations submitted by them are the result of mutual concession, after a long and careful comparison of conflicting opinions. Upon a question of such magnitude, infinitely important as it is to the future of the Republic, it was not to be expected that all should think alike. Sensible of the imperfections of the scheme, your committee submit it to Congress as the best they could agree upon, in the hope that its imperfections may be cured, and its deficiencies supplied, by legislative wisdom; and that, when finally adopted, it may tend to restore peace and harmony to the whole country, and to place our republican institutions on a more stable foundation.

W. P. FESSENDEN,
JAMES W. GRIMES,
IRA HARRIS,
J. M. HOWARD,
GEORGE H. WILLIAMS,
THADDEUS STEVENS,
ELLIHU B. WASHBURNE,
JUSTIN S. MORRILL,
JNO. A. BINGHAM,
ROSCOE CONKLING,
GEORGE S. BOUTWELL,
HENRY T. BLOW.

**Minority Report.**

June 22—Mr. JOHNSON in the Senate and Mr. ROGERS in the House, submitted this
REPORT:
The undersigned, a minority of the joint com-

mittee of the Senate and House of Representatives, constituted under the concurrent resolution of the 13th of December, 1865, making it their duty to "inquire into the condition of the States which formed the so-called Confederate States of America, and to report whether they or any of them are entitled to be represented in either House of Congress, with leave to report by bill or otherwise," not being able to concur in the measures recommended by the majority, or in the grounds upon which they base them, beg leave to report :

In order to obtain a correct apprehension of the subject, and as having a direct bearing upon it, the undersigned think it all important clearly to ascertain what was the effect of the late insurrection upon the relations of the States where it prevailed to the General Government, and of the people collectively and individually of such States. To this inquiry they therefore first address themselves.

First, as to the States. Did the insurrection at its commencement, or at any subsequent time, legally dissolve the connection between those States and the General Government? In our judgment, so far from this being a "profitless abstraction," it is a vital inquiry. For if that connection was not disturbed, such States during the entire rebellion were as completely component States of the United States as they were before the rebellion, and were bound by all the obligations which the Constitution imposes, and entitled to all its privileges. Was not this their condition?

The opposite view alone can justify the denial of such rights and privileges. That a State of the Union can exist without possessing them is inconsistent with the very nature of the Government and terms of the Constitution. In its nature the Government is formed of and by States possessing equal rights and powers. States unequal are not known to the Constitution. In its original formation perfect equality was secured. They were granted the same representation in the Senate, and the same right to be represented in the House of Representatives; the difference in the latter being regulated only by a difference in population. But every State, however small its population, was secured one Representative in that branch. Each State was given the right, and the same right, to participate in the election of President and Vice President, and all alike were secured the benefit of the judicial department. The Constitution, too, was submitted to the people of each State separately, and adopted by them in that capacity. The convention which framed it considered, as they were bound to do, each as a separate sovereignty, that could not be subjected to the Constitution except by its own consent. That consent was consequently asked and given. The equality, therefore, of rights was the condition of the original thirteen States before the Government was formed, and such equality was not only not interfered with, but guaranteed to them as well in regard to the powers conferred upon the General Government, as to those reserved to the States or to the people of the States.

The same equality is secured to the States which have been admitted into the Union since the Constitution was adopted. In each instance the State admitted has been "declared to be one of the United States, on an *equal footing with the original States in all respects whatever*."

The Constitution, too, so far as most of the powers it contains are concerned, operates directly upon the people in their individual and aggregate capacity, and on all alike. Each citizen, therefore, of every State owes the same allegiance to the General Government, and is entitled to the same protection. The obligation of this allegiance it is not within the legal power of his State or of himself to annul or evade. It is made paramount and perpetual, and for that very reason it is equally the paramount duty of the General Government to allow to the citizens of each State, and to the State, the rights secured to both, and the protection necessary to their full enjoyment. A citizen may, no doubt, forfeit such rights by committing a crime against the United States upon conviction of the same, where such forfeiture by law antecedently passed is made a part of the punishment. But a State cannot in its corporate capacity be made liable to such a forfeiture, for a State, as such, under the Constitution, cannot commit or be indicted for a crime. No legal proceeding, criminal or civil, can be instituted to deprive a State of the benefits of the Constitution, by forfeiting as against her any of the rights it secures. Her citizens, be they few or many, may be proceeded against under the law and convicted, but the State remains a State of the Union. To concede that, by the illegal conduct of her own citizens, she can be withdrawn from the Union, is virtually to concede the right of secession. For what difference does it make as regards the result whether a State can rightfully secede, (a doctrine, by-the-by, heretofore maintained by statesmen North as well as South,) or whether by the illegal conduct of her citizens she ceases to be a State of the Union? In either case the end is the same. The only difference is that by the one theory she ceases by law to be such a State, and by the other by crime, without and against law. But the doctrine is wholly erroneous. A State once in the Union must abide in it forever. She can never withdraw from or be expelled from it. A different principle would subject the Union to dissolution at any moment. It is, therefore, alike perilous and unsound.

Nor do we see that it has any support in the measures recommended by the majority of the committee. The insurrectionary States are by these measures conceded to be States of the Union. The proposed constitutional amendment is to be submitted to them as well as to the other States. In this respect each is placed on the same ground. To consult a State not in the Union on the propriety of adopting a constitutional amendment to the government of the Union, and which is necessarily to affect those States only composing the Union, would be an absurdity ; and to allow an amendment, which States in the Union might desire, to be defeated by the votes of States not in the Union, would be alike nonsensical and unjust. The very measure, therefore, of submitting to all the States forming the Union before the insurrection a constitutional amendment, makes the inquiry, whether all at this time are in or out of the Union, a vital one. If they are not, all should not be consulted; if they are, they should be, and should be only because they are. The very fact, therefore, of such a submission concedes that the Southern States are, and never ceased to be, States of the Union.

Tested, therefore, either by the nature of our Government or by the terms of the Constitution, the insurrection, now happily and utterly suppressed, has in no respect changed the relations of the States, where it prevailed, to the General Government. On the contrary, they are to all intents and purposes as completely States of the Union as they ever were. In further support of this proposition, if it needed any, we may confidently appeal to the fact just stated, that the very measure recommended, a constitutional amendment to be submitted to such States, furnishes such support; for, looking to and regarding the rights of the other States, such a submission has no warrant or foundation except upon the hypothesis that they are as absolutely States of the Union as any of the other States. It can never be under any circumstances a "profitless abstraction" whether under the Constitution a State is or is not a State of the Union. It can never be such an abstraction whether the people of a State once in the Union can voluntarily or by compulsion escape or be freed from the obligations it enjoins, or be deprived of the rights it confers or the protection it affords.

A different doctrine necessarily leads to a dissolution of the Union. The Constitution supposes that insurrections may exist in a State, and provides for their suppression by giving Congress the power to "call forth the militia" for the purpose. The power is not to subjugate the State within whose limits the insurrection may prevail, and to extinguish it as a State, but to preserve it as such by subduing the rebellion, by acting on the individual persons engaged in it, and not on the State at all. The power is altogether conservative; it is to protect a State, not to destroy it; to prevent her being taken out of the Union by individual crime, not, in any contingency, to put her out or keep her out. The continuance of the Union of all the States is necessary to the intended existence of the Government. The Government is formed by a constitutional association of States, and its integrity depends on the continuance of the entire association. If one State is withdrawn from it by any cause, to that extent is the Union dissolved. Those that remain may exist as a government, but it is not the very government the Constitution designs. That consists of all; and its character is changed and its power is diminished by the absence of any one.

A different principle leads to a disintegration that must sooner or later result in the separation of all, and the consequent destruction of the Government. To suppose that a power to preserve may, at the option of the body to which it is given, be used to destroy, is a proposition repugnant to common sense; and yet, as the late insurrection was put down by means of that power, that being the only one conferred upon Congress to that end, that proposition is the one on which alone it can be pretended that the Southern States are not in the Union now as well as at first.

The idea that the war power, as such, has been used, or could have been used, to extinguish the rebellion, is, in the judgment of the undersigned utterly without foundation. That power was given for a different contingency—for the contingency of a conflict with other governments, an international conflict. If it had been thought that that power was to be resorted to to suppress a domestic strife, the words "appropriate to that object" would have been used. But so far from this having been done, in the same section that confers it, an express provision is inserted to meet the exigency of a domestic strife or insurrection. To subdue that, authority is given to call out the militia. Whether, in the progress of the effort to suppress an insurrection, the rights incident to war as between the United States and foreign nations may not arise, is a question which in no way changes the character of the contest as between the Government and the insurrectionists. The exercise of such rights may be found convenient, or become necessary for the suppression of the rebellion, but the character of the conflict is in no way changed by a resort to them. That remains, as at first, and must from its very nature during its continuance remain, a mere contest in which the Government seeks, and can only seek, to put an end to the rebellion. That achieved, the original condition of things is at once restored. Two judicial decisions have been made, by judges of eminent and unquestioned ability, which fully sustain our view. In one, that of Amy Warwick, before the United States district court of Massachusetts, Judge Sprague, referring to the supposed effect of the belligerent rights which it was conceded belonged to the Government during the rebellion, by giving it, when suppressed, the rights of conquest, declared:

"It has been supposed that if the Government have the right of a belligerent, then, after the rebellion is suppressed, it will have the rights of conquest; that a State and its inhabitants may be permanently divested of all political advantages, and treated as foreign territory conquered by arms. This is an error, a grave and dangerous error. Belligerent rights cannot be exercised where there are no belligerents. Conquest of a foreign country gives absolute, unlimited sovereign rights, but no nation ever makes such a conquest of its own territory. If a hostile power, either from without or within, takes and holds possession and dominion over any portion of its territory, and the nation, by force of arms, expel or overthrow the enemy, and suppresses hostilities, it acquires no new title, and merely regains the possession of that of which it has been temporarily deprived. The nation acquires no new sovereignty, but merely maintains its previous rights.

"When the United States take possession of a rebel district, they merely vindicate their pre-existing title. Under despotic governments confiscation may be unlimited, but under our Government *the right of sovereignty over any portion of a State is given and limited by the Constitution*, and will be the same after the war as it was before."

In the other, an application for *habeas corpus* to Mr. Justice Nelson, one of the judges of the

Supreme Court of the United States, by James Egan, to be discharged from an imprisonment to which he had been sentenced by a military commission in South Carolina, for the offence of murder alleged to have been committed in that State, and the discharge was ordered, and, in an opinion evidently carefully prepared, among other things, said:

"For all that appears, the civil local courts of the State of South Carolina were in the full exercise of their judicial functions at the time of this trial, as restored by the suppression of the rebellion, some seven months previously, and by the revival of the laws and the reorganization of the State in obedience to, and in conformity with, its constitutional duties to the Union. Indeed, long previous to this the provisional government had been appointed by the President, who is commander-in-chief of the army and navy of the United States, (and whose will under martial law constituted the only rule of action,) for the special purpose of changing the existing state of things, and restoring the civil government over the people. In operation of this appointment, a new constitution had been formed, a governor and legislature elected under it, *and the State placed in the full enjoyment, or entitled to the full enjoyment, of all her constitutional rights and privileges.* The constitutional laws of the Union were thereby enjoyed and obeyed, and were as authoritative and binding over the people of the State as in any other portion of the country. Indeed, the moment the rebellion was suppressed, and the government growing out of it subverted, *the ancient laws resumed their accustomed sway, subject only to the new reorganization by the appointment of the proper officer to give them operation and effect.* This organization and appointment of the public functionaries, which was under the superintendence and direction of the President, the commander-in-chief of the army and navy of the country, and who, as such, had previously governed the State, from imperative necessity, by the force of martial law, had already taken place, and the necessity no longer existed."

This opinion is the more authoritative than it might possibly be esteemed otherwise, from its being the first elaborate statement of the reasons which governed the majority of the Supreme Court at the last term in their judgment in the case of Milligan and others, that military commissions for the trial of civilians are not constitutional. Mr. Justice Nelson was one of that majority, and of course was advised of the grounds of their decision. We submit that nothing could be more conclusive in favor of the doctrine for which they are cited than these judgments. In the one, the preposition of conquest of a State as a right under the war to suppress the insurrection is not only repudiated by Judge Sprague, but, because of the nature of our Government, is considered to be legally impossible. "The right of sovereignty over any portion of a State will," he tells us, "only be the same after the war as it was before." In the other, we are told "that the suppression of the rebellion restores the courts of the State," and that when her government is reorganized she at once is "in the full enjoyment, or entitled to the

full enjoyment, of all her constitutional rights and privileges."

Again, a contrary doctrine is inconsistent with the obligation which the Government is under to each citizen of a State. Protection to each is a part of that obligation—protection not only as against a foreign, but a domestic foe. To hold that it is in the power of any part of the people of a State, whether they constitute a majority or minority, by engaging in insurrection and adopting any measure in its prosecution to make citizens who are not engaged in it, but opposed to it, enemies of the United States, having no right to the protection which the Constitution affords to citizens who are true to their allegiance, is as illegal as it would be flagrantly unjust. During the conflict the exigency of the strife may justify a denial of such protection, and subject the unoffending citizen to inconvenience or loss; but the conflict over, the exigency ceases, and the obligation to afford him all the immunities and advantages of the Constitution, one of which is the right to be represented in Congress, becomes absolute and imperative. A different rule would enable the Government to escape a clear duty, and to commit a gross violation of the Constitution. It has been said that the Supreme Court have entertained a different doctrine in the prize cases. This, in the judgment of the undersigned, is a clear misapprehension. One of the questions in those cases was, whether in such a contest as was being waged for the extinguishment of the insurrection, belligerent rights, as *between the United States and other nations,* belonged to the former. The Court properly held that they did; but the parties engaged in the rebellion were designated as traitors, and liable to be tried as traitors when the rebellion should terminate. If the Confederate States, by force of insurrection, became foreign States and lost their character as States of the Union, then the contest was an international one, and treason was no more committed by citizens of the former against the latter, than by those of the latter against the former. Treason necessarily assumes allegiance to the government, and allegiance necessarily assumes a continuing obligation to the government. Neither predicament was true, except upon the hypothesis that the old state of things continued. In other words, that the States, notwithstanding the insurrection, were continuously, and are now, States of the United States, and their citizens responsible to the Constitution and the laws. Second: what is there, then, in the present political condition of such States that justifies their exclusion from representation in Congress? Is it because they are without organized governments, or without governments republican in point of form? In fact, we know that they have governments completely organized with legislative, executive, and judicial functions. We know that they are now in successful operation; no one within their limits questions their legality, or is denied their protection. How they were formed, under what auspices they were formed, are inquiries with which Congress has no concern. The right of the people of a State to form a government for themselves has never been questioned. In the absence of any restriction that right would be absolute; any form could be adopted that they might determine upon. The Constitution imposes but a single restriction—that the government adopted shall be "of a republican form," and this is done in the obligation to guarantee every State such a form. It gives no power to frame a constitution for a State. It operates alone upon one already formed by the State. In the words of the Federalist, (No. 44,) "it supposes a pre-existing government of the form which is to be guaranteed." It is not pretended that the existing governments of the States in question are not of the required form. The objection is that they were not legally established. But it is confidently submitted that that is a matter with which Congress has nothing to do. The power to establish or modify a State government belongs exclusively to the people of the State. When they shall exercise it, how they shall exercise it, what provisions it shall contain, it is their exclusive right to decide, and when decided, their decision is obligatory upon everybody, and independent of all congressional control, if such government be *republican.* To convert an obligation of guarantee into an authority to interfere in any way in the formation of the government to be guaranteed is to do violence to language. If it be said that the President did illegally interfere in the organization of such governments, the answers are obvious: First. If it was true, if the people of such States not only have not, but do not, complain of it, but, on the contrary, have pursued his advice, and are satisfied with and are living under the governments they have adopted, and those governments are republican in form, what right has Congress to interfere or deny their legal existence? Second. Conceding, for argument's sake, that the President's alleged interference was unauthorized, does it not, and for the same reason, follow that any like interference by Congress would be equally unauthorized? A different view is not to be maintained because of the difference in the nature of the powers conferred upon Congress and the President, the one being legislative and the other executive; for it is equally, and upon the same ground, beyond the scope of either to form a government for a people of a State once in the Union, or to expel such a State from the Union, or to deny, temporarily or permanently, the rights which belong to a State and her people under the Constitution.

Congress may admit new States, but a State once admitted ceases to be within its control, and can never again be brought within it. What changes her people may at any time think proper to make in her constitution is a matter with which neither Congress nor any department of the General Government can interfere, unless such changes make the State government anti-republican, and then it can only be done under the obligation to guarantee that it be republican. Whatever may be the extent of the power conferred upon Congress in the 3d section, article 4, of the Constitution, to admit new States—in what manner and to what extent they can, under that power, interfere in the formation and character of the Constitution of such States preliminary to admission into the Union, no one has ever pretended that when that is had, the State can again be brought within its influence. The power is exhausted when once executed, the subject forthwith passing out of its reach. The State admitted, like the original thirteen States, becomes at once and forever independent of congressional control. A different view would change the entire character of the Government as its framers and their contemporaries designed and understood it to be. They never intended to make the State governments subordinate to the General Government. Each was to move supreme within its own orbit; but as each would not alone have met the exigencies of a government adequate to all the wants of the people, the two, in the language of Mr. Jefferson, constituted "co-ordinate departments of one single and integral whole;" the one having the power of legislation and administration "in affairs which concerned their own citizens only;" the other, "whatever concerned foreigners, or citizens of other States." Within their respective limits each is paramount. The States, as to all powers not delegated to the General Government, are as independent of that government as the latter, in regard to all powers that are delegated to it, is independent of the governments of the States. The proposition, then, that Congress can, by force or otherwise, under the war or insurrectionary or any other power, expel a State from the Union, or reduce it to a territorial condition and govern it as such, is utterly without foundation. The undersigned deem it unnecessary to examine the question further. They leave it upon the observations submitted, considering it perfectly clear that States, notwithstanding occurring insurrections, continue to be States of the Union.

Thirdly. If this is so, it necessarily follows that the rights of States under the Constitution, as originally possessed and enjoyed by them, are still theirs, and those they are now enjoying, as far as they depend upon the executive and judicial departments of the government. By each of these departments they are recognized as States. By the one, all officers of the government required by law to be appointed in such States have been appointed, and are discharging, without question, their respective functions. By the other they are, as States, enjoying the benefit, and subjected to the powers of that department; a fact conclusive to show that, in the estimation of the judiciary, they are, as they were at first, States of the Union, bound by the laws of the Union, and entitled to all the rights incident to that relation. And yet, so far they are denied that right which the Constitution properly esteems as the security of all the others—that right, without which government is anything but a republic—is indeed but a tyranny—the right of having a voice in the legislative department, whose laws bind them in person and in property;—this, it is submitted, is a state of things without example in a representative republican government; and Congress, as long as it denies this right, is a mere despotism. Citizens may be made to submit to it by force, or dread of force, but a fraternal spirit and good feeling toward those who impose it, so important to the peace and prosperity of the country, are not to be hoped for, but rather unhappiness, dissatisfaction, and enmity. There is but one ground on which such conduct can find any excuse—a supposed public necessity; the peril of destruction to which the government would be subjected, if the right was allowed. But for such a supposition there is not, in the opinion of the undersigned, even a shadow of foundation.

The representatives of the States in which there was no insurrection, if the others were represented, would in the House, under the present apportionment, exceed the latter by a majority of seventy-two votes, and have a decided preponderance in the Senate. What danger to the Government, then, can possibly arise from southern representation? Are the present Senators and Representatives fearful of themselves? Are they apprehensive that they might be led to the destruction of our institutions by the persuasion, or any other influence, of southern members? How disparaging to themselves is such an apprehension. Are they apprehensive that those who may succeed them from their respective States may be so fatally led astray? How disparaging is that supposition to the patriotism and wisdom of their constituents. Whatever effect on mere party success in the future such a representation may have we shall not stop to inquire. The idea that the country is to be kept in turmoil, States to be reduced to bondage, and their rights under the Constitution denied, and their citizens degraded, with a view to the continuance in power of a mere political party, cannot for a moment be entertained without imputing gross dishonesty of purpose and gross dereliction of duty to those who may entertain it. Nor do we deem it necessary to refer particularly to the evidence taken by the committee to show that there is nothing in the present condition of the people of the southern States that even excuses on that ground a denial of representation to them. We content ourselves with saying that in our opinion the evidence most to be relied upon, whether regarding the character of the witnesses or their means of information, shows that representatives from the southern States would prove perfectly loyal. We specially refer for this only to the testimony of Lieutenant General Grant. His loyalty and his intelligence no one can doubt. In his letter to the President of the 18th of December, 1865, after he had recently visited South Carolina, North Carolina, and Georgia, he says:

"*Both in travelling and while stopping, I saw much and conversed freely with the citizens of those States, as well as with officers of the army who have been among them.* The following are the conclusions come to by me:

"I am satisfied that *the mass of thinking men of the South accept the present situation of affairs in good faith.* The questions which have heretofore divided the sentiments of the people of the two sections—slavery and State rights, or the right of a State to secede from the Union —they regard as having been settled forever by the highest tribunal, arms, that man can resort to. *I was pleased to learn from the leading men whom I met that they not only accepted the decision arrived at as final, but that now, the smoke of battle has cleared away and time has been* given for reflection, that this decision has been a fortunate one for the whole country, they receiving the like benefits from it with those who opposed them in the field and in the cause. * *

"My observations lead me to the conclusion that the citizens of the southern States *are anxious to return to self-government within the Union* as soon as possible; that while reconstructing, they *want and require protection from the Government; that they are in earnest in wishing to do what they think is required by the Government, not humiliating to them as citizens;* and that if such a course was pointed out, they would pursue it in good faith. *It is to be regretted that there cannot be a greater commingling at this time between the citizens of the two sections, and particularly of those intrusted with the law-making power.*"

Secession, as a practical doctrine ever hereafter to be resorted to, is almost utterly abandoned. It was submitted to and failed before the ordeal of battle. Nor can the undersigned imagine why, if its revival is anticipated as possible, the committee have not recommended an amendment to the Constitution guarding against it in terms. Such an amendment, it cannot be doubted, the southern as well as northern States would cheerfully adopt. The omission of such a recommendation is pregnant evidence that secession, as a constitutional right, is thought by the majority of the committee to be, practically, a mere thing of the past, as all the proof taken by them shows it to be, in the opinion of all the leading southern men who hitherto entertained it. The desolation around them, the hecatombs of their own slain, the stern patriotism of the men of the other States, exhibited by unlimited expenditure of treasure and of blood, and their love of the Union so sincere and deep-seated that it is seen they will hazard all to maintain it, have convinced the South that, as a practical doctrine, secession is extinguished forever. State secession, then, abandoned, and slavery abolished by the southern States themselves, or with their consent, upon what statesmanlike ground can such States be denied all the rights which the Constitution secures to States of the Union? All admit that to do so at the earliest period is demanded by every consideration of duty and policy, and none deny that the actual interest of the country is to a great extent involved in such admission. The staple productions of the Southern States are as important to the other States as to themselves. Those staples largely enter into the wants of all alike, and they are also most important to the financial credit of the Government. Those staples will never be produced as in the past until real peace, resting, as it can alone rest, on the equal and uniform operation of the Constitution and laws on all, is attained. To suppose that a brave and sensitive people will give an undivided attention to the increase of mere material wealth while retained in a state of political inferiority and degradation is mere folly. They desire to be again in the Union, to enjoy the benefits of the Constitution, and they invoke you to receive them. They have adopted constitutions free from any intrinsic objection, and have agreed to every stipulation thought by the President to be necessary for the protection and benefit of all, and in the opinion of the undersigned they are amply sufficient. Why exact, as a preliminary condition to representation, more? What more are supposed to be necessary? First, the repudiation of the rebel debt; second, the denial of all obligation to pay for manumitted slaves; third, the inviolability of our own debt. If these provisions are deemed necessary, they cannot be defeated, if the South were disposed to defeat them, by the admission into Congress of their representatives. Nothing is more probable, in the opinion of the undersigned, than that many of the southern States would adopt them all; but those measures the committee connect with others which we think the people of the South will never adopt. They are asked to disfranchise a numerous class of their citizens, and also to agree to diminish their representation in Congress, and of course in the electoral college, or to admit to the right of suffrage their colored males of twenty-one years of age and upwards, (a class now in a condition of almost utter ignorance,) thus placing them on the same political footing with white citizens of that age. For reasons so obvious that the dullest may discover them, the right is not directly asserted of granting suffrage to the negro. That would be obnoxious to most of the Northern and Western States, so much so that their consent was not to be anticipated; but as the plan adopted, because of the limited number of negroes in such States, will have no effect on their representation, it is thought it may be adopted, while in the southern States it will materially lessen their number. That these latter States will assent to the measure can hardly be expected. The effect, then, if not the purpose, of the measure is forever to deny representatives to such States, or, if they consent to the condition, to weaken their representative power, and thus, probably, secure a continuance of such a party in power as now control the legislation of the Government. The measure, in its terms and its effect, whether designed or not, is to degrade the southern States. To consent to it will be to consent to their own dishonor.

The manner, too, of presenting the proposed constitutional amendment, in the opinion of the undersigned, is impolitic and without precedent. The several amendments suggested have no connection with each other; each, if adopted, would have its appropriate effect if the others were rejected; and each, therefore, should be submitted as a separate article, without subjecting it to the contingency of rejection if the States should refuse to ratify the rest. Each by itself, if an advisable measure, should be submitted to the people, and not in such a connection with those which they may think unnecessary or dangerous as to force them to reject all. The repudiation of the rebel debt, and all obligation to compensate for the loss of slave property, and the inviolability of the debts of the Government, no matter how contracted, provided for by some of the sections of the amendment, we repeat, we believe would meet the approval of many of the southern States; but these no State can sanction without sanctioning others, which we think will not be done by them or by some of the northern States.

To force negro suffrage upon any State by means of a penalty of a loss of part of its representation, will not only be to impose a disparaging condition, but virtually to interfere with the clear right of each State to regulate suffrage for itself, without the control of the Government of the United States. Whether that control be exerted directly or indirectly, it will be considered, as it is, a fatal blow to the right which every State in the past has held vital, the right to regulate her franchise.

To punish a State for not regulating it in a particular way, so as to give to all classes of the people the privilege of suffrage, is but seeking to accomplish incidentally what, if it should be done at all, should be done directly. No reason, in the view of the undersigned, can be suggested for the course adopted, other than a belief that such a direct interference would not be sanctioned by the northern and western States, while, as regards such States, the actual recommendation, because of the small proportion of negroes within their limits, will not in the least lessen their representative power in Congress or their influence in the presidential election, and they may therefore sanction it. This very inequality in its operation upon the States renders the measure, in our opinion, most unjust, and, looking to the peace and quiet of the country, most impolitic. But the mode advised is also not only without but against all precedent. When the Constitution was adopted it was thought to be defective in not sufficiently protecting certain rights of the States and the people. With the view of supplying a remedy for this defect, on the 4th March, 1789, various amendments by a resolution constitutionally passed by Congress were submitted for ratification to the States. They were twelve in number. Several of them were even less independent of each other than are those recommended by the committee. But it did not occur to the men of that day that it was right to force the States to adopt or reject all. Each was, therefore, presented as a separate article. The language of the resolution was, "that the following articles be proposed to the legislatures of the several States as amendments of the Constitution of the United States, ALL OR ANY OF WHICH ARTICLES, when ratified by three-fourths of the said legislatures, to be valid to all intents and purposes as parts of the Constitution. The Congress of that day was willing to obtain either of the submitted amendments—to get a part, if not able to procure the whole. They thought (and in that we submit they but conformed to the letter and spirit of the amendatory clause of the Constitution,) that the people have the right to pass severally on any proposed amendments. This course of our fathers is now departed from, and the result will probably be that no one of the suggested amendments, though some may be approved, will be ratified. This will certainly be the result, unless the States are willing practically to relinquish the right they have always enjoyed, never before questioned by any recognized statesman, and all-important to their interest and security—the right to regulate the franchise in all their elections.

There are, too, some general considerations

that bear on the subject, to which we will now refer.

First. One of the resolutions of the Chicago convention, by which Mr. Lincoln was first nominated for the presidency, says, "that the maintenance inviolate of *the rights of the States* is essential to the balance of power on which the prosperity and endurance of our political fabric depend." In his inaugural address of 4th March, 1861, which received the almost universal approval of the people, among other things he said, "*no State of its own mere motion can lawfully get out of the Union;*" and that "in view of the Constitution and the laws, the Union is unbroken, and to the extent of my ability I shall take care, as the Constitution itself expressly enjoins upon me, that the laws of the Union be faithfully executed in all the States."

Second. Actual conflict soon afterwards ensued. The South, it was believed, misapprehended the purpose of the Government in carrying it on, and Congress deemed it important to dispel that misapprehension by declaring what the purpose was. This was done in July, 1861, by their passing the following resolution, offered by Mr. Crittenden: "That in this national emergency, Congress, banishing all feeling of mere passion or resentment, will recollect only its duty to the whole country; that this war is not waged, upon our part, in any spirit of oppression, nor for any purpose of conquest or subjugation, nor purpose of overthrowing or interfering with the rights or established institutions of those States, but to defend and maintain the supremacy of the Constitution, and to preserve the Union, with all the dignity, equality, and rights of the several States unimpaired; that as soon as these objects are accomplished, the war ought to cease." The vote in the House was 119 for and 2 against it, and in the Senate 30 for and 5 against it. The design to conquer or subjugate, or to curtail or interfere in any way with the rights of the States, is in the strongest terms thus disclaimed, and the only avowed object asserted to be "to defend and maintain the spirit of the Constitution, and to preserve the Union, AND THE DIGNITY, EQUALITY, AND RIGHTS OF THE SEVERAL STATES UNIMPAIRED." Congress, too, by the act of 13th July, 1861, empowered the President to declare, by proclamation, "that the inhabitants of such State or States where the insurrection existed are in a state of insurrection against the United States," and thereupon to declare that "all commercial intercourse by and between the same, by the citizens thereof and the citizens of the United States, shall cease and be unlawful *so long as such condition of hostility shall continue.*" Here, also, Congress evidently deals with the States as being in the Union and to remain in the Union. It seeks to keep them in by forbidding commercial intercourse between their citizens and the citizens of the other States so long, and so long only, as *insurrectionary hostility shall continue.* That ended, they are to be, as at first, entitled to the same intercourse with citizens of other States that they enjoyed before the insurrection. In other words, in this act, as in the resolution of the same month, the dignity, equality, and rights of such States (the insurrection ended) were not to be held in any respect impaired. The several

proclamations of amnesty issued by Mr. Lincoln and his successor under the authority of Congress are also inconsistent with the idea that the parties included within them are not to be held, in the future, restored to all rights belonging to them as citizens of their respective States. A power to pardon is a power to restore the offender to the condition in which he was before the date of the offence pardoned.

It is now settled that a pardon removes not only the punishment, but *all* the legal disabilities consequent on the crime. (7 Bac. Ab. Tit. Par.) Bishop on Criminal Law (vol. 1, p. 713) states the same doctrine. The amnesties so declared would be but false pretences if they were, as now held, to leave the parties who have availed themselves of them in almost every particular in the condition they would have been in if they had rejected them. Such a result, it is submitted, would be a foul blot on the good name of the nation. Upon the whole, therefore, in the present state of the country, the excitement which exists, and which may mislead legislatures already elected, we think that the matured sense of the people is not likely to be ascertained on the subject of the proposed amendment by its submission to existing State legislatures. If it should be done at all, the submission should either be to legislatures hereafter to be elected, or to conventions of the people chosen for the purpose. Congress may select either mode, but they have selected neither. It may be submitted to legislatures already in existence, whose members were heretofore elected with no view to the consideration of such a measure; and it may consequently be adopted, though a majority of the people of the States disapprove of it. In this respect, if there were no other objections to it, we think it most objectionable.

Whether regard be had to the nature or the terms of the Constitution, or to the legislation of Congress during the insurrection, or to the course of the judicial department, or to the conduct of the executive, the undersigned confidently submit that the southern States are States in the Union, and entitled to every right and privilege belonging to the other States. If any portion of their citizens be disloyal, or are not able to take any oath of office that has been or may be constitutionally prescribed, is a question irrespective of the right of the States to be represented. Against the danger, whatever that may be, of the admission of disloyal or disqualified members into the Senate or House, it is in the power of each branch to provide against by refusing such admission. Each by the Constitution is made the judge of the election returns and qualifications of its own members. No other department can interfere with it. Its decision concludes all others. The only corrective, when error is committed, consists in the responsibility of the members to the people. But it is believed by the undersigned to be the clear duty of each house to admit any Senator or Representative who has been elected according to the constitutional laws of the State, and who is able and willing to subscribe the oath required by constitutional law.

It is conceded by the majority that "it would

undoubtedly be competent for Congress to waive all formalities, and to admit those Confederate States at once, trusting that time and experience would set all things right." It is not, therefore, owing to a want of constitutional power that it is not done. It is not because such States are not States with republi an forms of government. The exclusion must therefore rest on considerations of safety or of expediency alone. The first, that of safety, we have already considered, and, as we think, proved it to be without foundation. Is there any ground for the latter expediency? We think not. On the contrary, in our judgment, their admission is called for by the clearest expediency. Those States include a territorial area of 850,000 square miles, an area larger than that of five of the leading nations of Europe. They have a coast line of 3,000 miles, with an internal water line, including the Mississippi, of about 36,000 miles. Their agricultural products in 1850 were about $560,000,000 in value, and their population 9,664,656. Their staple productions are of immense and growing importance and are almost peculiar to that region. That the North is deeply interested in having such a country and people restored to all the rights and privileges that the Constitution affords no sane man, not blinded by mere party considerations, or not a victim of disordering prejudice, can for a moment doubt. Such a restoration is also necessary to the peace of the country. It is not only important but vital to the potential wealth of which that section of our country is capable, that cannot otherwise be fully developed. Every hour of illegal political restraint, every hour the possession of the rights the Constitution gives is denied, is not only in a political but a material sense of great injury to the North as well as to the South. The southern planter works for his northern brethren as well as for himself. His labors heretofore inured as much if not more to their advantage than to his. Whilst harmony in the past between the sections gave to the whole a prosperity, a power, and a renown of which every citizen had reason to be proud, the restoration of such harmony will immeasurably increase them all. Can it, will it be restored as long as the South is kept in political and dishonoring bondage? and can it not, will it not be restored by an opposite policy? By admitting her to all the rights of the Constitution, and by dealing with her citizens as equals and as brothers, not as inferiors and enemies, such a course as this will, we are certain, soon be seen to bind them heart and soul to the Union, and inspire them with confidence in its government, by making them feel that all enmity is forgotten, and that justice is being done to them. The result of such a policy, we believe, will at once make us in very truth one people, as happy, as prosperous, and as powerful as ever existed in the tide of time; while its opposite cannot fail to keep us divided, injuriously affect the particular and general welfare of citizen and Government, and, if long persisted in, result in danger to the nation. In the words of an eminent British whig statesman, now no more, "A free constitution and large exclusions from its benefit cannot subsist together; the constitution will destroy them, or they will destroy the constitution." It is hoped that, heeding the warning, we will guard against the peril by removing its cause.

The undersigned have not thought it necessary to examine into the legality of the measures adopted, either by the late or the present President, for the restoration of the southern States. It is sufficient for their purpose to say that, if those of President Johnson were not justified by the Constitution, the same may at least be said of those of his predecessor. We deem such an examination to be unnecessary, because, however it might result, the people of the several States who possessed, as we have before said, the exclusive right to decide for themselves what constitutions they should adopt, have adopted those under which they respectively live. The motives of neither President, however, whether the measures were legal or not, are liable to censure. The sole object of each was to effect a complete and early union of all the States, to make the General Government, as it did at first, embrace all, and to extend its authority and secure its privileges and blessings to all alike. The purity of motive of President Johnson in this particular, as was to have been expected, is admitted by the majority of the committee to be beyond doubt; for, whatever was their opinion of the unconstitutionality of his course, and its tendency to enlarge the executive power, they tell us that they "do not for a moment impute to him any such design but cheerfully concede to him the most patriotic motives." And we cannot forbear to say, in conclusion, upon that point, that he sins against light, and closes his eyes to the course of the President during the rebellion, from its inception to its close, who ventures to impeach his patriotism. Surrounded by insurrectionists, he stood firm. His life was almost constantly in peril, and he clung to the Union, and discharged all the obligations it imposed upon him, even the closer because of the peril. And now that he has escaped unharmed, and by the confidence of the people has had devolved upon him the executive functions of the Government, to charge him with disloyalty is either a folly or a slander folly in the fool who believes it; slander in the man of sense, if any such there be, who utters it.

REVERDY JOHNSON,
A. J. ROGERS,
HENRY GRIDER

# VOTES ON PROPOSED CONSTITUTIONAL AMENDMENTS.

**The Constitutional Amendment, as Finally Adopted and Submitted to the Legislatures of the States.**

### IN SENATE.

1866, June 8—The Amendment in these words, as finally amended, was brought to a vote:

Joint resolution proposing an amendment to the Constitution of the United States.

*Resolved by the Senate and House of Representatives of the United States of America in Congress assembled,* (two-thirds of both Houses concurring,) That the following article be proposed to the legislatures of the several States as an amendment to the Constitution of the United States, which, when ratified by three-fourths of said legislatures, shall be valid as part of the Constitution, namely:

### ARTICLE 14.

SECTION 1. All persons born or naturalized in the United States, and subject to the jurisdiction thereof, are citizens of the United States and of the State wherein they reside. No State shall make or enforce any law which shall abridge the privileges or immunities of citizens of the United States; nor shall any State deprive any person of life, liberty, or property, without due process of law, nor deny to any person within its jurisdiction the equal protection of the laws.

SEC. 2. Representatives shall be apportioned among the several States according to their respective numbers, counting the whole number of persons in each State, excluding Indians not taxed. But when the right to vote at any election for the choice of electors for President and Vice-President of the United States, representatives in Congress, the executive and judicial officers of a State, or the members of the legislature thereof, is denied to any of the male inhabitants of such State, being twenty-one years of age, and citizens of the United States, or in any way abridged, except for participation in rebellion or other crime, the basis of representation therein shall be reduced in the proportion which the number of such male citizens shall bear to the whole number of male citizens twenty-one years of age in such State.

SEC. 3. No person shall be a senator or representative in Congress, or elector of President and Vice-President, or hold any office, civil or military, under the United States, or under any State, who, having previously taken an oath, as a member of Congress, or as an officer of the United States, or as a member of any State legislature, or as an executive or judicial officer of any State, to support the Constitution of the United States, shall have engaged in insurrec-tion or rebellion against the same, or given aid or comfort to the enemies thereof. But Congress may, by a vote of two-thirds of each house, remove such disability.

SEC. 4. The validity of the public debt of the United States, authorized by law, including debts incurred for payment of pensions and bounties for services in suppressing insurrection or rebellion, shall not be questioned. But neither the United States nor any State shall assume or pay any debt or obligation incurred in aid of insurrection or rebellion against the United States, or any claim for the loss or emancipation of any slave; but all such debts, obligations and claims shall be held illegal and void

SEC. 5. The Congress shall have power to enforce, by appropriate legislation, the provisions of this article.

It passed—yeas 33, nays 11, as follow:

YEAS—Messrs. Anthony, Chandler, Clark, Conness, Cragin, Creswell, Edmunds, Fessenden, Foster, Grimes, Harris. Henderson, Howard, Howe, Kirkwood. Lane of Kansas, Lane of Indiana, Morgan, Morrill, Nye, Poland, Pomeroy, Ramsey, Sherman, Sprague, Stewart, Sumner, Trumbull, Wade, Willey, Williams, Wilson, Yates—33.

NAYS—Messrs. Cowan, *Davis*, Doolittle, *Guthrie*, *Hendricks, Johnson, McDougall*, Norton, *Riddle, Saulsbury*, Van Winkle—11.

ABSENT—Messrs. Brown, *Buckalew*, Dixon, *Nesmith*, *Wright*—5.

### IN HOUSE.

June 13—The Amendment passed—yeas 138, nays 36, as follow:

YEAS—Messrs. Alley, Allison, Ames, Anderson, Delos R. Ashley, James M. Ashley, Baker, Baldwin, Banks, Barker, Baxter, Beaman, Benjamin, Bidwell, Bingham, Blaine, Blow, Boutwell, Brandegee, Bromwell, Broomall, Buckland, Bundy, Reader W. Clarke, Sidney Clarke, Cobb, Conkling, Cook, Cullom, Darling. Davis, Dawes, Defrees, Delano, Deming, Dixon, Dodge, Donnelly, Driggs, Dumont, Eckley, Eggleston, Eliot, Farnsworth, Farquhar, Ferry, Garfield, Grinnell, Griswold, Hale, Abner C. Harding, Hart, Hayes, Henderson, Higby, Holmes, Hooper, Hotchkiss, Asahel W. Hubbard, Chester D. Hubbard, Demas Hubbard, jr., John H. Hubbard, James R. Hubbell, Hulburd, Ingersoll, Jenckes, Julian, Kasson, Kelley, Kelso, Ketcham, Kuykendall, Laflin, Latham, George V. Lawrence, William Lawrence, Loan, Longyear, Lynch, Marston, Marvin, McClurg, McKee, McRuer, Mercur, Miller, Moorhead, Morrill, Morris, Moulton, Myers, Newell, O'Neill, Orth, Paine, Patterson, Perham, Phelps, Pike, Plants, Pomeroy, Price, William H. Randall, Raymond, Alexander H. Rice, John H. Rice, Rollins, Sawyer, Schenck, Scofield, Shellabarger, Sloan, Smith, Spalding, Stevens, Stillwell, Thayer, Francis Thomas, John L. Thomas, Trowbridge, Upson, Van Aernam, Burt Van Horn, Robert T. Van Horn, Ward, Warner, Ellihu B. Washburne, Henry D. Washburn, William B. Washburn, Welker, Wentworth, Whaley, Williams, James F. Wilson, Stephen F. Wilson, Windom, Woodbridge, the Speaker—138.

NAYS—Messrs. *Ancona, Bergen, Boyer, Chanler, Coffroth, Dawson, Denison, Eldridge, Finck, Glossbrenner, Grider, Aaron Harding, Hogan, Edwin N. Hubbell, James M. Humphrey, Johnson, Kerr, Le Blond, Marshall, McCullough, Niblack, Nicholson, Radford, Samuel J. Randall, Ritter, Rogers, Ross, Shanklin, Sitgreaves, Strouse, Taber, Taylor, Thornton, Trimble, Winfield, Wright*—36.

NOT VOTING—Messrs. Culver, *Goodyear, Harris*, Hill, James Humphrey, *Jones, McIndoe, Noell*, Rousseau, Starr—10.

## Preliminary Proceedings.

Prior to the adoption of the joint resolution in the form above stated, these reports were made from the Joint Committee, and these votes were taken in the two Houses:

### IN HOUSE.

April 30—Mr. Stevens, from the Joint Select Committee on Reconstruction reported a joint resolution, as follows:

A joint resolution proposing an amendment to the Constitution of the United States.

*Be it resolved, &c.,* (two-thirds of both Houses concurring,) That the following article be proposed to the legislatures of the several States as an amendment to the Constitution of the United States, which, when ratified by three-fourths of said legislatures, shall be valid as part of the Constitution, namely:

ARTICLE —.

SEC. 1. No State shall make or enforce any law which shall abridge the privileges or immunities of citizens of the United States; nor shall any State deprive any person of life, liberty, or property without due process of law, nor deny to any person within its jurisdiction the equal protection of the laws.

SEC. 2. Representatives shall be apportioned among the several States which may be included within this Union, according to their respective numbers, counting the whole number of persons in each State, excluding Indians not taxed. But whenever in any State the elective franchise shall be denied to any portion of its male citizens not less than twenty-one years of age, or in any way abridged, except for participation in rebellion or other crime, the basis of representation in such State shall be reduced in the proportion which the number of such male citizens shall bear to the whole number of male citizens not less than twenty-one years of age.

SEC. 3. Until the 4th day of July, in the year 1870, all persons who voluntarily adhered to the late insurrection, giving it aid and comfort, shall be excluded from the right to vote for representatives in Congress and for electors for President and Vice-President of the United States.

SEC. 4. Neither the United States nor any State shall assume or pay any debt or obligation already incurred, or which may hereafter be incurred, in aid of insurrection or of war against the United States, or any claim for compensation for loss of involuntary service or labor.

SEC. 5. The Congress shall have power to enforce, by appropriate legislation, the provisions of this article.

Objection having been made to its being a special order for Tuesday, May 8, and every day thereafter until disposed of, Mr. Stevens moved a suspension of the rules to enable him to make that motion; which was agreed to—yeas 107, nays 20.

The NAYS were: Messrs. *Ancona, Bergen, Boyer, Coffroth, Dawson, Eldridge, Finck, Grider, Aaron Harding, James M. Humphrey,* Latham, *Marshall, Niblack, Nicholson, Ritter, Ross, Strouse, Taylor, Thornton, Winfield*—20.

May 10—Mr. Stevens demanded the previous question; which was seconded, on a count, 85 to 57; and the main question was ordered—yeas 84, nays 79, as follow:

YEAS—Messrs. Allison, Ames, Anderson, Banks, Baxter, Bidwell, Boutwell, Bromwell, Broomall, *Chanler,* Reader W. Clarke, Sidney Clarke, Cobb, Conkling, Cook, Defrees, Dixon, Driggs, Dumont, Eckley, Eggleston, *Eldridge,* Eliot, *Grider,* Grinnell, *Aaron Harding,* Abner C. Harding, *Harris,* Hart, Higby, Holmes, Hooper, Hotchkiss, Asahel W. Hubbard, Demas Hubbard, Ingersoll, Julian, Kelley, Kelso, *Kerr,* William Lawrence, *Le Blond,* Loan, Lynch, Marston, McClurg, *McCullough,* McIndoe, Mercur, Morrill, Moulton, *Niblack,* O'Neill, Orth, Paine, Patterson, Perham, Pike, Price, John H Rice, *Ritter, Rogers,* Rollins, *Ross,* Rousseau, Sawyer, Schenck, Scofield, *Shanklin,* Shellabarger, Spalding, Stevens, Francis Thomas, John L. Thomas, *Thornton,* Trowbridge, Upson, Ward, Ellihu B. Washburne, Welker, James F. Wilson, Stephen F. Wilson, Windom, Woodbridge—84.

NAYS—Messrs. Alley, *Ancona,* Delos R. Ashley, James M. Ashley, Baker, Baldwin, Barker, Beaman, Benjamin, *Bergen,* Bingham, Blaine, Blow, *Boyer,* Buckland, Bundy, *Coffroth,* Cullom, Darling, Davis, Dawes, *Dawson,* Delano, Deming, Dodge, Donnelly, Farnsworth, Ferry, Finck, Garfield. *Glossbrenner,* Goodyear, Griswold, Hayes, Henderson, Chester D. Hubbard, James R. Hubbell, Hulburd, James Humphrey, Jenckes, Kasson, Ketcham, Kuykendall, Laflin, Latham, George V. Lawrence, Longyear, *Marshall,* McKee, McRuer, Miller, Moorhead, Morris, Myers, Newell, Phelps, Plants, *Radford, Samuel J. Randall,* William H. Randall, Raymond, Alexander H. Rice, *Sitgreaves,* Smith, Stillwell, *Strouse, Taber, Taylor,* Thayer, *Trimble,* Burt Van Horn, *Robert T.* Van Horn, Warner, Henry D. Washburn, William B. Washburn, Whaley, Williams, *Winfield, Wright*—79.

The joint resolution, as above printed, then passed—yeas 128, nays 37, as follow:

YEAS—Messrs. Alley, Allison, Ames, Anderson, Delos R. Ashley, James M. Ashley, Baker, Baldwin, Banks, Barker, Baxter, Beaman, Benjamin, Bidwell, Bingham, Blaine, Blow, Boutwell, Bromwell, Broomall, Buckland, Bundy, Reader W. Clarke, Sidney Clarke, Cobb, Conkling, Cook, Cullom, Darling, Davis, Dawes, Defrees, Delano, Deming, Dixon, Dodge, Donnelly, Driggs, Dumont, Eckley, Eggleston, Eliot, Farnsworth, Ferry, Garfield, Grinnell, Griswold, Abner C. Harding, Hart, Hayes, Henderson, Higby, Holmes, Hooper, Hotchkiss, Asahel W. Hubbard, Chester D. Hubbard, Demas Hubbard, James R. Hubbell, Hulburd, James Humphrey, Ingersoll, Jenckes, Julian, Kasson, Kelley, Kelso, Ketcham, Kuykendall, Laflin, George V. Lawrence, William Lawrence, Loan, Longyear, Lynch, Marston, McClurg, McIndoe, McKee, McRuer, Mercur, Miller, Moorhead, Morrill, Morris, Moulton, Myers, Newell, O'Neill, Orth, Paine, Patterson, Perham, Pike, Plants, Price, William H. Randall, Raymond, Alexander H. Rice, John H. Rice, Rollins, Sawyer, Schenck, Scofield, Shellabarger, Spalding, Stevens, Stillwell, Thayer, Francis Thomas, John L. Thomas, Trowbridge, Upson, Van Aernam, Burt Van Horn, Robert T. Van Horn, Ward, Warner, Ellihu B. Washburne, Henry D. Washburn, William B. Washburn, Welker, Williams, James F. Wilson, Stephen F. Wilson, Windom, Woodbridge, the Speaker—128.

NAYS—Messrs. *Ancona, Bergen, Boyer, Chanler, Coffroth, Dawson, Eldridge, Finck, Glossbrenner, Goodyear, Grider, Aaron Harding, Harris, Kerr,* Latham, *Le Blond, Marshall, McCullough, Niblack,* Phelps, *Radford, Samuel J. Randall, Ritter, Rogers, Ross,* Rousseau, *Shanklin, Sitgreaves,* Smith, *Strouse, Taber, Taylor, Thornton, Trimble,* Whaley, *Winfield, Wright*—37.

The amendments of the Senate were made to this proposition, when it was finally adopted by each House, in the form first stated.

### The Accompanying Bills.

April 30—Mr. Stevens, from the same committee, also reported this bill:

A Bill to provide for restoring the States lately in insurrection to their full political rights.

Whereas it is expedient that the States lately in insurrection should, at the earliest day consistent with the future peace and safety of the Union, be restored to full participation in all political rights; and whereas the Congress did, by joint resolution, propose for ratification to the legislatures of the several States, as an amendment to the Constitution of the United States, an article in the following words, to wit:

[For article, see page 102.]

Now, therefore,

*Be it enacted, &c.,* That whenever the above-recited amendment shall have become part of the

Constitution of the United States, and any State lately in insurrection shall have ratified the same, and shall have modified its constitution and laws in conformity therewith, the Senators and Representatives from such State, if found duly elected and qualified, may, after having taken the required oaths of office, be admitted into Congress as such.

SEC. 2. *And be it further enacted,* That when any State lately in insurrection shall have ratified the foregoing amendment to the Constitution, any part of the direct tax under the act of August 5, 1861, which may remain due and unpaid in such State may be assumed and paid by such State; and the payment thereof, upon proper assurances from such State to be given to the Secretary of the Treasury of the United States, may be postponed for a period not exceeding ten years from and after the passage of this act.

April 30—Mr. Stevens, from the same committee, also reported this bill:

A Bill declaring certain persons ineligible to office under the Government of the United States.

*Be it enacted, &c.,* That no person shall be eligible to any office under the Government of the United States who is included in any of the following classes, namely:

1. The president and vice president of the confederate States of America, so called, and the heads of departments thereof.

2. Those who in other countries acted as agents of the confederate States of America, so called.

3. Heads of Departments of the United States, officers of the army and navy of the United States, and all persons educated at the Military or Naval Academy of the United States, judges of the courts of the United States, and members of either House of the Thirty-Sixth Congress of the United States who gave aid or comfort to the late rebellion.

4. Those who acted as officers of the confederate States of America, so called, above the grade of colonel in the army or master in the navy, and any one who, as Governor of either of the so-called confederate States, gave aid or comfort to the rebellion.

5. Those who have treated officers or soldiers or sailors of the army or navy of the United States, captured during the late war, otherwise than lawfully as prisoners of war.

Neither of these bills has been voted on up to the time this page goes to press.

---

### The Negatived Amendment on Representation and Direct Taxes.
#### IN HOUSE.

January 22, 1866—Mr. Stevens reported this proposition from the Joint Select Committee:

*Resolved, &c.,* (two-thirds of both Houses concurring,) That the following article be proposed to the legislatures of the several States as an amendment to the Constitution of the United States; which, when ratified by three-fourths of the said legislatures, shall be valid as part of said Constitution, namely:

ARTICLE —. Representatives and direct taxes shall be apportioned among the several States which may be included within this Union, according to their respective numbers, counting the whole number of persons in each State, excluding Indians not taxed: *Provided,* That whenever the elective franchise shall be denied or abridged in any State on account of race or color, all persons of such race or color shall be excluded from the basis of representation.

Mr. Stevens moved to insert the word "therein" after the word "persons" where it last occurs.

Sundry propositions of amendment were offered, and

January 30—The report was recommitted, without instructions—the motion of Mr. Le Blond to commit it to the Committee of the Whole having been lost, yeas 37, nays 133. (Messrs. McRuer and Rousseau and 35 Democrats made up the affirmative vote.)

---

### The Negatived Constitutional Amendment on Representation.
#### IN HOUSE.

January 31, 1866—Mr. Stevens reported from the Committee on Reconstruction this joint resolution:

Joint Resolution proposing to amend the Constitution of the United States.

*Resolved, &c.,* (two-thirds of both Houses concurring,) That the following article be proposed to the legislatures of the several States as an amendment to the Constitution of the United States, which, when ratified by three-fourths of said legislatures, shall be valid as part of said Constitution, namely:

#### ARTICLE —.

Representatives shall be apportioned among the several States which may be included within this Union according to their respective numbers, counting the whole number of persons in each State, excluding Indians not taxed: *Provided,* That whenever the elective franchise shall be denied or abridged in any State on account of race or color, all persons therein of such race or color shall be excluded from the basis of representation.

Mr. Schenck submitted this as a substitute for the "Article:"

Representatives shall be apportioned among the several States which may be included within this Union according to the number of male citizens of the United States over twenty-one years of age having the qualifications requisite for electors of the most numerous branch of the State legislature. The Congress, at their first session after the ratification of this amendment by the required number of States, shall provide by law for the actual enumeration of such voters; and such actual enumeration shall be separately made in a general census of the population of all the States within every subsequent term of ten years, in such manner as the Congress may by law direct. The number of Representatives shall not exceed one for every one hundred and twenty-five thousand of actual population, but each State shall have at least one Representative.

Mr. Schenck's substitute was disagreed to—yeas 29, nays 131, as follow:

YEAS—Messrs. Anderson, Bromwell, Bundy, Reader W. Clarke. Sidney Clarke, Darling, Davis, Defrees, Farnsworth, Abner C. Harding, Hayes, Hill, Chester D. Hubbard, James R. Hubbell, Jas. Humphrey, Ingersoll, Kuykendall, William Lawrence, *Marshall, McCullough*, Miller, Orth, Pike, *Ross*, Schenck, Shellabarger, Sloan, *Thornton*, Van Horn—29.

NAYS—Messrs. Alley, Allison, Ames, James M. Ashley, Baker, Banks, Barker, Baxter, Beaman, Benjamin, *Bergen*, Bidwell, Bingham, Blaine, Blow, Boutwell, *Boyer*, Brandegee, *Brooks*, Broomall, Buckland. *Chanler*, Cobb, Conkling, Cook, Cullom. Dawes. *Dawson*, Delano, Deming, *Denison*, Dixon, Donnelly, Eckley, Eggleston, *Eldridge*, Eliot, Farquhar, Ferry, *Finck*, Garfield, *Grider*, Grinnell, Griswold, Hale, *Aaron Harding*, Harris, Hart, *Hogan*, Holmes, Hooper, Hotchkiss, Asahel W. Hubbard, Demas Hubbard, jr., John H. Hubbard, *Edwin N. Hubbell*, Hulburd, *James M. Humphrey*, Jenckes, *Johnson*, Julian, Kasson, Kelley, Kelso, *Kerr*, Ketcham, Laflin, Latham, George V. Lawrence, *Le Blond*, Longyear, Lynch, Marston, Marvin, McClurg, McIndoe, McKee, Mercur, Moorhead, Morrill, Morris. Moulton, Myers, *Niblack*, Nicholson, *Noell*, O'Neill, Paine, Patterson, Perham, Phelps, Plants, Pomeroy, Price, *Samuel J. Randall*, William H. Randall, Alexander H. Rice, John H. Rice, *Ritter*, *Rogers*, Rollins, Sawyer, Scofield, *Shanklin*, Smith, Spalding, Starr, Stevens, *Strouse*, *Taber*, *Taylor*, Thayer, Francis Thomas, John L. Thomas, jr., *Trimble*, Upson, Van Aernam, Burt Van Horn, *Voorhees*, Ward, Warner, Elihu B. Washburne, William B. Washburn, Welker, Wentworth, Whaley, Williams, James F. Wilson, Stephen F. Wilson, Windom, *Wright*—131.

The joint resolution, as reported, was then agreed to—yeas 120, nays 46, as follow:

YEAS—Messrs. Alley, Allison, Ames, Anderson, James M. Ashley, Baker, Banks, Barker, Baxter, Beaman, Benjamin, Bidwell, Bingham, Blaine, Blow, Boutwell, Brandegee, Bromwell, Broomall, Buckland, Bundy, Reader W. Clarke, Sidney Clarke, Cobb, Conkling, Cook, Cullom, Darling, Davis, Dawes, Defrees, Delano, Deming, Dixon, Donnelly, Eckley, Eggleston, Farnsworth, Farquhar, Ferry, Garfield, Grinnell, Griswold, Abner C. Harding, Hart, Hayes, Hill, Holmes, Hooper, Hotchkiss, Asahel W. Hubbard, Chester D. Hubbard, Demas Hubbard, jr., John H. Hubbard, James R. Hubbell, Hulburd, Jas. Humphrey, Ingersoll, Julian, Kasson, Kelley, Kelso, Ketcham, Kuykendall, Laflin, George V. Lawrence, William Lawrence, Longyear, Lynch, Marston, Marvin, McClurg, McIndoe, McKee, Mercur, Miller, Moorhead, Morrill, Morris, Moulton, Myers, O'Neill, Orth, Paine, Patterson, Perham, Pike, Plants, Pomeroy, Price, Alexander H. Rice, John H. Rice, Rollins, Sawyer, Schenck, Scofield, Shellabarger, Sloan, Spalding, Starr, Stevens, Stillwell, Thayer, Francis Thomas, John L. Thomas, jr., Upson, Van Aernam, Burt Van Horn, Robert T. Van Horn, Ward, Warner, Elihu B. Washburne, William B. Washburn, Welker, Wentworth, Williams, James F. Wilson, Stephen F. Wilson, Windom, Woodbridge—120.

NAYS—Messrs. Baldwin, *Bergen*, *Boyer*, *Brooks*, *Chanler*, *Dawson*, *Denison*, *Eldridge*, Eliot, *Finck*, *Grider*, Hale, *Aaron Harding*, *Harris*, *Hogan*, *Edwin N. Hubbell*, *M. Humphrey*, Jenckes, *Johnson*, *Kerr*, Latham, *Le Blond*, *Marshall*, *McCullough*, *Niblack*, *Nicholson*, *Noell*, Phelps, *Samuel J. Randall*, William H. Randall, Raymond, *Rogers*, *Ross*, Rousseau, *Shanklin*, *Sitgreaves*, Smith, *Strouse*, *Taber*, *Taylor*, *Thornton*, *Trimble*, *Voorhees*, Whaley, *Wright*, —46.

[Messrs. Driggs and Newell, February 1, stated they would have voted aye, if present.]

IN SENATE.

March 9, 1866—The resolution of the House was rejected—yeas 25, nays 22, as follow, (two-thirds being necessary:)

YEAS—Messrs. Anthony, Chandler, Clark, Conness, Cragin, Creswell, Fessenden, Foster, Grimes, Harris, Howe, Kirkwood, Lane of Indiana, McDougall, Morgan, Morrill, Nye, Poland, Ramsey, Sherman, Sprague, Trumbull, Wade, Williams, Wilson—25.

NAYS—Messrs. Brown, *Buckalew*, Cowan, *Davis*, Dixon, Doolittle, *Guthrie*, Henderson, *Hendricks, Johnson*, Lane of Kansas, *Nesmith*, Norton, Pomeroy, *Riddle, Saulsbury*, Stewart, *Stockton*, Sumner, Van Winkle, Willey, Yates—22.

## Report on Privileges and Immunities of Citizens.

IN HOUSE.

February 13, 1866—Mr. Bingham reported from the Joint Reconstruction Committee, this joint resolution, which was re-committed and ordered to be printed:

Joint Resolution proposing an amendment to the Constitution of the United States.

*Resolved, &c.,* (two-thirds of both Houses concurring,) That the following article be proposed to the legislatures of the several States as an amendment to the Constitution of the United States, which, when ratified by three-fourths of the said legislatures, shall be valid as part of said Constitution, viz:

ARTICLE —.

The Congress shall have power to make all laws which shall be necessary and proper to secure to the citizens of each State all privileges and immunities of citizens in the several States, and to all persons in the several States equal protection in the rights of life, liberty, and property.

February 26—Mr. Bingham reported it back, without amendment.

February 28—Mr. Eldridge moved that it lie on the table; which was disagreed to—yeas 41, nays 110, as follow:

YEAS—Messrs. *Ancona, Bergen, Brooks, Chanler, Coffroth, Davis, Dawson, Denison, Eldridge, Finck, Glossbrenner, Goodyear, Grider*, Griswold, Hale, *A. Harding, Hogan, E. N. Hubbell, Kerr*, Kuykendall, *Marshall*, Marvin, *McCullough, Niblack, Nicholson, Noell*, Phelps, *S. J. Randall, Ritter, Rogers, Ross*, Rousseau, *Shanklin, Sitgreaves, Strouse, Taber, Taylor, Thornton, Trimble, Winfield, Wright*—41.

NAYS—Messrs. Alley, Allison, Ames, Anderson, Delos R. Ashley, James M. Ashley, Baker, Baldwin, Banks, Barker, Baxter, Benjamin, Bidwell, Bingham, Blaine, Blow, Boutwell, Brandegee, Broomall, Buckland, Bundy, Reader W. Clarke, Sidney Clarke, Cobb, Conkling, Cook, Cullom, Darling, Defrees, Delano, Deming, Donnelly, Dumont, Eckley, Eggleston, Eliot, Farnsworth, Farquhar, Ferry, Garfield, Grinnell, Abner C. Harding, Hart, Hayes, Higby, Holmes, Hooper, Hotchkiss, Demas Hubbard, jr., John H. Hubbard, James R. Hubbell, Hulburd, James Humphrey, Ingersoll, Jenckes, Julian, Kelley, Kelso, Ketcham, Laflin, Latham, George V. Lawrence, William Lawrence, Loan, Longyear, Lynch, Marston, McClurg, McKee, McRuer, Mercur, Moorhead, Morrill, Morris, Moulton, Myers, Newell, O'Neill, Orth, Paine, Patterson, Perham, Pike, Price, Raymond, Alexander H. Rice, John H. Rice, Sawyer, Schenck, Shellabarger, Sloan, Spalding, Stevens, Thayer, Francis Thomas, John L. Thomas, jr., Trowbridge, Van Aernam, Burt Van Horn, Warner, Elihu B. Washburne, Henry D. Washburn, Wm. B. Washburn, Welker, Wentworth, Williams, James F. Wilson, Stephen F. Wilson, Windom, Woodbridge—110.

And on motion of Mr. Conkling, its further consideration was postponed until the second Tuesday in April.

There was no further vote on it.

IN SENATE.

February 13—Mr. Fessenden reported the same resolution, which was laid over, and not again considered.

## Report Concerning Tennessee.

IN HOUSE.

March 5, 1866—Mr. Bingham reported from the Select Joint Committee on Reconstruction this

Joint Resolution concerning the State of Tennessee.

*Resolved, &c.,* That whereas the people of Tennessee have made known to the Congress of the United States their desire that the constitutional relations heretofore existing between them and the United States may be fully established, and did, on the twenty-second day of February, eighteen hundred and sixty-five, by a large popular vote, adopt and ratify a constitution of government, republican in form and not inconsistent with the Constitution and laws of the United States, and a State government has been organized under the provisions thereof, which said provisions and the laws passed in pursuance thereof proclaim and denote loyalty to the Union; and whereas the people of Tennessee are found to be in a condition to exercise the functions of a State within this Union, and can only exercise the same by the consent of the law-making power of the United States: Therefore, the State of Tennessee is hereby declared to be one of the United States of America, on an equal footing with the other States, upon the express condition that the people of Tennessee will maintain and enforce, in good faith, their existing constitution and laws, excluding those who have been engaged in rebellion against the United States from the exercise of the elective franchise, for the respective periods of time therein provided for, and shall exclude the same persons for the like respective periods of time from eligibility to office; and the State of Tennessee shall never assume or pay any debt or obligation contracted or incurred in aid of the late rebellion; nor shall said State ever in any manner claim from the United States or make any allowance or compensation for slaves emancipated or liberated in any way whatever; which conditions shall be ratified by the Legislature of Tennessee, or the people thereof, as the Legislature may direct, before this act shall take effect.

The resolution was ordered to be printed, and was recommitted to the committee, and has not been voted on, up to the time this page goes to press.

### Payment of Rebel Debt.

December 19, 1865—Mr. James F. Wilson reported from the Committee on the Judiciary the following joint resolution to amend the Constitution of the United States:

*Be it resolved by the Senate and House of Representatives of the United States in Congress assembled,* (two-thirds of both Houses concurring,) That the following article be proposed to the legislatures of the several States as an amendment to the Constitution of the United States, which, when ratified by three-fourths of said legislatures, shall be valid to all intents and purposes as a part of said Constitution, namely:

ARTICLE —. No tax, duty, or impost shall be laid, nor shall any appropriation of money be made, by either the United States, or any one of the States thereof, for the purpose of paying, either in whole or in part, any debt, contract, or liability whatsoever, incurred, made, or suffered by any one or more of the States, or the people thereof, for the purpose of aiding rebellion against the Constitution and laws of the United States.

Which was passed—yeas 151, nays 11, as follow:

YEAS—Messrs. Alley, Allison, Ames, Anderson, James M. Ashley, Baker, Baldwin, Banks, Barker, Baxter, Beaman, Benjamin, *Bergen,* Bidwell, Bingham, Blow, Boutwell, *Boyer,* Brandegee, Bromwell, Broomall, Buckland, Bundy, *Chanler,* Reader W. Clarke, Sidney Clarke, Cobb, Conkling, Cook, Cullom, Darling, Dawes, Defrees, Delano, Deming, Dixon, Donnelly, Driggs, Dumont, Eckley, Eggleston, Eliot, Farnsworth, Farquhar, Ferry, *Finck,* Garfield, Grinnell, Griswold, Hale, Abner C. Harding, Hart, Hayes, Henderson, Higby, Hill, *Hogan,* Holmes, Hooper, Hotchkiss, Asahel W. Hubbard, Chester D. Hubbard, Demas Hubbard, jr., John H. Hubbard, James R. Hubbell, Hulburd, Ingersoll, Jenckes, *Johnson,* Julian, Kasson, Kelley, Kelso, *Kerr,* Ketcham, Kuykendall, Laflin, Latham, George V. Lawrence, William Lawrence, Loan, Longyear, Lynch, *Marshall,* Marston, Marvin, McClurg, McKee, McRuer, Mercur, Miller, Morrill, Moulton, Myers, Newell, *Niblack, Noell,* O'Neill, Orth, Paine, Patterson, Perham. Phelps, Pike, Plants, Price, *Radford, Samuel J. Randall,* William H. Randall, Raymond, Alexander H. Rice, John H. Rice, Rollins, *Ross,* Rousseau, Sawyer, Schenck, Scofield, Shellabarger, *Sitgreaves,* Sloan, Smith, Spalding, Starr, Stevens, Stillwell, *Strouse, Taber, Taylor,* Thayer, Francis Thomas, John L. Thomas, *Thornton,* Trowbridge, Upson, Van Aernam, Burt Van Horn, Robert T. Van Horn, *Voorhees,* Ward, Warner, Ellihu B. Washburne, William B. Washburn, Welker, Wentworth, Whaley, Williams, James F. Wilson, Stephen F. Wilson, Windom, *Wright*—151.

NAYS—Messrs. *Brooks, Denison, Eldridge, Grider, Aaron Harding, McCullough, Nicholson, Ritter, Rogers, Shanklin, Trimble*—11.

It was not acted on in the Senate; but the substance of it is included in the amendment as finally adopted.

# IX.

# MEMBERS OF THE CABINET OF PRESIDENT JOHNSON,

### AND OF THE

# THIRTY-NINTH CONGRESS,

### WITH

# NAMES OF CLAIMANTS FROM THE INSURRECTIONARY STATES.

### PRESIDENT JOHNSON'S CABINET.

*Secretary of State*—WILLIAM H. SEWARD, of New York.

*Secretary of Treasury*—HUGH McCULLOCH, of Indiana.

*Secretary of War*—EDWIN M. STANTON, of Ohio.

*Secretary of Navy*—GIDEON WELLES, of Connecticut.

*Postmaster General*—WILLIAM DENNISON, of Ohio.

*Secretary of Interior*—JAMES HARLAN, of Iowa.

*Attorney General*—JAMES SPEED, of Kentucky.

---

### THIRTY-NINTH CONGRESS.
#### Senate.

LAFAYETTE S. FOSTER, of Connecticut, *President of the Senate, and Acting Vice President.*

John W. Forney, of Pennsylvania, *Secretary.*

*Maine*—William Pitt Fessenden, Lot M. Morrill.

*New Hampshire*—Daniel Clark, Aaron H. Cragin.

*Vermont*—Solomon Foot,* Luke P. Poland.

*Massachusetts*—Charles Sumner, Henry Wilson.

*Rhode Island*—Henry B. Anthony, William Sprague.

*Connecticut*—James Dixon, Lafayette S. Foster.

*New York*—Ira Harris, Edwin D. Morgan.

*New Jersey*—William Wright, John P. Stockton.†

*Pennsylvania*—Charles R. Buckalew, Edgar Cowan.

*Delaware*—George Read Riddle, Willard Saulsbury.

*Maryland*—John A. J. Creswell, Reverdy Johnson.

*Ohio*—John Sherman, Benjamin F. Wade.

*Kentucky*—James Guthrie, Garrett Davis.

*Indiana*—Henry S. Lane, Thomas A. Hendricks.

*Illinois*—Lyman Trumbull, Richard Yates.

* Died March 28, 1866. His successor, George F. Edmunds, qualified April 5, 1866.

† Voted—yeas 22, nays 21—not entitled to a seat in the Senate, March 27, 1866. The vote on the amendment declaring him not-entitled was as follow :

YEAS—Messrs. Brown, Chandler, Clark, Conness, Cragin, Creswell, Fessenden, Grimes, Howard, Howe, Kirkwood, Lane of Indiana, Nye, Pomeroy, Ramsey, Sherman, Sprague, Sumner, Wade, Williams, Wilson, Yates—22.

NAYS—Messrs. Anthony, *Buckalew*, Cowan, *Davis*, Doolittle, *Guthrie*, Harris, Henderson, *Hendricks*, *Johnson*, Lane of Kansas, *McDougall*, Morgan, *Nesmith*, Norton, Poland, *Riddle*, *Saulsbury*, Trumbull, Van Winkle, Willey—21.

*Missouri*—B. Gratz Brown, John B. Henderson.

*Michigan*—Zachariah Chandler, Jacob M. Howard.

*Iowa*—James W. Grimes, Samuel J. Kirkwood.*

*Wisconsin*—James R. Doolittle, Timothy O. Howe.

*California*—John Conness, James A. McDougall.

*Minnesota*—Daniel S. Norton, Alexander Ramsey.

*Oregon*—James W. Nesmith, George H. Williams.

*Kansas*—Samuel C. Pomeroy, James H. Lane.

*West Virginia*—Peter G. Van Winkle, Waitman T. Willey.

*Nevada*—James W. Nye, William M. Stewart.

#### Senators Chosen from the late Insurrectionary States.

*Alabama*—Lewis E. Parsons, George S. Houston.

*Arkansas*—Elisha Baxter, William D. Snow.

*Florida*—William Marvin, Wilkerson Call.

*Georgia*—Alexander H. Stephens, Herschel V. Johnson.

*Louisiana*—Randall Hunt, Henry Boyce. (R. King Cutler and Michael Hahn also claim under a former election in October, 1864.)

*Mississippi*—William L. Sharkey, James L. Alcorn.

*North Carolina*—William A. Graham, John Pool.

*South Carolina*—Benjamin F. Perry, John L. Manning.

*Tennessee*—David T. Patterson, Joseph S. Fowler.

*Texas*—

*Virginia*—John C. Underwood, Joseph Segar.

#### MEMORANDUM.

Mr. A. H. Stephens was a delegate from Georgia to the convention which framed the "Confederate" constitution, and was Vice President of the "Confederacy" until its downfall. Mr. H. V. Johnson was a senator in the rebel congress in the first and second congresses, as was Mr. Graham, from North Carolina. Mr. Pool was a senator in the Legislature of North Carolina. Mr. Perry was a "Confederate States" judge. Mr. Manning was a volunteer aid to

*Credentials presented January 20, 1866, and he took his seat January 24, 1866.

General Beauregard at Fort Sumter and Manassas. Mr. Alcorn was in the Mississippi militia.

### House of Representatives.

SCHUYLER COLFAX, of Indiana, *Speaker.*
Edward McPherson, of Pennsylvania, *Clerk.*
*Maine*—John Lynch, Sidney Perham, James G. Blaine, John H. Rice, Frederick A. Pike.
*New Hampshire*—Gilman Marston, Edward H. Rollins, James W. Patterson.
*Vermont*—Frederick E. Woodbridge, Justin S. Morrill, Portus Baxter.
*Massachusetts*—Thomas D. Eliot, Oakes Ames, Alexander H. Rice, Samuel Hooper, John B. Alley, Nathaniel P. Banks, George S. Boutwell, John D. Baldwin, William B. Washburn, Henry L. Dawes.
*Rhode Island*—Thomas A. Jenckes, Nathan F. Dixon.
*Connecticut*—Henry C. Deming, Samuel L. Warner, Augustus Brandegee, John H. Hubbard.
*New York*—Stephen Taber, Teunis G. Bergen, James Humphrey*, Morgan Jones, Nelson Taylor, Henry J. Raymond, John W. Chanler, James Brooks†, William A. Darling, William Radford, Charles H. Winfield, John H. Ketcham, Edwin N. Hubbell, Charles Goodyear, John A. Griswold, Robert S. Hale, Calvin T. Hulburd, James M. Marvin, Demas Hubbard, Jr., Addison H. Laflin, Roscoe Conkling, Sidney T. Holmes, Thomas T. Davis, Theodore M. Pomeroy, Daniel Morris, Giles W. Hotchkiss, Hamilton Ward, Roswell Hart, Burt Van Horn, James M. Humphrey, Henry Van Aernam.
*New Jersey*—John F. Starr, William A. Newell, Charles Sitgreaves, Andrew J. Rogers, Edwin R. V. Wright.
*Pennsylvania*—Samuel J. Randall, Charles O'Neill, Leonard Myers, William D. Kelley, M. Russell Thayer, Benjamin M. Boyer, John M. Broomall, Sydenham E. Ancona, Thaddeus Stevens, Myer Strouse, Philip Johnson, Charles Denison, Ulysses Mercur, George F. Miller, Adam J. Glossbrenner, Alexander H. Coffroth‡, Abraham A. Barker, Stephen F. Wilson, Glenni W. Scofield, Charles V. Culver, John L. Dawson, James K. Moorhead, Thomas Williams, George V. Lawrence.
*Delaware*—John A. Nicholson.
*Maryland*—Hiram McCullough, John L. Thomas, Jr., Charles E. Phelps, Francis Thomas, Benjamin G. Harris.
*Ohio*—Benjamin Eggleston, Rutherford B. Hayes, Robert C. Schenck, William Lawrence, Francis C. Le Blond, Reader W. Clarke, Samuel Shellabarger, James R. Hubbell, Ralph P. Buckland, James M. Ashley, Hezekiah S. Bundy, William E. Finck, Columbus Delano, Martin Welker, Tobias A. Plants, John A. Bingham, Ephraim R. Eckley, Rufus P. Spalding, James A. Garfield.
*Kentucky*—Lawrence S. Trimble, Burwell C. Ritter, Henry Grider, Aaron Harding, Lovell H. Rousseau, Green Clay Smith, George S. Shanklin, William H. Randall, Samuel McKee.

*Indiana*—William E. Niblack, Michael C. Kerr, Ralph Hill, John H. Farquhar, George W. Julian, Ebenezer Dumont, Daniel W. Voorhees,* Godlove S. Orth, Schuyler Colfax, Joseph H. Defrees, Thomas N. Stillwell.
*Illinois*—John Wentworth, John F. Farnsworth, Ellihu B. Washburne, Abner C. Harding, Ebon C. Ingersoll, Burton C. Cook, Henry P. H. Bromwell, Shelby M. Cullom, Lewis W. Ross, Anthony Thornton, Samuel S. Marshall, Jehu Baker, Andrew J. Kuykendall, Samuel W. Moulton.
*Missouri*—John Hogan, Henry T. Blow, Thomas E. Noell, John R. Kelso, Joseph W. McClurg, Robert T. Van Horn, Benjamin F. Loan, John F. Benjamin, George W. Anderson.
*Michigan*—Fernando C. Beaman, Charles Upson, John W. Longyear, Thomas W. Ferry, Rowland E. Trowbridge, John F. Driggs.
*Iowa*—James F. Wilson, Hiram Price, William B. Allison, Josiah B. Grinnell, John A. Kasson, Asahel W. Hubbard.
*Wisconsin*—Halbert E. Paine, Ithamar C. Sloan, Amasa Cobb, Charles A. Eldridge, Philetus Sawyer, Walter D. McIndoe.
*California*—Donald C. McRuer, William Higby, John Bidwell.
*Minnesota*—William Windom, Ignatius Donnelly.
*Oregon*—James H. D. Henderson.
*Kansas*—Sidney Clarke.
*West Virginia*—Chester D. Hubbard, George R. Latham, Kellian V. Whaley.
*Nevada*—Delos R. Ashley.

### Members chosen in the late Insurrectionary States.

*Alabama*—C. C. Langdon, George C. Freeman, Gen. Cullen A. Battle, Joseph W. Taylor, B. T. Pope, Thomas J. Foster.
*Arkansas*—William Byers, George H. Kyle, James M. Johnson.
*Florida*—F. McLeod.
*Georgia*—Solomon Cohen, Gen. Philip Cook, Hugh Buchanan, E. G. Cabaniss, J. D. Matthews, J. H. Christy, Gen. W. T. Wofford.
*Louisiana*—Louis St. Martin, Jacob Barker, Robert C. Wickliffe, John E. King, John S. Ray. (Henry C. Warmoth claims seat as *delegate,* under universal suffrage election.)
*Mississippi*—Col. Arthur E. Reynolds, Col. Richard A. Pinson, James T. Harrison, A. M. West, E. G. Peyton.
*North Carolina*—Jesse R. Stubbs, Charles C. Clark, Thomas C. Fuller, Col. Josiah Turner, Jr., Lewis Hanes, S. H. Walkup, Alex. H. Jones.
*South Carolina*—Col. John D. Kennedy, William Aiken, Gen. Samuel McGowan, James Farrow.
*Tennessee*—Nathaniel G. Taylor, Horace Maynard, William B. Stokes, Edmund Cooper, William B. Campbell, Samuel M. Arnell, Isaac R. Hawkins, John W. Leftwich.
*Texas*—
*Virginia*—W. H. B. Custis, Lucius H. Chandler, B. Johnson Barbour, Robert Ridgway, Beverly A. Davis, Alex. H. H. Stuart, Robert Y. Conrad, Daniel H. Hoge.

---

* Died June 16, 1866.
† Unseated April 6, 1866, and William E. Dodge qualified as his successor.
‡ Admitted to a seat on *prima facie* case February 19, 1866. July 9.—Committee reported in favor of Wm. H. Koontz, contestant.

* Unseated February 23, 1866, and Henry D. Washburn qualified as his successor; July 18, Mr. Koontz admitted.

MEMORANDUM.

Of the *Alabama* delegation, Mr. Battle was a general in the rebel army, and Mr. Foster a representative in the first and second rebel congresses.

Of the *Georgia* delegation, Messrs. Cook and Wofford were generals in the rebel service.

Of the *Mississippi* delegation, Messrs. Reynolds and Pinson were colonels in the rebel service; Mr. Harrison was a member of the rebel provisional congress.

Of the *North Carolina* delegation, Mr. Fuller was a representative in the first rebel congress, and Mr. Turner was a colonel in the rebel army,

and a representative in the second rebel congress; Mr. Brown was a member of the State convention which passed the secession ordinance in 1861, and voted for it.

Of the *South Carolina* delegation, Mr. Kennedy was colonel and Mr. McGowan brigadier general in the rebel army; Mr. Farrow was a representative in the first and second rebel congresses.

Of the *Virginia* delegation, Messrs. Stuart and Conrad were members of the secession convention of Virginia, in 1861, and continued to participate after the passage of the ordinance and the beginning of hostilities.

---

# X.

# VOTES IN THE HOUSE OF REPRESENTATIVES

## ON VARIOUS POLITICAL DECLARATORY RESOLUTIONS.

### Payment of the Public Debt.

December 5, 1865—Mr. Samuel J. Randall offered this resolution:

*Resolved*, That, as the sense of this House, the public debt created during the late rebellion was contracted upon the faith and honor of the nation; that it is sacred and inviolate, and must and ought to be paid, principal and interest; that any attempt to repudiate or in any manner to impair or scale the said debt shall be universally discountenanced, and promptly rejected by Congress if proposed.

Which was agreed to—yeas 162, nays 1, as follow:

YEAS—Messrs. Alley, Allison, Ames, *Ancona*, Anderson, James M. Ashley, Baker, Baldwin, Banks, Barker, Baxter, Beaman, Benjamin, *Bergen*, Bidwell, Bingham, Blaine, Blow, Boutwell, *Boyer*, Brandegee, Bromwell, Broomall, Buckland, Bundy, *Chanler*, Reader W. Clarke, Sidney Clarke, Cobb, Conkling, Cook, Cullom, Culver, Darling, Davis, *Dawson*, Defrees, Delano, Deming, *Denison*, Dixon, Donnelly, Driggs, Dumont, Eckley, Eggleston, Eliot, Farnsworth, Farquhar, Ferry, *Finck*, Garfield, *Glossbrenner*, *Goodyear*, Grinnell, Griswold, Hale, Abner C. Harding, Hart, Hayes, Henderson, Higby, Hill, *Hogan*, Holmes, Hooper, Hotchkiss, Asahel W. Hubbard, Chester D. Hubbard, Demas Hubbard, jr., John H. Hubbard, *Edwin N. Hubbell*, James R. Hubbell, Hulburd, James Humphrey, *James M. Humphrey*, Ingersoll, Jenckes, *Johnson*, Julian, Kasson, Kelley, Kelso, *Kerr*, Ketcham, Kuykendall, Laflin, Latham, George V. Lawrence, William Lawrence, Loan, Longyear, Marston, Marvin, McClurg, *McCullough*, McIndoe, McKee, McRuer, Mercur, Miller, Moorhead, Morrill, Morris, Moulton, Myers, Newell, *Niblack*, *Nicholson*, *Noell*, O'Neill, Orth, Paine, Patterson, Perham, Phelps, Pike, Plants, Pomeroy, Price, *Radford*, *Samuel J. Randall*, William H. Randall, Raymond, Alexander H. Rice, *Rogers*, Rollins, *Ross*, Sawyer, Schenck, Scofield, *Shanklin*, Shellabarger, Sitgreaves, Sloan, Smith, Spalding, Starr, Stevens, Stillwell, *Strouse*, *Taber*, Thayer, Francis Thomas, John L. Thomas, jr., *Thornton*, Trowbridge, Upson, Burt Van Horn, Ward, Warner, Elihu B. Washburne, William B. Washburn, Welker, Wentworth, Whaley, Williams, Wilson, Windom, *Winfield*, Wright—162.

NAY—Mr. Trimble.

NOT VOTING—Messrs. Brooks, *Eldridge*, *Grider*, *Aaron Harding*, *Le Blond*, Lynch, *Marshall*, John H. Rice, *Ritter*, *Taylor*, Van Aernam, R. T. Van Horn, S. F. Wilson, F. E. Woodbridge—14.

### "Treason Ought to be Punished."

December 14, 1865—Mr. Henderson, of Oregon, submitted the following resolution:

*Resolved*, That treason against the United States Government is a crime that ought to be punished.

Mr. Hale moved it be laid on the table which was disagreed to; and, under the previous question, it was then passed—yeas 153, nays none, as follow:

YEAS—Messrs. Alley, Ames, *Ancona*, Anderson, James M. Ashley, Baker, Baldwin, Banks, Barker, Beaman, Benjamin, *Bergen*, Bidwell, Bingham, Blaine, Blow, Boutwell, *Boyer*, Bromwell, *Brooks*, Broomall, Buckland, Bundy, Reader W. Clarke, Sidney Clarke, Cobb, Conkling, Cook, Cullom, Darling, Davis, Dawes, *Dawson*, Defrees, Deming, *Denison*, Dixon, Donnelly, Driggs, Eckley, Eggleston, *Eldridge*, Eliot, Farquhar, Ferry, *Finck*, *Glossbrenner*, *Grider*, Grinnell, Griswold, Hale, *Aaron Harding*, Abner C. Harding, Hart, Hayes, Henderson, Higby, *Hogan*, Holmes, Hooper, Hotchkiss, Asahel W. Hubbard, Chester D. Hubbard, Demas Hubbard, jr., John H. Hubbard, *Edwin N. Hubbell*, James R. Hubbell, Hulburd, James Humphrey, *James M. Humphrey*, Ingersoll, Jenckes, *Johnson*, Julian, Kasson, Kelley, Kelso, *Kerr*, Ketcham, Kuykendall, George V. Lawrence, William Lawrence, *Le Blond*, Loan, Longyear, Lynch, *Marshall*, Marston, Marvin, McClurg, *McCullough*, McIndoe, McKee, McRuer, Mercur, Moorhead, Morrill, Morris, Myers, *Nicholson*, *Noell*, O'Neill, Orth, Paine, Perham, Pike, Plants, Price, *Radford*, *Samuel J. Randall*, William H. Randall, Alexander H. Rice, John H. Rice, *Ritter*, *Rogers*, Rollins, *Ross*, Rousseau, Sawyer, Scofield, *Shanklin*, Shellabarger, *Sitgreaves*, Sloan, Smith, Spalding, Starr, Stevens, *Strouse*, *Taber*, *Taylor*, Thayer, John L. Thomas, jr., *Thornton*, Trimble, Trowbridge, Upson, Van Aernam, Burt Van Horn, *Voorhees*, Ward, Warner, Ellihu B. Washburne, William B. Washburn, Welker, Wentworth, Whaley, Williams, James F. Wilson, Stephen F. Wilson, Windom, *Winfield*, Woodbridge—153.

NAYS—None.

### Representation of the late so-called Confederate States.

December 14, 1865—Mr. James F. Wilson submitted this resolution:

*Resolved*, That all papers which may be offered relative to the representation of the late so-called Confederate States of America, or either of them, shall be referred to the joint committee of fifteen without debate, and no members shall be admitted from either of said so-called States, until Congress shall declare such States or either of them entitled to representation.

Which was passed—yeas 107, nays 56, as follow:

YEAS—Messrs. Alley, Allison, Ames, Anderson, James M. Ashley, Baker, Baldwin, Banks, Barker, Baxter, Beaman, Benjamin, Bidwell, Bingham, Blaine, Boutwell, Brandegee, Bromwell, Broomall, Buckland, Bundy, Reader W. Clarke, Sidney Clarke, Cobb, Conkling, Cook, Cullom, Defrees, Deming, Dixon, Donnelly, Driggs, Eckley, Eliot, Ferry, Grinnell, Abner C. Harding, Hart, Hayes, Henderson, Higby, Holmes, Hooper, Hotchkiss, Asahel W. Hubbard, Chester D. Hubbard, Demas Hubbard, jr., John H. Hubbard, Hulburd, Ingersoll, Jenckes, Julian, Kelley, Kelso, Ketcham, Kuykendall, Laflin, George V. Lawrence, William Lawrence, Loan, Longyear, Marston, Marvin, McClurg, McIndoe, McKee, McRuer, Mercur, Moorhead, Morrill, Morris, Moulton, Myers, Newell, O'Neill, Orth, Paine, Patterson, Perham, Pike, Plants, Price, Alexander H. Rice, John H. Rice, Rollins, Sawyer, Scofield, Shellabarger, Sloan, Spalding, Starr, Stevens, Thayer, Trowbridge, Upson, Van Aernam, Burt Van Horn, Ward, Warner, Ellihu B. Washburne, William B. Washburn, Welker, Wentworth, Williams, James F. Wilson, Stephen F. Wilson, Windom—107.

NAYS—Messrs. Ancona, Bergen, Blow, Boyer, Brooks, Darling, Davis, Dawson, Denison, Eldridge, Farquhar, Finck, Glossbrenner, Grider, Griswold, Hale, Harding, Hill, Hogan, Edwin N. Hubbell, James R. Hubbell, James Humphrey, James M. Humphrey, Johnson, Kasson, Kerr, Latham, Le Blond, Marshall, Niblack, Nicholson, Noell, Phelps, Radford, Samuel J. Randall, William H. Randall, Raymond, Ritter, Rogers, Ross, Rousseau, Shanklin, Sitgreaves, Smith, Stillwell, Strouse, Taber, Taylor, Francis Thomas, John L. Thomas, jr., Thornton, Trimble, Voorhees, Whaley, Winfield, Wright—56.

### Elective Franchise in the States.

December 18, 1865—Mr. Thornton submitted this resolution:

Whereas, at the first movement toward independence, the Congress of the United States instructed the several States to institute governments of their own, and left each State to decide for itself the conditions for the enjoyment of the elective franchise; and whereas during the period of the confederacy there continued to exist a very great diversity in the qualifications of electors in the several States; and whereas the Constitution of the United States recognizes these diversities when it enjoins that in the choice of members of the House of Representatives the electors in each State shall have the qualifications requisite for the electors of the most numerous branch of the State legislatures; and whereas, after the formation of the Constitution, it remained, as before, the uniform usage of each State to enlarge the body of its electors according to its own judgment; and whereas so fixed was the reservation in the habits of the people, and so unquestioned has been the interpretation of the Constitution, that during the civil war the late President never harbored the purpose, certainly never avowed the purpose, of disregarding it: Therefore,

Resolved, That any extension of the elective franchise to persons in the States, either by act of the President or of Congress, would be an assumption of power which nothing in the Constitution of the United States would warrant, and that, to avoid every danger of conflict, the settlement of this question should be referred to the several States.

Mr. Ellihu B. Washburne moved that it be laid on the table; which was agreed to—yeas 111, nays 46, as follow:

YEAS—Messrs. Alley, Allison, Ames, Anderson, James M.

Ashley, Baker, Baldwin, Banks, Barker, Baxter, Beaman, Benjamin, Bidwell, Bingham, Blow, Boutwell, Brandegee, Broomall, Buckland, Bundy, Reader W. Clarke, Sidney Clarke, Conkling, Cook, Darling, Dawes, Defrees, Delano, Deming, Dixon, Driggs, Dumont, Eckley, Eggleston, Eliot, Farnsworth, Garfield, Grinnell, Hale, Abner C. Harding, Hart, Hayes, Henderson, Higby, Holmes, Hooper, Hotchkiss. Asahel W. Hubbard, Demas Hubbard, jr., John H. Hubbard. James R. Hubbell, Hulburd, James Humphrey, Jenckes, Julian, Kelley, Kelso, Ketcham, Laflin, Latham, George V Lawrence, William Lawrence, Loan, Longyear, Lynch, Marston, Marvin, McClurg, McIndoe, McKee, McRuer, Mercur, Miller, Moorhead, Morrill, Moulton, Myers, Newell, O'Neill, Paine, Patterson, Perham, Pike, Plants, Price, Raymond, Alexander H. Rice, John H. Rice, Rollins, Sawyer, Schenck, Scofield, Shellabarger, Spalding, Starr, Stevens, Thayer, Trowbridge, Upson, Van Aernam, Burt Van Horn, Robert T. Van Horn, Ward, Warner, Ellihu B. Washburne, William B. Washburn, Welker, Wentworth, Williams, James F. Wilson, Stephen F. Wilson—111.

NAYS—Messrs. Ancona, Bergen, Boyer, Bromwell, Brooks, Chanler, Dawson, Denison, Eldridge, Farquhar, Finck, Goodyear, Grider, Aaron Harding, Hill. Hogan, Chester D. Hubbard, Edwin D. Hubbell, Ingersoll, Johnson, Kerr, Kuykendall, Marshall, McCullough, Niblack, Nicholson, Noell, Orth, Radford, Samuel J. Randall, William H. Randall, Ritter, Rogers, Ross, Rousseau, Shanklin, Sitgreaves, Smith, Stillwell, Strouse, Taber, Taylor, Thornton, Trimble, Whaley, Wright—46.

February 26, 1866—Mr. Defrees offered this resolution, which was laid over:

Resolved, That it is the opinion of this House that Congress has no constitutional right to fix the qualification of electors in the several States.

May 21—It was referred to the Committee on the Judiciary—yeas 86, nays 30. The nays were:

Messrs. Ancona, Dawson, Defrees, Denison, Eldridge, Glossbrenner, Goodyear, Grider, Aaron Harding, Hogan, Edwin N. Hubbell, James M. Humphrey, Kerr, Kuykendall, George V. Lawrence, Le Blond, McCullough, Niblack, Nicholson, Samuel J. Randall, Ritter, Rogers, Ross, Sitgreaves, Stillwell, Taber, Taylor, Henry D. Washburn, Winfield, Wright—30.

### Test Oath.

December 18, 1865—Mr. Hill submitted this resolution:

Resolved, That the act of July 2, 1862, prescribing an oath to be taken and subscribed by persons elected or appointed to office under the Government of the United States before entering upon the duties of such office, is of binding force and effect on all departments of the public service, and should in no instance be dispensed with.

Mr. Finck moved that it be tabled; which was disagreed to—yeas 32, nays 126, as follow:

YEAS—Messrs. Ancona, Bergen, Boyer, Brooks, Chanler, Dawson, Denison, Eldridge, Finck, Grider, Aaron Harding, Harris, Hogan, Edwin N. Hubbell, Johnson, Kerr, Latham, Marshall, McCullough, Niblack, Nicholson, Noell, Samuel J. Randall, Ritter, Rogers, Ross, Shanklin, Sitgreaves, Strouse, Taber, Thornton, Trimble—32.

NAYS—Messrs. Alley, Allison, Ames, Anderson, James M. Ashley, Baker, Baldwin, Banks, Barker, Baxter. Beaman, Benjamin, Bidwell, Bingham, Blow, Boutwell, Brandegee, Bromwell, Broomall, Buckland, Bundy, Reader W. Clarke, Sidney Clarke, Conkling, Cook, Cullom, Darling, Davis, Dawes, Defrees, Delano, Deming, Dixon, Driggs, Dumont, Eggleston, Eliot, Farnsworth, Farquhar, Ferry, Garfield, Grinnell, Hale, Abner C. Harding, Hart, Hayes, Henderson, Higby, Hill, Holmes, Hooper, Hotchkiss, Asahel W. Hubbard, Demas Hubbard, jr., John H. Hubbard, James R. Hubbell, Hulburd, James Humphrey, Ingersoll, Jenckes, Julian, Kasson, Kelley, Kelso, Ketcham, Kuykendall, Laflin, George V. Lawrence, William Lawrence, Loan, Longyear, Lynch, Marston, Marvin, McClurg, McIndoe, McKee, McRuer, Mercur, Miller, Moorhead, Morrill, Myers, Newell, O'Neill, Orth, Paine, Patterson, Perham, Phelps, Pike, Plants, Price, William H. Randall, Raymond, Alexander H. Rice, John H. Rice, Rollins, Rousseau, Sawyer, Schenck. Scofield, Shellabarger, Smith, Spalding, Starr, Stevens, Stillwell, Thayer, John L. Thomas, Trowbridge, Upson, Van

Aernam, Burt Van Horn, Robert T. Van Horn, Ward, Warner, Ellihu B. Washburne, William B. Washburn, Welker, Wentworth, Whaley, Williams, James F. Wilson, Stephen F. Wilson—125.

It then passed.

### Test Oath for Lawyers.

January 15, 1866—Mr. Stevens offered this resolution:

*Resolved*, That the Committee on the Judiciary be instructed to inquire into the expediency of so amending the act of January 24, 1865, relative to the test oath, as to allow attorneys-at-law to practice their profession without taking said oath, on an equal footing with the members of all other professions.

Which was agreed to—yeas 82, nays, 77, as follow:

YEAS—Messrs. Alley, Ames, *Ancona, Bergen,* Blow, *Boyer, Brooks,* Buckland, Bundy, *Chanler,* Cobb. Cook, Darling, Davis, *Dawson, Denison,* Driggs, *Eldridge,* Farquhar, Ferry, *Finck. Glossbrenner, Goodyear, Grider,* Griswold, Hale, *Aaron Harding,* Abner C. Harding, Higby, Hill, *Hogan,* Hooper, John H. Hubbard, *Edwin N. Hubbell,* James R. Hubbell, James Humphrey, *James M. Humphrey,* Ingersoll, *Johnson,* Kasson, *Kerr,* Kuykendall, Latham, George V. Lawrence, *Le Blond. Marshall,* Marston, Marvin, *McCullough,* McRuer, Miller, Moorhead, *Niblack, Nicholson. Noell,* Orth, Phelps, Pike, Plants, Pomeroy, Price, *Radford, Samuel J. Randall,* Raymond, *Ritter, Rogers, Ross,* Sawyer, *Shanklin, Sitgreaves,* Smith, Stevens, Stillwell, *Strouse, Taber, Taylor,* Thayer, Francis Thomas, *Thornton, Trimble,* Trowbridge, *Winfield*—82.

NAYS—Messrs. Allison, Anderson, Delos R. Ashley, James M. Ashley, Baker, Banks, Barker, Baxter, Beaman, Benjamin, Bidwell, Bingham, Blaine, Boutwell, Brandegee, Bromwell, Reader W. Clarke, Sidney Clarke, Conkling, Dawes, Defrees, Delano, Deming, Dixon, Donnelly, Eckley, Eggleston, Eliot, Farnsworth, Grinnell, Hart, Hayes, Henderson, Holmes, Asahel W. Hubbard, Demas Hubbard, jr., Hulburd, Jenckes, Julian, Kelley, Kelso, Laflin, William Lawrence, Loan, Longyear, Lynch, McClurg, McKee, Mercur, Morrill, Morris, Moulton, O'Neill, Paine, Perham, Randall, Alexander H. Rice, John H. Rice, Rollins, Schenck, Scofield, Shellabarger, Sloan, Spalding, John L. Thomas, jr., Upson, Van Aernam, Burt Van Horn, Ward, Ellihu B. Washburne, William B. Washburn, Welker, Williams, James F. Wilson, Windom, Woodbridge—77.

### Endorsement of the President's Policy.

December 21, 1865—Mr. Voorhees submitted these resolutions, which were postponed till January 9, 1866:

*Resolved*, That the message of the President of the United States, delivered at the present Congress, is regarded by this body as an able and patriotic State paper.

2. That the principles therein advocated for the restoration of the Union are the safest and most practicable that can now be applied to our disordered domestic affairs.

3. That no State, or any number of States confederated together, can in any manner sunder their connection with the Federal Union, except by a total subversion of our present system of government; and that the President in enunciating this doctrine in his late message has but given expression to the sentiments of all those who deny the right or power of a State to secede.

4. That the President is entitled to the thanks of Congress and the country for his faithful, wise, and successful efforts to restore civil government, law, and order to those States whose citizens were lately in insurrection against the federal authority; and we hereby pledge ourselves to aid, assist, and uphold him in the policy which he has adopted to give harmony, peace, and union to the country.

January 9—Mr. Bingham offered this substitute:

*Resolved*, That this House has an abiding confidence in the President, and that in the future, as in the past, he will co-operate with Congress in restoring to equal position and rights with the other States in the Union all the States lately in insurrection.

Mr. Bingham moved to refer the resolutions and the substitute to the Committee on Reconstruction; which was agreed to—yeas 107, nays 42, as follow:

YEAS—Messrs. Allison, Ames, Anderson, James M. Ashley, Baker, Baldwin, Banks, Baxter, Beaman, Benjamin, Bidwell, Bingham. Blaine, Boutwell, Brandegee, Bromwell, Broomall, Buckland, Bundy, Reader W. Clarke, Sidney Clarke, Cobb, Conkling, Cook, Cullom, Davis, Dawes, Defrees, Deming, Donnelly, Driggs, Eggleston, Eliot, Ferry, Garfield, Grinnell, Hale, A. C. Harding, Hart, Hayes, Henderson, Higby, Hill, Holmes, Hooper, Asahel W. Hubbard, Chester D. Hubbard, John H. Hubbard, James R. Hubbell, Hulburd, Ingersoll, Jenckes, Julian, Kelley, Kelso, Ketcham, Kuykendall, Laflin, Latham, William Lawrence, Loan, Longyear, Lynch, Marvin, McClurg, McKee, McRuer, Mercur, Miller, Moorhead, Morrill, Morris, Moulton, Myers, Newell, O'Neill, Orth, Paine, Patterson, Perham, Phelps. Pike, Plants, Price, Alexander H. Rice, John H. Rice, Rollins, Sawyer, Scofield, Shellabarger, Smith, Spalding, Stevens, Stillwell, Thayer, John L. Thomas, jr., Trowbridge, Upson, Van Aernam, Burt Van Horn, Warner, Ellihu B. Washburne, William B. Washburn, Welker, Williams, S. F. Wilson, Windom—107.

NAYS—Messrs. *Ancona, Bergen, Boyer, Brooks, Chanler, Darling, Dawson, Denison, Eldridge, Glossbrenner, Grider, Aaron Harding, Hogan, J. M. Humphrey, Kerr, Le Blond, Marshall, Niblack, Nicholson, Noell, Radford, Simuel J. Randall, Raymond, Ritter, Rogers, Ross, Strouse, Taber, Taylor, Voorhees, Winfield, Wright*—42.

### Withdrawal of Military Force.

January 8, 1866—Mr. Thos. Williams submitted this resolution:

*Resolved*, That in order to the maintenance of the national authority and the protection of the loyal citizens of the seceding States, it is the sense of this House that the military forces of the Government should not be withdrawn from those States until the two Houses of Congress shall have ascertained and declared their further presence there no longer necessary.

Which was passed—yeas 94, nays 37, as follow:

YEAS—Messrs. Ames, Anderson, Delos R. Ashley, Baker, Banks, Baxter, Beaman, Benjamin, Bidwell, Bingham, Blaine, Boutwell, Brandegee, Bromwell, Broomall, Bundy, Reader W. Clarke, Sidney Clarke, Cobb, Conkling, Cook, Cullom, Defrees, Deming, Donnelly, Driggs, Eggleston, Eliot, Farnsworth, Farquhar, Ferry, Garfield, Grinnell, Abner C. Harding, Hart, Hayes, Henderson, Higby, Hill, Holmes, Hooper, Hubbard, Chester D. Hubbard, John H. Hubbard, James R. Hubbell, Hulburd, Jenckes, Julian, Kelley, Kelso, Ketcham, Kuykendall, Laflin, William Lawrence, Loan, Longyear, Lynch, Marvin, McClurg, McKee, McRuer, Mercur, Miller, Moorhead, Morrill, Morris, Moulton, Myers, O'Neill, Orth, Paine, Patterson, Plants, Price, Alexander H. Rice, Rollins, Sawyer, Scofield, Shellabarger, Spalding, Stevens, Thayer, Trowbridge, Upson, Van Aernam, Burt Van Horn, Robert T. Van Horn, Ward, Warner, Ellihu B. Washburne, Welker, Williams, Stephen F. Wilson, Windom—94.

NAYS—Messrs. *Ancona, Bergen, Boyer, Brooks, Chanler, Davis, Dawson,* Delano, *Denison, Eldridge, Glossbrenner, Grider, A. Harding, Hogan, Edwin N. Hubbell, James M. Humphrey, Kerr,* Latham, *Le Blond, Marshall, Niblack, Nicholson, Noell, Samuel J. Randall,* Raymond, *Ritter, Rogers, Ross,* Smith, Stillwell, *Strouse, Taber, Taylor, Voorhees, Winfield,* Woodbridge, *Wright*—37.

### The Legal Effect of Rebellion.

February 19, 1866—Mr. Longyear* submitted these resolutions:

*Resolved*, That in the language of the procla-

* The first two resolutions were offered at the request of Mr. BROOMALL, on previous notice.

mation of the President of May 29, 1865, "the rebellion which was waged by a portion of the people of the United States against the properly constituted authorities of the Government thereof in the most violent and revolting form, but whose organized and armed forces have now been almost entirely overcome, has in its revolutionary progress deprived the people" of the States in which it was organized "of all civil government."

2. That whenever the people of any State are thus "deprived of all civil government," it becomes the duty of Congress, by appropriate legislation, to enable them to organize a State government, and in the language of the Constitution "to guarantee to such State a republican form of government."

3. That it is the deliberate sense of this House that the condition of the rebel States fully justifies the President in maintaining the suspension of the writ of *habeas corpus* in those States.

4. That it is the deliberate sense of this House that the condition of the rebel States fully justifies the President in maintaining military possession and control thereof, and that the President is entitled to the thanks of the nation for employing the war power for the protection of Union citizens and the freedmen in those States.

Mr. Finck moved they be laid on the table: which was disagreed to—yeas 29, nays 119, as follow:

YEAS—Messrs. *Ancona. Bergen, Brooks, Chanler, Dawson, Eldridge, Finck, Glossbrenner, Goodyear, Grider, Aaron Harding, Hogan, James M. Humphrey, Kerr, Le Blond, Marshall, McCullough, Niblack, Nicholson, Radford, Samuel J. Randall, Ritter, Rogers, Ross, Shanklin, Taber, Thornton, Trimble, Voorhees*—29.

NAYS—Messrs. Allison, Anderson, Delos R. Ashley, James M. Ashley, Baker, Baldwin, Banks, Baxter, Beaman, Benjamin, Bidwell, Bingham, Blaine, Boutwell, Bromwell, Broomall, Reader W. Clarke, Sidney Clarke, Cobb, Conkling, Cook, Cullom, Dawes, Deming, Donnelly, Driggs, Eckley, Eggleston, Eliot, Farnsworth, Farquhar, Ferry, Garfield, Grinnell, Griswold, Hale, Abner C. Harding, Hayes, Henderson, Higby, Holmes, Hooper, Asahel W. Hubbard, Chester D. Hubbard, Demas Hubbard, John H. Hubbard, James R. Hubbell, Hulburd, James Humphrey, Ingersoll, Jenckes, Julian, Kasson, Kelley, Kelso, Ketcham, Kuykendall, Laflin, Latham, George V. Lawrence, William Lawrence, Loan, Longyear, Lynch, Marvin, McClurg, McIndoe, McKee, McRuer, Mercur, Moorhead, Morrill, Morris, Moulton, Myers, O'Neill, Orth, Paine, Patterson, Perham, Phelps, Pike, Plants, Pomeroy, Price, William H. Randall, Raymond, Alexander H. Rice, John H. Rice, Rollins, Rousseau, Sawyer, Schenck, Scofield, Shellabarger, Sloan, Smith, Spalding, Starr, Stevens, Thayer, John L. Thomas, Trowbridge, Upson, Van Aernam, Burt Van Horn, Robert T. Van Horn, Ward, Warner, Ellihu B. Washburne, William B. Washburn, Welker, Wentworth, Whaley, Williams, James F. Wilson, Stephen F. Wilson, Windom, Woodbridge—119.

A division of the question having been demanded, the *first* resolution was agreed to—yeas 102, nays 36, as follow:

YEAS—Messrs. Allison, Anderson, Delos R. Ashley, James M. Ashley, Baker, Baldwin, Banks, Baxter, Beaman, Benjamin, Bidwell, Bingham, Blaine, Boutwell, Brandegee, Bromwell, Broomall, Reader W. Clarke, Sidney Clarke, Cobb, Conkling, Cook, Defrees, Deming, Donnelly, Driggs, Eckley, Eggleston, Eliot, Farnsworth, Ferry, Garfield, Grinnell, Abner C. Harding, Hayes, Henderson, Higby, Holmes, Hooper, Asahel W. Hubbard, Demas Hubbard, John H. Hubbard, James R. Hubbell, Hulburd, Ingersoll, Jenckes, Julian, Kasson, Kelley, Kelso, Ketcham, Kuykendall, Laflin, William Lawrence, Loan, Longyear, Lynch, Marston, Marvin, McClurg, McIndoe, McKee, McRuer, Moorhead, Morrill, Morris, Moulton, Myers, O'Neill, Orth, Paine, Perham, Pike, Plants, Pomeroy, Price, William H. Randall, Alexander H. Rice, John H. Rice, Rollins, Schenck, Scofield, Shellabarger, Sloan, Spalding, Starr, Stevens, Thayer, Trowbridge, Upson, Van Aernam, Ward, Warner, Ellihu B.

Washburne, William B. Washburn, Welker, Wentworth, Williams, James F. Wilson, Stephen F. Wilson, Windom, Woodbridge—102.

NAYS.—Messrs. *Ancona, Bergen, Boyer, Brooks, Chanler, Dawson, Eldridge, Finck, Glossbrenner; Goodyear, Grider,* Hale, *Aaron Harding, Hogan,* Chester D. Hubbard, *Kerr,* Latham, *McCullough,* Mercur, *Niblack. Nicholson,* Phelps, *Radford, S muel J. Randall,* Raymond, *Ritter, R gers, Ross,* Rousseau, *Shanklin,* Smith, *Taber,* John L. Thomas, *Thornton, Trimble,* Whaley—36.

The *second* resolution was agreed to—yeas 104, nays 33, as follow:

YEAS—Messrs. Anderson, Delos R. Ashley, James M. Ashley, Baker, Baldwin, Banks, Baxter, Beaman, Benjamin, Bidwell, Bingham, Boutwell, Brandegee, Bromwell. Broomall, Reader W. Clarke, Cobb, Conkling, Cook, Cullom, Defrees, Deming, Donnelly, Driggs, Eckley, Eggleston, Eliot, Farnsworth, Ferry, Garfield, Grinnell, Griswold, Hale, Abner C. Harding, Hayes, Henderson, Higby. Holmes, Hooper, Hotchkiss, Asahel W. Hubbard, Chester D. Hubbard, Demas Hubbard, John H. Hubbard, James R. Hubbell, Hulburd, Ingersoll, Jenckes, Julian, Kelley, Kelso, Ketcham, Laflin, William Lawrence, Loan, Longyear, Lynch, Marvin, McClurg, McIndoe, McKee, McRuer, Mercur, Moorhead, Morrill, Morris, Moulton, Myers, O'Neill, Orth, Paine, Perham, Pike, Plants, Pomeroy, Price. William H. Randall, Alexander H. Rice, John H. Rice, Rollins, Sawyer, Schenck, Scofield, Shellabarger Sloan, Spalding, Starr, Stevens, Thayer, John L. Thomas, Trowbridge, Upson, Van Aernam, Burt Van Horn, Ward, Ellihu B. Washburne, William B. Washburn, Welker, Wentworth, Williams, James F. Wilson, Stephen F. Wilson, Windom, Woodbridge—104.

NAYS—Messrs. *Ancona, Bergen, Boyer, Brooks, Chanler, Dawson, Eldridge, Finck, Glossbrenner, Goodyear, Grider, Aaron Harding, Hogan,* Kasson, *Kerr,* Latham, *Le Blond, McCullough. Niblack, Nicholson,* Phelps, *Radford, Samuel J. Randall,* Raymond, *Ritter, Rogers, Ross, Shanklin,* Smith, *Taber, Thornton, Trimble,* Whaley—33.

The *third* resolution was agreed to—yeas 120, nays 26, as follow:

YEAS—Messrs. Allison. Anderson, James M. Ashley, Barker, Baldwin, Banks, Baxter, Beaman, Benjamin, Bidwell, Bingham, Blaine, Boutwell, Brandegee, Bromwell, Broomall, Reader W. Clarke, Sidney Clarke, Cobb, Conkling, Cook, Cullom, Dawes, Defrees, Deming, Donnelly, Driggs, Eckley, Eggleston, Eliot, Farnsworth, Farquhar, Ferry, Garfield, Grinnell, Griswold, Hale, Abner C. Harding, Hayes, Henderson, Higby, Holmes, Hooper, Hotchkiss, Chester D. Hubbard, Demas Hubbard, John H. Hubbard, James R. Hubbell, Hulburd, James Humphrey, Ingersoll, Jenckes. Julian, Kasson, Kelley, Kelso, Ketcham, Kuykendall, Laflin, Latham, George V. Lawrence, William Lawrence, Loan, Longyear, Lynch. Marston, Marvin, McClurg, McKee, McRuer, Mercur, Moorhead, Morrill, Morris, Moulton, Myers, O'Neill, Orth, Paine, Patterson, Perham, Phelps, Pike, Plants, Pomeroy. Price, William H. Randall, Raymond, Alexander H. Rice, John H. Rice, Rollins, Sawyer, Schenck, Scofield, Shellabarger, Sloan, Smith, Spalding, Starr, Stevens, Thayer, John L. Thomas, Trowbridge, Upson, Van Aernam, Burt Van Horn, Robert T. Van Horn, Ward, Warner, Ellihu B. Washburne, William B. Washburn, Welker, Wentworth, Whaley, Williams, James F. Wilson, Stephen F. Wilson, Windom, Woodbridge—120

NAYS—Messrs. *Ancona, Bergen, Boyer, Brooks, Chanler, Dawson, Eldridge, Finck, Glossbrenner. Goodyear, Grider, Aaron Harding, James M. Humphrey, Kerr, Le Blond. McCullough,* Newell, *Niblack, Radford, Ritter, Rogers, Ross, Shanklin, Taber, Thornton, Trimble*—26

The first clause of the *fourth* resolution was agreed to—yeas 118, nays 23, as follow:

YEAS—Messrs. Allison, Delos R. Ashley, James M. Ashley, Baker, Baldwin, Banks, I axter. Beaman, Benjamin, Bidwell, Bingham, Blaine, Boutwell, Brandegee, Bromwell, Broomall, Reader W. Clarke, Sidney Clarke, Cobb. Conkling, Cook, Cullom, Dawes, Defrees, Deming, Driggs, Eckley, Eggleston, Eliot, Farnsworth, Farquhar, Ferry, Garfield, Grinnell, Griswold, Hale, Abner C. Harding, Hayes, Henderson, Higby, Holmes, Hooper, Hotchkiss, Chester D. Hubbard, Demas Hubbard, jr., John H. Hubbard, James R. Hubbell, Hulburd, James Humphrey, Ingersoll, Jenckes, Julian, Kasson, Kelley, Kelso, Ketcham, Kuykendall, Laflin, Latham, George V. Lawrence, William Lawrence, Loan, Longyear, Lynch, Marston, Marvin, McClurg, McIndoe, McKee, McRuer, Mercur, Moorhead, Morris, Moulton, Myers, O'Neill, Orth, Paine, Patterson, Perham, Phelps, Plants, Pomeroy, Price, William H. Randall, Raymond, Alexander H. Rice, John H. Rice, Rollins, Rousseau, Sawyer, Schenck, Scofield, Shellabarger, Sloan, Smith, Starr, Stevens, Thayer, Francis Thomas, John L. Thomas, jr., Trowbridge, Upson, Van Aernam, Burt Van Horn, Robert T. Van Horn, Wa d,

Warner, Ellihu B. Washburne, William B. Washburn, Welker, Wentworth, Whaley, Williams, James F. Wilson, Stephen F. Wilson, Windom, Woodbridge—118.

NAYS—Messrs. *Ancona, Bergen, Boyer, Brooks, Dawson, Eldridge, Finck, Glossbrenner, Goodyear, Aaron Harding, James M. Humphrey, McCullough, Niblack, Nicholson, Radford, Samuel J. Randall, Ritter, Rogers, Ross, Shanklin, Taber, Thornton, Trimble—23.*

The second clause of the *fourth* resolution was agreed to—yeas 135, nays 8, as follow :

YEAS—Messrs. Allison, *Ancona,* Anderson, James M. Ashley, Baker, Baldwin, Banks, Baxter, Beaman, Benjamin, *Bergen,* Bidwell, Bingham, Blaine, Boutwell, *Boyer,* Brandegee, Bromwell, *Brooks,* Broomall, Reader W. Clarke, Sidney Clarke, Cobb, Conkling, Cook, Cullom, *Dawson.* Defrees, Deming, Donnelly, Driggs, Eckley, Eggleston, *Eldridge,* Eliot, Farnsworth, Farquhar, Ferry, *Finck,* Garfield, *Glossbrenner, Goodyear,* Griswold, Hale, Abner C. Harding, Hayes, Higby, Holmes, Hooper. Hotchkiss, Chester D. Hubbard, Demas Hubbard, John H. Hubbard, James R. Hubbell, Hulburd, James Humphrey. *James M. Humphrey,* Ingersoll, Jenckes, *Johnson,* Julian, Kasson, Kelley, Kelso, *Kerr,* Ketcham, Kuykendall, Laflin, Latham, George V. Lawrence, William Lawrence, Le Blond, Loan, Longyear, Lynch, Marston, Marvin, McClurg, McIndoe, McKee, Mercur, Moorhead, Morrill, Morris, Moulton, Myers, O'Neill, Orth, Paine, Patterson, Perham, Phelps, Pike, Plants, Pomeroy, Price, *Radford, Samuel J. Randall,* William H. Randall, Raymond, Alexander H. Rice, John H. Rice, Rollins, Rousseau, Sawyer, Schenck, Scofield, Shellabarger, Sloan, Smith, Spalding, Starr, Stevens, *Taber,* Thayer, Francis Thomas, John L Thomas, *Thornton,* Trowbridge, Upson, Van Aernam, Burt Van Horn, Robert T. Van Horn, Ward, Warner, Ellihu B. Washburne, William B. Washburn, Welker, Wentworth, Whaley, Williams, James F. Wilson, Stephen F. Wilson, Windom, Woodbridge—135.

NAYS—Messrs. *Grider, Aaron Harding, McCullough, Nicholson, Ritter, Rogers, Shanklin, Trimble—8.*

## Recognition of State government of North Carolina.

March 5, 1866—The SPEAKER having proposed to lay before the House a communication signed Jonathan Worth, Governor of North Carolina, Mr. Stevens objected to its reception; and on the question, will the House receive the same, the yeas were 38, nays 100, as follow :

YEAS—Messrs. Delos R. Ashley, *Bergen, Brooks, Chanler, Davis, Denison, Eldridge, Finck, Goodyear, Grider,* Hale, *Aaron Harding, Hogan, Edwin N. Hubbell,* James Humphrey, *Kerr,* Kuykendall, Latham, *Marshall,* McRuer, Newell, *Niblack, Nicholson Noell,* Phelps, *Radford,* Raymond, *Ritter, Rogers, Ross,* Rousseau, *Shanklin, Taber, Taylor, Thornton, Trimble,* Whaley, *Winfield.*—38.

NAYS—Messrs. Alley, Allison, Ames, Anderson, James M. Ashley, Baker, Banks, Barker, Baxter, Beaman, Benjamin, Bidwell, Bingham, Blaine, Boutwell, Bandegee, Bromwell, Broomall, Buckland, Bundy, Sidney Clarke, Cobb, Cook, Cullom, Defrees, Deming, Donnelly, Driggs, Dumont, Eckley, Eliot, Farnsworth, Farquhar, Ferry, Grinnell, Abner C. Harding, Hayes, Henderson, Higby, Hill, Holmes, Hooper, Hotchkiss, Asahel W. Hubbard, Demas Hubbard, jr., John H. Hubbard, James R. Hubbell, Hulburd, Ingersoll. Jenckes, Julian, Kelley, Kelso, Ketcham, William Lawrence, Lynch, Marston, McClurg, McKee, Miller, Morris, Moulton, Myers, O'Neill, Orth, Paine, Patterson, Perham, Pike, Price, William H. Randall, Alexander H. Rice, John H. Rice, Rollins, Sawyer, Schenck, Scofield, Schellabarger, Sloan, Spalding, Stevens, Stillwell, Thayer, Francis Thomas, John L. Thomas, jr., Trowbridge, Upson, Van Aernam, Burt Van Horn, Robert T. Van Horn, Warner, Ellihu B. Washburne, Henry D. Washburn, Welker, Wentworth, Williams, James F. Wilson, Stephen F. Wilson, Windom, Woodbridge.—100.

## Trial of Jefferson Davis.

June 11, 1866—Mr. Boutwell offered this resolution.

Whereas it is notorious that Jefferson Davis was the leader of the late rebellion, and is guilty of treason under the laws of the United States ; and whereas by the proclamation of the President of May, 1865, the said Davis was charged with complicity in the assassination of President Lincoln, and said proclamation has not been revoked nor annulled : Therefore,

*Be it resolved,* As the opinion of the House of Representatives, that said Davis should be held in custody as a prisoner, and subjected to a trial according to the laws of the land.

Which was agreed to—yeas 105, nays 19, as follow :

YEAS—Messrs. Alley, Allison, James M. Ashley, Baker, Baldwin, Banks, Baxter, Beaman, Bidwell, Bingham, Blaine, Boutwell, Bromwell, Buckland, Bundy, Reader W. Clarke, Sidney Clarke, Cobb, Conkling, Cook, Cullom. Darling, Davis, Dawes, Defrees, Donnelly, Eckley, Eliot, Farnsworth, Farquhar, Ferry, Garfield, Grinnell, Griswold, Hale, Abner C. Harding, Hart, Hayes, Henderson, Higby, Holmes, Hooper, Hotchkiss, Chester D. Hubbard, John H. Hubbard, James R. Hubbell, Julian, Kelso, Ketcham, Kuykendall, Laflin, Latham, George V. Lawrence, William Lawrence, Loan, Longyear, Lynch, *Marshall,* Marvin, McClurg, McKee, McRuer, Mercur, Miller, Moorhead, Morrill, Morris, Moulton, Myers, O'Neill, Orth, Paine, Perham, Phelps, Pike, Plants, Pomeroy, Price, William H. Randall, Raymond, Alexander H. Rice, Sawyer, Schenck, Scofield, Shellabarger, Sloan. Smith, Spalding, Thayer, John L Thomas, *Thornton,* Trowbridge, Upson, Van Aernam, Ward, Warner, Henry D Washburn, Welker, Whaley, Williams, James F. Wilson Stephen F. Wilson, Windom, Winfield, Woodbridge—105.

NAYS—Messrs. *Ancona, Boyer, Coffroth, Eldridge, Finck, Glossbrenner, Grider, Harris, Hogan, Johnson, McCullough, Niblack, Samuel J. Randall, Ritter, Rogers, Sitgreaves, Taber, Trimble, Wright—19.*

## Neutrality—The Fenians.

June 11, 1866—Mr. Ancona offered this resolution :

Whereas the Irish people and their brothers and friends in this country are moved by a patriotic purpose to assert the independence and re-establish the nationality of Ireland ; and whereas the active sympathies of the people of the United States are naturally with all men who struggle to achieve such ends, more especially when those engaged therein are the acknowledged friends of our Government, as are the Irish race, they having shed their blood in defense of our flag in every battle of every war in which the republic has been engaged ; and whereas the British Government, against whom they are struggling, is entitled to no other or greater consideration from us as a nation than that demanded by the strict letter of international law, for the reason that during our late civil war she did in effect, by her conduct, repeal her neutrality laws ; and whereas when reparation is demanded for damages to our commerce, resulting from her willful neglect to enforce the same, she arrogantly denies all responsibility, and claims to be the judge in her own case ; and whereas the existence of our neutrality law of 1818 compels the executive department of this Government to discriminate most harshly against those who have ever been and are now our friends, and in favor of those who have been faithless, not only to the general principles of comity which should exist between friendly States, but also to the written law of their own nation upon this subject : Therefore,

*Be it resolved,* That the Committee on Foreign Affairs be, and they are hereby, instructed to report a bill repealing an act approved April 20, 1818, entitled "An act in addition to an act for the punishment of certain crimes against the United States," and to repeal the act therein mentioned, it being the neutrality law, under the terms of which the President's proclamation against the Fenians was issued.

Mr. Davis, of New York, moved to lay it on

the table, which was lost—yeas 5, (Messrs. Cobb, Davis, Grinnell, Hale, Trowbridge,) nays 112.

Mr. Schenck moved this as a substitute:

*Resolved,* That the President of the United States, in the opinion of this House, should reconsider the policy which has been adopted by him as between the British Government and that portion of the Irish people who, under the name of Fenians, are struggling for their independent nationality; and that he be requested to adopt as nearly as practicable that exact course of procedure which was pursued by the Government of Great Britain on the occasion of the late civil war in this country between the United States and rebels in revolt, recognizing both parties as lawful belligerents, and observing between them a strict neutrality.

Mr. Hale moved to table it; which was lost—yeas 8, (Messrs. Cobb, Davis, Dawes, Dodge, Griswold, Hale, Sloan, Trowbridge,) nays 113.

Mr. Banks moved to refer to the Committee on Foreign Affairs, stating that if referred the committee would report upon it. The motion was agreed to—yeas 87, nays 35, as follow:

YEAS—Messrs. Alley, Allison, Delos R. Ashley, James M. Ashley, Baker, Baldwin, Banks, Baxter, Beaman, Bidwell, Bingham, Blaine, Boutwell, Bromwell, Buckland, Bundy, Reader W. C'arke, Sidney Clarke, Cobb, Cook, Cullom, Dawes, Defrees, Delano, Dodge, Driggs, Eckley, Farnsworth, Farquhar, Grinnell, Harris, Hart, Hayes, Holmes, Demas Hubbard, Edwin N. Hubbell, Jenckes, *Jones,* Kasson, Kelley, Kuykendall, Laflin, Latham, George V. Lawrence, William Lawrence, Longyear, Marvin, McClurg, McKee, McRuer, Mercur, Miller, Morrill, Morris, Moulton, Myers, O'Neill, Orth, Paine, Perham, Phelps, Pike, Plants, Price, William H. Randall, Raymond, Alexander H. Rice, John H. Rice, Ross, Rousseau, Sawyer, Schenck, Scofield, Shellabarger, Sloan, Spalding, Thayer, Trowbridge, Upson, Ward, Welker, Whaley, Williams, James F. Wilson, Stephen F. Wilson, Windom, Woodbridge—87.

NAYS—Messrs. *Ancona, Bergen, Boyer, Chanler, Coffroth,* Darling, Davis, Dumont, *Eldridge, Finck, Glossbrenner, Grider,* Hale, *Aaron Harding, Hogan, James M. Humphrey, Johnson, Kerr,* Ketcham, *McCullough, Niblack,* Pomeroy, *Samuel J. Randall, Ritter, Rogers, Sitgreaves.* Smith, Stillwell, *Strouse, Taber, Taylor, Thornton, Trimble, Winfield, Wright*—35.

---

**XI.**

# VOTES ON SUFFRAGE IN THE DISTRICT OF COLUMBIA

## AND OTHER POLITICAL BILLS.

### Suffrage in District of Columbia.

#### IN HOUSE.

January 10, 1866—Pending this bill, offered by Mr. Kelley, December 5, 1865, and reported from the Judiciary Committee by Mr. James F. Wilson, December 18, and then postponed till this day:

A Bill extending the right of suffrage in the District of Columbia.

*Be it enacted, &c.,* That from all laws and parts of laws prescribing the qualifications of electors for any office in the District of Columbia the word "white" be, and the same is hereby, stricken out, and that from and after the passage of this act no person shall be disqualified from voting at any election held in the said District on account of color.

SEC. 2. That all acts of Congress and all laws of the State of Maryland in force in said District and all ordinances of the cities of Washington and Georgetown inconsistent with the provisions of this act are hereby repealed and annulled.

After debate, Mr. Wilson moved its recommitment.

Mr. Hale moved to amend by adding these words: with instructions to amend the bill so as to extend the right of suffrage in the District of Columbia to all persons coming within either of the following classes, irrespective of caste or color, but subject only to existing provisions and qualifications other than those founded on caste or color, to wit:

First. Those who can read the Constitution of the United States.

Second. Those who are assessed for and pay taxes on real or personal property within the District.

Third. Those who have served in and been honorably discharged from the military or naval service of the United States, and to restrict such right of suffrage to the classes above named, and to include proper provisions excluding from the right of suffrage those who have borne arms against the United States during the late rebellion, or given aid or comfort to said rebellion.

January 17, 1866—Mr. Wilson accepted Mr. Hale's amendment as part of his.

January 18—Mr. Darling moved to postpone the bill till April 3.

Mr. Niblack moved to lay the bill on the table, which was disagreed to—yeas 47, nays 123, as follow:

YEAS—Messrs. *Ancona,* Delos R. Ashley, *Bergen, Boyer, Brooks, Chanler, Dawson,* Denison, *Eldridge, Finck, Glossbrenner, Goodyear, Grider, Aaron Harding, Hogan,* Chester D. Hubbard, *Edwin N. Hubbell, James M. Humphrey, Johnson, Jones, Kerr,* Kuykendall, Latham, *Le Blond, Marshall, McCullough, Niblack, Nicholson, Noell,* Phelps, *Radford, Samuel J. Randall,* William H. Randall, *Ritter, Rogers, Ross, Shanklin, Sitgreaves,* Smith, *Strouse, Taber, Taylor,* John L. Thomas, jr., *Thornton, Trimble, Voorhees, Winfield*—47.

NAYS—Messrs. Alley, Allison, Ames, Anderson, James M. Ashley, Baker, Baldwin, Banks, Barker, Baxter, Beaman,

Bidwell, Bingham, Blaine, Blow, Boutwell, Brandegee, Bromwell, Broomall, Buckland, Bundy, Reader W. Clarke, Sidney Clarke, Cobb, Conkling, Cook, Cullom, Darling, Davis, Dawes. Defrees, Delano, Deming, Dixon, Donnelly, Driggs, Eckley, Eggleston, Eliot, Farnsworth, Farquhar, Ferry, Garfield, Grinnell, Griswold, Hale, Abner C. Harding, Hart, Hayes, Henderson, Higby, Hill, Holmes, Hooper, Asahel W. Hubbard, Demas Hubbard, jr., John H. Hubbard, Hulburd, James Humphrey, Ingersoll, Jenckes, Julian, Kasson, Kelley, Kelso, Ketcham, Laflin, George V. Lawrence, William Lawrence, Loan, Longyear, Lynch, Marston, Marvin, McClurg, McKee, Mercur, Miller, Moorhead, Morrill, Morris. Moulton, Myers, O'Neill, Orth, Paine, Patterson, Perham, Pike, Plants, Pomeroy, Price, Raymond, Alexander H. Rice, John H. Rice, Rollins, Sawyer, Schenck, Scofield, Shellabarger, Sloan, Spalding, Starr, Stevens, Stillwell, Thayer, Francis Thomas, Trowbridge, Upson, Van Aernam, Burt Van Horn, Robert T. Van Horn, Ward, Warner, Ellihu B. Washburne, William B. Washburn, Welker, Wentworth, Williams, James F. Wilson, Stephen F. Wilson, Windom, Woodbridge—123.

Mr. Darling modified his motion so as to postpone until the first Tuesday in March, which was disagreed to—yeas 34, nays 138, as follow :

YEAS—Messrs. Anderson, Banks, Conkling, Darling, Davis, Defrees, Eggleston, Farquhar, Ferry, Griswold, Hale, Hart, Henderson, Hill, *Hogan*, Jas. Humphrey, Kasson, Ketcham, Kuykendall, Laflin, Latham, George V. Lawrence, Marvin, Mercur, Miller, Orth, Phelps, William H. Randall, Raymond, Smith, Stillwell, John L. Thomas, jr., *Trimble*, Robert T. Van Horn—34.

NAYS—Messrs. Alley, Allison, Ames, *Ancona*, Delos R. Ashley, James M. Ashley, Baker, Baldwin, Barker, Baxter, Beaman, *Benjamin*, *Bergen*, Bidwell, Bingham, Blaine, Blow, Boutwell, *Boyer*, Brandegee, Bromwell, *Brooks*, Broomall, Bundy, *Chanler*, Reader W. Clarke, Sidney Clarke, Cobb, Cook, Cullom, Dawes, *Dawson*, Deming, *Denison*, Dixon, Donnelly, Driggs, Eckley, *Eldridge*, Eliot, Farnsworth, *Finck*, Garfield, *Glossbrenner*, *Goodyear*, *Grider*, Grinnell, *Aaron Harding*, Abner C. Harding, Hayes, Higby, Holmes, Hooper, A. W. Hubbard, Chester D. Hubbard, Demas Hubbard, jr., John H. Hubbard, *Edwin N. Hubbell*, Hulburd, *James M. Humphrey*, Ingersoll, Jenckes, *Johnson*, *Jones*, Julian, Kelley, Kelso, *Kerr*, William Lawrence, *Le Blond*, Loan, Longyear, Lynch, *Marshall*, Marston, McClurg, *McCullough*, McKee, Moorhead, Morrill, Morris, Moulton, Myers, *Niblack*, *Nicholson*, *Noell*, O'Neill, Paine, Patterson, Perham, Pike, Plants, Pomeroy, Price, *Radford*, *Samuel J. Randall*, Alexander H. Rice, John H. Rice, *Ritter*, *Rogers*, Rollins, *Ross*, Sawyer, Schenck, Scofield, *Shanklin*, Shellabarger, *Sitgreaves*, Sloan, Spalding, Starr, Stevens, *Strouse*, *Taber*, *Taylor*, Thayer, Francis Thomas, *Thornton*, Trowbridge, Upson, Van Aernam, Burt Van Horn, *Voorhees*, Ward, Warner, Ellihu B. Washburne, William B. Washburn, Welker, Wentworth, James F.Wilson, Stephen F. Wilson, Windom, *Winfield*, Woodbridge—135.

The question recurring on Mr. Wilson's motion to commit with instructions, Mr. Schenck moved to strike from the proposed instructions these words : "Those who are assessed for and pay taxes on real or personal property within the district ;" which was agreed to.

The motion to recommit as amended, was then disagreed to—yeas 53, nays, 117, as follow :

YEAS—Messrs. Anderson, Banks, Blow, Brandegee, Bromwell, Buckland, Reader W. Clarke, Conkling, Darling, Davis, Dawes, Defrees, Delano, Deming, Dixon, Driggs, Eckley, Eggleston, Ferry, Griswold, Hale, Hart, Hayes, Henderson, Hooper, Hulburd, James Humphrey, Jenckes, Kasson, Ketcham, Kuykendall, Laflin, Latham, George V. Lawrence, William Lawrence, Longyear, Marvin, Miller, Moorhead, Morris, Myers, O'Neill, Plants, Raymond, Alexander H. Rice, Schenck, Stillwell, Trowbridge, Burt Van Horn, Robert T. Van Horn, Warner, William B. Washburn, Woodbridge—53.

NAYS—Messrs. Alley, Allison, Ames, *Ancona*, Delos R. Ashley, James M. Ashley, Baker, Baldwin, Barker, Baxter, Beaman, Benjamin, *Bergen*, Bidwell, Bingham, Blaine, Boutwell, *Boyer*, *Brooks*, Broomall, Bundy, *Chanler*, Clarke, Cobb, Cook, Cullom, *Dawson*, *Denison*, Donnelly, *Eldridge*, Eliot, Farnsworth, Farquhar, *Finck*, Garfield, *Glossbrenner*, *Goodyear*, *Grider*, Grinnell, *Aaron Harding*, Abner C. Harding, Higby, Hill, *Hogan*, Holmes, Asahel W. Hubbard, Chester D. Hubbard, Demas Hubbard, jr., John H. Hubbard, *Edwin N. Hubbell*, *James M. Humphrey*, Ingersoll, *Johnson*, *Jones*, Julian, Kelley, Kelso, *Kerr*, *Le Blond*, Loan, Lynch, *Marshall*, Marston, McClurg. *McCullough*, McKee, Mercur, Morrill, Moulton, *Niblack*, *Nicholson*, *Noell*, Orth, Paine, Patterson, Perham, Phelps, Pomeroy, Price, *Radford*, *Samuel J. Randall*, William H. Randall, John H. Rice, *Ritter*, *Rogers*, Rollins, *Ross*, Sawyer, Scofield, *Shanklin*, Shellabarger, Sit-

greaves, Sloan, Smith, Spalding, *Starr*, Stevens, *Strouse*, *Taber*, *Taylor*, Thayer, Francis Thomas, John L. Thomas, jr., *Thornton*, *Trimble*, Upson, Van Aernam, *Voorhees*, Ward, Ellihu B. Washburne, Welker, Wentworth, Williams, James F. Wilson, Stephen F. Wilson, Windom, Winfield—117.

The bill was then passed—yeas 116, nays 54, as follow :

YEAS—Messrs. Alley, Allison, Ames, James M. Ashley, Baker, Baldwin, Banks, Barker, Baxter, Beaman, Bidweil, Bingham, Blaine, Blow, Boutwell, Brandegee, Bromwell, Broomall, Buckland, Bundy, Reader W. Clarke, Sidney Clarke, Cobb, Conkling, Cook, Cullom, Darling, Davis, Dawes, Defrees, Delano, Deming, Dixon, Donnelly, Driggs, Eckley, Eggleston, Eliot, Farnsworth, Ferry, Garfield, Grinnell, Griswold, Hale, Abner C. Harding, Hart, Hayes, Higby, Holmes, Hooper, Asahel W. Hubbard, Demas Hubbard, jr., John H. Hubbard, Hulburd, James Humphrey, Ingersoll, Jenckes, Julian, Kasson, Kelley, Kelso, Ketcham, Laflin, George V. Lawrence, William Lawrence, Loan, Longyear, Lynch, Marston, Marvin, McClurg, Mercur, Miller, Moorhead, Morrill, Morris, Moulton, Myers, O'Neill, Orth, Paine, Patterson, Perham. Pike, Plants, Pomeroy, Price, Raymond, Alexander H. Rice, John H. Rice, Rollins, Sawyer, Schenck, Scofield, Shellabarger, Sloan, Spalding, Starr, Stevens, Thayer, Francis Thomas, Trowbridge, Upson, Van Aernam, Burt Van Horn, Ward, Warner, Ellihu B. Washburne, William B. Washburn, Welker, Wentworth, Williams, James F. Wilson, Stephen F. Wilson, Windom, Woodbridge—116.

NAYS—Messrs. *Ancona*, Anderson, Delos R. Ashley, Benjamin, *Bergen*, *Boyer*, *Brooks*, *Chanler*, *Dawson*, *Denison*, *Eldridge*, Farquhar, *Finck*, *Glossbrenner*, *Goodyear*, *Grider*, *Harding*, Henderson, Hill, *Hogan*, Chester D. Hubbard, *Edwin N. Hubbell*, *James M. Humphrey*, Johnson, Jones, Kerr, Kuykendall, Latham, *Le Blond*, *Marshall*, *McCullough*, McKee, *Niblack*, *Nicholson*, *Noell*, Phelps, *Radford*, *Samuel J. Randall*, William H. Randall, *Ritter*, *Rogers*, *Ross*, *Shanklin*, *Sitgreaves*, Smith, Stillwell, *Strouse*, *Taber*, *Taylor*, *Thornton*, *Trimble*, Robert T. Van Horn, *Voorhees*, *Vinfield* —54.

## In Senate.

June 27, 1866—The bill, as reported to the Senate from its committee amended, was considered, the pending question. being Mr. Morrill's motion to insert in the first section the words in brackets, below :

That from and after the passage of this act, each and every male person, excepting paupers and persons under guardianship, of the age of twenty-one years and upwards, who has not been convicted of any infamous crime, or offence, and who is a citizen of the United States, and who shall have resided in the said district for the period of six months previous to any election therein, [and excepting persons who may have voluntarily left the District of Columbia to give aid and comfort to the rebels in the late rebellion,] shall be entitled to the elective franchise, and shall be deemed an elector and entitled to vote at any election in said District, without any distinction on account of color or race.

Mr Morrill moved further to amend by inserting, also, after "therein," the words "and who can read the Constitution of the United States in the English language, and write his name;" which was disagreed to—yeas 15, nays 19, as follow :

YEAS—Messrs. Anthony, Cragin, Edmunds, Fessenden, Foster, Harris, Kirkwood, Morrill, Poland, Pomeroy, Sherman, Trumbull, Wade, Willey, Williams—15.

NAYS—Messrs. Brown, *Buckalew*, Conness, *Davis*, Grimes, *Guthrie*, *Hendricks*, Howard, Howe, Morgan, Norton, Nye, Ramsey, Sprague, Stewart, Sumner, Van Winkle, Wilson, Yates—19.

Mr. Willey offered this substitute for the bill :

In all elections to be held hereafter in the District of Columbia, the following described persons, and those only, shall have the right to vote, namely : first, all those persons who were actually residents of said District and qualified to vote therein at the elections held therein in the year 1865, under the statutes then in force; second all persons residents of said District who have been duly mustered into the military or naval service of the United States during the late rebellion, and have been or shall hereafter be honorably discharged therefrom; third, male citizens of the United States who shall have attained the age of twenty-one years, (excepting paupers, persons *non compotes mentis*, or convicted of an infamous offence,) and who, being residents of the ward or district in which they shall offer to vote, shall have resided in said District for the period of one year next preceding any election, and who shall have paid the taxes assessed against them, and who can read, and who can write their names.

No further vote has been taken up to date of putting this page to press.

### West Virginia Bill.

February 6, 1866—The House passed a joint resolution giving the consent of Congress to the transfer of Berkeley and Jefferson counties to West Virginia—yeas 112, nays 24; (the latter all Democrats except Mr. Baker.) The Senate passed it, March 6—yeas 32, nays 5.—Mr. *Johnson,* of Maryland, voted aye; the other Democrats, voting, voted nay.

### Extending the Homestead Act.
#### In House.

February 7, 1866—A bill providing that all the public lands in Alabama, Mississippi, Louisiana, Arkansas, and Florida, shall be disposed of according to the stipulations of the homestead law of 1862, no entry to be made for more than eighty acres, and no discrimination to be made on account of race or color, and the mineral lands to be reserved, was considered.

Mr. Taber moved to add this proviso:

*And provided, also,* That nothing in this act shall be so construed as to preclude such persons as have been or shall be pardoned by the President of the United States for their participation in the recent rebellion from the benefit of this act.

Which was disagreed to—yeas 37, nays 104, as follow:

YEAS—Messrs. Delos R. Ashley, *Bergen, Boyer, Brooks,* Buckland, *Chanler, Eldridge, Finck, Glossbrenner, Grider, Aaron Harding, Hogan,* Chester D. Hubbard, *Edwin N. Hubbell, James M. Humphrey, Kerr,* Latham, *Le Blond, Marshall, McCullough,* McRuer, *Niblack, Nicholson, Noell,* Phelps, *Ritter, Rogers, Ross, Shanklin, Sitgreaves, Strouse, Taber,* Thayer, *Thornton, Trimble, Voorhees*—37.

NAYS—Messrs. Alley, Allison, Ames, James M. Ashley, Baker, Baldwin, Banks, Barker, Baxter, Beaman, Benjamin, Bidwell, Bingham, Blaine, Blow, Boutwell, Brandegee, Bromwell, Broomall, Bundy, Reader W. Clarke, Sidney Clarke, Cobb, Conkling, Cook, Cullom, Darling, Davis, Dawes, Defrees, Deming, Donnelly, Driggs, Eckley, Eggleston, Eliot, Farnsworth, Farquhar, Ferry, Garfield, Hale, Abner C. Harding, Hart, Hayes, Higby, Hill, Hooper, Hotchkiss, Demas Hubbard, jr., John H. Hubbard, Ingersoll, Jenckes, Julian, Kasson, Kelley, Kelso, Kuykendall, Laflin, George V. Lawrence, William Lawrence, Longyear, Lynch, Marston, Marvin, McClurg, McIndoe, Mercur, Miller, Moorhead, Morris, Moulton, Myers, Newell, O'Neill, Orth, Paine, Patterson, Perham, Price, William H. Randall, Alexander H. Rice, John H. Rice, Rollins, Sawyer, Schenck, Sloan, Smith, Spalding, Starr, Stevens, Trowbridge, Upson, Van Aernam, Burt Van Horn, Ward, Warner, Elihu B. Washburne, William B. Washburn, Welker, Wentworth,

James F. Wilson, Stephen F. Wilson, Windom, Woodbridge—104.

February 8—The bill passed—yeas 112, nays 29; the latter all Democrats, except Messrs. Driggs and Latham.

The bill as finally passed provided that until January 1, 1867, any person applying for the benefit of the act shall swear "that he has not borne arms against the United States, or given aid and comfort to its enemies"

### Habeas Corpus.
#### In House.

March 20—The bill to amend an act entitled "An act relating to *habeas corpus,* and regulating judicial proceedings in certain cases," approved March 3, 1863, was passed—yeas 113, nays 31, as follow:

YEAS—Messrs. Alley, Allison, Ames, Anderson, Delos R. Ashley, James M. Ashley, Baker, Baldwin, Banks, Barker, Baxter, Beaman, Bidwell, Bingham, Blaine, Blow, Boutwell, Bromwell, Broomall, Buckland, Bundy, Reader W. Clarke, Conkling, Cook, Cullom, Delano, Deming, Dixon, Driggs, Dumont, Eggleston, Eliot, Farnsworth, Farquhar, Ferry, Garfield, Grinnell, Abner C. Harding, Hart, Hayes, Henderson, Hill, Holmes, Hooper, Asahel W. Hubbard, Chester D Hubbard, Demas Hubbard, jr., John H. Hubbard, James R. Hubbell, Hulburd, Ingersoll, Jenckes, Kasson, Kelley, Kelso, Ketcham, Kuykendall, Laflin, Latham, George V. Lawrence, William Lawrence, Loan, Lynch, Marston, Marvin, McClurg, McKee, McRuer, Miller, Moorhead, Morrill, Morris, Moulton, Myers, Newell, Noell, O'Neill, Orth, Paine, Perham, Phelps, Pike, Plants, Price, William H. Randall, Raymond, John H. Rice, Rollins, Rousseau, Sawyer, Scofield, Shellabarger, Sloan, Smith, Stevens, Stillwell, Thayer, Trowbridge, Upson, Van Aernam, Burt Van Horn, Robert T. Van Horn, Ward, Warner, Elihu B. Washburne, William B. Washburn, Welker, Wentworth, Whaley, Williams, James F. Wilson, Windom, Woodbridge—113.

NAYS—Messrs. Ancona, *Bergen, Boyer, Brooks, Chanler, Coffroth, Dawson, Eldridge, Glossbrenner, Grider,* Hale, *Aaron Harding, Hogan, Edwin N. Hubbell, James M. Humphrey, Jones, Kerr, Le Blond, Marshall, McCullough, Nicholson, Samuel J. Randall, Ritter, Rogers, Ross, Sitgreaves, Strouse, Taber, Thornton, Trimble, Winfield*—31.

#### In Senate.

April 20—The bill passed—yeas 30, nays 4, as follow:

YEAS—Messrs. Anthony, Chandler, Clark, Conness, Cragin, Doolittle, Edmunds, Foster, Henderson, Howard, Howe, Johnson, Kirkwood, Lane of Indiana, Morgan, Norton, Nye, Poland, Pomeroy, Ramsey, Sprague, Stewart, Sumner, Trumbull, Van Winkle, Wade, Willey, Williams, Wilson, Yates—30.

NAYS—Messrs *Buckalew, Guthrie, Hendricks, Saulsbury*—4.

### No Denial of the Elective Franchise on Account of Color.
#### In House.

1866, May 15—Pending the bill to amend the organic acts of the territories of Nebraska, Colorado, Dakota, Montana, Washington, Idaho, Arizona, Utah, and New Mexico, of which this is the ninth section:

"That within the territories aforesaid there shall be no denial of the elective franchise to citizens of the United States because of race or color, and all persons shall be equal before the law. And all acts or parts of acts, either of Congress or the legislative assemblies of the territories aforesaid, inconsistent with the provisions of this act, are hereby declared null and void."

Mr. Le Blond moved to strike it out, which was disagreed to—yeas 36, nays 76, as follow:

YEAS—Messrs *Ancona*, Delos R. Ashley, *Bergen, Boyer, Chanler, Dawson, Denison, Eldridge, Finck, Glossbrenner, Goodyear, Grider, Aaron Harding,* Chester D. Hubbard, *Edwin N. Hubbell, Kerr,* Kuykendall, Latham, *Le Blond, Marshall, Niblack, Nicholson,* Phelps, William H. Randall, *Ritter, Rogers, Ross,* Rousseau, *Shanklin, Sitgreaves, Strouse, Taber, Taylor, Trimble,* Whaley, *Wright*—36.

NAYS—Messrs. Allison, Ames, Anderson, James M. Ashley, Baker, Baldwin, Banks, Baxter, Blaine, Blow, Boutwell, Brandegee, Broomall, Sidney Clarke, Cook, Cullom, Darling, Davis, Dawes, Deming, Donnelly, Dumont, Eggleston, Farnsworth, Ferry, Garfield, Griswold, Hart, Hayes, Higby, Holmes, Hooper, Hotchkiss, Asahel W. Hubbard, Demas Hubbard, John H. Hubbard, Hulburd, Ingersoll, Jenckes, Julian, Kelley, Kelso, William Lawrence, Loan, Longyear, Lynch, Marston, McClurg, McRuer, Mercur, Miller, Moorhead, Morrill, Orth, Paine, Patterson, Perham, Pike, Plants, Price, Rollins, Sawyer, Spalding, Thayer, Francis Thomas, Van Aernam, Burt Van Horn, Ward, Warner, Ellihu B. Washburne, William B. Washburn, Welker, Williams, James F. Wilson, Stephen F. Wilson, Windom—76.

The bill then passed—yeas 79, nays 43.

IN SENATE.

June 29—The bill was considered but **not** voted on.

---

# XII.

# POLITICAL AND MILITARY MISCELLANEOUS.

### Union National Platform, June, 1864.

*Resolved*, That it is the highest duty of every American citizen to maintain against all their enemies the integrity of the Union and the paramount authority of the Constitution and laws of the United States ; and that, laying aside all differences of political opinions, we pledge ourselves, as Union men, animated by a common sentiment and aiming at a common object, to do everything in our power to aid the Government in quelling by force of arms the Rebellion now raging against its authority, and in bringing to the punishment due to their crimes the Rebels and traitors arrayed against it.

*Resolved*, That we approve the determination of the Government of the United States not to compromise with Rebels, or to offer them any terms of peace, except such as may be based upon an unconditional surrender of their hostility and a return to their just allegiance to the Constitution and laws of the United States, and that we call upon the Government to maintain this position, and to prosecute the war with the utmost possible vigor to the complete suppression of the Rebellion, in full reliance upon the self-sacrificing patriotism, the heroic valor, and the undying devotion of the American people to the country and its free institutions.

*Resolved*, That as Slavery was the cause, and now constitutes the strength of this Rebellion, and as it must be, always and everywhere, hostile to the principles of Republican Government, justice, and the National safety demand its utter and complete extirpation from the soil of the Republic ; and that, while we uphold and maintain the acts and proclamations by which the Government, in its own defence, has aimed a death-blow at this gigantic evil, we are in favor, furthermore, of such an amendment to the Constitution, to be made by the people in conformity with its provisions, as shall terminate and forever prohibit the existence of Slavery within the limits or the jurisdiction of the United States.

*Resolved*, That the thanks of the American people are due to the soldiers and sailors of the Army and Navy, who have periled their lives in defence of their country and in vindication of the honor of its flag ; that the nation owes to them some permanent recognition of their patriotism and their valor, and ample and permanent provision for those of their survivors who have received disabling and honorable wounds in the service of the country ; and that the memories of those who have fallen in its defence shall be held in grateful and everlasting remembrance.

*Resolved*, That we approve and applaud the practical wisdom, the unselfish patriotism, and the unswerving fidelity to the Constitution and the principles of American Liberty, with which Abraham Lincoln has discharged, under circumstances of unparalleled difficulty, the great duties and responsibilities of the Presidential office ; that we approve and endorse, as demanded by the emergency and essential to the preservation of the nation and as within the provisions of the Constitution, the measures and acts which he has adopted to defend the nation against its open and secret foes ; that we approve, especially, the Proclamation of Emancipation, and the employment as Union soldiers of men heretofore held in slavery ; and that we have full confidence in his determination to carry these and all other Constitutional measures essential to the salvation of the country into full and complete effect.

*Resolved*, That we deem it essential to the general welfare that harmony should prevail in the National Councils, and we regard as worthy of public confidence and official trust those only who cordially endorse the principles proclaimed in these resolutions, and which should characterize the administration of the Government.

*Resolved*, That the Government owes to all men employed in its armies, without regard to distinction of color, the full protection of the laws of war ; and that any violation of these laws, or of the usages of civilized nations in time of war, by the Rebels now in arms, should be made the subject of prompt and full redress.

*Resolved*, That foreign immigration, which in the past has added so much to the wealth, development of resources, and increase of power to this nation—the asylum of the oppressed of all nations—should be fostered and encouraged by a liberal and just policy.

*Resolved,* That we are in favor of the speedy construction of the Railroad to the Pacific coast.

*Resolved,* That the National faith, pledged for the redemption of the public debt, must be kept inviolate, and that for this purpose we recommend economy and rigid responsibility in the public expenditures, and a vigorous and just system of taxation; and that it is the duty of every loyal State to sustain the credit and promote the use of the National currency.

*Resolved,* That we approve the position taken by the Government that the people of the United States can never regard with indifference the attempt of any European Power to overthrow by force or to supplant by fraud the institutions of any Republican Government on the Western Continent; and that they will view with extreme jealousy, as menacing to the peace and independence of their own country, the efforts of any such power to obtain new footholds for Monarchical Governments, sustained by foreign military force, in near proximity to the United States.

----

### Democratic National Platform, August, 1864.

*Resolved,* That in the future, as in the past, we will adhere with unswerving fidelity to the Union under the Constitution as the only solid foundation of our strength, security and happiness as a people, and as a framework of government equally conducive to the welfare and prosperity of all the States, both northern and southern.

*Resolved,* That this convention does explicitly declare, as the sense of the American people, that after four years of failure to restore the Union by the experiment of war, during which, under the pretence of a military necessity, or war power higher than the Contitution, the Constitution itself has been disregarded in every part, and public liberty and private right alike trodden down and the material prosperity of the country essentially impaired—justice, humanity, liberty and the public welfare demand that immediate efforts be made for a cessation of hostilities, with a view to an ultimate convention of the States, or other peaceable means, to the end that at the earliest practicable moment peace may be restored on the basis of the Federal Union of the States.

*Resolved,* That the direct interference of the military authorities of the United States in the recent elections held in Kentucky, Maryland, Missouri, and Delaware, was a shameful violation of the Constitution; and a repetition of such acts in the approaching election will be held as revolutionary, and resisted with all the means and power under our control.

*Resolved,* That the aim and object of the Democratic party is to preserve the Federal Union and the rights of the States unimpaired; and they hereby declare that they consider that the administrative usurpation of extraordinary and dangerous powers not granted by the constitution; the subversion of the civil by military law in States not in insurrection; the arbitrary military arrest, imprisonment, trial and sentence of American citizens in States where civil law exists in full force; the suppression of freedom of speech and of the press; the denial of the right of asylum; the open and avowed disregard of State rights; the employment of unusual test-oaths, and the interference with and denial of the right of the people to bear arms in their defence, is calculated to prevent a restoration of the Union and the perpetuation of a government deriving its just powers from the consent of the governed.

*Resolved,* That the shameful disregard of the Administration to its duty in respect to our fellow-citizens who now are, and long have been, prisoners of war in a suffering condition, deserves the severest reprobation, on the score alike of public policy and common humanity.

*Resolved,* That the sympathy of the Democratic party is heartily and earnestly extended to the soldiery of our army and sailors of our navy, who are, and have been in the field and on the sea, under the flag of their country; and, in the event of its attaining power, they will receive all the care, protection, and regard that the brave soldiers and sailors of the Republic have so nobly earned.

----

### Call for a National Union Convention, 1866.

A National Union Convention, of at least two delegates from each congressional district of all the States, two from each Territory, two from the District of Columbia, and four delegates at large from each State, will be held at the city of Philadelphia, on the second Tuesday (14th) of August next.

Such delegates will be chosen by the electors of the several States who sustain the Administration in maintaining unbroken the Union of the States under the Constitution which our fathers established, and who agree in the following propositions, viz:

The Union of the States is, in every case, indissoluble, and is perpetual; and the Constitution of the United States, and the laws passed by Congress in pursuance thereof, supreme, and constant, and universal in their obligation;

The rights, the dignity, and the equality of the States in the Union, including the right of representation in Congress, are solemnly guaranteed by that Constitution, to save which from overthrow so much blood and treasure were expended in the late civil war;

There is no right anywhere to dissolve the Union or to separate States from the Union, either by voluntary withdrawal, by force of arms, or by Congressional action; neither by the secession of the States, nor by the exclusion of their loyal and qualified representatives, nor by the National Government in any other form;

Slavery is abolished, and neither can, nor ought to be, re-established in any State or Territory within our jurisdiction ·

Each State has the undoubted right to prescribe the qualifications of its own electors, and no external power rightfully can, or ought to, dictate, control, or influence the free and voluntary action of the States in the exercise of that right;

The maintenence inviolate of the rights of the States, and especially of the right of each State to order and control its own domestic concerns, according to its own judgment exclusively, subject only to the Constitution of the United States, is essential to that balance of power on which the perfection and endurance of our political fabric depend, and the overthrow of that system by the usurpation and centralization of power in Congress would be a revolution, dangerous to republican government and destructive of liberty;

Each House of Congress is made by the Constitution the sole judge of the elections, returns, and qualifications of its members; but the exclusion of loyal Senators and Representatives, properly chosen and qualified under the Constitution and laws, is unjust and revolutionary;

Every patriot should frown upon all those acts and proceedings everywhere, which can serve no other purpose than to rekindle the animosities of war, and the effect of which upon our moral, social, and material interests at home, and upon our standing abroad, differing only in degree, is injurious like war itself;

The purpose of the war having been to preserve the Union and the Constitution by putting down the rebellion, and the rebellion having been suppressed, all resistance to the authority of the General Government being at an end, and the war having ceased, war measures should also cease, and should be followed by measures of peaceful administration, so that union, harmony, and concord may be encouraged, and industry, commerce, and the arts of peace revived and promoted; and the early restoration of all the States to the exercise of their constitutional powers in the national Government is indispensably necessary to the strength and the defence of the Republic, and to the maintenance of the public credit;

All such electors in the thirty-six States and nine Territories of the United States, and in the District of Columbia, who, in a spirit of patriotism and love for the Union, can rise above personal and sectional considerations, and who desire to see a truly National Union Convention, which shall represent all the States and Territories of the Union, assemble, as friends and brothers, under the national flag, to hold counsel together upon the state of the Union, and to take measures to avert possible danger from the same, are specially requested to take part in the choice of such delegates.

But no delegate will take a seat in such convention who does not loyally accept the national situation and cordially endorse the principles above set forth, and who is not attached, in true allegiance, to the Constitution, the Union, and the Government of the United States.

WASHINGTON, June 25, 1866.

A. W. RANDALL,
President.

J. R. DOOLITTLE,
O. H. BROWNING,
EDGAR COWAN,
CHARLES KNAP,
SAMUEL FOWLER,
*Executive Committee National Union Club.*

We recommend the holding of the above convention, and endorse the call therefor.

DANIEL S. NORTON,　JAMES DIXON,
J. W. NESMITH,　　T. A. HENDRICKS,

## Address of Democratic Congressmen, 1866.

*To the People of the United States:*

Dangers threaten. The Constitution––the citadel of our liberties—is directly assailed. The future is dark, unless the people will come to the rescue.

In this hour of peril National Union should be the watchword of every true man.

As essential to National Union we must maintain unimpaired the rights, the dignity, and the equality of the States, including the right of representation in Congress, and the exclusive right of each State to control its own domestic concerns, subject only to the Constitution of the United States.

After a uniform construction of the Constitution for more than half a century, the assumption of new and arbitrary powers in the Federal Government is subversive of our system and destructive of liberty.

A free interchange of opinion and kind feeling between the citizens of all the States is necessary to the perpetuity of the Union. At present eleven States are excluded from the national council. For seven long months the present Congress has persistently denied any right of representation to the people of these States. Laws, affecting their highest and dearest interests, have been passed without their consent, and in disregard of the fundamental principle of free government. This denial of representation has been made to all the members from a State, although the State, in the language of the President, "presents itself, not only in an attitude of loyalty and harmony, but in the persons of representatives whose loyalty cannot be questioned under any existing constitutional or legal test."

The representatives of nearly one-third of the States have not been consulted with reference to the great questions of the day. There has been no nationality surrounding the present Congress. There has been no intercourse between the representatives of the two sections, producing mutual confidence and respect. In the language of the distinguished lieutenant general,

"It is to be regretted that, at this time, there cannot be a greater commingling between the citizens of the two sections, and particularly of those intrusted with the law-making power."

This state of things should be removed at once and forever.

Therefore, to preserve the National Union, to vindicate the sufficiency of our admirable Constitution, to guard the States from covert attempts to deprive them of their true position in the Union, and to bring together those who are unnaturally severed, and for these great national purposes only, we cordially approve the call for a National Union Convention, to be held at the city of Philadelphia, on the second Tuesday (14th) of August next, and endorse the principles therein set forth.

We, therefore, respectfully, but earnestly, urge upon our fellow-citizens in each State and Territory and congressional district in the United States, in the interest of Union and in a spirit of harmony, and with direct reference to the principles contained in said call, to act promptly in the selection of wise, moderate, and conservative men to represent them in said Convention, to the end that *all* the States shall at once be restored to their practical relations to the Union, the Constitution be maintained, and peace bless the whole country.

| | |
|---|---|
| W. E. Niblack, | Reverdy Johnson, |
| Anthony Thornton, | Thos. A. Hendricks, |
| Michael C. Kerr, | Wm. Wright, |
| G. S. Shanklin, | James Guthrie, |
| Garrett Davis, | J. A. McDougall, |
| H. Grider, | Wm. Radford, |
| Thomas E. Noell, | S. S. Marshall, |
| Samuel J. Randall, | Myer Strouse, |
| Lewis W. Ross, | Chas. Sitgreaves, |
| Stephen Taber, | S. E Ancona, |
| J. M. Humphrey, | E. N. Hubbell, |
| John Hogan, | B. C. Ritter, |
| B. M. Boyer, | A. Harding. |
| Teunis G. Bergen, | A. J. Glossbrenner, |
| Chas. Goodyear, | E. R. V. Wright, |
| Chas. H. Winfield, | A. J. Rogers, |
| A. H. Coffroth, | H. McCullough, |
| Lovell H. Rousseau, | F. C. Le Blond, |
| Philip Johnson, | W. E. Finck, |
| Chas. A. Eldridge, | L. S. Trimble, |
| | John L. Dawson. |

WASHINGTON, *July* 4, 1866.

---

### The Elections of 1866.

NEW HAMPSHIRE—Smyth, Union, 35,018; Sinclair, Democrat, 30,176.

CONNECTICUT—Hawley, Union, 43,974; English, Democrat, 43,433.

RHODE ISLAND—Burnside, Union, 8,197; Pierce, Democrat, 2,816.

OREGON—Wood, Union, 327 majority.

At the special election in CONNECTICUT, in the fall of 1865, on suffrage, the vote stood:

For colored suffrage, 27,217; against, 33,489. majority against, 6,272.

In WEST VIRGINIA, a vote was taken in May, on ratifying this constitutional amendment:

"No person who, since the 1st day of June, 1861, has given or shall give voluntary aid or assistance to the rebellion against the United States, shall be a citizen of this State, or be allowed to vote at any election held therein, unless he has volunteered into the military or naval service of the United States, and has been or shall be honorably discharged therefrom."

The majority in its favor is 6,922.

In the Territory of NEBRASKA, a vote was taken, with this result: For the proposed State constitution, 3,938; against it, 3,838. *Congress*—Marquette, Union, 4,110; Brooke, Democrat, 3,-974. *Governor*—Butler, Union, 4,093; Morton, Democrat, 3,948.

---

### Correspondence between General Grant and General Lee.

APRIL 7, 1865.

Gen. R. E. LEE, *Commanding C. S. A.:*

GENERAL: The result of the last week must convince you of the hopelessness of further resistance on the part of the Army of Northern Virginia in this struggle. I feel that it is so, and regard it as my duty to shift from myself the responsibility of any further effusion of blood, by asking of you the surrender of that portion of the Confederate States army known as the Army of Northern Virginia.

Very respectfully, your obedient servant,
U. S. GRANT, *Lieut. Gen.,*
*Commanding Armies of the United States*

—

APRIL 7, 1865.

GENERAL: I have received your note of this date. Though not entirely of the opinion you express of the hopelessness of the further resistance on the part of the Army of Northern Virginia, I reciprocate your desire to avoid a useless effusion of blood, and therefore before considering your proposition I ask the terms you will offer on condition of its surrender.

R. E. LEE, *General.*
To Lieut. Gen. GRANT, *Commanding Armies of the United States.*

—

APRIL 8, 1865.

General R. E. LEE, *Commanding C. S. A.:*

GENERAL: Your note of last evening, in reply to mine of same date, asking conditions on which I will accept the surrender of the Army of Northern Virginia, is just received.

In reply I would say that peace being my first desire, there is but one condition I insist upon, viz: That the men surrendered shall be disqualified for taking up arms again against the Government of the United States, until properly exchanged. I will meet you, or designate officers to meet any officers you may name, for the same purpose, at any point agreeable to you, for the purpose of arranging definitely the terms upon which the surrender of the Army of Northern Virginia will be received.

Very respectfully, your obedient servant,
U. S. GRANT, *Lieut. Gen.,*
*Commanding Armies of the United States.*

—

APRIL 8, 1865.

GENERAL: I received, at a late hour, your note of to-day, in answer to mine of yesterday. I did not intend to propose the surrender of the Army of Northern Virginia, but to ask the terms of your proposition. To be frank, I do not think the emergency has arisen to call for the surrender of this army; but as the restoration of peace should be the sole object of all, I desire to know whether your proposal would tend to that end. I cannot, therefore, meet you with a view to surrender the Army of Northern Virginia; but as far as your proposition may affect the Confederate States forces under my command, and tend to the restoration of peace, I should be pleased to meet you at 10 A. M. to-morrow, on the old stage road to Richmond, between the picket lines of the two armies.

Very respectfully, your obedient servant,
R. E. LEE, *General, C. S. A.*
To Lieut. Gen. U. S. GRANT, *Commanding Armies U. S. A.*

—

APRIL 9.

General R. E. LEE, *Commanding C. S. A.:*

GENERAL: Your note of yesterday is received. As I have no authority to treat on the subject of peace, the meeting proposed for 10 A. M. to-day could lead to no good. I will state, however, General, that I am equally anxious for peace with yourself, and the whole North entertain the same feeling.

The terms upon which peace can be had are well understood. By the South laying down their arms they will hasten that most desirable event, save thousands of human lives, and hundreds of millions of property not yet destroyed. Sincerely hoping that all our difficulties may be settled without the loss of another life, I subscribe myself, very respectfully, your obedient servant,

U. S. GRANT, *Lieut. Gen. U. S. A.*

—

APRIL 9, 1865.

GENERAL: I received your note of this morning on the picket line, whither I had come to meet you and ascertain definitely what terms were embraced in your proposition of yesterday with reference to the surrender of this army. I now request an interview in accordance with the offer contained in your letter of yesterday for that purpose.

Very respectfully, your obedient servant,
R. E. LEE, *General.*
To Lieut. Gen. GRANT, *Com'g U. S. Armies.*

—

APRIL 9.

General R. E. LEE, *Commanding C. S. A.:*

Your note of this date is but this moment (11.50 A. M.) received, in consequence of my having passed from the Lynchburg road to the Farmville and Lynchburg road. I am at this writing about four miles west of Walter's Church, and will push forward to the front for the purpose of meeting you.

Notice sent to me on this road where you wish the interview to take place, will meet me.

Very respectfully, your obedient servant,
U. S. GRANT, *Lieut. Gen.,*
*Commanding Armies of United States.*

—

APPOMATTOX C. H., *April 9, 1865.*

General R. E. LEE, *Commanding C. S. A.:*

In accordance with the substance of my letter to you of the 8th instant, I propose to receive the surrender of the Army of Northern Virginia on the following terms, to wit:

Rolls of all the officers and men to be made in duplicate, one copy to be given to an officer designated by me, the other to be retained by such officer or officers as you may designate.

The officers to give their individual paroles not to take arms against the Government of the United States until properly exchanged, and each company or regimental commander sign a like parole for the men of their commands. The arms, artillery, and public property to be parked and stacked, and turned over to the officers appointed by me to receive them. This will not embrace the side-arms of officers, nor their private horses or baggage.

This done, each officer and man will be allowed to return to their homes, not to be disturbed by United States authority so long as they observe their parole and the laws in force where they may reside.

Very respectfully,
U. S. GRANT, *Lieut. Gen.*

HEADQ'RS ARMY OF NORTHERN VIRGINIA,
*April 9, 1865.*

Lieut. Gen. U. S. GRANT, *Com'g U. S. Armies* ·

GENERAL: I have received your letter of this date containing the terms of surrender of the Army of Northern Virginia, as proposed by you. As they are substantially the same as those expressed in your letter of the 8th instant, they are accepted. I will proceed to designate the proper officer to carry the stipulations into effect.

Very respectfully, your obedient servant,
R. E. LEE, *General.*

The other Rebel armies subsequently surrendered on substantially the same terms.

——

## Agreement between Generals Sherman and Johnston.

Memorandum, or Basis of Agreement, made this 18th day of April, A. D. 1865, near Durham's Station, in the State of North Carolina, by and between General Joseph E. Johnston, commanding Confederate army, and Major General William T. Sherman, commanding Army of the United States, both being present:

1. The contending armies now in the field to maintain the *status quo*, until notice is given by the commanding general of any one to its opponent, and reasonable time, say forty-eight hours, allowed.

2. The Confederate armies now in existence to be disbanded and conducted to their several State capitals, therein to deposit their arms and public property in the State arsenal, and each officer and man to execute and file an agreement to cease from acts of war, and to abide the action of both State and Federal authorities. The number of arms and munitions of war to be reported to the Chief of Ordnance at Washington city, subject to the future action of the Congress of the United States, and in the meantime to be used solely to maintain peace and order within the borders of the States respectively.

3. The recognition by the Executive of the United States of the several State governments, on their officers and legislatures taking the oath prescribed by the Constitution of the United States ; and where conflicting State governments have resulted from the war, the legitimacy of all shall be submitted to the Supreme Court of the United States.

4. The re-establishment of the Federal Courts in the several States, with powers as defined by the Constitution and laws of Congress.

5. The people and inhabitants of all these States to be guaranteed, so far as the Executive can, their political rights and franchise, as well as their rights of person and property, as defined by the Constitution of the United States, and of the States respectively.

6. The Executive authority of the Government of the United States not to disturb any of the people by reason of the late war, so long as they live in peace and quiet, and abstain from acts of armed hostility, and obey the laws in existence at the place of their residence.

7. In general terms, the war to cease, a general amnesty, so far as the Executive of the United States can command, on the condition of the disbandment of the Confederate armies, dis-

tribution of arms, and the resumption of peaceable pursuits by the officers and men hitherto composing such armies. Not being fully empowered by our respective principals to fulfil these terms, we individually and officially pledge ourselves to promptly obtain an answer thereto, and to carry out the above programme.

W. T. SHERMAN,
*Maj. Gen., Commanding Army U. S. in N. C.*
J. E. JOHNSTON,
*General, Commanding C. S. A. in N. C.*

—

The following official dispatch to the Associated Press gives the particulars of its disapproval, and the supposed reasons therefor:

WASHINGTON, April 22.—Yesterday evening a bearer of despatches arrived from General Sherman. An agreement for a suspension of hostilities, and a memorandum of what is called a basis for peace, had been entered into on the 18th inst., by General Sherman with the rebel General Johnston, the rebel General Breckinridge being present at the conference.

A Cabinet meeting was held at 8 o'clock in the evening, at which the action of General Sherman was disapproved by the President, the Secretary of War, by General Grant, and by every member of the Cabinet.

General Sherman was ordered to resume hostilities immediately, and he was directed that the instructions given by the late President, in the following telegram, which was penned by Mr. Lincoln himself, at the Capitol, on the night of the 3d of March, were approved by President Andrew Johnson, and were reiterated to govern the action of military commanders.

On the night of the 3d of March, while President Lincoln and his Cabinet were at the Capitol, a telegram from General Grant was brought to the Secretary of War, informing him that General Lee had requested an interview or conference to make an arrangement for terms of peace. The letter of General Lee was published in a message of Davis to the rebel Congress.

General Grant's telegram was submitted to Mr. Lincoln, who, after pondering a few minutes, took up his pen and wrote with his own hand the following reply, which he submitted to the Secretary of State and Secretary of War. It was then dated, addressed, and signed by the Secretary of War, and telegraphed to General Grant:

WASHINGTON, March 3, 1866, 12 P. M.—*Lieutenant General Grant:* The President directs me to say to you that he wishes you to have no conference with General Lee, unless it be for the capitulation of General Lee's army, or on some minor and purely military matter. He instructs me to say that you are not to decide, discuss, or confer upon any political question. Such questions the President holds in his own hands, and will submit them to no military conferences or conventions. Meantime, you are to press to the utmost your military advantages.

EDWIN M. STANTON,
*Secretary of War.*

After the Cabinet meeting last night, General Grant started for North Carolina to direct operations against Johnston's army.

EDWIN M. STANTON,
*Secretary of War.*

It is reported that this proceeding of General Sherman was disapproved for the following, among other, reasons:

1. It was an exercise of authority not vested in General Sherman, and on its face shows that both he and Johnston knew that General Sherman had no authority to enter into any such arrangement.

2. It was a practical acknowledgment of the rebel government.

3. It undertook to re-establish the rebel State governments that had been overthrown at the sacrifice of many thousand loyal lives and immense treasure, and placed the arms and munitions of war in the hands of the rebels at their respective capitals, which might be used as soon as the armies of the United States were disbanded, and used to conquer and subdue the loyal States.

4. By the restoration of rebel authority in their respective States they would be enabled to re-establish slavery.

5. It might furnish a ground of responsibility by the Federal Government to pay the rebel debt, and certainly subjects the loyal citizens of rebel States to debt contracted by rebels in the State.

6. It would put in dispute the existence of loyal State governments, and the new State of West Virginia, which had been recognized by every department of the United States Government.

7. It practically abolished the confiscation laws, and relieved the rebels, of every degree, who had slaughtered our people, from all pains and penalties for their crimes.

8. It gave terms that had been deliberately, repeatedly, and solemnly rejected by President Lincoln, and better terms than the rebels had ever asked in their most prosperous condition.

9. It formed no basis of true and lasting peace, but relieved the rebels from the pressure of our victories, and left them in condition to renew their efforts to overthrow the United States Government and subdue the loyal States whenever their strength was recruited and any opportunity should offer.

### General Grant's Orders.

[General Orders, No. 3.]

WAR DEPARTMENT,
ADJUTANT GENERAL'S OFFICE,
WASHINGTON, *January* 12, 1866.

TO PROTECT PERSONS AGAINST IMPROPER CIVIL SUITS AND PENALTIES IN LATE REBELLIOUS STATES.

Military division and department commanders, whose commands embrace or are composed of any of the late rebellious States, and who have not already done so, will at once issue and enforce orders protecting from prosecution or suits in the State, or municipal courts of such State, all officers and soldiers of the armies of the United States, and all persons thereto attached, or in anywise thereto belonging, subject to military authority, charged with offences for acts done in their military capacity, or pursuant to orders from proper military authority; and to protect from suit or prosecution all loyal citizens, or persons charged with offences done against the rebel forces, directly or indirectly, during the existence of the rebellion; and all persons, their agents and employés, charged with the occupancy of abandoned lands or plantations, or the possession or custody of any kind of property whatever, who occupied, used, possessed, or controlled the same pursuant to the order of the President, or any of the civil or military departments of the Government, and to protect them from any penalties or damages that may have been or may be pronounced or adjudged in said courts in any of such cases; and also protecting colored persons from prosecutions in any of said States charged with offences for which white persons are not prosecuted or punished in the same manner and degree.

By command of Lieutenant General Grant:
E. D. TOWNSEND,
*Assistant Adjutant General.*

---

### SUPPRESSION OF DISLOYAL NEWSPAPERS.

HEADQUARTERS ARMIES OF UNITED STATES,
WASHINGTON, *Feb.* 17, 1866.

You will please send to these headquarters as soon as practicable, and from time to time thereafter, such copies of newspapers published in your department as contain sentiments of disloyalty and hostility to the Government in any of its branches, and state whether such paper is habitual in its utterance of such sentiments. The persistent publication of articles calculated to keep up a hostility of feeling between the people of different sections of the country cannot be tolerated. This information is called for with a view to their suppression, which will be done from these headquarters only.

By order of Lieutenant General Grant:
T. S. BOWERS,
*Assistant Adjutant General.*

---

## Democratic Convention of Penn., March 5, 1866.

The Democracy of Pennsylvania, in Convention met, recognizing a crisis in the affairs of the Republic, and esteeming the immediate restoration of the Union paramount to all other issues, do resolve:

1. That the States, whereof the people were lately in rebellion, are integral parts of the Union and are entitled to representation in Congress by men duly elected who bear true faith to the Constitution and laws, and in order to vindicate the maxim that taxation without representation is tyranny, such representatives should be forthwith admitted.

2. That the faith of the Republic is pledged to the payment of the national debt, and Congress should pass all laws necessary for that purpose.

3. That we owe obedience to the Constitution of the United States, (including the amendment prohibiting slavery), and under its provisions will accord to those emancipated all their rights of person and property.

4. That each State has the exclusive right to regulate the qualifications of its own electors.

5. That the white race alone is entitled to the control of the Government of the Republic, and we are unwilling to grant the negroes the right to vote.

6. That the bold enunciation of the principles of the Constitution and the policy of restoration contained in the recent annual message and Freedmen's Bureau veto message of President Johnson entitle him to the confidence and support of all who respect the Constitution and love their country.

7. That the nation owes to the brave men of our armies and navy a debt of lasting gratitude for their heroic services in defence of the Constitution and the Union; and that while we cherish with a tender affection the memories of the fallen, we pledge to their widows and orphans the nation's care and protection.

8. That we urge upon Congress the duty of equalizing the bounties of our soldiers and sailors.

The following was also adopted:

*Resolved*, That the thanks of the Democracy of Pennsylvania be tendered to the Hon. Charles R. Buckalew and Hon. Edgar Cowan, for their patriotic support of the President's restoration policy: and that such thanks are due to all the democratic members of Congress for their advocacy of the restoration policy of President Johnson.

## Union Convention of Pennsylvania, March 7.

2. That the most imperative duty of the present is to gather the legitimate fruits of the war, in order that our Constitution may come out of the rebellion purified, our institutions strengthened, and our national life prolonged.

3. That failure in these grave duties would be scarcely less criminal than would have been an acquiescence in secession and in the treasonable machinations of the conspirators, and would be an insult to every soldier who took up arms to save the country.

4. That filled with admiration at the patriotic devotion and fearless courage with which Andrew Johnson resisted and denounced the efforts of the rebels to overthrow the National Government, Pennsylvania rejoiced to express her entire confidence in his character and principles, and appreciation of his noble conduct, by bestowing her suffrage upon him for the second position in honor and dignity in the country. His bold and outspoken denunciation of the crime of treason, his firm demands for the punishment of the guilty offenders, and his expressions of thorough sympathy with the friends of the Union, secured for him the warmest attachment of her people, who, remembering his great services and sacrifices, while traitors and their sympathizers alike denounced his patriotic action, appeal to him to stand firmly by the side, and to repose upon the support, of the loyal masses, whose votes formed the foundation of his promotion, and who pledge to him their unswerving support in all measures by which treason shall be stigmatized, loyalty recognized, and the freedom, stability, and unity of the National Union restored.

5. That the work of restoring the late insurrectionary States to their proper relations to the Union necessarily devolves upon the law-making power, and that until such action shall be taken no State lately in insurrection is entitled to representation in either branch of Congress; that, as preliminary to such action, it is the right of Congress to investigate for itself the condition of the legislation of those States, to inquire respecting their loyalty, and to prescribe the terms of restoration, and that to deny this necessary constitutional power is to deny and imperil one of the dearest rights belonging to our representative form of government, and that we cordially approve of the action of the Union representatives in Congress from Pennsylvania on this subject.

6. That no man who has voluntarily engaged in the late rebellion, or has held office under the rebel organization, should be allowed to sit in the Congress of the Union, and that the law known as the test oath should not be repealed, but should be enforced against all claimants for seats in Congress.

7. That the national faith is sacredly pledged to the payment of the national debt incurred in the war to save the country and to suppress rebellion, and that the people will not suffer this faith to be violated or impaired; but all debts incurred to support the rebellion were unlawful, void, and of no obligation, and shall never be assumed by the United States, nor shall any State be permitted to pay any evidences of so vile and wicked engagements.

15. That in this crisis of public affairs, full of grateful recollections of his marvellous and memorable services on the field of battle, we turn to the example of unfaltering and uncompromising loyalty of Lieutenant General Grant with a confidence not less significant and unshaken, because at no period of our great struggle has his proud name been associated with a doubtful patriotism, or used for sinister purposes by the enemies of our common country.

17. That the Hon. Edgar Cowan, Senator from Pennsylvania, by his course in the Senate of the United States, has disappointed the hopes and forfeited the confidence of those to whom he owes his place, and that he is hereby most earnestly requested to resign.

The following resolution was offered as a substitute for the fourth resolution, but after some discussion was withdrawn:

That, relying on the well-tried loyalty and devotion of Andrew Johnson to the cause of the Union in the dark days of treason and rebellion, and remembering his patriotic conduct, services, and sufferings, which in times past endeared his name to the Union party; and now reposing full confidence in his ability, integrity, and patriotism, we express the hope and confidence that the policy of his Administration will be so shaped and conducted as to save the nation from the perils which still surround it.

The fourth resolution was then adopted—yeas 109, nays 21.

## General Grant's Order for the Protection of Citizens.

HEADQUARTERS OF THE ARMY,
ADJUTANT GENERAL'S OFFICE,
WASHINGTON, July 6, 1866.

[General Orders, No. 44.]

Department, district, and post commanders in the States lately in rebellion are hereby directed to arrest all persons who have been or may hereafter be charged with the commission of crimes and offences against officers, agents, citizens, and inhabitants of the United States, irrespective of color, in cases where the civil authorities have failed, neglected, or are unable to arrest and bring such parties to trial, and to detain them in military confinement until such time as a proper judicial tribunal may be ready and willing to try them.

A strict and prompt enforcement of this order is required.

By command of Lieutenant General Grant:

E. D. TOWNSEND,
*Assistant Adjutant General.*

## Unconditional Union Convention of Maryland, June 6, 1866.

*Resolved,* That the registered loyal voters of Maryland will listen to no propositions to repeal or modify the registry law, which was enacted in conformity with the provisions of the constitution, and must remain in full force until such time as the registered voters of the State shall decree that the organic law shall be changed.

2. That the loyal people of the State are "the legitimate guardians and depositaries of its power," and that the disloyal "have no just right to complain of the hardships of a law which they have themselves deliberately provoked."

3. That it is the opinion of this convention, that if disloyal persons should be registered, it will be the duty of judges of election to administer the oath prescribed by the constitution to all whose loyalty may be challenged, and, in the language of the constitution, to "*carefully exclude from voting*" all that are disqualified.

4. That we cordially endorse the reconstruction policy of Congress, which excludes the leaders of the rebellion from all offices of profit or trust under the National Government, and places the basis of representation on the only just and honest principle, and that a white man in Virginia or South Carolina should have just as much representative power, and no more, than a white man in Pennsylvania or Ohio.

5. That the question of negro suffrage is not an issue in the State of Maryland, but is raised by the enemies of the Union party for the purpose of dividing and distracting it, and by this means to ultimately enable rebels to vote.

6. That we are pledged to the maintenance of the present constitution of Maryland, which expressly and emphatically prohibits both rebel suffrage and negro suffrage, and we are equally determined to uphold the registry law, which disfranchises rebels and excludes negroes from voting, and have no desire or intention of rescinding or abolishing either the constitution or the registry law.

7. That we warn the Union men of Maryland "that no Union man, high or low, should court the favor of traitors, as they can never win it—from the first they have held him as their enemy, and to the last they will be his; and that they should eschew petty rivalries, frivolous jealousies, and self-seeking cabals; so shall they save themselves falling one by one, an unpitied sacrifice, in a contemptible struggle."

The vote upon the adoption of each resolution was unanimous, with the exception of the sixth resolution, upon which a division was called, and the result showed 54 yeas to 14 nays.

The resolutions were then read as a whole, and adopted unanimously as the utterance of the Convention.

## Convention of Southern Unionists.

TO THE LOYAL UNIONISTS OF THE SOUTH:

The great issue is upon us! The majority in Congress, and its supporters, firmly declare that "the rights of the citizen enumerated in the Constitution, and established by the supreme law, must be maintained inviolate."

Rebels and rebel sympathizers assert that "the rights of the citizen must be left to the States alone, and under such regulations as the respective States choose voluntarily to prescribe."

We have seen this doctrine of State sovereignty carried out in its practical results until all authority in Congress was denied, the Union temporarily destroyed, the constitutional rights of the citizen of the South nearly annihilated, and the land desolated by civil war.

The time has come when the restructure of Southern State government must be laid on constitutional principles, or the despotism, grown up under an atrocious leadership, be permitted to remain. We know of no other plan than that Congress, under its constitutional powers, shall now exercise its authority to establish the principle whereby protection is made coextensive with citizenship.

We maintain that no State, either by its organic law or legislation can make transgression on the rights of the citizen legitimate. We demand and ask you to concur in demanding protection to every citizen of the great Republic on the basis of equality before the law; and further, that no State government should be recognized as legitimate under the Constitution in so far as it does not by its organic law make impartial protection full and complete.

Under the doctrine of "State sovereignty," with rebels in the foreground, controlling Southern legislatures, and embittered by disappointment in their schemes to destroy the Union, there will be no safety for the loyal element of the South. Our reliance for protection is now on Congress, and the great Union party that has stood and is standing by our nationality, by the constitutional rights of the citizen, and by the beneficent principles of the government.

For the purpose of bringing the loyal Unionists of the South into conjunctive action with the true friends of republican government in the North, we invite you to send delegates in goodly numbers from all the Southern States, including Missouri, Kentucky, West Virginia, Maryland, and Delaware, to meet at Independence Hall, in the city of Philadelphia, on the first Monday of September next. It is proposed that we should meet at that time to recommend measures for the establishment of such government in the South as accords with and protects the rights of all citizens. We trust this call will be responded to by numerous delegations of such as represent the true loyalty of the South. That kind of government which gives full protection to all rights of the citizen, such as our fathers intended, we claim as our birthright. Either the lovers of constitutional liberty must rule the nation or rebels and their sympathizers be permitted to misrule it. Shall loyalty or disloyalty have the keeping of the destinies of the nation? Let the responses to this call which is now in circulation for signatures, and is being numerously signed, answer. Notice is given that gentlemen at a distance can have their names attached to it by sending a request by letter directed to D. W. Bingham, Esq., of Washington, D. C.

| | |
|---|---|
| *Tennessee* | W. B. STOKES, |
| | JOS. S. FOWLER, |
| | JAMES GETTYS. |
| *Texas* | A. J. HAMILTON, |
| | GEO. W. PASCHAL, |
| | LORENZO SHERWOOD, |
| | C. B. SABIN. |
| *Georgia* | G. W. ASHBURN, |
| | HENRY G. COLE. |
| *Missouri* | J. W. McCLURG, |
| | JOHN R. KELSO, |
| | J. F. BENJAMIN, |
| | GEO. W. ANDERSON. |
| *Virginia* | JOHN B. TROTH, |
| | J. M. STEWART, |
| | WM. N. BERKLEY, |
| | ALLEN C. HARMON, |
| | LEWIS McKENZIE, |
| | J. W. HUNNICUTT, |
| | JOHN C. UNDERWOOD, |
| | BURNHAM WARDWELL, |
| | ALEX. M. DAVIS. |
| *North Carolina* | BYRON LAFLIN, |
| | DANIEL R. GOODLOE. |
| *Alabama* | GEORGE REESE, |
| | D. H. BINGHAM, |
| | M. R. SAFFOLD, |
| | J. H. LARCOMBE, |

WASHINGTON, *July* 4, 1866.

XIII.—*Interesting Figures chiefly from the Census of 1860, bearing on Representation.*

| STATES.* | White Population. | Free Colored. | Slaves. | Aggregate Population. | Representative Population. | White Males over 20. | Colored Males over 20. | Vote of 1860. | Apportionment under Census of 1860. | Based on three fifths Slave Population. | According to whole populat'n, including Colored. | According to White Suffrage. |
|---|---|---|---|---|---|---|---|---|---|---|---|---|
| California | †358,110 | 4,086 | | 379,994 | 362,196 | 206,442 | 2,339 | 108,840 | 3 | | 3 | 7 |
| Connecticut | 451,504 | 8,627 | | 460,147 | 460,147 | 127,996 | 2,091 | 77,246 | 4 | | 4 | 4 |
| Illinois | 1,704,291 | 7,628 | | 1,711,951 | 1,711,951 | 439,503 | 1,753 | 339,693 | 14 | | 13 | 15 |
| Indiana | 1,338,710 | 11,428 | | 1,350,428 | 1,350,428 | 316,804 | 2,565 | 272,143 | 11 | | 10 | 11 |
| Iowa | 673,779 | 1,069 | | 674,913 | 674,913 | 164,535 | 290 | 12,331 | 6 | | 5 | 6 |
| Kansas | 106,390 | 625 | 2 | 107,206 | 107,206 | 31,037 | 149 | | | | 1 | 1 |
| Maine | 626,947 | 1,327 | | 628,279 | 628,279 | 167,724 | 362 | 97,918 | 5 | | 5 | 6 |
| Massachusetts | 1,221,432 | 9,602 | | 1,231,066 | 1,231,066 | 339,086 | 2,512 | 169,175 | 10 | | 9 | 12 |
| Michigan | 736,142 | 6,799 | | 749,113 | 749,113 | 200,474 | 1,918 | 154,747 | 6 | | 6 | 7 |
| Minnesota | 169,395 | 259 | | 172,023 | 172,023 | 48,186 | 65 | 34,799 | 2 | | 2 | 2 |
| New Hampshire | 325,579 | 494 | | 326,073 | 326,073 | 91,954 | 149 | 65,953 | 3 | | 3 | 3 |
| New Jersey | 646,699 | 25,318 | 18 | 672,035 | 672,027 | 167,441 | 6,291 | 121,125 | 5 | | 5 | 6 |
| New York | 3,831,590 | 49,005 | | 3,880,735 | 3,880,735 | 1,027,344 | 12,989 | 675,156 | 31 | | 29 | 35 |
| Ohio | 2,302,808 | 36,673 | | 2,339,511 | 2,339,511 | 562,901 | 8,770 | 442,441 | 19 | | 18 | 19 |
| Oregon | 52,160 | 128 | | 52,465 | 52,465 | 17,736 | 53 | 14,410 | 1 | | 1 | 1 |
| Pennsylvania | 2,849,529 | 56,949 | | 2,906,215 | 2,906,215 | 702,316 | 13,631 | 476,442 | 24 | | 22 | 24 |
| Rhode Island | 170,649 | 3,952 | | 174,620 | 174,620 | 46,417 | 1,023 | 19,951 | 2 | | 2 | 2 |
| Vermont | 314,369 | 709 | | 315,098 | 315,098 | 87,462 | 194 | 42,844 | 3 | | 3 | 3 |
| Wisconsin | 773,693 | 1,171 | | 775,881 | 775,881 | 198,914 | 353 | 152,170 | 6 | | 6 | 7 |
| | 18,653,776 | 225,849 | 20 | 18,907,753 | 18,889,947 | 4,944,272 | 57,497 | 3,393,392 | 156 | | 147 | 171 |
| Alabama | 526,271 | 2,690 | 435,080 | 964,201 | 790,169 | 118,589 | 96,458 | 90,357 | 6 | 1 | 7 | 4 |
| Arkansas | 324,143 | 144 | 111,115 | 435,450 | 391,004 | 73,963 | 25,044 | 54,053 | 3 | 1 | 3 | 3 |
| Delaware | 90,589 | 19,829 | 1,798 | 112,216 | 111,496 | 22,429 | 4,679 | 16,039 | 1 | | 1 | 1 |
| Florida | 77,747 | 932 | 61,745 | 140,424 | 115,726 | 18,687 | 14,315 | 14,347 | 1 | | 1 | 1 |
| Georgia | 591,550 | 2,500 | 462,198 | 1,057,286 | 872,406 | 132,479 | 97,170 | 106,365 | 7 | 2 | 8 | 5 |
| Kentucky | 919,484 | 10,684 | 225,483 | 1,155,684 | 1,065,490 | 217,883 | 50,442 | 146,216 | 9 | 1 | 9 | 8 |
| Louisiana | 357,456 | 18,647 | 331,726 | 708,002 | 575,311 | 101,499 | 101,814 | 50,510 | 5 | 2 | 6 | 4 |
| Maryland | 515,918 | 83,942 | 87,189 | 687,049 | 652,173 | 128,371 | 38,039 | 92,502 | 5 | | 5 | 5 |
| Mississippi | 353,899 | 773 | 436,631 | 791,305 | 616,652 | 85,838 | 113,828 | 69,120 | 5 | 2 | 6 | 3 |
| Missouri | 1,063,489 | 3,572 | 114,931 | 1,182,012 | 1,136,039 | 288,262 | 21,872 | 165,518 | 9 | 1 | 9 | 9 |
| North Carolina | 629,942 | 30,463 | 331,059 | 992,622 | 860,197 | 143,443 | 74,356 | 47,691 | 7 | 2 | 8 | 5 |
| South Carolina | 291,300 | 9,914 | 402,406 | 703,708 | 542,745 | 68,154 | 87,781 | ‡36,090 | 4 | 1 | 5 | 2 |
| Tennessee | 826,722 | 7,300 | 275,719 | 1,109,801 | 999,513 | 189,470 | 56,770 | 145,333 | 8 | 2 | 8 | 7 |
| Texas | 420,891 | 355 | 182,566 | 604,215 | 531,188 | 109,625 | 38,704 | 62,986 | 4 | 1 | 5 | 4 |
| Virginia* | 1,047,299 | 58,042 | 490,865 | 1,596,318 | 1,399,972 | 245,683 | 123,613 | 167,223 | 11 | 2 | 12 | 9 |
| | 8,036,700 | 250,787 | 3,950,511 | 12,240,293 | 10,660,081 | 1,924,375 | 914,885 | 1,263,260 | 85 | 18 | 94 | 70 |
| Grand Total | 26,690,476 | 476,636 | 3,950,531 | 31,148,046 | 29,550,028 | 6,868,647 | 1,002,382 | 4,656,652 | 241 | 18 | 241 | 241 |
| Representative Ratio | | | | | | | | 127,000 | | | 133,700 | 29,300 |

* Nevada admitted since, with one Representative—making whole number, at present, 242.   West Virginia created since, with three Representatives—leaving Virginia 8, instead of 11 allowed in 1860.

† Estimated.   ‡ Including Asiatics.

## Votes in the U. S. House of Representatives on the Various Tariffs.

| STATES. | Tariff of 1816. | | Tariff of 1824. | | Tariff of 1828. | | Tariff of 1832. | | Tariff of 1842. | | Tariff of 1846. | | Tariff of 1857. | | Tariff of 1861. | | Tariff of 1864. | | Tariff Bill of 1866.* | |
|---|---|---|---|---|---|---|---|---|---|---|---|---|---|---|---|---|---|---|---|---|
| | Yeas. | Nays. | Yeas. | Nays. | Yeas. | Nays. | Yeas. | Nays. | Yeas. | Nays. | Yeas. | Nays. | Yeas. | Nays. | Yeas. | Nays. | Yeas. | Nays. | Yeas. | Nays. |
| **NEW ENGLAND STATES.** | | | | | | | | | | | | | | | | | | | | |
| Maine | | | 1 | 6 | 0 | 7 | 6 | 1 | 3 | 3 | 7 | 1 | 6 | 0 | 5 | 0 | 3 | 0 | 3 | 0 |
| New Hampshire | 1 | 3 | 1 | 5 | 4 | 2 | 5 | 0 | 0 | 4 | 4 | 0 | 1 | 1 | 3 | 0 | 2 | 1 | 3 | 0 |
| Vermont | 4 | 1 | 5 | 0 | 4 | 1 | 0 | 3 | 5 | 0 | 0 | 3 | 0 | 3 | 3 | 0 | 3 | 0 | 3 | 0 |
| Massachusetts | 7 | 4 | 1 | 11 | 2 | 11 | 4 | 8 | 10 | 1 | 0 | 9 | 9 | 0 | 9 | 0 | 8 | 0 | 10 | 0 |
| Connecticut | 2 | 2 | 5 | 1 | 4 | 2 | 2 | 3 | 6 | 0 | 0 | 4 | 4 | 0 | 4 | 0 | 1 | 0 | 2 | 0 |
| Rhode Island | 2 | 0 | 2 | 0 | 1 | 1 | 0 | 2 | 2 | 0 | 0 | 1 | 1 | 1 | 2 | 0 | 1 | 0 | 2 | 0 |
| | 16 | 10 | 15 | 23 | 15 | 24 | 17 | 17 | 26 | 8 | 11 | 18 | 21 | 5 | 26 | 0 | 18 | 1 | 23 | 0 |
| **MIDDLE STATES.** | | | | | | | | | | | | | | | | | | | | |
| New York | 20 | 2 | 26 | 8 | 27 | 6 | 27 | 2 | 23 | 9 | 14 | 16 | 16 | 12 | 18 | 2 | 14 | 2 | 16 | 4 |
| New Jersey | 5 | 0 | 6 | 0 | 5 | 0 | 3 | 3 | 6 | 0 | 0 | 5 | 2 | 1 | 4 | 0 | 1 | 1 | 1 | 3 |
| Pennsylvania | 17 | 3 | 24 | 1 | 23 | 0 | 14 | 12 | 19 | 0 | 2 | 23 | 3 | 15 | 22 | 0 | 15 | 0 | 19 | 1 |
| Delaware | | | 1 | 0 | 1 | 0 | 0 | 1 | 1 | 0 | 0 | 1 | 0 | 1 | 1 | 0 | 1 | 0 | 0 | 1 |
| Maryland | 2 | 5 | 3 | 6 | 1 | 5 | 8 | 0 | 4 | 3 | 1 | 2 | 4 | 1 | 2 | 2 | 1 | 0 | 1 | 4 |
| | 44 | 10 | 60 | 15 | 57 | 11 | 52 | 18 | 53 | 12 | 17 | 47 | 25 | 30 | 47 | 4 | 32 | 3 | 37 | 13 |
| **SOUTHERN STATES.** | | | | | | | | | | | | | | | | | | | | |
| Virginia | 7 | 13 | 1 | 21 | 3 | 15 | 11 | 8 | 3 | 17 | 14 | 1 | 13 | 0 | | | | | | |
| West Virginia | | | | | | | | | | | | | | | | | | | 3 | 0 |
| North Carolina | 0 | 11 | 0 | 13 | 0 | 13 | 8 | 4 | 0 | 11 | 5 | 3 | 6 | 0 | 0 | 4 | | | | |
| South Carolina | 4 | 3 | 0 | 9 | 0 | 8 | 3 | 6 | 0 | 6 | 7 | 0 | 4 | 0 | 0 | 4 | | | | |
| Georgia | 3 | 3 | 0 | 7 | 0 | 7 | 1 | 6 | 0 | 8 | 5 | 2 | 4 | 0 | 0 | 6 | | | | |
| Florida | | | | | | | | | | | 1 | 0 | 1 | 0 | 0 | 0 | | | | |
| Alabama | | | 0 | 3 | 0 | 3 | 2 | 1 | 0 | 4 | 7 | 0 | 7 | 0 | 0 | 8 | | | | |
| Mississippi | | | 0 | 1 | 0 | 1 | 1 | 0 | 0 | 2 | 4 | 0 | 4 | 0 | 0 | 3 | | | | |
| Louisiana | 0 | 1 | 0 | 3 | 0 | 3 | 1 | 2 | 2 | 1 | 3 | 1 | 4 | 0 | 0 | 2 | | | | |
| Texas | | | | | | | | | | | 2 | 0 | 1 | 0 | 0 | 1 | | | | |
| | 14 | 31 | 1 | 57 | 3 | 50 | 27 | 27 | 5 | 49 | 48 | 7 | 44 | 0 | 0 | 37 | | | 3 | 0 |
| **WESTERN STATES.** | | | | | | | | | | | | | | | | | | | | |
| Kentucky | 6 | 1 | 11 | 0 | 12 | 0 | 9 | 3 | 4 | 8 | 3 | 7 | 6 | 2 | 4 | 4 | 0 | 4 | 1 | 7 |
| Tennessee | 3 | 2 | 2 | 7 | 0 | 9 | 9 | 0 | 1 | 13 | 6 | 6 | 7 | 0 | 1 | 3 | | | | |
| Ohio | 5 | 0 | 14 | 0 | 13 | 0 | 13 | 0 | 9 | 6 | 12 | 8 | 5 | 14 | 13 | 5 | 4 | 10 | 15 | 8 |
| Indiana | | | 2 | 0 | 3 | 0 | 3 | 0 | 3 | 3 | 6 | 2 | 3 | 8 | 2 | 4 | 2 | 4 | 0 | 7 |
| Illinois | | | 1 | 0 | 1 | 0 | 1 | 0 | 1 | 2 | 4 | 0 | 4 | 4 | 4 | 2 | 3 | 4 | 0 | 12 |
| Missouri | | | 1 | 0 | 0 | 1 | 1 | 0 | 1 | 1 | 4 | 0 | 0 | 3 | 0 | 4 | 5 | 0 | 2 | 4 |
| Arkansas | | | | | | | | | 0 | 1 | | | 2 | 0 | 0 | 0 | | | | |
| Iowa | | | | | | | | | | | | | 1 | 1 | 1 | 0 | 6 | 0 | 2 | 3 |
| Michigan | | | | | | | | | 1 | 0 | 3 | 0 | 1 | 3 | 3 | 0 | 4 | 0 | 4 | 0 |
| Minnesota | | | | | | | | | | | | | 2 | 0 | 2 | 0 | 1 | 0 | 0 | 2 |
| Wisconsin | | | | | | | | | | | | | 1 | 2 | 2 | 0 | 2 | 2 | 2 | 2 |
| Kansas | | | | | | | | | | | | | | | 1 | 0 | 1 | 0 | 1 | 0 |
| | 14 | 3 | 31 | 7 | 29 | 10 | 36 | 3 | 24 | 34 | 38 | 23 | 30 | 37 | 32 | 22 | 28 | 24 | 27 | 40 |
| **PACIFIC STATES.** | | | | | | | | | | | | | | | | | | | | |
| California | | | | | | | | | | | | | 2 | 0 | 0 | 1 | 3 | 0 | 2 | 0 |
| Oregon | | | | | | | | | | | | | | | | | | | 1 | 0 |
| Nevada | | | | | | | | | | | | | | | | | | | 1 | 0 |
| | | | | | | | | | | | | | 2 | 0 | 0 | 1 | 3 | 0 | 4 | 0 |
| Grand Total | 88 | 54 | 107 | 102 | 105 | 94 | 132 | 65 | 104 | 103 | 114 | 95 | 122 | 72 | 105 | 64 | 81 | 28 | 94 | 53 |

## Statement of the Public Debt of the United States on the 1st of June, 1866.

| | | |
|---|---|---|
| Debt bearing Coin Interest | | $1,195,825,191 80 |
| Debt bearing Currency Interest | | 1,147,222,226 28 |
| Matured Debt not presented for payment | | 4,900,429 64 |
| Debt bearing no Interest.—U. S. Notes | $402,128,318 00 | |
|     Fractional Currency | 27,334,965 04 | |
|     Gold Certificates of Deposit | 22,568,320 00 | |
| | | 452,031,603 04 |
| Total Debt | | 2,799,979,450 76 |
| Amount in Treasury, Coin | 50,679,957 72 | |
|     "    "    Currency | 79,011,125 52 | |
| | | 129,691,083 24 |
| Amount of Debt, less Cash in Treasury | | $2,670,288,367 52 |

* July 12—In SENATE, postponed till December next—yeas 23, nays 17, as follow:

YEAS—Messrs. Brown, *Davis*, Doolittle, Foster, Grimes, *Guthrie*, Harris, Henderson, *Hendricks*, *Johnson*, Kirkwood, Lane, Morgan, *Nesmith*, Norton, Pomeroy, *Riddle*, *Sauls bury*, Sumner, Trumbull, Willey, Williams, Wilson—23.

NAYS—Messrs. Anthony, Chandler, Clark, Conness, Cowan, Cragin, Edmunds, Fessenden, Howard, Howe, Poland, Ramsey, Sherman, Sprague, Stewart, Van Winkle, Wade—17.

# PART II

# POLITICAL MANUAL FOR 1867.

## XIV.

## PRESIDENT JOHNSON'S SPEECHES.

**On receiving the Proceedings of the Philadelphia 14th of August Convention.**

1866, August 18—A committee of the Convention presented the proceedings through their Chairman, Hon. Reverdy Johnson, who made some remarks in so doing.

President JOHNSON replied:

MR. CHAIRMAN AND GENTLEMEN OF THE COMMITTEE: Language is inadequate to express the emotions and feelings produced by this occasion. Perhaps I could express more by permitting silence to speak and you to infer what I ought to say. I confess that, notwithstanding the experience I have had in public life and the audiences I have addressed, this occasion and this assemblage are calculated to, and do, overwhelm me. As I have said, I have not language to convey adequately my present feelings and emotions.

In listening to the address which your eloquent and distinguished chairman has just delivered, the proceedings of the Convention, as they transpired, recurred to my mind. Seemingly, I partook of the inspiration that prevailed in the Convention when I received a dispatch, sent by two of its distinguished members, conveying in terms the scene which has just been described, of South Carolina and Massachusetts, arm in arm, marching into that vast assemblage, and thus giving evidence that the two extremes had come together again, and that for the future they were united, as they had been in the past, for the preservation of the Union. When I was thus informed that in that vast body of men, distinguished for intellect and wisdom, every eye was suffused with tears on beholding the scene, I could not finish reading the dispatch to one associated with me in the office, for my own feelings overcame me. [Applause.] I think we may justly conclude that we are acting under a proper inspiration, and that we need not be mistaken that the finger of an overruling and unerring Providence is in this great movement.

The nation is in peril. We have just passed through a mighty, a bloody, a momentous ordeal; and yet do not find ourselves free from the difficulties and dangers that at first surrounded us. While our brave soldiers, both officers and men, [turning to General Grant, who stood at his right,] have by their heroism won laurels imperishable, there are still greater and more important duties to perform; and while we have had their co-operation in the field, now that they have returned to civil pursuits, we need their support in our efforts to restore the Government and perpetuate peace. [Applause.] So far as the executive department of the Government is concerned, the effort has been made to restore the Union, to heal the breach, to pour oil into the wounds which were consequent upon the struggle, and (to speak in common phrase) to prepare, as the learned and wise physician would, a plaster healing in character and coextensive with the wound. [Applause.] We thought, and we think, that we had partially succeeded; but as the work progresses, as reconciliation seemed to be taking place, and the country was becoming reunited, we found a disturbing and marring element opposing us. In alluding to that element I shall go no further than your Convention and the distinguished gentleman who has delivered to me the report of its proceedings. I shall make no reference to it that I do not believe the time and the occasion justify.

We have witnessed in one department of the Government every endeavor to prevent the restoration of peace, harmony, and Union. We have seen hanging upon the verge of the Government, as it were, a body called, or which assumes to be, the Congress of the United States, while in fact it is a Congress of only a part of the States. We have seen this Congress pretend to be for the Union, when its every step and act tended to perpetuate disunion and make a disruption of the States inevitable. Instead of promoting reconciliation and harmony, its legislation has partaken of the character of penalties, retaliation, and revenge. This has been the course and the policy of one portion of your Government.

The humble individual who is now addressing you stands the representative of another department of the Government. The manner in which he was called upon to occupy that position I shall not allude to on this occasion. Suffice it to say that he is here under the Constitution of the country, and being here by virtue of its provisions, he takes his stand upon that charter of our liberties as the great rampart of civil and religious liberty. [Prolonged cheering.] Having been taught in my early life to hold it sacred, and having done so during my whole public career, I shall ever continue to reverence the Constitution of my fathers, and to make it my guide. [Hearty applause.]

I know it has been said (and I must be permitted to indulge in the remark) that the executive department of the Government has been despotic and tyrannical. Let me ask this audience of distinguished gentlemen to point to a vote I ever gave, to a speech I ever made, to a single act of my whole public life, that has not been against tyranny and despotism. What position have I ever occupied, what ground have I ever assumed, where it can be truthfully charged that I failed to advocate the amelioration and elevation of the great masses of my countrymen? [Cries of "Never," and great applause.]

So far as charges of this kind are concerned, they are simply intended to delude the public mind into the belief that it is not the designing men who make such accusations, but some one else in power, who is usurping and trampling upon the rights and perverting the principles of the Constitution. It is done by them for the purpose of covering their own acts. ["That's so," and applause.] And I have felt it my duty, in vindication of principle, to call the attention of my countrymen to their proceedings. When we come to examine who has been playing the part of the tyrant, by whom do we find despotism exercised? As to myself, the elements of my nature, the pursuits of my life, have not made me, either in my feelings or in my practice, aggressive. My nature, on the contrary, is rather defensive in its character. But having taken my stand upon the broad principles of liberty and the Constitution, there is not power enough on earth to drive me from it. [Loud and prolonged applause.] Having placed myself upon that broad platform, I have not been awed or dismayed or intimidated by either threats or encroachments, but have stood there, in conjunction with patriotic spirits, sounding the tocsin of alarm when I deemed the citadel of liberty in danger. [Great applause.]

I said on a previous occasion, and repeat now, that all that was necessary in this great contest against tyranny and despotism was that the struggle should be sufficiently audible for the American people to hear and properly understand the issues it involved. They did hear, and looking on and seeing who the contestants were, and what the struggle was about, determined that they would settle this question on the side of the Constitution and of principle. [Cries of "That's so," and applause.] I proclaim here to-day, as I have on previous occasions, that my faith is in the great mass of the people. In the darkest moment of this struggle, when the clouds seemed to be most lowering, my faith, instead of giving way, loomed up through their gloom; for, beyond, I saw that all would be well in the end. My countrymen, we all know that, in the language of Thomas Jefferson, tyranny and despotism can be exercised and exerted more effectually by the many than the one. We have seen Congress gradually encroach step by step upon constitutional rights, and violate, day after day and month after month, fundamental principles of the Government. [Cries of "That's so," and applause.] We have seen a Congress that seemed to forget that there was a limit to the sphere and scope of legislation. We have seen a Congress in a minority assume to exercise power which, if allowed to be consummated, would result in despotism or monarchy itself. [Enthusiastic applause.] This is truth; and because others, as well as myself, have seen proper to appeal to the patriotism and republican feeling of the country, we have been denounced in the severest terms. Slander upon slander, vituperation upon vituperation, of the most virulent character, has made its way through the press. What, gentlemen, has been your and my sir what has been the cause of our offending? I will tell you. Daring to stand by the Constitution of our fathers.

Mr. Chairman, I consider the proceedings of this Convention equal to, if not more important than, those of any convention that ever assembled in the United States. [Great applause.] When I look upon that collection of citizens coming together voluntarily, and sitting in council, with ideas, with principles and views commensurate with all the States, and co extensive with the whole people, and contrast it with a Congress whose policy, if persisted in, will destroy the country, I regard it as more important than any convention that has sat—at least since 1787. [Renewed applause.] I think I may also say that the declarations that were there made are equal to those contained in the Declaration of Independence itself, and I here to-day pronounce them a second Declaration of Independence. [Cries of "Glorious!" and most enthusiastic and prolonged applause.] Your address and declarations are nothing more nor less than a reaffirmation of the Constitution of the United States. [Cries of "Good!" and applause.]

Yes, I will go further, and say that the declarations you have made, that the principles you have enunciated in your address, are a second proclamation of emancipation to the people of the United States. [Renewed applause.] For in proclaiming and reproclaiming these great truths you have laid down a constitutional platform on which all, without reference to party, can make common cause, engage in a common effort to break the tyranny which the dominant party in Congress has so unrelentingly exercised, and stand united together for the restoration of the States and the preservation of the Government. The question only is the salvation of the country; for our country rises above all party consideration or influences. [Cries of "Good!" and applause.] How many are there in the United States that now require to be free? They have the shackles upon their limbs and are bound as rigidly by the behests of party leaders in the National Congress as though they were in fact in slavery. I repeat, then, that your declaration is the second proclamation of emancipation to the people of the United States, and offers a common ground upon which all patriots can stand. [Applause.]

In this connection, Mr. Chairman and gentlemen, let me ask what have I to gain more than the advancement of the public welfare? I am as much opposed to the indulgence of egotism as any one; but here, in a conversational manner, while formally receiving the proceedings of this Convention, I may be permitted again to inquire, what have I to gain, consulting human ambition, more than I have gained, except one thing —the consummation of the great work of restoration? My race is nearly run. I have been placed in the high office which I occupy by the Constitution of the country, and I may say that I have held, from lowest to highest, almost every station to which a man may attain in our Government. I have passed through every position, from alderman of a village to the Presidency of the United States. And surely, gentlemen, this should be enough to gratify a reasonable ambition.

If I had wanted authority, or if I had wished to perpetuate my own power, how easily could I have held and wielded that which was placed in my hands by the measure called the Freedmen's Bureau bill. [Laughter and applause.] With an army, which it placed at my discretion, I could have remained at the capital of the nation, and with fifty or sixty millions of appropriations at my disposal, with the machinery to be unlocked by my own hands, with my satraps and dependants in every town and village, with the civil rights bill following as an auxiliary, [laughter,] and with the patronage and other appliances of the Government, I could have proclaimed myself dictator. ["That's true!" and applause.]

But, gentlemen, my pride and my ambition have been to occupy that position which retains all power in the hands of the people. [Great cheering.] It is upon them I have always relied; it is upon them I rely now. [A voice: "And the people will not disappoint you."] And I repeat, that neither the taunts nor jeers of Congress, nor of a subsidized, calumniating press, can drive me from my purpose. [Great applause.] I acknowledge no superior except my God, the author of my existence, and the people of the United States. [Prolonged and enthusiastic cheering.] The commands of the one I try to obey as best I can, compatible with poor humanity. As to the other, in a political and representative sense, the high behests of the people have always been, and ever will be, respected and obeyed by me. [Applause.]

Mr. Chairman, I have said more than I had intended to say. For the kind allusion to myself, contained in your address, I thank you. In this crisis, and at the present period of my public life, I hold above all price, and shall ever recur with feelings of profound gratification, to the resolution containing the endorsement of a convention emanating spontaneously from the great mass of the people. With conscientious conviction as my courage, the Constitution as my guide, and my faith in the people, I trust and hope that my future action may be such that you and the Convention you represent may not regret the assurance of confidence you have so generously expressed. ["We are sure of it."]

Before separating, my friends, one and all, please accept my heartfelt thanks for the kind manifestations of regard and respect you have exhibited on this occasion.

## In New York, August 29.

GENTLEMEN: The toast which has just been drank, and the kind sentiments which preceded it in the remarks of your distinguished representative, the mayor of this city, are peculiarly, under existing circumstances, gratifying to me; and in saying they are gratifying to me I wish not to indulge in any vanity. If I were to say less I should not speak the truth, and it is always best to speak the truth and to give utterance to our sincere emotions. In being so kindly attended to, and being received as I have been received on this occasion—here to-night, and in your city to-day by such a demonstration—I am free to confess that this overwhelms me. But the mind would be exceedingly dull and the heart almost without an impulse that could not give utterance to something responsive to what has been said and been done. [Cheers.] And believe me on this occasion, warm is the heart that feels and willing is the tongue that speaks, and I would to God it were in my power to reduce to sentences and to language the feelings and emotions that this day and this night have produced. [Cheers.] I shall not attempt, in reference to what has been said and the manifestations that have been made, to go into any speech, or to make any argument before you on this occasion, but merely to give utterance to the sincere sentiments of my heart. I would that I could utter what I do feel in response to this outpouring of the popular heart which has gone forth on this occasion, and which will as a legion spread itself and communicate with every heart throughout the Confederacy. [Cheers.] All that is wanting in the great struggle in which we are engaged is simply to develop the popular heart of the nation. It is like latent fire. All that is necessary is a sufficient amount of friction to develop the popular sentiment of the popular feeling of the American people. [Cheers.] I know, as you know, that we have just passed through a bloody, perilous conflict; that we have gentlemen who are associated with us on this occasion, who have shared their part and participated in these struggles for the preservation of the Union. [Great applause.] Here is the Army, [pointing to the right, where sat General Grant,] and here the Navy [pointing to the left in the direction of Admiral Farragut.] They have performed their part in restoring the Government to its present condition of safety and security; and will it be considered improper in me, on this occasion, to say that the Secretary of State has done his part; [Cheers.] As for the humble individual who now stands before you, and to whom you have so kindly and pleasantly alluded, as to what part he has performed in this great drama, in this struggle for the restoration of the Government and the suppression of rebellion, I will say that I feel, though I may be included in this summing up, that the Government has done its duty. [Cheers.] But though the Government has done its duty, the work is not yet complete. Though we have passed through fields of battle, and at times have almost been constrained and forced to the conclusion that we should be compelled to witness the Goddess of Liberty, as it were, go scourged through fields of carnage and of blood, and make her exit, and that our Government would be a failure, yet we are brought to a period and to a time in which the Government has been successful. While the enemy have been put down in the field there is still a greater and more important task for you.

and others to perform. [Cheers.] I must be permitted—and I shall not trespass upon you a moment—I must be permitted to remark in this connection, that the Government commenced the suppression of this rebellion for the express purpose of preserving the union of these States. [Cheers.] That was the declaration that it made, and under that declaration we went into the war and continued in it until we suppressed the rebellion The rebellion has been suppressed, and in the suppression of the rebellion it has declared and announced and established the great fact that these States had not the power, and it denied their right, by forcible or by peaceable means, to separate themselves from the Union. [Cheers. "Good."] That having been determined and settled by the Government of the United States in the field and in one of the departments of Government—the executive department of the Government—there is an open issue; there is another department of your Government which has declared by its officials acts, and by the position of the Government, notwithstanding the rebellion was suppressed, for the purpose of preserving the Union of the States and establishing the doctrine that the States could not secede, yet they have practically assumed and declared, and carried up to the present point, that the Government was dissolved and the States were out of the Union. [Cheers.] We who contend for the opposite doctrine years ago contended that even the States had not the right to peaceably secede; and one of the means and modes of possible secession was that the States of the Union might withdraw their representatives from the Congress of the United States, and that would be practical dissolution. We denied that they had any such right. [Cheers.] And now, when the doctrine is established that they have no right to withdraw, and the rebellion is at an end, and the States again assume their position and renew their relations, as far as in them lies, with the Federal Government, we find that when they present representatives to the Congress of the United States, in violation of the sacred charter of liberty, which declares that you cannot, even by amendment of the Constitution of the United States, deprive any one of them of their representation—we find that in violation of the Constitution, in express terms, as well as in spirit, that these States of the Union have been and still are denied their representation in the Senate and in the House of Representatives. Will we then, in the struggle which is now before us, submit, will the American people submit, to this practical dissolution, a doctrine that we have repudiated, a doctrine that we have declared as having no justice or right? The issue is before you and before the country. Will these States be permitted to continue and remain as they are in practical dissolution and destruction, so far as representation is concerned? It is giving the lie direct—it is subverting every single argument and position we have made and taken since the rebellion commenced. Are we prepared now, after having passed through this rebellion; are we prepared, after the immense amount of blood that has been shed; are we prepared, after having accumulated a debt of over three thousand millions of dollars; are we prepared, after all the injury that has been inflicted upon the people, North and South, of this Confederacy, now to continue this disrupted condition of the country? [Cries, "No, no!" "Never!" Cheers.] Let me ask this intelligent audience here to-night, in the spirit of Christianity and of sound philosophy, are we prepared to renew the scenes through which we have passed? ["No! no! no!"] Are we prepared again to see one portion of this Government arrayed in deadly conflict against another portion? Are we prepared to see the North arrayed against the South, and the South against the North? Are we prepared, in this fair and happy Government of freedom and of liberty, to see man again set upon man, and in the name of God lift his hand against the throat of his fellow? Are we again prepared to see these fair fields of ours, this land that gave a brother birth, again drenched in a brother's blood? ["Never, never." Cheers.] Are we not rather prepared to bring from Gilead the balm that has relief in its character and pour it into the wound? [Loud cheering.] Have not we seen enough to talk practically of this matter? Has not this array of the intelligence, the integrity, the patriotism, and the wealth a right to talk practically? Let us talk about this thing. We have known of feuds among families of the most respectable character, which would separate, and the contest would be angry and severe, yet when the parties would come together and talk it all over, and the differences were understood, they let their quarrel pass to oblivion; and we have seen them approach each other with affection and kindness, and felt gratified that the feud had existed, because they could feel better afterwards. [Laughter and applause.] They are our brethren. [Cheers.] They are part of ourselves. ["Hear! hear!"] They are bone of our bone and flesh of our flesh. [Cheers.] They have lived with us and been part of us from the establishment of the Government to the commencement of the rebellion. They are identified with its history, with all its prosperity, in every sense of the word. We have had a hiatus, as it were, but that has passed by and we have come together again; and now, after having understood what the feud was, and the great apple of discord removed; having lived under the Constitution of the United States in the past, they ask to live under it in the future. May I be permitted to indulge in a single thought here? I will not detain you a moment. ["Go on." "Go on." "Go on." Cheers.] You [turning to Mayor Hoffman] are responsible for having invoked it. [Laughter.] What is now said, gentlemen, after the Philadelphia Convention has met to pronounce upon the condition of the country? What is now said? Why, that these men who met in that Convention were insincere; that their utterances were worthless; that it is all pretense, and they are not to be believed. When you talk about it, and talk about red-handed rebels, and all that, who has fought these traitors and rebels with more constancy and determination than the individual now before you? Who has sacrificed and suffered more? [Cheers.] But because my sacrifices and sufferings have been great, and as an incident growing out of a great civil war, should I become dead or insensible to truth or principle? ["No, no." Cheers.] But these men, notwithstanding they may profess now loyalty and devotion to the union of the States, are said to be pretenders, not to be believed. What better evidence can you have of devotion to the Government than profession and action? Who dare, at this day of religious and political freedom, to set up an inquisition, and come into the human bosom to inquire what are the sentiments there? [Cheers.] How many men have lived in this Government from its origin to the present time that have been loyal, that have obeyed all its laws, that have paid its taxes, and sustained the Government in the hour of peril, yet in sentiment would have preferred a change, or would have preferred to live under some other form of government? But the best evidence you can have is their practical loyalty, their professions, and their actions. ["Good," "good," and applause.] Then, if these gentlemen in convention, from the North and South, come forward and profess devotion to the Union and the Constitution of these States, when their actions and professions are for loyalty, who dare assume the contrary? [Cheers.] If we have reached that point in our country's history, all confidence is lost in man. If we have reached that point that we are not to trust each other, and our confidence is gone, I tell you your Government is not as strong as a rope of sand. It has no weight; it will crumble to pieces. This Government has no tie, this Government has no binding and adhesive power, beyond the confidence and trust in the people. ["Hear, hear." Loud applause.] But these men who sit in convention, who sit in a city whose professions have been, in times gone by, that they were a peace-loving and war-hating people—they said there, and their professions should not be doubted, that they have reached a point at which they say peace must be made; they have come to a point at which they want peace on earth and good-will to men. [Loud cheers.] And now, what is the argument in excuse? We won't believe you, and therefore this dissolution, this practical dissolution, must be continued to exist. Your attention to a single point. Why is a southern man not to be believed? and I do not speak here to-night because I am a southern man, and because my infant view first saw the light of heaven in a southern State. ["They are to be believed."] Thank God, though I say it myself, I feel that I have attained opinions and notions that are coextensive with all these States, with all the people of them. [Great applause. The whole audience rose and waved their handkerchiefs at this sentiment. Voice—"That's the best thing to-night."] While I am a southern man, I am a northern man; that is to say, I am a citizen of the United States, [cheers,] and I am willing to concede to all other citizens what I claim for myself. ["Sound."] But I was going to bring to your attention, as I am up, and you must not encourage me too much, ["Good! good!"] for some of those men who have been engaged in this thing, and pretty well broken down, require sometimes a little effort to get them warmed. [Laughter.] I was going to call your attention to a point. The southern States or their leaders proposed a separation. Now, what

was the reason that they offered for that separation? Your attention. The time has come to think; the time has come to consult our brain, and not the impulses and passions of the heart. The time has come when reason should bear sway, and feeling and impulse should be subdued. [Cheers.] What was the reason, or one of the reasons at least, that the South gave for separation? It was that the Constitution was encroached upon, and that they were not secured in their rights under it. That was one of the reasons; whether it was true or false, that was the reason assumed. We will separate from this Government, they said, because we cannot have the Constitution executed; and, therefore, we will separate and set up the same Constitution, and enforce it under a government of our own. But it was separation. I fought then against those who proposed this. I took my position in the Senate of the United States, and assumed then, as I have since, that this Union was perpetual, that it was a great magic circle never to be broken. [Cheers.] But the reason the South gave was that the Constitution could not be enforced in the present condition of the country, and hence they would separate. They attempted to separate, but they failed. But while the question was pending, they established a form of government; and what form of government was it? What kind of Constitution did they adopt? Was it not the same, with a few variations, as the Constitution of the United States, [Cheers, and "That's so!"] the Constitution of the United States, under which they had lived from the origin of the Government up to the time of their attempt at separation? They made the experiment of an attempted separation under the plea that they desired to live under that Constitution in a government where it would be enforced. We said "You shall not separate, you shall remain with us, and the Constitution shall be preserved and enforced." [Cheers.] The rebellion has ceased. And when their arms were put down by the Army and Navy of the United States, they accepted the terms of the Government. We said to them, before the termination of the rebellion, "Disband your armies, return to your original position in the Government, and we will receive you with open arms." The time came when their armies were disbanded under the leadership of my distinguished friend on the right, [General Grant.] ["Three cheers for General Grant."] The Army and the Navy dispersed their forces. What were the terms of capitulation? They accepted the proposition of the Government, and said, "We have been mistaken; we selected the arbitrament of the sword, and that arbiter has decided against us; and that being so, as honorable and manly men, we accept the terms you offer us." The query comes up, will they be accepted? Do we want to humiliate them and degrade them, and tread them in the dust? ["No, no!" Cheers.] I say this, and I repeat it here to-night, I do not want them to come back into this Union a degraded and debased people. [Loud cheers.] They are not fit to be a part of this great American family if they are degraded and treated with ignominy and contempt. I want them when they come back to become a part of this great coun try, an honored portion of the American people. I want them to come back with all their manhood; then they are fit, and not without that, to be a part of these United States. [Cheers. "Three cheers for Andrew Johnson."] I have not, however, approached the point that I intended to mention, and I know I am talking too long. ["Go on," "go on," "go on."] Why should we distrust the southern people and say they are not to be believed? I have just called your attention to the Constitution under which they were desirous to live, and that was the Constitution of their fathers, yet they wanted it in a separate condition. Having been defeated in bringing about that separation, and having lost the institution of slavery, the great apple of discord, they now, in returning, take up that Constitution, under which they always lived, and which they established for themselves, even in a separate government. Where, then, is the cause for distrust? Where, then, is the cause for the want of confidence? Is there any? ["No, no."] I do not come here to-night to apologize for persons who have tried to destroy this Government; and if every act of my life, either in speeches or in practice, does not disprove the charge that I want to apologize for them, then there is no use in a man's having a public record. [Cheers.] But I am one of those who take the southern people, with all their heresies and errors, admitting that in rebellion they did wrong. The leaders coerced thousands and thousands of honest men into the rebellion who saw the old flag flap in the breeze for the last time with unfeigned sorrow, and welcomed it again with joy and thanksgiving. The leaders betrayed and led the southern people astray upon this great doctrine of secession. We have in the West a game called hammer and anvil, and anvil and hammer, and while Davis and others were talking about separation in the South, there was another class, Phillips, Garrison, and men of that kind, who were talking about dissolution in the North; and of these extremes one was the hammer and the other was the anvil; and when the rebellion broke out one extreme was carrying it out, and now that it is suppressed the other class are still trying to give it life and effect. I fought those in the South who commenced the rebellion, and now I oppose those in the North who are trying to break up the Union. [Cheers.] I am for the Union. I am against all those who are opposed to the Union. [Great applause.] I am for the Union, the whole Union, and nothing but the Union. [Renewed cheering.] I have helped my distinguished friend on my right, General Grant, to fight the rebels South, and I must not forget a peculiar phrase, that he was going to fight it out on that line. [Applause and laughter.] I was with him, and I did all that I could; and when we whipped them at one end of the line, I want to say to you that I am for whipping them at the other end of the line. [Great laughter and applause.] I thank God that if he is not in the field, militarily speaking, thank God! he is civilly in the field on the other side. [Cheers for Grant.] This is a contest and struggle for the Union, for the union of these States. [Applause.] The North can't get along without the South, and the South can't get along with-

out the North. ["That's so," and applause.] I have heard an idea advanced, that if we let the southern members of Congress in they will control the Government. Do you want to be governed by rebels? [Cries of "Never," "No, no."] We want to let loyal men in, [" Hear, hear."] and none but loyal men. [" Good, good."] But, I ask here to-night, in the face of this intelligent audience, upon what does the face of the observation rest, that men coming in from the South will control the country to its destruction? Taking the entire delegation of the South, fifty-eight members, what is it compared with the two hundred and forty-two members of the rest of the Union? [" Good boy!"] Is it complimentary to the North to say we are afraid of them? Would the free States let in fifty-eight members from the South that we doubt, that we distrust, that we have no confidence in? If we bring them into the Government, these fifty-eight representatives, are they to control the two hundred and forty-two? There is no argument that the influence and talent and the principles they can bring to bear against us, placing them in the worst possible light [A voice, "The Sumner argument"] can be a cause for alarm. We are represented as afraid of these fifty-eight men, afraid that they will repudiate our public debt; that they can go into the Congress of the United States under the most favorable conditions they could require, the most offensive conditions to us, and could overwhelm a majority of a hundred and fifty to a hundred and eighty, [a voice, "Ridiculous"]—that these men are going to take charge of the country. Why, it is croaking; it is to excite your fears, to appeal to your prejudice. Consider the immense sums of money that have been expended, the great number of lives that have been lost, and the blood that has been shed; that our bleeding arteries have been staved and tied up; that commerce, and mechanical industry, and agriculture, and all the pursuits of peace restored, and we are represented as cowards enough to clamor that if these fifty-eight men are admitted as the representatives of the South the Government is lost. We are told that our people are afraid of the people of the South; that we are cowards. [Cries of "We are not."] Did they control you before the rebellion commenced? Have they any more power now than they had then? Let me say to this intelligent audience here to-night, I am no prophet, but I predicted at different times, in the beginning of the late rebellion, what has been literally fulfilled. [Cries of " That's so."] I told the southern people years ago, that whenever they attempted to break up this Union, whenever they attempted to do that, even if they succeeded, that the institution of slavery would be gone. ["Good, good."] Yes, sir, [turning to Mr. Seward,] you know that I made that argument to Jeff Davis. You will bear witness to the position I then occupied.

Mr. SEWARD. I guess so. [Applause.]

Mr. JOHNSON. Yes, and you were among the few that gave me encouragement. [Applause.] I told them then that the institution of slavery could not survive an attempt to break up this Union. They thought differently. They put up a stake: what was it? It was four millions of slaves, in which they had invested their capital. Their investment in the institution of slavery amounted to $3,000,000,000. This they put up at stake, and said they could maintain it by separating these States That was the experiment; what are the facts of the result? The Constitution still exists. [Great cheering.] The Union is still preserved. [Cheers.] They have not succeeded in going out, and the institution of slavery is gone. [" Hear, hear."] Since it has been gone they have come up manfully and acknowledged the fact in their State conventions and organizations, and they ratify its fall now and forever. [Cheers.] I have got one other idea to put right alongside of this. [Applause and laughter.] You have got a debt of about $3,000,000,000. ["That's so."] How are you going to preserve the credit of that? Will you tell me. [Voices, "You tell us."] How are you to preserve the credit of this $3,000,000,000? Yes, perhaps when the account is made up your debt will be found $3,000,000,000 or $4,000,000,000. Will you tell me how you are to secure it, how the ultimate payment of the principal and interest of this sum is to be secured? Is it by having this Government disrupted? [Mr. Seward and others, "No, no."] Is it by the division of these States? ["No."] Is it by separating this Union into petty States? [" No."] Let me tell you here to-night, my New York friends, I tell you that there is no way by which these bonds can be ultimately paid, by which the interest can be paid, by which the national debt can be sustained, but by the continuity and perpetuity and by the complete union of these States. [Applause.] Let me tell you who fall into this fallacy, and into this great heresy, you will reap a more bitter reward than the southern brethren have reaped in putting their capital into slavery.

Mr. SEWARD, sotto voce. The argumentum ad hominem [" Good."]

Mr. JOHNSON. Pardon me, I do not exaggerate. I understand this question. You who play a false part, now the great issue is past, you who play into the hands of those who wish to dissolve the Government, to continue the disreputable conditions to impair and destroy the public credit, let us unite the Government and you will have more credit than you need. [Applause.] Let the South come back with its great mineral resources; give them a chance to come back and bear a part, and I say they will increase the national resources and the national capacity for meeting these national obligations. I am proud to say on this occasion, not by way of flattery, to the people of New York, but I am proud to find a liberal and comprehensive and patriotic view of this whole question on the part of the people of New York. I am proud to find, too, that here you don't believe that your existence depends upon aggression and destruction; that while you are willing to live, you are willing to let others live. [Applause.] You don't desire to live by the destruction of others. Some have grown fat, some have grown rich by the aggression and destruction of others. It is for you to make the application, and not me. These men talk about this thing, and ask what is before you? What is before you? New York, this great State, this great commercial

emporium—I was asking your mayor to-day the amount of your taxation, and he informs me it is $18,000,000! Where did your Government start from but the other day? Do you remember that when General Washington was inaugurated President, that your annual bill was $2,500,000 for the entire General Government. Yet to-day I am told that my distinguished friend on my left controls the destinies of a city whose taxes amount to $18,000,000, and whose population numbers four millions—double what the entire nation had at the time when it commenced its existence.

General SANDFORD. Our taxation by the General Government is $50,000,000.

Mr. JOHNSON. I am simply trying to get at the amount collected to sustain your municipal establishment. Thus may we advance, entertaining the principles which are coextensive with the States of this Union, feeling, like you, that our system of Government comprehends the whole people, not merely a part. [Applause.] New York has a great work to perform in the restoration of this great Union. As I have told you, they who talk about destroying the great elements that bind this Government together deny the power, the inherent power, of the Government, which will, when its capacities are put to the test, re-establish and readjust its position, and the Government be restored. [Applause.] I tell you that we shall be sustained in this effort to preserve the Union. It would be just about as futile to attempt the resistance of the ocean wave, or to check the wind, as to prevent the result I predict. You might as well attempt to turn the Mississippi back upon its source as to resist this great law of gravitation that is bringing these States back and be united with us as strong as ever. I have been called a demagogue, and would to God that there were more demagogues in the land to save it! [Applause.] The demonstration here to-day is the result of some of these demagogical ideas; that the great mass of the people, when called to take care of the people, will do right.

A voice. Sure as you are born. [Laughter.]

Mr. JOHNSON. I tell you, you have commenced the grand process now. I tell those present who are croaking and talking about individual aggrandizement and perpetuation of party, I tell them that they had better stand from under [laughter and cheers,] they had better get out of the way [cheers;] the Government is coming together, and they cannot resist it. Sometimes, when my confidence gives out, when my reason fails me, my faith comes to my rescue, and tells me that this Government will be perpetuated and this Union preserved. [Cheers.] I tell you here to-night, and I have not turned philanthropist and fanatic, that men sometimes err, and can again do right; that sometimes the fact that men have erred is the cause of making them better men. [Applause.] I am not for destroying all men, or condemning to total destruction all men who have erred once in their lives. I believe in the memorable example of Him who came with peace and healing on his wings; and when he descended and found men condemned unto the law, instead of executing it, instead of shedding the blood of the world, he placed himself upon the cross, and died, that man might be saved. If I have pardoned many, I trust in God that I have erred on the right side. If I have pardoned many, I believe it is all for the best interests of the country; and so believing, and convinced that our southern brethren were giving evidence by their practice and profession that they were repentant, in imitation of Him of old who died for the preservation of men, I exercised that mercy which I believed to be my duty. I have never made a prepared speech in my life, and only treat these topics as they occur to me. The country, gentlemen, is in your hands. The issue is before you. I stand here to-night, not in the first sense in the character of the Chief Magistrate of the nation, but as a citizen, defending the restoration of the Union and the perpetuation of the Constitution of my country. Since becoming the Chief Magistrate I have tried to fulfill my duty—to bring about reconciliation and harmony; my record is before you. You know how politicians will talk; and if you people will get right, don't trouble yourselves about the politicians, for when the people get right the politicians are very accommodating. [Cheers.] But let me ask this audience here to-night, What am I to gain by taking the course I am taking if it was not patriotic and for my country? Pardon me; I talk to you in plain parlance. I have filled every office in this Government. You may talk to me as you will, and slander—that foul whelp of sin—may subsidize, a mercenary press may traduce and vilify, mendacious and unprincipled writers may write and talk, but all of them cannot drive me from my purpose. [" Bravo!" and cheers.] What have I to gain? I repeat. From the position of the lowest alderman in your city to President of the United States, I have filled every office to the country. Who can do more? Ought not men of reasonable ambition to be satisfied with this? And ought not I to be willing to quit right here, so far as I am concerned? [Applause.] I tell this audience here to-night, that the cup of my ambition has been filled to overflowing, with the exception of one thing. Will you hear what that is? [Cries of ". Yes," and " What is it?"] At this particular crisis and period of our country's history I find the Union of these States in peril. If I can now be instrumental in keeping the possession of it in your hands, in the hands of the people; in restoring prosperity and advancement in all that makes a nation great, I will be willing to exclaim, as Simeon did of old—[Three cheers]—as Simeon did of old, of him who had been born in a manger, that I have seen the glory of thy salvation, let thy servant depart in peace. [Applause.] That being done, my ambition is complete. I would rather live in history, in the affections of my countrymen, as having consummated this great end, than to be President of the United States forty times. [General Sandford called for " Three cheers for Andrew Johnson, the restorer of the Union." The cheers were given.] In conclusion, gentlemen, let me tender to you my sincere thanks on this occasion. So long as reason continues to occupy her empire, so long as my heart shall beat with one kind emotion, so long as my memory shall contain or be capable of recurring to one event, so long will I remember the kindnesses, so long will I feel the good that has been done on this occasion, and so long will I cherish in my heart the kindness which has been manifested towards me by the citizens of New York. [Immense applause.]

The band played " The Star Spangled Banner," the audience enthusiastically joining in the chorus. President Johnson, having seated himself, again arose and said: " Gentlemen, in conclusion, after having consumed more of your time than I intended, I fear unprofitably, let me propose, in sincerity, ' The Union, the perpetual Union of these States.' " The toast was drunk with cheers.

### In Cleveland, September 3.

FELLOW-CITIZENS: It is not for the purpose of making a speech that I now appear before you. I am aware of the great curiosity which prevails to see strangers who have notoriety and distinction in all countries. I know a large number of you desire to see General Grant and to hear what he has to say. [A voice, " Three cheers for General Grant."] But you cannot see him to-night. He is extremely ill. I repeat, I am not before you now to make a speech, but simply to make your acquaintance, to say, "How are you?" and to bid you "Good-by." We are now on our way to Chicago, to participate in or witness the laying of the corner-stone of a monument to the memory of a distinguished fellow-citizen who is no more. It is not necessary for me to mention the name of Stephen A. Douglas to the people of Ohio. [Applause.] I am free to say that I am flattered by the demonstrations I have witnessed, and being flattered, I don't mean to think it personal, but an evidence of what is pervading the public mind. And this demonstration is nothing more nor less than an indication of the latent sentiment of feeling of the great masses of the people with regard to the proper settlement of this great question.

I come before you as an American citizen simply, and not as the Chief Magistrate, clothed in the insignia and paraphernalia of state. Being an inhabitant of a State of this Union, I know it has been said that I am an alien [laughter] and that I did not reside in one of the States of the Union, and therefore could not be the Chief Magistrate, though the Constitution declares that I must be a citizen to occupy that office; therefore, all that was necessary was to declare the office vacant, or, under a pretext, to prefer articles of impeachment, and thus the individual who occupies the Chief Magistracy was to be disposed of and driven from power. But a short time since you had a ticket before you for the Presidency. I was placed upon that ticket, with a distinguished fellow-citizen who is now no more. I know there are some who complain. [A voice, " Unfortunately."] Yes, unfortunate for some that God rules on high and deals in right. [Cheers.] Yes, unfortunately, the ways of Providence are mysterious and incomprehensible, controlling all those who exclaim "Unfortunate." [" Bully for you!"]

I was going to say, my countrymen, a short time since I was selected and placed upon the ticket. There was a platform proclaimed and adopted by those who placed me upon it. Notwithstanding the subsidized gang of hirelings and traducers, I have discharged all my duties and fulfilled all my pledges, and I say here to-night that if my predecessor had lived the vials of wrath would have been poured out upon him. [Cries of "Never." "Three cheers for the Congress of the United States!"] I came here as I was passing along, and have been called upon for the purpose of exchanging views, and ascertaining, if we could, who was wrong. [Cries of "It's you."] That was my object in appearing before you to-night, and I want to say this, that I have lived among the American people, and have represented them in some public capacity for the last twenty-five years, and where is the man or woman who can place his finger upon one single act of mine deviating from any pledge of mine or in violation of the Constitution of the country? [Cheers.] Who is he? What language does he speak? What religion does he profess? Who can come and place his finger on one pledge I ever violated, or one principle I ever proved false to? [A voice, "How about New Orleans?" Another voice, "Hang Jeff Davis."] Hang Jeff Davis, he says. [Cries of "No," and "Down with him!"] Hang Jeff Davis, he says. [A voice, "Hang Thad. Stevens and Wendell Phillips."] Hang Jeff Davis. Why don't you hang him? [Cries of "Give us the opportunity."] Have not you got the court? Have not you got the Attorney General? [A voice, "Who is your Chief Justice who has refused to sit upon the trial?" Cheers.] I am not the Chief Justice. I am not the prosecuting attorney. [Cheers.] I am not the jury.

I will tell you what I did do. I called upon your Congress that is trying to break up the Government. [Cries, "You be d—d!" and cheers mingled with hisses. Great confusion "Don't get mad, Andy."] Well, I will tell you who is mad. "Whom the Gods wish to destroy, they first make mad." Did your Congress order any of them to be tried? [Three cheers for Congress.] Then, fellow-citizens, we might as well allay our passions, and permit reason to resume her empire and prevail. [Cheers.] In presenting the few remarks that I designed to make, my intention was to address myself to your common sense, your judgment, and your better feeling, not to the passion and malignancy in your hearts. [Cheers.] This was my object in presenting myself on this occasion, and to tell you "How do you do," and at the same time to bid you "Good-by." In this assembly here to-night the remark has been made, "Traitor! traitor!" My countrymen, will you hear me? [Shouts of "Yes."] And will you hear me for my cause and for the Constitution of my country? [Applause.] I want to know when or where, or under what circumstances, Andrew Johnson, not as Chief Executive, but in any capacity, ever deserted any principle or violated the Constitution of his country. [Cries of "Never."] Let me ask this large and intelligent audience if your Secretary of State, who served four years under Mr. Lincoln, and who was placed upon the butcher's block, as it were, and hacked to pieces and scarred by the assassin's knife, when he turned traitor? [Cries of "Never."] If I were disposed to play the orator and deal in declamation to-night, I would

imitate one of the ancient tragedies, and would take William H. Seward, and bring him before you, and point you to the hacks and scars upon his person. [A voice, "God bless him!"] I would exhibit the bloody garments, saturated with gore from his gushing wounds. Then I would ask you, Why not hang Thad. Stevens and Wendell Phillips? I tell you, my countrymen, I have been fighting the South, and they have been whipped and crushed, and they acknowledge their defeat and accept the terms of the Constitution; and now, as I go around the circle, having fought traitors at the South, I am prepared to fight traitors at the North. [Cheers.] God willing, with your help we will do it. [Cries of "We won't."] It will be crushed North and South, and this glorious Union of ours will be preserved. [Cheers.] I do not come here as the Chief Magistrate of twenty-five States out of thirty-six. [Cheers.] I came here to-night with the flag of my country and the Constitution of thirty-six States untarnished. Are you for dividing this country? [Cries of "No."] Then I am President, and I am President of the whole United States. [Cheers.] I will tell you one other thing. I understand the discordant notes in this crowd to-night. He who is opposed to the restoration of this Government and the reunion of the States is as great a traitor as Jeff Davis or Wendell Phillips. [Loud cheers.] I am against both. [Cries of "Give it to them!"] Some of you talk about traitors in the South who have not courage to get away from your homes to fight them. [Laughter and cheers.] The courageous men, Grant, Sherman, Farragut, and the long list of the distinguished sons of the Union, were in the field and led on their gallant hosts to conquest and to victory, while you remained cowardly at home. [Applause, "Bully!"] Now, when these brave men have returned home, many of whom have left an arm, or a leg, or their blood, upon many a battle-field, they find you at home speculating and committing frauds on the Government. [Laughter and cheers.]

You pretend now to have great respect and sympathy for the poor brave fellow who has left an arm on the battle-field. [Cries, "Is this dignified?"] I understand you. You may talk about the dignity of the President. [Cries, "How was it about his making a speech on the 22d of February?"] I have been with you in the battles of this country, and I can tell you furthermore, to-night, who have to pay these brave men who shed their blood. You speculated, and now the great mass of the people have to work it out. [Cheers.] It is time that the great mass of the people should understand what your designs are. What did General Butler say? [Hisses.] What did General Grant say? [Cheers.] And what does General Grant say about General Butler? [Laughter and cheers.] What does General Sherman say? [A voice, "What does General Sheridan say?"] General Sheridan says that he is for the restoration of the Government that Sheridan fought for. ["Bully!" and renewed cries of "New Orleans," and confusion.] I care not for dignity. There is a portion of your countrymen who will always respect their fellow-citizens when they are entitled to respect, and there is a portion of them who have no respect for themselves, and consequently have no respect for others. [A voice, "Traitor!"] I wish I could see that man. I would bet you now, that if the light fell on your face, cowardice and treachery would be seen in it. Show yourself. Come out here where I can see you. [Shouts of laughter.] If you ever shoot a man you will do it in the dark, and pull the trigger when no one is by to see you. [Cheers.] I understand traitors. I have been fighting them at the south end of the line, and we are now fighting them in the other direction. [Laughter and cheers.] I come here neither to criminate or recriminate, but when attacked, my plan is to defend myself. [Cheers.] When encroached upon, I care not from what quarter it comes, it is entitled to resistance. As Chief Magistrate I felt so after taking the oath to support the Constitution, and when I saw encroachments upon your Constitution and rights, as an honest man I dared to sound the tocsin of alarm. [Three cheers for Andrew Johnson.] Then, if this be right, the head and front of my offending is in telling when the Constitution of your country has been trampled upon. Let me say to those who thirst for more blood, who are still willing to sacrifice human life, if you want a victory, and my country requires it, erect your altar and lay me upon it to give the last libation to human freedom. [Loud applause.] I love my country. Every public act of my life testifies that is so. Where is the man that can put his finger upon any one act of mine that goes to prove the contrary? And what is my offending? [A voice, "Because you are not a radical," and cry of "Veto."] Somebody says veto. Veto of what? What is called the Freedmen's Bureau bill? I can tell you what it is. Before the rebellion commenced there were four millions of slaves and about three hundred and forty thousand white people living in the South. These latter paid the expenses, bought the land and cultivated it, and after the crops were gathered pocketed the profits That's the way the thing stood up to the rebellion. The rebellion commenced, the slaves were liberated, and then came up the Freedmen's Bureau bill. This provides for the appointment of agents and sub-agents in all States, counties, and school districts, who have power to make contracts for the freedmen, and hire them out, and to use the military power to carry them into execution. The cost of this to the people was $12,000,000 at the beginning. The further expense would be greater, and you are to be taxed for it. That's why I vetoed it. I might refer to the civil rights bill, the results of which are very similar. I tell you, my countrymen, that though the powers of hell and Thad. Stevens and his gang were by, they could not turn me from my purpose. There is no power that could turn me except you and the God who spoke me into existence.

In conclusion, beside that, Congress had taken much pains to poison their constituents against him. But what had Congress done? Have they done anything to restore the Union of these States? No; on the contrary they had done everything to prevent it; and because he stood now where he did when the rebellion commenced, he had been denounced as a traitor. Who had run greater risks or made greater sacrifices than

himself? But Congress, factious and domineering, had taken to poison the minds of the American people. It was with them a question of power. Those who held an office—as assessor, collector, postmaster—wanted to retain their places. Rotation in office used to be thought a good doctrine by Washington, Jefferson, and Adams; and Andrew Jackson, God bless him! thought so. [Applause.] This gang of office-holders, these blood-suckers and cormorants, had got fat on the country. You have got them over your district. Hence you see a system of legislation proposed so that these men shall not be turned out; and the President, the only channel through which they can be reached, is called a tyrant. He thought the time had come when those who had enjoyed fat offices for four years should give way for those who had fought for the country. Hence it was seen why he was assailed and traduced. He had invited them in the field, and God willing, he would stand by them. He had turned aside from the thread of his remarks to notice the insult sought to be given him. When an insult was offered he would resent it in a proper manner. But he was free to say he had no revengeful or resentful feelings. All he wanted, when war was over and peace had come, was for patriotic and Christian men to rally round the flag of the country in a fraternal hug, and resolve that all shall perish rather than that the Union shall not be restored.

While referring to the question of suffrage some one in the crowd asked him "How about Louisiana?" To which he replied, "Let the negroes vote in Ohio before you talk about their voting in Louisiana." [Laughter, and cries of "Good."] Take the beam out of your own eye before you seek the mote in your brother's. [Renewed laughter.] In conclusion, after some further remarks, he invoked God's best blessing on his hearers. [Applause.] The interruptions were few.

### At St. Louis, September 8.

FELLOW-CITIZENS: In being introduced to you to-night, it is not for the purpose of making a speech. It is true I am proud to meet so many of my fellow-citizens here on this occasion, and under the favorable circumstances that I do. [Cries, "How about our British subjects?"] We will attend to John Bull after awhile, so far as that is concerned.

I have just stated that I am not here for the purpose of making a speech; but, after being introduced, I wish simply to tender my cordial thanks for the welcome that you have given to me in your midst. [A voice, "Ten thousand welcomes."] Thank you, sir! I wish it was in my power to address you under favorable circumstances upon some of the questions that agitate and distract the public mind at this time—questions that have grown out of the fiery ordeal we have passed through, and which I think as important as that we have just passed by, though the time has come when it seems to me that all ought to be prepared for peace. The rebellion being suppressed, and the shedding of blood being stopped, the sacrifice of life being suspended and stayed, it seems that the time has arrived when you should be at peace, when the bleeding arta. les should be tied up. [A voice, " New Orleans."] Go on; perhaps if you had a word or two on the subject of New Orleans you might understand more about it than you do. [Laughter.] And if you will go back—if you will go back and ascertain the cause of the riot at New Orleans, perhaps you would not be so prompt in calling out "New Orleans." If you will take up the riot at New Orleans, and trace it back to its source or its immediate cause, you will find out who was responsible for the blood that was shed there. If you will take up the riot at New Orleans and trace it back to the radical Congress, [cheers and cries of "Bully!"] you will find that the riot at New Orleans was substantially planned. If you will take up the proceedings in their caucuses you will understand that they there knew [cheers] that a Convention was to be called, which was extinct by its power having expired; that it was said that the intention was that a new government was to be organized, and on the organization of that government the intention was to enfranchise one portion of the population, called the colored population, who had just been emancipated, and at the same time disfranchise white men. When you design to talk about New Orleans [confusion] you ought to understand what you are talking about. When you read the speeches that were made, and take up the facts on the Friday and Saturday before that Convention sat, you will there find that speeches were there made incendiary in their character, exciting that portion of the population, the black population, to arm themselves and prepare for the shedding of blood. [A voice, "That's so," and cheers.] You will also find that that Convention did assemble in violation of law, and the intention of that Convention was to supersede the reorganized authorities in the State government of Louisiana, which had been recognized by the Government of the United States; and every man engaged in that rebellion in that Convention, with the intention of superseding and upturning the civil government which had been recognized by the Government of the United States, I say that he was a traitor to the Constitution of the United States, [cheers;] and hence you find that another rebellion was commenced, having its origin in the radical Congress. These men were to go there, a government was to be organized, and the one in existence in Louisiana was to be superseded, set aside, and overthrown. You talk to me about New Orleans. And there the question was to come up, when they had established their government—a question of political powers—which of the two governments was to be recognized, a new government, inaugurated under this defunct Convention, set up in violation of law and without the will of the people. Then when they had established their government and extended universal and impartial franchise, as they called it, to the colored population, then this radical Congress was to determine that a government established on negro votes was to be the government of Louisiana. [Voices, "Never!" Cheers and cries of "Hurrah for Andy!"]

So much for the New Orleans riot. And there was the cause and the origin of the blood that was shed; and every drop of blood that was

shed is upon their skirts, and they are responsible for it. I could test this thing a little closer, but will not do it here to-night. But when you talk about the causes and consequences that resulted from proceedings of that kind, perhaps as I have been introduced here, and you have provoked questions of this kind, though it does not provoke me, I will tell you a few wholesome things that have been done by this radical Congress [cheers] in connection with New Orleans and the extension of the elective franchise.

I know that I have been traduced and abused. I know it has come in advance of me here as elsewhere—that I have attempted to exercise an arbitrary power in resisting laws that were intended to be forced upon the Government, [cheers;] that I had exercised that power, [cries, "Bully for you!"] that I had abandoned the party that elected me, and that I was a traitor, [cheers,] because I exercised the veto power in attempting and did arrest for a time a bill that was called a "Freedmen's Bureau bill;" yes, that I was a traitor. And I have been traduced, I have been slandered, I have been maligned, I have been called Judas Iscariot and all that. Now, my countrymen here to-night, it is very easy to indulge in epithets; it is easy to call a man Judas, and cry out traitor; but when he is called upon to give arguments and facts he is very often found wanting. Judas Iscariot—Judas. There was a Judas, and he was one of the twelve apostles. Oh! yes, the twelve apostles had a Christ. [A voice, "And a Moses, too;" laughter.] The twelve apostles had a Christ, and he never could have had a Judas unless he had had twelve apostles. If I have played the Judas, who has been my Christ that I have played the Judas with? Was it Thad. Stevens? Was it Wendell Phillips? Was it Charles Sumner? [Hisses and cheers.] These are the men that stop and compare themselves with the Saviour; and everybody that differs with them in opinion, and to try to stay and arrest their diabolical and nefarious policy, is to be denounced as a Judas. [" Hurrah for Andy!" and cheers.]

In the days when there was a Christ, while there was a Judas, were there unbelievers? Yes, while there were Judases there were unbelievers. [Voices heard, "Three groans for Fletcher."] Yes, oh yes; unbelievers in Christ, men who persecuted and slandered, and brought Him before Pontius Pilate, and preferred charges, and condemned and put Him to death on the cross to satisfy unbelievers; and this same persecuting, diabolical, and nefarious clan to-day would persecute and shed the blood of innocent men to carry out their purposes. [Cheers.]

But let me tell you; let me give you a few words here to-night. But a short time since I heard some one say in the crowd that we had a Moses. [Laughter.] Yes, there is a Moses; and I know sometimes it has been said that I have said that I would be the Moses of the colored man. [Cries of "Never!" and cheers.] Why, I have labored as much in the cause of emancipation as any other mortal man living; but, while I have striven to emancipate the colored man, I have felt and now feel that we have a great many white men that want emancipation. There is a set amongst you that have got shackles on their limbs, and are as much under the heel and control of their masters as the colored man that was emancipated.

I call upon you here to-night, as freemen, as men, to favor the emancipation of the white men as well as the colored ones. I have been in favor of emancipation. I have nothing to disguise about that. I have tried to do as much, and have done as much—and when they talk about Moses, and the colored man being led into the promised land, where is the land that this clan proposes to lead them into? When we talk about taking them out from among the white population and sending them to other climes, what is it they propose? Why, it is to give us a Freedmen's Bureau. And after giving us a Freedmen's Bureau, what then? Why, here in the South it is not necessary for me to talk to you, where I have lived and you have lived, and understand the whole system and how it operates. We know how the slaves have been worked heretofore. Their original owners bought the land and raised the negroes, or purchased them, as the case might be, paid all the expense of carrying on the farm; and after producing tobacco, cotton, hemp, flax, and all the various products of the South, bringing them into the market without any profit on them, while their owners put it all into their pockets. This was their condition before the emancipation; this was their condition before we talked about their Moses. [Laughter.] I ask your attention. Come, as we have got to talking on this subject give me your attention for a few minutes. I am addressing myself to your brains and not to your prejudices, to your reason and not to your passions; and when reason and argument again resume their empire, this mist, this prejudice, that has been incrusted upon the public mind, must give way and reason become triumphant. Now, my countrymen, let me call your attention to a single fact, the Freedmen's Bureau. [Laughter and hisses.]

Slavery was an accursed institution until emancipation took place. It was an accursed institution while one set of men worked them and got the profits. But after emancipation took place they gave us the Freedmen's Bureau; they gave us these agents to go into every county, every township, and into every school district throughout the United States, and especially the southern States; they gave us commissioners; they gave us $12,000,000, and placed the power in the hands of the Executive, who was to work this machinery, with the army brought to his aid and to sustain it. They let us run it with $12,000,000 as a beginning, and in the end receive fifty or sixty millions, and let us work the four millions of slaves. In fine, the Freedmen's Bureau was a simple proposition to transfer four millions of slaves in the United States from their original owners to a new set of taskmasters. [A voice, "Never!" and cheers.] I have been laboring for years to emancipate them; and then I was opposed to seeing them transferred to a new set of taskmasters, to be worked with more rigor than they had been worked heretofore. [Cheers.] Yes, under this new system they would work the slaves, and call on the Govern-

ment to bear all the expenses, and if there were any profits left why they would pocket them. [Laughter and cheers.] Thus, you, the people, must pay the expense of running the machine out of your own pockets while they get the profits of it.

I simply intended to-night to tender you my sincere thanks; but as I go along, as we are talking about this Congress, and these respectable gentlemen who contend that the President is wrong because he vetoed the Freedmen's Bureau bill, and all this; because he chose to exercise the veto power, he committed a high offence, and therefore ought to be impeached. [Voice, "Never."] Yes, yes; they are ready to impeach him. [Voice, "Let them try it."] And if they were satisfied they had the next Congress by a decided majority, as this, upon some pretext or other—violating the Constitution, neglect of duty, or omitting to enforce some act of law—upon some pretext or other, they would vacate the executive department of the United States. [A voice, "Too bad, they don't impeach him."] Now, as we talk about this Congress, let me call the soldiers' attention to this immaculate Congress. Let me call your attention to—oh! yes; this Congress that could make war upon the Executive because he stands upon the Constitution and vindicates the rights of the people, exercising the veto power in their behalf. Because he dared to do this they can clamor and talk about impeachment; and by way of stimulating this increasing confidence with the soldiers throughout the country, they talk about impeachments. So far as offenses are concerned, upon this subject of offenses let me ask you [voice, "Plenty here to-night"] to go back into my history of legislation, and even when Governor of a State. Let me ask if there is a man here to-night who in the dark days of Know-Nothingism stood and battled more for their rights. [Voice, "Good," and cheers.]

It has been my peculiar misfortune to have fierce opposition because I have always struck my blows direct, and fought with right and the Constitution on my side. [Cheers.] Yes, I will come back to the soldiers again in a moment. Yes; here was a neutrality law. I was sworn, in support of the Constitution, to see that the law was faithfully executed. ["Why didn't you do it?"] The law was executed; and because it was executed, then they raised a clamor, and tried to make an appeal to the foreigners, and especially the Fenians. And what did they do? They introduced a bill to tickle and play with the fancy, pretending to repeal the law, and at the same time making it worse, and then left the law just where it is. [Voice, "That's so!"]

They knew that whenever a law was presented to me, proper in its provisions, ameliorating and softening the rigors of the present law, it would meet my hearty approbation. But as they were pretty well broken down and losing public confidence, at the heel of the session they found they must do something; and hence, what did they do? They pretended to do something for the soldiers. Who has done more for the soldiers than I have? Who has perilled more in this struggle than I have? [Cheers.] But then, to make them their peculiar friends and favorites of the soldier, they come forward with a proposition to do what? Why we will give the soldier $50 bounty— your attention to this—if he has served two years, and $100 if he has served three years. Now, mark you, the colored man that served two years can get his $100 bounty, but the white man must serve three years before he can get his. [Cheers.] But that is not the point. While they were tickling and attempting to please the soldiers, by giving them $300 for two years' service, they took it into their heads to give somebody else about [laughter], and they voted themselves not fifty dollars, two years' service. Your attention: I want to make a lodgment in your minds of the facts, because I want to put the nail in; and having put it in, I want to clinch it on the other side. [Cheers.] The brave boys, the patriotic young man who followed his gallant officers, slept in the tented field, and perilled his life and shed his blood, and left his limbs behind him, and came home mangled and maimed, he can get fifty dollars bounty, if he has served two years; but the members of Congress, who never smelt gunpowder, can get $4,000 extra pay. [Great cheering.] This is a faint picture, my countrymen, of what has transpired. [A voice, " Stick to that question."]

Fellow-citizens, you are all familiar with the work of restoration. You know that since the rebellion collapsed, since the armies were suppressed in the field, that everything that could be done has been done by the executive department of the Government for the restoration of the Government; everything has been done with the exception of one thing, and that is the admission of members from eleven States that went into the rebellion; and after having accepted the terms of the Government—having abolished slavery, having repudiated their debt and sent loyal representatives—everything has been done excepting the admission of representatives, to which all the States are entitled. [Cheers.]

When you turn and examine the Constitution of the United States, you find that you cannot even amend that Constitution so as to deprive any State of its equal suffrage in the Senate. [A voice, "They have never been out."] It is said before me they have never been out. I say so too. That is what I have always said. They have never been out, and they cannot go out. [Cheers.] That being the fact, under the Constitution they are entitled to equal representation in the Congress of the United States without violating the Constitution, [cheers;] and the same argument applies to the House of Representatives.

How, then, does the matter stand? It used to be one of the arguments, that if the States withdraw their Representatives and Senators, that was secession—a peaceable breaking up of the Government. Now the radical power in this Government turn round and assume that the States are out of the Union, that they are not entitled to representation in Congress. [Cheers.] That is to say, they are dissolutionists, and their position now is to perpetuate a disruption of the Government; and that, too, while they are denying the States the right of representation, they impose taxation upon them, a principle upon which, in the Revolution, you resisted the power

of Great Britain. We deny the right of taxation without representation; that is one of our great principles.

Let the Government be restored; let peace be restored among this people. I have labored for it; I am for it now. I deny this doctrine of secession, come from what quarter it may, whether from the North or from the South. I am opposed to it, and am for the union of the States. [Voices, "That's right," and cheers.] I am for the thirty-six States, representing thirty-six States, remaining where they are under the Constitution as your fathers made it and handed it down to you; and if it is altered or amended, let it be done in the mode and manner pointed out by that instrument itself, and in no other. [Cheers.] I am for the restoration of peace. Let me ask the people here to-night if we have not shed enough of blood. Let me ask, Are you prepared to go into another civil war? Let me ask this people here to-night, Are they prepared to set man upon man, and in the name of God lift his hand against the throat of his fellow? [Voice, " Never!"] Are you prepared to see our fields laid waste again, our business and our commerce suspended, and our trade stopped? Are you prepared to see this land again drenched in our brothers' blood? Heaven avert it! is my prayer. [Cheers.] I am one of those who believe that man does sin, and having sinned, I believe he must repent, and, sometimes, having repented makes him a better man than he was before. [Cheers.]

I know it has been said that I have exercised my pardoning power. Yes, I have. [Cheers, and " What about Drake's constitution?"] Yes I have; and don't you think it is to prevail? I reckon I have pardoned more men, turned more men loose, and set them at liberty that were imprisoned, I imagine, than any other living man on God's habitable globe. [Voice, "Bully for you!" cheers.] I turned forty-seven thousand of our men loose who engaged in this struggle, with the arms we captured with them, and who were then in prison. I turned them loose. [Voice, " Bully for you!" and laughter.] Large numbers have applied for pardon, and I have granted them pardon; yet there are some who condemn, and hold me responsible for doing wrong. Yes, there are some who staid at home, who did not go into the field, that can talk about others being traitorous and being treacherous. There are some who can talk about blood and vengeance and crime and everything to make treason odious, and all that, who never smelt gunpowder on either side. [Cheers.] Yes, they can condemn others, and recommend hanging and torture, and all that. If I have erred, I have erred on the side of mercy. Some of these croakers have dared to assume they are better than was the Saviour of men himself—a kind of over-righteous —better than anybody else; and, although wanting to do Deity's work, thinking He cannot do it as well as they can. [Laughter and cheers.]

Yes, the Saviour of men came on earth and found the human race condemned and sentenced under the law; but when they repented and believed, He said Let them live. Instead of executing and putting the whole world to death, He went upon the cross, and there was nailed by unbelievers, there shed his blood that you might live. [Cheers.] Think of it; to execute and hang and put to death eight millions of people. Never! It is an absurdity. Such a thing is impracticable, even if it were right; but it is the violation of all law, human and divine. [Voice, "Hang Jeff Davis. You call on Judge Chase to hang Jeff Davis, will you?" Great cheering.] I am not the court, I am not the jury, nor the judge. Before the case comes to me, and all other cases, it would have to come on application as a case for pardon. That is the only way the case can get to me. Why don't Judge Chase, the Chief Justice of the United States, in whose district he is—why don't he try him? [Loud cheers.] But perhaps I could answer the question, as sometimes persons want to be facetious and indulge in repartee. I might ask you a question, Why don't you hang Thad Stevens and Wendell Phillips? [Great cheering.] A traitor at one end of the line is as bad as a traitor at the other. I know that there are some who have got up their little pieces and sayings to repeat on public occasions—talking parrots that have been placed in their mouths by their superiors—who have not the courage and the manhood to come forward and tell them themselves, but have their understrappers to do their work for them. [Cheers.] I know there are some that talk about this universal elective franchise, upon which they wanted to upturn the Government of Louisiana and institute another, who contended that we must send men there to control, govern, and manage their slave population because they are incompetent to do it themselves. And yet they turn round, when they get there, and say they are competent to go to Congress and manage all the affairs of State. [Cheers.] Before you commence throwing your stones you ought to be sure you don't live in a glass house. Then why all this clamor? Don't you see, my countrymen, it is a question of power; and being in power, as they are, their object is to perpetuate their power, since, when you talk about turning any of them out of office, oh, they talk about bread and butter. [Laughter.] Yes, these men are the most perfect and complete bread and butter party that has ever appeared in this Government. [Great cheering.] When you make an effort or struggle to take the nipple out of their mouths, how they clamor. They have stayed at home here five or six years, held the offices, grown fat, and enjoyed all the emoluments of position; and now, when you talk about turning one of them out, oh, it is proscription; and hence they come forward and propose, in Congress, to do what? To pass laws to prevent the Executive from turning anybody out. [Voice, "Put 'em out."] Hence, don't you see what the policy was to be? I believe in the good old doctrine—advocated by Washington, Jefferson, and Madison—of rotation in office. These people who have been enjoying these offices seem to have lost sight of this doctrine. I believe that one set of men have enjoyed the emoluments of office long enough. They should let another portion of the people have a chance. [Cheers.] How are these men to be got out—[Voice, "Kick 'em out!" Cheers and laughter.]—unless your Executive can put them out, unless

you can teach them through the President? Congress says he shall not turn them out, and they are trying to pass laws to prevent it being done. Well, let me say to you, if you will stand by me in this action, [cheers,] if you will stand by me in trying to give the people a fair chance —soldiers and citizens—to participate in these offices, God being willing, I will kick them out. I will kick them out just as fast as I can. Let me say to you, in concluding, that what I have said I intended to say. I was provoked into this, and I care not for their menaces, the taunts and the jeers. I care not for threats. I do not intend to be bullied by my enemies nor overawed by my friends. But, God willing, with your help, I will veto their measures whenever any of them come to me. I place myself upon the ramparts of the Constitution when I see the enemy approaching; so long as I have eyes to see, or ears to hear, or a tongue to sound the alarm, so help me God, I will do it, and call on the people to be my judges. [Cheers.]

I tell you here to-night that the Constitution of this country is being encroached upon. I tell you here to-night that the citadel of liberty is being endangered. [A voice, "Go it, Andy!"] Say to them, "Go to work; take the Constitution as your palladium of civil and religious liberty; take it as your chief ark of safety." Just let me ask you here to-night to cling to the Constitution, in this great struggle for freedom and for its preservation, as the shipwrecked mariner clings to the mast when the midnight tempest closes around him.

So far as my humble life has been advanced, the people of Missouri, as well as other States, know that all my efforts have been devoted in that direction. Why, where is the speech, where is the vote to be got of mine but which has always had a tendency to elevate the great working classes of this people? When they talk about tyranny and despotism, where is one act of Andy Johnson's that ever encroached upon the rights of a freeman in this land? But because I have stood, as a faithful sentinel, upon the watch-tower of freedom to sound the alarm, hence all this traducing and detraction that has been heaped upon me. [Cries of "Bully for Andy Johnson!"]

I now, in conclusion, my countrymen, hand over to you the flag of your country with thirty-six stars upon it. I hand over to you your Constitution, with the charge and responsibility of preserving it intact. I hand over to you to-day the Union of these States, the great magic circle which embraces them all. I hand them all over to you, the people, in whom I have always trusted in all great emergencies. I hand them over to you, men who can rise above party, who can stand around the altar of a common country with their faces uplifted to heaven, swearing by Him who lives forever and ever, that the altar and all shall sink in the dust, but that the Constitution of the Union shall be preserved.

Let us stand by the Union of these States; let us fight the enemies of the Government, come from what quarter they may. My stand has been taken. You understand what my position is. And parting with you now, I leave the Government in your hands, with the confidence I have always had, that the people will ultimately redress all wrongs and set the Government right. Then, gentlemen, in conclusion, for the cordial welcome you have shown me in this great city of the South, whose destiny none can foretell, now, in bidding you good night, I leave all in your charge and thank you for the cordial welcome you have given in this spontaneous outpouring of the people of your city.

---

### Interview with Chas. G. Halpine, March 5, 1867.

And now, apart from the directly political, [continued the President,] what is the main issue looming up in the immediate future? What issue is clearly foreshadowed to be the Aaron's rod which must swallow up all minor questions? It is the great financial issue, the issue of the national debt; whether it shall be paid or repudiated. This issue has fibres extending into the pockets of every citizen; for wherever a man has a dollar, or can earn a dollar, the Government is now compelled to go for its portion of his substance; and with the vast machinery under its control, the money is fetched.

There were four millions of slaves in the southern States before the rebellion, representing a capital of three, or possibly four billions of dollars; but let us call it three billions, or three thousand millions, as you may please. These slaves represented that amount of property, men put their savings into purchasing or raising them, and they represented as property whatever were the surplus profits of their labor, after due allowance for food, clothing, medicine, and interest on the capital invested.

On this property in slaves gradually grew up that slave oligarchy or aristocracy, against which the leaders of the anti-slavery party so successfully thundered during the twelve years preceding the rebellion; and after the first mad plunge into rebellion, the fate of that aristocracy was sealed. It is now a thing of the past. With its virtues—for it had virtues, courage, and hospitality eminently—and with its crimes of pride and lawless revolution, it has entered into history, and is a thing of the past.

But what do we find? The aristocracy based on $3,000,000,000 of property in slaves south of Mason and Dixon's line has disappeared; but an aristocracy, based on over $2,500,000,000 of national securities, has arisen in the northern States, to assume that political control which the consolidation of great financial with political interests formerly gave to the slave oligarchy of the late rebel States. The aristocracy based on negro property disappears at the southern end of the line, but only to reappear in an oligarchy of bonds and national securities in the States which suppressed the rebellion.

We have all read history, and is it not certain that of all aristocracies, that of mere wealth is the most odious, rapacious, and tyrannical? It goes for the last dollar the poor and helpless have got; and with such a vast machine as this Government under its control, that dollar will be fetched. It is an aristocracy that can see in the people only a prey for extortion. It has no political or military relations with them, such as the old feudal system created between liege lord and vassal; it has no intimate social and domestic ties, and no such strong bond of self-interest with the people as existed of necessity between the extinct slaveholders of our country and their slaves. To an aristocracy existing on the annual interest of a national debt, the people are only of value in proportion to their docility and power of patiently bleeding golden blood under the tax-gatherer's thumb-screw.

To the people the national debt is a thing of debt to be paid; but to the aristocracy of bonds and national securities it is a property of more than $2,500,000,000, from which a revenue of $180,000,000 a year is to be received into their pockets. So we now find that an aristocracy of the South, based on $3,000,000,000 in negroes, who were a productive class, has disappeared, and their place in political control of the country is assumed by an aristocracy based on nearly $3,000,000,000 of national debt—a thing which is not producing anything, but which goes on steadily every year, and must go on for all time until the debt is paid, absorbing and taxing at the rate of six or seven per cent. a year for every $100 bond that is represented in its aggregation.

Now, I am not speaking of this to do anything but deprecate the fearful issue which the madness of partisan hatred and the blindness of our new national-debt aristocracy to their own true interests is fast forcing upon the country. But is it not clear that the people, who have to pay $180,000,000 a year to this consolidated moneyed oligarchy, must, sooner or later, commence asking each other " How much was actually loaned to our Government during the civil war by these bondholders, who now claim that we owe them nearly $3,000,000,000?" You know what the popular answer must be—I do not say the right answer—" Less than half the amount they claim, for gold ranged at an average of one hundred premium while this debt was being incurred."

Just think of the annual tax of $180,000,000 for payment of interest on our national debt! This Government we have, with its enormous machinery, is a pretty hefty business in itself, costing more *per capita* to the people than the Government of England, which we always heretofore regarded as the most tax-devouring on earth. But over and beyond the expenses of the Government proper, as it should stand in the scale of peace at about $60,000,000 a year, we have, in the $180,000,000 of interest paid yearly on our national debt, enough to support three such Governments as this, with all their vast machinery and disbursements! We have not only, under the present system, one Government for the people to support, but, over and beyond this, we have to raise by taxation from the people sufficient to support three similar establishments every year!

All property is based upon and can only be sustained by law; and it is for a return to law and the guide of fixed constitutional principles that my whole course has been contending. But so short-sighted is this aristocracy of bonds and paper currency, this Plutocracy of the national debt, that my efforts in behalf of their true interests (which are certainly involved in the maintenance of law and the Constitution) have been everywhere encountered, and almost everywhere overwhelmed, by the preponderating influence which they have acquired from the natural force of capital and the agency of our national banks.

And what has been the course of that Congress which has just ended, and which this blind aristocracy of national debt sustained in overriding my efforts for a return to sound principles of internal government? Look at the bill giving from $480,000,000 to $600,000,000, nominally for back bounty, or as an equalization of bounties to the soldiers, but really, as all intelligent men must be aware, to be parcelled out as a prey among the bounty sharks and claim agents, who are the most reckless and clamorous adherents of the dominant majority in Congress. Then look at appropriations amounting to another $100,000,000, for internal improvements, which should properly be left to the laws governing private industry and the progress of our national development. Look also at the increase of all salaries with a prodigal hand, this virtuous Congress first setting an example against retrenchment by voting to themselves an increase of salaries. Everywhere, and in an ever-increasing ratio, the motto seems to be, "Always spend and never spare," a fresh issue from the paper-mill over yonder [slightly pointing his pencil to the Treasury Department] being the panacea prescribed for every evil of our present situation.

Every effort to increase our annual taxation is resisted, for increased taxes might help to awaken the people from their false dream of prosperity under the sway of revolutionary and radical ideas; but no addition to the national debt can be proposed, no further inflation of our inflated currency, which the preponderating votes of the western States will not be certain to favor. The war of finance is the next war we have to fight; and every blow struck against my efforts to uphold a strict construction of the laws and the Constitution is in reality a blow in favor of repudiating the national debt. The manufacturers and men of capital in the eastern States and the States along the Atlantic seaboard —a mere strip or fringe on the broad mantle of our country, if you will examine the map—these are in favor of high protective, and, in fact, prohibitory tariffs, and also favor a contraction of the currency. But against both measures the interests and votes of the great producing and non-manufacturing States of the West stand irrevocably arrayed, and a glance at the map and the census statistics of the last twenty years will tell every one who is open to conviction how that war must end.

The history of the world gives no example of a war debt that has ever been paid; but we have an exceptional country, and present an exceptional case. Our debt might easily be paid, provided the brakes against excessive expenditures could be turned on quickly enough; but now is the appointed time, and now or never the work must be commenced. If that debt is ever to be paid we need economy in every branch of the public service—the reduction, not an increase of salaries to Congressmen and other officials; the systematic reduction of our national debt; and not its increase by such monstrous bills as this last demagogue measure for the pretended equalization of bounties. The Congress, forsooth, is so patriotic, so loyal, that it "can refuse our gallant soldiers nothing." But you must have seen how promptly it rejected the names of nearly every gallant veteran sent in by me for confirmation to any civil office, a majority of our extremely "loyal Senators" using their guillotine without remorse in nearly every instance.

And whither is all this drifting? To intelligent men there can be but one answer. We are drifting towards repudiation, and the moneyed aristocracy of the national debt, the very men whose interests are most jeopardized, are so blind that they are practically helping to accelerate, not check our course in this downward direction. We need the industry and enormous possible products of the lately revolted States to help us in bearing our heavy burden; we need confidence and calm; we need internal harmony; and above all, we need a return to the unquestioned supremacy of the civil laws and constitutional restraints, if our debt is not to be repudiated within the next half score of years.

Financial prosperity was secured up to within a recent period; but already the delicate fabric of public credit—a house of cards' at best—begins to totter under the concussion of the various revolutionary ideas which have been recently exploited on the floors of Congress. Who now talks of the Constitution with respect? Who is not now made a laughing-stock in the papers and speeches of the violent revolutionary party, if he shall be so hardy as to claim that, being again at peace, the sway of civil over military law should be immediately resumed, if we desire to maintain our liberties? "The Constitution is played out," we hear on every hand; and every effort to advocate the just ascendency of the civil law only furnishes fresh food for ridicule.

No party as yet, and possibly no party for some years, will openly hoist the banner of repudiation. But a majority of those who shaped the legislation of this last Congress must know, unless they deceive themselves, or are too ignorant to appreciate their own acts, that we are drifting in that direction, and that it is by their votes we have been swung out into the downward stream. Doubtless, some of them would either be, or affect to feel, horrified if to-day branded as repudiationists, just as, in the infancy of the free-soil agitation, it was considered a bitter slander if the "freesoiler" should be styled an "abolitionist." There are steps in everything, and the term of reproach to-day will be worn as a feather in the cap some years from now, unless the true conservative wisdom of the country can be awakened, and rapidly, from its asphyxiating dream that our "national debt is a national blessing."

And look at the effect of the reconstruction bill just passed over my unavailing veto. I mean its peculiar effect as a step in the direction of repudiation, and not its general effect as a high-handed measure of congressional usurpation, striking out of existence so many States, and establishing a military despotism over more than one-third of our geographical Union. This bill suddenly adds four millions of ignorant and penniless negroes to the voting force of the country, an accession of just so much strength to the party whose interest it is, and must increasingly become, to favor repudiation as a policy. To secure the public creditor, our efforts should be, if that were possible, to restrict rather than to extend the right of suffrage; for money rapidly aggregates in a few hands; and whenever the men who have an interest in seeing that our national debt is paid shall have become out of all proportion few, compared with those who have an interest in its repudiation, the votes of the many will carry it, and the debt of $3,000,000,000 will be struck out of existence by ballots, just as rapidly and utterly as the similar amount invested in southern negroes has been abolished during the recent war under showers of bullets. At least, this is possible.

That we are to have a great financial crash this year I hold to be inevitable, though deprecating it, and having used every effort for its avoidance. To say that it can be staved off by any legislation, if the violated laws of trade and public economy call for it, is to assert that water can be made to run up hill, or shall cease to seek its own level under the compulsion of a congressional enactment. Perhaps, for so violent a disease, this violent cure may be the only remedy. It is like a man sustaining his strength on brandy; so long as he can increase the dose daily, he may get along in high good humor, just as we have been prospering on an irredeemable paper currency and fresh issues of public securities. But sooner or later, the day will come in which brandy no longer can stimulate; nor can irredeemable promises to pay pass current as a circulating medium forever. To the man will come a severe fit of sickness, teaching him that the laws of temperance can only be violated under fearful penalties, and to the nation will come a financial crash, teaching it that paper is only a representative of value, not value itself; and that the only true securities for our public credit must be looked for in a system of rigidly exacted obedience to all constitutional restraints, and a thorough system of economy in all branches of the public service.

For the slights and indignities, the unconstitutional curtailments and dishonors which the recent Congress has attempted to cast upon me for my unflinching and unalterable devotion to my constitutional oath, and to the best interests of the whole country, according to my best judgment and experience, I am only sorry as regards the indignities sought to be imposed on my high office, but unmoved as regards myself. Conscious of only having executed my duty, conscious of being denounced for "usurpation" only because refusing to accept unconstitutional powers and patronage, and satisfied that the day of wiser thought and sounder estimate cannot now be far distant, I look with perfect confidence for my vindication to the justice of that future which I am convinced cannot long be delayed. Unless all the senses are deceptive, unless all truth be a lie, unless God has ceased to live, I tell you that the folly and fraud now dominating the councils of this distracted country in Congress cannot endure forever.

It is, perhaps, but right to add that the foregoing is a report from memory of remarks made by Mr. Johnson in an extended conversation yesterday afternoon, and that the original did not take the form of a set speech, here unavoidably given to it. It should also be added that a few points embraced in the report, and attributed exclusively to the President, may have been, more or less, suggested by interjectional remarks of the person to whom he was speaking; but nothing has been here set down to which the full assent of Mr. Johnson was not given, always provided, of course, that his listener understood him, and remembers correctly.

---

# XV.

# PRESIDENT JOHNSON'S MESSAGES.

**The Annual Message, December 4, 1866.**

The following portions relate to reconstruction, and kindred subjects:

*Fellow-citizens of the Senate and House of Representatives:*

After a brief interval the Congress of the United States resumes its annual legislative labors. An all-wise and merciful Providence has abated the pestilence which visited our shores, leaving its calamitous traces upon some portions of our country. Peace, order, tranquillity, and civil authority have been formally declared to exist throughout the whole of the United States. In all of the States civil authority has superseded the coercion of arms, and the people, by their voluntary action, are maintaining their governments in full activity and complete operation. The enforcement of the laws is no longer "obstructed in any State by combinations too powerful to be suppressed by the ordinary course of judicial proceedings;" and the animosities engendered by the war are rapidly yielding to the beneficent influences of our free institutions, and to the kindly effects of unrestricted social and commercial intercourse. An entire restoration of fraternal feeling must be the earnest wish of every patriotic heart; and we will have accomplished our grandest national achievement when, forgetting the sad events of the past, and remembering only their instructive lessons, we resume our onward career as a free, prosperous, and united people.

In my message of the 4th of December, 1865, Congress was informed of the measures which had been instituted by the Executive with a view to the gradual restoration of the States in which the insurrection occurred to their relations with the General Government. Provisional Governors had been appointed, conventions called, Governors elected, Legislatures assembled, and Senators and Representatives chosen to the Congress of the United States. Courts had been opened for the enforcement of laws long in abeyance. The blockade had been removed, custom-houses re-established, and the internal revenue laws put in force, in order that the people might contribute to the national income. Postal operations had been renewed, and efforts were being made to restore them to their former condition of efficiency. The States themselves had been asked to take part in the high function of amending the Constitution, and of thus sanctioning the extinction of African slavery as one of the legitimate results of our internecine struggle.

Having progressed thus far, the executive department found that it had accomplished nearly all that was within the scope of its constitutional authority. One thing, however, yet remained to be done before the work of restoration could be completed, and that was the admission to Congress of loyal Senators and Representatives from the States whose people had rebelled against the lawful authority of the General Government. This question devolved upon the respective Houses, which, by the Constitution, are made the judges of the elections, returns, and qualifications of their own members; and its consideration at once engaged the attention of Congress.

In the mean time, the executive department —no other plan having been proposed by Congress—continued its efforts to perfect, as far as was practicable, the restoration of the proper relations between the citizens of the respective States, the States, and the Federal Government, extending, from time to time, as the public interests seemed to require, the judicial, revenue, and postal systems of the country. With the advice and consent of the Senate, the necessary officers were appointed, and appropriations made by Congress for the payment of their salaries. The proposition to amend the Federal Constitution so as to prevent the existence of slavery within the United States or any place subject to their jurisdiction, was ratified by the requisite number of States, and, on the 18th day of December, 1865, it was officially declared to have become valid as a part of the Constitution of the United States. All of the States in which the insurrection had existed promptly amended their constitutions so as to make them conform to the great change thus effected in the organic law of the land; declared null and void all ordinances and laws of secession; repudiated all pretended debts and obligations created for the revolutionary purposes of the insurrection; and proceeded, in good faith, to the enactment of measures for the protection and amelioration of the condition of the colored race. Congress, however, yet hesitated to admit any of these States to representation; and it was not until towards the close of the eighth month of the session that an exception was made in favor of Tennessee by the admission of her Senators and Representatives.

I deem it a subject of profound regret that Congress has thus far failed to admit to seats loyal Senators and Representatives from the other States whose inhabitants, with those of Tennessee, had engaged in the rebellion. Ten States—more than one-fourth of the whole number—remain without representation! The seats of fifty members in the House of Representatives and of twenty members in the Senate are yet vacant—not by their own consent, not by a failure of election, but by the refusal of Congress to accept their credentials. Their admission, it is believed, would have accomplished much towards the renewal and strengthening of our relations as one people, and removed serious cause for discontent on the part of the inhabitants of those States. It would have accorded with the great principle enunciated in the Declaration of American Independence, that no people ought to bear the burden of taxation and yet be denied the right of representation. It would have been in consonance with the express provisions of the Constitution, that "each State shall have at least one Representative," and "that no State, without its consent, shall be deprived of its equal suffrage in the Senate." These provisions were intended to secure to every State, and to the people of every State, the right of representation in each House of Congress; and so important was it deemed by the framers of the Constitution that the equality of the States in the Senate should be preserved, that not even by an amendment of the Constitution can any State, without its consent, be denied a voice in that branch of the national Legislature.

It is true, it has been assumed that the existence of the States was terminated by the rebellious acts of their inhabitants, and that the insurrection having been suppressed, they were thenceforward to be considered merely as conquered territories. The legislative, executive, and judicial departments of the Government have, however, with great distinctness and uniform consistency, refused to sanction an assumption so incompatible with the nature of our republican system and with the professed objects of the war. Throughout the recent legislation of Congress, the undeniable fact makes itself apparent, that these ten political communities are nothing less than States of this Union. At the very commencement of the rebellion each House declared, with a unanimity as remarkable as it was significant, that the war was not "waged, upon our part, in any spirit of oppression, nor for any purpose of conquest or subjugation, nor purpose of overthrowing or interfering with the rights or established institutions of those States, but to defend and maintain the supremacy of the Constitution and all laws made in pursuance thereof, and to preserve the Union with all the dignity, equality, and rights of the several States unimpaired; and that as soon as these objects" were "accomplished the war ought to cease." In some instances Senators were permitted to continue their legislative functions, while in other instances Representatives were elected and admitted to seats after their States had formally declared their right to withdraw from the Union, and were endeavoring to maintain that right by force of arms. All of the States whose people were in insurrection, as States, were included in the apportionment of the direct tax of $20,000,000 annually, laid upon the United States by the act approved 5th August, 1861. Congress, by the act of March 4, 1862. and by the apportionment of representation thereunder, also recognized their presence as States in the Union; and they have, for judicial purposes, been divided into districts, as States alone can be divided. The same recognition appears in the recent legislation in reference to Tennessee, which evidently rests upon the fact that the functions of the State were not destroyed by the rebellion, but merely suspended; and that principle is of course applicable to those States which, like Tennessee, attempted to renounce their place in the Union.

The action of the executive department of the Government upon this subject has been equally definite and uniform, and the purpose of the war was specifically stated in the proclamation issued by my predecessor on the 22d day of September, 1862. It was then solemnly proclaimed and declared that "hereafter, as heretofore, the war will be prosecuted for the object of practically restoring the constitutional relation between the United States and each of the States and the people thereof, in which States that relation is or may be suspended or disturbed."

The recognition of the States by the judicial department of the Government has also been clear and conclusive in all proceedings affecting them as States, had in the Supreme, Circuit, and District Courts.

In the admission of Senators and Representatives from any and all of the States, there can be no just ground of apprehension that persons who are disloyal will be clothed with the powers of legislation; for this could not happen when the Constitution and the laws are enforced by a vigilant and faithful Congress. Each House is made the "judge of the elections, returns, and qualifications of its own members," and may, "with the concurrence of two-thirds, expel a member." When a Senator or Representative presents his certificate of election, he may at once be admitted or rejected; or, should there be any question as to his eligibility, his credentials may be referred for investigation to the appropriate committee. If admitted to a seat, it must be upon evidence satisfactory to the House of which he thus becomes a member, that he possesses the requisite constitutional and legal qualifications. If refused admission as a member, for want of due allegiance to the Government, and returned to his constituents, they are admonished that none but persons loyal to the United States will be allowed a voice in the legislative councils of the nation, and the political power and moral influence of Congress are thus effectively exerted in the interests of loyalty to the Government and fidelity to the Union. Upon this question, so vitally affecting the restoration of the Union and the permanency of our present form of government, my convictions, heretofore expressed, have undergone no change; but, on the contrary, their correctness has been confirmed by reflection and time. If the admission of loyal members to seats in the respective Houses of Congress was wise and expedient a year ago, it is no less wise and expedient now. If this anomalous condition is right now—if, in the exact condition of these States at the present

time, it is lawful to exclude them from representation, I do not see that the question will be changed by the efflux of time. Ten years hence. if these States remain as they are, the right of representation will be no stronger, the right of exclusion will be no weaker.

The Constitution of the United States makes it the duty of the President to recommend to the consideration of Congress "such measures as he shall judge necessary or expedient." I know of no measure more imperatively demanded by every consideration of national interest, sound policy, and equal justice, than the admission of loyal members from the now unrepresented States. This would consummate the work of restoration, and exert a most salutary influence in the re-establishment of peace, harmony, and fraternal feeling. It would tend greatly to renew the confidence of the American people in the vigor and stability of their institutions. It would bind us more closely together as a nation, and enable us to show to the world the inherent and recuperative power of a Government founded upon the will of the people, and established upon the principles of liberty, justice, and intelligence. Our increased strength and enhanced prosperity would irrefragably demonstrate the fallacy of the arguments against free institutions drawn from our recent national disorders by the enemies of republican government. The admission of loyal members from the States now excluded from Congress, by allaying doubt and apprehension, would turn capital, now awaiting an opportunity for investment, into the channels of trade and industry. It would alleviate the present troubled condition of those States, and, by inducing emigration, aid in the settlement of fertile regions now uncultivated, and lead to an increased production of those staples which have added so greatly to the wealth of the nation and the commerce of the world. New fields of enterprise would be opened to our progressive people, and soon the devastations of war would be repaired, and all traces of our domestic differences effaced from the minds of our countrymen.

In our efforts to preserve "the unity of government," which constitutes us one people, by restoring the States to the condition which they held prior to the rebellion, we should be cautious, lest, having rescued our nation from perils of threatened disintegration, we resort to consolidation, and in the end absolute despotism, as a remedy for the recurrence of similar troubles. The war having terminated, and with it all occasion for the exercise of powers of doubtful constitutionality, we should hasten to bring legislation within the boundaries prescribed by the Constitution, and to return to the ancient landmarks established by our fathers for the guidance of succeeding generations. "The Constitution which at any time exists, until changed by an explicit and authentic act of the whole people, is sacredly obligatory upon all." "If, in the opinion of the people, the distribution or modification of the constitutional powers be, in any particular, wrong, let it be corrected by an amendment in the way in which the Constitution designates. But let there be no change by usurpation; for" "it is the customary weapon by which free Governments are destroyed." Washington spoke these words to his countrymen when, followed by their love and gratitude, he voluntarily retired from the cares of public life. "To keep in all things within the pale of our constitutional powers, and cherish the Federal Union as the only rock of safety," were prescribed by Jefferson as rules of action to endear to his "countrymen the true principles of their Constitution, and promote a union of sentiment and action equally auspicious to their happiness and safety." Jackson held that the action of the General Government should always be strictly confined to the sphere of its appropriate duties, and justly and forcibly urged that our Government is not to be maintained nor our Union preserved "by invasions of the rights and powers of the several States. In thus attempting to make our General Government strong, we make it weak. Its true strength consists in leaving individuals and States as much as possible to themselves; in making itself felt, not in its power, but in its beneficence; not in its control, but in its protection; not in binding the States more closely to the centre, but leaving each to move unobstructed in its proper constitutional orbit." These are the teachings of men whose deeds and services have made them illustrious, and who, long since withdrawn from the scenes of life, have left to their country the rich legacy of their example, their wisdom, and their patriotism. Drawing fresh inspiration from their lessons, let us emulate them in love of country and respect for the Constitution and the laws.

The report of the Secretary of the Treasury affords much information respecting the revenue and commerce of the country. His views upon the currency, and with reference to a proper adjustment of our revenue system, internal as well as impost, are commended to the careful consideration of Congress. In my last annual message I expressed my general views upon these subjects. * * * * *

The report presents a much more satisfactory condition of our finances than one year ago the most sanguine could have anticipated. During the fiscal year ending the 30th June, 1865, the last year of the war, the public debt was increased $941,902,537, and on the 31st of October, 1865, it amounted to $2,740,854,750. On the 31st day of October, 1866, it had been reduced to $2,551,310,006, the diminution, during a period of fourteen months, commencing September 1, 1865, and ending October 31, 1866, having been $206,379,565. In the last annual report on the state of the finances, it was estimated that during the three-quarters of the fiscal year ending the 30th of June last, the debt would be increased $112,194,947. During that period, however, it was reduced $31,196,387, the receipts of the year having been $89,905,905 more, and the expenditures $200,529,235 less than the estimates. Nothing could more clearly indicate than these statements the extent and availability of the national resources, and the rapidity and safety with which, under our form of government, great military and naval establishments can be disbanded, and expenses reduced from a war to a peace footing.

During the fiscal year ending the 30th of June, 1866, the receipts were $558,032,620, and the expenditures $520,750,940, leaving an available surplus of $37,281,680. It is estimated that the receipts for the fiscal year ending the 30th June 1867, will be $475,061,386 and that the expenditures will reach the sum of $316,428,078, leaving in the Treasury a surplus of $158,633,308. For the fiscal year ending June 30, 1868, it is estimated that the receipts will amount to $436,000,000, and that the expenditures will be $350,247,641—showing an excess of $85,752,359 in favor of the Government. These estimated receipts may be diminished by a reduction of excise and import duties; but after all necessary reductions shall have been made, the revenue of the present and of following years will doubtless be sufficient to cover all legitimate charges upon the Treasury, and leave a large annual surplus to be applied to the payment of the principal of the debt. There seems now to be no good reason why taxes may not be reduced as the country advances in population and wealth, and yet the debt be extinguished within the next quarter of a century * * * *

In the month of April last, as Congress is aware, a friendly arrangement was made between the Emperor of France and the President of the United States for the withdrawal from Mexico of the French expeditionary military forces. This withdrawal was to be effected in three detachments, the first of which, it was understood, would leave Mexico in November, now past, the second in March next, and the third and last in November, 1867. Immediately upon the completion of the evacuation, the French Government was to assume the same attitude of non-intervention, in regard to Mexico, as is held by the Government of the United States. Repeated assurances have been given by the Emperor, since that agreement, that he would complete the promised evacuation within the period mentioned, or sooner.

It was reasonably expected that the proceedings thus contemplated would produce a crisis of great political interest in the Republic of Mexico. The newly appointed Minister of the United States, Mr. Campbell, was therefore sent forward, on the 9th day of November last, to assume his proper functions as Minister Plenipotentiary of the United States to that Republic. It was also thought expedient that he should be attended in the vicinity of Mexico by the Lieutenant General of the Army of the United States, with the view of obtaining such information as might be important to determine the course to be pursued by the United States in re-establishing and maintaining necessary and proper intercourse with the Republic of Mexico. Deeply interested in the cause of liberty and humanity, it seemed an obvious duty on our part to exercise whatever influence we possessed for the restoration and permanent establishment in that country of a domestic and republican form of government.

Such was the condition of affairs in regard to Mexico, when, on the 22d of November last, official information was received from Paris that the Emperor of France had some time before decided not to withdraw a detachment of his forces in the month of November past, according to engagement, but that this decision was made with the purpose of withdrawing the whole of those forces in the ensuing spring. Of this determination, however, the United States had not received any notice or intimation; and, so soon as the information was received by the Government, care was taken to make known its dissent to the Emperor of France.

I cannot forego the hope that France will reconsider the subject, and adopt some resolution in regard to the evacuation of Mexico which will conform as nearly as practicable with the existing engagement, and thus meet the just expectations of the United States. The papers relating to the subject will be laid before you. It is believed that, with the evacuation of Mexico by the expeditionary forces, no subject for serious differences between France and the United States would remain. The expressions of the Emperor and people of France warrant a hope that the traditionary friendship between the two countries might, in that case, be renewed and permanently restored.

A claim of a citizen of the United States for indemnity for spoliations committed on the high seas by the French authorities, in the exercise of a belligerent power against Mexico, has been met by the Government of France with a proposition to defer settlement until a mutual convention for the adjustment of all claims of citizens and subjects of both countries, arising out of the recent wars on this Continent, shall be agreed upon by the two countries. The suggestion is not deemed unreasonable, but it belongs to Congress to direct the manner in which claims for indemnity by foreigners, as well as by citizens of the United States, arising out of the late civil war, shall be adjudicated and determined. I have no doubt that the subject of all such claims will engage your attention at a convenient and proper time. *    *    *    *    *

In the performance of a duty imposed upon me by the Constitution, I have thus submitted to the representatives of the States and of the people such information of our domestic and foreign affairs as the public interests seem to require. Our Government is now undergoing its most trying ordeal, and my earnest prayer is that the peril may be successfully and finally passed, without impairing its original strength and symmetry. The interests of the nation are best to be promoted by the revival of fraternal relations, the complete obliteration of our past differences, and the reinauguration of all the pursuits of peace. Directing our efforts to the early accomplishment of these great ends, let us endeavor to preserve harmony between the co-ordinate Departments of the Government, that each in its proper sphere may cordially co-operate with the other in securing the maintenance of the Constitution, the preservation of the Union, and the perpetuity of our free institutions.

ANDREW JOHNSON.

WASHINGTON, *December* 3, 1866.

---

## Veto of the Second Freedmen's Bureau Bill, July 16, 1866.*

*To the House of Representatives :*

A careful examination of the bill passed by the two Houses of Congress, entitled "An act to continue in force and to amend 'An act to establish a Bureau for the relief of Freedmen and Refugees,'

---

* For veto of freedmen's bill of February 29, 1866, see pages 68–74 of Political Manual for 1866.

and for other purposes," has convinced me that the legislation which it proposes would not be consistent with the welfare of the country, and that it falls clearly within the reasons assigned in my message of the 19th of February last, returning, without my signature, a similar measure which originated in the Senate. It is not my purpose to repeat the objections which I then urged. They are yet fresh in your recollection, and can be readily examined as a part of the records of one branch of the national Legislature. Adhering to the principles set forth in that message, I now reaffirm them and the line of policy therein indicated.

The only ground upon which this kind of legislation can be justified is that of the war-making power. The act of which this bill is intended as amendatory was passed during the existence of the war. By its own provisions, it is to terminate within one year from the cessation of hostilities and the declaration of peace. It is therefore yet in existence, and it is likely that it will continue in force as long as the freedmen may require the benefit of its provisions. It will certainly remain in operation, as a law, until some months subsequent to the meeting of the next session of Congress, when, if experience shall make evident the necessity of additional legislation, the two Houses will have ample time to mature and pass the requisite measures. In the mean time the questions arise, why should this war measure be continued beyond the period designated in the original act; and why, in time of peace, should military tribunals be created to continue until each "State shall be fully restored in its constitutional relations to the Government, and shall be duly represented in the Congress of the United States?"

It was manifest, with respect to the act approved March 3, 1865, that prudence and wisdom alike required that jurisdiction over all cases concerning the free enjoyment of the immunities and rights of citizenship, as well as the protection of person and property, should be conferred upon some tribunal in every State or district where the ordinary course of judicial proceedings was interrupted by the rebellion, and until the same should be fully restored. At that time, therefore, an urgent necessity existed for the passage of some such law. Now, however, war has substantially ceased; the ordinary course of judicial proceedings is no longer interrupted; the courts, both State and Federal, are in full, complete, and successful operation, and through them every person, regardless of race and color, is entitled to and can be heard. The protection granted to the white citizen is already conferred by law upon the freedman; strong and stringent guards, by way of penalties and punishments, are thrown around his person and property, and it is believed that ample protection will be afforded him by due process of law, without resort to the dangerous expedient of "military tribunals," now that the war has been brought to a close. The necessity no longer existing for such tribunals, which had their origin in the war, grave objections to their continuance must present themselves to the minds of all reflecting and dispassionate men. Independently of the danger, in representative republics, of conferring upon the military, in time of peace, extraordinary powers—so carefully guarded against by the patriots and statesmen of the earlier days of the Republic, so frequently the ruin of Governments founded upon the same free principles, and subversive of the rights and liberties of the citizen—the question of practical economy earnestly commends itself to the consideration of the law-making power. With an immense debt already burdening the incomes of the industrial and laboring classes, a due regard for their interests, so inseparably connected with the welfare of the country, should prompt us to rigid economy and retrenchment,.and influence us to abstain from all legislation that would unnecessarily increase the public indebtedness. Tested by this rule of sound political wisdom, I can see no reason for the establishment of the "military jurisdiction" conferred upon the officials of the bureau by the fourteenth section of the bill.

By the laws of the United States and of the different States, competent courts, Federal and State, have been established, and are now in full practical operation. By means of these civil tribunals ample redress is afforded for all private wrongs, whether to the person or the property of the citizen, without denial or unnecessary delay. They are open to all, without regard to color or race. I feel well assured that it will be better to trust the rights, privileges, and immunities of the citizen to tribunals thus established, and presided over by competent and impartial judges, bound by fixed rules of law and evidence, and where the right of trial by jury is guarantied and secured, than to the caprice or judgment of an officer of the bureau, who, it is possible, may be entirely ignorant of the principles that underlie the just administration of the law. There is danger, too, that conflict of jurisdiction will frequently arise between the civil courts and these military tribunals, each having concurrent jurisdiction over the person and the cause of action, the one judicature administered and controlled by civil law, the other by the military. How is the conflict to be settled, and who is to determine between the two tribunals when it arises? In my opinion, it is wise to guard against such conflict by leaving to the courts and juries the protection of all civil rights and the redress of all civil grievances.

The fact cannot be denied that, since the actual cessation of hostilities, many acts of violence—such, perhaps, as had never been witnessed in their previous history—have occurred in the States involved in the recent rebellion. I believe, however, that public sentiment will sustain me in the assertion that such deeds of wrong are not confined to any particular State or section, but are manifested over the entire country, demonstrating that the cause that produced them does not depend upon any particular locality, but is the result of the agitation and derangement incident to a long and bloody civil war. While the prevalence of such disorders must be greatly deplored, their occasional and temporary occurrence would seem to furnish no necessity for the extension of the bureau beyond the period fixed in the original act.

Besides the objections which I have thus briefly stated, I may urge upon your consideration the additional reason, that recent develop-

ments in regard to the practical operations of the bureau in many of the States show that in numerous instances it is used by its agents as a means of promoting their individual advantage, and that the freedmen are employed for the advancement of the personal ends of the officers instead of their own improvement and welfare, thus confirming the fears originally entertained by many, that the continuation of such a bureau for any unnecessary length of time would inevitably result in fraud, corruption, and oppression. It is proper to state that in cases of this character investigations have been promptly ordered, and the offender punished whenever his guilt has been satisfactorily established.

As another reason against the necessity of the legislation contemplated by this measure, reference may be had to the "civil rights bill," now a law of the land, and which will be faithfully executed so long as it shall remain unrepealed and may not be declared unconstitutional by courts of competent jurisdiction. By that act is enacted "that all persons born in the United States, and not subject to any foreign Power, excluding Indians not taxed, are hereby declared to be citizens of the United States; and such citizens, of every race and color, without regard to any previous condition of slavery or involuntary servitude, except as a punishment for crime whereof the party shall have been duly convicted, shall have the same right, in every State and Territory in the United States, to make and enforce contracts, to sue, be parties, and give evidence, to inherit, purchase, lease, sell, hold, and convey real and personal property, and to full and equal benefit of all laws and proceedings for the security of person and property, as is enjoyed by white citizens, and shall be subject to like punishment, pains, and penalties, and to none other, any law, statute, ordinance, regulation, or custom to the contrary notwithstanding."

By the provisions of the act full protection is afforded, through the district courts of the United States, to all persons injured, and whose privileges, as thus declared, are in any way impaired; and heavy penalties are denounced against the person who wilfully violates the law. I need not state that that law did not receive my approval; yet its remedies are far more preferable than those proposed in the present bill, the one being civil and the other military.

By the sixth section of the bill herewith returned, certain proceedings by which the lands in the "parishes of St. Helena and St. Luke, South Carolina," were sold and bid in, and afterwards disposed of by the tax commissioners, are ratified and confirmed. By the seventh, eighth, ninth, tenth, and eleventh sections provisions by law are made for the disposal of the lands thus acquired to a particular class of citizens. While the quieting of titles is deemed very important and desirable, the discrimination made in the bill seems objectionable, as does also the attempt to confer upon the commissioners judicial powers, by which citizens of the United States are to be deprived of their property in a mode contrary to that provision of the Constitution which declares that no person "shall be deprived of life, liberty, or property without due process of law." As a general principle, such legislation is unsafe, unwise, partial, and unconstitutional. It may deprive persons of their property who are equally deserving objects of the nation's bounty as those whom, by this legislation, Congress seeks to benefit. The title to the land thus to be portioned out to a favored class of citizens must depend upon the regularity of the tax sales, under the law as it existed at the time of the sale, and no subsequent legislation can give validity to the rights thus acquired, as against the original claimants. The attention of Congress is therefore invited to a more mature consideration of the measures proposed in these sections of the bill.

In conclusion, I again urge upon Congress the danger of class legislation, so well calculated to keep the public mind in a state of uncertain expectation, disquiet, and restlessness, and to encourage interested hopes and fears that the national Government will continue to furnish to classes of citizens in the several States means for support and maintenance, regardless of whether they pursue a life of indolence or of labor, and regardless also of the constitutional limitations of the national authority in times of peace and tranquillity.

The bill is herewith returned to the House of Representatives, in which it originated, for its final action.　　ANDREW JOHNSON.

WASHINGTON, D. C., *July* 16, 1866.

## Copy of the Vetoed Bill.

AN ACT to continue in force and to amend "An act to establish a Bureau for the relief of Freedmen and Refugees," and for other purposes.

*Be it enacted, &c.*, That the act to establish a Bureau for the relief of Freedmen and Refugees, approved March third, eighteen hundred and sixty-five, shall continue in force for the term of two years from and after the passage of this act.

SEC. 2. That the supervision and care of said bureau shall extend to all loyal refugees and freedmen, so far as the same shall be necessary to enable them as speedily as practicable to become self-supporting citizens of the United States, and to aid them in making the freedom conferred by proclamation of the Commander-in-Chief, by emancipation under the laws of States, and by constitutional amendment, available to them and beneficial to the Republic.

SEC. 3. That the President shall, by and with the advice and consent of the Senate, appoint two assistant commissioners, in addition to those authorized by the act to which this is an amendment, who shall give like bonds and receive the same annual salaries provided in said act; and each of the assistant commissioners of the bureau shall have charge of one district containing such refugees or freedmen, to be assigned him by the Commissioner, with the approval of the President. And the Commissioner shall, under the direction of the President, and so far as the same shall be, in his judgment, necessary for the efficient and economical administration of the affairs of the bureau, appoint such agents, clerks, and assistants as may be required for the proper conduct of the bureau. Military officers or enlisted men may be detailed for service and assigned to duty under this act; and the President may, if in his judgment safe and judicious so to do, detail from the Army all the officers and agents of this bureau; but no officer so assigned shall have increase of pay or allowances. Each agent or clerk, not heretofore authorized by law, not being a military officer, shall have an annual salary of not less than $500, nor more than $1,200, according to the service required of him. And it shall be the duty of the Commissioner, when it can be done consistently with public interest, to appoint, as assistant commissioners, agents, and clerks, such men as have proved their loyalty by faithful service in the armies of the Union during the rebellion. And all persons appointed to service under this act and the act to which this is an amendment, shall be so far deemed in the military service of the United States as to be under the military jurisdiction and entitled to the military protection of the Government while in discharge of the duties of their office.

SEC. 4. That officers of the Veteran Reserve Corps or of the volunteer service, now on duty in the Freedmen's Bureau as assistant commissioners, agents, medical officers, or in other capacities, whose regiments or corps have been or may hereafter be mustered out of service, may be retained upon such duty as officers of said bureau, with the same compensation as is now provided by law for their respective grades; and the Secretary of War shall have power to fill vacancies until other officers can be detailed in their places without detriment to the public service.

SEC. 5. That the second section of the act to which this is an amendment shall be deemed to authorize the Secretary of War to issue such medical stores or other supplies and transportation, and afford such medical or other aid as may be needful for the purposes named in said section: *Provided*, That no person shall be deemed "destitute," "suffering," or "dependent upon the Government for support," within the meaning of this act, who is able to find employment, and could, by proper industry or exertion, avoid such destitution, suffering, or dependence.

SEC. 6 Whereas, by the provisions of an act approved February sixth, eighteen hundred and sixty-three, entitled "An act to amend an act entitled 'An act for the collection of direct taxes in insurrectionary districts within the United States, and for other purposes,' approved June seventh, eighteen hundred and sixty-two," certain lands in the parishes of St. Helena and St. Luke, South Carolina, were bid in by the United States at public tax sales, and by the limitation of said act the time of redemption of said lands has expired; and whereas, in accordance with instructions issued by President Lincoln on the sixteenth day of September, eighteen hundred and sixty-three, to the United States direct tax commissioners for South Carolina, certain lands bid in by the United States in the parish of St. Helena, in said State, were in part sold by the said tax commissioners to "heads of families of the African race," in parcels of not more than twenty acres to each purchaser; and whereas, under the said instructions, the said tax commissioners did also set apart as "school farms" certain parcels of land in said parish, numbered on their plats from one to thirty-three, inclusive, making an aggregate of six thousand acres, more or less: Therefore, *be it further enacted*, That the sales made to "heads of families of the African race," under the instructions of President Lincoln to the United States direct tax commissioners for South Carolina, of date of September sixteenth, eighteen hundred and sixty-three, are hereby confirmed and established; and all leases which have been made to such "heads of families" by said direct tax commissioners, shall be changed into certificates of sale in all cases wherein the lease provides for such substitution; and all the lands now remaining unsold, which come within the same designation, being eight thousand acres, more or less, shall be disposed of according to said instructions.

SEC. 7. That all other lands bid in by the United States at tax sales, being thirty-eight thousand acres, more or less, and now in the hands of the said tax commissioners as the property of the United States, in the parishes of St. Helena and St. Luke, excepting the "school farms," as specified in the preceding section, and so much as may be necessary for military and naval purposes at Hilton Head, Bay Point, and Land's End, and excepting also the city of Port Royal, on St. Helena island, and the town of Beaufort, shall be disposed of in parcels of twenty acres, at one dollar and fifty cents per acre, to such persons, and to such only, as have acquired and are now occupying lands under and agreeably to the provisions of General Sherman's special field order, dated at Savannah, Georgia, January sixteen, eighteen hundred and sixty-five, and the remaining lands, if any, shall be disposed of in like manner to such persons as had acquired lands agreeably to the said order of General Sherman, but who have been dispossessed by the restoration of the same to former owners: *Provided*, That the lands sold in compliance with the provisions of this and the preceding section shall not be alienated by their purchasers within six years from and after the passage of this act.

SEC. 8. That the "school farms" in the parish of St. Helena, South Carolina, shall be sold, subject to any leases of the same, by the said tax commissioners, at public auction, on or before the first day of January, eighteen hundred and sixty-seven, at not less than ten dollars per acre; and the lots in the city of Port Royal, as laid down by the said tax commissioners, and the lots and houses in the town of Beaufort, which are still held in like manner, shall be sold at public auction; and the proceeds of said sales, after paying expenses of the surveys and sales, shall be invested in United States bonds, the interest of which shall be appropriated, under the direction of the Commissioner, to the support of schools, without distinction of color or race, on the islands in the parishes of St. Helena and St. Luke.

SEC. 9. That the assistant commissioners for South Carolina and Georgia are hereby authorized to examine all claims to lands in their respective States which are claimed under the provisions of General Sherman's special field order, and to give each person having a valid claim a warrant upon the direct tax commissioners for South Carolina for twenty acres of land; and the

said direct tax commissioners shall issue to every person, or to his or her heirs, but in no case to any assigns, presenting such warrant, a lease of twenty acres of land, as provided for in section seven, for the term of six years; but at any time thereafter, upon the payment of a sum not exceeding one dollar and fifty cents per acre, the person holding such lease shall be entitled to a certificate of sale of said tract of twenty acres from the direct tax commissioner or such officer as may be authorized to issue the same; but no warrant shall be held valid longer than two years after the issue of the same.

SEC. 10. That the direct tax commissioners for South Carolina are hereby authorized and required, at the earliest day practicable, to survey the lands designated in section seven into lots of twenty acres each, with proper metes and bounds distinctly marked, so that the several tracts shall be convenient in form, and as near as practicable have an average of fertility and woodland; and the expense of such surveys shall be paid from the proceeds of sales of said lands, or, if sooner required, out of any moneys received for other lands on these islands, sold by the United States for taxes, and now in the hands of the direct tax commissioners.

SEC. 11. That restoration of lands occupied by freedmen under General Sherman's field order dated at Savannah, Georgia, January sixteenth, eighteen hundred and sixty-five, shall not be made until after the crops of the present year shall have been gathered by the occupants of said lands, nor until a fair compensation shall have been made to them by the former owners of such lands, or their legal representatives, for all improvements or betterments erected or constructed thereon, and after due notice of the same being done shall have been given by the assistant commissioner.

SEC. 12. That the Commissioner shall have power to seize, hold, use, lease, or sell all buildings, and tenements, and any lands appertaining to the same, or otherwise, formerly held under color of title by the late so-called Confederate States, and not heretofore disposed of by the United States, and any buildings or lands held in trust for the same by any person or persons, and to use the same or appropriate the proceeds derived therefrom to the education of the freed people; and whenever the bureau shall cease to exist, such of said so-called Confederate States as shall have made provision for the education of their citizens without distinction of color shall receive the sum remaining unexpended of such sales or rentals, which shall be distributed among said States for educational purposes in proportion to their population.

SEC. 13. That the Commissioner of this bureau shall at all times co-operate with private benevolent associations of citizens in aid of freedmen, and with agents and teachers, duly accredited and appointed by them, and shall hire or provide by lease, buildings for purposes of education whenever such associations shall, without cost to the Government, provide suitable teachers and means of instruction; and he shall furnish such protection as may be required for the safe conduct of such schools.

SEC. 14. That in every State or district where

the ordinary course of judicial proceedings has been interrupted by the rebellion, and until the same shall be fully restored, and in every State or district whose constitutional relations to the Government have been practically discontinued by the rebellion, and until such State shall have been restored in such relations, and shall be duly represented in the Congress of the United States, the right to make and enforce contracts, to sue, be parties, and give evidence, to inherit, purchase, lease, sell, hold, and convey real and personal property, and to have full and equal benefit of all laws and proceedings concerning personal liberty, personal security, and the acquisition, enjoyment, and disposition of estate, real and personal, including the constitutional right to bear arms, shall be secured to and enjoyed by all the citizens of such State or district without respect to race or color, or previous condition of slavery. And whenever in either of said States or districts the ordinary course of judicial proceedings has been interrupted by the rebellion, and until the same shall be fully restored, and until such State shall have been restored in its constitutional relations to the Government, and shall be duly represented in the Congress of the United States, the President shall, through the Commissioner and the officers of the bureau, and under such rules and regulations as the President, through the Secretary of War, shall prescribe, extend military protection and have military jurisdiction over all cases and questions concerning the free enjoyment of such immunities and rights; and no penalty or punishment for any violation of law shall be imposed or permitted because of race or color, or previous condition of slavery, other or greater than the penalty or punishment to which white persons may be liable by law for the like offense. But the jurisdiction conferred by this section upon the officers of the bureau shall not exist in any State where the ordinary course of judicial proceedings has not been interrupted by the rebellion; and shall cease in every State when the courts of the State and the United States are not disturbed in the peaceable course of justice, and after such State shall be fully restored in its constitutional relations to the Government, and shall be duly represented in the Congress of the United States.

SEC 15. That all officers, agents, and employees of this bureau, before entering upon the duties of their office, shall take the oath prescribed in the first section of the act to which this is an amendment; and all acts or parts of acts inconsistent with the provisions of this act are hereby repealed.

The votes on this bill were:

May 29—The HOUSE passed its bill, differing in some details from the above—yeas 96, nays 32, as follow :

YEAS—Messrs. Allison, Ames, Anderson, Delos R. Ashley, James M. Ashley, Baker, Baldwin, Banks, Baxter, Beaman, Bidwell, Blaine, Bromwell, Buckland, Reader W. Clarke, Sidney Clarke, Cobb, Cook, Cullom, Dawes, Defrees, Deming, Dixon. Dodge, Donnelly, Dumont, Eckley, Eggleston, Eliot, Farquhar, Ferry, Garfield, Abner C. Harding, Hart, Henderson, Higby, Holmes, Hooper, Asahel W. Hubbard, Chester D. Hubbard, Demas Hubbard, jr., John H. Hubbard, James R. Hubbell, Ingersoll. Jenckes, Julian, Kelley, Latham, George V. Lawrence, William Lawrence, Loan, Longyear, Lynch. Marston, McClurg, McKee, McRuer, Mercur, Moorhead, Morrill, Morris, Myers, O'Neill, Orth, Paine, Patter-

son, Perham, Pike, Plants, Price, Alexander H. Rice, John H. Rice, Rollins, Sawyer, Schenck, Scofield, Shellabarger, Sloan, Starr, Stevens, Stillwell, Thayer, Francis Thomas, Trowbridge, Upson, Van Aernam, Burt Van Horn, Ward, Henry D. Washburn, William B. Washburn, Welker, Whaley, Williams, James F. Wilson, Stephen F. Wilson, Woodbridge—96.

NAYS—Messrs. Ancona, Bergen, Chanler, Darling, Davis, Dawson, Eldridge, Glossbrenner, Goodyear, Grider, Hale, Aaron Harding, Hogan, Edwin N. Hubbell, James M. Humphrey, Kuykendall, Le Blond, Marshall, Marvin, McCullough, Niblack, Nicholson, Radford, S. J. Randall, Raymond, Ritter, Ross, Sitgreaves, Strouss, Taylor, Trimble, Wright —32.

June 26—SENATE amended and passed it, there being no division on the final vote. A motion to postpone it till the next December was lost— yeas 6, (Messrs. Buckalew, Davis, Doolittle, Guthrie, Hendricks, Riddle,) nays 27.

July 2—In SENATE, the report of the Committee of Conference, being the above law, was agreed to, without a division.

July 3—IN HOUSE, a motion to table the report was lost—yeas 25, nays 102. The yeas were :

YEAS—Messrs. Ancona, Boyer, Coffroth, Dawson, Eldridge, Finck, Glossbrenner, Aaron Harding, Johnson, Kerr, Le Blond, Marshall, Niblack, Noell, Ritter, Rogers, Ross, Rousseau, Shanklin, Sitgreaves, Strouse, Taber, Taylor, Thornton, Trimble.

It was then agreed to.

July 16—The bill was vetoed.

Same day—The HOUSE re-passed the bill— yeas 103, nays 33, as follow :

YEAS—Messrs. Alley, Allison, Ames, Anderson, Delos R. Ashley. James M. Ashley, Baker, Banks, Barker, Baxter, Benjamin, Bidwell, Bingham, Boutwell, Bromwell, Buckland, Bundy, Reader W. Clarke, Sidney Clarke, Cobb, Conkling Cook. Dawes, Defrees, Delano, Deming, Donnelly, Driggs, Eckley, Eggleston, Eliot, Ferry, Garfield, Grinnell, Griswold, Hale, Hart, Henderson, Higby, Holmes, Hooper, Hotchkiss, Asahel W. Hubbard, Chester D. Hubbard, John H. Hubbard, James R. Hubbell, Hulburd, Julian, Kasson, Kelley, Ketcham, Laflin, Latham, George V. Lawrence, William Lawrence, Loan, Longyear, Lynch, Marston. Marvin, McClurg, McKee, McRuer, Mercur, Miller, Moorhead, Morrill, Morris, Moulton, Myers, Newell, O'Neill, Orth, Perham, Pike, Plants, Price, William H. Randall, Alexander H. Rice, Rollins, Sawyer, Scofield, Shellabarger, Spalding, Stevens, Thayer, John L. Thomas, jr., Trowbridge, Van Aernam, Burt Van Horn, Robert T. Van Horn, Ward, Warner, Ellihu B. Washburne, William B. Washburn, Welker, Wentworth, Whaley, Williams, James F. Wilson, Stephen F. Wilson, Windom, Woodbridge—103.

NAYS—Messrs. Ancona, Boyer, Dawson, Eldridge. Finck, Glossbrenner, Grider, Aaron Harding, Hogan, J. M. Humphrey, Johnson, Kerr, Kuykendall, LeBlond, Marshall, Niblack, Nicholson, Noell, Phelps, Samuel J. Randall, Raymond, Ritter, Rogers, Ross, Rousseau, Shanklin, Sitgreaves. Taber, Taylor, Thornton, Trimble, Henry D. Washburn, Wright— 33.

Same day—The SENATE re-passed it—yeas 33, nays 12, as follow :

YEAS—Messrs. Anthony, Brown, Chandler, Clark, Conness, Cragin, Creswell, Edmunds, Fessenden, Foster, Grimes, Harris, Henderson, Howard, Howe, Kirkwood, Lane of Indiana, Morgan, Morrill, Nye, Poland, Pomeroy, Ramsey, Sherman, Sprague, Stewart, Sumner, Trumbull, Wade, Willey, Williams, Wilson, Yates—33.

NAYS—Messrs. Buckalew, Davis, Doolittle, Guthrie, Hendricks, Johnson, McDougall, Nesmith, Norton, Riddle, Saulsbury, Van Winkle—12.

Whereupon the PRESIDENT of the Senate declared the bill a law.

### Restoring Tennessee to her Relations to the Union.

1866, March 5—Mr. BINGHAM reported from the Select Joint Committee on Reconstruction a joint resolution concerning the State of Tennessee, (for which see Political Manual for 1866. p. 105, 106.) No vote was taken upon it.

1866, July 20—The HOUSE passed the resolution in these words :

Joint Resolution declaring Tennessee again entitled to Senators and Representatives in Congress.

Whereas the State of Tennessee has in good faith ratified the article of amendment to the Constitution of the United States, proposed by the Thirty-Ninth Congress to the Legislatures of the several States, and has also shown to the satisfaction of Congress, by a proper spirit of obedience in the body of her people, her return to her due allegiance to the Government, laws, and authority of the United States: Therefore,

*Be it resolved by the Senate and House of Representatives of the United States of America in Congress assembled,* That the State of Tennessee is hereby restored to her former proper, practical relations to the Union, and is again entitled to be represented by Senators and Representatives in Congress, duly elected and qualified, upon their taking the oaths of office required by existing laws.

The preamble was agreed to—yeas 86, nays 48; and the resolution passed—yeas 126, nays 12, as follow:

YEAS—Messrs. Allison, Ames, *Ancona,* George W. Anderson, Delos R. Ashley, James M. Ashley, Baker, Banks, Baxter, Bidwell, Bingham, *Boyer,* Bromwell, Buckland, Bundy, Reader W. Clarke, Sidney Clarke, Cobb, Colfax, Conkling, Davis, Dawes, *Dawson,* Defrees, Delano, Deming, Donnelly, Driggs, Eckley, Eggleston, *Eldridge,* Farnsworth, Farquhar, Ferry, *Finck,* Garfield, *Glossbrenner, Aaron Harding,* Abner C. Harding, Hart, *Hogan,* Holmes, Hooper, Hotchkiss, Asahel W. Hubbard, Chester D. Hubbard, John H. Hubbard, James R. Hubbell, Hulburd, *James M. Humphrey,* Ingersoll, *Johnson,* Kasson, *Kerr,* Ketcham, Koontz, Kuykendall, Laflin, Latham, George V. Lawrence, William Lawrence, Lynch, Marston, *McCullough,* McRuer, Mercur, Miller, Moorhead, Morrill, Morris, Moulton, Myers, Newell, *Niblack, Nicholson, Noell,* O'Neill, Orth, Patterson, Perham, Phelps, Pike, Plants, Price, *Radford, Samuel J. Randall,* William H. Randall, Raymond, Alexander H. Rice, John H. Rice, *Ritter, Rogers,* Rollins, *Ross,* Rousseau, Sawyer, Schenck, Scofield, Shellabarger, *Sitgreaves,* Spalding, Stevens, *Strouse,* Taber, Taylor, Thayer, Francis Thomas, John L. Thomas, jr., *Thornton, Trimble,* Trowbridge, Van Aernam, Burt Van Horn, Robert T. Van Horn, Ward, Warner, Henry D. Washburn, William B. Washburn, Welker, Wentworth, Whaley, James F. Wilson, Stephen F. Wilson, Windom, Woodbridge, *Wright—126.*

NAYS—Messrs. Alley, Benjamin, Boutwell, Eliot, Higby, Jenckes, Julian, Kelley, Loan, McClurg, Paine, Williams—12.

July 23, 1866—The SENATE amended and passed it in these words:

Joint Resolution restoring Tennessee to her relations to the Union.

Whereas, in the year eighteen hundred and sixty-one, the government of the State of Tennessee was seized upon and taken possession of by persons in hostility to the United States, and the inhabitants of said State, in pursuance of an act of Congress, were declared to be in a state of insurrection against the United States; and whereas said State government can only be restored to its former political relations in the Union by the consent of the law-making power of the United States; and whereas the people of said State did, on the twenty-second day of February, eighteen hundred and sixty-five, by a large popular vote, adopt and ratify a constitution of government whereby slavery was abolished and all ordinances and laws of secession, and debts contracted under the same, were declared void; and whereas a State government has been organized under said constitution which has ratified the amendment to the Constitution

of the United States abolishing slavery, also the amendment proposed by the Thirty-Ninth Congress, and has done other acts proclaiming and denoting loyalty: Therefore,

*Be it resolved by the Senate and House of Representatives of the United States of America in Congress assembled,* That the State of Tennessee is hereby restored to her former proper, practical relations to the Union, and is again entitled to be represented by Senators and Representatives in Congress.

The vote was—yeas 28, nays 4, as follow:

YEAS—Messrs. Anthony, Chandler, Clark, Conness, *Cowan,* Creswell, *Doolittle,* Edmunds, Foster, *Hendricks,* Howard, Howe, Lane, Morgan, Morrill, *Nesmith,* Nye, Poland, Pomeroy, Sprague, Stewart, Trumbull, Van Winkle, Wade, Willey, Williams, Wilson, Yates—28.

NAYS—Messrs. Brown, *Buckalew, McDougall,* Sumner—4.

July 23—The HOUSE agreed to the Senate amendments, yeas 93, nays 26, as follow:

YEAS—Messrs. Allison, Ames, Anderson, Delos R. Ashley, Baker, Banks, Barker, Baxter, Benjamin, Bidwell, Bingham, Boutwell, Bromwell, Broomall, Buckland, Reader W. Clarke, Cobb, Conkling, Defrees, Dixon, Donnelly, Driggs, Eckley, Eggleston, Eliot, Farnsworth, Farquhar, Ferry, Garfield, Abner C. Harding, Hart, Hayes, Higby, Holmes, Hooper, Hotchkiss, Asahel W. Hubbard, Chester D. Hubbard, John H. Hubbard, James R. Hubbell, Hulburd, Ingersoll, Julian, Kelley, Ketcham, Koontz, Kuykendall, Laflin, George V Lawrence, William Lawrence, Loan, Lynch, Marston, McClurg, McRuer, Mercur, Miller, Moorhead, Morrill, Morris, Moulton, Myers, Newell, O'Neill, Orth, Paine, Perham, Plants, Price, William H. Randall, Alexander H. Rice, John H. Rice, Rollins, Sawyer, Schenck, Scofield, Shellabarger, Spalding, Stevens, John L. Thomas, jr., Trowbridge, Van Aernam, Burt Van Horn, Robert T. Van Horn, Ward, Welker, Wentworth, Whaley, Williams, James F. Wilson, Stephen F. Wilson, Windom, Woodbridge—93.

NAYS—Messrs. *Ancona, Bergen, Boyer, Dawson, Eldridge, Finck, Glossbrenner, Aaron Harding,* Jenckes, *Johnson,* Latham, *Le Blond, Marshall, Niblack, Nicholson, Radford, Samuel J. Randall,* Raymond, *Ritter, Ross, Shanklin, Strouse, Taber, Taylor, Thornton, Trimble—26.*

July 24—The PRESIDENT approved the bill, sending to the House this message:

*To the House of Representatives:*

The following "joint resolution, restoring Tennessee to her relations to the Union," was last evening presented for my approval:

"Whereas, in the year eighteen hundred and sixty-one, the government of the State of Tennessee was seized upon and taken possession of by persons in hostility to the United States, and the inhabitants of said State, in pursuance of an act of Congress, were declared to be in a state of insurrection against the United States; and whereas said State government can only be restored to its former political relations in the Union by the consent of the law-making power of the United States; and whereas the people of said State did, on the twenty-second day of February, eighteen hundred and sixty-five, by a large popular vote, adopt and ratify a constitution of government whereby slavery was abolished and all ordinances and laws of secession, and debts contracted under the same, were declared void; and whereas a State government has been organized under said constitution, which has ratified the amendment to the Constitution of the United States abolishing slavery, also the amendment proposed by the Thirty-Ninth Congress, and has done other acts proclaiming and denoting loyalty; Therefore,

"*Be it resolved by the Senate and House of Representatives of the United States in Congress assembled,* That the State of Tennessee is hereby restored to her former practical relations to the Union, and is again entitled to be represented by Senators and Representatives in Congress."

The preamble simply consists of statements, some of which are assumed, while the resolution is merely a declaration of opinion. It comprises no legislation, nor does it confer any power which is binding upon the respective Houses, the Executive, or the States. It does not admit to their seats in Congress the Senators and Representatives from the State of Tennessee; for, notwithstanding the passage of the resolution, each House, in the exercise of the constitutional right to judge for itself of the elections, returns, and qualifications of its members, may, at its discretion, admit them, or continue to exclude them. If a joint resolution of this character were necessary and binding as a condition precedent to the admission of members of Congress, it would happen, in the event of a veto by the Executive, that Senators and Representatives could only be admitted to the halls of legislation by a two-thirds vote of each of the two Houses.

Among other reasons recited in the preamble for the declarations contained in the resolution is the ratification, by the State government of Tennessee, of "the amendment to the Constitution of the United States abolishing slavery, and also the amendment proposed by the Thirty-Ninth Congress." If, as is also declared in the preamble, "said State government can only be restored to its former political relations in the Union by the consent of the law-making power of the United States," it would really seem to follow that the joint resolution which, at this late day, has received the sanction of Congress, should have been passed, approved, and placed on the statute books before any amendment to the Constitution was submitted to the Legislature of Tennessee for ratification. Otherwise, the inference is plainly deducible that while, in the opinion of Congress, the people of a State may be too strongly disloyal to be entitled to representation, they may, nevertheless, during the suspension of their "former proper practical relations to the Union," have an equally potent voice with other and loyal States in propositions to amend the Constitution, upon which so essentially depend the stability, prosperity, and very existence of the nation.

A brief reference to my annual message of the 4th of December last will show the steps taken by the Executive for the restoration to their constitutional relations to the Union of the States that had been affected by the rebellion.

Upon the cessation of active hostilities, provisional governors were appointed, conventions called, Governors elected by the people, Legislatures assembled, and Senators and Representatives chosen to the Congress of the United States. At the same time the courts of the United States were reopened, the blockade removed, the customhouses re-established, and postal operations resumed. The amendment to the Constitution abolishing slavery forever within the limits of the country was also submitted to the States, and they were thus invited to, and did participate in its ratification, thus exercising the highest functions pertaining to a State. In addition, nearly all of these States, through their conventions and

Legislatures, had adopted and ratified constitutions "of government, whereby slavery was abolished, and all ordinances and laws of secession, and debts contracted under the same, were declared void."

So far, then, the political existence of the States and their relations to the Federal Government had been fully and completely recognized and acknowledged by the executive department of the Government; and the completion of the work of restoration, which had progressed so favorably, was submitted to Congress, upon which devolved all questions pertaining to the admission to their seats of the Senators and Representatives chosen from the States whose people had engaged in the rebellion.

All these steps had been taken, when, on the fourth day of December, eighteen hundred and sixty-five, the Thirty-Ninth Congress assembled. Nearly eight months have elapsed since that time; and no other plan of restoration having been proposed by Congress for the measures instituted by the Executive, it is now declared in the joint resolution submitted for my approval, "that the State of Tennessee is hereby restored to her former proper practical relations to the Union, and is again entitled to be represented by Senators and Representatives in Congress." Thus, after the lapse of nearly eight months, Congress proposes to pave the way to the admission to representation of one of the eleven States whose people arrayed themselves in rebellion against the constitutional authority of the Federal Government.

Earnestly desiring to remove every cause of further delay, whether real or imaginary, on the part of Congress to the admission to seats of loyal Senators and Representatives from the State of Tennessee, I have, notwithstanding the anomalous character of this proceeding, affixed my signature to the resolution. My approval, however, is not to be construed as an acknowledgment of the right of Congress to pass laws preliminary to the admission of duly qualified representatives from any of the States. Neither is it to be considered as committing me to all the statements made in the preamble, some of which are, in my opinion, without foundation in fact, especially the assertion that the State of Tennessee has ratified the amendment to the Constitution of the United States proposed by the Thirty-Ninth Congress. No official notice of such ratification has been received by the Executive, or filed in the Department of State; on the contrary, unofficial information from most reliable sources induces the belief that the amendment has not yet been constitutionally sanctioned by the Legislature of Tennessee. The right of each House, under the Constitution, to judge of the elections, returns, and qualifications of its own members is undoubted, and my approval or disapproval of the resolution could not in the slightest degree increase or diminish the authority in this respect conferred upon the two branches of Congress.

In conclusion, I cannot too earnestly repeat my recommendation for the admission of Tennessee, and all other States, to a fair and equal participation in national legislation, when they present themselves in the persons of loyal Sena-

tors and Representatives, who can comply with all the requirements of the Constitution and the laws. By this means, harmony and reconciliation will be effected, the practical relations of all the States to the Federal Government re-established, and the work of restoration, inaugurated upon the termination of the war, successfully completed.                ANDREW JOHNSON.
WASHINGTON, D. C., *July* 24, 1866.

### Veto of the District of Columbia Suffrage Bill, January 7, 1867.

*To the Senate of the United States:*

I have received and considered a bill entitled "An act to regulate the elective franchise in the District of Columbia," passed by the Senate on the 13th of December, and by the House of Representatives on the succeeding day. It was presented for my approval on the 26th ultimo, six days after the adjournment of Congress, and is now returned with my objections to the Senate, in which House it originated.

Measures having been introduced, at the commencement of the first session of the present Congress, for the extension of the elective franchise to persons of color in the District of Columbia, steps were taken by the corporate authorities of Washington and Georgetown to ascertain and make known the opinion of the people of the two cities upon a subject so immediately affecting their welfare as a community. The question was submitted to the people at special elections, held in the month of December, 1865, when the qualified voters of Washington and Georgetown, with great unanimity of sentiment, expressed themselves opposed to the contemplated legislation. In Washington, in a vote of 6,556—the largest, with but two exceptions, ever polled in that city—only thirty-five ballots were cast for negro suffrage; while in Georgetown, in an aggregate of 813 votes—a number considerably in excess of the average vote at the four preceding annual elections—but one was given in favor of the proposed extension of the elective franchise. As these elections seem to have been conducted with entire fairness, the result must be accepted as a truthful expression of the opinion of the people of the District upon the question which evoked it. Possessing, as an organized community, the same popular rights as the inhabitants of a State or Territory to make known their will upon matters which affect their social and political condition, they could have selected no more appropriate mode of memorializing Congress upon the subject of this bill than through the suffrages of their qualified voters.

Entirely disregarding the wishes of the people of the District of Columbia, Congress has deemed it right and expedient to pass the measure now submitted for my signature. It therefore becomes the duty of the Executive, standing between the legislation of the one and the will of the other, fairly expressed, to determine whether he should approve the bill, and thus aid in placing upon the statute-books of the nation a law against which the people to whom it is to apply have solemnly and with such unanimity protested, or whether he should return it with his objections, in the hope that, upon reconsideration,

Congress, acting as the representatives of the inhabitants of the seat of Government, will permit them to regulate a purely local question as to them may seem best suited to their interests and condition.

The District of Columbia was ceded to the United States by Maryland and Virginia, in order that it might become the permanent seat of Government of the United States. Accepted by Congress, it at once became subject to the " exclusive legislation" for which provision is made in the Federal Constitution. It should be borne in mind, however, that in exercising its functions as the law-making power of the District of Columbia, the authority of the National Legislature is not without limit, but that Congress is bound to observe the letter and spirit of the Constitution, as well in the enactment of local laws for the seat of Government as in legislation common to the entire Union. Were it to be admitted that the right "to exercise exclusive legislation in all cases whatsoever" conferred upon Congress unlimited power within the District of Columbia, bills of attainder and *ex post facto* laws might be passed, and titles of nobility granted within its boundaries. Laws might be made "respecting an establishment of religion, or prohibiting the free exercise thereof; or abridging the freedom of speech or of the press; or the right of the people peaceably to assemble and to petition the Government for a redress of grievances." "The right of the people to be secure in their persons, houses, papers, and effects against unreasonable searches and seizures" might with impunity be violated. The right of trial by jury might be denied, excessive bail required, excessive fines imposed, and cruel and unusual punishments inflicted. Despotism would thus reign at the seat of government of a free republic, and, as a place of permanent residence, it would be avoided by all who prefer the blessings of liberty to the mere emoluments of official position.

It should also be remembered that in legislating for the District of Columbia, under the Federal Constitution, the relation of Congress to its inhabitants is analogous to that of a Legislature to the people of a State, under their own local constitution. It does not, therefore, seem to be asking too much that, in matters pertaining to the District, Congress should have a like respect for the will and interest of its inhabitants as is entertained by a State Legislature for the wishes and prosperity of those for whom they legislate. The spirit of our Constitution and the genius of our Government require that, in regard to any law which is to affect and have a permanent bearing upon a people, their will should exert at least a reasonable influence upon those who are acting in the capacity of their legislators. Would, for instance, the Legislature of the State of New York, or of Pennsylvania, or of Indiana, or of any State in the Union, in opposition to the expressed will of a large majority of the people whom they were chosen to represent, arbitrarily force upon them, as voters, all persons of the African or negro race, and make them eligible for office without any other qualification than a certain term of residence within the State? In neither of the States named would the colored population, when acting together, be able to produce any great social or political result. Yet, in New York, before he can vote, the man of color must fulfill conditions that are not required of the white citizen; in Pennsylvania the elective franchise is restricted to white freemen; while in Indiana negroes and mulattoes are expressly excluded from the right of suffrage. Nor does it seem consistent with the principles of right and justice that representatives of States where suffrage is either denied the colored man, or granted to him on qualifications requiring intelligence or property, should compel the people of the District of Columbia to try an experiment which their own constituents have thus far shown an unwillingness to test for themselves. Nor does it accord with our republican ideas that the principle of self government should lose its force when applied to the residents of the District, merely because their legislators are not, like those of the States, responsible, through the ballot, to the people for whom they are the law-making power.

The great object of placing the seat of Government under the exclusive legislation of Congress was to secure the entire independence of the General Government from undue State influence, and to enable it to discharge, without danger of interruption or infringement of its authority, the high functions for which it was created by the people. For this important purpose it was ceded to the United States by Maryland and Virginia, and it certainly never could have been contemplated, as one of the objects to be attained by placing it under the exclusive jurisdiction of Congress, that it would afford to propagandists or political parties a place for an experimental test of their principles and theories. While, indeed, the residents of the seat of Government are not citizens of any State, and are not therefore allowed a voice in the Electoral College, or representation in the councils of the nation, they are, nevertheless, American citizens, entitled as such to every guaranty of the Constitution, to every benefit of the laws, and to every right which pertains to citizens of our common country. In all matters, then, affecting their domestic affairs, the spirit of our democratic form of government demands that their wishes should be consulted and respected, and they taught to feel that, although not permitted practically to participate in national concerns, they are nevertheless under a paternal Government, regardful of their rights, mindful of their wants, and solicitous for their prosperity. It was evidently contemplated that all local questions would be left to their decision, at least to an extent that would not be incompatible with the object for which Congress was granted exclusive legislation over the seat of Government. When the Constitution was yet under consideration, it was assumed by Mr. Madison that its inhabitants would be allowed "a municipal legislature for local purposes, derived from their own suffrages." When, for the first time, Congress, in the year 1800, assembled at Washington, President Adams, in his speech at its opening, reminded the two Houses that it was for them to consider whether the local powers over the District of Columbia, vested by the Consti-

tution in the Congress of the United States, should be immediately exercised, and he asked them to "consider it as the capital of a great nation, advancing with unexampled rapidity in arts, in commerce, in wealth, and in population, and possessing within itself those resources which, if not thrown away or lamentably misdirected, would secure to it a long course of prosperity and self-government." Three years had not elapsed when Congress was called upon to determine the propriety of retroceding to Maryland and Virginia the jurisdiction of the territory which they had respectively relinquished to the Government of the United States. It was urged on the one hand that exclusive jurisdiction was not necessary or useful to the Government; that it deprived the inhabitants of the District of their political rights; that much of the time of Congress was consumed in legislation pertaining to it; that its government was expensive; that Congress was not competent to legislate for the District, because the members were strangers to its local concerns; and that it was an example of a government without representation—an experiment dangerous to the liberties of the States. On the other hand, it was held, among other reasons, and successfully, that the Constitution, the acts of cession of Virginia and Maryland, and the act of Congress accepting the grant, all contemplated the exercise of exclusive legislation by Congress, and that its usefulness, if not its necessity, was inferred from the inconvenience which was felt for want of it by the Congress of the Confederation; that the people themselves, who, it was said, had been deprived of their political rights, had not complained, and did not desire a retrocession; that the evil might be remedied by giving them a representation in Congress when the District should become sufficiently populous, and, in the mean time, a local legislature; that, if the inhabitants had not political rights, they had great political influence; that the trouble and expense of legislating for the District would not be great, but would diminish, and might, in a great measure, be avoided by a local legislature; and that Congress could not retrocede the inhabitants without their consent. Continuing to live substantially under the laws that existed at the time of the cession, and such changes only having been made as were suggested by themselves, the people of the District have not sought, by a local legislature, that which has generally been willingly conceded by the Congress of the nation.

As a general rule, sound policy requires that the Legislature should yield to the wishes of a people, when not inconsistent with the Constitution and the laws. The measures suited to one community might not be well adapted to the condition of another; and the persons best qualified to determine such questions are those whose interests are to be directly affected by any proposed law. In Massachusetts, for instance, male persons are allowed to vote without regard to color, provided they possess a certain degree of intelligence. In a population in that State of 1,231,066, there were, by the census of 1860, only 9,602 persons of color; and of the males over twenty years of age, there were 339,086 white to 2,602 colored. By the same official enumeration, there were in the District of Columbia 60,764 whites to 14,316 persons of the colored race. Since then, however, the population of the District has largely increased, and it is estimated that at the present time there are nearly a hundred thousand whites to thirty thousand negroes. The cause of the augmented numbers of the latter class needs no explanation. Contiguous to Maryland and Virginia, the District, during the war, became a place of refuge for those who escaped from servitude, and it is yet the abiding place of a considerable proportion of those who sought within its limits a shelter from bondage. Until then held in slavery, and denied all opportunities for mental culture, their first knowledge of the Government was acquired when, by conferring upon them freedom, it became the benefactor of their race; the test of their capability for improvement began when, for the first time, the career of free industry and the avenues to intelligence were opened to them. Possessing these advantages but a limited time—the greater number perhaps having entered the District of Columbia during the later years of the war, or since its termination, we may well pause to inquire whether, after so brief a probation, they are as a class capable of an intelligent exercise of the right of suffrage, and qualified to discharge the duties of official position. The people who are daily witnesses of their mode of living, and who have become familiar with their habits of thought, have expressed the conviction that they are not yet competent to serve as electors, and thus become eligible for office in the local governments under which they live. Clothed with the elective franchise, their numbers, already largely in excess of the demand for labor, would be soon increased by an influx from the adjoining States. Drawn from fields where employment is abundant, they would in vain seek it here, and so add to the embarrassments already experienced from the large class of idle persons congregated in the District. Hardly yet capable of forming correct judgments upon the important questions that often make the issues of a political contest, they could readily be made subservient to the purposes of designing persons. While in Massachusetts, under the census of 1860, the proportion of white to colored males over twenty years of age was one hundred and thirty to one, here the black race constitutes nearly one-third of the entire population, whilst the same class surrounds the District on all sides, ready to change their residence at a moment's notice, and with all the facility of a nomadic people, in order to enjoy here, after a short residence, a privilege they find nowhere else. It is within their power in one year to come into the District in such numbers as to have the supreme control of the white race, and to govern them by their own officers, and by the exercise of all the municipal authority, among the rest, of the power of taxation over property in which they have no interest. In Massachusetts, where they have enjoyed the benefits of a thorough educational system, a qualification of intelligence is required, while here suffrage is extended to all, without discrimination, as well to the most incapable, who can prove a residence in the District of one

year, as to those persons of color who, comparatively few in number, are permanent inhabitants, and having given evidence of merit and qualification, are recognized as useful and responsible members of the community. Imposed upon an unwilling people, placed, by the Constitution, under the exclusive legislation of Congress, it would be viewed as an arbitrary exercise of power, and as an indication by the country of the purpose of Congress to compel the acceptance of negro suffrage by the States. It would engender a feeling of opposition and hatred between the two races, which, becoming deep-rooted and ineradicable, would prevent them from living together in a state of mutual friendliness. Carefully avoiding every measure that might tend to produce such a result, and following the clear and well-ascertained popular will, we should assiduously endeavor to promote kindly relations between them, and thus, when that popular will leads the way, prepare for the gradual and harmonious introduction of this new element into the political power of the country.

It cannot be urged that the proposed extension of suffrage in the District of Columbia is necessary to enable persons of color to protect either their interests or their rights. They stand here precisely as they stand in Pennsylvania, Ohio, and Indiana. Here, as elsewhere, in all that pertains to civil rights, there is nothing to distinguish this class of persons from citizens of the United States; for they possess the "full and equal benefit of all laws and proceedings for the security of person and property as is enjoyed by white citizens," and are made "subject to like punishment, pains, and penalties, and to none other, any law, statute, ordinance, regulation, or custom to the contrary notwithstanding." Nor, as has been assumed, are their suffrages necessary to aid a loyal sentiment here; for local governments already exist of undoubted fealty to the Government, and are sustained by communities which were among the first to testify their devotion to the Union, and which, during the struggle, furnished their full quotas of men to the military service of the country.

The exercise of the elective franchise is the highest attribute of an American citizen, and, when guided by virtue, intelligence, patriotism, and a proper appreciation of our institutions, constitutes the true basis of a democratic form of government, in which the sovereign power is lodged in the body of the people. Its influence for good necessarily depends upon the elevated character and patriotism of the elector; for if exercised by persons who do not justly estimate its value, and who are indifferent as to its results, it will only serve as a means of placing power in the hands of the unprincipled and ambitious, and must eventuate in the complete destruction of that liberty of which it should be the most powerful conservator. Great danger is, therefore, to be apprehended from an untimely extension of the elective franchise to any new class in our country, especially when the large majority of that class, in wielding the power thus placed in their hands, cannot be expected correctly to comprehend the duties and responsibilities which pertain to suffrage. Yesterday, as it were, four millions of persons were held in a condition of slavery that had existed for generations; to-day they are freemen, and are assumed by law to be citizens. It can not be presumed, from their previous condition of servitude, that as a class they are as well inf :med as to the nature of our Government as the intelligent foreigner who makes our land the home of his choice. In the case of the latter, neither a residence of five years, and the knowledge of our institutions which it gives, nor attachment to the principles of the Constitution, are the only conditions upon which he can be admitted to citizenship. He must prove, in addition, a good moral character, and thus give reasonable ground for the belief that he will be faithful to the obligations which he assumes as a citizen of the Republic. Where a people—the source of all political power—speak, by their suffrages, through the instrumentality of the ballot-box, it must be carefully guarded against the control of those who are corrupt in principle and enemies of free institutions, for it can only become to our political and social system a safe conductor of healthy popular sentiment when kept free from demoralizing influences. Controlled, through fraud and usurpation, by the designing, anarchy and despotism must inevitably follow. In the hands of the patriotic and worthy, our Government will be preserved upon the principles of the Constitution inherited from our fathers. It follows, therefore, that in admitting to the ballot-box a new class of voters not qualified for the exercise of the elective franchise, we weaken our system of government instead of adding to its strength and durability.

In returning this bill to the Senate, I deeply regret that there should be any conflict of opinion between the legislative and executive departments of the Government in regard to measures that vitally affect the prosperity and peace of the country. Sincerely desiring to reconcile the States with one another, and the whole people to the Government of the United States, it has been my earnest wish to co-operate with Congress in all measures having for their object a proper and complete adjustment of the questions resulting from our late civil war. Harmony between the co-ordinate branches of the Government, always necessary for the public welfare, was never more demanded than at the present time, and it will therefore be my constant aim to promote, as far as possible, concert of action between them. The differences of opinion that have already occurred have rendered me only the more cautious, lest the Executive should encroach upon any of the prerogatives of Congress; or, by exceeding in any manner the constitutional limit of his duties, destroy the equilibrium which should exist between the several co-ordinate departments, and which is so essential to the harmonious working of the Government. I know it has been urged that the executive department is more likely to enlarge the sphere of its action than either of the other two branches of the Government, and especially in the exercise of the veto power conferred upon it by the Constitution. It should be remembered, however, that this power is wholly negative and conservative in its character, and was intended to operate as a check upon unconstitutional, hasty, and improvident legislation, and as a means of protection against invasions of the just powers of the executive and judicial departments. It is remarked by Chancellor Kent that "to enact laws is a transcendent power; and, if the body that possesses it be a full and equal representation of the people, there is danger of its pressing with destructive weight upon all the other parts of the machinery of government. It has, therefore, been thought necessary, by the most skillful and most experienced artists in the science of civil polity, that strong barriers should be erected for the protection and security of the other necessary powers of the Government. Nothing has been deemed more fit and expedient for the purpose than the provision that the head of the executive department should be so constituted as to secure a requisite share of independence, and that he should have a negative upon the passing of laws; and that the judiciary power, resting on a still more permanent basis, should have the right of determining upon the validity of laws by the standard of the Constitution."

The necessity of some such check in the hands of the Executive is shown by reference to the most eminent writers upon our system of government, who seem to concur in the opinion that encroachments are most to be apprehended from the department in which all legislative powers are vested by the Constitution. Mr. Madison, in referring to the difficulty of providing some practical security for each against the invasion of the others, remarks that "the legislative department is everywhere extending the sphere of its activity, and drawing all power into its impetuous vortex." "The founders of our republics * * * seem never to have recollected the danger from legislative usurpations, which, by assembling all power in the same hands, must lead to the same tyranny as is threatened by executive usurpations." "In a representative republic, where the executive magistracy is carefully limited, both in the extent and the duration of its power, and where the legislative power is exercised by an assembly which is inspired by a supposed influence over the people with an intrepid confidence in its own strength; which is sufficiently numerous to feel all the passions which actuate a multitude, yet not so numerous as to be incapable of pursuing the objects of its passions by means which reason prescribes—it is against the enterprising ambition of this department that the people ought to indulge all their jealousy and exhaust all their precautions." "The legislative department derives a superiority in our governments from other circumstances. Its constitutional powers being at once more extensive and less susceptible of precise limits, it can with the greater facility mask, under complicated and indirect measures, the encroachments which it makes on the co-ordinate departments." "On the other side, the executive power being restrained within a narrower compass, and being more simple in its nature, and the judiciary being described by landmarks still less uncertain, projects of usurpation by either of these departments would immediately betray and defeat themselves. Nor is this all. As the legislative department alone has access to the pockets of the people, and has, in some constitutions, full discretion, and in all a prevailing influence over the pecuniary rewards of those who fill the other departments, a dependence is thus created in the latter which gives still greater facility to encroachments of the former." "We have seen that the tendency of republican governments is to an aggrandizement of the legislative, at the expense of the other departments."

Mr. Jefferson, in referring to the early constitution of Virginia, objected that by its provisions all the powers of government, legislative, executive, and judicial, resulted to the legislative body, holding that "the concentrating these in the same hands is precisely the definition of despotic government. It will be no alleviation that these powers will be exercised by a plurality of hands, and not by a single one. One hundred and seventy-three despots would surely be as oppressive as one." "As little will it avail us that they are chosen by ourselves. An elective despotism was not the government we fought for, but one which should not only be founded on free principles, but in which the powers of government should be so divided and balanced among several bodies of magistracy as that no one could transcend their legal limits without being effectually checked and restrained by the others. For this reason, that Convention which passed the ordinance of government laid its foundation on this basis, that the legislative, executive, and judiciary departments should be separate and distinct, so that no person should exercise the powers of more than one of them at the same time. But no barrier was provided between these several powers. The judiciary and executive members were left dependent on the legislative for their subsistence in office, and some of them for their continuance in it. If, therefore, the legislature assumes executive and judiciary powers, no opposition is likely to be made, nor, if made, can be effectual; because in that case they may put their proceedings into the form of an act of assembly, which will render them obligatory on the other branches. They have accordingly, in many instances, decided rights which should have been left to judiciary controversy; and the direction of the executive, during the whole time of their session, is becoming habitual and familiar."

Mr. Justice Story, in his Commentaries on the Constitution, reviews the same subject, and says:

"The truth is, that the legislative power is the great and overruling power in every free government." "The representatives of the people will watch with jealousy every encroachment of the executive magistrate, for it trenches upon their own authority. But who shall watch the encroachment of these representatives themselves? Will they be as jealous of the exercise of power by themselves as by others?" "There are many reasons which may be assigned for the engrossing influence of the legislative department. In the first place, its constitutional powers are more extensive, and less capable of being brought within precise limits than those of either of the other departments. The bounds of the executive authority are easily marked out and defined. It reaches few objects, and those are known. It cannot transcend them without being brought in contact with the other departments. Laws may check and restrain and bound its exercise. The same remarks apply with still greater force to the judiciary. The jurisdiction is, or may be, bounded to a few objects or persons; or, however general and unlimited, its operations are necessarily confined to the mere administration of private and public justice. It cannot punish without law. It cannot create controversies to act upon. It can decide only upon rights and cases as they are brought by others before it. It can do nothing for itself. It must do everything for others. It must obey the laws; and if it corruptly administers them, it is subjected to the power of impeachment. On the other hand, the legislative power, except in the few cases of constitutional prohibition, is unlimited. It is forever varying its means and its ends. It governs the institutions and laws and public policy of the country. It regulates all its vast interests. It disposes of all its property. Look but at the exercise of two or three branches of its ordinary powers. It levies all taxes; it directs and appropriates all supplies; it gives the rules for the descent, distribution, and devises of all property held by individuals. It controls the sources and the resources of wealth. It changes at its will the whole fabric of the laws. It moulds at its pleasure almost all the institutions which give strength and comfort and dignity to society. In the next place, it is the direct, visible representative of the will of the people in all the changes of times and circumstances. It has the pride as well as the power of numbers. It is easily moved and steadily moved by the strong impulses of popular feeling and popular odium. It obeys, without reluctance, the wishes and the will of the majority for the time being. The path to public favor lies open by such obedience; and it finds not only support, but impunity, in whatever measures the majority advises, even though they transcend the constitutional limits. It has no motive, therefore, to be jealous or scrupulous in its own use of power; and it finds its ambition stimulated and its arm strengthened by the countenance and the courage of numbers. These views are not alone those of men who look with apprehension upon the fate of republics; but they are also freely admitted by some of the strongest advocates for popular rights and the permanency of republican institutions." "Each department should have a will of its own." "Each should have its own independence secured beyond the power of being taken away by either or both of the others. But at the same time the relations of each to the other should be so strong that there should be a mutual interest to sustain and protect each other. There should not only be constitutional means, but personal motives to resist encroachments of one on either of the others. Thus, ambition would be made to counteract ambition; the desire of power to check power; and the pressure of interest to balance an opposing interest." "The judiciary is naturally and almost necessarily, (as has been already said,) the weakest department. It can have no means of influence by patronage. Its powers can never be wielded for itself. It has no command over the purse or the sword of the nation. It can neither lay taxes, nor appropriate money, nor command armies, nor appoint to office. It is never brought into contact with the people by constant appeals and solicitations, and private intercourse, which belong to all the other departments of Government. It is seen only in controversies, or in trials and punishments. Its rigid justice and impartiality give it no claims to favor, however they may to respect. It stands solitary and unsupported except by that portion of public opinion which is interested only in the strict administration of justice. It can rarely secure the sympathy or zealous support either of the executive or the legislature. If they are not (as is not unfrequently the case) jealous of its prerogatives, the constant necessity of scrutinizing the acts of each, upon the application of any private person, and the painful duty of pronouncing judgment that these acts are a departure from the law or Constitution, can have no tendency to conciliate kindness or nourish influence. It would seem, therefore, that some additional guards would, under the circumstances, be necessary to protect this department from the absolute dominion of the others. Yet rarely have any such guards been applied; and every attempt to introduce them has been resisted with a pertinacity which demonstrates how slow popular leaders are to introduce checks upon their own power, and how slow the people are to believe that the judiciary is the real bulwark of their liberties." "If any department of the Government has undue influence or absorbing power, it certainly has not been the executive or judiciary."

In addition to what has been said by these distinguished writers, it may also be urged that the dominant party in each House may, by the expulsion of a sufficient number of members, or by the exclusion from representation of a requisite number of States, reduce the minority to less than one-third. Congress, by these means, might be enabled to pass a law, the objections of the President to the contrary notwithstanding, which would render impotent the other two departments of the Government, and make inoperative the wholesome and restraining power which it was intended by the framers of the Constitution should be exerted by them. This would be a practical concentration of all power in the Congress of the United States; this, in the language of the author of the Declaration of Independence, would be "precisely the definition of despotic government."

I have preferred to reproduce these teachings of the great statesmen and constitutional lawyers of the early and later days of the Republic rather than to rely simply upon an expression of my own opinions. We cannot too often recur to them, especially at a conjuncture like the present. Their application to our actual condition is so apparent that they now come to us a living voice, to be listened to with more attention than at any previous period of our history. We have been and are yet in the midst of popular commotion. The passions aroused by a great civil war are still dominant. It is not a time favorable to that calm and deliberate judgment which is the only safe guide when radical changes in our institutions are to be made. The measure now before me is one of those changes. It initiates an untried experiment for a people who have said, with one voice, that it is not for their good. This alone should make us pause; but it is not all. The experiment has not been tried, or so much as demanded, by the people of the several States for themselves. In but few of the States has such an innovation been allowed as giving the ballot to the colored population without any other qualification than a residence of one year, and in most of them the denial of the ballot to this race is absolute, and by fundamental law placed beyond the domain of ordinary legislation. In most of those States the evil of such suffrage would be partial; but, small as it would be, it is guarded by constitutional barriers. Here the innovation assumes formidable proportions, which may easily grow to such an extent as to make the white population a subordinate element in the body politic.

After full deliberation upon this measure, I cannot bring myself to approve it, even upon local considerations, nor yet as the beginning of an experiment on a larger scale. I yield to no one in attachment to that rule of general suffrage which distinguishes our policy as a nation. But there is a limit, wisely observed hitherto, which makes the ballot a privilege and a trust, and which requires of some classes a time suitable for probation and preparation. To give it indiscriminately to a new class, wholly unprepared by previous habits and opportunities to perform the trust which it demands, is to degrade it, and finally to destroy its power; for it may be safely assumed that no political truth is better established than that such indiscriminate and all-embracing extension of popular suffrage must end at last in its destruction.

ANDREW JOHNSON.
WASHINGTON, *January* 5, 1867.

### Copy of the Bill Vetoed.

AN ACT to regulate the elective franchise in the District of Columbia.

*Be it enacted, &c.*, That from and after the passage of this act each and every male person, excepting paupers and persons under guardian-ship, of the age of twenty-one years and upwards, who has not been convicted of any infamous crime or offense, and excepting persons who may have voluntarily given aid and comfort to the rebels in the late rebellion, and who shall have been born or naturalized in the United States, and who shall have resided in the said District for the period of one year, and three months in the ward or election precinct in which he shall offer to vote, next preceding any election therein, shall be entitled to the elective franchise, and shall be deemed an elector and entitled to vote at any election in said District, without any distinction on account of color or race.

SEC. 2. That any person whose duty it shall be to receive votes at any election within the District of Columbia, who shall wilfully refuse to receive, or who shall wilfully reject, the vote of any person entitled to such right under this act, shall be liable to an action of tort by the person injured, and shall be liable, on indictment and conviction, if such act was done knowingly, to a fine not exceeding five thousand dollars, or to imprisonment for a term not exceeding one year, in the jail of said District, or to both.

SEC. 3. That if any person or persons shall wilfully interrupt or disturb any such elector in the exercise of such franchise, he or they shall be deemed guilty of a misdemeanor, and, on conviction thereof, shall be fined in any sum not to exceed one thousand dollars, or be imprisoned in the jail in said District for a period not to exceed thirty days, or both, at the discretion of the court.

SEC. 4. That it shall be the duty of the several courts having criminal jurisdiction in said District to give this act in special charge to the grand jury at the commencement of each term of the court next preceding the holding of any general or city election in said District.

SEC. 5. That the mayors and aldermen of the cities of Washington and Georgetown, respectively, on or before the first day of March in each year, shall prepare a list of the persons they judge to be qualified to vote in the several wards of said cities in any election; and said mayors and aldermen shall be in open session to receive evidence of the qualification of persons claiming the right to vote in any election therein, and for correcting said list, on two days in each year, not exceeding five days prior to the annual election for the choice of city officers, giving previous notice of the time and place of each session in some newspaper printed in said District.

SEC. 6. That on or before the first day of March the mayors and aldermen of said cities shall post up a list of voters thus prepared in one or more public places in said cities, respectively, at least ten days prior to said annual election.

SEC. 7. That the officers presiding at any election shall keep and use the check-list herein required at the polls during the election of all officers, and no vote shall be received unless delivered by the voter in person, and not until the presiding officer has had opportunity to be satisfied of his identity, and shall find his name on the list, and mark it, and ascertain that his vote is single.

SEC. 8. That it is hereby declared unlawful

for any person, directly or indirectly, to promise, offer, or give, or procure or cause to be promised, offered, or given, any money, goods, right in action, bribe, present, or reward, or any promise, understanding, obligation, or security for the payment or delivery of any money, goods, right in action, bribe, present, or reward, or any other valuable thing whatever, to any person, with intent to influence his vote to be given at any election hereafter to be held within the District of Columbia; and every person so offending shall, on conviction thereof, be fined in any sum not exceeding two thousand dollars, or imprisoned not exceeding two years, or both, at the discretion of the court.

SEC. 9. That any person who shall accept, directly or indirectly, any money, goods, right in action, bribe, present, or reward, or any promise, understanding, obligation, or security for the payment or delivery of any money, goods, right in action, bribe, present, or reward, or any other valuable thing whatever, to influence his vote at any election hereafter to be held in the District of Columbia, shall, on conviction, be imprisoned not less than one year and be forever disfranchised.

SEC. 10. That all acts and parts of acts inconsistent with this act be, and the same are hereby, repealed.

The votes on this bill were:

1866, December 14—The SENATE passed it—yeas 32, nays 13, as follow:

YEAS—Messrs. Anthony, Brown, Cattell, Chandler, Conness, Creswell, Edmunds, Fessenden, Fogg, Frelinghuysen, Grimes, Harris, Henderson, Howard, Howe, Kirkwood, Lane, Morgan, Morrill, Poland, Pomeroy, Ramsey, Ross, Sherman, Sprague, Stewart, Sumner, Trumbull, Wade, Willey, Williams, Wilson—32.

NAYS—Messrs. *Buckalew, Cowan, Davis, Dixon, Doolittle, Foster, Hendricks, Nesmith, Norton, Patterson, Riddle, Saulsbury, Van Winkle*—13.

1866, December 14—The HOUSE passed it—yeas 128, nays 46, as follow:

YEAS—Messrs. Alley, Allison, Ames, Anderson, Arnell, Delos R. Ashley, James M. Ashley, Baker, Baldwin, Banks, Barker, Baxter, Beaman, Bidwell, Bingham, Blaine, Blow, Boutwell, Brandégee, Bromwell, Broomall, Buckland, Bundy, Reader W. Clarke, Sidney Clarke, Cobb, Conkling, Cook, Culver, Dawes, Defrees, Delano, Deming, Dixon, Dodge, Donnelly, Driggs, Eckley, Eggleston, Eliot, Farnsworth, Ferry, Garfield, Grinnell, Griswold, Hale, Abner C. Harding, Hart, Hawkins, Hayes, Henderson, Higby, Hill, Holmes, Hooper, Hotchkiss, Demas Hubbard, jr., John H. Hubbard, James R. Hubbell, Hulburd, Ingersoll, Jenckes, Julian, Kasson, Kelley, Kelso, Ketcham, Koontz, Laflin, George V. Lawrence, William Lawrence, Loan, Longyear, Lynch, Marston, Marvin Maynard, McClurg, McIndoe, McRuer, Mercur, Miller, Moorhead, Morrill, Morris, Moulton, Myers, Newell, O'Neill, Orth, Paine, Patterson, Perham, Pike, Pomeroy, Price, Raymond, Alexander H. Rice, John H. Rice, Rollins, Sawyer, Schenck, Scofield, Shellabarger, Sloan, Spalding, Starr, Stevens, Stokes, Thayer, Francis Thomas, Trowbridge, Upson, Van Aernam, Burt Van Horn, Robert T. Van Horn, Hamilton Ward, Warner, Ellihu B. Washburne, William B. Washburn, Welker, Wentworth, Williams, James F. Wilson, Stephen F. Wilson, Windom, Woodbridge, and SPEAKER COLFAX—128.

NAYS—Messrs. *Ancona, Bergen, Boyer, Campbell, Chanler, Cooper, Dawson, Denison, Eldridge, Finck, Glossbrenner, Goodyear, Aaron Harding, Harris, Hise, Hogan.* Chester D. Hubbard, *Edwin N. Hubbell, Hunter, Kerr,* Kuykendall, Latham, *LeBlond, Leftwich, Marshall,* McKee, *Niblack, Nicholson, Noell,* Phelps, *Samuel J. Randall,* William H. Randall, *Ritter, Rogers, Ross, Rousseau, Shanklin, Sitgreaves,* Stillwell, *Strouse, Taber, Nathaniel G. Taylor, Nelson Taylor, Thornton, Andrew H. Ward,* Whaley—46.

1867, January 7—The bill was vetoed.

Same day, the SENATE passed it, notwithstanding the President's objections, by a two-thirds vote—yeas 29, nays 10, as follow:

YEAS—Messrs. Anthony, Cattell, Chandler, Conness, Cragin, Creswell, Edmunds, Fessenden, Fogg, Fowler, Frelinghuysen, Grimes, Henderson, Howard, Howe, Kirkwood, Lane, Morgan, Morrill, Poland, Ramsey, Ross, Sherman, Stewart, Sumner, Trumbull, Wade, Willey, Williams—29.

NAYS—Messrs. *Cowan, Dixon, Doolittle, Foster, Hendricks, Johnson, Nesmith, Norton, Patterson,* Van Winkle—10.

January 8—The House passed it—yeas 113, nays 38, as follow:

YEAS—Messrs. Alley, Allison, Ames, Arnell, Delos R. Ashley, James M. Ashley, Baker, Baldwin, Banks, Barker, Baxter, Beaman, Benjamin, Bidwell, Bingham, Blaine, Boutwell, Brandegee, Bromwell, Broomall, Buckland, Bundy, Reader W. Clarke, Sidney Clarke, Cobb, Cook, Cullom, Culver, Darling, Dawes, Defrees, Delano, Deming, Dixon, Dodge, Donnelly, Driggs, Eckley, Eggleston, Farnsworth, Farquhar, Ferry, Garfield, Grinnell, Abner C. Harding, Hart, Hawkins, Hayes, Henderson, Higby, Hill, Holmes, Hooper, John H. Hubbard, James R. Hubbell, Ingersoll, Jenckes, Julian, Kasson, Kelley, Kelso, Ketcham, Koontz, George V. Lawrence, William Lawrence, Loan, Longyear, Lynch, Marston, Marvin, Maynard, McClurg, McRuer, Mercur, Miller, Morrill, Moulton, Myers, Newell O'Neill, Orth, Paine, Patterson, Perham, Pike, Plants. Price, Raymond, Alexander H. Rice, John H. Rice, Sawyer, Schenck, Scofield, Spalding, Starr, Stokes, Thayer, Francis Thomas, John L. Thomas, jr., Trowbridge, Upson, Van Aernam, Burt Van Horn, Hamilton Ward, Warner, Ellihu B. Washburne, Welker, Wentworth, Williams, James F. Wilson, Stephen F. Wilson, Windom, and SPEAKER COLFAX—113.

NAYS—Messrs. *Ancona, Bergen, Campbell, Chanler. Cooper, Dawson, Eldridge, Finck, Glossbrenner, Aaron Harding, Hise, Hogan.* Chester D. Hubbard, *Humphrey, Hunter, Kerr,* Kuykendall, Latham, *Leftwich, McCullough, Niblack, Nicholson, Noell,* Phelps, *Radford, Samuel J. Randall,* William H. Randall, *Ritter, Rogers, Ross, Shanklin, Strouse, Taber, Nathaniel G. Taylor, Nelson Taylor, Trimble, Andrew H. Ward, Winfield*—38.

Whereupon the SPEAKER of the House declared the bill a law.

---

## Veto of the Colorado Bill, January 29, 1867.

*To the Senate of the United States:*

I return to the Senate, in which House it originated, a bill entitled "An act to admit the State of Colorado into the Union," to which I cannot, consistently with my sense of duty, give my approval. With the exception of an additional section, containing new provisions, it is substantially the same as the bill of a similar title passed by Congress during the last session, submitted to the President for his approval, returned with the objections contained in a message bearing date the 15th of May last, and yet awaiting the reconsideration of the Senate.

A second bill, having in view the same purpose, has now passed both Houses of Congress, and been presented for my signature. Having again carefully considered the subject, I have been unable to perceive any reason for changing the opinions which have already been communicated to Congress. I find, on the contrary, that there are many objections to the proposed legislation, of which I was not at that time aware; and that while several of those which I then assigned have, in the interval, gained in strength, yet others have been created by the altered character of the measure now submitted.

The constitution under which this State government is proposed to be formed very properly contains a provision that all laws in force at the time of its adoption, and the admission of the State into the Union, shall continue as if the constitution had not been adopted. Among those laws is one absolutely prohibiting negroes and mulattoes from voting. At the recent session of the Territorial Legislature a bill for the repeal of this law, introduced into the council, was almost unanimously rejected; and at the very time when Congress was engaged in enacting the bill now under consideration, the Legislature passed an act excluding negroes and mulattoes from the right to sit as jurors. This bill was vetoed by the Governor of the Territory, who held that by the laws of the United States negroes and mulattoes are citizens, and subject to the duties, as well as entitled to the rights of citizenship. The bill, however, was passed, the objections of the Governor to the contrary notwithstanding, and is now a law of the Territory. Yet in the bill now before me, by which it is proposed to admit the Territory as a State, it is provided that "there shall be no denial of the elective franchise, or any other rights, to any person, by reason of race or color, excepting Indians not taxed."

The incongruity thus exhibited between the legislation of Congress and that of the Territory, taken in connection with the protest against the admission of the State hereinafter referred to, would seem clearly to indicate the impolicy and injustice of the proposed enactment.

It might indeed be a subject of grave inquiry, and doubtless will result in such inquiry if this bill become a law, whether it does not attempt to exercise a power not conferred upon Congress by the Federal Constitution. That instrument simply declares that Congress may admit new States into the Union. It nowhere says that Congress may make new States for the purpose of admitting them into the Union, or for any other purpose; and yet this bill is as clear an attempt to make the institutions as any in which the people themselves could engage.

In view of this action of Congress, the House of Representatives of the Territory have earnestly protested against being forced into the Union without first having the question submitted to the people. Nothing could be more reasonable than the position which they thus assume; and it certainly cannot be the purpose of Congress to force upon a community, against their will, a government which they do not believe themselves capable of sustaining.

The following is a copy of the protest alluded to, as officially transmitted to me:

"Whereas it is announced in the public prints that it is the intention of Congress to admit Colorado as a State into the Union: Therefore,

"*Resolved by the House of Representatives of this Territory,* That, representing as we do the last and only legal expression of public opinion on this question, we earnestly protest against the passage of a law admitting the State, without first having the question submitted to a vote of the people, for the reasons, first, that we have a right to a voice in the selection of the character of our government; second, that we have not a sufficient population to support the expenses of a State government. For these reasons we trust Congress will not force upon us a government against our will."

Upon information which I considered reliable, I assumed in my message of the 15th of May last that the population of Colorado was not more than thirty thousand, and expressed the opinion that this number was entirely too small either to assume the responsibilities or to enjoy the privileges of a State.

It appears that previous to that time the Legislature, with a view to ascertain the exact condition of the Territory, had passed a law authorizing a census of the population to be taken. The law made it the duty of the assessors in the several counties to take the census in connection with the annual assessments, and, in order to secure a correct enumeration of the population, allowed them a liberal compensation for the service by paying them for every name returned, and added to their previous oath of office an oath to perform this duty with fidelity.

From the accompanying official report it appears that returns have been received from fifteen of the eighteen counties into which the State is divided, and that their population amounts in the aggregate to twenty-four thousand nine hundred and nine. The three remaining counties are estimated to contain three thousand, making a total population of twenty-seven thousand nine hundred and nine, (27,909.)

This census was taken in the summer season, when it is claimed that the population is much larger than at any other period, as in the autumn miners, in large numbers, leave their work and return to the East, with the results of their summer enterprise.

The population, it will be observed, is but slightly in excess of one-fifth of the number required as the basis of representation for a single congressional district in any of the States, that number being one hundred and twenty-seven thousand.

I am unable to perceive any good reason for such great disparity in the right of representation, giving, as it would, to the people of Colorado, not only this vast advantage in the House of Representatives, but an equality in the Senate, where the other States are represented by millions. With perhaps a single exception, no such inequality as this has ever before been attempted. I know that it is claimed that the population of the different States at the time of their admission has varied at different periods, but it has not varied much more than the population of each decade and the corresponding basis of representation for the different periods.

The obvious intent of the Constitution was, that no State should be admitted with a less population than the ratio for a Representative at the time of application. The limitation in the second section of the first article of the Constitution, declaring that "each State shall have at least one Representative," was manifestly designed to protect the States which originally composed the Union from being deprived, in the event of a waning population, of a voice in the popular branch of Congress, and was never intended as a warrant to force a new State into the Union with a representative population far below that which might at the time be required of sister members of the Confederacy. This bill, in view of the prohibition of the same section, which declares that "the number of Representatives shall not exceed one for every thirty thousand," is at least a violation of the spirit, if not the letter of the Constitution.

It is respectfully submitted that however Congress, under the pressure of circumstances, may have admitted two or three States with less than a representative population at the time, there has been no instance in which an application for admission has even been entertained when the population, as officially ascertained, was below thirty thousand.

Were there any doubt of this being the true construction of the Constitution, it would be dispelled by the early and long-continued practice of the Federal Government. For nearly sixty years after the adoption of the Constitution no State was admitted with a population believed at the time to be less than the current ratio for a Representative, and the first instance in which there appears to have been a departure from the principle was in 1845, in the case of Florida. Obviously the result of sectional strife, we would do well to regard it as a warning of evil rather than as an example for imitation, and I think candid men of all parties will agree that the inspiring cause of the violation of this wholesome principle of restraint is to be found in a vain attempt to balance those antagonisms which refused to be reconciled except through the bloody arbitrament of arms. The plain facts of our history will attest that the great and leading States admitted since 1845, viz., Iowa, Wisconsin, California, Minnesota, and Kansas, including Texas, which was admitted that year, have all come with an ample population for one Representative, and some of them with nearly or quite enough for two.

To demonstrate the correctness of my views on this question, I subjoin a table containing a list of the States admitted since the adoption of the Federal Constitution, with the date of admission, the ratio of representation, and the representative population when admitted, deduced from the United States census tables, the calculation being made for the period of the decade corresponding with the date of admission:

| States. | Admitted. | Ratio. | Population. |
|---|---|---|---|
| Vermont | 1791 | 33,000 | 92,320 |
| Kentucky | 1792 | 33,000 | 95,638 |
| Tennessee | 1796 | 33,000 | 73,864 |
| Ohio | 1802 | 33,000 | 82,443 |
| Louisiana | 1812 | 35,000 | 75,212 |
| Indiana | 1816 | 35,000 | 98,110 |
| Mississippi | 1817 | 35,000 | 53,677 |
| Illinois | 1818 | 35,000 | 46,374 |
| Alabama | 1819 | 35,000 | 111,150 |
| Maine | 1820 | 35,000 | 298,335 |
| Missouri | 1821 | 35,000 | 69,260 |
| Arkansas | 1836 | 47,700 | 65,175 |
| Michigan | 1837 | 47,700 | 158,072 |
| Florida | 1845 | 70,680 | 57,951 |
| Texas | 1845 | 70,680 | *189,327 |
| Iowa | 1846 | 70,680 | 132,572 |
| Wisconsin | 1848 | 70,680 | 250,497 |
| California | 1850 | 70,680 | 92,597 |
| Oregon | 1858 | 93,492 | 44,630 |
| Minnesota | 1858 | 93,492 | 138,909 |
| Kansas | 1861 | 93,492 | 107,206 |
| West Virginia | 1862 | 93,492 | 349,628 |
| Nevada | 1864 | 127,000 | Not known. |

Colorado, which it is now proposed to admit as a State, contains, as has already been stated, a population less than twenty-eight thousand, while the present ratio of representation is one hundred and twenty-seven thousand.

There can be no reason, that I can perceive, for the admission of Colorado that would not apply with equal force to nearly every other Territory now organized; and I submit whether, if this bill become a law, it will be possible to resist the logical conclusion that such Territories as Dakota, Montana, and Idaho, must be received as States whenever they present themselves, without regard to the number of inhabitants they may respectively contain. Eight or ten new Senators, and four or five new members of the House of Representatives would thus be admitted to represent a population scarcely exceeding that which, in any other portion of the nation, is entitled to but a single member of the House of Representatives, while the average for two Senators in the Union, as now constituted, is at least one million of people. It would surely be unjust to all other sections of the Union to enter upon a policy with regard to admission of new States which might result in conferring such a disproportionate share of influence in the national Legislature upon communities which, in pursuance of the wise policy of our fathers, should for some years to come be retained under the fostering care and protection of the national Government. If it is deemed just and expedient now to depart from the settled policy of the nation during all its history, and to admit all the Territories to the rights and privileges of States, irrespective of their population or fitness for such government, it is submitted whether it would not be well to devise such measures as will bring the subject before the country for consideration and decision. This would seem to be evidently wise, because, as has already been stated, if it is right to admit Colorado now, there is no reason for the exclusion of the other Territories.

It is no answer to these suggestions that an enabling act was passed authorizing the people of Colorado to take action on this subject. It is well known that that act was passed in consequence of representations that the population reached, according to some statements, as high as eighty thousand, and to none less than fifty thousand, and was growing with a rapidity which by the time the admission could be consummated would secure a population of over a hundred thousand. These representations prove to have been wholly fallacious, and in addition, the people of the Territory, by a deliberate vote, decided that they would not assume the responsibilities of a State government. By that decision they utterly exhausted all power that was conferred by the enabling act, and there has been no step taken since in relation to the admission that has had the slightest sanction or warrant of law.

The proceeding upon which the present application is based was in the utter absence of all law in relation to it, and there is no evidence that the votes on the question of the formation of a State government bear any relation whatever to the sentiment of the Territory. The protest of the House of Representatives, previously quoted, is conclusive evidence to the contrary.

But if none of these reasons existed against this proposed enactment, the bill itself, besides being inconsistent in its provisions in conferring power upon a person unknown to the laws, and who may never have a legal existence, is so framed as to render its execution almost impossible. It is, indeed, a question whether it is not in itself a nullity. To say the least, it is of exceedingly doubtful propriety to confer the power proposed in the bill upon the "Governor elect;" for, as by its own terms the constitution is not to take effect until after the admission of

---

* In 1850.

the State, he, in the mean time, has no more authority than any other private citizen. But, even supposing him to be clothed with sufficient authority to convene the Legislature, what constitutes the "State Legislature," to which is to be referred the question of submission to the conditions imposed by Congress? Is it a new body, to be elected and convened by proclamation of the "Governor elect," or is it that body which met more than a year ago, under the provisions of the State constitution? By reference to the second section of the schedule, and to the eighteenth section of the fourth article of the State constitution, it will be seen that the term of the members of the House of Representatives, and that of one-half of the members of the Senate, expired on the first Monday of the present month. It is clear that if there were no intrinsic objections to the bill itself in relation to the purposes to be accomplished, this objection would be fatal; as it is apparent that the provisions of the third section of the bill to admit Colorado have reference to a period and a state of facts entirely different from the present, and affairs as they now exist, and, if carried into effect, must necessarily lead to confusion.

Even if it were settled that the old and not a new body were to act, it would be found impracticable to execute the law, because a considerable number of the members, as I am informed, have ceased to be residents of the Territory, and in the sixty days within which the Legislature is to be convened after the passage of the act there would not be sufficient time to fill the vacancies by new elections, were there any authority under which they could be held. It may not be improper to add that if these proceedings were all regular, and the result to be attained were desirable, simple justice to the people of the Territory would require a longer period than sixty days within which to obtain action on the conditions proposed by the third section of the bill. There are, as is well known, large portions of the Territory with which there is and can be no general communication, there being several counties which, from November to May, can only be reached by persons travelling on foot, while with other regions of the Territory, occupied by a large portion of the population, there is very little more freedom of access. Thus, if this bill should become a law, it would be impracticable to obtain any expression of public sentiment in reference to its provisions, with a view to enlighten the Legislature, if the old body were called together; and, of course, equally impracticable to procure the election of a new body. This defect might have been remedied by an extension of the time, and a submission of the question to the people, with a fair opportunity to enable them to express their sentiments.

The admission of a new State has generally been regarded as an epoch in our history, marking the onward progress of the nation; but, after the most careful and anxious inquiry on the subject, I cannot perceive that the proposed proceeding is in conformity with the policy which, from the origin of the Government, has uniformly prevailed in the admission of new States. I therefore return the bill to the Senate without my signature.        ANDREW JOHNSON.
WASHINGTON, *January* 28, 1867.

### Copy of the Bill Vetoed.

AN ACT to admit the State of Colorado into the Union.

Whereas, on the twenty-first day of March, anno Domini eighteen hundred and sixty-four, Congress passed an act to enable the people of Colorado to form a constitution and State Government, and offered to admit said State ,when so formed, into the Union upon compliance with certain conditions therein specified; and whereas it appears by message of the President of the United States, dated January     , eighteen hundred and sixty-six, that the said people have adopted a constitution, which, upon due examination, is found to conform to the provisions and comply with the conditions of said act, and to be republican in its form of government, and that they now ask for admission into the Union:

*Be it enacted by the Senate and House of Representatives of the United States of America in Congress assembled,* That the constitution and State government which the people of Colorado have formed for themselves be, and the same is hereby, accepted, ratified, and confirmed; and that the said State of Colorado shall be, and hereby is declared to be, one of the United States of America, and is hereby admitted into the Union upon an equal footing with the original States in all respects whatsoever.

SEC. 2. *And be it further enacted,* That the said State of Colorado shall be, and is hereby declared to be, entitled to all the rights, privileges, grants, and immunities, and to be subject to all the conditions and restrictions, of an act entitled "An act to enable the people of Colorado to form a constitution and State government, and for the admission of such State into the Union on an equal footing with the original States," approved March twenty-first, eighteen hundred and sixty-four.

SEC. 3. *And be it further enacted,* That this act shall not take effect except upon the fundamental condition that within the State of Colorado there shall be no denial of the elective franchise, or any other rights, to any person by reason of race or color, excepting Indians not taxed; and upon the further fundamental condition that the Legislature elected under said State constitution, by a solemn public act, shall declare the assent of said State to the said fundamental condition, and shall transmit to the President of the United States an authentic copy of said act; upon receipt whereof the President, by proclamation, shall forthwith announce the fact, whereupon said fundamental condition shall be held as a part of the organic law of the State; and thereupon, and without any further proceeding on the part of Congress, the admission of said State into the Union shall be considered as complete. Said State Legislature shall be convened by the Governor elect of said State within sixty days after the passage of this act, to act upon the condition submitted herein.

The votes on this bill were:

1867, January 9—The bill passed the SENATE, yeas 23, nays 11, with the third section in these words:

That this act shall take effect with the fundamental and perpetual condition that within said State of Colorado there shall be no abridgment or denial of the exercise of the elective franchise, or of any other right, to any person by reason of race or color, (excepting Indians not taxed.)

YEAS—Messrs Anthony, Cattell, Chandler, Conness, Cragin, Creswell, Edmunds, Fowler, Henderson, Howard, Kirkwood, Lane, Morrill, Poland, Ramsey, Ross, Sherman, Stewart, Sumner, Van Winkle, Wade, Willey, Williams—23.

NAYS—Messrs. *Buckalew, Doolittle,* Foster, Grimes, *Hendricks, Johnson,* Morgan, *Nesmith, Norton, Patterson, Riddle*—11.

January 16—The SENATE agreed to the bill with the third section as it stands—yeas 27, nays 12, as follows:

YEAS—Messrs. Anthony, Cattell, Chandler, Conness, Cragin, Fessenden, Fowler, Frelinghuysen, Grimes, Harris, Henderson, Howard, Kirkwood, Lane, Morrill, Poland, Ramsey, Sherman, Sprague, Stewart, Sumner, Van Winkle, Wade, Willey, Williams, Wilson, Yates—27.

NAYS—Messrs. *Buckalew, Dixon, Doolittle,* Edmunds, Foster, *Hendricks, Johnson, Nesmith, Norton, Patterson, Riddle, Saulsbury*—12.

### IN HOUSE.

1867, January 15—The bill passed—yeas 90, nays 60, as follow:

YEAS—Messrs. Alley, Allison, Ames, Anderson, Delos R. Ashley, James M. Ashley, Baldwin, Banks, Baxter, Benjamin, Boutwell, Brandegee, Bromwell, Broomall, Bundy, Reader W. Clarke, Cobb, Cook, Cullom, Culver, Dawes, Delano, Deming, Dixon, Dodge, Donnelly, Driggs, Eckley, Eliot, Farquhar, Ferry, Garfield, Grinnell, Griswold, Henderson, Higby, Hill, Holmes, Hooper, Demas Hubbard, jr., John H. Hubbard, J. R. Hubbell, Ingersoll, Jenckes, Julian, Kelley, Koontz, George V. Lawrence, Longyear, Marston, Marvin, McClurg, McIndoe, McRuer, Mercur, Miller, Moorhead, Morris, Moulton, Newell, O'Neill, Orth, Paine, Perham, Plants, Price, Alexander H. Rice, John H. Rice, Rollins, Sawyer, Schenck, Shellabarger, Spalding, Stokes, Thayer, Francis Thomas, John L. Thomas, jr., Trowbridge, Upson, Van Aernam, Burt Van Horn, Warner, Henry D. Washburn, William B. Washburn, Welker, Wentworth, Williams, James F. Wilson, Stephen F. Wilson, Windom—90.

NAYS—Messrs. *Ancona,* Baker, *Bergen,* Bingham, Blaine, *Boyer,* Buckland, *Campbell, Cooper,* Davis, Defrees, *Denison, Eldridge, Finck, Glossbrenner, Goodyear,* Hale, *Aaron Harding,* Abner C. Harding, Hart, Hawkins, *Hise, Hogan,* Chester D. Hubbard, *Edwin N. Hubbell, Humphrey,* Hunter, *Johnson,* Kelso, *Kerr,* Kuykendall, Latham, *Le Blond, Leftwich,* Lynch, *Marshall,* Maynard, McKee, Morrill, *Niblack, Nicholson,* Pike, *Radford, Samuel J. Randall,* Raymond, *Ritter, Rogers, Ross, Shanklin, Sitgreaves,* Stillwell, *Strouse, Taber, Nathaniel G. Taylor, Nelson Taylor, Thornton, Andrew H. Ward,* Hamilton Ward, Ellihu B. Washburne, *Whaley*—60.

The vote on substituting the third section as it stands for that of the Senate, taken previously to the above vote, was yeas 84, nays 65, being substantially the same as on the Nebraska bill, below.

January 29—The bill was vetoed, and no votes were subsequently taken on it.

### Veto of the Nebraska Bill, January 30, 1867.

*To the Senate of the United States:*

I return, for reconsideration, a bill entitled "An act for the admission of the State of Nebraska into the Union," which originated in the Senate, and has received the assent of both Houses of Congress. A bill having in view the same object was presented for my approval a few hours prior to the adjournment of the last session; but, submitted at a time when there was no opportunity for a proper consideration of the subject, I withheld my signature, and the measure failed to become a law.

It appears, by the preamble of this bill, that the people of Nebraska, availing themselves of the authority conferred upon them by the act passed on the 19th day of April, 1864, "have adopted a constitution which, upon due examination, is found to conform to the provisions and comply with the conditions of said act, and to be republican in its form of government, and that they now ask for admission into the Union." This proposed law would, therefore, seem to be

based upon the declaration contained in the enabling act, that, upon compliance with its terms, the people of Nebraska should be admitted into the Union upon an equal footing with the original States. Reference to the bill, however, shows that while, by the first section, Congress distinctly accepts, ratifies, and confirms the constitution and State government which the people of the Territory have formed for themselves, declares Nebraska to be one of the United States of America, and admits her into the Union upon an equal footing with the original States in all respects whatsoever, the third section provides that this measure "shall not take effect except upon the fundamental condition that within the State of Nebraska there shall be no denial of the elective franchise, or of any other right, to any person, by reason of race or color, excepting Indians not taxed; and upon the further fundamental condition that the Legislature of said State, by a solemn public act, shall declare the assent of said State to the said fundamental condition, and shall transmit to the President of the United States an authentic copy of said act, upon receipt whereof the President, by proclamation, shall forthwith announce the fact, whereupon said fundamental condition shall be held as a part of the organic law of the State; and thereupon, and without any further proceeding on the part of Congress, the admission of said State into the Union shall be considered as complete." This condition is not mentioned in the original enabling act; was not contemplated at the time of its passage; was not sought by the people themselves; has not heretofore been applied to the inhabitants of any State asking admission, and is in direct conflict with the constitution adopted by the people, and declared in the preamble "to be republican in its form of government," for in that instrument the exercise of the elective franchise, and the right to hold office, are expressly limited to white citizens of the United States. Congress thus undertakes to authorize and compel the Legislature to change a constitution which it is declared in the preamble has received the sanction of the people, and which by this bill is "accepted, ratified, and confirmed" by the Congress of the nation.

The first and third sections of the bill exhibit yet further incongruity. By the one Nebraska is "admitted into the Union upon an equal footing with the original States, in all respects whatsoever," while by the other Congress demands, as a condition precedent to her admission, requirements which in our history have never been asked of any people when presenting a constitution and State government for the acceptance of the law-making power. It is expressly declared by the third section that the bill "shall not take effect except upon the fundamental condition that within the State of Nebraska there shall be no denial of the elective franchise, or of any other right, to any person, by reason of race or color, except Indians not taxed." Neither more nor less than the assertion of the right of Congress to regulate the elective franchise of any State hereafter to be admitted, this condition is in clear violation of the Federal Constitution, under the provisions of which, from the very foundation of the Government, each State has been left free to determine for itself the qualifications necessary for the exercise of suffrage within its limits. Without precedent in our legislation, it is in marked contrast with those limitations which, imposed upon States that, from time to time, have become members of the Union had for their object the single purpose of preventing any infringement of the Constitution of the country.

If Congress is satisfied that Nebraska, at the present time, possesses sufficient population to entitle her to full representation in the councils of the nation, and that her people desire an exchange of a territorial for a State government, good faith would seem to demand that she should be admitted without further requirements than those expressed in the enabling act, with all of which, it is asserted in the preamble, her inhabitants have complied. Congress may, under the Constitution, admit new States or reject them, but the people of a State can alone make or change their organic law and prescribe the qualifications requisite for electors. Congress, however, in passing the bill in the shape in which it has been submitted for my approval, does not merely reject the application of the people of Nebraska for present admission as a State into the Union, on the ground that the constitution which they have submitted restricts the exercise of the elective franchise to the white population, but imposes conditions which, if accepted by the Legislature, may, without the consent of the people, so change the organic law as to make electors of all persons within the State, without distinction of race or color. In view of this fact, I suggest for the consideration of Congress, whether it would not be just, expedient, and in accordance with the principles of our government, to allow the people, by popular vote, or through a convention chosen by themselves for that purpose, to declare whether or not they will accept the terms upon which it is now proposed to admit them into the Union. This course will not occasion much greater delay than that which the bill contemplates when it requires that the Legislature shall be convened within thirty days after this measure shall have become a law, for the purpose of considering and deciding the conditions which it imposes, and gains additional force when we consider that the proceedings attending the formation of the State constitution were not in conformity with the provisions of the enabling act, that in an aggregate vote of seven thousand, seven hundred and seventy-six, the majority in favor of the constitution did not exceed one hundred; and that it is alleged that, in consequence of frauds, even this result cannot be received as a fair expression of the wishes of the people. As upon them must fall the burdens of a State organization, it is but just that they should be permitted to determine for themselves a question which so materially affects their interests. Possessing a soil and a climate admirably adapted to those industrial pursuits which bring prosperity and greatness to a people, with the advantage of a central position on the great highway that will soon connect the Atlantic and Pacific States, Nebraska is rapidly gaining in numbers and wealth, and may within a very brief period claim admission on grounds which will challenge and secure universal assent. She can therefore wisely and patiently afford to wait. Her population is said to be steadily and even rapidly increasing, being now generally conceded as high as forty thousand, and estimated by some, whose judgment is entitled to respect, at a still greater number. At her present rate of growth, she will, in a very short time, have the requisite population for a Representative in Congress, and, what is far more important to her own citizens, will have realized such an advance in material wealth as will enable the expenses of a State government to be borne without oppression to the tax-payer. Of new communities it may be said with special force—and it is true of old ones—that the inducement to emigrants, other things being equal, is in almost the precise ratio of the rate of taxation. The great States of the Northwest owe their marvellous prosperity largely to the fact that they were continued as Territories until they had grown to be wealthy and populous communities.

ANDREW JOHNSON.

WASHINGTON, *January* 29, 1867.

---

### Copy of the Bill Vetoed.

AN ACT for the admission of the State of Nebraska into the Union.

Whereas, on the twenty-first day of March, anno Domini eighteen hundred and sixty-four, Congress passed an act to enable the people of Nebraska to form a constitution and State government, and offered to admit said State, when so formed, into the Union upon compliance with certain conditions therein specified; and whereas it appears that the said people have adopted a constitution which, upon due examination, is found to conform to the provisions and comply with the conditions of said act, and to be republican in its form of government, and that they now ask for admission into the Union: Therefore,

*Be it enacted by the Senate and House of Representatives of the United States of America in Congress assembled*, That the constitution and State government which the people of Nebraska have formed for themselves be, and the same is hereby, accepted, ratified, and confirmed, and that the said State of Nebraska shall be, and is hereby declared to be, one of the United States of America, and is hereby admitted into the Union upon an equal footing with the original States in all respects whatsoever.

SEC. 2. *And be it further enacted*, That the said State of Nebraska shall be, and is hereby declared to be, entitled to all the rights, privileges, grants, and immunities, and to be subject to all the conditions and restrictions of an act entitled "An act to enable the people of Nebraska to form a constitution and State government, and for the admission of such State into the Union on an equal footing with the original States."

SEC. 3. *And be it further enacted*, That this act shall not take effect except upon the fundamental condition that within the State of Nebraska there shall be no denial of the elective franchise, or of any other right, to any person by reason of race or color, except Indians not taxed, and upon the further fundamental condition that the Legislature of said State, by a solemn public act, shall declare the assent of said State to the said fundamental condition, and shall transmit to the President of the United States an authentic copy of said act. Upon receipt whereof the President, by proclamation, shall forthwith announce the fact; whereupon said fundamental condition shall be held as a part of the organic law of the State; and thereupon, and without any further proceeding on the part of Congress, the admission of said State into the Union shall be considered as complete. Said State Legislature shall be convened by the Territorial Governor within thirty days after the passage of this act, to act upon the condition submitted herein.

The votes on this bill were:

1867, January 9—A bill passed in SENATE—yeas 24, nays 15, with the third section in these words:

"That this act shall take effect with the fundamental and perpetual condition that within said State of Nebraska there shall be no abridgment or denial of the exercise of the elective franchise, or of any other right, to any person by reason of race or color, excepting Indians not taxed."

YEAS—Messrs. Anthony, Cattell, Chandler, Conness, Cragin, Creswell, Edmunds. Fogg, Fowler, Henderson, Howard, Kirkwood, Lane, Morrill, Poland, Ramsey, Ross, Sherman, Stewart, Sumner, Van Winkle, Wade, Willey, Williams—24.

NAYS—Messrs. Buckalew, Cowan, Dixon, Doolittle, Foster, Grimes, Hendricks, Howe, Johnson, Morgan, Nesmith, Norton, Patterson, Riddle, Saulsbury—15.

January 16—The SENATE agreed to the third section as it stands—yeas 28, nays 14, as follow:

YEAS—Messrs. Anthony, Cattell, Chandler, Conness, Cragin, Fessenden, Fogg, Fowler, Frelinghuysen, Grimes, Henderson, Howard, Kirkwood, Lane, Morgan, Morrill, Poland, Ramsey, Sherman. Sprague, Stewart, Sumner, Van Winkle, Wade, Willey, Williams, Wilson, Yates—28.

NAYS—Messrs. Buckalew, Cowan, Dixon, Doolittle, Edmunds. Foster, Harris, Hendricks, Johnson, Nesmith, Norton, Patterson, Riddle, Saulsbury—14.

IN HOUSE.

January 15—The third section, as it stands, was substituted for that adopted above by the Senate—yeas 88, nays 70, as follow:

YEAS—Messrs. Alley, Allison, Ames, Anderson, James M. Ashley, Baldwin, Banks, Baxter, Blaine, Boutwell, Brandegee, Broomall, Cobb, Cook, Cullom, Culver, Dawes, Deming, Dixon, Dodge, Donnelly, Driggs, Eckley, Eliot, Ferry, Garfield, Grinnell, Griswold, Hart, Higby, Holmes, Hooper, Demas Hubbard, jr., John H. Hubbard, Ingersoll, Jenckes, Julian, Kelley, Kelso, Ketcham, Koontz, Kuykendall, Loan, Longyear, Lynch, Marston, Marvin, Maynard, McClurg, McIndoe, McRuer, Mercur, Moorhead, Morrill, Morris. Moulton, Newell, O'Neill, Orth, Paine, Patterson, Perham, Pike, Price, Raymond, Alexander H. Rice, John H. Rice, Rollins, Sawyer, Schenck, Scofield, Spalding, Stevens, Thayer, Trowbridge, Upson, Van Aernam, Burt Van Horn, Hamilton Ward, Warner, Ellihu B. Washburne, William B. Washburn, Welker, Wentworth, Williams, James F. Wilson. Stephen F. Wilson, Windom—88.

NAYS—Messrs. Ancona, Delos R. Ashley, Baker, Benjamin, Bergen, Bingham, Boyer, Bromwell, Buckland, Bundy, Campbell, Chanler, Reader W. Clarke, Cooper, Davis, Dawson, Defrees, Delano, Denison, Eldridge, Farnsworth, Farquhar, Finck, Glossbrenner, Goodyear, Hale, Aaron Harding, Abner C. Harding, Hawkins, Henderson, Hill, Hise, Hogan, Chester D. Hubbard, Edwin N. Hubbell, J. R. Hubbell, Humphrey, Hunter, Johnson, Kerr, Latham, George V. Lawrence, Le Blond, Leftwich, Marshall, McKee, Miller, Niblack, Nicholson, Plants, Radford, Samuel J. Randall, William H. Randall, Ritter, Rogers, Shanklin, Shellabarger, Sitgreaves, Stillwell, Stokes, Strouse, Taber, Nathaniel G. Taylor, Nelson Taylor, Francis Thomas, John L. Thomas, jr., Thornton, Andrew H. Ward, Henry D. Washburn, Whaley—70.

Same day—The bill passed—yeas 103, nays 55, as follow:

YEAS—Messrs. Alley, Allison, Ames, Anderson, Delos R.

Ashley, James M. Ashley, Baldwin, Banks, Baxter, Benjamin, Blaine, Boutwell, Brandegee, Bromwell, Broomall, Bundy, Reader W. Clarke, Cobb, Cook, Cullom, Culver, Dawes, Delano, Deming, Dixon, Dodge, Donnelly, Driggs, Eckley, Eliot, Farnsworth, Farquhar, Ferry. Garfield, Grinnell, Griswold, Hart, Henderson, Higby, Hill, Holmes, Hooper, Demas Hubbard, jr., John H. Hubbard, James R. Hubbell. Ingersoll, Jenckes, Julian, Kelley, Ketcham, Koontz, George V. Lawrence, Loan, Longyear. Lynch, Marston, Marvin, Maynard, McClurg. McIndoe, McRuer, Mercur, Miller, Moorhead, Morrill, Morris, Moulton, Newell, O'Neill, Orth, Paine, Patterson, Perham, Plants, Price, Alexander H. Rice, John H. Rice, Rollins, Sawyer, Schenck, Scofield, Shellabarger, Spalding, Stevens, Stokes, Thayer, Francis Thomes, John L. Thomas, jr., Trowbridge, Upson, Van Aernam, Burt Van Horn, Hamilton Ward, Warner, Ellihu B. Washburne, Henry D. Washburn, William B. Washburn, Welker, Wentworth, Williams, James F. Wilson, Stephen F. Wilson, Windom—103.

NAYS—Messrs. Ancona, Baker, Bergen, Bingham, Boyer, Buckland, Campbell, Chanler, Cooper, Davis, Dawson, Defrees, Denison, Eldridge, Finck, Glossbrenner, Goodyear, Hale, Aaron Harding, Abner C. Harding, Hawkins, Hise, Hogan, Chester D. Hubbard, Edwin N. Hubbell, Humphrey, Hunter, Johnson. Kelso, Kerr, Kuykendall, Latham, Le Blond, Leftwich, Marshall, McKee, Niblack, Nicholson, Radford, Samuel J. Randall, William H. Randall, Raymond, Ritter, Rogers, Ross, Shanklin, Sitgreaves, Stillwell, Strouse, Taber, Nathaniel G. Taylor, Nelson Taylor, Thornton, Andrew H. Ward, Whaley—55.

The bill then passed, as above.

January 30—The bill was vetoed.

February 8—The SENATE passed it over the veto—yeas 30, nays 9, as follow:

YEAS—Messrs. Anthony, Brown, Chandler, Cragin, Creswell, Fogg, Fowler, Frelinghuysen, Grimes. Harris, Henderson, Howard, Howe, Kirkwood, Lane, Morrill, Poland, Pomeroy, Ramsey, Ross, Sherman, Sprague, Stewart, Sumner, Trumbull, Van Winkle, Wade, Willey Wilson, Yates—30.

NAYS—Messrs. Buckalew, Davis, Doolittle, Foster, Hendricks, Morgan. Norton, Patterson, Saulsbury—9.

February 9—The HOUSE passed the bill—yeas 120, nays 44, as follow:

YEAS—Messrs. Allison, Anderson, James M. Ashley, Banks, Barker, Baxter, Beaman, Bidwell, Blaine, Blow, Boutwell, Brandegee. Bromwell, Broomall, Buckland, Reader W. Clarke, Sidney Clarke, Cobb, Cook, Cullom, Darling, Dawes, Delano, Deming, Dixon, Dodge, Donnelly, Driggs, Dumont, Eckley, Eggleston, Eliot, Farnsworth, Farquhar, Ferry, Garfield, Grinnell, Griswold, Abner C. Harding, Hart, Hayes, Henderson, Higby, Hill, Holmes, Hooper, Hotchkiss, John H. Hubbard, James R. Hubbell, Hulburd, Ingersoll, Jenckes, Julian, Kasson, Kelley, Kelso, Ketcham, Koontz, Laflin, George V. Lawrence, William Lawrence, Loan, Longyear, Marston, Marvin, Maynard, McClurg, McIndoe. McKee, McRuer, Mercur, Miller, Moorhead, Morrill, Morris, Moulton, Myers, Newell, O'Neill, Orth, Paine, Patterson, Perham, Pike, Plants, Pomeroy, Price, William H. Randall, Alexander H. Rice, John H. Rice, Rollins, Sawyer, Schenck, Scofield, Shellabarger, Sloan, Spalding, Starr, Stevens, Stokes, Thayer, Francis Thomas, Trowbridge, Upson, Van Aernam, Burt Van Horn, Robert T. Van Horn, Hamilton Ward, Warner, Henry D. Washburn, William B. Washburn, Welker, Wentworth, Whaley, Williams, James F. Wilson, Stephen F. Wilson, Windom, Woodbridge, and SPEAKER COLFAX—120.

NAYS—Messrs. Campbell, Chanler, Cooper, Davis, Dawson, Denison, Eldridge, Finck, Glossbrenner, Goodyear, Aaron Harding, Harris, Hawkins, Hise, Edwin N Hubbell, Humphrey, Hunter, Kerr. Kuykendall, Le Blond, Leftwich, Marshall, McCullough, Niblack, Nicholson, Noell, Radford, Samuel J. Randall, Raymond, Ritter, Rogers, Ross, Rousseau, Shanklin, Sitgreaves, Stillwell, Strouse, Taber, Nathaniel G. Taylor, Nelson Taylor, Thornton, Trimble, Andrew H. Ward, Winfield—44.

Whereupon the SPEAKER of the House declared the bill to be a law.

## Veto of the Reconstruction Bill, March 2, 1867.[*]

*To the House of Representatives:*

I have examined the bill "to provide for the more efficient government of the rebel States" with the care and anxiety which its transcendant importance is calculated to awaken. I am

---

[*] For copy of the bill vetoed, see chap. xviii

unable to give it my assent for reasons so grave, that I hope a statement of them may have some influence on the minds of the patriotic and enlightened men with whom the decision must ultimately rest.

The bill places all the people of the ten States therein named under the absolute domination of military rulers; and the preamble undertakes to give the reason upon which the measure is based, and the ground upon which it is justified. It declares that there exists in those States no legal governments, and no adequate protection for life or property, and asserts the necessity of enforcing peace and good order within their limits. Is this true as matter of fact?

It is not denied that the States in question have each of them an actual Government, with all the powers, executive, judicial, and legislative, which properly belong to a free State. They are organized like the other States of the Union, and, like them, they make, administer, and execute the laws which concern their domestic affairs. An existing *de facto* government, exercising such functions as these, is itself the law of the State upon all matters within its jurisdiction. To pronounce the supreme law-making power of an established State illegal is to say that law itself is unlawful.

The provisions which these Governments have made for the preservation of order, the suppression of crime, and the redress of private injuries, are in substance and principle the same as those which prevail in the northern States and in other civilized countries. They certainly have not succeeded in preventing the commission of all crime, nor has this been accomplished anywhere in the world. There, as well as elsewhere, offenders sometimes escape for want of vigorous prosecution, and occasionally, perhaps, by the inefficiency of courts or the prejudice of jurors. It is undoubtedly true that these evils have been much increased and aggravated, North and South, by the demoralizing influences of civil war, and by the rancorous passions which the contest has engendered. But that these people are maintaining local governments for themselves which habitually defeat the object of all government and render their own lives and property insecure, is in itself utterly improbable, and the averment of the bill to that effect is not supported by any evidence which has come to my knowledge. All the information I have on the subject convinces me that the masses of the southern people and those who control their public acts, while they entertain diverse opinions on questions of Federal policy, are completely united in the effort to reorganize their society on the basis of peace, and to restore their mutual prosperity as rapidly and as completely as their circumstances will permit.

The bill, however, would seem to show upon its face that the establishment of peace and good order is not its real object. The fifth section declares that the preceding sections shall cease to operate in any State where certain events shall have happened. These events are—First, the selection of delegates to a State Convention by an election at which negroes shall be allowed to vote. Second, the formation of a State Constitution by the Convention so chosen. Third, the insertion into the State Constitution of a provision which will secure the right of voting at all elections to negroes, and to such white men as may not be disfranchised for rebellion or felony. Fourth, the submission of the Constitution for ratification to negroes and white men not disfranchised, and its actual ratification by their vote. Fifth, the submission of the State Constitution to Congress for examination and approval, and the actual approval of it by that body. Sixth, the adoption of a certain amendment to the Federal Constitution by a vote of the Legislature elected under the new Constitution. Seventh, the adoption of said amendment by a sufficient number of other States to make it a part of the Constitution of the United States. All these conditions must be fulfilled before the people of any of these States can be relieved from the bondage of military domination; but when they are fulfilled, then immediately the pains and penalties of the bill are to cease, no matter whether there be peace and order or not, and without any reference to the security of life or property. The excuse given for the bill in the preamble is admitted by the bill itself not to be real. The military rule which it establishes is plainly to be used, not for any purpose of order or for the prevention of crime, but solely as a means of coercing the people into the adoption of principles and measures to which it is known that they are opposed, and upon which they have an undeniable right to exercise their own judgment.

I submit to Congress whether this measure is not, in its whole character, scope, and object, without precedent and without authority, in palpable conflict with the plainest provisions of the Constitution, and utterly destructive to those great principles of liberty and humanity for which our ancestors on both sides of the Atlantic have shed so much blood and expended so much treasure.

The ten States named in the bill are divided into five districts. For each district an officer of the Army, not below the rank of brigadier general, is to be appointed to rule over the people; and he is to be supported with an efficient military force to enable him to perform his duties and enforce his authority. Those duties and that authority, as defined by the third section of the bill, are, "to protect all persons in their rights of person and property, to suppress insurrection, disorder, and violence, and to punish, or cause to be punished, all disturbers of the public peace or criminals." The power thus given to the commanding officer over all the people of each district is that of an absolute monarch. His mere will is to take the place of all law. The law of the States is now the only rule applicable to the subjects placed under his control, and that is completely displaced by the clause which declares all interference of State authority to be null and void. He alone is permitted to determine what are rights of person or property, and he may protect them in such way as in his discretion may seem proper. It places at his free disposal all the lands and goods in his district, and he may distribute them without let or hindrance to whom he pleases. Being bound by no State law, and there being no other law to regulate the subject, he may make a criminal code of his own; and he can make it as bloody as any recorded in history, or he can reserve the privilege of acting upon the impulse of his private passions in each case that arises. He is bound by no rules of evidence; there is indeed no provision by which he is authorized or required to take any evidence at all. Everything is a crime which he chooses to call so, and all persons are condemned whom he pronounces to be guilty. He is not bound to keep any record, or make any report of his proceedings. He may arrest his victims wherever he finds them, without warrant, accusation, or proof of probable cause. If he gives them a trial before he inflicts the punishment, he gives it of his grace and mercy, not because he is commanded so to do.

To a casual reader of the bill, it might seem that some kind of trial was secured by it to persons accused of crime; but such is not the case. The officer "may allow local civil tribunals to try offenders," but of course this does not require that he shall do so. If any State or Federal court presumes to exercise its legal jurisdiction by the trial of a malefactor without his special permission, he can break it up, and punish the judges and jurors as being themselves malefactors. He can save his friends from justice, and despoil his enemies contrary to justice.

It is also provided that "he shall have power to organize military commissions or tribunals;" but this power he is not commanded to exercise. It is merely permissive, and is to be used only " when in his judgment it may be necessary for the trial of offenders." Even if the sentence of a commission were made a prerequisite to the punishment of a party, it would be scarcely the slightest check upon the officer, who has authority to organize it as he pleases, prescribe its mode of proceeding, appoint its members from among his own subordinates, and revise all its decisions. Instead of mitigating the harshness of his single rule, such a tribunal would be used much more probably to divide the responsibility of making it more cruel and unjust.

Several provisions, dictated by the humanity of Congress, have been inserted in the bill, apparently to restrain the power of the commanding officer; but it seems to me that they are of no avail for that purpose. The fourth section provides—First. That trials shall not be unnecessarily delayed; but I think I have shown that the power is given to punish without trial, and if so, this provision is practically inoperative. Second. Cruel or unusual punishment is not to be inflicted; but who is to decide what is cruel and what is unusual? The words have acquired a legal meaning by long use in the courts. Can it be expected that military officers will understand or follow a rule expressed in language so purely technical, and not pertaining in the least degree to their profession? If not, then each officer may define cruelty according to his own temper, and if it is not usual, he will make it usual. Corporal punishment, imprisonment, the gag, the ball and chain, and the almost insupportable forms of torture invented for military punishment, lie within the range of choice. Third. The sentence of a commission is not to be executed without being approved by the commander, if it affects life or liberty, and a

sentence of death must be approved by the President This applies to cases in which there has been a trial and sentence. I take it to be clear, under this bill, that the military commander may condemn to death without even the form of a trial by a military commission, so that the life of the condemned may depend upon the will of two men instead of one.

It is plain that the authority here given to the military officer amounts to absolute despotism. But, to make it still more unendurable, the bill provides that it may be delegated to as many subordinates as he chooses to appoint; for it declares that he shall "punish or cause to be punished." Such a power has not been wielded by any monarch in England for more than five hundred years. In all that time no people who speak the English language have borne such servitude. It reduces the whole population of the ten States—all persons, of every color, sex, and condition, and every stranger within their limits—to the most abject and degrading slavery. No master ever had a control so absolute over his slaves as this bill gives to the military officers over both white and colored persons.

It may be answered to this that the officers of the Army are too magnanimous, just, and humane to oppress and trample upon a subjugated people. I do not doubt that Army officers are as well entitled to this kind of confidence as any other class of men. But the history of the world has been written in vain, if it does not teach us that unrestrained authority can never be safely trusted in human hands. It is almost sure to be more or less abused under any circumstances, and it has always resulted in gross tyranny where the rulers who exercise it are strangers to their subjects, and come among them as the representatives of a distant power, and more especially when the power that sends them is unfriendly. Governments closely resembling that here proposed have been fairly tried in Hungary and Poland, and the suffering endured by those people roused the sympathies of the entire world. It was tried in Ireland, and, though tempered at first by principles of English law, it gave birth to cruelties so atrocious that they are never recounted without just indignation. The French Convention armed its deputies with this power, and sent them to the southern departments of the republic. The massacres, murders, and other atrocities which they committed show what the passions of the ablest men in the most civilized society will tempt them to do when wholly unrestrained by law.

The men of our race in every age have struggled to tie up the hands of their Governments and keep them within the law, because their own experience of all mankind taught them that rulers could not be relied on to concede those rights which they were not legally bound to respect. The head of a great empire has sometimes governed it with a mild and paternal sway; but the kindness of an irresponsible deputy never yields what the law does not extort from him. Between such a master and the people subjected to his domination there can be nothing but enmity; he punishes them if they resist his authority, and, if they submit to it, he hates them for their servility.

I come now to a question which is, if possible, still more important. Have we the power to establish and carry into execution a measure like this? I answer, certainly not, if we derive our authority from the Constitution, and if we are bound by the limitations which it imposes.

This proposition is perfectly clear—that no branch of the Federal Government, executive, legislative, or judicial, can have any just powers except those which it derives through and exercises under the organic law of the Union. Outside of the Constitution we have no legal authority more than private citizens, and within it we have only so much as that instrument gives us. This broad principle limits all our functions, and applies to all subjects. It protects not only the citizens of States which are within the Union, but it shields every human being who comes or is brought under our jurisdiction. We have no right to do in one place, more than in another, that which the Constitution says we shall not do at all. If, therefore, the southern States were in truth out of the Union, we could not treat their people in a way which the fundamental law forbids.

Some persons assume that the success of our arms in crushing the opposition which was made in some of the States to the execution of the Federal laws reduced those States and all their people—the innocent as well as the guilty—to the condition of vassalage, and gave us a power over them which the Constitution does not bestow or define or limit. No fallacy can be more transparent than this. Our victories subjected the insurgents to legal obedience, not to the yoke of an arbitrary despotism. When an absolute sovereign reduces his rebellious subjects, he may deal with them according to his pleasure, because he had that power before. But when a limited monarch puts down an insurrection, he must still govern according to law. If an insurrection should take place in one of our States against the authority of the State government, and end in the overthrow of those who planned it, would that take away the rights of all the people of the counties where it was favored by a part or a majority of the population? Could they, for such a reason, be wholly outlawed and deprived of their representation in the Legislature? I have always contended that the Government of the United States was sovereign within its constitutional sphere; that it executed its laws, like the States themselves, by applying its coercive power directly to individuals; and that it could put down insurrection with the same effect as a State, and no other. The opposite doctrine is the worst heresy of those who advocated secession, and cannot be agreed to without admitting that heresy to be right.

Invasion, insurrection, rebellion, and domestic violence were anticipated when the Government was framed, and the means of repelling and suppressing them were wisely provided for in the Constitution; but it was not thought necessary to declare that the States in which they might occur should be expelled from the Union. Rebellions, which were invariably suppressed, occurred prior to that out of which these questions grow; but the States continued to exist and the Union remained unbroken. In Massachusetts, in Pennsylvania, in Rhode Island, and in New York, at different periods in our history, violent and armed opposition to the United States was carried on; but the relations of those States with the Federal Government were not supposed to be interrupted or changed thereby, after the rebellious portions of their population were defeated and put down. It is true that in these earlier cases there was no formal expression of a determination to withdraw from the Union, but it is also true that in the southern States the ordinances of secession were treated by all the friends of the Union as mere nullities, and are now acknowledged to be so by the States themselves. If we admit that they had any force or validity, or that they did in fact take the States in which they were passed out of the Union, we sweep from under our feet all the grounds upon which we stand in justifying the use of Federal force to maintain the integrity of the Government.

This is a bill passed by Congress in time of peace. There is not in any one of the States brought under its operation either war or insurrection. The laws of the States and of the Federal Government are all in undisturbed and harmonious operation. The courts, State and Federal, are open, and in the full exercise of their proper authority. Over every State comprised in these five military districts life, liberty, and property are secured by State laws and Federal laws, and the national Constitution is everywhere in force and everywhere obeyed. What, then, is the ground on which this bill proceeds? The title of the bill announces that it is intended "for the more efficient government" of these ten States. It is recited by way of preamble that no legal State governments "nor adequate protection for life or property," exist in those States, and that peace and good order should be thus enforced. The first thing which arrests attention upon these recitals, which prepare the way for martial law, is this: that the only foundation upon which martial law can exist under our form of government is not stated or so much as pretended. Actual war, foreign invasion, domestic insurrection—none of these appear; and none of these in fact exist. It is not even recited that any sort of war or insurrection is threatened. Let us pause here to consider, upon this question of constitutional law and the power of Congress, a recent decision of the Supreme Court of the United States in *ex parte* Milligan.

I will first quote from the opinion of the majority of the Court: "Martial law cannot arise from a threatened invasion. The necessity must be actual and present, the invasion real, such as effectually closes the courts and deposes the civil administration." We see that martial law comes in only when actual war closes the courts and deposes the civil authority; but this bill, in time of peace, makes martial law operate as though we were in actual war, and become the *cause*, instead of the *consequence* of the abrogation of civil authority. One more quotation: "It follows from what has been said on this subject that there are occasions when martial law can be properly applied. If, in foreign invasion or civil war, the courts are actually closed, and it is impossible to administer criminal justice according to law, then, on the theatre of active military operations, where war really prevails, there is a necessity to furnish a substitute for the civil authority thus overthrown, to preserve the safety of the Army and society; and as no power is left but the military, it is allowed to govern by martial rule until the laws can have their free course."

I now quote from the opinion of the minority of the Court, delivered by Chief Justice Chase: "We by no means assert that Congress can establish and apply the laws of war where no war has been declared or exists. Where peace exists, the laws of peace must prevail." This is sufficiently explicit. Peace exists in all the territory to which this bill applies. It asserts a power in Congress, in time of peace, to set aside the laws of peace and to substitute the laws of war. The minority, concurring with the majority, declares that Congress does not possess that power. Again, and, if possible, more emphatically, the Chief Justice, with remarkable clearness and condensation, sums up the whole matter as follows:

"There are under the Constitution three kinds of military jurisdiction—one to be exercised both in peace and war; another to be exercised in time of foreign war without the boundaries of the United States, or in time of rebellion and civil war within States or districts occupied by rebels treated as belligerents; and a third to be exercised in time of invasion or insurrection within the limits of the United States, or during rebellion within the limits of the States maintaining adhesion to the national Government, when the public danger requires its exercise. The first of these may be called jurisdiction under MILITARY LAW, and is found in acts of Congress prescribing rules and articles of war, or otherwise providing for the government of the national forces; the second may be distinguished as MILITARY GOVERNMENT, superseding, as far as may be deemed expedient, the local law, and exercised by the military commander, under the direction of the President, with the express or implied sanction of Congress; while the third may be denominated MARTIAL LAW PROPER, and is called into action by Congress, or temporarily, when the action of Congress cannot be invited, and in the case of justifying or excusing peril, by the President, in times of insurrection or invasion, or of civil or foreign war, within districts or localities where ordinary law no longer adequately secures public safety and private rights."

It will be observed that of the three kinds of military jurisdiction which can be exercised or created under our Constitution, there is but one that can prevail in time of peace, and that is the code of laws enacted by Congress for the government of the national forces. That body of military law has no application to the citizen, nor even to the citizen soldier enrolled in the militia in time of peace. But this bill is not a part of that sort of military law, for that applies only to the soldier, and not to the citizen, whilst, contrariwise, the military law provided by this bill applies only to the citizen and not to the soldier.

I need not say to the Representatives of the American people that their Constitution forbids the exercise of judicial power in any way but one; that is, by the ordained and established courts. It is equally well known that in all criminal cases a trial by jury is made indispensable by the express words of that instrument. I will not enlarge on the inestimable value of the right thus secured to every freeman, or speak of the danger to public liberty in all parts of the country which must ensue from a denial of it anywhere or upon any pretense. A very

recent decision of the Supreme Court has traced the history, vindicated the dignity, and made known the value of this great privilege so clearly that nothing more is needed. To what extent a violation of it might be excused in time of war or public danger may admit of discussion; but we are providing now for a time of profound peace, where there is not an armed soldier within our borders except those who are in the service of the Government It is in such a condition of things that an act of Congress is proposed which, if carried out, would deny a trial by the lawful courts and juries to nine millions of American citizens, and to their posterity for an indefinite period. It seems to be scarcely possible that any one should seriously believe this consistent with a Constitution which declares, in simple, plain, and unambiguous language, that all persons shall have that right, and that no person shall ever in any case be deprived of it. The Constitution also forbids the arrest of the citizen without judicial warrant, founded on probable cause. This bill authorizes an arrest without warrant, at the pleasure of a military commander. The Constitution declares that "no person shall be held to answer for a capital or otherwise infamous crime unless on presentment by a grand jury." This bill holds every person, not a soldier, answerable for all crimes and all charges without any presentment. The Constitution declares that "no person shall be deprived of life, liberty, or property without due process of law." This bill sets aside all process of law, and makes the citizen answerable in his person and property to the will of one man, and as to his life to the will of two. Finally, the Constitution declares that "the privilege of the writ of *habeas corpus* shall not be suspended unless when, in case of rebellion or invasion, the public safety may require it;" whereas this bill declares martial law (which of itself suspends this great writ) in time of peace, and authorizes the military to make the arrest, and gives to the prisoner only one privilege, and that is a trial "without unnecessary delay." He has no hope of release from custody, except the hope, such as it is, of release by acquittal before a military commission.

The United States are bound to guarantee to each State a republican form of government. Can it be pretended that this obligation is not palpably broken if we carry out a measure like this, which wipes away every vestige of republican government in ten States, and puts the life, property, liberty, and honor of all the people in each of them under the domination of a single person clothed with unlimited authority?

The Parliament of England, exercising the omnipotent power which it claimed, was accustomed to pass bills of attainder; that is to say, it would convict men of treason and other crimes by legislative enactment. The person accused had a hearing, sometimes a patient and fair one; but generally party prejudice prevailed, instead of justice. It often became necessary for Parliament to acknowledge its error and reverse its own action. The fathers of our country determined that no such thing should occur here. They withheld the power from Congress, and thus forbade its exercise by that body; and they provided in the Constitution that no State should pass any bill of attainder. It is, therefore, impossible for any person in this country to be constitutionally convicted or punished for any crime by a legislative proceeding of any sort. Nevertheless, here is a bill of attainder against nine millions of people at once. It is based upon an accusation so vague as to be scarcely intelligible, and found to be true upon no credible evidence. Not one of the nine millions was heard in his own defense. The representatives of the doomed parties were excluded from all participation in the trial. The conviction is to be followed by the most ignominious punishment ever inflicted on large masses of men. It disfranchises them by hundreds of thousands, and degrades them all, even those who are admitted to be guiltless, from the rank of freemen to the condition of slaves.

The purpose and object of the bill, the general intent which pervades it from beginning to end, is to change the entire structure and character of the State governments, and to compel them by force to the adoption of organic laws and regulations which they are unwilling to accept if left to themselves. The negroes have not asked for the privilege of voting; the vast majority of them have no idea what it means. This bill not only thrusts it into their hands, but compels them, as well as the whites, to use it in a particular way. If they do not form a Constitution with prescribed articles in it, and afterwards elect a Legislature which will act upon certain measures in a prescribed way, neither blacks nor whites can be relieved from the slavery which the bill imposes upon them. Without pausing here to consider the policy or impolicy of Africanizing the southern part of our territory, I would simply ask the attention of Congress to that manifest, well-known, and universally acknowledged rule of constitutional law which declares that the Federal Government has no jurisdiction, authority, or power to regulate such subjects for any State. To force the right of suffrage out of the hands of the white people and into the hands of the negroes is an arbitrary violation of this principle.

This bill imposes martial law at once, and its operations will begin so soon as the general and his troops can be put in place. The dread alternative between its harsh rule and compliance with the terms of this measure is not suspended, nor are the people afforded any time for free deliberation. The bill says to them, take martial law first, *then* deliberate. And when they have done all that this measure requires them to do, other conditions and contingencies, over which they have no control, yet remain to be fulfilled before they can be relieved from martial law. Another Congress must first approve the constitutions made in conformity with the will of this Congress, and must declare these States entitled to representation in both Houses. The whole question thus remains open and unsettled, and must again occupy the attention of Congress, and in the meantime the agitation which now prevails will continue to disturb all portions of the people.

The bill also denies the legality of the governments of ten of the States which participated in the ratification of the amendment to the Federal Constitution abolishing slavery forever within the jurisdiction of the United States, and practically excludes them from the Union. If this assumption of the bill be correct, their concurrence cannot be considered as having been legally given, and the important fact is made to appear that the consent of three-fourths of the States—the requisite number—has not been constitutionally obtained to the ratification of that amendment, thus leaving the question of slavery where it stood before the amendment was officially declared to have become a part of the Constitution.

That the measure proposed by this bill does violate the Constitution in the particulars mentioned, and in many other ways which I forbear to enumerate, is too clear to admit of the least doubt. It only remains to consider whether the injunctions of that instrument ought to be obeyed or not. I think they ought to be obeyed, for reasons which I will proceed to give as briefly as possible.

In the first place, it is the only system of free government which we can hope to have as a nation. When it ceases to be the rule of our conduct, we may perhaps take our choice between complete anarchy, a consolidated despotism, and a total dissolution of the Union; but national liberty, regulated by law will have passed beyond our reach.

It is the best frame of government the world ever saw. No other is or can be so well adapted to the genius, habits, or wants of the American people. Combining the strength of a great empire with unspeakable blessings of local self-government, having a central power to defend the general interests, and recognizing the authority of the States as the guardians of industrial rights, it is "the sheet-anchor of our safety abroad and our peace at home." It was ordained "to form a more perfect union, establish justice, insure domestic tranquillity, promote the general welfare, provide for the common defense, and secure the blessings of liberty to ourselves and to our posterity." These great ends have been attained heretofore, and will be again, by faithful obedience to it; but they are certain to be lost if we treat with disregard its sacred obligations.

It was to punish the gross crime of defying the Constitution, and to vindicate its supreme authority, that we carried on a bloody war of four years' duration. Shall we now acknowledge that we sacrificed a million of lives and expended billions of treasure to enforce a Constitution which is not worthy of respect and preservation?

Those who advocated the right of secession alleged in their own justification that we had no regard for law, and that their rights of property, life, and liberty would not be safe under the Constitution, as administered by us. If we now verify their assertion, we prove that they were in truth and in fact fighting for their liberty, and instead of branding their leaders with the dishonoring name of traitors against a righteous and legal Government, we elevate them in history to the rank of self-sacrificing patriots, consecrate them to the admiration of the world, and place them by the side of Washington, Hampden, and Sydney. No; let us leave them to the infamy they deserve, punish them as they should be punished, according to law, and take upon ourselves no share of the odium which they should bear alone.

It is a part of our public history, which can never be forgotten, that both Houses of Congress, in July, 1861, declared, in the form of a solemn resolution, that the war was and should be carried on for no purpose of subjugation, but solely to enforce the Constitution and laws; and that when this was yielded by the parties in rebellion, the contest should cease, with the constitutional rights of the States and of individuals unimpaired. This resolution was adopted and sent forth to the world unanimously by the Senate,* and with only two dissenting voices in the House. It was accepted by the friends of the Union in the South, as well as in the North, as expressing honestly and truly the object of the war. On the faith of it, many thousands of persons in both sections gave their lives and their fortunes to the cause. To repudiate it now by refusing to the States and to the individuals within them the rights which the Constitution and laws of the Union would secure to them, is a breach of our plighted honor for which I can imagine no excuse, and to which I cannot voluntarily become a party.

The evils which spring from the unsettled state of our Government will be acknowledged by all. Commercial intercourse is impeded, capital is in constant peril, public securities fluctuate in value, peace itself is not secure, and the sense of moral and political duty is impaired. To avert these calamities from our country, it is imperatively required that we should immediately decide upon some course of administration which can be steadfastly adhered to. I am thoroughly convinced that any settlement, or compromise, or plan of action which is inconsistent with the principles of the Constitution will not only be unavailing, but mischievous; that it will but multiply the present evils, instead of removing them. The Constitution, in its whole integrity and vigor, throughout the length and breadth of the land, is the best of all compromises. Besides, our duty does not, in my judgment, leave us a choice between that and any other. I believe that it contains the remedy that is so much needed, and that if the co-ordinate branches of the Government would unite upon its provisions, they would be found broad enough and strong enough to sustain in time of peace the nation which they bore safely through the ordeal of a protracted civil war. Among the most sacred guaranties of that instrument are those which declare that "each State shall have at least one Representative," and that "no State, without its consent, shall be deprived of its equal suffrage in the Senate." Each House is made the "judge of the elections, returns, and qualifications of its own members," and may, "with the concurrence of two-thirds, expel a member." Thus, as heretofore urged, "in the admission of Senators and Representatives from any and all of the States, there can

be no just ground of apprehension that persons who are disloyal will be clothed with the powers of legislation; for this could not happen when the Constitution and the laws are enforced by a vigilant and faithful Congress." "When a Senator or Representative presents his certificate of election, he may at once be admitted or rejected; or, should there be any question as to his eligibility, his credentials may be referred for investigation to the appropriate committee. If admitted to a seat, it must be upon evidence satisfactory to the House of which he thus becomes a member, that he possesses the requisite constitutional and legal qualifications. If refused admission as a member for want of due allegiance to the Government, and returned to his constituents, they are admonished that none but persons loyal to the United States will be allowed a voice in the legislative councils of the nation, and the political power and moral influence of Congress are thus effectively exerted in the interests of loyalty to the Government and fidelity to the Union." And is it not far better that the work of restoration should be accomplished by simple compliance with the plain requirements of the Constitution, than by a recourse to measures which in effect destroy the States, and threaten the subversion of the General Government? All that is necessary to settle this simple but important question, without further agitation or delay, is a willingness on the part of all to sustain the Constitution and carry its provisions into practical operation. If to-morrow either branch of Congress would declare that, upon the presentation of their credentials, members constitutionally elected and loyal to the General Government would be admitted to seats in Congress, while all others would be excluded, and their places remain vacant until the selection by the people of loyal and qualified persons; and if, at the same time, assurance were given that this policy would be continued until all the States were represented in Congress, it would send a thrill of joy throughout the entire land, as indicating the inauguration of a system which must speedily bring tranquillity to the public mind.

While we are legislating upon subjects which are of great importance to the whole people, and which must affect all parts of the country, not only during the life of the present generation, but for ages to come, we should remember that all men are entitled at least to a hearing in the councils which decide upon the destiny of themselves and their children. At present ten States are denied representation, and when the Fortieth Congress assembles on the fourth day of the present month, sixteen States will be without a voice in the House of Representatives. This grave fact, with the important questions before us, should induce us to pause in the course of legislation which, looking solely to the attainment of political ends, fails to consider the rights it transgresses, the law which it violates, or the institutions which it imperils.

ANDREW JOHNSON.

WASHINGTON, *March* 2, 1867.

The votes on this bill were as follow :

IN HOUSE.

1867, February 20—The bill passed finally, as above—yeas 128, nays 46, as follow :

---

* This is not quite accurate. There were five negative votes in the Senate. (See Senate Journal, 1st Sess. 39th Congress, page 92.)

YEAS—Messrs. Alley, Allison, Ames, Anderson, Arnell, Delos R. Ashley, James M. Ashley, Baker, Baldwin, Banks, Barker, Baxter, Beaman, Benjamin, Bidwell, Bingham, Blaine, Blow, Boutwell, Brandegee, Bromwell, Broomall, Buckland, Bundy, Reader W. Clarke, Sidney Clarke, Cobb, Cook, Cullom, Darling, Davis, Dawes, Defrees, Delano, Deming, Dixon, Dodge, Donnelly, Dumont, Eggleston, Eliot, Farnsworth, Farquhar, Ferry, Garfield, Grinnell, Griswold, Abner C. Harding, Hart, Hayes, Henderson, Higby, Hill, Holmes, Hooper, Hotchkiss, Chester D. Hubbard, Demas Hubbard, jr., John H. Hubbard, Hulburd, Ingersoll, Julian, Kasson, Kelley, Kelso, Ketcham, Koontz, Laflin, George V. Lawrence, William Lawrence, Loan, Longyear, Lynch, Marvin, Maynard, McClurg, McIndoe, McKee, McRuer, Mercur, Miller, Moorhead, Morris, Moulton, Myers, Newell, O'Neill, Orth, Paine, Patterson, Perham. Pike, Plants, Pomeroy, Price, Raymond, Alexander H. Rice, John H. Rice, Rollins, Sawyer, Schenck, Scofield, Shellabarger, Sloan, Spalling, Starr, Stevens, Stokes, Thayer, Francis Thomas, John L. Thomas, jr., Trowbridge, Upson, Van Aernam, Burt Van Horn, Robert T. Van Horn, Hamilton Ward, Warner, Henry D. Washburn, William B. Washburn, Welker, Wentworth, Whaley, Williams, James F. Wilson, Stephen F. Wilson, Windom, Woodbridge—128.

NAYS—Messrs. *Ancona, Bergen, Boyer, Campbell, Chanler, Cooper, Dawson, Denison, Eldridge, Finck, Glossbrenner, Goodyear, Aaron Harding,* Hawkins, *Hise, Edwin N. Hubbell,* James R. Hubbell, *Humphrey, Hunter, Kerr,* Kuykendall, *LeBlond, Leftwich, Marshall, McCullough, Niblack, Nicholson,* Noell, *Phelps, Radford, Samuel J. Randall, Ritter, Rogers, Ross, Rousseau, Shanklin, Sitgreaves, Strouse, Taber, Nathaniel G. Taylor, Nelson Taylor, Thornton, Trimble, Andrew H. Ward, Winfield, Wright*—46.

Same day—The SENATE passed the bill—yeas 35, nays 7, as follow:

YEAS—Messrs. Brown, Cattell, Chandler, Conness, Cragin, Creswell, Edmunds, Fessenden, Fogg, Foster, Fowler, Frelinghuysen, Harris, Henderson, Howard, Howe, *Johnson,* Kirkwood, Lane, Morgan, Morrill, Poland, Pomeroy, Ramsey, Ross, Sherman, Stewart, Sumner, Trumbull, Van Winkle, Wade, Willey, Williams, Wilson, Yates—35.

NAYS—Messrs. *Buckalew, Cowan, Davis, Hendricks, Nesmith, Patterson, Saulsbury*—7.

March 2—The bill was vetoed.

Same day—The HOUSE re-passed the bill—yeas 138, nays 51, as follow:

YEAS—Messrs. Alley, Allison, Ames, Anderson, Arnell, Delos R. Ashley, James M. Asley, Baker, Baldwin, Banks, Barker, Baxter, Beaman, Benjamin, Bidwell, Bingham, Blaine, Blow, Boutwell, Brandegee, Bronwell, Broomall, Buckland, Bundy, Reader W. Clarke, Sidney Clarke, Cobb, Conkling, Cook, Cullom, Darling, Davis, Dawes, Defrees, Delano, Deming, Dixon, Dodge, Donnelly, Driggs, Dumont, Eckley, Eggleston, Eliot, Farnsworth, Farquhar, Ferry, Garfield, Grinnell, Griswold, Abner C. Harding, Hart, Hayes, Henderson, Higby, Hill, Holmes, Hooper, Hotchkiss, Asahel W. Hubbard, Chester D. Hubbard, Demas Hubbard, jr., John H. Hubbard, James R. Hubbell, Hulburd, Ingersoll, Jenckes, Julian, Kasson, Kelley, Kelso, Ketcham, Koontz, Laflin, George V. Lawrence, William Lawrence, Loan, Longyear, Lynch, Marquette, Marston, Marvin, Maynard. McClurg, McIndoe, McKee, McRuer, Mercur, Miller, Moorhead, Morrill, Morris, Moulton, Myers, Newell, O'Neill, Orth, Paine, Patterson, Perham, Pike, Plants, Pomeroy, Price, Raymond, Alexander H. Rice, John H. Rice, Rollins, Sawyer, Schenck, Scofield, Shellabarger, Sloan, Spalding. Starr, Stevens, Stokes. Thayer, Francis Thomas, John L. Thomas, jr., Trowbridge, Upson, Van Aernam, Burt Van Horn, Robert T. Van Horn, Hamilton Ward, Warner, Henry D. Washburn, William B. Washburn, Welker, Wentworth. Whaley, Williams, James F. Wilson, Stephen F. Wilson, Windom, Woodbridge, and SPEAKER COLFAX—138.

NAYS—Messrs. *Ancona, Bergen, Boyer, Campbell, Chanler, Cooper, Dawson, Denison, Eldridge, Finck, Glossbrenner, Goodyear,* Hale, *Aaron Harding, Harris,* Hawkins, *Hise, Hogan, Edwin N. Hubbell, Humphrey, Hunter, Jones, Kerr,* Kuydendall, Latham, *Le Blond, Leftwich, Marshall, McCullough, Niblack, Nicholson,* Noell, *Phelps, Radford, Samuel J. Randall, Ritter, Rogers, Ross,* Rousseau, *Shanklin, Sitgreaves,* Stillwell, *Strouse, Taber, Nathaniel G. Taylor, Nelson Taylor, Thornton, Trimble, Andrew H. Ward, Winfield, Wright*—51.

Same day—The SENATE re-passed it—yeas 38, nays 10, as follow:

YEAS—Messrs. Anthony, Cattell, Chandler, Conness, Cragin. Creswell, Edmunds. Fessenden, Fogg, Foster, Fowler, Frelinghuysen, Grimes, Harris, Henderson, Howard, Howe, *Johnson,* Kirkwood, Lane, Morgan, Morrill, Nye, Poland, Pomeroy, Ramsey, Ross, Sherman, Sprague, Stewart, Sumner, Trumbull, Van Winkle, Wade, Willey, Williams, Wilson, Yates—38.

NAYS—Messrs. *Buckalew, Cowan, Davis, Dixon, Doolittle, Hendricks, Nesmith, Norton, Patterson, Saulsbury*—10.

Whereupon the PRESIDENT of the Senate declared the bill to be a law.

---

### Veto of the Civil Tenure Bill, March 2, 1867.

*To the Senate of the United States:*

I have carefully examined the bill " to regulate the tenure of certain civil offices." The material portion of the bill is contained in the first section, and is of the effect following, namely: " That every person holding any civil office to which he has been appointed by and with the advice and consent of the Senate, and every person who shall hereafter be appointed to any such office and shall become duly qualified to act therein, is and shall be entitled to hold such office until a successor shall have been appointed by the President, with the advice and consent of the Senate, and duly qualified; and that the Secretaries of State, of the Treasury, of War, of the Navy, and of the Interior, the Postmaster General, and the Attorney General, shall hold their offices respectively for and during the term of the President by whom they may have been appointed. and for one month thereafter, subject to removal by and with the advice and consent of the Senate."

These provisions are qualified by a reservation in the fourth section, "that nothing contained in the bill shall be construed to extend the term of any office the duration of which is limited by law." In effect the bill provides that the President shall not remove from their places any of the civil officers whose terms of service are not limited by law, without the advice and consent of the Senate of the United States. The bill in this respect conflicts, in my judgment, with the Constitution of the United States. The question, as Congress is well aware, is by no means a new one. That the power of removal is constitutionally vested in the President of the United States is a principle which has been not more distinctly declared by judicial authority and judicial commentators than it has been uniformly practiced upon by the legislative and executive departments of the Government. The question arose in the House of Representatives so early as the 16th of June, 1789, on the bill for establishing an executive department denominated " The Department of Foreign Affairs." The first clause of the bill, after recapitulating the functions of that officer and defining his duties, had these words: " to be removable from office by the President of the United States " It was moved to strike out these words, and the motion was sustained with great ability and vigor. It was insisted that the President could not constitutionally exercise the power of removal exclusively of the Senate; that the Federalist so interpreted the Constitution when arguing for its adoption by the several States; that the Constitution had nowhere given the President power of removal, either expressly or by strong implication, but, on the contrary, had distinctly provided for removals from office by impeachment only.

A construction which denied the power of removal by the President was further maintained by arguments drawn from the danger of the abuse of the power; from the supposed tendency of an exposure of public officers to capricious removal to impair the efficiency of the civil service; from the alleged injustice and hardship of displacing incumbents dependent upon their official stations, without sufficient consideration; from a supposed want of responsibility on the part of the President; and from an imagined defect of guaranties against a vicious President who might incline to abuse the power. On the other hand, an exclusive power of removal by the President was defended as a true exposition of the text of the Constitution. It was maintained that there are certain causes for which persons ought to be removed from office without being guilty of treason, bribery, or malfeasance, and that the nature of things demands that it should be so. "Suppose," it was said, "a man becomes insane by the visitation of God, and is likely to ruin our affairs, are the hands of the Government to be confined from warding off the evil? Suppose a person in office, not possessing the talents he was judged to have at the time of the appointment, is the error not to be corrected? Suppose he acquires vicious habits and incurable indolence, or total neglect of the duties of his office, which shall work mischief to the public welfare, is there no way to arrest the threatened danger? Suppose he becomes odious and unpopular, by reason of the measures he pursues—and this he may do without committing any positive offense against the law—must he preserve his office in despite of the popular will? Suppose him grasping for his own aggrandizement and the elevation of his connections by every means short of the treason defined by the Constitution, hurrying your affairs to the precipice of destruction, endangering your domestic tranquillity, plundering you of the means of defense, alienating the affection of your allies, and promoting the spirit of discord; must the tardy, tedious, desultory road by way of impeachment be travelled to overtake the man who, barely confining himself within the letter of the law, is employed in drawing off the vital principle of the Government? The nature of things, the great objects of society, the express objects of the Constitution itself, require that this thing should be otherwise. To unite the Senate with the President in the exercise of the power," it was said, "would involve us in the most serious difficulty. Suppose a discovery of any of those events should take place when the Senate is not in session, how is the remedy to be applied? The evil could be avoided in no other way than by the Senate sitting always." In regard to the danger of the power being abused if exercised by one man, it was said "that the danger is as great with respect to the Senate, who are assembled from various parts of the continent, with different impressions and opinions;" "that such a body is more likely to misuse the power of removal than the man whom the united voice of America calls to the presidential chair. As the nature of government requires the power of removal," it was maintained "that it should be exercised in this way by the hand capable of exerting itself with effect; and the power must be conferred on the President by the Constitution, as the executive officer of the Government."

Mr. Madison, whose adverse opinion in the Federalist had been relied upon by those who denied the exclusive power, now participated in the debate. He declared that he had reviewed his former opinions, and he summed up the whole case as follows:

"The Constitution affirms that the executive power is vested in the President. Are there exceptions to this proposition? Yes, there are. The Constitution says that in appointing to office the Senate shall be associated with the President, unless in the case of inferior officers, when the law shall otherwise direct. Have we (that is, Congress) a right to extend this exception? I believe not. If the Constitution has invested all executive power in the President, I venture to assert that the legislature has no right to diminish or modify his executive authority. The question now resolves itself into this: Is the power of displacing an executive power? I conceive that if any power whatsoever is in the Executive it is the power of appointing, overseeing, and controlling those who execute the laws. If the Constitution had not qualified the power of the President in appointing to office by associating the Senate with him in that business, would it not be clear that he would have the right, by virtue of his executive power, to make such appointment? Should we be authorized, in defiance of that clause in the Constitution—'The executive power shall be vested in the President'—to unite the Senate with the President in the appointment to office? I conceive not. If it is admitted that we should not be authorized to do this, I think it may be disputed whether we have a right to associate them in removing persons from office, the one power being as much of an executive nature as the other; and the first one is authorized by being excepted out of the general rule established by the Constitution in these words: 'The executive power shall be vested in the President.'"

The question thus ably and exhaustively argued was decided by the House of Representatives, by a vote of thirty-four to twenty, in favor of the principle that the executive power of removal is vested by the Constitution in the Executive, and in the Senate by the casting vote of the Vice President.

The question has often been raised in subsequent times of high excitement, and the practice of the Government has nevertheless conformed in all cases to the decision thus early made.

The question was revived during the administration of President Jackson, who made, as is well recollected, a very large number of removals, which were made an occasion of close and rigorous scrutiny and remonstrance. The subject was long and earnestly debated in the Senate, and the early construction of the Constitution was nevertheless freely accepted as binding and conclusive upon Congress.

The question came before the Supreme Court of the United States in January, 1839, *ex parte Hennen*. It was declared by the Court on that occasion, that the power of removal from office was a subject much disputed, and upon which a great diversity of opinion was entertained in the early history of the Government. This related, however, to the power of the President to remove officers appointed with the concurrence of the Senate; and the great question was whether the removal was to be by the President alone, or with the concurrence of the Senate, both constituting the appointing power. No one denied the power of the President and Senate jointly to remove where the tenure of the office was not fixed by the Constitution, which was a full recognition of the principle that the power of removal was incident to the power of appointment; but it was very early adopted as a practical construction of the Constitution, that this power was vested in the President alone; and such would appear to have been the legislative construction of the Constitution, for in the organization of the three great Departments of State, War, and Treasury, in the year 1789, provision was made for the appointment of a subordinate officer by the head of the Department, who should have charge of the records, books, and papers appertaining to the office when the head of the Department should be removed from office by the President of the United States. When the Navy Department was established, in the year 1798, provision was made for the charge and custody of the books, records, and documents of the Department in case of vacancy in the office of Secretary by removal or otherwise. It is not here said "by removal of the President," as is done with respect to the heads of the other Departments, yet there can be no doubt that he holds his office with the same tenure as the other Secretaries, and is removable by the President. The change of phraseology arose, probably, from its having become the settled and well-understood construction of the Constitution that the power of removal was vested in the President alone in such cases, although the appointment of the officer is by the President and Senate. (13 Peters, page 139.)

Our most distinguished and accepted commentators upon the Constitution concur in the construction thus early given by Congress, and thus sanctioned by the Supreme Court. After a full analysis of the congressional debate to which I have referred, Mr. Justice Story comes to this conclusion: "After a most animated discussion, the vote finally taken in the House of Representatives was affirmative of the power of removal in the President, without any co-operation of the Senate, by the vote of thirty-four members against twenty. In the Senate, the clause in the bill affirming the power was carried by the casting vote of the Vice President. That the final decision of this question so made was greatly influenced by the exalted character of the President then in office, was asserted at the time, and has always been believed, yet the doctrine was opposed as well as supported by the highest talents and patriotism of the country. The public have acquiesced in this decision, and it constitutes, perhaps, the most extraordinary case in the history of the Government of a power conferred by implication on the Executive by the assent of a bare majority of Congress, which has not been questioned on many other occasions." The commentator adds: "Nor is this general acquiescence and silence without a satisfactory explanation."

Chancellor Kent's remarks on the subject are as follows:

"On the first organization of the Government it was made a question whether the power of removal in case of officers appointed to hold at pleasure resided nowhere but in the body which appointed, and, of course, whether the consent of the Senate was not requisite to remove. This was the construction given to the Constitution while it was pending for ratification before the State conventions, by the author of the Federalist. But the construction which was given to the Constitution by Congress, after great consideration and discussion, was different. The words of the act (establishing the Treasury Department) are: 'And whenever the same shall be removed from office by the President of the United States, or in any other case of vacancy in the office, the assistant shall act.' This amounted to a legislative construction of the Constitution, and it has ever since been acquiesced in and acted upon as a decisive authority in the case. It applies equally to every other officer of the Gov

ernment appointed by the President, whose term of duration is not specially declared. It is supported by the weighty reason that the subordinate officers in the executive department ought to hold at the pleasure of the head of the department, because he is invested generally with the executive authority, and the participation in that authority by the Senate was an exception to a general principle and ought to be taken strictly. The President is the great responsible officer for the faithful execution of the law, and the power of removal was incidental to that duty, and might often be requisite to fulfill it."

Thus has the important question presented by this bill been settled, in the language of the late Daniel Webster, (who, while dissenting from it, admitted that it was settled,) by construction, settled by precedent, settled by the practice of the Government, and settled by statute. The events of the last war furnished a practical confirmation of the wisdom of the Constitution as it has hitherto been maintained, in many of its parts, including that which is now the subject of consideration. When the war broke out. rebel enemies, traitors, abettors, and sympathizers, were found in every Department of the Government, as well in the civil service as in the land and naval military service. They were found in Congress and among the keepers of the Capitol; in foreign missions; in each and all of the executive Departments; in the judicial service; in the post office, and among the agents for conducting Indian affairs. Upon probable suspicion they were promptly displaced by my predecessor, so far as they held their offices under executive authority, and their duties were confided to new and loyal successors. No complaints against that power or doubts of its wisdom were entertained in any quarter. I sincerely trust and believe that no such civil war is likely to occur again. I cannot doubt, however, that in whatever form, and on whatever occasion, sedition can raise an effort to hinder, or embarrass, or defeat, the legitimate action of this Government, whether by preventing the collection of revenue, or disturbing the public peace, or separating the States, or betraying the country to a foreign enemy, the power of removal from office by the Executive, as it has heretofore existed and been practiced, will be found indispensable.

Under these circumstances, as a depository of the executive authority of the nation, I do not feel at liberty to unite with Congress in reversing it by giving my approval to the bill. At the early day when this question was settled, and, indeed, at the several periods when it has subsequently been agitated, the success of the Constitution of the United States, as a new and peculiar system of free representative government, was held doubtful in other countries, and was even a subject of patriotic apprehension among the American people themselves. A trial of nearly eighty years, through the vicissitudes of foreign conflicts and of civil war, is confidently regarded as having extinguished all such doubts and apprehensions for the future. During that eighty years the people of the United States have enjoyed a measure of security, peace, prosperity, and happiness never surpassed by any nation. It cannot be doubted that the triumphant success of the Constitution is due to the wonderful wisdom with which the functions of government were distributed between the three principal Departments—the legislative, the executive, and the judicial—and to the fidelity with which each has confined itself or been confined by the general voice of the nation within its peculiar and proper sphere. While a just, proper, and watchful jealousy of executive power constantly prevails as it ought ever to prevail, yet it is equally true that an efficient Executive, capable, in the language of the oath prescribed to the President, of executing the laws, and, within the sphere of executive action, of preserving, protecting, and defending the Constitution of the United States, is an indispensable security for tranquility at home, and peace, honor, and safety abroad. Governments have been erected in many countries upon our model. If one or many of them have thus far failed in fully securing to their people the benefits which we have derived from our system, it may be confidently asserted that their misfortune has resulted from their unfortunate failure to maintain the integrity of each of the three great departments while preserving harmony among them all.

Having at an early period accepted the Constitution in regard to the executive office in the sense in which it was interpreted with the concurrence of its founders, I have found no sufficient grounds in the arguments now opposed to that construction or in any assumed necessity of the times for changing those opinions. For these reasons I return the bill to the Senate, in which house it originated, for the further consideration of Congress which the Constitution prescribes. Insomuch as the several parts of the bill which I have not considered are matters chiefly of detail, and are based altogether upon the theory of the Constitution from which I am obliged to dissent, I have not thought it necessary to examine them with a view to make them an occasion of distinct and special objections.

Experience, I think, has shown that it is the easiest, as it is also the most attractive of studies to frame constitutions for the self-government of free States and nations. But I think experience has equally shown that it is the most difficult of all political labors to preserve and maintain such free constitutions of self-government when once happily established. I know no other way in which they can be preserved and maintained, except by a constant adherence to them through the various vicissitudes of national existence, with such adaptations as may become necessary, always to be effected, however, through the agencies and in the forms prescribed in the original constitutions themselves.

Whenever administration fails, or seems to fail, in securing any of the great ends for which republican government is established, the proper course seems to be to renew the original spirit and forms of the Constitution itself.

ANDREW JOHNSON.
WASHINGTON, *March 2, 1867.*

---

### Copy of the Bill Vetoed.

AN ACT regulating the tenure of certain civil offices.

*Be it enacted by the Senate and House of Representatives of the United States of America in Congress assembled,* That every person holding any civil office to which he has been appointed by and with the advice and consent of the Senate and every person who shall hereafter be appointed to any such office, and shall become duly qualified to act therein, is, and shall be, entitled to hold such office until a successor shall have been in like manner appointed and duly qualified, except as herein otherwise provided: *Provided,* That the Secretaries of State, of the Treasury, of War, of the Navy, and of the Interior, the Postmaster General, and the Attorney General shall hold their offices respectively for and during the term of the President by whom they may have been appointed, and for one month thereafter, subject to removal by and with the advice and consent of the Senate.

SEC. 2. That when any officer appointed as aforesaid, excepting judges of the United States courts, shall, during the recess of the Senate, be shown, by evidence satisfactory to the President, to be guilty of misconduct in office, or crime, or for any reason shall become incapable or legally disqualified to perform its duties, in such case, and in no other, the President may suspend such officer, and designate some suitable person to perform temporarily the duties of such office until the next meeting of the Senate, and until the case shall be acted upon by the Senate; and such person, so designated, shall take the oaths and give the bonds required by law to be taken and given by the person duly appointed to fill such office; and in such case it shall be the duty of the President, within twenty days after the first day of such next meeting of the Senate, to report to the Senate such suspension, with the evidence and reasons for his action in the case and the name of the person so designated to perform the duties of such office. And if the Senate shall concur in such suspension, and advise and consent to the removal of such officer, they shall so certify to the President, who may thereupon remove such officer, and, by and with the advice and consent of the Senate, appoint another person to such office. But if the Senate shall refuse to concur in such suspension, such officer so suspended shall forthwith resume the functions of his office, and the powers of the person so performing its duties in his stead shall cease, and the official salary and emoluments of such officer shall, during such suspension, belong to the person so performing the duties thereof, and not to the officer so suspended: *Provided, however,* That the President, in case he shall become satisfied that such suspension was made on insufficient grounds, shall be authorized, at any time before reporting such suspension to the Senate as above provided, to revoke such suspension and reinstate such officer in the performance of the duties of his office.

SEC. 3. That the President shall have power to fill all vacancies which may happen during the recess of the Senate, by reason of death or resignation, by granting commissions which shall expire at the end of their next session thereafter. And if no appointment, by and with the advice and consent of the Senate, shall be made to such office so vacant or temporarily filled as aforesaid during such next session of the Senate, such office shall remain in abeyance without any salary, fees, or emoluments attached thereto, until the same shall be filled by appointment thereto, by and with the advice and consent of the Senate; and during such time all the powers and duties belonging to such office shall be exercised by such other officer as may by law exercise such powers and duties in case of a vacancy in such office

Sec. 4. That nothing in this act contained shall be construed to extend the term of any office the duration of which is limited by law.

Sec. 5. That if any person shall, contrary to the provisions of this act, accept any appointment to or employment in any office, or shall hold or exercise, or attempt to hold or exercise, any such office or employment, he shall be deemed, and is hereby declared to be, guilty of a high misdemeanor, and, upon trial and conviction thereof, he shall be punished therefor by a fine not exceeding ten thousand dollars, or by imprisonment not exceeding five years, or both said punishments, in the discretion of the court.

Sec. 6. That every removal, appointment, or employment made, had, or exercised, contrary to the provisions of this act, and the making, signing, sealing, countersigning, or issuing of any commission or letter of authority for or in respect to any such appointment or employment, shall be deemed, and are hereby declared to be, high misdemeanors, and, upon trial and conviction thereof, every person guilty thereof shall be punished by a fine not exceeding ten thousand dollars, or by imprisonment not exceeding five years, or both said punishments, in the discretion of the court : *Provided,* That the President shall have power to make out and deliver, after the adjournment of the Senate, commissions for all officers whose appointment shall have been advised and consented to by the Senate.

Sec. 7. That it shall be the duty of the Secretary of the Senate, at the close of each session thereof, to deliver to the Secretary of the Treasury, and to each of his assistants, and to each of the Auditors, and to each of the Comptrollers in the Treasury, and to the Treasurer, and to the Register of the Treasury, a full and complete list, duly certified, of all persons who shall have been nominated to and rejected by the Senate during such session, and a like list of all the offices to which nominations shall have been made and not confirmed and filled at such session.

Sec. 8. That whenever the President shall, without the advice and consent of the Senate, designate, authorize, or employ any person to perform the duties of any office, he shall forthwith notify the Secretary of the Treasury thereof, and it shall be the duty of the Secretary of the Treasury thereupon to communicate such notice to all the proper accounting and disbursing officers of his Department.

Sec. 9. That no money shall be paid or received from the Treasury, or paid or received from or retained out of any public moneys or funds of the United States, whether in the Treasury or not, to or by or for the benefit of any person appointed to or authorized to act in or holding or exercising the duties or functions of any office contrary to the provisions of this act ; nor shall any claim, account, voucher, order, certificate, warrant, or other instrument providing for or relating to such payment, receipt, or retention, be presented, passed, allowed, approved, certified, or paid by any officer of the United States, or by any person exercising the functions or performing the duties of any office or place of trust under the United States, for or in respect to such office, or the exercising or performing the functions or duties thereof ; and every person who shall violate any of the provisions of this section shall be deemed guilty of a high misdemeanor, and, upon trial and conviction thereof, shall be punished therefor by a fine not exceeding ten thousand dollars, or by imprisonment not exceeding ten years, or both said punishments, in the discretion of the court.

The votes on this bill were :

February 18—The Senate passed it, as agreed upon by a committee of conference—yeas 22, nays 10, as follow :

Yeas—Messrs. Anthony, Brown, Chandler, Conness, Fogg, Fowler, Henderson, Howard, Howe, Lane, Morgan, Morrill, Ramsey, Ross, Sherman, Stewart, Sumner, Trumbull, Wade, Williams, Wilson, Yates—22.

Nays—Messrs. *Buckalew, Davis, Dixon, Doolittle, Hendricks, Johnson, McDougall, Patterson, Van Winkle, Willey*—10.

February 19—The House passed it—yeas 112, nays 41, as follow :

Yeas—Messrs. Alley, Allison, Ames, Anderson, Arnell, Delos R. Ashley, James M. Ashley, Baker, Baldwin, Banks, Baxter, Beaman, Benjamin, Bidwell, Blaine, Blow, Boutwell, Brandegee, Bromwell, Broomall, Buckland, Reader W. Clarke, Sidney Clarke, Cobb, Cook, Cullom, Darling, Deming, Dodge, Donnelly, Driggs, Dumont, Eggleston, Eliot, Farnsworth, Farquhar, Ferry, Grinnell, Abner C. Harding, Hart, Hayes, Henderson, Higby, Hill, Holmes, Hooper, Hotchkiss, Demas Hubbard, jr., John H. Hubbard, Hulburd. Ingersoll, Julian, Kasson, Kelley, Kelso, Ketcham, Koontz, Kuykendall, Laflin, George V. Lawrence, William Lawrence, Loan, Longyear, Lynch, Marvin, Maynard, McIndoe, McKee, McRuer, Mercur, Miller, Myers, Newell, Orth, Paine, Patterson, Perham, Pike, Plants, Pomeroy, Price, William H. Randall, Raymond, Alexander H. Rice, John H. Rice, Rollins, Sawyer, Schenck, Scofield, Shellabarger, Sloan, Spalding, Starr, Stevens, Stokes, Thayer, John L. Thomas, jr., Trowbridge, Upson, Van Aernam, Burt Van Horn, Robert T. Van Horn, Hamilton Ward, Warner, William B. Washburn, Welker, Wentworth, Williams, James F. Wilson, Stephen F. Wilson, Windom, Woodbridge—112.

Nays—Messrs. *Ancona, Bergen, Boyer, Campbell, Chanler, Cooper, Dawson, Denison, Eldridge, Finck, Glossbrenner, Aaron Harding, Harris,* Hawkins, *Hise, Humphrey, Hunter, Kerr, Latham, Le Blond, Leftwich, McCullough, Niblack, Nicholson, Radford, Samuel J. Randall, Ritter, Rogers, Ross,* Rousseau, *Shanklin, Sitgreaves, Stillwell, Taber, Nathaniel G. Taylor, Nelson Taylor, Thornton, Trimble, Andrew H. Ward,* Whaley, *Wright*—41.

March 2—The bill was vetoed.

Same day—The Senate re-passed it—yeas 35, nays 11, as follow :

Yeas—Messrs. Anthony, Cattell, Chandler, Conness, Cragin, Edmunds, Fessenden, Fogg, Foster, Fowler, Frelinghuysen, Grimes, Harris, Henderson, Howard, Kirkwood, Lane, Morgan, Morrill, Nye, Poland, Pomeroy, Ramsey, Ross, Sherman, Sprague, Stewart, Sumner, Trumbull, Van Winkle, Wade, Willey, Williams, Wilson, Yates—35.

Nays—Messrs. *Buckalew, Cowan, Davis, Dixon, Doolittle, Hendricks, Johnson, Nesmith, Norton, Patterson, Saulsbury*—11.

Same day—The House re-passed it—yeas 138, nays 40, as follow :

Yeas—Messrs. Alley, Allison, Ames, Anderson, Arnell, Delos R. Ashley, James M. Ashley, Baker, Baldwin, Banks, Barker, Baxter, Beaman, Benjamin, Bidwell, Bingham, Blaine, Blow, Boutwell, Brandegee, Bromwell, Broomall, Buckland, Bundy, Reader W. Clarke, Sidney Clarke, Cobb, Conkling, Cook, Cullom, Darling, Davis, Dawes, Defrees, Delano, Deming, Dixon, Dodge, Donnelly, Driggs, Dumont, Eckley, Eggleston, Eliot, Farnsworth, Farquhar, Ferry, Garfield, Grinnell, Griswold, Hale, Abner C. Harding, Hart, Hawkins, Hayes, Henderson, Higby, Hill, Holmes, Hooper, Hotchkiss, Asahel W. Hubbard, Chester D. Hubbard, John H. Hubbard, James R. Hubbell, Hulburd, Ingersoll, Jenckes, Julian, Kasson, Kelley, Kelso, Ketcham, Koontz, Laflin, George V. Lawrence, William Lawrence, Loan, Longyear, Lynch, Marquette, Marston, Marvin, Maynard, McClurg, McIndoe, McKee, McRuer, Mercur, Miller, Moorhead, Morrill, Morris, Moulton, Myers, Newell, O'Neill, Orth, Paine,

Patterson, Perham, Pike, Plants, Pomeroy, Price, William H. Randall, Raymond, Alexander H. Rice, John H. Rice, Rollins, Sawyer, Schenck, Scofield, Shellabarger, Sloan, Spalding, Starr, Stokes, Thayer, Francis Thomas, Trowbridge, Upson, Van Aernam, Burt Van Horn, Robert T. Van Horn, Hamilton Ward, Warner, Henry D. Washburn, William B. Washburn, Welker, Wentworth, Whaley, Williams, James F. Wilson, Stephen F. Wilson, Windom, Woodbridge, and SPEAKER COLFAX—138.

NAYS—Messrs. *Ancona, Bergen, Boyer, Campbell, Chanler, Cooper. Dawson, Eldridge, Finck, Glossbrenner, Goodyear, Aaron Harding, Hise, Hogan, Edwin N. Hubbell, Humphrey, Hunter, Jones,* Latham, *Le Blond, Leftwich, Marshall, McCullough, Niblack, Nicholson, Radford, Samuel J. Randall, Ritter, Rogers, Ross, Shanklin, Sitgreaves, Strouse, Taber, Nelson Taylor, Thornton, Trimble, Andrew H. Ward, Winfield, Wright*—40.

Whereupon the SPEAKER of the House declared the bill to be a law.

### Message Accompanying the Approval of the Army Appropriation Bill, March 2, 1867.

*To the House of Representatives:*

The act entitled "An act making appropriations for the support of the Army for the year ending June 30, 1868, and for other purposes," contains provisions to which I must call attention.

These provisions are contained in the second section, which in certain cases virtually deprives the President of his constitutional functions as Commander-in-Chief of the Army, and in the sixth section, which denies to ten States of the Union their constitutional right to protect themselves, in any emergency, by means of their own militia. These provisions are out of place in an appropriation act. I am compelled to defeat these necessary appropriations if I withhold my signature from the act. Pressed by these considerations, I feel constrained to return the bill with my signature, but to accompany it with my protest against the sections which I have indicated.                    ANDREW JOHNSON.
WASHINGTON, *March* 2, 1867.

The sections complained of are these.

SEC. 2. That the headquarters of the General of the Army of the United States shall be at the city of Washington; and all orders and instructions relating to military operations, issued by the President or Secretary of War, shall be issued through the General of the Army, and, in case of his inability, through the next in rank. The General of the Army shall not be removed, suspended, or relieved from command, or assigned to duty elsewhere than at said headquarters, except at his own request, without the previous approval of the Senate; and any orders or instructions relating to military operations issued contrary to the requirements of this section shall be null and void; and any officer who shall issue orders or instructions contrary to the provisions of this section shall be deemed guilty of a misdemeanor in office; and any officer of the Army who shall transmit, convey, or obey any orders or instructions so issued, contrary to the provisions of this section, knowing that such orders were so issued, shall be liable to imprisonment for not less than two nor more than twenty years, upon conviction thereof in any court of competent jurisdiction.

SEC. 6. That all militia forces now organized or in service in either of the States of Virginia, North Carolina, South Carolina, Georgia, Florida, Ala-

bama, Louisiana, Mississippi, and Texas, be forthwith disbanded, and that the further organization, arming, or calling into service of the said militia forces, or any part thereof, is hereby prohibited under any circumstances whatever, until the same shall be authorized by Congress.

### IN HOUSE.

Pending this bill,

February 20—Mr. BINGHAM moved to strike out from the second section the words in the second sentence, prohibiting the removal, suspension, &c., of the General without the previous approval of the Senate; which was disagreed to —yeas 62, nays 69, as follow:

YEAS—Messrs. *Ancona, Bergen,* Bingham, Buckland, *Campbell, Cooper,* Darling, Davis, Dawes, *Dawson, Denison, Eldridge, Farquhar, Finck. Glossbrenner, Goodyear, Aaron Harding,* Hawkins, *Hise, Hogan, Edwin N. Hubbell,* James R. Hubbell, *Humphrey, Hunter,* Ketcham, Kuykendall. Laflin, George V. Lawrence, *Le Blond, Leftwich,* Loan, *Marshall,* Marvin, *McCullough.* McRuer, Moorhead, *Niblack, Nicholson, Noell,* Phelps, Pike, Pomeroy, *Radford, Samuel J. Randall,* Raymond, *Ritter.Rogers, Ross,* Rousseau, Schenck, *Shanklin, Sitgreaves, Taber, Nathaniel G. Taylor,* Thayer, *Thornton, Trimble, Andrew H. Ward,* William B. Washburn, Whaley, *Winfield, Wright*—62.

NAYS—Messrs. Alley, Allison, Ames, Arnell, James M. Ashley, Baker, Baldwin, Barker, Beaman, Benjamin, Bidwell, Blaine, Blow, Boutwell, Brandegee, Bromwell, Broomall, Bundy, Reader W. Clarke. Sidney Clarke, Cullom, Dodge, Donnelly, Eggleston, Eliot, Abner C. Harding, Hart, Henderson, Higby, Hill, Holmes, Hooper, Hotchkiss, Demas Hubbard, jr., John H. Hubbard, Hulburd, Ingersoll, Julian, Kelley, Koontz, William Lawrence, Longyear, Maynard, McClurg, Mercur, Miller, Moulton, Myers, O'Neill, Orth, Paine, Perham, Price, Rollins, Scofield, Shellabarger. Spalding, Starr, Stevens, Stokes, Upson, Hamilton Ward, Warner, Henry D. Washburn, Welker, Wentworth, Williams, Stephen F. Wilson, Windom—69.

Same day—Mr. LEBLOND moved to strike out the second section; which was disagreed to— yeas 41, nays 88, as follow:

YEAS—Messrs. *Ancona, Bergen,* Bingham, *Campbell, Cooper,* Davis, *Dawson, Denison, Eldridge, Finck, Glossbrenner, Goodyear, Aaron Harding, Hise, Hogan, Humphrey. Hunter,* Kuykendall, *LeBlond, Leftwich,* Loan. *Marshall,* Marvin, *Niblack, Nicholson, Noell,* Phelps, *Radford, Samuel J. Randall,* Raymond, *Ritter,* Rousseau, *Sitgreaves, Nathaniel G. Taylor, Nelson Taylor, Thornton, Trimble, Andrew H. Ward,* Whaley, *Winfield, Wright.*—41.

NAYS—Messrs. Alley, Allison, Ames, Arnell, Delos R. Ashley, James M. Ashley, Baker, Barker, Baxter, Beaman, Benjamin, Bidwell. Blaine, Boutwell, Brandegee, Bromwell, Broomall, Bundy, Reader W. Clarke, Sidney Clarke, Cook, William A. Darling, Dodge, Donnelly, Eggleston, Eliot, Farnsworth, Farquhar, Abner C. Harding, Hart, Henderson. Higby, Hill, Holmes, Hooper, Hotchkiss, Demas Hubbard. jr., John H. Hubbard, James R. Hubbell, Ingersoll, Julian, Kelley, Kelso, Koontz, Laflin, George V. Lawrence, William Lawrence, Longyear, Lynch, Marston, Maynard, McClurg, McIndoe, McRuer, Mercur, Miller, Moorhead, Moulton, Myers, Newell, O'Neill, Orth, Paine, Patterson, Perham, Pike, Plants, Pomeroy, Price, John H. Rice, Rollins, Scofield, Shellabarger, Sloan, Spalding, Starr, Stevens, Stokes, John L. Thomas, jr., Trowbridge, Upson, Burt Van Horn, Hamilton Ward, Warner, Welker, Wentworth, Williams, Windom—88.

February 26—In SENATE, a motion to strike out the second section was lost—yeas 8, nays 28, as follow:

YEAS—Messrs. *Buckalew, Dixon, Doolittle,* Henderson, *Hendricks, Johnson, Norton, Patterson*—8.

NAYS—Messrs. Anthony, Chandler, Conness, Cragin, Creswell, Edmunds, Fessenden, Fogg, Foster, Frelinghuysen, Kirkwood, Morgan, Nye, Poland, Pomeroy, Ramsey, Ross, Sherman, Sprague, Stewart, Sumner, Trumbull, Van Winkle, Wade, Willey, Williams, Wilson, Yates—28.

### Veto of the Supplemental Reconstruction Bill, March 23, 1867.

*To the House of Representatives:*

I have considered the bill entitled "An act supplementary to an act entitled 'An act to provide for the more efficient government of the rebel States,' passed March 2, 1867, and to facilitate restoration," and now return it to the House of Representatives, with my objections.*

This bill provides for elections in the ten States brought under the operation of the original act to which it is supplementary. Its details are principally directed to the elections for the formation of the State constitutions, but by the sixth section of the bill "all elections" in these States occurring while the original act remains in force are brought within its purview. Referring to the details, it will be found that, first of all, there is to be a registration of the voters. No one whose name has not been admitted on the list is to be allowed to vote at any of these elections. To ascertain who is entitled to registration, reference is made necessary, by the express language of the supplement, to the original act and to the pending bill. The fifth section of the original act provides, as to voters, that they shall be "male citizens of the State, twenty-one years old and upward, of whatever race, color, or previous condition, who have been resident of said State for one year." This is the general qualification, followed, however, by many exceptions. No one can be registered, according to the original act, "who may be disfranchised for participation in the rebellion," a provision which left undetermined the question as to what amounted to disfranchisement, and whether, without a judicial sentence, the act itself produced that effect. This supplemental bill superadds an oath, to be taken by every person before his name can be admitted upon the registration, that he has "not been disfranchised for participation in any rebellion or civil war against the United States." It thus imposes upon every person the necessity and responsibility of deciding for himself, under the peril of punishment by a military commission, if he makes a mistake, what works disfranchisement by participation in rebellion, and what amounts to such participation. Almost every man—the negro as well as the white—above twenty-one years of age, who was resident in these ten States, during the rebellion, voluntarily or involuntarily, at some time and in some way, did participate in resistance to the lawful authority of the General Government. The question with the citizen to whom this oath is to be proposed must be a fearful one; for while the bill does not declare that perjury may be assigned for such false swearing, nor fix any penalty for the offense, we must not forget that martial law prevails; that every person is answerable to a military commission, without previous presentment by a grand jury for any charge that may be made against him; and that the supreme authority of the military commander determines the question as to what is an offense, and what is to be the measure of punishment.

The fourth section of the bill provides "that the commanding general of each district shall appoint as many boards of registration as may be necessary, consisting of three loyal officers or persons." The only qualification stated for these officers is that they must be "loyal" They may be persons in the military service or civilians,

residents of the State or strangers. Yet these persons are to exercise most important duties, and are vested with unlimited discretion. They are to decide what names shall be placed upon the register, and from their decision there is to be no appeal. They are to superintend the elections, and to decide all questions which may arise. They are to have the custody of the ballots, and to make returns of the persons elected. Whatever frauds or errors they may commit must pass without redress. All that is left for the commanding general is to receive the returns of the elections, open the same, and ascertain who are chosen "according to the returns of the officers who conducted said elections." By such means, and with this sort of agency, are the conventions of delegates to be constituted.

As the delegates are to speak for the people, common justice would seem to require that they should have authority from the people themselves. No convention so constituted will in any sense represent the wishes of the inhabitants of these States; for, under the all-embracing exceptions of these laws, by a construction which the uncertainty of the clause as to disfranchisement leaves open to the board of officers, the great body of the people may be excluded from the polls, and from all opportunity of expressing their own wishes, or voting for delegates who will faithfully reflect their sentiments.

I do not deem it necessary further to investigate the details of this bill. No consideration could induce me to give my approval to such an election law for any purpose, and especially for the great purpose of framing the constitution of a State. If ever the American citizen should be left to the free exercise of his own judgment, it is when he is engaged in the work of forming the fundamental law under which he is to live. That work is his work, and it cannot properly be taken out of his hands. All this legislation proceeds upon the contrary assumption that the people of each of these States shall have no constitution, except such as may be arbitrarily dictated by Congress and formed under the restraint of military rule. A plain statement of facts makes this evident.

In all these States there are existing constitutions, formed in the accustomed way by the people. Congress, however, declares that these constitutions are not "loyal and republican," and requires the people to form them anew. What then, in the opinion of Congress, is necessary to make the constitution of a State "loyal and republican?" The original act answers the question. It is universal negro suffrage—a question which the Federal Constitution leaves to the States themselves. All this legislative machinery of martial law, military coercion, and political disfranchisement is avowedly for that purpose, and none other. The existing constitutions of the ten States conform to the acknowledged standards of loyalty and republicanism. Indeed, if there are degrees in republican forms of government, their constitutions are more republican now than when these States—four of which were members of the original thirteen—first became members of the Union.

Congress does not now demand that a single provision of their constitutions be changed, except such as confine suffrage to the white population. It is apparent, therefore, that these provisions do not conform to the standard of republicanism which Congress seeks to establish. That there may be no mistake, it is only necessary that reference should be made to the original act, which declares "such constitution shall provide that the elective franchise shall be enjoyed by all such persons as have the qualifications herein stated for electors of delegates." What class of persons is here meant clearly appears in the same section. That is to say, " the male citizens of said State, twenty-one years old and upward, of whatever race, color, or previous condition, who have been resident in said State for one year previous to the day of such election."

Without these provisions no constitution which can be framed in any one of the ten States will be of any avail with Congress. This, then, is the test of what the constitution of a State of this Union must contain to make it republican. Measured by such a standard, how few of the States now composing the Union have republican constitutions! If, in the exercise of the constitutional guaranty that Congress shall secure to every State a republican form of government, universal suffrage for blacks as well as whites is a *sine qua non*, the work of reconstruction may as well begin in Ohio as in Virginia, in Pennsylvania as in North Carolina.

When I contemplate the millions of our fellow-citizens of the South, with no alternative left but to impose upon themselves this fearful and untried experiment of complete negro enfranchisement, and white disfranchisement it may be almost as complete, or submit indefinitely to the rigor of martial law, without a single attribute of freemen, deprived of all the sacred guaranties of our Federal Constitution, and threatened with even worse wrongs, if any worse are possible, it seems to me their condition is the most deplorable to which any people can be reduced. It is true that they have been engaged in rebellion, and that, their object being a separation of the States and a dissolution of the Union, there was an obligation resting upon every loyal citizen to treat them as enemies, and to wage war against their cause.

Inflexibly opposed to any movement imperiling the integrity of the Government, I did not hesitate to urge the adoption of all measures necessary for the suppression of the insurrection. After a long and terrible struggle, the efforts of the Government were triumphantly successful, and the people of the South, submitting to the stern arbitrament, yielded forever the issues of the contest. Hostilities terminated soon after it became my duty to assume the responsibilities of the Chief Executive officer of the Republic, and I at once endeavored to repress and control the passions which our civil strife had engendered, and no longer regarding these erring millions as enemies, again acknowledged them as our friends and our countrymen. The war had accomplished its objects. The nation was saved, and that seminal principle of mischief which, from the birth of the Government, had gradually but inevitably brought on the rebellion, was totally eradicated. Then, it seemed to me, was the auspicious time to commence the work of

reconciliation; then, when the people sought once more our friendship and protection, I considered it our duty generously to meet them in the spirit of charity and forgiveness, and to conquer them even more effectually by the magnanimity of the nation than by the force of its arms. I yet believe that if the policy of reconciliation then inaugurated, and which contemplated an early restoration of these people to all their political rights, had received the support of Congress, every one of these ten States, and all their people, would at this moment be fast anchored in the Union, and the great work which gave the war all its sanction, and made it just and holy, would have been accomplished. Then, over all the vast and fruitful regions of the South peace and its blessing would have prevailed, while now millions are deprived of rights guarantied by the Constitution to every citizen, and, after nearly two years of legislation, find themselves placed under an absolute military despotism. "A military republic—a Government formed on mock elections and supported daily by the sword," was nearly a quarter of a century since pronounced by Daniel Webster, when speaking of the South American States, as a "movement indeed, but a retrograde and disastrous movement from the regular and old-fashioned monarchical systems," and he added:

" If men would enjoy the blessings of republican government, they must govern themselves by reason, by mutual counsel and consultation, by a sense and feeling of general interest, and by the acquiescence of the minority in the will of the majority, properly expressed ; and, above all, the military must be kept, according to the language of our bill of rights, in strict subordination to the civil authority. Wherever this lesson is not both learned and practised, there can be no political freedom. Absurd, preposterous is it, a scoff and a satire on free forms of constitutional liberty, for forms of government to be prescribed by military leaders, and the right of suffrage to be exercised at the point of the sword."

I confidently believe that a time will come when these States will again occupy their true positions in the Union. The barriers which now seem so obstinate must yield to the force of an enlightened and just public opinion, and sooner or later unconstitutional and oppressive legislation will be effaced from our statute-books. When this shall have been consummated, I pray God that the errors of the past may be forgotten, and that once more we shall be a happy, united and prosperous people, and that at last, after the bitter and eventful experience through which the nation has passed, we shall all come to know that our only safety is in the preservation of our Federal Constitution, and in according to every American citizen and to every State the rights which that Constitution secures.

ANDREW JOHNSON.

WASHINGTON, *March*, 23, 1867.

The votes on this bill were :

IN HOUSE.

March 19—The test vote was on Mr. ELDRIDGE's motion to table the report; which was disagreed to—yeas 26, nays 101, as follow :

YEAS—Messrs. *Archer, Barnes, Boyer, Brooks, Burr, Eldridge, Fox, Getz, Glossbrenner, Haight, Holman, Humphrey, Kerr, Marshall, Morrissey, Mungen, Niblack, Nicholson, Noell, Pruyn, Randall, Robinson, Ross, Taber, Van Auken, Wood—26.*

NAYS—Messrs. Allison, Ames, Anderson, Delos R. Ashley, James M. Ashley, Baker, Baldwin, Banks, Beaman, Bingham, Blaine, Blair, Boutwell, Broomall, Buckland, Butler, t ke, Churchill, Reader W. Clarke, Sidney Clarke, Cobb, Coburn, Cook, Cornell. Covode, Cullom, Dodge, Donnelly, Driggs, Eckley, Eggleston. Ela, Farnsworth, Ferriss, Ferry, Fields, Gravely, Halsey, Hamilton, Hooper, Hopkins, Asahel W. Hubbard, Chester D. Hubbard, Hunter, Ingersoll, Judd, Julian, Kelley, Ketcham, Kitchen, Koontz, Laflin, William Lawrence, Lincoln. Loan, Logan, Loughridge, Mallory, Marvin, McClurg. Mercur, Miller, Moore, Morrell, Myers, Newcomb, O'Neill, Orth, Paine, Perham, Pile, Polsley, Robertson, Sawyer, Schenck, Scofield, Shanks, Shellabarger, Spalding, Aaron F. Stevens, Stewart, Taffe, Thomas, Trowbridge, Twichell, Upson, Van Aernam, Burt Van Horn, Robert T. Van Horn, Van Wyck, Ward, Cadwalader C. Washburn. Henry D. Washburn, Welker, Thomas Williams, William Williams, James F. Wilson, John T. Wilson, Stephen F. Wilson, Windom, Woodbridge—101.

IN SENATE.

March 19—It passed without division.

March 23—The bill was vetoed.

Same day—The HOUSE re-passed it—yeas 114, nays 25, as follow :

YEAS—Messrs. Allison, Ames, Anderson, Delos R. Ashley, James M Ashley, Baker, Baldwin, Banks, Beaman, Benjamin, Benton, Blaine, Blair, Boutwell, Broomall, Buckland, Butler, Cake, Churchill, Reader W. Clarke, Sidney Clarke, Cobb, Coburn, Cook, Cornell, Covode, Cullom, Dodge, Donnelly, Driggs, Eckley, Eggleston, Ela, Farnsworth, Ferriss, Ferry, Fields, Finney, Garfield, Gravely, Halsey, Hamilton, Hayes. Hill, Hooper, Hopkins, Chester D. Hubbard, Hulburd, Hunter, Ingersoll, Judd, Julian, Kelley, Kelsey, Ketcham, Kitchen, Koontz, Laflin, William Lawrence, Lincoln, Loan, Logan, Loughridge, Mallory, Marvin, McCarthy, McClurg, Mercur, Miller, Moore, Morrell, Myers, Newcomb, O'Neill, Orth, Paine, Perham, Peters, Pile, Plants, Poland, Polsley, Robertson, Sawyer, Schenck, Scofield. Selye, Shanks, Shellabarger, Smith. Spalding, Aaron F. Stevens. Thaddeus Stevens, Stewart, Taffe, Thomas, Trowbridge, Twichell, Upson, Van Aernam, Burt Van Horn, Robert T. Van Horn, Van Wyck, Ward, Cadwalader C. Washburn, Henry D. Washburn, Welker, Thomas Williams, William Williams, James F. Wilson, John T. Wilson, Stephen F. Wilson, Windom, Woodbridge—114.

NAYS—Messrs Barnes, Boyer, Brooks, Burr, Chanler, Eldridge, Fox, Getz, Glossbrenner, Haight, Holman, Humphrey, Marshall, Morrissey, Mungen, Niblack, Nicholson, Noell, Pruyn, Randall, Robinson, Ross, Taber, Van Auken, Van Trump—25.

Same day—The SENATE re-passed it—yeas 40, nays 7, as follow :

YEAS—Messrs. Anthony, Cameron, Chandler, Cattell, Cole, Conkling, Conness, Corbett, Cragin, Drake, Edmunds, Fessenden, Fowler, Frelinghuysen, Harlan, Howard, Howe, Johnson, Morgan, Lot M. Morrill, Justin S. Morrill, Morton, Nye, Jas. W. Patterson, Pomeroy, Ramsey, Ross, Sherman, Sprague, Stewart, Sumner, Thayer, Tipton, Trumbull, Van Winkle, Wade, Willey, Williams, Wilson, Yates—40.

NAYS—Messrs. Buckalew, Davis, Dixon, Doolittle, Norton, David T. Patterson, Saulsbury—7.

Whereupon the PRESIDENT of the Senate declared the bill to be a law.

---

**Message accompanying the Approval of a Bill relating to Reconstruction, March 30, 1867.**

*To the House of Representatives:*

In giving my approval to the "Joint resolution providing for the expenses of carrying into full effect an act entitled 'An act to provide for the more efficient government of the rebel States,'" I am moved to do so for the following reason : The seventh section of the act supplementary to the act "for the more efficient government of the rebel States" provides that all expenses incurred under or by virtue of that act shall be paid out of any moneys in the Treasury not otherwise appropriated. This provision is wholly unlimited as to the amount to be expended, whereas the resolution now before me limits the appropriation to $500,000. I consider this limitation as a very necessary check against unlimited expenditures and liabilities. Yielding to that consideration, I feel bound to approve this resolution, without modifying in any manner my objections heretofore stated against the original and supplementary acts. ANDREW JOHNSON.

WASHINGTON, *March* 30, 1867.

---

# XVI.

# MEMBERS OF THE CABINET OF PRESIDENT JOHNSON,

### AND OF THE

## THIRTY-NINTH AND FORTIETH CONGRESSES.

### PRESIDENT JOHNSON'S CABINET.

*Secretary of State*—WILLIAM H. SEWARD, of New York.

*Secretary of the Treasury*—HUGH McCULLOCH, of Indiana.

*Secretary of War*—EDWIN M. STANTON, of Ohio.

*Secretary of the Navy*—GIDEON WELLES, of Connecticut.

*Postmaster General*—ALEXANDER W. RANDALL, of Wisconsin, *vice* WILLIAM DENNISON, of Ohio, resigned July 11, 1866.

*Secretary of the Interior*—ORVILLE H. BROWNING. of Illinois, *vice* JAMES HARLAN, of Iowa, resigned September 30, 1866.

*Attorney General*—HENRY STANBERY, of Kentucky, *vice* JAMES SPEED, of Kentucky, resigned July 16, 1866.

### THIRTY-NINTH CONGRESS.

**Second Session, December 3, 1866–March 2, 1867.**

The following changes took place from the list at the First Session, as printed on pages 107 and 108 of the Manual for 1866 :

### SENATE.

*New Hampshire*—George G. Fogg, *vice* Daniel Clark, resigned August 9, 1866.

*New Jersey*—Frederick T. Frelinghuysen, *vice* William Wright, deceased; Alexander G. Cattell, *vice* John P. Stockton, seat vacated.

*Tennessee*—David T. Patterson (admitted July 28, 1866;) Joseph S. Fowler (admitted July 25, 1866.)

*Kansas*—Edmund G. Ross, (qualified July 25, 1866, as successor to James H. Lane.)

## HOUSE OF REPRESENTATIVES.

*New York*—John W. Hunter, *vice* James Humphrey, deceased.

*Pennsylvania*—Philip Johnson, died January 31, 1867.

*Kentucky*—Elijah Hise, *vice* Henry Grider, deceased; Lovell H. Rousseau elected to fill the vacancy caused by his resignation July 20, 1866; Andrew H. Ward, *vice* Green Clay Smith, resigned.

*Tennessee*—Nathaniel G. Taylor, Horace Maynard, William B. Stokes, Edmund Cooper, William B. Campbell, Samuel M. Arnell, Isaac R. Hawkins, John W. Leftwich. (Messrs. Campbell, Arnell, and Hawkins qualified December 3, 1866, the others July 24 and 25, 1866.)

*Nebraska*—Thomas M. Marquette, (qualified March 2, 1867.)

## CLAIMANTS FROM THE INSURRECTIONARY STATES —THIRTY-NINTH CONGRESS.

In SENATE, same as at first session, except James B. Campbell, of South Carolina, *vice* John L. Manning, resigned; and David G. Burnett and O. M. Roberts, of Texas, recently chosen.

In HOUSE, J. McCaleb Wiley, of Alabama, *vice* George C. Freeman, deceased; and James P. Hambleton, of Georgia, *vice* W. T. Wofford; TEXAS—George W. Chilton, Benj. H. Epperson, A. M. Branch, C. Herbert. (Mr. Branch and Mr. Herbert were Representatives in the Rebel Congress.)

## FORTIETH CONGRESS.

### First Session, March 4-30, 1867.

#### SENATE.

BENJAMIN F. WADE, of Ohio, *President of the Senate, and acting Vice President.*

John W. Forney, of Pennsylvania, *Secretary.*

*Maine*—Lot M. Morrill, William Pitt Fessenden.

*New Hampshire*—Aaron H. Cragin, James W. Patterson.

*Vermont*—George F. Edmunds, Justin S. Morrill.

*Massachusetts*—Charles Sumner, Henry Wilson.

*Rhode Island*—William Sprague, Henry B. Anthony.

*Connecticut*—James Dixon, Orris S. Ferry.

*New York*—Edwin D. Morgan, Roscoe Conkling.

*New Jersey*—Frederick T. Frelinghuysen, Alexander G. Cattell.

*Pennsylvania*—Charles R. Buckalew, Simon Cameron.

*Delaware*—George Read Riddle,* Willard Saulsbury.

*Maryland*—Reverdy Johnson, Philip Francis Thomas.†

*Ohio*—Benjamin F. Wade, John Sherman.

*Kentucky*—Garrett Davis, James Guthrie.

*Tennessee*—David T. Patterson, Joseph S. Fowler.

*Indiana*—Thomas A. Hendricks, Oliver P. Morton.

*Illinois*—Richard Yates, Lyman Trumbull.

*Missouri*—John B. Henderson, Charles D. Drake.

*Michigan* — Zachariah Chandler, Jacob M. Howard.

*Iowa*—James W. Grimes, James Harlan.

*Wisconsin*—James R. Doolittle, Timothy O. Howe.

*California*—John Conness, Cornelius Cole.

*Minnesota*—Alexander Ramsey, Daniel S. Norton.

*Oregon*—George H. Williams, Henry W. Corbett.

*Kansas*—Edmund G. Ross, Samuel C. Pomeroy.

*West Virginia*—Peter G. Van Winkle, Waitman T. Willey.

*Nevada*—William M. Stewart, James W. Nye.

*Nebraska*—T. W. Tipton, John M. Thayer.

#### HOUSE OF REPRESENTATIVES.

SCHUYLER COLFAX, of Indiana, *Speaker.*

Edward McPherson, of Pennsylvania, *Clerk.*

*Maine*—John Lynch, Sidney Perham, James G. Blaine, John A. Peters, Frederick A. Pike.

*New Hampshire**—Jacob H. Ela, Aaron F. Stevens, Jacob Benton.

*Vermont*—Frederick E. Woodbridge, Luke P. Poland, Worthington C. Smith.

*Massachusetts*—Thomas D. Eliot, Oakes Ames, Ginery Twichell, Samuel Hooper, Benjamin F. Butler, Nathaniel P. Banks, George S. Boutwell, John D. Baldwin, William B. Washburn, Henry L. Dawes.

*Rhode Island*—(Not elected.)

*Connecticut*—(Not elected.)

*New York*—Stephen Taber, Demas Barnes, William E. Robinson, John Fox, John Morrissey, Thomas E. Stewart, John W. Chanler, James Brooks, Fernando Wood, William H. Robertson, Charles H. Van Wyck, John H. Ketcham, Thomas Cornell, John V. L. Pruyn, John A. Griswold, Orange Ferriss, Calvin T. Hulburd, James M. Marvin, William C. Fields, Addison H. Laflin, John C. Churchill, Dennis McCarthy, Theodore M. Pomeroy, William H. Kelsey, William S. Lincoln, Hamilton Ward, Lewis Selye, Burt Van Horn, James M. Humphrey, Henry Van Aernam, one vacancy.

*New Jersey*—William Moore, Charles Haight, Charles Sitgreaves, John Hill, George A. Halsey.

*Pennsylvania*—Samuel J. Randall, Charles O'Neill, Leonard Myers, William D. Kelley, Caleb N. Taylor, Benjamin M. Boyer, John M. Broomall, J. Lawrence Getz, Thaddeus Stevens, Henry L. Cake, Daniel M. Van Auken, Charles Denison, Ulysses Mercur, George F. Miller, Adam J. Glossbrenner, William H. Koontz, Daniel J. Morrell, Stephen F. Wilson, Glenni W. Scofield, Darwin A. Finney, John Covode, James K. Moorhead, Thomas Williams, George V. Lawrence.

*Delaware*—John A Nicholson.

*Maryland*—Hiram McCullough, Stevenson Archer, Charles E. Phelps, Francis Thomas, Frederick Stone.

*Ohio*—Benjamin Eggleston, Rutherford B. Hayes, Robert C Schenck, William Lawrence,

---

* Died March 30, 1867.
† Not admitted to a seat, his credentials having been referred to the Committee on the Judiciary.

* Members qualified—the first two, March 18, 1867, the last, March 20.

William Mungen, Reader W. Clarke, Samuel Shellabarger, Cornelius S. Hamilton, Ralph P. Buckland, James M. Ashley, John T. Wilson, Philadelph Van Trump, George W. Morgan, Martin Welker, Tobias A. Plants, John A. Bingham, Ephraim R. Eckley, Rufus P. Spalding, James A. Garfield.

*Kentucky*—(Not elected.)
*Tennessee*—(Not elected.)

*Indiana*—William E. Niblack, Michael C. Kerr, Morton C. Hunter, William S. Holman, George W. Julian, John Coburn, Henry D. Washburn, Godlove S. Orth, Schuyler Colfax, William Williams, John P. C Shanks.

*Illinois*—Norman B Judd, John F. Farnsworth, Ellihu B. Washburne, Abner C. Harding, Ebon C. Ingersoll, Burton C. Cook, Henry P. H. Bromwell, Shelby M. Cullom, Lewis W. Ross, Albert G. Burr, Samuel S. Marshall, Jehu Baker, Green B. Raum, John A. Logan.

*Missouri*—William A. Pile, Carman A. Newcomb, Thomas E. Noell, Joseph J. Gravely, Joseph W. McClurg, Robert T. Van Horn, Benjamin F. Loan, John F. Benjamin, George W. Anderson.

*Michigan*—Fernando C. Beaman, Charles Upson, Austin Blair, Thomas W. Ferry, Rowland E. Trowbridge, John F. Driggs.

*Iowa*—James F. Wilson, Hiram Price, William B. Allison, William Loughridge, Grenville M. Dodge, Asahel W. Hubbard.

*Wisconsin*—Halbert E. Paine, Benjamin F. Hopkins, Amasa Cobb, Charles A. Eldridge, Philetus Sawyer, Cadwalader C. Washburn.

*California*—(Not elected.)
*Minnesota*—William Windom, Ignatius Donnelly
*Oregon*—Rufus Mallory.
*Kansas*—Sidney Clarke.
*West Virginia*—Chester D. Hubbard, Bethuel M. Kitchen, Daniel Polsley.
*Nevada*—Delos R. Ashley.
*Nebraska*—John Taffe.

CLAIMANTS FROM INSURRECTIONARY STATES— FORTIETH CONGRESS.

IN SENATE—John A. Winston, of Alabama, *vice* George S. Houston; John T. Jones, and Augustus H. Garland, of Arkansas, *vice* William D. Snow,* and Elisha Baxter; G. Williamson, of Louisiana, *vice* Henry Boyce; Mathias A. Manley, of North Carolina, *vice* John Pool. (Of these, Mr. Winston and Mr. Williamson served in the rebel army, the former as colonel of a regiment, the latter as major on General Polk's staff; Mr. Garland was in all the Rebel Congresses.)

*Seat declared vacant by the Legislature.

---

# XVII.

# VOTES ON POLITICAL BILLS AND RESOLUTIONS.

### Repeal of Pardon by Proclamation.
#### IN HOUSE.

1866, December 3—Mr. ELIOT introduced a bill, under a suspension of the rules, to repeal the thirteenth section of the act of July 17, 1862, which thirteenth section is in these words: "That the President is hereby authorized, at any time hereafter, by proclamation, to extend to persons who may have participated in the existing rebellion, in any State or part thereof, pardon and amnesty, with such exceptions, and at such time, and on such conditions, as he may deem expedient for the public welfare."

The bill passed—yeas 112, nays 29. The NAYS were:

Messrs. *Ancona. Boyer, Campbell, Chanler, Dawson, Eldridge, Glossbrenner,* Hale, *Aaron Harding, Hise, Kerr, Le Blond, Leftwich, Marshall, Niblack, Nicholson, Noell,* Phelps, *Samuel J. Randall. Ritter, Rogers,* Rousseau, *Shanklin, Sitgreaves,* Stillwell, *Nathaniel G. Taylor,* Nelson Taylor, *Trimble, Andrew H. Ward.*

1867, January 7—The SENATE passed it—yeas 27, nays 7, as follow:

YEAS—Messrs. Cattell, Chandler, Conness, Cragin, Creswell, Edmunds, Fessenden, Foster, Fowler, Henderson, Howard, Howe, Kirkwood, Lane, Morgan, Morrill, Poland, Ramsey, Ross, Sherman, Stewart, Sumner, Trumbull, Wade, Willey, Williams, Wilson—27.

NAYS—Messrs. *Dixon.* Doolittle, *Hendricks, Johnson, Norton, Patterson, Saulsbury*—7.

NOTE.—This bill became a law by reason of the failure of the President to sign, or return it with his objections, within ten days after presentation to him.

---

### Representation of Rebel States.
#### IN HOUSE.

1866, December 11—A bill passed, of which this is the chief section:

"That before the first meeting of the next Congress, and of every subsequent Congress, the Clerk of the next preceding House of Representatives shall make a roll of the representatives elect, and place thereon the names of all persons claiming seats as representatives elect from States which were represented in the next preceding Congress, and of such persons only, and whose credentials show that they were regularly elected in accordance with the laws of their States respectively, or the laws of the United States."

The vote was—yeas 124, nays 31, as follow:

YEAS—Messrs. Alley, Allison, Anderson, Arnell, Delos R. Ashley, James M. Ashley, Baker, Baldwin, Barker, Baxter, Beaman, Benjamin, Bidwell, Bingham, Blaine, Blow, Boutwell, Brandegee, Bromwell, Broomall, Buckland, Bundy, Reader W. Clarke, Sidney Clarke, Cobb, Conkling, Cook, Cullom, Darling, Dawes, Defrees, Delano, Deming, Dixon, Donnelly, Eckley, Eggleston, Eliot, Farnsworth, Farquhar, Ferry, Garfield, Grinnell, Hale, Abner C. Harding, Hart, Hayes, Henderson, Higby, Hill, Holmes, Hooper, Chester D. Hubbard, John H. Hubbard, James R. Hubbell, Hulburd, Ingersoll, Jenckes, Julian, Kasson, Kelley, Kelso, Ketcham, Koontz, Kuykendall, Laflin, Latham, George V. Lawrence, William Lawrence, Longyear, Lynch, Marston, Marvin, Maynard, McClurg, McIndoe, McKee, McRuer, Mercur, Miller, Moorhead, Morrill, Morris, Moulton, O'Neill, Orth, Paine, Patterson, Perham, Pike, Plants, Pomeroy, Price, William H. Randall, Raymond, Alexander H. Rice, John H. Rice, Rollins, Sawyer, Schenck, Scofield, Shellabarger, Sloan, Spalding, Starr, Stevens, Stokes, Thayer, Francis Thomas,

John L. Thomas, jr., Trowbridge, Upson, Van Aernam, Burt Van Horn, Hamilton Ward, Ellihu B. Washburne, William B. Washburn, Welker, Wentworth, Williams, James F. Wilson, Stephen F. Wilson, Windom, Woodbridge—104.

NAYS—Messrs. *Ancona, Bergen, Boyer, Campbell, Cooper, Dawson, Eldridge, Finck, Glossbrenner, Goodyear, Aaron Harding, Hise, Edwin N. Hubbell, Hunter, Le Blond, Marshall, Niblack, Nicholson, Samuel J. Randall, Ritter, Rogers, Ross,* Rousseau, *Shanklin, Sitgreaves,* Stillwell, *Taber, Nathaniel G. Taylor, Nelson Taylor, Trimble, Andrew H. Ward* —51.

### IN SENATE.

1867, February 1—The bill passed—yeas 31, nays 6, as follow:

YEAS—Messrs. Cattell, Chandler, Conness, Cragin, Edmunds, Fessenden, Fogg, Foster, Fowler, Grimes, Harris, Henderson, Howe, *Johnson,* Kirkwood, Lane, Morgan, Morrill, *Norton,* Poland, Ramsey, Ross, Sherman, Sprague, Stewart, Sumner, Trumbull, Van Winkle, Williams, Wilson, Yates—31.

NAYS—Messrs. *Buckalew, Davis, Hendricks, Nesmith, Patterson, Saulsbury*—6.

NOTE.—This bill became a law by reason of the failure of the President to sign or return it with his objection, within ten days after presentation to him.

---

### Elective Franchise in the Territories.

#### IN SENATE.

1867, January 10—Pending the bill to amend the organic acts of the Territories,

This substitute was adopted:

That from and after the passage of this act there shall be no denial of the elective franchise in any of the Territories of the United States, now or hereafter to be organized, to any citizen thereof, on account of race, color, or previous condition of servitude, and all acts or parts of acts, either of Congress or the legislative assemblies of said Territories, inconsistent with the provisions of this act, are hereby declared null and void.

The vote was—yeas 24, nays 8, as follow:

YEAS—Messrs. Anthony, Conness, Cragin, Creswell, Edmunds, Fessenden, Fogg, Foster, Fowler, Grimes, Henderson, Howard, Howe, Kirkwood, Lane, Morgan, Morrill, Poland, Sherman, Stewart, Sumner, Wade, Willey, Williams —24.

NAYS—Messrs. *Buckalew, Hendricks, Johnson, Norton, Patterson, Riddle, Saulsbury, Van Winkle*—8.

Same day—The HOUSE concurred—yeas 104, nays 38, as follow:

YEAS—Messrs. Alley, Allison, Ames, Arnell, James M. Ashley, Baker, Baldwin, Banks, Barker, Baxter, Beaman, Benjamin, Bidwell, Bingham, Blaine, Boutwell. Bromwell, Broomall, Buckland, Bundy, Reader W. Clarke, Sidney Clarke, Cobb, Cook, Cullom, Culver, Davis, Defrees, Delano, Deming, Dixon, Dodge, Donnelly, Driggs, Eckley, Eggleston, Farnsworth, Farquhar, Ferry, Garfield, Grinnell, Abner C. Harding, Hart, Hawkins, Higby, Hill, Holmes, Hooper, Demas Hubbard, jr., John H. Hubbard, James R. Hubbell, Ingersoll, Jenckes, Julian, Kasson, Kelso, Ketcham, Koontz, George V. Lawrence, William Lawrence, Loan, Longyear, Lynch, Marston, Marvin, Maynard, McClurg, McRuer, Mercur, Miller, Morrill, Moulton, Myers, O'Neill, Orth, Paine, Perham, Plants, Price, Raymond, John H. Rice, Rollins, Sawyer, Schenck, Scofield, Spalding, Stokes, Thayer, John L. Thomas, jr., Trowbridge, Upson, Van Aernam, Burt Van Horn, Hamilton Ward, Elihu B. Washburne, Henry D. Washburn, William B. Washburn, Welker, Wentworth, Williams, James F. Wilson, Stephen F. Wilson, Windom —104.

NAYS—Messrs. *Ancona, Bergen, Boyer, Campbell, Chanler, Cooper, Dawson, Denison, Eldridge, Finck, Glossbrenner, Aaron Harding, Hise, Hogan,* Chester D. Hubbard, *Edwin N. Hubbell, Humphrey, Johnson,* Latham, *Le Blond, Leftwich, Niblack, Nicholson, Noell, Samuel J. Randall,* William H. Randall, *Ritter, Rogers, Ross, Shanklin, Sitgreaves, Taber, Nathaniel G. Taylor, Thornton, Trimble, Andrew H. Ward, Whaley, Winfield*—38.

NOTE.—This bill became a law by reason of the failure of the President to sign, or return it with his objections, within ten days after presentation to him.

### Female Suffrage and Intelligence Suffrage.

Pending the District of Columbia Suffrage **bill** in the SENATE—

1866, December 12—Mr. COWAN moved to strike from it the word "male," which was lost —yeas 9, nays 37, as follow:

YEAS—Messrs. Anthony, Brown, *Buckalew, Cowan,* Foster, *Nesmith, Patterson, Riddle.* Wade—9.

NAYS—Messrs. Cattell. Chandler, Conness, Creswell, *Davis, Dixon,* Doolittle, Edmunds, Fessenden, Fogg, Frelinghuysen, Grimes, Harris, Henderson, *Hendricks,* Howard, Howe, Kirkwood, Lane, Morgan, Morrill, *Norton,* Poland, Pomeroy, Ramsey, Ross, *Saulsbury,* Sherman, Sprague, Stewart, Sumner, Trumbull, Van Winkle, Willey, Williams, Wilson, Yates—37.

Mr. DIXON moved to add to first section this proviso:

"That no person who has not heretofore voted in this District shall be permitted to vote, unless he shall be able at the time of offering to vote, to read, and also to write his own name."

Which, December 13, was lost—yeas 11, nays 34, as follow:

YEAS—Messrs. Anthony, *Buckalew, Dixon, Doolittle,* Fogg, Foster, *Hendricks, Nesmith, Patterson, Riddle,* Willey—11.

NAYS—Messrs Brown, Cattell, Chandler, Conness, *Cowan,* Creswell, *Davis,* Edmunds, Fessenden, Frelinghuysen, Grimes, Harris, Henderson, Howard, Howe, Kirkwood, Lane, Morgan, Morrill, *Norton,* Poland, Pomeroy, Ramsey, Ross, *Saulsbury,* Sherman, Sprague, Stewart, Sumner, Trumbull, Van Winkle, Wade, Williams, Wilson—34.

#### IN HOUSE.

January 28—Mr. NOELL introduced a bill to abolish all disqualification from voting in the District of Columbia, on account of sex, and moved it be referred to a select committee, which was lost—yeas 49, nays 74, as follow:

YEAS—Messrs. *Ancona,* Baker, Barker, Baxter, Benjamin, *Boyer,* Broomall, Bundy, *Campbell, Cooper,* Defrees, *Denison, Eldridge,* Farnsworth, Ferry, *Finck,* Garfield, Hale, Hawkins, *Hise,* Chester D. Hubbard, *Edwin N. Hubbell, Humphrey,* Julian, Kasson, Kelley, Kelso, *Le Blond,* Loan, McClurg, McKee, Miller, Newell, *Niblack, Noell,* Orth, *Ritter, Rogers, Ross, Sitgreaves,* Starr, Stevens, *Strouse, Taber, Nathaniel G. Taylor, Trimble, Andrew H. Ward,* Henry D. Washburn, *Winfield*—49.

NAYS—Messrs. Allison, Anderson, James M. Ashley, Baldwin, Beaman, Bidwell, Bingham, Blaine, Boutwell, Brandegee, Buckland, Reader W. Clarke, Conkling, Cook, Cullom, Darling, Dawes, Deming, Donnelly, Dumont, Eckley, Eggleston, Eliot, Farquhar, Grinnell, Higby, Holmes, Hooper, John H. Hubbard, Ingersoll, Jenckes, Koontz, Laflin, Lynch, Marvin, McIndoe, McRuer, Mercur, Moorhead, Morrill, Myers, O'Neill, Paine, Patterson, Perham, Phelps, Pike, Plants, Price, *Samuel J. Randall,* Raymond, Rollins, Sawyer, Schenck, Scofield, Shellabarger, Sloan, Spalding, Stokes, Francis Thomas, John L. Thomas, jr., Trowbridge, Upson, Van Aernam, Burt Van Horn, Hamilton Ward, Warner, William B. Washburn, Welker, Wentworth, Williams, James F. Wilson, Windom, Woodbridge—74.

### Test Oath of Attorneys.

#### IN HOUSE.

1867, January 22—Mr. BOUTWELL reported this bill:

*Be it enacted, &c.,* That no person shall be permitted to act as an attorney or counsellor in any court of the United States who has been guilty of treason, bribery, murder, or other felony, or who has been engaged in any rebellion against the Government of the United States, or who has given aid, comfort, or encouragement to the enemies of the United States in armed hostility thereto.

SEC. 2. That the first section of this act is hereby declared to be a rule of every court of the United States.

SEC. 3. That it shall be the duty of the judge or judges of any such court, when the suggestion is made in open court that any person acting as an attorney or counsellor of said court, or offering or proposing to so act, is barred by the provisions of this act, or whenever said judge or judges shall believe that such person is so barred, to inquire and ascertain whether such person has been guilty of treason, bribery, murder, or other felony, or whether he has been engaged in any rebellion against the Government of the United States, or whether he has given aid, comfort, or encouragement to the enemies of the United States in armed hostility thereto; and if the court shall be of opinion that such person has been guilty of treason, bribery, murder, or other felony, or that he has been engaged in any rebellion against the Government of the United States, or that he has given aid, comfort, or encouragement to the enemies of the United States in armed hostility thereto, to exclude and debar such person from the office of attorney or counsellor of said court. And any person who shall testify falsely in any examination made by any court, as aforesaid, shall be guilty of perjury, and liable to the pains and penalties of perjury.

January 23—The bill passed—yeas 119, nays 43, as follow:

YEAS—Messrs. Anderson, Delos R. Ashley, James M. Ashley, Baker, Baldwin, Banks, Barker, Baxter, Beaman, Benjamin, Bidwell, Bingham, Blaine, Boutwell, Brandegee, Bromwell, Broomall, Buckland, Bundy, Reader W. Clarke, Cobb, Conkling, Cook, Cullom, Darling, Dawes, Defrees, Delano, Deming, Dixon, Donnelly, Driggs, Dumont, Eckley, Eggleston, Eliot, Farnsworth, Farquhar, Ferry, Garfield, Grinnell, Griswold, Abner C. Harding, Hart, Hayes, Higby, Hill, Holmes, Hooper, Hotchkiss, Chester D. Hubbard, Demas Hubbard, jr., John H. Hubbard, Ingersoll, Jenckes, Julian, Kasson, Kelley, Kelso, Ketcham, Koontz, Kuykendall, Laflin, George V. Lawrence, William Lawrence, Loan, Longyear, Lynch, Marston, Marvin, Maynard, McClurg, McIndoe, McKee, Mercur, Miller, Moorhead, Morrill, Morris, Moulton, Myers, Newell, O'Neill, Orth, Paine, Patterson, Perham, Pike, Plants, Price, William H. Randall, Raymond, Alexander H. Rice, John H. Rice, Rollins, Sawyer, Scofield, Shellabarger, Sloan, Spalding, Starr, Stokes, Francis Thomas, John L. Thomas, jr., Trowbridge, Upson, Van Aernam, Burt Van Horn, Hamilton Ward, Warner, Henry D. Washburn, William B. Washburn, Welker, Wentworth, Williams, James F. Wilson, Stephen F. Wilson, Windom, Woodbridge—119.

NAYS—Messrs. Ancona, Bergen, Boyer, Campbell, Chanler, Cooper, Dawson, Denison, Eldridge, Finck, Glossbrenner, Goodyear, Hale, Aaron Harding, Hogan, Edwin N. Hubbell, Humphrey, Hunter, Kerr, Latham, Le Blond, Leftwich, Marshall, McCullough, McRuer, Niblack, Nicholson, Phelps, Radford, Samuel J. Randall, Ritter, Rogers, Ross, Shanklin, Sitgreaves, Stillwell, Taber, Nathaniel G. Taylor, Nelson Taylor, Thornton, Trimble, Andrew H. Ward, Winfield—43.

The bill was not acted upon in the Senate.

## Validating Certain Proclamations and Acts of the President, and Others.

### IN HOUSE.

1867, January 22—Pending this bill, introduced by Mr. BINGHAM, and reported from the Judiciary Committee, with amendments, by Mr. JAMES F. WILSON,

AN ACT to declare valid and conclusive certain proclamations of the President, and acts done in pursuance thereof, or of his orders, in the suppression of the late rebellion against the United States.

Be it enacted by the Senate and House of Representatives of the United States of America in Congress assembled, That all acts, proclamations, and orders of the President of the United States, or acts done by his authority or approval after the fourth of March, anno Domini eighteen hundred and sixty-one, and before the first day of July, anno Domini eighteen hundred and sixty-six, respecting martial law, military trials by courts-martial or military commissions, or the arrest, imprisonment, and trial of persons charged with participation in the late rebellion against the United States, or as aiders or abettors thereof, or as guilty of any disloyal practice in aid thereof, or of any violation of the laws or usages of war, or of affording aid and comfort to rebels against the authority of the United States, and all proceedings and acts done or had by courts-martial or military commissions, or arrests and imprisonments made in the premises by any person by the authority of the orders or proclamations of the President, made as aforesaid, or in aid thereof, are hereby approved in all respects, legalized and made valid, to the same extent and with the same effect as if said orders and proclamations had been issued and made, and said arrests, imprisonments, proceedings, and acts had been done under the previous express authority and direction of the Congress of the United States, and in pursuance of a law thereof previously enacted and expressly authorizing and directing the same to be done. And no civil court of the United States, or of any State, or of the District of Columbia, or of any district or Territory of the United States, shall have or take jurisdiction of, or in any manner reverse any of the proceedings had or acts done as aforesaid, nor shall any person be held to answer in any of said courts for any act done or omitted to be done in pursuance or in aid of any of said proclamations or orders, or by authority or with the approval of the President within the period aforesaid, and respecting any of the matters aforesaid; and all officers or other persons in the service of the United States, or who acted in aid thereof, acting in the premises, shall be held prima facie to have been authorized by the President; and all acts and parts of acts heretofore passed, inconsistent with the provisions of this act, are hereby repealed.

On the motion to insert the clause beginning " and all officers and other persons," the yeas were 109, the nays 37, (Messrs. Ancona, Bergen, Boyer, Campbell, Chanler, Cooper, Dawson, Denison, Eldridge, Finck, Glossbrenner, Goodyear, Aaron Harding, Hise, Edwin N. Hubbell, Humphrey, Hunter, Johnson, Kerr, Le Blond, Leftwich, Marshall, Niblack, Nicholson, Noell, Radford, Samuel J. Randall, Ritter, Rogers, Ross, Shanklin, Sitgreaves, Strouse, Taber, Nelson Taylor, Thornton, Trimble.)

February 23—The bill passed—yeas 112, nays 32, as follow:

YEAS—Messrs. Allison, Ames, Anderson, Arnell, Delos R. Ashley, James M. Ashley, Baker, Baldwin, Baxter, Beaman, Bidwell, Bingham, Blaine, Brandegee, Bromwell, Broomall, Buckland, Bundy, Reader W. Clarke, Sidney Clarke, Cobb, Conkling, Cook, Cullom, Davis, Dawes, Delano, Deming, Dixon, Dodge, Donnelly, Eggleston, Eliot, Farnsworth, Farquhar, Garfield, Grinnell, Abner C. Harding, Hawkins, Hayes, Henderson, Higby, Hill, Holmes, Hooper, Chester D. Hubbard, Demas Hubbard, jr., John H. Hubbard, James R. Hubbell, Hulburd, Ingersoll, Jenckes, Julian, Kasson, Kelley, Ketcham, Koontz, Kuykendall, Laflin, George V. Lawrence, William Lawrence, Loan, Longyear, Lynch, Marvin, Maynard, McClurg, McIndoe, McKee, McRuer, Mercur, Miller, Moorhead, Morris, Moulton, Myers, Newell, O'Neill, Orth, Paine, Perham, Plants, Price, William H. Randall, John H. Rice, Rollins, Sawyer, Scofield, Shellabarger, Sloan, Spalding, Starr, Stevens, Stillwell, Stokes, Thayer, Trowbridge, Upson,

Van Aernam, Burt Van Horn, Hamilton Ward, Warner, Henry D. Washburn, William B. Washburn, Welker, Wentworth, Whaley, Williams, James F. Wilson, Stephen F. Wilson, Windom, Woodbridge—112.

NAYS—Messrs. *Ancona, Bergen, Boyer, Campbell, Chanler, Cooper, Dawson, Eldridge, Finck, Glossbrenner, Aaron Harding, Harris, Hise, Edwin N. Hubbell, Humphrey, Hunter, Kerr, LeBlond, Marshall, McCullough, Niblack, Nicholson, Samuel J. Randall, Ritter, Shanklin, Sitgreaves, Strouse, Taber, Thornton, Trimble, Andrew H. Ward, Wright*—32.

### IN SENATE.

March 2—The bill passed—yeas 36, nays 8, as follow:

YEAS—Messrs. Anthony, Cattell, Chandler, Conness, Cragin, *Dixon, Doolittle,* Edmunds, Fessenden, Fogg, Foster, Fowler, Frelinghuysen, Grimes, Harris, Howard, Howe, Kirkwood, Lane, Morgan, Morrill, Nye, *Patterson,* Pomeroy, Ramsey, Ross, Sherman, Sprague, Stewart, Sumner, Trumbull, Van Winkle, Wade, Willey, Williams, Wilson, Yates—36.

NAYS—Messrs. *Buckalew, Cowan, Davis, Hendricks, Johnson, McDougall, Norton, Saulsbury*—8.

### Homesteads in Southern States.

1867, February 28—Mr. JULIAN reported a bill amending the act of June 21, 1866, respecting homesteads in Alabama, Mississippi, Louisiana, Arkansas, and Florida, so that any person applying for the benefit of said act shall be required to make oath that he has not voluntarily borne arms against the United States or given aid or comfort to its enemies; *Provided,* That said oath shall not be required of any person who during the late war enlisted in the military or naval service of the United States, and who shall have been honorably discharged therefrom, and not thereafter rendered any aid or comfort to the rebellion.

The bill was passed—yeas 97, nays 30, as follow:

YEAS—Messrs. Alley, Allison, Ames, Arnell, James M. Ashley, Baker, Banks, Baxter, Beaman, Bingham, Blaine, Brandegee, Bromwell, Broomall, Buckland, Reader W. Clarke, Cobb, Conkling, Cook, Darling, Davis, Dawes, Defrees, Delano, Dixon, Dodge, Dumont, Eliot, Farquhar, Griswold, Hawkins, Hayes, Higby, Hill, Holmes, Hooper, Chester D. Hubbard, Demas Hubbard, jr., John H. Hubbard, Hulburd, Jenckes, Julian, Kelley, Kelso, Koontz, George V. Lawrence, William Lawrence, Loan, Longyear, Lynch, Marvin, Maynard, McClurg, McIndoe, McKee, McRuer, Mercur, Miller, Morrill, Morris, Moulton, Myers, Newell, O'Neill, Orth, Paine, Perham, Pike, Plants, Pomeroy, W. H. Randall, Rollins, Sawyer, Schenck, Scofield, Shellabarger, Sloan, Spalding, Starr, Stokes. Thayer, Francis Thomas, John L. Thomas, jr., Trowbridge, Upson, Van Aernam, Burt Van Horn, Hamilton Ward, Warner, Henry D. Washburn, William B. Washburn, Welker, Wentworth. Whaley, Stephen F. Wilson, Windom—97.

NAYS—Messrs. *Ancona, Bergen, Campbell, Chanler, Cooper, Dawson, Finck, Glossbrenner, Goodyear, Aaron Harding, Hise, Hogan, Edwin N. Hubbell, Humphrey, Kerr, Kuydendall, Latham, Le Blond, Leftwich, Marshall, Niblack, Nicholson, Ritter, Shanklin, Sitgreaves, Taber, Trimble, Andrew H. Ward, Winfield, Wright*—30.

The bill was not acted upon in the Senate.

### To Suspend the Payment of Bounty to former Owners of Colored Volunteers.

#### IN HOUSE.

1867, January 14—Mr. COOK reported, under a suspension of the rules, from the Judiciary Committee this bill:

That so much of section twenty-four of an act approved February twenty-fourth, eighteen hundred and sixty-four, entitled "An act to amend an act entitled 'An act for enrolling and calling out the national forces, and for other purposes,'" approved March third, eighteen hundred and sixty-three, as provides that the Secretary of War should appoint a commission in each of the slave States then represented in Congress, charged to award to each loyal person to whom a colored volunteer might owe service a just compensation, not exceeding three hundred dollars for such colored volunteer, be suspended until otherwise provided by law, and that the duties and compensation of the commissioners heretofore appointed under said section, shall cease from the date of the passage of this resolution.

Which was passed—yeas 107, nays 36, as follow:

YEAS—Messrs. Alley, Allison, Ames, Anderson, Delos R. Ashley, James M. Ashley, Baker, Baldwin, Banks, Baxter, Benjamin, Bidwell, Bingham, Blaine, Boutwell, Bromwell, Broomall, Buckland, Bundy, Reader W. Clarke, Cobb, Cook, Cullom, Culver, Davis, Dawes, Defrees, Delano, Deming, Dixon, Donnelly, Driggs, Eckley, Eliot, Farnsworth, Farquhar, Ferry, Griswold, Abner C. Harding, Henderson, Higby, Hill, Holmes, Hooper, Chester D. Hubbard, Demas Hubbard, jr., John H. Hubbard, James R. Hubbell, Ingersoll, Jenckes, Julian, Kasson, Kelso, Ketcham, Koontz, Kuykendall, George V. Lawrence, Loan, Longyear, Lynch, Marston, Marvin, Maynard, McClurg, McKee, McRuer, Mercur, Morrill, Morris, Moulton, O'Neill, Orth, Paine, Patterson, Perham, Pike, Plants, Pomeroy, Price, Raymond, John H. Rice, Rollins, *Ross,* Sawyer, Schenck, Scofield, Shellabarger, Spalding, Stevens, Stokes, Thayer, Trowbridge, Upson, Van Aernam, Burt Van Horn, Hamilton Ward, Warner, Ellihu B. Washburne, Henry D. Washburn, William B. Washburn, Welker, Wentworth. Whaley. Williams, James F. Wilson, Stephen F. Wilson, Windom—107.

NAYS—Messrs. *Ancona, Bergen, Boyer, Campbell, Chanler, Dawson, Denison, Finck, Glossbrenner, Aaron Harding, Hawkins, Hise, Hogan, Edwin N. Hubbell, Humphrey, Johnson, Latham, Le Blond, Leftwich, Marshall, Niblack, Nicholson, Noell, Radford, Samuel J. Randall, William H. Randall, Ritter, Rogers, Shanklin, Sitgreaves, Strouse, Taber, Nathaniel G. Taylor, Nelson Taylor, Thornton, Andrew H. Ward*—36.

The bill was not acted upon in the Senate.

### To Suspend all Proceedings in relation to the Payment for Slaves drafted or received as Volunteers in the Military Service.

#### IN HOUSE.

1867, March 18—The bill passed, providing that all further proceedings under the twenty-fourth section of the act of Congress approved February twenty-fourth, eighteen hundred and sixty-four, "to award compensation to the masters of slaves drafted into the military service of the United States, and award compensation to persons to whom colored volunteers may owe service," and under the second section of the act approved July twenty-eighth, eighteen hundred and sixty-six, "making appropriation for payment to persons claiming service or labor from colored volunteers or drafted men," be, and the same is hereby suspended. And the Secretary of War is directed to dissolve the commissions appointed under the said sections, and make payment to the commissioners and clerks for the services rendered, upon their making report of their proceedings to the War Department.

March 18—The vote on Mr. SCHENCK's motion to suspend the rules to allow the consideration of the bill, was the only vote taken—and was yeas 92, nays 24, as follow:

YEAS—Messrs. Ames, Anderson, Delos R. Ashley, James M. Ashley, Baker, Baldwin, Beaman, Benjamin, Bingham, Blaine, Blair, Boutwell, Bromwell, Broomall, Buckland, Butler, Churchill, Reader W. Clarke, Sidney Clarke, Cobb, Cook, Cornell, Covode, Cullom, Dodge, Donnelly, Driggs, Eckley, Ela, Farnsworth, Ferriss, Ferry, Fields, Garfield, Gravely, Hamilton, Hayes, Hooper, Hopkins, Asahel W. Hubbard, Chester D. Hubbard. Hulburd, Hunter, Judd, Julian, Kelley, Kitchen, Koontz, Laflin, William Lawrence, Logan, Marvin. McClurg, Miller, Moore, Myers, Newcomb, O'Neill, Orth, Paine, Perham, Peters, Pile, Plants, Poland, Polsley, Pomeroy, Robertson, *Ross,* Sawyer, Schenck, Scofield, Shanks, Shellabarger, Smith, Spalding, Taylor, Twichell, Upson, Van Aernam, Burt Van Horn, Robert T. Van Horn, Van Wyck, Ward, Cadwalader C. Washburn, Henry D. Washburn, Welker, Thomas Williams, William Williams, James F Wilson, John T. Wilson, Windom—92.

NAYS—Messrs. *Boyer, Brooks, Burr, Eldridge, Fox, Getz, Glossbrenner, Holman, Kerr, Marshall, Morgan, Morrissey, Mungen, Niblack, Nicholson, Noell, Pruyn, Randall, Robinson, Sitgreaves, Taber, Van Auken, Van Trump, Wood*—24.

### IN SENATE.

March 21—The resolution passed—yeas 32, nays 7, as follow:

YEAS—Messrs. Anthony, Cameron, Cattell, Chandler, Cole, Conkling, Conness, Corbett, Cragin, Drake, Edmunds, Fowler, Harlan, Henderson, Howe, Morgan, Morrill of Vt., Morton, Nye, Patterson of N. H., Pomeroy, Ramsey, Ross, *Saulsbury*, Sherman, Sumner, Thayer, Tipton, Trumbull, Wade, Williams, Wilson—32.

NAYS—Messrs. *Buckalew, Davis, Doolittle, Johnson, Patterson* of Tenn., Van Winkle, Willey—7.

### A Bill to Restore the Possession of Lands Confiscated by the Authorities of the States lately in Rebellion.

### IN HOUSE.

1866, July 24—Mr. WILLIAMS reported from the Committee on the Judiciary the following bill :

That in all cases where any loyal citizen of the United States may have been disseized or dispossessed of any lands or tenements belonging to him or her, within any of the States lately in rebellion, by any order, proceeding, or decree, under the pretended authority of the so-called Confederate government, or of any of the States comprising the same, on the ground of his or her adherence to the cause of the Union, or his or her absence, or failure or refusal to give support to the said rebellion, it shall be the duty of the President of the United States, or the commanding officer of the military forces stationed within the particular State or District, on complaint made to either of them in writing, by the party or parties so disseized or dispossessed, their heirs or assigns, accompanied by satisfactory evidence that the title or possession of any such property is claimed by the person or persons occupying the same under or by virtue of any such order, proceeding, or decree, to restore the person or persons so interested and aggrieved to the possession and rights of which they have been thus unjustly deprived, and to protect them in the enjoyment of said rights by the application of so much force as may be necessary for that purpose.

Mr. TRIMBLE moved that it be laid on the table, which was disagreed to—yeas 24, nays 81, as follow :

YEAS—Messrs. *Ancona, Bergen, Boyer, Cooper, Eldridge, Finck, Glossbrenner, Aaron Harding, Hogan, Johnson, Kerr, Le Blond, McCullough, Niblack, Nicholson, Radford, Samuel J. Randall, Ritter, Ross, Strouse, Taber, Thornton, Trimble, Winfield*—24.

NAYS—Messrs. Allison, Baker, Banks, Barker, Baxter, Benjamin, Bidwell, Bingham, Buckland, Sidney Clarke, Cobb, Conkling, Cullom, Davis, Dawes, Defrees, Dixon, Driggs, Eckley, Eggleston, Eliot, Farnsworth, Farquhar, Ferry, Abner C. Harding, Hart, Hayes, Higby, Holmes, Hooper, Hotchkiss, Chester D. Hubbard, John H. Hubbard, James R. Hubbell, Hulburd, Jenckes. Julian, Kelley, Ketcham, Koontz, Laflin, George V Lawrence, William Lawrence, Loan, Lynch, Maynard McClurg, McRuer, Mercur, Miller, Moorhead, Morris, Myers, Newell. O'Neill, Orth, Paine, Perham, Plants, Price, Raymond, Rollins, Sawyer, Scofield, Shellabarger, Spalding, Stevens, Stokes, *Nathaniel G. Taylor*, John L. Thomas, jr., Burt Van Horn, Robert T. Van Horn, Hamilton Ward, Welker, Wentworth, Whaley, Williams, James F. Wilson, Stephen F. Wilson, Windom, Woodbridge—81.

The bill was then passed.

### IN SENATE.

1867, February 21—Mr. FRELINGHUYSEN reported it from the Committee on the Judiciary, with an amendment as to the form of proceeding, but it was not reached before adjournment.

---

## PROPOSED IMPEACHMENT OF PRESIDENT JOHNSON.

### In Thirty-Ninth Congress.

1866, December 17—Mr. JAMES M. ASHLEY moved a suspension of the rules to enable him to report, from the Committee on Territories, this resolution:

*Resolved,* That a select committee to consist of seven members of this House be appointed by the Speaker, whose duty it shall be to inquire whether any acts have been done by any officer of the Government of the United States which in contemplation of the Constitution are high crimes or misdemeanors, and whether said acts were designed or calculated to overthrow, subvert, or corrupt the Government of the United States, or any department thereof, and that said committee have power to send for persons and papers and to administer the customary oath to witnesses, and that they have leave to report by bill or otherwise.

Which was not agreed to, (two-thirds being necessary,) yeas 90, nays 49, as follow:

YEAS—Messrs. Alley, Allison, Anderson, Arnell, Delos R. Ashley, James M. Ashley, Baker, Baldwin, Banks, Barker, Baxter, Benjamin, Bidwell, Bingham, Blow, Boutwell, Brandegee, Bromwell, Buckland, Bundy, Reader W. Clarke, Sidney Clarke, Cobb, Conkling, Cullom, Dixon, Driggs, Eckley, Farnsworth, Farquhar, Ferry, Garfield, Grinnell, Abner C, Harding, Hart, Hawkins, Hayes, Henderson, Hill, Holmes, Hotchkiss, Demas Hubbard, jr., John H. Hubbard, Ingersoll, Julian, Kelley, Kelso, Koontz, Kuykendall, Laflin, William Lawrence, Loan, Longyear, Lynch, Marston, Marvin, McClurg, McIndoe, McKee, McRuer, Mercer, Morrill, Moulton, Myers, O'Neill, Orth, Paine, Patterson, Perham, Pike, Pomeroy, Price, William H. Randall, Schenck, Scofield, Sloan, Stevens, Thayer, Francis Thomas, Trowbridge, Upson, Van Aernam, Burt Van Horn, Robert T. Van Horn, Ellihu B. Washburne Welker, Wentworth, Williams, James F. Wilson, Windom - 90.

NAYS— Messrs. Ames, *Ancona, Bergen, Boyer, Campbell, Chanler, Cooper,* Dawes, Defrees, Deming, *Denison, Dodge, Eldridge, Finck. Glossbrenner,* Hale, *Aaron Harding, Hise,* Hogan, Chester D. Hubbard, *E. N. Hubbell, Hunter,* Jenckes *Kerr, Latham, LeBlond, Leftwich, Marshall,* Maynard, *Niblack, Nicholson, Noell, Samuel J. Randall,* Raymond, *Ritter, Rogers, Ross, Shanklin, Sitgreaves.* Spalding, Stokes, *Strouse, Taber, Nathaniel G. Taylor, Nelson Taylor, Thornton, Andrew H. Ward,* Warner, *Whaley*—49.

1867, January 7—Mr. LOAN offered this resolution, which was referred to the Committee on Reconstruction :

*Resolved,* That for the purpose of securing the fruits of the victories gained on the part of the Republic during the late war, waged by rebels and traitors against the life of the nation, and of giving effect to the will of the people as expressed at the polls during the recent elections by a majority numbering in the aggregate more than four hundred thousand votes, it is the imperative duty of the Thirty-Ninth Congress to take without delay such action as will accomplish the following objects:

1. The impeachment of the officer now exercising the functions pertaining to the office of President of the United States of America, and his removal from said office upon his conviction, in due form of law, of the high crimes and misdemeanors of which he is manifestly and notori-

ously guilty, and which render it unsafe longer to permit him to exercise the powers he has unlawfully assumed.

2. To provide for the faithful and efficient administration of the executive department of the Government within the limits prescribed by law.

3. To provide effective means for immediately reorganizing civil governments in those States lately in rebellion, excepting Tennessee, and for restoring them to their practical relations with the Government upon a basis of loyalty and justice; and to this end,

4. To secure, by the direct intervention of Federal authority, the right of franchise alike, without regard to color, to all classes of loyal citizens residing within those sections of the Republic which were lately in rebellion.

Same day—Mr. KELSO offered this resolution:

*Resolved*, That for the purpose of securing the fruits of the victories gained on the part of the Republic during the late war, waged by rebels and traitors against the life of the nation, and of giving effect to the will of the people, as expressed at the polls during the late elections by majorities numbering in the aggregate more than four hundred thousand votes, it is the imperative duty of the Thirty-Ninth Congress to take, without delay, such action as will accomplish the following objects:

1. The impeachment of the officer now exercising the functions pertaining to the office of the President of the United States of America, and his removal from office, upon his conviction, in due form, of the crimes and high misdemeanors of which he is manifestly and notoriously guilty, and which render it unsafe longer to permit him to exercise the powers he has unlawfully assumed.

2. To provide for the faithful and efficient administration of the executive department within the limits prescribed by law.

Mr. DAVIS moved it be tabled; which was disagreed to—yeas 40, nays, 104. The YEAS were:

Messrs. *Ancona*, Delos R. Ashley, Baldwin, *Bergen, Campbell, Chanler, Cooper*, Davis, *Dawson, Eldridge, Finck, Glossbrenner, Aaron Harding*, Hawkins, *Hise, Hogan, Humphrey, Hunter, Kerr*, Kuykendall, Latham, *Leftwich, McCullough, Niblack, Nicholson, Noell, Phelps, Samuel J. Randall*, William H. Randall, *Ritter, Ross, Shanklin, Strouse, Taber, Nathaniel G. Taylor, Nelson Taylor, Trimble, Ward*, Whaley, *Winfield*—40.

They were subsequently referred to the Committee on the Judiciary.

Same day—Mr. JAMES M. ASHLEY, as a question of privilege, submitted the following:

I do impeach Andrew Johnson, Vice-President and acting President of the United States, of high crimes and misdemeanors.

I charge him with a usurpation of power and violation of law:

In that he has corruptly used the appointing power;

In that he has corruptly used the pardoning power;

In that he has corruptly used the veto power;

In that he has corruptly disposed of public property of the United States;

In that he has corruptly interfered in elections, and committed acts which, in contempla-

tion of the Constitution, are high crimes and misdemeanors: Therefore,

*Be it resolved*, That the Committee on the Judiciary be, and they are hereby, authorized to inquire into the official conduct of Andrew Johnson, Vice-President of the United States, discharging the powers and duties of the office of President of the United States, and to report to this house whether, in their opinion, the said Andrew Johnson, while in said office, has been guilty of acts which were designed or calculated to overthrow, subvert, or corrupt the Government of the United States, or any department or officer thereof; and whether the said Andrew Johnson has been guilty of any act, or has conspired with others to do acts, which, in contemplation of the Constitution, are high crimes or misdemeanors, requiring the interposition of the constitutional power of this house; and that said committee have power to send for persons and papers, and to administer the customary oath to witnesses.

Mr. SPALDING moved to lay the subject on the table; which was disagreed to—yeas 39, nays 106.

The proposition of Mr. ASHLEY was then agreed to—yeas 108, nays 39, as follow:

YEAS—Messrs. Alley, Allison, Ames, Arnell, Delos R. Ashley, James M. Ashley, Baker, Baldwin, Banks, Barker, Baxter, Beaman, Benjamin, Bidwell, Bingham, Blaine, Boutwell, Brandegee, Bromwell, Broomall, Buckland, Bundy, Chanler, Reader W. Clarke, Sidney Clarke, Cobb, Cook, Cullom, Culver, Darling, Defrees, Delano, Deming, Dixon, Donnelly, Driggs, Eckley, Farnsworth, Farquhar, Ferry, Garfield, Grinnell, Abner C. Harding, Hart, Hayes, Henderson, Higby, Hill, Holmes, Hooper, Chester D. Hubbard, John H. Hubbard, Ingersoll, Jenckes, Julian, Kasson, Kelley, Kelso, Ketcham, Kuykendall, George V. Lawrence, William Lawrence, Loan, Longyear. Lynch, Marston. Marvin, Maynard, McClurg, McKee, McRuer, Mercur, Miller, Moorhead, Morrill, Moulton, Myers, O'Neill, Orth, Paine, Patterson, Perham, Pike, Price, William H. Randall, Alexander H. Rice, John H. Rice, Sawyer, Schenck, Scofield, Starr, Stevens, Stokes, Thayer, John L. Thomas, jr., Trowbridge, Upson, Van Aernam, Hamilton Ward, Warner, Ellihu B. Washburne, Henry D. Washburn, Welker, Wentworth, Williams, James F. Wilson, Stephen F. Wilson. Windom—108.

NAYS—Messrs. *Ancona, Bergen, Campbell. Cooper*, Davis, *Dawson*, Dodge, *Eldridge, Finck, Glossbrenner, Aaron Harding*, Hawkins, *Hise. Hogan*, James R. Hubbell. *Humphrey, Hunter, Kerr*, Latham, *Leftwich, McCullough, Niblack, Nicholson, Noell*, Phelps. *Samuel J. Randall*, Raymond, *Ritter, Ross, Shanklin*, Spalding, *Strouse, Taber, Nathaniel G. Taylor, Nelson Taylor, Trimble, Andrew H. Ward*, Whaley, *Winfield*—39.

---

### Report of the Committee, February 28, 1867.

*The Committee on the Judiciary, charged by the House with the examination of certain allegations of high crimes and misdemeanors against the President of the United States, submit the following report:*

On the seventh day of January, 1867, the House, on motion of Hon. James M. Ashley, a representative from the State of Ohio, adopted the following preamble and resolution, to wit:

"I do impeach Andrew Johnson, Vice President and acting President of the United States, of high crimes and misdemeanors.

"I charge him with a usurpation of power and violation of law: in that he has corruptly used the appointing power; in that he has corruptly used the pardoning power; in that he has corruptly used the veto power; in that he has corruptly disposed of public property of the United States; in that he has corruptly interfered in elections, and committed acts, and conspired with others to commit acts, which, in contemplation of the Constitution, are high crimes and misdemeanors.

"*Therefore, be it resolved*, That the Committee on the Judiciary be, and they are hereby. authorized to inquire into the official conduct of Andrew Johnson, Vice President of the United States, discharging the powers and duties of the office of President of the United States, and to report to this House whether, in their opinion. the said Andrew Johnson, while in said office, has been guilty of acts which were designed or calculated to overthrow, subvert, or corrupt the Government of the United States, or any department or officer thereof; and whether the said Andrew Johnson has been guilty of any act, or has conspired with others to do acts, which, in contemplation of the Constitution, are high crimes or misdemeanors, requiring the interposition of the constitutional powers of this House; and that said committee have power to send for persons and papers and to administer the customary oath to witnesses."

The duty imposed on the committee, by this action of the House, was of the highest and gravest character. No committee during the entire history of the Government had ever been charged with a more important trust. The responsibility which it imposed was of oppressive weight, and of most unpleasant nature. Gladly would the committee have escaped from the arduous labors imposed on it by the resolution of the House; but, once imposed, prompt, deliberate, and faithful action, with a view to correct results, became its duty, and to this end it has directed its efforts.

Soon after the adoption of the resolution by the House, the Hon. James M. Ashley communicated to the committee, in support of his charges against the President of the United States, such facts as were in his possession, and the investigation was proceeded with, and has been continued almost without a day's interruption. A large number of witnesses has been examined, many documents collected, and everything done which could be done to reach a conclusion of the case. But the investigation covers a broad field, embraces many novel and interesting and important questions, and involves a multitude of facts; while most of the witnesses are distant from the capital; owing to which, the committee, in view of the magnitude of the interests involved in this action, has not been able to conclude its labors, and is not, therefore, prepared to submit a definite and final report.

If the investigation had even approached completeness, the committee would not feel authorized to present the result to the House at this late period of the session, unless the charges had been so entirely negatived as to admit of no discussion, which, in the opinion of the committee, is not the case. Certainly, no affirmative report could be properly considered in the expiring hours of this Congress.

The committee not having fully investigated all the charges preferred against the President of the United States, it is deemed inexpedient to submit any conclusion, beyond the statement that sufficient testimony has been brought to its notice to justify and demand a further prosecution of the investigation.

The testimony which the committee has taken will pass into the custody of the Clerk of the House, and can go into the hands of such committee as may be charged with the duty of bringing this investigation to a close, so that the labor expended upon it may not have been in vain.

The committee regrets its inability definitely to dispose of the important subject committed to its charge, and presents this report for its own justification, and for the additional purpose of notifying the succeeding Congress of the incom-

pleteness of its labors, and that they should be completed.　　　JAMES F. WILSON, *Chairman.*
　　　　　.G. S. BOUTWELL,
　　　　　THOS. WILLIAMS,
　　　　　BURTON C. COOK,
　　　　　WM. LAWRENCE,
　　　　　FRANCIS THOMAS,
　　　　　D. MORRIS,
　　　　　F. E. WOODBRIDGE.

### MINORITY REPORT.

Mr. ROGERS, the minority of the committee, submits the following as his views:

The subscriber, one of the Judiciary Committee, to whom was referred by the House the inquiry to inquire into the official conduct of his Excellency the President of the United States, with a view to his impeachment upon certain charges made by the Hon. James M. Ashley, begs leave to submit the following report:

The committee refuse to allow a report to be made giving the evidence to the House at this time, upon grounds which are no doubt satisfactory to themselves. Therefore, I cannot report the evidence upon which my conclusion is based, which I would gladly do, did the committee deem it expedient. The examination of witnesses and the records was commenced, as appears by the majority report, about the time of the reference, to wit, on the 7th of January, 1867, and continued daily. A large number of witnesses has been examined, and everything done that could be to bring the case to a close, as appears by the majority report; and the majority came to the conclusion "that sufficient testimony has been brought to its notice to justify and demand a further prosecution of the investigation." I have carefully examined all the evidence in the case, and do report that there is not one particle of evidence to sustain any of the charges which the House charged the committee to investigate, and that the case is wholly without a particle of evidence upon which an impeachment could be founded, and that with all the effort that has been made, and the mass of evidence that has been taken, the case is entirely bald of proof. I furthermore report that the most of the testimony that has been taken is of a secondary character, and such as would not be admitted in a court of justice. In view of this conclusion, I can see no good in a continuation of the investigation. I am convinced that all the proof that can be produced has been before the committee, as no pains have been spared to give the case a full investigation. Why, then, keep the country in a feverish state of excitement upon this question any longer, as it is sure to end, in my opinion, in a complete vindication of the President, if justice be done him by the committee, of which I have no doubt.
　　　　　　　　　　　A. J. ROGERS.

### Impeachment in Fortieth Congress.
#### IN HOUSE.

1867, March 7—Mr. JAMES M. ASHLEY rose to a question of privilege, and submitted these resolutions:

Whereas the House of Representatives of the Thirty-Ninth Congress adopted, on the 7th of January, 1867, a resolution authorizing an inquiry into certain charges preferred against the President of the United States; and whereas the Judiciary Committee, to whom said resolution and charges were referred, with authority to investigate the same, were unable for want of time to complete said investigation before the expiration of the Thirty-Ninth Congress; and whereas in the report submitted by said Judiciary Committee on the 2d of March they declare that the evidence taken is of such a character as to justify and demand a continuation of the investigation by this Congress: Therefore,

*Be it resolved by the House of Representatives,* That the Judiciary Committee, when appointed, be, and they are hereby, instructed to continue the investigation authorized in said resolution of January 7, 1867, and that they have power to send for persons and papers, and to administer the customary oath to witnesses; and that the committee have authority to sit during the sessions of the House and during any recess which Congress or this House may take.

*Resolved,* That the Speaker of the House be requested to appoint the Committee on the Judiciary forthwith, and that the committee so appointed be directed to take charge of the testimony taken by the committee of the last Congress; and that said committee have power to appoint a clerk at a compensation not to exceed six dollars per day, and employ the necessary stenographer.

*Resolved,* That the Clerk of the House of Representatives be directed to pay out of the contingent fund of the House, on the order of the Committee of the Judiciary, such sum or sums of money as may be required to enable the said committee to prosecute the investigation above directed, and such other investigations as it may be ordered to make.

Mr. Holman moved to table the resolutions, which was disagreed to—yeas 32, nays 119, as follow:

YEAS—Messrs. *Archer, Barnes, Boyer, Brooks, Burr, Chanler, Denison, Eldridge, Fox, Getz, Haight, Holman, Humphrey, Kerr, Marshall, McCullough, Morgan, Morrissey, Mungen, Niblack, Nicholson,* Phelps, *Pruyn, Randall, Robinson, Ross, Sitgreaves,* Stewart, *Stone, Taber, Van Auken, Van Trump, Wood*—32.

NAYS—Messrs. Allison, Ames, Anderson, Delos R. Ashley, James M. Ashley, Baker, Baldwin, Banks, Beaman, Benjamin, Bingham, Blaine, Blair, Boutwell, Bromwell, Broomall, Buckland, Butler, Cake, Churchill, Reader W. Clarke, Sidney Clarke, Cobb, Coburn, Cook, Cornell, Covode, Cullom, Dawes, Dodge, Donnelly, Driggs, Eckley, Eggleston, Eliot, Farnsworth, Ferriss, Ferry, Fields, Finney, Garfield, Gravely, Halsey, Hamilton, Harding, Hayes, Hill, Hooper, Hopkins, Chester D. Hubbard, Hulburd, Hunter, Ingersoll, Judd, Julian, Kelley, Ketcham, Kitchen, Koontz, Laflin, George V. Lawrence, William Lawrence, Lincoln, Loan, Logan, Loughridge, Lynch, Marvin, McCarthy, McClurg, Mercur, Miller, Moore, Moorhead, Morrell, Myers, Newcomb, Noell, O'Neill, Orth, Paine, Perham, Peters, Pile, Plants, Poland, Polsley, Pomeroy, Price, Raum, Robertson, Sawyer, Schenck, Scofield, Shanks, Shellabarger, Smith, Stevens, Taffe, Taylor, Thomas, Trowbridge, Twichell, Upson, Van Aernam, Burt Van Horn, Robert T. Van Horn, Van Wyck, Ward, Cadwalader C. Washburn, William B. Washburn, Welker, Thomas Williams, William Williams, James F. Wilson, John T. Wilson, Stephen F. Wilson, Windom, Woodbridge—119.

March 29—Mr. Sidney Clarke offered this preamble and resolution:

Whereas upon charges preferred in the House of Representatives of the Thirty-Ninth Congress against the President of the United States of high crimes and misdemeanors, alleged to have been committed by him in the execution of his official trust, the Committee on the Judiciary of the said House, to which the same was referred, did report that for want of sufficient time they were unable to conclude their investigation, but that upon the facts disclosed it was in their judgment required and demanded that the inquiry should be prosecuted to a conclusion by the present Congress; and whereas in accordance with the said opinion this House did commit the said subject anew to its Committee on the Judiciary, which is now diligently engaged in the examination thereof; and whereas, in view of the report and recommendation of the Judiciary Committee of the last House, it would be dangerous to the public interest and failure of duty on the part of the present Congress, to adjourn and abdicate its practical control over the administration of the Government by surrendering its destinies, in the present critical condition of affairs, into the hands of an officer thus impeached before the nation, and well known not only to be hostile to the policy of its Congress, and to entertain the opinion that all the acts of that Congress looking to a restoration of the Union are unconstitutional: Therefore,

*Resolved,* That the Committee on the Judiciary be requested to report on the charges preferred against the President, as aforesaid, on the first day of the meeting of the House after the recess hereafter to be determined.

Mr. Robinson moved to table the resolution; which was disagreed to—yeas 38, nays 63, as follow:

YEAS—Messrs. *Archer,* Bingham, Blair, *Brooks,* Buckland, *Burr, Chanler,* Reader W. Clarke, Cornell, *Denison, Eldridge,* Ferriss, Fields, *Getz, Glossbrenner,* Griswold, *Holman,* Chester D. Hubbard, *Humphrey, Kerr,* Ketcham, Laflin, *Marshall,* Marvin, *Morrissey, Mungen, Niblack, Nicholson,* Phelps, Plants, *Robinson, Ross, Sitgreaves,* Stewart, *Taber, Van Auken, Van Trump, Wood*—38.

NAYS—Messrs. Allison, James M. Ashley, Baker, Benton, Boutwell, Broomall, Butler, Cake, Churchill, Sidney Clarke, Coburn, Cook, Covode, Cullom, Donnelly, Driggs, Eckley, Eggleston, Ela, Farnsworth, Garfield, Gravely, Halsey, Hamilton, Hayes, Hooper, Hopkins, Hulburd, Ingersoll, Judd, Kelley, Koontz, William Lawrence, Loan, Logan, Loughridge, Mallory, McClurg, Mercur, Miller, Morrell, Myers, O'Neill, Perham, Pile, Polsley, Robertson, Sawyer, Schenck, Scofield, Shanks, Thaddeus Stevens, Taylor, Trowbridge, Upson, Robert T. Van Horn, Ward, Welker, Thomas Williams, William Williams, John T. Wilson, Windom, Woodbridge—63.

The preamble was laid on the table, on a division by tellers—ayes 54, noes 32. The resolution was then adopted.

The committee, it is understood, will make a report upon the 3d of July, on the reassembling of Congress.

# XVIII.

# TEXT OF THE RECONSTRUCTION MEASURES.

### 14th Constitutional Amendment.

Joint Resolution proposing an Amendment to the Constitution of the United States.

*Be it resolved by the Senate and House of Representatives of the United States of America, in Congress assembled,* (two-thirds of both Houses concurring,) That the following article be proposed to the Legislatures of the several States as an amendment to the Constitution of the United States, which, when ratified by three-fourths of said Legislatures, shall be valid as part of the Constitution, namely :

#### ARTICLE XIV.

SECTION 1. All persons born or naturalized in the United States, and subject to the jurisdiction thereof, are citizens of the United States and of the State wherein they reside. No State shall make or enforce any law which shall abridge the privileges or immunities of citizens of the United States; nor shall any State deprive any person of life, liberty, or property, without due process of law, nor deny to any person within its jurisdiction the equal protection of the laws.

SEC. 2. Representatives shall be apportioned among the several States according to their respective numbers, counting the whole number of persons in each State, excluding Indians not taxed. But when the right to vote at any election for the choice of electors for President and Vice President of the United States, representatives in Congress, the executive and judicial officers of a State, or the members of the Legislature thereof, is denied to any of the male inhabitants of such State, being twenty-one years of age, and citizens of the United States, or in any way abridged, except for participation in rebellion or other crime, the basis of representation therein shall be reduced in the proportion which the number of such male citizens shall bear to the whole number of male citizens twenty-one years of age in such State.

SEC. 3. No person shall be a Senator or Representative in Congress, or elector of President and Vice President, or hold any office, civil or military, under the United States, or under any State, who, having previously taken an oath as a member of Congress, or as an officer of the United States, or as a member of any State Legislature, or as an executive or judicial officer of any State, to support the Constitution of the United States, shall have engaged in insurrection or rebellion against the same, or given aid or comfort to the enemies thereof. But Congress may, by a vote of two thirds of each House, remove such disability.

SEC. 4. The validity of the public debt of the United States, authorized by law, including debts incurred for payment of pensions and bounties for services in suppressing insurrection or rebellion, shall not be questioned. But neither the United States nor any State shall assume or pay any debt or obligation incurred in aid of insur-

rection or rebellion against the United States, or any claim for the loss or emancipation of any slave; but all such debts, obligations, and claims shall be held illegal and void.

SEC. 5. That Congress shall have power to enforce, by appropriate legislation, the provisions of this article.

Passed June 13, 1866.

---

### Reconstruction Act of Thirty-Ninth Congress.

AN ACT to provide for the more efficient government of the rebel States.

Whereas no legal State governments or adequate protection for life or property now exists in the rebel States of Virginia, North Carolina, South Carolina, Georgia, Mississippi, Alabama, Louisiana, Florida, Texas, and Arkansas ; and whereas it is necessary that peace and good order should be enforced in said States until loyal and republican State governments can be legally established : Therefore

*Be it enacted, &c.,* That said rebel States shall be divided into military districts and made subject to the military authority of the United States, as hereinafter prescribed, and for that purpose Virginia shall constitute the first district ; North Carolina and South Carolina the second district ; Georgia, Alabama, and Florida the third district; Mississippi and Arkansas the fourth district; and Louisiana and Texas the fifth district.

SEC. 2. That it shall be the duty of the President to assign to the command of each of said districts an officer of the army, not below the rank of brigadier general, and to detail a sufficient military force to enable such officer to perform his duties and enforce his authority within the district to which he is assigned.

SEC. 3. That it shall be the duty of each officer assigned as aforesaid to protect all persons in their rights of person and property, to suppress insurrection, disorder, and violence, and to punish, or cause to be punished, all disturbers of the public peace and criminals, and to this end he may allow local civil tribunals to take jurisdiction of and to try offenders, or, when in his judgment it may be necessary for the trial of offenders, he shall have power to organize military commissions or tribunals for that purpose; and all interference under color of State authority with the exercise of military authority under this act shall be null and void.

SEC. 4. That all persons put under military arrest by virtue of this act shall be tried without unnecessary delay, and no cruel or unusual punishment shall be inflicted ; and no sentence of any military commission or tribunal hereby authorized, affecting the life or liberty of any person, shall be executed until it is approved by the officer in command of the district, and the laws and regulations for the government of the army shall not be affected by this act, except in so far as they conflict with its provisions: *Pro*

191

*vided,* That no sentence of death under the provisions of this act shall be carried into effect without the approval of the President.

Sec. 5. That when the people of any one of said rebel States shall have formed a constitution of government in conformity with the Constitution of the United States in all respects, framed by a convention of delegates elected by the male citizens of said State twenty-one years old and upward, of whatever race, color, or previous condition, who have been resident in said State for one year previous to the day of such election, except such as may be disfranchised for participation in the rebellion, or for felony at common law, and when such constitution shall provide that the elective franchise shall be enjoyed by all such persons as have the qualifications herein stated for electors of delegates, and when such constitution shall be ratified by a majority of the persons voting on the question of ratification who are qualified as electors for delegates, and when such constitution shall have been submitted to Congress for examination and approval, and when said State, by a vote of its legislature elected under said constitution, shall have adopted the amendment to the Constitution of the United States, proposed by the Thirty-ninth Congress, and known as article fourteen, and when said article shall have become a part of the Constitution of the United States, said State shall be declared entitled to representation in Congress, and Senators and Representatives shall be admitted therefrom on their taking the oaths prescribed by law, and then and thereafter the preceding sections of this act shall be inoperative in said State: *Provided,* That no person excluded from the privilege of holding office by said proposed amendment to the Constitution of the United States shall be eligible to election as a member of the convention to frame a constitution for any of said rebel States, nor shall any such person vote for members of such convention.

Sec. 6. That until the people of said rebel States shall be by law admitted to representation in the Congress of the United States, any civil governments which may exist therein shall be deemed provisional only, and in all respects subject to the paramount authority of the United States at any time to abolish, modify, control, or supersede the same; and in all elections to any office under such provisional governments all persons shall be entitled to vote, and none others, who are entitled to vote under the provisions of the fifth section of this act; and no person shall be eligible to any office under any such provisional governments who would be disqualified from holding office under the provisions of the third article of said constitutional amendment.

Passed March 2, 1867.

### Supplemental Reconstruction Act of Fortieth Congress.

An Act supplementary to an act entitled "An act to provide for the more efficient government of the rebel States," passed March second, eighteen hundred and sixty-seven, and to facilitate restoration.

*Be it enacted, &c.,* That before the first day of September, eighteen hundred and sixty-seven, the commanding general in each district defined by an act entitled "An act to provide for the more efficient government of the rebel States," passed March second, eighteen hundred and sixty-seven, shall cause a registration to be made of the male citizens of the United States, twenty-one years of age and upwards, resident in each county or parish in the State or States included in his district, which registration shall include only those persons who are qualified to vote for delegates by the act aforesaid, and who shall have taken and subscribed the following oath or affirmation: " I, ——, do solemnly swear, (or affirm,) in the presence of Almighty God, that I am a citizen of the State of ——; that I have resided in said State for —— months next preceding this day, and now reside in the county of ——, or the parish of ——, in said State, (as the case may be;) that I am twenty-one years old; that I have not been disfranchised for participation in any rebellion or civil war against the United States, nor for felony committed against the laws of any State or of the United States; that I have never been a member of any State legislature, nor held any executive or judicial office in any State and afterwards engaged in insurrection or rebellion against the United States, or given aid or comfort to the enemies thereof; that I have never taken an oath as a member of Congress of the United States, or as an officer of the United States, or as a member of any State legislature, or as an executive or judicial officer of any State, to support the Constitution of the United States, and afterwards engaged in insurrection or rebellion against the United States or given aid or comfort to the enemies thereof; that I will faithfully support the Constitution and obey the laws of the United States, and will, to the best of my ability, encourage others so to do, so help me God;" which oath or affirmation may be administered by any registering officer.

Sec. 2. That after the completion of the registration hereby provided for in any State, at such time and places therein as the commanding general shall appoint and direct, of which at least thirty days' public notice shall be given, an election shall be held of delegates to a convention for the purpose of establishing a constitution and civil government for such State loyal to the Union, said convention in each State, except Virginia, to consist of the same number of members as the most numerous branch of the State legislature of such State in the year eighteen hundred and sixty, to be apportioned among the several districts, counties, or parishes of such State by the commanding general, giving to each representation in the ratio of voters registered as aforesaid, as nearly as may be. The convention in Virginia shall consist of the same number of members as represented the territory now constituting Virginia in the most numerous branch of the legislature of said State in the year eighteen hundred and sixty, to be apportioned as aforesaid.

Sec. 3. That at said election the registered voters of each State shall vote for or against a convention to form a constitution therefor under this act. Those voting in favor of such a convention shall have written or printed on the ballots by which they vote for delegates, as aforesaid, the words "For a convention," and those voting against such a convention shall have written or printed on such ballots the words "Against a convention." The person appointed to superintend said election, and to make return of the votes given thereat, as herein provided, shall count and make return of the votes given for and against a convention; and the commanding general to whom the same shall have been returned shall ascertain and declare the total vote in each State for and against a convention. If a majority of the votes given on that question shall be for a convention, then such convention shall be held as hereinafter provided; but if a majority of said votes shall be against a convention, then no such convention shall be held under this act: *Provided*, That such convention shall not be held unless a majority of all such registered voters shall have voted on the question of holding such convention.

SEC. 4. That the commanding general of each district shall appoint as many boards of registration as may be necessary, consisting of three loyal officers or persons, to make and complete the registration, superintend the election, and make return to him of the votes, lists of voters, and of the persons elected as delegates by a plurality of the votes cast at said election; and upon receiving said returns he shall open the same, ascertain the persons elected as delegates according to the returns of the officers who conducted said election, and make proclamation thereof; and if a majority of the votes given on that question shall be for a convention, the commanding general, within sixty days from the date of election, shall notify the delegates to assemble in convention, at a time and place to be mentioned in the notification, and said convention, when organized, shall proceed to frame a constitution and civil government according to the provisions of this act and the act to which it is supplementary; and when the same shall have been so framed, said constitution shall be submitted by the convention for ratification to the persons registered under the provisions of this act at an election to be conducted by the officers or persons appointed or to be appointed by the commanding general, as hereinbefore provided, and to be held after the expiration of thirty days from the date of notice thereof, to be given by said convention; and the returns thereof shall be made to the commanding general of the district.

SEC. 5. That if, according to said returns, the constitution shall be ratified by a majority of the votes of the registered electors qualified as herein specified, cast at said election, (at least one half of all the registered voters voting upon the question of such ratification,) the president of the convention shall transmit a copy of the same, duly certified, to the President of the United States, who shall forthwith transmit the same to Congress, if then in session, and if not in session, then immediately upon its next assembling; and if it shall, moreover, appear to Congress that the election was one at which all the registered and qualified electors in the State had an opportunity to vote freely and without restraint, fear, or the influence of fraud, and if the Congress shall be satisfied that such constitution meets the approval of a majority of all the qualified electors in the State, and if the said constitution shall be declared by Congress to be in conformity with the provisions of the act to which this is supplementary, and the other provisions of said act shall have been complied with, and the said constitution shall be approved by Congress, the State shall be declared entitled to representation, and Senators and Representatives shall be admitted therefrom as therein provided.

SEC. 6. That all elections in the States mentioned in the said "Act to provide for the more efficient government of the rebel States," shall, during the operation of said act, be by ballot; and all officers making the said registration of voters and conducting said elections shall, before entering upon the discharge of their duties, take and subscribe the oath prescribed by the act approved July second, eighteen hundred and sixty-two, entitled "An act to prescribe an oath of office:" * *Provided*, That if any person shall knowingly and falsely take and subscribe any oath in this act prescribed, such person so offending and being thereof duly convicted, shall be subject to the pains, penalties, and disabilities which by law are provided for the punishment of the crime of wilful and corrupt perjury.

SEC. 7. That all expenses incurred by the several commanding generals, or by virtue of any orders issued, or appointments made, by them, under or by virtue of this act, shall be paid out of any moneys in the treasury not otherwise appropriated.

SEC. 8. That the convention for each State shall prescribe the fees, salary, and compensation to be paid to all delegates and other officers and agents herein authorized or necessary to carry into effect the purposes of this act not herein otherwise provided for, and shall provide for the levy and collection of such taxes on the property

* This act is in these words:

*Be it enacted, &c.,* That hereafter every person elected or appointed to any office of honor or profit under the Government of the United States either in the civil, military, or naval departments of the public service, excepting the President of the United States, shall, before entering upon the duties of such office, and before being entitled to any of the salary or other emoluments thereof, take and subscribe the following oath or affirmation: "I, A B, do solemnly swear (or affirm) that I have never voluntarily borne arms against the United States since I have been a citizen thereof; that I have voluntarily given no aid, countenance, counsel, or encouragement to persons engaged in armed hostility thereto; that I have never sought nor accepted nor attempted to exercise the functions of any office whatever, under any authority or pretended authority, in hostility to the United States; that I have not yielded a voluntary support to any pretended government, authority, power, or constitution within the United States, hostile or inimical thereto; and I do further swear (or affirm) that, to the best of my knowledge and ability, I will support and defend the Constitution of the United States, against all enemies, foreign and domestic; that I will bear true faith and allegiance to the same; that I take this obligation freely, without any mental reservation or purpose of evasion, and that I will well and faithfully discharge the duties of the office on which I am about to enter; so help me God;" which said oath, so taken and signed, shall be preserved among the files of the Court, House of Congress, or Department to which the said office may appertain. And any person who shall falsely take the said oath shall be guilty of perjury, and on conviction, in addition to the penalties now prescribed for that offense, shall be deprived of his office, and rendered incapable forever after, of holding any office or place under the United States.

in such State as may be necessary to pay the same.

Sec. 9 That the word article, in the sixth section of the act to which this is supplementary, shall be construed to mean section.

Passed March 23, 1867.

## Votes of State Legislatures on the Fourteenth Constitutional Amendment.

### LOYAL STATES.

#### RATIFIED—TWENTY-ONE STATES.

*Maine—*
SENATE, January 16, 1867, yeas 31, nays 0.
HOUSE, January 11, 1867, yeas 126, nays 12.
*New Hampshire—*
SENATE, July 6, 1866, yeas 9, nays 3.
HOUSE, June 28, 1866, yeas 207, nays 112.
*Vermont—*
SENATE, October 23, 1866, yeas 28, nays 0.
HOUSE, October 30, 1866, yeas 199, nays 11.
*Massachusetts—*
SENATE, March 20, 1867, yeas 27, nays 6.
HOUSE, March 14, 1867, yeas 120, nays 20.
*Rhode Island—*
SENATE, February 5, 1867, yeas 26, nays 2.
HOUSE, February 7, 1867, yeas 60, nays 9.
*Connecticut—*
SENATE, June 25, 1866, yeas 11, nays 6.
HOUSE, June 29, 1866, yeas 131, nays 92.
*New York—*
SENATE, January 3, 1867, yeas 23, nays 3.
HOUSE, January 10, 1867, yeas 76, nays 40.
*New Jersey—*
SENATE, September 11, 1866, yeas 11, nays 10.
HOUSE, September 11, 1866, yeas 34, nays 24.
*Pennsylvania—*
SENATE, January 17, 1867, yeas 20, nays 9.
HOUSE, February 6, 1867, yeas 58, nays 29.
*West Virginia—*
SENATE, January 15, 1867, yeas 15, nays 3.
HOUSE, January 16, 1867, yeas 43, nays 11.
*Ohio—*
SENATE, January 3, 1867, yeas 21, nays 12.
HOUSE, January 4, 1867, yeas 54, nays 25.
*Tennessee—*
SENATE, July 11, 1866, yeas 15, nays 6.
HOUSE, July 12, 1866, yeas 43, nays 11.
*Indiana—*
SENATE, January 16, 1867, yeas 29, nays 18.
HOUSE, January 23, 1867, yeas —, nays —.
*Illinois—*
SENATE, January 10, 1867, yeas 17, nays 7.
HOUSE, January 15, 1867, yeas 59, nays 25.
*Michigan—*
SENATE, —— 1867, yeas 25, nays 1.
HOUSE, —— 1867, yeas 77 nays 15.
*Missouri—*
SENATE, January 5, 1867, yeas 26, nays 6.
HOUSE, January 8, 1867, yeas 85, nays 34.

*Minnesota—*
SENATE, January 16, 1867, yeas 16 nays 5.
HOUSE, January 15, 1867, yeas 40, nays 6.
*Kansas—*
SENATE, January 11, 1867, unanimously.
HOUSE, January 10, 1867, yeas 75, nays 7.
*Wisconsin—*
SENATE, January 23, 1867, yeas 22, nays 10.
HOUSE, February 7, 1867, yeas 72, nays 12.
*Oregon—*
*SENATE, ——, 1866, yeas 13, nays 7.
HOUSE, September 19, 1866, yeas 25, nays 22
*Nevada—*
*SENATE, January 22, 1867, yeas 14, nays 2.
HOUSE, January 11, 1867, yeas 34, nays 4.
*Unofficial.

#### REJECTED—THREE STATES.

*Delaware—*
SENATE.
HOUSE, February 6, 1867, yeas 6, nays 15.
*Maryland—*
SENATE, March 23, 1867, yeas 4, nays 13.
HOUSE, March 23, 1867, yeas 12, nays 45.
*Kentucky—*
SENATE, January 8, 1867, yeas 7, nays 24.
HOUSE, January 8, 1867, yeas 26, nays 62.

#### NOT ACTED—THREE STATES.
Iowa, California, Nebraska.

### INSURRECTIONARY STATES.

#### REJECTED—TEN STATES.

*Virginia—*
SENATE, January 9, 1867, unanimously.
HOUSE, January 9, 1867, 1 for amendment.
*North Carolina—*
SENATE, December 13, 1866, yeas 1, nays 44.
HOUSE, December 13, 1866, yeas 10, nays 93.
*South Carolina—*
SENATE, —— ——.
HOUSE, December 20, 1866, yeas 1, nays 95.
*Georgia—*
SENATE, November 9, 1866, yeas 0, nays 36.
HOUSE, November 9, 1866, yeas 2, nays 131.
*Florida—*
SENATE, December 3, 1866, yeas 0, nays 20.
HOUSE, December 1, 1866, yeas 0, nays 49.
*Alabama—*
SENATE, December 7, 1866, yeas 2, nays 27.
HOUSE, December 7, 1866, yeas 8, nays 69.
*Mississippi—*
SENATE, January 30, 1867, yeas 0, nays 27.
HOUSE, January 25, 1867, yeas 0, nays 88.
*Louisiana—*
SENATE, February 5, 1867, unanimously.
HOUSE, February 6, 1867, unanimously.
*Texas—*
SENATE, —— ——.
HOUSE, October 13, 1866, yeas 5, nays 67.
*Arkansas—*
SENATE, December 15, 1866, yeas 1, nays 24.
HOUSE, December 17, 1866, yeas 2, nays 68.

## XIX.

# PROCLAMATIONS AND ORDERS.

**PRESIDENT JOHNSON'S PROCLAMATIONS, ORDERS, AND TELEGRAMS ON RECONSTRUCTION.** ——

**Declaring the Insurrection at an End in Texas, and Civil Authority existing throughout the whole of the United States, August 20, 1866.**

Whereas, by proclamation of the fifteenth and nineteenth of April, eighteen hundred and sixty-one, the President of the United States, in virtue of the power vested in him by the Constitution and the laws, declared that the laws of the United States were opposed and the execution thereof obstructed in the States of South Carolina, Georgia, Alabama, Florida, Mississippi, Louisiana, and Texas, by combinations too powerful to be suppressed by the ordinary course of judicial proceedings, or by the powers vested in the marshals by law;

And whereas, by another proclamation, made on the sixteenth day of August, in the same year, in pursuance of an act of Congress approved July thirteen, one thousand eight hundred and sixty-one, the inhabitants of the States of Georgia, South Carolina, Virginia, North Carolina, Tennessee, Alabama, Louisiana, Texas,

Arkansas, Mississippi, and Florida, (except the inhabitants of that part of the State of Virginia lying west of the Alleghany mountains, and except also the inhabitants of such other parts of that State, and the other States before named, as might maintain a loyal adhesion to the Union and the Constitution, or might be, from time to time, occupied and controlled by forces of the United States engaged in the dispersion of insurgents,) were declared to be in a state of insurrection against the United States ;

And whereas, by another proclamation, of the first day of July, one thousand eight hundred and sixty-two, issued in pursuance of an act of Congress approved June seventh, in the same year, the insurrection was declared to be still existing in the States aforesaid, with the exception of certain specified counties in the State of Virginia ;

And whereas, by another proclamation made on the second day of April, one thousand eight hundred and sixty-three, in pursuance of the act of Congress of July thirteen, one thousand eight hundred and sixty one, the exceptions named in the proclamation of August sixteen, one thousand eight hundred and sixty-one, were revoked, and the inhabitants of the States of Georgia, South Carolina, North Carolina, Tennessee, Alabama, Louisiana, Texas, Arkansas, Mississippi, Florida, and Virginia (except the forty-eight counties of Virginia designated as West Virginia, and the ports of New Orleans, Key West, Port Royal, and Beaufort, in North Carolina) were declared to be still in a state of insurrection against the United States ;

And whereas, by another proclamation of the fifteenth day of September, one thousand eight hundred and sixty-three, made in pursuance of the act of Congress approved March third, one thousand eight hundred and sixty-three, the rebellion was declared to be still existing, and the privilege of the writ of *habeas corpus* was in certain specified cases suspended throughout the United States, said suspension to continue throughout the duration of the rebellion, or until said proclamation should, by a subsequent one to be issued by the President of the United States, be modified or revoked ;

And whereas the House of Representatives, on the twenty-second day of July, one thousand eight hundred and sixty-one, adopted a resolution in the words following, namely :

*Resolved by the House of Representatives of the Congress of the United States,* That the present deplorable civil war has been forced upon the country by the disunionists of the southern States, now in revolt against the constitutional Government, and in arms around the capital ; that in this national emergency, Congress, banishing all feelings of mere passion or resentment, will recollect only its duty to the whole country ; that this war is not waged upon our part in any spirit of oppression, nor for any purpose of conquest or subjugation, nor purpose of overthrowing or interfering with the rights or established institutions of those States, but to defend and maintain the supremacy of the Constitution, and to preserve the Union with all the dignity, equality, and rights of the several States unimpaired, and that as soon as these objects are accomplished the war ought to cease.

And whereas the Senate of the United States on the twenty-fifth day of July, one thousand eight hundred and sixty-one, adopted a resolution in the words following, to wit:

*Resolved,* That the present deplorable civil war has been forced upon the country by the disunionists of the southern States, now in revolt against the constitutional Government, and in arms around the capital ; that in this national emergency, Congress, banishing all feeling of mere passion or resentment, will recollect only its duty to the whole country ; that this war is not prosecuted upon our part in any spirit of oppression, nor for any purpose of conquest or subjugation, nor purpose of overthrowing or interfering with the rights or established institutions of those States, but to defend and maintain the supremacy of the Constitution, and all laws made in pursuance thereof, and to preserve the Union with all the dignity, equality, and rights of the several States unimpaired; that as soon as these objects are accomplished the war ought to cease.

And whereas these resolutions though not joint or concurrent in form, are substantially identical, and as such have hitherto been and yet are regarded as having expressed the sense of Congress upon the subject to which they relate ;

And whereas the President of the United States, by proclamation of the thirteenth of June, eighteen hundred and sixty-five, declared that the insurrection in the State of Tennessee had been suppressed, and that the authority of the United States therein was undisputed, and that such United States officers as had been duly commissioned were in the undisturbed exercise of their official functions ;

And whereas the President of the United States, by further proclamation issued on the second day of April, one thousand eight hundred and sixty-six, did promulgate and declare that there no longer existed any armed resistance of misguided citizens or others to the authority of the United States in any or in all the States before mentioned, excepting only the State of Texas, and did further promulgate and declare that the laws could be sustained and enforced in the several States before mentioned, except Texas, by the proper civil authorities, State or Federal, and that the people of the said States, except Texas, are well and loyally disposed, and have conformed or will conform in their legislation to the condition of affairs growing out of the amendment to the Constitution of the United States prohibiting slavery within the limits and jurisdiction of the United States ;

And did further declare in the same proclamation that it is the manifest determination of the American people that no State, of its own will, has a right or power to go out of, or separate itself from, or be separated from the American Union ; and that, therefore, each State ought to remain and constitute an integral part of the United States ;

And did further declare in the same last mentioned proclamation that the several afore-mentioned States, excepting Texas, had, in the manner aforesaid, given satisfactory evidence that they acquiesce in this sovereign and important resolution of national unity ;

And whereas the President of the United States, in the same proclamation, did further declare that it is believed to be a fundamental principle of government that the people who have revolted, and who have been overcome and subdued, must either be dealt with so as to induce them voluntarily to become friends, or else they must be held by absolute military power, or devastated, so as to prevent them from ever again doing harm as enemies, which last named policy is abhorrent to humanity and to freedom ;

And whereas the President did, in the same proclamation, further declare that the Constitution of the United States provides for constituent communities only as States, and not as Territories, dependencies, provinces, or protectorates;

And further, that such constituent States must necessarily be, and by the Constitution and laws of the United States are made equals, and placed upon a like footing as to political rights, immunities, dignity, and power with the several States with which they are united;

And did further declare that the observance of political equality as a principle of right and justice is well calculated to encourage the people of the before-named States, except Texas, to be and to become more and more constant and persevering in their renewed allegiance;

And whereas the President did further declare, that standing armies, military occupation, martial law, military tribunals, and the suspension of the writ of *habeas corpus* are, in time of peace, dangerous to public liberty, incompatible with the individual rights of the citizen, contrary to the genius and spirit of our free institutions, and exhaustive of the national resources, and ought not, therefore, to be sanctioned or allowed, except in cases of actual necessity, for repelling invasion or suppressing insurrection or rebellion;

And the President did further, in the same proclamation, declare that the policy of the Government of the United States, from the beginning of the insurrection to its overthrow and final suppression, had been conducted in conformity with the principles in the last-named proclamation recited;

And whereas the President, in the said proclamation of the thirteenth of June, one thousand eight hundred and sixty-five, upon the grounds therein stated and hereinbefore recited, did then and there proclaim and declare that the insurrection which heretofore existed in the several States before named, except in Texas, was at an end, and was henceforth to be so regarded;

And whereas, subsequently to the said second day of April, one thousand eight hundred and sixty-six, the insurrection in the State of Texas has been completely and everywhere suppressed and ended, and the authority of the United States has been successfully and completely established in the said State of Texas, and now remains therein unrestricted and undisputed, and such of the proper United States officers as have been duly commissioned within the limits of the said State are now in the undisturbed exercise of their official functions;

And whereas the laws can now be sustained and enforced in the said State of Texas by the proper civil authority, State or Federal, and the people of the said State of Texas, like the people of other States before named, are well and loyally disposed, and have conformed or will conform in their legislation to the condition of affairs growing out of the amendment of the Constitution of the United States prohibiting slavery within the limits and jurisdiction of the United States;

And whereas all the reasons and conclusions set forth in regard to several States therein specially named now apply equally and in all respects to the State of Texas, as well as to the other States which had been involved in insurrection:

And whereas adequate provision has been made by military orders to enforce the execution of the acts of Congress and the civil authorities, and secure obedience to the Constitution and laws of the United States within the State of Texas, if a resort to military force for such purpose should at any time become necessary;

Now, therefore, I, Andrew Johnson, President of the United States, do hereby proclaim and declare that the insurrection which heretofore existed in the State of Texas is at an end, and is to be henceforth so regarded in that State, as in the other States before named, in which the said insurrection was proclaimed to be at an end by the aforesaid proclamation of the second day of April, one thousand eight hundred and sixty-six.

And I do further proclaim that the said insurrection is at an end, and that peace, order, tranquillity, and civil authority now exist in and throughout the whole of the United States of America.

In testimony whereof I have hereunto set my hand and caused the seal of the United States to be affixed.

Done at the city of Washington, this twentieth day of August, in the year of our [L. S.]  Lord one thousand eight hundred and sixty-six, and of the independence of the United States of America the ninety-first.
                                  ANDREW JOHNSON.

By the President:
   WM. H. SEWARD, *Secretary of State.*

## Respecting American Merchant Vessels Stopping or Anchoring in Certain Ports of Japan, January 12, 1867.

Whereas in virtue of the power conferred by the act of Congress approved June 22, 1860, sections 15 and 24 of which act were designed by proper provisions to secure the strict neutrality of citizens of the United States residing in or visiting the empires of China and Japan, a notification was issued on the 4th of August last by the Legation of the United States in Japan, through the consulates of the open ports of that empire, requesting American shipmasters not to approach the coasts of Lucoa and Nagato pending the then contemplated hostilities between the Tycoon of Japan and the Daimio of the said provinces;

And whereas authentic information having been received by the said Legation that such hostilities had actually commenced, a regulation, in furtherance of the aforesaid notification and pursuant to the act referred to, was issued by the Minister Resident of the United States in Japan forbidding American merchant vessels from stopping or anchoring at any port or roadstead in that country except the three open ports, viz: Kanagawha, (Yokohama,) Nagasaki, and Hakodate, unless in distress or forced by stress of weather, as provided by treaty, and giving notice that masters of vessels committing a breach of the regulation would thereby render themselves liable to prosecution and punishment, and also to forfeiture of the protection of the United States if the visit to such non-opened port or roadstead should either involve a breach of treaty or be construed as an act in aid of insurrection or rebellion:

Now, therefore, be it known that I, Andrew Johson, President of the United States of America, with a view to prevent acts which might injuriously affect the relations existing between the Government of the United States and that of Japan, do hereby call public attention to the aforesaid notification and regulation, which are hereby sanctioned and confirmed.

In testimony whereof I have hereunto set my hand and caused the seal of the United States to be affixed.

Done at the city of Washington, this twelfth day of January, in the year of our Lord [SEAL.] one thousand eight hundred and sixty-seven, and of the independence of the United States the ninety-first.

ANDREW JOHNSON,

By the President:

WILLIAM H. SEWARD, *Secretary of State.*

## Respecting Decree of Maximilian, August 17, 1866.

Whereas a war is existing in the Republic of Mexico, aggravated by foreign military intervention;

And whereas the United States, in accordance with their settled habits and policy, are a neutral Power in regard to the war which thus afflicts the Republic of Mexico;

And whereas it has become known that one of the belligerents in the said war—namely, the Prince Maximilian—who asserts himself to be Emperor in Mexico, has issued a decree in regard to the port of Matamoros, and other Mexican ports which are in the occupation and possession of another of the said belligerents—namely, the United States of Mexico—which decree is in the following words:

"The port of Matamoros, and all those of the northern frontier which have withdrawn from their obedience to the Government, are closed to foreign and coasting traffic during such time as the empire of the law shall not be therein reinstated.

"ART. 2. Merchandise proceeding from the said ports, on arriving at any other where the excise of the empire is collected, shall pay the duties on importation, introduction, and consumption, and, on satisfactory proof of contravention, shall be irremissibly confiscated. Our Minister of the Treasury is charged with the punctual execution of this decree.

"Given at Mexico, the 9th of July, 1866."

And whereas the decree thus recited, by declaring a belligerent blockade unsupported by competent military or naval force, is in violation of the neutral rights of the United States, as defined by the law of nations, as well as of the treaties existing between the United States of America and the aforesaid United States of Mexico:

Now, therefore, I, Andrew Johnson, President of the United States, do hereby proclaim and declare, that the aforesaid decree is held, and will be held, by the United States, to be absolutely null and void, as against the Government and citizens of the United States; and that any attempt which shall be made to enforce the same against the Government or citizens of the United States will be disallowed.

In witness whereof I have hereunto set my hand, and caused the seal of the United States to be affixed.

Done at the city of Washington, the seven-

teenth day of August, in the year of our [L. S.] Lord one thousand eight hundred and sixty-six, and of the independence of the United States of America the ninety-first.

ANDREW JOHNSON.

By the President:

WILLIAM H. SEWARD, *Secretary of State.*

## Declaring the Suspension of Tonnage and Impost Duties, as respects the Vessels of the Hawaiian Islands, January 29, 1867.

Whereas by an act of the Congress of the United States of the twenty-fourth day of May, one thousand eight hundred and twenty-eight, entitled "An act in addition to an act, entitled 'An act concerning discriminating duties of tonnage and impost,' and to equalize the duties on Prussian vessels and their cargoes," it is provided that upon satisfactory evidence being given to the President of the United States by the government of any foreign nation that no discriminating duties of tonnage or impost are imposed or levied in the ports of said nation upon vessels wholly belonging to citizens of the United States, or upon the produce, manufactures, or merchandise imported to the same from the United States or from any foreign country, the President is thereby authorized to issue his proclamation, declaring that the foreign discriminating duties of tonnage and imposts within the United States are and shall be suspended and discontinued, so far as respects the vessels of the said foreign nation, and the produce, manufactures, or merchandise imported into the United States in the same from the said foreign nation, or from any other foreign country, the said suspension to take effect from the time of such notification being given to the President of the United States, and to continue so long as the reciprocal exemption of vessels belonging to citizens of the United States and their cargoes, as aforesaid, shall be continued, and no longer;

And whereas satisfactory evidence has lately been received by me from his Majesty the King of the Hawaiian Islands, through an official communication of his Majesty's Minister of Foreign Relations, under date of the 10th of December, 1866, that no other or higher duties of tonnage and impost are imposed or levied in the ports of the Hawaiian Islands upon vessels wholly belonging to citizens of the United States, and upon the produce, manufactures, or merchandise imported in the same from the United States, and from any foreign country whatever, than are levied on Hawaiian ships and their cargoes in the same ports under like circumstances;

Now, therefore, I, Andrew Johnson, President of the United States of America, do hereby declare and proclaim that so much of the several acts imposing discriminating duties of tonnage and impost within the United States are, and shall be, suspended and discontinued, so far as respects the vessels of the Hawaiian Islands, and the produce, manufactures, and merchandise imported into the United States in the same, from the dominions of the Hawaiian Islands, and from any other foreign country whatever, the said suspension to take effect from the said 10th day of December, and to continue thenceforward, so long as the reciprocal exemption of the vessels of the United States, and the produce, manufactures, and merchandise imported into the Hawaiian Islands in the same, as aforesaid, shall be continued on the part of the Government of his Majesty the King of the Hawaiian Islands.

In testimony whereof I have hereunto set my hand and caused the seal of the United States to be affixed.

Done at the city of Washington, the twenty-ninth day of January, in the year of our Lord one thousand eight hundred and [L. S.] sixty-seven, and of the independence of the United States of America, the ninety-first.                    ANDREW JOHNSON.

By the President:
WM. H. SEWARD, *Secretary of State.*

### Declaring Nebraska a State in the Union, March 1, 1867.

Whereas the Congress of the United States did, by an act approved on the nineteenth day of April, one thousand eight hundred and sixty-four, authorize the people of the Territory of Nebraska to form a constitution and State government, and for the admission of such State into the Union on an equal footing with the original States, upon certain conditions in said act specified ; and whereas said people did adopt a constitution conforming to the provisions and conditions of said act, and ask admission into the Union ; and whereas the Congress of the United States did, on the eighth and ninth days of February, one thousand eight hundred and sixty-seven, in mode prescribed by the Constitution, pass a further act for the admission of the State of Nebraska into the Union, in which last-named act it was provided that it should not take effect except upon the fundamental condition that within the State of Nebraska there should be no denial of the elective franchise or of any other right to any person by reason of race or color, excepting Indians not taxed, and upon the further fundamental condition that the Legislature of said State, by a solemn public act, should declare the assent of said State to the said fundamental condition, and should transmit to the President of the United States an authenticated copy of said act of the Legislature of said State, upon receipt whereof the President, by proclamation, should forthwith announce the fact, whereupon said fundamental condition should be held as a part of the organic law of the State, and thereupon, and without any further proceeding on the part of Congress, the admission of said State into the Union should be considered as complete; and whereas within the time prescribed by said act of Congress of the eighth and ninth of February, one thousand eight hundred and sixty-seven, the Legislature of the State of Nebraska did pass an act ratifying the said act of Congress of the eighth and ninth of February, one thousand eight hundred and sixty-seven, and declaring that the afore-named provisions of the third section of said last-named act of Congress should be a part of the organic law of the State of Nebraska; and whereas a duly authenticated copy of said act of the Legislature of Nebraska has been received by me:

Now, therefore, I, Andrew Johnson, President of the United States of America, do, in accordance with the provisions of the act of Congress last herein named, declare and proclaim the fact that the fundamental conditions imposed by Congress on the State of Nebraska to entitle that State to admission to the Union have been ratified and accepted, and that the admission of the said State into the Union is now complete.

In testimony whereof I have hereto set my hand, and have caused the seal of the United States to be affixed.

Done at the city of Washington, this first day of March, in the year of our Lord one [SEAL.] thousand eight hundred and sixty-seven, and of the independence of the United States of America the ninety-first.                    ANDREW JOHNSON.

By the President:
WILLIAM H. SEWARD, *Secretary of State.*

### Withdrawing reward for John H. Surratt, and others.*

WAR DEPARTMENT,
ADJUTANT GENERAL'S OFFICE,
WASHINGTON, *November* 24, 1865.

General Orders, No. 164.

*Ordered,* That—I. All persons claiming reward for the apprehension of John Wilkes Booth, Lewis Payne, G. A. Atzerodt, and David E. Herold, and Jefferson Davis, or either of them, are notified to file their claims and their proofs with the Adjutant General for final adjudication by the special commission appointed to award and determine upon the validity of such claims, before the first day of January next, after which time no claims will be received.

II. The rewards offered for the arrest of Jacob Thompson, Beverley Tucker, George N. Sanders, William C. Cleary, and John H. Surratt are revoked.

By order of the President of the United States:
E. D. TOWNSEND,
*Assistant Adjutant General.*

### Release of Convicts.

WAR DEPARTMENT,
ADJUTANT GENERAL'S OFFICE,
WASHINGTON, *July* 13, 1866.

General Orders, No 46.

*Ordered:* That all persons who are undergoing sentence by military courts, and have been imprisoned six months, except those who are under sentence for the crimes of murder, arson, or rape, and excepting those who are under sentence at the Tortugas, be discharged from imprisonment and the residue of their sentence remitted.

---

* Respecting this order, Secretary Stanton testified before a Congressional Committee, January 10, 1867, as follow:

Q. What was the reason for revoking the order offering a reward for the arrest of Surratt?

A. The reasons that influenced my mind, were in the first place, that many months had elapsed without accomplishing the arrest of these parties. I was entirely satisfied that they were not in the United States, and that if any arrest was made it would have to be by government officials, who ought not to have any pretence of claiming the reward ; besides, I thought that if the proclamation was withdrawn it would probably induce these parties to believe that pursuit was over, and they might return to the United States and be arrested. For these reasons I thought it expedient to revoke the order. It was done on my own responsibility, the President left it at my discretion to do as I thought best in the matter.

Those who belong to the military service, and their term unexpired, will be returned to their command, if it is still in service, and their release is conditional upon their serving their full term and being of good behavior.

By order of the President of the United States:

E. D. TOWNSEND,
*Assistant Adjutant General.*

---

### Reconstruction in Texas.

STATE DEPARTMENT,
AUSTIN, TEXAS, *July* 26, 1866.

HON. W. H. SEWARD:

Please inform me by telegram whether or not it is the will of the President that the Legislature of Texas shall meet on the 6th day of August, and General Throckmorton be inaugurated on the 9th? Will the Legislature be permitted to assemble without the inauguration of the Governor-elect? If so, what am I expected to do? You will perceive by reference to your dispatch of July 17 that my instructions are not definite. My solicitude increases as the time for the meeting of the Legislature approaches.

Your obedient servant,

JAMES H. BELL,
*Secretary of State of Texas.*

---

WAR DEPARTMENT,
WASHINGTON, *July* 28, 1866.

To JAMES H. BELL:

Your telegrams of the 21st and 26th of July, received. The President directs me to say that the Legislature of Texas will assemble and organize on the 6th of August without hindrance. The Governor-elect, Mr. Throckmorton, will be inaugurated on the 9th without hindrance. When you have reported the organization and inauguration to this Department, by telegraph or otherwise, the provisional governor will be relieved, and the government will be transferred to the elected authorities of Texas. Until the receipt of such notice by yourself, or by the Governor-elect, the condition of affairs will remain in the provisional government, as heretofore, except the organization and inauguration aforestated.

WM. H. SEWARD,
*Secretary of State.*

---

WASHINGTON, D. C., *October* 30, 1866.

Governor THROCKMORTON:

Your telegram of the 29th instant just received. I have nothing further to suggest than urging upon the Legislature to make all laws involving civil rights as complete as possible, so as to extend equal and exact justice to all persons, without regard to color, if it has not been done. We should not despair of the Republic. My faith is strong. My confidence is unlimited in the wisdom, prudence, virtue, intelligence, and magnanimity of the great mass of the people; and that their ultimate decision will be uninfluenced by passion and prejudice, engendered by the recent civil war, for the complete restoration of the Union by the admission of loyal Representatives and Senators from all the States to the respective Houses of the Congress of the United States. ANDREW JOHNSON.

### To Gov. Brownlow, of Tennessee.*

WASHINGTON, *July* 20, 1865.

HON. W. G. BROWNLOW:

I hope and have no doubt you will see that the recent amendments to the Constitution of the State, as adopted by the people, and all laws passed by the last Legislature in pursuance thereof, are faithfully and fairly executed, and that all illegal votes in the approaching election be excluded from the polls, and the election for members of Congress be legally and fairly conducted. When and wherever it becomes necessary to employ force for the execution of the laws and the protection of the ballot-box from violence and fraud, you are authorized to call upon Major General Thomas for sufficient force to sustain the civil authorities of the State. I have received your recent address to the people, and think it well-timed, and hope it will do much good in reconciling the opposition to the amendment of the constitution and the laws passed by the last Legislature. The law must be executed and the civil authority sustained. In your efforts to do this, if necessary, General Thomas will afford a sufficient military force. You are at liberty to make what use you think proper of this dispatch. ANDREW JOHNSON.

### To Montgomery Blair, Postmaster General.

NASHVILLE, *November* 24, 1863.

To Hon. M. BLAIR, *Postmaster General:*

I hope that the President will not be committed to the proposition of States relapsing into territories and held as such. If he steers clear of this extreme, his election to the next Presidency is without a reasonable doubt. I expected to have been in Washington before this time, when I could have conversed freely and fully in reference to the policy to be adopted by the Government; but it has been impossible for me to leave Nashville. I will be there soon. The institution of slavery is gone, and there is no good reason now for destroying the States to bring about the destruction of slavery.

ANDREW JOHNSON.

### General Grant's Revocation of Order Respecting Disloyal Newspapers.†

HEADQUARTERS ARMIES OF THE UNITED STATES,
WASHINGTON, *July* 24, 1866.

The order of February 17, 1866, from these headquarters directing department commanders to forward copies of such newspapers published within their respective commands, as contained sentiments of disloyalty, &c., is hereby revoked.

By command of Lieut. Gen. Grant,

GEO. K. LEET,
*Assistant Adjutant General.*

---

### Assigning Commanders to Military Districts, March 11, 12, and 15, 1867.

HEADQUARTERS OF THE ARMY,
ADJUTANT GENERAL'S OFFICE,
WASHINGTON, *March* 11, 1867.

General Orders No. 10.

\*          \*          \*          \*          \*

II. In pursuance of the act of Congress en-

---

*An incomplete copy of this telegram is printed on page 27 of the Political Manual for 1866.

†For original order see Manual for 1866, p. 123.

titled " An act to provide for the more efficient government of the rebel States," the President directs the following assignments to be made:

First District, State of Virginia, to be commanded by Brevet Major General J. M. Schofield. Headquarters, Richmond, Va.

Second District, consisting of North Carolina and South Carolina, to be commanded by Major General D. E. Sickles. Headquarters, Columbia, S. C.

Third District, consisting of the States of Georgia, Florida, and Alabama, to be commanded by Major General G. H. Thomas. Headquarters, Montgomery, Ala.

Fourth District, consisting of the States of Mississippi and Arkansas, to be commanded by Brevet Major General E. O. C. Ord. Headquarters, Vicksburg, Miss.

Fifth District, consisting of the States of Louisiana and Texas, to be commanded by Major General P. H. Sheridan. Headquarters, New Orleans, La.

The powers of departmental commanders are hereby delegated to the above-named district commanders.

By command of General Grant.
E. D. TOWNSEND,
*Assistant Adjutant General.*

—

HEADQUARTERS OF THE ARMY,
ADJUTANT GENERAL'S OFFICE,
WASHINGTON, *March* 12, 1867.
General Orders No. 14.

By direction of the President, the following changes are made in Geographical Departments as now constituted.

1. The States of West Virginia, Tennessee, and Kentucky to constitute the Department of the Cumberland, Brigadier and Brevet Major General John Pope to command. Headquarters, Louisville, Ky.

2. The counties of Alexandria and Fairfax, Virginia, are annexed to the command of the First District.

3. Indian Territory is attached to the Department of the Missouri.

By command of General Grant.
E. D. TOWNSEND,
*Assistant Adjutant General.*

—

HEADQUARTERS OF THE ARMY,
ADJUTANT GENERAL'S OFFICE,
WASHINGTON, *March* 15, 1867.

The President directs that the following changes be made, at the request of Major General Thomas, in the assignment announced in General Orders No. 10, of March 11, 1867, of commanders of districts under the act of Congress entitled "An act to provide for the more efficient government of the rebel States," and of the Department of the Cumberland created in General Orders No. 14, of March 12, 1867: Brevet Major General John Pope to command the Third District, consisting of the States of Georgia, Florida, and Alabama, and Major General George H. Thomas to command the Department of the Cumberland.

By command of General Grant.
E. D. TOWNSEND,
*Assistant Adjutant General.*

## Orders in First Military District.

HEADQUARTERS FIRST DISTRICT,
STATE OF VIRGINIA,
RICHMOND, *March* 13, 1867.
General Orders No. 1:

1. In compliance with the order of the President, the undersigned hereby assumes command of the First District, State of Virginia, under the act of Congress of March 2, 1867.

2 All officers under the existing provisional government of the State of Virginia will continue to perform the duties of their respective offices, according to law, unless otherwise hereafter ordered in individual cases, until their successors shall be duly elected and qualified, in accordance with the above-named act of Congress.

3. It is desirable that the military power conferred by the before-mentioned act be exercised only so far as may be necessary to accomplish the objects for which that power was conferred, and the undersigned appeals to the people of Virginia, and especially to magistrates and other civil officers, to render the necessity for the exercise of this power as slight as possible, by strict obedience to the laws, and by impartial administration of justice to all classes.

4. The staff officers now on duty at headquarters Department of the Potomac are assigned to corresponding duties at headquarters First District, State of Virginia.     J. M. SCHOFIELD,
*Brevet Major General, U. S. A.*

—

HEADQUARTERS FIRST DISTRICT,
STATE OF VIRGINIA,
RICHMOND, VA., *March* 15, 1867.
General Orders No. 2.

I. The following extract of an act of Congress is re-published for the information and government of all concerned:

[Public—No. 85.]

An Act making appropriations for the support of the army for the year ending June thirtieth, eighteen hundred and sixty-eight, and for other purposes. *     *     *     *     *

SEC. 5. *And be it further enacted,* That it shall be the duty of the officers of the army and navy and of the Freedmen's Bureau to prohibit and prevent whipping or maiming of the person, as a punishment for any crime, misdemeanor, or offence, by any pretended civil or military authority, in any State lately in rebellion, until the civil government in such State shall have been restored, and shall have been recognized by the Congress of the United States. *     *     *

Approved March 2, 1867.

II. In pursuance of the provisions of the 5th section of the act, as above cited, whipping or maiming of the person, as a punishment of any crime, misdemeanor, or offence, is hereby prohibited in this district.

By Command of Brig. and Bvt. Maj. Gen. J. M. Schofield, U. S. A.

S. F. CHALFIN, *A. A. G.*

—

HEADQUARTERS FIRST DISTRICT,
STATE OF VIRGINIA,
RICHMOND, VA., *March* 15, 1867.

I. The following extract of an act of Congress is re-published for the information and government of all concerned:

[Public—No 85.]
An Act making appropriations for the support of the army for the year ending June thirtieth, eighteen hundred and sixty-eight, and for other purposes.    *    *    *    *

SEC. 6. *And be it further enacted*, That all militia forces now organized or in service in either of the States of Virginia, North Carolina, South Carolina, Georgia, Florida, Alabama, Louisiana, Mississippi, and Texas, be forthwith disbanded, and that the further organization, arming, or calling into service of the said militia forces, or any part thereof, is hereby prohibited under any circumstances whatever, until the same shall be authorized by Congress.    *    *    *

Approved March 2, 1867.

By command of Brig. and Bvt. Maj. Gen. J. M. Schofield, U. S. A.    S. F. CHALFIN, *A. A. G.*

—

HEADQUARTERS FIRST DISTRICT,
STATE OF VIRGINIA,
RICHMOND, VA., *April* 2, 1867.
Special Orders, No. 16.
[Extract.]

1. A board of officers is hereby appointed to select and recommend to the commanding general for appointment persons to form boards of registration throughout the district, as required by the act of March 23, 1867.

The persons required will be one registering officer for each magisterial district of a county, or ward of a city at large, and two, four, or six for the county or city at large, according to the size of the county or city, so as to form with the registering officers of the several districts or wards, one, two, or three boards of registration for the county or city.

An officer of the army or Freedmen's Bureau will, if possible, be selected as a member of each board; and the other two will be selected from the following classes of persons, viz: 1st, Officers of the United States army, or of volunteers who have been honorably discharged after meritorious services during the late war. 2d, Loyal citizens of the county or city, for which they are selected. 3d, Any other loyal citizens having the proper qualifications.

These boards must be composed of men who not only are now, but always have been, loyal to the Government of the United States; men of high character, and sound, impartial judgment, and, as far as possible, men who have the confidence of all classes of citizens.

No registering officer shall be a candidate for any elective office while holding the office of registering officer.

With their recommendations for appointment, the board will report to the commanding general a brief of the testimonials and other evidence upon which their selections are based.

The board will appoint from time to time their selections for particular counties or cities, without waiting to complete the list.

DETAIL FOR THE BOARD.

Brevet Lieutenant Colonel George Gibson, jr., Captain 11th U. S. Infantry; Brevet Major C. R. Layton, Captain 11th U. S. Infantry; Brevet Major D. M. Vance, Captain 11th U. S. Infantry; Captain Garrick Mallery, 43d U. S. Infantry; Captain J. A. Bates, 43d U. S. Infantry.

By command of Brigadier and Brevet Major General J. M. Schofield, U. S. A.
S. F. CHALFIN, *A. A. G.*

—

HEADQUARTERS FIRST DISTRICT,
STATE OF VIRGINIA,
RICHMOND, VA., *April* 2, 1867.
General Orders, No. 8.

All elections, whether State, county, or municipal, under the provisional government of Virginia, are hereby ordered to be suspended until the registration provided for by the act of Congress of March 23, 1867, shall be completed.

Vacancies which may occur in the meantime will be filled by temporary appointments, to be made by the Commanding General.

By command of Brigadier and Brevet Major General J. M Schofield, U. S A.
S. F. CHALFIN, *A. A. G.*

—

HEADQUARTERS FIRST DISTRICT,
STATE OF VIRGINIA,
RICHMOND, VA., *April* 5, 1867.
General Orders, No. 9.

In pursuance of the acts of Congress of March 2 and 23, 1867, all officers hereafter to be elected or appointed under the provisional government of Virginia will, in addition to the oath of office prescribed by the laws of the State, be required to take and subscribe the following oath:

" I, ——, do solemnly ——, in the presence of Almighty God, that I have not been disfranchised for participation in any rebellion or civil war against the United States, nor for felony committed against the laws of any State or of the United States; that I have never been a member of any State Legislature, nor held any executive or judicial office in any State, and afterward engaged in insurrection or rebellion against the United States, or given aid or comfort to the enemies thereof; that I have never taken an oath as a member of Congress of the United States, or as an officer of the United States, or as a member of any State Legislature, or as an executive or judicial officer of any State, to support the Constitution of the United States, and afterward engaged in insurrection or rebellion against the United States, or given aid or comfort to the enemies thereof; that I will faithfully support the Constitution and obey the laws of the United States, and will, to the best of my ability, encourage others so to do; so help me God."

By order of Brigadier and Brevet Major General J. M. Schofield, U. S. A.
S. F. CHALFIN, *A. A. G.*

—

**Orders in Second Military District.**
HEADQUARTERS DEP'T OF THE SOUTH,
CHARLESTON, S. C., *March* 8, 1867.
General Orders, No. 26.

Whipping or maiming of the person, as a punishment for any crime, misdemeanor, or offence, being now prohibited by the laws of the United States, all officers of the army and Freedmen's Bureau on duty in this Department, are hereby directed to prevent the infliction of such punishment by any authority whatever.

By command of Brevet Maj. Gen. Robinson.
JNO. R. MYRICK, *A. A. A. G.*

A like order was issued in each of the other Districts.

HEADQUARTERS DEP'T OF THE SOUTH,
CHARLESTON, S. C., *March* 13, 1867.

General Orders, No. 27.

An official copy of the law, entitled "An act to provide for the more efficient government of the rebel States," having been received at these headquarters, it is hereby announced, for the information and government of all concerned, that the said law is in force within the military district composed of North Carolina and South Carolina, from this date.

By command of Brevet Maj. Gen. J. C. Robinson.

JNO. R. MYRICK, *A. A. A. G.*

HEADQUARTERS SECOND MILITARY DISTRICT,
(NORTH CAROLINA AND SOUTH CAROLINA,)
COLUMBIA, S. C., *March* 21, 1867.

General Orders, No. 1.

I. In compliance with General Orders No. 10, Headquarters of the Army, March 11, 1867, the undersigned hereby assumes command of the Second Military District, constituted by the act of Congress, Public No. 68, 2d March, 1867, entitled "An act for the more efficient government of the rebel States."

II. In the execution of the duty of the commanding general to maintain the security of the inhabitants in their persons and property, to suppress insurrection, disorder, and violence, and to punish or cause to be punished all disturbers of the public peace and criminals, the local and civil tribunals will be permitted to take jurisdiction of and try offenders, excepting only such cases as may, by the order of the commanding general, be referred to a commission or other military tribunal for trial.

III. The civil government now existing in North Carolina and South Carolina is provisional only, and in all respects subject to the paramount authority of the United States, at any time to abolish, modify, control, or supersede the same. Local laws and municipal regulations not inconsistent with the Constitution and laws of the United States, or the proclamations of the President, or with such regulations as are or may be prescribed in the orders of the commanding general, are hereby declared to be in force; and in conformity therewith, civil officers are hereby authorized to continue the exercise of their proper functions, and will be respected and obeyed by the inhabitants.

IV. Whenever any civil officer, magistrate, or court neglects or refuses to perform an official act properly required of such tribunal or officer, whereby due and rightful security to person or property shall be denied, the case will be reported by the post commander to these headquarters.

V. Post commanders will cause to be arrested persons charged with the commission of crimes and offenses when the civil authorities fail to arrest and bring such offenders to trial, and will hold the accused in custody for trial by military commission, provost court, or other tribunal organized pursuant to orders from these headquarters. Arrests by military authority will be reported promptly. The charges preferred will be accompanied by the evidence on which they are founded.

VI. The commanding general desiring to pre-

serve tranquillity and order by means and agencies most congenial to the people, solicits the zealous and cordial co-operation of civil officers in the discharge of their duties, and the aid of all good citizens in preventing conduct tending to disturb the peace; and to the end that occasion may seldom arise for the exercise of military authority in matters of ordinary civil administration, the commanding general respectfully and earnestly commends to the people and authorities of North and South Carolina unreserved obedience to the authority now established, and the diligent, considerate, and impartial execution of the laws enacted for their government.

VII. All orders heretofore published to the Department of the South are hereby continued in force.

VIII. The following-named officers are announced as the staff of the major general commanding:      *      *      *      *

D. E. SICKLES,
*Major General Commanding.*

HEADQUARTERS SECOND MILITARY DISTRICT,
(NORTH CAROLINA AND SOUTH CAROLINA,)
CHARLESTON, S. C., *April* 1, 1867.

General Orders, No. 5.

When an election for district, county, municipal, or town officers is required to take place, in accordance with the provisions of the local law, within the limits of any post in this command, command officers will promptly report to these headquarters the time and place of such election and the designation of the offices to be filled.

If the present incumbents be ineligible to hold office, or any objection exists, arising out of their misconduct in office, to the continuance of their functions, the facts will be reported by the post commander with his suggestions, having in view the interests of the service and the welfare of the locality immediately concerned.

By command of Major General D. E. Sickles.
J. W. CLOUS, *A. A. A. G.*

[By Telegraph.]
CHARLESTON, S. C., *April* 1, 1867.

Brvt. Brig. Gen. GREEN, *Commanding Richland District:*

The election [for sheriff] will not be held. When will the term of the present incumbent expire? A successor will be appointed.

By command of Gen. Sickles.
J. W. CLOUS, *A. A. A. G.*

HEADQUARTERS SECOND MILITARY DISTRICT,
CHARLESTON, S. C., *April* 11, 1867.

General Orders, No. 10.

The general destitution prevailing among the population of this military district cannot be relieved without affording means for the development of their industrial resources. The nature and extent of the destitution demand extraordinary measures. The people are borne down by a heavy burden of debt, the crops of grain and garden produce failed last year, many families have been deprived of shelter, many more need food and clothing, needful implements and auxiliaries of husbandry are very scarce; the laboring population in numerous localities are threatened with starvation unless supplied with food by the Government of the United States; the inability of a large portion of the people to pay taxes leaves the local authorities without adequate means of relief, and the gravity of the situation is increased by the general disposition shown by creditors to enforce upon an impoverished people the immediate collection of all claims. To suffer all this to go on without restraint or remedy is to sacrifice the general good. The rights of creditors shall be respected, but the appeal of want and suffering must be heeded. Moved by these considerations, the following regulations are announced. They will continue in force with such modification as the occasion may require until the civil government of the respective States shall be established in accordance with the requirements of the Government of the United States. The commanding general earnestly desires and confidently believes that the observance of these regulations and the co-operation of all persons concerned in employing fairly and justly the advantages still remaining to them, will mitigate the distress now existing, and that the avenues of industry, enterprise, and organization thus opened will contribute to the permanent welfare and future happiness of the people.

I. Imprisonment for debt is prohibited, unless the defendant in execution shall be convicted of a fraudulent concealment or disposition of his property with intent to hinder, delay, and prevent the creditor in the recovery of his debt or demand, and the proceedings now established in North and South Carolina respectively, for the trial and determination of such questions, may be adopted.

II. Judgments or decrees for the payment of money on causes of action arising between the 19th of December, 1860, and the 15th of May, 1865, shall not be enforced by execution against the property or the person of the defendant. Proceedings in such causes of action now pending shall be stayed, and no suit or process shall be hereafter instituted or commenced for any such causes of action.

III. Sheriffs, coroners, and constables are hereby directed to suspend for twelve calendar months the sale of all property upon execution or process on liabilities contracted prior to the 19th of December, 1860, unless upon the written consent of the defendants, except in cases where the plaintiff, or in his absence his agent or attorney, shall upon oath, with corroborative testimony, allege and prove that the defendant is removing or intends fraudulently to remove his property beyond the territorial jurisdiction of the court. The sale of real or personal property by foreclosure of mortgage is likewise suspended for twelve calendar months, except in cases where the payment of interest money accruing since the 15th day of May, 1865, shall not have been made before the day of sale.

IV. Judgments or decrees entered or enrolled on causes of action arising subsequent to the 15th of May, 1865, may be enforced by execution against the property of the defendant, and in the application of the money arising under such executions, regard shall be had to the priority of liens, unless in cases where the good faith of any lien shall be drawn in question. In such cases the usual mode of proceeding adopted in North and South Carolina respectively to determine that question shall be adopted.

V. All proceedings for the recovery of money under contracts, whether under seal or by parole, the consideration for which was the purchase of negroes, are suspended. Judgments or decrees entered or enrolled for such causes of action shall not be enforced.

VI. All advances of moneys, subsistence, implements, and fertilizers, loaned, used, employed, or required for the purpose of aiding the agricultural pursuits of the people, shall be protected, and the existing laws which have provided the most efficient remedies in such cases for the lender will be supported and enforced; wages for labor performed in the production of the crops shall be a lien on the crop, and payment of the amount due for such wages shall be enforced by the like remedies provided to secure advances of money and other means for the cultivation of the soil.

VII. In all sales of property under execution or by order of any court there shall be reserved out of the property of any defendant who has a family dependent upon his or her labor a dwelling-house and appurtenances and twenty acres of land for the use and occupation of the family of the defendant, and necessary articles of furniture, apparel, subsistence, implements of trade, husbandry or other employment of the value of $500. The homestead exemption shall inure only to the benefit of families—that is to say, to parent or parents and child or children—in other cases the exemption shall extend only to clothing, implements of trade or other employment usually followed by the defendant, of the value of $100. The exemption hereby made shall not be waived or defeated by the act of the defendant. The exempted property of the defendant shall be ascertained by the sheriff or other officer enforcing the execution, who shall specifically describe the same, and make a report thereof in each case to the court.

VIII. The currency of the United States declared by the Congress of the United State to be a legal tender in the payment of all debts, dues, and demands, shall be so recognized in North and South Carolina, and all cases in which the same shall be tendered in payment and refused by any public officer will be at once reported to these headquarters or to the commanding officer of the post within which such officer resides.

IX. Property of an absent debtor or one charged as such without fraud, whether consisting of money advanced for the purposes of agriculture or appliances for the cultivation of the soil, shall not be taken under the process known as foreign attachment; but the lien created by any existing law shall not be disturbed, nor shall the possession or the use of the same be in any wise interfered with, except in the execution of a judgment or final decree, in cases where they are authorized to be enforced.

X. In suits brought to recover ordinary debts known as actions *ex contractu*, bail, as heretofore authorized, shall not be demanded by the suitor nor taken by the sheriff or other officer serving the process; in suits for trespass, libel, wrongful conversion of property, and other cases, known as actions *ex delicto*, bail, as heretofore authorized, may be demanded and taken. The prohibition of bail in cases *ex contractu* shall not extend to persons about to leave the State, but the fact of intention must be clearly established by proof.

XI. In criminal proceedings the usual recognizances shall be required and taken by the proper civil officers heretofore authorized by law to take the same, provided that upon complaint being made to any magistrate or other person authorized by law to issue a warrant for breach of the peace or any criminal offense it shall be the duty of such magistrate or officer to issue his warrant upon the recognizance of the complainant to prosecute, without requiring him to give security on such recognizance.

XII. The practice of carrying deadly weapons, except by officers and soldiers in the military service of the United States, is prohibited. The concealment of such weapons on the person will be deemed an aggravation of the offence. A violation of this order will render the offender amenable to trial and punishment by military commission. Whenever wounding or killing shall result from the use of such weapons, proof that the party carried or concealed a deadly weapon shall be deemed evidence of a felonious attempt to take the life of the injured person.

XIII. The orders heretofore issued in this military department prohibiting the punishment of crimes and offenses by whipping, maiming, branding, stocks, pillory, or other corporal punishment is in force and will be obeyed by all persons.

XIV. The punishment of death in certain cases of burglary and larceny imposed by the existing laws of the provisional governments in this military district is abolished. Any person convicted of burglary or of larceny, when the property stolen is of the value of $25, of assault and battery with intent to kill, or of any assault with a deadly weapon, shall be deemed guilty of felony, and shall be punished by imprisonment at hard labor for a term not exceeding ten years nor less than two years, in the discretion of the court having jurisdiction thereof. Larceny, when the value of the property stolen is less than $25, shall be punished by imprisonment at hard labor for a term not exceeding one year, in the discretion of the court.

XV. The Governors of North and South Carolina shall have authority within their jurisdictions respectively to reprieve or pardon any person convicted and sentenced by a civil court, and to remit fines and penalties.

XVI. Nothing in this order shall be construed to restrain or prevent the operation of proceedings in bankruptcy in accordance with the acts of Congress in such cases made and provided, nor with the collection of any tax, impost, excise, or charge levied by authority of the United States, or of the provisional governments of North and South Carolina; but no imprisonment for over due taxes shall be allowed, nor shall this order or any law of the provisional governments of North and South Carolina operate to deny to minor children or children coming of age, or their legal representatives, nor to suspend as to them any right of action, remedy, or proceeding against executors, administrators, trustees, guardians, masters, or clerks of equity courts, or other officers or persons holding a fiduciary relation to the parties or the subject matter of the action or proceeding.

XVII. Any law or ordinance heretofore in force in North or South Carolina inconsistent with the provisions of this general order is hereby suspended and declared inoperative.

By command of Major Gen. D. E. Sickles.

　　　　　　　　　J. W. CLOUS, *A. A A. G.*

## Orders in Third Military District.

HEADQ'RS SUB-DIST. OF ALABAMA,
　　MONTGOMERY, ALA., *March* 28, 1867.
General Orders, No. 1.

I. By direction of General Grant, all State and local elections in this State are disallowed, pending the arrival of the district commander appointed for this district, and his order in the premises.

II. In default of certain information that municipal or other corporate elections have not occurred since the passage of "An act to provide for the more efficient government of the rebel States," all persons chosen to public office in this State during this month will report the fact by letter to these headquarters, for the action of the district commander.

　　　WAGER SWAYNE, *Major General.*

—

HEADQ'RS THIRD MILITARY DISTRICT,
　　MONTGOMERY, ALA., *April* 1, 1867.
Orders No. 1.

In compliance with General Orders No. 18, dated Headquarters of the Army, March 15, 1867, the undersigned assumes command of the Third Military District, which comprises the States of Alabama, Georgia, and Florida.

I. The districts of Georgia and Alabama will remain as at present constituted, and with their present commanders, except that the headquarters of the district of Georgia will be forthwith removed to Milledgeville.

The district of Key West is hereby merged into the District of Florida, which will be commanded by Colonel John T. Sprague, Seventh United States Infantry. The headquarters of the District of Florida are removed to Tallahassee, to which place the district commander will transfer his headquarters without delay.

II. The civil officers at present in office in Georgia, Florida, and Alabama will retain their offices until the expiration of their terms of service, unless otherwise directed in special cases, so long as justice is impartially and faithfully administered. It is hoped that no necessity may arise for the interposition of the military authorities in the civil administration, and such necessity can only arise from the failure of the civil tribunals to protect the people, without distinction, in their rights of person and property.

III. It is to be clearly understood, however, that the civil officers thus retained in office shall confine themselves strictly to the performance of their official duties, and whilst holding their offices they shall not use any influence whatever to deter or dissuade the people from taking an active part in reconstructing their State government, under the act of Congress to provide for the more efficient government of the rebel States and the act supplementary thereto.

IV. No elections will be held in any of the States comprised in this military district, except such as are provided for in the act of Congress, and in the manner therein established; but all vacancies in civil offices which now exist, or which may occur by expiration of the terms of office of the present incumbents, before the prescribed registration of voters is completed, will be filled by appointment of the general commanding the district. JOHN POPE, *Major General Commanding.*

HEADQ'RS THIRD MILITARY DISTRICT,
MONTGOMERY, ALA., *April* 8, 1867.
General Orders, No. 5.

I. The following extract from the recent acts of Congress in relation to reconstruction in the Southern States is published for the information of all concerned:

[PUBLIC—No. 6.]

An act supplementary to an act entitled "An act to provide for the more efficient government of the rebel States," passed March 2, 1867, and to facilitate restoration.

*Be it enacted, &c.*, That before the first day of September, 1867, the commanding general in each district (defined by an act entitled "An act to provide for the more efficient government of the rebel States," passed March 2, 1867) shall cause a registration to be made of the male citizens of the United States, twenty-one years of age and upwards, resident in each county or parish in the State or States included in his district, which registration shall include only those persons who are qualified to vote for delegates by the act aforesaid, and who shall have taken and subscribed the following oath or affirmation:

"I, —— do solemnly swear or affirm, in the presence of Almighty God, that I am a citizen of the State of ——; that I have resided in the State for——next preceding this day, and now reside in the county of ——, or the parish of ——, in said State, as the case may be; that I am twenty-one years old; that I have not been disfranchised for participation in any rebellion or civil war against the United States, nor for felony committed against the laws of any State or the United States; that I have never been a member of any State legislature, nor held any executive or judicial office in any State, and afterward engaged in insurrection or rebellion against the United States, or given aid or comfort to the enemies thereof; that I have never taken an oath as a member of Congress of the United States, or as an officer of the United States, or as a member of any State legislature, or as an executive or judicial officer of any State, to support the Constitution of the United States and afterward engaged in insurrection or rebellion against the United States, or given aid or comfort to the enemies thereof; that I will faithfully support the Constitution and obey the laws of the United States, and will to the best of my ability encourage others so to do. So help me God"—which oath or affimation may be administered by any registering officer.

SEC. 4. That the commanding general of each district shall appoint as many boards of registration as may be necessary, consisting of three loyal officers or persons, to make and complete the registration, superintend the election, and make return to him of the votes, list of voters,

and of the persons elected as delegates by a plurality of the votes cast at said election. * *

II. In order to execute this provision of the the act referred to with as little delay as possible, the commanding officers of the districts of Alabama, Georgia, and Florida will proceed immediately to divide those States into convenient districts for registration, aided by such information on the subject as they have or can obtain. It is suggested that the election districts in each State which in 1860 sent a member to the most numerous branch of the State legislature will be found a convenient division for registration.

It is desirable that in all cases the registers shall be civilians where it is possible to obtain such as come within the provisions of the act, and are otherwise suitable persons; and that military officers shall not be used for the purpose except in case of actual necessity. The compensation for registers will be fixed hereafter, but the general rule will be observed of graduating the compensation by the number of recorded voters. To each list of voters shall be appended the oath of the register or registers that the names have been faithfully recorded and represent actual legal voters, and that the same man does not appear under different names. The registers are specifically instructed to see that all information concerning their political rights is given to all persons entitled to vote under the act of Congress; and they are made responsible that every such legal voter has the opportunity to record his name.

III. As speedily as possible, the names of persons chosen for registers shall be communicated to these headquarters for the approval of the commanding general.

IV. The district commanders in each of the States comprised in this military district is authorized to appoint one or more general supervisors of registration, whose business it shall be to visit the various points where registration is being carried on, to inspect the operations of the registers, and to assure themselves that every man entitled to vote has the necessary information concerning his political rights, and the opportunity to record his name.

V. A general inspector, either an officer of the army or a civilian, will be appointed at these headquarters, to see that the provisions of these orders are fully and carefully executed.

VI. District commanders may, at their discretion, appoint civil officers of the United States as registers, with such additional compensation as may seem reasonable and sufficient.

VII. The commanding officer of each district will give public notice when and where the registers will commence the registration, which notice will be kept public by the registers in each district during the whole time occupied in registration.

VIII. Interference by violence, or threats of violence, or other oppressive means to prevent the registration of any voter, is positively prohibited; and any person guilty of such interference shall be arrested and tried by the military authorities.

By command of Brevet Major General Pope.
J. F. CONYNGHAM, *A. A. A. G.*

HEADQUARTERS DISTRICT OF ALABAMA,
MONTGOMERY, ALA., *April* 2, 1867.
General Orders, No. 1.

By direction of General Pope, the undersigned is charged with the administration of the military reconstruction bill of this State.

The principles which will control its execution have already been announced.

A literal compliance with the requirements of the civil rights bill will be exacted.

All payments on account of services rendered during the war to the pretended State organization, or any of its branches, are peremptorily forbidden.                         WAGER SWAYNE,
                                  *Major General.*

HEADQUARTERS POST OF AUGUSTA,
AUGUSTA, GA., *April* 9, 1867.
General Orders, No. 28.

It having been reported to me that the mayor and city council of this city construe General Order No. 1, issued from Headquarters Third Military District, dated Montgomery, Ala., April 1, 1867, to mean that their duties as public officers shall cease on the expiration of their term of service, and believing that it was not contemplated by the commanding general of this military district that the city should be left without a civil government, I, therefore, by the power vested in me as commanding officer of this post, do hereby order said civil authorities to continue to perform their civil duties until such time as the appointments referred to in section 4 of said General Order No. 1 be received and duly promulgated at this post.
                                  T. W. SWEENY,
                           *Brevet Col. U. S. A. Com'g.*

### Orders in Fourth Military District.
HEADQUARTERS FOURTH MILITARY DISTRICT,
MISSISSIPPI AND ARKANSAS,
VICKSBURG, *March* 26, 1867.
General Orders, No. 1.

1. The undersigned having been appointed by the President to command the Fourth Military District, consisting of the States of Mississippi and Arkansas, hereby assumes command thereof.

2. Competent civil officers in this District are expected to arrest and punish all offenders against the law, so as to obviate as far as possible, necessity for the exercise of military authority under the law of Congress, passed March 2, 1867, creating military districts.

3. Such other orders as may become necessary to carry out the above-named act, and an act supplemental thereto, will be duly published.
                                  E. O. C. ORD,
                           *Brev. Major and Brig. Gen. U. S. A.*

### Orders in Fifth Military District.
HEADQUARTERS FIFTH MILITARY DISTRICT,
NEW ORLEANS, LA., *March* 9, 1867.
General Orders, No. 13.

No commander having yet been appointed for the military district of Louisiana and Texas, created by the recent law of Congress, entitled "An act to provide for the more efficient government of the rebel States," and Brevet Major-General Mower, commanding in this city, and the mayor and chief of police of the city of New Orleans having all expressed to me personally their fears that the public peace may be dis-

turbed by the election for some of the city officers ordered by an act of the legislature of Louisiana, to take place on Monday, the 11th instant, and that body, at a special session, having refused to postpone said election, thereby rendering it necessary that measures for the preservation of the peace should be taken, I hereby assume the authority conferred upon the district commanders provided for in the act of Congress above cited, so far as it is necessary to declare that no such election shall take place. It is, therefore, ordered that for the preservation of the public peace, no polls shall be opened on that day, and that the elections shall be postponed until the district commander, under the law, is appointed, or special instructions are received covering the case.
                                  P. H. SHERIDAN,
                             *Major General Commanding.*

HEADQUARTERS FIFTH MILITARY DISTRICT,
NEW ORLEANS, LA., *March* 19, 1867.
General Orders, No. 1.

I. The act of Congress entitled "An act to provide for the more efficient government of the rebel States" having been officially transmitted to the undersigned in an order from the Headquarters of the Army, which assigns him to the command of the Fifth Military District created by that act, consisting of the States of Louisiana and Texas, he hereby assumes command of the same.

II. According to the provisions of the sixth section of the act of Congress above cited, the present State and municipal governments in the States of Louisiana and Texas are hereby declared to be provisional only, and subject to be abolished, modified, controlled, or superseded.

III. No general removals from office will be made, unless the present incumbents fail to carry out the provisions of the law, or impede the reorganization, or unless a delay in reorganizing should necessitate a change. Pending the reorganization, it is desirable and intended to create as little disturbance in the machinery of the various branches of the provisional governments as possible, consistent with the law of Congress and its successful execution; but this condition is dependent upon the disposition shown by the people, and upon the length of time required for reorganization.

IV. The States of Louisiana and Texas will retain their present military designations, viz: "District of Louisiana," and "District of Texas." The officers in command of each will continue to exercise all their military powers and duties as heretofore, and will, in addition, carry out all the provisions of the law within their respective commands, except those which specifically require the action of the military district commander, and except in cases of removals from and appointments to office.                         P. H. SHERIDAN,
                             *Major General Commanding.*

HEADQUARTERS FIFTH MILITARY DISTRICT,
NEW ORLEANS, LA., *March* 27, 1867.
General Orders, No. 5.

Andrew S. Herron, attorney general of the State of Louisiana; James T. Monroe, mayor of New Orleans; Edmund Abell, judge of the first district court of the city of New Orleans, are hereby removed from their respective offices from 12 m., to-day. The following appointments have been made to take effect from the same date: B. L. Lynch, attorney general of the State of Louisiana; Edward Heath, mayor of New Orleans; W. W. Howe, judge of the first district court of New Orleans Each person removed will turn over all the books, papers, and records, &c., pertaining to his office, to the one appointed thereto. The authority of the latter will be duly respected and enforced.

By command of Major General Sheridan.

GEO. L. HARTSUFF, *A. A. G.*

HEADQUARTERS FIFTH MILITARY DISTRICT, NEW ORLEANS, LA., *April* 10, 1867.

Special Orders, No. 15.

2. In obedience to the directions contained in the first section of the law of Congress, entitled " An act supplemental to an act entitled ' An act to provide for the more efficient government of the rebel States,' " the registration of the legal voters, according to the law of the parish of Orleans, will be commenced on the 15th instant, and must be completed by the 15th of May.

The four municipal districts of the city of New Orleans, and the parish of Orleans, right bank, (Algiers,) will each constitute a registration district. Election precincts will remain as at present constituted.

The following appointments of boards of registers is hereby made—to continue in office until further orders, viz:

First District—John A. Roberts, Wm. Baker, and W. M. Geddes.

Second District—Edward Ames, T. C. Thomas, and Michael Vidal.

Third District—Charles F. Berens, John McWhorter, and H. Stiles.

Fourth District—John L. Davies, Henry Bensel, Jr., and Edmund Flood.

Orleans Parish, right bank—W. H. Seymour, Thomas Kenefec, and George Herbert.

Each member of the board of registers, before commencing his duties, will file in the office of the assistant inspector general at these headquarters the oath required in the sixth section of the act referred to, and be governed in the execution of his duty by the provisions of the first section of that act, faithfully administering the oath therein prescribed to each person registered.

Boards of registers will immediately select suitable offices, within their respective districts, having reference to convenience and facility of registration, and will enter upon their duties on the day designated. Each board will be entitled to two clerks. Office hours for registration will be from 8 o'clock till 12 a. m., and from 4 till 7 p. m.

When elections are ordered the board of registers for each district will designate the number of polls and the places where they shall be opened in the election precincts within its district, appoint the commissioners and other officers necessary for properly conducting the elections, and will superintend the same.

They will also receive from the commissioners of elections of the different precincts the result of the vote, consolidate the same, and forward it to the commanding general.

Registers and all officers connected with elections will be held to a rigid accountability, and will be subject to trial by military commission for fraud, or unlawful or improper conduct in the performance of their duties. Their rate of compensation and manner of payment will be in accordance with the provisions of sections 6 and 7 of the supplemental act.

Brevet Brigadier General J. W. Forsyth, assistant inspector general of the Fifth Military District, is hereby directed to supervise the boards of registration for the parish of Orleans, to listen to and adjust, or refer to this office, all just causes of complaint. He is authorized to employ such experts as may be necessary to detect fraud in registration or elections.

Every male citizen of the United States twenty-one years old and upward, of whatever race, color, or previous condition, who has been resident in the State of Louisiana for one year and parish of Orleans for three months previous to the date at which he presents himself for registration, and who has not been disfranchised by act of Congress or for felony at common law, shall, after having taken and subscribed the oath prescribed in the first section of the act herein referred to, be entitled to be, and shall be, registered as a legal voter in the parish of Orleans and State of Louisiana.

Pending the decision of the Attorney General of the United States on the question as to who are disfranchised by law, registers will give the most rigid interpretation to the law, and exclude from registration every person about whose right to vote there may be a doubt. Any person so excluded who may, under the decision of the Attorney General, be entitled to vote, shall be permitted to register after that decision is received, due notice of which will be given.

By command of Major General P. H. Sheridan

GEO. L. HARTSUFF, *A. A. G.*

## A MILITARY COMMISSION APPOINTED.

The New Orleans *Republican* of the 13th of April, says:

General Sheridan has ordered a military commission to meet in this city on Monday next, 15th instant, for the trial of Mr. —— Walker, and such other persons as may be properly brought before it. The following is the detail for the commission : Brevet Major General A. Beckwith, Brevet Brigadier General C. G. Sawtelle, Brevet Colonel M. Maloney, Brevet Colonel A. D. Nelson, Brevet Major M. J. Asch, Captain J. D. DeRussey, First Lieutenant John Hamilton. Brevet Major Leslie Smith, judge advocate.

## Texas.

### ORDER OF GEN. GRIFFIN.

Gen. Griffin, in command of the State, issued the following order on the 5th inst. :

Under the act of Congress passed March 2, 1867, to provide for a more efficient government of the rebel States, and the supplementary act thereto, the district commander is required to protect all persons in their rights of person and property, to suppress insurrection, disorder, and violence, and to punish or cause to be punished all disturbers of the public peace and criminals. Jurisdiction of offenses may be taken, and offenders tried by the local civil tribunals, but w it is evident that local civil tribunals will not impartially try cases brought before them, and render decisions according to law and evidence, the immediate military commander will arrest or cause the arrest of the offenders or criminals, and hold them in confinement, presenting their cases in writing, with all the facts, to these headquarters, with the view to the said parties being brought before and tried by a military commission or tribunal, as provided in section three of the military bill.

### Proclamation of Gov. Brownlow, of Tennessee, February 25, 1867.

Whereas, it has been made known to me, the Governor of the State of Tennessee, that certain atrocious murders and numerous outrages have been committed in certain counties in this State, by violent and disloyal men, upon the persons and property of Union men, whose only offense has been their unswerving devotion to the national flag, and their uniform support of the State government; and whereas these bad men are banding themselves together in some localities, and notifying Union men to leave within a given time: Now, therefore, I, William G. Brownlow, Governor as aforesaid, by virtue of the authority and power in me vested, do hereby proclaim, that I intend to put a stop to all such outrages, by calling into active service a sufficient number of loyal volunteers, under the following recent act, which is now the law of Tennessee:

An Act to organize and equip a State Guard, and for other purposes.

*Be it enacted by the General Assembly of the State of Tennessee,* That the Governor is hereby authorized and empowered to organize, equip, and call into active service a volunteer force, to be known as the Tennessee State Guard, to be composed of one or more regiments from each congressional district of the State: *Provided always,* that the Tennessee State Guard shall be composed of loyal men, who shall take and subscribe the oath prescribed in the franchise act.

Sec. 2. That the Governor shall be commander-in-chief, and any member of said force shall be subject to his order, when in his opinion the safety of life, property, liberty, or the faithful execution of law require it; to be organized, armed, equipped, regulated, and governed by the rules and articles of war, and the revised army regulations of the United States, so far as applicable, and shall receive pay and allowances according to grade of rank, as provided for the United States Army while in active service, to be paid out of any money in the State treasury not otherwise appropriated: *Provided,* That the force provided for by this act shall not be armed and equipped until called into active service by the Governor.

Sec. 3. That this act shall take effect from and after its passage.

Standing, as I do, on the broad principles of the Constitution, and sworn to enforce the laws, I have no concessions to make to traitors; no compromises to offer assassins and robbers; and if, in the sweep of coming events, retributive justice shall overtake the lawless and violent, their own temerity will have called it forth. The outrages enumerated must and shall cease. Having reached the foregoing conclusion I feel justified in expressing the opinion that the present State government in Tennessee—so generally acquiesced in by loyal and law-abiding people—will be sustained and preserved, despite all the efforts of disappointed traitors and disloyal newspapers.

The interests of trade, of agricultural pursuits, of commercial intercourse between this State and others—of the development of our vast resources, of immigration, as well as justice to loyal sufferers—all require that these outrages at once cease in every county in the State. Disloyal men are giving forth their vile utterances in railroad cars, in public hotels, on the streets, and through the newspapers, damaging the material interests of the State, those of commerce, those of the mechanic arts, of religion and education, as well as bringing reproach upon the Commonwealth.

I cannot, however, close this brief proclamation without endeavoring to impress upon my fellow-citizens of all parties the importance, the absolute necessity, of remaining quiet, of preserving good order, and a quiet submission to, and a rigid enforcement of, the laws everywhere within the limits of our State. Outrages upon loyal citizens, whether white or black, and the setting aside of the franchise law, are all the work of bad men, who desire to foment strife, and will not be tolerated.

Prudent and experienced men will be placed in charge of the "State Guard" in every county where they are placed, who will be required to protect all good citizens, irrespective of political parties, and to punish murderers, robbers, and all violators of law. And the number of troops called into active service will be increased or diminished as the good or bad conduct of the people shall be developed. Hoping this proclamation will strengthen the hands and inspire the hearts of the loyal people of our State, as to the future, and deter the disloyal from further acts of violence, I respectfully submit it, with a repetition of the assurance that I mean what I say, and that the General Assembly was in earnest in the passage of this military law.

In testimony whereof I have hereunto set my hand and caused the great seal of the State to be affixed at the executive department in Nashville, on the twenty fifth day of February, 1867.

[L.S.]                WILLIAM G. BROWNLOW,
                    *Commander-in-Chief, &c.*

# XX.

# JUDICIAL OPINIONS.

## THE SUPREME COURT.

### On Trial by Military Commissions, Dec. 17, 1866.

No. 350.—December Term, 1865.

*Ex parte in matter of Lambdin P. Milligan, petitioner. On a certificate of division of opinion between the judges of the Circuit Court of the United States for the District of Indiana.*

Mr. Justice Davis delivered the opinion of the Court.

On the 10th day of May, 1865, Lambdin P. Milligan presented a petition to the circuit court of the United States for the district of Indiana to be discharged from an alleged unlawful imprisonment. The case made by the petition is this: Milligan is a citizen of the United States; has lived for twenty years in Indiana, and at the time of the grievances complained of was not, and never had been, in the military or naval service of the United States. On the 5th day of October, 1864, while at home, he was arrested by order of General Alvin P. Hovey, commanding the military district of Indiana, and has ever since been kept in close confinement.

On the 21st day of October, 1864, he was brought before a military commission, convened at Indianapolis by order of General Hovey, tried on certain charges and specifications, found guilty, and sentenced to be hanged, and the sentence ordered to be executed on Friday, the 19th day of May, 1865.

On the 2d day of January, 1865, after the proceedings of the military commission were at an end, the circuit court of the United States for Indiana met at Indianapolis and empanneled a grand jury, who were charged to inquire whether the laws of the United States had been violated, and if so, to make presentments. The court adjourned on the 27th day of January, having prior thereto discharged from further service the grand jury, who did not find any bill of indictment or make any presentment against Milligan for any offense whatever, and, in fact, since his imprisonment no bill of indictment has been found or presentment made against him by any grand jury of the United States.

Milligan insists that said military commission had no jurisdiction to try him upon the charges preferred, or upon any charges whatever; because he was a citizen of the United States and the State of Indiana, and had not been, since the commencement of the late rebellion, a resident of any of the States whose citizens were arrayed against the Government, and that the right of trial by jury was guaranteed to him by the Constitution of the United States.

The prayer of the petition was, that under the act of Congress approved March 3, 1863, entitled "An act relating to *habeas corpus*, and regulating judicial proceedings in certain cases," he may be brought before the court, and either turned over to the proper civil tribunal, to be proceeded against according to the law of the land, or discharged from custody altogether.

With the petition were filed the order for the commission, the charges and specifications, the findings of the court, with the order of the War Department, reciting that the sentence was approved by the President of the United States, and directing that it be carried into execution without delay. The petition was presented and filed in open court by the counsel for Milligan; at the same time the district attorney of the United States for Indiana appeared, and, by the agreement of counsel, the application was submitted to the court. The opinions of the judges of the circuit court were opposed on three questions, which are certified to the Supreme Court:

1st. "On the facts stated in said petition and exhibits, ought a writ of *habeas corpus* to be issued?"

2d. "On the facts stated in said petition and exhibits, ought the said Lambdin P. Milligan to be discharged from custody, as in said petition prayed?"

3d. "Whether, upon the facts stated in said petition and exhibits, the military commission mentioned therein had jurisdiction legally to try and sentence said Milligan, in manner and form as in said petition and exhibit is stated?"

The importance of the main question presented by this record cannot be overstated; for it involves the very framework of the Government and fundamental principles of American liberty.

During the late wicked rebellion, the temper of the times did not allow that calmness in deliberation and discussion so necessary to a correct conclusion of a purely judicial question. Then considerations of safety were mingled with the exercise of power, and feelings and interests prevailed which are happily terminated. Now that the public safety is assured, this question, as well as all others, can be discussed and decided without passion or the admixture of any element not required to form a legal judgment. We approach the investigation of this case, fully sensible of the magnitude of the inquiry and the necessity of full and cautious deliberation. But we are met with a preliminary objection. It is insisted that the Circuit Court of Indiana had no authority to certify these questions, and that we are without jurisdiction to hear and determine them. The sixth section of the "Act to amend the judicial system of the United States," approved April 29, 1802, declares "that whenever any question shall occur before a circuit court, upon which the opinions of the judges shall be opposed, the point upon which the disagreement shall happen shall, during the same term, upon the request of either party or their counsel, be stated under the direction of the judges, and certified, under the seal of the court, to the Supreme Court, at their next session to be held thereafter, and shall by the said Court be finally decided; and the decision of the Supreme Court and their order in the premises shall be remitted to the circuit court and be there entered of record, and shall have effect according to the nature of the said judgment and order: *Provided*, That nothing herein contained shall prevent the cause from proceeding, if, in the opinion of the court, further proceedings can be had without prejudice to the merits."

It is under this provision of law that a circuit court has authority to certify any question to the Supreme Court for adjudication. The inquiry, therefore, is, whether the case of Milligan is brought within its terms. It was admitted at the bar that the circuit court had jurisdiction to entertain the application for the writ of *habeas corpus* and to hear and determine it; and it could not be denied, for the power is expressly given in the 14th section of the judiciary act of 1789, as well as in the later act of 1863. Chief Justice Marshall, in Bollman's case, (4 Cranch,) construed this branch of the judiciary act to authorize the courts as well as the judges to issue the writ for the purpose of inquiring into the cause of the commitment; and this construction has never been departed from. But it is maintained with earnestness and ability that a certificate of division of opinion can occur only in a cause; and that the proceeding by a party moving for writ of *habeas corpus* does not become a cause until after the writ has been issued and a return made.

Independently of the provisions of the act of Congress of March 3, 1863, relating to *habeas corpus*, on which the petitioner bases his claim for relief, and which we will presently consider, can this position be sustained?

It is true that it is usual for a court, on application for a writ of *habeas corpus*, to issue the writ, and on the return to dispose of the case; but the court can elect to waive the issuing of the writ and consider whether, upon the facts presented in the petition, the prisoner, if brought before it, could be discharged. One of the very points on which the case of Tobias Watkins, reported in 3 Peters, turned was, whether, if the writ was issued, the petitioner would be remanded upon the case which he had made.

The Chief Justice, in delivering the opinion of the Court, said: "The cause of imprisonment is shown as fully by the petitioner as it could appear on the return of the writ; consequently the writ ought not to be awarded if the court is satisfied that the prisoner would be remanded to prison."

The judges of the circuit court of Indiana were therefore warranted by an express decision of this Court in refusing the writ, if satisfied that the prisoner, on his own showing, was rightfully detained; but, it is contended, if they differed about the lawfulness of the imprisonment, and could render no judgment, the prisoner is remediless, and cannot have the disputed question certified under the act of 1802. His remedy is complete by writ of error or appeal, if the court renders a final judgment refusing to discharge him; but if he should be so unfortunate as to be placed in the predicament of having the court divided on the question whether he should live or die, he is hopeless and without

remedy. He wishes the vital question settled, not by a single judge at his chambers, but by the highest tribunal known to the Constitution; and yet the privilege is denied him, because the circuit court consists of two judges instead of one. Such a result was not in the contemplation of the Legislature of 1802, and the language used by it cannot be construed to mean any such thing. The clause under consideration was introduced to further the ends of justice by obtaining a speedy settlement of important questions where the judges might be opposed in opinion.

The act of 1802 so changed the judicial system that the circuit court, instead of three, was composed of two judges; and without this provision, or a kindred one, if the judges differed, the difference would remain, the question be unsettled, and justice denied. The decisions of this court upon the provisions of this section have been numerous. In United States *vs.* Daniel, (6 Wheaton) the court, in holding that a division of the judges on a motion for a new trial could not be certified, say: "That the question must be one which arises in a case depending before the court relative to a proceeding belonging to the cause." Testing Milligan's case by this rule of law, is it not apparent that it is rightfully here, and that we are compelled to answer the questions on which the judges below were opposed in opinion? If, in the sense of the law, the proceeding for the writ of *habeas corpus* was the "*cause*" of the party applying for it, then it is evident that the "cause" was pending before the court and that the questions certified arose out of it, belonged to it, and were matters of right and not of discretion.

But it is argued that the proceeding does not ripen into a cause until there are two parties to it. This we deny. It was the *cause* of Milligan when the petition was presented to the circuit court. It would have been the *cause* of both parties, if the court had issued the writ and brought those who held Milligan in custody before it. Webster defines the word "cause" thus: "A suit or action in court; any legal process which a party institutes to obtain his demand, or by which he seeks his right, or supposed right"—and he says, "this is a legal, scriptural, and popular use of the word, coinciding nearly with case, from *cado*, and action, from *ago*, to urge and drive."

In any legal sense, action, suit, and cause are convertible terms. Milligan supposed he had a right to test the validity of his trial and sentence; and the proceeding which he set in operation for that purpose was his "cause" or "suit." It was the only one by which he could recover his liberty. He was powerless to do more; he could neither instruct the judges nor control their action, and should not suffer, because, without fault of his, they were unable to render a judgment. But the true meaning to the term "suit" has been given by this Court. One of the questions in Weston *vs.* City Council of Charleston (2 Peters) was, whether a writ of prohibition was a suit; and Chief Justice Marshall says: "The term is certainly a comprehensive one and is understood to apply to any proceeding in a court of justice by which an individual pursues that remedy which the law affords him."

Certainly Milligan pursued the only remedy which the law afforded him.

Again, in Cohens *vs.* Virginia, (6 Wheaton,) he says: " In law language a suit is the prosecution of some demand in a court of justice." Also, " to commence a suit is to demand something by the institution of process in a court of justice; and to prosecute the suit is to continue that demand." When Milligan demanded his release by the proceeding relating to *habeas corpus* he commenced a suit, and he has since prosecuted it in all the ways known to the law. One of the questions in Holmes *vs.* Jennison (14 Peters) was, whether under the 25th section of the judiciary act a proceeding for a writ of *habeas corpus* was a "suit." Chief Justice Taney held that, " if a party is unlawfully imprisoned, the writ of *habeas corpus* is his appropriate legal remedy. It is his suit in court to recover his liberty." There was much diversity of opinion on another ground of jurisdiction, but on this, that in the sense of the 25th section of the judiciary act, the proceeding by *habeas corpus* was a suit, was not controverted by any except Baldwin, Justice, and he thought that "suit" and " cause," as used in the section, mean the same thing.

The court do not say that a return must be made and the parties appear and begin to try the case before it is a suit. When the petition is filed and the writ prayed for, it is a *suit*—the suit of the party making the application. If it is a suit under the 25th section of the judiciary act, when the proceedings are begun, it is, by all the analogies of the law, equally a suit under the 6th section of the act of 1802.

But it is argued that there must be *two* parties to the suit, because the point is to be stated upon the request of " either party or their counsel." Such a literal and technical construction would defeat the very purpose the Legislature had in view, which was to enable any party to bring the case here, when the point in controversy was a matter of right and not of discretion; and the words " either party," in order to prevent a failure of justice, must be construed as words of *enlargement*, and not of *restriction*. Although this case is here *ex parte*, it was not considered by the court below without notice having been given to the party supposed to have an interest in the detention of the prisoner. The statements of the record show that this is not only a fair, but conclusive inference. When the counsel for Milligan presented to the court the petition for the writ of *habeas corpus*, Mr. Hanna, the district attorney for Indiana, also appeared; and, by agreement, the application was submitted to the court, who took the case under advisement, and on the next day announced their inability to agree, and made the certificate. It is clear that Mr. Hanna did not represent the petitioner, and why is his appearance entered? It admits of no other solution than this—that he was informed of the application, and appeared on behalf of the Government to contest it. The Government was the prosecutor of Milligan, who claimed that his imprisonment was illegal, and sought, in the only way he could, to recover his liberty. The case was a grave one; and the court, unquestionably, directed that the law officer of the Government should be informed of it. He very properly appeared, and as the facts were uncontroverted and the difficulty was in the application of the law, there was no useful purpose to be obtained in issuing the writ. The cause was, therefore, submitted to the court, for their consideration and determination. But Milligan claimed his discharge from custody by virtue of the act of Congress "relating to *habeas corpus*, and regulating judicial proceedings in certain cases," approved March 3, 1863. Did that act confer jurisdiction on the circuit court of Indiana to hear this case? In interpreting a law, the motives which must have operated with the legislature in passing it are proper to be considered. This law was passed in a time of great national peril, when our heritage of free government was in danger. An armed rebellion against the national authority, of greater proportions than history affords an example, was raging; and the public safety required that the privilege of the writ of *habeas corpus* should be suspended. The President had practically suspended it, and detained suspected persons in custody without trial; but his authority to do this was questioned. It was claimed that Congress alone could exercise this power, and that the legislature, and not the President, should judge of the political considerations on which the right to suspend it rested. The privilege of this great writ had never before been withheld from the citizen; and, as the exigence of the times demanded immediate action, it was of the highest importance that the lawfulness of the suspension should be fully established. It was under these circumstances, which were such as to arrest the attention of the country, that this law was passed. The President was authorized by it to suspend the privilege of the writ of *habeas corpus* whenever, in his judgment, the public safety required; and he did, by proclamation, bearing date the 15th of September, 1863, reciting among other things the authority of this statute, suspend it. The suspension of the writ does not authorize the arrest of any one, but simply denies to one arrested the privilege of this writ in order to obtain his liberty.

It is proper, therefore, to inquire under what circumstances the courts could rightfully refuse to grant this writ, and when the citizen was at liberty to invoke its aid.

The second and third sections of the law are explicit on these points. The language used is plain and direct, and the meaning of the Congress cannot be mistaken. The public safety demanded, if the President thought proper to arrest a suspected person, that he should not be required to give the cause of his detention on return to a writ of *habeas corpus*. But it was not contemplated that such person should be detained in custody, beyond a certain fixed period, unless certain judicial proceedings known to the common law were commenced against him. The Secretaries of State and War were directed to furnish to the judges of the courts of the United States a list of the names of all parties, not prisoners of war, resident in their respective jurisdictions, who then were or afterwards should be held in custody by the authority of the President, and who were citizens of States in which the administration of the laws in the Federal tribunals was unimpaired. After the list was furnished, if a grand jury of the district convened and adjourned, and did not indict or present one of the persons thus named, he was entitled to his discharge; and it was the duty of the judge of the court to order him brought before him to be discharged, if he desired it. The refusal or omission to furnish the list could not operate to the injury of any one who was not indicted or presented by the grand jury; for if twenty days had elapsed from the time of his arrest and the termination of the session of the grand jury, he was equally entitled to his discharge as if the list were furnished; and any credible person, on petition verified by affidavit, could obtain the judge's order for that purpose.

Milligan, in his application to be released from imprisonment, averred the existence of every fact necessary under the terms of this law to give the circuit court of Indiana jurisdiction. If he was detained in custody by the order of the President, otherwise than as a prisoner of war; if he was a citizen of Indiana, and had never been in the military or naval service, and the grand jury of the district had met, after he had been arrested for a period of twenty days, and adjourned without taking any proceedings against him, *then* the court had the right to entertain his petition and determine the lawfulness of his imprisonment. Because the word "court" is not found in the body of the second section, it was argued at the bar that the application should have been made to a judge of the court, and not to the court itself; but *this is not so;* for power is expressly conferred in the last proviso of the section on the court equally with a judge of it to discharge from imprisonment. It was the manifest design of Congress to secure a certain remedy by which any one deprived of liberty could obtain it, if there was a judicial failure to find cause of offence against him. Courts are not always in session, and can adjourn on the discharge of the grand jury; and before those who are in confinement could take proper steps to procure their liberation. To provide for this contingency, authority was given to the judges out of court to grant relief to any party who could show that, under the law, he should be no longer restrained of his liberty. It was insisted that Milligan's case was defective, because it did not state that the list was furnished to the judges, and, therefore, it was impossible to say under which section of the act it was presented.

It is not easy to see how this omission could affect the question of jurisdiction. Milligan could not know that the list was furnished, unless the judges volunteered to tell him; for the law did not require that any record should be made of it, or anybody but the judges informed of it. Why aver the fact, when the truth of the matter was apparent to the court without an averment? How can Milligan be harmed by the absence of the averment when he states that he was under arrest for more than sixty days before the court and grand jury, which should have considered his case, met at Indianapolis? It is apparent, therefore, that under the *habeas corpus* act of 1863, the circuit court of Indiana had complete jurisdiction to adjudicate upon this case, and if

the judges could not agree on questions vital to the progress of the cause they had the authority, (as we have shown in a previous part of this opinion,) and it was their duty to certify those questions of disagreement to this Court for final decision. It was agreed that a final decision on the questions presented ought not to be made, because the parties who were directly concerned in the arrest and detention of Milligan were not before the court; and their rights might be prejudiced by the answer which should be given to those questions. But this court cannot know what return will be made to the writ of *habeas corpus* when issued; and it is very clear that no one is concluded upon any question that may be raised to that return. In the sense of the law of 1802, which authorized a certificate of division, a final decision means final upon the points certified; final upon the court below, so that it is estopped from any adverse ruling in all the subsequent proceedings of the cause. But it is said that this case is ended, as the presumption is that Milligan was hanged in pursuance of the order of the President. Although we have no judicial information on the subject; yet the inference is that he is alive; for otherwise learned counsel would not appear for him and urge the Court to decide his case.

It can never be in this country of written constitution and laws, with a judicial department to interpret them, that any Chief Magistrate would be so far forgetful of his duty as to order the execution of a man who denied the jurisdiction that tried and convicted him, after his case was before federal judges, with power to decide it, who, being unable to agree on the grave questions involved, had, according to known law, sent it to the Supreme Court of the United States for decision. But even the suggestion is injurious to the Executive, and we dismiss it from further consideration. There is, therefore, nothing to hinder this Court from an investigation of the merits of this controversy.

The controlling question in the case is this: Upon the facts stated in Milligan's petition, and the exhibits filed, had the military commission mentioned in it jurisdiction legally to try and sentence him? Milligan, not a resident of one of the rebellious States, or a prisoner of war, but a citizen of Indiana for twenty years past, and never in the military or naval service, is, while at his home, arrested by the military power of the United States, imprisoned, and, on certain criminal charges preferred against him, tried, convicted, and sentenced to be hanged by a military commission, organized under the direction of the military commander of the military district of Indiana. Had this tribunal the legal power and authority to try and punish this man? No graver question was ever considered by this Court, nor one which more nearly concerns the rights of the whole people; for it is the birthright of every American citizen, when charged with crime, to be tried and punished according to law. The power of punishment is alone through the means which the laws have provided for that purpose, and if they are ineffectual there is an immunity from punishment, no matter how great an offender the individual may be, or how much his crimes may have shocked the sense of justice of the country or endangered its safety. By the protection of the law human rights are secured; withdraw that protection, and they are at the mercy of wicked rulers, or the clamor of an excited people. If there was law to justify this military trial, it is not our province to interfere; if there was not, it is our duty to declare the nullity of the whole proceedings. The decision of this question does not depend on argument or judicial precedents, numerous and highly illustrative as they are. These precedents inform us of the extent of the struggle to preserve liberty and to relieve those in civil life from military trials. The founders of our Government were familiar with the history of that struggle, and secured in a written constitution every right which the people had wrested from power during a contest of ages. By that Constitution, and the laws authorized by it, this question must be determined. The provisions of that instrument on the administration of criminal justice are too plain and direct to leave room for misconstruction or doubt of their true meaning. Those applicable to this case are found in that clause of the original Constitution which says, "that the trial of all crimes, except in case of impeachment, shall be by jury;" and in the fourth, fifth, and sixth articles of the amendments. The fourth proclaims the right to be secure in person and effects against unreasonable search and seizure; and directs that a judicial warrant shall not issue "without proof of probable cause supported by oath or affirmation." The fifth declares " that no person shall be held to answer for a capital or otherwise infamous crime unless on presentment by a grand jury, except in cases arising in the land or naval forces or in the militia when in actual service in time of war or public danger, nor be deprived of life, liberty, or property without due process of law." And the sixth guaranties the right of trial by jury in such manner and with such regulations that with upright judges, impartial juries, and an able bar, the innocent will be saved and the guilty punished. It is in these words: " In all criminal prosecutions the accused shall enjoy the right to a speedy and public trial by an impartial jury of the State and district wherein the crime shall have been committed, which district shall have been previously ascertained by law, and to be informed of the nature and cause of the accusation, to be confronted with the witnesses against them, to have compulsory process for obtaining witnesses in his favor, and to have the assistance of counsel for his defence." These securities for personal liberty thus embodied, were such as wisdom and experience had demonstrated to be necessary for the protection of those accused of crime. And so strong was the sense of the country of their importance, and so jealous were the people that these rights, highly prized, might be denied them by implication, that when the original Constitution was proposed for adoption, it encountered severe opposition, and, but for the belief that it would be so amended as to embrace them, it would never have been ratified.

Time has proven the discernment of our ancestors; for even these provisions, expressed in such plain English words that it would seem the ingenuity of man could not evade them, are now, after the lapse of more than seventy years, sought to be avoided. Those great and good men foresaw that troublous times would arise, when rulers and people would become restive under restraint, and seek, by sharp and decisive measures, to accomplish ends deemed just and proper, and that the principles of constitutional liberty would be in peril, unless established by irrepealable law. The history of the world had taught them that what was done in the past might be attempted in the future. The Constitution of the United States is a law for rulers and people, equally in war and in peace, and covers with the shield of its protection all classes of men, at all times, and under all circumstances. No doctrine involving more pernicious consequences was ever invented by the wit of man than that any of its provisions can be suspended during any of the great exigencies of Government. Such a doctrine leads directly to anarchy or despotism, but the theory of necessity on which it is based is false; for the Government, within the Constitution, has all the powers granted to it which are necessary to preserve its existence, as has been happily proved by the result of the great effort to throw off its just authority.

Have any of the rights guarantied by the Constitution been violated in the case of Milligan? and, if so, what are they? Every trial involves the exercise of judicial power; and from what source did the military commission that tried him derive their authority? Certainly no part of the judicial power of the country was conferred on them, because the Constitution expressly vests it " in the Supreme Court and such inferior courts as the Congress may, from time to time, ordain and establish," and it is not pretended that the commission was a court ordained and established by Congress. They cannot justify on the mandate of the President, because he is controlled by law, and has his appropriate sphere of duty, which is to execute, not to make the laws; and there is " no unwritten criminal code to which resort can be had as a source of jurisdiction." But it is said that the jurisdiction is complete under the "laws and usages of war." It can serve no useful purpose to inquire what those laws and usages are, whence they originated, where found, and on whom they operate; they can never be applied to citizens in States which have upheld the authority of the Government, and where the courts are open and their process unobstructed. This Court has judicial knowledge that in Indiana the Federal authority was always unopposed, and its courts always open to hear criminal accusations and to redress grievances; and no usage of war could sanction a military trial there, for any offence whatever, of a citizen in civil life, in no wise connected with the military service. Congress could grant no such power; and, to the honor of our National Legislature be it said, it has never been provoked by the state of the country even to attempt its exercise. One of the plainest constitutional provisions was, therefore, infringed when Milligan was tried by a court not ordained and established by Congress, and not composed of judges appointed during good behavior. Why was he not delivered to the circuit court of Indiana, to be proceeded against according to law?

No reason of necessity could be urged against it, because Congress had declared penalties against the offences charged, provided for their punishment, and directed that court to hear and determine them. And soon after this military tribunal was ended the circuit court met, peacefully transacted its business, and adjourned. It needed no bayonets to protect it, and required no military aid to execute its judgments. It was held in a State eminently distinguished for patriotism by judges commissioned during the rebellion, who were provided with juries, upright, intelligent, and selected by a marshal appointed by the President. The Government had no right to conclude that Milligan, if guilty, would not receive in that court merited punishment, for its records disclose that it was constantly engaged in the trial of similar offences, and was never interrupted in its administration of criminal justice. If it was dangerous in the distracted condition of affairs to leave Milligan unrestrained of his liberty because he "conspired against the Government, afforded aid and comfort to rebels, and incited the people to insurrection," the law said arrest him, confine him closely, render him powerless to do further mischief, and then present his case to the grand jury of the district, with proofs of his guilt, and, if indicted, try him according to the course of the common law. If this had been done the Constitution would have been vindicated, the law of 1863 enforced, and the securities for personal liberty preserved and defended.

Another guaranty of freedom was broken when Milligan was denied a trial by jury. The great minds of the country have differed on the correct interpretation to be given to various provisions of the Federal Constitution; and judicial decision has been often invoked to settle their true meaning; but until recently no one ever doubted that the right of trial by jury was fortified in the organic law against the power of attack. It is never assailed; but, if ideas can be expressed in words, and language has any meaning, this right—one of the most valuable in a free country—is preserved to every one accused of crime who is not attached to the army or navy, or militia in actual service. The sixth amendment affirms that " in all criminal prosecutions the accused shall enjoy the right to a speedy and public trial by an impartial jury," language broad enough to embrace all persons and cases; but the fifth, recognizing the necessity of an indictment, or presentment, before any one can be held to answer for high crimes "excepts cases arising in the land or naval forces, or in the militia, when in actual service, in time of war or public danger;" and the framers of the Constitution doubtless meant to limit the right of trial by jury, in the sixth amendment, to those persons who were subject to indictment or presentment in the fifth.

The discipline necessary to the efficiency of the army and navy required other and swifter modes of trial than are furnished by the common law courts; and, in pursuance of the power conferred by the Constitution, Congress has declared the kinds of trial, and the manner in which they shall be conducted, for offences committed while the party is in the military or naval service.

Every one connected with these branches of the public service is amenable to the jurisdiction which Congress has created for their government, and while thus serving, surrenders his right to be tried by the civil courts. All other persons, citizens of States where the courts are open, if charged with crime, are guarantied the inestimable privilege of trial by jury. This privilege is a vital principle, underlying the whole administration of criminal justice; it is not held by sufferance, and cannot be frittered away on any plea of State or political necessity. When peace prevails, and the authority of the Government is undisputed, there is no difficulty of preserving the safeguards of liberty; for the ordinary modes of trial are never neglected, and no one wishes it otherwise. But if society is disturbed by civil commotion—if the passions of men are aroused and the restraints of law weakened, if not disregarded—these safeguards need, and should receive, the watchful care of those entrusted with the guardianship of the Constitution and laws. In no other way can we transmit to posterity unimpaired the blessings of liberty, consecrated by the sacrifices of the Revolution.

It is claimed that martial law covers with its broad mantle the proceedings of this military commission. The proposition is this: That in a time of war the commander of an armed force (if, in his opinion, the exigencies of the country demand it, and of which he is to judge,) has the power, within the lines of his military district, to suspend all civil rights and their remedies, and subject citizens as well as soldiers to the rule of his will; and in the exercise of his lawful authority cannot be restrained, except by his superior officer or the President of the United States. If this position is sound to the extent claimed, then when war exists, foreign or domestic, and the country is subdivided into military departments for mere convenience, the commander of one of them can, if he chooses, within his limits, on the plea of necessity, with the approval of the Executive, substitute military force for and to the exclusion of the laws, and punish all persons as he thinks right and proper, without fixed or certain rules

The statement of this proposition shows its importance; for, if true, republican government is a failure, and there is an end of liberty regulated by law. Martial law, established on such a basis, destroys every guarantee of the Constitution, and effectually renders the "military independent of and superior to the civil power" —the attempt to do which by the King of Great Britain was deemed by our fathers such an offence that they assigned it to the world as one of the causes which impelled them to declare their independence. Civil liberty and this kind of martial law cannot endure together; the antagonism is irreconcilable, and in the conflict one or the other must perish.

This nation, as experience has proved, cannot always remain at peace, and has no right to expect that it will always have wise and humane rulers, sincerely attached to the principles of the Constitution. Wicked men, ambitious of power, with hatred of liberty, and contempt of law, may fill the place once occupied by Washington and Lincoln; and, if this right is conceded, and the calamities of war again befall us, the dangers to human liberty are frightful to contemplate. If our fathers had failed to provide for just such a contingency, they would have been false to the trust reposed in them. They knew —the history of the world told them—the nation they were founding, be its existence short or long, would be involved in war—how often, or how long continued, human foresight could not tell—and that unlimited power, wherever lodged at such a time, was especially hazardous to freemen. For this and other equally weighty reasons, they secured the inheritance they had fought to maintain, by incorporating in a written constitution the safeguards which time had proved essential to its preservation. Not one of these safeguards can the President, or Congress, or the judiciary disturb, except the one concerning the writ of *habeas corpus*.

It is essential to the safety of every government that, in a great crisis like the one we have just passed through, there should be a power somewhere of suspending the writ of *habeas corpus*. In every war there are men of previously good character wicked enough to counsel their fellow citizens to resist the measures deemed necessary by a good government to sustain its just authority and overthrow its enemies, and their influence may lead to dangerous combinations. In the emergency of the times an immediate public investigation, according to law, may not be possible, and yet the peril to the country may be too imminent to suffer such persons to go at large. Unquestionably, there is then an exigency which demands that the Government, if it should see fit, in the exercise of a proper discretion, to make arrests, should not be required to produce the persons arrested in answer to a writ of *habeas corpus*. The Constitution goes no further. It does not say after a writ of *habeas corpus* is denied a citizen, that he shall be tried otherwise than by the course of the common law; if it had intended this result, it was easy by the use of direct words to have accomplished it. The illustrious men who framed that instrument were guarding the foundations of civil liberty against the abuses of unlimited power; they were full of wisdom, and the lessons of history informed them that a trial by an established court, assisted by an impartial jury, was the only sure way of protecting the citizen against oppression and wrong. Knowing this, they limited the suspension to one great right, and left the rest to remain forever inviolable. But it is insisted that the safety of the country in time of war demands that this broad claim for martial law shall be sustained. If this were true, it could be well said that a country preserved at the sacrifice of all the cardinal principles of liberty is not worth the cost of preservation. Happily it is not so.

It will be borne in mind that this is not a question of the power to proclaim martial law, when war exists in a community and the courts and civil authorities are overthrown. Nor is it a question what rule a military commander, at the head of his army can impose on States in rebellion to cripple their resources and quell the insurrection. The jurisdiction claimed is much more extensive  The necessities of the service during the late rebellion required that the loyal States should be placed within the limits of certain military districts, and commanders appointed in them; and it is urged that this, in a military sense, constituted them the theatre of military operations, and, as in this case, Indiana had been and was again threatened with invasion by the enemy, the occasion was furnished to establish martial law. The conclusion does not follow from the premises. If armies were collected in Indiana, they were to be employed in another locality, where the laws were obstructed and the national authority disputed. On her soil there was no hostile foot; if once invaded, that invasion was at an end, and with it all pretext for martial law. Martial law cannot arise from a threatened invasion. The necessity must be actual and present, the. invasion real—such as effectually closes the courts and deposes the civil administration.

It is difficult to see how the safety of the country required martial law in Indiana. If any of her citizens were plotting treason, the power of arrest could secure them until the Government was prepared for their trial, when the courts were open and ready to try them. It was as easy to protect witnesses before a civil as a military tribunal; and, as there could be no wish to convict, except upon sufficient legal evidence, surely an ordained and established court was better able to judge of this than a military tribunal, composed of gentlemen not trained to the profession of the law.

It follows, from what has been said on this subject, that there are occcasions when martial rule can be properly applied. If in foreign invasion or civil war the courts are actually closed, and it is impossible to administer criminal justice according to law, then on the theater of active military operations, where war really prevails, there is a necessity to furnish a substitute for the civil authority thus overthrown to preserve the safety of the army and society; and as no power is left but the military, it is allowed to govern by martial rule until the laws can have their free course. As necessity creates the rule, so it limits its duration; for if this government is continued after the courts are reinstated, it is a gross usurpation of power. Martial rule can never exist where the courts are open, and in the proper and unobstructed exercise of their jurisdiction. It is also confined to the locality of actual war. Because during the late rebellion it could have been enforced in Virginia, where the national authority was overturned and the courts driven out, it does not follow that it should obtain in Indiana, where that authority was never disputed, and justice was always administered. And so in the case of a foreign invasion, martial rule may become a necessity in one State, when in another it would be "mere lawless violence." We are not without precedents in English and American history illustrating our views of this question; but it is hardly necessary to make particular reference to them.

From the first year of the reign of Edward the Third, when the Parliament of England reversed the attainder of the Earl of Lancaster, because he could have been tried by the courts of the realm, and declared "that in time of peace n<sub></sub>

man ought to be adjudged to death for treason or any other offence without being arraigned and held to answer, and that regularly when the king's courts are open it is a time of peace in judgment of law," down to the present day, martial law, as claimed in this case, has been condemned by all respectable English jurists as contrary to the fundamental laws of the land, and subversive of the liberty of the subject.

During the present century, an instructive debate on this question occurred in Parliament, occasioned by the trial and conviction by court martial at Demarara of the Rev. John Smith, a missionary to the negroes, on the alleged ground of aiding and abetting a formidable rebellion in that colony. Those eminent statesmen, Lord Brougham and Sir James Macintosh, participated in that debate, and denounced the trial as illegal, because it did not appear that the courts of law in Demarara could not try offences, and that "when the laws can act every other mode of punishing supposed crimes is itself an enormous crime."

So sensitive were our Revolutionary fathers on this subject, although Boston was almost in a state of siege when General Gage issued his proclamation of martial law, they spoke of it as an "attempt to supersede the course of the common law, and instead thereof to publish and order the use of martial law." The Virginia Assembly also denounced a similar measure on the part of Governor Dunmore "as an assumed power, which the king himself cannot exercise, because it annuls the law of the land and introduces the most execrable of all systems, martial law."

In some parts of the country, during the war of 1812, our officers made arbitrary arrests, and by military tribunals tried citizens who were not in the military service. These arrests and trials, when brought to the notice of the courts, were uniformly condemned as illegal. The cases of Smith *vs.* Shaw, and McConnell *vs.* Hampton, (reported in 12 Johnson,) are illustrations which we cite, not only for the principles they determine, but on account of the distinguished jurists concerned in the decisions, one of whom for many years occupied a seat on this bench.

It is contended that Luther *vs.* Borden, decided by this court, is an authority for the claim of martial law advanced in this case. The decision is misapprehended. *That case* grew out of the attempt in Rhode Island to supersede the old colonial government by a revolutionary proceeding. Rhode Island at that period had no other form of local government than the charter granted by King Charles II in 1663, and as that limited the right of suffrage, and did not provide for its own amendment, many citizens became dissatisfied because the Legislature would not afford the relief in their power, and without the authority of law formed a new and independent constitution, and proceeded to assert its authority by force of arms. The old government resisted this, and as the rebellion was formidable, called out the militia to subdue it, and passed an act declaring martial law.

Borden, in the military service of the *old* government, broke open the house of Luther, who upported the *new* in order to arrest him. Lu-

ther brought suit against Borden, and the question was, whether, under the constitution and laws of the State, Borden was justified. This court held that a State "may use its military power to put down an armed insurrection too strong to be controlled by the civil authority," and if the Legislature of Rhode Island thought the peril so great as to require the use of its military forces and the declaration of martial law, there was no ground on which *this court* could question its authority, and as Borden acted under military orders of the charter government, which had been recognized by the political power of the country, and was upheld by the State judiciary, he was justified in breaking into and entering Luther's house. This is the extent of the decision. There was no question in issue about the power of declaring martial law under the Federal Constitution, and the court did not consider necessary even to inquire "to what extent nor under what circumstances that power may be exercised by a State."

We do not deem it important to examine further the adjudged cases; and shall, therefore, conclude without any additional reference to authorities. To the third question, then, on which the judges below were opposed in opinion, an answer in the negative must be returned.

It is proper to say, although Milligan's trial and conviction by a military commission was illegal, yet, if guilty of the crimes imputed to him, and his guilt had been ascertained by an established court and impartial jury, he deserved severe punishment. Open resistance to measures deemed necessary to subdue a great rebellion by those who enjoy the protection of government, and have not the excuse even of prejudice of section to plead in their favor, is wicked; but that resistance becomes an enormous crime when it assumes the form of a secret political organization armed to oppose the laws, and seeks by stealthy means to introduce the enemies of the country into peaceful communities, there to light the torch of civil war, and thus overthrow the power of the United States. Conspiracies like these, at such a juncture, are extremely perilous; and those concerned in them are dangerous enemies to their country, and should receive the heaviest penalties of the law, as an example to deter others from similar criminal conduct. It is said the severity of the laws caused them; but Congress was obliged to enact severe laws to meet the crisis; and as our highest civil duty is to serve our country, when in danger, the late war has proved that rigorous laws, when necessary, will be cheerfully obeyed by a patriotic people, struggling to preserve the rich blessings of a free government.

The two remaining questions in this case must be answered in the affirmative. The suspension of the privilege of the writ of *habeas corpus* does not suspend the writ itself. The writ issues as a matter of course; and on the return made to it, the court decides whether the party applying is denied the right of proceeding any further with it.

If the military trial of Milligan was contrary to law, then he was entitled on the facts stated in his petition, to be discharged from custody by the terms of the act of Congress of March 3, 1863

The provisions of this law having been considered in a previous part of this opinion, we will not restate the views there presented. Milligan avers he was a citizen of Indiana, not in the military or naval service, and was detained in close confinement, by order of the President, from the 5th day of October, 1864, until the 2d day of January, 1865, when the circuit court for the district of Indiana, with a grand jury, convened in session at Indianapolis, and afterwards, on the 27th day of the same month, adjourned without finding an indictment or presentment against him. If these averments were true, (and their truth is conceded for the purposes of this case,) the court was required to liberate him on taking certain oaths prescribed by the law, and entering into recognizance for his good behavior. But it is insisted that Milligan was a prisoner of war, and, therefore, excluded from the privileges of the statute. It is not easy to see how he can be treated as a prisoner of war, when he lived in Indiana for the past twenty years, was arrested there, and had not been, during the late troubles, a resident of any of the States in rebellion. If, in Indiana, he conspired with bad men to assist the enemy, he is punishable for it in the courts of Indiana; but, when tried for the offence, he cannot plead the rights of war, for he was not engaged in legal acts of hostility against the Government, and only such persons, when captured, are prisoners of war. If he cannot enjoy the immunities attaching to the character of a prisoner of war, how can he be subject to their pains and penalties?

This case, as well as the kindred cases of Bowles and Horsey, were disposed of at the last term, and the proper orders were entered of record. There is, therefore, no additional entry required.

### DISSENTING OPINION.

Mr. Chief Justice CHASE delivered the following opinion:

Four members of the court concurring with their brethren in the order heretofore made in this cause, but unable to concur in some important particulars with the opinion which has just been read, think it their duty to make a separate statement of their views of the whole case.

We do not doubt that the circuit court for the district of Indiana had jurisdiction of the petition of Milligan for the writ of *habeas corpus.*

Whether this Court has jurisdiction upon the certificate of division admits of more question. The construction of the act authorizing such certificates which has hitherto prevailed here, denies jurisdiction in cases where the certificate brings up the whole cause before the court. But none of the adjudicated cases are exactly in point, and we are willing to resolve whatever doubt may exist in favor of the earliest possible answers to questions involving life and liberty. We agree, therefore, that this Court may properly answer questions certified in such a case as that before us.

The crimes with which Milligan was charged were of the gravest character, and the petition and exhibits in the record, which must here be taken as true, admit his guilt. But whatever his desert of punishment may be, it is more important to the country and to every citizen that he should not be punished under an illegal sentence, sanctioned by this Court of last resort, than that he should be punished at all. The laws which protect the liberties of the whole people must not be violated or set aside in order to inflict even upon the guilty, unauthorized, though merited justice.

The trial and sentence of Milligan were by military commission convened in Indiana during the fall of 1864. The action of the commission had been under consideration by President Lincoln for some time, when he himself became the victim of an abhorred conspiracy. It was approved by his successor in May, 1865, and the sentence was ordered to be carried into execution. The proceedings, therefore, had the fullest sanction of the executive department of the Government.

This sanction requires the most respectful and the most careful consideration of this Court The sentence which it supports must not be set aside except upon the clearest conviction that it cannot be reconciled with the Constitution and the constitutional legislation of Congress.

We must inquire, then, what constitutional or statutory provisions have relation to this military proceeding.

The act of Congress of March 3d, 1863, comprises all the legislation which seems to require consideration in this connection. The constitutionality of this act has not been questioned, and is not doubted.

The first section authorized the suspension during the rebellion of the writ of *habeas corpus* throughout the United States by the President. The two next sections limited this authority in important respects.

The second section required that lists of all persons, being citizens of States in which the administration of the laws had continued unimpaired in the Federal courts, who were then held or might thereafter be held as prisoners of the United States, under the authority of the President, otherwise than as prisoners of war, should be furnished to the judges of the circuit and district courts. The lists transmitted to the judges were to contain the names of all persons residing within their respective jurisdictions, charged with violation of national law. And it was required, in cases where the grand jury in attendance upon any of these courts should terminate its session without proceeding by indictment or otherwise against any prisoner named in the list, that the judge of the court should forthwith make an order that such prisoner, desiring a discharge, should be brought before him or the court to be discharged, on entering into recognizance, if required, to keep the peace and for good behavior, or to appear, as the court may direct, to be further dealt with according to law. Every officer of the United States, having custody of such prisoners, was required to obey and execute the judge's order, under penalty, for refusal or delay, of fine and imprisonment.

The third section provided, in case lists of persons other than prisoners of war then held in confinement, or thereafter arrested, should not be furnished within twenty days after the passage of the act, or, in cases of subsequent arrest, within twenty days after the time of arrest, that any citizen, after the termination of a session of the grand jury without indictment or present-ment, might, by petition alleging the facts, and verified by oath, obtain the judge's order of discharge in favor of any person so imprisoned, on the terms and conditions prescribed in the second section.

It was made the duty of the district attorney of the United States to attend examinations on petitions for discharge.

It was under this act that Milligan petitioned the circuit court for the district of Indiana for discharge from imprisonment.

The holding of the circuit and district courts of the United States in Indiana had been uninterrupted. The administration of the laws in the Federal courts had remained unimpaired, Milligan was imprisoned under the authority of the President, and was not a prisoner of war. No list of prisoners had been furnished to the judges either of the district or circuit courts, as required by the law. A grand jury had attended the circuit courts of the Indiana district while Milligan was there imprisoned, and had closed its session without finding any indictment or presentment, or otherwise proceeding against the prisoner.

His case was thus brought within the precise letter and intent of the act of Congress, unless it can be said that Milligan was not imprisoned by authority of the President, and nothing of this sort was claimed in argument on the part of the Government.

It is clear upon this statement that the circuit court was bound to hear Milligan's petition for the writ of *habeas corpus*, called in the act an order to bring the prisoner before the judge or the court, and to issue the writ, or, in the language of the act, to make the order.

The first question therefore—Ought the writ to issue?—must be answered in the affirmative.

And it is equally clear that he was entitled to the discharge prayed for.

It must be borne in mind that the prayer of the petition was not for an absolute discharge, but to be delivered from military custody and imprisonment, and if found probably guilty of any offence, to be turned over to the proper tribunal for inquiry and punishment; or, if not found thus probably guilty, to be discharged altogether.

And the express terms of the act of Congress required this action of the court. The prisoner must be discharged on giving such recognizance as the court should require, not only for good behavior, but for appearance, as directed by the court, to answer and be further dealt with according to law.

The first section of the act authorized the suspension of the writ of *habeas corpus* generally throughout the United States. The second and third sections limited this suspension in certain cases within States where the administration of justice by the Federal courts remained unimpaired. In these cases the writ was still to issue, and under it the prisoner was entitled to his discharge by a circuit or district judge or court, unless held to bail for appearance to answer charges. No other judge or court could make an order of discharge under the writ. Except under the circumstances pointed out by the act, neither circuit

nor district judge or court could make such an order. But under those circumstances the writ must be issued, and the relief from imprisonment directed by the act must be afforded. The commands of the act were positive, and left no discretion to court or judge.

An affirmative answer must, therefore, be given to the second question, namely, Ought Milligan to be discharged according to the prayer of the petition?

That the third question, namely, Had the military commission in Indiana, under the facts stated, jurisdiction to try and sentence Milligan? must be answered negatively, is an unavoidable inference from affirmative answers to the other two.

The military commission could not have jurisdiction to try and sentence Milligan, if he could not be detained in prison under his original arrest or under sentence, after the close of a session of the grand jury, without indictment or other proceedings against him.

Indeed, the act seems to have been framed on purpose to secure the trial of all offences of citizens by civil tribunals in States where these tribunals were not interrupted in the regular exercise of their functions.

Under it, in such States, the privilege of the writ might be suspended. Any person regarded as dangerous to the public safety might be arrested and detained until after the session of a grand jury. Until after such session no person arrested could have the benefit of the writ, and even then no such person could be discharged, except on such terms as to future appearance as the court might impose. These provisions obviously contemplate no other trial or sentence than that of a civil court, and we could not assert the legality of a trial and sentence by a military commission, under the circumstances specified in the act and described in the petition, without disregarding the plain directions of Congress.

We agree, therefore, that the two first questions certified must receive affirmative answers, and the last a negative. We do not doubt that the positive provisions of the act of Congress require such answers. We do not think it necessary to look beyond these provisions. In them we find sufficient and controlling reasons for our conclusions.

But the opinion which has just been read goes further, and, as we understand it, asserts not only that the military commission held in Indiana was not authorized by Congress, but that it was not in the power of Congress to authorize it, from which it may be thought to follow that Congress has no power to indemnify the officers who composed the commission against liability in civil courts for acting as members of it.

We cannot agree to this.

We agree in the proposition that no department of the Government of the United States— neither President nor Congress nor the courts —possess any power not given by the Constitution.

We assent fully to all that is said in the opinion of the inestimable value of trial by jury and of the other constitutional safeguards of civil liberty; and we concur also in what is said of the writ of *habeas corpus* and of its suspension, with two reservations: (1.) That, in our judgment, when the writ is suspended, the Executive is authorized to arrest as well as to detain; and, (2,) that there are cases in which, the privilege of the writ being suspended, trial and punishment by military commission, in States where civil courts are open, may be authorized by Congress, as well as arrest and detention. We think that Congress had power, though not exercised, to authorize the military commission which was held in Indiana.

We do not think it necessary to discuss at large the grounds of our conclusions. We will briefly indicate some of them.

The Constitution itself provides for military government as well as for civil government; and we do not understand it to be claimed that the civil safeguards of the Constitution have application in cases within the proper sphere of the former.

What, then, is that proper sphere? Congress has power to raise and support armies; to provide and maintain a navy; to make rules for the government and regulation of the land and naval forces, and to provide for governing such part of the militia as may be in the service of the United States.

It is not denied that the power to make rules for the government of the army and navy is a power to provide for trial and punishment by military courts without a jury. It has been so understood and exercised from the adoption of the Constitution to the present time.

Nor, in our judgment, does the fifth or any other amendment abridge that power. "Cases arising in the land and naval forces, or in the militia in actual service in time of war or public danger," are expressly excepted from the fifth amendment, "that no person shall be held to answer for a capital or otherwise infamous crime unless on a presentment or indictment of a grand jury," and it is admitted that the exception applies to the other amendments as well as to the fifth.

Now we understand this exception to have the same import and effect as if the powers of Congress in relation to the government of the army and navy and the militia had been recited in the amendment, and cases within those powers had been expressly excepted from its operation. The States, most jealous of encroachments upon the liberties of the citizen when proposing additional safeguards in the form of amendments, excluded specifically from their effect cases arising in the government of the land and naval forces. Thus Massachusetts proposed that "no person shall be tried for any crime by which he would incur an infamous punishment or loss of life until he be first indicted by a grand jury, except in such cases as may arise in the government and regulation of the land forces." The exception in similar amendments proposed by New York, Maryland, and Virginia, was in the same or equivalent terms. The amendments proposed by the States were considered by the First Congress, and such as were approved in substance were put in form, and proposed by that body to the States. Among those thus proposed, and subsequently ratified, was that which now

stands as the fifth amendment of the Constitution. We cannot doubt that this amendment was intended to have the same force and effect as the amendment proposed by the States. We cannot agree to a construction which will impose on the exception in the fifth amendment a sense other than that obviously indicated by action of the State conventions.

We think, therefore, that the power of Congress in the government of the land and naval forces and of the militia, is not at all affected by the fifth or any other amendment. It is not necessary to attempt any precise definition of the boundaries of this power. But may it not be said that government includes protection and defence as well as the regulation of internal administration? And is it impossible to imagine cases in which citizens conspiring or attempting the destruction or great injury of the national forces may be subjected by Congress to military trial and punishment in the just exercise of this undoubted constitutional power? Congress is but the agent of the nation, and does not the security of individuals against the abuse of this, as of every other power, depend on the intelligence and virtue of the people, on their zeal for public and private liberty, upon official responsibility secured by law, and upon the frequency of elections, rather than upon doubtful constructions of legislative powers?

But we do not put our opinion, that Congress might authorize such a military commission as was held in Indiana, upon the power to provide for the government of the national forces.

Congress has the power not only to raise and support and govern armies, but to declare war. It has, therefore, the power to provide by law for carrying on war. This power necessarily extends to all legislation essential to the prosecution of war with vigor and success, except such as interferes with the command of the forces and the conduct of campaigns. That power and duty belong to the President as Commander-in-Chief. Both these powers are derived from the Constitution, but neither is defined by that instrument. Their extent must be determined by their nature, by the laws of nations, and by the principles of our institutions.

The power to make the necessary laws is in Congress; the power to execute, in the President. Both powers imply many subordinate and auxiliary powers. Each includes all authorities essential to its due exercise. But neither can the President, in war more than in peace, intrude upon the proper authority of Congress, nor Congress upon the proper authority of the President. Both are servants of the people, whose will is expressed in the fundamental law. Congress cannot direct the conduct of campaigns, nor can the President, or any commander under him, without the sanction of Congress, institute tribunals for the trial and punishment of offences, either of soldiers or civilians, unless in cases of a controlling necessity, which justifies what it compels, or at least ensures acts of indemnity from the justice of the Legislature.

We by no means assert that Congress can establish and apply the laws of war where no war has been declared or exists.

Where peace exists the laws of peace must

prevail. What we do maintain is, that when the nation is involved in war, and some portions of the country are invaded, and all are exposed to invasion, it is within the power of Congress to determine in what States or districts such great and imminent public danger exists as justifies the authorization of military tribunals for the trial of crimes and offences against the discipline or security of the army, or against the public safety.

In Indiana, for example, at the time of the arrest of Milligan and his co-conspirators, it is established by the papers in the record, that the State was a military district, was the theatre of military operations, had been actually invaded, and was constantly threatened with invasion. It appears, also, that a powerful secret association, composed of citizens and others, existed within the State, under military organization, conspiring against the draft, and plotting insurrection, the liberation of the prisoners of war at various depots, the seizure of the State and national arsenals, armed co-operation with the enemy, and war against the National Government.

We cannot doubt that, in such a time of public danger, Congress had power, under the Constitution, to provide for the organization of a military commission, and for trial by that commission of persons engaged in this conspiracy. The fact that the Federal courts were open was regarded by Congress as a sufficient reason for not exercising the power; but that fact could not deprive Congress of the right to exercise it. Those courts might be open and undisturbed in the execution of their functions, and yet wholly incompetent to avert threatened danger, or to punish, with adequate promptitude and certainty, the guilty conspirators.

In Indiana the judges and officers of the courts were loyal to the Government. But it might have been otherwise. In times of rebellion and civil war it may often happen, indeed, that judges and marshals will be in active sympathy with the rebels, and courts their most efficient allies.

We have confined ourselves to the question of power. It was for Congress to determine the question of expediency. And Congress did determine it. That body did not see fit to authorize trials by military commission in Indiana, but by the strongest implication prohibited them. With that prohibition we are satisfied, and should have remained silent if the answers to the questions certified had been put on that ground, without denial of the existence of a power which we believe to be constitutional and important to the public safety—a denial which, as we have already suggested, seems to draw in question the power of Congress to protect from prosecution the members of military commissions who acted in obedience to their superior officers, and whose action, whether warranted by law or not, was approved by that upright and patriotic President under whose administration the Republic was rescued from threatened destruction.

We have thus far said little of martial law, nor do we propose to say much. What we have already said sufficiently indicates our opinion that there is no law for the government of the citizens, the armies, or the navy of the United States, within American jurisdiction, which is not contained in or derived from the Constitution. And wherever our army or navy may go, beyond our territorial limits, neither can go beyond the authority of the President or the legislation of Congress.

There are under the Constitution three kinds of military jurisdiction—one to be exercised both in peace and war; another to be exercised in time of foreign war without the boundaries of the United States, or in time of rebellion and civil war within States or districts occupied by rebels treated as belligerents; and a third to be exercised in time of invasion or insurrection within the limits of the United States, or during rebellion within the limits of States maintaining adhesion to the National Government, when the public danger requires its exercise. The first of these may be called jurisdiction under MILITARY LAW, and is found in acts of Congress prescribing rules and articles of war, or otherwise providing for the government of the national forces; the second may be distinguished as MILITARY GOVERNMENT, superseding, as far as may be deemed expedient, the local law, and exercised by the military commander under the direction of the President, with the express or implied sanction of Congress; while the third may be denominated MARTIAL LAW PROPER, and is called into action by Congress, or temporarily, when the action of Congress cannot be invited, and in the case of justifying or excusing peril, by the President, in times of insurrection or invasion, or of civil or foreign war, within districts or localities where ordinary law no longer adequately secures public safety and private rights.

We think that the power of Congress, in such times and in such localities, to authorize trials for crimes against the security and safety of the national forces, may be derived from its constitutional authority to raise and support armies and to declare war, if not from its constitutional authority to provide for governing the national forces.

We have no apprehension that this power, under our American system of government, in which all official authority is derived from the people, and exercised under direct responsibility to the people, is more likely to be abused than the power to regulate commerce or the power to borrow money. And we are unwilling to give our assent by silence to expressions of opinion which seem to us calculated, though not intended, to cripple the constitutional powers of the Government, and to augment the public dangers in times of invasion and rebellion.

Mr. Justice Wayne, Mr. Justice Swayne, and Mr. Justice Miller concur with me in these views.

## On the Missouri Constitutional Test Oath of Loyalty, January 14, 1867.

Mr. Justice FIELD delivered the opinion of the Court in the case of *John A. Cummings* vs. *The State of Missouri.*

This case comes before us on a writ of error to the supreme court of Missouri, and involves a consideration of the test oath imposed by the constitution of that State. The plaintiff in error is a priest of the Roman Catholic Church, and was indicted and convicted, in one of the circuit courts of that State, of the crime of teaching and preaching, as a priest and minister of that religious denomination, without having first taken the oath, and was sentenced to pay a fine of $500, and to be committed to jail until the same was paid. On appeal to the supreme court of the State, the judgment was affirmed.

The oath prescribed by the constitution, divided into its separable parts embraces more than thirty distinct affirmations or tests. Some of the acts against which it is directed constitute offences of the highest grade, to which, upon conviction, heavy penalties are attached. Some of the acts have never been classed as offences in the laws of any State, and some of the acts under many circumstances would not even be blameworthy. It requires the affiant to deny not only that he has ever been in armed hostility to the United States or the lawful authorities thereof, but, among other things, that he has ever, "by act or word," manifested his adherence to the cause of the enemies of the United States, foreign or domestic, or his desire for their triumph over the arms of the United States, or his sympathy with those engaged in rebellion, or that he has ever harbored or aided any person engaged in guerrilla warfare against the loyal inhabitants of the United States, or has ever entered or left the State for the purpose of avoiding enrollment or draft in the military service of the United States, or to escape the performance of duty in the militia of the United States, or has ever indicated in any terms his disaffection to the Government of the United States in its contest with rebellion.

Every person who is unable to take this oath is declared incapable of holding in the State "any office of honor, trust, or profit under its authority, or of being an officer, counselor, director, or trustee, or other manager of any incorporation, public or private, now existing or hereafter established by its authority, or of acting as a professor or teacher in any educational institution, or in any common or other school, or of holding any real estate or other property in trust for the use of any church, religious society, or congregation." And every person holding any of the offices, trusts, or positions mentioned, at the time the constitution takes effect, is required within sixty days thereafter to take the oath, and if he fail to comply with this requirement, it is declared that his office, trust, or position shall *ipso facto* become vacant. And no person after the expiration of the sixty days is permitted, without taking the oath, "to practice as an attorney or counselor at law, nor, after that period, can any person be competent as a bishop, priest, deacon, minister, elder, or other clergyman of any religious persuasion, sect, or denomination, to teach or preach or solemnize marriage." Fine and imprisonment are prescribed as a punishment for holding or exercising any of the offices, positions, trusts, professions or functions specified without having taken the oath, and false swearing or affirmation to the oath is declared to be perjury, and punishable by imprisonment in the penitentiary.

The oath thus required is without any precedent that we can discover for its severity. In the first place, it is retrospective. It embraces all the past from this day, and if taken years hence, it will also cover all the intervening period. In its retrospective feature, it is peculiar to this country. In England and France there have been test oaths, but they have always been limited to an affirmation of present belief or present disposition towards the Government, and were never exacted with reference to particular instances of past misconduct. In the second place, the oath is directed not merely against overt and visible acts of hostility to the Government, but is intended to reach words, desires, and sympathies also; and, in the third place, it allows no distinction between acts springing from malignant enmity and acts which may have been prompted by charity or affection or relationship. If one has ever expressed sympathy with any who were drawn into the rebellion, even if the recipients of that sympathy were connected by the closest ties of blood, he is as unable to subscribe to the oath as the most active and most cruel of rebels, and is equally debarred from the offices of honor and trust and the positions and employments specified.

But, as it was observed by the learned counsel who appeared on behalf of the State of Missouri, this Court cannot decide this case upon the justice or hardship of these provisions. Its duty is to determine whether they are in conflict with the Constitution of the United States. On behalf of Missouri, it is urged that these provisions only prescribe a qualification for holding certain offices and practicing certain callings, and are therefore within the power of the State to adopt. On the other hand, it is contended that these provisions are in conflict with that clause of the Constitution which forbids any State to pass a bill of attainder or *ex post facto* law.

We admit the propositions of the counsel for Missouri, that the States which existed previous to the adoption of the Federal Constitution possessed originally all the attributes of sovereignty; that they still retain those attributes, except as they have been surrendered by the formation of the Constitution and the amendments thereto; that the new States, upon their admission into the Union, became invested with equal rights, and were thereafter subject only to similar restrictions; and that among the rights reserved to the States is the right of each State to determine the qualifications for office, and the conditions upon which its citizens may exercise their various callings and pursuits within its jurisdiction. These are general propositions, and involve principles of the highest moment. But it by no means follows that under the form of creating a qualification or attaching a condition, the States can in effect inflict a punishment for a past act which was not punishable at the time it was committed. The question is not as to the existence of the power of the State over matters of internal police, but whether that power has been made in the present case an instrument for the infliction of punishment against the inhibition of the Constitution.

Qualifications relate to the fitness or capacity of the party for a particular pursuit or profession. Webster defines the term to mean "any natural endowment or any acquirement which fits a person for a place, office, or employment, or enables him to sustain any character with success." It is evident from the nature of the pursuits and professions of the parties placed under disabilities by the constitution of Missouri, that the acts from the taint of which they must purge themselves have no possible relation to their fitness for those pursuits and professions. There can be no connection between the fact that Mr. Cummings entered or left the State of Missouri to avoid enrollment or draft in the military service of the United States, and his fitness to teach the doctrines or administer the sacraments of his church. Nor can a fact of this kind, or the expression of words of sympathy with persons drawn into the rebellion, constitute any evidence of the unfitness of the attorney or counselor to practice his profession, or of the professor to teach the ordinary branches of education, or of the want of business knowledge or business capacity in the manager of a corporation, or in its directors or trustees. It is manifest, upon the simple statement of the acts and the professions and pursuits, that there is no such relation between them as to render a denial of the commission of the acts at all appropriate as a condition of allowing the exercise of the professions and pursuits. The oath could not, therefore, have been required as a means of ascertaining whether parties were qualified or not for their respective callings or the trusts with which they are charged. It was required in order to reach the person, not the calling. It was exacted not from any notion that the acts designated indicated unfitness for the calling, but because the acts were thought to deserve punishment, and there was no way to punish the persons who had committed them but by depriving them of some of the rights and privileges of the citizen.

The disabilities created by the constitution of Missouri must be regarded as penalties. They constitute punishment. We do not agree with the counsel of Missouri that "to punish one is to deprive him of life, liberty, or property, and that to take from him anything less than these is no punishment at all." The learned counsel does not use these terms, "life, liberty, and property," as comprehending every right known to the law. He does not include under "liberty" freedom from outrage on the feelings as well as restraints on the person. He does not include under "property" those estates which one may acquire in professions, though they are often the source of the highest emoluments and honors.

The deprivation of any rights, civil or political, may be punishment, the circumstances attending and the causes of deprivation determining this fact. Disqualification from office may be punishment, as in cases of conviction upon impeachment. Disqualification from the pursuit of a lawful avocation, or from positions of trust, or from the privilege of appearing in the courts, or acting as executor, administrator, or guardian, may also, and often has been, imposed as punishment. By the statute of 9 and 10 William III, if any person educated in or having made a profession of the Christian religion did, by writing, printing, teaching or advised speaking, deny the truth of the religion or the Divine authority of the Scriptures, he was for the first offence rendered incapable to hold any office or

place of trust, and for the second he was rendered incapable of bringing any action, being guardian, executor, legatee, or purchaser of lands, beside being subjected to imprisonment without bail. By statute 2 George I, contempts against the king's title were punished by incapacity to hold a public office or place of trust, to prosecute any suit, to be guardian or executor, to take any legacy or deed of gift, and to vote at any election for members of Parliament, and also by forfeiture of £500 to any one who would sue for the same.

" Some punishments," says Blackstone, " consist in exile or banishment, by abjuration of the realm or transportation : others in loss of liberty, by perpetual or temporary imprisonment. Some extend to confiscation by forfeiture of lands or movables, or both, or of the profits of lands for life. Others induce a disability of holding office or employments, being heirs and executors, and the like." Among the Romans, loss of the privilege of membership of the family or of citizenship were punishments inflicted by her laws. In France, deprivation or suspension of civil rights, or of some of them, are punishments prescribed by her code, and among civil rights are included the right of voting, of eligibility to office, of taking part in family councils, of being guardian and trustee, of bearing arms, or being employed in a school or seminary of learning.

The theory upon which our political institutions rest is, that all men have certain inalienable rights; that among these are life, liberty, and the pursuit of happiness; and that in the pursuit of happiness, all avocations, all honors, all positions, are alike open to every one, and that in the protection of these rights all are equal before the law. Any deprivation or suspension of any of these rights for past conduct or acts is punishment, and can in no otherwise be defined.

Punishment not being therefore restricted, as contended by counsel, to the deprivation of life, liberty, or property, but also embracing deprivation or suspension of political or civil rights, and the disabilities prescribed by the provisions of the Missouri constitution being in effect punishment, we proceed to consider whether there is any inhibition in the Constitution of the United States against their enforcement.

The counsel from Missouri closed his argument in this case by presenting a striking picture of the struggle for ascendency in that State during the recent rebellion between the friends and the enemies of the Union, and of the fierce passions which that struggle aroused. It was in the midst of the struggle that the present constitution was framed, although it was not adopted by the people until the war had ceased. It would have been strange, therefore, had it not exhibited in its provisions some traces of the excitement amid which the convention held its deliberations. It was against the excited action of the States, under such influences as these, that the framers of the Federal Constitution intended to guard. In Fletcher vs. Peck, Mr. Chief Justice Marshall, speaking of such action, uses this language :

" Whatever respect might have been felt for the State sovereignties, it is not to be disguised that the framers of the Constitution viewed, with some apprehension, the violent acts which might grow out of the feelings of the moment; and that the people of the United States, in adopting that instrument, have manifested a determination to shield themselves and their property from the effects of those sudden and strong passions to which men are exposed. The restrictions on the legislative power of the States are obviously founded in this sentiment; and the Constitution of the United States contains what may be deemed a bill of rights for the people of each State :

"'No State shall pass any bill of attainder, *ex post facto* law, or law impairing the obligation of contracts.'"

A bill of attainder is a legislative act which inflicts punishment without a judicial trial. If the punishment be less than death the act is termed a bill of pains and penalties. Within the meaning of the Constitution bills of attainder include bills of pains and penalties. In these cases the legislative body, in addition to its legitimate functions, exercises the powers and office of judge. It assumes, in the language of the text books, judicial magistracy. It pronounces upon the guilt of the parties without any of the forms or safeguards of trial. It determines the sufficiency of the proofs produced, whether conformable to the rules of evidence or otherwise. It fixes the degree of punishment in accordance with its own notion of the enormity of the offence. "Bills of this sort," says Mr. Justice Story, "have been usually passed in England in times of rebellion, or gross subserviency to the crown, or of violent political excitement—periods in which all nations are most liable, as well the free as the enslaved, to forget their duties and trample upon the rights and liberties of others."

These bills are generally directed against individuals by name, but they may be directed against a whole class. The bill against the Earl of Kildare, passed in the reign of Henry VIII, enacted "that all such persons which be or heretofore have been comforters, abettors, partakers, confederates or adherents of the said late Earl in his or their false and traitorous acts and purposes shall in likewise stand, be attainted, adjudged and convicted of high treason, and that the same attainder, judgment and conviction against the said comforters, aiders, abettors, undertakers, confederates, and adherents shall be as strong and effectual in the law against them and every one of them as though they and every one of them had been specially, singularly, and particularly named by their proper names in the said act."

These bills may inflict punishment absolutely or may inflict it conditionally. The bill against the Earl of Clarendon, passed in the reign of Charles II, enacted that the Earl should suffer perpetual exile and be forever banished from the realm, and that if he returned or was found in England, or in any other of the king's dominions after the first of February, 1667, he should suffer the pains and penalties of treason, with a proviso, however, that if he surrendered himself before the said first day of February for trial, the penalties and disabilities declared should be void and of no effect.

"A British act of Parliament," to cite the language of the supreme court of Kentucky, "might declare that if certain individuals failed to do a given act by a named day they should be deemed to be and treated as convicted felons and traitors, and the act would come precisely within the definition of a bill of attainder, and the English courts would enforce it without indictment

or trial by jury." If the clauses of the third article of the constitution of Missouri, to which we have referred, had in terms declared that Mr. Cummings was guilty, or should be held guilty, of having been in armed hostility to the United States, or of having entered that State to avoid being enrolled or drafted into the military service, and thereafter should be deprived of the right to preach as a priest of the Catholic Church or to teach in any institution of learning, there would be no question but that the clauses would constitute a bill of attainder within the meaning of the Federal Constitution. If these clauses, instead of mentioning his name, had declared that priests and clergymen within the State of Missouri were guilty of these acts, or should be held guilty of them, and hence should be subjected to the like deprivation, the clauses would be equally open to objection. And further, if these clauses had declared that all such priests and clergymen should be held guilty, and be thus deprived, provided they did not by a day designated do certain specified acts, they would be no less within the inhibition of the Federal Constitution.

In all these cases there would be the legislative enactment creating the deprivation, without any of the ordinary forms and guards provided for the security of the citizen in the administration of justice by the established tribunals.

The results which would follow from clauses of the character mentioned do follow from the clauses actually adopted. The difference between the last case supposed and the case actually presented is one of form only, and not of substance. The existing clauses presume the guilt of the priests and clergymen, and adjudge the deprivation of their right to preach or teach unless the presumption be first removed by their expurgatory oath. In other words, they assume the guilt and adjudge the punishment conditionally. The clauses supposed differ only in that they declare the guilt, instead of assuming it. The deprivation is effected with equal certainty in the latter case as it would be in the former, but not with equal directness. The purpose of the law-maker in the case supposed would be openly avowed; in the case existing it is only disguised. The legal result must be the same, for what cannot be done directly cannot be done indirectly. The Constitution deals with substance, not shadows. Its inhibition was leveled at the thing, not the name. It intended that the rights of the citizen should be secured against deprivation for past conduct by legislative enactment, however disguised. If the inhibition can be avoided by the form of the enactment, its insertion in the fundamental law was a vain and futile proceeding.

We proceed to consider the second clause of what Mr. Chief Justice Marshall terms "a bill of rights for the people of each State," the clause which inhibits the passage of an *ex post facto* law. By an *ex post facto* law is meant one which imposes a punishment for an act which was not punishable at the time it was committed, or imposes additional punishment to that then prescribed, or changes the rules of evidence, by which less or different testimony is required to convict than was then exacted. In Fletcher *vs.*

Peck, Mr. Chief Justice Marshall defined an *ex post facto* law to be "one which makes an act punishable in a manner in which it was not punishable when it was committed." "Such a law," said that eminent judge, "may inflict penalties on the person, or may inflict pecuniary penalties which swell the public treasury. The legislature is, then, prohibited from passing a law by which a man's estate, or any part of it, shall be seized for a crime which was not declared by some previous law to render him liable to that punishment. Why, then, should violence be done to the natural meaning of the words for the purpose of leaving to the Legislature the power of seizing for public use the estate of an individual in the form of a law annulling the title by which he holds the estate? The Court can perceive no sufficient grounds for making this distinction. The rescinding act would have the effect of an *ex post facto* law. It forfeits the estate of Fletcher for a crime not committed by himself, but by those from whom he purchased. This could not be effected in the form of an *ex post facto* law or bill of attainder. Why, then, is it allowable in the form of a law annulling the original grant?

The act to which reference is here made was one passed by the State of Georgia repealing a previous act under which land had been granted. The repealing act, divesting the title of the grantees, did not in terms define any crimes or inflict any punishment or direct any judicial proceedings; yet, inasmuch as the Legislature was forbidden from passing any law by which a man's estate could be seized for a crime which was not declared by some previous law to render him liable to that punishment, the Chief Justice was of opinion that the repealing act had the effect of an *ex post facto* law, and was within the constitutional inhibition.

Now, the clauses in the Missouri constitution which are the subject of consideration do not in terms define any crime or declare that any punishment shall be inflicted, but they produce the same result upon the parties against whom they are directed as though the crimes were defined and the punishment declared. They assume that there are persons in Missouri who are guilty of some of the acts designated. They would have no meaning in the constitution were not such the fact. They are aimed at past acts, and not future facts. They were intended to operate upon parties who, in some form or manner, by action or words, directly or indirectly, had aided or countenanced the rebellion, or sympathized with parties engaged in the rebellion, or had endeavored to escape the proper responsibilities and duties of a citizen in time of war. And they were intended to operate by depriving such persons of the right to hold certain offices and trusts, and to pursue their ordinary and regular avocations. This deprivation is punishment; nor is it any less so because a way is opened for escape from it by the expurgatory oath. The framers of the constitution of Missouri knew at the time that whole classes of individuals would be unable to take the oath prescribed. To them there is no escape provided. To them the deprivation was intended to be and is absolute and perpetual. To make the enjoyment of a right dependent upon an impossible condition is equivalent to an absolute denial of the right under any condition, and such denial enforced for a past act is nothing else than punishment imposed for that act; it is a misapplication of terms to call it anything else.

Now, some of the acts to which the expurgatory oath is directed were not offences at the time they were committed. It was no offence against any law to enter or leave the State of Missouri for the purpose of avoiding enrollment or draft in the military service, however much the evasion of such service might be the subject of moral censure. Clauses which prescribe a penalty for an act of this nature are within the terms of the definition of an *ex post facto* law. They impose a punishment for an act not punishable at the time it was committed. Some of the acts at which the oath is directed constituted high offences at the time they were committed, to which, upon conviction, fine and imprisonment or other heavy penalties were attached. The clauses which provide a further penalty for these acts are also within the definition of an *ex post facto* law. They impose additional punishment to that prescribed when the act was committed. And this is not all. The clauses in question subvert the presumptions of innocence and alter the rules of evidence which heretofore, under the universally recognized principles of the common law, have been supposed to be fundamental and unchangeable. They assume that the parties are guilty; they call upon the parties to show their innocence, and they declare that such innocence can be shown only in one way, by an inquisition in the form of an expurgatory oath into the consciences of the parties.

The objectionable character of these clauses will be more apparent if we put them in the ordinary form of a legislative act. Thus, if instead of the general provisions in the Constitution, the convention had provided as follows: "Be it enacted, that all persons who have been in armed hostility to the United States shall, upon conviction thereof, not only be punished as the laws provided at the time the offences were committed, but shall also be thereafter rendered incapable of holding any of the offices, trusts, and positions, and of exercising any of the pursuits mentioned in the third article of the constitution of Missouri," no one could have any doubt of the nature of the act. It would be an *ex post facto* law, and void, for it would add a new punishment to an old offence. So, too, if the convention had passed an enactment of a similar kind with reference to those acts which do not constitute offences. Thus, had it provided as follows: "Be it enacted, that all persons who have heretofore at any time entered or left the State of Missouri with intent to avoid enrollment or draft in the military service of the United States, shall, upon conviction thereof, be forever rendered incapable of holding any office of honor, trust, or profit in the United States, or of teaching in any seminary of learning, or of preaching as a minister of the Gospel of any denomination, or exercising any of the professions or pursuits mentioned in the third article of the Constitution," there would be no question of the character of the enactment. It would be an *ex pos-*

*facto* law, because it would impose a punishment for an act not punishable at the time it was committed.

The provisions of the constitution of Missouri accomplish precisely what enactments like those supposed would accomplish. They impose the same penalty without the formality of a judicial trial and conviction, for the parties embraced by the supposed enactments would be incapable of taking the oath prescribed. To them its requirements would be an impossible condition. Now, as the State, had she attempted the course supposed, would have failed, it must follow that any other mode producing the same result must equally fail. The provisions of the Federal Constitution intended to secure the liberty of the citizen cannot be evaded by the form in which the power of the State is exerted. If this be not so, if that which cannot be accomplished by means looking directly to the end can be accomplished by indirect means, the inhibition may be evaded at pleasure. No kind of oppression can be named against which the framers of the Constitution supposed they had guarded, which may not be effected. Take the case supposed by counsel, that of a man tried for treason and acquitted, or, if convicted, pardoned.

The legislature then may pass an act that if the person thus acquitted or pardoned does not take an oath that he never has committed the acts charged against him, he shall not be permitted to hold any office of honor or trust or profit, or pursue any avocation in the State. Take the case before us: The constitution of Missouri excludes, on failure to take the oath we have described, a large class of persons within her borders from numerous offices and pursuits. It would have been equally within the power of the State to have extended the exclusion so as to deprive the parties who were unable to take the oath from any avocations whatever in the State. Suppose, again, in the progress of events, persons now in the minority in the State should obtain the ascendency, and secure the control of the Government; nothing could prevent, if the constitutional prohibition can be evaded, the enactment of a provision requiring every person, as a condition of holding any office of honor or trust, or of pursuing any avocation in the State, to take an oath that he had never advocated or advised or supported the imposition of the present expurgatory oath. Under this form of legislation the most flagrant invasions of private rights in periods of excitement may be enacted, and individuals, and even whole classes, may be deprived of political and civil rights.

A question arose in New York, soon after the treaty of peace of 1783, upon a statute of that State, which involved a discussion of the nature and character of these expurgatory oaths when used as a means of inflicting punishment. The subject was regarded as so important, and the requirement of the oath such a violation of the fundamental principles of civil liberty and the rights of the citizen, that it engaged the attention of eminent lawyers and distinguished statesmen of the time, and among others, of Alexander Hamilton. We will cite some passages of a paper left by him on the subject, in which, with his characteristic fullness and ability, he examines the oath and demonstrates that it is not only a mode of inflicting punishment, but a mode in violation of all the constitutional guaranties secured by the Revolution of the rights and liberties of the people:

"If we examine it," (the measure requiring the oath,) said this great lawyer, "with an unprejudiced eye, we must acknowledge not only that it was an evasion of the treaty, but a subversion of one great principle of social security, to wit, that every man shall be presumed innocent until he is proved guilty. This was to invert the order of things, and instead of obliging the State to prove the guilt in order to inflict the penalty, it was to oblige the citizen to show his own innocence to avoid the penalty. It was to excite scruples in the honest and conscientious, and to hold out a bribe to perjury." * * * "It was a mode of inquiring who had committed any of those crimes to which the penalty of disqualification was annexed, with this aggravation, that it deprived the citizen of the benefit of that advantage which he would have enjoyed by leaving, as in all other cases, the burden of proof upon the prosecution. To place this matter in a still clearer light, let it be supposed that instead of the mode of indictment and trial by jury, the Legislature was to declare that every citizen who did not swear that he had never adhered to the King of Great Britain should incur all the penalties which our treason laws prescribe, would this not be a palpable evasion of the treaty, and a direct infringement of the Constitution? The principle is the same in both cases, with only this difference in the consequences, that in the instance already acted upon the citizen forfeits a part of his rights, in the one supposed, he would forfeit the whole. The degree of punishment is all that distinguishes the cases. In either, justly considered, it is substituting a new and arbitrary mode of prosecution for that ancient and highly esteemed one recognized by the laws and the constitution of the State—I mean the trial by jury.

"Let us not forget that the constitution declares that trial by jury in all cases in which it has been formerly used should remain inviolate forever, and that the legislature should at no time erect any new jurisdiction which should not proceed according to the course of the common law. Nothing can be more repugnant to the true genius of the common law than such an inquisition as has been mentioned into the consciences of men." * * * "If any oath with respect to past conduct had been made the condition on which individuals who have resided within the British lines should hold their estates, we should immediately see that this proceeding would be tyrannical and a violation of the treaty; and yet, when the same oath is employed to divest that right which ought to be deemed still more sacred, many of us are so infatuated as to overlook the mischief.

"To say that the persons who will be affected by it have previously forfeited their right, and that therefore nothing is taken away from them is a begging of the question. How do we know who are the parties in this situation? If it be answered this is the mode taken to ascertain it, the objection returns, it is an improper mode, because it puts the most essential interests of the citizen upon a worse footing than we should be willing to tolerate where inferior interests are concerned, and because, if allowed, it substitutes for the established and legal mode of investigating crimes and inflicting forfeitures one that is unknown to the constitution and repugnant to the genius of our law."

Similar views have frequently been expressed by the judiciary in cases involving analogous questions. They are presented with great force in the matter of Dorsey, (7 Porter,) but we do not deem it necessary to pursue the subject further. The judgment of the supreme court of Missouri must be reversed and the cause remanded, with directions to enter a judgment reversing the judgment of the circuit court, and directing that court to discharge the defendant from imprisonment and suffer him to depart without day, and it is so ordered.

### On the Test Oath of Lawyers, Jan. 14, 1867.

Mr. Justice FIELD delivered the opinion of the Court:

I am also instructed by the Court to deliver its opinion in the matter of the petition of A. H. Garland.

On the 2d of July, 1862, Congress passed an act prescribing an oath to be taken by every person elected or appointed to any office of honor or profit under the Government of the United States, either in the civil, military, or naval departments of the public service, except the President of the United States, before entering upon the duties of his office, and before being entitled to its salary or other emoluments. On the 24th of January, 1865, Congress passed a supplementary act, extending its provisions so as to embrace attorneys and counselors of the courts of the United States, which provides that after its passage no person shall be admitted as an attorney or counselor to the bar of the Supreme Court, and, after the 4th of March, 1865, to the bar of any circuit or district court of the United States, or of the Court of Claims, or be allowed to appear and be heard by virtue of any previous admission or any special power of attorney ; unless he shall have first taken and subscribed the oath prescribed in the act of July 2, 1862. The act also provides that the oath shall be preserved among the files of the court; and if any person take it falsely, he shall be guilty of perjury, and, upon conviction, shall be subject to the pains and penalties of that offence.

At the December term of 1860, the petitioner was admitted as an attorney and counselor of this Court, and took and subscribed the oath then required. By the second rule, as it then existed, it was only requisite to the admission of attorneys and counselors of this Court that they should have been such officers for the three previous years in the highest courts of the States to which they respectively belonged, and that their private and professional character should appear to be fair. In March, 1865, this rule was changed by the addition of a clause* requiring the admin-

istration of an oath, in conformity with the act of Congress.

In May, 1861, the State of Arkansas, of which the petitioner was a citizen, passed an ordinance of secession which purported to withdraw the State from the Union, and afterwards, in the same year, by another ordinance, attached herself to the so-called Confederate States, and by act of the Congress of that Confederacy she was received as one of its members. The petitioner followed the State and was one of her representatives, first in the lower House, and afterwards in the Senate, of the Congress of that Confederacy, and was a member of the Senate at the time of the surrender of the Confederate forces to the armies of the United States.

In July, 1865, he received from the President of the United States a full pardon for all offences committed by him by participation, direct or implied, in the rebellion. He now produces this pardon, and asks permission to continue to practice as an attorney and counselor of the court, without taking the oath required by the act of January 24, 1865, and the rule of this court, which he is unable to take by reason of the offices he held under the Confederate government.

He rests his application principally upon two grounds: First, that the act of January 24, 1865, so far as it affects his status in the court, is unconstitutional and void; second, that if the act be unconstitutional, he is released from compliance with its provisions by the pardon of the President. The oath prescribed by the act is as follows: 1. That the deponent has never voluntarily borne arms against the United States since he has been a citizen thereof. 2. That he has not voluntarily given aid, countenance, counsel, or encouragement to persons engaged in armed hostility thereto. 3. That he has never sought, accepted, or attempted to exercise the functions of any office whatsoever under any authority or pretended authority in hostility to the United States. 4. That he has not yielded a voluntary support to any pretended government, authority, power, or constitution within the United States hostile or inimical thereto. 5. That he will support and defend the Constitution of the United States against all enemies, foreign and domestic, and will bear true faith and allegiance to the same.

This last clause is promissory only, and requires no consideration. The questions presented for our determination arise from the other

---

* The rule, adopted without dissent, is as follows:
SUPREME COURT OF THE UNITED STATES.
December Term, 1864.—*Friday, March 10, 1865.*
AMENDMENT TO 2D RULE.
*Ordered,* That the last clause of the second rule of this Court be amended so as to read as follows:

They shall respectively take and subscribe the following oath or affirmation:

I, ———— ————, do solemnly swear that I have never voluntarily borne arms against the United States since I have been a citizen thereof; that I have voluntarily given no aid, countenance, counsel, or encouragement to persons engaged in armed hostility thereto; that I have neither sought, nor accepted, nor attempted to exercise the functions of any office whatever, under any authority, or pretended authority, in hostility to the United States; that I have not yielded a voluntary support to any pretended government, authority, power, or constitution, within the United States, hostile or inimical thereto. And I do further swear, (or affirm,) that, to the best of my knowledge and ability, I will support and defend the Constitution of the United States against all enemies, foreign and domestic; that I will bear true faith and allegiance to the same; that I take this obligation freely, without any mental reservation or purpose of evasion.

And I do further solemnly swear, (or affirm, as the case may be,) that I will demean myself as an attorney and counsellor of this Court uprightly and according to law: So help me God.

clauses. These all relate to past acts. Some of these acts constituted, when they were committed, offences against the criminal laws of the country, and some of them may or may not have been offences, according to the circumstances under which they were committed and the motives of the parties. The first clause covers one form of the crime of treason, and the affiant must declare that he has not been guilty of this crime, not only during the war of rebellion, but during any period of his life since he has been a citizen. The second clause goes beyond the limits of treason, and embraces not only the giving of aid and encouragement of a treasonable nature to a public enemy, but also the giving of assistance of any kind to persons engaged in armed hostility to the United States The third clause applies to the seeking, acceptance, or exercise, not only of offices created for the purpose of more effectually carrying on hostilities, but also of any of those offices which are required in every community, whether in peace or war, for the administration of justice and the preservation of order. The fourth clause not only includes those who gave a cordial and active support to the hostile government, but also those who yielded a reluctant obedience to the existing order established without their co-operation.

The statute is directed against parties who have offended in any of the particulars embraced by these clauses, and its object is to exclude them from the profession of the law, or at least from its practice in the courts of the United States. As the oath prescribed cannot be taken by these parties, the act as against them operates as a legislative decree of perpetual exclusion. An exclusion from any of the professions or any of the ordinary avocations of life for past conduct can be regarded in no other light than as a punishment for such conduct. The exaction of the oath is the mode provided for ascertaining the parties upon whom the act is intended to operate, and, instead of lessening, increases its objectionable character. All enactments of this kind partake of the nature of bills of pains and penalties, and are subject to the constitutional inhibition against the passage of bills of attainder, under which general designation they are included. In the exclusion which the statute adjudges, it imposes a punishment for some of the acts specified, which were not punishable, or may not have been punishable at the time they were committed; and for other acts it adds a new punishment to that then prescribed, and it is thus brought within the further inhibition of the Constitution against the passage of an *ex post facto* law.

In the case of Cummings *vs.* The State of Missouri, just decided, we had occasion to consider the meaning of a bill of attainder and an *ex post facto* law in the clause of the Constitution forbidding their passage by the States, and it is unnecessary to repeat here what we there said. A like prohibition is contained in the Constitution against enactments of this kind by Congress, and the argument presented in that case against certain clauses of the constitution of Missouri is equally applicable to the act of Congress under consideration in this case.

The profession of an attorney and counselor is not like an office created by an act of Congress, which depends for its continuance, its powers, and its emoluments on the will of its creator, and the possession of which may be burdened with any conditions not prohibited by the Constitution. Attorneys and counselors are not officers of the United States. They are not elected or appointed in the manner prescribed by the Constitution for the election or appointment of such officers. They are officers of the court, admitted as such by its order upon evidence of their possessing sufficient legal learning and fair character. Since the statute of 4 Henry IV, it has been the practice in England, and it has always been the practice in this country, to obtain this evidence by an examination of the parties. In this Court the fact of the admission of such officers in the highest court of the States to which they respectively belong for three years preceding their application is regarded as sufficient evidence of the possession of the requisite legal learning, and the statement of counsel moving their admission sufficient evidence that their private and professional character is fair. The order of admission is the judgment of the court that the parties possess the requisite qualifications as attorneys and counselors, and are entitled to appear as such and conduct causes therein From its entry the parties become officers of the court, and are responsible to it for professional misconduct.

They hold their office during good behavior, and can only be deprived of it for misconduct, ascertained and declared by the judgment of the court, after opportunity to be heard has been afforded. Their admission and their exclusion are not the exercise of a mere ministerial power. The court is not in this respect the register of the edicts of any other body. It is the exercise of judicial powers, and has been so held in numerous cases. It was so held by the court of appeals of New York in the matter of the application of Cooper for admission. "Attorneys and counselors," said that court, "are not only officers of the court, but officers whose duties relate almost exclusively to proceedings of a judicial nature, and hence their appointment may, with propriety, be entrusted to the courts ; and the latter, in performing this duty, may very justly be considered as engaged in the exercise of their appropriate judicial functions." In *ex parte* Secomb, a *mandamus* to the supreme court of the Territory of Minnesota to vacate an order removing an attorney and counselor was denied by this court on the ground that the removal was a judicial act.

"We are not aware of any case," said the court, " where a *mandamus* was issued to an inferior tribunal commanding it to reverse or annul its decision, where the decision was in its nature a judicial act, and within the scope of its jurisdiction and discretion." And in the same case the court observed that " it has been well settled by the rules and practice of common-law courts that it rests exclusively with the court to determine who is qualified to become one of its officers as an attorney and counselor, and for what causes he ought to be removed." The attorney and counselor, being by the solemn judicial act of the court clothed with his office, does not hold it as a matter of grace and favor; the right which it confers upon him to appear for suitors, and to argue causes, is something more than a mere indulgence, revokable at the pleasure of the court or at the command of the legislature; it is a right of which he can only be deprived by the judgment of the court for moral or professional delinquency. The legislature may undoubtedly prescribe qualifications for the office, with which he must conform, as it may, where it has exclusive jurisdiction, prescribe qualifications for the pursuit of any of the ordinary avocations of life; but to constitute a qualification, the condition or thing prescribed must be attainable, in theory at least, by every one. That which from the nature of things, or the past condition or conduct of the party, cannot be attained by every citizen, does not fall within the definition of the term. To all those by whom it is unattainable it is a disqualification which operates as a perpetual bar to the office. The question in this case is not as to the power of Congress to prescribe qualifications, but whether that power has been exercised as a means for the infliction of punishment against the prohibition of the Constitution. That this result cannot be effected indirectly by a State under the form of creating qualifications, we have held in the case of Cummings vs. The State of Missouri, and the reasoning upon which that conclusion was reached applies equally to similar action on the part of Congress.

These views are further strengthened by a consideration of the effect of the pardon produced by the petitioner and the nature of the pardoning power of the President. The Constitution provides that the President "shall have power to grant reprieves and pardons for offences against the United States, except in cases of impeachment." The power thus conferred is unlimited, with the exception stated; it extends to every offence known to the law, and may be exercised at any time after its commission, either before legal proceedings are taken, or during their pendency, or after conviction and judgment. This power of the President is not subject to legislative control. Congress can neither limit the effect of his pardon, nor exclude from its exercise any class of offenders. The benign prerogative of mercy reposed in him cannot be fettered by any legislative restriction. Such being the case, the inquiry arises as to the effect and operation of a pardon. On this point all the authorities concur: a pardon reaches both the punishment prescribed for the offense, and the guilt of the offender, and when the pardon is full it releases the punishment and blots out of existence the guilt, so that in the eye of the law the offender is as innocent as if he had never committed the offence. If granted before conviction, it prevents any of the penalties and disabilities consequent upon conviction, from attaching. If granted after conviction it removes the penalties and disabilities, and restores him to all his civil rights. It makes him, as it were, a new man, and gives him a new credit and capacity. There is only this limitation to its operation: it does not restore offices forfeited, or property, or interests vested in others in conse-

quence of the conviction and judgment. The pardon produced by the petitioner is a full pardon for all offences by him committed arising from participation direct or implied in the rebellion, and is subject to certain conditions which have been complied with. The effect of this pardon is to relieve the petitioner from all penalties and disabilities attached to the offence of treason committed by his participation in the rebellion. So far as that offence is concerned he is thus placed beyond the reach of punishment of any kind; but to exclude him by reason of that offence from continuing in the enjoyment of previously acquired right is to enforce a punishment for that offence notwithstanding the pardon. If such exclusion can be effected by the exaction of an expurgatory oath covering the offence, the pardon may be avoided, and that accomplished indirectly which cannot be reached by direct legislation. It is not within the constitutional power of Congress thus to inflict punishment beyond the reach of executive clemency.

From the petitioner, therefore, the oath required by the act of January 24, 1865, cannot be exacted, even were that act not subject to any other objection than the one just stated. It follows, from the views expressed, that the prayer of the petitioner must be granted.

The case of R. H. Marr is similar in its main features to that of the petitioner, and his petition must be granted; and the amendment to the second rule of the court, which requires the oath prescribed by the act of January 24, 1865, to be taken by attorneys and counselors, having been unadvisedly adopted, must be rescinded, and it is so ordered.*

### DISSENTING OPINION.

Mr. Justice MILLER. I dissent from both the opinions of the Court just announced. It may be hoped that the exceptional circumstances which give present importance to these cases will soon pass away, and that those who make the laws, both State and national, will find in the conduct of the persons affected by the legislation just declared to be void sufficient reason to repeal or essentially modify it. For the speedy return of that better spirit which shall leave no cause for such laws all good men look with anxiety, and with a hope, I trust, not altogether unfounded.

But the question involved, relating, as it does, to the right of the legislatures of the nation and the States to exclude from offices and places of high public trust, the administration of whose functions is essential to the very existence of the Government, those of its own citizens who engaged in the recent effort to destroy that Government by force, can never cease to be one of profound interest. It is at all times the exercise of an extremely delicate power for this Court to declare that the Congress of the nation or the

---

*The new order, made by a majority, is as follows:
	SUPREME COURT OF THE UNITED STATES.
December Term, 1866.—*Monday, January 14, 1867.*
		ORDER OF COURT.
	It is now here ordered by the Court that the amendment to the second rule of this Court, which requires the oath prescribed by the act of Congress of January 24, 1865, to be taken by attorneys and counselors, be, and the same is, hereby rescinded and annulled.

legislative body of a State has assumed an authority not belonging to it, and, by violating the Constitution, has rendered void its attempt at legislation. In the case of an act of Congress, which expresses the sense of the members of a co-ordinate department of the Government, as much bound by their oath of office as we are to respect that Constitution, and whose duty it is, as much as it is ours, to be careful that no statute is passed in violation of it, the incompatibility of the act with the Constitution should be so clear as to leave little reason for doubt before we pronounce it to be invalid. Unable to see this incompatibility either in the act of Congress or in the provision of the constitution of Missouri upon which the Court has just passed, but entertaining a strong conviction that both were within the competency of the bodies which enacted them, it seems to me an occasion which demands that my dissent from the judgment of the Court and the reasons for that dissent should be placed on its records.

In the comments which I have to make on these cases, I shall speak of principles equally applicable to both, although I shall refer more directly to that which involves the oath required of attorneys by the act of Congress, reserving to the close some remarks more especially applicable to the oath prescribed by the constitution of the State of Missouri.

The Constitution of the United States makes ample provision for the establishment of courts of justice, to administer its laws and protect and enforce the rights of its citizens. Article 3, section 1, of that instrument says that "the judicial power of the United States shall be vested in one supreme court and such inferior courts as Congress may from time to time ordain and establish." Section 8 of article 1, closes its enumeration of the powers conferred on Congress by the broad declaration that it shall have authority "to make all laws which shall be necessary and proper for carrying into execution the foregoing powers and all other powers vested by this Constitution in the Government of the United States, or in any department thereof." Under these provisions, Congress has ordained and established circuit courts, district courts, and Territorial courts, and has, by various statutes, fixed the number of the judges of the Supreme Court; it has limited and defined the jurisdiction of all these and determined the salaries of the judges who hold them. It has provided for their necessary officers, as marshals, clerks, prosecuting attorneys, bailiffs, commissioners, and jurors; and by the act of 1789, commonly called the judiciary act, passed by the first Congress assembled under the Constitution, it is, among other things, enacted "that in all the courts of the United States parties may plead and manage their causes personally, or by the assistance of such counsel or attorneys at law as by the rules of the said courts respectively shall be permitted to manage and conduct causes therein." It is believed that no civilized nation of modern times has been without a class of men intimately connected with the courts and with the administration of justice, called variously attorneys, counselors, solicitors, proctors, or other terms of similar import. The enactment which we have just cited

recognizes this body of men and their utility in the judicial system of the United States, and imposes upon the courts the duty of providing rules by which persons entitled to become members of this class may be permitted to exercise the privilege of managing and conducting causes in those courts. They are as essential to the successful working of the courts as clerks, sheriffs, and marshals, and, perhaps, as the judges themselves, since no instance is known of a court of law without a bar. The right to practice law in the courts as a profession is a privilege granted by the law under such limitations or conditions in each State or government as the law-making power may prescribe. It is a privilege, and not an absolute right

The distinction may be illustrated by the difference between the right of a party to a suit in court to defend his own cause, and the right of another party to appear and defend for him. The one, like the right to life, liberty, and the pursuit of happiness, is inalienable; the other is the privilege conferred by law on a person who complies with the prescribed conditions. Every State in the Union, and every civilized government, has laws by which the right to practice in its courts may be granted, and makes that right to depend upon the good moral character and professional skill of the party upon whom the privilege is conferred. This is not only true in reference to the first grant of license to practice law, but the continuance of the right is made by these laws to depend upon the continued possession of these qualities. Attorneys are often deprived of this right upon evidence of bad moral character, or specific acts of immorality or dishonesty, which show that they no longer possess the requisite qualifications. All this is done by law, either statutory or common, and, whether the one or the other, equally the expression of the legislative will, for the common law exists in this country only as it is adopted or permitted by legislatures or by constitutions.

No reason is perceived why this body of men, in their important relations to the courts of the nation, are not subject to the action of Congress to the same extent that they are under the legislative control in the States, or in any other Government, and to the same extent that the judges, clerks, marshals, and other officers of the court are subject to congressional legislation. Having the power to establish the courts, to provide for and regulate the practice in those courts, to create their officers, and to prescribe their functions, can it be doubted that Congress has the full right to prescribe terms for the admission, rejection, and expulsion of attorneys, and for requiring of them an oath to show whether they have the proper qualifications for the discharge of their duties.

The act which has just been declared to be unconstitutional is nothing more than a statute which requires of all lawyers who propose to practice in the national courts that they shall take the same oath which is exacted of every officer of the Government, civil or military. This oath has two aspects—one which looks to the past conduct of the party, and one to his future conduct—but both have reference to his disposition to support or to overturn the Government in whose functions he proposes to take a part. In substance, he is required to swear that he has not been guilty of treason to that Government in the past, and that he will bear faithful allegiance to it in the future. That fidelity to the Government under which he lives, and true and loyal attachment to it, and a sincere desire for its preservation, are among the most essential qualifications which should be required in a lawyer, seems to me too clear for doubt. The history of the Anglo-Saxon race shows that for ages past the members of the legal profession have been powerful for good or evil in the Government. They are by the nature of their duties the moulders of public sentiment on questions of government, and are every day engaged in aiding in the construction and enforcement of the laws. From among their numbers are necessarily selected the judges who expound the laws and the Constitution. To suffer treasonable sentiments to spread here unchecked is to permit the stream on which the life of the nation depends to be poisoned at its source. In illustration of this truth, I venture to affirm that if all the members of the legal profession in the States lately in insurrection had possessed the qualification of a loyal, faithful allegiance to the Government, we should have been spared the horrors of that rebellion. If, then, this qualification be so essential in a lawyer, it cannot be denied that the statute under consideration was eminently calculated to secure that result.

The majority of the Court, however, do not base their decision on the mere absence of authority in Congress and the States to enact the laws which are the subject of consideration, but insist that the Constitution of the United States forbids in prohibitory terms the passage of such laws, both to Congress and to the States. The provisions of that instrument relied on to sustain this doctrine are those which forbid Congress and the States respectively from passing bills of attainder and *ex post facto* laws. It is said that the act of Congress and the provision of the constitution of the State of Missouri under review are in conflict with both these provisions, and are therefore void.

I will examine this proposition in reference to these two clauses of the Constitution in the order in which they occur in that instrument. First, in regard to bills of attainder. I am not aware of any judicial decision by a court of Federal jurisdiction which undertakes to give a definition of that term. We are therefore compelled to recur to the bills of attainder passed by the English Parliament, that we may learn so much of their peculiar characteristics as will enable us to arrive at a sound conclusion as to what was intended to be prohibited by the Constitution. The word "attainder" is derived by Sir Thomas Tomlyn in his law dictionary from the words *attincto* and *attinctura*, and is defined to be the stain or corruption of the blood of a criminal capitally condemned, the immediate, inseparable consequence, by the common law, of the pronouncing of the sentence of death, and the effect of this corruption of the blood was that the party attainted lost all inheritable quality, and could neither receive nor transmit any property or other rights by inheritance. This attainder or corruption of blood, as a consequence of judicial sentence of death, continued to be the law of England in all cases of treason to the time when our Constitution was framed, and, for aught that is known to me, is the law of that country on condemnation for treason at this day. Bills of attainder, therefore, or acts of attainder, as they were called after they were passed into statutes, were laws which declared certain persons attainted and their blood corrupted, so that it had lost all inheritable quality. Whether it declared other punishments or not, it was an act of attainder if it declared this. This also seems to have been the main feature at which the authors of the Constitution were directing their prohibition; for, after having in article 1 prohibited the passage of bills of attainder, in section 9 to Congress, and in section 10 to the States, there still remained to the judiciary the power of declaring attainders. Therefore, to still further guard against this odious form of punishment, it has provided in section 3, article 3, concerning the judiciary, that, while Congress shall have power to declare the punishment of treason, no attainder of treason shall work corruption of blood or forfeiture, except during the life of the person attainted.

This, however, while it was the chief, was not the only peculiarity of bills of attainder which was intended to be included within the constitutional restriction. Upon an attentive examination of the distinctive features of this kind of legislation, I think it will be found that the following comprise the essential elements of bills of attainder, in addition to the one already mentioned, which distinguished them from other legislation, and which made them so obnoxious to the statesmen who organized our Government: First, they were convictions and sentences pronounced by the legislative department of the Government instead of the judiciary; second, the sentences pronounced and the punishments inflicted were determined by no previous law or fixed rule; third, the investigation into the guilt of the accused, if any such were made, was not necessarily or generally conducted in his presence or that of his counsel, and no recognized rule of evidence governed the inquiry. (See Story on the Constitution, section 1,344.)

It is no cause for wonder that the men who had just passed successfully through a desperate struggle in behalf of civil liberty should feel a detestation for legislation of which these were the prominent features. The framers of our political system had a full appreciation of the necessity of keeping separate and distinct the primary departments of the Government. Mr. Hamilton, in the seventy-eighth number of the Federalist, says that he agrees with the maxim of Montesquieu, that there is no liberty if the power of judging be not separated from the legislative and executive powers; and others of the ablest numbers of that publication are devoted to the purpose of showing that in our Constitution these powers are so justly balanced and restrained that neither will probably be able to make much encroachment upon the others. Nor was it less repugnant to their views of the security of personal rights that any person should be condemned without a hearing and punished with out a law previously prescribing the nature and extent of that punishment. They therefore struck boldly at all this machinery of legislative despotism, by forbidding the passage of bills of attainder and *ex post facto* laws, both to Congress and to the States.

It remains to inquire whether in the act of Congress under consideration—and the remarks apply with equal force to the Missouri constitution—there is found any of these features of bills of attainder, and, if so, whether there is sufficient in the act to bring it fairly within the description of that class of bills. It is not claimed that the law works a corruption of blood. It will therefore be conceded at once that the act does not contain this leading feature of bills of attainder. Nor am I capable of seeing that it contains a conviction or sentence of any designated person or persons. It is said that it is not necessary to a bill of attainder that the party to be affected should be named in the act, and the attainder of the Earl of Kildare and his associates is referred to as showing that the act was aimed at a class. It is very true that bills of attainder have been passed against persons by some description when their names were unknown but in such cases the law leaves nothing to be done to render its operation effectual but to identify those persons. Their guilt, its nature, and its punishment are fixed by the statute, and only their personal indentity remains to be made out. Such was the case alluded to. The act declared the guilt and punishment of the Earl of Kildare and all who were associated with him in his enterprise, and all that was required to insure their punishment was to prove that association. If this were not so, then it was mere *brutum fulmen*, and the parties other than the Earl of Kildare could only be punished, notwithstanding the act, by proof of their guilt before some competent tribunal.

No person is pointed out in the act of Congress, either by name or by description, against whom it is to operate. The oath is only required of those who propose to accept an office or to practice law, and as a prerequisite to the exercise of the functions of the lawyer or the officer it is demanded of all persons alike. It is said to be directed, as a class, to those alone who were engaged in the rebellion; but this is manifestly incorrect, as the oath is exacted alike from the loyal and disloyal under the like circumstances, and none are compelled to take it. Neither does the act declare any conviction either of persons or classes. If so, who are they, and of what crime are they declared to be guilty? Nor does it pronounce any sentence or inflict any punishment. If by any possibility it can be said to provide for conviction and sentence, though not found in the act itself, it leaves the party himself to determine his own guilt or innocence, and pronounce his own sentence. It is not, then, the act of Congress, but the party interested, that tries and condemns. We shall see, when we come to the discussion of this act in its relation to *ex post facto* laws, that it inflicts no punishment. A statute which designates no criminal either by name or by description, which declares no guilt, pronounces no sentence, and inflicts no punishment, can in no case be called a bill of attainder.

Passing now to the consideration, whether this statute is an *ex post facto* law, we find that the meaning of that term, as used in the Constitution, is a matter which has been frequently before this Court, and it has been so well defined as to leave no room for controversy. The only doubt which can arise is as to the character of the particular acts claimed to come within the definition, not as to the definition of the phrase itself. All the cases agree that the term is to be applied to criminal causes alone, and not to civil proceedings. In the language of Justice Story in the case of Watson *vs.* Mercer, 8 Peters, 88, "*ex post facto* laws relate to penal and criminal proceedings which impose punishments and forfeitures, and not to civil proceedings, which affect private rights retrospectively." (Calder *vs.* Bull, 3 Dallas, 386; Fletcher *vs.* Peck, 6 Cranch, 87; Ogden *vs.* Saunders, 12 Wheaton, 266; Satterlee *vs.* Matthewson, 2 Peters, 380.)

The first case on the subject is that of Calder *vs.* Bull, and it is the case in which the doctrine concerning *ex post facto* law is most fully expounded. The Court divides all laws which come within the meaning of that clause of the Constitution into four classes: 1. Every law that makes an action done before the passing of the law, and which was innocent when done, criminal, and punishes such action. 2. Every law that aggravates a crime, or makes it greater than it was when committed. 3. Every law that changes the punishment, and inflicts a greater punishment than the law annexed to the crime when committed. 4. Every law that alters the rule of evidence, and receives less or different testimony than the law required at the time of the commission of the offence to convict the offender.

Again, the Court draws, in the same opinion, the true distinction as between *ex post facto* laws and retrospective laws, and proceeds to show that however unjust the latter may be, they are not prohibited by the Constitution, while the former are. This exposition of the nature of an *ex post facto* law has never been denied, nor has any court or any commentator on the Constitution added to the classes of laws here set forth as coming within that clause of the organic law. In looking carefully at these four classes of laws, two things strike the mind as common to them all: First, that they contemplate the trial of some person charged with an offence; second, that they contemplate a punishment of a person found guilty of such offence.

Now, it seems to me impossible to show that the law in question contemplates either the trial of a person for an offence committed before its passage, or the punishment of any person for such an offence. It is true the act requiring an oath provides a penalty for falsely taking it, but this provision is prospective, as no one is supposed to take the oath until after the passage of the law. This prospective penalty is the only thing in the law which partakes of a criminal character. It is in all other respects a civil proceeding. It is simply an oath of office, and it is required of all office-holders alike. As far as I am informed, this is the first time in the history of jurisprudence that taking an oath of office has been called a criminal proceeding. If it is not a criminal proceeding, then, by all the authorities, it is not an *ex post facto* law. No trial of any person is contemplated by the act for any past offence; nor is any party supposed to be charged with any offence in the only proceeding which the law provides. A person proposing to appear in the court as an attorney is asked to take a certain oath. There is no charge made against him that he has been guilty of any of the crimes mentioned in that oath; there is no prosecution. There is not even an implication of guilt by reason of tendering him the oath; for it is required of the man who has lost everything in defence of the Government, and whose loyalty is written in the honorable scars which cover his body, the same as of the guiltiest traitor in the land. His refusal to take the oath subjects him to no prosecution; his taking it clears him of no guilt and acquits him of no charge.

Where, then, is this *ex post facto* law which tries and punishes a man for a crime committed before it was passed? It can only be found in those elastic rules of construction which cramp the powers of the Federal Government when they are to be exercised in certain directions, and enlarge them when they are to be exercised in others. No more striking example of this could be given than the cases before us, in one of which the Constitution of the United States is held to confer no power on Congress to prevent traitors from practicing in our courts, while in the other it is held to confer power on this Court to nullify a provision of the constitution of the State of Missouri relating to a qualification required of ministers of religion.

But the fatal vice in the reasoning of the majority is in the meaning which they attach to the word "punishment," in its application to this law, and in its relation to the definitions which have been given of the phrase *ex post facto* law. Webster's second definition of the word "punish" is this: "In a loose sense, to afflict with pain, &c., with a view to amendment; to chasten;" and it is in this loose sense that the word is used by the Court as synonymous with "chastisement," "correction," "loss or suffering to the party supposed to be punished," and not in the legal sense, which signifies a penalty inflicted for the commission of a crime. So in this sense it is said, that whereas persons who have been guilty of the offences mentioned in the oath were, by the laws then in force, only liable to be punished with death and confiscation of all their property, they are, by a law passed since those offences were committed, made liable to the enormous additional punishment of being deprived of the right to practice law. The law in question does not in reality deprive a person guilty of the acts therein mentioned of any right which he possessed before, for it is equally sound law, as it is the dictate of good sense, that a person who, in the language of the act, has voluntarily borne arms against the Government of the United States while a citizen thereof, and who has voluntarily given aid, comfort, counsel, or encouragement to persons engaged in armed hostility to the Government, has, by doing those things, forfeited his right to appear in her courts and take part in the administration of her laws. Such a person has exhibited a trait of character which, without the aid of the law in question, authorizes the court to declare him unfit to practice before it, and to strike his name from the roll of its attorneys, if it be found there. I have already shown that this act provides for no indictment or other charge, that it contemplates and admits of no trial, and I now proceed to show that even if the right of the court to prevent an attorney guilty of the acts mentioned from appearing in its forum depended upon the statute, still it inflicts no punishment in the legal sense of that term.

"Punishment," says Mr. Wharton in his Law Lexicon, "is a penalty for transgression of the law," and this is perhaps as comprehensive and at the same as accurate a definition as can be given. Now, what law is it whose transgression is punished in the case before us? None is referred to in the act, and there is nothing on its face to show that it was intended as an additional punishment for any offence described in any other act. A part of the matters of which the applicant is required to purge himself on oath may amount to treason, and surely there could be no intention or desire to inflict this small additional punishment for a crime whose penalty was already death and confiscation of property. In fact, the word "punishment" is used by the court in a sense which would make a great number of laws, partaking in no sense of a criminal character, laws for punishment, and therefore *ex post facto*. A law, for instance, which increases the facility for detecting frauds, by compelling a party to a civil proceeding to disclose his transactions under oath, would result in his punishment in this sense if it compelled him to pay an honest debt which could not be coerced from him before; but this law comes clearly within the class described by this Court in Watson *vs.* Mercer, as a civil proceeding which affects private rights retrospectively.

Again, let us suppose that several persons afflicted with a form of insanity heretofore deemed harmless shall be found all at once to be dangerous to the lives of persons with whom they associate. The State, therefore, passes a law that all persons so affected shall be kept in close confinement until their recovery is assured. Here is a case of punishment, in the sense used by the Court, for a matter existing before the passage of the law. Is it an *ex post facto* law; and, if not, in what does it differ from one? Just in the same manner that the act of Congress does—namely, that the proceeding is a civil, and not a criminal proceeding, and that the imprisonment in the one case, and the prohibition to practice law in the other, are not punishments in the legal meaning of that term.

The civil law maxim, *nemo debet bis vexari pro una et eadem causâ*, has long since been adopted in the common law as applicable both to civil and criminal proceedings; and one of the amendments of the Constitution incorporates this principle into that instrument so far as punishment affects life or limb.

It results from this rule that no man can be twice lawfully punished for the same offence. We have already seen that the acts of which the party is required to purge himself on oath constitute the crime of treason. Now, if the judgment of the Court in the cases before us, instead of permitting parties to appear without taking the oath, had been the other way, here would have been the case of a person who, on the reasoning of the majority, is punished by the judgment of this Court for the same acts which constitute the crime of treason; and yet, if the applicant here should be afterwards indicted for treason on account of those same acts, no one would pretend that the proceeding here could be successfully pleaded in bar of that indictment. But why not? Simply because there is here neither trial nor punishment within the legal meaning of these terms.

I maintain that the purpose of the act of Congress was to require loyalty as a qualification of all who practice law in the national courts. The majority say that the purpose was to impose a punishment for past acts of disloyalty. In pressing this argument, it is asserted by the majority that no requirement can be justly said to be a qualification which is not attainable by all, and that to demand a qualification not attainable by all is a punishment. The Constitution of the United States provides as a qualification for the office of President and Vice President that the person elected must be a native-born citizen. Is this a punishment to all those naturalized citizens who can never attain that qualification? The constitution of nearly all the States requires as a qualification for voting that the voter shall be a white male citizen. Is this a punishment for all the blacks who can never become white? It was a qualification required by some of the State constitutions for the office of judge that the person should not be over sixty years of age. To a very large number of the ablest lawyers in any State this is a qualification which they can never attain, for every year removes them further away from the designated age. Is it a punishment? The distinguished commentator on American law and chancellor of the State of New York was deprived of that office by this provision of the constitution of that State. He was, just in the midst of his usefulness, not only turned out of office, but he was forever disqualified from holding it again by a law passed after he had accepted the office. Here is a much stronger case than that of a disloyal attorney forbid by law to practice in the courts, yet no one ever thought that the law was *ex post facto* in the sense of the Constitution of the United States.

Illustrations of this kind could be multiplied indefinitely, but they are unnecessary. The history of the time when this statute was passed, the darkest hour of our great struggle, the necessity for its existence, the humane character of the President who signed the bill, and the face of the law itself, all show that it was purely a qualification exacted in self-defence of all who took part in administering the Government in any of its departments, and that it was not passed for the purpose of inflicting punishment, however merited, for past offences.

I think I have now shown that the statute in question is within the legislative power of Congress in its control over the courts and their officers, and that it is not void as being either a bill of attainder or an *ex post facto* law. If I am right on the question of qualification and punishment, that discussion disposes also of the proposition that the pardon of the President relieves the party accepting it of the necessity of taking the oath, even if the law be valid. I am willing to concede that the presidential pardon relieves the party from all penalties, or, in other words, from all the punishment which the law inflicts for his offence; but it relieves him from nothing more. If the oath required as a condition to practicing law is not a punishment, as I think I have shown it is not, then the pardon of the President has no effect in relieving him from the requirement to take it. If it is a qualification which Congress had a right to prescribe as necessary to an attorney, then the President cannot, by pardon or otherwise, dispense with the law requiring such qualification. This is not only the plain rule as between the legislative and executive departments of the Government, but it is the declaration of common sense. The man who, by counterfeiting, by theft, or by murder, or by treason, is rendered unfit to exercise the functions of an attorney or counsellor at law may be saved by the Executive pardon from the penitentiary or the gallows, but is not thereby restored to the qualifications which are essential to admission to the bar. No doubt it would be found that very many persons among those who cannot take this oath deserve to be relieved from the prohibition of the law, but this in nowise depends upon the act of the President in giving or refusing a pardon; it remains to the legislative power alone to prescribe under what circumstances this relief shall be extended.

In regard to the case of Cummings *vs.* The State of Missouri, allusions have been made in argument to the sanctity of the ministerial office and to the inviolability of religious freedom in this country; but no attempt has been made to show that the Constitution of the United States interposes any such protection between the State governments and their own citizens; nor can anything of the kind be shown. The Federal Constitution contains but two provisions on this subject. One of these forbids Congress to make any law respecting the establishment of religion or prohibiting the free exercise thereof; the other is, that no religious test shall ever be required as a qualification to any office or public trust under the United States. No restraint is placed by that instrument on the action of the States; but, on the contrary, in the language of Story, (Commentaries on the Constitution, section 1878,) the whole power over the subject of religion is left exclusively to the State governments, to be acted upon according to their own sense of justice and the State constitution. If there ever was a case calling for this Court to exercise all the power on this subject which properly belonged to it, it was the case of the Rev. B. Permoli, reported in 3 Howard, 589. An ordinance of the first municipality of the city of New Orleans imposed a penalty on any priest who should officiate at any funeral in any other church than the Obituary Chapel. Mr. Permoli, a Catholic priest, performed the funeral services of his Church over the body of one of his parishioners enclosed in a coffin in the Roman Catholic Church of St. Augustin. For this he was fined, and relying upon the vague idea advanced here, that the Federal Constitution protected him in the exercise of his holy functions, he brought the case to this Court; but, hard as the case was, the Court replied to him in the following language: "The Constitution of the United States makes no provision for protecting the citizens of the respective States in their religious liberties; this is left to the State constitutions and laws; nor is there any inhibition imposed by the Constitution of the United States in this respect on the States." Mr. Permoli's writ of error was therefore dismissed for want of jurisdiction. In that case an ordinance of a mere local corporation forbade a priest loyal to his Government from performing what he believed to be the necessary rites of his Church over the body of his departed friend. This Court said it could give him no relief. In this case the constitution of the State of Missouri, the fundamental law of the people of that State, adopted by their popular vote, declares that no priest of any Church shall exercise his ministerial functions unless he will show by his own oath that he has borne true allegiance to his Government; and this Court now holds this constitutional provision void, on the ground that the Federal Constitution forbids it. I leave the two cases to speak for themselves.

In the discussion of these cases I have said nothing, on the one hand, of the great evils inflicted on the country by the voluntary action of many of those persons affected by the laws under consideration, nor, on the other hand, of the hardships which they are now suffering much more as a consequence of that action than of any laws which Congress could possibly frame; but I have endeavored to bring to the examination of the grave questions of constitutional law involved in this inquiry those principles alone which are calculated to assist in determining what the law is, rather than what in my private judgment it ought to be.

I am requested to say that the Chief Justice and Justices Swayne and Davis concur in this opinion.

### Opinion of the Supreme Court of the District of Columbia in a like Case, February 12, 1867

Chief Justice CARTTER said:

This is a motion on the application of Mr. Allen B. Magruder and others for admission to the bar of this court, connected with a motion to rescind the rule which provides that each applicant for admission to bar shall, before being admitted, take and subscribe the following oath·

"I, ——, do solemnly —— that I have never voluntarily borne arms against the United States since I have been a citizen thereof; that I have voluntarily given no aid, countenance, counsel, or encouragement to persons engaged in armed hostility thereto; that I have neither sought, nor accepted, nor attempted to exercise, the functions of any office whatever, under any authority, or pretended authority, in hostility to the United States; that I have not yielded a voluntary support to any pretended government, authority, power, or constitution within the United States, hostile or inimical thereto. And I do further —— that, to the best of my knowledge and ability, I will support and defend the Constitution of the United States against all enemies, foreign and domestic; that I will bear true faith and allegiance to the same; that I take this obligation freely, without any mental reservation or purpose of evasion, and that I will well and faithfully discharge the duties of the office on which I am about to enter: so help me God. Sworn to and subscribed before me this —— day of ——, 186—."

The consideration of the subject in the order of the application suggests the inquiry, whether the applicant is eligible to admission irrespective of the oath. His history in this connection, as rendered by himself, makes him a citizen of the District of Columbia immediately antecedent to the outbreak of the rebellion, and a member of the bar of the former circuit court, and as such attorney under the obligation of the following oath, which he took and subscribed on the 12th of December, 1857:

"I do solemnly swear that I will support the Constitution of the United States; that I do not hold myself in allegiance to the king or queen of Great Britain; and that I will well and truly behave and demean myself in the office of attorney of this court in all things appertaining to the duties thereof, to the best of my skill and judgment; so help me God. And I declare that I believe in the Christian religion."

It also appears, from his own statement, that about the time of the inauguration of the rebellion, and before the secession of Virginia, he transferred himself from this jurisdiction to that State, where he became an officer in the rebel army, doubtless, as such, binding himself under oath to do all in his power to destroy this Government.

The reason he assigns for the violation of his oath to support the Constitution of the United States, as an attorney of the former circuit court, as we understand him, is that he was a native of Virginia, and owed to Virginia a paramount fealty. The mere statement of his case, as given by himself, would seem to make it impossible for any federal court to incorporate him among its officers.

The assumption of State sovereignty and the paramount duty of the citizen to the State is old as a pretence in justification for resistance to federal authority, having been chiefly used as a means to that end; but as an honest conviction of intelligent judgment it has been entertained but by few. The proposition that a part is greater than the whole, and that the Government of the United States only existed at the will of one of its members, is incapable of belief, and simply argues that the Government of the United States never existed, or if it had existence, had not vitality for self-preservation. The disqualification of the applicant for admission is made more significant if possible by his disinclination and failure to say that in taking the oath to support the Constitution of the United States in contemplation of admission to the bar of this court, he would regard it as binding him and his conscience in paramount duty to this Government. The essential absurdity of the position, that a State in conflict with the federal power is greater than the nation, and duty to the State greater than duty to the nation, which was put forth prior to the rebellion chiefly as a speculative means to the destruction of the Federal Government, seems still to afflict him, notwithstanding it has been persuaded and whipped out of nearly everybody else of similar hallucination by five years of bloody war and the sacrifice of about a million of men. It will be perceived, from this view of his case, that if the oath in question did not exist, it would still be impossible for the court to give the applicant admission to this bar.

This leads us to the consideration of the motion to rescind the first rule of this court, adopted March 23, 1863, in order that the several parties named in the motion may be admitted as members of the bar without first taking the oath prescribed by that rule.

We understand the motion to be based substantially upon the assumption that the oath is unconstitutional, that its unconstitutionality has been determined by the Supreme Court, and that that determination is mandatory upon the judgment of this court; that it is unconstitutional because it is *ex post facto* and in the nature of a penalty. It is a fundamental rule, that to authorize a court to pronounce a law unconstitutional the fault of the law should be clear, and its violation of the Constitution unembarrassed by doubt. Deference to the deliberations and judgment of the law-making and co-ordinate branch of the Government not only recommends this rule, but makes it imperative. Up to the time of the publication of the recent opinion of the majority of the Supreme Court, this court, from the time of the adoption of the rule, has entertained no doubt of its constitutionality, or of its propriety and necessity. The only doubt now existing in this regard has been raised by the expression of the opinion of the majority of that Court.

It is said to be *ex post facto* and in the nature of a penalty. Let us inquire. The penalty for what act? A law after what act? Does it propose to inflict an additional penalty for the treason committed, or simply to leave the traitor where the treason left him—in the enjoyment of all the ordinary and natural estate of the citizen? The *ex post facto* penalty contemplated by law is a new penalty prescribed for previous crimes— a new punishment for an old transgression. Does this rule do that? If it does, it is by withholding a privilege that the party never had, and that does not pertain to the estate of ordinary citizenship. The fact in the premises which it is objected is *ex post facto* is the office of attorney, with its privileges and immunities as a member of this bar—a fact which the party never had, and is now for the first time seeking. The condition to the enjoyment of the office complained of here, instead of being after the fact, precedes it, and is really complained of as an obstacle to it. The oath, instead of being a penalty, is simply among the evidences of fitness for the enjoyment of the estate in prospect, which, among other tests, this court has seen fit to impose for the protection of the *morale* of the bar and the integrity of the Government.

This view of the nature and constitutional character of this rule is sufficiently satisfactory to our mind without the aid even of the acknowledged constitutional power of Congress to make retroactive laws.

It is unnecessary to discuss in the light of this argument the effect of the pardon, inasmuch as it is not part of the office of a pardon to create in a criminal new rights disconnected with his crime and which he did not before possess.

But it is insisted that the unconstitutionality of this rule has been determined by the Supreme Court, which determination is mandatory upon this court. In ascertaining what the Supreme Court has determined, the first guide to judgment is the consideration of the case that the Supreme Court had before them. If the case before them defines the limits of their opinion, that Court has not decided the case before us. The case decided by the Supreme Court was the case of an existing member of their bar. The case before us is the case of the application of parties for admission to the bar. The case in the Supreme Court was a privilege in possession. The case before us is a privilege in prospect. The decision in the Supreme Court involved a dismemberment from the bar. The decision here involves admission to the bar. It may be said of the case in the Supreme Court that the pardon of the President, so far as the legal disabilities of Garland were concerned, removed them. It cannot be said that a similar pardon in the case before us would create the privilege. If the law expounded by the majority of the Supreme Court is simply an exposition of the case they had before them, it is not analogous with the case at bar; and it may be well questioned whether it would be authority beyond the limits of the legitimate issue presented. Outside of the issue, at most, it could only be considered as the expression of opinion by eminent judges.

The question remaining to be considered in this connection is, conceding the decision of the Supreme Court to be in point, whether it is mandatory upon the judgment of this court. This question is to be determined by the legal relation of this tribunal to that. To make their decision mandatory upon the judgment of this court in the strict definition of their authority, they must have the power to execute it upon the deliberation of this court. The only power they possess in this behalf is given by act of Congress, and regulated by the right of appeal, and confessedly does not extend to the subject under consideration. If there was any doubt upon this point, that doubt has been removed·by the repeated decisions of that eminent tribunal. In *ex parte* Burr, 9 Wheaton, 529, Chief Justice Marshall, delivering the opinion of the Court, said:

"On one hand the profession of an attorney is of great importance to an individual, and the prosperity of his whole life may depend on its exercise. The right to exercise it ought not to be lightly or capriciously taken from him. On the other hand it is extremely desirable that the respectability of the bar should be maintained, and that its harmony with the bench should be preserved. For these objects some controlling power, some discretion, ought to reside in the court."

"This discretion ought to be exercised with great moderation and judgment, but it must be exercised; and no other tribunal can decide in a case of removal from the bar with the same means of information as the court itself. If there be a revising tribunal, which possesses controlling authority, that tribunal will always feel the delicacy of interposing its authority, and would do so only in a plain case."

In *ex parte* John L. Tillinghast, 4 Peters, 108, the Court said:

"When, on a former occasion, a *mandamus* was applied for to restore Mr. Tillinghast to the roll of counsellors to the district court, this Court refused to interfere with the matter, not considering the same within their cognizance."

And in *ex parte* Secomb, 19 Howard, page 13, Chief Justice Taney said:

"In the case of Tillinghast *vs.* Conkling, which came before this Court in January term, 1829, a similar motion was overruled by the Court. The case is not reported to the Court, but a brief written opinion remains on the files of the Court, in which the Court says that the motion is overruled upon the ground that it had not jurisdiction in the case. The removal of the attorney and counsellor in that case took place in a district court of the United States, exercising the power of a circuit court in a court of that character, and the relations between the court and the attorneys and counsellors who practise in it, and their respective rights and duties, are regulated by the common law; and it has been well settled by the common rules and practice of the common law courts that it rests *exclusively* with the court to determine who is qualified to become one of its officers as an attorney and counsellor, and for what cause he ought to be removed."

After these repeated decisions this question may be said to be *res judicata.*

The inherent right of each court to regulate its own rules of practice, including the terms of admission of attorneys to and dismissions from the bar, has come down to us unquestioned through the long life of the common law. With regard to this court, and its inherent power of making its rules of admission to and dismission from the bar, Congress, the law-maker of this court, has not only confirmed the common law power of the court, hitherto deemed almost necessary to the existence of the court, but made it the duty of the court, in the organic act of its creation, to exercise that power, leaving the court in its discretion the sole tribunal to pass upon the question, subject only to the penalty of impeachment for the abuse of the power. These considerations are conclusive of the assumption that the opinion referred to is authority with this court. While we deny to this decision of the Supreme Court the office of such authority, we acknowledge the potency of that tribunal as the instructor of judgment, and if it had united its great wisdom in the pronunciation of opinion invalidating the rule in controversy we should feel disposed to bow to it.

But it comes to us as advisory, and we must receive it upon the conditions upon which it is sent. These conditions in the way of advice are that a majority of one of that Court counsels the condemnation of the rule, while a minority of one less than the majority counsels its support, leaving this court to form its own opinion without any substantial aid from the decision.

If we were to adopt the conclusion of the majority, it would be at the expense of condemning a law of Congress in defiance of the rule of judgment already referred to, and substantially upon the opinion of a single justice of the Supreme Court, for the judgment, after all, weighed in the balance, is reduced to the opinion of one justice, a result, however binding, not very impressive of wisdom when applied to the condemnation of a law.

In January term, 1835, the Supreme Court, through Chief Justice Marshall, refused to take up the cases of the Mayor of New York *vs.* George Miln and George Bricer *vs.* the Commonwealth's Bank of Kentucky (9 Peters, 85) because the Court was "not full," in consequence of the resignation of Justice Duvall.

This controversy of judicial opinion, largely attributable to political excitement, demonstrates to our judgment that the question in controversy is so involved with political considerations as to render it eminently proper that it should be referred back to the political power of the nation, and the law-making power which created it be consulted in its modification or repeal.

Without suggesting what would be our judgment as to the modification of the rule, or whether any, let it be sufficient to say that it is a question for legislation, and not for adjudication. The motions are denied.

## JUDGE WYLIE'S OPINION.

Matter of the application of Allen B. Magruder to be admitted to the bar of the supreme court of the District of Columbia.

Also, motion made by Mr. Bradley, that said court rescind its rule requiring applicants for admission to the bar to take the oath commonly called the test-oath, prescribed and adopted 23d March, 1863.

This application and this motion, though in some respects distinct subjects, have been argued together.

I shall first proceed to consider the motion to rescind our rule.

By the act of the 3d March, 1863, the late circuit court and the late criminal court of this District were abolished, and their powers and jurisdiction transferred to the supreme court of the District of Columbia, which was established by the same act. That act also conferred upon this court full power to make all rules which it might think proper relating to the practice of the court.

At the first meeting of the new court, held on the 23d of March, 1863, it was ordered that all applicants for admission to the bar should take and subscribe, as a condition of their admission, the oath, which the judges had themselves voluntarily taken, prescribed by the act of Congress approved July 2, 1862.

That act is in the following words:

"That hereafter every person elected or appointed to any office of honor or profit under the Government of the United States, either in the civil, military, or naval department of the public service, excepting the President of the United States, shall, before entering upon the duties of such office, and before being entitled to any of the salary or other emoluments thereof, take and subscribe the following oath or affirmation: 'I, A B, do solemnly swear (or affirm) that I have never voluntarily borne arms against the United States since I have been a citizen thereof; that I have voluntarily given no aid, countenance, counsel, or encouragement to persons engaged in armed hostility thereto; that I have neither sought nor accepted nor attempted to exercise the functions of any office whatever, under any authority or pretended authority, in hostility to the United States; that I have not yielded a voluntary support to any pretended government, authority, power, or constitution within the United States hostile or inimical thereto; and I do further swear (or affirm) that, to the best of my knowledge and ability, I will support and defend the Constitution of the United States against all enemies, foreign or domestic; that I will bear true faith and allegiance to the same; that I take this obligation freely, without any mental reservation or purpose of evasion, and that I will well and faithfully discharge the duties of the office on which I am about to enter; so help me God."

This oath has been taken and subscribed by every one who has since been admitted to the bar of this court.

The act, however, was not of itself obligatory upon the court or any of its officers, but only upon persons in the civil, military, or naval departments of the public service.

But we were in the midst of a terrible civil war; surrounded by a large population, many of whom were, in sentiment at least, disloyal to the Government; we were a court created by the United States, to stand if it stood, and be destroyed if it were overthrown; we were at the capital of the nation, and yet in sight of the armed forces of the rebellion. Treason walked our very streets defiantly, and encouraged its partisans amongst us with the promise of a speedy triumph of the rebellion.

It was at a time like this that the court felt

Itself called upon to exert its whole power to exclude the traitors to their country from admission to the bar of one of that country's courts, and we ordained the rule which we now have under consideration.

Its constitutionality was not then called in question, nor was its propriety doubted.

The office of attorney at law is one known to the common law, and with us is regulated in part by that law, partly by several acts of the Assembly of Maryland yet in force in this District, and partly by the act of Congress of 3d March, 1863, creating this court. The English statutes relating to attorneys at law are not in force here.

At common law no one was allowed to practice law in any court till after examination and admission, and every court possessed the exclusive power of prescribing the qualifications and conditions for admission to its bar. Blackstone says:

"No one can practice as an attorney in any of the courts of Westminster Hall but such as is admitted and sworn an attorney of that particular court; an attorney of the court of king's bench cannot practice in the common pleas, nor *vice versa.*"

The statute of Maryland of April, 1715 ch. 41, sec. 2, conferred upon the courts of that State full powers to make "such rules and orders from time to time for the well-governing and regulating the said courts, and the officers and suitors thereof, as to the courts, in their discretion, shall seem meet."

By another act of Maryland of the same year and month, ch. 48, sec. 12, the justices of the courts of that State were invested with authority to admit and to suspend attorneys at the bar without qualification or restriction, (*salvo jure coronæ*,) except that no court should admit any attorney to its bar without requiring of him the oath of allegiance prescribed by the act of Parliament, passed in the 6th of Queen Ann, entitled "An act for the security of her majesty's person and government, and of the succession to the crown of Great Britain in the Protestant line."

These acts, though more than a hundred and fifty years old, are still the law of this District, except that the Government of the United States has succeeded to the allegiance which was formerly sworn to the queen of Great Britain; and our rule has furnished a fitting substitute for that oath, accommodated to the changes of governments which have taken place in this country since the reign of Queen Ann.

Being that as a court of the United States, vested with full power to establish our own rules for the admission of members to the bar, and for governing and regulating the court and the officers and suitors thereof, without accountability to any other court, it would seem that we should ourselves be the ultimate judges of all the law upon these subjects. And, in my judgment, this principle has been affirmed and settled by the Supreme Court of the United States in Secomb's case, 19 Howard R., 9.

It is not to be inferred from this, however, that we are at liberty, in regard to these matters, to transgress against the Constitution of the United States at our pleasure. On the contrary, it is the sworn obligation and duty of the court faithfully to support that Constitution. As it regards the question of the constitutionality of our test-rule, it is not my intention to discuss that subject on this occasion. I have as yet heard no arguments which have disturbed my original convictions on that point.

The recent decision of the Supreme Court of the United States in Garland's case has been made the occasion of the present motion, and has been cited as settling the question against the rule. But I do not so understand that decision. On the contrary, it seems to my apprehension plainly inapplicable to the case under consideration. In compliance with the act of Congress of January 24, 1865, the Supreme Court had adopted a rule to carry out the provisions of that act, which were as follows: "That no person, after the date of this act, shall be admitted to the bar of the Supreme Court of the United States, or at any time after the 4th of March next shall be admitted to the bar of any circuit or district court of the United States, or of the Court of Claims, as an attorney or counsellor of such court, or shall be allowed to appear and be heard in any such court by virtue of any previous admission, or any special power of attorney, unless he shall have first taken the oath prescribed in an act to prescribe an oath of office, and for other purposes, approved July 2, 1862, according to the forms and in the manner in the said act prescribed."

Garland had been admitted an attorney and counsellor of that Court at the December term, 1860. He subsequently committed treason against the United States by taking part in the late rebellion, but was pardoned by the President. He then presented his petition to the Court, asking permission to appear and continue to practice there under his admission of 1860 and the pardon of the President, without being required to make the oath prescribed by the act of January 24, 1865, and the rule of court made in pursuance of said act. The decision of the Court was that his application should be granted; and the grounds of this decision were, that the pardon granted by the President had blotted out the sins of his rebellion, as though they had never been committed, and that being thus innocent of all offence in the eye of the law, he could not be a proper subject for punishment, or of exclusion from the privileges of the court, which had formerly belonged to him.

Mr. Justice Field, who delivered the opinion of the Court, says: "The effect of this pardon is to relieve the petitioner from all penalties and disabilities attached to the offence of treason committed by his participation in the rebellion. So far as that offence is concerned, he is thus placed beyond the reach of punishment of any kind; but to exclude him, by reason of that offence, from continuing in the enjoyment of a *previously acquired right,* is to enforce a punishment for that offence notwithstanding the pardon."

I can have no controversy with the Supreme Court as to that doctrine. It merely teaches that Garland, having been already admitted to the bar before the commencement of the war, and having received perfect absolution for his offences committed during the rebellion, he was not subject to the operation of either the act of

Congress or the rule of the court any otherwise than one who had been loyal to the Government throughout the war.

The facts in Garland's case required the Court to go no farther than this, but the opinion does go farther, and pronounces, in effect, that Garland would have been entitled to continue to practice in that Court, even without having been pardoned by the President for his treason, on the ground that to deprive him of the right to pursue his profession in that Court would have been a penalty inflicted for his offence, to which he was not liable at the time of its commission.

Although there is one passage in this opinion which seems to go even beyond this, and to advance the doctrine that the Court had no right to debar a man from admission to the profession on account of crimes previously committed, yet I am not disposed to believe that the Court intended to advance or to advocate, even *obiter*, a doctrine so extreme as that. If such, however, be the fair construction of the opinion, (and nothing short of such construction will answer the object of either of the motions now under our consideration,) I am constrained to avow my unwillingness to obey the doctrine thus promulged.

In the first place, the facts in the case of Garland called for no such decision; and, in the second place, having the absolute right ourselves to prescribe our own rules for admission to the bar, as has been already shown, we are not required to do violence to our convictions, in following such an interpretation of the Constitution, when given even by the eminent justices who concurred in that opinion. The opinion, in that respect, not coming to us with mandatory authority, I must for myself be permitted to look upon it only as the opinion of five gentlemen, learned in the law, weighed against the contrary opinion of the four other gentlemen, equally learned and able, and against the judgment of the whole legislative branch of the Government, by which the law was enacted; and whilst I acknowledge the importance of the principle that *res adjudicata pro veritate accipitur*, yet in this matter I am at perfect liberty to test the opinion of these five gentlemen by the application of that other maxim of the law, *testimonia ponderanda sunt, non numeranda*. Tried by this test, it appears to me that the preponderance of authority is not on the side of the doctrine of the Court's opinion on this point. In Fletcher *vs.* Peck, 6 Cranch, 87, Chief Justice Marshall says: "The question whether a law be void for its repugnancy to the Constitution is at all times a question of much delicacy, which ought seldom, if ever, to be decided in the affirmative in a doubtful case."

I am of the opinion, therefore, that the decision of the Supreme Court in Garland's case, even if received as authority and interpreted in its widest latitude, falls far short of requiring us to declare our rule void for unconstitutionality. Our rule applies only to persons not yet admitted to the bar, and who, therefore, possess no "previously acquired right" of which its enforcement can deprive them.

The rule of the Supreme Court was different from ours. It required persons already members of that bar to take the oath, under penalty of forfeiture of their "previously acquired right." Ours has no such operation.

It is true that one branch of the rule of the Supreme Court applied, like ours, also to persons asking for admission to that bar, and we are told that the rule has been wholly rescinded —no part of it preserved—in consequence of the decision in Garland's case. This may be true, but we have received no judicial evidence to convince our minds of the fact, and if it has been done, it must have been for other reasons than those furnished by the opinion of the court in that case.

In respect to the application of Magruder, the case is this: He is a native of Virginia, but for several years previous to the rebellion was a citizen of the United States, having his domicile in this District, and was a member of the bar of the late circuit court of this District. In April or May, 1861, he left us, and entered into the rebellion on the call of Virginia, and continued until the close of the war in armed hostility to the United States.

He has since received the pardon of the President for his offence, and been admitted to practice in the Supreme Court of the United States since the decision in Garland's case was made.

But the fatal objection to his admission to our bar is that he is now only applying for admission for the first time, and cannot furnish the requisite evidence of a previously acquired right whose *continued enjoyment* he might demand at the hands of the court, and is unable to take the oath required by our rule.

In his case, too, there is an additional reason, of great force in our judgment, which forbids his admission, and it is this: On being admitted to the bar of the late circuit court, he was sworn, among other things, "to support the Constitution of the United States," and should he be admitted to practice in the bar of this court, would be required to take the same oath again. This oath has a meaning, and was prescribed for an object. We understand that it requires him who takes it to support the Constitution of the United States as the supreme law of the land, in all cases in which its provisions come into conflict with the constitution or laws of any of the States, and in this sense to require a primary and paramount allegiance to the Government of the United States.

Mr. Magruder has told us that in taking up arms against the United States he acted conscientiously, and indignantly repels the imputation that he had violated his oath to support the Constitution. He says that he regarded himself as under "duality of allegiance;" that his first and paramount allegiance was due to his native State, and his secondary and subordinate allegiance was due to the United States; and that it was in this belief, honestly entertained, he went into the rebellion, in obedience to the call of his State, although he was himself of the opinion that the rebellion was without any just cause.

He acknowledges to have had no change of opinion on these points to the present hour.

Were we now, with a full knowledge of these facts, to admit him to take this oath, the ceremony would be a meaningless farce; we should swear him in one sense, whilst he would take the oath in another.

It would be well, perhaps, that our rule on this subject should be so amended as to enable gentlemen whose native States may hereafter rush into rebellion without just cause to see at once the path of their duty, and so relieve their consciences from any embarrassments originating in fanciful theories about a "duality of allegiance."

## Opinion of the Supreme Court on the Mississippi Application for an Injunction against the President and other officers, April 15, 1867.

Chief Justice CHASE delivered the opinion of the Court, as follows:

A motion was made some days since on behalf of the State of Mississippi, for leave to file a bill in the name of the State, praying this Court perpetually to enjoin and restrain Andrew Johnson, President of the United States, and E. O. C. Ord, general commanding in the district of Mississipi and Arkansas, from executing or in any manner carrying out certain acts of Congress therein named.

The acts referred to are those of March 2 and March 25, 1867, commonly called the reconstruction acts.

The Attorney General objected to the leave asked for upon the ground that no bill which makes the President a defendant and seeks an injunction against him to restrain the performance of his duties as President, should be allowed to be filed in this Court.

This point has been fully argued, and we will now dispose of it.

We shall limit our inquiry to the question presented by the objection, without expressing any opinion on the broader issues discussed in argument, whether in any case the President of the United States may be required by the process of this Court to perform a purely ministerial act required by law, or may be held answerable, in any case, otherwise than by impeachment, for crime.

The single point which requires consideration is this: Can the President be restrained from carrying into effect an act of Congress alleged to be unconstitutional?

It is assumed by the counsel for the State of Mississippi that the President, in the execution of the reconstruction acts, is required to perform a mere ministerial duty. In this assumption there is, we think, a confounding of the terms "ministerial" and "executive," which are by no means equivalent in import.

A ministerial duty, the performance of which may in proper cases be required of the head of a department by judicial process, is one in respect to which nothing is left to discretion. It is a simple, definite duty, arising under conditions admitted or proved to exist or imposed by law.

The case of Marbury vs. Madison, Secretary of State, furnishes an illustration. A citizen had been nominated, confirmed, and appointed a justice of the peace for the District of Columbia, and his commission had been made out, signed, and sealed. Nothing remained to be done except delivery, and the duty of delivery was imposed by law on the Secretary of State. It was held

that the performance of this duty might be enforced by mandamus issued from a court having jurisdiction.

So in the case of Kendall, Postmaster General, vs. Stockton and Stokes, (12 Peters, 527.) An act of Congress had directed the Postmaster General to credit Stockton and Stokes with such sums as the Solicitor of the Treasury should find due to them, and that officer refused to credit them with certain sums so found due. It was held that the crediting of this money was a mere ministerial duty, the performance of which might be judicially enforced.

In each of these cases nothing was left to discretion. There was no room for the exercise of judgment. The law required the performance of a single specific act; and that performance, it was held, might be required by mandamus.

Very different is the duty of the President in the exercise of the power to see that the laws are faithfully executed, and among those laws the acts named in the bill. By the first of these acts he is required to assign generals to command in the several military districts, and to detail sufficient military force to enable such officers to discharge their duties under the law. By the supplementary act other duties are imposed on the several commanding generals, and their duties must necessarily be performed under the supervision of the President, as Commander-in-Chief. The duty thus imposed on the President is in no just sense ministerial. It is purely executive and political.

An attempt on the part of the judicial department of the Government to enjoin the performance of such duties by the President might be justly characterized, in the language of Chief Justice Marshall, as "an absurd and excessive extravagance."

It is true that in the instance before us the interposition of the Court is not sought to enforce action by the Executive under constitutional legislation, but to restrain such action under legislation alleged to be unconstitutional.

But we are unable to perceive that this circumstance takes the case out of the general principle which forbids judicial interference with the exercise of executive discretion.

It was admitted in the argument that the application now made to us is without a precedent, and this is of much weight against it. Had it been supposed at the bar that this Court would in any case interpose to arrest the execution of an unconstitutional act of Congress, it can hardly be doubted that applications with that object would have been heretofore addressed to it. Occasions have not been infrequent.

The constitutionality of the act for the annexation of Texas was vehemently denied. It made important and permanent changes in the relative importance of States and sections, and was by many supposed to be pregnant with disastrous results to large interests in particular States. But no one seems to have thought of an application for an injunction against the execution of the act by the President.

And yet it is difficult to perceive upon what principle the application now before us can be allowed, and similar applications in that and other cases could have been denied.

The fact that no such application was ever before made in any case indicates the general judgment of the profession that no such application should be entertained.

It will hardly be contended that Congress can interpose, in any case, to restrain the enactment of an unconstitutional law, and yet how can the right to judicial interposition to prevent such an enactment, when the purpose is evident and the execution of that purpose certain, be distinguished in principle from the right to such interposition against the execution of such a law by the President?

The Congress is the legislative department of the Government; the President is the executive department. Neither can be restrained in its action by the judicial department, though the acts of both, when performed, are in proper cases subject to its cognizance.

The impropriety of such interference will be clearly seen upon consideration of its probable consequences.

Suppose the bill filed and the injunction prayed for be allowed. If the President refuse obedience, it is needless to observe that the Court is without power to enforce its process. If, on the other hand, the President complies with the order of the Court, and refuses to execute the act of Congress, is it not clear that a collision may occur between the executive and legislative departments of the Government? May not the House of Representatives impeach the President for such refusal? And in that case could this Court interpose in behalf of the President, thus endangered by compliance with its mandate, and restrain by injunction the Senate of the United States from sitting as a court of impeachment? Would the strange spectacle be offered to the public wonder of an attempt by this Court to arrest proceedings in that court?

These questions answer themselves. It is true that a State may file an original bill in this Court; and it may be true, in some cases, such a bill may be filed against the United States. But we are fully satisfied that this Court has no jurisdiction of a bill to enjoin the President in the performance of his official duties, and that no such bill ought to be received by us.

It has been suggested that the bill contains a prayer that if the relief sought cannot be had against Andrew Johnson as President, it may be granted against Andrew Johnson as a citizen of Tennessee. But it is plain that relief against the execution of an act of Congress by Andrew Johnson is relief against its execution by the President. A bill praying an injunction against the execution of an act of Congress by the incumbent of the presidential office cannot be received, whether it describes him as President or simply as a citizen of a State. The motion for leave to file the bill is therefore denied.

In the case of The State of Georgia against certain officers, the Attorney General makes no objection to the policy of the bill, and we will, therefore, grant leave to file that bill.

Mr. Sharkey. If the Court please, the objection to the bill which I attempted to file seems to be that it is an effort to enjoin the President. The bill is not filed, and I can reform it to suit the views of the Court, and present it again.

The Chief Justice. Leave to file the bill is refused. When another bill is presented it will be considered.

Mr. Sharkey. Do I understand the Court to say that the application can be made on Thursday?

The Chief Justice. On Thursday.

This subpoena was issued in the case, April 16, 1867:

The State of Georgia, complainant *vs.* Edwin M. Stanton, Ulysses S. Grant, and John Pope, defendants. In equity.

*The President of the United States to Edwin M. Stanton, Ulysses S. Grant, and John Pope, greeting:*

For certain causes offered before the Supreme Court of the United States, holding jurisdiction in equity, you are hereby commanded that, laying all other matters aside, and notwithstanding any excuse, you be and appear before the said Supreme Court, holding jurisdiction in equity, on the first Monday in December next, at the city of Washington, in the District of Columbia, being the present seat of the National Government of the United States, to answer unto the bill of complaint of the State of Georgia in the said Court exhibited against you. Hereof you are not to fail at your peril.

Witness: The Honorable SALMON P. CHASE, Chief Justice of the said Supreme Court, at the city of Washington, the first Monday of December, in the year of our Lord one thousand eight hundred and sixty-six, and of the Independence of the United States of America the ninety-first.

D. W. MIDDLETON,
*Clerk of the Supreme Court of the U. S.*

---

# XXI.

# RESOLUTIONS OF NATIONAL AND STATE CONVENTIONS.

**Of the Philadelphia Fourteenth of August Convention.**

They were reported August 17th, by Hon. Edgar Cowan, chairman of the committee on resolutions, and were unanimously adopted:

DECLARATION OF PRINCIPLES.

The National Union Convention, now assembled in the city of Philadelphia, composed of delegates from every State and Territory in the Union, admonished by the solemn lessons which, for the last five years, it has pleased the Supreme Ruler of the Universe to give to the American people; profoundly grateful for the return of peace; desirous, as are a large majority of their countrymen, in all sincerity, to forget and forgive the past; revering the Constitution as it comes to us from our ancestors; regarding the Union in its restoration as more sacred than ever; looking with deep anxiety into the future, as of instant and continuing trials, hereby issues and proclaims the following declaration of principles and purposes, on which they have, with perfect unanimity, agreed:

1. We hail with gratitude to Almighty God the end of the war and the return of peace to our afflicted and beloved land

2. The war just closed has maintained the authority of the Constitution, with all the powers which it confers, and all the restrictions which it imposes upon the General Government, unabridged and unaltered, and it has preserved the Union, with the equal rights, dignity, and authority of the States perfect and unimpaired.

3. Representation in the Congress of the United States and in the electoral college is a right recognized by the Constitution as abiding in every State, and as a duty imposed upon the people, fundamental in its nature, and essential to the existence of our republican institutions, and neither Congress nor the General Government has any authority or power to deny this right to any State or to withhold its enjoyment under the Constitution from the people thereof.

4. We call upon the people of the United States to elect to Congress as members thereof none but men who admit this fundamental right of representation, and who will receive to seats therein loyal representatives from every State in allegiance to the United States, subject to the constitutional right of each House to judge of the elections, returns, and qualifications of its own members.

5. The Constitution of the United States, and the laws made in pursuance thereof, are the supreme law of the land, anything in the constitution or laws of any State to the contrary notwithstanding. All the powers not conferred by the Constitution upon the General Government, nor prohibited by it to the States, are reserved to the States, or to the people thereof; and among the rights thus reserved to the States is the right to prescribe qualifications for the elective franchise therein, with which right Congress cannot interfere. No State or combination of States has the right to withdraw from the Union, or to exclude, through their action in Congress or otherwise, any other State or States from the Union. The Union of these States is perpetual.

6. Such amendments to the Constitution of the United States may be made by the people thereof as they may deem expedient, but only in the mode pointed out by its provisions; and in proposing such amendments, whether by Congress or by a convention, and in ratifying the same, all the States of the Union have an equal and an indefeasible right to a voice and a vote thereon.

7. Slavery is abolished and forever prohibited, and there is neither desire nor purpose on the part of the southern States that it should ever be re-established upon the soil, or within the jurisdiction of the United States; and the enfranchised slaves in all the States of the Union should receive, in common with all their inhabitants, equal protection in every right of person and property.

8. While we regard as utterly invalid, and never to be assumed or made of binding force, any obligations incurred or undertaken in making war against the United States, we hold the debt of the nation to be sacred and inviolable; and we proclaim our purpose in discharging this, as in performing all other national obligations, to maintain unimpaired and unimpeached the honor and the faith of the Republic.

9. It is the duty of the national Government to recognize the services of the Federal soldiers and sailors in the contest just closed, by meeting promptly and fully all their just and rightful claims for the services they have rendered the nation, and by extending to those of them who have survived, and to the widows and orphans of those who have fallen, the most generous and considerate care.

10. In Andrew Johnson, President of the United States, who, in his great office, has proved steadfast in his devotion to the Constitution, the laws, and interests of his country, unmoved by persecution and undeserved reproach, having faith unassailable in the people and in the principles of free government, we recognize a Chief Magistrate worthy of the nation, and equal to the great crisis upon which his lot is cast; and we tender to him in the discharge of his high and responsible duties, our profound respect and assurance of our cordial and sincere support.

## Of the Philadelphia Convention of Southern Loyalists.

They were reported by Hon. Andrew J. Hamilton, of Texas, chairman of the committee on resolutions, and unanimously adopted:

1. That the loyal people of the South cordially unite with the people of the North in thanksgiving to Almighty God, through whose will a rebellion unparalleled for its causelessness, its cruelty, and its criminality has been overruled to the vindication of the supremacy of the Federal Constitution over every State and Territory of the Republic.

2. That we demand now, as we have demanded at all times since the cessation of hostilities, the restoration of the States in which we live to their old relations with the Union, on the simplest and fewest conditions consistent with the protection of our lives, property, and political rights, now in jeopardy from the unquenched enmity of rebels lately in arms.

3. That the unhappy policy pursued by Andrew Johnson, President of the United States, is, in its effects upon the loyal people of the South, unjust, oppressive, and intolerable; and accordingly, however ardently we desire to see our respective States once more represented in the Congress of the nation, we would deplore their restoration on the inadequate conditions prescribed by the President, as tending not to abate, but only to magnify the perils and sorrows of our condition.

4. That with pride in the patriotism of the Congress, with gratitude for the fearless and persistent support they have given to the cause of loyalty, and their efforts to restore all the States to their former condition as States in the American Union, we will stand by the positions taken by them, and use all means consistent with a

peaceful and lawful course to secure the ratification of the amendments to the Constitution of the United States, as proposed by the Congress at its recent session, and regret that the Congress, in its wisdom, did not provide by law for the greater security of the loyal people in the States not yet admitted to representation.

5. That the political power of the Government of the United States in the administration of public affairs, is, by its Constitution, confided to the popular or law-making department of the Government.

6. That the political status of the States lately in rebellion to the United States Government, and the rights of the people of such States, are political questions, and are therefore clearly within the control of Congress to the exclusion of the independent action of any and every other department of the Government.

7. That there is no right, political, legal, or constitutional, in any State to secede or withdraw from the Union; that they may, by wicked and unauthorized revolution and force, sever the relations which they have sustained to the Union; and when they do so. and assume the attitude of public enemies at war with the United States, they subject themselves to all the rules and principles of international law, and the laws which are applicable to belligerents, according to modern usage.

8. That we are unalterably in favor of the Union of the States, and earnestly desire the legal and speedy restoration of all the States to their proper places in the Union and the establishment in each of them of influences of patriotism and justice by which the whole nation shall be combined to carry forward triumphantly the principles of freedom and progress, until all men of all races shall everywhere beneath the flag of our country have accorded to them freely all that their virtues, intelligence, industry, patriotism and energy may entitle them to attain.

9. That the organizations of the unrepresented States, assuming to be State governments, not having been legally established, are not legitimate governments until reorganized by Congress.

10. That the welcome we have received from the loyal citizens of Philadelphia, under the roof of the time-honored Hall in which the Declaration of Independence was adopted, inspires us with an animating hope that the principles of just and equal government, which were made the foundation of the Republic at its origin, shall become the corner-stone of reconstruction.

11. That we cherish with tender hearts the memory of the virtues, patriotism, sublime faith, upright Christian life, and generous nature of the martyr President, Abraham Lincoln.

12. That we are in favor of universal liberty the world over, and feel the deepest sympathy with the oppressed peoples of all countries in their struggles for freedom and the inherent right of all men to decide and control for themselves the character of the government under which they live.

13. That the lasting gratitude of the nation is due the men who bore the hardships of the battle, and, in covering themselves with imperishable glory, have saved to the world its hope of free government; and relying upon the "invincible soldiers and sailors" who made the grand army and navy of the Republic to be true to the principles for which they fought, we pledge them that we will stand by them in maintaining the honor due the saviors of the nation, and in securing the fruits of their victories.

14. That, remembering with profound gratitude and love the precepts of Washington, we should accustom ourselves to consider the Union as the primary object of our patriotic desire, which has heretofore sustained us with great power in our love of the Union, when so many of our neighbors in the South were waging war for its destruction; our deep and abiding love for the memory of the Father of his Country and for the Union is more deeply engraven upon our hearts than ever.

After the adjournment of this convention, the loyalists of the non-reconstructed States met and adopted an address, closing with this declaration:

"We affirm that the loyalists of the South look to Congress with affectionate gratitude and confidence, as the only means to save us from persecution, exile, and death itself; and we also declare that there can be no security for us or our children; there can be no safety for the country against the fell spirit of slavery, now organized in the form of serfdom, unless the Government, by national and appropriate legislation, enforced by national authority, shall confer on every citizen in the States we represent the American birthright of impartial suffrage and equality before the law. This is the one all-sufficient remedy. This is our great need and pressing necessity."

The vote was as follows: TEXAS, 10 yeas; LOUISIANA, 14 yeas; VIRGINIA, 28 yeas, 3 nays; GEORGIA, 8 yeas, 1 nay; ALABAMA, 2 yeas, 3 nays; MISSISSIPPI, 1 yea; ARKANSAS, 2 yeas; NORTH CAROLINA, 1 yea, 2 nays; FLORIDA, 2 yeas, 1 nay.

## Pittsburgh Convention of Soldiers and Sailors, September 26, 1866.

General Benjamin F. Butler reported these resolutions, which were adopted unanimously:

By the soldiers and sailors of the army and navy of the United States, in convention assembled, be it

*Resolved,* That the action of the present Congress in passing the pending constitutional amendment is wise, prudent, just. It clearly defines American citizenship, and guaranties all his rights to every citizen. It places on a just and equal basis the right of representation, making the vote of a man in one State equally potent with the vote of another man in any State. It righteously excludes from places of honor and trust the chief conspirators, guiltiest rebels, whose perjured crimes have drenched the land in fraternal blood. It puts into the very frame of our Government the inviolability of the national debt and the nullity forever of all obligations contracted in support of the rebellion.

2. That it is unfortunate for the country that these propositions have not been received in the spirit of conciliation, clemency, and fraternal feeling in which they were offered, as they are the mildest terms ever granted to subdued rebels.

3. That the President, as an executive officer,

has no right to a policy as against the legislative department of the Government; that his attempt to fasten his scheme of reconstruction upon the country is as dangerous as it is unwise; his acts in sustaining it have retarded the restoration of peace and unity; they have converted conquered rebels into impudent claimants to rights which they have forfeited, and places which they have desecrated. If consummated, it would render the sacrifices of the nation useless, the loss of the lives of our buried comrades vain, and the war in which we have so gloriously triumphed, what his present friends at Chicago in 1864 declared to be a failure.

4. That the right of the conqueror to legislate for the conquered has been recognized by the public law of all civilized nations; by the operation of that law for the conservation of the good of the whole country, Congress has the undoubted right to establish measures for the conduct of the revolted States, and to pass all acts of legislation that are necessary for the complete restoration of the Union.

5. That when the President claims that by the aid of the army and navy he might have made himself dictator, he insulted every soldier and sailor in the Republic. He ought distinctly to understand that the tried patriots of this nation can never be used to overthrow civil liberty or popular government.

6. That the neutrality laws should be so amended as to give the fullest liberty to the citizen consistent with the national faith; that the great Union Republican party is pledged to sustain liberty and equality of rights everywhere, and therefore we tender to all peoples struggling for freedom our sympathy and cordial co-operation.

7. That the Union men of the South, without distinction of race or color, are entitled to the gratitude of every loyal soldier and sailor who served his country in suppressing the rebellion, and that in their present dark hours of trial, when they are being persecuted by thousands, solely because they are now, and have been, true to the Government, we will not prove recreant to our obligations, but will stand by and protect with our lives, if necessary, those brave men who remain true to us when all around are false and faithless.

8. That in reorganizing the Army justice to the volunteer officers and soldiers demands that faithful and efficient service in the field ought ever to have place in the army and navy of the Union.

### Cleveland Convention of Soldiers and Sailors, September 18, 1866.

Col. L. D. CAMPBELL reported these resolutions, which were adopted unanimously:

The Union soldiers and sailors who served in the army and navy of the United States in the recent war for the suppression of the insurrection, the maintenance of the Constitution, the Government, and the flag of the Union, grateful to Almighty God for His preservation of them through the perils and hardships of war, and for His mercy in crowning their efforts with victory, freedom, and peace; deploring the absence from their midst of many brave and faithful comrades who had sealed with their life-blood their devotion to the sacred cause of American nationality, and determined now as heretofore, to stand by the principles for which their glorious dead have fallen, and by which the survivors have triumphed, being assembled in National Mass Convention in the city of Cleveland, Ohio, this 17th day of September, 1866, do resolve and declare—

1. That we heartily approve the resolutions adopted by the National Union Convention held in the city of Philadelphia, on the 14th day of August last, composed of delegates representing all the States and Territories of the United States.

2. That our object in taking up arms to suppress the late rebellion was to defend and maintain the supremacy of the Constitution, and to preserve the Union with all the dignity, equality, and rights of the several States unimpaired, and not in any spirit of oppression, nor for any purpose of conquest and subjugation; and that whenever there shall be any armed resistance to the lawfully constituted authorities of our national Union, either in the South or in the North, in the East or in the West, emulating the self-sacrificing patriotism of our revolutionary forefathers, we will again pledge to its support "our lives, our fortunes, and our sacred honor."

## STATE CONVENTIONS, 1867.

### Connecticut.

#### REPUBLICAN, JANUARY 24.

1. That the result of the elections of the last autumn affords new proof of the devotion of the American people to the fundamental principles of free government, and of their determination to establish and confirm a Union based upon those principles only; that we congratulate each other and the country upon that auspicious result, and pledge ourselves that Connecticut, in this respect, shall emulate the example of her loyal sister States.

2. That the pending amendment to the Federal Constitution, in the generous magnanimity of the terms which it proposed to the late insurgents, deserved and should have received their grateful recognition; that its rejection by them proceeds from a still prevailing spirit of rebellion, and imposes upon the national authority the duty of establishing the Union upon none other than just and durable foundations; that, in so doing, loyalty to the Republic should be recognized as the first of political virtues, and disloyalty as the worst of political crimes, and that the protection of all citizens throughout the Republic in the exercise of all the rights and immunities guarantied by the Constitution should be inviolably secured.

3. That the only just basis of human governments is the consent of the governed; that, in a representative republic, such a consent is expressed through the exercise of the suffrage by the individual citizen, and that the right to that exercise should not be limited by distinctions of race or color.

4. That in any revision of the revenue system the duties upon imports should be adjusted with a view to the encouragement of American industry, without impairing the public revenue, and

that the burdens now imposed by internal taxation should be alleviated as far as possible, and especially by the reduction of existing taxes upon incomes and sales.

5. That in the administration of State policy we are in favor of a rigid economy in expenditures, and permanent provision for the steady reduction and final payment of the State debt.

6. That the Republican party is identified in its history, and by its essential principles, with the rights, the interests, and the dignity of labor; that by all the record of that history and all the sanctity of those principles it is bound in sympathy with the toiling masses of society, of whom is composed the great proportion of its number, and that the workingmen of Connecticut will receive at its hands every needed legislative remedy of the evils of which they complain.

7. That the present salutary law concerning the employment of children in manufactories and education of such children should be rendered more efficient in its operation and more rigidly enforced.

8. That the Republican party regards with earnest solicitation the struggles of oppressed nationalities toward independence and purer liberty, and that it extends its earnest sympathy to Crete, to Ireland, and to Mexico, in their heroic efforts to liberate themselves from hated foreign dominion.

9. That the so-called Democratic Convention at New Haven, by its malignant spirit of hostility to the Federal authority, its deliberate attempt to renew the horrors of civil war, and its sanction of the treasonable utterances of its more prominent members, deserves, and should receive, the unqualified condemnation of every lover of of the National Union.

10. That a grateful people will never forget or cease to revere the heroic soldiers and sailors who, during the dark days of the rebellion, devoted their strength, their constancy, and their valor to the overthrow of an unholy rebellion, and rescued the country from its peril, and established the Government on the rock of universal liberty.

11. That we heartily recommend to the people of this commonwealth the gentlemen nominated by this Convention for State officers, and pledge ourselves to their cordial support and triumphant election.

### DEMOCRATIC, JANUARY 8.

Whereas, it becomes a free and intelligent people, justly jealous of their rights and liberties, to frankly and fearlessly assert their views upon all great and important public questions; and

Whereas, when armed resistance to the authority of the United States ceased each of the several States that had been in antagonism to the Government became, by the inherent force of the Constitution and the fundamental principles upon which our system of government is based, reinstated and restored to all their rights and privileges; and

Whereas, the Supreme Court of the United States has declared "that if military government is continued after the courts are reinstated, it is a gross usurpation of power. Martial rule can never exist where the courts are open and in the proper and unobstructed exercise of their jurisdiction:" Therefore,

*Resolved,* That each and all of the States that were arrayed in armed opposition to the authority of the Government of the United States, having ceased such opposition, are now entitled to representation in the Congress of the United States, and to all other rights and privileges appertaining to the States of the Union.

2. That the Congress of the United States, in its present exclusion of the Senators and Representatives of said States; in its open and avowed determination to destroy the organization and subvert the authorities of said States, violates and undermines the Constitution of the United States, attacks the very principles that lie at the foundation of our system of government, and strikes a fatal blow at the financial and commercial and industrial interests of the entire people of the Union.

3. That the Congress of the United States, in all its legislation, in its act levying internal taxes upon all the States, including the said States expressly by name; in its act prescribing the number of Representatives in Congress for all the States; in its act in submitting the constitutional amendment abolishing slavery to all the States; in its act of last session, submitting another proposed constitutional amendment to all the States; in its joint resolution, passed with almost entire unanimity, declaring the object of the war to be "to defend and maintain the supremacy of the Constitution, and to preserve the Union with all the dignity, equality and rights of the several States unimpaired;" and in other acts has uniformly, from the commencement of the civil war to the present time, in the most deliberate manner, recognized said States as existing States, and as States in the Union.

4. That the executive department of the United States, by its proclamations, its administrative action, and in its diplomatic intercourse with foreign Powers, has uniformly recognized all the said States as existing States, and as States in the Union.

5. That the judicial department of the United States, including the Supreme Court at Washington, the circuit courts in the several circuits, and the district courts in their respective districts, has uniformly recognized the said States as existing States, and as States in the Union.

6. That this repeated recognition of said States as existing States, and as States in the Union, by the executive, judicial, and legislative departments of the Government, leaves no question that the exclusion of these States from Congress, governing them and taxing them without representation, is not only a violation of the Federal Constitution in its most essential part, and tyranny as defined by the Declaration of Independence, but a most flagrant breach of public faith, alike prejudicial to the best interests and to the honor of the country.

7. That in the Supreme Court of the United States we possess a tribunal that may be justly termed the bulwark of republican liberty, and in the language of its eminent jurists,

"The Constitution of the United States is law for rulers and people, *equally in war and in peace,* and covers with its shield of protection all classes of men under all circumstances." * * "No doctrine involving more pernicious consequences was ever invented by the wit of man, than that any of its provisions can be suspended during any of the great exigencies of government. Such a doctrine leads directly to anarchy or despotism. But the theory of *necessity*, upon which this is based, is *false*, for the government within the Constitution has the powers granted to it which are necessary to preserve its existence."

Thus, the Supreme Court of the United States in 1866, vindicates and sustains the positions assumed and announced by the Democracy of Connecticut in convention in 1863.

8. That after solemn deliberation, it is the opinion of this convention that the suggestion of our conservative brethren of Kentucky, that a convention of the Democracy and all constitutional Union men of the thirty-six States should be called without delay by the National Democratic Committee; and we respectfully suggest that said convention meet in the city of New York on the 4th day of March next, to advise and counsel upon the great questions that agitate the public mind; to protest against the revolutionary and unconstitutional acts of the present majority of Congress; to announce the determination of the conservative men of the Union; to resist and oppose by constitutional exercise of power the disorganization of States and the destruction of State authority.

9. That the thanks of every patriotic citizen are eminently due the President of the United States for his repeated exercise of the Executive power in behalf of the Constitution and the rights of the States; and we pledge to him our support in all his future efforts to the same noble end.

### Rhode Island.
#### DEMOCRATIC, MARCH 11.

1. That frequent innovations upon our laws are pernicious, as tending to confuse the minds of the people and destroy that reverence for legal authority which is essential to the perpetuity of the State and the safety of the citizen.

2. That we regard the judiciary as the shield of the people against the unwise or arbitrary acts of popular or official passion, and that any attempt to weaken or override the authority of our courts, or to detract from their dignity, imperils the very existence of the Republic.

3. That after an exhausting war our whole energy should be turned to the development of all our internal resources and to the increase of our commerce; that our system of taxation ought to be so adjusted as to bear equally upon all classes of the community and all sections of the country, to necessitate the least expense in collection, and relieve as rapidly as possible the burden of debt; that our laws ought to be so framed as to require the smallest possible number of officials in their execution, since a multiplicity of offices begets arrogance and corruption in the holders, and discontent in the people, who unwillingly lavish that money upon the leeches on the body politic which should go to nourish the body itself.

4. That the Democratic party, having spent much of its blood in a struggle to preserve the Union, will watch earnestly and anxiously and labor patiently for the same great end in the present not less terrible, though bloodless, contest. We believe it to be the duty of all people,

in all sections of the Republic, to accept the circumstances which have resulted from war; to endeavor by all means consistent with honor to adapt themselves to the new status thus created, and to conform to it both in legislation and in personal and official regard for each other. As to political supremacy, we are content to await the hour when the fury of passion gives place to the temperance of reason, and the bitterness of hate is lost in the lapse of time.

### Maryland.
#### REPUBLICAN, FEBRUARY 27.

Whereas the present state of national affairs, and the action of the coalition which, by the treachery of Governor Swann, now usurps the power of the State, have caused this assembling of the Unconditional Union men of Maryland, and render proper a clear utterance on all the issues of the times: Therefore,

*Resolved, by the Republican Union party of Maryland, in State Convention assembled,* That we cordially approve the reconstruction bill which has been passed by Congress, and that we declare the principles of impartial manhood suffrage contained therein to be the only secure basis of reconstruction, and that the time has come when its adoption by every State is demanded by every consideration of right and interest.

2. That we hail the result of the late election in Georgetown as a practical proof of the wisdom of Congress, and as the omen of loyal control over all the South.

3. That the convention bill now before the Legislature is in conflict with the existing constitution, and can be made valid only by the assent of the people of the State and the Government of the United States; and that no change of the existing constitution can or shall be made, or ought to be recognized by Congress, which is not made by impartial manhood suffrage, without respect to color.

4. That we request the Republican members of the State Senate to prepare an amendment to said bill basing representation upon population and submitting the question of a convention to all the male citizens of the State, and providing for a new State government on the basis of impartial manhood suffrage; and that we shall insist that any change in the constitution shall be made upon this basis, and that no State government now erected without impartial manhood suffrage ought to be considered republican; and that, in the event of the passage of the oppressive and anti-republican bill now before the Legislature, we will appeal to Congress to provide for the assembling of a convention in this State on the basis of the reconstruction bill, and to organize a loyal State government with impartial suffrage.

5. That further to carry out the object of the foregoing resolutions, this convention, when it adjourns, stands adjourned to meet at the call of its president, on such early day after the adjournment of the Legislature as the president may by public notice direct, and in the event of the president being prevented by any cause from acting, the chairman of the State Central Committee be empowered to make such call.

REPUBLICAN, MARCH 27.

Whereas the Legislature of Maryland has since the adjournment of this Republican State Convention on the 27th of February, passed the convention bill, in regard to which this convention has already in previous resolutions declared its judgment, and this convention is now reassembled as provided for by its fifth resolution on the contingency of the passage of said convention bill: Therefore,

*Resolved*, That we return our thanks to the Republican members of the General Assembly for their memorial to Congress presented to that body on the 25th of March, and this convention in behalf of the majority of the people of Maryland appeal hereby to the Congress of the United States to grant the request of that memorial.*

* The memorial is as follows:

" *To the Honorable Senate and House of Representatives of the "United States:*

"The undersigned, members of the General Assembly of Maryland, respectfully present this memorial to your honorable body on the condition of public affairs in this State, to which they ask the immediate consideration of the national legislature. The General Assembly of Maryland is about to adjourn, after a session as memorable for evil and as important to the country as that which consigned the legislature of 1861 to the casemates of Fort Warren. Elected in great part by the deliberate violation of the election laws of the State by the votes of men who were in active acco d with the rebellion, and whose hatred to the Government rendered the presence of military force during the war necessary to prevent their active aid to the rebels in arms, and in spite of which they did give large aid in men and money, they have marked their session by a series of acts to which we desire to call your attention.

" The rebels of Maryland sent South during the war some 20,000 soldiers to the rebel army These men have nearly all returned, and an emigration from the South since the war has largely added to their number. By doubtful construction of a clause of the existing constitution, this General Assembly, thus elected, has enfranchised all white men, no matter what treason they have committed, and thus have added to the voting population about 30,000 persons who have only lately ceased an armed resistance to the Government Not satisfied with this, they have just passed a militia bill, which, in direct defiance to the present constitution of the State, has made all white rebels, no matter what their previous treason, part of the militia force. They have, by deliberate vote, refused to exclude, even from the highest office under this law, any person, no matter what his rank in the rebel army, and they are about to put in force this law, the effect of which is against our own constitution and the army laws of Congress, and which puts in the rear of the capital an armed force, composed largely of the same men who have just been forced to cease armed attempts to capture the capital.

"One great object of this bill is to better carry out the scheme of revolutionizing the government of the State, abolishing the existing constitution, and making another, still more firmly fastening on the necks of loyal people the yoke of rebel control. The present constitution of Maryland, while it does not allow colored suffrage, does not give to the late masters the right to represent in the legislature their disfranchised freedmen. It bases representation on white population. These conspirators, not satisfied with controlling the legislative and executive departments, have passed a bill calling an election for a constitutional convention on the 10th day of April, the convention to meet on the second Monday of May, 1867. This they have done, although the constitution provides that the legislature shall pass no laws providing for a change in the existing constitution except in the mode therein prescribed; and although the constitution regulates the representation in any convention called to make a new constitution by fixing it the same as that of each county in the General Assembly, they having fixed an arbitrary basis of representation which, while it excludes the colored man from the ballot-box, gives to the old worn-out counties, which were as rebellious as South Carolina, an increased representation, by which the oppressor is to represent the oppressed against his will, and by which a minority of the people of the State are to hold in their proposed convention the same power as the majority. The State of Maryland has at present a colored population of at least 200,000, and by emigration since the war perhaps 250,000, making a voting population of from 40,000 to 50,000. In most of the counties whose representation has thus been

2. That we will oppose any new constitution set up in subversion of the existing constitution under the convention bill which does not express the will of the majority of the people without regard to color, and that we will, with the aid of the loyal representatives of the nation, and by all means in our power, resist and destroy any such constitution as a revolutionary usurpation.

3. That we will take no part in the approaching election for delegates to a constitutional convention further than to recommend a general vote of the Republicans of the State against the call for a convention, and to use every lawful means in their power to defeat the call.

4. That should the call be sustained by a ma-

illegally increased, the colored population is equal to or greater than the white. The House of Representatives of the United States has already passed a resolution of inquiry whether the present constitution of this State is now republican, and since the colored man is now a citizen, it may well be doubtful whether a State which excludes for no crime one-fourth of its population who are citizens is republican. This General Assembly has inaugurated, however, a movement which, from the illegal representations made in the bill itself, actually now accomplishes not only the exclusion of this population from suffrage, but also gives the disloyal population a representation for them

"The present judiciary of the State is for the most part loyal, and one object of this movement is to legislate out all the remaining loyal officers whom they have not already removed, and place ex-rebels, perhaps brigadiers and colonels of the rebel army, in their places. Not satisfied with the pardon and the charity which Union men have extended, they have commenced a reaction against the results of the war, and determined on a policy which, if unchecked. destroys a loyal constitution, and puts in its place one made by traitors, and flagrantly anti-republican, and places an armed militia of disloyal men and a minority government of rebel sympathizers and rebels in the complete possession of this State.

"While the South is about to commence a career of freedom and progress, these men, untaught by the lessons of the past, have determined, by the forms of law, but in real violation of both the State and Federal law, to put this State back into a condition of darkness and slavery. These acts, we submit, are in violation of State and national law, oppressive, revolutionary, and dangerous to the order and peace of this nation. The Union men of Maryland are groaning under this tyranny: they are now oppressed by verdicts of disloyal juries in many counties; immigration to the State, except from the South, is stopped, and many loyal men are deliberating upon leaving the State. The most, however, are ready, by all personal means, and at all personal hazards, to resist this infamous attempt at oppression.

"The danger of bloodshed is imminent and the times are perilous. We call upon Congress not to adjourn before settling this grave matter, which, if not settled, may startle them in their recess by something worse than the massacre at New Orleans, although not so unequal and one-sided. We earnestly ask, on the part of the majority of the people of Maryland, deprived of legal voice except through us, a minority of the General Assembly, that Congress will guaranty to us a republican form of government on the only basis of right, truth, and peace—impartial suffrage, without respect to race or color, as it has already guarantied it to the southern States.

CURTIS DAVIS, Senator from Caroline.
CHARLES E. TRAIL, Senator from Frederick.
JACOB TOME, Senator from Cecil.
ELIAS DAVIS, Senator from Washington.
HART B. HOLTON, Senator from Howard.
JAMES L. BILLINGSLEA, Senator from Carroll.
EDWARD P. PHILPOT, Senator from Baltimore county
DANIEL C. BRUCE, Delegate from Allegany.
JONATHAN TOBEY, Delegate from Washington.
A. R. APPLEMAN, Delegate from Washington.
THOMAS GORSUCH, Delegate from Frederick.
J. P. BISHOP, Delegate from Washington.
BENJAMIN POOL, Delegate from Carroll.
JAMES V CRISWELL, Delegate from Carroll.
JOHN L. LINTHICUM, Delegate from Frederick.
J. R. ROUZER, Delegate from Frederick.
HENRY BAKER, Delegate from Frederick.
R. C. BAMFORD, Delegate from Washington,
S. R. GORE, Delegate from Carroll."
This memorial was signed by all the Republican members who were present at Annapolis when it was signed.

jority of the voters, that the State Central Committee, on ascertaining that result, issue a call for district meetings to be held in every election district in the State, for the choice by ballot, on the basis of universal manhood suffrage, of delegates to a State constitutional convention, each county and the city of Baltimore to elect the number to which they may be entitled under the present constitution of the State.

5. That said State constitutional convention, if called, shall assemble in the city of Baltimore on the first Wednesday in June, and proceed to form a constitution based on universal manhood suffrage.

6. That courage, wisdom, and action are all that is necessary to success, and we call on the tried Union veterans of the State, who have been hardened by the conflicts of six years of battle and agitation, to fly high the banner of liberty and Union, and know no end but victory.

This memorial was presented, and referred to the Committee on the Judiciary.

CALL FOR STATE REPUBLICAN CONVENTION.

At a meeting of the Republican Union State central committee of Maryland, held on Wednesday, April 17, 1867, the following resolutions were unanimously adopted:

*Resolved.* That all male citizens of Maryland, who are opposed to the organized conspiracy about to assemble at Annapolis on the 8th day of May, are requested to meet in primary assemblages in the various counties and the city of Baltimore, at such time as may be most convenient, to elect delegates to a State Republican convention, which shall assemble in Baltimore city on Tuesday, May 14, at 12 o'clock, m.

*Resolved,* That the State convention will be expected to take into consideration the present condition of political affairs in the State, and to deliberate upon the best method of guaranteeing to the people a republican form of government. To the primary meetings, the county conventions, and the State convention are invited all loyal citizens, without regard to past political differences, race, or color, who subscribe to the doctrine of the Republican Union party. The number of delegates to the State convention will not be limited; but the counties and the city of Baltimore shall be entitled to the same number of votes in the convention as they have representatives in both houses of the General Assembly. The members of the State central committee of the different counties will announce the day for holding the primary meetings, county conventions, or mass conventions, in the several counties, and the executive committee will fix the day for the aforesaid purposes in the city of Baltimore.          Thomas J. Wilson, *Chairman.*

J. W. Clayton, *Secretary.*

---

## Ohio.

### Democratic, January 8.

1. *Resolved,* That the democracy of Ohio steadfastly adhere to the principles of the party as expounded by the fathers, and approved by experience; that in accordance with these principles we declare that the Federal Government is a government of limited powers, and that it possesses no powers but such as are expressly, or by necessary implication, delegated to it in the federal Constitution; that all other powers are reserved to the States or the people; that a strict construction of the Constitution is indispensable to the preservation of the reserved rights of the States and the people; that all grants of power to Government, whether State or federal, should be strictly construed, because all such grants abridge the natural rights of men; that the preservation of the equality and rights of the State and the rights of the people is necessary to the preservation of the Union; that the Federal Government is unfitted to legislate for, or administer the local concerns of, the States; that it would be monstrous that the local affairs of Ohio should be regulated by a federal Congress in which she has but two Senators, and the New England States, with but a little greater population, have twelve; that the tendency of the Federal Government is to usurp the reserved rights of the States and of the people; and that, therefore, a centralization of power in its hands is an ever-pending danger; that such an absorption of power would, while it lasted, be destructive of the liberties and interests of the people, and would end either in despotism or a destruction of the Union; that a national debt, besides impoverishing the people, fosters an undue increase of the powers of the Federal Government; that high protective tariffs have a like effect, sacrificing the interests of the many for the emoluments of the few, and plainly violating the equity and spirit of the Constitution; that the collection and disbursement of the enormous revenues by the Federal Government have the same tendency, besides corrupting the Government, and that, therefore, economy is essential not only to the prosperity, but also to the liberties of the people; that unequal taxation is a plain violation of justice, of which no government can safely be guilty; that to each State belongs the right to determine the qualification of its electors, and all attempts to impair this right, either by congressional legislation or constitutional amendment, are unwise and despotic; that the tendency of power is to steal from the many to the few, and that, therefore, "eternal vigilance is the price of liberty;" that the tendency of the Government is to enlarge its authority by usurpation, and therefore the Government needs to be watched; that another of its tendencies is to govern too much—unnecessarily and vexatiously interfering with the business and habits of the people; that the freedom of speech and of the press is essential to the existence of liberty; that no person not in the military or naval service, or where the civil courts are prevented by war or insurrection from exercising their functions, can lawfully be deprived of life, liberty, or property, without due process of civil law; that the courts should always be open for the redress of grievances; that no *ex post facto* law should ever be made; that, in the language of the Supreme Court, "the Constitution of the United States is a law for the rulers and the people, equal in war and in peace, and covers with the shield of its protection all classes of men, at all times and under all circumstances    No doctrine involving more pernicious consequences was ever invented by the wit of man than that any of its provisions

can be suspended during any of the great exigencies of government. Such a docrine leads directly to anarchy or despotism ;" that the right of the people to peaceably assemble and consult upon public affairs is inviolable; that the military should be held in due subjection to the civil power; that while the majority, as prescribed by the Constitution, have the right to govern, the minority have indefeasible rights; and that a frequent recurrence to first principles is essential to the welfare of the State and the people.

2. That the States lately in rebellion are States in the Union, and have been recognized as such by every department of the Government, and by President Lincoln, who, in the midst of war, invited them to elect members of Congress; by President Johnson, in various proclamations and official acts; by Congress, which permitted Andrew Johnson to sit in the Senate as a Senator from Tennessee, and members from Virginia, Tennessee, and Louisiana to sit in the House of Representatives after those States had seceded, and while the war was being carried on, and which further recognized them as States in the Union by the congressional apportionment act, providing for their due representation in Congress; by various tax laws, and especially by the direct tax; by the resolutions submitting amendments to the Constitution for their approval, and by various other acts and resolutions imparting the same recognition, all of which were passed since the attempted secession of those States; by the judiciary of the United States, which holds federal courts in all those States, and especially by the Supreme Court, which entertains jurisdiction of cases coming from them, which it could not do were they not in the Union. That being thus in the Union, they stand on an equal footing with their sister States—States with unequal rights being a thing unknown to the Constitution; that, by the express terms of the Constitution, each State is entitled to have two Senators and a fair proportion of Representatives in the Congress, and to vote in all elections of President and Vice President; that, though these rights are subject to interruption by a state of civil war, they cannot, in time of peace, be suspended, much less destroyed, without a plain violation of the Constitution; that the assent of three-fourths of all the States, whether represented in Congress or not, is essential to the validity of constitutional amendments; that Congress has no power to deprive a State of its reserved rights and reduce it to a territorial condition; that, therefore, the exclusion, by the so-called Congress, of all representation from ten States, the proposed exclusion of those States from all voice in the next presidential election, the threatened overthrow of their State governments, and the reduction of their States to the condition of Territories, are each and every one of them unconstitutional, revolutionary, and despotic measures, destructive not merely of the rights of those States, but also of the rights of every other State in the Union. That those measures are parts of a plan to nullify the Constitution, to virtually overthrow the State governments, to erect a consolidated despotism on their ruins, and to establish and perpetuate a tyrannical rule of a minority over a majority of the American people. That the people cannot, without a loss of their liberties, prosperity, and honor, submit to such a result; and, therefore, in the hope that the warning will be heeded, and the danger to our institutions be peaceably averted, we do solemnly warn the advocates of the plan that it will not be submitted to.

3. That Congress is not an omnipotent law-making power; that the Constitution provides that no bill shall become a law without the approval of the President, unless it be passed by two-thirds of each House of Congress; that one of the objects of the present so-called Congress in excluding ten States from representation is to pass bills by a two-thirds vote, which, were all the States represented, could not pass, and thus to abolish the constitutional provision aforesaid; that if the precedent be acquiesced in there will be nothing to prevent a bare majority of Congress, at any time in the future, from nullifying the constitutional veto of the President, and usurping uncontrolled legislative power by an exclusion of the minority from their seats; that the exclusion of a single State might give this control, and a pretext for such an exclusion would never be wanting to an unscrupulous and revolutionary party.

4. That the people, and especially those of the agricultural States, have suffered too long the exactions of high protective tariffs, and as the representatives of an agricultural and laboring population, we demand that their substance shall no longer be extorted from them in order to fill the pockets of eastern monopolists.

5. That unequal taxation is contrary to the first principles of justice and sound policy, and we call upon our Government, Federal and State, to use all necessary constitutional means to remedy this evil.

6. That the radical majority in the so-called Congress have proved themselves to be in favor of negro suffrage, by forcing it upon the people of the District of Columbia against their wish, solemnly expressed at the polls; by forcing it upon the people of all the Territories, and by their various devices to coerce the people of the South to adopt it; that we are opposed to negro suffrage, believing it would be productive of evil to both whites and blacks, and tend to produce a disastrous conflict of races.

7. That for their efforts to uphold the Constitution, we tender to the President and to the majority of the judges of the Supreme Court of the United States our hearty thanks.

8. That we are in favor of a Democratic convention of delegates from all the States, to be held at such time and place as may be agreed upon, and that the State central committee be authorized to concur with other proper committees in fixing time and place, and that we prefer Louisville, Kentucky, as the place.

9. That the Democratic newspapers of Ohio deserve our earnest and liberal support, and that an early and thorough organization of the party is indispensable.

### Tennessee.

REPUBLICAN, FEBRUARY 22, 1867.

We, the representatives of the loyal people of Tennessee, in convention assembled, are thankful to Almighty God for the success of the arms of the United States over the army of traitors, who sought to destroy the best government ever known to man, thereby saving us and our posterity the blessings and privileges of our republican institutions, and a solution of the heretofore doubtful problem that man is capable of self-government.

"We hold these truths to be self-evident:"

1. "That all men are created equal, endowed with certain inalienable rights," and therefore the law should afford equal protection to all in the exercise of these rights, and, so far as it can, insure perfect equality under the law.

2. That a State or a nation should be governed, controlled, and directed by those who have saved it in times of peril, and who seek to preserve it with friendly hands from foes and dangers, external and internal.

3. That a wis are for the public safety sometimes renders it necessary that those who have sought resolutely to overthrow a government should not hastily be restored to the privileges of which they have deprived themselves by their crime of treason; certainly not until they have shown evidence of sincere repentance, and a disposition as energetically to support as they have in times past sought to destroy.

4. That rebellion is disfranchisement, and armed attempts to overthrow our common government treasonable expatriation; and the present franchise organic law is but the declaration of the handiwork of secession and rebellion. Those who have sought our country's ruin cannot be intrusted with its safety.

5. That lawless violence, reckless disregard of the rights of person and property, murder, assassination, arson, and kindred crimes, must be put down by the strong arm of power, and be made to feel that law is indeed a terror to evil-doers.

6 Therefore, in accordance with the above principles, we fully indorse the policy and action of the General Assembly of the State of Tennessee, in restricting the elective franchise to those who are not hostile to the Government, in extending it to those who proved their loyalty by imperiling their lives, and who need this privilege for their own protection, and in establishing a military organization which shall give necessary physical support to the moral power of the State government, becoming a salutary terror to evil-doers and a cheerful hope to those who do well.

7. That the "privileges and immunities" guarantied under the Constitution of our Union to the loyal from other States, and the pledge of freedom and equality in the declaration of American Independence, shall be *living truths* and *practical maxims* in Tennessee, for the protection of "life, liberty, and the pursuit of happiness."

8. That we have entire confidence in the integrity, wisdom, and ability of the Republican Union majority of Congress, and deem it signally fortunate that they, in whom alone the power resides to restore, preserve, and govern the country, have shown themselves so eminently fitted for these high duties, that no State should be admitted to representation in Congress without adopting the constitutional amendment.

9. That the Republican Union party of Tennessee are in favor of free speech and free discussion, and to this end we invite our friends from other States to come among us, and discuss the great issues now before the people, and we pledge the Republican Union party of Tennessee to tolerate all legitimate discussion, and at the same time claiming equal privileges on our part; and that any interference to prevent this will be regarded as an unwarranted act, and resisted to the last extremity.

10. That we honor the firmness, courage, and wisdom which have characterized the administration of our Chief Magistrate, the Hon. Wm. G. Brownlow, and while we sympathize with him in his bodily suffering, we admire the healthy mind, conscious to itself of rectitude, which bears with like equanimity the throes of pain and the perilous cares of State; and that we declare him the unanimous choice of the loyal people of Tennessee for our next Governor.

11. That we cover our faces with shame when we contemplate the disgrace brought upon our beloved State by the defection and degeneracy of her unprincipled adopted son, who by the bullet of an assassin has ascended to the Chief Magistracy of the nation; and we shall cordially endorse any action of Congress which shall legitimately deprive him of continued power to disturb the peace of the country.

"CONSERVATIVE," APRIL 17, 1867.

We, the Conservative men of Tennessee, adopt the following platform of principles:

1. We are in favor of the Union of the States under the Constitution of the United States.

2. We are the friends of peace and civil law, and that these great objects can be best promoted by legislation recognizing equal and exact justice to all—exclusive privileges to none.

3. We are in favor of the immediate restoration of our disfranchised fellow-citizens to all rights, privileges, and immunities of full and complete citizenship.

4. That our colored fellow-citizens, being now citizens of the United States and citizens of the State of Tennessee and voters of this State, are entitled to all the rights and privileges of citizens under the laws and Constitution of United States and of the State of Tennessee.

5. We are opposed to the repudiation of the national debt, and are in favor of equal taxation as the proper method of paying the same.

6. That the establishment of a standing army in our State, in time of peace, is a flagrant and dangerous encroachment upon the rights and liberties of the citizen, heavily oppressive to the tax-payer, and evidently designed to overawe the voters at the ballot-box.

7. We cordially approve of the patriotic efforts of Andrew Johnson, President of the United States, in defending the Constitution, preserving the Union of the States, and maintaining the supremacy of the laws.

## Alabama.

RESOLUTIONS OF THE GRAND COUNCIL OF THE UNION LEAGUE, APRIL, 1867.

*Resolved,* That the Alabama Grand Council of the Union League of America return thanks to the Congress of the United States for its patriotic action in affording to all the people an opportunity, on fair terms, to re-organize the government of the State, to put her destinies into the hands of true Union men, and to unite her again to her sister States by the only enduring bond of unswerving loyalty.

2. That we hail with joy the recurrence to the fundamental principle on which our forefathers achieved their independence—"that all men are created equal;" that we welcome its renewed proclamation as a measure of simple justice to a faithful and patriotic class of our fellow-men, and that we firmly believe that there could be no lasting pacification of the country under any system which denied to a large class of our population that hold upon the laws which is given by the ballot.

3. That while we believe that participation in rebellion is the highest crime known to the law, and that those guilty of it hold their continued existence solely by the clemency of an outraged but merciful Government, we are nevertheless willing to imitate that Government in forgiveness of the past, and to welcome to the Republican Union party all who, forsaking entirely the principles on which the rebellion was founded, will sincerely and earnestly unite with us in establishing and maintaining for the future a government of equal rights and unconditional loyalty.

4. That we consider willingness to elevate to power the men who preserved unswerving adherence to the Government during the war as the best test of sincerity in professions for the future.

5. That if the pacification now proposed by Congress be not accepted in good faith by those who staked and forfeited " their lives, their fortunes, and their sacred honor " in rebellion, it will be the duty of Congress to enforce that forfeiture by the confiscation of the lands, at least, of such a stiff-necked and rebellious people.

6. That the assertion that there are not enough intelligent loyal men in Alabama to administer the government is false in fact, and mainly promulgated by those who aim to keep treason respectable, by retaining power in the hands of its friends and votaries.

---

### Arkansas.

REPUBLICAN, APRIL 5, 1867.

The people of the State of Arkansas, willing to associate together for the purpose of co-operating with the National Union Republican party of the nation in securing and maintaining equal legal and political rights to all the citizens of the Republic and restore the State to its political relations in the Union, now here in State convention assembled, do proclaim and declare the following declaration of principles on which they have unanimously agreed:

I. That we will ever defend the Constitution of the United States thereunder as the sacred palladium of our rights and liberties. That the Union of the States under the Constitution constitutes a national Republic, and not a mere league of independent States, and that the Constitution of the United States and the laws made in pursuance thereof are the supreme laws of the land, anything in the constitution or laws of any State to the contrary notwithstanding.

II. That we arraign the unprincipled and corrupt demagogues who for so many years held every office and exercised a despotic control over its legislation as the sole authors of the present deplorable condition of the State and its people. To convict them of the folly and crime of having brought upon the people of the State their present woes, let facts be stated.

1. They appropriated to their own use and squandered the grants of money and lands made to the State by the National Government for educational purposes, and then refused to provide free schools or make sufficient provision for the education of the youth of the State.

2. They in like manner appropriated to their own use and otherwise squandered the swamp land grant and all other grants of land made by the National Government to the State for internal improvements and other purposes; and refusing to make any provision therefor, the State is left to this day without a completed railroad or other work of internal improvement within her borders.

3. They issued the bonds of the State as a pretended basis for a banking capital, and having negotiated the bonds and appropriated the proceeds to their own use, the State is left to pay their bonds, with years of accumulated interest, amounting in the aggregate to millions of dollars.

4. In a time of profound peace, and when the people of the State were enjoying a degree of prosperity and happiness unparalleled in any country on the globe, these unscrupulous and reckless demagogues, actuated by none but the most selfish purposes and wicked ambition, with a design of founding a government based on human slavery, and governed and controlled by an aristocracy of office-holders and slave-owners, and in defiance of the expressed will of the people at the ballot-box, and in violation of their own pledges, passed an ordinance of secession, proclaimed the State out of the Union, made war upon the National Government, and by the use of vigorous conscription laws and a military rule, the despotism of which is without a parallel in the history of the world, they forced an unwilling and loyal people, who loved their country and its flag, to join in an effort to destroy the Government that had showered blessings on them and their fathers.

Having inaugurated the rebellion for these hateful purposes, they secured to themselves all the civil and military offices of their insurrectionary government, and they used the power thus usurped over the lives, liberty, and property of the people to coerce them to join in their treason and rebellion, and wickedly and wantonly protracted the struggle until one-third of their victims were in their graves, and the property of all impressed, wasted away, or destroyed.

6. Failing to destroy the Republic and rob the people of their liberty by force of arms, they returned and at once demanded to be restored to the offices and control of the State, and speedily possessed themselves of the legislative department. the supreme court, and other important offices. Again in power in the State they renewed the atrocious system of plunder and oppression. The brief respite enjoyed by the people of the State from the despotic control of these

political vampires, who fled the State in 1863 to avoid a just punishment for their crimes, had enabled a loyal provisional government, by an honest and economical administration, to accumulate in the treasury of the State over $150,000 in cash. The treasury is at once plundered by these men of this hard-earned money of the people; extravagance, corruption, favoritism, and oppression mark their every act; the loyal men of the State are wronged and oppressed, and denied redress; treason is made a virtue and loyalty a crime; the constitution of the State is set at defiance, and the pretended laws and decrees of the now defunct rebel government declared to be in full force and binding on loyal people living under the Constitution of the United States. The obligations and evidence of indebtedness of the rebel State government which these men issued to themselves, and obtained fraudulently and without consideration, and of which the most unscrupulous of these men hold large amounts, are declared to be binding on a loyal State and a loyal people; they refuse to take the necessary, reasonable, and just steps to restore the State to the Union and representation in Congress, and contemptuously reject terms of settlement the most magnanimous and liberal ever offered to men in their position, and up to the present moment continue to present an attitude of hostility to the National Government, its authority, and supporters, bordering on open rebellion, and dangerous alike to the peace of the nation and State, and the safety of loyal and law-abiding men. And Congress wisely and justly judged that reconstruction was impossible while such constitutional and chronic traitors, plunderers of the public treasury and oppressors of the people, were permitted to exercise the political power of the State, which they have usurped and so long held by fraud, deceit, and oppression.

III. That we recognize the power and right of the National Government to determine the method and apply the means of reconstructing the rebel States, and of providing lawful governments for the same, and do willingly abide by and heartily accept the measures adopted, or which may hereafter be necessarily prescribed by Congress for a full, perfect, and final reconstruction of said States; and to the end that the State may be admitted to its wonted position in the Union and representation in Congress; that the liberty and rights of every citizen may be secured and sacredly guarded and protected under an honest, competent, and loyal State government; that the credit of the State may be restored, and economy in the public expenditures secured; that the construction of railroads and other internal improvements so necessary to the prosperity of the State may be commenced and vigorously prosecuted; that an enlightened and judicious system of free common schools, providing for the education of all the children of the State, may be inaugurated; that emigration and capital from every quarter may be invited and induced to enter our State, and that peace, security, and prosperity may be restored to the State and all its people, we declare that we are in favor of immediate action under and in conformity to the acts of Congress, and we hereby tender to the major general command-

ing this district our hearty and cordial support and co-operation in the honest and faithful execution of the same.

IV. That we denounce the guilty authors of the late rebellion who refuse to acquiesce in the necessary, legitimate, and just results of their own folly and crime, and who are now counseling the people to renewed opposition and resistance to the legitimate and lawful authority of the National Government, as enemies of the Union, and all the dearest and best interests of the State and her people, and they deserve and should receive the scorn of every honest citizen who desires to see law, and order, and peace, security, and prosperity secured to the State.

V. That the most dangerous enemies of the nation and State are the disloyal newspapers and political demagogues, who, while they denounce the late action of Congress as illegal, unconstitutional, and despotic, nevertheless declare it to be their purpose to control, if they can, all action thereunder, with the declared purpose, as soon as representation in Congress is secured, of immediately repudiating their compact with the National Government, and by a change of the constitution of the State disfranchise the recently enfranchised citizens of the State, prohibit the education of their children, and adopt other reactionary and revolutionary measures.

VI. That the Congress of the nation is solemnly pledged not to recognize any State government made by and in the hands of open and declared enemies of the great principles of liberty and justice embraced in the measures of reconstruction; and more especially will Congress refuse to recognize a government in the hands of men who avow it to be their purpose to overthrow these great principles the moment they obtain congressional recognition of their dishonest and hypocritical action; and we warn every good citizen of the State who favors reconstruction and wishes to enjoy the blessings and benefits to be derived from our early restoration to the Union against the criminal folly of intrusting the work to such hands.

VII. That we heartily indorse all meetings and conventions heretofore held in the State which had in view the reconstruction of this State in harmony with the will of Congress.

VIII. That State taxation shall be equal and uniform, and that no discrimination should be made in favor of one species of property at the expense of another.

IX. That all the citizens of every county in the State who approve of the declaration of principles and purposes here announced are earnestly urged to meet in their respective counties and organize, and report their organization to the chairman of the State central committee, at Little Rock, in order that a united and harmonious effort may be made to secure equal rights and justice to all, just and good government, wisely and honestly administered, by loyal men.

### North Carolina.

REPUBLICAN, MARCH 27, 1867.

Having assembled in the city of Raleigh, on the 27th of March, 1867, in conformity with a timely and patriotic call, reflecting the sentiments of the loyal men of the State, and i elieving the time is at hand when an open and fearless expression of sentiment, opinion, and purpose is urgently demanded : Therefore,

1. *Resolved,* That in view of our present political condition, our relations to the National Government, and the people of all sections of the country, we do this day with proud satisfaction unfurl the brilliant and glorious banner of the Republican party, and earnestly appeal to every true and patriotic man in the State to rally to its support.

The splendid and patriotic record made by this great political organization, in standing by the General Government with an inflexible resolution, in carrying forward profound measures of statesmanship to a successful issue, and the powerful aid given by it in finally overthrowing and prostrating the most gigantic rebellion of ancient or modern times, should command the respect and challenge the admiration of every candid man.

2. That the American Congress is eminently entitled to the profound thanks of the whole country for its persevering, persistent, and heroic devotion to the great principles of human rights as enunciated in the Declaration of Independence ; that in the name of the patriotic people of this State we feel warranted in cordially assenting to and accepting the reconstruction plan recently and finally adopted by that body; and to the end that peace and order may be permanently secured, and every industrial pursuit resumed and encouraged, we pledge ourselves to use every fair and legitimate means to influence public sentiment to the nearest possible approach to unanimity on this subject.

3. That we rejoice that the dogma, long propagated, of the right of peaceable secession under the Constitution, has been forever overthrown by the majestic uprising of the American people, in crushing out the late rebellion by force of arms, and that the doctrine of the supremacy of the General Government has been established, and that the paramount allegiance of the citizen has been acknowledged as due to the United States.

4. That we sincerely exult in the fact that as a nation we are now absolutely a nation of freemen, and that the sun in all his course over our wide-spread country no longer shines upon the brow of a slave. Without reservation, we heartily indorse the great measures of civil rights and impartial enfranchisement, without any property qualification, conferred without distinction of color, and that we are ready to unite in the early practical attainment of these inestimable privileges. Although the mortal remains of Abraham Lincoln now rest silently beneath the soil of his adopted State, yet his voice still rings like a clarion through the land, ʻearnestly summoning every American citizen to the support of the great party of liberty and emancipation.

5. That as the most potent and efficient means by which the South can speedily regain her lost prosperity, we earnestly advocate the spreading of knowledge and education among all men, and that to the attainment of this great end, we demand and shall persistently and firmly insist

upon the absolute right of free discussion and free speech on all subjects of public interest

6. That we join in an earnest wish for the maintenance, untarnished and undimmed, of the public credit and plighted faith of the nation

7. That in the maintenance of the position taken and the principles this day avowed, we earnestly invite the influence and co-operation of men of all political persuasions, who regard and cordially support the recent action of Congress as a solution of our present political difficulties ; that we deprecate partizan violence, and desire peace and good-will toward all men ; and if in an open and fearless effort, which we propose to make on every suitable occasion, to persuade and convince the people that our highest duty and truest interest are to be subserved by maintaining the principles of the Republican party, an earnest interest should be awakened, it will be from no other cause than a rigid adherence to what we regard as a sacred right and a solemn public duty.

## South Carolina.

OF CHARLESTON REPUBLICANS, MARCH 22, 1867.

1. *Resolved,* That we give our cordial and entire sanction to the action of Congress for the restoration of the Union, and to the wise and just principles of the Republican party.

2. That in order to make the labors of all our loyal fellow-citizens more effectual for carrying out the provisions of Congress for the restoration of law and order in our State, as well as for the peace and prosperity of our entire country, we do form an association to be known as the "Union Republican party of South Carolina."

3. That we pledge our sacred honor, our fortunes, and our lives to serve our country, to preserve her institutions, and especially to aid her in keeping inviolate the national faith, which has been sacredly pledged to the payment of the national debt incurred to save the liberties of the country and to suppress rebellion, and that the people will not suffer this faith to be violated or impaired ; but all debts incurred to support the rebellion, as they were unlawful, void, and of no obligation, shall never be assumed by the United States, nor shall South Carolina be permitted to pay any debt whatever which was contracted to aid the rebellion in any form.

4. That the nation owes to the brave men, white and colored, of our army and navy a debt of lasting gratitude for their heroic services in defence of the Constitution and the Union, and that, while we cherish with a tender affection the memories of the fallen, we pledge to their widows and orphans the nation's care and protection.

5. That as republican institutions cannot be preserved unless intelligence be generally diffused among all classes, we will demand of our legislature a uniform system of common schools, which shall be open to all, without distinction of race, color, or previous condition ; such system to be supported by a general tax upon all kinds of property.

6. That we will favor a liberal system of public improvements, such as railroads, canals, and other works, and also such a system of awarding contracts for the same as will give all our fel-

low-citizens an equal and fair chance to share in them.

7. That we will also insist on such modification of the laws of the State as will do away with imprisonment for debt, except for fraud; and imprisonment of witnesses, except for willful absence; and especially to abolish, entirely and forever, the barbarous custom of corporal punishment for crime or any other cause.

8. That, as large land monopolies tend only to make the rich richer and the poor poorer, and are ruinous to the agricultural, commercial, and social interests of the State, the legislature should offer every practicable inducement for the division and sale of unoccupied lands among the poorer classes and as an encouragement to emigrants to settle in our State.

9. That the law of ejectment and distraint should be so modified as to protect equally the landlord and the tenant.

10. That provision should be made for the exemption of the poor man's homestead.

11. That the interests of the State demand a revision of the entire code of laws and the reorganization of the courts.

12. That the interests not only of the State, but of the whole country, demand every possible guaranty for the perpetuity of all the rights conferred upon the newly enfranchised portion of our fellow-citizens, and that, in the use of the sacred right of the elective franchise, we will seek to elevate to offices of trust and honor only those who are truly loyal, honest, and capable, irrespective of race, color, or previous condition.

13. The consideration of justice and humanity demand provision by the legislature for the protection and support of the aged, infirm, and helpless poor, irrespective of race, color, or previous condition.

14. That we will not support any candidate for office who will not openly indorse, advocate, and defend the principles adopted by the Union Republican party.

15. Relying upon Divine Providence for wisdom in our counsels, efficiency in our action, harmony among ourselves, with malice toward none and charity to all, we pledge our earnest and best efforts for the return of peace and prosperity to all our people, and for an early representation of our beloved State in the Congress of the United States.

### Virginia Republican State Convention,
APRIL 17 AND 18, 1867.

Whereas, having for the first time in the history of Virginia assembled at her State capital, at the call of a Union Republican State committee, as a convention of Union men, for the purpose of ratifying the acts of the 39th and 40th Congresses, and adopting measures to unite all parties who earnestly and honestly desire that this legislation should be perfected in accordance with the express desire of Congress and carried out in good faith by the people of this State, we, therefore, in convention assembled, do

First. *Resolve*, That we return our sincere and heartfelt thanks to the 39th Congress for their recent legislation resulting in the passage of the Sherman-Shellabarger bill and its supplement, and certify with gratitude that the

beneficial effects of such legislation are already visible in the increased security of loyal men, and in inducing immediate efforts toward reconstruction on the part of all classes; and that we do hereby pledge our earnest and persistent efforts to carry out in good faith, without evasion, with honesty of purpose, unflinching courage, and never-tiring energy, all its provisions, believing that by this course alone can permanent peace and prosperity be restored to the State and an early admission to the Union be secured.

2. That in the principles of the National Republican party of the United States we recognize all we can desire as a guide in our political future; that we adopt them as our platform, and pledge ourselves to their support, and cordially invite the co-operation of all classes of our fellow-citizens, without distinction of race or color, without regard to former political opinions or action, induced by such convictions. We invite them to join us, and pledge them a warm welcome to our ranks, and a full and free participation in all the advantages of our organization. And firmly believing that in the present condition of public affairs the Republican party offers the most available means through its organization for the speedy attainment of permanent reconstruction, we do hereby adopt its principles and platform as the basis and platform of the Union Republican party of Virginia.

3. That we adopt as part of our platform and as cardinal points in the policy of the Union Republican party of Virginia the following propositions: first, equal protection to all men before the courts, and equal political rights in all respects, including the right to hold office; second, a system of common-school education, which shall give to all classes free schools and a free and equal participation in all its benefits; third, a more just and equitable system of taxation, which shall apportion taxes to property, and require all to pay in proportion to their ability; fourth, a modification of the usury laws sufficient to induce foreign capital to seek investment in the State; fifth, encouragement to internal improvements and every possible inducement to immigration.

4. That in the noble utterances of the founders of our Constitution, we recognize a true appreciation of the great fact that parties or governments, to be prosperous or successful, must be founded or administered on the basis of exact and equal justice to all men; and we accept as our guides the great principles enunciated by them, first and most important of which is the great and glorious truth "that all men are created free and equal, are endowed with certain inalienable rights, and that among these are life, liberty, and the pursuit of happiness;" and we solemnly pledge, on the part of this convention and the party it represents, a strict adhesion to these sentiments, which, for the first time in the history of Virginia, a political organization is in a position to adopt in spirit and action as in name.

5. That believing the principles enunciated in the foregoing resolutions can be objectionable to no man who really loves the Union, and that they are the only true principles which can give to Virginia an early restoration to the Union

and enduring peace and prosperity, we solemnly pledge ourselves to support no man for an elective office who fails to join us in their adoption and enforcement, who fails to identify himself with the Union Republican party in spirit and action, or hesitates to connect himself openly and publicly with its platform as adopted here to-day.

6. That we recognize the great fact that the interests of the laboring classes of the State are identical, and that, without regard to color, we desire to elevate them to their true position; that the exaltation of the poor and humble, the restraint of the rapacious and the arrogant, the lifting up of the poor and degraded without humiliation or degradation to any; that the attainment of the greatest amount of happiness and prosperity to the greatest number is our warmest desire, and shall have our earnest and persistent efforts in their accomplishment; that while we desire to see all men protected in full and equal proportions, and every political right secured to the colored man that is enjoyed by any other class of citizens, we do not desire to deprive the laboring white men of any rights or privileges which they now enjoy, but do propose to extend those rights and privileges by the organization of the Republican party in this State.

## KENTUCKY AND VIRGINIA RESOLUTIONS.

### Kentucky Resolutions, November, 1798.

1. *Resolved*, That the several States composing the United States of America are not united on the principle of unlimited submission to their General Government; but that, by compact, under the style and title of a Constitution for the United States and of Amendments thereto, they constituted a general government for special purposes, delegated to that Government certain definite powers, reserving each State to itself the residuary mass of right to their own self-government; and that whensoever the General Government assumes undelegated powers, its acts are unauthoritative, void, and of no force: That to this compact each State acceded as a State, and is an integral party, its co-States forming as to itself the other party: That the government created by this compact was not made the exclusive or final *judge* of the extent of the powers delegated to itself; since that would have made its discretion, and not the constitution, the measure of its powers; but that, as in all other cases of compact among parties having no common judge, each party has an equal right to judge for itself, as well of infractions, as of the mode and measure of redress.

2. That the Constitution of the United States having delegated to Congress a power to punish treason, counterfeiting the securities and current coin of the United States, piracies and felonies committed on the high seas, and offences against the laws of nations, and no other crimes whatever, and it being true as a general principle, and one of the amendments to the Constitution having also declared, " that the powers not delegated to the United States by the Constitution, nor prohibited by it to the States, are reserved to the States respectively or to the people;" therefore, also the same act of Congress, passed on the 14th day of July, 1798, and entitled, "An

act in addition to the act entitled, 'an act for the punishment of certain crimes against the United States," as also the act passed by them on the 27th day of June, 1798, entitled "An act to punish frauds committed on the Bank of the United States,' " (and all other their acts which assume to create, define, or punish crimes other than those enumerated in the Constitution,) are altogether void and of no force, and that the power to create, define, and punish such other crimes is reserved, and of right appertains solely and exclusively, to the respective States, each within its own territory.

3. That it is true as a general principle, and is also expressly declared by one of the amendments to the Constitution, that " the powers not delegated to the United States by the Constitution, nor prohibited by it to the States, are reserved to the States respectively or to the people;" and that no power over the freedom of religion, freedom of speech, or freedom of the press, being delegated to the United States by the Constitution, nor prohibited by it to the States, all lawful powers respecting the same did of right remain, and were reserved, to the States or to the people: That thus was manifested their determination to retain to themselves the right of judging how far the licentiousness of speech and of the press may be abridged without lessening their useful freedom, and how far those abuses which cannot be separated from their use should be tolerated rather than the use be destroyed; and thus, also, they guarded against all abridgment by the United States of the freedom of religious opinions and exercises, and retained to themselves the right of protecting the same, as this State, by a law passed on the general demand of its citizens, had already protected them from all human restraint or interference: And that, in addition to this general principle and express declaration, another and more special provision has been made by one of the amendments to the Constitution, which expressly declares that "Congress shall make no law respecting an establishment of religion or prohibiting the free exercise thereof, or abridging the freedom of speech or of the press," thereby guarding in the same sentence, and under the same words, the freedom of religion, of speech, and of the press, insomuch that whatever violates either throws down the sanctuary which covers the others, and that libels, falsehoods, and defamation, equally with heresy and false religion, are withheld from the cognizance of federal tribunals: That therefore the act of the Congress of the United States, passed on the 14th day of July, 1798, entitled "An act in addition to the act for the punishment of certain crimes against the United States," which does abridge the freedom of the press, is not law, but is altogether void and of no effect.

4. That alien friends are under the jurisdiction and protection of the laws of the State wherein they are; that no power over them has been delegated to the United States nor prohibited to the individual States distinct from their power over citizens; and it being true, as a general principle, and one of the amendments to the Constitution having also declared that " the powers not delegated to the United States by the Constitution, nor prohibited by it to the States,

are reserved to the States respectively or to the people," the act of the Congress of the United States, passed on the 22d day of June,1798, entitled "An act concerning aliens," which assumes power over alien friends not delegated by the Constitution, is not law, but is altogether void and of no force.

5. That in addition to the general principle as well as the express declaration that powers not delegated are reserved, another and more special provision inserted in the Constitution from abundant caution has declared "that the *migration* or importation of such persons as any of the States now existing shall think proper to admit shall not be prohibited by the Congress prior to the year 1808:" That this Commonwealth does admit the migration of alien friends described as the subject of the said act concerning aliens; that a provision against prohibiting their migration is a provision against all acts equivalent thereto, or it would be nugatory; that to remove them when migrated is equivalent to a prohibition of their migration, and is therefore contrary to the said provision of the Constitution and void.

6. That the imprisonment of a person under the protection of the laws of this Commonwealth on his failure to obey the simple *order* of the President to depart out of the United States, as is undertaken by the said act, entitled "an act concerning aliens," is contrary to the Constitution, one amendment to which has provided, that "no person shall be deprived of liberty without due process of law," and that another having provided "that in all criminal prosecutions the accused shall enjoy the right to a public trial by an impartial jury, to be informed of the nature and cause of the accusation, to be confronted with the witnesses against him, to have compulsory process for obtaining witnesses in his favor, and to have the assistance of counsel for his defence," the same act undertaking to authorize the President to remove a person out of the United States who is under the protection of the law, on his own suspicion, without accusation, without jury, without public trial, without confrontation of the witnesses against him, without having witnesses in his favor, without defence, without counsel, is contrary to these provisions also of the Constitution, is therefore not law, but utterly void and of no force. That transferring the power of judging any person, who is under the protection of the laws, from the courts to the President of the United States, as is undertaken by the same act concerning aliens, is against the article of the Constitution which provides that "the judicial power of the United States shall be vested in courts, the judges of which shall hold their offices during good behavior;" and that the said act is void for that reason also; and it is further to be noted, that this transfer of judiciary power is to that magistrate of the General Government who already possesses all the executive, and a qualified negative in all the legislative powers.

7. That the construction applied by the General Government (as is evinced by sundry of their proceedings) to those parts of the Constitution of the United States which delegates to Congress a power to lay and collect taxes, duties, imposts, and excises; to pay the debts, and pro-

vide for the common defence and general welfare of the United States, and to make all laws which shall be necessary and proper for carrying into execution the powers vested by the Constitution in the Government of the United States, or any department thereof, goes to the destruction of all the limits prescribed to their power by the Constitution. That words meant by that instrument to be subsidiary only to the execution of the limited powers ought not to be so construed as themselves to give unlimited powers, nor a part so to be taken as to destroy the whole residue of the instrument: That the proceedings of the General Government under color of these articles will be a fit and necessary subject for revisal and correction at a time of greater tranquillity, while those specified in the preceding resolutions call for immediate redress.

8. That the preceding resolutions be transmitted to the Senators and Representatives in Congress from this Commonwealth, who are hereby enjoined to present the same to their respective houses, and to use their best endeavors to procure, at the next session of Congress, a repeal of the aforesaid unconstitutional and obnoxious acts.

9. *Lastly*, That the Governor of this Commonwealth be, and is hereby, authorized and requested to communicate the preceding resolutions to the legislatures of the several States, to assure them that this Commonwealth considers union for specified national purposes, and particularly for those specified in their late federal compact, to be friendly to the peace, happiness, and prosperity of all the States: that faithful to that compact, according to the plain intent and meaning in which it was understood and acceded to by the several parties, it is sincerely anxious for its preservation: that it does also believe, that to take from the States all the powers of self-government, and transfer them to a general and consolidated government, without regard to the special obligations and reservations solemnly agreed to in that compact, is not for the peace, happiness, or prosperity of these States: And that therefore this Commonwealth is determined, as it doubts not its co-States are, tamely to submit to undelegated and consequently unlimited powers in no man or body of men on earth: that if the acts before specified should stand, these conclusions would flow from them; that the General Government may place any act they think proper on the list of crimes, and punish it themselves, whether enumerated or not enumerated by the Constitution as cognizable by them; that they may transfer its cognizance to the President or any other person, who may himself be the accuser, counsel, judge, and jury, whose *suspicions* may be the evidence, his order the sentence, his officer the executioner, and his breast the sole record of the transaction; that a very numerous and valuable description of the inhabitants of these States, being by this precedent reduced as outlaws to the absolute dominion of one man, and the barrier of the Constitution thus swept away from us all, no rampart now remains against the passions and the power of a majority of Congress to protect from a like exportation or other more grievous punishment the minority

of the same body, the legislatures, judges, governors, and counselors of the States, nor their other
peaceable inhabitants who may venture to reclaim the constitutional rights and liberties of
the States and people, or who for other causes,
good or bad, may be obnoxious to the views, or
marked by the suspicions of the President, or be
thought dangerous to his or their elections or
other interests, public or personal; that the
friendless alien has indeed been selected as the
safest subject of a first experiment; but the citizen will soon follow, or rather has already followed; for already has a sedition act marked
him as its prey: that these and successive acts
of the same character, unless arrested on the
threshold, may tend to drive these States into
revolution and blood and will furnish new calumnies against republican governments, and
new pretexts for those who wish it to be believed that man cannot be governed but by a
rod of iron: that it would be a dangerous delu-
sion, were a confidence in the men of our choice
to silence our fears for the safety of our rights:
that confidence is everywhere the parent of despotism; free government is founded in jealousy
and not in confidence; it is jealousy and not
confidence which prescribes limited constitutions to bind down those whom we are obliged
to trust with power: that our Constitution
has accordingly fixed the limits to which and
no further our confidence may go; and let the
honest advocate of confidence read the alien
and sedition acts, and say if the Constitution
has not been wise in fixing limits to the government it created, and whether we should be wise
in destroying those limits? Let him say what
the Government is if it be not a tyranny, which
the men of our choice have conferred on the
President, and the President of our choice has assented to and accepted over the friendly strangers, to whom the mild spirit of our country and
its laws had pledged hospitality and protection:
that the men of our choice have more respected
the bare suspicions of the President than the
solid rights of innocence, the claims of justification, the sacred force of truth, and the forms
and substance of law and justice In questions
of power, then, let no more be heard of confidence in man, but bind him down from mischief
by the chains of the Constitution. That this
Commonwealth does therefore call on its co-
States for an expression of their sentiments on
the acts concerning aliens and for the punishment of certain crimes hereinbefore specified,
plainly declaring whether these acts are or are
not authorized by the federal compact? And
it doubts not that their sense will be so announced as to prove their attachment unaltered
to limited government, whether general or particular, and that the rights and liberties of their
co-States will be exposed to no dangers by remaining embarked on a common bottom with
their own: That they will concur with this
Commonwealth in considering the said acts as so
palpably against the Constitution, as to amount
to an undisguised declaration that the compact
is not meant to be the measure of the powers of
the General Government, but that it will proceed
in the exercise over these States of all powers
whatsoever: That they will view this as seizing

the rights of the States, and consolidating them
in the hands of the General Government with a
power assumed to bind the States, (not merely
in cases made federal,) but in all cases whatsoever, by laws made, not with their consent, but
by others against their consent: That this would
be to surrender the form of government we have
chosen, and to live under one deriving its powers
from its own will, and not from our authority;
and that the co-States, recurring to their natural
right in cases not made federal, will concur in
declaring these acts void and of no force, and
will each unite with this Commonwealth in
requesting their repeal at the next session of
Congress.

## Virginia Resolutions, December, 1798.

*Resolved*, That the General Assembly of Virginia doth unequivocally express a firm resolution to maintain and defend the Constitution of
the United States and the constitution of this
State against every aggression, either foreign or
domestic; and that they will support the Government of the United States in all measures
warranted by the former.

2. That this Assembly most solemnly declares
a warm attachment to the Union of the States,
to maintain which it pledges its powers; and
that, for this end, it is their duty to watch over
and oppose every infraction of those principles
which constitute the only basis of that Union,
because a faithful observance of them can alone
secure its existence and the public happiness.

3. That this Assembly doth explicitly and
peremptorily declare, that it views the powers
of the Federal Government as resulting from the
compact to which the States are parties, as limited by the plain sense and intention of the instrument constituting that compact, as no further
valid than they are authorized by the grants
enumerated in that compact; and that, in case
of a deliberate, palpable, and dangerous exercise
of other powers, not granted by the said compact, the States, who are parties thereto, have
the right, and are in duty bound, to interpose for
arresting the progress of the evil, and for maintaining, within their respective limits, the authorities, rights, and liberties appertaining to
them

4. That the General Assembly doth also express its deep regret that a spirit has, in sundry
instances, been manifested by the Federal Government to enlarge its powers by forced constructions of the constitutional charter which defines
them; and that indications have appeared of a
design to expound certain general phrases (which,
having been copied from the very limited grant
of powers in the former Articles of Confederation,
were the less liable to be misconstrued) so as to
destroy the meaning and effect of the particular
enumeration which necessarily explains and limits the general phrases, and so as to consolidate
the States, by degrees, into one sovereignty, the
obvious tendency and inevitable result of which
would be to transform the present republican
system of the United States into an absolute, or,
at best, a mixed monarchy.

5. That the General Assembly doth particularly protest against the palpable and alarming
infractions of the Constitution in the two late

cases of the "alien and sedition acts," passed at the last session of Congress; the first of which exercises a power nowhere delegated to the Federal Government, and which, by uniting legislative and judicial powers to those of executive, subverts the general principles of free government, as well as the particular organization and positive provisions of the Federal Constitution; and the other of which acts exercises, in like manner, a power not delegated by the Constitution, but, on the contrary, expressly and positively forbidden by one of the amendments thereto—a power which, more than any other, ought to produce universal alarm, because it is levelled against the right of freely examining public characters and measures, and of free communication among the people thereon, which has ever been justly deemed the only effectual guardian of every other right.

6. That this State, having by its convention, which ratified the Federal Constitution, expressly declared that, among other essential rights, "the liberty of conscience and the press cannot be cancelled, abridged, restrained, or modified, by any authority of the United States," and from its extreme anxiety to guard these rights from every possible attack of sophistry and ambition, having, with other States, recommended an amendment for that purpose, which amendment was, in due time, annexed to the Constitution—it would mark a reproachful inconsistency, and criminal degeneracy if an indifference were now shown to the most palpable violation of one of the rights thus declared and secured, and to the establishment of a precedent which may be fatal to the other.

7. That the good people of this Commonwealth, having ever felt, and continuing to feel, the most sincere affection for their brethren of the other States, the truest anxiety for establishing and perpetuating the union of all, and the most scrupulous fidelity to that Constitution, which is the pledge of mutual friendship and the instrument of mutual happiness, the General Assembly doth solemnly appeal to the like dispositions in the other States, in confidence that they will concur with this Commonwealth in declaring, as it does hereby declare, that the acts aforesaid are unconstitutional, and that the necessary and proper measures will be taken by each for co-operating with this State in maintaining unimpaired the authorities, rights, and liberties reserved to the States respectively, or to the people.

8. That the Governor be desired to transmit a copy of the foregoing resolutions to the executive authority of each of the other States, with a request that the same may be communicated to the legislature thereof, and that a copy be furnished to each of the Senators and Representatives representing this State in the Congress of the United States.

---

# XXII.

# POLITICAL MISCELLANY.

## ELECTIVE FRANCHISE IN THE STATES.

### In Tennessee.

1867, February 6—The HOUSE passed a bill striking the word "white" from the franchise law of the State*—yeas 38, nays 25. The yeas were Messrs. Anderson of Hamilton, Anderson of White, Baker, Blackman, Clements, Clingan, Donaldson, Doughty, Dowdy, Elliott, Fuson, Garner, Gilmer, Hudson, Hale, Kerchival, Maxwell, McNair, Morris, Murphy, Norman, Patton, Porter, Puckett, Raulston, Richards, Shepherd, Smith of Hardeman, Smith of Obion, Taylor, Thornburgh, Underwood, Waters, Welsh, Wines, Woodcock, Woods, and Speaker (*pro tem.*) Mulloy—38.

February 18—The SENATE concurred—yeas 14, nays 7.

March 21—The supreme court of the State unanimously sustained the constitutionality of the franchise law.

A law was also passed containing this provision:

"That in all State, district, county, and all other elections, such aliens as have resided more than one year in the United States, and more than six months in the State of Tennessee, shall have the right of the elective franchise: *Provided*, That such persons shall have previously declared their intention to become citizens of the United States, and that they shall not have participated in the late rebellion."

---

### In Ohio.

1867, April 6—This joint resolution passed:

A RESOLUTION

Relative to an amendment of the constitution, providing for the extension of the elective franchise:

*Resolved*, By the General Assembly of the State of Ohio, three-fifths of the members elected to each house agreeing thereto, that it be and is hereby proposed to the electors of this State, to vote at the next annual October election upon the approval or rejection of the following amendment as a substitute for the first section of the fifth article of the constitution of this State, to wit: "Every male citizen of the United States of the age of twenty-one years, who shall have been a resident of the State one year next preceding the election, and of the county, township, or ward in which he resides such time as may be provided by law, except such persons as have borne arms in support of any insurrection or rebellion against the Government of the United States, or have fled from their places of residence to avoid being drafted into the military service thereof, or have deserted the military or naval service of said Government in time of war, and

* For copy of the law see Political Manual for 1866, pp. 27, 28.

had not subsequently been honorably discharged from the same, shall have the qualifications of an elector, and be entitled to vote at all elections."

In the SENATE, the vote was yeas 23, nays 11, strictly party vote except that Mr. Combs (Republican) voted in the negative.

### In Wisconsin.

Both houses have agreed to proposing an amendment to the constitution so as to extend suffrage to *all persons** over the age of twenty-one years. The vote in the Senate was 18 to 9, not voting 6.

### In New Jersey.

A proposition to strike the word "white" from the constitution was defeated in the house —yeas 20, nays 38, as follow:

YEAS—Messrs. Atwater, Sayre, Murphy, Edwards, Baldwin, Voorhees, Runyon, A. P. Condit, Bruere, Stansbury, Mount, Estler, J. D. Condit, Wolsieffer, Moore, Custis, Ball, Trimble, Morris, Falkenbury—20.

NAYS—Messrs. *Allen, Taylor, Iliff, Davenport,* W. W. Clark, *Vail, Lippincott,* Fort, *Christie, White, Pickel, Henry,* Coles, Crozer, Ayres, Tyrrell, *W. J. Iliff, Evans,* H. F. Clark, *Vliet,* Nixon, Garrison, Collings, *Wilson, Thompson,* Hendrickson, *Hedden, Dwyer,* Beesley, *Van Emburgh,* Jarrard, *Fulmer, Corlies, Ward, Perrine, Givens,* Coate, *Yawger*—38.

### In New York.

The Republican State convention to nominate delegates at large for a constitutional convention unanimously adopted this resolution:

*Resolved,* That the delegates to the coming constitutional convention, this day appointed, be instructed to support by every honorable means an amendment to the constitution giving to the black man the same rights of ballot as to the white man.

### In Kansas.

A proposition to extend the elective franchise to women is pending.

### A PROPOSED SUBSTITUTE FOR THE CONSTITUTIONAL AMENDMENT.

In February, 1867, an effort was made to prepare a constitutional amendment to be substituted for that proposed by Congress. The plan given below was published, and was declared to be approved by President Johnson, and submitted to the Legislature of North Carolina, but was not favorably received:

*The following paragraph from the *New York Tribune* is apposite:

Lucy Stone and H. B. Blackwell, citizens of New Jersey, have made an investigation, the result of which is remarkable, and proves that previously to 1776 only men voted, but that in 1776 the original State constitution conferred the franchise on "*all inhabitants*" (men or women, white or black) possessing the prescribed qualifications of £50 clear estate and twelve months' residence, and this constitution remained in force until 1814. In 1790, the Legislature, in an act regulating elections, used the words "he or she" in reference to voters. In 1797, another act relative to elections repeatedly designates the voters as "he or she." In the same year, 1797, seventy-five women voted in Elizabethtown for the Federal candidate. In 1800 women generally voted throughout the State in the presidential contest between Jefferson and Adams. In 1802 a member of the legislature from Hunterdon county was actually elected, in a closely contested election, by the votes of two or three women of color. In 1807, at a local election in Essex county for the location of the county seat, men and women generally participated, and were jointly implicated in very extensive frauds. In the winter of 1807-8, the legislature, in violation of the terms of the constitution, passed an act restricting suffrage to free white male adult citizens, and, in reference to these, virtually abolished the property qualification of £50, thus extending it to all white male tax-payers, while excluding all women and negroes. In 1820 the same provisions were repeated, and remained unchanged until the adoption of the present constitution in 1844.

Whereas it has been announced by persons high in authority that propositions from the southern States having in view the adjustment of our present political troubles would be received and considered, &c: Therefore,

*Resolved by the Legislature of the State of* ——, That the Congress of the United States be requested to propose to the legislatures of the several States the following amendment to the Constitution of the United States:

ARTICLE 14, SEC. 1. No State under the Constitution has a right of its own will to renounce its place in or to withdraw from the Union; nor has the Federal Government any right to eject a State from the Union, or to deprive it of its equal suffrage in the Senate or of representation in the House of Representatives. The Union under the Constitution shall be perpetual.

SEC. 2. The public debt of the United States, authorized by law, shall ever be held sacred and inviolate; but neither the United States nor any State shall assume or pay any debt or obligation incurred in aid of insurrection or rebellion against the Government or authority of the United States.

SEC. 3. All persons born or naturalized in the United States, and subject to the jurisdiction thereof, are citizens of the United States and of the States in which they reside; and the citizens of each State shall be entitled to all the privileges and immunities of citizens in the several States. No State shall deprive any person of life, liberty, or property without due process of law, nor deny to any person within its jurisdiction the equal protection of the laws.

SEC. 4. Representatives shall be apportioned among the several States according to their respective numbers, counting the whole number of persons in each State, excluding Indians not taxed. But when any State shall, on account of race or color or previous condition of servitude, deny the exercise of the franchise at any election for the choice of electors for President and Vice President of the United States, Representatives in Congress, members of the legislature, and other officers elected by the people, to any of the male inhabitants of such State being twenty-one years of age and citizens of the United States, then the entire class of persons so excluded from the exercise of the elective franchise shall not be counted in the basis of representation.

*And whereas, &c., be it further resolved by the Legislature of* ——, That the following article shall be adopted as an amendment to, and become a part of the constitution of the State of ——.

ARTICLE ——. Every male citizen who has resided in this State for one year, and in the county in which he offers to vote six months immediately preceding the day of election, and who can read the Declaration of Independence and the Constitution of the United States in the English language and write his name; or who may be the owner of two hundred and fifty dollars' worth of taxable property, shall be entitled to vote at all elections for governor of the State, members of the legislature and all other officers the election of whom may be by the people of the State: *Provided,* That no person by reason of this article shall be excluded from voting who has heretofore exercised the elective franchise under the constitution or laws of this State, or who, at the time of the adoption of this amendment, may be entitled to vote under said constitution and laws.

## THE ELECTIONS OF 1867.

In NEW HAMPSHIRE, the vote stood: *Governor*—Harriman, Republican, 35,776; Sinclair, Democrat, 32,733. Republican majority in Legislature, about 75.

In CONNECTICUT, the vote stood: *Governor*—Hawley, Republican, 46,585; English, Democrat, 47,575. *State Legislature:* SENATE—Republicans 11, Democrats 10. HOUSE—Republicans 124, Democrats 114. Republican majority on joint ballot, 11.

In RHODE ISLAND, the vote stood: *Governor*—Burnside, Republican, 7,554; Pierce, Democrat, 3,350. The legislature is largely Republican.

In MARYLAND, the vote on calling a convention to revise the constitution of the State, was: For a convention, 34,534; against, 24,136.

In Maryland, a new registry law was passed, directing the registering of "all white male persons" over twenty-one, not criminals or lunatics, and possessing sufficient residence. The legislature also passed an act authorizing and directing the comptroller of that State to examine, adjust, and pay all claims presented to him for settlement by the officers and members, and others of the General Assembly of 1861. It rejected a bill to authorize colored persons to testify in the courts. It provided for the appointment by the governor, by the advice and consent of the senate, in each county, of a "commissioner of slave statistics," to prepare statements of the names, number, age, sex, and physical condition of the slaves in the respective counties at the time of the adoption of the State constitution in 1864, to state whether they were slaves for life or term of years, and whether they were enlisted or drafted into the military service of the United States, so far as is known to said owners or others, and in what regiment they were placed, and what compensation, if any, has been received by such owners from the State or General Government for such slaves—the lists to be preserved among the public records of the counties, and declared to be legal evidence of ownership, &c. The commissioners are to receive twenty-five cents *per capita* for each slave, to be paid by the former owner.

## CONSTITUTIONAL CONVENTIONS.

A convention has recently been chosen in NEW YORK by the votes of all persons qualified to vote for members of the Assembly; but no person was allowed to vote who could not, if challenged, take and subscribe this oath:

"I (A. B.) do solemnly swear (or affirm) that I have never voluntarily borne arms against the United States since I have been a citizen thereof; that I have voluntarily given no aid, countenance, counsel, or encouragement to persons engaged in armed hostility thereto; that I have neither sought nor accepted, nor attempted to exercise, the functions of any office whatever under any authority or pretended authority in hostility to the United States; that I have not yielded a voluntary support to any pretended government, authority, power, or constitution within the United States, hostile or inimical thereto, and did not wilfully desert from the military or naval service of the United States, or leave this State to avoid the draft during the late rebellion."

The convention is to meet in Albany on the first Tuesday in June. The new constitution is to be submitted in November next—as a whole or otherwise, as the convention may determine —to a vote of those qualified to vote for delegates. The convention stands, politically, Republicans 100, Democrats 60.

A convention was chosen in MARYLAND, "by the registered voters thereof," on the second Wednesday of April, in which St. Mary's county has three delegates; Kent, 4; Calvert, 3; Charles, 3; Baltimore county, 7; Talbot, 4; Somerset, 5; Dorchester, 4; Cecil, 5; Prince George's, 4; Queen Anne's, 4; Worcester, 5; Frederick, 7; Harford, 5; Caroline, 4; Baltimore city, 21; Montgomery, 4; Allegany, 6; Carroll, 6; Howard, 4; Anne Arundel, 4; and Washington, 6. Said constitution it is provided, shall contain a "clause prohibiting the legislature from making any law providing for payment by this State for persons heretofore held as slaves." The convention is to meet in Annapolis, on the second Wednesday of May, 1867, the compensation of members to be five dollars per day and mileage, and the president of the convention is authorized to order the payment of the compensation above provided, and the treasurer required to pay the same, in conformity with said order. The constitution is to be submitted to the legal and qualified voters for their ratification or rejection, at such time, in such manner, and subject to such rules and regulations as the convention may prescribe. Judges of election, clerks of court, or sheriffs failing or neglecting to perform any duties required of them respecting these elections, are made liable to indictment, and fine of $1,000 and imprisonment of six months. The convention is unanimously Democratic and "Conservative," the Republicans declining to run candidates.

In MICHIGAN, a Convention has been chosen, with a large Republican supremacy.

---

*Statement of the Public Debt of the United States on the 1st of April, 1867.*

| | | |
|---|---:|---:|
| Debt bearing coin interest............................................................................... | | $1,499,381,591 80 |
| Debt bearing currency interest......................................................................... | | 734,280,780 00 |
| Matured debt not presented for payment............................................................. | | 12,825,658 32 |
| Debt bearing no interest.—U. S. Notes................................... | $375,417,249 00 | |
| Fractional currency........................................... | 29,217,494 96 | |
| Gold certificates of deposit................................. | 12,590,600 00 | |
| | | 417,225,343 96 |
| Total debt........................................................................ | | 2,663,713,374 18 |
| Amount in Treasury, Coin................................................. | 105,956,477 22 | |
| "       "       Currency......................................... | 34,328,826 52 | |
| | | 140,285,303 74 |
| Amount of Debt, less Cash in the Treasury.................................................................... | | $2,523,428,070 44 |

## PRESIDENT JOHNSON ON HABEAS CORPUS.

1865, July 7—Pending the execution of the order of President Johnson, given on page 7, respecting the convicted assassins of President Lincoln, an effort was made to stay the execution by the counsel of Mrs. Surratt, who obtained a writ of *habeas corpus* on that day from Judge Wylie, one of the justices of the supreme court of the District of Columbia.

This writ was served upon General Hancock by the marshal of the District, Mr. Gooding, and at 11 o'clock General Hancock, accompanied by Attorney General Speed, made his appearance in the criminal court room, and made the following return, to wit:

"HEADQUARTERS MIDDLE MILITARY DIVISION, "WASHINGTON, D. C., *July* 7, 1865.

"To Hon. ANDREW WYLIE, *Justice of the Supreme Court of the District of Columbia.*

" I hereby acknowledge the service of the writ hereto attached, and return the same, and respectfully say that the body of Mary E. Surratt is in my possession under and by virtue of an order of Andrew Johnson, President of the United States, and Commander-in-Chief of the army and navy, for the purposes of said order expressed, a copy of which is hereto attached and made part of this return; and that I do not produce said body by reason of the order of the President of the United States indorsed upon said writ, to which reference is hereby respectfully made, dated July 7, 1865.

"WINFIELD S. HANCOCK, " *Major General U. S. Vols., commanding.*"

The indorsement upon the writ is as follows:

"EXECUTIVE OFFICE, " *July* 7, 1865—10 A. M.

"To Major General W. S. HANCOCK, "*Commanding, &c.*

"I, Andrew Johnson, President of the United States, do hereby declare that the writ of *habeas corpus* has been heretofore suspended in such cases as this; and I do especially suspend this writ, and direct that you proceed to execute the order heretofore given you upon the judgment of the military commission; and you will give this order in return to this writ.

"ANDREW JOHNSON, *President.*"

When Attorney General Speed appeared he addressed the court briefly upon the action of the Government in the premises, and argued to show that the suspension of the writ of *habeas corpus* was absolutely necessary in a time of war. He declared that the Government had given the case anxious consideration, and had directed that the writ should not be complied with after mature deliberation.

The court responded by saying that no further action should be taken in the premises.

W. E. Doster, Esq., counsel for Payne and Atzerodt, also applied for a writ of *habeas corpus* in their behalf, but as the writ in the case of Mrs. Surratt had been of no avail, Judge Wylie declined to issue the writ.

## ADDITIONAL PROCLAMATIONS OF PRESIDENT JOHNSON.

1868, July 18—President Johnson issued a proclamation reciting the ratification of the XIVth amendment by South Carolina, in substantially the same terms as are used in the proclamation announcing the action in Florida and North Carolina, on page 379.

1868, July 18—President Johnson issued a like proclamation of the action in Louisiana.

1868, July 20—President Johnson issued a like proclamation of the action in Alabama.

1868, July 27—President Johnson issued a like proclamation of the action in Georgia.

### SECOND ELECTION IN MISSISSIPPI.

At the election held in Mississippi, November 30 and December 1, 1869, under the proclamation of President Grant, (see page 505,) the vote was as follows:

For the constitution, 113,735; against it, 955.

All of the separately-submitted portions (see page 505) were rejected, except section 5, article XII, which was ratified—yeas 70,427, nays 20,-834. Part of section 3, article VII, was rejected—yeas 2,206, nays 87,874. Section 5, article VII, was rejected—yeas 2,390, nays 87,253. Part of section 26, article XII, was rejected—yeas 2,171, nays 88,444. [For text of these sections see page 505.] The total registration was 176,-792, of whom 76,110 were white, and 100,682 colored. The total vote polled on constitution was 114,690. For Governor, James L. Alcorn, received 76,143 votes; Louis Dent 38,133. At the first election the constitution was defeated—June 22, 1868.

# PART III.

# POLITICAL MANUAL FOR 1868.

## XXIII.

### ORDERS, LETTERS, MESSAGE AND VOTES IN THE SENATE
#### RESPECTING SECRETARY STANTON.

**Request for Mr. Stanton's Resignation and Reply.**

1.—PRESIDENT JOHNSON TO SECRETARY STANTON.

EXECUTIVE MANSION,
WASHINGTON, *August 5, 1867.*

SIR: Public considerations of a high character constrain me to say that your resignation as Secretary of War will be accepted.

Very respectfully,
ANDREW JOHNSON.

To Hon. EDWIN M. STANTON,
*Secretary of War.*

2.—SECRETARY STANTON TO PRESIDENT JOHNSON.

WAR DEPARTMENT,
WASHINGTON, *August 5, 1867.*

SIR: Your note of this day has been received, stating that public considerations of a high character constrain you to say that my resignation as Secretary of War will be accepted.

In reply, I have the honor to say that public considerations of a high character, which alone have induced me to continue at the head of this Department, constrain me not to resign the office of Secretary of War before the next meeting of Congress. Very respectfully, yours,
EDWIN M. STANTON.

To the PRESIDENT.

**Secretary Stanton's Suspension.**

3.—PRESIDENT JOHNSON TO SECRETARY STANTON.

EXECUTIVE MANSION,
WASHINGTON, *August 12, 1867*

SIR: By virtue of the power and authority vested in me as President by the Constitution and laws of the United States, you are hereby suspended from office as Secretary of War, and will cease to exercise any and all functions pertaining to the same. You will at once transfer to General Ulysses S. Grant, who has this day been authorized and empowered to act as Secretary of War *ad interim*, all records, books, papers, and other public property now in your custody and charge.

Very respectfully, yours,
ANDREW JOHNSON.

To Hon. EDWIN M STANTON,
*Secretary of War.*

A

4.—PRESIDENT JOHNSON TO GENERAL GRANT.

EXECUTIVE MANSION,
WASHINGTON, *August 12, 1867.*

SIR: The honorable Edwin M. Stanton having been this day suspended as Secretary of War, you are hereby authorized and empowered to act as Secretary of War *ad interim*, and will at once enter upon the discharge of the duties of that office.

The Secretary of War has been instructed to transfer to you all records, books, papers, and other public property now in his custody and charge. Very respectfully, yours,
ANDREW JOHNSON.

To General ULYSSES S. GRANT,
*Washington, D. C.*

5.—GENERAL GRANT TO SECRETARY STANTON.

HEADQ'RS ARMIES OF THE UNITED STATES,
WASHINGTON, D. C., *August 12, 1867.*

SIR: Enclosed herewith I have the honor to transmit to you a copy of a letter just received from the President of the United States, notifying me of my assignment as Acting Secretary of War, and directing me to assume those duties at once.

In notifying you of my acceptance. I cannot let the opportunity pass without expressing to you my appreciation of the zeal, patriotism, firmness, and ability with which you have ever discharged the duties of Secretary of War.

With great respect, your obedient servant,
U. S. GRANT, *General.*

To Hon. EDWIN M. STANTON,
*Secretary of War.*

6.—SECRETARY STANTON TO PRESIDENT JOHNSON.

WAR DEPARTMENT,
WASHINGTON CITY, *August 12, 1867.*

SIR: Your note of this date has been received, informing me that, by virtue of the power and authority vested in you as President by the Constitution and laws of the United States, I am suspended from office as Secretary of War, and will cease to exercise any and all functions pertaining to the same, and also directing me at once to transfer to General U. S. Grant, who has this day been authorized and empowered to act as Secretary of War *ad interim*, all records books, papers, and other public property now in my custody and charge.

Under a sense of public duty I am compelled to deny your right, under the Constitution and laws of the United States, without the advice and consent of the Senate, and without legal cause, to suspend me from office as Secretary of War, or the exercise of any or all functions pertaining to the same, or without such advice and consent to compel me to transfer to any person the records, books, papers, and public property in my custody as Secretary. But inasmuch as the General commanding the armies of the United States has been appointed *ad interim*, and has notified me that he has accepted the appointment, I have no alternative but to submit, under protest, to superior force.

Very respectfully, yours,
EDWIN M. STANTON,
*Secretary of War.*

To the PRESIDENT.

### 7.—SECRETARY STANTON TO GENERAL GRANT.

WAR DEPARTMENT,
WASHINGTON CITY, *August* 12, 1867.

GENERAL: Your note of this date, accompanied by a copy of a letter addressed to you, August 12, by the President, appointing you Secretary of War *ad interim*, and informing me of your acceptance of the appointment, has been received.

Under a sense of public duty I am compelled to deny the President's right, under the Constitution and laws of the United States, to suspend me from office as Secretary of War, or to authorize any other person to enter upon the discharge of the duties of that office, or to require me to transfer to you or any other person the records, books, papers, and other property in my official custody and charge as Secretary of War.

But, inasmuch as the President has assumed to suspend me from office as Secretary of War, and you have notified me of your acceptance of the appointment of Secretary of War *ad interim*, I have no alternative but to submit, under protest, to the superior force of the President.

You will please accept my acknowledgment of the kind terms in which you have notified me of your acceptance of the President's appointment, and my cordial reciprocation of the sentiments expressed.

I am, with sincere regard, truly yours,
EDWIN M. STANTON,
*Secretary of War.*
General ULYSSES S. GRANT.

### Action of the Senate, January 13, 1868.

January 13—The Senate resumed consideration of the following resolution, reported by the Committee on Military Affairs and the Militia, the 10th instant:

*Resolved*, That having considered the evidence and reasons given by the President in his report of the 12th December, 1867, for the suspension from the office of Secretary of War of Edwin M. Stanton, the Senate do not concur in such suspension.

Which was determined in the affirmative—yeas 35, nays 6, as follow:

YEAS—Messrs. Anthony, Cameron, Cattell, Chandler, Cole, Conkling, Conness, Corbett, Cragin, Drake, Edmunds, Ferry, Fessenden, Fowler, Frelinghuysen, Harlan, Howard, Howe, Morgan, Morrill of Maine, Morrill of Vermont, Morton, Nye, Patterson of New Hampshire, Pomeroy, Ramsey, Stewart, Sumner, Thayer, Tipton, Trumbull, Wade, Willey, Williams, Wilson—35.

NAYS—Messrs. *Bayard, Buckalew, Davis, Dixon, Doolittle, Patterson* of Tennessee—6.

NOT VOTING—Messrs. Grimes, *Guthrie,* Henderson, *Hendricks, Johnson. Norton,* Ross, *Saulsbury,* Sherman, Sprague, Van Winkle, *Vickers,* Yates—13.

[The *National Intelligencer* stated, in its news columns, that Messrs. Henderson and Hendricks were paired, and that Mr. Ross, though present, declined to vote.]

### Action of General Grant.

HEADQUARTERS ARMIES UNITED STATES.
WASHINGTON, D. C., *January* 14, 1868.

SIR: I have the honor to enclose herewith copy of official notice received by me last evening of the action of the Senate of the United States in the case of the suspension of Hon. E. M. Stanton, Secretary of War. According to the provisions of section two of "An act regulating the tenure of certain civil offices," my functions as Secretary of War *ad interim* ceased from the moment of the receipt of the within notice.

I have the honor to be, very respectfully, your obedient servant,
U. S. GRANT, *General.*

His Excellency A. JOHNSON,
*President of the United States.*

### Subsequent Action of President Johnson.

1868, February 21—President Johnson sent this message to the Senate:

WASHINGTON, D. C., *February* 21, 1868.
*To the Senate of the United States:*

On the 12th day of August, 1867, by virtue of the power and authority vested in the President by the Constitution and laws of the United States, I suspended Edwin M. Stanton from the office of Secretary of War. In further exercise of the power and authority so vested in the President, I have this day removed Mr. Stanton from the office, and designated the Adjutant General of the Army as Secretary of War *ad interim*.

Copies of the communications upon this subject, addressed to Mr. Stanton and the Adjutant General, are herewith transmitted for the information of the Senate. ANDREW JOHNSON.

[For copies of these orders, see the first and second Articles of Impeachment.]

### Further Proceedings in the Senate.

February 21—Mr. Edmunds submitted the following resolution for consideration:

*Resolved*, That, having received and considered the communication of the President stating that he had removed from office Edwin M. Stanton, Secretary of War, the Senate disapprove the action of the President.

The Senate, by unanimous consent, proceeded to consider the said resolution.

Mr. Dixon moved to amend the resolution, by striking out all after the word "Resolved," and inserting as follows: *That the President be requested to inform the Senate by what authority he has removed Edwin M. Stanton from the office of Secretary of War.*

Mr. Drake moved to amend the amendment of Mr. Dixon, by inserting a preamble, as follows: *The Senate having received and considered the communication of the President of the United States, stating that he had removed Edwin M. Stanton from the office of Secretary of War, it is.*

Which was disagreed to.

The amendment of Mr. Dixon was disagreed to—yeas 4, nays 33, as follow:

YEAS—Messrs. *Buckalew, Dixon, Doolittle, Hendricks*—4.

NAYS—Messrs. Anthony, Cameron, Cattell, Chandler, Conkling, Conness, Corbett, Cragin, Drake, Edmunds, Ferry, Fessenden, Frelinghuysen, Harlan, Henderson, Howard, Howe, Morrill of Maine, Morrill of Vermont, Patterson of New Hampshire, Pomeroy, Ramsey, Sprague, Stewart, Sumner, Thayer, Tipton, Trumbull, Van Winkle, Willey, Williams, Wilson, Yates—33.

NOT VOTING—Messrs. *Bayard*, Cole, *Davis*, Fowler, Grimes, *Johnson, McCreery*, Morgan, Morton, *Norton*, Nye, *Patterson* of Tennessee, Ross, *Saulsbury*, Sherman, *Vickers*, Wade—17.

Mr. Chandler moved to amend the resolution of Mr. Edmunds, by adding thereto the words: *as a violation of the rights of the Senate, and unauthorized by law.*

Which was disagreed to.

Mr. Wilson moved to amend the resolution, by inserting a preamble, as follows: *Whereas the Senate have received and considered the communication of the President of the United States, stating that he had removed Edwin M. Stanton, Secretary of War, and had designated the Adjutant General of the Army to act as Secretary of War ad interim;* and by striking out all after the word "Resolved," and inserting, as follows: *by the Senate of the United States that, under the Constitution and laws of the United States, the President has no power to remove the Secretary of War and designate any other officer to perform the duties of that office ad interim.*

Mr. Yates moved to amend the amendment of Mr. Wilson, by striking out all after the word "Resolved," and inserting, as follows: *That the removal of Edwin M. Stanton, Secretary of War, and the appointment of a Secretary of War ad interim, during the session of the Senate, is simple resistance to law and revolutionary in character, and that the Senate disapproves of the same, and advises the said Edwin M. Stanton, Secretary of War, not to surrender the office to any person whomsoever.*

Which was disagreed to.

Mr. Corbett moved to amend the amendment of Mr. Wilson, by striking out all after the word "Whereas" in the preamble, and inserting the words: *The President has informed the Senate that he has removed the Secretary of War, Hon. E. M. Stanton, and appointed Adjutant General Thomas to act as Secretary of War ad interim, therefore be it;* and by striking out all after the word "Resolved," and inserting in lieu thereof the words: *That we do not concur in the action of the President in removing the Secretary of War and appointing the Adjutant General to act as Secretary of War ad interim; that we deny the right of the President so to act, under the existing laws, without the consent of the Senate.*

Which was disagreed to.

The amendment of Mr. Wilson to the resolution of Mr. Edmunds was then agreed to—yeas 28, nays 6, as follow:

YEAS—Messrs. Anthony, Cameron, Cattell, Cole, Conkling, Cragin, Drake, Ferry, Harlan, Morrill of Maine, Morrill of Vermont, Morton, Patterson of New Hampshire, Pomeroy, Ramsey, Ross, Sprague, Stewart, Sumner, Thayer, Tipton, Trumbull, Van Winkle, Wade, Willey, Williams, Wilson, Yates—28.

NAYS—Messrs. *Buckalew, Davis, Doolittle,* Edmunds, Hendricks, *Patterson* of Tennessee—6.

NOT VOTING—Messrs. *Bayard*, Chandler, Conness, Corbett, *Dixon,* Fessenden, Fowler, Frelinghuysen, Grimes, Henderson, Howard, Howe, *Johnson, McCreery*, Morgan, *Norton*, Nye, *Saulsbury,* Sherman, *Vickers*—20.

The resolution, as amended, was then agreed to without a division.

---

### Acceptance of General Lorenzo Thomas.

WAR DEPARTMENT,
ADJUTANT GENERAL'S OFFICE,
WASHINGTON, *February 21,* 1868.

His Excellency ANDREW JOHNSON, *President of the United States.*

SIR: I have the honor to report that I have delivered the communication addressed by you to the honorable Edwin M. Stanton, removing him from the office of Secretary of the War Department, and also to acknowledge the receipt of your letter of this date authorizing and empowering me to act as Secretary of War *ad interim.* I accept this appointment with gratitude for the confidence reposed in me, and will endeavor to discharge the duties to the best of my ability.

I have the honor to be, sir, your obedient servant, L. THOMAS, *Adjutant General.*

---

### Secretary Stanton "Relinquished Charge" of the War Department.

Secretary Stanton remained in possession of the War Office till after the vote in the Senate, sitting as a court of impeachment, on the 26th of May, on which day he addressed this communication to President Johnson:

WAR DEPARTMENT,
WASHINGTON CITY, *May 26,* 1868.

SIR: The resolution of the Senate of the United States, of the 21st of February last, declaring that the President "has no power to remove the Secretary of War and designate any other officer to perform the duties of that office *ad interim,*" having this day failed to be supported by two-thirds of the Senators present and voting on the articles of impeachment preferred against you by the House of Representatives, I have relinquished charge of the War Department, and have left the same, and the books, archives, papers, and property, heretofore in my custody as Secretary of War, in care of Brevet Major General Townsend, the senior Assistant Adjutant General, subject to your direction. EDWIN M. STANTON,
*Secretary of War.*

To the PRESIDENT *of the United States.*

Secretary Stanton's order to Gen. Townsend is as follows:

WAR DEPARTMENT,
WASHINGTON CITY, *May 26,* 1868.

GENERAL: You will take charge of the War Department, and the books and papers, archives and public property, belonging to the same, sub-

ject to the disposal and direction of the President.
EDWIN M. STANTON,
*Secretary of War.*
Brevet Major Gen. E. D. TOWNSEND,
*Assistant Adjutant General.*

### Action of the Senate upon the Nomination of General Schofield.

1868, May 29—Mr. Edmunds offered the following preamble and resolution:

Whereas, on the 23d of April, 1868, the President nominated John M. Schofield to be Secretary of War, in place of Edwin M. Stanton, removed; and whereas, in the opinion of the Senate, the said Stanton has not been legally removed from his office, but inasmuch as the said Stanton has relinquished his place as Secretary of War, for causes stated in his note to the President: Therefore

*Resolved,* That the Senate advise and consent to the appointment of John M. Schofield to be Secretary of War.

Mr. Willey moved to amend Mr. Edmunds's resolution, by striking out all after "Resolved," and inserting *That the Senate advise and consent to the appointment of John M. Schofield to be Secretary for the Department of War, in the place of Edwin M. Stanton, hereby removed.*

Which was debated and withdrawn by him.

Mr. Frelinghuysen moved to amend Mr. Edmunds's resolution, by striking out all after "Resolved," and inserting *That the Senate advise and consent to the appointment of John M. Schofield to be Secretary for the Department of War, in the place of Edwin M. Stanton, who has relinquished that office.*

Mr. Henderson moved to amend the amendment of Mr. Frelinghuysen, by striking out the words "in the place of Edwin M. Stanton, who has relinquished that office."

Which was rejected.

Mr. Stewart moved to amend Mr. Frelinghuysen's amendment, by striking out all after "Resolved," and inserting *That the Senate advise and consent to the appointment of John M. Schofield as Secretary of War, in place of Edwin M. Stanton, who has been forced to retire from the discharge of the duties of said office by reason of the illegal and unconstitutional acts of the President of the United States.*

Which was rejected—yeas 19, nays 21, as follow:

YEAS—Messrs. Cameron, Cattell, Cole, Conkling, Conness, Cragin, Drake, Morrill of Vermont, Patterson of New Hampshire, Pomeroy, Ramsey, Stewart, Sumner, Thayer, Tipton, Wade, Williams, Wilson, Yates—19.

NAYS—Messrs. Anthony, *Buckalew,* Corbett, *Doolittle,* Edmunds, Fowler, Frelinghuysen, Henderson, *Hendricks, Johnson, McCreery,* Morgan, Morton, *Norton, Patterson* of Tennessee, Ross, Sprague, Trumbull, Van Winkle, *Vickers,* Willey—21.

NOT VOTING—Messrs. *Bayard,* Chandler, *Davis, Dixon,* Ferry, Fessenden, Grimes, Harlan, Howard, Howe, Morrill of Maine, Nye, *Saulsbury,* Sherman—14.

The amendment of Mr. Frelinghuysen was then rejected—yeas 15, nays 22, as follow:

YEAS—Messrs. *Buckalew,* Corbett, *Doolittle,* Fowler, Frelinghuysen, *Hendricks, Johnson, McCreery, Norton, Patterson* of Tennessee, Ross, Sprague, Tipton, Van Winkle, *Vickers*—15.

NAYS—Anthony, Cameron, Cattell, Cole, Conkling, Conness, Cragin, Drake, Edmunds, Morgan, Morton, Patterson of New Hampshire, Pomeroy, Ramsey, Stewart, Sumner, Thayer, Wade, Willey, Williams, Wilson, Yates—22.

NOT VOTING—Messrs. *Bayard,* Chandler, *Davis, Dixon,* Ferry, Fessenden, Grimes, Harlan, Henderson, Howard, Howe, Morrill of Maine, Morrill of Vermont, Nye, *Saulsbury,* Sherman, Trumbull—17.

The resolution offered by Mr. Edmunds was then agreed to—yeas 35, nays 2, as follow:

YEAS—Messrs. Anthony, *Buckalew,* Cameron, Cattell, Cole, Conness, Corbett, *Doolittle,* Drake, Edmunds, Fowler, Frelinghuysen, Harlan, Henderson, *Hendricks, Johnson,* Morgan, Morrill of Vermont, Morton, Patterson of New Hampshire, *Patterson* of Tennessee, Pomeroy, Ramsey, Ross, Sprague, Stewart, Thayer, Tipton, Trumbull, Van Winkle, *Vickers,* Willey, Williams, Wilson, Yates—35.

NAYS—Messrs. *McCreery, Norton*—2.

NOT VOTING—Messrs. *Bayard,* Chandler, Conkling, Cragin, *Davis, Dixon,* Ferry, Fessenden, Grimes, Howard, Howe, Morrill of Maine, Nye, *Saulsbury,* Sherman, Sumner, Wade—17.

The preamble was then agreed to—yeas 28, nays 13, as follow:

YEAS—Messrs. Anthony, Cameron, Cragin, Cole, Conkling, Conness, Corbett, Cragin, Drake, Edmunds, Frelinghuysen, Harlan, Morgan, Morrill of Vermont, Morton, Patterson of New Hampshire, Pomeroy, Ramsey, Sprague, Stewart, Sumner, Thayer, Tipton, Wade, Willey, Williams, Wilson, Yates—28.

NAYS—*Buckalew, Doolittle,* Fowler, Henderson, *Hendricks, Johnson, McCreery, Norton, Patterson* of Tennessee, Ross, Trumbull, Van Winkle, *Vickers*—13.

NOT VOTING—Messrs. *Bayard,* Chandler, *Davis, Dixon,* Ferry, Fessenden, Grimes, Howard, Howe, Morrill of Maine, Nye, *Saulsbury,* Sherman—13.

## XXIV.

# THE ARTICLES OF IMPEACHMENT AND REPLY,
## VOTES IN THE HOUSE, AND JUDGMENT OF THE SENATE.

**Proposed Impeachment of President Johnson.***

1867, November 25—Mr. Boutwell, from the Committee on the Judiciary, submitted a report, representing the views of the majority, (Messrs. Boutwell, Thomas, Williams, Lawrence, and Churchill,) and closing with this resolution:

* Continued from page 64 of the Manual of 1867, or page 190 of the combined Manuals. [No report was made at the July session.]

*Resolved,* That Andrew Johnson, President of the United States, be impeached for high crimes and misdemeanors.

Mr. Wilson, for himself and Mr. Woodbridge, and Mr. Marshall, for himself and Mr. Eldridge, submitted minority reports.

December 7—The resolution above recited was disagreed to—yeas 57, nays 108, as follow:

YEAS—Messrs. Anderson, Arnell, J. M. Ashley, Boutwell, Bromwell, Broomall, Benjamin F. Butler, Churchill, Reader

W. Clarke. Sidney Clarke, Cobb, Coburn, Covode, Cullom, Donnelly, Eckley, Ela, Farnsworth,Gravely. Harding, Higby, Hopkins, Hunter, Judd, Julian, Kelley, Kelsey, William Lawrence, Loan, Logan, Longhridge, Lynch, Maynard, McClurg, Mercur, Mullins. Myers, Newcomb, Nunn, O'Neill, Orth. Paine. Pile, Price. Schenck, Shanks. Aaron F. Stevens, Thaddeus Stevens, Stokes, Thomas, John Trimble, Trowbridge, Robert T. Van Horn, Ward, Thomas Williams, William Williams, Stephen F. Wilson—57.

NAYS—Messrs. *Adams,* Allison, Ames, *Archer,* Delos R. Ashley, *Axtell,* Bailey, Baker, Baldwin, Banks, *Barnum,* Beaman, *Beck,* Benjamin. Benton, Bingham, Blaine, *Boyer, Brooks,* Buckland, *Burr, Cary, Chanler.* Cook, Dawes, Dixon, Dodge, Driggs, Eggleston, *Eldridge,* Eliot, Ferriss, Ferry, Fields. Garfield, *Getz, Glossbrenner, Golladay,* Griswold, *Grover, Haight,* Halsey, Hamilton, Hawkins, Hill, *Holman,* Hooper, *Hotchkiss.* Asahel W. Hubbard, Chester D. Hubbard, *Richard D Hubbard,* Hulburd, *Humphrey,* Ingersoll, *Johnson, Jones, Kerr,* Ketcham. *Knott,* Koontz, Laflin, George V. Lawrence, Lincoln, *Marshall,* Marvin, McCarthy, *McCullough.* Miller, Moorhead, *Morgan, Mungen, Niblack, Nicholson.* Perham, Peters, *Phelps,* Pike. Plants. Poland. Polsley, *Pruyn, Randall.* Robertson, *Robinson, Ross,* Sawyer, *Sitgreaves,* Smith, Spalding, Starkweather, *Stewart, Stone, Taber,* Taylor. Upson. Van Aernam, *Van Auken, Van Trump,* Van Wyck. Cadwalader C.Washburn, Elihu B. Washburne, Henry D. Washburn, William B.Washburn, Welker, James F. Wilson, John T. Wilson, Woodbridge, *Woodward* - 108.

### RESOLUTION OF INQUIRY.

1868, January 27—Mr. Spalding moved a suspension of the rules, to allow him to offer this resolution:

*Resolved,* That the Committee on Reconstruction be authorized to inquire what combinations have been made or attempted to be made to obstruct the due execution of the laws, and to that end the committee have power to send for persons and papers, and to examine witnesses on oath, and report to this House what action, if any, they may deem necessary, and that said committee have leave to report at any time.

Which was agreed to—yeas 103, nays 37, and the resolution was adopted—yeas 99, nays 31.

### OTHER MATTERS REFERRED

February 10—The evidence taken on Impeachment by the Committee on the Judiciary was, on motion of Mr. Thaddeus Stevens, referred to the Committee on Reconstruction, and the committee was given leave to report at any time.

February 11—The correspondence between General Grant and President Johnson, relating to the retirement of the former from the War Office. was also referred to the Committee on Reconstruction.

February 13-The Committee on Reconstruction are reported to have voted down resolutions of impeachment offered by Mr. Thaddeus Stevens.

The vote on a motion to lay them on the table was, yeas 6, nays 3, as follow:

YEAS—Messrs. Beaman, *Beck,* Bingham, *Brooks,* Hulburd, Paine—6.

NAYS—Messrs. Boutwell, Farnsworth, T. Stevens—3.

### The Final Effort at Impeachment.

#### IN HOUSE.

1868, February 21—The Speaker, by unanimous consent, laid before the House the following communication from the Secretary of War:

WAR DEPARTMENT,
WASHINGTON CITY, *February* 21, 1868.

SIR: General Thomas has just delivered to me a copy of the enclosed order, which you will please communicate to the House of Representatives. E. M. STANTON.
*Secretary of War.*

Hon. SCHUYLER COLFAX,
*Speaker House of Representatives.*

EXECUTIVE MANSION,
WASHINGTON, D. C., *February* 21, 1868.

SIR: By virtue of the power and authority vested in me as President by the Constitution and laws of the United States you are hereby removed from office as Secretary for the Department of War, and your functions as such will terminate upon the receipt of this communication.

You will transfer to Brevet Major General Lorenzo Thomas, Adjutant General of the Army, who has this day been authorized and empowered to act as Secretary of War *ad interim,* all records, books, papers, and other public property now in your custody and charge.

Respectfully, yours,
ANDREW JOHNSON.

To the Hon. EDWIN M. STANTON,
*Washington, D. C.*

Which was referred to the Committee on Reconstruction, with authority to report at any time, together with a resolution offered by Mr. Covode, as follows:

*Resolved,* That Andrew Johnson, President of the United States, be impeached of high crimes and misdemeanors.

### REPORT OF COMMITTEE.

1868, February 22—Mr. Thaddeus Stevens, from the Committee on Reconstruction, made the following report:

The Committee on Reconstruction, to whom was referred, on the 27th day of January last, the following resolution:

*Resolved,* That the Committee on Reconstruction be authorized to inquire what combinations have been made or attempted to be made to obstruct the due execution of the laws; and to that end the committee have power to send for persons and papers and to examine witnesses on oath, and report to this House what action, if any, they may deem necessary, and that said committee have leave to report at any time;

And to whom was also referred, on the 21st day of February, instant, a communication from Hon. Edwin M. Stanton, Secretary of War, dated on said 21st day of February, together with a copy of a letter from Andrew Johnson, President of the United States, to the said Edwin M. Stanton, as follows:

EXECUTIVE MANSION,
WASHINGTON, D. C., *February* 21, 1868.

SIR: By virtue of the power and authority vested in me as President by the Constitution and laws of the United States you are hereby removed from office as Secretary for the Department of War, and your functions as such will terminate upon the receipt of this communication.

You will transfer to Brevet Major General Lorenzo Thomas, Adjutant General of the Army, who has this day been authorized and empowered to act as Secretary of War *ad interim,* all records, books, papers, and other public property now in your custody and charge.

Respectfully, yours, ANDREW JOHNSON.

To the Hon. EDWIN M. STANTON,
*Washington. D. C*

And to whom was also referred by the House of Representatives the following resolution, namely:

*Resolved,* That Andrew Johnson, President of the United States, be impeached of high crimes and misde-

Have considered the several subjects referred to them, and submit the following report:

That, in addition to the papers referred to the committee, the committee find that the President, on the 21st day of February, 1868, signed and issued a commission or letter of authority to one Lorenzo Thomas, directing and authorizing said Thomas to act as Secretary of War *ad interim*, and to take possession of the books, records, and papers, and other public property in the War Department, of which the following is a copy:

EXECUTIVE MANSION,
WASHINGTON, *February* 21, 1868.

SIR: Hon. Edwin M. Stanton having been this day removed from office as Secretary for the Department of War, you are hereby authorized and empowered to act as Secretary of War *ad interim*, and will immediately enter upon the discharge of the duties pertaining to that office. Mr. Stanton has been instructed to transfer to you all the records, books, papers, and other public property now in his custody and charge.

Respectfully, yours, ANDREW JOHNSON.
To Brev. Maj. Gen. LORENZO THOMAS,
*Adjutant General U. S. A., Washington, D. C.*

Official copy respectfully furnished to Hon. Edwin M. Stanton. L. THOMAS,
*Secretary of War ad interim.*

Upon the evidence collected by the committee, which is herewith presented, and in virtue of the powers with which they have been invested by the House, they are of the opinion that Andrew Johnson, President of the United States, be impeached of high crimes and misdemeanors. They therefore recommend to the House the adoption of the accompanying resolution.

THADDEUS STEVENS,
GEORGE S. BOUTWELL,
JOHN A. BINGHAM,
C. T. HULBURD,
JOHN F. FARNSWORTH,
F. C. BEAMAN,
H. E. PAINE.

Resolution providing for the impeachment of Andrew Johnson, President of the United States.

*Resolved*, That Andrew Johnson, President of the United States, be impeached of high crimes and misdemeanors in office.

February 24—This resolution was adopted—yeas 128, nays 47, as follow:

YEAS—Messrs. Allison, Ames, Anderson, Arnell, Delos R. Ashley, James M. Ashley, Bailey, Baker, Baldwin, Banks, Beaman, Beatty, Benton, Bingham, Blaine, Blair, Boutwell, Bromwell, Broomall, Buckland, Butler, Cake, Churchill, Reader W. Clarke, Sidney Clarke, Cobb, Coburn, Cook, Cornell, Covode, Cullom, Dawes, Dodge, Driggs, Eckley, Eggleston, Eliot, Farnsworth, Ferriss, Ferry, Fields, Gravely, Griswold, Halsey, Harding, Higby, Hill, Hooper, Hopkins, Asahel W. Hubbard, Chester D. Hubbard, Hulburd, Hunter, Ingersoll, Jenckes, Judd, Julian, Kelley, Kelsey, Ketcham, Kitchen, Koontz, Laflin, George V. Lawrence, William Lawrence, Lincoln, Loan, Logan, Loughridge, Lynch, Mallory, Marvin, McCarthy, McClurg, Mercur, Miller, Moore, Moorhead, Morrell, Mullins, Myers, Newcomb Nunn, O'Neill, Orth, Paine, Perham, Peters, Pike, Pile, Plants, Poland, Polsley, Price, Raum, Robertson, Sawyer, Schenck, Scofield, Selye, Shanks, Smith, Spalding, Starkweather, Aaron F. Stevens, Thaddeus Stevens, Stokes, Taffe, Taylor, Thomas, Trowbridge, Twichell, Upson, Van Aernam, Burt Van Horn, Van Wyck, Ward, Cadwalader C. Washburn, Ellihu B. Washburne, William B. Washburn, Welker, Thomas Williams, James F. Wilson, John T. Wilson, Stephen F. Wilson, Windom, Woodbridge, Mr. Speaker Colfax—128.

NAYS—Messrs. Adams, Archer, Axtell, Barnes, Barnum, Beck, Boyer, Brooks, Burr, Cary, Chanler, Eldridge, Fox, Getz, Glossbrenner, Golladay, Grover, Haight, Holman, Hotchkiss, Richard D. Hubbard, Humphrey, Johnson, Jones, Kerr, Knott, Marshall, McCormick, McCullough, Morgan, Morrissey, Mungen, Niblack, Nicholson, Phelps, Pruyn, Randall. Ross, Sitgreaves, Stewart, Stone, Taber, Lawrence S. Trimble, Van Auken, Van Trump, Wood, Woodward—47.

NOT VOTING—Messrs. Benjamin, Dixon, Donnelly, Ela, Finney, Garfield, Hawkins, Maynard, Pomeroy, Robinson, Shellabarger, John Trimble, Robert T. Van Horn, Henry D. Washburn, William Williams—15.

Same day — On motion of Mr. Thaddeus Stevens, the appointment of a committee of two to notify the Senate, and of a committee of seven to prepare and report Articles of Impeachment against Andrew Johnson, President of the United States, was ordered, with power to send for persons, papers, and records, and to take testimony under oath.

Which was agreed to—yeas 124, nays 42

The Speaker appointed Messrs. Thaddeus Stevens and John A. Bingham on the former, and Messrs. Boutwell, Thaddeus Stevens, Bingham, James F. Wilson, Logan, Julian, and Ward, on the latter.

February 25—Mr. Thaddeus Stevens and Mr. John A. Bingham appeared at the bar of the Senate and delivered the following message:

Mr. PRESIDENT: By order of the House of Representatives, we appear at the bar of the Senate, and in the name of the House of Representatives, and of all the people of the United States, we do impeach Andrew Johnson, President of the United States, of high crimes and misdemeanors in office; and we do further inform the Senate that the House of Representatives will in due time exhibit particular articles of impeachment against him, and make good the same; and in their name we DO DEMAND that the Senate take order for the appearance of the said Andrew Johnson to answer to said impeachment.

The President of the Senate *pro tempore* replied that the Senate would take order in the premises, and the committee withdrew.

Same day—The committee reported to the House the response received at the bar of the Senate.

---

**Articles of Impeachment and Votes thereon, the Answer of President Johnson, the Replication of the House, the Progress of the Trial, and the Judgment of the Senate.**

FORTIETH CONGRESS, SECOND SESSION,
IN THE HOUSE OF REPRESENTATIVES U. S.,
*March* 2, 1868.

*Articles exhibited by the House of Representatives of the United States, in the name of themselves and all the people of the United States, against Andrew Johnson, President of the United States. in maintenance and support of their impeachment against him for high crimes and misdemeanors in office.*

ARTICLE I.—That the said Andrew Johnson, President of the United States, on the 21st day of February, in the year of our Lord 1868, at Washington, in the District of Columbia, unmindful of the high duties of his office, of his oath of office, and of the requirements of the Constitution that he should take care that the laws be faithfully executed, did unlawfully, and in violation of the Constitution and laws of the United

States, issue an order in writing for the removal of Edwin M. Stanton from the office of Secretary for the Department of War, said Edwin M. Stanton having been theretofore duly appointed and commissioned, by and with the advice and consent of the Senate of the United States, as such Secretary, and said Andrew Johnson, President of the United States, on the 12th day of August, in the year of our Lord 1867, and during the recess of said Senate, having suspended by his order Edwin M. Stanton from said office, and within twenty days after the first day of the next meeting of said Senate, that is to say, on the 12th day of December, in the year last aforesaid, having reported to said Senate such suspension with the evidence and reasons for his action in the case and the name of the person designated to perform the duties of such office temporarily until the next meeting of the Senate, and said Senate thereafterwards on the 13th day of January, in the year of our Lord 1868, having duly considered the evidence and reasons reported by said Andrew Johnson for said suspension, and having refused to concur in said suspension, whereby and by force of the provisions of an act entitled " An act regulating the tenure of certain civil offices," passed March 2, 1867, said Edwin M. Stanton did forthwith resume the functions of his office, whereof the said Andrew Johnson had then and there due notice, and said Edwin M. Stanton, by reason of the premises, on said 21st day of February, being lawfully entitled to hold said office of Secretary for the Department of War, which said order for the removal of said Edwin M. Stanton is in substance as follows, that is to say :

EXECUTIVE MANSION,
WASHINGTON, D. C., *February* 21, 1868.
SIR : By virtue of the power and authority vested in me as President by the Constitution and laws of the United States you are hereby removed from office as Secretary for the Department of War, and your functions as such will terminate upon receipt of this communication.
You will transfer to Brevet Major General Lorenzo Thomas, Adjutant General of the Army, who has this day been authorized and empowered to act as Secretary of War *ad interim*, all records, books, papers, and other public property now in your custody and charge.
Respectfully, yours,     ANDREW JOHNSON.
To the Hon. EDWIN M. STANTON, *Washington, D. C.*

Which order was unlawfully issued with intent then and there to violate the act entitled " An act regulating the tenure of certain civil offices," passed March 2, 1867, and with the further intent, contrary to the provisions of said act, in violation thereof, and contrary to the provisions of the Constitution of the United States, and without the advice and consent of the Senate of the United States, the said Senate then and there being in session, to remove said Edwin M. Stanton from the office of Secretary for the Department of War, the said Edwin M. Stanton being then and there Secretary for the Department of War, and being then and there in the due and lawful execution and discharge of the duties of said office, whereby said Andrew Johnson, President of the United States, did then and there commit, and was guilty of a high misdemeanor in office.

ARTICLE II.—That on the said 21st day of February, in the year of our Lord one thousand eight hundred and sixty-eight, at Washington, in the District of Columbia, said Andrew Johnson, President of the United States, unmindful of the high duties of his office, of his oath of

office, and in violation of the Constitution of the United States, and contrary to the provisions of an act entitled "An act regulating the tenure of certain civil offices," passed March 2, eighteen hundred and sixty-seven, without the advice and consent of the Senate of the United States, said Senate then and there being in session, and without authority of law, did, with intent to violate the Constitution of the United States, and the act aforesaid, issue and deliver to one Lorenzo Thomas a letter of authority in substance as follows, that is to say :

EXECUTIVE MANSION,
WASHINGTON, D. C., *February* 21, 1868.
SIR : The Hon. Edwin M. Stanton having been this day removed from office as Secretary for the Department of War, you are hereby authorized and empowered to act as Secretary of War *ad interim*, and will immediately enter upon the discharge of the duties pertaining to that office.
Mr. Stanton has been instructed to transfer to you all the records, books, papers, and other public property now in his custody and charge.     Respectfully, yours,
ANDREW JOHNSON.
To Brevet Major General LORENZO THOMAS,
*Adjutant General U. S. Army, Washington, D. C.*

Then and there being no vacancy in said office of Secretary for the Department of War, whereby said Andrew Johnson, President of the United States, did then and there commit and was guilty of a high misdemeanor in office.

ARTICLE III.—That said Andrew Johnson, President of the United States, on the 21st day of February, in the year of our Lord 1868, at Washington, in the District of Columbia, did commit and was guilty of a high misdemeanor in office, in this, that, without authority of law, while the Senate of the United States was then and there in session, he did appoint one Lorenzo Thomas to be Secretary for the Department of War *ad interim*, without the advice and consent of the Senate, and with intent to violate the Constitution of the United States, no vacancy having happened in said office of Secretary for the Department of War during the recess of the Senate, and no vacancy existing in said office at the time, and which said appointment so made by said Andrew Johnson, of said Lorenzo Thomas, is in substance as follows, that is to say :

EXECUTIVE MANSION,
WASHINGTON, D. C., *February* 21, 1868.
SIR : The Hon. Edwin M. Stanton having been this day removed from office as Secretary for the Department of War, you are hereby authorized and empowered to act as Secretary of War *ad interim*, and will immediately enter upon the discharge of the duties pertaining to that office.
Mr. Stanton has been instructed to transfer to you all the records, books, papers, and other public property now in his custody and charge.     Respectfully, yours,
ANDREW JOHNSON.
To Brevet Major Gen. LORENZO THOMAS,
*Adjutant General U. S. Army, Washington, D. C.*

ARTICLE IV.—That said Andrew Johnson, President of the United States, unmindful of the high duties of his office and of his oath of office, in violation of the Constitution and laws of the United States, on the 21st day of February, in the year of our Lord 1868, at Washington, in the District of Columbia, did unlawfully conspire with one Lorenzo Thomas, and with other persons to the House of Representatives unknown, with intent, by intimidation and threats, unlawfully to hinder and prevent Edwin M. Stanton, then and there the Secretary for the Department of War, duly appointed under the laws of the United States, from holding said office of Secretary for the Depart meat of War, contrary to and in violation of the Constitution of the United States, and of the provisions of an act entitled "An act to define and punish certain conspiracies," approved July 31, 1861, whereby said Andrew Johnson, President of the United States, did then and there commit and was guilty of a high crime in office.

ARTICLE V.—That said Andrew Johnson, President of the United States, unmindful of the high duties of his office and of his oath of office, on the 21st day of February, in the year of our Lord 1868, and on divers other days and times in said year, before the 2d day of March, in the year of our Lord 1868, at Washington, in the District of Columbia, did unlawfully conspire with one Lorenzo Thomas, and with other persons to the House of Representatives unknown, to prevent and hinder the execution of an act entitled "An act regulating the tenure of certain civil offices," passed March 2, 1867, and in pursuance of said conspiracy did unlawfully attempt to prevent Edwin M. Stanton, then and there being Secretary for the Department of War, duly appointed and commissioned under the laws of the United States, from holding said office, whereby the said Andrew Johnson, President of the United States, did then and there commit and was guilty of a high misdemeanor in office.

ARTICLE VI.—That said Andrew Johnson, President of the United States, unmindful of the high duties of his office and of his oath of office, on the 21st day of February, in the year of our Lord 1868, at Washington, in the District of Columbia, did unlawfully conspire with one Lorenzo Thomas, by force to seize, take, and possess the property of the United States in the Department of War, and then and there in the custody and charge of Edwin M. Stanton, Secretary for said Department, contrary to the provisions of an act entitled "An act to define and punish certain conspiracies," approved July 31, 1861, and with intent to violate and disregard an act entitled "An act regulating the tenure of certain civil offices," passed March 2, 1867, whereby said Andrew Johnson, President of the United States, did then and there commit a high crime in office.

ARTICLE VII.—That said Andrew Johnson, President of the United States, unmindful of the high duties of his office and of his oath of office, on the 21st day of February, in the year of our Lord 1868, at Washington, in the District of Columbia, did unlawfully conspire with one Lorenzo Thomas, with intent unlawfully to seize, take, and possess the property of the United States in the Department of War, in the custody and charge of Edwin M. Stanton, Secretary for said Department, with intent to violate and disregard the act entitled "An act regulating the tenure of certain civil offices," passed March 2, 1867, whereby said Andrew Johnson, President of the United States, did then and there commit a high misdemeanor in office.

ARTICLE VIII.—That said Andrew Johnson, President of the United States, unmindful of the high duties of his office and of his oath of office, with intent unlawfully to control the disburse-

ments of the moneys appropriated for the military service and for the Department of War, on the 21st day of February, in the year of our Lord 1868, at Washington, in the District of Columbia, did unlawfully and contrary to the provisions of an act entitled "An act regulating the tenure of certain civil offices," passed March 2, 1867, and in violation of the Constitution of the United States, and without the advice and consent of the Senate of the United States, and while the Senate was then and there in session, there being no vacancy in the office of Secretary for the Department of War, and with intent to violate and disregard the act aforesaid, then and there issue and deliver to one Lorenzo Thomas a letter of authority in writing, in substance as follows, that is to say:

EXECUTIVE MANSION,
WASHINGTON, D. C., *February* 21, 1868.

SIR: The Hon. Edwin M. Stanton having been this day removed from office as Secretary for the Department of War, you are hereby authorized and empowered to act as Secretary of War *ad interim*, and will immediately enter upon the discharge of the duties pertaining to that office.

Mr. Stanton has been instructed to transfer to you all the records, books, papers, and other public property now in his custody and charge. Respectfully, yours,
ANDREW JOHNSON.

To Brevet Major Gen. LORENZO THOMAS,
*Adjutant General U. S. Army, Washington, D. C.*

Whereby said Andrew Johnson, President of the United States, did then and there commit and was guilty of a high misdemeanor in office.

ARTICLE IX.—That said Andrew Johnson, President of the United States, on the 22d day of February, in the year of our Lord 1868, at Washington, in the District of Columbia, in disregard of the Constitution and the laws of the United States duly enacted, as commander-in-chief of the army of the United States, did bring before himself then and there William H. Emory, a major general by brevet in the army of the United States, actually in command of the department of Washington and the military forces thereof, and did then and there, as such commander-in-chief, declare to and instruct said Emory that part of a law of the United States, passed March 2, 1867, entitled "An act making appropriations for the support of the army for the year ending June 30, 1868, and for other purposes," especially the second section thereof, which provided, among other things, that, "all orders and instructions relating to military operations issued by the President or Secretary of War shall be issued through the General of the army, and in case of his inability through the next in rank" was unconstitutional, and in contravention of the commission of said Emory, and which said provision of law had been theretofore duly and legally promulgated by General Order for the government and direction of the army of the United States, as the said Andrew Johnson then and there well knew, with intent thereby to induce said Emory in his official capacity as commander of the department of Washington, to violate the provisions of said act, and to take and receive, act upon, and obey such orders as he, the said Andrew Johnson, might make and give, and which should not be issued through the General of the army of the United States, according to the provisions of said act, and with the further intent thereby to enable him, the said Andrew Johnson, to prevent the execution of the act entitled "An act regulating the tenure of certain civil offices," passed March 2, 1867, and to unlawfully prevent Edwin M. Stanton, then being Secretary for the Department of War, from holding said office and discharging the duties thereof, whereby said Andrew Johnson, President of the United States, did then and there commit and was guilty of a high misdemeanor in office.

And the House of Representatives, by protestation, saving to themselves the liberty of exhibiting at any time hereafter any further articles or other accusation, or impeachment against the said Andrew Johnson, President of the United States, and also of replying to his answers which he shall make unto the articles herein preferred against him, and of offering proof to the same, and every part thereof, and to all and every other article, accusation, or impeachment which shall be exhibited by them, as the case shall require, DO DEMAND that the said Andrew Johnson may be put to answer the high crimes and misdemeanors in office herein charged against him, and that such proceedings, examinations, trials, and judgments may be thereupon had and given as may be agreeable to law and justice.

SCHUYLER COLFAX,
*Speaker of the House of Representatives.*

Attest:

EDWARD McPHERSON,
*Clerk of the House of Representatives.*

—

IN THE HOUSE OF REPRESENTATIVES U. S.
*March* 3, 1868.

The following additional articles of impeachment were agreed to, viz:

ARTICLE X.—That said Andrew Johnson, President of the United States, unmindful of the high duties of his office and the dignity and proprieties thereof, and of the harmony and courtesies which ought to exist and be maintained between the executive and legislative branches of the government of the United States, designing and intending to set aside the rightful authority and powers of Congress, did attempt to bring into disgrace, ridicule, hatred, contempt and reproach the Congress of the United States, and the several branches thereof, to impair and destroy the regard and respect of all the good people of the United States for the Congress and legislative power thereof, (which all officers of the Government ought inviolably to preserve and maintain,) and to excite the odium and resentment of all the good people of the United States against Congress and the laws by it duly and constitutionally enacted; and in pursuance of his said design and intent, openly and publicly, and before divers assemblages of the citizens of the United States convened in divers parts thereof to meet and receive said Andrew Johnson as the Chief Magistrate of the United States, did, on the 18th day of August, in the year of our Lord 1866, and on divers other days and times, as well before as afterward, make and deliver with a loud voice certain intemperate, inflammatory, and scandalous harangues, and did therein utter loud threats and bitter menaces as well against Congress as the laws of the United States duly enacted thereby, amid the cries, jeers and laughter of the multitudes then assembled and in hearing, which are set forth in the several specifications hereinafter written, in substance and effect, that is to say:

SPECIFICATION FIRST.—In this, that at Washington, in the District of Columbia, in the Executive Mansion, to a committee of citizens who called upon the President of the United States, speaking of and concerning the Congress of the United States, said Andrew Johnson, President of the United States, heretofore, to wit, on the 18th day of August, in the year of our Lord 1866, did, in a loud voice, declare in substance and effect, among other things, that is to say:

"So far as the executive department of the government is concerned, the effort has been made to restore the Union, to heal the breach, to pour oil into the wounds which were consequent upon the struggle, and (to speak in common phrase) to prepare as the learned and wise physician would, a plaster healing in character and coextensive with the wound. We thought, and we think, that we had partially succeeded; but as the work progresses, as reconstruction seemed to be taking place, and the country was becoming reunited, we found a disturbing and marring element opposing us. In alluding to that element, I shall go no further than your convention and the distinguished gentleman who has delivered to me the report of its proceedings. I shall make no reference to it that I do not believe the time and the occasion justify.

"We have witnessed in one department of the Government every endeavor to prevent the restoration of peace, harmony, and Union. We have seen hanging upon the verge of the Government, as it were, a body called, or which assumes to be, the Congress of the United States, while in fact it is a Congress of only a part of the States. We have seen this Congress pretend to be for the Union, when its every step and act tended to perpetuate disunion and make a disruption of the States inevitable. * * * We have seen Congress gradually encroach step by step upon constitutional rights, and violate, day after day and month after month, fundamental principles of the government. We have seen a Congress that seemed to forget that there was a limit to the sphere and scope of legislation. We have seen a Congress in a minority, assume to exercise power which, allowed to be consummated, would result in despotism or monarchy itself."

SPECIFICATION SECOND.—In this, that at Cleveland, in the State of Ohio, heretofore, to wit, on the 3d day of September, in the year of our Lord 1866, before a public assemblage of citizens and others, said Andrew Johnson, President of the United States, speaking of and concerning the Congress of the United States, did, in a loud voice, declare in substance and effect, among other things, that is to say:

"I will tell you what I did do. I called upon your Congress, that is trying to break up the government. * * * "In conclusion, beside that, Congress had taken much pains to poison their constituents against him. But what had Congress done? Have they done anything to restore the union of these states? No; on the contrary, they had done everything to prevent it; and because he stood now where he did when the rebellion commenced, he had been denounced as a traitor. Who had run greater risks or made greater sacrifices than himself? But Congress, factions and domineering, had undertaken to poison the minds of the American people."

SPECIFICATION THIRD.—In this, that at St. Louis, in the State of Missouri, heretofore, to wit, on the 8th day of September, in the year of our Lord 1866, before a public assemblage of citizens and others, said Andrew Johnson, President of the United States, speaking of and concerning the Congress of the United States, did, in a loud voice, declare, in substance and effect, among other things, that is to say:

"Go on. Perhaps if you had a word or two on the subject of New Orleans you might understand more about it than you do. And if you will go back—if you will go back and ascertain the cause of the riot at New Orleans perhaps you will not be so prompt in calling out 'New Orleans.' If you will take up the riot at New Orleans, and trace it back to its source or its immediate cause, you will find out who was responsible for the blood that was shed there. If you will take up the riot at New Orleans and trace it back to the radical Congress, you will find that the riot at New Orleans was substantially planned. If you will take up the proceedings in their caucuses you will understand that they there knew that a convention was to be called which was extinct by its power having expired; that it was said that the intention was that a new government was to be organized, and on the organization of that government the intention was to enfranchise one portion of the population, called the colored population, who had just been emancipated, and at the same time disfranchise white men. When you design to talk about New Orleans, you ought to understand what you are talking about. When you read the speeches that were made, and take up the facts on the Friday and Saturday before that convention sat, you will there find that speeches were made incendiary in their character, exciting that portion of the population, the black population, to arm themselves and prepare for the shedding of blood. You will also find that that convention did assemble in violation of law, and the intention of that convention was to supersede the reorganized authorities in the State government of Louisiana, which had been recognized by the Government of the United States; and every man engaged in that rebellion in that convention, with the intention of superseding and upturning the civil government which had been recognized by the Government of the United States, I say that he was a traitor to the Constitution of the United States, and hence you find that another rebellion was commenced, *having its origin in the radical Congress.* * * * *

"So much for the New Orleans riot. And there was the cause and the origin of the blood that was shed; and every drop of blood that was shed is upon their skirts, and they are responsible for it. I could test this thing a little closer, but will not do it here to-night. But when you talk about the causes and consequences that resulted from proceedings of that kind, perhaps, as I have been introduced here, and you have provoked questions of this kind, though it does not provoke me, I will tell you a few wholesome things that have been done by this radical Congress in connection with New Orleans and the extension of the elective franchise.

"I know that I have been traduced and abused. I know it has come in advance of me here as elsewhere—that I have attempted to exercise an arbitrary power in resisting laws that were intended to be forced upon the Government; that I had exercised that power; that I had abandoned the party that elected me, and that I was a traitor, because I exercised the veto power in attempting, and did arrest for a time, a bill that was called a 'Freedman's Bureau' bill; yes, that I was a traitor. And I have been traduced, I have been slandered, I have been maligned, I have been called Judas Iscariot, and all that. Now, my countrymen, here to-night, it is very easy to indulge in epithets; it is easy to call a man Judas and cry out traitor, but when he is called upon to give arguments and facts, he is very often found wanting. Judas Iscariot—Judas. There was a Judas, and he was one of the twelve apostles. Oh! yes, the twelve apostles had a Christ. The twelve apostles had a Christ, and he never could have had a Judas unless he had had twelve apostles. If I have played the Judas, who has been my Christ that I have played the Judas with? Was it Thad. Stevens? Was it Wendell Phillips? Was it Charles Sumner? These are the men that stop and compare themselves with the Saviour; and everybody that differs with them in opinion, and to try to stay and arrest their diabolical and nefarious policy, is to be denounced as a Judas. * * * *

"Well, let me say to you, if you will stand by me in this action, if you will stand by me in trying to give the people a fair chance—soldiers and citizens—to participate in these offices, God being willing, I will kick them out. I will kick them out just as fast as I can.

"Let me say to you, in concluding, that what I have said I intended to say. I was not provoked into this, and I care not for their menaces, the taunts, and the jeers. I care not for threats. I do not intend to be bullied by my enemies nor overawed by my friends. But, God willing, with your help, I will veto their measures whenever any of them come to me."

Which said utterances, declarations, threats, and harangues, highly censurable in any, are peculiarly indecent and unbecoming in the Chief Magistrate of the United States, by means whereof said Andrew Johnson has brought the high office of the President of the United States into contempt, ridicule, and disgrace, to the great scandal of all good citizens, whereby said Andrew Johnson, President of the United States, did commit, and was then and there guilty of a high misdemeanor in office.

ARTICLE XI.—That said Andrew Johnson, President of the United States, unmindful of the high duties of his office, and of his oath of office, and in disregard of the Constitution and laws of the United States, did, heretofore, to wit, on the 18th day of August, A. D. 1866, at the city of Washington, and the District of Columbia, by public speech, declare and affirm, in substance, that the Thirty-Ninth Congress of the United States was not a Congress of the United States authorized by the Constitution to exercise legislative power under the same, but, on the contrary, was a Congress of only part of the States, thereby denying, and intending to deny, that the legislation of said Congress was valid or obligatory upon him, the said Andrew Johnson, except in so far as he saw fit to approve the same, and also thereby denying, and intending to deny, the power of the said Thirty-Ninth Congress to propose amendments to the Constitution of the United States; and, in pursuance of said declaration, the said Andrew Johnson, President of the United States, afterwards, to wit, on the 21st day of February, A. D. 1868, at the city of Washington, in the District of Columbia, did, unlawfully, and in disregard of the requirement of the Constitution, that he should take care that the laws be faithfully executed, attempt to prevent the execution of an act entitled "An act regulating the tenure of certain civil offices," passed March 2, 1867, by unlawfully devising and contriving, and attempting to devise and contrive means by which he should prevent Edwin M. Stanton from forthwith resuming the functions of the office of Secretary for the Department of War, notwithstanding the refusal of the Senate to concur in the suspension theretofore made by said Andrew Johnson of said Edwin M. Stanton from said office of Secretary for the Department of War; and, also, by further unlawfully devising and contriving, and attempting to devise and contrive, means, then and there, to prevent the execution of an act entitled "An act making appropriations for the support of the army for the fiscal year ending June 30, 1868, and for other purposes," approved March 2, 1867; and, also, to prevent the execution of an act entitled "An act to provide for the more efficient government of the rebel States," passed March 2, 1867, whereby the said Andrew Johnson, President of the United States, did then, to wit, on the 21st day of February, A. D. 1868, at the city of Washington, commit, and was guilty of, a high misdemeanor in office.

SCHUYLER COLFAX,
*Speaker of the House of Representatives.*

Attest:

EDWARD MCPHERSON,
*Clerk of the House of Representatives.*

### Votes on the Articles in the House.

1868, March 2—The *first* article was agreed to—yeas 127, nays 42, as follow:

YEAS—Messrs. Allison, Ames, Anderson, Arnell, Delos R. Ashley, James M. Ashley, Bailey, Baldwin, Banks, Beaman, Beatty, Benton, Bingham, Blaine, Blair, Boutwell, Bromwell, Broomall, Buckland, Butler, Cake, Churchill, Reader W. Clarke, Sidney Clarke, Cobb, Coburn, Cook, Cornell Covode, Cullom, Dawes, Dixon, Dodge, Donnelly, Driggs, Eggleston, Eliot, Farnsworth, Ferriss, Ferry, Fields, Garfield, Gravely, Griswold, Halsey, Harding, Higby, Hill, Hooper, Hopkins, C. D. Hubbard, Hulburd, Hunter, Ingersoll, Jenckes, Judd,

Julian, Kelley, Kelsey, Ketcham, Kitchen, Koontz, Laflin, Geo.V. Lawrence, William Lawrence, Lincoln, Loan, Logan, Loughridge, Lynch, Mallory, Marvin, Maynard, McCarthy, McClurg, Mercur, Miller, Moore, Morrell, Mullins, Myers, Newcomb, Nunn, O'Neill, Orth, Paine, Perham, Peters, Pike, Plants, Poland, Polsley, Pomeroy, Price, Raum, Robertson, Sawyer, Schenck, Scofield, Shanks, Smith, Spalding, Starkweather, Thaddeus Stevens, Stokes, Taffe, Taylor, Thomas, Trimble, Trowbridge, Twichell, Upson, Van Aernam, Burt Van Horn, Robert T. Van Horn, Van Wyck, Ward, Cadwalader C. Washburn, Elliha B.Washburne, William B. Washburn, Welker, Thomas Williams, James F. Wilson, John T. Wilson, Stephen F. Wilson, Windom, Woodbridge—127.

NAYS—Messrs. *Adams, Archer, Axtell, Barnum, Beck, Boyer, Brooks, Burr, Cary, Chanler, Eldridge, Fox, Getz, Glossbrenner, Golladay, Grover, Haight, Holman, Hotchkiss, Humphrey, Johnson, Jones, Kerr, Knott, Marshall, McCormick, Morgan, Mungen, Niblack, Nicholson, Pruyn, Randall, Ross, Sitgreaves, Stewart, Stone, Taber, Trimble, Van Auken, Van Trump, Wood, Woodward*—42

NOT VOTING—Messrs. *Baker, Barnes, Benjamin, Eckley, Eli, Finney, Hawkins, Asahel W. Hubbard, Richard D. Hubbard, McCullough, Moorhead, Morrissey, Phelps, Pile, Robinson, Selye, Shellabarger, Aaron F. Stevens, Henry D. Washburn, William Williams*—20.

The *second* article was agreed to—yeas 124, nays 41, not voting 24.

The *third* article was agreed to—yeas 124, nays 41, not voting 24.

The *fourth* article was agreed to—yeas 117, nays 40, not voting 32.

The *fifth* article was agreed to—yeas 127, nays 42, not voting 20.

The *sixth* article was agreed to—yeas 127, nays 42, not voting 20.

The *seventh* article was agreed to—yeas 127, nays 42, not voting 20.

The *eighth* article was agreed to—yeas 127, nays 42, not voting 20.

The *ninth* article was agreed to—yeas 108, nays 41, not voting 40.

The *tenth* article was agreed to—yeas 88, nays 44, not voting 57.

The *eleventh* article was agreed to—yeas 109, nays 32, not voting 48.

Messrs. John A. Bingham, George S. Boutwell, James F. Wilson, Benjamin F. Butler, Thomas Williams, John A. Logan, and Thaddeus Stevens were elected managers to conduct the impeachment.

March 4—The articles were read to the Senate by the Managers.

March 5—Chief Justice Chase took the chair, Associate Justice Nelson having administered the following oath:

"I do solemnly swear that in all things appertaining to the trial of the impeachment of Andrew Johnson, President of the United States, I will do impartial justice according to the Constitution and laws: So help me God."

March 5 and 6—The Chief Justice administered the same oath to the various Senators. On the 6th, an order was adopted, directing a summons on Andrew Johnson to file answer to the articles, returnable on the 13th instant.

March 13—The President's counsel entered this appearance:

*In the matter of the impeachment of Andrew Johnson, President of the United States.*

Mr. CHIEF JUSTICE: I, Andrew Johnson, President of the United States, having been served with a summon to appear before this honorable court, sitting as a court of impeachment, to answer certain articles of impeachment found and presented against me by the honorable the House of Representatives of the United States, do hereby enter my appearance by my counsel, Henry Stanbery, Benjamin R. Curtis, Jeremiah S. Black,* William M. Evarts, and Thomas A. R. Nelson, who have my warrant and authority therefor, and who are instructed by me to ask of this honorable court for a reasonable time for the preparation of my answer to said articles.

After a careful examination of the articles of impeachment, and consultation with my counsel, I am satisfied that at least forty days will be necessary for the preparation of my answer, and I respectfully ask that it be allowed.

ANDREW JOHNSON.

The counsel also read a "professional statement" in support of the request. The Senate retired for consultation, and, after some time, adopted, without a division, an order that the respondent file answer on or before the 23d inst. An order was also adopted—yeas 40, nays 10—that unless otherwise ordered by the Senate for cause shown, the trial shall proceed immediately after replication shall be filed.

### AN "ILLEGAL AND UNCONSTITUTIONAL COURT."

March 23—Mr. Davis, a member of the Senate and of the Court of Impeachment, from the State of Kentucky, moved the court to make this order:

The Constitution having vested the Senate with the sole power to try the articles of impeachment of the President of the United States preferred by the House of Representatives, and having also declared that "the Senate of the United States shall be composed of two Senators from each State, chosen by the legislatures thereof," and the States of Virginia, North Carolina, South Carolina, Georgia, Alabama, Mississippi, Arkansas, Louisiana, and Texas having, each by its legislature, chosen two Senators, who have been and continue to be excluded by the Senate from their seats respectively, without any judgment by the Senate against them personally and individually on the points of their elections, returns, and qualifications, it is

*Ordered,* That a Court of Impeachment for the trial of the President cannot be legally and constitutionally formed while the Senators from the States aforesaid are thus excluded from the Senate; and this case is continued until the Senators from these States are permitted to take their seats in the Senate, subject to all constitutional exceptions to their elections, returns, and qualifications severally.

Which was rejected—yeas 2, nays 49, as follow:

YEAS—Messrs. *Davis, McCreery*—2.

NAYS—Messrs. Anthony, *Buckalew,* Cameron, Cattell, Chandler, Cole, Conkling, Conness, Corbett, Cragin, *Dixon, Doolittle,* Drake, Edmunds, Ferry, Fessenden, Fowler, Frelinghuysen, Grimes, Harlan, Henderson, *Hendricks,* Howard, Howe, *Johnson,* Morgan, Morrill of Maine, Morrill of Vermont, Morton, *Norton,* Nye, Patterson of New Hampshire, *Patterson* of Tennessee, Pomeroy, Ramsey, Ross, Sherman, Sprague, Stewart, Sumner, Thayer, Tipton, Trumbull, Van Winkle, *Vickers,* Willey, Williams, Wilson, Yates—49.

NOT VOTING—Messrs. *Bayard, Saulsbury,* Wade—3.

### Answer of President Johnson.

Mr. Curtis then proceeded to read the answer to the close of that portion relative to the first article of impeachment.

---

* Mr. Black did not appear in the trial. March 23, Hon. William S. Groesbeck of Ohio appeared in his stead.

Mr. Stanbery read that portion of the answer beginning with the reply to the second article to the close of the response to the ninth article.

Mr. Evarts read the residue of the answer.

*Senate of the United States, sitting as a Court of Impeachment for the trial of Andrew Johnson, President of the United States.*

The answer of the said Andrew Johnson, President of the United States, to the articles of impeachment exhibited against him by the House of Representatives of the United States.

### ANSWER TO ARTICLE I.

For answer to the first article he says: That Edwin M. Stanton was appointed Secretary for the Department of War on the 15th day of January, A. D. 1862, by Abraham Lincoln, then President of the United States, during the first term of his presidency, and was commissioned, according to the Constitution and laws of the United States, to hold the said office during the pleasure of the President; that the office of Secretary for the Department of War was created by an act of the first Congress in its first session, passed on the 7th day of August, A. D. 1789, and in and by that act it was provided and enacted, that the said Secretary for the Department of War shall perform and execute such duties as shall from time to time be enjoined on and intrusted to him by the President of the United States, agreeably to the Constitution, relative to the subjects within the scope of said department; and, furthermore, that the said Secretary shall conduct the business of the said Department in such a manner as the President of the United States shall from time to time order and instruct.

And this respondent, further answering, says that by force of the act aforesaid and by reason of his appointment aforesaid the said Stanton became the principal officer in one of the executive departments of the Government within the true intent and meaning of the second section of the second article of the Constitution of the United States, and according to the true intent and meaning of that provision of the Constitution of the United States; and, in accordance with the settled and uniform practice of each and every President of the United States, the said Stanton then became, and so long as he should continue to hold the said office of Secretary for the Department of War must continue to be, one of the advisers of the President of the United States, as well as the person intrusted to act for and represent the President in matters enjoined upon him or intrusted to him by the President touching the department aforesaid, and for whose conduct in such capacity, subordinate to the President, the President is by the Constitution and laws of the United States, made responsible.

And this respondent, further answering, says he succeeded to the office of President of the United States upon, and by reason of, the death of Abraham Lincoln, then President of the United States, on the 15th day of April, 1865, and the said Stanton was then holding the said office of Secretary for the Department of War under and by reason of the appointment and commission aforesaid; and not having been re-moved from the said office by this respondent, the said Stanton continued to hold the same under the appointment and commission aforesaid, at the pleasure of the President, until the time hereinafter particularly mentioned; and at no time received any appointment or commission save as above detailed.

And this respondent, further answering, says that on and prior to the 5th day of August, A. D. 1867, this respondent, the President of the United States, responsible for the conduct of the Secretary for the Department of War, and having the constitutional right to resort to and rely upon the person holding that office for advice concerning the great and difficult public duties enjoined on the President by the Constitution and laws of the United States, became satisfied that he could not allow the said Stanton to continue to hold the office of Secretary for the Department of War without hazard of the public interest; that the relations between the said Stanton and the President no longer permitted the President to resort to him for advice, or to be, in the judgment of the President, safely responsible for his conduct of the affairs of the Department of War, as by law required, in accordance with the orders and instructions of the President; and thereupon, by force of the Constitution and laws of the United States, which devolve on the President the power and the duty to control the conduct of the business of that executive department of the government, and by reason of the constitutional duty of the President to take care that the laws be faithfully executed, this respondent did necessarily consider and did determine that the said Stanton ought no longer to hold the said office of Secretary for the Department of War. And this respondent, by virtue of the power and authority vested in him as President of the United States, by the Constitution and laws of the United States, to give effect to such his decision and determination, did, on the 5th day of August, A. D. 1867, address to the said Stanton a note, of which the following is a true copy:

SIR: Public considerations of a high character constrain me to say that your resignation as Secretary of War will be accepted.

To which note the said Stanton made the following reply:

WAR DEPARTMENT, *Washington, August* 5, 1867.
SIR: Your note of this day has been received, stating that "public considerations of a high character constrain you" to say "that my resignation as Secretary of War will be accepted."

In reply, I have the honor to say that public considerations of a high character, which alone have induced me to continue at the head of this Department, constrain me not to resign the office of Secretary of War before the next meeting of Congress.

Very respectfully, yours,
EDWIN M. STANTON.

This respondent, as President of the United States, was thereon of opinion that, having regard to the necessary official relations and duties of the Secretary for the Department of War to the President of the United States, according to the Constitution and laws of the United States, and having regard to the responsibility of the President for the conduct of the said Secretary, and having regard to the permanent executive authority of the office which the respondent holds under the Constitution and laws of the United States, it was impossible, consistently with the public interests, to allow the said Stanton to continue to hold the said office of Secretary for the Department of War; and it then became the official duty of the respondent, as President of the United States, to consider and decide what act or acts should and might lawfully be done by him, as President of the United States, to cause the said Stanton to surrender the said office.

This respondent was informed and verily believed that it was practically settled by the first Congress of the United States, and had been so considered, and, uniformly and in great numbers of instances, acted on by each Congress and President of the United States, in succession, from President Washington to, and including, President Lincoln, and from the First Congress to the Thirty-Ninth Congress, that the Constitution of the United States conferred on the President, as part of the executive power and as one of the necessary means and instruments of performing the executive duty expressly imposed on him by the Constitution of taking care that the laws be faithfully executed, the power at any and all times of removing from office all executive officers for cause to be judged of by the President alone. This respondent had, in pursuance of the Constitution, required the opinion of each principal officer of the executive departments upon this question of constitutional executive power and duty, and had been advised by each of them, including the said Stanton, Secretary for the Department of War, that under the Constitution of the United States this power was lodged by the Constitution in the President of the United States, and that, consequently, it could be lawfully exercised by him, and the Congress could not deprive him thereof; and this respondent, in his capacity of President of the United States, and because in that capacity he was both enabled and bound to use his best judgment upon this question, did, in good faith and with an earnest desire to arrive at the truth, come to the conclusion and opinion, and did make the same known to the honorable the Senate of the United States by a message dated on the 2d day of March, 1867, (a true copy whereof is hereunto annexed and marked A,) that the power last mentioned was conferred and the duty of exercising it, in fit cases, was imposed on the President by the Constitution of the United States, and that the President could not be deprived of this power or relieved of this duty, nor could the same be vested by law in the President and the Senate jointly, either in part or whole; and this has ever since remained and was the opinion of this respondent at the time when he was forced as aforesaid to consider and decide what act or acts should and might lawfully be done by this respondent, as President of the United States, to cause the said Stanton to surrender the said office.

This respondent was also then aware that by the first section of "An act regulating the tenure of certain civil offices," passed March 2, 1867, by a constitutional majority of both houses of Congress, it was enacted as follows:

That every person holding any civil office to which he has been appointed by and with the advice and consent of the Senate, and every person who shall hereafter be appointed to any such office, and shall become duly qualified to act therein, is and shall be entitled to hold such office until a successor shall have been in like manner appointed and duly qualified, except as herein otherwise provided: *Provided,* That the Secretaries of State, of the Treasury, of War, of the Navy, and of the Interior, the Postmaster General and the Attorney General, shall hold their offices respectively for and during the term of the President by whom they may have been appointed, and one month thereafter, subject to removal by and with the advice and consent of the Senate.

This respondent was also aware that this act was understood and intended to be an expression of the opinion of the Congress by which that act was passed, that the power to remove executive officers for cause might, by law, be taken from the President and vested in him and the Senate jointly; and although this respondent had arrived at and still retained the opinion above expressed, and verily believed, as he still believes, that the said first section of the last-mentioned act was and is wholly inoperative and void by reason of its conflict with the Constitution of the United States, yet, inasmuch as the same had been enacted by the constitutional majority in each of the two houses of that Congress, this respondent considered it to be proper to examine and decide whether the particular case of the said Stanton, on which it was this respondent's duty to act, was within or without the terms of that first section of the act; or, if within it, whether the President had not the power, according to the terms of the act, to remove the said Stanton from the office of Secretary for the Department of War, and having, in his capacity of President of the United States, so examined and considered, did form the opinion that the case of the said Stanton and his tenure of office were not affected by the first section of the last-named act.

And this respondent, further answering, says, that although a case thus existed which, in his judgment as President of the United States, called for the exercise of the executive power to remove the said Stanton from the office of Secretary for the Department of War, and although this respondent was of opinion, as is above shown, that under the Constitution of the United States the power to remove the said Stanton from the said office was vested in the President of the United States; and although this respondent was also of the opinion, as is above shown, that the case of the said Stanton was not affected by the first section of the last named act; and although each of the said opinions had been formed by this respondent upon an actual case, requiring him, in his capacity of President of the United States, to come to some judgment and determination thereon, yet this respondent, as President of the United States, desired and determined to avoid, if possible, any question of the construction and effect of the said first section of the last-named act, and also the broader question of the executive power conferred on the President of the United States, by the Constitution of the United States, to remove one of the principal officers of one of the executive departments for cause seeming to him sufficient; and this respondent also desired and determined that, if from causes over which he could exert no control, it should become absolutely necessary to raise and have, in some way, determined either or both of the said last-named questions,

it was in accordance with the Constitution of the
United States and was required of the President
thereby, that questions of so much gravity and
importance, upon which the legislative and executive departments of the Government had disagreed, which involved powers considered by all
branches of the Government, during its entire
history down to the year 1867, to have been
confided by the Constitution of the United
States to the President, and to be necessary for
the complete and proper execution of his constitutional duties, should be in some proper way
submitted to that judicial department of the
government intrusted by the Constitution with
the power, and subjected by it to the duty, not
only of determining finally the construction of
and effect of all acts of Congress, but of comparing them with the Constitution of the United
States and pronouncing them inoperative when
found in conflict with that fundamental law
which the people have enacted for the government of all their servants. And to these ends,
first, that through the action of the Senate of
the United States, the absolute duty of the President to substitute some fit person in place of Mr.
Stanton as one of his advisers, and as a principal
subordinate officer whose official conduct he was
responsible for and had lawful right to control,
might, if possible, be accomplished without the
necessity of raising any one of the questions
aforesaid; and, second, if this duty could not be
so performed, then that these questions, or such
of them as might necessarily arise, should be
judicially determined in manner aforesaid, and
for no other end or purpose this respondent, as
President of the United States, on the 12th day
of August, 1867, seven days after the reception
of the letter of the said Stanton of the 5th of
August, hereinbefore stated, did issue to the said
Stanton the order following, namely:

EXECUTIVE MANSION,
WASHINGTON, August 12, 1867.
SIR: By virtue of the power and authority vested in me
as President by the Constitution and laws of the United
States, you are hereby suspended from office as Secretary of
War, and will cease to exercise any and all functions per-
taining to the same.
You will at once transfer to General Ulysses S. Grant,
who has this day been authorized and empowered to act as
Secretary of War ad interim, all records, books, papers, and
other public property now in your custody and charge.
The Hon. EDWIN M. STANTON, Secretary of War.

To which said order the said Stanton made
the following reply:
WAR DEPARTMENT,
WASHINGTON CITY, August 12, 1867.
SIR: Your note of this date has been received, informing me that, by virtue of the powers vested in you as President by the Constitution and laws of the United States, I
am suspended from office as Secretary of War, and will
cease to exercise any and all functions pertaining to the
same, and also directing me at once to transfer to General
Ulysses S. Grant, who has this day been authorized and
empowered to act as Secretary of War ad interim, all
records, books, papers, and other public property now in
my custody and charge. Under a sense of public duty I
am compelled to deny your right, under the Constitution
and laws of the United States, without the advice and consent of the Senate, and without legal cause, to suspend me
from office as Secretary of War, or the exercise of any or
all functions pertaining to the same, or without such advice and consent, to compel me to transfer to any person
the records, books, papers, and public property in my custody as Secretary. But inasmuch as the General commanding the armies of the United States has been appointed ad
interim, and has notified me that he has accepted the appointment, I have no alternative but to submit, under protest, to superior force.
To the PRESIDENT.

And this respondent, further answering, says,
that it is provided in and by the second section
of "An act to regulate the tenure of certain
civil offices," that the President may suspend
an officer from the performance of the duties of
the office held by him, for certain causes therein
designated, until the next meeting of the Senate, and until the case shall be acted on by the
Senate; that this respondent, as President of
the United States, was advised, and he verily
believed and still believes, that the executive
power of removal from office confided to him by
the Constitution as aforesaid includes the power
of suspension from office at the pleasure of the
President, and this respondent, by the order
aforesaid, did suspend the said Stanton from
office, not until the next meeting of the Senate,
or until the Senate should have acted upon the
case, but by force of the power and authority
vested in him by the Constitution and laws of
the United States, indefinitely and at the pleasure of the President, and the order, in form
aforesaid, was made known to the Senate of the
United States on the 12th day of December, A. D.
1867, as will be more fully hereinafter stated.

And this respondent, further answering, says,
that in and by the act of February 13, 1795, it
was, among other things, provided and enacted
that, in case of vacancy in the office of Secretary for the Department of War, it shall be lawful for the President, in case he shall think it
necessary, to authorize any person to perform
the duties of that office until a successor be appointed or such vacancy filled, but not exceeding
the term of six months; and this respondent,
being advised and believing that such law was
in full force and not repealed, by an order dated
August 12, 1867, did authorize and empower
Ulysses S. Grant, General of the armies of the
United States, to act as Secretary for the Department of War ad interim, in the form in which
similar authority had theretofore been given,
not until the next meeting of the Senate and
until the Senate should act on the case, but at
the pleasure of the President, subject only to
the limitation of six months in the said last-
mentioned act contained; and a copy of the
last-named order was made known to the Senate
of the United States on the 12th day of December, A. D. 1867, as will be hereinafter more fully
stated; and in pursuance of the design and intention aforesaid, if it should become necessary
to submit the said questions to a judicial determination, this respondent, at or near the date
of the last-mentioned order, did make known
such his purpose to obtain a judicial decision of
the said questions, or such of them as might be
necessary.

And this respondent, further answering, says,
that in further pursuance of his intention and
design, if possible, to perform what he judged
to be his imperative duty, to prevent the said
Stanton from longer holding the office of Secretary for the Department of War, and at the
same time avoiding, if possible, any question
respecting the extent of the power of removal
from executive office confided to the President
by the Constitution of the United States, and
any question respecting the construction and
effect of the first section of the said "act regu-

lating the tenure ot certain civil offices," while he should not, by any act of his, abandon and relinquish, either a power which he believed the Constitution had conferred on the President of the United States, to enable him to perform the duties of his office, or a power designedly left to him by the first section of the act of Congress last aforesaid, this respondent did, on the 12th day of December, 1867, transmit to the Senate of the United States a message, a copy whereof is hereunto annexed and marked B, wherein he made known the orders aforesaid and the reasons which had induced the same, so far as this respondent then considered it material and necessary that the same should be set forth, and reiterated his views concerning the constitutional power of removal vested in the President, and also expressed his views concerning the construction of the said first section of the last-mentioned act, as respected the power of the President to remove the said Stanton from the said office of Secretary for the Department of War, well hoping that this respondent could thus perform what he then believed, and still believes, to be his imperative duty in reference to the said Stanton, without derogating from the powers which this respondent believed were confided to the President by the Constitution and laws, and without the necessity of raising judicially any questions respecting the same.

And this respondent, further answering, says, that this hope not having been realized, the President was compelled either to allow the said Stanton to resume the said office and remain therein, contrary to the settled convictions of the President, formed as aforesaid, respecting the powers confided to him and the duties required of him by the Constitution of the United States, and contrary to the opinion formed as aforesaid, that the first section of the last-mentioned act did not affect the case of the said Stanton, and contrary to the fixed belief of the President that he could no longer advise with or trust or be responsible for the said Stanton, in the said office of Secretary for the Department of War, or else he was compelled to take such steps as might, in the judgment of the President, be lawful and necessary to raise, for a judicial decision, the questions affecting the lawful right of the said Stanton to resume the said office, or the power of the said Stanton to persist in refusing to quit the said office, if he should persist in actually refusing to quit the same; and to this end, and to this end only, this respondent did, on the 21st day of February, 1868, issue the order for the removal of the said Stanton, in the said first article mentioned and set forth, and the order authorizing the said Lorenzo Thomas to act as Secretary of War *ad interim*, in the said second article set forth.

And this respondent, proceeding to answer specifically each substantial allegation in the said first article, says: He denies that the said Stanton, on the 21st day of February, 1868, was lawfully in possession of the said office of Secretary for the Department of War. He denies that the said Stanton, on the day last mentioned, was lawfully entitled to hold the said office against the will of the President of the United

States. He denies that the said order for the removal of the said Stanton was unlawfully issued. He denies that the said order was issued with intent to violate the act entitled "An act to regulate the tenure of certain civil offices." He denies that the said order was a violation of the last-mentioned act. He denies that the said order was a violation of the Constitution of the United States, or of any law thereof, or of his oath of office. He denies that the said order was issued with an intent to violate the Constitution of the United States, or any law thereof, or this respondent's oath of office; and he respectfully, but earnestly, insists that not only was it issued by him in the performance of what he believed to be an imperative official duty, but in the performance of what this honorable court will consider was, in point of fact, an imperative official duty. And he denies that any and all substantive matters in the first article contained, in manner and form as the same are therein stated and set forth, do by law constitute a high misdemeanor in office, within the true intent and meaning of the Constitution of the United States.

### ANSWER TO ARTICLE II.

And for answer to the second article, this respondent says, that he admits he did issue and deliver to said Lorenzo Thomas the said writing set forth in said second article, bearing date at Washington, District of Columbia, February 21, 1868, addressed to Brevet Major General Lorenzo Thomas, Adjutant General United States army, Washington, District of Columbia, and he further admits that the same was so issued without the advice and consent of the Senate of the United States, then in session; but he denies that he thereby violated the Constitution of the United States, or any law thereof, or that he did thereby intend to violate the Constitution of the United States or the provisions of any act of Congress; and this respondent refers to his answer to said first article for a full statement of the purposes and intentions with which said order was issued, and adopts the same as part of his answer to this article; and he further denies that there was then and there no vacancy in the said office of Secretary for the Department of War, or that he did then and there commit or was guilty of a high misdemeanor in office; and this respondent maintains and will insist:

1. That at the date and delivery of said writing there was a vacancy existing in the office of Secretary for the Department of War.

2. That, notwithstanding the Senate of the United States was then in session, it was lawful and according to long and well-established usage to empower and authorize the said Thomas to act as Secretary of War *ad interim*.

3. That if the said act regulating the tenure of civil offices be held to be a valid law, no provision of the same was violated by the issuing of said order or by the designation of said Thomas to act as Secretary of War *ad interim*.

### ANSWER TO ARTICLE III.

And for answer to said third article, this respondent says, that he abides by his answer to said first and second articles, in so far as the same are responsive to the allegations contained in the said third article, and, without here again repeating the same answer, prays the same be taken as an answer to this third article as fully as if here again set out at length; and as to the new allegation contained in said third article, that this respondent did appoint the said Thomas to be Secretary for the Department of War *ad interim*, this respondent denies that he gave any other authority to said Thomas than such as appears in said written authority set out in said article, by which he authorized and empowered said Thomas to act as Secretary for the Department of War *ad interim;* and he denies that the same amounts to an appointment, and insists that it is only a designation of an officer of that Department to act temporarily as Secretary for the Department of War *ad interim*, until an appointment should be made. But, whether the said written authority amounts to an appointment or to a temporary authority or designation, this respondent denies that in any sense he did thereby intend to violate the Constitution of the United States, or that he thereby intended to give the said order the character or effect of an appointment in the constitutional or legal sense of that term. He further denies that there was no vacancy in said office of Secretary for the Department of War existing at the date of said written authority.

### ANSWER TO ARTICLE IV.

And for answer to said fourth article, this respondent denies that on the said 21st day of February, 1868, at Washington aforesaid, or at any other time or place, he did unlawfully conspire with the said Lorenzo Thomas, or with the said Thomas and any other person or persons, with intent, by intimidations and threats, unlawfully to hinder and prevent the said Stanton from holding said office of Secretary for the Department of War, in violation of the Constitution of the United States, or of the provisions of the said act of Congress in said article mentioned, or that he did then and there commit or was guilty of a high crime in office. On the contrary thereof, protesting that the said Stanton was not then and there lawfully the Secretary for the Department of War, this respondent states that his sole purpose in authorizing the said Thomas to act as Secretary for the Department of War *ad interim* was, as is fully stated in his answer to the said first article, to bring the question of the right of the said Stanton to hold said office, notwithstanding his said suspension, and notwithstanding the said order of removal, and notwithstanding the said authority of the said Thomas to act as Secretary of War *ad interim*, to the test of a final decision by the Supreme Court of the United States, in the earliest practicable mode by which the question could be brought before that tribunal.

This respondent did not conspire or agree with the said Thomas, or any other person or persons, to use intimidation or threats to hinder or prevent the said Stanton from holding the said office of Secretary for the Department of War, nor did this respondent at any time command or advise the said Thomas or any other person or persons to resort to or use either threats or intimidations for that purpose. The only means in the contemplation or purpose of respondent to be used are set forth fully in the said orders

of February 21, the first addressed to Mr. Stanton and the second to the said Thomas.

By the first order, the respondent notified Mr. Stanton that he was removed from the said office, and that his functions as Secretary for the Department of War were to terminate upon the receipt of that order; and he also thereby notified the said Stanton that the said Thomas had been authorized to act as Secretary for the Department of War *ad interim*, and ordered the said Stanton to transfer to him all the records, books, papers, and other public property in his custody and charge; and, by the second order, this respondent notified the said Thomas of the removal from office of the said Stanton, and authorized him to act as Secretary for the Department of War *ad interim*, and directed him to immediately enter upon the discharge of the duties pertaining to that office, and to receive the transfer of all the records, books, papers, and other public property from Mr. Stanton then in his custody and charge.

Respondent gave no instructions to the said Thomas to use intimidation or threats to enforce obedience to these orders. He gave him no authority to call in the aid of the military or any other force to enable him to obtain possession of the office, or of the books, papers, records, or property thereof. The only agency resorted to or intended to be resorted to was by means of the said executive orders requiring obedience. But the Secretary of the Department of War refused to obey these orders, and still holds undisturbed possession and custody of that Department, and of the records, books, papers, and other public property therein. Respondent further states that, in execution of the orders so by this respondent given to the said Thomas, he, the said Thomas, proceeded in a peaceful manner to demand of the said Stanton a surrender to him of the public property in the said Department, and to vacate the possession of the same, and to allow him, the said Thomas, peaceably to exercise the duties devolved upon him by authority of the President. That, as this respondent has been informed and believes, the said Stanton peremptorily refused obedience to the orders so issued. Upon such refusal, no force or threat of force was used by the said Thomas, by authority of the President or otherwise, to enforce obedience, either then or at any subsequent time.

This respondent doth here except to the sufficiency of the allegations contained in said fourth article, and states for ground of exception, that it is not stated that there was any agreement between this respondent and the said Thomas, or any other person or persons, to use intimidation and threats, nor is there any allegation as to the nature of said intimidation and threats, or that there was any agreement to carry them into execution, or that any step was taken or agreed to be taken to carry them into execution, and that the allegation in said article that the intent of said conspiracy was to use intimidation and threats is wholly insufficient, inasmuch as it is not alleged that the said intent formed the basis or became a part of any agreement between the said alleged conspirators, and, furthermore, that there is no allegation of any conspiracy or agreement to use intimidation or threats.

### ANSWER TO ARTICLE V.

And for answer to the said fifth article, this respondent denies that on the said 21st day of February, 1868, or at any other time or times in the same year before the said 2d day of March, 1868, or at any prior or subsequent time, at Washington aforesaid, or at any other place, this respondent did unlawfully conspire with the said Thomas, or with any other person or persons, to prevent or hinder the execution of the said act entitled "An act regulating the tenure of certain civil offices," or that, in pursuance of said alleged conspiracy, he did unlawfully attempt to prevent the said Edwin M. Stanton from holding said office of Secretary for the Department of War, or that he did thereby commit, or that he was thereby guilty of, a high misdemeanor in office. Respondent, protesting that said Stanton was not then and there Secretary for the Department of War, begs leave to refer to his answer given to the fourth article and to his answer given to the first article, as to his intent and purpose in issuing the orders for the removal of Mr. Stanton and the authority given to the said Thomas, and prays equal benefit therefrom as if the same were here again repeated and fully set forth.

And this respondent excepts to the sufficiency of the said fifth article, and states his ground for such exception, that it is not alleged by what means or by what agreement the said alleged conspiracy was formed or agreed to be carried out, or in what way the same was attempted to be carried out, or what were the acts done in pursuance thereof.

### ANSWER TO ARTICLE VI.

And for answer to the said sixth article, this respondent denies that on the said 21st day of February, 1868, at Washington aforesaid, or at any other time or place, he did unlawfully conspire with the said Thomas by force to seize, take, or possess, the property of the United States in the Department of War, contrary to the provisions of the said acts referred to in the said article, or either of them, or with intent to violate either of them. Respondent, protesting that said Stanton was not then and there Secretary for the Department of War, not only denies the said conspiracy as charged, but also denies any unlawful intent in reference to the custody and charge of the property of the United States in the said Department of War, and again refers to his former answers for a full statement of his intent and purpose in the premises.

### ANSWER TO ARTICLE VII.

And for answer to the said seventh article, respondent denies that on the said 21st day of February, 1868, at Washington aforesaid, or at any other time and place, he did unlawfully conspire with the said Thomas with intent unlawfully to seize, take, or possess the property of the United States in the Department of War with intent to violate or disregard the said act in the said seventh article referred to, or that he did then and there commit a high misdemeanor in office. Respondent, protesting that the said Stanton was not then and there Secretary for the Department of War, again refers to his former answers, in so far as they are applicable, to show the intent with which he proceeded in the premises, and prays equal benefit therefrom as if the same were here again fully repeated. Respondent further takes exception to the sufficiency of the allegations of this article as to the conspiracy alleged, upon the same grounds as stated in the exception set forth in his answer to said article fourth.

### ANSWER TO ARTICLE VIII.

And for answer to the said eighth article, this respondent denies that on the 21st day of February, 1868, at Washington aforesaid, or at any other time and place, he did issue and deliver to the said Thomas the said letter of authority set forth in the said eighth article, with the intent unlawfully to control the disbursements of the money appropriated for the military service and for the Department of War. This respondent, protesting that there was a vacancy in the office of Secretary for the Department of War, admits that he did issue the said letter of authority, and he denies that the same was with any unlawful intent whatever, either to violate the Constitution of the United States or any act of Congress. On the contrary, this respondent again affirms that his sole intent was to vindicate his authority as President of the United States, and by peaceful means to bring the question of the right of the said Stanton to continue to hold the said office of Secretary of War to a final decision before the Supreme Court of the United States, as has been hereinbefore set forth; and he prays the same benefit from his answer in the premises as if the same were here again repeated at length.

### ANSWER TO ARTICLE IX.

And for answer to the said ninth article the respondent states that on the said 22d day of February, 1868, the following note was addressed to the said Emory by the private secretary of respondent:

EXECUTIVE MANSION,
WASHINGTON, D. C., *February* 22, 1868.

GENERAL: The President directs me to say that he will be pleased to have you call upon him as early as practicable.
Respectfully and truly, yours,
WILLIAM G. MOORE,
*United States Army.*

General Emory called at the Executive Mansion according to this request. The object of respondent was to be advised by General Emory as commander of the department of Washington, what changes had been made in the military affairs of the department. Respondent had been informed that various changes had been made, which in nowise had been brought to his notice or reported to him from the Department of War, or from any other quarter, and desired to ascertain the facts. After the said Emory had explained in detail the changes which had taken place, said Emory called the attention of respondent to a general order which he referred to and which this respondent then sent for, when it was produced. It is as follows:

[General Orders No. 17.]
WAR DEPARTMENT, ADJUTANT GENERAL'S OFFICE,
WASHINGTON, *March* 14, 1867.

The following acts of Congress are published for the information and government of all concerned:
II—PUBLIC—No. 85.
AN ACT making appropriations for the support of th

army for the year ending June 30, 1868, and for other purposes.

SEC. 2. *And be it further enacted,* That the headquarters of the General of the army of the United States shall be at the city of Washington, and all orders and instructions relating to military operations issued by the President or Secretary of War shall be issued through the General of the army, and in case of his inability, through the next in rank. The General of the army shall not be removed, suspended, or relieved from command or assigned to duty elsewhere than at said headquarters, except at his own request, without the previous approval of the Senate; and any orders or instructions relating to military operations issued contrary to the requirements of this section shall be null and void; and any officer who shall issue orders or instructions contrary to the provisions of this section shall be deemed guilty of a misdemeanor in office; and any officer of the army who shall transmit, convey, or obey any orders or instructions so issued contrary to the provisions of this section, knowing that such orders were so issued, shall be liable to imprisonment for not less than two nor more than twenty years, upon conviction thereof in any court of competent jurisdiction.

Approved March 2, 1867.

By order of the Secretary of War:

E. D. TOWNSEND,<br>*Assistant Adjutant General.*

General Emory not only called the attention of respondent to this order, but to the fact that it was in conformity with a section contained in an appropriation act passed by Congress. Respondent, after reading the order, observed: "This is not in accordance with the Constitution of the United States, which makes me commander-in-chief of the army and navy, or of the language of the commission which you hold." General Emory then stated that this order had met respondent's approval. Respondent then said in reply, in substance, "Am I to understand that the President of the United States cannot give an order but through the General-in-chief, or General Grant?" General Emory again reiterated the statement that it had met respondent's approval, and that it was the opinion of some of the leading lawyers of the country that this order was constitutional. With some further consideration, respondent then inquired the names of the lawyers who had given the opinion, and he mentioned the names of two. Respondent then said that the object of the law was very evident, referring to the clause in the appropriation act upon which the order purported to be based. This, according to respondent's recollection, was the substance of the conversation had with General Emory.

Respondent denies that any allegations in the said article of any instructions or declarations given to the said Emory, then or at any other time, contrary to or in addition to what is hereinbefore set forth, are true. Respondent denies that, in said conversation with said Emory, he had any other intent than to express the opinions then given to the said Emory; nor did he then, or at any time, request or order the said Emory to disobey any law or any order issued in conformity with any law, or intend to offer any inducement to the said Emory to violate any law. What this respondent then said to General Emory was simply the expression of an opinion which he then fully believed to be sound, and which he yet believes to be so—and that is, that by the express provisions of the Constitution, this respondent, as President, is made the commander-in-chief of the armies of the United States, and as such he is to be respected; and that his orders, whether issued through the War Department or through the

General-in-chief, or by any other channel of communication, are entitled to respect and obedience; and that such constitutional power cannot be taken from him by virtue of any act of Congress. Respondent doth therefore deny that by the expression of such opinion he did commit or was guilty of a high misdemeanor in office. And this respondent doth further say that the said article nine lays no foundation whatever for the conclusion stated in the said article, that the respondent, by reason of the allegations therein contained, was guilty of a high misdemeanor in office.

In reference to the statement made by General Emory, that this respondent had approved of said act of Congress containing the section referred to, the respondent admits that his formal approval was given to said act, but accompanied the same by the following message, addressed and sent with the act to the House of Representatives, in which House the said act originated, and from which it came to respondent:

*To the House of Representatives:*

The act entitled "An act making appropriations for the support of the army for the year ending June 30, 1868, and for other purposes," contains provisions to which I must call attention. These provisions are contained in the 2d section, which, in certain cases, virtually deprives the President of his constitutional functions as commander-in-chief of the army, and in the sixth section, which denies to ten states of the Union their constitutional right to protect themselves, in any emergency, by means of their own militia. These provisions are out of place in an appropriation act, but I am compelled to defeat these necessary appropriations if I withhold my signature from the act. Pressed by these considerations, I feel constrained to return the bill with my signature, but to accompany it with my earnest protest against the sections which I have indicated.

WASHINGTON, D. C., *March 2, 1867.*

Respondent, therefore, did no more than to express to said Emory the same opinion which he had expressed to the House of Representatives.

ANSWER TO ARTICLE X.

And in answer to the tenth article and specifications thereof, the respondent says that on the 14th and 15th days of August, in the year 1866, a political convention of delegates from all or most of the States and Territories of the Union was held in the city of Philadelphia, under the name and style of the National Union Convention, for the purpose of maintaining and advancing certain political views and opinions before the people of the United States, and for their support and adoption in the exercise of the constitutional suffrage, in the election of representatives and delegates in Congress, which were soon to occur in many of the States and Territories of the Union; which said convention, in the course of its proceedings and in furtherance of the objects of the same, adopted a "declaration of principles" and "an address to the people of the United States," and appointed a committee of two of its members from each State and of one from each Territory and one from the District of Columbia to wait upon the President of the United States and present to him a copy of the proceedings of the convention; that on the 18th day of said month of August, this committee waited upon the President of the United States at the Executive Mansion, and was received by him in one of the rooms thereof, and by their chairman, Hon. Reverdy Johnson, then and now a Senator of the United States, acting and speaking in their behalf, presented a copy of the proceedings of the convention, and addressed the President of the United States in a speech, of which a copy (according to a published report of the same, and, as the respondent believes, substantially a correct report) is hereto annexed as a part of this answer, and marked Exhibit C.

That thereupon, and in reply to the address of said committee by their chairman, this respondent addressed the said committee so waiting upon him in one of the rooms of the Executive Mansion; and this respondent believes that this his address to said committee is the occasion referred to in the first specification of the tenth article; but this respondent does not admit that the passages therein set forth, as if extracts from a speech or address of this respondent upon said occasion, correctly or justly present his speech or address upon said occasion, but, on the contrary, this respondent demands and insists that if this honorable court shall deem the said article and the said specification thereof to contain allegation of matter cognizable by this honorable court as a high misdemeanor in office, within the intent and meaning of the Constitution of the United States, and shall receive or allow proof in support of the same, that proof shall be required to be made of the actual speech and address of this respondent on said occasion, which this respondent denies that said article and specification contain or correctly or justly represent.

And this respondent, further answering the tenth article and the specifications thereof, says that at Cleveland, in the State of Ohio, and on the 3d day of September, in the year 1866, he was attended by a large assemblage of his fellow-citizens, and in deference and obedience to their call and demand he addressed them upon matters of public and political consideration; and this respondent believes that said occasion and address are referred to in the second specification of the tenth article; but this respondent does not admit that the passages therein set forth, as if extracts from a speech of this respondent on said occasion, correctly or justly present his speech or address upon said occasion; but, on the contrary, this respondent demands and insists that if this honorable court shall deem the said article and the second specification thereof to contain allegation of matter cognizable by this honorable court as a high misdemeanor in office, within the intent and meaning of the Constitution of the United States, and shall receive or allow proof in support of the same, that proof shall be required to be made of the actual speech and address of this respondent on said occasion, which this respondent denies that said article and specification contain or correctly or justly represent.

And this respondent, further answering the tenth article and the specifications thereof, says that at St. Louis, in the State of Missouri, and on the 8th day of September, in the year 1866, he was attended by a numerous assemblage of his fellow-citizens, and in deference and obedience to their call and demand he addressed them upon matters of public and political consideration; and this respondent believes that said occasion and address are referred to in the third specification of the tenth article; but this respondent does not admit that the passages therein set forth, as if extracts from a speech of this respondent on said occasion, correctly or justly present his speech or address upon said occasion; but, on the contrary, this respondent demands and insists that if this honorable court shall deem the said article and the said third specification thereof to contain allegation of matter cognizable by this honorable court as a high misdemeanor in office, within the intent and meaning of the Constitution of the United States, and shall receive or allow proof in support of the same, that proof shall be required to be made of the actual speech and address of this respondent on said occasion, which this respondent denies that the said article and specification contain or correctly or justly represent.

And this respondent, further answering the tenth article, protesting that he has not been unmindful of the high duties of his office, or of the harmony or courtesies which ought to exist and be maintained between the executive and legislative branches of the Government of the United States, denies that he has ever intended or designed to set aside the rightful authority or powers of Congress, or attempted to bring into disgrace, ridicule, hatred, contempt, or reproach the Congress of the United States or either branch thereof, or to impair or destroy the regard or respect of all or any of the good people of the United States for the Congress or the rightful legislative power thereof, or to excite the odium or resentment of all or any of the good people of the United States against Congress and the laws by it duly and constitutionally enacted. This respondent further says, that at all times he has, in his official acts as President, recognized the authority of the several Congresses of the United States as constituted and organized during his administration of the office of President of the United States.

And this respondent, further answering, says that he has, from time to time, under his constitutional right and duty as President of the United States, communicated to Congress his views and opinions in regard to such acts or resolutions thereof as, being submitted to him as President of the United States in pursuance of the Constitution, seemed to this respondent to require such communications; and he has, from time to time, in the exercise of that freedom of speech which belongs to him as a citizen of the United States, and, in his political relations as President of the United States to the people of the United States, is upon fit occasions a duty of the highest obligation, expressed to his fellow-citizens his views and opinions respecting the measures and proceedings of Congress; and that in such addresses to his fellow-citizens and in such his communications to Congress he has expressed his views, opinions, and judgment of and concerning the actual constitution of the two houses of Congress without representation therein of certain States of the Union, and of the effect that in wisdom and justice, in the opinion and judgment of this respondent, Congress, in its legislation and proceedings, should give to this political circumstance; and whatsoever he has thus communicated to Congress or addressed to his fellow-citizens or any assemblage thereof, this respondent says was and is within and according to his right and privilege as an American citizen and his right and duty as President of the United States.

And this respondent, not waiving or at all disparaging his right of freedom of opinion and of freedom of speech, as hereinbefore or hereinafter more particularly set forth, but claiming and insisting upon the same, further answering the said tenth article, says that the views and opinions expressed by this respondent in his said addresses to the assemblages of his fellow-citizens, as in said article or in this answer thereto mentioned, are not and were not intended to be other or different from those expressed by him in his communications to Congress—that the eleven States lately in insurrection never had ceased to be States of the Union, and that they were then entitled to representation in Congress by loyal Representatives and Senators as fully as the other States of the Union, and that, consequently, the Congress, as then constituted, was not, in fact, a Congress of all the States, but a Congress of only a part of the States. This respondent, always protesting against the unauthorized exclusion therefrom of the said eleven States, nevertheless gave his assent to all laws passed by said Congress which did not, in his opinion and judgment, violate the Constitution, exercising his constitutional authority of returning bills to said Congress with his objections when they appeared to him to be unconstitutional or inexpedient.

And, further, this respondent has also expressed the opinion, both in his communications to Congress and in his addresses to the people, that the policy adopted by Congress in reference to the States lately in insurrection did not tend to peace, harmony, and union, but, on the contrary, did tend to disunion and the permanent disruption of the States; and that in following its said policy, laws had been passed by Congress in violation of the fundamental principles of the government, and which tended to consolidation and despotism; and, such being his deliberate opinions, he would have felt himself unmindful of the high duties of his office if he had failed to express them in his communications to Congress, or in his addresses to the people when called upon by them to express his opinions on matters of public and political consideration.

And this respondent, further answering the tenth article, says that he has always claimed and insisted, and now claims and insists, that both in his personal and private capacity of a citizen of the United States, and in the political relations of the President of the United States to the people of the United States, whose servant, under the duties and responsibilities of the Constitution of the United States, the President of the United States is, and should always remain, this respondent had and has the full right, and in his office of President of the United States is held to the high duty of forming, and, on fit occasions, expressing, opinions of and concerning the legislation of Congress, proposed or completed, in respect of its wisdom, expediency, justice. worthiness, objects, purposes, and public and political motives and tendencies; and within and as a part of such right and duty to form, and on fit occasions to express, opinions of and concerning the public character and conduct, views, purposes, objects, motives, and tendencies of all men engaged in the public service, as well in Congress as otherwise, and under no other rules or limits upon this right of freedom of opinion and of freedom of speech, or of responsibility and amenability for the actual exercise of such freedom of opinion and freedom of speech, than attend upon such rights and their exercise on the part of all other citizens of the United States, and on the part of all their public servants.

And this respondent, further answering said tenth article, says that the several occasions on which, as is alleged in the several specifications of said article, this respondent addressed his fellow-citizens on subjects of public and political consideration, were not, nor was any one of them, sought or planned by this respondent; but, on the contrary, each of said occasions arose upon the exercise of a lawful and accustomed right of the people of the United States to call upon their public servants and express to them their opinions, wishes, and feelings, upon matters of public and political consideration, and to invite from such, their public servants, an expression of their opinions, views, and feelings on matters of public and political consideration; and this respondent claims and insists before this honorable court, and before all the people of the United States, that of or concerning this his right of freedom of opinion and of freedom of speech, and this his exercise of such rights on all matters of public and political consideration, and in respect of all public servants or persons whatsoever engaged in or connected therewith, this respondent, as a citizen or as President of the United States, is not subject to question, inquisition, impeachment, or inculpation in any form or manner whatsoever.

And this respondent says that neither the said tenth article nor any specification thereof, nor any allegation therein contained, touches or relates to any official act or doing of this respondent in the office of President of the United States or in the discharge of any of its constitutional or legal duties or responsibilities; but said article and the specifications and allegations thereof, wholly and in every part thereof, question only the discretion or propriety of freedom of opinion or freedom of speech as exercised by this respondent as a citizen of the United States in his personal right and capacity, and without allegation or imputation against this respondent of the violation of any law of the United States touching or relating to freedom of speech or its exercise by the citizens of the United States or by this respondent as one of the said citizens or otherwise; and he denies that, by reason of any matter in said article or its specifications alleged, he has said or done anything indecent or unbecoming in the Chief Magistrate of the United States, or that he has brought the high office of the President of the United States into contempt, ridicule, or disgrace, or that he has committed or has been guilty of a high misdemeanor in office.

### ANSWER TO ARTICLE XI.

And in answer to the eleventh article, this respondent denies that on the 18th day of August, in the year 1866, at the city of Washington, in the District of Columbia, he did, by public speech or otherwise, declare or affirm, in substance or at all, that the Thirty-Ninth Congress of the United States was not a Congress of the United States authorized by the Constitution to exercise legislative power under the same, or that he did then and there declare or affirm that the said Thirty-Ninth Congress was a Congress of only part of the States in any sense or meaning other than that ten States of the Union were denied representation therein; or that he made any or either of the declarations or affirmations in this behalf, in the said article alleged, as denying or intending to deny that the legislation of said Thirty-Ninth Congress was valid or obligatory upon this respondent, except so far as this respondent saw fit to approve the same; and as to the allegation in said article, that he did thereby intend or mean to be understood that the said Congress had not power to propose amendments to the Constitution, this respondent says that in said address he said nothing in reference to the subject of amendments of the Constitution, nor was the question of the competency of the said Congress to propose such amendments, without the participation of said excluded States at the time of said address, in any way mentioned or considered or referred to by this respondent, nor in what he did say had he any intent regarding the same, and he denies the allegation so made to the contrary thereof. But this respondent, in further answer to, and in respect of, the said allegations of the said eleventh article hereinbefore traversed and denied, claims and insists upon his personal and official right of freedom of opinion and freedom of speech, and his duty in his political relations as President of the United States to the people of the United States in the exercise of such freedom of opinion and freedom of speech, in the same manner, form, and effect as he has in this behalf stated the same in his answer to the said tenth article, and with the same effect as if he here repeated the same; and he further claims and insists, as in said answer to said tenth article he has claimed and insisted, that he is not subject to question, inquisition, impeachment, or inculpation, in any form or manner, of or concerning such rights of freedom of opinion of freedom of speech or his said alleged exercise thereof.

And this respondent further denies that on the 21st of February, in the year 1868, or at any other time, at the city of Washington, in the District of Columbia, in pursuance of any such declaration as is in that behalf in said eleventh article alleged, or otherwise, he did unlawfully, and in disregard of the requirement of the Constitution that he should take care that the laws should be faithfully executed, attempt to prevent the execution of an act entitled "An act regulating the tenure of certain civil offices," passed March 2, 1867, by unlawfully devising or contriving, or attempting to devise or contrive, means by which he should prevent Edwin M. Stanton from forthwith resuming the functions of Secretary for the Department of War; or by unlawfully devising or contriving, or attempting to devise or contrive, means to prevent the execution of an act entitled "An act making appropriations for the support of the army for the fiscal year ending June 30, 1868, and for other purposes," approved March 2, 1867, or to prevent the execution of an act entitled "An act to provide for the more efficient government of the rebel States," passed March 2, 1867.

And this respondent, further answering the said eleventh article, says that he has, in his answer to the first article, set forth in detail the acts, steps, and proceedings done and taken by this respondent to and toward or in the matter of the suspension or removal of the said Edwin M. Stanton in or from the office of Secretary for the Department of War, with the times, modes, circumstances, intents, views, purposes, and opinions of official obligation and duty under and with which such acts, steps, and proceedings were done and taken; and he makes answer to this eleventh article of the matters in his answer to the first article, pertaining to the suspension or removal of said Edwin M. Stanton, to the same intent and effect as if they were here repeated and set forth.

And this respondent, further answering the said eleventh article, denies that by means or reason of anything in said article alleged, this respondent, as President of the United States, did, on the 21st day of February, 1868, or at any other day or time, commit, or that he was guilty of, a high misdemeanor in office.

And this respondent, further answering the said eleventh article, says that the same and the matters therein contained do not charge or allege the commission of any act whatever by this respondent, in his office of President of the United States, nor the omission by this respondent of any act of official obligation or duty in his office of President of the United States; nor does the said article nor the matters therein contained name, designate, describe, or define any act or mode or form of attempt, device, contrivance, or means, or of attempt at device, contrivance or means, whereby this respondent can know or understand what act or mode or form of attempt, device, contrivance or means, or of attempt at device, contrivance, or means, are imputed to or charged against this respondent, in his office of President of the United States, or intended so to be, or whereby this respondent can more fully or definitely make answer unto the said article than he hereby does.

And this respondent, in submitting to this honorable court this his answer to the Articles of Impeachment exhibited against him, respectfully reserves leave to amend and add to the same from time to time, as may become necessary or proper, and when and as such necessity and propriety shall appear.

ANDREW JOHNSON

HENRY STANBERY,
B. R. CURTIS,
THOMAS A. R. NELSON,
WILLIAM M. EVARTS,
W. S. GROESBECK,
*Of Counsel.*

Same day—The President's counsel asked for thirty days for preparation before the trial shall proceed; which was debated and disagreed to— yeas 12, nays 41.

March 24—The Managers presented the replication adopted — yeas 116, nays 36 — by the House of Representatives, as follows :

IN THE HOUSE OF REPRESENTATIVES, UNITED STATES, *March 24, 1868.*

*Replication by the House of Representatives of the United States to the answer of Andrew Johnson, President of the United States, to the Articles of Impeachment exhibited against him by the House of Representatives.*

The House of Representatives of the United States have considered the several answers of Andrew Johnson, President of the United States, to the several articles of impeachment against him by them exhibited in the name of themselves and of all the people of the United States, and reserving to themselves all advantage of exception to the insufficiency of his answer to each and all of the several articles of impeachment exhibited against said Andrew Johnson, President of the United States, do deny each and every averment in said several answers, or either of them, which denies or traverses the acts, intents, crimes, or misdemeanors charged against said Andrew Johnson in the said articles of impeachment, or either of them ; and for replication to said answer do say that said Andrew Johnson, President of the United States, is guilty of the high crimes and misdemeanors mentioned in said articles, and that the House of Representatives are ready to prove the same.

SCHUYLER COLFAX,
*Speaker of the House of Representatives.*
EDWARD McPHERSON,
*Clerk of the House of Representatives.*

Same day—An order was adopted, finally without a division, that the Senate will commence the trial on the 30th inst., and proceed with all convenient despatch.

March 30 — Opening argument by Mr. Butler, one of the Managers, and some testimony introduced.

March 31, April 1, 2, 3, and 4, the testimony for the prosecution continued, and the case on the part of the House substantially closed. Adjourned till April 9, at the request of the President's counsel.

April 9 and 10—Occupied by Judge Curtis's opening argument for the defence, and in presenting testimony.

April 11, 13, 14, 15, 16, 17, 18, 20, testimony presented.

April 22—Argument begun, and continued on April 23, 24, 25, 27, 28, 29, 30, May 1, 2, 4, 5, and 6.

May 7 and 11 spent in determining rules, form of question, &c. May 12, adjourned in consequence of the sickness of Senator Howard, till May 16.

### The Judgment of the Senate.

May 16—By a vote of 34 to 19, it was ordered that the question on the eleventh article be taken first. [For Article XI, see page 10.]

The vote was 35 "guilty," 19 "not guilty," as follow :

GUILTY — Messrs. Anthony, Cameron, Cattell, Chandler, Cole, Conkling, Conness, Corbett, Cragin, Drake, Edmunds, Ferry, Frelinghuysen, Harlan, Howard, Howe, Morgan, Morrill of Maine, Morrill of Vermont, Morton, Nye, Patterson of New Hampshire, Pomeroy, Ramsey, Sherman, Sprague, Stewart, Sumner, Thayer, Tipton, Wade, Willey, Williams, Wilson, Yates—35.

NOT GUILTY—Messrs. *Bayard, Buckalew, Davis, Dixon, Doolittle,* Fessenden, Fowler, Grimes, Henderson, *Hendricks, Johnson, McCreery, Norton, Patterson* of Tennessee, Ross, *Saulsbury,* Trumbull, Van Winkle, *Vickers*—19.

May 26—The second and third articles were voted upon, *with the same result as on the eleventh :* GUILTY 35 ; NOT GUILTY, 19.

A motion that the court do now adjourn *sine die* was then carried—yeas 34, nays 16, as follow :

YEAS—Messrs. Anthony, Cameron, Cattell, Chandler, Cole, Conkling, Corbett, Cragin, Drake, Edmunds, Ferry, Frelinghuysen, Harlan, Howard, Morgan, Morrill of Maine, Morrill of Vermont, Morton, Nye, Patterson of New Hampshire, Pomeroy, Ramsey, Sherman, Sprague, Stewart, Sumner, Thayer, Tipton, Van Winkle, Wade, Willey, Williams, Wilson, Yates—34.

NAYS—Messrs. *Bayard, Buckalew, Davis, Dixon, Doolittle,* Fowler, Henderson, *Hendricks, Johnson, McCreery, Norton, Patterson* of Tennessee, Ross, *Saulsbury,* Trumbull, *Vickers*—16.

NOT VOTING—Conness, Fessenden, Grimes, Howe—4.

Judgment of acquittal was then entered by the Chief Justice on the three articles voted upon, and the Senate sitting as a court for the trial of Andrew Johnson, President of the United States, upon Articles of Impeachment exhibited by the House of Representatives, was declared adjourned without day.

---

# XXV.

## CORRESPONDENCE BETWEEN GEN. GRANT AND PRESIDENT JOHNSON,

### GROWING OUT OF SECRETARY STANTON'S SUSPENSION.

WAR DEPARTMENT,
WASHINGTON CITY, *February 4,* 1868.

SIR : In answer to the resolution of the House of Representatives of the 3d instant, I transmit herewith copies furnished me by General Grant of correspondence between him and the President, relating to the Secretary of War, and which he reports to be all the correspondence he has had with the President on the subject.

I have had no correspondence with the President since the 12th of August last. After the

action of the Senate on his alleged reason for my suspension from the office of Secretary of War, I resumed the duties of that office as required by the act of Congress, and have continued to discharge them without any personal or written communication with the President. No orders have been issued from this department in the name of the President, with my knowledge, and I have received no orders from him.

The correspondence sent herewith embraces all the correspondence known to me on the subject referred to in the resolution of the House of Representatives.

I have the honor to be, sir, with great respect, your obedient servant, EDWIN M. STANTON, Secretary of War.

Hon. SCHUYLER COLFAX, Speaker of the House of Representatives.

---

### 1.—GENERAL GRANT TO THE PRESIDENT.

HEADQUARTERS ARMY OF THE UNITED STATES, WASHINGTON, January 24, 1868.

SIR : I have the honor, very respectfully, to request to have, in writing, the order which the President gave me verbally on Sunday, the 19th instant, to disregard the orders of the Hon. E. M. Stanton, as Secretary of War, until I knew, from the President himself, that they were his orders.

I have the honor to be, very respectfully, your obedient servant, U. S. GRANT, General.

His Excellency A. JOHNSON, President of the United States.

---

### 2.—GENERAL GRANT TO THE PRESIDENT.

HEADQUARTERS ARMY OF THE UNITED STATES, WASHINGTON, D. C., January 28, 1868.

SIR: On the 24th instant, I requested you to give me in writing the instructions which you had previously given me verbally, not to obey any order from Hon. E. M. Stanton, Secretary of War, unless I knew that it came from yourself. To this written request I received a message that has left doubt in my mind of your intentions. To prevent any possible misunderstanding, therefore, I renew the request that you will give me written instructions, and, till they are received, will suspend action on your verbal ones.

I am compelled to ask these instructions in writing, in consequence of the many and gross misrepresentations affecting my personal honor, circulated through the press for the last fortnight. purporting to come from the President, of conversations which occurred either with the President privately in his office, or in cabinet meeting. What is written admits of no misunderstanding.

In view of the misrepresentations referred to, it will be well to state the facts in the case.

Some time after I assumed the duties of Secretary of War ad interim, the President asked me my views as to the course Mr. Stanton would have to pursue, in case the Senate should not concur in his suspension, to obtain possession of his office. My reply was, in substance, that Mr. Stanton would have to appeal to the courts to reinstate him, illustrating my position by citing the ground I had taken in the case of the Baltimore police commissioners.

In that case I did not doubt the technical right of Governor Swann to remove the old commissioners and to appoint their successors. As the old commissioners refused to give up, however, I contended that no resource was left but to appeal to the courts.

Finding that the President was desirous of keeping Mr. Stanton out of office, whether sustained in the suspension or not, I stated that I had not looked particularly into the tenure of office bill, but that what I had stated was a general principle, and if I should change my mind in this particular case I would inform him of the fact.

Subsequently, on reading the tenure of office bill closely, I found that I could not, without violation of the law, refuse to vacate the office of Secretary of War the moment Mr. Stanton was reinstated by the Senate, even though the President should order me to retain it, which he never did.

Taking this view of the subject, and learning on Saturday, the 11th instant. that the Senate had taken up the subject of Mr. Stanton's suspension, after some conversation with Lieutenant General Sherman and some members of my staff, in which I stated that the law left me no discretion as to my action, should Mr. Stanton be reinstated, and that I intended to inform the President, I went to the President for the sole purpose of making this decision known, and did so make it known.

In doing this I fulfilled the promise made in our last preceding conversation on the subject.

The President, however, instead of accepting my view of the requirements of the tenure of office bill, contended that he had suspended Mr. Stanton under the authority given by the Constitution, and that the same authority did not preclude him from reporting, as an act of courtesy, his reasons for the suspension to the Senate. That, having appointed me under the authority given by the Constitution, and not under any act of Congress, I could not be governed by the act. I stated that the law was binding on me, constitutional or not, until set aside by the proper tribunal. An hour or more was consumed, each reiterating his views on this subject, until, getting late, the President said he would see me again.

I did not agree to call again on Monday, nor at any other definite time, nor was I sent for by the President until the following Tuesday.

From the 11th to the cabinet meeting on the 14th instant, a doubt never entered my mind about the President's fully understanding my position, namely, that if the Senate refused to concur in the suspension of Mr. Stanton, my powers as Secretary of War ad interim would cease, and Mr. Stanton's right to resume at once the functions of his office would under the law be indisputable, and I acted accordingly. With Mr. Stanton I had no communication, direct nor indirect, on the subject of his reinstatement, during his suspension.

I knew it had been recommended to the President to send in the name of Governor Cox, of Ohio, for Secretary of War, and thus save all embarrassment—a proposition that I sincerely hoped he would entertain favorably; General Sherman seeing the President at my particular request to urge this, on the 13th instant.

On Tuesday, (the day Mr. Stanton re-entered the office of the Secretary of War,) General Comstock, who had carried my official letter announcing that, with Mr. Stanton's reinstatement by the Senate, I had ceased to be Secretary of War ad interim, and who saw the President open and read the communication, brought back to me from the President a message that he wanted to see me that day at the cabinet meeting, after I had made known the fact that I was no longer Secretary of War *ad interim.*

At this meeting, after opening it as though I were a member of the cabinet, when reminded of the notification already given him that I was no longer Secretary of War *ad interim,* the President gave a version of the conversations alluded to already. In this statement it was asserted that in both conversations I had agreed to hold on to the office of Secretary of War until displaced by the courts, or resign, so as to place the President where he would have been had I never accepted the office. After hearing the President through, I stated our conversations substantially as given in this letter. I will add that my conversation before the cabinet embraced other matter not pertinent here, and is therefore left out.

I in nowise admitted the correctness of the President's statement of our conversations, though, to soften the evident contradiction my statement gave, I said (alluding to our first conversation on the subject) the President might have understood me the way he said, namely, that I had promised to resign if I did not resist the reinstatement. I made no such promise.

I have the honor to be, very respectfully, your obedient servant,

U. S. GRANT, *General.*

His Excellency A. JOHNSON,
   *President of the United States.*

### No. 3.—ENDORSEMENT OF THE PRESIDENT ON GENERAL GRANT'S NOTE OF JANUARY 24, 1868.

JANUARY 29, 1868.

As requested in this communication, General Grant is instructed, in writing, not to obey any order from the War Department, assumed to be issued by the direction of the President, unless such order is known by the General commanding the armies of the United States to have been authorized by the Executive.

ANDREW JOHNSON.

### No. 4.—GENERAL GRANT TO THE PRESIDENT.

HEADQUARTERS ARMY OF THE UNITED STATES,
   WASHINGTON, *January* 30, 1868.

SIR: I have the honor to acknowledge the return of my note of the 24th instant, with your endorsement thereon, that I am not to obey any order from the War Department assumed to be issued by the direction of the President, unless such order is known by me to have been authorized by the Executive; and in reply thereto to say, that I am informed by the Secretary of War that he has not received from the Executive any order or instructions limiting or impairing his authority to issue orders to the army as has heretofore been his practice under the law and the customs of the department. While this authority to the War Department is not countermanded, it will be satisfactory evidence to me that any orders issued from the War Department, by direction of the President, are authorized by the Executive.

I have the honor to be, very respectfully, your obedient servant,        U. S. GRANT,
   *General.*

His Excellency A. JOHNSON,
   *President of the United States.*

### No. 5.—THE PRESIDENT TO GENERAL GRANT.

EXECUTIVE MANSION,
   *January* 31, 1868.

GENERAL: I have received your communication of the 28th instant, renewing your request of the 24th, that I should repeat in a written form my verbal instructions of the 19th instant, viz: That you obey no order from the honorable Edwin M. Stanton, as Secretary of War, unless you have information that it was issued by the President's directions.

In submitting this request, (with which I complied on the 29th instant,) you take occasion to allude to recent publications in reference to the circumstances connected with the vacation, by yourself, of the office of Secretary of War *ad interim,* and, with the view of correcting statements, which you term "gross misrepresentations," give at length your own recollection of the facts under which, without the sanction of the President, from whom you had received and accepted the appointment, you yielded the Department of War to the present incumbent.

As stated in your communication, some time after you had assumed the duties of Secretary of War *ad interim,* we interchanged views respecting the course that should be pursued in the event of non-concurrence by the Senate in the suspension from office of Mr. Stanton. I sought that interview, calling myself at the War Department. My sole object in then bringing the subject to your attention was to ascertain definitely what would be your own action should such an attempt be made for his restoration to the War Department. That object was accomplished, for the interview terminated with the distinct understanding that if, upon reflection, you should prefer not to become a party to the controversy, or should conclude that it would be your duty to surrender the department to Mr. Stanton, upon action in his favor by the Senate, you were to return the office to me prior to a decision by the Senate, in order that, if I desired to do so, I might designate some one to succeed you. It must have been apparent to you that, had not this understanding been reached, it was my purpose to relieve you from the further discharge of the duties of Secretary of War *ad interim,* and to appoint some other person in that capacity.

Other conversations upon this subject ensued, all of them having, on my part, the same object, and leading to the same conclusion, as the first. It is not necessary, however, to refer to any of them, excepting that of Saturday, the 11th instant, mentioned in your communication. As it was then known that the Senate had proceeded to consider the case of Mr. Stanton, I was anxious to learn your determination. After a protracted interview, during which the provisions of the tenure of office bill were freely discussed, you said that, as had been agreed upon in our first conference, you would either return the office to my possession in time to enable me to appoint a successor before final action by the Senate upon Mr. Stanton's suspension, or would remain as its head, awaiting a decision of the question by judicial proceedings. It was then understood that there would be a further conference on Monday, by which time I supposed you would be prepared to inform me of your final decision. You failed, however, to fulfill the engagement, and on Tuesday notified me, in writing, of the receipt by you of official notification of the action of the Senate in the case of Mr. Stanton, and at the same time informed me that according to the act regulating the tenure of certain civil offices your functions as Secretary of War *ad interim* ceased from the moment of the receipt of the notice. You thus, in disregard of the understanding between us, vacated the office without having given me notice of your intention to do so. It is but just, however, to say that in your communication you claim that you did inform me of your purpose, and thus "fulfilled the promise made in our last preceding conversation on this subject." The fact that such a promise existed is evidence of an arrangement of the kind I have mentioned. You had found in our first conference "that the President was desirous of keeping Mr. Stanton out of office, whether sustained in the suspension or not." You knew what reasons had induced the President to ask from you a promise; you also knew that in case your views of duty did not accord with his own convictions, it was his purpose to fill your place by another appointment. Even ignoring the existence of a positive understanding between us, these conclusions were plainly deducible from our various conversations. It is certain, however, that even under these circumstances, you did not offer to return the place to my possession, but, according to your own statement, placed yourself in a position where, could I have anticipated your action, I would have been compelled to ask of you, as I was compelled to ask of your predecessor in the War Department, a letter of resignation, or else to resort to the more disagreeable expedient of superseding you by a successor.

As stated in your letter, the nomination of Governor Cox, of Ohio, for the office of Secretary of War was suggested to me. His appointment, as Mr. Stanton's successor, was urged in your name, and it was said that his selection would save further embarrassment. I did not think that in the selection of a cabinet officer I should be trammelled by such considerations. I was prepared to take the responsibility of deciding the question in accordance with my ideas of constitutional duty, and, having determined upon a course which I deemed right and proper, was anxious to learn the steps you would take should the possession of the War Department be demanded by Mr. Stanton. Had your action been in conformity to the understanding between us, I do not believe that the embarrassment would have attained its present proportions, or that the probability of its repetition would have been so great.

I know that, with a view to an early termination of a state of affairs so detrimental to the public interests, you voluntarily offered, both on Wednesday, the 15th instant, and on the succeeding Sunday, to call upon Mr. Stanton, and urge upon him that the good of the service required his resignation. I confess that I considered your proposal as a sort of reparation for the failure, on your part, to act in accordance

with an understanding more than once repeated, which I thought had received your full assent, and under which you could have returned to me the office which I had conferred upon you, thus saving yourself from embarrassment, and leaving the responsibility where it properly belonged—with the President, who is accountable for the faithful execution of the laws.

I have not yet been informed by you whether, as twice proposed by yourself, you have called upon Mr. Stanton, and made an effort to induce him voluntarily to retire from the War Department.

You conclude your communication with a reference to our conversation at the meeting of the cabinet held on Tuesday, the 14th instant. In your account of what then occurred, you say that after the President had given his version of our previous conversations, you stated them substantially as given in your letter; that you in nowise admitted the correctness of his statement of them, "though, to soften the evident contradiction my statement gave, I said (alluding to our first conversation on the subject) the President might have understood me in the way he said, namely: that I had promised to resign if I did not resist the reinstatement. I made no such promise."

My recollection of what then transpired is diametrically the reverse of your narration. In the presence of the cabinet I asked you:

First. If, in a conversation which took place shortly after your appointment as Secretary of War *ad interim*, you did not agree either to remain at the head of the War Department and abide any judicial proceedings that might follow non-concurrence by the Senate in Mr. Stanton's suspension; or, should you wish not to become involved in such a controversy, to put me in the same position with respect to the office as I occupied previous to your appointment, by returning it to me in time to anticipate such action by the Senate. This you admitted.

Second. I then asked you if, at our conference on the preceding Saturday, I had not, to avoid misunderstanding, requested you to state what you intended to do, and further, if, in reply to that inquiry, you had not referred to our former conversations, saying that from them I understood your position, and that your action would be consistent with the understanding which had been reached. To these questions you also replied in the affirmative.

Third. I next asked if, at the conclusion of our interview on Saturday it was not understood that we were to have another conference on Monday, before final action by the Senate in the case of Mr. Stanton. You replied that that such was the understanding, but that you did not suppose the Senate would act so soon; that on Monday you had been engaged in a conference with General Sherman, and were occupied with "many little matters," and asked if General Sherman had not called on that day. What relevancy General Sherman's visit to me on Monday had with the purpose for which you were then to have called, I am at a loss to perceive, as he certainly did not inform me whether you had determined to retain possession of the office, or to afford me an opportunity to appoint a successor in advance of any attempted reinstatement of Mr. Stanton.

This account of what passed between us at the cabinet meeting on the 14th instant widely differs from that contained in your communication, for it shows that instead of having "stated our conversations as given in the letter," which has made this reply necessary, you admitted that my recital of them was entirely accurate. Sincerely anxious, however, to be correct in my statements, I have to-day read this narration of what occurred on the 14th instant to the members of the cabinet who were then present. They, without exception, agree in its accuracy.

It is only necessary to add that on Wednesday morning, the 15th instant, you called on me, in company with Lieutenant General Sherman. After some preliminary conversation, you remarked that an article in the National Intelligencer of that date did you much injustice. I replied that I had not read the Intelligencer of that morning. You then first told me that it was your intention to urge Mr. Stanton to resign his office.

After you had withdrawn, I carefully read the article of which you had spoken, and found that its statements of the understanding between us were substantially correct. On the 17th, I caused it to be read to four of the five members of the cabinet who were present at our conference on the 14th, and they concurred in the general accuracy of its statements respecting our conversation upon that occasion.

In reply to your communication, I have deemed it proper, in order to prevent further misunderstanding, to make this simple recital of facts. Very respectfully, yours,

ANDREW JOHNSON.

General U. S. GRANT,
*Commanding U. S Armies.*

---

No. 6.—GENERAL GRANT TO THE PRESIDENT.

HEADQ'RS ARMY OF THE UNITED STATES,
WASHINGTON, *February* 3, 1868.

SIR: I have the honor to acknowledge the receipt of your communication of the 31st ultimo, in answer to mine of the 28th ultimo. After a careful reading and comparison of it with the article in the National Intelligencer of the 15th ultimo, and the article over the initials J. B. S., in the New York World of the 27th ultimo, purporting to be based upon your statement and that of the members of your cabinet therein named, I find it to be but a reiteration, only somewhat more in detail, of the "many and gross misrepresentations" contained in these articles, and which my statement of the facts set forth in my letter of 28th ultimo was intended to correct; and I here reassert the correctness of my statements in that letter, anything in yours in reply to it to the contrary notwithstanding.

I confess my surprise that the cabinet officers referred to should so greatly misapprehend the facts in the matter of admissions alleged to have been made by me at the cabinet meeting of the 14th ultimo as to suffer their names to be made the basis of the charges in the newspaper article referred to, or agree in the accuracy, as you affirm they do, of your account of what occurred at that meeting.

You know that we parted on Saturday, the 11th ultimo, without any promise on my part, either express or implied, to the effect that I would hold on to the office of Secretary of War *ad interim* against the action of the Senate, or, declining to do so myself, would surrender it to you before such action was had, or that I would see you again at any fixed time on the subject.

The performance of the promises alleged by you to have been made by me would have involved a resistance to law, and an inconsistency with the whole history of my connection with the suspension of Mr. Stanton.

From our conversations, and my written protest of August 1, 1867, against the removal of Mr. Stanton, you must have known that my greatest objection to his removal or suspension was the fear that some one would be appointed in his stead who would, by opposition to the laws relating to the restoration of the southern States to their proper relations to the government, embarrass the army in the performance of duties especially imposed upon it by these laws; and it was to prevent such an appointment that I accepted the office of Secretary of War *ad interim*, and not for the purpose of enabling you to get rid of Mr. Stanton by my withholding it from him in opposition to law, or not doing so myself, surrendering it to one who would, as the statement and assumptions in your communication plainly indicate was sought. And it was to avoid the same danger, as well as to relieve you from this personal embarrassment in which Mr. Stanton's reinstatement would place you, that I urged the appointment of Governor Cox, believing that it would be agreeable to you and also to Mr. Stanton—satisfied as I was that it was the good of the country, and not the office, the latter desired.

On the 15th ultimo, in presence of General Sherman, I stated to you that I thought Mr. Stanton would resign, but did not say that I would advise him to do so. On the 18th I did agree with General Sherman to go and advise him to that course, and on the 19th I had an interview alone with Mr. Stanton, which led me to the conclusion that any advice to him of the kind would be useless, and I so informed General Sherman.

Before I consented to advise Mr. Stanton to resign, I understood from him, in a conversation on the subject immediately after his reinstatement, that it was his opinion that the act of Congress, entitled "An act temporarily to supply vacancies in the executive departments in certain cases," approved February 20, 1863, was repealed by subsequent legislation, which materially influenced my action. Previous to this time I had had no doubt that the law of 1863 was still in force, and notwithstanding my action, a fuller examination of the law leaves a question in my mind whether it is or is not repealed. This being the case, I could not now advise his resignation, lest the same danger I apprehended on his first removal might follow.

The course you would have it understood I agreed to pursue was in violation of law, and without orders from you; while the course I did pursue, and which I never doubted you fully understood, was in accordance with law, and not in disobedience of any orders of my superior.

And now, Mr. President, when my honor as a soldier and integrity as a man have been so violently assailed, pardon me for saying that I can but regard this whole matter, from the beginning to the end, as an attempt to involve me in the resistance of law, for which you hesitated to assume the responsibility in orders, and thus to destroy my character before the country. I am in a measure confirmed in this conclusion by your recent orders directing me to disobey orders from the Secretary of War—my superior and your subordinate—without having countermanded his authority to issue the orders I am to disobey.

With the assurance, Mr. President, that nothing less than a vindication of my personal honor and character could have induced this correspondence on my part,

I have the honor to be, very respectfully, your obedient servant, U. S. GRANT, *General.*

His Excellency A. JOHNSON,
*President of the United States.*

---

### No. 7.—THE PRESIDENT TO GENERAL GRANT.

EXECUTIVE MANSION,
*February* 10, 1868.

GENERAL: The extraordinary character of your letter of the 3d instant would seem to preclude any reply on my part; but the manner in which publicity has been given to the correspondence of which that letter forms a part, and the grave questions which are involved, induce me to take this mode of giving, as a proper sequel to the communications which have passed between us, the statements of the five members of the cabinet who were present on the occasion of our conversation on the 14th ultimo. Copies of the letters, which they have addressed to me upon the subject, are accordingly herewith enclosed.

You speak of my letter of the 31st ultimo as a reiteration of the "many and gross misrepresentations" contained in certain newspaper articles, and reassert the correctness of the statements contained in your communication of the 28th ultimo, adding—and here I give your own words—"anything in yours in reply to it to the contrary notwithstanding."

When a controversy upon matters of fact reaches the point to which this has been brought, further assertion or denial between the immediate parties should cease, especially where, upon either side, it loses the character of the respectful discussion which is required by the relations in which the parties stand to each other, and degenerates in tone and temper. In such a case, if there is nothing to rely upon but the opposing statements, conclusions must be drawn from those statements alone, and from whatever intrinsic probabilities they afford in favor of or against either of the parties. I should not shrink from this test in this controversy, but, fortunately, it is not left to this test alone. There were five cabinet officers present at the conversation, the detail of which, in my letter of the 28th ultimo, you allow yourself to say, contains "many and gross misrepresentations." These gentlemen heard that conversation and have read my statement. They speak for themselves, and I leave the proof without a word of comment.

I deem it proper, before concluding this communication, to notice some of the statements contained in your letter.

You say that a performance of the promises alleged to have been made by you to the President "would have involved a resistance to law, and an inconsistency with the whole history of my connection with the suspension of Mr. Stanton." You then state that you had fears the President would, on the removal of Mr. Stanton, appoint some one in his place who would embarrass the army in carrying out the reconstruction acts, and add:

"It was to prevent such an appointment that I accepted the office of Secretary of War *ad interim*, and not for the purpose of enabling you to get rid of Mr. Stanton, by my withholding it from him in opposition to law, or not doing so myself, surrendering it to one who would, as the statements and assumptions in your communication plainly indicate was sought."

First of all, you here admit that from the very beginning of what you term "the whole history" of your connection with Mr. Stanton's suspension, you intended to circumvent the President. It was to carry out that intent that you accepted the appointment. This was in your mind at the time of your acceptance. It was not, then, in obedience to the order of your superior, as has heretofore been supposed, that you assumed the duties of the office. You knew it was the President's purpose to prevent Mr. Stanton from resuming the office of Secretary of War, and you intended to defeat that purpose. You accepted the office, not in the interest of the President, but of Mr. Stanton. If this purpose, so entertained by you, had been confined to yourself—if, when accepting the office, you had done so with a mental reservation to frustrate the President—it would have been a tacit deception. In the ethics of some persons such a course is allowable. But you cannot stand even upon that questionable ground. The "history" of your connection with this transaction, as written by yourself, places you in a different predicament, and shows that you not only concealed your design from the President, but induced him to suppose that you would carry out his purpose to keep Mr. Stanton out of office, by retaining it yourself after an attempted restoration by the Senate, so as to require Mr. Stanton to establish his right by judicial decision.

I now give that part of this "history," as written by yourself in your letter of the 28th ult.:

"Sometime after I assumed the duties of Secretary of War *ad interim*, the President asked me my views as to the course Mr. Stanton would have to pursue, in case the Senate should not concur in his suspension, to obtain possession of his office. My reply was, in substance, that Mr. Stanton would have to appeal to the courts to reinstate him, illustrating my position by citing the ground I had taken in the case of the Baltimore police commissioners."

Now, at that time, as you admit in your letter of the 3d instant, you held the office for the very object of defeating an appeal to the courts. In that letter you say that in accepting the office one motive was to prevent the President from appointing some other person who would retain possession, and thus make judicial proceedings necessary. You knew the President was unwilling to trust the office with any one who would not, by holding it, compel Mr. Stanton to resort to the courts. You perfectly understood that in this interview "sometime" after you accepted the office, the President, not content with your silence, desired an expression of your views, and you answered him, that Mr. Stanton "would have to appeal to the courts" If the President had reposed confidence *before* he knew your views, and that confidence had been violated, it might have been said he made a mistake; but a violation of confidence reposed *after* that conversation was no mistake of his, nor of yours. It is the fact only that needs be stated, that at the date of this conversation you did not intend to hold the office with the purpose of forcing Mr. Stanton into court, but did hold it then, and had accepted it, to prevent that course from being carried out. In other words, you said to the President, "that is the proper course;" and you said to yourself, " I have accepted this office, and now hold it, to defeat that course." The excuse you make in a subsequent paragraph of that letter of the 26th ultimo, that afterwards you changed your views as to what would be a proper course, has nothing to do with the point now under consideration. The point is, that *before* you changed your views you had secretly determined to do the very thing which at last you did—surrender the office to Mr. Stanton. You may have changed your views as to the law, but you certainly did not change your views as to the course you had marked out for yourself from the beginning.

I will only notice one more statement in your letter of the 3d instant—that the performance of the promises which it is alleged were made by you would have involved you in the resistance of law. I know of no statute that would have been violated had you—carrying out your promises in good faith—tendered your resignation when you concluded not to be made a party in any legal proceedings You add:

" I am in a measure confirmed in this conclusion by your recent orders directing me to disobey orders from the Secretary of War, my *superior* and your subordinate, without having countermanded his authority to issue the orders I am to disobey."

On the 24th ultimo you addressed a note to the President, requesting, in writing, an order, given to you verbally five days before, to disregard orders from Mr. Stanton as Secretary of War, until you "knew from the President himself that they were his orders."

On the 29th, in compliance with your request, I did give you instructions in writing "not to obey any order from the War Department assumed to be issued by the direction of the President, unless such order is known by the General commanding the armies of the United States to have been authorized by the Executive."

There are some orders which a Secretary of War may issue without the authority of the President; there are others which he issues simply as the agent of the President, and which purport to be "by direction" of the President. For such orders the President is responsible, and he should, therefore, know and understand what they are before giving such "direction." Mr. Stanton states in his letter of the 4th instant, which accompanies the published correspondence, that he " has had no correspondence with the President since the 12th of August last;"

and he further says, that since he resumed the duties of the office he has continued to discharge them " without any personal or written communication with the President;" and he adds: " No orders have been issued from this Department in the name of the President with my knowledge, and I have received no orders from him."

It thus seems that Mr. Stanton now discharges the duties of the War Department without any reference to the President, and without using his name. My order to you had only reference to orders " assumed to be issued by the direction of the President." It would appear from Mr. Stanton's letter that you have received no such orders from him. However, in your note to the President of the 30th ultimo, in which you acknowledge the receipt of the written order of the 29th, you say that you have been informed by Mr. Stanton that he has not received any order limiting his authority to issue orders to the army, according to the practice of the Department, and state that " while this authority to the War Department is not countermanded, it will be satisfactory evidence to me that any orders issued from the War Department by direction of the President are authorized by the Executive."

The President issues an order to you to obey no order from the War Department, purporting to be made " by the direction of the President," until you have referred it to him for his approval. You reply that you have received the President's order, and will not obey it, but will obey an order purporting to be given by his direction, *if it comes from the War Department.* You will not obey the direct order of the President, but will obey his indirect order. If, as you say, there has been a practice in the War Department to issue orders in the name of the President without his direction, does not the precise order you have requested, and have received, change the practice as to the General of the army? Could not the President countermand any such order issued to you from the War Department? If you should receive an order from that Department, issued in the name of the President, to do a special act, and an order directly from the President himself not to do the act, is there a doubt which you are to obey? You answer the question when you say to the President, in your letter of the 3d instant, the Secretary of War is " my superior and your subordinate;" and yet you refuse obedience to the superior out of deference to the subordinate.

Without further comment upon the insubordinate attitude which you have assumed, I am at a loss to know how you can relieve yourself from obedience to the orders of the President, who is made by the Constitution the Commander-in-Chief of the army and navy, and is, therefore, the official superior, as well of the General of the army as of the Secretary of War.

Respectfully, yours,   ANDREW JOHNSON.
General U. S. GRANT, *Commanding Armies of the United States, Washington, D. C.*

———

Copy of a letter addressed to each of the members of the cabinet present at the conversation between the President and General Grant on the 14th of January, 1868:

EXECUTIVE MANSION,
WASHINGTON, D. C., *February* 5, 1868.

SIR: The Chronicle of this morning contains a correspondence between the President and General Grant, reported from the War Department, in answer to a resolution of the House of Representatives. I beg to call your attention to that correspondence, and especially to that part of it which refers to the conversation between the President and General Grant at the cabinet meeting on the 14th of January, and to request you to state what was said in that conversation.

Very respectfully, yours,

ANDREW JOHNSON.

---

#### LETTER OF THE SECRETARY OF THE NAVY.

WASHINGTON, D. C., *February* 5, 1868.

SIR: Your note of this date was handed to me this evening. My recollection of the conversation at the cabinet meeting on Tuesday, the 14th of January, corresponds with your statement of it in the letter of the 31st ultimo, in the published correspondence. The three points specified in that letter, giving your recollection of the conversation, are correctly stated.

Very respectfully,

GIDEON WELLES.

To the PRESIDENT.

---

#### LETTER OF THE SECRETARY OF THE TREASURY.

TREASURY DEPARTMENT,
*February* 6, 1868.

SIR: I have received your note of the 5th inst., calling my attention to the correspondence between yourself and General Grant, as published in the Chronicle of yesterday, especially to that part of it which relates to what occurred at the cabinet meeting on Tuesday, the 14th ultimo, and requesting me to state what was said in the conversation referred to.

I cannot undertake to state the precise language used; but I have no hesitation in saying that your account of that conversation, as given in your letter to General Grant under date of the 31st ultimo, substantially and in all important particulars, accorded with my recollection of it.

With great respect, your obedient servant,

HUGH McCULLOCH.

The PRESIDENT.

---

#### LETTER OF THE POSTMASTER GENERAL.

POST OFFICE DEPARTMENT,
WASHINGTON, *February* 6, 1868.

SIR: I am in receipt of your letter of the 5th February, calling my attention to the correspondence published in the Chronicle, between the President and General Grant, and especially to that part of it which refers to the conversation between the President and General Grant at the cabinet meeting on Tuesday, the 14th of January, with a request that I "state what was said in that conversation."

In reply, I have the honor to state that I have read carefully the correspondence in question, and particularly the letter of the President to General Grant, dated January 31, 1868. The following extract from your letter of the 31st of January to General Grant, is, according to my recollection, a correct statement of the conversation that took place between the President and General Grant at the cabinet meeting on the 14th of January last. In the presence of the cabinet, the President asked General Grant whether, "in a conversation which took place after his appointment as Secretary of War *ad interim*, he did not agree either to remain at the head of the War Department and abide any judicial proceedings that might follow the nonconcurrence by the Senate in Mr. Stanton's suspension; or, should he wish not to become involved in such a controversy, to put the President in the same position with respect to the office as he occupied previous to General Grant's appointment, by returning it to the President in time to anticipate such action by the Senate.

This General Grant admitted.

The President then asked General Grant if, at the conference on the preceding Saturday, he had not, to avoid misunderstanding, requested General Grant to state what he intended to do; and, further, if in reply to that inquiry he, General Grant, had not referred to their former conversations, saying that from them the President understood his position, and that his (General Grant's) action would be consistent with the understanding which had been reached.

To these questions General Grant replied in the affirmative.

The President asked General Grant, if, at the conclusion of their interview on Saturday, it was not understood that they were to have another conference on Monday, before final action by the Senate in the case of Mr. Stanton.

General Grant replied that such was the understanding, but that he did not suppose the Senate would act so soon; that on Monday, he had been engaged in a conference with General Sherman, and was occupied with "many little matters," and asked if "General Sherman had not called on that day."

I take this mode of complying with the request contained in the President's letter to me, because my attention had been called to the subject before, when the conversation between the President and General Grant was under consideration.

Very respectfully, your obedient servant,

ALEX. W. RANDALL,
*Postmaster General.*

To the PRESIDENT.

---

#### LETTER OF THE SECRETARY OF THE INTERIOR.

DEPARTMENT OF THE INTERIOR,
WASHINGTON, D. C., *February* 6, 1868.

SIR: I am in receipt of yours of yesterday, calling my attention to a correspondence between yourself and General Grant, published in the Chronicle newspaper, and especially to that part of said correspondence "which refers to the conversation between the President and General Grant at the cabinet meeting on Tuesday, the 14th of January," and requesting me "to state what was said in that conversation."

In reply, I submit the following statement: At the cabinet meeting on Tuesday, the 14th of January, 1868, General Grant appeared and took his accustomed seat at the Board. When he had been reached in the order of business, the

President asked him, as usual, if he had anything to present.

In reply, the General, after referring to a note which he had that morning addressed to the President, enclosing a copy of the resolution of the Senate refusing to concur in the reasons for the suspension of Mr. Stanton, proceeded to say that he regarded his duties as Secretary of War *ad interim* terminated by that resolution, and that he could not lawfully exercise such duties for a moment after the adoption of the resolution by the Senate; that the resolution reached him last night, and that this morning he had gone to the War Department, entered the Secretary's room, bolted one door on the inside, locked the other on the outside, delivered the key to the Adjutant General, and proceeded to the headquarters of the army, and addressed the note above mentioned to the President, informing him that he (General Grant) was no longer Secretary of War *ad interim*.

The President expressed great surprise at the course which General Grant had thought proper to pursue, and, addressing himself to the General, proceeded to say, in substance, that he had anticipated such action on the part of the Senate, and being very desirous to have the constitutionality of the tenure-of-office bill tested, and his right to suspend or remove a member of the cabinet decided by the judicial tribunals of the country, he had some time ago, and shortly after General Grant's appointment as Secretary of War *ad interim*, asked the General what his action would be in the event that the Senate should refuse to concur in the suspension of Mr. Stanton, and that the General had then agreed either to remain at the head of the War Department till a decision could be obtained from the court, or resign the office into the hands of the President before the case was acted upon by the Senate, so as to place the President in the same situation he occupied at the time of his (Grant's) appointment.

The President further said that the conversation was renewed on the preceding Saturday, at which time he asked the General what he intended to do if the Senate should undertake to reinstate Mr. Stanton; in reply to which the General referred to their former conversation upon the same subject, and said you understand my position, and my conduct will be conformable to that understanding; that he (the General) then expressed a repugnance to being made a party to a judicial proceeding, saying, that he would expose himself to fine and imprisonment by doing so, as his continuing to discharge the duties of Secretary of War *ad interim*, after the Senate should have refused to concur in the suspension of Mr. Stanton, would be a violation of the tenure-of-office bill; that in reply to this he (the President) informed General Grant he had not suspended Mr. Stanton under the tenure-of-office bill, but by virtue of the powers conferred on him by the Constitution; and that as to the fine and imprisonment, he (the President) would pay whatever fine was imposed, and submit to whatever imprisonment might be adjudged against him, (the General;) that they continued the conversation for some time, discussing the law at length; and that they finally separated, without having reached a definite conclusion, and with the understanding that the General would see the President again on Monday.

In reply, General Grant admitted that the conversations had occurred, and said that at the first conversation he had given it as his opinion to the President, that in the event of non-concurrence by the Senate in the action of the President in respect to the Secretary of War, the question would have to be decided by the court; that Mr. Stanton would have to appeal to the court to reinstate him in office; that the *ins* would remain in till they could be displaced, and the *outs* put in by legal proceedings; and that he *then* thought so, and had agreed that if he should change his mind, he would notify the President in time to enable him to make another appointment; but that at the time of the first conversation he had not looked very closely into the law—that it had recently been discussed by the newspapers, and that this had induced him to examine it more carefully, and that he had come to the conclusion that if the Senate should refuse to concur in the suspension, Mr. Stanton would thereby be reinstated, and that he (Grant) could not continue thereafter to act as Secretary of War *ad interim* without subjecting himself to fine and imprisonment, and that he came over on Saturday to inform the President of this change in his views, and did so inform him; that the President replied that he had not suspended Mr. Stanton under the tenure of-office bill, but under the Constitution, and had appointed him (Grant) by virtue of the authority derived from the Constitution, &c.; that they continued to discuss the matter some time, and, finally, he left without any conclusion having been reached, expecting to see the President again on Monday. He then proceeded to explain why he had not called on the President on Monday, saying that he had had a long interview with General Sherman, that various little matters had occupied his time till it was late, and that he did not think the Senate would act so soon, and asked: "Did not General Sherman call on you on Monday?"

I do not know what passed between the President and General Grant on Saturday, except as I learned it from the conversation between them at the cabinet meeting on Tuesday, and the foregoing is substantially what then occurred. The precise words used on the occasion are not, of course, given exactly in the order in which they were spoken, but the ideas expressed and the facts stated are faithfully preserved and presented.

I have the honor to be, sir, with great respect, your obedient servant,     O. H. BROWNING.

The PRESIDENT.

---

### LETTER OF THE SECRETARY OF STATE.

DEPARTMENT OF STATE,
WASHINGTON, *February* 6, 1868.

SIR: The meeting to which you refer in your letter was a regular cabinet meeting. While the members were assembling, and before the President had entered the council chamber, General Grant, on coming in, said to me that he was in attendance there not as a member of the cabinet, but upon invitation, and I replied by the inquiry whether there was a change in the War Department. After the President had taken his seat business went on in the usual way of hearing matters submitted by the several secretaries. When the time came for the Secretary of War, General Grant said that he was now there, not as Secretary of War, but upon the President's invitation; that he had retired from the War Department. A slight difference then appeared about the supposed invitation, General Grant saying that the officer who had borne his letter to the President that morning, announcing his retirement from the War Department, had told him that the President desired to see him at the cabinet; to which the President answered, that when General Grant's communication was delivered to him, the President simply replied that he supposed General Grant would be very soon at the cabinet meeting. I regarded the conversation thus begun as an incidental one. It went on quite informally, and consisted of a statement on your part of your views in regard to the understanding of the tenure upon which General Grant had assented to hold the War Department *ad interim*, and of his replies by way of answer and explanation. It was respectful and courteous on both sides. Being in this conversational form, its details could only have been preserved by verbatim report. So far as I know, no such report was made at the time. I can only give the general effect of the conversation. Certainly you stated that although you had reported the reasons for Mr. Stanton's suspension to the Senate, you nevertheless held that he would not be entitled to resume the office of Secretary of War, even if the Senate should disapprove of his suspension, and that you had proposed to have the question tested by judicial process, to be applied to the person who should be the incumbent of the Department, under your designation of Secretary of War *ad interim*, in the place of Mr. Stanton. You contended that this was well understood between yourself and General Grant; that when he entered the War Department as Secretary *ad interim*, he expressed his concurrence in the belief that the question of Mr. Stanton's restoration would be a question for the courts; that in a subsequent conversation with General Grant you had adverted to the understanding thus had, and that General Grant expressed his concurrence in it; that at some conversation which had been previously held General Grant said he still adhered to the same construction of the law, but said if he should change his opinion he would give you seasonable notice of it, so that you should, in any case, be placed in the same position in regard to the War Department that you were while General Grant held it *ad interim*. I did not understand General Grant as denying, nor as explicitly admitting these statements in the form and full extent to which you made them. His admission of them was rather indirect and circumstantial, though I did not understand it to be an evasive one. He said that reasoning from what occurred in the case of the police in Maryland, which he regarded as a parallel one, he was of opinion, and so assured you, that it would be his right and duty, under your instructions, to hold the War Office after

the Senate should disapprove of Mr. Stanton's suspension, until the question should be decided upon by the courts; that he remained until very recently of that opinion, and that on the Saturday before the cabinet meeting a conversation was held between yourself and him, in which the subject was generally discussed. General Grant's statement was, that in that conversation he had stated to you the legal difficulties which might arise, involving fine and imprisonment under the civil-tenure bill, and that he did not care to subject himself to those penalties; that you replied to this remark that you regarded the civil-tenure bill as unconstitutional, and did not think its penalties were to be feared, or that you would voluntarily assume them; and you insisted that General Grant should either retain the office until relieved by yourself, according to what you claimed was the original understanding between yourself and him, or, by seasonable notice of change of purpose on his part, put you in the same situation in which you would be if he adhered. You claimed that General Grant finally said in that Saturday's conversation that you understood his views, and his proceedings thereafter would be consistent with what had been so understood. General Grant did not controvert, nor can I say that he admitted this last statement. Certainly General Grant did not at any time in the cabinet meeting insist that he had, in the Saturday's conversation, either distinctly or finally advised you of his determination to retire from the charge of the War Department otherwise than under your own subsequent direction. He acquiesced in your statement that the Saturday's conversation ended with an expectation that there would be a subsequent conference on the subject, which he, as well as yourself, supposed could seasonably take place on Monday. You then alluded to the fact that General Grant did not call upon you on Monday, as you had expected from that conversation. General Grant admitted that it was his expectation or purpose to call upon you on Monday. General Grant assigned reasons for the omission. He said he was in conference with General Sherman; that there were many little matters to be attended to; he had conversed upon the matter of the incumbency of the War Department with General Sherman, and he expected that General Sherman would call upon you on Monday. My own mind suggested a further explanation; but I do not remember whether it was mentioned or not, namely: that it was not supposed by General Grant on Monday that the Senate would decide the question so promptly as to anticipate further explanation between yourself and him, if delayed beyond that day. General Grant made another explanation, that he was engaged on Sunday with General Sherman, and I think also on Monday, in regard to the War Department matter, with a hope, though he did not say in an effort, to procure an amicable settlement of the affair of Mr. Stanton, and he still hoped that it would be brought about.

I have the honor to be, with great respect, your obedient servant, WILLIAM H. SEWARD.
To the PRESIDENT.

## 8.—GENERAL GRANT TO THE PRESIDENT.

HEADQU'RS ARMY OF THE UNITED STATES,
WASHINGTON, D.C., *February* 11, 1868.

His Excellency A. JOHNSON,
*President of the United States.*

SIR: I have the honor to acknowledge the receipt of your communication of the 10th instant, accompanied by statements of five cabinet ministers, of their recollection of what occured in cabinet meeting on the 14th of January. Without admitting anything in these statements where they differ from anything heretofore stated by me, I propose to notice only that portion of your communication wherein I am charged with insubordination. I think it will be plain to the reader of my letter of the 30th of January, that I did not propose to disobey any legal order of the President, distinctly given; but only gave an interpretation of what would be regarded as satisfactory evidence of the President's sanction to orders communicated by the Secretary of War. I will say here that your letter of the 10th instant contains the first intimation I have had that you did not accept that interpretation.

Now, for reasons for giving that interpretation: It was clear to me, before my letter of January 30th was written, that I, the person having more public business to transact with the Secretary of War than any other of the President's subordinates, was the only one who had been instructed to disregard the authority of Mr. Stanton where his authority was derived as agent of the President.

On the 27th of January I received a letter from the Secretary of War, (copy herewith,) directing me to furnish escort to public treasure from the Rio Grande to New Orleans, &c., at the request of the Secretary of the Treasury to him. I also send two other enclosures, showing recognition of Mr. Stanton as Secretary of War by both the Secretary of the Treasury and the Postmaster General, in all of which cases the Secretary of War had to call upon me to make the orders requested, or give the information desired, and where his authority to do so is derived, in my view, as agent of the President.

With an order so clearly ambiguous as that of the President, here referred to, it was my duty to inform the President of my interpretation of it, and to abide by that interpretation until I received other orders.

Disclaiming any intention, now or heretofore, of disobeying any legal order of the President, distinctly communicated, I remain, very respectfully, your obedient servant,

U. S. GRANT, *General.*

---

## LETTER OF SECRETARY STANTON.

WAR DEPARTMENT,
WASHINGTON CITY, *January* 27, 1868.

GENERAL: The Secretary of the Treasury has requested this department to afford A. F. Randall, special agent of the Treasury Department, such military aid as may be necessary to secure and forward for deposit from Brownsville, Texas, to New Orleans, public moneys in possession of custom-house officers at Brownsville, and which are deemed insecure at that place.

You will please give such directions as you may deem proper to the officer commanding at Brownsville to carry into effect the request of the Treasury Department, the instructions to be sent by telegraph to Galveston, to the care of A. F. Randall, special agent, who is at Galveston waiting telegraphic orders, there being no telegraphic communication with Brownsville, and the necessity for military protection to the public moneys being represented as urgent.

Please favor me with a copy of such instructions as you may give, in order that they may be communicated to the Secretary of the Treasury. Yours, truly,

EDWIN M. STANTON,
*Secretary of War.*

To General U. S. GRANT,
*Commanding Army United States.*

---

## LETTER OF SECRETARY M'CULLOCH.

TREASURY DEPARTMENT,
*January* 29, 1868.

SIR: It is represented to this department that a band of robbers has obtained such a foothold in the section of country between Humboldt and Lawrence, Kansas, committing depredations upon travellers, both by public and private conveyance, that the safety of the public money collected by the receiver of the land office at Humboldt requires that it should be guarded during its transit from Humboldt to Lawrence. I have, therefore, the honor to request that the proper commanding officer of the district may be instructed by the War Department, if in the opinion of the Hon. Secretary of War it can be done without prejudice to the public interests, to furnish a sufficient military guard to protect such moneys as may be *in transitu* from the above office for the purpose of being deposited to the credit of the Treasury of the United States. As far as we are now advised, such service will not be necessary oftener than once a month. Will you please advise me of the action taken, that I may instruct the receiver and the Commissioner of the General Land Office in the matter.

Very respectfully, your obedient servant,

H. McCULLOCH,
*Secretary of the Treasury.*

To the Hon. SECRETARY OF WAR.

Respectfully referred to the General of the army to give the necessary orders in this case, and to furnish this department a copy for the information of the Secretary of the Treasury.

By order of the Secretary of War.

ED. SCHRIVER, *Inspector General.*

---

## LETTER OF THE SECOND ASSISTANT POSTMASTER GENERAL.

POST OFFICE DEPARTMENT,
CONTRACT OFFICE,
WASHINGTON, *February* 3, 1868.

SIR: It has been represented to this department that in October last a military commission was appointed to settle upon some general plan of defence for the Texas frontiers, and that the said commission has made a report recommending a line of posts from the Rio Grande to the Red river.

An application is now pending in this department for a change in the course of the San Antonio and El Paso mail, so as to send it by way of Forts Mason, Griffin, and Stockton, instead of by camps Hudson and Lancaster. This application requires immediate decision, but before final action can be had thereon it is desired to have some official information as to the report of the commission above referred to.

Accordingly, I have the honor to request that you will cause this department to be furnished, as early as possible, with the information desired in the premises, and also with a copy of the report, if any has been made by the commission. Very respectfully, &c., &c.,
GEORGE W. McLELLAN,
*Second Assistant Postmaster General.*
The Honorable the SECRETARY OF WAR.
Referred to the General of the army for report.
EDWIN M. STANTON,
FEBRUARY 3, 1868. *Secretary of War.*

# XXVI.

# LETTERS, PAPERS, TESTIMONY, POLITICO-MILITARY ORDERS,

## AND REPORT OF GENERAL GRANT.*

**General Grant's Orders respecting Slaves, issued in the Field.**

HEADQUARTERS DIST. OF WEST TENNESSEE,
FORT DONELSON, *February* 26, 1862.
General Orders, No. 14.

I. General Order No. 3, series 1861, from headquarters department of the Missouri, is still in force and must be observed. The necessity of its strict enforcement is made apparent by the numerous applications from citizens for permisson to pass through the camps to look for fugitive slaves. In no case whatever will permission be granted to citizens for this purpose.

II. All slaves at Fort Donelson at the time of its capture, and all slaves within the line of military occupation that have been used by the enemy in building fortifications, or in any manner hostile to the Government, will be employed by the quartermaster's department for the benefit of the Government, and will under no circumstances be permitted to return to their masters.

III. It is made the duty of all officers of this command to see that all slaves above indicated are promptly delivered to the chief quartermaster of the district.

By order of Brig. Gen. U. S. GRANT.
JNO. A. RAWLINS, *A. A. G.*

HEADQUARTERS DIST. OF WEST TENNESSEE,
CORINTH, MISS., *August* 11, 1862.
General Orders, No. 72.

Recent acts of Congress prohibit the army from returning fugitives from labor to their claimants, and authorize the employment of such persons in the service of the Government. The following orders are therefore published for the guidance of the army in this military district in this matter.

I. All fugitives thus employed must be registered, the names of the fugitives and claimants given, and must be borne upon morning reports of the command in which they are kept, showing how they are employed.

II. Fugitive slaves may be employed as laborers in the quartermaster's, subsistence, and engineer departments, and wherever by such employment a soldier may be saved to the ranks. They may be employed as teamsters, as company cooks (not exceeding four to a company,) or as hospital attendants or nurses. Officers may employ them as private servants, in which latter case the fugitive will not be paid or rationed by the Government. Negroes not thus employed will be deemed unauthorized persons, and must be excluded from the camps.

III. Officers and soldiers are prohibited from enticing slaves to leave their masters. When it becomes necessary to employ this kind of labor, commanding officers of posts or troops must send details (always under the charge of a suitable non-commissioned officer) to press into service the slaves of disloyal persons to the number required.

IV. Citizens within the reach of any military station, known to be disloyal and dangerous, may be ordered away or arrested, and their crops and stocks taken for the benefit of the Government or the use of the army.

V. All property taken from rebel owners must be duly reported and used for the benefit of Government, and be issued to troops through the proper departments, and, when practicable, the act of taking should be avowed by the written certificate of the officer taking, to the owner or agent of such property.

It is enjoined on all commanding officers to see that this order is strictly executed. The demoralization of troops consequent on being left to execute laws in their own way, without a proper head, must be avoided.

By order of Maj. Gen. U. S. GRANT.
JNO. A. RAWLINS, *A. A. G.*

HEADQUARTERS DEPART. OF THE TENNESSEE,
MILLIKEN'S BEND, LA., *April* 22, 1863.
General Orders, No. 25. [Extract.]

I. Corps, division, and post commanders will afford all facilities for the completion of the negro regiments now organizing in this department. Commissaries will issue supplies and

---

* For other papers of General Grant, see pages 67, 68, 120, 121, 122, 123 of the Manual of 1866, and 73, 74, and 78 of the Manual of 1867 ; or 67, 68, 120, 121, 122, 123, 199, 200, and 204 of the combined Manuals.

quartermasters will furnish stores on the same requisitions and returns as are required from other troops.

It is expected that all commanders will especially exert themselves in carrying out the policy of the administration, not only in organizing colored regiments and rendering them efficient, but also in removing prejudice against them. * *

By order of Maj. Gen. U S. GRANT.
JNO. A. RAWLINS, *A. A. G.*

HEADQUARTERS DEPART. OF THE TENNESSEE,
VICKSBURG, MISS., *August* 10, 1863.
General Orders, No. 51.

I. At all military posts in States within the department where slavery has been abolished by the proclamation of the President of the United States, camps will be established for such freed people of color as are out of employment.

II. Commanders of posts or districts will detail suitable officers from the army as superintendents of such camps. It will be the duty of such superintendents to see that suitable rations are drawn from the subsistence department for such people as are confided to their care.

III. All such persons supported by the Government will be employed in every practicable way, so as to avoid, as far as possible, their becoming a burden upon the Government. They may be hired to planters, or other citizens, on proper assurances that the negroes so hired will not be run off beyond the military jurisdiction of the United States; they may be employed on any public works; in gathering crops from abandoned plantations; and generally in any manner local commanders may deem for the best interests of the Government, in compliance with law and the policy of the administration.

IV. It will be the duty of the provost marshal at every military post to see that every negro within the jurisdiction of the military authority is employed by some white person, or is sent to the camps provided for freed people.

V. Citizens may make contracts with freed persons of color for their labor, giving wages per month in money, or employ families of them by the year on plantations, &c., feeding, clothing, and supporting the infirm as well as the able-bodied, and giving a portion—not less than one-twentieth—of the commercial part of their crops in payment for such service.

VI. Where the negroes are employed under this authority, the parties employing will register with the provost marshal their names, occupation, and residence, and the number of negroes employed. They will enter into such bonds as the provost marshal, with the approval of the local commander, may require, for the kind treatment and proper care of those employed, and as security against their being carried beyond the employer's jurisdiction.

VII. Nothing in this order is to be construed to embarrass the employment of such colored persons as may be required by the Government.

By order of Major General U. S. GRANT,
T. S. BOWERS, *A. A. A. G.*

HEADQUARTERS DEPART. OF THE TENNESSEE,
VICKSBURG, MISS., *August* 23, 1863.
General Orders, No. 53.

I. Hereafter, negroes will not be allowed in or about the camps of white troops, except such as are properly employed and controlled.

II. They may be employed in the quartermaster's department, subsistence department, medical department, as hospital nurses and laundresses, in the engineer department as pioneers. As far as practicable, such as have been or may be rejected as recruits for colored regiments by the examining surgeon will be employed about hospitals and in pioneer corps.

III. In regiments and companies they may be employed as follows : One cook to each fifteen men, and one teamster to each wagon. Officers may employ them as servants, but not in greater number than they are entitled to commutation for.

IV. Commanders of regiments and detachments will see that all negroes in or about their respective camps, not employed as provided in this order, are collected and turned over to the provost marshal of the division, post, or army corps to which their regiment or detachment belongs.

V. Provost marshals will keep all negroes thus coming into their hands from straggling and wandering about until they can be put in charge of the superintendent of the camp for colored people nearest them; and all negroes unemployed, in accordance with this or previous orders, not in and about camps of regiments and detachments, will be required to go into the camps established for negroes, and it is enjoined upon provost marshals to see that they do so.

VI. Recruiting for colored regiments in negro camps will be prohibited, except when special authority to do so is given.

VII. All able-bodied negro men who are found, ten days after publication of this order, without a certificate of the officer or person employing them, will be regarded as unemployed, and may be pressed into service. Certificates given to negroes must show how, when, and by whom they are employed, and if as officers' servants, that the officer employing them has not a greater number than by law he is entitled to commutation for.

By order of Major General U. S. GRANT.
JNO. A. RAWLINS, *A. A. G.*

## Letter on Slavery and Reconstruction.

VICKSBURG, MISSISSIPPI,
*August* 30, 1863.

Hon. E. B. WASHBURNE.

DEAR SIR : * * * The people of the North need not quarrel over the institution of slavery. What Vice President Stephens acknowledges the corner-stone of the Confederacy is already knocked out. Slavery is already dead, and cannot be resurrected. It would take a standing army to maintain slavery in the South, if we were to make peace to-day, guaranteeing to the South all their former constitutional privileges. I never was an abolitionist, not even what could be called anti-slavery; but I try to judge fairly and honestly, and it became patent to my mind early in the rebellion that the North and South could never live at peace with each other except as one nation, and that without slavery. As anxious as I am to see peace established, I would not, therefore, be willing to see any settlement until this question is forever settled. Your sincere friend,

U. S. GRANT.

## On being a Candidate for Political Office.

NASHVILLE, TENNESSEE,
*January 20, 1864.*

Hon. I. N. MORRIS.

DEAR SIR: Your letter of the 29th of December I did not receive until two days ago. I receive many such, but do not answer. Yours, however, is written in such a kindly spirit, and as you ask for an answer, confidentially, I will not withhold it. Allow me to say, however, that I am not a politician, never was, and hope never to be, and could not write a political letter. My only desire is to serve the country in her present trials. To do this efficiently it is necessary to have the confidence of the army and the people. I know no way to better secure this end than by a faithful performance of my duties. So long as I hold my present position, I do not believe that I have the right to criticize the policy or orders of those above me, or to give utterance to views of my own except to the authorities at Washington, through the General-in-Chief of the army. In this respect, I know I have proven myself a "good soldier."

In your letter you say that I have it in my power to be the next President. This is the last thing in the world I desire. I would regard such a consummation as being highly unfortunate for myself, if not for the country. Through Providence I have attained to more than I ever hoped, and with the position I now hold in the regular army, if allowed to retain it, will be more than satisfied. I certainly shall never shape a sentiment, or the expression of a thought, with a view of being candidate for office. I scarcely know the inducement that could be held out to me to accept office, and unhesitatingly say that I infinitely prefer my present position to that of any civil office within the gift of the people.

This is a private letter to you, not intended for others to see or read, because I want to avoid being heard from by the public except through acts in the performance of my legitimate duties.

I have the honor to be, very respectfully, your obedient servant, U. S. GRANT.

## On Results of "Peace on any Terms."

HEADQ'RS ARMIES OF THE UNITED STATES,
CITY POINT, *Va., August* 16, 1864.

Hon. E. B. WASHBURNE.

DEAR SIR: I state to all citizens who visit me that all we want now to insure an early restoration of the Union, is a determined unity of sentiment North. The rebels have now in their ranks their last man. The little boys and old men are guarding prisons, guarding railroad bridges, and forming a good part of their garrisons for entrenched positions.

A man lost by them cannot be replaced. They have robbed alike the cradle and the grave to get their present force. Besides what they lose in frequent skirmishes and battles, they are now losing, from desertions and other causes at least one regiment per day. With this drain upon them the end is not far distant if we will only be true to ourselves. Their only hope now is in

a divided North. This might give them reinforcements from Tennessee, Kentucky, Maryland, and Missouri, while it would weaken us. With the draft quietly enforced, the enemy would become despondent and would make but little resistance.

I have no doubt but the enemy are exceedingly anxious to hold out until after the Presidential election. They have many hopes from its effects. They hope a counter revolution; they hope the election of a peace candidate; in fact, like Micawber, they hope for something to turn up. Our peace friends, if they expect peace from separation, are much mistaken. It would be but the beginning of war, with thousands of northern men joining the South, because of our disgrace in allowing separation. To have "peace on any terms," the South would demand the restoration of their slaves already freed. They would demand indemnity for losses sustained, and they would demand a treaty which would make the North slave-hunters for the South. They would demand pay or the restoration of every slave escaping to the North.

Yours, truly, U. S. GRANT.

## On Filling the Armies.

CITY POINT, *September* 13, 1864,
10.30, a. m.

Hon. EDWIN M. STANTON, *Secretary of War.*

We ought to have the whole number of men called for by the President in the shortest possible time. Prompt action in filling our armies will have more effect upon the enemy than a victory over them. They profess to believe, and make their men believe, there is such a party North in favor of recognizing southern independence, that the draft cannot be enforced. Let them be undeceived. Deserters come into our lines daily, who tell us that the men are nearly universally tired of the war, and that desertions would be much more frequent, but that they believe peace will be negotiated after the fall election.

The enforcement of the draft and prompt filling up of our armies will save the shedding of blood to an immense degree.

U. S. GRANT, *Lieutenant General.*

## On Protecting Colored Soldiers.

HEADQ'RS ARMIES OF THE UNITED STATES,
*October* 29, 1864.

General R. E. LEE, C. S. A.,
*Commanding Army Northern Virginia.*

GENERAL: Understanding from your letter of the 19th that the colored prisoners who are employed at work in the trenches near Fort Gilmer have been withdrawn, I have directed the withdrawal of the Confederate prisoners employed in the Dutch Gap canal.

I shall always regret the necessity of retaliating for wrongs done our soldiers; but regard it my duty to protect all persons received into the army of the United States, regardless of color or nationality. When acknowledged soldiers of the Government are captured they must be treated as prisoners of war, or such treatment as they receive will be inflicted upon an equal number of prisoners held by us.

I have nothing to do with the discussion of

the slavery question : therefore decline answering the arguments adduced to show the right to return to former owners such negroes as are captured from our army.

In answer to the question at the conclusion of your letter, I have to state that all prisoners of war falling into my hands shall receive the kindest treatment possible, consistent with securing them, unless I have good authority for believing any number of our men are being treated otherwise. Then, painful as it may be to me, I shall inflict like treatment on an equal number of Confederate prisoners.

Hoping that it may never become my duty to order retaliation upon any man held as a prisoner of war, I have the honor to be, very respectfully, your obedient servant,

U. S. GRANT, *Lieutenant General.*

### General Grant's Testimony before the Committee on the Conduct of the War, on Exchange of Prisoners, February 11, 1865.

Q. It is stated, upon what authority I do not know, that you are charged entirely with the exchange of prisoners. A. That is correct. And what is more, I have effected an arrangement for the exchange of prisoners, man for man and officer for officer, or his equivalent, according to the old cartel, until one or the other party has exhausted the number they now hold. I get a great many letters daily from friends of prisoners in the South, every one of which I cause to be answered, telling them that this arrangement has been made, and that I suppose exchanges can be made at the rate of about 3,000 a week. The fact is, that I do not believe the South can deliver our prisoners to us as fast as that, on account of want of transportation on their part. But just as fast as they can deliver our prisoners to us, I will receive them, and deliver their prisoners to them.

Q. There is no impediment in the way? A. No, sir; I will take the prisoners as fast as they can deliver them. And, I would add, that after I have caused the letters to be answered, I refer the letters to Colonel Mulford, the commissioner of exchanges, so that he may effect special exchanges in those cases wherever he can do so. The Salisbury prisoners will be coming right on. I myself saw Colonel Hatch, the assistant commissioner of exchanges on the part of the South, and he told me that the Salisbury and Danville prisoners would be coming on at once. He said that he could bring them on at the rate of 5,000 or 6,000 a week. But I do not believe he can do that. Their roads are now taxed to their utmost capacity for military purposes, and are becoming less and less efficient every day. Many of the bridges are now down. I merely fixed, as a matter of judgment, that 3,000 a week will be as fast as they can deliver them.

Q. The fact is, that there is no impediment now in the way except the lack of transportation ? A. That is all. There is no impediment on our side. I could deliver and receive every one of them in a very short time, if they will deliver those they hold. We have lost some two weeks lately on account of the ice in the river.

Q. It has been said that we refused to ex-change prisoners because we found ours starved, diseased, and unserviceable when we received them, and did not like to exchange sound men for such men ? A. There never has been any such reason as that. That has been a reason for making exchanges. I will confess that if our men who are prisoners in the South were really well taken care of, suffering nothing except a little privation of liberty, then, in a military point of view, it would not be good policy for us to exchange, because every man they get back is forced right into the army at once, while that is not the case with our prisoners when we receive them. In fact, the half of our returned prisoners will never go into the army again, and none of them will until after they have had a furlough of thirty or sixty days. Still, the fact of their suffering as they do is a reason for making this exchange as rapidly as possible.

Q. And never has been a reason for not making the exchange ? A. It never has. Exchanges having been suspended by reason of disagreement on the part of agents of exchange on both sides before I came in command of the armies of the United States, and it then being near the opening of the spring campaign, I did not deem it advisable or just to the men who had to fight our battles to reinforce the enemy with thirty or forty thousand disciplined troops at that time. An immediate resumption of exchanges would have had that effect without giving us corresponding benefits. The suffering said to exist among our prisoners South was a powerful argument against the course pursued, and so I felt it.

### General Grant and the Proposed Mission to Mexico.

GENERAL GRANT TO SECRETARY STANTON.

HEADQ'RS ARMIES OF THE UNITED STATES, WASHINGTON, *October* 27, 1866.

Your letter of this date, enclosing one from the President of the United States of the 26th instant, asking you to request me " to proceed to some point on our Mexican frontier most suitable and convenient for communication with our minister ; or (if General Grant deems it best) to accompany him to his destination in Mexico, and to give him the aid of his advice in carrying out the instructions of the Secretary of State," is received. Also, copy of instructions to Hon. Lewis D. Campbell, minister to Mexico, accompanying your letter, is received.

The same request was made of me one week ago to-day, verbally, to which I returned a written reply, copy of which is herewith enclosed.

On the 23d instant, the same request was renewed in cabinet meeting, where I was invited to be present, when I again declined respectfully as I could the mission tendered me, with reasons.

I now again beg most respectfully to decline the proposed mission for the following additional reasons, to wit :

Now, whilst the army is being reorganized, and troops distributed as fast as organized, my duties require me to keep within telegraphic communication of all the department commanders, and of this city, from which orders must emanate. Almost the entire frontier between the United States and Mexico is embraced in the departments commanded by Generals Sheridan and Hancock, the command of the latter being embraced in the military division under Lieutenant General Sherman, three officers in whom the entire country has unbounded confidence.

Either of these general officers can be instructed to accompany the American minister to the Mexican frontier, or the one can through whose command the minister may propose to pass in reaching his destination.

If it is desirable that our minister should communicate with me he can do so through the officer who may accompany him, with but very little delay beyond what would be experienced if I were to accompany him myself. I might add that I would not dare counsel the minister in any matter beyond stationing of troops on the United States soil, without the concurrence of the administration. That concurrence could be more speedily had with me here than if I were upon the frontier, The stationing of troops would be as fully within the control of the accompanying officer as it would of mine.

I sincerely hope I may be excused from undertaking a duty so foreign to my office and tastes as that contemplated.

U. S. GRANT, *General.*

Hon. E. M. STANTON,
*Secretary of War.*

## General Grant and the Baltimore Troubles of October, 1866.

### 1.—GENERAL GRANT TO PRESIDENT JOHNSON.

HEADQ'RS ARMIES OF THE UNITED STATES,
WASHINGTON, *October* 24, 1866.

His Excellency A. JOHNSON,
*President of the United States.*

I have the honor to enclose to you the within report from General Canby, commander of this military department, upon the threatened violence in the city of Baltimore previous to the approaching elections. Upon receiving your verbal instructions of the 20th instant, to look into the nature of the threatened difficulties in Baltimore, to ascertain what course should be pursued to prevent it, I gave General Canby, whose department embraces the State of Maryland, instructions, also verbal, to proceed to Baltimore in person, to ascertain as nearly as he could the cause which threatened to lead to riot and bloodshed. The report submitted is given in pursuance of these instructions.

Since the rendition of General Canby's report I had a long conversation with him, and also with Governor Swann, of the State of Maryland. It is the opinion of General Canby and the statement of Governor Swann, that no danger of riot need be apprehended unless the latter should find it necessary to remove the present police commissioners of Baltimore from office and to appoint their successors. No action in this direction has been taken yet, nor will there be until Friday next, when the trial of the commissioners before the governor is set to take place. I cannot see the possible necessity for calling in the aid of the military in advance of even the cause, (the removal of said commissioners,) which is to induce riot.

The conviction is forced on my mind that no reason now exists for giving or promising the military aid of the government to support the laws of Maryland. The tendency of giving such aid or promise would be to produce the very result intended to be averted. So far there seems to be merely a very bitter contest for political ascendancy in the State.

Military interference would be interpreted as giving aid to one of the factions, no matter how pure the intentions or how guarded and just the instructions. It is a contingency I hope never to see arise in this country, while I occupy the position of general-in-chief of the army, to have to send troops into a State, *in full relations with the general government,* on the eve of an election, to preserve the peace. If insurrection does come, the law provides the method of calling out forces to suppress it. No such condition seems to exist now.     U. S. GRANT, *General.*

October 25—The President asked for the number of troops at convenient stations; to which General Grant replied, on the 27th, giving them. November 1, President directed Secretary Stanton: " In view of the prevalence in various portions of the country of a revolutionary and turbulent disposition, which might at any moment assume insurrectionary proportions and lead to serious disorders, and of the duty of the government to be at all times prepared to act with decision and effect, this force is not deemed adequate for the protection and security of the seat of government. I therefore request that you will at once take such measures as will insure its safety, and thus discourage any attempt for its possession by insurgent or other illegal combinations."

November 2—The President gave Secretary Stanton this order:

EXECUTIVE MANSION,
WASHINGTON, D. C., *November* 2, 1866.

SIR: There is ground to apprehend danger of an insurrection in Baltimore against the constituted authorities of the State of Maryland, on or about the day of the election soon to be held in that city, and that in such contingency the aid of the United States might be invoked under the acts of Congress which pertain to that subject. While I am averse to any military demonstration that would have a tendency to interfere with the free exercise of the elective franchise in Baltimore, or be construed into any interference in local questions, I feel great solicitude that, should an insurrection take place, the government should be prepared to meet and promptly put it down. I accordingly desire you to call General Grant's attention to the subject, leaving to his own discretion and judgment the measures of preparation and precaution that should be adopted.

Very respectfully, yours,
ANDREW JOHNSON.

Hon EDWIN M. STANTON,
*Secretary of War.*

Same day, General Grant sent this telegram to General Canby:

General E. R. S. CANBY,
*Comm'g Depart. of Washington.*

Enclosed I send you orders just received from the President of the United States. They fully explain themselves. As commander of the military department including the State of Mary-

land, you will take immediate steps for carrying them into execution. There are now six or eight companies of infantry ready organized in New York that have been ordered to Baltimore, on their way to their regiments here in Washington and in Virginia. Either visit Baltimore or send a staff officer there to stop these troops at Fort McHenry until further orders. Also hold one of the infantry regiments on duty in this city in readiness to move at a moment's notice. By having cars ready to take a regiment all at once, they will be practically as near Baltimore here as if in camp a few miles from that city. These are all the instructions deemed necessary in advance of troops being legally called out to suppress insurrection or invasion. Having the greatest confidence, however, in your judgment and discretion, I wish you to go to Baltimore in person and to remain there until the threatened difficulties have passed over. Proper discretion will no doubt go further towards preventing conflict than force. U. S. GRANT,
*General.*

P. S.—The orders referred to have not as yet been received. When received they will be forwarded to your address, which you will please communicate.

November 3—A copy of the President's instructions was sent to General Canby.

November 5—General Grant reported as follows:

HEADQ'RS ARMIES OF THE UNITED STATES,
BALTIMORE, MD., *November* 5, 1866.
Secretary STANTON,
*Washington, D. C.*

This morning collision looked almost inevitable. Wiser counsels now seem to prevail, and I think there is strong hope that no riot will occur. Propositions looking to the harmonizing of parties are now pending. U. S. GRANT,
*General.*

### General Grant on Martial Law in Texas.

HEADQUARTERS ARMIES UNITED STATES,
*January* 29, 1867.

Respectfully forwarded to the Secretary of War.* Attention is invited to that part of the within communication which refers to the condition of Union men and freedmen in Texas, and to the powerlessness of the military in the present state of affairs to afford them protection. Even the moral effect of the presence of troops is passing away, and a few days ago a squad of soldiers on duty was fired on by citizens in Brownsville, Texas; a report of which is this

---

* This is the report referred to:

HEADQUARTERS DEPARTMENT OF THE GULF,
NEW ORLEANS, LA., *January* 25, 1867.
GENERAL: The condition of freedmen and Union men in remote parts of Texas is truly horrible. The Government is denounced, the freedmen are shot, and Union men are persecuted if they have the temerity to express their opinion.

This condition exists in the northeastern counties of the State to an alarming extent.

Applications come to me from the most respectable authorities for troops, but troops have so little power that they are sufficient only in the moral effect which their presence has. * * * * * *

I am, General, very respectfully, your obedient servant,
P. H. SHERIDAN,
*Major General United States Army.*
General U. S. GRANT,
*Commanding Armies of the U. S., Washington, D. C.*

day forwarded. In my opinion the great number of murders of Union men and freedmen in Texas, not only as a rule unpunished, but uninvestigated, constitute practically a state of insurrection, and believing it to be the province and duty of every good government to afford protection to the lives, liberty, and property of her citizens, I would recommend the declaration of martial law in Texas to secure these ends.

The necessity for governing any portion of our territory by martial law is to be deplored. If resorted to, it should be limited in its authority, and should leave all local authorities and civil tribunals free and unobstructed, until they prove their inefficiency or unwillingness to perform their duties.

Martial law would give security, or comparatively so, to all classes of citizens, without regard to race, color, or political opinions, and could be continued until society was capable of protecting itself, or until the State is returned to its full relation with the Union.

The application of martial law to one of these States would be a warning to all, and, if necessary, could be extended to others.
U. S. GRANT, *General.*

No action was had by the civil authorities upon the foregoing recommendation.

---

### General Grant's Testimony before the House Committee on the Judiciary, July 18, 1867.

By Mr. Eldridge: Q. At what time were you made general of the army by your present title? A. In July, 1866.

Q. Did you after that time have interviews with the President in reference to the condition of affairs in the rebel States? A. I have seen the President very frequently on the subject, and have heard him express his views very frequently; but I cannot call to mind any special interview. I have been called to cabinet meetings a number of times.

Q. With reference to those matters? A. Generally, when I was asked to be at a cabinet meeting, it was because some question was up in which, as General of the army, I would be interested.

Q. Did you have any interviews with him on the subject of granting amnesty or pardon to the officers of the Confederate army, or to the people of those States? A. Not that I am aware of. I have occasionally recommended a person for amnesty. I do not recollect any special interview that I have had on the subject. I recollect speaking to him once or twice about the time that he issued his proclamation. I thought myself at that time that there was no reason why, because a person had risen to the rank of general, he should be excluded from amnesty any more than one who had failed to reach that rank. I thought his proclamation all right so far as it excluded graduates from West Point or from the Naval Academy, or persons connected with the government, who had gone into the rebellion; but I did not see any reason why a volunteer who happened to rise to the rank of general should be excluded any more than a colonel. I recollect speaking on that point. Neither did I see much reason for the twenty-thousand-dollar clause. These are the only two points that I remember to have spoken of at the time. I afterwards, however, told him that I thought he was much nearer right on the twenty-thousand-dollar clause than I was.

Q. Do you recollect, when you had that interview with him, when you expressed those opinions? A. About the time of the proclamation.

Q. Did the President, previous to issuing that proclamation, ask your opinion on the various points of it? A. I do not recollect. I know that I was present when it was read, before it was issued. I do not think that I was asked my views at all. I had the privilege, of course, being there, to express my views.

Q. Was not that the purpose of your attendance—to get your views on the subject? A. I cannot say that it was. About that time I was frequently asked to be present at cabinet meetings.

Q. Were there other subjects discussed before you at the meetings referred to? A. Yes, sir. Whenever I was there all the subjects that were up that day were discussed.

Q. I speak of that time. A. I imagine not. My recollection is that it was solely to hear the proclamation read; but I would not be positive as to that. It is my recollection.

Q. Did you give your opinion to the President that it would be better at that time to issue a proclamation of general amnesty? A. No, sir; I never gave any such opinion as that. By general amnesty I mean universal amnesty.

Q. Did you give your opinion to the President that his proclamation interfered with the stipulations between yourself and General Lee? A. No, sir. I frequently had to intercede for General Lee and other paroled officers, on the ground that their parole, so long as they obeyed the laws of the United States, protected them from arrest and trial. The President at that time occupied exactly the reverse grounds, viz., that they should be tried and punished. He wanted to know when the time would come that they should be punished. I told him, not so long as they obeyed the laws and complied with the stipulation. That was the ground that I took.

Q. Did you not also insist that that applied as well to the common soldiers? A. Of course it applied to every one who took the parole; but that matter was not canvassed except in case of some of the leaders. I claimed that, in surrendering their armies and arms, they had done what they could not all of them have been compelled to do, as a portion of them could have escaped. But they surrendered in consideration of the fact that they were to be exempt from trial so long as they conformed to the obligations which they had taken; and they were entitled to that.

Q. You looked on that in the nature of a parole, and held that they could only be tried when they violated that parole? A. Yes; that was the view I took of the question.

Q. That is your view still? A. Yes, sir, unquestionably.

Q. Did you understand that to apply to General Lee? A. Certainly.

Q. That was your understanding of the arrangement which you made with General Lee? A. That was my understanding of an arrangement which I gave voluntarily. General Lee's army was the first to surrender, and I believed that with such terms all the rebel armies would surrender, and that we would thus avoid bushwhacking and a continuation of the war in a way that we could make very little progress with, having no organized armies to meet.

Q. You considered that the like terms were given by General Sherman to the armies which surrendered to him? A. Yes, sir; to all the armies that surrendered after that.

Q. And you held that so long as they kept their parole of honor and obeyed the laws they were not subject to be tried by courts? A. That was my opinion. I will state here that I am not quite certain whether I am being tried, or who is being tried, by the questions asked.

Mr. Eldridge. I am not trying anybody; I am inquiring in reference to the President's proclamation, and as to the views he entertained.

Q. Did you give those views to the President? A. I have stated those views to the President frequently, and, as I have said, he disagreed with me in those views. He insisted on it that the leaders must be punished, and wanted to know when the time would come that those persons could be tried. I told him, when they violated their parole.

Q. Did you consider that that applied to Jefferson Davis? A. No, sir; he did not take any parole.

Q. He did not surrender? No, sir. It applied to no person who was captured—only to those who were paroled.

Q. Did the President insist that General Lee should be tried for treason? A. He contended for it.

Q. And you claimed to him that the parole which General Lee had given would be violated in such trial? A. I did. I insisted on it that General Lee would not have surrendered his army, and given up all their arms, if he had supposed that after surrender he was going to be tried for treason and hanged. I thought we got a very good equivalent for the lives of a few leaders in getting all their arms and getting themselves under control, bound by their oaths to obey the laws. That was the consideration which, I insisted upon, we had received.

Q. Did the President argue that question with you? A. There was not much argument about it; it was merely assertion.

Q. After you had expressed your opinion upon it did he coincide with you? A. No, sir; not then. He afterwards got to agreeing with me on that subject. I never claimed that the parole gave those prisoners any political rights whatever. I thought that that was a matter entirely with Congress, over which I had no control; that, simply, as general-in-chief commanding the army, I had a right to stipulate for the surrender on terms which protected their lives. That is all I claimed. The parole gave them protection and exemption from punishment for all offences not in violation of the rules of civilized warfare, so long as their parole was kept.

Q. Do you recollect at what time you had

those conversations? Can you state any particular time, or up to any particular time, when they were finished? A. The conversations were frequent after the inauguration of Mr. Johnson. I cannot give the time. He seemed to be anxious to get at the leaders to punish them. He would say that the leaders of the rebellion must be punished, and that treason must be made odious. He cared nothing for the men in the ranks—the common men. He would let them go, for they were led into it by the leaders.

Q. Was that said to you in conversation? A. I have heard him say it a number of times. He said it to me, and he said it in my presence at the time that delegations were coming up to him from the South.

Q. What persons do you recollect as being present at those conversations—I mean what southern men? A. I did not know them at all. I recollect that on one occasion he talked to a delegation from Richmond in that way.* I do not know any of their names.

Q. Was that prior or subsequent to his proclamation? A. It was subsequent, I think.

Q. Do you recollect at any time urging the President to go further in granting amnesty than he had gone in his proclamation? A. Just as I said before, I could not see any reason why the fact of a volunteer rising to the rank of general should exclude him any more than any other grade. And with reference to the twenty-thousand-dollar clause, I thought that a man's success in this world was no reason for his being excluded from amnesty; but I recollect afterwards saying to the President that I thought he was right in that particular, and I was wrong. In reference to the other, I never changed my views. If he was going to give amnesty to a soldier at all, I did not see why the fact of a man's having risen to the rank of a general should be reason for excluding him.

Q. Did you not advise the President that it was proper and right he should grant amnesty? A. I do not think I said anything on that subject. I only looked at the proclamation as one which he was determined to issue, and as a thing susceptible to amendment or improvement.

Q. Did you not give your opinion at all that amnesty ought to be granted to those people to any extent? A. I know that I was in favor of some proclamation of the sort, and perhaps I may have said so. It was necessary to do something to establish governments and civil law there. I wanted to see that done, but I do not think I ever pretended to dictate what ought to be done.

Q. Did you not advise? A. I do not think I ever did. I have given my opinions, perhaps, as to what has been done, but I do not think I advised any course myself any more than that I was very anxious to see something done to restore civil governments in those States.

Q. Did you not give your opinion at all to the President as to what should be done? A. I do not think I did. After matters were done, I was willing to express an opinion for or against particular clauses.

* See pages 47, 48 of the Manual for 1866.

Q. I suppose the President called on you for advice on those questions? A. I say I was in favor, and so expressed myself, of something being done to restore civil rule there immediately, as near as it could be done under the circumstances.

Q. Did you suggest anything? A. No, sir.

By Mr. Woodbridge: Q. I understand your position to be this: that you did not assume to originate or inaugurate any policy; but that when any question came up, and your opinion was asked as to what the President was going to do or had done, you gave an opinion? A. That was it, exactly; and I presumed the whole committee so understood me. I have always been attentive to my own duties, and tried not to interfere with other people's. I was always ready to originate matters pertaining to the army, but I never was willing to originate matters pertaining to the civil government of the United States. When I was asked my opinion about what had been done, I was willing to give it. I originated no plan and suggested no plan for civil government. I only gave my views on measures after they had been originated. I simply expressed an anxiety that something should be done to give some sort of control down there. There were no governments there when the war was over, and I wanted to see some governments established, and wanted to see it done quickly. I did not pretend to say how it should be done, or in what form.

By Mr. Eldridge: Q. I confined my questions entirely to war and peace. In expressing the opinion that something ought to be done and done quickly, did you make a suggestion of what ought to be done? A. No, sir. I will state here that, before Mr. Lincoln's assassination, the question about issuing a proclamation of some sort, and establishing some sort of civil government there, was up; and what was done then was continued after Mr. Johnson came into office.

Q. Did you give your opinion on that after it was done? A. I was present, I think, twice during Mr. Lincoln's administration, when a proclamation which had been prepared was read. After his assassination it continued right along, and I was there with Mr. Johnson.

Q. Did you give President Johnson your opinion on the subject of the proclamation, which you say was up before Mr. Lincoln's death, and was continued afterwards? A. I say I have given my opinion on particular passages of it.

Q. Tell us what conversations you had with President Johnson on the subject, so far as you can recollect it? A. I have stated once or twice that, so far as I can recollect, I disagreed with two clauses of the proclamation. As to the plan of establishing provisional governors there, that was a question which I knew nothing about, and which I do not recollect having expressed an opinion about. The only opinion I recollect having expressed on that subject at all was to the Secretary of War. I thought there would be some difficulty in getting people down there to accept offices, but I found afterwards they were ready enough to take them.

By the Chairman: Q. If I understand you

correctly, the only opinion that you expressed, and the only advice that you gave, were in reference to the military side of the question, and not in reference to the civil side? A. Nothing further than that I was anxious that something should be done to restore some sort of government.

Q. But you gave no advice as to what should be done? A. I gave no advice as to what should be done.

By Mr. Eldridge: Q. State the conversation that you had on that subject? A. I have had repeated conversations with the President, but I cannot specify what those conversations were any more than I have already done.

Q. Did you recommend certain generals of the Confederate army to the President for pardon who fell within the exemptions? A. Yes, sir. I recommended General Longstreet, I think, a year and a half ago; and although I cannot recollect the names of anybody else, I think I recommended several others.

Q. Do you recollect recommending J. G. French, a graduate of West Point? A. Yes, sir.

Q. What part did he take in the rebellion? A. He was a brigadier general.

Q. Was he a graduate of West Point? A. He was; and a class-mate of mine.

Q. Do you recollect recommending the pardon of George H. Stuart? A. Yes, sir.

Q. What part did he take in the Confederate service? A. He was a general, and commanded a brigade or division. He took no very conspicuous part.

Q. Was he a graduate of West Point? A. I think so.

Q. He was not a class-mate of yours? A. No, sir; he came long after me.

Q. Was there any special circumstance in his case which you considered? A. Yes, sir. I did that at the instance of General Hunter, and as a special favor to him, and I did it because it affected an inheritance. Stuart's wife was a staunch, consistent Union woman throughout the war, notwithstanding her husband was in the rebel army. I think she never went South. She was as devoted to the Union cause as any woman whose husband was on our side. There was considerable property in Maryland which had not been confiscated, which he inherits, and I thought that his wife and his children were entitled to that property. General Hunter thought so too. My recommendation was not out of any favor to General Stuart.

Q. Were those circumstances presented to the President as a reason for the pardon? A. I do not know that they were, and I do not know that they were not. I think I merely signed a recommendation.

Q. Did that contain the statement you have given? A. I do not recollect whether it did or not. I do not know that I stated the circumstances to the President.

Q. Do you recollect signing the recommendation of M. D. Ector, a rebel brigadier general? A. No, sir; I do not recollect there being such a brigadier general in the rebel service.

Q. The report in the House is that he was pardoned on the recommendation of Lieutenant General Grant and John Hancock. A. I do not recollect any such person as John Hancock, or the general named.

Q. Do you recollect —— Lloyd J. Dean? (Beall?) A. Yes, sir.

Q. Did you sign a recommendation, or make an application to the President for his pardon? A. I do not think that the record will show that I recommended his pardon, but I am not sure as to that. I know that he sent his application through me, with the request that I should forward it to the President with some endorsement. My recollection is that I made an endorsement as to his general character, which was as high, up to the breaking out of the rebellion, as any man's could be.

Q. Were you acquainted with him previous to the breaking out of the rebellion? A. Oh, yes, sir, for many years. I do not think that I recommended him, but still I may have done so. My recollection is that I simply endorsed his character on the application. The application was to the President, but sent through me.

Q. Do you recollect P. D. Roddy, said to be a rebel brigadier general? A. Yes, sir. I do not recollect what my endorsement was in Roddy's case, but I know that if I had it to do over again I would recommend his pardon very quickly, and I presume I did so. If he is not pardoned yet, I would be very glad to sign a recommendation for him now.

Q. Do you recollect any other officers of the rebel army who were recommended to the President for pardon by you? A. No, sir; I cannot mention any. You have already gone over a bigger list than I thought I recommended.

Q. Do you recollect the case of General Pickett? A. I know that I was urged in that case over and over again, and I can send you from the office exactly what I did in the matter.

Q. Did you sign a recommendation in his case? A. I do not think I did. I recollect receiving letter after letter from him, and letters were sent to me time and again on his behalf. He was specially uneasy lest he would be tried by a military commission on account of some men who were executed in North Carolina.

Q. Do you recollect talking to the President about him? A. I do not recollect ever mentioning his name to the President. I will furnish whatever is in my office about him. I received one appeal after another, not only from Pickett himself and his relatives, but from officers in the army who knew him very well and favorably prior to the war.

Q. Do you know whether he has been pardoned yet? A. I do not know.

Q. State what the circumstances of his case were, and whether you are in favor of his pardon. A. I was not in favor of his pardon. I was not in favor, however, of his being tried by a military commission. I think that his great anxiety was to receive some assurance that he would not be taken up and imprisoned for offences alleged against him as commander in North Carolina. He wanted to be able to go to work and make a living. It is likely I may have recommended that he be given assurance that he would not be arrested and imprisoned. I do not think that I ever, under any circumstances, signed a recommendation for his pardon. You have no right to ask what my opinion is now.

Q. Was he an active rebel officer? A. Yes, sir. He was charged with executing a number of North Carolina refugees who were captured with a garrison under General Wessels in North Carolina. Those men had gone there to evade the rebel conscription, or it may be had deserted from the rebel army, and they were tried as deserters, and quite a number of them executed. Pickett was commanding officer at that time, and there was a good deal said of his having approved the proceedings.

Q. Was this man French an active rebel officer? He served in the field. I never heard much of him during the rebellion. He was not generally in the army against which I was personally engaged. He was at one time on the James river, when General McClellan was in command, and was afterwards in the West, but he never filled a conspicuous place.

Q. Did you ever advise the pardon of General Lee? A. Yes, sir.

Q. Were you ever consulted on that question by the President? A. General Lee forwarded his application for amnesty through me, and I forwarded it to the President, approved

Q. Did you have any conversation about it with the President? A. I do not recollect having had any conversation with him on the subject. I think it probable that I recommended verbally the pardon of General Johnston, immediately after the surrender of his army, on account of the address he delivered to his army. I thought it in such good tone and spirit that we should distinguish between him and others who did not appear so well. I recollect speaking of that, and saying that I should be glad if General Johnston received his pardon, on account of the manly manner in which he addressed his troops.

By the Chairman: Q. You supposed his pardon would have a good effect? A. Yes; I thought it would have a good effect. I am not sure whether I spoke on the subject to the Secretary of War or to the President.

By Mr. Eldridge: Q. Do you recollect having a conversation with the President at any time when General Hillyer was present? A. I remember going with General Hillyer to see the President, but it was on the subject of an appointment which he wanted. I went to state to the President what I knew of General Hillyer. I do not recollect the conversation going beyond that range at all, though still it might have done so.

Q. You do not recollect any other meeting with the President when General Hillyer was present? A. I do not know. I think I met him twice, perhaps, but it was on a subject in which General Hillyer himself was personally interested. Whether the President conversed on any other subjects at that time I do not recollect.

Q. Do you not recollect any conversation with the President, in the presence of General Hillyer, on the subject of granting amnesty to the people of the South? A. No, sir; I do not recollect any conversation on the subject of gen-

eral amnesty, and I know that I never was in favor of general amnesty. I do not recollect any conversation at that time on the subject of amnesty at all. I have stated here that I never recommended general amnesty, and never was in favor of it, until the time shall come when it is safe to give it.

By Mr. Williams: Q. When you say that you did not recommend general amnesty, you mean universal amnesty? A. I do not recollect of ever having any conversation on the subject of universal amnesty. I know I could not have recommended such a thing, because I never was in favor of it, until the time shall come when it is safe.

Q. I merely put the question in reference to your use of the term "general," because it might be supposed from that that the amnesty in the proclamation was not a general amnesty? A. I meant universal amnesty, of course.

Q. You state that you differed with the President as to two points in his proclamation, but that his views afterwards changed. State when the President's mind underwent a change? A. It would be very hard, I reckon, to fix any period for it.

Q. Was it in the summer of 1865? A. Yes, sir; along in the summer of 1865.

Q. How long after the North Carolina proclamation of the 29th of May? A. It is impossible for me to say.

Q. Was it more than two or three months? A. I should think not.

By Mr. Woodbridge: What did you mean by saying that the President's views afterwards changed? A. I meant to say that while I was contending for the rights which those rebel paroled soldiers had, he was insisting on it that they should be punished. My remark was confined to that particular subject.

By Mr. Eldridge: Q. Did you have any correspondence with the President in writing? A. Any correspondence I ever had with the President is official, and can be furnished. I had to make frequent endorsements on the subject of the rights of those paroled prisoners. The only correspondence that I could have had on the subject of amnesty was where I recommended men for pardon, as in the case of French and others.

Q. Did you keep copies of them? A. Yes, sir, and will furnish them.

Q. Do you recollect the proclamation that is called the "North Carolina proclamation?" A. Yes, sir; that was the first one published giving a State government.

Q. Did you have any conversation with the President as to the terms or purport of that proclamation? A. I was, as I say, present when it was read. It was in the direction that I wanted. I was anxious to see something done to give some sort of temporary government there. I did not want to see anarchy.

Q. Did you give any opinion in favor of that proposition? A. I did not give any opinion against it. I was in favor of that or anything else which looked to civil government until Congress could meet and establish governments there. I did not want all chaos left there, and no form of civil government whatever. I was not in favor of anything or opposed to anything particularly. I was simply in favor of having a government there; that was all I wanted. I did not pretend to give my judgment as to what it should be. I was perfectly willing to leave that to the civil department. I asked no person what I should do in my duties; I was willing to take all the responsibilities; and I did not want to give my views as to what the civil branch of the government should do.

Q. Some of those governors were military officers and held rank in the army? A. That was during the rebellion. Mr. Johnson was military governor in Tennessee and General Hamilton in Texas. I do not recollect that there were any other military governors; the others were provisional governors. I did not care whether they were called provisional or military governors. I looked upon them as equally provisional.

By Mr. Thomas: Q. You have stated your opinion as to the rights and privileges of General Lee and his soldiers; did you mean that to include any political rights? A. I have explained that I did not.

Q. Was there any difference of opinion on that point between yourself and President Johnson at any time? A. On that point there was no difference of opinion; but there was as to whether the parole gave them any privileges or rights.

By Mr. Eldridge: Q. He claiming that it did not, and you claiming that it did? A. He claiming that the time must come when they could be tried and punished, and I claiming that that time could not come except by a violation of their parole. I claimed that I gave them no political privileges, but that I had a right, as military commander, to arrange terms of surrender which should protect the lives of those prisoners. I believe it is conceded by everybody that I had that right. I know that Mr. Lincoln conceded it at the time.

By Mr. Boutwell: Q. How recently has the President expressed to you the opinion that General Lee, or others who had the benefit of the parole, ought to be tried and punished? A. Not since about two years ago.

Q. Have you at any time heard the President make any remark in reference to admission of members of Congress from the rebel States into either house? A. I cannot say positively what I have heard him say on that subject I have heard him say as much, perhaps, in his published speeches last summer, as I ever heard him say at all upon that subject. I have heard him say —and I think I have heard him say it twice in his speeches — that if the North carried the elections by members enough to give them, with the southern members, a majority, why would they not be the Congress of the United States? I have heard him say that several times.

By Mr. Williams: Q. When you say "the North," you mean the democratic party of the North, or, in other words, the party favoring his policy? A. I mean if the North carried enough members in favor of the admission of the South. I did not hear him say that he would recognize them as the Congress. I merely heard him ask the question, "why would they not be the Congress?"

By the Chairman: Q. When did you hear him say that? A. I heard him say that in one or two of his speeches. I do not recollect where.

By Mr. Boutwell: Q. Have you heard him make a remark kindred to that elsewhere? A. Yes; I have heard him say that, aside from his speeches, in conversation. I cannot say just when. It was probably about that same time.

Q. Have you heard him, at any time, make any remark or suggestion concerning the legality of Congress with the southern members excluded? A. He alluded to that subject frequently on his tour to Chicago and back last summer. His speeches were generally reported with considerable accuracy. I cannot recollect what he said, except in general terms; but I read his speeches at the time, and they were reported with considerable accuracy.

Q. Did you hear him say anything in private on that subject, either during that trip or at any other time? A. I do not recollect specially.

Q. Did you at any time hear him make any remark concerning the executive department, or the government? A. No. I never heard him allude to that.

Q. Did you ever hear him make any remark looking to any controversy between Congress and the Executive? A. I think not.

By Mr. Marshall: Q. I understand you to say that you were very anxious, at the close of the war, that civil governments should be established in some form as speedily as possible, and that you so advised the President? A. I so stated frequently in his presence.

Q. But that you advised no particular form or mode of proceeding? A. I did not.

Q. Were you present when this North Carolina proclamation was read in the cabinet? A. I would not be certain, but my recollection is that the first time I heard it read was in the presence only of the President, the Secretary of War, and myself.

Q. Did you give your assent to that plan? A. I did not dissent from it. That is just in accordance with what I have stated. It was a civil matter, and, although I was anxious to have something done, I did not intend to dictate any plan. I do not think I said anything about it, or expressed any opinion about it at that time. I looked upon it simply as a temporary measure, to establish a sort of government, until Congress should meet and settle the whole question, that it did not make much difference how it was and done, so there was a form of government there.

Q. Were you present that time by invitation of the President or the Secretary of War? A. I must have been.

Q. Were you not invited for the purpose of getting your views as to whether it was a judicious plan to be adopted for the time? A. I suppose I was free to express my views. I suppose the object was, perhaps, that I might express my views if I could suggest any change.

Q. Were you at the time asked your views in reference to it? A. I do not think I was. I think it was merely read over.

Q. You think you neither assented nor dissented? A. I know that if I had been asked the question I would have assented to that or almost anything else that would have given stable government there.

Q. In reference to the amnesty proclamation, I wish to know whether you ever gave your opinion to the President as to whether it was too liberal or not liberal enough in its clauses? A. I think I have answered that question pretty fully. When the proclamation was published, I told the President that there were two points on which I disagreed with him—that is, as to excluding volunteer generals, and as to the $20,000 clause. I do not say anything as to whether the rest of it was too liberal or too stringent. I can state what I thought about it, but not what I said about it.

Q. I wish to know whether, at or about the time of the war being ended, you advised the President that it was, in your judgment, best to extend a liberal policy towards the people of the South, and to restore as speedily as possible the fraternal relations which existed prior to the war between the two sections? A. I know that immediately after the close of the rebellion there was a very fine feeling manifested in the South, and I thought we ought to take advantage of it as soon as possible; but since that there has been an evident change there. I may have expressed my views to the President.

Q. What is your recollection in reference to that? A. I may have done so, and it is probable that I did; I do not recollect particularly. I know that I conversed with the President very frequently. I do not suppose that there were any persons engaged in that consultation who thought of what was being done at that time as being lasting—any longer than until Congress would meet and either ratify that or establish some other form of government. I know it never crossed my mind that what was being done was anything more than temporary.

By Mr. Churchill: Q. You understood that to be the view of the President? A. I understood that to be the view of the President and of everybody else. I did not know of any difference of opinion on that subject.

Q. Did you understand that to be his view as other proclamations appeared from time to time? A. I cannot say as to that. It would seem that he was very anxious to have Congress ratify his own views.

By Mr. Woodbridge: Q. I understood you to say that Mr. Lincoln, prior to his assassination, had inaugurated a policy intended to restore those governments? A. Yes, sir.

Q. You were present when the subject was before the cabinet? A. I was present, I think, twice before the assassination of Mr. Lincoln, when a plan was read.

Q. I want to know whether the plan adopted by Mr. Johnson was substantially the plan which had been inaugurated by Mr. Lincoln as the basis for his future action? A. Yes, sir, substantially. I do not know but that it was verbatim the same.

Q. I suppose the very paper of Mr. Lincoln was the one acted on? A. I should think so. I think that the very paper which I heard read twice while Mr. Lincoln was President was the one which was carried right through.

By Mr. Churchill: Q. What paper was that? A. The North Carolina proclamation.

By Mr. Boutwell: Q. You understood that Mr. Lincoln's plan was temporary, to be either confirmed or a new government set up by Congress? A. Yes; and I understood Mr. Johnson's to be so too.

By Mr. Williams: Q. Was there anything said on that subject, or was that your inference? A. That was my inference.

Q. You never heard the President say the plan was to be temporary? A. No; but I was satisfied that everybody looked on it as simply temporary until Congress met.

Q. You stated that the North Carolina proclamation was a continuation of the project submitted by Mr. Lincoln. I wish to inquire of you whether you ever compared them to ascertain whether they were the same or not? A. No, sir; I never compared them. I took them to be the very same papers. The papers were substantially the same, if not the very same.

RECALLED AND EXAMINED, JULY 20, 1867.

By Mr. Boutwell: Q. Do you recollect having an interview with the President in company with General Hillyer, on the return of General Hillyer from the South? A. Since my attention was called to it I do. I did not remember it when I gave my testimony the last day here.

Q. What is your recollection of what transpired and was said at that interview? A. My recollection is that General Hillyer called to explain to the President what he had seen in the South, and what he had heard of the views and opinions of the people there; and that what he had seen was an acquiescence on the part of the southern people, and favorable to peace, harmony, and good will. That was said in general terms, but the language I do not remember.

Q. Do you recollect whether, at that interview, there was any expression by the President as to any political policy? A. No, sir, I do not; I remember General Hillyer said something of having been invited to make a speech in New York, or some place, I do not remember where, and that he should do so, and send me a copy of his speech. I am very sure that he mentioned that in the presence of the President. What he said in that speech I do not remember now. but I presume the speech could be procured. I remember that General Hillyer gave the substance of what leading men said to him in the South. He particularly mentioned Judge Hale, of Alabama. He said that Judge Hale very candidly said that when they went into the rebellion they took their lives, property, &c., in their hands, and that when they were defeated, they should accept such conditions as the government chose to give; and that they claim now that what they did they did in good faith, and would not take it back again. Judge Hale claimed no right whatever after the failure of the rebellion, except such as was granted to them. That was the point he made. The conversation was made up considerably of instances of that sort. I recollect his mentioning meeting a special party in Mobile, and what occurred there.

RICHMOND, VIRGINIA, *June* 13, 1865.
LEE, GENERAL R. E.—For benefits, and full restoration of all rights and privileges extended to those included in amnesty proclamation of the President of 29th May, 1865.

HEADQ'RS ARMY OF THE UNITED STATES,
16th *June*, 1865.

Respectfully forwarded through the Secretary of War to the President, with earnest recommendation that the application of General Robert E. Lee for amnesty and pardon may be granted him.

The oath of allegiance, required by recent order of the President to accompany application, does not accompany this, for the reason, as I am informed by General Ord, the order requiring it had not reached Richmond when this was forwarded.                U. S. GRANT,
*Lieutenant General.*

—

RICHMOND, VA., *June* 13, 1865.
LEE, GENERAL ROBERT E.—Understanding that he and other officers are to be indicted by grand jury at Norfolk, Virginia, states his readiness to be brought to trial, but had supposed the terms of his surrender protected him; therefore prays, &c.

HEADQ'RS ARMIES OF THE UNITED STATES,
16th *June*, 1865.

In my opinion, the officers and men paroled at Appomattox Court House, and since, upon the same terms given to Lee, cannot be tried for treason so long as they observe the terms of their parole. This is my understanding. Good faith as well as true policy dictates that we should observe the conditions of that convention. But faith on the part of the government, or a construction of that convention subjecting officers to trial for treason, would produce a feeling of insecurity in the minds of all the paroled officers and men. If so disposed they might even regard such an infraction of terms by the government as an entire release from all obligations on their part.

I will state, further, that the terms granted by me met with the hearty approval of the President at the time, and of the people generally.

The action of Judge Underwood in Norfolk has had an injurious effect, and I would ask that he be ordered to quash all indictments found against paroled prisoners of war, and to desist from further prosecution of them.

U. S. GRANT, *Lieut. General.*

—

[Cipher.]
HEADQ'RS ARMIES OF THE UNITED STATES,
WASHINGTON, *May* 6, 1865—1 P. M.
Major General HALLECK,
*Richmond, Virginia.*

Since receipt of your despatch of 3d, I think it will be advisable to leave Hunter alone for the present.

Although it would meet with opposition in the North to allow Lee the benefit of amnesty, I think it would have the best possible effect towards restoring good feeling and peace in the South to have him come in. All the people except a few political leaders in the South will accept whatever he does as right, and will be guided to a great extent by his example.*

U. S. GRANT, *Lieut. General.*

WASHINGTON, D. C., *March* 12, 1866.
PICKETT, GENERAL GEORGE E.—Presents history of his case, refers to surrender and agreement of April 9, 1865, and asks for protection from prosecution for treason.

HEADQUARTERS ARMIES UNITED STATES,
*March* 16, 1866.

Respectfully forwarded to his excellency the President of the United States, with the recommendation that clemency be extended in this case, or assurance given that no trial will take place for the offence charged against George E. Pickett.

During the rebellion belligerent rights were acknowledged to the enemies of our country, and it is clear to me that the parole given by the armies, laying down their arms, protects them against punishment for acts lawful to any other belligerent. In this case, I know it is claimed that the men tried and convicted for crime of desertion were Union men from North Carolina who had found refuge within our lines and in our service. The punishment was a hard one, but it was in time of war, and upon the enemy; they no doubt felt it necessary to retain by some power the service of every man within their reach.

General Pickett I know, personally, to be an honorable man, but in this case his judgment prompted him to do what cannot well be sustained, though I do not see how good, either to the friends of the deceased, or by fixing an example for the future, can be secured by his trial now. It would only open up the question whether or not the government did not disregard its contract entered into to secure the surrender of an armed enemy.                U. S. GRANT,
*Lieutenant General.*

—

ST. LOUIS, MISSOURI, *March* 26, 1866.
BEALL, W. H. R.—Application for pardon.

HEADQUARTERS ARMIES UNITED STATES,
2d *April*, 1866.

Respectfully submitted to his excellency the President, through the honorable Secretary of War, and recommended.        U. S. GRANT,
*Lieutenant General.*

—

RECALLED AND EXAMINED, JULY 18, 1867.

By Mr. Thomas: Q. Did the President propose, at any time, to use the military power for the adjustment of the controversy in Baltimore between the police commissioners appointed by Governor Swann and those who claimed authority independent of Governor Swann? A. I understood that he wanted to use it, and I called his attention to the law on the subject, which changed his views and determination evidently. I called his attention to the only circumstances in which the military forces of the United States can be called out to interfere in State matters. It was his intention to send troops there to enable Governor Swann, as he termed it, to enforce his decision in the case of those police commissioners.

Q. Did the President, on account of your opinion, change that purpose? A. I made a communication to him on the subject, which led to the Attorney General giving an opinion as to the power to use the military forces of the

United States to interfere in State affairs; and that led to a change of what was intended to be done. After this whole question was settled as to sending the military there, there were six companies of new troops organized in New York harbor, which belonged to regiments south of here, and I ordered them to their regiments, and to stop at Fort McHenry on their way down, in order to keep them there until after the election, with a view to have a force there in case there was a bloody riot.

Q. Do I understand you to say that the President changed his purpose in that respect before the difficulty had been adjusted in Baltimore? A. Yes, sir.

Q. That was in accord with your opinion, endorsed by the Attorney General? A. Yes, sir.

By Mr. Williams: Q. Have you a copy of the letter addressed by you to the President? A. I have a copy of everything official except conversation.

(Witness was directed to furnish the official documents on the subject.)

By Mr. Thomas: Q. Did the President signify his wish concerning the army in writing or verbally? A. Verbally and in writing.

Q. Were you sent for formally? A. Yes, sir. I was sent for several times—twice, I think, while Governor Swann was there in consultation with the President. Finding that the President wanted to send the military to Baltimore, I objected to it.

Q. Are you distinct in your recollection as to when the President acquiesced in your views? A. It was prior to the election, two or three days. When the matter was left entirely with me, I ordered those troops down to join their regiments, and to halt at Fort McHenry until after the election.

Q. Was it before or after the arrest of the commissioners appointed by Governor Swann, that the President withdrew his request to you to use the army in that controversy? A. I cannot state precisely as to that. It was before I ordered the troops from New York. What took place was in conversation, until I found that there was rather a determination to send troops there, and then I communicated officially to the Secretary of War my objection to using troops in that way. That called out the opinion of the Attorney General, and it was then that what I proposed was acquiesced in. I thought this was in writing, but do not find the paper.

By Mr. Marshall: Q. The President seemed to think he had a right to send the army under the circumstances? A. Yes, sir; he seemed to think so.

Q. After you sent your written communication, giving your views in reference to it, the President then left the subject entirely in your hands? A. Yes, sir; he left it entirely in my hands. I think that is in writing.

(Witness was directed to furnish a copy of the communication.)

By Mr. Eldridge: Q. That was a formal withdrawal of his first opinion? A. Yes, sir. I think I was sent a copy of the Attorney General's opinion as a sort of order in the matter, virtually leaving it to me.

Q. After that time you did have the manage-

ment of it? A. Yes, sir. I sent General Canby to Baltimore, and went there twice myself, and had troops stop there on their way to the South.

Q. It was entirely within your control? A. Yes, sir.

By the Chairman: Q. They were solely for the purpose of being used in the case of a riot? A. Solely for that purpose.

By Mr. Marshall: Q. Merely as a police force? A. Yes, sir.

I desire to make the following explanation of my evidence: On examination of the record I find there is more matter, in writing, from the President than, from memory, I thought there was. Also, that I have either misplaced or never wrote objections which I made verbally to what was asked of the President by Governor Swann, of Maryland, in the way of services of United States troops, and which the President seemed desirous of giving. Governor Swann visited the President, to my knowledge, (how often I do not know,) before the trial of the Baltimore police commissioners, to get the promise of military aid in case he should remove them. During the trial, and before the promulgation of his findings, he also visited the President for the same purpose. At least once before the trial, and once during the progress of the trial of the police commissioners, I was sent for to meet Governor Swann at the Executive mansion. Much was said by me on those occasions, but, as before stated, I have confused, in my evidence, what was verbal with what was written.

(The documents following are on pages 37, 38.)

## General Grant on the Removal of General Sheridan and Secretary Stanton.

### 1.—PRESIDENT JOHNSON TO GENERAL GRANT.

EXECUTIVE MANSION,
WASHINGTON, D. C., *August* 17, 1867.

DEAR SIR: Before you issue instructions to carry into effect the enclosed order I would be pleased to hear any suggestions you may deem necessary respecting the assignments to which the order refers.     Truly, yours,
ANDREW JOHNSON.

General U. S. GRANT,
*Secretary of War ad interim.*

### 2.—THE PRESIDENT'S ORDER.

EXECUTIVE MANSION,
WASHINGTON, D. C., *August* 17, 1867.

Major General Geo. H. Thomas is hereby assigned to the command of the fifth military district, created by the act of Congress passed on the 2d day of March, 1867.

Major General P. H. Sheridan is hereby assigned to the command of the department of the Missouri.

Major General Winfield S. Hancock is hereby assigned to the command of the department of the Cumberland.

The Secretary of War *ad interim* will give the necessary instructions to carry this order into effect.     ANDREW JOHNSON.

### 3.—GENERAL GRANT TO PRESIDENT JOHNSON.

HEADQ'RS ARMIES OF THE UNITED STATES,
WASHINGTON, D. C., *August* 17, 1867.

SIR: I am in receipt of your order of this

date, directing the assignment of General G. H. Thomas to the command of the fifth military district, General Sheridan to the department of the Missouri, and General Hancock to the department of the Cumberland; also of your note of this date, (enclosing these instructions,) saying: " Before you issue instructions to carry into effect the enclosed order, I would be pleased to hear any suggestions you may deem necessary respecting the assignments to which the order refers."

I am pleased to avail myself of this invitation to urge, earnestly urge, urge in the name of a patriotic people who have sacrificed hundreds of thousands of loyal lives, and thousands of millions of treasure to preserve the integrity and union of this country, that this order be not insisted on. It is unmistakably the expressed wish of the country that General Sheridan should not be removed from his present command.

This is a republic where the will of the people is the law of the land. I beg that their voice may be heard.

General Sheridan has performed his civil duties faithfully and intelligently. His removal will only be regarded as an effort to defeat the laws of Congress. It will be interpreted by the unreconstructed element in the South, those who did all they could to break up this government by arms, and now wish to be the only element consulted as to the method of restoring order, as a triumph. It will embolden them to renewed opposition to the will of the loyal masses, believing that they have the Executive with them.

The services of General Thomas in battling for the Union entitle him to some consideration. He has repeatedly entered his protest against being assigned to either oft he five military districts, and especially to being assigned to relieve General Sheridan.

There are military reasons, pecuniary reasons, and above all patriotic reasons, why this should not be insisted upon.

I beg to refer to a letter marked "private" which I wrote to the President, when first consulted on the subject of the change in the War Department. It bears upon the subject of this removal, and I had hoped would have prevented it.*

I have the honor to be, with great respect, your obedient servant,       U. S. GRANT,
General U. S. A., Secretary of War ad interim.
His Excellency A. JOHNSON,
    President of the United States.

_____

[*Private.]
HEADQ'RS ARMIES OF THE UNITED STATES,
    WASHINGTON, D. C., August 1, 1867.

SIR: I take the liberty of addressing you privately on the subject of the conversation we had this morning, feeling, as I do, the great danger to the welfare of the country should you carry out the designs then expressed.

First. On the subject of the displacement of the Secretary of War. His removal cannot be effected against his will without the consent of the Senate. It is but a short time since the United States Senate was in session, and why not then have asked for his removal if it was

5.—GENERAL GRANT TO PRESIDENT JOHNSON

OFFICE U. S. MIL. TEL., WAR DEPARTMENT,
    WASHINGTON, D. C., August 21, 1867.
To General U. S. GRANT.

General Thomas is absent in West Virginia, and has probably not yet seen his orders. He has been under medical treatment this summer for an affection of his liver, and it would be a great risk for him to go South at this time.
ALEXANDER B. HASSON,
    Surgeon U. S. A. and Med. Director,
        Department of the Cumberland.

Respectfully forwarded to the President for his information, and recommending a suspension of the order making change in military commanders.       U. S. GRANT, General.

_____

desired? It certainly was the intention of the legislative branch of government to place cabinet ministers beyond the power of executive removal, and it is pretty well understood that, so far as cabinet ministers are affected by the " tenure-of-office bill," it was intended specially to protect the Secretary of War, whom the country felt great confidence in. The meaning of the law may be explained away by an astute lawyer, but common sense and the views of loyal people will give to it the effect intended by its framers.

On the subject of the removal of the very able commander of the fifth military district, let me ask you to consider the effect it would have upon the public. He is universally and deservedly beloved by the people who sustained this government through its trials, and feared by those who would still be enemies of the government. It fell to the lot of but few men to do as much against an armed enemy as General Sheridan did during the rebellion, and it is within the scope of the ability of but few in this or other country to do what he has. His civil administration has given equal satisfaction. He has had difficulties to contend with which no other district commander has encountered. Almost if not quite from the day he was appointed district commander to the present time, the press has given out that he was to be removed; that the administration was dissatisfied with him, &c. This has emboldened the opponents to the laws of Congress within his command to oppose him in every way in their power, and has rendered necessary measures which otherwise may never have been necessary. In conclusion, allow me to say, as a friend desiring peace and quiet, the welfare of the whole country North and South, that it is in my opinion more than the loyal people of this country (I mean those who supported the government during the great rebellion) will quietly submit to, to see the very men of all others whom they have expressed confidence in removed.

I would not have taken the liberty of addressing the Executive of the United States thus but for the conversation on the subject alluded to in this letter, and from a sense of duty, feeling that I know I am right in this matter.

With great respect, your obedient servant,
    U. S. GRANT, General.
His Excellency A. JOHNSON,
    President of the United States.

**6.—PRESIDENT JOHNSON'S MODIFICATION OF THE ORDER.**

HEADQ'RS ARMIES OF THE UNITED STATES,
*August 22, 1867.*

In view of the precarious condition of General Thomas's health, as represented in the within despatch of Surgeon Hasson, General Thomas will, until further orders, remain in command of the department of the Cumberland.

AUGUST 23, 1867. _____ ANDREW JOHNSON.

**7.—GENERAL GRANT TO GENERAL SHERIDAN.**

[By Telegraph, in cipher.]

HEADQ'RS ARMIES OF THE UNITED STATES,
WASHINGTON, D. C., *August 24, 1867.*

General Thomas's orders to relieve you are suspended for the present. Orders will be sent by mail. Relax nothing in consequence of probable change of commands.

U. S. GRANT, *General.*

Maj. Gen. P. H. SHERIDAN,
*New Orleans, Louisiana.*

**8.—PRESIDENT JOHNSON'S SECOND MODIFICATION OF THE ORDER.**

EXECUTIVE MANSION,
WASHINGTON, D. C., *August 26, 1867.*

SIR: In consequence of the unfavorable condition of the health of Major General George H. Thomas, as reported to you in Surgeon Hasson's despatch of the 21st instant, my order dated August 17, 1867, is hereby modified so as to assign Major General Winfield S. Hancock to the command of the fifth military district, created by the act of Congress passed March 2, 1867, and of the military department comprising the States of Louisiana and Texas. On being relieved from the command of the department of the Missouri by Major General P. H. Sheridan, Major General Hancock will proceed directly to New Orleans, Louisiana, and assuming the command to which he is hereby assigned, will, when necessary to a faithful execution of the laws, exercise any and all powers conferred by acts of Congress upon district commanders, and any and all authority pertaining to officers in command of military depart-ments.

Major General P. H. Sheridan will at once turn over his present command to the officer next in rank to himself, and proceeding without delay to Fort Leavenworth, Kansas, will relieve Major General Hancock of the command of the department of the Missouri.

Major General George H. Thomas will, until further orders, remain in command of the department of the Cumberland.

Very respectfully, yours,    ANDREW JOHNSON
General U. S. GRANT,
*Secretary of War ad interim.*

**General Grant's Orders and Telegrams to Military Commanders in the Unreconstructed States.**

**1.—GENERAL GRANT TO GENERAL FOSTER, RESPECTING GENERAL ORDER 44.***

HEADQ'RS ARMIES OF THE UNITED STATES,
WASHINGTON, D. C., *August 7, 1866.*

Major General J. G. FOSTER, *Tullahoma, Fla.*

General Order No. 44* is not intended to

----

* See page 122 of Manual of 1866.

apply to offences committed prior to the close of hostilities. As a rule, no arrests should be made under it except where the civil authorities refuse to make them. Release all prisoners you may now have whose offences were committed previous to May, 1865.

U. S. GRANT, *General.*

**2.—GENERAL GRANT TO GENERAL SHERIDAN.**

HEADQ'RS ARMIES OF THE UNITED STATES,
WASHINGTON, D. C., *August 18, 1866.*

Major General SHERIDAN,
*New Orleans, Louisiana.*

Instructions to General Foster given some months ago prevent citizens of Florida appealing to other than the United States courts for recovery of property sold for taxes. Those instructions will be now annulled, and purchasers will look to civil courts and the civil-rights bill for protection.    U. S. GRANT, *General.*

**3.—GENERAL GRANT TO SECRETARY STANTON.**

HEADQ'RS ARMIES OF THE UNITED STATES,
WASHINGTON, *November 22, 1866.*

Hon. E. M. STANTON, *Secretary of War.*

Enclosed please find copy of a communication addressed to Major General Sheridan, under date of October 17, 1866, giving my construction of the President's proclamations upon certain military orders. The construction is the same that I understood you to entertain at the time. The orders referred to have not yet been revoked, nor has any construction of the effect of the President's proclamation upon these orders been officially announced to any but General Sheridan's command.

I would therefore submit whether my construction of the proclamation as above stated is correct, so that we may have a uniformity of action upon this matter throughout the different commands.

It is evident to my mind that the provisions of the civil-rights bill cannot be properly enforced without the aid of Order No. 44, or a similar one. Even in the State of Kentucky, General Jeff. C. Davis states that he cannot enforce it without the aid of this order.

U. S. GRANT, *General.*

To the foregoing communication no answer was ever received; but in answer to a Senate resolution, dated January 8, 1867, asking for information in relation to violations of the act entitled "An act to protect all persons in the United States in their civil rights and furnish the means of their vindication," and what steps had been taken to enforce the same, the President with his message of February 19, 1867, submitted, among other papers, Order No. 44, which led me to suppose that he regarded it as still in force. At this time Congress was discussing and maturing plans of legislation for the maintenance and enforcement of law and order in the States lately in rebellion. I therefore deemed it unnecessary to take further action in the premises, but await the result of congressional action.

The preceding correspondence and orders show briefly and generally the condition of the fifth military district (Florida, Texas, and Louisiana) prior to the passage of the military reconstruction bill. As the basis in part of this correspondence, and exhibiting more in detail the condition of affairs in different localities, the reports of subordinate commanders, so far as they are on file in this office, are also herewith submitted. All of these reports have reached here through the regular military channel.

### 4.—GENERAL GRANT TO GENERAL SHERIDAN.

HEADQ'RS ARMIES OF THE UNITED STATES,
WASHINGTON, D. C., *October* 17, 1866.
SIR: Referring to your endorsement upon communications of General J. G. Foster, commanding district of Florida, of date September 18 and 20, relative to the effect of the President's proclamation, &c., I am directed by the general-in-chief to enclose you a copy of the same, and to say that he construes the proclamation as nullifying General Order No. 3,* War Department, Adjutant's General's office, January 12, and General Order No. 44,† headquarters of the army, July 6, 1866.‡

I have the honor to be, very respectfully, your obedient servant,　　GEO. K. LEET, *A. A. G.*
Major General P. H. SHERIDAN,
*Commanding Depart. of the Gulf.*

### 5.—GENERAL GRANT TO GENERAL SHERIDAN.

HEADQ'RS ARMIES OF THE UNITED STATES,
WASHINGTON, *November* 1, 1866.
You will instruct General Foster to refrain from interference with the execution of civil law in Florida, when the laws of the State are not in conflict with laws of the United States. It is alleged that orders given by Colonel Sprague to officers in Fernandina practically prevent the execution of civil law. The duty of the military is to encourage the enforcement of the civil law and order to the fullest extent.
By command of General Grant.
　　　　　　　　　GEO. K. LEET, *A. A. G.*
General SHERIDAN,
*Commanding Depart. of the Gulf.*

---

\* See page 124 of Manual of 1866.
† See page 122 of Manual of 1866.
‡ General Foster's report is as follows, with General Sheridan's indorsement:

HEADQUARTERS DISTRICT OF FLORIDA,
ASSIST. ADJ. GENERAL'S OFFICE,
TALLAHASSEE, FLA., *September* 20, 1866.
GENERAL: I have the honor to make the following semi-monthly report of the condition of affairs in this district:

The state of feeling toward the government and Union and northern men has not improved since my last report, and there have been indications that the old bitter feeling engendered by the war still rankles in the hearts of many of the old secessionists, and that it will find vent in words and actions as soon as a favorable opportunity offers.

In this town, the intendant, assuming that the proclamation of the President, of August 20, fully restored the supremacy of the civil law over the military, essayed to arrest soldiers and employés of the United States, while in the performance of their duties, for trifling infractions of the municipal ordinance. I was obliged to order him peremptorily to desist. To allow he

### 6.—GENERAL GRANT TO GENERAL SHERIDAN.

HEADQ'RS ARMIES OF THE UNITED STATES,
WASHINGTON, D. C., *Sept.* 21, 1866.
Major General SHERIDAN, *New Orleans, La.*
Despatches of 20th received. Your course in regard to riot in Brenham, Texas, right, only I think troops to defend themselves should be sent there without delay. If arms are used against peaceable soldiers, disarm citizens.
　　　　　　　　　U. S. GRANT, *General.*

### 7.—GENERAL GRANT TO GENERAL SHERIDAN.

HEADQ'RS ARMIES OF THE UNITED STATES,
WASHINGTON, D. C., *October* 8, 1866.
Major General SHERIDAN, *New Orleans, La.*
Your despatch of 3d instant just received. Your views about not authorizing volunteers to be raised in Texas, ostensibly to put down Indian hostilities, are sustained. With the military at your command, as full protection can be given to the people of Texas as to any other exposed settlements. You may so instruct Governor Throckmorton.　U. S. GRANT, *General.*

### 8.—GENERAL GRANT TO GENERAL SHERIDAN.

HEADQ'RS ARMIES OF THE UNITED STATES,
WASHINGTON, D. C., *October* 11, 1866.
Major General SHERIDAN,
　　*Com'g Depart. of the Gulf, New Orleans.*
Despatches from the Governor of Texas to the President, and newspaper extracts, show Indian

---

State or municipal authorities the power of arresting and trying our officers and soldiers will be to give into the hands of our late enemies the power of retaliation for past injuries and present dislikes. I therefore hope that the supremacy of the military in all matters of conflict between the United States and municipal authorities, and in all actions under express laws of Congress, may be preserved.

I have some trouble in carrying out the provisions of the "homestead law;" in some localities combinations have been formed to resist the settlement of the negroes, and to drive them off. The freedmen are doing well.

I have the honor to be, very respectfully, your obedient servant,　　　　J. G. FOSTER,
　　　　　　*Bvt. Maj. Gen. U. S. Army,*
　　　　　　　　　*Commanding District.*
Bvt. Maj. Gen. GEO. L. HARTSUFF, *A. A. G.*,
　　　　　　*Depart. of the Gulf, N. O., La.*

---

[Endorsement.]
HEADQUARTERS DEPARTMENT OF THE GULF,
NEW ORLEANS, LA., *October* 6, 1866.
Respectfully forwarded for the information of the general-in-chief.

There has been increased indolence on the part of the functionaries of the civil law in Florida and Texas, growing out of the proclamation of the President.

In Louisiana it has not been so, as the proclamation has never been officially promulgated, and as General Orders Nos. 3 and 44, from headquarters of the army, have not been rescinded, I have gone on in Louisiana as though no proclamation had been issued.　P. H. SHERIDAN,
　　　　　　　*Maj. Gen. U. S. Army.*

hostilities to exist on the frontier of that State to an extent requiring immediate attention. Your despatches on the same subject have been received and shown to the President. Please report again the latest information you have on the subject, and in the meantime give such protection as you can with the means at hand. If it is necessary to break up any interior posts, take such as you think may be best spared.

U. S. GRANT, *General.*

---

#### 9.—GENERAL GRANT TO GENERAL SHERIDAN.

HEADQ'RS ARMIES OF THE UNITED STATES, WASHINGTON, D. C., *October* 12, 1866.

GENERAL: My despatch of yesterday was sent to you on receipt of the enclosed, which is forwarded for your information. Great care will have to be observed to see that no just cause of complaint can be urged against the army for not giving proper protection to the citizens of Texas against Indian hostilities; at the same time it is equally important that loyal and law-abiding citizens should have protection against the violently disposed in their midst. I am satisfied that you have done and are doing the very best that can be done. Your attention, however, is called to the enclosed, that you may know the apprehensions and desire of the President, and cause such inspection as will enable you to report satisfactorily on the points that give him uneasiness.

Very respectfully, your obedient servant, U. S. GRANT, *General.*

Major General P. H. SHERIDAN, *Com'g Depart. of the Gulf, New Orleans, La.*

---

#### 10.—GENERAL SHERIDAN TO GENERAL GRANT.

HEADQ'RS DEPARTMENT OF THE GULF, NEW ORLEANS, LA., *October* 12, 1866.

GENERAL: I have the honor to acknowledge the receipt of your despatch of the 11th.

I have no additional news regarding hostility on the Texas frontier, and still believe that there is a great deal of buncombe in the reports.

I have a company of cavalry stationed within a few miles of where the alleged massacre took place, and have no reports from it, and doubt whether it really occurred.

I will, however, send additional troops to the frontier without delay, and hope that the nine (9) companies of the seventeenth infantry, which are now in the north, will be sent to me at once.

I have notified the Governor of Texas that I would send an inspector to the frontier, and that I would render such protection as the forces within my control would permit of, and would establish posts in the early spring.

I do not doubt but that the secret of all this fuss about Indian troubles is the desire to have all the troops removed from the interior, and the desire of the loose and lazy adventurers to be employed as volunteers against the Indians under the acts of the State Legislature.

P. H. SHERIDAN, *Major General U. S. Army.*

General U. S. GRANT, *Com'ng Armies of the U. S., Washington, D. C.*

---

#### 11.—GENERAL GRANT TO SECRETARY OF WAR.

OCTOBER 13, 1866.

Respectfully referred to the Secretary of War for information. More troops will be sent to General Sheridan immediately—if, indeed, some are not already on the way—which will enable him to give all the protection that troops can give against Indian hostilities. Occasional murders will take place on our frontiers, and would if our people were all soldiers.

U. S. GRANT, *General.*

---

#### 12.—GENERAL GRANT TO GOV. THROCKMORTON.

HEADQ'RS ARMIES OF THE UNITED STATES, WASHINGTON, D C., *October* 20, 1866.

SIR: I have the honor to acknowledge the receipt of your communication of 5th instant, urging upon the general government the acceptance of a regiment of volunteers from the State of Texas, to be used in defending the frontier of that State against the incursions of hostile Indians, &c. In reply thereto I would state that General Sheridan has already sent as large a force to the portion of the frontier of Texas infested by Indians as probably can be supplied with forage and provisions during the coming winter. If a large force should still prove necessary, there are enough United States troops on their way or under orders to report to General Sheridan to supply the deficiency. It is deemed, therefore, unadvisable to accept the service of volunteers, whose pay and maintenance would have to be provided for hereafter by a special appropriation of Congress.

Very respectfully, your obedient servant, U. S. GRANT, *General.*

His Excellency J. W. THROCKMORTON, *Governor State of Texas, Austin, Texas.*

---

#### 13.—GENERAL GRANT TO GENERAL SHERIDAN.

HEADQ'RS ARMIES OF THE UNITED STATES, WASHINGTON, D. C., *August* 3, 1866.

Major General SHERIDAN, *New Orleans, Louisiana:*

Continue to enforce martial law so far as may be necessary to preserve the peace, and do not allow any of the civil authorities to act if you deem such action dangerous to the public safety. Lose no time in investigating and reporting the causes that led to the riot and the facts which occurred.

U. S. GRANT, *General.*

---

#### 14.—GENERAL GRANT TO GENERAL POPE.

WASHINGTON, D. C., *April* 21, 1867.

MY DEAR GENERAL: Having read Governor Jenkins's address to the citizens of Georgia, I was on the eve of writing you a letter advising his suspension and trial before a military commission, when your despatch announcing that the Governor had given such assurances as to render your order, in his case, unnecessary, was received. I am now in receipt of the order itself, and your accompanying letter, and have just prepared the enclosed endorsement to go with it.

My views are that district commanders are responsible for the faithful execution of the reconstruction act of Congress, and that in civil matters I cannot give them an order. I can give them my views, however, for what they are worth. * * * *

I presume the Attorney General will give a written opinion on the subject of the power of district commanders to remove civil officers and appoint their successors. When he does, I will forward it to all the district commanders.

It is very plain that the power of district commanders to try offenders by military commissions exists. I would advise that commissions be resorted to, rather than arbitrary removals, until an opinion is had from the Attorney General, or it is found that he does not intend to give one. * * * *

Yours, truly, U. S. GRANT, *General.*
Brevet Major General J. POPE,
　　*Commanding Third District.*

### 15.—GENERAL GRANT TO GENERAL POPE.

ATLANTA, GA, *April* —, 1867.

General John Pope, commanding third military district, submits copy of special order which he intends issuing so soon as he ascertains whether Governor Charles J. Jenkins, at the time he issued his address, was aware of his (General P.'s) Order No. 1.*

---

[Endorsement.]
HEADQ'RS ARMIES OF THE UNITED STATES,
　　*April* —, 1867.

Respectfully forwarded to the Secretary of War for his information. The telegraphic despatch herein enclosed shows that Governor Jenkins, of Georgia, has given such pledges to the commander of the third district as to induce him to withhold for the present his order suspending the governor. The conduct of the governor (Jenkins) demonstrates, however, how possible it is for a discontented civil officer of the unreconstructed States to defeat the laws of Congress if the power does not exist with district commanders to suspend their function for cause in some way. It seems clear to me that the power is given, in the bill "for the more efficient government of the rebel States," to use or not, at the pleasure of district commanders, the provisional machinery set up without the authority of Congress in the States to which the reconstruction acts applies. There being doubt, however, on this point, I would respectfully ask an early opinion on the subject.

If the power of removal does not exist with district commanders, then it will become necessary for them to take refuge under that section of the bill which authorizes military commissions. U. S. GRANT, *General.*

### 16.—GENERAL GRANT TO GENERAL POPE.

HEADQ'RS ARMY OF THE UNITED STATES,
　　WASHINGTON D. C. *May* 22, 1867.

The following is sent to district commanders for their guidance:

WAR DEPARTMENT,
WASHINGTON CITY, D. C., *May* 18, 1867.

GENERAL: Recent occurrences in some of the military districts indicate a necessity of great vigilance on the part of military commanders to be prepared for the prevention and prompt suppression of riots and breaches of the public peace, especially in towns and cities, and that they should have their forces in hand and so posted, on all occasions when disturbances may be apprehended, as to promptly check, and, if possible, to prevent outbreaks and violence endangering public or individual safety.

You will please, therefore, call the attention of the commanders of military districts to this subject, and issue such precautionary orders as may be found necessary for the purpose indicated. Yours truly, EDWIN M. STANTON,
　　　　　　　　　　　　*Secretary of War.*
General U. S. GRANT,
　　*Commanding Armies United States.*

The above conveys all the instructions deemed necessary, and will be acted upon by district commanders, making special reports of the precautionary orders issued by them to prevent a recurrence of mobs or other unlawful violence.

By command of General Grant.
GEO. K. LEET,
　　*Assistant Adjutant General.*
Brevet Major General JOHN POPE,
　　*Commanding Third Military District.*

### 17.—GENERAL POPE TO GENERAL GRANT.

General U. S. GRANT,
　　*Commanding Armies United States.*

Day before yesterday I received a copy of the opinion of the Attorney General on registration, sent me for my information, through the Assistant Adjutant General, by order of the President.

Ten days ago I had made, and published, instructions to registers, which will have to be dropped if the Attorney General's opinion is enforced. The opinion sent by the President's order does not seem to be an order to me on the subject; but, as there may be room for doubt, I ask that I be informed by telegraph whether or not I am ordered by the President to conform my action to the Attorney General's opinion. I stand ready to obey the President's orders on the subject, but I wrote you fully on the subject yesterday, the probable result of enforcing the Attorney General's opinion in this district; enclosing also copies of my orders and instructions about registration. JNO POPE,
　　*Major General Commanding.*

### 18.—GENERAL GRANT TO GENERAL POPE.

WASHINGTON, *June* 28, 1867.
Major General J. POPE, *Atlanta, Georgia.*

Your despatch of yesterday received. Enforce your own construction of the military bill, until ordered to do otherwise. The opinion of the Attorney General has not been distributed to district commanders in language or manner entitling it to the force of an order; nor can I suppose that the President intended it to have such force. U. S. GRANT, *General.*

### 19.—GENERAL GRANT TO GENERAL ORD.

WASHINGTON, *June* 23, 1867.
Brevet Major General E. O. C. ORD,
　　*Commanding the Fourth District.*

GENERAL: A copy of your final instructions to boards of registration of June 10, 1867, is

---

* For order, see page 78 of Manual of 1867, or page 204 of the combined Manual.

just received. I entirely dissent from the views contained in paragraph four. Your view as to the duty of registrars to register every man who will take the required oath, though they may know the applicant perjures himself, is sustained by the views of the Attorney General. My opinion is, that it is the duty of the board of registration to see, so far as it lies in their power, that no unauthorized person is allowed to register. To secure this end, registrars should be allowed to administer oaths and examine witnesses. The law, however, makes district commanders their own interpreters of their power and duty under it, and, in my opinion, the Attorney General or myself can do no more than give our opinion as to the meaning of the law; neither can enforce his views against the judgment of those made responsible for the faithful execution of the law, the district commanders.

Very respectfully, your obedient servant,
U. S. GRANT, *General.*

### 20.—GENERAL GRANT TO GENERAL POPE.

HEADQ'RS ARMY OF THE UNITED STATES,
WASHINGTON, D. C., *August* 3, 1867.

DEAR GENERAL: Your official letter on the subject of reconstruction in the third district, and your private letter accompanying it, are received, and I have read both with care. I think your views are sound, both in the construction which you give to the laws of Congress and the duties of the supporters of good government, to see that, when reconstruction is effected, no loop-hole is left open to give trouble and embarrassment hereafter. It is certainly the duty of district commanders to study what the framers of the reconstruction laws wanted to express, as much as what they do express, and to execute the law according to that interpretation. This, I believe, they have generally done, and, so far, have the approval of all who approve the congressional plan of reconstruction.

\*　　\*　　\*　　\*

Very truly, yours,
U. S. GRANT, *General.*
Brevet Major General JNO. POPE,
*Commanding Third Mil. Dist., Atlanta, Ga.*

### 21.—GENERAL POPE TO GENERAL GRANT.

General U. S. GRANT, *Commanding Armies.*

Shall I publish the order requiring jurors in this district to take the test-oath as by your instructions, or on my own authority? I had just made an order, but, fortunately, not distributed it, to require jurors to be drawn from the list of registered voters.

JOHN POPE, *Major General.*

### 22.—GENERAL GRANT TO GENERAL POPE.

WASHINGTON, *August* 14, 1867.
Brevet Major General J. POPE,
*Atlanta, Georgia.*

Publish the jury order which you had prepared. The only object in distributing General Griffin's order was to secure a jury system which will give protection to all classes.

U. S. GRANT, *General.*

### 23.—GENERAL GRANT TO PRESIDENT JOHNSON.

WASHINGTON, D. C., *October*, 1867.

Andrew Johnson, President of the United States, refers letter of Hon. Charles J. Jenkins, of Georgia, dated October 18, 1867, relative to apportionment of delegates to counties, instead of senatorial districts, in State of Georgia.

[Endorsement.]
HEADQUARTERS UNITED STATES ARMY,
*October* 24, 1867.

Respectfully returned to the President of the United States. It seems to me it would have been better to have apportioned delegates to counties instead of senatorial districts in the State of Georgia, but in view of the nearness of the election in that State, (on the 29th inst.,) I do not see how the matter can be corrected now. I have, however, sent the following despatch to General Pope:

WASHINGTON, D. C., *October* 24, 1867.
Major General JOHN POPE, *Atlanta, Georgia.*

Should not delegates to convention in Georgia be chosen by counties instead of by senatorial districts, to comply fully with the law? Could not a change be made in your election order in time for election in that State?

U. S. GRANT, *General.*

### 24.—GENERAL POPE TO GENERAL GRANT.

ATLANTA, GEORGIA, *October* 25, 1867.
General U. S. GRANT:

If you will examine the returns of registration sent you for Georgia, you will see that the apportionments cannot be made by counties without giving very unequal representation. The counties are small and numerous, and in many cases two or three would have to be united to make voters enough for one delegate. Please try and make the apportionment by counties, and you will see that it is not practicable. I tried it for two days. The districts are precisely as they were established by State laws, and on examination you will find that the apportionment is based precisely on voters, and is in all respects the fairest that could be made on the basis of registered voters. It is too late now to change, and certainly no man in Georgia can complain because I have taken the districts established by State laws. I wrote you fully on the subject day before yesterday. My purpose was to make as little change as possible in local divisions in the State known and recognized by State laws. You will receive my letter to-morrow. I send to-day a map of Georgia, with number of registered voters for each county written on face of county. Please see if it be possible to make fairer apportionment than we have done.

JOHN POPE,
*Bvt. Major General.*

### 25.—GENERAL GRANT TO GENERAL POPE.

HEADQ'RS ARMY OF THE UNITED STATES,
WASHINGTON, D. C., *October* 30, 1867.

GENERAL: Your reply to my letter suggesting a revocation of your order suspending State aid to the Georgia University, or rather your reply to B. H. Hill (and others') application for such revocation, is received. I am abundantly satisfied myself with your explanation and hope no more will be heard about it. But your reply which I real to the President and cabinet, was sent for last evening, and may result in some letter, suggestion, or opinion.

In your letter you say that the subject of the Georgia University controversy will be submitted to the convention. I would advise that you submit nothing to it officially except the laws of Congress authorizing the convention and defining its duties. A convention is a sort of original body to enact laws, or rather to frame restrictions and to establish powers within which legislative bodies may act. Under such circumstances, it would seem out of place for any authority to submit questions to such conventions as are now being elected in the military districts.

Yours, truly, U. S. GRANT, *General.*

Bvt. Maj. Gen. JOHN POPE,
　　　*Com. Third Mil. Dist.*

#### 26.—GENERAL GRANT TO GENERAL POPE.

WASHINGTON, *December* 23, 1867.
Bvt. Maj. Gen. JOHN POPE, *Atlanta, Ga.*

The constitutions adopted by the conventions now in session are not the law of the States until submitted to the people and ratified by them. I do not see, therefore, how you can enforce laws enacted by them until so ratified.
　　　　　U. S. GRANT, *General.*

#### 27.—GENERAL GRANT TO GENERAL POPE.

ATLANTA, GEORGIA, *December* 27, 1867.
General John Pope, commanding third district, relative to refusal of State treasurer, John Jones, of Georgia, to pay the members of convention in Georgia.

[Endorsement.]
HEADQ'RS OF THE ARMY UNITED STATES,
　　　　　*January* 6, 1868.

Respectfully returned. The convention is authorized by act of Congress passed March 23, 1867, supplementary to an act entitled "An act to provide for the more efficient government of the rebel States," of March 2, 1867, to levy upon and collect a sufficient amount of taxes on the property of the State as was necessary to pay the expenses of the same. The ordinance passed by the convention for the purpose, and the order of the military commander to the State treasurer endorsed thereon, is in conformity to the letter and spirit of said acts and the acts supplementary thereto, of July 19, 1867. The government, under the constitution of the State of Georgia, adopted in 1865, which said treasurer sets up as a bar to his compliance with said ordinance, is by the said acts of Congress specifically declared, with the governments of other States lately in rebellion, therein named, to be "not legal State governments; and that thereafter, said governments, if continued, were to be continued subject in all respects to the military commanders of the respective districts and the paramount authority of Congress."

Section 11 of said supplementary act of July 19, provides: "That all the provisions of this act and of the acts to which this is supplementary shall be construed liberally, to the end that all the interests thereof may be fully and perfectly carried out."

It is clear, from the correspondence between General Pope and the treasurer, that the proper administration of the military reconstruction acts requires the removal of said treasurer, and the appointment of some person in his stead, under section 2 of said supplementary act of July 19, who will respect the authority of Congress, the orders of military commanders, and the ordinance of the convention under the same.

Should the comptroller general of the State, as General Pope seems to fear he may, decline to execute the ordinance of the convention, then he, too, should be removed. U. S. GRANT,
　　　　　　　　　　　　　*General.*

#### 28.—GENERAL MEADE TO GENERAL GRANT.

General U. S. GRANT.

The passage of ordinances by the convention of Alabama and Georgia enacting stay-laws is producing great suffering in these States, by causing expedition to be made in making levies, in anticipation of these ordinances having the force of law.

Advantage is being taken of the interval of time before these ordinances are laws to hurry levies and executions, thus causing these ordinances, intended as measures of relief, to become in reality the means of increasing and greatly aggravating the burden of the people. I am, therefore, inclined to adopt these ordinances as the act of the military authority, and declare them to have force until the question is settled as to the adoption or rejection of the constitution enacting them. I refer to you, because your telegram of December 23 is adverse to enforcing any of the ordinances of the convention prior to the adoption of the constitution, and to obtain your approval of my proposed action.

Please answer immediately.
　　　　　G. G. MEADE, *Major General.*

#### 29.—GENERAL GRANT TO GENERAL MEADE.

WASHINGTON, *January* 10, 1868.
Major General G. G. MEADE, *Atlanta, Georgia.*

As district commander, I think you will be perfectly justifiable in adopting as your own order the stay-laws proposed in the constitutions to be submitted to the people of Alabama and Georgia. This course is different from adopting as law the provisions of the constitutions in advance of their ratification.

　　　　　　　U. S. GRANT, *General.*

#### 30.—GENERAL MEADE TO GENERAL GRANT.

General U. S. GRANT.

I have had a conference with Governor Jenkins, and exerted all my influence to induce him to consider the appropriation by the convention as an appropriation made by law and not inconsistent with the provisions of the Georgia constitution, and urged him to sign the warrant required by the treasury. The governor declined, and there is no other alternative but the exercise of my power to obtain control of the State treasury. To avoid making any more changes than are required to effect the object, and also the difficulty of finding a suitable person, and the question of bonds, I propose to remove only the treasurer, and to assign to the duty Brevet Brigadier General Ruger, with instructions to continue payments as heretofore, in accordance with the existing laws of the

State, and to make such payments to the convention as I shall authorize, checking thus unnecessary expenditures. I see no other mode of supplying the wants of the convention, and the continuance in session is dependent upon its wants being immediately supplied. It is probable other steps may have to be taken before the money can be secured, as it is intimated that an issue will be made with the view of testing the invalidity of my power.

Your approval or disapproval is asked at once.

GEO. G. MEADE, *Major General.*

#### 31.—GENERAL GRANT TO GENERAL MEADE.

WASHINGTON, *January* 10, 1868.

Major General G. G. MEADE, *Atlanta, Ga.*

Plan proposed in your despatch of last evening to remove State treasurer of Georgia is approved.                                        U. S. GRANT, *General.*

#### 32.—GENERAL GRANT TO GENERAL MEADE.

WASHINGTON, *January* 13, 1868.

Major General G. G. MEADE, *Atlanta, Ga.*

I would not advise interference with elections ordered by the Alabama convention, unless very satisfactory reasons exist for doing so.

U. S. GRANT, *General.*

#### 33.—GENERAL GRANT TO GENERAL MEADE.

WASHINGTON, *January* 13, 1868.

Major General G. G. MEADE, *Atlanta, Ga.*

You will perceive by the reconstruction acts that " conventions are to frame constitutions and civil governments for their respective States," which clearly implies authority to order the election of officers thereunder, and in fixing the day of election Alabama has only followed a well-established precedent. The governments elected cannot assume authority, except under orders from the district commander or after action of Congress upon their constitution.

U. S. GRANT, *General.*

#### 34.—GENERAL GRANT TO GENERAL MEADE.

WASHINGTON, *January* 17, 1868.

Major General G. G. MEADE, *Atlanta, Ga.*

Congress unquestionably can determine upon the questions presented by the governor of Florida, whatever may be the authority of district commanders over such cases. General Pope having practically settled the matter complained of by his action before you assumed command of the third district, it is deemed judicious not to interfere with the meeting of the convention at the time ordered by him, but leave the whole matter to Congress in its final action.                                        U. S. GRANT, *General.*

#### 35.—GENERAL GRANT TO GENERAL MEADE.

WASHINGTON, *January* 25, 1868.

Major General G. G MEADE, *Atlanta, Ga.*

Will it not be well to extend the number of days the polls are to be kept open at the Alabama election, in order to give full opportunity to all who register to vote? Two days will hardly give sufficient time. It would be better to amend General Pope's order now than after the election had commenced.

U. S. GRANT, *General.*

#### 36.—GENERAL GRANT TO GENERAL MEADE.

HEADQUARTERS ARMY OF THE UNITED STATES,
WASHINGTON, *April* 29, 1868.

Major General G. G. MEADE,
*Atlanta, Georgia.*

I have carefully read your letter of 16th of April and its enclosures. I see nothing in them to change my opinion as expressed to you in my despatch of March 2, 1868. The officers elected under the new constitution of Georgia are not officers of the provisional government referred to in the reconstruction acts, nor are they officers elected under any so-called State authority, and are not, therefore, required to take the oath prescribed in section 9, act of July 19, 1867. The eligibility to hold office must be determined by the new constitution and the amendment to the Constitution of the United States, designated as article 14.                                        U. S. GRANT, *General.*

#### General Grant's Order Respecting the Restoration of Removed Civil Officers.

HEADQUARTERS OF THE ARMY,
ADJUTANT GENERAL'S OFFICE,
WASHINGTON, *August* 29, 1867.

Special Orders, No. 420.

Commanders of the military districts created under the act of March 2, 1867, will make no appointments to civil office of persons who have been removed by themselves or their predecessors in command.

By command of General GRANT.

E. D. TOWNSEND,
*Assistant Adjutant General.*

#### Extract from General Grant's Report as Secretary of War ad interim, Referring to Reconstruction, November, 1867.

By act of Congress the ten southern States which have no representation in the national councils are divided into five military districts, each commanded by an officer of the army of not less rank than brigadier general. The powers of these commanders are both civil and military. So far as their military duties are concerned, they are under the same subordination to the General of the army and Secretary of War that department commanders are. In their civil capacity they are entirely independent of both the General and Secretary, except in the matters of removals, appointment, and detail, where the General of the army has the same powers as have district commanders. It is but fair to the district commanders, however, to state that, while they have been thus independent in their civil duties, there has not been one of them who would not yield to a positively expressed wish, in regard to any matter of civil administration, from either of the officers placed over them by the Constitution or acts of Congress, so long as that wish was in the direction of a proper execution of the law for the execution of which they alone are responsible. I am pleased to say that the commanders of the five military districts have executed their difficult trust faithfully and without bias from any judgment of their own as to the merit or demerit of the law they were executing

### FIRST MILITARY DISTRICT

Comprises the State of Virginia, Brevet Major General J. M. Schofield commanding. In assuming command, the principle was announced by General Schofield that the military power conferred by act of Congress on the district commander would be used only so far as was necessary to accomplish the purposes for which the power was conferred. The civil government was interfered with only when necessary, and the wisdom of the policy has been demonstrated by the result. The instances of complaint of the action of the civil courts became exceedingly rare. Still the evil which existed prior to the act of Congress of March 2, 1867, though mitigated by the increased efficiency of civil officers, was not removed. It was an evil in the jury system, apparent at all times, and fully developed by the natural antagonism between loyalist and rebel, or the prejudice between white and black, existing throughout the South since the rebellion. The first idea was to admit blacks on juries and prescribe a test of loyalty. But as the requirement of a unanimous verdict must give very inadequate protection where strong prejudice of class or caste exists, and as a military change of jury system would be but temporary, it was determined to leave its change to the convention soon to meet, and be content with a system of military commissions. Such commissioners were appointed from officers of the army and Freedmen's Bureau in the different cities and counties of the State, with powers of justices of the peace, while the State was divided into sub-districts, under commanders whose powers were ultimately increased to those of circuit judges, taking jurisdiction only in cases where civil authorities failed to do justice. The system has given a large measure of protection to all classes of citizens, with slight interference with the civil courts.

Since the publication of the act of March 23, 1867, all elections have been suspended. Existing State, county, and municipal officers were continued in office. Vacancies have been filled by the district commander. The number of removals has been five, and of appointments to fill vacancies one hundred and five.

In executing the registration a board of officers was first appointed to select registering officers. The selections were made with great care, and the officers so selected have, with few exceptions, done their duty in the most satisfactory manner. Carefully prepared regulations for the boards of registration were issued, being made as specific as possible, so as to secure a uniform rule of disfranchisement throughout the State. In prescribing them, the district commander was controlled by the belief that the law made him responsible for its correct interpretation, as well as its faithful execution.

The results of the first session of the registering boards were all received on September 15. One hundred and fifteen thousand and sixty-eight whites, and one hundred and one thousand three hundred and eighty-two colored, registered; one thousand six hundred and twenty whites, and two hundred and thirty-two colored, being rejected. The tax list of 1866-'67 (not quite complete) returns about one hundred and thirty-six thousand white male adults, and eighty-seven thousand colored male adults. This indicates that the number of whites disfranchised, or who have failed to register, is about nineteen thousand, and that about fifteen thousand more colored men have registered than were on the tax lists. Hence it may be inferred that nearly all male adults, white or colored, not disfranchised, have registered.

The principle upon which the apportionment was made was to give separate representations to the smallest practicable subdivisions of the State, and where fractions remained over so to combine counties in election districts as to justly represent those portions. This is believed to be the fairest mode of apportionment practicable under the law.

### SECOND MILITARY DISTRICT

Comprises the States of North Carolina and South Carolina, Brevet Major General E. R. S. Canby, commanding. Major General Daniel E. Sickles, who was originally assigned to the command of this district, was relieved, and General Canby assigned by the following order of the President:

(General Orders No. 80.—See Chap. Proclamations and Orders.)

"In order to secure a more efficient administration of justice it was deemed necessary to place all sheriffs and other municipal officers under the immediate control of a military officer. Accordingly all such officers were directed to report to the Provost Marshal General, and to make monthly reports of 'crimes committed' and 'prisoners confined.' The reports of prisoners confined has aided materially in detecting illegal imprisonments or punishments, and has enabled the district commander to secure the release of many Union men and freedmen, against whom much gross injustice had been committed.

"A bureau of civil affairs was established, to take charge of all matters pertaining to registration; and its duties were afterwards extended to include all questions of protection to person or property arising under the laws of Congress. One hundred and seventy registration precincts were established in North Carolina, and one hundred and nine in South Carolina.

"In North Carolina there were registered 103,060 whites, and 71,657 blacks; and in South Carolina, 45,751 whites, and 79,585 blacks. Registration proceeded very slowly on account of slowness of communication with distant parts of the district.

"Of the appropriation made by Congress, $54,802 87 have been expended, and outstanding liabilities will exceed the balance on hand $194,802 87.

"The present condition of the district is so satisfactory as to warrant the belief that after elections the number of military posts in both States can be diminished."

### THIRD MILITARY DISTRICT

Comprises the States of Georgia, Florida, and Alabama, Brevet Major General John Pope, commanding.

"On assuming command an order was issued" by General Pope "continuing in office State officials, but forbidding their opposing the reconstruction acts, prohibiting elections except under those acts, and giving notice that all vacancies in civil offices would be filled by the district commander. Becoming satisfied subsequently that State officials, while obeying the order personally, yet officially, by their patronage, encouraged papers opposing the reconstruction act, an order was issued forbidding official patronage to such papers.

"In consequence of the riot at Mobile, an order was issued holding city and county officers responsible for the preservation of peace at all public meetings, and requiring the United States troops to assist them when called on. No disturbances have since occurred.

"Under the laws of the State no colored person could be admitted to the jury-box, and there was no surety of justice to Union men, to people from the North, (and especially ex-Union soldiers,) or to colored persons, from juries inflamed with hostility towards such classes.

"There is a very large number of cases of wrong perpetrated by such juries in the district on file.

"Accordingly an order was issued directing all juries to be drawn indiscriminately from the list of voters registered by the boards of registration.

"Very few civil officers have been removed, and those, in almost every case, were removed for refusing to comply with orders. Appointments to fill vacancies have only been made where the daily business of the people demanded it.

"The State treasurers of Georgia, Alabama, and Florida have been ordered to make no payments after the appropriations of the present fiscal year have expired, save on warrants approved by the district commander, as it is believed that a new Legislature will not continue or approve many of the appropriations made.

"In executing the registration, it was deemed advisable that no officer nor soldier of the United States should be employed, and accordingly each board of registration was appointed from among the citizens living in the district, and to consist of two white men and one colored. A fixed sum was paid for registering each name, the average for the district being twenty-six cents per name.

"There were registered in Georgia 95,214 whites, and 93,457 colored; in Alabama 74,450 whites, and 90,350 colored, and in Florida 11,180 whites, and 15,357 colored. The amount expended in registration, &c., has been $162,325.

"The apportionment of delegates was made in Georgia for State senatorial districts, and in Alabama for Representative districts, fixed by an order. Polls were ordered to be opened at each county seat."

### FOURTH MILITARY DISTRICT

Comprises the States of Mississippi and Arkansas, Brevet Major General E. O. C. Ord, commanding.

"The reconstruction measures of Congress are unpopular with a majority of the white people, but their execution has met with slight opposition, the ignorant and lawless, from whom alone trouble was to be apprehended, having been kept in order by the troops distributed through the States.

"The civil laws have not been interfered with when equally administered, except to remove from the civil courts cases of crime charged against persons who, being opposed to the rebellion, had reason to fear prejudice. Also freedmen's cases, where the courts were practically closed against them; and cases of horse-stealing, and violations of acts of Congress, for all of which military commissions have been organized.

"The officers of the provisional State government have continued in office, except where they have failed to perform their duties. It is difficult to find competent men who can qualify to fill vacancies in civil offices, some of which are consequently vacant.

"In consequence of the indisposition (as manifested of late) of the civil authorities in Arkansas to take action in offences of an aggravated nature against freedmen, orders have been issued for the trial of all such cases by military commission, and for prompt action to be taken for the punishment of civil officers who fail to issue writs against offenders committing assaults, &c., against freedmen, and prohibiting bail for the appearance of such criminals."

The extension of suffrage to freedmen has evidently aroused a sentiment of hostility to the colored race, and to northern men in many parts of the district, which did not exist before; and General Ord is convinced that a larger force than is now stationed in those States will be required hereafter to protect them and secure the freedmen the use of the suffrage.

"In a majority of the counties of this district there are very few men who can take the test-oath, and these are not disposed to defy public opinion by accepting office, unless supported by a military force afterwards.

"The will of the colored people may be in favor of supporting loyal office-holders, but their intelligence is not now sufficient to enable them to combine for the execution of their will. All their combinations are now conducted by white men, under the protection of the military; if the protection is withdrawn, the white men now controlling would withdraw with it; and some of the southern people, now exasperated at what they deem the freedmen's presumption, would not be very gentle towards them, so that the presence of a larger military force will be required for some time to maintain the freedmen in the right of suffrage."

### FIFTH MILITARY DISTRICT

Comprises the States of Louisiana and Texas, Brevet Major General J. A. Mower, commanding.

No report has yet been received from General Mower, but it is expected in time for the meeting of Congress.

Major General P. H. Sheridan, who was originally assigned to the command of this district, was relieved, and General Hancock assigned, by the following orders of the President. On the decease of Brevet Major General Charles Griffin, designated as the officer next in rank to whom General Sheridan should turn over the command until General Hancock assumed it, General Mower succeeded to the command:

(General Orders 77 and 81.—For which see Proclamations and Orders.)

Generals Sheridan and Sickles having been relieved before the period for submitting their annual reports, none have been received from them. They have, however, been called on recently to submit reports, which may be expected before the meeting of Congress.

# XXVII.

# DIGEST OF ORDERS OF THE MILITARY COMMANDERS,

## AND GENERAL ACTION UNDER THE RECONSTRUCTION ACTS.*

### First Military District—Virginia.

1867, March 15—General Schofield prohibited whipping or maiming of the person as a punishment for any crime, misdemeanor, or offence. An order was issued, same day, disbanding and prohibiting any further organization of the militia forces of the State.

* For previous Orders referring to Reconstruction, see pages 73–81 of the Manual of 1867, or pages 190–207 of the combined Manual.

April 2—Board of officers appointed to select boards of registration, one to be an officer of the army or Freedmen's Bureau if possible, and the others either army officers or honorably discharged volunteer officers, or loyal citizens of the proper city or county, or any other loyal citizen. No registering officer to be a candidate for any elective office. All elections suspended till the completion of registration, vacancies to be filled by the commanding general. All officers under the provisional government to take the test oath of March 23, 1867. In registering, whites and colored to be entered in separate columns.

May 28—Where civil authorities fail to give adequate protection to all persons in their rights of person and property, it was announced that military commissioners would be appointed; trials by the civil courts preferred in all cases where there is satisfactory reason to believe that justice will be done.

June 3—It was held, respecting the right to be registered, that persons who *voluntarily* joined the rebel army, or persons who in that army committed *voluntarily* any hostile act, were disqualified; but persons who were *forced* into it, but avoided, as far as possible, doing hostile acts, and escaped from it as soon as possible, were not disqualified. Persons who voted for the secession ordinances were disqualified. Giving individual soldiers food or clothing enough to relieve present suffering did not work disqualification.

June 26—It was decided that, as the laws of Congress declared there was no legal government in Virginia, the Alexandria constitution does not disfranchise any persons.

July 13—It was decided that the President's pardon does not restore political rights, but merely civil; and, July 15, that it does not remove disfranchisement which exists without it.

July 26—All persons hereafter appointed to take the test oath of July 2, 1862, in lieu of that of March 23, 1867. Sub-district commanders directed to report names of all State, county and municipal officers who are "disloyal to the United States, and use their official influence to prevent reconstruction under acts of Congress."

August 16—A fine imposed by court, April 27, 1867, of two thousand dollars in "Confederate currency," was ordered scaled at the then rate, and $88 80, in lawful currency of United States, directed to be accepted by the court, in payment.

September 12—Election ordered for October 22, on a convention; 105 delegates to be elected at the same time.

September 21—Persons subject to parole upon the surrender, who have avoided giving it, are directed to take the prescribed parole within thirty days.

September 24—Delegates to the State convention not required to take the oath prescribed for officers of the United States.

September 25—A person who held no office prior to the war, and who was elected and served as a member of the secession convention, and was afterwards engaged in rebellion, is not thereby disfranchised.

October 3—Armed secret societies forbidden.

October 31—The regular session of the Legislature elected in 1866 dispensed with.

November 2—Vote on convention announced: 169,229 votes cast, of which 107,342 were for, and 61,887 against, a convention. December 3d fixed as the time, and hall of House of Delegates, Richmond, as the place of meeting.

December 2—General O. O. Howard instructs General O. Brown, of Freedmen's Bureau, to allow no man to suffer for food, and to assist to a home and employment those who he ascertains may have been, or may be, discharged for having voted as they pleased.

December 3—Convention met. Adjourned April 17, 1868, having adopted a constitution.

1868, March 12—Sales of property under deeds of trust suspended where such sales would result in a ruinous sacrifice or leave infirm persons without support.

April 4—The office of Governor of Virginia having become vacant by the expiration of Governor Pierpoint's term, and he being ineligible for the next term, Henry H. Wells was appointed.

June 2—General Stoneman assumed command.

No provision has thus far been made for submitting the constitution to a popular vote.

___

## Second Military District—North and South Carolina.

1867, April 18—General Sickles issued an order that, it having become apparent that justice to freedmen cannot be obtained in the civil Courts of Edgefield and Barnwell districts, a provost court be established, with jurisdiction of any case to which a person of color is a party, except murder, arson, and rape.

April 20—No sentence of such court, affecting the liberty of any person, to be executed till approved by the commanding general.

April 27—Local election in Newbern suspended; and officers appointed, and required to take the oath of March 23, 1867.

May 8—Registration announced to be begun on the third Monday in July; registering officers to be appointed, and required to take the test oath of July 2, 1862.

May 15—Commanding officers of posts authorized, upon sufficient cause shown, to grant permission to public officers to carry arms when necessary in the discharge of their duties.

May 20—Distillation of spirits from grain prohibited; violation of this order to be considered a misdemeanor.

May 30—Any citizen, a qualified voter under the reconstruction laws, declared to be eligible to office in the provisional government of North and South Carolina. All citizens who have paid assessed taxes for the current year declared qualified as jurors; and juries to be hereafter drawn from such persons. All citizens are eligible to follow any licensed calling, employment or avocation, subject to impartial regulations prescribed by municipal or other competent authority, the bond required as security not to exceed $100, with one or more sureties worth double the amount of the bond All contracts for the manufacture, sale, or transportation, storage, or insurance of intoxicating liquors to be treated as against public policy. In public conveyances, on railroads, highways, streets, or navigable waters, no discrimination because of color or caste shall be made, and the common rights of all citizens therein shall be recognized and respected; a violation of this regulation to be deemed a misdemeanor, and to render the offender liable to arrest and trial by a military tribunal, besides such damages as may be recovered in the civil courts. The remedy by distress for rent is abolished, where lands are leased or let out for hire or rent. No license for the sale of intoxicating liquors in quantities less than one gallon, or to be drank on the premises, shall be granted to any person other than an inn-keeper.

June 19—General Sickles asked to be relieved from command of the district, and asked a court that he might vindicate himself from the accusation of the Attorney General.

August 1—The session of the Legislature of North Carolina, elected in 1866, indefinitely postponed.

August 10—Order of May 30 suspended in its application to the superior and county courts of North Carolina, on account of the inability of the latter to revise the jury lists.

August 17—The finding of a court-martial confirmed, fining the captain of a steamer $250 for refusing a person a first-class ticket on account of color. It was added: "So long as the laws imposed civil and political disabilities because of servitude or color, carriers were permitted to enforce the same discrimination among passengers. Such disabilities and usages have ceased, with slavery, to have any legal sanction. Whatever belongs of common right to citizens, necessarily follows the recognition of the blacks as citizens, and belongs to them."

September 5—The act of the Legislature of North Carolina, of March 7, 1867, "for the relief of executors, administrators, &c.," annulled as in violation of the Constitution of the United States, and in violation of the acts of Congress passed prohibiting all acts in aid of the late rebellion. Courts directed to dismiss judgments, orders, and decrees, under said legislation.

September 5—General Canby assumed command.

September 13—General Canby ordered that all citizens assessed for taxes, and who shall have paid taxes for the current year, and who are qualified and have been or may be duly registered as voters, are declared qualified to serve as jurors. Any requirement of a property qualification for jurors is hereby abrogated. The collection of certain illegal and oppressive taxes, imposed in parts of North and South Carolina, was suspended.

October 16—An election ordered in South Carolina, November 19 and 20, for or against a "convention," and for delegates to constitute the Convention. Violence, or threats of violence, or of discharge from employment, or other oppressive agencies against the free exercise of the right of suffrage, prohibited. All bar-rooms, saloons, &c., ordered closed from 6 on the evening of November 18 to 6 on the morning of November 21. Military interference, unless "necessary to repel the armed enemies of the United States or to keep the peace at the polls," prohibited.

October 18—A similar order issued for North Carolina, fixing the election November 19 and 20.

October 19—Order issued suspending Hon. A. P. Aldrich from the exercise of all functions as judge of the court of common pleas and general sessions; and Gov. Orr authorized to provide for holding his term of court, by assigning another judge. The election of municipal officers in Charleston forbidden.

November 27—Prosecutions instituted in some of the courts of North Carolina for acts of war committed during the existence of hostilities, in violation of the true intent of the amnesty act of that State of Dec. 22, 1866, were prohibited. Also, ordered, that all parol "contracts, between any persons whatever, whereof one or more of them shall be a person of color," shall be of the same validity, be established by the same evidence, be determined by the same rules, and be enforced in the same manner as in like contracts where all the parties thereto are whites.

December 3—A system of taxation established, for the support of the provisional government of South Carolina for the year from October 1, 1867, to September 30, 1868. Appropriations ordered for the various offices and expenses of the State.

December 28—The election declared to have resulted in favor of a convention; and the delegates notified to meet in Charleston, January 14, 1868.

December 31—Convention declared carried in North Carolina; and the delegates notified to meet in Raleigh, January 14, 1868.

December 31—Judgments or decrees for money, or causes of action, from May 20, 1861, to April 20, 1865, in North Carolina, and from December 19, 1860, to April 29, 1865, in South Carolina, ordered not to be enforced, &c. All proceedings for the recovery of money for the purchase of slaves, made after January 1, 1863, suspended. Proceedings in any court in either State, recognizing or sanctioning the investment of the funds of minor heirs, or females, or insane persons in the securities of the late rebel government, or the war securities of either State, will be suspended till the validity of such investments shall be determined by United States courts or by additional legislation. Power to grant licenses for the sale of liquors remitted to local authorities.

1868, January 14—Conventions of both States met, and adjourned March 17.

February 6—Ordinance of South Carolina Convention for the collection of taxes, promulgated, and the assessors ordered to collect the taxes therein levied. State Treasurer authorized to pay the expenses of the Convention.

February 12—Same with regard to the North Carolina Convention.

February 27—Where advances are made by General R. K. Scott, assistant commissioner of Bureau of Refugees, in behalf of the Government of the United States, in aid of the depressed agriculture of South Carolina, these advances shall be a lien upon the produce of the plantation.

March 13—An election to be held in South Carolina, April 14 and 16, for or against the constitution, and on the same ballot for State officers, and Representatives in Congress, one for each of the four districts and two at large.

March 23—An election ordered for North Carolina, April 21, 22, 23; regulations prescribed.

April 8—Quarantine of ports of South Carolina established.

May 2—Constitution announced ratified by a majority of the votes actually cast by the qualified electors of South Carolina.

May 12—Constitution of North Carolina announced similarly ratified.

June 15—W. W. Holden, Governor elect of North Carolina, called a meeting of the Legislature for July 1.

### Third Military District—Georgia, Alabama, and Florida.

1867, April 4—General Pope issued an order directing post commanders to report acts of local or State authorities or tribunals which discriminate against persons on account of race, color, or political opinion.

April 8—Registration order issued. It provides, among other sections:

"It is desirable that in all cases the registers shall be civilians where it is possible to obtain such as come within the provisions of the act and are otherwise suitable persons; and that military officers shall not be used for the purpose, except in case of actual necessity.

"The registers are specifically instructed to see that all information concerning their political rights is given to all persons entitled to vote under the act of Congress; and they are made responsible that every such legal voter has the opportunity to record his name.

"Interference by violence, or threats of violence, or other oppressive means to prevent the registration of any voter, is positively prohibited; and any person guilty of such interference shall be arrested and tried by the military authorities."

April 11—Headquarters removed to Atlanta.

April 12—General Wager Swayne issued this order at Montgomery, Alabama:

General Orders, No. 3.

I. Complaints of hardship in the needless apprenticing of minors, particularly in pursuance of the preference given to the "former owner" in the law, have been almost incessant. It is enjoined upon probate judges, upon application, to revise the action taken in such cases, and as a rule to revoke indentures made within the past two years of minors who were capable of self-support.

II. The attention of magistrates is called to the repeal by the last Legislature of the "vagrant law," approved December 15, 1865, and published with the code. Attempts which are still made to put it into execution will hereafter be the subject of military cognizance.

III. The use of "chain-gangs" as a mode of legal punishment being found to involve serious abuses, will be henceforth discontinued, except in connection with the penitentiary.

May 1—The use of the "chain-gang" as a mode of legal punishment in Georgia is ordered discontinued, except in cases connected with prisoners sentenced to the penitentiary.

May 21—The States of Georgia and Alabama divided into registration districts, the boards of registration for each district to consist of two white registers and one colored, each to take the test oath of July 2, 1862. Violence and threats prohibited.

May 29—The duties of mayor, chief of police, &c., defined, in view of the riot at Mobile.

June 17—Special instructions given to registering boards in Florida.

August 2—No civil court will entertain any action against officers or soldiers, or others, for acts performed in accordance with the orders of the military authorities. All such suits now pending to be dismissed.

August 12—Ordered, that all advertisements or other official publications under State or municipal authority shall be made in such newspapers only as have not opposed and do not oppose reconstruction under acts of Congress, nor attempt to obstruct the civil officers appointed by the military authorities.

August 19—Grand and petit jurors, and all other jurors, shall hereafter be taken exclusively from the lists of voters without discrimination, as registered. Sheriffs to require jurors to swear that they have been registered. Jurors already drawn shall take this oath or be replaced by those who can.

August 26—General Pope disclaimed the purpose to interfere with the relation of debtor and creditor under State laws, not considering a stay law to be within his province to adjust.

August 31—An election ordered in Alabama on a convention, and for delegates, October 1, to continue three days.

September 19—A like election ordered for Georgia, October 29, to continue three days.

October 30—Polls ordered to be kept open till 6 p. m., November 2.

October 5—A like election for Florida, November 14, to continue three days.

October 18—Convention declared carried in Alabama, names of delegates announced, and convention directed to meet in Montgomery, November 5.

October 19—Post and detachment commanders directed to furnish to the proper civil officers such military aid as may be needed to enable them to collect taxes imposed by the laws of the State.

November 5—Alabama Convention met; adjourned December 6.

November 7—General Swayne ordered, for the purpose of securing to agricultural laborers payment for the labor of this year, a lien in their favor upon the crops grown on the farms on which they are respectively employed, said lien to attach from date and be subordinate to prior liens.

November 19—Convention declared carried in Georgia, names of delegates announced, and Convention directed to meet in Atlanta, December 9.

November 26—Payment of expenses of Alabama Convention by State treasurer authorized.

December 9—Georgia Convention met; adjourned March 11, 1868.

December 20—Election on Alabama constitution ordered for February 4, 1868, to continue four days. Lists of voters to be revised for fourteen days prior to election. State officers and Representatives in Congress to be voted for at same time, as provided by the election ordinance.

December 27—All military organizations expressly prohibited; and no parading of armed men permitted, except of United States troops.

December 28—Convention declared carried in Florida; delegates announced, and called to meet at Tallahassee, January 20, 1868.

1868, January 6—General Meade assumed command.

January 10—The ordinance of the Alabama Convention, to stay the collection of debts, was announced as to be deemed to have taken effect from this date, and continue in full force unless the pending constitution should not be accepted; but if it be adopted, the ordinance to be valid till Congress shall act on the constitution.

January 11—State officers admonished not to interfere, under color of State authority, with the exercise of military authority in the States composing this district.

January 12—General Meade sent this telegram:

"General U. S. GRANT:
"Unless the pending bill in Congress, directing military commanders to fill all offices in the State under their command, rescinds the test oath and provides for selection from qualified voters, I am informed its execution in this district will be entirely impracticable."

January 13—This order was issued: "Charles J. Jenkins, Provisional Governor, and Jno. Jones, provisional treasurer, of the State of Georgia, having declined to respect the instructions of and failed to co-operate with the major general commanding the third military district, are hereby removed from office." Brevet Brigadier General Thomas H. Ruger appointed Governor, and Brevet Captain Charles F. Rockwell to be treasurer of Georgia.

January 15—Order issued, that the frequency of reported outrages, and the accompanying expression of opinion of subordinate officers, that no justice is to be expected from the civil authorities, require notice and action on the part of the major general commanding, who instructs the military to co-operate with the civil in detecting and capturing criminals, but states that where the civil authorities fail to do their duty, he will take prompt action for the punishment of criminals and the removal from office of derelict civil officers.

January 16—The Georgia ordinance of relief, of December 12, 1867, was announced as having taken effect, till the Convention take further action, or further orders are issued.

January 17—John T. Burns removed as comptroller, and Captain Charles Wheaton appointed his successor, who was also appointed secretary of State, vice N. C. Barnett, removed.

January 20—Florida Convention met; adjourned February 25.

January 29—The Florida ordinance of relief, of January 21, 1868, given effect as in the case of Georgia.

February 2—The order of August 12 last modified so as to apply only to such newspapers as attempt to obstruct in any manner the civil officers appointed by the military, in the discharge of their duty, by threats of violence, prosecution, or other penalty to be enforced as soon as military protection is withdrawn.

February 3—Registered voters may vote anywhere in the State on constitution, on proof of registration.

February 4—8,114 less than half the registered vote of Alabama cast for the constitution.

February 11—The assistant commissioner of freedmen's affairs urged freedmen to make contracts for the present year, and to disregard the bad advice given them by others not to make contracts but await relief from the Atlanta Convention.

February 22—Imprisonment for debt in Georgia prohibited, in accordance with an ordinance of the Convention.

February 28—All civil courts and officers whose duty it is to provide for the relief of paupers, shall extend relief to all persons entitled to relief, as such, without any discrimination as to race or color.

March 14—An election ordered in Georgia, to commence April 20, 1868, to continue four days, on the ratification of the constitution adopted by the Convention; State officers and Representatives in Congress to be voted for at same time.

March 16—An election ordered in Florida, first Monday, Tuesday, and Wednesday of May, for like purposes.

March 18—In all the jails and other prisons, colored prisoners are to receive the same food, in quality and quantity, as white prisoners, and the sheriffs shall get the same fees for victualling all classes of prisoners.

March 26—Freedmen being threatened with discharge, "for the purpose of controlling their votes, or of restraining them from voting," bureau officers were directed by the superintendent of registration, E. Hulbert, to report all cases of interference with their political rights.

April 3—General Meade, on being applied to, expressed the opinion that Judge Irwin was ineligible for the governorship of Georgia. April 4, he gave the opinion that General John B. Gordon was eligible, under the acts of Congress.

April 4—General Meade issued an order, of which this is the first paragraph:

"I. The recent assassination at Columbus, Ga., of the Hon. G. W. Ashburn, late a member of the Constitutional Convention of said State, and other acts of violence and atrocity committed about the same time in various parts of this district, and the simultaneous publication of incendiary articles, and the receipt by many persons of threatening letters, indicating a concert of action, by violence and intimidation, to alarm and overawe a large part of the population, and by this means affect the results of pending elections in this district, all of which acts apparently emanate from a secret organization, for no good purpose, which seems to be rapidly spreading through these States, make it necessary for the commanding general to warn all persons against the commission of such acts, the publication of such articles, the sending of such letters, or connecting themselves with such evil organizations, and to assure all the good people of this district that he will use all the powers he possesses to protect them in the peaceable enjoyment of their homes and property, and in the exercise of their personal rights and political privileges.

"Military and civil officers are directed to arrest and bring to trial persons who may print and circulate incendiary papers or threatening letters; and conductors of newspapers and other printing offices are prohibited from publishing articles tending to produce intimidation, riot, or bloodshed; public writers and speakers are enjoined to refrain from inflammatory appeals, and military and municipal officers required to organize patrols to detect such persons as avail themselves of the secrecy of the night for executing their criminal purposes. Good citizens are called on to aid in preserving the peace, and are admonished that if intimidation and violence are not checked, bloody retaliation may be provoked."

April 6—General Meade ordered an election in Georgia, April 20, for Governor, General Assembly, county officers, and Representatives in Congress.

### Fourth Military District—Mississippi and Arkansas.

1867, April 5—Headquarters transferred to Vicksburg.

April 13—General orders or circulars of the assistant commissioner of refugees to be submitted, prior to promulgation, to General Ord.

April 15—No elections to be held for any purpose, till a registration of voters be made. Freedmen urged not to neglect their business to engage in political discussions, but to continue to provide for themselves and families, lest "a famine may come and they have no food." Due notice will be given of the times and places for registration.

May 6—Attention called to the prevalence of horse-stealing, and post commanders directed to exert themselves to break it up.

May 13—Instructions to registering officers directed the exclusion of all persons who held an office under the General Government prior to the war, and who afterwards engaged in or gave aid and comfort to rebellion. Registers not permitted to be candidates for Convention, or to make speeches, or electioneer for or against any candidate for office.

June 12—Sales of land, implements, stock, &c., under authority of State courts, where the cause of action accrued prior to January 1, 1866, stayed till December 30, 1867, to go into effect in Mississippi June 20, and in Arkansas June 30. Illicit distilling of corn into whiskey, prohibited; property seized for violation of this order to be sold for the benefit of the poor.

June 17—A poll-tax having been imposed upon freedmen by the county boards of police in Mississippi, under Section II of the act of Legislature of November 24, 1865,* "An act to amend the vagrant laws," it being, so far as it discriminates against freedmen, manifestly contrary to the civil rights act, all civil officers are forbidden to collect it.

June 29—An order issued, reciting that, as mistaken ideas on the subject of registering and voting may spread or arise among the freedmen in this district, which, if not corrected, would tend to prevent them from registering and voting, sub-district commanders will direct the agents of the Bureau of Refugees, Freedmen, and Abandoned Lands to visit every important plantation within their reach and instruct the freedmen upon these points. They and registers will inform the freedmen that the registration, where their names have to be entered and an oath taken, is not for the purpose of imposing any tax, or holding them to any military or

* See page 30 of Manual of 1866.

other service, but simply to enable them to share equally with the white men in the privilege of choosing who shall hold office in the county, State, and United States wherein they reside, and that unless they register they may be deprived of this privilege.

Whenever freedmen are interfered with, threatened or deprived of any advantage, place, or hire, on account of their registering or showing a wish to register, they will be informed it is their duty to report, such interference or deprivation, so that the party offending may be dealt with according to law. Registers and officers of the army throughout the district will report all such offenders to the assistant adjutant general at these headquarters, with the names of witnesses, date, and places given carefully, so that the offence may be punished.

July 29—An order issued notifying all State and municipal officers that any attempt to render nugatory the action of Congress designed to promote the better government of the rebel States, by speeches or demonstrations at public meetings in opposition thereto, will be deemed sufficient cause for their summary removal. The same prohibition in regard to speeches will be applied to all officers holding appointments from these headquarters, and to officers of the army in this district.

August 13—An order issued, that the general commanding having been credibly informed that in some instances land-holders within this district are, without legal cause, but upon frivolous pretexts, driving off their laborers, with a view to withhold their arrears of wages, or share in the growing crops, assistant commissioners of the Bureau of Refugees, Freedmen, and Abandoned Lands will instruct their subordinates carefully to investigate every such case which may come to their knowledge, affording all the parties a full hearing, so that, should the circumstances as developed disclose, on the part of the employers, cruel treatment of the laborer, or an attempt to defraud him of his wages, the offender may be brought to trial before a military commission.

Where laborers on the crop of 1866 have not been paid, the removal of the crop is prohibited till the claim can be adjusted by three referees, (one to be selected by each party and the third by them,) "the courts of the States in this district not being open to persons too poor to give bonds."

August 31—It was held that an attorney or counsellor at law is *not* an officer in the sense of the acts of Congress relating to registration, and voting for secession *was* giving aid and comfort to the enemies of the United States.

September 6—Where a person, indicted for a criminal offence, can prove by two credible witnesses that he was a loyal man during the rebellion, believes that he cannot by reason of that fact get a fair and impartial trial by jury, the court will not proceed to try the case, but the papers shall be transmitted to these headquarters. As freed people bear their share of taxation, no denial to them of the benefit of those laws will be tolerated, and a refusal or neglect to provide properly for colored paupers will be treated as a dereliction of official duty.

September 9—The assembling of *armed* organizations or bodies of citizens, under any pretence whatever, is prohibited.

September 10—Persons connected with the rebel armies, who have avoided taking the parole oath, will, within 30 days, report, and take it.

September 26—Registration having been completed, an election for or against a convention, and for delegates, will be held on the first Tuesday in November. Judges and clerks of election to take the test oath; registration to be revised for fourteen days prior to election; sheriff of each county made responsible for good order; public bar rooms closed; no register, judge, or clerk, to be a candidate.

September 27—Election for convention ordered in Arkansas, first Tuesday in November.

December 5—It was ordered that, in consequence of stolen goods being sold or delivered after dark, traders and all other parties are forbid purchasing or delivering country supplies after sunset till market hour in the morning, and making such sale or delivery a military offence.

December 5—A "Convention" declared carried by a majority of the registered vote in each State. The delegates for Mississippi are called to meet at Jackson, on January 7, and of Arkansas at Little Rock on January 7. All persons not in the military service, and not properly engaged in executing the laws, are prohibited from carrying concealed weapons.

December 12—Whenever a citizen is arrested by the military, he will be at once furnished with a written copy of the charges. Writs of *habeas corpus* by United States courts will be in all cases obeyed and respected by all officers of the military service in this command.

December 14—Sheriffs and other peace officers are requested to be prepared, with the aid of the *posse comitatus*, to arrest, disarm, and confine offenders against the peace and good order of the community; vagrancy and crime are to be suppressed. This order covered a proclamation of Governor Humphreys, of December 9, to this effect:

Whereas communications have been received at this office, from gentlemen of high official and social position in different portions of the State, expressing serious apprehensions that combinations and conspiracies are being formed among the blacks, " to seize the lands and establish farms, expecting and hoping that Congress will arrange a plan of division and distribution," " but unless this is done by January next, they will proceed to help themselves, and are determined *to go to war*, and are confident that they will be victors in any conflict with the whites," and furnish names of persons and places; and

Whereas similar communications have been received at headquarters fourth military district, and referred to me for my action, and the co-operation of the civil authorities of the State, with the United States military, in suppressing violence and maintaining order and peace—

Now, therefore, I, Benjamin G. Humphreys, Governor of Mississippi, do issue this my proclamation, admonishing the black race, that if any such hopes or expectations are entertained, you have been grossly deceived, and if any com-

binations or conspiracies have been formed, to carry into effect such purposes by lawless violence, I now warn you that you cannot succeed.

Upon the reference of the papers referred to in this proclamation to General Ord, he, under date of November 2, instructed General Gillem to learn what white men have been advising the freedmen to take arms, seize lands, or do any other illegal act, and to instruct the leading freedmen that Congress has no intention to take land from the late masters for the benefit of former slaves. General Gillem ordered promptly to arrest all incendiaries. Gov. Humphreys, in his proclamation, admonished the whites that, as they prized constitutional liberty for themselves, they must accord to the black race the full measure of their rights, privileges, and liberties secured to them by the Constitution and laws of the land; that they must deal justly with the blacks, and in no case undertake to redress wrongs, except in the mode and manner authorized by law.

December 16—It was declared that boards of arbitration for the protection of laborers, would be hereafter appointed only where a laborer may complain that his wages or share of the crop is wrongfully withheld from him, and where a landlord or merchant may complain that the planter has fraudulently assigned to the laborer an undue share of the crop, to the injury of the complainant.

December 17—All freedmen who are able will be required to earn their support during the coming year. Those who can, but will not work, will be liable to arrest as vagrants.

December 19—County courts in Arkansas directed to make immediate provision for their poor.

December 21—Result of election in Arkansas on convention officially declared, and convention directed to assemble.

1868, January 7—Arkansas Convention met; adjourned February 11. Same day—Mississippi Convention met; adjourned May 18.

January 9—An order was issued restoring to the civil courts of Mississippi the jurisdiction of general cases of horse-stealing, &c.; though, should it appear that any person charged with this crime could not obtain an impartial trial by reason of his political sentiments or his race, the jurisdiction shall still remain in the hands of the military.

January 27—Hereafter all questions arising from settlements of crops, and generally the relations of debtors and creditors of civil suitors, will be left to the proper civil courts, except such cases affecting the rights of freedmen, or others, as by acts of Congress are specially committed to the care of the Bureau of Refugees, Freedmen, and Abandoned Lands.

February 4—The general commanding refused to issue an order for the relief of debtors, believing that the homestead and exemption laws of Mississippi placed every one beyond the necessity of such protection.

February 14—Election on constitution of Arkansas, State officers, and Representatives in Congress, ordered for March 14.

March 14—Election held in Arkansas

April 13—Remits to civil courts jurisdiction of any violation of the laws of the State of Mississippi in relation to carrying concealed weapons.

May 19— An election was ordered to be held in Mississippi, June 22, on the ratification of the constitution and for the election of members of Congress and State officers.

June 4—General McDowell assumed command of the department.

June 16—He removed Governor Humphreys of Mississippi and Attorney General Hooker, and appointed General Adelbert Ames military governor, and Captain Jasper Myers attorney general.

### Fifth Military District—Louisiana and Texas.

March 28—No elections will be held till the reconstruction laws shall have been complied with.

April 8—An election in the parish of Livingston, Louisiana, annulled.

April 20—Registration boards appointed.

April 27—General Griffin, reciting that persons disqualified by law are drawn to serve as jurors in the civil courts of Texas, directed that hereafter no person shall be eligible to serve as a juryman until he shall have taken the test-oath of July 2, 1862. The second section of the civil rights act was published for the guidance of officials authorized to impannel jurors. [General Griffin vindicated this order, May 29, stating it was not his intention to prescribe whether jurors should be white or black; but to prevent the filling the jury-boxes with men of secession antecedents, inimical to the General Government, and hostile towards Union citizens, who were applying from all parts of the State for protection against the unjust action of the courts.]

May 2—An order issued, reciting that an act of the Legislature of Louisiana, of February 12, 1866, providing that officers and men of the police force of New Orleans shall read and write the English language, and have resided upwards of *five* consecutive years in the city, having been passed for the purpose of excluding ex-Union soldiers from the police force, and every ex-Union soldier had been discharged from it to make room for those of rebellious antecedents, so much of the act as requires the five years' residence was suspended, and a residence of two years adopted. The mayor, Edward Heath, ordered to adjust the police force so that at least one-half shall be composed of ex-Union soldiers.

May 3—New board of levee commissioners appointed.

May 11—Registration boards notified that false certificates of naturalization have been issued from some of the district courts of New Orleans, and to report them whenever found.

May 16—The carrying of fire-arms in New Orleans prohibited except by those authorized or required by law to do so in discharging official duties.

May 25—Collection of taxes in Texas levied during the rebellion prohibited.

June 3—The order appointing a new board of levee commissioners suspended, under President Johnson's directions. J. Madison Wells having made himself an impediment to the faithful execution of the reconstruction act, was removed as Governor of Louisiana, and Thomas J. Durant appointed thereto. William Baker appointed street commissioner of New Orleans, in place of the incumbent, removed for neglecting to keep the streets of the city clean.

June 6—Benjamin F. Flanders appointed Governor, in place of Mr. Durant declined.

June 10—The act of the Legislature of Texas, October 11, 1866, passed to get rid of Judge Thomas H. Stribling and W. P. Bacon, Union men, because of their political opinions, was annulled.

June 29—Registration extended till further orders, by direction of President Johnson.

July 19—Registration ordered to cease on the 31st instant.

July 27—The old board of levee commissioners reinstated.

July 30—J. W. Throckmorton, Governor of Texas, removed as an impediment to reconstruction, and E. M Pease appointed.

August 3—Civil tribunals in Texas ordered to disregard an act of legislation, November 1, 1866, regulating contracts for labor.

August 8—Judge Edward Dougherty, 12th district of Texas, removed for denying the supremacy of the laws of Congress, and Edward Basse appointed.

August 17—Election ordered in Louisiana on a convention and for delegates, September 27 and 28, the Convention to consist of 98 members. Commissioners of election ordered to do everything requisite to secure a full and impartial expression of the opinions and wishes of the people through the ballot-box.

August 22—General Griffin issued an order, at Galveston, that all distinctions on account of color, race, or previous condition, by railroads, or other chartered companies, that are common carriers, are forbidden in the district of Texas.

August 24—Registration being complete, no person not registered in accordance with law shall be considered "a duly qualified voter of the State of Louisiana." Only those duly registered are eligible, under the laws of Louisiana, as jurors; and the necessary revision of the jury lists is ordered to be made immediately, the State exemption from jury duty to remain in force.

September 1—General Sheridan relieved.

September 6—General Charles Griffin, upon whom the command temporarily devolved, telegraphed General Hartsuff, A. A. G., from Galveston, to transact all business as if General Sheridan had remained in command and received his anticipated leave of absence.

September —General Joseph A. Mower assumed command.

September 17—The assembling of armed men for political and other purposes, and posting them as sentinels or videttes, prevalent in various parts of Louisiana, are prohibited.

September 19—All persons subject to parole, now domiciled in Louisiana and Texas, ordered to give their paroles within thirty days.

September 28—All persons duly registered in Texas, and no others, will be eligible as jurors.

October 21—Convention declared carried, and delegates ordered to meet in New Orleans November 23.

November 16—Harry T. Hays removed as Sheriff of New Orleans, and George W. Avery appointed.

November 12—R. King Cutler appointed judge, in place of A. Cazabat, resigned.

November 21—Albert Voorhies removed as Lieutenant Governor, and several other State officers; and, November 22, this order was suspended.

November 29—General Winfield S. Hancock assumed command. He issued this order:

II. The general commanding is gratified to learn that peace and quiet reign in this department. It will be his purpose to preserve this condition of things. As a means to this great end, he regards the maintenance of the civil authorities in the faithful execution of the laws as the most efficient, under existing circumstances.

In war it is indispensable to repel force by force, and overthrow and destroy opposition to lawful anthority. But when insurrectionary force has been overthrown and peace established, and the civil authorities are ready and willing to perform their duties, the military power should cease to lead, and the civil administration resume its natural and rightful dominion. Solemnly impressed with these views, the general announces that the great principles of American liberty still are the lawful inheritance of this people and ever should be. The right of trial by jury, the habeas corpus, the liberty of the press, the freedom of speech, and the natural rights of persons, and the rights of property, must be preserved.

Free institutions, while they are essential to the prosperity and happiness of the people, always furnish the strongest inducements to peace and order. Crimes and offenses committed in this district must be referred to the consideration and judgment of the regular civil tribunals, and those tribunals will be supported in their lawful jurisdiction.

Should there be violations of existing laws, which are not inquired into by the civil magistrates or should failures in the administration of justice by the courts be complained of, the cases will be reported to these headquarters, when such orders will be made as may be deemed necessary.

While the general thus indicates his purpose to respect the liberties of the people, he wishes all to understand that armed insurrections or forcible resistance to the law will be instantly suppressed by arms.

By command of Major General W. S. Hancock.

W. G. MITCHELL,
*Bvt. Lieut. Col., Acting Assist. Adj't Gen.*

December 2—R King Cutler's appointment as judge revoked; and, December 3, A. Cazabat appointed.

December 5—This order was issued by General Hancock:

The true and proper use of military power, besides defending the national honor against foreign nations, is to uphold the laws and civil government, and to secure to every person residing among us the enjoyment of life, liberty, and property. It is accordingly made, by act of Congress, the duty of the commander of this district to protect all persons in these rights, to suppress disorder and violence, and to punish, or cause to be punished, all disturbers of the public peace and criminals.

The commanding general has been officially informed that the administration of justice, and especially of criminal justice, in the courts is clogged, if not entirely frustrated, by the enforcement of paragraph No. 2 of the military order numbered: Special Orders 125, current series, from these headquarters, issued on the 24th of August, A. D. 1867, relative to the qualifications of persons to be placed on the jury lists of the State of Louisiana.

To determine who shall and who shall not be jurors appertains to the legislative power; and until the laws in existence regulating this subject shall be amended or changed by that department of the civil government, which the constitutions of all the States under our republican system vest with that power, it is deemed best to carry out the will of the people as expressed in the last legislative act upon this subject.

The qualification of a juror under the law is a proper subject for the decision of the courts. The commanding general, in the discharge of the trust reposed in him, will maintain the just power of the judiciary, and is unwilling to permit the civil authorities and laws to be embarrassed by military interference; and as it is an established fact that the administration of justice in the ordinary tribunals is greatly embarrassed by the operations of Paragraph No. 2, Special Orders No. 125, current series, from these headquarters, it is ordered that said paragraph, which relates to the qualifications of jurors to be placed on the jury-lists of the State of Louisiana, be, and the same is hereby. revoked, and that the trial by jury be henceforth regulated and controlled by the Constitution and civil laws, without regard to any military orders heretofore issued from these headquarters.

December 18—Election ordered in Texas on a convention, and for delegates, February 10, 11, 12, 13, and 14, 1868.

1868, January 1—General Hancock issued this order:

Applications have been made at these headquarters implying the existence of an arbitrary authority in the commanding general touching purely civil controversies. One petitioner solicits this action, another that, and each refers to some special consideration of grace or favor, which he supposes to exist and which should influence this department. The number of such applications, and the waste of time they involve, make it necessary to declare that the administration of civil justice appertains to the regular courts. The rights of litigants do not depend on the views of the general. They are to be adjudged and settled according to the laws. Arbitrary power, such as he has been urged to assume, has no existence here. It is not found in the laws of Louisiana or Texas. It cannot be derived from any act or acts of Congress. It is restrained by a constitution, and prohibited from action in many particulars.

The major general commanding takes occasion to repeat that, while disclaiming judicial functions in civil cases, he can suffer no forcible resistance to the execution of processes of the courts.

By command of Major General Hancock.

G. L. HARTSUFF, *A. A. G.*

January 2—Mr. Joshua Baker appointed Governor in place of Hon. B. F. Flanders, resigned.

January 8—Mr. Baker took the oath of office as Governor of Louisiana.

In May, 1867, General Sheridan distributed memoranda of disqualifications, and questions to be proposed for the registers. Their substance was to declare disqualified all who had acted as United States Senators or Representatives, electors, officers of the army and navy, civil officers of the United States, and all State officers provided for by the constitution of the State prior to January 26, 1861, who had afterwards engaged in the rebellion, and all who, in 1862 and 1864, claimed protection of foreign Powers. If any person applying to be registered, having held such office, declared that he had been engaged in the rebellion, or if the registers knew them to have been so, they must not be registered.

On the 11th of January, 1868, General Hancock set aside these memoranda, declaring that he dissented from the construction given to the reconstruction laws therein, inasmuch as it applied to the officers of municipal and charitable corporations, which were not included in the act of March 23, 1867, and whose exclusion is directly contrary to that of July 19. Orders the registers to be guided by their own interpretation of the laws and the XIVth Constitutional Amendment.

February 7—For proceeding to hold an election, in contempt of orders from headquarters, certain members of the board of aldermen of New Orleans were removed and others appointed in their place.

February 27—The preceding order was revoked by direction of General Grant.

March 11—Election ordered in Louisiana on April 17 and 18, on the constitution adopted by the Convention.

March 13—It was decided that a pardon did not entitle a person to be registered, if he would have been disqualified without the pardon.

March 25—Election ordered for State officers and Representatives in Congress at the same time with the vote on the constitution.

May 13—The result of the election declared, 17,413 majority for the constitution.

June 2—The names of the members of the General Assembly, State officers, parish officers, and judicial officers were announced. The General Assembly was forbidden to convene till the commanding general was officially notified of the acceptance by Congress of the constitution, after which he would appoint a day for their meeting to act on the XIVth constitutional amendment. The civil government hereby provided for is provisional in its character until after the adoption of the XIVth constitutional amendment. Article 158 of the new constitu-

tion of the State provides that the terms of office of all civil officers elected under it shall date from the first Monday in November following the election. Therefore, the officers whose election is herein announced will only enter upon and hold their offices from that date. A vacancy occurring in any office in the meantime will be filled preferably by the person who has been elected to it.

If any of the officers whose election is herein announced shall be disqualified on the first Monday in November, 1868, to hold office, the incumbent at that date will hold over until the disability shall have been removed or a new election held.

June 6—The municipal officers chosen were announced and ordered to be installed in New Orleans on the 10th inst., and in other places on the seventh day after the receipt of the order.

June 6—The chairman of the board of registration, S. B. Packard, issued a proclamation reciting the provisons of the constitution requiring all civil officers to enter on their duties on the second Monday after the official promulgation of the election returns, and requiring the General Assembly to meet on the third Monday after such promulgation; declaring that the commanding general had violated such provision, and that to the board of registration had been delegated by the Convention the power to inaugurate the new State government; notifies all officers to take possession of their offices, and the General Assembly to meet, on the days above named.

The same day Mr. Packard was arrested, but released on recognizance to appear before a military commission to be immediately organized.

June 8—General Grant telegraphed to General Buchanan as follows:

In view of the legislation now pending relative to the admission of Louisiana, I would suggest suspension of all action in case of Packard's arrest and trial.

U. S. GRANT, *General.*

Same day—General Buchanan accordingly announced a suspension of arrest and further action respecting Packard and the other members of the board of registration.

June 16—The Constitutional Convention of Texas passed a resolution urging upon Congress the necessity of authorizing the organization by that body of a military force in the several counties of Texas, to act in conjunction with, and under the direction of, the military commander therein, for the protection of the lives and property of the citizens now every day being preyed upon by assassins and robbers to an extent unparalleled in the history of civilized communities in times of peace, and which, if not speedily arrested, must result in the destruction of social order; and that if protection be not speedily provided in some form by the national Government to the loyal and law-abiding citizens of Texas, they will be compelled, in the sacred right of self-defence, to organize for their own protection

# XXVIII.

## ABSTRACTS OF THE NEW CONSTITUTIONS

### OF MARYLAND AND NEW YORK, ALABAMA, ARKANSAS, FLORIDA, LOUISIANA, GEORGIA, NORTH CAROLINA, SOUTH CAROLINA, VIRGINIA AND MISSISSIPPI.

**Constitution of Maryland adopted in 1867.**

In the declaration of rights are the following:
That the people of this State have the sole and xclusive right of regulating the internal government and police thereof, as a free, sovereign, and independent State.

That the levying of taxes by the poll is grievous and oppressive, and ought to be prohibited; that paupers ought not to be assessed for the support of the government.

That slavery shall not be re-established in this State; but having been abolished under the policy and authority of the United States, compensation in consideration thereof is due from the United States.

That no religious test ought ever to be required, as a qualification for any office of profit or trust in this State, other than a declaration of belief in the existence of God; nor shall the Legislature prescribe any other oath of office than the oath prescribed by the constitution.

All elections by ballot; voters are white male citizens of the United States, twenty-one years of age and upwards, who have resided in the State one year and six months in the district in which he offers to vote. Sec. 5 provides a uniform registration of voters. Sec. 6 fixes the oath of office to support the Constitution of United States, and bear true allegiance to the State of Maryland, and support its constitution and laws, &c.

Art. 2, sec. 17 gives governor the veto power; a three-fifths vote of the members elected to each house necessary to pass a bill over the veto.

Art. 3, sec. 3, gives each county a senator, and Baltimore city 3, one for each district. Allegany county, till the next census, is to have five delegates in the house of delegates; Anne Arundel, 3; Baltimore county, 6; Baltimore city 18, elected in three districts; Calvert, 2; Caroline, 2; Carroll, 4; Cecil, 4; Charles, 2; Dorchester, 3; Frederick, 6; Harford, 4; Howard, 2; Kent, 2; Montgomery, 3; Prince George's, 3; Queen Anne's, 2; St. Mary's, 2; Somerset, 3; Talbot, 2; Washington, 5; Worcester, 3. Sect. 4 provides that after the next census each county with a population of 18,000 souls, or less, shall have two delegates; of 18,000 and less than 28,000, 3; of 28,000 and less than 40,000, 4; of 40,000 and less than 55,000, 5; of 55,000 and upwards, 6, and each of the legislative districts of Baltimore shall have a number of delegates equal to the largest county. The term of senators is fixed at four years and delegates two. Three years' citizenship in Maryland necessary to make a person eligible as senator or delegate.

Art. 4, sec. 28, requires a majority of the whole number of members elected to each house to pass a bill, and by yeas and nays. Sec. 37 is in these words:

The general assembly shall pass no law providing for payment by this State for slaves emancipated from servitude in this State; but they shall adopt such measures as they may deem expedient to obtain from the United States compensation for such slaves, and to receive and distribute the same equitably to the persons entitled.

Sec. 41 disqualifies from office of profit or trust any person fighting a duel or participating as second, or knowingly aiding or assisting those offending. Sec. 43 protects the property of the wife from the debts of her husband. Sec. 44 protects $500 worth of property from execution. Sec. 46 is in these words:

The general assembly shall have power to receive from the United States any grant or donation of land, money, or securities for any purpose designated by the United States, and shall administer or distribute the same according to the conditions of the said grant.

Sec. 53 provides that no person shall be incompetent, as a witness, on account of race or color, unless hereafter so declared by act of general assembly. Sec. 55 prohibits the general assembly from passing any law suspending the privilege of the writ of *habeas corpus.*

### Constitution of the State of New York.

Adopted in convention, but not yet submitted for ratification.

The privilege of the writ of *habeas corpus* shall not be suspended, unless when, in cases of rebellion or invasion, the public safety may require its suspension.

Every male inhabitant, of the age of twenty-one years, who shall have been a citizen for ten days and a resident of the State for one year next preceding an election, and for the last four months a resident of the county where he may offer his vote, shall be entitled to vote at such election in the election district of which he shall be at the time a resident, and not elsewhere, for all officers that now are or hereafter may be elective by the people, and upon all questions which may be submitted to the vote of the people of the State; provided that such citizen shall have been for thirty days next preceding the election a resident of the town or ward, and, for ten days, of the election district in which he offers his vote.

Registration of voters authorized. Thirty-two senators, and one hundred and thirty-nine assemblymen. No bill shall pass except upon the assent of a majority of the members elected to each house. Governor has veto, with two-thirds vote of members elected necessary to repass the vetoed bill. Legislature shall not authorize the consolidation of railroad corporations owning parallel or competing lines of road. No law shall be passed authorizing or sanctioning the suspension of specie payments. All able-bodied male citizens, between eighteen and forty-five, shall be annually enrolled, as a militia

66

force, to be divided into active and reserve forces—the active to be called the National Guard of the State of New York, and not to exceed, in peace, thirty thousand men.

## Constitution of Alabama.

Adopted in convention, November 5, 1867, voted on by the people, February 4, 1868.

The declaration of rights provides that all persons resident in the State, born in the United States, or naturalized, or who shall have legally declared their intention to become citizens of the United States, are citizens of the State, possessing equal civil and political rights and public privileges. Freedom of speech and press is guaranteed, with responsibility for its abuse; also the right to bear arms in defence of himself and the State. Prohibits any form of slavery or involuntary servitude except as punishment for crime. Asserts that the State has no right to sever its relations to the Federal Union, or to pass any law in derogation of the paramount allegiance of the citizens of this State to the Government of the United States.

The president of the senate and speaker of the house shall hold their offices until their successors shall be qualified. The legislature has power to suppress duelling. The State shall not engage in any internal improvements. The governor has the veto power, but a majority of the whole number of members of each house may pass a bill over the veto. The governor shall have a pardoning power in all cases except treason, but his pardon shall not relieve from civil or political disability.

Art. 7, sec. 2.—Every male person, born in the United States, and every male person who has been naturalized, or who has legally declared his intention to become a citizen of the United States, twenty-one years old or upwards, who shall have resided in this State six months next preceding the election, and three months in the county in which he offers to vote, except as hereinafter provided, shall be deemed an elector; provided that no soldier, or sailor, or marine, in the military or naval service of the United States, shall hereafter acquire a residence by reason of being stationed on duty in this State.

Sec. 3. It shall be the duty of the general assembly to provide, from time to time, for the registration of all electors, but the following classes of persons shall not be permitted to register, vote, or hold office: 1st. Those who, during the late rebellion, inflicted, or caused to be inflicted, any cruel or unusual punishment upon any soldier, sailor, marine, employé, or citizen of the United States, or who, in any other way, violated the rules of civilized warfare. 2d. Those who may be disqualified from holding office by the proposed amendment of the Constitution of the United States, known as "Article XIV," and those who have been disqualified from registering to vote for delegates to the Convention to frame a constitution for the State of Alabama, under the act of Congress "to provide for the more efficient government of the rebel States," passed by Congress March 2, 1867, and the acts supplementary thereto, except such persons as aided in the reconstruction proposed by Congress, and accept the political equality of all

men before the law; provided, that the general assembly shall have power to remove the disabilities incurred under this clause. 3d. Criminals. 4th. Idiots and insane persons.

All persons, before registering, must take and subscribe the following oath:

I, ——, do solemnly swear (or affirm) that I will support and maintain the Constitution and laws of the United States, and the constitution and laws of the State of Alabama; that I am not excluded from registering by any of the clauses in sec. 3, article 7, of the constitution of the State of Alabama; that I will never countenance or aid in the secession of this State from the United States; that I accept the civil and political equality of all men; and agree not to attempt to deprive any person or persons, on account of race, color, or previous condition, of any political or civil right, privilege, or immunity enjoyed by any other class of men; and, furthermore, that I will not in any way injure, or countenance in others any attempt to injure, any person or persons on account of past or present support of the Government of the United States, the laws of the United States, or the principle of political and civil equality of all men, or for affiliation with any political party.

The militia shall consist of all able-bodied male inhabitants between eighteen and forty-five, to be divided into two classes, volunteer and reserve. The common schools and other educational institutions shall be under the management of a board of education. Certain funds are inviolably appropriated to educational purposes. One fifth of the annual revenues of the State shall be devoted exclusively to the maintenance of public schools, the whole tax on real and personal property not, however, to exceed two per cent. of the assessed value. Corporations to be formed under general laws. Personal property to the value of $1,000 to be exempted from sale on execution for debt hereafter contracted; also every homestead in the country, not exceeding eighty acres of land, and the dwelling and appurtenances thereon; or, in lieu thereof, a lot in a city, town, or village, with the appurtenances thereon, and occupied by the owner, not exceeding $2,000 in value, such exemption not to extend to any mortgage lawfully obtained.

## Constitution of Arkansas.

Adopted by convention February 11, 1868, and ratified by the people March 13, 1868.

It provides, among other things, that the paramount allegiance of every citizen is due to the Federal Government, in the exercise of all its constitutional powers, as the same may have been or may be defined by the Supreme Court of the United States, and no power exists in the people of this or any other State of the Federal Union to dissolve their connection therewith, or perform any act tending to impair, subvert, or resist the supreme authority of the United States. The equality of all persons before the law is recognized and shall ever remain inviolate; nor shall any citizen ever be deprived of any right, privilege, or immunity, nor exempted from any burden or duty, on account of race, color, or previous condition.

The general assembly shall not grant to any citizen or class of citizens privileges or immunities which, upon the same terms, shall not equally belong to all citizens. No religious or property test shall be required for voting or holding office.

Sec. 25 declares null and void the ordinance

of secession, and all action of the State under its constitution of 1861, and the State debt then incurred shall not be recognized as obligatory.

No citizen of this State shall be disfranchised, or deprived of any of the rights or privileges secured to any citizen thereof, unless the same is done by the law of the land, or the judgment of his peers, except as hereinafter provided. There shall be neither slavery nor involuntary servitude, either by indentures, apprenticeships, or otherwise, except as a punishment for crime. The general assembly shall have no power to make compensation for emancipated slaves. Taxes limited to two per cent. of assessed value.

Every male person born in the United States, and every male person who has been naturalized, or has legally declared his intention to become a citizen of the United States, who is twenty-one years old or upwards, and who shall have resided in the State six months next preceding the election, and who at the time is an actual resident of the county in which he offers to vote, except as hereinafter provided, shall be deemed an elector.

ART. 8. SEC. 3. The following classes shall not be permitted to register or hold office, viz:

*First.* Those who during the rebellion took the oath of allegiance, or gave bonds for loyalty and good behaviour to the United States Government, and afterwards gave aid, comfort, or countenance to those engaged in armed hostility to the Government of the United States, either by becoming a soldier in the rebel army, or by entering the lines of said army, or adhering in any way to the cause of rebellion, or by accompanying any armed force belonging to the rebel army, or by furnishing supplies of any kind to the same.

*Second.* Those who are disqualified as electors, or from holding office in the State or States from which they came.

*Third.* Those persons who during the late rebellion violated the rules of civilized warfare.

*Fourth.* Those who may be disqualified by the proposed amendment to the Constitution of the United States, known as Article XIV, and those who have been disqualified from registering to vote for delegates to the convention to frame a constitution for the State of Arkansas, under the act of Congress entitled " An act to provide for the more efficient government of the rebel States," passed March 2d, 1867, and the acts supplemental thereto.

*Fifth.* Criminals.

*Sixth.* Insane.

Provided, that all persons included in the 1st, 2d, 3d and 4th subdivisions of this section, who have openly advocated or who have voted for the reconstruction proposed by Congress, and accept the equality of all men before the law, shall be deemed qualified electors under this constitution

SEC. 4. The general assembly shall have power, by a two thirds vote of each house, approved by the governor, to remove the disabilities included in the 1st, 2d, 3d and 4th subdivisions of section three, of this article, when it appears that such person, applying for relief from such disabilities, has in good faith returned to his allegiance to the Government of the United States;

provided, the general assembly shall have no power to remove the disabilities of any person embraced in the aforesaid subdivisions who, after the adoption of this constitution by the convention, persists in opposing the acts of Congress and reconstruction thereunder.

All persons before registering or voting must take and subscribe the following oath:

I, ———, do solemnly swear (or affirm) that I will support and maintain the Constitution and laws of the United States, and the constitution and laws of the State of Arkansas; that I am not excluded from registering or voting by any of the clauses in the first, second, third, or fourth subdivisions of Article VIII of the constitution of the State of Arkansas; that I will never countenance or aid in the secession of this State from the United States; that I accept the civil and political equality of all men, and agree not to attempt to deprive any person or persons, on account of race, color, or previous condition, of any political or civil right, privilege, or immunity enjoyed by any other class of men; and, furthermore, that I will not in any way injure, or countenance in others any attempt to injure, any person or persons on account of past or present support of the Government of the United States, the laws of the United States, or the principle of the political and civil equality of all men, or for affiliation with any political party.

All contracts for the sale or purchase of slaves are null and void, and no court of this State shall take cognizance of any suit founded on such contracts; nor shall any amount ever be collected or recovered on any judgment or decree which shall have been, or which hereafter may be, rendered on account of any such contract or obligation on any pretext, legal or otherwise.

A system of free schools shall be established, for the gratuitous instruction of all persons between 5 and 21 years, the funds to be distributed to the counties in the proportion of persons between those ages. Certain funds are set apart to be sacredly preserved as a public school fund; also, a *per capita* tax of $1 on every male inhabitant over twenty-one, to be collected for the support of free schools and a university, the residue required to be furnished from the State treasury. The general assembly shall require by law that every child of sufficient mental and physical ability shall attend the public schools for a term equivalent to three years, between the ages of 5 and 18 years, unless educated by other means. Public schools to be open not less than three months in a year. No poll tax to be levied except for school purposes. All able-bodied electors liable to military duty. Personal property to the value of $2,000 to be exempt from sale for debt hereafter contracted. Homestead of a married man or head of a family not to be encumbered except for taxes, laborers' and mechanics' liens, and securities for the purchase-money thereof; a country homestead of 160 acres and a town property of $5,000 to be exempt, with similar exceptions as above. Only qualified electors shall be jurors. Indentures not to be valid, being for more than one year, except in the case of apprenticeships. Persons disqualified herein shall not vote for candidates, nor upon the ratification of the constitution. The judges of election shall administer to every voter the oath prescribed in the constitution.

### Constitution of Florida.

Adopted by Convention February 25, 1868, and ratified by the people May 6, 1868.

It provides, among other things, that slavery shall not exist.

This State shall ever remain a member of the American Union, the people thereof a part of the American nation, and any attempt, from whatever source or upon whatever pretence, to dissolve said Union, or to sever said nation, shall be resisted with the whole power of the State.

It is the paramount duty of the State to make ample provision for the education of all the children residing within its borders, without distinction or preference.

Every male person of the age of 21 years and upwards, of whatever race, color, nationality, or previous condition, or who shall, at the time of offering to vote, be a citizen of the United States, or who shall have declared his intention to become such in conformity to the laws of the United States, and who shall have resided and had his habitation, domicil, home, and place of permanent abode in Florida for one year, and in the county for six months, next preceding the election at which he shall offer to vote, shall in such county be deemed a qualified elector at all elections under this constitution. Every elector shall, at the time of his registration, take and subscribe to the following oath:

I, —— ——, do solemnly swear that I will support, protect, and defend the Constitution and Government of the United States, and the constitution and government of Florida, against all enemies, foreign or domestic; that I will bear true faith, loyalty, and allegiance to the same, any ordinances or resolution of any State convention or legislation to the contrary notwithstanding. So help me God.

Lotteries are prohibited. No person who is not a qualified elector, or any person who shall have been convicted of bribery, forgery, perjury, larceny, or other high crime, unless restored to civil rights, shall be permitted to serve on juries. The governor has the veto, subject to the subsequent action of two-thirds of each house. Grand and petit jurors shall be taken from the registered voters of their respective counties. A common school fund provided for, of which a tax of not less than one mill on all taxable property is a part. Homestead exemption provided.

All able-bodied male inhabitants between 18 and 45, who are citizens of the United States, or have declared their intention to become so, shall constitute the militia.

The legislature shall enact laws requiring educational qualifications for electors after the year 1880, but no such laws shall be made applicable to any elector who may have registered or voted at any election previous thereto.

Confederate and State war debt repudiated. All contracts in consideration of slaves declared null. Governor has the appointment, with the consent of the senate, of the judges of the supreme court, circuit judges, secretary of state, and like State officers, and he has the absolute appointment of justices of the peace.

All ordinances and resolutions heretofore passed by any convention of the people, and all acts and resolutions of the Legislature conflicting or inconsistent with the Constitution of the United States and the statutes thereof, and with this constitution, and in derogation of the existence or position of the State as one of the States of the United States of America, are hereby declared null and void, and of no effect.

Recognizes all laws and acts of the rebel State government not inconsistent with the Constitution and laws of the United States or this constitution.

Article 16, sec. 1, disables any person from holding office who is disabled by the 14th constitutional amendment, subject to the removal of such disability by Congress.

The following shall be the oath of office for each officer in the State, including members of the legislature:

I do solemnly swear that I will support, protect, and defend the Constitution and Government of the United States, and of the State of Florida, against all enemies, domestic or foreign, and that I will bear true faith, loyalty, and allegiance to the same, and that I am entitled to hold office under this constitution. That I will well and faithfully perform all the duties of the office of ——, on which I am about to enter. So help me God.

There shall be no civil or political distinction in this State on account of race, color, or previous condition of servitude, and the legislature shall have no power to prohibit, by law, any class of persons on account of race, color, or previous condition of servitude, to vote or hold any office, beyond the conditions prescribed by this constitution.

Ordinances were adopted by the Convention declaring it unlawful for any sheriff or other officer to sell, under execution or other legal process, any property, real or personal, and any sale so made shall be void. Suits, decrees, &c., made during the war in the courts, against a person absent from the State, are annulled. So much of the act of January 16, 1866, as levied a tax of one dollar upon each colored male between twenty-one and fifty-five was repealed. County criminal courts abolished, and duties transferred to circuit courts.

### Constitution of Louisiana.

Adopted by Convention March 2, 1868, and ratified by the people April 18, 1868. Provides, among other things, that slavery shall not exist.

All persons, without regard to race, color, or previous condition, born or naturalized in the United States, and subject to the jurisdiction thereof, and residents of this State for one year, are citizens of this State. The citizens of this State owe allegiance to the United States; and this allegiance is paramount to that which they owe to the State. They shall enjoy the same civil, political, and public rights and privileges, and be subject to the same pains and penalties.

All persons shall enjoy equal rights and privileges, upon any conveyance of a public character, and all places of business, or of public resort, or for which a license is required by either State, parish, or municipal authority, shall be deemed places of a public character, and shall be opened to the accommodation and patronage of all persons, without distinction or discrimination on account of race or color. Every elector shall be eligible to a seat in the House of Representatives and to the Senate, if twenty-five years old; and he shall be eligible to any municipal office.

Every male person, of the age of twenty-one years or upwards, born or naturalized in the United States, and subject to the jurisdiction thereof, and a resident of this State one year next preceding an election, and the last ten days within the parish in which he offers to vote, shall be deemed an elector, except those disfranchised by this constitution, and persons under interdiction.

The following persons shall be prohibited from voting and holding any office: All persons who shall have been convicted of treason, perjury, forgery, bribery, or other crime punishable in the penitentiary, and persons under interdiction.

All persons who are estopped from claiming the right of suffrage by abjuring their allegiance to the United States Government, or by notoriously levying war against it, or adhering to its enemies, giving them aid or comfort, but who have not expatriated themselves, nor have been convicted of any of the crimes mentioned in the first paragraph of this article, are hereby restored to the said right, except the following: Those who held office, civil or military, for one year or more, under the organization styled "the Confederate States of America;" those who registered themselves as enemies of the United States; those who acted as leaders of guerrilla bands during the late rebellion; those who, in the advocacy of treason, wrote or published newspaper articles or preached sermons during the late rebellion; and those who voted for and signed an ordinance of secession in any State. No person included in these exceptions shall either vote or hold office until he shall have relieved himself by voluntarily writing and signing a certificate setting forth that he acknowledges the late rebellion to have been morally and politically wrong, and that he regrets any aid and comfort he may have given it; and he shall file the certificate in the office of the secretary of State, and it shall be published in the official journal: *Provided*, That no person who, prior to the 1st of January, 1868, favored the execution of the laws of the United States popularly known as the reconstruction acts of Congress, and openly and actively assisted the loyal men of the State in their efforts to restore Louisiana to her position in the Union, shall be held to be included among those herein excepted. Registrars of voters shall take the oath of any such person as *prima facie* evidence of the fact that he is entitled to the benefit of this proviso.

Members of the General Assembly and all other officers, before they enter upon the duties of their offices, shall take the following oath or affirmation:

I, (A. B.) do solemnly swear (or affirm) that I accept the civil and political equality of all men, and agree not to attempt to deprive any person or persons, on account of race, color, or previous condition, of any political or civil right, privilege, or immunity enjoyed by any other class of men; that I will support the constitution and laws of the United States, and the constitution and laws of this State, and that I will faithfully and impartially discharge and perform all the duties incumbent on me as —— according to the best of my ability and understanding: so help me God.

No liability, either State, parochial, or municipal, shall exist for any debts contracted for or in the interest of the rebellion against the United States Government.

There shall be no property qualification for office.

All agreements, the consideration of which was Confederate money, notes, or bonds, are null and void, and shall not be enforced by the courts of this State.

Contracts for the sale of persons are null and void.

The State of Louisiana shall never assume nor pay any debt or obligation contracted or incurred in aid of the rebellion; nor shall this State ever, in any manner, claim from the United States, or make any allowance or compensation for slaves emancipated or liberated in any way whatever.

All contracts by which children were bound out without the knowledge or consent of their parents are null and void.

There shall be at least one free public school in each parish, for children between six and twenty-one, who shall be admitted to the public schools or other institutions of learning sustained or established by the State in common, without distinction of race, color, or previous condition. And no municipal corporation shall make rules contrary to the spirit and intention of this article. Public school fund provided for, of which one half of the poll-tax is a part.

The militia are all able-bodied male citizens, between eighteen and forty-five.

The ordinance of secession of the State of Louisiana, passed 26th of January, 1861, is hereby declared to be null and void. The constitution adopted in 1864, and all previous constitutions in the State of Louisiana, are declared to be superseded by this constitution.

An election for State officers provided for April 17 and 18, at the same time with the vote on the constitution. All civil officers thus elected shall enter upon the discharge of their duties on the second Monday after the return of their election shall have been officially promulgated, or as soon as qualified according to law, and shall continue in office for the terms of their respective offices herein prescribed, said terms to date from the first Monday in November following the election. The Legislature shall meet in New Orleans on the third Monday after the promulgation aforesaid, and proceed, after organization, to vote upon the adoption of the XIVth Amendment to the Constitution of the United States.

### Constitution of Georgia.

Adopted by Convention, March 11, 1868, and ratified by the people, April 20, 1868. Provides, among other things, that slavery shall not exist.

All persons born or naturalized in the United States, and resident in this State, are hereby declared citizens of this State, and no laws shall be made or enforced which shall abridge the privileges or immunities of citizens of the United States, or of this State, or deny to any person within its jurisdiction the equal protection of its laws. And it shall be the duty of the General Assembly, by appropriate legislation, to protect every person in the due enjoyment of the rights, privileges, and immunities guaranteed in this section.

The State of Georgia shall ever remain a member of the American Union; the people thereof are a part of the American nation; every citizen thereof owes paramount allegiance to the Constitution and government of the United States, and no law or ordinance of this State, in contravention or subversion thereof, shall ever have any binding force.

Electors shall, in all cases except treason, felony, or breach of the peace, be privileged from arrest for five days before an election, during the election, and two days subsequent thereto.

The social *status* of the citizens shall never be the subject of legislation. The power of the courts to punish for contempt shall be limited by legislative acts. No imprisonment for debt. Whipping, as a punishment for crime, prohibited. No poll-tax to be levied except for educational purposes, and it not to exceed $1 annually on each poll.

Every male person, born in the United States, and every male person who has been naturalized, or who has legally declared his intention to become a citizen of the United States, twenty-one years old or upward, who shall have resided in this State six months next preceding the election, and shall have resided thirty days in the county in which he offers to vote, and shall have paid all taxes which may have been required of him, and which he may have had an opportunity of paying, agreeably to law, for the year next preceding the election, (except as hereinafter provided), shall be deemed an elector; and every male citizen of the United States, of the age aforesaid, (except as hereinafter provided,) who may be a resident of the State at the time of the adoption of this constitution, shall be deemed an elector, and shall have all the rights of an elector, as aforesaid: *Provided*, That no soldier, sailor, or marine in the military or naval service of the United States shall acquire the rights of an elector by reason of being stationed on duty in this State; and no person shall vote, who, if challenged, shall refuse to take the following oath: "I do swear that I have not given, or received, nor do I expect to give, or receive, any money, treat, or other thing of value, by which my vote, or any vote, is affected, or expected to be affected, at this election; nor have I given or promised any reward, or made any threat, by which to prevent any person from voting at this election."

Every Senator or Representative, before taking his seat, shall take an oath or affirmation to support the Constitution of the United States, and of this State; that he has not practiced any unlawful means, directly or indirectly, to procure his election, and that he has not given, or offered, or promised, or caused to be given, or offered, or promised, to any person, any money, treat, or thing of value, with intent to affect any vote, or to prevent any person voting at the election at which he was elected.

The Governor has the veto power, subject to a two thirds vote of each House.

All contracts made, and not executed, during the late rebellion, in aid of it, are annulled.

Common school fund provided for. Militia to be all able-bodied males, between eighteen and forty-five.

Each head of a family, or guardian or trustee of a family of minor children, shall be entitled to a homestead of realty to the value of two thousand dollars, in specie, and personal property to the value of one thousand dollars,

in specie, both to be valued at the time they are set apart.

The laws of general operation in force in this State are:

1. As the supreme law—the Constitution of the United States, the laws of the United States in pursuance thereof, and all treaties made under the authority of the United States. 2. This constitution. 3. Acts of rebel legislation not inconsistent with the Constitution and laws of the United States.

The following sections are those referred to in the action of Congress on the restoration of the State:

SECTION XVII—I. No court in this State shall have jurisdiction to try or determine any suit against any resident of this State upon any contract or agreement made or implied, or upon any contract made in renewal of any debt existing prior to the 1st day of June, 1865. Nor shall any court or ministerial officer of this State have authority to enforce any judgment, execution, or decree rendered or issued upon any contract or agreement made or implied, or upon any contract in renewal of a debt existing prior to the 1st day of June, 1865, except in the following cases:

1. In suits against trustees, where the trust property is in the hands of the trustee, or has been invested by him in other specific effects now in his hands, and in suits by the vendor of real estate against the vendee, where not more than one-third of the purchase-money has been paid, and the vendee is in possession of the land or specific effects for which he has sold it, and he refuses to deliver the land or said effects to the vendor. In such cases, the courts and officers may entertain jurisdiction and enforce judgments against said trust-property, or land, or effects.

2. In suits for the benefit of minors by trustees appointed before the 1st day of June, 1865.

3. In suits against corporations in their corporate capacity, but not so as to enforce the debt against the stockholders or officers thereof in their individual capacity.

4. In suits by charitable or literary institutions for money loaned, property — other than slaves—sold, or services rendered by such institutions.

5. In suits on debts due for mechanical or manual labor, when the suit is by the mechanic or laborer.

6. In cases when the debt is set up by way of defence, and the debt set up exceeds any debt due by defendant to plaintiff, of which the courts are denied jurisdiction.

7. In all other cases in which the General Assembly shall by law give the said courts and officers jurisdiction: *Provided*, That no court or officer shall have, nor shall the General Assembly give, jurisdiction or authority to try or give judgment on or enforce any debt, the consideration of which was a slave or slaves, or the hire thereof.

III. It shall be in the power of the General Assembly to assess and collect upon all debts, judgments, or causes of action when due, founded on any contract made or implied before the 1st day of June, 1865, in the hands of any one in his own right, or trustee, agent, or attorney of another, on or after the 1st day of January, 1868, a tax of not exceeding twenty-five per cent., to be paid by the creditor, on pain of the forfeiture of the debt, but chargeable by him as to one-half thereof against the debtor, and collectable with the debt: *Provided*, That this tax shall not be collected if the debt or cause of action be abandoned or settled without legal process, or, if in judgment, be settled without levy and sale: *And provided further*, That this tax shall not be levied so long as the courts of this State shall not have jurisdiction of such debts or causes of action.

### Constitution of North Carolina.

Adopted by Convention March 16, 1868, and ratified by the people April 23, 1868. Provides, among other things:

SEC. 3. That the people of this State have the inherent, sole, and exclusive right of regulating the internal government and police thereof, and of altering and abolishing their constitution and form of government, whenever it may be necessary to their safety and happiness; but every such right should be exercised in pursuance of law, and consistently with the Constitution of the United States.

SEC. 4. That this State shall ever remain a member of the American Union; that the people thereof are part of the American nation; that there is no right on the part of this State to secede, and that all attempts, from whatever source or upon whatever pretext, to dissolve said Union, or to sever said nation, ought to be resisted with the whole power of the State.

SEC. 5. That every citizen of this State owes paramount allegiance to the Constitution and Government of the United States, and that no law or ordinance of the State in contravention or subversion thereof can have any binding force.

SEC. 6. To maintain the honor and good faith of the State untarnished, the public debt, regularly contracted before and since the rebellion, shall be regarded as inviolable and never be questioned; but the State shall never assume or pay, or authorize the collection of, any debt or obligation, express or implied, incurred in aid of insurrection or rebellion against the United States, or any claim for the loss or emancipation of any slave.

ART. 6. SEC. 1. Every male person born in the United States, and every male person who has been naturalized, twenty-one years old or upward, who shall have resided in this State twelve months next preceding the election, and thirty days in the county in which he offers to vote, shall be deemed an elector.

SEC. 4. Every voter, except as hereinafter provided, shall be eligible to office; but before entering upon the discharge of the duties of his office, he shall take and subscribe the following oath:

I, ——, do solemnly swear (or affirm) that I will support and maintain the Constitution and laws of the United States, and the constitution and laws of North Carolina not inconsistent therewith, and that I will faithfully discharge the duties of my office. So help me God.

The general assembly, at its first session, shall establish a uniform system of public schools, to be free to all the children of the State between six and twenty-one years. The University of North Carolina declared to be held to an inseparable connection with the free public school system.

Homestead exemption secured, realty to the value of $1,000, personal $500. All able-bodied male citizens, between twenty-one and forty, are liable to duty in the militia.

Duelling prohibited.

### Constitution of South Carolina.

Adopted by Convention March 17, 1868, and ratified by the people April 16, 1868.

Provides, among other things, that slavery shall never exist in this State.

Every citizen of this State owes paramount allegiance to the Constitution and Government of the United States, and no law or ordinance of this State in contravention or subversion thereof can have any binding force.

This State shall ever remain a member of the American Union, and all attempts, from whatever source, or upon whatever pretext, to dissolve the said Union, shall be resisted with the whole power of the State.

No person shall be disqualified as a witness, or be prevented from acquiring, holding, and transmitting property, or be hindered in acquiring education, or be liable to any other punishment for any offence, or be subjected in law to any other restraints or disqualifications in regard to any personal rights than such as are laid upon others under like circumstances.

No person shall be imprisoned for debt, except in cases of fraud; and a reasonable amount of property, as a homestead, shall be exempted from seizure or sale for the payment of any debts or liabilities, except for the payment of such obligations as are provided for in this constitution.

No property qualification shall be necessary for an election to or the holding of any office.

All elections shall be free and open, and every inhabitant of this Commonwealth possessing the qualifications provided for in this constitution, shall have an equal right to elect officers and be elected to fill public offices.

Representation shall be apportioned according to population, and no person in this State shall be disfranchised, or deprived of any of the rights or privileges now enjoyed, except by the law of the land or the judgment of his peers.

Distinction on account of race or color, in any case whatever, shall be prohibited, and all classes of citizens shall enjoy equally all common, public, legal, and political privileges.

Members of the general assembly, and all officers, before they enter upon the execution of the duties of their respective offices, and all members of the bar, before they enter upon the practice of their profession, shall take and subscribe the following oath:

I, ——, do solemnly swear (or affirm, as the case may be) that I am duly qualified, according to the Constitution of the United States and of this State, to exercise the duties of the office to which I have been elected, (or appointed,) and that I will faithfully discharge, to the best of my abilities, the duties thereof; that I recognize the supremacy of the Constitution and laws of the United States over the constitution and laws of any State; and that I will support, protect, and defend the Constitution of the United States and the constitution of South Carolina, as ratified by the people on the —— day of ——, 1868. So help me God.

Every male citizen of the United States, of the age of twenty-one years and upwards, not laboring under the disabilities named in this constitution, without distinction of race, color, or former condition, who shall be a resident of this State at the time of the adoption of this constitution, or who shall thereafter reside in this State one year, and in the county in which he offers to vote sixty days next preceding any election, shall be entitled to vote for all officers that are now, or hereafter may be, elected by the people, and upon all questions submitted to the electors at any elections: *Provided*, That no person shall be allowed to vote or hold office who is now, or hereafter may be, disqualified therefor by the Constitution of the United States, until such disqualification shall be removed by the Congress of the United States.

Homestead exemption secured.

The general assembly shall never pass any law that will deprive any of the citizens of this State of the right of suffrage, except for treason, murder, robbery, or duelling, whereof the persons shall have been duly tried and convicted.

No person shall be disfranchised for felony or other crimes committed while such person was a slave.

All the public schools, colleges, and universities of this State, supported in whole or in part by the public funds, shall be free and open to all the children and youths of the State, without regard to race or color.

Governor has the veto, but two-thirds of *each* house may pass a bill over the veto. Judges shall not charge juries in respect to matters of fact, but may state the testimony and declare the law.

All contracts, whether under seal or not, the consideration of which were for the purchase of slaves, are declared null and void; and all proceedings under them annulled.

Elections shall be by ballot. All voters shall be eligible to elective offices, except as otherwise provided in this constitution or the Constitution and laws of the United States. Presidential electors shall be elected by the people.

The general assembly may levy a poll-tax of $1 per year, for the public school fund. No additional poll-tax shall be levied by any municipal corporation, and no person to be deprived of suffrage for non-payment of this tax.

No debt contracted by this State in behalf of the late rebellion, in whole or in part, shall ever be paid.

A liberal and uniform system of free public schools shall be established, for all children between six and sixteen, for a term equivalent to twenty-four months at least, facilities to be afforded to all the inhabitants for the free education of their children. School fund established.

The militia shall consist of all able-bodied male citizens between eighteen and forty-five. No person shall be elected or appointed to any office unless he possesses the qualifications of an elector.

### Constitution of Virginia.

Adopted by Convention April 7, 1868. Provides, among other things—

That this State shall ever remain a member of the United States of America, and that the people thereof are part of the American nation, and that all attempts, from whatever source or upon whatever pretext, to dissolve said Union or to sever said nation, are unauthorized and ought to be resisted with the whole power of the State.

The Constitution of the United States, and the laws of Congress passed in pursuance thereof, constitute the supreme law of the land, to which paramount allegiance and obedience are due from every citizen, anything in the constitution, ordinances, or laws of any State to the contrary notwithstanding.

Slavery shall not exist. All citizens of the State are declared to possess equal civil and political rights and public privileges. Duelling is prohibited. Only persons qualified to hold office shall be jurors.

Every male citizen of the United States, twenty-one years old, who shall have been a resident of this State twelve months, and of the county, city, or town in which he shall offer to vote three months next preceding any election, shall be entitled to vote upon all questions submitted to the people at such election.

Among the excepted persons are all those who have been Senators or Representatives in Congress, or electors of President or Vice President, or who held any office, civil or military, under the United States, or under any State, who, having previously taken an oath, as member of Congress or officer of the United States, or as a member of any legislature, or as an executive or judicial officer of any State, shall have engaged in insurrection or rebellion against the same, or given aid or comfort to the enemies thereof. This clause shall include the following officers: Governor, Lieutenant Governor, secretary of State; auditor of public accounts, second auditor, register of the land office, State treasurer, attorney general, sheriffs, sergeant of a city or town, commissioner of the revenue, county surveyors, constables, overseers of the poor, commissioner of the board of public works, judges of the supreme court, judges of the circuit court, judges of the court of hustings, justices of the county courts, mayor, recorder, alderman, councilmen of a city or town, coroners, escheators, inspectors of tobacco, flour, &c., clerks of the supreme, district, circuit, and county courts, and of the court of hustings, and attorneys for the Commonwealth: *Provided*, That the Legislature may, by a vote of three-fifths of both houses, remove the disabilities incurred by this clause from any person included therein, by a separate vote in each case.

All persons, before entering upon the discharge of any function as officers of the State, shall take the following oath:

I, ——, do solemnly swear (or affirm) that I will support and maintain the Constitution and laws of the United States, and the constitution and laws of the State of Virginia; that I recognize and accept the civil and political equality of all men before the laws; and that I will faithfully perform the duty of ——, to the best of my ability. So help me God.

In addition to this, all State, city and county officers shall take the test oath prescribed by the act of July 2, 1862.

The Legislature shall enact a registry law, and persons applying to register shall take this oath:

I, ——, do solemnly swear (or affirm) that I am not disqualified from exercising the right of suffrage by the constitution framed by the convention which assembled in the city of Richmond on the 3d day of December, 1867, and that I will support and defend the same to the best of my ability.

The Governor has the veto power, subject to the passage by two-thirds. Lotteries prohibited. A uniform system of public free schools to be established, and to be introduced into all the counties by 1876. Capitation tax and an annual tax on property not less than one mill nor more than five for the support of schools. The militia to consist of all able-bodied males between eighteen and forty-five. Homestead exemption provided.

Ordinance passed that the constitution be submitted for ratification June 2, when State officers and Representatives in Congress are to be chosen; the Assembly to meet June 24. [General Schofield recommended that the section prescribing the test-oath of 1862 for all State, city and county officers be submitted separately, and that the election be fixed not less than forty days after the passage by Congress of the necessary appropriation to pay the expense.]

### Constitution of Mississippi.

Adopted by convention May 15, 1868, and submitted to popular vote, June 22,

Provides, among other things, slavery shall not exist; no property qualification shall be required for jurors or for eligibility to office.

All persons resident in this State, citizens of the United States, are hereby declared citizens of the State of Mississippi.

No property or educational qualification shall ever be required for any person to become an elector.

The right to withdraw from the Federal Union on account of any real or supposed grievances shall never be assumed by this State, nor shall any law be passed in derogation of the paramount allegiance of the citizens of this State to the Government of the United States.

No public money or moneys shall be appropriated for any charitable or other public institutions in this State, making any distinction among the citizens thereof; *Provided*, That nothing herein contained, shall be so construed as to prevent the Legislature from appropriating the school fund in accordance with the article in this constitution relating to public schools.

The right of all citizens to travel upon all public conveyances shall not be infringed upon nor in any manner abridged in this State.

The Governor has the veto power, subject to two-thirds vote of each house.

All male inhabitants of this State, except idiots and insane persons, and Indians not taxed, citizens of the United States, or naturalized, twenty-one years old and upwards, who have resided in this State six months, and in the county one month next preceding the day of election at which said inhabitant offers to vote, and who are duly registered according to the requirements of section three of this article, and who are not disqualified by reason of any crime, are declared to be qualified electors.

The Legislature shall provide by law for the registration of all persons entitled to vote at any election, and all persons entitled to register shall take and subscribe to the following oath or affirmation:

I, ——, do solemnly swear (or affirm) in the presence of Almighty God, that I am twenty-one years old; that I have resided in this State six months, and in —— county one month; that I will faithfully support and obey the Constitution and laws of the United States, and of the State of Mississippi, and will bear true faith and allegiance to the same; that I am not disfranchised in any of the provisions of the acts known as the reconstruction acts of the Thirty-Ninth and Fortieth Congress; and that I admit the political and civil equality of all men. So help me God.

*Provided*, That if Congress shall, at any time, remove the disabilities of any person disfranchised in the said reconstruction acts of the said Thirty-Ninth and Fortieth Congress, (and the Legislature of this State shall concur therein,) then so much of this oath, and so much only, as refers to the said reconstruction acts, shall not be required of such person, so pardoned, to entitle him to be registered.

No person shall be eligible to any office of profit or trust, or to any office in the militia of this State, who is not a qualified elector.

No person shall be eligible to any office of profit or trust, civil or military, in this State, who, as a member of the Legislature, voted for the call of the convention that passed the ordinance of secession, or who, as a delegate to any convention, voted for or signed any ordinance of secession, or who gave voluntary aid, countenance, counsel or encouragement to persons engaged in armed hostility to the United States, or who accepted or attempted to exercise the functions of any office, civil or military, under any authority or pretended government, authority, power, or constitution, within the United States, hostile or inimical thereto, except all persons who aided reconstruction by voting for this convention, or who have continuously advocated the assembling of this convention, and shall continuously and in good faith advocate the acts of the same; but the Legislature may remove such disability; *Provided*, That nothing in this section, except voting for or signing the ordinance of secession, shall be so construed as to exclude from office the private soldier of the late so-called Confederate States army.

The State of Mississippi shall never assume nor pay any debt or obligation contracted in aid of the rebellion, nor shall this State ever in any manner claim from the United States, or make any allowance or compensation for slaves emancipated or liberated in any way whatever, since the 9th day of January, 1861.

Members of the Legislature, and all other officers elected or appointed to any office in this State, shall, before entering upon the discharge of the duties thereof, take and subscribe the following oath of office:

I, ——, do solemnly swear (or affirm) that I will faithfully support and true allegiance bear the Constitution of the United States and the State of Mississippi, and obey the laws thereof; that I am not disqualified from holding office by the Constitution of the United States or the State of Mississippi; that I have neve-

as a member of any convention voted for or signed any ordinance of secession; that I have never as a member of any State Legislature voted for the call of any convention that passed any such ordinance; that I will faithfully discharge the duties of the office upon which I am about to enter. So help me God.

The ordinance of secession of the State of Mississippi, passed January 9, 1866, is hereby declared to be null and void. The present and all previous constitutions of the State of Mississippi are hereby declared to be repealed and annulled by this constitution.

All laws now in force in this State, not enacted in furtherance of secession and rebellion, and not repugnant to this constitution, shall continue in force.

Common school fund provided for; the poll-tax in its aid not to exceed $2 annually.

All able-bodied males, between eighteen and forty-five, shall be liable to military duty in the militia.

Lotteries and sale of lottery tickets prohibited.

All lands sold in pursuance of decree of courts or execution shall be divided into tracts not to exceed one hundred and sixty acres.

All persons who have not been married, but are now living together and cohabiting as husband and wife, shall be taken and held for all purposes in law as married, and their children, whether born before or after the ratification of this constitution, shall be legitimate, and the Legislature may by law punish adultery and concubinage.

1868, March 13—An ordinance adopted, as follows:

SEC. 1. That no contracts shall be valid which in any manner abridge or affect the right of franchise of either party; and any person or persons demanding such conditions shall, upon conviction thereof before any court having competent jurisdiction, be disfranchised for the term of five years, and pay a fine of not less than five hundred dollars.

SEC. 2. Whoever shall dismiss from employment any person or persons for having exercised the right of franchise, or for offering to exercise such right, shall, on conviction, be fined not less than two hundred and fifty dollars, and be disfranchised for the term of five years.

# XXIX.

## SUPPLEMENTAL RECONSTRUCTION MEASURES.*

### Act of July 19, 1867.

An act supplementary to an act entitled "An act to provide for the more efficient government of the rebel States," passed on the second day of March, 1867, and the act supplementary thereto, passed on the 23d day of March, 1867.

*Be it enacted, &c.*, That it is hereby declared to have been the true intent and meaning of the act of the 2d day of March, 1867, entitled "An act to provide for the more efficient government of the rebel States," and of the act supplementary thereto, passed on the 23d day of March, 1867, that the governments then existing in the rebel States of Virginia, North Carolina, South Carolina, Georgia, Mississippi, Alabama, Louisiana, Florida, Texas, and Arkansas, were not legal State governments; and that thereafter said governments, if continued, were to be continued subject in all respects to the military commanders of the respective districts, and to the paramount authority of Congress.

SEC. 2. That the commander of any district named in said act shall have power, subject to the disapproval of the General of the army of the United States, and to have effect till disapproved, whenever in the opinion of such commander the proper administration of said act shall require it, to suspend or remove from office, or from the performance of official duties and the exercise of official powers, any officer or person holding or exercising, or professing to

hold or exercise, any civil or military office or duty in such district under any power, election, appointment, or authority derived from, or granted by, or claimed under, any so-called State or the government thereof, or any municipal or other division thereof; and upon such suspension or removal such commander, subject to the disapproval of the General as aforesaid, shall have power to provide from time to time for the performance of the said duties of such officer or person so suspended or removed, by the detail of some competent officer or soldier of the army, or by the appointment of some other person to perform the same, and to fill vacancies occasioned by death, resignation, or otherwise.

SEC. 3. That the General of the army of the United States shall be invested with all the powers of suspension, removal, appointment, and detail granted in the preceding section to district commanders.

SEC. 4. That the acts of the officers of the army already done in removing in said districts persons exercising the functions of civil officers, and appointing others in their stead, are hereby confirmed: *Provided*, That any person heretofore or hereafter appointed by any district commander to exercise the functions of any civil office, may be removed either by the military officer in command of the district, or by the General of the army. And it shall be the duty of such commander to remove from office, as aforesaid, all persons who are disloyal to the Government of the United States, or who use their official influence in any manner to hinder,

---

* For preceding Reconstruction Measures see pages 191–194 of Manual of 1867.

delay, prevent, or obstruct the due and proper administration of this act and the acts to which it is supplementary.

SEC. 5. That the boards of registration provided for in the act entitled "An act supplementary to an act entitled 'An act to provide for the more efficient government of the rebel States,' passed March 2, 1867, and to facilitate restoration," passed March 23, 1867, shall have power, and it shall be their duty, before allowing the registration of any person, to ascertain, upon such facts or information as they can obtain, whether such person is entitled to be registered under said act, and the oath required by said act shall not be conclusive on such question, and no person shall be registered unless such board shall decide that he is entitled thereto; and such board shall also have power to examine, under oath, (to be administered by any member of such board,) any one touching the qualification of any person claiming registration; but in every case of refusal by the board to register an applicant, and in every case of striking his name from the list as hereinafter provided, the board shall make a note or memorandum, which shall be returned with the registration list to the commanding general of the district, setting forth the grounds of such refusal or such striking from the list: *Provided,* That no person shall be disqualified as member of any board of registration by reason of race or color.

SEC. 6. That the true intent and meaning of the oath prescribed in said supplementary act is, (among other things,) that no person who has been a member of the Legislature of any State, or who has held any executive or judicial office in any State, whether he has taken an oath to support the Constitution of the United States or not, and whether he was holding such office at the commencement of the rebellion, or had held it before, and who has afterwards engaged in insurrection or rebellion against the United States, or given aid or comfort to the enemies thereof, is entitled to be registered or to vote; and the words "executive or judicial office in any State" in said oath mentioned shall be construed to include all civil offices created by law for the administration of any general law of a State, or for the administration of justice.

SEC. 7. That the time for completing the original registration provided for in said act may, in the discretion of the commander of any district, be extended to the 1st day of October, 1867; and the boards of registration shall have power, and it shall be their duty, commencing fourteen days prior to any election under said act, and upon reasonable public notice of the time and place thereof, to revise, for a period of five days, the registration lists, and, upon being satisfied that any person not entitled thereto has been registered, to strike the name of such person from the list, and such person shall not be allowed to vote. And such board shall also, during the same period, add to such registry the names of all persons who at that time possess the qualifications required by said act who have not been already registered; and no person shall, at any time, be entitled to be registered or to vote, by reason of any executive pardon or amnesty, for

any act or thing which, without such pardon or amnesty, would disqualify him from registration or voting.

SEC. 8. That section four of said last-named act shall be construed to authorize the commanding general named therein, whenever he shall deem it needful, to remove any member of a board of registration and to appoint another in his stead, and to fill any vacancy in such board.

SEC. 9. That all members of said boards of registration, and all persons hereafter elected or appointed to office in said military districts, under any so-called State or municipal authority, or by detail or appointment of the district commanders, shall be required to take and to subscribe the oath of office prescribed by law for officers of the United States.

SEC. 10. That no district commander or member of the board of registration, or any of the officers or appointees acting under them, shall be bound in his action by any opinion of any civil officer of the United States.

SEC. 11. That all the provisions of this act and of the acts to which this is supplementary shall be construed liberally, to the end that all the intents thereof may be fully and perfectly carried out.

[This bill passed the House, July 13, yeas 111, nays 23; and the Senate, the same day, yeas 31, nays 6—the Republicans voting yea, and the Democrats nay. July 19, the bill was vetoed by President Johnson, and the same day it was re-passed by both Houses—in the House, yeas 109, nays 25; in the Senate, yeas 30, nays 6; a party vote, as before.]

---

### Act of March 11, 1868.

AN ACT to amend the act passed March 23, 1867, entitled "An act supplementary to 'An act to provide for the more efficient government of the rebel States,' passed March 2, 1867, and to facilitate their restoration."

*Be it enacted, &c.,* That hereafter any election authorized by the act passed March 23, 1867, entitled "An act supplementary to 'An act to provide for the more efficient government of the rebel States,' passed March 2, 1867, and to facilitate their restoration," shall be decided by a majority of the votes actually cast; and at the election in which the question of the adoption or rejection of any constitution is submitted, any person duly registered in the State may vote in the election district where he offers to vote when he has resided therein for ten days next preceding such election, upon presentation of his certificate of registration, his affidavit, or other satisfactory evidence, under such regulations as the district commanders may prescribe.

SEC. 2. That the constitutional convention of any of the States mentioned in the acts to which this is amendatory may provide that at the time of voting upon the ratification of the constitution, the registered voters may vote also for members of the House of Representatives of the United States, and for all elective officers provided for by the said constitution; and the same election officers, who shall make the return of the votes cast on the ratification or rejection of the constitution, shall enumerate and certify the votes cast for members of Congress.

Became a law, March 11, 1868, by lapse of time, the President not having signed or returned it with his objections within ten days after its presentation to him.

[This bill passed the House, February 26, yeas 96, nays 32; and the Senate, February 25, yeas 28, nays 6; the Republicans voting for the bill, and the Democrats against it.]

### An Act to admit the State of Arkansas to Representation in Congress, June 22, 1868.

Whereas the people of Arkansas, in pursuance of the provisions of an act entitled "An act for the more efficient government of the rebel States," passed March 2, 1867, and the acts supplementary thereto, have framed and adopted a constitution of State government, which is republican, and the Legislature of said State has duly ratified the amendment to the Constitution of the United States proposed by the Thirty-Ninth Congress, and known as Article XIV; Therefore,

*Be it enacted, &c.*, That the State of Arkansas is entitled and admitted to representation in Congress, as one of the States of the Union, upon the following fundamental condition: That the constitution of Arkansas shall never be so amended or changed as to deprive any citizen or class of citizens of the United States of the right to vote who are entitled to vote by the constitution herein recognized, except as a punishment for such crimes as are now felonies at common law, whereof they shall have been duly convicted, under laws equally applicable to all the inhabitants of said State; *Provided*, That any alteration of said constitution prospective in its effect may be made in regard to the time and place of residence of voters.

[This bill passed the House, May 8—yeas 110, nays 32; the nays being all Democrats, except Messrs. Baker, Loan, Spalding, and Thomas Williams, the "fundamental condition" therein being "that the constitution of Arkansas shall never be so amended or changed as to deprive any citizen or class of citizens of the United States of the right to vote who are entitled to vote by the constitution herein recognized, except as a punishment for such crimes as are now felonies at common law, whereof they shall have been duly convicted." June 1, the bill was amended in the Senate, on motion of Mr. Drake, so that the "fundamental condition" should read: "That there shall never be in said State any denial or abridgment of the elective franchise, or of any other right, to any person by reason or on account of race or color, except Indians not taxed;" which was agreed to, yeas 26, nays 14, and was then passed, yeas 34, nays 8. A committee of conference agreed upon the bill as printed above, and their report passed the Senate, June 6, without a division, and the House also, a motion to table the report having been lost, yeas 27, (all Democrats,) nays 108, (all Republicans, except Mr. Stewart, of New York.) June 20, the bill was vetoed by the PRESIDENT, and passed in the House, yeas 111, nays 31; June 22, it passed the Senate, yeas 30, nays 7. In the House, on re-passing the bill, Mr. Stewart voted *aye* with the Republicans, and Mr. Cary voted *nay* with the Democrats. In the Senate the vote was:

YEAS—Messrs. Chandler, Cole, Conkling, Conness, Corbett, Cragin, Edmunds, Ferry, Fessenden, Harlan, Howard, Morgan, Morrill of Vermont, Nye, Patterson of New Hampshire, Pomeroy, Ramsey, Ross, Sherman, Sprague, Stewart, Sumner, Thayer, Tipton, Trumbull, Van Winkle, Wade, Willey, Wilson, Yates—30.

NAYS—Messrs. *Bayard, Davis, Doolittle, Hendricks, McCreery, Patterson* of Tennessee, *Saulsbury*—7.

### An Act to Admit the States of North Carolina, South Carolina, Louisiana, Georgia, Alabama, and Florida to Representation in Congress, June 25, 1868.

Whereas the people of North Carolina, South Carolina, Louisiana, Georgia, Alabama, and Florida have, in pursuance of the provisions of an act entitled "An act for the more efficient government of the rebel States," passed March 2, 1867, and the acts supplementary thereto, framed constitutions of State government which are republican, and have adopted such constitutions by large majorities of the votes cast at the elections held for the ratification or rejection of the same: therefore,

*Be it enacted, &c.*, That each of the States of North Carolina, South Carolina, Louisiana, Georgia, Alabama, and Florida, shall be entitled and admitted to representation in Congress as a State of the Union when the Legislature of such State shall have duly ratified the amendment to the Constitution of the United States proposed by the Thirty-Ninth Congress, and known as Article XIV, upon the following fundamental conditions: That the constitution of neither of said States shall ever be so amended or changed as to deprive any citizen, or class of citizens, of the United States of the right to vote in said State who are entitled to vote by the constitution thereof, herein recognized, except as a punishment for such crimes as are now felonies at common law, whereof they shall have been duly convicted under laws equally applicable to all the inhabitants of said State; *Provided*, That any alteration of said constitutions may be made with regard to the time and place of residence of voters. And the State of Georgia shall only be entitled and admitted to representation upon this further fundamental condition: That the first and third subdivisions of section seventeen of the fifth article of the constitution of said State, except the proviso to the first subdivision, shall be null and void, and that the general assembly of said State, by solemn public act, shall declare the assent of the State to the foregoing fundamental condition.*

SEC. 2. That if the day fixed for the first meeting of the Legislature of either of said States, by the constitution or ordinance thereof, shall have passed, or have so nearly arrived before the passage of this act that there shall not be time for the Legislature to assemble at the period fixed, such Legislature shall convene at the end of twenty days from the time this act takes effect unless the Governor-elect shall sooner convene the same.

SEC. 3. That the first section of this act shall take effect as to each State, except Georgia, when such State shall by its Legislature duly ratify Article XIV of the amendments to the Constitution of the United States, proposed by the Thirty-Ninth Congress, and as to the State of

* See page 331.

Georgia when it shall in addition give the assent of said State to the fundamental condition hereinbefore imposed upon the same; and thereupon the officers of each State, duly elected and qualified under the constitution thereof, shall be inaugurated without delay; but no person prohibited from holding office under the United States or under any State by section three of the proposed amendment to the Constitution of the United States known as Article XIV, shall be deemed eligible to any office in either of said States unless relieved from disability as provided in said amendment; and it is hereby made the duty of the President, within ten days after receiving official information of the ratification of said amendment by the Legislature of either of said States, to issue a proclamation announcing that fact.

[This bill passed the House, May 14, yeas 110, nays 35; the Senate, June 9, yeas 31, nays 5—Republicans *for*, Democrats *against* it. June 25, it was vetoed by President Johnson, and passed over the veto, same day, in the House, yeas 107, nays 31; and in the Senate, yeas 35, nays 8.]

## IMPORTANT VOTES DURING THE CONSIDERATION OF THE ABOVE BILLS.

### Votes prior to Passage of Act of March 11, 1868.

During the pendency in the Senate of the act of March 11, 1868—

February 25—Mr. Doolittle moved to amend by adding to the second section this proviso:

" *Provided, nevertheless*, That upon an election for the ratification of any constitution, or of officers under the same, previous to its adoption in any such State, no person not having the qualifications of an elector under the constitution and laws of such State, previous to the late rebellion, shall be allowed to vote, unless he shall possess one of the following qualifications, viz.:

"1st. He shall have served as a soldier in the Federal army for one year or more; or, 2d He shall have sufficient education to read the Constitution of the United States, and to subscribe his name to an oath to support the same; or, 3d. He shall be seized in his own right, or in the right of his wife, of a freehold of the value of two hundred and fifty dollars."

Which was not agreed to—yeas 3, nays 33, as follow:

YEAS—Messrs. *Dixon, Doolittle, Hendricks*—3.

NAYS—*Buckalew*, Chandler, Cole, Conkling, Corbett, Cragin, *Davis*, Drake, Ferry, Fowler, Harlan, Henderson, Howe, Morgan, Morrill of Maine, Morrill of Vermont, Nye, Patterson of New Hampshire, Pomeroy, Ramsey, Ross, Sherman, Stewart, Sumner, Thayer, Tipton, Trumbull, Van Winkle, Wade, Willey, Williams, Wilson, Yates—33.

1867, December 18—The House passed a bill modifying the fifth section of the act of March 23, 1867, so that a majority of the votes cast at the election shall be sufficient to ratify the constitution, and authorizing an election for members of Congress at the same time with the vote on the constitution, according to the districts as they existed in 1858 and 1859. On this the yeas were 104, nays 37, Republicans and Messrs. *Cary* and *Stewart* in the affirmative, and Democrats in the negative.

1868, January 21—The House passed a bill declaring that in the ten rebel States there are no civil State governments republican in form, and that the so-called civil governments in said States shall not be recognized as valid or legal State governments either by the executive or judicial power or authority of the United States. The General of the army was authorized and required to enjoin, by special orders, upon all officers in command within those States the performance of all acts authorized by the reconstruction acts, and authorized to remove from command any or all of said commanders, and detail other officers of the United States army, not below the rank of colonel, to the end that the people of said several States may speedily reorganize civil governments and be restored to political power in the Union. The General of the army was authorized to remove any or all civil officers now acting under the several provisional governments within said several disorganized States, and appoint others, and to do any and all acts which are authorized to be done by the several commanders of the military departments within said States; and the law which authorizes the President to detail the military commanders to said military departments, or to remove any officers who may be detailed as herein provided, is hereby repealed. It was provided that it shall be unlawful for the President of the United States to order any part of the army or navy of the United States to assist, by force of arms, the authority of either of said provisional governments in said disorganized States to oppose or obstruct the authority of the United States, as provided in this act and the acts to which this is supplementary. Fine and imprisonment were provided for violation of this act.

The vote was—yeas 124, nays 45, as follow:

YEAS—Messrs. Allison, Ames, Anderson, Arnell, Delos R. Ashley, James M. Ashley, Bailey, Baker, Baldwin, Banks, Beaman, Benjamin, Benton, Bingham, Blaine, Blair, Boutwell, Bromwell, Broomall, Buckland, Cake, Churchill, Reader W. Clarke, Sidney Clarke, Cobb, Coburn, Cook, Cullom, Dawes, Dixon, Dodge, Donnelly, Driggs, Eckley, Eggleston, Ela, Eliot, Farnsworth, Ferriss, Ferry, Fields, Garfield, Gravely, Griswold, Halsey, Harding, Higby, Hooper, Hopkins, Asahel W. Hubbard, Chester D. Hubbard, Hulburd, Hunter, Ingersoll, Jenckes, Judd, Julian, Kelley, Kelsey, Ketcham, Kitchen, Koontz, William Lawrence, Lincoln, Logan, Loughridge, Marvin, Maynard, McCarthy, McClurg, Mercur, Miller, Moore, Moorhead, Mullins, Myers, Newcomb, Nunn, O'Neill, Orth, Paine, Perham, Peters, Pike, Pile, Plants, Poland, Polsley, Pomeroy, Price, Raum, Robertson, Sawyer, Schenck, Scofield, Selye, Shanks, Smith, Spalding, Starkweather, Aaron F. Stevens, Thaddeus Stevens, Taylor, Thomas, Trowbridge, Twichell, Upson, Van Aernam, Burt Van Horn, Robert T. Van Horn, Van Wyck, Ward, Cadwalader C. Washburn, Elihu B. Washburne, Henry D. Washburn, William B. Washburn, Welker, Thomas Williams, William Williams, James F. Wilson, John T. Wilson, Stephen F. Wilson, Windom, Woodbridge—124.

NAYS—Messrs. *Adams, Archer, Axtell, Barnes, Barnum, Beck, Boyer, Brooks, Burr, Cary, Chanler, Eldridge, Fox, Getz, Glossbrenner, Holladay, Grover, Haight, Holman, Hotchkiss, Richard D. Hubbard, Humphrey, Johnson, Jones, Kerr, Knott, Marshall, McCormick, Morrissey, Mungen, Niblack, Nicholson, Phelps, Pruyn, Robinson, Ross, Sitgreaves, Stewart, Stone, Taber, L. S. Trimble, Van Auken, Van Trump, Wood, Woodward*—45.

Pending this bill,

1868, January 21—Mr. Butler offered a substitute that, in order to supply the place of these illegal governments, the constitutional conventions of each of said States, as soon as such conventions, respectively, shall have submitted to the people a constitution or frame of government for their ratification, shall have power to appoint all civil officers. It shall be the duty of the several district commanders to confirm the appointment of such officers by the convention; to install each officer in his office; to cause to be put into the possession and control of each officer the records and archives and other property of the State pertaining to his office, and to do all other acts which may be necessary to enable such State officers, respectively, to perform the functions of their offices. These governments to continue until each State shall be represented in Congress and other State officers shall have been elected and qualified under the constitution thereof.

Which was disagreed to—yeas 53, nays 112. The yeas were:

Messrs. Allison, Anderson, Arnell, Delos R. Ashley, James M. Ashley, Banks, Broomall, Butler, Cake, *Cary*, Churchill, Reader W. Clarke, Sidney Clarke, Cobb, Coburn, Donnelly, Driggs, Eckley, Ela, Ferry, Fields, Gravely, Harding, Higby, Hunter, Judd, Julian, Kelley, Kelsey, Kitchen, William Lawrence, Logan, Loughridge, Maynard, McClurg, Mercur, Mullins, Newcomb, Nunn, Perham, Raum, Schenck, Shanks, Thaddeus Stevens, Taylor, Thomas, John Trimble, Robert T. Van Horn, Van Wyck, Ward, William Williams, Stephen F. Wilson, Windom.

This bill was not taken up in the Senate.

## VOTES SUBSEQUENT TO THE PASSAGE OF THE ACT OF MARCH 11, 1868, AND PRIOR TO THE ACTS OF JUNE 22, AND JUNE 25, 1868.

### The Alabama Bill.

1868, March 26—The House Committee on Reconstruction reported a bill to admit the State of Alabama to representation in Congress, as soon as the Legislature, then recently elected, shall have duly ratified the XIVth Amendment, for which a substitute was offered by Mr. Spalding, making the constitution recently framed the fundamental law for a provisional government, also providing that the officers elected at the recent election should qualify on the 1st of May, 1868, and enter on their duties; and the Governor was authorized to convene the Legislature recently elected, who were given authority to submit said constitution for ratification, with such amendments as a majority of the Legislature may adopt. It was further provided that, whenever the people, by a majority vote of the electors of Alabama, qualified under the act of Congress of March 23, 1867, to vote for delegates to frame a constitution, and actually voting upon said ratification, shall have ratified a constitution submitted as aforesaid, and the Legislature of the proposed State organization shall have adopted the amendment to the Constitution of the United States proposed by the Thirty-Ninth Congress, and known as Article XIV, the constitution of Alabama may be presented to Congress for its approval.

This substitute was agreed to—yeas 77, nays 55, as follow:

YEAS—Messrs. Ames, Anderson, Delos R. Ashley, James M. Ashley, Baker, Baldwin, Banks, Beatty, Benjamin, Bromwell, Broomall, Churchill, Sidney Clarke, Coburn, Cook, Covode, Cullom, Dawes, Dixon, Dodge, Driggs, Eckley, Eggleston, Eliot, Ferriss, Ferry, Halsey, Hawkins, Hill, Hopkins, Hunter, Ingersoll, Judd, Julian, Kelsey, Ketcham, Koontz, Laflin, William Lawrence,

Loan, Loughridge, Maynard, McClurg, Mercur, Moore, Moorhead, Morrell, Mullins, Myers, Nunn, O'Neill, Orth, Poland, Polsley, Pomeroy, Price, Raum, Sawyer, Scofield, Shanks, Smith, Spalding, Thaddeus Stevens, Taffe, Twichell, Upson, Burt Van Horn, Robert T. Van Horn, Ward, Ellihu B. Washburne, William B. Washburn, Welker, Thomas Williams, James F. Wilson, John T. Wilson, Stephen F. Wilson, Woodbridge—77.

NAYS—Messrs. *Adams*, Arnell, Bailey, Beaman, *Beck*, Bingham, Blaine, Boutwell, *Brooks*, Buckland, *Burr*, *Cary*, *Eldridge*, Farnsworth, Fields, *Fox*, *Glossbrenner*, *Golladay*, Gravely, *Grover*, *Haight*, *Holman*, *Richard D. Hubbard*, Hulburd, *Humphrey*, *Johnson*, *Jones*, *Kerr*, *Knott*, Lincoln, Mallory, *Marshall*, Miller, *Mungen*, Newcomb, *Niblack*, *Nicholson*, Paine, Perham, Peters, Pile, Plants, *Pruyn*, *Ross*, *Sitgreaves*, *Taber*, Taylor, Thomas, John Trimble, *Lawrence S. Trimble*, *Van Auken*, *Van Trump*, Van Wyck, Windom, *Woodward*—55.

The bill then passed—yeas 102, nays 29; the nays all Democrats, including Mr. *Cary*.

The bill was not taken up in the Senate.

### The Arkansas Bill.

During the pendency of the bill admitting the State of Arkansas to representation, in the Senate as in Committee of the Whole—

1868, June 1—Mr. Henderson moved this as a substitute for Mr. Drake's "fundamental condition," previously noticed (page 337:)

That said State, in fixing the qualifications of electors therein, shall not be authorized to discriminate against any person on account of race, color, or previous condition; and also, on the further condition, that no person on account of race or color shall be excluded from the benefits of education, or be deprived of an equal share of the moneys or other funds created or used by public authority to promote education in said State.

Which was disagreed to—yeas 5, nays 30, as follow:

YEAS—Messrs. *Buckalew*, *Doolittle*, Henderson, *Hendricks*, *Ross*—5.

NAYS—Messrs. *Bayard*, Cameron, Cattell, Chandler, Cole, Conkling, Corbett, Drake, Ferry, Frelinghuysen, Harlan, Howe, *Johnson*, *McCreery*, Morrill of Maine, Morrill of Vermont, Nye, *Patterson* of Tennessee, Pomeroy, Ramsey, Stewart, Thayer, Tipton, Trumbull, Van Winkle, *Vickers*, Wade, Willey, Williams, Yates—30.

The amendment of Mr Drake was then agreed to—yeas 26, nays 14, as follow:

YEAS—Messrs. Cameron, Cattell, Chandler, Cole, Conkling, Cragin, Drake, Fessenden, Frelinghuysen, Harlan, Henderson, Howe, *Johnson*, Morrill of Maine, Morrill of Vermont, Nye, Patterson of New Hampshire, Ramsey, Stewart, Sumner, Thayer, Tipton, Trumbull, Wade, Wilson, Yates—26.

NAYS—Messrs. *Bayard*, *Buckalew*, Corbett, *Doolittle*, Ferry, Fowler, *Hendricks*, *McCreery*, Patterson of Tennessee, Ross, Van Winkle, *Vickers*, Willey, Williams—14.

Mr. Hendricks moved to strike out all of the preamble and bill after the enacting clause, and insert: "That the State of Arkansas is hereby declared restored to her former proper practical relations to the Union, and is again entitled to be represented by Senators and Representatives in Congress."

Which was disagreed to—yeas 15, nays 26, as follow:

YEAS—Messrs. *Bayard*, *Buckalew*, Corbett, *Doolittle*, Ferry, Fowler, *Hendricks*, *Johnson*, *McCreery*, Patterson of New Hampshire, *Patterson* of Tennessee, Ross, Van Winkle, *Vickers*, Willey—15.

NAYS—Messrs. Cameron, Cattell, Chandler, Cole, Conkling, Cragin, Drake, Fessenden, Frelinghuysen, Henderson, Howe, Morrill of Maine, Morrill of Vermont, Nye, Pomeroy, Ramsey, Sherman, Stewart, Sumner, Thayer, Tipton, Trumbull, Wade, Williams, Wilson, Yates—26.

The bill being then reported to the Senate, Mr. Ferry offered an amendment to strike out all after the enacting clause, and insert the words: "That the State of Arkansas is entitled and admitted to representation in Congress as one of the States of the Union." Which was disagreed to—yeas 18, nays 22, as follow:

YEAS—Messrs. *Bayard, Buckalew,* Conkling, Corbett, *Doolittle,* Ferry, Fessenden, *Hendricks, McCreery,* Patterson of New Hampshire, *Patterson* of Tennessee, Ross, *Saulsbury,* Trumbull, Van Winkle, *Vickers,* Willey, Williams—18.

NAYS—Messrs. Cameron, Cattell, Chandler, Cole, Cragin, Drake, Frelinghuysen, Harlan, Henderson, Howe, Morrill of Vermont, Nye, Pomeroy, Ramsey, Sherman, Stewart, Sumner, Thayer, Tipton, Wade, Wilson, Yates —22.

The bill then passed—yeas 34, nays 8, as follows:

YEAS—Messrs. Anthony, Cameron, Cattell, Chandler, Cole, Conkling, Corbett, Cragin, Drake, Edmunds, Fessenden, Frelinghuysen, Harlan, Henderson, Howe, Morrill of Maine, Morrill of Vermont, Nye, Patterson of New Hampshire, Pomeroy, Ramsey, Ross, Sherman, Stewart, Sumner, Thayer, Tipton, Trumbull, Van Winkle, Wade, Willey, Williams, Wilson, Yates—34.

NAYS—Messrs. *Bayard, Buckalew, Doolittle, Hendricks, McCreery, Patterson* of Tennessee, *Saulsbury, Vickers*—8.

### The Bill to Admit North Carolina, South Carolina, Louisiana, Georgia, Alabama, and Florida to Representation in Congress.

In this bill, as originally passed by the House, May 14, this provision was inserted at the close of the first section:

So much of the seventeenth section of the fifth article of the constitution of the State of Georgia as gives authority to Legislatures or courts to repudiate debts contracted prior to the 1st day of June, 1865, and similar provisions in all other of the constitutions mentioned in this bill, shall be null and void as against all men who were loyal during the whole time of the rebellion, and who during that time supported the Union, and they shall have the same rights in the courts and elsewhere as if no rebellion had ever existed.

This section was agreed to—yeas 79, nays 50, as follow:

YEAS—Messrs. *Adams,* Ames, Anderson, Arnell, James M. Ashley, Beaman, Beatty, Benjamin, Benton, Blair, Bromwell, Broomall, Buckland, Cake, Reader W. Clarke, Sidney Clarke, Cobb, Coburn, Donnelly, Driggs, Eckley, Eggleston, Farnsworth, Fields, Gravely, Harding, Higby, Hill, *Holman,* Hooper, Hopkins, Chester D. Hubbard, Hunter, Julian, Kelley, Kelsey, Kitchen, Koontz, George V. Lawrence, William Lawrence, Loan, Loughridge, Marvin, McCarthy, McClurg, Miller, Morrell, Myers, Newcomb, Nunn, O'Neill, Orth, Perham, Peters, Plants, Polsley, Price, Raum, Robertson, Sawyer, Shanks, Smith, Thaddeus Stevens, *Stewart,* Stokes, Taffe, Thomas, John Trimble, Trowbridge, Twichell, Upson, Van Wyck, Ward, Welker, William Williams, Stephen F. Wilson, Windom, Woodbridge, *Woodward*—79.

NAYS—Messrs. Allison, Delos R. Ashley, Bailey, Baker, Banks, Bingham, Boutwell, *Boyer,* Cullom, Ela, *Eldridge,* Eliot, Ferriss, Ferry, Garfield, *Getz, Glossbrenner, Golladay,* Grover, Ingersoll, *Johnson,* Judd, *Kerr,* Ketcham, *Knott,* Laflin. Lincoln. Logan, Mallory, *McCormick,* Moore, *Morgan, Mungen, Niblack, Nicholson,* Paine, Pile, *Pruyn, Randall, Ross,* Schenck, *Sitgreaves,* Aaron F. Stevens, Taylor. *Van Auken,* Burt Van Horn, *Van Trump,* Elihu B. Washburne, Henry D. Washburn, William B. Washburn—50.

A motion by Mr. Woodbridge to strike "Alabama" from the bill, was disagreed to—yeas 60, nays 74, as follow:

YEAS—Messrs. Delos R. Ashley, Baker, Baldwin, *Beck,* Blair, *Boyer, Brooks, Burr,* Coburn, **Driggs,** *Eld-*

*ridge,* Ferry, Garfield, *Getz, Glossbrenner, Golladay, Grover,* Hawkins, Higby, Hopkins, *Hotchkiss, Humphrey,* Ingersoll, Jenckes, *Johnson,* Julian, *Kerr,* Ketcham, *Knott,* George V. Lawrence, Loan, *Marshall,* Marvin, *McCormick, Morgan, Mungen,* Myers, *Niblack, Nicholson,* Orth, *Phelps,* Poland, *Pruyn, Randall,* Robertson, *Robinson, Ross,* Sawyer, *Sitgreaves,* Smith, *Stewart, Stone,* Taylor, *Van Auken, Van Trump,* Ward, Ellihu B. Washburne, William B. Washburn, Woodbridge, *Woodward*—60.

NAYS—Messrs. Allison, Ames, Anderson, Arnell, James M. Ashley, Bailey, Beaman, Beatty, Benjamin, Benton, Bingham, Boutwell, Bromwell, Broomall, Buckland, Reader W. Clarke, Sidney Clarke, Cobb, Covone, Cullom, Eckley, Ela, Farnsworth, Ferriss, Fields, Gravely, Harding, Chester D. Hubbard, Hunter, Judd, Kelley, Kelsey, Kitchen, Koontz, William Lawrence, Lincoln, Loughridge, Mallory, McCarthy, McClurg, Miller, Moore, Morrell, Newcomb, Nunn, O'Neill, Paine, Perham, Peters, Pike, Pile, Plants, Polsley, Price, Raum, Schenck, Scofield, Shanks, Aaron F. Stevens, Thaddeus Stevens, Stokes, Taffe, Thomas, John Trimble, Trowbridge, Twichell, Upson, Burt Van Horn, Van Wyck, Henry D. Washburn, Welker, William Williams, Stephen F. Wilson, Windom—74.

### IN SENATE.

June 2—The bill was reported with amendments. As reported it excluded Alabama, and added Florida.

June 9—Mr. Wilson moved to insert Alabama; which was agreed to—yeas 22, nays 21, as follow:

YEAS—Nessrs. Anthony, Chandler, Conness, Corbett, Ferry, Fowler, Harlan, Morrill of Maine, Morton, Nye, Pomeroy, Ramsey, Sherman, Stewart, Sumner, Thayer, Tipton, Van Winkle, Wade, Willey, Williams, Wilson —22.

NAYS—Messrs. *Bayard, Buckalew,* Cole, Conkling, *Davis, Doolittle,* Edmunds, Fessenden, Frelinghuysen, *Hendricks,* Howard, Howe, *Johnson, McCreery,* Morgan, Morrill of Vermont, *Patterson* of Tennessee, *Saulsbury,* Trumbull, *Vickers,* Yates—21.

June 10—Mr. Sherman moved to strike from the first section the words:

And the State of Georgia shall only be entitled and admitted to representation upon this further fundamental condition: that the first and third subdivisions of section seventeen of the fifth article of the constitution of said State, except the proviso to the first subdivision, shall be null and void, and that the general assembly of said State, by solemn public act, shall declare the assent of the State to the foregoing fundamental condition.

Which was disagreed to—yeas 8, nays 35, as follow:

YEAS—Messrs. Cameron, Ferry, Howe, Ramsey, Sherman, Thayer, Williams, Wilson—8.

NAYS—Messrs. Anthony, *Buckalew,* Chandler, Cole, Conkling, Conness, Corbett, Cragin, *Davis,* Drake, Edmunds, Fessenden, Frelinghuysen, Harlan, *Hendricks,* Howard, *Johnson, McCreery,* Morgan, Morrill of Maine, Morrill of Vermont, Morton, Nye, Patterson of New Hampshire, *Patterson* of Tennessee, **Ross,** *Saulsbury,* Sumner, Tipton, Trumbull, Van Winkle, *Vickers,* Wade, Willey, Yates—35.

Mr. Williams moved to strike out of the first section all after the words "fundamental condition," and insert as follows:

That so much of the seventeenth section of the fifth article of the constitution of the State of Georgia as suspends the collection of debts contracted prior to the 1st day of June, 1865, shall be void as against all persons who were loyal during the late rebellion, and who, during that time, supported the Union.

Which was rejected.

Mr. Williams moved to insert this clause after the word "same" in the third section, and before what is now the last clause of the bill:

And thereupon the officers of each State, duly elected and qualified under the constitution thereof, shall be inaugurated without delay; but no person prohibited from holding office under the United States, or under any State, by section three of the proposed amendment to the Constitution of the United States, known as article fourteen, shall be deemed eligible to any office in either of said States.

The first clause of the amendment, closing with "delay," was agreed to—yeas 23, nays 18, as follow:

YEAS—Messrs. Cameron, Chandler, Conness, Corbett, Cragin, Drake, Edmunds, Howard, Morrill of Maine, Morrill of Vermont, Morton, Nye, Patterson of New Hampshire, Pomeroy, Ramsey, Stewart, Sumner, Thayer, Tipton, Wade, Williams, Wilson, Yates—23.

NAYS—Messrs. *Bayard, Buckalew,* Cole, Conkling, *Davis,* Fowler, Frelinghuysen, Harlan, *Hendricks, McCreery,* Morgan, *Patterson* of Tennessee, Ross, *Saulsbury,* Trumbull, Van Winkle, *Vickers,* Willey—18.

The second clause was agreed to—yeas 26, nays 15, as follow:

YEAS—Messrs. Cameron, Chandler, Cole, Conness, Corbett, Cragin, Drake, Harlan, Howard, Morrill of Maine, Morrill of Vermont, Morton, Nye, Patterson of New Hampshire, Pomeroy, Ramsey, Stewart, Sumner, Thayer, Tipton, Van Winkle, Wade, Willey, Williams, Wilson, Yates—26.

NAYS—Messrs. *Bayard, Buckalew,* Conkling, *Davis,* Edmunds, Fowler, Frelinghuysen, *Hendricks, McCreery,* Morgan, *Patterson* of Tennessee, Ross, *Saulsbury,* Trumbull, *Vickers*—15.

Mr. Trumbull moved to strike out "Alabama," which had been inserted in Committee of the Whole; which was disagreed to—yeas 16, nays 24, as follow:

YEAS—Messrs. *Bayard, Buckalew,* Conkling, *Davis,* Edmunds, Frelinghuysen, *Hendricks,* Howe, *McCreery,* Morgan, Morrill of Vermont, *Patterson* of Tennessee, *Saulsbury,* Trumbull, *Vickers,* Yates—16.

NAYS—Messrs. Cameron, Chandler, Conness, Corbett, Cragin, Drake, Ferry, Harlan, Morrill of Maine, Morton, Nye, Pomeroy, Ramsey, Ross, Sherman, Stewart, Sumner, Thayer, Tipton, Van Winkle, Wade, Willey, Williams—24.

Mr. Conkling offered the following additional proviso:

And the State of Alabama shall be entitled and admitted to representation only upon this further fundamental condition: that section twenty-six of the first article of the constitution of said State, except so much thereof as makes navigable waters public highways, shall be null and void, and that the general assembly of said State, by a solemn public act, shall declare the assent of the State to the foregoing fundamental condition.

Which was disagreed to—yeas 16, nays 23, as follow:

YEAS—Messrs. Anthony, *Buckalew,* Conkling, Corbett, Edmunds, Frelinghuysen, *Hendricks,* Howe, *McCreery,* Morgan, Morrill of Maine, Morrill of Vermont, Nye, *Patterson* of Tennessee, Ross, *Vickers*—16.

NAYS—Messrs. Chandler, Cole, Conness, Cragin, Drake, Ferry, Harlan, Howard, Morton, Pomeroy, Ramsey, *Saulsbury,* Sherman, Stewart, Sumner, Thayer, Tipton, Van Winkle, Wade, Willey, Williams, Wilson, Yates—23.

Mr. Williams offered to add to his amendment

adopted above, the words: "Unless relieved from disability, as provided in said amendment;" which was agreed to.

The bill then passed—yeas 31, nays 5; as follow:

YEAS—Messrs. Anthony, Cameron, Chandler, Cole, Conkling, Conness, Cragin, Drake, Ferry, Frelinghuysen, Harlan, Howard, Howe, Morgan, Morrill of Maine, Morrill of Vermont, Nye, Patterson of New Hampshire, Pomeroy, Ramsey, Ross, Sherman, Stewart, Sumner, Thayer, Tipton, Trumbull, Wade, Williams, Wilson, Yates—31.

NAYS—Messrs. *Bayard, Buckalew, McCreery, Patterson* of Tennessee, *Vickers*—5.

## IN HOUSE.

June 12—The Committee on Reconstruction recommended concurrence in the Senate amendments.

Mr. Farnsworth moved to strike Florida from the bill; which was disagreed to—yeas 45, nays 99, as follow:

YEAS—Messrs. *Archer, Axtell, Barnes, Beck, Boyer,* Bromwell, *Brooks, Burr,* Cobb, *Eldridge,* Eliot, Farnsworth, *Getz, Glossbrenner, Golladay, Grover,* Harding, *Holman,* Hopkins, *Hotchkiss,* Julian, *Knott, Marshall,* Maynard, *McCormick, McCullough, Morrissey, Niblack, Nicholson,* Paine, *Phelps,* Pike, Price, *Randall, Robinson,* Sawyer, *Stewart, Stone, Taber,* Taffe, *Lawrence S. Trimble, Van Auken, Van Trump,* Ellihu B. Washburne, *Woodward*—45.

NAYS—Messrs. Allison, Ames, Delos R. Ashley, James M. Ashley, Bailey, Baker, Baldwin, Banks, Beaman, Beatty, Benjamin, Benton, Bingham, Blaine, Blair, Broomall, Buckland, Butler, Cake, Churchill, Reader W. Clarke, Sidney Clarke, Coburn, Cook, Cornell, Covode, Cullom, Dawes, Delano, Dixon, Dodge, Donnelly, Driggs, Eckley, Eggleston, Ela, Ferriss, Ferry, Fields, Garfield, Gravely, Griswold, Halsey, Hawkins, Higby, Chester D. Hubbard, Hulburd, Ingersoll, Judd, Kelsey, Ketcham, Kitchen, Koontz, Laflin, Lincoln, Loan, Logan, Loughridge, Lynch, Mallory, Marvin, McClurg, Mercur, Miller, Moore, Morrell, Mullins, Myers, Newcomb, O'Neill, Pile, Plants, Polsley, Pomeroy, Raum, Robertson, Schenck, Scofield, Selye, Shellabarger, Spalding, Starkweather, Aaron F. Stevens, Stokes, Taylor, Thomas, John Trimble, Trowbridge, Twichell, Upson, Van Aernam, Robert T. Van Horn, Ward, Henry D. Washburn, William B. Washburn, Welker, William Williams, John T. Wilson, Windom—99.

The amendments were then concurred in— yeas 111, nays 28; as follow:

YEAS—Messrs. Allison, Ames, Delos R. Ashley, James M. Ashley, Bailey, Banks, Beaman, Beatty, Benjamin, Benton, Bingham, Blaine, Blair, Bromwell, Broomall, Buckland, Butler, Churchill, Reader W. Clarke, Sidney Clarke, Cobb, Coburn, Cook, Cornell, Covode, Cullom, Dawes, Delano, Dixon, Dodge, Donnelly, Driggs, Eckley, Eggleston, Ela, Eliot, Ferriss, Ferry, Fields, Garfield, Gravely, Griswold, Halsey, Harding, Hawkins, Higby, Hopkins, Chester D. Hubbard, Hulburd, Ingersoll, Judd, Julian, Kelsey, Ketcham, Kitchen, Koontz, Laflin, Lincoln, Loan, Logan, Loughridge, Lynch, Mallory, Marvin, Maynard, McClurg, Mercur, Miller, Moore, Morrell, Mullins, Myers, Newcomb, O'Neill, Paine, Peters, Pike, Pile, Plants, Polsley, Pomeroy, Price, Raum, Robertson, Sawyer, Schenck, Scofield, Selye, Shellabarger, Spalding, Starkweather, Aaron F. Stevens, *Stewart,* Stokes, Taffe, Taylor, Thomas, John Trimble, Trowbridge, Twichell, Upson, Van Aernam, Robert T. Van Horn, Ward, Ellihu B. Washburne, Henry D. Washburn, William B. Washburn, Welker, William Williams, John T. Wilson, Windom—111.

NAYS—Messrs. *Archer, Axtell, Barnes, Boyer, Brooks, Burr, Eldridge, Getz, Glossbrenner, Golladay, Grover, Holman, Hotchkiss, Marshall, McCormick, McCullough, Morrissey, Niblack, Nicholson, Phelps, Randall, Robinson, Stone, Taber, Lawrence S. Trimble, Van Auken, Van Trump, Woodward*—28.

# XXX.

## PRESIDENT JOHNSON'S PROCLAMATIONS AND ORDERS.*

### Enjoining Obedience to the Constitution and Laws, September 3, 1867.

Whereas, by the Constitution of the United States, the executive power is vested in a President of the United States of America, who is bound by solemn oath faithfully to execute the office of President, and to the best of his ability to preserve, protect, and defend the Constitution of the United States, and is by the same instrument made Commander-in-Chief of the army and navy of the United States, and is required to take care that the laws be faithfully executed;

And whereas, by the same Constitution, it is provided that the said Constitution and the laws of the United States which shall be made in pursuance thereof shall be the supreme law of the land, and the judges in every State shall be bound thereby;

And whereas in and by the same Constitution the judicial power of the United States is vested in one Supreme Court and in such inferior courts as Congress may from time to time ordain and establish, and the aforesaid judicial power is declared to extend to all cases in law and equity arising under the Constitution, the laws of the United States, and the treaties which shall be made under their authority;

And whereas all officers, civil and military, are bound by oath that they will support and defend the Constitution against all enemies, foreign and domestic, and will bear true faith and allegiance to the same;

And whereas all officers of the army and navy of the United States, in accepting their commissions under the laws of Congress and the rules and articles of war, incur an obligation to observe, obey, and follow such directions as they shall from time to time receive from the President or the General, or other superior officers set over them, according to the rules and discipline of war;

And whereas it is provided by law that whenever, by reason of unlawful obstructions, combinations, or assemblages of persons, or rebellion against the authority of the Government of the United States, it shall become impracticable, in the judgment of the President of the United States, to enforce, by the ordinary course of judicial proceedings, the laws of the United States within any State or Territory, the Executive in that case is authorized and required to secure their faithful execution by the employment of the land and naval forces;

And whereas impediments and obstructions, serious in their character, have recently been interposed in the States of North Carolina and South Carolina, hindering and preventing for a time a proper enforcement there of the laws of the United States, and of the judgments and decrees of a lawful court thereof, in disregard of the command of the President of the United States;

And whereas reasonable and well-founded apprehensions exist that such ill-advised and unlawful proceedings may be again attempted there or elsewhere:

Now, therefore, I, Andrew Johnson, President of the United States, do hereby warn all persons against obstructing or hindering in any manner whatsoever the faithful execution of the Constitution and the laws; and I do solemnly enjoin and command all officers of the Government, civil and military, to render due submission and obedience to said laws, and to the judgments and decrees of the courts of the United States, and to give all the aid in their power necessary to the prompt enforcement and execution of such laws, decrees, judgments, and processes.

And I do hereby enjoin upon the officers of the army and navy to assist and sustain the courts and other civil authorities of the United States in the faithful administration of the laws thereof, and in the judgments, decrees, mandates, and processes of the courts of the United States; and I call upon all good and well-disposed citizens of the United States to remember that upon the said Constitution and laws, and upon the judgments, decrees, and processes of the courts made in accordance with the same, depend the protection of the lives, liberty, property, and happiness of the people. And I exhort them everywhere to testify their devotion to their country, their pride in its prosperity and greatness, and their determation to uphold its free institutions by a hearty co-operation in the efforts of the Government to sustain the authority of the law, to maintain the supremacy of the Federal Constitution, and to preserve unimpaired the integrity of the National Union.

In testimony whereof, I have caused the seal of the United States to be affixed to these presents, and sign the same with my hand.

Done at the city of Washington the 3d day of [L. S.] September, in the year 1867.

ANDREW JOHNSON.

By the President:
Wm. H. Seward, Secretary of State.

---

### Extending Full Pardon to Certain Persons who were Engaged in the late Rebellion, September 7, 1867.

Whereas, in the month of July, anno Domini 1861, the two houses of Congress, with extraordinary unanimity, solemnly declared that the war then existing was not waged on the part of the Government in any spirit of oppression, nor for any purpose of conquest or subjugation, nor purpose of overthrowing or interfering with the rights or established institutions of the States, but to defend and maintain the supremacy of the Constitution, and to preserve the Union with all the dignity, equality, and rights of the several States unimpaired, and that as soon as these objects should be accomplished the war ought to cease;

---

* For other proclamations and orders, see pages 7–18 of the Manual of 1866, and pages 68–74 of the Manual of 1867 or 194–200 of the Combined Manual.

And whereas the President of the United States, on the eighth day of December, anno Domini 1863, and on the twenty-sixth day of March, anno Domini 1864, did, with the objects of suppressing the then existing rebellion, of inducing all persons to return to their loyalty, and of restoring the authority of the United States, issue proclamations offering amnesty and pardon to all persons who had directly or indirectly participated in the then existing rebellion, except as in those proclamations was specified and reserved;

And whereas the President of the United States did, on the twenty-ninth day of May, anno Domini 1865, issue a further proclamation with the same objects before mentioned, and to the end that the authority of the Government of the United States might be restored, and that peace, order, and freedom might be established, and the President did, by the said last-mentioned proclamation, proclaim and declare that he thereby granted to all persons who had directly or indirectly participated in the then existing rebellion, except as therein excepted, amnesty and pardon, with restoration of all rights of property, except as to slaves, and except in certain cases where legal proceedings had been instituted, but upon condition that such persons should take and subscribe an oath therein prescribed, which oath should be registered for permanent preservation;

And whereas, in and by the said last-mentioned proclamation of the twenty-ninth day of May, anno Domini 1865, fourteen extensive classes of persons, therein specially described, were altogether excepted and excluded from the benefits thereof;

And whereas the President of the United States did, on the second day of April, anno Domini 1866, issue a proclamation declaring that the insurrection was at an end, and was thenceforth to be so regarded;

And whereas there now exists no organized armed resistance of misguided citizens or others to the authority of the United States in the States of Georgia, South Carolina, Virginia, North-Carolina, Tennessee, Alabama, Louisiana, Arkansas, Mississippi, Florida, and Texas, and the laws can be sustained and enforced therein by the proper civil authority, State or Federal, and the people of said States are well and loyally disposed, and have conformed, or, if permitted to do so, will conform in their legislation to the condition of affairs growing out of the amendment to the Constitution of the United States prohibiting slavery within the limits and jurisdiction of the United States;

And whereas there no longer exists any reasonable ground to apprehend, within the States which were involved in the late rebellion, any renewal thereof, or any unlawful resistance by the people of said States to the Constitution and laws of the United States;

And whereas large standing armies, military occupation, martial law, military tribunals, and the suspension of the privilege of the writ of *habeas corpus* and the right of trial by jury, are, in time of peace, dangerous to public liberty, incompatible with the individual rights of the citizen, contrary to the genius and spirit of our free institutions, and exhaustive of the national resources, and ought not, therefore, to be sanctioned or allowed, except in cases of actual necessity for repelling invasion, or suppressing insurrection or rebellion;

And whereas a retaliatory or vindictive policy, attended by unnecessary disqualifications, pains, penalties, confiscations, and disfranchisements, now, as always, could only tend to hinder reconciliation among the people and national restoration, while it must seriously embarrass, obstruct, and repress popular energies and national industry and enterprise;

And whereas, for these reasons, it is now deemed essential to the public welfare, and to the more perfect restoration of constitutional law and order, that the said last-mentioned proclamation, so as aforesaid issued on the 29th day of May, A. D. 1865, should be modified, and that the full and beneficent pardon conceded thereby should be opened and further extended to a large number of the persons who, by its aforesaid exceptions, have been hitherto excluded from executive clemency:

Now, therefore, be it known that I, Andrew Johnson, President of the United States, do hereby proclaim and declare that the full pardon described in the said proclamation of the 29th day of May, A. D. 1865, shall henceforth be opened and extended to all persons who, directly or indirectly, participated in the late rebellion, with the restoration of all privileges, immunities, and rights of property, except as to property with regard to slaves, and except in cases of legal proceedings under the laws of the United States; but upon this condition, nevertheless: that every such person who shall seek to avail himself of this proclamation shall take and subscribe the following oath, and shall cause the same to be registered for permanent preservation, in the same manner and with the same effect as with the oath prescribed in the said proclamation of the 29th day of May, 1865, namely:

"I, ——, do solemnly swear, (or affirm,) in presence of Almighty God, that I will henceforth faithfully support, protect, and defend the Constitution of the United States, and the Union of the States thereunder; and that I will, in like manner, abide by and faithfully support all laws and proclamations which have been made during the late rebellion with reference to the emancipation of slaves: So help me God."

The following persons, and no others, are excluded from the benefits of this proclamation, and of the said proclamation of the twenty-ninth day of May, 1865, namely:

First. The chief or pretended chief executive officers, including the President, Vice President, and all heads of departments of the pretended Confederate or rebel Government, and all who were agents thereof in foreign States and countries, and all who held, or pretended to hold, in the service of the said pretended Confederate Government, a military rank or title above the grade of brigadier general, or naval rank or title above that of captain, and all who were or pretended to be Governors of States, while maintaining, aiding, abetting, or submitting to and acquiescing in the rebellion.

Second. All persons who in any way treated otherwise than as lawful prisoners of war persons who in any capacity were employed or engaged in the military or naval service of the United States.

Third. All persons who, at the time they may seek to obtain the benefits of this proclamation, are actually in civil, military, or naval confinement or custody, or legally held to bail, either before or after conviction, and all persons who were engaged directly or indirectly in the assassination of the late President of the United States, or in any plot or conspiracy in any manner therewith connected.

In testimony whereof, I have signed these presents with my hand, and have caused the seal of the United States to be hereunto affixed.

Done at the city of Washington, the seventh day of September, in the year of our Lord one thousand eight hundred and [SEAL.] sixty-seven, and of the Independence of the United States of America the ninety-second.

ANDREW JOHNSON.

By the President:
WILLIAM H. SEWARD,
*Secretary of State.*

### Of General Amnesty, July 4, 1868.

Whereas in the month of July, A. D. 1861, in accepting the condition of civil war, which was brought about by insurrection and rebellion in several of the States which constitute the United States, the two houses of Congress did solemnly declare that the war was not waged on the part of the Government in any spirit of oppression, nor for any purpose of conquest or subjugation, nor for any purpose of overthrowing or interfering with the rights or established institutions of the States, but only to defend and maintain the supremacy of the Constitution of the United States, and to preserve the Union with all the dignity, equality, and rights of the several States unimpaired; and that so soon as these objects should be accomplished, the war on the part of the Government should cease;

And whereas the President of the United States has heretofore, in the spirit of that declaration, and with the view of securing for it ultimate and complete effect, set forth several proclamations, offering amnesty and pardon to persons who had been or were concerned in the aforesaid rebellion, which proclamations, however, were attended with prudential reservations and exceptions, then deemed necessary and proper, and which proclamations were respectively issued on the 8th day of December, 1863, on the 26th day of March, 1864, on the 29th day of May, 1865, and on the 7th day of September, 1867;

And whereas the said lamentable civil war has long since altogether ceased, with an acknowledged guarantee to all the States of the supremacy of the Federal Constitution and the Government thereunder; and there no longer exists any reasonable ground to apprehend a renewal of the said civil war, or any foreign interference, or any unlawful resistance by any portion of the people of any of the States to the Constitution and laws of the United States;

And whereas it is desirable to reduce the standing army, and to bring to a speedy termination military occupation, martial law, military tribunals, abridgement of freedom of speech and of the press, and suspension of the privilege of *habeas corpus,* and the right of trial by jury—such encroachments upon our free institutions in times of peace being dangerous to public liberty, incompatible with the individual rights of the citizen, contrary to the genius and spirit of our republican form of government, and exhaustive of the national resources;

And whereas it is believed that amnesty and pardon will tend to secure a complete and universal establishment and prevalence of municipal law and order, in conformity with the Constitution of the United States, and to remove all appearances or presumptions of a retaliatory or vindictive policy on the part of the Government attended by unnecessary disqualifications, pains, penalties, confiscations, and disfranchisements; and, on the contrary, to promote and procure complete fraternal reconciliation among the whole people, with due submission to the Constitution and laws:

Now, therefore, be it known that I, Andrew Johnson, President of the United States, do, by virtue of the Constitution and in the name of the people of the United States, hereby proclaim and declare, unconditionally and without reservation, to all and to every person who directly or indirectly participated in the late insurrection or rebellion, excepting such person or persons as may be under presentment or indictment in any court of the United States having competent jurisdiction upon a charge of treason or other felony, a full pardon and amnesty for the offence of treason against the United States, or of adhering to their enemies during the late civil war, with restoration of all rights of property, except as to slaves, and except also as to any property of which any person may have been legally divested under the laws of the United States.

In testimony wherof I have signed these presents with my hand, and have caused the seal of the United States to be hereunto affixed.

Done at the city of Washington, the fourth day of July, in the year of our Lord one [SEAL.] thousand eight hundred and sixty-eight, and of the independence of the United States of America the ninety-third.

ANDREW JOHNSON.

By the President:
WILLIAM H. SEWARD, *Sec'y of State.*

### Order Respecting the Transaction of Public Business, December 17, 1867.

It is desired and advised that all communications in writing intended for the executive department of the Government, and relating to public business, of whatever kind, including suggestions for legislation, claims, contracts, employment, appointments and removals from office, and pardons, be transmitted directly, in the first instance, to the head of the department to which the care of the subject-matter of the communication properly belongs. This regulation has become necessary for the more convenient, punctual, and regular despatch of the public business.

By order of the President:
WILLIAM H. SEWARD, *Sec'y of State.*
WASHINGTON, *December* 17, 1867.

**Correcting an Error of Date in previous Proclamation,\* October 7, 1867.**

Whereas it has been ascertained that in the nineteenth paragraph of the proclamation of the President of the United States, of the 20th of August, 1866, declaring the insurrection at an end which had theretofore existed in the State of Texas, the previous proclamation of the 13th of June, 1865, instead of that of the 2d of April, 1866, was referred to. Now, therefore, be it known that I, Andrew Johnson, President of the United States, do hereby declare and proclaim, that the said words "thirteenth of June, one thousand eight hundred and sixty-five" are to be regarded as erroneous in the paragraph adverted to, and that the words "second day of April, one thousand eight hundred and sixty-six" are to be considered as substituted therefor.

In testimony whereof, I have hereunto set my hand, and caused the seal of the United States to be affixed.

Done at the city of Washington, this 7th day of October, in the year of our Lord 1867,
[SEAL.] and of the Independence of the United States of America, the ninety-second.
ANDREW JOHNSON.

By the President:
WILLIAM H. SEWARD, *Sec'y of State.*

**Orders Referring to Reconstruction.†**

[General Orders No. 77.]
HEADQ'RS OF ARMY, ADJ'T GEN'S OFFICE,
WASHINGTON, *August* 19, 1867.

I. The following orders have been received from the President:

(For these orders see page 306.)

II. In pursuance of the foregoing order of the President of the United States, Major General G. H. Thomas will, on receipt of the order, turn over his present command to the officer next in rank to himself, and proceed to New Orleans, Louisiana, to relieve Major General P. H. Sheridan of the command of the fifth military district.

III. Major General P. H. Sheridan, on being relieved from the command of the fifth military district by Major General G. H. Thomas, will proceed to Fort Leavenworth, Kansas, and will relieve Major General W. S. Hancock in the command of the department of the Missouri.

IV. Major General W. S. Hancock, on being relieved from the command of the department of the Missouri by Major General Sheridan, will proceed to Louisville, Kentucky, and will assume command of the department of the Cumberland.

V. Major General G. H. Thomas will continue to execute all orders he may find in force in the fifth military district at the time of his assuming command of it, unless authorized by the General of the army to annul, alter, or modify them.

VI. Major General Sheridan, before relieving Major General Hancock, will report in person at these headquarters.

By command of General Grant.
E. D. TOWNSEND, *A. A. G.*

---

\* See page 70 of the Manual for 1867, or page 196 of the combined Manual for the proclamation referred to.
† For previous order see page 73 of Political Manual of 1867, or page 199 of the combined Manual.

[General Orders No. 81.]
HEADQUARTERS OF THE ARMY,
ADJUTANT GENERAL'S OFFICE,
WASHINGTON, *August* 27, 1867.

I. The following orders have been received from the President:

(For these orders see page 308.)

II. In compliance with the foregoing instructions of the President of the United States, Major General P. H. Sheridan will, on receipt of this order, turn over his present command to Brevet Major General Charles Griffin, the officer next in rank to himself, and proceed, without delay, to Fort Leavenworth, Kansas, and will relieve Major General Hancock in command of the department of the Missouri.

III. On being relieved by Major General Sheridan, Major General Hancock will proceed, without delay, to New Orleans, Louisiana, and assume command of the fifth military district, and of the department composed of the States of Louisiana and Texas.

IV. Major General George H. Thomas will continue in command of the department of the Cumberland.

By command of General Grant.
E. D. TOWNSEND,
*Assistant Adjutant General.*

---

HEADQUARTERS OF THE ARMY,
ADJUTANT GENERAL' OFFICE,
WASHINGTON, *August* 27, 1867.

I. The following orders have been received from the President:

EXECUTIVE MANSION,
WASHINGTON, D. C., *August* 26, 1867.

Brevet Major General Edward R. S. Canby is hereby assigned to the command of the second military district, created by the act of Congress of March 2, 1867, and of the military department of the South, embracing the States of North Carolina and South Carolina. He will, as soon as practicable, relieve Major General Daniel E. Sickles, and, on assuming the command to which he is hereby assigned, will, when necessary to a faithful execution of the laws, exercise any and all powers conferred by acts of Congress upon district commanders, and any and all authority pertaining to officers in command of military departments.

Major General Daniel E. Sickles is hereby relieved from the command of the second military district.

The Secretary of War *ad interim* will give the necessary instructions to carry this order into effect.
ANDREW JOHNSON.

II. In pursuance of the foregoing order of the President of the United States, Brevet Major General Canby will, on receipt of the order, turn over his present command to the officer next in rank to himself, and proceed to Charleston, South Carolina, to relieve Major General Sickles of the command of the second military district.

III. Major General Sickles, on being relieved, will repair to New York city, and report by letter to the Adjutant General.

By command of General Grant.
E. D. TOWNSEND,
*Assistant Adjutant General.*

---

HEADQUARTERS OF THE ARMY,
ADJUTANT GENERAL'S OFFICE,
WASHINGTON, *December* 28, 1867.

[General Orders, No. 104.]

By direction of the President of the United States the following orders are made:

I. Brevet Major General E. O. C. Ord will turn over the command of the fourth military discrict to Brevet Major General A. C. Gillem, and proceed to San Francisco, California, to take command of the department of California.

II. On being relieved by Brevet Major General Ord, Brevet Major General Irvin Mc-Dowell will proceed to Vicksburg, Mississippi, and relieve General Gillem in command of the fourth military district.

III. Brevet Major General John Pope is hereby relieved of the command of the third military district, and will report, without delay, at the headquarters of the army for further orders, turning over his command to the next senior officer until the arrival of his successor.

IV. Major General George G. Meade is assigned to the command of the third military district, and will assume it without delay. The department of the East will be commanded by the senior officer now on duty in it until a commander is named by the President.

V. The officers assigned in the foregoing order to command of military districts will exercise therein any and all powers conferred by act of Congress upon district commanders, and also any and all powers pertaining to military department commanders.

VI. Brevet Major General Wager Swayne, colonel 45th United States infantry, is hereby relieved from duty in the Bureau of Refugees, Freedmen, and Abandoned Lands, and will proceed to Nashville, Tennessee, and assume command of his regiment.

By command of General Grant.
E. D. TOWNSEND,
*Assistant Adjutant General.*

---

HEADQUARTERS OF THE ARMY,
ADJUTANT GENERAL'S OFFICE,
WASHINGTON, *June 30,* 1868.

[General Orders No. 33.]

By direction of the President of the United States, the following orders are made:

I. Brevet Major General Irvin McDowell is relieved from the command of the fourth military district, and will report in person, without delay, at the War Department.

II. Brevet Major General Alvan C. Gillem is assigned to the command of the fourth military district, and will assume it without delay.

By command of General Grant
E. D. TOWNSEND, *A. A. G.*

---

**Establishing a new Military Division, February 12, 1868.**

[General Orders No. 10.]

HEADQUARTERS OF THE ARMY,
ADJUTANT GENERAL'S OFFICE,
WASHINGTON, *Feb.* 12, 1868.

The following orders are published for the information and guidance of all concerned:

EXECUTIVE MANSION,
WASHINGTON, D. C., *February* 12, 1868.

GENERAL: You will please issue an order creating a military division, to be called the military division of the Atlantic, to be composed of the department of the Lakes, the department of the East, and the department of Washington, and to be commanded by Lieutenant General William T. Sherman, with his headquarters at Washington.

Until further orders from the President, you will assign no officer to the permanent command of the military division of the Missouri.

Respectfully yours,                 ANDREW JOHNSON.
General U. S. GRANT,
*Commd'g Armies of United States, Washington, D. C.*

Major General P. H. Sheridan, the senior officer in the military division of the Missouri, will temporarily perform the duties of commander of the military division of the Missouri, in addition to his duties of department commander.

By command of General Grant.
E. D. TOWNSEND,
*Assistant Adjutant General.*

---

February 13—The President nominated Lieut. General Sherman for the brevet rank of general, for distinguished gallantry, skill, and ability during the war of the rebellion, to which he responded, as follows:

ST. LOUIS, *February* 14, 1868.
Hon. JOHN SHERMAN.

Oppose confirmation of myself as brevet general, on ground that it is unprecedented and that it is better not to extend the system of brevets above major generals. If I can't avoid coming to Washington, I may have to resign.
W. T. SHERMAN,
*Lieutenant General.*

February 19—The President relieved Lieut. General Sherman from this order.

February 21—The President nominated Major General George H. Thomas as brevet lieutenant general and brevet general, with supposed reference to this command; whereupon General Thomas declined in these terms:

LOUISVILLE, *February* 22, 1868.
Hon. B. F. WADE, *President of the Senate.*

The morning papers of Louisville announced officially that my name was yesterday sent to the Senate for confirmation as brevet lieutenant general and brevet general. For the battle of Nashville I was appointed major general United States army. My services since the war do not merit so high a compliment, and it is now too late to be regarded as a compliment if conferred for services during the war. I, therefore, earnestly request that the Senate will not confirm the nomination.                   GEO. H. THOMAS,
*Major General*

---

March 28—Major General Hancock was assigned as follows:

[General Orders No. 17.]

HEADQUARTERS OF THE ARMY,
ADJUTANT GENERAL'S OFFICE,
WASHINGTON, *March* 28, 1868.

By direction of the President of the United States, Major General W. S. Hancock is relieved from command of the fifth military district and assigned to command of the military division of the Atlantic, created by General Orders No. 10, of February 12, 1868.

By command of General Grant.
E. D. TOWNSEND,
*Assistant Adjutant General.*

# XXXI

# MEMBERS OF THE CABINET OF PRESIDENT JOHNSON,
## AND OF THE FORTIETH CONGRESS.

### PRESIDENT JOHNSON'S CABINET.

*Secretary of State*—WILLIAM H. SEWARD, of New York.

*Secretary of the Treasury*—HUGH McCULLOCH, of Indiana.

*Secretary of War*—JOHN M. SCHOFIELD, of New York, from June 1, 1868, *vice* EDWIN M. STANTON, of Ohio, who was suspended by the President, August 12, 1867, when General ULYSSES S. GRANT was appointed Secretary of War *ad interim*, and served from that date to January 14, 1868, at which time he vacated the office, and Mr. STANTON resumed the functions thereof, the Senate having on the previous evening voted a non-concurrence in the said suspension. Mr. STANTON remained in the office till May 26, when he "relinquished charge."

*Secretary of the Navy*—GIDEON WELLES, of Connecticut.

*Postmaster General*—ALEXANDER W. RANDALL, of Wisconsin.

*Secretary of the Interior*—ORVILLE H. BROWNING, of Illinois.

*Attorney General*— *vice* HENRY STANBERY, of Kentucky, who resigned, March 12, 1868, to act as one of the President's counsel, Mr. Secretary BROWNING having been the same day appointed Acting Attorney General. (Mr. Stanbery was nominated for re-appointment, after the trial, but the Senate rejected the nomination.)

### MEMBERS OF THE FORTIETH CONGRESS.

Adjourned sessions of First Session—July 3-20, November 21-December 2, 1867. Second Session, December 4, 1867-July , 1868.

#### Senate.

BENJAMIN F. WADE, of Ohio, *President of the Senate, and Acting Vice President.*

George C. Gorham, of California, *Secretary,* from June 6, 1868, *vice* John W. Forney, of Pennsylvania, resigned.

*Maine*—Lot M. Morrill, William Pitt Fessenden.

*New Hampshire*—Aaron H. Cragin, James W. Patterson.

*Vermont*—George F. Edmunds, Justin S. Morrill.

*Massachusetts*—Charles Sumner, Henry Wilson.

*Rhode Island*—William Sprague, Henry B. Anthony.

*Connecticut*—James Dixon, Orris S. Ferry.

*New York*—Edwin D. Morgan, Roscoe Conkling.

*New Jersey*—Frederick T. Frelinghuysen, Alexander G. Cattell.

*Pennsylvania*—Charles R. Buckalew, Simon Cameron.

*Delaware*—James A. Bayard,* Willard Saulsbury.

*Maryland*—Reverdy Johnson, George Vickers.[a]

*Ohio*—Benjamin F. Wade, John Sherman.

*Kentucky*—Garrett Davis, Thomas C. McCreery.[†]

*Tennessee*—David T. Patterson, Joseph S. Fowler.

*Indiana*—Thomas A. Hendricks, Oliver P. Morton.

*Illinois*—Richard Yates, Lyman Trumbull.

*Missouri*—John B. Henderson, Charles D. Drake.

*Arkansas*[‡]—Alexander McDonald, Benjamin F. Rice.

*Michigan*—Zachariah Chandler, Jacob M. Howard.

*Florida*—Adonijah S. Welch, (qualified July 2, 1868,) Thomas W. Osborn, (qualified June 30.)

*Iowa*—James W. Grimes, James Harlan.

*Wisconsin*—James R. Doolittle, Timothy O. Howe.

*California*—John Conness, Cornelius Cole.

*Minnesota*—Alexander Ramsey, Dan'l S. Norton.

*Oregon*—George H. Williams, Henry W. Corbett.

*Kansas*—Edmund G. Ross, Samuel C. Pomeroy.

*West Virginia*—Peter G. Van Winkle, Waitman T. Willey.

*Nevada*—William M. Stewart, James W. Nye.

*Nebraska*—Thomas W. Tipton, John M. Thayer.

#### House of Representatives.

SCHUYLER COLFAX, of Indiana, *Speaker.*

Edward McPherson, of Pennsylvania, *Clerk.*

*Maine*—John Lynch, Sidney Perham, James G. Blaine, John A. Peters, Frederick A. Pike.

*New Hampshire*—Jacob H. Ela, Aaron F. Stevens, Jacob Benton.

*Vermont*—Frederick E. Woodbridge, Luke P. Poland, Worthington C. Smith.

*Massachusetts*—Thomas D. Eliot, Oakes Ames, Ginery Twichell, Samuel Hooper, Benjamin F. Butler, Nathaniel P. Banks, George S. Boutwell, John D. Baldwin, William B. Washburn, Henry L. Dawes.

*Rhode Island*‖—Thomas A. Jenckes, Nathan F. Dixon.

*Connecticut*§—Richard D. Hubbard, Julius Hotchkiss, Henry H. Starkweather, William H. Barnum.

*New York*—Stephen Taber, Demas Barnes, William E. Robinson, John Fox, John Morrissey, Thomas E. Stewart, John W. Chanler, James Brooks, Fernando Wood, William H. Robertson, Charles H. Van Wyck, John H. Ketcham, Thomas Cornell, John V. L. Pruyn, John A. Griswold, Orange Ferriss, Calvin T. Hulburd

*Qualified April 11, 1867, at special session, in place of George Read Riddle, deceased.

[a]Qualified March 9, 1868, in place of Philip Francis Thomas, who was denied admission, February 19, 1868—yeas 21, nays 28.

†Qualified February 28, 1868, in place of James Guthrie, resigned February 10, 1868.

‡Qualified June 23, 1868.

‖Qualified July 3, 1867.

§ Messrs. Hotchkiss and Starkweather qualified July 3, 1867; Messrs. Barnum and Hubbard, July 11, 1867.

James M. Marvin, William C. Fields, Addison H. Laflin, Alexander H. Bailey,* John C. Churchill, Dennis McCarthy, Theodore M. Pomeroy, William H. Kelsey, William S. Lincoln Hamilton Ward, Lewis Selye, Burt Van Horn, James M. Humphrey, Henry Van Aernam.

*New Jersey*—William Moore, Charles Haight, Charles Sitgreaves, John Hill, George A. Halsey.

*Pennsylvania*—Samuel J. Randall, Charles O'-Neill, Leonard Myers, William D. Kelley, Caleb N. Taylor, Benjamin M. Boyer, John M. Broomall, J. Lawrence Getz, Thaddeus Stevens, Henry L. Cake, Daniel M. Van Auken, George W. Woodward.† Ulysses Mercur, George F. Miller, Adam J. Glossbrenner, William H. Koontz, Daniel J. Morrell, Stephen F Wilson, Glenni W. Scofield, Darwin A. Finney, John Covode, James K. Moorhead, Thomas Williams, George V. Lawrence.

*Delaware*—John A. Nicholson.

*Maryland*—Hiram McCullough, Stevenson Archer, Charles E. Phelps, Francis Thomas, Frederick Stone.

*Ohio*—Benjamin Eggleston, Samuel F. Cary,‡ Robert C. Schenck, William Lawrence, William Mungen, Reader W. Clarke, Samuel Shellabarger, John Beatty,‖ Ralph P. Buckland, James M. Ashley, John T. Wilson, Philadelph Van Trump, Columbus Delano,§ Martin Welker, Tobias A. Plants, John A. Bingham, Ephraim R. Eckley, Rufus P. Spalding, James A. Garfield.

*Kentucky*¶—Lawrence S. Trimble, (vacancy,) Jacob S. Golladay, J. Proctor Knott, Asa P. Grover, Thomas L. Jones, James B. Beck, George M. Adams, Samuel McKee.

*Tennessee*\*\*—Roderick R. Butler, Horace Maynard, William B. Stokes, James Mullins, John Trimble, Samuel M. Arnell, Isaac R. Hawkins, David A. Nunn.

---

* Qualified November 30, 1867.
† Qualified November 21, 1867, **in place of Charles** Denison. deceased.
‡ Qualified November 21, 1867, in place of Rutherford B. Hayes, resigned.
‖ Qualified February 5, 1868, in place of Cornelius S. Hamilton, killed December 22, 1867.
§ June 3, 1868, Mr. Delano qualified, in place of George W. Morgan, the House having voted—36 to 79—that Mr. Morgan was not entitled, and—80 to 38—that Mr. Delano was entitled to the seat.
¶ Mr. Adams qualified July 8, 1867. Messrs. Beck, Grover, and Jones qualified Dec. 3, Mr. Knott Dec. 4, Mr. Golladay Dec. 5, and Mr. Trimble January 10, 1868. Mr. John Young Brown, claiming a seat for the second district, was voted, February 13—43 to 108—not entitled thereto, by reason of having voluntarily given aid, countenance, counsel, and encouragement to persons engaged in armed hostility to the United States; and February 15, the House voted—30 to 102—that Samuel E. Smith, not having received a majority of the votes cast for Representative, was not elected. The Speaker was directed to notify the Governor of Kentucky of the vacancy in the second district, but no election was called by him. Mr. McKee qualified June 22, 1868, the House having, June 22, voted—90 to 30—that John D. Young was not entitled to the seat, and that Samuel McKee was entitled to it.
\*\* Messrs. Maynard, Stokes, Mullins, John Trimble, Hawkins, and Nunn qualified November 21, 1867; Mr. Arnell, November 25; Mr. Butler, June 26, 1868.

*Indiana*—William E. Niblack, Michael C. Kerr, Morton C. Hunter, William S. Holman, George W. Julian, John Coburn, Henry D. Washburn, Godlove S. Orth, Schuyler Colfax, William Williams, John P. C. Shanks.

*Illinois*—Norman B. Judd, John F. Farnsworth, Elihu B. Washburne,* Abner C. Harding, Ebon C. Ingersoll, Burton C. Cook, Henry P. H. Bromwell, Shelby M. Cullom, Lewis W. Ross, Albert G. Burr, Samuel S. Marshall, Jehu Baker, Green B. Raum, John A. Logan.

*Missouri*—William A. Pile, Carman A. Newcomb, James R. McCormick,† Joseph J. Gravely, Joseph W. McClurg, Robert T. Van Horn, Benjamin F. Loan, John F. Benjamin, George W. Anderson.

*Arkansas*‡—Logan H. Roots, James Hinds, Thomas Boles.

*Michigan*—Fernando C. Beaman, Charles Upson, Austin Blair, Thomas W. Ferry, Rowland E. Trowbridge, John F. Driggs.

*Florida*—Charles M. Hamilton, (qualified July 1, 1868.)

*Iowa*—James F. Wilson, Hiram Price, William B. Allison, William Loughridge, Grenville M. Dodge, Asahel W. Hubbard.

*Wisconsin*—Halbert E. Paine, Benjamin F. Hopkins, Amasa Cobb, Charles A Eldridge, Philetus Sawyer, Cadwalader C. Washburn.

*California*‖—Samuel B. Axtell, William Higby, James A. Johnson.

*Minnesota*—William Windom, Ignatius Donnelly.

*Oregon*—Rufus Mallory.

*Kansas*—Sidney Clarke.

*West Virginia*—Chester D. Hubbard, Bethuel M. Kitchen, Daniel Polsley.

*Nevada*—Delos R. Ashley.

*Nebraska*—John Taffe.

The following persons were elected to the House of Representatives at the election held on the constitutions of their respective States:

*North Carolina*—John R. French, David Heaton, Oliver H. Dockery, John T. Deweese, Israel G. Lash, Nathaniel Boyden, Alexander H. Jones.

*South Carolina*—Benjamin F. Whittemore, C C. Bowen, Simon Corley, James H. Goss. (Also two elected at large: J. P. M. Epping, Elias H. Dickson.)

*Georgia*—J. W. Clift, Nelson Tift, William P. Edwards, Samuel F. Gove, Charles H. Prince, John H. Christy, P. M. B. Young.

*Louisiana*—J. Hale Sypher, James Mann, Joseph P. Newsham. Michel Vidal, W. Jasper Blackburn.

*Alabama*—Francis W. Kellogg, Charles W. Buckley, Benjamin W. Norris, Charles W. Pierce, John B. Callis, Thomas Haughey.

---

* Mr. Washburne having been absent at the previous session, qualified November 21, 1867.
† Qualified December 17, 1867, vice Thomas E. Noell, deceased.
‡ Qualified June 23, 1868, the bill declaring Arkansas entitled to representation having become a law June 22, 1868.
‖ Qualified November 21, 1867.

# XXXII

# VOTES ON POLITICAL BILLS AND RESOLUTIONS.

## To Continue the Bureau for the Relief of Freedmen and Refugees.

*Be it enacted,* &c., That the act entitled "An act to establish a Bureau for the relief of Freedmen and Refugees," approved March 3, 1865,* and the act entitled "An act to continue in force and to amend 'An act to establish a Bureau for the relief of Freedmen and Refugees, and for other purposes,'" passed on the 16th of July, 1866† shall continue in force for the term of one year from and after the 16th of July, in the year 1868, excepting so far as the same shall be herein modified. And the Secretary of War is hereby directed to re-establish said bureau where the same has been wholly or in part discontinued: *Provided,* He shall be satisfied that the personal safety of freedmen shall require it.

SEC. 2. That it shall be the duty of the Secretary of War to discontinue the operations of the bureau in any State whenever such State shall be fully restored in its constitutional relations with the Government of the United States, and shall be duly represented in the Congress of the United States, unless, upon advising with the Commissioner of the bureau and upon full consideration of the condition of freedmen's affairs in such State, the Secretary of War shall be of opinion that the further continuance of the bureau shall be necessary: *Provided, however,* That the educational division of said bureau shall not be affected or in any way interfered with, until such State shall have made suitable provision for the education of the children of freedmen within said State.

SEC. 3. That unexpended balances ‡ in the

---

\* See page 72 of Manual of 1866.

† See page 150 of Manual of 1867.

‡ The financial affairs of the bureau are as follow, as appears from a recent report on the subject in the House of Representatives, the figures in which were taken from the books of the bureau:

From the establishment of the bureau, on the 15th of May, 1865, there have been appropriated by Congress for its support .......................................................$10,780,750 00

The total expenditure from this appropriation, from 15th of May, 1865, to January 1, 1868, was as follows:

| | |
|---|---:|
| Salaries of assistant and sub-assistant commissioners ............................................. | $302,244 88 |
| Salaries of clerks....................................... | 509,833 80 |
| Stationery and printing.............................. | 78,306 14 |
| Quarters and fuel...................................... | 196,906 54 |
| Clothing for distribution............................ | 143,735 99 |
| Commissary stores. ................................... | 1,245,271 76 |
| Medical department.................................... | 470,834 37 |
| Transportation of officers and agents........ | 131,052 54 |
| Transportation of freedmen and refugees.. | 115,979 87 |
| Transportation of stores............................ | 87,490 36 |
| Forage ...................................................... | 53,096 28 |
| School superintendents.............................. | 28,247 61 |
| Building for schools and asylums,including construction, rental, and repairs.............. | 558,914 91 |
| Telegraphing and postage.......................... | 35,546 98 |
| Internal revenue (tax withheld on salaries) | 4,981 55 |
| Southern relief ......................................... | 385,410 81 |
| Agricultural Bureau (transferred).............. | 50,000 00 |

Total expended......................................$4,397,854 39

Balance in hands of agents, August 31, 1867.. 645,911 33
Undrawn from Treasury......... ..................... 5,736,984 28

Amount on hand December 31, 1867.....$6,382,895 61

---

hands of the Commissioner, not required otherwise for the due execution of the law, may be, in the discretion of the Commissioner, applied for the education of freedmen and refugees, subject to the provisions of law applicable thereto.

SEC. 4. That officers of the veteran reserve corps, or of the volunteer service, now on duty in the Freedmen's Bureau as assistant commissioners, agents, medical officers, or in other capacities, who have been or may be mustered out of service, may be retained by the Commissioner when the same shall be required for the proper execution of the laws, as officers of the bureau, upon such duty and with the same pay, compensation, and all allowances, from the date of their appointment, as now provided by law for their respective grades and duties at the dates of their muster-out and discharge; and such officers so retained shall have, respectively, the same authority and jurisdiction as now conferred upon "officers of the bureau" by act of Congress passed on the 16th of July, 1866.

SEC. 5. That the Commissioner is hereby empowered to sell for cash, or by instalments with ample security, school buildings and other buildings constructed for refugees and freedmen by the bureau, to the associations, corporate bodies, or trustees who now use them for purposes of education or relief of want, under suitable guarantees that the purposes for which said buildings were constructed shall be observed: *Provided,* That all funds derived therefrom shall be returned to the bureau appropriations and accounted for to the Treasury of the United States.

IN HOUSE.

1868, March 19—The bill passed—yeas 97, nays 38, as follow:

YEAS—Messrs. Allison, Ames, Arnell, Delos R. Ashley, James M. Ashley, Bailey, Baker, Baldwin, Banks, Beaman, Bingham, Blaine, Blair, Bromwell, Broomall, Buckland, Butler, Cake, Churchill, Sidney Clarke, Coburn, Cook, Cullom, Dawes, Dixon, Dodge, Donnelly, Driggs, Eckley, Eliot, Farnsworth, Ferriss, Ferry, Fields, Garfield, Gravely, Higby, Hill, Hooper, Hopkins, Chester D. Hubbard, Hulburd, Hunter, Ingersoll, Jenckes, Judd, Julian, Kelley, Kelsey,

---

Besides this appropriation by Congress, the bureau came into the possession of certain funds belonging to the "department of negro affairs" which had previously existed in the rebel States, and from rents, fines, conscript fund, and miscellaneous sources, amounting to .................... ........................$1,605,694 19

Of which, there were expended, for labor, schools, rents, repairs, clothing, fuel, subsistence, &c........... ................................ 1,544,092 80

Leaving a balance on hand, Dec. 31, 1867... $61,601 39

Of this amount of $4,397,854 39 expended, $500,000 were applied, by a resolution of Congress, for the relief of destitute people in the South who were starving by reason of failure of the crops, and $50,000 were transferred to the Agricultural Department for seeds for the South—making $550,000.

With these sums deducted from the expense account of the Bureau, the whole expenditure from appropriations by Congress, for the use of the Bureau from its establishment, amount to $3,847,854 39.

No further appropriation was asked or made for the ensuing fiscal year, and the appropriations previously made of $10,780,750 will carry the Bureau from May, 1865, to July, 1869.

Koontz, Laflin, William Lawrence, Loan, Logan, Lynch, Maynard, Miller, Moore, Morrell, Myers, Newcomb, O'Neill, Orth, Paine, Peters, Pike, Pile, Plants, Polsley, Pomeroy, Price, Raum, Robertson, Sawyer, Schenck, Selye, Shanks, Spalding, Aaron F. Stevens, Thaddeus Stevens, Taffe, Thomas, John Trimble, Trowbridge, Twichell, Upson, Robert T. Van Horn, Ward, Cadwalader C. Washburn, Ellihu B. Washburne, Henry D. Washburn, William B. Washburn, Welker, Thomas Williams, James F. Wilson, Stephen F. Wilson, Windom—97.

NAYS—Messrs. *Adams, Axtell, Barnes, Beck, Boyer, Brooks, Burr, Chanler, Eldridge, Getz, Golladay, Grover, Haight, Holman, Hotchkiss, Johnson, Kerr, Knott,* George V. Lawrence, *Marshall, McCormick, McCullough,* Mercur, Moorhead, *Morgan, Mungen, Niblack, Nicholson, Phelps, Randall, Ross, Sitgreaves, Taber, Lawrence S. Trimble, Van Auken, Van Trump, Wood, Woodward*—38.

### In Senate.

June 11—The bill passed without a division.

### Vote of Thanks to Ex-Secretary Stanton.

#### In Senate.

1868, May 28—Mr. Edmunds offered this resolution:

*Resolved by the Senate,* (the House of Representatives concurring,) That the thanks of Congress are due, and are hereby tendered, to Hon. Edwin M. Stanton for the great ability, purity, and fidelity to the cause of the country with which he has discharged the duties of Secretary of War, as well amid the open dangers of a great rebellion as at a later period when assailed by the Opposition, inspired by hostility to the measures of justice and pacification provided by Congress for the restoration of a real and permanent peace.

June 1—Mr. Hendricks moved to strike out the latter clause, beginning with the words "as well."

Mr. Henderson moved to amend so as to make the resolution read as follows:

That the thanks of Congress are due, and are hereby tendered, to Hon. Edwin M Stanton, for the great ability, purity, and fidelity to the cause of the country with which he discharged the duties of Secretary of War amid the open dangers of a great rebellion.

Which was rejected without a count; also, the amendment offered by Mr. Hendricks.

Mr. Henderson moved to amend by adding to the resolution these words:

And Congress takes this occasion to tender its thanks to Chief Justice Chase for the great ability, purity, and distinguished learning which have illustrated his position on the bench of the Supreme Court.

Which was disagreed to—yeas 11, nays 30, as follow:

YEAS—Messrs. *Buckalew, Doolittle,* Fowler, Henderson, *Hendricks, Johnson, McCreery, Norton, Patterson of* Tennessee, Ross, *Vickers*—11.

NAYS—Messrs. Cameron, Cattell, Chandler, Cole, Conkling, Conness, Cragin, Drake, Edmunds, Frelinghuysen, Harlan, Howard, Howe, Morgan, Morrill of Maine, Morrill of Vermont, Morton, Nye, Patterson of New Hampshire, Pomeroy, Ramsey, Stewart, Sumner, Thayer, Tipton, Van Winkle, Wade, Williams, Wilson, Yates—30.

The resolution was then adopted—yeas 37, nays 11, as follow:

YEAS—Messrs. Anthony, Cameron, Cattell, Chandler, Cole, Conkling, Conness, Cragin, Drake, Edmunds, Ferry, Fessenden, Frelinghuysen, Harlan, Howard, Howe, Morgan, Morrill of Maine, Morrill of Vermont, M·rton, Nye, Patterson of New Hampshire, Pomeroy, Ramsey, Sherman, Sprague, Stewart, Sumner, Thayer,

Tipton, Trumbull, Van Winkle, Wade, Willey, Williams, Wilson, Yates—37.

NAYS—Messrs. *Buckalew, Doolittle,* Fowler, Henderson, *Hendricks, Johnson, McCreery, Norton, Patterson of* Tennessee, Ross, *Vickers*—11.

### In House.

June 19—The resolution passed—yeas 102, nays 25, as follow:

YEAS—Messrs. Allison, Ames, Delos R. Ashley, Bailey, Baldwin, Beatty, Benjamin, Benton, Blaine, Blair, Boutwell, Buckland, Butler, Cake, Sidney Clarke, Cobb, Coburn, Cook, Cornell, Covode, Cullom, Delano, Donnelly, Driggs, Eckley, Eggleston, Ela, Eliot, Farnsworth, Ferriss, Fields, Garfield, Gravely, Griswold, Halsey, Harding, Higby, Hill, Hooper, Chester D. Hubbard, Hulburd, Jenckes, Judd, Julian, Kelsey, Ketcham, Kitchen, Koontz, Lincoln, Loan, Logan, Loughridge, Lynch, Mallory, Maynard, McCarthy, McClurg, Mercur, Miller, Moore, Moorhead, Morrell, Mullins, Myers, O'Neill, Orth, Paine, Peters, Pike, Pile, Polsley, Pomeroy, Price, Raum, Robertson, Sawyer, Schenck, Scofield, Shanks, Shellabarger, Smith, Starkweather, Aaron F. Stevens, Stokes, Taffe, Taylor, Twichell, Upson, Van Aernam, Van Wyck, Ward, Cadwalader C. Washburn, Henry D. Washburn, William B. Washburn, Welker, Thomas Williams, William Williams, James F. Wilson, John T. Wilson, Windom, Woodbridge, and Mr. Speaker Colfax—102.

NAYS—Messrs. *Archer, Beck, Brooks, Cary, Chanler, Eldridge, Getz, Golladay, Grover, Haight, Holman, Hotchkiss, Humphrey, Johnson, Jones, Kerr, Knott, McCormick, Mungen, Niblack, Nicholson, Phelps, Pruyn, Stone, Taber*—25.

### Quorum of Supreme Court.

1867, December 4—The SENATE passed, without a division, this bill:

*Be it enacted, &c.,* That any number of the justices of the Supreme Court of the United States, not less than five, and being a majority thereof, shall constitute a quorum.

### In House.

1868, January 13—The rules were suspended, (yeas 114, nays 38,) and the above bill with an amendment was reported to the House from the Judiciary Committee. The amendment was a new section, to which the proviso was added in the House, the whole being as follows:

SEC. 2. That no cause pending before the Supreme Court of the United States, involving the action or effect of any law of the United States, shall be decided adversely to the validity of such law without the concurrence of two-thirds of all the members of said court in the decision upon the several points in which said law or any part thereof may be deemed invalid: *Provided, however,* That if any circuit or district court of the United States shall adjudge any act of Congress to be unconstitutional or invalid, the judgment, before any further proceedings shall be had upon it, shall be certified up to the Supreme Court of the United States, and shall be considered therein; and if upon the consideration thereof two-thirds of all the members of the Supreme Court shall not affirm said judgment below, the same shall be declared and held reversed.

Pending this new section,

Mr. Thomas Williams moved to substitute for it these words:

In all cases of writs of error from and appeals to the Supreme Court of the United States, where is drawn in question the validity of a statute or an authority exercised by the United States, or the construction of any clause of the Constitution of the United States, or the validity of a statute of or an authority exercised under any State on the ground of repugnance to the Constitution or laws of the United States, the hearing shall be had only before a full bench of the judges of said court, and no judgment shall be rendered or decision made against the validity of any statute or of any authority exercised by the United States except with the concurrence of all the judges of the said court.

Which was disagreed to—yeas 25, nays 124. The yeas were:

Messrs. Arnell, Delos R. Ashley, James M. Ashley, Bingham, Cake, Sidney Clarke, Covode, Farnsworth, Harding, Judd, William Lawrence, Loan, Logan, Maynard, McCarthy, McClurg, Mullins, Pile, Price, John Trimble, Van Aernam, Robert T. Van Horn, Ward, Thomas Williams, William Williams.

Mr. James F. Wilson submitted the proviso in the section printed above, which was agreed to —yeas 111, nays 38 (all Democrats except Mr. Hawkins.) The amendment as amended was agreed to; and the bill then passed—yeas 116, nays 39, a party vote, except that Mr. Hawkins of Tennessee voted against the bill; which was not again considered in the Senate.

## Another Judiciary Act.

March 11—The Senate passed, without objection, the first section of the bill found below.

March 12—The House passed it, with the second section added, as an amendment, without a division.

AN ACT to amend an act entitled "An act to amend the judiciary act," passed the 24th of September, 1789.

*Be it enacted, &c.,* That final judgment in any circuit court of the United States, in any civil action against a collector or other officer of the revenue, for any act done by him in the performance of his official duty, or for the recovery of any money exacted by or paid to him, which shall have been paid into the Treasury of the United States, may, at the instance of either party, be re-examined and reversed or affirmed in the Supreme Court of the United States, upon writ of error, without regard to the sum or value in controversy in such action.

SEC. 2. That so much of the act approved February 5, 1867, entitled "An act to amend an act to establish the judicial courts of the United States," approved September 24, 1789, as authorizes an appeal from the judgment of the circuit court to the Supreme Court of the United States, or the exercise of any such jurisdiction by said Supreme Court on appeals which have been or may hereafter be taken, be, and the same is hereby, repealed.

March 12—The Senate concurred in the House amendment—yeas 32, nays 6, as follow:

YEAS—Messrs. Anthony, Cameron, Cattell, Chandler, Cole, Conkling, Conness, Drake, Edmunds, Ferry, Fessenden, Frelinghuysen, Grimes, Harlan, Henderson, Howard, Howe, Morgan, Morrill of Maine, Morrill of Vermont, Pomeroy, Ramsey, Ross, Sprague, Stewart, Sumner, Tipton, Trumbull, Van Winkle, Wade, Willey, Williams—32.

NAYS—Messrs. *Buckalew,* Fowler, *Hendricks, McCreery, Norton, Vickers*—6.

March 25—The bill was returned with the objections of the President.

March 27—The bill passed the Senate, over the veto—yeas 33. nays 9, as follow:

YEAS—Messrs. Cameron, Cattell, Chandler, Cole, Conkling, Cragin, Edmunds, Ferry, Frelinghuysen,

Harlan, Henderson, Howard, Howe, Morgan, Morrill of Maine, Morrill of Vermont, Morton, Nye, Patterson of New Hampshire, Pomeroy, Ramsey, Ross, Stewart, Sumner, Thayer, Tipton, Trumbull, Van Winkle, Wade, Willey, Williams, Wilson, Yates—33.

NAYS—Messrs. *Bayard, Buckalew, Davis, Dixon, Hendricks, McCreery, Norton, Patterson* of Tennessee, *Saulsbury*—9.

Same day—The House passed the bill—yeas 115, nays 34, as follow:

YEAS—Messrs. Ames, Anderson, Arnell, Delos R. Ashley, James M. Ashley, Bailey, Baker, Baldwin, Banks, Beaman, Beatty, Benjamin, Benton, Bingham, Blaine, Boutwell, Bromwell, Broomall, Buckland, Cake, Churchill, Reader W. Clarke, Sidney Clarke, Coburn, Cook, Covode, Cullom, Dawes, Dixon, Dodge, Driggs, Eckley, Eggleston, Eliot, Farnsworth, Ferriss, Ferry, Fields, Gravely, Halsey, Higby, Hill, Hooper, Hopkins, Chester D. Hubbard, Hulburd, Hunter, Ingersoll, Jenckes, Judd, Julian, Kelley, Kelsey, Ketcham, Kitchen, Koontz, Laflin, William Lawrence, Lincoln, Loan, Logan, Loughridge, Mallory, Maynard, McClurg, Mercur, Miller, Moore, Moorhead, Morrell, Mullins, Myers, Newcomb, O'Neill, Orth, Paine, Perham, Peters, Pike, Pile, Plants, Poland, Polsley, Pomeroy, Price, Raum, Sawyer, Schenck, Scofield, Selye, Shanks, Smith, Spalding, Aaron F. Stevens, Thaddeus Stevens, Taffe, Taylor, Thomas, John Trimble, Twichell, Upson, Burt Van Horn, Robert T. Van Horn, Van Wyck, Ward, Cadwalader C. Washburn, Ellihu B. Washburne, William B. Washburn, Welker, Thomas Williams, James F. Wilson, John T. Wilson, Stephen F. Wilson, Windom, Woodbridge—115.

NAYS—Messrs. *Adams, Archer, Axtell, Barnes, Beck, Brooks, Burr, Cary, Chanler, Eldridge, Fox, Getz, Glossbrenner, Golladay, Holman, Hotchkiss, Hubbard, Humphrey, Johnson, Kerr, Knott, Marshall, McCormick, Mungen, Niblack, Nicholson, Pruyn, Ross, Sitgreaves, Stone, Taber, Lawrence S. Trimble, Van Auken, Woodward*—34.

Whereupon the Speaker declared it to be a law.

## For the Further Security of Equal Rights in the District of Columbia.

The following were the proceedings in Congress on this bill:

### IN SENATE.

1867, July 17—This bill was passed:

*Be it enacted, &c.,* That in the District of Columbia no person shall be excluded from any office by reason of race or color, and so much of all laws making any such discrimination are hereby repealed.

Yeas 25, nays 5, as follow:

YEAS—Messrs. Cattell, Chandler, Cole, Edmunds, Fessenden, Frelinghuysen, Harlan, Henderson, Howard, Howe, Morgan, Morrill of Maine, Nye, Patterson of New Hampshire, Pomeroy, Ramsey, Sherman, Sprague, Sumner, Thayer, Tipton, Wade, Willey, Wilson, Yates—25.

NAYS—Messrs. *Bayard, Buckalew, Davis, Hendricks, Johnson*—5.

### IN HOUSE.

July 18—The bill was amended by substituting after the word "that" the following:

The word "white," wherever it occurs in the laws relating to the District of Columbia, or in the charter or ordinances of the city of Washington or Georgetown, and operates as a limitation on the right of any elector of said District, or either of said cities, to hold any office, or to be selected and to serve as a juror, be, and the same is hereby, repealed, and it shall be unlawful for any person or officer to enforce or attempt to enforce said limitation after the passage of this act.

And passed—yeas 90, nays 20, as follow:

YEAS—Messrs. Allison, Anderson, James M. Ashley, Baker, Baldwin, Banks, Beaman, Benjamin, Benton, Bingham, Blair, Boutwell, Broomall, Buckland, Butler, Churchill, Reader W. Clarke, Sidney Clarke, Cobb,

Coburn, Cook, Cornell, Covode, Dawes, Dixon, Driggs, Ferriss, Ferry, Fields, Finney, Gravely, Halsey, Hamilton, Hooper, Hopkins, Hotchkiss, Asahel W. Hubbard, Chester D. Hubbard, Hunter, Ingersoll, Jenckes, Judd, Julian, Kelley, Kelsey, Ketcham, Kitchen, Koontz, William Lawrence, Lincoln, Loan, Logan, Loughridge, McClurg, Mercur, Moore, Morrell, Myers, Newcomb, O'Neill, Paine, Perham, Pike, Plants, Polsley, Price, Raum, Robertson, Schenck, Scofield, Selye, Shanks, Smith, Aaron F. Stevens, Trowbridge, Twichell, Upson, Van Aernam, Burt Van Horn, Robert T. Van Horn, Ward, Cadwalader C. Washburn, Henry D. Washburn, William B. Washburn, Welker, Thomas Williams, William Williams, James F. Wilson, John T. Wilson, Woodbridge—90.

NAYS—Messrs. *Adams, Archer, Barnes, Boyer, Brooks, Burr, Eldridge, Getz, Glossbrenner, Haight, Holman, Kerr, Niblack, Nicholson, Noell, Pruyn, Robinson, Stone, Van Auken, Van Trump*—20.

July 19—The Senate concurred without division, adding an amendment about juries for 1867, which was also agreed to without division, and likewise concurred in by the House.

The bill was presented to the President the day of the adjournment, and was not acted upon by him before adjournment.

1867, December 5—The same bill again passed the Senate—yeas 32, nays 8, as follow:

YEAS—Messrs. Anthony, Cameron, Cattell, Chandler, Conkling, Corbett, Cragin, Drake, Edmunds, Ferry, Fessenden, Fowler, Harlan, Henderson, Howard, Howe, Morgan, Morrill of Maine, Morrill of Vermont, Morton, Ramsey, Ross, Sherman, Stewart, Sumner, Thayer, Tipton, Trumbull, Wade, Willey, Williams, Wilson—32.

NAYS—Messrs. *Buckalew, Davis, Dixon, Doolittle, Hendricks, Johnson, Norton, Patterson* of Tennessee—8.

December 9—The House passed it—yeas 104, nays 39, as follow:

YEAS—Messrs. Allison, Ames, Arnell, James M. Ashley, Bailey, Baker, Baldwin, Banks, Beaman, Benjamin, Benton, Bingham, Blaine, Boutwell, Bromwell, Broomall, Buckland, Butler, Churchill, Reader W. Clarke, Cobb, Coburn, Cook, Cullom, Dawes, Dixon, Dodge, Donnelly, Driggs, Eckley, Eggleston, Ela, Eliot, Farnsworth, Ferriss, Ferry, Fields, Garfield, Halsey, Hamilton, Harding, Hawkins, Hooper, Hopkins, Hubbard, Hulburd, Hunter, Ingersoll, Jenckes, Judd, Julian, Kelley, Kelsey, Ketcham, Koontz, Laflin, William Lawrence, Lincoln, Logan, Loughridge, Lynch, Maynard, McClurg, Mercur, Moorhead, Mullins, Myers, Newcomb, Nunn, O'Neill, Orth, Paine, Perham, Peters, Pike, Plants, Poland, Polsley, Price, Robertson, Sawyer, Schenck, Shanks, Smith, Starkweather, Aaron F. Stevens, Thaddeus Stevens, *Stewart*, Stokes, Thomas Trimble, Trowbridge, Upson, Van Aernam, Robert T. Van Horn, Cadwalader C. Washburn, Henry D. Washburn, William B. Washburn, Welker, Thomas Williams, William Williams, James F. Wilson, John T. Wilson, Windom—104.

NAYS—Messrs. *Adams, Archer, Axtell, Barnes, Beck,*

Boyer, Brooks, Burr, Chanler, Eldridge, Getz, Glossbrenner, Golladay, Grover, Haight, Holman, Richard D. Hubbard, Humphrey, Johnson, Jones, Kerr, Knott, Mallory, Marshall, Morgan, Mungen, Niblack, Nicholson, Phelps, Pruyn, Randall, Robinson, Ross, Sitgreaves, Taber, Van Auken, Van Trump, Wood, Woodward*—39.

The ten days within which the President was required to act having expired during the Christmas adjournment, the President held that the bill fell, and he neither returned it with his objections, nor proclaimed it a law by reason of non-action. The *law* of the case is a disputed point, and led to a message from him January 23, 1868, in reply to a resolution of the Senate of January 8.

## The Eight-Hour Bill.

1868, January 6—The House passed this bill, without a division:

*Be it enacted, &c.*, That eight hours shall constitute a day's work for all laborers, workmen, and mechanics now employed, or who may be hereafter employed, by or on behalf of the government of the United States; and that all acts and parts of acts inconsistent with this act be, and the same are hereby, repealed.

June 24—The Senate considered it, and Mr. Sherman moved to add a proviso:

"Unless otherwise provided by law, the rate of wages paid by the United States shall be the current rate for the same labor, for the same time, at the place of employment;"

Which was disagreed to—yeas 16, nays 21, as follow:

YEAS—Messrs. Cattell, Corbett, *Davis*, Edmunds, Ferry, Fessenden, Howard, Morgan, Morrill of Maine, Morrill of Vermont, Patterson of New Hampshire, Ross, Sherman, Sumner, Van Winkle, Williams—16.

NAYS—Messrs. *Buckalew,* Cole, Conkling, Conness, *Cragin, Dixon, Doolittle,* Harlan, *Hendricks, Johnson,* McDonald, *McCreery,* Morton, Nye, *Patterson* of Tennessee, Pomeroy, Ramsey, Stewart, Tipton, Wade, Wilson—21.

The bill then passed—yeas 26, nays 11, as follow:

YEAS—Messrs. *Buckalew*, Chandler, Cole, Conness, *Cragin, Dixon, Doolittle,* Fowler, Harlan, *Hendricks,* Howard, *McCreery,* McDonald, Morton, Nye, Patterson of New Hampshire, *Patterson* of Tennessee, Ramsey, Ross, Stewart, Thayer, Tipton, Wade, Williams, Wilson, Yates, —26.

NAYS—Messrs. Corbett, *Davis*, Edmunds, Ferry, Fessenden, Morgan, Morrill of Vermont, Pomeroy, Sherman, Sumner, Van Winkle—11.

# XXXIII.

# GENERAL POLITICAL MISCELLANY.

**Votes of State Legislatures on the Fourteenth Amendment.**

In Political Manual for 1867, p. 68, and in the combined Manual, p. 194, is given the action of the States up to April, 1867. The record then stood:

RATIFYING STATES.—Maine, New Hampshire, Vermont, Massachusetts, Rhode Island, Connecticut, New York, New Jersey, Pennsylvania, West Virginia, Ohio, Tennessee, Indiana, Illinois, Michigan, Missouri, Minnesota, Kansas, Wisconsin, Oregon, Nevada—21.

REJECTING STATES—Delaware, Maryland, and Kentucky—3. Besides the ten insurrectionary States of Virginia, North Carolina, South Carolina, Georgia, Florida, Alabama,* Mississippi,

* President Johnson's telegram to ex-Provisional Governor Parsons, of Alabama, on the ratification of the Fourteenth Amendment:

EX-GOVERNOR PARSONS'S TELEGRAM.

MONTGOMERY, ALABAMA,
*January 17, 1867.*

Legislature in session. Efforts making to reconsider vote on constitutional amendment. Re-

Louisiana, Texas, Arkansas, as reorganized under the Presidential plan—13 in all.

Not Acted—Iowa, California, Nebraska—3.

### Subsequent Action of State Legislatures.

Since that date, Iowa and Nebraska ratified the amendment and California rejected it, thus increasing the ratifying States to 23, and the rejecting to 4, excluding the insurrectionary States, or 14 with them.

The Legislatures of Ohio and New Jersey of 1868 passed resolutions for the withdrawal of their previous ratification.

In Ohio the vote on withdrawing, January 13, 1868, was as follow:

In Senate—yeas 19, nays 17, as follow:

Yeas—Messrs. *Berry, Campbell, Carter, Dickey, Dowdney, Emmitt, Evans, Godfrey, Golden, Hutcheson, Jamison, Kenney, Lawrence, Linn, May, Rex, Scribner, Stambaugh, Winner*—19.

Nays—Messrs. Biggs, Brooks, Burrows, Conant, Corey, Everett, Griswold, Hall, Jones, Keifer, Kessler, Kraner, Potts, Simmons, Torrence, Woodworth, Yeoman—17.

In House—yeas 56, nays 46, as follow:

Yeas—Messrs. *Acker, Baker, Ball, Belville, Bœhmer, Branch, Buell, Callen, Cockerill, Cusac, Denman, Dilworth, Dungan, Fielding, Finley, Fitch, Gaston, Gerhart, Gordon, Headley, Henricks, Hill of Defiance, Hord, Hughes of Butler, Hughes of Highland, Jewett, Jones, Kemp, Kennon, Larwill, Lawson, Leete, Mann, McMarrell, Moffett, Neal, Newman, Nichol, Parks, Parr, Pennisten, Read, Richardson, Robinson, Ross, Rutter, Shaw, Stickney, Swaim, Swetland, Thompson of Stark, Thornhill, Walling, Wilson, Worth,* Mr. Speaker *Follett*—56.

Nays—Messrs. Anderson, Betts, Borden, Bronson, Brooke, Canfield, Cannon, Carpenter, Coleman, Dennis, Dickson, Dunn, Eames, Gallup, Hare, Hill of Erie, Hill of Fulton, Howard, Johnson, Kain, Kennett, Kerr of Fayette, Kerr of Jefferson, Lawrence, Lee, Lewton, McMorran, Moore, Parker, Pond, Ritezell, Rough, Rukenbrod, Saylor, Scott of Hamilton, Scott of Warren, Sherwin, Sinclair, Sisler, Skaats, Thompson of Columbiana, Ullery, Warnking, Warren, Welsh, Wolf—46.

In New Jersey, the resolution of withdrawal

port from Washington says it is probable an enabling act will pass. We do not know what to believe. I find nothing here.

Lewis E. Parsons.<br>
Exchange Hotel.

His Excellency Andrew Johnson, *President.*

### REPLY OF THE PRESIDENT.

United States Military Telegraph,
Executive Office,

Washington, D. C., *January* 17, 1867.

What possible good can be obtained by reconsidering the constitutional amendment? I know of none in the present posture of affairs; and I do not believe the people of the whole country will sustain any set of individuals in attempts to change the whole character of our Government by enabling acts or otherwise. I believe, on the contrary, that they will eventually uphold all who have the patriotism and courage to stand by the Constitution, and who place their confidence in the people. There should be no faltering on the part of those who are honest in their determination to sustain the several co-ordinate departments of the Government, in accordance with its original design.

Andrew Johnson

Hon. Lewis E. Parsons,
Montgomery, Alabama.

passed the Senate February 19, 1868, and the House February 20, but was vetoed by the Governor.

The resolution was repassed over the Governor's veto, in the Senate, March 5—yeas 11, nays 9, as follow:

Yeas—Messrs. *Anderson, Bowne, Dater, Edsall, Gaskill, Hopper, Little,* (President,) *Rice, Robins, Wildrick, Winfield*—11.

Nays—Messrs. Bettle, Blackman, Clark, Cobb, Hays, Horner, Plummer, Richey, Warwick—9.

The vote on passing in the House, March 25, was yeas 45, nays 13, as follow:

Yeas—Messrs. *Albertson, Allen, J. L. Baldwin, Bergen, Brown, Christie, H. C. Clark, H. F. Clark, Coghlan, Collins, Corlies, Corson, Cox, Duryer, Evans,* (Speaker,) *Fulmer, Givens, Hedden, Hendrickson, Henry, Hering, Hood, Hough, Huff, Hunt, Jones, Lanning, Lippincott, Magonagle, Maxwell, Molony, Pearce, Pickel, Price, Probasco, Rosenbaum, Sharp, Smith, Strong, Taylor, Van Vorst, Vliet, Westcott, Whelan, Wills*—45. (One Democrat absent.)

Nays—Messrs. Atwater, J. R. Baldwin, Cowperthwaite, Gage, Keim, Kennedy, Lord, Mackin, Nixon, Peck, Reeves, Speer, Van Voorhies—13. (One Republican absent.)

### Of the Insurrectionary States,

Arkansas ratified the amendment, April 6, Senate, yeas 23, nays 0; and, April 3, House, yeas 56, nays 0.

Florida ratified the amendment, June 9, in Senate, yeas 10, nays 3; and in House of Representatives, yeas 25, nays 14.

North Carolina ratified it, July 1, in the Senate 36 to 2, in the House 72 to 23.

With the ratification by the Legislatures of the remaining States whose restoration to representation is dependent upon that condition, as set forth in the act of June 25, 1868, the requisite three-fourths of the thirty-seven States will be secured, even conceding the right of Ohio and New Jersey to withdraw.

## Votes on Constitutional Amendments in the States.

### IN MICHIGAN.

The vote in April 1868, on the new constitution, as officially declared by the State board of canvassers, was as follow:

| | |
|---|---:|
| Vote for the Constitution | 71,733 |
| Against the Constitution | 110,582 |
| Majority against the Constitution | 38,849 |
| For prohibition | 72,462 |
| Against prohibition | 86,143 |
| Majority against prohibition | 13,681 |
| For annual sessions | 24,482 |
| For biennial sessions | 100,314 |
| Majority for biennial sessions | 75,832 |

The vote on the constitution is larger by about 18,000 than the vote on Governor in 1866.

| | |
|---|---:|
| Total vote on constitution | 182,315 |
| "  "  prohibition | 158,605 |
| "  "  sessions | 124,796 |

### IN OHIO.

In October, 1867, the vote was taken on the proposed constitutional amendment respecting suffrage, for which see Political Manual for 1867, page 131, or the combined Manual, page 257. The result was:

Against the amendment................................... 255,340
For the amendment......................................... 216,987

Total vote....................................................... 472,327
Majority against on vote cast........................... 38,353
Not voting on amendment................................ 12,276

Constitutional majority against...................... 50,629

### IN KANSAS.

In November, 1867, the vote was taken on three proposed amendments respecting voters: *First.* To strike out the word "white." *Second.* To strike out the word "male." *Third.* To disfranchise rebels. The votes were as follows:

On striking out "white," the yeas were 10,483, nays 19,421. Majority against, 8,938.

On striking out "male," the yeas were 9,070, nays 19,857. Majority against, 10,787.

On disfranchising rebels, the yeas were 15,672, nays 12,990. Majority for, 2,682.

### IN MINNESOTA.

In November, 1867, on a vote to amend the constitution so as to extend suffrage without regard to color, the yeas were 27,461, the nays 28,759.

### IN ILLINOIS.

In November, 1868, a vote is to be taken for or against calling a convention to form a new constitution.

## FINANCIAL LEGISLATION.

### Act Authorizing the 6's of 1881.

July 17. 1861—An act to authorize a national loan, and for other purposes.

SEC. 1. *Be it enacted, &c.,* That the Secretary of the Treasury be, and he is hereby, authorized to borrow on the credit of the United States, within twelve months from the passage of this act, a sum not exceeding $250,000,000, or so much thereof as he may deem necessary for the public service, for which he is authorized to issue coupon bonds, or registered bonds, or treasury notes, in such proportions of each as he may deem advisable; the bonds to bear interest not exceeding 7 per cent. per annum, payable semi-annually, irredeemable for twenty years, and after that period redeemable at the pleasure of the United States; and the treasury notes to be of any denomination fixed by the Secretary of the Treasury, not less than $50, and to be payable three years after date, with interest at the rate of seven and three-tenths per cent. per annum, payable semi-annually.

### Act Authorizing the 5.20's.

February 25, 1862—An act to authorize the issue of United States notes, and for the redemption or funding thereof, and for funding the floating debt of the United States.

\* \* \* \* \* \* \*

SEC. 2. That to enable the Secretary of the Treasury to fund the treasury notes and floating debt of the United States, he is hereby authorized to issue, on the credit of the United States, coupon bonds, or registered bonds, to an amount not exceeding $500,000,000, redeemable at the pleasure of the United States after five years,

and payable twenty years from date, and bearing interest at the rate of 6 per cent. per annum, payable semi-annually. And the bonds herein authorized shall be of such denominations, not less than $50, as may be determined upon by the Secretary of the Treasury. And the Secretary of the Treasury may dispose of such bonds at any time, at the market value thereof, for the coin of the United States, or for any of the treasury notes that have been or may hereafter be issued under any former act of Congress, or for United States notes that may be issued under the provisions of this act; and all stocks, bonds, and other securities of the United States held by individuals, corporations, or associations, within the United States, shall be exempt from taxation by or under State authority.

### Act Creating a Sinking Fund, &c.

SEC. 5. That all duties on imported goods shall be paid in coin, or in notes payable on demand heretofore authorized to be issued and by law receivable in payment of public dues, and the coin so paid shall be set apart as a special fund, and shall be applied as follows:

*First.* To the payment in coin of the interest on the bonds and notes of the United States.

*Second.* To the purchase or payment of one per centum of the entire debt of the United States, to be made within each fiscal year after the 1st day of July, 1862, which is to be set apart as a sinking-fund, and the interest of which shall in like manner be applied to the purchase or payment of the public debt as the Secretary of the Treasury shall from time to time direct

*Third.* The residue thereof to be paid into the Treasury of the United States.

### Act Authorizing the 10.40's.

March 3, 1864—An act supplementary to an act entitled "An act to provide ways and means for the support of the Government," approved March 3, 1863.

SEC. 1. *Be it enacted, &c.* That in lieu of so much of the loan authorized by the act of March 3, 1863, to which this is supplementary, the Secretary of the Treasury is authorized to borrow, from time to time, on the credit of the United States, not exceeding $200,000,000 during the current fiscal year, and to prepare and issue therefor coupon or registered bonds of the United States, bearing date March 1, 1864, or any subsequent period, redeemable at the pleasure of the government after any period not less than five years, and payable at any period not more than forty years from date, in coin, and of such denominations as may be found expedient, not less than $50, bearing interest not exceeding six per centum a year, payable on bonds not over $100 annually, and on all other bonds semi-annually, in coin; and he may dispose of such bonds at any time, on such terms as he may deem most advisable, for lawful money of the United States, or, at his discretion, for treasury notes, certificates of indebtedness, or certificates of deposit, issued under any act of Congress; and all bonds issued under this act shall be exempt from taxation by or under State or municipal authority. And the Secretary of the Treasury shall pay the necessary expenses of the preparation, issue, and disposal of such bonds out of any money in the treasury not otherwise appropriated, but the amount so paid shall not exceed one-half of one per centum of the amount of the bonds so issued and disposed of. ————

## Act Authorizing the Consolidated Loan of 1865.

March 3, 1865—An act to provide ways and means to support the government.

SEC. 1. *Be it enacted, &c.*, That the Secretary of the Treasury be, and he is hereby, authorized to borrow, from time to time, on the credit of the United States, in addition to the amounts heretofore authorized, any sums not exceeding in the aggregate $600,000,000, and to issue therefor bonds or treasury notes of the United States, in such form as he may prescribe; and so much thereof as may be issued in bonds shall be of denominations not less than $50, and may be made payable at any period not more than forty years from date of issue, or may be made redeemable, at the pleasure of the government, at or after any period not less than five years nor more than forty years from date, or may be made redeemable and payable as aforesaid, as may be expressed upon their face; and so much thereof as may be issued in treasury notes may be made convertible into any bonds authorized by this act, and may be of such denominations —not less than $50—and bear such dates and be made redeemable or payable at such periods as in the opinion of the Secretary of the Treasury may be deemed expedient. And the interest on such bonds shall be payable semi-annually; and on treasury notes authorized by this act the interest may be made payable semi-annually, or annually, or at maturity thereof; and the principal or interest, or both, may be made payable in coin or in other lawful money: *Provided*, That the rate of interest on any such bonds or treasury notes, when payable in coin, shall not exceed six per cent. per annum; and when not payable in coin shall not exceed seven and three-tenths per cent. per annum; and the rate and character of interest shall be expressed on all such bonds or treasury notes.

## Act Creating Legal Tenders.

February 25, 1862—An act to authorize the issue of United States notes and for the redemption or funding thereof, and for funding the floating debt of the United States.

SEC. 1. * * * *And provided further*, That the amount of the two kinds of notes together shall at no time exceed the sum of $150,000,000, and such notes herein authorized shall be receivable in payment of all taxes, internal duties, excises, debts, and demands of every kind due to the United States, except duties on imports, and of all claims and demands against the United States of every kind whatsoever, except for interest upon bonds and notes, which shall be paid in coin, and shall also be lawful money and a legal tender in payment of all debts, public and private, within the United States, except duties on imports and interest as aforesaid.

## Act Limiting the Amount of "Greenbacks."

June 30, 1864.—An act to provide ways and means for the support of the government, and for other purposes.

SEC. 1. *Be it enacted, &c.*, That the Secretary of the Treasury be, and he is hereby, authorized to borrow, from time to time, on the credit of the United States, $400,000,000, and to issue therefor coupon or registered bonds of the United States, redeemable at the pleasure of the Government, after any period not less than five, nor more than thirty years, or, if deemed expedient, made payable at any period not more than forty years from date. And said bonds shall be of such denominations as the Secretary of the Treasury shall direct, not less than fifty dollars, and bear an annual interest not exceeding six per centum, payable semi-annually in coin. And the Secretary of the Treasury may dispose of such bonds, or any part thereof, and of any bonds commonly known as five-twenties remaining unsold, in the United States, or if he shall find it expedient, in Europe, at any time, on such terms as he may deem most advisable, for lawful money of the United States, or, at his discretion, for treasury notes, certificates of indebtedness, or certificates of deposit issued under any act of Congress. And all bonds, treasury notes, and other obligations of the United States, shall be exempt from taxation by or under State or municipal authority.

SEC. 2 That the Secretary of the Treasury may issue on the credit of the United States, and in lieu of an equal amount of bonds authorized by the preceding section, and as a part of said loan, not exceeding $200,000,000 in treasury notes, of any denomination not less than ten dollars, payable at any time not exceeding three years from date, or, if thought more expedient, redeemable at any time after three years from date, and bearing interest not exceeding the rate of seven and three tenths per centum, payable in lawful money at maturity, or, at the discretion of the Secretary, semi-annually. And the said treasury notes may be disposed of by the Secretary of the Treasury on the best terms that can be obtained, for lawful money; and such of them as shall be made payable, principal and interest, at maturity, shall be a legal tender to the same extent as United States notes for their face value, excluding interest, and may be paid to any creditor of the United States at their face value, excluding interest, or to any creditor willing to receive them at par, including interest; and any treasury notes issued under the authority of this act may be made convertible, at the discretion of the Secretary of the Treasury, into any bonds issued under the authority of this act. And the Secretary of the Treasury may redeem and cause to be cancelled and destroyed any treasury notes or United States notes heretofore issued under authority of previous acts of Congress, and substitute, in lieu thereof, an equal amount of treasury notes such as are authorized by this act, or of other United States notes: *Provided*, That the total amount of bonds and treasury notes authorized by the first and second sections of this act shall not exceed $400,000,000, in addition to the amounts heretofore issued; nor shall the total amount of United States notes, issued or to be issued, ever exceed $400,000,000, and such additional sum, not exceeding $50,000,000, as may be temporarily required for the redemption of temporary loan; nor shall any treasury note bearing interest, issued under this act, be a legal tender in payment or redemption of any notes issued by any bank, banking association, or banker, calculated or intended to circulate as money.

### Important Military Order in Texas.

AUSTIN, TEXAS, *June* 11, 1868.

[General Orders, No. 13.]

Trustworthy information received at these headquarters shows that in many counties in Texas organized bands of lawless men are committing murders, and otherwise violating the laws and disturbing the peace of the country: It is therefore ordered, that all civil officers use increased diligence to arrest parties so offending. For this purpose, military aid will be rendered on application to any post commander in this State. Information with regard to offenders is requested from all citizens. Such information may be sent direct to these headquarters, or to the most convenient military post. When civil officers fail to discharge their duty, evidence to that effect is requested, to the end that proper steps may be taken in the premises. Where prisoners cannot be safely kept by the civil authorities, they may be taken to the most convenient military post, the commander whereof will receive the same, and hold them subject to orders from these headquarters. Full report and list of witnesses will be promptly forwarded in each case, in accordance with General Orders No. 41, from these headquarters, of November 22, 1867.

By command of Bvt. Maj. Gen. J. J. Reynolds.
C. E. MORSE, 1*st Lieut. 26th Inf.,*
*A. D. C. and A. A. A. G.*

---

# XXXIV.

## NATIONAL PLATFORMS OF 1852, 1856, 1860 AND 1864.

### NATIONAL PLATFORMS OF 1852.

#### Democratic, at Baltimore, June.

*Resolved,* That the American Democracy place their trust in the intelligence, the patriotism, and the discriminating justice of the American people.

II. *Resolved,* That we regard this as a distinctive feature of our political creed, which we are proud to maintain before the world as the great moral element in a form of government springing from and upheld by the popular will; and we contrast it with the creed and practice of Federalism, under whatever name or form, which seeks to palsy the will of the constituent, and which conceives no imposture too monstrous for the popular credulity.

III. *Resolved, therefore,* That, entertaining these views, the Democratic party of this Union, through their delegates assembled in a general convention of the States, coming together in a spirit of concord, of devotion to the doctrines and faith of a free representative government, and appealing to their fellow-citizens for the rectitude of their intentions, renew and re-assert before the American people the declarations of principles avowed by them when, on former occasions, in general convention, they presented their candidates for the popular suffrage:

1. That the Federal Government is one of limited powers, derived solely from the Constitution, and the grants of power made therein ought to be strictly construed by all the departments and agents of the Government; and that it is inexpedient and dangerous to exercise doubtful constitutional powers.

2. That the Constitution does not confer upon the General Government the power to commence and carry on a general system of internal improvements.

3. That the Constitution does not confer authority upon the Federal Government, directly or indirectly, to assume the debts of the several States, contracted for local internal improvements or other State purposes; nor would such assumption be just and expedient.

4. That justice and sound policy forbid the Federal Government to foster one branch of industry to the detriment of any other, or to cherish the interests of one portion to the injury of another portion of our common country; that every citizen, and every section of the country, has a right to demand and insist upon an equality of rights and privileges, and to complete and ample protection of persons and property from domestic violence or foreign aggression.

5. That it is the duty of every branch of the Government to enforce and practice the most rigid economy in conducting our public affairs, and that no more revenue ought to be raised than is required to defray the necessary expenses of the Government, and for the gradual but certain extinction of the public debt.

6. That Congress has no power to charter a national bank; that we believe such an institution one of deadly hostility to the best interests of the country, dangerous to our republican institutions and the liberties of the people, and calculated to place the business of the country within the control of a concentrated money power, and above the laws and the will of the

people; and that the results of democratic legislation, in this and all other financial measures upon which issues have been made between the two political parties of the country, have demonstrated, to candid and practical men of all parties, their soundness, safety, and utility, in all business pursuits.

7. That the separation of the moneys of the Government from banking institutions is indispensable for the safety of the funds of the Government and the rights of the people.

8. That the liberal principles embodied by Jefferson in the Declaration of Independence, and sanctioned in the Constitution, which makes ours the land of liberty and the asylum of the oppressed of every nation, have ever been cardinal principles in the democratic faith ; and every attempt to abridge the present privilege of becoming citizens and the owners of soil among us, ought to be resisted with the same spirit which swept the alien and sedition laws from our statute-books.

9. That Congress has no power under the Constitution to interfere with or control the domestic institutions of the several States, and that such States are the sole and proper judges of everything appertaining to their own affairs, not prohibited by the Constitution; that all efforts of the abolitionists or others, made to induce Congress to interfere with questions of slavery, or to take incipient steps in relation thereto, are calculated to lead to the most alarming and dangerous consequences; and that all such efforts have an inevitable tendency to diminish the happiness of the people, and endanger the stability and permanency of the Union, and ought not to be countenanced by any friend of our political institutions.

IV. *Resolved*, That the foregoing proposition covers, and was intended to embrace, the whole subject of slavery agitation in Congress; and, therefore, the Democratic party of the Union, standing upon this national platform, will abide by and adhere to a faithful execution of the acts known as the compromise measures settled by the last Congress, " the act for reclaiming fugitives from service or labor" included ; which act, being designed to carry out an express provision of the Constitution, cannot, with fidelity thereto, be repealed or so changed as to destroy or impair its efficiency.

V. *Resolved*, That the Democratic party will resist all attempts at renewing, in Congress or out of it, the agitation of the slavery question, under whatever shape or color the attempt may be made.

VI. *Resolved*, That the proceeds of the public lands ought to be sacredly applied to the national objects specified in the Constitution ; and that we are opposed to any law for the distribution of such proceeds among the States, as alike inexpedient in policy and repugnant to the Constitution.

VII. *Resolved*, That we are decidedly opposed to taking from the President the qualified veto power, by which he is enabled, under restrictions and responsibilities amply sufficient to guard the public interest, to suspend the passage of a bill whose merits can not secure the approval of two-thirds of the Senate and House of Representa-

tives, until the judgment of the people can be obtained thereon, and which has saved the American people from the corrupt and tyrannical domination of the Bank of the United States, and from a corrupting system of general internal improvements.

VIII. *Resolved*, That the Democratic party will faithfully abide by and uphold the principles laid down in the Kentucky and Virginia resolutions of 1798* and in the report of Mr. Madison to the Virginia Legislature in 1799; that it adopts those principles as constituting one of the main foundations of its political creed, and is resolved to carry them out in their obvious meaning and import.

IX. *Resolved*, That the war with Mexico, upon all the principles of patriotism and the laws of nations, was a just and necessary war on our part, in which every American citizen should have shown himself on the side of his country, and neither morally nor physically, by word or deed, have given "aid and comfort to the enemy."

X. *Resolved*, That we rejoice at the restoration of friendly relations with our sister Republic of Mexico, and earnestly desire for her all the blessings and prosperity which we enjoy under republican institutions; and we congratulate the American people upon the results of that war, which have so manifestly justified the policy and conduct of the Democratic party, and insured to the United States " indemnity for the past, and security for the future."

XI. *Resolved*, That, in view of the condition of popular institutions in the Old World, a high and sacred duty is devolved, with increased responsibility, upon the Democratic party of this country, as the party of the *people*, to uphold and maintain the rights of every State, and thereby the Union of the States, and to sustain and advance among us constitutional liberty, by continuing to resist all monopolies and exclusive legislation for the benefit of the few at the expense of the many, and by a vigilant and constant adherence to those principles and compromises of the Constitution, which are broad enough and strong enough to embrace and uphold the Union as it was, the Union as it is, and the Union as it shall be, in the full expansion of the energies and capacity of this great and progressive people.

---

### Whig, at Baltimore, June.

The Whigs of the United States, in convention assembled, firmly adhering to the great conservative republican principles by which they are controlled and governed, and now, as ever, relying upon the intelligence of the American people, with an abiding confidence in their capacity for self-government and their continued devotion to the Constitution and the Union, do proclaim the following as the political sentiments and determinations for the establishment and maintenance of which their national organization as a party is effected:

I. The Government of the United States is of a limited character, and it is confined to the ex-

---

* For these resolutions, see pages 128–131 of the Manual for 1867, or pages 254–257 of the Combined Manual.

ercise of powers expressly granted by the Constitution, and such as may be necessary and proper for carrying the granted powers into full execution, and that all powers not thus granted or necessarily implied are expressly reserved to the States respectively and to the people.

II. The State Governments should be held secure in their reserved rights, and the General Government sustained in its constitutional powers, and the Union should be revered and watched over as "the palladium of our liberties."

III. That, while struggling freedom everywhere enlists the warmest sympathy of the Whig party, we still adhere to the doctrines of the Father of his Country, as announced in his Farewell Address, of keeping ourselves free from all entangling alliances with foreign countries, and of never quitting our own to stand upon foreign ground. That our mission as a republic is not to propagate our opinions, or impose on other countries our form of government by artifice or force, but to teach by example, and show by our success, moderation, and justice, the blessings of self-government and the advantages of free institutions.

IV. That where the people make and control the government, they should obey its constitution, laws, and treaties, as they would retain their self-respect, and the respect which they claim and will enforce from foreign powers.

V. Government should be conducted upon principles of the strictest economy, and revenue sufficient for the expenses thereof in time of peace ought to be mainly derived from a duty on imports, and not from direct taxes; and in levying such duties, sound policy requires a just discrimination and protection from fraud by specific duties, when practicable, whereby suitable encouragement may be assured to American industry, equally to all classes and to all portions of the country.

VI. The Constitution vests in Congress the power to open and repair harbors and remove obstructions from navigable rivers, and it is expedient that Congress should exercise that power whenever such improvements are necessary for the common defence or for the protection and facility of commerce with foreign nations or among the States, such improvements being, in every instance, national and general in their character.

VII. The Federal and State Governments are parts of one system, alike necessary for the common prosperity, peace, and security, and ought to be regarded alike with a cordial, habitual, and immovable attachment. Respect for the authority of each, and acquiescence in the constitutional measures of each, are duties required by the plainest considerations of National, of State, and of individual welfare.

VIII. The series of acts of the 31st Congress, commonly known as the compromise or adjustment, (the act for the recovery of fugitives from labor included,) are received and acquiesced in by the Whigs of the United States as a final settlement, in principle and substance, of the subjects to which they relate; and, so far as these acts are concerned, we will maintain them, and insist on their strict enforcement, until time and experience shall demonstrate the necessity of further legislation to guard against the evasion of the laws on the one hand, and the abuse of their powers on the other, not impairing their present efficiency to carry out the requirements of the Constitution; and we depre cate all further agitation of the questions thus settled, as dangerous to our peace, and will discountenance all efforts to continue or renew such agitation, whenever, wherever, or however made; and we will maintain this settlement as essential to the nationality of the Whig party and the integrity of the Union.

## NATIONAL PLATFORMS OF 1856.

### Republican, at Philadelphia, June.

This convention of delegates assembled in pursuance of a call addressed to the people of the United States, without regard to past political differences or divisions, who are opposed to the repeal of the Missouri compromise, to the policy of the present Administration, to the extension of slavery into free territory, in favor of admitting Kansas as a free State, of restoring the action of the Federal Government to the principles of Washington and Jefferson, and who purpose to unite in presenting candidates for the offices of President and Vice President, do resolve as follows:

1. That the maintenance of the principles promulgated in the Declaration of Independence and embodied in the Federal Constitution is essential to the preservation of our republican institutions, and that the Federal Constitution, the rights of the States, and the union of the States, shall be preserved; that, with our republican fathers, we hold it to be a self-evident truth, that all men are endowed with the inalienable rights to life, liberty, and the pursuit of happiness, and that the primary object and ulterior design of our Federal Government were to secure these rights to all persons within its exclusive jurisdiction; that, as our republican fathers, when they had abolished slavery in all our national territory, ordained that no person should be deprived of life, liberty, or property without due process of law, it becomes our duty to maintain this provision of the Constitution against all attempts to violate it for the purpose of establishing slavery in the United States by positive legislation prohibiting its existence or extension therein; that we deny the authority of Congress, of a Territorial Legislature, of any individual or association of individuals, to give legal existence to slavery in any Territory of the United States while the present Constitution shall be maintained.

2. That the Constitution confers upon Congress sovereign power over the Territories of the United States for their government, and that in the exercise of this power it is both the right and the duty of Congress to prohibit in the Territories those twin relics of barbarism, polygamy and slavery.

3. That, while the Constitution of the United States was ordained and established by the people "in order to form a more perfect union, establish justice, insure domestic tranquility, provide for the common defence, promote the general welfare, and secure the blessings of

liberty," and contains ample provisions for the protection of the life, liberty, and property of every citizen, the dearest constitutional rights of the people of Kansas have been fraudulently and violently taken from them; their territory has been invaded by an armed force; spurious and pretended legislative, judicial, and executive officers have been set over them, by whose usurped authority, sustained by the military power of the Government, tyrannical and unconstitutional laws have been enacted and enforced; the right of the people to keep and bear arms has been infringed; test-oaths of an extraordinary and entangling nature have been imposed as a condition of exercising the right of suffrage and holding office; the right of an accused person to a speedy and public trial by an impartial jury has been denied; the right of the people to be secure in their persons, houses, papers, and effects, against unreasonable searches and seizures, has been violated; they have been deprived of life, liberty, and property without due process of law; that the freedom of speech and of the press has been abridged; the right to choose their representatives has been made of no effect; murders, robberies, and arsons have been instigated and encouraged, and the offenders have been allowed to go unpunished; that all these things have been done with the knowledge, sanction, and procurement of the present Administration, and that for this high crime against the Constitution, the Union, and humanity, we arraign the Administration, the President, his advisers, agents, supporters, apologists, and accessories either *before* or *after* the fact, before the country and before the world; and that it is our fixed purpose to bring the actual perpetrators of these atrocious outrages and their accomplices to a sure and condign punishment hereafter.

4. That Kansas should be immediately admitted as a State of the Union, with her present free constitution, as at once the most effectual way of securing to her citizens the enjoyment of the rights and privileges to which they are entitled, and of ending the civil strife now raging in her territory.

5. That the highwayman's plea that "might makes right," embodied in the Ostend circular, was in every respect unworthy of American diplomacy, and would bring shame and dishonor upon any Government or people that gave it their sanction.

6. That a railroad to the Pacific ocean by the most central and practicable route is imperatively demanded by the interests of the whole country, and that the Federal Government ought to render immediate and efficient aid in its construction; and, as an auxiliary thereto, to the immediate construction of an emigrant route on the line of the railroad.

7. That appropriations by Congress for the improvement of rivers and harbors of a national character, required for the accommodation and security of our existing commerce, are authorized by the Constitution and justified by the obligation of Government to protect the lives and property of its citizens.

8. That we invite the affiliation and co-operation of freemen of all parties, however differing from us in other respects, in support of the principles herein declared; and, believing that the spirit of our institutions, as well as the Constitution of our country, guaranties liberty of conscience and equality of rights among citizens, we oppose all legislation impairing their security.

### Democratic, at Cincinnati, June.

The platform reiterates in detail the resolutions adopted in 1852, down to and including the VIIIth resolution, and added the following:

And whereas since the foregoing declaration was uniformly adopted by our predecessors in national conventions an adverse political and religious test has been secretly organized by a party claiming to be exclusively American, it is proper that the American Democracy should clearly define its relation thereto, and declare its determined opposition to all secret political societies, by whatever name they may be called

*Resolved*, That the foundation of this Union of States having been laid in, and its prosperity, expansion, and pre-eminent example in free government built upon, entire freedom in matters of religious concernment, and no respect of person in regard to rank or place of birth, no party can justly be deemed national, constitutional, or in accordance with American principles, which bases its exclusive organization upon religious opinions and accidental birth-place. And hence a political crusade in the nineteenth century, and in the United States of America, against Catholic and foreign-born, is neither justified by the past history or the future prospects of the country, nor in unison with the spirit of toleration and enlarged freedom which peculiarly distinguishes the American system of popular government.

And that we may more distinctly meet the issue on which a sectional party, subsisting exclusively on slavery agitation, now relies to test the fidelity of the people, North and South, to the Constitution and the Union:

1. *Resolved*, That claiming fellowship with, and desiring the co-operation of all who regard the preservation of the Union under the Constitution as the paramount issue, and repudiating all sectional parties and platforms concerning domestic slavery, which seek to embroil the States and incite to treason and armed resistance to law in the Territories, and whose avowed purpose, if consummated, must end in civil war and disunion, the American Democracy recognize and adopt the principles contained in the organic laws establishing the Territories of Kansas and Nebraska, as embodying the only sound and safe solution of the "slavery question" upon which the great national idea of the people of this whole country can repose in its determined conservatism of the Union—NON-INTERFERENCE BY CONGRESS WITH SLAVERY IN STATE AND TERRITORY, OR IN THE DISTRICT OF COLUMBIA.

2. That this was the basis of the compromises of 1850, confirmed by both the Democratic and Whig parties in national conventions, ratified by the people in the election of 1852, and rightly applied to the organization of Territories in 1854.

3. That by the uniform application of this democratic principle to the organization of Territories, and to the admission of new States, with

or without domestic slavery, as they may elect, the equal rights of all the States will be preserved intact, the original compacts of the Constitution maintained inviolate, and the perpetuity and expansion of this Union insured to its utmost capacity of embracing, in peace and harmony, every future American State that may be constituted or annexed with a republican form of government.

*Resolved,* That we recognize the right of the people of all the Territories, including Kansas and Nebraska, acting through the legally and fairly-expressed will of a majority of actual residents, and wherever the number of their inhabitants justifies it, to form a constitution, with or without domestic slavery, and be admitted into the Union upon terms of perfect equality with the other States.

*Resolved, finally,* That in the view of the condition of popular institutions in the Old World (and the dangerous tendencies of sectional agitation, combined with the attempt to enforce civil and religious disabilities against the rights of acquiring and enjoying citizenship in our own land,) a high and sacred duty is devolved with increased responsibility upon the Democratic party of this country, as the party of the Union, to uphold and maintain the rights of every State, and thereby the Union of the States; and to sustain and advance among us constitutional liberty, by continuing to resist all monopolies and exclusive legislation for the benefit of the few at the expense of the many, and by a vigilant and constant adherence to those principles and compromises of the Constitution, which are broad enough and strong enough to embrace and uphold the Union as it was, the Union as it is, and the Union as it shall be, in the full expansion of the energies and capacity of this great and progressive people.

1. *Resolved,* That there are questions connected with the foreign policy of this country, which are inferior to no domestic question whatever. The time has come for the people of the United States to declare themselves in favor of free seas and progressive free trade throughout the world, by solemn manifestations, to place their moral influence at the side of their successful example. [Adopted—yeas 230, nays 29.]

2. *Resolved,* That our geographical and political position with reference to the other States of this continent, no less than the interest of our commerce and the development of our growing power, requires that we should hold as sacred the principles involved in the Monroe doctrine; their bearing and import admit of no misconstruction; they should be applied with unbending rigidity. [Adopted—yeas 239, nays 21.]

3. *Resolved,* That the great highway which nature as well as the assent of the States most immediately interested in its maintenance has marked out for a free communication between the Atlantic and the Pacific oceans, constitutes one of the most important achievements realized by the spirit of modern times and the unconquerable energy of our people. That result should be secured by a timely and efficient exertion of the control which we have the right to claim over it, and no power on earth should be suffered to impede or clog its progress by any

interference with the relations it may suit our policy to establish between our Government and the governments of the States within whose dominions it lies. We can, under no circumstance, surrender our preponderance in the adjustment of all questions arising out of it. [Adopted—yeas 180, nays 56.]

4. *Resolved,* That, in view of so commanding an interest, the people of the United States cannot but sympathize with the efforts which are being made by the people of Central America to regenerate that portion of the continent which covers the passage across the interoceanic isthmus. [Adopted—yeas 221, nays 38.]

5. *Resolved,* That the Democratic party will expect of the next Administration that every proper effort be made to insure our ascendancy in the Gulf of Mexico, and to maintain a permanent protection to the great outlets through which are emptied into its waters the products raised out of the soil and the commodities created by the industry of the people of our western valleys and of the Union at large. [Adopted—yeas 229, nays 33.]

The following resolution, reported from the committee on resolutions, was laid on the table—yeas 154, nays 120:

*Resolved,* That the Democratic party recognizes the great importance, in a political and commercial point of view, of a safe and speedy communication by military and postal roads, through our own territory, between the Atlantic and Pacific coasts of this Union, and that it is the duty of the Federal Government to exercise promptly all its constitutional power for the attainment of that object. On tabling, the vote was:

YEAS—Maine 1, New Hampshire 4, Massachusetts 17, Rhode Island 4, Connecticut 6, New Jersey 7, Pennsylvania 27, Delaware 3, Virginia 15, North Carolina 10, South Carolina 8, Georgia 6, Alabama 9, Mississippi 7, Ohio 16, Kentucky 8, Tennessee 3, Florida 3—154.

NAYS—Maine 7, New Hampshire 1, Vermont 5, Massachusetts 12, Maryland 6, Georgia 4, Louisiana 6, Ohio 6, Kentucky 4, Tennessee 9, Indiana 13, Illinois 11, Missouri 9, Arkansas 4, Michigan 6, Texas 4, Iowa 4, Wisconsin 5, California 4—120.

The second day thereafter the rules were suspended—yeas 208, nays 88—and this resolution was adopted—yeas 205, nays 87:

*Resolved,* That the Democratic party recognizes the great importance, in a political and commercial point of view, of a safe and speedy communication through our own territory between the Atlantic and Pacific coasts of the Union, and that it is the duty of the Federal Government to exercise all its constitutional power to the attainment of that object, thereby binding the Union of these States in indissoluble bonds, and opening to the rich commerce of Asia an overland transit from the Pacific to the Mississippi river, and the great lakes of the North.

## NATIONAL PLATFORMS OF 1860.

### Republican, at Chicago, May.

*Resolved,* That we, the delegated representatives of the Republican electors of the United States, in Convention assembled, in discharge of the duty we owe to our constituents and our country, unite in the following declarations:

1. That the history of the nation, during the

last four years, has fully established the propriety and necessity of the organization and perpetuation of the Republican party, and that the causes which called it into existence are permanent in their nature, and now, more than ever before, demand its peaceful and constitutional triumph.

2. That the maintenance of the principles promulgated in the Declaration of the Independence and embodied in the Federal Constitution, "That all men are created equal; that they are endowed by their Creator with certain inalienable rights; that among these are life, liberty, and the pursuit of happiness; that to secure these rights, governments are instituted among men, deriving their just powers from the consent of the governed," is essential to the preservation of our republican institutions; and that the Federal Constitution, the rights of the States, and the Union of the States, must and shall be preserved.

3. That to the Union of the States this nation owes its unprecedented increase in population, its surprising development of material resources, its rapid augmentation of wealth, its happiness at home, and its honor abroad; and we hold in abhorrence all schemes for disunion, come from whatever source they may: and we congratulate the country that no Republican member of Congress has uttered or countenanced the threats of disunion so often made by Democratic members, without rebuke and with applause from their political associates; and we denounce those threats of disunion, in case of a popular overthrow of their ascendency, as denying the vital principles of a free government, and as an avowal of contemplated treason, which it is the imperative duty of an indignant people sternly to rebuke and forever silence.

4. That the maintenance inviolate of the rights of the States, and especially the right of each State to order and control its own domestic institutions according to its own judgment exclusively is essential to that balance of power on which the perfection and endurance of our political fabric depends; and we denounce the lawless invasion by armed force of the soil of any State or Territory, no matter under what pretext, as among the gravest of crimes.

5. That the present Democratic Administration has far exceeded our worst apprehensions, in its measureless subserviency to the exactions of a sectional interest, as especially evinced in its desperate exertions to force the infamous Lecompton constitution upon the protesting people of Kansas; in construing the personal relation between master and servant to involve an unqualified property in persons; in its attempted enforcement everywhere, on land and sea, through the intervention of Congress and of the Federal courts, of the extreme pretensions of a purely local interest; and in its general and un. varying abuse of the power intrusted to it by a confiding people.

6. That the people justly view with alarm the reckless extravagance which pervades every department of the Federal Government; that a return to rigid economy and accountability is indispensable to arrest the systematic plunder of the public treasury by favored partisans,

while the recent startling developments of frauds and corruptions at the Federal metropolis show that an entire change of administration is imperatively demanded.

7. That the new dogma, that the Constitution, of its own force, carries slavery into any or all of the Territories of the United States, is a dangerous political heresy, at variance with the explicit provisions of that instrument itself, with contemporaneous exposition, and with legislative and judicial precedent; is revolutionary in its tendency, and subversive of the peace and harmony of the country.

8. That the normal condition of all the territory of the United States is that of freedom; that as our republican fathers, when they had abolished slavery in all our national territory, ordained that "no person should be deprived of life, liberty, or property, without due process of law," it becomes our duty, by legislation, whenever such legislation is necessary, to maintain this provision of the Constitution against all attempts to violate it; and we deny the authority of Congress, of a territorial legislature, or of any individuals, to give legal existence to slavery in any Territory of the United States.

9. That we brand the recent re-opening of the African slave-trade, under the cover of our national flag, aided by perversions of judicial power, as a crime against humanity and a burning shame to our country and age; and we call upon Congress to take prompt and efficient measures for the total and final suppression of that execrable traffic.

10. That in the recent vetoes, by their Federal governors, of the acts of the legislatures of Kansas and Nebraska, prohibiting slavery in those Territories, we find a practical illustration of the boasted democratic principle of nonintervention and popular sovereignty, embodied in the Kansas-Nebraska bill, and a demonstration of the deception and fraud involved therein.

11. That Kansas should of right be immediately admitted as a State under the constitution recently formed and adopted by her people and accepted by the House of Representatives.

12. That, while providing revenue for the support of the General Government by duties upon imports, sound policy requires such an adjustment of these imposts as to encourage the development of the industrial interests of the whole country; and we commend that policy of national exchanges which secures to the workingmen liberal wages, to agriculture remunerative prices, to mechanics and manufacturers an adequate reward for their skill, labor, and enterprise, and to the nation commercial prosperity and independence.

13. That we protest against any sale or alienation to others of the public lands held by actual settlers, and against any view of the free homestead policy which regards the settlers as paupers or suppliants for public bounty; and we demand the passage by Congress of the complete and satisfactory homestead measure which has already passed the House.

14. That the Republican party is opposed to any change in our naturalization laws, or any State legislation by which the rights of citizen-

ship hitherto accorded to immigrants from foreign lands shall be abridged or impaired ; and in favor of giving a full and efficient protection to the rights of all classes of citizens, whether native or naturalized, both at home and abroad.

15. That appropriations by Congress for river and harbor improvements of a national character, required for the accommodation and security of an existing commerce, are authorized by the Constitution and justified by the obligation of Government to protect the lives and property of its citizens.

16. That a railroad to the Pacific ocean is imperatively demanded by the interests of the whole country ; that the Federal Government ought to render immediate and efficient aid in its construction ; and that, as preliminary thereto, a daily overland mail should be promptly established.

17. Finally, having thus set forth our distinctive principles and views, we invite the co-operation of all citizens, however differing on other questions, who substantially agree with us in their affirmance and support.

### Democratic (Douglas) Platform, adopted at Charleston and Baltimore, June.

1. *Resolved,* That we, the Democracy of the Union, in convention assembled, hereby declare our affirmance of the resolutions unanimously adopted and declared as a platform of principles by the Democratic Convention in Cincinnati, in the year 1856, believing that Democratic principles are unchangeable in their nature, when applied to the same subject-matters; and we recommend, as the only further resolutions, the following :

2. *Resolved,* That it is the duty of the United States to afford ample and complete protection to all its citizens, whether at home or abroad, and whether native or foreign.

3. *Resolved,* That one of the necessities of the age, in a military, commercial, and postal point of view, is speedy communication between the Atlantic and Pacific States ; and the Democratic party pledge such constitutional Government aid as will insure the construction of a railroad to the Pacific coast at the earliest practicable period.

4. *Resolved,* That the Democratic party are in favor of the acquisition of the Island of Cuba, on such terms as shall be honorable to ourselves and just to Spain.

5. *Resolved,* That the enactments of State legislatures to defeat the faithful execution of the fugitive-slave law are hostile in character, subversive of the Constitution, and revolutionary in their effect.

6. *Resolved,* That it is in accordance with the true interpretation of the Cincinnati platform that, during the existence of the territorial governments, the measure of restriction, whatever it may be, imposed by the Federal Constitution on the power of the territorial legislature over the subject of the domestic relations, as the same has been, or shall hereafter be, finally determined by the Supreme Court of the United States, should be respected by all good citizens, and enforced with promptness and fidelity by every branch of the General Government.

### Democratic (Breckinridge) Platform, adopted at Charleston and Baltimore, June.

*Resolved,* That the platform adopted by the Democratic party at Cincinnati be affirmed, with the following explanatory resolutions :

1. That the government of a territory organized by an act of Congress is provisional and temporary, and during its existence all citizens of the United States have an equal right to settle with their property in the territory, without their rights, either of person or property, being destroyed or impaired by congressional or territorial legislation.

2. That it is the duty of the Federal Government, in all its departments, to protect, when necessary, the rights of persons and property in the territories, and wherever else its constitutional authority extends.

3. That when the settlers in a territory, having an adequate population, form a State constitution, the right of sovereignty commences, and, being consummated by admission into the Union, they stand on an equal footing with the people of other States ; and the State thus organized ought to be admitted into the Federal Union, whether its constitution prohibits or recognizes the institution of slavery.

4. That the Democratic party are in favor of the acquisition of the Island of Cuba, on such terms as shall be honorable to ourselves and just to Spain, at the earliest practicable moment.

5. That the enactments of State legislatures to defeat the faithful execution of the fugitive-slave law are hostile in character, subversive of the Constitution, and revolutionary in their effect.

6. That the Democracy of the United States recognize it as the imperative duty of this Government to protect the naturalized citizen in all his rights, whether at home or in foreign lands, to the same extent as its native-born citizens.

Whereas one of the greatest necessities of the age, in a political, commercial, postal, and military point of view, is a speedy communication between the Pacific and Atlantic coasts; therefore, be it

*Resolved,* That the National Democratic party do hereby pledge themselves to use every means in their power to secure the passage of some bill, to the extent of the constitutional authority of Congress, for the construction of a Pacific railroad from the Mississippi river to the Pacific ocean, at the earliest practicable moment.

### NATIONAL PLATFORMS OF 1864.

### Republican, at Baltimore, June.

*Resolved,* That it is the highest duty of every American citizen to maintain against all their enemies the integrity of the Union and the paramount authority of the Constitution and laws of the United States ; and that, laying aside all differences of political opinions, we pledge ourselves as Union men, animated by a common sentiment, and aiming at a common object, to do everything in our power to aid the Government, in quelling by force of arms the rebellion now raging against its authority, and in bringing to the punishment due to their crimes the rebels and traitors arrayed against it.

2. That we approve the determination of the Government of the United States not to compromise with rebels, or to offer them any terms of peace, except such as may be based upon an unconditional surrender of their hostility and a return to their just allegiance to the Constitution and laws of the United States; and that we call upon the Government to maintain this position and to prosecute the war with the utmost possible vigor to the complete suppression of the rebellion, in full reliance upon the self-sacrificing patriotism, the heroic valor, and the undying devotion of the American people to the country and its free institutions.

3. That as slavery was the cause, and now constitutes the strength of this rebellion, and as it must be always and everywhere hostile to the principles of republican government, justice and the national safety demand its utter and complete extirpation from the soil of the republic; and that while we uphold and maintain the acts and proclamations by which the Government, in its own defence, has aimed a death-blow at this gigantic evil, we are in favor, furthermore, of such an amendment to the Constitution, to be made by the people in conformity with its provisions, as shall terminate and forever prohibit the existence of slavery within the limits of the jurisdiction of the United States.

4. That the thanks of the American people are due to the soldiers and sailors of the army and navy, who have perilled their lives in defence of their country and in vindication of the honor of its flag; that the nation owes to them some permanent recognition of their patriotism and their valor, and ample and permanent provision for those of their survivors who have received disabling and honorable wounds in the service of the country; and that the memories of those who have fallen in its defence shall be held in grateful and everlasting remembrance.

5. That we approve and applaud the practical wisdom, the unselfish patriotism, and the unswerving fidelity to the Constitution and the principles of American liberty, with which Abraham Lincoln has discharged, under circumstances of unparalleled difficulty, the great duties and responsibilities of the presidential office; that we approve and endorse, as demanded by the emergency and essential to the preservation of the nation and as within the provisions of the Constitution, the measures and acts which he has adopted to defend the nation against its open and secret foes; that we approve especially the proclamation of emancipation and the employment as Union soldiers of men heretofore held in slavery; and that we have full confidence in his determination to carry these and all other constitutional measures essential to the salvation of the country into full and complete effect.

6. That we deem it essential to the general welfare that harmony should prevail in the national councils, and we regard as worthy of public confidence and official trust those only who cordially endorse the principles proclaimed in these resolutions, and which should characterize the administration of the Government.

7. That the Government owes to all men employed in its armies, without regard to distinction of color, the full protection of the laws of war; and that any violation of these laws, or of the usages of civilized nations in time of war by the rebels now in arms, should be made the subject of prompt and full redress.

8. That foreign immigration, which in the past has added so much to the wealth, development of resources and increase of power to the nation—the asylum of the oppressed of all nations—should be fostered and encouraged by a liberal and just policy.

9. That we are in favor of the speedy construction of the railroad to the Pacific coast.

10. That the national faith, pledged for the redemption of the public debt, must be kept inviolate, and that for this purpose we recommend economy and rigid responsibility in the public expenditures, and a vigorous and just system of taxation; and that it is the duty of every loyal State to sustain the credit and promote the use of the national currency.

11. That we approve the position taken by the Government that the people of the United States can never regard with indifference the attempt of any European power to overthrow by force, or to supplant by fraud, the institutions of any republican government on the western continent; and that they will view with extreme jealousy, as menacing to the peace and independence of their own country, the efforts of any such power to obtain new footholds for monarchical governments, sustained by foreign military force, in near proximity to the United States.

---

### Democratic, at Chicago, August.

*Resolved,* That in the future, as in the past, we will adhere with unswerving fidelity to the Union under the Constitution as the only solid foundation of our strength, security, and happiness as a people, and as a framework of government equally conducive to the welfare and prosperity of all the States, both northern and southern.

*Resolved,* That this convention does explicitly declare, as the sense of the American people, that after four years of failure to restore the Union by the experiment of war, during which, under the pretence of a military necessity or war-power higher than the Constitution, the Constitution itself has been disregarded in every part, and public liberty and private right alike trodden down, and the material prosperity of the country essentially impaired, justice, humanity, liberty, and the public welfare demand that immediate efforts be made for a cessation of hostilities, with a view to an ultimate convention of the States, or other peaceable means, to the end that, at the earliest practicable moment, peace may be restored on the basis of the Federal Union of the States.

*Resolved,* That the direct interference of the military authorities of the United States in the recent elections held in Kentucky, Maryland, Missouri, and Delaware was a shameful violation of the Constitution, and a repetition of such acts in the approaching election will be held as revolutionary, and resisted with all the means and power under our control.

*Resolved*, That the aim and object of the Democratic party is to preserve the Federal Union and the rights of the States unimpaired, and they hereby declare that they consider that the administrative usurpation of extraordinary and dangerous powers not granted by the Constitution—the subversion of the civil by military law in States not in insurrection; the arbitrary military arrest, imprisonment, trial, and sentence of American citizens in States where civil law exists in full force; the suppression of freedom of speech and of the press; the denial of the right of asylum; the open and avowed disregard of State rights; the employment of unusual test-oaths; and the interference with and denial of the right of the people to bear arms in their defence is calculated to prevent a restoration

of the Union and the perpetuation of a Government deriving its just powers from the consent of the governed.

*Resolved*, That the shameful disregard of the Administration to its duty in respect to our fellow-citizens who now are and long have been prisoners of war in a suffering condition deserves the severest reprobation on the score alike of public policy and common humanity.

*Resolved*, That the sympathy of the Democratic party is heartily and earnestly extended to the soldiery of our army and sailors of our navy, who are and have been in the field and on the sea under the flag of our country, and, in the event of its attaining power, they will receive all the care, protection, and regard that the brave soldiers and sailors of the republic so nobly earned.

---

# XXXV.

## NATIONAL PLATFORMS OF 1868,

### THE LETTERS OF ACCEPTANCE OF CANDIDATES, AND SUNDRY PROCEEDINGS OF THE CONVENTIONS.

### Republican, at Chicago, May.*

The National Republican party of the United States, assembled in National Convention in the city of Chicago, on the 21st day of May, 1866, make the following declaration of principles:

1. We congratulate the country on the assured success of the reconstruction policy of Congress, as evinced by the adoption, in the majority of the States lately in rebellion, of constitutions securing equal civil and political rights to all; and it is the duty of the Government to sustain those institutions and to prevent the people of such States from being remitted to a state of anarchy.

2. The guaranty by Congress of equal suffrage to all loyal men at the South was demanded by every consideration of public safety, of gratitude, and of justice, and must be maintained; while the question of suffrage in all the loyal States properly belongs to the people of those States.

\* Reported from the following committee on resolutions: *Alabama*—D. C. Humphreys. *Arkansas*—H. B. Morse. *Colorado*—G. M. Chilcott. *Connecticut*—J. M. Woodward. *Delaware*—C. S. Layton. *Florida*—R. G. Roder. *Georgia*—R. H. McCoy. *Illinois*—Herman Raster. *Indiana*—Richard W. Thompson. *Iowa*—G. M. Dodge. *Kansas*—B. F. Simpson. *Kentucky*—Charles Eginton. *Louisiana*—William R. Fish. *Maine*—Eugene Hall. *Maryland*— *Massachusetts*—F. W. Bird. *Michigan*—R. R. Beecher. *Minnesota*—R. M. McClelland. *Mississippi*—A. R. Howe. *Missouri*—Robert T. Van Horn. *Nebraska*—R. W. Furniss. *Nevada*—C. E. De Long. *New Hampshire*—J. F. Briggs. *New Jersey*—John Davidson. *New York*—Charles Andrews. *North Carolina*—L. G. Estes. *Ohio*—J. C. Lee. *Oregon*—H. R. Kincaid. *Pennsylvania*—Samuel E. Dimmick. *Rhode Island*—R. G. Hazard. *South Carolina*—B. O. Duncan. *Tennessee*—W. G. Elliott. *Texas*—George W. Paschal. *Vermont*—W. H. Johnson. *Virginia*—L. Bill. *West Virginia*—R. S. Brown. *Wisconsin*—H. Rublee.

The thirteenth and fourteenth were added to the committee's resolutions on motion of General Carl Schurz.

3. We denounce all forms of repudiation as a national crime; and the national honor requires the payment of the public indebtedness in the uttermost good faith to all creditors at home and abroad, not only according to the letter, but the spirit of the laws under which it was contracted.

4. It is due to the labor of the nation that taxation should be equalized, and reduced as rapidly as the national faith will permit.

5. The national debt, contracted as it has been for the preservation of the Union for all time to come, should be extended over a fair period for redemption; and it is the duty of Congress to reduce the rate of interest thereon, whenever it can be honestly done.

6. That the best policy to diminish our burden of debt is to so improve our credit that capitalists will seek to loan us money at lower rates of interest than we now pay, and must continue to pay so long as repudiation, partial or total, open or covert, is threatened or suspected.

7. The Government of the United States should be administered with the strictest economy; and the corruptions which have been so shamefully nursed and fostered by Andrew Johnson call loudly for radical reform.

8. We profoundly deplore the untimely and tragic death of Abraham Lincoln, and regret the accession to the Presidency of Andrew Johnson, who has acted treacherously to the people who elected him and the cause he was pledged to support; who has usurped high legislative and judicial functions; who has refused to execute the laws; who has used his high office to induce other officers to ignore and violate the laws; who has employed his executive powers to render insecure the property, the peace, liberty and life, of the citizen; who has abused the pardoning power; who has denounced the national

legislature as unconstitutional : who has persistently and corruptly resisted, by every means in his power, every proper attempt at the reconstruction of the States lately in rebellion ; who has perverted the public patronage into an engine of wholesale corruption ; and who has been justly impeached for high crimes and misdemeanors, and properly pronounced guilty thereof by the vote of thirty-five Senators.

9. The doctrine of Great Britain and other European powers, that because a man is once a subject he is always so, must be resisted at every hazard by the United States, as a relic of feudal times, not authorized by the laws of nations, and at war with our national honor and independence. Naturalized citizens are entitled to protection in all their rights of citizenship, as though they were native-born ; and no citizen of the United States, native or naturalized, must be liable to arrest and imprisonment by any foreign power for acts done or words spoken in this country ; and, if so arrested and imprisoned, it is the duty of the Government to interfere in his behalf.

10. Of all who were faithful in the trials of the late war, there were none entitled to more especial honor than the brave soldiers and seamen who endured the hardships of campaign and cruise, and imperilled their lives in the service of the country ; the bounties and pensions provided by the laws for these brave defenders of the nation are obligations never to be forgotten ; the widows and orphans of the gallant dead are the wards of the people—a sacred legacy bequeathed to the nation's protecting care.

11. Foreign immigration, which in the past has added so much to the wealth, development, and resources, and increase of power to this republic, the asylum of the oppressed of all nations, should be fostered and encouraged by a liberal and just policy.

12. This convention declares itself in sympathy with all oppressed peoples struggling for their rights.

13. That we highly commend the spirit of magnanimity and forbearance with which men who have served in the rebellion, but who now frankly and honestly coöperate with us in restoring the peace of the country and reconstructing the southern State governments upon the basis of impartial justice and equal rights, are received back into the communion of the loyal people ; and we favor the removal of the disqualifications and restrictions imposed upon the late rebels in the same measure as the spirit of disloyalty will die out, and as may be consistent with the safety of the loyal people.

14. That we recognize the great principles laid down in the immortal Declaration of Independence, as the true foundation of democratic government ; and we hail with gladness every effort toward making these principles a living reality on every inch of American soil.

## Soldiers and Sailors' National Convention, at Chicago, May.

1. *Resolved*, That the soldiers and sailors, steadfast now as ever to the Union and the flag, and fully recognizing the claims of General Ulysses S.

Grant to the confidence of the American people, and believing that its victories under his guidance in war will be illustrated by him in peace by such measures as shall secure the fruits of our exertions and the restoration of the Union upon a loyal basis, we declare it as our deliberate conviction that he is the choice of the soldiers and sailors of the Union for the office of President of the United States.

2. That in the maintenance of those principles which underlie our Government, and for which we fought during four years, we pledge our earnest and active support to the Republican party as the only political organization which, in our judgment, is true to the principles of loyalty and equality before the law.

3. That speaking for ourselves and the soldiers and sailors who imperilled their lives to preserve the Union, we believe that the impeachment of Andrew Johnson by the House of Representatives, for high crimes and misdemeanors in office, and his trial before the United States Senate, have presented unmistakable proofs of his guilt, and that whatever may be the judgment of the tribunal before which he is arraigned, the verdict of guilty has been rendered by the people, and we regard any Senator who has voted for acquittal as falling short of the proper discharge of his duty in this hour of the nation's trial, and as unworthy of the confidence of a brave and loyal people.

4. That the soldiers and sailors recognize no difference between native and adopted citizens, and they demand that the Government shall protect naturalized citizens abroad as well as those of native birth.

## LETTERS OF ACCEPTANCE OF THE REPUBLICAN NOMINEES.

### General Grant's Letter.

WASHINGTON, D. C., *May* 29, 1868.

General JOSEPH R. HAWLEY,
    *President Nat. Union Republican Convention :*

In formally accepting the nomination of the National Union Republican Convention of the 21st of May instant, it seems proper that some statement of views beyond the mere acceptance of the nomination should be expressed.

The proceedings of the convention were marked with wisdom, moderation, and patriotism, and I believe express the feelings of the great mass of those who sustained the country through its recent trials. I endorse their resolutions. If elected to the office of President of the United States, it will be my endeavor to administer all the laws in good faith, with economy, and with the view of giving peace, quiet, and protection everywhere. In times like the present it is impossible, or at least eminently improper, to lay down a policy to be adhered to, right or wrong, through an administration of four years. New political issues, not foreseen, are constantly arising ; the views of the public on old ones are constantly changing, and a purely administrative officer should always be left free to execute the will of the people. I always have respected that will and always shall.

Peace and universal prosperity, its sequence, with economy of administration, will lighten the burden of taxation, while it constantly reduces the national debt. Let us have peace.

With great respect, your obedient servant,
U. S. GRANT.

### Mr. Colfax's Letter.

WASHINGTON, *May 30, 1868.*

Hon. J. R. HAWLEY,
*President Nat. Union Republican Convention.*

DEAR SIR: The platform adopted by the patriotic convention over which you presided, and the resolutions which so happily supplement it, so entirely agree with my views as to a just national policy, that my thanks are due to the delegates, as much for this clear and auspicious declaration of principles as for the nomination with which I have been honored, and which I gratefully accept.

When a great rebellion, which imperilled the national existence, was at last overthrown, the duty of all others devolving on those intrusted with the responsibilities of legislation evidently was to require that the revolted States should be readmitted to participation in the Government against which they had warred only on such a basis as to increase and fortify, not to weaken or endanger, the strength of the nation.

Certainly no one ought to have claimed that they should be readmitted under such rules that their organization as States could ever again be used, as at the opening of the war, to defy the national authority, or to destroy the national unity. This principle has been the pole-star of those who have inflexibly insisted on the congressional policy your convention so cordially endorsed. Baffled by executive opposition, and by persistent refusals to accept any plan of reconstruction proffered by Congress, justice and public safety at last combined to teach us that only by an enlargement of suffrage in those States could the desired end be attained, and that it was even more safe to give the ballot to those who loved the Union than to those who had sought ineffectually to destroy it. The assured success of this legislation is being written on the adamant of history, and will be our triumphant vindication. More clearly, too, than ever before does the nation now recognize that the greatest glory of a republic is, that it throws the shield of its protection over the humblest and the weakest of its people, and vindicates the rights of the poor and the powerless as faithfully as those of the rich and the powerful.

I rejoice, too, in this convention, to find in your platform the frank and fearless avowal that the naturalized citizens must be protected abroad, "at every hazard, as though they were native-born." Our whole people are foreigners or descendants of foreigners. Our fathers established by arms their right to be called a nation. It remains for us to establish the right to welcome to our shores all who are willing by oaths of allegiance to become American citizens. Perpetual allegiance, as claimed abroad, is only another name for perpetual bondage, and would make all slaves to the soil where first they saw the light. Our national cemeteries prove how faithfully these oaths of fidelity to their adopted land have been sealed in the life blood of thousands upon thousands. Should we not then be faithless to the dead if we did not protect their living brethren in the enjoyment of that nationality, for which, side by side with the native-born, our soldiers of foreign birth laid down their lives.

It was fitting, too, that the representatives of a party which had proved so true to national duty in time of war should speak so clearly in time of peace for the maintenance untarnished of national honor, national credit, and good faith as regards its debt, the cost of our national existence.

I do not need to extend this reply by further comment on a platform which has elicited such hearty approval throughout the land. The debt of gratitude it acknowledges to the brave men who saved the Union from destruction—the frank approval of amnesty based on repentance and loyalty—the demand for the most thorough economy and honesty in the Government—the sympathy of the party of liberty with all throughout the world who long for the liberty we here enjoy—and the recognition of the sublime principles of the Declaration of Independence, are worthy of the organization on whose banners they are to be written in the coming contest.

Its past record cannot be blotted out or forgotten. If there had been no Republican party, slavery would to-day cast its baleful shadow over the republic. If there had been no Republican party, a free press and free speech would be as unknown from the Potomac to the Rio Grande as ten years ago. If the Republican party could have been stricken from existence when the banner of rebellion was unfurled, and when the response of "no coercion" was heard at the North, we would have had no nation to-day. But for the Republican party daring to risk the odium of tax and draft laws, our flag could not have been kept flying on the field till the long-looked-for victory came. Without a Republican party, the civil rights bill, the guarantee of equality under the law to the humble and the defenceless as well as to the strong, would not be to-day upon our national statute-book.

With such inspirations from the past, and following the example of the founders of the republic, who called the victorious general of the Revolution to preside over the land his triumphs had saved from its enemies, I cannot doubt that our labors will be crowned with success. And it will be a success that will bring restored hope, confidence, prosperity and progress, South as well as North, West as well as East, and above all, the blessings under Providence of national concord and peace.

Very truly, yours,    SCHUYLER COLFAX.

The nomination of General Grant was made on the first ballot. That of Mr. Colfax occurred on the fifth ballot, as follows:

|  | 1st. | 2d. | 3d. | 4th. | 5th. |
|---|---|---|---|---|---|
| Schuyler Colfax, of Indiana. | 115 | 145 | 165 | 186 | 541 |
| Benj. F. Wade, of Ohio........ | 147 | 170 | 178 | 206 | 38 |
| Reuben E. Fenton, of N. Y. | 126 | 144 | 139 | 144 | 69 |
| Henry Wilson, of Mass...... | 119 | 114 | 101 | 87 | - |
| Andrew G. Curtin, of Pa..... | 51 | 45 | 40 | - | - |
| Hannibal Hamlin, of Maine. | 28 | 30 | 25 | 25 | - |
| James Speed, of Kentucky. | 22 | - | - | - | - |
| James Harlan, of Iowa....... | 16 | - | - | - | - |
| John A. J. Creswell, of Md.... | 14 | - | - | - | - |
| William D. Kelley, of Pa...... | 4 | - | - | - | - |
| Samuel C. Pomeroy, of Kas.. | 6 | - | - | - | - |

**Democratic, at New York, July.***

The Democratic Party, in National Convention assembled, reposing its trust in the intelligence, patriotism, and discriminating justice of the people, standing upon the Constitution as the foundation and limitation of the powers of the Government, and the guarantee of the liberties of the citizen, and recognizing the questions of slavery and secession as having been settled, for all time to come, by the war or the voluntary action of the Southern States in constitutional conventions assembled, and never to be renewed or reagitated, do with the return of peace, demand:

*First*—Immediate restoration of all the States to their rights in the Union under the Constitution, and of civil government to the American people.

*Second*—Amnesty for all past political offences, and the regulation of the elective franchise in the States by their citizens.

*Third*—Payment of the public debt of the United States as rapidly as practicable; all moneys drawn from the people by taxation, except so much as is requisite for the necessities of the Government, economically administered, being honestly applied to such payment, and where the obligations of the Government do not expressly state upon their face, or the law under which they were issued does not provide that they shall be paid in coin, they ought, in right and in justice, to be paid in the lawful money of the United States.

*Fourth*—Equal taxation of every species of property according to its real value, including Government bonds and other public securities.

*Fifth*—One currency for the Government and the people, the laborer and the office-holder, the pensioner and the soldier, the producer and the bondholder.

*Sixth*—Economy in the administration of the Government; the reduction of the standing army and navy; the abolition of the Freedmen's Bureau and all political instrumentalities designed to secure negro supremacy; simplification of the system, and discontinuance of inquisitorial modes of assessing and collecting Internal Revenue, so that the burden of taxation may be equalized and lessened; the credit of the Government and the currency made good; the repeal of all enactments for enrolling the State militia into national forces in time of peace; and a tariff for revenue

* Unanimously reported from this Committee on Resolutions: *Alabama*—Charles C. Langdon. *Arkansas*—A. H. Garland. *California*—A. H. Rose. *Connecticut*—Tilton E. Doolittle. *Delaware*—James A. Bayard. *Florida*—Wilkerson Call. *Georgia*—Henry S. Fitch. *Illinois*—Wiliam J. Allen. *Indiana*—Joseph E. McDonald. *Iowa*—John H. O'Neil. *Kansas*—George W. Glick. *Kentucky*—William Preston. *Louisiana*—James B. Eustis. *Maine*—Richard D. Rice. *Maryland*—Stevenson Archer. *Massachusetts*—Edward Avery. *Michigan*—Charles E. Stuart. *Minnesota*—James J. Green. *Mississippi*—Ethelbert Barksdale. *Missouri*—Charles Mansur. *Nebraska*—Charles F. Porter. *Nevada*—J. A. St. Clair. *New Hampshire*—J. M. Campbell. *New Jersey*—Jacob R. Wortendyke. *New York*—Henry C. Murphy. *North Carolina*—Robert Strange. *Ohio*—William G. Gilmore. *Oregon*—R. D. Fitch. *Pennsylvania*—Franklin W. Hughes. *Rhode Island*—Thomas Steere. *South Carolina*—Wade Hampton. *Tennessee*—Edmund Cooper. *Texas*—George W. Smith. *Vermont*—Charles N. Davenport. *Virginia*—Thomas S. Bocock. *West Virginia*—John Davis. *Wisconsin*—James A. Mallory

upon foreign imports, and such equal taxation under the Internal Revenue laws as will afford incidental protection to domestic manufactures, and as will, without impairing the revenue, impose the least burden upon and best promote and encourage the great industrial interests of the country.

*Seventh*—Reform of abuses in the administration, the expulsion of corrupt men from office, the abrogation of useless offices, the restoration of rightful authority to, and the independence of, the executive and judicial departments of the Government, the subordination of the military to the civil power, to the end that the usurpations of Congress and the despotism of the sword may cease.

*Eighth*—Equal rights and protection for naturalized and native-born citizens at home and abroad, the assertion of American nationality which shall command the respect of foreign powers, and furnish an example and encouragement to people struggling for national integrity, constitutional liberty, and individual rights and the maintenance of the rights of naturalized citizens against the absolute doctrine of immutable allegiance, and the claims of foreign powers to punish them for alleged crime committed beyond their jurisdiction.

In demanding these measures and reforms, we arraign the Radical party for its disregard of right, and the unparalleled oppression and tyranny which have marked its career.

After the most solemn and unanimous pledge of both Houses of Congress to prosecute the war exclusively for the maintenance of the Government and the preservation of the Union under the Constitution, it has repeatedly violated that most sacred pledge under which alone was rallied that noble volunteer army which carried our flag to victory. Instead of restoring the Union it has, so far as in its power, dissolved it, and subjected ten States, in time of profound peace, to military despotism and negro supremacy. It has nullified there the right of trial by jury; it has abolished the *habeas corpus*, that most sacred writ of liberty; it has overthrown the freedom of speech and the press; it has substituted arbitrary seizures and arrests, and military trials and secret star-chamber inquisitions for the constitutional tribunals; it has disregarded in time of peace the right of the people to be free from searches and seizures; it has entered the post and telegraph offices, and even the private rooms of individuals, and seized their private papers and letters without any specific charge or notice of affidavit, as required by the organic law; it has converted the American Capitol into a bastile; it has established a system of spies and official espionage to which no constitutional monarchy of Europe would now dare to resort; it has abolished the right of appeal on important constitutional questions to the supreme judicial tribunals, and threatens to curtail or destroy its original jurisdiction, which is irrevocably vested by the Constitution, while the learned Chief Justice has been subjected to the most atrocious calumnies, merely because he would not prostitute his high office to the support of the false and partisan charges preferred against the President. Its corruption and extravagance have exceeded anything known in history, and, by its frauds and monopolies, it has nearly doubled the burden of the debt created by the war. It has stripped the President of his constitutional power of appointment, even of his own cabinet. Under its repeated assaults the pillars of the Government are rocking on their base, and should it succeed in November next and inaugurate its President, we will meet as a subjected and conquered people, amid the ruins of liberty and the scattered fragments of the Constitution.

And we do declare and resolve that ever since the people of the United States threw off all subjection to the British Crown the privilege and trust of suffrage have belonged to the several States, and have been granted, regulated, and controlled exclusively by the political power of each State respectively, and that any attempt by Congress, on any pretext whatever, to deprive any State of this right, or interfere with its exercise, is a flagrant usurpation of power which can find no warrant in the Constitution, and, if sanctioned by the people, will subvert our form of government, and can only end in a single centralized and consolidated government, in which the separate existence of the States will be entirely absorbed, and an unqualified despotism be established in place of a Federal union of co-equal States.

And that we regard the reconstruction acts (so called) of Congress, as such, as usurpations and unconstitutional, revolutionary, and void. That our soldiers and sailors, who carried the flag of our country to victory against a most gallant and determined foe, must ever be gratefully remembered, and all the guarantees given in their favor must be faithfully carried into execution.

That the public lands should be distributed as widely as possible among the people, and should be disposed of either under the pre-emption of homestead lands, or sold in reasonable quantities, and to none but actual occupants, at the minimum price established by the Government. When grants of the public lands may be allowed, necessary for the encouragement of important public improvements, the proceeds of the sale of such lands, and not the lands themselves, should be so applied.

That the President of the United States, Andrew Johnson, in exercising the power of his high office in resisting the aggressions of Congress upon the constitutional rights of the States and the people, is entitled to the gratitude of the whole American people, and in behalf of the Democratic party we tender him our thanks for his patriotic efforts in that regard.

Upon this platform the Democratic party appeal to every patriot, including all the Conservative element and all who desire to support the Constitution and restore the Union, forgetting all past differences of opinion, to unite with us in the present great struggle for the liberties of the people; and that to all such, to whatever party they may have heretofore belonged, we extend the right hand of fellowship, and hail all such co-operating with us as friends and brethren.

*Resolved,* That this convention sympathize cordially with the workingmen of the United States in their efforts to protect the rights and interests of the laboring classes of the country.

[Offered by Mr. Vallandigham, and adopted the last day of the convention.]

*Resolved,* That the thanks of the convention are tendered to Chief Justice Salmon P. Chase, for the justice, dignity, and impartiality with which he presided over the court of impeachment on the trial of President Andrew Johnson.

[This last was offered by Mr. Kernan, of New York, after the nominations and immediately before the final adjournment, and was carried by acclamation.]

## Soldiers and Sailors, at New York, July.

Whereas a mutual interchange of views between members of this Convention and delegates to the Democratic National Convention, has fully confirmed us in our previously entertained opinion of the purity and patriotism of that body, and fully justifies the belief that in the selection of candidates and in the construction of a platform the Convention will be governed by the spirit of the address adopted by this body on the 6th inst.; therefore, relying upon this belief,

*Resolved,* That we will support its nominees for President and Vice President of the United States, and that on our return home we will induce our late comrades in arms to unite with us in yielding to them a united support.

[Reported from the Committee on Resolutions and adopted—yeas 287, nays 7.]

*Resolved,* That the declaration of principles adopted by the Democratic National Convention be and the same is hereby ratified and approved, and that the secretary communicate to that Convention a copy of this resolution forthwith.

*Resolved,* That the President of the Convention appoint a committee of five to wait upon General George B. McClellan, and assure him that although we are called upon by duty to support the nominee for the Presidency of the National Democratic party now in Convention, our confidence in him is unimpaired, and that our love for him is as ardent as ever, and that the highest honor that this Convention could confer upon him would but poorly express our esteem for him. Also, that the said committee be requested to ask him to come and assist us with all his ability during the coming campaign.

*Resolved,* That the thanks of this Convention, and of all patriotic and right-minded citizens, are due to the President of the United States for the removal of E. M. Stanton from the War Department of the Government, a position which the said Stanton has disgraced and dishonored ever since his appointment to that office, by his many acts of cruelty—both to the Union and Confederate soldiers—and by his official acts of tyranny; and that the soldiers and sailors should, on all occasions, meet him with the same feelings of outraged dignity and patriotism that he was received with, on an ever-memorable occasion, in the city of Washington, from that great and glorious soldier—General William Tecumseh Sherman.

[The last three resolutions were offered in the Convention, and adopted unanimously, under a suspension of the rule requiring the reference of all resolutions to the committee on resolutions.]

Pending the resolutions reported from the committee above, General Thomas Ewing, jr., of Kansas, offered this resolution:

*Resolved*, That the faith of the republic to its creditors, as pledged in its laws, is inviolable, and the public burdens should be lightened by vigilant economy in expenditures, and never by repudiation; that all the bonds of the United States issued after the passage of the legal tender act, and not by law expressly payable in coin, should be paid when redeemable in legal-tender notes, but without undue inflation of the currency, or at the option of the holders, converted into bonds bearing a low rate of interest; that the national bank currency should be retired and its place supplied by legal tenders, so as to save to the Government interest upon the amount of that circulation, and that the policy of permitting banks to supply nearly half of the national currency — allowing the five-twenty bonds, bearing, as they do, interest at the rate of nearly nine per cent. per annum, to run beyond the date when they become redeemable, and of contracting the currency until it shall rise to the value of gold, is a policy which favors the few against the many, is oppressive to the laboring and the debtor classes, and tends to bring upon the country the dishonor of repudiation.

[He moved for the suspension of the rule requiring reference to the committee, which was lost—yeas 78, nays 197; and the resolution was accordingly referred, and not again considered.]

### General Blair's Letter.

OMAHA, NEBRASKA, July 13, 1868.
General GEORGE W. MORGAN, *Chairman Committee National Democratic Convention.*

GENERAL: I take the earliest opportunity of replying to your letter, notifying me of my nomination for Vice President of the United States by the National Democratic Convention, recently held in the city of New York.

I accept without hesitation the nomination tendered in a manner so gratifying, and give you and the committee my thanks for the very kind and complimentary language in which you have conveyed to me the decision of the convention.

I have carefully read the resolutions adopted by the convention, and most cordially concur in every principle and sentiment they announce.

My opinion upon all of the questions which discriminate the great contending parties have been freely expressed on all suitable occasions, and I do not deem it necessary at this time to reiterate them.

The issues upon which the contest turns are clear, and cannot be obscured or distorted by the sophistries of our adversaries. They all resolve themselves into the old and ever-renewing struggle of a few men to absorb the political power of the nation. This effort, under every conceivable name and disguise, has always characterized the opponents of the Democratic party, but at no time has the attempt assumed a shape so open and daring as in this contest. The adversaries of free and constitutional government,

in defiance of the express language of the Constitution, have erected a military despotism in ten of the States of the Union, have taken from the President the powers vested in him by the supreme law, and have deprived the Supreme Court of its jurisdiction. The right of trial by jury, and the great writ of right, the *habeas corpus*—shields of safety for every citizen, and which have descended to us from the earliest traditions of our ancestors, and which our revolutionary fathers sought to secure to their posterity forever in the fundamental charter of our liberties—have been ruthlessly trampled under foot by the fragment of a Congress. Whole States and communities of people of our own race have been attainted, convicted, condemned, and deprived of their rights as citizens, without presentment, or trial, or witnesses, but by congressional enactment of *ex post facto* laws, and in defiance of the constitutional prohibition denying even to a full and legal Congress the authority to pass any bill of attainder or *ex post facto* law. The same usurping authority has substituted as electors in place of the men of our own race, thus illegally attainted and disfranchised, a host of ignorant negroes, who are supported in idleness with the public money, and combined together to strip the white race of their birthright, through the management of freedmen's bureaus and the emissaries of conspirators in other States; and, to complete the oppression, the military power of the nation has been placed at their disposal, in order to make this barbarism supreme.

The military leader under whose prestige this usurping Congress has taken refuge since the condemnation of their schemes by the free people of the North in the elections of the last year, and whom they have selected as their candidate to shield themselves from the result of their own wickedness and crime, has announced his acceptance of the nomination, and his willingness to maintain their usurpations over eight millions of white people at the South, fixed to the earth with his bayonets. He exclaims: "Let us have peace." "Peace reigns in Warsaw" was the announcement which heralded the doom of the liberties of a nation. "The empire is peace," exclaimed Bonaparte, when freedom and its defenders expired under the sharp edge of his sword. The peace to which Grant invites us is the peace of despotism and death.

Those who seek to restore the Constitution by executing the will of the people condemning the reconstruction acts, already pronounced in the elections of last year, and which will, I am convinced, be still more emphatically expressed by the election of the Democratic candidate as the President of the United States, are denounced as revolutionists by the partisans of this vindictive Congress. Negro suffrage, which the popular vote of New York, New Jersey, Pennsylvania, Ohio, Michigan, Connecticut, and other States have condemned as expressly against the letter of the Constitution, must stand, because their Senators and Representatives have willed it. If the people shall again condemn these atrocious measures by the election of the Democratic candidate for President, they must not be disturbed, although decided to be unconstitutional by the Supreme Court, and although the President is sworn to maintain and support the Constitution. The will of a fraction of a Congress, reinforced with its partisan emissaries sent to the South and supported there by the soldiery, must stand against the will of the people and the decision of the Supreme Court, and the solemn oath of the President to maintain and support the Constitution.

It is revolutionary to execute the will of the people! It is revolutionary to execute the judgment of the Supreme Court! It is revolutionary in the President to keep inviolate his oath to sustain the Constitution! This false construction of the vital principle of our Government is the last resort of those who would have their arbitrary reconstruction sway and supersede our time-honored institutions. The nation will say the Constitution must be restored, and the will of the people again prevail.

The appeal to the peaceful ballot to attain this end is not war, is not revolution. They make war and revolution who attempt to arrest this quiet mode of putting aside military despotism and the usurpations of a fragment of a Congress, asserting absolute power over that benign system of regulated liberty left us by our fathers. This must be allowed to take its course. This is the only road to peace. It will come with the election of the Democratic candidate, and not with the election of that mailed warrior, whose bayonets are now at the throats of eight millions of people in the South, to compel them to support him as a candidate for the Presidency, and to submit to the domination of an alien race of semi-barbarous men. No perversion of truth or audacity of misrepresentation can exceed that which hails this candidate in arms as an angel of peace.

I am, very respectfully, your most obedient servant,                     FRANK P. BLAIR.

The nomination of Ex-Governor Seymour was made, July 9, on the 22d ballot, as follows:

| *Candidates.* | 1. | 2. | 3. | 4. | 5. | 6. | 7. | 8. | 9. | 10. | 11. |
|---|---|---|---|---|---|---|---|---|---|---|---|
| Horatio Seymour | ... | ... | ... | 9 | ... | ... | ... | ... | ... | ... | ... |
| George H. Pendleton | 105 | 104 | 119½ | 118½ | 122 | 122½ | 137½ | 156½ | 144 | 147½ | 144½ |
| Andrew Johnson | 65 | 52 | 34½ | 32 | 24 | 21 | 12½ | 6 | 5½ | 6 | 5½ |
| Winfield S. Hancock | 33½ | 40½ | 45½ | 43½ | 46 | 47 | 42½ | 28 | 34½ | 34 | 33½ |
| Sanford E, Church | 33 | 33 | 33 | 33 | 33 | 33 | 33 | ... | ... | .. | ... |
| Asa Packer | 26 | 26 | 26 | 26 | 27 | 27 | 26 | 26 | 26½ | 27½ | 26 |
| Joel Parker | 13 | 15½ | 13 | 13 | 13 | 13 | 7 | 7 | 7 | 7 | 7 |
| James E. English | 16 | 12½ | 7½ | 7½ | 7 | 6 | 6 | 6 | 6 | ... | ... |
| James R. Doolittle | 13 | 12½ | 12 | 12 | 15 | 12 | 12 | 12 | 12 | 12 | 12½ |
| Reverdy Johnson | 8½ | 8 | 11 | 8 | 9½ | ... | ... | ... | ... | ... | ... |
| Thomas A. Hendricks | 2½ | 2 | 9½ | 11½ | 19½ | 30 | 39½ | 75 | 80½ | 82½ | 88 |
| F. P. Blair, Jr. | ½ | 10½ | 4½ | 2 | ... | 5 | ½ | ½ | ½ | ½ | ½ |
| Thomas Ewing | ... | ½ | 1 | 1 | ... | ... | ... | ... | ... | ... | ... |
| J. Q. Adams | ... | ... | ... | ... | 1 | ... | ... | ... | ... | ... | ... |
| George B. McClellan | ... | ... | ... | ... | ... | ... | ... | ... | ... | ... | ... |
| Salmon P. Chase | ... | ... | ... | ... | ... | ... | ... | ... | ... | ... | ... |
| Franklin Pierce | ... | ... | ... | ... | ... | ... | ... | ... | ... | ... | ... |
| John T. Hoffman | ... | ... | ... | ... | ... | ... | ... | ... | ... | ... | ... |
| Stephen J. Field | ... | ... | ... | ... | ... | ... | ... | ... | ... | ... | ... |
| Thomas H. Seymour | ... | ... | ... | ... | ... | ... | ... | ... | ... | ... | ... |

| *Candidates.* | 12. | 13. | 14. | 15. | 16. | 17. | 18. | 19. | 20. | 21. | 22. |
|---|---|---|---|---|---|---|---|---|---|---|---|
| Horatio Seymour | ... | ... | ... | ... | ... | ... | ... | ... | ... | ... | 317 |
| George H. Pendleton | 145½ | 134½ | 130 | 129½ | 107½ | 70½ | 56½ | ... | ... | ... | ... |
| Andrew Johnson | 4½ | 4½ | ... | 5½ | 5½ | 6 | 10 | ... | ... | 5 | ... |
| Winfield S. Hancock | 30 | 48½ | 56 | 79½ | 113½ | 137½ | 144½ | 135½ | 142½ | 135½ | ... |
| Sanford E. Church | ... | ... | ... | ... | ... | ... | ... | ... | ... | ... | ... |
| Asa Packer | 26 | 26 | 26 | ... | ... | ... | ... | 22 | ... | ... | ... |
| Joel Parker | 7 | 7 | 7 | 7 | 7 | 7 | 3½ | ... | ... | ... | ... |
| James E. English | ... | ... | ... | ... | ... | ... | ... | 6 | 16 | 19 | ... |
| James R. Doolittle | 12½ | 13 | 13 | 12 | 12 | 12 | 12 | 12 | 12 | 12 | ... |
| Reverdy Johnson | ... | ... | ... | ... | ... | ... | ... | ... | ... | ... | ... |
| Thomas A. Hendricks | 89 | 81 | 84½ | 82½ | 70½ | 80 | 87 | 107½ | 121 | 132 | ... |
| F. P. Blair, Jr. | ½ | ½ | ... | ... | ... | ... | ... | 13½ | 13 | ... | ... |
| Thomas Ewing | ... | ... | ... | ... | ... | ... | ... | ... | ... | ... | ... |
| J. Q. Adams | ... | ... | ... | ... | ... | ... | ... | ... | ... | ... | ... |
| George B. McClellan | 1 | ... | ... | ... | ... | ... | ... | ... | ... | ½ | ... |
| Salmon P. Chase | ½ | ½ | ... | ... | ... | ½ | ½ | ½ | ... | 4 | ... |
| Franklin Pierce | ... | 1 | ... | ... | ... | ... | ... | ... | ... | ... | ... |
| John T. Hoffman | ... | ... | ... | ... | ... | 3 | 3 | ... | ... | ... | ... |
| Stephen J. Field | ... | ... | ... | ... | ... | ... | ... | 15 | 9 | 8 | ... |
| Thomas H. Seymour | ... | ... | ... | ... | ... | ... | ... | 4 | 2 | ... | ... |

Necessary to a choice..................212

General Blair was nominated unanimously on the first ballot.

## CHAP. XXXVI.—Election Returns from 1860.

| STATES | Presidential Election of 1860 | | | | Presidential Election of 1864, Including army vote | | State Elections | | | | | | Electoral College | | |
|---|---|---|---|---|---|---|---|---|---|---|---|---|---|---|---|
| | Lincoln | Bell | Douglas | Breckinridge | Lincoln | McClellan | 1866 Rep. | 1866 Dem. | 1867 Rep. | 1867 Dem. | 1868 Rep. | 1868 Dem. | 1864 Linc'n | 1864 McCl'n | At the present time. |
| Maine | 62,811 | 2,046 | 26,693 | 6,368 | 72,278 | 47,736 | 69,696 | 41,939 | 57,649 | 45,948 | | | 7 | | 7 |
| New Hampshire | 37,519 | 441 | 25,881 | 2,112 | 36,595 | 33,034 | 35,137 | 30,481 | 35,809 | 32,663 | 39,724 | 37,098 | 5 | | 5 |
| Massachusetts | 106,533 | 22,331 | 34,372 | 5,939 | 126,742 | 48,745 | 91,980 | 26,671 | 98,306 | 70,360 | | | 12 | | 12 |
| Rhode Island | 12,244 | | *7,707 | | 14,343 | 8,718 | 8,197 | 2,816 | 7,372 | 3,178 | 10,044 | 5,709 | 4 | | 4 |
| Connecticut | 43,792 | 3,291 | 15,522 | 14,641 | 44,693 | 42,288 | 43,974 | 43,433 | 46,578 | 47,565 | 48,777 | 50,541 | 6 | | 6 |
| Vermont | 33,808 | 1,969 | 6,849 | 218 | 42,422 | 13,325 | 34,117 | 11,292 | 31,094 | 11,510 | | | 5 | | 5 |
| New York | 362,646 | | *312,510 | | 368,726 | 361,996 | 366,315 | 352,526 | 325,099 | 373,029 | | | 33 | | 33 |
| New Jersey | 58,324 | | *62,801 | | 60,723 | 68,014 | 65,542 | 63,947 | 51,114 | 67,468 | | | | 7 | 7 |
| Pennsylvania | 268,030 | 12,776 | 16,785 | *178,871 | 296,389 | 276,308 | 307,274 | 290,096 | 266,824 | 287,746 | | | 26 | | 26 |
| Delaware | 3,815 | 3,864 | 1,023 | 7,337 | 8,155 | 8,767 | 8,598 | 9,810 | No State election. | | | | | 3 | 3 |
| Maryland | 2,294 | 41,760 | 5,966 | 42,482 | 40,153 | 32,739 | 27,351 | 40,264 | 21,890 | 63,602 | | | 7 | | 7 |
| Virginia | 1,929 | 74,681 | 16,290 | 74,323 | | | | | | | | | | | |
| North Carolina | | 44,990 | 2,701 | 48,539 | | | | | | | | | | | 9 |
| South Carolina | No popular vote. | | | | | | | | | | | | | | 6 |
| Georgia | | 42,886 | 11,590 | 51,889 | | | 10,749 | 34,345 | | | | | | | 9 |
| Kentucky | 1,364 | 66,058 | 25,651 | 53,143 | 27,786 | 64,301 | 58,035 | 95,979 | †33,939 | 90,225 | | | | 11 | 11 |
| Tennessee | | 69,274 | 11,350 | 64,709 | | | | | 74,484 | 22,548 | | | | | 10 |
| Ohio | 231,610 | 12,194 | 187,232 | 11,405 | 265,154 | 205,568 | 256,302 | 213,606 | 243,605 | 240,622 | | | 21 | | 21 |
| Louisiana | | 20,204 | 7,625 | 22,681 | | | | | | | | | | | 7 |
| Mississippi | | 25,040 | 3,283 | 40,797 | | | | | | | | | | | |
| Indiana | 139,033 | 5,306 | 115,509 | 12,295 | 150,422 | 130,233 | 169,601 | 155,399 | No State election. | | | | 13 | | 13 |
| Illinois | 172,161 | 4,913 | 160,215 | 2,404 | 189,487 | 158,349 | 203,045 | 147,058 | No State election. | | | | 16 | | 16 |
| Alabama | | 27,875 | 13,651 | 48,831 | | | | | | | | | | | 8 |
| Missouri | 17,028 | 58,372 | 58,801 | 31,317 | 72,991 | 31,026 | 62,187 | 40,958 | No State election. | | | | 11 | | 11 |
| Arkansas | | 20,094 | 5,227 | 28,732 | | | 6,476 | 27,931 | | | | | | | 5 |
| Michigan | 88,480 | 405 | 65,057 | 805 | 85,352 | 67,370 | 96,746 | 67,708 | 80,819 | 55,865 | | | 8 | | 8 |
| Florida | | 5,437 | 367 | 8,543 | | | | | | | | | | | 3 |
| Texas | | *15,438 | | 47,548 | | | 12,051 | 48,631 | No gen'l election. | | | | | | |
| Iowa | 70,409 | 1,763 | 55,111 | 1,048 | 87,331 | 49,260 | 91,227 | 55,815 | 90,789 | 58,880 | | | 8 | | 8 |
| Wisconsin | 86,110 | 161 | 65,021 | 888 | 79,564 | 43,875 | 79,323 | 55,416 | 73,637 | 68,873 | | | 8 | | 8 |
| California | 39,173 | 6,817 | 38,516 | 34,334 | 62,134 | 43,841 | No gen'l election. | | ‡40,359 | 49,905 | §72,279 | 65,142 | 5 | | 5 |
| Minnesota | 22,069 | 62 | 38,516 | 748 | 25,060 | 17,375 | 25,983 | 15,775 | 34,870 | 29,543 | | | 4 | | 4 |
| Oregon | 5,270 | 183 | 3,951 | 5,006 | 9,888 | 8,457 | 10,283 | 9,956 | No State election. | | | | 3 | | 3 |
| Kansas | Admitted since 1860. | | | | 14,228 | 3,871 | 19,370 | 8,151 | | | | | 3 | | 3 |
| West Virginia | Included in Virginia in 1860. | | | | 23,223 | 10,457 | 28,802 | 17,158 | No State election. | | ‖10,300 | 11,500 | 5 | | 5 |
| Nevada | Admitted since 1860. | | | | 9,826 | 6,594‡ | 5,126 | 4,036 | | | | | ¶2 | | 3 |
| Nebraska | Admitted since 1860. | | | | | | 4,093 | 3,948 | | | | | | | 3 |
| Total | 1,866,452 | 590,631 | 1,375,157 | 847,953 | 2,213,665 | 1,802,237 | | | | | | | 212 | 21 | 294 |

* Fusion ticket.  † Third party, 13,167.  ‡ Third party, 2,088.  § Judicial.  ‖ Estimated.  ¶ One elector having died, but two votes were polled from Nevada.
Not yet restored: Virginia 10, Mississippi 7, Texas 6—23.  Total of college 317.  Majority of full college 159.  Majority of actual college 148.

*Statement showing the amount and rate of taxation (U. S. and State) of the National Banks, for the year ending December 31, 1867.*

| STATES AND TERRITORIES. | Capital. | Amount of taxes paid United States. | Paid to and assessed by State authorities. | Rate per cent. U.S. taxation. | Rate per cent. State taxati'n. | Taxes paid to U. S. and State authorities. | Rate of tax (U. S. & State) on capital |
|---|---|---|---|---|---|---|---|
| Maine | $9,085,000 00 | $180,119 00 | $141,225 64 | 2. | 1.5 | $321,344 64 | 3.5 |
| New Hampshire | 4,735,000 00 | 88,772 90 | 93,178 83 | 1.9 | 1.9 | 181,951 75 | 3.8 |
| Vermont | 6,510,012 50 | 122,213 57 | 144,163 50 | 1.9 | 2.2 | 266,377 07 | 4.1 |
| Massachusetts | 79,932,000 00 | 1,616,824 50 | 1,562,128 10 | 2.02 | 2. | 3,178,952 60 | 4.02 |
| Rhode Island | 20,364,800 00 | 324,844 25 | 195,355 32 | 1.5 | 1. | 520,199 57 | 2.5 |
| Connecticut | 24,684,220 00 | 434,440 35 | 387,146 26 | 1.7 | 1.6 | 821,586 61 | 3.2 |
| New York | 116,494,941 00 | 3,022,662 16 | 4,058,705 11 | 2.61 | 3.48 | 7,081,368 27 | 6.09 |
| New Jersey | 11,333,350 00 | 253,359 31 | 223,106 28 | 2.2 | 2. | 476,465 59 | 4.2 |
| Pennsylvania | 50,277,990 00 | 1,242,037 40 | 278,268 04 | 2.47 | 0.55 | 1,520,305 44 | 3.02 |
| Delaware | 1,428,185 00 | 32,620 68 | 1,260 61 | 2.28 | 0.08 | 33,881 29 | 2.36 |
| Maryland | 12,590,202 50 | 260,261 25 | 166,054 11 | 2.06 | 1.31 | 426,315 36 | 3.37 |
| District of Columbia | 1,350,000 00 | 15,329 45 | 3,285 94 | 1.33 | 0.28 | 18,615 39 | 1.61 |
| Virginia | 2,500,000 00 | 48,344 81 | 13,925 66 | 1.93 | 0.55 | 62,270 47 | 2.48 |
| West Virginia | 2,216,400 00 | 46,966 34 | 51,457 38 | 2.1 | 2.3 | 98,423 72 | 4.4 |
| North Carolina | 583,300 00 | 9,048 71 | 5,144 31 | 1.55 | 0.88 | 14,193 02 | 2.43 |
| Georgia | 1,700,000 00 | 40,844 75 | 6,050 46 | 2.5 | 0.4 | 46,895 21 | 2.9 |
| Alabama | 500,000 00 | 8,762 52 | 3,829 49 | 1.75 | 0.95 | 12,592 01 | 2.7 |
| Louisiana | 1,300,000 00 | 35,894 28 | 20,041 58 | 2.76 | 1.54 | 55,935 86 | 4.3 |
| Texas | 576,450 00 | 6,865 36 | 2,149 34 | 1.19 | 0.37 | 9,014 70 | 1.56 |
| Arkansas | 200,000 00 | 5,745 38 | 1,350 99 | 2.87 | 0.68 | 7,096 37 | 3.55 |
| Kentucky | 2,885,000 00 | 59,816 01 | 17,466 77 | 2.1 | 0.6 | 77,282 78 | 2.7 |
| Tennessee | 2,100,000 00 | 52,459 82 | 27,974 80 | 2.7 | 1.4 | 80,434 62 | 4.1 |
| Ohio | 22,404,700 00 | 514,681 46 | 520,951 20 | 2.29 | 2.32 | 1,035,632 66 | 4.61 |
| Indiana | 12,867,000 00 | 278,797 60 | 200,372 29 | 2.16 | 1.55 | 479,169 89 | 3.71 |
| Illinois | 11,620,000 00 | 321,406 24 | 231,917 40 | 2.76 | 2. | 553,323 24 | 4.76 |
| Michigan | 5,070,010 00 | 111,789 56 | 68,061 41 | 2.2 | 1.34 | 179,850 97 | 3.54 |
| Wisconsin | 2,935,000 00 | 76,583 25 | 62,011 51 | 2.61 | 2.1 | 138,594 76 | 4.71 |
| Minnesota | 1,660,000 00 | 39,132 43 | 29,522 20 | 2. | 1.3 | 68,654 63 | 3.3 |
| Iowa | 3,992,000 00 | 106,349 34 | 88,281 27 | 2.66 | 2.21 | 194,630 61 | 4.87 |
| Missouri | 7,559,300 00 | 133,141 77 | 189,247 69 | 1.4 | 2. | 322,389 46 | 3.4 |
| Kansas | 400,000 00 | 10,229 23 | 7,801 08 | 2.5 | 2. | 18,030 31 | 4.5 |
| Nebraska | 250,000 00 | 10,734 67 | 7,014 39 | 4.29 | 2.8 | 17,749 06 | 7.09 |
| Oregon | 100,000 00 | 1,623 86 | | 2.4 | | 1,623 86 | 2.4 |
| Territories | 700,000 00 | 12,005 10 | 4,677 36 | 1.33 | 0.078 | 17,582 46 | 2.12 |
| Totals | $423,304,861 00 | $9,525,007 26 | $8,812,823 92 | 2.25 | 2.08 | $18,338,431 18 | 4.33 |

*Receipts of Internal Revenue for the fiscal years ending June 30, 1867, and June 30, 1868.*

| | Manufactures & Productions. | Gross rec'ts | Sales. | Spec'l Taxes. | Income. | Legacies and Successions. | Articles in Schedule A. | Bk. Cir. & Dep. | Pass-ports, &c. | Penalties, &c. | Total. |
|---|---|---|---|---|---|---|---|---|---|---|---|
| 1867 | *$145,794,732 55 | $7,397,120 75 | $4,103,513 20 | $18,103,615 69 | $64,895,314 01 | $1,861,429 16 | $2,116,495 22 | $2,028,193 29 | $263,115 04 | $854,650 73 | $247,418,179 64 |
| 1868 { To March 31, 1868. | 83,446,918 72 | 4,787,422 51 | 3,509,947 88 | 8,527,745 96 | 24,426,435 18 | 2,031,296 55 | 629,475 44 | 1,474,539 22 | 6,158 10 | 842,291 89 | 129,682,231 45 |
| Estimated for last quarter. | 16,641,000 00 | 1,244,000 00 | 912,400 00 | 9,536,320 00 | 20,074,800 00 | 676,200 00 | 332,100 00 | 401,400 00 | 1,900 00 | 280,400 00 | 50,190,620 00 |

* Of this, $29,151,339 78 were from distilled spirits, and $23,769,076 80 from cotton. The tax derived from distilled spirits during the last fiscal year was about $14,000,000. The act exempting cotton from internal tax was approved February 3, 1868, and the act to exempt certain manufactures from internal taxes was approved March 31, 1868. The total expense of collecting Internal Revenue, including stamps and all contingencies, for the year ending June 30, 1866, was $7,089,700 46; for 1867, $7,712,089 02. The expenses of the next fiscal year (ending June 30, 1869) are estimated at $8,500,000.

## Registration, Disfranchisement, and Election Returns in the Rebel States, under the Reconstruction Acts.

| STATES. | Registration Returns. | | | Number Disfranchised. | | Votes on calling Constitutional Conventions. | | | | | | | Votes on Ratification of Constitutions recommended by Conventions. | | | |
|---|---|---|---|---|---|---|---|---|---|---|---|---|---|---|---|---|
| | Whites. | Colored. | Total. | Whites. | Col'd. | For. Whites. | For. Colored. | For. Total. | Against. Whites. | Against. Col'd. | Against. Total. | Total Vote. | Adoption. | Rejection. | Total Vote. | Date of Election. |
| Alabama | 61,295 | 104,518 | 165,813 | | | 18,553 | 71,730 | 90,283 | 5,583 | | 5,583 | 95,866 | 70,812 | 1,005 | 71,817 | Feb'y 4, 1868. |
| *Arkansas | | | 66,831 | | | | | 27,576 | | | 13,558 | 41,134 | 27,913 | 26,597 | 54,510 | Mar. 15, 1868. |
| Florida | 11,914 | 16,089 | 28,003 | 350 | ‡200 | 1,220 | 13,080 | 14,300 | 203 | | 203 | 14,503 | 14,520 | 9,491 | 24,011 | May 4, 1868. |
| Georgia | 96,333 | 95,168 | 191,501 | 10,500 | | 32,000 | 70,283 | 102,283 | 4,000 | 127 | 4,127 | 106,410 | 89,007 | 71,309 | 160,316 | April 20, 1868. |
| Louisiana | 45,218 | 84,436 | 129,654 | | | | | *75,083 | | | §4,006 | 79,174 | 66,152 | 48,739 | 114,891 | April 17, 1868. |
| *Mississippi | | | 139,690 | | | | | 69,739 | | | 6,277 | 76,016 | † | | | June 22, 1868. |
| North Carolina | 106,721 | 72,932 | 179,653 | 11,688 | 493 | 31,284 | 61,722 | 93,006 | 32,961 | | 32,961 | 125,967 | 93,084 | 74,015 | 167,099 | April 21, 1868. |
| South Carolina | 46,882 | 80,550 | 127,432 | 8,244 | 625 | 2,350 | 66,418 | 68,708 | 2,278 | | 2,278 | 71,046 | 70,758 | 27,288 | 98,046 | April 14, 1868. |
| Texas | 59,633 | 49,497 | 109,130 | | | 7,757 | 36,932 | 44,689 | 10,622 | 818 | 11,440 | 56,129 | | | | |
| Virginia | 120,101 | 105,832 | 225,933 | †16,343 | | 14,835 | 92,507 | 107,342 | 61,249 | 638 | 61,887 | 169,229 | | | | |

* No distinction between white and colored. ¶ No election held.

† "Failed to register from any cause."—*Report of Maj. Gen. J. M. Schofield, December 13, 1867.* ‡ Chiefly for felony.

NOTE.—The revised registration made before voting on the constitution was, in North Carolina 196,873, in Arkansas 73,784, in Florida 31,498. § 85 blanks.

## Statement of the Public Debt on the 1st of July, 1857, and subsequent years.

| | |
|---|---|
| On 1st of July, 1857 | $29,060,386 90 |
| 1858 | 44,910,777 66 |
| 1859 | 58,754,699 33 |
| 1860 | 64,769,703 08 |
| 1861 | 90,867,828 68 |
| 1862 | 514,211,371 92 |
| 1863 | 1,098,793,181 37 |
| 1864 | 1,740,690,489 49 |
| 1865 | 2,682,593,026 53 |
| 1866 | 2,783,425,789 21 |
| 1867 | 2,692,199,215 12 |
| 1868, (1st June) | 2,510,245,886 74 |

## Statement of the Public Debt of the United States, on the 1st of June, 1868.

| | |
|---|---|
| Debt bearing coin interest—5 per cent. bonds | $220,812,400 00 |
| 6 per cent. bonds of 1867 and 1868 | 8,582,641 80 |
| 6 per cent. bonds, 1881 | 283,677,200 00 |
| 6 per cent. 5-20 bonds | 1,494,755,600 00 |
| Navy pension fund | 13,000,000 00 |
| | $2,020,827,841 80 |
| Debt bearing currency interest—6 per cent. bonds | $25,902,000 00 |
| 3-year compound interest notes | 21,604,890 00 |
| 3-year 7.30 notes | 105,610,650 00 |
| 3 per cent. certificates | 50,000,000 00 |
| | 203,117,540 00 |
| Matured debt not presented for payment | 10,834,222 64 |
| Debt bearing no interest—United States notes | $356,144,212 00 |
| Fractional currency | 32,531,589 94 |
| Gold certificates of deposit | 20,298,180 00 |
| | 408,973,981 94 |
| Total debt | $2,643,753,566 38 |
| Amount in Treasury—Coin | $90,228,559 31 |
| " Currency | 43,279,120 33 |
| | 133,507,679 64 |
| Amount of debt, less cash in Treasury | $2,510,245,886 74 |

### Statement of the annual revenue collected by the Government from each source since 1860.

| Years. | *From customs: duties, imposts, and tonnage. | From internal revenue. | From direct taxes. | From public lands. | From miscellaneous sources. | Total, exclusive of loans and treasury notes. | From loans and treasury notes. | Total receipts. |
|---|---|---|---|---|---|---|---|---|
| 1860 | $53,187,511 87 | .......... | .......... | $1,778,557 71 | $1,088,530 25 | $56,054,599 83 | $20,786,808 00 | $76,841,407 83 |
| 1861 | 39,582,125 64 | .......... | .......... | 870,658 54 | 1,023,515 31 | 41,476,299 49 | 41,895,340 65 | 83,371,640 13 |
| 1862 | 49,056,397 62 | .......... | .......... | 152,203 77 | 931,787 64 | 51,935,720 76 | 529,092,460 50 | 581,628,181 26 |
| 1863 | 69,059,642 40 | $37,640,787 95 | $1,795,331 73 | 167,617 17 | 4,344,139 82 | 112,687,290 95 | 776,082,361 57 | 889,379,652 52 |
| 1864 | 102,316,152 99 | 109,741,134 10 | 475,648 96 | 583,333 29 | 51,505,502 26 | 264,626,771 60 | 1,121,131,842 98 | 1,385,758,614 58 |
| 1865 | 84,928,260 60 | 209,464,215 25 | 1,200,573 03 | 996,553 31 | 37,125,002 89 | 333,714,605 08 | 1,472,224,740 85 | 1,805,939,345 93 |
| 1866 | 179,046,651 58 | 309,226,813 42 | 1,974,754 12 | 665,031 03 | 67,119,369 91 | 558,032,620 06 | 712,851,553 05 | 1,270,884,173 11 |
| 1867 | 176,417,810 88 | 266,027,537 43 | 4,200,233 70 | 1,163,575 76 | 42,824,852 50 | 490,634,010 27 | 640,426,910 29 | 1,131,060,920 16 |
| 1868 | | | | | | | | |
| To Jan. 1 | 81,065,212 69 | 99,182,232 33 | 1,029,685 66 | 666,519 69 | 25,277,787 51 | 207,221,437 88 | 332,557,102 00 | 539,778,539 88 |

### Statement of the annual expenditures of the Government from 1860.

| Years. | Civil list. | Foreign intercourse. | Navy Department. | War Department. | Pensions. | Indians. | Miscellaneous. | Total of ordinary expenditures. | Interest on public debt. | Principal of public debt. | Total debts and loans. | Total expenditures. |
|---|---|---|---|---|---|---|---|---|---|---|---|---|
| 1860 | $6,077,008 95 | $1,146,143 79 | $11,514,649 83 | $16,472,202 72 | $1,100,802 32 | 2,991,121 54 | $20,708,183 43 | $60,010,112 58 | $3,144,620 94 | $13,900,392 13 | $17,045,013 07 | $77,055,125 65 |
| 1861 | 6,074,141 83 | 1,147,786 91 | 12,387,156 52 | 23,001,530 67 | 1,034,599 73 | 2,865,481 17 | 16,026,574 79 | 62,637,171 62 | 4,034,157 30 | 18,815,984 16 | 22,850,141 46 | 86,387,313 08 |
| 1862 | 5,939,009 29 | 1,339,710 35 | 42,674,569 69 | 394,368,407 36 | 879,583 23 | 2,223,402 27 | 14,129,771 52 | 461,554,453 71 | 13,190,324 45 | 96,096,922 09 | 109,287,246 54 | 570,841,700 25 |
| 1863 | 6,350,618 78 | 1,231,413 06 | 63,211,105 27 | 599,298,600 83 | 3,140,194 44 | 1,076,326 35 | 15,671,890 24 | 689,980,148 97 | 24,729,846 61 | 181,086,635 07 | 205,816,481 68 | 895,796,630 65 |
| 1864 | 8,059,177 23 | 1,290,691 92 | 85,733,292 77 | 690,791,842 97 | 4,979,633 17 | 2,538,297 80 | 18,155,730 31 | 811,548,666 17 | 53,685,421 65 | 430,197,114 03 | 483,882,535 72 | 1,298,144,656 00 |
| 1865 | 10,833,944 87 | 1,260,818 08 | 122,567,776 12 | 1,031,323,360 79 | 9,291,610 48 | 4,966,964 90 | 32,670,795 17 | 1,212,911,270 41 | 77,397,712 00 | 607,361,241 68 | 684,758,953 68 | 1,897,674,224 09 |
| 1866 | 12,287,828 55 | 1,338,388 18 | 43,324,118 52 | 284,449,701 82 | 15,605,352 35 | 3,247,064 56 | 27,430,744 81 | 387,683,198 79 | 133,067,741 69 | 620,321,725 61 | 753,389,467 30 | 1,141,072,666 09 |
| 1867 | 15,585,489 55 | 1,548,589 26 | 31,034,011 04 | 95,224,415 63 | 20,936,551 71 | 4,642,531 77 | 33,975,948 46 | 202,947,537 42 | 143,781,591 91 | 746,350,525 94 | 890,132,117 85 | 1,093,079,655 27 |
| 1868 | | | | | | | | | | | | |
| To Jan. 1 | †27,191,353 54 | .......... | 13,151,168 92 | 61,910,561 13 | ‡13,875,648 60 | | | 116,128,712 19 | 71,145,554 03 | 388,470,185 66 | 459,615,739 69 | 575,744,461 88 |

NOTE.—The revenues and expenditures of the fiscal year ending June 30, 1868, are not yet officially ascertained, but the following is an accurate statement of them:

Revenue.

| | |
|---|---|
| Customs, (gold)................................ | $163,500,000 |
| Internal revenue, (currency)................ | 193,000,000 |
| Public lands and direct tax................ | 2,800,000 |
| Miscellaneous................................ | 47,000,000 |
| | $406,300,000 |

Expenditures.

| | |
|---|---|
| Civil list, (including foreign)................ | $53,009,846 95 |
| Navy Department............................ | 25,775,502 72 |
| War Department............................ | 123,246,648 62 |
| Interior Department........................ | 27,882,576 07 |
| Total of ordinary expenses................ | 229,914,674 36 |
| Interest on public debt.................... | 141,635,551 00 |
| | $371,550,225 36 |

☞ Of the War Department payments, $38,000,000 were for bounties.

*Gold.   †Includes foreign and miscellaneous.   ‡Includes Indians.

*Statement of the expenditures of the United States during the fiscal years ending appropriations for the fiscal year ending June*

| | Year ending June 30, 1866. | Year ending |
|---|---|---|
| Civil expenses | | $12,287,828 55 | |
| Foreign intercourse | | 1,338,388 18 | |
| **Interior Department—** | | |
| Indian department | $3,242,688 04 | $4,586,393 40 |
| Pensions, military | 12,905,847 93 | 19,016,263 21 |
| " naval | 2,699,504 42 | 1,920,288 50 |
| Relief of sundry individuals | 4,376 52 | 56,138 37 |
| | 18,852,416 91 | |
| **War Department—** | | |
| *Pay department | $205,934,240 70 | †30,700,776 08 |
| Commissary department | 7,430,606 67 | 10,331,174 87 |
| Quartermaster's department | 49,856,986 39 | 35,438,367 31 |
| Ordnance " | 9,932,402 63 | 4,690,677 09 |
| Engineer's " | 2,651,903 37 | 3,233,414 08 |
| Provost Marshal General | 6,779,114 77 | 105,658 39 |
| Adjutant General | 243,539 74 | 1,495,788 53 |
| Secretary's office, (army expenditures) | 3,594,375 28 | 8,514,008 23 |
| Relief of sundry individuals | 30,009 80 | 756,466 41 |
| | 286,453,179 35 | 95,266,330 88 |
| Deduct excess of repayment from Surgeon General's dept | 2,003,477 53 | 41,915 25 |
| | 284,449,701 82 | |
| **Navy Department—** | | |
| Secretary's bureau | $10,831,260 08 | 10,545,843 51 |
| Marine Corps | 1,492,617 83 | 1,440,993 68 |
| Bureau of Yards and Docks | 4,777,868 83 | 3,828,198 13 |
| " Equipment and Recruiting | 5,103,661 99 | 3,577,311 08 |
| " Navigation | 351,061 92 | 551,981 35 |
| " Ordnance | 3,494,216 32 | 1,921,788 99 |
| " Construction and Repair | 8,675,216 81 | 4,545,509 72 |
| " Steam Engineering | 6,154,888 23 | 2,940,665 19 |
| " Provisions and Clothing | 2,244,775 99 | 1,440,642 70 |
| " Medicine and Surgery | 95,708 73 | 88,099 72 |
| Relief of sundry individuals | 102,841 79 | 152,976 97 |
| | 43,324,118 52 | |
| Interest on the public debt, including Treasury notes | 133,067,741 69 | |
| Principal of public debt | 620,321,725 61 | |
| Miscellaneous | 27,430,744 81 | |
| Total for year | 1,141,072,666 09 | |

* Bounties (report Secretary of War, 1866, p. 391,) $7,662,736

† Of this there were paid for bounties and arrears by "Division of Referred Claims," as shown on p. 6, Report of Paymaster General, 1867...$12,706,000 00

‡ Includes *foreign* and *miscellaneous*.

‖ General and staff officers ..... $1,329,805 50
Signal corps ..... 2,580 00
Engineers ..... 358,327 50
Ordnance ..... 502,113 50
Cavalry ..... 3,084,738 00
Artillery ..... 2,233,622 50
Infantry ..... 12,970,063 50
Scouts and bands ..... 300,540 00

*June* 30, 1858, *June* 30, 1866, 1867, *and till January* 1, 1868, *together with the* 30, 1869, *and the estimates for the same year.*

| June 30, 1867. | 1868, to Jan. 1. | Appropriated for year ending June 30, 1869. | ‡Estimates for year ending June 30, 1869. | ¶Expenditures for year ending June 30, 1858. | |
|---|---|---|---|---|---|
| $15,585,489 55 | ‡$27,191,353 54 | $18,357,549 69 | $23,891,292 03 | $7,052,196 75 | |
| 1,548,589 26 | | ‡‡8,411,634 00 | 1,423,454 00 | 1,321,407 91 | |
| | | $3,989,163 45 | $3,240,152 86 | $4,812,815 09 | |
| | | 30,000,000 00 | 30,000,000 00 | 1,075,837 14 | |
| | | 350,000 00 | 330,000 00 | 143,246 17 | |
| | | | | 20,224 98 | |
| 25,579,083 48 | 12,875,648 60 | 34,339,163 45 | 33,570,152 86 | | 6,051,923 38 |
| | | 17,792,120 00 | ‖22,600,775 00 | *17,455,976 85 | |
| | | 14,299,000 00 | 28,280,066 20 | | |
| | | 381,680 00 | 1,533,084 00 | 1,443,235 74 | |
| | | 1,800,000 00 | 10,528,769 88 | 5,540,276 26 | |
| | | | | ††411,844 20 | |
| | | 100,000 00 | 300,000 00 | ‡‡164,301 31 | |
| | | 376,805 00 | 193,305 00 | 469,748 24 | |
| 95,224,415 63 | 61,910,551 13 | 34,749,605 00 | 63,436,000 08 | | 25,485,333 60 |
| | | 8,000,000 00 | 10,760,560 00 | 5,665,315 34 | |
| | | 482,000 00 | 1,614,978 05 | 587,242 25 | |
| | | 1,493,600 00 | 11,512,412 25 | 1,982,923 62 | |
| | | 1,268,000 00 | 3,536,000 00 | ‖3,394,646 29 | |
| | | 413,250 00 | 650,999 40 | 43,731 22 | |
| | | 279,500 00 | 2,370,135 75 | 202,849 14 | |
| | | 3,039,000 00 | 8,737,120 00 | 841,323 37 | |
| | | 674,000 00 | 4,448,800 00 | 885,322 20 | |
| | | 1,626,000 00 | 3,451,603 50 | | |
| | | 90,000 00 | 204,575 00 | 71,346 70 | |
| | | | | 301,300 46 | 13,976,000 54 |
| 31,034,011 04 | 13,151,158 92 | 17,365,350 00 | 47,317,183 95 | | |
| 143,781,591 91 | 71,145,554 03 | 103,961,958 50 | 103,961,958 50 | | 1,567,055 67 |
| 746,350,525 94 | 388,470,185 66 | | 25,716,120 00 | | 8,417,462 32 |
| 33,975,948 46 | | 10,289,606 76 | 12,545,654 00 | | 17,937,217 54 |
| 1,093,079,655 27 | 575,744,451 88 | 227,474,267 40 | 311,861,815 42 | | 81,585,667 76 |

‡ Besides these specific estimates, the Secretary of the Treasury stated that there may be required—
For bounties, under act of July, 1866......$25,500,000 00
For miscellaneous .................................9,969,000 00

Total ...............................$35,469,000 00

¶ In gold.
** Includes heads of Pay, Commissary, and Quarter master's departments.
†† Miscellaneous.
‡‡ West Point.
‖ Includes heads of repair and ordnance.
‡‡ $7,200,000 00 of this are for the purchase of Alaska.

# ADDENDA.

## A Bill relating to the Freedmen's Bureau and Providing for its Discontinuance.

*Be it enacted, &c.*, That the duties and powers of commissioner of the bureau for the relief of freedmen and refugees shall continue to be discharged by the present commissioner of the bureau, and in case of a vacancy in said office occurring by reason of his death or resignation, the same shall be filled by appointment of the President, on the nomination of the Secretary of War, and with the advice and consent of the Senate ; and no officer of the army shall be detailed for service as commissioner, or shall enter upon the duties of commissioner, unless appointed by and with the advice and consent of the Senate; and all assistant commissioners, agents, clerks, and assistants shall be appointed by the Secretary of War, on the nomination of the commissioner of the bureau. In case of vacancy in the office of commissioner happening during the recess of the Senate, the duties of the commissioner shall be discharged by the acting assistant adjutant general of the bureau until such vacancy can be filled.

SEC. 2. That the commissioner of the bureau shall, on the 1st day of January next, cause the said bureau to be withdrawn from the several States within which said bureau has acted, and its operations shall be discontinued. But the educational department of the said bureau, and the collection and payment of moneys due to soldiers, sailors, and marines, or their heirs, shall be continued, as now provided by law, until otherwise ordered by act of Congress : *Provided, however*, That the provisions of this section shall not apply to any State which shall not, on the 1st of January next, be restored to its former political relations with the Government of the United States, and be entitled to representation in Congress.

Passed both Houses.

## Joint Resolution excluding from the Electoral College Votes of States lately in Rebellion which shall not have been Reorganized.

*Resolved, &c.*, That none of the States whose inhabitants were lately in rebellion shall be entitled to representation in the electoral college for the choice of President or Vice President of the United States, nor shall any electoral votes be received or counted from any of such States, unless at the time prescribed by law for the choice of electors the people of such State, pursuant to the acts of Congress in that behalf, shall have, since the 4th day of March, 1867, adopted a constitution of State government, under which a State government shall have been organized and shall be in operation ; nor unless such election of electors shall have been held under the authority of such constitution and government, and such State shall have also become entitled to representation in Congress pursuant to the acts of Congress in that behalf: *Provided*, That nothing herein contained shall be construed to apply to any State which was represented in Congress on the 4th day of March, 1867.

July 20—The PRESIDENT sent a veto, of which these are the most important paragraphs :

" The mode and manner of receiving and counting the electoral votes for President and Vice President of the United States are in plain and simple terms prescribed by the Constitution. That instrument imperatively requires that the President of the Senate " shall, in the presence of the Senate and House of Representatives, open all the certificates, and the votes shall then be counted." Congress has, therefore, no power, under the Constitution, to receive the electoral votes or reject them. The whole power is exhausted when, in the presence of the two Houses, the votes are counted and the result declared. In this respect the power and duty of the President of the Senate are, under the Constitution purely ministerial. When, therefore, the joint resolution declares that no electoral votes shall be received or counted from States that, since the 4th of March, 1867, have not "adopted a constitution or State government under which a State government shall have been organized," a power is assumed which is nowhere delegated to Congress, unless upon the assumption that the State governments organized prior to the 4th of March, 1867, were illegal and void.

"The joint resolution, by implication at least, concedes that these States were States by virtue of their organization, prior to the 4th of March, 1867, but denies to them the right to vote in the election of President and Vice President of the United States. It follows either that this assumption of power is wholly unauthorized by the Constitution, or that the States so excluded from voting were out of the Union by reason of the rebellion, and have never been legitimately restored. Being fully satisfied that they were never out of the Union, and that their relations thereto have been legally and constitutionally restored, I am forced to the conclusion that the joint resolution which deprives them of the right to have their vote for President and Vice President received and counted is in conflict with the Constitution, and that Congress has no more power to reject their votes than those of the States which have been uniformly loyal to the Federal Union.

"It is worthy of remark that if the States whose inhabitants were recently in rebellion were legally and constitutionally organized and restored to their rights prior to the 4th of March, 1867, as I am satisfied they were, the only legitimate authority under which the election for President and Vice President can be held therein must be derived from the governments instituted before that period.

"It clearly follows that all the State governments organized in those States under acts of Congress for that purpose, and under military control, are illegitimate and of no validity whatever; and, in that view, the votes cast in those States for President and Vice President, in pursuance of acts passed since the 4th of March, 1867, and in obedience to the so-called reconstruction acts of Congress, cannot be legally received and counted; while the only votes in those States that can be legally cast and counted will be those cast in pursuance of the laws in force in the several States prior to the legislation by Congress upon the subject of reconstruction."

Same day—The bill re-passed the SENATE—yeas 45, nays 8, as follow:

YEAS—Messrs. Abbott, Anthony, Cameron, Cattell, Chandler, Cole, Conkling, Conness, Corbett, Cragin, Drake, Edmunds, Ferry, Fessenden, Frelinghuysen, Harlan, Harris, Henderson, Howard, Howe, Kellogg, McDonald, Morgan, Morrill of Maine, Morrill of Vermont, Morton, Nye, Osborn, Patterson of New Hampshire, Pomeroy, Rice, Ross, Sherman, Sprague, Stewart, Sumner, Tipton, Van Winkle, Wade, Welch, Willey, Williams, Wilson, Yates—45.

NAYS—Messrs. Buckalew, Davis, Doolittle, Hendricks, McCreery, Patterson of Tennessee, Vickers, Whyte—8.

Same day—It passed the HOUSE—yeas 134, nays 36; and the Speaker proclaimed it to be a law. The NAYS were—

Messrs. Adams, Archer, Axtell, Barnes, Beck, Boyden, Boyer, Brooks, Cary, Eldridge, Fox, Getz, Glossbrenner, Golladay, Grover, Haight, Holman, Hotchkiss, Johnson, Thomas L. Jones, Kerr, Knott, Marshall, McCullough, Niblack, Nicholson, Phelps, Randall, Ross, Sitgreaves, Stone, Taber, Lawrence S. Trimble, Van Auken, Wood, Woodward—36.

**Proclamation of President Johnson respecting the Ratification of the XIVth Amendment by Florida and North Carolina, July 11, 1868.**

Whereas by an act of Congress, entitled "An act to admit the States of North Carolina, South Carolina, Louisiana, Georgia, Alabama, and Florida to representation in Congress," passed on the 25th of June, 1868, it is declared that it is made the duty of the President within ten days after receiving official information of the ratification by the legislature of either of said States of a proposed amendment to the Constitution known as article XIV, to issue a proclamation announcing that fact;

And whereas the said act seems to be prospective;

And whereas a paper, purporting to be a resolution of the Legislature of Florida, adopting the amendment of the XIIIth and XIVth articles of the Constitution of the United States, was received at the Department of State on the 16th of June, 1868, prior to the passage of the act of Congress referred to, which paper is attested by the names of Horatio Jenkins, Jr., as president pro tem. of the Senate, and W. W. Moore as speaker of the Assembly, and of William L. Apthoop as secretary of the Senate, and William Forsyth Bynum as clerk of the Assembly, and which paper was transmitted to the Secretary of State in a letter dated Executive Office, Tallahassee, Florida, June 10, 1868, from Harrison Reed, who therein signs himself Governor;

And whereas, on the 6th day of July, 1868, a paper was received by the President, which paper being addressed to the President, bears date of the 4th of July, 1868, and was transmitted by and under the name of W. W. Holden, who therein writes himself Governor of North Carolina, which paper certifies that the said proposed amendment, known as article XIV, did pass the Senate and House of Representatives of the General Assembly of North Carolina on the second day of July instant, and is attested by the names of John H. Boner or Bower, as secretary of the House of Representatives, and T. A. Byrnes, as secretary of the Senate, and its ratification on the 4th of July, 1868, is attested by Tod R. Caldwell as Lieutenant Governor, president of Senate, and J. W. Holden as speaker of House of Representatives;

Now, therefore, be it known that I, Andrew Johnson, President of the United States of America, in compliance with and execution of the act of Congress aforesaid, do issue this proclamation, announcing the fact of the ratification of the said amendment by the Legislature of the State of North Carolina, in the manner hereinbefore set forth.

In testimony whereof I have signed these presents with my hand, and have caused the seal of the United States to be hereto affixed.

Done at the city of Washington, this eleventh day of July, in the year of our Lord [SEAL.] one thousand eight hundred and sixty-eight, and of the Independence of the United States of America the ninety-third. ANDREW JOHNSON.

By the President:
WM. H. SEWARD,
Secretary of State.

**Certificate of Mr. Secretary Seward respecting the Ratification of the Fourteenth Amendment to the Constitution, July 20, 1868.**

William H. Seward, Secretary of State of the United States, to all to whom these presents may come, greeting:

Whereas the Congress of the United States, on or about the sixteenth of June, in the year one thousand eight hundred and sixty-six, passed a resolution which is in the words and figures following, to wit:

[For text of XIVth Amendment, see page 68 of Manual of 1867, or 194 of the combined Manual.]

And whereas by the second section of the act of Congress, approved the twentieth of April, one thousand eight hundred and eighteen, entitled "An act to provide for the publication of the laws of the United States, and for other purposes," it is made the duty of the Secretary of State forthwith to cause any amendment to the Constitution of the United States, which has been adopted according to the provisions of the said Constitution, to be published in the newspapers authorized to promulgate the laws, with his certificate specifying the States by which the same may have been adopted, and that the same has become valid, to all intents and purposes, as a part of the Constitution of the United States;

And whereas neither the act just quoted from, nor any other law, expressly or by conclusive implication, authorizes the Secretary of State to determine and decide doubtful questions as to the authenticity of the organization of State legislatures, or as to the power of any State legislature to recall a previous act or resolution of ratification of any amendment proposed to the Constitution;

And whereas it appears from official documents on file in this Department that the amendment to the Constitution of the United States, proposed as aforesaid, has been ratified by the legislatures of the States of Connecticut, New Hampshire, Tennessee, New Jersey, Oregon, Vermont, New York, Ohio, Illinois, West Virginia, Kansas, Maine, Nevada, Missouri, Indiana, Minnesota, Rhode Island, Wisconsin, Pennsylvania, Michigan, Massachusetts, Nebraska, and Iowa;

And whereas it further appears, from documents on file in this Department, that the amendment to the Constitution of the United States, proposed as aforesaid, has also been ratified by newly-constituted and newly-established bodies avowing themselves to be, and acting as, the legislatures, respectively, of the States of Arkansas, Florida, North Carolina, Louisiana, South Carolina, and Alabama;

And whereas it further appears from official documents on file in this Department that the legislatures of two of the States first above enumerated, to wit: Ohio and New Jersey, have since passed resolutions respectively withdrawing the consent of each of said States to the aforesaid amendment; and whereas it is deemed a matter of doubt and uncertainty whether such resolutions are not irregular, invalid, and therefore ineffectual for withdrawing the consent of the said two States, or of either of them, to the aforesaid amendment;

And whereas the whole number of States in the United States is thirty-seven, to wit: New Hampshire, Massachusetts, Rhode Island, Connecticut, New York, New Jersey, Pennsylvania, Delaware, Maryland, Virginia, North Carolina, South Carolina, Georgia, Vermont, Kentucky, Tennessee, Ohio, Louisiana, Indiana, Mississippi, Illinois, Alabama, Maine, Missouri, Arkansas, Michigan, Florida, Texas, Iowa, Wisconsin, Minnesota, California, Oregon, Kansas, West Virginia, Nevada, and Nebraska;

And whereas the twenty-three States first hereinbefore named, whose legislatures have ratified the said proposed amendment, and the six States next thereafter named, as having ratified the said proposed amendment by newly-constituted and established legislative bodies, together constitute three-fourths of the whole number of States in the United States:

Now, therefore, be it known, that I, William H. Seward, Secretary of State of the United States, by virtue and in pursuance of the second section of the act of Congress, approved the twentieth of April, eighteen hundred and eighteen, hereinbefore cited, do hereby certify that if the resolutions of the legislatures of Ohio and New Jersey ratifying the aforesaid amendment are to be deemed as remaining in full force and effect, notwithstanding the subsequent resolutions of the legislatures of those States which purport to withdraw the consent of said States from such ratification, then the aforesaid amendment has been ratified in the manner hereinbefore mentioned, and so has become valid, to all intents and purposes, as a part of the Constitution of the United States.

In testimony whereof, I have hereunto set my hand, and caused the seal of the Department of State to be affixed.

Done at the City of Washington this 20th day of July, in the year of our Lord [SEAL.] 1868, and of the independence of the United States of America the ninety-third. WILLIAM H. SEWARD, *Secretary of State.*

## Concurrent Resolution of Congress on the same Subject, July 21, 1868.

Whereas the legislatures of the States of Connecticut, Tennessee, New Jersey, Oregon, Vermont, West Virginia, Kansas, Missouri, Indiana, Ohio, Illinois, Minnesota, New York, Wisconsin, Pennsylvania, Rhode Island, Michigan, Nevada, New Hampshire, Massachusetts, Nebraska, Maine, Iowa, Arkansas, Florida, North Carolina, Alabama, South Carolina, and Louisiana, being three-fourths and more of the several States of the Union, have ratified the fourteenth article of amendment to the Constitution of the United States, duly proposed by two-thirds of each House of the Thirty-Ninth Congress; therefore

*Resolved by the Senate, (the House of Representatives concurring,)* That said fourteenth article is hereby declared to be a part of the Constitution of the United States, and it shall be duly promulgated as such by the Secretary of State.

July 21—Passed the SENATE without a count.

Same day—Passed the HOUSE—the resolution—yeas 126, nays 32; the preamble—yeas 127, nays 35.

Georgia has ratified it since, by a majority of ten in the Senate, and twenty-four in the House.

## General Blair's Letter to Colonel Brodhead.

WASHINGTON, *June 30,* 1868.

Colonel JAMES O. BRODHEAD.

DEAR COLONEL: In reply to your inquiries, I beg leave to say, that I leave to you to determine, on consultation with my friends from Missouri, whether my name shall be presented to the Democratic Convention, and to submit the following as what I consider the real and only issue in this contest.

The reconstruction policy of the Radicals will be complete before the next election; the States so long excluded will have been admitted, negro suffrage established, and the carpet-baggers installed in their seats in both branches of Congress. There is no possibility of changing the political character of the Senate, even if the Democrats should elect their President and a majority of the popular branch of Congress. We cannot, therefore, undo the Radical plan of reconstruction by congressional action; the Senate will continue a bar to its repeal. Must we submit to it? How can it be overthrown? It can only be overthrown by the authority of the Executive, who is sworn to maintain the Constitution, and who will fail to do his duty if he allows the Constitution to perish under a series of congressional enactments which are in palpable violation of its fundamental principles.

If the President elected by the Democracy enforces or permits others to enforce these reconstruction acts, the Radicals, by the accession of twenty spurious Senators and fifty Representatives, will control both branches of Congress, and his administration will be as powerless as the present one of Mr. Johnson.

There is but one way to restore the Government and the Constitution, and that is for the President elect to declare these acts null and void, compel the army to undo its usurpations at the South, disperse the carpet-bag State governments, allow the white people to reorganize their own governments, and elect Senators and Representatives. The House of Representatives will contain a majority of Democrats from the North, and they will admit the Representatives elected by the white people of the South, and, with the co-operation of the President, it will not be difficult to compel the Senate to submit once more to the obligations of the Constitution. It will not be able to withstand the public judgment, if distinctly invoked and clearly expressed on this fundamental issue, and it is the sure way to avoid all future strife to put the issue plainly to the country.

I repeat, that this is the real and only question which we should allow to control us: Shall we submit to the usurpations by which the Government has been overthrown; or shall we exert ourselves for its full and complete restoration? It is idle to talk of bonds, greenbacks, gold, the public faith, and the public credit. What can a Democratic President do in regard to any of these, with a Congress in both branches controlled by the carpet-baggers and their allies? He will be powerless to stop the supplies by which idle negroes are organized into political clubs—by which an army is maintained to protect these vagabonds in their outrages upon the ballot. These, and things like these, eat up the revenues and resources of the Government and destroy its credit—make the difference between gold and greenbacks. We must restore the Constitution before we can restore the finances, and to do this we must have a President who will execute the will of the people by trampling into dust the usurpations of Congress known as the reconstruction acts. I wish to stand before the convention upon this issue, but it is one which embraces everything else that is of value in its large and comprehensive results. It is the one thing that includes all that is worth a contest, and without it there is nothing that gives dignity, honor, or value to the struggle.      Your friend,      FRANK P. BLAIR.

---

**Speeches of Horatio Seymour and Francis P. Blair, Jr., Accepting the Nominations, July 10, 1868.**

[From the N. Y. World, July 11, 1868.]

SPEECH OF GOVERNOR SEYMOUR.

MR. CHAIRMAN AND GENTLEMEN OF THE COMMITTEE: I thank you for the courteous terms in which you have communicated to me the action of the Democratic National Convention. I have no words adequate to express my gratitude for the good-will and kindness which that body has shown to me. Its nomination was unsought, and unexpected. It was my ambition to take an active part, from which I am now excluded, in the great struggle going on for the restoration of good government, of peace and prosperity to our country. But I have been caught up by the whelming tide that is bearing us on to a great political change, and I find myself unable to resist its pressure. You have also given to me a copy of the resolutions put forth by the convention, showing its position upon all the great questions which now agitate the country. As the presiding officer of that convention, I am familiar with their scope and import, and as one of its members, I am a party to their terms; they are in accord with my views, and I stand upon them in the contest upon which we are now entering; and I shall strive to carry them out in future, wherever I may be placed, in public or private life. I congratulate you, and all conservative men, who seek to restore order, peace, prosperity, and good government to our land, upon the evidences everywhere shown that we are to triumph at the next election. Those who are politically opposed to us flattered themselves there would be discord in our councils; they mistook the uncertainties of our views as to the best methods of carrying out our purposes, for difference of opinion with regard to those purposes. They mistook an intense anxiety to do no act which should not be wise and judicious, for a spirit of discord; but during the lengthened proceedings and earnest discussions of the convention there has prevailed an entire harmony of intercourse, a patient forbearance, and a self-sacrificing spirit, which are the sure tokens of a coming victory. Accept for yourselves, gentlemen, my wishes for your future welfare and happiness. In a few days I will answer the communication you have just handed me by letter, as is the customary form.

SPEECH OF GENERAL BLAIR.

MR. CHAIRMAN: I accept the platform of resolutions passed by the late Democratic Convention, and I accept their nomination with feelings of profound gratitude; and, sir, I thank you for the very kind manner in which you have already conveyed to me the decision of the Democratic Convention. I accept the nomination with the conviction that your nomination for the Presidency is one which will carry us to certain victory, and because I believe that the nomination is the most proper nomination that could be made by the Democratic party. The contest which we wage is for the restoration of constitutional government, and it is proper that we should make this contest under the lead of one who has given his life to the maintenance of constitutional government. We are to make the contest for the restoration of those great principles of government which belong to our race. And, my fellow-citizens, it is most proper that we should select for our leader a man not from military life, but one who has devoted himself to civil pursuits; who has given himself to the study and the understanding of the Constitution and its maintenance with all the force of reason and judgment. My fellow-citizens, I have said that the contest before us was one for the restoration of our government; it is also one for the restoration of our race. It is to prevent the people of our race from being exiled from their homes—exiled from the government which they formed and created for themselves and for their children, and to prevent them from being driven out of the country or trodden under foot by an inferior and semi-barbarous race. In this country we shall have the sympathy of every man who is worthy to belong to the white race. What civilized people on earth would refuse to associate with themselves in all the rights and honors and dignity of their country such men as Lee and Johnston? What civilized country on earth would fail to do honor to those who, fighting for an erroneous cause, yet distinguished themselves by gallantry in that service? In that contest, for which they are sought to be disfranchised and to be exiled from their homes—in that contest, they have proved themselves worthy to be our peers. My fellow-citizens, it is not my purpose to make any long address, (cries of " go on,") but simply to express my gratitude for the great and distinguished honor which has been conferred upon me——

A voice. " You are worthy of it."

General Blair——and from my heart to reiterate the words of thanks that fell from my lips when I arose.

---

### The Funding Bill, July 25, 1868.

An Act providing for payment of the national debt, and for the reduction of the rate of interest thereon.

*Be it enacted, &c.,* That the Secretary of the Treasury is hereby authorized to issue coupon or registered bonds of the United States, in such form as he may prescribe, and of denominations of one hundred dollars, or any multiple of that sum, redeemable in coin at the pleasure of the United States after thirty and forty years, respectively, and bearing the following rates of yearly interest, payable semi-annually in coin, that is to say: The issue of bonds falling due in

thirty years shall bear interest at four and a half per centum; and bonds falling due in forty years shall bear interest at four per centum; which said bonds and the interest thereon shall be exempt from the payment of all taxes or duties to the United States, other than such income tax as may be assessed on other incomes, as well as from taxation in any form by or under State, municipal, or local authority, and the said bonds shall be exclusively used, par for par, for the redemption of or in exchange for an equal amount of any of the present outstanding bonds of the United States known as the five-twenty bonds, and may be issued to an amount, in the aggregate, sufficient to cover the principal of all such five-twenty bonds, and no more.

Sec. 2. That there is hereby appropriated out of the duties derived from imported goods the sum of one hundred and thirty-five millions of dollars annually, which sum, during each fiscal year, shall be applied to the payment of the interest and to the reduction of the principal of the public debt in such a manner as may be determined by the Secretary of the Treasury, or as Congress may hereafter direct; and such reduction shall be in lieu of the sinking fund contemplated by the fifth section of the act entitled " An act to authorize the issue of United States notes, and for the redemption or funding thereof, and for funding the floating debt of the United States," approved February twenty-fifth, eighteen hundred and sixty-two.

Sec. 3. That from and after the passage of this act no percentage, deduction, commission, or compensation of any amount or kind shall be allowed to any person for the sale, negotiation, redemption or exchange of any bonds or securities of the United States, or of any coin or bullion disposed of at the Treasury Department or elsewhere on account of the United States; and all acts or parts of acts authorizing or permitting, by construction or otherwise, the Secretary of the Treasury to appoint any agent, other than some proper officer of his department, to make such sale, negotiation, redemption, or exchange of bonds and securities are hereby repealed.

# PART I.

# POLITICAL MANUAL FOR 1869.

## XXXVII.

### MEMBERS OF THE CABINET OF PRESIDENT JOHNSON,

### AND OF THE FORTIETH CONGRESS, THIRD SESSION.

**PRESIDENT JOHNSON'S CABINET.**

*Secretary of State*—WM. H. SEWARD, of New York.
*Secretary of the Treasury*—HUGH McCULLOCH, of Indiana.
*Secretary of War*—JOHN M. SCHOFIELD, of New York.
*Secretary of the Navy*—GIDEON WELLES, of Connecticut.
*Secretary of the Interior*—ORVILLE H. BROWNING, of Illinois.
*Postmaster General*—ALEXANDER W. RANDALL, of Wisconsin.
*Attorney General*—WM. M. EVARTS, of New York.

**MEMBERS OF THE FORTIETH CONGRESS.**

Third Session, December 7, 1868—March 3, 1869.

### Senate.

BENJAMIN F. WADE, of Ohio, *President of the Senate, and Acting Vice President.*
George C. Gorham, of California, *Secretary.*
*Maine*—Lot M. Morrill, William Pitt Fessenden.
*New Hampshire*—Aaron H. Cragin, James W. Patterson.
*Vermont*—George F. Edmunds, Justin S. Morrill.
*Massachusetts*—Charles Sumner, Henry Wilson.
*Rhode Island*—William Sprague, Henry B. Anthony.
*Connecticut*—James Dixon, Orris S. Ferry.
*New York*—Edwin D. Morgan, Roscoe Conkling.
*New Jersey*—Frederick T. Frelinghuysen, Alexander G. Cattell.
*Pennsylvania*—Charles R. Buckalew, Simon Cameron.
*Delaware*—James A. Bayard, Willard Saulsbury.
*Maryland*—William Pinckney Whyte, George Vickers.
*North Carolina*—John C. Abbott, John Pool.
*South Carolina*—Thomas J. Robertson, Frederick A. Sawyer.
*Alabama*—Willard Warner, George E. Spencer.
*Louisiana*—John S. Harris, William P. Kellogg.
*Ohio*—Benjamin F. Wade, John Sherman.
*Kentucky*—Thomas C. McCreery, Garrett Davis.
*Tennessee*—David T. Patterson, Joseph S. Fowler.
*Indiana*—Thomas A. Hendricks, Oliver P. Morton.
*Illinois*—Richard Yates, Lyman Trumbull.
*Missouri*—John B. Henderson, Charles D. Drake.
*Arkansas*—Alexander McDonald, Benjamin F Rice.
*Michigan*—Zachariah Chandler, Jacob M. Howard.
*Florida*—Adonijah S. Welch, Thomas W. Osborn.
*Iowa*—James W. Grimes, James Harlan.
*Wisconsin*—James R. Doolittle, Timothy O. Howe.
*California*—John Conness, Cornelius Cole.
*Minnesota*—Alexander Ramsey, Dan'l S. Norton.
*Oregon*—George H. Williams, Henry W. Corbett.
*Kansas*—Edmund G. Ross, Samuel C. Pomeroy.
*West Virginia*—Peter G. Van Winkle, Waitman T. Willey.
*Nevada*—William M. Stewart, James W. Nye.
*Nebraska*—Thomas W. Tipton, John M. Thayer.

### House of Representatives.

SCHUYLER COLFAX, of Indiana, *Speaker.*
Edward McPherson, of Pennsylvania, *Clerk.*
*Maine*—John Lynch, Sidney Perham, James G. Blaine, John A. Peters, Frederick A. Pike.
*New Hampshire*—Jacob H. Ela, Aaron F. Stevens, Jacob Benton.
*Vermont*—Frederick E. Woodbridge, Luke P. Poland, Worthington C. Smith.
*Massachusetts*—Thomas D. Eliot, Oakes Ames, Ginery Twichell, Samuel Hooper, Benjamin F. Butler, Nathaniel P. Banks, George S. Boutwell, John D. Baldwin, William B. Washburn, Henry L. Dawes.
*Rhode Island*—Thomas A. Jenckes, Nathan F. Dixon.
*Connecticut*—Richard D. Hubbard, Julius Hotchkiss, Henry H. Starkweather, William H. Barnum.
*New York*—Stephen Taber, Demas Barnes, William E. Robinson, John Fox, John Morrissey, Thomas E. Stewart, John W. Chanler, James Brooks, Fernando Wood, William H. Robertson, Charles H. Van Wyck, John H. Ketcham, Thomas Cornell, John V. L. Pruyn, John A. Griswold, Orange Ferriss, Calvin T. Hulburd, James M. Marvin, William C. Fields, Addison H. Laflin, Alexander H. Bailey, John C. Churchill, Dennis McCarthy, Theodore M. Pomeroy, William H. Kelsey, William S. Lincoln, Hamilton Ward, Lewis Selye, Burt Van Horn, James M. Humphrey, Henry Van Aernam.

*New Jersey*—William Moore, Charles Haight, Charles Sitgreaves, John Hill, George A. Halsey.

*Pennsylvania*—Samuel J. Randall, Charles O'-Neill, Leonard Myers, William D. Kelley, Caleb N. Taylor, Benjamin M. Boyer, John M. Broomall, J. Lawrence Getz, O. J. Dickey,* Henry L. Cake, Daniel M. Van Auken, George W. Woodward, Ulysses Mercur, George F. Miller, Adam J. Glossbrenner, William H. Koontz, Daniel J. Morrell, Stephen F. Wilson, Glenni W. Scofield, S. Newton Pettis,† John Covode, James K. Moorhead, Thomas Williams, George V. Lawrence.

*Delaware*—John A. Nicholson.

*Maryland*—Hiram McCullough, Stevenson Archer, Charles E. Phelps, Francis Thomas, Frederick Stone.

*North Carolina*—John R. French, David Heaton, Oliver H Dockery, John T. Deweese, Israel G. Lash, Nathaniel Boyden, Alexander H. Jones.

*South Carolina*—B. F. Whittemore, C. C. Bowen, Simeon Corley, James H. Goss.

*Georgia*—J. W. Clift, Nelson Tift, W. P. Edwards, Samuel F. Gove, C. H. Prince, (vacancy,) P. M. B. Young.

*Alabama*—Francis W. Kellogg, Charles W. Buckley, Benjamin W. Norris, Charles W. Pierce, John B. Callis, Thomas Haughey.

*Louisiana*—J. Hale Sypher, (vacancy,) Joseph P. Newsham, Michel Vidal, W. Jasper Blackburn.

*Ohio*—Benjamin Eggleston, Samuel F. Cary, Robert C. Schenck, William Lawrence, William Mungen, Reader W. Clarke, Samuel Shellabarger, John Beatty, Ralph P. Buckland, James M. Ashley, John T. Wilson, Philadelph Van Trump, Columbus Delano, Martin Welker, Tobias A. Plants, John A. Bingham, Ephraim R. Eckley, Rufus P. Spalding, James A. Garfield.

*Kentucky*—Lawrence S. Trimble, (vacancy,) J. S. Golladay, J. Proctor Knott, Asa P. Grover, Thomas L. Jones, James B. Beck, George M. Adams, Samuel McKee.

*Tennessee*—Roderick R. Butler, Horace Maynard, William B. Stokes, James Mullins, John Trimble, Samuel M. Arnell, Isaac R. Hawkins, David A. Nunn.

*Indiana*—William E. Niblack, Michael C. Kerr, Morton C. Hunter, William S. Holman, George W. Julian, John Coburn, Henry D. Washburn, Godlove S. Orth, Schuyler Colfax, William Williams, John P. C. Shanks.

*Illinois*—Norman B. Judd, John F. Farnsworth, Ellihu B. Washburne, Abner C. Harding, Ebon C. Ingersoll, Burton C. Cook, Henry P. H. Bromwell, Shelby M. Cullom, Lewis W. Ross, Albert G. Burr, Samuel S. Marshall, Jehu Baker, Green B. Raum, John A. Logan.

*Missouri*—William A. Pile, Carman A. Newcomb, James R. McCormick, Joseph J. Gravely, John H. Stover,* Robert T. Van Horn, Benjamin F. Loan, John F. Benjamin, George W. Anderson.

*Arkansas*—Logan H. Roots, James T. Elliott, Thomas Boles.

*Michigan*—Fernando C. Beaman, Charles Upson, Austin Blair, Thomas W. Ferry, Rowland E. Trowbridge, John F. Driggs.

*Florida*—Charles M. Hamilton.

*Iowa*—James F. Wilson, Hiram Price, William B. Allison, William Loughridge, Grenville M. Dodge, Asahel W. Hubbard.

*Wisconsin*—Halbert E. Paine, Benjamin F. Hopkins, Amasa Cobb, Charles A. Eldridge, Philetus Sawyer, Cadwalader C. Washburn.

*California*—Samuel B. Axtell, William Higby, James A. Johnson.

*Minnesota*—William Windom, Ignatius Donnelly.

*Oregon*—Rufus Mallory.

*Kansas*—Sidney Clarke.

*West Virginia*—Chester D. Hubbard, Bethuel M. Kitchen, Daniel Polsley.

*Nevada*—Delos R. Ashley.

*Nebraska*—John Taffe.

---

\* In place of Thaddeus Stevens, deceased.

† In place of Darwin A. Finney, deceased.

\* In place of Joseph W. McClurg, resigned.

---

## XXXVIII.

## PRESIDENT JOHNSON'S LAST ANNUAL MESSAGE,

### DECEMBER 7, 1868.

The following extracts relate to reconstruction and other controverted subjects:

*Fellow-Citizens of the Senate
　　and House of Representatives:*

Upon the reassembling of Congress, it again becomes my duty to call your attention to the state of the Union, and to its continued disorganized condition under the various laws which have been passed upon the subject of reconstruction.

It may be safely assumed, as an axiom in the government of States, that the greatest wrongs inflicted upon a people are caused by unjust and arbitrary legislation, or by the unrelenting decrees of despotic rulers, and that the timely revocation of injurious and oppress-ive measures is the greatest good that can be conferred upon a nation. The legislator or ruler who has the wisdom and magnanimity to retrace his steps, when convinced of error, will sooner or later be rewarded with the respect and gratitude of an intelligent and patriotic people.

Our own history, although embracing a period less than a century, affords abundant proof that most, if not all, of our domestic troubles are directly traceable to violations of the organic law and excessive legislation. The most striking illustrations of this fact are furnished by the enactments of the past three years upon the question of reconstruction. After a fair trial they have substantially failed and proved pernicious in their results, and there seems to be no good reason why they should remain longer upon the statute-book. States to which the Constitution guaranties a republican form of government have been reduced to military dependencies, in each of which the people have been made subject to the arbitrary will of the commanding general. Although the Constitution requires that each State shall be represented in Congress, Virginia, Mississippi, and Texas are yet excluded from the two Houses, and, contrary to the express provisions of that instrument, were denied participation in the recent election for a President and Vice President of the United States. The attempt to place the white population under the domination of persons of color in the South has impaired, if not destroyed, the kindly relations that had previously existed between them; and mutual distrust has engendered a feeling of animosity which, leading in some instances to collision and bloodshed, has prevented that co-operation between the two races so essential to the success of industrial enterprises in the Southern States. Nor have the inhabitants of those States alone suffered from the disturbed condition of affairs growing out of these congressional enactments. The entire Union has been agitated by grave apprehensions of troubles which might again involve the peace of the nation; its interests have been injuriously affected by the derangement of business and labor, and the consequent want of prosperity throughout that portion of the country.

The Federal Constitution—the *magna charta* of American rights, under whose wise and salutary provisions we have successfully conducted all our domestic and foreign affairs, sustained ourselves in peace and in war, and become a great nation among the Powers of the earth—must assuredly be now adequate to the settlement of questions growing out of the civil war waged alone for its vindication. This great fact is made most manifest by the condition of the country when Congress assembled in the month of December, 1865. Civil strife had ceased; the spirit of rebellion had spent its entire force; in the Southern States the people had warmed into national life, and throughout the whole country a healthy reaction in public sentiment had taken place. By the application of the simple yet effective provisions of the Constitution the executive department, with the voluntary aid of the States, had brought the work of restora-

tion as near completion as was within the scope of its authority, and the nation was encouraged by the prospect of an early and satisfactory adjustment of all its difficulties. Congress, however, intervened, and, refusing to perfect the work so nearly consummated, declined to admit members from the unrepresented States, adopted a series of measures which arrested the progress of restoration, frustrated all that had been so successfully accomplished, and after three years of agitation and strife has left the country further from the attainment of union and fraternal feeling than at the inception of the congressional plan of reconstruction. It needs no argument to show that legislation which has produced such baneful consequences should be abrogated, or else made to conform to the genuine principles of republican government

Under the influence of party passion and sectional prejudice, other acts have been passed not warranted by the Constitution. Congress has already been made familiar with my views respecting the "tenure-of-office bill." Experience has proved that its repeal is demanded by the best interests of the country, and that while it remains in force the President cannot enjoin that rigid accountability of public officers so essential to an honest and efficient execution of the laws. Its revocation would enable the executive department to exercise the power of appointment and removal in accordance with the original design of the Federal Constitution.

The act of March 2, 1867, making appropriations for the support of the army for the year ending June 30, 1868, and for other purposes, contains provisions which interfere with the President's constitutional functions as Commander-in-Chief of the Army, and deny to States of the Union the right to protect themselves by means of their own militia. These provisions should be at once annulled; for while the first might, in times of great emergency, seriously embarrass the Executive in efforts to employ and direct the common strength of the nation for its protection and preservation, the other is contrary to the express declaration of the Constitution, that, "a well-regulated militia being necessary to the security of a free State, the right of the people to keep and bear arms shall not be infringed."

It is believed that the repeal of all such laws would be accepted by the American people as at least a partial return to the fundamental principles of the Government, and an indication that hereafter the Constitution is to be made the nation's safe and unerring guide. They can be productive of no permanent benefit to the country, and should not be permitted to stand as so many monuments of the deficient wisdom which has characterized our recent legislation.

The condition of our finances demands the early and earnest consideration of Congress. Compared with the growth of our population, the public expenditures have reached an amount unprecedented in our history.

The population of the United States in 1790 was nearly four millions of people. Increasing each decade about thirty-three per cent., it reached in 1860 thirty-one millions—an increase of seven hundred per cent. on the population in

1790. In 1869 it is estimated that it will reach thirty-eight millions, or an increase of eight hundred and sixty-eight per cent. in seventy-nine years.

The annual expenditures of the Federal Government in 1791 were $4,200,000; in 1820, $18,200,000; in 1850, $41,000,000; in 1860, $63,000,000; in 1865, nearly $1,300,000,000; and in 1869 it is estimated by the Secretary of the Treasury, in his last annual report, that they will be $372,000,000.

By comparing the public disbursements of 1869, as estimated, with those of 1791, it will be seen that the increase of expenditure since the beginning of the Government has been eight thousand six hundred and eighteen per cent., while the increase of the population for the same period was only eighteen hundred and sixty-eight per cent. Again: the expenses of the Government in 1860, the year of peace immediately preceding the war, were only $63,000,000; while in 1869, the year of peace three years after the war, it is estimated they will be $372,000,000—an increase of four hundred and eighty-nine per cent., while the increase of population was only twenty-one per cent. for the same period.

These statistics further show, that in 1791 the annual national expenses, compared with the population, were little more than $1 *per capita*, and in 1860 but $2 *per capita;* while in 1869 they will reach the extravagant sum of $9 78 *per capita.*

It will be observed that all of these statements refer to and exhibit the disbursements of peace periods. It may, therefore, be of interest to compare the expenditures of the three war periods—the war with Great Britain, the Mexican war, and the war of the rebellion.

In 1814 the annual expenses incident to the war of 1812 reached their highest amount—about thirty-one millions; while our population slightly exceeded eight millions, showing an expenditure of only $3 80 *per capita.* In 1847 the expenditures growing out of the war with Mexico reached $55,000,000, and the population about twenty-one millions, giving only $2 60 *per capita* for the war expenses of that year. In 1865 the expenditures called for by the rebellion reached the vast amount of $1,290,000,000, which, compared with a population of thirty-four millions, gives $38 20 *per capita.*

From the 4th day of March, 1789, to the 30th of June, 1861, the entire expenditures of the Government were $1,700,000,000. During that period we were engaged in wars with Great Britain and Mexico, and were involved in hostilities with powerful Indian tribes; Louisiana was purchased from France at a cost of $15,000,000; Florida was ceded to us by Spain for $5,000,000; California was acquired from Mexico for $15,-000,000; and the Territory of New Mexico was obtained from Texas for the sum of $10,000,000. Early in 1861 the war of the rebellion commenced; and from the 1st of July of that year to the 30th of June, 1865, the public expenditures reached the enormous aggregate of $3,300,000,000. Three years of peace have intervened, and during that time the disbursements of the Government have successively been $520,000,000, $346,000,000, and $393,000,000. Adding to these amounts

$372,000,000, estimated as necessary for the fiscal year ending the 30th of June, 1869, we obtain a total expenditure of $1,600,000,000 during the four years immediately succeeding the war, or nearly as much as was expended during the seventy-two years that preceded the rebellion, and embraced the extraordinary expenditures already named.

These startling facts clearly illustrate the necessity of retrenchment in all branches of the public service. Abuses which were tolerated during the war for the preservation of the nation will not be endured by the people, now that profound peace prevails. The receipts from internal revenues and customs have during the past three years gradually diminished, and the continuance of useless and extravagant expenditures will involve us in national bankruptcy, or else make inevitable an increase of taxes, already too onerous, and in many respects obnoxious on account of their inquisitorial character. One hundred millions annually are expended for the military force, a large portion of which is employed in the execution of laws both unnecessary and unconstitutional; $150,000,000 are required each year to pay the interest on the public debt; an army of tax-gatherers impoverishes the nation; and public agents, placed by Congress beyond the control of the Executive, divert from their legitimate purposes large sums of money which they collect from the people in the name of the Government. Judicious legislation and prudent economy can alone remedy defects and avert evils which, if suffered to exist, cannot fail to diminish confidence in the public councils, and weaken the attachment and respect of the people toward their political institutions. Without proper care the small balance which it is estimated will remain in the Treasury at the close of the present fiscal year will not be realized, and additional millions be added to a debt which is now enumerated by billions.

It is shown by the able and comprehensive report of the Secretary of the Treasury that the receipts for the fiscal year ending June 30, 1868, were $405,638,083, and that the expenditures for the same period were $377,340,284, leaving in the Treasury a surplus of $28,297,799. It is estimated that the receipts during the present fiscal year ending June 30, 1869, will be $341,392,868, and the expenditures $336,152,470, showing a small balance of $5,240,398 in favor of the Government. For the fiscal year ending June 30, 1870, it is estimated that the receipts will amount to $327,000,000, and the expenditures to $303,-000,000, leaving an estimated surplus of $24,-000,000.

It becomes proper, in this connection, to make a brief reference to our public indebtedness, which has accumulated with such alarming rapidity and assumed such colossal proportions.

In 1789, when the Government commenced operations under the Federal Constitution, it was burdened with an indebtedness of $75,000,000 created during the war of the Revolution. This amount had been reduced to $45,000,000 when, in 1812, war was declared against Great Britain. The three years' struggle that followed largely increased the national obligations, and in 1816 they had attained the sum of $127,000,000. Wise and economical legislation, however, enabled the Government to pay the entire amount within a period of twenty years, and the extinguishment of the national debt filled the land with rejoicing, and was one of the great events of President Jackson's administration. After its redemption a large fund remained in the Treasury, which was deposited for safe-keeping with the several States, on condition that it should be returned when required by the public wants. In 1849—the year after the termination of an expensive war with Mexico—we found ourselves involved in a debt of $64,000,000; and this was the amount owed by the Government in 1860, just prior to the outbreak of the rebellion. In the spring of 1861 our civil war commenced. Each year of its continuance made an enormous addition to the debt; and when, in the spring of 1865, the nation successfully emerged from the conflict, the obligations of the Government had reached the immense sum of $2,873,992,-909. The Secretary of the Treasury shows that on the 1st day of November, 1867, this amount had been reduced to $2,491,504,450; but at the same time his report exhibits an increase during the past year of $35,625,102; for the debt on the 1st day of November last is stated to have been $2,527,129,552. It is estimated by the Secretary that the returns for the past month will add to our liabilities the further sum of $11,000,000—making a total increase during thirteen months of $46,500,000.

In my message to Congress of December 4, 1865, it was suggested that a policy should be devised, which, without being oppressive to the people, would at once begin to effect a reduction of the debt, and if persisted in discharge it fully within a definite number of years. The Secretary of the Treasury forcibly recommends legislation of this character, and justly urges that the longer it is deferred the more difficult must become its accomplishment. We should follow the wise precedents established in 1789 and 1816, and without further delay make provision for the payment of our obligations at as early a period as may be practicable. The fruits of their labor should be enjoyed by our citizens, rather than used to build up and sustain moneyed monopolies in our own and other lands. Our foreign debt is already computed by the Secretary of the Treasury at $850,000,000; citizens of foreign countries receive interest upon a large portion of our securities, and American tax-payers are made to contribute large sums for their support. The idea that such a debt is to become permanent should be at all times discarded, as involving taxation too heavy to be borne and payment once in every sixteen years at the present rate of interest of an amount equal to the original sum. This vast debt, if permitted to become permanent and increasing, must eventually be gathered into the hands of a few, and enable them to exert a dangerous and controlling power in the affairs of the Government. The borrowers would become servants to the lenders —the lenders the masters of the people. We now pride ourselves upon having given freedom to four millions of the colored race; it will then be our shame that forty million people, by their own toleration of usurpation and profligacy,

have suffered themselves to become enslaved, and merely exchanged slave-owners for new task-masters in the shape of bond-holders and tax-gatherers. Besides, permanent debts pertain to monarchical governments, and tending to monopolies, perpetuities, and class legislation, are totally irreconcilable with free institutions. Introduced into our republican system, they would gradually but surely sap its foundations, eventually subvert our governmental fabric, and erect upon its ruins a moneyed aristocracy. It is our sacred duty to transmit unimpaired to our posterity the blessings of liberty which were bequeathed to us by the founders of the Republic, and by our example teach those who are to follow us carefully to avoid the dangers which threaten a free and independent people.

Various plans have been proposed for the payment of the public debt. However they may have varied as to the time and mode in which it should be redeemed, there seems to be a general concurrence as to the propriety and justness of a reduction in the present rate of interest. The Secretary of the Treasury, in his report, recommends five per cent.; Congress, in a bill passed prior to adjournment, on the 27th of July last, agreed upon four and four and a half per cent.; while by many three per cent. has been held to be an amply sufficient return for the investment. The general impression as to the exorbitancy of the existing rate of interest has led to an inquiry in the public mind respecting the consideration which the Government has actually received for its bonds, and the conclusion is becoming prevalent that the amount which it obtained was in real money three or four hundred per cent. less than the obligations which it issued in return. It cannot be denied that we are paying an extravagant percentage for the use of the money borrowed, which was paper currency, greatly depreciated below the value of coin. This fact is made apparent, when we consider that bond-holders receive from the Treasury, upon each dollar they own in Government securities, six per cent. in gold, which is nearly or quite equal to nine per cent. in currency; that the bonds are then converted into capital for the national banks, upon which those institutions issue their circulation, bearing six per cent. interest; and that they are exempt from taxation by the Government and the States, and thereby enhanced two per cent. in the hands of the holders. We have thus an aggregate of seventeen per cent. which may be received upon each dollar by the owners of Government securities.

A system that produces such results is justly regarded as favoring a few at the expense of the many, and has led to the further inquiry, whether our bondholders, in view of the large profits which they have enjoyed, would themselves be averse to a settlement of our indebtedness upon a plan which would yield them a fair remuneration, and at the same time be just to the tax-payers of the nation. Our national credit should be sacredly observed; but in making provision for our creditors we should not forget what is due to the masses of the people. It may be assumed that the holders of our securities have already received upon their bonds a larger amount than their original investment.

measured by a gold standard. Upon this statement of facts it would seem but just and equitable that the six per cent. interest now paid by the Government should be applied to the reduction of the principal in semi-annual installments, which in sixteen years and eight months would liquidate the entire national debt. Six per cent. in gold would at present rates be equal to nine per cent. in currency, and equivalent to the payment of the debt one and a half time in a fraction less than seventeen years. This, in connection with all the other advantages derived from their investment, would afford to the public creditors a fair and liberal compensation for the use of their capital, and with this they should be satisfied. The lessons of the past admonish the lender that it is not well to be over anxious in exacting from the borrower rigid compliance with the letter of the bond.*

If provision be made for the payment of the indebtedness of the Government in the manner suggested, our nation will rapidly recover its wonted prosperity. Its interests require that some measure should be taken to release the large amount of capital invested in the securities of the Government. It is not now merely unproductive, but in taxation annually consumes $150,000,000, which would otherwise be used by our enterprising people in adding to the wealth of the nation. Our commerce, which at one time successfully rivaled that of the great maritime Powers, has rapidly diminished, and our industrial interests are in a depressed and languishing condition. The development of our inexhaustible resources is checked, and the fertile fields of the South are becoming waste for want of means to till them. With the release of capital, new life would be infused into the paralyzed energies of our people, and activity and vigor imparted to every branch of industry. Our people need encouragement in their efforts to recover from the effects of the rebellion and of injudicious legislation; and it should be the aim of the Government to stimulate them by the prospect of an early release from the burdens which impede their prosperity. If we cannot take the burdens from their shoulders, we should at least manifest a willingness to help to bear them.

In referring to the condition of the circulating medium, I shall merely reiterate, substantially, that portion of my last annual message which relates to that subject.

The proportion which the currency of any country should bear to the whole value of the annual produce circulated by its means is a question upon which political economists have not agreed. Nor can it be controlled by legislation, but must be left to the irrevocable laws which everywhere regulate commerce and trade. The circulating medium will ever irresistibly flow to those points where it is in greatest demand. The law of demand and supply is as unerring as that which regulates the tides of the ocean; and indeed currency, like the tides, has its ebbs and flows throughout the commercial world.

At the beginning of the rebellion the bank-note circulation of the country amounted to not

much more than $200,000,000; now the circulation of national bank notes and those known as "legal-tenders" is nearly $700,000,000 While it is urged by some that this amount should be increased, others contend that a decided reduction is absolutely essential to the best interests of the country. In view of these diverse opinions, it may be well to ascertain the real value of our paper issues, when compared with a metallic or convertible currency. For this purpose let us inquire how much gold and silver could be purchased by the $700,000,000 of paper money now in circulation. Probably not more than half the amount of the latter, showing that when our paper currency is compared with gold and silver its commercial value is compressed into $350,000,000. This striking fact makes it the obvious duty of the Government, as early as may be consistent with the principles of sound political economy, to take such measures as will enable the holder of its notes and those of the national banks to convert them, without loss, into specie or its equivalent. A reduction of our paper-circulating medium need not necessarily follow. This, however, would depend upon the law of demand and supply; though it should be borne in mind that by making legal-tender and bank notes convertible into coin or its equivalent, their present specie value in the hands of their holders would be enhanced one hundred per cent.

Legislation for the accomplishment of a result so desirable is demanded by the highest public considerations. The Constitution contemplates that the circulating medium of the country shall be uniform in quality and value. At the time of the formation of that instrument the country had just emerged from the war of the Revolution, and was suffering from the effects of a redundant and worthless paper currency. The sages of that period were anxious to protect their posterity from the evils which they themselves had experienced. Hence, in providing a circulating medium, they conferred upon Congress the power to coin money and regulate the value thereof, at the same time prohibiting the States from making anything but gold and silver a tender in payment of debts.

The anomalous condition of our currency is in striking contrast with that which was originally designed. Our circulation now embraces, first, notes of the national banks, which are made receivable for all dues to the Government, excluding imposts, and by all its creditors, excepting in payment of interest upon its bonds and the securities themselves; second, legal-tender notes issued by the United States, and which the law requires shall be received as well in payment of all debts between citizens as of all Government dues, excepting imposts; and, third, gold and silver coin. By the operation of our present system of finance, however, the metallic currency, when collected, is reserved only for one class of Government creditors, who, holding its bonds. semi-annually receive their notes in coin from the national Treasury. There is no reason which will be accepted as satisfactory by the people why those who defend us on the land and protect us on the sea; the pensioner upon the gratitude of the nation, bearing the scars and wounds received while

---

* See resolutions of Senate and House of Representatives thereon, pp. 391.

in its service; the public servants in the various Departments of the Government; the farmer who supplies the soldiers of the army and the sailors of the navy; the artisan who toils in the nation's workshops, or the mechanics and laborers who build its edifices and construct its forts and vessels of war, should, in payment of their just and hard-earned dues, receive depreciated paper, while another class of their countrymen, no more deserving, are paid in coin of gold and silver. Equal and exact justice requires that all the creditors of the Government should be paid in a currency possessing a uniform value. This can only be accomplished by the restoration of the currency to the standard established by the Constitution; and by this means we would remove a discrimination which may, if it has not already done so, create a prejudice that may become deeprooted and wide-spread, and imperil the national credit.

The feasibility of making our currency correspond with the constitutional standard may be seen by reference to a few facts derived from our commercial statistics.

The aggregate product of precious metals in the United States from 1849 to 1867 amounted to $1,174,000,000, while for the same period the net exports of specie were $741,000,000. This shows an excess of product over net exports of $433,000,000. There are in the Treasury $103,407,985 in coin, in circulation in the States on the Pacific coast about $40,000,000, and a few millions in the national and other banks—in all less than $160,000,000. Taking into consideration the specie in the country prior to 1849 and that produced since 1867, and we have more than $300,000,000 not accounted for by exportation or by the returns of the Treasury, and therefore most probably remaining in the country.

These are important facts, and show how completely the inferior currency will supersede the better, forcing it from circulation among the masses, and causing it to be exported as a mere article of trade, to add to the money capital of foreign lands. They show the necessity of retiring our paper money, that the return of gold and silver to the avenues of trade may be invited, and a demand created which will cause the retention at home of at least so much of the productions of our rich and inexhaustible goldbearing fields as may be sufficient for purposes of circulation. It is unreasonable to expect a return to a sound currency so long as the Government and banks, by continuing to issue irredeemable notes, fill the channels of circulation with depreciated paper. Notwithstanding a coinage by our mints, since 1849, of $874,000,000, the people are now strangers to the currency which was designed for their use and benefit, and specimens of the precious metals bearing the national device are seldom seen, except when produced to gratify the interest excited by their novelty. If depreciated paper is to be continued as the permanent currency of the country, and all our coin is to become a mere article of traffic and speculation, to the enhancement in price of all that is indispensable to the comfort of the people, it would be wise economy to abolish our mints, thus saving the nation the care and expense incident to such establishments, and let all our precious metal be exported in bullion. The time has come, however, when the Government and national banks should be required to take the most efficient steps and make all necessary arrangements for a resumption of specie payments. Let specie payments once be earnestly inaugurated by the Government and banks, and the value of the paper circulation would directly approximate a specie standard.

Specie payments having been resumed by the Government and banks, all notes or bills of paper issued by either of a less denomination than twenty dollars should by law be excluded from circulation, so that the people may have the benefit and convenience of a gold and silver currency which, in all their business transactions, will be uniform in value at home and abroad.

"Every man of property or industry, every man who desires to preserve what he honestly possesses, or to obtain what he can honestly earn, has a direct interest in maintaining a safe circulating medium—such a medium as shall be real and substantial, not liable to vibrate with opinions, not subject to be blown up or blown down by the breath of speculation, but to be made stable and secure. A disordered currency is one of the greatest political evils. It undermines the virtues necessary for the support of the social system, and encourages propensities destructive of its happiness. It wars against industry, frugality, and economy, and it fosters the evil spirits of extravagance and speculation." It has been asserted by one of our profound and most gifted statesmen, that "of all the contrivances for cheating the laboring classes of mankind none has been more effectual than that which deludes them with paper money. This is the most effectual of inventions to fertilize the rich man's fields by the sweat of the poor man's brow. Ordinary tyranny, oppression, excessive taxation—these bear lightly on the happiness of the mass of the community compared with a fraudulent currency and the robberies committed by depreciated paper. Our own history has recorded for our instruction enough and more than enough of the demoralizing tendency, the injustice, and the intolerable oppression on the virtuous and well-disposed of a degraded paper currency authorized by law or in any way countenanced by Government." It is one of the most successful devices, in times of peace or war, of expansions or revulsions, to accomplish the transfer of all the precious metals from the great mass of the people into the hands of the few, where they are hoarded in secret places or deposited under bolts and bars, while the people are left to endure all the inconvenience, sacrifice, and demoralization resulting from the use of depreciated and worthless paper. * * *

During the fiscal year ending June 30, 1868, six million six hundred and fifty-five thousand seven hundred acres of public land were disposed of. * * *

On the 30th of June, 1868, one hundred and sixty-nine thousand six hundred and forty-three names were borne on the pension rolls, and during the year ending on that day the total amount paid for pensions, including the expenses of disbursement, was $24,010,982, being $5,391,-025 greater than that expended for like purposes during the preceding year.   *   *   *

Treaties with various Indian tribes have been concluded, and will be submitted to the Senate for its constitutional action.   *   *   *

The strength of our military force on the 30th of September last was forty-eight thousand men, and it is computed that, by the 1st of January next, this number will be decreased to forty-three thousand.   It is the opinion of the Secretary of War that within the next year a considerable diminution of the infantry force may be made without detriment to the interests of the country; and in view of the great expense attending the military peace establishment, and the absolute necessity of retrenchment wherever it can be applied, it is hoped that Congress will sanction the reduction which his report recommends. While in 1860 sixteen thousand three hundred men cost the nation $16,472,000, the sum of $65,682,000 is estimated as necessary for the support of the army during the fiscal year ending June 30, 1870.  The estimates of the War Department for the last two fiscal years were, for 1867, $33,814,461; and for 1868, $25,205,669. The actual expenditures during the same periods were, respectively, $95,224,415 and $123,246,648. The estimate submitted in December last for the fiscal year ending June 30, 1869, was $77,124,707; the expenditures for the first quarter, ending the 30th of September last, were $27,219,117, and the Secretary of the Treasury gives $66,000,000 as the amount which will probably be required during the remaining three quarters, if there should be no reduction of the army—making its aggregate cost for the year considerably in excess of $93,000,000.  The difference between the estimates and expenditures for the three fiscal years which have been named is thus shown to be $175,545,343 for this single branch of the public service.   *   *   *

The total number of vessels in the navy is two hundred and six, mounting seventeen hundred and forty-three guns.  Eighty-one vessels of every description are in use, armed with six hundred and ninety-six guns.  The number of enlisted men in the service, including apprentices, has been reduced to eight thousand five hundred.   *   *   *

The ordinary postal revenue for the fiscal year ending June 30, 1868, was $16,292,600, and the total expenditures, embracing all the service for which special appropriations have been made by Congress, amounted to $22,730,592, showing an excess of expenditures of $6,437,991.  *  *  *

Comprehensive national policy would seem to sanction the acquisition and incorporation into our Federal Union of the several adjacent continental and insular communities as speedily as it can be done peacefully, lawfully, and without any violation of national justice, faith, or honor. Foreign possession or control of those communities has hitherto hindered the growth and impaired the influence of the United States.  Chronic revolution and anarchy there would be equally injurious.  Each one of them, when firmly established as an independent republic, or when incorporated into the United States, would be a new source of strength and power.  Conforming my administration to these principles, I have on no occasion lent support or toleration to unlawful expeditions set on foot upon the plea of republican propagandism or of national extension or aggrandizement.  The necessity, however, of repressing such unlawful movements clearly indicates the duty which rests upon us of adapting our legislative action to the new circumstances of a decline of European monarchical power and influence, and the increase of American republican ideas, interests, and sympathies.

It cannot be long before it will become necessary for this Government to lend some effective aid to the solution of the political and social problems which are continually kept before the world by the two republics of the Island of St. Domingo, and which are now disclosing themselves more distinctly than heretofore in the Island of Cuba.  The subject is commended to your consideration with all the more earnestness because I am satisfied that the time has arrived when even so direct a proceeding as a proposition for an annexation of the two republics of the Island of St. Domingo would not only receive the consent of the people interested, but would also give satisfaction to all other foreign nations.

I am aware that upon the question of further extending our possessions it is apprehended by some that our political system cannot successfully be applied to an area more extended than our continent; but the conviction is rapidly gaining ground in the American mind that, with the increased facilities for intercommunication between all portions of the earth, the principles of free government, as embraced in our Constitution, if faithfully maintained and carried out, would prove of sufficient strength and breadth to comprehend within their sphere and influence the civilized nations of the world.   *   *   *

I renew the recommendation contained in my communication to Congress dated the 18th July last, a copy of which accompanies this message, that the judgment of the people should be taken on the propriety of so amending the Federal Constitution that it shall provide—

*First.* For an election of President and Vice President by a direct vote of the people, instead of through the agency of electors, and making them ineligible for re-election to a second term.

*Second.* For a distinct designation of the person who shall discharge the duties of President in the event of a vacancy in that office by the death, resignation, or removal of both the President and Vice President.

*Third.* For the election of Senators of the United States directly by the people of the several States, instead of by the legislatures; and

*Fourth.* For the limitation to a period of years of the terms of federal judges.

Profoundly impressed with the propriety of making these important modifications in the Constitution, I respectfully submit them for the early and mature consideration of Congress.  We should as far as possible remove all pretext for violations of the organic law, by remedying such imperfections as time and experience may develop, ever remembering that "the Constitution which at any time exists, until changed by an explicit and authentic act of the whole people, is sacredly obligatory upon all."

In the performance of a duty imposed upon me by the Constitution, I have thus communicated to Congress information of the state of the Union, and recommended for their consideration such measures as have seemed to me necessary and expedient. If carried into effect, they will hasten the accomplishment of the great and beneficent purposes for which the Constitution was ordained, and which it comprehensively states were "to form a more perfect Union, establish justice, insure domestic tranquillity, provide for the common defense, promote the general welfare, and secure the blessings of liberty to ourselves and our posterity." In Congress are vested all legislative powers, and upon them devolves the responsibility as well for framing unwise and excessive laws, as for neglecting to devise and adopt measures absolutely demanded by the wants of the country. Let us earnestly hope that before the expiration of our respective terms of service, now rapidly drawing to a close, an all-wise Providence will so guide our counsels as to strengthen and preserve the Federal Union, inspire reverence for the Constitution, restore prosperity and happiness to our whole people, and promote "on earth peace, good will toward men." ANDREW JOHNSON.

WASHINGTON, *December* 9, 1868.

## XXXIX.

## POLITICAL VOTES IN THIRD SESSION OF FORTIETH CONGRESS.

### CONDEMNATION OF PRESIDENT JOHNSON'S PROPOSITION RESPECTING THE PAYMENT OF THE PUBLIC DEBT.

**Condemnatory Resolutions.**

#### IN SENATE.

1868, December 14—Mr. Willey submitted this resolution, which was reported from the Committee on Finance by Mr. Cattell, December 16:

*Resolved,* That the Senate, properly cherishing and upholding the good faith and honor of the nation, do hereby utterly disapprove of and condemn the sentiments and propositions contained in so much of the late annual message of the President of the United States as reads as follows:

"It may be assumed that the holders of our securities have already received upon their bonds a larger amount than their original investment, measured by a gold standard. Upon this statement of facts, it would seem but just and equitable that the six per cent. interest now paid by the Government should be applied to the reduction of the principal in semi-annual installments, which in sixteen years and eight months would liquidate the entire national debt. Six per cent. in gold would at present rates be equal to nine per cent. in currency, and equivalent to the payment of the debt one and a half times in a fraction less than seventeen years. This, in connection with all the other advantages derived from their investment, would afford to the public creditors a fair and liberal compensation for the use of their capital, and with this they should be satisfied. The lessons of the past admonish the lender that it is not well to be over-anxious in exacting from the borrower rigid compliance with the letter of the bond."

Mr. Hendricks moved this as a substitute:

That the Senate cordially endorse the sentiment in the President's message, "that our national credit should be sacredly observed," and declare that the public debt should be paid as rapidly as practicable, exactly in accordance with the terms of the contracts under which the several loans were made, and where the obligations of the Government do not expressly state upon their face, or the law under which they were issued does not provide, that they shall be paid in coin, they ought in right and justice to be paid in the lawful money of the United States.

Which was disagreed to—yeas 7, nays 44, as follow:

YEAS—Messrs. *Buckalew, Davis, Hendricks, McCreery, Saulsbury, Vickers, Whyte*—7.

NAYS—Messrs. Abbott, Anthony, Cattell, Chandler, Cole, Conkling, Corbett, *Dixon,* Drake, Edmunds, Ferry, Fessenden, Frelinghuysen, Grimes, Harris, Henderson, Howard, Howe, Kellogg, Morgan, Morrill of Maine, Morrill of Vermont, Nye, Osborn, Pool, Ramsey, Rice, Robertson, Ross, Sawyer, Sherman, Spencer, Stewart, Sumner, Thayer, Trumbull, Van Winkle, Wade, Warner, Welch, Willey, Williams, Wilson, Yates—44.

December 18—The resolution was adopted—yeas 43, nays 6, as follow:

YEAS—Messrs. Abbott, Anthony, Cameron, Cattell, Chandler, Cole, Conkling, Corbett, Cragin. Dixon, Edmunds, Ferry, Fessenden, Frelinghuysen, Grimes, Harlan, Harris, Henderson, Howard, Howe, Kellogg, Morgan, Morrill of Vermont, Nye, Osborn, Pomeroy, Ramsey, Robertson, Ross, Sawyer, Sherman, Spencer, Stewart, Sumner, Thayer, Van Winkle, Wade, Warner. Willey, Williams, Wilson. Yates—43.

NAYS—Messrs. *Davis, McCreery, Patterson* of Tennessee, *Saulsbury, Vickers, Whyte*—6.

## In House.

1868, December 14.—Mr. Broomall moved that the rules be suspended, so as to enable him to submit the following preamble and resolution:

Whereas the President of the United States, in his annual message to the Fortieth Congress, at its third session, says: "It may be assumed that the holders of our securities have already received upon their bonds a larger amount than their original investment, measured by a gold standard. Upon this statement of facts it would seem but just and equitable that the six per cent. interest now paid by the Government should be applied to the reduction of the principal in semi-annual installments. which in sixteen years and eight months would liquidate the entire national debt. Six per cent. in gold would at present rates be equal to nine per cent. in currency, and equivalent to the payment of the debt one and a half time in a fraction less than seventeen years. This, in connection with all the other advantages derived from their investment, would afford to the public creditors a fair and liberal compensation for the use of their capital, and with this they should be satisfied. The lessons of the past admonish the lender that it is not well to be over anxious in exacting from the borrower rigid compliance with the letter of the bond;" and whereas such sentiments, if permitted to go to the world without immediate protest, may be understood to be the sentiments of the people of the United States and their Representatives in Congress: therefore,

*Resolved*, That all forms and degrees of repudiation of national indebtedness are odious to the American people. And that under no circumstances will their Representatives consent to offer the public creditor, as full compensation, a less amount of money than that which the Government contracted to pay him.

The rules were suspended—yeas 135, nays 29.

A division of the question was called, the first division to include the preamble and the first sentence of the resolution. The previous question was called and seconded, and the main question ordered. A motion to reconsider the vote ordering the main question was tabled, yeas 134, nays 37. The question recurring on the first division of the question, a motion to table the preamble was lost—yeas 37, nays 133.

The first division of the question—being the preamble and the first sentence of the resolution—was then agreed to, yeas 155, nays 6, not voting 60, as follow:

Yeas—Messrs. Allison, Ames, Arnell, James M. Ashley, *Axtell*, Bailey, Baker, Baldwin, Banks, *Barnum*, Beaman, Beatty, Benjamin, Benton, Bingham, Blair, Boutwell, Bowen, Boyden, *Boyer*, Broomall, Buckley, Roderick R. Butler, Callis, *Cary*, *Chanler*, Churchill, Reader W. Clarke, Sidney Clarke, Coburn, Cook, Corley, Covode, Cullom, Dawes, Deweese, Dickey, Dixon, Donnelly, Driggs, Eckley, Edwards, Eggleston, Ela, Thomas D. Eliot, Farnsworth, Ferriss, Ferry, Fields, French, Garfield, *Getz, Glossbrenner*, Goss, Gove, Griswold, Haughey, Hawkins, Higby, Hooper, Hopkins, *Hotchkiss*, Chester D. Hubbard, *Richard D. Hubbard*, Hulburd, Hunter, Ingersoll, Jenckes, Alexander H. Jones, Judd, Julian, Kelley, Kellogg, Kelsey, Ketcham, Kitchen, Koontz, Lash, George V. Lawrence, Wm. Lawrence, Lincoln, Loan, Loughridge, Lynch, Mallory, Marvin, McCarthy, McKee, Mercur, Miller, Moore, Moorhead, Morrell, *Morrissey*, Mullins, Myers, Newsham, Norris, O'Neill, Orth, Paine, Perham, Peters, Pettis, *Phelps*, Pike, Pile, Plants. Po-land, Polsley, Price, Prince, *Pruyn, Randall*, Raum, Robertson, *Robinson*, Schenck, Scofield, Shanks, *Sitgreaves*, Smith, Spalding, Starkweather, Stevens, Stewart, Stokes, Stover, Sypher, *Taber*, Taffe, Taylor-Thomas, *Tift*, Trowbridge, Twichell, Upson, Van Aernam, Burt Van Horn, Van Wyck, Ward, Cadwalader C. Washburn, Ellihu B. Washburne, Henry D. Washburn, Wm. B. Washburn, Welker, Whittemore, William Williams, James F. Wilson, John T. Wilson, Stephen F. Wilson, Windom, *Wood*, Woodbridge, *Woodward*—155.

Nays—Messrs. *Adams, Archer*, Grover, Thomas L. *Jones*, Mungen, *Lawrence S. Trimble*—6.

Not Voting—Messrs. Anderson, Delos R. Ashley, *Barnes, Beck*, Blackburn, Blaine, Boles, Bromwell, *Brooks*, Buckland, *Burr*, Benjamin F. Butler, Cake, Clift, Cobb, Cornell, Delano, Dockery, Dodge, *Eldridge, Fox, Golladay*, Gravely. Haight, Halsey, Hamilton, Harding, Heaton, Hill, *Holman*, Asahel W. Hubbard, *Humphrey, Johnson, Kerr, Knott*, Laflin, Logan, *Marshall*, Maynard, *McCormick, McCullough*, Newcomb, *Niblack, Nicholson*, Nunn, Pierce, Pomeroy, Roots, *Ross*, Sawyer, Selye, Shellabarger, *Stone*, John Trimble, *Van Auken*, Robert T. Van Horn, *Van Trump*, Vidal, Thomas Williams, *Young*—60.

The second division of the question—being the remaining portion of the preamble and resolution—was agreed to without a division.

## Vote on Minority Representation.

### In House.

1869, January 19—Pending a bill (H. R. 1824) to preserve the purity of elections in the several Territories, Mr. Phelps moved this as an additional section:

"That the legislatures of the Territories hereinbefore named shall, at their first session after the passage of this act, provide by law for a re-apportionment of the members of the several legislatures as nearly equal as may be among council and legislative districts, entitled each to elect three members of council and three representatives; and that the outlying districts, if any, to which it may be necessary that a less number than three shall be apportioned, shall be located in the least populous portions of said Territories; and that at the next legislative elections thereafter in said Territories every qualified voter shall be entitled to three votes for member of council, and three votes for member of the house of representatives, with the privilege of cumulating said votes upon any one or two of the candidates for either house respectively, it being the intent and meaning of this act to secure an equitable and just representation to minorities in said Territories in all cases where minority parties exceed in number two-fifths of the electoral body."

Which was disagreed to—yeas 49, nays 116, as follow, (not voting, 57):

Yeas—Messrs. Anderson, *Archer, Axtell*, Baker, *Barnes, Barnum, Beck*, Benjamin, Boyden, *Boyer*, Roderick R. Butler, *Chanler*, Cook, Deweese, *Getz, Glossbrenner*, Golladay, Gove, *Grover*, Hawkins, Heaton, *Holman, Hotchkiss, Humphrey*, Jenckes, Alexander H. Jones, *Thomas L. Jones, Kerr, Knott*, Lash, George V. Lawrence, Mallory, *Marshall*, McCormick, *McCullough, Mungen*, Newsham, *Nicholson, Phelps, Ross*, Spalding, *Stone, Taber*, Taffe, *Van Trump*, Ellihu B. Washburne, Stephen F. Wilson, *Woodward, Young*—49.

Nays—Messrs. Allison, James M. Ashley, Bailey, Baldwin, Banks, Beaman, Beatty, Benton, Blaine, Blair, Boutwell, Bowen, Broomall, Buckland, Buckley, Callis, *Cary*, Reader W. Clarke, Sidney Clarke, Clift, Cobb, Coburn, Corley, Cornell, Covode, Cullom, Dawes, Dickey, Dodge, Eggleston, Ela, Thomas D. Eliot, James T. Elliott, Farnsworth, Ferriss, Fields, French, Goss, Gravely, Harding, Haughey, Higby, Hill, Hopkins,

Hunter, Ingersoll, *Johnson*, Judd, Julian, Kellogg, Kelsey, Kitchen, Koontz, William Lawrence, Lincoln, Loughridge, Marvin, Maynard, McCarthy, McKee, Mercur, Miller, Moore, Moorhead, Mullins, Myers, Newcomb, *Niblack*, Norris, O'Neill, Orth, Paine, Perham, Pettis, Pierce, Pike, Pile, Plants, Poland, Polsley, Price, Prince, *Randall*, Raum, *Robinson*, Roots, Sawyer, Schenck, Scofield, Shanks, Shellabarger, *Sitgreaves*, Smith, Starkweather, Stevens, Stokes, Stover, Thomas, *Tift*, John Trimble, *Lawrence S. Trimble*, Upson, Van Aernam, *Van Auken*, Burt Van Horn, Vidal, Ward, Henry D. Washburn, William B. Washburn, Welker, Whittemore, Thomas Williams, William Williams, James F. Wilson, John T. Wilson, Windom —116.

## Removal of Disabilities.

### IN SENATE.

1868, December 9—Pending the bill to relieve from disabilities Franklin J. Moses, of South Carolina—

Mr. GARRETT DAVIS moved to add the words, " and all other citizens of the State of South Carolina."

Which was disagreed to—yeas 9, nays 44, as follow :

YEAS—Messrs. *Bayard, Davis, Dixon, Doolittle,* Ferry, *McCreery, Norton, Patterson* of Tennessee, *Saulsbury*—9.

NAYS—Messrs. Anthony, Cameron, Cattell, Chandler, Cole, Conkling, Conness, Corbett, Cragin, Drake, Edmunds, Fessenden, Fowler, Frelinghuysen, Grimes, Harlan, Harris, Howe, Kellogg, Morgan, Morrill of Maine, Morrill of Vermont, Nye, Osborn, Patterson of New Hampshire, Pomeroy, Ramsey, Rice, Robertson, Sherman, Spencer, Stewart, Sumner, Thayer, Tipton, Trumbull, Van Winkle, Wade, Warner, Welch, Willey, Williams, Wilson, Yates—44.

[No general disability bill was passed at either the third session of the Fortieth Congress or the first session of the Forty-First.]

## The Representation of Georgia.

### IN HOUSE.

1869, January 28—Mr. Paine, from the Committee on Reconstruction, reported the following preamble and resolution:

Whereas it is provided by the reconstruction act, passed March 2, 1867, that until the people of the lately rebellious States shall be by law admitted to representation in Congress, any civil government which may exist therein shall be deemed provisional only, and that no persons shall be eligible to office in such provisional governments who are disqualified for office by the fourteenth amendment of the Constitution of the United States ; and whereas it is reported that the legislature of Georgia has expelled the colored members thereof, and admitted to their seats white men who received minorities of votes at the polls, and that members of said legislature who had been elected thereto by the votes of colored men joined in such action, and that twenty-seven disqualified white men hold seats in said legislature in violation of the fourteenth amendment of the Constitution and of the reconstruction acts of Congress; and whereas Senators from Georgia have not yet been admitted to the Senate of the United States : therefore,

*Resolved*, That the Committee on Reconstruction be ordered to inquire and report whether any, and if any, what, further action ought to be taken during the Fortieth Congress respecting the representation of Georgia in this House.

Under the operation of the previous question,

the resolution was agreed to—yeas 128, nays 34, not voting 60.

The NAYS were : Messrs. *Archer*, Baker, *Barnes, Beck, Boyer, Brooks, Burr, Cary, Chanler, Fox, Getz, Golladay, Grover, Haight, Hotchkiss, Humphrey, Thomas L. Jones, Kerr, Knott, Marshall, Niblack, Phelps, Pruyn, Randall, Ross, Sitgreaves,* Spalding, *Stone, Taber, Tift, Van Auken, Wood, Woodward, Young*—34.

The preamble was then agreed to—yeas 135, nays 34, not voting 53.

The NAYS were : Messrs. *Archer, Barnes, Beck, Boyer, Brooks, Burr, Chanler, Fox, Getz, Glossbrenner, Golladay, Grover, Haight, Hotchkiss, Richard D. Hubbard, Humphrey, Thomas L. Jones, Kerr, Knott, Marshall, Niblack, Phelps, Pruyn, Randall, Robinson, Ross, Sitgreaves, Stone, Taber, Tift, Van Auken, Wood, Woodward, Young*—34.

The Committee made no report.

## Counting the Electoral Vote.

### IN SENATE.

1869, February 6—Mr. Edmunds submitted this concurrent resolution :

Whereas the question whether the State of Georgia has become and is entitled to representation in the two houses of Congress is now pending and undetermined ; and whereas by the joint resolution of Congress passed July 20, 1868, entitled " A resolution excluding from the electoral college votes of States lately in rebellion which shall not have been reorganized," it was provided that no electoral votes from any of the States lately in rebellion should be received or counted for President or Vice President of the United States until, among other things, such State should have become entitled to representation in Congress, pursuant to acts of Congress in that behalf : therefore,

*Resolved by the Senate,* (the House of Representatives concurring,) That on the assembling of the two houses on the second Wednesday of February, 1869, for the counting of the electoral votes for President and Vice President, as provided by law and the joint rules, if the counting or omitting to count the electoral votes, if any, which may be presented, as of the State of Georgia, shall not essentially change the result, in that case they shall be reported by the President of the Senate in the following manner : " Were the votes presented as of the State of Georgia to be counted, the result would be for —— ——, for President of the United States, —— votes; if not counted, for —— ——, for President of the United States, —— votes ; but in either case —— —— is elected President of the United States ; and in the same manner for Vice President.

February 8—It was adopted—yeas 34, nays 11, as follow :

YEAS—Messrs. Abbott, Anthony, Cameron, Cattell, Cole, Conkling, Corbett, Cragin, Drake, Edmunds, Frelinghuysen, Howard, McDonald, Morgan, Morrill of Maine, Morrill of Vermont, Morton, Nye, Pool, Ramsey, Rice, Robertson, Ross, Sherman, Stewart, Sumner, Thayer, Tipton, Warner, Welch, Willey, Williams, Wilson, Yates—34.

NAYS—Messrs. *Buckalew, Davis,* Fowler, *Hendricks, McCreery, Norton, Patterson* of Tennessee, *Saulsbury,* Trumbull, *Vickers, Whyte*—11.

### IN HOUSE.

February 8—The rules were suspended—yeas 97, nays 18, not voting 107—so as to enable the House to take up this resolution. The vote was as follows :

YEAS—Messrs. Allison, Ames, Banks, Beaman, Beatty, Benjamin, Benton, Blaine, Blair, Boles, Bowen, Broomall, Buckland, Benjamin F. Butler, Roderick R. Butler, Churchill, Clift, Cobb, Coburn, Corley, Cullom, Dawes, Delano, Deweese, Dickey, Dixon, Dodge, Eckley, Ela, Ferriss, Ferry, Garfield, Halsey, Harding, Heaton, Higby, Hill, Hooper, Hopkins, Chester D. Hubbard, Hulburd, Jenckes, Julian, Kelley, Kellogg, Kelsey, Koontz, Laflin, William Lawrence, Loan, Logan, Loughridge, Marvin, Maynard, McCarthy, McKee, Miller, Moore, Moorhead, Mullins, Norris, Paine, Perham, Peters, Pierce, Pile, Plants, Price, Prince, Raum, Roots, Sawyer, Schenck, Scofield. Shanks, Shellabarger, Starkweather, Stevens, Stewart, Stokes, Stover, Sypher, Taylor, Thomas, Trowbridge, Twichell, Upson, Robert T. Van Horn, Vidal, Henry D. Washburn, William B. Washburn. Welker, Whittemore, William Williams, James F. Wilson, John T. Wilson, Windom—97.

NAYS—Messrs. Baker, Boyden, *Boyer*, Farnsworth, *Getz, Holman, Hotchkiss, Johnson, Thomas L. Jones, Niblack, Phelps, Randall, Ross, Taber, Van Auken, Van Trump, Woodward, Young*—18.

The resolution was then taken up, and concurred in.

### PROCEEDINGS UNDER THIS RESOLUTION.

On Wednesday, February 10, the two houses met in the Hall of the House for the purpose of opening and counting the votes for President and Vice President.

The President of the Senate then proceeded to open the certificates of the electors of the several States, authorized to be represented in the electoral college,* for President and Vice President. Upon the certificate of the electors of Louisiana being read—

Mr. Mullins objected to the counting of the vote of Louisiana, upon the ground that no valid election of electors had been held in said State.

The SENATE withdrew, and voted

That the votes of the electors of the State of Louisiana be counted—yeas 51, nays 7, as follow:

YEAS—Messrs. Abbott, Anthony, *Buckalew*, Cameron, Cattell, Cole, Conkling, Conness, Corbett, Cragin, *Davis, Dixon, Doolittle*, Drake, Edmunds, Ferry, Fessenden, Fowler, Frelinghuysen, Grimes, Harlan, Harris, *Hendricks*, Howe, Kellogg, *McCreery*, McDonald, Morgan, Morrill of Vermont, Osborn, Patterson of New Hampshire, *Patterson* of Tennessee, Pool, Ramsey, Rice, Ross, *Saulsbury*, Sawyer, Sherman, Spencer, Sprague, Stewart, Tipton, Trumbull, Van Winkle, *Vickers*, Warner, *Whyte*, Willey, Williams, Yates—51.

NAYS—Messrs. Chandler, Howard, Nye, Robertson, Sumner, Thayer, Wilson—7.

The HOUSE voted to count the vote of Louisiana—yeas 137 nays 63, not voting 22, as follow:

YEAS—Messrs. Allison, Ames, *Axtell*, Baker, *Barnes, Barnum*, Beaman, Beatty, *Beck*, Benjamin, Bingham, Blaine, Blair, Boyden, *Boyer*, Bromwell, *Brooks*, Broomall, Buckland, *Burr*, Roderick R. Butler, *Cary, Chanler*, Churchill, Coburn, Cullom, Delano, Deweese, Dickey, Dixon, Dockery, Dodge, Eggleston, *Eldridge*, Farnsworth, Ferriss, Ferry, Garfield, *Getz, Glossbrenner, Golladay*, Gove, Gravely, *Grover, Haight*, Halsey, Hawkins, Heaton, Higby, Hill, *Holman*, Hooper, Hopkins, *Hotchkiss*, Asahel W. Hubbard, *Humphrey*, Ingersoll, Jenckes, *Johnson*, Alexander H. Jones, *Thomas L. Jones*, Judd, Kelley, Kellogg, *Kerr*, Ketcham, Kitchen, *Knott*, Koontz, Laflin, Lash, George V. Lawrence, William Lawrence, Lincoln, Logan, Loughridge, *Mallory, Marshall*, Marvin, McCarthy, *McCormick, McCullough*, Miller, Moore, Moorhead, Mungen, Newcomb, *Niblack, Nicholson*, Norris, Nunn, Peters, *Phelps*, Pike, Pile, Plants, Poland, Polsley, Price, *Pruyn, Randall*, Raum, Robertson, *Ross*, Sawyer, Schenck, Scofield, Selye, Shellabarger, *Sitgreaves*, Smith, Spalding, Starkweather, Stewart, Stokes, *Stone, Taber*, Taffe, Taylor, Thomas, Tift, John Trimble, Trowbridge, Twichell, *Van Auken*, Burt Van Horn, *Van Trump*, Ellihu B. Washburne, William B. Washburn, Welker, James F. Wilson, John T. Wilson, Windom, *Wood*, Woodbridge, *Woodward, Young*—137.

NAYS—Messrs. Delos R. Ashley, James M. Ashley,

Banks, Benton, Blackburn, Boles, Boutwell, Bowen, Buckley, Benjamin F. Butler, Cake, Callis, Reader W. Clarke, Sidney Clarke, Clift, Cobb, Corley, Covode, Dawes, Donnelly, Driggs, Eckley, Edwards, Ela, Thomas D. Eliot, James T. Elliott, Fields, French, Hamilton, Harding, Haughey, Chester D. Hubbard, Hulburd, Hunter, Julian, Kelsey, Loan, Maynard, McKee, Morrell, Mullins, Newsham, O'Neill, Orth, Paine, Perham, Pettis, Pierce, Prince, Roots, Shanks, Stevens, Stover, Upson, Van Aernam, R. T. Van Horn, Van Wyck, Vidal, Ward, Henry D. Washburn, Whittemore, Thomas Williams, William Williams—63.

The SENATE returned, and the vote of Louisiana was then counted.

The certificates of all the States except Georgia having been read, and that of Georgia having been read,

Mr. Benjamin F. Butler submitted the following objection to counting the vote of Georgia:

*First.* I object, under the joint rule, that the vote of the State of Georgia for President and Vice President ought not to be counted, and object to the counting thereof because, among other things, the vote of the electors in the electoral college was not given on the first Wednesday of December, as required by law, and no excuse or justification for the omission of such legal duty is set forth in the certificate of the action of the electors.

*Second.* Because, at the date of the election of said electors, the State of Georgia had not been admitted to representation as a State in Congress since the rebellion of her people, or become entitled thereto.

*Third.* That at said date said State of Georgia had not fulfilled, in due form, all the requirements of the Constitution and laws of the United States known as the "reconstruction acts," so as to entitle said State of Georgia to be represented as a State in the Union in the electoral vote of the several States in the choice of President and Vice-President.

*Fourth.* That the election pretended to have been held in the State of Georgia, on the first Tuesday of November last past, was not a free, just equal, and fair election, but the people of the State were deprived of their just rights therein by force and fraud.

The SENATE withdrew; and voted

That, under the special order of the two Houses respecting the electoral votes from the State of Georgia, the objections made to the counting of the electors for the State of Georgia are not in order—yeas 31, nays 26, as follow:

YEAS—Messrs. Abbott, Anthony, *Buckalew*, Cattell, Conness, Corbett, Cragin, *Davis, Dixon, Doolittle*, Edmunds, Fowler, Frelinghuysen, Grimes, *Hendricks*, Kellogg, *McCreery*, Morrill of Maine, Morrill of Vermont, Morton, Patterson of New Hampshire, *Patterson* of Tennessee, Ross, *Saulsbury*, Sawyer, Sherman, Sprague, Stewart, Tipton, *Vickers, Whyte*, Williams—31.

NAYS—Messrs. Cameron, Chandler, Cole, Conkling, Drake, Ferry, Fessenden, Harlan, Harris, Howe, McDonald, Morgan, Nye, Pool, Ramsey, Rice, Robertson, Spencer, Sumner, Thayer, Trumbull, Van Winkle, Wade, Warner, Willey, Yates—26.

Mr. Howard offered this resolution:

*Resolved,* That the electoral vote of Georgia ought not to be counted.

Which, being entertained as in order, was disagreed to—yeas 25, nays 34, as follow:

YEAS—Messrs. Abbott, Cameron, Chandler, Cole, Conkling, Drake, Harlan, Harris, Howard, Howe, Kellogg, McDonald, Nye, Osborn, Ramsey, Rice, Robertson, Sawyer, Spencer, Stewart, Sumner, Thayer, Wade, Wilson, Yates—25.

NAYS—*Buckalew*, Conness, Corbett, Cragin, *Davis,*

Dixon, *Doolittle*, Edmunds, Ferry, Fessenden, Fowler, *Frelinghuysen*, Grimes, *Hendricks, McCreery*, Morgan, Morrill of Maine, Morrill of Vermont, Morton, Patterson of New Hampshire, *Patterson* of Tennessee, Pool, Ross, *Saulsbury*, Sherman, Sprague, Tipton, Trumbull, Van Winkle, *Vickers*, Warner, *Whyte*, Willey, Williams—34.

The House voted on the question, Shall the vote of Georgia be counted? Yeas 41, nays 150, (not voting 31,) as follow:

YEAS—Messrs *Axtell*, Baker, *Barnes, Barnum, Beck, Boyer, Brooks, Burr, Cary, Chanler, Eldridge,* Farnsworth, *Getz, Glossbrenner, Golladay, Grover, Haight,* Hawkins, *Holman, Hotchkiss, Humphrey, Johnson, T. L. Jones, Kerr, Knott, Marshall, McCormick, Mungen, Nicholson, Phelps, Pruyn, Randall, Ross, Sitgreaves, Taber, Tift, Van Auken, Van Trump, Wood, Woodward, Young—41.*

NAYS—Messrs. Allison, D. R. Ashley, J. M. Ashley, Baldwin, Banks, Beaman, Beatty, Benjamin, Benton, Bingham, Blaine, Blair, Boles, Boutwell, Bowen, Boyden, Bromwell, Broomall, Buckland, Buckley, Benj. F. Butler, Roderick R. Butler, Cake, Callis, Churchill, Reader W. Clarke, Sidney Clarke, Clift, Cobb, Coburn, Corley, Covode, Cullom, Dawes, Deweese, Dickey, Dixon, Dodge, Donnelly, Driggs, Eckley, Edwards, Eggleston, Ela, Thomas D. Eliot, James T. Elliott, Ferriss, Ferry, Fields, French, Garfield, Goss, Gove, Gravely, Halsey, Hamilton, Harding, Haughey, Heaton, Higby, Hill, Hooper, Hopkins, Chester D. Hubbard, Hulburd, Hunter, Ingersoll, Jenckes, Alexander H. Jones, Judd, Julian, Kelley, Kellogg, Kelsey, Ketcham, Kitchen, Koontz, Laflin, Lash, George V. Lawrence, William Lawrence, Lincoln, Loan, Logan, Loughridge, Mallory, Marvin, Maynard, McCarthy, McKee, Miller, Moore, Moorhead, Morrell, Mullins, Newcomb, Newsham, Norris, O'Neill, Orth, Paine, Perham, Peters, Pettis, Pierce, Pike, Pile, Plants, Poland, Polsley, Price, Prince, Raum, Robertson, Roots, Sawyer, Schenck, Scofield, Selye, Shanks, Shellabarger, Starkweather, Stevens, Stewart, Stokes, Stover, Sypher, Taffe, Taylor, Thomas, Trimble, Trowbridge, Twichell, Upson, Van Aernam, Burt Van Horn, Robert T. Van Horn, Van Wyck, Vidal, Ward, Ellihu B. Washburne, Henry D. Washburn, William B. Washburn, Welker, Whittemore, Thomas Williams, James F. Wilson, John T. Wilson, Stephen F. Wilson, Windom—150.

The SENATE returned, and the vote of Georgia was counted in the manner provided by the concurrent resolution, and Ulysses S. Grant was declared duly elected President, and Schuyler Colfax Vice-President of the United States for four years, commencing on the 4th day of March, 1869.

---

## For the Further Security of Equal Rights in the District of Columbia.

1869, February 11—The Senate passed the following bill without division:

FORTIETH CONGRESS, THIRD SESSION.

*Be it enacted, &c.,* That the word "white," wherever it occurs in the laws relating to the District of Columbia, or in the charter or ordinances of the cities of Washington or Georgetown, and operates as a limitation on the right of any elector of such District, or of either of the cities, to hold any office, or to be selected and to serve as a juror, be, and the same is hereby, repealed; and it shall be unlawful for any person or officer to enforce or attempt to enforce said limitation after the passage of this act.

IN HOUSE.

March 2—It passed, without a call of the yeas and nays.

March 3—It was presented to the President (Johnson), and "pocketed."

FORTY-FIRST CONGRESS, FIRST SESSION.

March 8—The SENATE passed the same bill, without a division.

March 16—The HOUSE passed it—yeas 111, nays 46, (not voting 39,) as follow:

YEAS—Messrs. Ambler, Armstrong, Arnell, Asper, Bailey, Banks, Beaman, Beatty, Benjamin, Benton, Bingham, Blair, Boles, Boyd, Buffinton, Burdett, Benjamin F Butler, Roderick R. Butler, Cessna, Churchill, Clarke, Amasa Cobb, Clinton L. Cobb, Conger, Cullom, Davis, Dawes, Deweese, Dockery, Donley, Duval, Dyer, Ela, Ferriss, Ferry, Finkelnburg, Fisher, Fitch, Garfield, Gilfillan, Hale, Heaton, Hoar, Hooper, Hopkins, Hotchkiss, Ingersoll, Jenckes, Alexander H. Jones, Judd, Julian, Kelley, Kelsey, Ketcham. Knapp, Laflin, Lash, Lawrence, Loughridge, Maynard. McCarthy, McCrary, McGrew, Mercur, Eliakim H. Moore, Jesse H. Moore, William Moore, Morrell, Morrill, Negley, O'Neill, Orth, Packard, Paine, Palmer, Peters, Phelps, Poland, Pomeroy, Prosser, Roots, Sanford, Sargent, Sawyer, Schenck, Scofield, Shanks, John A. Smith, William J. Smith, William Smyth, Stevenson, Stokes, Stoughton, Strickland, Taffe, Tanner, Tillman, Townsend, Twichell, Tyner, Upson, Van Horn, Cadwalader C. Washburn, William B. Washburn, Welker, Wheeler, Whittemore, Wilkinson, Willard, Williams, Winans—111.

NAYS—Messrs. Archer, *Axtell*, Beck, *Biggs, Bird, Brooks, Burr, Calkin, Crebs, Dickinson, Eldridge, Getz, Golladay, Haight, Haldeman, Hamill, Holman, Johnson, Thomas L. Jones, Knott, Marshall, Mayham, McCormick, McNeely, Moffet, Morgan, Mungen, Niblack, Potter, Reading, Reeves, Rice, Slocum, Joseph S. Smith, Stone, Strader, Swann, Sweeney, Trimble, Van Auken, Van Trump, Wells, Eugene M. Wilson, Winchester,* Witcher, *Wood—46.*

The bill was approved by President Grant, March 18, 1869.

---

## BILL TO STRENGTHEN THE PUBLIC CREDIT.

### Fortieth Congress.

IN HOUSE.

1869, February 24—This bill passed:

AN ACT to strengthen the public credit, and relating to contracts for the payment of coin.

*Be it enacted, &c.,* That in order to remove any doubt as to the purpose of the Government to discharge all just obligations to the public creditors, and to settle conflicting questions and interpretations of the laws by virtue of which such obligations have been contracted, it is hereby provided and declared, that the faith of the United States is solemnly pledged to the payment in coin, or its equivalent, of all the interest-bearing obligations of the United States, except in cases where the law authorizing the issue of any such obligation has expressly provided that the same may be paid in lawful money or other currency than gold and silver: *Provided, however,* That before any of said interest-bearing obligations not already due shall mature, or be paid before maturity, the obligations not bearing interest, known as United States notes. shall be made convertible into coin at the option of the holder.

SEC. 2. That any contract hereafter made specifically payable in coin, and the consideration of which may be a loan of coin, or a sale of property, or the rendering of labor or service of any kind, the price of which, as carried into the contract, may have been adjusted on the basis of the coin value thereof at the time of such sale or the rendering of such service or labor, shall be legal and valid, and may be enforced according to its terms; and on the trial of a suit brought for the enforcement of any such contract, proof of the real consideration may be given.

Yeas 121, nays 60, (not voting 41,) as follow:

YEAS—Messrs. Allison, Ames, Anderson, Arnell, Delos R. Ashley, James M. Ashley, *Axtell*, Baldwin, Banks,

Barnum,Beaman,Benjamin, Benton, Blackburn, Blaine, Blair, Boyden, *Boyer*, *Brooks*, Broomall, Buckley, Callis, *Chanler*, Churchill, Reader W. Clarke, Sidney Clarke, Clift, Corley, Cornell, Cullom, Dawes, Delano, Dixon, Dodge, Driggs, Eckley, Thomas D. Eliot, James T. Elliott, Ferriss, Ferry, Fields, Garfield, *Getz*, *Glossbrenner*, Gove, Griswold, Halsey, Harding, Heaton, Higby, Hill, Hooper, *Hotchkiss*, Chester D. Hubbard, *Richard D. Hubbard*, Hulburd, Jenckes, Alexander H. Jones, Judd, Julian, Kellogg, Kelsey, Ketcham, Kitchen, Koontz, Laflin, Lash, George V. Lawrence, Lynch, Marvin, Maynard, McKee, Mercur, Miller, Moore, Moorhead, Morrell, Mullins, Myers, Newcomb, Newsham, Norris, O'Neill, Paine, Perham, Peters, Pettis, *Phelps*, Plants, Poland, Pomeroy, Price, Raum, Robertson, *Robinson*, Roots. Sawyer, Schenck, Scofield, Shellabarger, Smith, Spalding, Starkweather, Stewart, Stover, *Taber*, Taylor, Trowbridge, Twichell, Upson, Van Aernam, Burt Van Horn, Robert T. Van Horn, Ward, Cadwalader C. Washburn, William B. Washburn, Welker, Whittemore, Thomas Williams, James F. Wilson, Windom—121.

Nays—Messrs. *Archer*, Baker, Beatty, *Beck*, Bowen, *Burr*, Benjamin F. Butler, Roderick R. Butler, Cake, *Cobb*, Coburn, Cook, Covode, Deweese, Donnelly, Eggleston, Ela, *Eldridge*, Farnsworth, *Fox*, French, *Golladay*, Goss, *Grover*, *Haight*, Hawkins, *Holman*, Hopkins, *Humphrey*, Hunter, Ingersoll, *Johnson*, *Thomas L. Jones*, Kelley, *Kerr*, *Knott*, William Lawrence, Loughridge, *Marshall*, *McCormick*, *Mungen*, *Niblack*, Nunn, Orth, Pike, *Ross*, Shanks, Stevens, Stokes, *Stone*, Taffe, Thomas, *Tift*, *Van Trump*, Henry D. Washburn, William Williams, John T. Wilson, *Wood*, *Young*—60.

Pending the passage,

Mr. Niblack moved to strike out the first section, which was lost—yeas 54, nays 130, (not voting 38,) as follow :

Yeas—Messrs. *Archer*, Baker, *Barnes*, Beatty, *Beck*, Bowen, *Burr*, Roderick R. Butler, Cobb, Coburn, Deweese, Donnelly, Eggleston, Ela, *Eldridge*, Farnsworth, *Fox*, *Getz*, *Golladay*, Goss, Gravely, *Grover*, *Haight*, Hawkins, *Holman*, Hopkins, *Humphrey*, Hunter, Ingersoll, *Johnson*, *Thomas L. Jones*, *Kerr*, *Knott*, Loan, *Marshall*, *McCormick*, *Mungen*, *Niblack*, Orth, Pike, *Pruyn*, *Ross*, Shanks, Stevens, Stokes, *Stone*, Taffe, *Tift*, *Van Auken*, *Van Trump*, Henry D. Washburn, John T. Wilson, *Wood*, *Young*—54.

Nays—Messrs. Allison, Ames, Anderson, Arnell, Delos R. Ashley, James M. Ashley, *Axtell*, Baldwin, Banks, *Barnum*, Beaman, Benjamin, Benton, Bingham, Blackburn, Blaine, Blair, Boutwell, Boyden, *Boyer* Bromwell, *Brooks*, Broomall, Buckley, Cake, *Chanler*, Churchill, Reader W. Clarke, Sidney Clarke, Clift, Corley, Cornell, Covode, Cullom, Delano, Dickey, Dixon, Dockery, Dodge, Driggs, Eckley, Thomas D. Eliot, James T. Elliott, Ferriss, Ferry, Fields, *Glossbrenner*, Gove, Griswold, Halsey, Harding, Heaton, Higby, Hill, Hooper, *Hotchkiss*, Chester D. Hubbard, *Richard D. Hubbard*, Hulburd, Jenckes, Alexander H. Jones, Judd, Julian, Kelley, Kellogg, Kelsey, Ketcham, Kitchen, Koontz, Laflin, Lash, George V. Lawrence, William Lawrence, Logan, Lynch, Mallory, Marvin, Maynard, McKee, Mercur, Miller, Moore, Moorhead, Mullins, Myers, Newsham, Norris, O'Neill, Paine, Perham, Peters, Pettis, *Phelps*, Pierce, Pile, Plants, Poland, Pomeroy, Price, Prince, Raum, Robertson, Roots, Sawyer, Schenck, Scofield, Shellabarger, Smith, Spalding, Starkweather, Stewart, Stover, Taber, Taylor, Thomas, Trimble, Trowbridge, Twichell, Upson, Van Aernam, Burt Van Horn, Ward, Cadwalader C. Washburn, William B. Washburn, Welker, Whittemore, Thomas Williams, William Williams, James F. Wilson, Windom—130.

Mr. Allison moved to strike out the second section, which was lost—yeas 72, nays 100, (not voting 50,) as follow :

Yeas—Messrs. Allison, Baker, Beatty, *Beck*, Benton, Bowen, Bromwell, Benjamin F. Butler, Cake, Clift, Cobb, Coburn, Cook, Cornell, Cullom, Deweese, Dickey, Donnelly, Eckley, Ela, *Eldridge*, Farnsworth, Ferriss, Ferry, *Fox*, *Golladay*, Goss, Gravely, Hawkins, *Holman*, Hooper, Hopkins, Hunter, Ingersoll, Kelley, Kelsey, *Knott*, Koontz, William Lawrence, Loan, Loughridge, Lynch, Maynard, Miller, Moore, Morrell, Mullins, *Mungen*, Myers, *Niblack*, Nunn, O'Neill, Orth, Peters, Robertson, *Ross*, Sawyer, Shanks, Shellabarger, Smith, Stevens, Stokes, Taffe, Thomas, *Tift*, Upson, *Van Trump*, Henry D. Washburn, Thomas Williams, William Williams, John T. Wilson, *Young*—72.

Nays—Messrs. Ames, Anderson, *Archer*, Arnell, Delos R. Ashley, James M. Ashley, *Axtell*, Baldwin, Banks,

Barnes, *Barnum*, Beaman, Benjamin, Blackburn, Blair, Boyden, *Boyer*, *Brooks*, Broomall, Buckley, Roderick R. Butler, Callis, *Chanler*, Churchill, Reader W. Clarke, Corley, Covode, Dawes, Delano, Dixon, Dodge, Driggs, Edwards. Thomas D. Eliot, James T. Elliott, Fields, *Getz*, *Glossbrenner*, Gove, Griswold, *Grover*, *Haight*, Halsey, Harding, Heaton, *Hotchkiss*, Chester D. Hubbard, *Richard D. Hubbard*, Hulburd, Jenckes, *Johnson*, Alexander H. Jones, *Thomas L. Jones*, Judd, Julian, *Kerr*, Ketcham, Kitchen, Laflin, Lash, George V. Lawrence, Mallory, Marvin, McCormick, McKee, Mercur, Moorhead, Newsham, Norris, Paine, Perham, *Phelps*, Pierce, Pike, Plants, Poland, Pomeroy, Price, *Pruyn*, Raum, Schenck, Scofield, Spalding, Starkweather, Stewart, *Stone*, Stover, *Taber*, Taylor, Trowbridge, Twichell, Van Aernam, *Van Auken*, Burt Van Horn, Hamilton, Ward, William B. Washburn, Welker, Whittemore, James F. Wilson, *Wood*—100.

### In Senate.

February 26—The bill was reported back from the Committee on Finance, amended so as to read as follows :

An Act relating to the public debt.

*Be it enacted, &c.*, That in order to remove any doubt as to the purpose of the Government to discharge all just obligations to the public creditors, and to settle conflicting questions and interpretations of the laws by virtue of which such obligations have been contracted, it is hereby provided and declared, that the faith of the United States is solemnly pledged to the payment in coin, or its equivalent, of all the obligations of the United States, except in cases where the law authorizing the issue of any such obligation has expressly provided that the same may be paid in lawful money or other currency than gold and silver.

Sec. 2. That any contract hereafter made specifically payable in coin, and the consideration of which may be a loan of coin, or a sale of property, or the rendering of labor or service of any kind, the price of which, as carried into the contract, may have been adjusted on the basis of the coin value thereof at the time of such sale or the rendering of such service or labor, shall be legal and valid, and may be enforced according to its terms.

February 27—Mr. Henderson moved to amend the first clause of the second section by making it read as follow :

That any contract hereafter made specifically payable in coin shall be legal and valid, and may be enforced according to its terms.

Which was not agreed to—yeas 10, nays 35, as follow :

Yeas—Messrs. Cole, Conkling, Corbett, *Dixon*, Fessenden, Henderson, Pomeroy, Ross, Stewart, Trumbull—10.

Nays—Messrs. Abbott, Anthony, Cameron, Cattell, Chandler, Conness, Cragin, *Davis*, *Doolittle*, Drake, Edmunds, Ferry, Frelinghuysen, Harlan, Howe, Kellogg, *McCreery*, McDonald, Morgan, Morrill of Vermont, Morton, Nye, Osborn, Patterson of New Hampshire, Ramsey, Rice, Sawyer, Sherman, Sumner, Thayer, Wade, Welch, Willey, Williams, Wilson—35.

Mr. Bayard moved to strike out the second section, which was not agreed to—yeas 7, nays 36, as follow :

Yeas—Messrs. Chandler, Cole, *Davis*, *Doolittle*, Fowler, Howe, Wade—7.

Nays—Messrs. Abbott, Anthony, Cameron, Cattell, Conkling, Conness, Corbett, Cragin, *Dixon*, Drake, Edmunds, Ferry, Fessenden, Frelinghuysen, Harlan, Kellogg, *McCreery*, McDonald, Morgan, Morrill of Vermont, Morton, Nye, Osborn, Patterson of New Hampshire, Pomeroy, Ramsey, Ross, Sherman, Stewart, Sumner, Thayer, Trumbull, Welch, Willey, Williams, Wilson—36.

Mr. Henderson moved to amend the first section so as to make it read as follows:

That it is hereby provided and declared that the faith of the United States is solemnly pledged to an early resumption of specie payment by the Government in order that conflicting questions touching the mode of discharging the public indebtedness may be settled and that the same may be paid in gold.

Which was not agreed to—yeas 8, nays 34, as follow:

YEAS—Messrs. Cole, *Davis*, Henderson, Morton, Pomeroy, Robertson, Ross, Spencer—8.

NAYS—Anthony, Cattell, Conkling, Conness, Corbett, Cragin, *Dixon*, Edmunds, Ferry, Fessenden, Frelinghuysen, Grimes, Harlan, Harris, Howard, McDonald, Morgan, Morrill of Maine, Morrill of Vermont, Nye, Osborn, Patterson of New Hampshire, Sawyer, Sherman, Stewart, Sumner, Thayer, Tipton, Wade, Warner, Welch, Willey, Williams, Wilson—34.

The bill, as amended by the report of the Committee on Finance, was then passed—yeas 30, nays 16, as follow:

YEAS—Messrs. Abbott, Cattell, Conkling, Conness, Corbett, Cragin, *Dixon*, Edmunds, Ferry, Fessenden, Frelinghuysen, Grimes, Harlan, Harris, Howard, Morgan, Morrill of Maine, Morrill of Vermont, Nye, Patterson of New Hampshire, Robertson, Sawyer, Sherman, Stewart, Sumner, Thayer, Tipton, Willey, Williams, Wilson—30.

NAYS—Messrs. Cole, *Davis, Doolittle*, Fowler, Henderson, *Hendricks, McCreery*, McDonald, Morton, Osborn, *Patterson* of Tennessee, Pomeroy, Ross, Spencer, Wade, Welch—16.

The title was amended so as to read "An act in relation to the public debt."

March 2—The House non-concurred in the amendments of the Senate, and a committee of conference (Messrs. Schenck, Allison, and Niblack) appointed.

Same day—The Senate insisted on its amendments, and appointed Messrs. Sherman, Williams, and Morton a conference committee.

March 3—The committee reported the following bill:

AN ACT to strengthen the public credit, and relating to contracts for the payment of coin.

*Be it enacted, &c.*, That in order to remove any doubt as to the purpose of the Government to discharge all just obligations to the public creditors, and to settle conflicting questions and interpretations of the laws by virtue of which such obligations have been contracted, it is hereby provided and declared, that the faith of the United States is solemnly pledged to the payment in coin, or its equivalent, of all the obligations of the United States not bearing interest, known as United States notes, and of all the interest-bearing obligations of the United States, except in cases where the law authorizing the issue of any such obligation has expressly provided that the same may be paid in lawful money or other currency than gold and silver. But none of said interest-bearing obligations not already due shall be redeemed or paid before maturity, unless at such time United States notes shall be convertible into coin at the option of the holder, or unless at such time bonds of the United States bearing a lower rate of interest than the bonds to be redeemed can be sold at par in coin. And the United States also solemnly pledges its faith to make provision at the earliest practicable period for the redemption of the United States notes in coin.

SEC. 2. That any contract hereafter made specifically payable in coin, and the consideration of which may be a loan of coin, or a sale of property, or the rendering of labor or service of any kind, the price of which, as carried into the contract, may have been adjusted on the basis of the coin value thereof at the time of such sale or the rendering of such service or labor, shall be legal and valid, and may be enforced according to its terms; and on the trial of a suit brought for the enforcement of any such contract, proof of the real consideration may be given.

Same day—The Senate agreed to the report—yeas 31, nays 24, as follow:

YEAS—Messrs. Abbott, Anthony, Cameron, Cattell, Chandler, Conkling, Conness, Corbett, Cragin, *Dixon*, Drake, Edmunds, Ferry, Fessenden, Frelinghuysen, Harris, Howard, Morgan, Morrill of Maine, Morrill of Vermont, Nye, Patterson of New Hampshire, Ramsey, Sherman, Stewart, Sumner, Trumbull, Van Winkle, Warner, Willey, Williams—31.

NAYS—Messrs. *Bayard, Buckalew*, Cole, *Davis, Doolittle*, Fowler, *Hendricks*, Kellogg, *McCreery*, McDonald, Morton, *Norton*, Osborn, *Patterson* of Tennessee, Robertson, Ross, Sawyer, Spencer, Sprague, Thayer, Tipton, *Vickers*, Wade, *Whyte*—24.

Same day—The House adopted the report—yeas 117, nays 59, (not voting 48,) as follow:

YEAS—Messrs. Allison, Ames, Arnell, Delos R. Ashley, James M. Ashley, *Axtell*, Bailey, *Barnes, Barnum*, Beaman, Benjamin, Benton, Bingham, Blair, Boutwell, Bowen, Boyden, *Brooks*, Broomall, Buckley, Cake, Callis, *Chanler*, Churchill, Reader W. Clarke, Sidney Clarke, Clift, Corley, Cornell, Cullom, Dawes, Dickey, Dixon, Dodge, Eckley, Thomas D. Eliot, James T. Elliott, Ferriss, Ferry, Fields, Garfield, Gove, Griswold, Halsey, Haughey, Heaton, Higby, Hill, Hooper, *Hotchkiss, Richard D. Hubbard*, Hulburd, Jenckes, Alexander H Jones, Judd, Julian, Kellogg, Kelsey, Ketcham, Laflin, Lash, George V. Lawrence, Lincoln, Logan, Lynch, Mallory, Marvin, Maynard, McCarthy, McKee, Mercur, Miller, Moore, Moorhead, Morrell, Mullins, Myers, Newsham, Norris, O'Neill, Paine, Perham, Peters, *Phelps*, Pile, Plants, Poland, Price, Prince, Raum, Robertson, *Robinson*, Roots, Sawyer, Schenck, Scofield, Shellabarger, Smith, Starkweather, Stevens, Stewart, Stover, Sypher, *Taber*, Taylor, Trowbridge, Twichell, Upson, Burt Van Horn, Van Wyck, Ward, Cadwalader C. Washburn, William B. Washburn, Welker, Whittemore, James F. Wilson, Woodbridge—117.

NAYS—Messrs. *Adams, Archer*, Baker, Beatty, *Beck, Boyer*, Bromwell, *Burr*, Benjamin F. Butler, Roderick R. Butler, *Cary*, Cobb, Coburn, Cook, Deweese, Dockery, Donnelly, Eggleston, *Eldridge*, Farnsworth, *Getz, Golladay*, Goss, *Haight*, Harding, Hawkins, *Holman*, Hopkins, Hunter, Ingersoll, *Johnson, Thomas L. Jones, Kerr, Knott*, William Lawrence, *Marshall, McCormick, McCullough, Mungen, Niblack*, Orth, *Pruyn, Randall, Ross*, Shanks, *Sitgreaves, Stone*, Thomas, *Tift, Trimble*, Van Aernam, *Van Auken, Van Trump*, Henry D. Washburn, William Williams, Stephen F. Wilson, *Wood, Woodward, Young*—59.

The President (Johnson) "pocketed" the bill.

[For other votes on this subject in first session, Forty-First Congress, see a subsequent chapter.]

### TENURE-OF-OFFICE ACT.

#### Fortieth Congress, Third Session.

##### IN HOUSE.

1869, January 11—A bill to repeal an act regulating the tenure of certain civil offices, passed March 2, 1867,[*] was introduced by Mr. H. D. Washburn, and read a first and second time. The previous question on the engrossment of the

---

[*] For copy of the act, and votes on passage, see Political Manual for 1867, pp. 50, 51; and Hand Book of Politics, pp. 176, 177.

bill was ordered—yeas 116, nays 47; and the bill was ordered engrossed, and was read a third time. It was then passed—yeas 121, nays 47, not voting 53, as follow:

YEAS—Messrs. Allison, Anderson, *Axtell*, Bailey, Baldwin, Banks, *Barnum*, Beaman, *Beck*, Bingham, Blaine, Blair, Boutwell, Bowen, Boyden, Buckley, *Burr*, Benjamin F. Butler, Roderick R. Butler, Callis, *Cary*, *Chanler*, Reader W. Clarke, Sidney Clarke, Clift, Cobb, Coburn, Cook, Corley, Cornell, Cullom, Dawes, Deweese, Dixon, Driggs, Eckley, *Eldridge*, Thomas D. Eliot, Fields, *Fox*, *Getz*, *Glossbrenner*, *Golladay*, Goss, Gove, Griswold, *Grover*, *Haight*, Halsey, Haughey, Heaton, Hooper, Hopkins, *Hotchkiss*, *Humphrey*, Hunter, Ingersoll, *Johnson*, Alexander H. Jones, *Thomas L. Jones*, Judd, Julian, Kelley, Kellogg, *Kerr*, Ketcham, *Knott*, Lash, George V. Lawrence, Lincoln, Loughridge, Mallory, Marvin, *McCormick*, *McCullough*, Miller, *Mungen*, Newcomb, *Niblack*, *Nicholson*, Norris, O'Neill, Paine, Peters, Pettis, *Phelps*, Plants, Price, Prince, Robertson, *Robinson*, Roots, Sawyer, Scofield, *Sitgreaves*, Spalding, Starkweather, Stevens, Stewart, *Stone*, Stover, Sypher, *Taber*, Thomas, *Tift*, *Trimble*, Trowbridge, Twichell, *Van Auken*, *Van Trump*, Vidal, Ellihu B. Washburne, Henry D. Washburn, William Williams, James F. Wilson, John T. Wilson, Stephen F. Wilson, Windom, Woodbridge, *Woodward*, *Young*—121.

NAYS—Messrs. Ames, Arnell, Delos R. Ashley, Baker, Beatty, Benjamin, Benton, Boles, Bromwell, Buckland, Churchill, Delano, Ela, Farnsworth, Ferriss, French, Garfield, Harding, Higby, Jenckes, Kelsey, Kitchen, Laflin, Maynard, McCarthy, McKee, Mercur, Moore, Moorhead, Morrell, Mullins, Newsham, Perham, Pike, Poland, Polsley, Pomeroy, Schenck, Shanks, Shellabarger, Stokes, Taffe, John Trimble, Upson, Ward, Welker, Whittemore—47.

NOT VOTING—Messrs. *Adams*, *Archer*, James M. Ashley, *Barnes*, Blackburn, *Boyer*, *Brooks*, Broomall, Cake, Covode, Dickey, Dockery, Dodge, Donnelly, Edwards, Eggleston, Ferry, Gravely, Hamilton, Hawkins, Hill, *Holman*, Asahel W. Hubbard, Chester D. Hubbard, *Richard D. Hubbard*, Hulburd, Koontz, William Lawrence, Loan, Logan, Lynch, *Marshall*, *Morrissey*, Myers, Nunn, Orth, Pierce, Pile, *Pruyn*, *Randall*, Raum, *Ross*, Selye, Smith, Taylor, Van Aernam, Burt Van Horn, Robert T. Van Horn, Van Wyck, Cadwalader C. Washburn, William B. Washburn, Thomas Williams, *Wood*—53.

## IN SENATE.

No direct vote was reached on the above bill in the Senate. And pending the legislative appropriation bill—

March 2—Mr. Morton moved as an additional section the House repealing bill.

Mr. Sumner offered the following substitute for that amendment:

That the first section of the act entitled "An act regulating the tenure of certain civil offices," passed March 2, 1867, is hereby amended so as to read as follows: " That every person holding any civil office to which he has been appointed by and with the advice and consent of the Senate, and every person who shall hereafter be appointed to any such office and shall become duly qualified to act therein, is and shall be entitled to hold such office until a successor shall have been in like manner appointed and duly qualified, except as herein otherwise provided.

" SEC. —. That the second section of such act is hereby amended so as to read as follows: That it shall be lawful for the President, whenever, during a recess of the Senate, in his opinion the public good shall require it, to suspend any officer appointed as aforesaid, excepting judges of the United States courts, and to designate some suitable person to perform temporarily the duties of such office until the next meeting of the Senate, and until the matter shall be acted upon by the Senate; and such person so designated shall take the oaths and give the bonds required by law to be taken and given by the person duly appointed

to fill such office; and in case of such suspension, it shall be the duty of the President, within twenty days after the first day of such next meeting of the Senate, to report to the Senate such suspension, with the name of the person so designated to perform the duties of such office; and if the Senate shall concur in such suspension, and advise and consent to the removal of such officer, they shall so certify to the President, who may thereupon remove such officer, and, by and with the advice and consent of the Senate, appoint another person to such office; but if the Senate shall refuse to concur in such suspension the officer so suspended shall forthwith resume the functions of his office, and the powers of the person so performing its duties in his stead shall cease; and the official salary and emoluments of such officer shall during such suspension belong to the person so performing the duties thereof and not to the officer so suspended: *Provided,* however, that the President may, in his discretion, before reporting such suspension to the Senate as above provided, revoke the same, and reinstate such officer in the performance of the duties of his office.

" SEC. —. That no person shall hold nor shall he receive salary or compensation for performing the duties of more than one office or place of trust or profit under the Constitution or laws of the United States at the same time, whether such office or place be civil, military, or naval; and any person holding any such office or place who shall accept or hold any other office or place of trust or profit under the Constitution or laws of the United States shall be deemed to have vacated the office or place which he held at the time of such acceptance.

"SEC. —. That nothing in the foregoing section shall be construed to prevent such designations or appointments of officers to perform temporarily the duties of other officers as are or may be authorized by law, nor to prevent such appointments or designations to office or duty as are required by law to be made from the army or navy.

" SEC. —. That the penalties provided in the act to which this is an amendment shall apply to violations of this act.

Which was not agreed to—yeas 17, nays 32, as follow:

YEAS—Messrs. Chandler, Conkling, Cragin, Harlan, Harris, Howard, Howe, Morrill of Maine, Morrill of Vermont, Patterson of New Hampshire, Ramsey, Sawyer, Sprague, Sumner, Welch, Willey, Williams—17.

NAYS—Messrs. Abbott, Cameron, Cattell, Cole, Conness, Corbett, *Dixon*, Drake, Ferry, Frelinghuysen, Grimes, Henderson, McDonald, Morgan, Morton, Nye, Osborn, Pomeroy, Pool, Robertson, Ross, Sherman, Spencer, Thayer, Tipton, Trumbull, Van Winkle, *Vickers*, Wade, Warner, *Whyte*, Wilson—32.

The amendment offered by Mr. Morton was then disagreed to—yeas 22, nays 26, as follow:

YEAS—Messrs. Cole, Conness, *Dixon*, Drake, Grimes, Henderson, Kellogg, McDonald, Morgan, Morton, Osborn, Pomeroy, Pool, Ramsey, Robertson, Ross, Sherman, Thayer, Van Winkle, *Vickers*, Warner, *Whyte*—22.

NAYS—Messrs. Abbott, Anthony, Cameron, Chandler, Corbett, Cragin, Ferry, Frelinghuysen, Harlan, Harris, Howard, Howe, Morrill of Maine, Morrill of Vermont, Patterson of New Hampshire, Sawyer, Spencer, Sprague, Sumner, Tipton, Trumbull, Wade, Welch, Willey, Williams, Wilson—26.

[For further votes on this subject, see a subsequent chapter.]

# XL.

## XVTH CONSTITUTIONAL AMENDMENT.

A RESOLUTION proposing an amendment to the Constitution of the United States.

*Resolved by the Senate and House of Representatives of the United States of America in Congress assembled,* (two-thirds of both houses concurring,) That the following article be proposed to the legislatures of the several States as an amendment to the Constitution of the United States, which, when ratified by three-fourths of said legislatures, shall be valid as part of the Constitution, namely:

### ARTICLE XV.

SEC. 1. The right of citizens of the United States to vote shall not be denied or abridged by the United States or by any State on account of race, color, or previous condition of servitude.

SEC. 2. The Congress shall have power to enforce this article by appropriate legislation.

SCHUYLER COLFAX,
*Speaker of the House of Representatives.*
B. F. WADE,
*President of the Senate pro tempore.*
Attest:
EDWD. MCPHERSON,
*Clerk of House of Representatives.*
GEO. C. GORHAM,
*Secretary of Senate United States.*

### The Final Vote

#### IN SENATE.

1869, February 26—The report of the committee of conference, recommending the passage of the amendment as printed above was agreed to—yeas 39, nays 13, as follow:

YEAS—Messrs. Anthony, Cattell, Chandler, Cole, Conkling, Conness, Cragin, Drake, Ferry, Fessenden, Frelinghuysen, Harlan, Harris, Howard, Howe, Kellogg, McDonald, Morgan, Morrill of Maine, Morrill of Vermont, Morton, Nye, Osborn, Patterson of New Hampshire, Ramsey, Rice, Robertson, Sherman, Stewart, Thayer, Tipton, Trumbull, Van Winkle, Wade, Warner, Welch, Willey, Williams, Wilson—39.

NAYS—Messrs. *Bayard, Buckalew, Davis, Dixon, Doolittle,* Fowler, *Hendricks, McCreery, Norton, Patterson* of Tennessee, Pool, *Vickers, Whyte*—13.

February 25—The House concurred—yeas 144, nays 44, (not voting 35,) as follow:

YEAS—Messrs. Allison, Ames, Anderson, Arnell, Delos R. Ashley, James M. Ashley, Bailey, Baker, Banks, Beaman, Beatty, Benjamin, Benton, Bingham, Blaine, Blair, Boutwell, Bowen, Boyden, Bromwell, Broomall, Buckley, Benjamin F. Butler, Roderick R. Butler, Callis, Churchill, Reader W. Clarke, Sidney Clarke, Clift, Cobb, Coburn, Cook, Corley, Cornell, Covode, Cullom, Dawes, Dickey, Dodge, Donnelly, Driggs, Eckley, Eggleston, Ela, Thomas D. Eliot, James T. Elliott, Farnsworth, Ferriss, Ferry, Fields, French, Garfield, Goss, Gove, Gravely, Griswold, Hamilton, Harding, Haughey, Heaton, Higby, Hill, Hooper, Hopkins, Chester D. Hubbard, Hulburd, Hunter, Ingersoll, Jenckes, Alexander H. Jones, Judd, Julian, Kelley, Kellogg, Kelsey, Ketcham, Kitchen, Koontz, Laflin, Lash, William Lawrence, Logan, Lynch, Marvin, Maynard, McCarthy, McKee, Mercur, Miller, Moore, Moorhead, Morrell, Mullins, Myers, Newsham, Norris, Nunn, O'Neill, Orth,

Paine, Perham, Peters, Pettis, Pike, Plants, Poland, Pomeroy, Price, Prince, Raum, Robertson, Roots, Sawyer, Scofield, Shanks, Shellabarger, Smith, Spalding, Starkweather, Stevens, Stewart, Stokes, Stover, Taffe, Thomas, Trimble, Trowbridge, Twichell, Upson, Van Aernam, Burt Van Horn, Robert T. Van Horn, Ward, Cadwalder C. Washburn, Henry D. Washburn, William B. Washburn, Welker, Whittemore, Thomas Williams, William Williams, James F. Wilson, John T. Wilson, Windom, Mr. Speaker Colfax—144.

NAYS—Messrs. *Archer, Axtell, Barnes, Beck, Boyer, Brooks, Burr, Cary, Chanler, Eldridge, Fox, Getz, Glossbrenner, Golladay, Grover, Haight,* Hawkins, *Holman, Hotchkiss, Richard D. Hubbard, Humphrey,* Johnson, *Thomas L. Jones, Kerr, Knott,* Loughridge, Mallory, Marshall, *McCormick, McCullough, Mungen, Niblack, Nicholson, Phelps, Pruyn, Robinson, Ross, Stone, Taber, Van Auken, Van Trump, Wood, Woodward, Young*—44.

This subject engaged a large share of attention during the third session of the Fortieth Congress. The various votes and proceedings upon it are subjoined in the order of the date of occurrence.

### The House Joint Resolution, (H. R. 402.)

#### IN HOUSE.

1869, January 30—The House passed the amendment in these words:

JOINT RESOLUTION proposing an amendment to the Constitution of the United States.

*Be it resolved by the Senate and House of Representatives of the United States of America in Congress assembled,* (two-thirds of both houses concurring,) That the following article be proposed to the legislatures of the several States as an amendment to the Constitution of the United States, which, when ratified by three-fourths of said legislatures, shall be held as part of said Constitution, namely:

#### ARTICLE —

SEC. 1. The right of any citizen of the United States to vote shall not be denied or abridged by the United States or any State by reason of race, color, or previous condition of slavery of any citizen or class of citizens of the United States.

SEC. 2. The Congress shall have power to enforce by appropriate legislation the provisions of this article.

The vote was yeas 150, nays 42, not voting 31, as follow:

YEAS—Messrs. Allison, Arnell, Delos R. Ashley, James M. Ashley, Bailey, Baldwin, Banks, Beaman, Beatty, Benjamin, Benton, Blackburn, Blaine, Blair, Boles, Boutwell, Bowen, Boyden, Bromwell, Broomall, Buckland, Buckley, Benjamin F. Butler, Cake, Callis, Churchill, Sidney Clarke, Clift, Cobb, Coburn, Cook, Corley, Covode, Cullom, Dawes, Delano, Deweese, Dockery, Dodge, Donnelly, Driggs, Eckley, Edwards, Eggleston, Ela, Thomas D. Eliot, James T. Elliott, Farnsworth, Ferriss, Ferry, Fields, French, Garfield, Goss, Gove, Gravely, Griswold, Halsey, Hamilton, Harding, Haughey, Heaton, Higby, Hooper, Hopkins, Chester D. Hubbard, Hulburd, Hunter, Jenckes, Alexander H. Jones, Judd, Julian, Kelley, Kellogg, Kelsey, Ketcham, Koontz, Laflin, Lash, George V. Lawrence, William Lawrence, Lincoln, Loan, Logan, Loughridge, Lynch, Marvin, Maynard, McKee, Mercur, Miller,

'Moore, Moorhead, Morrell, Mullins, Myers, Newcomb, Newsham, Norris, Nunn, O'Neill, Orth, Paine, Perham, Peters, Pierce, Pike, Pile, Plants, Poland, Price, Prince, Raum, Robertson, Roots, Sawyer, Scofield, Selye. Shanks, Shellabarger, Smith, Spalding, Starkweather, Stewart, Stokes, Stover, Taffe, Taylor, Thomas, John Trimble, Trowbridge, Twichell, Upson, Van Aernam, Burt Van Horn, Robert T. Van Horn, Van Wyck, Ward, Cadwalader C. Washburn, Henry D. Washburn, William B. Washburn, Welker, Whittemore, Thomas Williams, William Williams, James F. Wilson, John T. Wilson, Stephen F. Wilson, Windom, and Mr. Speaker Colfax —150.

NAYS—Messrs. *Archer, Axtell,* Baker, *Barnum, Beck,* Bingham, *Boyer,* Brooks, Burr, *Cary Chanler, Fox, Getz, Golladay, Grover, Haight,* Hawkins, *Hotchkiss, Humphrey, Johnson, Thomas L. Jones, Kerr, Knott, Marshall, McCormick, Mungen, Niblack, Nicholson, Phelps,* Polsley, *Pruyn, Randall, Robinson, Ross, Sitgreaves, Stone, Taber, Tift, Van Auken, Van Trump, Woodward, Young*—42.

NOT VOTING—Messrs. *Adams,* Ames, Anderson, *Barnes,* Roderick R. Butler, Reader W. Clarke, Cornell, Dickey, Dixon, *Eldridge, Glossbrenner,* Hill, *Holman,* Asahel W. Hubbard, *Richard D. Hubbard,* Ingersoll, Kitchen, Mallory, McCarthy, *McCullough, Morrissey,* Pettis, Pomeroy, Schenck, Stevens, Sypher, *Lawrence S. Trimble,* Vidal, Ellihu B. Washburne, *Wood,* Woodbridge—31.

---

### The Previous Votes.

Same day—An amendment by Mr. Bingham, and an amendment to the amendment by Mr, Shellabarger pending, the House voted as follows upon them:

Mr. Bingham's amendment was to substitute the following for the first section of the said joint resolution:

No State shall make or enforce any law which shall abridge or deny to any male citizen of the United States of sound mind and twenty-one years of age or upward the exercise of the elective franchise at all elections in the State wherein he shall have actually resided for a period of one year next preceding such election, (subject to such registration laws and laws prescribing local residence as the State may enact,) except such of said citizens as shall engage in rebellion or insurrection, or who may have been, or shall be, duly convicted of treason or other infamous crimes.

Mr. Shellabarger's amendment to the amendment was to strike out the above, and insert what follows:

No State shall make or enforce any law which shall deny or abridge to any male citizen of the United States of the age of twenty-one years or over, and who is of sound mind, an equal vote at all elections in the State in which he shall have such actual residence as shall be prescribed by law, except to such as have engaged or may hereafter engage in insurrection or rebellion against the United States, and to such as shall be duly convicted of treason, felony, or other infamous crime.

Mr. Shellabarger's amendment to the amendment was disagreed to—yeas 62, nays 125, not voting 35, as follow:

YEAS—Messrs. Delos R. Ashley, Baldwin, Beamen, Beatty, Benton, Boles, Bowen, Broomall, Buckland, Cake, Clift, Cobb, Coburn, Cullom, Dawes, Delano, Eckley, Eggleston, Ela, James T. Elliott, French, Gravely, Hamilton, Hawkins, Hooper, Chester D. Hubbard, Judd, Julian, Kelley, Kelsey, George V. Lawrence, William Lawrence, Loan, Logan, Maynard, Mullins, Newsham, Norris, O'Neill, Orth, Paine, Plants, Polsley, Price, Prince, Sawyer, Schenck, Scofield, Shanks, Shellabarger, Starkweather, Stokes, Sypher, Twichell, Robert T. Van Horn, Ward, Cadwalader C. Washburn, Henry D. Washburn, William B. Washburn, Welker, Whittemore, Thomas Williams—62.

NAYS—Messrs. Allison, *Archer,* Arnell, James M. Ash-

ley, *Axtell,* Bailey, Baker, Banks, *Barnum, Beck,* Benjamin, Bingham, Blaine, Blair, Boutwell, Boyden, *Boyer,* Bromwell, *Brooks, Burr,* Benjamin F. Butler, Callis, *Cary, Chanler,* Churchill, Sidney Clarke, Cook, Corley, Covode, Deweese, Dockery, Dodge, Donnelly, Driggs, Edwards, *Eldridge,* Thomas D. Eliot, Ferriss, Ferry, Fields, *Fox,* Garfield, *Getz, Golladay,* Goss, Gove, Griswold, *Grover, Haight,* Halsey, Harding, Haughey, Heaton, Higby, Hopkins, *Hotchkiss,* Hulburd, *Humphrey,* Hunter, Jenckes, *Johnson,* Alexander H. Jones, *Thomas L. Jones, Kerr,* Ketcham. *Knott,* Koontz, Laflin, Lash, Lincoln, Loughridge, *Marshall,* Marvin, *McCormick, McCullough,* McKee, Mercur, Miller, Moore, Morrell, *Mungen,* Myers, Newcomb, *Niblack, Nicholson,* Nunn, Perham, Peters, *Phelps,* Pierce, Pike, Pile, Poland, *Pruyn, Randall,* Raum, Robertson, *Robinson,* Roots. *Ross, Sitgreaves,* Smith, Spalding, Stewart, *Stone,* Stover, Taber, Taffe, Taylor, Thomas, *Tift,* John Trimble, Trowbridge, Upson, Van Aernam, *Van Auken.* Burt Van Horn, *Van Trump,* Van Wyck, John T. Wilson, Stephen F. Wilson, Windom, Woodbridge, *Woodward, Young*—128.

NOT VOTING—Messrs. *Adams,* Ames, Anderson, *Barnes,* Blackburn, Buckley, Roderick R. Butler, Reader W. Clarke, Cornell, Dickey, Dixon, Farnsworth, *Glossbrenner,* Hill, *Holman.* Asahel W. Hubbard, *Richard D. Hubbard,* Ingersoll, Kellogg, Kitchen, Lynch, Mallory, McCarthy, Moorhead, *Morrissey,* Pettis, Pomeroy, Selye, Stevens, *Lawrence S. Trimble,* Vidal, Ellihu B. Washburne, William Williams, James F. Wilson, *Wood*—35.

The amendment of Mr. Bingham was then disagreed to—yeas 24, nays 160, not voting 38, as follow:

YEAS—Messrs. *Axtell,* Baker, Bingham, *Brooks,* Deweese, Dockery, *Eldridge,* Garfield, *Haight,* Heaton, *Hotchkiss,* Alexander H. Jones, *McCullough, Phelps,* Plants, *Robinson, Ross,* Spalding, Stewart, *Stone, Tift,* John T. Wilson, *Woodward, Young*—24.

NAYS—Messrs. Allison, Arnell, Delos R. Ashley, James M. Ashley, Bailey, Banks, Beaman, Beatty, *Beck,* Benjamin, Benton, Blaine, Blair, Boles, Boutwell, Bowen, Boyden, *Boyer,* Bromwell, Broomall, Buckland, Buckley, *Burr,* Benjamin F. Butler, Cake, Callis, *Cary, Chanler,* Churchill, Sidney Clarke, Clift, Cobb, Coburn, Cook, Corley, Covode, Cullom, Dawes, Delano, Donnelly, Driggs, Eckley, Eggleston, Ela, Thomas D. Eliot, James T. Elliott, Ferriss, Ferry, Fields, *Fox,* French, *Getz, Golladay,* Goss, Gove, Gravely, Griswold, *Grover,* Halsey, Hamilton, Harding, Hawkins, Higby, Hooper, Hopkins, Chester D. Hubbard, Hulburd, *Humphrey,* Hunter, Jenckes, *Johnson, Thomas L. Jones,* Judd, Julian, Kelley, Kellogg, Kelsey, *Kerr,* Ketcham, Koontz, Laflin, Lash, George V. Lawrence, William Lawrence, Lincoln, Loan, Logan, Loughridge, Lynch, *Marshall,* Marvin, Maynard, *McCormick,* McKee, Mercur, Miller, Moore, Moorhead, Morrell, Mullins, *Mungen,* Myers, Newcomb, Newsham, *Niblack, Nicholson,* Norris, Nunn, O'Neill, Orth, Paine, Perham, Peters, Pierce, Pike, Poland, Polsley, Price, Prince, *Pruyn, Randall,* Raum, Robertson, Roots, Sawyer, Schenck, Scofield, Selye, Shanks, Shellabarger, *Sitgreaves,* Smith, Starkweather, Stokes, Stover, Sypher, *Taber,* Taffe, Taylor, Thomas, Trowbridge, Twichell, Upson, Van Aernam, *Van Auken,* Burt Van Horn, Robert T. Van Horn, *Van Trump,* Van Wyck, Ward, Cadwalader C. Washburn, Henry D. Washburn, William B. Washburn, Welker, Whittemore, Thomas Williams, William Williams, Stephen F. Wilson, Windom, Woodbridge—160.

NOT VOTING—Messrs. *Adams,* Ames, Anderson, *Archer,* Baldwin, *Barnes, Barnum,* Blackburn, Roderick R. Butler, Reader W. Clarke, Cornell, Dickey, Dixon, Dodge, Edwards, Farnsworth, *Glossbrenner,* Haughey, Hill, *Holman,* Asahel W. Hubbard, *Richard D. Hubbard,* Ingersoll, Kitchen, *Knott,* Mallory, McCarthy, *Morrissey,* Pettis, Pile, Pomeroy, Stevens, John Trimble, *Lawrence S. Trimble,* Vidal, Ellihu B. Washburne, James F. Wilson, *Wood*—38.

The resolution was then engrossed and read a third time—yeas 144, nays 45, not voting 33, and passed as above.

---

### Proceedings upon it in the Senate

#### IN SENATE.

In Committee of the Whole,

February 3—Mr. Stewart moved to amend by substituting the following in place of the House resolution:

SEC. 1. The right of citizens of the United

States to vote and hold office shall not be denied or abridged by the United States or by any State on account of race, color, or previous condition of servitude.

February 8—Mr. Williams moved to amend the amendment by striking out all after the words " section 1," and inserting:

Congress shall have power to abolish or modify any restrictions upon the right to vote or hold office prescribed by the constitution or laws of any State.

Which was disagreed to.

Mr. Drake moved to substitute for the amendment of Mr. Stewart the following:

No citizen of the United States shall, on account of race, color, or previous condition of servitude be, by the United States or by any State, denied the right to vote or hold office.

Which was disagreed to.

Mr. Howard moved to substitute for the amendment of Mr. Stewart the following:

Citizens of the United States of African descent shall have the same right to vote and hold office in States and Territories as other citizens, electors of the most numerous branch of their respective legislatures.

Which was disagreed to—yeas 16, nays 35, as follow :

Yᴇᴀs—Messsrs. Anthony, Chandler, Cole, Corbett, Cragin, Ferry, Harlan, Howard, Norton, Patterson of New Hampshire, Sumner, Thayer, Tipton, Wade, Welch, Williams—16.

Nᴀʏs—Messrs. Abbott, *Bayard*, *Buckalew*, Cameron, Cattell, *Doolittle*, Drake, Edmunds, Frelinghuysen, Harris, *Hendricks*, Howe, Kellogg, *McCreery*, McDonald, Morgan, Morrill of Maine, Morrill of Vermont, Nye, *Patterson* of Tennessee, Ramsey, Rice, *Saulsbury*, Sawyer, Sherman, Spencer, Stewart, Trumbull, Van Winkle, *Vickers*, Warner, *Whyte*, Willey, Wilson, Yates—35.

Mr. Warner moved to substitute for the amendment of Mr. Stewart the following:

The right of citizens of the United States to hold office shall not be denied or abridged by the United States or any State on account of property, race, color, or previous condition of servitude ; and every male citizen of the United States of the age of twenty-years or over, and who is of sound mind, shall have an equal vote at all elections in the State in which he shall have actually resided for a period of one year next preceding such election, except such as may hereafter engage in insurrection or rebellion against the United States, and such as shall be duly convicted of treason, felony, or other infamous crime.

Which was disagreed to.

February 9—Mr. Wilson moved to amend by substituting the following :

There shall be no discrimination in any State among the citizens of the United States in the exercise of the elective franchise in any election therein, or in the qualifications for office in any State, on account of race, color, nativity, property, education, or religious belief.

Which was disagreed to—yeas 19, nays 24, as follow :

Yᴇᴀs—Messrs. Cattell, Conness, Grimes, Harlan, Harris, Howe, McDonald, Morton, Ramsey, Ross, Sawyer, Sherman, Sumner, Van Winkle, Wade, Welch, Williams, Wilson, Welker—19.

Nᴀʏs—Messrs. Abbott, Anthony, *Bayard*, Cole, Conkling, Corbett, *Davis*, *Dixon*, Fessenden, Fowler, Frelinghuysen, Howard, Morgan, Morrill of Vermont, *Norton*, Nye, *Patterson* of Tennessee, Rice, Robertson, Spencer, Stewart, Trumbull, *Vickers*, Willey—24.

Mr. Sawyer moved to amend by substituting the following :

The right to vote and hold office in the United States and the several States and Territories shall belong to all male citizens cf the United States who are twenty-one years old, and who have not been, and shall not be, duly convicted of treason or other infamous crime: *Provided*, That nothing herein contained shall deprive the several States of the right to make such registration laws as shall be deemed necessary to guard the purity of elections, and to fix the terms of residence which shall precede the exercise of the right to vote : *And provided*, That the United States and the several States shall have the right to fix the age and other qualifications for office under their respective jurisdictions, which said registration laws, terms of residence, age, and other qualifications shall be uniformly applicable to all male citizens of the United States.

Which was disagreed to.

Mr. Henderson moved to add to Mr. Stewart's amendment the following :

Nor shall such right to vote, after the first day of January, 1872, be denied or abridged for offences now committed, unless the party to be affected shall have been duly convicted thereof.

Which was disagreed to.

Mr. Fowler moved to amend by substituting the following :

All the male citizens of the United States, residents of the several States now or hereafter comprehended in the Union, of the age of twenty-one years and upward, shall be entitled to an equal vote in all elections in the State wherein they shall reside, the period of such residence as a qualification for voting to be decided by each State, except such citizens as shall engage in rebellion or insurrection, or shall be duly convicted of treason or other infamous crime.

Which was disagreed to—yeas 9, nays 35, as follow :

Yᴇᴀs—Messrs. *Bayard*, Cragin, *Dixon*, Fowler, *Patterson* of Tennessee, Ross, Sherman, Van Winkle, Wilson—9.

Nᴀʏs—Messrs. Abbott, Anthony, Cattell, Cole, Conkling, Conness, Corbett, *Davis*, Drake, Ferry, Frelinghuysen, Harlan, Harris, Howard, McDonald, Morgan, Morrill of Vermont, Morton, Nye, Patterson of New Hampshire, Pool, Ramsey, Rice, Robertson, Sawyer, Spencer, Stewart, Tipton, Trumbull, *Vickers*, Wade, Welch, Willey, Williams, Yates—35.

On motion of Mr. Conness, the word "or" after the words " United States," where it occurs the second time in the pending amendment, was made to read " nor."

Mr. Vickers moved to add to Mr. Stewart's amendment the following : '

Nor shall the right to vote be denied or abridged because of participation in the recent rebellion.

Which was disagreed to—yeas 21, nays 32, as follow :

Yᴇᴀs—Messrs. *Bayard*, *Buckalew*, *Davis*, *Dixon*, *Doolittle*, Ferry, Fowler, Grimes, Harlan, *Hendricks*, *McCreery*, *Norton*, *Patterson* of Tennessee, Pool, Ramsey, Robertson, Sawyer, Trumbull, Van Winkle, *Vickers*, Wilson—21.

Nᴀʏs—Messrs. Abbott, Anthony, Cattell, Cole, Conkling, Conness, Corbett, Cragin, Drake, Fessenden, Frelinghuysen, Harris, Howard, Howe, Morgan, Morrill of Vermont, Morton, Nye, Patterson of New Hampshire, Rice, Ross, Sherman, Spencer, Stewart, Sumner, Thayer, Tipton, Wade, Welch, Willey, Williams, Yates—32.

Mr. Bayard moved to amend Mr. Stewart's amendment so as to make it read:

The right of citizens of the United States to vote for electors of President and Vice President, and members of the House of Representatives of the United States, and hold office under the United States, shall not be denied or abridged by the United States nor by any State, on account of race, color, or previous condition of servitude.

Which was disagreed to—yeas 12, nays 42, as follow:

YEAS—Messrs. Anthony, *Bayard*, *Buckalew*, *Davis*, *Dixon*, *Doolittle*, Grimes, *Hendricks*, *McCreery*, *Norton*, *Saulsbury*, *Van Winkle*—12.

NAYS—Messrs. Abbott, Cattell, Cole, Conkling, Conness, Corbett, Cragin, Drake, Ferry, Frelinghuysen, Harlan, Harris, Howard, Howe, McDonald, Morgan, Morrill of Maine, Morrill of Vermont, Morton, Nye, Patterson of New Hampshire, Pool, Ramsey, Rice, Robertson, Ross, Sawyer, Sherman, Spencer, Stewart, Sumner, Thayer, Tipton, Trumbull, *Vickers*, Wade, Warner, Welch, Willey, Williams, Wilson, Yates—42.

Mr. Wilson moved to amend Mr. Stewart's amendment by substituting for it the following:

No discrimination shall be made in any State among the citizens of the United States in the exercise of the elective franchise, or in the right to hold office in any State, on account of race, color, nativity, property, education, or creed.

Which was agreed to—yeas 31, nays 27, as follow:

YEAS—Messrs. Abbott, Cameron, Cattell, Conness, Cragin, Ferry, Grimes, Harlan, Harris, *Hendricks*, Howe, McDonald, Morton, Osborn, Pool, Rice, Robertson, Ross, Sawyer, Sherman, Sumner, Thayer, Tipton, Van Winkle, Wade, Warner, Welch, Willey, Williams, Wilson, Yates—31.

NAYS—Messrs. Anthony, *Buckalew*, Chandler, Cole, Conkling, Corbett, *Dixon*, *Doolittle*, Drake, Edmunds, Fessenden, Frelinghuysen, *McCreery*, Morgan, Morrill of Maine, Morrill of Vermont, Nye, Patterson of New Hampshire, *Patterson* of Tennessee, Ramsey, *Saulsbury*, Spencer, Sprague, Stewart, Trumbull, *Vickers*, *Whyte*—27.

The amendment as amended was then agreed to.

Mr. Corbett moved to add to the first section the words:

But Chinamen not born in the United States, and Indians not taxed, shall not be deemed or made citizens.

Which was disagreed to.

Mr. Buckalew moved to add the following new section:

SEC. 3. That the foregoing amendment shall be submitted for ratification to the legislatures of the several States the most numerous branches of which shall be chosen next after the passage of this resolution.

Which was disagreed to—yeas 13, nays 43, as follow:

YEAS—Messrs. Bayard, Buckalew, Davis, Dixon, Doolittle, Fowler, Hendricks, McCreery, Patterson of Tennessee, Saulsbury, Van Winkle, Vickers, Whyte—13.

NAYS—Messrs. Abbott, Cameron, Cattell, Chandler, Cole, Conkling, Conness, Corbett, Cragin, Drake, Edmunds, Ferry, Fessenden, Frelinghuysen, Harlan, Harris, Howe, Morgan, Morrill of Maine, Morrill of Vermont, Morton, Nye, Patterson of New Hampshire, Pool, Ramsey, Rice, Robertson, Ross, Sawyer, Sherman, Spencer, Stewart, Sumner, Thayer, Tipton, Trumbull, Wade, Warner, Welch, Willey, Williams, Wilson, Yates—43.

Mr. Dixon moved to amend so as to refer the amendments to "conventions" in the States instead of the legislatures; which was disagreed to—yeas 11, nays 45, as follow:

YEAS—Messrs. Bayard, Buckalew, Davis, Dixon, Doolittle, Hendricks, McCreery, Patterson of Tennessee, Saulsbury, Vickers, Whyte—11.

NAYS—Messrs. Abbott, Cameron, Cattell, Chandler, Cole, Conkling, Conness, Corbett, Cragin, Drake, Edmunds, Ferry, Fessenden, Frelinghuysen, Harlan, Harris, Howe, Kellogg, McDonald, Morgan, Morrill of Maine, Morrill of Vermont, Nye, Patterson of New Hampshire, Pool, Ramsey, Rice, Robertson, Ross, Sawyer, Sherman, Spencer, Stewart, Sumner, Thayer, Tipton, Trumbull, Van Winkle, Wade, Warner, Welch, Willey, Williams, Wilson, Yates—45.

Mr. Morton moved to amend by adding the following as article XVI:

The second clause, first section, second article of the Constitution of the United States shall be amended to read as follows: Each State shall appoint, by a vote of the people thereof qualified to vote for representatives in Congress, a number of electors equal to the whole number of senators and representatives to which the State may be entitled in the Congress; but no senator or representative, or person holding an office of trust or profit under the United States, shall be appointed an elector; and the Congress shall have power to prescribe the manner in which such electors shall be chosen by the people.

Which was disagreed to—yeas 27, nays 29, as follow:

YEAS—Messrs. *Buckalew*, Cattell, *Dixon*, *Doolittle*, Ferry, Fessenden, Fowler, Grimes, *Hendricks*, Kellogg, McDonald, Morton, Patterson of New Hampshire, Pool, Rice, Ross, Sawyer, Spencer, Van Winkle, *Vickers*, Wade, Warner, Welch, *Whyte*, Willey, Williams, Wilson—27.

NAYS—Messrs. Abbott, Cameron, Chandler, Cole, Conkling, Conness, Corbett, Cragin, *Davis*, Drake, Frelinghuysen, Harlan, Harris, Howe, *McCreery*, Morgan, Morrill of Maine, Morrill of Vermont, Nye, *Patterson* of Tennessee, Ramsey, Robertson, Sherman, Sprague, Stewart, Sumner, Tipton, Trumbull, Yates—29.

Mr. Sumner then moved to strike out all after the enacting clause, and insert as follows:

That the right to vote, to be voted for, and to hold office, shall not be denied or abridged anywhere in the United States under any pretence of race or color; and all provisions in any State constitutions, or in any laws, State, territorial, or municipal, inconsistent herewith, are hereby declared null and void.

SEC. 2. *And be it further enacted,* That any person who, under any pretence of race or color, wilfully hinders or attempts to hinder any citizen of the United States from being registered, or from voting, or from being voted for, or from holding office, or who attempts by menaces to deter any such citizen from the exercise or enjoyment of the rights of citizenship above mentioned, shall be punished by a fine not less than one hundred nor more than three thousand dollars, or by imprisonment in the common jail for not less than thirty days nor more than one year.

SEC. 3. *And be it further enacted,* That every person legally engaged in preparing a register of voters, or in holding or conducting an election, who wilfully refuses to register the name or to receive, count, return, or otherwise give the proper legal effect to the vote of any citizen under any pretence of race or color, shall be punished by a fine not less than five hundred nor more than four thousand dollars, or by imprisonment in the common jail for not less than three calendar months nor more than two years.

SEC. 4. *And be it further enacted,* That the district courts of the United States shall have exclusive jurisdiction of all offences against this act; and the district attorneys, marshals, and deputy marshals, the commissioners appointed by the circuit and territorial courts of the United States, with powers of arresting, imprisoning, or bailing offenders, and every other officer specially empowered by the President of the United States, shall be, and they are hereby, required, at the expense of the United States, to institute proceedings against any person who violates this act, and cause him to be arrested and imprisoned or bailed, as the case may be, for trial before such court as by this act has cognizance of the offence.

SEC. 5. *And be it further enacted,* That every citizen unlawfully deprived of any of the rights of citizenship secured by this act under any pretence of race or color, may maintain a suit against any person so depriving him, and recover damages in the district court of the United States for the district in which such person may be found.

Which was disagreed to—yeas 9, nays 46, as follow:

YEAS—Messrs. Edmunds, McDonald, Nye, Ross, Sumner, Thayer, Wade, Wilson, Yates—9.
NAYS—Messrs. Abbott, Anthony, *Bayard,* Cameron, Chandler, Cole, Conkling, Conness, Corbett, Cragin, *Davis, Dixon, Doolittle,* Drake, Ferry, Fessenden, Fowler, Frelinghuysen, Grimes, Harlan, Harris, *Hendricks,* Howe, *McCreery,* Morgan, Morrill of Maine, Morrill of Vermont, Morton, Patterson of New Hampshire, Pool, Ramsey, Rice, Robertson, *Saulsbury,* Sawyer, Sherman, Spencer, Sprague, Stewart, Trumbull, Van Winkle, *Vickers,* Warner, *Whyte,* Willey, Williams—46.

The resolution was then reported to the Senate, and the question being on concurring in the amendment made in Committee of the Whole,

Mr. Warner moved to substitute for the article adopted in committee the following:

SEC. 1. No State shall make or enforce any law which shall abridge or deny to any male citizen of the United States of sound mind and over twenty-one years of age the equal exercise of the elective franchise at all elections in the State wherein he shall have such actual residence as shall be prescribed by law, except to such of said citizens as have engaged or shall hereafter engage in rebellion or insurrection, or who may have been, or shall be, duly convicted of treason or other crime of the grade of felony at common law, nor shall the right to hold office be denied or abridged on account of race, color, nativity, property, religious belief, or previous condition of servitude.

SEC. 2. The Congress shall have power to enforce this article by appropriate legislation.

Which was disagreed to—yeas 5, nays 47, as follow:

YEAS—Messrs. Conkling, Kellogg, McDonald, Spencer, Warner—5.
NAYS—Messrs. Abbott, Anthony, *Buckalew,* Cameron, Cattell, Chandler, Cole, Conness, Corbett, Cragin, *Davis, Dixon, Doolittle,* Drake, Ferry, Fessenden, Fowler, Frelinghuysen, Harlan, Harris, *Hendricks,* Howe, *McCreery,* Morgan, Morrill of Maine, Morrill of Vermont, Nye, Osborn, *Patterson* of Tennessee, Ramsey, Rice, Robertson, Ross, *Saulsbury,* Sawyer, Sherman, Sprague, Stewart, Thayer, Trumbull, Van Winkle, *Vickers, Whyte,* Willey, Williams, Wilson, Yates—47.

Mr. Morton then offered the amendment offered by him in Committee of the Whole, proposing an additional article as Article XVI, and rejected, as follows:

The second clause, first section, second article of the Constitution of the United States shall be amended to read as follows: Each State shall appoint, by a vote of the people thereof qualified to vote for representatives in Congress, a number of electors equal to the whole number of senators and representatives to which the State may be entitled in the Congress; but no senator or representative, or person holding an office of trust or profit under the United States, shall be appointed an elector, and the Congress shall have power to prescribe the manner in which such electors shall be chosen by the people.

Which was agreed to—yeas 37, nays 19, as follow:

YEAS—Messrs. *Buckalew,* Cameron, Cattell, Cole, Conkling, Conness, Corbett, *Dixon, Doolittle,* Ferry, Fessenden, Fowler, Grimes, Harlan, Howe, Kellogg, McDonald, Morrill of Maine, Morton, Osborn, Patterson of New Hampshire, Pool, Ramsey, Rice, Robertson, Ross, Sawyer, Spencer, Thayer, *Vickers,* Wade, Warner, Welch, *Whyte,* Willey, Williams, Wilson—37.
NAYS—Messrs. Abbott, Chandler, Cragin, *Davis,* Drake, Edmunds, Frelinghuysen, Harris, *Hendricks, McCreery,* Morgan, Morrill of Vermont, *Patterson* of Tennessee, *Saulsbury,* Sherman, Stewart, Trumbull, Van Winkle, Yates—19.

Mr. Wilson moved to reconsider this vote; which was disagreed to—yeas 26, nays 28, as follow:

YEAS—Messrs. Cameron, Cattell, Chandler, Cole, Conness, Cragin, Drake, Edmunds, Ferry, Fessenden, Frelinghuysen, Harris, Howe, Kellogg, Morgan, Morrill of Maine, Morrill of Vermont, Nye, Ramsey, Sherman, Stewart, Thayer, *Whyte,* Willey, Wilson, Yates—26.
NAYS—Messrs. Abbott, *Buckalew,* Conkling, Corbett, *Davis, Dixon, Doolittle,* Fowler, Grimes, Harlan, *Hendricks,* McDonald, Morton, Osborn, Patterson of New Hampshire, *Patterson* of Tennessee, Pool, Rice, Robertson, Ross, Sawyer, Spencer, Sprague, Van Winkle, *Vickers,* Wade, Warner, Williams—28.

The resolution as amended—being the substitute offered by Mr. Wilson and the additional article offered by Mr. Morton—was then passed —yeas 40, nays 16, as follow:

YEAS—Messrs. Abbott, Cameron, Cattell, Chandler, Cole, Conkling, Conness, Cragin, Drake, Ferry, Harlan, Harris, Howe, Kellogg, McDonald, Morgan, Morrill of Maine, Morrill of Vermont, Morton, Nye, Osborn, Patterson of New Hampshire, Pool, Ramsey, Rice, Robertson, Ross, Sawyer, Sherman, Spencer, Stewart, Thayer, Van Winkle, Wade, Warner, Welch, Willey, Williams, Wilson, Yates—40.
NAYS—Messrs. Anthony, *Bayard,* Corbett, *Davis, Dixon, Doolittle,* Edmunds, Fowler, Grimes, *Hendricks, McCreery, Patterson* of Tennessee, *Saulsbury,* Sprague, *Vickers, Whyte*—16.

### IN HOUSE

February 15—The House—having suspended the rules, yeas 126, nays 31, not voting 65—disagreed to the amendments made by the Senate. The first question was on the amendment substituting the following for the first section:

"No discrimination shall be made in any State among citizens of the United States in the exercise of the elective franchise or in the right to hold office in any State on account of race, color, nativity, property, education, or creed."

Yeas 37, nays 133, (not voting 52,) as follow:

YEAS—Messrs. *Axtell,* Baker, Beatty, Bingham, Buckland, Sidney Clarke, Coburn, Cullom, Deweese, Dickey, Dockery, Donnelly, Eggleston, Haughey, Heaton, Asahel W. Hubbard, Ingersoll, Kitchen, George V. Lawrence, William Lawrence, Nunn, Orth, Pile, Plants, Poland, Scofield, Shanks, Spalding, Stover, Thomas, John

Trimble, Robert P. Van Horn, Ward, Welker, James F. Wilson, John T. Wilson, Stephen F. Wilson—37.

NAYS—Messrs. Anderson, Delos R. Ashley, James M. Ashley, Banks, *Barnum*, Beaman, *Beck*, Benjamin, Benton, Blaine, Blair, Boutwell, Bowen, Boyden, *Boyer*, Bromwell, *Brooks*, Buckley, *Burr*, Benjamin F. Butler, Roderick R. Butler, Callis, *Cary*, *Chanler*, Churchill, Reader W. Clarke, Clift, Cobb, Corley, Cornell, Covode, Dawes, Driggs, Edwards, *Eldridge*, Thomas D. Eliot, James T. Elliott, Farnsworth, Ferriss, Ferry, Fields, *Fox*, *Glossbrenner*, Gove, Gravely, *Grover*, *Haight*, Hamilton, Hawkins, Higby, *Holman*, Hopkins, *Hotchkiss*, Chester D. Hubbard, Hulburd, *Humphrey*, Hunter, Jenckes, *Johnson*, Alexander H. Jones, *Thomas L. Jones*, Julian, Kelley, Kellogg, Kelsey, *Kerr*, Ketcham, *Knott*, Koontz, Laflin, Lash, Loan, Loughridge, Lynch, Mallory, *Marshall*, Marvin, McCarthy, *McCormick*, McKee, Miller, Moore, Moorhead, Morrell, *Mungen*, Myers, Newcomb, Newsham, *Niblack*, *Nicholson*, Norris, O'Neill, Paine, Perham, Peters, *Phelps*, Pierce, Polsley, Pomeroy, Price, Prince, *Pruyn*, *Randall*, Raum, Robertson, *Robinson*, Roots, *Ross*, Sawyer, Shellabarger, *Sitgreaves*, Smith, Starkweather, Stewart, Stokes, *Stone*, *Taber*, Taffe, Trowbridge, Twichell, Upson, Burt Van Horn, *Van Trump*, Van Wyck, Cadwalader C. Washburn, Henry D. Washburn, William B. Washburn, Whittemore, William Williams, Windom, *Wood*, *Woodward*, *Young*—133.

The other amendments were then disagreed to without a division.

### IN SENATE.

February 17—Mr. Stewart moved that the Senate recede from its amendments disagreed to by the House; which was agreed to—yeas 33, nays 24, as follow:

YEAS—Messrs. Anthony, Cameron, Cattell, Chandler, Cole, Conkling, Corbett, Cragin, Drake, Edmunds, Ferry, Fessenden, Frelinghuysen, Harris, Howard, Kellogg, McDonald, Morgan, Morrill of Maine, Morrill of Vermont, Morton, Nye, Patterson of New Hampshire, Pomeroy, Robertson, Stewart, Thayer, Trumbull, Van Winkle, Welch, Willey, Williams, Yates—33.

NAYS—Messrs. Abbott, *Bayard, Buckalew, Davis, Dixon, Doolittle,* Fowler, Harlan, *Hendricks, McCreery, Norton,* Osborn, *Patterson* of Tennessee, Pool, Rice, Ross, *Saulsbury,* Sherman, Spencer, *Vickers,* Wade, Warner, *Whyte,* Wilson—24.

Mr. Wilson moved to lay the resolution on the table; which was disagreed to—yeas 28, nays 30, as follow:

YEAS—Messrs. Abbott, Anthony, *Bayard, Buckalew, Davis, Dixon, Doolittle,* Edmunds, Fowler, Grimes, *Hendricks,* Howe, *McCreery, Norton, Patterson* of Tennessee, Pool, Ross, *Saulsbury,* Sawyer, Spencer, Sumner, Trumbull, Van Winkle, *Vickers,* Warner, *Whyte,* Wilson, Yates—28.

NAYS—Messrs. Cameron, Cattell, Chandler, Cole, Conkling, Cragin, Drake, Ferry, Fessenden, Frelinghuysen, Harlan, Harris, Howard, Kellogg, McDonald, Morgan, Morrill of Maine, Morrill of Vermont, Nye, Osborn, Patterson of New Hampshire, Ramsey, Rice, Robertson, Sherman, Stewart, Thayer, Wade, Willey, Williams—30.

Mr Morton moved to reconsider the vote of the Senate receding from its amendments; which was disagreed to—yeas 24, nays 32, as follow:

YEAS—Messrs. Abbott, Cragin, Drake, Grimes, Harlan, Harris, McDonald, Morton, Osborn, Pomeroy, Pool, Rice, Robertson, Ross, Sawyer, Sherman, Spencer, Sumner, Thayer, Van Winkle, Wade, Warner, Welch, Willey—24.

NAYS—Messrs. Anthony, *Buckalew,* Cameron, Cattell, Chandler, Cole, Conkling, *Davis, Doolittle,* Edmunds, Ferry, Fessenden, Fowler, Frelinghuysen, *Hendricks,* Howard, Kellogg, *McCreery,* Morgan, Morrill of Vermont, *Norton,* Nye, Patterson of Tennessee, Ramsey, *Saulsbury,* Stewart, Trumbull, *Vickers, Whyte,* Williams, Yates—32.

On the question, shall the resolution (as originally passed by the House) pass, it was determined in the negative, (two-thirds not having voted in the affirmative)—yeas 31, nays 27, as follow:

YEAS—Messrs. Anthony, Cameron, Cattell, Chandler, Cole, Conkling, Cragin, Drake, Ferry, Fessenden, Frelinghuysen, Harlan, Harris, Howard, Kellogg, Morgan,

Morrill of Vermont, Morton, Nye, Patterson of New Hampshire, Pool, Ramsey, Rice, Robertson, Sherman, Stewart, Trumbull, Van Winkle, Wade, Williams, Yates—31.

NAYS—Messrs. Abbott, *Bayard, Buckalew, Davis, Dixon, Doolittle,* Edmunds, Fowler, *Grimes, Hendricks, McCreery,* McDonald, *Norton,* Osborn, *Patterson* of Tennessee, Pomeroy, Ross, *Saulsbury.* Sawyer, Spencer, Sumner, Thayer, *Vickers,* Warner, Welch, *Whyte,* Wilson—27.

And the House proposition fell.

### The Senate Joint Resolution. (S. 8.)

#### IN SENATE.

On the same day (February 17), and immediately after the failure of the House proposition, the Senate resolved itself into Committee of the Whole on a joint resolution reported January 15, 1869, from the Committee on the Judiciary, and amended by the Senate without division, January 28, so as to make it read as follows:

JOINT RESOLUTION proposing an amendment to the Constitution of the United States.

*Resolved by the Senate and House of Representatives of the United States of America in Congress assembled,* (two-thirds of both houses concurring,) That the following article be proposed to the legislatures of the several States as an amendment to the Constitution of the United States, which, when ratified by three-fourths of said legislatures, shall be valid as part of the Constitution, namely:

##### ARTICLE XV.

The right of citizens of the United States to vote and hold office shall not be denied or abridged by the United States or by any State on account of race, color, or previous condition of servitude.

The Congress shall have power to enforce this article by appropriate legislation.

The question being on concurring in the amendment made in Committee of the Whole,

Mr. Drake moved to amend it by striking out all after the words "section 1," and inserting the following:

No citizen of the United States shall, on account of race, color, or previous condition of servitude be, by the United States or by any State, denied the right to vote or hold office.

Which was disagreed to.

Mr. Bayard moved to amend the amendment by striking out the words "vote and," so that it would read:

The right of citizens of the United States to hold office shall not be denied or abridged by the United States or any State, &c.

Which was disagreed to—yeas 6, nays 29, as follows:

YEAS—Messrs. *Bayard, Buckalew, Davis, Hendricks, Vickers, Whyte*—6.

NAYS—Messrs. Abbott, Cattell, Cole, Drake, Edmunds, Ferry, Fessenden, Frelinghuysen, Howard, Kellogg, McDonald, Morton, Nye, Osborn, Patterson of New Hampshire, Pomeroy, Ramsey, Rice, Ross, Sawyer, Spencer, Stewart, Trumbull, Van Winkle, Wade, Warner, Willey, Wilson, Yates—29.

Mr. Howard moved to amend the amendment made in Committee of the Whole by striking out the words "the United States or by."

Which was disagreed to—yeas 18, nays 22, as follow:

YEAS—Messrs. *Buckalew,* Conkling, Cragin, *Davis, Dixon, Doolittle,* Ferry, Fowler, *Hendricks,* Howard, *Norton,* Patterson of New Hampshire, Robertson, *Saulsbury,* Trumbull, Van Winkle, *Vickers, Whyte*—18.

NAYS—Messrs. Abbott, Cattell, Cole, Drake, Edmunds, Fessenden, Frelinghuysen, Harris, Kellogg, McDonald, Morrill of Vermont, Morton, Pomeroy, Ramsey, Rice, Sawyer, Stewart, Wade, Warner, Willey, Wilson, Yates—22.

Mr. Doolittle moved to add to the amendment made in Committee of the Whole the words:

Nor shall any citizen be so denied by reason of any alleged crime unless duly convicted thereof according to law.

Which was disagreed to—yeas 13, nays 30, as follow:

YEAS—Messrs. *Buckalew, Davis, Dixon, Doolittle,* Ferry, Fowler, *Hendricks, McCreery, Norton, Saulsbury, Vickers, Whyte,* Wilson—13.

NAYS—Messrs. Abbott, Cattell, Cole, Conkling, Cragin, Drake, Edmunds, Fessenden, Frelinghuysen, Harris, Howard, McDonald, Morrill of Vermont, Morton, Nye, Patterson of New Hampshire, Pomeroy, Ramsey, Rice. Robertson, Sawyer, Spencer, Stewart, Trumbull, Wade, Warner, Welch, Willey, Williams, Yates—30.

Mr. Fowler moved to amend the amendment of the Committee of the Whole by striking out the words "on account of race, color, or previous condition of servitude."

Which was disagreed to—yeas 5, nays 30. The yeas were Messrs. *Doolittle,* Fowler, *Hendricks, Vickers, Whyte.*

The amendment made in Committee of the Whole was then concurred in, without a division.

Mr. Howard moved to amend the resolution by striking out all after the word "that," where it first occurs, and substituting the following:

The following article be proposed to the legislatures of the several States as an amendment to the Constitution of the United States:

### ARTICLE XV.

Citizens of the United States of African descent shall have the same right to vote and hold office in States and Territories as other electors.

Mr. Davis moved to amend so as to provide for the submission of this to legislatures "hereafter to be chosen;" which was disagreed to.

Mr. Howard's amendment was then disagreed to—yeas 22, nays 28, as follow:

YEAS—Messrs. Abbott, Cole, Conkling, Conness, Drake, Ferry, Harlan, Harris, Howard, Nye, Osborn, Patterson of New Hampshire, Pomeroy, Ramsey, Robertson, Spencer, Thayer, Tipton, Warner, Welch, Willey, Williams—22.

NAYS—Messrs. Bayard, *Buckalew,* Cattell, Cragin, *Davis, Dixon,* Edmunds, Fessenden, Fowler. Frelinghuysen, *Hendricks,* Howe, *McCreery,* McDonald, Morgan, Morrill of Maine, Morrill of Vermont, Morton, Rice, Ross, *Saulsbury,* Stewart, Trumbull, Van Winkle, *Vickers, Whyte,* Wilson, Yates—28.

Mr. Hendricks moved to amend by adding to the resolution the following words:

The foregoing amendment shall be submitted for ratification to the legislatures of the several States the most numerous branches of which shall be chosen next after the passage of this resolution.

Which was disagreed to—yeas 12, nays 40, as follow:

YEAS—Messrs. *Bayard, Buckalew, Davis, Dixon,* Fowler, *Hendricks, McCreery, Norton, Patterson* of Tennessee, *Saulsbury, Vickers, Whyte*—12.

NAYS—Messrs. Abbott, Cameron, Cole, Conkling, Cragin, Drake, Edmunds, Ferry, Frelinghuysen, Harlan, Harris, Howard, Howe, Kellogg, McDonald, Morgan, Morrill of Maine, Morrill of Vermont, Morton, Nye, Osborn, Patterson of New Hampshire, Pomeroy, Pool, Ramsey, Rice, Robertson, Ross, Sawyer, Spencer, Stewart, Thayer, Tipton, Van Winkle, Wade, Warner, Welch, Willey, Williams, Wilson—40.

Mr. Dixon moved to amend by submitting the article to *conventions* instead of *legislatures*; which was disagreed to—yeas 10, nays 39. [The affirmative vote was the same as above, except that Messrs. Fowler and *McCreery* did not vote. The negative also the same, except that Messrs. Sawyer and Wade did not vote, and Mr. Yates did.]

Mr. Davis moved a reconsideration of the vote disagreeing to the last amendment offered by Mr. Howard, which was disagreed to—yeas 16, nays 29, as follow:

YEAS—Messrs. Chandler, Cole, Conkling, Harlan, Howard, Nye, Osborn, Patterson of New Hampshire, Pomeroy, Ramsey, Robertson, Sawyer, Tipton, Warner, Welch, Williams—16.

NAYS—Messrs. Abbott, *Buckalew,* Cragin, *Davis,* Drake, Edmunds, Ferry, Frelinghuysen, Harris, *Hendricks,* Kellogg, *McCreery.* McDonald, Morgan, Morrill of Vermont, Morton, *Patterson* of Tennessee, Pool, Rice, Ross, *Saulsbury.* Spencer, Stewart, Thayer, *Vickers,* Wade, *Whyte,* Wilson, Yates—29.

The resolution was then engrossed and read a third time, and passed—yeas 35, nays 11, as follow:

YEAS—Messrs. Abbott, Chandler, Cole, Conkling, Cragin, Drake, Edmunds, Ferry, Frelinghuysen, Harlan, Harris, Kellogg, McDonald, Morgan, Morrill of Vermont, Morton, Osborn, Patterson of New Hampshire, Pomeroy, Pool, Ramsey, Rice, Robertson, Ross, Sawyer, Spencer, Stewart, Thayer, Van Winkle, Wade, Warner, Welch, Willey, Williams, Wilson—35.

NAYS—Messrs. *Bayard, Buckalew, Davis,* Fowler, *Hendricks, McCreery, Norton, Patterson* of Tennessee, *Saulsbury, Vickers, Whyte*—11.

### IN HOUSE.

February 20—On motion of Mr. Boutwell, the rules were suspended, (yeas 139, nays 35, not voting 48,) and the joint resolution of the Senate was taken up.

Messrs Logan, Shellabarger, and Bingham submitted amendments.

Mr. Boutwell moved to suspend the rules, and that the House proceed to vote on the pending amendments and the joint resolution without dilatory motions; which was agreed to—yeas 144, nays 37, not voting 41.

Mr. Logan's amendment—to strike from the first section the words "and hold office"—was disagreed to—yeas 70, nays 95, (not voting 57,) as follow:

YEAS—Messrs. *Archer,* Delos R. Ashley, *Axtell, Barnum, Beck,* Benton, Bingham, *Boyer, Burr, Cary, Chanler,* Churchill, Coburn, Dockery, Eckley, *Eldridge,* Fields, *Fox,* Garfield, *Getz, Golladay, Grover, Haight,* Halsey, Higby, *Holman, Hotchkiss,* Chester D. Hubbard, *Humphrey,* Hunter, *Johnson,* Thomas L. *Jones,* Judd, Ketcham, *Knott,* George V. Lawrence, Logan. Marvin, *McCormick, McCullough.* Mercur, Miller, Moore, Moorhead, Morrell, *Mungen,* Myers, *Niblack, Nicholson,* O'Neill, *Phelps,* Pile, *Pruyn, Randall,* Raum, Robertson, Schenck, Scofield, Selye, Smith, Spalding, Starkweather, Stevens, *Stone, Taber, Tift, Van Trump,* William Williams, Woodbridge, *Woodward*—70.

NAYS—Messrs. Allison, Ames, James M. Ashley, Baker, Banks, Beaman, Beatty, Benjamin, Blaine, Blair, Boutwell, Bowen, Bromwell, Broomall, Buckland, Buckley, Roderick R. Butler, Cake, Callis, Reader W. Clarke, Sidney Clarke, Clift, Cobb, Cook, Corley, Cullom, Dawes, Dickey, Dodge. Donnelly, Driggs, Eggleston, Ela, Thomas D. Eliot, James T. Elliott. Ferriss, French, Goss, Gove, Gravely, Hamilton, Haughey, Heaton, Hooper, Hopkins. Hulburd, Jenckes, Alexander H. Jones, Julian, Kelley, Kellogg, Kelsey, Kitchen, Koontz, Laflin, Lash, William Lawrence, Loughridge, Lynch, Maynard, McKee, Newcomb, Nunn, Orth, Paine, Perham, Peters, Pettis, Pike, Plants, Poland, Pomeroy, Prince, Roots, Sawyer, Shanks, Shellabarger, Stokes, Stover, Sypher. Taffe, Thomas, John Trimble, Trowbridge, Twichell, Upson, Van Aernam, Burt Van Horn, Ward, William B. Washburn. Welker, Whittemore, Thomas Williams, Stephen F. Wilson, Windom—95.

Mr. Bingham's amendment, to strike out the words "by the United States or," and insert the words "nativity, property, creed," so that it will read as follows:

The right of citizens of the United States to vote and hold office shall not be denied or abridged by any State on account of race, color, nativity, property, creed, or previous condition of servitude,

Was agreed to—yeas 92, nays 71, (not voting 59) as follow:

YEAS—Messrs. Allison, *Archer*, James M. Ashley, *Axtell*, Baker, *Barnum*, Beatty, *Beck*, Benton, Bingham, Blaine, *Boyer*, Buckland, *Burr*, Reader W. Clarke, Cobb, Coburn, Cullom, Dockery, Dodge, Donnelly, Driggs, Eckley, Eggleston, Ela, *Eldridge*, Farnsworth, Ferry, *Fox*, Garfield, *Getz*, Gravely, Griswold, *Haight*, Hamilton, Haughey, Heaton, *Holman*, Hopkins, *Hotchkiss*, Chester D. Hubbard, *Humphrey*, Hunter, Alexander H. Jones, Judd, Julian, Kitchen, *Knott*, Koontz, George V. Lawrence, William Lawrence, Marvin, *McCormick, McCullough*, Mercur, Moore, Moorhead, *Mungen*, Myers, Newcomb, *Niblack, Nicholson*, Orth, Paine, Pettis, Pile, Plants, *Randall*, Raum, *Robinson*, Ross, Schenck, Scofield, Shanks, Smith, Spalding, Starkweather, Stevens, *Stone*, Stover, Taylor, Upson, Robert T. Van Horn, Cadwalader C. Washburn, William B. Washburn, Welker, Whittemore, William Williams, James F. Wilson, John T. Wilson, Woodbridge, *Woodward*—92.

NAYS—Messrs. Delos R. Ashley, Banks, Beaman, Blair, Boutwell, Bowen, Bromwell, Broomall, Buckley, Benjamin F. Butler, Roderick R. Butler, Cake, *Cary*, Churchill, Sidney Clarke, Cook, Corley, Covode, Dawes, Dickey, Thomas D. Eliot, James T. Elliott, Ferriss, Fields, French, *Golladay*, Goss, Gove, *Grover*, Halsey, Higby, Hooper, Hulburd, Jenckes, *Johnson*, Kelley, Kelsey, Ketcham, Laflin, Lash, Loughridge, Maynard, McKee, Miller, Morrell, Nunn, O'Neill, Perham, *Phelps*, Pike, Poland, Pomeroy, Price, Prince, *Pruyn*, Robertson, Roots, Sawyer, Selye, Shellabarger, Stokes, Sypher, Taffe, Thomas, John Trimble, Trowbridge, Twichell, Van Aernam, Burt Van Horn, Ward, Thomas Williams—71.

Mr. Shellabarger then withdrew his amendment, and the joint resolution passed—yeas 140, nays 37, (not voting 46,) as follow:

YEAS—Messrs. Allison, Ames, Arnell, Delos R. Ashley, James M. Ashley, Baker, Banks, Beaman, Beatty, Benjamin, Benton, Bingham, Blaine, Blair, Boutwell, Bowen, Bromwell, Broomall, Buckland, Buckley, Benjamin F. Butler, Roderick R. Butler, Cake, Churchill, Reader W. Clarke, Sidney Clarke, Clift, Cobb, Coburn, Cook, Corley, Covode, Cullom, Dawes, Dickey, Dockery, Dodge, Donnelly, Driggs, Eckley, Eggleston, Ela, Thomas D. Eliot, James T. Elliott, Farnsworth, Ferriss, Ferry, Fields, French, Garfield, Goss, Gove, Gravely, Griswold, Halsey, Hamilton, Haughey, Hea-

ton, Higby, Hill, Hooper, Hopkins, Chester D. Hubbard, Hulburd, Hunter, Alexander H. Jones, Judd, Julian, Kelley, Kellogg, Kelsey, Ketcham, Kitchen, Koontz, Laflin, Lash, George V. Lawrence, William Lawrence, Logan, Loughridge, Lynch, Marvin, Maynard, McKee, Mercur, Miller, Moore, Moorhead, Morrell, Myers, O'Neill, Orth, Paine, Perham, Peters, Pettis, Pile, Plants, Poland, Pomeroy, Price, Prince, Raum, Roots, Sawyer, Schenck, Scofield, Selye, Shanks, Shellabarger, Smith, Starkweather, Stevens, Stokes, Stover, Sypher, Taffe, Taylor, Thomas, Tift, John Trimble, Trowbridge, Twichell, Upson, Van Aernam, Burt Van Horn, Robert T. Van Horn, Ward, Cadwalader C. Washburn, William B. Washburn, Welker, Whittemore, Thomas Williams, William Williams, James F. Wilson, John T. Wilson, Stephen F. Wilson, Windom, Woodbridge, and Mr. Speaker Colfax—140.

NAYS—Messrs. *Archer, Axtell, Barnum, Beck, Boyer, Burr, Cary, Chanler, Eldridge, Fox, Getz, Golladay, Grover, Haight, Hawkins, Holman, Hotchkiss, Humphrey*, Jenckes, *Johnson, Knott, Marshall, McCormick, McCullough, Mungen, Niblack, Nicholson, Phelps, Pruyn, Randall, Robinson, Ross, Stone, Taber, Van Trump, Woodward, Young*—37.

### IN SENATE.

February 23—The Senate disagreed to the amendment of the House, and asked a conference on the disagreeing votes of the two Houses thereon; which was agreed to—yeas 32, nays 17, as follow:

YEAS—Messrs. Anthony, Cattell, Chandler, Cole, Conkling, Cragin, Drake, Edmunds, Ferry, Frelinghuysen, Grimes, Harris, Howard, Howe, Morgan, Morrill of Maine, Morrill of Vermont, Morton, Nye, Osborn, Pomeroy, Ramsey, Sherman, Sprague, Stewart, Thayer, Tipton, Trumbull, Van Winkle, Willey, Williams, Wilson—32.

NAYS—Messrs. Abbott, *Buckalew, Davis, Dixon, Doolittle*, Kellogg, *McCreery, Norton, Patterson* of Tennessee, Pool, Rice, Robertson, Ross, Sawyer, *Vickers*, Warner, *Whyte*—17.

Messrs. Stewart, Conkling, and Edmunds were appointed the managers of the conference on the part of the Senate; and Messrs. Boutwell, Bingham, and Logan were appointed on the part of the House, the House having agreed to the conference—yeas 117, nays 37, not voting 68.

February 25—The conference reported, recommending that the House recede from their amendment, and agree to the resolution of the Senate, with an amendment, as follows: In section 1, line 2, strike out the words "and hold office," and the Senate agree to the same.

February 26—The Senate agreed to the report—yeas 39, nays 13, as printed on page 399.

February 25—The House agreed to the report—yeas 144, nays 44, not voting 35, as printed on page 399.

---

# XLI.

## MEMBERS OF THE CABINET OF PRESIDENT GRANT,

### AND OF THE FORTY-FIRST CONGRESS.

**PRESIDENT GRANT'S CABINET.***

*Secretary of State*—HAMILTON FISH, of New York, *vice* ELLIHU B. WASHBURNE, of Illinois, resigned March 10, 1869.

*Secretary of the Treasury*—GEORGE S. BOUT- WELL, of Massachusetts.
*Secretary of War*—JOHN A. RAWLINS, of Illinois.
*Secretary of the Navy*—GEORGE M. ROBESON, of

---

*Mr. Washburne was nominated and confirmed as Secretary of State March 5, and resigned March 10, to take effect upon the qualification of his successor, which took place March 16. Mr. Alexander T. Stewart, of New

York, was nominated and confirmed as Secretary of the Treasury March 5, and resigned March 9, being found disqualified by the act of Congress of September 2, 1789, providing that the Secretary of the Treasury, with

New Jersey, *vice* ADOLPH E. BORIE, of Pennsylvania, resigned June 25, 1869.

*Postmaster General*—JOHN A. J. CRESWELL, of Maryland.

*Secretary of the Interior*—JACOB D. COX, of Ohio.

*Attorney General*—E. ROCKWOOD HOAR, of Massachusetts.

## MEMBERS OF THE FORTY-FIRST CONGRESS.

First Session, March 4, 1869—April 10, 1869.

### Senate.

SCHUYLER COLFAX, of Indiana, *Vice-President of the United States and President of the Senate.*

George C. Gorham, of California, *Secretary.*

*Maine*—William Pitt Fessenden, Hannibal Hamlin.

*New Hampshire*—Aaron H. Cragin, James W. Patterson.

*Vermont*—Justin S. Morrill, George F. Edmunds.

*Massachusetts*—Henry Wilson, Charles Sumner.

*Rhode Island*—Henry B. Anthony, William Sprague.

*Connecticut*—Orris S. Ferry, William A. Buckingham.

*New York*—Roscoe Conkling, Reuben E. Fenton.

*New Jersey*—Alexander G. Cattell, John P. Stockton.

*Pennsylvania*—Simon Cameron, John Scott.

*Delaware*—Willard Saulsbury, Thomas F. Bayard.

*Maryland*—George Vickers, William T. Hamilton.*

*North Carolina*—John C. Abbott, John Pool.

*South Carolina*—Thomas J. Robertson, Frederick A. Sawyer.

*Alabama*—Willard Warner, George E. Spencer.

*Louisiana*—John S. Harris, William P. Kellogg.

*Ohio*—John Sherman, Allen G. Thurman.

*Kentucky*—Thomas C. McCreery, Garrett Davis.

*Tennessee*—Joseph S. Fowler, William G. Brownlow.

*Indiana*—Oliver P. Morton, Daniel D. Pratt.

*Illinois*—Richard Yates, Lyman Trumbull.

*Missouri*—Charles D. Drake, Carl Schurz.

*Arkansas*—Alexander McDonald, Benjamin F. Rice.

*Michigan*—Jacob M. Howard, Zachariah Chandler.

*Florida*—Thomas W. Osborn, Abijah Gilbert.

*Iowa*—James W. Grimes, James Harlan.

*Wisconsin*—Timothy O. Howe, Matthew H. Carpenter.

*California*—Cornelius Cole, Eugene Casserly.

*Minnesota*—Daniel S. Norton, Alexander Ramsey.

*Oregon*—George H. Williams, Henry W. Corbett.

*Kansas*—Edmund G. Ross, Samuel C. Pomeroy.

*West Virginia*—Waitman T. Willey, Arthur I. Boreman

*Nevada*—James W. Nye, William M. Stewart.

*Nebraska*—John M. Thayer, Thomas W. Tipton.

### House of Representatives.

JAMES G. BLAINE, of Maine, *Speaker.*

Edward McPherson, of Pennsylvania, *Clerk*

*Maine*—John Lynch, Samuel P. Morrill, James G. Blaine, John A. Peters, Eugene Hale.

*New Hampshire*\*—Jacob H. Ela, Aaron F. Stevens, Jacob Benton.

*Vermont*—Charles W. Willard, Luke P. Poland, Worthington C. Smith.

*Massachusetts*—James Buffinton, Oakes Ames, Ginery Twichell, Samuel Hooper, Benjamin F. Butler, Nathaniel P. Banks, George S. Boutwell,† George F. Hoar, William B. Washburn, Henry L. Dawes.

*Rhode Island*—Thomas A. Jenckes, Nathan F. Dixon.

*Connecticut*‡—Julius Strong, Stephen W. Kellogg, Henry H. Starkweather, William H. Barnum.

*New York*—Henry A. Reeves, John G. Schumaker, Henry W. Slocum, John Fox, John Morrissey, Samuel S. Cox,§ Hervey C Calkin, James Brooks, Fernando Wood, Clarkson N. Potter, George W. Greene, John H. Ketcham, John A. Griswold, Stephen L Mayham, Adolphus H. Tanner, Orange Ferriss, William A. Wheeler, Stephen Sanford, Charles Knapp, Addison H. Laflin, Alexander H. Bailey, John C. Churchill, Dennis McCarthy, George W. Cowles, William H. Kelsey, Giles W. Hotchkiss, Hamilton Ward, Noah Davis, John Fisher, David S. Bennett, Porter Sheldon.

*New Jersey*—William Moore, Charles Haight, John T. Bird, John Hill, Orestes Cleveland.

*Pennsylvania*—Samuel J. Randall, Charles O'Neill, Leonard Myers,‖ William D. Kelley, John R. Reading, John D. Stiles, Washington Townsend, J. Lawrence Getz, Oliver J. Dickey, Henry L. Cake, Daniel M. Van Auken, George W. Woodward, Ulysses Mercur, John B. Packer, Richard J. Haldeman, John Cessna, Daniel J. Morrell, William H. Armstrong, Glenni W. Scofield, Calvin W. Gilfillan (vacancy), James S. Negley, Darwin Phelps, Joseph B. Donley.

*Delaware*—Benjamin T. Biggs.

*Maryland*—Samuel Hambleton, Stevenson Archer, Thomas Swann, Patrick Hamill, Frederick Stone.

*North Carolina*—Clinton L. Cobb, David Heaton, Oliver H. Dockery, John T. Deweese, Israel G. Lash, Francis E. Shober,¶ Alexander H. Jones.

*South Carolina*—B. F. Whittemore, C. C. Bowen, Solomon L. Hoge,\*\* (vacancy.)

*Louisiana*—(Vacancy,) Lionel A. Sheldon, \*\*\* (vacancy,) (vacancy.)

*Ohio*—Peter W. Strader, Job E. Stevenson,

---

other officers described, shall not be, directly or indirectly, concerned or interested in carrying on the business of trade or commerce, or be owner, in whole or in part, of any sea vessel, or purchase, by himself or another in trust for him, any public lands or other public property, or be concerned in the purchase or disposal of any public securities of any State or of the United States, or take or apply to his own use any emolument or gain for negotiating or transacting any business in the said Department other than what shall be allowed by law. Mr. Boutwell qualified March 12, 1869. Mr. Schofield remained Secretary of War until March 12, when Mr. Rawlins qualified

\*Qualified March 25, 1869.

\* Qualified March 15.

† Resigned March 12.

‡ Messrs. Strong, Kellogg, and Starkweather qualified April 9, 1869; Mr. Barnum did not appear.

§ Did not qualify, by reason of absence from the country.

‖ Qualified April 9, 1869, in place of John Moffet, unseated.

¶ Did not qualify, disabilities not having been relieved.

\*\* Admitted on *prima facie*, yeas 101, nays 39, and qualified April 8.

\*\*\* Qualified April 8, having been voted entitled to the seat, yeas 85, nays 38.

Robert C. Schenck, William Lawrence, William Mungen, John A. Smith, James J. Winans, John Beatty, Edward F. Dickinson, Truman H. Hoag, John T. Wilson, Philadelph Van Trump, George W. Morgan, Martin Welker, Eliakim H. Moore, John A. Bingham, Jacob A. Ambler, William H. Upson, James A. Garfield.

*Kentucky*—Lawrence S. Trimble, William N. Sweeney, J. S. Golladay, J. Proctor Knott, Boyd Winchester, Thomas L. Jones, James B. Beck, George M. Adams, John M. Rice.

*Tennessee*—Roderick R. Butler, Horace Maynard, William B. Stokes, Lewis Tillman, William F. Prosser, Samuel M. Arnell, Isaac R. Hawkins, William J. Smith.

*Indiana*—William E. Niblack, Michael C. Kerr, William S. Holman, George W. Julian, John Coburn, Daniel W. Voorhees, Godlove S. Orth, James N. Tyner, John P. C. Shanks, William Williams, Jasper Packard.

*Illinois*—Norman B. Judd, John F. Farnsworth, Ellihu B. Washburne,* John B. Hawley, Ebon C. Ingersoll, Burton C. Cook, Jesse H. Moore, Shelby M. Cullom, Thompson W. McNeely, Albert G. Burr, Samuel S. Marshall, John B. Hay, John M. Crebs, John A. Logan.

*Missouri*—Erastus Wells, Gustavus A. Finkelnburg, James R. McCormick, Sempronius H. Boyd, Samuel S Burdett, Robert T. Van Horn, Joel F. Asper, John F. Benjamin, David P. Dyer.

*Arkansas*—Logan H. Roots, A. A. C. Rogers, Thomas Boles.

*Michigan*—Fernando C. Beaman, William L. Stoughton, Austin Blair, Thomas W. Ferry, Omar D. Conger, Randolph Strickland.

*Florida*—Charles M. Hamilton.

*Iowa*—George W. McCrary, William Smyth, William B. Allison, William Loughridge, Frank W. Palmer, Charles Pomeroy.

*Wisconsin*—Halbert E. Paine, Benjamin F. Hopkins, Amasa Cobb, Charles A. Eldridge, Philetus Sawyer, Cadwalader C. Washburn.

*California*—Samuel B. Axtell, Aaron A. Sargent, James A. Johnson.

*Minnesota*—Morton S. Wilkinson, Eugene M. Wilson.

*Oregon*—Joseph S. Smith.

*Kansas*—Sidney Clarke.

*West Virginia*—Isaac H. Duval, James C. McGrew, John S. Witcher.

*Nevada*—Thomas Fitch.

*Nebraska*—John Taffe.

*Resigned March 6.

# XLII.

## POLITICAL VOTES IN FIRST SESSION OF FORTY-FIRST CONGRESS.

### Additional Reconstruction Legislation.

AN ACT authorizing the submission of the constitutions of Virginia, Mississippi, and Texas to a vote of the people, and authorizing the election of State officers, provided by the said constitutions, and members of Congress.

*Be it enacted, &c.,* That the President of the United States, at such time as he may deem best for the public interest, may submit the constitution which was framed by the convention which met in Richmond, Virginia, on Tuesday, the 3d day of December, 1867, to the voters of said State, registered at the date of said submission, for ratification or rejection, and may also submit to a separate vote such provisions of said constitution as he may deem best, such vote to be taken either upon each of the said provisions alone, or in connection with the other portions of said constitution, as the President may direct.

SEC. 2. That at the same election the voters of said State may vote for and elect members of the General Assembly of said State, and all the officers of said State provided for by the said constitution, and members of Congress; and the officer commanding the district of Virginia shall cause the lists of registered voters of said State to be revised, enlarged, and corrected prior to such election, according to law, and for that purpose may appoint such registrars as he may deem necessary. And said elections shall be held, and returns thereof made, in the manner provided by the acts of Congress commonly called the reconstruction acts.

SEC. 3. That the President of the United States may in like manner submit the constitution of Texas to the voters of said State at such time and in such manner as he may direct, either the entire constitution, or separate provisions of the same, as provided in the 1st section of this act, to a separate vote; and at the same election the voters may vote for and elect the members of the Legislature and all the State officers provided for in said constitution, and members of Congress: *Provided, also,* That no election shall be held in said State of Texas for any purpose until the President so directs.

SEC. 4. That the President of the United States may in like manner re-submit the constitution of Mississippi to the voters of said State at such time and in such manner as he may direct, either the entire constitution or separate provisions of the same, as provided in the 1st section of this act, to a separate vote; and at the same election the voters may vote for and elect the members of the legislature and all the State officers provided for in said constitution, and members of Congress.

Sec. 5 That if either of said constitutions shall be ratified at such election, the Legislature of the State so ratifying, elected as provided for in this act, shall assemble at the capital of said State on the fourth Tuesday after the official promulgation of such ratification by the military officer commanding in said State.

Sec. 6. That before the States of Virginia, Mississippi, and Texas shall be admitted to representation in Congress, their several legislatures, which may be hereafter lawfully organized, shall ratify the fifteenth article which has been proposed by Congress to the several States as an amendment to the Constitution of the United States.

Sec. 7. That the proceedings in any of the said States shall not be deemed final, or operate as a complete restoration thereof, until their action, respectively, shall be approved by Congress.

Approved April 10, 1869.

The final votes on this act were as follow:

### In SENATE, *April 9.*

YEAS—Messrs. Abbott, Boreman, Brownlow, Buckingham, Carpenter, Cattell, Chandler, Cole, Conkling, Corbett, Cragin, Drake, Fenton, Ferry, Fessenden, Hamlin, Harris, Howard, Howe, McDonald, Morrill, Morton, Nye, Patterson, Pomeroy, Pratt, Ramsey, Rice, Robertson, Ross, Sawyer, Schurz. Scott, Sherman, Spencer, Stewart, Sumner, Thayer, Tipton, Trumbull, Warner, Willey, Williams, Wilson—44.

NAYS—Messrs. *Bayard, Casserly, Davis,* Fowler; *McCreery, Norton,* Sprague, *Stockton, Thurman*—9.

### In HOUSE, *April 9.*

YEAS—Messrs. Ambler, Ames, Armstrong, Asper, Banks, Beaman, Benton, Bingham, Blair, Boles, Bowen, Boyd, Buffinton, B. F. Butler, Cake, Cessna, Churchill, Amasa Cobb, Clinton L. Cobb, Coburn, Cook, Conger, Cullom, Dawes, Deweese, Dockery, Duval, Ela, Farnsworth, Ferriss, Ferry, Finkelnburg, Fitch, Gilfillan, Hale, Hawley, Hay, Heaton, Hoar, Hooper, Hopkins, Hotchkiss, Ingersoll, Alexander H. Jones, Judd, Julian, Kelley, Kellogg, Ketcham, Knapp, Laflin. Lash, Logan, Loughridge. Lynch, Maynard, McCarthy, McCrary, McGrew, Mercur, William Moore, Morrell, Myers, Negley, O'Neill, Orth, Packard, Paine, Palmer. Phelps, Poland, Pomeroy, Prosser, Roots, Sargent, Sawyer, Scofield, Shanks, Lionel A. Sheldon, Porter Sheldon, John A. Smith, William J. Smith, William Smyth, Starkweather, Stevens, Stevenson, Stokes, Stoughton, Strickland, Strong, Tanner, Tillman, Townsend, Twichell, Tyner, Upson, Van Horn, Ward, Cadwalder C, Washburn, Welker, Wheeler, Whittemore, Wilkinson, Willard, Williams, John T. Wilson, Winans, Witcher—108.

NAYS—Messrs. *Adams, Archer, Axtell, Biggs, Bird, Brooks, Burr, Cleveland, Crebs, Eldridge, Getz, Golladay, Griswold, Haldeman, Hamill,* Hawkins, *Holman, Thomas L. Jones, Kerr, Knott, Marshall, Mayham, McCormick, McNeely, Niblack, Potter, Reeves, Slocum. Stone, Swann, Sweeney, Trimble, Van Auken, Van Trump, Voorhees, Wells, Eugene M. Wilson, Winchester, Woodward*—39.

---

### Previous Votes.

### In HOUSE.

1869, April 8—The House passed the following bill:

An ACT authorizing the submission of the constitutions of Virginia, Mississippi, and Texas to a vote of the people, and authorizing the election of State officers, provided by the said constitutions, and members of Congress.

*Be it enacted, &c.,* That the President of the United States, at such time as he may deem best for the public interest, may submit the constitution which was framed by the convention which met in Richmond, Virginia, on Tuesday, the 3d day of December, 1867, to the registered voters of said State for ratification or rejection, and may also submit to a separate vote such provisions of said constitution as he may deem best, such vote to be taken either upon each of the said provisions alone, or in connection with the other portions of said constitution, as the President may direct.

Sec. 2. That at the same election the voters of said State may vote for and elect members of the general assembly of said State, and all the officers of said State provided for by the said constitution, and members of Congress; and the officer commanding the district of Virginia shall cause the lists of registered voters of said State to be revised and corrected prior to such election, and for that purpose may appoint such registrars as he may deem necessary. And said election shall be held and returns thereof made in the manner provided by the election ordinance adopted by the convention which framed said constitution.

Sec. 3. That the President of the United States may in like manner submit the constitution of Texas to the voters of said State at such time and in such manner as he may direct, either the entire constitution, or separate provisions of the same, as provided in the 1st section of this act, to a separate vote; and at the same election the voters may vote for and elect the members of the legislature and all the State officers provided for in said constitution, and members of Congress: *Provided, also,* That no election shall be held in said State of Texas for any purpose until the President so directs.

Sec. 4. That the President of the United States may in like manner re-submit the constitution of Mississippi to the voters of said State, at such time and in such manner as he may direct, either the entire constitution or separate provisions of the same, as provided in the 1st section of this act, to a separate vote; and at the same election the voters may vote for and elect the members of the legislature and all the State officers provided for in said constitution, and members of Congress.

Sec. 5. That if either of said constitutions shall be ratified at such election, the legislature of the State so ratifying, elected as provided for in this act, shall assemble at the capital of said States, respectively, on the fourth Tuesday after the official promulgation of such ratification by the military officer commanding in said State.

Sec. 6. That in either of said States the commanding general, subject to the approval of the President of the United States, may suspend, until the action of the legislature elected under the constitution respectively, all laws that he may deem unjust and oppressive to the people.

Yeas 125, nays 25, (not voting 47,) as follow:

YEAS—Messrs. Allison, Ambler, Armstrong. Arnell, *Axtell,* Bailey, Banks, Beaman, Beatty, *Beck,* Bingham, Blair, Boles. Bowen, *Brooks,* Buffinton, Burdett, Benjamin F. Butler, Roderick R. Butler, *Calkin,* Cessna, Churchill, Clarke, Amasa Cobb, Clinton L. Cobb, Coburn, Cook, Conger, *Crebs,* Cullom. Davis, Dawes, Deweese, Dickey, *Dickinson,* Dixon, Dockery, Donley, Duval, Ela, Farnsworth, Ferriss, Ferry, Finckelnburg, Fisher, Fitch, Garfield, Gilfillan, Hale, Hawley, Hay, Heaton, Hill, Hoar, Hoge. Hopkins, Hotchkiss, Ingersoll, Jenckes, Alexander H. Jones, Judd, Julian, Kelley, Kelsey, Ketcham, Knapp, Laflin. Lash, Lawrence, Logan, Loughridge, Lynch, McCarthy, *McCormick,* McCrary, McGrew, William Moore, *Morgan,* Morrell, Morrill,

Negley, O'Neill, Orth, Packard, Packer, Paine, Palmer, Phelps, Poland, Pomeroy, Prosser, Roots, Sanford, Sawyer, Schenck, Scofield, Shanks, Sheldon, *Slocum*, John A. Smith, William J. Smith, William Smyth, Stevens, Stevenson, Stokes, Stoughton, Strickland, Tanner, Tillman, Townsend, Tyner, Upson, Ward, Cadwalader C. Washburn, William B. Washburn, Welker, Wheeler, Whittemore, Wilkinson, Willard, Williams, John T. Wilson, Winans, Witcher, *Woodward*—125.

NAYS—Messrs. *Adams, Archer, Biggs, Bird, Burr, Cleveland, Eldridge, Getz, Golladay, Haldeman, Hamill, Holman, Thomas L. Jones, Kerr, Knott, McNeely, Moffet, Niblack, Potter, Randall, Reeves, Sweeney, Trimble, Wells, Winchester*—25.

## IN SENATE.

1869, April 9 - The House bill pending,

Mr. Morton moved this as a new section:

That, before the States of Virginia, Mississippi, and Texas shall be admitted to representation in Congress, their several legislatures, which may be hereafter lawfully organized, shall ratify the fifteenth article which has been proposed by Congress to the several States as an amendment to the Constitution of the United States.

Which was agreed to—yeas 30, nays 20, as follow:

YEAS—Messrs. Abbott, Brownlow, Buckingham, Carpenter, Chandler, Cole, Drake, Harris, Howard, McDonald, Morrill, Morton, Nye, Osborn, Pool, Pratt, Ramsey, Rice, Robertson, Ross, Schurz, Sherman, Stewart, Sumner, Thayer, Tipton, Warner, Williams, Wilson, Yates —30.

NAYS—Messrs. Anthony, *Bayard*, Boreman, *Casserly*, Conkling, *Davis*, Edmunds, Fenton, Ferry, Fessenden, Fowler, *McCreery, Norton*, Patterson, Sawyer, Sprague, *Stockton, Thurman*, Trumbull, Willey—20.

A few unimportant changes were made, and the bill passed both Houses, as above.

[A bill passed the House of Representatives, December 9, 1868, providing for an election in Virginia on the 27th of May, 1869, on the constitution and for State officers, and for members of Congress, the legislature to meet September 7. It passed without a division. The bill was reported in Senate from the Judiciary Committee, with amendments, February 10, 1869, but was not called up.

The general provisions of the bill were these: That the constitution adopted by the convention which met in Richmond, Virginia, on the 3d day of December, A. D. 1867, be submitted for ratification on the day above named to the voters of the State of Virginia, who shall then be registered and qualified as such in compliance with the acts of Congress known as the reconstruction acts. The vote on said constitution shall be "for the constitution," or "against the constitution." The said election shall be held at the same places where the election for delegates to said convention was held, and under the regulations to be prescribed by the commanding general of the military district, and the returns made to him as directed by law.

It is provided by the second section that an election shall be held at the same time and places for members of the general assembly and for all State officers to be elected by the people under said constitution; the election for State officers to be conducted under the same regulations as the election for the ratification of the constitution and by the same persons. The returns of this election shall be in duplicate; one copy to the commanding general and one copy to the president of said convention, who shall give certificates of election to the persons elected.

The officers elected shall enter upon the duties of the offices for which they are chosen as soon as elected and qualified in compliance with the provisions of said constitution, and shall hold their respective offices for the term of years prescribed by the constitution, counting from the 1st day of January next, and until their successors are elected and qualified.

The third section provides that an election for members of the United States Congress shall be held in the congressional districts as established by said convention, one member of Congress being elected in the State at large, at the same time and places as the election for State officers; said election to be conducted by the same persons and under the same regulations before mentioned in this act; the returns to be made in the same manner provided for State officers.

By the fourth section it is provided that no person shall act either as a member of any board of registration to revise and correct the registration of voters as provided in section seven of the act of July 19, 1867, amendatory of the act of March 2, 1867, entitled "An act for the more efficient government of the rebel States," &c., or as a judge, commissioner, or other officer, at any election to be held under the provisions of this act, who is a candidate for any office at the elections to be held as herein provided for.

The fifth section provides that the general assembly elected under and by virtue of this act shall assemble at the capitol, in the city of Richmond, on first Tuesday in September, 1869.

The Senate committee's amendments were: To submit, at the same election, to a separate vote of said voters, the question whether the fourth subdivision of the first section of the third article and the seventh section of the third article of said constitution shall constitute a part thereof, and the vote on said question shall be "for disqualification" or "against disqualification." Also, to substitute the following for the fifth section:

In case a majority of all the votes cast on the ratification of the constitution shall be "for the constitution," the general assembly elected under and by virtue of this act shall assemble at the capitol, in the city of Richmond, on the first Tuesday of July, 1869; but if a majority of the votes cast on the question of ratification be against said constitution, said general assembly shall not convene nor shall any person elected to office under the provisions of this act enter upon the discharge of the duties thereof in pursuance of said election. The provision of the constitution voted upon separately shall constitute a part of the constitution if a majority of the votes cast upon it be "for disqualification;" but if a majority of the votes cast on that question be "against disqualification," it shall not constitute part of the constitution.]

### The Mississippi Bill.

#### IN HOUSE.

1869, March—Mr. Benjamin F. Butler, from the Committee on Reconstruction, reported the following bill:

A BILL to provide for the organization of a provisional government for the State of Mississippi.

*Be it enacted, &c.,* That for the better security of persons and property in Mississippi, the constitutional convention of said State, heretofore elected under and in pursuance of an act of Congress, passed March 2, 1867, entitled "An act for the more efficient government of the rebel States," and the several acts of Congress supplementary thereto and amendatory thereof, and as organized at the time of its adjournment, is hereby authorized to assemble forthwith upon the call of the president thereof; and in case of his failure for thirty days to summon said convention, then the commanding general of the fourth military district is hereby authorized and required to summon by proclamation said convention to assemble at the capital of said State; and said convention shall have, and it is hereby authorized to exercise, the following powers in addition to the powers now authorized by law, to wit: to appoint a provisional governor; to authorize the provisional governor of said State to remove and appoint registrars and judges of elections under said acts of Congress, who shall not be voted for at elections within their own precincts; to submit to the people of said State the constitution heretofore framed by said convention, either with or without amendments; to provide by ordinance that the votes for and against said constitution and for and against the clauses thereof submitted by this act to a separate vote, together with the votes cast for and against all State and local officers voted for under said constitution, shall be forwarded to the provisional governor by the judges of election, and shall be counted in the presence of the provisional governor, the general commanding the military district of Mississippi, and such committee as the convention may appoint for that purpose; and it shall be the duty of said provisional governor, commanding general, and committee to make proclamation of the result of such elections; to pass laws exempting a homestead not exceeding $1,000 in value, and household furniture, mechanical and farming tools, provisions, and other articles of personal property necessary for the support of a family, not exceeding $500 in value, from seizure or sale upon process for the collection of debts; which laws shall continue in force until repealed or modified by the legislature to be elected under the Constitution; and to pass such ordinances, not inconsistent with the Constitution and laws of the United States, as it may deem necessary to protect all persons in their lives, liberty, and property: *Provided,* That said convention shall not continue in session for more than sixty days: *And provided further,* That the districts unrepresented from any cause in the convention at the time of its adjournment shall at once proceed to elect duly qualified persons to take seats in said convention. The election of such delegates shall be held under the direction of the commanding general, in accordance with the provisions of the act of Congress approved March 2, 1867, entitled "An act for the more efficient government of the rebel States," and the acts supplementary thereto; and certificates of election shall be awarded to the candidates receiving the highest number of votes: *And provided, also,* That said convention may submit any one or more provisions of said proposed constitution to a separate vote.

SEC. 2. That the several ordinances which may be passed by the constitutional convention of said State within the limitations as herein provided, shall be in force in said State until disapproved by Congress, or until Mississippi shall have adopted a constitution of State government and the same shall have been approved by Congress: *Provided,* That nothing in this act contained shall deprive any person of trial by jury in the courts of said State for offences against the laws of said State.

SEC. 3. That the military commander in said State, upon the requisition of the provisional governor thereof, shall give aid to the officers of the provisional government of said State in preserving the peace and enforcing the laws, and especially in suppressing unlawful obstructions and forcible resistance to the execution of the laws.

SEC. 4. That the said provisional governor may remove from office in said State any person holding office therein, and may appoint a successor in his stead, and may also fill all vacancies that may occur by death, resignation, or otherwise, subject, however, in all removals and appointments, to the orders and directions of the President of the United States; and the President of the United States may at any time remove the said provisional governor and appoint a successor in his stead.

SEC. 5. That if at any election authorized in the State of Mississippi any person shall knowingly personate and falsely assume to vote in the name of any other person, whether such other person shall then be living or dead, or if the name of the said other person be the name of a fictitious person, or vote more than once at the same election for any candidate for the same office, or vote at a place where he may not be lawfully entitled to vote, or without having a lawful right to vote, or falsely register as a voter, or do any unlawful act to secure a right or an opportunity for himself or other person to vote, or shall, by force, fraud, threat, menace, intimidation, bribery, reward, offer, or promise of any valuable thing whatever, or by any contract for employment, or labor, or for any right whatever, or otherwise attempt to prevent any voter who may at any time be qualified from freely exercising the right of suffrage, or shall by either of such means induce any voter to refuse or neglect to exercise such right, or compel or induce, by either of such means, or otherwise, any officer of an election to receive a vote from a person not legally qualified or entitled to vote, or interfere to hinder or impede in any manner any officer in any election in the discharge of his duties, or by either of such means, or otherwise, induce any officer in any election, or officer whose duty it is to ascertain, announce, or declare the result of any vote, or give or make any certificate, document, or evidence in relation thereto, to violate or refuse to comply with his duty or any law regulating the same, or if any such officer shall neglect or refuse to perform any duty required of him by law, or violate any duty imposed by law, or do any act unauthorized by law relating to or affecting any such vote, election, or the result thereof, or if any person shall aid, counsel, procure, or advise any such voter, person, or officer to do any act herein made a crime, or to omit to do any duty the omission of which is hereby made a crime, or attempt so to do, or if any person shall by force, threat, menace, intimidation, or otherwise prevent any citizen or citizens from assembling in public meeting to discuss or hear discussed any subject whatever, or if any person shall by any means break up, disperse, or molest any assemblage, or any citizen in or of such assemblage when met or meeting to discuss or hear discussion, as aforesaid, or shall by any means prevent any citizen from attending any such assemblage, every person so offending shall be deemed guilty of a crime, and shall for such crime be liable to indictment in any court of the United States of competent jurisdiction, and on conviction thereof shall be adjudged to pay a fine not exceeding five hundred dollars or less than one hundred dollars, and suffer imprisonment for a term not exceeding three years nor less than six months, in the discretion of the court, and pay the costs of prosecution.

SEC. 6. That no officer of Mississippi shall buy or sell treasury warrants, or claims of any sort upon the treasury of the State, or of any county or district thereof. All taxes and moneys collected by any officer shall be paid into the appropriate treasury; and any collector who may receive warrants in payment of taxes shall file with the treasurer a schedule, made under oath, of such warrants, with the name and residence of each person from whom any such warrant may have been received. Any person who shall violate this section shall be deemed guilty of a misdemeanor, and upon conviction thereof shall be punished as is prescribed in the fifth section of this act.

SEC. 7. That the courts of the United States shall have jurisdiction of cases arising under this act.

SEC. 8. That the poll-tax levied in any one year upon any citizen of Mississippi shall not exceed $1 50, and all laws in said State for the collection of taxes and debts shall be uniform, and every citizen shall be entitled to all the exemptions and immunities in these respects of the most favored citizen or class of citizens.

SEC. 9. That all lands which shall hereafter be forfeited and sold for non-payment of any tax, impost, or assessment whatever, in the State of Mississippi, or under proceedings in bankruptcy, or by virtue of the judgment or decree of any court in the said State of Mississippi, shall be disposed of only by sale in separate sub-divisions not exceeding forty acres each: *Provided, however,* That such portion of said land shall first be offered for sale as can be sold with the least injury to the remainder.

April 1—Its further consideration was postponed till the first Monday in December next—yeas 103, nays 62, (not voting 31,) as follow:

YEAS—Messrs. Allison, *Archer,* Armstrong, *Axtell,* Bailey, *Beck, Biggs, Bird,* Blair, *Brooks, Burr, Calkin, Cleveland,* Cowles, *Crebs,* Cullom, Dawes, Deweese,,*Dickinson,* Dixon, Dockery, *Eldridge,* Farnsworth, Ferriss, Finkelnburg, Fitch, Garfield, *Getz,* Gilfillan, *Golladay,* Griswold, *Haldeman,* Hale, *Hambleton, Hamill,* Hawkins, Hawley, *Hoag, Holman,* Hopkins, *Hotchkiss,* Jenckes, *Johnson, Thomas L. Jones, Kerr,* Laflin, Loughridge,

Lynch, *Marshall, Mayham,* McCarthy, *McCormick,* McCrary, *McNeely,* Mercur, *Moffet,* Jesse H. Moore, William Moore, *Morgan,* Morrell, Morrill, *Mungen, Niblack,* O'Neill, Packer, Palmer, Peters, Poland, Pomeroy, *Potter, Randall, Reading, Reeves, Rice,* Rogers, Schenck, *Schumaker,* Scofield, Shanks, *Slocum,* Worthington C. Smith, William Smyth, Stevens, *Stiles,* Stokes, *Stone,* Strickland, *Swann, Sweeney,* Taffe, Tanner, *Trimble,* Twichell, *Van Auken, Voorhees,* Cadwalader C. Washburn, William B. Washburn, *Wells,* Wilkinson, Willard, *Eugene M. Wilson,* Winans, *Woodward*—103.

NAYS—Messrs. Ambler, Arnell, Asper, Beaman, Beatty, Benton, Bingham, Bowen, Boyd, Buffinton, Burdett, Benjamin F. Butler, Roderick R. Butler, Cake, Cessna, Churchill, Amasa Cobb, Clinton L. Cobb, Coburn, Cook, Conger, Donley, Duvall, Ela, Fisher, Hay, Heaton, Hill, Hoar, Alexander H. Jones, Judd, Julian, Kelley, Kelsey, Knapp, Lash, Lawrence, Maynard, Eliakim H. Moore, Negley, Orth, Packard, Paine, Phelps, Prosser, Roots, Sargent, Sheldon, John A. Smith, William J. Smith, Stevenson, Stoughton, Tillman, Tyner, Upson, Van Horn, Ward, Welker, Whittemore, Williams, John T. Wilson, Witcher—62.

## The Public Credit Act.

This bill became a law March 18, 1869, being the first act approved by President GRANT:

*Be it enacted, &c.,* That in order to remove any doubt as to the purpose of the Government to discharge all just obligations to the public creditors, and to settle conflicting questions and interpretations of the laws by virtue of which such obligations have been contracted, it is hereby provided and declared, that the faith of the United States is solemnly pledged to the payment in coin or its equivalent of all the obligations of the United States not bearing interest, known as United States notes, and of all the interest-bearing obligations of the United States, except in cases where the law authorizing the issue of any such obligation has expressly provided that the same may be paid in lawful money or other currency than gold and silver. But none of said interest-bearing obligations not already due shall be redeemed or paid before maturity unless at such time United States notes shall be convertible into coin at the option of the holder, or unless at such time bonds of the United States bearing a lower rate of interest than the bonds to be redeemed can be sold at par in coin. And the United States also solemnly pledges its faith to make provision at the earliest practicable period for the redemption of the United States notes in coin.

March 12—It passed the House—yeas 97, nays 47, (not voting 49,) as follow:

YEAS—Messrs. Allison, Ambler, Ames, Armstrong, Arnell, Asper, *Axtell,* Bailey, Banks, Beaman, Benjamin, Bennett, Bingham, Blair, Boles, Boyd, Buffinton, Burdett, Cessna, Churchill, Clinton L. Cobb, Cook, Conger, Cowles, Cullom, Dawes, Donley, Duval, Dyer, Farnsworth, Ferriss, Ferry, Finkelnburg, Fisher, Fitch, Gilfillan, Hale, Hawley, Heaton, Hoar, Hooper, Hotchkiss, Jenckes, Alexander H. Jones, Judd, Julian, Kelsey, Ketcham, Knapp, Laflin, Lash, Lawrence, Lynch, Maynard, McCrary, McGrew, Mercur, Jesse H. Moore, William Moore, Morrill, Negley, O'Neill, Packard, Paine, Palmer, Phelps, Poland, Pomeroy, Prosser, Roots, Sanford, Sargent, Sawyer, Schenck, Scofield, Sheldon, John A. Smith, Worthington C. Smith, William Smyth, Stokes, Stoughton, Tanner, Tillman, Twichell, Upson, Van Horn, Ward, Cadwalader C. Washburn, William B. Washburn, Welker, Wheeler, Whittemore, Wilkinson, Willard, Williams, Winans—97.

NAYS—Messrs. *Archer,* Beatty, *Beck, Biggs, Bird, Burr,* Benjamin F. Butler, Roderick R. Butler, Amasa Cobb, Coburn, *Crebs,* Deweese, *Dickinson, Eldridge, Getz, Golladay,* Hawkins, *Holman,* Hopkins, *Johnson, Thomas L. Jones, Kerr, Knott, Marshall, Mayham, McCormick, McNeely, Moffet, Mungen, Niblack,* Orth, *Reading, Reeves, Rice,* Shanks, *Joseph S. Smith, Stiles, Stone, Strader, Sweeney,*

Taffe, *Trimble*, Tyner, *Van Trump*, John T. Wilson, *Winchester*, *Woodward*—47.

March 16—It passed the Senate—yeas 42, nays 13, as follow:

YEAS—Messrs. Abbott, Anthony, Boreman, Brownlow, Cameron, Cattell, Chandler, Conkling, Corbett, Cragin, Drake, Edmunds, Fenton, Ferry, Fessenden, Gilbert, Grimes, Harris, Howard, Kellogg, McDonald, Morrill, Nye, Patterson, Pool, Pratt, Ramsey, Robertson, Sawyer, Schurz, Scott, Sherman, Stewart, Sumner, Thayer, Tipton, Trumbull, Warner, Willey, Williams, Wilson, Yates—42.

NAYS—Messrs. *Bayard*, Carpenter, *Casserly*, Cole, *Davis*, Morton, Osborn, Rice, Ross, Spencer, *Stockton*, *Thurman*, *Vickers*—13.

Pending the consideration of this subject, the following proceedings took place:

### IN HOUSE.

1869, March 12—Mr. Schenck introduced the bill passed at third session of Fortieth Congress, and "pocketed" by President JOHNSON. (See page 13–395.)

Mr. Allison moved to strike out the second section; which was agreed to—yeas 87, nays 56, as follow:

YEAS—Messrs. Allison, Ames, *Archer*, Bailey, Beaman, Beatty, *Beck*, *Biggs*, Bingham, *Bird*. Bowen, *Burr*, Benjamin F. Butler, Cake, Cessna, Amasa Cobb, Coburn, Cullom, Davis, Deweese, *Dickinson*, Dyer, *Eldridge*, Farnsworth, Ferriss, Ferry, Fitch, *Getz*, *Golladay*, Haldeman, Hale, *Hamill*, Hawkins, Hay, *Hoag*, Holman, Hooper, Hopkins, Ingersoll, Jenckes, *Thomas L. Jones*, Kelsey, *Kerr*, Knapp, *Knott*, Lawrence, Loughridge, Lynch, *Marshall*, *Mayham*, McCormick, *McNeely*, *Moffet*, Jesse H. Moore, Morrill, *Mungen*, *Niblack*, O'Neill, Orth, *Reading*, Sawyer, Scofield, Shanks, Worthington C. Smith, Stevenson, *Stiles*, *Stone*, Stoughton, *Strader*, *Swann*, *Sweeney*, Taffe, *Trimble*, Tyner, Van Horn, William B. Washburn, Welker, *Wells*, Wilkinson, Willard, Williams, *Eugene M. Wilson*, John T. Wilson, Winans, *Winchester*, Witcher, *Woodward*—87.

NAYS—Messrs. Armstrong, Asper, *Axtell*, Banks, Benjamin, Bennett, Blair, Boles, Boyd, Buffinton, Burdett, Roderick R. Butler, Churchill, Clinton L. Cobb, Conger, Cowles, Dawes, Dockery, Donley, Finkelnburg, Fisher, Garfield, Gilfillan, Heaton, Hoar, *Johnson*, Alexander H. Jones, Judd, Julian, Ketcham, Laflin, Lash, Logan, McGrew, Mercur, William Moore, Packard, Paine, Palmer, Poland, Pomeroy, Prosser, Roots, Sanford, Sargent, Schenck, Sheldon, John A. Smith, Stokes, Strickland, Tanner, Twichell, Ward, Cadwalader C. Washburn, Wheeler, Whittemore—56.

The bill was then passed by the vote previously given.

### IN SENATE.

March 9—The following bill was reported from the Committee on Finance:

A BILL to strengthen the public credit, and relating to contracts for the payment of coin.

*Be it enacted, &c.*, That in order to remove any doubt as to the purpose of the Government to discharge all just obligations to the public creditors, and to settle conflicting questions and interpretations of the laws by virtue of which such obligations have been contracted, it is hereby provided and declared, that the faith of the United States is solemnly pledged to the payment in coin, or its equivalent, of all the interest-bearing obligations of the United States, except in cases where the law authorizing the issue of any such obligation has expressly provided that the same may be paid in lawful money or other currency than gold and silver: *Provided, however,* That before any of said interest-bearing obligations not already due shall mature or be paid before maturity, the obligations not bearing interest, known as United States notes, shall be made convertible into coin at the option of the holder.

SEC. 2. That any contract hereafter made specifically payable in coin, and the consideration of which may be a loan of coin, or a sale of property, or the rendering of labor or service of any kind, the price of which, as carried into the contract, may have been adjusted on the basis of the coin value thereof at the time of such sale or the rendering of such service or labor, shall be legal and valid, and may be enforced according to its terms.

March 11—Mr. Howard moved to insert the word "written" before "contract" in the 2d section where it first occurs; which was agreed to.

Mr. Sumner moved to strike out the 2d section; which was agreed to—yeas 28, nays 15, as follow:

YEAS—Messrs. *Bayard*, Boreman, Carpenter, *Casserly*, Conkling, Corbett, Cragin, Ferry, Fessenden, Gilbert, Harris, Kellogg, McDonald, *Norton*, Nye, Pratt, Robertson, Sawyer, Schurz, Scott, Sprague, Stewart, *Stockton*, Sumner, *Thurman*, Trumbull, *Vickers*, Wilson—28.

NAYS—Messrs. Abbott, Anthony, Brownlow, Drake, Grimes, Hamlin, Morrill, Morton, Osborn, Patterson, Ramsey, Ross, Sherman, Warner, Williams—15.

Mr. Thurman moved to add to the 1st section the following proviso:

*Provided,* That nothing herein contained shall apply to the obligations commonly called five-twenty bonds.

Which was not agreed to—yeas 12, nays 31, as follow:

YEAS—Messrs. *Bayard*, Boreman, *Casserly*, Morton, *Norton*, Osborn, Pratt, Ross, Sprague, *Stockton*, *Thurman*, *Vickers*—12.

NAYS—Messrs. Abbott, Anthony, Brownlow, Carpenter, Conkling, Corbett, Cragin, Drake, Fenton, Ferry, Gilbert, Grimes, Hamlin, Harris, Kellogg, McDonald, Morrill, Nye, Patterson, Ramsey, Sawyer, Schurz, Scott, Sherman, Stewart, Sumner, Tipton, Trumbull, Warner, Williams, Wilson—31.

Mr. Morton moved to strike from section 1st the words, "authorizing the issue of any such obligation;" which was not agreed to—yeas 14, nays 32, as follow:

YEAS—Messrs. *Bayard*, Brownlow, *Casserly*, Morton, *Norton*, Pomeroy, Pratt, Robertson, Ross, Spencer, Sprague, *Stockton*, *Thurman*, *Vickers*—14.

NAYS—Messrs. Abbott, Anthony, Boreman, Carpenter, Cattell, Corbett, Cragin, Drake, Fenton, Ferry, Fessenden, Gilbert, Grimes, Hamlin, Howard, Howe, Morrill, Patterson, Ramsey, Sawyer, Schurz, Scott, Sherman, Stewart, Sumner, Thayer, Tipton, Warner, Willey, Williams, Wilson, Yates—32.

March 15—This bill was then laid aside, and the House bill taken up and passed by the vote given above.

### Amendment to the Tenure-of-Office Act.

This bill passed both Houses, and became a law:

AN ACT to amend "An act regulating the tenure of certain civil offices."

*Be it enacted by the Senate and House of Representatives of the United States of America in Congress assembled,* That the first and second sections of an act entitled "An act regulating the tenure of certain civil offices," passed March 2, 1867, be, and the same are hereby, repealed, and in lieu of said repealed sections the following are hereby enacted:

That every person holding any civil office to which he has been or hereafter may be appointed, by and with the advice and consent of the Senate, and who shall have become duly qualified to act therein, shall be entitled to hold such office during the term for which he shall have been appointed, unless sooner removed by and with the advice and consent of the Senate, or by the appointment, with the like advice and consent, of a successor in his place, except as herein otherwise provided.

SEC. 2. *And be it further enacted*, That during any recess of the Senate the President is hereby empowered, in his discretion, to suspend any civil officer appointed by and with the advice and consent of the Senate, except judges of the United States courts, until the end of the next session of the Senate, and to designate some suitable person, subject to be removed in his discretion by the designation of another, to perform the duties of such suspended officer in the meantime; and such person so designated shall take the oaths and give the bonds required by law to be taken and given by the suspended officer, and shall, during the time he performs his duties, be entitled to the salary and emoluments of such office, no part of which shall belong to the officer suspended; and it shall be the duty of the President within thirty days after the commencement of each session of the Senate, except for any office which in his opinion ought not to be filled, to nominate persons to fill all vacancies in office which existed at the meeting of the Senate, whether temporarily filled or not, and also in the place of all officers suspended; and if the Senate during such session shall refuse to advise and consent to an appointment in the place of any suspended officer, then, and not otherwise, the President shall nominate another person as soon as practicable to said session of the Senate for said office.

SEC. 3. *And be it further enacted*, That section three of the act to which this is an amendment be amended by inserting after the word "resignation," in line three of said section, the following: " or expiration of term of office."

Approved, April 5, 1869.

The final vote was as follows:

### IN HOUSE, March 31.

YEAS—Messrs. Allison, Ambler, Ames, Armstrong, Arnell, Asper, Bailey, Banks, Beaman, Bennett, Bingham, Blair, Boles, Bowen, Buffinton, Burdett, Benjamin F. Butler, Roderick R. Butler, Cake, Cessna, Churchill, Amasa Cobb, Clinton L. Cobb, Coburn, Cook, Conger, Cowles, Cullom, Dawes, Dixon, Dockery, Donley, Duval, Ela, Ferriss, Finkelnburg, Fisher, Fitch, Garfield, Gilfillan, Hale, Hawley, Hay, Heaton, Hill, Hooper, Hopkins, Ingersoll, Jenckes, Alexander H. Jones, Judd, Kelsey, Knapp, Laflin, Lash, Logan, Lynch, Maynard, McCarthy, McCrary, McGrew, Mercur, Eliakim H. Moore, Jesse H. Moore, William Moore, Morrell, Morrill, O'Neill, Packard, Packer, Paine, Palmer, Peters, Phelps, Pomeroy, Prosser, Roots, Sanford, Sargent, Sawyer, Schenck, Scofield, Shanks, Sheldon, John A. Smith, William J. Smith, William Smyth, Stevens, Stevenson, Stokes, Stoughton, Strickland, Taffe, Tanner, Tillman, Twichell, Tyner, Upson, Van Horn, Ward, Cadwalader C. Washburn, William B. Washburn, Welker, Wheeler, Williams, John T. Wilson, Winans, Witcher—108.

NAYS—Messrs. *Archer, Axtell*, Beatty, *Beck*, Benton, *Biggs, Bird*, Boyd, *Brooks, Burr, Calkin*, Clarke, *Cleveland, Crebs*, Davis, Deweese, *Dickinson, Eldridge*, Ferry, *Getz, Golladay, Griswold, Haldeman, Hambleton. Hamill*, Hawkins, *Hoag*, Hoar, *Holman, Johnson, Thomas L.* Jones, Julian, *Kerr*, Loughridge, *Marshall, Mayham, McCormick, McNeely, Moffet, Morgan, Mungen, Niblack*, Orth, Poland, *Potter, Randall, Reading. Reeves*, Rice, Rogers, *Schumaker, Slocum*, Worthington C. Smith, *Stiles, Stone, Swann, Sweeney, Trimble, Van Auken, Voorhees, Wells*, Whittemore, Wilkinson, Willard, *Eugene M. Wilson, Wood, Woodward* —67.

### IN SENATE, March 31.

YEAS—Messrs. Abbott, Anthony, Boreman, Brownlow, Buckingham, Cameron, Carpenter, Chandler, Conkling, Corbett, Cragin, Drake, Edmunds, Fenton, Ferry, Gilbert, Grimes, Hamlin, Harlan, Harris, Howard, Kellogg, Morrill, Nye, Osborn, Patterson, Pomeroy, Pool, Pratt, Ramsey, Rice, Sawyer, Schurz, Scott, Spencer, Sumner, Tipton, Trumbull, Willey, Williams, Wilson, Yates—42.

NAYS—Messrs. *Bayard, Casserly, Davis, McCreery*, Sprague, *Stockton, Thurman, Vickers*—8.

### PRELIMINARY VOTES.

The following is the action of each House in detail:

### IN HOUSE.

1869, March 9—The bill to repeal the tenure-of-office act was introduced by Mr. Benjamin F. Butler, and read a first and second time and passed—yeas 138, nays 16, (not voting 39,) as follow:

YEAS—Messrs. *Adams*, Allison, Ambler, *Archer*, Asper, *Axtell*, Bailey, Banks, Beaman, *Beck*, Bennett, *Biggs*, Bingham, Blair, Boutwell, Bowen, Boyd, Buffinton, Burdett, *Burr*, Benjamin F. Butler, Roderick R. Butler, Cake, Cessna, Churchill, Clarke, *Cleveland*, Amasa Cobb, Clinton L. Cobb, Coburn, Cook, Conger, *Crebs*, Cullom, Davis, Dawes, Deweese, Dickey, *Dickinson*, Dyer, *Eldridge*, Ferry, Finckelnburg, Fisher, Fitch, Gilfillan, *Golladay, Griswold, Haldeman*, Hale, *Hamill*, Hawkins, Hawley, Hay, Heaton, Hill, *Hoag*, Hoar, *Holman*, Ingersoll, *Johnson*, Alexander H. Jones, *Thomas L. Jones*, Judd, Julian, Kelley, Kelsey, *Kerr*, Ketcham, Knapp, *Knott*, Lash, Logan, Loughridge, *Marshall, Mayham, McCormick*, McCrary, McGrew, *McNeely, Moffet*, Eliakim H. Moore, Jesse H. Moore, Morrill, Negley, *Niblack*, O'Neill, Orth, Packard, Packer, Paine, Palmer, Peters, Phelps, Pomeroy, *Potter*, Prosser, *Randall, Reading, Rice*, Rogers, Sargent, *Schumaker*, Scofield, Shanks, Sheldon, *Slocum*, John A. Smith, William J. Smith, Stevenson, *Stiles, Stone*, Stoughton, *Strader*, Strickland, *Swann, Sweeney. Trimble*, Twichell, Tyner, Upson, *Van Auken*, Van Horn, *Van Trump, Voorhees*, Cadwalader C. Washburn, William B. Washburn, Welker, *Wells*, Wheeler, Williams, *Eugene M. Wilson*, John T. Wilson, Winans, *Winchester*, Witcher, *Wood, Woodward*—138.

NAYS—Messrs. Arnell, Boles, Farnsworth, Ferriss, Hotchkiss, Jenckes, Lawrence, Maynard, Schenck, Worthington C. Smith, Stokes, Taffe, Tillman, Ward, Whittemore, Willard—16.

### IN SENATE.

March 11—It was referred to the Committee on the Judiciary—yeas 34, nays 25, as follow:

YEAS—Messrs. Abbott, Anthony, Brownlow, Buckingham, Carpenter, Cattell, Chandler, Conkling, Cragin, Drake, Edmunds, Ferry, Gilbert, Hamlin, Harris, Howard, Howe, Morrill, *Norton*, Nye, Patterson, Pomeroy, Ramsey. Rice, Sawyer, Schurz, Scott, Stewart. Sumner, Tipton, Trumbull, Williams, Wilson, Yates—34.

NAYS—Messrs. *Bayard*, Boreman, Cameron, *Casserly*, Corbett, *Davis*, Fenton, Fessenden, Fowler, Grimes, *McCreery*, McDonald, Morton, Pool, Pratt, Robertson, Ross, Sherman, Spencer, Sprague, Stockton, Thayer, *Thurman, Vickers*, Warner—25.

March 24—Mr. Trumbull reported the bill from the Committee on the Judiciary, amended so as to strike out all after the enacting clause and insert as follows:

That the 1st and 2d sections of an act entitled "An act regulating the tenure of certain civil officers," passed March 2, 1867, be, and the same are hereby, repealed, and in lieu of said repealed sections the following are hereby enacted: That every person holding any civil office to which he has been or may hereafter be appointed, by and with the advice and consent of the Senate, and who shall have become qualified to act therein, shall be entitled to hold such office during the term for which he shall have been appointed, unless sooner removed by and with the advice and consent of the Senate, or by the appointment, with the like advice and consent, of a successor in his place, except as herein otherwise provided.

SEC. 2. *And be it further enacted,* That during any recess of the Senate the President is hereby empowered, in his discretion, to suspend any civil officer appointed by and with the advice and consent of the Senate, except judges of the United States courts, until the end of the next session of the Senate, and to designate some suitable person subject to be removed in his discretion by the designation of another to perform the duties of such suspended officer in the meantime; and such person so designated shall take oaths and give bonds required by law to be taken and given by the suspended officer, and shall during the time he performs his duties be entitled to the salary and emoluments of such office, no part of which shall belong to the officer suspended. It shall be the duty of the President within thirty days after the commencement of each session of the Senate, except for any office which in his opinion ought not to be filled, to nominate persons to fill all vacancies in office which existed at the meeting of the Senate, whether temporarily filled or not, and also in the place of all officers suspended, and if the Senate during such session shall refuse to advise and consent to an appointment in the place of any suspended officer, and shall also refuse by vote to assent to his suspension, then, and not otherwise, such officer, at the end of the session, shall be entitled to resume the possession of the office from which he was suspended, and afterwards to discharge its duties and receive its emoluments as though no such suspension had taken place.

Which was agreed to—yeas 37, nays 15, as follow:

YEAS—Messrs. Abbott, Anthony, Boreman, Brownlow, Buckingham, Carpenter, Cattell, Chandler, Conkling, Cragin, Drake, Edmunds, Ferry, Gilbert, Hamlin, Harlan, Harris, Howard, Kellogg, Morrill, Osborn, Patterson, Pratt, Ramsey, Rice, Sawyer, Schurz, Scott, Spencer, Stewart, Sumner, Tipton, Trumbull, Willey, Williams, Wilson, Yates—37.

NAYS—Messrs. Bayard, *Casserly, Davis,* Fessenden, Fowler, Grimes, *McCreery,* McDonald, *Norton,* Ross, Sprague, *Stockton, Thurman, Vickers,* Warner—15.

### IN HOUSE.

March 25—A motion to refer to the Committee on the Judiciary was agreed to—yeas 94, nays 79, not voting 23.

March 26—This vote was reconsidered, without a division, and the House refused to concur in the amendment of the Senate—yeas 70, nays 99, (not voting 27,) as follow:

YEAS—Messrs. Ames, Armstrong, Asper, Bailey, Beaman, Beatty, Benton, Bingham, Boles, Burdett, Roderick R. Butler, Cessna, Churchill, Clinton L. Cobb, Coburn, Cowles, Dixon, Dockery, Donley, Duval, Ela, Farnsworth, Ferriss, Finkelnburg, Garfield, Gilfillan, Hawley, Hill, Hooper, Hotchkiss, Ingersoll, Jenckes, Kelley, Kelsey, Ketcham, Knapp, Laflin, Lash, William Lawrence, Lynch, Maynard, McCarthy, McGrew, Mercur, Eliakim H. Moore, William Moore. Packer, Poland, Pomeroy, Prosser, Roots, Sanford, Sargent, Sawyer, Schenck, Scofield, Shanks, William J. Smith, William Smyth, Stevens, Stoughton, Strickland, Taffe. Tillman,

Twichell, Ward, Welker, Wheeler, John T. Wilson, Winans—70.

NAYS—Messrs. Allison, Ambler, *Archer, Axtell,* Banks, *Beck, Biggs, Bird,* Blair, Boyd, *Brooks,* Buffinton, *Burr,* Benjamin F. Butler, *Calkin,* Clarke, *Cleveland,* Amasa Cobb, Cook, Conger, *Crebs,* Cullom, Davis, Dawes, Deweese, Dickey, *Dickinson,* Dyer, *Eldridge,* Ferry, Fisher, *Fox, Getz, Golladay, Griswold,* Haight, *Haldeman, Hambleton,* Hawkins, Hay, Heaton, *Hoag,* Hoar, *Holman,* Hopkins, *Johnson,* Alexander H. Jones, *Thomas L. Jones,* Julian, *Kerr, Knott,* Logan, Loughridge, *Marshall, Mayham,* McCrary, *McNeely, Moffet,* Jesse H. Moore, *Morgan, Mungen, Niblack,* O'Neill, Orth, Packard, Paine, Palmer, Phelps, *Randall, Reading,* Reeves, Rice, Rogers, *Schumaker,* Sheldon, *Slocum,* John A. Smith, *Joseph S. Smith,* Stevenson, *Swann, Sweeney,* Tanner, Townsend, *Trimble,* Tyner, Upson, Van Horn, *Van Trump,* Cadwalader C. Washburn, William B. Washburn, *Wells,* Whittemore, Wilkinson, Williams, *Eugene M. Wilson, Winchester,* Witcher, *Wood, Woodward*—99.

### IN SENATE.

March 30—A motion to recede from its amendments was lost—yeas 20, nays 37, as follow:

YEAS—Messrs. Bayard, *Casserly,* Cole, *Davis,* Fenton, Fessenden, Fowler, Grimes, *McCreery,* McDonald, Morton, Pool, Robertson, Ross, Sprague, *Stockton,* Thayer, *Thurman, Vickers,* Warner—20.

NAYS—Messrs. Abbott, Anthony, Boreman, Brownlow, Buckingham, Cameron, Carpenter, Cattell, Conkling, Cragin, Drake, Edmunds, Ferry, Gilbert, Hamlin, Harlan, Harris, Howard, Howe, Kellogg, Morrill, Nye, Patterson, Pomeroy, Pratt, Ramsey, Rice, Sawyer, Schurz, Scott, Spencer, Sumner, Tipton, Trumbull, Willey, Williams, Wilson—37.

A committee of conference was then voted, and Messrs. Trumbull, Edmunds, and Grimes appointed conferees.

### IN HOUSE.

March 30—A motion that the House recede from its disagreement was lost—yeas 61, nays 106. The conference was granted, and Messrs Benjamin F. Butler, Cadwalader C. Washburn, and Bingham were appointed the managers.

March 31—The committee of conference reported, recommending certain amendments, (to make the bill stand as it finally passed,) and the report was adopted—in the House, yeas 108, nays 67; in the Senate, yeas 42, nays 8, as printed above.

---

### On the Effect of the XVth Amendment.

1869, March 22—Mr. Johnson moved a suspension of the rules so as to enable him to submit this resolution:

*Resolved,* That in passing the resolution for the fifteenth amendment to the Constitution of the United States this house never intended that Chinese or Mongolians should become voters.

The motion to suspend the rules was lost—yeas 42, nays 106, not voting 48. The YEAS were Messrs. *Archer, Axtell, Bird, Brooks, Burr, Calkin, Crebs, Dickinson, Eldridge,* Fitch, *Golladay,* Haight, *Haldeman, Hambleton, Hamill,* Hawkins, *Holman, Johnson, Thomas L. Jones, Kerr, Knott, Mayham, McNeely, Potter, Randall, Reading, Reeves,* Sargent, *Slocum, Joseph S. Smith,* William J. Smith, *Stiles, Stone, Strader, Swann, Van Auken, Van Trump, Wells, Eugene M. Wilson, Winchester, Wood, Woodward.*

# XLIII.

## PRESIDENT GRANT'S INAUGURAL ADDRESS,

### AND MESSAGE ON RECONSTRUCTION, AND THE OFFICIAL PROCLAMATIONS OF THE YEAR.

**President Grant's Inaugural Address, March 4th, 1869.**

*Citizens of the United States:*

Your suffrages having elected me to the office of President of the United States, I have, in conformity to the Constitution of our country, taken the oath of office prescribed therein. I have taken this oath without mental reservation, and with the determination to do to the best of my ability all that it requires of me. The responsibilities of the position I feel, but accept them without fear. The office has come to me unsought; I commence its duties untrammelled. I bring to it a conscious desire and determination to fill it to the best of my ability to the satisfaction of the people.

On all leading questions agitating the public mind I will always express my views to Congress, and urge them according to my judgment; and, when I think it advisable, will exercise the constitutional privilege of interposing a veto to defeat measures which I oppose. But all laws will be faithfully executed whether they meet my approval or not.

I shall on all subjects have a policy to recommend, but none to enforce against the will of the people. Laws are to govern all alike, those opposed as well as those who favor them. I know no method to secure the repeal of bad or obnoxious laws so effective as their stringent execution.

The country having just emerged from a great rebellion, many questions will come before it for settlement in the next four years which preceding Administrations have never had to deal with. In meeting these it is desirable that they should be approached calmly, without prejudice, hate or sectional pride, remembering that the greatest good to the greatest number is the object to be attained.

This requires security of person, property, and free religious and political opinion in every part of our common country, without regard to local prejudice. All laws to secure these ends will receive my best efforts for their enforcement.

A great debt has been contracted in securing to us and our posterity the Union. The payment of this, principal and interest, as well as the return to a specie basis, as soon as it can be accomplished without material detriment to the debtor class or to the country at large, must be provided for. To protect the national honor every dollar of government indebtedness should be paid in gold, unless otherwise expressly stipulated in the contract. Let it be understood that no repudiator of one farthing of our public debt will be trusted in public place, and it will go far towards strengthening a credit which ought to be the best in the world, and will ultimately enable us to replace the debt with bonds bearing less interest than we now pay. To this should be added a faithful collection of the revenue, a strict accountability to the treasury for every dollar collected, and the greatest practicable retrenchment in expenditure in every department of government.

When we compare the paying capacity of the country now—with the ten States in poverty from the effects of war, but soon to emerge, I trust, into greater prosperity than ever before—with its paying capacity twenty-five years ago, and calculate what it probably will be twenty-five years hence, who can doubt the feasibility of paying every dollar then with more ease than we now pay for useless luxuries? Why, it looks as though Providence had bestowed upon us a strong box in the precious metals locked up in the sterile mountains of the far west, and which we are now forging the key to unlock, to meet the very contingency that is now upon us.

Ultimately it may be necessary to insure the facilities to reach these riches, and it may be necessary also that the general government should give its aid to secure this access. But that should only be when a dollar of obligation to pay secures precisely the same sort of dollar to use now, and not before. Whilst the question of specie payments is in abeyance, the prudent business man is careful about contracting debts payable in the distant future. The nation should follow the same rule. A prostrate commerce is to be rebuilt and all industries encouraged.

The young men of the country, those who from their age must be its rulers twenty-five years hence, have a peculiar interest in maintaining the national honor. A moment's reflection as to what will be our commanding influence among the nations of the earth in their day, if they are only true to themselves, should inspire them with national pride. All divisions, geographical, political, and religious, can join in this common sentiment. How the public debt is to be paid, or specie payments resumed, is not so important as that a plan should be adopted and acquiesced in.

A united determination to do is worth more than divided counsels upon the method of doing. Legislation upon this subject may not be necessary now, nor even advisable, but it will be when the civil law is more fully restored in all parts of the country, and trade resumes its wonted channels.

It will be my endeavor to execute all laws in good faith, to collect all revenues assessed, and to h    em properly accounted for and economically disbursed. I will, to the best of my ability, appoint to office those only who will carry out this design.

In regard to foreign policy, I would deal with nations as equitable law requires individuals to deal with each other, and I would protect the law-abiding citizen, whether of native or foreign birth, wherever his rights are jeopardized or the flag of our country floats. I would respect the rights of all nations, demanding equal respect for our own. If others depart from this rule in their dealings with us, we may be compelled to follow their precedent.

The proper treatment of the original occupants of this land, the Indians, is one deserving of careful study. I will favor any course toward them which tends to their civilization and ultimate citizenship.

The question of suffrage is one which is likely to agitate the public so long as a portion of the citizens of the nation are excluded from its privileges in any State. It seems to me very desirable that this question should be settled now, and I entertain the hope and express the desire that it may be by the ratification of the fifteenth article of amendment to the Constitution.

In conclusion, I ask patient forbearance one toward another throughout the land, and a determined effort on the part of every citizen to do his share toward cementing a happy Union, and I ask the prayers of the nation to Almighty God in behalf of this consummation.

----

### President Grant's Message respecting the Reconstruction of Virginia and Mississippi, April 7, 1869.     —

*To the Senate and House of Representatives:*

While I am aware that the time in which Congress proposes now to remain in session is very brief, and that it is its desire, as far as is consistent with the public interest, to avoid entering upon the general business of legislation, there is one subject which concerns so deeply the welfare of the country that I deem it my duty to bring it before you.

I have no doubt that you will concur with me in the opinion that it is desirable to restore the States which were engaged in the rebellion to their proper relations to the Government and the country at as early a period as the people of those States shall be found willing to become peaceful and orderly communities, and to adopt and maintain such constitutions and laws as will effectually secure the civil and political rights of all persons within their borders. The authority of the United States, which has been vindicated and established by its military power, must undoubtedly be asserted for the absolute protection of all its citizens in the full enjoyment of the freedom and security which is the object of a republican government. But whenever the people of a rebellious State are ready to enter in good faith upon the accomplishment of this object, in entire conformity with the constitutional authority of Congress, it is certainly desirable that all causes of irritation should be

removed as promptly as possible, that a more perfect union may be established, and the country be restored to peace and prosperity.

The convention of the people of Virginia which met in Richmond on Tuesday, December 3, 1867, framed a constitution for that State, which was adopted by the convention on the 17th of April, 1868, and I desire respectfully to call the attention of Congress to the propriety of providing by law for the holding of an election in that State at some time during the months of May and June next, under the direction of the military commander of that district, at which the question of the adoption of that constitution shall be submitted to the citizens of the State; and if this should seem desirable, I would recommend that a separate vote be taken upon such parts as may be thought expedient, and that at the same time and under the same authority there shall be an election for the officers provided under such constitution, and that the constitution, or such parts thereof as shall have been adopted by the people, be submitted to Congress on the first Monday of December next for its consideration, so that if the same is then approved the necessary steps will have been taken for the restoration of the State of Virginia to its proper relations to the Union. I am led to make this recommendation from the confident hope and belief that the people of that State are now ready to co-operate with the national government in bringing it again into such relations to the Union as it ought as soon as possible to establish and maintain and to give to all its people those equal rights under the law which were asserted in the Declaration of Independence in the words of one of the most illustrious of its sons.

I desire also to ask the consideration of Congress to the question whether there is not just ground for believing that the constitution framed by a convention of the people of Mississippi for that State, and once rejected,* might not be again submitted to the people of that State in like manner, and with the probability of the same result.

U. S. GRANT.

WASHINGTON, D. C., *April* 7, 1869.

### Final Certificate of Mr. Secretary Seward respecting the Ratification of the Fourteenth Amendment to the Constitution, July 28, 1868.

BY WILLIAM H. SEWARD, SECRETARY OF STATE OF THE UNITED STATES.

*To all to whom these presents may come, greeting:*

Whereas by an act of Congress passed on the 20th of April, 1818, entitled "An act to provide for the publication of the laws of the United States and for other purposes," it is declared, that whenever official notice shall have been received at the Department of State that any amendment which heretofore has been and hereafter may be proposed to the Constitution of the United States has been adopted according to the provisions of the Constitution, it shall be the duty of the said Secretary of State forthwith to cause the said amendment to be published in the newspapers authorized to promulgate the laws,

----

*The vote was taken June 22, 1868, and, as transmitted by Gen. Gillem, was as follows: For the constitution, 56,231; against it, 63,860. Number of registered voters, 155,351.

with his certificate, specifying the States by which the same may have been adopted, and that the same has become valid to all intents and purposes as a part of the Constitution of the United States;

And whereas the Congress of the United States, on or about the 16th day of June, 1866, submitted to the legislatures of the several States a proposed amendment to the Constitution in the following words, to wit:

JOINT RESOLUTION proposing an amendment to the Constitution of the United States.

*Be it resolved by the Senate and House of Representatives of the United States of America, in Congress assembled,* (two-thirds of both Houses concurring,) That the following article be proposed to the legislatures of the several States as an amendment to the Constitution of the United States, which, when ratified by three-fourths of said legislatures, shall be valid as part of the Constitution, namely:

### ARTICLE XIV.

SEC. 1. All persons born or naturalized in the United States, and subject to the jurisdiction thereof, are citizens of the United States, and of the States wherein they reside. No State shall make or enforce any law which shall abridge the privileges or immunities of citizens of the United States; nor shall any State deprive any person of life, liberty, or property, without due process of law, nor deny to any person within its jurisdiction the equal protection of the laws.

SEC. 2. Representatives shall be apportioned among the several States according to their respective numbers, counting the whole number of persons in each State, excluding Indians not taxed. But when the right to vote at any election for the choice of electors for President and Vice-President of the United States, representatives in Congress, the executive and judicial officers of a State, or the members of the legislature thereof, is denied to any of the male inhabitants of such State, being twenty-one years of age, and citizens of the United States, or in any way abridged, except for participation in rebellion or other crime, the basis of representation therein shall be reduced in the proportion which the number of such male citizens shall bear to the whole number of male citizens twenty-one years of age in such State.

SEC. 3. No person shall be a senator or representative in Congress, or elector of President and Vice-President, or hold any office, civil or military, under the United States, or under any State, who, having previously taken an oath as a member of Congress, or as an officer of the United States, or as a member of any State Legislature, or as an executive or judicial officer of any State, to support the Constitution of the United States, shall have engaged in insurrection or rebellion against the same, or given aid or comfort to the enemies thereof. But Congress may by a vote of two-thirds of each House remove such disability.

SEC. 4. The validity of the public debt of the United States, authorized by law, including debts incurred for payment of pensions and bounties for services in suppressing insurrection or rebellion, shall not be questioned. But neither the United States nor any State shall assume or pay any debt or obligation incurred in aid of insurrection or rebellion against the United States, or any claim for the loss or emancipation of any slave; but all such debts, obligations, and claims shall be held illegal and void.

SEC. 5. The Congress shall have power to enforce, by appropriate legislation, the provisions of this article. SCHUYLER COLFAX,
*Speaker of the House of Representatives.*
LA FAYETTE S. FOSTER,
*President of the Senate pro tempore.*
Attest:
EDWD. McPHERSON,
*Clerk of the House of Representatives.*
J. W. FORNEY,
*Secretary of the Senate.*

And whereas the Senate and House of Representatives of the Congress of the United States, on the 21st day of July, 1868, adopted and transmitted to the Department of State a concurrent resolution, which concurrent resolution is in the words and figures following, to wit:

IN SENATE OF THE UNITED STATES,
*July* 21, 1868.

Whereas the Legislatures of the States of Connecticut, Tennessee, New Jersey, Oregon, Vermont, West Virginia, Kansas, Missouri, Indiana, Ohio, Illinois, Minnesota, New York, Wisconsin, Pennsylvania, Rhode Island, Michigan, Nevada, New Hampshire, Massachusetts, Nebraska, Maine, Iowa, Arkansas, Florida, North Carolina, Alabama, South Carolina, and Louisiana, being three-fourths and more of the several States of the Union, have ratified the fourteenth article of amendment to the Constitution of the United States, duly proposed by two-thirds of each House of the Thirty-Ninth Congress; therefore,

*Resolved by the Senate,* (the House of Representatives concurring,) That said fourteenth article is hereby declared to be a part of the Constitution of the United States, and it shall be duly promulgated as such by the Secretary of State.

Attest: GEORGE C. GORHAM,
*Secretary.*

And whereas official notice has been received at the Department of State that the legislatures of the several States next hereinafter named have, at the times respectively herein mentioned, taken the proceedings hereinafter recited upon or in relation to the ratification of the said proposed amendment, called article fourteenth, namely:

The Legislature of Connecticut ratified the amendment June 30, 1866; the Legislature of New Hampshire ratified it July 7, 1866; the Legislature of Tennessee ratified it July 19, 1866; the Legislature of New Jersey ratified it September 11, 1866, and the Legislature of the same State passed a resolution in April, 1868, to withdraw the consent to it; the Legislature of Oregon ratified it September 19, 1866; the Legislature of Texas rejected it November 1, 1866; the Legislature of Vermont ratified it on or previous to November 9, 1866; the Legislature of Georgia rejected it November 13, 1866, and the Legislature of the same State ratified it July 21, 1868; the Legislature of North Carolina rejected it December 4, 1866, and the Legislature of the same State ratified it July 4, 1868; the Legislature of South Carolina rejected it December 20, 1866, and the Legislature of the same State ratified it July 9, 1868; the Legislature of Virginia rejected it January 9, 1867; the Legislature of Kentucky rejected it January 10, 1867; the Legislature of New York ratified it January 10, 1867; the Legislature of Ohio ratified it January 11, 1867, and the Legislature of the same State passed a resolution in January, 1868, to withdraw its consent to it; the Legislature of Illinois ratified it January 15, 1867; the Legislature of West Virginia ratified it January 16, 1867; the Legislature of Kansas ratified it January 18, 1867; the Legislature of Maine ratified it January 19, 1867; the Legislature of Nevada ratified it January 22, 1867; the Legislature of Missouri ratified it on or previous to January 26, 1867; the Legislature of Indiana ratified it January 29, 1867; the Legislature of Minnesota ratified it February 1, 1867; the Legislature of Rhode Island ratified it February 7, 1867; the Legislature of Delaware rejected it February 7, 1867; the Legislature of Wisconsin ratified it February 13, 1867; the Legislature of Pennsylvania ratified it February 13, 1867; the Legislature of Michigan ratified it February 15, 1867; the Legislature of Massachusetts ratified it March 20, 1867; the Legislature of Maryland rejected it March 23, 1867; the Legislature of Nebraska ratified it June 15, 1867; the Legislature of Iowa ratified it April 3, 1868; the Legislature of Arkansas ratified it April 6, 1868; the Legislature of Florida ratified it June 9, 1868; the Legislature of Louisiana ratified it July 9, 1868; and the Legislature of Alabama ratified it July 13, 1868.

Now, therefore, be it known that I, William H. Seward, Secretary of State of the United States, in execution of the aforesaid act, and of the aforesaid concurrent resolution of the 21st of July, 1868, and in conformance thereto, do hereby direct the said proposed amendment to the Constitution of the United States to be published in the newspapers authorized to promulgate the laws of the United States, and I do hereby certify that the said proposed amendment has been adopted in the manner hereinbefore mentioned by the States specified in the said concurrent resolution, namely, the States of Connecticut, New Hampshire, Tennessee, New Jersey, Oregon, Vermont, New York, Ohio, Illinois, West Virginia, Kansas, Maine, Nevada, Missouri, Indiana, Minnesota, Rhode Island, Wisconsin, Pennsylvania, Michigan, Massachusetts, Nebraska, Iowa, Arkansas, Florida, North Carolina, Louisiana, South Carolina, Alabama, and also by the Legislature of the State of Georgia; the States thus specified being more than three-fourths of the States of the United States.

And I do further certify, that the said amendment has become valid to all intents and purposes as a part of the Constitution of the United States.

In testimony whereof I have hereunto set my hand and caused the seal of the Department of State to be affixed.

Done at the city of Washington, this 28th day of July, in the year of our Lord 1868, and of the independence of the [SEAL.] United States of America the ninety-third.

WILLIAM H. SEWARD,
*Secretary of State.*

[For previous certificates see Manual of 1868, p. 121, or Hand-Book of Politics, p. 379.]

## President Johnson's Proclamation of General Amnesty, December 25, 1868.

Whereas the President of the United States has heretofore set forth several proclamations, offering amnesty and pardon to persons who had been or were concerned in the late rebellion against the lawful authority of the Government of the United States, which proclamations were severally issued on the 8th day of December, 1863, on the 26th day of March, 1864, on the 29th day of May, 1865, on the 7th day of September, 1867, and on the 4th day of July, in the present year;

And whereas the authority of the federal government having been re-established in all the States and Territories within the jurisdiction of the United States, it is believed that such prudential reservations and exceptions as of the dates of said several proclamations were deemed necessary and proper may now be wisely and justly relinquished, and that a universal amnesty and pardon for participation in said rebellion extended to all who have borne any part therein will tend to secure permanent peace, order, and prosperity throughout the land, and to renew and fully restore confidence and fraternal feeling among the whole people, and their respect and attachment to the national government, designed by its patriotic founders for general good:

Now, therefore, be it known that I, ANDREW JOHNSON, President of the United States, by virtue of the power and authority in me vested by the Constitution, and in the name of the sovereign people of the United States, do hereby proclaim and declare unconditionally, and without reservation, to all and to every person who directly or indirectly participated in the late insurrection or rebellion, a full pardon and amnesty for the offence of treason against the United States, or of adhering to their enemies during the late civil war, with restoration of all rights, privileges, and immunities under the Constitution and the laws which have been made in pursuance thereof.

In testimony whereof I have signed these presents with my hand, and have caused the seal of the United States to be hereunto affixed.

Done at the city of Washington, the 25th day of December, in the year of our Lord 1868, and of the independence of the [SEAL.] United States of America the ninety-third. ANDREW JOHNSON.

By the President:
F. W. SEWARD,
*Acting Secretary of State.*

[For previous proclamations of amnesty, see Manual of 1867, p. 9; Manual of 1868, pp. 82-84, or Hand-Book of Politics, pp. 9, 342-344.]

**Message Respecting this Proclamation, January 19, 1869.**

*To the Senate of the United States:*

The resolution adopted on the 5th instant, requesting the President "to transmit to the Senate a copy of any proclamation of amnesty made by him since the last adjournment of Congress, and also to communicate to the Senate by what authority of law the same was made," has been received.

I accordingly transmit herewith a copy of a proclamation dated the 25th day of December last. The authority of law by which it was made is set forth in the proclamation itself, which expressly affirms that it was issued " by virtue of the power and authority in me vested by the Constitution and in the name of the sovereign people of the United States," and proclaims and declares "unconditionally, and without reservation, to all and to every person who directly or indirectly participated in the late insurrection or rebellion, a full pardon and amnesty for the offence of treason against the United States, or of adhering to their enemies during the late civil war, with restoration of all rights, privileges, and immunities under the Constitution, and the laws which have been made in pursuance thereof."

The federal Constitution is understood to be, and is regarded by the Executive, as the supreme law of the land. The second section of article second of that instrument provides that the President "shall have power to grant reprieves and pardons for offences against the United States, except in cases of impeachment." The proclamation of the 25th ultimo is in strict accordance with the judicial expositions of the authority thus conferred upon the Executive, and, as will be seen by reference to the accompanying papers, is in conformity with the precedent established by Washington in 1795, and followed by President Adams in 1800, Madison in 1815, and Lincoln in 1863, and by the present Executive in 1865, 1867, and 1868.

ANDREW JOHNSON.

WASHINGTON, D. C., *January* 18, 1869.

---

**President Grant's Proclamation for the Election in Virginia, May 14, 1869.**

In pursuance of the provisions of the act of Congress approved April 10, 1869, I hereby designate the 6th day of July, 1869, as the time for submitting the constitution passed by the convention which met in Richmond, Virginia, on Tuesday, the 3d day of December, 1867, to the voters of said State registered at the date of such submission, viz., July 6, 1869, for ratification or rejection.

And I submit to a separate vote the fourth clause of section 1, article III, of said constitution, which is in the following words:

Every person who has been a senator or representative in Congress, or elector of President or Vice-President, or who held any office, civil or military, under the United States, or under any State, who, having previously taken an oath as a member of Congress, or as an officer of the United States, or as a member of any State legislature, or as an executive or judicial officer of any State, shall have engaged in insurrection or rebellion against the same, or given aid or comfort to the enemies thereof This clause shall include the following officers: Governor, lieutenant governor, secretary of State, auditor of public accounts, second auditor, register of the land office, State treasurer, attorney general, sheriffs, sergeant of a city or town, commissioner of the revenue, county surveyor, constables, overseers of the poor, commissioner of the board of public works, judges of the supreme court, judges of the circuit court, judge of the court of hustings, justices of the county courts, mayor, recorder, aldermen, councilmen of a city or town, coroners, escheators, inspectors of tobacco, flour, &c., and clerks of the supreme, district, circuit, and county courts, and of the court of hustings, and attorneys for the Commonwealth; provided that the legislature may, by a vote of three-fifths of both houses, remove the disabilities incurred by this clause from any person included therein by a separate vote in each case.

And I also submit to a separate vote the 7th section of article III of the said constitution, which is in the words following:

In addition to the foregoing oath of office, the governor, lieutenant governor, members of the General Assembly, Secretary of State, auditor of public accounts, State treasurer, attorney general, and all persons elected to any convention to frame a constitution for this State, or to amend or revise this constitution in any manner, and the mayor and council in any city or town shall, before they enter on the duties of their respective offices, take and subscribe to the following oath or affirmation, provided the disabilities therein contained may be individually removed by a three-fifths vote of the General Assembly: "I, ———, do solemnly swear (or affirm) that I have never voluntarily borne arms against the United States since I have been a citizen thereof; that I have voluntarily given no aid, countenance, counsel, or encouragement to persons engaged in armed hostility thereto; that I have never sought or accepted, or attempted to exercise, the functions of any office whatever under any authority or pretended authority in hostility to the United States; that I have not yielded a voluntary support to any pretended government, authority, power or constitution within the United States hostile or inimical thereto. And I do further swear (or affirm) that to the best of my knowledge and ability I will support and defend the Constitution of the United States against all enemies, foreign and domestic; that I will bear true faith and allegiance to the same; that I take this obligation freely, without any mental reservation or purpose of evasion, and that I will well and faithfully discharge the duties of the office on which I am about to enter, so help me God." The above oath shall also be taken by all the city and county officers before entering upon their duties, and by all other State officers not included in the above provision.

I direct the vote to be taken upon each of the above-cited provisions alone, and upon the other portions of the said constitution in the following manner, viz.:

Each voter favoring the ratification of the constitution (excluding the provisions above quoted) as framed by the convention of December 3, 1867, shall express his judgment by voting

### FOR THE CONSTITUTION.

Each voter favoring the rejection of the constitution (excluding the provisions above quoted) shall express his judgment by voting

### AGAINST THE CONSTITUTION.

Each voter will be allowed to cast a separate ballot for or against either or both of the provisions above quoted.

In testimony whereof I have hereunto set my hand and caused the seal of the United States to be affixed.

Done at the city of Washington, this 14th day of May, in the year of our Lord 1869, [SEAL.] and of the independence of the United States of America the ninety-third.

U. S. GRANT.

By the President:
HAMILTON FISH,
*Secretary of State.*

---

### Respecting Wages of Labor, May 19, 1869.

Whereas the act of Congress, approved June 25, 1868, constituted on and after that date eight hours a day's work for all laborers, workmen, and mechanics employed by or on behalf of the Government of the United States, and repealed all acts and parts of acts inconsistent therewith:

Now, therefore, I, Ulysses S. Grant, President of the United States, do hereby direct that, from and after this date, no reduction shall be made in the wages paid by the Government by the day to such laborers, workmen, and mechanics on account of such reduction of the hours of labor.

In testimony whereof I have hereto set my hand and caused the seal of the United States to be affixed.

Done at the city of Washington, this 19th day of May, in the year of Lord 1869, and [SEAL.] of the independence of the United States the ninety-third. U. S. GRANT.

By the President:
HAMILTON FISH,
*Secretary of State.*

---

### Relative to Duties upon Merchandize in French Vessels, June 12, 1869.

Whereas satisfactory evidence has been received by me from his majesty the Emperor of France, through the Count Faverney, his chargé d'affaires, that on and after this date the discriminating duties heretofore levied in French ports upon merchandize imported from the countries of its origin in vessels of the United States are to be discontinued and abolished:

Now, therefore, I, U. S. Grant, President of the United States of America, by virtue of the authority vested in me by an act of Congress of the 7th day of January, 1824, and by an act in addition thereto of the 24th day of May, 1828,

do hereby declare and proclaim, that on and after this date, so long as merchandize imported from countries of its origin into French ports in vessels belonging to citizens of the United States is admitted into French ports on the terms aforesaid, the discriminating duties heretofore levied upon merchandize imported from the countries of its origin into ports of the United States in French vessels shall be, and are hereby, discontinued and abolished.

In testimony whereof I have hereunto set my hand and caused the seal of the United States to be affixed.

Done at the city of Washington, this 12th day of June, in the year of our Lord 1869, [SEAL.] and of the independence of the United States of America the ninety-third.

U. S. GRANT.

By the President:
HAMILTON FISH,
*Secretary of State.*

---

The following is the official notification containing the evidence upon which the foregoing proclamation was issued:

[Translation.]

LEGATION OF FRANCE TO THE U. S.,
WASHINGTON, *June 12, 1869.*

MR. SECRETARY OF STATE: In conformity with the desire expressed in the note addressed by you to M. Berthemy, of the 19th of March last, I have requested of the Emperor's government to be informed by telegraphic dispatch of the abolition of discriminating duties on merchandize imported into France from the countries of its origin in American vessels.

I have the honor to send you herewith a copy of the notice which I have just received on this subject from his excellency the Minister of Foreign Affairs. This shows that discriminating duties upon merchandize imported into the empire under the American flag have been abolished from and after the 12th of June, 1869. Consequently, pursuant to what has been agreed between us, I pray your excellency to have the goodness to take the necessary measures in order that reciprocal treatment may at once be granted France by the Government of the United States.

Accept, Mr. Secretary of State, the assurances of my high consideration.

COUNT DE FAVERNEY.

To Hon. HAMILTON FISH,
*Secretary of State.*

---

[Translation.]

DATED —, 1869. RECEIVED IN WASHINGTON JUNE 12.

*To the Chargé d'Affaires of France, Washington:*

Discriminating duties on merchandize imported from the countries of its origin in American vessels have this day been discontinued in the ports of the empire. Ask for reciprocity.

THE MINISTER
PARIS. *for Foreign Affairs.*

# XLIV.

## ORDERS AND PAPERS ON RECONSTRUCTION.

### ADDITIONAL MILITARY ORDERS UNDER THE RECONSTRUCTION ACTS, AND THE NEW CONSTITUTION OF TEXAS.

**Orders and Papers relating to Reconstruction, and General Action under the Reconstruction Laws.***

HEADQUARTERS OF THE ARMY,
ADJUTANT GENERAL'S OFFICE,
WASHINGTON, *July* 28, 1868.

General Orders, No. 55:

The following orders from the War Department, which have been approved by the President, are published for the information and government of the army and of all concerned:

The commanding generals of the second, third, fourth, and fifth military districts having officially reported that the States of Arkansas, North Carolina, South Carolina, Louisiana, Georgia, Alabama, and Florida have fully complied with the acts of Congress known as the reconstruction acts, including the act passed June 22, 1868, entitled "An act to admit the State of Arkansas to representation in Congress," and the act passed June 25, 1868, entitled "An act to admit the States of North Carolina, South Carolina, Louisiana, Georgia, Alabama, and Florida to representation in Congress," and that, consequently, so much of the act of March 2, 1867, and the acts supplementary thereto, as provide for the organization of military districts, subject to the military authority of the United States, as therein provided, has become inoperative in said States, and that the commanding generals have ceased to exercise in said States the military powers conferred by said acts of Congress: therefore, the following changes will be made in the organization and command of military districts and geographical departments:

I. The second and third military districts having ceased to exist, the States of North Carolina, South Carolina, Georgia, Alabama, and Florida, will constitute the department of the South; Major General George G. Meade to command. Headquarters at Atlanta, Georgia.

II. The fourth military district will now consist only of the State of Mississippi, and will continue to be commanded by Brevet Major General A. C. Gillem.

III. The fifth military district will now consist of the State of Texas, and will be commanded by Brevet Major General J. J. Reynolds. Headquarters at Austin, Texas.

IV. The States of Louisiana and Arkansas will constitute the department of Louisiana. Brevet Major General L. H. Rousseau is assigned

---

*Continuation of the record from p. 346 Hand-Book of Politics for 1868, or p. 87 Political Manual of 1868.

40

to the command. Headquarters at New Orleans, Louisiana. Until the arrival of General Rousseau at New Orleans, Brevet Major General Buchanan will command the department.

V. Brevet Major General George Crooke is assigned, according to his brevet of major general, to command the department of the Columbia, in place of Rousseau, relieved.

VI. Brevet Major General E. R. S. Canby is reassigned to command the department of Washington.

VII. Brevet Major General Edward Hatch, colonel 9th cavalry, will relieve General Buchanan as assistant commissioner of the Bureau of Refugees, Freedmen, and Abandoned Lands in Louisiana.

By command of General Grant.

E. D. TOWNSEND,
*Assistant Adjutant General*

---

ATTORNEY GENERAL'S OFFICE,
*August* 20, 1868.

ALEXANDER MAGRUDER, Esq.,
*United States Marshal Northern District of Florida, St. Augustine, Florida.*

SIR: Your letter of the 12th instant reached me yesterday, and has received an attentive consideration. Colonel Sprague's information to you must have been based upon his own construction of General Meade's order lately issued, and not upon any special instructions from the President to Colonel Sprague, through General Meade or otherwise, as no such special instructions have been issued by the President. You add: "Under some circumstances I should be glad to have the aid of the military, and, if practicable, would be pleased to have instructions given to the military to aid me when necessary. I ask this, as Colonel Sprague informs me under his instructions he cannot do so."

This desire and request for the aid of the military under certain circumstances I understand to refer to the occasional necessity which may arise that the marshal should have the means of obtaining the aid and assistance of a more considerable force than his regular deputies supply for execution of legal process in his district.

The 27th section of the judiciary act of 1789 establishes the office of marshal, and names among his duties and powers the following: "And to execute throughout the district all lawful precepts directed to him and issued under the authority of the United States, and he shall have power to command all necessary assistance in the execution of his duty, and to appoint, as there may be occasion, one or more deputies."—(1st ¶ 87.)

You will observe from this that the only measure of the assistance which you have power to command is its necessity for the execution of your duty, and upon your discreet judgment, under your official responsibility, the law reposes the determination of what force each particular necessity requires. This power of the marshal is equivalent to that of a sheriff, and with either embraces, as a resort in necessity, the whole power of the precinct (county or district) over which the officer's authority extends. In defining this power Attorney General Cushing—and, as I understand the subject, correctly—says it "comprises every person in the district or county above the age of fifteen years, whether civilians or not, and including the military of all denominations—militia, soldiers, marines—all of whom are alike bound to obey the commands of a sheriff or marshal."

While, however, the law gives you this "power to command all necessary assistance," and the military within your district are not exempt from obligation to obey, in common with all the citizens, your summons, in case of necessity, you will be particular to observe that this high and responsible authority is given to the marshal only in aid of his duty "to execute throughout the district all lawful precepts directed to him and issued under the authority of the United States," and only in case of *necessity* for this extraordinary aid. The military persons obeying this summons of the marshal will act in subordination and obedience to the civil officer, the marshal, in whose aid in the execution of process they are called, and only to the effect of securing its execution.

The special duty and authority in the execution of process issued to you must not be confounded with the duty and authority of suppressing disorder and preserving the peace, which, under our Government, belongs to the civil authorities of the States, and not to the civil authorities of the United States. Nor are this special duty and authority of the marshal in executing process issued to him to be confounded with the authority and duty of the President of the United States in the specific cases of the Constitution and under the statutes to protect the States against domestic violence, or with his authority and duty under special statutes to employ military force in subduing combinations in resistance to the laws of the United States; for neither of these duties or authorities is shared by the subordinate officers of the Government, except when and as the same may be specifically communicated to them by the President.

I have thus called your attention to the general considerations bearing upon the subject to which your letter refers, for the purpose of securing a due observance of the limits of your duty and authority in connection therewith. Nothing can be less in accordance with the nature of our Government or the disposition of our people than a frequent or ready resort to military aid in the execution of the duties confided to civil officers. Courage, vigor, and intrepidity are appropriate qualities for the civil service which the marshals of the United States are expected to perform, and a reinforcement of their power by extraordinary means is permitted by the law only in extraordinary emergencies.

If it shall be thought that any occasion at any time exists for instructions to the military authorities of the United States within any of the States in connection with the execution of process of the courts of the United States, these instructions will be in accordance with the exigency then appearing.

I am, sir, very respectfully, your obedient servant,
WM. M. EVARTS,
*Attorney General.*

---

HEADQUARTERS OF THE ARMY,
ADJUTANT GENERAL'S OFFICE,
WASHINGTON, *August* 25, 1868.
Major General G. G. MEADE, *U. S. A.,*
*Commanding Department of South,*
*Atlanta, Georgia.*

GENERAL: In reply to your request for instruction relative to the use of troops under your command in aid of the civil authorities, the Secretary of War directs to be furnished for your information and government the enclosed copies of a letter of instructions to Brevet Major General Buchanan, commanding department of Louisiana, dated August 10, 1868, and of a letter from the Attorney General of the United States to Alexander Magruder, esq., United States marshal, northern district of Florida, dated August 20, 1868.

The letter to General Buchanan indicates the conditions under which the military power of the United States may be employed to suppress insurrection against the government of any State, and prescribes the duties of the department commander in reference thereto.

The letter of the Attorney General sets forth the conditions under which the marshals and sheriffs may command the assistance of the troops in the respective districts or counties to execute lawful precepts issued to them by competent authority.

The obligation of the military, (individual officers and soldiers,) in common with all citizens, to obey the summons of a marshal or sheriff, must be held subordinate to their paramount duty as members of a permanent military body. Hence the troops can act only in their proper organized capacity, under their own officers, and in obedience to the immediate orders of their officers. The officer commanding troops summoned to the aid of a marshal or sheriff must also judge for himself, and upon his own official responsibility, whether the service required of him is lawful and necessary, and compatible with the proper discharge of his ordinary military duties, and must limit the action absolutely to proper aid in execution of the lawful precept exhibited to him by the marshal or sheriff.

If time will permit, every demand from a civil officer for military aid, whether it be for the execution of civil process or to suppress insurrection, shall be forwarded to the President, with all the material facts in the case, for his orders; and in all cases the highest commander whose orders can be given in time to meet the emergencies will alone assume the responsibility of action.

By a timely disposition of troops where there is reason to apprehend a necessity for their use, and by their passive interposition between hostile parties, dangers of collision may be averted.

Department commanders, and in cases of necessity their subordinates, are expected, in this regard, to exercise, upon their own responsibility, a wise discretion, to the end that in any event the peace may be preserved.

By command of General Grant.

J. C. KELTON,
*Assistant Adjutant General.*

HEADQUARTERS OF THE ARMY,
ADJUTANT GENERAL'S OFFICE,
WASHINGTON, *October* 31, 1868.
General Orders, No. 90.

The following order has been received from the War Department, and is published for the information and guidance of all concerned:

Soldiers may, for certain offences not strictly military, be sentenced by general court-martial to confinement in a penitentiary.

If any State in a military department has made provision by law for confinement in a penitentiary thereof of prisoners under sentence by courts-martial of the United States, the department commander may designate such penitentiary as a place for the execution of any such sentence to penitentiary confinement; but if no such provision has been made by any State in the department, the record will be forwarded to the Secretary of War for designation of a prison.

The authority which has designated the place of confinement, or higher authority, can change the place of confinement, or mitigate or remit the sentence.

The same rules apply to prisoners sentenced by military commission, so long as the law under which the military commission acted is in force; but when that law ceases to be operative, the President alone can change the place of confinement, or mitigate or remit the sentence.

By command of General Grant.

E. D. TOWNSEND,
*Assistant Adjutant General.*

HEADQUARTERS OF THE ARMY,
ADJUTANT GENERAL'S OFFICE,
WASHINGTON, *November* 4, 1868.
General Orders, No. 91.

I. The following orders have been received from the War Department:

WAR DEPARTMENT,
WASHINGTON CITY, *November* 4, 1868.

By direction of the President, Brevet Major General E. R. S. Canby is hereby assigned to the command of the fifth military district, created by the act of Congress of March 2, 1867, and of the military department of Texas, consisting of the State of Texas. He will, without unnecessary delay, turn over his present command to the next officer in rank, and proceed to the command to which he is hereby assigned, and, on assuming the same, will, when necessary to a faithful execution of the laws, exercise any and all powers conferred by acts of Congress upon district commanders, and any and all authority pertaining to officers in command of military departments.

Brevet Major General J. J. Reynolds is hereby relieved from the command of the fifth military district.       J. M. SCHOFIELD,
*Secretary of War.*

II. In pursuance of the foregoing order of the President of the United States, Brevet Major General Canby will, on receipt of this order, turn over his present command to the officer next in rank to himself, and proceed to Austin, Texas, to relieve Brevet Major General Reynolds of the command of the fifth military district.

By command of General Grant.

E. D. TOWNSEND,
*Assistant Adjutant General.*

HEADQUARTERS OF THE ARMY,
ADJUTANT GENERAL'S OFFICE,
WASHINGTON, *March* 5, 1869.
General Orders, No. 10.

The President of the United States directs that the following orders be carried into execution as soon as practicable:

1. The department of the South will be commanded by Brigadier and Brevet Major General A. H. Terry.

2. Major General G. G. Meade is assigned to command the military division of the Atlantic, and will transfer his headquarters to Philadelphia, Pennsylvania. He will turn over his present command temporarily to Brevet Major General T. H. Ruger, colonel 33d infantry, who is assigned to duty according to his brevet of major general while in the exercise of this command.

3. Major General P. H. Sheridan is assigned to command the department of Louisiana, and will turn over the command of the department of the Missouri temporarily to the next senior officer.

4. Major General W. S. Hancock is assigned to command the department of Dacotah.

5. Brigadier and Brevet Major General E. R. S. Canby is assigned to command the first military district, and will proceed to his post as soon as relieved by Brevet Major General Reynolds.

6. Brevet Major General A. C. Gillem, colonel 24th infantry, will turn over the command of the fourth military district to the next senior officer, and join his regiment.

7. Brevet Major General J. J. Reynolds, colonel 26th infantry, is assigned to command the fifth military district, according to his brevet of major general.

8. Brevet Major General W. H. Emory, colonel 5th cavalry, is assigned to command the department of Washington, according to his brevet of major general.

By command of the general of the army.

E. D. TOWNSEND,
*Assistant Adjutant General.*

HEADQUARTERS OF THE ARMY,
ADJUTANT GENERAL'S OFFICE,
WASHINGTON, *March* 16, 1869.
General Orders, No. 18.

By direction of the President of the United States, the following changes are made in military divisions and department commands:

I. Lieutenant General P. H. Sheridan is assigned to command the military division of the Missouri.

II. Major General H. W. Halleck is assigned to the command of the military division of the South, to be composed of the departments of the South and Louisiana, of the fourth military district, and of the States composing the present department of the Cumberland, headquarters Louisville, Kentucky. Major General Halleck will proceed to his new command as soon as relieved by Major General Thomas.

III. Major General G. H. Thomas is assigned to command the military division of the Pacific.

IV. Major General J. M. Schofield is assigned to command the department of the Missouri The State of Illinois and post of Fort Smith, Arkansas, are transferred to this department.

V. Brigadier and Brevet Major General O. O. Howard is assigned to command the department of Louisiana. Until his arrival, the senior officer, Brevet Major General J. A. Mower, will command according to his brevet of major general.

VI. The department of Washington will be discontinued and merged in the department of the East. The records will be sent to the adjutant general of the army.

VII. The first military district will be added to the military division of the Atlantic.

VIII. As soon as Major General Thomas is ready to relinquish command of the department of the Cumberland, the department will be discontinued, and the States composing it will be added to other departments, to be hereafter designated. The records will be forwarded to the adjutant general of the army.

By command of General Sherman:
E. D. TOWNSEND,
*Assistant Adjutant General.*

HEADQUARTERS OF THE ARMY,
ADJUTANT GENERAL'S OFFICE,
WASHINGTON, *March* 31, 1869.
Special Orders, No. 75.
Extract.

\* \* \* \* \* \*

16. By direction of the President of the United States, Brevet Major General A. S. Webb, U. S. army, is assigned to command the first military district, according to his brevet of major general, until the arrival of Brevet Major General Canby to relieve him. He will accordingly repair to Richmond, Virginia, without delay. \* \*

By command of General Sherman:
E. D. TOWNSEND,
*Assistant Adjutant General.*

HEADQUARTERS OF THE ARMY,
ADJUTANT GENERAL'S OFFICE,
WASHINGTON, *April* 3, 1869.
General Orders, No. 29.

I. By direction of the President of the United States, paragraph VIII of General Orders, No. 18, of March 16, 1869, is hereby revoked.

II. Brigadier and Brevet Major General P. St. G. Cooke, U. S. army, is assigned to the command of the department of the Cumberland when it shall be relinquished by Major General Thomas.

By command of General Sherman:
E. D. TOWNSEND,
*Assistant Adjutant General.*

## ORDERS OF THE DISTRICT COMMANDERS.*

### First Military District—Virginia.

HEADQUARTERS DEPARTMENT OF VIRGINIA,
RICHMOND, VA., *June* 23, 1869.
General Order, No. 77.

The laws of the State of Virginia and the or-

dinances of the different municipalities within the State having especial reference to and made to restrain the personal liberty of free colored persons were designed for the government of such persons while living amid a population of colored slaves; they were enacted in the interests of slave-owners, and were designed for the security of slave property: they were substantially parts of the slave code.

Slavery has been abolished in Virginia; and, therefore, upon the principle that where the reason of the law ceases the law itself ceases, these laws and ordinances have become obsolete. People of color will henceforth enjoy the same personal liberty that other citizens and inhabitants enjoy; they will be subject to the same restraints and to the same punishments for crime that are imposed on whites, and to no others.

Vagrancy, however, will not be permitted; neither whites nor blacks can be allowed to abandon their proper occupations, to desert their families, or roam in idleness about this department; but neither whites nor blacks will be restrained from seeking employment elsewhere, when they cannot obtain it with just compensation at their homes, nor from travelling from place to place on proper and legitimate business.

Until the civil tribunals are re-established, the administration of criminal justice must of necessity be by military courts. Before such courts the evidence of colored persons will be received in all cases.

By command of Major General A. H. Terry.
ED. W. SMITH, *A. A. G*
Official: A. R. S. FOOTE, *A. A. G.*

1869, February 8—All civil officers, corporations, &c., required to make returns to the legislature, ordered to make the same to headquarters.

March 15—The joint resolution respecting the provisional governments of Virginia and Texas was promulgated, and all officers unable to take the test oath removed, to take effect the 18th instant.

March 18—Removal in accordance with above order suspended till the 21st instant.

March 21—General Stoneman submitted his report, which showed that there were 5,446 offices in the State, 532 of which had been filled by General Schofield, 1,972 by General Stoneman, 329 could take the oath, and 2,613 were unfilled, owing to the difficulty in finding men able to take the test-oath.

March 22—The mayor of Richmond asked the commanding officer if the appointment of colored policemen would meet his approval, who on the 23d answered that it would, and so would their appointment to all positions to which they were eligible and for which they were competent.

March 27—General Stoneman took upon himself the duties of governor, removing Governor Wells.

March 30—In compliance with Special Order, 75, A. G. O., Brevet Major General A. G. Webb assumed command.

April 2—Governor Wells was reinstated.

April 3—It appearing that the organization of civil government under the reconstruction laws in certain counties proved to be impossible, since suitable persons to qualify and assume the duties of the various offices of this district, under the

*Continued from p. 325 Hand-Book of Politics for 1868, or p. 65 Political Manual for 1868.

laws of the United States, had not been found, military officers were again appointed in some sections of the State.

April 20—General E. R. S. Canby assumed command.

April 22—All officers of the provisional government ordered to take the test-oath.

May 7—Orders that "all persons elected or appointed to civil office who have subscribed the oath of office of July 2, 1862, and filed the same with county clerks or with other civil officers, as required by law, will cause duly certified copies of said oath to be made and filed at these headquarters, that their ability to qualify under the joint resolution of Congress passed February 6, 1869, (Public, No. 6,) may be definitely ascertained. A failure to send forward such oath will be an indication that the office is vacated under the resolution before cited."

May 27—Assigns military commissioners and superintendents of registration and election; invests the military commissioners with all the powers of justices of the peace and police magistrates, to be "governed in the execution of their duties by the laws of Virginia, except so far as those laws may conflict with the laws of the United States or with the orders issued from these headquarters;" places at their disposition all peace officers, in addition to troops; makes it their duty to promptly report to headquarters all cases, and when parties are held for trial, either in confinement or under bail, the cases to be so fully reported as to enable the commanding general to decide whether they shall be tried by a military commission or a civil court; declares that the powers herein conferred upon military commissioners are not to be construed as extending to the inhabitants in their ordinary personal relations, but to the end that United States laws be duly executed and full protection given to all parties in their rights of person and property, and that they will only be exercised where the civil authorities refuse or fail to act, or exact and impartial justice from the civil courts cannot be secured; all persons required to obey and execute all lawful orders of the military commissioners. Civil officers not relieved from duty—this order being intended to aid and not supersede them—except in cases of necessity. The superintendents of registration and election districts are invested with similar but subordinate powers to those of military commissioners, to or through whom they must report.

June 29—The stay of executions against personal property extended until January 1, 1870: *Provided*, That between January 1 and August 1, 1869, the debtor shall have paid one year's interest upon the principal sum due.

June 30—To guard against fraud, two ballot-boxes at each polling place: one to receive ballots for or against the constitution as a whole, the other, for or against the separate clauses to be voted on; a committee of not more than three persons from each political party to witness ballot counting, but none save sworn election officers to examine or handle poll-lists, ballot-boxes, or ballots.

---

In justification of his test-oath order, General Canby wrote the following letter:

HEADQUARTERS FIRST MILITARY DISTRICT,
STATE OF VIRGINIA,
RICHMOND, VA., *June 26*, 1869.

Mr. B. W. GILLIS, *Richmond, Va.*

SIR: I have received your note of the 23d instant, and will state in reply to the inquiries therein made—

First. That I have uniformly held that members of the general assembly and State officers to be elected on the 6th proximo would be required to take, before entering upon the duties of their offices, the oath prescribed by the law of July 2, 1862, unless the constitution should first be approved by Congress, or the oath be otherwise dispensed with by law.

Second. That this decision is in conformity with the action heretofore taken upon the same subject in another district, and was based upon a careful consideration of all the laws bearing upon the question now presented.

The 6th section of the law of March 2, 1867, provides "That until the people of the said rebel States shall be by law admitted to representation in the Congress of the United States, any government which may exist therein shall be deemed provisional only, and in all respects subject to the paramount authority of the United States to abolish, modify, control, or supersede the same." The conditions that must precede this admission to representation are prescribed by the 5th section of the same law, the 5th section of the law of March 23, 1867, and the 6th section of the law of April 10, 1869. The same section prescribes the qualifications of voters in all elections to office, and the qualifications (eligibility) of officers under such provisional governments. The supplementary law of March 23, 1867, modified the qualifications of voters by prescribing registration and determining the conditions essential to registration, and the amendatory law of March 13, 1868, section 2, applied the same qualifications (registered voters) to the voters for members of the House of Representatives of the United States, and all elective offices provided for by those constitutions, at the elections to be held upon the questions of ratifying or rejecting the proposed constitutions, and the 9th section of the law of July 19, 1867, imposes an additional qualification upon the officers, by requiring that they shall take the oath of office prescribed by the law of July 2, 1862.

Under the original law of March 2, 1867, (section 5,) it was in the power of the district commander to prescribe an oath of office, conforming to the conditions of eligibility prescribed by that section, and this in fact was done by several of the district commanders in this district by General Orders, No. 9, of April 5, 1867; and these oaths continued in force until they were superseded by the oath required by the law of July 19, 1867. That law placed the subject beyond the discretion and control of the district commander, and he cannot now prescribe or adopt any different oath without disregarding or annulling a positive and controlling law. I have heretofore held, and do now hold, that the approval by Congress of any proposed constitution makes it a part of the reconstruction laws, and, to the extent that Congress directs or authorizes any action under it in advance of the admission of the State, dispenses with the provisions of any previous laws that conflict with it. In all other respects the constitutions and the governments organized under them remained inoperative until all the conditions of restoration were satisfied. It has been suggested recently that this decision is in conflict with a decision made by the general of the army in relation to the State of Georgia; on the 2d of March, 1868. The only decision of that date which I have been able to find relates to the State of Florida, and is in reply to a specific inquiry as to the qualifications of voters for offices under the constitution, "and to take office on the adoption of the constitution," and the answer is to be interpreted by the decision of January 13, 1868, that "The governments elected cannot assume authority except under the orders of the district commander, or after action of Congress on their constitutions." The decision in relation to Georgia is dated on the 29th of April, 1868. It is similar in import, and refers to the dispatch of March 2, and this has probably led to the confusion of dates. It is in answer to a communication from the commander of the third military district, and applies directly and apparently exclusively to the 2d paragraph of General Orders, No. 61, third military district, of May 15, 1868, which provides that "inasmuch as said general assembly, should the constitution now submitted to the people of the State be ratified by them, and be approved by Congress, is required to convene and adopt the proposed amendment to the Constitution designated as Article XIV before the State can be admitted to representation in Congress, it may be decided that the members of the said general assembly are, while taking this preliminary action, officers of a provisional government, and as such required, under the 9th section of the act of Congress, of July 19, 1867, to take the "test oath."

This decision must also be interpreted by the decision of January 13th, and this I apprehend to be the proper rule of interpretation of all the correspondence upon this subject, as I have been unable to find any case in which the inquiry and answer did not relate to the status of these officers *after* the approval by Congress of the constitution under which they were elected. The law of June 25, 1868, approving the constitutions of several States, and authorizing specific action under them, was regarded by me as dispensing with the oath of office prescribed by the law of July 2, 1862, first as to the members of the general assembly, and after the ratification of the constitutional amendment to the other State officers duly elected and qualified under those constitutions. This construction, in its first application, did not include the governor and lieutenant governor; but as the organization of the legislature would have been incomplete without the lieutenant governor, and as the legislative action required by the law might have been embarrassed by the action of the old incumbents, the general of the army directed that they should be removed, and the governor and lieutenant governor elect should be appointed in their places. They were so appointed in North and South Carolina, qualified under their military appointment, and after the ratification of the constitutional amendment again qualified under the constitutions of their States.

The action taken in the first case was approved, and in the second, directed by the general of the army. It has also been suggested that the reconstruction laws are silent as to the qualification of officers to be elected under the proposed constitutions and of voters at such elections, and that the laws under which the decision has been made are in conflict with the recent legislation of Congress (act of April 10, 1869) and with the XIVth article of the amendments to the Constitution of the United States. The question with regard to the qualification of voters was raised in the case of the (then) proposed constitution of the State of Florida, and was settled by the 2d section of the law of March 13, 1868, which provides "That the constitutional conventions of any of the States named in the acts to which this is amendatory may provide, that at the time of voting upon the ratification of the constitution, the *registered voters* may vote also for members of the House of Representatives of the United States and for all elective officers provided by said constitution." The "voters" at the election to be held in this State for "members of the general assembly," "State officers," and "members of Congress," under the authority of the 2d section of the law of April 10, 1869, are determined by the 1st section of that law to be the "voters of said State registered at the date of said submission (of the constitution) for ratification or rejection." The qualification of the officers rests upon the same basis, and must be governed by the reconstruction laws until the constitution becomes the controlling law, and this does not obtain until it has been approved by Congress. Over the remaining suggestions the district commander has no control, and the question whether the laws are or are not in conflict with the constitution must be determined by the Supreme Court of the United States.

Very respectfully, your obedient servant,

Ed. R. S. Canby,
*Brevet Major General, commanding.*

---

## Second Military District—North Carolina and South Carolina.

1868, July 2—Various appointments of railroad directors, &c., made by Governor Worth annulled.

July 2—Legislature of North Carolina ratified the XIVth constitutional amendment.

July 3—General Canby telegraphed to Governor Holden, "Your telegram announcing the ratification of the constitutional amendment by the Legislature of North Carolina has been received, and instructions will be sent to-day to the military commanders in North Carolina to abstain from the exercise of any authority under the reconstruction laws, except to close up unfinished business, and not to interfere in any civil matters unless the execution of the law of June 25, 1868, should be obstructed by unlawful or forcible opposition to the inauguration of the new State government."

July 6—Issued instructions as to the course to be pursued by commanding officers on ratification of XIVth amendment in North Carolina and issue of the President's proclamation.

July 9—The Legislature of South Carolina ratified the XIVth constitutional amendment.

July 13—Order similar to that of July 6 in relation to South Carolina.

July 24—All authority conferred upon and heretofore exercised by the commander of the said second military district, by and under the aforecited law of March 2, 1867, remitted to the civil authorities constituted and organized in the said States of North Carolina and South Carolina under the constitutions adopted by the people thereof and approved by the Congress of the United States.

### Third Military District—Georgia, Florida, and Alabama.

1868, April 10—The resignations of sheriffs in Georgia being very numerous on account of the near approach of the election, their resignations were not received, and they were required to continue in the discharge of their duties till relieved by further orders.

Forbade the attempts of employers to control the action or will of their laborers as to voting, by threats of discharge or other oppressive means, under the penalty of fine and imprisonment. Announced it as the intention of the commanding general to secure to all duly registered voters an opportunity to vote "freely and without restraint, fear, or the influence of fraud."

April 11—Forbade all municipal elections in Georgia on the general election day. Forbade the assembling of any armed bodies to discuss political questions. Forbade the carrying of arms at or near polling places on election day. Enjoined the superintendents of registration and officers of Freedmen's Bureau to instruct the freedmen as to their rights.

April 13—It having been reported that many names have been stricken from the registered list of voters in Georgia without any cause, and it being the determination of the commanding general that all the candidates shall be able to show, from official data, that the election was honestly and fairly conducted, all managers of elections were ordered to receive the votes of all such persons, to be sent in a separate envelope with the returns of the election.

April 15—Members of the General Assembly of Georgia taking their seats before the ratification of the XIVth constitutional amendment are officers of a provisional government, and required to take the test-oath.

April 24—Allowed the employment on the highway of such persons as had been convicted of minor offences, permitted the use of the ball and chain where there was danger of escape, but the chain-gang not to be revived.

May 11—Declared the constitution of Georgia ratified by a majority of 17,699.

June 2—Declared the constitution of Florida ratified by a majority of 5,050.

June 9—Legislature of Florida ratified the XIVth constitutional amendment.

June 28—Rufus B. Bullock appointed Governor of Georgia, vice Brevet Brigadier General T. H. Ruger, to date from July 5. William H. Smith, Governor, vice R. M. Patton removed, and A. J. Applegate, Lieutenant Governor, of Alabama, both to date from July 13.

June 29—All civil officers in Florida ordered to turn over all public property, &c., to duly elected officers, and the district commander, on notification of the inauguration of civil government, to transfer everything appertaining to the government of said State to the proper civil officers, and to abstain in future upon any pretext whatever from any interference with or control over the civil authorities of the State in the persons and property of the citizens thereof.

July 2—Forbade any court or ministerial officer in Georgia to enforce any judgment, decree, or execution against any real estate, except for taxes, money borrowed and expended in the improvement of the homestead or for the purchase-money of the same, and for labor done thereon or material furnished therefor, or removal of incumbrance thereon, until the legislature should have time to provide for the setting apart and valuation of such property.

July 3—Governor R. B. Bullock ordered to effect organization of the two houses of the legislature of Georgia on the 4th inst.

July 9—Governor Wm. H. Smith ordered to organize the two houses of the legislature of Alabama on the 13th inst., having required beforehand that each house shall be purged of those who were obnoxious to the XIVth constitutional amendment.

July 13—The legislature of Alabama ratified the XIVth constitutional amendment.

July 14—Military rule withdrawn from the State of Alabama. All prisoners ordered to be turned over to civil courts. Writs from State courts to be answered by stating that the prisoners are prisoners of the United States, and writ must come from United States court.

July 21—Legislature of Georgia ratified the XIVth constitutional amendment.

July 22—Military rule withdrawn from Georgia.

HEADQUARTERS THIRD MILITARY DISTRICT, (DEPT. OF GEORGIA, FLORIDA, AND ALABAMA,) ATLANTA, GA., *July* 30, 1868.

General Orders, No. 108.

I. The several States comprising this military district having, by solemn acts of their Assemblies, conformed to the requisitions of the act of Congress which became a law June 25, 1868, and civil government having been inaugurated in each, the military power vested in the district commander by the reconstruction laws, by the provisions of these laws ceases to exist, and hereafter all orders issued from these headquarters, and bearing upon the rights of persons and property, will have in the several States of Georgia, Alabama, and Florida only such force as may be given to them by the courts and legislatures of the respective States.          *          *

By order of Major General Meade:

S. F. BARSTOW, *A. A. A. G.*

### Fourth Military District—Mississippi and Arkansas.

1868, June 22—Arkansas admitted to representation in Congress.

June 22—Election in Mississippi, constitution defeated.

June 30—Military rule withdrawn from Arkansas.

August 5—Arkansas detached from the fourth military district and attached to the department of Louisiana.

1869, March 23—All offices held by persons unable to take the test-oath and whose disabilities have not been removed declared vacant.

April 9—Annuls an act of the legislature of Mississippi of 1867 in regard to poll-tax, fixing it at one dollar instead of two. No city or town allowed to levy a poll-tax.

April 27—Ordered that all persons, without respect to race, color, or previous condition of servitude, who possess the qualifications prescribed by article 135, page 499, of the Revised Code of 1857, shall be competent jurors.

### Fifth Military District—Louisiana and Texas.

1868, July 9—Legislature of Louisiana ratified the XIVth constitutional amendment.

July 13—Military rule withdrawn from Louisiana.

August 4—Louisiana detached from the fifth military district.

September 18—The constitutional convention of the State of Texas, on the 25th day of August, 1868, levied a tax of one-fifth of one per cent. on the assessment of 1868; which tax the assessors and collectors now have instructions to collect. It is hereby ordered that the tax be promptly paid. Any obstruction or resistance to the collection of said tax will be a violation of the law of Congress, and as such will be punished by military authority.

September 29—No election for electors of President and Vice President of the United States will be held in the State of Texas on the 3d of November next. Any assemblages, proceedings, or acts for such purposes are hereby prohibited, and all citizens are admonished to remain at home, or attend to their ordinary business on that day.

November 4—General Reynolds removed from command. General E. R. S. Canby assigned to the fifth military district.

December 7—The constitutional convention reassembled,

1869, January 16—Divided the State into posts, giving instructions as to the duties of the commanding officers of each, and calling on all good citizens to unite in enforcing the law and establishing a good government.

January 20—Forbids all military interference where civil power is sufficient to insure justice and order, and requires all things to be done as nearly in accordance with the laws of the States as may be, and promises the support of the military in every case of need to the civil authorities.

January 21—Authorizes post commanders to admit to bail persons not subject to Articles of War held in military arrest. Prescribes the form of bond.

"II. The commanding general is advised that in some of the counties of this State it has been the practice of the sheriff, in calling for assistance in the execution of legal process, to summon only persons who are of the same political party. The administration of justice should not only be impartial, but its agents should be free from the suspicion of political or partisan bias; and it is made the duty of all sheriffs and peace officers

in all cases where they may lawfully require assistance, to summon substantial citizens of the county, whose social and material interests are involved in the peace and prosperity of the community, without reference to their political opinions.

"For like reasons, no person who is personally or pecuniarily interested in any issue to be tried will hereafter be deputed to serve or be summoned to aid in the service of any legal process connected with the particular cause of action."

HEADQ'RS FIFTH MILITARY DISTRICT,
AUSTIN, TEXAS, *April* 7, 1869.
General Orders, No. 68.

The provisions of chapter 63, general laws of the 11th legislature, State of Texas, passed October 27, 1866, are so modified, that hereafter no county judge or county court shall apprentice any child whose relatives, either by consanguinity or affinity, take such care of it as to prevent its becoming a charge upon the public; and in every case where a child has been apprenticed by the county court since the 19th day of June, 1865, the indentures shall be cancelled by the court that ordered them, when the relatives of such child, either by consanguinity or affinity, apply to the county court for the custody and care of it.

It is further ordered, that the bond required by section 5 of said act shall, in addition to the conditions therein prescribed, provide for the tuition of such child in some private or public school for three months in every year of the apprenticeship.     *     *

In any case where a sale of real estate may be made under execution or other judicial process, or "under a mortgage or deed of trust," and the proceeds of such sale are for the benefit of the State of Texas, the Governor and attorney general may direct that such real estate shall be bid in for the State, if in their judgment the interest of the State will thereby be promoted; and the deed in such case shall be executed to the State of Texas in the same manner and with like effect as if the purchase had been made by an individual.

The State of Texas shall in no case be required to give any bond or other security in the prosecution of its suits or remedies in the courts of the State.

The operation of the act of the 11th legislature of Texas, providing "for the education of indigent white children of the several counties of the State," passed November 12, 1866, is hereby suspended until the legislature shall provide for an equal system of common schools. All moneys collected for the purposes named in the act above cited, and not paid out or due under existing contracts or agreements, are hereby directed to be paid to the treasurers of the several counties wherein the same shall have been collected, and said treasurers are directed and required to receipt and account for the same as by law required with reference to other moneys not applicable to any special fund or purpose.

By command of Bvt. Maj. Gen. E. R. S. Canby:
LOUIS V. CAZIARC,
*A. D. C. A. A. A. G.*

April 8.—Gen. Canby relinquished command, and Gen. J. J. Reynolds resumed it.

April 12.—All civil officers in the State who cannot take the test-oath will cease to perform official duties on the 25th instant.

### New Constitution of Texas.

The constitution of the State of Texas, adopted by the convention, and to be submitted to a vote of the people at a time to be indicated by the President, contains in the preamble an acknowledgment, with gratitude, of the grace of God in permitting them to make a choice of our form of government.

In the bill of rights are these declarations:

That the heresies of nullification and secession, which brought the country to grief, may be eliminated from political discussion, that public order may be restored, private property and human life protected, and the great principles of liberty and equality secured to us and our posterity, we declare that—

The Constitution of the United States, and the laws and treaties made and to be made in pursuance thereof, are acknowledged to be the supreme law; that this constitution is framed in harmony with and in subordination thereto; and that the fundamental principles embodied herein can only be changed subject to the national authority.

All freemen, when they form a social compact, have equal rights, and no man or set of men is entitled to exclusive separate public emoluments or privileges.

No law shall be passed depriving a party of any remedy of the enforcement of a contract which existed when the contract was made.

No person shall ever be imprisoned for debt.

No citizen of this State shall be deprived of life, property, or privileges, outlawed, exiled, or in any manner disfranchised, except by due course of the law of the land.

Perpetuities and monopolies are contrary to the genius of a free government, and shall never be allowed; nor shall the law of primogeniture or entailment ever be in force in this State.

The equality of all persons before the law is herein recognized, and shall ever remain inviolate; nor shall any citizen ever be deprived of any right, privilege, or immunity, nor be exempted from any burdens or duty, on account of race, color, or previous condition.

Importations of persons under the name of "coolies," or any other designation, or the adoption of any system of peonage, whereby the helpless and unfortunate may be reduced to partial bondage, shall never be authorized or tolerated by the laws of the State; and neither slavery nor involuntary servitude, except as a punishment for crime, whereof the party shall have been duly convicted, shall ever exist in the State.

Every male person who shall have attained the age of twenty-one years, and who shall be (or who shall have declared his intention to become) a citizen of the United States, or who is at the time of the acceptance of this constitution by the Congress of the United States a citizen of Texas, and shall have resided in the State one year next preceding an election, and the last six months within the district or county in which he offers to vote and is duly registered, (Indians not taxed excepted,) shall be deemed a qualified elector; and should such qualified elector happen to be in any other county, situated in the district in which he resides, at the time of an election, he shall be permitted to vote for any district officer; provided that the qualified elector shall be permitted to vote anywhere in the State for State officers; and provided further, that no soldier, seaman, or marine in the army or navy of the United States shall be entitled to vote at any election created by this constitution.

Senators shall be chosen for six years, and representatives for two. The governor for four.

The legislature shall not authorize any lottery, and shall prohibit the sale of lottery tickets.

It shall be the duty of the legislature to immediately expel from the body any member who shall receive or offer a bribe, or suffer his vote influenced by promise of preferment or reward; and every person so offending and so expelled shall thereafter be disabled from holding any office of honor, trust, or profit in this State.

The legislature shall proceed, as early as practicable, to elect senators to represent this State in the Senate of the United States; and also provide for future elections of representatives to the Congress of the United States; and on the second Tuesday after the first assembling of the legislature after the ratification of this constitution the legislature shall proceed to ratify the XIIIth and XIVth articles of amendment to the Constitution of the United States of America.

The governor may at all times require information in writing from all the officers of the executive department on any subject relating to the duties of their offices, and he shall have a general supervision and control over them. He shall have the power of removal of each of said officers, except the lieutenant governor, for misfeasance, malfeasance, or nonfeasance; but the reasons and causes of such removal shall be communicated in writing by him to the senate at the first meeting of the legislature which occurs after such removal, for its approval or disapproval; if disapproved by the senate, it may restore the displaced incumbent by a vote of that body.

The governor has the veto power, subject to an overriding vote of two-thirds of each House.

The supreme judges to be appointed by the governor, with approval of the senate, to serve for nine years.

Every male citizen of the United States, of the age of twenty-one years and upwards, not laboring under the disabilities named in this constitution, without distinction of race, color, or former condition, who shall be a resident of this State at the time of the adoption of this constitution, or who shall hereafter reside in this State one year, and in the county in which he offers to vote sixty days next preceding any election, shall be entitled to vote for all officers that are now or hereafter may be elected by the people, and upon all questions submitted to the electors at any election; provided, that no person shall be allowed to vote or hold office who is now or hereafter may be disqualified thereby by the Constitution of the United States, until such disqualification shall be removed by the Congress of the United States; provided, further, that no person while kept in any asylum, or confined in prison, or who has been convicted of felony, or who is of unsound mind, shall be allowed to vote or hold office.

It shall be the duty of the legislature of the State to make suitable provisions for the support and maintenance of a system of public free schools, for the gratuitous instruction of all the inhabitants of this State between the ages of six and eighteen years.

The legislature shall establish a uniform system of public free schools throughout the State.

The legislature at its first session (or as soon thereafter as may be possible) shall pass such laws as will require the attendance on the public free schools of the State of all the scholastic population thereof for the period of at least four months of each and every year; provided, that whenever any of the scholastic inhabitants may be shown to have received regular instruction for said period of time in each and every year from any private teacher having a proper certificate of competency, this shall exempt them from the operation of the laws contemplated by this section.

As a basis for the establishment and endowment of said public free schools, all the funds, lands, and other property heretofore set apart and appropriated for the support and maintenance of public schools shall constitute the public school fund; and all sums of money that may come to this State hereafter from the sale of any portion of the public domain of the State of Texas shall also constitute a part of the public school fund. And the legislature shall appropriate all the proceeds resulting from sales of public lands of this State to such public school fund. And the legislature shall set apart, for the benefit of public schools, one-fourth of the annual revenue derivable from general taxation, and shall also cause to be levied and collected an annual poll-tax of one dollar on all male persons in this State between the ages of twenty-one and sixty years for the benefit of public schools. And said fund and the income derived therefrom, and the taxes herein provided for school purposes, shall be a perpetual fund, to be applied, as needed, exclusively for the education of all the scholastic inhabitants of this State, and no law shall ever be made appropriating such fund for any other use or purpose whatever.

The legislature shall, if necessary, in addition to the income derived from the public school fund and from the taxes for school purposes provided for in the foregoing section, provide for the raising of such amount, by taxation, in the several school districts in the State, as will be necessary to provide the necessary school-houses in each district and insure the education of all the scholastic inhabitants of the several districts.

The public lands heretofore given to counties shall be under the control of the legislature, and may be sold under such regulations as the legislature may prescribe, and in such case the proceeds of the same shall be added to the public school fund.

The legislature shall, at its first session, (and from time to time thereafter, as may be found necessary,) provide all needful rules and regulations for the purpose of carrying into effect the provisions of this article. It is made the imperative duty of the legislature to see to it that all the children in the State, within the scholastic age, are without delay provided with ample means of education. The legislature shall annually appropriate for school purposes, and to be equally distributed among all the scholastic population of the State, the interest accruing on the school fund and the income derived from taxation for school purposes, and shall, from time to time, as may be necessary, invest the principal of the school fund in the bonds of the United States Government, and in no other security.

To every head of a family, who has not a homestead, there shall be donated one hundred and sixty acres of land out of the public domain, upon the condition that he will select, locate, and occupy the same for three years, and pay the office fees on the same. To all single men twenty-one years of age there shall be donated eighty acres of land out of the public domain, upon the same terms and conditions as are imposed upon the head of a family.

Members of the legislature, and all officers, before they enter upon the duties of their offices, shall take the following oath or affirmation: "I (A. B.) do solemnly swear (or affirm), that I will faithfully and impartially discharge and perform all duties incumbent on me as ——, according to the best of my skill and ability, and that I will support the Constitution and laws of the United States and of this State. And I do further swear (or affirm), that since the acceptance of this constitution by the Congress of the United States, I, being a citizen of this State, have not fought a duel with deadly weapons, or committed an assault upon any person with deadly weapons, or sent or accepted a challenge to fight a duel with deadly weapons, or acted as second in fighting a duel, or knowingly aided or assisted any one thus offending, either within the State or out of it; that I am not disqualified from holding office under the 14th amendment to the Constitution of the United States, (or, as the case may be, my disability to hold office under the XIV amendment to the Constitution of the United States has been removed by act of Congress;) and, further, that I am a qualified elector in this State."

Laws shall be made to exclude from office, serving on juries, and from the right of suffrage, those who shall hereafter be convicted of bribery, perjury, forgery, or other high crimes. The privilege of free suffrage shall be supported by laws regulating elections, and prohibiting under adequate penalties all undue influence thereon from power, bribery, tumult, or other improper practice.

The legislature shall provide by law for the compensation of all officers, servants, agents, and public contractors, not provided for by this constitution, and shall not grant extra compensation to any officer, agent, servant, or public contractor, after such public service shall have been performed, or contract entered into for the performance of the same; nor grant, by appropriation or otherwise, any amount of money out of the treasury of the State, to any individual, on a claim, real or pretended, where the same shall not have been provided for by pre-existing law.

General laws, regulating the adoption of children, emancipation of minors, and the granting of divorces, shall be made; but no special law shall be enacted relating to particular or individual cases.

The rights of married women to their separate property, real and personal, and the increase of the same, shall be protected by law; and married women, infants, and insane persons, shall not be barred of their rights of property by adverse possession or law of limitation of less than seven years from and after the removal of each and all of their respective legal disabilities.

The legislature shall have power, and it shall be their duty, to protect by law from forced sale a certain portion of the property of all heads of families. The homestead of a family, not to exceed two hundred acres of land, (not included in a city, town, or village,) or any city, town, or village lot or lots, not to exceed five thousand dollars in value at the time of their designation as a homestead, and without reference to the value of any improvements thereon, shall not be subject to forced sales for debts, except they be for the purchase thereof, for the taxes assessed thereon, or for labor and materials expended thereon; nor shall the owner, if a married man, be at liberty to alienate the same unless by the consent of the wife, and in such manner as may be prescribed by law.

All persons who at any time heretofore lived together as husband and wife, and both of whom, by the law of bondage, were precluded from the rites of matrimony, and continued to live together until the death of one of the parties, shall be considered as having been legally married, and the issue of such cohabitation shall be deemed legitimate, and all such persons as may be now living together in such relation shall be considered as having been legally married, and the children heretofore or hereafter born of such cohabitations shall be deemed legitimate.

No minister of the Gospel, or priest of any denomination whatever, who accepts a seat in the legislature as representative, shall, after such acceptance, be allowed to claim exemption from military service, road duty, or serving on juries, by reason of his said profession.

The ordinance of the convention passed on the first day of February, A. D. 1861, commonly known as the ordinance of secession, was in contravention of the Constitution and laws of the United States, and therefore null and void from the beginning; and all laws and parts of laws founded upon said ordinance were also null and void from the date of their passage. The legislatures which sat in the State of Texas from the 18th day of March, A. D. 1861, until the 6th day of August, A. D. 1866, had no constitutional authority to make laws binding upon the people of the State of Texas: *Provided,* That this section shall not be construed to inhibit the authorities of this State from re-pecting and enforcing such rules and regulations as were prescribed by the said legislatures which were not in violation of the Constitution and laws of the United States, or in aid of the rebellion against the United States, or prejudicial to citizens of this State who were loyal to the United States, and which have been actually in force or observed in Texas during the above period of time, nor to affect prejudicially private rights which may have grown up under such rules and regulations, nor to invalidate official acts not in aid of the rebellion against the United States during said period of time. The legislature which assembled in the city of Austin on the 6th day of August, A. D. 1866, was provisional only, and its acts are to be respected only so far as they were not in violation of the Constitution and laws of the United States, or were not intended to reward those who participated in the rebellion or discriminate between citizens on account of race or color, or to operate prejudicially to any class of citizens.

All debts created by the so-called State of Texas from and after the 28th day of January, A. D. 1861, and prior to the 5th day of August, 1865, were and are null and void, and the legislature is prohibited from making any provision for the acknowledgment or payment of such debts. All unpaid balances, whether of salary, per diem, or monthly allowance due to employees of the State, who were in the service thereof on the said 28th day of January, 1861, civil or military, and who gave their aid, countenance, or support to the rebellion then inaugurated against the Government of the United States, or turned their arms against the said Government, thereby forfeited the sums severally due to them. All the ten per cent. warrants issued for military services, and exchanged during the rebellion at the treasury for non-interest warrants, are hereby declared to have been fully paid and discharged: *Provided,* That any loyal person, or his or her heirs or legal representatives, may, by proper legal proceedings, to be commenced within two years after the acceptance of this constitution by the Congress of the United States, show proof in avoidance of any contract made, or revise or annul any decree or judgment rendered since the said 28th day of January, 1861, when, through fraud practiced or threats of violence used towards such persons, no adequate consideration for the contract has been received; or when, through absence from the State of such person, or through political prejudice against such person, the decision complained of was not fair or impartial.

All the qualified voters of each county shall also be qualified jurors of such county.

Four congressional districts are established, to continue till otherwise provided by law.

The election on the adoption of the constitution to be held on the first Monday in July, 1869, at the places and under the regulations to be prescribed by the commanding general of the military district.

# XLV.

# JUDICIAL DECISIONS, AND THE OPINION OF THE ATTORNEY GENERAL OF THE UNITED STATES ON THE JURISDICTION OF MILITARY COMMISSIONS.

## SUPREME COURT OF THE UNITED STATES.

### On the Right of a State to Tax Passengers Passing through it.

No. 85, DECEMBER TERM, 1867.

William H. Crandall, pl'ff in error, *vs.* The State of Nevada. } In error to the supreme court of the State of Nevada.

Mr. Justice Miller delivered the opinion of the court.

The question for the first time presented to the court by this record is one of importance. The proposition to be considered is the right of a State to levy a tax upon persons residing in the State who may wish to get out of it, and upon persons not residing in it who may have occasion to pass through it.

It is to be regretted that such a question should be submitted to our consideration with neither brief nor argument on the part of plaintiff in error. But our regret is diminished by the reflection, that the principles which must govern its determination have been the subject of much consideration in cases heretofore decided by this court.

The plaintiff in error, who was the agent of a stage company engaged in carrying passengers through the State of Nevada, was arrested for refusing to report the number of passengers that had been carried by the coaches of his company, and for refusing to pay the tax of one dollar imposed on each passenger by the law of that State. He pleaded in good form that the law of the State under which he was prosecuted was void, because it was in conflict with the Constitution of the United States; and his plea being overruled, the case came into the supreme court of the State, where it was decided against the claim thus set up under the Federal Constitution.

The provisions of the statute charged to be in violation of the Constitution are to be found in sections 90 and 91 of the revenue act of 1865, page 271 of the statutes of Nevada for that year. Section 90 enacts, that "there shall be levied and collected a capitation tax of one dollar upon every person leaving the State by any railroad, stage-coach, or other vehicle engaged or employed in the business of transporting passengers for hire;" and that the proprietors, owners, and corporations so engaged shall pay said tax of one dollar for each and every person so conveyed or transported from the State. Section 91, for the purpose of collecting the tax, requires from persons engaged in such business, or their agents, a report every month, under oath, of the number of passengers so transported, and the payment of the tax to the sheriff or other proper officer.

It is claimed by counsel for the State that the tax thus levied is not a tax upon the passenger, but upon the business of the carrier who transports him.

If the act were much more skillfully drawn to sustain this hypothesis than it is, we should be very reluctant to admit that any form of words which had the effect to compel every person traveling through the country by the common and usual modes of public conveyance to pay a specific sum to the State was not a tax upon the right thus exercised. The statute before us is not, however, embarrassed by any nice difficulties of this character. The language which we have just quoted is, that there shall be levied and collected a capitation tax upon every person leaving the State by any railroad or stage-coach, and the remaining provisions of the act, which refer to this tax, only provide a mode of collecting it. The officers and agents of the railroad companies and the proprietors of the stage-coaches are made responsible for this, and so become the collectors of the tax.

We shall have occasion to refer hereafter somewhat in detail to the opinions of the judges of this court in the Passenger Cases, 7 Howard, in which there were wide differences on several points involved in the case before us. In the case from New York then under consideration the statute provided that the health commissioner should be entitled to demand and receive from the master of every vessel that should arrive in the port of New York from a foreign port $1 50 for every cabin passenger and $1 for each steerage passenger, and from each coasting vessel twenty-five cents for every person on board. That statute does not use language so strong as the Nevada statute, indicative of a personal tax on the passenger, but merely taxes the master of the vessel according to the number of his passengers; but the court held it to be a tax upon the passenger, and that the master was the agent of the State for its collection. Chief Justice Taney, while he differed from the majority of the court, and held the law to be valid, said of the tax levied by the analogous statute of Massachusetts, that "its payment is the condition upon which the State permits the alien passenger to come on shore and mingle with its citizens and to reside among them. It is demanded of the captain, and not from every separate passenger, for convenience of collection. But the burden evidently falls upon the passenger, and he in fact pays it, either in the enhanced price of his passage or directly to the captain before he is allowed to embark for the voyage.

The nature of the transaction and the ordinary course of business show that this must be so."

Having determined that the statute of Nevada imposes a tax upon the passenger for the privilege of leaving the State, or passing through it by the ordinary mode of passenger travel, we proceed to inquire if it is for that reason in conflict with the Constitution of the United States.

In the argument of the counsel for the defendant in error, and in the opinion of the supreme court of Nevada, which is found in the record, it is assumed that this question must be decided by an exclusive reference to two provisions of the Constitution, namely : that which forbids any State, without the consent of Congress, to lay any imposts or duties on imports or exports, and that which confers on Congress the power to regulate commerce with foreign nations and among the several States.

The question as thus narrowed is not free from difficulties. Can a citizen of the United States traveling from one part of the Union to another be called an export? It was insisted in the Passenger Cases, to which we have already referred, that foreigners coming to this country were imports within the meaning of the Constitution, and the provision of that instrument that the migration or importation of such persons as any of the States then existing should think proper to admit should not be prohibited prior to the year 1808, but that a tax might be imposed on such importation was relied on as showing that the word import applied to persons as well as to merchandize. It was answered that this latter clause had exclusive reference to slaves, who were property as well as persons, and therefore proved nothing. While some of the judges who concurred in holding those laws to be unconstitutional gave as one of their reasons that they were taxes on imports, it is evident that this view did not receive the assent of a majority of the court. The application of this provision of the Constitution to the proposition which we have stated in regard to the citizen is still less satisfactory than it would be to the case of foreigners migrating to the United States.

But it is unnecessary to consider this point further in the view which we have taken of the case.

As regards the commerce clause of the Constitution, two propositions are advanced on behalf of the defendant in error : 1. That the tax imposed by the State on passengers is not a regulation of commerce. 2. That if it can be so considered it is one of those powers which the States can exercise until Congress has so legislated as to indicate its intention to exclude State legislation on the same subject.

The proposition that the power to regulate commerce, as granted to Congress by the Constitution, necessarily excludes the exercise by the States of any of the power thus granted, is one which has been much considered in this court, and the earlier discussions left the question in much doubt. As late as the January term, 1849, the opinions of the judges in the Passenger Cases show that the question was considered to be one of much importance in those cases, and was even then unsettled, though previous decisions of the court were relied on by the judges themselves as deciding it in different ways. It was certainly, so far as those cases affected it, left an open question.

In the case of Cooley vs. Board of Wardens, 12 Howard, 299, four years later, the same question came directly before the court in reference to the local laws of the port of Philadelphia concerning pilots. It was claimed that they constituted a regulation of commerce, and were therefore void. The court held that they did come within the meaning of the term "to regulate commerce," but that until Congress made regulations concerning pilots the States were competent to do so.

Perhaps no more satisfactory solution has ever been given of this vexed question than the one furnished by the court in that case. After showing that there are some powers granted to Congress which are exclusive of similar powers in the States, because they are declared to be so, and that other powers are necessarily so from their very nature, the court proceeds to say, that the authority to regulate commerce with foreign nations and among the States includes within its compass powers which can only be exercised by Congress, as well as powers which, from their nature, can best be exercised by the State legislatures, to which latter class the regulation of pilots belongs. "Whatever subjects of this power are in their nature national, or admit of one uniform system or plan of regulation, may justly be said to be of such a nature as to require exclusive legislation by Congress." In the case of Gillman vs. Philadelphia, 3 Wallace, 713, this doctrine is reaffirmed, and under it a bridge across a stream navigable from the ocean, authorized by State law, was held to be well authorized in the absence of any legislation by Congress affecting the matter.

It may be that under the power to regulate commerce among the States, Congress has authority to pass laws, the operation of which would be inconsistent with the tax imposed by the State of Nevada, but we know of no such statute now in existence. Inasmuch, therefore, as the tax does not itself institute any regulation of commerce of a national character, or which has a uniform operation over the whole country, it is not easy to maintain, in view of the principles on which those cases were decided, that it violates the clause of the Federal Constitution which we have had under review.

But we do not concede that the question before us is to be determined by the two clauses of the Constitution which we have been examining.

The people of these United States constitute one nation. They have a Government in which all of them are deeply interested. This Government has necessarily a capital established by law, where its principal operations are conducted. Here sits its legislature, composed of senators and representatives from the States and from the people of the States. Here resides the President, directing through thousands of agents the execution of the laws over all this vast country. Here is the seat of the supreme judicial power of the nation, to which all its citizens have a right to resort to claim justice at its hands. Here are the great executive departments, administering the offices of the mails, of the public lands, of the collection and distribution of the public revenues, and of our foreign relations. These are all established and conducted under the admitted powers of the Federal Government. That Government has a right to call to this point any or all of its citizens to aid in its service, as members of the Congress, of the courts, of the executive departments, and to fill all its other offices; and this right cannot be made to depend upon the pleasure of a State, over whose territory they must pass to reach the point where these services must be rendered. The Government also has its offices of secondary importance in all other parts of the country. On the seacoasts and on the rivers it has its ports of entry. In the interior it has its land offices, its revenue offices, and its sub-treasuries. In all these it demands the services of its citizens, and is entitled to bring them to those points from all quarters of the nation, and no power can exist in a State to obstruct this right that would not enable it to defeat the purposes for which the Government was established.

The federal power has a right to declare and prosecute wars, and, as a necessary incident, to raise and transport troops through and over the territory of any State of the Union.

If this right is dependent in any sense, however limited, upon the pleasure of a State, the Government itself may be overthrown by an obstruction to its exercise. Much the largest part of the transportation of troops during the late rebellion was by railroads, and largely through States whose people were hostile to the Union. If the tax levied by Nevada on railroad passengers had been the law of Tennessee, enlarged to meet the wishes of her people, the treasury of the United States could not have paid the tax necessary to enable its armies to pass through her territory.

But if the Government has these rights on her own account, the citizen also has correlative rights. He has the right to come to the seat of Government to assert any claim he may have upon that Government, or to transact any business he may have with it; to seek its protection, to share its offices, to engage in administering its functions. He has a right to free access to its sea-ports, through which all the operations of foreign trade and commerce are conducted, to the sub-treasuries, the land offices, the revenue offices, and the courts of justice in the several States, and this right is in its nature independent of the will of any State over whose soil he must pass in the exercise of it.

The views here advanced are neither novel nor unsupported by authority. The question of the taxing power of the States, as its exercise has affected the functions of the Federal Government, has been repeatedly considered by this court, and the right of the States in this mode to impede or embarrass the constitutional operations of that Government, or the rights which its citizens hold under it, has been uniformly denied.

The leading case of this class is that of McCulloch vs. Maryland, (4 Wheaton, 316.) The case is one every way important, and is familiar to the statesman and the constitutional lawyer. The Congress, for the purpose of aiding the fiscal operations of the Government, had chartered the Bank of the United States, with authority to establish branches in the different States, and to issue notes for circulation. The legislature of Maryland had levied a tax upon these circulating notes, which the bank refused to pay, on the ground that the statute was void by reason of its antagonism to the Federal Constitution. No particular provision of the Constitution was pointed to as prohibiting the taxation by the State. Indeed, the authority of Congress to create the bank, which was strenuously denied, and the discussion of which constituted an important element in the opinion of the court, was not based by that opinion on any express grant of power, but was claimed to be necessary and proper to enable the Government to carry out its authority to raise a revenue, and to transfer and disburse the same. It was argued also that the tax on the circulation operated very remotely, if at all, on the only functions of the bank in which the Government was interested. But the court, by a unanimous judgment, held the law of Maryland to be unconstitutional.

It is not possible to condense the conclusive argument of Chief Justice Marshall in that case, and it is too familiar to justify its reproduction here; but an extract or two, in which the results of his reasoning are stated, will serve to show its applicability to the case before us. " That the power of taxing the bank by the States," he says, " may be exercised so as to destroy it is too obvious to be denied. But taxation is said to be an absolute power, which acknowledges no other limits than those prescribed by the Constitution, and, like sovereign power of any description, is trusted to the discretion of those who use it. But the very terms of this argument admit that the sovereignty of the State in the article of taxation is subordinate to and may be controlled by the Constitution of the United States." Again he says : " We find then on just theory a total failure of the original right to tax the means employed by the Government of the Union for the execution of its powers. The right never existed, and the question of its surrender cannot arise. * * " That the power to tax involves the power to destroy: that the power to destroy may defeat and render useless the power to create; that there is a plain repugnance in conferring on one government a power to control the constitutional measures of another, which other, with respect to those very means, is declared to be supreme over that which exerts the control are propositions not to be denied. If the States may tax one instrument employed by the Government in the execution of its powers, they may tax any and every other instrument. They may tax the mail; they may tax the mint; they may tax patent rights; they may tax the papers of the custom-house; they may tax judicial process; they may tax all the means employed by the Government to an excess which would defeat all the ends of Government. This was not intended by the American people. They did not design to make their Government dependent on the States."

It will be observed that it was not the extent of the tax in that case which was complained of, but the right to levy any tax of that character. So, in the case before us, it may be said that a tax of one dollar for passing through the State of Nevada, by stage coach or by railroad, cannot sensibly affect any function of the Government, or deprive a citizen of any valuable right. But if the State can tax a railroad passenger one dollar, it can tax him one thousand dollars. If one State can do this, so can every other State. And thus one or more States, covering the only practicable routes of travel from the east to the west, or from the north to the south, may totally prevent or seriously burden all transportation of passengers from one part of the country to the other.

A case of another character, in which the taxing power, as exercised by a State, was held void, because repugnant to the Federal Constitution, is that of Brown vs. The State of Maryland, (12 Wheaton, 412.)

The State of Maryland required all importers of foreign merchandize who sold the same by wholesale, by bale or by package, to take out a license, and this act was claimed to be unconstitutional. The court held it to be so on three different grounds: first, that it was a duty on imports; second, that it was a regulation of commerce; and, third, that the importer who had paid the duties imposed by the United States had acquired a right to sell his goods in the same original packages in which they were imported. To say nothing of the first and second grounds, we have in the third a tax of a State declared to be void because it interfered with the exercise of a right derived by the importer from the laws of the United States. If the right of passing through a State by a citizen of the United States is one guarantied to him by the Constitution, it must be as sacred from State taxation as the right derived by the importer from the payment of duties to sell the goods on which the duties were paid.

In the case of Weston vs. The City of Charleston, (2 Peters, 447,) we have a case of State taxation of still another class, held to be void as an interference with the rights of the Federal Government. The tax in that instance was imposed on bonds or stocks of the United States, in common with all other securities of the same character. It was held by the court that the free and successful operation of the Government required it at times to borrow money; that to borrow money it was necessary to issue this class of national securities, and that if the States could tax these securities, they might so tax them as to seriously impair or totally destroy the power of the Government to borrow. This case, itself based on the doctrines advanced by the court in McCulloch vs. The State of Maryland, has been followed in all the recent cases involving State taxation of Government bonds, from that of The People of New York vs. Tax Commissioners, (2 Black, 620,) to the decisions of the court at this term.

In all these cases the opponents of the taxes levied by the States were able to place their opposition oh no express provision of the Constitution, except in that of Brown vs. Maryland. But in all the other cases; and in that case also, the court distinctly placed the invalidity of the State taxes on the ground that they interfered with an authority of the Federal Government, which was itself only to be sustained as necessary and proper to the exercise of some other power expressly granted.

In the Passenger Cases, to which reference has already been made, Justice Grier, with whom Justice Catron concurred, makes this one of the four propositions on which they held the tax void in those cases. Judge Wayne expresses his assent to Judge Grier's views; and perhaps this ground received the concurrence of more of the members of the court who constituted the majority than any other.

But the principles here laid down may be found more clearly stated in the dissenting opinion of the Chief Justice in those cases, and with more direct pertinency to the case now before us, than anywhere else.

After expressing his views fully in favor of the validity of the tax, which he said had exclusive reference to foreigners, so far as those cases were concerned, he proceeds to say, for the purpose of preventing misapprehension, that so far as the tax affected American citizens it could not in his opinion be maintained. He then adds: "Living as we do under a common government, charged with the great concerns of the whole Union, every citizen of the United States, from the most remote States or Territories, is entitled to free access, not only to the principal departments established at Washington, but also to its judicial tribunals and public offices in every State in the Union. * * * For all the great purposes for which the Federal Government was formed we are one people, with one common country. We are all citizens of the United States, and as members of the same community must have the right to pass and repass through every part of it without interruption as freely as in our own States. And a tax imposed by a State for entering its territories or harbors is inconsistent with the rights which belong to citizens of other States as members of the Union, and with the objects which that Union was intended to attain. Such a power in the States could produce nothing but discord and mutual irritation, and they very clearly do not possess it."

Although these remarks are found in a dissenting opinion, they do not relate to the matter on which the dissent was founded. They accord with the inferences which we have already drawn from the Constitution itself, and from the decisions of this court in exposition of that instrument.

Those principles, as we have already stated them in this opinion, must govern the present case.

The judgment of the Supreme Court of the State of Nevada is therefore reversed, and the case remanded to that court, with directions to discharge the plaintiff in error from custody.

Mr. Justice Clifford: I agree that the State law in question is unconstitutional and void, but I am not able to concur in the principal reasons assigned in the opinion of the court in support of that conclusion.

On the contrary, I hold that the act of the State legislature is inconsistent with the power conferred upon Congress to regulate commerce among the several States, and I think the judgment of the court should have been placed exclusively upon that ground.

Strong doubts are entertained by me whether Congress possesses the power to levy any such tax; but whether so or not, I am clear that the State legislature cannot impose any such burden upon commerce among the several States. Such commerce is secured against such legislation in the States by the Constitution, irrespective of any congressional action.

The Chief Justice also dissents, and concurs in the views I have expressed.

### On State Taxation of United States Certificates of Indebtedness.

#### December Term, 1868.

The People of the State of New York, *ex rel.* The Bank of New York National Banking Association, plaintiffs in error,
No. 246.      *vs.*
Richard B. Connolly, comptroller, and John T. Hoffman, mayor, &c., *et al.*

The People of the State of New York, *ex rel.* The National Broadway Bank, plaintiffs in error,
No. 248.      *vs.*
John T. Hoffman, mayor, and Richard T. Connolly, comptroller, etc.,
and
The People of the State of New York, *ex rel.* The National Bank of the Republic of the city of New York, plaintiffs in error,
No. 252.      *vs.*
John T. Hoffman, mayor, Richard B. Connolly, comptroller of the city of New York, *et al.*

In error to the court of appeals of the State of N. York.

Mr. Chief Justice Chase delivered the opinion of the court in these causes.

These three cases present, under somewhat different forms, the same question, namely: Are the obligations of the United States, known as certificates of indebtedness, liable to be taxed by State legislation?

These three cases were argued and will be considered together.

In 1863 and in 1864 the proper officers of the State, acting under the laws of New York, assessed certain taxes upon the capital stock of the several banking associations in that State. Some of these banking associations resisted the collection of the tax on the ground that, though nominally imposed upon their respective capitals, it was in fact imposed upon the bonds and obligations of the United States, in which a large proportion of these capitals was invested, and which, under the Constitution and laws of the United States, were exempt from State taxation.

This question was brought before the court of appeals, which sustained the assessments, and disallowed the claim of the banking associations.

From this decision an appeal was taken to this court, upon the hearing of which, at the December term, 1864, it was adjudged that the taxes imposed upon the capitals of the associations were a tax upon the national bonds and obligations in which they were invested, and, therefore, so far, contrary to the Constitution of the United States.[*]

A mandate in conformity with this decision was sent to the court of appeals of New York, which court thereupon reversed its judgment, and entered a judgment agreeably to the mandate.

---

[*] 2 Wall., 210.

Afterwards, on the 30th of April, 1866, the legislature of New York provided by law for refunding to the banking associations and other corporations in like condition the taxes of 1863 and 1864 collected upon that part of their capitals invested in securities of the United States exempt by law from taxation. The board of supervisors of the county of New York was charged with the duty of auditing and allowing, with the approval of the mayor of the city and the corporation counsel, the amount collected from each corporation for taxes on the exempt portion of its capital, together with costs, damages, and interest. Upon such auditing and allowance the sums awarded were to be paid to the corporations severally entitled by the issue to each of New York county seven per cent. bonds of equal amounts. These bonds were to be signed by the comptroller of the city of New York, countersigned by the mayor, and sealed with the seal of the board of supervisors, and attested by the clerk of the board.

Under this act the board of supervisors audited and allowed to the several institutions represented in the three cases under consideration their several claims for taxes collected upon the national securities held by them, including in this allowance the taxes paid on certificates of indebtedness, which the corporations claimed to be securities of the United States exempt from taxation.

But the comptroller, mayor, and clerk refused to sign, countersign, seal, and attest the requisite amount of bonds for payment, insisting that certificates of indebtedness were not exempt from taxation.

A writ of mandamus was thereupon sued out of the supreme court of New York for the purpose of compelling these officials to perform their alleged duties in this respect. An answer was filed, and the court, by its judgment, sustained the refusal. An appeal was taken to the court of appeals of New York, by which the judgment of the supreme court was affirmed. Writs of error, under the 25th section of the judiciary act, bring these judgments here for revision.

The first question to be considered is one of jurisdiction. It is insisted in behalf of the defendants in error that the judgment of the New York court of appeals is not subject to review in this court.

But is it not plain that, under the act of the legislature of New York, the banking associations were entitled to reimbursement by bonds of the taxes illegally collected from them in 1863 and 1864?

No objection was made in the State court to the process by which the associations sought to enforce the issue of the bonds to which they asserted their right. Mandamus to the officers charged with the execution of the State law seems to have been regarded on all hands as the appropriate remedy.

But it was objected on the part of those officers that the particular description of obligations, of the tax on which the associations claimed reimbursement, were not exempt from taxation. The associations, on the other hand, insisted that these obligations were exempt under the Constitution and laws of the United States. If they were so exempt, the associations were entitled to the relief which they sought. The judgment of the court of appeals denied the relief, upon the ground that certificates of indebtedness were not entitled to exemption. Is it not clear that in the case before the State court a right, privilege, or immunity was claimed under the Constitution or a statute of the United States, and that the decision was against the right, privilege, or immunity claimed, and, therefore, that the jurisdiction of this court to review that decision is within the express words of the amendatory act of February 5, 1867? There can be but one answer to this question. We can find no ground for doubt on the point of jurisdiction.

The general question upon the merits is this: Were the obligations of the United States known as certificates of indebtedness liable to State taxation?

If this question can be affirmatively answered, the judgments of the court of appeals must be affirmed; if not, they must be reversed.

Evidences of the indebtedness of the United States, held by individuals or corporations, and sometimes called stock or stocks, but recently better known as bonds or obligations, have uniformly been held by this court not to be liable to taxation under State legislation.

The authority to borrow money on the credit of the United States is, in the enumeration of the powers expressly granted by the Constitution, second in place, and only second in importance, to the authority to lay and collect taxes. Both are given as means to the exercise of the functions of Government under the Constitution, and both, if neither had been expressly conferred, would be necessarily implied from other powers; for no one will assert that without them the great powers—mentioning no others—to raise and support armies, to provide and maintain a navy, and to carry on war, could be exercised at all, or, if at all, with adequate efficiency.

And no one affirms that the power of the Government to borrow, or the action of the Government in borrowing, is subject to taxation by the States.

There are those, however, who assert that, although the States cannot tax the exercise of the powers of the Government, as for example in the conveyance of the mails, the transportation of troops, or the borrowing of money, they may tax the indebtedness of the Government when it assumes the form of obligations held by individuals, and so becomes in a certain sense private property.

This court, however, has constantly held otherwise.

Forty years ago, in the case of Weston vs. The City of Charleston, this court, speaking through Chief Justice Marshall, said :*

"The American people have conferred the power of borrowing money upon their Government, and by making that Government supreme have shielded its action in the exercise of that power from the action of the local governments. The grant of the power is incompatible with a restraining or controlling power, and the declaration of supremacy is a declaration that no such restraining or controlling power shall be exercised."

And, applying these principles, the court proceeded to say :

"The right to tax the contract to any extent, when made, must operate on the power to borrow before it is exercised and have a sensible influence on the contract. The extent of this influence depends on the will of a distinct government. To any extent, however inconsiderable, it is a burden upon the operations of the Government. It may be carried to an extent which shall arrest them entirely."

And finally:

" A tax on Government stock is thought by this court to be a tax on the contract, a tax on the power to borrow money on the credit of the United States, and consequently repugnant to the Constitution."

Nothing need be added to this, except that in no case decided since have these propositions been retracted or qualified. The last cases in which the power of the States to tax the obligations of the Government came directly in question were those of the Bank of Commerce vs. The City of New York, in 1862,* and the Bank Tax Case,† in 1865, in both of which the power was denied.

An attempt was made at the bar to establish a distinction between the bonds of the Government expressed for loans of money and the certificates of indebtedness for which the exemption was claimed. The argument was ingenious, but failed to convince us that such a distinction can be maintained. It may be admitted that these certificates were issued in payment of supplies and in satisfaction of demands of public creditors. But we fail to perceive either that there is a solid distinction between certificates of indebtedness issued for money borrowed and given to creditors and certificates of indebtedness issued directly to creditors in payment of their demands; or that such certificates, issued as a means of executing constitutional powers of the Government, other than of borrowing money, are not as much beyond control and limitation by the States through taxation as bonds or other obligations issued for loans of money.

The principle of exemption is, that the States cannot control the national Government within the sphere of its constitutional power , for there it is supreme; and cannot tax its obligations for payment of money issued for purposes within that range of powers, because such taxation necessarily implies the assertion of the right to exercise such control.

The certificates of indebtedness in the case before us are completely within the protection of this principle. For the public history of the country and the acts of Congress show that they were issued to creditors for supplies necessary to the Government in carrying on the recent war for the integrity of the Union and the preservation of our republican institutions. They were received instead of money at a time when full money payment for supplies was impossible, and, according to the principles of the cases to which we have referred, are as much beyond the taxing

---

*2 Peters, 467.                    * 2 Black., 628.        † 2 Wall., 200.

power of the States as the operations themselves in furtherance of which they were issued.

It results that the several judgments of the court of appeals must be reversed.

## On State Taxation of United States Notes.

No. 247.—December Term, 1868.

The People of the State of New York, ex rel. the Bank of New York, plaintiffs in error, vs. The Board of Supervisors of the County of New York.

In error to the court of appeals of the State of New York.

Mr. Chief Justice Chase delivered the opinion of the court.

This case differs from those just disposed of in two particulars: (1) That the board of supervisors, which in the other cases allowed and audited the claims of the banking associations, refused to allow the claim made in this case; and (2) that the exemption from State taxation claimed in this case was of United States notes, while in the other cases it was of certificates of indebtedness.

The mandamus in the State court was therefore directed, in the case now before us, to the board of supervisors, instead of the officers authorized to issue bonds, as in the cases already decided.

The judgment of the court of appeals sustained the action of the board, and the case is brought here by writ of error to that court.

The general question requiring consideration is, whether United States notes come under another rule in respect of taxation than that which applies to certificates of indebtedness.

The issues of United States notes were authorized by three successive acts. The first was the act of February 25, 1862;* the second the act of July 11, 1862;† and the third that of March 3, 1863.‡

Before either of these acts received the sanction of Congress the Secretary of the Treasury had been authorized by the act of July 17, 1861,§ to issue treasury notes not bearing interest, but payable on demand by the assistant treasurers at New York, Philadelphia, or Boston; and about three weeks later these notes, by the act of August 5, 1861,‖ had been made receivable generally for public dues. The amount of notes to be issued of this description was originally limited to fifty millions, but was afterwards, by the act of February 12, 1862,¶ increased to sixty millions.

These notes, made payable on demand and receivable for all public dues, including duties on imports always payable in coin, were practically equivalent to coin; and all public disbursements, until after the date of the act last mentioned, were made in coin or these notes.

In December, 1861, the State banks (and no others then existed) suspended payment in coin; and it became necessary to provide by law for the use of State bank notes, or to authorize the issue of notes for circulation under the authority of the national Government. The latter alternative was preferred, and in the necessity thus recognized originated the legislation providing

at first for the emission of United States notes, and at a later period for the issue of the national bank currency.

Under the exigencies of the times it seems to have been thought inexpedient to attempt any provision for the redemption of the United States notes in coin. The law, therefore, directed that they should be made payable to bearer at the treasury of the United States, but did not provide for payment on demand. The period of payment was left to be determined by the public exigencies. In the meantime the notes were receivable in payment of all loans, and were, until after the close of our civil war, always practically convertible into bonds of the funded debt, bearing not less than five per cent. interest, payable in coin.

The act of February 25, 1862, provided for the issue of these notes to the amount of $150,000,000. The act of July 11, 1862, added another $150,000,000 to the circulation, reserving, however, $50,000,000 for the redemption of temporary loan, to be issued and used only when necessary for that purpose. Under the act of March 3, 1863, another issue of $150,000,000 was authorized, making the whole amount authorized $450,000,000, and contemplating a permanent circulation, until resumption of payment in coin, of $400,000,000.

It is unnecessary here to go further into the history of these notes, or to examine their relation to the national bank currency. That history belongs to another place, and the quality of these notes, as legal tenders, belongs to another discussion. It has been thought proper only to advert to the legislation by which these notes were authorized in order that their true character may be clearly perceived.

That these notes were issued under the authority of the United States, and as a means to ends entirely within the constitutional power of the Government, was not seriously questioned upon the argument.

But it was insisted that they were issued as money; that their controlling quality was that of money; and that therefore they were subject to taxation in the same manner and to the same extent as coin issued under like authority.

And there is certainly much force in the argument. It is clear that these notes were intended to circulate as money, and, with the national bank notes, to constitute the credit currency of the country.

Nor is it easy to see that taxation of these notes, used as money and held by individual owners, can control or embarrass the power of the Government in issuing them for circulation more than like taxation embarrasses its power in coining and issuing gold and silver money for circulation.

Apart from the quality of legal tender impressed upon them by acts of Congress, of which we now say nothing, their circulation as currency depends on the extent to which they are received in payment, on the quantity in circulation, and on the credit given to the promises they bear. In these respects they resemble the bank notes formerly issued as currency.

But, on the other hand, it is equally clear that these notes are obligations of the United States.

---

*12 U. S. Stat., 345.   †12 U. S. Stat., 532.   ‡12 U. S. Stat., 709.   §12 U. S. Stat., 259, §6.   ‖12 U. S. Stat., 313, §5.   ¶12 U. S. Stat., 338.

Their name imports obligation. Every one of them expresses upon its face an engagement of the nation to pay to the bearer a certain sum. The dollar note is an engagement to pay a dollar, and the dollar intended is the coined dollar of the United States—a certain quantity in weight and fineness of gold or silver, authenticated as such by the stamp of the Government. No other dollars had before been recognized by the legislation of the national Government as lawful money

Would, then, their usefulness and value as means to the exercise of the functions of government be injuriously affected by State taxation?

It cannot be said, as we have already intimated, that the same inconveniences as would arise from the taxation of bonds and other interest-bearing obligations of the Government would attend the taxation of notes issued for circulation as money. But we cannot say that no embarrassment would arise from such taxation. And we think it clearly within the discretion of Congress to determine whether, in view of all the circumstances attending the issue of the notes, their usefulness as a means of carrying on the Government would be enhanced by exemption from taxation; and within the constitutional power of Congress, having resolved the question of usefulness affirmatively, to provide by law for such exemption.

There remains, then, only this question: Has Congress exercised the power of exemption?

A careful examination of the acts under which they were issued has left no doubt in our minds upon that point.

The act of February, 1862,* declares that "all United States bonds and other securities of the United States held by individuals, associations, or corporations, within the United States, shall be exempt from taxation by or under State authority."

We have already said that these notes are obligations. They bind the national faith. They are, therefore, strictly securities. They secure the payment stipulated to the holders by the pledge of the national faith, the only ultimate security of all national obligations, whatever form they may assume.

And this provision is re-enacted in application to the second issue of United States notes by the act of July 11, 1863.†

And, as if to remove every possible doubt from the intention of Congress, the act of March 3, 1863,‡ which provides for the last issue of these notes, omits in its exemption clause the word "stocks," and substitutes for "other securities" the words, "Treasury notes or United States notes issued under the provisions of this act."

It was insisted at the bar that a measure of exemption in respect to the notes issued under this, different from that provided in the former acts in respect to the notes authorized by them, was intended. But we cannot yield our assent to this view. The rule established in the last act is in no respect inconsistent with that previously established. It must be regarded, therefore, as explanatory. It makes specific what was before expressed in general terms.

*12 U. S. Stat., 346, §2.    †12 U. S. Stat., 546.    ‡12 Stat., 709.

Our conclusion is, that United States notes are exempt, and, at the time the New York statutes were enacted, were exempt from taxation by or under State authority. The judgment of the court of appeals must therefore be reversed.

## Clause making United States Notes a Legal Tender for Debts has no reference to State Taxes.

### No. 5.—DECEMBER TERM, 1868.

The County of Lane, pl'ff in error, } In error to the supreme court of the
				vs.
The State of Oregon.           } State of Oregon.

Mr. Chief Justice Chase delivered the opinion of the court.

The State of Oregon, in April, 1865, filed a complaint against the county of Lane, in the circuit court of the State for that county, to recover $5,460 96 in gold and silver coin, which sum was alleged to have become due as State revenue from the county to the State on the 1st Monday of February, 1864.

To this complaint an answer was put in by the county, alleging a tender of the amount claimed by the State, made on the 23d day of January, 1864, to the State treasurer, at his office, in United States notes, and averring that the lawful money so tendered and offered was, in truth and fact, part of the first moneys collected and paid into the county treasury after the assessment of taxes for the year 1862.

To this answer there was a demurrer, which was sustained by the circuit court, and judgment was given that the plaintiff recover of the defendent the sum claimed in gold and silver coin, with costs of suit, and this judgment was affirmed upon writ of error by the supreme court of the State.

The case is brought here by writ of error to that court; and two propositions have been pressed upon our attention, ably and earnestly, in behalf of the plaintiff in error.

The *first* is, that the laws of Oregon did not require the collection in coin of the taxes in question, and that the treasurer of the county could not be required to pay to the treasurer of the State any other money than that in which the taxes were actually collected.

The *second* is, that the tender of the amount of taxes made to the treasurer of the State by the treasurer of the county in United States notes, was warranted by the acts of Congress authorizing the issue of these notes, and that the law of the State, if it required collection and payment in coin, was repugnant to these acts, and therefore void.

The first of these propositions will be first considered.

The answer avers substantially that the money tendered was part of the first moneys collected in Lane county after the assessment of 1863, and the demurrer admits the truth of the answer.

The fact therefore may be taken as established, that the taxes for that year in Lane county were collected in United States notes.

But was this in conformity with the laws of Oregon?

In this court the construction given by the State courts to the laws of a State relating to local affairs is uniformily received as the true construction, and the question first stated must have been passed upon, in reaching a conclusion upon the demurrer, both by the circuit court for the county and by the supreme court of the State. Both courts must have held that the statutes of Oregon, either directly or by clear implication, required the collection of taxes in gold and silver coin.

Nor do we perceive anything strained or unreasonable in this construction. The laws of Oregon, as quoted in the brief for the State, provided that "the sheriff shall pay over to the county treasurer the full amount of the State and school taxes in gold and silver coin;"* and that "the several county treasurers shall pay over to the State treasurer the State tax in gold and silver coin."†

It is certainly a legitimate if not a necessary inference that these taxes were required to be collected in coin. Nothing short of express words would warrant us in saying that the laws authorized collection in one description of money from the people and required payment over of the same taxes into the county and State treasuries in another.

If, in our judgment, however, this point were otherwise, we should still be bound by the soundest principles of judicial administration and by a long train of decisions in this court to regard the judgment of the supreme court of Oregon, so far as it depends on the right construction of the statutes of that State, as free from error.

The second proposition remains to be examined, and this inquiry brings us to the consideration of the acts of Congress authorizing the issue of the notes in which the tender was made.

The first of these was the act of February 25, 1862, which authorized the Secretary of the Treasury to issue, on the credit of the United States, $150,000,000 in United States notes, and provided that these notes "shall be receivable in payment of all taxes, internal duties, excises, debts, and demands due to the United States, except duties on imports, and of all claims and demands against the United States of every kind whatsoever, except interest on bonds and notes, which shall be paid in coin; and shall also be lawful money and legal tender in payment of all debts, public and private, within the United States, except duties on imports and interest as aforesaid."

The second act contains a provision nearly in the same words with that just recited, and under these two acts two-thirds of the entire issue was authorized. It is unnecessary, therefore, to refer to the third act, by which the notes to be issued under it are not in terms made receivable and payable, but are simply declared to be lawful money and a legal tender.

In the first act no emission was authorized of any notes under five dollars, nor in the other two of any under one dollar. The notes, authorized by different statutes, for parts of a dollar, were never declared to be lawful money or a legal tender.‡

It is obvious, therefore, that a legal tender in United States notes of the precise amount of taxes admitted to be due to the State could not

be made. Coin was then and is now the only legal tender for debts less than one dollar.

In the view which we take of this case this is not important. It is mentioned only to show that the general words "all debts" were not intended to be taken in a sense absolutely literal.

We proceed then to inquire whether, upon a sound construction of the acts, taxes imposed by a State government upon the people of a State are debts within their true meaning.

In examining this question it will be proper to give some attention to the constitution of the States and to their relations as United States.

The people of the United States constitute one nation, under one government; and this government, within the scope of the powers with which it is invested, is supreme. On the other hand, the people of each State compose a State, having its own government, and endowed with all the functions essential to separate and independent existence. The States disunited might continue to exist. Without the States in union there could be no such political body as the United States.

Both the States and the United States existed before the Constitution. The people, through that instrument, established a more perfect union, by substituting a national Government, acting, with ample power, directly upon the citizens, instead of the confederate government which acted with powers, greatly restricted, only upon the States. But in many articles of the Constitution the necessary existence of the States, and, within their proper spheres, the independent authority of the States, is distinctly recognized. To them nearly the whole charge of interior regulation is committed or left; to them and to the people all powers not expressly delegated to the national Government are reserved. The general condition was well stated by Mr. Madison, in the Federalist, thus: "The federal and State governments are in fact but different agents and trustees of the people, constituted with different powers and designated for different purposes."

Now, to the existence of the States, themselves necessary to the existence of the United States, the power of taxation is indispensable. It is an essential function of government.

It was exercised by the colonies; and when the colonies became States, both before and after the formation of the confederation, it was exercised by the new governments.

Under the articles of confederation the Government of the United States was limited in the exercise of this power to requisitions upon the States, while the whole power of direct and indirect taxation of persons and property, whether by taxes on polls, or duties on imports, or duties on internal production, manufacture, or use, was acknowledged to belong exclusively to the States, without any other limitation than that of non-interference with certain treaties made by Congress.

The Constitution, it is true, greatly changed this condition of things. It gave the power to tax, both directly and indirectly, to the national Government, and, subject to the one prohibition of any tax upon exports and to the conditions of uniformity in respect to indirect and of propor-

---

*Statutes of Oregon, 438, §32. †Ibid., 441, §46. ‡12 U. S. Stat., 592; Ibid., 711.

tion in respect to direct taxes, the power was given without any express reservation.

On the other hand, no power to tax exports, or imports except for a single purpose and to an insignificant extent, or to lay any duty on tonnage, was permitted to the States. In respect, however, to property, business, and persons within their respective limits, their power of taxation remained and remains entire. It is indeed a concurrent power, and in the case of a tax on the same subject by both Governments, the claim of the United States, as the supreme authority, must be preferred; but with this qualification it is absolute.

The extent to which it shall be exercised, the subjects upon which it shall be exercised, and the mode in which it shall be exercised are all equally within the discretion of the legislatures to which the States commit the exercise of the power. That discretion is restrained only by the will of the people expressed in the State constitutions or through elections, and by the condition that it must not be so used as to burden or embarrass the operations of the national Government.

There is nothing in the Constitution which contemplates or authorizes any direct abridgement of this power by national legislation. To the extent just indicated it is as complete in the States as the like power, within the limits of the Constitution, is complete in Congress.

If, therefore, the condition of any State, in the judgment of its legislature, requires the collection of taxes in kind, that is to say, by the delivery to the proper officers of a certain proportion of products, or in gold and silver bullion, or in gold and silver coin, it is not easy to see upon what principle the national legislature can interfere with the exercise, to that end, of this power, original in the States, and never as yet surrendered.

If this be so, it is certainly a reasonable conclusion that Congress did not intend, by the general terms of the currency acts, to restrain the exercise of this power in the manner shown by the statutes of Oregon.

Other considerations strengthen this conclusion. It cannot escape observation that the provision intended to give currency to the United States notes in the two acts of 1862 consists of two quite distinguishable clauses. The first of these clauses makes those notes receivable in payment of all dues to the United States, and payable in satisfaction of all demands against the United States, with specified exceptions; the second makes them lawful money, and a legal tender in payment of debts, public and private, within the United States, with the same exceptions.

It seems quite probable that the first clause only was in the original bill, and that the second was afterwards introduced during its progress into an act.

However this may be, the fact that both clauses were made part of the act of February, and were retained in the act of July, 1862, indicates clearly enough the intention of Congress that both shall be construed together. Now, in the first clause, taxes are plainly distinguished, in enumeration, from debts; and it is not an unreasonable infer-

ence that the word debts in the other clause was not intended to include taxes.

It must be observed that the first clause, which may be called the receivability and payability clause, imposes no restriction whatever upon the States in the collection of taxes. It makes the notes receivable for national taxes, but does not make them receivable for State taxes. On the contrary, the express reference to receivability by the national Government, and the omission of all reference to receivability by the State governments, excludes the hypothesis of an intention on the part of Congress to compel the States to receive them as revenue.

And it must also be observed that any construction of the second, or, as it may well enough be called, legal-tender clause, that includes dues for taxes under the words debts, public and private, must deprive the first clause of all effect whatever. For if those words, rightly apprehended, include State taxes, they certainly include national taxes also; and if they include national taxes, the clause making them receivable for such taxes was wholly unnecessary and superfluous.

It is also proper to be observed that a technical construction of the words in question might defeat the main purpose of the act, which doubtless was to provide a currency in which the receipts and payments incident to the exigencies of the then existing civil war might be made.

In his work on the Constitution, the late Mr. Justice Story, whose praise as a jurist is in all civilized lands, speaking of the clause in the Constitution giving to Congress the power to lay and collect taxes, says of the theory which would limit the power to the object of paying the debts, that, thus limited, it would be only a power to provide for the payment of debts *then existing.*[*] And certainly, if a narrow and limited interpretation would thus restrict the word debts in the Constitution, the same sort of interpretation would in like manner restrict the same word in the act.

Such an interpretation needs only to be mentioned to be rejected. We refer to it only to show that a right construction must be sought through larger and less technical views.

We may, then, safely decline either to limit the word debts to existing dues, or to extend its meaning so as to embrace all dues of whatever origin and description.

What then is its true sense? The most obvious, and, as it seems to us, the most rational answer to this question is, that Congress must have had in contemplation debts originating in contract or demands carried into judgment, and only debts of this character. This is the commonest and most natural use of the word. Some strain is felt upon the understanding when an attempt is made to extend it so as to include taxes imposed by legislative authority, and there should be no such strain in the interpretation of a law like this.

We are the more ready to adopt this view, because the greatest of English elementary writers upon law, when treating of debts in their various descriptions, gives no hint that

---

*1 Story on Cons., 639, §921.

taxes come within either:* while American State courts of the highest authority have refused to treat liabilities for taxes as debts, in the ordinary sense of that word, for which actions of debt may be maintained.

The first of these cases was that of Pierce vs. The City of Boston,† 1842, in which the defendant attempted to set off against a demand of the plaintiff certain taxes due to the city. The statute allowed mutual debts to be set off, but the court disallowed the right to set off taxes. This case went, indeed, upon the construction of the statute of Massachusetts, and did not turn on the precise point before us; but the language of the court shows that taxes were not regarded as debts within the common understanding of the word.

The second case was that of Shaw vs. Pickett,‡ in which the supreme court of Vermont said: "The assessment of taxes does not create a debt that can be enforced by suit, or upon which a promise to pay interest can be implied. It is a proceeding *in invitum*."

The next case was that of the City of Camden vs. Allen,‖ 1857. That was an action of debt brought to recover a tax by the municipality to which it was due. The language of the supreme court of New Jersey was still more explicit: "A tax, in its essential characteristics," said the court, "is not a debt, nor in the nature of a debt. A tax is an impost levied by authority of government upon its citizens or subjects for the support of the State. It is not founded on contract or agreement. It operates *in invitum*. A debt is a sum of money due by certain and express agreement. It originates in and is founded upon contracts express or implied."

These decisions were all made before the acts of 1862 were passed, and they may have had some influence upon the choice of the words used.

Be this as it may, we all think that the interpretation which they sanction is well warranted.

We cannot attribute to the legislature an intent to include taxes under the term debts without something more than appears in the acts to show that intention.

The supreme court of California, in 1862, had the construction of these acts under consideration in the case of Perry vs. Washburn.§ The decisions which we have cited were referred to by Chief Justice Field, now holding a seat on this bench, and the very question we are now considering, "What did Congress intend by the act?" was answered in these words: "Upon this question we are clear, that it only intended by the terms debts, public and private, such obligations for the payment of money as are founded upon contract."

In whatever light, therefore, we consider this question, whether in the light of the conflict between the legislation of Congress and the taxing power of the States to which the interpretation insisted on in behalf of the county of Lane would give occasion, or in the light of the language of the acts themselves, or in the light of the decisions to which we have referred, we find ourselves brought to the same conclusion, that the

clause making the United States notes a legal tender for debts has no reference to taxes imposed by State authority, but relates only to debts, in the ordinary sense of the word, arising out of simple contracts or contracts by specialty, which include judgments and recognizances.*

Whether the word debts, as used in the act, includes obligations expressly made payable, or adjudged to be paid in coin, has been argued in another case. We express at present no opinion on that question.

The judgment of the supreme court of Oregon must be affirmed.

---

## Express Contracts to Pay Coined Dollars can only be satisfied by the Payment of Coined Dollars.

### No. 89.—DECEMBER TERM, 1868.

| | |
|---|---|
| Frederick Bronson, executor of the last will and testament of Arthur Bronson, deceased, plaintiff in error, vs. Peter Rodes. | In error to the court of appeals of the State of New York. |

**Mr. Chief Justice Chase** delivered the opinion of the court.

This case comes before us upon a writ of error to the supreme court of New York.

The facts shown by the record may be briefly stated.

In December, 1851, one Christian Metz, having borrowed of Frederick Bronson, executor of Arthur Bronson, $1,400, executed his bond for the repayment to Bronson of the principal sum borrowed on the 18th day of January, 1857, in gold and silver coin, lawful money of the United States, with interest also in coin until such repayment, at the yearly rate of seven per cent.

To secure these payments, according to the bond, at such place as Bronson might appoint, or, in default of such appointment, at the Merchants' Bank of New York, Metz executed a mortgage upon certain real property, which was afterwards conveyed to Rodes, who assumed to pay the mortgage debt, and did, in fact, pay the interest until and including the 1st day of January, 1864.

Subsequently, in January, 1865, there having been no demand of payment nor any appointment of a place of payment by Bronson, Rodes tendered to him United States notes to the amount of $1,507, a sum nominally equal to the principal and interest due upon the bond and mortgage.

At that time one dollar in coin was equivalent in market value to two dollars and a quarter in United States notes.

This tender was refused, whereupon Rodes deposited the United States notes in the Merchants' Bank to the credit of Bronson, and filed his bill in equity praying that the mortgaged premises might be relieved from the lien of the mortgage, and that Bronson might be compelled to execute and deliver to him an acknowledgment of the full satisfaction and discharge of the mortgage debt.

The bill was dismissed by the supreme court sitting in Erie county; but, on appeal to the supreme court in general term, the decree of dismissal was reversed, and a decree was entered adjudging that the mortgage had been satisfied

---

* 2 Black. Com., 475, 476. † 3 Met., 520. ‡ 26 Vt., 486. ‖ 2 Dutch., 398. § 20 California, 350.

*1 Parsons on Contracts, 7.

by the tender, and directing Bronson to satisfy the same of record; and this decree was affirmed by the court of appeals.

The question which we have to consider, therefore, is this:

Was Bronson bound by law to accept from Rodes United States notes equal in nominal amount to the sum due him as full performance and satisfaction of a contract which stipulated for the payment of that sum in gold and silver coin, lawful money of the United States?

It is not pretended that any real payment and satisfaction of an obligation to pay fifteen hundred and seven coined dollars can be made by the tender of paper money worth in the market only six hundred and seventy coined dollars. The question is, does the law compel the acceptance of such a tender for such a debt?

It is the appropriate function of courts of justice to enforce contracts according to the lawful intent and understanding of the parties.

We must, therefore, inquire what was the intent and understanding of Frederick Bronson and Christian Metz when they entered into the contract under consideration in December, 1851.

And this inquiry will be assisted by reference to the circumstances under which the contract was made.

Bronson was an executor, charged as a trustee with the administration of an estate. Metz was a borrower from the estate. It was the clear duty of the former to take security for the full repayment of the money loaned to the latter.

The currency of the country at the time consisted mainly of the circulating notes of State banks, convertible, under the laws of the States, into coin, on demand. This convertibility, though far from perfect, together with the acts of Congress which required the use of coin for all receipts and disbursements of the national Government, insured the presence of some coin in the general circulation; but the business of the people was transacted almost entirely through the medium of bank notes. The State banks had recently emerged from a condition of great depreciation and discredit, the effects of which were still widely felt, and the recurrence of a like condition was not unreasonably apprehended by many. This apprehension was, in fact, realized by the general suspension of coin payments, which took place in 1857, shortly after the bond of Metz became due.

It is not to be doubted, then, that it was to guard against the possibility of loss to the estate, through an attempt to force the acceptance of a fluctuating and perhaps irredeemable currency in payment, that the express stipulation for payment in gold and silver coin was put into the bond. There was no necessity in law for such a stipulation, for at that time no money, except of gold or silver, had been made a legal tender. The bond, without any stipulation to that effect, would have been legally payable only in coin. The terms of the contract must have been selected, therefore, to fix definitely the contract between the parties, and to guard against any possible claim that payment in the ordinary currency ought to be accepted.

The intent of the parties is, therefore, clear. Whatever might be the forms or the fluctuations

of the note currency. this contract was not to be affected by them. It was to be paid, at all events, in coined lawful money.

We have just adverted to the fact that the legal obligation of payment in coin was perfect without express stipulation. It will be useful to consider somewhat further the precise import in law of the phrase "dollars payable in gold and silver coin, lawful money of the United States."

To form a correct judgment on this point, it will be necessary to look into the statutes regulating coinage. It would be instructive, doubtless, to review the history of coinage in the United States, and the succession of statutes by which the weight, purity, forms, and impressions of the gold and silver coins have been regulated; but it will be sufficient for our purpose if we examine three only—the acts of April 2, 1792,* of January 18, 1837,† and March 3, 1849.‡

The act of 1792 established a mint for the purpose of a national coinage. It was the result of very careful and thorough investigations of the whole subject, in which Jefferson and Hamilton took the greatest parts; and its general principles have controlled all subsequent legislation. It provided that the gold of coinage, or standard gold, should consist of eleven parts fine and one part alloy, which alloy was to be of silver and copper in convenient proportions, not exceeding one-half silver, and that the silver of coinage should consist of fourteen hundred and eighty-five parts fine and one hundred and seventy-nine parts of an alloy wholly of copper.

The same act established the dollar as the money unit, and required that it should contain four hundred and sixteen grains of standard silver. It provided further for the coinage of half-dollars, quarter-dollars, dimes, and half-dimes, also of standard silver, and weighing respectively a half, a quarter, a tenth, and a twentieth of the weight of the dollar. Provision was also made for a gold coinage, consisting of eagles, half-eagles, and quarter-eagles, containing, respectively, two hundred and ninety, one hundred and thirty-five, and sixty-seven and a half grains of standard gold, and being of the value, respectively, of ten dollars, five dollars, and two-and-a-half dollars.

These coins were made a lawful tender in all payments, according to their respective weights of silver or gold; if of full weight, at their declared values, and if of less, at proportional values. And this regulation as to tender remained in full force until 1837.

The rule prescribing the composition of alloy has never been changed; but the proportion of alloy to fine gold and silver, and the absolute weight of coins, have undergone some alteration, partly with a view to the better adjustment of the gold and silver circulations to each other, and partly for the convenience of commerce.

The only change of sufficient importance to require notice, was that made by the act of 1837.‖ That act directed that standard gold, and standard silver also, should thenceforth consist of nine parts pure and one part alloy; that the weight of standard gold in the eagle should be two hun-

*1 U. S. Stat., 246.   †5 U. S. Stat., 136.   ‡9 U. S. Stat., 397.   ‖5 U. S. Stat., 137.

dred and fifty-eight grains, and in the half-eagle and quarter-eagle, respectively, one-half and one-quarter of that weight precisely; and that the weight of standard silver should be in the dollar four hundred twelve and a half grains, and in the half dollar, quarter-dollar, dimes, and half-dimes, exactly one-half, one-quarter, one-tenth, and one-twentieth of that weight.

The act of 1849* authorized the coinage of gold double-eagles and gold dollars conformably in all respects to the established standards, and, therefore, of the weights respectively of five hundred and sixteen grains and twenty-five and eight-tenths of a grain.

The methods and machinery of coinage had been so improved before the act of 1837 was passed, that unavoidable deviations from the prescribed weight became almost inappreciable; and the most stringent regulations were enforced to secure the utmost attainable exactness, both in weight and purity of metal.

In single coins the greatest deviation tolerated in the gold coins was half a grain in the double-eagle, eagle, or half-eagle, and a quarter of a grain in the quarter eagle or gold dollar ;† and in the silver coins, a grain and a half in the dollar and half-dollar, and a grain in the quarter-dollar, and half a grain in the dime and half-dime.‡

In 1849 the limit of deviation in weighing large numbers of coins on delivery by the chief coiner to the treasurer and by the treasurer to depositors was still further narrowed.

With these and other precautions against the emission of any piece inferior in weight or purity to the prescribed standard, it was thought safe to make the gold and silver coins of the United States legal tender in all payments according to their nominal or declared values. This was done by the act of 1837. Some regulations as to the tender, for small loans, of coins of less weight and purity have been made; but no other provision than that made in 1837, making coined money a legal tender in all payments, now exists upon the statute-books.

The design of all this minuteness and strictness in the regulation of coinage is easily seen. It indicates the intention of the legislature to give a sure guaranty to the people that the coins made current in payments contain the precise weight of gold or silver of the precise degree of purity declared by the statute. It recognizes the fact, accepted by all men throughout the world, that value is inherent in the precious metals; that gold and silver are in themselves values, and being such, and being in other respects best adapted to the purpose, are the only proper measures of value; that these values are determined by weight and purity; and that form and impress are simply certificates of value, worthy of absolute reliance only because of the known integrity and good faith of the Government which gives them.

The propositions just stated are believed to be incontestible. If they are so in fact, the inquiry concerning the legal import of the phrase "dollars payable in gold and silver coin, lawful money of the United States," may be answered without much difficulty. Every such dollar is a piece of gold or silver, certified to be of a certain weight and purity by the form and impress given to it at the mint of the United States, and therefore declared to be legal tender in payments. Any number of such dollars is the number of grains of standard gold or silver in one dollar multiplied by the given number.

Payment of money is delivery by the debtor to the creditor of the amount due. A contract to pay a certain number of dollars in gold or silver coins is, therefore, in legal import, nothing else than an agreement to deliver a certain weight of standard gold, to be ascertained by a count of coins, each of which is certified to contain a definite proportion of that weight. It is not distinguishable, as we think, in principle, from a contract to deliver an equal weight of bullion of equal fineness. It is distinguishable, in circumstance, only by the fact that the sufficiency of the amount to be tendered in payment must be ascertained, in the case of bullion, by assay and the scales, while in the case of coin it may be ascertained by count.

We cannot suppose that it was intended by the provisions of the currency acts to enforce satisfaction of either contract by the tender of depreciated currency of any description equivalent only in nominal amount to the real value of the bullion or of the coined dollars. Our conclusion, therefore, upon this part of the case is, that the bond under consideration was in legal import precisely what it was in the understanding of the parties, a valid obligation, to be satisfied by a tender of actual payment according to its terms, and not by an offer of mere nominal payment. Its intent was that the debtor should deliver to the creditor a certain weight of gold and silver, of a certain fineness, ascertainable by count of coins made legal tender by statute, and this intent was lawful.

Arguments and illustrations of much force and value in support of this conclusion might be drawn from the possible case of the repeal of the legal-tender laws relating to coin, and the consequent reduction of coined money to the legal condition of bullion, and also from the actual condition of partial demonetization to which gold and silver money was reduced by the introduction into circulation of the United States notes and national bank currency; but we think it unnecessary to pursue this branch of the discussion further.

Nor do we think it necessary now to examine the question whether the clauses of the currency acts making the United States notes a legal tender are warranted by the Constitution. But we will proceed to inquire whether, upon the assumption that those clauses are so warranted, and upon the further assumption that engagements to pay coined dollars may be regarded as ordinary contracts to pay money rather than as contracts to deliver certain weights of standard gold, it can be maintained that a contract to pay coined money may be satisfied by a tender of United States notes.

Is this a performance of the contract within the true intent of the acts?

It must be observed that the laws for the coinage of gold and silver have never been repealed or modified. They remain on the statute-

*9 U. S. Stat., 793.   †19 U. S. Stat., 398.   ‡15 U. S. Stat., 137.

book in full force; and the emission of gold and silver coins from the mint continues, the actual coinage during the last fiscal year having exceeded, according to the report of the director of the mint, $19,000,000.

Nor have those provisions of law which make these coins a legal tender in all payments been repealed or modified.

It follows that there were two descriptions of money in use at the time the tender under consideration was made, both authorized by law, and both made legal tender in payments. The statute denomination of both descriptions was dollars; but they were essentially unlike in nature. The coined dollar was, as we have said, a piece of gold or silver of a prescribed degree of purity, weighing a prescribed number of grains. The note dollar was a promise to pay a coined dollar; but it was not a promise to pay on demand nor at any fixed time, nor was it, in fact, convertible into a coined dollar. It was impossible, in the nature of things, that these two dollars should be the actual equivalents of each other, nor was there anything in the currency acts purporting to make them such. How far they were, at that time, from being actual equivalents has been already stated.

If, then, no express provision to the contrary be found in the acts of Congress, it is a just, if not a necessary inference, from the fact that both descriptions of money were issued by the same Government, that contracts to pay in either were equally sanctioned by law. It is, indeed, difficult to see how any question can be made on this point. Doubt concerning it can only spring from that confusion of ideas which always attends the introduction of varying and uncertain measures of value into circulation as money.

The several statutes relating to money and legal tender must be construed together. Let it be supposed then that the statutes providing for the coinage of gold and silver dollars are found among the statutes of the same Congress which enacted the laws for the fabrication and issue of note dollars, and that the coinage and note acts, respectively, make coined dollars and note dollars legal tender in all payments, as they actually do. Coined dollars are now worth more than note dollars; but it is not impossible that note dollars actually convertible into coin at the chief commercial centres, receivable everywhere for all public dues, and made, moreover, a legal tender everywhere for all debts, may become, at some points, worth more than coined dollars. What reason can be assigned now for saying that a contract to pay coined dollars must be satisfied by the tender of an equal number of note dollars, which will not be equally valid then for saying that a contract to pay note dollars must be satisfied by the tender of an equal number of coined dollars?

It is not easy to see how difficulties of this sort can be avoided except by the admission that the tender must be according to the terms of the contract.

But we are not left to gather the intent of these currency acts from mere comparison with the coinage acts. The currency acts themselves provide for payments in coin. Duties on imports must be paid in coin, and interest on the public debt, in the absence of other express provisions, must also be paid in coin. And it hardly requires argument to prove that these positive requirements cannot be fulfilled if contracts between individuals to pay coin dollars can be satisfied by offers to pay their nominal equivalent in note dollars. The merchant who is to pay duties in coin must contract for the coin which he requires; the bank which receives the coin on deposit contracts to repay coin on demand; the messenger who is sent to the bank or the custom-house contracts to pay or deliver the coin according to his instructions. These are all contracts, either express or implied, to pay coin. Is it not plain that duties cannot be paid in coin if these contracts cannot be enforced?

An instructive illustration may be derived from another provision of the same acts. It is expressly provided that all dues to the Government, except for duties on imports, may be paid in United States notes. If, then, the Government, needing more coin than can be collected from duties, contracts with some bank or individual for the needed amount, to be paid at a certain day, can this contract for coin be performed by the tender of an equal amount in note dollars? Assuredly it may, if the note dollars are a legal tender to the Government for all dues except duties on imports. And yet a construction which will support such a tender will defeat a very important intent of the act.

Another illustration, not less instructive, may be found in the contracts of the Government with the depositors of bullion at the mint to pay them the ascertained value of their deposits in coin. These are demands against the Government other than for interest on the public debt; and the letter of the acts certainly makes United States notes payable for all demands against the Government except such interest. But can any such construction of the act be maintained? Can judicial sanction be given to the proposition that the Government may discharge its obligation to the depositors of bullion by tendering them a number of note dollars equal to the number of gold or silver dollars which it has contracted by law to pay?

But we need not pursue the subject further. It seems to us clear beyond controversy, that the act must receive the reasonable construction, not only warranted, but required by the comparison of its provisions with the provisions of other acts, and with each other; and that upon such reasonable construction it must be held to sustain the proposition that express contracts to pay coined dollars can only be satisfied by the payment of coined dollars. They are not "*debts*" which may be satisfied by the tender of United States notes.

It follows that the tender under consideration was not sufficient in law, and that the decree directing satisfaction of the mortgage was erroneous.

Some difficulty has been felt in regard to the judgments proper to be entered upon contracts for the payment of coin. The difficulty arises from the supposition that damages can be assessed only in one description of money. But the act of 1792 provides that "the money of account of the United States shall be expressed in dollars, dimes, cents, and mills, and that all accounts in the public offices, and all proceedings in the courts of the United States, shall be kept and had in conformity to these regulations."

This regulation is part of the first coinage act, and doubtless has reference to the coins provided for by it. But it is a general regulation, and relates to all accounts and all judicial proceedings. When, therefore, two descriptions of money are sanctioned by law, both expressed in dollars and both made current in payments, it is necessary, in order to avoid ambiguity and prevent a failure of justice, to regard this regulation as applicable alike to both. When, therefore, contracts made payable in coin are sued upon, judgments may be entered for coined dollars and parts of dollars: and when contracts have been made payable in dollars generally, without specifying in what description of currency payment is to be made, judgments may be entered generally, without such specification.

We have already adopted this rule as to judgments for duties by affirming a judgment of the circuit court for the district of California,* in favor of the United States, for $1,388 10, payable in gold and silver coin, and judgments for express contracts between individuals for the payment of coin may be entered in like manner.

It results that the decree of the court of appeals of New York must be reversed, and the cause remanded to that court for further proceedings.

Mr. Justice Davis, concurring in the result, said:

I assent to the result which a majority of the court have arrived at, that an express contract to pay coin of the United States, made before the act of February 25, 1862, commonly called the legal-tender act, is not within the clause of that act which makes treasury notes a legal tender in payment of debts; but I think it proper to guard against all possibility of misapprehension, by stating that if there be any reasoning in the opinion of the majority which can be applicable to any other class of contracts, it does not receive my assent.

Mr. Justice Swayne said:

I concur in the conclusion announced by the Chief Justice.

My opinion proceeds entirely upon the language of the contract and the construction of the statutes.

The question of the constitutional power of Congress, in my judgment, does not arise in the case.

### Dissenting Opinion.

Mr. Justice Miller, dissenting:

I do not agree to the judgment of the court in this case, and shall, without apology, make a very brief statement of my reasons for believing that the judgment of the court of appeals of New York should be affirmed. The opinion just read correctly states that the contract in this case, made before the passage of the act or acts commonly called the legal-tender acts, was an agreement to pay $1,400 "in gold and silver coin, lawful money of the United States." And I agree that it was the intention of both parties to this contract that it should be paid in coin.

* Cheang-Kee vs. U. S., 3 Wall., 320.

I go a step further than this, and agree that the legal effect of the contract, as the law stood when it was made, was that it should be paid in coin, and could be paid in nothing else. This was the conjoint effect of the contract of the parties and the law under which that contract was made.

But I do not agree that in this respect the contract under consideration differed, either in intention of the parties, or in its legal effect, from a contract to pay $1,400 without any further description of the dollars to be paid.

The only dollars which, by the laws then in force, or which ever had been in force since the adoption of the federal Constitution, could have been lawfully tendered in payment of any contract simply for dollars, were gold and silver.

These were the "lawful money of the United States" mentioned in the contract, and the special reference to them gave no effect to that contract beyond what the law gave.

The contract then did not differ, in its legal obligation, from any other contract payable in dollars. Much weight is attached in the opinion to the special intent of the parties in using the words gold and silver coin, but as I have shown that the intent thus manifested is only what the law would have implied if those words had not been used, I cannot see their importance in distinguishing this contract from others which omit these words. Certainly every man who at that day received a note payable in dollars, expected and had a right to expect to be paid "in gold and silver coin, lawful money of the United States," if he chose to demand it. There was therefore no difference in the intention of the parties to such a contract, and an ordinary contract for the payment of money, so far as the right of the payee to exact coin is concerned. If I am asked why these words were used in this case I answer, that they were used out of abundant caution by some one not familiar with the want of power in the States to make legal-tender laws. It is very well known that under the system of State banks, which furnished almost exclusively the currency in use for a great many years prior to the issue of legal-tender notes by the United States, there was a difference between the value of that currency and gold, even while the bank notes were promptly redeemed in gold. And it was doubtless to exclude any possible assertion of the right to pay this contract in such bank notes that the words gold and silver coin were used, and not with any reference to a possible change in the laws of legal tender established by the United States, which had never, during the sixty years that the Government had been administered under the present Constitution, declared anything else to be a legal tender or lawful money but gold and silver coin.

But if I correctly apprehend the scope of the opinion delivered by the chief justice, the effort to prove for this contract a special intent of payment in gold is only for the purpose of bringing it within the principle there asserted, both by express words and by strong implication, that all contracts must be paid according to the intention of the parties making them. I think I am not mistaken in my recollection that it is broadly stated that it is the business of courts of justice to enforce contracts as they are intended by the parties, and that the tender must be according to the intent of the contract.

Now, if the argument used to show the intent of the parties to the contract is of any value in this connection, it is plain that such intent must enter into, and form a controlling element in, the judgment of the court in construing the legal tender acts.

I shall not here consume time by any attempt to show that the contract in this case is a debt, or that when Congress said that the notes it was about to issue should be received as a legal tender in payment for *all private debts*, it intended that which these words appropriately convey. To assume that Congress did not intend by that act to authorize a payment by a medium differing from that which the parties intended by the contract is in contradiction to the express language of the statute, to the sense in which it was acted on by the people who paid and received those notes in discharge of contracts for incalculable millions of dollars, where gold dollars alone had been in contemplation of the parties, and to the decisions of the highest courts of fifteen States in the Union, being all that have passed upon the subject.

As I have no doubt that it was intended by those acts to make the notes of the United States to which they applied a legal tender for all private debts then due, or which might become due on contracts then in existence, without regard to the intent of the parties on that point, I must dissent from the judgment of the court, and from the opinion on which it is founded.

---

### The Status of the State of Texas.

No. 6 (ORIGINAL.)—DECEMBER TERM, 1868.

The State of Texas, complainant,

*vs.*

George W. White, John Chiles, John A. Hardenberg, Samuel Wolf, George W. Stewart, The Branch of the Commercial Bank of Kentucky, Western F. Birch, Byron Murray, jr., and —— Shaw.  }  Bill in equity.

Mr. Chief Justice Chase delivered the opinion of the court.

This is an original suit in this court, in which the State of Texas, claiming certain bonds of the United States as her property, asks an injunction to restrain the defendants from receiving payment from the national Government, and to compel the surrender of the bonds to the State.

It appears from the bill, answers, and proofs, that the United States, by act of September 9, 1850, offered to the State of Texas, in compensation for her claims connected with the settlement of her boundary, $10,000,000 in five-per-cent. bonds, each for the sum of $1,000, and that this offer was accepted by Texas.

One-half of these bonds were retained for certain purposes in the national treasury, and the other half were delivered to the State.

The bonds thus delivered were dated January 1, 1851, and were all made payable to the State of Texas, or bearer, and redeemable after the 31st day of December, 1864.

They were received, in behalf of the State, by the comptroller of public accounts, under author-ity of an act of the legislature, which, besides giving that authority, provided that no bond should be available in the hands of any holder until after endorsement by the governor of the State.

After the breaking out of the rebellion, the insurgent legislature of Texas, on the 11th of January, 1862, repealed the act requiring the endorsement of the governor,[*] and on the same day provided for the organization of a military board, composed of the governor, comptroller, and treasurer, and authorized a majority of that board to provide for the defence of the State by means of any bonds in the treasury, upon any account, to the extent of $1,000,000.[†]

The defence contemplated by the act was to be made against the United States by war.

Under this authority the military board entered into an agreement with George W. White and John Chiles, two of the defendants, for the sale to them of one hundred and thirty-five of these bonds, then in the treasury of the State, and seventy-six more, then deposited with Droege & Co., in England, in payment for which they engaged to deliver to the board a large quantity of cotton cards and medicines. This agreement was made on the 12th of January, 1865.

On the 12th of March, 1865, White and Chiles received from the military board one hundred and thirty-five of these bonds, none of which were endorsed by any governor of Texas.

Afterward, in the course of the years 1865 and 1866, some of the same bonds came into the possession of others of the defendants by purchase, or as security for advances of money.

Such is a brief outline of the case. It will be necessary hereafter to refer more in detail to some particular circumstances of it.

The first inquiries to which our attention was directed by counsel arose upon the allegations of the answer of Chiles, (1,) that no sufficient authority is shown for the prosecution of the suit in the name and on the behalf of the State of Texas; and, (2,) that the State having severed her relations with a majority of the States of the Union, and having by her ordinance of secession attempted to throw off her allegiance to the Constitution and Government of the United States, has so far changed her status as to be disabled from prosecuting suits in the national courts.

The first of these allegations is disproved by the evidence. A letter of authority, the authenticity of which is not disputed, has been produced; in which J. W. Throckmorton, elected governor under the constitution adopted in 1866, and proceeding under an act of the State legislature relating to these bonds, expressly ratifies and confirms the action of the solicitors who filed the bill, and empowers them to prosecute this suit; and it is further proved by the affidavit of Mr. Paschal, counsel for the complainant, that he was duly appointed by Andrew J. Hamilton, while provisional governor of Texas, to represent the State of Texas in reference to the bonds in controversy, and that his appointment has been renewed by E. M. Pease, the actual governor. If Texas was a State of the Union at the time of these acts, and these persons, or either of them, were competent to represent the State, this proof

---

[*] Acts of Texas, 1862, p. 45.　　[†] Texas Laws, p. 55.

leaves no doubt upon the question of authority.

The other allegation presents a question of jurisdiction. It is not to be questioned that this court has original jurisdiction of suits by States against citizens of other States, or that the States entitled to invoke this jurisdiction must be States of the Union. But it is equally clear that no such jurisdiction has been conferred upon this court of suits by any other political communities than such States.

If, therefore, it is true that the State of Texas was not at the time of filing this bill, or is not now, one of the United States, we have no jurisdiction of this suit, and it is our duty to dismiss it.

We are very sensible of the magnitude and importance of this question, of the interest it excites, and of the difficulty, not to say impossibility, of so disposing of it as to satisfy the conflicting judgments of men equally enlightened, equally upright, and equally patriotic. But we meet it in the case, and we must determine it in the exercise of our best judgment, under the guidance of the Constitution alone.

Some not unimportant aid, however, in ascertaining the true sense of the Constitution, may be derived from considering what is the correct idea of a State, apart from any union or confederation with other States. The poverty of language often compels the employment of terms in quite different significations; and of this hardly any example more signal is to be found than in the use of the word we are now considering. It would serve no useful purpose to attempt an enumeration of all the various senses in which it is used. A few only need be noticed.

It describes sometimes a people or community of individuals united more or less closely in political relations, inhabiting temporarily or permanently the same country; often it denotes only the country or territorial region inhabited by such a community; not unfrequently it is applied to the government under which the people live; at other times it represents the combined idea of people, territory, and government.

It is not difficult to see that in all these senses the primary conception is that of a people or community. The people, in whatever territory dwelling, either temporarily or permanently, and whether organized under a regular government, or united by looser and less definite relations, constitute the State.

This is undoubtedly the fundamental idea upon which the republican institutions of our own country are established. It was stated very clearly by an eminent judge* in one of the earliest cases adjudicated by this court, and we are not aware of anything in any subsequent decision of a different tenor.

In the Constitution the term State most frequently expresses the combined idea just noticed, of people, territory, and government. A State, in the ordinary sense of the Constitution, is a political community of free citizens, occupying a territory of defined boundaries, and organized under a government sanctioned and limited by a written constitution, and established by the consent of the governed. It is the union of such States under a common constitution which forms the distinct and greater political unit which that Constitution designates as the United States, and makes of the people and States which compose it one people and one country.

The use of the word in this sense hardly requires further remark. In the clauses which impose prohibitions upon the States in respect to the making of treaties, emitting of bills of credit, laying duties of tonnage, and which guaranty to the States representation in the House of Representatives and in the Senate, are found some instances of this use in the Constitution. Others will occur to every mind.

But it is also used in its geographical sense, as in the clauses which require that a representative in Congress shall be an inhabitant of the State in which he shall be chosen, and that the trial of crimes shall be held within the State where committed.

And there are instances in which the principal sense of the word seems to be that primary one to which we have adverted, of a people or political community, as distinguished from a government.

In this latter sense the word seems to be used in the clause which provides that the United States shall guaranty to every State in the Union a republican form of government, and shall protect each of them against invasion.

In this clause a plain distinction is made between a State and the government of a State.

Having thus ascertained the senses in which the word State is employed in the Constitution, we will proceed to consider the proper application of what has been said.

The republic of Texas was admitted into the Union as a State on the 27th of December, 1845. By this act the new State, and the people of the new State, were invested with all the rights, and became subject to all the responsibilities and duties, of the original States under the Constitution.

From the date of admission until 1861, the State was represented in the Congress of the United States by her Senators and Representatives, and her relations as a member of the Union remained unimpaired. In that year, acting upon the theory that the rights of a State under the Constitution might be renounced, and her obligations thrown off at pleasure, Texas undertook to sever the bond thus formed, and to break up her constitutional relations with the United States.

On the 1st of February* a convention, called without authority, but subsequently sanctioned by the legislature regularly elected, adopted an ordinance to dissolve the union between the State of Texas and the other States under the Constitution of the United States, whereby Texas was declared to be " a separate and sovereign State," and "her people and citizens" to be " absolved from all allegiance to the United States or the Government thereof."

It was ordered by a vote of the convention† and by an act of the legislature,‡ that this ordinance should be submitted to the people, for approval or disapproval, on the 23d of February, 1861.

---

*Mr. Justice Paterson, in Penhallow vs. Doane's Admrs. 3 Dall., 93.

* Paschal's Digest Laws of Texas, 78.   † Paschal's Digest, 80.   ‡ Laws of Texas, 1859–61, p. 11.

Without awaiting, however, the decision thus invoked, the convention, on the 4th of February, adopted a resolution, designating seven delegates to represent the State in the convention of seceding States at Montgomery, "in order," as the resolution declared, "that the wishes and interests of the people of Texas may be consulted in reference to the constitution and provisional government that may be established by said convention."

Before the passage of this resolution the convention had appointed a committee of public safety, and adopted an ordinance giving authority to that committee to take measures for obtaining possession of the property of the United States in Texas, and for removing the national troops from her limits. The members of the committee, and all officers and agents appointed or employed by it, were sworn to secrecy and to allegiance to the State.* Commissioners were at once appointed, with instructions to repair to the headquarters of General Twiggs, then representing the United States in command of the department, and to make the demands necessary for the accomplishment of the purposes of the committee. A military force was organized in support of these demands, and an arrangement was effected with the commanding general by which the United States troops were engaged to leave the State, and the forts and all the public property, not necessary to the removal of the troops, were surrendered to the commissioners.†

These transactions took place between the 2d and the 18th of February, and it was under these circumstances that the vote upon the ratification or rejection of the ordinance of secession was taken on the 23d of February. It was ratified by a majority of the voters of the State.

The convention, which had adjourned before the vote was taken, reassembled on the 2d of March, and instructed the delegates already sent to the congress of the seceding States to apply for admission into the confederation, and to give the adhesion of Texas to its provisional constitution.

It proceeded, also, to make the changes in the State constitution which this adhesion made necessary. The words "United States" were stricken out wherever they occurred, and the words "Confederate States" substituted; and the members of the legislature, and all officers of the State, were required by the new constitution to take an oath of fidelity to the constitution and laws of the new confederacy.

Before, indeed, these changes in the constitution had been completed, the officers of the State had been required to appear before the committee and take an oath of allegiance to the Confederate States.

The governor and secretary of state, refusing to comply, were summarily ejected from office.

The members of the legislature, which had also adjourned and reassembled on the 18th of March, were more compliant. They took the oath, and proceeded, on the 8th of April, to provide by law for the choice of electors of president and vice president of the Confederate States.

The representatives of the State in the Congress of the United States were withdrawn, and, as soon as the seceded States became organized under a constitution, Texas sent senators and representatives to the confederate congress.

In all respects, so far as the object could be accomplished by ordinances of the convention, by acts of the legislature, and by votes of the citizens, the relations of Texas to the Union were broken up, and new relations to a new government were established for them.

The position thus assumed could only be maintained by arms, and Texas accordingly took part with the other Confederate States in the war of the rebellion which these events made inevitable. During the whole of that war there was no governor, or judge, or any other State officer in Texas who recognized the national authority. Nor was any officer of the United States permitted to exercise any authority whatever under the national Government within the limits of the State, except under the immediate protection of the national military forces.

Did Texas in consequence of these acts cease to be a State? Or, if not, did the State cease to be a member of the Union?

It is needless to discuss at length the question whether the right of a State to withdraw from the Union for any cause regarded by herself as sufficient is consistent with the Constitution of the United States.

The Union of the States never was a purely artificial and arbitrary relation. It began among the colonies, and grew out of common origin, mutual sympathies, kindred principles, similar interests, and geographical relations. It was confirmed and strengthened by the necessities of war, and received definite form, and character, and sanction, from the Articles of Confederation. By these the Union was solemnly declared to "be perpetual." And, when these articles were found to be inadequate to the exigencies of the country, the Constitution was ordained "to form a more perfect Union." It is difficult to convey the idea of indissoluble unity more clearly than by these words. What can be indissoluble, if a perpetual Union made more perfect is not?

But the perpetuity and indissolubility of the Union by no means implies the loss of distinct and individual existence, or of the right of self-government, by the States. Under the Articles of Confederation each State retained its sovereignty, freedom, and independence, and every power, jurisdiction, and right,· not expressly delegated to the United States. Under the Constitution, though the powers of the States were much restricted, still all powers not delegated to the United States, nor prohibited to the States, are reserved to the States respectively, or to the people. And we have already had occasion to remark at this term, that "the people of each State compose a State, having its own government, and endowed with all the functions essential to separate and independent existence;" and that "without the States in union there could be no such political body as the United States."* Not only, therefore, can there be no loss of separate and independent autonomy to

*Paschal's Digest, 80. † Texan Reports of the Committee, (Lib. of Con.,) p. 45.

*County of Lane vs. The State of Oregon.

the States, through their union under the Constitution, but it may be not unreasonably said that the preservation of the States and the maintenance of their governments are as much within the design and care of the Constitution as the preservation of the Union and the maintenance of the national Government. The Constitution, in all its provisions, looks to an indestructible Union, composed of indestructible States.

When, therefore, Texas became one of the United States, she entered into an indissoluble relation. All the obligations of perpetual union, and all the guaranties of republican government in the Union, attached at once to the State. The act which consummated her admission into the Union was something more than a compact—it was the incorporation of a new member into the political body, and it was final. The union between Texas and the other States was as complete, as perpetual, and as indissoluble as the union between the original States. There was no place for reconsideration or revocation, except through revolution or through consent of the States.

Considered, therefore, as transactions under the Constitution, the ordinance of secession adopted by the convention and ratified by a majority of the citizens of Texas, and all the acts of her legislature intended to give effect to that ordinance, were absolutely null. They were utterly without operation in law. The obligations of the State as a member of the Union, and of every citizen of the State as a citizen of the United States, remained perfect and unimpaired. It certainly follows that the State did not cease to be a State nor her citizens to be citizens of the Union. If this were otherwise, the State must have become foreign and her citizens foreigners; the war must have ceased to be a war for the suppression of rebellion, and must have become a war for conquest and subjugation.

Our conclusion, therefore, is, that Texas continued to be a State, and a State of the Union, notwithstanding the transactions to which we have referred. And this conclusion, in our judgment, is not in conflict with any act or declaration of any department of the national Government, but entirely in accordance with the whole series of such acts and declarations since the first outbreak of the rebellion.

But in order to the exercise by a State of the right to sue in this court, there needs to be a State government competent to represent the State in its relations with the national Government, so far, at least, as the institution and prosecution of a suit is concerned.

And it is by no means a logical conclusion, from the premises which we have endeavored to establish, that the governmental relations of Texas to the Union remained unaltered. Obligations often remain unimpaired, while relations are greatly changed. The obligations of allegiance to the State and of obedience to her laws, subject to the Constitution of the United States, are binding upon all citizens, whether faithful or unfaithful to them; but the relations which subsist while these obligations are performed are essentially different from those which arise when they are disregarded and set at nought.

And the same must necessarily be true of the obligations and relations of States and citizens to the Union. No one has been bold enough to contend that, while Texas was controlled by a Government hostile to the United States, and, in affiliation with a hostile confederation, waging war upon the United States, senators chosen by her legislature, or representatives elected by her citizens, were entitled to seats in Congress; or that any suit instituted in her name could be entertained in this court. All admit that, during this condition of civil war, the rights of the State as a member and of her people as citizens of the Union, were suspended. The Government and the citizens of the State refusing to recognize their constitutional obligations assumed the character of enemies and incurred the consequences of rebellion.

These new relations imposed new duties upon the United States. The first was that of suppressing the rebellion. The next was that of re-establishing the broken relations of the State with the Union. The first of these duties having been performed, the next necessarily engaged the attention of the national Government.

The authority for the performance of the first had been found in the power to suppress insurrection and carry on war; for the performance of the second, authority was derived from the obligation of the United States to guaranty to every State in the Union a republican form of government. The latter, indeed, in the case of a rebellion, which involves the government of a State, and, for the time, excludes the national authority from its limits, seems to be a necessary complement to the former.

Of this the case of Texas furnishes a striking illustration. When the war closed there was no government in the State except that which had been organized for the purpose of waging war against the United States. That government immediately disappeared. The chief functionaries left the State. Many of the subordinate officials followed their example. Legal responsibilities were annulled or greatly impaired. It was inevitable that great confusion should prevail. If order was maintained, it was where the good sense and virtue of the citizens gave support to local acting magistrates, or supplied more directly the needful restraints.

A great social change increased the difficulty of the situation. Slaves in the insurgent States, with certain local exceptions, had been declared free by the proclamation of emancipation, and whatever questions might be made as to the effect of that act under the Constitution, it was clear from the beginning that its practical operation, in connection with legislative acts of like tendency, must be complete enfranchisement. Wherever the national forces obtained control, the slaves became freemen. Support to the acts of Congress and the proclamation of the President concerning slaves was made a condition of amnesty* by President Lincoln, in December, 1863, and by President Johnson, in May, 1865.† And emancipation was confirmed, rather than ordained, in the insurgent States, by the amendment to the Constitution prohibiting slavery throughout the

*13 U. S. Stat., 737.    †13 U. S. Stat., 758

Union, which was proposed by Congress in February, 1865, and ratified before the close of the following autumn by the requisite three-fourths of the States.*

The new freemen necessarily became part of the people, and the people still constituted the State; for States, like individuals, retain their identity, though changed to some extent in their constituent elements. And it was the State, thus constituted, which was now entitled to the benefit of the constitutional guaranty.

There being, then, no government in Texas, in constitutional relations with the Union, it became the duty of the United States to provide for the restoration of such a government. But the restoration of the government which existed before the rebellion, without a new election of officers, was obviously impossible; and before any such election could be properly held, it was necessary that the old constitution should receive such amendments as would conform its provisions to the new conditions created by emancipation, and afford adequate security to the people of the State.

In the exercise of the power conferred by the guaranty clause, as in the exercise of every other constitutional power, a discretion in the choice of means is necessarily allowed. It is essential only that the means must be necessary and proper for carrying into execution the power conferred, through the restoration of the State to its constitutional relations, under a republican form of government, and that no acts be done, and no authority exerted, which is either prohibited or unsanctioned by the Constitution.

It is not important to review at length the measures which have been taken under this power by the executive and legislative departments of the national Government. It is proper, however, to observe, that almost immediately after the cessation of organized hostilities, and while the war yet smouldered in Texas, the President of the United States issued his proclamation appointing a provisional governor for the State, and providing for the assembling of a convention, with a view to the re-establishment of a republican government, under an amended constitution, and to the restoration of the State to her proper constitutional relations. A convention was accordingly assembled, the constitution amended, elections held, and a State government acknowledging its obligations to the Union established.

Whether the action then taken was in all respects warranted by the Constitution it is not now necessary to determine. The power exercised by the President was supposed doubtless to be derived from his constitutional functions as commander-in-chief; and, so long as the war continued, it cannot be denied that he might institute temporary government within insurgent districts occupied by the national forces, or take measures in any State for the restoration of State government faithful to the Union, employing, however, in such efforts, only such means and agents as were authorized by constitutional laws.

But the power to carry into effect the clause of guaranty is primarily a legislative power and resides in Congress. "Under the fourth article of the Constitution, it rests with Congress to decide what government is the established one in a State. For, as the United States guaranty to each State a republican government, Congress must necessarily decide what government is established in the State before it can determine whether it is republican or not."

This is the language of the late Chief Justice, speaking for this court, in a case from Rhode Island,* arising from the organization of opposing governments in that State. And we think that the principle sanctioned by it may be applied with even more propriety to the case of a State deprived of all rightful government by revolutionary violence, though necessarily limited to cases where the rightful government is thus subverted or in imminent danger of being overthrown by an opposing government set up by force within the State.

The action of the President must, therefore, be considered as provisional, and in that light it seems to have been regarded by Congress. It was taken after the term of the 38th Congress had expired. The 39th Congress, which assembled in December, 1865, followed by the 40th Congress, which met in March, 1867, proceeded, after long deliberation, to adopt various measures for reorganization and restoration. These measures were embodied in proposed amendments to the Constitution, and in the acts known as the reconstruction acts, which have been so far carried into effect, that a majority of the States which were engaged in the rebellion have been restored to their constitutional relations, under forms of government adjudged to be republican by Congress, through the admission of their "Senators and Representatives into the councils of the Union."

Nothing in the case before us requires the court to pronounce judgment upon the constitutionality of any particular provision of these acts.

But it is important to observe, that these acts themselves show that the governments which had been established, and had been in actual operation under executive direction, were recognized by Congress as provisional, as existing, and as capable of continuance.

By the act of March 2, 1867,† the first of the series, these governments were, indeed, pronounced illegal, and were subjected to military control, and were declared to be provisional only; and by the supplementary act of July 19, 1867, the third of the series, it was further declared, that it was the true intent and meaning of the act of March 2 that the governments then existing were not legal State governments, and, if continued, were to be continued subject to the military commanders of the respective districts and to the paramount authority of Congress. We do not inquire here into the constitutionality of this legislation so far as it relates to military authority, or to the paramount authority of Congress. It suffices to say, that the terms of the acts necessarily imply recognition of actually existing governments, and that, in

---

*13 U. S. Stat., 774–5.

*Luther *vs.* Borden, 7 How., 42. †U. S. Stat., 428.

point of fact, the governments thus recognized, in some important respects, still exist.

What has thus been said generally describes with sufficient accuracy the situation of Texas. A provisional governor of the State was appointed by the President in 1865, in 1866 a governor was elected by the people under the constitution of that year, at a subsequent date a governor was appointed by the commander of the district. Each of the three exercised executive functions, and actually represented the State in the executive department.

In the case before us each has given his sanction to the prosecution of the suit, and we find no difficulty, without investigating the legal title of either to the executive office, in holding that the sanction thus given sufficiently warranted the action of the solicitor and counsel in behalf of the State. The necessary conclusion is that the suit was instituted and is prosecuted by competent authority.

The question of jurisdiction being thus disposed of, we proceed to the consideration of the merits as presented by the pleadings and the evidence.

And the first question to be answered is, whether or not the title of the State to the bonds in controversy was divested by the contract of the military board with White and Chiles?

That the bonds were the property of the State of Texas on the 11th of January, 1862, when the act prohibiting alienation without the endorsement of the governor was repealed, admits of no question and is not denied. They came into her possession and ownership through public acts of the General Government and of the State, which gave notice to all the world of the transaction consummated by them. And we think it clear that, if a State by a public act of her legislature imposes restrictions upon the alienation of her property, every person who takes a transfer of such property must be held affected by notice of them. Alienation in disregard of such restrictions can convey no title.

In this case, however, it is said that the restriction imposed by the act of 1851 was repealed by the act of 1862. And this is true if the act of 1862 can be regarded as valid. But was it valid?

The legislature of Texas, at the time of the repeal, constituted one of the departments of a State government established in hostility to the Constitution of the United States. It cannot be regarded, therefore, in the courts of the United States, as a lawful legislature, or its acts as lawful acts. And, yet it is a historical fact that the government of Texas, then in full control of the State, was its only actual government; and, certainly, if Texas had been a separate State, and not one of the United States, the new government, having displaced the regular authority, and having established itself in the customary seats of power, and in the exercise of the ordinary functions of administration, would have constituted, in the strictest sense of the words, a *de facto* government, and its acts, during the period of its existence as such, would be effectual, and in almost all respects valid. And to some extent this is true of the actual government of Texas, though unlawful and revolutionary as to the United States.

It is not necessary to attempt any exact definitions within which the acts of such a State government must be treated as valid or invalid. It may be said, perhaps with sufficient accuracy, that acts necessary to peace and good order among citizens, such, for example, as acts sanctioning and protecting marriage and the domestic relations, governing the course of descents, regulating the conveyance and transfer of property, real and personal, and providing remedies for injuries to person and estate, and other similar acts, which would be valid if emanating from a lawful government, must be regarded in general as valid when proceeding from an actual, though unlawful government; and that acts in furtherance or support of rebellion against the United States, or intended to defeat the just rights of citizens, and other acts of like nature, must, in general, be regarded as invalid and void.

What, then, tried by these general tests, was the character of the contract of the military board with White and Chiles?

That board, as we have seen, was organized, not for the defence of the State against a foreign invasion, or for its protection against domestic violence, within the meaning of these words as used in the national Constitution, but for the purpose, under the name of defence, of levying war against the United States. This purpose was undoubtedly unlawful, for the acts which it contemplated are, within the express definition of the Constitution, treasonable.

It is true that the military board was subsequently reorganized. It consisted thereafter of the governor and two other members, appointed and removable by him; and was, therefore, entirely subordinate to executive control. Its general object remained without change, but its powers were "extended to the control of all public works and supplies, and to the aid of producing within the State, by the importation of articles necessary and proper for such aid."

And it was insisted in argument on behalf of some of the defendants that the contract with White and Chiles, being for the purchase of cotton cards and medicines, was not a contract in aid of the rebellion, but for obtaining goods capable of a use entirely legitimate and innocent, and therefore that payment for those goods by the transfer of any property of the State was not unlawful. We cannot adopt this view. Without entering at this time upon the inquiry whether any contract made by such a board can be sustained, we are obliged to say that the enlarged powers of the board appear to us to have been conferred in furtherance of its main purpose of war against the United States, and that the contract under consideration, even if made in the execution of these enlarged powers, was still a contract in aid of the rebellion, and therefore void. And we cannot shut our eyes to the evidence which proves that the act of repeal was intended to aid rebellion by facilitating the transfer of these bonds. It was supposed, doubtless, that negotiation of them would be less difficult if they bore upon their face no direct evidence of having come from the possession of any insurgent State government.

We can give no effect, therefore, to this repealing act.

It follows that the title of the State was not divested by the act of the insurgent government in entering into this contract.

But it was insisted further, in behalf of those defendants who claim certain of these bonds by purchase, or as collateral security, that however unlawful may have been the means by which White and Chiles obtained possession of the bonds, they are innocent holders without notice, and entitled to protection as such under the rules which apply to securities which pass by delivery. These rules were fully discussed in Murray vs. Lardner.* We held in that case that the purchase of coupon bonds, before due, without notice and in good faith, is unaffected by want of title in the seller, and that the burden of proof in respect to notice and want of good faith is on the claimant of the bonds as against the purchaser. We are entirely satisfied with this doctrine.

Does the State, then, show affirmatively notice to these defendants of want of title to the bonds in White and Chiles?

It would be difficult to give a negative answer to this question, if there were no other proof than the legislative acts of Texas. But there is other evidence which might fairly be held to be sufficient proof of notice, if the rule to which we have adverted could be properly applied to this case.

But these rules have never been applied to matured obligations. Purchasers of notes or bonds past due take nothing but the actual right and title of the vendors.†

The bonds in question were dated January 1, 1851, and were redeemable after the 31st of December, 1864. In strictness, it is true they were not payable on the day when they became redeemable; but the known usage of the United States to pay all bonds as soon as the right of payment accrues, except where a distinction between redeemability and payability is made by law and shown on the face of the bonds, requires the application of the rule respecting over-due obligations to bonds of the United States which have become redeemable, and in respect to which no such distinction has been made.

Now, all the bonds in controversy had become redeemable before the date of the contract with White and Chiles; and all bonds of the same issue which have the endorsement of a governor of Texas made before the date of the secession ordinance—and there were no others endorsed by any governor—had been paid in coin on presentation at the Treasury Department; while, on the contrary, applications for the payment of bonds, without the required endorsement, and of coupons detached from such bonds, made to that department, had been denied.

As a necessary consequence, the negotiation of these bonds became difficult. They sold much below the rates they would have commanded had the title to them been unquestioned. They were bought in fact, and under the circumstances could only have been bought, upon speculation. The purchasers took the risk of a bad title,

* 2 Wall., 118. † Brown vs. Davis, 37 R., 80; Goodman vs. Symonds, 20 How., 366.

hoping, doubtless, that, through the action of the national Government or of the government of Texas, it might be converted into a good one. And it is true that the first provisional governor of Texas encouraged the expectation that these bonds would be ultimately paid to the holders. But he was not authorized to make any engagement in behalf of the State, and in fact made none. It is true, also, that the Treasury Department, influenced perhaps by these representations, departed to some extent from its original rule, and paid bonds held by some of the defendants without the required endorsement. But it is clear that this change in the action of the department could not affect the rights of Texas as a State of the Union, having a government acknowledging her obligations to the national Constitution.

It is impossible upon this evidence to hold the defendants protected by absence of notice of the want of title in White and Chiles. As these persons acquired no right to payment of these bonds as against the State, purchasers could acquire none through them.

On the whole case, therefore, our conclusion is, that the State of Texas is entitled to the relief sought by her bill, and a decree must be made accordingly.

—

## DISSENTING OPINION.

Mr. Justice Grier dissenting, delivered the following opinion:

I regret that I am compelled to dissent from the opinion of the majority of the court on all the points raised and decided in this case.

The first question in order is the jurisdiction of the court to entertain this bill in behalf of the State of Texas.

The original jurisdiction of this court can be invoked only by one of the United States. The Territories have no such right conferred on them by the Constitution, nor have the Indian tribes who are under the protection of the military authorities of the Government.

Is Texas one of these United States? Or was she such at the time this bill was filed, or since? This is to be decided as *a political fact*, not as a *legal fiction*. This court is bound to know and notice the public history of the nation.

If I regard the truth of history for the last eight years, I cannot discover the State of Texas as one of these United States. I do not think it necessary to notice any of the very astute arguments which have been advanced by the learned counsel in this case to find the definition of a State, when we have the subject treated in a clear and common-sense manner, and without any astute judicial abstractions, by Chief Justice Marshall, in the case of Hepburn & Dundass *vs* Elzey, 2 Cranch, 452. As the case is short and clear, I hope to be excused for a full report of the case as stated and decided by the court. "The question," says Marshall, C. J., "is whether the plaintiffs, as residents of the District of Columbia, can maintain an action in the circuit court of the United States for the district of Virginia. This depends on the act of Congress describing the jurisdiction of that court. The act gives jurisdiction to the circuit courts in cases between a citizen of the State in which the suit is brought, and a citizen of another State. To support the jurisdiction in this case, it must appear that Columbia is a State. On the part of the plaintiff it has been urged that Columbia is a distinct political society, and is, therefore, a 'State' according to the definition of writers on general law. This is true; but as the act of Congress obviously uses the word 'State' in reference to that term as used in the Constitution, it becomes necessary to inquire whether Columbia is a State in the sense of that instrument. The result of that examination is a conviction that the members of the American confederacy *only* are the States contemplated in the Constitution. The House of Representatives is to be composed of members chosen by the people of the several States, and each State shall have at least one representative. 'The Senate of the United States shall be composed of two senators from each State.' Each State shall appoint for the election of the executive a number of electors equal to its whole number of senators and representatives. These clauses show that the word 'State' is used in the Constitution as designating a member of the Union, and excludes from the term the signification attached to it by writers on the law of nations."

Now we have here a clear and well defined test by which we may arrive at a conclusion with regard to the questions of fact now to be decided.

Is Texas a State, now represented by members chosen by the people of that State and received on the floor of Congress? Has she two senators to represent her as a State in the Senate of the United States? Has her voice been heard in the late election of President? Is she not now held and governed as a conquered province by military force? The act of Congress of March 28, 1867, declares Texas to be a "rebel State," and provides for its government until a legal and republican State government could be legally established. It constituted Louisiana and Texas the fifth military district, and made it subject, not to the civil authority, but to the "military authorities of the United States."

It is true that no organized rebellion now exists there, and the courts of the United States now exercise jurisdiction over the people of that province. But this is no test of the State's being in the Union: Dacotah is no State, and yet the courts of the United States administer justice there as they do in Texas. The Indian tribes, who are governed by military force, cannot claim to be States of the Union. Wherein does the condition of Texas differ from theirs?

Now, by assuming or admitting *as a fact* the present *status* of Texas as a State not in the Union *politically*, I beg leave to protest against any charge of inconsistency as to judicial opinions heretofore expressed as a member of this court or silently assented to. I do not consider myself bound to express any opinion judicially as to the constitutional right of Texas to exercise the rights and privileges of a State of this Union, or the power of Congress to govern her as a conquered province, to subject her to military domination and keep her in pupilage. I can only submit to *the fact* as decided by the political position of the government; and I am not disposed to join in any essay of judicial subtlety to prove Texas to be a State of the Union, when Congress have decided that she is not. It is a question of fact, I repeat, and of fact only. *Politically*, Texas is not *a State in this Union*. Whether rightfully out of it or not is a question not before the court, and I am not called on to confute a fact with syllogisms.

But conceding now the fact to be as judicially assumed by my brethren, the next question is whether she has a right to repudiate her contracts? Before proceeding to answer this question, we must notice a fact in this case that was forgotten in the argument. I mean that the United States are no party to this suit, and refusing to pay the bonds because the money paid would be used to advance the interests of the rebellion. It is a matter of utter insignificance to the Government of the United States to whom she makes the payment of these bonds. They are payable to the bearer. The Government is not bound to inquire into the *bona fides* of the holder, nor whether the State of Texas has parted with the bonds wisely or foolishly. And, although by the reconstruction acts she is required to repudiate all debts contracted for the purposes of the rebellion, this does not annul all acts of the State government during the rebellion or contracts for other purposes, nor authorize the State to repudiate them.

Now, whether we assume the State of Texas to be judicially in the Union (though actually out of it) or not, it will not alter the case. The contest is now between the State of Texas and her own citizens. She seeks to annul a contract with the respondents based on the allegation that there was no authority in Texas competent to enter into an agreement during the rebellion. Having relied upon one judicial fiction, namely, that she *is* a state in the Union, she now relies upon a second one, which she wishes this court to adopt, that she was not a State at all during the five years that she was in rebellion. She now sets up the plea of *insanity*, and asks the court to treat all her acts made during the disease as void.

We have had some very astute logic to prove that judicially she was not a State at all, although governed by her own legislature and executive as "a distinct political body."

The ordinance of secession was adopted by the convention on the 18th February, 1861, submitted to a vote of the people, and ratified by an overwhelming majority.

I admit that this was a very ill-advised measure. Still, it was the sovereign act of a sovereign State, and the verdict on the trial of this question "by battle," (Prize Cases, 2 Black, 673,) as to her right to secede, has been against her. But that verdict did not settle any question not involved in the case. It did not settle the question of her right to plead insanity and set aside all her contracts, made during the pending of the trial, with her own citizens, for food, clothing, or medicines. The same "organized political body," exercising the sovereign power of the State, which required the endorsement of these bonds by the governor, also passed the laws authorizing the disposal of them without such endorsement. She cannot, like the chameleon, assume the color of the object to which she adheres, and ask this court to involve itself in the contradictory positions that she is a State in the Union and was never out of it, and yet not a State at all for four years, during which she acted and claims to be "an organized political body," exercising all the powers and functions of an independent sovereign State. Whether a State *de facto* or *de jure*, she is estopped from denying her identity in disputes with her own citizens. If they have not fulfilled their contract, she can have her legal remedy for the breach of it in her own courts.

But the case of Hardenberg differs from that of the other defendants. He purchased the bonds in open market, *bona fide*, and for a full consideration. Now, it is to be observed that these bonds are payable to bearer, and that this court is appealed to as a court of equity. The argument to justify a decree in favor of the Commonwealth of Texas as against Hardenberg is simply this: these bonds, though payable to bearer, are redeemable fourteen years from date. The Government has exercised her privilege of paying the interest for a term without redeeming the principal, which gives an additional value to the bonds. *Ergo*, the bonds are dishonored. *Ergo*, the former owner has a right to resume the possession of them, and reclaim them from a *bona fide* owner by a decree of a court of equity.

This is the legal argument, when put in the form of a logical sorites, by which Texas invokes our aid to assist her in the perpetration of this great wrong.

A court of chancery is said to be a court of conscience; and however astute may be the argument introduced to defend this decree, I can only say that neither my reason nor my conscience can give assent to it. Of course I am justly convicted by my brethren of an erroneous use of both; but I hope I may say, without offence, that I am not convinced of it.

Mr. Justice Swayne delivered the following opinion:

I concur with my brother Grier as to the incapacity of the State of Texas, in her present condition, to maintain an original suit in this court. The question, in my judgment, is one in relation to which this court is bound by the action of the legislative department of the Government.

Upon the merits of the case I agree with the majority of my brethren.

I am authorized to say that my brother Miller unites with me in these views.

The decree in this case was, on motion of William M. Evarts and J. M. Carlisle, suspended in so far as it affects the rights of any holders or purchasers of the coupon bonds who obtained them in open market, and a re-argument of the case was ordered for October next.

## The McCardle Case.

No. 223, DECEMBER TERM, 1868.

*Ex parte* William H. McCardle, appellant.
Appeal from the circuit court of the United States for the southern district of Mississippi.

Mr. Chief Justice Chase delivered the opinion of the court.

This cause came here by appeal from the circuit court for the southern district of Mississippi.

A petition for the writ of *habeas corpus* was preferred in that court by the appellant, alleging unlawful restraint by military force.

The writ was issued, and a return was made by the military commander, admitting the restraint, but denying that it was unlawful.

It appeared that the petitioner was not in the military service of the United States, but was held in custody by military authority for trial before a military commission upon charges founded upon the publication of articles alleged to be incendiary and libelous, in a newspaper of which he was editor.

Upon the hearing the petitioner was remanded to the military custody; but upon his prayer an appeal was allowed him to this court, and, upon filing the usual appeal bond for costs, he was admitted to bail upon recognizance, with sureties, conditioned for his future appearance in the circuit court, to abide by and perform the final judgment of this court.

A motion to dismiss this appeal was made at the last term, and, after argument, was denied. A full statement of the case may be found in the report of this decision;* and it is unnecessary to repeat it here.

Subsequently the case was argued very thoroughly and ably upon the merits, and was taken under advisement. While it was thus held, and before conference in regard to the decision proper to be made, an act was passed by Congress,† returned with objections by the President, and re-passed by the constitutional majority, which it is insisted takes from this court juridiction of the appeal.

The second section of this act was as follows:

"*And be it further enacted*, That so much of the act approved February 5, 1867, entitled an act to amend an act to establish the judicial courts of the United States, approved September 24, 1789, as authorized an appeal from the judgment of the circuit court to the Supreme Court of the United States, or the exercise of any such jurisdiction by said Supreme Court on appeals which have been or may hereafter be taken, be, and the same is hereby, repealed."

The attention of the court was directed to this statute at the last term, but counsel having expressed a desire to be heard in argument upon its effect, and the Chief Justice being detained from his place here by his duties in the court of impeachment, the cause was continued under advisement.

At this term we have heard argument upon the effect of the repealing act, and will now dispose of the case.

The first question necessarily is that of jurisdiction; for, if the act of March, 1868, takes away the jurisdiction defined by the act of February, 1867, it is useless, if not improper, to enter into any discussion of other questions.

It is quite true, as was argued by the counsel for the petitioner, that the appellate jurisdiction of this court is not derived from acts of Congress. It is, strictly speaking, conferred by the Consti-

*Ex-parte* McCardle, 6 Wall., 318. †Act March 27, 1868, 15 U. S. Stat. 44.

tution. But it is conferred "with such exceptions and under such regulations as Congress shall make."

It is unnecessary to consider whether, if Congress had made no exceptions and no regulations, this court might not have exercised general appellate jurisdiction under rules prescribed by itself. For among the earliest acts of the 1st Congress, at its 1st session, was the act of September 24, 1789, to establish the judicial courts of the United States. That act provided for the organization of this court, and prescribed regulations for the exercise of its jurisdiction.

The source of that jurisdiction, and the limitations of it by the Constitution and by statute, have been on several occasions subjects of consideration here. In the case of Durousseau vs. The United States,* particularly, the whole matter was carefully examined, and the court held that, while "the appellate powers of this court are not given by the judicial act, but are given by the Constitution," they are nevertheless "limited and regulated by that act, and by such other acts as have been passed on the subject." The court said further, that the judicial act was an exercise of the power given by the Constitution to Congress " of making exceptions to the appellate jurisdiction of the Supreme Court." "They have described affirmatively," said the court, "its jurisdiction, and this affirmative description has been understood to imply a negation of the exercise of such appellate power as is not comprehended within it."

The principle that the affirmation of appellate jurisdiction implies the negation of all such jurisdiction not affirmed having been thus established, it was an almost necessary consequence that acts of Congress, providing for the exercise of jurisdiction, should come to be spoken of as acts granting jurisdiction, and not as acts making exceptions to the constitutional grant of it.

The exception to appellate jurisdiction in the case before us, however, is not an inference from the affirmation of other appellate jurisdiction. It is made in terms. The provision of the act of 1867, affirming the appellate jurisdiction of this court in cases of *habeas corpus*, is expressly repealed. It is hardly possible to imagine a plainer instance of positive exception.

We are not at liberty to inquire into the motives of the legislature. We can only examine into its power under the Constitution ; and the power to make exceptions to the appellate jurisdiction of this court is given by express words.

What, then, is the effect of the repealing act upon the case before us ? We cannot doubt as to this. Without jurisdiction the court cannot proceed at all in any cause. Jurisdiction is power to declare the law, and when it ceases to exist, the only function remaining to the court is that of announcing the fact and dismissing the cause.

And this is not less clear upon authority than upon principle.

Several cases were cited by the counsel for the petitioner in support of the position that jurisdiction of this case is not affected by the repealing act. But none of them, in our judgment, afford any support to it. They are all cases of

the exercise of judicial power by the legislature, or of legislative interference with courts in the exercising of continuing jurisdiction.*

On the other hand, the general rule, supported by the best elementary writers,† is, that "when an act of the legislature is repealed, it must be considered, except as to transactions past and closed, as if it never existed." And the effect of repealing acts upon suits under acts repealed has been determined by the adjudications of this court. The subject was fully considered in Norris *vs.* Crocker,‡ and more recently in Insurance Company *vs.* Ritchie.§ In both of these cases it was held that no judgment could be rendered in a suit after the repeal of the act under which it was brought and prosecuted.

It is quite clear, therefore, that this court cannot proceed to pronounce judgment is this case, for it has no longer jurisdiction of the appeal ; and judicial duty is not less fitly performed by declining ungranted jurisdiction than in exercising firmly that which the Constitution and the laws confer.

Counsel seem to have supposed, if effect be given to the repealing act in question, that the whole appellate power of the court in cases in *habeas corpus* is denied. But this is an error. The act of 1868 does not except from that jurisdiction any cases but appeals from circuit courts under the act of 1867. It does affect the jurisdiction which was previously exercised.‖

The appeal of the petitioner in this case must be dismissed for want of jurisdiction.

## Opinions in the Cæsar Griffin Case—Virginia.

Opinion of Chief Justice Chase, May 10, 1869.

Circuit court of the United States for the district of Virginia, in the matter of Cæsar Griffin—Petition for habeas corpus.

This is an appeal from an order of discharge from imprisonment made by the district judge, acting as a judge of the circuit court, upon a writ of *habeas corpus*, allowed upon the petition of Cæsar Griffin.

The petition alleged unlawful restraint of the petitioner, in violation of the Constitution of the United States, by the sheriff of Rockbridge county, Virginia, in virtue of a pretended judgment rendered in the circuit court of that county by Hugh W. Sheffey, present and presiding therein as judge, though disabled from holding any office whatever by the XIVth amendment of the Constitution of the United States.

Upon this petition a writ of *habeas corpus* was allowed and served, and the body of the petitioner, with a return showing the cause of detention, was produced by the sheriff, in conformity with its command.

The general facts of the case, as shown to the district judge, may be briefly stated as follows :

The circuit court of Rockbridge county is a court of record of the State of Virginia, having civil and criminal jurisdiction. In this court, the petitioner, Cæsar Griffin, indicted in the

---

* De Chastellux *vs.* Fairchild, 15 Pa., 18 ; The State *vs.* Fleming, 7 Humph., 152 ; Lewis *vs.* Webb, 3 Greene, 326 ; Lanier *vs.* Gallatus, 13 La. An., 175.
† Dwarris on Statutes, 538. ‡ 13 How., 429. § 5 Wall., 541.
‖ *Ex parte* McCardle, 6 Wall,, 324.

---

* 6 Cranch, 312 ; Wiscart *vs.* Dauchy, 3 Dall., 321.

county court for shooting, with intent to kill, was regularly tried in pursuance of his own election; and, having been convicted, was sentenced according to the finding of the jury, to imprisonment for two years, and was in the custody of the sheriff to be conveyed to the penitentiary, in pursuance of this sentence.

Griffin is a colored man; but there was no allegation that the trial was not fairly conducted, or that any discrimination was made against him, either in indictment, trial, or sentence, on account of color.

It was not claimed that the grand jury by which he was indicted, or the petit jury by which he was tried, was not in all respects lawful and competent. Nor was it alleged that Hugh W. Sheffey, the judge who presided at the trial and pronounced the sentence, did not conduct the trial with fairness and uprightness.

One of the counsel for the petitioner, indeed, upon the hearing in this court, pronounced an eulogium upon his character both as a man and as a magistrate, to deserve which might well be the honorable aspiration of any judge.

But it was alleged and was admitted that Judge Sheffey, in December, 1849, as a member of the Virginia house of delegates, took an oath to support the Constitution of the United States, and also that he was a member of the legislature of Virginia during the late rebellion in 1862, and as such voted for measures to sustain the so-called Confederate States in their war against the United States; and it was claimed in behalf of the petitioner that he thereby became, and was at the time of the trial of the petitioner, disqualified to hold any office, civil or military, under the United States, or under any State; and it was specially insisted that the petitioner was entitled to his discharge upon the ground of the incapacity of Sheffey under the XIVth amendment to act as judge and pass sentence of imprisonment.

Upon this showing and argument it was held by the district judge that the sentence of Cæsar Griffin was absolutely null; that his imprisonment was in violation of the Constitution of the United States, and an order for his discharge from custody was made accordingly.

The general question to be determined on the appeal from this order is whether or not the sentence of the circuit court of Rockbridge county must be regarded as a nullity, because of the disability to hold any office under the State of Virginia imposed by the XIVth amendment on the person who in fact presided as judge in that court.

It may be properly borne in mind that the disqualification did not exist at the time that Sheffey became judge.

When the functionaries of the State government existing in Virginia at the commencement of the late civil war took part, together with a majority of the citizens of the State, in rebellion against the Government of the United States, they ceased to constitute a State government for the State of Virginia which could be recognized as such by the national Government. Their example of hostility to the Union, however, was not followed throughout the State. In many counties the local authorities and majorities of the people adhered to the national Government; and representatives from those counties soon after assembled in convention at Wheeling, and organized a government for the State. This government was recognized as the lawful government of Virginia by the executive and legislative departments of the national Government, and this recognition was conclusive upon the judicial department.

The government of the State thus recognized was, in contemplation of law, the government of the whole State of Virginia, though excluded, as the Government of the United States was itself excluded, from the greater portion of the territory of the State. It was the legislature of the reorganized State which gave the consent of Virginia to the formation of the State of West Virginia. To the formation of that State the consent of its own legislature and of the legislature of the State of Virginia and of Congress was indispensable. If either had been wanting, no State within the limits of the old could have been constitutionally formed; and it is clear, that if the government instituted at Wheeling was not the government of the whole State of Virginia, no new State has ever been constitutionally formed within her ancient boundaries.

It cannot admit of question, then, that the government which consented to the formation of the State of West Virginia, remained, in all national relations, the government of Virginia, although that event reduced to very narrow limits the territory acknowledging its jurisdiction, and not controlled by insurgent force. Indeed, it is well known, historically, that the State and the government of Virginia, thus organized, was recognized by the national Government. Senators and Representatives from the State occupied seats in Congress, and when the insurgent force which held possession of the principal part of the territory was overcome, and the government recognized by the United States was transferred from Alexandria to Richmond, it became in fact, what it was before in law, the government of the whole State. As such it was entitled, under the Constitution, to the same recognition and respect, in national relations, as the government of any other State.

It was under this government that Hugh W. Sheffey was, on the 22d February, 1866, duly appointed judge of the circuit court of Rockbridge county, and he was in the regular exercise of his functions as such when Griffin was tried and sentenced.

More than two years had elapsed, after the date of his appointment, when the ratification of the XIVth amendment by the requisite number of States was officially promulgated by the Secretary of State, on the 28th of July, 1868.

That amendment, in its 3d section, ordains that "no person shall be a senator or representative in Congress, or elector of President and Vice President, or hold any office, civil or military, under the United States, or under any State, who, having previously taken an oath as a member of Congress, or as an officer of the United States, or as a member of any State legislature, or as an executive or judicial officer of any State, to support the Constitution of the United States, shall have engaged in insurrection or rebellion against the same, or given aid or comfort to the enemies thereof."

And it is admitted that the office held by Judge Sheffey, at the time of the trial of Griffin, was an office under the State of Virginia, and that he was one of the persons to whom the prohibition to hold office pronounced by the amendment applied.

The question to be considered, therefore, is whether, upon a sound construction of the amendment, it must be regarded as operating directly, without any intermediate proceeding whatever, upon all persons within the category of prohibition, and as depriving them at once and absolutely of all official authority and power.

One of the counsel for the petitioner suggested that the amendment must be construed with reference to the act of 1867, which extends the writ of *habeas corpus* to a large class of cases in which the previous legislation did not allow it to be issued. And it is proper to say a few words of this suggestion here.

The judiciary act of 1789 expressly denied the benefit of the writ of *habeas corpus* to prisoners not confined under or by color of the authority of the United States. Under that act, no person confined under State authority could have the benefit of the writ. Afterwards, in 1833 and 1842, the writ was extended to certain cases, specially described, of imprisonment under State process; and in 1867, by the act to which the counsel referred, the writ was still further extended "to all cases where any person may be restrained of liberty in violation of the Constitution, or of any treaty or law of the United States."

And the learned counsel was doubtless correct in maintaining that without the act of 1867 there would be no remedy for *habeas corpus* in the case of the petitioner, nor, indeed, in any case of imprisonment in violation of the Constitution of the United States, except in the possible case of an imprisonment not only within the provisions of this act, but also within the provisions of some one of the previous acts of 1789, 1833, and 1842.

But if, in saying that the amendment must be construed with reference to the act, the counsel meant to affirm that the existence of the act throws any light whatever upon the construction of the amendment, the court is unable to perceive the force of his observation.

It is not pretended that imprisonment for shooting with intent to kill is unconstitutional, and it will hardly be affirmed that the act of 1867 throws any light whatever upon the question, whether such imprisonment in any particular case is unconstitutional. The case of unconstitutional imprisonment must be established by appropriate evidence. It cannot be inferred from the existence of a remedy for such a case. And, surely, no construction, otherwise unwarranted, can be put upon the amendment more than upon any other provision of the Constitution, to make a case of violation out of acts which, otherwise, must be regarded as not only constitutional, but right.

We come then to the question of construction. What was the intention of the people of the United States in adopting the XIVth amendment? What is the true scope and purpose of the prohibition to hold office contained in the third section?

The proposition maintained in behalf of the petitioner is, that this prohibition instantly, on the day of its promulgation, vacated all offices held by persons within the category of prohibition, and made all official acts performed by them since that day null and void.

One of the counsel sought to vindicate this construction of the amendment upon the ground that the definitions of the verb "to hold," given by Webster, in his dictionary, are "to stop; to confine; to restrain from escape; to keep fast; to retain;" of which definitions the author says that "to hold rarely or never signifies the first act of seizing or falling on, but the act of retaining a thing when seized on or confined."

The other counsel seemed to be embarrassed by the difficulties of this literal construction, and sought to establish a distinction between sentences in criminal cases and judgments and decrees in civil cases. He admitted, indeed, that the latter might be valid when made by a court held by a judge within the prohibitive category of the amendment, but insisted that the sentences of the same court in criminal cases must be treated as nullities. The ground of the distinction, if we correctly apprehend the argument, was found in the circumstance that the act of 1867 provided a summary redress in the latter class of cases; while in the former no summary remedy could be had, and great inconvenience would arise from regarding decrees and judgments as utterly null and without effect.

But this ground of distinction seems to the court unsubstantial. It rests upon the fallacy already commented on. The amendment makes no such distinction as is supposed. It does not deal with cases, but with persons. The prohibition is general. No person in the prohibitive category can hold office. It applies to all persons and to all offices, under the United States or any State. If upon a true construction it operates as a removal of a judge, and avoids all sentences in criminal cases pronounced by him after the promulgation of the amendment it must be held to have the effect of removing all judges and all officers, and annulling all their official acts after that date.

The literal construction, therefore, is the only one upon which the order of the learned district judge, discharging the prisoner, can be sustained, and was, indeed, as appears from his certificate, the construction upon which the order was made. He says expressly, "the right of the petitioner to his discharge appeared to me to rest solely on the incapacity of the said Hugh W. Sheffey to act, (that is, as judge,) and so to sentence the prisoner, under the XIVth amendment."

Was this a correct construction?

In the examination of questions of this sort, great attention is properly paid to the argument from inconvenience. This argument, it is true, cannot prevail over plain words or clear reason. But, on the other hand, a construction which must necessarily occasion great public and private mischief must never be preferred to a construction which will occasion neither, or neither in so great degree, unless the terms of the instrument absolutely require such preference.

Let it then be considered what consequences would spring from the literal interpretation contended for in behalf of the petitioner.

The amendment applies to all the States of the Union, to all offices under the United States or under any State, and to all persons in the category of prohibition, and for all time, present and future. The offences for which exclusion from office is denounced are not merely engaging in insurrection or rebellion against the United States, but the giving of aid or comfort to their enemies. They are offences not only of civil, but of foreign war.

Now, let it be supposed that some of the persons described in the third section, during the war with Mexico, gave aid and comfort to the enemies of their country, and nevertheless held some office on the 28th of July, 1868, or subsequently. Is it a reasonable construction of the amendment which will make it annul every official act of such an officer?

But let another view be taken. It is well known that many persons engaged in the late rebellion have emigrated to States which adhered to the national Government, and it is not to be doubted that not a few among them, as members of Congress, or officers of the United States, or as members of State legislatures, or as executive or judicial officers of a State, had before the war taken an oath to support the Constitution of the United States. In their new homes, capacity, integrity, fitness, and acceptability, may very possibly have been more looked to than antecedents. Probably some of these persons have been elected to office in the States which have received them. It is not unlikely that some of them held office on the 28th July, 1868. Must all their official acts be held to be null under the inexorable exigencies of the amendment?

But the principal intent of the amendment was, doubtless, to provide for the exclusion from office in the lately insurgent States of all persons within the prohibitive description.

Now, it is well known that before the amendment was proposed by Congress, governments acknowledging the constitutional supremacy of the national Government had been organized in all these States. In some these governments had been organized through the direct action of the people, encouraged and supported by the President, as in Tennessee, Louisiana and Arkansas, and in some through similar action in pursuance of Executive proclamation, as in North Carolina, Alabama, and several other States. In Virginia such a State government had been organized as has been already stated, soon after the commencement of the war; and this government only had been fully recognized by Congress, as well as by the President.

This government, indeed, and all the others, except that of Tennessee, were declared by Congress to be provisional only.

But in all these States all offices had been filled, before the ratification of the amendment, by citizens who at the time of the ratification were actively engaged in the performance of their several duties. Very many, if not a ma-

jority of these officers, had, in one or another of the capacities described in the third section, taken an oath to support the Constitution and had afterwards engaged in the late rebellion; and most, if not all, of them continued in the discharge of their functions after the promulgation of the amendment, not supposing that by its operation their offices could be vacated without some action of Congress.

If the construction now contended for be given to the prohibitive section, the effect must be to annul all official acts performed by these officers. No sentence, no judgment, no decree, no acknowledgment of a deed, no record of a deed, no sheriff's or commissioner's sale—in short, no official act is of the least validity. It is impossible to measure the evils which such a construction would add to the calamities which have already fallen upon the people of these States.

The argument from inconveniences, great as these, against the construction contended for, is certainly one of no light weight.

But there is another principle which, in determining the construction of this amendment, is entitled to equal consideration with that which has just been stated and illustrated. It may be stated thus: Of two constructions, either of which is warranted by the words of an amendment of a public act, that is to be preferred which best harmonizes the amendment with the general tenor and spirit of the act amended.

This principle forbids a construction of the amendment not clearly required by its terms, which will bring it into conflict or disaccord with the other provisions of the Constitution.

And here it becomes proper to examine somewhat more particularly the character of the third section of the amendment

The amendment itself was the first of the series of measures proposed or adopted by Congress with a view to the reorganization of State governments acknowledging the constitutional supremacy of the national Government in those States which had attempted to break up their constitutional relations with the Union, and to establish an independent confederacy.

All citizens who had, during its earlier stages, engaged in or aided the war against the United States, which resulted inevitably from this attempt, had incurred the penalties of treason under the statute of 1790.

But by the act of July 17, 1862, while the civil war was flagrant, the death penalty for treason committed by engaging in rebellion was practically abolished. Afterwards, in December, 1863, full amnesty, on conditions which now certainly seem to be moderate, was offered by President Lincoln, in accordance with the same act of Congress; and, after organized resistance to the United States had ceased, amnesty was again offered, in accordance with the same act, by President Johnson, in May, 1865. In both these offers of amnesty extensive exceptions were made.

In June, 1866, little more than a year later, the XIVth amendment was proposed, and was ratified in July, 1868. The only punitive section contained in it is the third, now under consideration. It is not improbable that one of the objects of this section was to provide for the security of the nation and of individuals by the exclusion of a class of citizens from office; but it can hardly be doubted that its main purpose was to inflict upon the leading and most influential characters who had been engaged in the rebellion, exclusion from office as a punishment for the offence.

It is true that, in the judgment of some enlightened jurists, its legal effect was to remit all other punishment, for it led to the general amnesty of December 25, of the same year, and to the order discontinuing all prosecutions for crime and proceedings for confiscation originating in the rebellion. Such certainly was its practical effect. But this very effect shows distinctly its punitive character.

Now, it is undoubted that those provisions of the Constitution which deny to the legislature power to deprive any person of life, liberty, or property without due process of law, or to pass a bill of attainder, or an *ex post facto* law, are inconsistent, in their spirit and general purpose, with any provision which at once, without trial, deprives a whole class of persons of offices held by them for cause, however grave. It is true that no limit can be imposed on the people when exercising their sovereign power in amending their own constitution of government. But it is a necessary presumption that the people, in the exercise of that power, seek to confirm and improve, rather than to weaken and impair, the general spirit of the Constitution.

If there were no other grounds than these for seeking another interpretation of the amendment than that which we are asked to put upon it, we should feel ourselves bound to hold them sufficient.

But there is another and sufficient ground, and it is this, that the construction demanded in behalf of the petitioner is nugatory except for mischief.

In the language of one of the counsel, "the object had in view by us is not to unseat Hugh W. Sheffey, and no judgment of the court can effect that."

Now, the object of the amendment is to unseat every officer, whether judicial or executive, who holds civil or military office in contravention of the terms of the amendment. Surely, a construction which fails to accomplish the main purpose of the amendment and yet necessarily works the mischiefs and inconveniences which have been described, and is repugnant to the first principles of justice and right embodied in other provisions of the Constitution, is not to be favored if any other reasonable construction can be found.

Is there, then, any other reasonable construction? In the judgment of the court there is another, not only reasonable, but very clearly warranted by the terms of the amendment, and recognized by the legislation of Congress.

The object of the amendment is to exclude from certain offices a certain class of persons. Now, it is obviously impossible to do this by a simple declaration, whether in the Constitution or in an act of Congress, that all persons included within a particular description shall not hold office. For, in the very nature of things, it must be ascertained what particular individuals are embraced by the definition before

any sentence of exclusion can be made to operate. To accomplish this ascertainment and insure effective results, proceedings, evidence, decisions, and enforcement of decisions, more or less formal, are indispensable; and these can only be provided for by Congress.

Now, the necessity of this is recognized by the amendment itself, in its fifth and final section, which declares that "Congress shall have power to enforce, by appropriate legislation, the provisions of this article."

There are, indeed, other sections than the third, to the enforcement of which legislation is necessary; but there is no one which more clearly requires legislation in order to give effect to it. The fifth section qualifies the third to the same extent as it would if the whole amendment consisted of these two sections.

And the final clause of the third section itself is significant: it gives to Congress absolute control of the whole operation of the amendment These are its words: "But Congress may, by a vote of two-thirds of each House, remove such disability." Taking the third section then in its completeness, with this final clause, it seems to put beyond reasonable question the conclusion that the intention of the people of the United States in adopting the XIVth amendment was to create a disability, to be removed in proper cases by a two thirds vote, and to be made operative in other cases by the legislation of Congress in its ordinary course. The construction gives certain effect to the undoubted intent of the amendment to insure the exclusion from office of the designated class of persons, if not relieved from their disabilities, and avoids the manifold evils which must attend the construction insisted upon by the counsel for the petitioner.

It results from this examination that persons in office by lawful appointment, or elected before the promulgation of the XIVth amendment, are not removed therefrom by the direct and immediate effect of the prohibition to hold office contained in the third section; but that legislation by Congress is necessary to give effect to the prohibition, by providing for such removal. And it results further, that the exercise of their several functions by these officers, until removed in pursuance of such legislation, is not unlawful.

The views which have been just stated receive strong confirmation from the action of Congress and of the executive department of the Government. The decision of the district judge, now under revision, was made in December, 1868, and two months afterwards, in February, 1869, Congress adopted a joint resolution, entitled "A resolution respecting the provisional governments of Virginia and Texas." In this resolution it was provided, that persons "holding office in the provisional governments of Virginia and Texas," but unable to take and subscribe the test-oath prescribed by the act of July 2, 1862, except those relieved from disability, "be removed therefrom;" but a provision was added, suspending the operation of the resolution for thirty days from its passage. The joint resolution was passed and received by the President on the 6th of February, and, not having been returned in ten days, became a law without his approval.

It cannot be doubted that this joint resolution recognized persons unable to take the oath required, to which class belonged all persons within the description of the third section of the XIVth amendment, as holding office in Virginia at the date of its passage, and provided for their removal from office.

It is not clear whether it was the intent of Congress that this removal should be effected in Virginia by the force of the joint resolution itself, or by the commander of the first military district. It was understood by the executive or military authorities as directing the removal of the persons described by military order. The resolution was published by command of the general of the army, for the information of all concerned, on the 22d of March, 1869. It had been previously published by direction of the commander of the first military district, accompanied by an order, to take effect on the 18th of March, 1869, removing the persons described from office. The date at which this order was to take effect was afterwards changed to the 21st of March.

It is plain enough from this statement that persons holding office in Virginia, and within the prohibition of the XIVth amendment, were not regarded by Congress, or by the military authority, in March, 1869, as having been already removed from office.

It is unnecessary to discuss here the question whether the government of Virginia, which seems to have been not provisional, but permanent, when transferred from Alexandria to Richmond, became provisional under the subsequent legislation of Congress, or to express any opinion concerning the validity of the joint resolution, or of the proceedings under it. The resolution and proceedings are referred to here only for the purpose of showing that the amendment had not been regarded by Congress or the executive, so far as represented by the military authorities, as effecting an immediate removal of the officers described in the third section.

After the most careful consideration, I find myself constrained to the conclusion that Hugh W. Sheffey had not been removed from the office of judge at the time of the trial and sentence of the petitioner; and, therefore, that the sentence of the circuit court of Rockbridge county was lawful.

In this view of the case, it becomes unnecessary to determine the question relating to the effect of the sentence of a judge *de facto*, exercising the office with the color, but without the substance of right. It is proper to say, however, that I should have no difficulty in sustaining the custody of the sheriff under the sentence of a court held by such a judge.

Instructive argument and illustration of this branch of the case might be derived from an examination of those provisions of the Constitution ordaining that no person shall be a representative, or senator, or President, or Vice President, unless having certain prescribed qualifications. These provisions, as well as those which ordain that no senator or representative shall, during his term of service, be appointed to any office under the United States, under certain circum-

stances, and that no person holding any such office shall, while holding such office, be a member of either House, operate on the capacity to take office. The election or appointment itself is prohibited and invalidated; and yet no instance is believed to exist where a person has been actually elected, and has actually taken the office, notwithstanding the prohibition, and his acts while exercising its functions have been held invalid.

But it is unnecessary to pursue the examination. The cases cited by counsel cover the whole ground, both of principle and authority.*

This subject received the consideration of the judges of the Supreme Court at the last term with reference to this and kindred cases in this district, and I am authorized to say that they unanimously concurred in the opinion, that a person convicted by a jury, and sentenced in court held by a judge *de facto*, acting under color of office, though not *de jure*, and detained in custody in pursuance of his sentence, cannot be properly discharged upon *habeas corpus*.

It follows that the order of the district judge must be reversed, and that the petitioner must be remanded to the custody of the sheriff of Rockbridge county.

## OPINION OF JUDGE UNDERWOOD.

### In the matter of Cæsar Griffin—Petition for habeas corpus.

In entering upon the consideration of this case, I am oppressed by the gravity of the principles and consequences it involves. The history of civilization has established the fact that the liberties of the people in all modern nations depend upon the restraints which courts of justice have succeeded in opposing to the oppressions of tyrants and usurpers. And no device for this purpose can be compared with the writ of *habeas corpus*, which we have inherited from our English ancestors.

That great scholar and writer, Dr. Samuel Johnson, well said to his friend Boswell, "the *habeas corpus* is the single advantage which our government has over that of other countries."

The historian Macaulay, in his graphic description of the tyrant James the Second, has well written: "One of his objects was to obtain a repeal of the *habeas corpus* act, which he hated, as it was natural that a tyrant should hate the most stringent curb that ever legislation imposed on tyranny. This feeling remained deeply fixed in his mind to the last, and appears in the instructions which he drew up, when in exile, for the guidance of his son. But the *habeas corpus* act, though passed during the ascendancy of the whigs, was not more dear to the whigs than to the tories. It is, indeed, not wonderful that this great law should be highly prized by all Englishmen, without distinction of party; for it is a law which, not by circuitous, but by direct operation, adds to the security and happiness of every inhabitant of the realm."

The petition in the present case alleges that the petitioner is deprived of his liberty in violation of the Constitution of the United States, and the evidence proves that he is imprisoned

* Taylor *vs.* Skinner, 2 S. C., 696; State *vs.* Bloom, 17 Wis., 521, *Ex rel.* Ralston *vs.* Bangs, 24 Ill., 184.

under color of a sentence pronounced against him by a person pretending to be a judge of the circuit court of Rockbridge county, in the State of Virginia; that the said pretended judge, having previously taken an oath as a member of the State legislature to support the Constitution of the United States, had engaged in insurrection or rebellion against the same, or given aid or comfort to the enemies thereof; whereas the Constitution of the United States (amendments, Art. XIV) provides that no such person as aforesaid shall hold any civil office under any State; and, consequently, the said pretended judge had no jurisdiction over the person or alleged offence of the petitioner, and all his proceedings in the case were invalid and absolutely void.

Two questions are before the court. They are both of a legal, not of a political character, and I propose to consider them strictly upon legal principles and judicial authority. They are

1. Did the writ properly issue in this case?

2. Ought the petitioner, on the consideration of the whole case, to be discharged?

1st. Did the writ properly issue?

The act of Congress of February 5, 1867, provides as follows:

"*Be it enacted*, &c., &c., That the several courts of the United States and the several justices and judges of said courts within their respective jurisdictions, in addition to the authority already conferred by law, shall have power to grant writs of *habeas corpus* in all cases where any person may be restrained of his or her liberty in violation of the Constitution, or of any treaty or law of the United States; and it shall be lawful for such person so restrained of his or her liberty to apply to either of said justices or judges for a writ of *habeas corpus*, which application shall be in writing and verified by affidavit, and shall set forth the facts concerning the detention of the party applying, in whose custody he or she is detained, and by virtue of what claim or authority, if known; and the said justice or judge to whom such application shall be made shall forthwith award a writ of *habeas corpus*, unless it shall appear from the petition itself that the party is not deprived of his or her liberty in contravention of the Constitution and laws of the United States."

The petition, in form, complied with the requirements of the statute; and it did not appear from the petition itself that the party is not deprived of his liberty in contravention of the Constitution of the United States. Therefore the obligation would seem to have been imperative on the judge to whom the application was made to issue the writ. The language of the statute is sufficiently plain, even without the aid of judicial construction. But it has had judicial construction by the highest authority in the land. In McCardle's case the Supreme Court of the United States, in an opinion delivered by its learned Chief Justice, with his usual force and elegance of expression, said:

"This legislation is of the most comprehensive character. It brings within the *habeas corpus* jurisdiction of every court and of every judge every possible case of privation of liberty contrary to the national Constitution, treaties, or laws. It is impossible to widen this jurisdiction."

A judge capable of understanding the plainest English language could entertain no doubt, under the statute, of his duty to issue the writ, on a petition such as was presented in this case; and if any doubt could have arisen under the statute standing alone, this decision of the Supreme Court of the United States would have removed it.

2d. Ought the petitioner, on the return, answer, and evidence, to be discharged?

The XIVth amendment to the Constitution provides:

"SEC. 3. No person shall be a senator or representative in Congress, or elector of President and Vice President, or hold any office, civil or military, under the United States, or any State, who, having previously taken an oath, as a member of Congress, or as an officer of the United States, or as a member of any State legislature, or as an executive or judicial officer of any State, to support the Constitution of the United States, shall have been engaged in insurrection or rebellion against the same, or given aid or comfort to the enemies thereof."

The fact that the person who pronounced the sentence was disqualified, under the XIVth amendment of the Constitution of the United States, is not controverted, and I believe to be incontrovertible. But it is argued that the court was a court *de facto*, and that the disqualification of the judge cannot be availed of in a collateral proceeding.

Let us examine these two points:

First. That it was a court *de facto*. It is hardly worth our while to be frightened, at this day, by a little law Latin. *De facto* means of or from the fact, or, more properly, as used here, in fact; that is to say, the objection urged is, that this was a court in fact, if not in law.

Now, let us ask what makes it a court in fact? Is that a court in fact which the Constitution of the United States says shall not be a court? Then the Constitution is a dead letter—a mat to wipe our feet upon—not a shield to protect our breasts. There can be no such thing, in time of peace, when the national authority is everywhere re-established, as a court prohibited by the plain letter of the Constitution, (and a court composed of such judges is so prohibited,) and yet having power to deprive citizens of their life or their liberty. Such a proposition seems to me the most unmaintainable of absurdities on its very face.

If the doctrine here urged is correct, and is the doctrine on which our practice is to be based, it might be advantageously incorporated into this XIVth amendment and made a part of it. We will see how this amendment would then read. I know no better way to exhibit the untenableness of the proposition than thus to put it into the shape of that organic law which, it is contended, it ought to control.

"No person shall hold any civil office" in theory, though he may in fact, and as a rebel pretended judge may sentence loyal men to be imprisoned and to be hanged, "who, having previously taken an oath as a member of Congress, or as an officer of the United States, or as a member of any State legislature, or as an executive or judicial officer of any State, to support the Constitution of the United States, shall have engaged in insurrection or rebellion against the same, or given aid or comfort to the enemies thereof."

How would such a provision as that read? And yet, if it is to be the law administered by the court, it might as well be in the Constitution or on the statute-book.

As a judge of one of the courts of the United States I am sworn to support the Constitution of the United States. If, after having taken that oath, I were to hold that he shall be a judge of whom that Constitution says, "He shall hold no civil office," I could not look upon myself as other than a perjured man.

This great nation has spoken in the most solemn and authoritative manner in which its voice is ever heard, and has said, Such a man shall not be a judge; and am I, as an exponent of its will and power, to presume to answer back, I agree that in theory it shall be according to your command; but, in defiance of your express decree, he shall in fact, or, as lawyers say, *de facto*, be a judge, and he shall exercise all the power and authority of a judge over your lives and over your liberties?

If this thing can be, then a single judge, sitting here in this court-room, has the power, attempted in vain by armies, to nullify the Constitution and set the laws enacted by the national legislature at defiance.

What says the illustrious Chief Justice Marshall on the nature and obligation of the oath administered to judges?

He says: "It is apparent that the framers of the Constitution contemplated that instrument as a rule for the government of courts as well as of the legislatures." And he asks:

"Why otherwise does it direct the judges to take an oath to support it? This oath certainly applies in an especial manner to their conduct in their official character. How immoral to impose it on them if they were to be used as the instruments, and the knowing instruments, for violating what they swear to support!" * *

Again he says:

"Why does a judge swear to discharge his duties agreeably to the Constitution of the United States, if that Constitution forms no rule for his government? If it is closed upon him, and cannot be inspected by him; if such be the real state of things, this is worse than solemn mockery. To prescribe or to take this oath become equally a crime."

But it is contended that though the petitioner has raised a question of constitutional law, it is not our duty to look into the Constitution to determine it. What said Chief Justice Marshall to such an argument, when it was addressed to him and to the Supreme Court of the United States? He replied:

"The judicial power of the United States is extended to all cases arising under the Constitution.

"Could it be the intention of those who gave this power to say that in using it the Constitution should not be looked into? That a case arising under the Constitution should be decided without examining that instrument under which it arises?

"This is too extravagant to be maintained. In some cases, then, the Constitution must be looked into by the judges. And if they can open it at all, what part of it are they forbidden to read or to obey?" * * "It is declared that no 'tax or duty shall be laid on articles exported from any State.'

"Suppose a duty on the export of cotton, of tobacco, or of flour, and a suit instituted to recover it. Ought judgment to be rendered in such a case? Ought the judges to close their eyes on the Constitution, and only see the law?

"The Constitution declares 'that no bill of attainder or *ex post facto* law shall be passed.'

"If, however, such a bill should be passed, and a person should be prosecuted under it, must the court condemn to death those victims whom the Constitution endeavors to preserve?"

And the Constitution endeavors to preserve all men from the official acts of all those whom the XIVth amendment disqualifies for holding civil office. And if we are thus bound to obey the Constitution, even when we might shield ourselves by a law in violation of it, as Chief Justice Marshall declares, with what triple bonds are we bound to obey it, when, as in this case, there is not only no law against it, but when we have a law aiding and enforcing our obedience. enacted by the same Congress which submitted this provision of the Constitution to the people, and for the very purpose of making our duty so plain that to err would seem impossible.

What is called a court *de facto* in this case was not, in any proper and legal sense, a court. Nothing expressly prohibited by the Constitution was ever so called. A court is defined to be "an incorporeal political being, which requires for its existence the presence of the judges, or a competent member of them, a clerk, or prothonotary," &c. There was no judge present at that court, unless a man can be a judge of whom the Constitution declares he shall not be a judge. And I certainly shall never rule that the Constitution of this country is impotent, effete, and not to be obeyed. I have neither the will nor the courage to attempt, by a judicial opinion, to overturn that Constitution which all the rebel armies assailed in vain, and which their cannon, though it shook the continent, could never shake.

"If," asks Chief Justice Marshall, "an act of the legislature repugnant to the Constitution is void, does it, notwithstanding its invalidity, bind the courts and oblige them to give it effect? Or, in other words, though it be not law, does it constitute a rule as operative as if it was a law?" And he remarks: "This would be to overthrow in fact what was established in theory; and would seem, at first view, an absurdity too gross to be insisted on."

So, I ask, if the Constitution has declared that a person disqualified in a certain manner shall hold no civil office, and a person so disqualified attempts to exercise the office of judge, shall I hold that his acts, notwithstanding his constitutional disqualifications, bind this court, and oblige its judges to give them effect? And I say further, in the language of that illustrious chief justice: "This would be to overthrow in fact what was established in theory, and would seem to be an absurdity too gross to be insisted on."

From the earliest period in the history of the writ of *habeas corpus* it has been uniformly held, that one of the most conclusive grounds for discharging a prisoner under that great writ was that he was held under color of the authority of a court not of competent jurisdiction, although, ordinarily, the writ would not lie for a prisoner in execution; yet it would lie for such a prisoner if the execution issued out of a court not of competent jurisdiction.

Says the great Lord Chief Justice Wilmot, in his masterly exposition of the law of *habeas corpus*, contained in a series of learned and profound answers to questions propounded to him by the house of lords:

"If it appears clearly that the act for which the party is committed is no crime, or that it is a crime, but he is committed for it by a person who has no jurisdiction, the court discharges."

Now, what jurisdiction has ɩ judge who is declared by the Constitution incapable of being a judge? Not a particle more than judge lynch, a modern committee of vigilance, or a town mob?

If he has any jurisdiction, then we have no constitution. Either all his official acts are void, or the Constitution is void. The two cannot both stand valid together; and if this court is bound blindly to consider such a court a court *de facto*, then this court is not itself a court *de facto*, but only in name.

The reports are full of cases in which proceedings of courts have been held to be void because the courts were composed, even in part, of disqualified magistrates.

In Regina *vs.* The Aberdale Canal Company, the proceedings of the commissioners were held to be void by the queen's bench of England, because a few, out of a large body of commissioners, were disqualified by one of the provisions of the statute known as the canal act. (14 Q. B., 854.)

In Regina *vs.* The Cheltenham Commissioners, the proceedings of the commissioners were quashed by the queen's bench, "because a question in the cause had been decided by a court improperly constituted." (12 Q. B., 467.)

Indeed, it is an old maxim of law, *judicum a non suo judice dictum*—judgment, if not pronounced by the proper judge, is of no effect.

I therefore conclude, that on general and long-established legal principles the petitioner is entitled to his discharge. But our duty in the case is not left to the guidance of general principles, although according to them it would seem to be plain enough. But it is specifically pointed out by the statute—the habeas corpus act of 1867. That act provides, that the "court or judge shall proceed in a summary way to determine the facts in the case, by hearing testimony and the arguments of the parties interested, and if it shall appear that the petitioner is deprived of his or her liberty in contravention of the Constitution or laws of the United States, he or she shall forthwith be discharged and set at liberty."

Now, it does appear in this case that the prisoner is deprived of his liberty in contravention of the Constitution, and it seems to me that nothing can be plainer than that we must discharge him, or violate an act of Congress and our oath of office.

Some other points in the argument in opposition it may be well enough to notice.

It is asserted that legislation by Congress is necessary to give effect to this constitutional provision—that it cannot act "*proprio vigore.*"

The provision, like that which says no bill of attainder or *ex post facto* law shall be passed, is a mere negation. It says no person disqualified, as this pretended judge is admitted to be, shall hold any office, and it no more needs additional legislation for the application of the writ of *habeas corpus*, than legislation is needed to understand and apply the simplest axioms of Euclid, the ten commandments, or the Lord's prayer.

It is said that the character or jurisdiction of the court cannot be examined in a collateral proceeding. But if this is a collateral proceeding I should like to know what is a direct one! We examine nothing but the exact point at issue. The petitioner alleges that he is imprisoned under color of authority of an unconstitutional tribunal. Under this allegation, which is denied by the opposing party, certainly the question whether it is an unconstitutional tribunals is the direct and only issue and in no sense collateral.

The writ of *habeas corpus*, as it applies to this case, is no collateral proceeding. It demands by no indirection, but in the most positive and direct manner possible, to know whether the petitioner is held in confinement by legal authority, and if at the time of the demand it can be shown that he is restrained of his liberty without lawful, much less constitutional authority, it requires immediate deliverance. It is the people's great writ of right and liberty, and cannot be abridged or defeated by any forms or pretences of precedent, by any legal quibbles, technicalities, or presumptions, which would prevent the most speedy, thorough, and rigid investigation.

To the prisoner, loaded with chains or pining within the bolts and bars of the most filthy dungeon, it proclaims the privilege of a hearing. It says to the jailor: Tyrant, oppressor, and usurper, stand back; let me know for what cause and by what authority you presume to hold this man, made in the image of his Maker, in this durance, shut from the common air and sunlight bestowed by almighty Goodness as the common inheritance of the human race.

In the name of Runnymede, of British bills of rights, of the revolutions of 1688 and 1776, of the laws and Constitution of the United States, and of the God of liberty, of law, of justice, and equality, it demands the most thorough investigation of this case, and claims that no imprisonment is legal by any order, either of judge lynch, of a committee of vigilance, town mob, or of any person who is not at the time fully qualified to act in so solemn a transaction as that of imprisoning a fellow man.

And clearly every man, under constitutional prohibition, is as incapable of rightful, valid, official action as if he was physically dead.

Moreover, it is contended that great inconvenience will result from the enforcement of the Constitution and the laws. That argument is one which I think ought not to be very popular in this community. Whatever inconvenience may result from the maintenance of the Constitution and the laws, I think the experience of the last few years shows that much greater inconvenience results from attempting their overthrow.

Where the words of the statute are clear, the argument of inconvenience is only for the legislature, and cannot be considered by the court. "Arguments drawn from impolicy or inconvenience," says Mr. Justice Story, "ought to have little weight. The only sound principle is to declare *ita lex scripta est*—to follow and to obey." (Conflict of Laws, 17.)

"Where the language is clear, and where, of course, the intent is manifest," says Mr. Chief Justice Shaw, "the court is not at liberty to be governed by considerations of inconvenience." (11 Pick., 407.)

In this case the language of the statute is perfectly clear, and the court is not at liberty to be governed by considerations of inconvenience.

The Constitution declares that "This Constitution, and the laws and treaties enacted in pursuance thereof, shall be the supreme law of the land. It does not say that they shall be the supreme law of the land when they are not found inconvenient. Had it so declared, the rebellion could have been accomplished without so much as a resort to arms.

As to any inconvenience which may arise, as is alleged, from turning criminals loose upon the community, an intelligent people will place the responsibility for that where it belongs, upon those who have presumed, in open defiance of the Constitution, to assume functions prohibited to them by that instrument, and not upon this court.

This circuit, in which the former circuit judge, Mr. Chief Justice Taney, spent almost his expiring breath in defence of the *habeas corpus*, is the last one in the country in which it should ever be shorn of its efficacy.

In that most celebrated case of James Sommerset, published in the English State Trials, Lord Mansfield well answered the argument of inconvenience, where it was urged that to discharge the petitioner would be to destroy the commercial supremacy of Great Britain.

In that case Charles Stewart, a Virginia planter, had, in 1769, just a hundred years ago, taken his slave Sommerset to England, where, incited perhaps by some Quaker or abolitionist, the slave ran away and claimed his freedom. The next year, when Stewart desired to sail for America, he caused the slave to be seized and put upon a vessel in the Thames. Lord Mansfield issued the writ of *habeas corpus*, and the case, after a second argument, the first not being entirely satisfactory, was decided in favor of the petitioner. Sergeant Davy closed his masterly speech in behalf of liberty in these magnificent words: "This air is too pure for a slave to breathe in."

Lord Mansfield, in his final disposition of the case, on the 22d June, 1772: "Whatever inconvenience therefore may follow from the decision, I cannot say this case is allowed or approved by the law of England; and, therefore, the black must be discharged."

In respectful imitation of these sublime authorities I will only add, the soil of Virginia, soaked with so much patriotic blood, poured out in the cause of constitutional, national sovereignty, should be fruitful in the products of peace, union, and fraternal concord, sustaining law-abiding men, implicitly obeying the Constitution of the country, and the proposition that no citizen, however humble, can be deprived of his liberty by the action of any pretended judge or other person in open defiance of a plain, palpable, clearly defined provision of that Constitution; and therefore, in my judgment, the petitioner should be discharged.

## Can a Negro hold Office in Georgia?

DECISION AND OPINIONS OF THE JUSTICES OF THE SUPREME COURT OF THAT STATE.

Before announcing the judgment of the court, Judge McCay said:

The case of Richard W. White, plaintiff in error, against the State of Georgia, on the relation of Wm. J. Clements, defendant in error, comes before this court on the following state of facts:

Wm. J. Clements applied to the judge of the superior court of Chatham county, alleging that, at an election which had been held in that county for a clerk of the superior court, he and Richard W. White were the sole candidates. That Richard W. White had got a majority of the votes, but that he, Clements, had also got a good many votes, and that no other persons were running. The petition further stated, that Richard W. White had been declared elected, and had been commissioned, and was in the actual performance of the duties of the office, and that Richard W. White was a person of color, having one-eighth or more of African blood in his veins. That, therefore, under the laws of Georgia, he was ineligible to office; and further, that under the laws of Georgia, as White, the person having the majority of votes, was ineligible, he, Clements, having received the next highest number of votes, was entitled to the position. He prayed the court for leave to file an information for a *quo warranto*. To that petition, of which White was notified, he (White) filed a demurrer. Subsequently, however, he withdrew the demurrer to that petition, and the information issued in the name of the State of Georgia. The court passed an order directing the solicitor general for that circuit to make out an information in the name of the State, reciting, in effect, the facts which had been recited in Clements' petition, and calling upon White to show cause why a *mandamus absolute* should not issue against him, depriving him of the office and putting Clements in. White, at the proper time fixed by the information for answering, filed a demurrer to the information, and at the same time filed an answer denying that he was a person of color, or that he had one-eighth or more of African blood in his veins.

On this the court summoned a jury for the purpose of trying the issue. When the jury had been sworn, the defendant below (the plaintiff here) called up his demurrer to the information. It is stated in the record that the plaintiff, in the information, made no objection to taking up the demurrer at that time, but consented; and the court heard the motion, as an independent motion, before the case was submitted to the jury. The court decided that in the argument upon that motion—that demurrer—Clements, the movant in the general proceeding, was entitled to open and conclude the argument; that, the matter being before the jury, the general rule which gives to the party moving in a demurrer the right to open and conclude did not apply.

The court heard the argument on the demurrer and overruled the demurrer. The case then went to the jury on the issue of fact, whether or not White had one-eighth or more of African blood in his veins. On the trial there were various questions made as to the testimony. One witness testified that the defendant, White, was reputed in the neighborhood to be a colored person. Another witness testified that he (the witness) was a registrar of voters; that when White registered, he, the registrar, had affixed opposite White's name the letter "C," to denote that he was a person of color; that he subsequently posted the lists in a public place, and that they had remained there two or three weeks, without any application having been made to him to have that letter "C" erased or changed. It did not appear, however, that there was any notice to White that this letter "C" had been placed opposite to his name, nor did it appear that it was the law or the practice that, if he had applied to have it corrected, they would have corrected it; in other words, that it was the part or the duty of the officer at all to make that entry. At least it has not so been made to appear to us.

This evidence was objected to by the defence, but admitted by the court. The court also admitted as evidence the statement by a physician, an examining physician of an insurance company, that at a previous time he had examined White, and had pronounced him a mulatto. There was no testimony by the physician of what his opinion was at the time of the trial. The testimony was that at some previous time he had examined him, and was at that previous time of opinion that he was a mulatto.

In the further progress of the trial they proposed to introduce a copy of an application for a life insurance on the life of White in favor of his wife, which application purported to be signed by White. The application does not seem to have a word in it as to whether White was a white man or black man, it gave no indication as to his color; but on the back of it there was an entry, by a person who purported to be an examining physician, that White was a mulatto. The witness swore at first that he thought White signed the paper, but swore afterwards that he didn't know whether White had signed it or whether his wife had signed it for him. Objection was made to this paper on three grounds: one, that it was a copy-paper, though it was proven that the original was in New York; the other that there was no proof that the original had been executed; and, third, that in any event the paper amounted to nothing.

Another witness, also a physician, swore that he was a practicing physician, and that he had studied the science of ethnology; that that science taught men the rules by which the race of a man was ascertained, and this witness gave his opinion upon the point. The court admitted his opinion, that White was a person of color,

as being the opinion of an expert. The case went to the jury on this testimony. There were some objections to the charge of the court, which we however have not noticed, because we didn't think the point very material. The jury found for the plaintiff in the information. Thereupon the court passed judgment, deposing White from his position as clerk of the superior court, and declaring that Clements was entitled to hold that office.

This case has been argued before us with a great deal of learning and ability.

This court has agreed upon the judgment which it will deliver in this case, but not upon the reasons upon which this judgment is founded. The court all agree that the judgment in the court below ought to be reversed, this court being unanimously of opinion that the court below erred in various of its rulings on the trial and on the question of the argument on the demurrer.

A majority of the court—the chief justice and myself—agree in the judgment that the court below erred in overruling the demurrer, it being our opinion that, under the Code of Georgia, a person of color is eligible to office in Georgia. My brother Brown, however, and myself do not exactly agree upon the grounds upon which we base that judgment. The statutes of the State of Georgia require that the court shall agree in the *decision* which it makes—the principle upon which it puts the case which it decides; and as my brother Warner, whilst he agrees to the general judgment, puts his opinion upon one set of grounds, and my brother the chief justice puts his upon another, while I put mine upon a third, we are unable to agree upon a statement of general principles upon which we put our judgment. Hence, under the statute, we shall each give a statement of the ground upon which we assent to the judgment of this court.

I will, therefore, now read the grounds upon which the whole court bases its decision, the ground upon which the majority of the court bases its decision, and I shall also announce the principles upon which I myself hold that the court below erred.

As this is a case of a good deal of public importance, involving not only the rights of the defendant and this plaintiff in error, but of a very large portion of the people of this State, and one in which there is a great deal of interest taken, I have reduced to writing, in detail, my opinion; and I will preface the reading of the judgment of the whole court and of the majority of the court with some written remarks, preferring to do that rather than make a parol introduction.

Whatever may have been, under the Constitution of the United States, the abstract truth as to the political condition and status of the people of Georgia at the close of the late war, from the stand-point of a mere observer, it seems to me perfectly conclusive that the several branches of the present State government are shut up in the doctrine that the constitution and frame of civil government in existence in this State on the 1st of January, 1861, with all its disabilities and restrictions, was totally submerged in the great revolution which from 1861 to 1865 swept over the State. Early in June, 1865, the governor of 1860 was in prison at Washington, and there was not in the whole State a single civil officer in the exercise of the functions of his office.

The whole body lately acting had been chosen under the laws of the Confederate States, and the incumbents of 1860 had all either died or resigned or renounced their positions as officers under the Consitution of the United States, by swearing fealty to the confederacy and repudiating the Government of the Union.

The people of the State were, in the language of the President, without civil government of any kind—in anarchy. The State, as a State of the federal Union, still existed, but without any frame of civil government regulating, restraining, and directing the exercise of its functions. From that time until the present State government went into operation, the government of the State was, with more or less completeness, in the hands of the military authorities of the United States, and the entire ancient civil polity of the State was totally ignored. Directly in the teeth of the old constitution, the people of color were recognized as freemen, and as entitled to equal legal and political rights with the whites. The convention of 1867 met under the laws of the United States, and was elected and composed in total disregard of all the provisions and presumptions, qualifications, disqualifications, and distinctions of the old organization.

The black people participated in its election and in its composition on equal terms, in theory at least, with the white, and nothing can to my mind be plainer, than that by the whole theory then acted upon they were recognized as forming an integral part of the sovereign people then assembled in convention to form for their common benefit a constitution and frame of civil government.

Such being the facts of the case, it appears to me that this court, deriving its whole authority from the constitution then framed, and sworn to support it, is, from the very nature of the case, absolutely prohibited from recognizing, as then or now in force, either the constitution of 1860 or 1865, or any of the legal or political disabilities or distinctions among the people dependent upon them or either of them.

The convention met under the laws of the United States to form a constitution for a people without civil government.

It had nothing to repeal, nothing to modify, nothing to grant. None of the old constitutions of the State were at the time in operation—the convention met under entirely new ideas and new presumptions. It represented a new people—a people among whom slavery had ceased, and among whom black people as well as white were recognized as forming part of the political society, and entitled to equal participation in its rights, privileges, and immunities.

It is not necessary, for the purposes of this argument, that this theory shall be proven to have been a legal one under the Constitution of the United States. It is sufficient to state that it is true as a fact, and that the present state government is based upon it.

If, when the convention met in December,

1867, the ancient constitution of the State or any of its legal or political disabilities or disqualifying distinctions upon persons of color, were of force, then the convention itself was illegal, the present state government is illegal, this court is illegal? His honor the chief justice has his proper place in the executive chair, my respected associate and myself are private citizens, the plaintiff in error is a slave, and the whole political history of the State, since the imprisonment of Governor Brown, in June, 1865, a gigantic illegality.

I am aware that a very large class of our most intelligent people so at this moment honestly believe: to them this argument is not directed. But it seems to me that to a judge, holding his office under the present State government, forming an essential part of its machinery, these views must be of overwhelming force. If he assumes the power to decide at all, he must, it seems to me, base his judgment upon principles which do not, if adopted in his own case, utterly subvert his own authority.

I make these remarks with the greatest deference to the integrity and to the sound legal acumen of my associates. Honest men see things in different lights, and it is as presumptuous as it is uncharitable for one man to set up his convictions as the necessary guide of the conscience of another. These are my convictions, and as a matter of course I must act upon them, and accordingly, under the rules prescribed by the statute, I announce, as the general principles controlling my judgment in this case, the following :

By the whole court :

1. The statement of a registrar of voters that he had marked a registered person's name with a "C," to denote that he was colored, and had posted his lists for some time in a public place, and that no application had been made to have the said "C" erased, is no evidence that the person is a colored person, it not being shown that the person knew of the entry and that it was the subject of correction.

2. Although a copy of a paper proven to be beyond the jurisdiction of the court is good secondary evidence of its contents, yet it must be shown that the original was duly executed.

3. An application for a life insurance, though signed by the applicant, upon the back of which was an entry by the examining physician that the applicant was a mulatto, is no evidence, unless it be proven that the person signed the paper after the entry on it was made by the physician, and with knowledge of the entry and with intent to adopt it, or that he used the paper after the entry was made with a knowledge that such entry was there.

4. The statement by an examining physician that he had at a certain time examined a person, and had then been of the opinion that the person was a mulatto, is not evidence. If the physician is an expert, he must give his present opinion, and if not, he must state the facts upon which he bases his opinion. Whether or not one is a person of color, that is, has African blood in his veins, is matter of opinion, and a witness may give his opinion, if he states the facts upon which it is based. But whether the

fact that he has one-eighth or more of such blood be matter of opinion or not, query?

5. One who testifies that he has studied the science of ethnology may give his opinion as an expert on the question of race. Its weight is for the jury.

Pedigree, relationship, and race may be proven by evidence of reputation among those who know the person whose pedigree or race is in question.

The whole court agree upon those propositions.

The majority of the court agree upon this proposition: Where a *quo warranto* was issued charging that a person holding an office was ineligible when chosen because of his having in his veins one-eighth or more of African blood, and there was a demurrer to the information, as well as an answer denying the fact, upon which denial there was an issue and a trial before the jury: held, that, by the Code of Georgia, a person having one-eighth or more of African blood in his veins is not ineligible to office in this State, and it was error in the court to overrule the demurrer and to charge the jury that if the plaintiff proved the defendant to have one-eighth or more of African blood he was ineligible to office in this State.

Whilst I agree that the Code of Georgia—the law of Georgia, as separate from the constitution—does make persons of color eligible to office, my opinion is that eligibility is guaranteed by the constitution of the State; and I announce these propositions as the general principles upon which my opinion is based:

1st. The constitution of Georgia, known as the constitution of 1868, is a new constitution, made by and formed for a people who at the time were by the facts of the case and by the laws of the United States without any legal civil government; and as the people of Georgia, without regard to past political distinctions, and without regard to distinctions of color, participated on equal terms in the election for the convention and in its composition and deliberations, as well as in the final ratification of the constitution it framed, in the construction of that constitution, and in the investigation of what rights it guarantees or denies, such distinctions are equally to be ignored.

2d. The rights of the people of this State, white and black, are not granted to them by the constitution thereof. The object and effect of that instrument is not to give, but to restrain, deny, regulate, and guarantee rights; and all persons recognized by that constitution as citizens of the State have equal legal and political rights, except as otherwise expressly declared.

3d. It is the settled and uniform sense of the word "citizen," when used in reference to the citizens of the several States of the United States and to their rights as such citizens, that it describes a person entitled to every right, legal and political, enjoyed by any person in that State, unless there be some express exception, made by positive law, covering the particular person, or class of persons, whose rights are in question.

4th. Words used in a statute or constitution have their ordinary signification, unless they be words of art, when they have the sense placed upon them by those skilled in the art, or unless their meaning be defined and fixed by law; in which latter case the legal meaning must prevail.

5th. By the 1648th and 1649th sections of Irwin's Revised Code, it is expressly declared, that among the rights of citizens is the right to hold office, and that all citizens are entitled to exercise all their rights as such, unless expressly prohibited by law; and as the constitution of 1868 expressly adopts said Code as the law of the State, when that constitution uses the word "citizen," it uses it in the sense put upon it by the express definition of the Code it adopted.

6th. Article 1 and section 2 of the constitution of 1868 expressly declares that all persons born in the United States, or naturalized therein, resident in this State, are citizens of this State; and as the Code adopted by the convention in express terms declares that among the rights of citizens is the right to hold office, a colored person born in the United States, and resident in this State, is by that section of the constitution guaranteed eligibility to office, except when otherwise prohibited.

7th. Nor would the repeal of those sections of the Code or their alteration deprive a colored person of the right thus guaranteed, since it is a settled rule that it is not in the power of the legislature to divest a right or change a constitutional guaranty by altering the legal meaning of the word by which that guaranty was made.

8th. The right to vote involves the right to be voted for, unless otherwise expressly provided, since it is not to be presumed, without an express enactment, that the principal is of less dignity or rights than the agent.

9th. There being in the constitution of 1868 various special disqualifications of electors for particular offices, and four separate sections detailing disqualifications for any office, and a black skin not being mentioned as one of these disqualifications, under the rule that the expression, &c., of one thing is the exclusion of others, persons of color electors are not disqualified from holding office.

10th. There never has been in this State, at any period of its history, any denial in terms of the right to vote or to hold office to colored persons, as such. By the old law, they were either slaves or free persons of color, and these rights were denied them, by declaring that they were not and could not be citizens of the State; and when article 1 section 2 of the constitution of 1868 recognized them as citizens, the right to vote and to hold office, except as otherwise provided by the constitution, was, *ex vi termini*, also guaranteed to them.

11th. Ineligibility to office involves not only the denial to the person claiming the place the right to be chosen, but, what is of far greater moment, the right of the selecting power to choose; and to make out a case of ineligibility there must be such a state of affairs as established not only the want of power to be chosen, but a denial of power in the selecting party to choose.

12th. The people of a State, in their collective capacity, have every right a political society can have, except such as they have conferred upon the United States, or on some department of the State government, or have expressly denied to themselves by their constitution; and as the right to select a public officer is a political right, the people, or that branch of the government clothed by the constitution with the power to choose, may select whomsoever it will, unless the right to choose a particular person or class of persons is expressly taken away by the constitution. —

Chief Justice Brown then read from his written opinion, as follows:

The view which I take of the rights of the parties litigant in this case, under the Code of Georgia, renders it unnecessary for me to enter into an investigation of the question, whether the XIVth amendment of the Constitution of the United States, or the second section of the first article of the constitution of Georgia, which in substance is identical with the XIVth amendment, confers upon colored citizens the right to hold office. If the respondent in this case acquires the right by grant found in either of the said Constitutions, or in the Code of this State, it is sufficient for all the purposes of the case at bar, and entitles him to a reversal of the judgment of the court below, which was adverse to his right.

The third paragraph of the 9th article of the constitution of this State adopts, in subordination to the Constitution of the United States and the laws and treaties made in pursuance thereof, and in subordination to the said constitution of this State, the "body of laws known as the Code of Georgia, and the acts amendatory thereof, which said Code and acts are embodied in the printed book known as Irwin's Code," "except so much of the said several statutes, Code, and laws, as may be inconsistent with the supreme law herein recognized."

The Code, section 1646, classifies natural persons into four classes: 1st, citizens; 2d, residents; 3d, aliens; 4th, persons of color.

Section 46 of the Code declares that all *white* persons born in this State, or in any other State of this Union, who are or may become residents of this State with the intention of remaining herein; all *white* persons naturalized under the laws of the United States, and who are or may become residents of this State with the intention of remaining herein; all persons who have obtained a right to citizenship under former laws, and all children, wherever born, whose father was a citizen of this State at the time of the birth of such children, or in case of posthumous children at the time of his death, are held and deemed citizens of this State.

By the Code the distinction is therefore clearly drawn between citizens who are *white* persons and persons of color.

In other words, none are citizens under the "printed book known as Irwin's Code" but white persons. Having specified the class of persons who are citizens, the Code proceeds, in section 1648, to define some of the rights of citizens, as follows:

"Among the rights of citizens are the enjoyment of personal security, of personal liberty, private property and the disposition thereof, the elective franchise, *the right to hold office*, to appeal to the courts, to testify as a witness, to perform any civil function, and to keep and bear arms."

Section 1649 declares that "*All* citizens are entitled to exercise *all* their rights as such unless specially prohibited by law."

Section 1650 prohibits females from exercising the elective franchise or holding civil office.

Section 1651 prohibits minors from the exercise of civil functions till they are of legal age.

Sections 1652 and 1653 prohibit certain criminals, and persons *non compos mentis*, from exercising certain rights of citizens.

Article 3, chapter 1, title 1, part 2, of the Code, defines the rights of the 4th class of natural persons, designated as persons of color, giving them the right to make contracts; sue and be sued, give evidence, inherit, purchase and sell property; and to have marital rights, security of person, estate, &c., embracing the usual civil rights of citizens, but does not confer citizenship. Thus the Code stood prior to its adoption by the new constitution.

As already shown, it was adopted in subordination to the constitution, and must yield to the fundamental law whenever in conflict with it. In so far as the Code had conferred rights on the colored race, there is no conflict and no repeal. The constitution took away no right then possessed by them under the Code, but it enlarged their rights, as defined in the Code, by conferring upon them the right of citizenship. It transferred them from the 4th class of natural persons, under the above classification, who were denied citizenship by the Code, to the 1st class, as citizens.

The 46th section of the Code limited citizenship to white persons. The constitution struck out the word white, and made all persons born or naturalized in the United States, and resident in this State, citizens, without regard to race or color. It so amended section 46 of the Code as greatly to enlarge the class of citizens; but it repealed no part of section 1648, which defines the rights of citizens.

It did not undertake to define the rights of a citizen. It left that to the legislature, subject to such guarantees as are contained in the constitution itself, which the legislature cannot take away. It declares expressly that no law shall be made or enforced which shall "abridge the privileges or immunities of citizens of the United States or of this State." It is not necessary to the decision of this case to inquire what are the "privileges and immunities" of a citizen which are guaranteed by the XIVth amendment to the Constitution of the United States and by the constitution of this State. Whatever they may be, they are protected against all abridgment by legislation. This is the full extent of the constitutional guaranty. All rights of the citizen not embraced within these terms, if they do not embrace all, are subject to the control of the legislature.

Whether the "privileges and immunities" of the citizen embrace political rights, including the right to hold office, I need not now inquire. If they do, that right is guaranteed alike by the Constitution of the United States, and the constitution of Georgia, and is beyond the control of legislation. If not, that right is subject to the control of the legislature, as the popular voice may dictate; and in that case the legislature would have power to grant or restrict it at pleasure, in case of white persons as well as of persons of color. The constitution of Georgia has gone as far as the XIVth amendment has gone, but no further. An authoritative construction of the XIVth amendment by the Supreme Court of the United States upon this point would be equally binding as a construction of the constitution of the State of Georgia, which is in the same words.

Georgia has complied fully with the terms dictated by Congress in the formation of her constitution. She has stopped nothing short, and gone nothing beyond. The highest judicial tribunal of the Union will no doubt finally settle the meaning of the terms "privileges and immunities" of the citizen, which legislation cannot abridge; and the people of Georgia, as well as those of all the other States, must conform to, and in good faith abide by, and carry out, the decision. All the rights, of all the citizens of every State, which are included in the phrase "privileges and immunities," are protected against legislative abridgment by the fundamental law of the Union. Those not so embraced, unless included within some other constitutional guarantee, are subject to legislative action. These same rights which the XIVth amendment to the Constitution of the United States confers upon, and guarantees to, a colored citizen of Ohio, are conferred upon and guaranteed to every colored citizen of Georgia, by the same amendment, and by the constitution of the State, made in conformity to the reconstruction acts of Congress.

Whatever may or may not be the privileges and immunities guaranteed to the colored race by the Constitution of the United States and of this State, it cannot be questioned that both Constitutions make them citizens. And I think it very clear that the Code of Georgia, upon which alone I base this opinion, which is binding upon all her inhabitants while of force, confers upon all her citizens the right to hold office, unless they are prohibited by some provision found in the Code itself. I find no such prohibition in the Code affecting the rights of this respondent. I am, therefore, of the opinion that the judgment of the court below is erroneous, and I concur in the judgment of reversal.

___

DISSENTING OPINION OF JUDGE HIRAM WARNER.

The defendant is a person of color, having, as the record states, one-eighth of negro or African blood in his veins, who claims to be lawfully entitled to hold and exercise the duties of the office of clerk of the superior court of Chatham county, and the question presented for our consideration and judgment is, whether a person of color, of the description mentioned in the record, is legally entitled to hold office in this State, under the constitution and laws thereof?

The XIVth amendment to the Constitution of the United States declares that "all persons born or naturalized in the United States, and subject to the jurisdiction thereof, are citizens of the United States and the State wherein they reside. No State shall make or enforce any law which shall abridge the privileges or immunities of citizens of the United States."

The constitution of this State declares that "all persons born or naturalized in the United States, and resident in this State, are hereby declared citizens of this State, and no laws shall be made or enforced which shall abridge the privileges or immunities of citizens of the United States, or of this State."

From the time of the adoption of the XIVth amendment and the adoption and ratification of the constitution of this State in 1868, the defendant became (notwithstanding his color and African blood) a citizen of the United States and of this State, and is entitled to have all the privileges and immunities of a citizen.

Does the fact that the defendant was made a citizen of the State, with all the privileges or immunities of a citizen thereof, confer upon him the legal right to hold office in this State as such citizen? When we take into consideration the definition and object of creating an office, and by what authority it is conferred upon a citizen, the distinction between the privileges and immunities of a citizen, as such, and his right to hold office, will be at once apparent. It will be seen that the privileges and immunities of a citizen, as such, is one thing, and that his legal right to hold office as such citizen, under the authority of the State, is another and quite a different question. What is an office? "An office," says Bacon, "is a right to exercise a public function or employment, and to take the fees and emoluments belonging to it. An officer is one who is lawfully invested with an office. It is said that the word *officium* principally implies a duty, and in the next place the charge of such duty, and that it is a rule that, where one man hath to do with another's affairs against his will, and without his leave, that this is an office, and he who is in it is an officer. By the ancient common law officers ought to be honest men, legal and sage, *et qui melius sciant et possint officis in intendre*, and this, says my Lord Coke was the policy of prudent antiquity, that officers did even give grace to the place, and not the place only to grace the officer." (7th Bacon's Ab., 270, title Offices and Officers.) Blackstone says, the king, in England, is the fountain of honor and of office, and the reason given is, that the law supposes that no one can be so good a judge of an officer's merits and services as the king, who employs him.

"From the same principle also arises the prerogative of creating and disposing of offices, for honors and offices are in their nature convertible and synonymous. All officers under the crown carry, in the eye of the law, an honor along with them, because they imply a superiority of parts and abilities, being supposed to be always filled with those that are most able to execute them." (1 Bl. Com., 271, 272.) Officers, says Blackstone, have a right to exercise a public or private employment, and to take the fees and emoluments thereunto belonging, and are also incorporeal hereditaments. (2 Bl. Com., 36.)

All citizens of the State, whether white or colored, male or female, minors or adults, idiot or lunatic, are entitled to have all the privileges and immunities of citizens, but it does not follow that all of these different classes of citizens are entitled to hold office under the public authority of the State because the privileges and immunities of citizens are secured to them. The State in this country, as the crown in England, is the fountain of honor and of office, and she who desires to employ any class of her citizens in her service is the best judge of their fitness and qualifications therefor. An officer of the State, as we have shown, "hath to do with another's affairs against his will and without his leave," and such officer must have the authority of the State to perform these public duties against the will of the citizen and without his leave. This authority must be conferred upon the citizen by some public law of the State from that class of her citizens which, in her judgment, will best promote the general welfare of the State. The right to have and enjoy the privileges and immunities of a citizen of the State does not confer upon him the right to serve the State in any official capacity until that right is expressly granted to him by law. Mr. Justice Curtis, in his dissenting opinion in the case of Dred Scott *v.* Sanford, 19 How., pp. 3 and 5, says: "So in all the States, numerous persons, though citizens, cannot vote or cannot hold office, either on account of their age or sex, or the want of the necessary legal qualifications." (Corfield *v.* Corvell, 4 Wash. C. C. Rep., 1 and 3, to the same point.)

The defendant, therefore, cannot legally claim any right to hold office either under the XIVth amendment of the Constitution of the United States or the constitution of this State, which make him a citizen, and guarantee unto him the privileges or immunities of a citizen, for he may well have and enjoy all the privileges and immunities of a citizen in the State without holding any office, or exercising any public or official duty under the authority of the State.

The privileges and immunities of a citizen of the State do not confer the legal right to hold office under the public authority of the State and receive the emoluments thereof. Does the public law of the State, recognized and adopted by the constitution of 1868, (known as Irwin's Code,) confer upon the defendant the legal right to hold office in this State?

The Code took effect as the public law of this State on the 1st day of January, 1863. By the 46th section thereof it is declared, " All white persons born in this State, or in any other State of this Union, who are or may become residents of this State, with the intention of remaining herein; all white persons naturalized under the laws of the United States, and who are or may become residents of this State, with the intention of remaining herein; all persons who have obtained a right to citizenship under former laws; and all children wherever born whose father was a citizen of this State at the time of the birth of such children, or in case of posthumous children at the time of his death, are held and deemed citizens of this State. Persons having one-eighth or more of negro or African blood in their veins are not 'white persons in the meaning of this Code. The 1646th section declares, that 'Natural persons are distinguished

according to their rights and status, into, 1st, citizens; 2d, residents, not citizens; 3d, aliens; 4th, persons of color."

The persons to whom belong the rights of citizenship and the mode of acquiring and losing the same have been specified in a former article, (referring to article 46, before cited. Among the rights of citizens are the enjoyment of personal security, of personal liberty, private property and the disposition thereof, the elective franchise, the right to hold office, to appeal to the courts, to testify as a witness, to perform any civil function, and to keep and bear arms. All citizens are entitled to exercise all these rights, as such, unless specially prohibited by law. (Sections 1647, 1648, 1649, 1650, 1651, 1652, 1653 of the Code.)

It will be remembered that, at the time of the adoption of the Code, in 1863, the defendant was not a citizen of this State, and was not recognized by the Code as a citizen thereof. By the 1646th section the status of the defendant is defined to be that of a person of color, and not that of a citizen.

The revised Code, adopted by the constitution of 1868, includes the act of 1866, which declares that "all negroes, mulattoes, mestizoes, and their descendants, having one-eighth of negro or African blood in their veins, shall be known in this State as persons of color," and especially defines their legal rights, but the right to hold office is not one of them. (Revised Code, section 1661.)

It is true that since the adoption of the Code the defendant has been made a citizen, but all the legal rights conferred upon citizens by the Code were conferred upon that class of persons only who are declared and recognized by the Code as citizens of the State at the time of its adoption. When the Code declares that it shall be the right of a citizen to hold office, such right is confined to that class of persons who are recognized and declared therein to be citizens of the State, and not to any other class of persons who might thereafter become citizens. So, where the Code declares that "all citizens are entitled to exercise all their rights as such, unless prohibited by law," it is applicable to that class of persons only who were declared to be citizens of the State at that time, and not to any other class of persons who might thereafter be made citizens of the State, such as Chinese, Africans, or persons of color. The truth is that the public will of the State has never been expressed by any legislative enactment in favor of the right of the colored citizen to hold office in this State since they became citizens thereof.

Although these several classes of persons might be made citizens of the State, with the privileges and immunities of citizens, still they could not legally hold office under the authority of the State until that right shall be conferred upon them by some public law of the State, subsequent to the time at which they became citizens, so as to include them in its provisions. The public will of the State, as to the legal right of that class of her citizens to hold office, has never been affirmatively expressed; but, on the contrary, when the proposition was distinctly made in the convention which formed the present constitution to confer the right upon colored citizens to hold office in this State, it was voted down by a large majority. (See Journal of Convention, p. 312.) So far as there has been any expression of the public will of the State as to the legal right of that class of citizens known as colored citizens, and since they became such, to hold office in this State, it is against that right now claimed by the defendant.

The insurmountable obstacle in the way of the defendant claiming a legal right to hold office in this State under the provisions of the Code is the fact that he was not a citizen of the State at the time of its adoption. The class of persons to which he belongs were not recognized by it as citizens, and therefore he is not included in any of its provisions which confer the right to hold office upon the class of citizens specified in the Code. The Code makes no provision whatever for colored citizens to hold office in this State; all its provisions apply exclusively to white citizens and to no other class of citizens.

The convention which framed the present State constitution, and declared persons of color to be citizens, could have conferred the right upon them to hold office, but declined to do so by a very decided vote of that body, and went before the people claiming its ratification upon the ground that colored citizens were not entitled to hold office under it; and there can be no doubt that the people of the State voted for its ratification at the ballot-box with that understanding.

But now it is contended that the defendant, though a colored person, is made a citizen of the State and of the United States, and that no enabling act has ever been passed to allow a naturalized citizen to hold office in this State when he possessed the other requisite qualifications prescribed by law; that the defendant, having been made a citizen of the State, is entitled to hold office in the same manner as a naturalized citizen could do. The reply is, that naturalized citizens were white persons, and as such had a common-law right to hold office—a right founded upon immemorial usage and custom, which has existed so long that "the memory of man runneth not to the contrary." The 1644th section of the Code simply affirms the common law as to the right of a white citizen to hold office in this State. No such common-law right, however, can be claimed in this State in favor of persons of color to hold office. They have but recently become entitled to citizenship, and have never held office in this State. In 1848, in the case of Cooper and Worsham *against* The Mayor and Aldermen of the City of Savannah, (4 Ga. Reps. 72,) it was unanimously held and decided by this court, that free persons of color were not entitled to hold any civil office in this State. The naturalized white citizen can claim his common-law right to hold office in this State; the colored citizen cannot claim any such common-law right, for the reason that he has never exercised and enjoyed it; and that constitutes the difference between the legal right of a naturalized white citizen to hold office in this State, and a person of color who has recently been made a citizen "since the adoption of the Code, and who is not embraced within its provisions."

The one can claim his common-law right to hold office in the State, the other cannot; and until the State shall declare by some legislative enactment that it is her will and desire that her colored citizens shall hold office under her authority, they cannot claim the legal right to do so, for we must not forget that the State is the fountain and parent of office, and may confer or refuse to confer the right to hold office upon any class of her citizens she may think proper and expedient.

When a new class of persons are introduced into the body politic of the State and made citizens thereof, who cannot claim a common-law right to hold office therein, it is incumbent on them to show affirmatively that such right has been conferred upon them by some public law of the State since they were made citizens thereof, to entitle them to have and enjoy such right. In other words, they must show the public law of the State enacted since they became citizens thereof, which confers the legal right claimed, before they can demand a judgment of the court in favor of such legal right.

All male white citizens of the State, whether native born or naturalized citizens, (having the necessary legal qualifications,) have a common-law right to hold office in this State; and, in order to deprive them of that common-law right, a prohibitory statute is necessary. A naturalized citizen had a common-law right to hold the office of President of the United States; hence the prohibition in the Constitution of the United States. But colored citizens of the State, who have recently been made such, cannot claim a common-law right to hold office in the State, as no prohibitory statute is necessary to deprive them of a right which they never had under the common or statute law of the State. When, therefore, it is said that colored citizens have the right to hold office in the State, unless specially prohibited by law, it must be shown affirmatively that they had previously enjoyed that right. If they cannot show their right to hold office in the State, either under the common law, the constitution, or statutes of the State, the fact that they are not specially prohibited from exercising a right which they never had amounts to nothing, so far as investing them with the right to hold office is concerned.

When and where and by what public law of the State was the legal right to hold office therein conferred on the colored citizens thereof? If this question cannot be answered in the affirmative, and the legal authority under which the right is claimed cannot be shown, then the argument, that inasmuch as there is no special prohibition in the law against the right of colored citizens to hold office, falls to the ground. If there was no existing legal right to hold office to be prohibited, the fact that there is no prohibition does not confer such legal right. There was no legal necessity to prohibit that which did not exist.

It is not the business or duty of courts to make the laws, but simply to expound and enforce existing laws which have been prescribed by the supreme power of the State.

After the most careful examination of this question, I am clearly of the opinion that there is no existing law of this State which confers the right upon the colored citizens thereof to hold office therein, and, consequently, that the defendant has no legal right to hold and exercise the duties of the office which he claims under her authority, and that the judgment of the court below, overruling the demurrer, should be affirmed.

## Intermarriage of White and Colored Persons in Georgia.

Opinion of the Supreme Court of that State.

Charlotte Scott, plaintiff in error *vs.* The State of Georgia, defendant in error. Indictment for adultery and fornication, from Dougherty county.

Brown, C. J., delivering the opinion.

The record in this case presents a single question for the consideration and adjudication of this court: Have white persons and persons of color the right, under the constitution and laws of Georgia, to intermarry, and live together in this State as husband and wife? The question is distinctly made, and it is our duty to meet it fairly and dispose of it.

The Code of Georgia, as adopted by the new constitution, section 1707, forever prohibits the marriage relation between the two races, and declares all such marriages null and void.

With the policy of this law we have nothing to do. It is our duty to declare what the law is, not to make law. For myself, however, I do not hesitate to say that it was dictated by wise statesmanship, and has a broad and solid foundation in enlightened policy, sustained by sound reason and common sense. The amalgamation of the races is not only unnatural, but is always productive of deplorable results. Our daily observation shows us that the offspring of these unnatural connections are generally sickly and effeminate, and that they are inferior in physical development and strength to the full blood of either race. It is sometimes urged that such marriages should be encouraged for the purpose of elevating the inferior race. The reply is, that such connections never elevate the inferior race to the position of the superior, but they bring down the superior to that of the inferior. They are productive of evil and evil only, without any corresponding good.

I do not propose to enter into any elaborate discussion of the question of policy at this time, but only to express my opinion after mature consideration and reflection.

The power of the legislature over the subject matter, when the Code was adopted, will not, I suppose, be questioned. The legislature certainly had as much right to regulate the marriage relation, by prohibiting it between persons of different races, as they had to prohibit it between persons within the levitical degrees, or between idiots. Both are necessary and proper regulations. And the regulation now under consideration is equally so.

But it has been urged by the learned counsel for the plaintiff in error, that the section of the Code under consideration is in conflict with the eleventh section of the first article of the constitution of this State, which declares that "the social status of the citizen shall never be the subject of legislation."

In so far as the marriage relation is connected with the social status, the very reverse is true. That section of the constitution forever prohibits legislation of any character regulating or interfering with the social status.

It leaves social rights and status where it finds them. It prohibits the legislature from repealing any laws in existence which protect persons in the free regulation among themselves of matters properly termed social, and it also prohibits the enactment of any new laws on that subject in future.

As illustrations, the laws in force when the constitution was adopted left the churches in this State free to regulate matters connected with social status in their congregations as they thought proper. They could say who should enter their church edifices and occupy seats, and in what order they should be classified or seated. They could say that females should sit in one part of the church and males in another; and that persons of color should, if they attended, occupy such seats as were set apart for them. In all this they were protected by the common law of this State. The new constitution forever guarantees this protection, by denying to the legislature the power to pass any law withdrawing it or regulating the social status in such assemblages.

And I may here remark, that precisely the same protection is guaranteed to the colored churches, in the regulation of social status in their assemblages, which is afforded the whites. Neither can ever intrude upon the other, or interfere with social arrangements without their consent.

The same is true of railroad and steamboat companies and hotel keepers. By the law in existence at the time the constitution was adopted, they were obliged to furnish comfortable and convenient accommodations, to the extent of their capacity to accommodate, to all who applied, without regard to race or color. But they were not compelled to put persons of different races or of different sexes in the same cars or in the same apartments, or seat them at the same table. This was left to their own discretion. They had power to regulate it according to their own notions of propriety, and to classify their guests or passengers according to race or sex; and to place them at hotels in different houses or different parts of the same house; or on railroads, in different cars; or on steamboats, in different parts of the vessel; and to give them their meals at different tables. When they had made public these regulations, all persons patronizing them were bound to conform to them, and those who did not like their regulations must seek accommodations elsewhere. There was no law to compel them to group together, in social connection, persons who did not recognize each other as social equals.

To avoid collisions and strife, and to preserve peace, harmony, and good order in society, the new constitution has wisely prohibited the legislature from enacting laws compelling these companies to make new social arrangements among their patrons, or to disturb those in existence. The law shall stand as it is, says the constitution, leaving each to regulate such matters as they think best, and there shall be no legislative interference. All shall be comfortably accommodated, but you shall not be compelled by law to force social equality, either upon your trains, your boats, or in your hotels.

The same remarks apply to the regulation of social status among families, and to the social intercourse of society generally.

This, in my opinion, is one of the wisest provisions in the constitution, as it excludes from the halls of the legislature a question which was likely to produce more unprofitable agitation, wrangling, and contention than any other subject within the whole range of their authority.

Government has full power to regulate civil and political rights, and to give to each citizen of the State, as our Code has done, equal civil and equal political rights, as well as equal protection of the laws. But government has no power to regulate social status. Before the laws the Code of Georgia makes all citizens equal, without regard to race or color; but it does not create, nor does any law of the State attempt to enforce, moral or social equality between the different races or citizens of the State. Such equality does not in fact exist and never can. The God of nature made it otherwise, and no human law can produce it, and no human tribunal can enforce it. There are gradations and classes throughout the universe. From the tallest archangel in heaven down to the meanest reptile on earth moral and social inequalities exist, and must continue to exist throughout all eternity.

While the great mass of the conquering people of the States which adhered to the Union during the late civil strife have claimed the right to dictate the terms of settlement, and have maintained in power those who demand that the people of the States lately in rebellion shall accord to the colored race equality of civil rights, including the ballot, with the same protection under the law which is offered the white race, they have neither required of us the practice of miscegenation, nor have they claimed for the colored race social equality with the white race. The fortunes of war have compelled us to yield to the freedmen the legal rights above mentioned, but we have neither authorized nor legalized the marriage relation between the races, nor have we enacted laws or placed it in the power of the legislature hereafter to make laws regarding the social status, so as to compel our people to meet the colored race on terms of social equality. Such a state of things could never be desired by the thoughtful and reflecting portion of either race. It could never promote peace, quiet, or social order in any State or community. No such laws are of force in any of the northern States, so far as I know, and it is supposed no considerable part of the people of any State desires to see them enacted. Indeed, the most absolute and despotic governments do not attempt to regulate social status by fixed laws, or to enforce social equality among races or classes without their consent.

As already stated, we are of the opinion that the section of the Code which forbids intermarriages between the races is neither inconsistent with, nor is it repealed by, the section of the constitution now under consideration. It therefore stands upon the statute-book of the State forever prohibiting all such marriages, and declaring them to be *null* and *void*.

Let the judgment of the court below be affirmed.

---

## Opinion of Attorney General Hoar as to the Jurisdiction of Military Commissions in Texas.

ATTORNEY GENERAL'S OFFICE,
*May 31, 1869.*

Hon. JOHN A. RAWLINS,
*Secretary of War.*

SIR: Your letter of March 24, 1869, submitting for my opinion as to proper action to be had in the premises in the case of James Weaver, a citizen of Texas, who was tried before a military commission appointed by the commanding general of the fifth military district, under authority of section 3 of the act of March 2, 1867, to provide for the more efficient government of rebel States, and found guilty of murder and sentenced to be hanged, the record having been forwarded for the action of the President, as required by section 4 of said act, and returned by him to your department upon the 1st day of February last, without any action upon the same, was received on the 26th March last.

The grave importance of the questions involved required such careful and deliberate consideration, that, under the pressure of other official duties, I have not been able, until this time, to give it sufficient attention. Having now carefully examined it, I proceed to state the conclusions to which I have arrived from the papers accompanying your letter. It appears that James Weaver, a citizen of Bastrop county, in Texas, was indicted for murder in that county. By request of J. J. Thornton, district judge of the second district in Texas, made to General Reynolds, the commander of the fifth military district, accompanied by statement that a trial could not probably be had in the State courts, and asking that he may be tried by the military authorities, a military commission was organized at Austin, Texas, before which, on the 17th of September, 1868, and days following, Weaver was arraigned and tried. He was defended by counsel and found guilty, and sentenced to be hanged, and the question on which you wish my opinion seems to be this: Whether the general commanding the fifth military district had authority to take a man from a civil power and try him by military law, or, in other words, whether a military commission in Texas, in September, 1868, had jurisdiction over a citizen, not in the naval or military service, charged with the murder of another citizen, and under indictment and arrest therefor. From the letter of Judge Thornton to General Reynolds, above referred to, which is made a part of the record in this case, it appears Weaver was under indictment in the district court for the second judicial district of Texas for murder, and that the civil courts were so badly situated and managed that if left with them no trial could probably be had. Exceptions to the jurisdiction of the commission were filed by Weaver, who objected, firstly, that he was entitled to a trial by jury; secondly, that the Constitution of the United States provides that no person shall be twice put in jeopardy of life or limb for the same offence, that the offence with which he was charged belonged entirely to the civil courts of the State of Texas, and that he would be unable to plead the finding of the commission in bar in the district court in Bastrop county; thirdly, that before the date of the order convening the commission he was under indictment in civil courts and was under arrest to await trial therein, and that the said indictment for the same offence was still pending against him; fourthly, because the district court of Bastroy county was fully organized and prepared to pass upon all cases brought before it; fifthly, because he, the said Weaver, was a citizen, not connected with the army of the United States, and deceased was also a citizen. These exceptions were overruled by the commission. The statute of March 2, 1867, entitled "An act to provide for the more efficient government of the rebel States," declares in its preamble that no legal State governments or adequate protection for life or property then existed in the rebel States therein enumerated, including among them the State of Texas, and that it was necessary that peace and good order should be enforced in said States until loyal and republican State governments could be legally established: it is therefore enacted, that said rebel States should be made into military districts, and made subject to the military authority of the United States, as thereinafter prescribed; that it should be the duty of the President to assign to the command of each of said districts an officer of the army, and to detail a sufficient military force to enable such officer to perform his duties and enforce his authority in the district to which he was assigned. The 3d and 4th sections of said act are as follows:

"SEC. 3. *And be it further enacted*, That it shall be the duty of each officer assigned as aforesaid to protect all persons in their rights of person and property; to suppress insurrection, disorder, and violence, and to punish, or cause to be punished, all disturbers of the public peace and criminals; and to this end he may allow local civil tribunals to take jurisdiction of and to try offenders; or, when in his judgment it may be necessary for the trial of offenders, he shall have power to organize military commissions or tribunals for that purpose; and all interference under the color of State authority with the exercise of military authority under this act shall be null and void.

"SEC. 4. *And be it further enacted*, That all persons put under military arrest by virtue of this act shall be tried without unnecessary delay, and no cruel or unusual punishment shall be inflicted; and no sentence of any military commission or tribunal hereby authorized, affecting the life or liberty of any person, shall be executed until it is approved by the officer in command of the district. And the laws and regulations for the government of the army shall not be affected by this act except in so far as they conflict with its provisions: *Provided*, That no sentence of death under the provisions of this act shall be carried into effect without the approval of the President.".

The act also provided that its provisions should become inoperative when the States had adopted constitutions approved by Congress and senators and representatives were admitted therefrom;

and that until the people of said States should be by law admitted to representation in Congress, any civil governments which may exist therein shall be deemed provisional only, and in all respects subject to the paramount authority of the United States at any time to abolish, modify, control, or supersede the same. As the State of Texas had not in September, 1868, and has not since, adopted a constitution in conformity with the provisions of the act, and has not become entitled to representation in the Congress of the United States, the act was operative in Texas at the time the military commission was organized for the trial of Weaver, and the commanding general exercised this discretion intrusted to him by 3d section, by deciding that it was necessary for the trial of an offender to organize a military commission for that purpose. If, therefore, this statute of March 2, 1867, is a constitutional and valid statute, it then appears the jurisdiction of military commissions was complete, and that there is no legal obstacle to the execution of its sentence. It is obvious, in the first place, that, under the Constitution, the United States Congress has no right to subject any citizen of a State to trial and punishment by military power in time of peace; but the power to declare war is, by the Constitution, expressly vested in Congress; it has also power to suppress insurrection, and to make all laws necessary and proper for carrying into execution all the powers vested by the Constitution in the Government of the United States, or in any department or office thereof. The power to declare war undoubtedly includes not only the power to commence a war, but to recognize its existence when commenced by others; to declare that there is a war, and thereupon to make provision for waging war; to determine, so far as the nation can assert and enforce its will, how long the war shall continue and when peace is restored. The Constitution has made no provision in terms for a rebellion of the magnitude of that which has occurred, involving destruction of all the legitimate and constitutional governments in the States of the Union and involving a war between those States and the national Government. But the Constitution is a frame of government, and clearly implies the endowment of that Government with all powers necessary to maintain its own existence and the vindication of its authority within the scope of its appropriate functions. When war was waged upon the United States by States of the Union as organized communities, Congress could and must recognize the existence of that war, and apply itself, by the means belonging to war, to the vindication of the national authority, the preservation of the national territory, and the restoration of a republican government, under the national Constitution, in each of the rebellious States. As was said by the Supreme Court in the Prize Cases, (2 Black, p. 673,) it is a proposition never doubted, that the belligerent party who claims to be sovereign may exercise both belligerent and sovereign rights. The territory possessed by the rebels might lawfully and constitutionally be treated by the United States as enemies' territory. In the language of the court, in the same case, all persons residing within this territory, whose property may be used to increase the revenues of the hostile power, are in this contest liable to be treated as enemies, though not foreigners. They have cast off their allegiance and made war on their Government, and are none the less enemies because they are traitors. Where all lawful governments have been extinguished by the rebellion on the theatre of active military operations, where war really prevailed, there is a necessity to furnish a substitute for the civil authority thus overthrown, to preserve the safety of the army and society; and as no power is left but the military, it is allowed to govern by martial rule until the laws can have their free course. The right to govern by military law under such circumstances was fully conceded in the opinion of the Supreme Court of the United States in *ex parte* Milligan, (4 Wall., p. 127.) The test is there suggested that the right to govern by military power depends upon the fact that the courts are actually closed, and that it is impossible to administer criminal justice according to law. But while the war continues, although military power may be the only government in territory held by force of arms, the military commander may make use of such local tribunals already existing as he may find it convenient to employ in subjection to his paramount authority. It then remains to consider: First, whether the State of Texas has been, during rebellion, so deprived of all constitutional and lawful government as a State, and so in armed hostility to the Government of the United States, as to be subject to military law when possession of her territory was regained by the military power of the United States; and, secondly, whether the right to hold and govern the State by military power has terminated. To the first question there can be but one answer. In language of Chief Justice Chase, in Texas vs. White *et al.*, decided at the present term of the Supreme Court, no one has been bold enough to contend that, while Texas has been controlled by a government hostile to the United States and in affiliation with a hostile confederation waging war upon the United States, senators chosen by her legislature or representatives elected by her citizens, were entitled to seats in Congress, or that any suit instituted in her name would be entertained in this court. All admit that during this condition of civil war the right of the State as a member, and of her people as citizens, of the Union, was suspended. The government and the citizens of the State, refusing to recognize their constitutional obligations, assumed the character of enemies, and incurred the consequences of rebellion. The second question is one of more importance and difficulty. Having suppressed the rebellion as far as it was maintained by an armed force, it became the duty of Congress to re-establish the broken relations of the State with the Union; and the same authority which recognized the existence of the war is, in my judgment, the only authority having the constitutional right to determine when, for all purposes, the war has ceased. The rights of war do not necessarily terminate with the cessation of actual hostilities. I can have no doubt that it is competent for the nation to retain the territory and the people which have once assumed a hostile and belligerent character (within the grasp of war) until the work of restoring the relations of peace can be accomplished; that it is for Congress, the department of the national Government to which the power to declare war is intrusted by the Constitution, to determine when the war has so far ended that this work can be safely and successfully completed. The act of Congress of March 2, 1867, is, in my opinion, a legislative declaration that in Texas the war, which sprang from the rebellion, is not, to all intents and purposes, ended; and that it shall be held to continue until, in conformity with the legislative will, a State government republican in form and subordinate to the Constitution and laws of the United States, for which the act makes provision, shall have been re-established. It is true that in several acts of Congress the suppression of the rebellion and the end of the war have in express terms or by implication been recognized, but it will be found on examination that these phrases have been used in regard to special subjects, which do not seem to me inconsistent with the proposition that for some purposes the rights of war are not ended; while, in respect to captured and abandoned property, a limitation of the right to commence suits in the Court of Claims has been fixed by statute, and for the purpose of settling the question of the pay of officers in the volunteer army the date of the President's proclamation declaring the insurrection at an end has been adopted to interpret the phrase "close of the war."

It does not seem to me inconsistent with either of these enactments that Congress should declare that the States whose civil governments have been destroyed should continue under military authority until such governments could be restored. Every act of Congress is to be presumed to be constitutional unless the contrary plainly appears. It is to be also presumed that Congress will provide for the restoration, through constitutional government, of the rebellious States, as speedily as in its judgment the public safety will allow; but until civil authority is restored, and the rights of persons and property can be protected in the region which has been the theatre of war by organized governments, the direction by Congress to employ a military force to give that protection and preserve the peace would seem to be the only alternative with anarchy. It appears by the papers submitted that the trial of Weaver before the military commission was fairly and carefully conducted, and that the murder of which he was convicted was wanton and cruel. A freedman who had been at work for Weaver, having chosen to leave his employment to go to work for another man, went to him in a field near his house on that morning to ask for the wages which were due him. Weaver seized an ox-band, beat him severely with that, and then sent his hired man to his house for a double-barreled gun, loaded with buckshot, and on his return with it shot the freedman through the head, killing him instantly. There appears to have been neither provocation nor resistance; and this atrocious act was committed in the sight of the wife of the man murdered, who stood by her own door. The finding of the commission has been approved by the military commander, and has been certified to be regular and proper by the Judge Advocate General. I find no reason in law for the President's with-

holding his approval. The papers which were sent me are returned herewith.

Very respectfully, your obedient servant,
E. R. Hoar, *Attorney General.*

# XLVI.

# STATE PLATFORMS OF 1869.*

## CALIFORNIA, IOWA, MISSISSIPPI, OHIO, PENNSYLVANIA, VERMONT, VIRGINIA, WASHINGTON TERRITORY.

### CALIFORNIA.

#### Republican, July 22, 1869.

*Resolved,* That the Republican party of California gives its earnest support to the administration of President Grant, and do hereby endorse the acts and policy of his administration. We recognize the earnest effort of the Government to secure an economical administration of its affairs, to reduce expenses, to honestly pay the national debt, to prevent peculation and fraud upon the treasury, to enforce the collection of the revenue, and to cause the speedy restoration of public confidence in our financial strength and integrity.

2. That the negro question has ceased to be an element in American politics, and that the ratification of the XVth amendment to the Constitution ought to be followed by an act of universal amnesty and enfranchisement of the southern people.

3. That we regard with pride and satisfaction the evidences of an increasing immigration to this State of industrious and intelligent people from the Atlantic States and Europe, with whom we are anxious to share the benefits of a fruitful soil, a genial climate, and an advancing civilization; but, while giving preference to the immigration of people of our own race, we hold that unoffending emigrants from China to this State are entitled to full protection for their lives, liberty, and property, and due process of law to enforce the same, but we are opposed to Chinese suffrage in any form, and to any change in the naturalization laws of the United States.

4. That we recognize the power of the general Government to restrict or prevent Chinese immigration whenever the welfare of the nation demands such a measure, by terminating our commercial relations with China, but it should be considered that the adoption of a non-intercourse policy in respect to China surrenders to Europe the commerce of the empire of Asia. We believe that the general prosperity will be greatly enhanced by fostering commercial intercourse with Asia, and that the closing of our ports at this time against Chinese would be most injurious to

the material interests of this coast, a reproach upon the intelligence of the American people, and contrary to the spirit of the age.

5. That the Republican party having ever had in its especial keeping the rights of labor and of the laborer, and removed therefrom the blighting curse of slavery, and inaugurated a new era, in which the wages of labor have greatly advanced, while the hours therefor have been correspondingly diminished, claim to have originated in this State and steadily supported what is known as the "eight-hour law," the sound policy of which has been proclaimed by a Republican Congress, and by a proclamation of a Republican President made applicable to the public works of the United States.

6. That we endorse the action of the Senate of the United States in rejecting the so-called "Alabama treaty," and consider it the duty of the general Government to demand full reparation for the injuries inflicted by the British Government and her people upon our commerce during the late rebellion.

7. That we are in favor of imposing upon all kinds and classes of taxable property in the State an equal share of the burdens of taxation, and to that end favor the organization of a State board of equalization or review, that the inequalities now existing under the present system of assessment and collection of the State revenues may be avoided.

8. That we are opposed to grants of State aid to railroads, and are in favor of limiting taxation to the amount of revenues absolutely requisite to pay the actual expenses of the State Government, and to maintain the financial credit of the State.

9. That we hail with joy the return of peace, and the promising signs of an increasing development of the country and the permanent prosperity of the whole people. We earnestly invite the co-operation at the ballot-box of all who agree to the foregoing declarations, regardless of old party ties or previous differences of opinion upon the now settled questions of slavery, rebellion, reconstruction, and negro suffrage.

---

* It is deemed inadvisable to enlarge this chapter and volume by presenting all the State platforms. Such only are given as are of most significance and recent date.

### Democratic, June 29, 1869.

Whereas upon the eve of a political canvass the time-honored usages of our party require that a platform of principles be announced for the government of those who may be elected to political office; and whereas new questions have arisen since the meeting of the last Democratic convention, making such action eminently proper: therefore,

*Resolved*, That the Democracy of California now and always confide in the intelligence, patriotism, and discriminating justice of the white people of the country to administer and control their Government, without the aid of either negroes or Chinese.

2. That the Democratic party view with alarm the action of an unscrupulous majority in Congress in their attempts to absorb the powers of the executive and judicial departments of the federal Government, and to annihilate the rights and functions reserved to the State Governments.

3. That the subjection of the white population of the southern States to the rule of a mass of ignorant negroes, their disfranchisement, and the denial to them of all those sacred rights guaranteed to every freeman, is an outrage and a wrong for which the history of free governments in modern times may be searched in vain for a parallel.

4. That the Democratic party is opposed to the policy of lending the credit of the State and squandering the State property upon railway or other corporations, to the detriment of the public interests, and the overwhelming increase of the State debt and taxation.

5. That the Democratic party ever has been, is now, and ever will be, the champion of the rights of the mechanic and workingman; that all the reforms having for their object the reduction of the hours of his labor, the enlargement of his privileges, and the protection of his personal liberty, have ever been demanded, enacted, and enforced by the Democracy; that we point with pride to the fact that in California it was the Democratic element in the legislature that passed and a Democratic governor that approved the eight hour law, and that we pledge ourselves to use our utmost exertions to carry the provisions of that law into full force and effect, as well as to labor in other directions for the cause of the sons of toil.

6. That we are opposed to the adoption of the proposed XVth amendment of the United States Constitution, believing the same to be designed, and if adopted, certain to degrade the right of suffrage, to ruin the laboring white man, by bringing untold hordes of Pagan slaves (in all but name) into direct competition with his efforts to earn a livelihood; to build up an aristocratic class of oligarchs in our midst, created and maintained by Chinese votes; to give the negro and Chinaman the right to vote and hold office; and that its passage would be inimical to the best interests of our country, in direct opposition to the teachings of Washington, Adams, Jefferson, and the other founders of the republic; in flagrant violation of the plainest principles upon which the superstructure of our liberties was raised, subversive of the dearest rights of the different States, and a direct step toward anarchy and its

natural sequence, the erection of an empire upon the ruins of constitutional liberty.

7. That the Democracy of California believe that the labor of our white population should not be brought into competion with the labor of a class of inferior people, whose living costs comparatively nothing, and who add nothing to the wealth of our churches, schools, societies, and social and political institutions.

8. That we arraign the Radical party for its profligacy, corruption, and extravagance in public expenditures; for its tyranny, extortion, and disfranchisement; for its contempt of constitutional obligations; for placing the city of Washington in the hands of semi-civilized Africans; and we particularly condemn the appointment of healthy and able-bodied negroes to office while the land is filled with capable white citizens who are suffering for the common necessaries of life.

9. That we heartily endorse and approve of the manner in which the Democracy have administered the State government, and point with pride to the acts to protect the wages of labor, to lessen public and official expenses, and to the fact that, during the present State administration, the State debt has been reduced nearly $1,000,000, and taxation reduced from $1 18 on $100 to 97 cents.

10. That the so-called Alabama treaty having been rejected by the treaty-making power of the Government, the Democratic party, true to its record as the only political party which on such issues has uniformly proved itself faithful to our own country, will now, as heretofore, be found ready to sustain all measures demanded by the honest dignity and rights of the republic in its relations with all foreign Powers.

11. That all voters in the State of California who are opposed to the radical measures of Congress, including the proposed XVth amendment to the Constitution of the United States, and who are opposed to the appointment of negroes to office, be invited to unite with the Democracy in the coming contest.

12. That the Western Union Telegraph Company, which controls all the wires connecting the Atlantic with the Pacific, has, in instituting a tariff designed to give a virtual monopoly of eastern news to a few newspapers of one political party in this State, been guilty of a great public wrong, has betrayed the trust confided to it, and effectually restricted the liberties of the press, and that its action in this regard calls loudly for such legislative interference as shall prohibit discriminations, prevent the use of the telegraph as a political engine, and make it, like the mails, free to all.

13. That Hon. Eugene Casserly, by his manly and statesmanlike course in the United States Senate, deserves the confidence of the people of the State of California.

## IOWA.

### Republican, June 10, 1869.

*Resolved*, That we cordially endorse the administration of Governor Merril as wise, economical, and honest, and that it deserves, as it has received, the hearty approval of the people of Iowa.

2. That we insist upon a continuance of strict and close economy in all departments of our State government, in order to the maintenance of the happy and unexceptional financial condition to which our State has attained under Republican rule.

3. That the means now in the State treasury, and which may become available, ought to be used for the purpose of defraying the necessary expenditures of the State government economically administered, and for no other purposes; and no State taxes, or only the minimum absolutely required, should be levied or collected until such means are exhausted, to the end that the burden of taxation may be made as light as possible.

4. That we rejoice in the glorious national victory of 1868, which has brought peace and happiness and prosperity to our nation, and we heartily endorse the administration of General Grant.

5. That the Republican party of Iowa, being among the first since the rebellion to incorporate in a State constitution the great principle of impartial suffrage, cordially accepts the opportunity presented by adopting the XVth amendment to the Constitution of the United States of making the principle national.

6. That the public expenditures of the national Government should be reduced to the lowest sum which can be reached by a system of the most rigid economy; that no money should be taken from the national Treasury for any work of internal improvement, or for the erection of any public buildings not clearly necessary to be made or erected until the national debt is paid or greatly reduced; that all the money that can be saved from the national revenue honestly collected should be applied to the reduction of the national debt, to the end that the people may be relieved from the burden of taxation as rapidly as practicable.

7. That we endorse and approve the policy which the present Secretary of the Treasury of the United States has pursued.

### Democratic, July 14, 1869.

Whereas upon the eve of a political canvass the time-honored usage of our party requires that a platform of principles be announced for the government of those who may be elected to office:

*Resolved,* That the Democratic party view with alarm the action of an unscrupulous majority in Congress, in their attempt to absorb the powers of the executive and judicial departments of the Government, and to annihilate the rights and functions reserved to the State governments.

2. That we favor a reform in the national banking system looking to an ultimate abolishment of that pernicious plan for the aggrandizement of a few at the expense of the many.

3. That now, as in times past, we are opposed to a high protective tariff, and that we will use every effort to prevent and defeat that system of national legislation which would enrich a small class of manufacturers at the expense of the great mass of producers and consumers, and that we are in favor of such reforms in our tariff

system as shall promote commerce with every nation of the world.

4. That the pretended trial, conviction, and execution of persons not belonging to the military or naval service of the United States, by military commission, is in direct conflict with the Constitution, and we denounce the same as unworthy of a free people, and disgraceful to the American Government.

5. That we demand no more, and will submit to nothing less, than the settlement of the Alabama claims according to the recognized rules of international law, and that we declare it to be the duty of the government to protect every citizen, whether naturalized or native, in every right of liberty and property throughout the world, without regard to the pretended claims of foreign nations to their allegiance.

6. That we are in favor of, and insist upon, an economical administration of the national and State Governments, that the people may be as speedily as possible relieved from the load of taxation with which they are now oppressed, and that the public officers should be held to a strict accountability to the people for all their official acts.

7. That a national debt is a national curse, and that while we favor the payment of our present indebtedness according to the strict letter of the contract, we would rather repudiate the same than see it made the means for the establishment of an empire upon the ruins of constitutional law and liberty.

8. That in the opinion of this convention the so-called Maine liquor law, that now disgraces the statute-books of the State of Iowa ought to be repealed at the earliest possible moment.

The following resolutions were offered and rejected:

*Resolved,* That we are in favor of the repeal of the present prohibitory liquor law, believing it inadequate to accomplish the purposes designed by it, and as a substitute for the same we are in favor of the enactment of a stringent license law.

2. That we are opposed to the proposed XVth amendment to the Federal Constitution.

### MISSISSIPPI.

### Republican, July 2, 1869.

The Republicans of Mississippi, in convention assembled, in a spirit of amity and peace toward their opponents, and of justice to themselves, make the following declaration of principles and policy:

1. Unfaltering devotion to the Union, first, last, and forever.

2. Faith in and fidelity to the principles, objects, and aims of the great national Republican party, with which and with the President and Congress we are in full accord and sympathy.

3. A fair, impartial, just, and economical administration of the Government, national and State.

4. Full and unrestricted right of speech to all men, at all times and all places, with the most complete and unrestrained freedom of the ballot, including protection to citizens in the exercise of the suffrage.

5. A system of free schools which shall place the means of liberal education within the reach of every child in the State.

6. Reformation of the iniquitous and unequal taxation and assessments which, discriminating against labor and laborers, have borne so unjustly and unequally upon the people.

7. That all men, without regard to race, color, or previous condition, are equal before the law; and that to be a freeman is to possess all the civil and political rights of a citizen, are not only enduring truths, but the settled and permanent doctrines of the Republican party.

8. This convention recognizes but two great national parties; that under the administration of the one, the material and industrial resources of the country will languish, whilst under the liberal and fostering care of the national Republican party, commerce, manufactures, and internal improvements by the General Government will surely make the people of Mississippi what nature, soil, and climate intend they should be —rich, prosperous, and contented.

9. Recognizing as peculiarly American and republican the sentiment that the true basis of government is the "consent of the governed," which, in a republic, is expressed through the ballot-box, we, in the language of the Chicago platform, "favor the removal of the disqualifications and restrictions imposed upon the late rebels in the same measure as the spirit of disloyalty may die out, and as may be consistent with the safety of the loyal people;" and we shall hail with unfeigned delight the day when the spirit of toleration now dawning upon our State shall be so firmly established as to warrant Congress and the nation in declaring disabilities and restrictions forever at an end—when there shall be no citizen of Mississippi clamoring for his rights.

10. That the present modified condition of public sentiment in this State renders it wise and expedient that the Republican party should embrace the opportunity which is to be presented in the approaching election of ratifying the new constitution, so far modified in the franchise and general provisions thereof as to conform to the Constitution of the United States and the reconstruction laws; and that, as soon as Mississippi shall be fully reconstructed, according to the true intent of the laws, all disabilities imposed upon the late rebels should be entirely removed.

11. That we favor the prompt ratification by this State of article XV as an amendment to the Constitution of the United States at the earliest practicable opportunity.

12. We declare for universal amnesty and universal suffrage, the enlightened spirit of the age demanding that the fossil remains of proscription must be numbered with the things of the past.

13. The languishing condition of our State, notwithstanding her genial climate and productive soil, capable of sustaining and inviting a population of 15,000,000, reminds us not only of the necessity of reconstruction on a proper basis, but of the need of immigration. Schemes designed for class immigration, such as laborers only, or favoring one section, or country, or people, or portions of people, over another, on account of political or any other causes, will meet with no success; plans to increase our population must embrace all countries, climes, people, professions, politics, and religious beliefs; any plan stopping short of this, or hesitating to give a practical, earnest, cordial welcome to settlers, without regard to race, color, locality, politics, or religion, will meet with merited failure, because indicating the existence of bigotry and intolerance.

14. We recognize in General Grant the chosen leader of our party and cause, as well as the representative man of the age. As Washington was in his time, so is Grant now "first in war, first in peace, and first in the hearts of his countrymen." Through his election, peace, toleration and prosperity at last dawn upon Mississippi, and ere long throughout these States the old flag and the ancient principles he and it represent, will be respected, adopted, and adored. The magic words, "Let us have peace," possess a power, and have a mission, which will embrace the whole world, and will cease only with time.

15. We endorse and adopt his language, "that the question of suffrage is one which is likely to agitate the public so long as a portion of the citizens of the nation are excluded from its privileges," and, in his own words, we "favor such constitution and laws as will effectually secure the civil and political rights of all persons," a consummation we devoutly desire at the earliest practicable moment, with safety and justice to all.

16. We confide in and will support Major General Adelbert Ames, military commander and governor of this State. We look to him as the representative of the President and of Congress, and regard him as able and firm in peace as in war; his quiet yet decided administration commands our confidence and admiration. For his order relieving the poor of a heavy burden and unequal taxes, and for the order abolishing distinction of color for the jury, and for the marked ability and independence displayed by him, the loyal people owe him a debt of gratitude which they can never repay, save by a life of like devotion to the principles he represents.

17. We look to Congress as the assembled wisdom and expressed will of the nation. At whatever cost of obloquy or life, we shall in the future, as in the past, yield our unwavering fidelity to the laws and policy of the national legislature. A united nation and the principles of liberty owe their existence to-day to the firmness, patriotism, and wisdom of a Republican Congress.

---

### Conservative Republican, June 23.

*Resolved*, That this convention now proceed to organize the National Union Republican party of the State of Mississippi.

2. That we express our unfaltering devotion to the great principles of the National Union Republican party, and that we look forward with hope and confidence to the early restoration of our State government in accordance with the reconstruction laws of the Congress of the United States.

3. That the repeated failures of all former and existing organizations to restore the State and to meet the requirements of the republican spirit

of our institutions, by insisting upon measures of proscription far exceeding the provisions of the Constitution of the United States and the reconstruction acts of Congress, have rendered them unworthy of the respect and confidence of the voters of Mississippi.

4. That, in the language of President Grant, "the question of suffrage is one which is likely to agitate the public so long as a portion of the citizens of the nation are excluded from its privileges in any State;" and therefore we sincerely favor the addition of the proposed XVth amendment to the Constitution of the United States.

5. That we deprecate any attempt to impose upon the people of this State any greater disabilities than the Constitution and laws of the United States already recognize, and that we believe it to be the duty of all good citizens to use every effort to obliterate the animosities of the past, and to unite in the restoration of a State government based on the equal rights, civil and political, of men of every race.

6. That we express our thanks to the President and the Congress of the United States for rejecting the scheme to impose the rejected constitution upon the people of this State, and affirm our unwavering support of the administration of General Grant.

7. That we announce ourselves unqualifiedly in favor of universal suffrage, and universal amnesty, upon the restoration of the State to her federal relations, and pledge ourselves in good faith to urge upon Congress the removal of all political disabilities incurred by participation in the late rebellion.

8. That the State executive committee be authorized and instructed to issue, in behalf of this convention, an address to the people of this State, declaratory of the principles and sentiments of the National Union Republican party of Mississippi.

9. That the State executive committee be authorized and instructed to issue a call for a State convention, composed of delegates representing the different counties of the State, to meet at such time and place as they may deem expedient, for the purpose of nominating a State and congressional ticket.

## OHIO.

### Republican, June 23, 1869.

*Resolved,* That as citizens of the nation, representing the republican sentiment of an honored commonwealth, we regard with sincere satisfaction the fidelity evinced by General Grant to the Republican party, and his policy, both foreign and domestic, and of his national administration, and pledge our cordial support to the measures inaugurated to insure conciliation, economy, and justice at home, and command consideration and respect abroad.

2. That we hail with the profoundest satisfaction the patriotic and constitutional declaration of President Grant, in his inaugural address, that while he will, on all subjects, have a policy to recommend to Congress, he will have none to enforce against the will of the people; a sentiment which assures the country of an executive administration founded on the models of the administrations of Washington and Madison, and that will insure to Congress the unrestricted exercise of its constitutional functions, and to the people their rightful control of the Government.

3. That the abolishment of slavery was a natural and necessary consequence of the war of the rebellion, and that the reconstruction measures of Congress were measures well adapted to effect the reconstruction of the southern States and secure the blessings of liberty and a free government; and as a completion of those measures, and firmly believing in its essential justice, we are in favor of the adoption of the XVth amendment to the Constitution.

4. That the late Democratic general assembly, in its reckless expenditure of public money; its utter neglect of the business interests of the State by failing to enact the wise and much needed financial measures providing for the assessment and equalization of taxation prepared by the commission appointed by the preceding general assembly; its hostility to our benevolent and literary institutions; its failure to carry out the repeated pledges of the Democratic party to secure economy in the State; its extraordinary length of session in time of peace, resulting in an expense to the State amounting, for the pay of its members alone, to more than double that of the previous general assembly; its malignant attempts to disfranchise disabled soldiers and other citizens of the State; its attempt to take from the general Government the right to pursue, arrest, and punish those who violate the laws made in pursuance of the Constitution of the United States, and the vicious acts intended to destroy the power of the nation to preserve and protect the liberty and safety of its citizens, has shown the Democratic party unworthy of the trust, confidence, and support of an honest and patriotic people.

5. That the Republican party of Ohio is in favor of a speedy establishment of a soldiers' orphans' home in Ohio, not only as an act of justice to the many poor and helpless orphans of deceased soldiers, but as a recognition of the patriotic services of their fathers in the late war, and for the purpose of redeeming the pledges made by all loyal people to protect the families of those who fought and fell in the cause of human liberty and right.

### Democratic, July 7, 1869.

*Resolved,* That exemption from tax of over $2,500,000,000 Government bonds and securities is unjust to the people, and ought not be tolerated, and that we are opposed to any appropriation for the payment of the interest on the public bonds until they are made subject to taxation.

2. That the claim of the bondholders, that the bonds which were bought with greenbacks, and the principal of which is by law payable in currency, should, nevertheless, be paid in gold, is unjust and extortionate, and if persisted in will force upon the people the question of repudiation.

3. That we denounce the high protective tariff which was designed only in the interests of the New England manufacturers; that said tariff is

also, by its enormous impositions on salt, sugar, tea, coffee, and the necessaries of life, unendurable and oppressive, especially upon the people of the West, and that we demand its repeal and the substitution of another based upon revenue principles alone, upon the closest possible approximation to absolute free trade.

4. That the Democratic party of the United States have always been pre-eminently friendly to the rights and interests of the laboring men; that they are in favor of a limited number of hours in all manufacturing workshops, the hours dictated by the physical and mental well-being of the laborer; that they favor the most liberal laws in regard to household and homestead exemption from sale and execution; that they are also in favor of liberal grants of land from the public domain to actual settlers, without any cost, and are opposed to the donation of them to swindling railroad corporations; and that they are generally friendly to a system of measures advocated by the labor and industrial congresses, and we pledge the democratic party, if restored to power, to exercise their influence in giving them practical application.

5. That the attacks of Governor Hayes and Lee upon the doings of the late general assembly are false in fact, malicious in spirit, and unworthy of gentlemen occupying their elevated positions.

6. That the late general assembly were called upon to make large and extraordinary appropriations to rebuild the burned lunatic asylum, to provide a reform school for girls, to construct a new blind asylum, to make appropriations to pay over $80,000 of a judgment obtained in the supreme court of the State in favor of a life insurance and trust company, and to meet a deficiency of over $500,000 of the preceding Republican legislature, which, together with the extra compensation paid to the members, under the law passed by the Republican legislature, were provided for without an increase of the State levy; and the appropriations in the aggregate are much less than those of the preceding Republican legislature, without abstracting $800,000 from the relief fund for the maimed and disabled soldiers and their families.

7. That we hereby return our thanks to the fifty-eighth general assembly for their economical expenditure in the administration of the State government and the exposal of wholesale frauds in the erection of State buildings, whereby the people were swindled out of half a million of dollars by the negligence of the Republican State officials and the dishonesty of others.

8. That it is th right of each State to decide for itself who shall possess the elective franchise within it; that the attempt to regulate suffrage in Ohio by means of the so-called XVth constitutional amendment is subversive of the federal Constitution.

9. That the policy and legislation of the Radical party directly tend to destroy all the reserved rights of the States, and convert the Republic into a consolidated despotism; that whether such despotism be exercised by an emperor, a president, a congress, the result would be fatal to liberty and good government; that consolidation in this country means the absolute dominion of monopoly and aggregate capital over the lives, the liberty, and the property of the toiling masses.

10. That we denounce the national banking system as one of the worst out-growths of the bonded debt, which unnecessarily increases the burden of the people $30,000,000 annually, and that we demand its immediate repeal.

11. That the trial and sentence to death by military commissions of citizens of Texas not in the military or naval service, when the civil courts were in unobstructed exercise of their functions in that State and in the time of profound peace, and the approval of that sentence by President Grant, are violations of the most sacred rights of American citizens guaranteed by their constitution, State and federal, and deserve and should receive the earnest condemnation of every lover of liberty and constitutional government.

12. That the numerous palpable and high-handed usurpations of the party in power; their many public and private acts of tyranny, trampling under foot the civil law and the guarantees of the Constitution; their continuing to deprive sovereign States of representation in Congress, and to govern said States by military rule, show them to be the party of despotism, and unworthy the confidence and support of a free people.

13. That we extend the right hand of fellowship, and recognize as brethren in a common cause, all conservative men, not heretofore Democrats, who will unite with us in rescuing the Government from the unworthy hands into which it has fallen; and we pledge the united and cordial support of the two hundred and fifty thousand Democrats in Ohio, whom we represent, to the ticket nominated by this convention, and presented by us to the suffrages of the people of Ohio.

## PENNSYLVANIA.

### Republican, June 23, 1869.

*Resolved*, That we rejoice in the glorious national victory of 1868, which is bringing peace, happiness, and prosperity to us as a nation.

2. That we wholly approve of the principles and policy of the administration of General Grant, and we heartily endorse every sentiment contained in his inaugural address, and especially do hereby ratify and approve the late amendment proposed by Congress to the Constitution of the United States, and known as the XVth amendment.

3. That we have confidence that the general administration will wisely and firmly protect the interests and dignity of the nation in respect to our just claims against Great Britain, and that we endorse the action of the Senate in rejecting the Johnson-Clarendon treaty, known as the Alabama claims.

4. That we heartily sympathize with the struggling peoples of all nations in their efforts to attain universal freedom and the invaluable rights of man.

5. That we confidently endorse the administration of General John W. Geary as wise, economical, and honest, and that it deserves, as it

has received, the approval of the people of Pennsylvania; and we especially commend his uniform efforts to restrain the evils of special legislation.

6. That in Hon. Henry W. Williams, our candidate for the supreme court, we present a learned, pure, and patriotic jurist, who will adorn the high position to which we purpose to elect him.

7. That we reiterate and affirm our adherence to the doctrine of protection, as proclaimed in the 9th resolution of the platform adopted at the State convention of March 7, 1866.

8. That we endorse the ticket this day nominated, and pledge to it our hearty and cordial support.

## Democratic, July 14, 1869.

*Resolved*, That the federal government is limited in power to the grants contained in the federal Constitution; that the exercise of doubtful constitutional powers is dangerous to the stability of the Government and the safety of the people, and the Democratic party will never consent that the State of Pennsylvania shall surrender her right of local self-government.

2. That the attempted ratification of the proposed XVth amendment to the federal Constitution by the Radical members of the last legislature, and their refusal to submit the same to a vote of the people, was a deliberate breach of their official duty and an outrage upon every citizen of the State, and the resolution making such ratification should be promptly repealed, and the amendment committed to the people at the polls for acceptance or rejection.

3. That the Democratic party of Pennsylvania is opposed to conferring upon the negro the right to vote, and we do emphatically deny that there is any right or power in Congress, or elsewhere, to impose negro suffrage upon the people of this State in opposition to their will.

4. That reform in the administration of the federal and State governments, and in the management of their financial affairs, is imperatively demanded.

5. That the efforts now being made for the amelioration of the condition of the laboring man have our most cordial co-operation.

6. That the legislation of the late Republican Congress outside of the Constitution, the disregard of the majority therein of the will of the people and the sanctity of the ballot-box in the exclusion from their seats in Congress of representatives clearly elected, the establishment of military governments in the States of the Union, and the overthrow of all civil governments therein, are acts of tyranny and usurpation that tend directly to the destruction of all republican government and the creation of the worst forms of despotism.

7. That our soldiers and sailors who carried the flag of our country to victory must be gratefully remembered, and all the guarantees given in their favor must be faithfully carried into execution.

8 Equal rights and protection for naturalized and native born citizens at home and abroad. The assertion of American nationality, which shall command the respect of foreign powers and furnish an example and encouragement to people struggling for national integrity, constitutional liberty, and individual rights.

9. That the present internal revenue and taxing system of the general Government is grossly unjust, and means ought at once to be adopted to cause a modification thereof.

## VERMONT.

### Republican, June, 1869.

*Resolved*, That the Republican Union party of Vermont hereby affirms its adherence to the cardinal principles of the party, and especially the exclusion of traitors from the positions of public trust, the right of impartial suffrage, and the integrity of the public credit.

2. That we have confidence that the administration will wisely and firmly protect the interests and dignity of the nation in respect to our just claims against Great Britain, and that, in our judgment, we can afford to wait until her majesty's government finds it for her interest to make settlement.

3. That we wholly approve the principles and policy of the administration of President Grant, and we particularly commend that point of his inaugural address wherein he declares, "I would protect the law-abiding citizen, whether of native or foreign birth, wheresoever his rights are jeopardized, or the flag of our country floats, and would protect the rights of all nations, demanding equal respect for our own."

4. That we cordially commend the State ticket this day nominated, and pledge to its support such a majority as shall show that Vermont takes no step backward in her Republican course.

### Democratic, June 17, 1869.

*Resolved*, That the practical workings of the general Government, as administered by the opposition to the Democratic party, renews our zeal and love for the principles of our party.

2. That we are still in favor of a strict adherence to the Constitution of the United States, as the safeguard of the States.

3. That the Democracy, now as ever, make no distinction between citizens, whether of native or of foreign birth, and that we sympathize now as ever, with men of all nationalities striving for self-government.

4. That we are opposed to the present unequal system of taxation of the general Government, and to the corrupt and wasteful expenditures of the proceeds of such taxation.

5. That we prefer a system of government in accordance with the principles of the Democratic party rather than the present system of Radical rule.

6. That we will heartily support the nominees this day made.

## VIRGINIA.

### Republican, March 11, 1869.

*Resolved*, That the early restoration of the State of Virginia to the federal Union, clothed with all the rights and privileges of the most favored States, is required by the obligations which the Government owes to the several States, is necessary to the just independence, dignity, and character of the State, is demanded by every consideration of patriotism as well as of interest; but that this return can now take place only under the authority of Congress, in the way pointed out by the reconstruction acts, and by the adoption, without change or modification, of the constitution soon to be submitted to the people, and an election by them of their chosen officials, public servants, and representatives, which election ought to be immediately held, nor can it be longer delayed without serious danger of final disaster.

2. That the election of General Grant has given a new guarantee and awakened new confidence in the full and final triumph of the principles of the Republican party. The sublime truth that all men are free and equal will now become a great living fact. All persons born in the United States and subject to its jurisdiction are citizens not only of the United States, but of any State in which they may choose to reside. Nor can any State deny to any citizen within its jurisdiction the equal protection of the laws, or the possession or enjoyment of any right or privilege on account of race, prior condition, or religious faith. We hail with gratitude the President's inaugural address, and will never cease to thank him for telling the American people that while suffrage is denied to a portion of the citizens of the nation there cannot be peace. We pray Almighty God that the hope which is expressed for the ratification of the XVth article of amendment may be shortly realized, so that hereafter no State of the federal Union can deny to any citizen the blessed boon of suffrage on account of the accident of color, nor ever deny to him who has the right to vote the twin privilege, the right to be voted for. We thank the President, too, for that prompt act of retributive justice which has restored Sheridan and Reynolds to the commands from which they were removed by an unjust Executive, because of their faithful discharge of duty, their noble homage to the rights of humanity, and the manly enforcement of the reconstruction laws of Congress. In this act of justice we recognize another sure ground for confident hope, that tried fidelity to the Government is to be regarded as a virtue, and the support of the Union is to be honorable. We promise to his administration our earnest support. We invoke his best powers and wisest counsels to aid us in an early, just, and lasting reconstruction of our commonwealth.

3. That the equality in rights of all the citizens, a just and proper provision for the education of the people through public schools open to all, a more equal system of taxation, a reasonable provision to secure a home, the necessaries of life, and the means of earning a support exempt from forced levy and sale; to preserve the plighted faith of the State by the payment of her honest debts; to do justly by making and impartially enforcing just and equal laws; to enrich the State by developing her resources; to secure an impartial jury trial by opening the jury-box to all the male citizens, without regard to race or color; to soothe animosities and strife by removing the causes of irritation; to create friendship and harmony by burying enmities; the right of the people to frame their own organic

law, and the right of the real party of reconstruction to determine the manner in which, as well as the constitution and laws under which the State shall be restored, are all fundamental principles, vital to the success of the great work of reconstruction, and to which we now again pledge our faith, allegiance, and earnest support.

4. That no republican form of government can long exist, or be wisely administered, where a considerable portion of the people are disfranchised, and that the Republican party of the State of Virginia is not in favor of the creation of permanent disabilities, but pledges its influence and efforts to secure the removal of all the disabilities incurred by participation in the late rebellion from all the citizens of this State, who, accepting in good faith the results of the war by their acts and influence, shall cordially co-operate in an earnest effort for the restoration of the State under the reconstruction laws. We believe, however, that such disabilities should not be removed solely on the application of personal friends, nor from mere personal considerations, but because the individual himself possesses such superior claims for amnesty as are not possessed by the great body of disfranchised persons.

5. That the Republican party is the real party of reconstruction; that there can be no permanent and just restoration of the State excepting through its instrumentality. That all efforts for its destruction or demoralization are dangerous to the best interests of the State, fraught with most serious consequences to the Union men, and, if successful, must finally defeat reconstruction itself; to the preservation of the party and its organization in their integrity, to its most complete consolidation and its higher elevation, we pledge our utmost efforts, while at the same time we open its doors wide, and cordially invite to its support, labors, and triumphs, all citizens who, rising above mere partizanship, and standing upon the higher level of statesmanship, embrace the common faith and vital principles which lie at the foundation of true reconstruction, just equality, lasting peace, and State and national prosperity.

6. That five members of the State central committee, including the chairman thereof, be requested to wait on General Canby, when he shall assume command of this district, and request him to issue such orders to his officers as shall secure the abrogation of all distinctions as to race, color, or previous condition, in the selection of juries.

—

### Conservative,* April 29, 1869.

Whereas the people of the State of Virginia,

*These resolutions were reported April 28, by Messrs. Robert Ould, J. B. Baldwin, J. K. Edmunds, F. McMullen, L. B. Anderson, Jas. C. Campbell, A. Mosely, W. D. Haskins, and W. T. Sutherlin—a majority of the committee. Messrs. John Goode, Jr., Hugh Latham, and J. G. Mason presented the following minority report:

Whereas the people of Virginia, by their delegates duly chosen, met in convention in this city in the month of December, 1868, and. after solemn and mature deliberation adopted their "declaration of principles," setting forth and defining the policy of the white people of the State;

And whereas in the said "declaration of principles," in its own language, did distinctly declare by their delegates in convention duly chosen,

that the government of the State and of the Union were formed by white men to be subject to their control, and that suffrage should be so regulated by the States as to continue the system under the control and direction of the white race, and that in the opinion of this convention the people of Virginia will sincerely co-operate with all men throughout the Union, of whatever name or party, who will labor to restore the constitutional Union of the States, and to continue its government and those of the States under the control of the white race;

And whereas the organization of the conservative party of the State of Virginia exists by authority of the said convention and the action of the people thereunder;

And whereas the Congress of the United States have directed an election in this State to be ordered by the President, whose proclamation is daily expected, at which election the Underwood constitution is to be submitted to the people for ratification or rejection, and at the same time an election is to be held for State officers;

And whereas, for the purpose of consolidating and making effective the entire strength of the Conservative party in the State in opposition to the said constitution, the State executive committee and the county and city superintendents, in the exercise of the powers confided in them on the —— day of ——, 1868, did nominate a State ticket: Now, therefore, be it

*Resolved,* That the declaration of principles unanimously adopted by the said convention, composed of the representatives of the white men of all parts of the State, is binding upon the body until it shall have been revoked or modified by another convention of equal powers, and this meeting has no right to abandon the same.

2. That this meeting earnestly recommend to the people of Virginia to adhere steadfastly to the declaration of principles, and to the plan of organization adopted by themselves in convention assembled, and to continue to follow the leadership of their nominees, who have upheld the principles of their organization with such conspicuous gallantry and devotion.

3. That the clauses of the Underwood constitution proposed to be submitted to a separate vote are immaterial and insignificant compared to the leading features of that instrument: Universal negro suffrage, negro eligibility to office. That the same number of votes that will strike out the clauses to be submitted to a separate vote, will, if polled to that effect, defeat the whole constitution.

4. That the military rule of one of our own race, responsible to his superiors, is far preferable to the domination of an irresponsible multitude of ignorant negroes; and that, impelled by these considerations, we call upon all white men, whether native or adopted citizens, to vote down the constitution, and thereby save themselves and their posterity from negro suffrage, negro office-holding, and its legitimate consequence— negro social equality.

5. That even were an abandonment of the above-mentioned principles to be agreed on by this body, the 7th section of the election law,

met in convention in this city in the month of

entitled an act authorizing the submission of the constitution, &c., to the vote of the people, holds the restoration of the State subject to the subsequent action of Congress, and that in this fact we find abundant reason to believe other conditions may be imposed upon us.

6. That the act in question imposes a condition precedent in the adoption of the XVth amendment, which is in violation of every principle of constitutional law, and should not of right be endorsed by the people of Virginia.

Mr. Shackelford, of Culpeper, objected to both reports, and moved the following:

*Resolved,* That this meeting adjourn, to meet again ten days after the proclamation of the President of the United States fixing the day of voting on the constitution for Virginia and of election of officers under said constitution.

2. That the people of the counties of the State be requested to send delegates to the said adjourned meeting, to act in conjunction with the present representatives, for the purpose of considering and definitely acting upon the said constitution, or such modifications as may be presented by the President to the people for their adoption or rejection.

The convention refused, by yeas 29, nays 36, to lay the reports on the table; and, April 29th, the minority report having been withdrawn to give opportunity for the renewal of Mr. Shackelford's motion to postpone, the latter was debated and rejected by yeas 24, nays 54; after which, without a division, the majority report was adopted.

Resolutions unanimously adopted by the Conservative convention, December 12, 1867, were as follows:

1. This convention doth recognize that, by the results of the late war, slavery has been abolished; and it doth declare that it is not the purpose or desire of the people of Virginia to reduce or subject again to slavery the people emancipated by the events of the war, and by the amendment to the Constitution of the United States.

2. This convention doth declare, that Virginia of right should be restored to her federal relations with the Government of the United States, and that it is not in the contemplation of the people of Virginia to violate or impair her obligations to the federal Union, but to perform them in good faith.

3. This convention doth solemnly declare and assert, that the people of Virginia are entitled to all the rights of freedom, and all the guarantees therefor, provided by the Constitution of the United States; and they insist on the same as unquestionable, and that the said Constitution, which all are sworn to support, does not justify the governing of Virginia by any power not delegated by it, nor ought she, under it, to be controlled by the federal Government, except in strict accordance with its terms and limitations.

4. This convention doth declare, in the language of a resolution adopted by a public meeting held at the Cooper Institute, in the city of New York, "That the policy which continues to subject the people of ten States of the Union to an irresponsible government, carried on by military

December, 1867, and appointed an executive committee to organize the counties and cities of the State with a view to consolidate the strength of the conservative party;

And whereas the State executive committee and city and county superintendents did in the month of May, 1868, meet in this city and nominate a State ticket for the suffrage of the people;

And whereas said executive committee and superintendents have again assembled to consider the present state of affairs, and each candidate, with patriotic desire to promote the prosperity and welfare of the State, has resigned his candidacy: Now, therefore, be it

*Resolved,* That this meeting accepts the said resignations of said candidates, and hereby expresses its high appreciation of their devotion to the best interests of the State, and of their zeal and ability in the discharge of those duties which their candidacy imposed on them.

2. That notwithstanding the accepted resignations of our nominees, the conservative voters of the State are urged to organize for the purpose of defeating such obnoxious provisions of

---

power, is inconsistent with the express provisions of the Constitution of the United States, and is subversive of the fundamental ideas of our Government and of civil liberty; and the object for which this great wrong has been persisted in, as now being disclosed to the people of this country and to the world, to-wit, to subject the white people of these States to the absolute supremacy, in their local governments and in their representation in the Senate and House of Representatives, of the black race, just emerged from personal servitude, is abhorrent to the civilization of mankind, and involves us and the people of the northern States, in consequence of surrendering one-third of the Senate and one-quarter of the House of Representatives, which are to legislate over us, to the dominion of an organized class of emancipated slaves, who are without any of the training, habits, or traditions of self government.

5. This convention, for the people of Virginia, doth declare that they disclaim all hostility to the black population; that they sincerely desire to see them advance in intelligence and national prosperity, and are willing to extend to them a liberal and generous protection. But that while, in the opinion of this convention, any constitution of Virginia ought to make all men equal before the law; and should protect the liberty and property of all, yet this convention doth distinctly declare, that the governments of the States and of the Union were formed by white men, to be subject to their control; and that the suffrage should still be so regulated by the States as to continue the federal and State systems under the control and direction of the white race.

6. That, in the opinion of this convention, the people of Virginia will sincerely co-operate with all men throughout the Union, of whatever name or party, who will labor to restore the constitutional union of the States, and to continue its government and those of the States under the control of the white race.

the constitution framed by the late convention in Richmond as may be separately submitted, and to that end, as well as to secure the election of proper persons to the legislature, the organizations already in existence are exhorted to increased activity, and in those localities where no organizations have been formed the people are earnestly requested to meet together and adopt measures for the purpose of preventing the incorporation of such iniquities in the organic law of the State.

3. That this convention, while expressing its hostility to the leading and general features of said constitution, and while urging the necessity of organization for the purpose of defeating such provisions as may be submitted separately, declines to make any recommendation to the conservative voters of the State as to their suffrages upon the constitution expurgated of said provisions, or as to the candidates that may be before the people, feeling well assured that their good sense and patriotism will lead them to such results as will best subserve the true and substantial interests of the Commonwealth.

## WASHINGTON TERRITORY.

### Republican.

*Resolved,* That the principles of the Republican party, as declared by the last National Republican convention at Chicago, meet with our hearty approval, and adherence thereto by the national, State, and territorial legislatures, will secure the peace and prosperity of our country.

2. That we recognize the great principles laid down in the immortal Declaration of Independence as the true foundation of democratic government, and we hail with gladness every effort toward making these principles a living reality on every inch of American soil.

3. That we regard with great pride and satisfaction the accession of the wise, efficient, and victorious leader of the American army, General Grant, to the high and honorable position of President of the United States, and confidently rely upon the earnest co-operation of the different branches of the Government for the enactment and enforcement of such measures as shall secure the rights and liberty of every American citizen, upon principles of justice and equality, and that respect for the laws by the people that will insure the peace and progress of the entire country.

4. That the interests of Washington Territory can best be promoted by the election of an able Republican representative of our people as delegate to Congress, who will exert himself to obtain the fostering care and material aid of the general Government for our territory, and secure the just rights of each and all of our citizens, and who, as opportunity offers, will make known to the people of the States, by public addresses, the great advantages and inducements our territory presents to capital and population.

5. That a system of internal improvements in our territory should receive the encouragement and support of the general Government, in order that our important resources may be developed and the prosperity of the country promoted.

Among these internal improvements the construction of the Northern Pacific, Columbia River and Puget Sound, and Walla Walla and Columbia River railroads are of great and paramount importance, and their early completion highly necessary for the interests of not only this Territory, but also those of the entire country.

6. That the nominee of this convention can, and by the hearty and united efforts of the Union Republican party will, be triumphantly elected, and to that end all personal preferences and prejudices should be waived for the general good, and the present as well as future success of the Republican party and its principles be thereby effectually maintained.

---

### Democratic.

*Resolved,* That the Democracy of Washington Territory rely upon the justice and patriotism of the American people for the ultimate triumph of democratic principles, which alone can effect the full and complete restoration of the American Union, and restore to the people and the States respectively their rights under the constitution.

2. That this Government was founded by white men, and that we are opposed to the extension of the elective franchise or citizenship to negroes, Indians, or Chinamen.

3. That the recent attempt on the part of the Radical party in Congress to disfranchise the people of the Territory indicates a purpose in that party to destroy the liberties of the people.

4. That we are opposed to the proposed XVth amendment of the Constitution of the United States.

5. That the exclusion of any State from representation in Congress in time of peace is a dangerous assault upon the liberties of the people, in violation of the principles of our Union, and subversive of the rights of the Constitution.

6. That we are opposed to the present system of Government taxation, and are in favor of raising the necessary revenue for Government purposes by an *ad valorem* tax on the entire imports and property of the country.

7. That we favor the construction of railroads, the development of the vast resources of our Territory, and believe that Government should aid the construction of the same, and we acknowledge the important services rendered to our Territory in projecting the North Pacific railroad by the late I. I. Stevens.

---

# XLVII.

## VOTES OF STATE LEGISLATURES

### ON THE PROPOSED XVTH AMENDMENT TO THE CONSTITUTION OF THE UNITED STATES.

#### Alabama.

[Not yet voted.]

---

#### Arkansas.

SENATE, *March* 13, 1869.

YEAS—Messrs. Barber, Beldin, V. Dell, Evans, Hadley, Harbison, Hunt, Hemingway, Keeton, Mallory, Martin, Mason, Portis, Rogers, Sarber, Snyder, Vance, Wheeler, Young—19.

NAYS—Messrs. Sanders, Ray—2.

HOUSE OF REPRESENTATIVES, *March* 15, 1869.

YEAS—Messrs. John G. Price, [Speaker,] Isaac Ayres, Samuel Bard, Joseph Brooks, Wm. A. Britton, James A. Butler, Abraham T. Carroll, Jeremiah Clem, Robert S. Curry, Charles C. Farrelly, Edgar D. Fenno, George M. French, John H. Fitzwater, Jerome W. Ferguson, Solomon Exon, John J. Gibbons, James M. Gray, William H. Grey, Arthur Gunther, John W. Harrison, Asa Hodges, Jeffrey A. Houghton, Jacob Hufstedler, Daniel Hunt, Daniel R. Lee, James M. Livesay, Z. Henry Manees, Alfred M. Merrick, Solomon Miller, Jesse Millsaps, Saml. F. Mitchell, Wm. T. Morrow, Peter Moseley, Wm. S. McCullough, Nathan M. Newell, *David Nicholls,* Marville M. Olive, John F. Owen, Newton L. Pears, Nathan N. Rawlings, Moses Reed, Anderson L. Rush, Richard Samuels, Ephraim Sharp, Daniel J. Smith, Wm. W. Stansberry, John B. C. Turman, Daniel P. Upham, Benj. Vaughan, Jas. T. White, John K. Whitson, Wm. H. Wills, Wm. H. Wright—53.

NAYS—0.

#### California.

[Not yet voted.]

---

#### Connecticut.

SENATE, *May* 7, 1869.

YEAS—Messrs. Calvin O. King, Samuel W. Dudley, Erasmus D. Avery, Henry W. Kingsley, Aaron E. Emmons, Heusted W. R. Hoyt, David Gallup, Joseph D. Barrows, Charles B. Andrews, Oscar Leach, Carnot O. Spencer, Chas. Underwood, Edwin D. Alvord—13.

NAYS—Messrs. *George M. Landers, N. Webster Holcomb, Lucian W. Sperry, Alfred B. Judd, Owen B. King, E. Grove Lawrence*—6.

NOT VOTING—Edward N. Shelton, *James S. Taylor*—2.

HOUSE OF REPRESENTATIVES, *May* 13, 1869.

YEAS—Messrs. Henry Woodford, Henry Sage, Albert C. Raymond, James F. Comstock, Daniel Phelps, Caleb Leavitt, George S. Miller, Rufus Stratton, Thomas Cowles, Samuel Q. Porter,

Abira Merriam, Byron Goddard, Charles H. Arnold, Horace Eddy, Samuel Rockwell, Robert Sugden, Benjamin F. Hastings, Samuel N. Reid, John M. G. Brace, Joseph J. Francis, Joseph T. Hotchkiss, Julius A. Dowd, Stephen R. Bartlett, Jonathan Willard, Clinton Clark, T. Andrew Smith, Daniel A. Patten, George A. Bryan, John R. Platt, Israel Holmes, William A. Warner, Seth Smith, Benjamin B. Thurston, Edward Harland, George Pratt, William W. Smith, Joseph N. Adams, John D. Watrous, Paul Couch, William H. Potter, Robert Palmer, David Geer, Daniel Bailey, Israel Allyn, Henry S. Lord, John F. Laplace, Willet R. Wood, Alfred Clarke, Roger G. Avery, Gurdon F. Allyn, David D. Mallory, Benjamin B. Hewitt, Amos S. Treat, Walker B. Bartram, Ebenezer S. Judd, Ira Scofield, Charles Judson, Francis L. Aiken, Israel M. Bullock, William H. Hill, Aaron H. Davis, William O. Seymour, Phineas S. Jacobs, Alfred Hoyt, Lewis W. Burritt, Hiram St. John, William Woodbridge, Joseph E. Marcy, George R. Hammond, Edwin H. Bugbee, Charles Burton, Isaac K. Cutler, Lucius Fits, John W. Clapp, Hezekiah Babbitt, Henry H. Cary, James Pike, Eden Davis, Franklin H. Converse, Albert Campbell, Lewis Burlingham, Charles Larabee, Ezra Dean, William H. Church, Norman A. Wilson, Lyman Gridley, Seth K. Priest, Frederic Merrill, William W. Welch, William E. Phelps, Edward Dailey, Charles Hotchkiss, Edward B. Birge, Augustine T. Peck, Charles A. Warren, John T. Rockwell, Charles J. York, Stephen A. Loper, Martin L. Roberts, George Jones, James L. Davis, Henry Tucker, Samuel M. Comstock, Phineas M. Augur, Samuel H. Lord, Daniel Strong, Oliver C. Carter, Gilbert F. Buckingham, Edwin Kirkland, George H. Kingsbury, C. B. Pomeroy, Henry W. Mason, Isaac Mason, Guy P. Collins, John M. Way, George B. Armstrong, Meenelly H. Hanks. Elijah Cutter, R. W. Andrews, J. R. Washburn, George D. Colburn, Chauncey Paul, A. Park Hammond, Hezekiah Eldridge, William Shaffer —125.

NAYS—Messrs *Elisha Johnson, Norman Smith, William J. Gabb, Edward B. Dunbar, George J. Hinman, Henry A. Case, Benjamin Taylor, William M. Bates, Flavel S. Newton, Joseph Thompson, Roland O. Buell, William C. Case, Horace Belden, Roswell A. Neal, Noah H. Byington, Francis Jones, Samuel W. Goodrich, Alva Fenton, Alexander Clapp, Timothy C. Coogan, Samuel L. Bronson, Michael Williams, Asa C. Woodward, William D. Hendrick. Burritt Bradley, Mark Bishop, Gilbert S. Benham, Selah Strong, James Sweet, John A. Peck, Egbert L. Warner, Philo Holbrook, John C. Wooster, Hezekiah Hall, John Roach, Amos S. Blake, Isaac Hough, Enoch L. Beckwith, Thomas H. C. Kingsbury, Sanford Bromley, Robert F. Chapman, Daniel S. Guile, Prentice Avery, Geo. D. Loveland, Savilion Chapman, David H. Meekes, Edwin Wheeler, Cyrus Sherwood, Bern L. Budd, Jonathan A. Close, Jno. G. Wellstood, Eli D. Beardsley, Hinman Knapp, Philo H. Skidmore, Cyrus F. Fairchild, Asa Smith, Harvey K. Smith, Jarvis H. Wanzer, Sherman French. 2d, Matthew Buckley, James Smibert, Joseph Phillips, William R. James, Henry A. Kimball, Lyman N. Appley, George C. Martin, Josiah G. Beckwith, John B. Hopkins, Arbert E. Merrill,*

*Calvin Aldrich, Marshall E. Beecher. Austin H. Gillett, Lorenzo H. Hakes, William G. Kinney, John S. Wheeler, William H. Harrison, Mija A. Nickerson, Fred. A. Lucas, Enos B. Pratt, Sidney Peck, Isaac B. Bristol, Albert S. Hill, James A. Root, Eliott Beardsley, Pliney S. Barton, Erastus D. Goodwin, Edgar J. Reed, David L. Smith, John B. Newton, Henry S. Wheaton, Robert Bacon, Edwin Scovill, Hezekiah Scovil, JAMES C. WALKLEY,* Charles Kirby, Huntington Southmayd, Charles E. Brownell, Edwin A. Emmons, Randolph P. Stevens, Charles D. Kelsey, John S. Topliff, Thos. J. White, Samuel A. Collins, Thompson Strickland—105.*

NOT VOTING—Addison O. Mills, Jeremiah H. Bartholomew, James Baldwin, Fred. A. Mallory, Edwin Roberts, James M. Kibbe—6.

## Delaware

[The Senate voted down the resolution to adopt amendment by a strict party vote, the particulars of which were not received in time for publication.]

## Florida.

### SENATE, *June* 14, 1869.

YEAS—Messrs. Bradwell, Cruse, Hillyer, Katzenberg, Krimminger. Meacham, Pearce, Purman, Smith, Underwood, Vaughan, Walls, Wentworth —13.

NAYS—Messrs. *Atkins, Crawford, Ginn, Henderson, Kendrick, Moragne, McCaskill, Weeks*—8.

### HOUSE, *June* 11, 1869.

YEAS—Mr. Speaker, Messrs. Butler, Bogue, Black, Cox, Cruce, DeLaney, Erwin, Fortune, Graham, Harman, Harris, Hill, Hodges, Keene, Lee, Mills, Moore of Columbia, Pons, Powell, Robinson, Scott, Simpson, Thompson, Walker, Wells—26.

†NAYS—Messrs. *Bostick, Bradwell, Cheshire, Forward, McKinnon, Moore* of Hillsborough, *Oliver, Pittman, Raney, Steward, Stone, Urquhart, Watson*—13.

## Georgia.

### ‡SENATE, *March* 18, 1869.

YEAS—Messrs. Joseph Adkins, B. F. Bruton, J. J. Collier, William Griffin, McW. Hungerford, W. F. Jordan, W. W. Merrill, *B. R. McCutchen, R. T. Nesbit. M. C. Smith, C. J. Wellborn, F. O. Welch, W. T. Winn*—13.

---

* Independent Republican.

†June 12—Mr. Filer, of Monroe, sent the following communication to the Speaker:

"Having unintentionally been absent from the Assembly when the vote was taken yesterday on the joint resolution ratifying the XVth amendment of the Constitution of the United States, I respectfully ask that this communication be placed upon the Journal, that my disapprobation of the measure and desire to vote against it may be publicly known and placed on record. This is asked in justice to myself and my constituency."

The request was granted.

‡ March 10, a motion to lay joint resolution to ratify proposed XVth amendment to the Constitution on the table was lost by yeas 13, nays 16; March 12, the joint resolution was adopted by yeas 21, nays 16; March 13, a motion to reconsider prevailed, by yeas 19, nays 14; March 17. the resolution was indefinitely postponed, by yeas 18, nays 17—the chair giving the casting vote. March 18, this vote was reconsidered, by yeas 17, nays 14; but a direct vote upon adoption of the amendment resulted in yeas 13, nays 16, as above.

NAYS—Messrs. *W. J. Anderson*, W. F. Bowers, *J. T. Burns*, *M. A. Candler*, J. M. Colman, *J. C. Fain*, J. Griffin, John Harris, *B. B. Hinton*, *R. E. Lester*, *W. T. McArthur*, *C. R. Moore*, *A. D. Nunally*, Josiah Sherman, W. C. Smith, T. J. Speer—16.

*HOUSE OF REPRESENTATIVES, March 16, 1869.

YEAS—Messrs. *W. D. Anderson*, Benjamin Ay-*ar*, Edwin Belcher, Marion Bethune, *P. H. Brassell*, *T. F. Brewster*, *G. S. Carpenter*, W. C. Carson, P. H. Chambers, *W. H. Clarke*, *Clower*, *A. E. Cloud*, James Cunningham, S. A. Darnell, Madison Davis, *R. A. Donaldson*, *J. T. Ellis*, *W. S. Erwin*, J. R. Evans, *F. M. Ford*, *A. M. George*, *N. N. Gober*, *W. B. Gray*, *W. W. Grieger*, *J. E. Gullatt*, *R. B. Hall*, *W. D. Hamilton*, J. F. Harden, *G. R. Harper*, *J. N. Harris*, Heard, W. F. Holden, *G. M. Hooks*, Darling Johnson, *H. C. Kellogg*, *C. H. Kytle*, W. A. Lane, Aug. H. Lee, *John Long*, *J. J. McArthur*, J. A. Madden, *J. A. Maxwell*, *J. C. Nesbit*, J. W. O'Neal, C. K. Osgood, *R. M. Parks*, *J. B. Parke*, Joseph L. Perkins, *W. P. Price*, *M. Rawles*, *James M. Rouse*, *G. W. Rumph*, Pierce Sewell, *M. Shackelford*, *J. E. Shumate*, *J. A. Smith*, *J. R. Smith*, *Smith*, S. L. Strickland, *E. M. Taliaferro*, W. W. Watkins, *Hiram Williams*, W. S. Zellers, B. H. Zelner—64.

NAYS — Messrs. *M. R. Ballanger*, Richard Bradford, *W. G. Brown*, *Wm. M. Butt*, *J. M. Burtz*, *C. C. Cleghorn*, *J. A. Cobb*, *J. M. Crawford*, *John C. Drake*, *H. R. Felder*, *McK. Fincannon*, James Fitzpatrick, *R. W. Flournoy*, *A. S. Fowler*, *David Goff*, *Thomas W. Grimes*, *T. M. Harkness*, *James A. Harrison*, *W. B. Hill*, Virgil Hillyer, *W. L. Hitchcock*, *G. M. Hook*, *Haywood Hughes*, *C. C. Humber*, *J. R. Kimbrough*, *J. J. Kelley*, Samuel McComb, *W. T. McCullough*, Platte Madison, *J. W. Matthews*, *J. W. Meadows*, *Henry Morgan*, *Lewis Nash*, *J. M. Nunn*, *S. E. Pearson*, *J. H. Penland*, *F. L. Pepper*, *N. J. Perkins*, *R. W. Phillips*, *G. S. Rosser*, *J. R. Saussey*, *F. M. Scroggins*, *Dunlap Scott*, *V. P. Sisson*, *J. B. Sorrell*, *W. M. Tumlin*, *R. A. Turnipseed*, *L. H. Walthal*, *L. C. A. Warren*, *Ware*, *Frank Wilcher*, *Wilcox*, *J. C. Wilson*—53.

### Illinois.
—
### SENATE, May, 1869.

YEAS—Messrs. John H. Addams, Thomas A. Boyd, Andrew Crowford, John C. Dore, William C. Flagg, Greenbury L. Fort, Allen C. Fuller, Isaac McManus, John McNulta, Dan. W. Munn, A. B. Nicholson, William Patten, Daniel J. Pinckney, Henry Snapp, J. W. Strevell, John L. Tincker, John P. Van Dorston, Jasper D. Ward—18.

NAYS—Messrs. *S. K. Casey*, *S. R. Chittenden*, *James M. Epler*, *Edwin H. Harlan*, *William Sheppard*, *Joseph J. Turney*, *John M. Woodson*—7.

*March 11, a joint resolution to ratify the amendment was adopted by 67 yeas to 60 nays, three other members protesting that if the proposed amendment does not confer upon the colored man the right to hold office, then they vote "aye," otherwise "no." March 12, this vote was reconsidered by 60 yeas to 45 nays. Subsequently, March 16, a substitute ratifying the amendment was offered and adopted by the above vote.

HOUSE OF REPRESENTATIVES, *March 5*, 1869.

YEAS—Messrs. Joseph M. Bailey, L. L. Bond, Alexander W. Bothwell, Thomas H. Burgess, James E. Callaway, Samuel H. Challis, Henry C. Child, Philip Collins, Ansel B. Cook, John Cook, Franklin Corwin, Irus Coy, Peter W. Deitz, James Dinsmoor, Silas H. Elliott, David M. Findley, Calvin H. Frew, W. Selden Gale, George Gaylord, George Gundlach, Philip K. Hanna, Joel W. Hopkins, Humphrey Horrabin, Daniel Kerr, Alonzo Kinyon, J. C. Knickerbocker, Iver Lawson, Charles W. Marsh, John M. McCutcheon, James R. Miller, William B Miller, Francis Munson, Adam Nase, George W. Parker, James M. Perry, William E. Phelps, John Porter, N. N. Ravlin, Chas. G. Reed, J. S. Reynolds, Alexander Ross, John W. Scroggs, Hiram F. Sickles, William M. Smith, Wilson M. Stanley, William Strawn, Ephraim Sumner, Jacob Swigart, H. H. Talbott, E. S. Taylor, Bradford F. Thompson, L. D. Whiting, Samuel Wiley, Jonathan C. Willis, Ogden B. Youngs—55.

NAYS—Messrs. *Silas Beason*, *Andrew J. D. Bradshaw*, *Lewis Brookhart*, *Beatty F. Burke*, *Charles Burnett*, *Newton R. Casey*, *Joseph Cooper*, Edward L. Denison, *James E. Downing*, *John Ewing*, *Thomas B. Fuller*, *E. M. Gilmore*, John *Halley*, *Thomas Jasper*, *John Landrigan*, *Edward Lanning*, *Thomas E. Merritt*, *Abraham Mittower*, *D. H. Morgan*, *Timothy M. Morse*, *Smith M. Palmer*, *C. C. M. V. B. Paine*, *James G. Phillips*, *John W. Ross*, *Leonard Rush*, *S. R. Saltonstall*, *Charles Voris*, *David M. Woodson*—28.

NOT VOTING—*Henry Dresser*, Henry Green—2.

### Indiana.
—
### SENATE.

YEAS—Messrs Alanson Andrews, F. G. Armstrong, J. Rufus Beardsley, Fabius Josephus Bellamy, A. S. Case, John Carew, Firmin Church, John R. Cravens, James Elliott, Sternes Fisher, E. W. Fosdick, Isaac P. Gray, John Green, John V. Hadley, Thomas M. Hamilton, L. W. Hess, A. Y. Hooper, David F. Johnson, Isaac Kinley, Thomas N. Rice, John Reynolds, Milton S. Robinson, William J. Robinson, Harvey D. Scott, John A. Stein, Anson Wolcott, Samuel F. Wood—27.

PRESENT BUT NOT VOTING—*James Bradley*, *William W. Carson*, *George W. Denbo*, *Thomas Gifford*, *E. C. Henderson*, *Archibald Johnston*, *Charles B. Laselle*, *Thomas G. Lee*, *David Morgan*, *William F. Sherrod*, *Wilson Smith*—11.

ABSENT—Messrs. *Oehmig Bird*, Sims A. Calley, *James M. Hanna*, *George V. Howk*, *Robert Huey*, *Elijah Huffman*, James Hughes. *J. M. Humphreys*, *William H. Montgomery*, *William Taggart*, *William S. Turner*—11.

*HOUSE OF REPRESENTATIVES, *May 14*, 1869.

YEAS—Messrs. George A. Buskirk, (Speaker,)

*On this day a message from the governor announced the resignations of the following members of the House:
*James F. Mock*, *C. R. Cory*, *W. D. Hutchings*, *J. R. Bobo*, *D. Montgomery*, *S. A. Shoaff*, *B. S. Fuller*, *J. G. Johnson*, *Isaac Odell*, *T. H. Palmer*, *J. C. McGregor*, *C. R. McBride*, *L. Carr*, *S. Wile*, *J. D. Williams*, *W. E. Dittemore*, *D. W. Cunningham*, *R. Logan*, *J. Addison*, *L. Calvert*, *D. H. Long*, *W. K. Admire*, *J. C. Lawler*, *W. Tebbs*, *J. D. Cox*, *J. Hyatt*, *S. J. Barritt*, *J. L. Bates*, *D. McDonald*, *A. Zollars*, *N. D.*

Reuben Baker, John P. Barnett, Samuel Beatty, Fielding Beeler, Wm. C. Bowen, Robert Breckenridge, George W. Chapman, George F. Chittenden, Stephen Davidson, Henry G. Davis, Moses F. Dunn, Reuben W. Fairchild, Timothy Field, E. C. Field, Allen Furnas, Oliver P. Gilham, A. E. Gordon, Samuel Greene, Colbarth Hall, E. W. Hamilton, E. S. Higbee, John Higgins, Austin Hutson, Amasa Johnson, James T. Johnson, Samuel V. Jump, Robert T. Kercheval, Jonathan Lamborn, Thomas Mason, John Millekan, Robert Miller, William Y. Monroe, Milton A. Osborn, John Overmyer, Gilbert A. Pierce, Isaac N. Pierce, John Ratcliff, James Ruddell, Stephen Sabin, William Skidmore, Allen W. Smith, A. P. Stanton, Richard Stephenson, Stephen H. Stewart, David M. Stewart, Freeman Tabor, John J. Underwood, J. T. Vardeman, T. J. Vater, J. A. Wildman, Isaac Williams, Benjamin F. Williams, William Wilson—54.

PRESENT BUT NOT VOTING—Messrs. *John R. Coffroth, J. S. Davis,* and James V. Mitchell—3.

---

## Iowa.

[Not yet voted.]

---

## Kansas.

### SENATE, *February* 27, 1869.

YEAS—Abner Arrowsmith, J. C. Bailey, J. C. Broadhead, A. A. Carnahan, J. C. Carpenter, S. A. Cobb, W. H. Fitzgerald, W. H. Grimes, O. J. Grover, E. J. Jenkins, William Larimer, O. E. Learnard, James R. Mead, M. M. Murdock, John McKee, E. S. Niccolls, J. H. Prescott, Martin Schmitt, W. H. Smallwood, S. J. H. Snyder, A. G. Speer, E. Tucker, M. V. Voss, H. H. Williams, Levi Woodward—25.

NAYS—0.

ABSENT AND NOT VOTING—0.

HOUSE OF REPRESENTATIVES, *February* 27, 1869.

YEAS—Messrs. N. J. Allen, L. D. Bailey, P. Y. Baker, James Blood, M. B. Bowers, F. C. Bowles, Aaron Brundage, John Buterbaugh, Alexander E. Case, H. W. Cook, E. B. Crocker, William Crosby, I. N. Dalrymple, Rufus Darby, C. Drake, A. J. Evans, F. Gilluly, Charles Gregg, Joel Grover, John Guthrie, W. M. Hamm, H. C. Hawkins, D. Helphrey, Joseph Howell, J. M. Hunter, M. B. Hupp, Samuel Hymer, George E. Irwin, Z. Jackson, J. L. Jones, J. B. Johnson, D. B. Johnson, B. F. Johnson, Josiah Kellogg, Cyrus Kilgore, W. W. Lambert, Samuel Lappin, J. S. Larimer, Joseph Logan, J. H. Madden, Joel Maltby, J. B. Moore, John McClenahan, C. C. McDowell, J. A. McGinnis, H. W. McNay, W. F. Osborne, A. C. Pierce, J. Q. Porter, J. T. Rankin, M. H. Ristine, D. D. Roberts, L. Rob-

*Miles, T. W. Lemman, W. G. Neff, J. C. Shoemaker, M. T. Carnahan, P. M. Zenor, J. M. Sleeth, J. S. Cotton, J. F. Welborn, L. D. Britton, B. D. Miner—41.*

After the message, a vote was taken upon the adoption of the proposed XVth amendment, with above result. The Speaker ruled, that for ordinary legislation the State constitution prescribes that two-thirds of the House (or 67 members present and answering to their names) constitutes a quorum, but it does not define what number of members, more than a simple majority of the legislature, shall be sufficient to act upon a proposed amendment to the United States Constitution. He therefore declared the resolution adopted.

---

erts, A. G. Seaman, E. Secrest, William Simpson, W. H. Smith, J. D. Snoddy, R. E. Stevenson, Jacob Stotler, J. S. Taylor, Perry Tice, W. F. Travis, Wm. J. Uhler, James Walmsley, Amos Walton, Saml. R. Weed, R. P. West, David Whitaker, J. L. Williams, T. R. Wilson, George W Wood, M. S. Adams, (Speaker)—73.

NAYS—Messrs. *Thomas Feeny, R. V. Flora N. Humber, R. E. Palmer, P. H. Tiernan, Geo W. Thompson, John F. Wright*—7.

NOT VOTING—Messrs. T. H. Butler, E. E. Coffin, Oliver Davis, S. K. Hungerford, G. B. Inge, J. S. Martin, A. J. Mowry, McGrath, McIntosh, R. Smith—10.

---

### Kentucky.*

### SENATE, *March* 12, 1869.

YEAS—R. T. Baker, Robert Boyd, John B. Bruner, O. P. Johnson, Henry C. Lilly, W. J. Worthington—6.

NAYS—Mr. Speaker, (*Wm. Johnson,*) *Joseph M. Alexander, F. M. Allison, A. K. Bradley, Jno. G. Carlisle, Jos. H. Chandler. Jno. B. Clarke, Lyttleton Cooke, A. D. Crosby, Wm. A. Dudley, A. H. Field, Joseph Gardner, Evan M. Garriott, P. H. Leslie, W. Lindsay, Isaac T. Martin, W. H. Payne, I. A. Spalding, E. D. Standeford, Philip Swigert, Harrison Thompson, Oscar Turner, A. C. Vallandigham, W. L. Vories, Benj. J. Webb, I. C. Winfrey, C. T. Worthington*—27.

HOUSE OF REPRESENTATIVES, *March* 11, 1869.

YEAS—Robert Bird, Alexander Bruce, Dempsey King, Zachariah Morgan, Hiram S. Powell—5.

NAYS—Mr. Speaker, (*John T. Bunch,*) *Peter Abell, John J. Allnutt, George W. Anderson, Robert C. Beauchamp, Higgason G. Boone, Orlando C. Bowles, Jeremiah W. Bozarth, Jesse D. Bright, Richard J. Browne, William W. Bush, B. F. Camp, Patrick Campion, George M. Caywood, A. T. Chenault, Thomas T. Cogar, John N. Conkwright, Thomas H. Corbett, Robert T. Davis, John Deaton, Francis U. Dodds, Michael A. Downing, O. L. Drake, George W. Drye, Thomas J. Eades, George R. Fearons, Manlius T. Flippin, Hart Gibson, Robert T. Glass, Wm. O. Hall, George Hamilton, Mortimer D. Hay, JAMES R. HINDMAN,† Smith M. Hobbs, Basil Holland, Richard C. Hudson, Thomas L. Jefferson, Alfred M. Jones, Francis Justice, Alfred Kendall, Gabriel A. Lackey, J. Fry Lawrence, John W. Leathers, Charles H. Lee, Wm. Lusby, Wm. J. Lusk, Beriah Magoffin, Samuel I. M Major, Andrew J. Markley, Alexander L. Martin, Mortimer D. Martin, Jas. M. McFerran, W. Estill McHenry, James A. McKenzie, Guy S. Miles, John Wesley Mosely, John Allen Murray, John W. Ogilvie, William N. Owens, Thompson S. Parks, Henry L. Perry, George G. Perkins, Julian N. Phelps, Elijah S. Phister, Wm. Preston, Wm. B. Read, John D. Russell, Culvin Sanders, Robert Simmons, Fenton Sims, Alexander B. Smith, Richard M. Spalding, Barton W. Stone, David P. Stout, Hezekiah K. Thomas, James White, Robert K.*

---

\* The vote actually taken was on a joint resolution to *reject* the amendment; but I have made the record to correspond in form with the other States, in which the question was on ratifying.

† Conservative.

*White, James A. Wilson, Samuel M. Wrather, J. Hall Yowell*—80.

## Louisiana.

### SENATE, *February 27, 1869.*

YEAS—Messrs. C. C. Antoine, H. J. Campbell, F. V. Coupland, L. B. Jenks, G. Y. Kelso, J. Lynch, J. J. Monette, C. C. Packard, P. B. S. Pinchback, R. Poindexter, C. Pollard, J. Randall, J. Ray, M. F. Smith, S. M. Todd, C. Wilcox, J. R. Williams, J. Wittgenstein—18.

NAYS—Messrs. *G. H. Braughn,* J. C. Egan, W. L. Thompson—3.

HOUSE OF REPRESENTATIVES, *March 1, 1869.*

YEAS— Messrs. Charles W. Lowell, *(Speaker,)* Isaac A. Abbott, Frank Alexander, F. C. Antoine, C. J. Adolphe, Octave Belot, O. H. Brewster, Dennis Burrell, B. Collins, W. S. Calhoun, M. Carr, Sam E. Cuny, P. G. Deslonde, E. W. Dewees, P. L Dufresne, A. J. Demarest, N. Douglas, T. B. W. Evans, A. W. Faulkner, P. Guigonet, John Gair, J. Garstkamp. Chas. Gray, Paul Guidry. J. A. Hall, J. T. Hanlon, H. Heidenhain, G. H. Hill, E. Honore, J. W. Hutchinson, R. H. Isabelle, J. Lange, V. M. Lange, E. Le Blanc, Chas. Le Roy, Milton Morris, J. H. Mo Vean, Wm. Murrel, W. C. Melvin, F. Morey, R. J. Moran, James S. Mathews, John Page, M. Raymond, D. H. Reese, Henry L. Rey, Moses Sterrett, Robert J. Taylor, A. Tureaud, H. C. Tounoir, S. Umphreys, James J. Walsh, Geo. Washington, E. S. Wilson, David Young—55.

NAYS—Messrs. *L. P. Bryant, James R. Currell, Wm. Haskell, James McCullen, W. Pope Noble, C. B. Pratt, J. E. Rengstorff, P. H. Waters, Jacob Zoelly*—9.

NOT VOTING—Messrs. Leslie Barbee, W. W. Bennett, J. B Bergerson, F. Borge, J. A. Crawford, Jos. H. Degrange, Ulger Dupart, Charles A. Eager, J. B. Esnard, David C. Fouts, Peter Harper, W. M. Holland, J. M. Judice, Amos Kent, J. B. Landers, A. L. Lee, E. F. L'Haste, Harry Lott, Jacob Magee, Theophile Mahier, W. L. McMillen, Joseph Mansion, C. R. May, S. C. Mollere, John Pearce, William H. Pierce, S. Prejean, Willis Prescott, J. Simms, H. C. Slaton, Henderson Williams, William C. Williams, L. A. Wiltz, B. C. Wren, P. Jones Yorke, Nicholas Young—36.

## Maine.

### SENATE, *March 11, 1869.*

YEAS—Messrs. William W. Balster, John A. Buck, George Cary, T. H. Cushing, Reuel B. Fuller, Lorenzo Garcelon, Charles E. Gibbs, George Goodwin, Thomas R. Kingsbury, M. D. L. Lane, Thomas S. Lang, Stephen D. Lindsay, Manderville T. Ludden, Frederick G. Messer, Benjamin D. Metcalf, Jeremiah Mitchell, Jacob P. Morse, Benjamin B. Murray, jr., Sumner A. Patten, William B. Snell, John L. Stevens, F. Loring Talbot, Samuel Tyler, Luther H. Webb, Joseph H. West—25.

NAY—Mr. *Moses R. Mathews*—1.

HOUSE, *March 11, 1869.*

ADOPTED UNANIMOUSLY—The members present being: Charles B. Abbot, Nathaniel Averill,

John W. Barker, *E. K. Bennett,* W. H. Bigelow, Francis Blackman, Granville Blake, E. P. Blaisdell, Hiram Bliss, jr., Uranus O. Brackett, Alden Bradford, Edmund Bragdon, jr., Henry Brawn, George E. Brickett, John R. Bridges, John A. Briggs, Jethro Brown, James M. Buzzell, *G. W. Caldwell,* E. A. Calderwood, *P. J. Carleton,* Hanson T. Carver, John S. Case, J. H. Chamberlain, Andrew C. Chandler, D. W. Chapman, F. A. Chase, George A. Clark, James M. Coffin, Cyrus Cole, Marshall Cram, *Joseph Crandon, jr.,* G. F. Danforth, *William Dickey, Abner Dinsmore,* William S. Dodge, William Dolbier, J. H. Drummond, (Speaker,) Edwin A. Duncan, Cyrus Dunn, James Dunning, Parker G. Eaton, *Robert Edes,* E. C Farrington, *J. A. Farrington,* A. B. Farwell, W. B. Ferguson, Levi H. Folsom, Francis H Foss, Isaac Foster, Jacob F. Frederic, Washington Gilbert, D. T. Giveen, Isaac B. Goodwin, G. C. Goss, *A. Greely, Seward B. Gunnison, James R. Haley,* John S. P. Ham, *G. A. Hammond.* G. W. Hammond, Austin Harris, A. J. Hatch, *Joseph W. Holland, George S. Holman,* Caleb Holyoke, William Hopkins, *G. W. Howe,* Wales Hubbard, Aaron W. Huntress, William Irish, *Charles Junkins,* Eleazer Kelley, Ezra Kempton, I. G. Kimball, Thomas Knowlton, Francis B. Lane, Andrew Leighton, Jonathan Libby, William L. Longley, Tobias Lord, Leonard Lord, William W. Lucas, George C. Lynam, John G. Mayo, A. B. McCausland, Orrin McFadden, Mason J. Metcalf, Charles V. Minot, Charles J. Morris, S. M. Newhall, Stillman Noyes, jr., Lyndon Oak, G. S. Palmer, J. W. Palmer, George Parcher, Jere G. Patten, *David Patterson, Andrew M. Peables,* Henry O. Perry, *Oscar Pike,* Stanley A. Plummer, Daniel F. Potter, C. M. Powers, A. C. Pray, Joseph C. Purinton, Thomas B. Reed, Samuel A. Rendell, S. D. Richardson, William M. Rust, Edmund Russell, John Russell, D. W. Sawyer, Whitman Sawyer, Stillman W. Shaw, *Reuben Small,* Joseph O. Smith, Thaddeus S. Somes, Pliny B. Soule, Jas. M. Stone, *L. H. Storer,* Ira D. Sturgis, Judah D. Teague, *N. Thompson,* E. W. Thompson, J. P. Thwing, Philander Tolman, Abner Toothaker, *Eastman H. Tripp,* Charles Y. Tuell, *Ellery Turner,* Thomas E. Twitchell, *Alfred Watts,* Cyrus Waugh, E. W. Wedgewood, Andrew J. Weston, Charles R. Whidden, Daniel White, *Joshua Whitney,* Elijah Wyman.

## Maryland.

[Not yet voted.]

## Massachusetts.

### SENATE, *March 9, 1869.*

YEAS—Messrs. Nathl. E. Atwood, Nathl. J. Holden, Joshua N. Marshall, George M. Rice, George O. Brastow, Estes Howe, George H. Monroe, H. H. Coolidge, Richmond Kingman, Daniel Needham, George S. Taylor, Samuel D. Crane, Lucius J. Knowles, Julius A. Palmer, Whiting Griswold, John H. Lockey, Richard Plumer, Gershom B. Weston, John B. Hathaway Chas. R. McLean, Joseph G. Pollard, O. H. P. Smith, George M. Buttrick, George A. King, Edwin L. Morton, George H. Sweetser, J. Scott Todd, Edmund Dowse, Charles R. Ladd, Robert C. Pitman,

Harrison Tweed, Charles A. Whirlock, Francis A. Hobart, Charles Marsh, Joseph G. Ray, Jonathan White—36.

NAYS—Messrs. *Benjamin Dean, Alonzo M. Giles*—2.

HOUSE OF REPRESENTATIVES, *March* 12, 1869.

YEAS—Messrs. William T. Adams, Alexander H. Allen, John A. P. Allen, William W. Amadon, Frank M. Ames, Isaac A. Anthony, John I. Baker, Life Baldwin, John Barlow, William E. Barnes, William Bartlett, Ezra Batcheller, Jacob Bates, Loring Bates, Marcus A. Bates, Alfred Belden, Francis W. Bird, Saml. G. Bowdlear, Charles Bradley, Samuel P. Breed, Ezra C Brett, Benjamin A Bridges, Jethro C. Brock, William G. Brooks, John Brown, Werden R. Brown, Ferdinand L. Burley, Alvah A. Burrage, Alfred A. Burrill, Rodney French, Josiah O. Friend, jr., Chauncey G Fuller, Geo. L. Gibbs, Edwin Gilbert, Kimball C. Gleason, Abijah W. Goddard, Stephen D. Goddard, John B. Goodrich, Thomas H. Goodspeed, Levi S. Gould, Sam. H. Gould, Wesley A. Gove, Wm. T. Grammer, Calvin S. Greenwood, Charles H. Guild, Moses H. Hale, Lyman S. Hapgood, Rich. P. A. Harris, Abraham G. Hart, Edward H. Hartshorn, Andrew L. Haskell, Wm. H. Haskell, James A. Hervey, James Hewes, Chas. A. Hewins, Elmer Hewitt, Wm. Hichborn, Levi W. Hobart, Thorndike D. Hodges, Ambrous Hodgkins, Alvah Holway, James Horswell, Samuel Horton, Charles H. Hovey, Geo. F. Howland, James Humphrey, Theodore C. Hurd, Harvey Jewell, (Speaker,) Henri L. Johnson, Robert Johnson, Herbert C. Joyner, Shubael B. Kelley, William W. Kellogg, Thos. G. Kent. Moses Kimball, Dexter S. King, Enoch King, Daniel W. Knight, Jos. S. Knight, Oliver S. Butler, Solomon Carter, Albert Chamberlin, Linus M. Child, Wm. M. Child, Horace Choate, Le Baron B. Church, Joseph N. Clark, Asa Clement, Samuel Cloon, Aurj G. Coes, Benjamin F. Cook, George P. Cox, Freeborn W. Cressy, James M. Cunliff, Robt. S. Daniels, Elnathan Davis, William W. Davis, Ebenezer Dawes, John Dean, Avery J. Denison, Benjamin Dupar, J. Franklin Dyer, Wm. I. Edwards, Thos. Ellis, Jacob Fisher, Charles A. Fiske, Wm Fletcher, James B. Francis, Franklin C. Knox, Albert Langdon, Roger H. Leavitt, Manning Leonard, Nahum Leonard, jr., William Livermore, Caleb Lombard, Josiah Lor., jr, Marcus M. Luther; Charles N. Marsh, Wm. Melcher, Wm. R. Melden, Chas. H. Merriam, John M. Merrick, Moody Merrill, Wm. H. Merritt, Lansing Millis, Eben Mitchell, Elliott Montague, Lyman E. Moore, Asa P. Morse, Newton Morse, Edwin Mudge, Nathaniel C. Nash, Henry J. Nazro, Thomas L. Nelson, Daniel H. Newton, Jeremiah L. Newton, Geo. K. Nichols, John P. Ober, Weaver Osborn, Rufus S. Owen, Samuel S. Paine, John C. Peak, Joseph D. Peirce, Francis A. Perry, Avery Plumer, A. A. Plimpton, M. C Phipps, Augustus Pratt, Joseph A. Priest, Asahel D. Puffer, Edgar H. Reed, Ezra Rice, James Ritchie, James H. Roberts, Ensign B. Rogers, Joseph N. Rolfe, Augustine K. Russell, George J Sanger, Joseph L. Sargent, Samuel D. Sawin, Clark Sears, John N. Sherman, Rufus S. Slade, Edward Smith, Horace Smith, Iram Smith, John J. Smith, Martin L. Smith, Willis Smith, Welcome W. Sprague, Charles W. Soule, L. Miles Standish, Haynes K. Starkweather, Eliphalet Stone, Ruel F. Thayer, Justus Toner, S. K. Towle, Welcome H. Wales, Royal S. Warren, Thos. S. Waters, Henry White, D Dwight Whitmore, Emerson Wight, Charles Wilcox, Salem Wilder, Alfred M. Williams, Warren Williams, William D. Witherell, George M. Woodward, D. T. Woodwell, Luther A. Wright, P. Ambrose Young—192.

NAYS—Messrs. *Rich. D. Blinn, Dennis Cawley, jr, Samuel Clark, Alanson Crittenden, Benjamin Franklin, Dennis J. Gorman, Hugh A. Madden, Murdock Matheson, Charles J. McIntyre, F. H. Morse, Thomas F. Plunkett, Thomas K. Plunkett, Caleb Rand, James Wilson, Orlow Wolcott*—15.

* NOT VOTING—33.

---

### Michigan.

#### SENATE, 1869.

YEAS—Charles Andrews, John K. Boies, Evan J. Bonine, Henry C. Conkling, John C. Fitzgerald, Bela W. Jenks, John H. Jones, Ezra L. Koon, Charles Blunt Mills, Stephen Pearl, Peter R. L. Peirce, Delos Phillips, Abraham C. Prutyman, Hampton Rich, Elliott T. Slocum, Amos Smith, Thaddeus G. Smith, John H. Standish, George Thomas, Jerome W. Turner, P. Dean Walker, William B. Williams, (President, *pro tem.,*) Richard Winsor, Alfred B. Wood, Hiel Woodward—25.

NAYS— *William Adair, Lorenzo M. Mason, Edward G. Morton, Lyman Deeatur Norris, William Willard, jr.*—5.

#### HOUSE OF REPRESENTATIVES, 1869.

YEAS—John Avery, Horace T. Barnaby, Benjamin L. Baxter, Isaac D. Beall, John E. Blake, Ezra Bostwick. Nathan S. Boynton, George, G. Briggs, Ellery A. Bronnell, Alexander Cameron, Benjamin Clark, Archer H. Crane, Daniel L. Crossman, James L. Curry, William R. Davis, Philo Doty, William R. Eck, Adam Elliott, George H. Fenner, Ceylon C. Fuller, Milo E. Gifford, Levi N. Goodrich, William W. Hartson, Henry H. Holt, Dexter Horton, Edmund W. Hunt, William H. Hurlbut, Benjamin W. Huston, jr., Loomis Hutchinson, John N. Ingersoll, Charles A. Jewell, Peter Lane, Enos T. Lovell, James W. Mandigo, Edward M. Mason, Henry McCowen, Norton L. Miller, Charles R. Millington, William H. C. Mitchell, Lyman Murray, Orlando Newman, Henry A. Norton, John M. Osborn, Emory M. Plimpton, Uzziel Putnam, jr., Almond B. Riford, Harvey B. Rowlson, George P. Sanford, Brackley Shaw, jr., Charles Shier, Aaron Sickels, Thomas J. Slayton, Robert B. Smith, Jos. W. Snell, Abiel S. Stannard, Frank B. Stockbridge, George W. Swift, Almon A.

* Under an order of the House, permitting absentees to record how they would have voted had they been present, the following were recorded:

YEAS—Messrs. George H. Barrett, Wm. W. Nichols, S. H. Walker, Henry Chase, O. S. Brown, E. Foster Bailey, Lewis S. Judd, Addison G. Fay, Henry Blake, Jos. A. Stranger, Francis A. Nye, Samuel B. Simmons, Stephen M. Crosby, S. S. Willson, Charles P. Lyon, Shepard Thayer, Tilly Haynes, Frank M. Ames, W. A. Russell, Edward Stowell—20.

NAY—*Patrick A. Collins.*

Thompson, George Vowles, John Wagner, John Walker, Jacob Walton, Edgar B. Ward, Luther Westover, Hubert G. Williams, James A. Williams, Jonathan J. Woodman, (Speaker,) Samuel W. Yawkey—68.

NAYS—*Robert V. Briggs, Orman Clark, Bela Cogshall, Jerome B. Eaton, Thomas W. Harris, John H. Hubbard, Frederick G. Kendrick, James Kingsley, Peter Klein, James B. Lee, John Q. McKernan, Cyrus Miles, William Purcell, Claude N. Riopelle, James W. Romeyn, James Stewart, Newton Shelton, Peter Ternes, Joseph Weier, Jacob A. T. Wendall, Darwin O. White, Elliott R. Wilcox, William D. Williams, David A. Woodard—24.*

### Minnesota.

[Not yet voted—the legislature declining to act upon a telegram, and adjourning prior to receipt of an official copy of proposed amendment.]

### Mississippi.

[Not yet voted.]

### Missouri.

#### SENATE, *March* 1, 1869.

YEAS—Messrs. Wells H. Blodgett, George W. Boardman, C. S. Brown of Shelby, Theodore ·Bruere, John S. Corender, John B. Clark, sr., David R. Conrad, Lewellyn Davis, Isam B. Dodson, Ellis G. Evans, John M. Filler, Louis Gottschalk, Minor T. Graham, Thos. Harbine, Samuel W. Headlee, George H. Rea, Stephen Ridgley, Wm. B. Rogers, M. G. Roseberry, William A. Shelton, James H. Todd, David A. Waters, Eugene Williams - 23.

NAYS—Messrs. *James H. Birch, jr., Joseph Brown* of St. Louis, *Thomas M. Carroll, Thomas Essex, Thomas J. O. Morrison, John H. Morse, James S. Rollins, Thomas B. Reed, Henry J. Spannhorst—9.*

NOT VOTING—George W. Elwell, John C. Human.

#### HOUSE OF REPRESENTATIVES, *March* 1, 1869.

YEAS—Messrs. John C. Orrick, (Speaker,) J. J. Akard, Ben Alsup, T. W. Allred, A. Jackson Baker, T. S. Benefiel, Tarlton Brewster, W. P. Browning, Henry Bruihl, C. C. Byrne, Daniel Clark, M. S. Courtright, D. S. Crumb, W. H. H. Cundiff, E. S. Davis, R. B. Denny, R. T. Dibble, J. H. Dolle, D. S. Donegan, W. B. Elliot, A. M. Ellison, Frank Eno, J. W. Enoch, W. J. Ferguson, E. P. Ferrell, J. B. Freeman, A. L. Gibbs, J. H. Glenn, Richard Gladney, A. Hackman, J. B. Harper, Samuel Hayes, J. T. K. Hayward, A. F. Heely, N. P. Howe, Anthony Iltner, Jesu Jennings, R. F. Johnson, T. H. Jones of Laclede, W. A. Jones of Nodaway, R. D. Keeney, G. R. King, Oscar Kirkham, N. B. Klaine, M. L. Laughlin, Wm. Lawson, F. T. Ledergerber, F. E. Lombar, J. M. Magner, M. J. Manville, J. C. McGinnis, J. F. McKernan, W. H. McLane, R S. Moore, H. G. Mullings, A. Munch, W. N. Nalle, T. D. Neal, W. H. Norris, C. R. Peck, Anthony Perry, J. L. Powell, J. M. Quigley, Constance Riek, J. P. Robertson, L. A. Rountree, F. T. Russell, Louis Schulenberg, W. L. Snidow, James Southard, T. J. Stauber, E. Stinson, L. A. Thompson, J. S. Todd, J. L. Vickers,

G. H. Walser, *H. Winchester,* Jacob Yankee, J. M. Young—79.

NAYS—Messrs. *J. F. Adams, Joseph Bogy, W. H. Bowles, A. F. Brown* of Callaway, *L. A. Brown* of Howard, *A. Burge, J. G. Burton, Thomas Byrns, D. L. Caldwell, R. A. Campbell, Tyree Harris, Garland Hurt, William Key, F. L. Marchand, Andrew McElvain, J. M. McMichael, C. J. Miller, A. W. Mitchell* of St. Louis, *J. P. Murphy, A. R. Phillips; Lucius Salisbury, J. Salyer, E. C. Sebastian, M. Sides, G. D. Sloan, C. R. Smythe, J. H. Terry, Robert Waide, T. F. Warner,* C. Weinrich—30.

### Nebraska

[Not yet voted.]

### Nevada.

#### SENATE, *March* 1, 1869.

YEAS—Messrs. David H. Brown, T. W. Abraham, T. D. Edwards, C. H. Eastman, O. H. Grey, Wm. N. Hall, James W. Haynes, M. S. Hurd, David L. Hastings, Benjamin S. Mason, Thomas B. Shamp, C. C. Stevenson, Frederick A. Tritle, D. W. Welty—14.

NAYS—Messrs. *M. S. Bonnifield, Eugene B. Hazard,* Jacob J. Linn, *Robert Mullan, Wm. G. Monroe,* Samuel Wilson—6.

#### HOUSE OF REPRESENTATIVES, *March* 1, 1869.

YEAS—Messrs. D. O. Adkison, (Speaker,) J. K. Barney, Wilmer Brown, N. E. Bunker, J. S. Burson, J. A. Burlingame, William H. Corbett, H. F. Dangberg, S. J. Davis, William Doolin, J. S. Ford, W. D. Gray, J. M. Handford, John Hanson, C. J. Hillyer, C. D. King, George J. Lammon, J. L. Richardson, C. P. Shakespere, E. R. Schimmin, John Welch, J. M. Woodworth, S. C. Wright—23.

NAYS—Messrs. Anderson, John Bowman, *E. Clark,* A. C. Cleveland, G. D. Coburn, J. S. Mayhugh, *G. F. Mills,* R. J. Moody, S. A. Moulton, A. K. Potter, F. W. Randall, T. W. Rule, R. H. Scott, J. W. Small, T. J. Tennant, *A. B. Waller* 16.

### New Hampshire.

#### *SENATE, 1869.

#### HOUSE OF REPRESENTATIVES, 1869.

YEAS—Messrs. William C. Noyes, Jacob Lufkin, John W. Dudley, Rufus W. Moore, Daniel Clifford, Harvey P. Hood, George Moore, 2d., Sebastian A. Brown, Andrew J. Hoyt, Ebenezer Folsom, George Beebe, John D. Ordway, Dewitt C. Durgin, Emery Batchelder, Andrew W. Mack, Matthew Holmes, Joshua M. Bickford, Charles Wingate, William H. Y. Hackett, Edward D. Coffin, Daniel J. Vaughn, Isaiah Wilson, Wm. P. Jones, Charles Robinson, William H. Henderson, Frank W. Miller, John W. Wheeler, Joel C. Carey, George Marston, Patrick Quinn, Leonard Lang, Rei Hills, John S. Buzzell, Jos. Daniels, William T. Wentworth, Hiram F. Snow, Alvah Moulton, Samuel M. Wheeler, George Wadleigh, Oliver Wyatt, Charles H. Sawyer, Jonas H. Colony, John Hill, George Lyman,

* Adopted the amendment, but returns not received in time for insertion.

Samuel G. Chamberlain, Larkin Harrington, John Crockett, Silas Hussey, jr., Jos. N. Hayes, John Drew, Daniel Chadbourne, George Stevens, Daniel J. Holmes, Charles F. Montgomery, Chas. Hayes, Walter G. C. Emerson, Rufus G. Morrill, Enoch Franders, Stephen B. Cole, Rufus E. Gale, Geo. W. Sanborn, Sam'l. Emerson, Aaron Clarke, Wm. Blake, jr., Mark Nickerson, Wm. M. Weed, Enoch Q. Fellows, Jas. M. Pease, Sam'l. W. Roberts, Blake Folsom, Nehemiah Butler, Wm. H. Allen, Henry Farnum, John West, Benjamin E. Badger, Augustine C. Pierce, Ephraim W. Woodward, Jos. W. Prescott, Calvin C. Webster, Geo. F. Whittrege, John B. Ireland, Arthur S. Nesmith, George W. Rice, Moses Favor, Benjamin J. Gile, Thomas B. Jones, Reuben E. French, Nahum T. Greenwood, Nathaniel G. Foote, Chas. E. Perkins, Cyrus French, David A. Macurdy, William A. Mack, William N. Tuttle, James H. Hall, Samuel D. Downes, John Greer, Lucien D. Hunkins, Avery M. Clark, Chas. B. Richardson, Daniel M. Greeley, Luther Cram, Joseph L. Stephens, Nathan P. Kidder, Timothy W. Challis, Geo. S. Andrews, Jas. O. Adams, Albert H. Daniels, William Flanders, Herman Foster, Benjamin Currier, Samuel D. Lord, James P. Eaton, Robert Hall, Robert M. Shirley, Elisha B. Barrett, Benj. Ela, Samuel G. Dearborn, Bainbridge Wadleigh, Archibald H. Dunlap, George A. Ramsdell, Caleb Burbank, Amos Webster, Chas. Holman, William A. Preston, Riley B. Hatch, Chas. Wilder, Stephen H. Bacon, Isaiah Wheeler, Charles O. Ballou, Alonzo H. Wood, Aaron Smith, John N. Richardson, George S. Wilder, Frederick W. Bailey, John Humphrey, Solon S. Wilkinson, Robert Wilson, Charles Bridgman, Solon A. Carter, Wm. French, Jairus Collins, Geo. A. Whitney, Alba C. Davis, Charles Mason, William H. Porter, Augustus Hodgkins, Henry Abbott, Edward Alexander, Chas. H. Whitney, Chapin K. Brooks, Nathan W. Howard, Franklin W. Putnam, William Ellis, Hiram Webb, Edward L. Goddard, George N. Farwell, Joseph B. Comings, Albina Hall, William H. Eastman, Martin Bascom, Benjamin F. Sawyer, John B. Cooper, Levi F. Hill, Thos. N. Hughes, Abner Fowler, Sam'l. K. Mason, Erastus Dole, Converse G. Morgan, Herbert Bailey, Jacob S. Perley, Jas. S. Adams, Harlow S. Nash, Joseph W. Cleveland, Jesse C. Sturtevant, Hiram Noyes, Horace B. Savage, Isaac D. Miner, Theodore M. Franklin, Frank Paddleford, Reuben Batchelder, Henry H. Palmer, Willard Spencer, Henry O. Kent, Ossian Ray, Charles E. Philbrook, George W. Libbey—187.

NAYS—Messrs. *John W. Cate, Jesse W. Sargent, Joseph R Garrish, George W. Sanborn, Jas. L. Rundlett, Stephen G. Sleeper, Chas. W. Pickering, Josiah D. Presscott, Charles B. Clark, Wm. A. Shackford, Nathan H. Leavitt, jr., Levi Wilson, Samuel S. Warner, Pike H. Harvey, John R. Reading, Samuel Langdon, David Griffin, Thos. Green, Joseph Chase. Lafayette Hall, Harry S. Parker, Hosea B. Snell, Franklin Colbath, Chas. H. Boody, William Proctor, Jacob W. Evans, Ebenezer P. Osgood, John W. Busiel, John Neally, Nathan B. Wadleigh, Lyman B. Ames, William S. Woodman, Benjamin B. Lamprey, Harrison C. Smith, Thomas J. Allard, George W. M. Pitman, Daniel Chandler, 2d, Christopher W. Wil-*

*der, Charles H. Osgood, Thomas Lovering, Jonathan Gale, William H. H. Mason, Henry J. Banks, Sanborn B. Carter, Elisha Goodwin, jr., Henry Dowst, Henry A. Weymouth, Samuel C. Clement, William O. Heath, Joseph Ayers, John S. Sherburne, Charles Smith, Samuel Martin, Archelaus Moore, James M. Sawyer, Hiram Cilley, Charles O. Rogers, Christopher G. McAlpine, Lemuel W. Collins, Jason Walker, Jno. C. Dodge, Augustus Wilson. Alfred W Savage, Brooks W. Webber, Ephraim Dutton, John W. Griffin, Andrew W. Raymond, George Edgecomb, Dennis D. Sullivan, Eldridge P. Brown Andrew J. Bennett, William G. Butler, Francis Green, Joel Hesselton, Silas Chapman, Asa H. Burge, James H. Goodrich, Aaron D. Hammond, Ezra G. Huntley, Asa H. Bullock, Edward E. Upton, Philip D. Angier, David Parsons, Leonard B. Holland, George Rust, Charles Knight. John Chase, Abram Bean, Daniel A. George, Ora M. Huntoon, Weld D. Proctor, Luke Gale, John Bedel, Chase Whitcher, Thomas J. Spooner, James C. Felch, Joseph D. Weeks, John A. Butrick, Elias M. Blodgett, James M. Dristen, Nathaniel W. Cheney, Alvah Stevens, Joseph Wheat, George F. Putnam, Charles M. Weeks, Thomas Muzzey, George F. Cummings, Daniel Whitcher, Samuel A. Edson, Charles C. Smith, Richard Smith, Joseph A. Dodge, Horace B. Perkins, George W. Garland, Samuel B. Page, Joseph Savage, Joseph W. Campbell, Daniel Green, Charles S. Leavitt, Benjamin Young, William S. Rolfe, Lucius Bond, Charles L. Heywood, Rufus F. Ingalls, Charles L. Plaisted, Moses Hodgdon, jr., Wayne Cobleigh, Thomas C. Hart, Cyrus E. Bickford, Sylvanus M. Jordan, Sam. C. Brown—* 131.

### New Jersey.

[Late in the session, the Senate, by a party vote, passed a resolution postponing all action on the amendment till the third Tuesday of January, 1870—the Republicans voting no. The House did not act on the resolution.]

### New York.

SENATE, *April* 14, 1869.

YEAS—Messrs. Samuel Campbell, Orlow W. Chapman, Richard Crowley, Charles J. Volger, Matthew Hale, Wolcott J. Humphrey, George N. Kennedy, Abner C. Mattoon, Lewis H. Morgan, John I. Nicks, John O'Donnell, Abiah W. Palmer, Abraham X. Parker, Charles Stanford, Francis S. Thayer, John B. Van Petten, Stephen K. Williams—17.

NAYS—Messrs. *A. Bleecker Banks, Geo. Beach, John J. Bradley, William Cauldwell, Thomas J. Creamer, Lewis A. Edwards, Henry W. Genet, William M. Graham, John F. Hubbard, jr., Lewis Morris, Henry C. Murphy, Asher P. Nichols, Michael Norton, James F. Pierce, William M Tweed—*15.

HOUSE, *March* 17, 1869.

YEAS—James R. Allaban, A. H. Andrews, Clifford S. Arms, Eli Avery, Isaac V. Baker, jr., W. F. Barker, C. V. B. Barse, Benjamin J. Bassett, P. H. Bender, D. V. Berry, Monroe Brundage, W. W. Butterfield, Albert C. Calkins, Winfield S. Cameron, W. W. Campbell, Wesley M. Carpenter, James A. Chase, G. Clark, W. A. Coannt,

Hugh Conger, George Cook, H. M. Crane, J. C. Bancroft Davis, Erasmus W. Day, J. Dimick, B. Doolittle, E. Ely, W. M. Ely, Benjamin Farley, J. Ferris, Sanford Gifford, George M. Gleason, Elijah M. K. Glenn, David R. Gould, Miles B. Hackett, Marvin Harris, W. W. Hegeman, F. A. Hixson, A. B. Hodges, C. Dewitt Hoyt, Marcus A. Hull, James A. Husted, James V. Kendall, E. C. Kilham, Nicholas B. La Bau, James D. Lasher, S. Mitchell, J. M. Palmer, C. Pearsall, William I. Perry, Andrew J. Randall, C. Ray, Charles B. Rich, Silas Richardson, James A. Richmond, Samuel Root, E. F. Sargent, J. O. Schoonmaker, John H. Selkreg, L. E. Smith, N. B. Smith, D. Stewart, W. H. Stuart, Moses Summer., Merritt Thornton, Lyman Truman, Addison B. Tuttle, Edward C. Walker, C. H. Weed, Hiram Whitmarsh, C. S. Wright, Truman G. Younglove—72.

Nays—*G. J. Bramler, W. G. Bergen, N. C. Bradstreet, Denis Burns, T. J. Campbell, Owen Cavanagh, H. M. Clark, Henry J. Cullen, jr., P. R. Dyckman, C. Ferris, A. J. Flynn, John Galvin, Baldwin Griffin, William Halpin, Anthony Hartman, A. E. Hasbrouck, William Hitchman, Morgan Horton, H. B. Howard, James Irving, John C. Jacobs, Law. D. Kiernan, John M. Kimball, J. L. La Moree, E. D. Lawrence, Thomas Y. Lyon, Josiah T. Miller, P. Mitchell, William W. Moseley, M. C. Murphy, Martin Nachtmann, D. O'Keeffe, Edward L. Patrick, J. B. Pearsall, George W. Plunkitt, Josiah Porter, R. M. Skeels, A. W. Smith, James Stevens, Edward Sturges, James Suffern, John Tighe, Moses Y. Tilden, D. W. C. Tower, Peter Trainer, Charles H. Whalen, Henry Woltman*—47.

Not Voting—Edward Akin, Matthew P. Bemus, *John Decker, John L. Flagg, George L. Fox, Alexander Frear, John Keegan, John B. Madden,* H. Ray—9.

### North Carolina.

#### Senate, March 4, 1869.

Yeas—Messrs. William Barrow, J. W. Beasley, P. T. Beeman, N. B. Bellamy, C. H. Brogden, Silas Burns, Jas. Blythe, D. D. Colgrove, J. B. Cook, J. H. Davis, J. B. Eaves, Henry Eppes, Samuel Forkner, A. H. Galloway, O. S. Hayes, J. S. Harrington, J. A. Hyman, A. J. Jones, W. D. Jones, R. W. Lassiter, Edwin Legg, J. M. Lindsay, P. A. Long, *W. L. Love, L. A. Mason,* F. G. Martindale, W. A. Moore, W. M. Moore, *J. W. Osborne,* W. B. Richardson, J. B. Respass, T. M. Shoffner, S. P. Smith, J. W. Stephens, W. H. S. Sweet, G. W. Welker, E. A. White, R. J. Wynne, C. S. Winstead, Peter Wilson—40.

Nays—Messrs. *Joshua Barnes, R. L. Beall, J. W. Graham, C. Melchor, W. M. Robbins, J. G. Scott*—6.

#### House, March 4, 1869.

Yeas—Messrs Joseph W. Holden, (Speaker,) Wallace Ames, *Thomas M. Argo,* J. Ashworth, Louis Banner, S. C. Barnett, E. T. Blair, J. W. Bowman, W. G. Candler, M. Carson, W. Carey, Wm. Cawthorn, H. C. Cherry, J. H. Crawford, Joseph Dixon. Hugh Downing, D. S. Ellington, L. G. Estes, R. Falkenor, F. W. Foster, S. D. Franklin, George Z. French, Geo. W. Gahagan, W. W. Gilbert, George A. Graham, *W. W. Grier,*

W. T. Gunter, J. T. Harris, J. H. Harris, W T. J. Hayes, A. L. Hendrix, R. H. Hilliard, B. R. Hinnaut, David Hodgin, *P. Hodnett,* J. Hoffman S. G. Horney, *T. C. Humphries,* Ivey Hudgings, Dixon Ingram, *T. J. Jarvis,* W. D. Justus, J. M. Justice, *J A. Kelly.* Geo. Kinney, Byron Laflin, J. S. Leary, J. B. Long, C. Mayo, W. W. McCanless. J. R. Mendenhall, F. G. Moring, *J. A. Moore,* W. A. Moore, B. D. Morrill, B. W. Morris, R. C. Parker, J. T. Pearson, E. W. Pou, Geo. W. Price, jr., E. K. Proctor, J. W. Ragland, J. J. Red, John W. Renfrow, P. D. Robbins, *J. L. Robinson.* J. T. Reynolds, A. T. Seymour, W. B. Siegrist, James Sinclair, J. R. Simonds, J. J. Smith, E. T. Snipes, *George W. Stanton,* Hiram E. Stilley, J. S. Sweat. T. A. Sykes, T. M. Vestal, J. P. Vest, J. E. Waldrop, *W. P. Welch,* J. White, *R. D. Whitley,* L. D. Wilkie, J. H. Williamson, S. C. Wilson, A. C. Wiswall—87.

Nays—Messrs. *J. J. Allison, N. E. Armstrong, W. W. Boddie, J. W. Clayton, Plato Durham, T. Farrow, W. B. Ferebee, J. P. Gibson, J. A. Hawkins, D. P. High, W. H. Malone, J. C. McMillan, T. A. Nicholson, E. M. Painter, David Proffit, Isaac M. Shaver, J. L. Smith, D. E. Smith, F. Thompson, B. C. Williams*—20.

### Ohio.*

#### Senate, April 30, 1869.

Yeas—Messrs. Thomas R. Biggs, J. Twing Brooks, J. B. Burrows, Abel M. Corey, David A Dangler, Homer Everett, L. D. Griswold, J. Francis Keifer, Henry Kessler, King, Solomon Kraner, Abraham Simmons, William Stedman, Samuel N. Yeoman—14.

Nays—Messrs. *Curtis Berry, jr., W. H. H. Campbell, Wm Carter, S. F. Dowdney. J. Emmitt, Louis Evans, T. J. Godfrey, W. Reed Golden, Harmount. Robert Hutcheson, James B. Jamison, Jonathan Kenney, William Lawrence, Daniel B. Linn, Manuel May, Henry W. Onderdonk, Geo. Rex, Charles M. Scribner, John L. Winner*—19.

#### House, April 1, 1869.

Yeas—Messrs. Ross W. Anderson, Madison Betts, Hiram Bronson, Delos Canfield, Reuben P. Cannon. S. C. Carpenter, George Crist, Robert B. Dennis, Joseph H. Dickson, Jeremiah M. Dunn, William M. Eames, Morris E. Gallup, Benjamin L. Hill, Amos Hill, William P. Johnson, Samuel F. Kerr, Samuel C. Kerr, M. C. Lawrence, Alfred E. Lee, Samuel T. McMorran, Fred. W. Moore, Welcome O. Parker, William Ritezel, Jonathan K. Rukenbrod, James Sayler, William H. Scott, John Lincoln, William Sinclair, Geo. W. Skaats, Perry Stewart, Josiah Thompson, Joseph C. Ullery, Henry Waruking, Marwin Warren, Thomas Welsh, Jacob Wolf—36.

Nays—Messrs. *William T. Acker, Jacob Baker, Edward Ball, Wilmer M. Belville, John W. Branch, Peres B. Buell, Bushnall, Daniel J. Callen, Joseph R. Cockerill, Elisha G. Denman, Joseph Dilworth, Levi Dungan, William Fielding, Isaac J. Finley, Elias W. Gaston, Robert B. Gordon, Eliel Headley, George Henricks, William D. Hill, Peyton Hord, John L. Hughes, Huyh*

*The vote actually taken was on a joint resolution to *reject*, but I have made the record correspond with other States, and stated it as if the motion had been to *ratify.*

J. Jewett, Richard E. Jones, John D. Kemp, Jno. M. Kennon, Wm. Larwill, John Lawson, Ralph Leete, C. T. Mann, Lawrence McMarrell, More, Lawrence T. Neal, James W. Newman, Thomas M. Nichol, Morgan N. Odell, James Parks, Jno. B. Read, James Robinson, William L. Ross, N. C. Rutter, William Shaw, Andrew J. Swain, Jeriah Swetland, Ansel T. Walling, William R. Wilson, Samuel M. Worth, and Speaker—47.

## Oregon.

[Not yet voted.]

## Pennsylvania.

SENATE, March 11, 1869.

YEAS—Messrs. Esaias Billingfelt, James C. Brown, G. Dawson Coleman, George Connell, Russell Errett James W. Fisher, James L. Graham, A. Wilson Henszey, James Kerr, Morrow B. Lowry, A. G. Olmsted, P. M. Osterhout, Jno. K. Robinson, C. H. Stinson, Alex. Stutzman, A. W. Taylor, H. White, Wilmer Worthington—18.

NAYS—Messrs. John B. Beck, R. S. Brown, Charlton Burnett, J. D. Davis, C. M. Duncan, George D. Jackson, R. J. Linderman, William McCandless, Charles J. T. McIntire, A. G. Miller, D. A. Nagle, William M. Randall, Thomas B. Searight, Samuel G. Turner, William A. Wallace—15.

HOUSE OF REPRESENTATIVES, March 25, 1869.

YEAS—Messrs. Alex. Adaire, Fred. W. Ames, William Beatty, Samuel T. Brown, Andrew J. Buffington, Wm. M. Bumd, Loren Burritt, John F. Chamberlain, Thos Church, Junius R. Clark, John Cloud, Elisha W. Davis, Allender P. Duncan, John Edwards, David Foy, Jacob C. Gatchell, Alex C. Hamilton, Jacob G. Heilman, A. Jackson Herr, Wm. G. Herrold, Robert Hervey, Henry B. Hoffman, Jas. Holgate, Marshall C. Hong. Washington W. Hopkins, Miles S. Humphreys, Jas. A. Hunter, Samuel M. Jackson, Samuel Kerr, Chas. Kleckner, Augustus B. Leedond, Alex. Leslie, Jacob H. Longenecker, David M. Marshall, Amos H. Martin, Stephen M. Meredith, Vincent Miller, George F. Morgan, George W. Myers, Thomas Nicholson, Jerome B. Niles, Wm. P. I. Painter, Jacob G. Peters, Jas. M. Phillips, Geo. P. Rea, Archimides Robb, Jos. Robison, David Robison, Almon P. Stephens, James V. Stokes, John D. Stranahan, Butler B. Strang, Jas. Subers, Aaron H. Summy, James Taylor, Harvey J. Vankirk, John H. Walker, James H. Webb, Jno. Weller, Geo. S. Westlake, Geo. Wilson, John Clark, (Speaker,)—62.

NAYS—Messrs. Joshua Beans, Michael Beard, Samuel F. Bossard, Phillip Breen, Henry Brobst, Robert B. Brown, Theodore Cornman, Daniel H. Creitz, Samuel D. Dailey, William J. Davis, Armstrong B Dill, James Eschbach, John H. Fogel, George H. Goundie. Henry S. Hottenstein, George R. Hursk, Richmond L. Jones, Samuel Josephs, William H. Kase, Thos. J. McCullough, John M. Ginnis, Edward C. McKinstry, Henry McMiller, P. Gray Meek, Michael Mullin, Wm. M. Nelson, Decatur E. Nice, Danl. L. O'Neill, Jas. Place, Wm. H. Playford, John Porter, Benjamin F. Porter, John I. Rogers, George Scott, Jos. Sedgwick, John Shirely, Lewis H. Stout, Nathan G. Westler—38.

## Rhode Island.

SENATE, May 27, 1869.

YEAS—Messrs. Wheaton Allen, Nicholas Ball, George L. Clark, George H. Corliss, Benoni Carpenter, Samuel W. Church, James S. Cook, Geo. B. Coggeshall, John M. Douglass, James T. Edwards, Benjamin Fessenden, Lysander Flagg, Charles H. Fisher, Albert G. Hopkins, David Hopkins, Asahel Matteson, Jos. Osborne, Daniel B. Pond, William C. Potter, Jethro Peekham, Isaac B. Richmond, Lewis B. Smith, Charles C. Van Zandt—23.

NAYS—Messrs Pardon W. Stevens, Alfred Anthony, William Butler, Stephen C. Browning, Silas C. Crandall, Samuel H. Cross, Alexander Eddy, Timothy A. Leonard, Nathaniel C. Peckham, John B. Pearce, Joseph W. Sweet, George W. Taylor—12.

HOUSE OF REPRESENTATIVES, May 29, 1869.

*Vote on postponing the question till the January session.*

FOR POSTPONEMENT—Messrs. William D. Aldrich, Ferdinand H. Allen, Emor J. Angell, Julius Baker, George N. Bliss. Theodore P. Bogert Baylies Bourne, John C. Brown, Ezra J. Cady, J. Hamilton Clarke, Nathaniel B. Durfee. Henry T. Grant, Richard W. Greene, Mason W. Hale, Stephen Harris, William S. Kent, Robert R. Knowles, Edward Lillibridge, John Loveland, Francis W Miner, Arlon Mowry, George H. Olney, Samuel B. Parker, John C. Pegram, Samuel Rodman, jr., William P. Shaffield, Nathaniel C. Smith, George T. Spicer, Joseph E. Speink Horatio A. Stone, Nathan T. Verry. Albert M Waite, John E. Weeden, Joseph D. Wilcox, Jas. M. Wright—35.

AGAINST POSTPONEMENT—Messrs. Benjamin T Eames, (Speaker,) William T. Adams, Edwin Aldrich, Lucius C. Ashley, John H. Barden, William W. Blodgett, Francis Brinley, Joseph F. Brown, Henry Bull, jr., John T. Bush, Thomas G. Carr, John G. Childs, Thomas Coggeshall, jr., James C. Collins, Davis Cook, jr., Saladin Cook, Ed. Dowling, Daniel E. Day, Henry F. Brown, Edwin L. Freeman, George W. Green, David S. Harris, Wm. Knowles. Nathan B. Lewis, Jesse Metcalf, Jabez W. Mowry, Charles H. Perkins, William H. Seagrave, Owen W. Simmons—29.

## South Carolina.

SENATE, March 6, 1869.

YEAS—Messrs. H. Luck, R. H. Cain, E. F Dickson, R. J. Donaldson, H. W. Duncan, J. A Greene, W. R. Hoyt, J. K. Jillson. C. P. Leslie, John Lunney, C. W. Montgomery, H. J. Maxwell, W. B. Nash, Y. J. P. Owens, J. H. Rainey, W. E. Rose, S. A. Swails, J. J. Wright—18.

NAY—Mr. Joel Foster—1.

HOUSE OF REPRESENTATIVES, March 11, 1869.

YEAS—Messrs. F. J. Moses. jr., (Speaker,) B. A. Boseman, B. F. Berry, W J. Brodie, S. Brown, John Boston, Joseph Boston, John A Boswell, Jason Bryant, W. A. Bishop, Lawrence Cain, E. J. Cain, Wilson Cooke, W. S. Collins, Joseph Crews, R. C. DeLarge, John B. Dennis, William Driffle, R. B. Elliott, J. H. Feriter. S. Farr W. H. W. Gray, John Gardner, Æsop Goodson, E.

Hayes, C. D. Hayne, James N. Hayne, B. Humphries, G. Hollinan, James Hutson, D. Harris, John B. Hyde, D. J. J. Johnson, W. E. Johnston, S. Johnson, B. F. Jackson, H. Jacobs, B. James, H. James, W. R. Jervay, J. H. Jones, W. H. Jones, C. S. Kuh, H. J. Lomax, George Lee, S. J. Lee, J. Long, J. Mayer, W. C. Morrison, W. J. McKinley, E. Mickey, G. F. McIntyre, H. McDaniels, J. S. Mobley, J. P. Mays, J. W. Mead, W. Nelson, J. W. Nash, J. L. Nagle, P. J. O'Connell, H. W. Purvis, W. Perrin, J. Prendegrass, A. J. Ransier, Thomas Richardson, T. Root, A. Rush, P. R. Rivers, E. M. Stoeber, C. J. Stolbranch, Robert Smalls, A. Smith, S. Saunders, H. L. Shrewsbury, P. Smythe, T. K. Serporlas, R. F. Scott, B. A. Thompson, S. B. Thompson, Reuben Tomlinson, W. M. Thomas, S. Tinsley, C. M. Wilder, John Wooley, W. J. Whipper, J. H. White, J. B. Wright, George M. Wells—88.

NAYS—Messrs. *O. M. Doyle, R. M. Smith, John Wilson*—3.

NOT VOTING—Messrs. B. Barton, *T. F. Clyburn,* John A. Chestnut, George Dusenberry, L. W. Duvall, F. De Mars, P. E. Ezekiel, John G. Grant, J. Henderson, J. H. Jenks, H. Johnson, G. Johnson, *W. C. Keith, F. A. Lewie, S. Littlejohn,* Wm. McKinley, *John B. Moore,* Y. B. Milford, F. F. Miller, W. J. Mixson, S. Nuckles, C. H. Pettengill, *B. F. Sloan, W. G. Stewart,* William Simons, J. Smiley, *C. C. Turner, W. W. Waller,* H. W. Webb—29.

----

### Tennessee.

[Not yet voted ]

----

### Texas.

[Not yet voted.]

----

### Vermont.

[Not yet voted.]

----

### Virginia.

[Not yet voted.]

----

### West Virginia.

SENATE, *March* 3, 1869.

YEAS—Messrs. Joseph T. Hoke, (President,) James Burley, H. K. Dix, Willis J. Drummond, Ephraim Doolittle, George K. Leonard, Z. D. Ramsdell, Alstorpheus Werninger, Wm. Workman, Samuel Young—10.

NAYS—Messrs. *Lewis Applegate,* Wm. J. Boreman, Jesse H. Cather, *Henry G. Davis,* John M. Phelps, *Andrew Wilson*—6.

HOUSE, *March* 2, 1869.

YEAS—Messrs. Solomon G. Fleming, (Speaker,) Joseph W. Allison, George W. Carpenter, James Carpenter, Benjamin F. Charlton, Elias Cunningham, George Edwards, Joseph H. Gibson, Sidney Haymond, Fenelon Howes, John S. Keever, Edward S. Mahon, Andrew W. Mann, William M. Powell, Thomas G. Putnam, John Reynolds, Barney J. Rollins, Owen G. Scofield,

John Rufus Smith, Jesse F. Snodgrass, Richard Thomas, William O. Wright—22.

NAYS—Messrs. *Rhodes B. Ballard,* John Bowyer, *Reuben Davisson,* Henry H. Dits, William M. French, Alpheus Garrison, *Benjamin F. Harrison, James Hervey, John A. Hutton, Alexander M. Jacob,* John J. Jacob, John Kincaid, *Daniel Lamb, Thomas W. Manion,* Jas. T. McClaskey, David S. Pinnell, Charles W. Smith, Louis C. Stifel, *John T. Vance*—19.

----

### Wisconsin.

SENATE, *March* 9, 1869.

YEAS—Messrs. Henry Adams, S. S. Barlow, W. J. Copp, J. W. Fisher, William M. Griswold, Geo. C. Hazelton, Lemuel W. Joiner, W. J. Kershaw, A. W. Newman, David Taylor, Anthony Van Wyck, Geo. D. Waring, Chas. M. Webb, C. G. Williams, Nelson Williams—15.

NAYS—Messrs. *W. J. Abrams, Satterlee Clarke, H. H. Gray, Carl Habich, Chas. H. Larkin, Wm. Pitt Lynde, Lyman Morgan, Geo. Reed, Adam Schantz, W. W. Woodman, Wm. Young* —11.

ABSENT AND NOT VOTING—*E. S. Bragg, C. M. Buth, William Ketcham,* N. M. Littlejohn, *M. W. Louder, Curtis Mann,* Henry Stevens—7.

HOUSE OF REPRESENTATIVES, *March,* 3, 1869.

YEAS—Messrs. Fayette Allen, Douglas Arnold, H. D. Barron, J. B. G. Baxter, J. Bennett, Van S. Bennett, Benjamin H. Bettis, J. M. Bingham, J. N. P. Bird, Thomas Blackstock, H. C. Bottum, G. H. Brock, Luther Buxton, Sylvester Calwell, Ben. M. Coutes, Joseph S. Curtis, W. P. Dewey, Seth Fisher, Jas. S. Foster, Hiram L. Gilmore, Geo. T. Graves, J. K. Hamilton, Joseph Harris, Andrew Henry, Robert Henry, Edwin L. Hoyt, Frederick Huntley, Edwin Hurlbut, Thos. A. Jackson, D. H. Johnson, J. E. Johnson, C. C. Kuntz, O. B. Lapham, A. R. McCartney, J. R. McDonald, John McLees, D. E. Maxson, Knute Nelson, C. C. Palmer, C. D. Parker, C. H. Parker, Cyrus Perry, A. L. Phillips, Thad. C. Pound, Abner Powell N. B. Richardson, Freeman M. Ross, Wm. E. Rowe, M. H. Sessions, Adelman Sherman, John A. Smith, S. E. Tarbell, Joseph M. Thomas, Thornton Thompson, Vernon Lichoner, G. W. Trask, A. J. Turner, N. P. Waller W. S. Warner, Jefferson F. Wescott, Samuel C. West, and Mr. Speaker A. M. Thomson—62.

NAYS—Messrs. *John Adams, John H. Bohne, A. K. Delaney. Andrew Dieringer, Richard Donovan, Patrick Drew, Rees Evans, B. F. Fay, John Fellenz, Charles Geisse, Job Haskell, James Woye, E. H. Ives, John Kastler, J. McDonald, C. E. McIntosh, D. W. Maxon, William Murphy, Eugene O'Connor, C. H. M. Peterson, J. Phillips, C. Pole, Jerome B. Potter, Henry Reed, Henry C. Rankel, John Ruttledge, John Scheffel, Geo. B. Smith, Joseph Winslow*—29.

NOT VOTING—Messrs. George Abert, P. J. Conklin, J. L. Fobes, John Gillespie, Daniel Hooper, A. G. Kellam, *Henry Roethe,* Parlan Semple, *Randall Wilcox*—9

# XLVIII.

## STATISTICAL TABLES.

### PRESIDENTIAL ELECTION RETURNS.—NATIONAL DEBT STATEMENT.

*Electoral and Popular Votes for President of the United States† for the Term Commencing March 4, 1869.

| Number of Votes. | STATES. | ‡FOR PRESIDENT OF THE UNITED STATES. | | POPULAR VOTE. | | |
|---|---|---|---|---|---|---|
| | | U. S. Grant, of Illinois. | Horatio Seymour, of New York. | Republican, Grant. | Democratic, Seymour. | Republican Majorities. |
| 5 | New Hampshire | 5 | | 38,191 | 31,224 | 6,967 |
| 12 | Massachusetts | 12 | | 136,477 | 59,408 | 77,069 |
| 4 | Rhode Island | 4 | | 12,993 | 6,548 | 6,445 |
| 6 | Connecticut | 6 | | 50,641 | 47,600 | 3,041 |
| 5 | Vermont | 5 | | 44,167 | 12,045 | 32,122 |
| 33 | New York | | 33 | 419,883 | 429,883 | ⸹10,⸹⸹0 |
| 7 | New Jersey | | 7 | 80,121 | 83,001 | ⸹2,880 |
| 26 | Pennsylvania | 26 | | 342,280 | 313,382 | 28,898 |
| 3 | Delaware | | 3 | 7,623 | 10,980 | ⸹3,357 |
| 7 | Maryland | | 7 | 30,438 | 62,357 | ⸹31,919 |
| | Virginia‖ | | | | | |
| 9 | North Carolina | 9 | | 96,226 | 84,090 | 12,136 |
| 6 | South Carolina | 6 | | 62,301 | 45,237 | 17,064 |
| 11 | Kentucky | | 11 | 39,566 | 115,889 | ⸹76,323 |
| 10 | Tennessee | 10 | | 56,757 | 26,311 | 30,446 |
| 21 | Ohio | 21 | | 280,128 | 238,700 | 41,428 |
| 7 | Louisiana | | 7 | 33,263 | 80,225 | ⸹46,962 |
| 13 | Indiana | 13 | | 176,552 | 166,980 | 9,572 |
| | Mississippi‖ | | | | | |
| 16 | Illinois | 16 | | 250,293 | 199,143 | 51,150 |
| 8 | Alabama | 8 | | 76,366 | 72,086 | 4,280 |
| 7 | Maine | 7 | | 70,426 | 42,396 | 28,030 |
| 11 | Missouri | 11 | | 85,671 | 59,788 | 25,883 |
| 5 | Arkansas | 5 | | 22,152 | 19,078 | 3,074 |
| 8 | Michigan | 8 | | 128,550 | 97,069 | 31,481 |
| 3 | Florida¶ | 3 | | | | |
| | Texas‖ | | | | | |
| 8 | Wisconsin | 8 | | 108,857 | 84,710 | 24,147 |
| 8 | Iowa | 8 | | 120,399 | 74,040 | 46,359 |
| 5 | California | 5 | | 54,592 | 54,078 | 514 |
| 4 | Minnesota | 4 | | 43,542 | 28,072 | 15,470 |
| 3 | Oregon | | 3 | 10,961 | 11,125 | ⸹164 |
| 3 | Kansas | 3 | | 31,049 | 14,019 | 17,030 |
| 5 | West Virginia | 5 | | 29,025 | 20,306 | 8,719 |
| 3 | Nevada | 3 | | 6,480 | 5,218 | 1,262 |
| 3 | Nebraska | 3 | | 9,729 | 5,439 | 4,290 |
| | Excluding Georgia | 214 | 71 | 2,955,699 | 2,600,427 | 355,272 |
| 9 | Georgia | | 9 | 57,134 | 102,822 | ⸹45,688 |
| | Including Georgia | 214 | 80 | 3,012,833 | 2,703,249 | 309,584 |

* The whole number of electors to vote for President and Vice President, including electors of Georgia, is 294, of which a majority is 148; and the whole number, excluding those of Georgia, is 285, of which a majority is 143.
† For presidential election returns of 1860 and 1864 see p. 111 Political Manual for 1868, or p. 372 Hand-Book of Politics.
‡ For Vice President, Schuyler Colfax, of Indiana, received 214 electoral votes; and F. P. Blair, Jr., of Missouri, 71 votes, excluding the vote of Georgia, or 80 including it.
⸹ Democratic majorities.
‖ No vote.
¶ By legislature.

## STATEMENT OF THE PUBLIC DEBT OF THE UNITED STATES.—JULY 1, 1869.

### Debt bearing Coin Interest.

| Authorizing Acts. | Character of Issue. | Rate of Interest. | Amount outstanding. | When Redeemable or Payable. | Accrued Interest. | When Payable. |
|---|---|---|---|---|---|---|
| June 14, 1858 | Bonds | 5 per cent | $20,000,000 00 | Payable after 15 years from January 1, 1859 | $500,000 00 | January and July. |
| June 22, 1860 | Bonds | 5 per cent | 7,022,000 00 | Payable after 10 years from January 1, 1861 | 175,550 00 | January and July. |
| February 8, 1861 | Bonds, 1881 | 6 per cent | 18,415,000 00 | Payable after December 31, 1880 | 552,450 00 | January and July. |
| March 2, 1861 | Bonds, (Oregon war,) 1881 | 6 per cent | 945,000 00 | Redeemable 20 years from July 1, 1861 | 28,350 00 | January and July. |
| July 17 and August 5, 1861. | Bonds, 1881 | 6 per cent | 189,317,500 00 | Payable at pleasure of Government after 20 years from June 30, 1861. | 5,679,525 00 | January and July. |
| February 25, 1862 | Bonds, (5-20's) | 6 per cent | 514,771,600 00 | Redeemable after 5 and payable 20 years from May 1, 1862 | 5,147,716 00 | May and November. |
| March 3, 1863 | Bonds, 1881 | 6 per cent | 75,000,000 0½ | Payable after June 30, 1881 | 2,250,000 00 | January and July. |
| March 3, 1864 | Bonds, (10-40's) | 5 per cent | 194,567,300 00 | Redeemable after 10 and payable 40 years from March 1, 1864 | 3,242,788 33 | March and September. |
| March 3, 1864 | Bonds, (5-20's) | 6 per cent | 3,882,500 00 | Redeemable after 5 and payable 20 years from Nov. 1, 1864 | 38,825 00 | May and November. |
| June 30, 1864 | Bonds, (5-20's) | 6 per cent | 125,561,300 00 | Redeemable after 5 and payable 20 years from Nov. 1, 1864 | 1,255,613 00 | May and November. |
| March 3, 1865 | Bonds, (5-20's) | 6 per cent | 203,327,250 00 | Redeemable after 5 and payable 20 years from Nov. 1, 1865 | 2,033,272 50 | May and November. |
| March 3, 1865 | Bonds, (5-20's) | 6 per cent | 332,998,950 00 | Redeemable after 5 and payable 20 years from July 1, 1865 | 9,989,968 50 | January and July. |
| March 3, 1865 | Bonds, (5-20's) | 6 per cent | 379,582,850 00 | Redeemable after 5 and payable 20 years from July 1, 1867 | 11,387,455 50 | January and July. |
| March 3, 1865 | Bonds, (5-20's) | 6 per cent | 42,539,350 00 | Redeemable after 5 and payable 20 years from July 1, 1868 | 1,276,210 50 | January and July. |
| Aggregate of debt bearing coin interest | | | 2,107,930,600 00 | | 43,557,724 33 | |
| | | | | Coupons payable May 1, 1869, not presented for payment | 2,938,388 00 | |
| | | | | | 46,496,112 33 | |
| | | | | Less amount paid in advance | 1,122,182 00 | |
| | | | | | 45,373,930 33 | |

### Debt bearing Interest in Lawful Money.

| Authorizing Acts. | Character of Issue. | Rate of Interest. | Amount outstanding. | When Redeemable or Payable. | Accrued Interest. | When Payable. |
|---|---|---|---|---|---|---|
| March 2, 1867, and July 2, 1868. | Certificates | 3 per cent | $52,120,000 00 | On demand, (interest estimated for 9 months) | $1,172,700 00 | Ann'ally or on redemption of certificate. |
| July 23, 1868. | Navy Pens'n Fund | 3 per cent | 14,000,000 00 | Interest only applicable to payment of pensions | 210,000 00 | January and July. |
| Aggregate of debt bearing interest in lawful money. | | | 66,120,000 00 | | 1,382,700 00 | |

## STATEMENT OF THE PUBLIC DEBT OF THE UNITED STATES, JULY 1, 1869.—Continued.

### Debt on which *Interest* has ceased *since maturity*.

| Authorizing Acts. | Character of Issue. | Rate of Interest. | Amount out- standing. | When Redeemable or Payable. | Accrued Interest. |
|---|---|---|---|---|---|
| April 15, 1842........ | Bonds ...... ......... | 6 per cent......... | $6,000 00 | Matured December 31, 1862............................ | $360 00 |
| January 28, 1847.... | Bonds ......... ...... | 6 per cent......... | 26,150 00 | Matured December 31, 1867............................ | 1,569 00 |
| March 31, 1848...... | Bonds............... | 6 per cent......... | 69,850 00 | Matured July 1, 1868, (9 months' interest)............ | 3,143 25 |
| September 9, 1850.. | Bonds, (Tex. ind.) | 5 per cent. ...... | 242,000 00 | Matured December 31, 1864............................ | 12,100 00 |
| Prior to 1857........ | Treasury notes.... | 1 mill to 6 per ct | 104,511 64 | Matured at various dates........... . .................. | 3,135 35 |
| December 23, 1857.. | Treasury notes.... | 5 to 5½ per ct... | 2,400 00 | Matured March 1, 1859................................ | 120 00 |
| March 2, 1861....... | Treasury notes.... | 6 per cent......... | 3,300 00 | Matured April and May, 1863......................... | 198 00 |
| July 17, 1867........ | Treasury notes, (3 years.) | 7 3-10 per cent.. | 34,900 00 | Matured August 19 and October 1, 1864............. | 2,547 70 |
| March 3, 1863........ | Treasury notes, (1 and 2 years.) | 5 per cent......... | 338,552 00 | Matured from January 7 to April 1, 1866............. | 16,927 60 |
| March 3, 1863........ | Certificates of ind. | 6 per cent......... | 12,000 00 | Matured at various dates in 1866.................... | 720 00 |
| March 3, 1863, and June 30, 1864. | Comp. int. notes... | 6 per cent......... | 2,871,410 00 | Matured June 10, 1867, and May 15, 1868............. | 557,053 08 |
| June 30, 1864........ | Temporary loan... | 4, 5, and 6 per ct. | 186,310 00 | Matured October 15, 1866............................ | 7,661 98 |
| June 30, 1864, and March 3, 1865. | Treasury notes, (3 years.) | 7 3-10 per cent.. | 1,166,500 00 | Matured August 15, 1867, and June 15, 1868........ | 85,154 50 |
| Aggregate of debt on which interest has ceased since maturity. | | | 5,063,883 64 | ....................................................... | 690,680 46 |

### Debt bearing *no Interest*.

| | | | | | |
|---|---|---|---|---|---|
| July 17, 1861....... February 12, 1862. | Demand notes...... | No interest........ | $121,637 50 | | |
| February 25, 1862. July 11, 1862...... March 3, 1863...... | U. S. legal-ten. nts. | No interest........ | 355,935,194 50 | | |
| July 17, 1862...... | Postal currency.... | No interest....... | 32,062,027 73 | | |
| March 3, 1863...... June 30, 1864...... | Fractional cur'cy.... | No interest....... | | | |
| March 3, 1863 | Cert. for gold dep. | No interest........ | 30,489,640 00 | | |
| Aggregate c⁻ debt bearing no interest................. | | | 418,608,499 73 | | |

## STATEMENT OF THE PUBLIC DEBT OF THE UNITED STATES, JULY 1, 1869.—Continued.

*Recapitulation.*

| | Amount outstanding. | Interest. | |
|---|---|---|---|
| **Debt bearing interest in coin, viz:** | | | |
| Bonds at 5 per cent, issued before March 3, 1864 | $27,022,000 00 | | |
| Bonds at 5 per cent, (10-40's,) issued under act of March 3, 1864 | 194,567,300 00 | | |
| Bonds of 1881, at 6 per cent | 283,677,500 00 | | |
| 5-20 Bonds, at 6 per cent | 1,602,663,800 00 | | |
| | $2,107,930,600 00 | 45,373,930 38 | |
| **Debt bearing interest in lawful money, viz:** | | | |
| Certificates, 3 per cent. interest | 52,120,000 00 | | |
| Navy pension fund, 3 per cent. interest | 14,000,000 00 | | |
| | 66,120,000 00 | 1,382,700 00 | |
| **Debt bearing no interest, viz:** | | | |
| Demand and legal-tender notes | 356,056,882 00 | | |
| Postal and fractional currency | 32,062,027 73 | | |
| Certificates of gold deposited | 30,489,640 00 | | |
| | 418,608,499 73 | 690,680 46 | |
| Debt on which interest has ceased since maturity | 5,063,883 64 | | |
| Total debt—Principal outstanding | 2,597,722,983 37 | | |
| Interest accrued, $48,569,493 79, less am't of interest paid in advance, $1,122,182 | | 47,447,310 79 | |
| Total debt—Principal and interest | | | $2,645,170,294 16 |
| **Amount in Treasury—**Coin, belonging to Government | | $79,713,072 62 | |
| Coin, for which certificates of deposit are outstanding | | 30,489,640 00 | |
| Currency | | 37,097,818 89 | |
| Sinking fund, in bonds bearing coin interest and accrued interest thereon | | 8,867,282 07 | |
| | | | 156,167,813 58 |
| Amount of public debt, less cash and sinking fund in Treasury | | | 2,489,002,480 58 |
| Amount of public debt, less cash and sinking fund in Treasury, on the 1st ultimo | | | 2,505,412,613 12 |
| Decrease of public debt during the past month | | | 16,410,132 54 |
| Decrease since March 1, 1869 | | | 36,460,779 43 |

STATEMENT OF THE PUBLIC DEBT OF THE UNITED STATES, JULY 1, 1869.—Continued.

*Bonds issued to the Union Pacific Railroad Company and Branches, Interest Payable in Lawful Money.*

| Authorizing Acts. | Character of Issue. | Rate of Interest. | Amount outstanding. | When Redeemable or Payable. | Interest Payable. | Interest Accrued and not yet paid. | Interest paid by United States. | Interest repaid by transporta'n of mails, &c. | Balance of interest paid by United States. |
|---|---|---|---|---|---|---|---|---|---|
| July 1, 1862, and July 2, 1864. | Bonds, (Union Pacific Co.) | 6 per cent. | $25,998,000 00 | Payable 30 years from date. | January 1 and July 1. | $768,104 87 | $1,313,765 52 | $906,446 11 | $407,319 41 |
| July 1, 1862, and July 2, 1864. | Bonds, (Union Pacific, Eastern Division.) | 6 per cent. | 6,303,000 00 | Payable 30 years from date. | January 1 and July 1. | 189,090 00 | 645,723 09 | 546,569 10 | 99,153 99 |
| July 1, 1862, and July 2, 1864. | Bonds, (Sioux City and Pacific.) | 6 per cent. | 1,628,320 00 | Payable 30 years from date. | Jan. 1 & July 1 | 43,454 93 | 52,963 76 | 16 27 | 52,947 49 |
| July 1, 1862, and July 2, 1864. | Bonds, (Central Pacific.) | 6 per ct. } | 2,362,000 00 / 20,427,000 00 | } Payable 30 years from date. | Jan.16 & July 16 / Jan. 1 & July 1 | 64,065 65 / 543,064 49 | 517,956 83 / 584,829 76 | } 72,666 99 | 1,030,119 60 |
| July 1, 1862, and July 2, 1864. | Bonds, (Central Bra'ch Union Pacific, assignees of Atchison and Pike's Peak.) | 6 per cent. | 1,600,000 00 | Payable 30 years from date. | January 1 and July 1. | 45,000 00 | 157,808 26 | 3,490 79 | 154,317 47 |
| July 1, 1862, and July 2, 1864. | Bonds, (Western Pacific.) | 6 per cent. | 320,000 00 | Payable 30 years from date. | January 1 and July 1. | 9,600 00 | 37,006 03 | ............ | 37,006 03 |
| Total issue ........ | | | 58,638,320 00 | | | 1,665,469 44 | 3,310,053 25 | 1,529,189 26 | 1,780,863 99 |

# XLIX.

## MISCELLANEOUS MATTERS.

### Letter from General Sherman.

THE SURRENDER OF GENERAL JOS. E. JOHNSTON.

*To the editor of the Tribune.*

SIR: In your issue of yesterday is a notice of Mr. Healy's picture, representing the interview between Mr. Lincoln, General Grant, Admiral Porter, and myself, which repeats substantially the account published some time ago in *Wilkes' Spirit of the Times* explanatory of that interview, and attributing to Mr. Lincoln himself the paternity of the terms to General Johnston's army at Durham, in April, 1865.*

I am glad you have called public attention to the picture itself, because I feel a personal interest that Mr. Healy should be appreciated as one of our very best American artists. But some friends here think by silence I may be construed as willing to throw off on Mr. Lincoln the odium of those terms. If there be any odium, which I doubt, I surely would not be willing that the least show of it should go to Mr. Lincoln's memory, which I hold in too much veneration to be stained by anything done or said by me. I understand that the substance of Mr. Wilkes's original article was compiled by him after a railroad conversation with Admiral Porter, who was present at that interview, as represented in the picture, and who made a note of the conversation immediately after we separated. He would be more likely to have preserved the exact words used on the occasion than I, who made no notes, then or since. I cannot now even pretend to recall more than the subjects touched upon by the several parties, and the impression left on my mind after we parted. The interview was in March, nearly a month before the final catastrophe, and it was my part of the plan of operations to move my army, reinforced by Schofield, then at Goldsboro', North Carolina, to Burkesville, Virginia, when Lee would have been forced to surrender in Richmond. The true move left to him was a hasty abandonment of Richmond, join his force to Johnston's, and strike me in the open country. The only question was, could I sustain this joint attack till General Grant came up in pursuit? I was confident I could; but at the very moment of our conversation General Grant was moving General Sheridan's heavy force of cavalry to his extreme left to prevent this very contingency. Mr. Lincoln, in hearing us speak of a final bloody battle, which I then thought would fall on me near Raleigh, did exclaim, more than once, that blood enough had already been shed, and he hoped that the war would end without any more. We spoke of what was to be done with Davis, other party

* For these terms, see Political Manual for 1866, and the Hand-Book of Politics for 1868, p. 121.

leaders, and the rebel army; and he left me under the impression that all he asked of us was to dissipate these armies, and get the soldiers back to their homes anyhow, the quicker the better, leaving him free to apply the remedy and the restoration of civil law. He (Mr. Lincoln) surely left upon my mind the impression, warranted by Admiral's Porter's account, that he had long thought of his course of action when the rebel armies were out of his way, and that he wanted to get civil governments reorganized at the South, the quicker the better, and strictly conforming with our general system.

I had been absent so long that I presumed, of course, that Congress had enacted all the laws necessary to meet the event of peace so long expected, and the near approach of which must then have been seen by the most obtuse, and all I aimed to do was to remit the rebel army surrendering to me to the conditions of the laws of the country as they then existed. At the time of Johnston's surrender at Durham, I drew up the terms with my own hand. Breckinridge had nothing at all to do with them more than to discuss their effect, and he knew they only applied to the military, and he forthwith proceeded to make his escape from the country; a course that I believe Mr. Lincoln wished that Mr. Davis should have succeeded in effecting, as well as all the other leading southern politicians against whom public indignation always turned with a feeling far more intense than against Generals Lee, Johnston, and other purely military men.

I repeat, that, according to my memory, Mr. Lincoln did not expressly name any specific terms of surrender, but he was in that kindly and gentle frame of mind that would have induced him to approve fully what I did, excepting, probably, he would have interlined some modifications, such as recognizing his several proclamations antecedent, as well as the laws of Congress, which would have been perfectly right and acceptable to me and to all parties.

I dislike to open this or any other old question, and do it for the reason stated, viz, lest I be construed as throwing off on Mr. Lincoln what his friends think should be properly borne by me alone.

If in the original terms I had, as I certainly meant, included the proclamations of the President, they would have covered the slavery question and all the real State questions which caused the war: and had not Mr. Lincoln been assassinated at that very moment, I believe those "terms" would have taken the usual course of approval, modification, or absolute disapproval, and been returned to me, like hundreds of other official acts, without the newspaper clamor and unpleasant controversies so unkindly and unpleasantly thrust upon me at the time.

I am, truly, yours,

W. T. SHERMAN, *General.*

WASHINGTON, D. C., *April* 11, 1869.

### *President Grant's Proclamation for the Election in Mississippi, issued July 13, 1869.

In pursuance of the provisions of the act of Congress approved April 10. 1869, I hereby designate Tuesday, the 30th day of November, as the time for submitting the constitution adopted on the 15th day of May, 1868, by the convention which met in Jackson, Mississippi, to the voters of said State registered at the date of such submission, viz, November 30, 1869.

And I submit to a separate vote that part of section 3 of article VII of said constitution, which is in the following words:

"That I am not disfranchised in any of the provisions of the act known as the reconstruction acts of the 39th and 40th Congresses, and that I admit the political and civil equality of all men; so help me God: *Provided,* That if Congress shall at any time remove the disabilities of any person disfranchised in the said reconstruction acts of the said 39th and 40th Congresses, (and the legislature of this State shall concur therein,) then so much of this oath, and so much only, as refers to the said reconstruction acts, shall not be required of such person so pardoned to entitle him to be registered."

And I further submit to a separate vote section 5 of the same article of said constitution, which is in the following words: "No person shall be eligible to any office of profit or trust, civil or military, in this State, who, as a member of the legislature, voted for the call of the convention that passed the ordinance of secession, or who, as a delegate to any convention, voted for or signed any ordinance of secession, or who gave voluntary aid, countenance, counsel, or encouragement to persons engaged in armed hostility to the United States, or who accepted or attempted to exercise the functions of any office, civil or military, under any authority or pretended government, authority, power, or constitution, within the United States, hostile or inimical thereto, except all persons who aided reconstruction by voting for this convention, or who have continuously advocated the assembling of this convention, and shall continuously and in good faith advocate the acts of the same; but the legislature may remove such disability: *Provided,* That nothing in this section, except voting for or signing the ordinance of secession, shall be so construed as to exclude from office the private soldier of the late so-called Confederate States army."

And I further submit to a separate vote section 5 of article XII of the said constitution, which is in the following words: "The credit of the State shall not be pledged or loaned in aid of any person, association, or corporation; nor shall the State hereafter become a stockholder in any corporation or association."

And I further submit to a separate vote part of the oath of office prescribed in section 26 of

article XII of the said constitution, which is in the following words: "'That I have never, as a member of any convention, voted for or signed any ordinance of secession; that I have never, as a member of any State legislature, voted for the call of any convention that passed any such ordinance' The above oath shall also be taken by all the city and county officers before entering upon their duties, and by all other State officers not included in the above provision."

I direct the vote to be taken upon each of the above cited provisions alone, and upon the other portions of the said constitution in the following manner, viz:

Each voter favoring the ratification of the constitution, (excluding the provisions above quoted,) as adopted by the convention of May 15, 1868, shall express his judgment by voting

FOR THE CONSTITUTION.

Each voter favoring the rejection of the constitution, (excluding the provisions above quoted,) shall express his judgment by voting

AGAINST THE CONSTITUTION.

Each voter will be allowed to cast a separate ballot for or against either or both of the provisions above quoted.

It is understood that sections 4, 5, 6, 7, 8, 9, 10, 11, 12, 13, 14, and 15, of article XIII, under the head of "Ordinance," are considered as forming no part of the said constitution.

In testimony whereof I have hereunto set my hand and caused the seal of the United States to be affixed.

Done at the city of Washington this thirteenth day of July, in the year of our Lord one thousand eight hundred and sixty-
[SEAL.] nine, and of the independence of the United States of America the ninety-fourth. U. S. GRANT.

By the President:

HAMILTON FISH,
*Secretary of State.*

### *President Grant's Proclamation for the Election in Texas, issued July 15, 1869.

In pursuance of the provisions of the act of Congress approved April 10, 1869, I hereby designate Tuesday, the 30th day of November, 1869, as the time for submitting the constitution adopted by the convention which met in Austin, Texas, on the 15th day of June, to the voters of said State, registered at the date of such submission, viz:

I direct the vote to be taken upon the said constitution in the following manner, viz:

Each voter favoring the ratification of the constitution, as adopted by the convention of the 15th of June, 1868, shall express his judgment by voting

FOR THE CONSTITUTION.

Each voter favoring the rejection of the constitution shall express his judgment by voting

AGAINST THE CONSTITUTION.

In testimony whereof I have hereunto set my hand and caused the seal of the United States to be affixed.

Done at the city of Washington, this fifteenth day of July, in the year of our Lord one thousand eight hundred and sixty-

---

* Received too late for insertion in proper place with other proclamations.

[SEAL.] nine, and of the independence of the United States of America the ninety-fourth.　　　　　U. S. GRANT.

By the President:
HAMILTON FISH,
*Secretary of State.*

## Female Suffrage.

The special committee of the Senate of Massachusetts has reported the following amendment to the constitution of that State:

*Article of amendment.*—"The word 'male' is hereby stricken from the 3d article of the amendment of the constitution. Hereafter women of this Commonwealth shall have the right of voting at elections and be eligible to office on the same terms, restrictions, and qualifications, and subject to the same restrictions and disabilities, as male citizens of this Commonwealth now are, and no other."

[This amendment must be approved by two successive legislatures, and then submitted to the men of the State.]

June 2.—It was voted down by the *Senate*—yeas 9, nays 22, as follows:

YEAS.—Messrs. Whiting Griswold, Francis A. Hobart, Nathaniel J. Holden, Richmond Kingman, Charles R. Ladd, Charles Marsh, Robert C. Pitman, (President,) Richard Plumer, Chas. U. Wheelock—9.

NAYS.—Messrs. Geo. O. Brastow, Geo. M. Buttrick, H. H. Coolidge, Sam'l D. Crane, Edmund Dowse, John B. Hathaway, Estes Howe, George A. King, C. J. Kittredge, J. N. Marshall, Geo. H. Monroe, E. W. Morton, J. R. Palmer, Jos. G. Pollard, O. H. P. Smith, George H. Sweetser, George S. Taylor, Edward Thomas, J. S. Todd, Harrison Tweed, G. B. Weston, Jonathan White—22.

NOT VOTING.—Messrs. Nathaniel E. Atwood, Benjamin Dean, A. M. Giles, L. J. Knowles, John H. Lockey, Charles R. McLean Daniel Needham, Jos. G. Ray, Geo. M. Rice—9.

## Proposed XVIth Amendment.

HOUSE OF REPRESENTATIVES U. S., 1869, *March* 16.—Mr. JULIAN introduced a joint resolution proposing the following as the XVIth amendment to the Constitution of the United States:

ARTICLE XVI. The right of suffrage in the United States shall be based on citizenship, and shall be regulated by Congress, and all citizens of the United States, whether native or naturalized, shall enjoy this right equally, without any distinction or discrimination whatever founded on sex.

## Proposed Amendment to Constitution of the United States.

At various public meetings the following amendment to the preamble of the Constitution of the United States has been proposed:

We, the people of the United States, acknowledging Almighty God as the source of all authority and power in civil government, the Lord Jesus Christ as the ruler among the nations, and His will, revealed in the Holy Scriptures, as of supreme authority, in order to constitute a christian government, form a more perfect union, establish justice, insure domestic tranquillity, provide for the common defence, promote the general welfare, do ordain and establish this Constitution for the United States of America.

## Elections of 1869.

In NEW HAMPSHIRE the vote was: for Governor, Onslow Stearns, (Rep.,) 35,733; John Bedel, (Dem.,) 32,001.

In RHODE ISLAND the vote was: for Governor, Seth Paddleford, (Rep.,) 7,359; Symon Pierce, (Dem.,) 3,390.

In CONNECTICUT the vote was; for Governor, Marshall Jewell, (Rep.,) 45,493; James E. English, (Dem.,) 45,082. Jewell's majority, 411.

In MICHIGAN, at the judicial election, Thomas M. Cooley was elected justice of the supreme court by 90,705 to 59,886 for O. Darwin Hughes.

In VIRGINIA the vote was: for Governor. Gilbert C. Walker, (Cons.,) 119,492; H. H. Wells, (Rep.,) 101,291—Walker's majority, 18,264. The vote on clauses was: for clause 4, sec. 1, art. III of constitution, (disfranchising,) 84,410, against 124,360—majority, 39,950; for sec. 7, art. III, (test oath.) 83,458, against 124,715—majority, 41,257. For the constitution, 210,585, against 9,136.

In WASHINGTON Territory the vote was: for Delegate to Congress, Garfield, (Rep.,) 2 742; Moore, (Dem.,) 2,595—Garfield's majority, 147.

## R. T. Daniel's Dispatch to President Grant.

RICHMOND, *July* 7, 1869.

Mr. PRESIDENT: On behalf of the State executive committee of the Walker party, I congratulate you upon the triumph of your policy in Virginia. The gratitude of the people for your liberality is greatly enlivened by the overwhelming majority by which that policy prevails.　　　　　R. T. DANIEL.
*Chairman*

His Excellency U. S. GRANT,
*President of the United States.*

# PART V.

# POLITICAL MANUAL FOR 1870.

## L.

## MEMBERS OF THE CABINET OF PRESIDENT GRANT,

### AND OF THE FORTY-FIRST CONGRESS, SECOND SESSION.

### PRESIDENT GRANT'S CABINET.

*Secretary of State*—HAMILTON FISH, of New York.

*Secretary of the Treasury*—GEORGE S. BOUTWELL, of Massachusetts.

*Secretary of War*—WM. W. BELKNAP, of Iowa.*

*Secretary of the Navy*—GEORGE M. ROBESON, of New Jersey.

*Secretary of the Interior*—JACOB D. COX, of Ohio.

*Postmaster General*—JOHN A. J. CRESWELL, of Maryland.

*Attorney General*—AMOS T. AKERMAN, of Georgia.†

### MEMBERS OF THE FORTY-FIRST CONGRESS.

Second Session, December 6, 1869—July 15, 1870.

#### Senate.

SCHUYLER COLFAX, of Indiana, *Vice President of the United States and President of the Senate.*

George C. Gorham, of California, *Secretary.*

*Maine*—Lot M. Morrill,‡ Hannibal Hamlin.

*New Hampshire*—Aaron H. Cragin, James W. Patterson.

*Vermont*—Justin S. Morrill, George F. Edmunds.

*Massachusetts*—Henry Wilson, Charles Sumner.

*Rhode Island*—Henry B. Anthony, William Sprague.

*Connecticut*—Orris S. Ferry, William A. Buckingham.

*New York*—Roscoe Conkling, Reuben E. Fenton.

*New Jersey*—Alexander G. Cattell, John P. Stockton.

*Pennsylvania*—Simon Cameron, John Scott.

*Delaware*—Willard Saulsbury, Thomas F. Bayard.

*Maryland*—George Vickers, William T. Hamilton.

*Virginia*§—John W. Johnston, John F. Lewis.

*North Carolina*—John C. Abbott, John Pool.

*South Carolina*—Thomas J. Robertson, Frederick A. Sawyer.

*Georgia.*—Not represented.

*Alabama*—Willard Warner, George E. Spencer.

*Mississippi*\*—Hiram R. Revels, Adelbert Ames.

*Louisiana*—John S. Harris, William P. Kellogg.

*Ohio*—John Sherman, Allen G. Thurman.

*Kentucky*—Thomas C. McCreery, Garrett Davis.

*Tennessee*—Joseph S. Fowler, William G. Brownlow.

*Indiana*—Oliver P. Morton, Daniel D. Pratt.

*Illinois*—Richard Yates, Lyman Trumbull.

*Missouri*—Charles D. Drake, Carl Schurz.

*Arkansas*—Alexander McDonald, Benjamin F. Rice.

*Michigan*—Jacob M. Howard, Zachariah Chandler.

*Florida*—Thomas W. Osborn, Abijah Gilbert.

*Texas*†—Morgan C. Hamilton, James W. Flanagan.

*Iowa*—James B. Howell,‡ James Harlan.

*Wisconsin*—Timothy O. Howe, Matthew H. Carpenter.

*California*—Cornelius Cole, Eugene Casserly.

*Minnesota*—Daniel S. Norton,§ Alex'r Ramsey.

*Oregon*—George H. Williams, Henry W. Corbett.

*Kansas*—Edmund G. Ross, Samuel C. Pomeroy.

*West Virginia*—Waitman T. Willey, Arthur I. Boreman.

*Nevada*—James W. Nye, William M. Stewart.

*Nebraska*—John M. Thayer, Thomas W. Tipton.

#### House of Representatives.

JAMES G. BLAINE, of Maine, *Speaker.*

Edward McPherson, of Pennsylvania, *Clerk.*

*Maine*—John Lynch, Samuel P. Morrill, James G. Blaine, John A. Peters, Eugene Hale.

*New Hampshire*—Jacob H. Ela, Aaron F. Stevens, Jacob Benton.

*Vermont*—Charles W. Willard, Luke P. Poland, Worthington C. Smith.

*Massachusetts*—James Buffinton, Oakes Ames,

---

* Qualified October 18, 1869, in place of John A. Rawlins, deceased September 6, 1869.

† Qualified July 8, 1870, in place of E. R. Hoar, resigned.

‡ Qualified December 6, 1869, in place of William Pitt Fessenden, deceased.

§ Mr. Lewis qualified January 27, 1870; Mr. Johnston, January 28.

* Mr. Revels qualified February 25, 1870; Mr. Ames, April 1, 1870.

† Qualified March 31, 1870.

‡ Qualified January 26, 1870, in place of James W Grimes, resigned.

§ Died July 14, 1870.

507

Ginery Twichell, Samuel Hooper, Benjamin F. Butler, Nathaniel P. Banks, George M. Brooks,* George F. Hoar, William B. Washburn, Henry L. Dawes.

*Rhode Island*—Thomas A. Jenckes, Nathan F. Dixon.

*Connecticut*—Julius L. Strong, Stephen W. Kellogg, Henry H. Starkweather, William H. Barnum.†

*New York*—Henry A. Reeves, John G. Schumaker, Henry W. Slocum, John Fox, John Morrissey, Samuel S. Cox,† Hervey C. Calkin, James Brooks, Fernando Wood, Clarkson N. Potter, Charles H. Van Wyck,‡ John H. Ketcham, John A. Griswold, Stephen L. Mayham, Adolphus H. Tanner, Orange Ferriss, William A. Wheeler, Stephen Sanford, Charles Knapp, Addison H. Laflin, Alexander H. Bailey, John C. Churchill, Dennis McCarthy, George W. Cowles, William H. Kelsey, Giles W. Hotchkiss, Hamilton Ward, Noah Davis, John Fisher, David S. Bennett, Porter Sheldon.

*New Jersey*—William Moore, Charles Haight, John T. Bird, John Hill, Orestes Cleveland.

*Pennsylvania*₂—Samuel J. Randall, Charles O'Neill, Leonard Myers, William D. Kelley, Caleb N. Taylor, John D. Stiles, Washington Townsend, J. Lawrence Getz, Oliver J. Dickey, Henry L. Cake, Daniel M. Van Auken, George W. Woodward, Ulysses Mercur, John B. Packer, Richard J. Haldeman, John Cessna, Daniel J. Morrell, William H. Armstrong, Glenni W. Scofield, Calvin W. Gilfillan, John Covode, James S. Negley, Darwin Phelps, Joseph B. Donley.

*Delaware*—Benjamin T. Biggs.

*Maryland*—Samuel Hambleton, Stevenson Archer, Thomas Swann, Patrick Hamill, Frederick Stone.

*Virginia*‖—Richard S. Ayer, James H. Platt, jr., Charles H. Porter, George W. Booker, Robert Ridgway, William Milnes, jr., Lewis McKenzie, James K. Gibson.

*North Carolina*¶—Clinton L. Cobb, (vacancy,) Oliver H. Dockery, (vacancy,) Israel G. Lash, Francis E. Shober, Alexander H. Jones.

*South Carolina***—(Vacancy,) C. C. Bowen, Solomon L. Hoge, Alexander S. Wallace.

*Georgia*—Not represented.

*Alabama*††—Alfred E. Buck, Charles W. Buckley, Robert S. Heflin, Charles Hays, Peter M. Dox, William C. Sherrod.

*Mississippi*‡‡—George E. Harris, J. L. Morphis,

Henry W. Barry, George C. McKee, Legrand W. Perce.

*Louisiana*\*—(Vacancy,) Lionel A. Sheldon, C. B. Darrall, Joseph P. Newsham (vacancy.)

*Ohio*—Peter W. Strader, Job E. Stevenson, Robert C. Schenck, William Lawrence, William Mungen, John A. Smith, James J. Winans, John Beatty, Edward F. Dickinson, Erasmus D. Peck,† John T. Wilson, Philadelph Van Trump, George W. Morgan, Martin Welker, Eliakim H. Moore, John A. Bingham, Jacob A. Ambler, William H. Upson, James A. Garfield.

*Kentucky*—Lawrence S. Trimble, William N. Sweeney, Joseph H. Lewis,‡ J. Proctor Knott, Boyd Winchester, Thomas L. Jones, James B. Beck, George M. Adams, John M. Rice.

*Tennessee*—Roderick R. Butler, Horace Maynard, William B. Stokes, Lewis Tillman, William F. Prosser, Samuel M. Arnell, Isaac R. Hawkins, William J. Smith.

*Indiana*—William E. Niblack, Michael C. Kerr, William S. Holman, George W. Julian, John Coburn, Daniel W. Voorhees, Godlove S. Orth, James N. Tyner, John P. C. Shanks, William Williams, Jasper Packard.

*Illinois*—Norman B. Judd, John F. Farnsworth, Horatio C. Burchard, ₂ John B. Hawley, Ebon C. Ingersoll, Burton C. Cook, Jesse H. Moore, Shelby M. Cullom, Thompson W. McNeely, Albert G. Burr, Samuel S. Marshall, John B. Hay, John M. Crebs, John A. Logan.

*Missouri*—Erastus Wells, Gustavus A. Finkelnburg, James R. McCormick, Sempronius H. Boyd, Samuel S. Burdett, Robert T. Van Horn, Joel F. Asper, John F. Benjamin, David P. Dyer.

*Arkansas*—Logan H. Roots, Anthony A. C. Rogers, Thomas Boles.

*Michigan*—Fernando C. Beaman, William L. Stoughton, Austin Blair, Thomas W. Ferry, Omar D. Conger, Randolph Strickland.

*Florida*—Charles M. Hamilton.

*Texas*‖—G. W. Whitmore, John C. Conner, W. T. Clark, Edward Degener.

*Iowa*—George W. McCrary, William Smyth, William B. Allison, William Loughridge, Frank W. Palmer, Charles Pomeroy.

*Wisconsin*—Halbert E. Paine, David Atwood, ¶ Amasa Cobb, Charles A. Eldridge, Philetus Sawyer, Cadwalader C. Washburn.

*California*—Samuel B. Axtell, Aaron A. Sargent, James A. Johnson.

*Minnesota*—Morton S. Wilkinson, Eugene M. Wilson.

*Oregon*—Joseph S. Smith.

*Kansas*—Sidney Clarke.

*West Virginia*—Isaac H. Duval, James C. McGrew, John S. Witcher.

*Nevada*—Thomas Fitch.

*Nebraska*—John Taffe.

---

* Qualified December 6, 1869, in place of George S. Boutwell, resigned.
† Qualified December 6, 1869.
‡ Qualified February 17, 1870, in place of George W. Greene, unseated February 16—yeas 120, nays 59.
₂ Mr. Covode qualified February 9, 1870. Mr. Taylor, April 13, 1870, in place of John R. Reading, unseated—yeas 112, nays 46.
‖ Messrs. Platt, Ridgway, Milnes, and Porter qualified January 27, 1870; Mr. Gibson, January 28; Messrs. Ayer and McKenzie, January 31; Mr. Booker, February 1.
¶ John T. Deweese resigned February 28, 1870. Mr. Shober qualified April 13, 1870. David Heaton died June 25, 1870.
** B. F. Whittemore resigned February 24, 1870; re-elected, and, June 21, refused admittance by a vote of 130 to 24. Mr. Wallace qualified May 27, 1870.
†† Messrs. Buck and Buckley qualified December 6, 1869. Messrs. Dox, Hays, Sherrod, and Heflin, December 7.
‡‡ Messrs. Harris, Morphis, McKee, and Perce, qualified February 23, 1870. Mr. Barry, April 8.

* Mr. Newsham admitted May 21, 1870—yeas 79, nays 71; qualified May 23. Mr. Darrall admitted July 6, 1870—yeas 96, nays 77; qualified same day.
† Qualified April 23, 1870, in place of Truman H. Hoag, deceased.
‡ Mr. Golladay resigned February 28, 1870. Mr. Lewis qualified as his successor May 10, 1870.
₂ Qualified December 6, 1869, in place of E. B. Washburne, resigned.
‖ Qualified March 31, 1870.
¶ Qualified February 23, 1870, in place of Benjamin F. Hopkins, deceased.

## LI.

# JUDICIAL DECISIONS.

## SUPREME COURT OF THE UNITED STATES.

**On the Validity of Contracts in Confederate Money.**

—

DECEMBER TERM, 1868.

Thorington } Appeal from the district court for the
vs. } middle district of Alabama.
Smith. }

The Chief Justice delivered the opinion of the court.

The questions before us upon this appeal are these:

(1.) Can a contract for the payment of Confederate notes, made during the late rebellion, between parties residing within the so-called Confederate States, be enforced at all in the courts of the United States?

(2.) Can evidence be received to prove that a promise expressed to be for the payment of dollars was, in fact, made for the payment of any other than lawful dollars of the United States?

(3.) Does the evidence in the record establish the fact that the note for the thousand dollars was to be paid, by agreement of the parties, in Confederate notes?

The first question is by no means free from difficulty. It cannot be questioned that the Confederate notes were issued in furtherance of an unlawful attempt to overthrow the Government of the United States by insurrectionary force. Nor is it a doubtful principle of law that no contracts made in aid of such an attempt can be enforced through the courts of the country whose government is thus assailed. But was the contract of the parties to this suit a contract of that character? Can it be fairly described as a contract in aid of the rebellion?

In examining this question, the state of that part of the country in which it was made must be considered. It is familiar history, that early in 1861 the authorities of seven States, supported, as was alleged, by popular majorities, combined for the overthrow of the national Union, and for the establishment within its boundaries of a separate and independent confederation. A governmental organization, representing these States, was established at Montgomery, in Alabama, first under a provisional constitution and afterwards under a constitution intended to be permanent. In the course of a few months four other States acceded to this confederation, and the seat of the central authority was transferred to Richmond, in Virginia. It was by the central authority thus organized, and under its direction, that civil war was carried on upon a vast scale against the Government of the United States for more than four years. Its power was recognized as supreme in nearly the whole of the territory of the States confederated in insurrec-

tion. It was the actual government of all the insurgent States, except those portions of them protected from its control by the presence of the armed forces of the national Government.

What was the precise character of this government in contemplation of law?

It is difficult to define it with exactness. Any definition that may be given may not improbably be found to require limitation and qualification. But the general principles of law relating to *de facto* government will, we think, conduct us to a conclusion sufficiently accurate.

There are several degrees of what is called *de facto* government.

Such a government, in its highest degree, assumes a character very closely resembling that of a lawful government. This is when the usurping government expels the regular authorities from their customary seats and functions, and establishes itself in their place, and so becomes the actual government of a country. The distinguishing characteristic of such a government is, that adherents to it in war against the government *de jure* do not incur the penalties of treason, and, under certain limitations, obligations assumed by it in behalf of the country, or otherwise, will, in general, be respected by the government *de jure* when restored.

Examples of this description of government *de facto* are found in English history. The statute 11 Henry VII, c. 1*, relieves from penalties for treason all persons who, in defense of the king, for the time being, wage war against those who endeavor to subvert his authority by force of arms, though warranted in so doing by the lawful monarch.† But this is where the usurper obtains actual possession of the royal authority of the kingdom, not when he has succeeded only in establishing his power over particular localities. Being in possession, allegiance is due to him as king *de facto*.

Another example may be found in the government of England under the Commonwealth, first by Parliament, and afterwards by Cromwell as protector. It was not, in the contemplation of law, a government *de jure*, but it was a government *de facto* in the most absolute sense. It incurred obligations and made conquests which remained the obligations and conquests of England after the restoration. The better opinion doubtless is, that acts done in obedience to this government could not be justly regarded as treasonable, though in hostility to the king *de jure*. Such acts were protected from criminal prosecution by the spirit, if not by the letter, of the statute of Henry VII. It was held otherwise by the judges by whom Sir Henry Vane was

* 2 British Stats. at Large, 82. † 4 Commentaries, 77.

509

tried for treason,* in the year following the restoration. But such a judgment, in such a time,
has little authority.

It is very certain that the Confederate government was never acknowledged by the United
States as a *de facto* government in this sense,
nor was it acknowledged as such by other powers. No treaty was made by it with any civilized State. No obligations of a national character
were created by it, binding after its dissolution
on the States which it represented, or on the
national Government. From a very early period
of the civil war to its close it was regarded as
simply the military representative of the insurrection against the authority of the United States.

But there is another description of government
called also by publicists a government *de facto*,
but which might perhaps be more aptly denominated a government of paramount force. Its
distinguishing characteristics are (1) that its existence is maintained by active military power
within the territories and against the rightful
authority of an established and lawful government; and (2) that while it exists it must necessarily be obeyed in civil matters by private
citizens, who, by acts of obedience, rendered in
submission to such force, do not become responsible as wrong-doers for those acts, though not
warranted by the laws of the rightful government. Actual governments of this sort are established over districts differing greatly in extent
and conditions. They are usually administered
directly by military authority, but they may be
administered also by civil authority, supported
more or less directly by military force.

One example of this sort of government is
found in the case of Castine, in Maine, reduced
to British possession during the war of 1812.
From the 1st of September, 1814, to the ratification of the treaty of peace in 1815, according to
the judgment of this court in United States *vs.*
Rice,† "the British government exercised all
civil and military authority over the place."
"The authority of the United States over the
territory was suspended, and the laws of the
United States could no longer be rightfully enforced there, or be obligatory upon the inhabitants
who remained and submitted to the conqueror.
By the surrender the inhabitants passed under a
temporary allegiance to the British government,
and were bound by such laws, and such only, as
it chose to recognize and impose." It is not to
be inferred from this that the obligations of the
people of Castine, as citizens of the United States,
were abrogated. They were suspended merely
by the presence, and only during the presence,
of the paramount force. A like example is found
in the case of Tampico, occupied during the war
with Mexico by the troops of the United States.
It was determined by this court, in Fleming *vs.*
Page,‡ that, although Tampico did not become a
part of the United States in consequence of that
occupation, still, having come, together with the
whole State of Tamaulipas, of which it was part,
into the exclusive possession of the national
forces, it must be regarded and respected by
other nations as the territory of the United

States. These were cases of temporary possession
of territory by lawful and regular governments
at war with the country of which the territory
so possessed was part.

The central government established for the
insurgent States differed from the temporary
governments at Castine and Tampico, in the circumstance that its authority did not originate
in lawful acts of regular war, but it was not on
that account less actual or less supreme. And
we think that it must be classed among the governments of which these are examples. It is to
be observed, that the rights and obligations of a
belligerent were conceded to it in its military
character very soon after the war began, from
motives of humanity and expediency, by the
United States. The whole territory controlled
by it was thereafter held to be enemies' territory,
and the inhabitants of that territory were held,
in most respects, for enemies. To the extent,
then, of actual supremacy, however unlawfully
gained, in all matters of government within its
military lines, the power of the insurgent government cannot be questioned. That supremacy
did not justify acts of hostility to the United
States. How far it should excuse them must be
left to the lawful government upon the reëstab-
lishment of its authority. But it made obedience
to its authority, in civil and local matters, not
only a necessity, but a duty. Without such obedience, civil order was impossible.

It was by this government exercising its power
throughout an immense territory that the Confederate notes were issued early in the war, and
these notes in a short time became almost exclusively the currency of the insurgent States.
As contracts in themselves, except in the contingency of successful revolution, these notes were
nullities; for, except in that event, there could
be no payer. They bore, indeed, this character
upon their face, for they were made payable
only "after the ratification of a treaty of peace
between the Confederate States and the United
States of America." While the war lasted, however, they had a certain contingent value, and
were used as money in nearly all the business
transactions of many millions of people. They
must be regarded, therefore, as a currency imposed on the community by irresistible force.

It seems to follow as a necessary consequence
from this actual supremacy of the insurgent
government, as a belligerent, within the territory
where it circulated, and from the necessity of
civil obedience on the part of all who remained
in it, that this currency must be considered in
courts of law in the same light as if it had been
issued by a foreign government temporarily
occupying a part of the territory of the United
States. Contracts stipulating for payments in
this currency cannot be regarded for that reason
only as made in aid of the foreign invasion in
the one case, or of the domestic insurrection in
the other. They have no necessary relations to
the hostile government, whether invading or
insurgent. They are transactions in the ordinary
course of civil society, and, though they may
indirectly and remotely promote the ends of the
unlawful government, are without blame, except
when proved to have been entered into with
actual intent to further invasion or insurrection.

---

* 6 State Trials, 119.     † 4 Wheaton, 253.
‡ 9 Howard, 614.

We cannot doubt that such contracts should be enforced in the courts of the United States, after the restoration of peace, to the extent of their just obligation. The first question, therefore, must receive an affirmative answer.

The second question, whether evidence can be received to prove that a promise made in one of the insurgent States, and expressed to be for the payment of dollars, without qualifying words, was in fact made for the payment of any other than lawful dollars of the United States? is next to be considered.

It is quite clear that a contract to pay dollars, made between citizens of any State of the Union, while maintaining its constitutional relations with the national Government, is a contract to pay lawful money of the United States, and cannot be modified or explained by parol evidence. But it is equally clear, if in any other country coins or notes denominated dollars should be authorized of different value from the coins or notes which are current here under that name, that, in a suit upon a contract to pay dollars, made in that country, evidence would be admitted to prove what kind of dollars were intended, and, if it should turn out that foreign dollars were meant, to prove their equivalent value in lawful money of the United States. Such evidence does not modify or alter the contract. It simply explains an ambiguity, which, under the general rules of evidence, may be removed by parol evidence.

We have already seen that the people of the insurgent States, under the Confederate government, were, in legal contemplation, substantially in the same condition as inhabitants of districts of a country occupied and controlled by an invading belligerent. The rules which would apply in the former case would apply in the latter; and as in the former case the people must be regarded as subjects of a foreign power, and contracts among them be interpreted and enforced with reference to the conditions imposed by the conquerer, so in the latter case the inhabitants must be regarded as under the authority of the insurgent belligerent power actually established as the government of the country, and contracts made with them must be interpreted and enforced with reference to the condition of things created by the acts of the governing power.

It is said, indeed, that under the insurgent government the word dollar had the same meaning as under the Government of the United States; that the Confederate notes were never made a legal tender, and, therefore, that no evidence can be received to show any other meaning of the word when used in a contract.

But it must be remembered that the whole condition of things in the insurgent States was matter of fact, rather than matter of law, and, as matter of fact, these notes, payable at a future and contingent day, which has not arrived and can never arrive, were forced into circulation as dollars, if not directly by the legislation, yet indirectly and quite as effectually by the acts of the insurgent government. Considered in themselves, and in the light of subsequent events, these notes had no real value, but they were made current as dollars by irresistible force. They were the only measure of value which the people had, and their use was a matter of almost absolute necessity; and this use gave them a sort of value, insignificant and precarious enough it is true, but always having a sufficiently definite relation to gold and silver, the universal measures of value, so that it was always easy to ascertain how much gold and silver was the real equivalent of a sum expressed in this currency. In the light of these facts it seems hardly less than absurd to say that these dollars must be regarded as identical in kind and value with the dollars which constitute the money of the United States. We cannot shut our eyes to the fact that they were essentially different in both respects; and it seems to us that no rule of evidence properly understood requires us to refuse, under the circumstances, to admit proof of the sense in which the word dollar is used in the contract before us. Our answer to the second question is, therefore, also in the affirmative. We are clearly of opinion that such evidence must be received in respect to such contracts, in order that justice may be done between the parties, and that the party entitled to be paid in these Confederate dollars can recover their actual value at the time and place of the contract in lawful money of the United States.

We do not think it necessary to go into a detailed examination of the evidence in the record in order to vindicate our answer to the third question. It is enough to say that it has left no doubt in our minds that the note for $10,000, to enforce payment of which suit was brought in the circuit court, was to be paid, by agreement of the parties, in Confederate notes.

It follows that the decree of the circuit court must be reversed, and the cause remanded, for further hearing and decree, in conformity with this opinion.

---

## On the Constitutionality of Legal-Tender Clause as relates to Contracts made prior to its adoption.

DECEMBER TERM, 1869.

Susan P. Hepburn and Henry H. P. Hepburn, pl'ffs in error, vs. Henry A. Griswold.  } In error to the court of appeals of the State of Kentucky.

(1.) Construed by the plain import of their terms and the manifest intent of the legislature, the statutes of 1862 and 1863, which make United States notes a legal tender in payment of debts, public and private, apply to debts contracted before as well as to debts contracted after enactment.

(2.) The cases of Lane County vs. Oregon, Bronson vs. Rodes, and Butler vs. Horwitz, in which it was held that, upon a sound construction of those statutes, neither taxes imposed by State legislation nor dues upon contracts for the payment or delivery of coin or bullion are included by legislative intent under the description of debts, public and private, are approved and reaffirmed.

(3.) When a case arises for judicial determination, and the decision depends on the alleged inconsistency of a legislative provision with the Constitution, it is the plain duty of the Supreme Court to compare the act with the fundamental law, and if the former cannot, upon a fair construction, be reconciled with the latter, to give effect to the Constitution rather than the statute.

(3½.) There is in the Constitution no express grant of legislative power to make any description of credit currency a legal tender in payment of debts.

(4.) The words "all laws necessary and proper for carrying into execution" powers expressly granted or vested have in the Constitution a sense equivalent to that of the words: laws, not absolutely necessary indeed, but appropriate, plainly adapted to constitutional and legitimate ends, which are not prohibited, but consistent with the letter and spirit of the Constitution; laws really calculated to effect objects intrusted to the Government.

(5.) Among means appropriate, plainly adapted, not inconsistent with the spirit of the Constitution, nor prohibited by its terms, the legislature has unrestricted choice; but no power can be derived by implication from any express power to enact laws as means for carrying it into execution unless such laws come within this description.

(6.) The making of notes or bills of credit a legal tender in payment of pre-existing debts is not a means appropriate, plainly adapted, or really calculated to carry into effect any express power vested in Congress, is inconsistent with the spirit of the Constitution, and is prohibited by the Constitution.

(7.) The clause in the acts of 1862 and 1863 which makes United States notes a legal tender in payment of all debts, public and private, is, so far as it applies to debts contracted before the passage of those acts, unwarranted by the Constitution.

(8.) Prior to the 25th of February, 1862, all contracts for the payment of money, not expressly stipulating otherwise, were, in legal effect and universal understanding, contracts for the payment of coin, and, under the Constitution, the parties to such contracts are respectively entitled to demand and bound to pay the sums due, according to their terms, in coin, notwithstanding the clause in that act, and the subsequent acts of like tenor, which make United States notes a legal tender in payment of such debts.

Mr. Chief Justice Chase delivered the opinion of the court.

The question presented for our determination by the record in this case is, whether or not the payee or assignee of a note, made before the 25th of February, 1862, is obliged by law to accept in payment United States notes, equal in nominal amount to the sum due according to its terms, when tendered by the maker or other party bound to pay it.

And this requires, in the first place, a construction of that clause of the first section of the act of Congress passed on that day which declares the United States notes, the issue of which was authorized by the statute, to be a legal tender in payment of debts.

The entire clause is in these words: "And such notes, herein authorized, shall be receivable in payment of all taxes, internal duties, excises, debts, and demands of every kind due to the

United States, except duties on imports, and of all claims and demands against the United States of every kind whatsoever, except for interest upon bonds and notes, which shall be paid in coin; and shall also be lawful money and a legal tender in payment of all debts, public and private, within the United States, except duties on imports and interest as aforesaid." *

This clause has already received much consideration here, and this court has held that, upon a sound construction, neither taxes imposed by State legislation,† nor demands upon contracts which stipulate in terms for the payment or delivery of coin or bullion,‡ are included by legislative intention under the description of debts public and private.

We are now to determine whether this description embraces debts contracted before as well as after the date of the act.

It is an established rule for the construction of statutes that the terms employed by the legislature are not to receive an interpretation which conflicts with acknowledged principles of justice and equity, if another sense, consonant with those principles, can be given to them.

But this rule cannot prevail where the intent is clear. Except in the scarcely supposable case, where a statute sets at naught the plainest precepts of morality and social obligation, courts must give effect to the clearly ascertained legislative intent, if not repugnant to the fundamental law ordained in the Constitution.

Applying the rule just stated to the act under consideration, there appears to be strong reason for construing the word *debts* as having reference only to debts contracted subsequent to the enactment of the law. For no one will question that the United States notes, which the act makes a legal tender in payment, are essentially unlike in nature, and, being irredeemable in coin, are necessarily unlike in value, to the lawful money intended by parties to contracts for the payment of money made before its passage.

The lawful money then in use and made a legal tender in payment consisted of gold and silver coin.

The currency in use under the act, and declared by its terms to be lawful money and a legal tender, consists of notes or promises to pay, impressed upon paper prepared in convenient form for circulation, and protected against counterfeiting by suitable devices and penalties.

The former possess intrinsic value, determined by the weight and fineness of the metal; the latter have no intrinsic value, but a purchasing value, determined by the quantity in circulation, by general consent to its currency in payments, and by opinion as to the probability of redemption in coin.

Both derive, in different degrees, a certain additional value from their adaptation to circulation by the form and impress given to them under national authority and from the acts making them respectively a legal tender.

Contracts for the payment of money, made before the act of 1862, had reference to coined money, and could not be discharged, unless by

* 12 United States Stats., 345.   † Lane County *vs.* Oregon, 7 Wall., 71.   ‡ Bronson *vs.* Rodes, 7 Wall., 229; Butler *vs.* Horwitz, 7 Wall., 258.

consent, otherwise than by tender of the sum due in coin. Every such contract, therefore, was in legal import a contract for the payment of coin.

There is a well-known law of currency, that notes or promises to pay, unless made conveniently and promptly convertible into coin at the will of the holder, can never, except under unusual and abnormal conditions, be at par in circulation with coin.

It is an equally well-known law that depreciation of notes must increase with the increase of the quantity put in circulation and the diminution of confidence in the ability or disposition to redeem. Their appreciation follows the reversal of these conditions. No act making them a legal tender can change materially the operation of these laws.

Their force has been strikingly exemplified in the history of the United States notes. Beginning with a very slight depreciation when first issued, in March, 1862, they sank in July, 1864, to the rate of two dollars and eighty-five cents for a dollar in gold, and then rose until recently a dollar and twenty cents in paper became equal to a gold dollar.

Admitting, then, that prior contracts are within the intention of the act, and assuming that the act is warranted by the Constitution, it follows that the holder of a promissory note, made before the act, for a thousand dollars, payable, as we have just seen, according to the law and according to the intent of the parties, in coin, was required, when depreciation reached its lowest point, to accept in payment a thousand note dollars, although with the thousand coin dollars, due under the contract, he could have purchased on that day two thousand eight hundred and fifty such dollars. Every payment, since the passage of the act, of a note of earlier date, has presented similar, though less striking, features.

Now, it certainly needs no argument to prove that an act compelling acceptance in satisfaction of any other than stipulated payment alters arbitrarily the terms of the contract and impairs its obligation, and that the extent of impairment is in the proportion of the inequality of the payment accepted under the constraint of the law to the payment due under the contract.

Nor does it need argument to prove that the practical operation of such an act is contrary to justice and equity.

It follows that no construction which attributes such practical operation to an act of Congress is to be favored, or indeed to be admitted, if any other can be reconciled with the manifest intent of the legislature.

What, then, is that manifest intent? Are we at liberty, upon a fair and reasonable construction of the act, to say that Congress meant that the word "debts" used in the act should not include debts contracted prior to its passage?

In the case of Bronson vs. Rodes we thought ourselves warranted in holding that this word, as used in the statute, does not include obligations created by express contracts for the payment of gold and silver, whether coined or in bullion. This conclusion rested, however, mainly on the terms of the act, which not only allow, but require, payments in coin by or to the Government, and may be fairly considered, independently of considerations belonging to the law of contracts for the delivery of specified articles, as sanctioning special private contracts for like payments, without which, indeed, the provisions relating to government payments could hardly have practical effect.

This consideration, however, does not apply to the matter now before us. There is nothing in the terms of the act which looks to any difference in its operation on different descriptions of debts payable generally in money, that is to say, in dollars and parts of a dollar. These terms, on the contrary, in their obvious import, include equally all debts not specially expressed to be payable in gold or silver, whether arising under past contracts and already due, or arising under such contracts and to become due at a future day, or arising and becoming due under subsequent contracts. A strict and literal construction, indeed, would, as suggested by Mr. Justice Story,[*] in respect to the same word used in the Constitution, limit the word "debts" to *debts existing;* and, if the construction cannot be accepted because the limitation sanctioned by it cannot be reconciled with the obvious scope and purpose of the act, it is certainly conclusive against any interpretation which will exclude existing debts from its operation.

The same conclusion results from the exception of interest on loans and duties on imports from the effect of the legal-tender clause. This exception affords an irresistible implication that no description of debts, whenever contracted, can be withdrawn from the effect of the act, if not included within the terms or the reasonable intent of the exception.

And it is worthy of observation in this connection that in all the debates to which the act gave occasion in Congress, no suggestion was ever made that the legal-tender clause did not apply as fully to contracts made before as to contracts made after its passage.

These considerations seem to us conclusive. We do not think ourselves at liberty, therefore, to say that Congress did not intend to make the notes authorized by it a legal tender in payment of debts contracted before the passage of the act.

We are thus brought to the question whether Congress has power to make notes issued under its authority a legal tender in payment of debts which when contracted were payable by law in gold and silver coin.

The delicacy and importance of this question has not been overstated in the argument. This court always approaches the consideration of questions of this nature reluctantly; and its constant rule of decision has been, and is, that acts of Congress must be regarded as constitutional unless clearly shown to be otherwise.

But the Constitution is the fundamental law of the United States. By it the people have created a government, defined its powers, prescribed their limits, distributed them among the different departments, and directed, in general, the manner of their exercise.

No department of the Government has any other powers than those thus delegated to it by

---

[*] 1 Story on Const., § 921.

the people. All the legislative power granted by the Constitution belongs to Congress; but it has no legislative power which is not thus granted. And the same observation is equally true in its application to the executive and judicial powers granted respectively to the President and the courts. All these powers differ in kind, but not in source or in limitation. They all arise from the Constitution and are limited by its terms.

It is the function of the judiciary to interpret and apply the law to cases between parties as they arise for judgment. It can only declare what the law is, and enforce, by proper process, the law thus declared.

But, in ascertaining the respective rights of parties, it frequently becomes necessary to consult the Constitution; for there can be no law inconsistent with the fundamental law. No enactment not in pursuance of the authority conferred by it can create obligations or confer rights. For such is the express declaration of the Constitution itself, in these words:

"The Constitution, and the laws of the United States which shall be *made in pursuance thereof*, and all treaties made, or which shall be made, under the authority of the United States, shall be the supreme law of the land; and the judges of every State shall be bound thereby, anything in the constitution or laws of any State to the contrary notwithstanding."

Not every act of Congress, then, is to be regarded as the supreme law of the land; nor is it by every act of Congress that the judges are bound. This character and this force belong only to such acts as are "made in pursuance of the Constitution."

When, therefore, a case arises for judicial determination, and the decision depends on the alleged inconsistency of a legislative provision with the fundamental law, it is the plain duty of the court to compare the act with the Constitution, and if the former cannot, upon a fair construction, be reconciled with the latter, to give effect to the Constitution rather than the statute. This seems so plain that it is impossible to make it plainer by argument. If it be otherwise, the Constitution is not the supreme law; it is neither necessary nor useful, in any case, to inquire whether or not any act of Congress was passed in pursuance of it; and the oath which every member of this court is required to take, that he "will administer justice without respect to persons, and do equal right to the poor and the rich, and faithfully perform the duties incumbent upon him to the best of his ability and understanding, agreeably to the Constitution and laws of the United States," becomes an idle and unmeaning form.

The case before us is one of private right. The plaintiff in the court below sought to recover of the defendants a certain sum expressed on the face of a promissory note. The defendants insisted on the right, under the act of February 25, 1862, to acquit themselves of their obligation by tendering in payment a sum nominally equal in United States notes. But the note had been executed before the passage of the act, and the plaintiff insisted on his right under the Constitution to be paid the amount due in gold and silver. And it has not been and cannot be denied, that the plaintiff was entitled to judgment according to his claim, unless bound by a constitutional law to accept the notes as coin.

Thus two questions were directly presented: Were the defendants relieved by the act from the obligation assumed in the contract? Could the plaintiff be compelled by a judgment of the court to receive in payment a currency of different nature and value from that which was in the contemplation of the parties when the contract was made?

The court of appeals resolved both questions in the negative, and the defendants in the original suit seek the reversal of that judgment by writ of error.

It becomes our duty, therefore, to determine whether the act of February 25, 1862, so far as it makes United States notes a legal tender in payment of debts contracted prior to its passage, is constitutional and valid or otherwise. Under a deep sense of our obligation to perform this duty to the best of our ability and understanding, we shall proceed to dispose of the case presented by the record.

We have already said, and it is generally, if not universally, conceded, that the Government of the United States is one of limited powers, and that no department possesses any authority not granted by the Constitution.

It is not necessary, however, in order to prove the existence of a particular authority to show a particular and express grant. The design of the Constitution was to establish a government competent to the direction and administration of the affairs of a great nation, and, at the same time, to mark, by sufficiently definite lines, the sphere of its operations. To this end it was needful only to make express grants of general powers, coupled with a further grant of such incidental and auxiliary powers as might be required for the exercise of the powers expressly granted. These powers are necessarily extensive. It has been found, indeed, in the practical administration of the government, that a very large part, if not the largest part, of its functions have been performed in the exercise of powers thus implied.

But the extension of power by implication was regarded with some apprehension by the wise men who framed and by the intelligent citizens who adopted the Constitution. This apprehension is manifest in the terms by which the grant of incidental and auxiliary powers is made. All powers of this nature are included under the description of "power to make all laws necessary and proper for carrying into execution the powers expressly granted to Congress or vested by the Constitution in the government or in. any of its departments or officers."

The same apprehension is equally apparent in the Xth article of the Amendments, which declares that "the powers not delegated to the United States by the Constitution, nor prohibited by it to the States, are reserved to the States or the people."

We do not mean to say that either of these constitutional provisions is to be taken as restricting any exercise of power fairly warranted by legitimate derivation from one of the enumerated or express powers. The first was undoubtedly introduced to exclude all doubt in respect to the existence of implied powers; while the words "necessary and proper" were intended to have a "sense," to use the words of Mr. Justice Story, "at once admonitory and directory," and to require that the means used in the execution of an express power "should be *bona fide* appropriate to the end."[*] The second provision was intended to have a like admonitory and directory sense, and to restrain the limited government established under the Constitution from the exercise of powers not clearly delegated or derived by just inference from powers so delegated.

It has not been maintained in argument, nor, indeed, would any one, however slightly conversant with constitutional law, think of maintaining, that there is in the Constitution any express grant of legislative power to make any description of credit currency a legal tender in payment of debts.

We must inquire then whether this can be done in the exercise of an implied power.

The rule for determining whether a legislative enactment can be supported as an exercise of an implied power was stated by Chief Justice Marshall, speaking for the whole court, in the case of McCullough *vs.* The State of Maryland,[†] and the statement then made has ever since been accepted as a correct exposition of the Constitution. His words were these: " Let the end be legitimate, let it be within the scope of the Constitution, and all means which are appropriate, which are plainly adapted to that end, which are not prohibited, but consistent with the letter and spirit of the Constitution, are constitutional." And in another part of the same opinion the practical application of this rule was thus illustrated: "Should Congress, in the execution of its powers, adopt measures which are prohibited by the Constitution, or should Congress, under the pretext of executing its powers, pass laws for the accomplishment of objects not intrusted to the government, it would be the painful duty of this tribunal, should a case requiring such a decision come before it, to say that such an act was not the law of the land. But where the law is not prohibited, and is really calculated to effect any of the objects intrusted to the government, to undertake here to inquire into the degree of its necessity would be to pass the line which circumscribes the judicial department, and tread on legislative ground."[‡]

It must be taken then as finally settled, so far as judicial decisions can settle anything, that the words "all laws necessary and proper for carrying into execution" powers expressly granted or vested, have in the Constitution a sense equivalent to that of the words: laws not absolutely necessary indeed, but appropriate, plainly adapted to constitutional and legitimate ends; laws not prohibited, but consistent with the letter and spirit of the Constitution; laws really calculated to effect objects intrusted to the government.

The question before us, then, resolves itself into this: Is the clause which makes United States notes a legal tender for debts contracted prior to its enactment a law of the description stated in the rule?

It is not doubted that the power to establish a standard of value by which all other values may be measured, or, in other words, to determine what shall be lawful money and a legal tender, is in its nature and of necessity a governmental power. It is in all countries exercised by the government. In the United States, so far as it relates to the precious metals, it is vested in Congress by the grant of the power to coin money. But can a power to impart these qualities to notes, or promises to pay money, when offered in discharge of pre-existing debts, be derived from the coinage power, or from any other power expressly given?

It is certainly not the same power as the power to coin money. Nor is it in any reasonable or satisfactory sense an appropriate or plainly adapted means to the exercise of that power. Nor is there more reason for saying that it is implied in, or incidental to, the power to regulate the value of coined money of the United States, or of foreign coins. This power of regulation is a power to determine the weight, purity, form, impression, and denomination of the several coins, and their relation to each other, and the relations of foreign coins to the monetary unit of the United States.

Nor is the power to make notes a legal tender the same as the power to issue notes to be used as currency. The old Congress, under the Articles of Confederation, was clothed by express grant with the power to emit bills of credit, which are in fact notes for circulation as currency ; and yet that Congress was not clothed with the power to make these bills a legal tender in payment. And this court has recently held that the Congress under the Constitution, possesses as incidental to other powers, the same power as the old Congress to emit bills or notes; but it was expressly declared at the same time that this decision concluded nothing on the question of legal tender. Indeed, we are not aware that it has ever been claimed that the power to issue bills or notes has any identity with the power to make them a legal tender. On the contrary, the whole history of the country refutes that notion. The States have always been held to possess the power to authorize and regulate the issue of bills for circulation by banks or individuals, subject, as has been lately determined, to the control of Congress, for the purpose of establishing and securing a national currency ; and yet the States are expressly prohibited by the Constitution from making anything but gold and silver coin a legal tender. This seems decisive on the point that the power to issue notes and the power to make them a legal tender are not the same power, and that they have no necessary connection with each other.

But it has been maintained in argument that the power to make United States notes a legal tender in payment of all debts is a means appropriate and plainly adapted to the execution of the power to carry on war, of the power to regulate commerce, and of the power to borrow money. If it is, and is not prohibited, nor inconsistent with the letter or spirit of the Constitution, then the act which makes them such legal tender must be held to be constitutional.

Let us, then, first inquire whether it is an appropriate and plainly adapted means for carry-

---

[*] 2 Story on the Const., p. 142, § 1253.   [†] 4 Wheaton 421.
[‡] 4 Wheat., 423.

ing on war? The affirmative argument may be thus stated: Congress has power to declare and provide for carrying on war; Congress has also power to emit bills of credit, or circulating notes receivable for government dues and payable, so far at least as parties are willing to receive them, in discharge of government obligations; it will facilitate the use of such notes in disbursements to make them a legal tender in payment of existing debts; therefore Congress may make such notes a legal tender.

It is difficult to say to what express power the authority to make notes a legal tender in payment of pre-existing debts may not be upheld as incidental, upon the principles of this argument. Is there any power which does not involve the use of money? And is there any doubt that Congress may issue and use bills of credit as money in the execution of any power? The power to establish post offices and post roads, for example, involves the collection and disbursement of a great revenue. Is not the power to make notes a legal tender as clearly incidental to this power as to the war power?

The answer to this question does not appear to us doubtful. The argument, therefore, seems to prove too much. It carries the doctrine of implied powers very far beyond any extent hitherto given to it. It asserts that whatever in any degree promotes an end within the scope of a general power, whether, in the correct sense of the word, appropriate or not, may be done in the exercise of an implied power.

Can this proposition be maintained?

It is said that this is not a question for the court deciding a cause, but for Congress exercising the power. But the decisive answer to this is, that the admission of a legislative power to determine finally what powers have the described relation as means to the execution of other powers plainly granted, and, then, to exercise absolutely and without liability to question, in cases involving private rights, the powers thus determined to have that relation, would completely change the nature of American government. It would convert the government, which the people ordained as a government of limited powers, into a government of unlimited powers. It would confuse the boundaries which separate the executive and judicial from the legislative authority. It would obliterate every criterion which this court, speaking through the venerated chief justice in the case already cited, established for the determination of the question whether legislative acts are constitutional or unconstitutional.

Undoubtedly, among means appropriate, plainly adapted, really calculated, the legislature has unrestricted choice. But there can be no implied power to use means not within the description.

Now, then, let it be considered what has actually been done in the provision of a national currency. In July and August, 1861, and February, 1862, the issue of $60,000,000 in United States notes, payable on demand, was authorized.* They were made receivable in payments, but were not declared a legal tender until March, 1862,† when the amount in circulation had been greatly reduced by receipt and cancellation. In

1862 and 1863* the issue of $450,000,000 in United States notes, payable not on demand, but in effect at the convenience of the Government, was authorized, subject to certain restrictious as to $50,000,000. These notes were made receivable for the bonds of the national loans, for all debts due to or from the United States, except duties on imports and interest on the public debt, and were also declared a legal tender. In March, 1863,† the issue of notes for parts of a dollar was authorized to an amount not exceeding $50,000,000. These notes were not declared a legal tender, but were made redeemable under regulations to be prescribed by the Secretary of the Treasury. In February, 1863,‡ the issue of $300,000,000 in notes of the national banking associations was authorized. These notes were made receivable to the same extent as United States notes, and provision was made to secure their redemption, but they were not made a legal tender.

These several descriptions of notes have since constituted, under the various acts of Congress, the common currency of the United States. The notes which were not declared a legal tender have circulated with those which were so declared without unfavorable discrimination.

It may be added, as a part of the history, that other issues, bearing interest at various rates, were authorized and made a legal tender, except in redemption of bank notes, for face amount, exclusive of interest. Such were the one and two years five per cent. notes and three years compound interest notes.‖ These notes never entered largely or permanently into the circulation; and there is no reason to think that their utility was increased or diminished by the act which declared them a legal tender for face amount. They need not be further considered here. They serve only to illustrate the tendency, remarked by all who have investigated the subject of paper money, to increase the volume of irredeemable issues, and to extend indefinitely the application of the quality of legal tender. That it was carried no further during the recent civil war, and has been carried no further since, is due to circumstances, the consideration of which does not belong to this discussion.

We recur, then, to the question under consideration. No one questions the general constitutionality, and not very many perhaps the general expediency, of the legislation by which a note currency has been authorized in recent years. The doubt is as to the power to declare a particular class of these notes to be a legal tender in payment of pre-existing debts.

The only ground upon which this power is asserted is, not that the issue of notes was an appropriate and plainly-adapted means for carrying on the war, for that is admitted, but that the making of them a legal tender to the extent mentioned was such a means.

Now, we have seen that of all the notes issued those not declared a legal tender at all constituted a very large proportion, and that they circulated freely and without discount.

It may be said that their equality in circula-

---

* 12 United States Stats., 259, 313, and 338.   † 12 United States Stats., 370.

* 12 United States Stats., 345, 532, and 709.   † 12 United States Stats., 711.   ‡ 12 United States Stats., 669.   † 13 United States Stats., 218, 425.

tion and credit was due to the provision made by law for the redemption of this paper in legal-tender notes. But this provision, if at all useful in this respect, was of trifling importance compared with that which made them receivable for government dues. All modern history testifies that, in time of war especially, when taxes are augmented, large loans negotiated, and heavy disbursements made, notes issued by the authority of the government, and made receivable for dues of the government, always obtain at first a ready circulation; and even when not redeemable in coin on demand are as little and usually less subject to depreciation than any other description of notes for the redemption of which no better provision is made. And the history of the legislation under consideration is, that it was upon this quality of receivability, and not upon the quality of legal tender, that reliance for circulation was originally placed; for the receivability clause appears to have been in the original draft of the bill, while the legal-tender clause seems to have been introduced at a later stage of its progress.

These facts certainly are not without weight as evidence that all the useful purposes of the notes would have been fully answered without making them a legal tender for pre-existing debts.

It is denied, indeed, by eminent writers, that the quality of legal tender adds anything at all to the credit or usefulness of government notes They insist, on the contrary, that it impairs both.

However this may be, it must be remembered that it is as a means to an end to be attained by the action of the government that the implied power of making notes a legal tender in all payments is claimed under the Constitution. Now, how far is the government helped by this means? Certainly it cannot obtain new supplies or services at a cheaper rate, for no one will take the notes for more than they are worth at the time of the new contract. The price will rise in the ratio of the depreciation; and this is all that could happen if the notes were not made a legal tender. But it may be said that the depreciation will be less to him who takes them from the government if the government will pledge to him its power to compel his creditors to receive them at par in payments. This is, as we have seen, by no means certain. If the quantity issued be excessive, and redemption uncertain and remote, great depreciation will take place; if, on the other hand, the quantity is only adequate to the demands of business, and confidence in early redemption is strong, the notes will circulate freely, whether made a legal tender or not.

But if it be admitted that some increase of availability is derived from making the notes a legal tender under new contracts, it by no means follows that any appreciable advantage is gained by compelling creditors to receive them in satisfaction of pre-existing debts. And there is abundant evidence that whatever benefit is possible from that compulsion to some individuals or to the government is far more than outweighed by the losses of property, the derangement of business, the fluctuations of currency and values, and the increase of prices to the people and the government, and the long train of evils which flow from the use of irredeemable paper money.

It is true that these evils are not to be attributed altogether to making it a legal tender. But this increases these evils. It certainly widens their extent and protracts their continuance.

We are unable to persuade ourselves that an expedient of this sort is an appropriate and plainly adapted means for the execution of the power to declare and carry on war. If it adds nothing to the utility of the notes it cannot be upheld as a means to the end in furtherance of which the notes are issued. Nor can it, in our judgment, be upheld as such if, while facilitating in some degree the circulation of the notes, it debases and injures the currency in its proper use to a much greater degree. And these considerations seem to us equally applicable to the powers to regulate commerce and to borrow money. Both powers necessarily involve the use of money by the people and by the government, but neither, as we think, carries with it, as an appropriate and plainly adapted means to its exercise, the power of making circulating notes a legal tender in payment of pre-existing debts.

But there is another view which seems to us decisive, to whatever express power the supposed implied power in question may be referred. In the rule stated by Chief Justice Marshall the words "appropriate," "plainly adapted," "really calculated," are qualified by the limitation that the means must be not prohibited, but consistent with the letter and spirit of the Constitution. Nothing so prohibited or inconsistent can be regarded as appropriate, or plainly adapted, or really calculated means to an end.

Let us inquire, then, first, whether making bills of credit a legal tender, to the extent indicated, is consistent with the spirit of the Constitution.

Among the great cardinal principles of that instrument no one is more conspicuous or more venerable than the establishment of justice. And what was intended by the establishment of justice in the minds of the people who ordained it is happily not a matter of disputation. It is not left to inference or conjecture, especially in its relations to contracts.

When the Constitution was undergoing discussion in the convention, the Congress of the confederation was engaged in the consideration of the ordinance for the government of the territory northwest of the Ohio, the only territory subject at that time to its regulation and control. By this ordinance certain fundamental articles of compact were established between the original States and the people and States of the territory, for the purpose, to use its own language, "of extending the fundamental principles of civil and religious liberty, whereon these republics," (the States united under the confederation) "their laws, and constitutions are erected." Among these fundamental principles was this: "And in the just preservation of rights and property it is understood and declared, that no law ought ever to be made or have force in the said territory that shall in any manner whatever interfere with or affect private contracts or engagements bona fide and without fraud previously formed."

The same principle found more condensed expression in that most valuable provision of the Constitution of the United States, ever recognized as an efficient safeguard against injustice, that "no State shall pass any law impairing the obligation of contracts."

It is true that this prohibition is not applied in terms to the Government of the United States. Congress has express power to enact bankrupt laws, and we do not say that a law made in the execution of any other express power, which incidentally only impairs the obligation of a contract, can be held to be unconstitutional for that reason.

But we think it clear that those who framed and those who adopted the Constitution intended that the spirit of this prohibition should pervade the entire body of legislation, and that the justice which the Constitution was ordained to establish was not thought by them to be compatible with legislation of an opposite tendency. In other words, we cannot doubt that a law not made in pursuance of an express power, which necessarily and in its direct operation impairs the obligation of contracts, is inconsistent with the spirit of the Constitution.

Another provision, found in the Vth Amendment, must be considered in this connection. We refer to that which ordains that private property shall not be taken for public use without compensation. This provision is kindred in spirit to that which forbids legislation impairing the obligation of contracts; but, unlike that, it is addressed directly and solely to the national government. It does not, in terms, prohibit legislation which appropriates the private property of one class of citizens to the use of another class; but if such property cannot be taken for the benefit of all without compensation, it is difficult to understand how it can be so taken for the benefit of a part without violating the spirit of the prohibition.

But there is another provision in the same amendment, which, in our judgment, cannot have its full and intended effect unless construed as a direct prohibition of the legislation which we have been considering. It is that which declares that "no person shall be deprived of life, liberty, or property without due process of law."

It is not doubted that all the provisions of this amendment operate directly in limitation and restraint of the legislative powers conferred by the Constitution. The only question is, whether an act which compels all those who hold contracts for the payment of gold and silver money to accept in payment a currency of inferior value deprives such persons of property without due process of law.

It is quite clear that, whatever may be the operation of such an act, due process of law makes no part of it. Does it deprive any person of property?

A very large proportion of the property of civilized men exists in the form of contracts. These contracts almost invariably stipulate for the payment of money. And we have already seen that contracts in the United States, prior to the act under consideration, for the payment of money, were contracts to pay the sums specified in gold and silver coin. And it is beyond doubt that the holders of these contracts were and are as fully entitled to the protection of this constitutional provision as the holders of any other description of property.

But it may be said that the holders of no description of property are protected by it from legislation which incidentally only impairs its value. And it may be urged in illustration that the holders of stock in a turnpike, a bridge, or a manufacturing corporation, or an insurance company, or a bank, cannot invoke its protection against legislation which, by authorizing similar works or corporations, reduces its price in the market. But all this does not appear to meet the real difficulty. In the cases mentioned, the injury is purely contingent and incidental. In the case we are considering, it is direct and inevitable.

If in the cases mentioned the holders of the stock were required by law to convey it on demand to any one who should think fit to offer half its value for it, the analogy would be more obvious. No one probably could be found to contend that an act enforcing the acceptance of fifty or seventy-five acres of land in satisfaction of a contract to convey a hundred would not come within the prohibition against arbitrary privation of property.

We confess ourselves unable to perceive any solid distinction between such an act and an act compelling all citizens to accept, in satisfaction of all contracts for money, half or three-quarters, or any other proportion less than the whole of the value actually due, according to their terms. It is difficult to conceive what act would take private property without process of law if such an act would not.

We are obliged to conclude that an act making mere promises to pay dollars a legal tender in payment of debts previously contracted is not a means appropriate, plainly adapted, really calculated to carry into effect any express power vested in Congress; that such an act is inconsistent with the spirit of the Constitution; and that it is prohibited by the Constitution.

It is not surprising that amid the tumult of the late civil war, and under the influence of apprehensions for the safety of the republic almost universal, different views, never before entertained by American statesmen or jurists, were adopted by many. The time was not favorable to considerate reflection upon the constitutional limits of legislative or executive authority. If power was assumed from patriotic motives, the assumption found ready justification in patriotic hearts. Many who doubted yielded their doubts; many who did not doubt were silent. Some who were strongly averse to making government notes a legal tender felt themselves constrained to acquiesce in the views of the advocates of the measure. Not a few who then insisted upon its necessity, or acquiesced in that view, have, since the return of peace and under the influence of the calmer time, reconsidered their conclusions, and now concur in those which we have just announced. These conclusions seem to us to be fully sanctioned by the letter and spirit of the Constitution.

We are obliged, therefore, to hold that the defendant in error was not bound to receive from the plaintiffs the currency tendered to him in payment of their note, made before the passage of the act of February 25, 1862. It follows that the judgment of the court of appeals of Kentucky must be affirmed.

It is proper to say that Mr. Justice Grier, who was a member of the court when this cause was decided in conference,* and when this opinion was directed to be read,† stated his judgment to be that the legal-tender clause, properly construed, has no application to debts contracted prior to its enactment; but that upon the construction given to the act by the other judges he concurred in the opinion that the clause, so far as it makes United States notes a legal tender for such debts, is not warranted by the Constitution.

### Dissenting Opinion.

Mr. Justice Miller dissenting:

The provisions of the Constitution of the United States which have direct reference to the function of legislation may be divided into three primary classes:

1. Those which confer legislative powers on Congress.

2. Those which prohibit the exercise of legislative powers by Congress.

3. Those which prohibit the States from exercising certain legislative powers.

The powers conferred on Congress may be subdivided into the positive and the auxiliary, or, as they are more commonly called, the express and the implied powers.

As instances of the former class may be mentioned the power to borrow money, to raise and support armies, and to coin money and regulate the value thereof.

The implied or auxiliary powers of legislation are founded largely on that general provision which closes the enumeration of powers granted in express terms, by the declaration that Congress shall also "have power to make all laws which shall be necessary and proper for carrying into execution the foregoing powers, and all other powers vested by this Constitution in the Government of the United States, or in any department or officer thereof."

The question which this court is called upon to consider is, whether the authority to make the notes of the United States a lawful tender in payment of debts is to be found in Congress under either of these classes of legislative powers.

As one of the elements of this question, and in order to negative any idea that the exercise of such a power would be an invasion of the rights reserved to the States, it may be as well to say at the outset, that this is among the subjects of legislation forbidden to the States by the Constitution. Among the unequivocal utterances of that instrument on this subject of legal tender is that which declares that "No State shall coin money, emit bills of credit, or make anything but gold and silver coin a tender in payment of debts;" thus removing the whole matter from the domain of State legislation.

No such prohibition is placed upon the power of Congress on this subject, though there are, as I have already said, matters expressly forbidden to Congress; but neither this of legal tender, nor of the power to emit bills of credit or to impair the obligation of contracts, is among them. On the contrary, Congress is expressly authorized to coin money and to regulate the value thereof

* Nov. 27, 1869.    † Jan. 29, 1870.

and of foreign coin, and to punish the counterfeiting of such coin and of the securities of the United States. It has been strongly argued by many able jurists that these latter clauses, fairly construed, confer the power to make the securities of the United States a lawful tender in payment of debts.

While I am not able to see in them, standing alone, a sufficient warrant for the exercise of this power, they are not without decided weight when we come to consider the question of the existence of this power as one necessary and proper for carrying into execution other admitted powers of the Government. For they show that so far as the framers of the Constitution did go in granting *express* power over the lawful money of the country, it was confided to Congress and forbidden to the States; and it is no unreasonable inference, that if it should be found necessary, in carrying into effect some of the powers of the Government essential to its successful operation, to make its securities perform the office of money in the payment of debts, such legislation would be in harmony with the power over money granted in express terms.

It being conceded, then, that the power under consideration would not, if exercised by Congress, be an invasion of any right reserved to the States, but one which they are forbidden to employ, and that it is not one in terms either granted or denied to Congress, can it be sustained as a law necessary and proper, at the time it was enacted, for carrying into execution any of these powers that are expressly granted, either to Congress or to the Government or to any department thereof?

From the organization of the Government under the present Constitution there have been from time to time attempts to limit the powers granted by that instrument by a narrow and literal rule of construction, and these have been specially directed to the general clause which we have cited as the foundation of the auxiliary powers of the Government. It has been said that this clause, so far from authorizing the use of any means which could not have been used without it, is a restriction upon the powers necessarily implied by an instrument so general in its language.

The doctrine is, that when an act of Congress is brought to the test of this clause of the Constitution, its necessity must be absolute, and its adaptation to the conceded purpose unquestionable.

Nowhere has this principle been met with more emphatic denial and more satisfactory refutation than in this court. That eminent jurist and statesman, whose official career of over thirty years as chief justice commenced very soon after the Constitution was adopted, and whose opinions have done as much to fix its meaning as those of any man, living or dead, has given this particular clause the benefit of his fullest consideration.

In the case of the United States *vs.* Fisher, (2 Cranch, 358,) decided in 1804, the point in issue was the priority claimed for the United States as a creditor of a bankrupt over all other creditors. It was argued mainly on the construction of the statutes, but the power of Congress to pass such a law was also denied. Chief Justice Marshall said: "It is claimed under the authority to make all·laws which shall be necessary and proper to carry into execution the powers vested by the Constitution in the Government or in any department thereof. In construing this clause, it would be incorrect and would produce endless difficulties, if the opinion should be maintained that no law was authorized which was not indispensably necessary to give effect to a specified power. Where various systems might be adopted for that purpose, it might be said with respect to each that it was not necessary, because the end might be attained by other means. Congress must possess the choice of means, and must be empowered to use any means which are in fact conducive to the exercise of the power granted by the Constitution."

It was accordingly held that, under the authority to pay the debts of the Union, it could pass a law giving priority for its own debts in cases of bankruptcy.

But in the memorable case of McCulloch vs. The State of Maryland, (4 Wheaton, 316,) the most exhaustive discussion of this clause is found in the opinion of the court by the same eminent expounder of the Constitution. That case involved, it is well known, the right of Congress to establish the Bank of the United States and to authorize it to issue notes for circulation. It was conceded that the right to incorporate or create such a bank had no specific grant in any clause of the Constitution, still less the right to authorize it to issue notes for circulation as money. But it was argued that, as a means necessary to enable the Government to collect, transfer, and pay out its revenues, the organization of a bank with this function was within the power of Congress. In speaking of the true meaning of the word "necessary" in this clause of the Constitution he says: "Does it always import an absolute physical necessity so strong that one thing to which another may be termed necessary cannot exist without it? We think it does not. If reference be had to its use, in the common affairs of the world or in approved authors, we find that it frequently imports no more than that one thing is convenient or useful or essential to another. To employ means necessary to an end is generally understood as employing any means calculated to produce the end, and not as being confined to those single means, without which the end would be entirely unattainable."

The word necessary admits, he says, of all degrees of comparison. "A thing may be necessary, very necessary, absolutely or indispensably necessary." * * * "This word, then, like others, is used in various senses, and in its construction the subject, the context, the intention of the person using them are all to be taken into view. Let this be done in the case under consideration. The subject is the execution of those great powers on which the welfare of a nation essentially depends. It must have been the intention of those who gave these powers to insure, as far as human prudence could insure, their beneficial execution. This could not be done by confining the choice of means to such narrow limits as not to leave it in the power of Congress

to adopt any which might be appropriate and which were conducive to the end. This provision is made in a constitution intended to endure for ages to come, and consequently to be adapted to various crises of human affairs. To have prescribed the means by which the government should in all future time execute its powers would have been to change entirely the character of the instrument, and give it the properties of a legal code. It would have been an unwise attempt to provide by immutable rules for exigencies which, if foreseen at all, must have been but dimly, and which can best be provided for as they occur. To have declared that the best means shall not be used, but those alone without which the power given would be nugatory, would have been to deprive the legislature of the capacity to avail itself of experience, to exercise its reason, and to accommodate its legislation to circumstances."

I have cited at unusual length these remarks of Chief Justice Marshall because, though made half a century ago, their applicability to the circumstances under which Congress called to its aid the power of making the securities of the Government a legal tender as a means of successfully prosecuting a war which without such aid seemed likely to terminate its existence, and to borrow money which could in no other manner be borrowed, and to pay the debt of millions due to its soldiers in the field, which could by no other means be paid, seem to be almost prophetic. If he had had clearly before his mind the future history of his country he could not have better characterized a principle which would in this very case have rendered the power to carry on war nugatory, which would have deprived Congress of the capacity to avail itself of experience, to exercise its reason, and to accommodate its legislation to circumstances by the use of the most appropriate means of supporting the Government in the crisis of its fate.

But it is said that the clause under consideration is admonitory as to the use of implied powers, and adds nothing to what would have been authorized without it.

The idea is not new, and is probably intended for the same which was urged in the case of McCulloch vs. The State of Maryland, namely, that instead of enlarging the powers conferred on Congress, or providing for a more liberal use of them, it was designed as a restriction upon the ancillary powers incidental to every express grant of power in general terms. I have already cited so fully from that case that I can only refer to it to say that this proposition is there clearly stated and refuted.

Does there exist, then, any power in Congress or in the Government, by express grant, in the execution of which this legal-tender act was necessary and proper, in the sense here defined, under the circumstances of its passage?

The power to declare war, to suppress insurrection, to raise and support armies, to provide and maintain a navy, to borrow money on the credit of the United States, to pay the debts of the Union, and to provide for the common defense and general welfare, are each and all distinctly and specifically granted in separate clauses of the Constitution.

We were in the midst of a war which called all these powers into exercise and taxed them severely; a war which, if we take into account the increased capacity for destruction introduced by modern science and the corresponding increase of its cost, brought into operation powers of belligerency more potent and more expensive than any that the world has ever known.

All the ordinary means of rendering efficient the several powers of Congress above mentioned had been employed to their utmost capacity, and with the spirit of the rebellion unbroken, with large armies in the field unpaid, with a current expenditure of over $1,000,000 per day, the credit of the Government nearly exhausted, and the resources of taxation inadequate to pay even the interest on the public debt, Congress was called on to devise some new means of borrowing money on the credit of the nation, for the result of the war was conceded by all thoughtful men to depend on the capacity of the Government to raise money in amounts previously unknown. The banks had already loaned their means to the treasury. They had been compelled to suspend the payment of specie on their own notes. The coin in the country, if it could all have been placed within the control of the Secretary of the Treasury, would not have made a circulation sufficient to answer army purchases and army payments, to say nothing of the ordinary business of the country. A general collapse of credit, of payment, and of business seemed inevitable, in which faith in the ability of the Government would have been destroyed, the rebellion would have triumphed, the States would have been left divided, and the people impoverished. The national government would have perished, and with it the Constitution which we are now called upon to construe with such nice and critical accuracy.

That the legal-tender act prevented these disastrous results, and that the tender clause was necessary to prevent them, I entertain no doubt. It furnished instantly a means of paying the soldiers in the field and filled the coffers of the commissary and quartermaster. It furnished a medium for the payment of private debts, as well as public, at a time when gold was being rapidly withdrawn from circulation and the State-bank currency was becoming worthless. It furnished the means to the capitalist of buying the bonds of the Government. It stimulated trade, revived the drooping energies of the country, and restored confidence to the public mind.

The results which followed the adoption of this measure are beyond dispute. No other adequate cause has ever been assigned for the revival of government credit, the renewed activity of trade, and the facility with which the Government borrowed in two or three years, at reasonable rates of interest, mainly from its own citizens, double the amount of money there was in the country, including coin, bank notes, and the notes issued under the legal-tender acts.

It is now said, however, in the calm retrospect of these events, that treasury notes suitable for circulation as money, bearing on their face the pledge of the United States for their ultimate payment in coin, would, if not equally efficient, have answered the requirement of the occasion without being made a lawful tender for debts.

But what was needed was something more than the credit of the Government. That had been stretched to its utmost tension, and was clearly no longer sufficient in the simple form of borrowing money. Is there any reason to believe that the mere change in the form of the security given would have revived this sinking credit? On the contrary, all experience shows that a currency not redeemable promptly in coin, but dependent on the credit of a promiser whose resources are rapidly diminishing, while his liabilities are increasing, soon sinks to the dead level of worthless paper. As no man would have been compelled to take it in payment of debts, as it bore no interest, as its period of redemption would have been remote and uncertain, this must have been the inevitable fate of any extensive issue of such notes.

But when by law they were made to discharge the function of paying debts, they had a perpetual credit or value equal to the amount of all the debts, public and private, in the country. If they were never redeemed, as they never have been, they still paid debts at their par value, and for this purpose were then, and always have been, eagerly sought by the people. To say, then, that this quality of legal tender was not necessary to their usefulness seems to be unsupported by any sound view of the situation.

Nor can any just inference of that proposition arise from a comparison of the legal-tender notes with the bonds issued by the Government about the same time. These bonds had a fixed period for their payment, and the Secretary of the Treasury declared that they were payable in gold. They bore interest, which was payable semi-annually in gold, by express terms on their face, and the customs duties, which by law could be paid in nothing but gold, were sacredly pledged to the payment of this interest. They can afford no means of determining what would have been the fate of treasury notes designed to circulate as money, but which bore no interest, and had no fixed time of redemption, and by law could pay no debts, and had no fund pledged for their payment.

The legal-tender clauses of the statutes under consideration were placed emphatically, by those who enacted them, upon their necessity to the further borrowing of money and maintaining the army and navy.

It was done reluctantly and with hesitation, and only after the necessity had been demonstrated and had become imperative. Our statesmen had been trained in a school which looked upon such legislation with something more than distrust. The debates of the two houses of Congress show that on this necessity alone could this clause of the bill have been carried, and they also prove, as I think, very clearly the existence of that necessity.

The history of that gloomy time, not to be forgotten by the lover of his country, will forever remain the full, clear, and ample vindication of the exercise of this power by Congress, as its results have demonstrated the sagacity of those who originated and carried through this measure.

Certainly it seems to the best judgment that I

can bring to bear upon the subject that this law was a necessity in the most stringent sense in which that word can be used. But if we adopt the construction of Chief Justice Marshall and the full court over which he presided, a construction which has never to this day been overruled or questioned in this court, how can we avoid this conclusion? Can it be said that this provision did not conduce towards the purpose of borrowing money, of paying debts, of raising armies, of suppressing insurrection? or that it was not calculated to effect these objects? or that it was not useful and essential to that end? Can it be said that this was not among the choice of means, if not the only means, which were left to Congress to carry on this war for national existence?

Let us compare the present with other cases decided in this court.

If we can say judicially that to declare, as in the case of the United States vs. Fisher, that the debt which a bankrupt owes the Government shall have priority of payment over all other debts is a necessary and proper law to enable the Government to pay its own debts, how can we say that the legal-tender clause was not necessary and proper to enable the Government to borrow money to carry on the war?

The creation of the United States Bank, and especially the power granted to it to issue notes for circulation as money, was strenuously resisted as without constitutional authority; but this court held that a bank of issue was necessary, in the sense of that word as used in the Constitution, to enable the Government to collect, to transfer, and to pay out its revenues.

It was never claimed that the Government could find no other means to do this. It could not then be denied, nor has it ever been, that other means more clearly within the competency of Congress existed, nor that a bank of deposit might possibly have answered without a circulation. But because that was the most fitting, useful, and efficient mode of doing what Congress was authorized to do, it was held to be necessary by this court. The necessity in that case is much less apparent to me than in the adoption of the legal-tender clause.

In the Veazie Bank vs. Fenno, decided at the present term, this court held, after full consideration, that it was the privilege of Congress to furnish to the country the currency to be used by it in the transaction of business, whether this was done by means of coin, or the notes of the United States, or of banks created by Congress; and that, as a means of making this power of Congress efficient, that body could make this currency exclusive by taxing out of existence any currency authorized by the States. It was said "that having, in the exercise of undoubted constitutional power, undertaken to provide a currency for the whole country, it cannot be questioned that Congress may constitutionally secure the benefit of it to the people by appropriate means." Which is the more appropriate and effectual means of making the currency established by Congress useful, acceptable, perfect —the taxing of all other currency out of existence, or giving to that furnished by the Government the quality of lawful tender for debts?

The latter is a means directly conducive to the end to be attained, a means which attains the end more promptly and more perfectly than any other means can do. The former is a remote and uncertain means in its effect, and is liable to the serious objection that it interferes with State legislation. If Congress can, however, under its implied power, protect and foster this currency by such means as destructive taxation on State bank circulation, it seems strange, indeed, if it cannot adopt the more appropriate and the more effectual means of declaring these notes of its own issue, for the redemption of which its faith is pledged, a lawful tender in payment of debts.

But it is said that the law is in conflict with the spirit if not the letter of several provisions of the Constitution. Undoubtedly it is a law impairing the obligation of contracts made before its passage. But while the Constitution forbids the States to pass such laws it does not forbid Congress. On the contrary, Congress is expressly authorized to establish a uniform system of bankruptcy, the essence of which is to discharge debtors from the obligation of their contracts; and in pursuance of this power Congress has three times passed such a law, which in every instance operated on contracts made before it was passed. Such a law is now in force, yet its constitutionality has never been questioned. How it can be in accordance with the spirit of the Constitution to destroy directly the creditor's contract for the sake of the individual debtor, but contrary to its spirit to affect remotely its value for the safety of the nation, it is difficult to perceive.

So it is said that the provisions, that private property shall not be taken for public use without due compensation, and that no person shall be deprived of life, liberty, or property without due course of law, are opposed to the acts under consideration.

The argument is too vague for my perception by which the indirect effect of a great public measure, in depreciating the value of lands, stocks, bonds, and other contracts, renders such a law invalid as taking private property for public use or as depriving the owner of it without due course of law.

A declaration of war with a maritime power would thus be unconstitutional, because the value of every ship abroad is lessened twenty-five or thirty per cent. and those at home almost as much. The abolition of the tariff on iron or sugar would in like manner destroy the furnaces, and sink the capital employed in the manufacture of these articles. Yet no statesmen, however warm an advocate of high tariff, has claimed that to abolish such duties would be unconstitutional as taking private property.

If the principle be sound, every successive issue of government bonds during the war was void, because by increasing the public debt it made those already in private hands less valuable.

This whole argument of the injustice of the law, an injustice which, if it ever existed, will be repeated by now holding it wholly void and of its opposition to the spirit of the Constitution, is too abstract and intangible for application to courts of justice, and is above all dangerous as a ground on which to declare the legislation of Congress void by the decision of a court. It would authorize this court to enforce theoretical views of the genius of the government, or vague notions of the spirit of the Constitution and of abstract justice, by declaring void laws which did not square with those views. It substitutes our ideas of policy for judicial construction, an undefined code of ethics for the Constitution, and a court of justice for the national legislature.

Upon the enactment of these legal-tender laws they were received with almost universal acquiescence as valid. Payments were made in the legal-tender notes for debts in existence when the law was passed to the amount of thousands of millions of dollars, though gold was the only lawful tender when the debts were contracted. A great if not larger amount is now due under contracts made since their passage, under the belief that these legal tenders would be valid payment.

The two houses of Congress, the President who signed the bill, and fifteen State courts, being all but one that has passed upon the question, have expressed their belief in the constitutionality of these laws.

With all this great weight of authority, this strong concurrence of opinion among those who have passed upon the question, before we have been called to decide it, whose duty it was as much as it is ours to pass upon it in the light of the Constitution, are we to reverse their action, to disturb contracts, to declare the law void because the necessity for its enactment does not appear so strong to us as it did to Congress, or so clear as it was to other courts?

Such is not my idea of the relative functions of the legislative and judicial departments of the Government. Where there is a choice of means, the selection is with Congress, not the court. If the act to be considered is in any sense essential to the execution of an acknowledged power, the degree of that necessity is for the legislature and not for the court to determine. In the case in Wheaton, from which I have already quoted so fully, the court says that "where the law is not prohibited, and is really calculated to effect any of the objects intrusted to the Government, to undertake here to inquire into the degree of its necessity would be to pass the line which circumscribes the judicial department, and to tread on legislative ground. This court disclaims all pretences to such a power." This sound exposition of the duties of the court in this class of cases relieves me from any embarrassment or hesitation in the case before me. If I had entertained doubts of the constitutionality of the law, I must have held the law valid until those doubts became convictions. But as I have a very decided opinion that Congress acted within the scope of its authority, I must hold the law to be constitutional, and dissent from the opinion of the court.

I am authorized to say that Mr. Justice Swayne and Mr. Justice Davis concur in this opinion.

NOTE.—When this decision was made the court consisted of eight judges, there being one vacancy, caused by the death of Judge Wayne, of Georgia. The five who concurred in the decision are Chief Justice Chase and Associate Justices Nelson, Clifford, Grier, and Field. Of these, the first three are understood to hold the legal-tender clause unconstitutional for all purposes, and the latter two as unconstitutional as to prior contracts only.

Since the decision was pronounced, Associate Justices Strong and Bradley have been added to the bench, the former in place of Associate Justice Grier, the latter in place of Associate Justice Wayne. There is a strong impression that the *full* court will reverse the above decision whenever a case involving the question may arise.—E. McP.

## On the Right of the United States Government to Tax State Banks.

### DECEMBER TERM, 1869

| | |
|---|---|
| The President, Directors, and Company of the Veazie Bank, plaintiffs,<br><br>*vs.*<br><br>Jeremiah Fenno, collector of internal revenue. | Certificate of division in opinion between the judges of the circuit court of the United States for the district of Maine. |

Mr. Chief Justice Chase delivered the opinion of the court.

The necessity of adequate provision for the financial exigencies created by the late rebellion suggested to the administrative and legislative departments of the Government important changes in the systems of currency and taxation which had hitherto prevailed. These changes, more or less distinctly shown in administrative recommendations, took form and substance in legislative acts. We have now to consider, within a limited range, those which relate to circulating notes and the taxation of circulation.

At the beginning of the rebellion the circulating medium consisted almost entirely of bank notes issued by numerous independent corporations variously organized under State legislation, of various degrees of credit, and very unequal resources, administered often with great, and not unfrequently with little skill, prudence, and integrity. The acts of Congress then in force prohibiting the receipt or disbursement, in the transactions of the national Government, of anything except gold and silver, and the laws of the States requiring the redemption of bank notes in coin on demand, prevented the disappearance of gold and silver from circulation. There was then no national currency except coin; there was no general* regulation of any other by national legislation, and no national taxation was imposed in any form on the State bank circulation.

The first act authorizing the emission of notes by the Treasury Department for circulation was that of July 17, 1861.† The notes issued under this act were treasury notes, payable on demand in coin. The amount authorized by it was fifty millions of dollars, and was increased by the act of February 12, 1862,‡ to sixty millions.

On the 31st of December, 1861, the State banks suspended specie payment. Until this time the expenses of the war had been paid in coin, or in the demand notes just referred to, and for sometime afterwards they continued to be paid in these notes, which, if not redeemed in coin, were received as coin in the payment of duties.

Subsequently, on the 25th of February, 1862,§ a new policy became necessary in consequence of the suspension and of the condition of the country, and was adopted. The notes hitherto issued, as has just been stated, were called treas-

*See the act of December 27, 1854, to suppress small notes in the District of Columbia, 10 U. S. Stats., 599. †12 U. S. Stats., 259. ‡12 U. S. Stats., 338. §12 U. S. Stats., 345.

ury notes, and were payable on demand in coin. The act now passed authorized the issue of bills for circulation under the name of United States notes, made payable to bearer, but not expressed to be payable on demand, to the amount of $150,000,000; and this amount was increased by subsequent acts to $450,000,000, of which $50,000,000 were to be held in reserve, and only to be issued for a special purpose, and under special directions as to their withdrawal from circulation.* These notes, until after the close of the war, were always convertible into or receivable at par for bonds payable in coin, and bearing coin interest, at a rate not less than five per cent., and the acts by which they were authorized declared them to be lawful money and a legal tender.

This currency, issued directly by the Government for the disbursement of the war and other expenditures, could not, obviously, be a proper object of taxation.

But on the 25th of February, 1863, the act authorizing national banking associations† was passed, in which, for the first time during many years, Congress recognized the expediency and duty of imposing a tax upon currency. By this act a tax of two per cent. annually was imposed on the circulation of the associations authorized by it. Soon after, by the act of March 3, 1863,‡ a similar but lighter tax of one per cent. annually was imposed on the circulation of State banks in certain proportions to their capital and of two per cent. on the excess; and the tax on the national associations was reduced to the same rates.

Both acts also imposed taxes on capital and deposits, which need not be noticed here.

At a later date, by the act of June 3, 1864,§ which was substituted for the act of February 25, 1863, authorizing national banking associations, the rate of tax on circulation was continued and applied to the whole amount of it, and the shares of their stockholders were also subjected to taxation by the States; and a few days afterwards, by the act of June 30, 1864,‖ to provide ways and means for the support of the Government, the tax on the circulation of the State banks was also continued at the same annual rate of one per cent., as before, but payment was required in monthly installments of one-twelfth of one per cent., with monthly reports from each State bank of the amount in circulation.

It can hardly be doubted that the object of this provision was to inform the proper authorities of the exact amount of paper money in circulation, with a view to its regulation by law.

The first step taken by Congress in that direction was by the act of July 17, 1862,¶ prohibiting the issue and circulation of notes under one dollar by any person or corporation. The act just referred to was the next, and it was followed some months later by the act of March 3, 1865, amendatory of the prior internal revenue acts, the 6th section of which provides: "That every national banking association, State bank, or State banking association, shall pay a tax of ten per centum on the amount of the notes of any State

bank or State banking association paid out by them after the 1st day of July, 1866."*

The same provision was re-enacted, with a more extended application, on the 13th of July, 1866, in these words: "Every national banking association, State bank, or State banking association, shall pay a tax of ten per centum on the amount of notes of any person, State bank, or State banking association, used for circulation and paid out by them after the 1st day of August, 1866, and such tax shall be assessed and paid in such manner as shall be prescribed by the Commissioner of Internal Revenue."†

The constitutionality of this last provision is now drawn in question, and this brief statement of the recent legislation of Congress has been made for the purpose of placing in a clear light its scope and bearing, especially as developed in the provisions just cited. It will be seen that when the policy of taxing bank circulation was first adopted in 1863, Congress was inclined to discriminate for, rather than against, the circulation of the State banks; but that when the country had been sufficiently furnished with a national currency by the issue of United States notes and of national bank notes, the discrimination was turned, and very decidedly turned, in the opposite direction.

The general question now before us is, whether or not the tax of ten per cent., imposed on State banks or national banks paying out the notes of individuals or State banks used for circulation, is repugnant to the Constitution of the United States.

It is presented by a certificate of division of opinion between the judges of the circuit court of the United States for the district of Maine, in a suit brought by the President, Directors, and Company of the Veazie Bank against Jeremiah Fenno, collector of internal revenue, for the recovery of the tax, penalty, and costs paid by the bank to the collector under protest and to avoid distraint.

The Veazie Bank is a corporation chartered by the State of Maine, with authority to issue bank notes for circulation, and the notes on which the tax imposed by the act was collected were issued under this authority. There is nothing in the case showing that the bank sustained any relation to the State as a financial agent, or that its authority to issue notes was conferred or exercised with any special reference to other than private interests.

The case was presented to the circuit court upon an agreed statement of facts; and upon a prayer for instructions to the jury the judges found themselves opposed in opinion on three questions, the first of which is this:

"Whether the second clause of the 9th section of the act of Congress of the 13th of July, 1866, under which the tax in this case was levied and collected, is a valid and constitutional law?"

The other two questions differ from this in form only, and need not be recited.

In support of the position that the act of Congress, so far as it provides for the levy and collection of this tax, is repugnant to the Constitution, two propositions have been argued with much force and earnestness.

---

* Act of July 11, 1862, 12 U. S. Stats., 532; act of March 3, 1863, 12 U. S. Stats., 710. † 12 U. S. Stats., 670. ‡ 12 U. S. Stats., 712. § 13 U. S. Stats., 111. ‖ 13 U. S. Stats., 277. ¶ 12 U. S. Stats, 592.

* 13 U. S. Stats., 484. † 14 U. S. Stats., 146.

The first is that the tax in question is a direct tax, and has not been apportioned among the States agreeably to the Constitution.

The second is that the act imposing the tax impairs a franchise granted by the State, and that Congress has no power to pass any law with that intent or effect.

The first of these propositions will be first examined.

The difficulty of defining with accuracy the terms used in the clause of the Constitution which confers the power of taxation upon Congress was felt in the convention which framed that instrument, and has always been experienced by courts when called upon to determine their meaning.

The general intent of the Constitution, however, seems plain. The general government, administered by the congress of the Confederation, had been reduced to the verge of impotency by the necessity of relying for revenue upon requisitions on the States, and it was a leading object in the adoption of the Constitution to relieve the government to be organized under it from this necessity, and confer upon it ample power to provide revenue by the taxation of persons and property. And nothing is clearer, from the discussions in the convention and the discussions which preceded final ratification by the necessary number of States, than the purpose to give this power to Congress, as to the taxation of everything except exports, in its fullest extent.

This purpose is apparent, also, from the terms in which the taxing power is granted. The power is "to lay and collect taxes, duties, imposts, and excises, to pay the debt and provide for the common defence and general welfare of the United States." More comprehensive words could not have been used. Exports only are by another provision excluded from its application.

There are, indeed, certain virtual limitations arising from the principles of the Constitution itself. It would undoubtedly be an abuse of the power if so exercised as to impair the separate existence and independent self-government* of the States, or if exercised for ends inconsistent with the limited grants of power in the Constitution.

And there are directions as to the mode of exercising the power. If Congress sees fit to impose a capitation or other direct tax, it must be laid in proportion to the census; if Congress determines to impose duties, imposts, and excises, they must be uniform throughout the United States. These are not strictly limitations of power. They are rules prescribing the mode in which it shall be exercised. It still extends to every object of taxation except exports, and may be applied to every object of taxation to which it extends in such measure as Congress may determine.

The comprehensiveness of the power thus given to Congress may serve to explain, at least, the absence of any attempt by members of the convention to define, even in debate, the terms of the grant. The words used certainly describe the whole power, and it was the intention of the convention that the whole power should be conferred. The definition of particular words therefore became unimportant.

It may be said, indeed, that this observation, however just in its application to the general grant of power, cannot be applied to the rules by which different descriptions of taxes are directed to be laid and collected.

Direct taxes must be laid and collected by the rule of apportionment; duties, imposts, and excises must be laid and collected under the rule of uniformity.

Much diversity of opinion has always prevailed upon the question, what are direct taxes? Attempts to answer it by reference to the definitions of political economists have been frequently made, but without satisfactory results. The enumeration of the different kinds of taxes which Congress was authorized to impose was probably made with very little reference to their speculations. The great work of Adam Smith, the first comprehensive treatise on political economy in the English language, had then been recently published; but in this work, though there are passages which refer to the characteristic difference between direct and indirect taxation, there is nothing which affords any valuable light on the use of the words direct taxes in the Constitution.

We are obliged, therefore, to resort to historical evidence, and to seek the meaning of the words in the use and in the opinion of those whose relations to the government and means of knowledge warranted them in speaking with authority.

And, considered in this light, the meaning and application of the rule as to direct taxes appears to us quite clear.

It is, as we think, distinctly shown in every act of Congress on the subject.

In each of these acts a gross sum was laid upon the United States, and the total amount was apportioned to the several States according to their respective numbers of inhabitants, as ascertained by the last preceding census. Having been apportioned, provision was made for the imposition of the tax upon the subjects specified in the act, fixing its total sum.

In 1798, when the first direct tax was imposed, the total amount was fixed at $2,000,000;* in 1813, the amount of the second direct tax was fixed at $3,000,000;† in 1815, the amount of the third at $6,000,000, and it was made an annual tax;‡ in 1816, the provision making the tax annual was repealed by the repeal of the 1st section of the act of 1815, and the total amount was fixed for that year at $3,000,000.§ No other direct tax was imposed until 1861, when a direct tax of $20,000,000 was laid and made annual;‖ but the provision making it annual was suspended, and no tax except that first laid was ever apportioned. In each instance the total sum was apportioned among the States by the constitutional rule, and was assessed at prescribed rates on the subjects of the tax. These subjects in 1798,¶ 1813,** 1815,†† 1816,‡‡ were lands, improvements, dwelling-houses, and slaves; and in 1861 lands, improvements, dwelling-houses only. Under the act of 1798, slaves were assessed at fifty

---

* County of Lane v. State of Oregon, 7 Wall., 73.

* Act of July 14, 1798, 1 U. S. Stats., 597. † Act of August 2, 1813, 3 U. S. Stats., 53. ‡ Act of July 9, 1815, 3 U. S. Stats., 164. ₰ Act of March 5, 1816, 3 U. S. Stats., 255. ‖ Act of August 5, 1861, 12 U. S. Stats., 294. ¶ Act of July 9, 1798, 1 U. S. Stats., 586. ** Act of July 22, 1813, 3 U. S. Stats., 26. †† 3 U. S. Stats., 166. ‡‡ 3 U. S. Stats., 255.

cents on eacn; under the other acts, according to valuation by assessors.

This review shows that personal property, contracts, occupations, and the like, have never been regarded by Congress as proper subjects of direct tax. It has been supposed that slaves must be considered as an exception to this observation. But the exception is rather apparent than real. As persons, slaves were proper subjects of a capitation tax, which is described in the Constitution as a direct tax; as property, they were by the laws of some, if not most, of the States classed as real property, descendible to heirs. Under the first view, they would be subject to the tax of 1798 as a capitation tax; under the latter, they would be subject to the taxation of the other years as realty. That the latter view was that taken by the framers of the acts after 1798 becomes highly probable, when it is considered that in the States where slaves were held much of the value which would otherwise have attached to land passed into the slaves. If indeed the land only had been valued without the slaves, the land would have been subject to much heavier proportional imposition in those States than in States where there were no slaves; for the proportion of tax imposed on each State was determined by population, without reference to the subjects on which it was to be assessed.

The fact, then, that slaves were valued under the acts referred to, far from showing, as some have supposed, that Congress regarded personal property as a proper object of direct taxation under the Constitution, shows only that Congress, after 1798, regarded slaves, for the purpose of taxation, as realty.

It may be rightly affirmed, therefore, that in the practical construction of the Constitution by Congress, direct taxes have been limited to taxes on land and appurtenances, and taxes on polls, or capitation taxes.

And this construction is entitled to great consideration, especially in the absence of anything adverse to it in the discussions of the convention which framed and of the conventions which ratified the Constitution.

What does appear in those discussions, on the contrary, supports the construction. Mr. Madison, says Mr. King, asked what was the precise meaning of direct taxation, and no one answered. On another day, when the question of proportioning representation to taxation, and both to the white and three-fifths of the slave inhabitants, was under consideration, Mr. Ellsworth said: "In case of a poll-tax, there would be no difficulty;" and, speaking doubtless of direct taxation, he went on to observe, "The sum allotted to a State may be levied without difficulty, according to the plan used in the State for raising its own supplies. All this doubtless shows uncertainty as to the true meaning of the term direct tax; but it indicates also an understanding that direct taxes were such as may be levied by capitation, and on lands and appurtenances; or, perhaps, by valuation and assessment of personal property upon general lists; for these were the subjects from which the States at that time usually raised their principal supplies.

This view received the sanction of this court

two years before the enactment of the first law imposing direct taxes *eo nomine.*

During the February term, 1796, the constitutionality of the act of 1794, imposing a duty on carriages, came under consideration in the case of Hylton *vs.* The United States.* Suit was brought by the United States against Daniel Hylton to recover the penalty imposed by the act for not returning and paying duty on a number of carriages for the conveyance of persons, kept by the defendant for his own use. The law did not provide for the apportionment of the tax, and, if it was a direct tax, the law was confessedly unwarranted by the Constitution. The only question in the case, therefore, was whether or not the tax was a direct tax.

The case was one of great expectation, and a general interest was felt in its determination. It was argued, in support of the tax, by Lee, Attorney General, and Hamilton, recently Secretary of the Treasury; in opposition to the tax, by Campbell, attorney for the Virginia district, and Ingersoll, attorney general of Pennsylvania.

Of the justices who then filled this bench, Ellsworth, Paterson, and Wilson had been members, and conspicuous members, of the constitutional convention, and each of the three had taken part in the discussions relating to direct taxation. Ellsworth, the chief justice, sworn into office that morning, not having heard the whole argument, declined taking part in the decision. Cushing, senior associate justice, having been prevented by indisposition from attending to the argument, also refrained from expressing an opinion. The other judges delivered their opinions in succession, the youngest in commission delivering the first, and the oldest the last.

They all held that the tax on carriages was not a direct tax within the meaning of the Constitution. Chase, J., was inclined to think that the direct taxes contemplated by the Constitution are only two: a capitation or poll tax, and a tax on land. He doubted whether a tax by a general assessment of personal property can be included within the term direct tax. Paterson, who had taken a leading part in the constitution convention, went more fully into the sense in which the words giving the power of taxation were used by that body. In the course of this examination he said:

"Whether direct taxes, in the sense of the Constitution, comprehend any other tax than a capitation tax and tax on land is a questionable point. If Congress, for instance, should tax, in the aggregate or mass, things that generally pervade all the States in the Union, then, perhaps, the rule of apportionment would be the most proper, especially if an assessment was to intervene. This appears from the practice of some of the States to have been considered as a direct tax. Whether it be so under the Constitution of the United States is a matter of some difficulty; but as it is not before the court, it would be improper to give any decisive opinion upon it. I never entertained a doubt that the principal—I will not say the only—objects that the framers of the Constitution contemplated as falling within the rule of apportionment were a capitation tax and a tax on land."†

*3 Dall., 171.                    † 3 Dall., 177.

Iredell, delivering his opinion at length, concurred generally in the views of Justices Chase and Paterson. Wilson had expressed his opinions to the same general effect when giving the decision upon the circuit, and did not now repeat them. Neither Chief Justice Ellsworth nor Justice Cushing expressed any dissent; and it cannot be supposed if, in a case so important, their judgments had differed from those announced, that an opportunity would not have been given them by an order for reargument to participate in the decision.

It may be safely assumed, therefore, as the unanimous judgment of the court, that a tax on carriages is not a direct tax. And it may further be taken as established, upon the testimony of Paterson, that the words direct taxes, as used in the Constitution, comprehended only capitation taxes and taxes on land, and perhaps taxes on personal property by general valuation and assessment of the various descriptions possessed within the several States.

It follows necessarily that the power to tax without apportionment extends to all other objects. Taxes on other objects are included under the heads of taxes not direct, duties, imposts, and excises, and must be laid and collected by the rule of uniformity. The tax under consideration is a tax on bank circulation, and may very well be classed under the head of duties. Certainly it is not in the sense of the Constitution a direct tax. It may be said to come within the same category of taxation as the tax on incomes of insurance companies, which this court, at the last term, in the case of Soule vs. the Insurance Company,* held not to be a direct tax.

Is it, then, a tax on a franchise granted by a State, which Congress, upon any principle exempting the reserved powers of the States from impairment by taxation, must be held to have no authority to lay and collect?

We do not say that there may not be such a tax. It may be admitted that the reserved rights of the States, such as the right to pass laws, to give effect to laws through executive action, to administer justice through the courts, and to employ all necessary agencies for legitimate purposes of State government, are not proper subjects of the taxing power of Congress. But it cannot be admitted that franchises granted by a State are necessarily exempt from taxation; for franchises are property, often very valuable and productive property; and, when not conferred for the purpose of giving effect to some reserved power of a State, seem to be as properly objects of taxation as any other property.

But in the case before us the object of taxation is not the franchise of the bank, but property created or contracts made and issued under the franchise or power to issue bank bills. A railroad company, in the exercise of its corporate franchises, issues freight receipts, bills of lading, and passenger tickets; and it cannot be doubted that the organization of railroads is quite as important to the State as the organization of banks. But it will hardly be questioned that these contracts of the company are objects of taxation

within the powers of Congress, and not exempted by any relation to the State which granted the charter of the railroad. And it seems difficult to distinguish the taxation of notes issued for circulation from the taxation of these railroad contracts. Both descriptions of contracts are means of profit to the corporations which issue them; and both, as we think, may properly be made contributory to the public revenue.

It is insisted, however, that the tax in the case before us is excessive, and so excessive as to indicate a purpose on the part of Congress to destroy the franchise of the bank, and is, therefore, beyond the constitutional power of Congress.

The first answer to this is that the judicial cannot prescribe to the legislative departments of the government limitations upon the exercise of its acknowledged powers. The power to tax may be exercised oppressively upon persons, but the responsibility of the legislature is not to the courts, but to the people by whom its members are elected. So if a particular tax bears heavily upon a corporation or a class of corporations, it cannot, for that reason only, be pronounced contrary to the Constitution.

But there is another answer which vindicates equally the wisdom and the power of Congress.

It cannot be doubted that under the Constitution the power to provide a circulation of coin is given to Congress. And it is settled by the uniform practice of the Government and by repeated decisions, that Congress may constitutionally authorize the emission of bills of credit. It is not important here to decide whether the quality of legal tender in payment of debts can be constitutionally imparted to these bills; it is enough to say that there can be no question of the power of the Government to emit them, to make them receivable in payment of debts to itself, to fit them for use by those who see fit to use them in all the transactions of commerce, to provide for their redemption, to make them a currency uniform in value and description, and convenient and useful for circulation. These powers until recently were only partially and occasionally exercised. Lately, however, they have been called into full activity, and Congress has undertaken to supply a currency for the entire country.

The methods adopted for the supply of this currency were briefly explained in the first part of this opinion. It now consists of coin, and of United States notes, and of the notes of the national banks. Both descriptions of notes may be properly described as bills of credit, for both are furnished by the government; both are issued on the credit of the government, and the government is responsible for the redemption of both; primarily as to the first description, and immediately upon default of the bank as to the second. When these bills shall be made convertible into coin at the will of the holder, this currency will perhaps satisfy the wants of the community in respect to a circulating medium as perfectly as any mixed currency that can be devised.

Having thus, in the exercise of undisputed constitutional powers, undertaken to provide a currency for the whole country, it cannot be questioned that Congress may constitutionally

---

* 7 Wall., 453.

secure the benefit of it to the people by appropriate legislation. To this end Congress has denied the quality of legal tender to foreign coins, and has provided by law against the imposition of counterfeit and base coin on the community. To the same end Congress may restrain by suitable enactments the circulation as money of any notes not issued under its own authority. Without this power, indeed, its attempts to secure a sound and uniform currency for the country must be futile.

Viewed in this light, as well as in the other light of a duty on contracts or property, we cannot doubt the constitutionality of the tax under consideration.

The three questions certified from the circuit court of the district of Maine must therefore be answered affirmatively.

### Dissenting Opinion.

Mr. Justice Nelson dissenting.

I am unable to concur in the opinion of a majority of the court in this case.

The Veazie Bank was incorporated by the Legislature of the State of Maine in 1848, with a capital of $200,000, and was invested with the customary powers of a banking institution; and among others the power of receiving deposits, discounting paper, and issuing notes or bills for circulation. The constitutional authority of the State to create these institutions, and to invest them with full banking powers, is hardly denied. But it may be useful to recur for a few moments to the source of this authority.

The Xth amendment to the Constitution is as follows: "The powers not delegated to the United States by the Constitution, nor prohibited by it to the States, are reserved to the States respectively or to the people." On looking into the Constitution it will be found that there is no clause or provision which, either expressly or by reasonable implication, delegates this power to the federal Government, which originally belonged to the States, nor which prohibits it to them. In the discussions on the subject of the creation of the first bank of the United States in the first Congress and in the Cabinet of Washington, in 1790 and 1791, no question was made as to the constitutionality of the State banks. The only doubt that existed, and which divided the opinion of the most eminent statesmen of the day, many of whom had just largely participated in the formation of the Constitution, the government under which they were then engaged in organizing, was, whether or not Congress possessed a concurrent power to incorporate a banking institution of the United States.

Mr. Hamilton, in his celebrated report on a national bank to the House of Representatives, discusses at some length the question whether or not it would be expedient to substitute the Bank of North America, located in Philadelphia, and which had accepted a charter from the Legislature of Pennsylvania, in the place of organizing a new bank. And, although he finally came to the conclusion to organize a new one, there is not a suggestion or intimation as to the illegality or unconstitutionality of this State bank.

The act incorporating this bank, passed February 25, 1791, prohibited the establishment of any other by Congress during its charter, but said nothing as to the State banks. A like prohibition is contained in the act incorporating the Bank of the United States of 1816. The constitutionality of a bank incorporated by Congress was first settled by the judgment of this court in McCulloch vs. The State of Maryland, in 1819. (4 Wheat., p. 316.) In that case both the counsel and the court recognize the legality and constitutionality of banks incorporated by the States.

The constitutionality of the Bank of the United States was again discussed and decided in the case of Osborn vs. United States Bank, (9 Wheat., 738.) And in connection with this was argued and decided a point in the case of the United States Bank vs. The Planters' Bank of Georgia, which was common to both cases. The question was whether the circuit courts of the United States had jurisdiction of a suit brought by the United States Bank against the Planters' Bank of Georgia, incorporated by that State, and in which the State was a stockholder. (9 Wheat., pp. 804–904.)

The court held in both cases that it had. Since the adoption of the Constitution down to the present act of Congress and the case now before us, the question in Congress and in the courts has been, not whether the State banks were constitutional institutions, but whether Congress had the power conferred on it by the States to establish a national bank. As we have said, that question was closed by the judgment of this court in McCulloch vs. The State of Maryland. At the time of the adoption of the Constitution there were four State banks in existence and in operation—one in each of the States of Pennsylvania, New York, Massachusetts, and Maryland. The one in Philadelphia had been originally chartered by the Confederation, but subsequently took a charter under the State of Pennsylvania. The framers of the Constitution were, therefore, familiar with these State banks and the circulation of their paper as money, and were also familiar with the practice of the States, that was so common, to issue bills of credit, which were bills issued by the State exclusively on its own credit, and intended to circulate as currency, redeemable at a future day. They guarded the people against the evils of this practice of the State governments by the provision in the 10th section of the first article, "that no State shall" "emit bills of credit," and in the same section guard against any abuse of paper money of the State banks, in the following words: "Nor make anything but gold and silver coin a tender in payment of debts." As bills of credit were thus entirely abolished, the paper money of the State banks was the only currency or circulating medium to which this prohibition could have had any application, and was the only currency, except gold and silver, left to the States. The prohibition took from this paper all coercive legislation, and left it to stand alone upon the credit of the banks.

It was no longer an irredeemable currency, as the banks were under obligation, and including, frequently, that of its stockholders, to redeem their paper in circulation in gold or silver at the counter. The State banks were left in this condition by the Constitution, untouched by any other provision. As a consequence they were gradually established in most or all of the States, and had not been encroached upon or legislated against, or in any other way interfered with by acts of Congress, for more than three-quarters of a century—from 1787 to 1864. But, in addition to the above recognition of the State banks, the question of their constitutionality came directly before this court in the case of Briscoe vs. The Bank of the Commonwealth of Kentucky. (11 Pet., 257.) The case was most elaborately discussed both by the counsel and the court. The court, after the fullest consideration, held that the States possessed the power to grant charters to State banks; that the power was incident to sovereignty; and that there was no limitation in the federal Constitution on its exercise by the States. The court observed that the Bank of North America and of Massachusetts, and some others, were in operation at the time of the adoption of the Constitution, and that it could not be supposed the notes of these banks were intended to be inhibited by that instrument, or that they were considered as bills of credit within its meaning. All the judges concurred in this judgment except Mr. Justice Story. The decision in this case was affirmed in Woodruff vs. Trapnall, (10 How., 205;) in Danington vs. the Bank of Alabama, (13 *ib.*, 12;) and in Curran vs. State of Arkansas, (15 *ib.*, 317.)

Chancellor Kent observes that Mr. Justice Story, in his Commentaries on the Constitution, (vol. 3, p. 19,) seems to be of opinion that, independent of the long-continued practice, from the time of the adoption of the Constitution, the States would not, upon a sound construction of the Constitution, if the question was *res integra*, be authorized to incorporate banks with a power to circulate bank paper as currency, inasmuch as they are expressly prohibited from coining money. He cites the opinions of Mr. Webster, of the Senate of the United States, and of Mr. Dexter, formerly Secretary of War, on the same side. But, the chancellor observes, the equal if not the greater authority of Mr. Hamilton, the earliest Secretary of the Treasury, may be cited in support of a different opinion; and the contemporary sense and uniform practice of the nation are decisive of the question. He further observes, the prohibition (of bills of credit) does not extend to bills emitted by individuals, singly or collectively, whether associated under a private agreement for banking purposes, as was the case with the Bank of New York prior to its earliest charter, which was in the winter of 1791, or acting under a charter of incorporation, so long as the State lends not its credit, or obligation, or coercion to sustain the circulation.

In the case of Briscoe vs. The Bank of the Commonwealth of Kentucky, he observes this question was put at rest by the opinion of the court, that there was no limitation in the Constitution on the power of the States to incorporate banks, and their notes were not intended nor were considered *as bills of credit.* (1 Kent's Com., p. 409, marg. note A, 10th ed.)

The constitutional power of the States being thus established by incontrovertible authority to create State banking institutions, the next question is whether or not the tax in question can be upheld consistently with the enjoyment of this power.

The act of Congress of July 13, 1866, (14 U. S. Stats., 146, § 9,) declares that the State banks shall pay ten per centum on the amount of their notes, or the notes of any person, or other State bank, used for circulation and paid out by them after the 1st of August, 1866. In addition to this tax there is also a tax of five per centum per annum upon all dividends to stockholders, (13 U. S. Stats., p. 283, § 120,) besides a duty of one twenty-fourth of one per centum monthly upon all deposits, and the same monthly duty upon the capital of the bank. (*Ib.*, 277, § 110.) This makes an aggregate of some sixteen per cent. imposed annually upon these banks. It will be observed the tax of ten per centum upon the bills in circulation is not a tax on the property of the institutions. The bills in circulation are not the property, but the debts of the bank, and, in their account of debits and credits, are placed to the debit side. Certainly no government has yet made the discovery of taxing both sides of this account, debit and credit, as the property of a taxable person or corporation. If both these items could be made available for this purpose a heavy national debt need not create any very great alarm, neither as it respects its pressure on the industry of the country, for the time being, or of its possible duration. There is nothing in the debts of a bank to distinguish them in this respect from the debts of individuals or persons. The discounted paper received for the notes in circulation is the property of the bank, and is taxed as such, as is the property of individuals received for their notes that may be outstanding.

The imposition upon the banks cannot be upheld as a tax upon property; neither could it have been so intended. It is simply a mode by which the powers or faculties of the States to incorporate banks are subjected to taxation, and which, if maintainable, may annihilate those powers.

No person questions the authority of Congress to tax the property of the banks, and of all other corporate bodies of a State, the same as that of individuals. They are artificial bodies, representing the associated pecuniary means of real persons, which constitute their business capital, and the property thus invested is open and subject to taxation with all the property, real and personal, of the State. A tax upon this property, and which, by the Constitution, is to be uniform, affords full scope to the taxing power of the federal Government, and is consistent with the power of the States to create the banks, and, in our judgment, is the only subject of taxation by this Government to which these institutions are liable.

As we have seen, in the forepart of this opinion, the power to incorporate banks was not surrendered to the federal Government, but reserved to the States; and it follows that the Constitution itself protects them, or should protect them, from any encroachment upon this right. As to the powers thus reserved, the

States are as supreme as before they entered into the Union, and are entitled to the unrestrained exercise of them. The question as to the taxation of the powers and faculties belonging to governments is not new in this court. The bonds of the federal Government have been held to be exempt from State taxation. Why? Because they were issued under the power in the Constitution to borrow money, and the tax would be a tax upon this power; and, as there can be no limitation to the extent of the tax, the power to borrow might be destroyed. So, in the instance of the United States notes or legal tenders, as they are called, issued under a constructive power to issue bills of credit, as no express power is given in the Constitution, they are exempt from State taxation for a like reason as in the case of Government bonds; and we learn from the opinion of the court in this case that one step further is taken, and that is, that the notes of the national banks are to be regarded as bills of credit, issued indirectly by the Government; and it follows of course from this that the banks used as instruments to issue and put in circulation these notes are also exempt. We are not complaining of this. Our purpose is to show how important it is to the proper protection of the reserved rights of the States that these powers and prerogatives should be exempt from federal taxation, and how fatal to their existence if permitted. And also that, even if this tax could be regarded as one upon property, still, under the decisions above referred to, it would be a tax upon the powers and faculties of the States to create these banks, and therefore unconstitutional.

It is true that the present decision strikes only at the power to create banks, but no person can fail to see that the principle involved affects the power to create any other description of corporations, such as railroads, turnpikes, manufacturing companies, and others.

This taxation of the powers and faculties of the State governments, which are essential to their sovereignty and to the efficient and independent management and administration of their internal affairs, is for the first time advanced as an attribute of federal authority. It finds no support or countenance in the early history of the government or in the opinions of the illustrious statesmen who founded it. These statesmen scrupulously abstained from any encroachment upon the reserved rights of the States, and within these limits sustained and supported them as sovereign States.

We say nothing as to the purpose of this heavy tax of some sixteen per centum upon the banks, ten of which we cannot but regard as imposed upon the power of the States to create them; indeed the purpose is scarcely concealed in the opinion of the court, namely, to encourage the national banks. It is sufficient to add, that the burden of the tax, while it has encouraged these banks, has proved fatal to those of the States; and, if we are at liberty to judge of the purpose of an action from the consequences that have followed it, it is not, perhaps, going too far to say that these consequences were intended.

[I am instructed to say that Mr. Justice Davis concurs in this opinion.]

## On the Right of the State Governments to Tax National Banks.

### December Term, 1869.

The First National Bank of Louisville, plaintiff in error, vs. The Commonwealth of Kentucky. } In error to the court of appeals of the State of Kentucky.

Mr. Justice Miller delivered the opinion of the court.

This is an action brought by the State of Kentucky in her own courts against the First National Bank of Louisville to recover the amount of a tax of fifty cents per share on the shares of its stock. The case resulted in a judgment in favor of the commonwealth in the court of appeals, to which this writ of error is prosecuted.

The suit is brought, according to the practice of the courts of that State, by a petition, setting forth the amount of the tax, and claiming a judgment for the same. The answer, by the same mode of practice, sets up four distinct defenses to the action. These are:

1. That defendant is not organized under the law of the State, but under the bank act of the United States, and is not, therefore, subject to State taxation.

2. That it has been selected and is acting as a depositary and financial agent of the Government of the United States, and, therefore, is not liable to any tax whatever, either on the bank, its capital, or its shares.

3. That its entire capital is invested in securities of the Government of the United States, and that its shares of stock represent but an interest in said securities, and therefore are not subject to State taxation.

4. That the shares of the stock are the property of the individual shareholders, and that the bank cannot be made responsible for a tax levied on those shares, and cannot be compelled to collect and pay such tax to the State.

In the several recent decisions concerning the taxation of the shares of the national banks, as regulated by sections forty and forty-one of the act of Congress of June 3, 1864, (13 U. S. Stats., 111,) it has been established as the law governing this court that the property or interest of a stockholder in an incorporated bank, commonly called a share, the shares in their aggregate totality being called sometimes the capital stock of the bank, is a different thing from the moneyed capital of the bank, held and owned by the corporation. This capital may consist of cash, or of bills and notes discounted, or of real estate combined with these. The whole of it may be invested in bonds of the Government, or in bonds of the States, or in bonds and mortgages. In whatever it may be invested it is owned by the bank as a corporate entity, and not by the stockholders. A tax upon this capital is a tax upon the bank, and we have held that when that capital was invested in the securities of the Government it could not be taxed, nor could the corporation be taxed as the owner of such securities.

On the other hand, we have held that the shareholders or stockholders, by which is meant the same thing, may be taxed by the States on stock or shares so held by them, although all the capital of the bank be invested in federal securities, provided the taxation does not violate the rule prescribed by the act of 1864.

It is not intended here to enter again into the argument by which this distinction is maintained, but to give a clear statement of the propositions that we have decided, that we may apply them to the case before us.

If, then, the tax for which the State of Kentucky recovered judgment in this case is a tax upon the shares of the stock of the bank, and is not a tax upon the capital of the bank owned by the corporation, the first, second, and third grounds of defence must fail.

There are, then, but two questions to be considered in the case before us:

1. Does the law of Kentucky, under which this tax is claimed, impose a tax upon the shares of the bank, or upon the capital of the bank, which is all invested in Government bonds?

2. If it is found to be a tax on the shares, can the bank be compelled to pay the tax thus levied on the shares by the State?

The revenue law of Kentucky imposes a tax "on bank stock, or stock in any moneyed corporation of loan and discount, of fifty cents on each share thereof, equal to one hundred dollars of stock therein, owned by individuals, corporations, or societies."

We entertain no doubt that this provision was intended to tax the shares of the stockholders, and that if no other provision had been made the amount of the tax would have been primarily collectible of the individual or corporation owning such shares, in the same manner that other taxes are collected from individuals. It is clear that it is the shares owned or held by individuals in the banking corporation which are to be taxed, and the measure of the tax is fifty cents per share of one hundred dollars. These shares may, in the market, be worth a great deal more or a great deal less than their par or nominal value, as its capital may have been increased or diminished by gains or losses, but the tax is the same in each case. This shows that it is the *share* which is intended to be taxed, and not the cash or other actual capital of the bank.

It is said that there may be, or that there really are, banks in Kentucky whose stock is not divided into shares of $100 each, but into shares of $50 or other amounts, and that this shows that the legislature did not intend a tax of fifty cents on the share, but a tax on the capital.

But the argument is of little weight. What the legislature intended to say was, that we impose a tax on the shares held by individuals or other corporations in banks in this State. The tax shall be at the rate of fifty cents per share of stock equal to $100. If the shares are only equal to $50, it will be twenty-five cents on each of such shares. If they are equal to $500, it will be $2 50 per share. The rate is regulated so as to be equal to fifty cents on each share of $100.

But it is strongly urged that it is to be deemed a tax on the capital of the bank, because the law requires the officers of the bank to pay this tax on the shares of its stockholders.

Whether the State has the right to do this we will presently consider; but the fact that it has attempted to do it does not prove that the tax is anything else than a tax on these shares. It has been the practice of many of the States for a long time to require of its corporations thus to pay the tax levied on their shareholders. It is the common, if not the only, mode of doing this in all the New England States, and in several of them the portion of this tax which should properly go as the shareholders' contribution to local or municipal taxation is thus collected by the State of the bank and paid over to the local municipal authorities.

In the case of shareholders not residing in the State, it is the only mode in which the State can reach their shares for taxation.

We are therefore of opinion that the law of Kentucky is a tax upon the share of the stockholder.

If the State cannot require of the bank to pay the tax on the shares of its stock it must be because the Constitution of the United States or some act of Congress forbids it. There is certainly no express provision of the Constitution on the subject. But it is argued that the banks, being instrumentalities of the federal Government, by which some of its important operations are conducted, cannot be subjected to such State legislation.

It is certainly true that the bank of the United States and its capital were held to be exempt from State taxation on the ground here stated, and this principle, laid down in the case of McCulloch *vs.* The State of Maryland, has been repeatedly reaffirmed by the court. But the doctrine has its foundation in the proposition that the right of taxation may be so used in such cases as to destroy the instrumentalities by which the Government proposes to effect its lawful purposes in the States, and it certainly cannot be maintained that banks or other corporations or instrumentalities of the Government are to be wholly withdrawn from the operation of State legislation. The most important agents of the federal Government are its officers, but no one will contend that when a man becomes an officer of the Government he ceases to be subject to the laws of the State. The principle we are discussing has its limitation, a limitation growing out of the necessity on which the principle itself is founded.

That limitation is, that the agencies of the federal Government are only exempted from State legislation so far as that legislation may interfere with or impair their efficiency in performing the functions by which they are designed to serve that Government.

Any other rule would convert a principle founded alone in the necessity of securing to the Government of the United States the means of exercising its legitimate powers into an unauthorized and unjustifiable invasion of the rights of the States. The salary of a federal officer may not be taxed; he may be exempted from any personal service which interferes with the discharge of his official duties, because those exemptions are essential to enable him to perform those duties. But he is subject to all the laws of the State which affect his family or social relations or his property, and he is liable to punishment for crime, though that punishment be imprisonment or death.

So of the banks. They are subject to the laws of the State, and are governed in their daily course of business far more by the laws of the State than of the nation. All their contracts are governed and construed by State laws. Their acquisition and transfer of property, their right to collect their debts, and their liability to be sued for debts, are all based on State law. It is only when the State law incapacitates the banks from discharging their duties to the Government that it becomes unconstitutional.

We do not see the remotest probability of this in their being required to pay the tax which their stockholders owe to the State for the shares of their capital stock, when the law of the federal Government authorizes the tax.

If the State of Kentucky had a claim against a stockholder of the bank who was a non-resident of the State it could undoubtedly collect the claim by legal proceeding, in which the bank could be attached or garnished, and made to pay the debt out of the means of its shareholder under its control. This is, in effect, what the law of Kentucky does in regard to the tax of the State on the bank shares. It is no greater interference with the functions of the bank than any other legal proceeding to which its business operations may subject it, and it in no manner hinders it from performing all the duties of financial agent of the Government.

A very nice criticism of the proviso to the forty-first section of the national-bank act, which permits the States to tax the shares of such banks, is made to us, to show that the tax must be collected of the shareholder directly, and that the mode we have been considering is by implication forbidden. But we are of opinion that while Congress intended to limit State taxation to the shares of the bank as distinguished from its capital, and to provide against a dis-crimination in taxing such bank shares unfavorable to them, as compared with the shares of other corporations and with other moneyed capital, it did not intend to prescribe to the States the mode in which the tax should be collected.

The mode under consideration is the one which Congress itself has adopted in collecting its tax on dividends and on the income arising from bonds of corporations. It is the only mode which, certainly and without loss, secures the payment of the tax on all the shares, resident or non-resident, and, as we have already stated, it is the mode which experience has justified in the New England States as the most convenient and proper in regard to the numerous wealthy corporations of those States. It is not to be readily inferred, therefore, that Congress intended to prohibit this mode of collecting a tax which they expressly permitted the States to levy.

It is said here in argument that the tax is void, because it is greater than the tax laid by the State of Kentucky on other moneyed capital in that State.

This proposition is not raised among the very distinct and separate grounds of defence set up by the bank in the pleading. Nor is there any reason to suppose that it was ever called to the attention of the court of appeals, whose judgment we are reviewing.

We have so often of late decided that when a case is brought before us by writ of error to a State court that we can only consider such alleged errors as are involved in the record and actually received the consideration of the State court, that it is only necessary to state the proposition now. As the question thus sought to be raised here was not raised in the court of appeals of Kentucky, we cannot consider it.

The judgment of that court is affirmed.

# LII.

## PRESIDENT GRANT'S

### FIRST ANNUAL AND SPECIAL MESSAGES AND PROCLAMATION.

**President Grant's First Annual Message,**

DECEMBER 6, 1869.

*To the Senate and House of Representatives:*

In coming before you for the first time as Chief Magistrate of this great nation, it is with gratitude to the Giver of all good for the many benefits we enjoy: we are blessed with peace at home, and are without entangling alliances abroad to forebode trouble; with a territory unsurpassed in fertility, of an area equal to the abundant support of five hundred millions of people, and abounding in every variety of useful mineral in quantity sufficient to supply the world for generations; with exuberant crops; with a variety of climate adapted to the production of every species of earth's riches, and suited to the habits, tastes, and requirements of every living thing; with a population of forty millions of free people, all speaking one language; with facilities for every mortal to acquire an education; with institutions closing to none the avenues to fame or any blessing of fortune that may be coveted; with freedom of the pulpit, the press, and the school; with a revenue flowing into the national treasury beyond the requirements of the Government. Happily, harmony is being rapidly restored within our own borders. Manufactures hitherto unknown in our country are springing up in all sections, producing a degree of national independence unequaled by that of any other power.

These blessings and countless others are intrusted to your care and mine for safe-keeping, for the brief period of our tenure of office. In a short time we must, each of us, return to the ranks of the people who have conferred upon us our honors, and account to them for our stewardship. I earnestly desire that neither you nor I may be condemned by a free and enlightened constituency, nor by our own consciences.

Emerging from a rebellion of gigantic magnitude, aided as it was by the sympathies and assistance of nations with which we were at peace, eleven States of the Union were four years ago left without legal State governments. A national debt had been contracted; American commerce was almost driven from the seas; the industry of one-half of the country had been taken from the control of the capitalist and placed where all labor rightfully belongs—in the keeping of the laborer. The work of restoring State governments loyal to the Union, of protecting and fostering free labor, and providing means for paying the interest on the public debt, has received ample attention from Congress. Although your efforts have not met with the success in all particulars that might have been desired, yet, on the whole, they have been more successful than could have been reasonably anticipated.

Seven States which passed ordinances of secession have been fully restored to their places in the Union. The eighth, Georgia, held an election at which she ratified her constitution, republican in form, elected a governor, members of Congress, a State legislature, and all other officers required. The governor was duly installed and the legislature met and performed all the acts then required of them by the reconstruction acts of Congress. Subsequently, however, in violation of the constitution which they had just ratified, (as since decided by the supreme court of the State,) they unseated the colored members of the legislature and admitted to seats some members who are disqualified by the third clause of the XIVth amendment to the Constitution, an article which they themselves had contributed to ratify. Under these circumstances, I would submit to you whether it would not be wise, without delay, to enact a law authorizing the governor of Georgia to convene the members originally elected to the legislature, requiring each member to take the oath prescribed by the reconstruction acts, and none to be admitted who are ineligible under the third clause of the XIVth amendment.

The freedmen, under the protection which they have received, are making rapid progress in learning, and no complaints are heard of lack of industry on their part where they receive fair remuneration for their labor. The means provided for paying the interest on the public debt, with all other expenses of government, are more than ample. The loss of our commerce is the only result of the late rebellion which has not received sufficient attention from you. To this subject I call your earnest attention. I will not now suggest plans by which this object may be effected, but will, if necessary, make it the subject of a special message during the session of Congress.

At the March term, Congress by joint resolution authorized the Executive to order elections in the States of Virginia, Mississippi, and Texas, to submit to them the constitutions which each had previously, in convention, framed, and submit the constitutions, either entire or in separate parts, to be voted upon at the discretion of the Executive. Under this authority elections were called. In Virginia the election took place on the 6th of July, 1869. The governor and lieutenant governor elected have been installed. The legislature met and did all required by this resolution and by all the reconstruction acts of Congress, and abstained from all doubtful authority. I recommend that her senators and representatives be promptly admitted to their seats, and that the State be fully restored to its place in the family of States. Elections were called in Mississippi and Texas, to commence on the 30th of November, 1869, and to last two days in Mississippi and four days in Texas. The elections have taken place, but the result is not known. It is to be hoped that the acts of the legislatures of these States when they meet will be such as to receive your approval and thus close the work of reconstruction.

Among the evils growing out of the rebellion, and not yet referred to, is that of an irredeemable currency. It is an evil which I hope will receive your most earnest attention. It is a duty, and one of the highest duties, of government to secure to the citizen a medium of exchange of fixed, unvarying value. This implies a return to a specie basis, and no substitute for it can be devised. It should be commenced now and reached at the earliest practicable moment consistent with a fair regard to the interests of the debtor class. Immediate resumption, if practicable, would not be desirable. It would compel the debtor class to pay, beyond their contracts, the premium on gold at the date of their purchase, and would bring bankruptcy and ruin to thousands. Fluctuation, however, in the paper value of the measure of all values (gold) is detrimental to the interests of trade. It makes the man of business an involuntary gambler, for, in all sales where future payment is to be made, both parties speculate as to what will be the value of the currency to be paid and received. I earnestly recommend to you, then, such legislation as will insure a gradual return to specie payments and put an immediate stop to fluctuations in the value of currency.

The methods to secure the former of these results are as numerous as are the speculators on political economy. To secure the latter I see but one way, and that is, to authorize the treasury to redeem its own paper, at a fixed price, whenever presented, and to withhold from circulation all currency so redeemed until sold again for gold.

The vast resources of the nation, both developed and undeveloped, ought to make our credit the best on earth. With a less burden of taxation than the citizen has endured for six years past, the entire public debt could be paid in ten years. But it is not desirable that the people should be taxed to pay it in that time. Year by year the ability to pay increases in a rapid ratio. But the burden of interest ought to be reduced as rapidly as can be done without the violation of contract. The public debt is represented in great part by bonds, having from five to twenty and from ten to forty years to run, bearing interest at the rate of six per cent. and five per cent., respectively. It is optional with the Government to pay these bonds at any period after the expiration of the least time mentioned upon their face. The time has already expired when a great part of them may be taken up, and is rapidly approaching when all may be. It is believed that all which are now due may be replaced by bonds bearing a rate of interest not exceeding four-and-a-half per cent., and as rapidly as the remainder become due that they may be replaced in the same way. To

accomplish this it may be necessary to authorize the interest to be paid at either of three or four of the money-centers of Europe, or by any assistant treasurer of the United States, at the option of the holder of the bond. I suggest this subject for the consideration of Congress, and also, simultaneously with this, the propriety of redeeming our currency, as before suggested, at its market value at the time the law goes into effect, increasing the rate at which currency shall be bought and sold from day to day or week to week, at the same rate of interest as Government pays upon its bonds.

The subjects of tariff and internal taxation will necessarily receive your attention. The revenues of the country are greater than its requirements, and may with safety be reduced. But, as the funding of the debt in a four or a four-and-a-half per cent. loan would reduce annual current expenses largely, thus, after funding, justifying a greater reduction of taxation than would be now expedient, I suggest postponement of this question until the next meeting of Congress.

It may be advisable to modify taxation and tariff in instances where unjust or burdensome discriminations are made by the present laws; but a general revision of the laws regulating this subject I recommend the postponement of for the present. I also suggest the renewal of the tax on incomes, but at a reduced rate, say of three per cent., and this tax to expire in three years.

With the funding of the national debt, as here suggested, I feel safe in saying that taxes and the revenue from imports may be reduced safely from sixty to eighty millions per annum at once, and may be still further reduced from year to year, as the resources of the country are developed.

The report of the Secretary of the Treasury shows the receipts of the Government for the fiscal year ending June 30, 1869, to be $370,943,-747, and the expenditures, including interest, bounties, &c., to be $321,490,597. The estimates for the ensuing year are more favorable to the Government, and will no doubt show a much larger decrease of the public debt.

The receipts in the Treasury, beyond expenditures, have exceeded the amount necessary to place to the credit of the sinking fund as provided by law. To lock up the surplus in the Treasury and withhold it from circulation would lead to such a contraction of the currency as to cripple trade and seriously affect the prosperity of the country. Under these circumstances the Secretary of the Treasury and myself heartily concurred in the propriety of using all the surplus currency in the Treasury in the purchase of government bonds, thus reducing the interest-bearing indebtedness of the country, and of submitting to Congress the question of the disposition to be made of the bonds so purchased. The bonds now held by the Treasury amount to about seventy-five millions, including those belonging to the sinking fund. I recommend that the whole be placed to the credit of the sinking fund.

Your attention is respectfully invited to the recommendations of the Secretary of the Treasury for the creation of the office of commissioner of customs revenue, for the increase of salaries to certain classes of officials, the substitution of increased national bank circulation to replace to outstanding three per cent. certificates, and most especially to his recommendation for the repeal of laws allowing shares of fines, penalties, forfeitures, &c., to officers of the Government or to informers.

The office of Commissioner of Internal Revenue is one of the most arduous and responsible under the Government. It falls but little, if any, short of a cabinet position in its importance and responsibilities. I would ask for it, therefore, such legislation as in your judgment will place the office upon a footing of dignity commensurate with its importance, and with the character and qualifications of the class of men required to fill it properly.

As the United States is the freest of all nations, so, too, its people sympathize with all peoples struggling for liberty and self-government. But, while so sympathizing, it is due to our honor that we should abstain from enforcing our views upon unwilling nations, and from taking an interested part, *without invitation*, in the quarrels between different nations or between governments and their subjects. Our course should always be in conformity with strict justice and law, international and local. Such has been the policy of the administration in dealing with these questions. For more than a year a valuable province of Spain, and a near neighbor of ours, in whom all our people cannot but feel a deep interest, has been struggling for independence and freedom. The people and Government of the United States entertain the same warm feelings and sympathies for the people of Cuba, in their pending struggle, that they manifested throughout the previous struggles between Spain and her former colonies in behalf of the latter. But the contest has at no time assumed the conditions which amount to a war in the sense of international law, or which would show the existence of a *de facto* political organization of the insurgents sufficient to justify a recognition of belligerency.

The principle is maintained, however, that this nation is its own judge when to accord the rights of belligerency, either to a people struggling to free themselves from a government they believe to be oppressive or to independent nations at war with each other.

The United States have no disposition to interfere with the existing relations of Spain to her colonial possessions on this continent. They believe that in due time Spain and other European powers will find their interest in terminating those relations, and establishing their present dependencies as independent powers— members of the family of nations. These dependencies are no longer regarded as subject to transfer from one European power to another. When the present relation of colonies ceases they are to become independent powers, exercising the right of choice and of self-control in the determination of their future condition and relations with other powers.

The United States, in order to put a stop to bloodshed in Cuba, and in the interest of a neighboring people, proposed their good offices to bring the existing contest to a termination. The offer, not being accepted by Spain on a basis which we

believed could be received by Cuba, was withdrawn. It is hoped that the good offices of the United States may yet prove advantageous for the settlement of this unhappy strife. Meanwhile a number of illegal expeditions against Cuba have been broken up. It has been the endeavor of the administration to execute the neutrality laws in good faith, no matter how unpleasant the task, made so by the sufferings we have endured from lack of like good faith toward us by other nations.

On the 26th of March last the United States schooner Lizzie Major was arrested on the high seas by a Spanish frigate, and two passengers taken from it and carried as prisoners to Cuba. Representations of these facts were made to the Spanish government as soon as official information of them reached Washington. The two passengers were set at liberty, and the Spanish government assured the United States that the captain of the frigate in making the capture had acted without law, that he had been reprimanded for the irregularity of his conduct, and that the Spanish authorities in Cuba would not sanction any act that could violate the rights or treat with disrespect the sovereignty of this nation.

The question of the seizure of the brig Mary Lowell at one of the Bahama Islands, by Spanish authorities, is now the subject of correspondence between this Government and those of Spain and Great Britain.

The captain general of Cuba, about May last, issued a proclamation authorizing search to be made of vessels on the high seas. Immediate remonstrance was made against this, whereupon the captain general issued a new proclamation limiting the right of search to vessels of the United States so far as authorized under the treaty of 1795. This proclamation, however, was immediately withdrawn.

I have always felt that the most intimate relations should be cultivated between the republic of the United States and all independent nations on this continent. It may be well worth considering whether new treaties between us and them may not be profitably entered into, to secure more intimate relations, friendly, commercial, and otherwise.

The subject of an inter-oceanic canal to connect the Atlantic and Pacific oceans, through the Isthmus of Darien, is one in which commerce is greatly interested. Instructions have been given to our minister to the republic of the United States of Colombia to endeavor to obtain authority for a survey by this Government, in order to determine the practicability of such an undertaking, and a charter for the right of way to build, by private enterprise, such a work, if the survey proves it to be practicable.

In order to comply with the agreement of the United States as to a mixed commission at Lima for the adjustment of claims, it became necessary to send a commissioner and secretary to Lima in August last. No appropriation having been made by Congress for this purpose, it is now asked that one be made covering the past and future expenses of the commission.

The good offices of the United States to bring about a peace between Spain and the South American republics, with which she is at war, having been accepted by Spain, Peru, and Chili, a congress has been invited to be held in Washington during the present winter.

A grant has been given to Europeans of an exclusive right of transit over the territory of Nicaragua, to which Costa Rica has given its assent, which, it is alleged, conflicts with vested rights of citizens of the United States. The Department of State has now this subject under consideration.

The minister of Peru having made representations that there was a state of war between Peru and Spain, and that Spain was constructing, in and near New York, thirty gunboats, which might be used by Spain in such a way as to relieve the naval force at Cuba, so as to operate against Peru, orders were given to prevent their departure. No further steps having been taken by the representative of the Peruvian government to prevent the departure of these vessels, and I not feeling authorized to detain the property of a nation with which we are at peace on a mere executive order, the matter has been referred to the courts to decide.

The conduct of the war between the allies and the republic of Paraguay has made the intercourse with that country so difficult that it has been deemed advisable to withdraw our representative from there.

Toward the close of the last administration a convention was signed at London for the settlement of all outstanding claims between Great Britain and the United States, which failed to receive the advice and consent of the Senate to its ratification. The time and the circumstances attending the negotiation of that treaty were unfavorable to its acceptance by the people of the United States, and its provisions were wholly inadequate for the settlement of the grave wrongs that had been sustained by this Government as well as by its citizens. The injuries resulting to the United States by reason of the course adopted by Great Britain during our late civil war, in the increased rates of insurance, in the diminution of exports and imports, and other obstructions to domestic industry and production, in its effect upon the foreign commerce of the country, in the decrease and transfer to Great Britain of our commercial marine, in the prolongation of the war and the increased cost (both in treasure and in lives) of its suppression, could not be adjusted and satisfied as ordinary commercial claims, which continually arise between commercial nations. And yet the convention treated them simply as such ordinary claims, from which they differ more widely in the gravity of their character than in the magnitude of their amount, great even as is that difference. Not a word was found in the treaty, and not an inference could be drawn from it, to remove the sense of the unfriendliness of the course of Great Britain in our struggle for existence, which had so deeply and universally impressed itself upon the people of this country.

Believing that a convention thus misconceived in its scope and inadequate in its provisions would not have produced the hearty, cordial settlement of pending questions, which alone is consistent with the relations which I desire to have firmly established between the United States and Great Britian, I regarded the action of the Senate, in rejecting the treaty, to have been wisely taken in the interest of peace, and as a necessary step in the direction of a perfect and cordial friendship between the two countries. A sensitive people, conscious of their power, are more at ease under a great wrong, wholly unatoned, than under the restraint of a settlement which satisfies neither their ideas of justice nor their grave sense of the grievance they have sustained. The rejection of the treaty was followed by a state of public feeling, on both sides, which I thought not favorable to an immediate attempt at renewed negotiations. I accordingly so instructed the minister of the United States to Great Britain, and found that my views in this regard were shared by her majesty's ministers. I hope that the time may soon arrive when the two governments can approach the solution of this momentous question with an appreciation of what is due to the rights, dignity, and honor of each, and with the determination not only to remove the causes of complaint in the past, but to lay the foundation of a broad principle of public law, which will prevent future differences and tend to firm and continued peace and friendship.

This is now the only grave question which the United States has with any foreign nation.

The question of renewing a treaty for reciprocal trade between the United States and the British provinces on this continent has not been favorably considered by the administration. The advantages of such a treaty would be wholly in favor of the British producer. Except, possibly, a few engaged in the trade between the two sections, no citizen of the United States would be benefited by reciprocity. Our internal taxation would prove a protection to the British producer, almost equal to the protection which our manufacturers now receive from the tariff. Some arrangement, however, for the regulation of commercial intercourse between the United States and the Dominion of Canada may be desirable.

The commission for adjusting the claims of the "Hudson's Bay and Puget Sound Agricultural Company" upon the United States has terminated its labors. The award of $650,000 has been made, and all rights and titles of the company on the territory of the United States have been extinguished. Deeds for the property of the company have been delivered. An appropriation by Congress to meet this sum is asked.

The commissioners for determining the northwestern land boundary between the United States and the British possessions, under the treaty of 1856, have completed their labors, and the commission has been dissolved.

In conformity with the recommendation of Congress, a proposition was early made to the British government to abolish the mixed courts created under the treaty of April 7, 1862, for the suppression of the slave trade. The subject is still under negotiation.

It having come to my knowledge that a corporate company, organized under British laws, proposed to land upon the shores of the United States and to operate there a submarine cable, under a concession from his majesty the emperor of the French, of an exclusive right, for twenty years, of telegraphic communication between the shores of France and the United States, with the very objectionable feature of subjecting all messages conveyed thereby to the scrutiny and control of the French government, I caused the French and British legations at Washington to be made acquainted with the probable policy of Congress on this subject, as foreshadowed by the bill which passed the Senate in March last. This drew from the representatives of the company an agreement to accept, as the basis of their operations, the provisions of that bill, or of such other enactment on the subject as might be passed during the approaching session of Congress; also, to use their influence to secure from the French government a modification of their concession, so as to permit the landing upon French soil of any cable belonging to any company incorporated by the authority of the United States or of any State in the Union, and, on their part, not to oppose the establishment of any such cable. In consideration of this agreement, I directed the withdrawal of all opposition by the United States authorities to the landing of the cable, and to the working of it, until the meeting of Congress. I regret to say that there has been no modification made in the company's concession, nor, so far as I can learn, have they attempted to secure one. Their concession excludes the capital and the citizens of the United States from competition upon the shores of France. I recommend legislation to protect the rights of citizens of the United States, as well as the dignity and sovereignty of the nation, against such an assumption I shall also endeavor to secure by negotiation an abandonment of the principle of monopolies in ocean telegraphic cables. Copies of this correspondence are herewith furnished.

The unsettled political condition of other countries, less fortunate than our own, sometimes induces their citizens to come to the United States for the sole purpose of becoming naturalized. Having secured this, they return to their native country and reside there, without disclosing their change of allegiance. They accept official positions of trust or honor, which can only be held by citizens of their native land; they journey under passports describing them as such citizens; and it is only when civil discord, after perhaps years of quiet, threatens their persons or their property, or when their native State drafts them into its military service, that the fact of their change of allegiance is made known. They reside permanently away from the United States, they contribute nothing to its revenues, they avoid the duties of its citizenship, and they only make themselves known by a claim of protection. I have directed the diplomatic and consular officers of the United States to scrutinize carefully all such claims for protection. The citizen of the United States, whether native or adopted, who discharges his duty to his country, is entitled to its complete protection. While I have a voice in the direction of affairs, I shall not consent to imperil this sacred right by conferring it upon fictitious or fraudulent claimants.

On the accession of the present administration it was found that the minister for North Germany had made propositions for the negotiation of a convention for the protection of emigrant passengers, to which no response had been given. It was concluded that, to be effectual, all the maritime powers engaged in the trade should join in such a measure. Invitations have been extended to the cabinets of London, Paris, Florence, Berlin, Brussels, The Hague, Copenhagen, and Stockholm, to empower their representatives at Washington to simultaneously enter into negotiations, and to conclude with the United States conventions identical in form, making uniform regulations as to the construction of the parts of vessels to be devoted to the use of emigrant passengers, as to the quality and quantity of food, as to the medical treatment of the sick, and as to the rules to be observed during the voyage, in order to secure ventilation, to promote health, to prevent intrusion, and to protect the females, and providing for the establishment of tribunals in the several countries for enforcing such regulations by summary process.

Your attention is respectfully called to the law regulating the tariff on Russian hemp, and to the question whether, to fix the charges on Russian hemp higher than they are fixed upon Manilla, is not a violation of our treaty with Russia, placing her products upon the same footing with those of the most favored nations.

Our manufactures are increasing with wonderful rapidity under the encouragement which they now receive. With the improvements in machinery already effected and still increasing, causing machinery to take the place of skilled labor to a large extent, our imports of many articles must fall off largely within a very few years. Fortunately, too, manufactures are not confined to a few localities, as formerly, and it is to be hoped will become more and more diffused, making the interest in them equal in all sections. They give employment and support to hundreds of thousands of people at home, and retain with us the means which otherwise would be shipped abroad. The extension of railroads in Europe and the East is bringing into competition with our agricultural products like products of other countries. Self-interest, if not self-preservation, therefore, dictates caution against disturbing any industrial interest of the country. It teaches us also the necessity of looking to other markets for the sale of our surplus. Our neighbors south of us, and China and Japan, should receive our special attention. It will be the endeavor of the administration to cultivate such relations with all these nations as to entitle us to their confidence, and make it their interest as well as ours to establish better commercial relations.

Through the agency of a more enlightened policy than that heretofore pursued toward China, largely due to the sagacity and efforts of one of our own distinguished citizens, the world is about to commence largely-increased relations with that populous and hitherto exclusive nation. As the United States have been the initiators in this new policy, so they should be the most earnest in showing their good faith in making it a success. In this connection I advise such legislation as will forever preclude the enslavement of the Chinese upon our soil under the name of coolies, and also prevent American vessels from engaging in the transportation of coolies to any country tolerating the system. I also recommend that the mission to China be raised to one of the first class.

On my assuming the responsible duties of Chief Magistrate of the United States, it was with the conviction that three things were essential to its peace, prosperity, and fullest development. First among these is strict integrity in fulfilling all our obligations. Second, to secure protection to the person and property of the citizen of the United States in each and every portion of our common country, wherever he may choose to move, without reference to original nationality, religion, color, or politics, demanding of him only obedience to the laws and proper respect for the rights of others. Third, union of all the States—with equal rights—indestructible by any constitutional means.

To secure the first of these, Congress has taken two essential steps: first, in declaring, by joint resolution, that the public debt shall be paid, principal and interest, in coin; and, second, by providing the means for paying. Providing the means, however, could not secure the object desired, without a proper administration of the laws for the collection of the revenues, and an economical disbursement of them. To this subject the administration has most earnestly addressed itself, with results, I hope, satisfactory to the country. There has been no hesitation in changing officials in order to secure an efficient execution of the laws, sometimes, too, when, in a mere party view, undesirable political results were likely to follow; nor any hesitation in sustaining efficient officials, against remonstrances wholly political.

It may be well to mention here the embarrassment possible to arise from leaving on the statute-books the so-called "tenure-of-office acts," and to earnestly recommend their total repeal. It could not have been the intention of the framers of the Constitution, when providing that appointments made by the President should receive the consent of the Senate, that the latter should have the power to retain in office persons placed there, by federal appointment, against the will of the President. The law is inconsistent with a faithful and efficient administration of the government. What faith can an executive put in officials forced upon him, and those, too, whom he has suspended for reason? How will such officials be likely to serve an administration which they know does not trust them?

For the second requisite to our growth and prosperity, time and a firm but humane administration of existing laws (amended from time to time as they may prove ineffective, or prove harsh and unnecessary) are probably all that are required.

The third cannot be attained by special legislation, but must be regarded as fixed by the Constitution itself, and gradually acquiesced in by force of public opinion.

From the foundation of the Government to the present, the management of the original inhabitants of this continent, the Indians, has been a subject of embarrassment and expense, and has been attended with continuous robberies, murders, and wars. From my own experience upon the frontiers and in Indian countries, I do not hold either legislation, or the conduct of the whites who come most in contact with the Indian, blameless for these hostilities. The past, however, cannot be undone, and the question must be met as we now find it. I have attempted a new policy toward these wards of the nation, (they cannot be regarded in any other light than as wards,) with fair results so far as tried, and which I hope will be attended ultimately with great success. The Society of Friends is well known as having succeeded in living in peace with the Indians, in the early settlement of Pennsylvania, while their white neighbors of other sects, in other sections, were constantly embroiled. They are also known for their opposition to all strife, violence, and war, and are generally noted for their strict integrity and fair dealings. These considerations induced me to give the management of a few reservations of Indians to them, and to throw the burden of the selection of agents upon the Society itself. The result has proven most satisfactory. It will be found more fully set forth in the report of the Commissioner of Indian Affairs. For superintendents and Indian agents not on the reservations officers of the army were selected. The reasons for this are numerous. Where Indian agents are sent, there, or near there, troops must be sent also. The agent and the commander of troops are independent of each other, and are subject to orders from different departments of the Government. The army officer holds a position for life; the agent one at the will of the President. The former is personally interested in living in harmony with the Indian, and in establishing a permanent peace, to the end that some portion of his life may be spent within the limits of civilized society. The latter has no such personal interest. Another reason is an economic one; and still another, the hold which the Government has upon a life officer to secure a faithful discharge of duties in carrying out a given policy.

The building of railroads, and the access thereby given to all the agricultural and mineral regions of the country, is rapidly bringing civilized settlements into contact with all the tribes of Indians. No matter what ought to be the relations between such settlements and the aborigines, the fact is they do not harmonize well, and one or the other has to give way in the end. A system which looks to the extinction of a race is too horrible for a nation to adopt, without entailing upon itself the wrath of all Christendom, and engendering in the citizen a disregard for human life and the rights of others dangerous to society. I see no substitute for such a system, except in placing all the Indians on large reservations, as rapidly as it can be done, and giving them absolute protection there. As soon as they are fitted for it, they should be induced to take their lands in severalty, and to set up territorial governments for their own protection. For full details on this subject I call your special attention to the reports of the Secretary of the Interior and the Commissioner of Indian Affairs.

The report of the Secretary of War shows the expenditures of the War Department, for the year ending June 30, 1869, to be $80,644,042, of which $23,882,310 was disbursed in the payment of debts contracted during the war, and is not chargeable to current army expenses. His estimate of $34,531,031 for the expenses of the army, for the next fiscal year, is as low as it is believed can be relied on. The estimates of bureau officers have been carefully scrutinized, and reduced wherever it has been deemed practicable. If, however, the condition of the country should be such, by the beginning of the next fiscal year, as to admit of a greater concentration of troops, the appropriation asked for will not be expended.

The appropriations estimated for river and harbor improvements and for fortifications are submitted separately. Whatever amount Congress may deem proper to appropriate for these purposes will be expended.

The recommendation of the General of the Army that appropriations be made for the forts at Boston, Portland, New York, Philadelphia, New Orleans, and San Francisco, if for no other, is concurred in. I also ask your special attention to the recommendation of the general commanding the military division of the Pacific for the sale of the seal islands of St. Paul and St. George, Alaska Territory, and suggest that it either be complied with, or that legislation be had for the protection of the seal fisheries, from which a revenue should be derived.

The report of the Secretary of War contains a synopsis of the reports of the heads of bureaus, of the commanders of military divisions, and of the districts of Virginia, Mississippi, and Texas, and the report of the General of the Army in full. The recommendations therein contained have been well considered, and are submitted for your action. I, however, call special attention to the recommendation of the Chief of Ordnance for the sale of arsenals and lands no longer of use to the Government; also, to the recommendation of the Secretary of War that the act of 3d March, 1869, prohibiting promotions and appointments in the staff corps of the army, be repealed. The extent of country to be garrisoned, and the number of military posts to be occupied, is the same with a reduced army as with a large one. The number of staff officers required is more dependent upon the latter than the former condition.

The report of the Secretary of the Navy, accompanying this, shows the condition of the navy when this administration came into office, and the changes made since. Strenuous efforts have been made to place as many vessels "in commission," or render them fit for service, if required, as possible, and to substitute the sail for steam while cruising, thus materially reducing the expenses of the navy and adding greatly to its efficiency. Looking to our future, I recommend a liberal though not extravagant policy toward this branch of the public service.

The report of the Postmaster General furnishes a clear and comprehensive exhibit of the operations of the postal service, and of the financial condition of the Post Office Department. The ordinary postal revenues for the year ending the 30th of June, 1869, amounted to $18,344,510, and the expenditures to $23,698,131, showing an excess of expenditures over receipts of $5,353,620. The excess of expenditures over receipts for the previous year amounted to $6,437,992. The increase of revenues for 1869 over those of 1868 was $2,051,909, and the increase of expenditures was $967,538. The increased revenue in 1869 exceeded the increased revenue in 1868 by $996,336; and the increased expenditure in 1869 was $2,527,570 less than the increased expenditure in 1868, showing by comparison this gratifying feature of improvement, that while the increase of expenditures over the increase of receipts in 1868 was $2,439,535, the increase of receipts over the increase of expenditures in 1869 was $1,084,371.

Your attention is repectfully called to the recommendations made by the Postmaster General for authority to change the rate of compensation to the main trunk railroad lines for their services in carrying the mails, for having post-route maps executed, for reorganizing and increasing the efficiency of the special agency service, for increase of the mail service on the Pacific, and for establishing mail service, under the flag of the Union, on the Atlantic; and most especially do I call your attention to his recommendation for the total abolition of the franking privilege. This is an abuse from which no one receives a commensurate advantage; it reduces the receipts for postal service from twenty-five to thirty per cent., and largely increases the service to be performed. The method by which postage should be paid upon public matter is set forth fully in the report of the Postmaster General.

The report of the Secretary of the Interior shows that the quantity of public lands disposed of during the year ending the 30th of June, 1869, was 7,666,152 acres, exceeding that of the preceding year by 1,010,409 acres. Of this amount 2,899,544 acres were sold for cash, and 2,737,365 acres entered under the homestead laws. The remainder was granted to aid in the construction of works of internal improvement, approved to the States as swamp land, and located with warrants and scrip. The cash receipts from all sources were $4,472,886, exceeding those of the preceding year $2,840,140.

During the last fiscal year 23,196 names were added to the pension rolls and 4,876 dropped therefrom, leaving at its close 187,963. The amount paid to pensioners, including the compensation of disbursing agents, was $28,422,884, an increase of $4,411,902 on that of the previous year. The munificence of Congress has been conspicuously manifested in its legislation for the soldiers and sailors who suffered in the recent struggle to maintain "that unity of government which makes us one people." The additions to the pension rolls of each successive year since the conclusion of hostilities result in a great degree from the repeated amendments of the act of the 14th of July, 1862, which extended its provisions to cases not falling within its original scope. The large outlay which is thus occasioned is further increased by the more liberal allowance bestowed since that date upon those who, in the line of duty, were wholly or permanently disabled. Public opinion has given an emphatic sanction to these measures of Congress, and it will be conceded that no part of our public burden is more cheerfully borne than that which is imposed by this branch of the service.

It necessitates for the next fiscal year, in addition to the amount justly chargeable to the naval pension fund, an appropriation of $30,000,000.

During the year ending the 30th of September, 1869, the Patent Office issued 13,762 patents, and its receipts were $686,389, being $213,926 more than the expenditures.

I would respectfully call your attention to the recommendation of the Secretary of the Interior for uniting the duties of supervising the education of freedmen with the other duties devolving upon the Commissioner of Education.

If it is the desire of Congress to make the census which must be taken during the year 1870 more complete and perfect than heretofore, I would suggest early action upon any plan that may be agreed upon. As Congress at the last session appointed a committee to take into consideration such measures as might be deemed proper in reference to the census, and report a plan, I desist from saying more.

I recommend to your favorable consideration the claims of the Agricultural Bureau for liberal appropriations. In a country so diversified in climate and soil as ours, and with a population so largely dependent upon agriculture, the benefits that can be conferred by properly fostering this bureau are incalculable.

I desire respectfully to call the attention of Congress to the inadequate salaries of a number of the most important offices of the Government. In this message I will not enumerate them, but will specify only the justices of the Supreme Court. No change has been made in their salaries for fifteen years. Within that time the labors of the court have largely increased, and the expenses of living have at least doubled. During the same time Congress has twice found it necessary to increase largely the compensation of its own members; and the duty which it owes to another department of the Government deserves, and will undoubtedly receive, its due consideration.

There are many subjects, not alluded to in this message, which might with propriety be introduced, but I abstain, believing that your patriotism and statesmanship will suggest the topics and the legislation most conducive to the interests of the whole people. On my part, I promise a rigid adherence to the laws and their strict enforcement. U. S. GRANT.

EXECUTIVE MANSION,
*Washington, D. C., December 6, 1869.*

## SPECIAL MESSAGES.

### Recommending early Action toward an Increase of the Commerce of the United States.

*To the Senate and House of Representatives:*

In the executive message of December 6, 1869, to Congress, the importance of taking steps to revive our drooping merchant marine was urged, and a special message promised at a future day, during the present session, recommending more specifically plans to accomplish this result. Now that the committee of the House of Representatives intrusted with the labor of ascertaining "the cause of the decline of American commerce" has completed its work and submitted its report to the legislative branch of the Government,

I deem this a fitting time to execute that promise.

The very able, calm, and exhaustive report of the committee points out the grave wrongs which have produced the decline in our commerce. It is a national humiliation that we are now compelled to pay from twenty to thirty millions of dollars annually (exclusive of passage-money, which we should share with vessels of other nations) to foreigners for doing the work which should be done by American vessels, American-built, American-owned, and American-manned. This is a direct drain upon the resources of the country of just so much money, equal to casting it into the sea, so far as this nation is concerned.

A nation of the vast and ever-increasing interior resources of the United States, extending, as it does, from one to the other of the great oceans of the world, with an industrious, intelligent, energetic population, must one day possess its full share of the commerce of these oceans, no matter what the cost. Delay will only increase this cost and enhance the difficulty of attaining the result. I therefore put in an earnest plea for early action in this matter, in a way to secure the desired increase of American commerce. The advanced period of the year, and the fact that no contracts for ship-building will probably be entered into until this question is settled by Congress, and the further fact that, if there should be much delay, all large vessels contracted for this year will fail of completion before winter sets in, and will therefore be carried over for another year, induces me to request your early consideration of this subject. I regard it of such grave importance, affecting every interest of the country to so great an extent, that any method which will gain the end will secure a great national blessing. Building ships and navigating them utilizes vast capital at home; it employs thousands of workmen in their construction and manning; it creates a home market for the products of the farm and the shop; it diminishes the balance of trade against us precisely to the extent of freights and passage-money paid to American vessels, and gives us a supremacy upon the seas of inestimable value in case of foreign war.

Our navy, at the commencement of the late war, consisted of less than one hundred vessels, of about one hundred and fifty thousand tons, and a force of about eight thousand men. We drew from the merchant marine, which had cost the Government nothing, but which had been a source of national wealth, six hundred vessels, exceeding one million tons, and about seventy thousand men to aid in the suppression of the rebellion.

This statement demonstrates the value of the merchant marine as a means of national defense in time of need.

The committee on the causes of the reduction of American tonnage, after tracing the causes of its decline, submit two bills which, if adopted, they believe will restore to the nation its maritime power. Their report shows with great minuteness the actual and comparative American tonnage at the time of its greatest prosperity; the actual and comparative decline since, together with the causes, and exhibits all other statistics of material interest in reference to the subject. As the report is before Congress, I will not recapitulate any of its statistics, but refer only to the methods recommended by the committee to give back to us our lost commerce.

As a general rule, when it can be adopted, I believe a direct money subsidy is less liable to abuse than an indirect aid given to the same enterprise. In this case, however, my opinion is that subsidies, while they may be given to specified lines of steamers or other vessels, should not be exclusively adopted; but, in addition to subsidizing very desirable lines of ocean traffic, a general assistance should be given in an effective way. I therefore commend to your favorable consideration the two bills proposed by the committee and referred to in this message.

U. S. GRANT.

EXECUTIVE MANSION, *March* 23, 1870.

### Urging the Ratification of the Treaty with San Domingo.

*To the Senate of the United States:*

I transmit to the Senate for consideration, with a view to its ratification, an additional article to the treaty of the 29th of November last for the annexation of the Dominican republic to the United States, stipulating for an extension of the time for exchanging the ratifications thereof, signed in this city on the 14th instant, by the plenipotentiaries of the parties. It was my intention to have also negotiated with the plenipotentiary of San Domingo, amendments to the treaty of annexation to obviate objections which may be urged against the treaty as it is now worded; but, on reflection, I deem it better to submit to the Senate the propriety of their amending the treaty as follows: First, to specify that the obligations of this Government shall not exceed the $1,500,000 stipulated in the treaty; secondly, to determine the manner of appointing the agents to receive and disburse the same; thirdly, to determine the class of creditors who shall take precedence in the settlement of their claims; and, finally, to insert such amendments as may suggest themselves to the minds of Senators to carry out in good faith the conditions of the treaty submitted to the Senate of the United States in January last, according to the spirit and intent of that treaty. From the most reliable information I can obtain the sum specified in the treaty will pay every just claim against the republic of San Domingo, and leave a balance sufficient to carry on a territorial government until such time as new laws for providing a territorial revenue can be enacted and put in force.

I feel an unusual anxiety for the ratification of this treaty, because I believe it will redound greatly to the glory of the two countries interested, to civilization, and to the extirpation of the institution of slavery. The doctrine promulgated by President Monroe has been adhered to by all political parties, and I now deem it proper to assert the equally important principle, that hereafter no territory on this continent shall be regarded as subject to transfer to a European Power. The government of San Domingo has voluntarily sought this annexation. It is a weak power, numbering probably less than one hundred and twenty thousand souls, and yet possessing one of the richest territories under the sun, capable of supporting a population of ten million of people in luxury. The people of San Domingo are not capable of maintaining themselves in their present condition, and must look for outside support. They yearn for the protection of our free institutions and laws, our progress, and civilization. Shall we refuse them? I have information, which I believe reliable, that a European power stands ready now to offer $2,000,000 for the possession of Samana bay alone if refused by us. With what grace can we prevent a foreign power from attempting to secure the prize?

The acquisition of San Domingo is desirable because of its geographical position. It commands the entrance to the Caribbean sea and the isthmus transit of commerce. It possesses the richest soil, best and most capacious harbors, most salubrious climate, and the most valuable products of the forest, mine, and soil, of any of the West India islands. Its possession by us will, in a few years, build up a coastwise commerce of immense magnitude, which will go far toward restoring to us our lost merchant marine. It will give to us those articles which we consume so largely and do not produce, thus equalizing our exports and imports. In case of foreign war it will give us command of all the islands referred to, and thus prevent an enemy from ever again possessing himself of a rendezvous upon our very coast. At present our coast trade between the States bordering on the Atlantic and those bordering on the Gulf of Mexico is cut in two by the Bahamas and the Antilles. Since we must, as it were, pass through foreign countries to get by sea from Georgia to the west coast of Florida, San Domingo, with a stable government, under which her immense resources can be developed, will give remunerative wages to tens of thousands of laborers not now upon the island. This labor will take advantage of every available means of transportation to abandon the adjacent islands and seek the blessings of freedom and its sequence, each inhabitant receiving the reward of his own labor. Porto Rico and Cuba will have to abolish slavery as a measure of self-preservation to retain their laborers. San Domingo will become a large consumer of the products of northern farms and manufactories. The cheap rate at which her citizens can be furnished with food, tools, and machinery, will make it necessary that the contiguous islands should have the same advantages in order to compete in the production of sugar, coffee, tobacco, tropical fruits, &c. This will open to us a still wider market for our products. The production of our own supply of these articles will cut off more than $100,000,000 of our annual imports, besides largely increasing our exports. With such a picture it is easy to see how our large debt abroad is ultimately to be extinguished. With a balance of trade against us, including interest on bonds held by foreigners, and money spent by our citizens traveling in foreign lands equal to the entire yield of the precious metals in this country, it is not so easy to see how this result is to be otherwise accomplished.

The acquisition of San Domingo is an adherence to the Monroe doctrine. It is a measure of national protection; it is asserting our just claim to a controlling influence over the great commercial traffic soon to flow from east to west by way of the Isthmus of Darien; it is to build up our merchant marine; it is to furnish new markets for the products of our farms, shops, and manufactories; it is to make slavery insupportable in Cuba and Porto Rico at once, and ultimately so in Brazil; it is to settle the unhappy condition of Cuba and end an exterminating conflict; it is to provide honest means of paying our honest debts without overtaxing the people; it is to furnish our citizens with the necessaries of every-day life at cheaper rates than ever before, and it is, in fine, a rapid stride toward that greatness which the intelligence, industry, and enterprise of the citizens of the United States entitle this country to assume among nations.          U. S. GRANT.

EXECUTIVE MANSION, *May* 31, 1870.

### Respecting Cuban Affairs.

*To the Senate and House of Representatives:*

In my annual message to Congress at the beginning of its present session I referred to the contest which had then for more than a year existed in the island of Cuba, between a portion of its inhabitants and the government of Spain, and to the feelings and sympathies of the people and Government of the United States for the people of Cuba, as for all people struggling for liberty and self-government, and said "that the contest has at no time assumed the conditions which amount to war in the sense of international law, or which would show the existence of a *de facto* political organization of the insurgents sufficient to justify a recognition of belligerency." During the six months which have passed since the date of that message the condition of the insurgents has not improved, and the insurrection itself, though not subdued, exhibits no signs of advance, but seems to be confined to an irregular system of hostilities, carried on by small and illy-armed bands of men roaming without concentration through the woods and the sparsely-populated regions of the island, attacking from ambush convoys and small bands of troops, burning plantations, and the estates of those not sympathizing with their cause. But, if the insurrection has not gained ground, it is equally true that Spain has not suppressed it. Climate, disease, and the occasional bullet have worked destruction among the soldiers of Spain, and although the Spanish authorities have possession of every seaport and every town on the island, they have not been able to subdue the hostile feeling which has driven a considerable number of the native inhabitants of the island to armed resistance against Spain, and still leads them to endure the dangers and privations of a roaming life of guerrilla warfare.

On either side the contest has been conducted and is still carried on with a lamentable disregard of human life and of the usages and practices which modern civilization has prescribed in mitigation of the necessary horrors of war. The torch of Spaniard and Cuban is alike busy in carrying devastation over fertile regions; murderous and revengeful decrees are issued and executed by both parties. Count Valmaseda and Colonel Boet, on the part of Spain, have each startled humanity and aroused the indignation of the civilized world by the execution, each, of a score of prisoners at a time, while General Quesada, the Cuban chief, coolly, and with apparent unconsciousness of aught else than a proper act, has admitted the slaughter by his own deliberate order, in one day, of upward of six hundred and fifty prisoners of war. A summary trial, with few if any escapes from conviction, followed by immediate execution, is the fate of those arrested on either side on suspicion of infidelity to the cause of the party making the arrest.

Whatever may be the sympathies of the people or of the Government of the United States for the cause or objects for which a part of the people of Cuba are understood to have put themselves in armed resistance to the Government of Spain, there can be no just sympathy in a conflict carried on by both parties alike in such barbarous violation of the rules of civilized nations, and with such continued outrage upon the plainest principles of humanity.

We cannot discriminate, in our censure of their mode of conducting their contest, between the Spaniards and the Cubans. Each commit the same atrocities and outrage alike the established rules of war.

The properties of many of our citizens have been destroyed or embargoed, the lives of several have been sacrificed, and the liberty of others has been restrained. In every case that has come to the knowledge of the Government an early and earnest demand for reparation and indemnity has been made; and most emphatic remonstrance has been presented against the manner in which the strife is conducted, and against the reckless disregard of human life, the wanton destruction of material wealth, and the cruel disregard of the established rules of civilized warfare. I have, since the beginning of the present session of Congress, communicated to the House of Representatives, upon their request, an account of the steps which I had taken in the hope of bringing this sad conflict to an end, and of securing to the people of Cuba the blessings and the right of independent self-government. The efforts thus made failed, but not without an assurance from Spain that the good offices of this Government might still avail for the objects to which they had been addressed.

During the whole contest the remarkable exhibition has been made of large numbers of Cubans escaping from the island and avoiding the risks of war, congregating in this country, at a safe distance from the scene of danger, and endeavoring to make war from our shores, to urge our people into the fight which they avoid, and to embroil this Government in complications and possible hostilities with Spain. It can scarce be doubted that this last result is the real object of these parties, although carefully covered under the deceptive and apparently plausible demand for a mere recognition of belligerency.

It is stated, on what I have reason to regard as good authority, that Cuban bonds have been prepared, to a large amount, whose payment is made dependent upon the recognition by the United States of either Cuban belligerency or independence. The object of making their value thus contingent upon the action of this Government is a subject for serious reflection.

In determining the course to be adopted on the demand thus made for a recognition of belligerency, the liberal and peaceful principles adopted by the Father of his Country and the eminent statesmen of his day, and followed by succeeding chief magistrates and the men of their day, may furnish a safe guide to those of us now charged with the direction and control of the public safety.

From 1789 to 1815 the dominant thought of our statesmen was to keep the United States out of the wars which were devastating Europe. The discussion of measures of neutrality begins with the State papers of Mr. Jefferson, when Secretary of State. He shows that they are measures of national right as well as of national duty; that misguided individual citizens cannot be tolerated in making war according to their own caprice, passions, interests, or foreign sympathies; that the agents of foreign governments, recognized or unrecognized, cannot be permitted to abuse our hospitality by usurping the functions of enlisting or equipping military or naval forces within our territory.

Washington inaugurated the policy of neutrality and of absolute abstinence from all foreign entangling alliances, which resulted, in 1794, in the first municipal enactment for the observance of neutrality.

The duty of opposition to fillibustering has been admitted by every President. Washington encountered the efforts of Genet and the French revolutionists; John Adams the projects of Miranda; Jefferson the schemes of Aaron Burr; Madison and subsequent Presidents had to deal with the question of foreign enlistment or equipment in the United States, and since the days of John Quincy Adams it has been one of the constant cares of government in the United States to prevent piratical expeditions against the feeble Spanish-American republics from leaving our shores. In no country are men wanting for any enterprise that holds out promise of adventure or of gain.

In the early days of our national existence the whole continent of America (outside of the limits of the United States) and all its islands, were in colonial dependence upon European powers. The revolutions which, from 1810, spread almost simultaneously through all the Spanish-American continental colonies, resulted in the establishment of new States, like ourselves, of European origin, and interested in excluding European politics and the questions of dynasty and of balances of power from further influence in the New World.

The American policy of neutrality, important before, became doubly so from the fact that it became applicable to the new republics as well as to the mother country.

It then devolved upon us to determine the great international question, at what time and under what circumstances to recognize a new power as entitled to a place among the family of nations, as well as the preliminary question of the attitude to be observed by this Government toward the insurrectionary party pending the contest.

Mr. Monroe concisely expressed the rule which has controlled the action of this Government with reference to revolting colonies, pending their struggle, by saying: "As soon as the movement assumed such a steady and constant form as to make the success of the provinces probable, the rights to which they were entitled by the laws of nations, as equal parties to a civil war, were extended to them."

The strict adherence to this rule of public policy has been one of the highest honors of American statesmanship, and has secured to this Government the confidence of the feeble powers on this continent, which induces them to rely upon its friendship and absence of designs of conquest, and to look to the United States for example and moral protection. It has given to this Government a position of prominence and of influence which it should not abdicate, but which imposes upon it the most delicate duties of right and of honor regarding American questions, whether those questions affect emancipated colonies or colonies still subject to European dominion.

The question of belligerency is one of fact, not to be decided by sympathy for or prejudice against either party. The relations between the parent State and the insurgents must amount, in fact, to war in the sense of international law. Fighting, though fierce and protracted, does not alone constitute war; there must be military forces acting in accordance with the rules and customs of war, flags of truce, cartels, exchange of prisoners, &c., &c.; and to justify a recognition of belligerency there must be, above all, a *de facto* political organization of the insurgents sufficient in character and resources to constitute it, if left to itself, a State among nations capable of discharging the duties of a State, and of meeting the just responsibilities it may incur as such toward other powers in the discharge of its national duties.

Applying the best information which I have been enabled to gather, whether from official or unofficial sources, including the very exaggerated statements which each party gives to all that may prejudice the opposite or give credit to its own side of the question, I am unable to see in the present condition of the contest in Cuba those elements which are requisite to constitute war in the sense of international law.

The insurgents hold no town or city; have no established seat of government; they have no prize courts; no organization for the receiving or collecting of revenue; no seaport to which a prize may be carried, or through which access can be had by a foreign power to the limited interior territory and mountain fastnesses which they occupy. The existence of a legislature representing any popular constituency is more than doubtful.

In the uncertainty that hangs around the entire insurrection, there is no palpable evidence of an election of any delegated authority, or of any government outside the limits of the camps occupied from day to day by the roving companies of insurgent troops. There is no commerce, no trade, either internal or foreign, no manufactures.

The late commander-in-chief of the insurgents, having recently come to the United States, publicly declared that "all commercial intercourse or trade with the exterior world has been utterly cut off," and he further added, "to-day we have not ten thousand arms in Cuba."

It is a well-established principle of public law that a recognition by a foreign State of belligerent rights to insurgents under circumstances such as now exist in Cuba, if not justified by necessity, is a gratuitous demonstration of moral support to the rebellion. Such necessity may yet hereafter arrive; but it has not yet arrived, nor is its probability clearly to be seen.

If it be war between Spain and Cuba, and be so recognized, it is our duty to provide for the consequences which may ensue in the embarrassment to our commerce and the interference with our revenue.

If belligerency be recognized, the commercial marine of the United States becomes liable to search and to seizure by the commissioned cruisers of both parties. They become subject to the adjudication of prize courts.

Our large coastwise trade between the Atlantic and the Gulf States, and between both and the Isthmus of Panama and the States of South America, (engaging the larger parts of our commercial marine,) passes, of necessity, almost in sight of the Island of Cuba. Under the treaty with Spain of 1795, as well as by the law of nations, our vessels will be liable to visit on the high seas.

In case of belligerency, the carrying of contraband, which now is lawful, becomes liable to the risks of seizure and condemnation. The parent government becomes relieved from responsibility for acts done in the insurgent territory, and acquires the right to exercise against neutral commerce all the powers of a party to a maritime war. To what consequences the exercise of those powers may lead is a question which I desire to commend to the serious consideration of Congress. In view of the gravity of this question, I have deemed it my duty to invite the attention of the war-making power of the country to all the relations and bearings of the question in connection with the declaration of neutrality and granting of belligerent rights.

There is not a *de facto* government in the Island of Cuba sufficient to execute law and maintain just relations with other nations. Spain has not been able to suppress the opposition to Spanish rule on the island, nor to award speedy justice to other nations, or citizens of other nations, when their rights have been invaded.

There are serious complications growing out of the seizure of American vessels upon the high seas, executing American citizens without proper trial, and confiscating or embargoing the property of American citizens. Solemn protests have been made against every infraction of the rights either of individual citizens of the United States or the rights of our flag upon the high seas, and all proper steps have been taken and are being pressed for the proper reparation of every indignity complained of.

The question of belligerency, however, which is to be decided upon definite principles and according to ascertained facts, is entirely different from and unconnected with the other questions of the manner in which the strife is carried on on both sides and the treatment of our citizens entitled to our protection.

The questions concern our own dignity and responsibility, and they have been made, as I have said, the subjects of repeated communications with Spain, and of protests and demands for redress on our part. It is hoped that these will not be disregarded; but should they be, these questions will be made the subject of a further communication to Congress.

U. S. GRANT.

EXECUTIVE MANSION, *June* 13, 1870.

## PROCLAMATION

**President Grant's Proclamation against the Fenian Invasion of Canada, issued May 24, 1870.**

Whereas it has come to my knowledge that sundry illegal military enterprises and expeditions are being set on foot within the territory and jurisdiction of the United States, with a view to carry on the same from such territory or jurisdiction against the people and district of the Dominion of Canada, within the dominions of her majesty the Queen of the United Kingdom of Great Britain and Ireland, with whom the United States are at peace:

Now, therefore, I, Ulysses S. Grant, President of the United States, do hereby admonish all good citizens of the United States, and all persons within the territory and jurisdiction of the United States, against aiding, countenancing, abetting, or taking part in such unlawful proceedings; and I do hereby warn all persons that, by committing such illegal acts, they will forfeit all right to the protection of this Government, or to its interference in their behalf to rescue them from the consequences of their own acts; and I do hereby enjoin all officers in the service of the United States to employ all their lawful authority and power to prevent and defeat the aforesaid unlawful proceedings, and to arrest and bring to justice all persons who may be engaged therein.

In testimony whereof I have hereunto set my hand and caused the seal of the United States to be affixed.

Done at the city of Washington, this 24th day of May, in the year of our Lord 1870, and [SEAL.] of the independence of the United States the ninety-fourth. U. S. GRANT.

By the President:

HAMILTON FISH,
*Secretary of State.*

# LIII.

## XVTH AMENDMENT,

### VOTES ON RATIFICATION, PROCLAMATION OF RATIFICATION, BILLS ENFORCING AND VOTES THEREON.

**Special Message of President Grant on Ratification of the XVth Amendment.**

*To the Senate and House of Representatives:*

It is unusual to notify the two houses of Congress, by message, of the promulgation, by proclamation of the Secretary of State, of the ratification of a constitutional amendment. In view, however, of the vast importance of the XVth Amendment to the Constitution, this day declared a part of that revered instrument, I deem a departure from the usual custom justifiable. A measure which makes at once four millions of people voters, who were heretofore declared by the highest tribunal in the land not citizens of the United States, nor eligible to become so, (with the assertion that, "at the time of the Declaration of Independence, the opinion was fixed and universal in the civilized portion of the white race, regarded as an axiom in morals as well as in politics, that black men had no rights which the white man was bound to respect,") is indeed a measure of grander importance than any other one act of the kind from the foundation of our free government to the present day.

Institutions like ours, in which all power is derived directly from the people, must depend mainly upon their intelligence, patriotism, and industry. I call the attention, therefore, of the newly-enfranchised race to the importance of their striving in every honorable manner to make themselves worthy of their new privilege. To the race more favored heretofore by our laws I would say, withhold no legal privilege of advancement to the new citizen. The framers of our Constitution firmly believed that a republican government could not endure without intelligence and education generally diffused among the people. The "Father of his Country," in his farewell address, uses this language: "Promote, then, as a matter of primary importance, institutions for the general diffusion of knowledge. In proportion as the structure of the Government gives force to public opinion, it is essential that public opinion should be enlightened." In his first annual message to Congress the same views are forcibly presented, and are again urged in his eighth message.

I repeat that the adoption of the XVth Amendment to the Constitution completes the greatest civil change and constitutes the most important event that has occurred since the nation came into life. The change will be beneficial in proportion to the heed that is given to the urgent recommendations of Washington. If these recommendations were important then, with a population of but a few millions, how much more important now, with a population of forty millions, and increasing in a rapid ratio.

I would therefore call upon Congress to take all the means within their constitutional powers to promote and encourage popular education throughout the country; and upon the people everywhere to see to it that all who possess and exercise political rights shall have the opportunity to acquire the knowledge which will make their share in the government a blessing and not a danger. By such means only can the benefits contemplated by this amendment to the Constitution be secured.　　　　U. S. GRANT.

EXECUTIVE MANSION, *March* 30, 1870.

**Certificate of Mr. Secretary Fish respecting the Ratification of the XVth Amendment to the Constitution, March 30, 1870.**

HAMILTON FISH, SECRETARY OF STATE OF THE UNITED STATES.

*To all to whom these presents may come, greeting:*

Know ye that the Congress of the United States, on or about the 27th day of February, in the year 1869, passed a resolution in the words and figures following, to wit:

A RESOLUTION proposing an amendment to the Constitution of the United States.

*Resolved by the Senate and House of Representatives of the United States of America in Congress assembled, (two-thirds of both houses concurring,)* That the following article be proposed to the legislatures of the several States as an amendment to the Constitution of the United States, which, when ratified by three-fourths of said legislatures, shall be valid as part of the Constitution, namely:

ARTICLE XV.

SECTION 1. The right of citizens of the United States to vote shall not be denied or abridged by the United States or by any State on account of race, color, or previous condition of servitude.

SEC. 2. The Congress shall have power to enforce this article by appropriate legislation.

And, further, that it appears, from official documents on file in this department, that the amendment to the Constitution of the United States, proposed as aforesaid, has been ratified by the legislatures of the States of North Carolina, West Virginia, Massachusetts, Wisconsin, Maine, Louisiana, Michigan, South Carolina, Pennsylvania, Arkansas, Connecticut, Florida, Illinois, Indiana, New York, New Hampshire, Nevada, Vermont, Virginia, Alabama, Missouri, Mississippi, Ohio, Iowa, Kansas, Minnesota, Rhode Island, Nebraska, and Texas; in all, twenty-nine States.

And, further, that the States whose legislatures

have so ratified the said proposed amendment constitute three-fourths of the whole number of States in the United States.

And, further, that it appears, from an official document on file in this department, that the legislature of the State of New York has since passed resolutions claiming to withdraw the said ratification of the said amendment which had been made by the legislature of that State, and of which official notice had been filed in this department.

And, further, that it appears, from an official document on file in this department, that the legislature of Georgia has by resolution ratified the said proposed amendment.:

Now, therefore, be it known that I, Hamilton Fish, Secretary of State of the United States, by virtue and in pursuance of the 2d section of the act of Congress, approved the 20th day of April, 1818, entitled "An act to provide for the publication of the laws of the United States, and for other purposes," do hereby certify, that the amendment aforesaid has become valid, to all intents and purposes, as part of the Constitution of the United States.

In testimony whereof I have hereunto set my hand and caused the seal of the Department of State to be affixed.

Done at the city of Washington, this 30th day of March, in the year of our Lord 1870, [SEAL.] and of the independence of the United States the ninety-fourth.

HAMILTON FISH.

### Enforcement of the Fourteenth and Fifteenth Amendments.

AN ACT to enforce the right of citizens of the United States to vote in the several States of this Union, and for other purposes.

Be it enacted, &c., That all citizens of the United States who are or shall be otherwise qualified by law to vote at any election by the people in any State, Terrritory, district, county, city, parish, township, school district, municipality, or other territorial subdivision, shall be entitled and allowed to vote at all such elections without distinction of race, color, or previous condition of servitude; any constitution, law, custom, usage, or regulation of any State or Territory, or by or under its authority, to the contrary notwithstanding.

SEC. 2. That if by or under the authority of the constitution or laws of any State, or the laws of any Territory, any act is or shall be required to be done as a prerequisite or qualification for voting, and by such constitution or laws persons or officers are or shall be charged with the performance of duties in furnishing to citizens an opportunity to perform such prerequisite, or to become qualified to vote, it shall be the duty of every such person and officer to give to all citizens of the United States the same and equal opportunity to perform such prerequisite, and to become qualified to vote, without distinction of race, color, or previous condition of servitude; and if any such person or officer shall refuse or knowingly omit to give full effect to this section, he shall, for every such offense, forfeit and pay the sum of $500 to the person aggrieved thereby,

to be recovered by an action on the case, with full costs and such allowance for counsel fees as the court shall deem just, and shall also, for every such offense, be deemed guilty of a misdemeanor, and shall, on conviction thereof, be fined not less than $500, or be imprisoned not less than one month and not more than one year, or both, at the discretion of the court.

SEC. 3. That whenever, by or under the authority of the constitution or laws of any State, or the laws of any Territory, an act is or shall be required to be done by any citizen as a prerequisite to qualify or entitle him to vote, the offer of any such citizen to perform the act required to be done as aforesaid shall, if it fail to be carried into execution by reason of the wrongful act or omission aforesaid of the person or officer charged with the duty of receiving or permitting such performance or offer to perform or acting thereon, be deemed and held as a performance in law of such act; and the person so offering and failing as aforesaid, and being otherwise qualified, shall be entitled to vote in the same manner and to the same extent as if he had in fact performed such act; and any judge, inspector, or other officer of election whose duty it is or shall be to receive, count, certify, register, report, or give effect to the vote of any such citizen who shall wrongfully refuse or omit to receive, count, certify, register, report, or give effect to the vote of such citizen, upon the presentation by him of his affidavit stating such offer and the time and place thereof, and the name of the officer or person whose duty it was to act thereon, and that he was wrongfully prevented by such person or officer from performing such act, shall for every such offense forfeit and pay the sum of $500 to the person aggrieved thereby, to be recovered by an action on the case, with full costs and such allowance for counsel fees as the court shall deem just, and shall also for every such offense be guilty of a misdemeanor, and shall, on conviction thereof, be fined not less than $500, or be imprisoned not less than one month and not more than one year, or both, at the discretion of the court.

SEC. 4. That if any person, by force, bribery, threats, intimidation, or other unlawful means, shall hinder, delay, prevent, or obstruct, or shall combine and confederate with others to hinder, delay, prevent, or obstruct, any citizen from doing any act required to be done to qualify him to vote or from voting at any election as aforesaid, such person shall for every such offense forfeit and pay the sum of $500 to the person aggrieved thereby, to be recovered by an action on the case, with full costs and such allowance for counsel fees as the court shall deem just, and shall also for every such offense be guilty of a misdemeanor, and shall, on conviction thereof, be fined not less than five hundred dollars, or be imprisoned not less than one month and not more than one year, or both, at the discretion of the court.

SEC. 5. That if any person shall prevent, hinder, control, or intimidate, or shall attempt to prevent, hinder, control, or intimidate, any person from exercising or in exercising the right of suffrage, to whom the right of suffrage is secured or guarantied by the XVth Amendment to the Constitution of the United States, by means of bribery, threats, or threats of depriving such person of employment or occupation, or of ejecting such person from rented house, lands, or other property, or by threats of refusing to renew leases or contracts for labor, or by threats of violence to himself or family, such person so offending shall be deemed guilty of a misdemeanor, and shall, on conviction thereof, be fined not less than five hundred dollars, or be imprisoned not less than one month and not more than one year, or both, at the discretion of the court.

SEC. 6. That if two or more persons shall band or conspire together, or go in disguise upon the public highway, or upon the premises of another, with intent to violate any provision of this act, or to injure, oppress, threaten, or intimidate any citizen with intent to prevent or hinder his free exercise and enjoyment of any right or privilege granted or secured to him by the Constitution or laws of the United States, or because of his having exercised the same, such persons shall be held guilty of felony, and, on conviction thereof, shall be fined or imprisoned, or both, at the discretion of the court, the fine not to exceed $5,000, and the imprisonment not to exceed ten years, and shall, moreover, be thereafter ineligible to, and disabled from holding, any office or place of honor, profit, or trust created by the Constitution or laws of the United States.

SEC. 7. That if, in the act of violating any provision in either of the two preceding sections, any other felony, crime, or misdemeanor shall be committed, the offender, on conviction of such violation of said sections, shall be punished for the same with such punishments as are attached to the said felonies, crimes, and misdemeanors by the laws of the State in which the offense may be committed.

SEC. 8. That the district courts of the United States, within their respective districts, shall have, exclusively of the courts of the several States, cognizance of all crimes and offenses committed against the provisions of this act, and also, concurrently with the circuit courts of the United States, of all causes, civil and criminal, arising under this act, except as herein otherwise provided, and the jurisdiction hereby conferred shall be exercised in conformity with the laws and practice governing United States courts; and all crimes and offenses committed against the provisions of this act may be prosecuted by the indictment of a grand jury, or, in cases of crimes and offenses not infamous, the prosecution may be either by indictment or information filed by the district attorney in a court having jurisdiction.

SEC. 9. That the district attorneys, marshals, and deputy marshals of the United States, the commissioners appointed by the circuit and territorial courts of the United States, with powers of arresting, imprisoning, or bailing offenders against the laws of the United States, and every other officer who may be specially empowered by the President of the United States, shall be, and they are hereby, specially authorized and required, at the expense of the United States, to institute proceedings against all and every person who shall violate the provisions of this act, and cause him or them to be arrested and imprisoned, or bailed, as the case may be, for trial before such court of the United States or territorial court as has cognizance of the offense.

And with a view to afford reasonable protection to all persons in their constitutional right to vote, without distinction of race, color, or previous condition of servitude, and to the prompt discharge of the duties of this act, it shall be the duty of the circuit courts of the United States, and the superior courts of the Territories of the United States, from time to time, to increase the number of commissioners, so as to afford a speedy and convenient means for the arrest and examination of persons charged with a violation of this act; and such commissioners are hereby authorized and required to exercise and discharge all the powers and duties conferred on them by this act, and the same duties with regard to offenses created by this act as they are authorized by law to exercise with regard to other offenses against the laws of the United States.

SEC. 10. That it shall be the duty of all marshals and deputy marshals to obey and execute all warrants and precepts issued under the provisions of this act, when to them directed; and should any marshal or deputy marshal refuse to receive such warrant or other process when tendered, or to use all proper means diligently to execute the same, he shall, on conviction thereof, be fined in the sum of $1,000, to the use of the person deprived of the rights conferred by this act. And the better to enable the said commissioners to execute their duties faithfully and efficiently, in conformity with the Constitution of the United States and the requirements of this act, they are hereby authorized and empowered, within their districts respectively, to appoint in writing, under their hands, any one or more suitable persons, from time to time, to execute all such warrants and other process as may be issued by them in the lawful performance of their respective duties, and the persons so appointed to execute any warrant or process as aforesaid shall have authority to summon and call to their aid the bystanders or posse comitatus of the proper county, or such portion of the land or naval forces of the United States, or of the militia, as may be necessary to the performance of the duty with which they are charged, and to insure a faithful observance of the XVth amendment to the Constitution of the United States; and such warrants shall run and be executed by said officers anywhere in the State or Territory within which they are issued.

SEC. 11. That any person who shall knowingly and willfully obstruct, hinder, or prevent any officer or other person charged with the execution of any warrant or process issued under the provisions of this act, or any person or persons lawfully assisting him or them from arresting any person for whose apprehension such warrant or process may have been issued, or shall rescue, or attempt to rescue, such person from the custody of the officer or other person or persons, or those lawfully assisting as aforesaid, when so arrested pursuant to the authority herein given and declared, or shall aid, abet, or assist any person so arrested as aforesaid, directly or indirectly, to escape from the custody of the officer or other person legally authorized as aforesaid, or shall harbor or conceal any person for whose arrest a warrant or process shall have been issued as aforesaid, so as to prevent his discovery and arrest after notice or knowledge of the fact that a warrant has been issued for the apprehension of such person, shall, for either of said offenses, be subject to a fine not exceeding one thousand dollars, or imprisonment not exceeding six months, or both, at the discretion of the court, on conviction before the district or circuit court of the United States for the district or circuit in which said offense may have been committed, or before the proper court of criminal jurisdiction, if committed within any one of the organized Territories of the United States.

SEC. 12. That the commissioners, district attorneys, the marshals, their deputies, and the clerks of the said district, circuit, and territorial courts, shall be paid for their services the like fees as may be allowed to them for similar services in other cases. The person or persons authorized to execute the process to be issued by such commissioners for the arrest of offenders against the provisions of this act shall be entitled to the usual fees allowed to the marshal for an arrest for each person he or they may arrest and take before any such commissioner as aforesaid, with such other fees as may be deemed reasonable by such commissioner for such other additional services as may be necessarily performed by him or them, such as attending at the examination, keeping the prisoner in custody, and providing him with food and lodging during his detention and until the final determination of such commissioner, and in general for performing such other duties as may be required in the premises; such fees to be made up in conformity with the fees usually charged by the officers of the courts of justice within the proper district or county, as near as may be practicable, and paid out of the treasury of the United States on the certificate of the judge of the district within which the arrest is made, and to be recoverable from the defendant as part of the judgment in case of conviction.

SEC. 13. That it shall be lawful for the President of the United States to employ such part of the land or naval forces of the United States, or of the militia, as shall be necessary to aid in the execution of judicial process issued under this act.

SEC. 14. That whenever any person shall hold office, except as a member of Congress or of some State legislature, contrary to the provisions of the 3d section of the XIVth article * of amendment

of the Constitution of the United States, it shall be the duty of the district attorney of the United States for the district in which such person shall hold office as aforesaid to proceed against such person by writ of *quo warranto*, returnable to the circuit or district court of the United States in such district, and to prosecute the same to the removal of such person from office; and any writ of *quo warranto*, so brought as aforesaid, shall take precedence of all other cases on the docket of the court to which it is made returnable, and shall not be continued unless for cause proved to the satisfaction of the court.

SEC. 15. That any person who shall hereafter knowingly accept or hold any office under the United States or any State, to which he is ineligible under the 3d section of the XIVth article of amendment of the Constitution of the United States, or who shall attempt to hold or exercise the duties of any such office, shall be deemed guilty of a misdemeanor against the United States, and upon conviction thereof before the circuit or district court of the United States shall be imprisoned not more than one year, or fined not exceeding $1,000, or both, at the discretion of the court.

SEC. 16. That all persons within the jurisdiction of the United States shall have the same right in every State and Territory in the United States to make and enforce contracts, to sue, be parties, give evidence, and to the full and equal benefit of all laws and proceedings for the security of person and property as is enjoyed by white citizens, and shall be subject to like punishment, pains, penalties, taxes, licenses, and exactions of every kind, and none other, any law, statute, ordinance, regulation, or custom to the contrary notwithstanding. No tax or charge shall be imposed or enforced by any State upon any person immigrating thereto from a foreign country which is not equally imposed and enforced upon every person immigrating to such State from any other foreign country, and any law of any State in conflict with this provision is hereby declared null and void.

SEC. 17. That any person who, under color of any law, statute, ordinance, regulation, or cus-

---

* XIVth Article of Amendment to the Constitution of the United States.

SECTION 1. All persons born or naturalized in the United States, and subject to the jurisdiction thereof, are citizens of the United States and of the State wherein they reside. No State shall make or enforce any law which shall abridge the privileges or immunities of citizens of the United States; nor shall any State deprive any person of life, liberty, or property, without due process of law, nor deny to any person within its jurisdiction the equal protection of the laws.

SEC. 2. Representatives shall be apportioned among the several States according to their respective numbers, counting the whole number of persons in each State, excluding Indians not taxed. But when the right to vote at any election for the choice of electors for President and Vice President of the United States, representatives in Congress, the executive and judicial officers of a State, or the members of the legislature thereof, is denied to any of the male inhabitants of such State, being twenty-one years of age and citizens

of the United States, or in any way abridged, except for participation in rebellion or other crime, the basis of representation therein shall be reduced in the proportion which the number of such male citizens shall bear to the whole number of male citizens twenty-one years of age in such State.

SEC. 3. No person shall be a senator or representative in Congress, or elector of President and Vice President, or hold any office, civil or military, under the United States, or under any State, who, having previously taken an oath, as a member of Congress, or as an officer of the United States, or as a member of any State legislature, or as an executive or judicial officer of any State, to support the Constitution of the United States, shall have engaged in insurrection or rebellion against the same, or given aid or comfort to the enemies thereof. But Congress may, by a vote of two-thirds of each house, remove such disability.

SEC. 4. The validity of the public debt of the United States, authorized by law, including debts incurred for payment of pensions and bounties for services in suppressing insurrection or rebellion, shall not be questioned. But neither the United States nor any State shall assume or pay any debt or obligation incurred in aid of insurrection or rebellion against the United States, or any claim for the loss or emancipation of any slave; but all such debts, obligations, and claims shall be held illegal and void.

SEC. 5. The Congress shall have power to enforce, by appropriate legislation, the provisions of this article.

tom, shall subject, or cause to be subjected, any inhabitant of any State or Territory to the deprivation of any right secured or protected by this act, or to different punishment, pains, or penalties, on account of such person being an alien, or by reason of his color or race, than is prescribed for the punishment of citizens, shall be deemed guilty of a misdemeanor, and, on conviction, shall be punished by fine not exceeding $1,000, or imprisonment not exceeding one year, or both, in the discretion of the court.

Sec. 18. That the act to protect all persons in the United States in their civil rights and furnish the means of their vindication, passed April 9, 1866, is hereby re-enacted; and sections 16 and 17 hereof shall be enforced according to the provisions of said act.

Sec. 19. That if at any election for representative or delegate in the Congress of the United States any person shall knowingly personate and vote, or attempt to vote, in the name of any other person, whether living, dead, or fictitious; or vote more than once at the same election for any candidate for the same office; or vote at a place where he may not be lawfully entitled to vote; or vote without having a lawful right to vote; or do any unlawful act to secure a right or an opportunity to vote for himself or any other person; or by force, threat, menace, intimidation, bribery, reward, or offer, or promise thereof, or otherwise unlawfully prevent any qualified voter of any State of the United States of America, or of any Territory thereof, from freely exercising the right of suffrage, or by any such means induce any voter to refuse to exercise such right; or compel or induce by any such means or otherwise any officer of an election in any such State or Territory to receive a vote from a person not legally qualified or entitled to vote; or interfere in any manner with any officer of said election in the discharge of his duties; or by any of such means, or other unlawful means, induce any officer of an election, or officer whose duty it is to ascertain, announce, or declare the result of any such election, or give or make any certificate, document, or evidence in relation thereto, to violate or refuse to comply with his duty, or any law regulating the same; or knowingly and willfully receive the vote of any person not entitled to vote, or refuse to receive the vote of any person entitled to vote; or aid, counsel, procure, or advise any such voter, person, or officer to do any act hereby made a crime, or to omit to do any duty the omission of which is hereby made a crime, or attempt to do so, every such person shall be deemed guilty of a crime, and shall for such crime be liable to prosecution in any court of the United States of competent jurisdiction, and, on conviction thereof, shall be punished by a fine not exceeding $500, or by imprisonment for a term not exceeding three years, or both, in the discretion of the court, and shall pay the costs of prosecution.

Sec. 20. That if, at any registration of voters for an election of representative or delegate in the Congress of the United States, any person shall knowingly personate and register, or attempt to register, in the name of any other person, whether living, dead, or fictitious, or fraudulently register, or fraudulently attempt to register, not having a lawful right so to do, or do any unlawful act to secure registration for himself or any other person; or by force, threat, menace, intimidation, bribery, reward, or offer, or promise thereof, or other unlawful means, prevent or hinder any person having a lawful right to register from duly exercising such right; or compel or induce, by any of such means, or other unlawful means, any officer of registration to admit to registration any person not legally entitled thereto, or interfere in any manner with any officer of registration in the discharge of his duties, or by any such means, or other unlawful means, induce any officer of registration to violate or refuse to comply with his duty, or any law regulating the same; or knowingly and willfully receive the vote of any person not entitled to vote, or refuse to receive the vote of any person entitled to vote, or aid, counsel, procure, or advise any such voter, person, or officer to do any act hereby made a crime, or to omit any act, the omission of which is hereby made a crime, every such person shall be deemed guilty of a crime, and shall be liable to prosecution and punishment therefor, as provided in section nineteen of this act for persons guilty of any of the crimes therein specified: *Provided*, That every registration made under the laws of any State or Territory, for any State or other election at which such representative or delegate in Congress shall be chosen, shall be deemed to be a registration within the meaning of this act, notwithstanding the same shall also be made for the purposes of any State, territorial, or municipal election.

Sec. 21. That whenever, by the laws of any State or Territory, the name of any candidate or person to be voted for as representative or delegate in Congress shall be required to be printed, written, or contained in any ticket or ballot with other candidates or persons to be voted for at the same election for State, territorial, municipal, or local officers, it shall be sufficient *prima facie* evidence, either for the purpose of indicting or convicting any person charged with voting, or attempting or offering to vote unlawfully, under the provisions of the preceding sections, or for committing either of the offenses thereby created, to prove that the person so charged or indicted voted, or attempted or offered to vote, such ballot or ticket, or committed either of the offenses named in the preceding sections of this act with reference to such ballot. And the proof and establishment of such fact shall be taken, held, and deemed to be presumptive evidence that such person voted, or attempted or offered to vote, for such representative or delegate, as the case may be, or that such offense was committed with reference to the election of such representative or delegate, and shall be sufficient to warrant his conviction, unless it shall be shown that any such ballot, when cast, or attempted or offered to be cast by him, did not contain the name of any candidate for the office of representative or delegate in the Congress of the United States, or that such offense was not committed with reference to the election of such representative or delegate.

Sec. 22. That any officer of any election at which any representative or delegate in the Congress of the United States shall be voted for, whether such officer of election be appointed or ᴄreated by or under any law or authority of the United States, or by or under any State, territorial, district, or municipal law or authority, who shall neglect or refuse to perform any duty in regard to such election required of him by any law of the United States, or of any State or Territory thereof; or violate any duty so imposed, or knowingly do any act thereby unauthorized, with intent to affect any such election, or the result thereof; or fraudulently make any false certificate of the result of such election in regard to such representative or delegate; or withhold, conceal, or destroy any certificate of record so required by law respecting, concerning, or pertaining to the election of any such representative or delegate; or neglect or refuse to make and return the same as so required by law; or aid, counsel, procure, or advise any voter, person, or officer to do any act by this or any of the preceding sections made a crime; oʀ to omit to do any duty the omission of which is by this or any of said sections made a crime, or attempt to do so, shall be deemed guilty of a crime, and shall be liable to prosecution and punishment therefor, as provided in the nineteenth section of this act for persons guilty of any of the crimes therein specified.

Sᴇᴄ. 23. That whenever any person shall be defeated or deprived of his election to any office, except elector of President or Vice President, representative or delegate in Congress, or member of a State legislature, by reason of the denial to any citizen or citizens who shall offer to vote of the right to vote, on account of race, color, or previous condition of servitude, his right to hold and enjoy such office, and the emoluments thereof, shall not be impaired by such denial; and such person may bring any appropriate suit or proceeding to recover possession of such office, and in cases where it shall appear that the sole question touching such office arises out of the denial of the right to vote to citizens who so offered to vote on account of race, color, or previous condition of servitude, such suit or proceeding may be instituted in the circuit or district court of the United States of the circuit or district in which such person resides. And said circuit or district court shall have, concurrently with the State courts, jurisdiction thereof so far as to determine the rights of the parties to such office by reason of the denial of the right guarantied by the XVth article of amendment to the Constitution of the United States and secured by this act.

### The Final Vote.

#### In Senate.

1870, May 25.—The report of the committee of conference, recommending the passage of the bill as printed above was agreed to—yeas 48, nays 11, as follow:

Yᴇᴀs—Messrs. Ames, Anthony, Boreman, Brownlow, Buckingham, Cameron, Chandler, Cole, Conkling, Cragin, Drake, Edmunds, Ferry, Flanagan, Gilbert, Hamilton of Texas, Hamlin, Harlan, Harris, Howard, Howe, Kellogg, Lewis, McDonald, Morrill of Maine, Morrill of Vermont, Morton, Nye, Osborn, Patterson, Pomeroy, Pool, Pratt, Ramsey, Rice, Ross, Sawyer, Scott, Sherman, Spencer, Sprague, Stewart, Sumner, Thayer, Tipton, Trumbull, Warner, Williams—48.

Nᴀʏs—Messrs. *Bayard, Casserly, Davis,* Fowler, *Hamilton* of Maryland, *Johnston, McCreery, Saulsbury, Stockton, Thurman, Vickers*—11.

May 27—The House concurred—yeas 133, nays 58, (not voting 39,) as follow:

Yᴇᴀs—Messrs. Allison, Ambler, Armstrong, Arnell, Asper, Atwood, Ayer, Bailey, Banks, Barry, Beatty, Bennett, Benton, Bingham, Blair, Boles, Bowen, Boyd, George M. Brooks, Buckley, Buffinton, Burchard, Burdett, Benjamin F. Butler, Roderick R. Butler, Cessna, Churchill, William T. Clark, Sidney Clarke, Amasa Cobb, Clinton L. Cobb, Coburn, Cook, Conger, Covode, Cowles, Cullom, Davis, Dawes, Degener, Dickey, Dixon, Dockery, Donley, Ferris, Finkelnburg, Fitch, Garfield, Hale, Harris, Hawley, Hay, Hays, Heflin, Hill, Hoar, Hooper, Hotchkiss, Ingersoll, Jenckes, Alexander H. Jones, Judd, Kelley, Kellogg, Kelsey, Ketcham, Knapp, Laflin, Lash, Lawrence, Logan, Lynch, Maynard, McCrary, McGrew, McKee, *McKenzie,* Mercur, Eliakim H. Moore, William Moore, Daniel H. Morrell, Samuel P. Morrill, Myers, Negley, O'Neill, Orth. Packard, Packer, Paine, Peck, Perce, Peters, Phelps, Poland, Pomeroy, Prosser, Roots, Sargent, Sawyer, Schenck, Scofield, Shanks, Lionel A. Sheldon, Porter Sheldon, John A. Smith, William J. Smith, Worthington C. Smith, William Smyth, Starkweather, Stevens, Stevenson, Stokes, Stoughton, Strickland, Strong, Taffe, Taylor, Tillman, Townsend, Twichell, Tyner, Upson, Wallace, Ward, William B. Washburn, Welker, Wheeler, Whitmore, Willard, Williams, John T. Wilson, Winans, Witcher—133.

Nᴀʏs—Messrs. *Adams, Archer, Axtell, Barnum, Beck, Biggs, Bird, Booker, James Brooks, Burr, Calkin, Cleveland, Conner, Cox, Crebs, Dickinson, Dox, Eldridge, Fox, Getz, Gibson, Haight, Haldeman, Hambleton,* Hawkins, *Holman, Johnson, Kerr, Knott. Lewis, Marshall, Mayham, McCormick, McNeely, Morgan, Morrissey, Mungen, Niblack, Potter, Randall, Reeves, Rice, Ridgway, Rogers, Schumaker, Sherrod, Shober, Slocum, Joseph S. Smith, Stiles, Stone, Swann, Sweeney, Trimble, Voorhees, Wells, Eugene M. Wilson, Woodward*—58.

### Previous Votes.

#### In House.

1870, May 16—Mr. Bingham, from the Committee on the Judiciary, reported the following bill:

*Be it enacted, &c.,* That any officer of the United States, or of any State, Territory, or district, and every officer of any city, county, town, township, borough, ward, parish, or hundred, in any State, Territory, or district, who shall by any official act whatever, or by the omission, neglect, or refusal to perform any official act or duty whatever, whether under color or pretext of any provision of any State constitution, or any law of any State, Territory, or district whatsoever, or of any local, municipal, or other law, rule, or ordinance, deny or abridge the right of any citizen of the United States to vote, on account of race, color, or previous condition of servitude, at any Federal, State, county, municipal, or other election, shall, upon conviction thereof, be adjudged guilty of a misdemeanor, and shall be punished by imprisonment of not less than one year and not exceeding three years, or by a fine not less than $500 nor exceeding $5,000, or both such fine and imprisonment, at the discretion of the court.

Sᴇᴄ. 2. That all colored citizens of the United States resident in the several States of the United States shall be entitled to vote at all elections in the State, county, parish, town, township, ward, or hundred of their residence, subject only to the same conditions which now are or may hereafter be required to qualify white citizens to vote therein. And any person who shall by force, fraud, intimidation, or other unlawful means whatsoever, prevent any colored citizen from voting at any such election, who possesses the qualifications, except in respect of color, requisite to enable a white citizen to vote thereat, shall, upon conviction thereof, be adjudged guilty of a misdemeanor, and shall be imprisoned not less than six months and not exceeding one year, or be fined not less than $100 nor more than $1,000, or be punished by both such fine and imprisonment, in the discretion of the court.

Sᴇᴄ. 3. That in case the constitution or law of any State shall require the assessment or payment of a tax as a qualification of an elector, if any assessor or other officer elected or appointed under the laws of such State, and authorized or required by the laws thereof to make any assessment of persons or property for the purpose of such taxation, shall refuse or willfully neglect to assess the person or property of any colored citizen of the United States qualified as aforesaid, and residing in the town, hundred, borough, township, parish, county, ward, or district for which said assessor or other officer shall have been elected or appointed as aforesaid, he shall, for every such offense, forfeit and pay the sum of $500 to any person who will sue for the same, and shall for every such offense be guilty of a misdemeanor, and shall be fined not less than $500, and be imprisoned not less than one month.

Sᴇᴄ. 4. That in case the constitution or law of any State shall require the assessment or payment of a tax as a qualification of an elector, if any officer or member of any levy court, or other body of officers, authorized or required by the laws of such State to make or correct any assessment of persons or property for the purpose of such taxation, or authorized or required by the laws of such State to assess or levy any such tax, shall refuse, or willfully neglect or advise, or shall participate, concur, or acquiesce in the refusal or willful neglect of such levy court, or other body of officers, to assess the person or property, or to assess or levy any such tax upon the person or property of any colored citizen of the United States, qualified as aforesaid, and residing in the county or district for which said officer, levy court, or other body of officers shall have been elected or appointed, he shall for every such offense forfeit and pay the sum of $500 to any person who will sue for the same, and shall for every such offense be deemed guilty of a misdemeanor, and shall be fined not less than $500 and be imprisoned not less than one month.

Sᴇᴄ. 5. That if any clerk or other officer required by the law of any State to register, record, or transcribe any list of persons upon whom taxes have been assessed, or to transcribe and certify any duplicate of such list to the collector of taxes, shall refuse or willfully neglect to register, record, transcribe, or enter upon the proper assessment list, or upon the proper duplicates of such assessment list, the name of any colored citizen of the United States who has been lawfully assessed to pay any tax, the payment of which tax is by the constitution or laws of such State a qualification of an elector of such State, every such clerk or officer shall for every such offense forfeit and pay the sum of $500 to any person who will sue for the same, and shall for every such offense be deemed guilty of a misdemeanor,

and shall be fined not less than $500 and be imprisoned not less than one month.

Sᴇᴄ. 6. That if any collector of taxes elected or appointed by authority of the laws of any State shall refuse or willfully neglect to receive from any colored citizen of the United States residing in such State any tax which he is required by law to collect from citizens of such State, and the payment of which tax is by the constitution or laws of such State a qualification of an elector of such State, or if any such collector shall refuse or willfully neglect to give to any such colored citizen a receipt for any such tax, when the amount thereof shall have been paid or tendered to him by such colored citizen, he shall for every such offense forfeit and pay the sum of $500 to any person who will sue for the same, and shall for every such offense be deemed guilty of a misdemeanor, and shall be fined not less than $200, and be imprisoned for not less than one month.

Sᴇᴄ. 7. That if at any State, county, township, hundred, or municipal election, held by the authority of any law of any State, or at any election for electors of President of the United States, or for members of the House of Representatives of the United States, any officer, inspector, or judge of the election shall refuse to receive, or shall advise or concur in refusing to receive, the vote of any person on account of his race, color, or previous condition of servitude, every such officer, inspector, or judge shall for every such offense forfeit and pay the sum of $500 to any person whose vote shall have been so refused, who may sue for the same in any court of the United States; and such officer, inspector, or judge shall for every such offense be deemed guilty of a misdemeanor, and on conviction thereof shall be fined not less than $200, nor more than $500, and be imprisoned not less than one month.

Sᴇᴄ. 8. That any register or officer who shall refuse to register or enter upon the list of voters or list of persons who will be entitled to vote at any election the name of any colored person having the qualifications of a white citizen entitled to vote or to be placed on such list in other respects except race or color, and any officer or member of any board for the admission of electors, who shall refuse to admit to the electors' oath, or to the privileges of an elector, any colored person on account of his race, color, or previous condition of servitude, or having the qualifications of a white citizen entitled to the privileges of an elector in other respects than race, color, or previous condition of servitude, shall be guilty of a misdemeanor, and on conviction thereof shall forfeit and pay a penalty of not less than $200 nor more than $500, and shall be imprisoned not less than one month nor more than six months, or both, at the discretion of the court.

Sᴇᴄ. 9. That if any person shall, by threats, violence, or intimidation, prevent, or attempt to prevent, any citizen of the United States from the free exercise of his right to vote in any election at which members of Congress or electors for President or Vice President of the United States may be voted for, such person so offending shall be liable to indictment, and on conviction thereof shall be subject to a fine not exceeding $1,000, or to imprisonment not less than one year nor more than three years, or both, at the discretion of the court.

SEC. 10. That the circuit courts of the United States shall have jurisdiction of the suits for forfeitures imposed and causes of action created by this act, and the circuit and district courts of the United States shall have jurisdiction of the misdemeanors created by this act.

Which was agreed to—yeas 131, nays 44, as follow:

YEAS—Messrs. Allison, Ambler, Ames, Armstrong, Arnell, Asper, Atwood, Ayer, Banks, Barry, Beaman, Beatty, Benjamin, Bennett, Benton, Bingham, Blair, *Booker*, Boyd, George M. Brooks, Buck, Buckley, Buffinton, Burchard, Benjamin F. Butler, Cake, Cessna, Churchill, William T. Clark, Sidney Clarke, Amasa Cobb, Coburn, Cook, Conger, Cowles, Dawes, Dickey, Dixon, Donley, Duval, Dyer, Ela, Farnsworth, Ferriss, Ferry, Finkelnburg, Fitch, Garfield, Gilfillan, Hale, Hamilton, Harris, Hawley, Hay, Heflin, Hill, Hoar, Hooper, Hotchkiss, Ingersoll, Julian, Kelley, Kellogg, Kelsey, Ketcham, Laflin, Lash, Logan, Loughridge, Lynch, Maynard, McCarthy, McCrary, McGrew, McKee, *McKenzie*, Mercur, Milnes, Eliakim H. Moore, Jesse H. Moore, William Moore, Morphis, Daniel J. Morrell, Myers, Negley, O'Neill, Packard, Packer, Peck, Perce, Peters, Platt, Poland, Pomeroy, Prosser, Roots, Sanford, Sargent, Sawyer, Schenck, Scofield, Shanks. Lionel A. Sheldon, Porter Sheldon, John A. Smith, William J. Smith, Worthington C. Smith, William Smyth, Starkweather, Stevens, Stevenson, Stokes, Stoughton, Strickland, Strong, Taffe, Tanner, Taylor, Tillman, Townsend, Twichell, Tyner, Upson, Cadwalader C. Washburn, Welker, Wheeler, Whitmore, Willard, Williams, John T. Wilson, Winans—131.

NAYS—Messrs. *Adams, Archer, Axtell, Barnum, Beck, Biggs, James Brooks, Burr, Conner, Crebs, Dickinson, Dox, Eldridge, Gibson, Griswold, Haight, Haldeman, Hamill, Hawkins, Holman, Knott, Lewis, Mayham, McNeely, Morgan, Mungen, Niblack, Potter, Randall, Rice, Rogers, Schumaker, Sherrod, Slocum, Joseph S. Smith, Stiles, Swann, Sweeney, Trimble, Van Trump, Voorhees, Eugene M. Wilson, Winchester, Wood*—44.

## IN SENATE.

1870, May 18—Mr. Stewart moved to substitute the following:

That all citizens of the United States who are or shall be otherwise qualified by law to vote at any election by the people in any State, Territory, district, county, city, parish, township, school district, municipality, or other territorial subdivision, shall be entitled and allowed to vote at all such elections, without distinction of race, color, or previous condition of servitude; any law, custom, usage, or regulation of any State or Territory, or by or under its authority, to the contrary notwithstanding.

SEC. 2. That if, by or under the authority of the constitution or laws of any State, or the laws of any Territory, any act is or shall be required to be done as a prerequisite or qualification for voting, and by such constitution or laws persons or officers are or shall be charged with the performance of duties in furnishing to citizens an opportunity to perform such prerequisite, or to become qualified to vote, it shall be the duty of every such person and officer to give to all citizens of the United States the same and equal opportunity to perform such prerequisite, and to become qualified to vote, without distinction of race, color, or previous condition of servitude; and if any such person or officer shall refuse or knowingly omit to give full effect to this section, he shall, for every such offense, forfeit and pay the sum of $500 to the person aggrieved thereby,

to be recovered by an action on the case, with full costs and such allowance for counsel fees as the court shall deem just, and shall also, for every such offense, be deemed guilty of a misdemeanor, and shall, on conviction thereof, be fined not less than $500, and be imprisoned not less than one month and not more than one year.

SEC. 3. That whenever, by or under the authority of the constitution or laws of any State or the laws of any Territory, any act is or shall be required to be done by any citizen as a prerequisite to qualify or entitle him to vote, the offer of any such citizen to perform the act required to be done as aforesaid shall, if it fail to be carried into execution by reason of the wrongful act or omission aforesaid of the person or officer charged with the duty of receiving or permitting such performance or offer to perform or acting thereon, be deemed and held as a performance in law of such act; and the person so offering and failing as aforesaid and being otherwise qualified, shall be entitled to vote in the same manner and to the same extent as if he had in fact performed such act; and any judge, inspector, or other officer of election whose duty it is or shall be to receive, count, certify, register, report, or give effect to the vote of any such citizen, who shall refuse or knowingly omit to receive, count, certify, register, report, or give effect to the vote of such citizen, upon the presentation by him of his affidavit stating such offer and the time and place thereof, and the name of the officer or person whose duty it was to act thereon, and that he was wrongfully prevented by such person or officer from performing such act, shall for every such offense forfeit and pay the sum of $500 to the person aggrieved thereby, to be recovered by an action on the case, with full costs and such allowance for counsel fees as the court shall deem just, and shall also, for every such offense, be guilty of a misdemeanor, and shall, on conviction thereof, be fined not less than $500, and be imprisoned not less than one month and not more than one year.

SEC. 4. That if any person, by force, bribery, threats, intimidation, or otherwise, shall hinder, delay, prevent, or obstruct, or attempt to hinder, delay, prevent, or obstruct any citizen from doing any act required to be done to qualify him to vote or from voting at any election as aforesaid, such person shall for every such offense forfeit and pay the sum of $500 to the person aggrieved thereby, to be recovered by an action on the case, with full costs and such allowance for counsel fees as the court shall deem just, and shall also for every such offense be guilty of a misdemeanor, and shall, on conviction thereof, be fined not less than $500, and be imprisoned not less than one month and not more than one year.

SEC. 5. That any person who shall be deprived of any office, except that of member of Congress or member of a State legislature, by reason of the violation of the provisions of this act, shall be entitled to recover possession of such office by writ of *mandamus* or other appropriate proceeding; and the circuit and district courts of the United States shall have concurrent jurisdiction with the proper State courts of all cases arising under this section.

Sᴇᴄ. 6. That the district courts of the United States, within their respective districts, shall have, exclusively of the courts of the several States, cognizance of all crimes and offenses committed against the provisions of this act, and also, concurrently with the circuit courts of the United States, of all causes, civil and criminal, arising under this act, except as herein otherwise provided; and the jurisdiction hereby conferred shall be exercised in conformity with the laws and practice governing United States courts; and all crimes and offenses committed against the provisions of this act may be prosecuted by the indictment of a grand jury, or in cases of crimes and offenses not infamous the prosecution may be either by indictment or information filed by the district attorney in a court having jurisdiction.

Sᴇᴄ. 7. That the district attorneys, marshals, and deputy marshals of the United States, the commissioners appointed by the circuit and territorial courts of the United States, with powers of arresting, imprisoning, or bailing offenders against the laws of the United States, and every other officer who may be specially empowered by the President of the United States, shall be, and they are hereby, specially authorized and required, at the expense of the United States, to institute proceedings against all and every person who shall violate the provisions of this act, and cause him or them to be arrested and imprisoned or bailed, as the case may be, for trial, before such court of the United States or territorial court as has cognizance of the offense. And with a view to afford reasonable protection to all persons in their constitutional right to vote, without distinction of race, color, or previous condition of servitude, and to the prompt discharge of the duties of this act, it shall be the duty of the circuit courts of the United States, and the superior courts of the Territories of the United States, from time to time, to increase the number of commissioners, so as to afford a speedy and convenient means for the arrest and examination of persons charged with a violation of this act; and such commissioners are hereby authorized and required to exercise and discharge all the powers and duties conferred on them by this act, and the same duties with regard to offenses created by this act, as they are authorized by law to exercise with regard to other offenses against the laws of the United States.

Sᴇᴄ. 8. That it shall be the duty of all marshals and deputy marshals to obey and execute all warrants and precepts issued under the provisions of this act when to them directed; and should any marshal or deputy marshal refuse to receive such warrant or other process when tendered, or to use all proper means diligently to execute the same, he shall, on conviction thereof, be fined in the sum of $1,000, to the use of the person deprived of the rights conferred by this act. And the better to enable the said commissioners to execute their duties faithfully and efficiently, in conformity with the Constitution of the United States and the requirements of this act, they are hereby authorized and empowered, within their districts respectively, to appoint, in writing, under their hands, any one or more suitable persons from time to time to execute all such warrants and other process as may be issued by them in the lawful performance of their respective duties; and the persons so appointed to execute any warrant or process as aforesaid shall have authority to summon and call to their aid the bystanders or *posse comitatus* of the proper county, or such portion of the land or naval forces of the United States or of the militia as may be necessary to the performance of the duty with which they are charged, and to insure a faithful observance of the XVth Amendment to the Constitution of the United States; and such warrants shall run and be executed by said officers anywhere in the State or Territory within which they are issued.

Sᴇᴄ. 9. That any person who shall knowingly and willfully obstruct, hinder, or prevent any officer or other person charged with the execution of any warrant or process issued under the provisions of this act, or any person or persons lawfully assisting him or them, from arresting any person for whose apprehension such warrant or process may have been issued, or shall rescue or attempt to rescue such person from the custody of the officer or other person or persons, or those lawfully assisting as aforesaid when so arrested, pursuant to the authority herein given and declared, or shall aid, abet, or assist any person so arrested as aforesaid, directly or indirectly, to escape from the custody of the officer or other person legally authorized as aforesaid, or shall harbor or conceal any person for whose arrest a warrant or process shall have been issued as aforesaid, so as to prevent his discovery and arrest after notice or knowledge of the fact that a warrant has been issued for the apprehension of such person, shall for either of said offenses be subject to a fine not exceeding $1,000 and imprisonment not exceeding six months, by indictment and conviction before the district or circuit court of the United States for the district or circuit in which said offense may have been committed, or before the proper court of criminal jurisdiction, if committed within any one of the organized Territories of the United States.

Sᴇᴄ. 10. That the commissioners, district attorneys, the marshals, their deputies, and the clerks of the said district, circuit, and territorial courts shall be paid for their services the like fees as may be allowed to them for similar services in other cases. The person or persons authorized to execute the process to be issued by such commissioners for the arrest of offenders against the provisions of this act shall be entitled to a fee of $10 for each person he or they may arrest and take before any such commissioner as aforesaid, with such other fees as may be deemed reasonable by such commissioner for such other additional services as may be necessarily performed by him or them, such as attending at the examination, keeping the prisoner in custody, and providing him with food and lodging during his detention, and until the final determination of such commissioner, and in general for performing such other duties as may be required in the premises; such fees to be made up in conformity with the fees usually charged by the officers of the courts of justice within the proper district or county, as near as may be practicable, and paid out of the Treasury of the United States on the certificate of the judge of the district within which the arrest is made, and to be recoverable from the defendant as part of the judgment in case of conviction.

SEC. 11. That whenever the President of the United States shall have reason to believe that offenses have been or are likely to be committed against the provisions of this act within any judicial district, it shall be lawful for him, in his discretion, to direct the judge, marshal, and district attorney of such district to attend at such place within the district, and for such time as he may designate, for the purpose of the more speedy arrest and trial of persons charged with a violation of this act; and it shall be the duty of every judge or other officer, when any such requisition shall be received by him, to attend at the place and for the time therein designated.

SEC. 12. That it shall be lawful for the President of the United States, or such person as he may empower for that purpose, to employ such part of the land or naval forces of the United States, or of the militia, as shall be deemed necessary to prevent the violation and enforce the due execution of this act.

SEC. 13. That whenever any person shall hold office, except as a member of Congress or of some State legislature, contrary to the provisions of the third section of the XIVth article of amendment of the Constitution of the United States, it shall be the duty of the district attorney of the United States for the district in which such person shall hold office as aforesaid to proceed against such person by writ of *quo warranto*, returnable to the circuit or district court of the United States in such district, and to prosecute the same to the removal of such person from office; and any writ of *quo warranto* so brought as aforesaid shall take precedence of all other cases on the docket of the court to which it is made returnable, and shall not be continued unless for cause proved to the satisfaction of the court.

SEC. 14. That any person who shall hereafter knowingly accept or hold any office under the United States or any State, to which he is ineligible under the third section of the XIVth article of amendment of the Constitution of the United States, or who shall attempt to hold or exercise the duties of any such office, shall be deemed guilty of a misdemeanor against the United States, and upon conviction thereof before the circuit or district court of the United States shall be imprisoned not more than one year and fined not exceeding $1,000, and shall forever be disqualified to hold any office of honor, trust, or profit under the United States or any State.

SEC. 15. That all persons within the jurisdiction of the United States shall have the same right in every State and Territory in the United States to make and enforce contracts, to sue, be parties, give evidence, and to the full and equal benefit of all laws and proceedings for the security of person and property as is enjoyed by white citizens, and shall be subject to like punishments, pains, penalties, taxes, licenses, and exactions of every kind, and none other, any law, statute, ordinance, regulation, or custom to the contrary notwithstanding. No tax or charge shall be imposed or enforced by any State upon any person emigrating thereto from a foreign country, which is not equally imposed and enforced upon every person emigrating to such State from any other foreign country, and any law of any State in conflict with this provision is hereby declared null and void.

SEC. 16. That any person who, under color of any law, statute, ordinance, regulation, or custom, shall subject, or cause to be subjected, any inhabitant of any State or Territory to the deprivation of any right secured or protected by this act, or to different punishment, pains, or penalties, on account of such person being an alien, or by reason of his color or race, than is prescribed for the punishment of citizens, shall be deemed guilty of a misdemeanor, and on conviction shall be punished by fine not exceeding $1,000, or imprisonment not exceeding one year, or both, in the discretion of the court.

SEC. 17. That the act to protect all persons in the United States in their civil rights, and furnish the means of their vindication, passed April 9, 1866, is hereby re-enacted; and said act, except the first and second sections thereof, is hereby referred to and made a part of this act; and section fifteen and section sixteen hereof shall be enforced according to the provisions of said act.

Mr. Sherman moved to amend the substitute by adding the following sections:

SEC. —. That if at any election for representative or delegate in the Congress of the United States any person shall knowingly personate and vote, or attempt to vote, in the name of any other person, whether living, dead, or fictitious; or vote more than once at the same election for any candidate for the same office; or vote at a place where he may not be lawfully entitled to vote; or vote without having a lawful right to vote; or do any unlawful act to secure a right or an opportunity to vote for himself or any other person; or by force, threat, menace, intimidation, bribery, reward, or offer, or promise thereof, or otherwise unlawfully prevent any qualified voter of any State of the United States of America, or of any Territory thereof, from freely exercising the right of suffrage, or by any such means induce any voter to refuse to exercise such right; or compel or induce by any such means, or otherwise, any officer of an election in any such State or Territory to receive a vote from a person not legally qualified or entitled to vote; or interfere in any manner with any officer of said elections in the discharge of his duties; or by any of such means or otherwise induce any officer of an election, or officer whose duty it is to ascertain, announce, or declare the result of any such election, or give or make any certificate, document, or evidence in relation thereto, to violate or refuse to comply with his duty or any law regulating the same; or knowingly and willfully receive the vote of any person not entitled to vote, or refuse to receive the vote of any person entitled to vote; or aid, counsel, procure, or advise any such voter, person, or officer to do any act hereby made a crime, or to omit to do any duty the omission of which is hereby made a crime, or attempt to do so, every such person shall be deemed guilty of a crime, and shall for such crime be liable to indictment in any court of the United States of competent jurisdiction, and on conviction thereof shall be punished by a fine not exceeding $500, or by imprisonment for a term not exceeding three years, or both, in the discretion of the court, and shall pay the costs of prosecution.

SEC. —. That if at any registration of voters for an election for representative or delegate in the Congress of the United States, any person shall knowingly personate or register, or attempt to register, in the name of any other person, whether living, dead, or fictitious, or attempt to register at a place where he shall not be lawfully entitled to register, or register or attempt to register not having a lawful right so to do, or do any unlawful act to secure registration for himself or any other person, or by force, threat, menace, intimidation, bribery, reward, or offer, or promise thereof, or otherwise, unlawfully prevent or hinder any person having a lawful right to register from duly exercising such right; or compel or induce by any such means, or otherwise, any officer of registration to admit to registration any person not legally entitled thereto; or interfere in any manner with any officer of registration in the discharge of his duties; or by any such means, or otherwise, induce any officer of registration to violate or refuse to comply with his duty or any law regulating the same; or knowingly and willfully receive the vote of any person not entitled to vote, or refuse to receive the vote of any person entitled to vote, or aid, counsel, procure, or advise any such voter, person, or officer to do any act hereby made a crime, or to omit any act the omission of which is made a crime, every such person shall be deemed guilty, of a crime, and shall be liable to indictment and punishment therefor, as provided in the first section of this act for persons guilty of any of the crimes therein specified.

SEC. —. That if any person shall, by force, threat, menace, intimidation, or otherwise, unlawfully prevent any citizen or citizens from assembling in public meeting, to freely discuss or hear discussed the claims or merits of any candidate for the office of President or Vice President or elector thereof, or representative or delegate in Congress, or of any officer of the Government of the United States; or the laws or measures of Congress, or any measure existing, pending, or proposed, affecting the Government of the United States, or any department or officer thereof; or if any person shall by any such means break up, disperse, or molest any such assemblage, or molest any citizen in or of such assemblage, every person so offending shall be deemed guilty of a crime, and shall be liable to indictment and punishment therefor, as provided in the first section of this act for persons guilty of any of the crimes therein specified.

Which was disagreed to.

Mr. Hamlin moved to add the first two sections proposed by Mr. Sherman, which was agreed to—yeas 31, nays 12, as follow:

YEAS—Messrs. Abbott, Carpenter, Chandler, Cole, Corbett, Cragin, Flanagan, Hamlin, Harlan, Harris, Howell, McDonald, Morrill of Maine, Morton, Nye, Osborn, Patterson, Pomeroy, Pratt, Ramsey, Revels, Rice, Sawyer, Scott, Spencer, Sprague, Stewart, Sumner, Thayer, Warner, Yates—31.

NAYS—Messrs. *Casserly, Davis,* Fowler, *Hamilton* of Maryland, *Johnston, McCreery,* Pool, Ross, *Stockton, Thurman, Vickers*—12.

Mr. Morton moved to insert the following, to come in as the fifth section of the bill:

That if any person shall prevent, hinder, control, or intimidate, or shall attempt to prevent, hinder, control, or intimidate, any person from exercising or in exercising the right of suffrage, to whom the right of suffrage is secured or guarantied by the XVth Amendment to the Constitution of the United States, by means of bribery, threats, or threats of depriving such person of employment or occupation, or of ejecting such person from rented house, lands, or other property, or by threats of refusing to renew leases or contracts for labor, or by threats of violence to himself or family, such person so offending shall be deemed guilty of a misdemeanor, and upon conviction thereof shall be fined not less than $500 and be imprisoned not less than one month and not more than one year.

Which was agreed to—yeas 36, nays 9, as follow:

YEAS—Messrs. Abbott, Anthony, Carpenter, Chandler, Cole, Corbett, Cragin, Flanagan, Hamlin, Harlan, Harris, Howell, McDonald, Morrill of Maine, Morton, Nye, Osborn, Patterson, Pomeroy, Pool, Pratt, Ramsey, Revels, Rice, Ross, Sawyer, Scott, Spencer, Sprague, Stewart, Sumner, Thayer, Warner, Willey, Williams, Yates—36.

NAYS—Messrs. *Casserly, Davis,* Fowler, *Hamilton* of Maryland, *Johnston, McCreery, Stockton, Thurman, Vickers*—9.

Mr. Davis moved to amend, by inserting the following additional section:

SEC. —. That no person shall enter into, hold, or attempt to exercise the powers or perform the duties of any office or public trust, which the Constitution or laws require to be filled by vote of the people, unless he shall have received at the election therefor a greater number of the votes of the electors entitled to vote at such election than any other candidate; and all persons entering into, holding, or attempting to exercise the powers or perform the duties of such office or public trust shall thereby commit a high misdemeanor, for which they shall be subject to indictment and punishment of imprisonment for not less than one or more than five years, and fine of not less than $1,000 or more than $5,000, one-half thereof to go to the informer; and all treasury officers settling, passing, or paying any claim or account for pay or compensation of any kind of any person entering into or holding, or attempting to exercise the powers or perform the duties of any office or public trust, against the provisions of this section, shall be guilty of a misdemeanor, thereby forfeit and be disqualified to hold his place, and be subject to indictment and punishment of imprisonment for not less than twelve months, and fine of $1,000, one-half to the informer. All persons entering into, holding, or attempting to exercise the powers or perform the duties of any office or public trust, against the provisions of this section, shall also be subject to the civil suit of any person injured thereby.

Which was disagreed to.

Mr. Pool moved to insert as sections 6 and 7 the following:

SEC. —. That if two or more persons shall band or conspire together, or go in disguise upon the public highway, or upon the premises of another, with intent to violate any provision of this act, or to injure, oppress, threaten, or intimidate any citizen with intent to prevent or hinder his free exercise and enjoyment of any right or privilege granted or secured to him by the Constitution or laws of the United States, or because of his having exercised the same, such person shall be held guilty of felony, and on conviction thereof shall be fined and imprisoned; the fine not to exceed $5,000, and the imprisonment not to exceed ten years; and shall, moreover, be thereafter ineligible to, and disabled from holding, any office or place of honor, profit, or trust, created by the Constitution or laws of the United States.

SEC. —. That if in the act of violating any provision in either of the two preceding sections, any other felony, crime, or misdemeanor shall be committed, the offender, on conviction of such violation of said sections, shall be punished for the same with such punishments as are attached to like felonies, crimes, and misdemeanors by the laws of the State in which the offense may be committed.

Which was agreed to.

Mr. Pool moved to strike out the twelfth section and insert as follows:

That the President of the United States may employ in any State such part of the land and naval forces of the United States, or of the militia, as he may deem necessary to enforce the complete execution of this act; and with such forces may pursue, arrest, and hold for trial all persons charged with the violation of any of the provisions of this act, and enforce the attendance of witnesses upon the examination or trial of such persons.

Which was disagreed to—yeas 6, nays 34, on a division.

Mr. Willey moved to strike out of the second section the following words:

For every such offense forfeit and pay the sum of $500 to the person aggrieved thereby, to be recovered by an action on the case, with full costs and such allowance for counsel fees as the court shall deem just, and shall also

Which was disagreed to—yeas 21, nays 27, as follow:

YEAS—Messrs. Anthony, *Casserly*, *Davis*, Fowler, *Hamilton* of Maryland, Hamlin, Harlan, Howell, *Johnston*, *McCreery*, Patterson, Pomeroy, Pratt, Ross, Scott, *Stockton*, *Thurman*, *Vickers*, Willey, Williams, Yates—21.

NAYS—Messrs. Abbott, Cameron, Carpenter, Chandler, Cole, Corbett, Cragin, Flanagan, Hamilton of Texas, Harris, Howard, Howe, McDonald, Nye, Osborn, Pool, Ramsey, Revels, Rice, Robertson, Sawyer, Spencer, Sprague, Stewart, Sumner, Thayer, Warner—27.

Mr. Carpenter moved to amend by adding the following section:

SEC. —. That any person who shall be deprived of or fail to be elected to any office, except that of member of Congress or member of a State legislature, by reason of a violation of any of the provisions of this act, or by reason of the denial to any citizen of the right to vote on account of his race, color, or previous condition of servitude, shall be entitled to hold such office and perform the duties and receive the emoluments thereof, and may recover the possession of such office by *quo warranto* or other appropriate proceeding in the circuit or district court of the United States for the proper district, or in any State court having jurisdiction of such proceedings.

Which was agreed to—yeas 24, nays 22, as follow:

YEAS—Messrs. Cameron, Carpenter, Chandler, Cole, Cragin, Flanagan, Gilbert, Hamilton of Texas, Harris, Howe, Howell, McDonald, Nye, Osborn, Ramsey, Revels, Rice, Robertson, Sawyer, Spencer, Stewart, Sumner, Thayer, Warner—24.

NAYS—Messrs. Abbott, *Casserly*, Corbett, *Davis*, *Hamilton* of Maryland, Harlan, Howard, *Johnston*, *McCreery*, Morton, Pomeroy, Pool, Pratt, Ross, Scott, *Stockton*, *Thurman*, Trumbull, *Vickers*, Willey, Williams, Yates—22.

Mr. Williams moved to strike out of the eighth section the words "or such portion of the land or naval forces of the United States or of the militia."

Which was disagreed to—yeas 12, nays 38, as follow:

YEAS—Messrs. *Casserly*, *Davis*, Fowler, *Hamilton* of Maryland, *Johnston*, *McCreery*, Ross, Sprague, *Stockton*, *Thurman*, *Vickers*, Williams—12.

NAYS—Messrs. Abbott, Brownlow, Cameron, Carpenter, Chandler, Cole, Corbett, Cragin, Flanagan, Hamilton of Texas, Hamlin, Harlan, Howard, Howe, Howell, McDonald, Morton, Nye, Osborn, Patterson, Pomeroy, Pool, Pratt, Ramsey, Revels, Rice, Robertson, Sawyer, Scott, Spencer, Stewart, Sumner, Thayer, Trumbull, Warner, Willey, Yates—38.

Mr. Scott moved to strike out the third section of the substitute, which was disagreed to—yeas 14, nays 33, as follow:

YEAS—Messrs. Anthony, *Casserly*, *Davis*, Fowler, *Hamilton* of Maryland, Howell, *Johnston*, *McCreery*, Ross, Scott, *Stockton*, *Thurman*, *Vickers*, Williams—14.

NAYS—Messrs. Abbott, Brownlow, Cameron, Carpenter, Chandler, Cole, Corbett, Cragin, Flanagan, Gilbert, Hamilton of Texas, Hamlin, Harlan, Harris, Howe, McDonald, Morrill of Maine, Nye, Osborn, Pomeroy, Pool, Pratt, Ramsey, Revels, Rice, Robertson, Sawyer, Spencer, Stewart, Sumner, Thayer, Warner, Yates—33.

Mr. Vickers moved to amend the fourth section by inserting in the first line after the words "That if," the words "under or by color of State authority;" which was disagreed to—yeas 9, nays 41, as follow:

YEAS—Messrs. *Casserly*, *Davis*, Fowler. *Hamilton* of Maryland, *Johnston*, *McCreery*, *Stockton*, *Thurman*, *Vickers*—9.

NAYS—Messrs. Abbott, Anthony, Brownlow, Cameron, Carpenter, Chandler, Cole, Corbett, Cragin, Flanagan, Gilbert, Hamilton of Texas, Hamlin, Harlan, Harris, Howard, Howe, Howell, McDonald, Morrill of Maine, Morton, Nye, Osborn, Patterson, Pomeroy, Pool, Pratt, Ramsey, Revels, Rice, Robertson, Sawyer, Scott, Spencer, Stewart, Sumner, Thayer, Trumbull, Warner, Williams, Yates—41.

Mr. Casserly moved to strike out the words "and such allowance for counsel fees as the court shall deem just" wherever they occur in the bill; which was disagreed to—yeas 10, nays 39, as follow:

YEAS—Messrs. *Casserly*, *Davis*, Fowler, *Hamilton* of Maryland, *Johnston*, *McCreery*, Ross, *Stockton*, *Thurman*, *Vickers*—10.

NAYS—Messrs. Abbott, Anthony, Brownlow, Cameron, Carpenter, Chandler, Cole, Corbett, Cragin, Flanagan, Gilbert, Hamilton of Texas, Hamlin, Harlan, Harris, Howard, Howe, Howell, McDonald, Morton, Nye, Osborn, Patterson, Pomeroy, Pool, Pratt, Ramsey, Revels, Rice, Robertson, Sawyer, Scott, Spencer, Stewart, Sumner, Thayer, Warner, Williams, Yates—39.

Mr. Howard moved to amend section four by striking out the word "attempt" and inserting the words "shall combine or confederate with others;" which was agreed to.

With some verbal amendments the bill was passed—yeas 43, nays 8, as follow:

YEAS—Messrs. Abbott, Anthony, Brownlow, Cameron, Carpenter, Chandler, Cole, Corbett, Cragin, Flanagan,

Gilbert, Hamilton of Texas, Hamlin, Harlan, Harris, Howard, Howe, Howell, McDonald, Morrill of Maine, Morton, Nye, Osborn, Patterson, Pomeroy, Pool, Pratt, Ramsey, Revels, Rice, Ross, Sawyer, Scott, Spencer, Sprague, Stewart, Sumner, Thayer, Trumbull, Warner, Willey, Williams, Yates—43.

Nays—Messrs. *Casserly, Davis,* Fowler, *Hamilton* of Maryland, *Johnston, McCreery, Thurman, Vickers*—8.

The Senate amendments were disagreed to by the House and a committee of conference asked and granted, which reported to both houses the bill as finally passed, as above.

## VOTES OF THE STATE LEGISLATURES ON THE PROPOSED XVth AMENDMENT TO THE CONSTITUTION OF THE UNITED STATES.*

### Alabama.

#### Senate, *November* 16, 1869.

Yeas—Messrs. R. N. Barr, F. G. Bromberg, W. M. Buckley, D. E. Coon, J. A. Farden, J. T. Foster, W. W. Glass, Burrell Johnston, W. B. Jones, Philip King, Thomas Lambert, Benjamin Lentz, G. T. McAfee, J. W. Mabry, J. W. Mahan, W. B. Martin, William Miller, J. F. Morton, John Oliver, J. L. Pennington, J. D. F. Richards, B. F. Royal, H. C. Sanford, D. V. Sevier, I. D. Sibley, J. P. Stow, H. H. Wise, C. O. Whitney, F. D. Wyman, J. A. Yordy—30.

Nay—Mr. *A. N. Worthy*—1.

#### House of Representatives, *November* 16, 1869.

Yeas—Messrs. Benjamin Alexander, T. W. Armstrong, William Alley, John R. Ard, ——— Austin, E. W. Attaway, Matt. Avery, Alfred Baker, M. R. Bell, Samuel Blanden, Warren A. Brantley, N. A. Brewington, Pierce Burton, Richard Burke, John Carraway, E. T. Childress, W. R. Chisholm, John W. Coleman, George W. Cox, J. W. Daniels, John W. Dereen, Thomas Diggs, Joseph Drawn, A. Emmons, Thomas D. Fister, J. R. Greene, G. W. Haley, John Hardy, R. E. Harris, John A. Hart, William Henderson, D. H. Hill, A. L. Holman, George Houston, D. C. Humphreys, E. F. Jennings, ——— Jones, P. A. Kendrick, S. F. Kenemer, Horace King, E. W. Lawrence, G. Lewis, Thomas Masterson, *G. W. Malone, Jeff. McCall,* T. W. Newsom, ——— Ninninger, ——— Rice, A. G. Richardson, Justin Ronayne, Edward Rose, Thomas Sanford, C. P. Simmons, W. G. W. Smith, S. Speed, H. J. Springfield, T. C. Steward, Paul Strobach, W. L. Taylor, John Taylor, William Taylor, H. Thompson, Charles T. Thweatt, William V. Turner, James Vanzandt, Spencer Weaver, George White, L. J. Williams, B. R. Wilson, Jack Wood, George F. Harrington, Speaker—71.

Nays—Messrs. *W. T. Brown, W. D. Humphrey, J. P. Hubbard, W. F. Hunt, Jacob Magee, William Mastin, J. G. Moore, E. J. Mansell, William Murrah, Adolph Proskauer, James A. Reeves, Ryland Randolph, H. C. Tompkins, C. Tucker, Jackson Tyner, J. M. Walker*—16.

### California.

Both houses rejected the amendment at the late session of the legislature, but an application for a copy of the vote was not granted. The vote is understood to have been a party one—the Republicans supporting, the Democrats rejecting, the amendment.

---

*See pp. 488 to 498, Manual of 1869, for the rest of the votes in State Legislatures.

### Delaware.

#### Senate, *March* 17, 1869.

Yᴇᴀs—Messrs. Curtis B. Ellison, John G. Jackson—2.

Nays—Messrs. *Jacob Bounds, Thomas H. Denney, Chas. Gooding, John W. Hall, John H. Paynter, Geo. Russell, James Williams,* Speaker—7.

#### House of Representatives, *March* 18, 1869.

Yᴇᴀs—0.

Nays—Messrs. *John G. Bacon, Geo. F. Brady, John A. Brown, Lot Cloud, Isaac Connoway, Jacob Deakyne, William Dean, Shepard P. Houslon, Thomas J. Marvel, Philip C. Matthews, Whiteley W. Meredith, Robert J. Reynolds, Peter Robinson, Albert H. Silver, William B. Tomlinson, Joseph W. Vandegrift, H. C. Wolcott, J. Hickman,* Speaker—19.

### Georgia.*

#### Senate, *February* 2, 1870.

Yᴇᴀs—Messrs. W. F. Bowers, H. A. Bradley, Walker Brock, T. G. Campbell, I. M. Coleman, N. Corbitt, John Dickey, J. L. Dunning, William Griffin, Joshua Griffin, John Harris, E. I. Higbee, McW. Hungerford, W. B. Jones, W. F. Jordan, J. H. McWhorter, J. C. Richardson, Josiah Sherman, W. C. Smith, T. I. Speer, A. M. Stringer, J. W. Traywick, George Wallace, F. O. Welch, Benjamin Conley, President—25.

Nays—Messrs. *John T. Burns, M. A. Candler, J. C. Fain, H. Hicks, A. W. Holcomb, W. T. McArthur, A. D. Nunnally, M. C. Smith, C. B. Wooten*—9.

#### House of Representatives.

Yᴇᴀs—Messrs. James Allen, T. M. Allen, J. W. Atkins, ——— Armstrong, W. R. Bell, I. M. Buchan, Marion Bethune, Eli Barnes, Richard Bradford, T. P. Beard, James Cunningham, W. C. Carson, M. Claiborne, A. Colby, J. T. Costin, G. H. Clower, T. G. Campbell, jr., J. H. Caldwell, Mat. Davis, J. M Ellis, James Fitzpatrick, Monday Floyd, W. A. Golden, Samuel Gardner, ——— Guilford, *N. N. Gober,* W. L. Goodman, *W. B. Gray,* Virgil Hillyer, H. C. Holcomb, W. H. Harrison, W. H. F. Hall, J. F. Harden, A. Haren, J. P. Hutchings, W. F. Holden, Charles H. Hooks, U. L. Houston, John Higdon, G. W. Johnson, Charles O. Johnson, P. Joiner, ——— Jackson, G. Lastinger, W. A. Lane, George Linder, J. A. Madden, R. Moore, Plate Madison, J. T. McCormick, John B. Nesbitt, *J. C. Nisbit,* Peter O'Neal, *R. M. Parks,* S. C. Prudden, James Porter, *W. P. Price,* J. L. Perkins, A. R. Reid, A. Richardson, J. Mason Rice, *P. Sewell,* F. M. Smith, Abram Smith, S. L. Strickland, J. M. Sims, S. F. Salter, E. Tweedy, W. W. Watkins, John Warren, Hiram Williams, W. N. Williams, A. J. Williams, B. H. Zellars, R. L. McWhorter, Speaker—75.

Nays—Messrs. *J. K. Barnum, M. R. Ballenger, W. G. Brown, J. A. Cobb, C. C. Cleghorn, A. E. Cloud, W. H. Clark, C. C. Duncan, W. S. Erwin, McK. Fincannon, H. R. Felder, J. E. Gullatt, W. D. Hamilton, G. M. Hook,* ——— *Harris, C. H. Kytle, J. J. McArthur, J. W. Mathews, R. W. Phillips, N. J. Perkins, F. L. Pepper, Thomas F. Rainey, V. P. Sisson, Dunlap Scott, W. M. Tumlin, U. O. Tate, W. G. Vinson, L. H. Walthal, L. C. A. Warren*—29.

---

*See p. 489 for a former vote on same proposition.

## Iowa.

SENATE, *January* 26, 1870.

YEAS—Messrs. Benjamin F. Allen, Charles Atkins, Charles Beardsley, G. G. Bennett, Edward M. Bill, Henry C. Bulis, Frank T. Campbell, John M. Cathcart, James Chapin, Hans R. Claussen, George W. Couch, John N. Dixon, William G. Donnan, Joseph Dysart, George E. Griffith, Joseph Grimes, A. H. Hamilton, Joseph W. Havens, Theodore Hawley, James S. Hurley, Alexander B. Ireland, Isaac W. Keller, William Larrabee, Matthew Long, Robert Lowry, John McKean, Samuel McNutt, I. J. Mitchell, Napoleon B. Moore, Benjamin F. Murray, Homer E. Newell, J. G. Patterson, Abial R. Pierce, Wells S. Rice, Robert Smith, Henry C. Traverse, Marcus Tuttle, Jacob G. Vale, W. F. Vermillion, John P. West, William P. Wolf, James D. Wright—42.

NAYS—Messrs. *J. P. Casady, Lewis B. Dunham, Samuel H. Fairall, Liberty E. Fellows, F. M. Knoll, E. S. McCulloch, M. B. Mulkern*—7.

HOUSE OF REPRESENTATIVES, *January* 20, 1870.

YEAS—Messrs. C. C. Applegate, Delos Arnold, Joseph Ball, James W. Beatty, John Beresheim, Peter G. Bonewitz, Aaron Brown, Joel Brown, Caleb Bundy, William Butler, G. W. Butterfield, William H. Campbell, T. B. Carpenter, John Carver, Aylett R. Colton, M. E. Cutts, Harwood G. Day, David Dickerson, Charles Dudley, Samuel B. Dumont, David T. Durham, Benjamin F. Elbert, William C. Evans, Amos S. Faville, John W. Green, William Harper, O. C. Harrington, George D. Harrison, B. F. Hartshorn, Benjamin A. Haycock, Joseph Hobson, John F. Hopkins, William Hopkirk, Henry L. Huff, John D. Hunter, George W. Jones, John A. Kasson, Benjamin F. Keables, James P. Ketcham, John F. Lacey, Daniel S. Lee, Anders O. Lommen, John Mahin, Constant R. Marks, L. T. McCoun, George H. McGavren, William W. Merritt, J. D. Miles, Lewis Miles, jr., John L. Millard, Claudius B. Miller, John D. Miracle, John Morrison, jr., Samuel Murdock, J. G. Newbold, Cole Noel, Timothy O. Norris, Galusha Parsons, Henry O. Pratt, Samuel H. Rogers, Matthias J. Rohlfs, George N. Rosser, Neal W. Rowell, John Russell, Cummings Sanborn, Thomas J. Sater, J. W. Satterthwait, Erastus Snow, Benjamin Spencer, O. O. Stanchfield, David Stewart, John Y. Stone, A. H. Stutsman, Alexander H. Swan, John H. Tait, Hamilton B. Taylor, Frederick Teale, Gillum S. Tolliver, John W. Traer, J. Q. Tufts, Edgar A. Warner, Jesse Wasson, Horace B. Williams, George H. Wright —84.

NAYS—Messrs. *David S. Bell, John Christoph, Theophilus Crawford, Emory DeGroat, James Dunne, Patrick Gibbons, Christian Hirschler, James M. Hood, John P. Irish, William Mills, Frederick O'Donnell, Pierce G. Wright*—12.

## Maryland.

SENATE, *February*, 1870.

YEAS—0.

NAYS—Messrs. *Joshua Biggs, Nathan Browne, John Lee Carroll, James C. Clarke, Barnes Compton, Isaac M. Denson, James T. Earle, Daniel Fields, James H. Grove, Eli J. Henkle, Daniel M. Henry, C. H. Hyland, Charles M. Jump, William Kimmell, G. Frederick Maddox, Lemuel*

*Malone, John M. Miller, John C. Parker, W. O. Sellman, Henry Snyder, Alfred Spates, William B. Stephenson, William E. Timmons, William Welsh, George W. Wilson*—25.

HOUSE OF DELEGATES, *February*, 1870.

YEAS—0.

NAYS—Messrs. *R. W. Baldwin, William Baldwin, Horatio Beck, George Biddle, Thomas R. Blake, Noah Bowlus, Robert F. Brattan, John B. Brown, Daniel W. Cameron, William E. Collins, George Colton, John H. Cooper, Andrew G. Chapman, Edward S. W. Choate, Andrew J. Crawford, William H. Crouse, Samuel K. Dennis, James I. Duke, Charles S. Duvall, John F. Ehlen, Isaiah Gardner, Robert J. W. Garey, William G. Gordy, Arthur P. Gorman, Thomas H. Hamilton, Alexander Hardcastle, E. L. F. Hardcastle, Benjamin H. Harrington, Henry R. Harris, F. S. Hoblitzell, J. T. C. Hopkins, John H. Jordan, Anthony Kean, E. G. Kilbourn, George A. Kirk, Benjamin Lankford, E. C. Latrobe, Jefferson D. Loker, Fendall Marbury, William T. Markland, John H. Marshall, Thomas Martin, John T. McCreery, James L. McLane, William M. Merrick, John W. Mitchell, Thomas W. Morse, Jacob Myers, Alexander Neill, John Owens, Henry Owings, George Percy, John R. Purnell, William Richards, J. Alfred Ritter, James B. Sauner, David Seibert, Columbus I. Shipley, George A. Shower, John M. Standish, J. M. Street, J. Monroe Sword, John B. Thomas, Joel Thomas, James Touchstone, Lewis Turner, jr., Greenbury M. Watkins, James Webb, George Wells, John Welty, William White, John F. Wiley, William B. Wilmer, James Wilson, Airheart Winters, Richard Wooton*—87.

## Minnesota.

SENATE, *January* 12, 1870.

YEAS—Messrs. George F. Batchelder, J. B. Crooker, Charles Hill, W. S. Jackson, D. E. King, J. A. Latimer, J. A. Leonard, Samuel Lord, C. H. Pettit, William Pfaender, B. F. Smith, B. D. Sprague, H. C. Wait—13.

NAYS—Messrs. *L. L. Baxter, George L. Becker, C. F. Buck, D. L. Buell, J. N. Castle, R. J. Chewning, William Henry, William Lochren*—8.

HOUSE OF REPRESENTATIVES, *January* 13, 1870.

YEAS—Messrs. B. Abbott, William Barton, Ole C. Bratrud, H. A. Brown, William L. Couplin, William Close, R. Crandall, Orin Densmore, Henry Drought, John Gage, S, W. Graham, A. R. Hall, B. S. Larsen, William Lowell, John Miller, William E. Potter, E. A. Rice, H. W. Rulifison, M. E. L. Shanks, Giles Slocum, Charles Stewart, P. H. Swift, Isaac Thorson, Nathan Vance, C. H. Waterman, A. C. Wedge, W. C. Young, John L. Merriam—28.

NAYS—Messrs. *John Bullen, G. M. Cameron, S. G. Canfield, John M. Cool, J. K. Cullen, John Flannegan, A. J. Fowler, A. M. Fridley, William Jones, John F. Meagher, J. S. Norris, John A. Pfaar, J. H. Pound, M. Scanlan, John L. Wilson*—15.

## Mississippi.

SENATE, *January* 15, 1870.

YEAS—Messrs. F. M. Abbott. Horatio N. Ballard, Charles Caldwell, *Thomas W. Castles, H. L. Duncan,* John Gartman, William H. Gibbs,

Robert Gleed, William Gray, William M. Hancock, *Thomas J. Hardy, Stephen Johnson,* Robert E. Leachman, Finis H. Little, Orange S. Miles, Green Millsaps, Albert T. Morgan, Alston Mygatt, Henry M. Paine, J. H. Pierce, Hiram R. Revels, W. S. Rushing, James C. Shoup, George S. Smith, *William T. Strieklin,* Thomas W. Stringer, Charles A. Sullivan, and Alexander Warner—28.

NAYS—0.

HOUSE OF REPRESENTATIVES, *January* 17, 1870.

YEAS—Mr. Speaker, F. E Franklin, Messrs. P. Balch, P. Barrow, *J. L. Bolton,* J. F. Boulden, C. M. Bowles, Rasselas Boyd, E. Buchanan, W. S. Cabell, M. Campbell, G. Charles, C. W. Clarke, J. S. B. Coggeshall, *V. A. Collins, J. P. Conner, E. Currie,* A. K Davis, W. H. Foote, H. M. Foley, C. A. Foster, O. C. French, *John Gillis,* T. R. Gowan, *H. C. Grier,* E. Handy, *W. W. Hart,* E. P. Hatch, C. P. Head, *W. L. Hemmingway,* A. Henderson, J. L. Herbert, D. Higgins, William Hodges, G. Holland, W. Holmes, M. Howard, *E. N. Hunt,* H. P. Jacobs, *R. A. Johns,* W. L. Jones of Marshall county, C. D. Landon, G. N. Langford, H. W. Lewis, J. R. Lynch, C. W. Loomis, Henry Mayson, *M. K. Mister,* J. A. Moore, J. Morgan, L. A. Munson, M. T. Newsom, C. F. Norris, I. N. Osborne, J. G. Owen, W. B. Owings, A. Parker, *E. Phillips,* J. H. Piles, *Henry Pitman,* D. N. Quinn, *A. S. Roane* of Calhoun, W. H. Roane of Pike, *J F. Sessions,* W. B. Snowden, J. J. Spelman, J. Stewart, E. H. Stiles, D. Stiles, J. M. Stone, *H. M. Street,* H. Taylor, B. G. Underwood, J. V. Walker, H. W. Warren, G. W. White, S. V. W. Whiting, W. B. Williams W. J. Willing, A. S. Wood—79.

NAYS—0.

### Missouri

HOUSE OF REPRESENTATIVES, *January* 7, 1870.*

YEAS—Messrs. J. J. Akard, Benjamin Alsup, Thomas W. Allred, A. J. Baker, Francis P. Becker, T. S. Benefiel, John Bitman, John H. Bohn, Jacob S. Boreman, Tarlton Brewster, William P. Browning, Henry Bruihl, C. C. Byrne, Daniel Clark, M. S. Courtright, D. S. Crumb, W. H. H. Cundiff, E. S. Davis, R. B. Denny, R. T. Dibble, John H. Dolle, W. B. Elliott, A. W. Ellison, Frank Eno, John W. Enoch, John F. Fassen, William J. Ferguson, E. P. Ferrell, John B. Freeman, A. L. Gibbs, James Gibson, John H. Glenn, R. T. Gladney, August Hackman, James B. Harper, Samuel Hays, J. T. K. Hayward, Asa F. Heely, Newton P. Howe, Anthony Ittner, Jesse Jennings, R. F. Johnson, T. H. Jones, Rufus D. Keeney, Oscar Kirkham, Milo S. Laughlin, Frank E. Lombar, J. M. Magner, James C. McGinnis, William H. McLane, G. W. L. Mitchell, Robert S. Moore, H. G. Mullings, Adolphus Munch, William N. Nalle, Thomas D. Neal, W. H. Norris, W. R. Pyle, C. R. Peck, James L. Powell, Joseph Pulitzer, J. M. Quigley, David C. Reed, John A. Rice, Constance Riek, J. P. Robertson, Samuel E. Roberts, Frederick Roever, L. A. Rountree, Ozias Ruark, F. T. Russell, Louis Schulenberg, Milton F. Simmons, Sam. L. Smith, James Southard, T. J. Stauber, Edmon Stinson, David K. Steele, L. A. Thompson, James S. Todd,

J. D. Vickers, B. J. Waters, Conrad Weinrich, Jacob Yankee, J. Morris Young, John C. Orrick, Speaker—86.

NAYS—Messrs. *James T. Adams, Emile P. Albert, W. H. Bennett, Joseph Bogy, W. H. Bowles, S. A. Brown, John G. Burton, Thomas Byrns, D. S. Caldwell, R. A. Campbell, N. C. Claiborne, G. William Colley, T. G. Harris, Jesse Huffman, Garland Hurt, William Key, W. J. Knott, William T. Leeper, F. L. Marchand, Andrew McElvain, John M. McMichael, C. J. Miller, John P. Murphy, Sidney S. Neely, M. H. Phelan, Amos R. Phillips, James H. Requa, Lucien Salisbury, John Salyer, Edwin S. Sebastian, Marion Sides, George D. Sloan, Robert Waide, Theodore F. Warner*—34.

### Nebraska.

SENATE, *February* 17, 1870.

YEAS—Messrs. Tolbert Ashton, E. E. Cunningham, William Daily, Geo. W. Frost, Samuel A. Fulton, Charles H. Gere, William F. Goodwill, Hiram D. Hathaway, Nathan S. Porter, Eugene L. Reed, Thomas B. Stevenson, Edward B. Taylor—12.

NAYS—Mr. *Guy C. Barnum*—1.

HOUSE OF REPRESENTATIVES, *February* 17, 1870.

YEAS—Messrs. Wells Brewer, Sardius C. Brewster, Jarvis C. Church, Samuel Carter, Jonathan Edwards, James Fitchie, Joseph Fox, J. F. Gardner, Joel T. Griffin, J. McF. Hagood, P C. Jones, Edwin Loveland, A. F. McCartney, David McCaig, Joseph McKeon, H. O. Minick, Daniel S. Parmelee, Watson Parish, L. W. Pattison, Christian Rathman, Hinman Rhodes, F. R. Roper, Geo. L. Seybolt, Geo. R. Shook, Henry Stinemann, A. S. Stewart, W. H. B. Stout, J. W. Talbot, Ezra Tullis, Anton Zimmerrer, William McLennan, Speaker—31.

NAYS—Messrs. *Marcus Brush, J. S. Hunt, C. A. Leary, C. A. Speice*—4.

### New Hampshire.*

SENATE, *July* 1, 1869.

The resolution ratifying the amendment was adopted without a division, there being eleven Senators in the body, as follow:

John H. Bailey, Nathaniel Gordon, Joseph F. Kennard, John Y. Mugridge, George C. Peavey, Ezra Gould, Gilman Scripture, *Jonas Livingston,* Ellery Albee, Ira Colby, jr., *John W. Barney.*

### New Jersey.

SENATE, *February* 7, 1870.

YEAS—Messrs. Jesse Adams, John C. Belden, Edward Bettle, George T. Cobb, Samuel Hopkins, James H. Nixon, John W. Taylor, John Torrey, jr.—8.

NAYS—Messrs. *Edward H. Bird, Joseph G. Bowne, James J. Brinkerhoff, Calvin Corle, Richard E. Edsall, Job H. Gaskill, John Hopper, Henry S. Little, Learning Rice, Amos Robins* (President,) *Noah D. Taylor, James T. Wiley, John Woolverton*—13.

HOUSE OF ASSEMBLY, *February* 1, 1870.

YEAS—Messrs. Thomas C. Alcott, William H.

---

*The former vote, on p. 494, Manual of 1869, was void through informality.

* For vote in House, see p. 494, Manual of 1869.

Barton, Columbus Beach, Thomas Beesley, Henry L. Bonsall, Albert M. Bradshaw, Albert A. Drake, David Evans, Charles F. H. Gray, C. P. Gurnee, James L. Gurney, Leonard F. Harding, William A. House, John Hunkele, Levi D. Jarrard, Farrand Kitchell, James C. Norris, Benjamin H. Overheiser, Theodore W. Phœnix, Albert L. Runyon, Joseph F. Sanxay, William R. Sayre, William C. Shinn, Abel I. Smith, John R. Staats, Henry W. Wilson, Nimrod Woolery—27.

NAYS—Messrs. *Leon Abbett, James W. Arrowsmith, S. B. Beraus, Ferdinand Blauck, William Brinkerhoff, George E. Brown, Herman D. Busch, Hiram C. Clark, James B. Doremus, Levi French, Charles O. Groscup, William W. Hawkins, Henry Hobbs, Henry A. Hopper, Charles O. Hudnut, Samuel H. Hunt, John Kugler, John P. Lair, John J. Maxwell, Mathew Murphy, Austin H. Patterson, Abraham Perkins, Theodore Probasco, Absalom B. Purcell, Hugh Reid, Jesse M. Sharp, William Silverthorn, Caleb H. Valentine, D. H. Van Mater, Samuel Whartman, Chauncey G. Williams, and Eben Winton*—32.

### Rhode Island.

HOUSE OF REPRESENTATIVES,* *January* 18, 1870.

YEAS—Mr. Speaker Benj. T. Eames, Messrs. William T. Adams, Edwin Aldrich, William D. Aldrich, Ferdinand H. Allen, *Emor J. Angell*, Lucius C. Ashley, Julius Baker, John H. Barden, William W. Blodgett, Baylies Bourne, Francis Brinley, Joseph F. Brown, Henry Bull, jr., John T. Bush, Ezra J. Cady, Thomas G. Carr, John G. Childs, J. Hamilton Clarke, William H. Clarke, James C. Collins, Davis Cook, jr., Saladin Cook, Edwin Darling, Daniel E. Day, Henry F. Drown, Edward L. Freeman, Henry T. Grant, George W. Greene, Richard W. Green, Mason W. Hale, David S. Harris, Stephen Harris, William S. Kent, Robert R. Knowles, William. Knowles, George W. Lewis, Nathan B. Lewis, John Loveland, Jesse Metcalf, *Francis W. Miner*, Arlon Mowry, Jabez W. Mowry, George H. Olney, *Samuel B. Parker*, Charles H. Perkins, DeWitt C. Remington, William H. Seagrave, Ira O. Seamans, William P. Sheffield, Orrin W. Simmons, George T. Spicer, *Joseph E. Spink*, Horatio A. Stone, Albert M. Waite, William R. Walker, John E. Weeden, Joseph D. Wilcox, James M. Wright—59.

NAYS—Messrs. *George N. Bliss*, Theodore P. Bogert, *Raymond P. Colwell*, Nathaniel B. Durfee, *Edward Lillibridge*, John C. Pegram, *William C. Rhodes, Samuel Rodman, jr.*, Nathaniel C. Smith, *Nathan T. Verry*—10.

### Tennessee.

SENATE, *November* 24, 1869.

The resolution ratifying the amendment was referred to the Committee on Federal Relations, from which it has never been reported.

HOUSE OF REPRESENTATIVES,† *November* 16, 1869.

YEAS—Messrs. J. H. Agee, Baker, Boyd, Eckel, Hunley, Layman, McConnell, McElwee, Scott, Singletary, Snodderly, and Yoakum—12.

* Question postponed from May, 1869, as shown on p. 487 Manual of 1869.
† The full names are not given here on account of inability to obtain them.

NAYS—Messrs. *Baber, Barry, Barton, Boyett, Bright, Caldwell, Cheatham, Clark* of Jackson, *Colville, Cox, Curl, Dunlap, Everett, Fleming, Glenn, Hampton, Harrison, Hinkle, Hornberger, James* of Hamilton, *James* of Smith, *Jones, Keeney, Kelley, Kenney, King, Knight, Longacre, McGaughey, Morrison, Neil, Nicks, Nixon, Pearson, Rhea, Roach, Rose, Rosson, Russell* of Rutherford, *Saddler, Saunders, Sherrod, Slack, Smith, Spears, Steale, Stephens, Thomas, Towsand, Tucker, Walker, Warren, West, White, Wilson, Young*, and Mr. Speaker *Pearkins*—57.

### Texas.

SENATE, *February* 18, 1870.

YEAS—Messrs. E. L. Alford, Thomas H. Baker, John G. Bell, *W. H. Bowers, E. T. Braughton*, Don Campbell, *D. W. Cole, E. L. Dohoney, J. P.* Douglass, W. Flanagan, S. W. Ford, A. K. Foster, A. J. Fountain, Matt. Gaines, P. W. Hall, Theodore Hertzberg, *H. R. Latimer*, J. S. Mills, W. H. Parsons, B. J. Pridgen, *E. L. Pyle*, Henry Rawson, G. T. Ruby, W. A. Saylor—24.

NAYS—Messrs. *Samuel Evans, G. R. Shannon*—2.

HOUSE OF REPRESENTATIVES, *February* 15, 1870.

YEAS—Messrs. J. O. Austin, J. A. Abney, C. L. Abbott, M. L. Armstrong, H. R. Allen, R. A. Allen, J. Abbott, J. D. Burnett, *E. J. Becton*, J. P. Butler, D. W. Burley, *T. J. Chambers*, L. W. Cooper, S. Cotton, *J. R. Cole*, L. B. Camp, A. M. Cox, G. Dupree, W. W. Davis, A. Dorris, T. G. Franks, C. W. Gardner, F. E. Grothaus, C. T. D. Harn, J. P. Hill, J. J. Hamilton, G. T. Haswell, *J. E. Hawkins*, J. W. Johnson, *C. Jenkins*, M. Kendal, *John W. Lane, A. F. Leonard*, W. J. Locke, M. Manning, J. H. Morrison, H. Moore, *W. P. McLean, J. R. McKee*, J. F. McKee, S. Mullins, D. Medlock, R. L. Moore, *J. W. Posey*, W. C. Pierson, B. R. Plumly, W. Prissie, W. G. Robinson, F. Schleckum, G. H. Slaughter, W. H. Sinclair, W. Sherriff, *W. B. Stirman, E. L. Smith*, C. J. Stockbridge, *B. S. Shelburn*, J. Schutze, F. Tegner, *S. S. Weaver*, B. F. Williams, H. W. Young, J. B. York, H. C. Youngkin, R. Zapp, and A. Zoller—65.

NAYS—Messrs. *S. J. Adams, H. C. Ellis, W. A. Gaston, W. E. Hughes, F. Kyle, B. B. Lacy, J. H. Miller, E. L. Robb, T. E. Ross, J. G. Smith*—10.

### Vermont.

SENATE, *October* 20, 1869.

YEAS—Messrs. Grenville G. Benedict, Asa R. Camp, William Collamer, Lucius Copeland, George N. Dale, Albert G. Dewey of Windsor, Jerry E. Dickerman, William G. Elkins, Roswell Farnham, David Goodell, Ezra B. Green, A. B. Halbert, Harley M. Hall, J. H. Hastings, Charles H. Heath, William R. Hutchinson, James Hutchinson, jr., Rollin J. Jones, Jedd P. Ladd, George A. Merrill, William P. Nash, Franklin H. Orvis, William M. Pingry, Homer E. Royce, Robert J. Saxe, Hoyt H. Wheeler—26.

NAYS—0.

HOUSE OF REPRESENTATIVES, *October* 19, 1869.

YEAS—Messrs. David C. Abbott, Stephen Alden, Andrew S. Allis, Joseph Andrew, Lyman

Batcheller, John Bailey, jr., Frederick H. Baldwin, George A. Ballard, J. Warren Barnes, Fayette Barney, George Barrett of Weathersfield, Jonas R. Bartlett, William H. Bebee, Julius B. Benedict, George Benton, John Bigelow, Lewis H. Bisbee, Saul Bishop, George O. Boyce. Caleb R. Brewer, George B. Brewster, Sumner Briggs, Asa Brigham, Charles W. Brigham, Jerome B. Bromley, Ebenezer B. Brown, William C. Brown, Horatio N Bull, Oscar E Butterfield, James Cardell, Hiram Carleton, Benjamin F. D. Carpenter, Charles Chamberlin, Charles Chase, T. Abel Chase, Howard Clark, Nathan S. Clark, Jason Clark, Lewis Cobb, James A. Coburn, Mason S. Colburn, Chauncey H. Conkey, David Cook, Edwin S. Cook, Seth F. Cowles, Sumner Curtis, Ezra F. Darling, Leonard W. Day, William Deming, Asa M. Dickey, Jonathan B. Dike, Josiah B. Divoll, Chester B. Dow, William P. Downing, Stephen L Dutton, Frederick P. Eaton, Alanson Edgerton, Ezra Edson, Jacob Estey, Edson Farman, Jona B Farnsworth, John Farrar, Joseph C. Fenn, James K. Foster, George P. Foster, Ezra S. Freeman, Barnes Frisbie, John H. Gambell, Nelson Gay, David N. Gibb, George Giffin, jr., Philip K. Gleed, William Goff, George Goodell, George S. Goodrich, Henry H. Goodsell, Marcus D. Grover, Emerson Hall. Josiah L. Hamblet, John O. Hamilton, Samuel Harrington, Royal D. Hedden, Rufus N. Hemenway, Charles Hewitt, Ansel L. Hill, Calvin Hill, Lyman G. Hinckley, Charles B. Holden, William C. Holman, Benjamin A. Holmes, Lyman W. Holmes of Waterville, Joel Holton, Orman P. Hooker, Heman Hopkins, jr., John P. Hoskison, A. S. Howard, Asahel H. Hubbard, Julius A. Humphrey, Samuel S Hunt of Guilford, Loyal Huntington, Elisha B. Hurd, Luther H. Hurlburt, John V. S. Isham, Lyman Jackson, Andrew Jackson, Samuel R Jenkins, Elias L. Jewett, John Johnson, William Johnson, Charles H. Joyce, George B. Keeler, Phineas A. Kemp, Isaac K. Kenaston, Silas G. King, Aaron N. King, Harvey N. Kingsbury, John Kinsley, Alfred H. Knapp, Willard Kneeland, Melvin A. Knowlton, Charles I. Ladd, James R. Langdon, Jabez W. Langdon, Martin Leonard, Joseph P. Long, Joel Lyman, Isaac A. Manning, Augustus M. Marsh, John L. Mason, Nathaniel C McKnight, Gardner Merrill, Timothy C. Miles, Ephraim Moore, Ira A. Morse, Lucius P. Mowry, Isaac J. Nichols, Luther A. Nichols, Joseph Nickerson, Julius N North, George N. Ober, Frank E. Ormsby, Carrol S. Page, —— Paine, Harry B. Parker, James Parker, Daniel P. Peabody, Francis Phelps, Horatio S. Pierce, Milo Pierce, Joseph H. Pratt, Joseph Purmort, Marcus S Reed, Philemon Remington, Edward J. Reynolds, Jotham S. Rice, Lorenzo Richmond, Jesse J. Ridley, Henry B. Ripley, Oscar P. Rixford, Abraham R. Ross, Noah B. Safford, Charles A. Scott, George Severance, William H. Silsby, Isaac M. Smith, Oliver Smith, Homer H. Southwick, Eugene H. Spaulding, Marshal W, Stoddard, Alpheus H. Stone, Cyrus W. Strong, Andrew J. Taylor, Albin L. Thompson, Joseph Underwood, Asahel Upham, Torrey E. Wales, William W. Walker, Henry A. Walker, George B. Warner, Edwin W. Washburn, Frederick A. Way, Walter A. Weed, Merrick Wentworth, Farwell Wetherby, Samuel E. Wheat, Eugene P. Wheeler, Joseph W. Wheelock, Edwin C. White, James E. White, Erastus Whitney, John Willey,

Henry B. Williams, Horace G. Wood, Albert Worcester, Pliney Wright, George W. Grandey, Speaker—196.

NAYS—Messrs. *G. W. Aiken, Patrick Barrett, Josiah F. Brigham, Almon L. Clark, Channing Hazeltine, Rollin W. Holbrook, Abial C. Palmer, Fred. Parks, James M. Peak, Thomas Pollard, James M. Soule, George Wooster* of Marshfield—12.

---

### Virginia.

#### SENATE, *October* 8, 1869.

YEAS—Messrs. *Abner Anderson, William A. Anderson,* William P. Austin, *R. S. Beazley,* J. W. D. Bland, *Charles Campbell,* David G. Carr, *A. R. Courtney, A. M. Davis, Thomas P. Fitzpatrick, James Milton French, James S. Greever, D. A. Grimsley, Marcus A. Harris,* F. W. Haskell, *Charles Herndon, George H. Kindrick, T. N. Latham, Meriwether Lewis,* William T. Martin, E. W. Massie, William P. Moseley, Frank Moss, *Robert L. Owen, James Patterson, W. K. Perrin, John E. Penn, Washington L. Riddick,* John Robinson, *John E. Roller,* J. Ambler Smith, *Normand Smith, William D. Smith, Edgar Snowden, jr., Thomas E. Taylor, W. H. Taylor,* George Teamoh, *William R. Terry, Joseph Waddell,* Franklin Wood—40.

NAYS—Messrs. *Abel T. Johnson,* Isaiah L. Lyons—2.

#### HOUSE OF REPRESENTATIVES, *October* 8, 1869.

YEAS—Messrs. William H. Andrews, *W. W. Arnett, John W. Ashby, George R. Atkinson, Jacob S. Atlee, Edmund R. Bagwell,* William Bartlett, *Henry Bell, H. M. Bell, Augustus Bodeker, Stith Bolling, Henry Bowen,* Henry M. Bowden, *Philo Bradley, Cary Breckinridge,* William H. Brisby, *L. C. Bristow, Lewis H. Bryant, William A. Bryant, Isaac D. Budd,* John W. Bullman, *Richard U. Burgess, Robert C. Burkholder, Josiah L. Campbell, J. T. Chase, M. H. Clark, A. B. Cochrane, Walter Coles,* Henry Cox, *John B. Crenshaw, John W. Daniel, Addison Davis,* S. M. Dodge, John Dugger, *Isaac Edmundson,* B. T. Edwards, George Fayerman, *L. H. Frayser,* A. N. Fretz, *J. H. Fulton, W. J. Fulton, George K. Gilman, T. H. Gosney, George Graham,* G. W. Graham, *George H. T. Greer, Marshall Hanger, Benjamin N. Hatcher, Job Hawxhurst, B. G. Haynie,* Henry B. *Hamsberger, J. C. Hill, James O. Hensley, John Henson,* C. E. Hodges, John Q. Hodges, *John M. Hudgin,* Thomas P. Jackson, *Reuben Johnson,* B. F. Jones, *James D. Jones,* R. G. W. Jones, *A. M. Keiley, James Keith,* John A. *Kelly, J. H. Kelly,* Luther Lee, jr., *Frank W. Lindsey,* James Lipscomb, *William Lovenstein,* F. W. *Mahood,* F. L. *Marshall,* Stephen Mason, *Joseph H. Massie, William Matthey, J. A. McCaull,* Bernard McCracken, *William McDonald, William McLaughlin, Robert A. Miller, David J. Miller,* J. B. Miller, jr., Peter G. Morgan, *Samuel B. Morrison, John R. Moss, Benjamin H. Moulton, Rufus A. Murrell,* J. H. Noble, F. S. Norton, Robert Norton, *Alexander Owen, David Pannill, Thomas C. Parramore, Robert O. Peatross,* Cæsar Perkins, F. M. *Perkins, Robert B. Poore, John R. Popham, W. A. J. Potts,* William H. Ragsdale, George L. Seaton, *Arthur S. Segar, Thomas M. Shearman, John H. A. Smith,* G. H. Southall, *S. V. Southall, J. C. Shelton,* L. R. Stewart, *John R. Strother,* Josiah Tattum, Wil-

liam F. B. Taylor, *John F. Terry, E. F. Tiller,*
James C. Toy, David Thayer, C. Y. Thomas, *John
R. Thurman, Smith S. Turner, George Walker,
James W. Walker, jr., William J. Wall,* John Wat-
son, Watson R. Wentworth, D. B. White, Ellis
Wilson, *William L. Williams, W. R. Winn, W. W.
Wood, B. L. Woodson,* A. L. Woodworth, *George
Young, Zeph. Turner,* Speaker—132.

NAYS—0.

## VOTES OF NEW YORK AND OHIO, THE FOR-MER ON RESCINDING A PREVIOUS RATIFI-CATION AND THE LATTER ON RATIFICA-TION AFTER A PREVIOUS REJECTION.*

### New York.

#### SENATE, *January* 5, 1870.

YEAS—Messrs. *A. Bleecker Banks, Isaiah Blood,
John T. Bradley, William Cauldwell, Thomas J.
Creamer, Samuel H. Frost, Henry W. Genet, Wil-
liam M. Graham, John F. Hubbard, jr., Jarv. Lord,
George Morgan, Henry C. Murphy, Christopher
F. Norton, Michael Norton, George H. Sanford,
William M. Tweed*—16.

NAYS—Messrs. George Bowen, William H.
Brand, Orlow W. Chapman, Augustus R. Elwood,
George N. Kennedy, Loren L. Lewis, Theodore
L. Minier, Abraham X. Parker, Allen D. Scott,
Francis S. Thayer, Norris Winslow, James Wood,
William B. Woodin—13.

#### ASSEMBLY, *January* 5, 1870,

YEAS—Messrs. *Seymour Ainsworth, Orson M.
Allaben, Francis B. Baldwin, George J. Bamler,
Gershon Bancker, Daniel D. Barnes, James G.
Bennett, William G. Bergen, John J. Blair,* John
Brown, Dennis Burns, *Timothy J. Campbell, John
Carey, Owen Cavanagh, Hugh M. Clark, Wil-
liam W. Cook, William C. Coon, Henry J. Cul-
len, jr., John Davis, Daniel G. Dodge, Joseph
Droll, John F. Empie,* John L. Flagg, *Richard
Flanagan, Patrick J. Flynn, Alexander Frear,
Isaiah Fuller, Abraham E. Hasbrouck, Odell S.
Hathaway, Bernard Haver, John R. Hennessey,
Morgan Horton,* Abraham Howe, James Irving,
*John C. Jacobs, St. Perrie Jerred, William C. Jones,
Lawrence D. Kiernan, Charles H. Krack, jr.,
John L. La Moree, Thomas J. Lanahan, Edward
D. Lawrence, Thomas J. Lyon, Godfrey R. Mar-
tine, Peter Mitchell, James J. Mooney, William
W. Moseley, Michael C. Murphy, Owen Murphy,
William D. Murphy, Martin Nachtmann, James
M. Nelson, Dennis O'Keeffe, Edward L. Patrick,
Lewis S. Payne, James B. Pearsall, George W.
Plunkitt, Harry B. Ransom, Edward D. Ronan,
James Shanahan, Brinley D. Sleight, William
W. Snow, Robert R. Steele, Edward Sturges, Silas
Sweet, John Tighe, Hiram Van Sturburgh, James
Young, William Hitchman,* Speaker—69.

NAYS—Messrs. Thomas G. Alvord, Isaac V.
Baker, jr., Matthew P. Bemus, John Berry, Al-
bert H. Blossom, Alpheus Bolt, William Brad-
ford, Samuel L. Brown, Volney P. Brown, Wil-
liam W. Butterfield, J. Thomas Davis, Clayton H.
De Lano, John H. Deming, Jay Dimick, William
H. Eaker, William M. Ely, Charles N. Flanagin,
Charles Foster, James Franklin, George M. Glea-
son, James S. Graham, Stephen S. Green, Amasa
Hall, Stephen S. Hewitt, Marcus A. Hull, James
W. Husted, Eugene Hyatt, Richard Johnson,
Leonard C. Kilham, De Witt C. Littlejohn, Sam-

uel S. Lowery, Samuel T. Maddox, T. Warren
Merchant, David M. Miner, David H. Mulford,
Daniel A. Northrop, Lyman Oatman, Julius M.
Palmer, John Parker, *Jay A. Pease,* James H.
Pierce, Henry Ray, William T. Remer, James
Roberts, Lee R. Sanborn, James A. Seward, Gus-
tavus Sniper, Thomas Stevenson, Nathan R.
Tefft, Edward C. Walker, George N. West, John
H. White, David E. Wilson, Orange S. Winans,
Anson S. Wood, Charles S. Wright—56.

### Ohio.

#### SENATE, *January* 14, 1870.

YEAS—Messrs. John Bartram, James A. Bell,
Abel M. Corey, Jerry Dunbar, Homer Everett,
Moses D. Gatch, Michael Goepper, A. P. Howard,
Homer C. Jones, Henry McKinney, Peter Odlin,
Benjamin F. Potts, Joseph M. Root, Rodney M.
Stimson, Worthy S. Streator, Deciers S. Wade,
Thomas A. Welsh, Laurin D. Woodworth, Thomas
H. Yeatman—19.

NAYS—Messrs. *James O Amos, Charles Boe-
sel, James M. Burt, Lewis D. Campbell, John
Cowan, M. A. Daugherty, James Emmitt, Samuel
T. Hunt, Adin G. Hibbs, William H. Holden,
James R. Hubbell, James B. Jamison, A. E. Jen-
ner, L. B. Leeds, Nathan C. Lord, Hinchman S.
Prophet, John L. Winner, John Woodbridge*—18.

#### HOUSE OF REPRESENTATIVES, *January* 20, 1870.

YEAS—Messrs William Adair, R. W. Anderson,
Bethel Bates, H. M. Bates, M. W. Beach, S. E.
Blakeslee, E. Bogardus, A. H. Brown, Samuel
C. Bowman, James Bradbury, George W. Brooke,
John A. Brown, R. P. Cannon, A. J. Cunning-
ham, H. W. Curtiss, R. B. Dennis, Joseph H.
Dickson, William H. Enochs, Ed. H. Fitch,
Samuel H. Ford, Robert C. Fulton, Thomas
Geffs, Elijah Glover, Wilson W. Griffith, Samuel
Hayward, A. Hill, B. L. Hill, George H. Hill,
Peter Hitchcock, George A. Hubbard, William
N. Hudson, Ellis N. Johnson, jr., Thomas F.
Joy, E. F. Kleinschmidt, A. P. Lacey, John Lit-
tle, J. K. Mower, A. Munson, W. O. Parker,
William Park, John A. Price, William Ritezel,
James Sayler, R. M. Stanton, George W. Steele,
James A. Sterling, Jarnin Strong, jr., Samuel N.
Titus, J. C. Ullery, N. H. Van Vorhees, M. J.
Williams, William S. Williams, John P. Wil-
liamson, William W. Wilson, J. K. Wing, Alfred
Wolcott, G. I. Young—57.

NAYS—Messrs. *William T. Acker, William
Armstrong, Isaac Anstill, R. P. L. Baber, George
S. Baker, John Baker, Edward Ball, John Bet-
telon, Daniel J. Callen, William T. Cessna, Joseph
R. Cockerill, James E. Chase, Levi Colby, Wil-
liam T. Conkling, Thomas A. Corcoran, James
W. Devose, Ozro J. Dodds, Elias Ellis, E. H.
Gaston, Lewis Green, Thomas I. Haldeman,
James H. Hambleton, S. M. Heller, John L.
Hughes, John D. Kemp, A. C. Kile, John Kisor,
Jesse Leohner, John K. Love, John G. Marshall,
Jason McVey, William Milligan, Samuel R. Mott,
jr., William Pace, Thomas W. Peckinpaugh,
Michael V. Ream, James Robinson, Henry
Schirck, Henry Schoenfeldt, John Seitz, Aaron B.
Shafer, William Shaw, Lewis W. Sifford, Gar-
ret B. Smith, A. Soule, E. T. Stickney, W. Still-
well, John D. Thompson, E. M. Walker, A. Ward,
John A. Weyer, Clark White, John C. Waldron,
William R. Wilson, Hiram W. Winslow*—55.

---

# LIV

# LAND SUBSIDIES, 1827–1870.

## Grant to tne State of Indiana in aid of the Wabash and Erie Canal.

The first grant of public lands for the purpose of aiding internal improvements was made to the State of Indiana for the Wabash and Erie canal, in 1827, by an act entitled "An act to grant a certain quantity of land to the State of Indiana for the purpose of aiding said State in opening a canal to connect the waters of the Wabash river with those of Lake Erie."*

It provides: "That there be, and hereby is, granted to the State of Indiana, for the purpose of aiding the said State in opening a canal to unite at navigable points the waters of the Wabash river with those of Lake Erie, a quantity of land equal to one-half of five sections in width on each side of said canal, and reserving each alternate section to the United States, to be selected by the Commissioner of the Land Office, under the direction of the President of the United States, from one end thereof to the other; and the said lands shall be subject to the disposal of the Legislature of said State for the purpose aforesaid, and no other: *Provided*, That the said canal, when completed, shall be and forever remain a public highway for the use of the Government of the United States, free from any toll or other charge whatever, for any property of the United States, or persons in their service, passing through the same: *Provided*, That said canal shall be commenced within five years, and completed in twenty years, or the State shall be bound to pay to the United States the amount of any lands previously sold, and that the title to purchasers under the State shall be valid."

This act granted to the State of Indiana 1,439,-279 acres.† The bill was reported from the Committee on Roads and Canals by William Hendricks, of Indiana, and passed both Houses by the following vote (politics not indicated):

IN SENATE, *February* 13, 1827.

YEAS—Messrs. David Barton, Ephraim Bateman, Samuel Bell, Thomas H. Benton, Dominique Bouligny, Ezekiel F. Chambers, Dudley Chase, John H. Eaton, William Henry Harrison, William Hendricks, John Holmes, Richard M. Johnson, Josiah S. Johnston, Elias K. Kane, William Rufus King, Nehemiah R. Knight, John McKinley, William Marks, James Noble, Thomas B. Reed, Henry M. Ridgely, Asher Robbins, Benjamin Ruggles, Horatio Seymour, Nathaniel Silsbee, Samuel Smith, Jesse B. Thomas, Calvin Willey—28.

NAYS—Messrs. John Branch, John Chandler, Thomas Clayton, Thomas W. Cobb, Mahlon Dickerson, Henry W. Edwards, William Findlay, Robert Y. Hayne, Nathaniel Macon, John Randolph, Nathan Sanford, William Smith, Littleton W. Tazewell, Levi Woodbury—14.

IN HOUSE OF REPRESENTATIVES, *March* 2, 1827.

The bill passed without a division, the yeas and nays having just before been taken on a precisely similar proposition, granting lands to aid in the construction of a canal between the Illinois river and Lake Michigan, which vote was as follows:

YEAS—Messrs. Parmenio Adams, Adam R. Alexander, Luther Badger, Mordecai Bartley, John Barney, Ratliff Boon, William L. Brent, Richard A. Buckner, John W. Campbell, James Clark, Lewis Condict, Benjamin W. Crowninshield, Clement Dorsey, Henry W. Dwight, Samuel Edwards, Edward Everett, John Findlay, James Findlay, Chauncey Forward, Henry H. Gurley, Abraham B. Hasbrouck, Moses Hayden, John F. Henry, Ebenezer Herrick, George Holcombe, Samuel Houston, Daniel Hugunin, jr., Charles Humphrey, Ralph J. Ingersoll, Jacob C. Isacks, Jonathan Jennings, Joseph Johnson, Francis Johnson, Samuel Lathrop, Joseph Lawrence, Joseph Lecompte, Robert P. Letcher, Peter Little, John Lock, Rollin C. Mallary, John H. Marable. Henry C. Martindale, Dudley Marvin, Robert McHatton, Samuel McKean, William McLean, Ezra Meech, Charles F. Mercer, Orange Merwin, Thomas Metcalf, John Miller, James S. Mitchell, John Mitchell, George E. Mitchell, James C. Mitchell, Thomas P. Moore, Thomas Newton, George W. Owen, George Peter, Timothy H. Porter, Alfred H. Powell, John Reed, Robert S. Rose, Henry H. Ross, Joshua Sands, John Scott, Thomas Shannon, Thomas H. Sill, John Sloane, Andrew Stewart, James Strong, Samuel Swan, John Test, Gideon Tomlinson, David Trimble, Ebenezer Tucker, Joseph Vance, Samuel F. Vinton, George E. Wales, Aaron Ward, Daniel Webster, John C. Weems, Thomas Whipple, jr., Barton White, Elisha Whittlesey, Charles A. Wickliffe, James Wilson, John Woods, John C. Wright, William S. Young—90.

NAYS—Messrs. William Addams, Mark Alexander, Willis Alston, William G. Angel, Henry Ashley, John Bailey, John Baldwin, Ichabod Bartlett, Noyes Barber, John S Barbour, Francis Baylies, John Blair, Titus Brown, Joseph H. Bryan, James Buchanan, William Burleigh, Samuel P. Carson, George Cary, Nathaniel H. Claiborne, John Cocke, Henry W. Conner, George W. Crump, Thomas Davenport, William Deitz, William Drayton, Nehemiah Eastman, John Forsyth, Andrew R. Govan, Robert Harris, Jonathan Harvey, Charles E. Haynes, Richard Hines, Aaron Hobart, Michael Hoffman, Jeromus Johnson, David Kidder, Thomas Kittera, Jacob Krebs, Edward Livingston, John Long, William McCoy, George McDuffie, William McManus, James Merriwether, Daniel H. Miller, Charles Miner, Jeremiah O'Brien, Robert Orr, Elisha Phelps. George Plumer, James K. Polk, James W. Ripley, William C. Rives, Lemuel Sawyer, James S. Stevenson, John Taliaferro, Starling Tucker, John Varnum, Gulian C. Verplanck, Elias Whittemore, Lewis Williams, John Wilson, George Wolf, Silas Wood, John Wurts—67.

It was then signed by the President, John Quincy Adams, on the same day.

## Grant to the State of Illinois in aid of the Illinois Central Railroad.

The first grant of public lands in aid of the construction of railroads was that made by "An act granting the right of way and making a grant of land to the States of Illinois, Mississippi, and Alabama, in aid of the construction of a railroad from Chicago to Mobile," in 1850.*

This act provided (sec. 2) "That there be, and is hereby granted to the State of Illinois, for the purpose of aiding in making the railroad and branches aforesaid, every alternate section of land designated by even numbers, for six sections in width on each side of said road and branches." It also provided, that in case any of the land so

---

*4 U. S. Stats., p. 236.   † Rep. Com. Land Office 1867, p. 257.

*9 U. S. Stats., p. 466.

granted should have been sold, or the right of pre-emption should have attached, before the line of the road was definitely ascertained, agents appointed by the Governor of Illinois should select other lands; none of such lands, however, to be farther than fifteen miles from the line of the road."

Sec. 3 provided that the land which shall remain "to the United States within six miles on each side of said road and branches shall not be sold for less than double the minimum price of the public lands."

Sec. 4 reserved the right to the United States to use the said road free from toll or other charge upon the transportation of any property or troops of the United States.

Sec. 7 extended the provisions of the act to the States of Alabama and Mississippi to aid in the continuation of the Central railroad from the mouth of the Ohio river to Mobile.

The estimated amount of land inuring under this grant was 2,595,053 acres,* all of which has been certified.

The bill was introduced by Stephen A. Douglas, of Illinois, reported from the Committee of Public Lands by Mr. Shields, of Illinois, and passed both houses by the following vote:

### In Senate, *May* 2, 1850.

YEAS†—Messrs. *David R. Atchison,* George E. Badger, John Bell, *Thomas H. Benton. Solon Borland, Jesse D. Bright, Lewis Cass,* Thomas Corwin, *Jefferson Davis, Henry Dodge, Augustus C. Dodge, Stephen A. Douglas, Solomon U. Downs, Henry S. Foote. Samuel Houston, George W. Jones,* William Rufus King, Willie P. Mangum, Jackson Morton, *William K. Sebastian,* William H Seward, *James Shields,* Truman Smith, *Daniel Sturgeon,* Joseph R. Underwood, *Isaac P. Walker*—26.

NAYS—Messrs. *James W. Bradbury, Andrew P. Butler,* SALMON P. CHASE, John H. Clarke. William C. Dawson, William L. Dayton, *Robert M. T. Hunter,* Jacob W. Miller, *Moses Norris, jr.,* Samuel S. Phelps. *Thomas G. Pratt,* Hopkins L. Turney, John Wales, *David L. Yulee*—14.

NOT VOTING—Messrs Roger S. Baldwin. John McP. Berrien, *John C. Calhoun,* Henry Clay, *Jere. Clemens,* James Cooper, John Davis, *Daniel S. Dickinson, Alpheus Felch,* Albert C. Greene, JOHN P. HALE, *Hannibal Hamlin, James M. Mason,* James A. Pearce, *Thomas J. Rusk, Pierre Soule, Presley Spruance,* William Upham, Daniel Webster, *James Whitcomb*—20.

Of those not voting Messrs. Greene and *Spruance* voted "aye" on the same proposition two years before, and Messrs. *Calhoun* and HALE voted "no."

### In House of Representatives, *Sept.* 17, 1850.

YEAS—Messrs. *Nathaniel Albertson,* CHARLES ALLEN, William J. Alston, Josiah M. Anderson, George R. Andrews, George Ashmun, Edward D. Baker, *Kingsley S. Bingham, William H Bissell,* David A. Bokee, *Franklin W. Bowden,* Richard I. Bowie, *James B. Bowlin,* George Briggs, James Brooks, *Albert G. Brown, William J. Brown, Alexander W. Buel.* Lorenzo Burrows, Thomas B. Butler, E. Carrington Cabell, Samuel Calvin, Joseph Casey, Joseph R. Chandler, *Chauncey F. Cleveland,* Thomas L. Clingman, *Williamson R. W. Cobb,* Orsamus Cole, Moses B. Corwin, John Crowell, *James Duane Doty,* James H. Duncan, *Cyrus L. Dunham,* CHARLES DURKEE, Samuel A. Eliot, *Winfield S. Featherston,* John Freedley, Meredith P. Gentry, Edward Gilbert, *Willis A. Gorman,* Daniel Gott, Herman D. Gould, *James S. Green.* Joseph Grinnell, *Willard P. Hall,* Ransom Halloway, *Andrew J. Harlan, Sampson W. Harris,* Thomas L. Harris, Andrew K. Hay, Thomas S. Haymond, *Moses Hoagland,* Volney E. Howard, David Hubbard, *Samuel W Inge,* Joseph W. Jackson, *Robert W. Johnson,* GEORGE W. JULIAN, *David S. Kaufman,* James G. King, John A. King, *Emile La Sere, Shepherd Leffler,* Horace

---

*Rep. Com. Land Office 1867, p. 253.

†Democrats in *italics,* Whigs in roman, Freesoilers in SMALL CAPS.

---

Mann, Orsamus B. Matteson, *John A. McClernand, Robert M. McLane, William McWillie,* Charles S. Morehead, *Isaac E. Morse.* James L. Orr, John Otis, *John S. Phelps,* J. Phillips Phœnix, Charles W. Pitman, Harvey Putnam, *William A. Richardson,* Elijah Risley, *John L. Robinson.* Robert L. Rose, Abraham M. Schermerhorn, John L. Schoolcraft, Elbridge G. Spaulding, William Sprague, Edward Stanley, *Frederick P. Stanton, Richard H. Stanton,* Alexander H. Stephens, John L. Taylor, *Jacob Thompson,* John R. Thurman, Walter Underhill, *Hiram Walden, Loren P. Waldo, John Wentworth,* Hugh White, *William A. Whittlesey,* Christopher H. Williams, *Amos E. Wood,* George W. Wright, *Timothy R. Young.*—101.

NAYS—Messrs. Henry P. Alexander, *William S. Ashe, Thomas H. Averett. James M. H. Beale,* WALTER BOOTHE, *Armistead Burt, Joseph Cable,* Joseph P. Caldwell, Lewis D. Campbell, *David K. Cartter,* Charles E. Clarke, *William F. Colcock,* Jesse C. Dickey, *Milo M. Dimmick, David T. Disney,* Nathan F. Dixon, William Duer, *Henry A. Edmundson.* Alexander Evans, Nathan Evans, Orin Fowler. *Thomas J. D. Fuller. Elbridge Gerry, Alfred Gilmore, William T. Hamilton,* Moses Hampton, *Hugh A. Haralson, Isham G. Harris. Harry Hibbard, Alexander R. Holladay,* JOHN W. HOWE, William F. Hunter, William T. Jackson, *Andrew Johnson, George W. Jones,* John B. Kerr. George G. King, PRESTON KING, *Nathaniel S. Littlefield, Job Mann,* Humphrey Marshall, *James McDowell,* Edward W. McGaughey, Thomas McKissock, *James X. McLanahan, Fayette McMullen, John McQueen, John K. Miller, John S. Millson,* Henry D. Moore, *Jonathan D. Morris.* William Nelson, David Outlaw, *Richard Parker,* Charles H. Peaslee, *Emery D. Potter,* Robert R. Reed, *John Robbins, jr., Thomas Ross,* David Rumsey, jr., *John H. Savage, Cullen Sawtelle,* Robert C. Schenck, *James A. Seddon,* Augustine H. Shepperd, Thaddeus Stevens, *Charles Stetson, James H. Thomas, James Thompson, Abraham W. Venable,* Samuel F. Vinton, *Daniel Wallace,* Albert G. Watkins, *Isaac Wildrick,* Joseph A. Woodward.—75.

The bill was signed by the President, Zachary Taylor, September 20, 1850.

---

### Grant to the Union Pacific Railroad Company.

The first grant of lands made to any corporation to aid it in building its railroad was to the Union Pacific Railroad, in 1862, by an act entitled "An act to aid in the construction of a railroad and telegraph line from the Missouri river to the Pacific ocean, and to secure to the Government the use of the same for postal, military, and other purposes."

Section 1 creates the corporation and provides regulations for its government.

Section 2 provides "That the right of way through the public lands be, and the same is hereby, granted to said company for the construction of said railroad and telegraph line; and the right, power, and authority is hereby given to said company to take from the public lands adjacent to the line of said road earth, stone, timber, and other materials for the construction thereof; said right of way is granted to said railroad to the extent of two hundred feet in width on each side of said railroad where it may pass over the public lands, including all necessary grounds for stations, buildings, workshops, and depots, machine-shops, switches, side tracks, turntables, and water stations. The United States shall extinguish as rapidly as may be the Indian titles to all lands falling under the operation of this act and required for the said right of way and grants hereinafter made."

Section 3 provides "That there be, and is hereby, granted to said company, for the purpose of aiding in the construction of said railroad and telegraph line, and to secure the safe and speedy transportation of the mails, troops, munitions of war, and public stores thereon, every alternate section of public land designated by odd numbers, to the amount of five alternate sections per mile on each side of said railroad, on the line thereof, and within the limits of ten miles on each side of said road, not sold, reserved, or otherwise disposed of by the United States, and to which a preëmption or homestead claim may not have attached at the time the line of said road is definitely fixed: *Provided*, That all mineral lands shall be excepted from the operation of this act; but where the same shall contain timber, the timber thereon is hereby granted to said company. And all such lands so granted by this section, which shall not be sold or disposed of by said company within three years after the entire road shall have been completed, shall be subject to settlement and preëmption, like other lands, at a price not exceeding one dollar and twenty-five cents per acre, to be paid to said company."

Section 5 authorizes the issue of bonds to the amount of $16,000 per mile, which shall constitute a first mortgage on the road.

Section 6 provides that all compensation for services rendered for the Government shall be applied to the payment of the bonds and interest, and that at least five per cent. of the net earnings of the road shall be applied annually to payment of the same.

Section 18 provides that when the net earnings of the road shall exceed ten per cent., exclusive of the five per cent. to be paid to the United States, Congress may reduce the rates of fare thereon.

It is estimated* that there inures to the Union Pacific Railroad Company, under this grant, 35,000,000 acres.

This act was reported in the House by Mr. Campbell, of Penn., from the Pacific Railroad Committee, and passed both Houses by the following vote:

IN HOUSE OF REPRESENTATIVES, *April* 8, 1862.†

YEAS—Messrs. Cyrus Aldrich, *William Allen*, John B. Alley, Isaac N. Arnold, James M. Ashley, Fernando C. Beaman, *Charles J Biddle*, John A Bingham, Francis P. Blair, jr., Harrison G. Blake, William G. Brown, James H. Campbell, Andrew J. Clements, Schuyler Colfax, Erastus Corning, John Covode, William P. Cutler, William Morris Davis, *Isaac C. Delaplaine*, R. Holland Duell, *George W. Dunlap*, Sidney Edgerton, Thomas D. Elliot, Alfred Ely, Reuben E. Fenton, Samuel C. Fessenden, George P. Fisher, Richard Franchot, Augustus Frank, Daniel W. Gooch, John N. Goodwin, Bradley F. Granger, John A. Gurley, *Edward Haight*, William A. Hall, Samuel Hooper, Valentine Horton, *John Hutchins*, George W. Julian, *William D. Kelley*, Francis W. Kellogg, John W. Killinger, William E. Lansing, Cornelius L. L. Leary, *William E. Lehman*, Dwight Loomis, *John W. Menzies*, James K. Moorehead, Anson P. Morrill, John T. Nixon, *John W. Noell, Elijah H. Norton*, Abraham B. Olin, Nehemiah Perry, Timothy G. Phelps, Thomas L. Price, Alexander H. Rice, Albert G. Riddle, *James S. Rollins*, Aaron A. Sargent, Charles B. Sedgwick, Samuel Shellabarger, *John B. Steele*, Thaddeus Stevens, Charles R. Train, Rowland E. Trowbridge, Burt Van Horn, John P. Verree, John W. Wallace, Charles W. Walton, *Elijah Ward*, Ellihu B. Washburne, *Edwin H. Webster*, William A. Wheeler, Kellian V. Whaley, James F. Wilson, William Windom, Samuel T. Worcester—79.

NAYS—Messrs. *Sydenham E. Ancona*, Elijah Babbitt, *Joseph Bailey*, Stephen Baker, Jacob B. Blair, George H. Browne, James Buffinton, *Charles B. Calvert*, Jacob P. Chamberlain, *George T. Cobb*, Frederick A. Conkling, *Samuel S. Cox*, James A. Cravens, John W. Crisfield, John

* Rep. Com. Land Office 1867, p. 255.
† This was the test vote, on the first passage of the bill in the House.

J. *Crittenden*, Alexander S. Diven, W. McKee Dunn, *James E. English, Henry Grider, Aaron Harding*, Richard A. Harrison, *Philip Johnson*, William Kellogg, *Anthony L. Knapp*, John Law, Owen Lovejoy, Robert McKnight, *Robert Mallory*, Justin S. Morrill, *James R. Morris, Warren P. Noble, Moses F. Odell*, Frederick A. Pike, Albert G. Porter, *William A. Richardson, James C. Robinson*, John P. C. Shanks, *William P. Sheffield*, William G. Steele, Benjamin F. Thomas, Francis Thomas, Carey A. Trimble, *Clement L. Vallandigham, Daniel W. Voorhees, William H. Wadsworth*, E. P. Walton, Albert S. White, *Charles A. Wickliffe, George C. Woodruff*—49.

IN SENATE, *June* 20, 1862.

YEAS—Messrs. Henry B. Anthony, Orville H. Browning, Zachariah Chandler, Daniel Clark, Jacob Collamer, Edgar Cowan, *Garrett Davis*, James Dixon, James R. Doolittle, Solomon Foot, Lafayette S. Foster, James W. Grimes, John P. Hale, James Harlan, Ira Harris, John B. Henderson, Jacob M. Howard, *Anthony Kennedy*, Henry S. Lane, James H. Lane, *Milton S. Latham*, Joseph A. McDougall, Lot M. Morrill, *George W. Nesmith*, Samuel C. Pomeroy. *Henry M. Rice*, John Sherman, *Benjamin Stark*, Charles Sumner, Lyman Trumbull, Benjamin F. Wade, Waitman T. Willey, David Wilmot, Henry Wilson, *Robert Wilson*—35.

NAYS—Messrs. Timothy O. Howe, Preston King, *James A. Pearce*, Morton S. Wilkinson, *Joseph A. Wright* —5.

---

## Grant to the Northern Pacific Railroad.

In 1864 an act was passed granting to the Northern Pacific railroad the right of way over the route proposed, and every alternate section, designated by odd numbers, to the amount of twenty alternate sections per mile, on each side of the road wherever the route lies through the Territories of the United States, and ten alternate sections per mile wherever the route lies through any State. It provided that no money should be drawn from the treasury of the United States to aid in the construction of the said road, and "that no mortgage or construction bonds shall ever be issued by said company on said road, or mortgage or lien made in any way, except by the consent of the Congress of the United States."

The route proposed was from a point on Lake Superior, in the State of Minnesota or Wisconsin, by the most eligible railroad route, within the territory of the United States, on a line north of the 45th degree of latitude, to some point on Puget's sound, with a branch, via the valley of the Columbia river, to a point at or near Portland, in Oregon, leaving the main trunk line at the most suitable place, not more than one hundred miles from its western terminus.

This bill passed both houses by the following vote:

IN HOUSE OF REPRESENTATIVES, *May* 31, 1864.

YEAS—Messrs. *James C. Allen*, William B. Allison, Lucien Anderson, *Augustus C. Baldwin*, John D. Baldwin, Fernando C. Beaman, James G. Blaine, Jacob B. Blair, Sempronius H. Boyd, John M. Broomall, *James S. Brown*, Amasa Cobb, *Alexander H. Coffroth*, Cornelius Cole, John A. J. Creswell, Henry Winter Davis, Ignatius Donnelly, John F. Driggs, *John R. Eden, Charles A. Eldridge*, John F. Farnsworth, Augustus Frank, James A. Garfield, Daniel W. Gooch, Josiah B. Grinnell, James T. Hale, *William A. Hall*, William Higby, Giles W. Hotchkiss, Asahel W. Hubbard, John H. Hubbard, William D. Kelley, Francis W. Kellogg, Orlando Kellogg, *Austin A. King, Anthony L. Knapp, Jesse Lazear*, Benjamin F. Loan, John W. Longyear, James M. Marvin, *Archibald McAllister*, Joseph W. McClurg, Daniel Morris, Leonard Myers, *Homer A. Nelson, Warren P. Noble, Moses F. Odell*, Charles O'Neill, James W. Patterson, Sidney Perham, Hiram Price, *John V. L. Pruyn*, William H. Randall, Alexander H. Rice, John H. Rice, Edward H. Rollins. *James S. Rollins, John G. Scott*, Thomas B. Shannon. Ithamar C. Sioan, *John E. Steele*, William G. Steele, Thaddeus Stevens, *Lorenzo D.*

*M. Sweat,* M. Russell Thayer, Charles Upson, *Daniel W. Voorhees, Elijah Ward,* William B. Washburn, Kellian V. Whaley, *Ezra Wheeler,* Thomas Williams, A. Carter Wilder, William Windom—74.

NAYS—Messrs. John B. Alley, *Sydenham E. Ancona,* Portus Baxter, *George Bliss,* James Brooks, John W. *Chanler, Samuel S. Cox,* James A. Cravens, *John L. Dawson, Charles Denison,* Ephraim R. Eckley, *Joseph K. Edgerton,* Thomas D. Eliot, Reuben E. Fenton, *William E. Finck,* John *Ganson,* Henry W. Harrington, Anson Herrick, *William S. Holman,* Calvin T. Hulburd, Ebon C. Ingersoll, *William Johnson, Martin Kalbfleisch, Francis Kernan, John Law. Francis C. LeBlond,* DeWitt C. Littlejohn, *Alexander Long, Robert Mallory, Daniel Marcy,* James F. McDowell, Justin S. Morrill, *William R. Morrison,* John O'Neill, Godlove S. Orth, *George H. Pendleton,* Frederick A. Pike, Theodore M. Pomeroy, *William Radford,* Lewis W. Ross, Robert C. Schenck, Glenni W. Scofield, Rufus P. Spalding, *John D. Stiles,* Henry W. Tracy, *William H. Wadsworth,* Ellihu B. Washburne, *Joseph W. White,* James F. Wilson, *Charles H. Winfield*—50.

In the Senate the bill passed without a division.

The estimated number of acres inuring under this grant is 47,000,000.

At the present session of Congress—the second session of the Forty-First Congress—the following act was passed:

A RESOLUTION authorizing the Northern Pacific Railroad Company to issue its bonds for the construction of its road and to secure the same by mortgage, and for other purposes.

*Resolved, &c.,* That the Northern Pacific Railroad Company be, and hereby is, authorized to issue its bonds to aid in the construction and equipment of its road, and to secure the same by mortgage on its property and rights of property of all kinds and descriptions, real, personal, and mixed, including its franchise as a corporation; and, as proof and notice of its legal execution and effectual delivery, said mortgage shall be filed and recorded in the office of the Secretary of the Interior; and also to locate and construct, under the provisions and with the privileges, grants, and duties provided for in its act of incorporation, its main road to some point on Puget sound, via the valley of the Columbia river, with the right to locate and construct its branch from some convenient point on its main trunk line across the Cascade mountains to Puget sound; and in the event of there not being in any State or Territory in which said main line or branch may be located, at the time of the final location thereof, the amount of lands per mile granted by Congress to said company, within the limits prescribed by its charter, then said company shall be entitled, under the directions of the Secretary of the Interior, to receive so many sections of land belonging to the United States, and designated by odd numbers, in such State or Territory, within ten miles on each side of said road beyond the limits prescribed in said charter, as will make up such deficiency, on said main line or branch, except mineral and other lands, as excepted in the charter of said company of 1864, to the amount of the lands that have been granted, sold, reserved, occupied by homestead settlers, pre-empted, or otherwise disposed of, subsequent to the passage of the act of July 2, 1864. And that twenty-five miles of said main line, between its western terminus and the city of Portland, in the State of Oregon, shall be completed by the 1st day of January, A. D. 1872,

and forty miles of the remaining portion thereof each year thereafter, until the whole shall be completed between said points: *Provided,* That all lands hereby granted to said company, which shall not be sold or disposed of or remain subject to the mortgage by this act authorized at the expiration of five years after the completion of the entire road, shall be subject to settlement and pre-emption, like other lands, at a price to be paid to said company not exceeding $2 50 per acre; and if the mortgage hereby authorized shall at any time be enforced by foreclosure or other legal proceeding, or the mortgaged lands hereby granted, or any of them, be sold by the trustees to whom such mortgage may be executed, either at its maturity or for any failure or default of said company under the terms thereof, such lands shall be sold at public sale, at places within the States and Territories in which they shall be situate, after not less than sixty days' previous notice, in single sections or subdivisions thereof, to the highest and best bidder: *Provided further,* That in the construction of the said railroad, American iron or steel only shall be used, the same to be manufactured from American ores exclusively.

SEC. 2. That Congress may at any time alter or amend this joint resolution, having due regard to the rights of said company and any other parties.

Approved, May 31, 1870.

The final vote on this bill was as follows:

IN SENATE, *April* 21, 1870.

YEAS—Messrs. Ames, Anthony, Brownlow, Buckingham, Cameron, Chandler, Cole, Corbett, Cragin, Fenton, Ferry, Flanagan, Hamilton of Texas. Hamlin, Harris, Howard, Howe, Kellogg, McDonald, Morrill of Maine, Morrill of Vermont, Norton, Nye, Osborn, Patterson, Pomeroy, Ramsey, Revels, Rice, Robertson, Sawyer, Scott, Spencer, Stewart, Sumner, Thayer, Trumbull, Williams, Wilson, Yates—40.

NAYS—Messrs. *Bayard,* Boreman, *Casserly,* Fowler, Harlan, *McCreery,* Morton, Pratt, *Saulsbury,* Schurz, Willey—11.

IN HOUSE OF REPRESENTATIVES, *May* 26, 1870.

YEAS—Messrs. Allison, Ames, *Archer,* Armstrong, Atwood, *Axtell,* Ayer, Bailey, Banks, *Barnum,* Barry, Bennett, Benton, Bingham, Blair, *Booker,* Bowen, Boyd, George M. Brooks, Buckley, Burdett, Roderick R. Butler, Cake, *Calkin,* Churchill, William T. Clark, Clinton L. Cobb, Conger, *Conner,* Covode, Cowles, Dawes, Degener, Dickey, Dixon, Dockery, *Dox,* Ferriss, Ferry, Fitch, *Fox,* Garfield, *Gibson,* Hamilton, Harris, Hays, Hoar, Hooper, Hotchkiss, *Johnson,* Alexander H. Jones, Kelley, Kellogg, Kelsey, Ketcham, Knapp, Laflin, Lash, Logan, Lynch, Maynard, McCarthy, McKee, *McKenzie,* Morphis, Daniel J. Morrell, *Morrissey,* Myers, Negley, Newsham, O'Neill, Peck, Perce, Peters, Phelps, Poland, Pomeroy, Prosser, Roots, Sawyer, Schenck, *Schumaker,* Lionel A. Sheldon, Porter Sheldon, *Sherrod, Shober, Joseph S. Smith,* William J. Smith, Worthington C. Smith, Wm. Smyth, Starkweather, Stokes, Stoughton, Strickland, Taffe, Tanner, Tillman, Townsend, *Trimble,* Twichell, *Van Auken,* Cadwalader C. Washburn, William B. Washburn, Wheeler, Whitmore, Wilkinson, Eugene M. Wilson—107.

NAYS—Messrs. Ambler, Arnell, Asper, Beatty, *Beck, Biggs, Bird,* James Brooks, Buffinton, Burchard, Cessna, Sidney Clarke, *Cleveland,* Amasa Cobb, Coburn, Cook, *Cox, Crebs,* Cullom, *Dickinson,* Donley, Duval, Dyer, Ela, *Eldridge,* Farnsworth, Finkelnburg, *Getz, Griswold, Haight, Haldeman,* Hale, *Hamill,* Hawkins, Hawley, Hay, Heflin, Hill, *Holman,* Ingersoll, *Kerr, Knott,* Lawrence, *Lewis, Marshall, Mayham,* McCrary, McGrew, *McNeely,* Mercur, Eliakim H. Moore, Jesse H. Moore, William Moore, *Morgan,* Orth, Packard, Packer, Paine, *Potter, Randall, Reeves, Rice, Rogers,* Sargent, Schofield, Shanks, John A. Smith, Stevens, Stevenson, *Stiles, Stone,* Strong, *Swann,* Taylor, Tyner, Upson, Van Wyck, *Voorhees,* Ward, Willard, Williams, John T. Wilson, Winans, Witcher, *Woodward*—85.

## Previous Votes.

### In Senate.

1870, February 8—Mr. Ramsey introduced the resolution which on February 22 was reported from the Committee on the Pacific Railroad, as follows:

*Be it resolved, &c.*, That the northern Pacific Railroad Company be, and hereby is, authorized to issue its bonds to aid in the construction and equipment of its road, and to secure the same by mortgage on its property and rights of property of all kinds and descriptions, real, personal, and mixed, including its franchise as a corporation; and, as proof and notice of its legal execution and effectual delivery, said mortgage shall be filed and recorded in the office of the Secretary of the Interior, and when so filed shall be deemed to be a good and sufficient conveyance of all the rights and property of said company as therein expressed, and also to locate and construct, under the provisions and with the privileges and duties provided for in its act of incorporation and the amendments thereto, its main road to its western terminus, *via* the valley of the Columbia River, with the right to locate and construct its branch from some convenient point on its main trunk line, across the Cascade mountains, to Puget Sound; and in the event of there not being in any State or Territory in which said main line or branch may be located, at the time of the final location thereof, the amount of lands per mile granted by Congress to said company, within the limits prescribed by its charter, then said company shall be entitled, under the directions of the Secretary of the Interior, to receive so many sections of land belonging to the United States, and designated by odd numbers, in such State or Territory, within ten miles on each side of said road beyond the limits prescribed in said charter, as will make up such deficiency on said main line or branch. And that twenty-five miles of said main line, between its western terminus and the city of Portland, in the State of Oregon, shall be completed by the 1st day of January, A. D. 1872, and forty miles of the remaining portion thereof each year thereafter, until the whole shall be completed between said points.

April 11—Mr. Thurman moved to insert at the end of the resolution the following:

And the rights and privileges hereby conferred upon said company, and the grants of land hereby made to it, are conferred and made upon the following express conditions, to wit:

First. That the alternate sections of land heretofore or hereby granted to said company, except such portions thereof as shall be laid out by said company in town or city lots, and such portions thereof as shall be used by it for depots, ditches, water-stations, round-houses, coal, wood, lumber, and cattle-yards, sites for workshops, and other buildings or structures necessary for said road or branch road, shall be sold by said company to actual settlers upon the same and to no other person or persons; and no such settler shall be entitled to purchase more than one hundred and sixty acres thereof, nor shall he or those claiming under him receive a deed therefor until the same shall have been actually occupied by him or by him and them at least two years.

Second. The price at which said lands shall be sold by said company to actual settlers, as aforesaid, shall not exceed $1 25 per acre, with interest at the rate of six per cent. per annum upon deferred payments.

Third. Such actual settlers shall respectively be entitled to purchase said lands, as aforesaid, in lots of forty, eighty, or one hundred and sixty acres.

Fourth. All said lands for sale to actual settlers, as aforesaid, that shall not be sold by said company within fifteen years from the passage of this joint resolution, shall revert to the United States.

Fifth. Any mortgage or mortgages of said lands or any part thereof that may be made or executed by said company shall be subject to the conditions aforesaid in favor of the actual settlers or of the United States, and no foreclosure of any such mortgage or sale thereunder by any trustee or trustees, or under any judicial judgment or decree, shall operate to deprive such actual settlers or the United States of the rights and privileges hereinbefore specified; nor shall anything in this resolution contained be held to waive the conditions upon which patents are to issue, specified in section four of the charter of said company.

Sixth. Within ninety days after the passage of this joint resolution said company shall file in the Department of the Interior its written assent to the foregoing conditions, and if it shall fail so to do, this joint resolution shall become null and void.

Mr. Wilson moved to strike out the words "heretofore or," in the first of the conditions, which was agreed to—yeas 30, nays 9, as follow:

Yeas—Messrs. Ames, Anthony, Chandler. Cole, Conkling, Corbett, Cragin, Flanagan, Fowler, Gilbert, Hamilton of Texas, Hamlin, Howard, Kellogg, McDonald, Morrill of Vermont, Nye, Osborn, Patterson, Pomeroy, Ramsey, Rice, Ross, Sawyer, Stewart, Sumner, Tipton, Trumbull, Williams, Wilson—30.

Nays—Messrs. *Bayard, Casserly, Davis*, Harlan, Howell, *Johnston, McCreery*, Pool, *Thurman*—9.

Mr. Thurman's amendment was then disagreed to—yeas 15, nays 26, as follow:

Yeas—Messrs. Anthony, *Bayard, Casserly*. Cragin, *Davis*, Fowler, Harlan, Howell, *Johnston, McCreery*, Pool, *Stockton, Thurman*, Tipton, Wilson—15.

Nays—Messrs. Ames, Chandler, Cole, Conkling, Corbett, Drake, Flanagan, Gilbert, Hamilton of Texas, Hamlin, Howard, Howe, Kellogg, McDonald, Morrill of Vermont, Nye, Osborn, Pomeroy, Ramsey, Rice, Ross, Sawyer, Stewart, Sumner, Trumbull, Williams—26.

Mr. Wilson moved to insert after the word "branch," in line 35, the following:

And the additional alternate sections of land granted by this resolution shall be sold by the company only to actual settlers, in quantities not exceeding one hundred and sixty acres or quarter-section to any one settler, and at prices not exceeding $2 50 per acre;

Which was disagreed to—yeas 15, nays 22, as follow:

Yeas—Messrs. Anthony, *Bayard, Casserly*, Cragin, *Davis*, Fowler, Harlan, Howell, *Johnston, McCreery*, Pool, *Thurman*. Tipton, Trumbull, *Vickers*—15.

Nays—Messrs. Ames, Chandler, Cole, Corbett, Drake, Flanagan, Gilbert, Hamlin, Howard, Howe. Kellogg, McDonald, Morrill of Vermont, Nye, Osborn, Pomeroy, Ramsey, Rice, Ross, Sawyer, Stewart, Williams—22.

April 20. Mr. Harlan moved to strike out the following words:

And in the event of there not being in any

State or Territory, in which said main line or branch may be located, at the time of the final location thereof, the amount of lands per mile granted by Congress to said company, within the limits prescribed by its charter, then said company shall be entitled, under the directions of the Secretary of the Interior, to receive so many sections of land belonging to the United States, and designated by odd numbers, in such State or Territory, within ten miles on each side of said road, beyond the limits prescribed in said charter, as will make up such deficiency on said main line or branch* to the amount of the lands that have been granted, sold, reserved, occupied by homestead settlers, pre-empted or otherwise disposed of subsequent to the passage of the act of July 2, 1864.

Which was disagreed to—yeas 11, nays 41, as follow:

YEAS—Messrs. Buckingham, *Casserly*, *Davis*, Harlan, Howell, *McCreery*, Pratt, *Saulsbury*, Schurz, *Thurman*, Willey—11.

NAYS—Messrs. Ames, Anthony, Brownlow, Chandler, Cole, Corbett, Cragin, Drake, Edmunds, Fenton, Ferry, Flanagan, Gilbert, Hamilton of Texas, Hamlin, Harris, Howard, Howe, Kellogg, McDonald, Morrill of Maine, Morrill of Vermont, Norton, Nye, Patterson, Pomeroy, Ramsey, Revels, Rice, Robertson, Ross, Sawyer, Scott, Sherman, Spencer, Stewart, Sumner, Thayer, Trumbull, Williams, Wilson—41.

Mr. Howell moved to insert the following proviso at the end of the resolution:

*Provided*, That all lands granted by this joint resolution, which shall not be sold or disposed of by said company within five years after the road shall have been completed, shall be subject to settlement and pre-emption like other lands, at a price not exceeding $1 25 per acre, to be paid to said company.

Which was disagreed to—yeas 13, nays 34, as follow:

YEAS—Messrs. Boreman, *Casserly*, *Davis*, Fowler, Harlan, Harris, Howe, Howell, *McCreery*, *Saulsbury*, *Thurman*, Willey, Wilson—13.

NAYS—Messrs. Ames, Anthony, Brownlow, Buckingham, Chandler, Cole, Corbett, Cragin, Edmunds, Fenton, Ferry, Flanagan, Gilbert, Hamilton of Texas, Hamlin, Howard, Kellogg, McDonald, Morrill of Maine, Morrill of Vermont, Norton, Nye, Osborn, Pomeroy, Ramsey, Revels, Robertson, Ross, Sawyer, Scott, Sherman, Stewart, Thayer, Williams—34.

Mr. Casserly moved to insert the following proviso:

*Provided*, That all lands granted by this joint resolution, which shall not be sold or disposed of by said company within ten years after the road shall have been completed, shall be subject to settlement and pre-emption like other lands, at a price not exceeding $1 25 cents per acre, to be paid to said company.

Which was disagreed to—yeas 16, nays 28, as follow:

YEAS—Messrs. Anthony, Boreman, Cameron, *Casserly*, *Davis*, Fowler, Hamlin, Harlan, Howe, Howell, *McCreery*, *Saulsbury*, *Thurman*, Warner, Willey, Wilson—16.

NAYS—Messrs. Ames, Brownlow, Buckingham, Chandler, Corbett, Cragin, Edmunds, Flanagan, Gilbert, Howard, Kellogg, McDonald, Morrill of Maine, Morrill of Vermont, Norton, Nye, Osborn, Patterson, Pomeroy, Ramsey, Rice, Robertson, Ross, Sawyer, Scott, Stewart, Thayer, Williams—28.

---

* The remainder of the section was not in the bill as reported from the committee, but seems to have been inserted informally; at what time the record does not show.

April 21.—Mr. Thurman moved to insert at the end of the resolution the following:

And the rights and privileges hereby conferred upon said company and the grants of land hereby made to it are conferred and made upon this condition: That said company, its successors and assigns, shall forever transport over said road and its branches, free from any toll or charge, all troops, produce, stores, and munitions of war that may belong to the United States.

Which was disagreed to—yeas 12, nays 35, as follow:

YEAS—Messrs. Ames, *Bayard*, Boreman, Cameron, *Casserly*, Harlan, *McCreery*, Morton, Pratt, *Saulsbury*, Willey, Yates—12.

NAYS—Messrs. Anthony, Brownlow, Chandler, Cole, Corbett, Cragin, Fenton, Flanagan, Fowler, Hamlin, Harris, Howard, Howe, Kellogg, McDonald, Morrill of Maine, Morrill of Vermont, Norton, Nye, Osborn, Patterson, Pomeroy, Ramsey, Revels, Rice, Robertson, Sawyer, Scott, Spencer, Stewart, Sumner, Thayer, Trumbull, Williams, Wilson—35.

Mr. Scott moved to insert at the end of the resolution the following:

*Provided*, That all lands hereby granted to said company which shall not be sold or disposed of or remain subject to the mortgage by this act authorized, at the expiration of five years after the completion of the entire road, shall be subject to settlement and pre-emption like other lands, at a price to be paid to said company not exceeding $2 50 per acre. And if the mortgage hereby authorized shall at any time be enforced by foreclosure or other legal proceeding, or the government lands hereby granted, or any of them, be sold by the trustees to whom such mortgage may be executed, either at its maturity or for any failure or default of said company under the terms thereof, such lands shall be sold at public sale at places within the States and Territories in which they shall be situate, after not less than sixty days' previous notice, in single sections or subdivisions thereof, to the highest and best bidders.

Which was agreed to—yeas 38, nays 8, as follow:

YEAS—Messrs. Anthony, *Bayard*, Boreman, Buckingham, Cameron, *Casserly*, Chandler, Cole, Corbett, Cragin, Fenton, Ferry, Fowler, Harlan, Harris, Howard, Howe, Kellogg, *McCreery*, McDonald, Morrill of Maine, Morrill of Vermont, Morton, Osborn, Patterson, Pratt, Ramsey, Revels, *Saulsbury*, Scott, Spencer, Sumner, Thayer, Trumbull, Willey, Williams, Wilson, Yates—38.

NAYS—Messrs. Ames, Brownlow, Flanagan, Hamilton of Texas, Nye, Pomeroy, Robertson, Stewart—8.

Mr. Cameron moved to insert at the end of the resolution the following:

*Provided further*, That in the construction of the said railroad American iron or steel only shall be used, the same to be manufactured from American ores exclusively.

Which was agreed to—yeas 27, nays 18, as follow:

YEAS—Messrs. Anthony, Boreman, Brownlow, Buckingham, Cameron, Chandler, Cragin, Fenton, Flanagan, Fowler, Hamlin, Harlan, Harris, Howard, Howe, McDonald, Morton, Nye, Osborn, Patterson, Pratt, Ramsey, Revels, Scott, Stewart, Thayer, Willey—27.

NAYS—Messrs. Ames, *Bayard*, *Casserly*, Cole, Corbett, Ferry, Kellogg, *McCreery*, Pomeroy, Rice, Robertson, *Saulsbury*, Spencer, Sumner, Trumbull, Williams, Wilson, Yates—18.

### IN HOUSE OF REPRESENTATIVES.

1870, May 25—Mr. Hawley moved to amend, by adding to the first section as follows:

*And provided further*, That the privileges herein granted are upon the following conditions, namely: all the lands herein or heretofore granted to said railroad company shall be sold to actual settlers only, and in quantities not greater than one hundred and sixty acres to any one person, and for a price not exceeding $2 50 per acre: *And provided further*, That no mortgage that may be given by said railroad company shall operate to prevent the sale to actual settlers only, upon the terms and conditions herein provided, of all the lands herein or heretofore granted by the United States to said railroad company, and any violation of this condition shall work a forfeiture of all the lands herein or heretofore granted by the United States to said railroad company.

Which was disagreed to—yeas 78, nays 106, as follow:

YEAS—Messrs. *Adams*, Ambler, Arnell, Asper, Ayer, Beatty, *Biggs*, Bird, *James Brooks*, Buffinton, Burchard, Sidney Clark, *Cleveland*, Amasa Cobb, Coburn, Cook, Cowles, *Cox*, *Crebs*, Cullom, Degener, *Dickinson*, Donley, Duval, Dyer, Ela, *Eldridge*, Farnsworth, Finkelnburg, *Haight*, *Haldeman*, Hawkins, Hawley, Hay, Hays, Heflin, Ingersoll, Judd, *Kerr*, *Knott*, Lawrence, *Lewis*, *Marshall*, McCrary, McGrew, *McNeely*, Mercur, Eliakim H. Moore, Jesse H. Moore, William Moore, *Morgan*, Packard, Packer, Paine, Pomeroy, *Potter*, *Randall*, *Reeves*, *Rice*, *Rogers*, Sargent, Shanks, *Slocum*, John A. Smith, William Smyth, Stevenson, *Stiles*, Tyner, Upson, Ward, Cadwalader C. Washburn, Willard, Williams, John T. Wilson, Winans, Witcher, *Woodward*—78.

NAYS—Messrs. Allison, Ames, *Archer*, Armstrong, Atwood, *Axtell*, Bailey, Banks, *Barnum*, Barry, Beaman, Bennett, Benton, Bingham, Blair, *Booker*, Bowen, Boyd, George M. Brooks, Buckley, Burdett, Roderick R. Butler, Cake, *Calkin*, Cessna, Churchill, William T. Clark, Clinton L. Cobb, Conger, *Conner*, Covode, Dawes, Dickey, Dixon, Dockery, *Dox*, Ferriss, Ferry, Fitch, *Fox*, Garfield, *Getz*, *Gibson*, Hale, *Hamill*, Hamilton, Harris, Hoar, Hooper, Hotchkiss, *Johnson*, Alexander H. Jones, Kelley, Kellogg, Kelsey, Ketcham, Knapp, Laflin, Lash, Logan, Lynch, *Mayham*, Maynard, McCarthy, McKee, *McKenzie*, Daniel J. Morrell, *Morrissey*, Myers, Negley, Newsham, O'Neill, Peck, Perce, Peters, Phelps, Poland, Prosser, Roots, Sawyer, Schenck, *Schumaker*, Lionel A. Sheldon, *Sherrod*, *Joseph S. Smith*, Worthington C. Smith, Starkweather, Stokes, *Stone*, Stoughton, Strickland, Strong, *Swann*, Taffe, Tanner, Taylor, Tillman, *Trimble*, Twichell, *Van Auken*, William B. Washburn, Welker, Wheeler, Whitmore, Wilkinson, *Eugene M. Wilson*—106.

Mr. Sargent moved to strike out the proviso inserted in the Senate on motion of Mr. Scott, and to insert as follows:

*Provided*, That all lands granted to said company shall be subject to settlement and pre-emption like other lands, at a price to be paid to said company, not exceeding $2 50 per acre; and if the mortgage hereby authorized shall at any time be enforced by foreclosure or other legal proceeding, or the mortgage lands hereby granted, or any of them, be sold by the trustees to whom such mortgage may be executed, either at its maturity or for any failure or default of said company under the terms thereof, such lands shall be sold at public sale at places within the States and Territories in which they shall be situate, after not less than sixty days' previous notice, in single sections or subdivisions thereof, to the highest and best bidder; and the purchasers at said sale, except actual settlers on not greater subdivisions than one hundred and sixty acres, shall acquire no higher interest in said lands than is by this act granted to said company; and as to all lands purchased under any such sale by any corporation or by other persons, greater in quantity than one quarter section for any one person, all such lands shall be and re-

main subject to the right of purchase by actual settlers at a price not exceeding $2 50 per acre, and in amounts not exceeding one quarter section by any one person, under such rules and regulations as the Secretary of the Interior may prescribe to carry this provision into effect.

Which was disagreed to—yeas 73, nays 104, as follow:

YEAS—Messrs. Ambler, Arnell, Asper, Ayer, Beatty, Beck, Bird, *James Brooks*, Buffinton, Burchard, Sidney Clarke, *Cleveland*, Amasa Cobb, Coburn, Cook, Cowles, *Cox*, *Crebs*, Cullom, Degener, *Dickinson*, Donley, Duval, Dyer, Ela, *Eldridge*, Farnsworth, Finkelnburg, *Haldeman*, Hawley, Hay, Hays, Heflin, Ingersoll, *Johnson*, Judd, *Kerr*, *Knott*, Lawrence, *Lewis*, *Marshall*, McCrary, McGrew, *McNeely*, Mercur, Eliakim H. Moore, William Moore, *Morgan*, Morphis, Packard, Paine, *Potter*, *Randall*, *Rice*, *Rogers*, Sargent, Shanks, *Slocum*, John A. Smith, William J. Smith, Stevenson, *Stiles*, Tyner, Upson, Van Wyck, Ward, Cadwalader C. Washburn, Willard, Williams, John T. Wilson, Winans, Witcher, *Woodward*—73.

NAYS—Messrs. Allison, Ames, *Archer*, Armstrong, Atwood, *Axtell*, Bailey, Banks, *Barnum*, Barry, Beaman, Bennett, Benton, Bingham, Blair, *Booker*, Bowen, Boyd, George M. Brooks, Buckley, Burdett, Roderick R. Butler, Cake, *Calkin*, Cessna, Churchill, William T. Clark, Clinton L. Cobb, Conger, *Conner*, Covode, Dawes, Dickey, Dixon, Dockery, *Dox*, Ferriss, Ferry, Fitch, *Fox*, Garfield, *Getz*, *Gibson*, *Hamill*, Hamilton, Harris, Hoar, Hooper, Hotchkiss, Alexander H. Jones, Kelley, Kellogg, Kelsey, Ketcham, Knapp, Laflin, Lash, Logan, Lynch, Maynard, McCarthy, McKee, *McKenzie*, Daniel J. Morrell, *Morrissey*, Myers, Negley, Newsham, O'Neill, Packer, Peck, Perce, Peters, Phelps, Poland, Pomeroy, Prosser, Roots, Sawyer, Schenck, *Schumaker*, Lionel A Sheldon, *Sherrod*, *Joseph S. Smith*, Worthington C. Smith, William Smyth, Starkweather, *Stone*, Stoughton, Strickland, Strong, Taffe, Tanner, Taylor, Tillman, *Trimble*, Twichell, *Van Auken*, William B. Washburn, Welker, Wheeler, Whitmore, Wilkinson, *Eugene M. Wilson*—104.

May 26—Mr. Welker moved to amend, by adding to the first section the following:

*Provided further*, That as to all new grants herein of additional lands, such lands, excepting pine and fir timber lands and mineral lands, shall be sold by said company to actual settlers at a price not exceeding $2 50 per acre, and in quantities not exceeding one hundred and sixty acres to any one person, under such regulations as may be prescribed by the Secretary of the Interior.

Which was disagreed to—ayes 87, nays 95, as follow:

YEAS—Messrs. Ambler, Arnell, Asper, Beatty, Beck, *Biggs*, Bingham, Bird, *James Brooks*, Buffinton, Burchard, Benjamin F. Butler, Cessna, Sidney Clarke, *Cleveland*, Amasa Cobb, Coburn, Cook, *Cox*, *Crebs*, Cullom, Dickey, *Dickinson*, Donley, Duval, Dyer, Ela, *Eldridge*, Farnsworth, Ferry, Finkelnburg, *Getz*, *Griswold*, *Haight*, *Haldeman*, Hawley, Hay, Hays, Heflin, *Holman*, Ingersoll, *Johnson*, Judd, *Kerr*, *Knott*, Lawrence, *Lewis*, *Marshall*, McCrary, McGrew, *McNeely*, Mercur, Eliakim H. Moore, Jesse H. Moore, William Moore, Morphis, *Niblack*, Orth, Packard, Packer, Paine, *Potter*, *Randall*, *Reeves*, *Rice*, *Ridgway*, Sargent, Shanks, John A. Smith, William Smyth, Stevens, Stevenson, *Stiles*, Strong, Townsend, Tyner, Upson, Van Wyck, *Voorhees*, Ward, Welker, Willard, Williams, John T. Wilson, Winans, Witcher, *Woodward*—87.

NAYS—Messrs. Allison, Ames, *Archer*, Armstrong, Atwood, *Axtell*, Ayer, Bailey, Banks, *Barnum*, Barry, Bennett, Benton, Blair, Boles, *Booker*, Boyd, George M. Brooks, Buckley, Burdett, Roderick R. Butler, Cake, *Calkin*, Churchill, William T. Clark, Clinton L. Cobb, Conger, *Conner*. Covode, Cowles, Dawes, Dixon, *Dox*, Ferriss, Fitch, *Fox*, Garfield, Hale, *Hamill*, Hamilton, Harris, Hoar, Hooper, Hotchkiss, Alexander H. Jones, Kelley, Kellogg, Kelsey, Ketcham, Knapp, Laflin, Lash, Logan, Lynch, *Mayham*, Maynard, McCarthy, McKee, *McKenzie*, Daniel J. Morrell, Samuel P. Morrill, *Morrissey*, Myers, Negley, Newsham, O'Neill, Peck, Perce, Peters, Phelps, Poland, Prosser, Roots, Sawyer, Schenck, *Schumaker*, Lionel A. Sheldon, Porter

Sheldon, *Sherrod, Joseph S. Smith,* Worthington C. Smith, Starkweather, Stokes, Stoughton, Strickland, Taffe, Tanner, Tillman, Twichell, *Van Auken,* William B. Washburn, Wheeler, Whitmore, Wilkinson, *Eugene M. Wilson—95.*

Mr. Randall moved to insert, after the words "Secretary of the Interior," in line eleven, the following:

*Provided,* That nothing in this act shall be construed as a guaranty by the United States of the bonds issued by said company or its agents, or of any bonds authorized or permitted by this act.

Which was disagreed to—yeas 89, nays 92, as follow:

YEAS—Messrs. *Adams,* Ambler, *Archer,* Arnell, Asper, Beatty, *Biggs, Bird, James Brooks,* Buffinton, Burchard, Benjamin F. Butler, Cessna, Sidney Clarke, *Cleveland,* Amasa Cobb, Coburn, Cook, Cowles, *Cox, Crebs,* Cullom, Dawes, Dickey, *Dickinson,* Donley, Duval, Dyer, Ela, *Eldridge,* Farnsworth, Finkelnburg, *Getz, Griswold, Haight,* Haldeman, Hale, *Hamill,* Hamilton, Hawley, Hay, Hays, Heflin, Hill, *Holman,* Ingersoll, Judd, *Kerr, Knott,* Lawrence, *Lewis, Marshall,* McCrary, McGrew, *McKenzie, McNeely,* Mercur, Eliakim H. Moore, Jesse H. Moore, William Moore, *Morgan,* Orth, Packard, Packer, Paine, *Randall, Reeves, Rice, Ridgway,* Sargent, Shanks, John A. Smith, Stevens, Stevenson, *Stiles, Swann,* Tillman, Tyner, Upson, Van Wyck, *Voorhees,* Ward, Welker, Willard, Williams, John T. Wilson, Winans, Witcher, *Woodward—89.*

NAYS—Messrs. Allison, Armstrong, Atwood, *Axtell,* Ayer, Bailey, Banks, *Barnum,* Barry, Bennett, Benton, Bingham, Blair, Boles, *Booker,* Boyd, George M. Brooks, Buckley, Burdett, Roderick R. Butler, Cake, *Calkin,* Churchill, William T. Clark, Clinton L. Cobb, Conger, *Conner,* Covode, Dixon, Dockery, *Dox,* Ferriss, Ferry, Fitch, *Fox,* Garfield, Harris, Hoar, Hooper, Hotchkiss, *Johnson,* Kelley, Kelsey, Ketcham, Knapp, Laflin, Lash, Logan, Maynard, McCarthy, McKee, Morphis, Daniel J. Morrell, *Morrissey,* Myers, Negley, Newsham, O'Neill, Peck, Perce, Peters, Phelps, Poland, Pomeroy, Prosser, Roots, Sawyer, Schenck, *Schumaker,* Lionel A. Sheldon, Porter Sheldon, *Sherrod, Joseph S. Smith,* Worthington C. Smith, William Smyth, Starkwether, Stokes, *Stone,* Stoughton, Strickland, Taffe, Tanner, Taylor, Townsend, *Trimble,* Twichell, *Van Auken,* William B. Washburn, Wheeler, Whitmore, Wilkinson, *Eugene M. Wilson—92.*

Mr. Sidney Clarke moved to amend, by adding the following additional section:

SEC. —. That the lands granted by this act and all previous acts to said company shall inure to the benefit of said company, its assigns and successors, in the manner following, that is to say: that all the lands shall be immediatley open to settlement, and shall be sold to actual settlers only, who shall be entitled to receive patents therefor in contiguous parcels not exceeding a quantity equal to one quarter section to any one person, and at the price of $2 50 per acre, under such rules and regulations as may be prescribed by the Secretary of the Interior, in accordance with the provisions of this act: *Provided, however,* That such persons shall be citizens of the United States, or shall have declared their intention to become such, before they shall be entitled to become actual settlers under the provisions of this act: *And provided further,* That when the company shall file with the Secretary of the Interior the certificate of the Governor of the State or Territory in which said road is located that any twenty consecutive miles of said road have been completed in a good, substantial, and workmanlike manner, together with a map designating by the public surveys the line of such completed portion, and the points of beginning and ending, the Secretary of the Interior shall there-

upon direct the proper district land officers to give public notice to all actual settlers under the provisions of this act residing on the granted lands opposite to and conterminous with said completed section, to make proof and payment to the district land officers for their claims within three months from the date of said notice; and the registers and receivers shall report the sale of said lands monthly, as in the sales of public lands; and the amount received shall be placed by the receivers to the credit of the railroad company, in such depository as they may designate: *Provided,* That if any settler shall fail to make proof and pay for his claim within the time herein specified, his right thereto shall become forfeited, and the land shall be patented to the said company: *And provided further,* That patents shall issue to said company for all lands which shall remain unsold after the expiration of three months from the date of completion of each section of said road: *And provided also,* That the railroad company may, at any time, sell, convey by deed, mortgage, or deed of trust, all of said land, to persons or corporations, and not actual settlers, and at such prices and on such terms as the parties may agree upon: *Provided,* That when so sold or conveyed the said lands in the hands of the purchaser, mortgagee, or trustee, or other grantees, shall be subject to sale to actual settlers within the time limited as aforesaid, and on the same terms as though the said deed, mortgage, or deed of trust had never been made: *Provided,* That if said road is not completed within ten years from the date of the acceptance of the grant herein made, the lands remaining along the uncompleted portions of the road shall revert to the Government and be open to pre-emption and homestead entry after due public notice by the district land officers, under instructions from the Secretary of the Interior, as provided in the case of public lands.

Which was disagreed to—yeas 68, nays 117, as follow:

YEAS—Messrs. Ambler, Arnell, Asper, Beatty, *Biggs, Bird,* Buffinton, Burchard, Cessna, Sidney Clarke, *Cleveland,* Amasa Cobb, Coburn, Cook, *Cox, Crebs,* Cullom, *Dickinson,* Donley, Duval, Dyer, Ela, *Eldridge,* Farnsworth, *Griswold, Haight, Haldeman,* Hawkins, Hawley, Hay, Heflin, *Holman,* Ingersoll, *Johnson,* Judd, *Kerr, Knott,* Lawrence, *Lewis, Marshall,* McCrary, McGrew, *McNeely,* Eliakim H. Moore, Jesse H. Moore, William Moore, *Morgan,* Orth, Packard, *Potter, Randall, Reeves, Rice,* Ridgway, *Rogers,* Sargent, Shanks, John A. Smith, Stevenson, *Stiles,* Tyner, Upson, Van Wyck, Ward, Williams, John T. Wilson, Winans, Witcher, *Woodward—68.*

NAYS—Messrs. Allison, Ames, *Archer,* Armstrong, Atwood, *Axtell,* Ayer, Bailey, Banks, *Barnum,* Barry, Bennett, Benton, Bingham, Blair, Boles, *Booker,* Bowen, Boyd, George M. Brooks, Buckley, Burdett, Roderick R. Butler, Cake, *Calkin,* Churchill, William T. Clark, Clinton L. Cobb, Conger, *Conner,* Covode, Cowles, Dawes, *Degener,* Dickey, Dixon, Dockery, *Dox,* Ferriss, Ferry, Finkelnburg, Fitch, *Fox,* Garfield, *Getz,* Hale, *Hamill,* Hamilton, Harris, Hays, Hoar, Hooper, Hotchkiss, Kelley, Kellogg, Kelsey, Ketcham, Knapp, Laflin, Lash, Logan, Lynch, *Mayham,* Maynard, McCarthy, McKee, *McKenzie,* Mercur, Morphis, Daniel J. Morrell, Samuel P. Morrill, *Morrissey,* Myers, Negley, Newsham, O'Neill, Packer, Paine, Peck, Perce, Peters, Phelps, Poland, Pomeroy, Prosser, Roots, Sawyer, Schenck, *Schumaker,* Lionel A. Sheldon, Porter Sheldon, *Sherrod, Shober, Joseph S. Smith,* Worthington C. Smith, William Smyth, Starkweather, Stokes, *Stone,* Stoughton, Strickland, Strong, *Swann,* Taffe, Tanner, Taylor, Tillman, Townsend, *Trimble,* Twichell, *Van Auken,* William B. Washburn, Welker, Wheeler, Whitmore, Wilkinson, *Eugene M. Wilson—117.*

Mr. Ela moved to add at the end of section one the following:

*And provided further*, That any railroad now authorized or which hereafter may be authorized to be built by competent State or national authority, whose line of road does or shall intersect the line of the said Northern Pacific Railroad Company, shall have the right of way to the extent of two hundred feet in width, with necessary grounds for depot purposes, over and across the lands of such company, now or heretofore granted to said Northern Pacific Railroad Company by act of Congress, free of any charge whatever.

Which was disagreed to—yeas 69, nays 112, as follow:

YEAS—Messrs. Ambler, Arnell, Asper, Beatty, *Beck, Bird, James Brooks*, Buffinton, Burchard, Cessna, Sidney Clarke, *Cleveland*, Amasa Cobb, Coburn, Cook, *Cox, Crebs*, Cullom, *Dickinson*, Donley, Duval, Dyer, Ela, *Eldridge*, Farnsworth, Finkelnburg, *Griswold, Haight, Haldeman*, Hawkins, Hawley, Hay, Heflin, *Holman*, Ingersoll, Judd, *Kerr, Knott*, Lawrence, *Lewis, Marshall*, McCrary, McGrew, McKee, *McNeely*, Jesse H. Moore, William Moore, *Morgan*, Orth, Packard, *Potter, Randall, Reeves, Rice*, Sargent, Shanks, John A. Smith, William J. Smith. Stevens, Stevenson. *Stiles*, Tyner, Upson, Van Wyck, Williams, John T. Wilson, Winans, Witcher, *Woodward*—69.

NAYS—Messrs. Allison, Ames, *Archer*, Armstrong, Atwood, *Axtell*, Ayer, Bailey, Banks, *Barnum*, Barry, Bennett, Benton, Bingham, Blair, Boles, *Booker*, Bowen, Boyd, George M. Brooks, Buckley, Burdett, Roderick R. Butler, Cake, *Calkin*, Churchill, William T. Clark, Clinton L. Cobb, Conger, *Conner*, Covode, Cowles, Dawes, Degener, Dixon, Dockery, *Dox*, Ferriss, Ferry, Fitch, *Fox*, Garfield, *Getz*, Hale, *Hamill*, Hamilton, Harris. Hays, Hoar, Hooper, Hotchkiss, *Johnson*, Kelley. Kellogg, Kelsey, Ketcham, Knapp, Laflin, Lash, Logan, Lynch, *Mayham*, Maynard, McCarthy, *McKenzie*, Mercur, Daniel J. Morrill, *Morrissey*, Myers, Negley, Newsham, Packer, Peck, Perce, Peters, Phelps, Poland, Pomeroy, Prosser, Roots, Sawyer, Schenck, *Schumaker*, Lionel A. Sheldon, Porter Sheldon, *Sherrod, Shober, Joseph S. Smith*, Worthington C. Smith, William Smyth, Starkweather, Stokes, *Stone*, Stoughton, Strickland, Strong, *Swann*, Taffe, Tanner, Taylor, Tillman, Townsend, *Trimble*, Twichell, *Van Auken, Voorhees*, Ward, William B. Washburn, Wheeler, Whitmore, Wilkinson, *Eugene M. Wilson*—112.

Mr. Lawrence moved to insert the following additional section:

SEC. —. That said railroad company shall make reports annually, or oftener, if required by the Secretary of the Interior, of its condition and transactions, and containing all such information as said Secretary may require, and in such form and verified in such manner as he may require.

Which was disagreed to—yeas 62, nays 95, as follow:

YEAS—Messrs. Ambler, *Archer*, Asper, Beatty, *Beck, Bird, James Brooks*, Buffinton, Burchard, Cessna, Sidney Clarke, Amasa Cobb, Coburn, Cook, *Cox, Crebs*, Cullom, *Dickinson*, Donley, Duval, Dyer, Farnsworth, Finkelnburg, *Getz, Haldeman*, Hawley, Hay, Heflin, *Holman, Kerr, Knott*, Lawrence, *Lewis, Marshall*, McGrew, *McNeely*, Mercur, Jesse H. Moore, William Moore, *Morgan*, Orth, Packard. Packer, *Potter, Randall, Reeves, Rice, Ridgway*, Sargent, Shanks, Stevenson, *Stiles*, Tyner, Van Wyck, *Voorhees*, Ward, Williams, John T. Wilson, Winans, Witcher, *Woodward*—62.

NAYS—Messrs. Allison, Armstrong, Atwood, *Axtell*, Ayer, Bailey, *Barnum*, Barry, Bennett, Benton, Bingham, Blair, *Booker*, Bowen, Boyd, George M. Brooks, Buckley, Burdett, Benjamin F. Butler, Roderick R. Butler, Cake, *Calkin*, Churchill, William T. Clark, Conger, *Conner*, Covode, Cowles, Degener, Dixon, Dockery, *Dox*, Ferriss, Ferry, Fitch, *Fox*, Garfield, Hale, Hamilton, Harris, Hays, Hoar, Hooper, Hotchkiss, *Johnson*, Kelley, Kellogg, Kelsey, Ketcham, Knapp, Laflin, Lash, Logan, Lynch, *Mayham*, Maynard, McCarthy, McKee, *McKenzie*, Morphis, Daniel J. Morrell, *Morrissey*, Myers, Negley, Newsham, O'Neill, Paine, Peck, Peters, Phelps, Poland, Pomeroy, Roots, Sawyer, *Schumaker*, Porter Sheldon, *Sherrod, Shober, Joseph S. Smith*, Wor-

thington C. Smith, William Smyth, Starkweather, Stokes, *Stone*, Stoughton, Strickland, Tanner, Taylor, Townsend, *Trimble*. Twichell, *Van Auken*, Wheeler, Wilkinson, *Eugene M. Wilson*—95.

Mr. Lawrence further moved to amend by adding the following:

And the United States shall have the right, at all times, to take possession of and own the road of said company, and all its appurtenances, on paying the actual and legitimate cost thereof, exclusive of the value of the lands granted to said company and the proceeds thereof.

Which was disagreed to—yeas 52, nays 115, as follow:

YEAS—Messrs. Ambler, Arnell, Asper, Beatty, *James Brooks*, Buffinton, Burchard, Cessna, Sidney Clarke, Coburn, Cook, *Cox, Crebs*, Cullom, *Dickinson*, Duval, Dyer, Ela, Farnsworth, Finkelnburg, *Haldeman*, Hawley, Hay, Heflin, *Holman*, Ingersoll, *Knott*, Lawrence, *Lewis, Marshall*, McGrew, *McNeely*, Eliakim H. Moore, William Moore, Morphis, Orth, Packard. Packer, *Potter, Randall, Reeves, Rice*, Sargent, Shanks, William J. Smith, *Stiles*, Tyner, Van Wyck, Williams, Winans, Witcher, *Woodward*—52.

NAYS—Messrs. Allison, Ames, *Archer*, Armstrong, Atwood, *Axtell*, Ayer, Bailey, *Barnum*, Barry, *Beck*, Bennett, Benton, *Biggs*, Bingham, *Bird*, Blair, *Booker*, Bowen, Boyd, George M. Brooks, Buckley, Burdett, Benjamin F. Butler, Roderick R. Butler, Cake, *Calkin*, Churchill, *Cleveland*, Clinton L. Cobb, Conger, *Conner*, Covode, Cowles, Davis, Dawes, Dixon, Dockery, Donley, *Dox*, Ferriss, Ferry, Fitch, Garfield, *Getz*, Hale, *Hamill*, Hamilton, Harris, Hays, Hoar, Hooper, Hotchkiss, *Johnson*, Kelley, Kellogg, Kelsey, *Kerr*, Ketcham, Knapp, Laflin, Lash, Logan, Lynch, Maynard, McCarthy, McKee, *McKenzie*, Mercur, Daniel J. Morrell, Samuel P. Morrill, *Morrissey*, Myers, Negley, Newsham, O'Neill, Paine, Peck, Perce, Phelps, Poland, Pomeroy, Prosser, Roots, Sawyer, Schenck, *Schumaker*, Lionel A. Sheldon, Porter Sheldon, *Sherrod, Shober*, John A. Smith, *Joseph S. Smith*, Worthington C. Smith, William Smyth, Starkweather, Stokes, *Stone*, Stoughton, Strickland, Strong, Taffe, Tanner, Taylor, Townsend, *Trimble*, Twichell, Upson, *Van Auken, Voorhees*, Ward, William B. Washburn, Wheeler, Wilkinson, *Eugene M. Wilson*—115.

Mr. Coburn moved to insert after the word "point," in line sixteen, these words: "not exceeding three hundred miles east of the western terminus," so as to provide that the branch shall not be over three hundred miles in length.

Which was disagreed to—yeas 68, nays 99, as follow:

YEAS—Messrs. Allison, Ambler, Arnell, Asper, Beatty, Bingham, *Bird, James Brooks*, Buffinton, Cessna, Sidney Clarke, *Cleveland*, Amasa Cobb, Coburn, Cook, *Cox, Crebs*, Cullom, *Dickinson*, Donley, Duval, Dyer, Ela, *Eldridge*, Farnsworth, Finkelnburg, *Griswold, Haight, Haldeman*, Hawley, Hay, Heflin, *Holman*, Ingersoll, Judd, *Knott*, Lawrence, *Lewis, Marshall*, McCrary, McGrew, *McNeely*, Mercur, William Moore, *Morgan*, Orth, Packard. Packer, Paine, *Potter, Randall, Reeves, Rice, Ridgway*, Sargent, Shanks, John A. Smith, William J. Smith, Stevenson, *Stiles*, Tyner, Upson, Van Wyck, *Voorhees*, Ward, Williams, Winans, Witcher—68.

NAYS—Messrs. Ames, *Archer*, Armstrong, *Axtell*, Ayer, Bailey, *Barnum*, Barry, Bennett, Benton, Blair, *Booker*, Bowen, Boyd, George M. Brooks, Buckley, Burdett, Roderick R. Butler, Cake, *Calkin*, Churchill, William T. Clark, Clinton L. Cobb, Conger, *Conner*, Covode, Dawes, Degener, Dixon, *Dox*, Ferriss, Ferry, Fitch, *Fox*, Garfield, *Getz, Hamill*, Harris, Hays, Hoar, Hooper, Hotchkiss, *Johnson*, Kelley, Kelsey, Ketcham, Knapp, Laflin, Lash, Logan, Lynch, Maynard, McCarthy, McKee, *McKenzie*, Morphis, Daniel J. Morrell, *Morrissey*, Myers, Negley, Newsham, O'Neill, Peck, Perce, Peters, Phelps, Poland, Pomeroy, *Rogers*, Roots, Sawyer, Schenck, *Schumaker*, Lionel A. Sheldon, Porter Sheldon, *Sherrod, Shober, Joseph S. Smith*, Worthington C. Smith, William Smyth, Starkweather, Stokes, *Stone*, Stoughton, *Swann*, Taffe, Tanner, Taylor, Tillman, Townsend, *Trimble*, Twichell, *Van Auken*, William B. Washburn, Wheeler, Whitmore, Wilkinson, *Eugene M. Wilson, Woodward*—99.

Mr. Coburn further moved to amend, by striking out the words, "and to secure the same by mortgage on its property and rights of property of all kinds and descriptions, real, personal, and mixed, including its franchise as a corporation;" and inserting these words: "and to secure the same by mortgage on its tracks, depots, rolling stock, and other personal property alone."

Which was disagreed to—yeas 59, nays 107, as follow:

YEAS—Messrs. Ambler, Arnell, Asper, Beatty, *Bird*, Buffinton, Burchard, Cessna, Sidney Clarke, *Cleveland*, Amasa Cobb, Coburn, Cook, *Crebs*, Cullom, *Dickinson*, Duval, Ela, *Eldridge*, Farnsworth, Finkelnburg, *Griswold, Haight, Haldeman*, Hawley, Hay, Heflin, *Holman*, Inger*s*oll, Judd, *Kerr, Knott*, Lawrence, *Lewis, Marshall*, McCrary, McGrew, *McNeely*, Jesse H. Moore, William Moore, *Morgan*, Orth, Packard, Packer, *Randall, Reeves, Rice*, Sargent, Shanks, William J. Smith, Stevenson, *Stiles*, Tyner, Upson, Van Wyck, *Voorhees*, Williams, Winans, Witcher—59.

NAYS—Messrs. Allison, Ames, *Archer*, Armstrong, Atwood, *Axtell*, Ayer, Bailey, *Barnum*, Barry, Bennett, Benton, Bingham, Blair, *Booker*, Bowen, Boyd, Buckley, Burdett, Roderick R. Butler, Cake, *Calkin*, Churchill, William T. Clark, Conger, *Conner*, Covode, Cowles, Dawes, Degener, Dixon, Dockery, *Dox*, Ferriss, Ferry, Fitch, *Fox*, Garfield, *Getz*, Hale, *Hamill*, Hamilton, Harris, Hays, Hoar, Hooper, Hotchkiss, Kelley, Kellogg, Kelsey, Ketcham, Knapp, Laflin, Lash, Logan, Lynch, Maynard, McCarthy, McKee, *McKenzie*, Mercur, Daniel J. Morrell, *Morrissey*, Myers, Negley, Newsham, O'Neill, Paine, Peck, Peters, Phelps, Poland, Pomeroy, Prosser, Roots, Sawyer, Schenck, *Schumaker*, Lionel A. Sheldon, Porter Sheldon, *Sherrod*, John A. Smith, *Joseph S. Smith*, Worthington C. Smith, William Smyth, Starkweather, Stokes, *Stone*, Stoughton, Strickland, *Swann*, Taffe, Tanner, Taylor, Tillman, Townsend, *Trimble*, Twichell, *Van Auken*, Ward, William B. Washburn, Wheeler, Whitmore, Wilkinson, *Eugene M. Wilson, Woodward*—107.

Mr. Williams moved to add to the 1st section the following:

*And be it further provided*, That the grants of lands herein stipulated to said company are made upon the express condition that the Congress of the United States reserves the right to regulate and limit the rates of freight and fare of passengers on said road, whenever, in the opinion of Congress, the same shall become necessary to protect commerce among the several States.

Which was disagreed to—yeas 72, nays 94, as follow:

YEAS—Messrs. Allison, Ambler, Arnell, Asper, Beatty, Buffinton, Burchard, Cessna, Sidney Clarke, Amasa Cobb, Cook, Cowles, *Cox, Crebs*, Cullom, Dawes, Degener, *Dickinson*, Donley, Duval, Dyer, Ela, *Eldridge*, Finkelnburg, Garfield, *Haldeman*, Hamilton, Hawkins, Hawley, Hay, Heflin, *Holman*, Ingersoll, *Johnson*. Judd, *Knott*, Lawrence, *Lewis*, McCrary, McGrew, *McNeely*, Mercur, Eliakim H. Moore, William Moore, Newsham, Orth, Packard, Packer, Paine, Pomeroy, *Potter, Randall, Reeves, Rice*, Sargent, Shanks. John A. Smith, William J. Smith, Stevens, Stevenson, *Stiles*, Streng, Tyner, Upson, Van Wyck, Ward, William B. Washburn, Williams, John T. Wilson, Winans, Witcher, *Woodward*—72.

NAYS—Messrs. Ames, Armstrong, *Axtell*, Ayer, Bailey, Banks, *Barnum*, Barry, Bennett, *Bird*, Blair, *Booker*, Bowen, Boyd, George M. Brooks, Buckley, Roderick R. Butler, Cake, *Calkin*, Churchill, William T. Clark, *Cleveland*, Clinton L. Cobb, Conger, *Conner*. Covode, Dixon, *Dox*, Ferriss, Ferry, Fitch, *Fox, Getz, Haight, Hamill*, Harris, Hays, Hoge, Hooper, Hotchkiss, Kelley, Kellogg, Kelsey, *Kerr*, Ketcham, Knapp, Laflin, Lash, Logan, Lynch, *Mayham*, Maynard, McCarthy, McKee, Morphis, Daniel J. Morrell, *Morrissey*, Myers, Negley, O'Neill, Peck, Perce, Peters, Phelps. Poland, Prosser, Roots, Sawyer, Schenck, *Schumaker*, Lionel A. Sheldon, Porter Sheldon, *Sherrod, Shober, Joseph S. Smith*, Worthington C. Smith, William Smyth, Starkweather, Stokes, *Stone*, Stoughton, Strickland, Taffe, Tanner, Taylor, Tillman, Townsend, *Trimble*, Twichell, *Van Auken*, Wheeler, Whitmore, Wilkinson, *Eugene M. Wilson*—94.

The bill then passed both Houses as above.

## IN HOUSE.

1870, March 21.—Mr. Holman submitted the following resolution, which was unanimously agreed to:

*Resolved*, That in the judgment of this House the policy of granting subsidies in public lands to railroad and other corporations ought to be discontinued; and that every consideration of public policy and equal justice to the whole people requires that the public lands of the United States should be held for the exclusive purpose of securing homesteads to actual settlers under the homestead and pre-emption laws, subject to reasonable appropriations of such lands for the purposes of education.

# LV.

# THE RESTORATION OF VIRGINIA, MISSISSIPPI, AND TEXAS.

**AN ACT to admit the State of Virginia to Representation in the Congress of the United States.**

Whereas the people of Virginia have framed and adopted a constitution of State government which is republican; and whereas the Legislature of Virginia elected under said constitution have ratified the XIVth and XVth amendments to the Constitution of the United States; and whereas the performance of these several acts in good faith was a condition precedent to the representation of the State in Congress: Therefore,

*Be it enacted, &c.*, That the said State of Virginia is entitled to representation in the Congress of the United States: *Provided*, That before any member of the Legislature of said State shall take or resume his seat, or any officer of said State shall enter upon the duties of his office, he shall take and subscribe and file in the office of the secretary of state of Virginia, for permanent preservation, an oath in the form following: "I, —— ——, do solemnly swear that I have never taken an oath as a member of Congress, or as an officer of the United States, or as a member of any State legislature, or as an executive or judicial officer of any State, to support the Constitution of the United States, and afterward engaged in insurrection or rebellion against the same, or given aid or comfort to the enemies thereof: so help me God;" or such person shall in like manner take, subscribe, and file the following oath: " I, —— ——, do solemnly swear that I have by act of Congress of the United States been relieved from the disabilities imposed upon me by the XIVth Amendment of the Constitution of the United States: so help me God;" which oaths shall be taken before and certified by any officer lawfully authorized to administer oaths. And any person who shall knowingly swear falsely in taking either of such oaths shall be deemed guilty of perjury, and shall be punished therefor by imprisonment not less than one year and not more than ten years, and shall be fined not less than $1,000 and not more than $10,000. And in all trials for any violation of this act the certificate of the taking of either of said oaths, with proof of the signature of the party accused, shall be taken and held as conclusive evidence that such oath was regularly and lawfully administered by competent authority: *And provided further,* That every such person who shall neglect for the period of thirty days next after the passage of this act to take, subscribe, and file such oath as aforesaid, shall be deemed and taken, to all intents and purposes, to have vacated his office: *And provided further,* That the State of Virginia is admitted to representation in Congress as one of the States of the Union upon the following fundamental conditions: First, That the constitution of Virginia shall never be so amended or changed as to deprive any citizen or class of citizens of the United States of the right to vote who are entitled to vote by the constitution herein recognized, except as a punishment for such crimes as are now felonies at common law, whereof they shall have been duly convicted under laws equally applicable to all the inhabitants of said State: *Provided,* That any alteration of said constitution, prospective in its effects, may be made in regard to the time and place of residence of voters. Second, That it shall never be lawful for the said State to deprive any citizen of the United States, on account of his race, color, or previous condition of servitude, of the right to hold office under the constitution and laws of said State, or upon any such ground to require of him any other qualifications for office than such as are required of all other citizens. Third, That the constitution of Virginia shall never be so amended or changed as to deprive any citizen or class of citizens of the United States of the school rights and privileges secured by the constitution of said State.

Approved, January 26, 1870.

The final votes on this act were as follow:

IN SENATE, *January* 24, 1870.

YEAS—Messrs. Abbott, Anthony, Boreman, Brownlow, Buckingham, Carpenter, Chandler, Cole, Conkling, Corbett, Cragin, Drake, Edmunds, Fenton, Ferry, Gilbert, Hamlin, Harlan, Harris, Howard, Howe, Kellogg, McDonald, Morrill of Maine, Morton, Nye, Osborn, Patterson, Pomeroy, Pratt, Ramsey, Rice, Robertson, Ross, Sawyer, Schurz, Scott, Sherman, Spencer, Stewart, Tipton, Trumbull, Warner, Willey, Williams, Wilson, Yates—47.

NAYS—Messrs. *Bayard, Casserly, Davis,* Fowler, *William T. Hamilton, Norton, Saulsbury, Stockton, Thurman, Vickers*—10.

IN HOUSE, *January* 24, 1870.

YEAS—Messrs. Allison, Ambler, Ames, Armstrong, Arnell, Asper, Bailey, Banks, Beaman, Beatty, Benjamin, Bennett, Benton, Bingham, Blair, Boles, Bowen, Boyd, George M. Brooks, Buck, Buckley, Buffinton,

Burchard, Burdett, Benjamin F. Butler, Roderick R. Butler, Cake, Cessna, Clarke, Amasa Cobb, Clinton L. Cobb, Coburn, Cook, Conger, Cowles, Cullom, Davis, Dawes, Dixon, Donley, Duval, Dyer, Ela, Farnsworth, Ferriss, Ferry, Finkelnburg, Fisher, Fitch, Garfield, Gilfillan, Hale, Hamilton, Hawley, Hay, Heaton, Heflin, Hill, Hoar. Sol. L. Hoge, Hooper, Ingersoll, Jenckes, Judd, Julian, Kelley, Kellogg, Kelsey, Ketcham, Knapp, Laflin, Lash, Lawrence, Logan, Loughridge, Lynch, Maynard, McCarthy, McCrary, McGrew, Eliakim H. Moore, Jesse H. Moore, William Moore, Daniel J. Morrell, Samuel P. Morrill, Myers, Negley, O'Neill, Orth, Packard, Paine, Palmer, Peters, Phelps, Poland, Pomeroy, Prosser, Roots, Sanford, Sargent, Sawyer, Schenck, Scofield, Shanks, Lionel A. Sheldon, Porter Sheldon, John A. Smith, William J. Smith, Worthington C. Smith, William Smyth, Starkweather, Stevens, Stevenson, Stokes, Stoughton, Strickland, Strong, Taffe, Tanner, Tillman, Townsend, Twichell, Tyner, Upson, Van Horn, Ward, Cadwalader C. Washburn, William B. Washburn, Welker, Wheeler, B. F. Whittemore, Wilkinson, Willard, Williams, John T. Wilson, Winans—136.

NAYS—Messrs. *Adams, Archer, Axtell, Beck, Bird, James Brooks, Burr, Calkin, Cleveland, Cox, Crebs, Deweese, Dickinson, Dox, Eldridge, Getz, Golladay, Greene, Griswold, Haldeman, Hambleton, Hamill,* Hawkins, *Holman, Johnson, Thomas L. Jones, Kerr, Knott, Marshall, Mayham, McCormick, McNeely, Morgan, Mungen, Niblack, Potter, Randall, Reeves, Rice, Rogers, Schumaker, Sherrod, Slocum, Joseph S. Smith, Stiles, Stone, Strader, Swann, Sweeney, Trimble, Van Auken, Van Trump, Voorhees, Wells, Eugene M. Wilson, Winchester, Wood, Woodward*—58.

### Previous Votes.

#### IN HOUSE.

1870, January 11—Mr. Farnsworth, from the Committee on Reconstruction, reported the following bill, to admit the State of Virginia to representation in the Congress of the United States:

Whereas the people of Virginia have adopted a constitution republican in form, and by its provisions assuring the equality of right in all citizens of the United States before the law; and whereas the Congress of the United States have received assurances and are assured that the people of Virginia, and especially those heretofore in insurrection against the United States, have renounced all claims of any right of secession in a State, and that they are now well-disposed to the Government of the United States, and will support and defend the Constitution thereof, and will carry out in letter and spirit the provisions and requirements of the constitution submitted under the reconstruction acts of Congress, and ratified by the people of Virginia; Therefore,

*Be it enacted, &c.,* That the State of Virginia is entitled to representation in Congress as a State of the Union, under the constitution ratified on the 6th day of July, 1869, upon the following fundamental conditions: First. That no persons shall hold any office, civil or military, in said State, who shall not have taken and subscribed one of the following oaths or affirmations, viz: "I do solemnly swear (or affirm) that I have never taken an oath as a member of Congress, or as an officer of the United States, or as a member of any State legislature, or as an executive or judicial officer of any State, to support the Constitution of the United States and thereafter engaged in insurrection or rebellion against the same or given aid or comfort to the enemies thereof;" or, "I do solemnly swear (or affirm) that I have been relieved from disability by an act of Congress, as provided for by the third section of the XIVth article of the amendments of the Constitution of the United States." Second. That the constitution of said State shall never be so amended or changed as to deprive any citizen or class of citizens of the United States of the right to vote or hold office in said State who are entitled to vote or hold office by said constitution, except as a punishment for such crimes as are now felonies at common law, whereof they shall have been duly convicted under laws equally applicable to all the inhabitants of said State; or to prevent any person on account of race, color, or previous condition of servitude from serving as a juror, or participating equally in the school fund or school privileges provided for in said constitution: *Provided,* That any alteration of said constitution equally applicable to all the voters of said State may be made with regard to the time and place of residence of said voters. Third. That all persons who shall at the time when said constitution shall take effect hold or exercise the functions of any executive, administrative, or judicial office in said State, by the appointment or authority of the district commander, shall continue to discharge the duties of their respective offices until their successors. or those upon whom such duties shall, under said constitution, devolve, are duly chosen or appointed and qualified.

SEC. 2. That the election of United States Senators by the general assembly of said State, on the 19th day of October, 1869, shall have the same validity as if made by previous authority of law.

January 14—Mr. Whittemore moved to amend by inserting in the first section, at the end of the first condition, as follows:

"And any person who shall falsely take either of the aforesaid oaths or affirmations shall be deemed guilty of perjury, and shall suffer the pains and penalties thereof, and may be tried, convicted, and punished therefor by the circuit court of the United States for the district in which said crime was committed, and the jurisdiction of said court shall be sole and exclusive for the purpose aforesaid;" which was agreed to—yeas 123, nays 70, as follow:

YEAS—Messrs. Ambler, Ames, Armstrong, Arnell, Asper, Beaman, Beatty, Benjamin, Bennett, Benton, Boles, Bowen, Boyd, George M. Brooks, Buck, Buckley, Buffinton, Burchard, Burdett, Roderick R. Butler, Cake, Cessna, Churchill, Clarke, Amasa Cobb, Clinton L. Cobb, Coburn, Cook, Conger, Cowles, Cullom, Dawes, Dickey, Dixon, Donley, Duval, Dyer, Ela, Ferriss, Ferry, Finkelnburg, Fisher, Fitch, Garfield, Gilfillan, Hale, Hamilton, Hawley, Hay, Heflin, Hill, Hoar, Solomon L. Hoge, Hooper, Ingersoll, Jenckes, Judd, Kelley, Kellogg, Kelsey, Ketcham, Knapp, Laflin, Lash, Lawrence, Logan, Loughridge, Maynard, McCarthy, McCrary, McGrew, Mercur, Eliakim H. Moore, Jesse H. Moore, William Moore, Daniel J. Morrell, Samuel P. Morrill, Myers, Negley, O'Neill, Orth, Packard, Packer, Paine, Palmer, Peters, Phelps, Pomeroy, Prosser, Roots, Sargent, Schenck, Scofield, Shanks, Lionel A. Sheldon, Porter Sheldon, John A. Smith, William J. Smith, Worthington C. Smith, William Smyth, Starkweather, Stevens, Stevenson, Stokes, Stoughton, Strong, Taffe, Townsend, Twichell, Tyner, Upson, Van Horn, Ward, Cadwalader C. Washburn, William B. Washburn, Wheeler, B. F. Whittemore, Willard, Williams, John T. Wilson, Winans, Witcher—123.

NAYS—Messrs. *Adams, Archer, Axtell,* Bailey, Banks, *Barnum, Beck, Biggs,* Bingham, *Bird,* Blair, *James Brooks, Burr, Calkin, Cleveland, Cox,* Deweese, *Dickinson,* Dockery, *Dox, Eldridge,* Farnsworth, *Fox, Getz, Golladay, Greene, Griswold, Haight,* Haldeman, *Hambleton, Hamill,* Hawkins, Heaton, *Holman, Johnson, Kerr, Knott, Mar-*

*shall, Mayham, McCormick, McNeely, Morgan, Mungen, Niblack, Potter, Randall, Reading, Reeves, Rice, Rogers, Schumaker, Slocum, Joseph S. Smith, Stiles, Stone, Strader, Swann, Sweeney,* Tanner, Tillman, *Trimble, Van Auken, Van Trump, Voorhees,* Welker, *Wells, Eugene M. Wilson, Winchester, Wood, Woodward*—70.

Same day Mr. Bingham offered the following substitute:

Whereas the people of Virginia have adopted a constitution republican in form, and have in all respects conformed to the requirements of the act of Congress entitled "An act authorizing the submission of the constitutions of Virginia, Mississippi, and Texas to a vote of the people, and authorizing the election of State officers, provided by the said constitutions, and members of Congress," approved April 10, 1869: Therefore,

*Be it resolved, &c.,* That the said State of Virginia is entitled to representation in the Congress of the United States.

Which was adopted—yeas 98, nays 95, as follow:

YEAS—Messrs. *Adams, Archer, Axtell,* Bailey, Banks, *Barnum, Beck, Biggs,* Bingham, *Bird,* Blair, George M. Brooks, *James Brooks,* Buckley, Burchard, *Burr, Calkin, Cleveland, Cox, Crebs,* Cullom, Dawes, Deweese, *Dickinson,* Dockery, *Dox, Eldridge,* Farnsworth, Ferry, Finkelnburg, Fitch, *Fox,* Garfield, *Getz, Golladay, Greene, Griswold, Haight, Haldeman,* Hale, *Hambleton, Hamill,* Hawkins, Hay, Heaton, *Holman,* Hooper, Ingersoll, Jenckes, *Johnson,* Kellogg, *Kerr,* Ketcham, *Knott,* Laflin, Logan, *Marshall, Mayham,* McCarthy, *McCormick, McNeely,* Jesse H. Moore, *Morgan, Mungen, Niblack,* Orth, Peters, *Potter, Randall, Reading, Reeves, Rice, Rogers,* Sanford, *Schumaker, Slocum, Joseph S. Smith,* Worthington C. Smith, *Stiles, Stone, Strader,* Strong, *Swann, Sweeney,* Tanner, Tillman, *Trimble, Van Auken, Van Trump, Voorhees; Wells, Eugene M. Wilson,* John T. Wilson, Winans, *Winchester,* Witcher, *Wood, Woodward* —98.

NAYS—Messrs. Ambler, Ames, Armstrong, Arnell, Asper, Beaman, Beatty, Benjamin, Bennett, Benton, Boles, Bowen, Boyd, Buck, Buffinton, Burdett, Roderick R. Butler, Cake, Cessna, Churchill, Clarke, Amasa Cobb, Clinton L. Cobb, Coburn, Cook, Conger, Cowles, Dickey, Dixon, Donley, Duval, Dyer, Ela, Ferriss, Fisher, Gilfillan, Hamilton, Hawley, Heflin, Hill, Hoar, Solomon L. Hoge, Judd, Kelley, Kelsey, Knapp, Lash, Lawrence, Loughridge, Maynard, McCrary, McGrew, Mercur, Eliakim H. Moore, William Moore, Daniel J. Morrell, Samuel P. Morrill, Myers, Negley, O'Neil, Packard, Packer, Paine, Palmer, Phelps, Pomeroy, Prosser, Roots, Sargent, Schenck, Scofield, Shanks, Porter Sheldon, John A. Smith, William J. Smith, William Smyth, Starkweather, Stevens, Stevenson, Stokes, Stoughton, Taffe, Townsend, Twichell, Tyner, Upson, Van Horn, Ward, Cadwalader C. Washburn, William B. Washburn, Welker, Wheeler, B. F. Whittemore, Willard, Williams—95.

The bill was then passed—yeas 142, nays 49, as follow:

YEAS—Messrs. *Adams,* Ames, *Archer,* Armstrong, *Axtell,* Bailey, Banks, *Barnum,* Beaman, *Beck,* Benjamin, Bennett, *Biggs,* Bingham, *Bird,* Blair, George M. Brooks, *James Brooks,* Buck, Buckley, Burchard, Burdett, *Burr,* Roderick R. Butler, Cake, *Calkin,* Churchill, Clinton L. Cobb, Cook, Conger, Cowles, *Cox, Crebs,* Cullom, Dawes, Deweese, *Dickinson,* Dockery, *Dox,* Duval, Dyer, *Eldridge,* Farnsworth, Ferry, Finkelnburg, Fitch, *Fox,* Garfield, *Getz,* Gilfillan, *Golladay, Greene, Griswold, Haight, Haldeman,* Hale, *Hambleton, Hamill,* Hawkins, Hay, Heaton, Heflin, Hill, *Holman,* Hooper, Ingersoll, Jenckes, *Johnson,* Judd, Kellogg, *Kerr,* Ketcham, *Knott,* Laflin, Lash, Logan, *Marshall, Mayham,* McCarthy, *McCormick,* McGrew, *McNeely,* Mercur, Eliakim H. Moore, Jesse H. Moore, *Morgan,* Daniel J. Morrell, Samuel P. Morrill, *Mungen,* Myers, *Niblack,* Orth, Packard, Packer, Paine, Peters, Poland, *Potter,* Prosser, *Randall, Reading, Reeves, Rice, Rogers,* Sanford, Sargent, Schenck, *Schumaker,* Scofield, Porter Sheldon, John A. Smith, *Joseph S. Smith,* Worthington C. Smith, Starkweather, *Stiles, Stone,* Stoughton, *Strader,* Strong, *Swann, Sweeney,* Tanner, Tillman, *Trimble,* Twichell, Tyner, Upson, *Van Auken, Van Trump, Voorhees,* William B. Washburn, Welker, *Wells,* Williams, *Eugene M. Wilson,* John T.

Wilson, Winans, *Winchester*, Witcher, *Wood*, *Woodward*—142.

NAYS—Messrs. Ambler, Arnell, Asper, Beatty, Benton, Boles, Bowen, Boyd, Buffinton, Cessna, Clarke, Amasa Cobb, Coburn, Dickey, Dixon, Donley, Ela, Ferriss, Fisher. Hamilton, Hawley, Hoar, Solomon L. Hoge, Kelley, Kelsey, Lawrence, Loughridge, Maynard, McCrary, William Moore, Negley, O'Neill, Palmer, Phelps, Pomeroy, Roots, Shanks, William J. Smith, William Smyth, Stevens, Stevenson, Stokes, Taffe, Townsend, Ward, Cadwalader C. Washburn, Wheeler, B. F. Whittemore, Willard—49.

## IN SENATE.

1870, January 17—Mr. Edmunds moved to amend by inserting at the end of the bill the following proviso:

*Provided*, That before any member of the legislature of said State shall take or resume his seat, or any officer of said State shall enter upon the duties of his office, he shall take and subscribe and file in the office of the secretary of state of Virginia, for permanent preservation, an oath in the form following: " I, ———— ——, do solemnly swear that I have never taken an oath as a member of Congress, or as an officer of the United States, or as a member of any State legislature, or as an executive or judicial officer of any State, to support the Constitution of the United States and afterward engaged in insurrection or rebellion against the same, or given aid or comfort to the enemies thereof: so help me God;" or such person shall in like manner take, subscribe, and file the following oath: " I, ———— ——, do solemnly swear that I have by act of Congress of the United States been relieved from the disabilities imposed upon me by the XIVth Amendment of the Constitution of the United States: so help me God;" which oaths shall be taken before and certified by any officer lawfully authorized to administer oaths. And any person who shall knowingly swear falsely in taking either of such oaths shall be deemed guilty of perjury, and shall be punished therefor by imprisonment not less than one year and not more than ten years, and shall be fined not less than $1,000 and not more than $10,000. And in all trials for any violation of this act the certificate of the taking of either of said oaths, with proof of the signature of the party accused, shall be taken and held as conclusive evidence that such oath was regularly and lawfully administered by competent authority: *And provided further*, That every such person who shall neglect for the period of thirty days next after the passage of this act to take, subscribe, and file such oath as aforesaid, shall be deemed and taken, to all intents and purposes, to have vacated his office;

Which (January 19) was agreed to—yeas 45, nays 16, as follow:

YEAS—Messrs. Abbott, Anthony, Boreman, Brownlow, Buckingham, Cameron, Carpenter, Chandler, Cole, Conkling. Corbett, Cragin, Drake, Edmunds, Fenton, Gilbert, Hamlin, Harlan, Harris, Howard, Howe, McDonald, Morrill of Maine, Morrill of Vermont, Morton, Nye, Osborn, Patterson, Pomeroy, Pratt, Ramsey, Rice, Robertson, Sawyer, Schurz, Scott, Sherman, Spencer, Sumner, Thayer, Tipton, Warner, Willey, Williams, Wilson—45.

NAYS—Messrs. *Bayard*, *Casserly*, *Davis*, Ferry, Fowler, *William T. Hamilton*, Kellogg, *McCreery*, *Norton*, Ross, *Saulsbury*, Stewart, *Stockton*, *Thurman*, Trumbull, *Vickers*—16.

January 21—Mr. Drake moved to insert at the end of the bill the following:

*And provided further*, That the State of Virginia is admitted to representation in Congress as one of the States of the Union, upon the following fundamental conditions: First. That the constitution of Virginia shall never be so amended or changed as to deprive any citizen or class of citizens of the United States of the right to vote who are entitled to vote by the constitution herein recognized, except as a punishment for such crimes as are now felonies at common law, whereof they shall have been duly convicted under laws equally applicable to all the inhabitants of said State: *Provided*, That any alteration of said constitution, prospective in its effects, may be made in regard to the time and place of residence of voters.

Mr. Schurz moved to amend the amendment by inserting after the word "vote," the words "or to hold office," which was not agreed to—yeas 28, nays 32, as follow:

YEAS—Messrs. Abbott, Anthony, Boreman, Brownlow, Buckingham, Chandler, Edmunds, Gilbert, Hamlin, Harlan, Harris, Howe, McDonald, Morrill of Vermont, Morton, Osborn, Pomeroy, Pratt, Ramsey, Rice, Robertson, Schurz, Spencer, Sumner, Thayer, Warner, Wilson, Yates—28.

NAYS—Messrs. *Bayard*, Carpenter, *Casserly*, Cole, Conkling, Corbett, Cragin, *Davis*, Drake, Fenton, Ferry, Fowler, *William T. Hamilton*, Howard, Kellogg, Morrill of Maine, *Norton*, Nye, Patterson, Ross, *Saulsbury*, Sawyer, Scott, Sherman, Stewart, *Stockton*, *Thurman*, Tipton, Trumbull, *Vickers*, Willey, Williams—32.

The amendment of Mr. Drake was agreed to—yeas 31, nays 28, as follow:

YEAS—Messrs. Abbott, Anthony, Boreman, Brownlow, Buckingham, Chandler, Cragin, Drake, Edmunds, Gilbert, Hamlin, Harlan, Harris, Howard, Howe, Kellogg, McDonald, Morrill of Vermont, Morton, Osborn, Patterson, Pomeroy, Pratt, Ramsey, Rice, Robertson, Spencer, Sumner, Thayer, Wilson, Yates—31.

NAYS—Messrs. *Bayard*, Carpenter, *Casserly*, Cole, Conkling, Corbett, *Davis*, Fenton, Ferry, Fowler, *William T. Hamilton*, Morrill of Maine, *Norton*, Nye, Ross, *Saulsbury*, Sawyer, Scott, Sherman, Stewart, *Stockton*, *Thurman*, Tipton, Trumbull, *Vickers*, Warner, Willey, Williams—28.

Same day, Mr. Drake moved further to amend by inserting at the end of the bill the following:

Second. That it shall never be lawful for the said State to deprive any citizen of the United States, on account of his race, color, or previous condition of servitude, of the right to hold office under the constitution and laws of said State, or upon any such ground to require of him any other qualifications for office than such as are required of all other citizens.

Which was agreed to—yeas 30, nays 29, as follow:

YEAS—Messrs. Abbott, Boreman, Brownlow, Buckingham, Chandler, Drake, Edmunds, Gilbert, Hamlin, Harlan, Harris, Howard, Howe, Kellogg, McDonald, Morrill of Vermont, Morton, Osborn, Patterson, Pomeroy, Pratt, Ramsey, Rice, Robertson, Schurz, Spencer, Sumner, Thayer, Wilson, Yates—30.

NAYS—Messrs. *Bayard*, Carpenter, *Casserly*, Cole, Conkling, Corbett, Cragin, *Davis*, Fenton, Ferry, Fowler, *William T. Hamilton*, Morrill of Maine, *Norton*, Nye, Ross, *Saulsbury*, Sawyer, Scott, Sherman, Stewart, *Stockton*, *Thurman*, Tipton, Trumbull, *Vickers*, Warner, Willey, Williams—29.

Same day, Mr. Wilson moved to amend by inserting at the end of the bill the following:

Third. That the constitution of Virginia shall never be so amended or changed as to deprive any citizen or class of citizens of the United States of the school rights and privileges secured by the constitution of said State.

Which was agreed to—yeas 31, nays 29, as follow:

YEAS—Messrs. Abbott, Anthony, Boreman, Brownlow, Buckingham, Chandler, Cragin, Drake, Edmunds, Gilbert, Hamlin, Harlan, Harris, Howard, Howe, McDonald, Morrill of Vermont, Morton, Osborn, Patterson, Pomeroy, Pratt, Ramsey, Rice, Robertson, Schurz, Spencer, Sumner, Thayer, Wilson, Yates—31.

NAYS—Messrs. *Bayard*, Carpenter, *Casserly*, Cole, Conkling, Corbett, *Davis*, Fenton, Ferry, Fowler, *William T. Hamilton*, Kellogg, Morrill of Maine, *Norton*, Nye, Ross, *Saulsbury*, Sawyer, Scott, Sherman, Stewart, *Stockton*, *Thurman*, Tipton, Trumbull, *Vickers*, Warner, Willey, Williams—29.

Same day Mr. Morton moved to amend the preamble as follows:

The people of Virginia have framed and adopted a constitution of State government which is republican; and whereas the Legislature of Virginia elected under said constitution have ratified the XIVth and XVth amendments to the Constitution of the United States; and whereas the performance of these several acts in good faith was a condition precedent to the representation of the State in Congress: Therefore

Which was agreed to—yeas 39, nays 20, as follow:

YEAS—Messrs. Abbott, Anthony, Boreman, Brownlow, Buckingham, Chandler, Cole, Cragin, Drake, Edmunds, Fenton, Gilbert, Hamlin, Harlan, Harris, Howard, Howe, McDonald, Morrill of Maine, Morrill of Vermont, Morton, Osborn, Patterson, Pomeroy, Pratt, Ramsey, Rice, Robertson, Sawyer, Schurz, Scott, Spencer, Sumner, Thayer, Tipton, Willey, Williams, Wilson, Yates—39.

NAYS—Messrs. *Bayard*, Carpenter, *Casserly*, Conkling, Corbett, *Davis*, Ferry, Fowler, *William T. Hamilton*, Kellogg, *Norton*, Nye, *Saulsbury*, Sherman, Stewart, *Stockton*, *Thurman*, Trumbull, *Vickers*, Warner—20.

The bill as amended passed the Senate and was concurred in by the House as above.

----

The following bill passed both houses without opposition; the House, January 27; the Senate, January 31:

AN ACT to amend an act entitled "An act to admit the State of Virginia to representation in the Congress of the United States."

*Be it enacted, &c.,* That wherever the word "oath" is used in the act entitled "An act to admit the State of Virginia to representation in the Congress of the United States," it shall be construed to include an affirmation; and every person required by said act to take either of the oaths therein prescribed, who has religious or conscientious scruples against taking an oath, may make and file an affirmation to the same purport and effect: *Provided,* That all the pains and penalties of perjury prescribed by said act shall apply also to any false affirmation taken thereunder.

Approved, February 1, 1870.

----

## AN ACT to admit the State of Mississippi to Representation in the Congress of the United States.

Whereas the people of Mississippi have framed and adopted a constitution of State government which is republican; and whereas the legislature of Mississippi elected under said constitution has ratified the XIVth and XVth amendments to the Constitution of the United States; and whereas the performance of these several acts in good faith is a condition precedent to the representation of the State in Congress: Therefore,

*Be it enacted, &c.,* That the said State of Mississippi is entitled to representation in the Congress of the United States: *Provided,* That before any member of the legislature of said State shall take or resume his seat, or any officer of said State shall enter upon the duties of his office, he shall take and subscribe and file in the office of the secretary of state of Mississippi, for permanent preservation, an oath or affirmation in the form following: "I, ———, do solemnly swear (or affirm) that I have never taken an oath as a member of Congress, or as an officer of the United States, or as a member of any State legislature, or as an executive or judicial officer of any State, to support the Constitution of the United States and afterward engaged in insurrection or rebellion against the same, or given aid or comfort to the enemies thereof: so help me God;" or under the pains and penalties of perjury, (as the case may be;) or such person shall in like manner take, subscribe, and file the following oath or affirmation: "I, ———, do solemnly swear (or affirm) that I have by act of Congress of the United States been relieved from the disabilities imposed upon me by the XIVth Amendment of the Constitution of the United States: so help me God;" or under the pains and penalties of perjury, (as the case may be;) which oaths or affirmations shall be taken before and certified by any officer lawfully authorized to administer oaths. And any person who shall knowingly swear or affirm falsely in taking either of such oaths or affirmations shall be deemed guilty of perjury, and shall be punished therefor by imprisonment not less than one year and not more than ten years, and shall be fined not less than $1,000 and not more than $10,000. And in all trials for any violation of this act the certificate of the taking of either of said oaths or affirmations, with proof of the signature of the party accused, shall be taken and held as conclusive evidence that such oath or affirmation was regularly and lawfully administered by competent authority: *And provided further,* That every such person who shall neglect for the period of thirty days next after the passage of this act to take, subscribe, and file such oath or affirmation as aforesaid shall be deemed and taken, to all intents and purposes, to have vacated his office: *And provided further,* That the State of Mississippi is admitted to representation in Congress as one of the States of the Union upon the following fundamental conditions: First, That the constitution of Mississippi shall never be so amended or changed as to deprive any citizen or class of citizens of the United States of the right to vote who are entitled to vote by the constitution herein recognized, except as a punishment for such crimes as are now felonies at common law, whereof they shall have been duly convicted under laws equally applicable to all the inhabitants of said State: *Provided,* That any alteration of said constitution, prospective in its effects, may be made in regard to the time and place of residence of voters. Second, That it shall never be lawful for the said State to deprive any citizen of the United States, on account of his race, color, or previous condition of servitude, of the right to hold office under the constitution and laws of said State, or upon any such ground to require of him any other qualifications for office than such as are required of all other citizens.

Third, That the constitution of Mississippi shall never be so amended or changed as to deprive any citizen or class of citizens of the United States of the school rights and privileges secured by the constitution of said State.

Approved, February 23, 1870.

The final votes on this act were as follow:

### In House, *February* 3, 1870.

YEAS—Messrs. Allison, Ambler, Ames, Armstrong, Arnell, Asper, Ayer, Banks, Beaman, Beatty, Benjamin, Bennett, Benton, Bingham, Blair, Boles, Booker, Bowen, Boyd, George M. Brooks, Buck, Buckley, Buffinton, Burchard, Burdett, Benjamin F. Butler, Roderick R. Butler, Cake, Cessna, Churchill, Clarke, Amasa Cobb, Clinton L. Cobb, Coburn, Cook, Conger, Cowles, Cullom, Davis, Dawes, Deweese, Dickey, Dixon, Dockery, Donley, Duval, Dyer, Ela, Farnsworth, Ferriss, Ferry, Finkelnburg, Fitch, Garfield, Gilfillan, Hale, Hamilton, Hawley, Hay, Heflin, Hill, Solomon L. Hoge, Hooper, Jenckes, Judd, Julian, Kelley, Kellogg, Kelsey, Ketcham, Knapp, Laflin, Lash, Lawrence, Logan, Loughridge, Lynch, Maynard, McCrary, McGrew, McKenzie, Mercur, Milnes, Eliakim H. Moore, William Moore, Daniel J. Morrell, Samuel P. Morrill, Myers, Negley, O'Neill, Orth, Packard, Packer, Paine, Peters, Phelps, Platt, Pomeroy, Prosser, Ridgway, Roots, Sargent, Sawyer, Scofield, Shanks, Lionel A. Sheldon, Porter Sheldon, John A. Smith, William Smyth, Starkweather, Stevens, Stevenson, Stokes, Stoughton, Strong, Taffe, Tanner, Tillman, Townsend, Twichell, Tyner, Upson, Van Horn, Ward, Cadwalader C. Washburn, William B. Washburn, Welker, Wheeler, B. F. Whittemore, Wilkinson, Willard, Williams, John T. Wilson, Winans—134.

NAYS—Messrs. *Adams, Archer, Beck, Biggs, Bird, James Brooks, Burr, Calkin, Cleveland, Cox, Crebs, Dickinson, Dox, Eldridge, Getz, Gibson, Golladay, Greene, Griswold, Haight, Hambleton, Hamill,* Hoar, *Holman, Johnson, Thomas L. Jones, Kerr, Knott, Marshall, Mayham, McCormick, McNeely, Morgan, Niblack,* Palmer, *Potter, Randall, Reading, Reeves, Rice, Rogers, Schumaker, Sherrod, Stiles, Stone, Strader, Swann, Sweeney, Van Auken, Van Trump, Voorhees, Wells, Winchester, Wood, Woodward*—56.

### In Senate, *February* 17, 1870.

YEAS—Messrs. Abbott, Anthony, Boreman, Brownlow, Buckingham, Cameron, Chandler, Cole, Conkling, Corbett, Cragin, Drake, Edmunds, Fenton, Gilbert, Hamlin, Harlan, Harris, Howard, Howe, Howell, Kellogg, McDonald, Morrill of Maine, Morrill of Vermont, Morton, Nye, Osborn, Patterson, Pomeroy, Pool, Pratt, Ramsey, Rice, Robertson, Ross, Sawyer, Scott, Spencer, Sprague, Stewart, Sumner, Thayer, Tipton, Trumbull, Warner, Willey, Williams, Wilson, Yates—50.

NAYS—Messrs. *Bayard, Casserly, Davis,* Fowler, *William T. Hamilton, Johnston, McCreery, Saulsbury, Stockton, Thurman, Vickers*—11.

---

### Previous Votes.

#### In House.

Mr. Beck offered as a substitute the following:

Whereas the people of Mississippi have framed and adopted a constitutional State government, which is republican in form: Therefore,

· *Be it enacted, &c.,* That the said State of Mississippi is entitled to representation in the Congress of the United States.

Which was not agreed to—yeas 83, nays 100, as follow:

YEAS—Messrs. *Adams, Axtell, Barnum, Beck, Biggs, Bird,* Blair, *James Brooks,* Burchard, *Burr, Calkin, Cleveland, Cox, Crebs,* Deweese, *Dickinson, Dockery, Dox, Eldridge,* Farnsworth, Ferry, Finkelnburg, Fitch, Garfield, *Getz, Gibson, Golladay, Griswold, Haight,* Hale, *Hambleton, Hamill,* Hawkins, Hay, Hill, *Holman,* Jenckes, *Johnson, Thomas L. Jones,* Kellogg, *Kerr,* Ketcham, *Knott,* Laflin, Logan, *Marshall, Mayham, McCormick,* McKenzie, *McNeely,* Milnes, *Morgan, Niblack,* Orth, *Potter, Randall, Reading, Reeves, Rice, Ridgway, Rogers, Schumaker, Sherrod, Slocum, Joseph S. Smith, Stiles, Stone,* Strong, *Swann, Sweeney,* Tanner, Tillman, *Trimble, Van Auken, Van Trump, Voorhees, Wells,* Eugene

M. *Wilson,* Winans, *Winchester,* Witcher, *Wood, Woodward*—83.

NAYS—Messrs. Allison, Ambler, Armstrong, Arnell, Asper, Ayer, Banks, Beaman, Beatty, Benjamin, Bennett, Benton, Boles, *Booker,* Boyd, George M. Brooks, Buck, Buckley, Buffinton, Burdett, Benjamin F. Butler, Roderick R. Butler, Cake, Cessna, Churchill, Clarke, Amasa Cobb, Clinton L. Cobb, Coburn, Cook, Conger, Cowles, Dickey, Dixon, Donley, Duval, Dyer, Ela, Ferriss, Hamilton, Hawley, Heflin, Hoar, Judd, Julian, Kelley, Kelsey, Knapp, Lash, Lawrence, Lynch, McCrary, McGrew, Mercur, Eliakim H. Moore, William Moore, Daniel J. Morrell, Samuel P. Morrill, Myers, Negley, O'Neill, Packard, Packer, Paine, Palmer, Peters, Phelps, Platt, Pomeroy, Prosser, Sargent, Sawyer. Schenck, Scofield, Shanks, Lionel A. Sheldon, Porter Sheldon, John A. Smith, William J. Smith, William Smyth, Starkweather, Stevens, Stevenson, Stokes, Stoughton, Taffe, Townsend, Twichell, Tyner, Upson, Van Horn, Ward, Cadwalader C. Washburn, William B. Washburn, Wheeler, B. F. Whittemore, Wilkinson, Willard, Williams, John T. Wilson—100.

#### In Senate.

February 17—Mr. Willey moved to strike out the third proviso and insert as follows:

So much of the act of Congress entitled "An act to admit the State of Virginia to representation in the Congress of the United States," approved January 26, 1870, as declares that Virginia is admitted to representation upon certain fundamental conditions therein expressed, be, and the same is hereby, repealed.

Which was disagreed to—yeas 23, nays 36, as follow:

YEAS—Messrs. *Bayard, Casserly,* Conkling, *Davis,* Ferry, Fowler, *William T. Hamilton, Johnston,* Kellogg, *McCreery,* Nye, Ross, *Saulsbury,* Sawyer, Sprague, Stewart, *Stockton, Thurman,* Trumbull, *Vickers,* Warner, Willey, Williams—23.

NAYS—Messrs. Abbott, Anthony, Boreman, Brownlow, Buckingham, Cameron, Chandler, Cole, Cragin, Drake, Edmunds, Fenton, Gilbert, Hamlin, Harlan, Harris, Howard, Howell, McDonald, Morrill of Vermont, Morton, Osborn, Patterson, Pomeroy, Pool, Pratt, Ramsey, Rice, Robertson, Scott, Spencer, Sumner, Thayer, Tipton, Wilson, Yates—36.

The Committee on the Judiciary recommended to amend by striking out all the provisos; which was disagreed to—yeas 27, nays 32, as follow:

YEAS—Messrs. *Bayard, Casserly,* Cole, Conkling, *Davis,* Fenton, Ferry, Fowler, *William T. Hamilton, Johnston,* Kellogg, *McCreery,* Morrill of Maine, Ross, *Saulsbury,* Sawyer, Scott, Sprague, Stewart, *Stockton, Thurman,* Tipton, Trumbull, *Vickers,* Warner, Willey, Williams—27.

NAYS—Messrs. Abbott, Anthony, Boreman, Brownlow, Buckingham, Cameron, Chandler, Cragin, Drake, Edmunds, Gilbert, Hamlin, Harlan, Harris, Howard, Howell, McDonald, Morrill of Vermont, Morton, Nye, Osborn, Pomeroy, Pool, Pratt, Ramsey, Rice, Robertson, Spencer, Sumner, Thayer, Wilson, Yates—32.

So the bill passed as above.

### AN ACT to admit the State of Texas to representation in the Congress of the United States.

Whereas the people of Texas have framed and adopted a constitution of State government which is republican; and whereas the Legislature of Texas elected under said constitution has ratified the XIVth and XVth amendments to the Constitution of the United States; and whereas the performance of these several acts in good faith is a condition precedent to the representation of the State in Congress: Therefore,

*Be it enacted, &c.,* That the said State of Texas is entitled to representation in the Congress of the United States: *Provided,* That before any member of the legislature of said State shall take or resume his seat, or any officer of said State

578                          POLITICAL MANUAL.

shall enter upon the duties of his office, he shall
take and subscribe and file in the office of the
secretary of state of Texas, for permanent preservation, an oath or affirmation in the form following: "I, —— ——, do solemnly swear (or
affirm) that I have never taken an oath as a
member of Congress, or as an officer of the United
States, or as a member of any State legislature,
or as an executive or judicial officer of any State,
to support the Constitution of the United States
and afterward engaged in insurrection or rebellion against the same, or given aid or comfort to
the enemies thereof: so help me God;" or under
the pains and penalties of perjury, (as the case
may be;) or such person shall, in like manner,
take, subscribe, and file the following oath or
affirmation: "I, —— ——, do solemnly swear
(or affirm) that I have, by act of Congress of the
United States, been relieved from the disabilities
imposed upon me by the XIVth Amendment of
the Constitution of the United States: so help me
God;" or under the pains and penalties of perjury, (as the case may be;) which oaths or affirmations shall be taken before and certified by
any officer lawfully authorized to administer
oaths. And any person who shall knowingly
swear or affirm falsely in taking either of such
oaths or affirmations shall be deemed guilty of
perjury, and shall be punished therefor by imprisonment not less than one year, and not more
than ten years, and shall be fined not less than
one thousand dollars, and not more than ten
thousand dollars. And in all trials for any violation of this act the certificate of the taking of
either of said oaths or affirmations, with proof of
the signature of the party accused, shall be taken
and held as conclusive evidence that such oath or
affirmation was regularly and lawfully administered by competent authority: *And provided further*, That every such person who shall neglect
for the period of thirty days next after the passage of this act to take, subscribe, and file such
oath or affirmation, as aforesaid, shall be deemed
and taken, to all intents and purposes, to have
vacated his office: *And provided further*, That
the State of Texas is admitted to representation
in Congress as one of the States of the Union,
upon the following fundamental conditions: First,
That the constitution of Texas shall never be so
amended or changed as to deprive any citizen or
class of citizens of the United States of the right
to vote who are entitled to vote by the constitution herein recognized, except as a punishment
for such crimes as are now felonies at common
law, whereof they shall have been duly convicted
under laws equally applicable to all the inhabitants of said State: *Provided*, That any alteration
of said constitution, prospective in its effects, may
be made in regard to the time and place of residence of voters. Second, That it shall never be
lawful for the said State to deprive any citizen
of the United States, on account of his race, color,
or previous condition of servitude, of the right to
hold office under the constitution and laws of said
State, or upon any such ground to require of him
any other qualifications for office than such as are
required of all other citizens. Third, That the
constitution of Texas shall never be so amended
or changed as to deprive any citizen or class of
citizens of the United States of the school rights

and privileges secured by the constitution of said
State.
   Approved, March 30, 1870.
   The final votes on this act were as follow:

IN SENATE, *March 29, 1870.*
   YEAS—Messrs. Abbott, Boreman, Brownlow, Buck-
ingham, Cameron, Cattell, Chandler, Cole, Corbett, Cragin, Drake, Fenton, Ferry, Gilbert, Hamlin, Harlan,
Harris, Howard, Howell, Lewis, McDonald, Morrill of
Maine, Morrill of Vermont, Morton, Nye, Osborn, Patterson, Pomeroy, Pratt, Ramsey, Revels, Rice, Robertson, Ross, Sawyer, Schurz, Scott, Sherman, Sprague,
Stewart, Sumner, Thayer, Tipton, Warner, Willey, Williams, Wilson—47.
   NAYS—Messrs. *Bayard, Casserly, Davis, William T.
Hamilton, Johnston, McCreery, Norton, Saulsbury, Stockton, Thurman, Vickers*—11.

IN HOUSE, *March 30, 1870.*
   YEAS—Messrs. Allison, Ambler, Ames, Arnell, Asper,
Atwood, Ayer, Beaman, Beatty, Benjamin, Bennett,
Benton, Blair, Boles, Boyd, George M. Brooks, Buck,
Buckley, Buffinton, Burchard, Burdett, Benjamin F.
Butler, Cake, Cessna, Sidney Clarke, Clinton L. Cobb,
Coburn, Cook, Conger, Covode, Cowles, Cullom, Davis,
Dawes, Dickey, Dixon, Dockery, Donley, Duval, Dyer,
Ela, Farnsworth, Ferriss, Ferry, Finkelnburg, Fisher,
Garfield, Gilfillan, Hale, Hamilton, Harris, Hawley, Hay,
Heaton, Heflin, Hill, Hoar, Hoge, Hooper, Ingersoll,
Jenckes, Alexander H. Jones, Judd, Julian, Kelley,
Kelsey, Knapp, Lash, Lawrence, Logan, Loughridge,
Lynch, Maynard, McCarthy, McCrary, McGrew, Mc-
Kenzie, Mercur, *Milnes*, Eliakim H. Moore, William
Moore, Morphis, D. J. Morrell, Myers, Negley, O'Neill,
Orth, Packard, Packer, Paine, Perce, Peters, Platt, Po-
land, Pomeroy, Prosser, Roots, Sanford, Sargent, Saw-
yer, Schenck, Scofield, Shanks, Lionel A. Sheldon, Por-
ter Sheldon, John A. Smith, William J. Smith, Worthing-
ton C. Smith, William Smyth, Stevens, Stevenson,
Stokes, Stoughton, Strickland, Taffe, Tillman, Tyner,
Upson, Van Horn, Van Wyck, Ward, Cadwalader C.
Washburn, William B. Washburn, Welker, Wheeler,
Wilkinson, Williams, John T. Wilson, Winans, Witch-
er—130.
   NAYS—Messrs. *Adams, Archer, Axtell, Beck, Biggs,
Bird, James Brooks, Burr, Calkin, Cleveland, Cox, Crebs,
Dickinson, Dox, Eldridge, Getz, Gibson, Griswold, Haight,
Haldeman, Hambleton, Hamill, Holman, Kerr, Knott,
Marshall, Mayham, McCormick, McNeely, Morgan, Mungen,
Niblack, Potter, Randall, Reading, Rice, Ridgway, Schu-
maker, Sherrod, Slocum, Joseph S. Smith, Stiles, Stone,
Swann, Sweeney, Trimble, Van Trump, Wells, Eugene M.
Wilson, Wood*—50.

### Previous Votes.
IN HOUSE.
   1870, March 15—Mr. B. F. Butler, from the
Committee on Reconstruction, reported the above
bill, with the addition of the following proviso:
   *Provided further*, That this act shall not affect
in any manner the conditions and guarantees
upon which the State of Texas was annexed and
admitted as a State.
   Mr. Wood moved to add to the end of the bill
the following:
   *And provided further*, That this act shall re-
admit the State of Texas to all the rights of
other States within the Union, without qualification or fundamental conditions, except as herein
stated.
   Which was disagreed to—yeas 49, nays 121,
as follow:
   YEAS—Messrs. *Adams, Archer, Barnum, Beck, Biggs,
Bird, James Brooks, Burr, Calkin, Crebs, Dickinson, Dox,
Eldridge, Getz, Griswold, Haight, Haldeman, Hamill, Hol-
man, Johnson, Kerr, Knott, Mayham, McCormick, McKen-
zie, McNeely, Morgan, Mungen, Niblack, Potter, Randall,
Reading, Reeves, Rice, Ridgway, Rogers, Scofield, Sherrod,
Slocum, Stiles, Stone, Swann, Trimble, Van Auken, Van
Trump, Voorhees, Wells, Eugene M. Wilson, Wood*—49.
   NAYS—Messrs. Allison, Ambler, Armstrong, Arnell,
Asper, Atwood, *Axtell*, Beatty, Benjamin, Blair, Boles,
Booker, Boyd, George M. Brooks, Buck, Buckley,

Buffinton, Burchard, Burdett, Benjamin F. Butler, Roderick R. Butler, Cake, Cessna, Churchill, Sidney Clarke, Amasa Cobb, Clinton L. Cobb, Coburn, Conger, Covode, Cullom, Dawes, Duval, Ela, Ferriss, Ferry, Finkelnburg, Fisher, Garfield, Hamilton, Harris, Hawkins, Hawley, Hay, Heaton, Heflin, Hill, Hoar, Hooper, Ingersoll, Jenckes, Alexander H. Jones, Judd, Julian, Kelley, Kellogg, Kelsey, Ketcham, Laflin, Logan, Loughridge, Lynch, Maynard, McCarthy, McCrary, McGrew, McKee, Jesse H. Moore, William Moore, Morphis, Morrell, Morrill, Myers, O'Neill, Orth, Packard, Packer, Paine, Palmer, Perce, Peters, Poland, Pomeroy, Prosser, Roots, Sanford, Sargent, Sawyer, Schenck, Schumaker, Shanks, Lionel A. Sheldon, Porter Sheldon, John A. Smith, William J. Smith, Worthington C. Smith, William Smyth, Starkweather, Stevens, Stevenson, Stokes, Stoughton, Strickland, Strong, Taffee, Tillman, Townsend, Twichell, Tyner, Upson, Van Horn, Ward, Cadwalader C. Washburn, William B. Washburn, Welker, Wheeler, Wilkinson, Willard, Williams, John T. Wilson, Winans—121.

Mr. Beck moved to amend by substituting as follows:

"Whereas the State of Texas has a constitution of State government republican in form: Therefore,

"Be it enacted by the Senate and House of Representatives of the United States of America in Congress assembled, that the said State of Texas is entitled to representation in the Congress of the United States."

Which was disagreed to—yeas 52, nays 106—as follow:

YEAS—Messrs. *Adams, Archer, Beck, Biggs, Bird,* Blair, *James Brooks, Burr, Calkin, Dickinson,* Dockery, *Dox, Eldridge,* Farnsworth, *Getz, Griswold, Haight, Haldeman, Hamill,* Hawkins, Hay, *Holman, Johnson, Kerr, Knott, Mayham, McCormick, McKenzie, McNeely, Morgan, Mungen, Niblack, Potter, Randall, Reading, Reeves, Rice, Ridgway, Rogers, Schumaker, Sherrod, Slocum, Stiles, Stone, Swann, Trimble, Van Auken, Van Trump, Voorhees, Wells, Eugene M. Wilson, Wood*—52.

NAYS—Messrs. Allison, Ambler, Armstrong, Arnell, Asper, Atwood, Ayer, Banks, Beaman, Beatty, Benjamin, Boles, *Booker,* Boyd, George M. Brooks, Buck, Buckley, Buffinton, Burdett, Benjamin F. Butler, Roderick R. Butler, Cessna, Sidney Clarke, Amasa Cobb, Coburn, Cook, Conger, Covode, Donley, Duval, Ferriss, Ferry, Finkelnburg, Hamilton, Harris, Hawley, Heaton, Heflin, Hill, Hoar, Ingersoll, Jenckes, Alexander H. Jones, Judd, Julian, Kelley, Kelsey, Loughridge, Lynch, Maynard, McCarthy, McCrary, McGrew, McKee, William Moore, Morphis, Morrell, Morrill, Myers, Neg-

ley, O'Neill, Orth, Packard, Packer, Paine, Palmer, Perce, Peters, Phelps, Poland, Pomeroy, Prosser, Roots, Sanford, Sargent, Sawyer, Schenck, Scofield, Shanks, Lionel A. Sheldon, Porter Sheldon, John A. Smith, William J. Smith, William Smyth. Starkweather, Stevenson, Stokes, Stoughton, Strickland, Strong, Taffe, Tillman, Townsend, Twichell, Tyner, Upson, Van Horn, Ward, Cadwalader C. Washburn, William B. Washburn. Welker, Wheeler, Wilkinson, Willard, Williams, Winans—106.

The bill was then passed as reported—yeas 127, nays 46, as follows:

YEAS—Messrs. Allison, Ambler, Armstrong, Arnell, Asper, Atwood, Bailey, Banks, Beaman, Beatty, Benjamin, Blair, Boles, *Booker,* Bowen, Boyd, George M. Brooks. Buck, Buckley, Buffinton, Burchard, Burdett, Benjamin F. Butler, Roderick R. Butler, Cake, Cessna, Churchill, Sidney Clarke, Amasa Cobb, Coburn, Cook, Conger, Covode, Cullom, Dawes, Dockery, Donley, Duval, Farnsworth, Ferriss, Ferry, Finkelnburg, Fitch, Garfield, Hale, Hamilton, Harris. Hawley, Hay, Heaton, Heflin, Hill, Hoar, Ingersoll, Jenckes, Alexander H. Jones, Judd, Julian, Kelley, Kellogg, Kelsey, Ketcham, Laflin, Logan, Loughridge, Lynch, Maynard, McCarthy, McGrew, McKee, *McKenzie.* William Moore, Morphis, Morrell, Morrill, Myers, Negley, O'Neill, Orth, Packard, Packer, Paine, Perce, Peters, Phelps, Poland, Pomeroy, Prosser, *Ridgway,* Roots, Sanford, Sargent, Sawyer. Schenck, Scofield, Shanks, Lionel A. Sheldon, Porter Sheldon, John A. Smith, William J. Smith, Worthington C. Smith, William Smyth, Starkweather, Stevens, Stevenson, Stokes, Stoughton, Strickland, Strong, *Sweeney,* Taffe, Tillman, Townsend. Twichell, Tyner, Upson, Van Horn, Ward, Cadwalader C. Washburn. William B. Washburn, Welker, Wheeler, Wilkinson, Willard, Williams. John T. Wilson, Winans—127.

NAYS—Messrs. *Adams, Archer,* Ayer, *Beck, Biggs, Bird, James Brooks, Burr, Calkin, Dickinson, Dox, Eldridge, Getz, Griswold, Haight, Haldeman, Hamill, Holman. Johnson, Kerr, Knott, Mayham, McCormick, McNeely, Morgan, Niblack, Potter, Randall, Reading, Reeves, Rice, Rogers, Schumaker, Sherrod, Slocum, Stiles. Stone, Strader, Swann, Trimble, Van Auken, Van Trump, Voorhees, Wells, Eugene M. Wilson, Wood*—46.

## IN SENATE.

1870, March 26—Mr. Sherman moved to amend by striking out the last proviso, which was agreed to, and the bill then passed both houses as above.

The State of Virginia was turned over by the military to the civil authorities January 28, 1870; the State of Mississippi, February 28, 1870; and the State of Texas, April 16, 1870.

# LVI.

# DECLARATORY RESOLUTIONS

ON REPUDIATION, PURCHASE OF U. S. BONDS, INCREASING THE CURRENCY. TARIFF, AMNESTY; AND THE VALIDITY OF THE XIVTH AND XVTH AMENDMENTS; AND THE BILL TO RE-APPORTION REPRESENTATIVES.

## IN HOUSE.

### On Repudiation.

1869, December 16—Mr. Garfield offered in Committee of the Whole the following resolution:

*Resolved,* That the proposition, direct or indirect, to repudiate any portion of the debt of the United States is unworthy of the honor and good name of the nation; and that this House, without distinction of party, hereby sets its seal of condemnation upon any and all such propositions.

Which was reported to the House and agreed to—yeas 124, nays 1, as follow:

YEAS—Messrs. *Adams,* Allison, Ambler, Ames, *Archer,* Armstrong, Arnell, Asper, *Barnum,* Beatty, Blair, Boles, Boyd, George M. Brooks, *James Brooks,* Buffinton, Burchard, Cessna, Churchill, Clarke, Amasa Cobb, Coburn, Conger, *Cox, Crebs,* Davis, Dawes, Dickey, *Dixon,* Donley, *Dox,* Duvall, Dyer, Ela, *Eldridge,* Farnsworth, Ferris, Finkelnburg, Fisher, Fitch, Garfield, *Getz,* Gilfillan. *Haldeman, Hambleton, Hamill,* Hawkins, Hawley, Hay, Heaton, Hill, Hoar, *Holman,* Hooper, Hotchkiss, Ingersoll, Jenckes, Alexander H. Jones, Julian, Kelley, Kellogg, Kelsey, *Kerr,* Ketcham, Knapp, Laflin, Lawrence, Lynch, *Mayham*, Maynard, McCarthy, *McCormick*, McGrew, Mercur, Jesse H. Moore, William Moore, Myers, *Niblack*, O'Neill, Orth, Packard, Packer, Paine, Palmer, Phelps, Pomeroy, *Potter*, *Randall*, Sanford, Sargent, Sawyer, Schenck, Scofield, Shanks, *Slocum*, John A. Smith, William J. Smith, Worthington C. Smith, William Smyth, Starkweather, Stevens, Stevenson, *Stiles*, Strong, *Swann*, Taffe, Tanner, Tillman, Twichell, Tyner, Upson, Van Horn, Ward, Cadwalader C. Washburn, William B. Washburn, Welker, B. F Whittemore, Wilkinson, Willard, Williams, *Eugene M. Wilson*, John T. Wilson, Witcher, *Woodward*—124.

NAYS—Mr. *Thomas L. Jones*—1.

## On Purchasing Bonds.

1870, January 31—Mr. McNeely submitted the following resolution:

*Resolved,* That the national debt should be paid in strict compliance with the contract, whether it is made payable in gold or greenbacks; that the five-twenty bonds are payable in greenbacks or their equivalent, and we condemn the policy of the administration, which is squandering millions of money by buying such bonds at a high rate of premium, when the Government had the clear right to redeem them at par.

Which was laid on the table—yeas 122, nays 42, as follow:

YEAS—Messrs. Allison, Ames, Arnell, Asper, *Axtell*, Bailey, Banks, Beaman, Benjamin, Bennett, Benton, Bingham, Blair, Boles, Bowen, Boyd, George M. Brooks, Buck, Buckley, Buffinton, Burchard, Cake, Cessna, Churchill, Clark, Amasa Cobb, Clinton L. Cobb, Coburn, Conger, Cowles, Cullom, Dawes, Deweese, Dickey, Dixon, Dockery, Donley, Duval, Farnsworth, Ferriss. Ferry, Finkelnburg, Fisher, Fitch, Garfield, Gilfillan, *Greene*, Hale, Hamilton, Hawley, Heaton, Heflin. Hill, Hoar, Hooper, Jenckes. Judd, Kelley, Kellogg, Kelsey, Ketcham, Knapp, Laflin, Lawrence, Logan, Loughridge, Lynch, Maynard, McCrary, McGrew, Mercur, Eliakim H. Moore, William Moore, Daniel J. Morrell, Samuel P. Morrill, Myers, O'Neill, Orth, Packard, Packer, Paine, Palmer, Peters, Phelps, Platt, Poland, Pomeroy, Roots, Sargent, Sawyer, Schenck, Scofield, Shanks, Lionel A. Sheldon, Porter Sheldon, *Slocum*, John A. Smith, William J. Smith, Worthington C. Smith. William Smyth, Starkweather, Stevens, Stevenson, Stokes, Stoughton, Strickland, Strong, Taffe, Tanner, Tillman, Townsend, Twichell, Tyner, Upson, Cadwalader C. Washburn, William B. Washburn, Welker, Wheeler, B. F. Whittemore, Wilkinson, Willard, Williams—122.

NAYS—Messrs *Adams*, Beatty, *Beck*, *Biggs*, *Bird*, *James Brooks*, *Burr*, *Crebs*. Dickinson, *Dox*, *Eldridge*, *Getz*, *Gibson*, *Golladay*, *Griswold*, *Holman*, *Johnson*, *Thomas L. Jones*, *Kerr*, *Knott*, *Marshall*, *McCormick*. *McNeely*, *Morgan*, *Niblack*, *Reading*, *Rice*, *Schumaker*, *Sherrod*, *Joseph S. Smith*, *Stiles*, *Strader*, *Sweeney*, *Trimble*, *Van Auken*, *Van Trump*, *Voorhees*, *Wells*, *Eugene M. Wilson*, *Winchester*, *Woodward* —42.

## On Increasing the Currency.

1870, February 14—Mr. Loughridge offered the following resolution:

*Resolved,* That in the opinion of the House the business interests of the country require an increase in the volume of circulating currency, and the Committee on Banking and Currency are instructed to report to the House, at as early a day as practicable, a bill increasing the currency to the amount of at least $50,000,000.

Mr. Ward moved to lay the resolution on the table, which was disagreed to—yeas 74, nays 92, as follow:

YEAS—Messrs. Ames, *Axtell*, Banks, *Barnum*, Beaman, Benton, *Bird*, George M. Brooks, *James Brooks*, Buckley, Buffinton, Burchard, Churchill, Cowles, *Cox*, Davis, Dawes, Dixon, Duval, Ela, Ferriss, Fisher, Fitch, Garfield, *Getz*, Gilfillan, *Haight*. Hale. Hill, Hoar, Hooper, Hotchkiss, Jenckes, Kelley, Kellogg, Kelsey, Knapp, Laflin. Lynch, McGrew, Mercur, Daniel J. Morrell, Samuel P. Morrill, Myers, Negley, O'Neill, Peters, Platt, Poland, *Potter*, *Randall*, *Reading*, Sargent, Sawyer, Schu-

maker, Scofield, Porter Sheldon, *Slocum*, Worthington C. Smith, Starkweather, Stevens, *Stiles*, Strong, Tanner, Tillman, Townsend, Twichell, *Van Auken*, Ward, Cadwalader C. Washburn, William B. Washburn, Wheeler, Willard, *Woodward*—74.

NAYS—Messrs. Allison, Armstrong, Asper, *Beck*, Benjamin, *Biggs*, Bingham, Boles, *Booker*, Boyd, Burdett, *Burr*, Amasa Cobb, Coburn, Cook, Conger, *Crebs*, Deweese, Dockery, *Dox*, Dyer, *Eldridge*, Farnsworth, Ferry, Finkelnburg, *Gibson*. *Golladay*, *Greene*, *Griswold*, Hawkins, Hawley, Hay, Heflin, Hoge, *Holman*, Ingersoll, *Johnson*, Alexander H. Jones, *Thomas L. Jones*, Judd, *Kerr*, *Knott*, Lash, Lawrence, Logan, Loughbridge, *Marshall*, *Mayham*, Maynard, *McCormick*, McCrary, *McKenzie*, *McNeely*, Eliakim H. Moore, *Morgan*, *Mungen*, *Niblack*, Orth, Packard, Packer, Paine, Palmer, Phelps, Pomeroy, Prosser, *Reeves*, *Rice*, *Ridgway*, *Rogers*, Schenck, Shanks, Lionel A. Sheldon, *Joseph S. Smith*, William Smyth, Stevenson, Stokes, *Stone*, Stoughton, *Strader*. *Swann*, Taffe, *Trimble*, Tyner, Van Horn, *Voorhees*, Welker, *Wells*, Wilkinson, *Eugene M. Wilson*, John T. Wilson, Witcher, *Wood*—92.

February 21—The resolution was agreed to—yeas 110, nays 73, as follow:

YEAS—Messrs. *Adams*, Allison, Armstrong, Asper, Ayer, Beatty, *Beck*, Benjamin, Bennett, Bingham, Boles, *Booker*, Boyd, Buck, Buckley, Burdett, *Burr*, Benjamin F. Butler, Roderick R. Butler, Cake, Clarke, Amasa Cobb, *Coburn*, Cook, *Conger*, *Crebs*, Cullom, Deweese, Dickey, *Dickinson*, Dockery, *Dox*, Dyer, *Eldridge*, Farnsworth, Ferry, Finkelnburg, *Gibson*, *Golladay*, *Hamill*, Hamilton, Hawkins, Hawley, Hay, Heaton, Heflin, Hoge, *Holman*, Ingersoll, *Johnson*, Alexander H. Jones, *Thomas L. Jones*, Judd, Julian, *Kerr*, *Knott*, Lash, Lawrence, Logan, Loughridge, *Marshall*, Maynard, McCarthy, *McCormick*, McCrary, *McNeely*, Eliakim H. Moore, Jesse H. Moore, *Morgan*, *Mungen*, *Niblack*, Orth, Packard, Packer, Paine, Palmer, Pomeroy, Prosser, *Rice*, *Rogers*, Roots, Schenck, Shanks, Lionel A. Sheldon, *Sherrod*, John A. Smith, William J. Smith, William Smyth, Stevenson, Stokes, Stoughton, Strader, Strickland, *Swann*, Taffe, *Trimble*, Tyner, Van Horn, *Van Trump*, Van Wyck, *Voorhees*, Welker, *Wells*, B. F. Whittemore, Wilkinson, Williams, *Eugene M. Wilson*, John T. Wilson, Witcher, *Wood*—110.

NAYS—Messrs. Ambler, Ames, Arnell, *Axtell*, Banks, *Barnum*, Beaman, Benton, *Bird*, Blair, Geo. M. Brooks, *James Brooks*, Buffinton, Burchard, Calkin, Cessna, Churchill, Cowles, *Cox*, Davis, Dawes, Duval, Ferriss, Fisher, Fitch, Garfield, *Getz*, Gilfillan, *Haight*, *Haldeman*, Hale, Hoar, Hooper, Hotchkiss, Jenckes, Kelley, Kellogg, Ketcham, Knapp, Laflin, *Mayham*, McGrew, William Moore, Samuel P. Morrill, Myers, O'Neill, Peters, Phelps, Platt, Poland, *Randall*, *Reading*, *Reeves*, Sargent, Sawyer, Scofield, *Slocum*, Worthington C. Smith, Starkweather, Stevens, Strong, Tanner, Tillman, Townsend, Twichell, Upson, Ward, Cadwalader C. Washburn, William B. Washburn, Wheeler, Willard, Winans, *Woodward*—73.

## IN SENATE.

1870, February 24—Mr. Williams submitted the following resolution; which was considered, by unanimous consent, and agreed to:

*Resolved,* That to add to the present irredeemable paper currency of the country would be to render more difficult and remote the resumption of specie payments, to encourage and foster the spirit of speculation, to aggravate the evils produced by frequent and sudden fluctuations of values, to depreciate the credit of the nation, and to check the healthful tendency of legitimate business to settle down upon a safe and permanent basis, and, therefore, in the opinion of the Senate, the existing volume of such currency ought not to be increased.

## IN HOUSE.

1870, March 21—Mr. Williams introduced the following resolution:

*Resolved,* That while it is the duty of Congress to provide for the funding of the national debt at a lower rate of interest, and to extend the time for its payment to a period at which it will be the least oppressive to the people, it is also the sense of this House that the interest-bearing debt of the United States should not be increased by causing a surrender of any part of our present circulating medium not bearing interest, and the substitution therefor of interest-bearing bonds.

Which was agreed to.

## On the Tariff.

1870, January 31 — Mr. Marshall offered the following resolution:

*Resolved,* That the power granted in the federal Constitution to levy and collect taxes, duties, imposts, and excises, to pay the debts and provide for the common defense and general welfare of the United States, does not include or embrace any power to levy duties for any purpose other than the collection of revenue for the uses therein indicated; that a tariff levied for any purpose other than revenue, and especially one levied to foster and enrich one section of our country at the expense of others, or to foster and enrich one class of citizens at the expense of others, is unauthorized by the Constitution, unjust to the great body of the American people, and in its results injurious eventually to nearly every industrial interest of the country.

*Resolved,* That in the preparation of a bill for the modification of existing tariff laws Congress should confine its action strictly to the preparation of a tariff for revenue exclusively; and that the duties on no article should be greater than that which will give the maximum of revenue on said article.

February 7 — On motion of Mr. Kelsey, it was laid on the table—yeas 90, nays 77, as follow:

YEAS—Messrs. Ambler, Ames, Asper, Banks, Beaman, Bennett, Benton, Bingham, Blair, Boles, Bowen, Buck, Buckley, Buffinton, Burdett, Cessna, Churchill, Clarke, Amasa Cobb, Conger, Cowles, Dawes, Dickey, Donley, Duval, Ela, Ferriss, Ferry, Fisher, Gilfillan, Hale, Hamilton, Heaton, Heflin, Hoar, Hoge, Hotchkiss, Jenckes, Kelley, Kelsey, Ketcham, Knapp, Laflin, Lash, Lynch, Maynard, McGrew, Mercur, Milnes, Eliakim H. Moore, William Moore, Daniel J. Morrell, Samuel P. Morrill, Myers, Negley, O'Neill, Paine, Palmer, Phelps, Poland, Prosser, Roots, Sanford, Schenck, Scofield, Lionel A. Sheldon, John A. Smith, William J. Smith, Worthington C. Smith, Starkweather, Stevens, Stokes, Stoughton, Strickland, Strong, Taffe, Tanner, Tillman, Twichell, Van Horn, Ward, Cadwalader C. Washburn, William B. Washburn, Welker, Wheeler, B. F. Whittemore, Willard, Williams, John T. Wilson, Witcher—90.

NAYS—Messrs. *Adams,* Allison, *Archer,* Arnell, *Axtell,* Beatty, *Beck,* Benjamin, *Biggs, Bird, Booker, James Brooks,* Burchard, *Burr,* Roderick R. Butler, Calkin, Coburn, *Cox, Crebs,* Cullom, Deweese, *Dickinson,* Dockery, *Dox,* Finkelnburg, *Getz, Gibson, Golladay, Griswold,* Haight, Haldeman, Hambleton, *Hamill,* Hawkins, Hay, Ingersoll, *Johnson, Thomas L. Jones,* Judd, Julian, *Kerr, Knott,* Lawrence, *Marshall, Mayham, McCormick,* McCrary, *McKenzie, McNeely, Niblack,* Orth, Packard, Pomeroy, *Reading, Reeves, Rogers,* Schumaker, Shanks, *Sherrod, Slocum,* William Smyth, Stevenson, *Stiles, Stone, Strader, Swann, Sweeney, Trimble,* Tyner, *Van Auken, Van Trump, Wells, Eugene M. Wilson,* Winans, *Winchester, Wood, Woodward*—77.

1870, March 14 — Mr. Marshall submitted the following resolution:

*Resolved,* That the present depressed condition of the business and the various industrial interests of the country demand of Congress prompt action in relieving the people of all burdens of taxation not absolutely necessary to provide for the wants of the Government economically administered, and that in reforming existing tariff laws legislation should be based upon these principles:

1. That no duty should be imposed on any article above the lowest rate which will yield the largest amount of revenue.

2. That the maximum revenue duty should be imposed on luxuries; and

3. That the duty should be so imposed as to operate as equally as possible throughout the Union, discriminating neither for nor against any class or section.

Mr. Holman moved that it lie on the table; which was disagreed to—yeas 38, nays 119, as follow:

YEAS—Messrs. Ambler, Armstrong, Ayer, Banks, Bennett, Blair, George M. Brooks, Buck, Buckley, Benjamin F. Butler, Cessna, Dawes, Ela, Fisher, Gilfillan, Hamilton, Harris, Hoar, Hoge, Jenckes, Kelsey, Maynard, McKee, Daniel J. Morrell, Negley, O'Neill, Packer, Perce, Roots, Sargent, Scofield, Lionel A. Sheldon, Porter Sheldon, Stoughton, Strickland, Tillman, Ward, Willard—38.

NAYS—Messrs *Adams,* Allison, *Archer,* Asper, Atwood, *Barnum,* Beatty, Benjamin, *Bird,* Boles, Boyd, *James Brooks,* Buffinton, Burchard, *Burdett, Burr, Calkin,* Churchill, Sidney Clarke, Amasa Cobb, Coburn, Cook, Conger, *Crebs,* Cullom, Dickey, *Dickinson,* Dockery, Donley, *Dox, Eldridge,* Ferriss, Ferry, Finkelnburg, Fitch, Garfield, *Getz, Griswold,* Haight, *Haldeman,* Hale, Hawkins, Hawley, Hay, Hays, Heflin, Hill, *Holman,* Ingersoll, *Johnson,* Alexander H. Jones, Judd, Kelley, *Kerr,* Ketcham, *Knott,* Laflin, Lash, Logan, Loughridge, *Marshall, Mayham,* McCarthy, *McCormick,* McCrary, *McKenzie, McNeely,* Jesse H. Moore, William Moore, *Morgan,* Morphis, Samuel P. Morrill, *Mungen,* Myers, *Niblack,* Orth, Packard, Paine, Peters, Pomeroy, *Potter, Randall, Reeves, Rice, Ridgway, Rogers,* Sawyer, Schenck, Schumaker, Shanks, *Sherrod, Slocum,* John A. Smith, Worthington C. Smith, Starkweather, Stevens, Stevenson, *Stiles,* Stokes, *Stone, Strader,* Strong, Taffe, Tanner, *Trimble,* Tyner, Upson, *Van Trump, Voorhees,* Cadwalader C. Washburn, William B. Washburn, Welker, *Wells,* Wheeler, Wilkinson, Williams, *Eugene M. Wilson,* John T. Wilson, *Wood*—119.

The resolution was then referred to the Committee of Ways and Means.

1870, February 28—Mr. Spink introduced the following resolution:

*Resolved,* That the interests of the country require such tariff for revenue upon foreign imports as will afford incidental protection to domestic manufacturers, and as will, without impairing the revenue, impose the lowest burden upon and best promote and encourage the great industrial interests of the country.

Mr. Wood moved that it lie on the table, which was disagreed to. It was then passed—yeas 108, nays 47, as follow:

YEAS—Messrs. Ambler, Ames, Atwood, *Axtell,* Beaman, Bingham, Blair, *James Brooks,* Buck, Buffinton, Burdett, Benjamin F. Butler, Roderick R. Butler, Cake, Cessna, Churchill, Clinton L. Cobb, Cook, Conger, Covode, Cullom, Davis, Donley, Dyer, Ferriss, Fisher, Garfield, *Getz, Hamill,* Harris, Hawley, Heaton, Hill, Hoar, Hoge, Hooper, Hotchkiss, Ingersoll, Jenckes, *Johnson,* Alexander H. Jones, Kelley, Kellogg, Kelsey, Ketcham, Knapp, Laflin, Lash, Lawrence, Loughridge, Maynard, McCrary, McGrew, Mercur, Milnes, Eliakim H. Moore, Jesse H. Moore. William Moore, Morphis, Morrell, Morrill, Myers, Negley, O'Neill, Packard, Paine, Palmer, Perce, Peters, Phelps, Platt, Pomeroy, Prosser, *Randall,* Sargent, Sawyer, Schenck, Scofield, Shanks, Lionel A. Sheldon, John A. Smith, William J. Smith, Worthington C. Smith, Starkweather, Stevens, Stevenson, *Stiles,* Stokes, Stoughton, Strickland, Strong, *Swann,* Taffe, Tanner, Tillman, Twichell, Upson, Van Horn, Cadwalader C. Washburn, William B. Washburn, Welker, Wheeler, Wilkinson, Willard, Williams, John T. Wilson, Witcher, *Woodward*—108.

NAYS—Messrs. Allison, *Archer, Biggs, Bird, Booker,* Boyd, George M. Brooks, Burchard, *Burr, Calkin, Cox, Crebs, Dickinson, Dox,* Finkelnburg, *Gibson, Griswold,* Haight, *Hambleton,* Hawkins, Hay, Hays, Heflin, *Holman,*

*Thomas L. Jones*, Judd, *Kerr*, *Marshall*, *Mayham*, *McCormick*, *McNeely*, *Mungen*, *Niblack* Orth, *Potter*, *Reeves*, *Ridgway*, *Rogers*, *Schumaker*, *Sherrod*, *Joseph S. Smith*, *Stone*, *Trimble*, Tyner, *Voorhees*, Winans, *Wood*—47.

1870, June 6—Mr. Ward submitted the following resolution:

*Resolved*, That the Committee of Ways and Means is hereby instructed, at the earliest practicable moment, to report a bill to this House abolishing the tariff on coal, so as to secure that important article of fuel to the people free from all taxation.

Which was agreed to—yeas 112, nays 78, as follow:

YEAS—Messrs. *Adams*, Allison, Ames, Atwood, Bailey, Banks, Beatty, *Beck*, Bennett, *Biggs*, Bird, Boyd, Geo. M. Brooks, *James Brooks*, Buffinton, Burchard, *Burr*, Benjamin F. Butler, Churchill, Sidney Clarke, Coburn, Cook, Conger, *Conner*, Cowles, *Cox*, *Crebs*, Cullom, Davis, Dawes, Degener, Dixon, *Dox*, Dyer, Ela, *Eldridge*, Farnsworth, Ferriss, Finkelnburg, Fisher, Fitch, *Fox*, *Griswold*, *Haight*, Hale, Hamilton, Harris, Hawley, Hay, Hays, Heflin, Hoar, *Holman*, Hotchkiss, Ingersoll, Jenckes, *Johnson*, Alexander H. Jones, Judd, Kellogg, *Kerr*, Ketcham, *Knott*, Laflin, Lash, Lawrence, Logan, Loughridge, Lynch, *Marshall*, *Mayham*, *McCormick*, McCrary, *McNeely*, Jesse H. Moore, *Morgan*, *Morrissey*, *Niblack*, Orth, *Packard*, Paine, Peck, Peters, Pomeroy, *Potter*, *Reeves*, Sargent, *Sherrod*, *Slocum*, *Joseph S. Smith*, William J. Smith, Worthington C. Smith, Wm. Smyth, Starkweather, Stevenson, Stoughton, Strong, *Sweeney*, Tanner, Twichell, Tyner, *Van Trump*, Ward, William B. Washburn, Wheeler, Whitmore, Wilkinson, Williams, *Eugene M. Wilson*, Winans, *Winchester*, *Wood*—112.

NAYS—Messrs. Ambler, Armstrong, *Axtell*, Ayer, Barry, Beaman, Benjamin, Benton, Bingham, Blair, Boles, Bowen, Buck, Cake, Cessna, Amasa Cobb, Covode, Dickey, Donley, Duval, Garfield, *Getz*, Gilfillan, *Haldeman*, *Hamill*, Hawkins, Hill, Kelley, Knapp, *Lewis*, Maynard, McCarthy, McGrew, *McKenzie*, Mercur, *Milnes*, Eliakim H. Moore, William Moore, Morphis, Daniel J. Morrell, Myers, Negley, Newsham, O'Neill, Packer, Phelps, Platt, Prosser, *Randall*, *Rice*, *Ridgway*, *Rogers*, Roots, Sanford, Sawyer, Schenck, Scofield, Lionel A. Sheldon, Porter Sheldon, John A. Smith, Stokes, *Stone*, *Strader*, Strickland, *Swann*, Taylor, Tillman, Townsend, *Trimble*, Upson, Van Wyck, Wallace, Welker, *Wells*, Willard, John T. Wilson, Witcher, *Woodward*—78.

June 27—Mr. Reeves offered the following resolution:

Whereas salt is an article of prime necessity and universal consumption, which, proportionally to numbers, forms a larger item in the domestic economy of families of small or moderate means than it does in those of the wealthier classes, and ought therefore at all times to be as lightly taxed as is consistent with a due regard to the revenue needed for an economical administration of the Government; and whereas in any genuine and well-considered scheme of revenue reform duties which tend directly and largely to augment the cost of such a commodity as salt should be reduced in preference to others which bear less heavily upon the resources of the great body of the people: Therefore,

*Be it resolved*, That the Committee of Ways and Means are hereby directed and instructed to report to this House forthwith a bill reducing the present duties on all classes of salt fifty per cent.

Which was agreed to—yeas 110, nays 49, as follow:

YEAS—Messrs. Allison, Asper, Beatty, *Beck*, Benjamin, *Biggs*, Bird, Boles, *Booker*, *James Brooks*, Buck, Buckley, Burchard, Burdett, *Burr*, Roderick R. Butler, William T. Clark, Sidney Clarke, *Cleveland*, Clinton L. Cobb, Coburn, *Conner*, Cook, *Cox*, *Crebs*, Cullom, Davis, Degener, *Dickinson*, Dyer, Ela, *Eldridge*, Farnsworth, Finkelnburg, Fitch, Garfield, *Haldeman*, Hawkins, Hawley, Hay, Hays, Heflin, *Holman*, Ingersoll, *Johnson*, *Thomas L. Jones*, Judd, Kellogg, *Kerr*, *Knott*, Lash, Lawrence, *Lewis*,

Logan, Loughridge, *Marshall*, *McCormick*, McCrary, McKenzie, *McNeely*. *Milnes*, Jesse H. Moore, *Morgan*, *Mungen*, Newsham, *Niblack*, Orth, Packard, Paine, Peck, Perce, Platt, Pomeroy, Prosser, *Reeves*, *Rice*, *Rogers*, Sargent, Shanks, *Shober*, John A. Smith, *Joseph S. Smith*, William J. Smith, Worthington C. Smith, William Smyth, Stevens, Stevenson, *Stiles*, Stokes, Stoughton, Strong, *Swann*, *Sweeney*, Taffe, *Trimble*. Twichell, Tyner, *Van Auken*, Van Horn, *Van Trump*, Ward, *Wells*. Whitmore, Wilkinson, Williams, *Eugene M. Wilson*, Winans, *Winchester*, *Wood*, *Woodward*—110.

NAYS—Messrs. Ambler, Ames, Armstrong, Atwood, Beaman, Bennett, Benton, Bingham, Blair, George M. Brooks, Buffinton, Benjamin F. Butler, Cessna, Amasa Cobb, Conger, Covode, Dixon, Donley. Ferriss, Ferry, Fisher, Hoar, Kelley, Kelsey, Knapp, Laflin, Maynard, McCarthy, McGrew, Eliakim H. Moore, William Moore, Daniel J. Morrell, Myers, Negley, O'Neill, Packer, Phelps, Poland, Sawyer, Schenck, Porter Sheldon, Strickland, Tanner, Taylor, Tillman, Townsend, Wheeler, Willard, John T. Wilson—49.

---

## On General Amnesty.

1870, May 16—Mr. Cox introduced the following resolution:

*Resolved*, That the Select Committee on Reconstruction be, and are hereby, instructed to report forthwith a bill for general amnesty.

Mr. Randall moved that it lie on the table, which was disagreed to—yeas 84, nays 87, as follow:

YEAS—Messrs. Ambler, Ames, Asper, Atwood, Banks, Beaman, Benjamin, Benton, Boyd, George M. Brooks, Buffinton, Burdett, Benjamin F. Butler, Cessna, Amasa Cobb, Coburn, Cook, Conger, Cowles, Dawes, Dixon, Donley, Duval, Dyer, Ferriss, Gilfillan, Hamilton. Hawley, Hoar, Hotchkiss, Judd, Julian, Kelley, Kelsey; Lash, Lawrence, Maynard, McCarthy, McGrew, Mercur, Eliakim H. Moore, Jesse H. Moore, William Moore, Daniel J. Morrell, Myers, Negley, O'Neill, Orth, Packard, Packer, Paine, Peck, Peters, Pomeroy, Prosser, Roots, Sanford, Sargent, Sawyer, Shanks, Porter Sheldon, John A. Smith, William J. Smith, William Smyth, Starkweather, Stevens, Stevenson, Stokes, Stoughton, Strickland, Taffe, Tanner, Taylor, Tillman, Townsend, Twichell, Tyner, Upson, Cadwalader C. Washburn, Wheeler, Wilkinson. Willard, Williams, John T. Wilson—84.

NAYS—Messrs. Allison, Arnell, *Axtell*, Ayer, Barry, Beatty, *Beck*, Bennett, *Biggs*, Bingham, Blair, *Booker*, Bowen, *James Brooks*, Buckley, Burchard, *Burr*, Cake, Churchill, Clarke, *Conner*, *Cox*, *Crebs*, Degener, *Dickinson*, *Dox*, *Eldridge*, Farnsworth, Ferry, Finkelnburg, Fitch, Garfield, *Getz*, Gibson, *Haight*, *Haldeman*, Hale. Harris, Hawkins, Heflin, Hill, *Holman*, Ingersoll, *Johnson*, Kellogg, Ketcham, Laflin *Lewis*, Logan, *Mayham*, McKee, *McKenzie*, *McNeely*, *Milnes*, *Morgan*, Morphis, *Mungen*, *Niblack*, Perce, Platt, Poland, *Potter*, *Randall*, *Rice*, *Rogers*, *Schumaker*, Scofield, Lionel A. Sheldon, *Sherrod*, *Shober*, *Slocum*, *Joseph S. Smith*, Worthington C. Smith, *Stiles*, Strong, *Swann*, *Sweeney*, *Trimble*. *Van Trump*, *Voorhees*, Welker, Whitmore, *Eugene M. Wilson*, Winans, *Winchester*, *Wood*, *Woodward*—87.

Mr. Cessna moved that the resolution be referred to the Committee on Reconstruction, which was agreed to—yeas 116, nays 55, as follow:

YEAS—Messrs. Allison, Ambler, Ames, Arnell, Atwood, Banks, Beaman, Beatty, Benjamin, Bennett, Benton, Bingham, Blair, Bowen, George M. Brooks, Buck, Buckley, Buffinton, Burchard, Burdett, Benjamin F. Butler, Cake, Cessna, Amasa Cobb, Coburn, Cook, Conger, Cowles, Dawes, Degener, Dickey, Dixon, Donley, Duval, Dyer, Ela, Farnsworth, Ferriss, Ferry, Finkelnburg, Fitch, Garfield, Gilfillan, Hale, Hawkins, Hawley, Heflin, Hill, Hoar, Hooper, Hotchkiss, Ingersoll, Judd, Kelley, Kellogg, Kelsey, Ketcham, Laflin, Lash, Logan, Maynard, McCarthy, McCrary, McGrew, McKee, Mercur, Eliakim H. Moore, Jesse H. Moore, William Moore, Morrell, Myers, Negley, O'Neill, Orth, Packard, Packer. Paine, Peck. Peters, Platt, Poland. Pomeroy, Prosser, Roots, Sanford, Sargent, Sawyer, Schenck, Scofield, Shanks, Lionel A. Sheldon, Porter Sheldon, John A. Smith, William J. Smith, Worthington C. Smith, William Smyth. Starkweather, Stevens, Stokes, Stoughton, Strickland, Strong, Tanner, Taylor, Tillman. Townsend, Twichell, Tyner, Upson, Cadwalader C. Washburn, Welker, Wheeler, Willard, Williams, John T. Wilson—116.

NAYS—Messrs. *Adams, Archer, Axtell, Ayer, Barnum, Barry, Beck, Biggs, Booker, James Brooks, Burr, Conner, Cox, Crebs, Dickinson, Dox, Eldridge, Getz, Haight, Haldeman, Hamill,* Harris, *Holman, Johnson, Knott,* Lawrence, *Lewis, Mayham, McKenzie, McNeely, Milnes,* Morphis, *Mungen, Niblack, Perce, Potter, Randall, Rice, Rogers, Schumaker, Sherrod, Shober, Joseph S. Smith, Stiles, Swann, Sweeney,* Taffe, *Trimble, Van Trump, Voorhees,* Wilkinson, Winans, *Winchester, Wood, Woodward*—55.

1870, June 13—Mr. Stokes moved to suspend the rules, and put upon its passage a bill to relieve every citizen of all political disabilities imposed by the provisions of the XIVth Amendment for participation in the late rebellion.

It provides, two-thirds of each House concurring, that all political disabilities imposed by the provisions of the XIVth Amendment to the Constitution of the United States upon citizens for participation in the late rebellion shall be, and the same are hereby, removed: *Provided,* That no person relieved by the provisions of this act shall be required to take or subscribe to what is known as the iron-clad or test oath.

The motion of Mr. Stokes was disagreed to—yeas 59, nays 112, as follow:

YEAS—Messrs. *Adams, Barry,* Beck, *Booker,* James Brooks, Buckley, *Burr, Calkin, Conner, Cox,* Crebs, *Dockery, Dox, Eldridge,* Fitch, *Fox, Gibson, Griswold, Hamill,* Harris, Hawkins, *Johnson, Kerr, Knott, Lewis,* Marshall, *Mayham,* McCormick, McKee, *McKenzie, McNeely,* Milnes, *Morgan, Mungen. Niblack,* Perce, Platt, *Randall, Reeves, Rice, Ridgway, Rogers,* Sargent, *Sherrod, Shober, Joseph S. Smith,* Stokes, *Strader, Swann, Sweeney,* Tillman, *Trimble, Van Trump,* Wells, *Eugene M. Wilson, Winchester, Wood, Woodward*—59.

NAYS—Messrs. Allison, Ambler, Ames, Armstrong, Arnell, Asper, Atwood, Bailey, Banks, Beaman, Beatty, Benjamin, Bennett, Benton, Bingham, Blair, Boles, Boyd, George M. Brooks, Buffinton, Burchard, Burdett, Benjamin F. Butler, Roderick R. Butler, Cessna, Churchill. William T. Clark, Amasa Cobb, Clinton L. Cobb, Coburn, Cook, Conger, Cullom, Davis, Dawes, Degener, Dickey, Dixon, Donley, Duval, Ela, Farnsworth, Ferriss, Ferry, Finkelnburg, Fisher, Garfield, Gilfillan. Hale, Hawley, Hill, Hoar, Hooper, Hotchkiss, Ingersoll, Judd, Julian. Kelley, Kellogg, Kelsey, Ketcham, Knapp, Laflin, Lash, Lawrence, Logan, Maynard, McCarthy, McCrary, McGrew, Mercur, Eliakim H. Moore, William Moore, Daniel J. Morrell, Samuel P. Morrill, Myers, Newsham, O'Neill, Orth, Packard, Paine, Palmer, Peck, Phelps, Pomeroy, Porter, Roots, Sanford, Sawyer, John A Smith, William Smyth, Starkweather, Stevenson, Stoughton, Strickland, Taffe, Tanner, Twichell, Tyner, Upson, Van Horn, Van Wyck, Ward, Cadwalader C. Washburn, William B. Washburn, Wheeler, Whitmore, Wilkinson, Willard, John T. Wilson, Winans, Witcher—112.

## On the Validity of the XIVth and XVth Amendments.

1870, July 11—Mr. Ferriss offered the following resolution:

*Resolved,* That the XIVth and XVth articles of amendment to the Constitution of the United States, having been duly ratified by the Legislatures of three-fourths of the several States, are valid to all intents and purposes as part of the Constitution of the United States, and, as such, binding and obligatory upon the Executive, the Congress, the judiciary, the several States and Territories, and all citizens of the United States.

Which was agreed to—yeas 138, nays 32, as follow:

YEAS—Messrs. Allison, Ambler, Ames, Armstrong, Arnell, Asper, Atwood, *Axtell,* Ayer, Bailey, Banks, Barry, Beatty, Benjamin, Bennett, Benton, Bingham, Blair, Boles, *Booker,* George M. Brooks, Buckley, Buffinton, Burchard, Burdett, Benjamin F. Butler, Roderick R. Butler, Churchill, William T. Clark, Sidney Clarke. Amasa Cobb, Coburn, Cook, Conger, Covode, Cowles, Cullom. Darrall, Davis, Dawes, Degener, Dickey, Dixon, Donley, Duval, Ela, Farnsworth, Ferriss,

Finkelnburg, Fisher, Fitch, Gilfillan, Harris, Hawley, Hay, Heflin, Hill, Hoar, Hooper, Ingersoll, Jenckes, Judd, Kelley, Kellogg, Kelsey, Ketcham, Knapp, Laflin, Lash, Lawrence, Logan, Loughridge, Maynard, McCarthy, McCrary, McGrew, McKee, *McKenzie.* Mercur. *Milnes,* Jesse H. Moore, William Moore, Morphis, Daniel J. Morrell, Myers, Negley, O'Neill, Orth, Packard, Packer, Paine, Palmer, Peck, Peters, Phelps, Platt, Poland, Porter, Roots, Sanford, Sargent, Sawyer, Schenck, Scofield, Shanks, Lionel A. Sheldon, Porter Sheldon, John A. Smith, William J. Smith, Worthington C. Smith, William Smyth, Starkweather, Stevens, Stokes. Stoughton, Strickland, Strong, Taffe, Tanner, Taylor, Tillman, Townsend, Twichell, Tyner, Upson, Van Horn, Van Wyck, Ward, Cadwalader C. Washburn, William B. Washburn, Welker, Wheeler. Whitmore, Wilkinson, Willard, Williams, John T. Wilson, Witcher—138.

NAYS—Messrs. *Adams, Barnum, Beck, Biggs. Bird, Burr, Dickinson, Fox, Getz, Griswold, Hawkins, Holman, Johnson, Thomas L. Jones, Knott, Lewis, Mayham. McNeely, Mungen, Niblack, Potter, Reeves, Rice, Joseph S. Smith, Stiles, Swann. Sweeney, Trimble, Van Trump, Voorhees, Winchester, Woodward*—32.

NOT VOTING—Messrs. *Archer,* Beaman, Bowen, Boyd, James Brooks, Buck, *Cake, Calkin,* Cessna, *Cleveland,* Clinton L. Cobb, *Conner, Cox, Crebs,* Dockery, *Dox,* Dyer, *Eldridge,* Ferry, Garfield, *Gibson, Haight, Haldeman,* Hale, *Hambleton, Hamill,* Hamilton, Hays, Hoge. Hotchkiss, Alexander H. Jones, Julian, *Kerr,* Lynch, *Marshall, McCormick,* Eliakim H. Moore, *Morgan,* Samuel P. Morrill, *Morrissey,* Newsham, Perce, Pomeroy, Prosser, *Randall, Ridgway, Rogers, Schumaker, Sherrod, Shober, Slocum,* Stevenson, *Stone, Strader, Van Auken,* Wallace, *Wells, Eugene M. Wilson,* Winans, *Wood*—60.

## On Apportionment of Representatives.

1870, April 18—Mr. A. H. Jones introduced the following bill:

To provide for the apportionment of representatives to Congress among the several States.

*Be it enacted, &c.,* That from and after the 3d day of March, 1871, the House of Representatives shall be composed of two hundred and seventy-five members, to be apportioned among the several States in accordance with the provisions of this act: *Provided,* That if, after such apportionment shall have been made, any new State shall be admitted into the Union, the representative or representatives of such new State shall be additional to the number of two hundred and seventy-five herein limited; and if the number of representatives of any State shall be reduced by such apportionment, such reduction shall not take effect in the Forty-Second Congress, but such State shall have the same number of representatives in the Forty-Second Congress to which it is by law entitled in the Forty-First Congress, and any representative or representatives which any State may have in the Forty-Second Congress, in excess of the number fixed by such apportionment, shall be additional to the number of two hundred and seventy-five herein limited; and if the representation of any State shall be increased by such apportionment, any additional representative or representatives of such State in the Forty-Second Congress shall be chosen by the State at large, and all other representatives for the Forty-Second Congress shall be chosen in the respective congressional districts now provided by law in the several States.

SEC. 2 That after the next enumeration of the inhabitants of the United States shall have been completed according to law, and before the 15th day of August, 1870, the Superintendent of the Census shall prepare and submit to the Secretary of the Interior a preliminary report of the results of such enumeration, embracing such statistics as shall be necessary to enable the Secretary of the Interior to perform the duties in this act prescribed.

SEC. 3. That after the preliminary report provided for in the foregoing section shall have been submitted to the Secretary of the Interior, he shall ascertain from such preliminary report the basis of representation of each State and the aggregate basis of representation of the United States, and he shall ascertain the basis of representation of the several congressional districts by dividing the aggregate basis of representation of the United States by the number two hundred and seventy-five, rejecting any fraction of a unit which may remain; and he shall ascertain the number of representatives to be apportioned to each State by dividing the basis of representation of such State by the basis of representation of the several congressional districts, rejecting any fraction of a unit which may remain; and he shall apportion so many additional representatives to the States having the largest rejected fractions, one to each, as shall make the whole number of representatives two hundred and seventy-five.

SEC. 4. That the Secretary of the Interior shall, on or before the 10th day of September, 1870, prepare and transmit, under the seal of his office, to the Speaker of the House of Representatives, and to the Governor of each of the States, a certified statement of his proceedings under the provisions of this act.

Sec. 5. That all acts and parts of acts in conflict with the provisions of this act are hereby repealed.

Mr. Kelsey moved that the bill be laid upon the table, which was disagreed to—yeas 77, nays 90.

The bill was then passed—yeas 86, nays 85, as follow:

YEAS—Messrs. Allison, Arnell, Asper, Atwood, *Axtell*, Ayer, Barry, Beatty, *Beck*, Benjamin, Bingham, Boles, *Booker*, Boyd, Buck, Buckley, Burchard, Burdett, Benjamin F. Butler, Roderick R. Butler, William T. Clark, Sidney Clarke, Amasa Cobb, Clinton L. Cobb, Coburn, Cook, Conger, *Conner*, Cullom, Degener, Dockery, *Dox*, Farnsworth, Ferry, Finkelnburg, Fitch, Hamilton, Harris, Hawkins, Hawley, Hay, Hays, Heflin, Hill, Hoge, Ingersoll, *Johnson*, Alexander H..Jones, Judd, Logan, Loughridge, *Marshall*, Maynard, McCrary, McKee, *McKenzie*, Jesse H. Moore, Orth, Paine, Palmer, Perce, Piatt, Pomeroy, Porter, Prosser, Roots, Sargent, Sawyer, Shanks, Lionel A. Sheldon, *Sherrod*, William Smyth, Stokes, *Sweeney*, Taffe, Tyner, Upson, Van Horn, Cadwalader C. Washburn, Welker, Whitmore, Williams, *Eugene M. Wilson*, Winans, *Winchester*, Witcher—86.

NAYS—Messrs. *Archer*, Banks, *Barnum*, Beaman, Benton, *Bird*, George M. Brooks, *James Brooks*, Buffinton, *Burr*, Cake, *Calkin*, Cessna, Cowles, Dawes, Dickey, *Dickinson*, Dixon, Ela, *Eldridge*, Ferriss, Fisher, Garfield, *Gibson*, *Griswold*, *Haldeman*, Hale, *Hambleton*, Hamill, Hoar, *Holman*, Hooper, Hotchkiss, Jenckes, *Thomas L. Jones*, Kelley, Kellogg, Kelsey, *Kerr*, Knapp, Lawrence, Lynch, *McCormick*, McGrew, *McNeely*, Mercur, William Moore, *Morgan*, Daniel J. Morrell, *Mungen*, Myers, Negley, *Niblack*, O'Neill, Packer, Peters, Phelps, Poland, *Potter*, *Randall*, *Reeves*, Schenck, *Schumaker*, Scofield, John A. Smith, *Joseph S. Smith*, Worthington C. Smith, Starkweather, Stevens, Stevenson, *Strader*, Strong, Tanner, Taylor, *Trimble*, Twichell, *Van Trump*, *Voorhees*, Ward, William B. Washburn, *Wells*, Wheeler, Willard, *Wood*, *Woodward*—85.

## IN SENATE.

1870, May 25—Mr. Trumbull, from the Committee on the Judiciary, reported the bill with amendments, as follows: Strike out the words "two hundred and seventy-five" wherever they occur, and insert the words "three hundred." Strike out all from the word "limited" in the 11th line to the word "limited" in the 23d line, and all of the first section after the words "at large" in the 27th line.

June 13.—The first amendment of the committee, striking out two hundred and seventy-five, and inserting three hundred, was agreed to, yeas 31, nays 21, as follow:

YEAS—Messrs. Abbott, *Bayard*, Boreman, Carpenter, *Casserly*, Chandler, Corbett, Fowler, Gilbert, Harlan, Howard, Howe, Howell. *Johnston*, Kellogg, *McCreery*, McDonald, Pomeroy, Ramsey, Rice, Ross, Schurz, Sprague, Stewart, *Stockton*, Thayer, *Thurman*, Tipton, Trumbull, Warner, Yates—31.

NAYS—Messrs. Ames, Brownlow, Buckingham, Cole, *Davis*, Drake, Fenton, *Hamilton* of Maryland, Hamilton of Texas, Hamlin, Morrill of Maine, Morrill of Vermont, Morton, Pratt, Robertson, *Saulsbury*, Scott, Sherman, Sumner, *Vickers*, Williams—21.

The next amendment of the committee, to strike out the following words—

"And if the number of representatives of any State shall be reduced by such apportionment, such reduction shall not take effect in the Forty-Second Congress, but such State shall have the same number of representatives in the Forty-Second Congress to which it is by law entitled in the Forty-First Congress, and any representative or representatives which any State may have in the Forty-Second Congress in excess of the number fixed by such apportionment shall be additional to the number of two hundred and seventy-five herein limited"—was agreed to.

The next amendment of the committee, to strike out the following words—

"And all other representatives for the Forty-Second Congress shall be chosen in the respective congressional districts now provided by law in the several States"—was agreed to.

Mr. Trumbull moved to amend, by inserting in the last clause of the first section the words "or diminished" after the word "increased;" the words "so increased and all the representatives of any State so diminished" after the words "o' such State;" and the words "unless otherwise provided by such State," at the end of the section, so that it would read:

"And if the representation of any State shal' be increased or diminished by such apportionment, any additional representative or repr' sentatives of such State so increased and all t. representatives of any State so diminished : the Forty-Second Congress shall be chosen b the State at large, unless otherwise provided by such State."

Mr. Drake moved to add thereto the following words: "but thereafter shall be elected by single districts;" which was disagreed to—yeas 24, nays 28, as follow:

YEAS—Messrs. Ames, Boreman, Buckingham, *Casserly*, Corbett, *Davis*, Drake, Edmunds, Fenton, *Hamilton* of Maryland, Howell, *Johnston*, *McCreery*, Morrill of Vermont, Morton, Pool, Pratt, Schurz, Scott, Spencer, *Stockton*, *Thurman*, *Vickers*, Warner—24.

NAYS—Messrs. Abbott, *Bayard*, Carpenter, Chandler, Cole, Gilbert, Hamilton of Texas, Hamlin, Harlan, Harris, Howard, Howe, Kellogg, McDonald, Morrill of Maine, Osborn, Pomeroy, Ramsey, Rice, Robertson, Ross, Sherman, Sprague, Stewart, Sumner, Tipton, Trumbull, Yates—28.

The amendment of Mr. Trumbull was then agreed to.

Mr. Edmunds moved to strike out "1871" in

the first line of the bill, and insert "1873;" which was disagreed to—yeas 9, nays 31, as follow:

YEAS—Messrs. *Bayard*, Cole, Hamlin, Morrill of Maine, Morrill of Vermont, Pratt, Scott, Sprague, Sumner—9.

NAYS—Messrs. Abbott, Ames, Boreman, *Casserly*, Chandler, *Davis*, Fowler, Gilbert, *Hamilton* of Maryland, Harlan, Howard, Howe, Howell, Lewis, *McCreery*, McDonald, Morton, Nye, Osborn, Pomeroy, Ramsey, Robertson, Ross. Sherman, Spencer, Stewart, *Stockton*, Thayer, Trumbull, *Vickers*, Warner—31.

The bill, some verbal amendments having been made, was then passed—yeas 30, nays 10, as follow:

YEAS—Messrs. Abbott, Ames, *Bayard*, Boreman, *Casserly*, Chandler, *Davis*, Fowler, Gilbert, Harlan, Howard, Howe, Howell, Lewis, *McCreery*, McDonald, Morton, Nye, Osborn, Pomeroy, Pratt, Ramsey, Robertson, Ross, Spencer, Sprague, Stewart, *Stockton*, Trumbull, Warner—30.

NAYS—Messrs. Cole, Drake, *Hamilton* of Maryland, Hamlin, Morrill of Maine, Morrill of Vermont, Scott, Sherman, Sumner, *Vickers*—10.

### In House.

June 22—Mr. Judd moved that the amendments of the Senate be concurred in. Mr. Marshall moved to add the following as an additional section:

SEC. 6. That in all cases at any election where there shall be two or more members of Congress elected in any State by general ticket, each qualified voter may, at such election, cast as many votes for one candidate as there are representatives to be thus elected, or may distribute the same, or equal parts thereof, among the candidates, as he shall see fit; and the candidates highest in votes shall be declared elected.

Mr. Scofield moved that the bill and amendments be laid on the table, which was disagreed to—yeas 78, nays 95, as follow:

YEAS — Messrs. Ames, *Archer*, Armstrong, Bailey, Banks, Blair. George M. Brooks, *James Brooks*, Buffinton, Benjamin F. Butler, Cessna, Churchill, Covode, *Cox*, *Crebs*, Davis, Dawes, Dickey, Dixon, Donley, Ela, *Eldridge*, Ferriss, Fisher, *Fox*, *Getz*, Gilfillan, *Haldeman*, Hale. *Hambleton*, *Hamill*, Hoar, Jenckes, *Thomas L. Jones*, Kelley, Kellogg, Kelsey, Ketcham, Knapp, Laflin, Lash, Lawrence, *Marshall*, *Mayham*, *McNeely*, William Moore, *Morgan*, Myers, Negley, *Niblack*, O'Neill, Packer, Phelps, Poland, *Potter*, Prosser, *Randall*. *Reeves*, Scofield. Porter Sheldon, *Shober*. *Slocum*, John A. Smith, *Joseph S. Smith*, Stevens. Stevenson, *Stiles*, Strong, *Swann*, Tanner, Taylor, Twichell, *Van Auken*, Van Wyck, Ward, William B. Washburn, Wheeler, *Wood*—78.

NAYS—Messrs. Allison, Arnell, Asper, Atwood, *Axtell*, Beatty, *Beck*, Benjamin, Bennett. Bingham, *Bird*, Boles, *Booker*, Boyd, Buck, Burchard, Burdett, *Calkin*, William T. Clark. Sidney Clarke, *Cleveland*, Amasa Cobb, Clinton L. Cobb, Coburn, Cook, Conger. Cullom, Degener, *Dickinson*, Dockery, Dyer. Farnsworth. Ferry, Finkelnburg. Garfield, *Haight*, Harris, Hawkins, Hay, Hays, Heflin, Ingersoll, *Johnson*, Judd, Julian. *Knott*, *Lewis*, Logan. Maynard, *McCormick*, McCrary, McGrew, McKee, *McKenzie*. Jesse H. Moore, Morphis, Daniel J. Morrell. Orth. Packard, Paine, Palmer, Peck, Perce, Platt, Pomeroy, *Rice*, *Rogers*, Roots, Sargent, Sawyer, Schenck, *Schumaker*, Shanks, Lionel A. Sheldon, *Sherrod*, William Smyth, Stoughton, *Strader*, Strickland. Taffe, *Trimble*. Tyner. Upson. Van Horn, Wallace, Cadwalader C. Washburn, Welker, *Wells*, Whitmore, Wilkinson, Williams, *Eugene M. Wilson*, John T. Wilson, Winans, *Winchester*—95.

June 23—Mr. Scofield moved that the bill and amendments be referred to the Committee on the Judiciary; which was agreed to—yeas 96, nays 94, as follow:

YEAS—Messrs. Ames, *Archer*, Armstrong, Arnell, Bailey, Banks, Beaman, Bennett, *Biggs*, *Bird*, Blair, George M. Brooks, *James Brooks*, Buffinton, *Burr*, Benjamin F. Butler, *Calkin*, Cessna, Churchill, William T. Clark, *Cleveland*, Covode, *Cox*, Davis, Dawes. Dickey, Donley, Ela, *Eldridge*, Ferriss, Fisher, *Getz*, Gilfillan. *Griswold*, *Haight*, *Haldeman*. Hale, *Hambleton*, *Hamill*, Hill. Hoar, *Holman*, Hooper, Jenckes, Julian, Kelley, Kellogg, Kelsey. Ketcham, Knapp. Laflin. Lash, Lawrence, *Lewis*, *Mayham*, Maynard, *McNeely*, William Moore, *Morgan*, Daniel J. Morrell, Samuel P. Morrill, *Morrissey*, Myers, Negley, *Niblack*, O'Neill, Packer, Phelps, Poland. Porter, *Randall*, *Reeves*, Sanford, Scofield, Porter Sheldon, *Shober*, *Slocum*, John A. Smith, William J. Smith, Starkweather, Stevens, Stevenson, *Stiles*, *Stone*, Strong, *Swann*, Taylor, Twichell, *Van Auken*, *Van Trump*, Van Wyck, Ward, William B. Washburn, Wheeler, *Wood*, Woodward—96.

NAYS—Messrs. *Adams*, Allison. Asper, Atwood, *Axtell*, Barry, Beatty, *Beck*, Benjamin, Bingham, Boles, *Booker*, Boyd, Buck, Buckley, Burchard, Burdett, Sidney Clarke, Amasa Cobb. Clinton L. Cobb, Coburn, Conger, *Conner*, Cook, Cullom, Degener. *Dickinson*, Dockery, *Dox*, Dyer, Farnsworth, Ferry, Finkelnburg, Garfield. *Gibson*, Hamilton, Harris, Hawkins, Hawley, Hay, Hays, Heflin, Ingersoll, *Johnson*. Alexander H. Jones. *Thomas L. Jones*, Judd, *Knott*, Logan. *Marshall*, *McCormick*, McCrary, McGrew, McKee. *McKenzie*, Jesse H. Moore, Morphis, Newsham, Orth, Packard, Paine, Palmer, Peck. Perce, Platt, Prosser, *Rice*, *Rogers*, Roots, Sargent, Sawyer. Shanks, Lionel A. Sheldon, *Sherrod*, *Joseph S. Smith*, William Smyth, Stoughton, *Strader*, Strickland. Taffe, Tillman, *Trimble*, Tyner, Upson, Van Horn, Wallace, Cadwalader C. Washburn, Welker, *Wells*, Whitmore, Wilkinson, Williams, John T. Wilson, *Winchester*—94.

### Present Apportionment.

The present apportionment is as follows:

| | | | |
|---|---|---|---|
| Maine | 5 | Kentucky | 9 |
| New Hampshire | 3 | Tennessee | 8 |
| Vermont | 3 | Indiana | 11 |
| Massachusetts | 10 | Illinois | 14 |
| Rhode Island | 2 | Missouri | 9 |
| Connecticut | 4 | Arkansas | 3 |
| New York | 31 | Michigan | 6 |
| New Jersey | 5 | Florida | 1 |
| Pennsylvania | 24 | Texas | 4 |
| Delaware | 1 | Iowa | 6 |
| Maryland | 5 | Wisconsin | 6 |
| Virginia | 8 | California | 3 |
| North Carolina | 7 | Minnesota | 2 |
| South Carolina | 4 | Oregon | 1 |
| Georgia | 7 | Kansas | 1 |
| Alabama | 6 | West Virginia | 3 |
| Mississippi | 5 | Nevada | 1 |
| Louisiana | 5 | Nebraska | 1 |
| Ohio | 19 | | |
| | | Whole number of representatives | 243 |
| | | Delegates | 9 |

Whole number of representatives and delegates 252

The original number fixed was 233. Eight were subsequently added for special States, making 241, and Nevada and Nebraska have since been admitted into the Union, increasing the representation to 243.

Another bill, containing the same provisions, with an amendment, providing that every State having a fraction exceeding one-half of the number required for a representative, shall have one representative added to its representation, was passed by the Senate on the 7th day of July, 1870, but was not reached in the House, a motion to suspend the rules for the purpose of considering it having been disagreed to July 13, 1870—yeas 93, nays 97.

A previous proposition on this subject was made in the House by Mr. Coburn, of Indiana, on the 13th day of December, 1869, as an amendment to the census bill; which, after discussion, was withdrawn

# LVII.

## BANKING AND CURRENCY.

**AN ACT to provide for the redemption of the three per centum temporary loan certificates, and for an increase of national bank notes.**

*Be it enacted, &c.*, That $54,000,000, in notes for circulation may be issued to national banking associations in addition to the $300,000,000 authorized by the 22d section of the "Act to provide a national currency secured by a pledge of United States bonds, and to provide for the circulation and redemption thereof," approved June 3, 1864; and the amount of notes so provided shall be furnished to banking associations organized or to be organized in those States and Territories having less than their proportion under the apportionment contemplated by the provisions of the "Act to amend an act to provide a national currency secured by a pledge of United States bonds, and to provide for the circulation and redemption thereof," approved March 3, 1865, and the bonds deposited with the Treasurer of the United States to secure the additional circulating notes herein authorized shall be of any description of bonds of the United States bearing interest in coin; but a new apportionment of the increased circulation herein provided for shall be made as soon as practicable, based upon the census of 1870: *Provided*, That if applications for the circulation herein authorized shall not be made within one year after the passage of this act, by banking associations organized or to be organized in States having less than their proportion, it shall be lawful for the Comptroller of the Currency to issue such circulation to banking associations applying for the same in other States or Territories having less than their proportion, giving the preference to such as have the greatest deficiency: *And Provided further*, That no banking association hereafter organized shall have a circulation in excess of $500,000.

SEC. 2. That at the end of each month after the passage of this act it shall be the duty of the Comptroller of the Currency to report to the Secretary of the Treasury the amount of circulating notes issued, under the provisions of the preceding section, to national banking associations during the previous month; whereupon the Secretary of the Treasury shall redeem and cancel an amount of the three per centum temporary loan certificates issued under the acts of March 2, 1867, and July 25, 1868, not less than the amount of circulating notes so reported, and may, if necessary, in order to procure the presentation of such temporary loan certificates for redemption, give notice to the holders thereof, by publication or otherwise, that certain of said certificates (which shall be designated by number, date, and amount) shall cease to bear interest from and after a day to be designated in such notice, and that the certificates so designated shall no longer be available as any portion of the lawful money reserve in possession of any national banking association, and after the day designated in such notice no interest shall be paid on such certificates, and they shall not thereafter be counted as a part of the reserve of any banking association,

SEC. 3. That upon the deposit of any United States bonds, bearing interest payable in gold, with the Treasurer of the United States, in the manner prescribed in the 19th and 20th sections of the national currency act, it shall be lawful for the Comptroller of the Currency to issue to the association making the same circulating notes of different denominations not less than $5, not exceeding in amount eighty per cent. of the par value of the bonds deposited, which notes shall bear upon their face the promise of the association to which they are issued to pay them upon presentation at the office of the association, in gold coin of the United States, and shall be redeemable upon such presentation in such coin: *Provided*, That no banking association organized under this section shall have a circulation in excess of $1,000,000.

SEC. 4. That every national banking association formed under the provisions of the preceding section of this act shall at all times keep on hand not less than twenty-five per cent. of its outstanding circulation in gold or silver coin of the United States, and shall receive at par in the payment of debts the gold notes of every other such banking association which at the time of such payments shall be redeeming its circulating notes in gold or silver coin of the United States.

SEC. 5. That every association organized for the purpose of issuing gold notes as provided in this act shall be subject to all the requirements and provisions of the national currency act, except the first clause of section 22, which limits the circulation of national banking associations to $300,000,000; the first clause of section 32, which, taken in connection with the preceding section, would require national banking associations organized in the city of San Francisco to redeem their circulating notes at par in the city of New York; and the last clause of section 32, which requires every national banking association to receive in payment of debts the notes of every other national banking association at par: *Provided*, That in applying the provisions and requirements of said act to the banking associations herein provided for the terms "lawful money" and "lawful money of the United States," shall be held and construed to mean gold or silver coin of the United States.

SEC. 6. That to secure a more equitable distribution of the national banking currency, there may be issued circulating notes to banking associations organized in States and Territories having less than their proportion, as herein set forth; and the amount of circulation in this section authorized shall, under the direction of the Secretary of the Treasury, as it may be required for this purpose, be withdrawn, as herein provided, from banking associations organized in States having a circulation exceeding that provided for by the act entitled "An act to amend an act entitled 'An act to provide for a national banking currency secured by pledge of United States bonds, and to provide for the circulation and redemption thereof,'" approved March 3, 1865, but the amount so withdrawn shall not exceed $25,-000,000. The Comptroller of the Currency shall, under the direction of the Secretary of the Treasury, make a statement showing the amount of circulation in each State and Territory, and the amount to be retired by each banking association in accordance with this section, and shall, when such redistribution of circulation is required, make a requisition for such amount upon such banks, commencing with the banks having a circulation exceeding $1,000,000 in States having an excess of circulation, and withdrawing their circulation in excess of $1,000,000, and then proceeding *pro rata* with other banks having a circulation exceeding $300,000 in States having the largest excess of circulation, and reducing the circulation of such banks in States having the greatest proportion in excess, leaving undisturbed the banks in States having a smaller proportion, until those in greater excess have been reduced to the same grade, and continuing thus to make the reduction provided for by this act until the full amount of $25,000,000 herein provided for shall be withdrawn; and the circulation so withdrawn shall be distributed among the States and Territories having less than their proportion, so as to equalize the same; and it shall be the duty of the Comptroller of the Currency, under the direction of the Secretary of the Treasury, forthwith to make a requisition for the amount thereof upon the banks above indicated as herein prescribed; and upon failure of such associations, or any of them, to return the amount so required within one year, it shall be the duty of the Comptroller of the Currency to sell at public auction, having given twenty days' notice thereof in one daily newspaper printed in Washington and one in New York city, an amount of bonds deposited by said association, as security for said circulation, equal to the circulation to be withdrawn from said association and not returned in compliance with such requisition; and the Comptroller of the Currency shall with the proceeds redeem so many of the notes of said banking association as they come into the treasury as will equal the amount required and not so returned, and shall pay the balance, if any, to such banking association: *Provided,* That no circulation shall be withdrawn under the provisions of this section until after the $54,000,000 granted in the first section shall have been taken up.

SEC. 7. That after the expiration of six months from the passage of this act any banking association located in any State having more than its proportion of circulation may be removed to any State having less than its proportion of circulation, under such rules and regulations as the Comptroller of the Currency, with the approval of the Secretary of the Treasury, may require: *Provided,* That the amount of the issue of said banks shall not be deducted from the amount of new issue provided for in this act.

Approved July 13, 1870.

### Final Vote.

#### IN SENATE, *July* 6, 1870.

The bill, as printed above, being the report of the committee of conference last appointed, was agreed to without a division.

#### IN HOUSE, *July* 7, 1870.

YEAS—Messrs. Allison, Ambler, Armstrong, Asper, Atwood, Ayer, Bailey, Banks, Benjamin, Bennett, Benton, Blair, Boles, *Booker*, Boyd, Buck, Buckley, Burchard, Burdett, Roderick R. Butler, Cake, Cessna, Churchill, William T. Clark, Sidney Clarke, Amasa Cobb, Coburn, Conger, Cook, Covode, Cowles, Darrall, Dickey, Donley, Duval, Dyer, Ferriss, Ferry, Finkelnburg, Fisher, Garfield, Gilfillan, Harris, Hawley, Hays, Hill, *Thomas L. Jones*, Judd, Kelley, Knapp, Lash, Logan, Loughridge, McCarthy, McCrary, McGrew, *McKenzie*, Mercur, Eliakim H. Moore, Jesse H. Moore, William Moore, Morphis, Daniel J. Morrell, Myers, Negley, O'Neill, Packard, Packer, Palmer, Peck, Poland, Porter, Prosser, Roots, Sawyer, Scofield, Lionel A. Sheldon, Porter Sheldon, John A. Smith, William J. Smith, Worthington C. Smith, William Smyth, Stevens, Stokes, Stoughton, Strickland, Taffe, Tanner, Taylor, Tillman, *Trimble*, Upson, Van Horn, Cadwalader C. Washburn, William B. Washburn, Wheeler, Whitmore, Wilkinson, Willard, John T. Wilson—100.

NAYS—Messrs. *Adams*, *Archer*, Arnell, *Axtell*, *Barnum*, Beatty, *Biggs*, Bingham, *Bird*, George M. Brooks, *James Brooks*, Buffinton, *Burr*, Benjamin F. Butler, *Calkin*, *Cleveland*, *Conner*, *Cox*, *Crebs*, Davis, *Dickinson*, Dixon, *Dox*, Ela, *Getz*, *Haldeman*, *Hamill*, Hawkins, Hay, Hoar, Hooper, Ingersoll, Jenckes, *Johnson*, Julian. Kellogg, *Kerr*, Lawrence, *Lewis*, *Marshall*, *Mayham*, *McCormick*, *McNeely*, *Morgan*, *Mungen*, *Niblack*, Orth, Paine, *Potter*, *Randall*, *Reeves*, *Rice*, Sanford, Sargent, *Schumaker*, Shanks, *Slocum*, *Joseph S. Smith*, Starkweather, Stevenson, *Stiles*, *Stone*, Strong, *Swann*, *Sweeney*, Townsend, Twichell, Tyner, *Van Auken*, *Van Trump*, Van Wyck, *Voorhees*, Ward, Welker, Williams, *Winchester*, *Woodward* —77.

### Previous Votes.

#### IN SENATE.

1870, January 11—Mr. Sherman, from the Committee on Finance, reported the following bill:

To provide a national currency of coin notes, and to equalize the distribution of circulating notes.

*Be it enacted, &c.,* That $45,000,000 in notes for circulation may be issued to national banking associations, in addition to the $300,000,000 authorized by the 22d section of the "Act to provide a national currency secured by a pledge of United States bonds, and to provide for the circulation and redemption thereof," approved June 4, 1864; and the amount of notes so provided shall be furnished to banking associations organized or to be organized in those States and Territories having less than their proportion under the apportionment contemplated by the provisions of the "Act to amend an act to provide a national currency secured by a pledge of United States bonds, and to provide for the circulation and redemption thereof," approved March 3, 1865; but a new apportionment shall be made as soon as practicable, based upon the census of 1870.

SEC. 2. That at the end of each month after the passage of this act it shall be the duty of the Comptroller of the Currency to report to the Secretary of the Treasury the amount of circulating notes issued to national banking associations during the previous month; whereupon the Secretary of the Treasury shall redeem and retire an amount of the three per centum temporory loan certificates issued under the acts of March 2, 1867, and July 25, 1868, not less than the amount of circulating notes so reported; and may, if necessary, in order to procure the presentation of such temporary loan certificates for redemption, give notice to the holders thereof, by publication or otherwise, that certain of said certificates, (which shall be designated by number, date, and amount,) shall cease to bear interest from and after the date of such notice, and that the certificates so designated shall no longer be available as any portion of the lawful money reserve in the possession of any national bank, and after such notice no interest shall be paid on such certificates, and they shall not be counted as a part of the reserve of any banking association.

SEC. 3. That upon the deposit of any United States bonds, bearing interest payable in gold, with the Treasurer of the United States, in the manner prescribed in the nineteenth and twentieth sections of the national currency act, it shall be lawful for the Comptroller of the Currency to issue to the association making the same circulating notes of different denominations, not less than five dollars, equal in amount to ninety per centum of the gold value of the bonds deposited, but not exceeding eighty per centum of their par value; which notes shall bear upon their face the promise of the association to which they are issued to pay them upon presentation at the office of the association in gold or silver coin of the United States, and shall be redeemable upon such presentation in such coin.

SEC. 4. That every national banking association formed under the provisions of section three of this act shall at all times keep on hand not less than twenty-five per centum of its outstanding circulation in gold or silver coin of the United States, and shall receive at par in the payment of debts the gold notes of every other banking association which at the time of such payment shall be redeeming its circulating notes in gold or silver coin of the United States.

SEC. 5. That every association organized for the purpose of issuing gold notes, as provided in the preceding section, shall be subject to all the requirements and provisions of the national currency act, except the first clause of section 22, which limits the circulation of national banking associations to $300,000,000; the first clause of section 32, which, taken in connection with the preceding section, would require national banking associations organized in the city of San Francisco to redeem their circulating notes at par in the city of New York; and the last clause of section 32, which requires every national banking association to receive in payment of debts the notes of every other national banking association at par: *Provided*, That in applying the provisions and requirements of said act to the banking associations herein provided for, the terms "lawful money" and "lawful money of the United States" shall be held and construed to mean gold or silver coin of the United States.

January 31—The Senate being in Committee of the Whole, Mr. Sherman, from the Committee on Finance, moved to strike out, in section three, the words "equal in amount to ninety per cent. of the gold value of the bonds deposited, but not exceeding eighty per cent. of their par value," and in lieu thereof to insert "not exceeding in amount eighty per cent. of the par value of the bonds deposited;" which was agreed to.

Mr. Sherman also moved to insert, as section three, the following:

SEC. 3. That any banking association located in any State having more than its proportion of circulation may be removed to any State having less than its proportion of circulation, under such rules and regulations as the Comptroller of the Currency, with the approval of the Secretary of the Treasury, may require.

Mr. Abbett moved to amend this amendment by adding the following:

*Provided*, That the amount to be issued by said banks shall not be deducted from the amount of new issue provided for in this act.

Which was agreed to.

Mr. Warner moved to insert at the beginning of the section the words, "after the expiration of six months from the passage of this act;" which was agreed to.

The amendment as amended was then agreed to—yeas 43, nays 12, as follow:

YEAS—Messrs. Abbott, *Bayard*, Brownlow, Cameron, Carpenter, *Casserly*, Chandler, Corbett, *Davis*, Drake, Gilbert, Harlan, Harris, Howe, Howell, *Johnston*, Kellogg, Lewis, *McCreery*, Morton, Osborn, Pomeroy, Pool, Pratt, Ramsey, Rice. Robertson, Ross, *Saulsbury*, Sawyer, Schurz, Scott, Sherman, Spencer, Stewart, *Stockton*, Thayer, Tipton, Trumbull, *Vickers*, Warner, Willey, Williams— 43.

NAYS—Messrs. Anthony, Buckingham, Conkling, Edmunds, Fenton, Ferry, McDonald, Morrill of Vermont, *Norton*, Nye, Sumner, Wilson—12.

February 1—Mr. Morton moved to amend the first section by striking out, in the first line, the words "forty-five," and inserting the words "fifty-two."

Which was agreed to—yeas 39, nays 21, as follow:

YEAS—Messrs. Abbott, *Bayard*, Boreman, Brownlow, Cameron, Carpenter, *Davis*, Drake, Fowler, Gilbert, *Hamilton* of Maryland, Harlan, Harris, Howard, Howe, Howell, *Johnston*, Kellogg, *McCreery*, McDonald, Morrill of Maine, Morton, *Norton*, Osborn, Pomeroy. Pool, Pratt, Ramsey, Rice, Robertson, Ross, Schurz, Scott, Spencer, Thayer, *Thurman*, Tipton, *Vickers*, Warner—39.

NAYS—Messrs. Anthony, Buckingham, *Casserly*, Chandler, Conkling, Corbett, Cragin, Edmunds, Fenton, Hamlin, Morrill of Vermont, Patterson, *Saulsbury*, Sherman, Stewart, *Stockton*, Sumner, Trumbull, Willey, Williams, Wilson—21.

Mr. Conkling moved to amend by inserting after the word "apportionment," where it last occurs in the first section, the words "of the fifty-two million dollars of circulating notes hereby authorized."

Which was disagreed to—yeas 23, nays 38, as follow:

YEAS—Messrs. Anthony, Boreman, Buckingham, Cameron, Chandler, Cole, Conkling, Corbett, Cragin, Edmunds, Fenton, Ferry, Hamlin, Morrill of Maine, Morrill of Vermont, Osborn, Patterson, Pomeroy. Rice, Scott, Stewart, Sumner, Wilson—23.

NAYS—Messrs. Abbott, *Bayard*, Brownlow, Carpenter, *Casserly*, *Davis*, Drake, Fowler, *Hamilton* of Maryland, Harlan, Harris, Howe, Howell, *Johnston*, Kellogg, *McCreery*, McDonald. Morton, *Norton*, Pool, Pratt, Ramsey, Robertson, Ross, *Saulsbury*, Sawyer, Schurz, Sherman,

Spencer. *Stockton*, Thayer. *Thurman*, Tipton, Trumbull, *Vickers*, Warner, Willey, Williams—38.

Mr. Conkling further moved to strike out the last part of the first section, as follows: " but a new apportionment shall be made as soon as practicable, based upon the census of 1870."

Which was disagreed to—yeas 16, nays 44, as follow:

YEAS—Messrs. Anthony, Boreman, Buckingham, Cole, Conkling Cragin, Edmunds, Fenton, Ferry, Hamlin, Howe, Morrill of Vermont, Patterson, Scott, Sumner, Wilson—16.

NAYS—Messrs. Abbott, *Bayard*, Cameron, Carpenter, *Casserly*, Corbett, *Davis*, Drake, Fowler, *Hamilton* of Maryland, Harlan, Harris, Howard, Howell, *Johnston*, *McCreery*, McDonald, Morrill of Maine, Morton, *Norton*, Osborn, Pomeroy, Pool, Pratt, Ramsey, Rice, Robertson, Ross, *Saulsbury*, Sawyer, Schurz, Sherman, Spencer, Stewart, *Stockton*, Thayer, *Thurman*, Tipton, Trumbull, *Vickers*, Warner, Willey, Williams—44.

Mr. Sumner offered an amendment, which was disagreed to without a division.

Mr. Saulsbury moved to add to the end of the bill the following:

SEC. —. That the sixth section of the act approved March 3, 1865, entitled " Act to amend an act entitled 'An act to provide internal revenue to support the Government, to pay the interest on the public debt, and for other purposes,' approved June 30, 1864," be, and the same is hereby, repealed.

(The section referred to imposed a tax of ten per cent. on State bank circulation;) which was disagreed to—yeas 18, nays 42, as follow:

YEAS—Messrs. *Bayard*, Cameron, *Casserly*, Cragin, *Davis*, Ferry, *Hamilton* of Maryland, *Johnston*, *McCreery*, *Norton*, Pool, Robertson, *Saulsbury*, Spencer, *Stockton*, *Thurman*, *Vickers*, Wilson—18.

NAYS—Messrs. Abbott, Anthony, Boreman, Brownlow. Carpenter, Chandler, Cole, Conkling, Corbett, Drake, Edmunds, Fenton, Hamlin, Harlan, Harris, Howard, Howe, Howell, Kellogg, McDonald, Morrill of Maine, Morrill of Vermont, Morton, Osborn, Patterson, Pomeroy, Pratt, Ramsey, Rice, Ross, Sawyer, Schurz, Scott, Sherman, Stewart, Sumner, Thayer, Tipton, Trumbull, Warner, Willey, Williams—42.

Mr. Morton moved to add the following to the bill:

SEC. —. That to secure a better distribution of the national banking currency, there may be issued circulation notes to banking associations organized in States and Territories having a less banking circulation than their *pro rata* share, as herein set forth. And the circulation in this section authorized shall within one year, if required, be withdrawn, as herein provided, from banks organized in States having a circulation exceeding that provided for by the act entitled "An act to amend an act entitled 'An act to provide for a national banking currency secured by pledge of United States bonds, and to provide for the circulation and redemption thereof,' approved March 3, 1865;" but the amount to be so withdrawn shall not exceed $13,000,000. The Comptroller of the Currency shall, under the direction of the Secretary of the Treasury, make a statement showing the amount of circulation in each State and the amount to be retired by each bank in accordance with this section, and shall, when circulation is required, make a requisition for such amount upon such banks, commencing with the banks having a circulation exceeding $1,000,-000 in States having an excess of circulation, and withdrawing one-third of their circulation in excess of $1,000,000, and then proceeding *pro*

*rata* with banks having a circulation exceeding $100,000 in States having the largest excess of circulation, and reducing the circulation of banks in States having the greatest proportion in excess, leaving undisturbed the banks in States having a smaller proportion, until those in greater excess have been reduced to the same grade, and continuing thus to make the reduction provided for by this act until the full amount of $13,000,000 herein provided for shall be withdrawn; and the circulation so withdrawn shall be distributed among the States and Territories having less than their proportion, and so as to equalize the distribution of such circulation among such States and Territories upon the basis provided by law. And upon failure of such bank to return the amount so required within ninety days after said requisition, it shall be the duty of the Comptroller of the Currency to sell at public auction, having given twenty days' notice in a newspaper published in Washington city and New York city, an amount of bonds deposited by said bank as security for its circulation equal to the circulation to be withdrawn from such bank, and with the proceeds to redeem so many of the notes of such bank, as they come into the treasury, as will equal the amount required from it, and shall pay the balance to such bank: *Provided*, That no circulation shall be withdrawn from States having an excess until after the $52,000,000 granted in the first section have been taken up.

Mr. Davis moved to strike out the word "thirteen," wherever it occurs in the amendment, and insert the words "twenty-five;" which was disagreed to.

The amendment of Mr. Morton was then agreed to—yeas 34, nays 27, as follow:

YEAS—Messrs. Abbott, *Bayard*, Brownlow, Carpenter, *Casserly*, Cole, *Davis*, Fowler, *Hamilton* of Maryland, Harlan, Harris, Howe, Howell, *Johnston*, Kellogg, *McCreery*, McDonald, Morton, *Norton*, Osborn, Pool, Pratt, Ramsey, Rice, Robertson, *Saulsbury*, Sawyer, Spencer, *Stockton*, Thayer, *Thurman*, Tipton, *Vickers*, Wilson—34.

NAYS—Messrs. Anthony, Boreman, Buckingham, Cameron, Chandler, Conkling, Corbett, Cragin, Drake, Edmunds, Fenton, Ferry, Gilbert, Hamlin, Howard, Morrill of Maine, Morrill of Vermont, Patterson, Pomeroy, Scott, Sherman, Stewart, Sumner, Trumbull, Warner, Willey, Williams—27.

Mr. Kellogg moved to amend by striking out the 4th, 5th, and 6th sections, which was disagreed to—yeas 24, nays 33, as follow:

YEAS—Messrs. *Bayard*, Boreman, Buckingham, Carpenter, *Casserly*, Conkling, Fowler, *Hamilton* of Maryland, Harris, Howe, Howell, Kellogg, McDonald, Morton, *Norton*, Rice, *Saulsbury*, Scott, Spencer, *Stockton*, Sumner, Thayer, *Thurman*, *Vickers*—24.

NAYS—Messrs. Abbott, Anthony, Brownlow, Cameron, Chandler, Cole, Corbett, Cragin, *Davis*, Drake, Edmunds, Fenton, Ferry, Harlan, Howard, *McCreery*, Morrill of Maine, Morrill of Vermont, Osborn, Patterson, Pomeroy, Pool, Pratt, Robertson, Sawyer, Sherman, Stewart, Tipton, Trumbull, Warner, Willey, Williams, Wilson—33.

Mr. Chandler moved to strike out the 1st section; which was disagreed to.

Mr. Vickers moved to insert at the end of section 4 the following:

*Provided*, That the aggregate amount of banking capital to be furnished under this section shall not exceed $50,000,000.

Which was disagreed to.

Mr. Sherman moved to insert in the 1st section, after the word "apportionment," where it last occurs, the words "of the circulation herein provided for."

Which was agreed to.

Mr. Casserly moved to strike out in section 5 the words "at all times keep on hand not less than twenty-five per centum of its outstanding circulation in gold or silver coin of the United States," and insert in lieu thereof:

Before the issue to it of any circulating notes, have a paid-up cash capital of not less than $400,000, which shall not thereafter be diminished. It shall at all times have on hand, in gold and silver coin of the United States, not less than thirty-three and one-third per cent. of its outstanding circulation, and two-thirds in specie funds, in bills, notes, and other securities. If at any time the gold and silver coin shall fall below the proportion above specified, such banking association shall not make any loan, discount, or issue of circulating notes until such proportion shall be restored; and a violation of this provision shall be an act of insolvency, and every director participating in such violation shall become individually liable for all debts and obligations of such banking association.

Which was disagreed to—yeas 11, nays 47, as follow:

YEAS—Messrs. *Bayard*, *Casserly*, *Davis*, Fowler, *Hamilton* of Maryland, *McCreery*, *Saulsbury*, Spencer, *Stockton*, *Thurman*, *Vickers*—11.

NAYS—Messrs. Abbott, Anthony, Boreman, Brownlow, Buckingham, Cameron, Carpenter, Chandler, Cole, Conkling, Corbett, Cragin, Drake, Edmunds, Fenton, Ferry, Hamlin, Harlan, Harris, Howard, Howe, McDonald, Morrill of Maine, Morrill of Vermont, Morton, Osborn, Patterson, Pomeroy, Pool, Pratt, Ramsey, Rice, Robertson, Ross, Sawyer, Schurz, Scott, Sherman, Stewart, Sumner, Thayer, Tipton, Trumbull, Warner, Willey, Williams, Wilson—47.

Mr. Casserly further moved to amend the bill by inserting at the end thereof the following as an additional section:

SEC. —. That bonds of the United States deposited by any bank or banking association under the provisions of this act shall cease to bear interest while they are so deposited, and the franchise of banking hereby granted shall be deemed to be payment and discharge of all interest accrued during the period of such deposit.

Which was disagreed to—yeas 9, nays 46, as follow:

YEAS—Messrs. *Bayard*, *Casserly*, *Davis*, Fowler, *Hamilton* of Maryland, *McCreery*, *Norton*, *Thurman*, *Vickers*—9.

NAYS—Messrs. Abbott, Anthony, Boreman, Brownlow, Buckingham, Cameron, Carpenter, Chandler, Conkling, Corbett, Cragin, Drake, Edmunds, Fenton, Ferry, Hamlin, Harlan, Harris, Howard, Howell, *Johnston*, McDonald, Morrill of Vermont, Morton, Osborn, Patterson, Pomeroy, Pool, Ramsey, Rice, Robertson, Ross, *Saulsbury*, Sawyer, Schurz, Scott, Sherman, Stewart, Sumner, Thayer, Tipton, Trumbull, Warner, Willey, Williams, Wilson—46.

Mr. Ross moved to amend section 1 by adding thereto the following:

*Provided*, That nothing in this section shall be construed to prevent the immediate distribution of $25,000,000 of the above sum under the provisions of this act.

Which was disagreed to.

Mr. Wilson moved to add to the bill the following:

SEC. —. That no banking association organized, or to be organized, under the act to provide a national currency secured by a pledge of United States bonds, and to provide for the circulation and redemption thereof, approved June 3, 1864, shall in any case charge or receive upon any loan or discount a higher rate of interest than seven per cent. per annum.

Which, being modified, on motion of Mr. Thurman, by adding the following:

And any contract upon which more than seven per cent. shall be reserved or received shall be void,

Was disagreed to—yeas 13, nays 48, as follow:

YEAS—Messrs. *Bayard*, Cameron, Carpenter, Conkling, Cragin, Edmunds, Patterson, Pratt, Rice, Ross, Spencer, *Thurman*. Wilson—13.

NAYS—Messrs. Abbott, Anthony, Boreman, Brownlow, Buckingham, Chandler, Cole, Corbett, *Davis*, Drake, Fenton, Ferry, Fowler, Gilbert, *Hamilton* of Maryland. Hamlin, Harlan, Harris, Howard, Howe, Howell, *Johnston*, Kellogg, *McCreery*, McDonald, Morrill of Maine, Morrill of Vermont, *Norton*, Osborn, Pomeroy, Pool, Ramsey, Robertson, *Saulsbury*, Sawyer, Schurz, Scott, Sherman, Stewart, *Stockton*, Sumner, Thayer, Tipton, Trumbull, *Vickers*, Warner, Willey, Williams—48.

February 2.—The bill having been reported to the Senate with the amendments, the first question being on concurring in the first amendment offered by Mr. Morton and adopted, it was disagreed to.

The second amendment, being that offered by Mr. Sherman as section 3, was agreed to—yeas 43, nays 20, as follow:

YEAS—Messrs. Abbott, *Bayard*, Boreman, Brownlow, Carpenter, *Casserly*, Chandler, Corbett, Drake, Gilbert, Harlan, Harris, Howard, Howe, Howell, *Johnston*, Kellogg, Lewis, Morrill of Maine, Morton, Osborn, Pomeroy, Pool, Pratt, Ramsey, Rice, Robertson, Ross, Sawyer, Schurz, Scott, Sherman, Spencer, Stewart, *Stockton*, Thayer, *Thurman*, Tipton, Trumbull, *Vickers*, Warner, Willey, Williams—43.

NAYS—Messrs. Anthony, Buckingham, Cameron, Conkling, Cragin, *Davis*, Edmunds, Fenton, Ferry, *Hamilton* of Maryland, Hamlin, *McCreery*, McDonald, Morrill of Vermont, *Norton*, Nye, Patterson, *Saulsbury*, Sumner, Wilson—20.

The first amendment offered by Mr. Sherman was then agreed to—yeas 44, nays 12, as follow:

YEAS—Messrs. Abbott, Anthony, Boreman, Brownlow, Buckingham, Cameron, Chandler, Cole, Conkling, Corbett, Edmunds, Fenton, Ferry, Gilbert, Hamlin, Harlan, Harris, Howard, Howell, Kellogg, Morrill of Maine, Morrill of Vermont, Nye, Osborn, Patterson, Pomeroy, Pratt, Ramsey, Rice, Robertson, Sawyer, Schurz, Scott, Sherman, Spencer, Stewart, Sumner, Thayer, Tipton, Trumbull, Warner, Willey, Williams, Wilson—44.

NAYS—Messrs. *Bayard*, Carpenter, *Casserly*, *Davis*, *Hamilton* of Maryland, Howe, McDonald, *Norton*, *Saulsbury*, *Stockton*, *Thurman*, *Vickers*—12.

Mr. Morton moved to amend the amendment offered by him and adopted, by striking out the word "thirteen" wherever it occurs therein and inserting the word "twenty," and by striking out the word "fifty-two" and inserting the word "forty-five;" which was agreed to—yeas 43, nays 15, as follow:

YEAS—Messrs. Abbott, *Bayard*, Boreman, Brownlow, Carpenter, *Casserly*, Cole, Corbett, *Davis*, Drake, Fowler, Gilbert, *Hamilton* of Maryland, Harlan, Harris, Howe, Howell, *Johnston*, Kellogg, *McCreery*, McDonald, Morton, *Norton*, Osborn, Pratt, Rice, Robertson, Ross, *Saulsbury*, Sawyer, Schurz, Scott, Sherman, Spencer, Stewart, *Stockton*, Thayer, *Thurman*, Tipton, Trumbull, *Vickers*, Warner, Wilson—43.

NAYS—Messrs. Anthony, Buckingham, Cameron, Chandler, Conkling, Cragin, Edmunds, Fenton, Ferry, Howard, Morrill of Maine, Morrill of Vermont, Patterson, Sumner, Willey—15.

The amendment of Mr. Morton as thus amended was then agreed to—yeas 39, nays 15, as follow:

YEAS—Messrs. Abbott, *Bayard*, Boreman, Brownlow,

Carpenter, *Casserly*, Corbett, *Davis*, Drake, Harlan, Harris, Howe, Howell, Kellogg, *McCreery*. McDonald, Morton, Osborn. Pool, Pratt, Ramsey, Rice, Robertson, Ross, Sawyer. Schurz, Scott, Sherman. Spencer. Stewart, *Stockton*, Thayer, *Thurman*. Tipton, Trumbull, *Vickers*. Warner, Willey. Wilson—39.

NAYS—Messrs. Anthony, Buckingham, Cameron, Conkling. Cragin, Edmunds, Fenton, Ferry, Fowler, Howard. Morrill of Maine, Morrill of Vermont, Nye, Patterson, Sumner—15.

Mr. Morrill, of Vermont, moved to insert at the end of section 3 the following:

But shall be accounted for as between the States from which and to which any banks may remove.

Which was disagreed to—yeas 21, nays 36, as follow:

YEAS—Messrs. Anthony, Buckingham, Cameron, Chandler, Conkling, Cragin, Edmunds, Fenton, Ferry, Gilbert, Hamlin, Morrill of Maine, Morrill of Vermont, Nye, Patterson, Sherman, Stewart, Sumner, *Vickers*, Williams, Wilson—21.

NAYS—Messrs. Abbott, Boreman, Brownlow, Carpenter, *Casserly*, Corbett, *Davis*, Drake, Fowler, Harlan, Harris, Howard, Howe, Howell, *Johnston*, Kellogg, *McCreery*. McDonald. Morton, *Norton*, Osborn, Pool, Pratt, Ramsey, Rice, Robertson, Ross, *Saulsbury*, Sawyer, Schurz. Scott, *Stockton*, Thayer, Tipton, Trumbull, Warner—36.

Mr. Howe moved to strike out the 4th, 5th, and 6th sections; which was disagreed to—yeas 29, nays 29, as follow:

YEAS—Messrs. Abbott *Bayard* Boreman, Buckingham, Carpenter, Casserly, Conkling, *Davis*, Drake, Ferry. Fowler, *Hamilton* of Maryland, Harris, Howe, Howell, *Johnston*, McDonald, Morton, *Norton*, Pomeroy, Rice, *Saulsbury*, Scott, Spencer, *Stockton*, Sumner, *Thurman*, *Vickers*—29.

NAYS—Messrs. Anthony, Brownlow, Cameron, Corbett, Edmunds, Gilbert, Hamlin, Harlan. Howard, *McCreery*, Morrill of Maine, Morrill of Vermont, Nye, Osborn, Patterson, Pool, Pratt, Robertson, Ross, Sawyer, Sherman, Stewart, Thayer, Tipton, Trumbull. Warner, Willey, Williams, Wilson–29.

The bill was then passed—yeas 39, nays 23, as follow:

YEAS—Messrs. Abbott, Boreman, Brownlow, Cameron, Chandler, Corbett, *Davis*, Drake, Gilbert, Hamlin, Harlan, Harris, Howard, Howell, *Johnston*, Kellogg, *McCreery*, Norton, Nye, Osborn, Pomeroy, Pool, Pratt, Ramsey, Rice, Robertson, Ross, Sawyer, Schurz, Sherman, Spencer. Stewart, Thayer, Tipton, Trumbull, Warner, Willey, Williams, Wilson—39.

NAYS—Messrs. Anthony, *Bayard*, Buckingham, Carpenter, *Casserly*, Cole, Conkling, Edmunds, Fenton, Ferry, Fowler, *Hamilton* of Maryland, Howe, McDonald, Morrill of Maine, Morrill of Vermont, *Norton*, *Saulsbury*, Scott, *Stockton*, Sumner, *Thurman*, *Vickers*—23.

### IN HOUSE OF REPRESENTATIVES.

1870, June 9—Mr. Garfield, from the Committee on Banking and Currency, offered the following substitute for the Senate bill:

That $95,000,000 in notes for circulation may be issued to national banking associations, in addition to the $300,000,000 authorized by the 22d section of the "Act to provide a national currency secured by a pledge of United States bonds, and to provide for the circulation and redemption thereof," approved June 3, 1864; and the amount of notes so provided shall be furnished to banking associations organized or to be organized in those States and Territories having less than their proportion under the apportionment contemplated by the provisions of the "Act to amend an act to provide a national currency secured by a pledge of United States bonds, and to provide for the circulation and redemption thereof," approved March 3, 1865, and the bonds deposited with the Treasurer of the United States

to secure the additional circulating notes herein authorized shall be of any description of bonds of the United States bearing interest in coin: *Provided*, That if applications for the circulation herein authorized shall not be made within one year after the passage of this act, by banking associations organized or to be organized in States having less than their proportion, it shall be lawful for the Comptroller of the Currency to issue such circulation to banking associations in other States or Territories not in excess applying for the same, giving the preference to such as have the geatest deficiency: *And provided further*, That no banking association hereafter organized shall have a circulation in excess of $500,000.

SEC. 2. That at the end of each month after the passage of this act it shall be the duty of the Comptroller of the Currency to report to the Secretary of the Treasury the amount of circulating notes issued under the provisions of the preceding section to national banking associations during the previous month; whereupon the Secretary of the Treasury shall redeem and cancel an amount of the three per centum temporary loan certificates issued under the acts of March 2, 1867, and July 25, 1868, not less than the amount of circulating notes so reported, and may, if necessary, in order to procure the presentation of such temporary loan certificates for redemption, give notice to the holders thereof, by publication or otherwise, that certain of said certificates (which shall be designated by number, date, and amount) shall cease to bear interest from and after a day to be designated in such notice, and that the certificates so designated shall no longer be available as any portion of the lawful money reserve in possession of any national banking association, and after the day designated in such notice no interest shall be paid on such certificates, and they shall not thereafter be counted as a part of the reserve of any banking association. And when the whole amount of additional circulating notes issued in accordance with the provisions of the preceding section of this act shall exceed the amount of the three per centum temporary loan certificates, the Secretary of the Treasury shall, at the beginning of each month, redeem and cancel an amount of United States notes equal to eighty per centum of the amount of additional circulating notes issued to national banking associations during the preceding month, in accordance with the provisions of this act.

SEC. 3. That to secure a more equitable distribution of the national banking currency, there may be issued circulating notes to banking associations organized in States and Territories having less than their proportion as herein set forth. And the amount of circulation in this section authorized shall, under the direction of the Secretary of the Treasury, as it may be required for this purpose, be withdrawn, as herein provided, from banking associations organized in States having a circulation exceeding that provided for by the act entitled "An act to amend an act entitled 'An act to provide for a national banking currency secured by pledge of United States bonds, and to provide for the circulation and redemption thereof,'" approved March 3, 1865;

but the amount so withdrawn shall not exceed $25,000,000. The Comptroller of the Currency shall, under the direction of the Secretary of the Treasury, make a statement showing the amount of circulation in each State and Territory, and the amount to be retired by each banking association in accordance with this section, and shall, when such redistribution of circulation is required, make a requisition for such amount upon such banks, commencing with the banks having a circulation exceeding $1,000,000 in States having an excess of circulation, and withdrawing their circulation in excess of $1,000,000, and then proceeding *pro rata* with other banks having a circulation exceeding $300,000 in States having the largest excess of circulation, and reducing the circulation of such banks in States having the greatest proportion in excess, leaving undisturbed the banks in States having a smaller proportion, until those in greater excess have been reduced to the same grade, and continuing thus to make the reduction provided for by this act until the full amount of $25,000,000 herein provided for shall be withdrawn; and the circulation so withdrawn shall be distributed among the States and Territories having less than their proportion, so as to equalize the same. And it shall be the duty of the Comptroller of the Currency, under the direction of the Secretary of the Treasury, forthwith to make a requisition for the amount thereof upon the banks above indicated, as herein prescribed. And upon failure of such associations, or any of them, to return the amount so required within one year, it shall be the duty of the Comptroller of the Currency to sell at public auction, having given twenty days' notice thereof in one daily newspaper printed in Washington, and one in New York city, an amount of bonds deposited by said association, as security for said circulation, equal to the circulation to be withdrawn from said association and not returned in compliance with such requisition; and the Comptroller of the Currency shall with the proceeds redeem so many of the notes of said banking association, as they come into the treasury, as will equal the amount required and not so returned, and shall pay the balance, if any, to such banking association: *Provided*, That no circulation shall be withdrawn under the provisions of this section until after the $95,000,000 granted in the 1st section shall have been taken up.

SEC. 4. That after the expiration of six months from the passage of this act any banking association located in any State having more than its proportion of circulation may be removed to any State having less than its proportion of circulation, under such rules and regulations as the Comptroller of the Currency, with the approval of the Secretary of the Treasury, may require: *Provided*, That the amount of the issue of said banks shall not be deducted from the amount of new issue provided for in this act.

June 14—Mr. Randall offered the following substitute:

That from and after the passage of this act it shall be unlawful for any individual, association, or corporation to issue as money any note or bill not authorized by act of Congress; and the Secretary of the Treasury is hereby authorized to issue, on the credit of the United States, such

sums as may be necessary for the purposes set forth in this act, not exceeding in aggregate amount $300,000,000 of United States notes, not bearing interest, of such denominations as he may deem expedient, not less than $5 each, which said notes shall be lawful money and a legal tender for debts in like manner as provided in the 1st section of an act entitled "An act to authorize the issue of United States notes, and for the redemption or funding thereof, and for funding the floating debt of the United States," passed February 25, 1862. And the provisions of the 6th and 7th sections of said act are hereby re-enacted and applied to the notes herein authorized.

SEC. 2. That the notes issued under this act shall be used only in exchange for the circulating notes issued to national banking associations under the provisions of an act of Congress approved March 3, 1864, entitled "An act to provide a national currency secured by a pledge of United States bonds," &c., and for the purchase of such amounts of United States bonds as may be necessary to carry out the true intent of this act.

SEC. 3. That all circulating notes of national banking associations which may hereafter be paid into the Treasury of the United States shall be retained in the treasury and not again put in circulation; and the Secretary of the Treasury may pay out for circulation, as the wants of the Government may require, an equal amount of the United States notes hereby authorized to be issued. And the Secretary of the Treasury may exchange United States notes, issued under authority of this act, with any person or persons for a like amount of circulating notes of national banking associations. And the Secretary of the Treasury shall notify any banking association of the amount of its notes so accumulated when such amount is not less than $900; and the said banking association is hereby required, within thirty days after the issuing of said notice, to redeem said notes at the Treasury of the United States in lawful money, and to present the notes so redeemed to the Secretary of the Treasury for cancellation. And the Secretary of the Treasury is hereby directed to cancel the said notes and to return to the said banking association the proportionate amount of United States bonds deposited as security for the same.

SEC. 4. That in case any national banking association shall neglect or decline to redeem its circulating notes as provided in the preceding section within the thirty days therein specified, the Secretary of the Treasury is hereby authorized and directed to cancel said notes, and to pay said banking association in the United States notes authorized by this act the market value of the United States bonds deposited as security for said circulating notes, after deducting therefrom the amount required for redeeming said national bank notes, and to cancel said bonds, first furnishing to said banking association a list of the numbers, dates, and denominations of the notes so canceled: *Provided*, That if it shall appear to the Secretary of the Treasury that any of such bonds, held by him on deposit as security for said notes, shall have matured, then it shall be his duty to take the same up at par with the notes authorized by this act to an extent of the proportion of the notes to be so redeemed and bonds held as security for the same.

SEC. 5. That when the circulating notes of any national banking association shall have been so far redeemed and canceled at the Treasury that the remaining notes shall not exceed three per cent. of the whole amount of circulating notes originally issued to said banking association, the Secretary of the Treasury is hereby authorized and directed to return to said bank the bonds deposited as security for its circulating notes, and said banking association shall be relieved from its obligation to pay said notes remaining in circulation, and the same shall be redeemed by the Secretary of the Treasury, and paid, on presentation to the Treasury, out of any money in the Treasury not otherwise appropriated.

SEC. 6. That so much of any law or laws as are inconsistent herewith shall be, and the same are hereby, repealed.

Which was disagreed to—yeas 51, nays 111, as follow:

YEAS—Messrs. *Adams, Axtell, Beck, Bird, Booker,* Benjamin F. Butler, *Calkin,* Clinton L. Cobb, Cook, Covode, *Cox, Crebs,* Dockery, *Dox, Eldridge,* Fitch, *Fox, Getz, Gibson, Hambleton, Hamill,* Hay, Hays, Heflin, *Holman, Johnson,* Lash, *Marshall,* McCormick, *McNeely, Milnes, Morgan, Morrissey, Mungen, Niblack, Randall, Reeves, Rice, Ridgway. Rogers, Schumaker, Sherrod, Shober, Joseph S. Smith, Stiles, Strader, Sweeney, Trimble, Wells, Winchester, Woodward*—51.

NAYS—Messrs. Allison, Ambler, Ames, Armstrong, Asper, Atwood, Bailey. Banks, Barry, Beaman, Beatty, Benjamin, Bennett, Benton, *Biggs,* Bingham, Blair, Boles. George M. Brooks, Buck, Buckley, Buffinton, Burchard, Burdett, Roderick R. Butler, Cessna, Churchill, Sidney Clarke. Amasa Cobb, Coburn, Conger, Cowles, Cullom, Dawes, Degener, Dickey, Dixon, Donley. Duval, Ferriss, Finkelnburg, Fisher, Garfield, Gilfillan, *Griswold,* Hawley, Hoar, Hooper, Hotchkiss, Judd, Julian, Kelley, Kellogg, Kelsey, Ketcham, Knapp, Laflin, Lawrence, *Lewis,* Logan, *Mayham,* Maynard. McCarthy, McCrary, McGrew, Mercur, Eliakim H. Moore. Jesse H. Moore, William Moore, Morphis, Daniel J. Morrell, Newsham, Orth, Packard, Paine, Palmer, Peck, Perce, Phelps, Platt, Poland, Pomeroy, Porter, *Potter,* Prosser, Sanford, Sargent, Sawyer, Lionel A. Sheldon, Porter Sheldon, John A. Smith, William Smyth, Starkweather, Stokes, Stoughton, Strickland, Taffe, Tanner, Taylor, Tillman, Townsend, Twichell. Upson, *Van Trump,* Van Wyck, Ward, Cadwalader C. Washburn, William B. Washburn, Wheeler. Whitmore, Winans—111.

Mr. Morgan moved to substitute the following:

That all acts and parts of acts authorizing the issue of national bank notes be, and the same are hereby, repealed.

SEC. 2. That in order to meet the demands of trade, to secure a currency in quantity and value corresponding to the development of the material wealth and population of the United States, and provide for the people a means of paying their taxes, the Secretary of the Treasury is hereby required to cause to be executed gold treasury notes, commonly called greenbacks, of convenient denominations, in manner and form as already prescribed by law, to the amount of $400,000,000.

SEC. 3. That the Secretary of the Treasury is hereby further required to cancel and destroy all matured United States bonds deposited by the national banks as security in the Treasury of the United States, and to redeem in said treasury notes the national bank notes issued on said bonds, and return to said banks, in redemption for their notes, the non-matured bonds deposited as aforesaid; and he shall cancel and destroy all such

bank notes which have been or may be received by the agents of the United States in payment of taxes, or otherwise, and substitute for the same an equal amount of gold treasury notes, and pay to the depositors of said bonds a sum at par in treasury notes equal to the difference between the nominal value of the bonds deposited and the amount of bank currency issued on them.

SEC. 4. That the Secretary of the Treasury is hereby also required to forthwith give notice, by publication, to the holders of the 5-20 bonds, so called, (which shall be designated by number, date, and amount,) of the largest denominations, and of such issues as have matured, that the same will be paid to the amount of $100,000,000, at par, in said treasury notes on presentation, and that on failure to present said bonds for payment within six weeks after said notice interest on the same shall cease from that date.

SEC. 5. That in order to secure a uniform and stable currency, from and after the passage of this act all taxes, duties, and imposts of every kind, payable to the Government of the United States, shall be receivable in gold, silver, or treasury notes, at the option of the person making the payment; and upon the redemption of the public debt all outstanding treasury notes shall be redeemed at par, in gold or silver, in a manner to be provided for by law. And all acts and parts of acts inconsistent with the provisions of this act are hereby repealed.

Which was disagreed to—yeas 37, nays 127, as follow:

YEAS—Messrs. *Adams, Axtell, Beck, Biggs, Bird, Burr, Conner, Crebs, Dox, Gibson, Hamill,* Hawkins, Hays, Heflin, *Holman, Johnson, Kerr, Knott, Lewis, Marshall,* McCormick, *McNeely, Morgan, Mungen, Niblack, Reeves, Rice, Ridgway, Rogers, Sherrod.* Shober, *Strader, Sweeney, Trimble, Van Trump, Wells, Winchester*—37.

NAYS—Messrs. Allison, Ambler, Ames, Armstrong, Asper, Atwood, Bailey, Banks, Barry, Beaman, Beatty, Benjamin, Bennett, Benton, Bingham, Blair, Boles, *Booker,* George M. Brooks, Buckley, Buffinton, Burchard, Burdett, Roderick R. Butler, *Calkin,* Cessna, Churchill, William T. Clark, Amasa Cobb, Clinton L. Cobb, Coburn, Cook, Conger, Cowles, *Cox,* Cullom, Dawes, Degener, Dickey, Dixon, Donley, Duval, Ela, Farnsworth, Ferriss, Ferry, Finkelnburg, Fisher, *Fox,* Garfield, *Getz,* Gilfillan, *Griswold,* Hale, *Hambleton,* Hamilton, Harris, Hawley, Hay, Hooper, Hotchkiss, Ingersoll, Judd, Julian, Kelley, Kellogg, Kelsey. Ketcham, Knapp, Laflin, Lash, Lawrence, Logan, Maynard, McCarthy, McCrary, McGrew, Mercur, *Milnes,* Eliakim H. Moore, Jesse H. Moore, William Moore, Morphis, Daniel J. Morrell, *Morrissey,* Newsham, Orth, Packard, Paine, Palmer, Peck, Perce, Phelps, Platt, Poland, Pomeroy, Porter, *Potter,* Prosser, *Randall,* Sanford, Sargent, Sawyer, Lionel A. Sheldon, Porter Sheldon, John A. Smith, William Smyth. Starkweather, Stiles, Stokes, Stoughton, Strickland, Taffe, Tanner, Taylor, Tillman, Townsend. Twichell, Upson, Van Horn, Van Wyck, Ward, Cadwalader C. Washburn, Whitmore, Willard, John T. Wilson, Winans—127.

June 15—Mr. Ingersoll moved to substitute the following:

That the Secretary of the Treasury, in addition to the United States legal-tender notes heretofore issued under former acts of Congress, be, and he is hereby, authorized and directed to issue like notes of the denominations heretofore issued, and in such proportions as he may deem best, to the amount of $44,000,000; $10,000,000 of said notes to be issued within thirty days after the passage of this act, and $10,000,000 within sixty days after the passage of this act; and $10,000,000 within ninety days after the passage of this act, and the remaining $14,900,000 within or e hundred and twenty days after the passage of this act.

Which was disagreed to—yeas. 51, nays 103, as follow:

YEAS—Messrs. *Adams, Archer,* Beatty, *Beck,* Bennett, *Burr,* Amasa Cobb, Coburn, Cook, *Conner, Crebs,* Cullom, *Dox, Eldridge, Gibson, Hambleton, Hamill,* Hamilton, Hawkins, Hay, Hays, Heflin, *Holman,* Ingersoll, *Kerr, Knott,* Lawrence, *Lewis,* Marshall, *McCormick, McKenzie, McNeely,* Milnes, *Morgan, Niblack,* Orth, Packard, *Reeves, Rice, Ridgway, Rogers,* Roots, Sherrod, *Strader, Trimble,* Tyner, *Van Trump,* Wells, *Winchester,* Witcher, *Wood*—51.

NAYS—Messrs. Allison, Ambler, Ames, Asper, Atwood, Bailey, Banks, Barry, Beaman, Benjamin, Benton, Bingham, *Bird,* Blair, *Booker,* George M. Brooks, Buck, Buckley, Buffinton, Burchard, Burdett, Roderick R. Butler, Cessna, Churchill, Sidney Clarke, *Cleveland,* Conger, Cowles, *Cox,* Degener, Dickey, Dixon, Donley, Duval, Dyer, Ela, Farnsworth, Ferriss, Finkelnburg, Fisher, Fitch, *Fox,* Garfield, *Getz, Haight,* Hale, Harris, Hawley, Hoar, Hooper, Hotchkiss, Judd, Julian, Kelley, Kellogg, Kelsey, Ketcham, Knapp, Laflin, Lash, Maynard, McCarthy, McCrary, McGrew, Mercur, William Moore, Morphis, Daniel J. Morrell, *Morrissey,* Newsham, Packer, Peck, Perce, Phelps, Poland, Pomeroy, *Potter, Randall,* Sargent, Sawyer, Schenck, *Schumaker,* Porter Sheldon, *Joseph S. Smith,* William Smyth, Starkweather, *Stiles,* Stokes, Strickland, Strong, *Swann,* Taffe, Tanner, Tillman, Twichell, Upson, *Van Auken,* Van Wyck, Ward, William B. Washburn, Willard, Winans, *Woodward*—103.

Messrs. Ingersoll and Lynch offered amendments in the nature of substitutes, which were disagreed to without a division.

Mr. Joseph S. Smith moved to insert as an additional section to the Senate bill:

SEC. —. That after the 1st day of January, A. D. 1871, no interest shall be paid to any national banking association on the bonds deposited by it in pursuance of law as security for its circulation, except on the excess of the par value of such bonds over and above the amount of national bank notes issued to it and not redeemed or canceled by the Government; and that after that date no tax shall be levied or collected on the circulation of any national banking association.

Which was disagreed to—yeas 37, nays 118, as follow:

YEAS—Messrs. *Adams, Beck, Bird, Burr, Calkin, Conner, Cox, Crebs, Dox, Hambleton, Holman, Knott,* Lewis, *Marshall, Mayham, McNeely,* Milnes, *Morgan, Morrissey, Mungen, Niblack, Randall, Reeves,* Rice, *Ridgway, Rogers, Schumaker, Sherrod, Shober, Joseph S. Smith, Stiles, Sweeney, Trimble, Van Auken, Van Trump, Winchester, Wood*—37.

NAYS—Messrs. Allison, Ames, Armstrong. Asper, Atwood, Bailey, Banks, Barry, Beaman, Beatty, Bennett, Benton, Blair, Boles, *Booker,* Boyd, George M. Brooks, Buck, Buckley, Buffinton, Burchard, Burdett, Benjamin F. Butler, Roderick R. Butler, Cessna, Churchill, William T. Clark, *Cleveland,* Amasa Cobb, Coburn, Cook, Conger, Cowles, Degener, Dickey, Dixon, Dockery, Donley, Duval, Ela, Farnsworth, Ferriss, Finkelnburg, Fisher, Garfield, *Getz, Haight,* Hale, Hamilton, Hawkins, Hawley, Hay, Hays, Hoar, Hooper, Hotchkiss, Ingersoll, Judd, Julian, Kelley, Kellogg, Kelsey, Ketcham, Knapp, Laflin, Lash, Lawrence, Logan, Maynard, McCarthy, McCrary, McGrew, Mercur, Eliakim H. Moore, Jesse H. Moore, William Moore, Morphis, Daniel J. Morrell, Orth, Packard, Packer, Paine, Palmer, Peck, Phelps, Platt, Poland, Pomeroy, *Potter,* Sargent, Sawyer, Schenck, Lionel A. Sheldon, John A. Smith, William Smyth, Starkweather, Stokes, Stoughton, *Strader,* Strickland, Strong, Taffe, Tanner, Taylor, Tillman, Twichell, Tyner, Upson, Van Wyck, Ward, Cadwalader C. Washburn, William B. Washburn. Wheeler, Willard, John T. Wilson, Winans, Witcher, *Woodward*—118.

Mr. Judd moved to strike out the following from the 2d section of the substitute:

And when the whole amount of additional circulating notes, issued in accordance with the provisions of the preceding section of this act, shall exceed the amount of three per cent. tem-

porary loan certificates, the Secretary of the Treasury shall, at the beginning of each month, redeem and cancel an amount of United States notes equal to eighty per cent. of the amount of additional circulating notes issued to national banking associations during the preceding month, in accordance with the provisions of this act.

Which was agreed to, upon a division—ayes 72, noes 44.

Mr. Allison moved to add to the last section of the substitute the following:

And from and after the passage of this act it shall be unlawful for any national banking association to pay interest on deposits received from and deposited by any other national banking association, or to pay interest on current deposits, or to include in its reserve of lawful money any deposits upon which interest is received or paid.

Which was disagreed to—yeas 69, nays 94, as follow:

YEAS—Messrs. *Adams,* Allison, Ames, *Archer,* Asper, *Axtell,* Barry, *Beck, Biggs,* Boles, Burchard, *Burr, Calkin,* Churchill, William T. Clark, *Cleveland,* Cook, Conger, *Conner, Crebs,* Degener, *Dox,* Dyer, Finkelnburg, *Fox,* Garfield, *Getz, Haight,* Harris, Hawkins, Hay, Heflin, *Holman,* Hooper, Judd, Kelley, *Knott, Marshall, Mayham,* Maynard, *McCormick, McKenzie, McNeely, Milnes, Morgan, Morrissey, Mungen, Niblack,* Perce, *Reeves, Rice, Ridgway, Rogers,* Schenck, *Sherrod, Shober, Joseph S. Smith. Stiles, Strader, Sweeney,* Taylor, *Trimble, Van Auken, Van Trump, Wells, Winchester,* Witcher, *Wood*—69.

NAYS—Messrs. Ambler, Armstrong, Atwood, Bailey, Banks, Beaman, Beatty, Benton, Bingham, *Bird,* Blair, *Booker,* Boyd, George M. Brooks, Buck, Buckley, Buffinton, Burdett, Roderick R. Butler, Cessna, Sidney Clarke, Amasa Cobb, Clinton L. Cobb, Coburn, Cowles, *Cox,* Cullom, Dawes, Dickey, Dixon, Donley, Duval, Farnsworth, Ferriss, Fisher, *Griswold,* Hawley, Hays, Hoar, Hotchkiss, Ingersoll, Julian, Kellogg, Kelsey, Ketcham, Knapp, Laflin, Lash, Lawrence, *Lewis,* McCarthy, McGrew, Mercur, Eliakim II. Moore, Jesse H. Moore, William Moore, Daniel J. Morrell, Samuel P. Morrill, Newsham, Orth, Packard, Packer, Paine, Peck, Phelps, Platt, Poland, Pomeroy, *Roots,* Sanford, Sargent, Sawyer, Lionel A. Sheldon, Porter Sheldon William Smyth, Starkweather, Stokes, Stoughton Strickland, Strong, Taffe, Tanner, Tillman, Twichell, Tyner, Upson, Van Wyck. Ward, Cadwalader C. Washburn, William B. Washburn, Wheeler, Willard, John T. Wilson, *Woodward*—94.

Mr. Burchard moved to amend the substitute by adding the following as a new section:

SEC. —. That hereafter every national banking association shall retain and keep in coin, or Treasury coin certificates, as part of its reserve, the interest falling due upon its bonds deposited as security for its circulation, until the reserve required to be kept by such bank at its place of business shall consist wholly of coin and coin certificates.

Which was disagreed to—yeas 33, nays not counted.

Mr. Coburn moved to add to the substitute of the committee the following, as a new section:

SEC. —. That the Secretary of the Treasury be, and he is hereby, authorized to issue on the credit of the United States the sum of $44,000,000 of United States notes, in addition to such as have been heretofore issued, in denominations of not less than $100, under the provisions of law for issuing such notes, and shall with them redeem the said three per cent. temporary loan certificates, used as a portion of the lawful money reserves by the national banks.

Which was disagreed to—yeas 77, nays 95, as follow:

YEAS—Messrs. *Adams*, Allison, Ames. *Archer*, Beatty, *Beck*, Bennett, Boles, *Booker*, Boyd. Buckley, Burr, Benjamin F. Butler, Roderick R. Butler, Sidney Clarke, Amasa Cobb, Clinton L. Cobb, Coburn, Cook, *Conner*, *Crebs*, Cullom, Dockery, *Dox*, Dyer, *Eldridge*, *Gibson*, Griswold, *Hambleton*, Hawkins, Hay, Hays, Heflin, *Holman*, Ingersoll, *Knott*, Lash, Lawrence, *Lewis*, *Marshall*, Maynard, *McCormick*, *McKenzie*, *McNeely*, Eliakim H. Moore, Jesse H. Moore, *Morgan*, Morphis, *Morrissey*, *Mungen*, Newsham, *Niblack*, Orth, Packard, Pomeroy, *Randall*, *Reeves*, *Rice*, *Ridgway*, *Rogers*, Roots, *Sherrod*, *Shober*, *Joseph S. Smith*, *Strader*, Taffe, *Trimble*, Tyner, Van Horn, *Van Trump*, VanWyck, *Wells*, John T. Wilson, *Winchester*, Witcher, *Wood*—77.

NAYS—Messrs. Ambler, Armstrong, Asper, Atwood, *Axtell*, Bailey, Banks, Barry, Beaman, Benjamin, Benton, Bingham, *Bird*, Blair, George M. Brooks, *James Brooks*, Buck, Buffinton, Burchard, Burdett, *Calkin*, Churchill, William T. Clark, *Cleveland*, Conger, Cowles, *Cox*, Dawes, Degener, Dickey, Dixon, Donley, Duval, Farnsworth, Ferriss, Finkelnburg, Fisher, *Fox*, Garfield, *Getz*, *Haight*, Hale, Hawley, Hooper, Hotchkiss, Judd, Julian, Kelley, Kellogg, Kelsey, Ketcham, Knapp, Laflin, *Mayham*, McCarthy, McGrew, Mercur, William Moore, Daniel J. Morrell, Samuel P. Morrill, Packer, Paine, Palmer, Peck, Perce, Phelps, Platt, Poland, Porter, *Potter*, Sanford, Sawyer, Schenck, *Schumaker*, Lionel A. Sheldon, Porter Sheldon, William Smyth, Starkweather, *Stiles*, Stokes, Stoughton, Strickland, Strong, Tanner, Taylor, Tillman, Twichell, Upson, *Van Auken*, Ward, Cadwalader C. Washburn, William B. Washburn, Wheeler, Willard, Winans, *Woodward*—95.

The bill was then passed—yeas 98, nays 80, as follow:

YEAS—Messrs. Allison, Ambler, Armstrong, Asper, Atwood, Bailey, Barry, Beaman, Beatty, Benjamin, Bennett, Bingham, Boles, *Booker*, Boyd, Buck, Buckley, Burchard, Burdett, Cessna, William T. Clark, Amasa Cobb, Clinton L. Cobb, Coburn, Cook, Conger, Cowles, Cullom, Degener, Dickey, Dockery, Donley, Duval, Dyer, Farnsworth, Finkelnburg, Garfield, *Gibson*, Hamilton, Harris, Hawkins, Hawley, Hay, Hays, Heflin, Judd, Julian, Kelley, Kelsey, Knapp, Lash, Lawrence, Logan, McCarthy, *McCormick*, McCrary, McGrew, McKee, *McKenzie*, Mercur, *Milnes*, Eliakim H. Moore, Jesse H. Moore, William Moore, Morphis, Newsham, Orth, Packard, Packer, Palmer, Peck, Perce, Phelps, Platt, Pomeroy, *Rogers*, Roots, Schenck, Shanks, Lionel A. Sheldon, Porter Sheldon, William Smyth, Stokes, Stoughton, Strickland, Taffe, Tillman, Tyner, Upson, Van Horn, Van Wyck, Welker, *Wells*, Wilkinson, Willard, John T. Wilson, Winans, Witcher—98.

NAYS—Messrs. *Adams*, Ames, *Archer*, *Axtell*, Banks, Benton, *Biggs*, *Bird*, Blair, George M. Brooks, *James Brooks*, Buffinton, *Burr*, *Calkin*, Churchill, *Cleveland*, *Conner*, *Cox*, *Crebs*, Dawes, Dixon, *Dox*, Ela, *Eldridge*, Ferriss, Fisher, *Fox*, *Getz*, *Griswold*, *Haight*, Hale, *Hambleton*, *Hamill*, Hoar, *Holman*, Hooper, Ingersoll, Ketcham, *Knott*, Laflin, *Lewis*, *Marshall*, *Mayham*, Maynard, *McNeely*, *Morgan*, Daniel J. Morrell, Samuel P. Morrill, *Morrissey*, *Mungen*, *Niblack*, Paine, Poland, *Potter*, *Randall*, *Reeves*, *Rice*, Sanford, Sargent, Sawyer, *Shober*, *Joseph S. Smith*, Starkweather, *Stiles*, *Strader*, Strong, *Swann*, *Sweeney*, Tanner, Taylor, Twichell, *Van Auken*, *Van Trump*, Ward, Cadwalader C. Washburn, William B. Washburn, Wheeler, *Winchester*, *Wood*, *Woodward*—80.

Mr. Garfield moved to amend the title, so as to read: "To provide for the redemption of the three per cent. temporary loan certificates and for the increase of national bank notes."

Which was agreed to.

1870, June 21—The SENATE refused to concur in the House amendments and asked a committee of conference, which was granted.

June 27—The COMMITTEE OF CONFERENCE, consisting of Senators Sherman, Warner, and Sprague, and Representatives Garfield, Thomas L. Jones, and Lionel A. Sheldon, made the following report:

That the Senate recede from their disagreement to the amendments of the House to the Senate bill, and agree to the same, with the following amendments:

Page 1, line 1, strike out "ninety-five" and insert in lieu thereof "forty-five." Page 1, line 18, after the word "coin" insert the following "but a new apportionment of the increased circulation herein provided for shall be made as soon as practicable, based upon the census of 1870."

After section — add the following sections:

SEC. —. That upon the deposit of any United States bonds, bearing interest payable in gold, with the Treasurer of the United States, in the manner prescribed in the 19th and 20th sections of the national currency act, it shall be lawful for the Comptroller of the Currency to issue to the association making the same circulating notes of different denominations not less than five dollars, not exceeding in amount eighty per cent. of the par value of the bonds deposited which notes shall bear upon their face the promise of the association to which they are issued to pay them upon presentation at the office of the association in gold coin of the United States, and shall be redeemable upon such presentation in such coin: *Provided*, That no banking association organized under this section shall have a circulation in excess of $1,000,000.

SEC. —. That every national banking association formed under the provisions of the preceding section of this act shall at all times keep on hand not less than twenty-five per cent. of its outstanding circulation in gold or silver coin of the United States, and shall receive at par in the payment of debts the gold notes of every other such banking association which at the time of such payments shall be redeeming its circulating notes in gold coin of the United States.

SEC. —. That every association organized for the purpose of issuing gold notes, as provided in this section, shall be subject to all the requirements and provisions of the national currency act, except the first clause of section 22, which limits the circulation of national banking associations to $300,000,000; the first clause of section 32, which, taken in connection with the preceding section, would require national banking associations organized in the city of San Francisco to redeem their circulating notes at par in the city of New York; and the last clause of section 32, which requires every national banking association to receive in payment of debts the notes of every other national banking association at par: *Provided*, That in applying the provisions and requirements of said act to the banking associations herein provided for, the terms "lawful money" and "lawful money of the United States" shall be held and construed to mean gold or silver coin of the United States.

That section 3 be amended as follows: page 4, line 3, after the word "withdrawing," insert "one-third of."

Same page, line 5, strike out the word "three" and insert in lieu thereof the word "two."

IN HOUSE, *June 29*, 1870.

The report of the committee of conference was disagreed to—yeas 53, nays 127, as follow:

YEAS—Messrs. Ames, Asper, Ayer, Bailey, Benton, Blair, Boles, Bowen, Buckley, Roderick R. Butler, Churchill, Dickey, Ela, Ferriss. Finkelnburg, Fitch, Garfield, Hale, Harris, Heflin, Hill, *Thomas L. Jones*, Kelsey, Knapp, Laflin, Lash, Mercur, Eliakim H. Moore, Palmer, Perce, Poland, Pomeroy, Roots, Sargent, Sawyer, Schenck, Scofield, Lionel A. Sheldon,

Porter Sheldon, *Shober*, John A. Smith, Worthington C. Smith. William Smyth, Stevens, Stokes, Tanner, Taylor, Tillman, Upson, Wallace, Ward, Willard, Winans—53.

NAYS—Messrs. *Adams*, Allison, Ambler, Armstrong, Atwood, Banks, *Barnum*, Beatty, *Beck*, Benjamin, Bennett, *Biggs*, Bingham, *Bird*, George M. Brooks, *James Brooks*, Buffinton, Burchard, *Burr*, Benjamin F. Butler, *Calkin*, Cessna, William T. Clark, Sidney Clarke. *Cleveland*, Amasa Cobb, Clinton L. Cobb, Coburn, Conger, Cook, *Cox*, *Crebs*, Cullom, Davis, Dawes, Degener, *Dickinson*, Dixon, Dockery, *Dox*, Dyer, *Eldridge*, Farnsworth, Ferry, Fisher, *Getz*, *Griswold*, Hambleton, Hamill, Hawkins, Hawley, Hay, Hoar, *Holman*, Hooper, Ingersoll, *Johnson*. Judd, Kelley, Kellogg, *Kerr*, Ketcham, *Knott*, Lawrence, *Lewis*, Loughridge, *Marshall*, Maynard, McCarthy, *McCormick*, McGrew, McKee, *McNeely*, *Milnes*, Jesse H. Moore, William Moore, *Morgan*, Morphis, Daniel J. Morrell, *Mungen*, Myers, Negley, *Niblack*, O'Neill, Orth, Packer. Paine, Peck, Phelps, Porter, Prosser, *Reeves*, *Rice*, *Rogers*, Sanford, *Schumaker*, Shanks *Slocum*, *Joseph S. Smith*. Starkweather, Stevenson, *Stiles*, *Stone*, Stoughton, *Strader*, Strickland, Strong, *Swann*, *Sweeney*, Taffe, Townsend, Twichell. Tyner, *Van Auken*, Van Horn, Van Wyck. Welker, *Wells*, Wheeler, Whitmore, Wilkinson, Williams. *Eugene M. Wilson*, John T. Wilson, *Winchester*, Wood, *Woodward*—127.

A second committee of conference, consisting of Senators Williams, Morton, and Bayard, and Representatives Judd, Packer, and Knott, agreed upon a report, being the bill as finally passed, and printed at the beginning of this chapter.

The following, it is understood, will be the apportionment of the additional circulation given in this act:

Virginia, $4,915,985; West Virginia, $457,770; Illinois, $1,079,592; Michigan, $786,776; Wisconsin, $2,117,939; Iowa, $681,363; Kansas, $174,712; Missouri, $3,000,412; Kentucky, $4,651,349; Tennessee, $4,331,759; Louisiana, $5,425,193; Mississippi, $2,980,470; Nebraska, $6,576; Georgia, $4,681,728; North Carolina, $4,098,628; South Carolina, $4,216,838; Alabama, $4,081,212; Oregon, $161,273; Texas, $2,032,194; Arkansas, $1,455,519; Utah, $58,332; California, $1,717,388; Florida, $546,442; Dakota, $15,441; New Mexico, $277,939; Washington Territory, $47,180. Total, $54,000,000.

The following is the apportionment of the existing circulation:

Maine, $5,415,000; New Hampshire, $3,312,000; Vermont, $2,989,500; Massachusetts, $21,795,000; Rhode Island, $4,794,000; Connecticut, $7,222,500; New York, $53,473,500; New Jersey, $6,690,000; Pennsylvania, $26,527,500; Maryland, $7,137,000; Delaware, $1,090,500; District of Columbia, $658,500; Virginia, $10,731,000; West Virginia, $2,788,500; Ohio, $17,623,500; Indiana, $9,615,000; Illinois, $11,838,000; Michigan, $5,200,500; Wisconsin, $6,211,500; Iowa, $4,408,500; Minnesota, $1,050,000; Kansas, $646,500; Missouri, $9,411,000; Kentucky, $10,500,000; Tennessee, $8,766,000; Louisiana, $10,581,000; Mississippi, $5,265,000; Nebraska, $181,500; Colorado, $193,500; Georgia, $9,420,500; North Carolina, $7,546,500; South Carolina, $7,566,000; Alabama, $7,425,000; Nevada, $48,000; Oregon, $370,500; Texas, $3,961,000; Arkansas, $2,724,000; Utah, $237,000; California, $3,003,000; Florida, $955,500; Dakota, $27,000; New Mexico, $486,000; Washington Territory, $82,500. Total, $299,968,500.

IN HOUSE, *December 11, 1869.*

Mr. Ingersoll introduced a "bill authorizing an additional issue of legal-tender notes to the amount of $44,000,000, and for other purposes;" which was referred to the Committee on Banking and Currency. Pending question of reference, Mr. Scofield moved to lay the bill on the table; which was disagreed to—yeas 65, nays 88, as follow:

YEAS—Messrs. Ambler. Ames, Asper, Bailey, Beaman, Benjamin, *Biggs*. *Bird*, Blair, Boyd, George M. Brooks, Buck, Buckley, Buffinton, *Cox*. Dawes, Dixon. Donley, Duval, Ferriss, Finkelnburg. Fisher, Garfield, *Getz*, Haldeman, Hoar, Hooper, Jenckes. Kelley, Kellogg, Kelsey, *Kerr*, Ketcham, Knapp, Laflin, Lash, McGrew, Mercur, William Moore, Samuel P. Morrill, *Mungen*, Myers, O'Neill, Poland, *Randall*, *Reading*, *Reeves*. Scofield, Porter Sheldon, John A. Smith, Worthington C Smith, Starkweather, Stevens. Stoughton, Strickland, Strong, Townsend, Twichell, Ward, Cadwalader C. Washburn. William B. Washburn, Wheeler, Willard, Winans, *Woodward*—65.

NAYS—Messrs. Allison, Armstrong, Arnell, Beatty, Bennett, Boles, Burchard, Burdett, *Burr*, Benjamin F. Butler, Roderick R. Butler, Calkin, Cessna, Amasa Cobb, Coburn, Cook, Cowles, *Crebs*, Cullom, Davis, Deweese, *Dickinson*, Dockery, *Dox*, Dyer, Eldridge, Farnsworth, Ferry, Fitch, Gilfillan, *Griswold*, Hamilton, Hawkins Hawley, Hay, Heaton, Heflin, Hoag. Solomon L. Hoge, *Holman*. Ingersoll, *Johnson*, Alexander H. Jones, Judd, Julian, *Knott*, Lawrence, Loughridge, *Mayham*, Maynard, McCarthy, *McCormick*, McCrary, *Morgan*, Negley, *Niblack*, Orth, Packard, Paine, Peters, Pomeroy, Prosser, *Rice*. *Rogers*, Sargent, Lionel A. Sheldon, *Joseph S. Smith*, William J. Smith, William Smyth, Stevenson, Stokes, *Stone*, *Strader*, *Sweeney*, Taffe, Tanner, Tillman, Tyner, Upson, Van Trump, Welker, *Wells*, B. F. Whittemore, Wilkinson, Williams, *Eugene M. Wilson*, Witcher, *Wood*—88.

1870, January 17—Mr. McNeely moved to suspend the rules to offer, and the House to adopt, the following resolution, viz:

*Resolved*, That the Committee on Banking and Currency be, and they are hereby, instructed to report at an early day a bill providing for withdrawing from circulation the national bank currency, and for issuing, instead of such currency, treasury notes, usually known as "greenbacks."

Which was disagreed to—yeas 56, nays 114, as follow:

YEAS—Messrs. *Adams*, *Archer*, *Axtell*, *Beck*, *Biggs*, *Bird*, *James Brooks*, *Burr*, Roderick R. Butler, *Calkin*, *Cox*, *Crebs*, *Dickinson*, *Dox*, *Eldridge*, *Getz*, *Golladay*, *Greene*, *Griswold*, *Haight*, *Haldeman*, *Hambleton*, *Hamill*, *Hawkins*, *Hay*, *Holman*, *Johnson*, *Thomas L. Jones*, *Kerr*, *Knott*, *Marshall*, *Mayham*, *McCormick*, *McNeely*, *Morgan*, *Mungen*, *Niblack*, *Randall*, *Reading*, *Reeves*, *Rogers*, *Schumaker*, *Sherrod*, *Joseph S. Smith*, *Stiles*, *Strader*, *Swann*, *Trimble*, *Van Auken*, *Van Trump*, *Voorhees*, *Wells*, *Eugene M. Wilson*, *Winchester*, *Wood*, *Woodward*—56.

NAYS—Messrs. Ambler, Ames, Armstrong, Asper, Bailey, Banks, *Barnum*, Beaman, Beatty, Benjamin, Benton, Bingham, Blair, Boles, Bowen, Boyd. G. M. Brooks, Buck, Buckley, Buffinton, Burchard, Burdett, Cake, Cessna, Sidney Clarke, Amasa Cobb, Clinton L. Cobb, Coburn, Cook, Conger, Cowles. Dawes, Deweese, Dickey, Dixon, Donley, Duval, Dyer. Ferriss, Finkelnburg, Fisher, Garfield, Gilfillan, Hale, Hamilton, Hawley, Heaton, Heflin, Hill, Hoar, Hooper, Jenckes, Judd, Julian, Kelley, Kellogg, Kelsey, Ketcham, Knapp, Lash, Lawrence, Logan, Lynch, McCarthy, McCrary, McGrew, Mercur, Eliakim H. Moore, Jesse H. Moore, William Moore. Daniel J. Morrell, Myers, Negley, O'Neill, Orth, Packard, Packer, Paine, Palmer, Peters, Phelps, Poland, Pomeroy, *Potter*, Prosser, Roots, Sargent, Sawyer, Scofield, Lionel A. Sheldon, Porter Sheldon, John A. Smith, William J. Smith, Worthington C. Smith, Starkweather, Stevens, Stokes, Stoughton, Strong, Taffe, Tanner, Tillman, Townsend. Twichell, Tyner, Upson, Cadwalader C. Washburn, William B. Washburn, Welker, Wheeler, Wilkinson, Willard, Williams, John T. Wilson—114.

# LVIII.

## THE FUNDING ACT.

**AN ACT to authorize the refunding of the national debt.**

*Be it enacted, &c.*, That the Secretary of the Treasury is hereby authorized to issue, in a sum or sums not exceeding in the aggregate $200,-000,000, coupon or registered bonds of the United States, in such form as he may prescribe, and of denominations of fifty dollars, or some multiple of that sum, redeemable in coin of the present standard value, at the pleasure of the United States, after ten years from the date of their issue, and bearing interest, payable semi-annually in such coin, at the rate of five per cent. per annum; also a sum or sums not exceeding in the aggregate $300,000,000 of like bonds, the same in all respects, but payable at the pleasure of the United States, after fifteen years from the date of their issue, and bearing interest at the rate of four and a half per cent. per annum; also a sum or sums not exceeding in the aggregate $1,000,000,000 of like bonds, the same in all respects, but payable at the pleasure of the United States, after thirty years from the date of their issue, and bearing interest at the rate of four per cent. per annum; all of which said several classes of bonds, and the interest thereon, shall be exempt from the payment of all taxes or duties of the United States, as well as from taxation in any form by or under State, municipal, or local authority; and the said bonds shall have set forth and expressed upon their face the above specified conditions, and shall, with their coupons, be made payable at the Treasury of the United States. But nothing in this act, or in any other law now in force, shall be construed to authorize any increase whatever of the bonded debt of the United States.

Sec. 2. That the Secretary of the Treasury is hereby authorized to sell and dispose of any of the bonds issued under this act at not less than their par value for coin, and to apply the proceeds thereof to the redemption of any of the bonds of the United States outstanding and known as 5-20 bonds at their par value; or he may exchange the same for such 5-20 bonds, par for par; but the bonds hereby authorized shall be used for no other purpose whatsoever. And a sum not exceeding one-half of one per cent. of the bonds herein authorized is hereby appropriated to pay the expense of preparing, issuing, advertising, and disposing of the same.

Sec. 3. That the payment of any of the bonds hereby authorized after the expiration of the said several terms of ten, fifteen, and thirty years shall be made in amounts to be determined from time to time by the Secretary of the Treasury at his discretion, the bonds so to be paid to be distinguished and described by the dates and numbers, beginning for each successive payment with the bonds of each class last dated and numbered, of the time of which intended payment or redemption the Secretary of the Treasury shall give public notice; and the interest on the particular bonds so selected at any time to be paid shall cease at the expiration of three months from the date of such notice.

Sec. 4. That the Secretary of the Treasury is hereby authorized, with any coin in the Treasury of the United States which he may lawfully apply to such purpose, or which may be derived from the sale of any of the bonds the issue of which is provided for in this act, to pay at par and cancel any six per cent. bonds of the United States of the kind known as 5-20 bonds which have become or shall hereafter become redeemable by the terms of their issue. But the particular bonds so to be paid and canceled shall in all cases be indicated and specified by class, date, and number, in order of their numbers and issue, beginning with the first numbered and issued, in public notice, to be given by the Secretary of the Treasury, and in three months after the date of such public notice the interest on the bonds so selected and advertised to be paid shall cease.

Sec. 5. That the Secretary of the Treasury is hereby authorized, at any time within two years from the passage of this act, to receive gold coin of the United States on deposit for not less than thirty days, in sums of not less than $100, with the Treasurer, or any assistant treasurer of the United States authorized by the Secretary of the Treasury to receive the same, who shall issue therefor certificates of deposit, made in such form as the Secretary of the Treasury shall prescribe, and said certificates of deposit shall bear interest at a rate not exceeding two and a half per cent. per annum; and any amount of gold coin so deposited may be withdrawn from deposit at any time after thirty days from the date of deposit, and after ten days' notice and on the return of said certificates: *Provided,* That the interest on all such deposits shall cease and determine at the pleasure of the Secretary of the Treasury. And not less than twenty-five per cent. of the coin deposited for or represented by said certificates of deposits shall be retained in the Treasury for the payment of said certificates; and the excess beyond twenty-five per cent. may be applied, at the discretion of the Secretary of the Treasury, to the payment or redemption of such outstanding bonds of the United States heretofore issued and known as the 5-20 bonds, as he may designate under the provisions of the 4th section of this act; and any certificates of deposit issued as aforesaid may be received at par, with the interest accrued thereon, in payment for any bonds authorized to be issued by this act.

Sec. 6. That the United States bonds purchased and now held in the Treasury in accordance with the provisions relating to a sinking fund, of section 5 of the act entitled "An act to authorize the issue of United States notes, and for the re-

597 .

demption or funding thereof, and for funding the floating debt of the United States," approved February 25, 1862, and all other United States bonds which have been purchased by the Secretary of the Treasury with surplus funds in the Treasury, and now held in the Treasury of the United States, shall be canceled and destroyed, a detailed record of such bonds so canceled and destroyed to be first made in the books of the Treasury Department. Any bonds hereafter applied to said sinking fund, and all other United States bonds, redeemed or paid hereafter by the United States, shall also in like manner be recorded, canceled, and destroyed, and the amount of the bonds of each class that have been canceled and destroyed shall be deducted respectively from the amount of each class of the outstanding debt of the United States. In addition to other amounts that may be applied to the redemption or payment of the public debt, an amount equal to the interest on all bonds belonging to the aforesaid sinking fund shall be applied, as the Secretary of the Treasury shall from time to time direct, to the payment of the public debt, as provided for in section 5 of the act aforesaid; and the amount so to be applied is hereby appropriated annually for that purpose out of the receipts for duties on imported goods.

Approved, July 14, 1870.

## Final Votes.

### In Senate, *July* 13, 1870.

The bill, being the report of the committee of conference last appointed, was agreed to without a division.

### In House, *July* 13, 1870.

YEAS—Messrs. Allison, Ambler, Ames, Armstrong, Arnell, Asper, Atwood, Ayer, Bailey, Banks, Barry, Benjamin, Bennett, Benton, Bingham, Blair, Boles, Boyd, George M. Brooks, Buck, Buckley, Buffinton, Burchard, Burdett, Roderick R. Butler, Cake, Cessna, Churchill, Sidney Clarke, William T. Clark, Amasa Cobb, Coburn, Conger, Cook, Covode, Cowles, Cullom, Darrall, Davis, Dawes, Degener, Dickey, Dixon, Donley, Duval, Ela, Farnsworth, Ferriss, Ferry, Finkelnburg, Fisher, Fitch, Garfield, Gilfillan, Hamilton, Harris, Hawley, Hays, Heflin, Hill, Hoar, Hooper, Hotchkiss, Jenckes, Judd, Julian, Kelley, Kellogg, Kelsey, Ketcham, Knapp, Laflin, Lash, Lawrence, Logan, Loughridge, Lynch, Maynard, McCarthy, McCrary, McGrew, Mercur, Eliakim H. Moore, Jesse H. Moore, William Moore, Morphis, Daniel J. Morrell, Myers, Negley, O'Neill, Orth, Packard, Packer, Paine, Palmer, Peck, Perce, Peters, Phelps, Poland, Porter, Prosser, Rogers, Roots, Sanford, Sargent, Sawyer, Schenck, Shanks, Lionel A. Sheldon, Porter Sheldon, John A. Smith, William J. Smith, Worthington C. Smith, William Smyth, Stevens, Stokes, Stoughton, Strickland, Taffe, Tanner, Taylor, Tillman, Townsend, Twichell, Tyner, Upson, Van Horn, Van Wyck, Ward, William B. Washburn, Welker, Wheeler, Whitmore, Wilkinson, Willard, Williams, John T. Wilson, Witcher—139.

NAYS—Messrs. *Adams, Archer, Axtell, Barnum,* Beatty, *Beck, Biggs, Bird, James Brooks, Burr, Calkin, Cleveland, Cox, Crebs, Dickinson, Eldridge, Fox, Getz, Griswold, Haight, Hambleton, Hamill, Hay, Holman, Johnson, Thomas L. Jones, Kerr, Knott, Lewis, Marshall, Mayham, McCormick, McKenzie, Morgan, Potter, Randall, Reeves, Rice, Schumaker, Sherrod, Slocum, Joseph S. Smith, Stiles, Stone, Swann, Sweeney, Trimble, Van Trump, Voorhees, Wells, Eugene M. Wilson, Winchester,* Wood, *Woodward*—54.

## Previous Votes.

### In Senate.

1870, February 7—Mr. Sherman, from the Committee on Finance, reported the following bill:

*Be it enacted, &c.,* That for the purpose of funding the debt of the United States and reducing the interest thereon, the Secretary of the Treasury be, and he is hereby, authorized to issue, on the credit of the United States, coupon or registered bonds of such denominations, not less than $50, as he may think proper, to an amount not exceeding $400,000,000, redeemable in coin at the pleasure of the Government at any time after ten years, and payable in coin at twenty years from date, and bearing interest at the rate of five per centum per annum, payable semi-annually in coin; and the bonds thus authorized may be disposed of, at the discretion of the Secretary, under such regulations as he shall prescribe, either in the United States or elsewhere, at not less than their par value for coin, or they may be exchanged for any of the outstanding bonds of an equal aggregate par value heretofore issued and known as the five-twenty bonds, and for no other purpose; and the proceeds of so much thereof as may be disposed of for coin shall be placed in the Treasury, to be used for the redemption of such six per centum bonds at par as may not be offered in exchange, or to replace such amount of coin as may have been used for that purpose.

SEC. 2. That the Secretary of the Treasury be, and he is hereby, authorized to issue on the credit of the United States, coupon or registered bonds to the amount of $400,000,000, of such denominations, not less than $50, as he may think proper, redeemable in coin at the pleasure of the Government at any time after fifteen years, and payable in coin at thirty years from date, and bearing interest not exceeding four and one-half centum per annum, payable semi-annually in coin; and the bonds authorized by this section may be disposed of under such regulations as the Secretary shall prescribe, in the United States or elsewhere, at not less than par for coin; or they may be exchanged at par for any of the outstanding obligations of the Government bearing a higher rate of interest in coin; and the proceeds of such bonds as may be sold for coin shall be deposited in the Treasury, to be used for the redemption of such obligations bearing interest in coin as by the terms of issue are or may become redeemable or payable, or to replace such coin as may have been used for that purpose.

SEC. 3. That the Secretary of the Treasury be, and he is hereby, authorized to issue, on the credit of the United States, from time to time, coupon or registered bonds of such denominations, not less than $50, as he may think proper, to the amount of $400,000,000, redeemable in coin at the pleasure of the Government at any time after twenty years, and payable in coin at forty years from date, and bearing interest at the rate of four per centum per annum, payable semi-annually in coin; and such bonds may be disposed of, either in the United States or elsewhere, at not less than their par value, for coin, or, at the discretion of the Secretary, for United States notes; or may be exchanged at not less than par for any of the obligations of the United States outstanding at the date of the issue of such bonds; and if in the opinion of the Secretary of the Treasury it is thought advisable to issue a larger amount of four per centum bonds for any of the purposes herein or hereinafter recited than would be otherwise authorized by this section of this act, such further issues are hereby authorized: *Provided*, That there shall be no increase in the aggregate debt of the United States in consequence of any issues authorized by this act.

SEC. 4. That the bonds authorized by this act shall be exempt from all taxation by or under national, State, municipal, or local authority.

SEC. 5. That the coupons of said bonds may be made payable at the Treasury of the United States, or at the office of an authorized agent of the United States, either in the cities of London, Paris, Berlin, Amsterdam, or Frankfort, in dollars, or the equivalent thereof in sterling money, in francs or in thalers.

SEC. 6. That the Secretary of the Treasury be, and he is hereby, authorized to appoint such agents in the United States and in Europe as he may deem necessary to aid in the negotiation of said bonds; and he may advertise the loan herein authorized and the conditions thereof in such newspapers and journals in this country and in Europe as he may select for that purpose; and a sum not exceeding one per centum of the bonds herein authorized is hereby appropriated to pay the expense of preparing, issuing, and disposing of the same.

SEC. 7. That in order to carry into execution the provisions of the 5th section of the act entitled "An act to authorize the issue of United States notes and for the redemption or funding thereof and for funding the floating debt of the United States," approved February 25, 1862, relating to the sinking fund, there is hereby appropriated out of the duties derived from imported goods the sum of $150,000,000 annually, which sum during each fiscal year shall be applied to the payment of the interest and to the reduction of the principal of the public debt. And the United States bonds now held as the sinking fund and the United States bonds now held in the Treasury shall be canceled and destroyed, a detailed record thereof being first made in the books of the Treasury Department. And the bonds hereafter purchased under this section shall in like manner be canceled and destroyed. And a full and detailed account of the application of the money herein appropriated shall be made by the Secretary of the Treasury to Congress with his annual report; and the aggregate amount of the bonds canceled and destroyed shall be stated in the monthly statements of the public debt.

SEC. 8. That on and after the 1st day of October, 1870, registered bonds of any denomination not less than $1,000, issued under the provisions of this act, and no others, shall be deposited with the Treasurer of the United States as security for the notes issued to national banking associations for circulation under an act entitled "An act to provide a national currency secured by a pledge of United States bonds, and to provide for the circulation and redemption thereof," approved June 3, 1864; and all national banking associations organized under said act, or any amendment thereof, are hereby required to deposit bonds issued under this act as security for their circulating notes within one year from the date of the

passage of this act, in default of which their right to issue notes for circulation shall be forfeited, and the Treasurer and the Comptroller of the Currency shall be authorized and required to take such measures as may be necessary to call in and destroy their outstanding circulation, and to return the bonds held as security therefor to the association by which they were deposited, in sums of not less than $1,000: *Provided*, That any such association now in existence may, upon giving thirty days' notice to the Comptroller of the Currency by resolution of its board of directors, deposit legal-tender notes with the Treasurer of the United States to the amount of its outstanding circulation, and take up the bonds pledged for its redemption: *And provided further*, That not more than one-third of the bonds deposited by any bank as such security shall be of either of the classes of bonds hereby authorized on which the maximum rate of interest is fixed at four and one-half or five per centum per annum.

SEC. 9. That the amount of circulating notes which any bank may receive from the Comptroller of the Currency, under the provisions of section 21 of said act, may equal but not exceed eighty per centum of the par value of the bonds deposited, but shall not exceed in the aggregate the amount to which such bank may be entitled under said section.

SEC. 10. That any banking association organized or to be organized under the national currency act and the acts amendatory thereof, may, upon depositing with the Treasurer United States notes to an amount not less than $100,000, receive an equal amount of registered bonds of the United States, of the kind and description provided for by section 3 of this act, and may deposit the same as the security for circulating notes, and thereupon such banking association shall be entitled to and shall receive circulating notes upon terms and conditions and to the extent provided in the said national currency acts, and without respect to the limitation of the aggregate circulation of national currency prescribed by said acts: *Provided, however*, That as circulating notes are issued under this section an equal amount of United States notes shall be canceled and destroyed.

March 8—Mr. Davis moved that the bill be recommitted to the Committee on Finance, with instructions to report a bill embodying the following provisions:

First, The reduction of the amount of each outstanding bond of the United States by the difference between the nominal amount thereof and its gold value, or the gold value of the bond of which it is the immediate or remote substitute, at the time of the sale thereof by the Government.

Second, By the amount of usury paid by the United States on said bond or any bond or bonds of which it is the immediate or remote substitute.

Third, To reduce the rate of interest upon all outstanding bonds to five per centum per annum.

Fourth, To tax all dividends received on United States bonds as so much income.

Fifth, To reduce the appropriations for the army to the reasonable cost of twenty thousand men, rank and file.

Sixth, To reduce the aggregate appropriation for the navy to $20,000,000.

Seventh, To reduce the aggregate appropriation for the civil and diplomatic service of the Government ten per centum.

Eighth, To reduce the aggregate amount of internal taxes and duties on imports each thirty-three and one-third per centum.

Which was disagreed to without a division.

March 9—Mr. Morrill, of Vermont, moved to amend the 2d section by striking out the words "four-and-a-half" and inserting the word "five."

Which was disagreed to—yeas 8, nays 40, as follow:

YEAS—Messrs. *Bayard*, Brownlow, Buckingham, *Casserly*, Ferry, *Johnston*, Morrill of Vermont, *Stockton*—8.

NAYS—Messrs. Boreman. Cameron, Chandler, Cole, Conkling, Corbett, *Davis*, Drake, Fenton, Fowler, Gilbert, Hamlin, Harris, Howard, Howe, Howell, Kellogg, *McCreery*, McDonald, *Norton*, Osborn, Pomeroy, Pool, Pratt, Ramsey, Revels, Rice, Ross, Schurz, Scott, Sherman, Sumner, Thayer, Tipton, Trumbull, *Vickers*, Warner, Willey, Williams, Wilson—40.

Mr. Sherman moved to amend the 5th section by striking out, in line 2, the word "may," and inserting "shall;" and in line 3 by striking out the word "or," and in lieu thereof inserting, "but the Secretary of the Treasury may, at his discretion, make the coupons of any portion of the bonds provided for by the 3d section of this act payable"—

Which was agreed to—yeas 30, nays 10, as follow:

YEAS—Messrs. Abbott, Anthony, *Bayard*, *Casserly*, Chandler, Cole, Fenton, Gilbert, Hamlin, Harlan, Howe, Howell, *Johnston*, Morrill of Maine, Morrill of Vermont. Morton, Pratt, Ramsey, Revels, Rice, Ross, Schurz, Sherman, Sumner, Tipton, Trumbull, *Vickers*, Warner, Williams, Wilson—30.

NAYS—Messrs. Buckingham, Cameron. Corbett, *Davis*, Fowler, Harris, Howard, Osborn, Sprague, *Stockton*—10.

Mr. Corbett moved to strike out the 5th section, which was agreed to—yeas 29, nays 11, as follow:

YEAS—Messrs. *Bayard*, Buckingham, Cameron, *Casserly*, Chandler. Cole, Conkling, Corbett, Fenton, Gilbert, Hamlin, Harlan, Harris, Howard, Howe, Howell, *Johnston*, Morrill of Maine, Osborn, Pratt, Ramsey, Ross, Schurz, Sprague, *Stockton*, Sumner, *Thurman*, Trumbull. Wilson—29.

NAYS—Messrs. Abbott, Anthony, Edmunds, Morrill of Vermont. Morton, Rice, Sherman, Tipton, *Vickers*, Warner, Williams—11.

Mr. Howard moved to amend the 8th section by inserting in the 14th line the following:

And any such banking association may, on such terms as may be prescribed by the Secretary of the Treasury and at the market price current in the city of New York, exchange its bonds now deposited as security under said act for bonds issued under this act, for the purpose aforesaid.

Which was disagreed to.

Mr. Buckingham moved to amend the 8th section, by striking out all after the words "eighteen hundred and sixty-four," which was disagreed to—yeas 15, nays 28, as follow:

YEAS—Messrs. Buckingham. Conkling, Corbett, Edmunds, Ferry, Gilbert, Hamlin, Howard, Howe. McDonald, Morrill of Maine, Morrill of Vermont, Pomeroy, Revels, Scott—15.

NAYS—Messrs. Abbott. *Bayard*, Boreman, *Casserly*, Chandler, Cole, Drake, Harlan, Howell, *Johnston*, Kellogg, *McCreery*, Osborn, Pratt. Ramsey, Rice, Ross, Sawyer, Sherman, Spencer, Stewart, *Stockton*, Sumner, *Thurman*, Trumbull, Warner, Willey, Williams, Wilson—28.

Mr. Hamlin moved to amend the 8th section by inserting in line 13, after the word "thereof," the words, "the bonds of which are then redeemable by their terms, and as they shall thereafter become redeemable;" which was disagreed to—yeas 16, nays 28, as follow:

YEAS—Messrs. Boreman, Buckingham, Conkling, Corbett, Edmunds, Ferry, Gilbert, Hamlin, Howard, Howe. McDonald, Morrill of Maine, Morrill of Vermont, Pomeroy, Revels, Scott—16.

NAYS—Messrs. Abbott, *Bayard*, *Casserly*, Chandler, Cole, Drake, Harlan, Howell, *Johnston*, Kellogg, *McCreery*, Osborn, Pratt, Rice, Ross, Sawyer, Schurz, Sherman, Spencer, Stewart, *Stockton*, Sumner, *Thurman*, Trumbull, Warner, Willey, Williams, Wilson—28.

March 11—Mr. Wilson moved to amend by striking out sections 1, 2, and 3, and inserting in lieu thereof the following:

That, for the purpose of reducing the interest on the five-twenty six per centum bonds of the United States, the Secretary of the Treasury be, and he is hereby, authorized to issue, on the credit of the United States, coupon or registered bonds of such denominations, not less than $50, as he may think proper, not exceeding in amount the five-twenty six per centum bonds of the United States, redeemable in coin at the pleasure of the Government, at any time after ten years, and payable at forty years from date, and bearing interest at the rate of five per centum per annum, or at any time after twenty years, and payable at forty years from date, and bearing interest at the rate of four and one-half per centum per annum, or payable at fifty years from date, and bearing interest at the rate of four per centum per annum, payable semi-annually in coin; and the bonds thus authorized may be exchanged for any of the outstanding five-twenty six per centum bonds of an equal aggregate par value, heretofore issued and known as the five-twenty bonds, and for no other purpose; or they may be disposed of at the discretion of the Secretary, under such regulations as he shall prescribe, either in the United States or elsewhere, at not less than their par value for coin; and the proceeds of so much thereof as may be disposed of for coin shall be placed in the Treasury, to be used for the redemption of such six per centum bonds at par as may not be offered in exchange, or to replace such amount of coin as may have been used for that purpose.

Which was disagreed to.

Mr. Sherman moved to amend by striking out in section 2, line 7, "thirty," and inserting "forty," which was disagreed to.

Mr. Morton moved to amend the 2d section by striking out in line 12 the words, "or, at the discretion of the Secretary, for United States notes," and by inserting in line 13, before the word "obligations," the words "interest-bearing," which was disagreed to—yeas 18, nays 32, as follow:

YEAS—Messrs. Boreman, Brownlow, Cole, Fowler, Howe, Howell. Kellogg, *McCreery*, McDonald, Morton, Pomeroy, Pool, Pratt, Ramsey, Revels, Sprague, *Thurman*, Tipton—18.

NAYS—Messrs. Anthony, *Bayard*, Buckingham, Cameron, *Casserly*, Chandler, Conkling, Corbett, Drake, Fenton, Ferry, Gilbert, Hamlin, Harlan, Harris, Howard, *Johnston*. Morrill of Vermont, Osborn, Rice, Sawyer, Schurz, Scott, Sherman, Stewart, *Stockton*, Sumner, Trumbull, Warner, Willey, Williams, Wilson—32.

Mr. Buckingham moved to strike out the 8th section, which was disagreed to—yeas 16, nays 32, as follow:

YEAS—Messrs. Anthony, Brownlow, Buckingham, Cameron, Conkling, Corbett. Ferry, Hamlin, Howard, Howe, McDonald, Morrill of Vermont, Pomeroy, Ramsey, Scott, Wilson—16.

NAYS—Messrs. *Bayard*, Boreman, *Casserly*, Chandler, Cole, Drake, Fowler, Gilbert, Harlan, Harris, Howell, *Johnston*, Kellogg, *McCreery*, Osborn, Pool, Pratt, Revels, Rice, Ross, Schurz, Sherman, Stewart, *Stockton*, Sumner, Thayer, *Thurman*, Tipton, Trumbull, Warner, Willey, Williams—32.

Mr. Howe moved to amend the 10th section by inserting in line 6, after the word "States," "one-third of which shall be," and in line 7 striking out the words "section 3" and inserting "each of the first three sections," which was disagreed to—yeas 16, nays 25, as follow:

YEAS—Messrs. Buckingham, Cameron, Corbett, Gilbert, Hamlin, Harlan, Howe, Howell, Morrill of Vermont, Pomeroy, Ramsey, Revels, Schurz, Scott, Sprague, Trumbull—16.

NAYS—Messrs. *Bayard*, *Casserly*, Chandler, Cole, Drake, Ferry, Fowler, Harris, Howard, *Johnston*, *McCreery*, Morton, Osborn, Pratt, Rice, Ross, Sherman, Stewart, *Stockton*, Sumner, *Thurman*, Warner, Willey, Williams, Wilson—25.

Mr. Boreman moved to amend by striking out in line 2, section 4, the words: "And the annual interest thereon."

Which was disagreed to—yeas 14, nays 29, as follow:

YEAS—Messrs. *Bayard*, Boreman, *Casserly*, Cole, Harlan, *Johnston*, *McCreery*, Pomeroy, Pratt, Sprague, *Stockton*, *Thurman*, Willey, Wilson—14.

NAYS—Messrs. Buckingham, Cameron, Chandler, Corbett, Drake, Fenton, Ferry, Fowler, Gilbert, Harris, Howard, Howell, Kellogg, McDonald, Morrill of Vermont, Osborn, Ramsey, Revels, Ross, Sawyer, Schurz, Scott, Sherman, Stewart, Sumner, Tipton, Trumbull, Warner, Williams—29.

Mr. Bayard moved to strike out the 4th section, which was disagreed to—yeas 7, nays 38, as follow:

YEAS—Messrs *Bayard*, Boreman, *Casserly*, *Johnston*, *McCreery*, *Stockton*, *Thurman*—7.

NAYS—Messrs. Buckingham, Cameron, Chandler, Cole, Corbett. Drake, Fenton, Ferry, Fowler, Gilbert, Hamlin, Harlan, Harris, Howard, Howell, Kellogg, McDonald, Morrill of Vermont, Morton, Osborn, Pomeroy, Pratt, Ramsey, Revels, Rice, Ross, Sawyer, Schurz, Scott, Sherman, Stewart, Sumner, Tipton, Trumbull, Warner, Willey, Williams, Wilson—38.

Mr. Cameron moved to amend by inserting at the end of the bill the following:

SEC. —. That it shall be the duty of the Secretary of the Treasury, on the 1st day of July, 1870, to redeem and fund in bonds hereby authorized all the fractional currency of the United States that may be offered for redemption at the Treasury or any of its branches, which he shall at once cause to be canceled; and it shall not be lawful for him after that date to issue any such paper fractional currency, but he shall make all payments of fractions of the dollar in the legal coin of the United States.

Which was disagreed to—yeas 18, nays 26, as follow:

YEAS—Messrs. *Bayard*, Buckingham, Cameron, *Casserly*, Corbett, Hamlin, Harlan, Howard, *Johnston*, Kellogg, Morrill of Vermont, Pomeroy, Scott, *Stockton*, Sumner, *Thurman*, Trumbull, Wilson—18.

NAYS—Messrs. Boreman, Chandler, Cole, Drake, Fenton, Ferry, Fowler, Gilbert, Harris, Howell, *McCreery*, McDonald, Morton, Osborn, Pratt, Ramsey, Revels, Ross, Sawyer, Schurz, Sherman, Stewart, Tipton, Warner, Willey, Williams—26.

Mr. Wilson moved to amend by inserting in line 8, section 6, after the word "exceeding," the words "one-half of;" which was agreed to—yeas 23, nays 20, as follow:

YEAS—Messrs. Boreman, Buckingham, *Casserly*, Cole, Corbett, Ferry, Fowler, Harlan, Harris, Howell, *Johnston*, *McCreery*, McDonald, Pratt, Ross, Sawyer, Schurz, Scott, Sprague, Sumner, Thayer, Tipton, Wilson—23.

NAYS—Messrs. Chandler, Conkling, Drake, Edmunds, Fenton, Gilbert, Hamlin, Howard, Kellogg. Morrill of Vermont, Osborn, Pomeroy, Ramsey, Revels, Rice, Sherman, Stewart, Warner, Willey, Williams—20.

Mr. Stewart moved to amend the 9th section by striking out the word "eighty" and inserting the word "ninety;" which was disagreed to—yeas 12, nays 30, as follow:

YEAS—Messrs. Boreman, Cole, Fenton, Fowler, Morton, Pomeroy, Ramsey, Ross, Scott, Sprague, Stewart, Warner—12.

NAYS—Messrs. Buckingham, *Casserly*, Chandler, Conkling, Corbett, Drake, Edmunds, Ferry, Hamlin, Harlan, Harris, Howard, Howell, *Johnston*, Kellogg, *McCreery*, McDonald, Morrill of Vermont, Osborn, Pratt, Revels. Rice, Sawyer, Schurz, Sherman, Sumner, Thayer, Tipton, Willey, Williams—30.

Mr. Morton moved to strike out the 10th section; which was disagreed to—yeas 12, nays 29, as follow:

YEAS—Messrs. Boreman, Cole, Fowler, Howell, *Johnston*, *McCreery*, Morton, Ramsey, Revels, Rice, Ross, Sprague—12.

NAYS—Messrs. Buckingham, Chandler, Conkling, Corbett, Drake, Edmunds, Fenton, Ferry, Hamlin, Harlan, Harris, Kellogg, McDonald, Morrill of Vermont, Osborn, Pomeroy, Sawyer, Schurz, Scott, Sherman, Spencer, Stewart, Sumner, Thayer, Tipton, Warner, Willey, Williams, Wilson—29.

The bill then passed—yeas 32, nays 10, as follow:

YEAS—Messrs. Chandler, Cole, Conkling. Edmunds, Fenton, Ferry, Fowler, Gilbert, Harlan, Harris, Howard, Howell, Kellogg, Morrill of Vermont, Morton, Osborn, Pomeroy, Pratt, Ramsey, Revels, Rice, Sawyer, Schurz, Scott, Sherman, Stewart, Sumner, Thayer, Tipton, Warner, Williams, Wilson—32.

NAYS—Messrs. *Bayard*, Boreman, Buckingham, *Casserly*, Corbett, *McCreery*, McDonald, Sprague, *Stockton*, *Thurman*—10.

## IN HOUSE OF REPRESENTATIVES.

1870, June 6—Mr. Schenck, from the Committee of Ways and Means, reported the following as a substitute for the Senate bill:

That the Secretary of the Treasury is hereby authorized to issue, in a sum or sums not exceeding in the aggregate $1,000,000,000, coupon or registered bonds of the United States, in such form as he may prescribe, and of denominations of $50 or some multiple of that sum, redeemable in coin of the present standard value at the pleasure of the United States after thirty years from the date of their issue, and bearing interest payable semi-annually in such coin at the rate of four per centum per annum, which said bonds and the interest thereon shall be exempt from the payment of all taxes or duties of the United States as well as from taxation in any form by or under State, municipal, or local authority; and the said bonds shall have set forth and expressed upon their face the above specified conditions, and shall, with their coupons, be made payable at the Treasury of the United States. But nothing in this act, or in any other law now in force, shall be construed to authorize any increase whatever of the bonded debt of the United States.

SEC. 2. That the Secretary of the Treasury is hereby authorized to sell and dispose of any of the bonds issued under this act at not less than their par value for coin, and to apply the proceeds thereof to the redemption of any of the bonds of the United States outstanding and known as five-twenty bonds at their par value, or he may exchange the same for such five-twenty bonds, par for par; but the bonds hereby authorized shall be used for no other purpose whatsoever.

SEC. 3. That the payment of any of the bonds hereby authorized after the expiration of the said term of thirty years shall be made in amounts to be determined from time to time by the Secretary of the Treasury at his discretion, and by classes to be distinguished and described by the dates and numbers, beginning for each successive payment with the bonds last dated and numbered, of the time of which intended payment or redemption the Secretary of the Treasury shall give public notice, and the interest on the particular bonds so selected at any time to be paid shall cease at the expiration of three months from the date of such notice.

SEC. 4. That the Secretary of the Treasury is hereby authorized and instructed, with any coin in the Treasury of the United States which in his opinion and discretion can be conveniently applied to that purpose, to pay at par and cancel any six per cent. bonds of the United States of the kind known as five-twenty bonds which have become or shall hereafter become redeemable by the terms of their issue. But the particular bonds so to be paid and canceled shall in all cases be indicated and specified by class, date, and number, in the order of their numbers and issue, beginning with the first numbered and issued, in public notice to be given by the Secretary of the Treasury, and in three months after the date of such public notice the interest on the bonds so selected and advertised to be paid shall cease. But it shall be competent for the holders and owners of any said bonds so specified for payment to exchange the same for bonds issued under the authority of this act at any time before the end of the notice provided for in the 2d section of this act.

SEC. 5. That the Secretary of the Treasury is hereby authorized to receive gold coin of the United States or bullion on deposit for not less than thirty days, in sums of not less than $100, with the Treasurer or any assistant treasurer of the United States authorized by the Secretary of the Treasury to receive the same, who shall issue therefor certificates of deposit made in such form as the Secretary of the Treasury shall prescribe, and said certificates of deposit shall bear interest at a rate not exceeding three per centum per annum; and any amount of gold coin or bullion so deposited may be withdrawn from deposit at any time after thirty days from the date of deposit, and after ten days' notice and on the return of said certificates: *Provided*, That the interest on all such deposits shall cease and determine at the pleasure of the Secretary of the Treasury. And not less than twenty-five per centum of the coin and bullion deposited for or represented by said certificates of deposits shall be retained in the Treasury for the payment of said certificates; and the excess beyond twenty-five per centum may be applied, at the discretion of the Secretary of the Treasury, to the payment or redemption of such outstanding bonds of the United States, heretofore issued and known as the five-twenty bonds, as he may designate under the provisions of the

4th section of this act; and any certificates of deposit issued as aforesaid may be received at par, with the interest accrued thereon, in payment for any bonds authorized to be issued by this act.

SEC. 6. That the United States bonds purchased and now held in the Treasury, in accordance with the provisions, relating to a sinking fund, of section 5 of the act entitled "An act to authorize the issue of United States notes and for the redemption or funding thereof and for funding the floating debt of the United States," approved February 25, 1862, and all other United States bonds which have been purchased by the Secretary of the Treasury with surplus funds in the Treasury and now held in the Treasury of the United States, shall be canceled and destroyed, a detailed record of such bonds so canceled and destroyed to be first made in the books of the Treasury Department. Any bonds hereafter applied to said sinking fund, and all other United States bonds redeemed or paid hereafter by the United States, shall also in like manner be canceled and destroyed; and the amount of the bonds of each class that have been canceled and destroyed shall be deducted respectively from the amount of each class of the outstanding debt of the United States. In addition to other amounts that may be applied to the redemption or payment of the public debt, an amount equal to the interest on all bonds belonging to the aforesaid sinking fund shall be applied, as the Secretary of the Treasury shall from time to time direct, to the payment of the public debt, as provided for in section 5 of the act aforesaid.

June 30—Mr. Blair moved to insert in the 1st section, before the last sentence, as follows:

And the amount of interest specified in each coupon shall be expressed in dollars, and the equivalent thereof in English sterling currency and in francs.

Which was disagreed to.

Mr. Mayham moved to strike out of the 1st section the words "of the United States, as well as from taxation;" so that portion of the section would read as follows:

Which said bonds and the interest thereon shall be exempt from the payment of all taxes or duties, in any form, by or under State, municipal, or local authority, &c.

Which was disagreed to—yeas 25, nays 97, on a division.

Mr. Ingersoll moved to amend the 1st section by striking out the words "in coin of the present standard of value," and the words "such coin," and inserting in lieu the words "lawful money of the United States;" which was disagreed to.

Mr. Marshall moved to amend the clause fixing the time these bonds shall run, by making it "twenty" instead of "thirty" years; which was disagreed to—yeas 22, nays 85, on a division.

Mr. Coburn moved to make the time fifty years; which was disagreed to.

Mr. Holman moved to add to the 1st section the following:

*Provided*, That no agent or agents shall be employed in the United States or elsewhere for the sale or exchange of such bonds.

Which was disagreed to—yeas 36, nays 87, on a division.

Mr. Wood moved to amend the 2d section by adding to it as follows:

But nothing in this act shall authorize the Secretary of the Treasury to allow or pay any commission or percentage for the sale of the bonds so issued, or any part thereof.

Mr. Ingersoll moved to amend this amendment by inserting before the words "sale of the bonds" the words "transfer, exchange, or" which Mr. Wood accepted. Mr. Wood's amendment was then disagreed to—yeas 57, nays 102, as follow:

YEAS—Messrs. Ambler, *Barnum, Beck, Biggs, Bird,* James Brooks, Burchard, *Calkin, Cleveland,* Amasa Cobb, Cox, *Crebs,* Degener, *Eldridge,* Farnsworth, Ferriss, *Getz, Griswold, Hamill,* Hawkins, Hay, *Holman,* Ingersoll, *Thomas L. Jones,* Kelley, *Kerr, Knott, Lewis,* Logan, *Mayham, McCormick,* McGrew, *Niblack,* Packer, *Randall, Reeves, Rice, Rogers,* Shanks, *Sherrod, Shober, Slocum, Joseph S. Smith,* William J. Smith, *Stiles, Sweeney,* Taffe, *Trimble, Van Trump,* Van Wyck, *Voorhees,* Ward, *Wells,* Williams, *Winchester, Wood, Woodward*—57.

NAYS—Messrs. Allison, Ames, Armstrong, Arnell, Asper, Atwood, Ayer, Bailey, Banks, Beatty, Benjamin, Benton, Bingham, Blair, Boles, *Booker,* Boyd, Buck, Buckley, Buffinton, Benjamin F. Butler, Roderick R. Butler, Cessna, Churchill, Sidney Clarke, Clinton L. Cobb, Coburn, Conger, Covode, Cullom, Davis, Dawes, Dockery, Donley, Ela, Finkelnburg, Fisher, Fitch, Hale, Hill, Hoar, Hooper, Jenckes, Judd, Julian, Kellogg, Kelsey, Ketcham, Knapp, Laflin, Lash, Lawrence, Loughridge, Marshall, McCarthy, *McKenzie,* Mercur, Eliakim H. Moore, Jesse H. Moore, William Moore, Daniel J. Morrell, Myers, Negley, O'Neill, Orth, Paine, Peck, Peters, Phelps, Poland, Porter, Prosser, Roots, Sargent, Sawyer, Schenck, Scofield, Lionel A. Sheldon, John A. Smith, Worthington C. Smith, William Smyth, Starkweather, Stevens, Stokes, Stoughton, Strickland, Strong, Tanner, Taylor, Tillman, Townsend, Twichell, Tyner, Upson, Van Horn, Wallace, Welker, Wheeler, Whitmore, Wilkinson, Willard, John T. Wilson—102.

July 1—Mr. Schenck, from the Committee of Ways and Means, moved to amend the 4th section by striking out the words "in the order of their numbers and issue, beginning with the first numbered and issued."

Which was agreed to.

Mr. Holman moved to amend the 4th section by striking out the words "coin in the Treasury of the United States," and inserting in lieu thereof the words "United States notes in the Treasury of the United States arising from the sale of bonds authorized to be issued by this act, or other such notes in the Treasury."

Which was disagreed to—yeas 41, nays 127, as follow:

YEAS—Messrs. *Adams,* Beatty, *Bird, Burr, Cleveland,* Coburn, *Crebs,* Dickinson, Dockery, *Dox, Eldridge, Getz, Griswold, Hamill, Holman, Thomas L. Jones, Kerr, Knott, Lewis, Marshall, Mayham, McCormick, McNeely,* Morgan, *Mungen, Niblack, Orth, Reeves, Rice, Rogers, Shober, Joseph S. Smith, Stiles, Sweeney, Trimble,* Tyner, *Van Trump, Voorhees, Wells, Winchester, Woodward*—41.

NAYS—Messrs. Allison, Ambler, Ames, *Archer,* Armstrong, Arnell, Asper, Atwood, *Axtell,* Ayer, Bailey, *Barnum,* Benjamin, Bennett, Benton, Bingham, Blair, Boles, *Booker,* Boyd, George M. Brooks, *James Brooks,* Buck, Buckley, Buffinton, Burchard, Burdett, Cessna, Churchill, William T. Clark, Amasa Cobb, Conger, Cullom, Davis, Dawes, Dickey, Donley, Dyer, Ferriss, Ferry, Finkelnburg, Fisher, Fitch, Hale, Harris, Hawley, Hay, Hays, Heflin, Hill, Hoar, Hooper, Jenckes, Alexander H. Jones, Judd, Julian, Kelley, Kellogg, Kelsey, Ketcham, Knapp, Laflin, Lash, Lawrence, Logan, Loughridge, Maynard, McCarthy, McCrary, McGrew, *McKenzie,* Mercur, Eliakim H. Moore, Jesse H. Moore, William Moore, Morphis, Daniel J. Morrell, Myers, O'Neill, Packard, Packer, Paine, Palmer, Peck, Peters, Poland, Pomeroy, Porter, Prosser, *Randall,* Roots, Sanford, Sargent, Sawyer, Schenck, Scofield, Lionel A. Sheldon, *Slocum,* John A. Smith, William J. Smith, Worthington C. Smith, William Smyth, Stevens, Stevenson, Stokes, *Stone,* Stoughton, Strickland, *Swann,* Taffe, Tanner, Taylor, Tillman, Townsend, Twichell, Upson, Van Horn, Van Wyck, Wallace, Welker, Wheeler, Whitmore, Wilkinson, Willard, Williams, Winans—127.

Mr. Judd moved to strike out from the 4th section the following words: "which in his opinion and discretion can be conveniently applied to that purpose," and insert the following words: "which may be derived from the sale of any of the bonds the issue of which is provided for in this act."

Mr. Schenck moved to amend this amendment by adding the words "or which he may lawfully apply to such purpose," which was agreed to. Mr. Judd's amendment was then agreed to.

Mr. B. F. Butler moved to amend the 4th section by adding to it the following:

But none of said interest-bearing obligations not already due shall be redeemed or paid before maturity, unless at such time United States notes shall be convertible into coin at the option of the holder, or unless at such time bonds of the United States bearing a lower rate of interest than the bonds to be redeemed can be sold at par in coin. And the United States also solemnly pledges its faith to make provision at the earliest practicable period for the redemption of the United States notes in coin.

Which was disagreed to—yeas 54, nays 98, as follow:

YEAS—Messrs. Allison, Ambler, Armstrong, Bennett, Boles, George M. Brooks, Burchard, Benjamin F. Butler, Cessna, Amasa Cobb, Coburn, Cullom, Dickey, *Dickinson,* Dockery, *Dox,* Dyer, Ferry, Finkelnburg, Fitch, *Griswold,* Hale, Hawkins, Hawley, Hay, Heflin, Hoar, Judd, Kelsey, Loughridge, *McCormick,* McCrary, Mercur, Jesse H. Moore, Orth, Packard, Packer, Paine, Poland, Pomeroy, *Rogers,* Shanks, Lionel A. Sheldon, *Shober,* John A. Smith, Worthington C. Smith, William Smyth, Stevenson, Stokes, Tyner, Wallace, Williams, John T. Wilson, *Woodward*—54.

NAYS—Messrs. *Adams,* Ames. *Archer,* Asper, *Axtell,* Ayer, Bailey, Beaman, Benjamin, Benton, Bingham, *Bird,* Blair, *Booker,* Boyd, *James Brooks,* Buck, Buckley, Buffinton. Burdett, *Burr,* Roderick R. Butler, *Calkin,* William T. Clark, Clinton L. Cobb, Conger, Cook, *Cox, Crebs,* Davis, Donley, Ferriss, Fisher, *Getz, Hamill,* Harris, Hill, *Holman,* Hooper, Ingersoll, Jenckes, *Thomas L. Jones,* Julian, Kelley, Ketcham, Knapp, *Knott,* Laflin, Lash, Lawrence, Maynard, McCarthy, McGrew, *McKenzie,* William Moore, Daniel J. Morrell, *Morrissey, Mungen,* Myers, Negley, *Niblack,* O'Neill, Peck, Peters, Phelps, Prosser, *Randall, Reeves, Rice,* Sanford, Sawyer, Schenck, *Schumaker, Scofield, Slocum, Joseph S. Smith,* William J. Smith, Stevens, *Stiles, Stone,* Stoughton, Strickland, *Swann, Sweeney,* Taffe, Tanner, Taylor, Tillman. Townsend, *Trimble,* Twichell, Upson, Welker, Wheeler, Whitmore, Willard, Winans, *Winchester*—98.

Mr. Griswold moved to strike out the 4th section; which was disagreed to.

Mr. Mungen moved to add to the 4th section the following: *Provided further,* That nothing in this act contained shall be construed to operate in conflict with the act of February 25, 1862, authorizing the issue of United States notes, bonds, &c.

Which was disagreed to.

Mr. Davis moved to amend the 5th section by inserting after the word "bullion," the words "assayed and stamped under the laws of the United States," which was agreed to. Mr. Davis also moved to reduce the interest on gold deposits from three per cent. to two per cent.; which was disagreed to.

Mr. Townsend moved to add to the 5th section the following: *Provided,* That if on a demand for payment of any of said certificates in coin there should not be sufficient gold coin in the Treasury arising under this act, then it shall be lawful for the Secretary of the Treasury to appropriate any other gold coin in the Treasury in payment of said certificates.

Which was disagreed to.

Mr. Ingersoll moved to add the following: That from and after the passage of this act it shall not be lawful for the Secretary of the Treasury to sell any gold coin on account of the United States; which was disagreed to.

Mr. Maynard moved to amend section 6 by inserting after the word "Department" the words "and a statement of the sinking fund shall be kept, so as to show the principal of the fund, with the current interest, as it would be if the bonds composing the said fund were kept to represent it."

Which was disagreed to.

Mr. Davis moved to add at the end of the bill the following sections:

SEC. 7. That the Secretary of the Treasury is hereby authorized and directed to issue registered bonds of the United States, in such form and of such denominations, of not less than fifty dollars and multiples thereof, as he shall think proper, payable in thirty years from date in gold, bearing interest at four per cent., payable semi-annually in gold, and free from all excise and taxation whatever, either on such bonds or the income derived therefrom, and redeemable in gold at the option of the United States after ten years, upon six months' public notice, which said bonds shall be known as the convertible bonds of the United States; and such bonds shall express on their face that they are convertible at any time into legal-tender notes.

SEC. 8. That whenever any person shall pay any legal-tender notes of the United States at the Treasury or at any assistant treasury of the United States, to the amount of fifty dollars or any multiple thereof, for that purpose he shall receive at par value an equal amount of such convertible bonds, and whoever shall present one or more of said convertible bands at the Treasury or at any assistant treasury of the United States, or at any public depository of the moneys of the United States which the Secretary of the Treasury shall have designated for that purpose, and demand redemption thereof, at any time before the maturity thereof, he shall receive the face of his bond or bonds in legal-tender notes at par value, and the accrued interest remaining unpaid up to the date of such demand in gold; and such bonds shall be immediately canceled and returned to the Treasurer of the United States as vouchers of the amount paid thereon.

SEC. 9. That the Secretary of the Treasury shall, as soon as practicable after receiving the same, use or invest at least eighty per cent., and as much more as he shall deem expedient, of all legal-tender notes received for such bonds, in buying up or redeeming the six per cent. gold interest bonds of the United States. And he shall have authority to make such regulations as he shall deem needful to carry the provisions of this act into effect.

Which was disagreed to.

The substitute was then agreed to and the bill passed—yeas 129, nays 42, as follow:

YEAS—Messrs. Allison, Ambler, Ames, Armstrong, Arnell, Asper, Atwood, *Axtell*, Ayer, Bailey, *Barnum*, Benjamin, Bennett, Benton, Bingham, Blair, Boles, *Booker*, Boyd, George M. Brooks, Buck, Buckley, Buffinton, Burchard, Burdett, Roderick R. Butler, Cessna, Churchill, William T. Clark, Sidney Clarke, Amasa

Cobb, Clinton L. Cobb, Coburn, Cook, Conger, Cullom, Dawes, Degener, Dickey, Dockery, Donley, Ela, Ferriss, Ferry, Finkelnburg, Fisher, Fitch, Hale, Harris, Hawley, Hay, Hill, Hoar, Hooper, Jenckes, Alexander H. Jones, Judd, Julian, Kelley, Kellogg, Kelsey, Ketcham, Knapp, Laflin, Lash, Lawrence, Logan, Loughridge, Maynard, McCarthy, McGrew, *McKenzie*, Mercur, Eliakim H. Moore, Jesse H. Moore, William Moore Morphis, Daniel J. Morrell, Myers, Negley, O'Neill, Orth, Packard, Packer, Paine, Palmer, Peck, Perce Peters, Phelps, Porter, Prosser, Roots, Sanford, Sargent, Sawyer, Schenck, *Schumaker*, Scofield, Shanks, Porter Sheldon, *Slocum*, John A. Smith, William J. Smith, William Smyth, Starkweather, Stevens, *Stone*, Stoughton, Strickland, Strong, Taffe, Tanner, Taylor, Tillman, Townsend, Twichell, Tyner, Upson, Van Horn, Var Wyck, Wallace, Cadwalader C. Washburn, Welker, *Wells*, Whitmore, Willard, Williams, John T. Wilson—129.

NAYS—Messrs. *Adams, Archer*, Beatty, *Beck, Bird, Calkin, Cleveland, Crebs*, Davis, *Dox, Eldridge, Getz, Griswold, Hamill*, Hawkins, Ingersoll, *Johnson, Thomas L. Jones Kerr, Knott, Lewis, Marshall, Mayham, McNeely, Morgan, Mungen, Niblack, Randall, Reeves, Rice, Sherrod, Shober* Stevenson, *Stiles, Sweeney, Trimble, Van Trump, Voorhees, Eugene M. Wilson, Winchester, Wood, Woodward*—42.

The Senate refused to concur in the amendments of the House, and asked and obtained a conference. The committee was composed of Messrs. Sherman, Sumner, and Davis, on the part of the Senate, and Messrs. Schenck, Hooper, and Marshall, on the part of the House.

July 12—The committee reported a bill precisely similar to that which finally passed, with the addition of the following section:

SEC. 7. That from and after the passage of this act the Treasurer of the United States shall receive no other than registered bonds issued under the provisions of this act as security for the circulating notes of national banking associations issued under the act entitled "An act to provide a national currency secured by a pledge of United States bonds, and to provide for the circulation and redemption thereof," approved June 3, 1864, or any act supplementary or amendatory thereof.

Which report was rejected by the House—yeas 88, nays 103, as follow:

YEAS—Messrs. Ambler, Ames, Armstrong, Atwood, Ayer, Bailey, Banks, Bennett, Benton, Bingham, Boles, G. M. Brooks, Buffinton, Burdett, Roderick R. Butler, Cake, Cessna, Churchill, Conger, Covode, Cowles, Davis, Dawes, Dixon, Donley, Duval, Ela, Ferriss, Ferry, Finkelnburg, Fisher, Fitch, Gilfillan, Hoar, Hooper, Jenckes, Julian, Kelley, Kellogg, Kelsey, Ketcham, Knapp, Laflin, Lawrence, Lynch, Maynard, McCarthy, McCrary, McGrew, Mercur, Eliakim H. Moore, William Moore, Myers, Negley, O'Neill, Orth, Packard, Peck, Peters, Phelps, Poland, Roots, Sanford, Sargent, Sawyer, Schenck, Scofield, Shanks, Porter Sheldon, John A. Smith, William J. Smith, William Smyth, Starkweather, Stevens, Stokes, Stoughton, Strickland, Strong, Tanner, Taylor, Twichell, Upson, Cadwalader C. Washburn, William B. Washburn, Welker, Wheeler, Willard, Williams—88.

NAYS—Messrs. *Adams*, Allison, *Archer*, Asper, *Axtell, Barnum*, Barry, Beatty, *Beck*, Benjamin, *Biggs, Bird*, Blair, *Booker*, Boyd, *James Brooks*, Buckley, *Burchard, Burr, Calkin*, William T. Clark, Sidney Clarke, *Cleveland*, Amasa Cobb, Coburn, *Conner, Cox, Crebs*, Cullom, Darrall, *Dickinson, Eldridge, Fox*, Garfield, *Getz, Griswold, Haight, Haldeman, Hambleton, Hamill*, Harris, Hawkins, Hawley, Hay, Hays, Heflin, *Holman*, Ingersoll, *Johnson, Thomas L. Jones*, Judd, *Kerr, Knott*, Lash, *Lewis*, Loughridge, *Marshall, Mayham, McCormick, McKenzie, McNeely*, Jesse H. Moore, *Morgan*, Morphis, Daniel J. Morrell, *Mungen, Niblack*, Packer, Paine, Palmer, Platt, Pomeroy, *Potter, Randall, Reeves, Rice, Rogers, Schumaker*, Lionel A. Sheldon, *Sherrod, Slocum, Joseph S. Smith*, Worthington C. Smith, *Stiles, Stone, Swann*, Taffe, Townsend, *Trimble*, Tyner, *Van Auken*, Van Horn, *Van Trump*, Van Wyck, *Voorhees*, Whitmore, Wilkinson, *Eugene M. Wilson*, John T. Wilson, *Winchester*, Witcher, *Wood, Woodward*—103.

The same committee was appointed on the second conference, and the bill, as finally passed and printed above, was agreed to.

# LIX.

## INTERNAL TAX AND TARIFF.

1870, May 27—Mr. Schenck, from the Committee of Ways and Means, reported "A bill to reduce internal taxes and for other purposes," which, he stated, reduced taxation about $34,-000,000. Among other things, it provided for an income tax of five per cent. on all incomes over $1,500.

June 1—Mr. Cox moved to reduce the tax from five to three per cent.

Which was agreed to—yeas 114, nays 76, as follow:

YEAS—Messrs. Allison, Ames, *Archer*, Armstrong, *Axtell*, Ayer, Banks, Barry, *Beck*, Bennett, *Biggs*, Bingham, *Bird*, Bowen, George M. Brooks, *James Brooks*, Buffinton, *Burr*, Sidney Clarke, *Cleveland*, Covode, Cowles, Davis, Dawes, Deweese. Degener, *Dickinson*, Donley, *Dox*, Duval, *Eldridge*, Ferriss, Finkelnburg, Fisher, Fitch, *Fox*, *Getz*, Gilfillan, *Griswold*. Haight, *Hambleton*, *Hamill*, Hamilton, Harris, Heflin, Hill, Hoar, *Holman*, Hooper, Hotchkiss, Jenckes, *Johnson*, Judd, Kelley, Kellogg, *Kerr*, Ketcham, Knapp, Laflin, Lawrence, Lynch, *Mayham*, McCarthy, McGrew, *McKenzie*, *McNeely*, *Milnes*, William Moore, *Morgan*, Daniel J. Morrell, *Morrissey*, Myers, Negley, Newsham, *Niblack*, O'Neill, Orth, Packer, Perce, Peters, *Potter*, Prosser, *Randall*. *Reeves*, *Ridgway*, Sargent, Sawyer, Scofield, Porter Sheldon, *Slocum*, *Joseph S. Smith*, Worthington C. Smith, Starkweather, Stevenson, *Stiles*, *Stone*, *Strader*, Strong, *Swann*, *Sweeney*, Tanner, Taylor, Townsend, *Trimble*, Twichell, Upson, William B. Washburn, Welker, *Wells*, Wheeler, John T. Wilson, Winans, *Winchester*, *Wood*—114.

NAYS—Messrs. Ambler, Arnell, Asper, Atwood, Bailey, Beaman, Beatty, Benjamin, Benton, Blair, Boles, *Booker*, Boyd, Burchard, Burdett, Benjamin F. Butler, Roderick R. Butler, William T. Clark, Amasa Cobb, Coburn, Cook, Conger, *Crebs*, Cullom, Dockery, Ela, Farnsworth, Garfield, *Gibson*, Hale, Hawkins, Hay, Hays, Ingersoll, Alexander H. Jones, Kelsey, Lash, *Lewis*, Logan, Loughridge, *Marshall*, Maynard, *McCormick*, McCrary, Mercur, Eliakim H. Moore, Jesse H. Moore, Morphis, Samuel P. Morrill, Packard, Paine, Peck, Phelps, Pomeroy, *Rice*, Roots, Schenck, Lionel A. Sheldon, *Sherrod*, John A. Smith, William J. Smith, William Smyth, Stokes, Stoughton, Strickland, Tillman, Tyner, *Van Auken*, Van Horn, Wallace, Ward, Wilkinson, Willard, Williams, *Eugene M. Wilson*, Witcher—76.

Mr. Hawley moved to amend by raising the amount exempted to $2,500.

Which amount Mr. Hale moved to reduce to $2,000; which was agreed to.

Mr. Hawley's amendment as amended was then agreed to—yeas 138, nays 52, as follow:

YEAS—Messrs. Allison, *Archer*, Armstrong, Atwood, *Axtell*, Ayer, Bailey, Banks, Barry, Beaman, *Beck*, Bennett, *Biggs*, *Bird*, Boles, Bowen, George M. Brooks, *James Brooks*, Buffinton, Burchard, *Burr*, William T. Clark, Sidney Clarke, *Cleveland*, Cook, Conger, Covode, Cowles, Cullom, Davis, Dawes, *Dickinson*. Dockery, Donley, *Dox*, Duval, *Eldridge*, Farnsworth, Ferriss, Fisher, Fitch, *Fox*, *Getz*, *Gibson*, Gilfillan, *Griswold*, *Haight*, Hale, *Hambleton*, *Hamill*, Harris, Hawkins, Hawley, Hay, Hays, Heflin, Hill, Hoar, *Holman*, Hooper, Hotchkiss, Ingersoll, *Johnson*, Judd, Kelley, Kellogg, *Kerr*, Ketcham, Laflin, Logan, Lynch, *Marshall*, *Mayham*, McCarthy, McGrew, *McKenzie*, *McNeely*, *Milnes*, Jesse H. Moore, William Moore, *Morgan*, *Morrissey*. Myers, Newsham, *Niblack*, O'Neill, Orth. Packard, Peck, Perce, Peters, Phelps, Platt, Pomeroy, Porter, *Potter*, Prosser, *Randall*, *Reeves*, *Ridgway*, Sargent, Sawyer, Scofield, Lionel A. Sheldon. Porter Sheldon, *Sherrod*, *Slocum*, John A. Smith, *Joseph S. Smith*, W. C. Smith, Starkweather. Stevenson, *Stiles*, *Stone*, Stoughton, *Strader*, Strickland, Strong, *Swann*, *Sweeney*, Tanner, Tillman, Townsend, *Trimble*, Twichell, Upson, *Van Auken*, William B. Washburn, *Wells*, Wheeler, Winans, *Winchester*, *Wood*, *Woodward*—138.

NAYS—Messrs. Ambler, Ames, Arnell, Asper, Beatty, Benjamin, Benton, Bingham, Blair, Boyd, Burdett, Benjamin F. Butler, Roderick R. Butler, Amasa Cobb, Coburn, *Crebs*, Dyer, Ela, Finkelnburg, Garfield, Alexander H. Jones, Kelsey, Knapp, *Knott*, Lash, *Lewis*, Loughridge, Maynard, *McCormick*, McCrary, Eliakim H. Moore, Samuel P. Morrill, Paine, *Rice*, Roots, Schenck, *Schumaker*, William J. Smith, William Smyth, Taffe, Taylor, Tyner, Van Horn, Wallace, Ward, Welker, Wilkinson, Willard, Williams, *Eugene M. Wilson*, John T. Wilson, Witcher—51.

Mr. Potter moved to amend by adding the following proviso:

*Provided*, That the tax imposed by this section shall not continue or be collected after the expiration of the year 1870.

Which was disagreed to—yeas 72, nays 107, as follow:

YEAS—Messrs. Ames, *Archer* Armstrong, Banks, Bennett, *Biggs*, *Bird*, Bowen, Buffinton, *Burr*, Benjamin F. Butler, *Cleveland*, Covode, Cowles, *Crebs*, Davis, *Dickinson*, *Dox*, *Eldridge*, Fisher, Fitch, *Fox*, Garfield, *Getz*, *Gibson*, *Haight*, *Hamill*, Hill, Hotchkiss, *Johnson*, Kelley, Kellogg, Laflin, Lynch, *Mayham*, McCarthy, *McKenzie*, *McNeely*, *Milnes*, William Moore, Daniel J. Morrell, *Morrissey*, Myers, Negley, Newsham, *Niblack*, O'Neill, Packer, Paine, Phelps, Platt, *Potter*, *Randall*, *Reeves*, Sargent, *Schumaker*, *Slocum*, *Joseph S. Smith*, Starkweather, Stevenson, *Stiles*, *Stone*. *Strader*. Strong, *Swann*, *Sweeney*, Taylor, *Trimble*, Upson, Whitmore, *Wood*, *Woodward*—72.

NAYS—Messrs. Allison, Ambler, Arnell, Asper, Atwood, Ayer, Bailey, Barry, Beaman, Beatty, Benjamin, Benton, Bingham, Blair, Boles. *Booker*, Boyd, George M. Brooks, Burchard, Roderick R. Butler, Sidney Clarke, Amasa Cobb, Coburn, Cook, Conger, Cullom, Dixon, Dockery, Donley, Duval, Dyer, Ela, Farnsworth, Ferriss, Finkelnburg, Gilfillan, Hale, *Hambleton*, Hamilton, Harris, Hawkins, Hawley, Hay, Hays, Heflin, Hoar, *Holman*, Hooper, Ingersoll, Alexander H. Jones, Judd, Kelsey, *Kerr*, *Knott*, Lash, Lawrence, *Lewis*, Loughridge, *Marshall*, Maynard, *McCormick*, McCrary, McGrew, Mercur. Eliakim H. Moore, Jesse H. Moore. Morphis, Samuel P. Morrill, Orth, Packard, Peck, Perce, Peters, *Rice*, *Ridgway*, Roots, Sawyer, Schenck, Scofield, Lionel A. Sheldon, *Sherrod*, John A. Smith, William J. Smith, Worthington C. Smith, William Smyth, Stokes, Stoughton, Strickland, Taffe, Tanner, Townsend, Twichell, Tyner, *Van Auken*, Van Horn, Wallace, Ward, William B. Washburn, Welker, Wheeler, Wilkinson, Williams, *Eugene M. Wilson*, John T. Wilson, Winans, Witcher—107.

Mr. Woodward moved to strike out all of section 35, levying the income tax, and insert the following:

That there shall be levied a tax at the rate of five per cent. per annum upon the interest of interest-bearing bonds issued or to be issued by the Government of the United States, to be deducted and retained from the payments of interest upon said bonds, under regulations to be prescribed by the Secretary of the Treasury.

Which was disagreed to.

Mr. Holman moved to add the following:

And a tax of ten per centum per annum on the interest and income accruing from all bonds, notes, and other securities of the United States, the same to be deducted and withheld from such

605

interest at the time of the payment thereof by the Treasurer of the United States.

Which was disagreed to—yeas 46, nays 135, as follow:

YEAS—Messrs. Adams, Axtell, Ayer, Beck, Biggs, Bird, Booker, Burr, Cleveland, Crebs, Dickinson, Dox, Farnsworth, Getz, Gibson, Hambleton, Hamill, Heflin, Holman, Johnson, Kerr, Knott, Lewis, McCormick, McNeely, Milnes, Morgan, Morrissey, Niblack, Potter, Randall, Reeves, Rice, Ridgway, Sherrod, Stiles, Stone, Strader, Sweeney, Trimble, Van Auken, Eugene M. Wilson, Winchester, Witcher, Wood, Woodward—46.

NAYS—Messrs. Allison, Ambler, Ames, Armstrong, Arnell, Asper, Atwood, Bailey, Banks, Barry, Beaman, Beatty, Benjamin, Benton, Bingham, Blair, Boyd, George M. Brooks, James Brooks, Buffinton, Burchard, Burdett, Benjamin F. Butler, Roderick R. Butler, William T. Clark, Sidney Clarke, Coburn, Cook, Conger, Covode, Cowles, Cullom, Davis, Dawes, Degener, Dockery, Donley, Duval, Dyer, Ferriss, Finkelnburg, Fisher, Fitch, Garfield, Gilfillan, Haight, Hale, Hamilton, Harris, Hawkins, Hawley, Hay, Hill, Hoar, Hooper, Hotchkiss, Ingersoll, Jenckes, Alexander H. Jones, Judd, Kelley, Kellogg, Kelsey, Ketcham, Knapp, Laflin, Lash, Lawrence, Logan, Loughridge, Lynch, Maynard, McCarthy, McCrary, McGrew, McKenzie, Mercur, Eliakim H. Moore, Jesse H. Moore, William Moore, Morphis, Daniel J. Morrell, Samuel P. Morrill, Myers, Negley, Newsham, O'Neill, Orth, Packard, Packer, Paine, Peck, Perce, Peters, Phelps, Pomeroy, Prosser, Roots, Sargent, Sawyer, Schenck, Schumaker, Scofield, Lionel A. Sheldon, Porter Sheldon, Slocum, John A. Smith, William J. Smith, Worthington C. Smith, William Smyth, Starkweather, Stevenson, Stokes, Stoughton, Strickland, Strong, Taffe, Tanner, Taylor, Tillman. Townsend, Twichell, Tyner, Upson, Van Horn, Wallace, Ward, William B. Washburn, Welker, Wheeler, Whitmore, Wilkinson, Willard, Williams, John T. Wilson, Winans—135.

Mr. McCarthy moved to strike out all the sections relating to income tax; which was disagreed to—yeas 61, nays 122, as follow:

YEAS—Messrs. Archer, Axtell, Bennett, Biggs, Bird, Bowen, Buffinton, Burr, Cleveland, Covode, Cowles, Crebs, Davis, Dickinson, Fitch, Fox, Garfield, Getz, Haight, Hamill, Hill, Hooper, Hotchkiss, Jenckes, Johnson, Kelley, Kellogg, Ketcham, Laflin, Lynch, Mayham, McCarthy, Milnes, Jesse H. Moore, William Moore, Daniel J. Morrell, Morrissey, Myers, Negley, Newsham, Niblack, O'Neill, Paine, Potter, Randall, Reeves, Ridgway, Sargent, Schumaker, Slocum, Joseph S. Smith, Starkweather, Stevenson, Stiles, Strong, Swann, Taylor, Trimble, Twichell, Upson, Wood—61.

NAYS—Messrs. Allison, Ambler, Armstrong, Arnell, Asper, Atwood, Baily, Barry, Beaman, Beatty, Beck, Benjamin, Benton, Bingham, Blair, Boles, Booker, Boyd, Geo. M. Brooks, Burchard, Burdett, Roderick R. Butler, William T. Clark, Sidney Clarke, Amasa Cobb, Coburn, Cook, Conger, Cullom, Dawes, Degener, Dockery, Donley, Dox, Duval, Dyer, Ela, Eldridge, Farnsworth, Ferriss, Finkelnburg, Fisher, Gibson, Gilfillan, Hale, Hambleton, Hamilton, Hawkins, Hawley, Hay, Hays, Heflin, Hoar, Holman, Ingersoll, Alexander H. Jones, Judd, Kelsey, Kerr, Knapp, Knott, Lash, Lawrence, Lewis, Logan, Loughridge, Marshall, Maynard, McCormick, McCrary, McGrew, McKenzie, McNeely, Mercur, Eliakim H. Moore, Morgan, Morphis, Samuel P. Morrill, Orth, Packard, Packer, Peck, Perce, Peters, Phelps, Platt, Pomeroy, Porter, Prosser, Rice, Roots, Sawyer, Schenck, Scofield, Lionel A. Sheldon, Porter Sheldon, John A. Smith, William J. Smith, Worthington C. Smith, William Smyth, Stokes, Stone, Stoughton, Strickland, Sweeney, Taffe, Tanner, Tillman, Townsend, Tyner, Van Auken, Wallace, Ward, William B. Washburn, Wheeler, Whitmore, Willard, Williams, John T. Wilson, Winans, Witcher, Woodward—122.

Mr. Beck moved to amend by levying a tax of five per cent. on the interest or coupons of all bonds or evidences of debt, including United States bonds; which was disagreed to—yeas 78, nays 111, as follow:

YEAS—Messrs. Adams, Archer, Axtell, Beck, Benjamin, Biggs, Bird, Booker, James Brooks, Burr, Benjamin F. Butler, Cleveland, Amasa Cobb, Coburn, Crebs, Cullom, Dickinson, Dockery, Dox, Dyer, Ela, Eldridge, Farnsworth, Fitch, Fox, Getz, Gibson, Griswold, Haight, Haldeman, Hambleton, Hamill, Hamilton, Hawkins, Hay,

Hays, Heflin, Holman, Ingersoll, Johnson, Alexander H. Jones, Kerr, Knott, Lewis, Logan, Marshall, Mayham, McCormick, McNeely, Milnes, Jesse H. Moore, Morgan, Morrissey, Niblack, Orth, Potter, Randall, Reeves, Rice, Sargent, Lionel A. Sheldon, Sherrod, Joseph S. Smith, Stiles, Stokes, Strader, Sweeney, Trimble, Tyner, Van Auken, Wells, Whitmore, Eugene M. Wilson, John T. Wilson, Winchester, Witcher, Wood, Woodward—78.

NAYS—Messrs. Allison, Ambler, Ames, Armstrong, Arnell, Asper, Atwood, Ayer, Bailey, Banks, Barry, Beaman, Beatty, Bennett, Benton, Bingham, Blair, Bowen, Boyd, George M. Brooks, Buffinton, Burchard, Burdett, Roderick R. Butler, Sidney Clarke, Conger, Covode, Cowles, Davis, Dawes, Degener, Donley, Duval, Ferriss, Finkelnburg, Fisher, Garfield, Gilfillan, Hale, Harris, Hawley, Hill, Hoar, Hooper, Hotchkiss, Jenckes, Judd, Kelley, Kellogg, Kelsey, Knapp, Laflin, Lash, Lawrence, Loughridge, Lynch, Maynard, McCarthy, McCrary, McGrew, McKenzie, Mercur, Eliakim H. Moore, William Moore, Morphis, Daniel J. Morrell, Samuel P. Morrill, Myers, Negley, Newsham, O'Neill, Packard, Packer, Peck, Perce, Peters, Phelps, Platt, Pomeroy, Porter, Roots, Sawyer, Schenck, Schumaker, Scofield, Porter Sheldon, Slocum, John A. Smith, William J. Smith, Worthington C. Smith, William Smyth, Starkweather, Stevenson, Stoughton, Strickland, Strong, Tanner, Taylor, Tillman, Townsend, Twichell, Upson, Ward, William B. Washburn, Welker, Wheeler, Wilkinson, Willard, Williams, Winans—111.

June 6—Mr. Schenck moved to amend by adding a new section, being a condensation of the tariff bill formerly reported to the House by the Committee of Ways and Means, and fixing the tariff, among other things, on tea at 15 cents per pound; coffee, 3 cents per pound; sugar, raw, 2 cents per pound, clarified 2¾ cents per pound, and refined 4 cents per pound; on pig iron $7 per ton; on steel railway bars 1½ cents per pound, and on all railway bars made in part of steel 1¼ cents per pound: *Provided,* That metal converted, cast, or made from iron by the Bessamer or pneumatic process, of whatever form or description, shall be classed as steel; on nickel 40 cents per pound.

Which was agreed to—yeas 137, nays 44, as follow:

YEAS—Messrs. Adams, Allison, Ambler, Ames, Armstrong, Arnell, Atwood, Ayer, Bailey, Banks, Beaman, Beatty, Bennett, Benton, Bingham, Blair, Boles, Booker, Bowen, Boyd, George M. Brooks, Buffinton, Burchard, Burdett, Roderick R. Butler, Cake, Cessna, Churchill, William T. Clark, Sidney Clarke, Amasa Cobb, Cook, Conger, Covode, Cowles, Cullom, Davis, Dawes, Degener, Dickey, Donley, Duval, Dyer, Ela, Farnsworth, Ferriss, Finkelnburg, Fisher, Garfield, Gilfillan, Hale, Hamilton, Harris, Hawkins, Hawley, Hay, Hill, Hoar, Hooper, Hotchkiss, Ingersoll, Alexander H. Jones, Kelley, Kellogg, Ketcham, Knapp, Knott, Laflin, Lash, Lawrence, Loughridge, Lynch, Maynard, McCrary, McGrew, McKenzie, Mercur, Milnes, Eliakim H. Moore, Jesse H. Moore, William Moore, Morphis, Daniel J. Morrell, Samuel P. Morrill, Myers, Negley, O'Neill, Orth, Packard, Packer, Peck, Perce, Peters, Phelps, Platt, Poland, Pomeroy, Rice, Roots, Sanford, Sawyer, Schenck, Scofield, Porter Sheldon, John A. Smith, William J. Smith, Worthington C. Smith, William Smyth, Starkweather, Stevenson, Stokes, Stone, Stoughton, Strickland, Strong, Taffe, Tanner, Taylor, Tillman, Townsend, Trimble, Twichell, Tyner, Upson, Van Wyck, Ward, William B. Washburn, Welker, Wheeler, Whitmore, Wilkinson, Willard, Williams, Winans, Witcher, Woodward—137.

NAYS—Messrs. Axtell, Benjamin, Biggs, Bird, James Brooks, Buck, Burr, Benjamin F. Butler, Conner, Cox, Crebs, Dox, Eldridge, Fox, Getz, Griswold, Haight, Haldeman, Hamill, Heflin, Holman, Kerr, Lewis, Marshall, Mayham, McNeely, Morgan, Niblack, Potter, Randall, Reeves, Ridgway, Rogers, Sargent, Schumaker, Sherrod, Stiles, Strader, Swann, Sweeney, Van Trump, Wells, Winchester, Wood—44.

Mr. Schenck also offered as an amendment another section, enlarging the free list, which, together with the tariff section, he stated, would decrease the revenue from the tariff about $20,-000,000. He also stated that the tax bill as amended in the House would decrease the revenue from internal taxes about $45,000,000.

This section was then agreed to, and the bill passed—yeas 152, nays 35, as follow:

YEAS—Messrs. *Adams*, Allison, Ambler, Ames, Armstrong, Arnell, Atwood, *Axtell*, Ayer, Bailey, Banks, Beaman, Beatty, Benjamin, Bennett, Benton, Bingham, Blair, Boles, *Booker*, Bowen, Boyd, George M. Brooks, Buck, Buffinton, Burchard, Burdett, Roderick R. Butler, Cake, Cessna, Churchill, William T. Clark, Sidney Clarke, Amasa Cobb, Coburn, Cook, Conger, Covode, Cowles, *Crebs*, Cullom, Dawes, Degener, Dickey, Donley, Duval, Dyer, Ela, Farnsworth, Ferriss, Finkelnburg, Fisher, Fitch, Garfield, Gilfillan, Hale, Hamilton, Harris, Hawkins, Hawley, Hay, Hill, Hoar, Hooper, Hotchkiss, Ingersoll, Kelley, Kellogg, Ketcham, Knapp, *Knott*, Laflin, Lash, Lawrence, *Lewis*, Logan. Loughridge, Lynch, Maynard, McCarthy, *McCormick*, McCrary, McKee, *McKenzie*, Mercur, *Milnes*, Eliakim H. Moore, Jesse H. Moore, William Moore, Morphis, Daniel J. Morrell, Samuel P. Morrill, Myers, Negley, Newsham, O'Neill, Orth, Packard, Packer, Paine, Peck, Perce, Peters, Phelps, Platt, Poland. Pomeroy, Prosser, *Rice*, *Rogers*, Roots, Sanford, Sargent, Sawyer, Schenck, Scofield, Lionel A. Sheldon, Porter Sheldon, John A. Smith, William J. Smith, Worthington C. Smith, William Smyth, Starkweather, Stevenson, Stokes, Stoughton, Strickland, Strong, Taffe, Tanner, Taylor, Tillman, Townsend, *Trimble*, Twichell, Tyner, Upson, Van Horn, Van Wyck, Ward, William B. Washburn, Welker, *Wells*, Wheeler, Whitmore, Wilkinson, Willard, Williams, John T. Wilson, Winans, Witcher, *Woodward*—152.

NAYS—Messrs. Bird, *James Brooks*, Burr, *Conner*, Cox, Dox, Eldridge, *Fox*, *Getz*, *Griswold*, Haight, Haldeman, Hamill, Hays, Heflin, *Holman*, *Johnson*, *Kerr*, *Mayham*, McNeely, *Morgan*, *Morrissey*, *Niblack*, *Potter*, *Randall*, *Reeves*, *Ridgway*, *Sherrod*, *Slocum*, *Stiles*, *Stone*, *Swann*, *Van Trump*, *Winchester*, *Wood*—35.

### IN SENATE.

1870, June 24—Mr. Conkling moved to strike out the 35th section, being that relating to the income tax; which was agreed to—yeas 34, nays 23, as follow:

YEAS—Messrs. Abbott, Ames, Anthony, *Bayard*, Buckingham, Cameron, Carpenter, *Casserly*, Cole, Conkling, Corbett, *Davis*, Fenton, Ferry, Fowler, Gilbert, *Hamilton* of Maryland, Harris, *Johnston*, Kellogg, *McCreery*, McDonald, Osborn, Pomeroy, Robertson, *Saulsbury*, Scott, Stewart, Sumner, *Thurman*, Trumbull, *Vickers*, Wilson, Yates—34.

NAYS—Messrs. Boreman, Brownlow, Chandler, Drake, Hamlin, Harlan, Howard, Howe, Howell, Morrill of Maine, Morrill of Vermont, Morton, Pratt, Ramsey, Rice, Ross, Schurz, Sherman, Sprague, Thayer, Warner, Willey, Williams—23.

June 29—The bill having been reported to the Senate, Mr. Hamilton, of Maryland, moved to amend by adding the following:

SEC. —. That hereafter there shall be annually deducted and withheld by the Treasurer of the United States five per cent. of all moneys payable as interest upon the public debt of the United States, the same being hereby imposed as a tax upon the property represented by the bonds heretofore issued under the laws of the United States.

Which was disagreed to—yeas 11, nays 25, as follow:

YEAS—Messrs. *Casserly*, Fenton, Fowler, *Hamilton* of Maryland, *McCreery*, Pratt, Rice, Ross, Sprague, *Thurman*, *Vickers*—11.

NAYS—Messrs. Anthony, Boreman, Cattell, Cole, Cragin, Gilbert, Hamlin, Harlan, Harris, Howe, Howell, McDonald, Morrill of Maine, Morrill of Vermont, Pomeroy, Ramsey. Sawyer, Schurz, Scott, Sherman, Stewart, Sumner, Willey, Williams, Wilson—25.

July 1—Mr. Bayard moved to amend by inserting the following:

SEC. —. That hereafter there shall be annually deducted and withheld by the Treasurer of the United States five per cent. of all moneys payable as interest upon the public debt of the United States, the same being hereby imposed as a tax upon the property represented by the bonds heretofore issued under the laws of the United States.

Which was disagreed to—yeas 12, nays 36, as follow:

YEAS—Messrs. *Bayard, Casserly, Davis*, Fowler, *Hamilton* of Maryland, *McCreery*, Pratt, Spencer, Sprague, *Stockton, Thurman, Vickers*—12.

NAYS—Messrs. Anthony, Boreman, Chandler, Corbett, Cragin, Drake, Edmunds, Fenton, Gilbert, Hamlin, Harlan, Harris, Howe, Howell, McDonald, Morrill of Maine, Morrill of Vermont, Morton, Nye, Osborn, Pomeroy, Ramsey, Revels, Rice, Sawyer, Schurz, Scott, Sherman, Sumner, Thayer, Tipton, Trumbull, Warner, Willey, Williams, Wilson—36.

Mr. Thurman moved to insert the following:

SEC.—That there shall be levied and collected, in the manner hereinafter specified, a tax of five per cent. upon the income of every person residing in the United States, and of every citizen of the United States residing abroad, derived from interest on the bonds of the United States; said tax to be collected by withholding the same in the payment of such interest.

Which was disagreed to—yeas 11, nays 35, as follow:

YEAS—Messrs. *Bayard, Casserly, Davis,* Fenton, *Hamilton* of Maryland, *McCreery*, Pratt, Sprague, *Stockton, Thurman, Vickers*—11.

NAYS—Messrs. Anthony, Boreman, Chandler, Corbett, Cragin, Drake, Edmunds, Fowler, Gilbert, Hamlin, Harris, Howe, Lewis, McDonald, Morrill of Maine, Morrill of Vermont, Morton, Osborn, Patterson, Pomeroy, Revels, Robertson, Ross, Sawyer, Schurz, Scott, Sherman, Stewart, Sumner, Tipton, Trumbull, Warner, Willey, Williams, Wilson—35.

Mr. Wilson moved to amend section 35, so that it should read:

That during the years 1871 and 1872, and no longer, there shall be levied and collected annually a tax of two and a half per cent. upon the gains, profits, and income of every person residing in the United States, &c.

Which was disagreed to—yeas 23, nays 28, as follow:

YEAS—Messrs. Abbott, Boreman, Cragin, Hamlin, Harlan, Howe, Howell, Morrill of Maine, Morrill of Vermont, Morton, Patterson, Pratt, Ramsey, Rice, Ross, Schurz, Spencer, Sprague, Tipton, Warner, Willey, Wilson—23.

NAYS—Messrs. Anthony, *Bayard*, Cameron, *Casserly*, Cole, Corbett, *Davis*, Edmunds, Fenton, Fowler, Gilbert, *Hamilton* of Maryland, Harris, Kellogg, Lewis, *McCreery*, McDonald, Nye, Osborn, Revels, Robertson, Scott, Stewart, *Stockton*, Sumner, *Thurman*, Trumbull, *Vickers*—28.

The amendment as agreed to in committee of the whole, striking out all the sections relating to income tax, was agreed to—yeas 26, nays 22, as follow:

YEAS—Messrs. Anthony, *Bayard, Casserly*, Cole, Corbett, *Davis*, Edmunds, Fenton, Fowler, Gilbert, *Hamilton* of Maryland, Harris, Kellogg, *McCreery*, McDonald, Osborn. Revels, Robertson, Scott, Stewart, *Stockton*, Sumner, *Thurman*, Trumbull, *Vickers*, Wilson—26.

NAYS—Messrs. Abbott, Boreman, Cragin, Drake, Hamlin, Harlan, Howe, Howell, Morrill of Maine, Morrill of Vermont, Morton, Patterson, Pratt, Ramsey, Ross, Schurz, Sherman, Spencer, Sprague, Tipton. Warner, Willey—22.

Mr. Sherman moved to strike out the words "gross receipts" from an amendment adopted by the committee of the whole, whereby that tax on gross receipts was abolished; which was disagreed to—yeas 25, nays 25, as follow:

YEAS—Messrs. Anthony, *Bayard*, Boreman, *Casserly*, Corbett, Edmunds, Fenton, Fowler, Gilbert, Harlan. Lewis, McDonald, Morrill of Maine, Morrill of Vermont,

Nye, Pratt, Ramsey, Schurz, Scott, Sherman, Sprague, Stewart, Thayer, Warner, Willey—25.

NAYS—Messrs. Cameron, Cole, *Cragin*, *Davis*, Drake, *Hamilton* of Maryland, Hamlin, Harris, Howe, Howell, Kellogg, *McCreery*, Osborn, Patterson, Pomeroy, Robertson, Ross, Spencer, *Stockton*, Sumner, *Thurman*, Trumbull, *Vickers*, Williams, Wilson—25.

Mr. Edmunds moved to reconsider the vote by which the income tax was stricken out; which was agreed to—yeas 26, nays 25, as follow:

YEAS—Messrs. Abbott, Anthony, Cragin, Drake, Edmunds, Hamlin, Harlan, Howe, Howell, Morrill of Maine, Morrill of Vermont, Nye, Patterson, Pool, Pratt, Ramsey, Rice, Schurz, Sherman, Spencer, Sprague, Tipton, Warner, Willey, Williams, Wilson—26.

NAYS—Messrs. *Bayard*, Cameron, *Casserly*, Corbett, *Davis*, Fenton, Gilbert, *Hamilton* of Maryland, Harris, *Johnston*, Kellogg, Lewis, *McCreery*, McDonald, Pomeroy, Revels, Robertson, Ross, Scott, Stewart, *Stockton*, Sumner, *Thurman*, Trumbull, *Vickers*—25.

Mr. Wilson's amendment was then agreed to—yeas 27, nays 21, as follow:

YEAS—Messrs. Abbott, Anthony, Chandler, Cragin, Drake, Edmunds, Hamlin, Harlan, Howell, Morrill of Maine, Morrill of Vermont, Patterson, Pomeroy, Pool, Pratt, Ramsey, Rice, Ross, Schurz, Sherman, Spencer, Thayer, Tipton, Warner, Willey, Williams, Wilson—27.

NAYS—Messrs. *Bayard*, *Casserly*, Corbett, *Davis*, Fenton, Gilbert, *Hamilton* of Maryland, Harris, Howe, *Johnston*, *McCreery*, McDonald, Revels, Robertson, Scott, Stewart, *Stockton*, Sumner, *Thurman*, Trumbull, *Vickers*—21.

The question then recurring on the amendment to strike out all concerning the income tax, it was disagreed to—yeas 22, nays 26, as follow:

YEAS—Messrs. *Bayard*, *Casserly*, Corbett, Fenton, Gilbert, *Hamilton* of Maryland, Harris, *Johnston*, Kellogg, Lewis, *McCreery*, McDonald, Osborn, Pomeroy, Robertson, Scott, Stewart, *Stockton*, Sumner, *Thurman*, Trumbull, *Vickers*—22.

NAYS—Messrs. Abbott, Anthony, Chandler, Cragin, Drake, Edmunds, Hamlin, Harlan, Howe, Howell, Morrill of Maine, Morrill of Vermont, Patterson, Pool. Pratt, Ramsey, Rice, Ross, Schurz, Sherman, Spencer, Tipton, Warner, Willey, Williams, Wilson—26.

July 5—Mr. Conkling moved to add as follows: That no such income tax shall be levied or collected until by act of Congress it shall be hereafter so directed.

Mr. Edmunds moved to amend this as follows: And all provisions of law providing for the assessment and collection of taxes on gross receipts are hereby continued until the further action of Congress.

Which was disagreed to—yeas 18, nays 33, as follow:

YEAS—Messrs. Anthony, *Bayard*, Boreman, Cole, Corbett, Drake, Edmunds, Fenton, Gilbert, Harlan, Morrill of Vermont, Nye, Ramsey, Shurz, Scott, Sherman, Stewart, Wilson—18.

NAYS—Messrs. Carpenter, Chandler, Conkling, Cragin, Fowler, *Hamilton* of Maryland, Hamilton of Texas, Hamlin, Harris, Howe, *Johnston*, Kellogg, *McCreery*, Morton, Patterson, Pomeroy, Pool, Revels, Rice, Robertson, Ross, *Saulsbury*, Sawyer, Spencer, Sprague, *Stockton*, Sumner, *Thurman*, Trumbull, *Vickers*, Warner, Willey, Williams—33.

Mr. Conkling's amendment was then disagreed to—yeas 26, nays 26, as follow:

YEAS—Messrs. *Bayard*, Carpenter, Cole, Conkling, Corbett, Fenton, Fowler, Gilbert, *Hamilton* of Maryland, Harris, *Johnston*, Kellogg, *McCreery*, McDonald, Pomeroy, Revels, Robertson, *Saulsbury*. Scott, Stewart, *Stockton*, Sumner, *Thurman*, Trumbull, *Vickers*, Wilson—26.

NAYS—Messrs. Anthony, Boreman, Chandler, Cragin, Drake, Edmunds, Hamilton of Texas, Hamlin, Harlan, Howe, Howell, Morrill of Vermont, Morton, Nye, Patterson, Pool, Ramsey, Rice, Ross, Sawyer, Schurz, Sherman, Spencer, Warner, Willey, Williams—26.

The bill was then passed—yeas 43, nays 6, as follow:

YEAS—Messrs. Antnony, Boreman, Carpenter, Chandler, Cole, Conkling, Corbett, Cragin, Drake, Edmunds, Fenton, Gilbert, Hamilton of Texas, Hamlin, Harlan, Howe, Howell, Kellogg, McDonald, Morrill of Vermont, Morton, Nye, Patterson, Pool, Ramsey, Rice, Robertson, Ross, Sawyer, Schurz, Scott, Sherman, Spencer, Sprague, Stewart, *Stockton*, Thayer, *Thurman*, Trumbull, Warner, Willey, Williams, Wilson—43.

NAYS—Messrs. *Bayard*, *Hamilton* of Maryland, Harris, *McCreery*, *Saulsbury*, *Vickers*—6.

IN HOUSE.

July 9—The bill having been returned from the Senate with amendments,

Mr. Davis moved to suspend the rules and strike out the income tax, which was disagreed to—yeas 67, nays 117, as follow:

YEAS—Messrs. Ambler, Ames, *Archer*, *Axtell*, Banks, Barnum, Bennett, *Biggs*, Bird, *James Brooks*, Buffinton, *Burr*, Benjamin F. Butler, *Calkin*, Covode, Cowles, *Cox*, Davis, *Dickinson*, Dixon, Fitch, Garfield, *Getz*, Gilfillan, *Griswold*, *Haight*, Hill, Hooper, Jenckes, Judd, Kelley, Kellogg, Ketcham, Lynch, Mayham, McCarthy, *McKenzie*, *Milnes*, William Moore, Daniel J. Morrell. *Morrissey*, Myers, Negley, *Niblack*, O'Neill, Paine, *Potter*, *Randall*, *Reeves*, Rogers, Sargent, *Schumaker*, Scofield, *Slocum*, *Joseph S. Smith*, Starkweather, Stevenson, *Stiles*, *Stone*, Strong, *Swann*, *Trimble*, Twichell, Upson, Van Wyck, *Winchester*, *Wood*—67.

NAYS—Messrs. *Adams*, Allison, Arnell, Asper, Atwood, Ayer, Bailey, Beatty, Benjamin, Benton, Bingham. Blair, Boles, *Booker*, Boyd, George M. Brooks, Buck, Buckley, Burchard, Roderick R Butler, Cake, Churchill, Sidney Clarke, Amasa Cobb, Coburn, Conger, *Conner*, *Crebs*, Cullom, Darrall. Dawes, Degener, Dickey, Donley, Duval, Dyer, Ela, Farnsworth, Ferriss, Ferry, Finkelnburg, Fisher, Hale, Hamilton, Harris, Hawkins, Hawley, Hay, Hoar, Ingersoll, *Thomas L. Jones*, Kelsey, *Knott*, Lash, Lawrence, *Lewis*, Logan, Loughridge, *Marshall*, Maynard, *McCormick*, McCrary, McGrew, McKee, *McNeely*, Mercur, Eliakim H. Moore. Morphis, Orth, Packard, Packer, Palmer, Peck, Perce, Phelps, Poland, Porter, Prosser, *Rice*. Roots. Sanford, Sawyer, Schenck, Shanks, Lionel A. Sheldon, Porter Sheldon, *Sherrod*, John A. Smith, Worthington C. Smith, William Smyth, Stevens, Stokes, Stoughton, Strickland, *Sweeney*, Taffe, Tanner, Tillman. Townsend. Tyner, *Van Auken*, Van Horn, Ward, Cadwalader C. Washburn, William B. Washburn. Welker, *Wells*. Wheeler, Whitmore, Wilkinson, Willard. Williams, *Eugene M. Wilson*, John T. Wilson, Winans, *Woodward*—117.

The amendment of the Senate abolishing all special taxes was agreed to—yeas 107, nays 73, as follow:

YEAS—Messrs. *Adams*, Allison, *Archer*, Ayer, *Barnum*, Beatty, *Beck*, *Biggs*, Bird, Boyd, Buck, Buckley, Burchard, *Burr*, Benjamin F. Butler, William T. Clark. Sidney Clarke, Coburn, Cook. *Conner*, *Cox*, *Crebs*, Cullom, Darrall, Davis. Dawes, *Dickinson*, Donley, Fitch, Garfield, *Getz*, Gilfillan, *Griswold*, *Haight*, *Haldeman*, Hale, Hamilton, Harris, Hawley, Hay, Hays, Heflin, Ingersoll, *Johnson*, *Thomas L. Jones*, Judd, Kellogg. *Kerr*, *Knott*, Lawrence, *Lewis*, Logan, Lynch, *Marshall*, *McCormick*, McCrary, *McKenzie*, *McNeely*, Mercur, *Milnes*, Jesse H. Moore. William Moore, *Morgan*, *Mungen*, Myers, *Niblack*, O'Neill, Orth, Packard, Packer, Paine, Perce, Poland, *Potter*, *Reeves*, *Rice*, *Rogers*, Sargent, Sawyer, *Schumaker*, Scofield, Shanks, Lionel A. Sheldon, *Sherrod*, *Slocum*, John A. Smith, *Joseph S. Smith*, Worthington C. Smith, Stevenson, *Stiles*, *Stone*, *Swann*, *Sweeney*, *Trimble*, Twichell, Tyner, *Van Auken*, Van Horn, Cadwalader C. Washburn, *Wells*, Williams, *Eugene M. Wilson*, Winans, *Winchester*, *Wood*, *Woodward*—107.

NAYS—Messrs. Ambler, Ames, Armstrong, Arnell, Asper, Atwood, Bailey, Barry, Benjamin, Bennett, Benton, Bingham, Blair, Boles, *Booker*, George M. Brooks, Buffinton, Burdett, Roderick R. Butler. Cake, Conger, Duval, Dyer, Ela, Farnsworth, Ferriss, Ferry, Finkelnburg, Fisher, Hawkins, Hill, Hooper. Kelley, Kelsey, Ketcham, Knapp, Lash, Loughridge. Maynard, McCarthy, McGrew, Eliakim H. Moore, Morphis. Daniel J. Morrell, Negley, Palmer, Peck, Platt, Porter, Roots, Sanford, Schenck, William J. Smith, William Smyth, Stevens, Stokes, Stoughton, Strickland. Taffe, Taylor, Tillman, Townsend, Upson, Van Wyck, Wallace, Ward, William B. Washburn, Welker, Wheeler, Whitmore, Wilkinson, Willard, John T. Wilson—73.

The Senate amendment fixing the income tax at $2\frac{1}{2}$ per cent. instead of 3 was agreed to.

The Senate amendments on Bessemer steel, reducing the rate on steel bars from 1½ cents per pound to 1¼, and on rails made partly of steel from 1¼ cents to 1 cent, were agreed to—the latter without a division; the former, yeas 99, nays 72, as follow:

YEAS—Messrs. *Adams*, Allison, *Archer*, Asper, Ayer, Beatty, *Beck*, Benjamin, *Biggs, Bird, James Brooks,* Buckley, *Burr*, Benjamin F. Butler, Sidney Clarke, Coburn, Cook, *Cox, Crebs,* Cullom, Darrall, *Dickinson, Eldridge,* Farnsworth, Finkelnburg, Fitch, Garfield, *Getz, Griswold, Haight, Haldeman,* Hale, Harris, Hawkins, Hawley, Hay, Hays, Heflin. Ingersoll. *Johnson, Thomas L. Jones,* Judd, *Kerr,* Ketcham, *Knott,* Lewis. Logan, Loughridge, Lynch, *Marshall, Mayham, McCormick,* McCrary. *McKenKie, McNeely,* Eliakim H. Moore, Jesse H. Moore, *Morgan, Mungen, Niblack,* Orth, Packard, Paine, *Potter, Reeves. Rice, Rogers,* Sargent, *Schumaker,* Shanks, Lionel A. Sheldon, *Sherrod, Slocum, Joseph S. Smith,* Worthington C. Smith. William Smyth, Stevenson, *Stiles, Stone,* Stoughton, Strong, *Swann, Sweeney,* Taffe, *Trimble,* Twichell, Tyner, *Van Auken,* Van Wyck, *Voorhees,* Cadwalader C. Washburn, *Wells,* Wilkinson, Williams, *Eugene M. Wilson,* Winans, *Winchester, Wood, Woodward—* 99.

NAYS—Messrs. Ambler, Ames, Armstrong, Arnell, Atwood, Bailey, Barry, Benton, Bingham, Blair, Buffinton. Roderick R. Butler, Cake, Churchill, Amasa Cobb, Conger, Covode, Cowles, Davis, Dawes, Donley, Duval, Ferriss, Ferry, Fisher, Gilfillan, Hill, Hoar, Hooper, Kelley, Kellogg, Kelsey, Knapp, Lash, Maynard, McCarthy, McGrew, Mercur, William Moore, Morphis, Daniel J. Morrell, Myers, Negley, O'Neill, Packer, Peck, Perce, Phelps, Porter, Prosser, Sanford, Sawyer, Schenck, Scofield, Porter Sheldon, John A. Smith, Stevens, Stokes, Strickland, Tanner, Taylor, Tillman, Townsend, Upson, Wallace, Ward, William B. Washburn, Welker, Wheeler, Whitmore, Willard, John T. Wilson—72.

A committee of conference appointed, consisting of Senators Sherman, Morrill of Vermont, and Hamilton of Maryland, and Representatives Schenck, Kelley, and James Brooks.

IN SENATE, *May* 13, 1870.

The report of the conference committee was agreed to without a division.

IN HOUSE, *July* 13, 1870.

YEAS—Messrs. Allison, Ambler, Ames, Armstrong, Arnell, Atwood, *Axtell.* Ayer, Bailey, *Barnum,* Beatty, Benjamin. Bennett, Benton, Bingham, Blair, Boles, *Booker,* Boyd, George M. Brooks, Buck, Buckley, Buffinton, Burchard, Burdett, Benjamin F. Butler, Roderick R. Butler, Cake, Cessna, Churchill, William T. Clark, Sidney Clarke, Amasa Cobb, Coburn, Conger, Covode, Cowles. Cullom, Davis, Dawes, Dickey, Dixon, Donley, Duval, Ela, Farnsworth, Ferriss, Ferry, Finkelnburg, Fitch, Garfield, Gilfillan, Hamilton, Harris, Hawkins, Hawley, Hay, Heflin, Hill, Hoar, Hooper, Hotchkiss, Ingersoll, Jenckes, Judd, Julian, Kelley,

Kellogg, Kelsey, Ketcham, Knapp, Laflin, Lash. Lawrence, Logan, Loughridge, Lynch, Maynard, McCarthy, McCrary, McGrew, *McKenzie,* Mercur, *Milnes,* Eliakim H. Moore, Jesse H. Moore, William Moore, Morphis, Daniel J. Morrell, Myers, Negley, O'Neill, Orth, Packard, Packer, Paine, Palmer, Peck, Perce, Peters, Phelps, Poland, Porter, Prosser, *Rice, Rogers,* Roots, Sargent. Sawyer, Schenck, Scofield, Shanks, Lionel A. Sheldon, Porter Sheldon, John A. Smith. William J. Smith, Worthington C. Smith, William Smyth, Stevens, Stevenson, Stokes, Stoughton, Strickland, Taffe, Tanner, Taylor, Tillman, Townsend, *Trimble.* Twichell, Tyner, Upson, Van Horn, Van Wyck, Ward, Cadwalader C. Washburn, William B. Washburn, Welker, Wheeler, Whitmore, Wilkinson, Willard, Williams, John T. Wilson—144.

NAYS—Messrs. *Adams, Archer.* Asper, *Beck, Biggs, Bird, James Brooks, Burr, Cleveland, Cox, Crebs, Dickinson, Eldridge, Fox. Getz, Griswold, Haight, Haldeman, Hambleton,* Hays, *Holman, Johnson, Thomas L. Jones, Kerr, Knott, Lewis, Marshall, Mayham, McNeely, Morgan, Niblack, Potter, Randall, Reeves, Schumaker, Sherrod, Slocum, Joseph S. Smith, Stiles, Stone, Swann, Sweeney, Van Auken, Voorhees, Wells, Eugene M. Wilson, Winchester. Wood, Woodward—*49.

In submitting the report of the conference committee, Mr. Schenck made the following statement as to the reduction of taxes made by the bill:

"Calculated upon the basis of the receipts of the fiscal year ending the 30th of June, 1869, which was at that time the only complete report we had before us, I made out by a close analysis of the bill, and as accurate a calculation as I could furnish to the House, a reduction of the internal taxes to the amount of $45,000,000, and of import duties to the amount of $20,000,000, making in the aggregate $65,000,000. After the bill had passed the House, however, and before any action upon it or change made by the Senate, the complete returns of internal revenue, but not of imports, were obtained for the year ending the 30th June, 1870, and the increase has been such that trying the bill by that standard it was found that the reduction of internal taxes as compared with those for last year was $50,000,000, and of import duties $27,000,000, making a reduction of $77,000,000, in the aggregate. By the striking off of some other taxes, including an additional deduction from the income tax, the tax on passports, and various other matters, I do not hesitate to say that the reduction by this bill, compared with the receipts of last year, will be to the people of this country an alleviation of the burdens of taxation from these two quarters, the internal taxes and import duties, of over $80,000,-000."

# LX.

# THE RESTORATION OF GEORGIA.

**AN ACT to promote the Reconstruction of the State of Georgia.**

*Be it enacted, &c.,* That the governor of the State of Georgia be, and hereby is, authorized and directed, forthwith, by proclamation, to summon all persons elected to the general assembly of said State, as appears by the proclamation of George G. Meade, the general commanding the military district including the State of Georgia,

dated June 25, 1868, to appear on some day certain, to be named in said proclamation, at Atlanta, in said State; and thereupon the said general assembly of said State shall proceed to perfect its organization in conformity with the Constitution and laws of the United States, according to the provisions of this act.

SEC. 2. That when the members so elected to said Senate and House of Representatives shall be convened, as aforesaid, each and every member and each and every person claiming to be elected as a member of said senate or house of representatives shall, in addition to taking the oath or oaths required by the constitution of Georgia, also take and subscribe and file in the office of the secretary of state of the State of Georgia one of the following oaths or affirmations, namely: " I do solemnly swear (or affirm, as the case may be) that I have never held the office, or exercised the duties of, a Senator or Representative in Congress, nor been a member of the legislature of any State of the United States, nor held any civil office created by law for the administration of any general law of a State, or for the administration of justice in any State or under the laws of the United States, nor held any office in the military or naval service of the United States and thereafter engaged in insurrection or rebellion against the United States, or gave aid or comfort to its enemies, or rendered, except in consequence of direct physical force, any support or aid to any insurrection or rebellion against the United States, nor held any office under, or given any support to, any government of any kind organized or acting in hostility to the United States, or levying war against the United States: so help me God, (or on the pains and penalties of perjury, as the case may be;") or the following oath or affirmation, namely: "I do solemnly swear (or affirm, as the case may be) that I have been relieved by an act of the Congress of the United States from disability as provided for by section three of the XIVth Amendment to the Constitution of the United States: so help me God, (or on the pains and penalties of perjury, as the case may be.") Which oath or affirmation, when so filed, shall be entered of record by the secretary of state of the State of Georgia, and said oath or affirmation, or a copy of the record thereof, duly certified by said secretary of state, shall be evidence in all courts and places. And every person claiming to be so elected, who shall refuse or decline or neglect or be unable to take one of said oaths or affirmations above provided, shall not be admitted to a seat in said Senate or House of Representatives, or to a participation in the proceedings thereof, but shall be deemed ineligible to such seats.

SEC. 3. That if any person claiming to be elected to said Senate or House of Representatives, as aforesaid, shall falsely take either of said oaths or affirmations above provided, he shall be deemed guilty of perjury, and shall suffer the pains and penalties thereof; and may be tried, convicted, and punished therefor by the circuit court of the United States for the district of Georgia in which district said crime was committed; and the jurisdiction of said court shall be sole and exclusive for the purpose aforesaid.

SEC. 4. That the persons elected, as aforesaid, and entitled to compose such legislature, and who shall comply with the provisions of this act, by taking one of the oaths or affirmations above prescribed, shall thereupon proceed, in said Senate and House of Representatives to which they have been elected respectively, to reorganize said Senate and House of Representatives, respectively, by the election and qualification of the proper officers of each house.

SEC. 5. That if any person shall, by force, violence, or fraud, willfully hinder or interrupt any person or persons elected as aforesaid from taking either of the oaths or affirmations prescribed by this act, or from participating in the proceedings of said Senate or House of Representatives, after having taken one of said oaths or affirmations, and otherwise complied with this act, he shall be deemed guilty of a felony, and may be tried, convicted, and punished therefor by the circuit or district court of the United States for the district of Georgia in which district said offense shall be committed; and shall be punished therefor by imprisonment at hard labor for not less than two nor more than ten years, in the discretion of the court; and the jurisdiction of said courts shall be sole and exclusive for the purpose aforesaid.

SEC. 6. That it is hereby declared that the exclusion of any person or persons elected as aforesaid, and being otherwise qualified, from participation in the proceedings of said Senate or House of Representatives, upon the ground of race, color, or previous condition of servitude, would be illegal and revolutionary, and is hereby prohibited.

SEC. 7. That upon the application of the Governor of Georgia, the President of the United States shall employ such military or naval forces of the United States as may be necessary to enforce and execute the preceding provisions of this act.

SEC. 8. That the Legislature shall ratify the XVth Amendment proposed to the Constitution of the United States before Senators and Representatives from Georgia are admitted to seats in Congress.

Approved December 22, 1869.

The final votes on this act were as follow:

IN SENATE, *December 17, 1869.*

YEAS—Messrs. Abbott, Anthony, Brownlow, Buckingham, Carpenter, Cattell, Chandler, Cole, Conkling, Corbett, Cragin, Drake, Edmunds, Fenton, Gilbert, Hamlin, Harlan, Harris, Howard, Kellogg, McDonald, Morrill of Maine, Morrill of Vermont, Morton, Nye, Osborn, Patterson, Pomeroy, Pratt, Ramsey, Rice, Robertson, Ross, Sawyer, Schurz, Scott, Sherman, Spencer, Stewart, Sumner, Thayer, Warner, Willey, Williams, Wilson—45.

NAYS—Messrs. *Bayard, Casserly, Davis,* Fowler, *William T. Hamilton, Saulsbury, Stockton, Thurman, Vickers*—9.

IN HOUSE, *December 21, 1869.*

YEAS—Messrs. Allison, Ambler, Armstrong, Arnell, Asper, Bailey, Beaman, Beatty, Benjamin, Bennett, Benton, Boles, Bowen, Boyd, George M. Brooks, Buck, Buckley, Buffinton, Burchard, Burdett, Benjamin F. Butler, Roderick R. Butler, Cessna, Amasa Cobb, Coburn, Cook, Conger, Cullom, Dawes, Deweese, Dickey, Dixon, Donley, Duval, Ela, Ferriss, Ferry, Finkelnburg, Fisher, Fitch, Garfield, Hale, Hamilton, Hawley, Hay, Heaton, Hill, Hoar, Solomon L. Hoge, Hooper, Hotchkiss, Ingersoll, Jenckes, Alexander H. Jones, Judd, Kelley, Kellogg, Kelsey, Knapp, Lash, Lawrence, Logan, Loughridge, Maynard, McCarthy, McCrary, McGrew, Mercur, Eliakim H. Moore, Jesse H. Moore, William Moore, Daniel J. Morrell, Samuel P. Morrill, Myers, Negley, O'Neill, Orth, Packard, Packer, Paine, Palmer, Peters, Phelps, Poland, Pomeroy, Prosser, Roots, Sanford, Sargent, Sawyer, Schenck, Scofield, Shanks, Lionel A. Sheldon, Porter Sheldon, John A. Smith, William J. Smith, Worthington C. Smith, William Smyth, Starkweather, Stevens, Stevenson, Stokes, Stoughton, Strickland, Strong, Taffe, Tanner, Townsend, Twichell, Tyner, Upson, Van Horn, Cadwalader C. Washburn, Welker, Wheeler, B. F. Whittemore, Wilkinson, William Williams, John T. Wilson, Winans—121.

NAYS—Messrs. *Adams, Archer, Axtell, Beck, Biggs,* Bingham, *Bird, Calkin, Cox, Crebs, Dickinson, Dox, Eldridge,* Farnsworth, *Getz, Greene, Griswold, Haldeman, Hambleton, Hamill,* Hawkins, *Holman, Johnson. Thomas L. Jones, Kerr, Knott,* Marshall, *Mayham, McCormick, McNeely, Morgan, Mungen, Niblack, Potter, Randall, Reeves, Rice, Rogers, Joseph S. Smith, Stone, Strader, Swann, Sweeney, Trimble, Van Trump, Voorhees, Wells, Eugene M. Wilson, Winchester,* Witcher, *Woodward*—51.

### Previous Votes.

#### IN SENATE.

1869, December 17—Mr. Morton moved to strike out the eighth section of the bill as reported from the Judiciary Committee, which was in these words:

"That the Legislature of Georgia shall be regarded as provisional only, until the further action of Congress,"

And to insert the section as in the text of the bill, which was agreed to—yeas 38, nays 15, as follows:

YEAS—Messrs. Abbott, Brownlow, Buckingham, Cattell, Chandler, Cole, Cragin, Drake, Fenton, Gilbert, Hamlin, Harlan, Harris, Howard, Kellogg, McDonald, Morrill of Maine, Morrill of Vermont, Morton, Nye, Osborn, Patterson, Pomeroy, Pratt, Ramsey, Robertson, Ross, Sawyer, Schurz, Scott, Sherman, Spencer, Stewart, Sumner, Thayer, Warner, Williams, Wilson—38.

NAYS.—Messrs. *Bayard,* Carpenter, *Casserly,* Conkling, Corbett, *Davis,* Fowler, *William T. Hamilton, Norton,* Rice, *Saulsbury, Stockton, Thurman, Vickers,* Willey—15.

A few unimportant changes were made, and the bill passed both Houses, as above.

### An act relating to the State of Georgia.

*Be it enacted, &c.,* That the State of Georgia, having complied with the reconstruction acts, and the XIVth and XVth articles of amendments to the Constitution of the United States having been ratified in good faith by a legal legislature of said State, it is hereby declared that the State of Georgia is entitled to representation in the Congress of the United States. But nothing in this act contained shall be construed to deprive the people of Georgia of the right to an election for members of the general assembly of said State, as provided for in the constitution thereof.

SEC. 2. That so much of the act entitled "An act making appropriations for the support of the army for the year ending June 30, 1868, and for other purposes," approved March 2, 1867, as prohibits the organization, arming, or calling into service of the militia forces in the States of Georgia, Mississippi, Texas, and Virginia, be, and the same is hereby, repealed; and nothing in this or any other act of Congress shall be construed to affect the term to which any officer has been appointed or any member of the general assembly elected, as prescribed by the constitution of the State of Georgia.

Approved July 15, 1870.

This act, being the report of the committee of conference, was adopted in both houses without a division July 14, 1870.

### Previous Votes.

#### IN HOUSE.

1870, February 25—Mr. B. F. Butler, from the Committee on Reconstruction, reported a bill for the restoration of Georgia, similar in terms to the Mississippi and Texas bills, (for which see chapter LV.)

Mr. Bingham moved to add the following proviso:

*Provided,* That nothing in this act contained shall be construed to vacate any of the offices now filled in the State of Georgia, either by the election of the people, or by the appointment of the governor thereof, by and with the advice and consent of the senate of said State; neither shall this act be construed to extend the official term of any officer of said State beyond the term limited by the constitution thereof, dating from the election or appointment of such officer; nor to deprive the people of Georgia of the right, under their constitution, to elect senators and representatives of the State of Georgia in the year 1870, but said election shall be held in the year 1870, either on the day named in the constitution of said State or such other day as the present legislature may designate by law.

Which was agreed to—yeas 115, nays 71, as follow:

YEAS—Messrs. *Adams,* Allison, Ambler, *Archer, Axtell,* Banks, Beaman, Beatty, *Beck, Biggs,* Bingham, *Bird,* Blair, *Booker,* Burchard, *Burr, Calkin,* Churchill, *Cleveland,* Coburn, Cook, *Cox, Crebs,* Cullom, Dawes, *Dickinson,* Dockery, *Dox,* Duval, *Eldridge,* Farnsworth, Ferriss, Ferry, Finkelnburg, Garfield, *Getz, Griswold,* Haight, *Haldeman,* Hale, *Hambleton, Hamill,* Hawkins, Hawley, Hay, Heaton, Hill, *Holman,* Ingersoll, Jenckes, *Johnson, Thomas L. Jones,* Judd, Kellogg, *Kerr,* Ketcham, *Knott,* Laflin, Logan, *Marshall, Mayham,* McCarthy, *McCormick,* McCrary, *McKenzie, McNeely, Milnes,* Eliakim H. Moore, Jesse H. Moore, *Niblack,* Orth, Packard, Packer, Platt, Pomeroy, *Potter, Randall, Reading, Reeves, Rice, Rogers,* Sargent, Schenck, *Schumaker, Sherrod, Slocum,* John A. Smith, Worthington C. Smith, Starkweather, *Stiles, Stone, Strader.* Strong, *Swann,* Taffe, Tanner, *Trimble,* Tyner, *Van Auken, Van Trump, Voorhees,* Cadwalader C. Washburn, William B. Washburn, Welker, *Wells,* Wheeler, Wilkinson, Willard, Williams, *Eugene M. Wilson,* John T. Wilson, Winans, Witcher, *Wood, Woodward*—115.

NAYS—Messrs. Arnell, Asper, Atwood, Ayer, Benjamin. Boles, Bowen, Boyd, George M. Brooks, Buck, Buckley, Buffinton, Burdett, Benjamin F. Butler, Roderick R. Butler, Cake, Cessna, Clarke, Amasa Cobb, Clinton L. Cobb, Conger, Covode, Davis, Dickey, Donley, Fisher, Gilfillan, Hamilton, Harris, Hays, Heflin, Hoar, Hoge, Hooper, Hotchkiss, Alexander H. Jones, Julian, Kelley, Knapp, Lash, Lawrence, Loughridge, Maynard, McKee, Mercur, William Moore, Morrell, Morrill, Myers, Negley, O'Neill, Paine, Palmer, Perce, Phelps, Prosser, Roots, Sanford, Sawyer, Shanks, William J. Smith, William Smyth, Stevenson, Stokes, Stoughton, Strickland, Tillman, Townsend, Twichell, Upson, Van Horn—71.

The bill was then passed—yeas 125, nays 55, as follow:

YEAS—Messrs. Allison, Ambler, Arnell, Asper, Atwood, Ayer, Banks, Beaman, Beatty, Benjamin, Bingham, Blair, *Boles, Booker,* Bowen, Boyd, George M, Brooks, Buck, Buckley, Buffinton, Burchard, Burdett. Benjamin F. Butler, Roderick R. Butler, Cake, Cessna. Churchill, Clarke, Amasa Cobb, Clinton L. Cobb, Coburn, Cook, Conger, Cullom, Davis, Dawes, Dickey, Dockery, Donley, Duval, Ferriss, Ferry, Finkelnburg, Fisher, Garfield, Gilfillan, Hale, Hamilton, Harris, Hawley, Hay, Heaton, Heflin, Hill, Hoar, Hoge, Hooper, Hotchkiss, Ingersoll, Jenckes, Alexander H. Jones. Judd, Julian, Kelley, Kellogg, Ketcham, Knapp, Laflin, Lash, Lawrence, Logan, Loughridge, Lynch, McCarthy, McCrary, *McKenzie,* Mercur, Eliakim H. Moore, Jesse H. Moore, William Moore, Morrell, Morrill, Myers, Negley, O'Neill, Orth, Packard, Packer, Paine, Phelps, Platt, Pomeroy, Prosser, Roots, Sanford, Sargent, Sawyer, Schenck, Scofield, Shanks, John A. Smith, William J. Smith, Worthington C. Smith, William Smyth, Starkweather, Stokes, Stoughton, Strickland, Strong, Tillman, Townsend, Twichell, Tyner, Upson, Van Horn, Cadwalader C. Washburn, William B. Washburn, Welker, Wheeler, Wilkinson, Willard, Williams, John T. Wilson, Winans, Witcher—125.

NAYS—Messrs. *Adams, Archer, Axtell, Beck, Biggs, Bird, Burr, Calkin, Cleveland, Cox, Crebs, Dickinson, Dox, Eldridge, Getz, Griswold, Haight, Haldeman, Hambleton, Hamill,* Hawkins, *Holman, Johnson, Thomas L. Jones, Kerr, Knott, Marshall, Mayham, McCormick, McNeely, Milnes Niblack, Potter, Randall, Reading, Reeves, Rice, Rogers, Schumaker, Sherrod, Slocum.* Stevenson, *Stiles, Stone, Strader, Swann,* Tanner, *Trimble, Van Auken, Van Trump, Voorhees, Wells, Eugene M. Wilson, Wood, Woodward*—55.

## IN SENATE.

1870, March 18—Mr. Morton moved to amend by inserting at the end of the bill as follows:

SEC. 2. That so much of the act entitled "An act making appropriations for the support of the army for the year ending June 30, 1868, and for other purposes," approved March 2, 1867, as prohibits the organization, arming, or calling into service of the militia forces in the State of Georgia, be, and the same is hereby, repealed.

Which was agreed to.

April 14—Mr. Williams moved to strike out the last clause of the Bingham proviso and insert as follows:

*Provided further,* That the next election for members of the general assembly of said State shall be held on the Tuesday after the first Monday of November, A. D. 1872, and the last clause of the second subdivision of the 1st section of the IIId article of said constitution, in the following words: "The general assembly may, by law, change the time of election, and the members shall hold until their successors are elected and qualified," shall never be by any legislature exercised so as to extend the term of any office beyond the regular period named in the said constitution; and the said general assembly shall, by joint resolution, consent to this proviso as a fundamental condition before this act shall take effect.

Which was disagreed to—yeas 24, nays 25, as follow:

YEAS—Messrs. Abbott, Ames, Boreman, Chandler, Cole, Drake, Fenton, Flanagan, Gilbert, Hamilton of Texas, Howard. Howell, Lewis, Nye, Osborn, Ramsey, Rice, Spencer, Stewart, Sumner, Thayer, Warner, Williams, Wilson—24.

NAYS—Messrs. Anthony, Buckingham. Carpenter, *Casserly,* Corbett, *Davis,* Ferry, Fowler, *William T. Hamilton,* Howe, *Johnston, McCreery,* Morrill of Maine, Morrill of Vermont, Patterson, Pratt, Schurz, Scott, Sherman, Sprague, *Stockton,* Tipton, Trumbull, *Vickers,* Willey—25.

April 19—Mr. Wilson moved to strike out the Bingham proviso, and to insert, "That in consequence of the failure of the general assembly of Georgia to effect a legal organization for a period of over eighteen months it be, and hereby is, declared that the term of service of the said general assembly as now organized shall date from the 26th of January, 1870, and shall continue until the persons to be chosen on the Tuesday after the 1st Monday of November, 1872, as members of the general assembly of said State, are qualified: *Provided,* That the last clause of the second subdivision of the first section of the third article of the constitution of Georgia, in the following words: 'The general assembly may by law change the time of election, and the members shall hold until their successors are elected and qualified,' shall never be by any legislature exercised so as to extend the term of any office beyond the regular period

named in the said constitution; and the said general assembly shall, by joint resolution, consent to this fundamental condition before this act shall take effect."

Mr. Pomeroy moved to amend the amendment of Mr. Wilson by striking out all after the word "that" in the first line and inserting as follows: "The existing government in the State of Georgia is hereby declared to be provisional; and the same shall continue subject to the provisions of the acts of Congress of March 2, 1867, and March 23, 1867, and of July 19, 1867, until the admission of said State, by law, to representation in Congress; and for this purpose the State of Georgia shall constitute the third military district.

"SEC. 2. That in accordance with the provisions of, and under the powers and limitations provided in, said acts, an election shall be held in said State on the 15th day of November, 1870, for all the members of the general assembly of said State provided for in the constitution of said State, adopted by its convention on the 11th day of March, 1868, at which election all persons who by said constitution are electors shall be entitled to vote. And said general assembly, so elected, shall assemble at the capitol of said State, on Tuesday, the 13th day of December, 1870, and organize, preparatory to the admission of the State to representation in Congress; and the powers and functions of the members of the existing general assembly shall cease and determine on the said 13th day of December, 1870."

Mr. Pomeroy's amendment was agreed to—yeas 37, nays 24, as follow:

YEAS—Messrs. Abbott, Ames, Anthony, Buckingham, Carpenter, *Casserly,* Cole, Corbett, Cragin, *Davis,* Edmunds, Ferry, Fowler, *Hamilton* of Maryland, Hamlin, Harlan, Howe, Kellogg, *McCreery,* Morrill of Maine, Morrill of Vermont, Patterson, Pomeroy, Pool, Pratt, Robertson, *Saulsbury,* Sawyer, Schurz, Scott, Sherman, *Stockton, Thurman,* Tipton, Trumbull, Warner, Willey—37.

NAYS—Messrs. Boreman, Brownlow, Drake, Fenton, Flanagan, Hamilton of Texas, Harris, Howard, Howell, McDonald, Morton. Nye, Osborn, Ramsey, Revels, Rice, Ross, Spencer, Stewart, Sumner, Thayer, Williams, Wilson, Yates—24.

Mr. Wilson's amendment as amended was agreed to—yeas 36, nays 23, as follow:

YEAS—Messrs. Abbott, Ames, Anthony, Brownlow, Buckingham, Carpenter, *Casserly,* Cole, Corbett, *Davis,* Edmunds, Ferry, Fowler, *Hamilton* of Maryland, Hamlin, Harlan, Howe, Kellogg, *McCreery,* Morrill of Maine, Morrill of Vermont, Patterson, Pomeroy, Pool, Pratt, Robertson, *Saulsbury,* Sawyer, Schurz, Scott, Sherman, *Stockton, Thurman,* Tipton, Warner, Willey—36.

NAYS—Messrs. Boreman, Drake, Fenton, Flanagan, Hamilton of Texas, Harris, Howard, Howell, McDonald, Morton, Nye, Osborn, Revels, Rice, Ross, Spencer, Stewart, Sumner, Thayer, Trumbull, Williams, Wilson, Yates—23.

Mr. Wilson then moved to postpone the bill indefinitely; which was disagreed to—yeas 23, nays 39, as follow:

YEAS—Messrs. Boreman, Chandler, Drake, Fenton, Flanagan, Hamilton of Texas, Harris, Howard, Howell, McDonald, Morton, Nye, Osborn, Ramsey, Revels, Rice, Spencer, Stewart, Sumner, Thayer, Williams, Wilson, Yates—23.

NAYS—Messrs. Abbott, Ames, Anthony, Brownlow, Buckingham, Carpenter, *Casserly,* Cole. Corbett, Cragin, *Davis,* Edmunds, Ferry, Fowler, *Hamilton* of Maryland, Hamlin, Harlan, Howe, Kellogg, *McCreery,* Morrill of Maine, Morrill of Vermont, Patterson, Pomeroy, Pool, Pratt, Robertson, Ross, *Saulsbury,* Sawyer, Schurz,

Scott, Sherman, *Stockton*, *Thurman*, Tipton, Trumbull, Warner, Willey—39.

Mr. Pomeroy moved further to amend by striking out all of the bill except the amendment just adopted; which was agreed to—yeas 38, nays 23, as follow:

YEAS—Messrs. Abbott, Ames, Anthony, Brownlow, Buckingham. Carpenter, *Casserly*, Cole, Corbett, Cragin, *Davis*, Drake, Edmunds, Ferry, Fowler, *Hamilton* of Maryland, Hamlin, Harlan, Howe, Kellogg, *McCreery*, Morrill of Maine, Morrill of Vermont. Patterson, Pomeroy, Pool, Pratt, Robertson, *Saulsbury*, Sawyer, Schurz, Scott, Sherman, *Stockton*, Tipton, Trumbull, Warner, Willey—38.

NAYS—Messrs. Boreman, Chandler, Fenton, Flanagan, Hamilton of Texas, Harris, Howard, Howell, McDonald, Morton, Nye, Osborn, Ramsey, Revels, Rice, Ross, Spencer, Stewart, Sumner, Thayer, Williams, Wilson, Yates—23.

Mr. Drake moved to add the following section:

SEC. —. That whenever it shall appear to the President, from an application by the legislature of any State, or by the governor of such State when the legislature cannot be convened, that there exist in such State organizations or combinations of men engaged in the perpetration of acts of violence against the persons or property of others, or in obstructing the due execution of the laws of such State, and that the government of such State is unable to suppress the perpetration of such acts of violence or obstruction, the county or district wherein such organizations or combinations exist shall be considered as in a state of rebellion, and it shall be the duty of the President to send into such county or district such number of the troops of the United States as may be necessary for the suppression of such acts of violence or obstruction and the subjugation and dispersion of such organizations and combinations; and the officer commanding such troops, upon arriving in such county or district, shall declare martial law over the same, with suspension of the writ of *habeas corpus*, if such declaration and suspension be authorized by the President, and in that case shall take all measures known to martial law for the suppression of such organizations and combinations and the punishment of parties engaged therein, and shall hold and maintain military jurisdiction over all persons arrested by his order until their cases shall be finally disposed of; and shall proceed to levy upon and collect from the inhabitants of such county or district a sum of money sufficient to pay the expenses of the transportation of such troops from the point whence they were ordered to the point of their operations in such county or district, and all other expenses of his command, except pay and clothing, while such command shall be there stationed for the purpose aforesaid. And this section shall apply to any case where the President may have heretofore sent a military force into any State, upon the request of the legislature or governor thereof, for the suppression of domestic violence. And if the army of the United States shall be so stationed or employed as that it cannot, in the judgment of the President, be advantageously used for this service, he shall call out and organize a sufficient number of the militia of States which have not at any time been in armed hostility to the United States to accomplish such suppression; and the provisions of this section shall apply to the militia so called out and organized.

Mr. Hamlin moved to strike out all of this amendment after the word "combinations" in the 19th line; which was agreed to—yeas 32, nays 24, as follow:

YEAS—Messrs. Anthony, Boreman, Buckingham, Carpenter, *Casserly*, Cole, Cragin, *Davis*, Edmunds, Ferry, Fowler, *Hamilton* of Maryland, Hamlin, Harlan, Howe, Howell, Morrill of Maine, Morrill of Vermont, Pomeroy, Pratt, Robertson, *Saulsbury*, Sawyer, Schurz, Scott, Sherman, Stewart, *Stockton*, *Thurman*, Tipton, Trumbull, Willey—32

NAYS—Messrs. Abbott, Ames, Brownlow, Chandler, Corbett, Drake, Flanagan, Hamilton of Texas, Harris, Howard, McDonald, Nye, Osborn, Pool, Ramsey, Revels, Rice, Ross, Spencer, Sumner, Thayer, Warner, Wilson, Yates—24.

Mr. Drake then asked and obtained consent to withdraw the remainder of his amendment.

Mr. Drake then moved to amend by inserting the following additional section:

SEC. —. That whenever it shall appear to the President, from an application by the legislature of any State, or by the governor of such State when the legislature cannot be convened, that domestic violence prevails in any city, county, or municipal organization in such State, tha cannot be suppressed by the local authorities, i¹ shall be the duty of the President to suppress such domestic violence; and for that purpose he is hereby authorized to suspend the privilege of the writ of *habeas corpus* within the limits of such municipality, and to employ the military force of the United States, and any portion of the militia of any State he may deem necessary, and to exercise all such powers and inflict such punishment as may by the laws or the rules and articles of war be exercised or inflicted in case of insurrection or invasion.

Which was disagreed to—yeas 30, nays 31, as follow:

YEAS—Messrs. Abbott, Ames, Brownlow, Chandler, Cragin, Drake, Fenton, Flanagan, Hamilton of Texas, Harris, Howard, Kellogg, McDonald, Morton, Nye, Osborn, Pool, Pratt, Ramsey, Revels, Rice, Robertson, Sherman, Spencer, Stewart, Sumner, Thayer, Warner, Wilson, Yates—30.

NAYS—Messrs. Anthony, Boreman, Buckingham, Carpenter, *Casserly*, Cole, Corbett, *Davis*, Edmunds, Ferry, Fowler, *Hamilton* of Maryland, Hamlin, Harlan. Howe, Howell, *McCreery*, Morrill of Maine, Morrill of Vermont, Pomeroy, Ross, *Saulsbury*, Sawyer, Schurz, Scott, *Stockton*, *Thurman*, Tipton, Trumbull, Willey, Williams—31.

The same section was again proposed, modified at the suggestion of Mr. Sherman, as follows:

SEC. —. That whenever it shall appear to the President, from an application by the legislature of any State, or by the governor of such State when the legislature cannot be convened, that domestic violence prevails in any city, county, or municipal organization in such State, that cannot be suppressed by the local authorities, it shall be the duty of the President to suppress such domestic violence, and for that purpose he is hereby authorized to employ the military force of the United States, and any portion of the militia of any State he may deem necessary, and to exercise all such powers and inflict such punishment as may by the laws or the rules and articles of war be exercised or inflicted in case of insurrection or invasion.

Which was agreed to—yeas 32, nays 26, as follow:

YEAS—Messrs. Abbott, Ames, Chandler, Drake, Fenton, Flanagan, Hamilton of Texas, Hamlin, Harlan, Harris, Howard, McDonald, Morton, Nye, Osborn, Patterson, Pool, Pratt, Ramsey, Revels, Rice, Robertson, Scott, Sherman, Spencer. Stewart, Sumner, Thayer, Warner, Williams, Wilson, Yates—32.

NAYS—Messrs. Anthony, Boreman, Buckingham, Carpenter, *Casserly*, Cole, Corbett, *Davis*, Edmunds, Ferry, Fowler, *Hamilton* of Maryland, Howe, Howell, *Mc-Creery*, Morrill of Maine, Morrill of Vermont, Pomeroy, Ross, *Saulsbury*, Sawyer, *Stockton*, *Thurman*, Tipton, Trumbull, Willey—26.

Mr. Pomeroy moved to amend the preamble to read as follows:

Whereas great irregularities have been practiced in the organization of the Legislature in the State of Georgia, both in its first organization and in the expulsion of certain members, as well also as in its reorganization since the act of December last: Therefore,

Which was agreed to.

Mr. Edmunds moved to insert at the end of Mr. Drake's amendment the words "but the provisions of this section shall not be construed to suspend the writ of *habeas corpus.*"

Which was disagreed to—yeas 29, nays 30, as follow:

YEAS—Messrs. Anthony, Buckingham, Carpenter, *Casserly*, Cole, *Davis*, Edmunds, Ferry, Fowler, *Hamilton* of Maryland, Hamlin, Howe, Howell, *McCreery*, Morrill of Maine, Morrill of Vermont, Patterson, Pomeroy, Ross, *Saulsbury*, Sawyer, Schurz, Scott, *Stockton*, *Thurman*, Tipton, Trumbull, Willey, Williams—29

NAYS—Messrs. Abbott, Ames, Boreman, Chandler, Corbett, Cragin, Drake, Fenton, Flanagan, Hamilton of Texas, Harris, Howard, McDonald, Morton, Nye, Osborn, Pool, Pratt, Ramsey, Revels, Rice, Robertson, Sherman, Spencer, Stewart, Sumner, Thayer, Warner, Wilson, Yates—30.

Mr. Pomeroy moved to insert the following additional section:

SEC. —. That so much of the act entitled "An act making appropriations for the support of the army for the year ending June 30, 1868, and for other purposes," approved March 2, 1867, as prohibits the organization, arming, or calling into service of the militia forces in the State of Georgia be, and the same is hereby, repealed.

Which was agreed to—yeas 48, nays 9, as follow:

YEAS—Messrs. Abbott, Ames, Anthony, Boreman, Buckingham, Carpenter, Chandler, Cole, Corbett, Drake, Edmunds, Fenton, Ferry, Flanagan, Hamilton of Texas, Harris, Howard, Howell, Kellogg, McDonald, Morrill of Maine, Morrill of Vermont, Morton, Nye, Osborn, Patterson, Pomeroy, Pool, Pratt, Ramsey, Revels, Rice, Robertson, Ross, Schurz, Scott, Sherman, Spencer, Stewart, Sumner, Thayer, Tipton, Trumbull, Warner, Willey, Williams, Wilson, Yates—48.

NAYS—Messrs. *Casserly*, Fowler, *Hamilton* of Maryland, Hamlin, Howe, *McCreery*, *Saulsbury*, Sawyer, *Stockton*—9.

The bill then passed—yeas 27, nays 25, as follow:

YEAS—Messrs. Ames, Anthony, Buckingham, Carpenter, Cole, Corbett, Cragin, Edmunds, Ferry, Hamlin, Howe, Kellogg, Morrill of Maine, Morrill of Vermont, Patterson, Pomeroy, Pool, Pratt, Robertson, Ross, Sawyer, Schurz, Scott, Sherman, Tipton, Warner, Willey—27.

NAYS—Messrs. Boreman, Chandler, Drake, Fenton, Flanagan, Fowler, Hamilton of Texas, Harris, Howard, Howell, McDonald, Morton, Nye, Osborn, Ramsey, Revels, Rice, Spencer, Stewart, Sumner, Thayer, Trumbull, Williams, Wilson, Yates—25.

The bill, as finally passed, stood as follows:

Whereas great irregularities have been practiced in the organization of the legislature in the State of Georgia, both in its first organization and in the expulsion of certain members, as well also as in its reorganization since the act of December last: Therefore,

*Be it enacted, &c.,* That the existing government in the State of Georgia is hereby declared to be provisional; and the same shall continue subject to the provisions of the acts of Congress of March 2, 1867, and March 23, 1867, and of

July 19, 1867, until the admission of said State, by law, to representation in Congress; and for this purpose the State of Georgia shall constitute the third military district.

SEC. 2. That in accordance with the provisions of, and under the powers and limitations provided in, said acts, an election shall be held in said State, commencing on the 15th of November, 1870, and continuing as the President may designate, for all the members of the general assembly of said State provided for in the constitution of said State, adopted by its convention on the 11th day of March, 1868; at which election all persons who by said constitution are electors shall be entitled to vote. And said general assembly so elected shall assemble at the capitol of said State, on Tuesday, the 13th day of December, 1870, and organize preparatory to the admission of the State to representation in Congress; and the powers and functions of the members of the existing general assembly shall cease and determine on the said 13th day of December, 1870.

SEC. 3. That whenever it shall appear to the President, from an application by the legislature of any State, or by the governor of such State when the legislature cannot be convened, that domestic violence prevails in any city, county, or municipal organization in such State, that cannot be suppressed by the local authorities, it shall be the duty of the President to suppress such domestic violence, and for that purpose he is hereby authorized to employ the military force of the United States, and any portion of the militia of any State he may deem necessary, and to exercise all such powers and inflict such punishment as may by the laws or the rules and articles of war be exercised or inflicted in case of insurrection or invasion.

SEC. 4. That so much of the act entitled "An act making appropriations for the support of the army for the year ending June 30, 1868, and for other purposes," approved March 2, 1867, as prohibited the organization, arming, or calling into service of the militia forces in the State of Georgia be, and the same is hereby, repealed.

IN HOUSE.

1870, June 24—Mr. B. F. Butler, from the Committee on Reconstruction, reported back the Senate amendment, with the recommendation that the bill previously reported by him be passed, with an addition to the 1st section, as follows: but nothing in this act shall be construed to deprive the people of Georgia of the right to elect members of the general assembly of said State in the year 1870, as provided in the constitution of said State; and also the following additional section:

SEC. 2. That so much of the act entitled "An act making appropriations for the support of the army for the year ending June 30, 1868, and for other purposes," approved March 2, 1867, as prohibits the organization, arming, or calling into service of the militia forces in the States of Georgia, Mississippi, Texas, and Virginia, be, and the same is hereby, repealed.

Mr. Dawes moved to amend by substituting for the Senate amendment as follows:

SEC. 1. That the State of Georgia, having complied with the reconstruction acts, and the XIVth and XVth amendments to the Constitution of the United States having been ratified in good faith by a legal legislature of said State, it is hereby declared that the State of Georgia is entitled to representation in the Congress of the United States.

SEC. 2. That so much of the act entitled "An act making appropriations for the support of the army for the year ending June 30, 1868, and for other purposes," approved March 2, 1867, as prohibits the organization, arming, or calling into service of the militia forces in the States of Georgia, Mississippi, Texas, and Virginia, be, and the same is hereby, repealed.

Mr. Farnsworth moved to amend Mr. Dawes's substitute by inserting at the end of the 1st section as follows:

But nothing in this act contained shall be construed to deprive the people of Georgia of the right to an election for members of the general assembly of said State in the year 1870, as provided for in the constitution of said State.

Mr. Dickey moved to amend Mr. Farnsworth's amendment by striking out the words "in the year 1870;" which was agreed to—yeas 122, nays 71, as follow:

YEAS—Messrs. Allison, Ambler, Ames, Armstrong, Arnell, Asper, Atwood, Bailey, Banks, Barry, Benjamin, Bennett, Benton, Boles, Boyd, George M. Brooks, Buck, Buckley, Buffinton, Burchard, Burdett, Benjamin F. Butler, Cessna, Churchill, William T. Clark, Sidney Clarke, Amasa Cobb, Clinton L. Cobb, Coburn, Conger, Cook, Covode, Cullom, Davis, Dawes, Degener, Dixon, Donley, Dyer, Ela, Ferriss, Ferry, Fisher, Fitch, Gilfillan, Hale, Hamilton, Harris, Hay, Hays, Heflin, Hill, Hoar, Hooper, Ingersoll, Alexander H. Jones, Judd, Julian, Kelley, Kelsey, Ketcham, Knapp, Lash, Lawrence, Logan, Loughridge, Maynard, McCrary, McKee, William Moore, Morphis, Daniel J. Morrell, Myers, Negley, Newsham, O'Neill, Packard, Packer, Paine, Palmer, Peck, Perce, Peters, Phelps, Platt, Poland, Pomeroy, Porter, Prosser, Roots, Sanford, Sargent, Sawyer, Scofield, Shanks, Lionel A. Sheldon, Porter Sheldon, William J. Smith, William Smyth, Starkweather, Stevens, Stevenson, Stokes, Stoughton, Strong, Taffe, Taylor, Tillman, Twichell, Tyner, Van Horn, Van Wyck, Wallace, Ward, Cadwalader C. Washburn, William B. Washburn, Welker, Wheeler, Whitmore, Wilkinson, Williams, John T. Wilson—122.

NAYS—Messrs. *Adams, Archer, Axtell*, Beaman, Beatty, *Beck, Biggs*, Bingham, *Bird*, Blair, *James Brooks, Burr, Calkin, Cleveland, Conner, Cox, Crebs, Dickinson*, Dockery, *Dox, Eldridge*, Farnsworth, Finkelnburg, Garfield, *Getz, Griswold, Haight, Haldeman, Hambleton*, Hawkins, *Holman*, Jenckes, *Johnson, Thomas L. Jones*, Kellogg, Knott, Laflin, *Lewis, Marshall, Mayham, McCormick, McKenzie, McNeely*, Jesse H. Moore, *Morgan, Morrissey, Mungen, Niblack*, Orth, *Potter, Reeves, Rice, Rogers, Schumaker, Sherrod, Shober*, Slocum, John A. Smith, *Joseph S. Smith, Stiles, Stone, Sweeney, Trimble*, Upson, *Van Auken, Van Trump, Wells, Eugene M. Wilson*, Winans, *Wood, Woodward*—71.

Mr. Farnsworth's amendment, as amended, was then agreed to—yeas 98, nays 90, as follow:

YEAS—Messrs. *Adams*, Allison, Ambler, *Archer, Axtell*, Beaman, Beatty, *Beck*, Benjamin, Bingham, *Bird*, Blair, Booker, *James Brooks*, Burchard, *Burr, Calkin, Cleveland, Conner*, Cook, *Crebs*, Cullom, *Dickinson*, Dockery, *Dox, Eldridge*, Farnsworth, Ferris, Ferry, Finkelnburg, Fitch, Garfield, *Getz, Griswold, Haight, Haldeman*, Hale, *Hambleton*, Hawkins, Hay, *Holman*, Ingersoll, Jenckes, *Johnson, Thomas L. Jones*, Judd, Kellogg, Ketcham, Knott, Laflin, *Lewis*, Logan, *Marshall, Mayham, McCormick, McKenzie, McNeely*, Jesse H. Moore, *Morgan*, Daniel J. Morrell, *Morrissey, Mungen, Niblack*, Orth, Packard, Paine, Peters, Poland, *Potter, Reeves, Rice, Rogers*, Sargent, *Schumaker, Sherrod, Shober*, Slocum, John A. Smith, *Joseph S. Smith*, Starkweather, *Stiles, Stone*, Strong, *Sweeney*, Taffe, *Trimble*, Tyner, Upson, *Van Auken, Van Trump*, Cadwalader C. Washburn, William B. Washburn, *Wells*, Williams, *Eugene M. Wilson*, Winans, *Wood*, Woodward—98.

NAYS—Messrs. Ames, Armstrong, Arnell, Asper, Atwood, Bailey, Barry, Bennett, Benton, Boles, G. M. Brooks, Buck, Buckley, Buffinton, Burdett, Benjamin F. Butler, Cessna, Churchill, William T. Clark, Sidney Clarke,

Amasa Cobb, Clinton L. Cobb, Coburn, Conger, Covode, Davis, Dawes, Degener, Dixon, Donley, Dyer, Ela, Fisher, Gilfillan, Hamilton, Harris, Hays, Heflin, Hill, Hoar, Hooper, Alexander H. Jones, Julian, Kelley, Kelsey, Knapp, Lash, Lawrence, Loughridge, Maynard, McCrary, McKee, William Moore, Morphis, Myers, Negley, Newsham, O'Neill, Palmer, Peck, Perce, Phelps, Platt, Pomeroy, Porter, Prosser, Sanford, Sawyer, Scofield, Shanks, Porter Sheldon, William J Smith, William Smyth, Stevens, Stevenson, Stokes, Stoughton, Strickland, Taylor, Tillman, Twichell, Van Horn, Van Wyck, Wallace, Ward, Welker, Wheeler, Whitmore, Wilkinson, John T. Wilson—90.

Mr. Lawrence moved to amend Mr. Dawes's substitute further by adding as follows:

SEC. —. That the State of Georgia is admitted to representation in Congress as one of the States of the Union, upon the following fundamental conditions: 1st, that it shall never be lawful for the said State to deprive any citizen of the United States, on account of his race, color, or previous condition of servitude, of the right to hold office under the constitution and laws of said State, or upon any such ground to require of him any other qualifications for office than such as are required of all other citizens; 2d, that the constitution of Georgia shall never be so amended or changed as to deprive any citizen or class of citizens of the United States of the school rights and privileges secured by the constitution of said State.

Which, on a division, was rejected—yeas 48, nays 74.

The amendment of Mr. Dawes was then substituted for the Senate amendment without a division—making the bill to stand as follows:

The State of Georgia having complied with the reconstruction acts, and the XIVth and XVth articles of amendments to the Constitution of the United States having been ratified in good faith by a legal legislature of said State, it is hereby declared that the State of Georgia is entitled to representation in the Congress of the United States. But nothing in this act contained shall be construed to deprive the people of Georgia of the right to an election for members of the general assembly of said State as provided for in the constitution thereof.

SEC. 2. That so much of the act entitled "An act making appropriations for the support of the army for the year ending June 30, 1868, and for other purposes," approved March 2, 1867, as prohibits the organization, arming, or calling into service of the militia forces in the States of Georgia, Mississippi, Texas, and Virginia, be, and the same is hereby, repealed.

IN SENATE.

July 8.—The amendments of the House were non-concurred in, and a committee of conference asked, by the following vote:

YEAS—Messrs. Abbott, *Bayard*, Buckingham, Carpenter, *Casserly*, Cole, Conkling, Corbett, Cragin, Fowler, *Hamilton* of Maryland, Hamlin, Harlan, Harris, Howe, *Johnston*, Kellogg, *McCreery*, Morrill of Vermont, Patterson, Pomeroy, Pratt, Ross, *Saulsbury*, Sawyer, Schurz, Scott, Sprague, *Stockton, Thurman*, Trumbull. Warner, Willey, Wilson—34.

NAYS—Messrs. Ames, Boreman, Cameron, Chandler, Drake, Gilbert, Hamilton of Texas, Howard, Howell, Lewis, Morton, Nye, Pool, Ramsey, Rice, Robertson, Spencer, Stewart, Sumner, Thayer, Williams, Yates—22.

Messrs. Howard, Hamlin, and Thurman were appointed such committee on the part of the Senate, and Messrs. B. F. Butler, Farnsworth, and Paine on the part of the House, who reported the bill as passed above.

# LXI.

## MISCELLANEOUS.

### President's Message on European war and American shipping.

*To the Senate and House of Representatives:*

Your attention is respectfully called to the necessity of passing an Indian appropriation bill before the members of Congress separate. Without such appropriation Indian hostilities are sure to ensue, and with them sufferings, loss of life, and expenditures, vast as compared with the amount asked for.

The latest intelligence from Europe indicates the imminence of a war between France and North Germany. In view of this a sound policy indicates the importance of some legislation tending to enlarge the commercial marine of this country

The vessels of this country at the present time are insufficient to meet the demand which the existence of a war in Europe will impose upon the commerce of the United States, and I submit to the consideration of Congress that the interests of the country will be advanced by the opportunity to our citizens to purchase vessels of foreign construction for the foreign trade of the country. An act to this effect may be limited in its duration to meet the immediate exigency.

The foreign mail service of the United States is in a large degree dependent upon the Bremen and Hamburg line of steamers. The Post Office Department has entered into contracts in writing with the two companies above named, and with the Williams and Guion lines respectively for a regular and continuous service of two years.

The only arrangement that could be made with the Inman and Cunard lines is temporary, and may be broken off at any time. The North German lines are first-class in point of speed and equipment, their steamers usually making the trip across the Atlantic in from twenty-four to thirty-six hours in advance of the Williams and Guion line. Should the North German steamers be blockaded or impeded by France, our postal intercourse with foreign nations will be greatly embarrassed, unless Congress shall interpose for its relief.

I suggest to Congress the propriety of further postponing the time for adjournment, with the view of considering the questions herein communicated.                     U. S. GRANT.

WASHINGTON, D. C., *July* 15, 1870.

This message was sent to Congress too late for insertion in the chapter of President Grant's messages.

---

### AN ACT to amend the naturalization laws and to punish crimes against the same.

*Be it enacted, &c.,* That in all cases where any oath, affirmation, or affidavit shall be made or taken under or by virtue of any act or law relating to the naturalization of aliens, or in any proceedings under such acts or laws, and any person or persons taking or making such oath, affirmation, or affidavit, shall knowingly swear or affirm falsely, the same shall be deemed and taken to be perjury, and the person or persons guilty thereof shall upon conviction thereof be sentenced to imprisonment for a term not exceeding five years and not less than one year, and to a fine not exceeding $1,000.

SEC. 2. That if any person applying to be admitted a citizen, or appearing as a witness for any such person, shall knowingly personate any other person than himself, or falsely appear in the name of a deceased person, or in an assumed or fictitious name, or if any person shall falsely make, forge, or counterfeit any oath, affirmation, notice, affidavit, certificate, order, record, signature, or other instrument, paper, or proceeding required or authorized by any law or act relating to or providing for the naturalization of aliens; or shall alter, sell, dispose of, or use as true or genuine, or for any unlawful purpose, any false, forged, ante-dated, or counterfeit oath, affirmation, notice, certificate, order, record, signature, instrument, paper, or proceeding as aforesaid; or sell or dispose of, to any person other than the person for whom it was originally issued, any certificate of citizenship or certificate showing any person to be admitted a citizen; or if any person shall in any manner use, for the purpose of registering as a voter, or as evidence of a right to vote, or otherwise, unlawfully, any order, certificate of citizenship, or certificate, judgment, or exemplifications showing such person to be admitted to be a citizen, whether heretofore or hereafter issued or made, knowing that such order or certificate, judgment, or exemplification has been unlawfully issued or made; or if any person shall unlawfully use, or attempt to use, any such order or certificate, issued to or in the name of any other person, or in a fictitious name, or the name of a deceased person; or use, or attempt to use, or aid, or assist or participate in the use of any certificate of citizenship, knowing the same to be forged, or counterfeit, or ante-dated, or knowing the same to have been procured by fraud, or otherwise unlawfully obtained; or if any person, and without lawful excuse, shall knowingly have or be possessed of any false, forged, ante-dated, or counterfeit certificate of citizenship, purporting to have been issued under the provisions of any law of the United States relating to naturalization, knowing such certificate to be false, forged, ante-dated, or counterfeit, with intent unlawfully to use the same; or if any person shall obtain, accept, or receive any certificate of citizenship known to such person to have been procured by fraud or by the use of any false name, or by means of any false statement made with intent to procure, or to aid in procuring, the issue of such certificate, or known to such person to be fraudulently altered or ante-dated; or if any person who has been or may be admitted to be a citizen shall, on oath or affirmation or by affidavit, knowingly deny that he has been so admitted, with intent to evade or avoid any duty or liability imposed or required by law, every person so offending shall be deemed and adjudged guilty of felony, and, on conviction thereof, shall be sentenced to be imprisoned and kept at hard labor for a period not less than one year nor more than five years, or be fined in a sum not less than $300 nor more than $1,000, or both such punishments may be imposed, in the discretion of the court. And every person who shall knowingly and intentionally aid or abet any person in the commission of any such felony, or attempt to do any act hereby made felony, or counsel, advise, or procure, or attempt to procure, the commission thereof, shall be liable to indictment and punishment in the same manner and to the same extent as the principal party guilty of such felony, and such person may be tried and convicted thereof without the previous conviction of such principal.

SEC. 3. That any person who shall knowingly use any certificate of naturalization heretofore granted by any court, or which shall hereafter be granted, which has been or shall be procured through fraud, or by false evidence, or has been or shall be issued by the clerk, or any other officer of the court, without any appearance and hearing of the applicant in court, and without lawful authority, and any person who shall falsely represent himself to be a citizen of the United States, without having been duly admitted to citizenship, for any fraudulent purpose whatever, shall be deemed guilty of a misdemeanor, and, upon conviction thereof in due course of law, shall be sentenced to pay a fine of not exceeding $1,000, or be imprisoned not exceeding two years, either or both, in the discretion of the court taking cognizance of the same.

SEC. 4. That the provisions of this act shall apply to all proceedings had or taken, or attempted to be had or taken, before any court in which any proceeding for naturalization shall be commenced, had, or taken, or attempted to be commenced; and the courts of the United States shall have jurisdiction of all offenses under the provisions of this act, in or before whatsoever court or tribunal the same shall have been committed.

SEC. 5. That in any city having upward of twenty thousand inhabitants, it shall be the duty of the judge of the circuit court of the United States for the circuit wherein said city shall be, upon the application of two citizens, to appoint in writing, for each election district or voting precinct in said city, and to change or renew said appointment as occasion may require, from time to time, two citizens resident of the district or precinct, one from each political party, who, when so designated, shall be, and are hereby, authorized to attend at all times and places fixed for the registration of voters, who being registered would be entitled to vote for representative in Congress, and at all times and places for holding elections of representatives in Congress, and for counting the votes cast at said elections, and to challenge any name proposed to be registered and any vote offered, and to be present and witness throughout the counting of all votes, and to remain where the ballot-boxes are kept at all times after the polls are open until the votes are finally counted; and said persons, and either of them, shall have the right to affix their signature or his signature to said register for purposes of identification, and to attach thereto, or to the certificate of the number of votes cast, and statement touching the truth or fairness thereof which they or he may ask to attach; and any one who shall prevent any person so designated from doing any of the acts authorized as aforesaid, or who shall hinder or molest any such person in doing any of the said acts, or shall aid or abet in preventing, hindering, or molesting any such person in respect of any such acts, shall be guilty of a misdemeanor, and on conviction shall be punished by imprisonment not less than one year.

SEC. 6. That in any city having upward of twenty thousand inhabitants, it shall be lawful for the marshal of the United States for the district wherein said city shall be to appoint as many special deputies as may be necessary to preserve order at any election at which representatives in Congress are to be chosen; and said deputies are hereby authorized to preserve order at such elections, and to arrest for any offense or breach of the peace committed in their view.

Sec. 7. That the naturalization laws are hereby extended to aliens of African nativity and to persons of African descent.

Approved July 14, 1870.

[Portions of this act and of the act to enforce the XIVth and XVth amendments are taken substantially from the report of the Committee on Alleged New York Election Frauds, 3d sess. 40th Cong., report 31, which treated of these questions.]

---

### Final Votes.

#### IN SENATE, *July* 4, 1870.

YEAS— Messrs. Anthony, Chandler, Conkling, Corbett, Cragin, Drake, Edmunds, Fenton, Gilbert, Hamlin, Harlan, McDonald, Morrill of Vermont, Morton, Nye, Osborn, Patterson, Pomeroy, Ramsey, Rice, Robertson, Sawyer, Scott, Spencer, Stewart, Sumner, Thayer, Tipton, Trumbull, Warner, Willey, Williams, Wilson—33.

NAYS—Messrs. *Bayard*, Boreman, *Hamilton* of Maryland, *McCreery, Saulsbury, Stockton, Thurman, Vickers*—8.

#### IN HOUSE, *June* 11, 1870.

YEAS—Messrs. Allison, Ambler, Ames, Armstrong, Asper, Atwood, Ayer, Bailey, Banks, Beatty, Benjamin, Benton, Bingham, Blair, Boles, Boyd, George M. Brooks, Buck, Buckley, Buffinton, Burchard, Burdett, Benjamin F. Butler, Roderick R. Butler, Cake, Churchill, William T. Clark, Sidney Clarke, Amasa Cobb, Coburn, Conger, Cook, Covode, Cowles, Cullom, Darrall, Davis, Dawes, Degener, Dickey, Donley, Duval, Ela, Farnsworth, Ferriss, Ferry, Finkelnburg, Fisher, Fitch, Garfield, Gilfillan, Hamilton, Harris, Hawley, Heflin, Hill, Hoar, Hooper, Ingersoll, Jenckes, Judd, Kelley, Kelsey, Ketcham, Knapp, Laflin, Lash, Lawrence, Logan, Loughridge, Maynard, McCarthy, McGrew, *McKenzie*, Mercur, Jesse H. Moore, William Moore, Morphis, Daniel J. Morrell, Myers, Negley, O'Neill, Orth, Packard, Packer, Paine, Palmer, Peck, Peters, Phelps, Platt, Poland, Porter, Prosser, Roots, Sargent, Sawyer, Schenck, Shanks, Lionel A. Sheldon, Porter Sheldon, John A. Smith, William J. Smith, Worthington C. Smith, William Smyth, Starkweather, Stevens, Stevenson, Stokes, Stoughton, Strickland, Taffe, Tanner, Tay lor, Tillman, Townsend, Twichell, Tyner, Upson, Van Horn, Van Wyck, Ward, Cadwalader C. Washburn, William B. Washburn, Welker, Wheeler, Whitmore, Wilkinson, Willard, Williams, John T. Wilson, Witcher—132.

NAYS—Messrs. *Axtell, Barnum, Beck, Bennett, Biggs, Bird, Booker, James Brooks, Burr, Calkin, Conner, Cox, Crebs, Dickinson. Fox, Getz, Griswold, Haight, Hay, Holman, Johnson, Thomas L. Jones, Kerr, Knott, Lewis, Marshall, Mayham, McCormick, McNeely, Milnes, Morgan, Mungen, Niblack, Potter, Randall, Reeves, Rice, Rogers, Schumaker, Sherrod, Slocum, Joseph S. Smith, Stiles, Stone, Swann, Sweeney, Trimble, Van Auken, Van Trump, Eugene M. Wilson, Winchester, Wood, Woodward—53.*

### Previous Votes.

1870, June 13—Mr. Davis introduced the bill, as finally passed, with the exception of the last three sections, which, under a suspension of the rules, was passed—yeas 130, nays 47, as follow:

YEAS—Messrs. Allison, Ambler, Ames, Armstrong, Arnell, Asper, Atwood, Bailey, Banks, Barry, Beaman, Beatty, Benjamin, Bennett, Benton, Bingham, Blair, *Booker*, Bowen, Boyd, George M. Brooks, Buck, Buckley, Buffinton, Burchard, Burdett, Benjamin F. Butler, Roderick R. Butler, Cessna, Churchill, William T. Clark, Sidney Clarke, Amasa Cobb, Clinton L. Cobb, Coburn, Cook, Conger, Cullom, Davis, Dawes, Dickey, Dixon, Dockery, Donley, Duval, Ela, Farnsworth, Ferriss, Ferry, Finkelnburg, Fisher, Fitch, Garfield, Gilfillan, Hale, Hamilton, Harris, Hawley, Hay, Heflin, Hill, Hoar, Hooper, Hotchkiss, Ingersoll, Alexander H. Jones, *Thomas L. Jones*, Judd, Julian, Kelley, Kellogg, Kelsey, Ketcham, Knapp, Laflin, Lash, Lawrence, Logan, Maynard, McCarthy, McCrary, McGrew, McKee, Mercur, Eliakim H. Moore, Jesse H. Moore, William Moore, Daniel J. Morrell, Samuel P. Morrill, Myers, Newsham, O'Neill, Orth, Packard, Paine, Palmer, Peck, Perce, Phelps, Platt, Poland, Pomeroy, Porter, *Roots*, Sanford, Sargent, Sawyer, Lionel A. Sheldon, John A. Smith, William Smyth, Stevenson, Stokes, Stoughton, Strickland, Taffe, Tanner, Tillman, Twichell, Tyner, Upson, Van Horn, Ward, Cadwalader C. Washburn, William B. Washburn, Wheeler, Whitmore, Wilkinson. Willard, Winans, Witcher—130.

NAYS—Messrs. *Adams, Axtell, Beck, James Brooks, Burr, Calkin, Conner, Cox, Crebs, Dox, Eldridge, Fox, Getz, Gibson, Griswold, Hamill, Holman, Johnson, Kerr, Knott, Lewis, Marshall, Mayham, McCormick, McNeely, Milnes, Morgan, Mungen, Niblack, Randall, Reeves, Rice, Ridgway, Sherrod, Shober, Joseph S. Smith, Strader, Swann, Sweeney, Trimble, Van Auken, Van Trump, Wells, Eugene M. Wilson, Winchester, Wood, Woodward—47.*

### IN SENATE.

1870, June 18—Mr. Conkling, from the Committee on the Judiciary, reported a bill with the recommendation that it be substituted for the House bill. It provided that all jurisdiction over naturalization should be in the United States courts; that the applicant must have resided in the United States four years and six months, and in the State one year prior to the application; that every certificate of naturalization issued since July 4, 1868, in any city of over 100,000 inhabitants, shall not be evidence of naturalization unless presented to the United States court, and by it approved; that the minor children of naturalized persons shall be citizens of the United States on attaining their majority; that in all cities of upward ·of 20,000 inhabitants the court shall select two persons from each precinct to act as judges of election and registration, and the marshal shall also appoint as many deputies as he shall deem necessary to keep the peace; provided for the punishment of the false and fraudulent issuing or using certificates of naturalization, or the disturbance of the court while sitting to grant certificates of naturalization.

July 2—Mr. Sumner moved to amend the proposed substitute by adding the following new section.

SEC. —. That all acts of Congress relating to naturalization be, and the same are hereby, amended by striking out the word "white" wherever it occurs, so that in naturalization there shall be no distinction of race or color.

Which was disagreed to—yeas 22, nays 23, as follow:

YEAS—Messrs. Anthony, Carpenter, Fowler, Hamlin, Harris, Kellogg, Lewis, McDonald, Morrill of Vermont, Pomeroy, Pratt, Ramsey, Revels, Rice, Robertson, Ross, Sawyer, Schurz, Scott, Sprague, Sumner, Trumbull—22.

NAYS—Messrs. *Bayard*, Boreman, *Casserly*, Corbett, Cragin, *Davis*, Drake, Edmunds, Gilbert, Harlan, Howe, Howell, *Johnston, McCreery*, Morton, Stewart, *Stockton, Thurman*, Tipton, *Vickers*, Warner, Williams, Wilson—23.

The substitute of the committee was then disagreed to—yeas 17, nays 33, as follow:

YEAS—Messrs. Anthony, Carpenter, Conkling, Cragin, Edmunds, Fenton, Hamlin, Morrill of Vermont, Patterson. Pomeroy, Rice, Sawyer, Scott, Stewart, Sumner, Trumbull. Wilson 17.

NAYS—Messrs. *Bayard*, Boreman, *Casserly*, Chandler, Corbett, *Davis*, Drake, Gilbert, Harlan, Harris, Howe, Howell, *Johnston*, Kellogg, Lewis, *McCreery*, McDonald, Morton, Pratt, Ramsey, Revels, Robertson, Ross, Shurz, Sprague, *Stockton*, Thayer, *Thurman*, Tipton, *Vickers*, Warner, Willey, Williams—33.

The question then recurring on the House bill, the Senate being in committee of the whole, Mr. Conkling moved to amend by the addition of the following sections, which were the last two sections of the committee's substitute:

SEC. —. That in any city having upward of twenty thousand inhabitants it shall be the duty of the judge of the circuit court of the United States for the circuit wherein said city shall be, upon the application of two citizens, to appoint in writing for each election district or voting precinct in said city, and to change or renew said appointment as occasion may require, from time to time, two citizens resident of the district or precinct, one from each political party, who, when so designated, shall be, and are hereby, authorized to attend at all times and places fixed for the registration of voters, who being registered would be entitled to vote for representative in Congress, and at all times and places for holding elections of representatives in Congress, and for counting the votes cast at said elections, and to challenge any name proposed to be registered and any vote offered, and to be present and witness throughout the counting of all votes, and to remain where the ballot-boxes are kept at all times after the polls are open until the votes are finally counted; and said persons and either of them shall have the right to affix their signature or his signature to said register for purposes of identification, and to attach thereto, or to the certificate of the number of votes cast, and statement touching the truth or fairness thereof which they or he may ask to attach; and any one who shall prevent any person so designated from doing any of the acts authorized as aforesaid, or who shall hinder or molest any such person in doing any of the said acts, or shall aid or abet in preventing, hindering, or molesting any such person in respect of any such acts, shall be guilty of a misdemeanor, and on conviction shall be punished by imprisonment not less than one year.

SEC. —. That in any city having upward of twenty thousand inhabitants, it shall be lawful for the marshal of the United States for the district wherein said city shall be to appoint as many special deputies as may be necessary to preserve order at any election at which representatives in Congress are to be chosen; and said deputies are hereby authorized to preserve order at such elections, and to arrest for any offense or breach of the peace committed in their view.

Which was agreed to—yeas 37, nays 9, as follow:

YEAS—Messrs. Anthony, Carpenter, Chandler, Conkling, Corbett, Cragin, Drake, Edmunds, Fenton, Gilbert, Hamlin, Harris, Howe, Howell, Kellogg, Lewis, McDonald. Morrill of Vermont, Morton, Patterson, Pomeroy, Pratt, Ramsey, Rice, Robertson, Sawyer, Scott, Sprague, Stewart, Sumner, Thayer, Tipton, Trumbull. Warner, Willey, Williams, Wilson—37.

NAYS—Messrs. *Bayard,* Boreman, *Casserly, Davis, Johnston, McCreery, Stockton, Thurman, Vickers—9.*

Mr. Sumner moved to amend by adding the following section:

SEC.—That all acts of Congress relating to naturalization be, and the same are hereby, amended by striking out the word "white" wherever it occurs; so that in naturalization there shall be no distinction of race or color.

Which was agreed to—yeas 27, nays 22, as follow:

YEAS—Messrs. Anthony, Carpenter, Conkling. Fenton, Fowler, Gilbert, Hamlin, Harris, Howe. Kellogg, Lewis. McDonald, Morrill of Vermont, Patterson, Pomeroy, Pratt, Ramsey, Rice, Robertson, Ross, Sawyer, Schurz, Scott, Sprague, Sumner, Thayer, Trumbull—27.

NAYS—Messrs. *Bayard,* Boreman, *Casserly,* Corbett, Cragin, *Davis,* Drake, Edmunds, Harlan, Howell, *Johnston, McCreery,* Morton, Stewart, *Stockton, Thurman,* Tipton, *Vickers,* Warner, Willey, Williams, Wilson—22.

July 4—Mr. Williams moved to add to the bill the following:

*Provided,* That nothing in this act shall be construed to authorize the naturalization of persons born in the Chinese empire.

Mr. Hamlin moved to reconsider the vote by which Mr. Sumner's amendment was adopted; which was agreed to—yeas 27, nays 14, as follow:

YEAS—Messrs. *Bayard,* Boreman, Chandler, Conkling, Corbett, Cragin, *Davis.* Drake, Edmunds, *Hamilton* of Maryland, Hamlin, Harlan, *McCreery,* Nye, Ramsey, *Saulsbury,* Scott, Stewart, *Stockton, Thurman,* Tipton, *Vickers,* Warner, Willey, Williams, Wilson—27.

NAYS—Messrs. Brownlow, Fenton, Harris, Kellogg, McDonald, Morrill of Maine, Pomeroy, Revels, Robertson, Ross, Spencer, Sprague, Sumner, Trumbull—14.

Mr. Howe moved to amend Mr. Sumner's amendment by adding as follows:

*Provided,* That nothing in this or any other act of Congress shall be so construed as to authorize the naturalization of any person born in a pagan country, unless with his oath of allegiance the applicant shall take and file an oath abjuring his belief in all forms of paganism.

Which was disagreed to.

Mr. Sumner's amendment was then disagreed to—yeas 14, nays 30, as follow:

YEAS—Messrs. Fenton, Fowler, Harris, Howe, McDonald, Morrill of Vermont, Pomeroy, Rice, Robertson, Ross, Spencer, Sprague, Sumner, Trumbull—14.

NAYS—Messrs. *Bayard,* Boreman, Chandler, Conkling, Corbett, Cragin, *Davis,* Drake, Edmunds, Gilbert, *Hamilton* of Maryland, Hamlin, Harlan, *McCreery,* Morton, Nye, Osborn, Ramsey, *Saulsbury,* Scott, Stewart, *Stockton,* Thayer, *Thurman,* Tipton, *Vickers,* Warner, Willey, Williams, Wilson—30.

Mr. Warner moved to add the following section:

SEC. —. That the naturalization laws are hereby extended to aliens of African nativity and to persons of African descent.

Which was agreed to—yeas 21, nays 20, as follow:

YEAS—Messrs. Chandler, Drake, Gilbert. Harris, Kellogg, McDonald, Morton, Osborn, Pomeroy, Rice, Robertson, Ross, Scott, Spencer, Sprague, Sumner, Thayer, Tipton, Trumbull, Warner, Willey—21.

NAYS—Messrs. *Bayard,* Boreman, Conkling, Corbett, Cragin, *Davis,* Edmunds. *Hamilton* of Maryland, Hamlin, Howe, *McCreery,* Nye, Ramsey, *Saulsbury,* Stewart, *Stockton, Thurman, Vickers,* Williams, Wilson—20.

The bill was then reported to the Senate, and the question being taken on Mr. Warner's amendment, it was agreed to—yeas 20, nays 17, as follow:

YEAS—Messrs. Chandler, Drake, Fenton, Harlan, McDonald, Morrill of Vermont, Morton, Osborn, Pomeroy, Rice, Robertson, Scott, Spencer, Sprague, Sumner, Thayer, Tipton, Trumbull, Warner, Willey—20.

NAYS—Messrs. *Bayard,* Boreman, Cragin, Edmunds, *Hamilton* of Maryland, Howe, *McCreery,* Nye, Ramsey, *Saulsbury,* Stewart, *Stockton, Thurman, Vickers,* Williams, Wilson—17.

Mr. Sumner again moved the following amendment:

SEC. —. That all acts of Congress relating to naturalization be, and the same are hereby, amended by striking out the word "white" wherever it occurs; so that in naturalization there shall be no distinction of race or color.

Which was disagreed to—yeas 12, nays 26, as follow:

YEAS—Messrs. Fenton, Fowler, Howe, McDonald, Morrill of Vermont, Osborn, Pomeroy, Rice, Robertson, Sprague, Sumner, Trumbull—12.

NAYS—Messrs. *Bayard,* Boreman, Chandler, Conkling, Corbett, Cragin, Drake, *Hamilton* of Maryland, Hamlin, Harlan, *McCreery,* Morton, Nye, Ramsey, *Saulsbury,* Scott, Stewart, *Stockton,* Thayer, *Thurman,* Tipton, *Vickers,* Warner, Willey, Williams, Wilson—26.

Mr. Trumbull moved to amend the amendment of Mr. Warner, which was adopted, by adding thereto the words "or persons born in the Chinese empire; which was disagreed to—yeas 9, nays 31, as follow:

YEAS—Messrs. Fenton, Fowler, McDonald, Pomeroy, Rice, Robertson, Sprague, Sumner, Trumbull—9.

NAYS—Messrs. *Bayard,* Boreman, Chandler, Conkling, Corbett, Cragin, Drake, Gilbert, *Hamilton* of Maryland, Hamlin, Harlan, Howe, *McCreery,* Morrill of Vermont, Morton, Nye, Osborn, Ramsey, *Saulsbury,* Sawyer, Scott, Stewart, *Stockton,* Thayer, *Thurman,* Tipton, *Vickers,* Warner, Willey, Williams, Wilson—31.

The bill as amended was then passed, and the Senate amendments were agreed to as above.

## The Cuban Question.

### IN HOUSE OF REPRESENTATIVES.

1870, June 14—Mr. Banks, from the Committee on Foreign Affairs, submitted the following:

Joint resolution in relation to the contest between the people of Cuba and the Government of Spain.

*Resolved, &c.,* That the President of the United States be, and hereby is, authorized and instructed to declare and maintain a strictly impartial neutrality on the part of the Government of the United States in the contest now existing between the people of Cuba and the Government of the kingdom of Spain.

SEC. 2. That all provisions of the statute approved 20th of April, 1818, entitled "An act in addition to the act for the punishment of certain crimes against the United States, and to repeal the acts therein mentioned," shall be construed to apply equally to each of the parties in the existing contest between the people of Cuba and the Government of Spain.

SEC. 3. That the President is hereby authorized and requested to remonstrate against the barbarous manner in which the war in Cuba has been conducted, and, if he shall deem it expedient, to solicit the co-operation of other governments in such measures as he may deem necessary to secure from both contending parties an observance of the laws of war recognized by all civilized nations.

The minority of the committee submitted as a substitute the following:

A joint resolution making it a misdemeanor to fit out or equip ships of war, with intent that they shall be employed in the service of any European prince or State for the purpose of subduing American colonists claiming independence, and providing for the forfeiture of such ship or vessel.

*Be it resolved, &c.,* That if any person shall, within the limits of the United States, fit out, arm, or equip, or attempt to fit out, arm, or equip, or procure to be fitted out, armed, or equipped, or shall knowingly be concerned in the fitting out, arming, or equipping, of any ship or vessel, with intent that such ship or vessel shall be employed in the service of any European prince or State, for the purpose of subduing American colonists claiming independence, or shall issue or deliver a commission within the territory of the United States for any ship or vessel, with the intent that she may be employed as aforesaid, every person so offending shall be guilty of a misdemeanor, and, upon conviction thereof, shall be fined in any sum not exceeding $5,000, and be imprisoned for a period not exceeding two years nor less than six months; and every such ship or vessel, with her tackle, apparel, and furniture, together with all materials, arms, ammunition, and stores, which may have been procured for the building and equipment thereof, shall be forfeited, one-half to the use of the informer and the other half to the United States.

SEC. 2. That in every case where a ship or vessel shall be fitted out, armed, or equipped, or attempted to be fitted out, armed, or equipped, contrary to the provisions of this joint resolution, it shall be lawful for the President of the United States, or such person as he shall have empowered for that purpose, to employ the land or naval forces or the militia of the United States, or any part thereof, for the purpose of taking possession of and detaining any such ship or vessel.

SEC. 3. That the provisions of the act approved April 20, 1818, entitled "An act in addition to the 'act for the punishment of certain crimes against the United States,' and to repeal the acts therein mentioned," shall be held to apply and be in force, as to all attempts of American colonies, or parts thereof, to assert their independence; and the words "colonies, districts, or peoples" in such act shall be held to apply to and include all such American colonists claiming independence, as described in the 1st section of this joint resolution.

The previous question having been ordered, it was by unanimous consent agreed that the following day should be devoted to debate, and the main question should be considered as having been ordered. On the following day—June 15 —after debate, Mr. Bingham moved to reconsider the vote by which the main question was ordered—

Mr. Eldridge moved that the motion lie on the table; which latter motion was disagreed to —yeas 82, nays 94, as follow :

YEAS—Messrs. *Adams, Archer,* Arnell, *Axtell,* Bailey, Banks, Beatty, *Beck, Bird, Booker,* Bowen, Boyd, *James Brooks, Burr, Calkin,* Sidney Clarke, *Cleveland,* Clinton L. Cobb, *Conner, Cox, Crebs,* Degener, *Dox, Eldridge,* Ferriss, Fitch, *Fox, Getz, Griswold, Haight, Hambleton, Hamill,* Hamilton, Hawkins, Hay, *Holman,* Hotchkiss, Ingersoll, *Johnson,* Julian, *Knott, Lewis,* Logan, *Marshall, Mayham, McKenzie, McNeely, Milnes,* Morphis, *Morrissey, Mungen,* Newsham, *Niblack,* Paine, Porter, *Potter, Randall, Reeves, Rice,* Roots, Sanford, *Schumaker,* Shanks, Porter Sheldon, *Sherrod, Shober, Joseph S. Smith, Stiles, Strader, Swann, Sweeney,* Taylor, *Trimble, Van Auken,* Van Horn, *Van Trump,* Van Wyck, *Wells,* Wilkinson, *Winchester, Wood, Woodward*—82.

NAYS—Messrs. Allison, Ambler, Ames, Armstrong, Asper, Atwood, Beaman, Bennett, Benton, Bingham, Blair, George M. Brooks, Buckley, Buffinton, Burchard, Burdett, Benjamin F. Butler, Roderick R. Butler, Cessna, Churchill, Amasa Cobb, Coburn, Cook, Conger, Dawes, Dickey, Dockery, Donley, Duval, Dyer, Ela, Farnsworth, Ferry, Finkelnburg, Fisher, Garfield, Hale, Harris, Hawley, Hays, Heflin, Hoar, Hooper, Judd, Kelley, Kellogg, Kelsey, Ketcham, Knapp, Laflin, Lawrence, Maynard, *McCormick,* McCrary, McGrew, McKee, Mercur, Eliakim H. Moore, Jesse H. Moore, William Moore, Daniel J. Morrell, Orth, Packard, Packer, Palmer, Peck, Perce, Phelps, Platt, Poland, Pomeroy, Sawyer, Schenck, John A. Smith, William Smyth, Starkweather, Stoughton, Strickland, Strong, Taffe, Tanner, Tillman, Twichell, Tyner, Upson, Ward, Cadwalader C. Washburn, William B. Washburn, Welker, Wheeler, Willard, John T. Wilson, Winans, Witcher—94.

The motion to reconsider was then agreed to— yeas 88, nays 70:

June 16 —Mr. Logan moved to amend the 2d section of the majority resolution by striking out the words "shall be construed to apply equally to each of the parties in the existing contest between the people of Cuba and the Government of Spain," and inserting in lieu thereof the following: "Shall be so construed as to give to both contending parties the same advantages of intercourse and trade with the United States, consistent with the law of nations, which have been or may be accorded to the Government of Spain."

Which was disagreed to—yeas 77, nays 101, as follow :

YEAS—Messrs. *Adams, Archer, Axtell,* Ayer, Banks, Beatty, *Beck, Bird, Booker,* Boyd, *James Brooks, Burr, Calkin,* William T. Clark, Sidney Clarke, *Cleveland,* Clinton L. Cobb, *Conner, Cox,* Degener, *Dickinson, Dox, Eldridge,* Ferriss, Fitch, *Fox, Getz, Gibson, Griswold, Haight, Hambleton, Hamill,* Hamilton, Hay, *Holman,* Ingersoll, *Johnson,* Julian, *Knott,* Lash, *Lewis,* Logan, *Marshall, Mayham, McKenzie, McNeely, Milnes, Morgan,* Morphis, *Morrissey, Mungen,* Newsham, *Niblack,* Prosser, *Randall, Reeves, Rice,* Roots, *Schumaker,* Lionel A. Sheldon, *Sherrod, Shober, Joseph S. Smith, Stiles,* Stokes, *Strader, Swann, Sweeney,* Van Horn, *Van Trump,* Ward, *Wells,* Whitmore, *Eugene M. Wilson, Winchester, Wood, Woodward*—77.

NAYS—Messrs. Allison, Ambler, Ames, Arnell, Asper, Atwood, Bailey, Beaman, Benjamin, Bennett, Benton, Bingham, Blair, George M. Brooks, Buckley, Buffinton, Burchard, Burdett, Benjamin F. Butler, Roderick R. Butler, Cake, Cessna, Churchill, Amasa Cobb, Cook, Conger, Cowles, Dawes, Dickey, Dixon, Dockery, Donley, Duval, Dyer, Farnsworth, Ferry, Finkelnburg, Fisher, Garfield, Gilfillan, Hale, Harris, Hawkins, Hill, Hoar, Hooper, Hotchkiss, Judd, Kelley, Kellogg, Kelsey, Ketcham, Knapp, Laflin, Lawrence, Maynard, McCarthy, McCrary, McGrew, Mercur, Eliakim H. Moore, William Moore, Daniel J. Morrell, Negley, O'Neill, Orth, Packard, Packer, Paine, Perce, Phelps, Platt, Poland,

Pomeroy, *Rogers*, Sargent, Sawyer, Schenck, Scofield, Shanks, Porter Sheldon, John A. Smith, William Smyth, Starkweather, Stoughton, Strickland, Strong, Taffe, Taylor, Townsend, Twichell, Tyner, Upson, Cadwalader C. Washburn, William B. Washburn, Welker, Willard, John T. Wilson, Winans, Witcher—101.

Mr. Bingham moved to substitute for the minority resolutions the following:

That the President is hereby authorized to remonstrate against the barbarous manner in which the war in Cuba has been conducted, and, if he shall deem it expedient, to solicit the co-operation of other governments in such measures as he may deem necessary to secure from both contending parties an observance of the laws of war recognized by all civilized nations.

Which was agreed to—yeas 100, nays 17, on a division.

The minority resolution, as amended by Mr. Bingham—being simply Mr. Bingham's proposition—was then substituted for that of the majority—yeas 101, nays 88, as follow:

YEAS—Messrs. Allison, Ambler, Ames, Armstrong, Asper, Atwood, Beaman, Benjamin, Benton, Bingham, George M. Brooks, Buckley, Buffinton, Burchard, Roderick R. Butler, Cake, Cessna, Churchill, William T. Clark, Coburn, Cook, Conger, Covode, Cowles, Dawes, Dickey, Dixon, Dockery, Donley, Duval, Dyer, Ela, Farnsworth, Ferry, Fisher, Garfield, Hale, Harris, Hawkins, Heflin, Hill, Hoar, Hooper, Hotchkiss, Judd, Kelley, Kellogg, Kelsey, Ketcham, Knapp, Laflin, Lawrence, Maynard, McCarthy, McCrary, McGrew, Mercur, Eliakim H. Moore, Jesse H. Moore, William Moore, Daniel J. Morrell, Negley, O'Neill, Orth, Packard, Packer, Palmer, Perce, Phelps, Platt, Poland, Pomeroy, Rogers, Sargent, Sawyer, Schenck, Scofield, John A. Smith, William J. Smith, William Smyth, Starkweather, Stokes. Stoughton, Strickland, Strong, Taffe, Tanner, Tillman, Townsend, Twichell, Tyner, Upson, Ward, Cadwalader C. Washburn, William B. Washburn, Welker, Wheeler. Whitmore, Willard, John T. Wilson, Winans—101.

NAYS—Messrs. *Adams, Archer, Axtell*, Bailey, Banks, Barry, Beatty, *Beck, Biggs, Bird*, Blair, *Booker*, Boyd, *James Brooks*, Buck, Burdett, *Burr*, Benjamin F. Butler, *Calkin*, Sidney Clarke, Amasa Cobb, Clinton L. Cobb, *Conner, Cox*, Cullom, Degener, *Dickinson, Dox, Eldridge*, Ferriss, Finkelnburg, Fitch, *Fox, Getz, Gibson, Griswold*, Haight, *Hamill*, Hamilton, Hay, *Holman*, Ingersoll, *Johnson*, Julian, *Kerr, Knott*, Lash, *Lewis*, Logan, *Marshall, Mayham*, McKee, *McKenzie, McNeely, Milnes. Morgan*, Morphis, *Morrissey, Mungen*, Newsham, *Niblack*, Paine, Porter, *Potter*, Prosser, *Randall, Reeves, Rice*, Roots, *Schumaker*, Shanks, Lionel A. Sheldon, Porter Sheldon, *Sherrod, Shober, Joseph S. Smith, Stiles, Strader, Swann, Sweeney*, Taylor, *Trimble, Van Trump, Wells, Eugene M. Wilson, Winchester, Wood, Woodward*—88.

The resolution was then agreed to without a division.

### Ratification of Constitutional Amendments.

1870, May 8—Mr. Bingham reported the following bill:

To regulate the mode of determining the ratification of amendments to the Constitution of the United States proposed by Congress, and for other purposes.

That whenever the legislature of any State shall have ratified an amendment to the Constitution of the United States heretofore proposed, or which shall be hereafter proposed, by Congress to the legislatures of the several States for ratification, it shall be the duty of the Executive of such State so ratifying to certify forthwith, under the seal of such State, such ratification and the date thereof to the Secretary of State of the United States, whose duty it shall be to file and record the same in the Department of State.

SEC. 2. That in all cases wherein official notice has been given, or shall hereafter be given to, and has been or shall hereafter be received by,

the Secretary of State of the United States, that the legislature of any State has ratified any amendment heretofore proposed by Congress, or which shall hereafter be proposed by Congress, to the Constitution of the United States, it shall be unlawful for any officer of such State to certify thereafter any repeal of such amendment, unless an amendment for the repeal thereof shall have been first proposed by the Congress of the United States, or by a convention called by Congress for proposing amendments; and if such certificate of repeal be made, said Secretary of State shall not receive or make any record thereof in the Department of State, but the same shall be void and of no effect.

SEC. 3. That whoever, after the legislatures of three-fourths of the States shall have ratified any amendment to the Constitution of the United States heretofore proposed, or which shall hereafter be proposed, by the Congress thereof, shall do any act declaring the repeal, either by color of State legislation or of State ordinance, of any ratification of such amendment, after the same shall have been certified to the Secretary of State of the United States, and before the Congress of the United States shall have proposed an amendment providing for the repeal thereof, or a convention called by Congress for proposing amendments shall have proposed such amendment, shall be guilty of a misdemeanor, and, upon conviction thereof in any court of the United States having jurisdiction in the premises, shall be subject to imprisonment not less than one nor more than ten years, or to a fine of not less than $2,000 nor more than $10,000, or to both, in the discretion of the court.

SEC. 4. That all acts or parts of acts inconsistent herewith are hereby repealed;

Which, the rules being suspended, under the operation of the previous question, was agreed to—yeas 130, nays 54, as follow:

YEAS—Messrs. Allison, Ambler, Ames, Armstrong, Arnell, Asper, Atwood, Bailey, Barry, Beatty, Benjamin, Bennett, Benton, Bingham, Blair, Boles, George M. Brooks. Buckley, Buffinton, Burchard, Burdett, Benjamin F. Butler, Roderick R. Butler, Cake, Cessna, Churchill, William T. Clark. Sidney Clarke, Amasa Cobb, Coburn, Conger, Cook, Cowles, Cullom, Darrall, Davis. Dawes, Degener, Dickey, Donley, Duval, Dyer, Ela, Ferriss, Finkelnburg, Fisher, Fitch, Garfield. Gilfillan, Hale, Hamilton, Harris, Hawley, Hay, Hays, Heflin, Hill, Hoar, Jenckes, Judd, Julian, Kelley, Kelsey, Ketcham, Knapp, Lash, Loughridge. Lynch, Maynard, McCarthy, McCrary, McGrew, McKee, *McKenzie*, Mercur, Eliakim H. Moore, Jesse H. Moore, William Moore, Myers, Negley, O'Neill, Orth, Packard, Paine, Palmer, Peck, Perce, Peters, Phelps, Poland, Porter, Prosser, Roots, Sanford, Sargent, Sawyer, Scofield, Shanks, Lionel A. Sheldon, Porter Sheldon, John A. Smith, William J. Smith, Worthington C. Smith. William Smyth, Starkweather, Stevens, Stevenson, Stokes, Stoughton, Strickland, Strong, Tanner, Taylor, Tillman, Townsend, Twichell, Tyner, Upson, Van Wyck, Wallace, Ward, Cadwalader C. Washburn, William B. Washburn, Welker, Wheeler, Whitmore, Willard, Williams, John T. Wilson, Winans—130.

NAYS—Messrs. *Archer, Beck. Biggs, Bird, Booker, James Brooks, Burr, Calkin, Cleveland, Conner, Cox, Crebs, Dickinson, Eldridge, Fox, Getz, Griswold, Haight, Haldeman, Hamill,* Hawkins, *Johnson, Thomas L. Jones, Kerr, Knott, Lewis, Mayham, McCormick, McNeely, Milnes, Morgan, Mungen, Niblack, Potter, Randall, Reeves, Rogers, Schumaker, Sherrod, Slocum, Joseph S. Smith, Stiles, Stone, Swann, Sweeney, Trimble, Van Auken, Voorhees, Wells, Eugene M. Wilson, Winchester, Wood, Woodward*—54.

### New Constitution of Illinois.

At the recent election, in July, this instrument was adopted by the majority of the people of the State. Among its features are the following:

## SUBMITTED SEPARATELY.

Divides the State into senatorial districts, and provides for the election of one senator and three representatives from the same district; gives each voter as many votes as there are representatives to be elected, and allows him to divide his vote among candidates as he sees fit.

## BOUNDARIES.

Same as the old.

## BILL OF RIGHTS.

No person shall be denied any civil or political right, privilege, or capacity, on account of his religious opinions. Grand juries may be abolished by law (when a better system is devised.)

The fee of land taken for railroad tracks shall remain with the owner, subject only to the use for which it is taken.

No irrevocable grant of special privileges shall be passed.

## OATH.

Members of the Legislature required to take an oath that they have not paid any bribe to secure their election, and that they will not accept any gift or bribe for any vote or influence they may give or withhold for any official act.

## APPROPRIATIONS.

No appropriation of money allowed in any private law, and bills making appropriations for the pay of any officer shall not contain any other provision.

The general assembly shall have no power to release or extinguish, in whole or in part, the indebtedness, liability, or obligation of any corporation or individual to this State, or to any municipal corporation therein.

The general assembly shall never grant or authorize extra compensation, fee, or allowance to any public officer, agent, servant, or contractor, after service has been rendered, or a contract made, nor authorize the payment of any claim, or part thereof, hereafter created against the State under any agreement or contract made without express authority of law; and all such authorized agreements or contracts shall be null and void.

The State shall never pay, assume, or become responsible for the debts or liabilities of, or in any manner give, loan, or extend its credits to, or in aid of, any puiblic or other corporation, association, or individual.

No law shall be passed which shall operate to extend the term of any public officer after his election or appointment.

No county, city, township, school district, or other municipal corporation, shall be allowed to become indebted in any manner, or for any purpose, to an amount, including existing indebtedness, in the aggregate exceeding five per centum of the value of the taxable property therein, to be ascertained by the last assessment of State and county taxes previous to the incurring of said indebtedness.

Railroads are forbidden to consolidate with a competing line.

General assembly to fix maximum rates of charges for the different railroads.

## INDIANA

### Republican, February 22, 1870.

1. We congratulate the country on the restoration of law and order in the late rebellious States under the reconstruction measures adopted by the General Government, and upon the prevalence of peace and return of fraternal feeling among the people of all the States under a constitution securing an equality of political and civil rights to all citizens, without distinction of race or color.

2. That we reverence the Constitution of the United States as the supreme law of the land and a wise embodiment of the principles of free government, and, following its teachings, we will adopt from time to time such amendments as are necessary more completely to establish justice, insure domestic tranquillity, and secure the blessings of liberty to ourselves and our posterity; and that we rejoice at the ratification of the XVth Amendment, which forever secures an equality of political rights to all men, and we extend to the colored man a helping hand to enable him in the race of life to improve and elevate his condition.

3. That the national debt created in the defense and preservation of the Union, however great the burden, must be cheerfully borne, until honorably and honestly extinguished in accordance with the letter and spirit of the several laws authorizing the debt; and that all attempts at repudiation of principal or interest should meet the scorn and denunciation of an honest and patriotic people.

4. That we demand in every department of the Government, from the highest to the lowest, the strictest economy in all expenditures, consistent with the requirements of the public service; the reduction and abolishment of all extravagant fees and salaries; the closing of all useless offices and the dismissal of their incumbents; and all efforts to these ends, in Congress or elsewhere, have our unqualified approval

5. That a reduction of taxation is demanded, both of tariff and internal taxes, until it reaches the lowest amount consistent with the credit and necessities of the Government; and that we are in favor of a tariff for revenue, believing that a proper adjustment of duties must necessarily afford all the incidental protection to which any interest is entitled.

6. That we are in favor of a currency founded on the national credit, as abundant as the trade and commerce of the country demand; and we disapprove of all laws in reference thereto which establish monopoly or inequality therein.

7. That we are opposed to the donation of the public lands, or the grant of subsidies in money to railroads and other corporations; and that we demand the reservations of the public domain for the use of actual settlers and educational purposes.

8. That we reaffirm that of "all who were faithful in the trials of the late war, there are none entitled to more especial honor than the brave soldiers and seamen who endured the hardships of campaign and cruise, and imperiled their lives in the service of their country, and the bounties and pensions provided by law for those brave defenders of the nation are obligations never to be forgotten, and should be paid with-

out cost to the recipient. The widows and orphans of the gallant dead are wards of the nation —a sacred legacy bequeathed to the nation's protecting care.

9. That we approve the general course of our Senators and Republican Representatives in Congress, and express our full and entire confidence that they will act with wisdom and integrity in all that concerns the welfare of the people; and that we tender thanks to Senator Morton for his exertions in so shaping the legislation of Congress on the reconstruction of the late rebel States as to secure the passage of the XVth Amendment.

10. That we indorse the administration of General Grant as President of the United States, accept the increased collection of revenue, the reduction of expenditures, and payment of a large portion of the public debt as a fulfillment of his promises of economy, and rejoice that the victorious general of the Union armies should, as a civil officer, receive the last of the rebel States in its return to the national family.

11. Inasmuch as all republican governments depend for their stability and perpetuity on the intelligence and virtue of the people, it is the right and duty of the State and national authorities to establish, foster, and secure the highest moral and intellectual development of the people.

12. That taxation for county and other local purposes has become so great as to be oppressive to the people; that our system of county administration needs reform, and we demand of our representatives in the legislature such changes in the statutes of the State as will protect the people from extravagant tax levies by local authorities; and as an aid to this needed reform, we favor a reduction of the fees of the county officers to a standard which will furnish a fair and reasonable compensation for the services rendered, and that no officer should be favored with salary, fees, or perquisites beyond such fair and reasonable compensation.

13. That the canal stocks issued under the legislation of 1846 and 1847, commonly called the "Butler bill," were, by the terms of the contract, charged exclusively upon the Wabash and Erie canal, its revenues and lands, and the faith of the State never having been, directly or indirectly, pledged for the payment or redemption thereof, said canal stocks therefore constitute no part of the outstanding debts or liabilities of the State; that the constitution of this State ought to be amended at the earliest practicable period, so as to prohibit the taking effect of any law or acts of the general assembly proposing to recognize or create any liability of the State for the said canal stocks, or any part thereof, until such proposition shall have been submitted to a direct vote of the people of the State and approved by them.

14. That we heartily indorse the administration of our State affairs by Governor Baker and his associate State officers, and especially congratulate the people that the time is so near when the State debt will be entirely liquidated.

### Democratic, January 8, 1870.

*Resolved*, That the federal Union, with all the rights and dignity of the several States, should be preserved; and to secure that great national blessing, the Constitution must be respected and observed, and every approach to centralized despotism defeated, whether attempted by Congress or the Executive.

2. That recent events have, more than ever, convinced us of the infamous and revolutionary character of the reconstruction measures as an invasion of the sovereign and sacred rights of the people and of all the States.

3. That the independence of the Supreme Court of the United States is essential to the safety and security of the States and the people; and we declare that the measures of Congress, having in view the destruction of the powers of that court to adjudicate on the constitutionality of the enactments of Congress is a dangerous evidence of the usurpations of the legislative over the judicial department of the Government.

4. That we are in favor of a tariff for revenue only; and we demand that the burdens of taxation shall be fairly and equally adjusted, and that such an adjustment cannot be made without striking from the statute book the present and odious tariff laws, a system of taxation based upon favoritism, and which has destroyed American shipping and commerce, oppressed the people of the great agricultural regions, which compels the many to pay tribute to the few, and which has built up monopolies that control not only every American market, but also the legislation of Congress; and we demand that the prime articles of necessity, such as tea, coffee, sugar, and salt, shall be placed upon the free list.

5. That we are willing to pay our national debt in strict compliance with our contracts, whether it was made payable in gold or greenbacks, but we are unwilling to do more than that; and we declare that the five-twenty bonds are payable in greenbacks, or their equivalent; and we condemn the policy of the administration, which is squandering millions of money by buying such bonds at a high rate of premium, when the Government has the clear right to redeem them at par.

6. That the national bank system, organized in the interest of the bondholders, ought to be abolished, and greenbacks issued in lieu of such bank paper, thus saving millions annually to the people, and giving to the whole people (instead of the few) the benefits of issuing a paper currency.

7. That the business interests of the country demand an increased and maintained volume of the currency; and the burden of the public debt, the high rate of interest and taxation, imperatively forbid the contraction of the currency in the interest of the bondholders.

8. That the shares of stock in the national banks ought to be subjected to school and municipal taxation on the same conditions as other property; and we demand of our State legislature that the shares of such banks shall be subjected to equal taxation with other property of the State.

9. That the bonds of the United States ought to be taxed by Congress for national purposes to such an extent as will substantially equalize the taxation of such bonds with other property subject to local taxation.

10. That we denounce the action of our last legislature in attempting to force upon the peo-

ple the proposed XVth Amendment to the Constitution of the United States as in palpable violation of our State constitution, and we solemnly protest against Indiana being counted for said amendment; and we hereby declare our unalterable opposition to its ratification.

11. That any attempt to regulate the moral ideas, appetites, or innocent amusements of the people by legislation is unwise and despotic.

12. That we are opposed to any change in the naturalization laws of the United States, whereby admission to citizenship will be made more difficult or expensive; and we especially denounce the proposed plan of transferring the naturalization of aliens to the courts of the United States, and abridging the powers of State courts in that respect, as a hardship and expense to the poor and friendless candidate for American citizenship: we recognize the proposed change as the off-shoot of intolerant "Know-Nothingism"— the "twin relic" of radicalism itself.

## OHIO.

### Democratic, June 1, 1870.

The democracy of Ohio, coming together in the spirit of devotion to the doctrines and faith of free representative government, and relying for success upon discussion and the intelligence of the people, deem the present convention a fitting occasion to reassert the following time-honored principles of the Democratic party:

That the federal Government is one of limited powers, derived solely from the Constitution; that the grants of power made therein ought to be strictly construed by all the dependents and agents of the Government, and that it is inexpedient and dangerous to exercise doubtful powers;

That the Constitution of the United States is founded on the fundamental principle of the entire and absolute equality of all the States of the Union, and it is not competent for Congress to impose upon them any conditions or restrictions in respect to their internal concerns which the federal Constitution has not imposed;

That the liberal principles embodied by Jefferson in the Declaration of Independence, and sanctioned in the Constitution, which make ours the land of liberty and the asylum of the oppressed of every nation, have ever been cardinal principles of the democratic faith, and every attempt to abridge the privileges of becoming citizens and the owners of soil among us ought to be resisted with the same spirit which swept the alien and sedition laws from the statute books;

And, in order that we may more distinctly declare our views of the measures and policy of the present administration,

*Resolved*, That we denounce the present tariff, as well as the substitute lately introduced in the House of Representatives by the Committee of Ways and Means, as a gigantic robbery of the labor and industry of the country; that they are solely designed to advance the interests of a few thousand monopolies, and that they should no longer be submitted to; and that no candidate for Congress, nor for any other office, is worthy of support who is not in favor of a low revenue tariff, which closely approximates to free trade;

that in the arrangement of any revenue tariff all the necessaries of life should be absolutely free of duty.

2. That the internal revenue system of the United States is unendurable in its oppressive exactions; that it should be immediately remodeled; that its annoyances of stamps and licenses and taxes upon sales and incomes should be abolished; that the tax itself should be collected by the State and county officials; and that the multiplication of officers is wholly unnecessary, except to eat out the resources of the tax-payers; and that we pledge ourselves to effect a thorough reform in this particular. We denounce the profligacy in the present administration of the federal Government, the corruption which has entered all the official stations, the favoritism which, overlooking fitness for office, has appointed to positions of public trust the friends or tools of those who control the public patronage, and the imbecility which directs the destinies of the republic, without an apparent purpose, and manages its affairs with such embarrassment and disaster to the material interests of the people at home, and with such disregard of the rights and liberties of its citizens abroad.

3. That land monopoly is one of the great evils of our country and against the spirit of our institutions; that the whole of our public lands ought to be held as a sacred trust to secure homesteads for actual settlers; we therefore denounce the recent action of Congress in making grants to mammoth railroad corporations, which are already too powerful, and may become dangerous to a free people.

4. That we regard the act recently passed by Congress to enforce the "Fifteenth Amendment," as unconstitutional, unjust and oppressive; an invasion of the rights of the States, subversive of the best interests of the people, and therefore demand its unconditional repeal.

5. That the power of the federal Government to assess and collect taxes on bonds of the United States is clear and unquestioned; and we demand of Congress that a share of taxation equal to the fair average amount levied in each State on money loaned shall be assessed and collected from all investments made in bonds.

6. That we are opposed to the system of national banks, and demand the immediate repeal of the law creating them, and that in place of the notes of such banks treasury notes of the United States should be substituted.

7. That the Democracy of Ohio sympathize with the efforts of all people struggling for self-government, and that we denounce the truckling of the federal Administration to Great Britain and Spain, and the efforts of the party in power to reduce whole States in our Union to a condition of vassalage to the general Government.

8. That the thanks of the Democracy of Ohio are extended to our Senator, Allen G. Thurman, and the Democratic Representatives in Congress, who, though in a small minority, have bravely contended for the principles of democracy and the interests of the people.

9. That upon the foregoing platform we invite all the electors of Ohio, without regard to past differences, to vote for the ticket this day nominated.

# LXII

# STATISTICAL TABLES.

## PUBLIC LANDS, REVENUE AND NATIONAL DEBT STATEMENTS.

**TABLE,** showing the area of the land States, the amount of land granted to railroads, sold, and otherwise disposed of, and the amount remaining on hand in each.

| States and Territories containing public land. | Areas of States and Territories containing public land. | Conveyed under grants in aid of railroads, &c. | Quantity sold. | Entered under homestead law and grant'd for military services. | Disposed of in all other ways. | Remaining on hand. |
|---|---|---|---|---|---|---|
| Ohio | 25,576,960.00 | | 12,805,971.08 | 1,823,494.67 | 10,947,374.25 | 220.00 |
| Indiana | 21,637,760.00 | | 16,122,244.78 | 1,311,956.65 | 4,504,559.50 | 1,920.93 |
| Illinois | 35,462,400.00 | 2,595,053.00 | 19,879,408.27 | 9,533,805.03 | 3,353,800.97 | 332.73 |
| Missouri | 41,824,000.00 | 1,715,435.00 | 22,924,661.21 | 8,030,532.06 | 8,826,407.67 | 1,181,129.30 |
| Alabama | 32,462,080.00 | 2,288,138.50 | 17,789,351.45 | 1,539,559.85 | 3,263,724.81 | 6,581,305.40 |
| Mississippi | 30,179,840.00 | 908,680.29 | 12,201,037.03 | 585,217.92 | 11,735,645.69 | 4,749,259.07 |
| Louisiana | 26,461,440.00 | 1,072,405.45 | 5,720,349.71 | 1,224,105.23 | 11,924,781.24 | 6,519,798.37 |
| Michigan | 36,128,640.00 | 5,686,109.51 | 12,381,774.87 | 5,962,634.77 | 8,835,790.22 | 4,162,330.61 |
| Arkansas | 33,406,720.00 | 1,793,167.10 | 8,235,726.57 | 2,691,011.98 | 9,308,870.87 | 11,377,943.78 |
| Florida | 37,931,520.00 | 1,760,468.39 | 1,832,431.49 | 768,181.58 | 21,710,248.78 | 17,349,167.32 |
| Iowa | 35,228,800.00 | 3,415,669.46 | 11,773,758.20 | 14,514,170.55 | 4,547,120.38 | 1,978,081.41 |
| Wisconsin | 34,511,360.00 | 1,729,710.05 | 10,043,685.78 | 7,154,420.58 | 6,889,226.79 | 8,694,316.80 |
| California | 120,947,840.00 | 161,892.56 | 2,925,668.80 | 907,600.02 | 15,549,079.62 | 101,403,599.00 |
| Minnesota | 53,459,840.00 | 2,510,283.64 | 2,255,884.10 | 8,649,550.51 | 5,212,089.70 | 34,732,032.05 |
| Oregon | 60,975,360.00 | 1,813,600.00 | 264,902.91 | 436,955.16 | 7,722,162.88 | 51,737,739.25 |
| Kansas | 52,043,520.00 | 2,908.92 | 285,029.73 | 5,115,316.03 | 4,257,993.47 | 42,482,271.85 |
| Nevada | 71,737,600.00 | | 62,064.36 | 21,774.55 | 4,572,264.99 | 67,081,496.10 |
| Nebraska | 48,636,800.00 | | 442,053.23 | 2,956,369.32 | 4,293,584.99 | 40,944,792.46 |
| Washington Ter. | 44,796,160.00 | | 300,530.80 | 336,914.47 | 2,781,590.77 | 41,377,123.96 |
| New Mexico " | 77,568,640.00 | | 480.00 | 480.00 | 6,763,122.00 | 70,704,558.00 |
| Utah " | 54,065,043.20 | | 51,638.26 | 104,244.65 | 5,088,733.00 | 48,820,427.29 |
| Dakota " | 96,596,128.00 | | 32,859.01 | 296,937.09 | 5,376,331.00 | 90,890,000.90 |
| Colorado " | 66,880,000.00 | | 82,502.09 | 292,087.98 | 3,716,755.93 | 62,788,654.00 |
| Montana " | 92,016,640.00 | | 9,335.96 | 7,952.28 | 5,112,035.00 | 86,887,316.76 |
| Arizona " | 72,906,240.00 | | | | 4,050,350.00 | 68,855,890.00 |
| Idaho " | 55,228,160.00 | | 10,270.69 | 13,829.51 | 3,068,231.00 | 52,135,828.80 |
| Wyoming " | 62,645,068.80 | | | | 3,480,281.00 | 59,164,787.80 |
| Indian " | 44,154,240.00 | | | | | 44,154,240.00 |
| Alaska " | 369,529,600.00 | | | | | 369,529,600.00 |
| **Total** | 1,834,998,400.00 | 27,453,521.87 | 158,433,620.38 | 73,278,902.44 | 179,546,191.37 | 1,396,286,163.94 |

The amount remaining on hand is subject to a reduction of 163,496,626.33 acres, granted by Congress to aid in the construction of railroad lines, and not yet selected and certified to them.

## REVENUE RECEIPTS AND REDUCTIONS.

*Statement showing the receipts from the several general sources of revenue for the years ending—*

| SOURCES OF REVENUE. | June 30, 1869. | July 31, 1869. | Aug. 31, 1869. | Sept. 30, 1869. | Oct. 31, 1869. | Nov. 30, 1869. | Dec. 31, 1869. | Jan. 31, 1870. | Feb. 28, 1870. | Mar. 31, 1870. | April 30, 1870. | May 31, 1870. |
|---|---|---|---|---|---|---|---|---|---|---|---|---|
| Spirits | $45,026,401 74 | $46,316,552 87 | $46,680,565 44 | $46,581,253 87 | $47,265,439 26 | $49,099,254 13 | $50,069,610 44 | $50,720,282 38 | $51,538,039 53 | $53,117,025 07 | $52,990,086 20 | $54,571,871 49 |
| Tobacco | 23,430,707 57 | 24,630,783 69 | 25,809,646 66 | 27,241,593 90 | 28,393,905 45 | 29,178,936 78 | 29,256,702 16 | 29,325,611 08 | 29,876,363 15 | 30,277,504 47 | 30,532,728 32 | 30,822,208 63 |
| Fermented liquors | 6,099,879 54 | 6,047,015 45 | 6,054,218 02 | 6,052,784 50 | 6,015,219 96 | 6,119,032 89 | 6,945,383 68 | 6,058,156 54 | 6,064,876 95 | 6,095,049 26 | 6,136,428 49 | 6,134,336 75 |
| Banks and bankers | 3,335,516 52 | 3,512,649 55 | 3,606,511 25 | 3,664,643 29 | 3,685,877 59 | 3,748,653 76 | 3,800,782 85 | 3,923,016 01 | 3,974,775 58 | 4,104,086 73 | 4,211,381 48 | 4,237,308 25 |
| Gross receipts | 6,300,908 82 | 6,366,686 90 | 6,402,907 00 | 6,504,004 66 | 6,527,512 01 | 6,539,774 09 | 6,631,924 31 | 6,691,924 40 | 6,704,227 48 | 6,806,874 01 | 6,807,597 32 | 6,828,197 33 |
| Sales | 8,206,839 03 | 8,383,564 83 | 8,494,278 64 | 8,503,543 54 | 8,587,421 73 | 8,705,785 35 | 8,762,956 69 | 8,811,310 21 | 8,762,823 16 | 8,817,362 90 | 8,795,208 19 | 8,782,429 76 |
| Special taxes not elsewhere enumerated | 8,801,454 67 | 8,892,468 56 | 9,014,096 23 | 9,106,772 37 | 9,189,369 18 | 9,262,870 62 | 9,308,035 46 | 9,352,591 92 | 9,377,541 24 | 9,425,066 39 | 9,428,034 45 | 9,553,655 50 |
| Income, includ'g salaries | 34,791,855 84 | 36,047,965 00 | 36,516,638 41 | 36,880,571 69 | 37,144,522 54 | 37,333,641 40 | 37,570,746 51 | 37,595,863 88 | 37,950,180 34 | 37,950,180 34 | 38,539,478 19 | 37,123,899 19 |
| Legacies | 1,244,837 01 | 1,248,264 94 | 1,276,960 33 | 1,306,937 25 | 1,447,500 45 | 1,454,221 04 | 1,523,523 36 | 1,612,191 58 | 1,609,070 97 | 1,619,606 97 | 1,636,863 56 | 1,647,728 07 |
| Successions | 1,189,756 22 | 1,180,402 90 | 1,181,121 22 | 1,202,355 19 | 1,229,829 29 | 1,270,963 96 | 1,325,842 98 | 1,423,399 06 | 1,393,137 41 | 1,363,812 96 | 1,374,112 40 | 1,414,378 33 |
| Articles in schedule A | 882,860 73 | 885,464 30 | 892,027 80 | 894,553 05 | 894,340 76 | 894,880 98 | 894,841 26 | 893,569 98 | 892,482 57 | 891,939 56 | 893,396 20 | 877,922 81 |
| Passports | 29,453 00 | 23,346 00 | 23,391 00 | 23,371 00 | 25,114 00 | 26,559 00 | 27,734 00 | 23,780 00 | 25,000 00 | 23,634 00 | 24,999 00 | 22,736 00 |
| Gas | 2,116,005 82 | 2,137,110 70 | 2,133,885 41 | 2,165,728 53 | 2,176,905 17 | 2,290,161 46 | 2,215,976 27 | 2,246,859 81 | 2,278,079 57 | 2,282,637 44 | 2,303,416 57 | 2,306,021 71 |
| Sources not elsewhere enumerated | 1,284,978 98 | 835,371 52 | 685,388 46 | 579,264 89 | 551,879 60 | 526,854 39 | 447,282 80 | 470,107 92 | 493,238 87 | 618,889 16 | 608,908 34 | 593,079 24 |
| Penalties | 877,088 79 | 771,849 47 | 703,491 95 | 701,496 33 | 673,157 24 | 709,073 96 | 696,392 64 | 692,504 77 | 762,321 38 | 662,638 76 | 637,790 95 | 815,776 90 |
| Net receipts from stamps | 15,505,493 01 | 15,619,281 47 | 15,711,668 97 | 15,796,699 47 | 15,701,030 50 | 15,829,332 76 | 15,882,306 80 | 15,923,065 14 | 15,894,350 16 | 15,768,557 51 | 15,718,125 35 | 15,663,364 18 |
| Total | 169,124,127 29 | 162,898,778 15 | 164,176,806 79 | 167,216,173 53 | 169,509,024 73 | 172,933,301 95 | 174,382,286 83 | 175,833,972 43 | 177,617,576 20 | 179,824,865 53 | 180,638,555 01 | 181,394,914 14 |

*Statement showing the aggregate of certificates of deposit received at the office of internal revenue for each month during the fiscal years ending June 30, 1869 and 1870.*

| | Fiscal year 1869. | Fiscal year 1870. |
|---|---|---|
| July | $16,990,649 92 | $21,583,359 34 |
| August | 13,899,385 70 | 15,015,396 81 |
| September | 9,760,796 29 | 13,022,303 87 |
| October | 10,092,335 34 | 12,056,399 77 |
| November | 9,641,304 63 | 13,145,569 70 |
| December | 10,201,800 33 | 11,719,642 56 |
| January | 11,127,801 66 | 12,496,092 48 |
| February | 10,272,257 89 | 12,115,566 39 |
| March | 11,512,002 47 | 12,735,195 70 |
| April | 12,060,053 91 | 13,543,885 92 |
| May | 20,642,280 00 | 21,164,996 07 |
| June | 22,088,470 99 | 25,431,939 42 |
| Total | 158,289,139 13 | 184,032,948 03 |

*Estimate of the annual reduction in internal revenue by the act approved July 14, 1870.*

| Source of Income. | Amount. |
|---|---|
| In special taxes | $10,674,000 |
| In gross receipts | 6,784,000 |
| In sales | 8,804,000 |
| In income | 23,700,000 |
| In legacies | 1,619,000 |
| In successions | 1,364,000 |
| In articles in schedule A | 892,000 |
| In passports | 25,000 |
| In stamps | 1,350,000 |
| Total | 55,212,000 |

*Estimate of the annual reduction in internal revenue by legislation since July 1866.*

| Under what law. | Amount. |
|---|---|
| By statute of July 13, 1866 | $65,000,000 |
| By statute of March 2, 1867 | 40,000,000 |
| By statute of February 2, 1868 | 23,000,000 |
| By statute of March 31, 1868 } | 45,000,000 |
| By statute of July 20, 1868 } | |
| By statute of July 14, 1870 | 55,000,000 |

# STATEMENT OF THE PUBLIC DEBT OF THE UNITED STATES, JULY 1, 1870.

## Debt bearing Interest in Coin.

| Authorizing Acts. | Character of issue. | Rate of Interest. | Registered. | Coupon. | Total outstanding. | Purchased by Treasury. | When Redeemable or Payable. | Accrued Interest. | When payable. |
|---|---|---|---|---|---|---|---|---|---|
| June 14, 1858 | Bonds | 5 per cent. | $5,250,000 | $14,750,000 | $20,000,000 | .......... | Payable after 15 years from January 1, 1859. | $500,000 00 | January and July. |
| June 22, 1860 | Bonds | 5 per cent. | 6,074,000 | 948,000 | 7,022,000 | .......... | Payable after 10 years from January 1, 1861. | 175,550 00 | January and July. |
| February 8, 1861 | Bonds, 1881 | 6 per cent. | 13,241,000 | 5,174,000 | 18,415,000 | .......... | Payable after December 31, 1880. | 552,450 00 | January and July. |
| March 2, 1861 | Bonds, (Oregon), 1881. | 6 per cent. | .......... | 945,000 | 945,000 | .......... | Redeemable 20 years from July 1, 1861. | 28,350 00 | January and July. |
| July 17 and August 5, 1861. | Bonds, 1881 | 6 per cent. | 118,381,300 | 70,936,800 | 189,318,100 | .......... | Payable at option of Government, after 20 years from June 30, 1861. | 5,679,543 00 | January and July. |
| February 25, 1862 | Bonds, (5-20's) | 6 per cent. | 129,752,500 | 385,019,100 | 514,771,600 | $15,063,700 | Redeemable after 5 and payable 20 years from May 1, 1862. | 5,147,716 00 | May and November. |
| March 3, 1863 | Bonds, 1881 | 6 per cent. | 51,519,550 | 23,480,450 | 75,000,000 | .......... | Payable after June 30, 1881. | 2,250,000 00 | January and July. |
| March 3, 1864 | Bonds, (10-40's) | 5 per cent. | 129,578,450 | 64,988,850 | 194,567,300 | .......... | Redeemable after 10 and payable 40 years from March 1, 1864. | 3,242,788 33 | March and Sept. |
| March 3, 1864 | Bonds, (5-20's) | 6 per cent. | 3,882,500 | .......... | 3,882,500 | 752,400 | Redeemable after 5 and payable 20 years from November 1, 1864. | 38,825 00 | May and November. |
| June 30, 1864 | Bonds, (5-20's) | 6 per cent. | 72,452,850 | 53,108,450 | 125,561,300 | 16,488,150 | Redeemable after 5 and payable 20 years from November 1, 1864. | 1,255,613 00 | May and November. |
| March 3, 1865 | Bonds, (5 20's) | 6 per cent. | 67,268,550 | 136,058,700 | 203,327,250 | 9,713,450 | Redeemable after 5 and payable 20 years from November 1, 1865. | 2,033,272 50 | May and November. |
| March 3, 1865..*.. | Bonds, (5-20's) | 6 per cent. | 121,663,550 | 211,335,400 | 332,998,950 | 47,740,750 | Redeemable after 5 and payable 20 years from July 1, 1865. | 9,989,968 50 | January and July. |
| March 3, 1865 | Bonds, (5-20's) | 6 per cent. | 109,185,200 | 270,417,150 | 379,602,350 | 28,926,650 | Redeemable after 5 and payable 20 years from July 1, 1867. | 11,388,070 50 | January and July. |
| March 3, 1865 | Bonds, (5-20's) | 6 per cent. | 11,728,500 | 30,810,850 | 42,539,350 | 2,744,000 | Redeemable after 5 and payable 20 years from July 1, 1868. | 1,276,180 50 | January and July. |
| Aggregate of debt bearing interest in coin... | | | 839,977,950 | 1,267,972,750 | 2,107,950,700 | 121,429,100 | | 43,558,327 33 | |
| | | | | | | | Interest due and unpaid. | 6,088,705 05 | |
| | | | | | | | | 49,647,032 38 | |

## Debt bearing Interest in Lawful Money.

| Authorizing Acts. | Character of issue. | Rate of Interest. | Total outstanding. | When Redeemable or Payable. | Accrued Interest. | When payable. |
|---|---|---|---|---|---|---|
| March 2, 1867, and July 25, 1868. | Certificates | 3 per cent. | $45,545,000 00 | On demand | $277,993 57 | Annually or on redemption of certificate. |
| July 23, 1868 | Navy Pension Fund. | 3 per cent. | 14,000,000 00 | Interest only applicable to payment of pensions | 210,000 00 | January and July. |
| Aggregate of debt bearing interest in lawful money. | | | 59,545,000 00 | | 487,993 57 | |

## STATEMENT OF THE PUBLIC DEBT OF THE UNITED STATES, JULY 1, 1870.—Continued.

### Debt on which Interest has ceased since maturity.

| Authorizing Acts. | Character of Issue. | Rate of Interest. | Amount outstanding. | When Redeemable or Payable. | Accrued Interest. |
|---|---|---|---|---|---|
| April 15, 1842 | Bonds | 6 per cent | $6,000 00 | Matured December 31, 1862 | $360 00 |
| January 28, 1847 | Bonds | 6 per cent | 12,350 00 | Matured December 31, 1867 | 741 00 |
| March 31, 1848 | Bonds | 6 per cent | 43,700 00 | Matured July 1, 1868 | 1,311 00 |
| September 9, 1850 | Bonds, (Texas indemnity.) | 5 per cent | 242,000 00 | Matured December 31, 1864 | 12,100 00 |
| Prior to 1857 | Treasury notes | 1 mill to 6 per cent | 89,625 35 | Matured at various dates | 2,938 76 |
| December 23, 1857 | Treasury notes | 3 to 5½ per cent | 2,000 00 | Matured March 1, 1859 | 108 00 |
| March 2, 1861 | Treasury notes | 6 per cent | 3,200 00 | Matured April and May, 1863 | 195 00 |
| July 17, 1861 | Treasury notes, (3 years.) | 7 3-10 per cent | 29,700 00 | Matured August 19, and October 1, 1864 | 1,084 06 |
| March 3, 1863 | Treasury notes, (1 and 2 years.) | 5 per cent | 248,272 00 | Matured from January 7 to April 1, 1866 | 12,266 28 |
| March 3, 1863 | Certificates of indebtedness. | 6 per cent | 5,000 00 | Matured at various dates in 1866 | 313 48 |
| March 3, 1863, and June 30, 1864 | Compound interest notes. | 6 per cent | 2,152,910 00 | Matured June 10, 1867, and May 15, 1868 | 410,568 61 |
| June 30, 1864 | Temporary loan. | 4, 5, and 6 per cent | 181,310 00 | Matured October 15, 1866 | 7,501 91 |
| June 30, 1864, and March 3, 1865 | Treasury notes, (3 years.) | 7 3-10 per cent | 631,300 00 | Matured August 15, 1867, and June 15 and July 15, 1868 | 23,042 47 |
| Aggregate of debt on which interest has ceased since maturity. | | | 3,647,367 35 | | 472,530 57 |

### Debt bearing no Interest.

| Authorizing Acts. | Character of Issue. | | Amount outstanding. | |
|---|---|---|---|---|
| July 17, 1861 | Demand notes | | | $106,256 00 |
| February 12, 1862 | U. S. legal-tender notes | {New issue | $289,145,032 00 | |
| February 25, 1862 | | {Series 1869 | 66,854,968 00 | 356,000,000 00 |
| July 11, 1862 | | | | |
| March 3, 1863 | | | | |
| July 17, 1862 | Fractional currency | {1st series | 4,476,995 87 | |
| March 3, 1863 | | {2d series | 3,273,191 03 | |
| June 30, 1864 | | {3d series | 10,666,556 52 | |
| | | {4th series | 21,461,941 06 | 39,878,684 48 |
| March 3, 1863 | Certifs. for gold deposited | | | 34,547,120 00 |
| Aggregate of debt bearing no interest. | | | | 430,532,060 48 |

## STATEMENT OF THE PUBLIC DEBT OF THE UNITED STATES, JULY 1, 1870.—Continued.

*Recapitulation.*

| | Amount outstanding. | Interest. | Totals. |
|---|---|---|---|
| Debt bearing interest in coin: | | | |
| Bonds at 5 per cent | $221,589,300 00 | | |
| Bonds at 6 per cent | 1,856,361,400 00 | | |
| | $2,107,950,700 00 | $49,647,032 38 | |
| Debt bearing interest in lawful money: | | | |
| Certificates at 3 per cent | 45,546,000 00 | | |
| Navy pension fund, at 3 per cent | 14,000,000 00 | | |
| | 59,545,000 00 | 487,993 57 | |
| Debt on which interest has ceased since maturity | 8,647,367 35 | 472,630 57 | |
| Debt bearing no interest: | | | |
| Demand and legal-tender notes | 356,106,256 00 | | |
| Fractional currency | 39,878,684 48 | | |
| Certificates of gold deposited | 34,547,120 00 | | |
| | 430,532,060 48 | | |
| Total debt, principal and interest, to date, including interest due and unpaid | 2,601,675,127 83 | 50,607,556 62 | $2,652,282,684 35 |
| Amount in Treasury: | | | |
| Coin | | $112,776,048 88 | |
| Currency | | 28,945,067 19 | |
| Sinking fund, in United States coin interest bonds, and accrued interest thereon | | 37,663,191 63 | |
| Other United States coin interest bonds purchased, and accrued interest thereon | | 86,837,776 91 | |
| | | | 265,924,084 61 |
| Debt, less amount in the Treasury | | | 2,386,358,599 74 |
| Debt, less amount in the Treasury on the 1st ultimo | | | 2,406,562,371 78 |
| Decrease of debt during the past month | | | 20,203,772 04 |
| Decrease of debt since March 1, 1870 | | | 51,969,877 43 |

## STATEMENT OF THE PUBLIC DEBT OF THE UNITED STATES, JULY 1, 1870.—Continued.

*Bonds issued to the Pacific Railroad Companies, Interest payable in Lawful Money.*

| Authorizing acts. | Character of Issue. | Rate of interest. | Amount outstanding. | When redeemable or payable. | Interest payable. | Interest accrued and not yet paid. | Interest paid by United States. | Interest repaid by transportat'n of mails, &c. | Balance of interest paid by United States. |
|---|---|---|---|---|---|---|---|---|---|
| July 1, 1862, and July 2, 1864. | Bonds, (Union Pacific Company.) | 6 per cent. | $27,075,000 00 | Payable 30 years from date. | January 1 and July 1. | $812,250 00 | $2,891,729 85 | $1,289,576 87 | $1,602,152 98 |
| July 1, 1862, and July 2, 1864. | Bonds, (Kansas Pacific, late U. P., E. D.) | 6 per cent. | 6,303,000 00 | Payable 30 years from date. | January 1 and July 1. | 189,090 00 | 1,023,903 09 | 684,359 12 | 339,543 97 |
| July 1, 1862, and July 2, 1864. | Bonds, (Sioux City and Pacific.) | 6 per cent. | 1,628,220 00 | Payable 30 years from date. | January 1 and July 1. | 48,849 60 | 145,358 29 | 396 08 | 144,962 21 |
| July 1, 1862, and July 2, 1864. | Bonds, (Central Pacific.) | 6 per cent. | 25,881,000 00 | Payable 30 years from date. | January 1 and July 1. | 770,605 78 | 2,491,744 26 | 164,054 17 | 2,327,690 09 |
| July 1, 1862, and July 2, 1864. | Bonds,(Cent'l Branch Union Pacific, assignees of Atchison and Pike's Peak.) | 6 per cent. | 1,600,000 00 | Payable 30 years from date. | January 1 and July 1. | 48,000 00 | 253,808 26 | 7,401 92 | 246,406 34 |
| July 1, 1862, and July 2, 1864. | Bonds, (Western Pacific.) | 6 per cent. | 1,970,000 00 | Payable 30 years from date. | January 1 and July 1 | 57,966 40 | 73,288 76 | .............. | 73,288 76 |
| Total issued ............ | | | 64,457,320 00 | | | 1,926,761 78 | 6,879,832 51 | 2,146,788 16 | 4,734,044 35 |

The foregoing is a correct statement of the public debt, as appears from the books and Treasurer's returns in the department at the close of business on the last day of June, 1870.

GEORGE S. BOUTWELL, *Secretary of the Treasury.*

# INDEX.